the

AMERICANA
ANNUAL

1970

AN ENCYCLOPEDIA OF THE EVENTS OF 1969
YEARBOOK OF THE ENCYCLOPEDIA AMERICANA

WALLACE S. MURRAY
Editorial Director

LOWELL A. MARTIN
Editorial Consultant

JOHN D. TEDFORD
Assistant to the
Editorial Director

ELIZABETH CHASE
Art and Production
Coordinator

THE AMERICANA ANNUAL
STAFF

contents

Charles Frankel

Wernher von Braun

Walter Sullivan

THE NEW YORK TIMES STUDIO

Thomas O. Paine

A Special Report

THE YEAR OF THE MOON   Page 14

In its special, front-of-the-book feature, THE AMERICANA ANNUAL presents the epic story of 1969's manned lunar landings. The five-part report opens with a perceptive analysis by **Charles Frankel,** Old Dominion professor of philosophy and public affairs at Columbia University, of the significance of the journey to the moon. The author of *The Case of Modern Man* and *The Uses of Philosophy,* Professor Frankel examines the towering achievement in the light of today's urgent human needs. Dr. Frankel served as assistant secretary of state for educational and cultural affairs in 1965-67. The second and third sections are devoted to detailed accounts of the Apollo 11 and Apollo 12 missions, contributed by **Wernher von Braun** in collaboration with Frederick I. Ordway, III. Dr. von Braun, as head of NASA's George C. Marshall Space Flight Center, Huntsville, Ala., directed the building of the giant Saturn launch vehicles that propelled the first men to the moon. In early 1970 he was named NASA deputy associate administrator for planning. Mr. Ordway is professor of science and technology applications, Research Institute, University of Alabama at Huntsville. In the fourth part of this special report, **Walter Sullivan,** science editor of *The New York Times,* discusses the great amount of scientific knowledge that has been gained to date from the Apollo landings. Mr. Sullivan has received numerous honors for his science writing, including the 1959 George Polk Memorial Award. His book, *We Are Not Alone,* won the International Non-Fiction Book Prize. The future of space exploration is the subject of the final section, prepared by **Thomas O. Paine,** NASA administrator since March 1969. Dr. Paine, who became acting administrator in October 1968, directed the vast Apollo program during the climactic months leading to the first manned landing. Before joining the space agency, he had worked on a number of scientific projects for the General Electric Company.

Classified Listing of Articles

(continued)

contents *(continued)*

MEDICINE AND HEALTH

MILITARY AFFAIRS

RELIGION

SCIENCE

SUPRANATIONAL ORGANIZATIONS

MISCELLANEOUS

(For nations of the world, Canadian provinces, and U. S. states and territories, see separate entries under alphabetical headings.)

preface

In 1969 man strode upon the surface of the moon, bringing to a climax the remarkable decade of the Sixties and realizing a dream that goes back to mankind's earliest days on earth.

In journeying to the moon, the astronauts also learned something of the singular beauty and hospitality of their home planet. And millions of their fellowmen, viewing the striking images of earth as seen from the vicinity of the moon, gained a new appreciation of the place that must remain man's home no matter where he may travel in the solar system.

The view from earth was somewhat less reassuring. For in addition to the customary ills of war, poverty, disease, and injustice with which he has always lived, man became increasingly aware in 1969 that his physical environment—the air, land, and water that sustain him—was rapidly being degraded by his own acts. And so the astronauts' view of earth, of a shimmering blue and white oasis in the hostile void of space, served to remind man how terribly he had disfigured his celestial home and with what abandon he had spent its irreplaceable resources.

There were other wrongs to lament in the year that man first set foot on the moon. The glittering technological success of the Apollo missions pointed up, by contrast, the continuing failure of society to provide a better life for millions of disadvantaged people throughout the world. It is this wide and growing gulf between capability and performance that Professor Charles Frankel speaks of in the special report, "The Year of the Moon," in this 48th edition of THE AMERICANA ANNUAL. In analyzing the significance to mankind of the Apollo triumphs, he writes: "The moon landings brought home to millions of people what has long been an aching paradox in American and indeed in much of Western civilization: its mastery of means and techniques, its thoughtlessness about ends and purposes."

But whatever questions may be raised concerning the wisdom of the costly space program, they cannot diminish the personal achievement of the crew of Apollo 11 and of those who followed. Neil Armstrong, Edwin Aldrin, Jr., and Michael Collins will always be numbered in that small company of men who have dared the unknown and thus enlarged the lives of all. By their courage, skill, and supreme dedication, they proved that man is equal to whatever challenge he chooses to accept.

S. J. F.

CHRONOLOGY 1969

Earl Warren administers presidential oath to Richard M. Nixon as Mrs. Nixon looks on.

JANUARY

S	M	T	W	T	F	S
			1	2	3	4
5	6	7	8	9	10	11
12	13	14	15	16	17	18
19	20	21	22	23	24	25
26	27	28	29	30	31	

NIXON INAUGURATED AS 37TH PRESIDENT

LODGE TAKES OVER AT PEACE TALKS

1 President Ludvík Svoboda of Czechoslovakia appoints the government that will direct the federal state created today. ● In Brazzaville, Maj. Marien Ngouab head of the National Council of the Revolution, becomes president of the Congo Republic.

2 Luis A. Ferré is inaugurated as governor of Puerto Rico ending the 28-year rule of Luis Muñoz Marín's Popular Democratic party.

3 Senator Edward M. Kennedy captures the post of Democratic whip of the U. S. Senate. ● Adam Clayton Powell is reseated in the House of Representatives but is fined $25,000 and denied seniority.

4 In Londonderry, Northern Ireland, 136 persons are injured as Protestants attack marching university students. ● President Suharto of Indonesia offers a new 5-year plan to the nation.

5 President-elect Nixon announces that effective January 20, Henry Cabot Lodge will become the chief U. S. negotiator at the Paris talks on the Vietnam War.

6 Pope Paul VI consecrates 12 new Roman Catholic bishops.

7 France and the Soviet Union end a week of negotiations by agreeing to double their trade by 1974.

10 Publication of the 148-year-old magazine *Saturday Evening Post* is discontinued.

12 The New York Jets upset the Baltimore Colts, 16–7, for the American Football League's first victory in the Super Bowl.

14 Fire and explosions aboard the U. S. carrier *Enterprise* in the Pacific kill 25 men and injure 85.

16 Former Premier Rashid Karami heads a new coalition cabinet in Lebanon, ending a 9-day government crisis.

20 Richard M. Nixon is inaugurated as the 37th president of the United States. Spiro T. Agnew becomes the nation's 39th vice president.

22 In Moscow a gunman fires at a motorcade including party leader Leonid I. Brezhnev and Soviet cosmonauts who escape injury.

25 Spanish police begin an intensive roundup of persons engaged in illegal opposition to the government. ● Czech student Jan Palach, who had burned himself to death, is given a hero's funeral as half a million persons line the streets of Prague.

27 Iraq hangs 14 persons, including 9 Jews, as spies.

Samuel M. Vauclain—William Hazlett Upson—James Warner Bellah
Wesley Stout—Eleanor Mercein—Samuel Crowther—Booth Tarkington

The defunct *Saturday Evening Post* was noted for covers by artist Norman Rockwell.

FEBRUARY

S	M	T	W	T	F	S
						1
2	3	4	5	6	7	8
9	10	11	12	13	14	15
16	17	18	19	20	21	22
23	24	25	26	27	28	

OIL LEAK CLOSES CALIFORNIA HARBOR

ISRAEL AIRLINER HIT BY TERRORISTS

2 French President Charles de Gaulle outlines a constitutional reform enlarging regional authority and curbing the powers of the Senate.

5 The harbor of Santa Barbara, Calif., is closed as a huge oil slick from offshore drilling operations contaminates 16 miles (26 km) of beaches. ● Italian workers disrupt the nation as they stage a one-day general strike for better pensions.

6 Peru seizes all local holdings of the International Petroleum Company.

7 The Soviet government announces stringent conservation measures to halt pollution of Lake Baikal, the world's deepest body of fresh water.

8 The government of Brazil suspends the legislatures of five states on the grounds of corruption.

10 The Canadian House of Commons is advised that the nation proposes to discuss with Communist China the establishment of diplomatic relations.

12 Indian Prime Minister Indira Gandhi's Congress party suffers a stunning defeat in West Bengal elections as the Communist-dominated United Front party sweeps to victory. ● The government of Thailand wins an impressive plurality in the first general election in 11 years.

14 Peruvian gunboats fire on U.S. fishing boats off the Peruvian coast; one vessel is captured but later released. ● More than 200 students of Kyoto University in Japan are injured in battle with police.

16 Allied forces in Vietnam observe a 24-hour cease-fire as the Vietnamese people celebrate Tet, the lunar new year.

18 Four Arab terrorists attack an Israeli airliner at Zürich, Switzerland; six passengers are wounded, and one of the attackers is killed. ● Communist China cancels a long-awaited meeting in Warsaw with the United States 48 hours before it was scheduled to take place.

21 Pakistani President Mohammad Ayub Khan announces that he will not seek reelection in 1970. ● The Chinese Communist party newspaper *Jen Min Jih Pao* announces government plans to make the year 1969 one of major growth in industry and agriculture.

25 Australia and New Zealand declare that they will keep military forces in Malaysia and Singapore after the British withdrawal in 1971.

27 Britain increases the bank rate from 7% to 8% to reinforce its credit squeeze on commercial banks.

UPI
Bridge over Tujunga Wash is among casualties of flooding rains in southern California.

WIDE WORLD

James Earl Ray is led to prison after conviction as slayer of Martin Luther King, Jr.

MAULDIN © CHICAGO SUN-TIMES

"It's Ike himself. Pass the word."

MARCH

S	M	T	W	T	F	S
						1
2	3	4	5	6	7	8
9	10	11	12	13	14	15
16	17	18	19	20	21	22
23	24	25	26	27	28	29
30	31					

EISENHOWER DEAD

CHINESE, SOVIETS FIGHT ON BORDER

RAY SENTENCED

1 Baseball's Mickey Mantle announces his retirement after 18 seasons with the New York Yankees.

2 Soviet and Chinese troops clash along the Ussuri River frontier in eastern Siberia, resulting in 31 Soviet and an unspecified number of Chinese dead. ● President Nixon returns to the United States after an 8-day tour through five western European countries.

5 West Germany elects Justice Minister Gustav Heinemann president of the Federal Republic.

6 The price of gold soars in European markets on speculation that the French franc will be devalued.

10 James Earl Ray pleads guilty to the murder of Martin Luther King, Jr., on April 4, 1968, and is sentenced to a prison term of 99 years.

11 Rafael Caldera Rodríguez of the Social Christian party is inaugurated as president of Venezuela.

13 U. S. spacecraft Apollo 9, carrying three astronauts, splashes down in the Pacific after 10 days in orbit around the earth. ● The U. S. Senate approves the international agreement to prevent the spread of nuclear weapons by a vote of 83 to 15.

14 President Nixon asks Congress to approve a modified Sentinel and antiballistic missile system.

16 A Venezuelan jetliner with 83 aboard crashes into a suburb of Maracaibo, killing a total of 155 persons and injuring 100 in history's worst air disaster.

17 A Yemeni National Assembly meets for the first time after almost 1,000 years of autocratic or colonial government. ● Mrs. Golda Meir is sworn in as Israel's fourth premier, succeeding the late Levi Eshkol.

19 British paratroopers and police occupy the Caribbean island of Anguilla, ending its claim to independence.

20 A UAR jetliner crashes at Aswan, killing 87 and injuring 14.

25 After two weeks of violence and rioting in Pakistan, President Mohammad Ayub Khan resigns; Gen. Agha Mohammed Yahya Khan, Army commander in chief, is placed in charge of the government.

28 Former U. S. President Dwight D. Eisenhower dies at 78.

31 In Syria, the peaceful selection of a 16-man executive group of the ruling Baathist party appears to end a period of political turbulence. ● Morocco signs an accord of association with the European Common Market. ● Explosions rip the Altos Hornos coal mines in northern Mexico, killing 156 miners.

APRIL

S	M	T	W	T	F	S
		1	2	3	4	5
6	7	8	9	10	11	12
13	14	15	16	17	18	19
20	21	22	23	24	25	26
27	28	29	30			

DE GAULLE RESIGNS

U.S. PLANE DOWNED BY NORTH KOREANS

SIRHAN GUILTY

1 President Nixon confers separately with 12 world leaders who are in Washington for the state funeral of former President Eisenhower.

3 Pope Paul VI states that dissent within the Roman Catholic Church is nearing schism. ● Prime Minister Pierre Trudeau announces that Canada will reduce its NATO forces but will continue its membership in the alliance.

6 A 4-man British expedition reaches the North Pole after a 14-month, 1,300-mile (2,100-km) trek by dogsled.

8 The Kuomintang party of the Republic of China (Taiwan) reelects Chiang Kai-shek president.

9 Greek Premier George Papadopoulos restores three basic constitutional rights that had been suspended by the government.

10 More than 400 police remove hundreds of demonstrating students at Harvard University in Cambridge, Mass.

14 The 9th Congress of the Chinese Communist party adopts a new charter stipulating that Defense Minister Lin Piao will be the eventual successor of Mao Tse-tung as China's leader.

15 North Korea shoots down a U.S. reconnaissance plane over the Sea of Japan; 31 men are lost.

17 Gustav Husák replaces Alexander Dubček as first secretary of the Czechoslovak Communist party. ● In Los Angeles, Calif., Sirhan B. Sirhan is convicted of murder in the first degree for the slaying of Sen. Robert Kennedy on June 5, 1968.

23 The Nigerian government reports that it has captured Umuahia, the administrative headquarters of secessionist Biafra. ● Argentina, Bolivia, Brazil, Paraguay, and Uruguay sign a treaty for the development of the Río de la Plata basin.

27 President René Barrientos Ortuño of Bolivia is killed in a helicopter crash; Vice President Luis Adolfo Siles Salinas is sworn in as his successor.

28 President Charles de Gaulle of France resigns as his government suffers defeat in a referendum on constitutional reform; Alain Poher, president of the Senate, becomes interim president of the republic. ● Pope Paul VI elevates 33 Roman Catholic prelates to the Sacred College of Cardinals.

WIDE WORLD
Harvard dean is evicted from administration building by student protesters.

UPI
Sirhan Sirhan talks to attorneys prior to sentencing for Robert Kennedy murder.

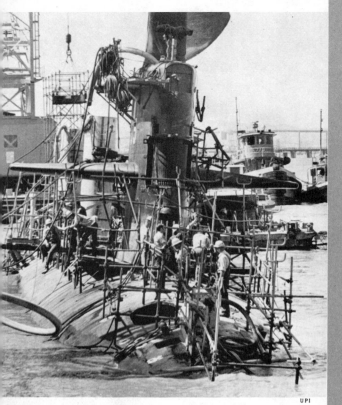

Salvage crews refloat submarine *Guittaro*, which sank at dockside in five minutes.

Thor Heyerdahl's papyrus boat *Ra* sails Atlantic to test ancient migration theory.

MAY

S	M	T	W	T	F	S
				1	2	3
4	5	6	7	8	9	10
11	12	13	14	15	16	17
18	19	20	21	22	23	24
25	26	27	28	29	30	31

FORTAS QUITS COURT

NAVY WON'T PUNISH CREW OF 'PUEBLO'

1 Maj. James D. Chichester-Clark becomes Northern Ireland's fifth prime minister, after the resignation of Capt. Terence O'Neill.

3 The 95th consecutive running of the Kentucky Derby at Churchill Downs, Ky., is won by Majestic Prince.

4 The Montreal Canadiens win their 16th Stanley Cup hockey title by sweeping the St. Louis Blues in four games. ● Negro militant leader James Forman interrupts services at Riverside Church in New York City to demand "reparations" to Negroes from religious organizations.

6 Navy Secretary John H. Chafee, overruling a naval court of inquiry, announces that no disciplinary action will be taken against the crew of the U. S. spy ship *Pueblo*.

9 In a sweeping reform of the liturgical calendar, the Roman Catholic Church removes 200 saints from the list of saints whose feast days are celebrated by the entire church.

11 At the request of President Nixon, New York Gov. Nelson Rockefeller begins a series of fact-finding missions to Latin America.

14 President Nixon proposes a mutual withdrawal of troops from South Vietnam over a period of 12 months. ● The Canadian House of Commons votes broad criminal code changes, including the legalization of abortion and homosexual acts under certain circumstances. ● U. S. Supreme Court Justice Abe Fortas resigns under fire because of his financial relationship with convicted financier Louis Wolfson.

16 Unmanned Soviet spacecraft Venera 5 completes a 4-month mission to Venus, transmitting information about the planet's atmosphere for 53 minutes.

17 The Yugoslav Federal Assembly confirms President Tito's nomination of Mitja Ribičič as federal premier.

23 Peru expels U. S. military missions and rejects the impending visit of President Nixon's fact-finder, Nelson Rockefeller.

25 Sudanese military officers overthrow the government. A new revolutionary council is headed by Col. Jaafar Muhammad al-Nimeiry.

26 U. S. spacecraft Apollo 10 splashes down in the South Pacific after a moon-orbiting flight and a successful descent of the lunar landing module to within 9.4 miles (15.1 km) of the moon's surface. ● Bolivia, Chile, Colombia, Ecuador, and Peru formally join an association intended to become an Andean common market.

30 Mario Andretti wins the 53d Memorial Day 500-mile auto race in Indianapolis, Ind., in record time.

JUNE

S	M	T	W	T	F	S
1	2	3	4	5	6	7
8	9	10	11	12	13	14
15	16	17	18	19	20	21
22	23	24	25	26	27	28
29	30					

NIXON ANNOUNCES TROOP WITHDRAWAL

BURGER HEADS COURT

POMPIDOU WINS

2 The Australian aircraft carrier *Melbourne* collides with the U. S. destroyer *Evans* in the South China Sea; 74 men from the *Evans* are killed as the vessel is sliced in half.

5 A study group of the National Commission on the Causes and Prevention of Violence states that the United States has become a "bloody-minded people in both action and reaction."

8 In a meeting on Midway Island with South Vietnamese President Nguyen Van Thieu, President Nixon announces that 25,000 U. S. troops will be withdrawn from Vietnam by Aug. 31, 1969.

10 Pope Paul VI visits Geneva, the home of the Swiss Reformation, and asks for an end to religious strife.

11 Communist China announces that Soviet and Chinese troops have clashed on the border of northwestern Sinkiang.

15 Orville Moody wins the U. S. Open golf championship in Houston, Texas. ● In San Rafael, near Madrid, Spain, 53 persons are killed and 142 are injured as a mountain restaurant collapses.

16 In presidential elections in France, Georges Pompidou, a Gaullist, wins 57% of the vote to defeat interim President Alain Poher and become Charles de Gaulle's successor for a 7-year term.

17 A 13-day meeting of delegates of 75 national Communist parties in Moscow ends with little result except emphasizing the Sino-Soviet rift.

19 Air transportation in the United States is snarled as about 240 federal air traffic controllers report that they are "sick."

20 The United States and Spain agree to extend the defense agreement of 1953 until Sept. 26, 1970.

23 Warren E. Burger becomes the 15th chief justice of the United States as Earl Warren retires after 16 years.

24 Millions of dead fish float in the northern Rhine River in the fifth day of spreading contamination by a chemical insecticide.

26 President Eduardo Frei Montalva of Chile announces a gradual nationalization of the Anaconda Company's Chilean copper mines, to be completed in 1972.

27 The six nations of the European Common Market agree to spend $900 million, over a period of 5½ years, in 18 African states associated with the Common Market.

28 New York City school teachers ratify a contract giving them the highest average salaries in the country.

RAYMOND DEPARDON—GAMMA—PIX
Georges Pompidou waves from balcony of his home after election as president of France.

7

Senator and Mrs. Edward Kennedy leave church after funeral of Mary Jo Kopechne.

JULY

S	M	T	W	T	F	S
		1	2	3	4	5
6	7	8	9	10	11	12
13	14	15	16	17	18	19
20	21	22	23	24	25	26
27	28	29	30	31		

ASTRONAUTS WALK ON LUNAR SURFACE

KENNEDY IN CRASH

POPE VISITS AFRICA

1 Britain's Queen Elizabeth II invests her 20-year-old son, Prince Charles, as the 21st prince of Wales in colorful ceremonies at Caernarvon Castle in Wales.

2 Prime Minister John Lynch of the Irish Republic is re-elected and names a new government, including Deputy Prime Minister Erskine Childers, the first non-Roman Catholic to hold the office.

5 In Nairobi, Kenya's Minister of Economic Affairs Tom Mboya is killed by an unknown assailant. ● Italian Premier Mariano Rumor's coalition cabinet resigns; President Saragat requests the government to continue on a caretaker basis.

7 The Canadian House of Commons approves a bill placing the French language on a par with English throughout the federal government.

8 Portuguese Premier Marcello Gaetano arrives in Brazil for a 5-day official visit in an effort to strengthen ties between the two Portuguese-speaking nations.

10 In a speech to the Supreme Soviet, Foreign Minister Andrei A. Gromyko of the Soviet Union calls for closer relations with the United States.

11 U. S. reconnaissance planes keep watch over a fleet of seven Soviet warships as they steam off the Florida coast en route to Havana, Cuba.

18 El Salvador and Honduras accept a four-point peace plan drafted by the Organization of American States to end the 6-day war resulting from a Salvadoran invasion of Honduras; approximately 2,400 lives are lost on both sides.

19 On Martha's Vineyard, Mass., an automobile driven by Sen. Edward M. Kennedy plunges off a bridge into a pond; passenger Mary Jo Kopechne is killed as Kennedy escapes. ● The Indian government nationalizes the country's 14 largest banks.

21 U. S. astronauts Neil A. Armstrong and Col. Edwin E. Aldrin, Jr., become the first men to walk on the surface of the moon; Lt. Col. Michael Collins remains in lunar orbit in the command ship of Apollo XI.

22 Francisco Franco, Spanish chief of state, designates Prince Juan Carlos of Bourbon as his eventual successor and the future king of Spain.

24 In Paris, 10 leading industrial powers reach a compromise agreement opening the way for a monetary reserve unit that would increase world financial liquidity.

31 Pope Paul VI arrives in Kampala, Uganda, to consecrate 12 African bishops and dedicate a shrine to African Christian martyrs.

President Nixon talks with U. S. troops in South Vietnam during visit to Asia in July.

AUGUST

S	M	T	W	T	F	S
					1	2
3	4	5	6	7	8	9
10	11	12	13	14	15	16
17	18	19	20	21	22	23
24	25	26	27	28	29	30
31						

**RUSH BRITISH TROOPS
TO NORTHERN IRELAND**

**ROCK FESTIVAL
ATTRACTS 300,000**

1 The government of Indonesia reports that West Irian, or West New Guinea, has voted to remain a part of Indonesia.

3 President Nixon returns to Washington after a 12-day, round-the-world tour to eight countries, including Rumania. ● Israeli leaders declare that the nation will permanently retain the Golan Heights, the Gaza Strip, and parts of the Sinai Peninsula, won in the June 1967 war.

5 Unmanned U.S. spacecraft Mariner 7 approaches to within 2,200 miles (3,500 km) of Mars and relays dramatic photographs of the planet's surface back to earth.

6 Rumanian President Nicolae Ceauşescu departs from principles of Soviet communism by setting forth a doctrine of full independence for individual Communist parties. ● In Italy, Mariano Rumor is sworn in as the new premier, heading a minority cabinet composed only of Christian Democrats.

8 The French government devalues the franc in an effort to help the nation's faltering economy. ● President Nixon proposes sweeping changes in the U.S. welfare system.

15 Britain begins airlifting troops to Northern Ireland as violence between Catholics and Protestants spreads. ● Communist China accuses the Soviet Union of mobilizing its troops and warns the Chinese people to prepare for conflict.

18 More than 300,000 young people depart from Bethel, N.Y., as the Woodstock Music and Art Fair closes after three days of rock music, mud, and drugs. ● Mississippi is declared a disaster area as hurricane Camille slams into the Gulf coast with winds of 190 mph, and into Virginia, leaving an estimated 300 persons dead and thousands homeless.

20 V. V. Giri, acting president of India since the death of Zakir Husain on May 3, is elected the fourth president of the nation.

21 In Jerusalem, the Mosque of Al Aksa, one of Islam's holiest shrines, is severely damaged in a fire reportedly set by an Australian Christian.

23 South Vietnamese President Thieu chooses Gen. Tran Thien Khiem to replace Tran Van Huong as premier.

29 In Ghana's first free general elections since 1956, the Progress party, led by Kofi A. Busia, is assured of control of the 140-member National Assembly.

31 Brazil's top military commanders announce that they have assumed control of the nation's government after President Artur da Costa e Silva is felled by a stroke.

LONDON DAILY EXPRESS—PICTORIAL PARADE
Belfast's Catholics and Protestants battle police in Northern Ireland's troubled city.

GILLES CARON, FROM GAMMA-PIX
Defiant students face troops in Prague on first anniversary of Soviet invasion of city.

9

SEPTEMBER

S	M	T	W	T	F	S
	1	2	3	4	5	6
7	8	9	10	11	12	13
14	15	16	17	18	19	20
21	22	23	24	25	26	27
28	29	30				

KOSYGIN, CHOU MEET

TANKER NEGOTIATES NORTHWEST PASSAGE

COUP IN LIBYA

WIDE WORLD

Islamic summit conference in Morocco draws heads of state from six Muslim countries.

TASS, FROM SOVFOTO

Soviet Premier Aleksei Kosygin meets with Red China's Premier Chou En-lai in Peking.

1 A junta composed of young army officers overthrows the Libyan government of King Idris I and proclaims the nation a socialist republic.

8 President Nixon and President Díaz Ordaz of Mexico dedicate the giant new Amistad dam on the Rio Grande

9 Norwegian Premier Per Borten's 4-party coalition wins a majority of seats in the Storting in a close general election. ● Israeli tanks and armored infantry engage in a 10-hour sweep of the UAR coast along the Gulf of Suez. ● A midair crash of a jetliner and a private plane kills 83 persons near Indianapolis, Ind.

10 The government of Alaska receives more than $900 million for northern coast oil leases in the greatest such competitive sale in U. S. history.

11 In a surprise visit to Peking, Soviet Premer Aleksei N. Kosygin confers with Communist Chinese Premier Chou En-lai.

14 The 1,005-foot (306-meter) tanker S. S. *Manhattan,* after 10 days of battling the northern ice pack, reaches open water and becomes the first commercial vessel to navigate the famed Northwest Passage to Alaska.

15 The British board of trade releases figures indicating that during August the nation had a surplus in its international trade for the first time in more than two years ● South Korea reports that 257 persons are dead and more than 60,000 homeless in the worst floods since 1959.

16 French Premier Jacques Chaban-Delmas urges sweeping social, economic, and administrative changes in "archaic" French society. ● Presdent Nixon announces that 35,000 more U. S. troops will be withdrawn from South Vietnam by December 15. ● Miss Angie E. Brooks of Liberia is elected president of the 24th General Assembly of the United Nations.

22 A conference of the heads of state of 25 Islamic countries opens in Rabat, Morroco. ● In the fifth day of rioting between Muslims and Hindus in the Indian state of Gujarat, more than 350 persons are dead and more than 2,000 have been arrested. ● Communist Warsaw Pact nations begin extensive military maneuvers in Poland.

23 North Vietnamese Vice President Ton Duc Thang is elected by the National Assembly to succeed President Ho Chi Minh, who died on September 3.

26 Bolivian President Luis Adolfo Siles Salinas is overthrown by a military junta.

OCTOBER

S	M	T	W	T	F	S
			1	2	3	4
5	6	7	8	9	10	11
12	13	14	15	16	17	18
19	20	21	22	23	24	25
26	27	28	29	30	31	

METS WIN SERIES

BRANDT ELECTED

MONTREAL POLICE, FIREMEN STRIKE

2 The United States conducts underground test of an H-bomb on Amchitka Island in Alaska, despite widespread criticism.

7 Communist China and the Soviet Union agree to hold talks in Peking on border disputes.

8 Montreal, Que., returns to normal after a one-day strike by police and firemen, during which lawlessness and looting required the summoning of army units.

10 President Nixon relieves Lt. Gen. Lewis B. Hershey of his post as director of the Selective Service System, effective Feb. 16, 1970.

12 General elections in Turkey result in victory for Premier Süleyman Demirel's conservative Justice party.

13 Swedish Minister of Education Olof Palme is sworn in as premier, succeeding retiring Tage Erlander.

15 A broad cross secton of the people of the United States engages in rallies and other activities in observance of a moratorium in opposition to the war in Vietnam.

16 The New York Mets became baseball's World Series champions by defeating the Baltimore Orioles, 5–3, in the fifth game.

18 South Korean President Chung Hee Park wins a resounding victory as the electorate approves a constitutional amendment enabling him to seek a third term.

21 The West German Bundestag elects Willy Brandt the fourth chancellor of the Federal Republic.

22 Lebanese Premier Rashid Karami submits his resignaton as government forces and Arab guerrillas battle in the southern part of the country.

23 Irish-born writer Samuel Beckett wins the 1969 Nobel Prize in literature.

24 West Germany revalues the mark upward by 9.29%.

27 Thirteen U.S. labor unions launch a nationwide strike against the General Electric Company.

28 The U.S. Supreme Court rules that school districts must end school segregation "at once." ● In Israeli general elections, Premier Golda Meir's ruling Labor party is returned to power but without an absolute majority.

30 Gen. Emílio Garrastazú Médici takes office as president of Brazil.

31 Spanish Chief of State Francisco Franco shuffles his cabinet, almost entirely eliminating Falangists and giving European-oriented "technocrats" the balance of power.

UPI
Willy Brandt takes oath of office as West Germany's first Social Democratic party chancellor, October 21.

UPI
Israeli Premier Golda Meir casts vote in nation's first general election since 1967 war.

 (continued — caption)

UPI

Washington Monument in nation's capital is site of vast gathering for Vietnam peace.

NOVEMBER

S	M	T	W	T	F	S
						1
2	3	4	5	6	7	8
9	10	11	12	13	14	15
16	17	18	19	20	21	22
23	24	25	26	27	28	29
30						

APOLLO 12 ON MOON

250,000 IN CAPITAL PROTEST THE WAR

ARMS TALKS BEGIN

3 President Nixon addresses the nation in an effort to rally support for his program of gradual "Vietnamization" of the war.

4 In U.S. elections Republicans gain governorships in New Jersey and Virginia; John Lindsay is re-elected mayor of New York City.

8 In Sapporo, Japan, a 2,000-man police force clears demonstrating students from buildings at Hokkaido University.

11 President Ferdinand Marcos of the Philippines wins decisive victory in presidential election.

13 Vice President Agnew assails television news coverage and calls on the networks to examine their practices.

15 Over 250,000 persons converge on Washington, D.C., to protest the Vietnam War in the largest antiwar demonstration in U.S. history.

17 The Soviet Union and the United States open preliminary strategic arms limitation talks (SALT) at Helsinki.

19 U.S. astronauts Charles Conrad, Jr., and Alan Bean begin an exploration of the lunar surface lasting more than 8½ hours of their 31½-hour stay on the moon; Richard Gordon, Jr., remains in lunar orbit in the Apollo 12 command ship.

20 Henry Cabot Lodge resigns as chief U.S. negotiator at the Paris talks on the Vietnam War.

21 Japan and the United States agree on the return of Okinawa to Japanese rule in 1972. ● The U.S. Senate defeats the nomination of Clement F. Haynsworth, Jr., to the Supreme Court by a vote of 55 to 45.

24 The Soviet Union and the United States sign the nuclear nonproliferation treaty. ● The U.S. Army announces that Lt. William L. Calley, Jr., will be given a general court-martial in connection with the alleged massacre of South Vietnamese civilians by U.S. soldiers at the hamlet of My Lai in March 1968.

25 President Nixon announces a ban on the use of biological weapons and orders the destruction of existing U.S. germ warfare stockpiles.

27 Pro-Arab Jordanian commandos bomb Israeli airline office in Athens, injuring 15 persons and causing extensive damage.

28 West Germany signs the nuclear nonproliferation treaty.

29 In New Zealand, the National party of Prime Minister Keith J. Holyoake wins its fourth successive election and is returned to power for another 3-year term.

DECEMBER

S	M	T	W	T	F	S
	1	2	3	4	5	6
7	8	9	10	11	12	13
14	15	16	17	18	19	20
21	22	23	24	25	26	27
28	29	30	31			

JUMBO JET IN FLIGHT

ARAB HEADS MEET

JAPANESE VOTERS BACK SATO PARTY

1 The first U.S. draft lottery since World War II is held in Washington, D. C., to determine the order of selection of draftees for 1970.

2 The European Economic Community (ECC) agrees to open negotiations on British membership in 1970. ● The 362-seat Boeing 747 jumbo jet makes its first public flight from Seattle, Wash., to New York City.

4 Warsaw Pact nations issue a communique praising West Germany's offer to improve relations with Poland. ● Central American countries meet in Managua, Nicaragua, to mediate hostilities between Honduras and El Salvador.

8 West Germany and the Soviet Union open talks in Moscow on mutual renunciation of force.

9 Gold prices on the free market sink to record lows.

10 President Emile Derlin Zinsou of Dahomey is ousted by a military junta in sixth coup since 1960.

12 Greece withdraws from the Council of Europe after 13 of the 18 member nations decide to vote for a resolution suspending Greece from the council until it restores democratic freedoms.

16 Brig. Gen. Omar Torrijos Herrera of Panama's National Guard executes successful countercoup following a one-day overthrow by rival officers. ● The British House of Commons votes to abolish capital punishment.

18 Major Hugh J. Addonizio of Newark, N.J., and other city administrators are indicted on charges including extortion, conspiracy, and tax evasion in inquiry into organized crime in the state.

19 President Milton Obote of Uganda is shot and wounded while leaving annual party convention at Kampala.

21 UAR President Gamal Abdel Nasser and 12 other Arab leaders gather in Rabat, Morocco, for 3-day conference to formulate policy toward Israel.

22 The Soviet Union and the United States end preliminary strategic arms limitation talks, agreeing to open full-scale negotiations at Vienna in April 1970 and return the talks to Helsinki at a later date. ● Israel denounces an 11-point U. S. peace formula for the Middle East submitted to France, Britain, and the Soviet Union.

26 Vice President Agnew embarks on a 25-day goodwill tour of 11 Asian nations, including South Vietnam.

27 The ruling Liberal Democratic party of Japanese Premier Eisaku Sato scores a resounding victory in elections for the House of Representatives, winning 288 seats in the 486-seat lower house.

© CHRONICLE PUBLISHING CO. 1969

WIDE WORLD
Premier Eisaku Sato (*left*) celebrates election victory with members of his Liberal-Democratic party.

13

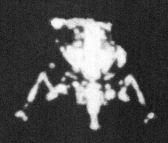

The Year of the Moon

By CHARLES FRANKEL
*Old Dominion Professor of Philosophy
and Public Affairs, Columbia University*

When two men walked on the moon in July 1969, many people who watched from the earth probably had the same thought: something as important as Columbus' discovery of America is taking place; the human race is crossing into a new world with different spatial, social, and moral horizons.

Yet the way in which men perceived the landing on the moon was different from the way in which, in all probability, Columbus' contemporaries perceived his achievement. Those who heard about his voyage were a small fraction of the world's population, and even the basic geographical fact that two vast new continents had been discovered was not recognized for some time. In contrast, the landing on the moon came after eight years of carefully staged preparations. Each step in

Historic journey of Apollo 11 begins on July 16, 1969, at Kennedy Space Center. About one million spectators watched the awesome lift-off.

the process constituted a public drama, in which thousands of people participated directly as workers in or contributors to the space program, and in which tens of millions on all continents participated vicariously. It is a banal but strange truth that no explorers ever traveled farther and yet were less alone than astronauts Neil Armstrong, Edwin Aldrin, and Michael Collins.

The most important of all the differences between 1492 and 1969 is the historical and psychological context in which the landing on the moon took place. Unlike Columbus' voyage, it came after five centuries of continued discovery; it was an apex to a prolonged era of human movement and exploration, not its beginning. It came, furthermore, after centuries of steadily accelerating scientific triumphs that had presented mankind with ideas about the universe that most men still find bewildering and many find upsetting. And it came after two hundred years of technological innovations that have created an environment in which the artifices of men have pushed the natural universe into the background—an environment that nevertheless seems somehow less human, less personal, less adapted to the human frame and nervous system. To land men on the moon, a dead and alien place in which the men must carry their earthly environment on their backs, was simply to have given this paradox a visible and dramatic form.

Moreover, the moon landing took place at the end of a decade of brutally disappointed hopes for progress in dealing with human issues such as poverty and war. It took place in a year in which the United States, the main center of power and wealth in the world, was going through a profound crisis of conscience and confidence and was perhaps more dangerously divided than it had been since the Civil War. When President John F. Kennedy, back in 1961, announced the inauguration of a program to put a man on the moon before the end of the decade, he spoke to a nation largely immersed in private concerns. Its public

NASA

(Overleaf) *The lunar module of Apollo 12, with Charles Conrad, Jr., and Alan Bean aboard, heads for a landing on the moon's Ocean of Storms in November 1969.*

problems, although serious, seemed manageable. It was possible to think at that time that the nation needed a heady challenge, a test of its will and capacities, that would renew its sense of the United States as an adventure in collective achievement. It was all the easier to think in such terms because the cold war psychology of competition with the Soviet Union was still in the ascendant.

But by the end of the decade, when the enterprise so launched had proved successful, the achievement (for all its excitement) was surrounded with ambiguities. The cold war had lost much of its plausibility; to large numbers of people, the cost of thoughtless competition with the Russians, in no matter what domain, had come to seem excessive. The war in Vietnam, furthermore, had greatly reduced public confidence in the wisdom of government policies. With the nation involved in the longest war in its history, a war with an uncertain beginning and an indefinitely postponed conclusion, not even those who supported the U. S. government's policies were inclined to say that the policies had been well conceived or implemented. The space program undoubtedly suffered some of the side effects of this general lack of enthusiasm for the government's activities.

Accordingly, the landing on the moon raised, as it should have done, basic questions about the meaning of American life and the guiding purposes of American civilization. It was an event that pointed in two directions. It turned loose as many thoughts about the past as about the future, making men rue lost opportunities even as they wondered about the new opportunities they faced. Was an expensive program to land men on the moon the best way to use American resources? Or was not a willingness to put so much effort into the exploration of outer space one sign of the unwillingness of the United States to deal with its own poisoned physical and social environment?

In brief, the moon landing brought home to millions of people what has long been an aching paradox in American and indeed in much of Western civilization: its mastery of means and techniques, its thoughtlessness about ends and purposes. The moon landing raised a moral question that is ultimate in the lives of individuals and societies everywhere: Should men multiply their resources and endlessly multiply their wants simply because the challenge and the possibility are there? Or should they try to limit their wants, to order them in terms of some criticized conception of the Good, and concentrate their powers on doing the central things that count? Should they follow the example of Odysseus and Faust, or of Socrates and Tolstoy?

The question is not easy to answer. Certainly it is not so easy as simplistic arguments for or against technological progress often appear to suggest. The case for technological progress usually is put in narrowly materialistic terms, the case against it in moralistic ones. But there is an impulse behind the history of technology that eludes both simple economic calculations and the neat divisions between good and evil, right and wrong, that schoolbook moralists make. Technology is in part the expression of the human desire to explore and tinker with, to readjust and tame, the human habitat. Its product may be greater human convenience and security, but, as the myth of Prometheus suggests, its origin often lies simply in impatience with what is ordained as the order of things—in the desire to take a chance and to use one's powers and ingenuity, even if it is at the expense of safety.

'The landing raised a moral question...'

ASTRONAUT EDWIN ALDRIN STANDS NEAR A FOOTPAD OF THE 'EAGLE' (NASA PHOTO)

'Faith and effort, and the faith
that grows from effort, are in many ways
their own solution to the problems
that call them forth.'

There is something to be said for the human impulse to climb a mountain just because it is there. It is the same impulse, in a more sublimated and less physical form, that explains major achievements in mathematics, in poetry, in the building of the great cathedrals of the Middle Ages. In the simple sense of the term these achievements are purposeless. They are, in a way, their own purpose; it is the achievement in itself that justifies the effort that went into it. A good portion of the achievements that have maintained the energies of the human race have been adventures of this sort—extravagant in terms of the resources available, wasteful in relation to the more commonplace and practical purposes to which attention might have been given. But they have expanded men's conception of the possibilities of their life on the planet earth; and, often, they have "solved" practical problems simply by bypassing them, creating circumstances in which the old problems no longer exist, or generating new needs and values in terms of which old concerns recede in importance.

It is frequently said by defenders of the space effort that its "spin-off" consequences are enough to justify its existence. It cannot be doubted that among its by-products have been technical refinements, new industries, and research systems whose economic potentialities are considerable. But the main case for the moon landings is psychological and moral: the space program has demonstrated the miracles that can be performed by careful planning, backed by adequate financial and political resources. However important the long-range scientific, technical, and economic implications of the moon landings may turn out to be, their most important immediate effect has been the renewed confidence they have generated in human intelligence and courage.

Another effect may or could be more momentous. The practical by-products of the space program have raised the question whether at least equally useful side effects might not have been produced by a comparably organized and financed program to deal with such problems as urban reorganization, slums, racial injustice, transportation, education, waste disposal, and air and water pollution. And the moral and psychological effects of such a program could have been even greater. These human problems are difficult to solve; few answers are known. But a concerted political and financial effort, launched with the same sense of purpose as that with which the space program was launched, could in itself have curative powers. Faith and effort, and the faith that grows from effort, are in many ways their own solution to the problems that call them forth.

At the beginning of the 1960's the United States made a decision to put men on the moon. It gave up many good and useful things it might otherwise have done in order to succeed in this effort. At the end of the decade, with the confidence of the nation in its technical powers still further increased but with its confidence in itself greatly reduced, what would a comparable effort to reduce human wretchedness and to produce a livable social and physical environment do? The dazzling success of the space missions has raised this question. Looking ahead to the 1970's, which are likely to be as unpredictable as the 1960's turned out to be, at least one thing is plain: more and more Americans are likely to think that their civilization makes no sense unless the country undertakes as serious an effort toward answering this question as the effort it made to reach the moon.

'Man Must Understand His Universe in Order to Understand His Destiny'

The following is a transcript of remarks made by Neil A. Armstrong, the first man on the moon, to a joint session of Congress, Sept. 16, 1969.

We landed on the Sea of Tranquility, in the cool of the early lunar morning, when the long shadows would aid our perception.

The sun was only ten degrees above the horizon. While the earth turned through nearly a full day during our stay, the sun at Tranquility Base rose barely eleven degrees—a small fraction of the month-long lunar day. There was a peculiar sensation of the duality of time—the swift rush of events that characterizes all our lives—and the ponderous parade which makes the aging of the universe.

Both kinds of time were evident—the first by the routine events of the flight—whose planning and execution were detailed to fractions of a second—the latter by rocks around us, unchanged throughout the history of man—whose three-billion-year-old secrets made them the treasure we sought.

The plaque on the Eagle which summarized our hopes bears this message: "Here men from the planet earth first set foot upon the moon July 1969 A.D. We came in peace for all mankind."

Those nineteen hundred and sixty-nine years had constituted the majority of the age of Pisces—a twelfth of the great year that is measured by the thousand generations the precession of the earth's axis requires to scribe a giant circle in the heavens.

In the next twenty centuries, the age of Aquarius of the great year, the age for which our young people have such high hopes, humanity may begin to understand its most baffling mystery—where are we going? The earth is, in fact, traveling many thousands of miles per hour in the direction of the constellation Hercules—to some unknown destination in the cosmos. Man must understand his universe in order to understand his destiny.

Mystery, however, is a very necessary ingredient in our lives.

Mystery creates wonder and wonder is the basis for man's desire to understand. Who knows what mysteries will be solved in our lifetime, and what new riddles will become the challenge of the new generations? Science has not mastered prophecy. We predict too much for next year yet far too little for the next ten. Responding to challenge is one of democracy's great strengths. Our successes in space lead us to hope that this strength can be used in the next decade in the solution of many of our planet's problems.

Several weeks ago, I enjoyed the warmth of reflection on the true meaning of the spirit of Apollo.

I stood in the highlands of this nation, near the continental divide, introducing to my sons the wonders of nature and pleasures of looking for deer and for elk.

In their enthusiasm for the view, they frequently stumbled on the rocky trails. But when they looked only to their footing, they did not see the elk. To those of you who have advocated looking high we owe our sincere gratitude, for you have granted us the opportunity to see some of the grandest views of the Creator.

Those of you who have been our honest critics we also thank, for you have reminded us that we dare not forget to watch the trail.

We carried on Apollo 11 two flags of this Union that had flown over the Capitol, one over the House of Representatives, one over the Senate. It is our privilege to return them now in these halls which exemplify man's highest purpose—to serve one's fellowman.

We thank you, on behalf of all the men of Apollo, for giving us the privilege of joining you in serving—for all mankind.

'One Giant Leap for Mankind'

By Wernher von Braun
*Deputy Associate Administrator
for Planning, NASA*

and Frederick I. Ordway, III
*Research Institute, University of Alabama
in Huntsville*

On July 20, 1969, two U. S. astronauts set foot on the moon—the first time any man had done so. The flight achieved an age-old dream of man: to leave his planetary cradle and stride on alien worlds. It will be the task of future historians to assess the full impact of the lunar landing on man's history, but even now it can be asserted with good reason that man's thinking about himself and his world can never again be quite the same.

The three astronauts who made up the crew of Apollo 11 were Neil A. Armstrong, a civilian, and Edwin E. Aldrin, Jr., and Michael Collins, both Air Force officers. Each of the men had made one previous flight into space and was a veteran pilot with several years of training. Aldrin was also a graduate of the Massachusetts Institute of Technology with the degree of doctor of science in astronautics. On the Apollo 11 flight, Armstrong was the mission commander, Aldrin served as the commander of the lunar module (code-named *Eagle* for the flight), and Collins was the pilot of the spacecraft's command module (code-named *Columbia*). Armstrong and Aldrin were the men who would descend to the surface of the moon.

THE JOURNEY TO THE MOON

The Apollo 11 mission got under way at 9:32 A. M. Eastern Daylight Time (EDT) on July 16. Approximately one million spectators in the Cape Kennedy, Fla., area and hundreds of millions of television viewers around the world watched the Saturn 5 rocket rise slowly from Launch Complex 39. The spacecraft entered a temporary "parking" orbit about 115 miles (185 km) above the earth, where the instrumentation unit's guidance system computed the exact moment for the S-4B stage of the rocket to reignite in order to insert the Apollo into its translunar path. This path was calculated so that, should the engine of the service module fail to place the Apollo in lunar orbit, the spacecraft would swing around the moon and return to earth along a so-called "free return" trajectory.

The firing of the S-4B stage took place on schedule, speeding the Apollo 11 to an initial velocity of nearly 24,300 miles (39,100 km) per hour. So accurate was the firing that three or four planned midcourse corrections were subsequently canceled. Early in the translunar period, however, several necessary maneuvers were carried out to reorient the spacecraft. The linked command and service modules were turned about so as to dock with the lunar module, after which *Eagle*'s four connections to its adapter and the S-4B stage were severed. Later, about 34 hours into the flight, the astronauts relayed their first scheduled color television broadcast to the world.

As Apollo 11 neared the moon on July 19, the time came to fire the service module's propulsion system. The engine burn reduced the spacecraft's velocity from approximately 6,500 to 3,700 miles (10,460 to 5,960 km) per hour and placed the astronauts in an elliptical lunar orbit. After two circuits the men reignited the engine to bring their craft into a roughly circular orbit between 62 and 75 miles (100 and 121 km) above the surface of the moon. On-board systems were checked out thoroughly; this completed, Armstrong and the Houston controllers agreed that it was time for the descent maneuver to begin. Armstrong and Aldrin pressurized the tunnel between *Eagle* and *Columbia*, opened the connective hatches, and crawled into the lunar module, where they made extensive reviews of all systems and subsystems before undocking. Collins remained aboard the command module. Armstrong reported to Houston: "The *Eagle* has wings."

FIRST MEN ON THE MOON

Tension now rose in *Eagle* and *Columbia*, at mission control in Houston, and in front of television receivers in homes and public places all around the world. *Eagle*'s descent engine was fired, first at 10% throttle and then at 40%. The lunar module's orbital path became highly elliptical. When the proper landing approach "corridor" had been identified, the engine was again fired, permitting the craft to sink downward to the moon. Everything now proceeded

"Red Carpet" by Franklin McMahon, one of a series of paintings on the space program.

NASA

under the automatic control of the on-board computer until *Eagle* was about 7,600 feet (2,320 meters) high and about 26,000 feet (7,930 meters) uprange from the planned touchdown site in the Sea of Tranquility, northwest of Crater Moltke. The craft was further braked at this point, and dropped to about 500 feet (150 meters) as the crew received visual cues from the landscape and assessed the terrain for the best place to land.

At about 450 feet (137 meters) Armstrong and Aldrin took over the controls, having decided against an automatic landing sequence in favor of a semi-automatic procedure. Because of a program alarm that indicated the on-board computer was being overworked, the astronauts and Houston brought *Eagle* down through a verbal exchange of instrument data and visual observations. The last few moments were extremely nervous ones for everyone involved, as besides the program alert, the module's guidance and navigation system was heading the crew toward a rocky crater. Armstrong had to burn the engines for another 70 seconds to reach a smoother landing site about 4 miles away.

The final moments came as Aldrin reported, "Forward, forward, good. Forty feet. Picking up some dust. . . . Drifting to the right. . . . Contact light. OK. Engine stop!" Armstrong delayed for one second; then, looking down onto

a sheet of moon soil blown away in all directions by the rocket exhaust, he shut off the engine. "Tranquility Base here. The *Eagle* has landed," the commander reported. The time was 4:17:41 P. M. (EDT), July 20. Men were on the moon.

Up until this moment, the millions of television viewers could only listen to words being passed between Apollo 11 and ground control. Soon they would be able to watch events on the moon as well. (Ironically, one man who could not see what was happening there until after the mission was completed was Collins, who had to be content with listening to the voices of his crewmates.) Originally, the mission plan had scheduled about eight hours for systems checkout, eating, and resting, before the astronauts were actually to leave their module. However, after assuring themselves that *Eagle* was in good shape, Armstrong and Aldrin requested permission to cancel or at least postpone their rest period. Houston agreed; it seemed unlikely that the two men would do much sleeping at this stage of their momentous journey.

Nevertheless, more than three hours were needed to get suited up for their extravehicular activities; the donning of portable life support system backpacks proved particularly time-consuming. In their suits at last, the astronauts depressurized their cabin—which proved to be

(*Continued on page 24*)

'THE EAGLE HAS LANDED'

On July 20, 1969, tens of millions of persons throughout the world listened intently to conversations between Eagle, *the Apollo 11 lunar module, and the Manned Spacecraft Center in Houston, Texas. The following are excerpts from the NASA transcript of messages between Neil A. Armstrong and Edwin E. Aldrin, Jr., aboard* Eagle, *and Houston, along with remarks by Apollo Control; Michael Collins in* Columbia, *the Apollo 11 command module; and President Nixon. The sequence begins in the final phase of the descent.*

HOUSTON: Eagle, you're looking great, coming up 9 minutes.

CONTROL: We're now in the approach phase of it, looking good. Altitude 5,200 feet.

HOUSTON: You're go for landing.

EAGLE: Roger, understand. Go for landing. 3,000 feet....

CONTROL: Altitude 1,600. 1,400 feet. Still looking very good.

EAGLE (Aldrin, calling out altitude readings to Armstrong): 35 degrees. 35 degrees. 750, coming down at 23. 700 feet, 21 down. 33 degrees. 600 feet, down at 19. 540 feet, down at 30—down at 15. 400 feet, down at 9. 8 forward. 350, down at 4. 330, 3½ down. We're pegged on horizontal velocity. 300 feet, down 3½. 47 forward . . . down 1 a minute. 1½ down. 70. Got the shadow out there. 50, down at 2½. 19 forward. Altitude-velocity lights. 3½ down, 220 feet. 13 forward. 11 forward, coming down nicely. 200 feet, 4½ down. 5½ down. 160, 6½ down, 5½ down, 9 forward. 5 percent. Quantity light. 75 feet, things looking good.

HOUSTON: 60 seconds.

EAGLE: Lights on. Down 2½. Forward. Forward. Good. 40 feet, down 2½. Picking up some dust. 30 feet, 2½ down. Faint shadow. 4 forward, drifting to the right a little.

HOUSTON: 30 seconds.

EAGLE: Drifting right. Contact light. OK, engine stop....

HOUSTON: We copy you down, Eagle.

EAGLE (Armstrong): Houston, Tranquility Base here. The Eagle has landed.

HOUSTON: Roger, Tranquility, we copy you on the ground. You've got a bunch of guys about to turn blue. We're breathing again. Thanks a lot.

Immediately after landing at 4:18 P.M. (EDT), Armstrong and Aldrin began putting the craft in readiness for the Eagle's *eventual ascent back to the* Columbia *spacecraft, still orbiting the moon. With that and other chores out of the way, Armstrong was ready, 6 hours and 21 minutes later (and 5 hours ahead of schedule), to open the hatch and start down the 9-step, 10-foot ladder. On the second step, he pulled a D-ring that deployed a TV camera on the spacecraft to depict his progress down the ladder.*

HOUSTON: Man, we're getting a picture on the TV. OK, Neil, we can see you coming down the ladder now....

ARMSTRONG: I'm at the foot of the ladder. The LM footpads are only depressed in the surface about 1 or 2 inches. Although the surface appears to be very, very fine grained, as you get close to it it's almost like a powder. Now and then, it's very fine.

[At 10:56 P.M.] I'm going to step off the LM now. That's one small step for a man, one giant leap for mankind.

The surface is fine and powdery. I can kick it up loosely with my toe. It does adhere in fine layers like powdered charcoal to the sole and sides of my boots. I go in only a small fraction of an inch, maybe an eighth of an inch, but I can see the footprints of my boots and the treads in the fine, sandy particles.

There seems to be no difficulty in moving around as we suspected. It's even perhaps easier than the simulations at one-sixth G that we performed on the ground.

It's quite dark here in the shadow and a little hard for me to see if I have good footing. I'll work my way over into the sunlight here without looking directly into the sun....

ARMSTRONG: ... This is very interesting. It's a very soft surface but here and there where I plug with a contingency sample collector I run into a very hard surface, but it appears to be very cohesive material of the same sort.

ALDRIN (from within *Eagle*): That looks beautiful from here, Neil.

ARMSTRONG: It has a stark beauty all its own. It's like much of the high desert of the United States. It's different, but it's very pretty out here.

At 11:11 P.M., Aldrin squeezes out of the hatch—a task made difficult by the bulk of his Portable Life Support System—and prepares to back down the ladder as Armstrong photographs him.

ARMSTRONG: The shoes are about to come over the sill.... There you go—you're clear.

ALDRIN: Now I want to back up and partially close the hatch, making sure not to lock it on my way out.

ARMSTRONG: A good thought.

ALDRIN: That's our home for the next couple of hours and I want to take good care of it....

ALDRIN (on lunar surface): Beautiful, beautiful!

ARMSTRONG: Isn't that something? Magnificent sight down here!

ALDRIN: Magnificent desolation!

ALDRIN: ...The rocks are rather slippery.... Very powdery surface when the sun hits.... We will attempt to slide over it rather easily....

COLUMBIA (Michael Collins, orbiting the moon): ... How's it going?

HOUSTON: The Eva [extravehicular activity] is progressing beautifully. I believe they are setting up the flag now.

COLUMBIA: Great.

HOUSTON, I guess you're about the only person around that doesn't have TV coverage of the scene.

COLUMBIA: That's right. That's all right, I don't mind a bit. How is the quality of the TV?

HOUSTON: Oh, it's beautiful, Mike. Really is.

COLUMBIA: Oh, gee, that's great. Is the lighting halfway decent?

HOUSTON: Yes, indeed. They've got the flag up and you can see the Stars and Stripes on the lunar surface.

COLUMBIA: Beautiful, just beautiful!

ALDRIN: ...You do have to be rather careful to keep track of where your center of mass is. Sometimes, it takes two or three paces to make sure you've got your feet underneath you. About two to three or maybe four easy paces can bring you to a nearly smooth stop. Next direction, like a football player, you have to split out to the side and cut a little bit. A kangaroo hop does work but it seems that your forward ability is not as good as it is in the conventional one foot after another....

HOUSTON: Tranquility Base, this is Houston. Could we get both of you on the camera for a minute, please?

ARMSTRONG: Say again, Houston.

HOUSTON. Roger. We'd like to get both of you in the field of view of the camera for a minute. Neil and Buzz, the President of the United States is in his office now and would like to say a few words to you....

PRESIDENT NIXON: Neil and Buzz, I am talking to you by telephone from the Oval Room at the White House. And this certainly has to be the most historic telephone call ever made.... For every American, this has to be the proudest day of their lives. And for people all over the world, I am sure they, too, join with Americans in recognizing what a feat this is. Because of what you have done, the heavens have become a part of man's world. And as you talk to us from the Sea of Tranquility, it inspires us to double our efforts to bring peace and tranquility to earth. For one priceless moment...in the whole history of man, all the people on earth are truly one.

another tedious process—and opened the hatch. It was 6½ hours since the lunar module had landed.

Armstrong slowly descended the nine-rung ladder leading down from the "porch" of the lunar module. At the second rung he released a fold-down equipment department on the side of the module, releasing a television camera. Soon the silhouetted figure of Armstrong could be seen by viewers back on earth, as he continued his descent of the ladder. When he took his first cautious step onto the lunar soil, at 10:56:20 P. M. (EDT), he paused to pronounce the now-familiar words: "That's one small step for a man, one giant leap for mankind."

Soon Armstrong began to give verbal descriptions of the material on which he walked. "The surface appears to be very, very fine grained . . . like a powder. . . . I can kick it up loosely with my toe . . . like powdered charcoal. . . . I can see the footprints of my boots . . . in the fine sandy particles . . . no trouble to walk around." Meanwhile Aldrin monitored the television camera inside the module and observed his companion's movements. Finally he asked, "Is it OK for me to come out?" A few minutes later he too stood on the moon.

Like tourists visiting a spectacular vacation area, the astronauts took dozens of photographs. They showed television viewers the plaque on *Eagle*'s descent stage, which read:

HERE MEN FROM THE PLANET EARTH
FIRST SET FOOT UPON THE MOON
JULY 1969 A. D.
WE CAME IN PEACE FOR ALL MANKIND

The plaque was signed by the astronauts and President Richard M. Nixon, who later made a telephone call to the moon from the White House. In the early minutes of their extravehicular activities Armstrong and Aldrin also erected a metallic U. S. flag at a site near the landing craft.

AT WORK ON THE LUNAR SURFACE

Surface activities involved three principal goals. First, the astronauts checked and photographed *Eagle* from all angles to determine if any flight or landing damage had occurred. They also studied the depressions—only 1 to 2 inches (about 2.5 to 5 cm) deep—made by *Eagle*'s footpads. Second, the astronauts had to familiarize themselves with the lunar environment by walking and running; their evaluations of clothing and equipment would be invaluable for later landing missions. Third, Aldrin and Armstrong collected as much operational and scientific data as possible during their stay.

Armstrong gathered about 48 pounds (22 kg) of rocks and soil samples, placing them in sealed bags, which were then inserted in two aluminum boxes. He also attempted to take core samples of subsurface materials. The astronauts set up three instrument systems for obtaining data: a solar-wind-composition detector, a seismic detector, and a laser reflector, from which scientists back on earth later "bounced" laser beams for a more accurate determination of the landing site and the motions of the earth and moon and the distance between them.

The solar wind device consisted simply of a very thin aluminum foil deployed so that the foil would be directly exposed to the sun's rays. In effect, it was a trap for the inert-gas constituents of the stream of particles constantly flowing outward from the sun. (The lunar soil itself was later found to be rich in solar wind particles.) Near the end of the stay on the moon, it was folded and placed in a sample container. The seismic detector was deployed to monitor possible "moonquakes," meteoroid impacts, free oscillations of the moon, and general signs of internal activity.

The astronauts provided interesting verbal descriptions of their new environment. Aldrin reported "literally thousands" of craters about 1 to 2 feet (0.3 to 0.6 meter) in diameter; there were also boulders of all shapes, up to 2 feet across, with some even larger. Many of them were above the ground, while others were partially or almost completely buried. The two men's footprints were about an eighth of an inch (0.3 cm) deep.

Armstrong and Aldrin found mobility was no problem, although both men described the ground as "slippery" (possibly as a result of the many tiny glass spherules later found in the soil samples). They quickly became accustomed to the low gravity, finding it best to anticipate their motions three or four steps in advance in order to compensate for the reduced length of time that the foot remains on the ground during a lunar stride.

The astronauts had to begin their return to the landing craft after about 2½ hours of work on the surface. They stowed the foil from the solar wind device, dusted off their extravehicular mobility units, kicked their boots clean against the footpad of the module, ascended the platform, swung open the hatch, disconnected the equipment conveyor, and jettisoned equipment and items no longer needed. Then they took a well-earned rest before their return the next day to *Columbia*.   (*Continued on page 26*)

FIRST MEN
ON THE MOON

"That's one small step for a man, one giant leap for mankind." With these words Neil Armstrong stepped down from the ladder of *Eagle*, the lunar module of Apollo 11, and set foot upon the surface of the moon. Thus July 20, 1969, entered history as the day when man, for the first time, walked on a world other than his native earth. Apollo 11 marked the climax of years of effort by the U.S. National Aeronautics and Space Administration to place a man on the moon by 1970.

(*Below*) Astronaut Edwin Aldrin is photographed by Armstrong in the glare of lunar day. Armstrong and the *Eagle* are reflected in Aldrin's helmet visor.

NASA PHOTO

PLATE 1

HEADING TOWARD THE MOON

On July 16; 1969, as millions of spectators viewed the event over television, the Apollo 11 astronauts began their historic eight-day journey. Below, an automatic camera high on the tower of Launch Complex 39 at Kennedy Space Center, Florida, records the early moments of liftoff. The mighty, 364-foot Saturn 5/Apollo 11 space vehicle slowly rises past the camera on a column of flame, its initial 7.5 million pounds of thrust generated by the burning of kerosine and liquid oxygen.

NASA PHOTOS

PLATE 2

Once in lunar trajectory, the astronauts use their cameras to photograph the earth they are leaving. North Africa and the Arabian peninsula are clearly visible in the midst of swirling patterns of clouds.

PLATE 3

Apollo 11 Emblem

ON THE LUNAR SURFACE

Four days after Apollo 11's launch, astronauts Neil Armstrong and Edwin Aldrin entered *Eagle*, the lunar module, and descended to the surface of the moon, while Michael Collins remained in lunar orbit in the command module *Columbia*. Armstrong's first words as the LM touched down in the Sea of Tranquility were: "Houston, Tranquility Base here. The Eagle has landed." (Above, the emblem worn by the crew of Apollo 11 symbolized the landing.) The two men spent 21½ hours working and resting on the moon before rising in *Eagle's* ascent stage to rejoin Collins in lunar orbit and return to earth.

NASA PHOTOS

(*Above*) Aldrin cautiously descends the ladder of *Eagle* as he is photographed by Armstrong, who had stepped out on the moon a few minutes earlier.

(*Right*) Walking around the rim of a small crater, Aldrin carries two of the instruments that were set up and left behind on the lunar surface to send back scientific information.

PLATE 4

Against a backdrop of "magnificent desolation," as he described the lunar landscape, Aldrin sets up a seismic detector to measure tremors on the moon's surface. The LM stands in the background, and beside it the U.S. flag.

Armstrong poses for a picture beside the metal U.S. flag. The prints made by the boots of the two astronauts in the fine, powdery surface material are clearly visible in the foreground—marks that may remain undisturbed indefinitely.

PLATE 5

PROJECT APOLLO—TRIP TO THE MOON

On these pages are shown the highlights of Apollo's lunar trip. Across the top, the various components (shown in greater detail below) are regrouped in space. At lower right, diagrams depict the moon landing and take-off.

COMMAND, SERVICE, AND LUNAR MODULES

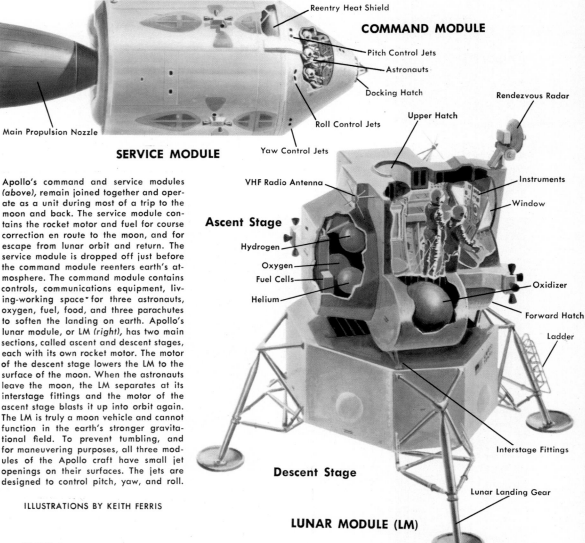

Reentry Heat Shield

COMMAND MODULE

Pitch Control Jets

Astronauts

Docking Hatch

Rendezvous Radar

Main Propulsion Nozzle

Roll Control Jets

Upper Hatch

SERVICE MODULE

Yaw Control Jets

VHF Radio Antenna

Instruments

Window

Ascent Stage

Hydrogen

Oxygen

Fuel Cells

Helium

Oxidizer

Forward Hatch

Ladder

Interstage Fittings

Descent Stage

Lunar Landing Gear

Apollo's command and service modules (above), remain joined together and operate as a unit during most of a trip to the moon and back. The service module contains the rocket motor and fuel for course correction en route to the moon, and for escape from lunar orbit and return. The service module is dropped off just before the command module reenters earth's atmosphere. The command module contains controls, communications equipment, living-working space for three astronauts, oxygen, fuel, food, and three parachutes to soften the landing on earth. Apollo's lunar module, or LM (right), has two main sections, called ascent and descent stages, each with its own rocket motor. The motor of the descent stage lowers the LM to the surface of the moon. When the astronauts leave the moon, the LM separates at its interstage fittings and the motor of the ascent stage blasts it up into orbit again. The LM is truly a moon vehicle and cannot function in the earth's stronger gravitational field. To prevent tumbling, and for maneuvering purposes, all three modules of the Apollo craft have small jet openings on their surfaces. The jets are designed to control pitch, yaw, and roll.

ILLUSTRATIONS BY KEITH FERRIS

LUNAR MODULE (LM)

PLATE 6

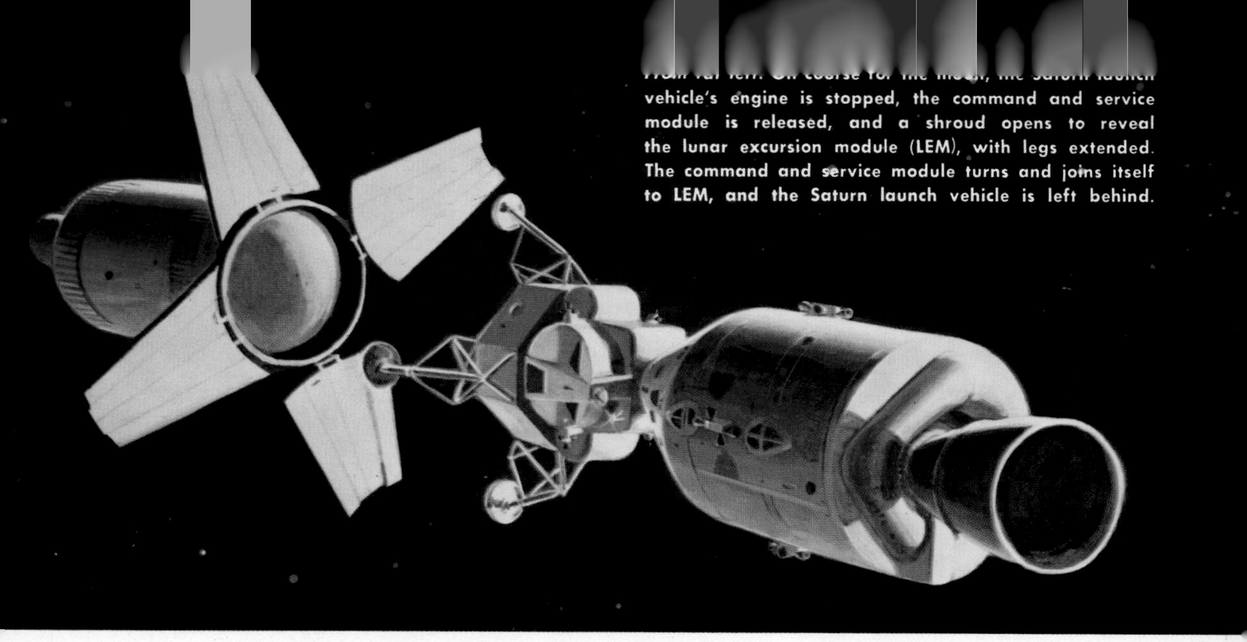

From far left. On course for the moon, the Saturn launch vehicle's engine is stopped, the command and service module is released, and a shroud opens to reveal the lunar excursion module (LEM), with legs extended. The command and service module turns and joins itself to LEM, and the Saturn launch vehicle is left behind.

AT THE MOON — LANDING AND TAKE-OFF

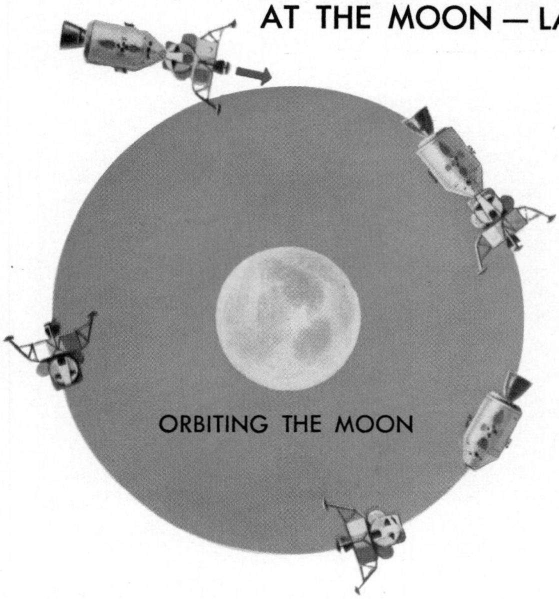

ORBITING THE MOON

LANDING ON THE MOON

While the command, service, and lunar modules are in unpowered orbit around the moon, there is a checkout of the crew and all equipment. Then two astronauts transfer from the command module into the LM and the two modules separate, with the third astronaut remaining in lunar orbit as the LM descends toward the surface. Once the module has landed, the two astronauts go outside their craft to explore the surface, perform experiments, and gather samples. At the proper time for rendezvous with the command and service modules, they blast off in the LM's upper stage, leaving the lower stage on the moon. With their main motor and attitude control jets they get into orbit, maneuver into position, and dock with the command module. The LM's upper stage then is jettisoned, and remains in lunar orbit. The astronauts fire the rocket of the service module to enter a trajectory back toward earth. The rocket is also used to make midcourse corrections along the way, if necessary. As the spacecraft nears the earth the service module is jettisoned and the command module turned around so that re-entry into the atmosphere takes place with its heat shield forward. The module then descends to the ocean surface with the aid of parachutes.

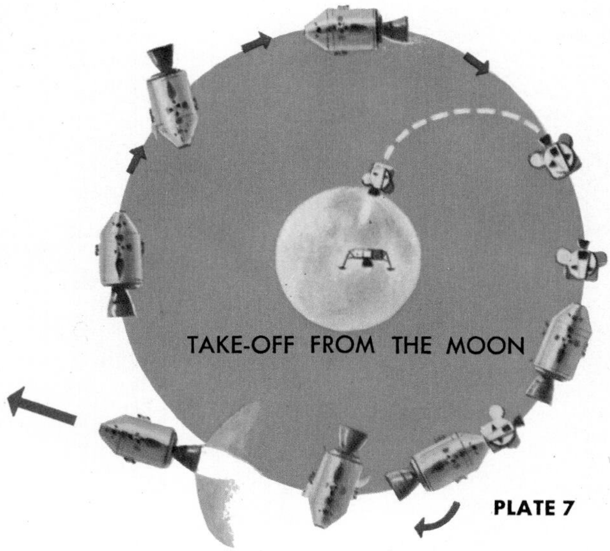

TAKE-OFF FROM THE MOON

PLATE 7

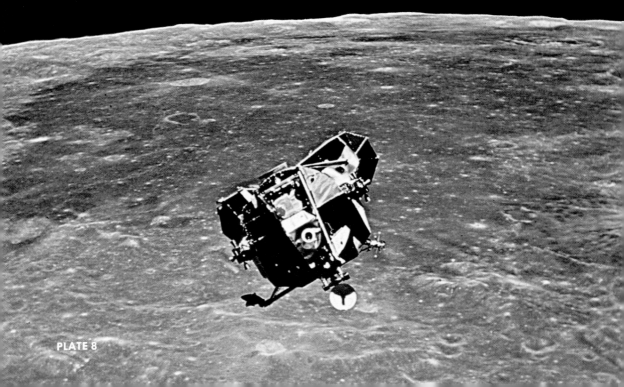

Rising rapidly from the moon, *Eagle* approaches *Columbia* for docking as the modules swing around to the moon's near side. Earth, the next target of the three astronauts, looms 235,000 miles away in the black sky.

NASA PHOTO

PLATE 8

The Crew of Apollo 11

NEIL A. ARMSTRONG, Apollo II commander, in 1969 became the first man to walk on another celestial body. Blond, blue-eyed, and looking much like the former Eagle Scout he is, Armstrong is a small-boned man standing 5 feet 11 and weighing 165 pounds. Associates find him reserved in demeanor and sparing in speech. He was born in Wapakoneta, Ohio, on Aug. 5, 1930, the son of a career civil servant (state of Ohio). With money earned as a mechanic's helper at the Wapakoneta airport, Neil took lessons and became a pilot at 16. He joined the Navy at 19 and eventually flew 76 combat missions in the Korean War, once nursing a damaged jet back to friendly territory before bailing out. He received his bachelor's degree in aeronautical engineering from Purdue University in 1955. As a test pilot at what later became the NASA Flight Research Center at Edwards Air Force Base, Calif., he flew experimental rocket planes, the X-1 and X-15, setting records for speed (3,989 mph) and altitude (207,500 feet). In the Gemini 8 mission in 1966, Armstrong performed the first docking of two vehicles in space and then averted disaster by landing his spacecraft safely in the Pacific after a thruster malfunctioned. He is married to the former Janet Shearon of Evanston, Ill., and has two sons, Eric and Mark. As a civil servant (Grade 16, Step 7), he earns a salary of $30,054 a year.

MICHAEL COLLINS, pilot of the *Columbia* command module in the Apollo 11 mission, flew in lonely orbit around the moon while Armstrong and Aldrin walked on the lunar surface. "Not since Adam," Houston control commented, "has any human known such solitude as Mike Collins is experiencing during the 47 minutes of each lunar revolution when he's behind the moon with no one to talk to." Collins, who was an Air Force lieutenant colonel during the mission and won promotion to colonel immediately afterward, stands 5 feet 11 inches tall and weighs 165 pounds. "Stay casual"—the motto attributed to him by the West Point yearbook of 1952—typifies his relaxed, affable manner even while performing exacting tasks. He was born in Rome, Italy, on Oct. 31, 1930, the son of a U. S. Army major general then serving as a military attaché. After graduating from the U. S. Military Academy, Collins became an experimental flight test officer at Edwards Air Force Base, primarily flying jet fighters. In the Gemini 10 mission in 1966, Collins and John Young staged a docking with an Agena target vehicle, and Collins made two space walks. He is married to the former Patricia Finnegan of Boston and they have three children—Kathleen, Ann, and Michael. In late 1969, President Nixon nominated Collins to be assistant secretary of state for public affairs.

EDWIN E. ALDRIN, JR., Apollo II lunar module pilot, joined Armstrong on the moon's surface. A former high school football player (he showed how to "cut" sharply in direction while running on the moon), Buzz Aldrin stands 5 feet 10 and weighs 165. He dresses well and is urbane in manner. Born in Montclair, N. J., on Jan. 20, 1930, he is the son of an Air Force colonel who was a famous flyer. Aldrin graduated third in a class of 475 at the U. S. Military Academy in 1951, and he received a doctor of science degree in astronautics from Massachusetts Institute of Technology in 1963. His dissertation dealt with guidance for manned orbital rendezvous. An Air Force colonel at the time of the moon mission, he is a veteran of 66 combat missions in F-86 jets in the Korean War and destroyed two MIG-15 aircraft. His wife is the former Joan Archer of Ho-Ho-Kus, N. J., and they have three children—Michael, Janice, and Andrew. In 1966, Aldrin and command pilot James Lovell closed the Gemini program with the spectacularly successful 4-day Gemini 12 flight. Aldrin spent more than 5½ hours in space outside the craft. His accomplishments included attaching a tether to an unmanned Agena; demonstrating the use of body restraints designed for completing work tasks in space; and taking the first photo in space of an eclipse of the sun.

(Continued from page 24)

THE RETURN TO EARTH

Lift-off from the lunar surface took place at 1:55 P. M. (EDT) on July 21. Despite their strenuous activities on the moon, the *Eagle* crewmen actually slept very little before the time of launch. When the ascent stage engine was fired, the stage soared rapidly upwards in what Armstrong described as a very smooth and quiet ride. The engine had to burn for more than seven minutes in order to produce a final velocity of 4,128 miles (6,646 km) per hour. Maneuvers brought the two ships within rendezvous distance of each other, and *Eagle* and *Columbia* began to dock. The ships suddenly gyrated—to the surprise of the astronauts—but docking was accomplished thereafter without mishap and only three minutes behind schedule. Aldrin and Armstrong crawled back into *Columbia,* and *Eagle* was jettisoned.

The return trip to earth took about 60 hours, during which time the astronauts again transmitted a television program to earth. Each of them, in turn, reflected on the meaning of their flight. Aldrin said, "This has been far more than three men on a voyage to the moon; more, even, than the efforts of one nation. We feel that this stands as a symbol of the insatiable curiosity of all mankind to explore the unknown."

On July 24, some 3½ hours before the Apollo began to reenter the atmosphere, the astronauts turned the command module's heat shield away from the sun to permit it to cool to the maximum extent. The service module was then separated, and at an altitude of about 24,000 feet (73,000 meters) the heat shield was jettisoned and parachutes deployed. The astronauts splashed down in the Pacific Ocean southwest of Hawaii at 12:40 P. M. (EDT), about 2 miles (3.2 km) away from their intended target and 13 miles (20 km) from the waiting recovery ship, the U. S. S. *Hornet*. The men and their capsule were quickly retrieved. Before they left their capsule, however, they were handed three biological isolation garments with plastic-visored face masks. This was the first of several steps taken to reduce to an absolute minimum any danger of contamination from lunar materials. As soon as they entered the waiting life rafts, the astronauts were thoroughly washed with a decontaminant, after which they in turn washed the frogman who performed this chore. The hatch of the Apollo was also scrubbed. These measures had been developed by an interagency committee prior to the flight, although most scientists felt that the possibility that microorganisms existed on the moon was remote.

Upon being delivered to the *Hornet,* where President Nixon waited to greet them, the astronauts were transferred to a quarantine van and flown back to the Manned Spacecraft Center at Houston, via Hawaii. There they and their precious cargo of lunar rocks and soil were transferred to a Lunar Receiving Laboratory, where the men remained in quarantine for 18 days. Having shown no sign of ill effects from having come in contact with the moon, Armstrong, Aldrin, and Collins were permitted to emerge on August 11. Now truly returned to the world of men, the astronauts had to prepare for another arduous mission: the days and weeks of parades, interviews, and acclamation that were to follow. The first explorers of the moon became earth's heroes.

The Happy Explorers of Apollo 12

The United States repeated the achievement of its Apollo 11 mission four months later, with additional scientific bonuses, when the Apollo 12 spacecraft journeyed to the moon.

THE FLIGHT

On November 14, 1969, at 11:22 A. M. Eastern Standard Time (EST), Saturn 5 AS-507 took off from Cape Kennedy under very poor atmospheric conditions with astronauts Charles (Pete) Conrad, Jr., Alan Bean, and Richard Gordon, Jr., aboard. There was considerable apprehension in the spacecraft cabin and on the ground when, 36½ seconds after lift-off, electrical discharges from the sullen clouds covering the region passed through Saturn 5 and its exhaust plume, causing a temporary loss of AC power in some of the vehicle's systems. At the same time, minor disturbances were recorded in the cabin. These events had no effect on the entry of the spacecraft into its "parking" orbit, however, and the astronauts soon restored power by resetting the circuit breakers.

Apollo 12's translunar trajectory differed from that of previous lunar missions in that it was not a "free return" but a "hybrid." That is, it did not provide for an automatic safe return to earth should the Apollo not be able to enter moon orbit. The so-called "hybrid transfer" midcourse correction took place about 31 hours

Alan Bean inspects Surveyor 3 spacecraft that landed on the moon in 1967. In the background, some 600 feet away, stands the Apollo 12 lunar module.

NASA

into the mission; however, reestablishment of a free-return trajectory was within the capability of both the service and the lunar modules' propulsion system.

En route, astronauts Conrad (the flight commander), Gordon (command module pilot), and Bean (lunar module pilot)—all Navy commanders—underwent the same routines as in earlier flights. On November 17, just before 11 P. M. (EST), their craft entered lunar orbit. About 25 hours later the lunar module, manned by Conrad and Bean, undocked from the command module; the two modules were henceforth referred to, respectively, as *Intrepid* and *Yankee Clipper*. As *Yankee Clipper* continued to orbit the moon, piloted by Gordon, *Intrepid* commenced its descent orbit insertion maneuver.

ON THE MOON

Conrad and Bean skillfully brought their craft down to the surface of the moon, although for a while there was some concern over the time taken in landing. Bean reported, "... Looking good, watch the dust. 32, 31, 30 feet. . . .

Pete, you got plenty of gas, plenty of gas, babe. Stay in there. He's got it made. . . . Contact light!" When the dust settled, Conrad found he had brought *Intrepid* down 1 minute and 43 seconds late, at 1:54:43 A. M., November 19. The ship was right on target, about 600 feet (180 meters) from where the Surveyor 3 moon probe had soft-landed on a crater's edge in April 1967.

The enthusiasm of the astronauts was evident from the moment they landed. "Holy cow," exclaimed Conrad as he looked out upon the Ocean of Storms, "it's beautiful out there." The two men rested, then commenced preparations for their first 4-hour walk on the moon. The hatch opened at 6:30 A. M. As Conrad made ready to step onto the surface about 10 minutes later, he referred jokingly to Neil Armstrong's historic words on the previous flight. Said Conrad, "That may have been a small step for Neil, but that's a long one for me! . . . Oh, is that soft! . . . I don't sink in too far. . . . Boy, that sun's bright! . . . you'll never believe it! Guess what I see sitting on the side of the crater? The old Surveyor. . . . How about that?" From Houston, 233,450 miles (375,850 km) away, came "Well planned, Pete." About half an hour later Bean, too, was out on the lunar surface.

The astronauts spent four hours outside during the first of two planned periods of extravehicular activity. Unfortunately, the television camera that was sending images back to viewers on earth failed shortly after it was deployed, while Conrad was wheeling it into position; thereafter only the voices of the two men were heard. Conrad and Bean gathered a contingency sample of lunar rocks and soil, set up a solar wind experiment to determine the elemental and isotopic composition of solar inert gases, took photographs, and examined the depressions made by *Intrepid*'s footpads. (In this somewhat different terrain, the pads went in a little deeper than had those of Apollo 11.)

After these preliminary activities it was time to deploy the Apollo lunar surface experiments package (ALSEP), designed to operate for about a year on the moon. During that time it would measure the strength of the solar wind, the solar magnetic field, and the earth's magnetic field on the moon, and study the physics of the moon's surface and interior. A dust detector was designed to measure the presence of dust or other debris that might impinge on the ALSEP.

Other experiments included a lunar ionosphere detector, a lunar atmosphere detector, and a solar wind spectrometer. The astronauts also performed field geological surveys, among their instruments being a close-up camera for taking high-resolution stereoscopic photographs of the surface. Conrad and Bean poked into everything they could find and reported back to earth. Although Houston overruled them, neither of the men wanted to go back inside *Intrepid* at the end of their first moon walk. Trotting back to their module, over 1,000 feet (300 meters) away, they picked up some additional samples and performed visual geological studies. Finally they reentered their temporary home, advising mission control that they were "not going to have any trouble sleeping tonight."

Some 12½ hours later they were back outside *Intrepid* for a second period of exploration that was to last more than 4½ hours. Both astronauts were as gleeful on their second excursion as on the first. They gathered additional samples, took more photographs, rolled a rock into "Head" Crater to test the operation of the seismometer, visited the ALSEP array, and noted some big fragments at the bottom of "Bench" Crater. Conrad remarked of the fragments, "It looks to me like the stuff is melted in the bottom" of the crater—that is, as if the crater had been flooded with once-molten material.

The major task of the astronauts was to visit the Surveyor 3 probe. Arriving there, they noted that the formerly white-painted spacecraft had turned tan because of exposure to the lunar environment; otherwise it seemed unaffected by 2½ years of standing on the moon. The men removed its television camera, some glass and tubing, and the mechanical scoop that was filled with soil. Among other things, scientists and engineers wanted to find out whether any terrestrial organisms carried by the craft had survived and what effects micrometeorites had on the structure.

THE JOURNEY HOME

Returning to *Intrepid* for the last time, Conrad and Bean made ready to blast off on November 20, after 31½ hours on the moon. The ascent and rendezvous maneuvers were executed flawlessly, and the men transferred back to *Yankee Clipper* in lunar orbit. Then, in a switch from the Apollo 11 practice, the *Intrepid* was ordered to crash back onto the moon's surface. When this was done, the resulting series of reverberations through the moon surprised the scientific world by continuing for nearly an hour. Geophysicist Frank Press said, "We've never seen anything like it on earth; it's beyond the range of anything we expected."

The astronauts spent one more day in lunar orbit, photographing future landing sites, before they headed back toward earth. En route, they held the first space-to-earth press conference, in which they reported further details of their experiences on the moon. Splashdown occurred at 3:58 P.M. (EST), November 24, within 3 miles (5 km) of the carrier U. S. S. *Hornet,* which was waiting some 400 miles (640 km) southeast of Pago Pago in the Pacific Ocean. The three astronauts had been away for more than 244 hours, and they arrived back on earth only 14 seconds behind schedule.

As on the preceding flight, the men were placed in isolation for several days. Meanwhile scientists everywhere were jubilant over the trip, praising the geological descriptions given by the men, the samples they brought back, and their ability to deploy the several scientific instruments. One scientist said, "The people who wonder at the involvement of man in this program must have learned a few lessons. The ability of man to correct faults, that you don't do by automation very handily, was clearly in evidence." As he spoke plans for the next Apollo mission were well under way. Less than nine years after the program had been announced, the reality of the manned exploration of the moon was firmly established.

NASA

The Crew of Apollo 12

CHARLES CONRAD, JR., Apollo 12 commander, was the third man on the moon. Known as Pete, he is one of the smallest astronauts at 5 feet 6½ inches and 138 pounds. Just after stepping off the ladder of the lunar module *Intrepid,* he recalled Armstrong's historic remark about "one small step" by quipping: "Whoopie, man, that may have been a small step for Neil, but that's a long one for me!" Conrad is known for his good cheer: he punctuated his moon talk with laughs and hummed ("dum de dum dum dum") while gathering rocks. He was born in Philadelphia on June 2, 1930, the son of an investment banker, and he earned a bachelor's degree in aeronautical engineering from Princeton University in 1953. Upon graduation he joined the Navy and over the years served as a project pilot, flight instructor, and performance engineer, rising to captain after the moon flight. In Gemini 5 in 1965, Conrad teamed with command pilot Gordon Cooper to set a space endurance record by staying aloft eight days. In Gemini 11 in 1966, Conrad, as command pilot, performed orbital maneuvers that permitted his craft to rendezvous and dock with an Agena. Also, he guided Gemini 11 to a record 850-mile altitude. His family consists of his wife, the former Jane DuBose of Uvalde, Texas, and sons Peter, Thomas, Andrew, and Christopher.

RICHARD F. GORDON, JR., pilot of the *Yankee Clipper* command module, orbited the moon alone in the Apollo 12 mission while Conrad and Bean walked the surface 60 miles below. A Navy captain, he is both highly social and highly competitive. In the latter area, Gordon established a transcontinental speed record in 1961 by winning the Bendix Trophy Race at an average speed of 869 mph, flying from Los Angeles to New York in 2 hours, 47 minutes. He stands 5 feet 7 inches and weighs 150 pounds. Born in Seattle, Wash., on Oct. 5, 1929, he earned a B. S. degree in chemistry from the University of Washington in 1951. After receiving his wings as a naval aviator in 1953, he eventually did flight test work on the Crusader, Tigercat, Fury, and Skyhawk. Joining Conrad in the Gemini 11 mission, Gordon performed two periods of activity outside the capsule. In the first, he linked Gemini with an unmanned Agena by a tether and was photographed riding astride the Agena. The tie-up task proved strenuous and Gordon had trouble seeing because of perspiration in his eyes. In his second extra-vehicular activity, he stood up in the craft and took pictures outside the hatch. Gordon and his wife, the former Barbara Field of Seattle, have six children, more than any other astronaut family —Carleen, Richard, Lawrence, Thomas, James, and Diane.

ALAN F. BEAN, Apollo 12 lunar module pilot, was the chatty, energetic companion of Pete Conrad in two exploratory walks on the moon. To the delight of listeners back on earth, Bean registered amazement and enthusiasm while examining craters ("Hey, you can see some little shiny glass, yeah, glass, in those rocks. . . . You can also see some pure glass if you look around.") He's a Navy captain, making the Apollo 12 crew all-Navy. Bean stands 5 feet 9½ and weighs 155 pounds. He was born in Wheeler, Texas, on March 15, 1932; graduated from high school in Fort Worth; and obtained a bachelor's degree in aeronautical engineering from the University of Texas in 1955. In that year he married a Texan, Sue Ragsdale of Dallas, and they have two children, Clay and Amy Sue. He received his Navy commission, via ROTC, upon graduation from college and soon was flying in an attack squadron. Later, as a test pilot, he flew jet, propeller, and helicopter models at the Naval Air Test Center, Patuxent River, Md. In all he has flown 27 kinds of aircraft and logged more than 3,500 hours of flying time, including about 3,000 hours in jet aircraft. Although he was backup command pilot for Gemini 10, Bean had to wait until Apollo 12 for his first voyage into space—a journey that took him all the way to the Ocean of Storms and its shiny rocks.

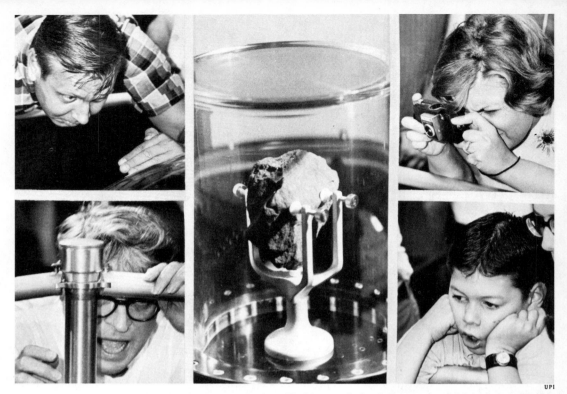

Moon rock on display at the Smithsonian Institution, Washington, D.C., drew crowds of interested spectators.

The Rocks Yield Some of Their Secrets

By Walter Sullivan
Science Editor, "The New York Times"

Until 1969, man's firsthand knowledge of materials from beyond the earth was essentially limited to a few meteorites that had survived their plunge through the earth's atmosphere. Even then, the sources of these meteorites could not be known with certainty. The flights of Apollo 11 and Apollo 12 introduced a whole new era of astronomy. For the first time, men could directly study the nature and the materials of another celestial body.

INVESTIGATIONS ON THE MOON

The primary and most important task assigned the astronauts of the first Apollo lunar landing mission was to collect rock and soil specimens and bring them back to earth. For this reason Neil Armstrong, almost immediately after stepping out on the moon's surface from his lunar module, had to gather "contingency" samples of rock—just in case an emergency should arise and a quick lift-off from the surface prove necessary.

Sample-Gathering. One of the major worries in planning the Apollo flights was how to protect the gathered samples from exposure to oxygen. The moon has virtually no atmosphere, and there was concern that any exposure of its rocks to the pure-oxygen atmosphere of the spacecraft would alter their chemical composition. Even more serious was the fear of an explosive reaction involving lunar dust in the spacecraft, since it was known from laboratory accidents on earth that some finely powdered substances (such as pure iron and nickel) oxidize with explosive speed when exposed to oxygen. Therefore, in order to isolate the samples from oxygen and other forms of contamination, the astronauts were provided with two vacuum-sealed "rock boxes" in which to bring home their specimens.

The astronauts carried tongs and a scoop to collect the samples from the surface. On earth a geologist records his observations in a field notebook, but this was impossible for the lunar pioneers. Instead they kept up a running commentary that was relayed by radio from their space suits to the lunar module and thence to giant receiving antennas on earth. There it was recorded for future reference at the Manned Spacecraft Center in Houston, Texas, 238,000 miles (383,000 km) away.

The men also were equipped with a special camera for making close-up pictures of the surface, since their inflated suits kept them from stooping with their hand-held cameras. The special camera viewed the surface through two lenses, producing images that could be viewed stereoscopically. It was mounted on an extension handle, making of the assembly a kind of walking stick whose lower end could be placed on a tiny crater or other feature to be photographed. The lower end was a hollow cylinder with a camera at its top, thus keeping the camera at the proper distance from the target area for perfect focus. A flashgun fired when a picture was taken and the film advanced for the next picture.

By the time the Apollo 11 manned exploration of the moon was completed, after 2 hours and 21 minutes of walking and setting up equipment, the astronauts had loaded 48 pounds (22 kg) of rock and soil into their sample boxes. The Apollo 12 crew collected even more material, returning with a total of 95 pounds (43 kg) of rock and soil.

Nature of the Surface. The lunar surface was a strange combination of slippery, powdery material and firm subsoil. The extremely fine powder of the surface clung to everything, including the rocks that were collected and the white space suits of the astronauts, and it was sufficiently slippery to require the men to walk carefully.

When the Apollo 11 lunar module landed, the blast of the descent engine blew up so much dust that, at an elevation of 100 feet (30 meters), the visibility of the astronauts was cut 75%. In fact, it was hard for them to judge their lateral motion during the last, critical seconds of their descent. Furthermore, the dust behaved in a most peculiar way in the airless, low-gravity environment, streaming away from the descending module in all directions and flying parallel to the lunar surface.

Yet the four legs of the Apollo 11 lunar module sank only 3 or 4 inches (about 8 to 9 cm) into the soil when it landed. (The Apollo 12 module sank in slightly farther.) When the astronauts tried to drive a flagpole into the ground, the staff would penetrate no more than about 7 inches (18 cm). So hard was the subsurface that when a tube was driven into the soil to collect a cross section of its top layers, hammering that was sufficient to dent the tube's upper rim drove the tube down only 8 or 9 inches (20 to 23 cm). Another pole was shoved into the ground, again with difficulty, in order to suspend a long scroll of aluminum foil for capturing particles of the "solar wind"—the stream of extremely thin and very high-velocity gases blowing out from the sun.

From the earth it had been observed that, as lunar craters of smaller and smaller size are cataloged, they become systematically more numerous. Photographs from unmanned spacecraft that preceded the Apollo flights to the moon showed that this pattern continued down to craters a few yards in diameter. Now the astronauts could see that the craters became even more numerous, down to the limits of their vision; some of the rocks were thoroughly pocked by tiny indentations. Armstrong compared these to craters made by BB shot.

Solder-like Deposits. However, what scientists in charge of the Apollo project classed as "the most interesting and unexpected" discovery on the surface was the coating of solder-like material on some small stones. These deposits, said the astronauts, "had a metallic luster and resembled blobs of solder splattered on an irregular surface." The rocks were found at the bottom of a half dozen small craters no more than 4 inches (10 cm) in diameter. Stereoscope pictures of the "solder" deposits made them appear even more remarkable—as though some little moon man had poured a little bit of the molten material here and there.

TABLE OF LUNAR DATA	
Diameter (linear)	2,160 mi
Average apparent (angular) diameter	0.5°
Average (mean) distance from earth	238,866 mi
Least distance from earth (at *perigee*)	221,463 mi
Greatest distance from earth (at *apogee*)	252,710 mi
Average *albedo* (reflectivity of surface)	0.07
Physical constants (earth = 1):	
Mass	0.0123
Surface area	0.074
Surface gravity	0.1645
Volume	0.02
Density	0.60
Mean geocentric horizontal *parallax*	57' 2.7"
Average daily angular motion in orbit	13°
Eccentricity of orbit	0.05490
Inclination of orbit to ecliptic plane	5° 8'
Inclination of orbit to earth's equator:	
Maximum	−28.5° to +28.5°
Minimum	−18.5° to +18.5°
Period of *sidereal* revolution and rotation—the time between two successive meridian transits of the same star	27^{d}7^{h}43^{m}11.5^s
Period of *synodical* revolution— from *conjunction* to *conjunction* (approximately new moon to new moon)	29^{d}12^{h}44^{m}2.8^s

Dr. Thomas Gold of Cornell University had a controversial explanation for the deposits. He suggested that, perhaps once every thousand years, the sun flares up to 100 times its normal brilliance for a period of 10 to 100 seconds. On the airless moon such a flare would melt the tops of rocks placed where the resulting heat would be most concentrated—namely, the centers of tiny craters.

However, the more conventional argument is that high-velocity impacts of small objects produce effects on the moon that are not seen on earth. Our planet is subjected to a constant rain of microscopic meteors moving at tremendous speed, but none of the small particles reach the surface except as slowly–falling dust. On the moon, such tiny particles hit the surface with as much velocity as the objects that carved some of the moon's giant craters. Material at the points of impact is melted and splashed in ways unknown on earth.

Seismic Studies. Two instrument packages set up with great care by the Apollo 11 astronauts were left behind on the moon. One of them was a unit designed to sense moonquakes, or tremors of the lunar surface, caused either by meteor impacts or by internal activities such as those that produce earthquakes on our own planet.

The seismic instrument package had to be levelled carefully and its adjustable antenna rod aimed so that its data would be radioed to earth. Then, in one of those remarkable feats characteristic of modern electronics, technicians in Houston sent a radio command to the instrument loosening the devices that had protected its four seismometers from vibration damage while in transit to the moon. Electrical energy was derived from sunlight by two solar panels unfolded by the astronauts from either side of the device, and the seismic package began radioing data back to earth. Scientists could monitor the jarring of the surface by the pounding of core tubes, the footfalls of the astronauts, the thumps of the life-support equipment units as the men threw them out of the lunar module before lift-off, and the shock of the lift-off itself.

In following days a succession of seismic "events" was observed. Some tremors were attributed to distant meteorite impacts and nearer landslides in craters. However, closer study of the data persuaded specialists that most of the tremors resulted from the periodic venting of remaining gases from tanks aboard the lunar module's lower stage, left behind when the astronauts took off in the upper stage. That is, as the sun climbed to the zenith after the astronauts had left, the lunar surface became very hot, and the expanding gas in the lower-stage tanks sought to escape.

The Apollo 11 seismometers, deriving their power from sunlight, could operate only during the two-week lunar day, and the working lifetime of the package was limited. The more elaborate instruments landed by the Apollo 12 team in November were powered by a nuclear battery, in which heat generated by radioactive decay was converted into electricity, so that the seismic unit of the Apollo 12 package was able to operate in lunar night as well as lunar day. It recorded a number of events assumed to be meteorite impacts. The strange thing about the tremors was that they grew in strength for a number of minutes, then gradually tapered off, lasting for remarkable lengths of time—sometimes close to an hour. It was as though something on the moon were ringing like a bell.

On earth the water content of soil and rock tends to absorb such tremors; but on the virtually waterless moon, when tremors are induced in an enclosed region (such as a sea of lava rock enclosed by mountains), seismic waves seem to flow back and forth across it like sound waves reverberating in a great hall.

When results from the Apollo 12 flight were at hand, it was possible to go back and reexamine the Apollo 11 seismic data and find similar events attributable to meteorite impacts. None were found that could be ascribed to internal activities such as those associated, on earth, with volcanoes and other quake-producing releases of tension.

Laser Experiment. The other instrument set up on the moon by the Apollo 11 astronauts was a device designed to reflect laser signals back to the earth. (The laser is an instrument that produces an extraordinarily narrow and intense light beam. Such a beam, aimed at the moon from the earth, illuminates only a few acres of the lunar surface; if directed by means of the optics of a large telescope, the beam would remain even narrower.) The purpose of the experiment was to attack a variety of problems that could be solved if very precise distance measurements were possible between points on the earth and a point on the moon.

With a laser reflector placed on the moon, the distances to that reflector from various observatories on earth could be obtained—it was hoped—to within a few inches by using laser pulses of extremely short duration (a few billionths of a second). By making the observations from different continents, it should be possible within a decade or so to determine whether the continents are in motion relative to one another, as proponents of the theory of continental drift now maintain. It should also be possible to determine whether or not the universal force of gravity is slowly weakening, as some theories propose; because if it is, the moon should be spiralling away from the earth slightly more than it would be merely as a result of purely dynamic factors (chiefly a by-product of tidal drag on the earth).

After some difficulties, the Lick Observatory in California and the McDonald Observatory in Texas both began to get laser flashes back from the reflector set up by the Apollo 11 astronauts. The observations will have to continue for several years before any results can be expected.

QUARANTINE TESTS AND RESULTS

One of the many worries of the men directing the Apollo program was that some harmful substance, or even a dangerous organism, might be brought back from this first venture to another celestial body. It was no coincidence that there appeared about this time a frightening science fiction novel by a Harvard Medical School student, *The Andromeda Strain*. The book described the almost total annihilation of a community by a "germ" brought back to earth by a returning spacecraft. Scientists feared that, even if the material brought back by the astronauts were harmless to human beings, it might attack other forms of life that constitute a vital link in the earth's

Close-up vew of the lunar surface was made by Apollo 11 crew. Half-inch lump at top is splashed with glassy material.

UPI

food chains—for example, the drifting plant life of the sea.

For this reason elaborate quarantine provisions were made for Apollo 11 (and repeated for Apollo 12). On returning to earth and before leaving their capsule as it bobbed in the Pacific Ocean, the astronauts were thrown isolation garments, including face masks. Their spacecraft and the specimen boxes were washed with disinfectant. The astronauts were hurried into a quarantine van that was unloaded from the ship in Hawaii, flown to Texas, and carried by truck to an elaborately equipped Lunar Receiving Laboratory in Houston. There the astronauts remained in isolation, along with the men attending and examining them, until specialists were satisfied that they harbored no dangerous germs.

Samples of lunar material were injected into (or otherwise exposed to) a wide range of plants and animals. The only notable discovery was that some plants grew better in soil enriched with moon dust than they did in ordinary earth soil. This, it was suspected, was because trace elements depleted in garden soil but needed by the plants were present in the moon dust.

ANALYSES OF LUNAR SOIL AND ROCK

While the astronauts were being checked out in their quarantine facility, the soil and rock specimens that they had collected were undergoing preliminary examination elsewhere in the same building. Specimen vacuum cabinets were used for this work, as were chambers filled with inert nitrogen gas. One of the tasks of the Lunar Receiving Laboratory, at this stage, was to select samples to be sent to laboratories in many parts of the world.

All told, more than 500 scientists in nine countries received samples of lunar material. The modern techniques of nuclear physics, electron microscopy, and magnetic and chemical analyses, among other kinds of investigation, enabled scientists to obtain a remarkably wide range of information from what looked like a heap of gray rocks and dust.

Age of the Moon. Probably the most exciting find, at least for its broad implications, was the antiquity of the lunar material. The dating of the Apollo 11 rocks showed that—as many scientists had hoped—the surface of the moon is extremely old and that its scars bear the record of events whose traces on earth have long been plowed under by mountain-building processes or worn away by weathering. The record may even go back to the final stages of planet formation, thus providing clues to how the earth itself was formed.

The ages of the samples were measured by using a variety of atomic "clocks" dependent on the decay of some radioactive substance into a staple product. In the lava-like rocks collected from the Sea of Tranquility, measurement was made of the extent to which rubidium 87 had turned into strontium 87; the rate of this process being known, it was possible to conclude that the specimens had not been heated substantially for the past 3.7 billion years. (Heating sets such "clocks" back to zero, like a stopwatch.) Another measurement, this time in terms of potassium 40's decay into argon 40, gave a similar age. This indicates that the catastrophic event that spread lava across the Sea of Tranquility occurred roughly 3.7 billion years ago, somewhat earlier than the formation of the oldest known rocks on the earth's surface. (A preliminary look at the Apollo 12 samples from the Sea of Storms seems to indicate that the area was flooded with lava a billion years later than the Apollo 11 site.)

Furthermore, the composite age of the lunar soil from the Sea of Tranquility was approximately 4.6 billion years, a billion years older than the lava-like rocks. The soil presumably is a collection of material thrown over the lunar surface by meteorite impacts or volcanic eruptions, and its age reflects the age of the moon as a whole. That age—4.6 billion years—is virtually identical to the age of many meteorites, and so it is assumed to represent the time that has elapsed since the planets, moons, and other bodies of the solar system coalesced from the cloud of dust and gas that also formed the sun.

Thus there begins to emerge a timetable of the moon's history. Its rugged highlands formed very early, and the outpourings that produced its dark "seas" occurred at widely spaced intervals later on. The vast extent of these level seas has been partially explained, as well, through analyses of the Apollo 11 rocks. That is, the composition of the rocks differs from that of similar lava flows, or basalts, on the earth, and the rocks were formed in an environment almost totally lacking in water and 100,000 times poorer in oxygen than the environment in which terrestrial basalts were produced. It has been calculated that such rock, when molten, would be ten times more fluid than a similar lava flow on earth, and hence would spread over great areas.

The very slow rate at which changes take place on the moon's surface was further indicated through the identification of radioactive elements synthesized, inside the rocks, by atomic nuclei—the so-called cosmic rays—hitting the moon almost at the speed of light. It was shown that one rock had lain on or near the lunar surface for 10 million years and within 6 feet (2

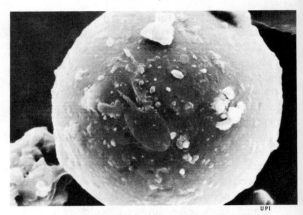

UPI

Glassy spherule (enlarged 6,600 times) was found among Apollo 11 lunar rocks. Shape indicates a former molten state.

meters) of the surface for at least 500 million years. It is estimated that the footprints of the astronauts may endure for thousands or even millions of years.

Composition of the Lunar Samples. From their chemistry it is evident that the Apollo 11 rocks originally crystallized at very high temperatures. Furthermore, the lunar material is poor in elements that melt at relatively low temperatures, such as potassium, chlorine, cesium, thallium, and rubidium; on the earth, these elements are thought to have made their way to the surface because of their relative volatility. One proposal based on these results of the Apollo studies is that the moon formed from a cloud of gas and dust at perhaps 2,000° F (nearly 1,100° C), so that many of the more volatile elements were driven from the cloud.

On the other hand, the lunar soil proved to be rich in gold, silver, copper, and zinc. These same elements are relatively plentiful in a remarkable class of meteorites known as carbonaceous chondrites, which, although found only rarely, are the most controversial meteorites because they contain a mixture of organic compounds, particularly hydrocarbons of the type found in petroleum. The compounds have been taken by some scientists as the residue of life that has evolved elsewhere in the solar system; however, the general view is that nature can manufacture such substances without any help from living organisms. In fact, it is suspected that this synthesis may have occurred very early in the life of the solar system, and the study of lunar soil has now encouraged an earlier suspicion that these peculiar meteorites are far more abundant wanderers through space than would be expected from their rarity on earth (they tend to disintegrate during passage through the atmosphere and dissolve in rain).

If, in fact, carbonaceous chondrites fall rather steadily on the moon and the earth, and have always done so, they may have contributed a substantial portion of the "starting material" that, on earth, eventually became organized into living structures. With respect to this possibility, although very few carbon compounds were found in the top inch or two of lunar soil, early Apollo 12 results indicated that the carbon content is considerably richer a foot or more down, where there is some protection from the devastating effects of solar and space radiation. It was found from laboratory tests that the lunar soil also serves as an effective thermal blanket, and there is probably little day-to-night temperature change three feet (about one meter) below the surface. (This fact, by the way, is an invitation for the construction of underground bases on the moon in the future.)

In studying the lunar samples, three minerals were identified that have not been seen on earth. However, all three were related to known minerals, and their existence on the moon could be explained in terms of the special environment there. Through analyses it was also found that the lunar rocks had about five times more magnetism than had been expected. This could be attributable to some past and unknown event or situation, such as the former existence of a core of churning molten rock within the moon, or the immersion of the moon within the earth's magnetic field.

Microscopic Studies. The lunar soil was observed to be extremely rich in glassy beads that, under the microscope, glittered in many colors: yellow, orange, purple, brown, and wine red. What a contrast to the drab appearance of the material when seen on a gross scale! Some of the beads were pocked on several sides by miniature craters. The supposition is that the beads were formed from splashes of molten rock that fell on the surface in a fiery rain after being thrown up by some cataclysmic event such as a meteorite impact or a volcanic explosion. As they spun in their flight (according to one proposition), they were bombarded by particles that produced the tiny craters.

Another remarkable discovery was that of candy-stripe patterns in the basalts known as pyroxenes. The bands were detected under a high-voltage electron microscope, and their machine-like uniformity and symmetry brought gasps from many of those who first saw them. Some scientists suggested that the bands represented a self-organization of iron atoms into crystal layers by some process unknown on earth. Others proposed that the banding was a so-called exsolution phenomenon that occurs when two substances that mix readily at high temperature are cooled and, becoming incompatible, separate into a series of uniform layers that alternate in composition.

Microscopic examinations of tiny tracks left in the moon rocks by high-energy particles from the sun inspired hopes for the birth of a new science—the "paleontology" of solar activity extending far into the solar system's past. Study of materials buried below the lunar surface revealed that they had once lain on the surface and been "wind-burned" by the solar wind, extending the possibilities of the sun's "fossil" record.

THE ACCOMPLISHMENT OF APOLLO 11

The results of the Apollo 11 mission did not resolve—nor are those of Apollo 12 likely to resolve—such basic questions concerning the moon as how it was formed, whether its interior is (or ever has been) hot, whether the great events that produced its seas have run their course or may recur, and whether those lunar events have been shared by the earth—for example, whether the earth has also been bombarded by gigantic meteors or asteroids. It is not clear whether the moon is a child or a sister of the earth, or whether the moon evolved elsewhere and was captured by the earth's gravity. Is the moon a heterogeneous collection of objects that were drawn together gravitationally and that never went through the melting and sorting processes that gave the earth its differentiated ores, granite mountains, and basaltic ocean basins? Or is the moon more like the earth in this respect?

A few answers can be proposed from what has been learned thus far. It seems unlikely that there has been extensive differentiation on the moon. Apollo 11 has also shown that, if the moon is indeed born of the earth, the event occurred more than 4.3 billion years ago—long before the time that has been suggested by some popular theories.

Thus, although the technological feat of Apollo 11 and the physical courage of the three men who flew the mission have not answered all the questions concerning the moon, they have greatly narrowed the choice of answers.

The moon remains one of the most challenging scientific puzzles confronted by man. Each new manned landing provides new clues to the puzzle, but each also imposes new constraints upon the theorist. "Now you must explain *this*," says the new specimen, the new laboratory finding. Perhaps, as with attempts to explain the origin of life or the nature of the universe, no complete answer ever will be forthcoming. But, to paraphrase a travel slogan, trying to get there is half the fun.

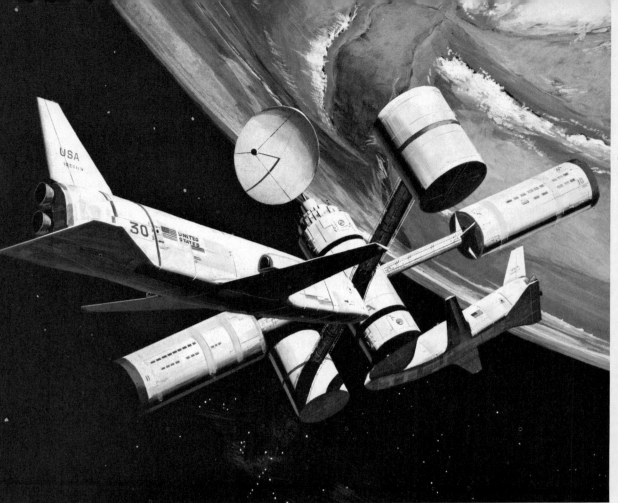

Winged giant shuttle craft, docked with space station in this drawing, unloads men and cargo before starting back to earth. Idea is one of several under study.

NASA Prepares for the Future

By Thomas O. Paine

Administrator, National Aeronautics and Space Administration

The National Aeronautics and Space Administration looks upon the manned lunar landings of 1969 as a beginning, rather than an end, of its program of space exploration. NASA planners already are busy with preliminary studies that will lead to bases on the moon as well as to permanent earth-orbital stations. From there they hope eventually to push out across the billions of miles of space that lie beyond in the solar system. Man, it is generally felt, will not be content to investigate the other planets with unmanned robot vehicles alone. The flights of Apollo 11 and Apollo 12 have brought a cautious confidence that man himself can play an increasingly useful and vital role in exploring this great new frontier.

Much must yet be learned, both about man and about the vehicles he is to use, before manned space exploration can attain its grander goals. Nevertheless, the achievements of the Apollo missions in setting up experiments on the moon's surface and bringing back lunar material for study already have provided more information about that celestial body than generations of astronomers had gained with earth-based telescopes and other instruments. These achievements are only a token of what human explorers could achieve in the future.

NASA currently has seven Apollo vehicles capable of flying to the moon. As part of the first phase of present plans for manned space exploration, the vehicles will be launched at the rate of two per year in 1970 and 1971, one in 1973, and two in 1974. Improved Apollo equipment will be introduced on the sixth flight to the moon, permitting the stay on the surface (now confined to about a day and a half) to be increased to three days. This will enable the astronauts to move about more effectively and carry out more ambitious studies and experiments.

In the second planned phase of exploration, emphasis will be placed on cost reduction. Lower costs may be brought about through a combination of means, one of the most important of which will be the development of reusable equipment, such as spacecraft that can make hundreds of flights. Another development will be the harnessing of nuclear power for space flights beyond the earth's orbit. In addition, a permanent orbiting space station can be constructed to serve as a research center and base of operations. Among other means, the launching of refueling stations also will be used to attain a more economical exploration program.

Space Shuttles. One crucial element in future plans is the development of a space shuttle that can run back and forth to earth for equipment and other necessary supplies. The shuttle will be the workhorse of the space program, performing a function equivalent to that of an elevator in a tall building. Its usefulness will extend to all three aspects of earth-moon space travel: between earth and earth orbit, between earth orbit and lunar orbit, and between lunar orbit and lunar surface.

Designed to be fully recoverable, the shuttle will be a two-stage vehicle that consists of a basic booster rocket and an upper-stage spacecraft capable of orbiting the earth. That is, it will be able to fly from the earth's surface into orbit, return to earth with people and items from the orbiting space station, make an airplane-type landing, be refueled, and go back into orbit, operating on a round-trip schedule between earth and space much as airplanes link cities and continents. Using a shuttle, orbital transportation costs are expected to be greatly reduced from what they are today. The aim will be to trim the cost of flying a payload into orbit from the present $1,000 or less per pound to perhaps 10% of that amount.

Preliminary studies on the space shuttle have already begun. Plans are proposed for a similar multipurpose "tug," a vehicle designed for use in outer space only. The tug would be used for communication from one spaceship to another.

Space Stations. Establishing a space station in orbit will make it possible for basic research to be carried out in a scientifically useful and stimulating environment. The first such station is planned for 1972 launching, in the form of a simple unit carrying three astronauts whose main task will be to see how the system works. This preliminary station would consist of three main parts: an Apollo spacecraft, a workshop made from an empty stage of a Saturn booster rocket, and a large astronomical telescope. The power source would be a panel of solar cells extending from the side of the workshop. Three of the four rooms in the workshop area would serve as sleeping compartments, with food preparation and waste management facilities also being housed in this section. Present plans call for at least 4,000 cubic feet (about 113 cubic meters) of living and working space for each man.

Bigger and more complex stations will be employed later on, such as a four-floor module capable of accommodating up to 12 men. Such stations will be designed so that they can be attached to one another. By the 1980's it may be possible to have as many as 100 scientists, engineers, and researchers in many disciplines engaged in activity at the same time in a permanent space station. The station would function as a laboratory where physical and biological experiments could be conducted on a continuing basis; the activities would include observational studies (including astronomy and earth-sensing) and onboard experiments in bioscience and high-energy physics. Astronomy, in particular, will benefit from being able to record celestial phenomena from outside the thick and increasingly polluted atmosphere of the earth. In addition the laboratory will be useful in testing advanced systems for further space exploration.

Large stations in the future will enable astronauts to travel to desired destinations in space and carry out other functions without having to return to earth after each mission. And, if the proposed search for fuel and other resources on the moon is successful, the moon could become a source of supplies for these large space stations, making unnecessary the more difficult and costlier flights from the earth to bring in such materials.

"Lunar Module White Room," a painting by Billy Morrow Jackson, depicts spacecraft being assembled.

NASA

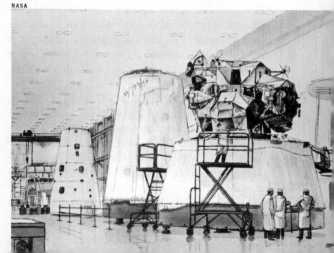

Lunar Bases. By studying the moon, scientists hope to understand the origin and evolution of the solar system and perhaps of life itself, and to gain more knowledge of the dynamic processes that shape the earth's environment. The eventual goal of manned lunar exploration is to utilize earth's nearest neighbor for the benefit of mankind; the moon, it is to be remembered, is a whole new world with a surface area of several million square miles. What actual uses will be made of the moon in the more immediate future will depend, of course, on a wide variety of developments here on earth.

In the meantime, NASA has prepared studies of possible semipermanent and permanent lunar bases that can be served by surface or near-surface transportation systems. As envisaged, the lunar base system would consist of a family of prefabricated modules flown to the moon and assembled. This manner of construction would be adaptable to a wide range of missions, from small outposts manned by from 2 to 18 men, to larger and more permanent installations.

Within available technology, provision could be made for men to remain on the lunar surface for as long as six months, but under present plans a lunar colony will not be developed very rapidly. It is expected to grow progressively from a few relatively simple modules—for shelter, laboratory facilities, power supply, and life support—to a larger complex of modules. The original module may be no more than the Apollo lunar landing craft together with other equipment placed on the moon before, after, or at the same time as the astronauts land. Next would come semipermanent scientific bases. Then, if a permanent colony does appear feasible, it would be built as an expansion of the scientific bases or at a new and carefully chosen site.

Future developments will decide the physical choices in setting up the lunar base. For example, a surface base would be more accessible, could be assembled and equipped easily, and would be adaptable to expansion, but it would offer poor protection against meteorites and cosmic and solar radiation and would otherwise be more vulnerable to environmental damage. On the other hand, subsurface bases would be better protected but would be more difficult to install and connect.

The answer to these alternatives may lie in excavating and backfilling with lunar materials. Under this plan, the modules would be placed on the surface and connected, after which they would be covered for protection. The basic module would be designed for a year of unattended storage prior to use. It would be a shelter capable of housing several men, and it would have integral life support, power, and communications equipment so arranged that it could function virtually alone as a small temporary outpost. However, all but the most temporary outposts eventually would also be served by a central life support system, and slightly larger outposts would have nuclear power plants as their basic source of energy.

The Uses of a Lunar Colony. The time schedule for setting up a lunar colony depends upon the attitude of Congress toward such a major venture into space, and the resulting size of the appropriations granted to such a program. Sufficient reasons for establishing a base on the moon would not appear difficult to find.

A permanent or semipermanent lunar colony will be essential to a really thorough exploration of the moon, because traverses and extended geological surveys will be needed to verify and refine data sent earlier by remote-sensor probes. The base would provide an environment for optical and radio astronomy installations that would be far superior to that of a space station, and could serve as an operational base for wide-ranging scientific investigations—for example, eventual manned missions to the other planets. Experiments in physics, chemistry, biology, physiology, and applied sciences that are difficult or impossible to perform on earth could be carried out easily in the airless and exposed lunar environment, without the restraints imposed by the size and limited facilities of a space station.

More practical applications also suggest themselves in the establishment of a lunar base. For example, earthly plants seem to thrive when placed in the samples of lunar soil brought back by the Apollo astronauts. If a source of water can be found on or below the lunar surface—possibly as a constituent of some minerals—the time may not be too far off when gardens can be cultivated and other food sources developed on the moon. Man's physical strength and other capabilities also are extended by the moon's lower gravity—one-sixth that of the earth. This fact suggests immediately useful applications in activities at a lunar base, and also suggests interesting new avenues of biomedical research to be explored.

Whatever man's fate is to be on the moon, it is fairly safe to predict that the next decade or two will bring great changes in the ease with which space flights are accomplished. The day seems to be drawing closer when it will be not only the trained astronaut who can go into space and stay for varying periods of time. The scientist, and perhaps even the ordinary tourist, may also become space travelers in increasing numbers in the not too distant future.

U. S. MARINES IN THE A SHAU VALLEY (UPI PHOTO)

PEACE DEMONSTRATORS IN WASHINGTON, D. C. (UPI PHOTO)

REVIEW OF THE YEAR

ACCIDENTS AND DISASTERS

Accidents are the leading cause of death for persons aged 1 to 37, and are the fourth largest killer in the United States.

Accidents in the United States. The National Safety Council reported 115,000 accidental deaths in 1968, an increase of 2% over 1967. Accidental deaths during the first nine months of 1969 totaled 86,300.

Motor-vehicle accidents claimed 41,160 U. S. lives during the first nine months of 1969. A total of 55,200 persons died in traffic accidents in 1968. Half of these deaths involved drinking drivers.

During the first nine months of 1969, home accidents killed 19,800 persons, public nonautomotive accidental deaths totaled 17,300, and work accidents claimed the lives of 10,700 persons.

New U. S. Highway Standards. In an effort to reduce deaths and injuries on U. S. highways, the National Highway Safety Bureau issued several new standards for motor vehicles and state highway safety programs. New standards promulgated for 1969 cars included lamps and reflective devices, hood latch systems for each hood, and head restraints. Other standards govern headlight concealment devices, door locks, and tires. New standards for state highway safety programs dealt with improvement of police traffic service, pedestrian safety, and post-crash hazard control and cleanup.

Drinking Drivers. The Department of Transportation's 1968 report to Congress on *Alcohol and Highway Safety* concluded that "alcohol has been the largest single factor leading to fatal crashes."

Legislation. Congress was considering several versions of the Occupational Safety and Health Act of 1969, designed to provide optimum on-the-job safety for the nation's employed. All versions included provisions to insure safe and healthful work-

ACCIDENT FATALITY TOLL IN THE UNITED STATES

Year	Total[1]	Motor vehicle	Public nonmotor vehicle	Home	Work
1962	97,139	40,804	17,000	28,500	13,700
1963	100,669	43,564	17,500	28,500	14,200
1964	105,000	47,700	18,500	28,000	14,200
1965	108,004	49,163	19,500	28,500	14,100
1966	113,563	53,041	20,000	29,500	14,500
1967	112,000	53,100	20,000	28,500	14,200
1968	115,000	55,290	20,500	28,500	14,300
1969 (Jan.–Sept.)	86,300	41,160	17,300	19,800	10,700

[1] Duplications among motor vehicle, work, and home accidents are eliminated in total. Sources: National Center for Health Statistics and National Safety Council.

ing conditions, authorized appropriate authorities to set health and safety standards, offered assistance to states in their efforts to eliminate on-the-job accidents, and provided for research, education, and training in the field of occupational safety and health.

The Clean Air Act was amended to provide for planning grants to air-pollution control agencies, establish interstate control agencies, and authorize establishment of air quality standards. The amendment increased federal responsibility for dealing with air pollution. Funds of $45 million were authorized for research on air pollution caused by fuel combustion.

Congress passed a new Federal Coal Mine Safety Act, extending federal jurisdiction to surface mines, establishing standards for coal dust levels, and streamlining enforcement procedures. (See also MINING.)

More Airports. The Federal Aviation Administration's National Airport Plan authorized construction of 808 new airports, 31 heliports, and four seaplane bases in the next five years to relieve congestion, a cause of air crashes.

HOWARD PYLE
President, National Safety Council

AUTO PILE-UP on the fog-shrouded New Jersey Turnpike on November 29, during the Thanksgiving weekend, resulted in 5 deaths. Twenty persons were injured.

UPI

HUMAN LIFELINE is formed by British soldiers to bring sailors ashore from a Greek tanker driven aground on a reef off Malta by a sudden gale, September 23. Only one of the crewmen was lost.

AIRPLANE CRASH on June 23 in a business district of Miami, near the airport, killed 10 persons, including 6 on the ground. The broken tail of the Dominican Airlines DC-4 can be seen at upper left.

MAJOR ACCIDENTS AND DISASTERS OF 1969

AVIATION

Jan. 5—Afghan jetliner crashes into house while attempting landing in fog in Gatwick, England, killing 50 persons, including 2 on ground, and injuring 15.

Jan. 18—Denver-bound United Air Lines Boeing 727 jetliner falls into Pacific during rainstorm after take-off from Los Angeles International Airport, killing all 38 persons on board.

Feb. 18—Airliner vanishes in Nevada desert during snowstorm while returning 35 persons from Nevada gambling resort to southern California.

March 16—In history's worst air disaster, Venezuelan airliner with 83 persons on board crashes into Maracaibo suburb, killing total of 155 persons and injuring 100.

March 20—UAR airliner crashes at Aswan, killing 87 persons and injuring 14.

April 2—Polish airliner crashes on mountain near Czech border, claiming 53 lives.

April 16—Congolese Air Force plane crashes into Congo River near Kinshasa, killing all 45 persons on board.

April 22—All 44 persons on board Indian aircraft die when plane crashes near Khulna, East Pakistan.

June 4—Mexican tennis star Rafael Osuna and political leader Carlos Madrazo are among 79 persons to die as Mexican jetliner crashes on mountain near Monterrey.

July 13—Royal Nepal Airlines DC-3 catches fire and crashes near Simra, Nepal, killing all 35 persons on board.

July 26—Two of 37 persons on board an Algerian airliner survive a crash in the desert near Algiers.

Sept. 9—Collision near Indianapolis, Ind., between Allegheny Airlines jet and small private plane kills all 82 persons on board airliner and pilot of small plane.

Sept. 12—Philippine Airlines jetliner crashes in Manila suburb, killing 45 of the 47 persons on board.

Sept. 21—U. S. military jet and Air Vietnam DC-4 collide near Danang airstrip, killing all 75 persons on airliner and 2 others on ground.

Sept. 21—Mexicana Airlines jet crash-lands in Mexico City, killing 27 of the 118 persons on board.

Dec. 3—Paris-bound Air France jetliner crashes into Caribbean after take-off from Caracas, Venezuela, killing all 62 persons on board.

Dec. 8—All 90 persons on board Olympics Airways DC-6B die in crash on Mt. Panelon near Athens.

HURRICANE CAMILLE battered the Gulf Coast in August. A house at Gulfport, Miss., was deposited on tracks.

WIDE WORLD

EARTHQUAKES

Jan. 3—Iranian province of Khurasan is struck by earthquake killing 50 persons and injuring 300.

March 28—Earthquake kills 53 persons and causes heavy damage in Alaşehir, Turkey.

July 25—Most destructive earthquake of 1969 strikes eastern China, south of Tientsin, killing approximately 3,000 persons.

Oct. 1—About 80 persons die and several villages are destroyed as earthquake strikes Huancayo, Peru.

Oct. 27—A major earthquake levels town of Banja Luka, Yugoslavia; 20 persons die and 400 are injured.

FLOODS AND LANDSLIDES

Jan. 18–26—Heavy rains cause flooding in southern California, killing 91 persons and causing $35 million damage.

Feb. 23—Tidal waves generated by earthquake kill 600 persons on western coast of island of Sulawesi, Indonesia.

March 17—At least 218 persons drown and hundreds are missing as flash flood sweeps Mundau Valley in Alagoas, Brazil.

April 23—Tidal wave swamps 680 square miles (1,760 sq km) in mainland China's Shantung province, endangering 100,000 persons; the number of casualties is unreported.

Aug. 25—Mountain slides in western Virginia, touched off by hurricane Camille, kill 189.

Sept. 15—At least 250 persons are dead, 90 are missing, and more than 60,000 are homeless as South Korea suffers worst floods in 10 years.

LAND AND SEA TRANSPORTATION

Jan. 14—Fire and explosions on U.S.S. *Enterprise* off Hawaii kill 27 men and injure 83.

March 21—Power failure causes crash of train and locomotive near São Paulo, Brazil, killing 30–40 persons and injuring more than 300.

March 25—Head-on train crash kills 20 and injures 70 persons in La Louvière, Belgium.

April 7—Freighter and string of oil barges collide and explode in Mississippi River at New Orleans, La., leaving 26 persons unaccounted for.

June 2—Australian aircraft carrier *Melbourne* collides with U. S. destroyer *Evans* in South China Sea, killing 74 men aboard the *Evans*.

June 16—Iranian troop ship sinks in Persian Gulf with loss of 480 officers and men.

June 21—Barge sinks in Zambezi River in Mozambique, with loss of 108 of 150 Portuguese troops on board.

July 15—Train carrying Hindu pilgrims collides with freight in Jaipur, India, killing 85 persons and injuring 130.

July 30—Train collides with tank cars in southern Yugoslavia, killing 29 persons and injuring 17.

July 30—Launch capsizes in Godavari River, Andhra, India, drowning 50 persons.

Sept. 8—Bus plunges into 600-foot ravine near Ankara, Turkey, killing 13 persons and injuring 50.

Oct. 2—Bus bursts into flames after collision with truck in Lima, Peru, killing 21 persons and severely burning 25.

Dec. 23—Bus crash in Erivan, Soviet Armenia, may have killed as many as 100 persons, although there is no announcement of official casualty figures.

STORMS

April 14—Cyclone strikes East Pakistan at 90 miles per hour, killing at least 540 persons and injuring more than 1,000.

July 4—Ohio's worst natural disaster leaves 41 dead, as severe storms and flooding from Lake Erie hit northern part of state.

July 7—Atlantic storm kills 23 along French coast in Brittany and Normandy and leaves 8 persons missing on British side of English Channel.

Aug. 18—Second strongest hurricane ever to reach United States, Camille, kills 149 persons in Gulf coast area.

Sept. 27—Typhoon Elsie, traveling at 120 miles per hour, kills at least 47 persons, injures 66, and leaves 2 missing in Taiwan.

MISCELLANEOUS

March 31—Explosions in the Altos Hornos coal mines in northern Mexico kill 156 miners.

June 15—Fifty-seven die and 139 are injured as mountain restaurant in San Rafael, near Madrid, Spain, collapses.

July 7—Coal dust explodes in mine near Taipei, Taiwan, leaving 24 miners dead and 53 injured.

Nov. 7—Dynamite explosion in gold mine near Johannesburg, South Africa, kills 64 miners and injures 14.

Dec. 2—Fire in home for aged at Notre-Dame-du-loc, Quebec, kills 54 persons; 22 others escape.

ADEN. See SOUTHERN YEMEN.

ADVERTISING

Although its practitioners and critics may think otherwise, advertising is largely a reflection of sociological and economic trends. Thus in 1969 there was more nudity in advertising, as there was on the bathing beaches and in the entertainment world. And expenditures on advertising increased 7% over 1968—a gain following the overall economy rather than leading it.

Revenues. Total spending on advertising in 1969 was $19.3 billion, compared with $18 billion in 1968. Television advertising again led the field. National advertising on network and spot television was $2.9 billion, up 8% over 1968. Expenditures on radio—network and spot—hit $440 million to post a 7.2% gain, the second highest among media.

The other media tagged along with the economy. National advertising in newspapers in 1969 was $1.1 billion, up 4%; in business papers (trade and merchandising publications), $725 million, up 1.5%; and in outdoor billboards and posters, $142 million, up 4%.

National advertising in all other media (including direct mail, point-of-purchase displays, and specialties such as matchbooks and ballpoint pens) increased 5.4% to $4.9 billion. That brought total spending by national advertisers to $11.5 billion, a gain of 5.7% over 1968. Local advertisers spent $7.9 billion, or 8.9% more than in 1968.

The continued growth of television as a medium for mass advertising was responsible for the demise in 1969 of the *Saturday Evening Post* and the *This Week* Sunday newspaper supplement, both of which had large readerships. They died for lack of adver-

KENYON & ECKHARDT, INC., FOR SHELL OIL CO.

PUBLIC-INTEREST advertising by large corporations is appearing more frequently, as in this appeal to preserve the nation's landscape by avoiding litter.

tising revenue in a society where most mass communications media depend on advertising for support. Magazines and newspapers have continued to post absolute gains in advertising revenue, although their share of the advertising dollar has decreased.

Cigarette Ads. Print media may benefit from restrictions on cigarette advertising on television and radio, which began to manifest themselves in 1969. Westinghouse's Group W stations imposed an outright ban. The National Association of Broadcasters decided to bar all cigarette advertising by September 1971, a major decision because $235 million in annual advertising revenue is involved. Cigarette advertisers, however, planned to withdraw from broadcast media even before that date, with the aim of forestalling a congressional ban on cigarette advertising in all media.

The official position of the advertising associations was that, if a product is legal, advertising for it is legitimate and productive. On the other hand, the Supreme Court in 1969 upheld the requirement by the Federal Communications Commission for broadcasters to carry anti-cigarette advertisements.

"Games" and the FTC. Also on the governmental front, the Federal Trade Commission ruled that advertisers promoting "sweepstakes" and "games" must disclose the odds of winning and the prizes that actually would be granted. (Many prizes offered in advertising have not actually been won, and the odds of winning have not been as encouraging as the public has thought.) After the FTC action, sweepstakes and games became less interesting to advertisers as a promotional tool.

Despite such activities, the FTC came under

TRAFFIC SAFETY received an eye-stopping, thought-provoking assist with this advertisement, created by the Advertising Council, an industry body.

NEEDHAM, HARPER & STEERS FOR THE ADVERTISING COUNCIL

Mrs. Gordon never bothered with safety belts just to go to the beauty shop.

What's *your* excuse?

Advertising contributed for the public good

Now Art

"Yellow Submarine" art sailed into many TV and print ads in 1969. The school traces its name and current popularity to the Beatles' movie that featured childlike drawings with exotic shapes and bright hues. Ad men also call it "now art" and "the art of today." Leading exponents of "Yellow Submarine" art include Milton Glaser and Peter Max.

heavy attack by consumer groups, crusader Ralph Nader, and an American Bar Association panel appointed by President Nixon. The panel found that the commission is ineffectual against many deceptive practices, and it advised the president either to strengthen the FTC or to disband it. Casper Weinberger, the new FTC chairman, vowed greater consumer protection.

The Brighter Side. On the whole, however, advertising continued to be regarded as a positive economic and social activity, and it flourished. Sears Roebuck, which specializes in private brands that would seem to need the least amount of advertising, increased its annual advertising expenditure to $50 million. Interpublic, Inc., the conglomerate of advertising agencies that had apparently overextended itself, reported a profit. J. Walter Thompson, the world's largest advertising agency, became a public corporation with a glowing profit picture.

WALTER JOYCE
Editor, "Marketing/Communications"

AEROSPACE INDUSTRY

The U. S. aerospace industry in 1969 achieved its greatest triumph—the landing of men on the moon—but, paradoxically, the industry was facing more difficulties than at perhaps any time since the late 1950's.

In 1969, for the first time since 1955, the industry's total sales declined below the level of the previous year. In Congress, the aerospace manufacturers were under heavy fire for their role in the so-called "military-industrial complex" and for extensive cost increases on several projects. A slight decline in the growth rate of air travel, coupled with an economic squeeze on the airline industry, caused a slow-up in the sale of commercial airliners. There were widespread layoffs among the aerospace manufacturers as sales slipped, and in the stock market the industry's problems were reflected by a continuing slump in the price of aerospace stocks.

Sales. Sales for the year were approximately $28.5 billion, a decline of about 3.4% from the 1968 record high of $29.5 billion. Military and commercial aircraft sales accounted for $15.6 billion; space systems and satellites, $4.9 billion; and missiles and nonaerospace products, $8 billion.

A major reason for the sales decline was a slow-up in the ordering of new airliners. Many airlines had placed large orders during 1968 for the new generation of large-capacity, wide-fuselage jumbo jets, such as the 362-passenger Boeing 747, and were awaiting their delivery before ordering additional planes. Also, generally depressed airline profits prompted some airlines to delay or cancel some orders for new jets. Of the industry's backlog for commercial jets at the close of 1969, about $2.9 billion represented orders from foreign airlines.

Sales of satellites and space vehicles declined by more than $300 million, reflecting a continued decline in U. S. government space expenditures after the outlay for the Project Apollo lunar landing program hit a peak in the 1965–67 period. Another factor was the cancellation of the Air Force's Manned Orbiting Laboratory, a two-man satellite that was to have been used for photographic reconnaissance and other intelligence-gathering missions over foreign countries. The MOL fell victim to congressional pressures on the Pentagon to cut spending.

One area of growing sales for the industry was "general aviation" aircraft. This term applies to private and business aircraft, or all planes except those used by the military or airlines. Sales of these planes, used for travel by corporate executives as well as by amateur pilots, increased by about 16% over 1968. This segment of the aerospace market is expected to continue its growth at a brisk rate. According to government projections, the 1969 fleet of 122,000 general aviation aircraft is expected to more than double by 1980.

Employment. Aerospace remained the nation's largest manufacturing industry. Because of the slowed pace in the space program, fewer orders for new airliners, and the cancellation of several major defense projects, total employment dropped by more than 5%, to about 1.2 million persons. Scientists and engineers compose about 16% of the industry's employment. The employment is heaviest along the West Coast, with 41% of the total, and in the New England-Mid-Atlantic region, with 19%.

Highlights of the Year. The first landings by men on the moon, close-up photography of Mars by two Mariner spacecraft, and the first flight of the giant Boeing 747 were the major successes of the nation's aerospace industry in 1969. The industry, together with two of its principal customers, the Department of Defense and the National Aeronautics and Space Administration, encountered mounting criticism in Congress and among some segments of the public about its operations and objectives.

The criticism reached a peak after a congressional investigation disclosed that the Air Force's C5A program to develop the world's largest airplane had exceeded its budget by $2 billion. Congressional pressure caused a cutback in orders for the F-111 fighter and a bomber version of the F-111, as well as cancellation of the MOL and a new Army helicopter known as the Cheyenne.

The Defense Department nevertheless weathered other congressional attacks and pushed ahead with some projects that lifted the fortunes of the aerospace industry. President Nixon's proposal to deploy

HOUND DOG missiles go through an IRAN (inspect and repair as necessary) line at an aerospace plant in Tulsa, Okla. Weapons are made for the U. S. Air Force.

NORTH AMERICAN ROCKWELL CORPORATION

the Safeguard antiballistic missile program was approved by a narrow margin. Development of a new Navy fighter, the F-14A, was authorized. Another step that promised to help the industry's sales on a long-term basis was the President's decision supporting development of a supersonic transport (SST).

Diversification. Because of its success at the frontiers of technology, the aerospace industry has sought to apply its skills to nonaerospace problems, using the "systems approach," the technique it developed for managing large missile and space projects. In essence, the systems approach involves dividing a large project into many small problems and, through extensive use of computers, planning and coordinating the multifaceted developments so that they mesh successfully within a manageable timeable. Although the industry's diversification programs so far produce less than 5% of its total sales, the sales are growing in such fields as marine technology and oceanography, education, medicine, law enforcement, computerized information systems, transportation, and waste management.

The Future. Aerospace industry economists expect the downward trend in aerospace sales to continue in 1970. They also expect that the industry will have to continue to face public questions about the value and role in society of some of its projects at a time when other urgent demands will be competing for tax dollars.

(See also AIR TRANSPORTATION; AIR FORCE; MISSILES; SPACE EXPLORATION.)

ROBERT H. LINDSEY
Aviation Reporter, "The New York Times"

AFGHANISTAN

In 1969, Afghanistan held its second free elections since the promulgation of the 1964 constitution. On the economic scene, there was a significant increase in private enterprise investments.

Political Developments. In May, student protests against nepotism in the Ibn Sena high school in Kabul resulted in repressive police action. Beginning in June, almost all students in Kabul joined in a 48-day strike led by Kabul University students. The protesters primarily demanded that the government punish those responsible for sending police and troops to the campus. The government closed the university on July 9, and it remained closed until November 6. Leftist student leaders then attempted to begin a new round of demonstrations but were only partly successful.

The "do-nothing" 12th Parliament was replaced by the more conservative 13th Parliament, after nation-wide elections held in August and September. Legally, Afghanistan has no political parties, although informal groupings cover the entire political spectrum. King Mohammed Zahir Shah asked Nur Ahmad Etemadi (prime minister since late 1967) to form a new government. The 13th Parliament approved the Etemadi cabinet on December 2, after two weeks of speeches broadcast by radio to all parts of the country.

The Economy. The third 5-year plan (1967–72) lies practically moribund as the government attempts to complete projects begun under the first two plans. There continued to be limited progress on the three major irrigation-land reclamation projects (U. S.-supported Helmand Valley, Soviet-supported Nangrahar project, and Communist Chinese-supported Parwan project).

AFGHANISTAN

Information Highlights

Area: 249,999 square miles (647,497 sq km).
Population: 16,113,000 (1968 est.).
Chief Cities (1967 census): Kabul, the capital, 456,342; Kandahar, 123,938; Herat (1964 census), 62,000; Mazar-i-sharif, 40,000.
Government: *King*—Mohammed Zahir Shah (acceded Nov. 8, 1933); *Prime Minister*—Nur Ahmad Etemadi (took office 1967). *Parliament* (Shura)—House of the Elders (Meshrano Jirga), 84 members, House of the People (Wolesi Jirga), 216 members.
Religious Faiths: Sunni Muslims, 99% of population.
Education: *Literacy rate* (1969), 10% of population. *Total school enrollment* (1968)—532,402 (primary, 447,347; secondary, 68,013; teacher-training, 6,296; technical/vocational, 7,320; university/higher, 3,426).
Finance (1969 est.): *Revenues*, $128,800,000; *expenditures*, $146,600,000; *monetary unit*, afghani (70-75 afghanis equal U. S.$1).
Gross National Product (1967): $1,355,000,000.
Economic Indexes (1967): *Agricultural production*, 130 (1952–56=100); *cost of living* (1961), 98 (1958=100).
Manufacturing (metric tons, 1967): Cement, 124,000; sugar, 10,000; cotton yarn, 900; lumber, 570,000 cubic meters; sawn wood, 90,000 cubic meters.
Crops (metric tons, 1967–68 crop year): Sugar beets, 60,000; cottonseed, 44,000; cotton (lint), 22,000.
Minerals (metric tons, 1967): Bituminous coal, 152,000; salt, 32,000.
Foreign Trade (1966): *Exports*, $69,530,000 (chief exports, 1967: fruits and nuts, $30,103,000; karakul skins, $23,945,-000; cotton, $13,197,000; carpets, $8,686,000); *imports*, $66,680,000 (chief imports, 1967: petroleum, $8,988,000; sugar, $8,760,000). *Chief trading partners* (1967): USSR (took 33% of exports, supplied 48% of imports); United States (took 8% of exports, supplied 30% of imports); India (took 16% of exports, supplied 5% of imports).
Transportation: *Roads* (1968), 9,000 miles (14,484 km); *motor vehicles* (1967), 45,100 (automobiles, 27,600); *national airline*, Ariana Afghan; *principal airports*, Kandahar, Kabul.
Communications: *Telephones* (1968): 9,800; *radios* (1965), 200,000; *newspapers* (1966), 18 (daily circulation, 101,000).

Decreased foreign assistance from the major powers was partly made up for by increased United Nations assistance.

The Private Investment Law of 1967 brought about a surprising increase in private investments. By October, 35 new companies had begun operation with Afghan capital amounting to about 85% of the total investment. Tax laws and collection procedures were still woefully inadequate, and the drive to increase foodstuff production lagged far behind earlier favorable predictions. Tourism continued to be a major industry, and a new Intercontinental Hotel opened in Kabul.

Foreign Affairs. Afghanistan, a non-aligned country, sent delegates to a consultative meeting of nonaligned nations in Belgrade, Yugoslavia, in July, and to the abortive summit meeting of Muslim states held in Rabat, Morocco, in September. Afghanistan's relations with neighboring states continued to be good during 1969.

King Mohammed Zahir Shah paid visits to Nepal in February and to Japan in April. Both Soviet Premier Aleksei Kosygin and U. S. Secretary of State William Rogers visited Kabul in May, and Mrs. Indira Gandhi, prime minister of India, arrived in June.

LOUIS DUPREE
NANCY HATCH DUPREE
American Universities Field Staff

MOHAMED AMIN, FROM KEYSTONE

Political assassination continued to mar the African scene in 1969. Mourners surround the coffin of Tom Mboya, Luo tribesman and secretary-general of Kenya's ruling KANU party, killed on July 5.

AFRICA

It is tempting to describe the year 1969 in Africa by the question-begging term "normal." In using such a term one refers primarily to the absence of any spectacular changes. Situations in Africa in recent years have developed a persistence that prolongs them in a substantially unchanged form, even when the situation itself is so critical that it would appear that it must be resolved one way or another in short order.

There were no major outbreaks of violence, apart from the appalling civil war in Nigeria, which continued all year, ending abruptly, after 30 months, early in 1970. Lesser civil wars continued in Chad and Sudan. In the Congo (Kinshasa), chief scene of civil strife earlier in the decade, public order seemed to be becoming more firmly established.

All in all, however, it would be an exaggeration to call 1969 a good year for Africa. The authority of existing states was being undermined almost everywhere by the divisive force of tribalism. As a method of changing governments, the coup d'etat was more common than the peaceful election, and there were several instances of political assassination. Economic advance was minimal, and in some states the economy was declining.

There was a widespread feeling of exasperation in Africa as the world's attention veered to other areas of immediate crisis, notably the Middle East and the Far East. This tendency to behave as if salvation must come from outside the continent was, itself, a symptom of African weakness. In general, the euphoria of the early 1960's in Africa had given way, inevitably but depressingly, to the workaday, grim realities of the late 1960's. Economic problems and the sometimes desperate attempts to maintain national unity were the primary order of business, rather than ambitious and flamboyant plans for international action or African unity.

POLITICAL TURMOIL

Tribalism. Events in 1969 underlined the extent to which the principal focus of the loyalty of the ordinary African remains the tribe, rather than that novel and often largely hypothetical entity, the nation-state to which he happens to belong. For the most part, the African states are somewhat artificial constructions. They were formed on a possibly inappropriate model—the European nation-state. Their boundaries are a legacy of the days of European imperialism; yet no African state wishes to lose territory in any boundary readjustment.

Tribalism in tropical Africa may be said to be *the* primary social and anthropological reality. It provides—particularly for the poor and uneducated—economic aid, security, continuity, and a sense of identity. These are great social boons, not lightly to be cast aside. Nevertheless, from the point of view of the governments of African states, tribalism is more and more turning into a divisive nightmare that undermines the possibility of state-wide cohesion. The sense of being a member of the whole nation rather than the tribe will take time to build up; meanwhile, the new state may fall apart. The seriousness of the question is increased by the fact that the generation of detribalized leaders who brought Africa to independence is tending to lose influence; indeed many of its leaders are dead.

The problem is ubiquitous in sub-Saharan Africa. The most glaring example is Nigeria, referred to below. Other striking instances are provided currently

47

GILLES CARON, GAMMA—PIX

ROADSIDE BURIAL is given a 6-year-old Biafran boy, one of thousands to die of hunger in the civil war.

by the states of Ghana, Chad, Sudan, and Kenya.

Ghana. The National Liberation Council, which has ruled Ghana since the overthrow of Nkrumah's dictatorship in 1966, actually did perform its promise to permit a return to civilian rule. In the election of August 29, the Progress party of Kofi Busia was overwhelmingly successful, taking three fourths of the 140 seats in the Legislature. Unfortunately, the tribal implications of the election cast a cloud over the picture of democracy in action. The National Alliance of Liberals (NAL), the main opposition party, led by the controversial Komla Gbedemah, won all of its 29 seats in areas not inhabited by the majority Akan tribes—in fact mostly in Ewe areas. No Ewe has been given office in the new cabinet. There is thus an unfortunate tendency for a correlation to arise between membership of the Akan tribes and support of the Busia government on one side, and Ewe affiliation and the opposition on the other. To make matters worse, the Ewe of Ghana live in areas adjacent to the Ewe of Togo. The movement for an independent Ewe state could reemerge at any time.

Chad. The rebellion of the northern, nomadic, Arabic tribes of Chad against the southerners who dominate the government in Fort-Lamy, which began in August 1968, continued in 1969 and claimed thousands of lives. The government of President Tombalbaye has been receiving military help under treaty from France, and about 2,000 French troops, half belonging to the Foreign Legion, have been involved in the struggle. The French were anxious to reduce their involvement if possible, but it was felt in both Fort-Lamy and Paris that Chad should be upheld as a buffer against the seepage of seditious influences southward from the radical Arab states of Sudan and Libya into French-speaking states such as Cameroon, Gabon, and Ivory Coast, all of which maintain excellect relations with France.

Sudan. In some respects the Sudanese political situation is the reverse of that in Chad. Here too, there is a great gulf between the Islamic, Arabic-speaking north and the negroid, Christian or pagan tribes of the south. But in Sudan the seat of political power is in the north. Since 1955, the year before Sudanese independence, the southerners have been waging a grueling war against what they regard as their northern oppressors. It was uncertain what would be the long-run effect on the Sudanese civil war of the leftist, military-backed takeover by a junta, which on May 25 overthrew the government of Mohammed Mahgoub and assumed absolute power. Since the tone of the new regime's first acts was harsh and struck a note of Arabic solidarity, it seemed unlikely that the change would mean improvement in the lot of the black tribes of the south. However, on June 10 it was announced that the new National Revolutionary Council was granting the three southern provinces "regional autonomy within the framework of a new integral Socialist Sudan."

Kenya. The appearance in Kenya of tendencies to political fission along tribal lines was of greater concern than similar developments in these other countries, precisely because the government of President Jomo Kenyatta hitherto had provided a model of success in building national unity without resort to extremism. The stability of Kenya, in its six years of independence, has rested on the fragile unity of the 1.6 million Kikuyu and 1.3 million Luo, the nation's two largest tribes, which between them compromise one third of the population. This unity was disrupted by the murder on July 5 of Tom Mboya, a detribalized Luo who was a cabinet minister and secretary-general of the ruling Kenya African National Union (KANU). Many Luos jumped to the conclusion that the murder was a Kikuyu plot aimed at preventing Mboya's succeeding the 79-year-old Kenyatta. Politics began to be shaped along rigid tribal lines. The Kikuyus revived the custom of bolstering Kikuyu unity by oath-taking. The Luos grouped themselves behind Oginga Odinga, leader of the opposition Kenya People's Union (KPU).

Kenyatta's October 25 visit to Luo country having touched off rioting there, the president took desperate measures: He banned the KPU and put Odinga and others into detention until after the general election of December 6. Kenya thus became a one-party state. The turn of events seemed to have a sobering effect, possibly temporary, on Luo dissent. The election, which became in effect a primary among KANU rivals, took place under quiet circumstances. However, voters rebuked the government by defeating most of the incumbents seeking reelection, including five cabinet ministers.

Military Coups. African countries continued to be susceptible to change of government by coup d'etat. As usual the ability to achieve such an overthrow depended upon control of the military, or

(*Continued on page 50*)

A NATION DIVIDED

Nigeria's devastating civil war raged over another 12 months in 1969. There was no longer any serious attempt at peace negotiations by the two sides. Although short of arms and near starvation, the Biafrans fought stubbornly. However, it became evident in late 1969 that they were steadily losing ground, and their sudden collapse in mid-January 1970 ended 30 months of bitter strife.

GILLES CARON, FROM GAMMA—PIX

Biafran soldiers of the Ibo tribe, poorly dressed and badly equipped, fought a brave but losing battle.

(Below) *General Gowon* (at left), *Nigerian leader, welcomes British Prime Minister Wilson in April.*

CENTRAL PRESS, FROM PICTORIAL PARADE

Nigerian federal troops display weapons used against rebels. Lagos received arms from Britain and the USSR.

ANNETTE LENA, FROM GAMMA—PIX

RHODESIA'S two societies meet but do not mix on a Salisbury street. The white women chat confidently while black women and children sit nearby, silent and ignored.

MARION KAPLAN, CAMERA PRESS—PIX

of an important part of the army located in the capital. Thus, fewer than 1,000 soldiers were able to take over Sudan in less than 3 hours on May 25.

The takeover in Mali in late 1968 (November 19) by a young military group was followed by four coups in African countries during 1969: the Sudan revolution, already mentioned; the overthrow of the royal government in Libya on September 1 and its replacement by a radical "National Revolutionary Council" much less cooperative toward the West (see MIDDLE EAST); and the coups in Somalia on October 21 and Dahomey on December 10.

In Somalia, Prime Minister Mohammed Egal and his cabinet were ousted by a military junta, which brought to an end nine years of democratic government while ironically proclaiming a "Somali Democratic Republic." This doubtless meant the end of the "Good Neighbor" policy toward Ethiopia and Kenya, which had looked quite promising early in 1969, and a reversion to policies of irredentism. In Dahomey the fifth military coup in six years overthrew the short-lived civilian government of President Emile Derlin Zinsou. A 3-man junta led by Lt. Col. Paul Emile de Souza took control.

The policies of the new regimes that have come into power in these coups are still in a formative stage and unclear. In general one can say, however, that whereas the Mali coup signified a turn away from a Communist-type military and political structure, an end to collectivization of agriculture, and a novel welcome for foreign capital, the new regimes in Sudan, Libya, and Somalia had an anti-conservative and anti-Western orientation. The situation in Dahomey was too confused to be evaluated.

Deaths with Political Significance. Political assassination continued to deface the African political scene. In an area where politics is highly personal, and where political experience is rare, a disproportionate amount of political change can be achieved by bringing about the death of a single man. Thus the murder, by means of an explosive parcel received in the post, in Dar es Salaam, Tanzania, on February 3, of Eduardo Mondlane, leader of *Frelimo* (the Mozambique Liberation Front) dealt *Frelimo* a serious blow because of the lack of any able successor who commands united support. The murder of Tom Mboya on July 5 altered the whole face of politics in Kenya. A third assassination in 1969 was that of the able and moderate president of Somalia,

Abdirashid Shermarke, on October 17, which preceded and facilitated the Somalia coup. Attempts were made on the lives of President Zinsou of Dahomey, before the coup there, and President Milton Obote of Uganda, in late December.

Deaths by natural causes also claimed prominent political leaders. Former President Kasavubu of the Congo (Kinshasa) died on March 24, having lived in retirement since the 1965 coup in which Mobutu replaced him. On November 21, Sir Edward Mutesa, the kabaka of the former kingdom of Buganda, who had been exiled since 1966, died in London in a state of poverty that the Labour government had not permitted even the British royal family to mitigate. In July there occurred the somewhat suspicious death in an Algerian prison of Moise Tshombe, the Katangese leader and former premier of the Congo.

TROUBLE SPOTS

Nigeria. In the summer of 1969 the civil war between Nigeria and the Ibo secessionist region of Biafra passed from its second into its third year. The Biafran case seemed truly desperate in April, when Nigerian troops captured Umuahia, but a Biafran rally recaptured Owerri along with a stretch of territory to the south.

Food supplies to avert mass starvation in Biafra were the subject of an acrimonious quarrel between the federal government of Nigeria, which seemed to regard starvation as a legitimate weapon, and the International Committee of the Red Cross. Throughout 1969, Biafran morale was high, and the traditional Ibo bravery and ingenuity were repeatedly demonstrated. The Soviet Union and Britain continued to give military aid to the Nigerian government, while the United States and the United Nations uneasily looked the other way. The war ended with the collapse of Biafra on Jan. 12, 1970.

Southern Africa. The condition of southern Africa did not alter substantively throughout the year. The Republic of South Africa was attempting, with some success, to establish friendly contacts with black Africa, beginning with its neighbor Malawi. Special *ad hoc* missions have been exchanged with Gabon and with the Malagasy Republic, which is in economic difficulties. These moves have led to a breakaway movement on the right wing of Premier Balthazar J. Vorster's ruling party in South Africa. In Rhodesia, the fourth anniversary of independence was observed on November 11. The constitutional proposals passed by referendum on June 20 authorized the establishment of a republic. International sanctions against Rhodesia remained theoretically in force, but the self-proclaimed nation was an established factor on the international scene.

AFRICAN INTERNATIONAL ORGANIZATIONS

OAU. The Organization of African Unity (OAU) failed to gain any prestige by its handling of the Nigerian issue—a crucial failure since this was a question squarely on its own doorstep, the kind of issue it was presumably invented to deal with. The OAU meeting in April at Monrovia, Liberia, marked the fourth abortive attempt of the OAU to mediate the civil war. The proposals of the six-nation OAU consultative committee were all based on the premise of "one Nigeria"—a premise that was unacceptable to the Biafrans.

In general, it was not a year of achievement for the OAU. The Council of Ministers meeting, held at Addis Ababa, Ethiopia, on February 17–22, accepted a lower budget for the coming year, made necessary by the failure of many member-states to pay their assessments. This meeting and others later in the year issued a number of pronouncements that expressed aspirations rather than policies.

OCAM. Meetings of the *Organisation Commune Africaine et Malgache* (OCAM) advanced a number of projects of technical cooperation. Twelve of the 14 members of OCAM were represented at the summit meeting held at Kinshasa, January 27–29, 10 by their heads of state. This meeting endorsed plans for sugar and meat marketing, technical training, and marine and insurance matters. The meeting also admitted a 15th member, Mauritius.

A good deal of OCAM activity throughout the year was concerned with attempts to patch up the diplomatic rift between Congo (Kinshasa) and its neighbor across the river, Congo (Brazzaville).

ARTHUR C. TURNER
University of California, Riverside

WIDE WORLD
VICE PRESIDENT AGNEW criticizes the news media before the Alabama Chamber of Commerce.

AGNEW, Spiro Theodore

Vice president of the United States: b. Baltimore, Md., Nov. 9, 1918.

Spiro T. Agnew, who had been the frequent butt of ridicule during the 1968 election campaign, established himself during his first year in the vice presidency as a figure to be seriously reckoned with on the national political scene.

Official Duties. Agnew began by conscientiously applying himself to the more routine duties of his new job. In fulfilling his responsibilities as presiding officer of the Senate he diligently sought to master the parliamentary intricacies of that body. At meetings of high-level government committees, such as the Urban Affairs Council, he proved to be a thoughtful participant and, in the president's absence, an efficient chairman.

It soon became apparent that Agnew enjoyed the confidence of President Nixon. He was given ample office space and a substantial personal staff and, moreover, in March was entrusted with supervision of a new federal agency, the Office of Inter-Governmental Relations. It was to the task of establishing liaison between Washington and the states and cities that Agnew devoted most of his energies.

Controversial Speeches. As he grew more accustomed to the vice presidency, Agnew seemed to gain self-confidence, and became more outspoken. After the first successful landing on the moon in July, Agnew was the first high administration official to urge publicly that Mars be selected as the next site for a manned space landing.

In a far more controversial vein, the vice president made a series of speeches in the fall in which he lashed out at critics of administration policy on the Vietnam War, particularly the young people who spearheaded the protest movement. Agnew characterized them as "an effete corps of impudent snobs." And he contended that the only purpose served by the October 15 Moratorium against the war was "as an emotional purgative."

Americans could not afford to be divided by "decadent-thinking" dissidents, Agnew said. "We can, however, afford to separate them from our society," he declared, "with no more regret than we should feel over discarding rotten apples from a barrel."

Broadening his assault to cover the communications media, Agnew charged that television news was controlled by "a tiny and closed fraternity of privileged men, elected by no one and enjoying a monopoly sanctioned and licensed by government." He also warned of concentration of power in the written press.

Predictably, the vice president's pungent oratory brought sharp rebuttals from his targets. But it also brought him a flood of favorable mail, and it was clear that Agnew would continue to serve as a vigorous spokesman for administration policies and for millions of American conservatives.

Background. Spiro Agnew entered public life as a member of the Baltimore County Board of Zoning Appeals. In 1962 he was elected Baltimore County executive, and in 1966 he won the governorship of Maryland on the Republican ticket. He and Mrs. Agnew, the former Elinor Isobel Judefind, have four children and one grandchild.

ROBERT SHOGAN
Washington Bureau, "Newsweek" Magazine

NEW RICE VARIETIES, capable of doubling or tripling harvests, were developed at this institute in the Philippines.

AGRICULTURE

Developments in agriculture—production trends in 1969, technological advances, and other news—are reviewed in this article under the following headings: (1) World Agriculture; (2) U. S. Agriculture; (3) U. S. Agricultural Research; (4) U. S. Farm Services; (5) Dairy Products; (6) Livestock; (7) Grains; (8) Fruits; and (9) Vegetables.

WORLD AGRICULTURE

World agricultural production in 1969 rose to record levels, slightly over the previous highs of 1968. Per capita output was up fractionally over the previous year.

Preliminary estimates in late 1969 indicated a strong rise in food and fiber output in lands of the Western Hemisphere, a third consecutive year of high farm output in western Europe, subpar production in the Soviet Union, eastern Europe, and mainland China, and record agricultural output in the Far East and Oceania. Production rose 4% in such developing lands as India, Pakistan, Indonesia, and Brazil.

Major exceptions to the general rise were lower production in Africa because of erratic weather conditions and just-average crops in such western Asian nations as Turkey, Iran, Iraq, Syria, Lebanon, Jordan, Israel, and Cyprus.

Weather conditions—the most important variable in world farm production—could sharply change final 1969 output data, but for at least the third year in a row world weather appeared to smile on food and fiber production with certain exceptions. Use of better-yielding varieties of plants, greater quantities of fertilizer, and better farming practices also contributed to the tremendous outpouring of farm products.

Surpluses. The short-term production outlook is so promising that the threat of price-depressing farm surpluses is beginning to worry some experts. These surpluses exist not only in the United States, Canada, and western Europe but also in such developing lands as Kenya and Mexico. The accumulation in surplus stocks tends to choke world trade channels and push down prices. This limits the ability of the developing countries to earn foreign exchange needed for heavy reinvestment in agriculture and industry.

Addeke H. Boerma, director general of the Food and Agriculture Organization of the United Nations, said that solutions to the problems of surplus "will increasingly have to take into account the growing self-sufficiency in many developing countries, which already has contributed to the emergence of surplus stocks in the developed exporting countries."

Surpluses consist mainly of wheat, rice, butter, dry skim milk, coffee, and sugar. Lack of markets for them helped to stagnate world agricultural trade late in 1969.

More importantly, however, the specter of even larger, more-difficult-to-control surpluses is haunting Boerma. He worries that if the richer nations of the world cannot control and dispose of their surpluses, many underdeveloped countries, on the brink of producing surpluses of their own for the first time in many years, will be even less able to cope with the staggering problems of building adequate storage, eliminating waste, and constructing transport facilities.

"The difficulties experienced by the developed countries," Boerma told an FAO meeting in Rome in November 1969, "in coming to grips with the problem of surplus production is indicative of the strength and tenacity of the economic, technological, social, and political factors that tend to make farm production in high-income countries grow faster than consumption. . . ." Matching output to demand will be difficult for these richer lands, he added, "but today even more seems to be required. An increasing number of developing countries are near a technological breakthrough in cereal production. Some of them will have exportable surpluses and will need markets for the commodities that they produce efficiently. In part they will have to find them by expanding trade among themselves." But, he said, the developing countries could help immensely if they could take the coming surpluses into account in adjusting their own farm economies.

World Trade Stalemate. Partly as a result of surpluses accumulating already, world trade in farm commodities failed to increase in value in 1968, the most recent year for which figures are available. Volume expanded somewhat, but preliminary data suggest that this was offset by lower average prices. In fact, the value of agricultural trade remained little changed for the four years through 1968. In contrast, the value of world trade as a whole since 1964 grew at a rate of about 8% a year.

However, there was one bright spot. Trade in forest products—such as lumber, pulp, paper, plywood, and other materials—increased by more than 13% in 1968. Export earnings from forest products for the developing countries rose by 20%.

In 1968 total world agricultural production—including cotton, tobacco, and other inedible output—registered an index number of about 143 (1952–56 average = 100). For 1969 the index number was estimated at about 147.

1969 Developments. World production of the two major bread grains, wheat and rye, is estimated by the U. S. Department of Agriculture at only about 323 million metric tons—5.3% below the record 341 million tons produced in 1968. U. S. output of these grains is off sharply because of government checkreins on plantings. Crops were also smaller in France and Australia. Wheat is the food most widely traded in international commerce.

World production of corn in 1969 was placed at about 241 million metric tons, nearly 5% more than in 1968. Output of the other feed grains, barley and oats, was estimated at 165 million metric tons, 2% more than the 1968 record. These feed grains are the raw materials for producing meat and milk.

The surging production of feed grains has led to larger production of red-meat animals. In 1968 per capita consumption of meat rose in most of the 39 major meat-producing and meat-consuming lands. New Zealand, with 224 pounds, became the world's leading per capita consumer of red meats. Uruguay formerly was first, but its per capita intake fell to 218 pounds in 1968 from 227 pounds in 1967.

Use of new high-yielding varieties of wheat, rice, corn, sorghum, and millet continued to expand rapidly, especially in the Far East, where food shortages have threatened in recent years. The Republic of China (Taiwan), Ceylon, India, South Korea, Malaysia, Pakistan, and the Philippines have been adopting high-yield grains rapidly.

Canada. Unusually high yields in Canada's vital wheat crop more than offset a sharp drop in planted areas. Output of other important grains and oilseeds was near a record. Livestock production, however, fell sharply from 1968. One reason was that higher prices encouraged producers to hold back cattle and hogs for breeding purposes so as to expand their herds. The seeded area for barley, flaxseed, soy-beans, and forage crops rose substantially and for rapeseed it reached a record. Canada's grain exports declined, and although there was some recovery near the end of 1969, the total volume of farm exports was down from the 1968 levels.

Latin America. Agricultural output in 1969 reached record levels. One exception was Mexico, where output was expected only to approach 1968 levels, the result of drought-blighted crops. Lower prices led to a sharp cutback in cotton plantings in Mexico and Central America. However, in Central America, the cotton decline was more than offset by larger harvests of coffee, sugar cane, and food crops. Near-normal growing conditions brought about a sharp recovery from the 1968 droughts in important areas of Central America, the Caribbean, and South America. Recovery came to El Salvador, Guatemala, and Honduras. Growing conditions were good in the Dominican Republic and Haiti, as well as in Jamaica and in Trinidad and Tobago. Cuba's sugar cane harvest was estimated at about 4.7 million tons, down one million tons below the 1965–68 average.

Farm output in Argentina, Brazil, Colombia, and Venezuela was expected to move to high levels. Substantial gains occurred in Ecuador, Guyana, and Uruguay. Farm output in South America, taken as a whole, attained record levels in 1969.

Europe and the Soviet Union. Agricultural production in this huge land mass was generally good in 1969. In western Europe, output just about matched the 1968 record. Output in eastern Europe was fair to good, but it did not reach the large production of 1968. The Soviet Union suffered damage to the winter grain crop, but spring wheat and other spring grains produced record output. Production of livestock and livestock products in Communist lands declined. Livestock and poultry output in western Europe declined slightly too, with beef production entering a cyclical downturn. Dairy output rose moderately, and dairy surpluses were becoming more troublesome.

Grain production in western Europe in 1969 fell somewhat short of the record 120 million tons of 1968. Most of the decline occurred in smaller-producing countries such as Portugal and those in Scandinavia. Nevertheless wheat production was well above normal needs.

In eastern Europe grain production in 1969 was greatly improved over the previous year in Bulgaria, Hungary, Rumania, and Yugoslavia. Production was also good in Czechoslovakia, but East Germany and Poland produced less grain than in 1968. For the entire region, grain output might turn out to have been an all-time high.

In the Soviet Union, the wheat crop was hit by extreme cold, high winds, and low rainfall in January, but spring-planted grains fared much better. Total grain output totaled perhaps 140 million tons, close to the record-breaking outputs in 1966 and 1968. Livestock product output was limited by short feed supplies, and a severe winter further curtailed livestock operations in early 1969. Most output was down as much as 8% from the previous year, and milk products were about equal to year-earlier levels.

Africa and Western Asia. In North Africa cereal grain crops failed to match the record 1968 production. Heavy rains in some areas and drought in others cut yields in Morocco, Algeria, Tunisia, and Libya. Output in the United Arab Republic and Sudan, however, was average or better. Both the

UAR and Sudan will have more cotton to export. The whole region will have exportable surpluses of olive oil, rice, wine, citrus fruit, and hides and skins.

In West and Central Africa widespread drought, especially in Niger, Upper Volta, Mali, Senegal, and Mauritania, caused a shortage in subsistence food crops. The United States donated food to these lands. In Liberia rubber output rose substantially. The Ivory Coast's coffee crop was up 14%. In the Democratic Republic of Congo (Kinshasa), several basic food crops have reached production levels that had been attained before independence. Southern Africa's corn crop set a record. East Africa's farm output equaled or exceeded that of 1968, with tea and cotton showing moderate gains. Kenya's corn and wheat surpluses swelled again.

Western Asia fared well in 1969. Turkey produced more wheat and cotton. Iran's wheat was down but cotton output may be record high. In Iraq increases were indicated for sugar beets, cotton, and grains. Syrian cotton and barley suffered from unfavorable weather. Israel's wheat crop was off from 1968. Cyprus recovered from a drought.

Asia and the Far East. The 1969 farm output in this region was excellent for a third consecutive year and probably exceeded the record levels of the previous year. Even mainland China, which suffered a setback in its farming operations in 1968, fared better in 1969.

This region's most important crop is rice, and the 1969 output broke all records. Wheat production also was at a record high, especially in India and Pakistan. Mainland China probably surpassed its 1968 wheat production. Australia's wheat output was expected to decline.

A rapid rise in rubber prices benefited Malaysia, Cambodia, Ceylon, Thailand, and Indonesia. Food-grain output in India was about 100 million tons, up from a record 95 million tons in 1968. Pakistan's wheat harvest totaled 7 million tons, up 8% in a year.

Per capita consumption of livestock and poultry products in this region, although very low by Western standards, reached record levels in 1969. It probably will continue to rise rapidly as feed-grain production expands.

JOE WESTERN
Kominus Agri-Info Associates

U. S. AGRICULTURE

Production of crops and livestock set records in the United States in 1969, the Department of Agriculture reported. Gross farm income attained a new high. But net income, although it rose substantially, remained below the near-record level of 1966.

Secretary of Agriculture Clifford M. Hardin sketched proposals for changes in farm policy. He favored reduction of restraints on production and advocated direct welfare aid to 400,000 marginal farmers.

Farm Income. Gross farm income increased to about $54.5 billion, up from the previous high of $51.1 billion in 1968. Mainly because the prices that farmers received for their products averaged about 6% higher than in 1968, net income rose to $15.9 billion, up from $14.8 billion in 1968 and trailing only the net-income figures in 1947, 1948, and 1966. Net income per farm rose to a record of about $5,300 from $4,841 in 1968. The previous record was $5,044 per farm in 1966.

The larger net farm income stemmed from higher prices received by farmers, especially for livestock products, fruits, and vegetables; continued high volume of marketings; and record high direct government payments to farmers. The gains in gross and net income were partly offset by an increase in production expenses to record highs.

Direct government payments to farmers totaled about $3.8 billion, up from the previous high of $3.5 billion in 1968. The increase stems mainly from larger payments made to farmers to persuade them to plant fewer acres of feed grains.

Average crop prices were about 2% below the 1968 average. But prices for livestock and livestock products were up 12%. Total volume of farm marketings was up at least 2% above the 1968 volume.

Cash receipts from meat animals were much higher than in 1968, reflecting strong demand despite ample supplies. Dairy product receipts also ran slightly larger, because 4.5% higher prices more than offset a 1.5% decline in the volume of milk marketed. Poultry and egg receipts were up substantially because of sharply higher prices.

Crop receipts were higher in 1969 because larger marketings more than offset the average lower prices. Prices were higher, however, for fresh vege-

UPI

PROTESTING their economic plight as grain farmers, more than 150 men mounted tractors in Paris, Ill., on July 19, 1969, and headed for Washington, 700 miles away. This "survival drive" was conducted by the United Grain Farmers of America.

tables and fruits—except for citrus fruits—as supplies expanded along with demand. Citrus-fruit marketings were so large that receipts offset lower prices. Receipts were larger from cotton, tobacco, soybeans, wheat, corn, barley, oats, and rye only because huge marketings made up for a slight price dip.

Production expenses climbed to about $38.6 billion in 1969, up from the previous high of $36.3 billion in 1968. Costs for feeder livestock were up sharply, by 12%; farm machinery and motor vehicle prices paid by farmers were up about 5%; and building and fencing materials were up 10%. Feed prices were about the same as in 1968, and fertilizer prices were down 4%. Interest, taxes, and wage rates were up an average of 8%. But wage rates jumped 12%, more than offsetting a 5% decline in the number of hired hands.

Food Production. The U. S. all-crop production index (1957–59 = 100) rose to a record high 121, up from the previous high of 120 in 1968. The per-acre yield for 28 leading crops at 132 was also a record high, up from the previous peak of 129 in 1968. The largest crops ever were harvested in oil seeds, potatoes, hay, sugar beets, and peanuts.

Crops planted in 1969 covered about 286 million acres, down from the 295 million acres of the previous year. Plantings were smaller for wheat, corn, barley, sorghum grain, rice, sugarcane, and hops, partly offset by larger acreages of oats, rye, cotton, flaxseed, dry field peas, soybeans, potatoes, sweet potatoes, tobacco, and sugar beets.

Wheat production at nearly 1.5 billion bushels was below the previous high of 1.6 billion in 1968. Per-acre yield of 30.6 bushels was higher than ever, up from the previous peak of 28.4 in 1968. Corn output at 4.6 billion bushels was up from 4.4 billion in 1968 but below the record of almost 4.8 billion in 1967. Per-acre yield of this key crop was also a record 83.9 bushels, up from the previous high of 78.6 bushels in 1967.

Supplies of fresh vegetables and eight principal vegetables for processing were down 22% from 1968 stocks. The citrus crop was moderately larger than in the previous year. The tonnage of noncitrus fruits was up substantially from 1968, mainly because of huge output of apples. Potato production was up 4%.

Soybean production in 1969 totaled a record of 1.1 billion bushels, 1% more than the previous record in 1968. Yield per acre, at 27.3 bushels, was also a record high.

Production of potatoes at 307.2 million hundredweight was 4% more than output in 1968. Per-acre yield of 219 hundredweight was up from 214 in 1968 and 210 in 1967.

Meat and poultry production rose to about 46 billion pounds, up from about 45 billion pounds in 1968. Milk marketed in 1969 totaled about 1% less than the previous year's output of around 117.3 billion pounds and was well below the record 124 billion pounds in 1964.

Farm Policy Proposals. Secretary of Agriculture Hardin presented proposals on farm policy before the House Agriculture Committee on Sept. 24, 1969. His testimony came as Congress was considering the future of agricultural-subsidy and planting-control programs that are scheduled to expire at the end of 1970. Wheat, feed grains, and cotton are the major commodities involved. Under existing programs, federal subsidies and price supports are available to farmers who hold out of production some land that was formerly devoted to producing surplus crops.

Hardin suggested that the commodity programs be continued, but he also said that government payments to any one farmer should have some legal limit. (Earlier, legislation that passed the House proposed a $20,000 limit.)

Hardin told the legislators that farmers ought to have more freedom to plant crops as they see fit. And he recommended that farmers receive some additional government aid for crops grown for export, so that U. S. commodities can compete in world markets, where prices generally are lower than they are in the United States.

As for the problems of marginal farmers, Hardin suggested that these growers be included in the President's proposed welfare plan in which low-income families would receive payments to supplement income.

In attempting to find long-range solutions for control of U. S. farm surpluses—which continue to plague farmers and push up federal costs in propping prices and storing the plentiful crops—many economists have proposed "soil-bank" programs. Under these plans, land owners are paid rent by the government if they take their land permanently out of production of surplus crops and use it for timber growing, grazing, and recreation. Hardin's proposal in his testimony was to begin a pilot program that would retire as many as 4 million acres a year. The pilot program would continue until farm economists had enough information to calculate the expected impact of large-scale land-retirement programs.

Food Consumption. The per-capita food consumption index (1957–59 = 100) remained at 105.6, about the same as in 1968 following three years of substantial increase. The index was 100.5 a decade earlier. Meat and poultry consumption per person rose to 228.2 pounds in 1969 from 227.8 pounds in the previous year. The average person in the United States ate about 109.7 pounds of beef, up slightly from the previous high of 109.4 pounds in 1968. Pork consumption declined to 64.7 pounds per capita from 66 pounds in 1968. Per-capita consumption rose for fats and oils, fruits, canned vegetables, and milled rice. Consumption declined for veal, eggs, ice cream, butter, and lard.

Agricultural Employment. The index of farm wage rates (1957–59 = 100) rose to a new high of about 173 in 1969, up from 160 in the previous year. Wages averaged approximately $1.35 an hour in 1969, up by about 14 cents—or about 12%—in a year. The farm work force declined perhaps 3% from 4,745,800 in 1968.

Farm Assets. The market value of farm real estate on Jan. 1, 1970, totaled an estimated $209 billion, up $6 billion from a year earlier. The value of agricultural assets, including crop and livestock inventories, was estimated at $308 billion on Jan. 1, 1970, up $11 billion a year. Liabilities against those assets, including debt on real estate and loans from other creditors, were estimated at $60 billion. This left a balance of $248 billion in agricultural equities, up $5.5 billion in a year.

Agricultural Exports. For the fiscal year that ended June 30, 1969, exports of U.S. farm commodities declined for the second consecutive year. They totaled about $5.7 billion, down 9% from the previous fiscal year. Lower prices for several major commodities and rising food production in some developing lands that formerly imported huge quantities of food and fiber contributed to the decline. Cotton exports tumbled 31% in value, wheat fell 30%, and feed grains nearly 25%. These losses more than offset increases in exports of soybeans, tobacco, fruits, vegetables, and animal products. The dip in total farm exports was deepened by a longshoreman's strike that began in December 1968 and closed all Atlantic and Gulf ports through March 1969.

JOE WESTERN
Kominus Agri-Info Associates

U. S. AGRICULTURAL RESEARCH

Agricultural Research Service (ARS), which is an agency of the U. S. Department of Agriculture, conducts research concerned with farming, human nutrition, consumer and food economics, marketing, and finding new uses for agricultural products. The agency also carries on regulatory activities to control pests of livestock and plants, to prevent the entry of animal and plant pests into the United States, and to assure that pesticides meet acceptable standards of safety and effectiveness. Much of this work is done in cooperation with state agricultural experiment stations.

Chemical Defleecing. Chemicals are being used experimentally to defleece sheep—with neither nicks nor cuts to the sheep, nor skills on the part of the defleecer. The chemicals are new drugs used in anti-

U.S. DEPARTMENT OF AGRICULTURE

DEFLEECING is speeded up by use of a drug that interrupts cell growth in the hair roots of a sheep.

cancer studies. They interrupt cell growth in the bulb of each wool fiber, causing a ringlike constriction. When the constriction moves up from the bulb of each wool fiber to a point just below the skin surface, in six or seven days, the fiber breaks easily and the entire fleece can be separated at the skinline. The compound is given to the sheep by mouth or injection.

New Wheat Flour. A new food, wheat flour fortified with wheat, was developed by ARS scientists in 1969. The product is 70% ordinary wheat flour and 30% high-protein wheat flour to which calcium and vitamin A have been added. The mixture has 25% to 30% more protein than ordinary flour, with higher quality protein.

Earth Resources Satellites. The first agricultural research space station may be orbited in 1972 or 1973. This station, the first of the earth resources

satellites to be sent up by the National Aeronautics and Space Administration, should hasten remote-sensing techniques that will aid the management of agricultural and other natural resources. Remote sensing involves getting information about things from a distance—the aircraft pilot's radar is an example. A remote-sensing satellite could provide information on vegetation, soil, and water infinitely faster and often more accurately than ground observation.

Milk-Storage Studies. Milk is apparently not as perishable as was thought. If the storage temperature is lowered to freezing or slightly above freezing, milk will keep as long as seven weeks. Research also showed that milk pasteurized under higher-than-normal temperatures would keep 20 weeks or more.

Livestock Research. Researchers are analyzing the fat composition of boar semen to find why the semen will not withstand freezing. Frozen bull semen has, for many years, done much to improve dairy cattle. The swine industry hopes for similar benefits from frozen boar semen. Fats, or lipids, make up a large proportion of the outer membrane of the sperm cell, and they may help protect the sperm cell against such adverse conditions as freezing.

Ice-cold milk can be used to raise orphan lambs. In tests, some 90% of lambs started on the cold formula survived to weaning, compared to a survival rate of 80% for lambs reared naturally.

Plant Research. A variety of tall fescue, Kentucky 31 (*Festuca arundinacea*), may solve lawn problems in the eastern areas of the United States not suitable to either northern or southern grasses. The area, called the transition region, covers an area extending roughly from Washington, D. C., to northeastern Kansas.

The discovery of several types of twin and triplet seedlings in a number of inbred lines of pearl millet has opened the way to new sources of gene pools for improving this crop.

Insect Pests. Cotton fragments from a Mexican cave have added 1,000 years to the history of the boll weevil. Found in Oaxaca, Mexico, the fragments had entombed a boll weevil that had failed to chew its way out of a cotton boll. Before discovery of the 1,000-year-old weevil, scientists inferred from lack of ancient history on the insect that its fondness for cotton was recently acquired.

Sexually sterile male codling moths are helping in the war against the wormy apple. In an experimental orchard, one million of them were released; they outnumbered native males by a ratio of 62 to 1. The released moths, sterilized by exposure to radioactive cobalt, retained their normal mating instincts, but eggs produced from matings of sterile and native moths were infertile. This technique poses no threat to crops or man—the moths do not become radioactive nor do they feed on fruit when released.

Of 535 new experimental repellents, scientists found 12 that held yellow-fever mosquitoes at bay for more than 100 days. Because mosquitoes have been becoming increasingly resistant to widely used insecticides, ARS entomologists seek better use of present insecticides while testing new materials.

Synergists and molting hormones have potential use as biochemical insect controls. Synergists, compounds in conventional insecticides, proved to have hormonal effects on insects, derailing normal growth and development. Molting hormones, vital to normal insect development, can kill or sterilize insects when too much is present at the wrong time. In tests, manmade molting hormones unexpectedly caused sterility in female house flies and death in immature stages of mosquitoes and houseflies.

Regulatory and Control Activities. Confirmed hog cholera outbreaks totaled 1,055 in fiscal year 1969, compared with 849 in the preceding year and an estimated 5,000 to 6,000 outbreaks yearly before the start of the eradication program. Forty-five states and Puerto Rico—containing over 98% of the country's hogs—have progressed to the final "stamping out" phases of the eradication program.

More than 96% of the U. S. counties—or 3,039 of them—have achieved modified-certified brucellosis area status by reducing the incidence of the disease in cattle to not more than 1% of the animals and to not more than 5% of the herds. More than 42% of the counties, or 1,339, have eradicated the disease. Certified as brucellosis-free are the Virgin Islands and all counties in 16 states—Arizona, California, Connecticut, Delaware, Maine, Maryland, Massachusetts, Michigan, Nevada, New Hampshire, New Jersey, New York, Rhode Island, Vermont, Washington and Wisconsin.

Efforts to eradicate swine brucellosis still continue, and more than 3,000 herds already have been validated brucellosis-free. There were 182 validated brucellosis-free counties in 12 states, the Virgin Islands, and Puerto Rico. This included all counties in Arizona, Nevada, Vermont, Utah, and the Virgin Islands.

In the campaign to eradicate bovine-type tuberculosis in cattle, 612 counties in 23 states, Puerto Rico, and the U. S. Virgin Islands have been accredited tuberculosis free. All counties in Maine, Connecticut, and New Hampshire, as well as the Virgin Islands, have achieved this status.

ROBERT B. RATHBONE
U. S. Agricultural Research Service

U. S. FARM SERVICES

Financial and technical assistance in a wide variety of rural economic undertakings is provided to farmers in the United States by the Farmers Home Administration, Farm Credit System, Rural Electrification Administration, and the Federal Crop Insurance Corporation.

Farmers Home Administration. This supervised-credit agency helped 5.2 million farm and other rural people during fiscal 1969 through more than $1.4 billion in loans and grants advanced. Some of the money was insured by FHA and actually lent by others. Family farm loans, for operating costs and for buying farm land, totaled more than $553.2 million in credit to 64,722 families. The FHA also advanced $117.7 million in emergency credit to help farmers restore their operations in areas hit by floods, drought, and other natural disasters.

Rural housing loans totaling $512 million for purchase, construction, and remodeling were advanced to 57,600 families in fiscal 1969. These included $17.3 million to construct or improve rental housing for senior citizens and low-income rural residents and $8.5 million in loans and grants to provide adequate housing for farm laborers and their families.

Loans amounting to $164.6 million and grants totaling $24.9 million went for the development of 989 water and sewage system projects in 48 states and Puerto Rico. This expanding program provided water and sewage service that benefited more than 2.8 million people in rural areas. Rural development efforts by FHA also included lending $18.3 million for community recreation facilities that benefited 193,000 people. The FHA also made $12.9 million in economic-opportunity loans that benefited 13,280 low-income rural families and 193 cooperatives serving low-income people.

Loans outstanding at the end of fiscal 1969 totaled nearly $5.5 billion, up from $4.8 billion a year earlier. Principal and interest repayments of $779.8 million in that fiscal year were the highest in FHA history.

Farm Credit System. The farmer-owned cooperative Farm Credit System, supervised by the Farm Credit Administration (an independent agency not a part of the Department of Agriculture), lent $10 billion to farmers and their cooperatives in fiscal 1969, up $800 million in a year.

The Farm Credit System comprises 12 federal land banks and 652 federal land bank associations, 12 federal intermediate credit banks and 451 production credit associations, and 13 banks for cooperatives. These are federally chartered but privately financed lending institutions. Funds lent are raised by selling bonds and debentures on the open market. The Farm Credit System had $12.9 billion in loans outstanding at the end of fiscal 1969, up $2.5 billion over a year earlier.

The federal land banks provided $1.18 billion in long-term mortgage loans for 41,164 farmers in fiscal 1969. Production credit associations lent $6.5 billion in seasonal-production and capital-improvement loans in fiscal 1969. The banks for cooperatives lent $1.6 billion to 2,957 cooperatives during the year.

Rural Electrification Administration. Nearly 200,000 rural consumers and subscribers will be added to electric and telephone systems financed by REA as a result of loans approved in fiscal 1969. The loans also help to meet service needs of the more than 25 million people already being served.

In fiscal 1969, REA approved 223 electric loans to bring initial service to 117,955 rural consumers or to build facilities necessary to keep pace with requirements of consumers. The loans amounted to nearly $345 million. By year's end, the 1,101 REA-financed electric systems were serving 6.1 million meters on 1.7 million miles of line in 46 states. About half of the 3 million electrified farms in the United States are served by REA-financed electric systems.

In its telephone program, REA made 153 loans in fiscal 1969. They will provide new and improved all-dial telephone service for 78,929 subscribers. The loans totaled nearly $125 million. Of the telephone systems financed by REA, 638 are commercial companies and 235 are cooperatives. The systems serve more than 2 million rural subscribers from 520,000 miles of line in 1,872 counties in 46 states.

Federal Crop Insurance Corporation. This corporation paid an estimated $38 million in 1969 to compensate farmers whose crops did not return production costs because of drought, freeze, storms, insects, plant diseases, and other unavoidable natural causes of crop loss. The corporation's $900 million worth of insurance covered 25 types of crops on 20 million acres.

JOE WESTERN
Kominus Agri-Info Associates

DAIRY PRODUCTS

Milk production in the United States in 1969 declined to about 116.2 billion pounds from 117.3 billion pounds in the previous year. Since the peak production of nearly 127 billion pounds in 1964, output of milk has decreased every year.

Output per cow continued to increase in 1969 as it has in nearly every year since the end of World War II. The average was estimated at 9,174 pounds, up from 9,006 pounds in 1968. Although year-to-year gains are slowing, the current average is far above the 5,314 pounds per cow produced 20 years earlier.

The downward trend in the number of milk cows on farms, begun in 1945, continued in 1969 but showed a slowing of the rate of decline. Milk cows on farms averaged 12.7 million, down from 13 million in 1968. This decline of about 2.5% compares with declines of 5% and 6% in 1965 and 1966. The slowdown appears to be associated with a falloff in the number of dairy-herd sales. "Improved dairy incomes have enhanced dairying's position relative to that of other occupations," the Department of Agriculture reported.

Use of milk in commercial markets decreased again, to about 109 billion pounds, from 109.5 billion pounds in 1968 and from the record high 115.6 billion in 1966.

Price-support purchases of dairy products from the domestic market totaled the equivalent of about 4.5 billion pounds of milk, down from 5.2 billion in 1968. Record U. S. government purchases were in 1962 when the total was 10.8 billion pounds.

The Department of Agriculture supports milk prices by standing ready to buy at fixed prices cheese, nonfat dry milk, and butter. For the first time, the department contracted in 1969 for the purchase of "instantized" nonfat dry milk for distribution in welfare programs. The overall decline in government purchases of dairy surpluses occurred because lower farm marketings of milk more than offset a decline in commercial consumption.

Dairy products in commercial and government stocks at the end of 1969 totaled the equivalent of perhaps little more than 5.4 billion pounds of milk, down from 6.7 billion pounds at the end of 1968. Civilian use of milk in 1969 was estimated at about 112.9 billion pounds, down from 113.8 billion a year earlier.

World Production. According to preliminary estimates, milk production in the 36 countries that normally produce about 85% of the world's supply of milk rose slightly in 1969 above the previous year's output of about 714 billion pounds. Output was about the same in most lands, with some declines offset by increases in France and eastern European countries.

JOE WESTERN
Kominus Agri-Info Associates

LIVESTOCK AND POULTRY

Cattle and calves on farms rose slightly to a record high in the United States in 1969. But the total number of pigs born declined in the year and sheep numbers fell to record lows. Production of broiler chickens rose significantly to a record high.

Throughout the world, cattle and sheep totals rose slightly, but hog numbers dipped.

United States. The number of cattle in the United States rose perhaps as much as 750,000 head by Jan. 1, 1970, over the year-earlier record total of 109.7 million. Slaughter totaled about 40.8 million head in 1969, down slightly from 41 million in the previous year.

The number of hogs slaughtered in the United States in 1969 declined slightly—to 85.2 million from 86.4 million in 1968. The number of pigs farrowed decreased about 3% from the 1968 total of nearly 94.5 million.

The number of sheep declined for the tenth year in a row, to a record low 4% below 21.1 million in 1968. The slaughter of sheep and lambs at 11 million head was down from 12.1 million in the previous year. The lamb crop of 13.6 million head declined from 14.4 million in 1968.

Egg production in 1969 totaled about 191 million cases, down from 193 million in the previous year. Broiler production jumped about 8% above the record 2.6 billion birds in 1968. The 1969 turkey crop just about matched the previous year's output of about 106.5 million birds.

World Livestock Populations. The world population of cattle and buffalo rose to a record high, 1,160,900,000 in 1969, from 1,159,800,000 in the previous year. The 1969 total was substantially above the 1961–65 average of 1,068,000,000. Cattle numbers rose in North America, western Europe, and some parts of Asia. It decreased in South America, eastern Europe, and the Soviet Union.

CENTER FOR INTERNATIONAL TROPICAL AGRICULTURE

MALNUTRITION may be prevented or overcome by new high-protein corn like that fed pig MS (*right*). Pig C got common corn and pig O, genetically improved corn. All were from same litter.

The total number of hogs, at 510 million, was slightly below the year-earlier total of 511.9 million but still well above the 1961–65 average of 445.9 million. Hog numbers rose in North America but decreased in South America, eastern Europe, and the Soviet Union.

The world total of sheep in 1969 was estimated at about 1,029,100,000, narrowly more than the year-earlier estimate of 1,027,600,000 but above the 1961–65 average of 978,500,000. Sheep numbers rose in Australia, New Zealand, South America, and the Soviet Union. They decreased in North America, western Europe, and eastern Europe.

JOE WESTERN
Kominus Agri-Info Associates

GRAINS

Total production of the feed grains—corn, oats, barley, and sorghum—in the United States increased in 1969. Production of the food grains—wheat, rye, and rice—declined.

Feed Grains. U. S. production of corn, oats, barley, and sorghum totaled 174.2 million tons, an increase of 3% from 1968 but 1.8 million tons under the record crop of 1967. Corn, oat, and sorghum production increased but barley production declined. The acreage harvested was 2% smaller than in 1968. Harvested acreages for corn, barley, and sorghum were smaller than in 1968. Record yields for corn and barley and near-record yields for sorghum and oats more than offset the decline in acreage.

World production of corn, oats, and barley totaled 406,360,000 metric tons in 1969, up from 392,240,000 tons in 1968.

Food Grains. In 1969 the United States produced 49.2 million tons of food grains—wheat, rye, and rice. Production was down 7% from 1968 and down 3% from 1967. Rye production increased, but wheat and rice production declined. Harvested acreage was 13% under 1968 and 17% under 1967. Record wheat yields partially offset the decline in acreage.

Wheat. The United States produced 1,458,872 bushels of wheat in 1969. The crop was 7% smaller than the record crop of 1968 and 4% smaller than the 1967 crop. Winter wheat production totaled 1,147,646 bushels, down 7% from the 1968 record. Producers harvested wheat from 47,555,000 acres, 14% fewer than were harvested in 1968.

The U. S. yield of wheat averaged a record 30.7 bushels per acre, 2.2 bushels more than the previous record yield set in 1968. Kansas led the states in wheat production, followed by North Dakota.

The world produced 293,491,000 metric tons or 10,783,900,000 bushels in 1969–70, a drop of 5% from the record production of 1968–69. About 529,007,000 acres were harvested, 18,025,000 fewer than in 1968–69. The world yield of wheat averaged 20.4 bushels per acre, $\frac{4}{10}$ of a bushel less than a year earlier.

Rye. Rye production in the United States totaled 31,405,000 bushels in 1969, up 34% from the preceding year. The 1969 crop yielded a record 23.5 bushels per acre, up from 23 bushels in 1968 and 22.6 bushels in 1967. Rye was harvested from 1,334,000 acres, 32% more than in 1968. South Dakota was the leading rye-producing state.

World rye production totaled 29,849,000 metric tons or 1,175,100,000 bushels in 1969–70. The crop was 7% smaller than a year earlier. Producers harvested 53,762,000 acres, 3% less than in 1968–69.

The yield of rye averaged 21.9 bushels per acre, a drop of one bushel from 1968–69.

Rice. Production of rice in the United States totaled 91,303,000 hundredweight in 1969, a drop of 12% from the record crop of 1968. The yield per acre averaged 4,290 pounds, compared to 4,422 pounds for 1968. The 1969 crop was harvested from 2,128,400 acres, 10% fewer than in 1968. Arkansas led the states in rice production.

Corn. The U. S. corn crop totaled 4,577,864 bushels in 1969—184,591,000 bushels more than in 1968 but 182,212,000 bushels fewer than in 1967. The 1969 crop yielded a record 83.9 bushels per

WORLD PRODUCTION OF GRAINS BY LEADING COUNTRIES

(In metric tons)

	5-year average ending 1965	1968–69	1969–70
Wheat			
USSR	50,000,000	78,500,000	. . .
United States	33,254,000	42,741,000	39,652,000
Canada	14,651,000	17,686,000	18,455,000
India	10,809,000	16,568,000	18,000,000
France	11,906,000	14,945,000	14,669,000
Australia	8,298,000	14,687,000	13,608,000
Italy	8,259,000	9,590,000	9,000,000
Turkey	6,940,000	8,400,000	8,600,000
Pakistan	4,065,000	6,478,000	6,879,000
West Germany	4,731,000	6,198,000	6,000,000
World total	231,758,000	309,254,000	293,491,000
Rye			
USSR	13,330,000	12,700,000	. . .
Poland	7,401,000	8,514,000	7,955,000
West Germany	3,225,000	3,347,000	2,950,000
East Germany	1,784,000	1,971,000	1,600,000
United States	827,000	590,000	814,000
Czechoslovakia	911,000	761,000	748,000
Canada	274,000	331,000	430,000
Austria	401,000	413,000	387,000
Spain	393,000	364,000	355,000
France	373,000	351,000	314,000
World total	32,331,000	32,160,000	29,849,000
Rice			
India	52,432,000	59,701,000	63,000,000
Pakistan	17,745,000	20,084,000	21,267,000
Japan	16,251,000	18,061,000	17,568,000
Indonesia	13,969,000	16,615,000	. . .
Thailand	11,469,000	12,410,000	14,000,000
Burma	7,762,000	8,023,000	8,350,000
South Korea	5,102,000	4,350,000	5,582,000
Philippines	4,113,000	4,583,000	5,131,000
South Vietnam	4,872,000	4,400,000	5,094,000
United States	3,575,000	4,777,000	4,090,000
World total	167,512,000	186,620,000	195,082,000
Corn			
United States	94,562,000	111,121,000	109,532,000
Brazil	10,112,000	11,500,000	. . .
Mexico	6,064,000	9,200,000	8,600,000
USSR	9,564,000	7,600,000	. . .
Yugoslavia	5,664,000	6,810,000	7,500,000
Rumania	5,784,000	7,105,000	7,475,000
India	4,402,000	6,500,000	7,000,000
Argentina	4,984,000	6,900,000	. . .
France	2,625,000	5,226,000	5,500,000
South Africa	5,147,000	4,962,000	. . .
World total	194,960,000	230,640,000	241,260,000
Oats			
United States	14,496,000	13,492,000	13,617,000
USSR	6,560,000	9,700,000	. . .
Canada	6,070,000	5,591,000	5,959,000
West Germany	2,211,000	2,893,000	3,000,000
Poland	2,700,000	2,890,000	2,660,000
France	2,628,000	2,506,000	2,345,000
United Kingdom	1,705,000	1,231,000	1,241,000
Sweden	1,272,000	1,523,000	1,133,000
Czechoslovakia	870,000	874,000	850,000
East Germany	900,000	850,000	810,000
World total	48,700,000	50,700,000	51,400,000
Barley			
USSR	16,117,000	22,400,000	. . .
United States	8,831,000	9,104,000	9,056,000
France	6,239,000	9,062,000	8,963,000
United Kingdom	5,891,000	8,415,000	8,931,000
Canada	3,752,000	7,084,000	8,474,000
West Germany	3,433,000	4,974,000	5,050,000
Denmark	3,241,000	5,059,000	4,950,000
Spain	1,893,000	3,708,000	3,938,000
Turkey	3,310,000	3,500,000	3,600,000
India	2,630,000	3,469,000	3,000,000
World total	84,600,000	110,900,000	113,700,000

Source: Foreign Agricultural Service, U.S. Department of Agriculture.

acre, exceeding by 5.3 bushels the record set in 1967. Corn was harvested from 54,573,000 acres, a drop of 1,307,000 acres from 1968 and the smallest acreage of record. Illinois was the leading corn-producing state, followed by Iowa.

World corn production totaled 241,260,000 metric tons or 9,498,000,000 bushels in 1969. The crop was 10.6 million tons larger than the 1968 crop. About 257.5 million acres were harvested, 6 milion more than a year earlier.

The world yield of corn averaged 36.9 bushels, nearly a bushel more than in 1968.

Oats. Oat production totaled 949,874,000 bushels in the United States in 1969, an increase of 1% from the 1968 crop and 20% from the 1967 crop. The 1969 crop was the largest since 1963. Producers harvested 18,003,000 acres in 1969—470,000 acres more than a year earlier. The crop yielded 52.8 bushels per acre, about a bushel less than in 1968. Minnesota ranked first among the states in oat production.

World oat production totaled 51.4 million metric tons or 3,541,200,000 bushels in 1969, up 1% from 1968. The crop was harvested from 78.8 million acres, 3% more than a year earlier.

The world yield of oats averaged 44.9 bushels, compared to 45.8 bushels in 1968.

Barley. The United States produced 417,156,000 bushels of barley in 1969, 1% less than a year earlier. The crop was harvested from 9,388,000 acres, 321,000 acres fewer than in 1968. The crop yielded a record 44.4 bushels per acre, up nearly a bushel from the preceding year. North Dakota led the states in barley production.

The world produced a record 113.7 million metric tons or 5,222,200,000 bushels of barley in 1969, 3% more than a year earlier. The crop was harvested from 173.1 million acres, up 5% from 1968. The world yield averaged 30.2 bushels per acre, slightly less than in 1968.

Sorghum Grain. Production of sorghum grain in the United States in 1969 totaled 743,124,000 bushels, 1% more than in 1968 but 2% less than the 1967 record crop. Producers harvested the crop from 13,463,000 acres, 4% fewer than a year earlier. The yield per acre averaged 55.2 bushels, second to the record 55.8 bushels of 1966. Texas was the leading grain sorghum-producing state.

NICHOLAS KOMINUS
Kominus Agri-Info Associates

FRUITS

Production of deciduous and citrus fruits increased in the United States in 1969. Deciduous fruit production totaled 11 million tons, an increase of 12% from 1968. Production of all deciduous fruits, except plums and prunes, increased in 1969. Citrus fruit production totaled 11.2 million tons, an increase of 34% from the 1967–68 crop.

Apples. The nation's apple growers produced the largest crop in over 30 years. The crop totaled 6,761,900,000 pounds, an increase of 24% from a year earlier. Large crops in Washington and Oregon accounted for more than half of the increase. The leading variety, Delicious, accounted for 30% of total production. Golden Delicious ranked second. Other leading varieties were McIntosh, Rome Beauty, Jonathan, and York Imperial.

Peaches. The peach crop totaled 3,695,400,000 pounds, an increase of 3% from 1968 and of 38% from 1967.

Pears. The nation produced 710,850 tons of pears in 1969, a gain of 15% over 1968 and of 57% over 1967. Washington, Oregon, and California accounted for over 90% of the crop. Over 75% of the pears produced in those states are Bartletts.

Cherries. The sweet cherry crop totaled 123,900 tons, which was an increase of 36% from 1968 and 12% from 1967. The seven Western producing states accounted for nearly 75% of the crop. The tart cherry crop totaled 150,050 tons, up 9% from 1968 and 70% from the small 1967 crop. New York, Pennsylvania, Ohio, Michigan, and Wisconsin produced 90% of the tart cherry crop.

U. S. PRODUCTION OF APPLES, PEACHES, AND PEARS, BY LEADING STATES
(In pounds)

	1967	1968	1969
Apples[1]			
Washington	1,240,000,000	1,025,000,000	1,690,000,000
New York	950,200,000	830,000,000	925,000,000
Michigan	555,000,000	555,000,000	680,000,000
California	348,000,000	620,000,000	560,000,000
Pennsylvania	359,000,000	390,000,000	500,000,000
Virginia	363,000,000	413,000,000	455,000,000
West Virginia	228,400,000	220,800,000	260,000,000
North Carolina	166,100,000	169,800,000	206,000,000
Oregon	124,000,000	87,000,000	160,000,000
Ohio	101,700,000	130,000,000	150,000,000
Total U.S.	5,394,900,000	5,441,900,000	6,761,900,000
Peaches			
California	1,788,000,000	2,208,000,000	2,270,000,000
South Carolina	171,000,000	400,000,000	350,000,000
Georgia	145,100,000	234,500,000	183,000,000
Pennsylvania	38,400,000	106,100,000	120,000,000
New Jersey	50,000,000	100,500,000	115,000,000
Michigan	68,500,000	34,500,000	95,000,000
North Carolina	40,000,000	77,800,000	56,000,000
Virginia	24,500,000	50,000,000	52,800,000
Alabama	50,000,000	39,000,000	50,000,000
Arkansas	52,000,000	36,400,000	42,000,000
Total U.S.	2,684,900,000	3,590,700,000	3,695,400,000
Pears	(In tons)		
California	117,000	344,000	354,000
Oregon	151,000	93,000	188,000
Washington	133,770	141,540	106,100
Michigan	21,000	11,000	24,000
New York	17,200	9,300	18,000
Colorado	1,500	5,700	7,800
Utah	4,130	6,300	5,500
Pennsylvania	2,600	3,250	3,000
Connecticut	1,880	1,600	2,150
Idaho	1,900	700	2,100
Total U.S.	451,980	616,390	710,850

[1] Estimates of the commercial crop refer to the total production of apples in the commercial orchards of 100 or more bearing-age trees.

U. S. CITRUS PRODUCTION BY LEADING STATES
(Number of boxes)[1]

	Average 1966–67[2]	1967–68	1968–69
Oranges			
Florida	139,500,000	100,500,000	129,700,000
California	36,800,000	19,150,000	44,300,000
Arizona	3,910,000	3,120,000	5,380,000
Texas	2,700,000	1,800,000	4,500,000
Total U. S.	182,910,000	124,570,000	183,880,000
Grapefruit			
Florida	43,600,000	32,900,000	39,900,000
Texas	5,400,000	2,800,000	6,700,000
California	4,996,000	4,618,000	5,060,000
Arizona	1,680,000	3,740,000	2,510,000
Total U. S.	55,676,000	44,058,000	54,170,000
Lemons			
California	15,100,000	13,600,000	12,300,000
Arizona	2,810,000	3,250,000	3,510,000
Total U. S.	17,910,000	16,850,000	15,810,000
Tangerines			
Florida	4,100,000	2,800,000	3,400,000
California	600,000	560,000	640,000
Arizona	200,000	150,000	170,000
Total U. S.	4,900,000	3,510,000	4,210,000

[1] Approximate weight per box varies as follows: Oranges—California and Arizona, 75 pounds; other states, 90 pounds. Grapefruit—California, Desert Valleys, and Arizona, 64 pounds; other California areas, 67 pounds; Florida, 85 pounds; Texas, 80 pounds. Lemons—76 pounds. Tangerines—California and Arizona, 75 pounds; Florida 95 pounds. [2] The crop year begins with the bloom of the first year shown and ends with completion of harvest the following year.

PLASTIC GREENHOUSES and water desalinizers may some day make deserts bloom and produce the needed food for earth's constantly growing population.

Grapes. The United States produced 3,874,300 tons of grapes in 1969, an increase of 9% from 1968 and of 27% from 1967. California accounted for more than 90% of the crop. The California crop was divided as follows: raisin varieties, 61%; table varieties, 17%; and wine varieties, 22%.

Apricots. Apricot production totaled 219,420 tons, up 47% from 1968 and 49% from 1967. The crop was the largest since 1960. The crop was produced in three states—California, Washington, and Utah.

Plums and Prunes. The California plum crop totaled 65,500 tons, a drop of 38% from a year earlier. The crop was the smallest since 1958. The California prune crop totaled 129,000 tons, 16% under 1968 and 21% under 1967. It was also the smallest crop since 1958. Production of plums and prunes increased in the four other important producing states—Michigan, Idaho, Washington, and Oregon. The crop in these four states totaled 81,500 tons, more than double 1968 production and 12% above 1967 production.

Cranberries. The nation produced 1,767,500 barrels of cranberries in 1969, up 20% from 1968 and 26% from 1967. The crop was produced in five states—Massachusetts (the leader with 43% of the crop), New Jersey, Wisconsin, Washington, and Oregon. Production was up in all states with the exception of Washington.

Avocados. Florida produced 12,600 tons of avocados in 1968–69, a drop of 14% from a year earlier but more than twice as large as the 1966–67 crop. California produced 61,000 tons, almost twice as large as the 1967–68 crop.

Citrus. The United States produced 265.1 million boxes of citrus fruit in 1968–69. The crop, the second largest of record, was 1% smaller than the record crop of 1966–67. Of the total crop, 69% was oranges, 21% grapefruit, 6% lemons, and 4% other citrus—tangerines, tangelos, temples, and limes.

Orange production increased 45% from a year earlier. Grapefruit production was up 24%, but lemon production was down 6%. Florida production accounted for 71% of the oranges and 74% of the grapefruit; California produced 24% of the oranges, and Texas and Arizona the remaining 5%. Texas ranked second in grapefruit production, followed by California and Arizona. California produced more than 75% of the lemons. Florida led the states in tangerine production.

About 70% of the citrus fruit produced in the United States was used by processors. Processors used 77% of the oranges, 59% of the grapefruit, and 43% of the lemons.

The 1968–69 citrus crop was valued at $668 million, up 10% from the preceding crop.

NICHOLAS KOMINUS
Kominus Agri-Info Associates

VEGETABLES

The United States produced fewer vegetables for the fresh market and for processing in 1969 than it did in 1968. The year did, however, produce a record potato crop and a larger sweet potato crop.

Vegetables for Processing. Production of the 10 principal vegetable crops grown for commercial processing totaled 9,388,030 tons in 1969. That was a drop of 22% from the record tonnage of 1968 and 6% under 1967 production.

Production of all 10 crops declined in 1969. Output of tomatoes, the most important crop for processing, slipped 29%. The other declines were as follows: beets, 20%; sweet corn, 16%; green lima beans, 15%; spinach, 12%; asparagus, 11%; snap beans, 10%; green peas, 10%; cucumbers for pickles, 8%; and cabbage for kraut, 4%.

The declines were brought about primarily by smaller acreages. Increases in yields were registered for lima beans, snap beans, and cucumbers for pickles. Yields for the other crops showed small declines over the previous year.

The crops were harvested from 1,723,320 acres, compared to 2,011,740 in 1968. More acres were planted to corn than any of the other crops. Wisconsin accounted for 18% of the acreage and Cali-

U. S. PRODUCTION OF COMMERCIAL VEGETABLES AND MELONS FOR FRESH MARKET
(In hundredweight)

	1967	1968	1969
Vegetables			
Artichokes	730,000	576,000	656,000
Asparagus	822,000	918,000	849,000
Beans, lima	288,000	259,000	n/a
Beans, snap	3,797,000	3,549,000	3,361,000
Beets	294,000	241,000	n/a
Broccoli	2,782,000	3,080,000	2,304,000
Brussels Sprouts	685,000	638,000	627,000
Cabbage	19,132,000	18,988,000	18,177,000
Carrots	17,724,000	19,346,000	18,275,000
Cauliflower	2,428,000	2,729,000	2,549,000
Celery	14,512,000	15,295,000	15,291,000
Corn, sweet	13,117,000	12,395,000	12,436,000
Cucumbers	4,980,000	4,466,000	4,678,000
Eggplant	575,000	453,000	529,000
Escarole	1,122,000	1,066,000	1,097,000
Garlic	506,000	800,000	840,000
Kale	72,000	70,000	n/a
Lettuce	42,630,000	44,130,000	44,457,000
Onions	28,562,000	28,849,000	28,017,000
Peas, green	68,000	59,000	n/a
Peppers, green	4,351,000	4,933,000	4,678,000
Shallots	32,000	37,000	n/a
Spinach	885,000	812,000	704,000
Tomatoes	20,588,000	19,651,000	19,633,000
Total vegetables	180,682,000	183,340,000	179,158,000
Melons			
Cantaloupes	12,552,000	13,535,000	13,725,000
Honeydew Melons	1,577,000	1,379,000	1,874,000
Watermelons	27,735,000	27,611,000	26,307,000
Total melons	41,864,000	42,525,000	41,906,000
Total vegetables and melons	222,546,000	225,865,000	221,064,000

Source: Statistical Reporting Service, U. S. Department of Agriculture.

U. S. PRODUCTION OF FROZEN VEGETABLES
(In pounds)

	1967	1968
Asparagus	32,460,000	34,355,000
Beans, green, regular cut	147,552,000	138,506,000
Beans, green, French cut	70,219,000	65,504,000
Beans, green, whole	7,077,000	3,900,000
Beans, green, Italian	6,345,000	7,073,000
Beans, wax	7,113,000	6,533,000
Beans, butter	5,190,000	2,397,000
Beans, butter, speckled	13,033,000	7,681,000
Broccoli	166,731,000	172,959,000
Brussels Sprouts	39,479,000	49,024,000
Carrots, diced	89,467,000	108,246,000
Carrots, sliced	43,870,000	27,774,000
Carrots, chips, chunks, Julienne and crinkle cut	n/a	26,262,000
Cauliflower	50,971,000	67,566,000
Celery	3,745,000	2,246,000
Collards	13,795,000	17,897,000
Corn, cut	316,100,000	334,549,000
Corn-on-Cob	43,973,000	76,358,000
Kale	5,459,000	4,721,000
Lima beans, baby	85,687,000	84,579,000
Lima beans, emerald	11,628,000	14,445,000
Lima beans, fordhook	63,950,000	66,513,000
Mustard greens	10,520,000	11,914,000
Okra	47,465,000	30,485,000
Onions	23,973,000	34,621,000
Peas, blackeyed	44,236,000	25,579,000
Peas, green	424,246,000	429,352,000
Potatoes	1,490,809,000	1,736,055,000
Pumpkin and Cooked Squash	23,298,000	24,672,000
Rhubarb	6,846,000	6,176,000
Spinach	153,228,000	153,960,000
Squash, summer	10,467,000	12,832,000
Sweet Potatoes and Yams	6,153,000	9,564,000
Turnip greens	25,123,000	20,622,000
Turnips, Turnip greens with Turnips	6,722,000	13,347,000
Miscellaneous vegetables	10,695,000	29,573,000
Total	3,507,625,000	3,857,840,000

Source: National Association of Frozen Food Packers.

U. S. PRODUCTION OF VEGETABLES FOR COMMERCIAL PROCESSING
(In tons)

	1967	1968	1969
Asparagus	110,950	115,850	103,400
Beans, lima	115,680	115,120	97,670
Beans, snap	636,790	626,700	565,530
Beets	206,350	269,200	215,750
Cabbage, for kraut	273,100	231,800	222,950
Corn, sweet	2,101,900	2,479,300	2,086,500
Cucumbers, for pickles	595,640	554,640	507,950
Peas, green	590,550	581,720	524,710
Spinach	157,030	153,780	134,720
Tomatoes	5,187,450	6,965,860	4,928,850
Total	9,975,440	12,093,970	9,388,030

Source: Statistical Reporting Service, U. S. Department of Agriculture.

fornia 14%. California, however, accounted for 39% of production, compared to 9% for Wisconsin. Those states, plus Minnesota, Oregon, and Ohio, accounted for more than 65% of the crop.

The total value of the 10 crops was $451,458,-000, a drop of 25% from 1968. The crops produced in California accounted for over 30% of the total value.

Fresh Vegetables and Melons. Production of vegetables and melons for the fresh market totaled 221,064,000 hundredweight in 1969, a decline of 2% from 1968. Increases in lettuce and sweet corn production were more than offset by declines in cabbage, carrot, celery, onion, and tomato production. Total melon production slipped as small increases in the cantaloupe and honeydew melon crops were offset by a decline in watermelon production.

California led the states in the production of vegetables for processing, accounting for 38% of the total. Five states—California, Florida, Texas, Arizona, and New York—accounted for more than 70% of the crop.

The vegetable crops were harvested from 1,211,-350 acres—11,885 acres fewer than a year earlier.

Despite the decline in production, the value of the vegetable and melon crop increased. It had a total value of $1,230,000, an increase of 4% from 1968. Lettuce and tomatoes accounted for 38% of the value of the total crop. The California crop accounted for 40% of the total value.

Strawberries. The 1969 strawberry crop totaled 485,676,000 pounds, a drop of 7% from 1968 but up 3% from 1967. Of the total, 35% was for processing.

Potatoes. The nation produced a record 307,-229,000 hundredweight of potatoes in 1969, an increase of 4% from 1968 and 1% more than the 1967 crop. The yield per acre, which averaged 219 hundredweight, was at a record high. The acreage harvested was 2% higher than in 1968.

Increases in the production of early spring, late spring, and fall potatoes more than offset the smaller winter, early summer, and late summer potato crops.

The winter crop totaled 3,828,000 hundredweight, slightly less than 1968. Early spring production totaled 5,687,000 hundredweight, up from 5,019,000 hundredweight in 1968. The late spring crop yielded 21,290,000 hundredweight, up 4% from 1968. A total of 13,487,000 hundredweight were produced from the early summer crop, a decline of 4% from a year earlier. The late summer crop totaled 29,-300,000 hundredweight, a drop of 2% from 1968. The fall potato crop totaled a record 233,637,000 hundredweight, up 6% from 1968.

The potato crop was harvested from 1,403,800 acres, 2% more than in 1968 but 4% less than in 1967. Idaho led in potato production, followed by Maine, Washington, and California.

Sweet Potatoes. Sweet potato production totaled 13,958,000 hundredweight in 1969, an increase of 1% from 1968 and 2% from 1967. A record yield of sweet potatoes per acre offset a decline in acreage. The average yield per acre was 95 hundredweight, compared to 92 hundredweight in 1968. The crop was harvested from 147,300 acres—the second smallest acreage of record. Louisiana led in sweet potato production, followed by North Carolina and Virginia.

NICHOLAS KOMINUS
Kominus Agri-Info Associates

FIRST FB-111A supersonic bomber was delivered to SAC on Oct. 8, 1969.

AIR FORCE

The U. S. bombing of North Vietnam, which had been halted by President Johnson on Nov. 1, 1968, was not resumed in 1969. Air Force activity in the Vietnam War consisted in the main of bombing infiltration routes from the north into South Vietnam, close air support for ground forces, troop airlift and medical evacuation, reconnaissance, air defense, and psychological warfare support.

Congressional budget-cutting caused cancellation of the Air Force's long-planned manned orbiting laboratory (MOL), and an investigation into the costs ($36 million per plane) of the giant C-5 Galaxy transport. Budget cuts cost the Air Force 50,000 service personnel, 13,000 civilians, and 209 aircraft. The swing-wing F-111 fighter became operational, and training began for crews of the FB-111 bomber. Bids were sought for a new bomber.

Vietnam War. The Seventh Air Force, with headquarters at Tan Son Nhut Air Base near Saigon, is the air arm of the Military Assistance Command, Vietnam (MACV). It has 59,000 combat and support personnel and more than 1,000 combat aircraft.

November 1965 saw the introduction of the unique AC-47 Dragonship into special operations warfare. The versatile "Gooney Bird," using three 7.62-mm Miniguns, is credited with saving many small allied outposts from falling. AC-119 gunships are equipped to detect concealed troop staging areas and supply depots. The AC-130 Gunship II, introduced to Vietnam in late 1968, is a 4-engine aircraft with four 7.62-mm Miniguns and four M-61 20-mm Vulcan cannons. It uses high-intensity lights and flares plus advanced detection devices.

Psychological warfare is credited with more than 100,000 defections from the Communist ranks since the war began. Air-dropped leaflets and broadcasts persuade the enemy to join the South Vietnamese.

After the bombing halt, reconnaissance over North Vietnam continued in order to record troop concentrations and construction of fortifications.

The Military Airlift Command's 3d Aerospace Rescue and Recovery Group, with headquarters at Tan Son Nhut Air Base, has completed more than 3,000 successful rescues in the Vietnam War.

More than 4 million passengers and combat troops are airlifted annually in Vietnam. For the year ending June 1969, approximately 920,000 tons of supplies and equipment were airlifted.

Strategic Air Command (SAC). The main mission of SAC is nuclear deterrence. Its weapons are intercontinental ballistic missiles (ICBM's) and 450 long-range B-52 bombers with their tankers.

The ICBM force has 54 Titan II and 1,000 Minuteman missiles. Titan II, with the heaviest warhead in the missile inventory, will be kept through June 1973. Minuteman I is being replaced by Minuteman II, which has increased throw weight, greater accuracy, and a larger number of target options. Minuteman III, being flight-tested in late 1969, will be able to carry Multiple Independent Reentry Vehicles (MIRV), also penetration aids to confuse enemy defenses. A much advanced ICBM, under study in 1969, will include a larger payload at maximum range.

Bids were invited for prototype models of the B-1 (formerly known as the AMSA—Advanced Manned Strategic Aircraft). Its design features include supersonic speed, long range at low altitude, low radar and infrared signatures, and improved bombing and navigation accuracy.

Tactical Air Command (TAC). The Vietnam War caused TAC's growth from 70,000 personnel and assets of $3 billion in 1961 to a strength of more than 120,000 and assets of $6 billion in 1969. TAC provides fully equipped quick-reaction forces and replacement crews for overseas use. Increased flexibility was achieved in 1969 by giving tactical fighter, airlift, and reconnaissance squadrons their own maintenance, supply, and medical capabilities.

The TAC unit that introduced the F-111 into the Air Force, the 4527th Combat Crew Training Squadron at Nellis Air Force Base, Nev., completed its 10,000th hour of training in the swing-wing fighter. The same unit began training a cadre of SAC pilots for the FB-111 bomber in late 1969.

Several deployments and exercises involving TAC units were held during the year. TAC C-130's teamed up with Reserve C-119's to open Exotic Dancer II, an exercise held in Puerto Rico during May and June 1969. Some 969 members of the 92d Airborne Division were airlifted by TAC C-130's from Fort Bragg, N. C., to an assault drop zone in the exercise area, the planes returning to Fort Bragg without stopping.

TAC C-130's airdropped 2,700 troops and equipment in Korea in the "longest airborne assault in history," Exercise Focus Retina, after an 8,500-mile flight from the United States east coast.

Air Reserve and Air Guard forces, called up in the wake of the *Pueblo* crisis, operated from Kunsan, South Korea, and Itazuke Air Base, Japan, but by June 1969 all these units had returned home.

Aerospace Defense Command (ADC). More than 70% of the North American Air Defense (NORAD) forces are provided by ADC. Advanced ground radars to detect ICBM's are being tested. In addition, coastal radars are being modified to detect missiles launched from the sea.

As of July 18, 1969, 1,743 manmade objects were in orbit around the earth. A limited capability exists for destroying orbiting satellites.

Military Airlift Command. Airlift requirements have been increasing: MAC moved more than 2.8 million passengers in the year ending June 30, 1969, compared with 2.7 million the previous year. In the same year, cargo movement increased from 679,079 tons to more than 700,000.

The major airlift burden fell on MAC's C-141

B-1 supersonic bomber is shown in an artist's conception. A go-ahead has been given for prototypes of the plane, formerly called the Advanced Manned Strategic Aircraft.

Starlifters in 1969, as the giant C-5 Galaxy entered its flight-test program. The C-5 lifted a record 762,-000 pounds in June 1969. The C-141's plus the C-5's will enable MAC to deliver an Army division —with almost all of its combat equipment—to any place on earth.

In 1969 MAC also received eight C-9 Nightingales, the first aircraft designed specifically for aeromedical evacuation. The number of patients moved by the international aeromedical operation was 98,-959 during the 11 months ending May 31, 1969, as compared with 87,414 for the full year ending June 30, 1968. The Aerospace Rescue and Recovery Service (ARRS) raised its total number of U. S. and allied servicemen saved in Vietnam during the past year to 2,527—1,702 in the face of enemy fire.

Considerable activity was recorded by the command's Reserve Forces, numbering about 50,000 in 345 flying and support units. Four Air Force Reserve Associate Airlift Groups were organized at MAC bases during 1969. Active duty for 10 Air Force Reserve units—some 3,200 officers and airmen—was terminated between May 27 and June 18, 1969. A total of 5,900 Reservists had been mobilized early in 1968 as a result of the *Pueblo* crisis.

Operation Reforger/Crested Cap saw more than 17,000 Army and Air Force personnel airlifted from the United States to Germany and returned during the four months ending in April. This exercise was to show that the number of U. S. personnel in Europe could be reduced without affecting readiness. Another movement took more than 4,500 troops and their equipment from Colorado to Vietnam.

Air Force Systems Command (AFSC). With some 9,900 officers, 18,000 airmen, and 30,000 civilians, AFSC develops modern weapons for the Air Force. Much of its research is to increase speeds, and to improve aircraft survivability and weapon accuracy. Under study are space, computers, high-lift devices, microelectronics, lasers, exotic materials, reliability, and human performance.

The Air Force and NASA announced in 1969 that they will cooperate in testing the world's fastest sustained-speed airplane—the YF-12A, a Mach 3 experimental long-range interceptor.

TACSAT I, the largest communications satellite, was boosted into a synchronous equatorial orbit by the Titan IIIC in February 1969, to provide worldwide communication among all U. S. armed forces.

The final launch in the Titan IIIC research and development program was accomplished on May 23, 1969, with the orbiting of two improved Vela satellites, to monitor nuclear detonations and detect solar flares and other hazards to manned space programs.

AFSC scientists are working on a voice-actuated control system for astronaut-maneuvering units which would respond to 14 verbal commands, such as *stop, back, right, up,* or *down,* thus freeing the astronaut's hands.

AFSC developed in 1969 such items as a television camera tube for low-light-level operation, allowing pinpoint target acquisition, identification, tracking, and weapons delivery. An electronic locating system was demonstrated: signals transmitted by a pocket radio, carried by all aircrewmen, are received in a rescue helicopter and position it directly over the man to be rescued, even when he is hidden by darkness or dense foliage.

Several air traffic control systems were under development or testing in 1969. One involved a tactical air control tower, transportable by helicopter, capable of converting an unattended airstrip into a high-capacity airfield within one hour. Another, Project Seek Dawn, was installed in Southeast Asia to monitor and direct combat air operations, using computers to process flight plans and keeping track of aircraft by radar.

Air Training Command (ATC). In the year ending June 30, 1969 technical training was provided for 561,000 students, including 144,000 in resident training, 370,000 by field training detachments, and 47,000 under other special training courses. More than 7,000 officers were graduated from flight training schools during the year, and nearly 10,000 men went through the survival school. The Officer Training School at Lackland Air Force Base, Texas, graduated some 4,900 new Air Force officers, 200 of them women, in the year ending June 30, 1969.

Administration and Command. Secretary Harold Brown left the Air Force on Feb. 15, 1969. He was replaced by Dr. Robert C. Seamans, Jr., former deputy administrator of the National Aeronautics and Space Administration. Gen. John P. McConnell, chief of staff, retired on Aug. 1, 1969, and was succeeded by Gen. John D. Ryan. See also DEFENSE FORCES; MISSILES; VIETNAM WAR.

HARRY M. ZUBKOFF
Office of the Secretary of the Air Force

AIR TRANSPORTATION

Against a backdrop of exciting technological strides and nagging economic problems, the U.S. airline industry in 1969 continued to grow at a vigorous rate—much faster than the nation's overall economy.

As U.S. airlines hauled record volumes of passengers and cargo, they sought to cope with inflationary pressures and falling profits, increasing airport congestion, and the challenges of introducing fleets of expensive new jumbo jets and selling enough tickets to fill the seats of these cavernous aircraft. They faced more militant opposition from airport-area residents over the noise and smoke output of jetliners and saw a relatively minor headache of previous years—hijacking—explode into a major safety crisis—the solution to which remained elusive.

Traffic Volume. The scheduled domestic airlines carried an estimated 164 million passengers in 1969, an increase of approximately 8% over 1968. This was a decline in the industry's recent rate of growth, which averaged 15% through the 1960's. The airlines' cargo volume increased by about 15%, to 5 billion ton miles. The domestic airlines added approximately 30,000 employees to their payrolls, bringing the total to about 325,000. They accepted delivery of 309 new aircraft valued at $1.9 billion, bringing their total investment in aircraft and facilities to $8.7 billion. Worldwide, it was estimated that scheduled airlines carried more than 300 million passengers, an increase of approximately 10% over 1968.

One of the fastest growing segments of the airline industry was a group of 12 U.S. airlines known as the supplemental carriers. They fly passengers on nonscheduled charter flights, often at half the price of scheduled airlines. Over the North Atlantic routes between the United States and Europe, the supplementals carried an estimated 700,000 people, up more than 70% from the total number carried during the previous year.

In 1970 supplemental carriers are expected to carry more than one million passengers, although the same economic pressures that are worrying the scheduled airlines are also affecting the supplementals and could stem some of their expected growth. Charter flight bargains divert many passengers from scheduled airline flights across the North Atlantic and in the intra-European vacation air travel market, evoking pressures by the regular airlines on governmental agencies to limit the supplementals' operating rights.

Fare Increases. The Civil Aeronautics Board permitted the scheduled airlines two fare increases during 1969—3.8% in February and 6.35% in October. The board granted the boosts after airlines argued that inflation had eaten deeply into their earnings. The industry contended that its rate of return on investment had dropped to 5%. A 10.5% return had been set as reasonable by the Civil Aeronautics Board.

Wage settlements given airline workers during 1969 averaged more than 25% over the term of three-year contracts and put additional pressure on the airlines' profits. Many airline leaders said additional fare increases might be sought in 1970.

The continuing economic problems of several airlines led to discussions about the possibility of airline mergers. On November 11, Northwest Airlines and Northeast Airlines announced an agreement in principle to merge, subject to a number of conditions, including CAB approval. Profitable Northwest flies from New York to the Pacific Northwest and on to the Orient; unprofitable Northeast flies

CONCORDE 001, the first French-British supersonic transport, hurtles into the air at Toulouse, France, in its maiden flight on March 2, 1969.

SUD AVIATION—BRITISH AIRCRAFT CORPORATION

THE PRESENT

The world's biggest commercial jetliner, the Boeing 747 (above), made its first test flight on Feb. 14, 1969, dwarfing an F-86. Meanwhile, the U.S. supersonic transport or SST (sketched below), designed to fly at 1,800 mph, was under development by Boeing.

AND THE FUTURE

throughout New England and from New York to Florida.

The airlines' falling profits appeared to be jeopardizing their ability to finance new planes and other equipment. According to an estimate of one bank, the domestic airlines will need to borrow $55 billion through 1980. The bank said that raising the money may be very difficult in a capital-short economy.

Fare levels were also the subject of brisk activity in international aviation. The International Air Transport Association, a 103-airline organization that sets fares between countries, introduced a new group fare to compete with the bargains of supplemental airlines and attract passengers to the jumbo jets. However, several IATA members objected to this fare plan, and late in the year they disavowed the agreement. This touched off a round of fare cutting that produced the best bargains in history for scheduled trans-Atlantic travel.

Technical Developments. In aeronautics the two high points of 1969 were the first flights of the Boeing 747 and the British-French Concorde supersonic airliner. The 747, the first of the jumbo jets,

ect because of its cost and criticisms about the sonic boom, the president asked Congress to authorize development of two prototype U. S. supersonic transports. These craft, under design by Boeing, are to streak through the sky at up to 1,800 mph (about 3,000 km per hour), but they are not expected to enter commercial service before 1978.

While the SST's promised to speed up air travel, the 747 and two slightly smaller craft, the McDonnell Douglas DC-10 and the Lockheed 1011, promised to make air travel in the 1970's more comfortable. With cabins up to twice as wide as the jets of the 1960's, these jets will give passengers more elbow room and less of the feeling of being cramped into a narrow tunnel. Airlines have ordered more than 180 four-engine 747's and more than 380 of the smaller, three-engine 250-to-300 passenger McDonnell Douglas and Lockheed "airbuses."

The French and West German governments decided in 1969 to move ahead with development of another airbus, called the A-300B.

Congestion. One of the unwelcome effects of the U. S. boom in air transportation has been congestion in the air and on the ground at many air-

NEW AIR TERMINAL capable of serving 8 million passengers a year will be built at Logan International Airport, Boston, beginning in 1970. The $75 million structure, known as the South Terminal Building (model at right), will double the airport's passenger capacity and be able to handle 34 jets simultaneously.

MASSACHUSETTS PORT AUTHORITY

is two and one half times larger than any airliner before it, with enough capacity to carry as many as 490 passengers. Pan American World Airways was scheduled to make the first commercial flight with the behemoth new plane in December. But, after an otherwise successful test program that began with a flight on February 9, problems emerged in production models of the plane's engines and the inaugural commercial service was delayed until 1970.

The Western world's first supersonic airliner, the 1,320-mph Concorde, logged more than 120 hours of successful test flights following its maiden flight on March 2. The Concorde is scheduled to enter airline service in 1973.

In the Soviet Union, pilots continued to test the 1,450-mph Tu-144, which may enter commercial service as early as the fall of 1970. The Soviet Union has indicated it wants to sell the plane to foreign airlines. A delegation of U. S. airline officials inspected the Tu-144 and came away impressed. However, they generally were skeptical about the possibility of placing orders for the plane.

Following a debate within the Nixon administration in which some advisers argued against the proj-

ports. For the first time, the Federal Aviation Administration rationed flights at major airports—Kennedy International, LaGuardia, and Newark in the New York area, Washington National, and Chicago's O'Hare Field—during 1969. Hourly quotas on take-offs and landings, coupled with other steps designed to ease congestion, reduced the number and length of flight delays during 1969 to a lower level than the crisis proportions of midsummer in 1968.

Air traffic controllers, whose slowdown tactics, designed to dramatize their complaints of an under-staffed and outmoded traffic control system had been one of the major causes of the 1968 tie-ups, caused massive delays for hundreds of jetliners from June 18 to 20. But otherwise the FAA handled the traffic without the kind of monumental delays experienced the previous summer.

Jammed terminal buildings and congested airport access roads continued to make air travel harrowing at many airports during the peak travel periods. However, the aviation world got some hope in 1969 that help was on the way to expand and modernize the overcrowded air transportation network. President Nixon proposed and the House approved a 10-

SMOKELESS ENGINES reduce airport pollution. A Boeing 727 (*top*), its engines modified, takes off cleanly. Another 727 (*bottom*) emits the usual exhaust.

TEST AIRCRAFT lifts off Lake Erie at Buffalo for the first take-off and landing on water by a plane with a landing system employing an air cushion.

MOST SPECTACULAR of the year's hijackings came on October 31 when a young U. S. Marine diverted a jet from California to Rome, stopping at New York (*below*).

year program to pump $5 billion into construction of new airport and air traffic control facilities. The projects were to be financed by new taxes, including an additional 3% levy (bringing the total to 8%) on passenger tickets, a $3 departure tax for overseas trips, and a 5% tax on air freight.

In a program to decongest the crowded airways, the FAA laid out blueprints to install computerized systems to ease the workload of controllers at all on-the-ground control centers by 1973.

The agency authorized the first operational use of "area navigation" systems. This will allow some airliners to fly off the crowded point-to-point airways that are marked across the country by radio navigation stations. By using the new computer-based navigation system, pilots will be able to fly off these regular routes and, in effect, open up multiple traffic lanes in the sky.

The Air Transport Association, the airlines' trade association, tested an experimental collision avoidance system to warn pilots of a possible mid-air collision. Several airlines indicated they may install the devices in jets beginning in 1970.

Noise Restrictions. Empowered by legislation passed by Congress in 1968, the FAA published the nation's first national standards limiting the noise output of airliners. They require new airliners to be at least 50% quieter than the jets of the 1960's, such as a Boeing 707.

Research by the National Aeronautics and Space Administration indicated use of sound-absorbing materials in early model jets such as the Boeing 707 can achieve substantial noise reductions. The FAA is to consider broadening its rule to cover these planes in 1970.

Route Expansion. The domestic airlines experienced one of the largest expansions of their route networks in history during 1969. The CAB and President Nixon made decisions that brought the 10-year-old trans-Pacific route case to an end. Trans World Airlines, Pan American World Airways, American Airlines, Northwest Airlines, and Flying Tiger cargo line were given major new international routes over the Pacific. TWA, Western, United, Continental, Northwest, Braniff, and American were allowed to link mainland cities and Hawaii.

As part of a move to divert some air traffic out of the congested New York area, National Airlines was given new rights to fly between Miami and London. The CAB gave several airlines new authority to fly between East and West Coast cities on routes across the southern part of the country.

Hijacking. More than 65 airliners were hijacked in 1969, exceeding the total for all the years since the first hijacking in 1952. More than 40 planes were diverted at gunpoint to Cuba. Airline and government officials agreed that the only way to stop the aerial piracy would be an international treaty requiring nations to extradite hijackers to the country from which a plane was diverted. A step in this direction was taken with the final ratification of the 1960 Tokyo Convention, which requires signatory nations to release passengers, crewmen, and planes involved in hijackings. The U. S. sought expansion of the treaty to require extradition or punishment of hijackers. But there was skepticism among some U. S. and other diplomats that it would ever be enacted because of an international tradition of extending asylum to political fugitives.

ROBERT H. LINDSEY
Aviation Reporter, "The New York Times"

ALABAMA

Albert P. Brewer, who succeeded to the Alabama governorship on the death of Mrs. George C. Wallace in 1968, continued in office in 1969. By the middle of the year, observers had noted the emergence of a distinctive Brewer style of administration characterized by close attention to gubernatorial duties and an emphasis on modernization of the state government, economy and efficiency in government operations, and industrial development in the state.

The prohibition against gubernatorial succession in office, which had been the reason behind Mrs. Wallace's candidacy, was eliminated from the state's constitution. The new amendment dealing with succession enables Alabama's constitutional executive officers to succeed themselves in office for one additional term.

Judicial Legislation. The legislature met in both regular and special sessions in 1969. One of the significant developments to come out of these sessions involved the state's system of appellate courts. The legislature increased the membership of the state supreme court from seven to nine. The one existing intermediate-level appellate court was abolished and two such courts were created in its stead. The new court of criminal appeals and the new court of civil appeals consist of three judges each, and their combined jurisdiction is considerably greater than that vested in the former intermediate court.

Education. Governor Brewer called the legislature into special session in April to consider the problem of obtaining additional financial support for education. The administration's revenue measures were passed, largely intact, by the legislature and were expected to contribute significantly toward the governor's goal of "quality education" for the state. In addition, the legislature proposed a constitutional amendment to alter the existing state educational organization, which consisted of an elective state superintendent and a state board appointed by the governor. The amendment, ratified in December, provided for an elective state board of education with the power to appoint the state superintendent.

As the school year began in September, federal departures from "freedom of choice" as a means of achieving school desegregation aroused some controversy. Former Gov. George Wallace urged parents to take their children to the school of their choice despite court orders to the contrary, and he asked the legislature to demonstrate its support of the freedom-of-choice system of desegregation. The legislature then responded with a resolution, but a substantial number of legislators protested the revival of this type of opposition to federal programs. Wallace's action was widely interpreted in the press as indicative of his interest in the gubernatorial election of 1970. Governor Brewer stated that, in his opinion, the action was not "politically motivated"; nevertheless speculation on Wallace's plans continued.

Elections. Only municipal and special elections were held in the state of Alabama during 1969. In Greene county, where Negroes have a voting superiority of about two to one, a special election was held in July by order of the U. S. Supreme Court after it had been determined that the names of six black candidates had been wrongfully omitted from the ballot in the prior election. The six Negroes won the positions, thereby gaining for Negroes a majority vote on the county governing board and the county board of education.

The total number of Negro officeholders continued to increase in 1969 as Negroes were elected to seats on city councils in Anniston and Birmingham.

Court Actions. U. S. court actions included decisions that (1) directed the administration of Auburn University to permit Rev. William S. Coffin, Jr., Yale University chaplain, to address a student meeting after an invitation had been extended by students and withdrawn by the administration; (2) invalidated the state's vagrancy statute; and (3) declared unconstitutional a 60-year-old state obscenity statute.

The incident that aroused the most interest in the state, however, concerned the expulsion of a state senator charged with misconduct involving payment to obtain favorable committee action on a legislative bill. A Montgomery county grand jury later indicted the senator, but he was acquitted in the subsequent trial.

Convinced that public opinion demanded action, Governor Brewer promulgated by executive order a code of ethics for state governmental personnel and created a blue-ribbon ethics commission to administer the code. The legislature created interim committees to study the question of legislative ethics and the modernization and improvement of legislative organization and procedure in general.

JAMES D. THOMAS
University of Alabama

ALABAMA • Information Highlights

Area: 51,609 square miles (133,667 sq km).

Population: 3,577,000 (Jan. 1, 1969, est.).

Chief Cities (1968 est.): Montgomery, the capital, 146,000; Birmingham, 325,000; Mobile, 220,000; Huntsville, 143,000; Tuscaloosa, 74,000; Gadsden, 54,000.

Government: *Chief Officers*—governor, Albert P. Brewer (Democrat); secy. of state, Mrs. Mabel Amos (D); atty. gen., MacDonald Gallion (D); treas., Mrs. Agnes Baggett (D); supt. of pub. instr., Ernest Stone; chief justice, J. Ed. Livingston. *Legislature*—Senate, 35 members (33 Democrats, 1 Republican, 1 vacancy); House of Representatives, 106 members (104 D, 1 R, 1 vacancy).

Education: *School enrollment* (1968–69)—public elementary, 460,000 pupils (16,600 teachers); public secondary, 390,000 pupils (16,400 teachers); nonpublic schools, 28,900 pupils (1,450 teachers); college and university (fall 1967), 88,575 students. *Public school expenditures* (1967–68)—$395,000 ($497 per pupil); average teacher's salary, $5,900.

Public Finance (fiscal year 1968): *Revenues*, $1,078,364,000 (general sales and gross receipts taxes, $180,358,000; motor fuel tax, $102,674,000; federal funds, $308,335,000). *Expenditures*, $1,117,439,000 (education, $478,212,000; health, welfare, and safety, $203,023,000; highways, $166,004,000). *State debt*, $608,755,000 (June 30, 1968).

Personal Income (1968): $8,316,000,000; average annual income per person, $2,337.

Public Assistance (fiscal year 1968): $129,343,138 to 154,544 recipients (aged, $99,703,057; dependent children, $15,513,271).

Labor Force (employed persons, July 1969): *Agricultural*, 70,700; *nonagricultural* (wage and salary earners), $1,156,000 (27.4% manufacturing, 15.7% trade, 16.9% government). *Unemployed persons* (July 1969)—54,500.

Manufacturing (1966): Value added by manufacture, $3,644,184,000 (primary metals, $896,858,000; food and products, $253,230,000; fabricated metals, $200,310,000; transportation equipment, $196,177,000; electrical machinery, $118,949,000).

Agriculture (1967): Cash farm income, $683,034,000 (livestock, $424,776,000; crops, $169,078,000; govt. payments, $89,180,000). *Chief crops* (tons)—Pecans, 10,500 (ranks 4th among the states); corn, 1,059,500.

Mining (1967): Production value, $251,391,000. *Chief minerals* (tons)—Stone, 18,317,000; bituminous coal, 15,486,000; sand and gravel, 7,229,000.

Fisheries (1967): *Commercial catch*, 32,400,000 pounds ($8,900,000). *Leading species*—Shrimp, 14,455,572 pounds ($6,048,511).

Transportation: *Roads* (1969), 77,278 miles (124,340 km); *motor vehicles* (1967), 1,800,000; *railroads* (1968), 5,008.96 track miles (8,059 km); airports (1969), 9.

Communications (1969): *Telephones* (1968), 1,338,100; *television stations*, 17; *radio stations*, 166; *newspapers*, 21 (daily circulation, 1,370,129).

STATE OF ALASKA 23RD OIL AND GAS LEASE SALE

Map Courtesy of ALASKA MAP SERVICE, INC.

$,900,220,590

UPI

NORTH SLOPE mineral rights in Alaska drew bids of over $900 million (*above*). Preparations for drilling oil began at Prudhoe Bay (*left*).

SIKORSKY AIRCRAFT

ALASKA

Oil fever dominated Alaska's affairs in 1969. It created transportation blocks and political snarls, meanwhile overshadowing—and accelerating—the remainder of the economy.

Petroleum. In September the oil activity culminated in the 23d oil and gas lease sale in Alaska. This one smashed all records for such sales in the state. Competitive bidding among the major oil companies for acreage in the oil-rich North Slope provided $900,457,027 for the treasury and yielded $207,000 per day in interest on the deposits.

The first barrel of oil from the wells of the North Slope (between the Brooks Range and the Arctic Sea) was delivered on September 20 to the 115,000-ton supertanker S. S. *Manhattan,* the first commercial vessel to transit the Northwest Passage. Meanwhile, on the southern shore, Alaska's oil industry established a new $18 million refinery at Kenai. It is expected to process 15,000 barrels of crude oil per day from the state's share of Cook Inlet oil.

To advise the state on how to handle its oil bonanza, the government hired two sets of experts from "outside." Gov. Keith H. Miller engaged the Stanford Research Institute to survey the needs and resources of the state and to make long-range recommendations. The Legislative Council employed the Brookings Institution to conduct a statewide series of seminars designed to formulate policies for the future use of Alaska's resources.

Transportation. Moving supplies and equipment to the North Slope oilfields occupied the energies of the state's planners, as did the question of getting the oil to market. A winter road costing $766,291 for construction and maintenance was constructed in the winter of 1968 and used for six weeks in 1969 to bear more than 7,000 tons of cargo. Governor Miller abandoned the road to save wildlife, but then decided to keep it. By sea the largest barging operation in history delivered almost 94,000 tons of equipment to the North Slope. In April, more cargo was dispatched from the Fairbanks International Airport than from any other single airport in the world.

For getting the oil to market, the U. S. Interior Department requested $3,150,000 of Congress for a study to devise guidelines for, and to supervise construction and operation of, a proposed 800-mile

ALASKA · Information Highlights

Area: 586,400 square miles (1,518,778 sq km).
Population: 281,000 (Jan. 1, 1969).
Chief Cities (Jan. 1, 1969 est.): Juneau, the capital, 7,500; Anchorage, 52,000; Fairbanks, 17,500.
Government: *Chief Officers*—governor, Keith H. Miller (Republican); secy. of state, Robert W. Ward; atty. gen., G. Kent Edwards; commissioner, dept. of revenue, George A. Morrison; commissioner, dept. of educ., Dr. Cliff R. Hartman; chief justice, Buell A. Nesbett. *Legislature*—Senate, 20 members (9 Democrats, 11 Republicans); House of Representatives, 40 members (22 D, 18 R).
Education: *School enrollment* (fall 1968)—public elementary, 47,222 pupils (1,995 teachers); public secondary, 24,247 pupils (1,274 teachers); nonpublic schools, 2,300 pupils (170 teachers); college and university (fall 1967), 5,836 students. *Public school expenditures* (1968–69)—$94,-100,000 ($987 per pupil); average teacher's salary, $10,427.
Public Finance (fiscal year 1968): *Revenues,* $263,609,000 (total sales and gross receipts taxes, $16,291,000; motor fuel tax, $7,806,000; federal funds, $124,358,000). *Expenditures,* $286,550,000 (education, $41,666,000; health, welfare, and safety, $18,266,000; highways, $89,955,000). *State debt,* $176,850,000.
Personal Income (1968): $1,136,000,000; average annual income per person, $4,146.
Public Assistance (fiscal year 1967): $4,977,228 to 84,756 recipients (aged, $2,672,908; dependent children, $2,304,-319).
Labor Force (employed persons, calendar year 1968): *Agricultural,* 100,114; *nonagricultural* (wage and salary), 90,-110 (8.7% manufacturing, 15.7% trade, 40.3% government). *Unemployed persons*—9,127.
Manufacturing (1966): Value added by manufacture, $131,-060,000 (food and products, $65,872,000; lumber, $16,-922,000).
Agriculture (1967): *Cash farm income,* $4,330,000 (livestock, $3,159,000; crops, $1,101,000; govt. payments, $70,000).
Mining (1968): Production value, $218,600,000. *Chief minerals*—crude petroleum, 66,148,000 bbls; sand and gravel, 17,585,000 tons; natural gas, 49,326,000,000 cubic feet; coal, 812,000 tons; gold (1967), 22,948 troy ounces; (1967), silver (1968), 6,000 troy ounces.
Fisheries (1967): *Commercial catch,* 369,000,000 pounds ($47,000,000). *Leading species* (1966)—salmon, 333,325,-300 pounds ($54,201,954); king crab, 159,201,700 pounds ($15,670,485).
Transportation: *Roads* (1966), 6,562 miles (10,560 km); *motor vehicles* (1969), 139,580; *railroads* (1968), 552.5 track miles (889.9 km); *public and military airports* (1967), 458.
Communications (1968): *Telephones* (1967), 64,000; *television stations,* 7; *radio stations,* 20; *newspapers,* 7.

pipeline to the North Slope wells. The projected Trans-Alaska Pipeline System (TAPS), organized by three major oil companies, has received 500,000 tons of 48-inch pipe at the Alaskan port of Valdez. An access road is being built from Livengood to the Yukon River in order to facilitate construction of the pipeline.

Politics. When Alaska's Gov. Walter J. Hickel became U. S. secretary of the interior, Alaskan Secretary of State Keith H. Miller, a Republican, became governor. Hickel had named Theodore Stevens, majority leader of the Alaska House of Representatives, to the U. S. Senate seat left vacant by the death of veteran Sen. E. L. (Bob) Bartlett.

The Legislature. The Alaskan legislature had in 1969 the longest session in its history. The session lasted 95 days, 35 of them after the governor had told the members to go home. Opposing parties held slim majorities in the two houses. The most significant legislation passed in 1969 was an $8.2 million revenue-sharing plan. Local political subdivisions now will receive state funds apportioned according to their responsibilities and can spend the funds as they see fit. The lawmakers also created a public defender system, enacted an air-pollution control program, and raised the legal interest rate. A record budget of $154 million was passed.

Amchitka Bomb Tests. On October 2 the Atomic Energy Commission (AEC) conducted underground calibration tests, detonating a 1.2 megaton hydrogen bomb, despite protests by Japan and Canada and by some scientists and conservationists in the United States. The purpose of the calibration tests was to determine the island's capacity to sus-

tain bigger tests to be carried out in the future.

The Economy. The number of out-of-state corporations authorized to do business in Alaska doubled between Jan. 1 and Sept. 1, 1969. Building permits in Alaska's largest city, Anchorage, rose 56% over 1968. The two-way trade with Japan through Alaskan ports climbed to $23.3 million for six months, a gain of $1.7 million over a similar period in 1968.

RONALD E. CHINN
University of Alaska

ALBANIA

The year 1969 marked the 25th anniversary of the Communist seizure of power in Albania.

The country's Chinese-inspired Ideological and Cultural Revolution entered its fourth year, with continuing emphasis on the elimination of all remaining "bourgeois" and "revisionist" traits in Albanian life.

Visibly shaken by the Soviet-led intervention in Czechoslovakia in 1968, the Albanian government increased its 1969 defense budget by 40%. During November and December 1968, Albania sought and received promises of additional Chinese military and economic assistance.

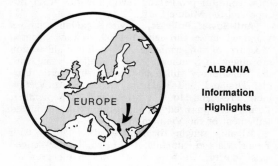

ALBANIA

Information Highlights

Area: 11,099 square miles (28,748 sq km).
Population: 2,019,000 (1968 est.).
Chief Cities (1964 est.): Tiranë, the capital, 156,950; Durrës, 45,935; Shkodër, 45,925.
Government: *President of the Presidium*—Haxhi Lleshi (took office in 1953); *Premier*—Maj. Gen. Mehmet Shehu (took office in 1954); *First Secretary of the Albanian Labor Party*—Gen. Enver Hoxha (took office in 1946). *Legislature* (unicameral)—People's Assembly, 240 members (all members of the Albanian Labor Party).
Education: *Literacy rate* (1965), 71.5% of the population aged 9 and over. *Total school enrollment* (1965)—453,254 (primary 361,241; secondary, 55,261; teacher-training, 5,417; technical/vocational, 18,574; university/higher, 12,-761).
Finance (1965 est.): *Revenues,* $684,000,000; *expenditures,* $672,000,000; *monetary unit,* lek; (5 leks equal U. S.$1).
Manufacturing (metric tons, 1966): Cement, 135,000; gasoline (1965), 45,000; sugar (1967), 15,000; olive oil, 4,000.
Crops (metric tons, 1967–68 crop year): Maize, 165,000; sugar beets, 150,000; wheat (1966), 115,000; cotton seed, 16,000; oats, 16,000.
Minerals (metric tons, 1967): Crude petroleum, 1,091,000; chromite (1965) 315,000; lignite, 340,000; copper (1966), 4,000; nickel ore (1965), 3,700.
Foreign Trade (1964): *Exports,* $59,924,000 (chief exports, 1964: Fuels, minerals, metals, $32,500,000; foodstuffs, $13,800,000; organic raw material, $10,000,000); *Imports,* $98,128,000 (chief imports, 1964: machinery and equipment, $48,680,000; fuels, minerals, metals, $14,680,000; raw material for food industry, $11,320,000). *Chief trading partners* (1964): Communist China (took 41% of exports, supplied 63% of imports); Czechoslovakia (took 19% of exports, supplied 9% of imports); Poland (took 10% of exports, supplied 8% of imports).
Transportation: *Motor vehicles* (1966), 9,900 (automobiles, 2,500); *railways* (1965), 65 miles (105 km); *merchant vessels* (1967), 8 (33,000 gross registered tons).
Communications: *Telephones* (1968): 4,813; *television stations* (1968), 1; *television sets* (1968), 1,000; *radios* (1967), 135,-000; *newspapers* (1966), 2 (daily circulation, 87,000).

Relations with China. In a new economic agreement signed in November, China agreed to supply a further loan and additional technical assistance that would enable Albania to undertake "several important projects" and to expand its industrial base.

Between Nov. 27 and Dec. 3, 1968, a Chinese military delegation visited the country to bolster Albanian morale. This morale had sagged markedly following the Soviet intervention in Czechoslovakia. The major by-product of this visit appears to have been a Chinese promise to aid Albania in the construction of a defensive missile system to improve its ability to resist potential Soviet aggression in the Balkans. Reports from Albania during 1969 indicated that the Chinese were fulfilling their pledge.

Albania supported the Chinese in their clash with the Soviet Union over the Ussuri River border in March. Albanian leaders endorsed the "correct and proven policies" of Mao Tse-tung and Lin Piao and joined with Peking in condemning the convocation of the Moscow meeting of world Communist parties in June. Radio Peking in June inaugurated a program of broadcasts to Albania.

During 1969, Albania's role as Peking's major propaganda base in Europe was expanded. In addition to utilizing the powerful radio transmitters that they had constructed in Albania, the Chinese were reported to have established a school in Tiranë to train youthful pro-Peking revolutionaries from Europe and the Middle East.

Anti-Soviet Policies. Soviet-Albanian relations remained tense throughout 1969. Tiranë accused Moscow of undermining the national liberation movement in Southeast Asia by collaborating with the "reactionary ruling cliques" of Indonesia, Burma, Thailand, and Malaysia. When North Vietnamese President Ho Chi Minh died in September, Tiranë reemphasized its opposition to a negotiated settlement of the Vietnam War.

Albania sought to improve its relations with Yugoslavia and Rumania. In March, Tiranë pledged its solidarity with both these states in the event of conflict with the USSR. Albania also continued to express its opposition to the Soviet hard-line policy toward Czechoslovakia.

Domestic Affairs. Albanian leaders devoted much attention to preparations for the silver jubilee of the Communist takeover in November. They stressed the importance of realizing the goals set in the 1969 economic plan, which called for an increase of 12.4% in industrial production; 22.1% in agricultural output; 16.4% in national income; 10.9% in domestic trade turnover; and 8.7% in exports.

For the 25th anniversary of the Communist regime, the government in November reduced the prices of consumer goods, abolished the income tax, and granted new economic concessions to the peasants.

NICHOLAS C. PANO
Western Illinois University

ALBERTA

Significant economic advances occurred in the northern part of Alberta in 1969. New Premier Harry E. Strom, who had taken office in December 1968, led the provincial government during the year.

Economy. The locally owned Alberta Resources Railway was completed at a cost of about $96 million. It provides access to great reserves of timber, oil, gas, coal, and other minerals in the northwestern part of the province. Exploitation of coal reserves began immediately, to fill Japanese orders, and the new town of Grande Cache experienced boom conditions.

There was much labor unrest in 1969, including a 15-day strike of transit workers in Edmonton.

Alberta had near-record grain harvests, but declining prices and shrinking markets caused serious storage problems. However, beef prices reached new highs, reflecting steady export demands.

Government. Harry E. Strom, a former municipal affairs minister, was elected leader of the Alberta Social Credit party on Dec. 6, 1968 and became premier on December 12. In May, he reorganized the entire cabinet, which he had named in December.

On July 1, Alberta joined most other provinces in the federally sponsored Medicare plan by introducing a compulsory health insurance program. The provincial government also established three agencies for the development of human resources.

Education. As a result of burgeoning enrollments, the three Alberta universities appealed to the public for capital assistance to supplement massive provincial grants for buildings and equipment.

In June there were scattered student demonstrations against the dismissals of some high school teachers. In September, a teachers' strike closed all schools in Minburn County.

JOHN W. CHALMERS
University of Alberta

--------- **ALBERTA · Information Highlights** ---------

Area: 255,285 square miles (661,189 sq km).

Population: 1,547,000 (Jan. 1, 1969 est.).

Chief Cities (1968): Edmonton, the capital (393,563); Calgary (354,856); Lethbridge (37,760); Red Deer (26,730); Medicine Hat (25,574).

Government: *Chief Officers*—lt. gov., J. W. Grant MacEwan; premier, Harry Edwin Strom (Social Credit party); prov. secy., Ambrose Holowach (SC); atty. gen., Edgar H. Gerhart (SC); prov. treas., Anders Olav Aalborg (SC); min. of educ., Robert Curtis Clark (SC); chief justice, Sidney Bruce Smith. *Legislature*—Legislative Assembly (convened Feb. 13, 1969); 65 members (54 Social Credit, 10 Progressive Conservative, 1 independent).

Education: School enrollment (1966–67 est.)—public elementary and secondary, 372,894 pupils (16,839 teachers); private schools, 5,324 pupils (310 teachers); Indian (federal) schools, 3,625 pupils (171 teachers); college and university (fall 1966), 16,983 students. *Public school expenditures* (1963)—$153,424,000 ($495 per pupil); medium teacher's salary (1967–68) $7,499.

Public Finance (fiscal year 1968 est.): *Revenues,* $522,000,000 (sales tax, $73,820,000; income tax, $135,225,000; federal funds, $50,914,000). *Expenditures,* $604,000,000 (education, $282,400,000; health and social welfare, $167,640,000; transport and communications, $94,930,000).

Personal Income (1967 est.): $3,535,000,000; average annual income per person, $2,372.

Social Welfare (fiscal year 1968 est.): $38,210,000 (aged and blind, $3,520,000; dependents and unemployed, $17,740,-000).

Manufacturing (1966): Value added by manufacture, $527,-197,000 (transportation equipment, $14,565,000; primary metals, $31,368,000; nonelectrical machinery, $11,844,000; electrical machinery, $7,852,000; food and beverages, $140,696,000; fabricated metals, $44,057,000; wood industries, $34,769,000).

Agriculture (1968): *Cash farm income,* $810,900,000 (livestock, $425,215,000; crops, $371,474,000; govt. payments (1966), $13,895,000). *Chief crops* (cash receipts)—wheat, $155,-941,000 (ranks 2d among the provinces); barley, $48,153,-000 (ranks 1st); rapeseed, $15,232,000 (ranks 1st); sugarbeets, $7,024,000 (ranks 1st); oats, $6,340,000 (ranks 2d).

Mining (1967 est.): *Production value,* $996,833,364. *Chief minerals:* sulphur, 2,220,000 tons (ranks 1st among the provinces); crude petroleum, 231,587,000 bbl. (ranks 1st); natural gas, 1,180,000,000,000 cubic feet (ranks 1st).

Transportation: *Roads* (1966), 74,563 miles (119,994 km); *motor vehicles* (1966), 638,852; *railroads* (1966) 5,680 track miles (9,141 km).

Communications: *Telephones* (1966), 577,827; *television stations* (1967), 7; *radio stations* (1967), 21; *daily newspapers* (1966), 7 (daily circulation, 290,951).

All figures given in Canadian dollars equal to U. S.93¢.

ALCOHOLIC BEVERAGES

Sales and production figures reflected continued growth in the brewing, distilling, and wine industries in the United States.

BREWING INDUSTRY

Beer sales in the United States set a record in the 1969 fiscal year, for the eighth successive year. Sales totaled 111,866,595 barrels of 31 gallons each —4,396,165 barrels higher than in fiscal 1968. The brewing industry set monthly record sales in 10 of the 12 months ending in June 1969.

About 7.4% of the U. S. population live where the sale of beer and ale is prohibited. The results of 1,180 local-option elections held in 1968 increased by 180,895 the number of persons living in areas where it is legal to sell malt beverages.

Brewers paid more than $1 billion in state and federal taxes in calendar year 1968, and they contributed more than $6 billion to the national economy. During 1968 brewers expended more than $285 million for agricultural products, $725 million for kegs, bottles, cans, and related materials, and $550 million in direct salaries and wages, as well as substantial amounts paid in a variety of employee benefits.

HENRY B. KING
United States Brewers Association, Inc.

DISTILLING INDUSTRY

Production of distilled spirits in the United States in fiscal 1969 amounted to 985,641,278 tax gallons, up from 905,459,342 gallons in 1968. Whiskey accounted for 179,943,428 gallons of the 1969 production. (A tax or proof gallon is a standard U. S. gallon of 231 cubic inches containing 50% of ethyl alcohol by volume; a wine gallon is a standard U. S. gallon regardless of proof.)

Rectified Spirits. In the 1969 fiscal year rectifying plants used 117,874,537 proof gallons (108,927,208 proof gallons in the 1968 fiscal year) of domestic and imported liquors. Production by rectification amounted to 117,169,116 proof gallons (109,558,682 proof gallons in 1968). Whiskey accounted for about 61% of the production by rectification.

Output for Consumption. In the 1968 calendar year the bottled output of domestic and imported distilled spirits was 292,638,855 wine gallons, an increase of 2.3% over the previous year. Whiskey represented 61.8% of all spirits bottled in 1968 and amounted to 181,157,247 gallons, an increase of 0.8% over 1967 bottling. Increased bottling in 1968 was reported for all other classes of spirits. Rum led the percentage increase at 11.1%, followed by cordials and liqueurs 7.2%; vodka, 6.9%; brandy, 2.6%; and gin, 0.6%.

Apparent Consumption. The apparent U. S. consumption of distilled spirits in 1968 rose 6.4% over 1967 to 345,487,825 wine gallons. This figure is based on wholesale and retail sales in the control states and on tax collections or shipments to wholesalers in the license states.

Imports and Exports. Dutiable imports of distilled spirits into the United States in 1968 amounted to 75,543,788 gallons, with whiskey making up 88% of the total. Exports of distilled spirits amounted to 3,206,862 gallons.

ROBERT W. COYNE, *President*
Distilled Spirits Institute, Inc.

WINE INDUSTRY

Widespread rains during ripening were detrimental to wine quality in Europe in 1968. Prolonged wet spells in South Africa's 1968–69 season caused their first serious outbreak of downy mildew, and drought depressed Argentina's wine production. In California, 1968 was one of the best years, overall, in the last three decades.

The increasing interest in good table wine in the United States has led to new plantings and new wineries, many of the latter small. But in 1969 several wineries were purchased by large companies having other beverage interests. New plantings in California are of varieties selected to upgrade wines and freed of the five known serious and widespread virus vine diseases.

Increasing wages and vineyard labor strife have hastened labor-saving developments in California (and also caused the uprooting of some table-grape vineyards). Mechanical harvesting of wine and juice grapes has made the transition from the trial stage to commercial acceptance. In 1969 about 40% of New York grapes were harvested mechanically, compared with only about 15% in 1968.

Production. World wine production in 1968 dropped 0.4% from 1967, but it was 4.1% above the average for the previous five years. Improved technology increased production in Greece and Chile; additional bearing acreage raised output in the USSR, United States, and South Africa. In spite of 1.4% increase in production, California saw its share of U. S. wine output decrease 2.2% to 80.4%.

WORLD WINE PRODUCTION
(Millions of U.S. gallons)

Region	1968	1967	Average 1963–67
Algeria	271.0	165.7	265.9
Argentina	578.4	744.2	564.9
Canada	11.4	10.8	...
Chile	141.6	129.1	118.8
France	1,720.3	1,611.5	1,614.1
Germany, West	159.8	160.3	153.9
Greece	126.4	117.9	98.2
Hungary	128.6	126.8	102.3
Italy	1,723.4	1,974.1	1,733.4
Portugal	315.6	260.8	321.6
Rumania	150.3	114.7	155.1
South Africa	130.1	114.2	106.7
Spain	631.4	619.5	745.9
USSR	489.1	447.1	405.7
United States	214.5	206.1	205.3
California	172.6	170.2	173.2
Yugoslavia	160.6	138.2	147.0
28 other countries	505.5	485.0	...
World total	7,398.1	7,426.1	7,109.7

Source: Office International de la Vigne et du Vin, Paris, and Wine Institute, San Francisco.

Consumption. U. S. wine consumption in 1968 was 1.069 gallons per capita, up 4% from 1967. Table wine constituted 44.8% of the total; sparkling wine, 5.9%; dessert wine and sherry, 37.4%; vermouth, 4.6%; and other flavored wines, 7.3%. For the first time, consumption of natural wines (12% alcohol) exceeded that of fortified wines (20% alcohol).

U. S. consumption of foreign wine increased by 14.6% to 10.4% of national consumption in 1968.

California accounted for 21.6% of U. S. wine consumption, at 2.42 gallons per capita. New York was the second-ranking state (13.5%, or 1.59 gallons per capita). Annual per capita wine consumption is about 32 gallons in France, 4.1 gallons in West Germany, and 7/10 of a gallon in England.

VERNON L. SINGLETON
University of California, Davis

ALGERIA

For Algeria, 1969 was a year of consolidation and economic progress, in contrast to the previous seven years of independence.

Domestic Affairs. The government of Col. Houari Boumedienne went ahead with its plans to strengthen state institutions and held elections in May for departmental assemblies. Members for each of the 15 assemblies were chosen from a list of names presented by the National Liberation Front (FLN), Algeria's only party. These consultative bodies, elected for 5 years, will give advice on economic matters to government-appointed prefects and will vote on departmental budgets.

During the past two years the provincial administration has been strengthened, while the influence of the army in decisions has declined. In late autumn FLN chief Kaïd Ahmed lost his post, and President Boumedienne showed interest in directly supervising party affairs, presumably because the party might be used to mobilize the population in government programs. The question in Algeria is still whether the people will respond enthusiastically and agree to aid development efforts on the regime's terms.

In the country's first political trials since Boumedienne came to power four years ago, exiled Belkacem Krim, deputy premier of the provisional government before independence, and others were found guilty of conspiring to assassinate Algeria's chief leaders. Participants in the attempted army coup of 1967 also received prison sentences.

In October severe floods hit parts of Algeria. There were 68 persons killed, and more than 100,-000 were left homeless.

Foreign Affairs. Algeria drew closer to the

ALGERIA • Information Highlights

Area: 919,590 square miles (2,381,741 sq km).
Population: 12,943,000 (1968 est.).
Chief Cities (April 4, 1966 est.): Algiers, the capital, 943,142; Oran, 328,257.
Government: *President*—Col. Houari Boumedienne (took office June 19, 1965).
Religious Faiths: Muslims, over 90% of population.
Education: *Literacy rate* (1954), 19% of population aged 15 and over. *School enrollment* (1967)—primary, 1,350,220; secondary, 170,000; university, 9,000.
Finance (1969 est.): Operating budget $794,000,000; *monetary unit,* dinar (4.937 dinars equal U. S.$1).
Gross National Product (1967): $3,600,000,000.
National Income (1965 est.): $2,259,000,000; average annual income per person, $193.
Economic Indexes (1965): *Industrial production,* 105 (1963 = 100); *agricultural production* (1967), 87 (1963 = 100); *cost of living* (1966), 103 (1958 = 100).
Manufacturing (metric tons, 1967): Wine, 6,821,000 hectoliters; cement, 731,000; natural gasoline, 688,000; wheat flour, 395,000; olive oil, 20,000.
Crops (metric tons, 1967–68 crop year): Grapes, 322,000; wheat, 1,266,000; citrus fruits (1966), 382,000; barley, 299,000; tobacco, 13,600.
Minerals (metric tons, 1967): Crude petroleum (1968), 43,000,-000; iron ore, 1,760,000; natural gas, 2,158,000,000 cubic meters.
Foreign Trade (1967): *Exports,* $724,000,000 (chief exports: crude petroleum, $502,228,000; wine, $54,425,000; citrus fruits, $22,908,000; iron ore, $23,290,000; *imports* (1968), $788,000,000 (chief imports, 1967: sugar, $25,805,000; iron & steel, $46,627,000; wheat, $53,169,000). *Chief trading partners* (1967): France (took 60% of exports, supplied 60% of imports); United States (took 2% of exports, supplied 8% of imports); Italy (took 3% of exports, supplied 3% of imports).
Transportation: *Roads* (1966), 55,000 miles (88,495 km); *motor vehicles* (1967), 178,000 (automobiles 98,000); *railways* (1965), 2,548 miles (4,100 km); *merchant vessels* (1967), 4 (15,000 gross registered tons); *national airline,* Air Algeria; *principal airports,* Algiers, Oran.
Communications: *Telephones* (1968): 145,000; *television stations* (1967), 9; *television sets* (1969), 250,000; *radios* (1967), 700,000; *newspapers* (1967), 8 (daily circulation, 185,000).

Soviet Union in most areas of foreign policy. The two states differed only on the Arab-Israeli crisis, as Algeria continued to insist on the necessity of escalating the guerrilla operations of Palestinian Arabs against Israel. About 3,000 Russians worked with the Algerian army, oil industry, and government agencies, while 600 Algerian pilots and other technicians attended courses in the USSR.

Algerian exports to Russia quadrupled between 1966 and 1968, and they should reach $100 million in 1969. In March, Russia agreed to import 132 million gallons (5 million hectoliters) of Algerian wine each year until 1975 and also agreed to participate in 82 development projects. Good relations were crowned by the visit of Soviet President Nikolai V. Podgorny to Algiers in the spring.

Despite the break in diplomatic relations with Washington, the Algerian ministry of industry turned to U. S. companies for investment capital and technical assistance to help develop the booming mining, oil, and natural gas industries. El Paso Natural Gas negotiated a $1 billion investment agreement, representing the largest single externally financed project in Africa.

Relations with France improved slightly with the visit in September of Foreign Minister Maurice Schumann to Algiers. France settled a point of contention by tentatively agreeing to import 105 million gallons (4 million hectoliters) of wine. Earlier in the year the French promised to contribute $150 million toward the development of the gas industry. Although Algeria has put emphasis on Arabizing education, 3,500 French teachers served in the country's schools as technical assistants.

Relations between Morocco and Algeria continued to improve. President Boumedienne visited Morocco in January. King Hassan II of Morocco and the Algerian leader discussed a 20-year treaty of solidarity and cooperation. Despite disagreement over the Arab-Israeli crisis (Morocco favored a negotiated settlement), Algeria sent a delegation to the Islamic conference in Rabat.

On June 29, exactly two years after being kidnapped, Moïse Tshombe, the former premier of Congo (Kinshasa), died in an Algerian prison. Relations with the Congo had been strained because of the Algerian government's refusal to extradite Tshombe (who had been sentenced to death in absentia), and his death allowed the Boumedienne government to avoid embarrassment at the Pan-African Cultural Festival held in Algiers in July. The Algerians used the event to promote the Palestinian Liberation Movement.

Economy. Budgetary receipts increased 18% between 1968 and 1969. All ministries received an increase in funds, except national defense, a positive result of the détente with Morocco.

On February 14 the government issued an ordinance favoring the agricultural development of 5,-700,000 acres (2,300,000 hectares) of nationalized land, and it increased investments in agriculture by nearly 30%. Nationalization acts in May and August brought most external commerce under state control. The completion of the $300 million state-owned steel plant near Annaba in June symbolized Algeria's new drive to develop its industries.

STUART SCHAAR
Brooklyn College, City University of New York

ALLEN, James E. See biographical sketch under EDUCATION.

ALLERGIES

Much of the important research in allergies during 1969 centered upon tests for allergens, the substances that cause allergies. Other research was concerned with methods of treating allergies and discovering new allergens. There was also a study of the effects of humidity on asthma.

Allergy Tests. Penicillin, a leading allergen, is known to cause more than 3,000 deaths a year, and so it is significant that skin tests for penicillin sensitivity were reported. One test uses a derivative of the drug penicilloyl polylysine (PPL) which, when injected into the skin of a susceptible person, causes the area to become reddish.

A blood test developed in England may prove useful in testing for allergies caused by foods and pollen. This test, called the radio-allergosorbent test (R.A.S.T.), uses a technique in which antibodies to specific allergens are absorbed out of the patient's serum and identified by radioactive antibodies. This test bolsters the belief that allergy antibodies are unique substances found in a specific (IgE) fraction of the blood's gamma globulin.

Provocation tests were reported as safe specific procedures for identifying allergens. In these tests the patient is exposed to offending substances by inhaling them into the nose or lungs. The resistance to the passage of air, which increases after exposure to known allergens, is then measured. This test also showed a "priming effect," in which smaller doses of allergen were needed each succeeding day to cause the same amount of airway resistance. This may explain why hay fever symptoms trouble more people as the season progresses.

Allergy Treatment. In treatment, further work with disodiumcromoglycate (Intal) continued to prove its effectiveness against asthma. However, this drug, which is administered through inhalation, is not yet available to the general public. From India came a report of relieving asthma by chewing the leaves of the plant *Tylophoria indica*. Another substance reported helpful in treating asthma is metraproternol, which can be taken by mouth.

Allergoids, injectable substances prepared by treating allergens with formalin, continued to be useful for treating allergies. Such treatment by injecting increasing amounts of allergen is called immunotherapy. Although immunotherapy has been demonstrated to be effective in allergy management, warnings were sounded about the use of gamma globulin injections since they have been shown to be both useless and potentially harmful.

New Allergens. The list of air-borne allergens increased during 1969 with the addition of a mite, *Dermatophagoides farinae*, and the German cockroach, *Blatella germanica*. The list of known mold spore allergens was also enlarged, and important cross reactions among various groups were shown. Green algae were also added to the roster of air-borne allergens.

Humidity and Asthma. In a well-executed study, children were kept in an environmental control room under conditions of stable temperature but changing humidity. No improvement was seen in the lung function of either normal or asthmatic children when the humidity was increased from 50% to 90%.

IRWIN J. POLK, M. D.
St. Luke's Hospital, New York City

ALUMINUM. See MINING.

AMBASSADORS AND ENVOYS

In 1969 the United States opened diplomatic relations with two countries—Cambodia, after a four-year break incited by problems over the Vietnam War, and the Islamic Republic of Mauritania, after a two-year break. On October 24, following two years of strained relations, Southern Yemen severed diplomatic relations with the United States, giving U. S. embassy personnel 24 hours to depart.

In the following list of ambassadors and envoys from and to the United States as of Dec. 31, 1969, A designates ambassador extraordinary and plenipotentiary; CA, chargé d'affaires; DCM, deputy chief of mission.

LIST OF AMBASSADORS AND ENVOYS

Country	From U. S.	To U. S.
Afghanistan	Robert G. Neumann (A)	Abdullah Malikyar (A)
Argentina	John Davis Lodge (A)	Rafael M. Vazquez (CA)
Australia	Walter L. Rice (A)	John Keith Waller (A)
Austria	John P. Hunes (A)	Karl Gruber (A)
Barbados	Eileen R. Donovan (A)	Valerie Theodore McComie (A)
Belgium	John S. D. Eisenhower (A)	Walter Loridan (A)
Bolivia	Ernest V. Siracusa (A)	Julio Sanjines-Goytia (A)
Botswana	Charles H. Pletcher (DCM)	Linchwe II Molefi Kgafela (A)
Brazil	C. Burke Elbrick (A)	Celso Diniz (CA)
Bulgaria	John M. McSweeney (A)	Luben Guerassimov (A)
Burma	Arthur W. Hummel, Jr. (A)	U San Maung (A)
Burundi	Thomas Patrick Melady (A)	Terence Nsanze (A)
Cambodia	Lloyd M. Rives (CA)	Thay Sok (CA)
Cameroon	Lewis Hoffacker (A)	Joseph N. Owono (A)
Canada	Adolph W. Schmidt (A)	A. Edgar Ritchie (A)
Central Afr. Rep.	Geoffrey W. Lewis (A)	Michel Gallin-Douathe (A)
Ceylon	Andrew V. Corry (A)	Oliver Weerasinghe (A)
Chad	Terence A. Todman (A)	Lazare Massibe (A)
Chile	Edward M. Korry (A)	Domingo Santa María (A)
China (Taiwan)	Walter P. McConaughy (A)	Chow Shu-Kai (A)
Colombia	Jack Hood Vaughn (A)	Douglas Botero-Bashell (A)
Congo (Kinshasa)	Sheldon B. Vance (A)	Justin-Marie Bomboko (A)
Costa Rica	Sandy MacGregor Pringle (DCM)	Luis Demetrio Tinoco (A)
Cyprus	David H. Popper (A)	Zenon Rossides (A)
Czechoslovakia	Malcolm Toon (A)	Ivan Rohal-Ilkiv (A)
Dahomey	Matthew J. Looram, Jr. (A)	Maxime-Leopold Zollner (A)
Denmark	Guilford Dudley, Jr. (A)	Torben Rønne (A)
Dominican Republic	Francis E. Meloy, Jr. (A)	Mario Read-Vittini (A)
Ecuador	Edson O. Sessions (A)	Carlos Mantilla-Ortega (A)
El Salvador	William Garton Bowdler (A)	Julio A. Rivera (A)
Equatorial Guinea	Lewis Hoffacker (A)	....
Ethiopia	William O. Hall (A)	Minasse Haile (A)
Finland	Val Peterson (A)	Olavi Munkki (A)
France	Robert Sargent Shriver, Jr. (A)	Charles Lucet (A)
Gabon	Richard Funkhouser (A)	Gaston R. Bouckat-Nziengui (A)
Gambia	L. Dean Brown (A)	....
Germany	Kenneth Rush (A)	Rolf Pauls (A)
Ghana	Thomas W. McElhiney (A)	Ebenezer Moses Debrah (A)
Great Britain	Walter H. Annenberg (A)	John Freeman (A)
Greece	Henry J. Tasca (A)	Basil George Vitsaxis (A)
Guatemala	Nathaniel Davis (A)	Francisco Linares Aranda (A)
Guinea	....	Fadiala Keita (A)

KIDNAPPED AMBASSADOR, C. Burke Elbrick, U. S. envoy to Brazil, returns to his wife (*below*) in the embassy in Rio de Janeiro on Sept. 7, 1969, after Brazil met captors' demands and freed 15 political prisoners, shown (*left*) arriving by jet airliner in Mexico City.

UPI

CLAUS MEYER, FROM BLACK STAR

LIST OF AMBASSADORS AND ENVOYS (continued)

Country	From U.S.	To U.S.
Guyana	Spencer M. King (A)	John Carter (A)
Haiti	Clinton E. Knox (A)	Arthur Bonhomme (A)
Honduras	Hewson A. Ryan (A)	Armando Alvarez Martinez (CA)
Hungary	Alfred Puhan (A)	Janos Nagy (A)
Iceland	Luther I. Replogle (A)	Magnus V. Magnusson (A)
India	Kenneth B. Keating	Nawab Ali Yavar Jung (A)
Indonesia	Francis J. Galbraith	Soedjatmoko (A)
Iran	Douglas MacArthur II (A)	Amir-Aslan Afshar (A)
Ireland	John D. J. Moore (A)	Séan O'hÉideain (CA)
Israel	Walworth Barbour (A)	Yitzhak Rabin (A)
Italy	Graham A. Martin (A)	Egidio Ortona (A)
Ivory Coast	John F. Root (A)	Timothée N'Guetta Ahoua (A)
Jamaica	Vincent de Roulet (A)	Egerton R. Richardson (A)
Japan	Armin H. Meyer (A)	Takeso Shimoda (A)
Jordan	Harrison M. Symmes (A)	Abdul Hamid Sharaf (A)
Kenya	Robinson McIlvaine	Leonard Oliver Kibinge (A)
Korea	William J. Porter (A)	Dong Jo Kim (A)
Kuwait	John Patrick Walsh (A)	Talat Al-Ghoussein (A)
Laos	G. McMurtrie Godley	Khamking Souvanlasy (A)
Lebanon	Dwight J. Porter (A)	Najati Kabbani (A)
Lesotho	Norman E. Barth (DCM)	Mothusi T. Mashologu (A)
Liberia	Samuel Z. Westerfield, Jr. (A)	S. Edward Peal (A)
Libyan Arab Republic	Joseph Palmer 2d	Fathi Abidia (A)
Luxembourg	Kingdon Gould, Jr. (A)	Jean Wagner (A)
Malagasy Republic	Anthony D. Marshall (A)	René Gilbert Ralison (CA)
Malawi	Marshall P. Jones (A)	Nyemba Wales Mbekeani (A)
Malaysia	Jack W. Lydman (A)	Tan Sri Ong Yoke Lin (A)
Maldives	Andrew V. Corry	Abdul Sattar (A)
Mali	G. Edward Clark (A)	Seydou Traore (A)
Malta	John C. Pritzlaff, Jr. (A)	Arvid Pardo (A)
Mauritania	....	....
Mauritius	Julian P. Fromer (DCM)	Pierre Guy Girald Balancy (A)

Country	From U.S.	To U.S.
Mexico	Robert H. McBride (A)	Hugo B. Margáin (A)
Morocco	....	Ahmed Osman (A)
Nepal	Carol C. Laise (A)	Kul Shekhar Sharma (A)
Netherlands	J. William Middendorf II (A)	Rijnhard B. Van Lynden (A)
New Zealand	Kenneth Franzheim II (A)	Frank Corner (A)
Nicaragua	Kennedy M. Crockett (A)	Guillermo Sevilla-Sacasa (A)
Niger	....	Adamou Mayaki (A)
Nigeria	William C. Trueheart (A)	Joe Iyalla (A)
Norway	Philip K. Crowe (A)	Arne Gunneng (A)
Pakistan	Joseph S. Farland (A)	Agha Hilaly (A)
Panama	Robert M. Sayre (A)	Roberto R. Aleman (A)
Paraguay	J. Raymond Ylitalo (A)	Roque J. Avila (A)
Peru	Taylor C. Belcher (A)	Fernando Berckemeyer (A)
Philippines	Henry A. Byroade (A)	Ernesto V. Lagdameo (A)
Poland	Walter J. Stoessel, Jr. (A)	Jerzy Michalowski (A)
Portugal	Ridgway B. Knight (A)	Vasco Vieira Garin (A)
Rumania	Leonard C. Meeker (A)	Corneliu Bogdan (A)
Rwanda	Leo G. Cyr (A)	Fidèle Nkundabagenzi (A)
Saudi Arabia	Hermann F. Eilts (A)	Ibrahim Al-Sowayel (A)
Senegal	L. Dean Brown (A)	Cheikh Ibrahima Fall (A)
Sierra Leone	Robert G. Miner (A)	John J. Akar (A)
Singapore	Charles T. Cross (A)	Ernest Steven Monteiro (A)
Somali Republic	Fred L. Hadsel (A)	Yusuf O. Azhari (A)
South Africa	William M. Rountree (A)	H. L. T. Taswell (A)
Spain	Robert C. Hill (A)	Marquis de Merry del Val (A)
Swaziland	Chris C. Pappas, Jr. (DCM)	S. T. Msindazwe Sukati (A)
Sweden	Turner C. Cameron, Jr. (DCM)	Hubert de Besche (A)
Switzerland	Shelby Davis (A)	Felix Schnyder (A)
Tanzania	Claude G. Ross	Gosbert Marcell Rutabanzibwa (A)
Thailand	Leonard Unger (A)	Sunthorn Hongladarom (A)
Togo	Albert W. Sherer, Jr. (A)	Alexandre J. Ohin (A)

LIST OF AMBASSADORS AND ENVOYS (continued)

Country	From U. S.	To U. S.
Trinidad and Tobago	J. Fife Symington, Jr. (A)	Ellis Emmanuel Innocent Clarke (A)
Tunisia	John A. Calhoun (A)	Hamed Ammar (CA)
Turkey	William J. Handley (A)	Melih Esenbel (A)
Uganda	....	E. Otema Allimadi (A)
USSR	Jacob D. Beam (A)	Anatoliy F. Dobrynin (A)
Upper Volta	William E. Schaufele, Jr. (A)	Paul Rouamba (A)
Uruguay	Charles W. Adair, Jr. (A)	Hector Luisi (A)
Venezuela	Francis W. Herron (DCM)	Julio Sosa-Rodriguez (A)
Vietnam	Ellsworth Bunker (A)	Bui Diem (A)
Yugoslavia	William Leonhart (A)	Bogdan Crnobrnja (A)
Zambia	Oliver L. Troxel, Jr. (A)	Mainza Chona (A)

AMERICAN INDIANS. See INDIANS, AMERICAN.

AMERICAN LIBRARY ASSOCIATION

The recommendations in 1968 of the National Advisory Commission on Libraries was the focus of congressional action in 1969. Thirty congressmen and 20 senators sponsored bills to establish a permanent National Commission of Libraries and Information Science. The bill in the Senate was passed; the House measure awaited action.

Conferences and Projects. The 88th annual Conference of the American Library Association (ALA) was held in Atlantic City, N. J., on June 22–28. Taking office were William S. Dix, Princeton University Library, president; Lillian M. Bradshaw, Dallas Public Library, first vice president and president-elect; and Hoyt R. Galvin, Charlotte and Mecklenburg County (N. C.) Public Library, second vice president.

The School Library Manpower Project, set up by a Knapp Foundation to the ALA, was reported to be working successfully after only six months in operation. The project's aim is to help provide qualified library personnel urgently needed by schools.

Plans have been made for a Conference on Inter-Library Communications and Networks. Three divisions of the ALA—Information Science and Automation, Reference Services, and Resources and Technical Services—will supervise the conference in its study of the present state of interlibrary communication, the technology it employs, and the tasks and goals to be set up that would insure the best possible libraries in the future. The conference was made possible through a grant of $124,678 by the U. S. Office of Education.

Following approval by the ALA Council, a program to promote the Library Bill of Rights was started by the Office for Intellectual Freedom and the Intellectual Freedom Committee of the ALA.

Publications. Among publications issued in 1969 were *Library Response to Urban Change: A Study of the Chicago Public Library; German Exile Literature in America 1933–50; A Bridge of Children's Books; Cataloging U. S. A.; Work Simplification in Danish Public Libraries; Historical Sets, Collected Editions, and Monuments of Music; Books for Junior College Libraries;* and *Standards for School Media Programs.*

Awards. The J. Morris Jones-World Book Encyclopedia-ALA Goals Award was given to a project to establish effective American Library Association chapter relationships and to cordinate ALA activities at the local, state, and national levels. The project was proposed by the Southwestern Library Association and the ALA Committee on Chapter Relationships. Ethel M. Fair, director of the Library School, New Jersey College for Women, received the Beta Phi Mu Award for distinguished service to education for librarianship.

Anne Rebecca Izard, children's consultant, Westchester, N. Y., library system, received the Grolier Award for her contributions in guiding the reading habits of children and young people.

The Joseph W. Lippincott Award for distinguished service in the library profession was presented to Germaine Krettek, associate executive director of the ALA Washington office. Vera S. Flandorf, Children's Memorial Hospital Library, Chicago, was the recipient of the Association of Hospital and Institution Libraries Award. The Armed Forces Librarians Achievement Citation went to Mary J. Carter, command librarian of the Pacific Air Forces. William S. Dix, ALA president and Princeton University librarian, received the Melvil Dewey Award for creative professional achievement.

A special project to coordinate and improve regional and state library meetings through the use of exhibits won the Exhibits Round Table Award. *The Missouri Library Association Quarterly,* the journal of the Missouri Library Association, won the H. W. Wilson Library Periodical Award. The California Library Association received the Halsey W. Wilson Library Recruitment Award.

Lloyd Alexander received the John Newbery Medal for *The High King.* The Randolph J. Caldecott Medal was presented to Uri Shulevitz, illustrator of *The Fool of the World and the Flying Ship.* The Mildred L. Batchelder Award for the most outstanding book published abroad in a foreign language and subsequently published in the United States was given to Charles S. Scribner's Sons for *Don't Take Teddy,* by Mrs. Babbis Friis-Baastad, translated by Elisa Holt Somme McKinnin.

The Clarence Day Award, for promoting the love of books and reading, was presented to Clifton Fadiman. Ralph McCoy, Southern Illinois University Library, received the Scarecrow Press Award for Library Literature for *Freedom of the Press: An Annotated Bibliography.* The Distinguished Library Service Award for School Administrators was presented to superintendents Paul W. Briggs, Cleveland public schools; Everette B. Stanley, Washington City (Va.) schools; and E. C. Stimbert, Memphis schools.

Alexander J. Skrzypek, Chicago Public Library, received the Francis Joseph Campbell Citation for contributions to the advancement of library service to the blind. The Margaret Mann Citation for achievement in cataloging went to Katharine L. Ball, University of Toronto School of Library Service. Trustee Citations were presented to Rachel Gross, Huntington Valley (Pa.) Public Library; and Alex P. Allain, trustee, St. Mary Parish, Franklin, La.

Scholarships. Betty Eisler, Swarthmore, Pa., received the Library Binding Institute Scholarship. The Frederic G. Melcher Scholarship was presented to Mrs. Linda Joan Brass, Seattle, Wash. The E. P. Dutton-John Macrae Award was given to Mrs. Rose H. Agree, Library Department, School District 30, Valley Stream, N. Y., and Bertha L. Parker, Countee Cullen Branch, New York Public Library. (See also LIBRARIES.)

CURTIS E. SWANSON
American Library Association

AMERICAN LITERATURE

The year 1969 produced a relatively small number of important new works by established writers, but it was marked by controversy over the increasing frankness of sexual material in literature.

Much of the criticism of the new freedom in handling such subjects was directed against popular novels intended for the mass market, many of them written by women. These included Jacqueline Susann's *The Love Machine,* Gwen Davis' *The Pretenders,* and the year's most successful hoax, *Naked Came the Stranger,* by "Penelope Ashe," the pen name of one of the book's several authors. Complaints about unnecessary preoccupation with sex also were lodged against a number of serious books, especially Philip Roth's *Portnoy's Complaint.* Vladimir Nabokov's *Ada,* Bernard Malamud's *Pictures of Fidelman,* and some of the new volumes of poetry also came under fire. For the present, public demand for books with sexual themes seems to outweigh the complaints of those whom they offend.

Novels. Certainly the most talked-about book of the year was Roth's third novel, *Portnoy's Complaint.* Roth's hero, the product of an urban Jewish environment, tells of his attempt to escape the clutches of one of the most fearsome Jewish mothers in literature and to attain sexual and emotional maturity. The novel is often very funny, but it is also tedious. Roth seems too preoccupied with the pleasure of providing new shocks for the reader to make the reader care very much whether Portnoy succeeds or fails in his efforts.

Nabokov's new novel, *Ada, or Ardor: A Family Chronicle* was well received by critics. It is part fantasy, part satire, part romance, and part sex. Because of his graceful and witty style, Nabokov is less likely to offend the reader than is Roth, but he is hardly less frank. *Ada* is, among other things, a pun-filled and disdainful critique of our society and culture. As in his earlier best-seller, *Lolita,* Nabokov relies on the sexual material and a dazzling style to condition the reader's response to his defense of aristocratic values and patterns of behavior. We are left with admiration for the author's display of pyrotechnic skill in writing and a certain apathy toward his ideas—and Nabokov probably planned it this way.

John Cheever's *Bullet Park* was another of the year's major novels. It is a low-keyed allegory of life in modern America. Cheever gives the reader a sense of the realities of suburban life, but he is chiefly concerned with the struggle between two symbolic characters. One of them is content to take life as it is, while the other feels a need for violent confrontations in order to break the grip of a dying society. Both men struggle for the soul of the conformist's son, who is a symbol of rootless youth. The fantastic elements that Cheever uses so well in short fiction do not work as well in this novel, which is less impressive than his earlier works.

Kurt Vonnegut, Jr., is usually associated with black humor and with science fiction. There are elements of both in his *Slaughterhouse-Five; Or, The Children's Crusade,* but it is also a very serious book. Vonnegut, when a prisoner of war in World War II, witnessed the destruction of Dresden by Allied bombers but, as he tells us, he was never able to write about the experience. He has done so now in a book that is to some degree flawed by mannerisms and a fantastic sub-plot, but which brings the terrors of mass destruction into sharp focus. *Slaughterhouse-Five* lacks the range and wildness of Joseph Heller's *Catch—22* (1961), but it has its own desperate power.

A number of other established writers produced noteworthy new novels. Bernard Malamud's *Pictures of Fidelman* is an episodic story of a modern man's search for reality. Hortense Calisher's *The New Yorkers* deals with the tangled social and personal lives of city dwellers, while Thomas Williams' *Whipple's Castle* focuses on similar problems in a small town. Calder Willingham wrote *Paradise Island,* another funny but overlong book on contemporary sexual mores, and Evan S. Connell, Jr., returned to the Midwestern setting and characters from an earlier novel in *Mr. Bridge.* Richard M. Elman completed *The Reckoning,* a bitter trilogy about Hungarian Jews in World War II.

Many younger writers produced interesting novels. Leonard Gardner's *Fat City* is a moving evocation of the life of an unsuccessful prizefighter. Ivan Gold's *Sick Friends* portrays the obstacles placed in the way of modern love by lovers themselves. D. Keith Mano writes of the improbable but revealing encounter of a white minister and a black political leader in *Horn,* an unsettling look into the future. Other promising books included John Leonard's *Crybaby of the Western World,* Lloyd Kropp's *The Drift,* L. Woiwode's *What I'm Going to Do, I Think,* Thomas McGuane's *The Sporting Club,* and Robert Canzoneri's *Men with Little Hammers.*

The achievement of black novelists continued to grow in stature in 1969. John A. Williams published another of his apocalyptic views of the racial struggle, *Sons of Darkness, Sons of Light,* which portrays the kind of racial civil war we may engage in if our problems in that area are not resolved. Ishmael Reed displays one of the most original new talents in *Yellow Back Radio Broke-Down,* a wild, surrealistic look at American culture which is only too close to reality. Nathan C. Heard, in *Howard Street,* depicts the struggle for existence in a Newark ghetto. Carlene Hatcher Polite's *The Flagellants* focuses on the barriers separating black men and women.

Several young women contributed important novels. The young but skillful historical novelist, Cecelia Holland, dealt with the Mongol conquerors of the 13th century in *Until the Sun Falls.* Joyce Carol Oates continued her prolific career with *them,* a novel combining Gothic horror with a strong sense of the daily lives of her tormented characters. Ilona Karmel's *An Estate of Memory* told of four women in a concentration camp and their efforts to save the life of a baby. Marilyn Hoff's *Rose* was a sympathetic account of the disaffected young and their life styles. Marjorie Kellogg contributed *Tell Me that You Love Me, Junie Moon,* a story of three misfits and the private world they share.

Short Fiction. *The Collected Stories of Peter Taylor* received more enthusiastic acclaim than any other literary work published in 1969. A critic wrote in *Newsweek* that "no one writing in English can do more with a story than this man." This recognition comes late but deservedly to an author, now in his fifties, who has been writing distinguished short fiction for over 25 years. His stories are often low-keyed and apparently lacking in intensity, but they have their own drama and they contain acute perceptions about human life. Taylor's style always seems perfectly suited to the demands of his material.

A much younger and very different talent was displayed in Robert Coover's *Pricksongs & Descants,* a worthy successor to his first two novels. Coover is fascinated by language, by the bizarre, and by fiction's ability to comment on itself as well as on human life. Where Taylor reveals the inevitability of human behavior, Coover is concerned with showing its variability; some of his stories manage to suggest the alternatives inherent in apparently cut-and-dried social situations. Coover's fiction with its verbal fireworks owes something to the work of John Barth and Donald Barthelme, but Coover is no imitator and his stories have originality.

Ernest Gaines' *Bloodline* and James Alan McPherson's *Hue and Cry* were two interesting collections of short stories by black writers. Among the veteran practitioners of the form, John O'Hara published yet another collection, *The O'Hara Generation,* while *The Collected Stories of Jean Stafford* brought together the work of a distinguished stylist. John Hawkes continued to write in a surrealistic vein in *Lunar Landscapes,* a volume containing three short novels and six other brief pieces.

Other books deserving attention included Nancy A. J. Potter's *We Have Seen the Best of Our Times,* Leonard Michael's *Going Places,* Harry Mark Petrakis' *The Waves of Light and Other Stories,* and Ronald Sukenick's *Up.*

Poetry. In 1969, Robert Lowell, long known for the variety and looseness of form of his poetry, turned to the unrhymed sonnet, a variation on one of the oldest poetic conventions, in *Notebooks 1967–1968.* While the unvarying verse form makes the poems seem somewhat repetitious, Lowell's tone and imagery provide variety, and he has a number of interesting and unconventional observations to make about the tempestuous modern era. The book will do no harm to Lowell's wide reputation.

Two retrospective collections were of special interest. *The Complete Poems of Randall Jarrell* demonstrates that this poet had a rather narrow range, and that his imaginative power was not great. A few of his poems have lasting value, but the body of his work, while large, is not as impressive as has generally been believed. *The Complete Poems of Elizabeth Bishop,* on the other hand, displays the steady craftsmanship of a distinguished minor poet. Miss Bishop's poems show a distinct point of view from which she makes acute observations about our civilization and modes of behavior.

Openings, by Wendell Berry, shows the work of a poet more at home with nature than any poet since Robert Frost. Berry's quiet but forceful poetry presents sharp contrasts between the virtues of land and the failings of urban society. Berry is not an innovative poet, but he convinces by strength of his quiet voice and his obvious familiarity with the natural world.

Richard Eberhart was represented by *Shifts of Being,* a collection of recent poems. When his imagination is engaged, Eberhart writes movingly of the mysteries and confusions of the world. However, some of these poems seem to be merely exercises. More conventional in technique than many of his contemporaries, Eberhart is also more concerned with theological questions, but, in the end, his poetry contains the tragic vision so often found in modern literature.

There was not a great deal of activity among other established poets during the year. Daniel Hoffman published *Striking the Stones,* and Howard

HALSMAN

VLADIMIR NABOKOV, novelist, poet, short story writer, playwright, essayist, and lepidopterist, again demonstrated his talents as a satirist and stylist and his flair for the unconventional in his novel *Ada, or Ardor: A Family Chronicle* (1969). He first created a sensation with his novel *Lolita* (1958), the story of a middle-aged intellectual's passion for a 12-year-old "nymphet." *Lolita* and the early novel *Laughter in the Dark* (1938) were made into motion pictures.

Nabokov was born in St. Petersburg (now Leningrad), Russia, on April 23, 1899. He emigrated to England in 1919 and graduated from Trinity College, Cambridge, in 1923. He moved to the United States in 1940 where he taught at Wellesley College (1941–48) and Cornell University (1949–58). Nabokov's works include the novels *Invitation to a Beheading* (1959), *Pale Fire* (1962), *Despair* (1966), and *King, Queen, Knave* (1968); and the memoir *Speak, Memory* (1951).

Moss was represented by *Second Nature.* The black poetess Gwendolyn Brooks produced some bitter commentary on the racial dilemma in *In the Mecca.* Interesting works by younger poets included Elie Siegel's *Hail, American Development,* Louise Gluck's *Firstborn,* and Diane Wakoski's *Inside the Blood Factory.*

Literary History and Criticism. Despite new experiments in fiction and poetry, this continues to be an age of criticism. Attention is now being focused on the major writers of the first half of the 20th century. A major biography of one of the most famous American novelists was Carlos Baker's *Ernest Hemingway: A Life Story.* The book is a thorough account of the writer's life, but it has been criticized for failing to show the connections between Hemingway's life and his art. Baker seems determined to maintain an icy objectivity, even when writing about the best and worst traits of his subject. Nevertheless, the book is certain to remain the standard biography of Hemingway for the foreseeable future. A less ambitious study, Robert O. Stephens' *Hemingway's Nonfiction: The Public Voice,* summarizes the author's journalistic work.

JOHN BERRYMAN (*right*), prize-winning U. S. poet, converses with new friends and quenches his thirst at a pub in Dublin, Ireland. In 1969, he received a National Book Award and shared the Bollingen Prize in Poetry with Karl Shapiro.

TERRENCE SPENCER © TIME INC.

John Unterecker's *Voyager: A Life of Hart Crane* was another exhaustive biographical study. Like Baker, Unterecker piles up an enormous amount of detail in an attempt to explain the tormented life of the inspired but undisciplined poet who took his own life while still a young man. Despite some stylistic lapses and the inept handling of notes (they are not included in the book and buyers must write to the author to obtain a copy), the biography is a sound, sympathetic, and definitive study of its subject.

Leon Edel's interest is in an earlier period of American literature. In 1969, he produced the fourth volume in a projected 5-volume biography, *Henry James: The Treacherous Years, 1895–1901.* Edel writes thorough biography combined with perceptive criticism. The new volume sympathetically chronicles the difficult years when James, a failure as a dramatist, found his way back to the writing of fiction. Louis O. Coxe, in *Edwin Arlington Robinson: The Life of Poetry,* presents a thorough, helpful study of a neglected but important poet.

Increasing attention is centering on the work of the doctor-poet William Carlos Williams, and two new studies deserve special attention. James Guimond's *The Art of William Carlos Williams: A Discovery and Possession of America* is the most detailed study to date of the whole range of Williams' work, including his fiction, drama, and criticism, as well as his poetry. In *The Music of Survival: A Biography of a Poem by William Carlos Williams,* Guimond's teacher, Sherman Paul, deals with a much narrower subject in his discussion of Williams' late poem *The Desert Music.* Other books that shed light on modern poets include an informal study by Jane Kramer, *Allen Ginsberg in America,* and *Selected Letters* of E. E. Cummings, edited by F. W. Dupee and George Stade.

Ellen Moers contributed an important work on the changes in the fictional methods of Theodore

JOHN BERRYMAN, poet, critic, and teacher, received the 1968 National Book Award for poetry in March 1969 for *His Toy, His Dream, His Rest,* described as a "witty and original medley of rhetorics." In January he was co-recipient, with Karl Shapiro, of the Bollingen Prize in Poetry, conferred by Yale University. Among his other honors are the Shelley Memorial Award (1949), the American Academy Award (1950), and the 1964 Pulitzer Prize in poetry for his *77 Dream Songs.*

Berryman was born in McAlester, Okla., on Oct. 25, 1914. He graduated from Columbia College in 1936. He taught at Wayne State University in Detroit (1939–40), Harvard University (1940–43), and Princeton University intermittently from 1943 to 1949. Noted for the wit and craftsmanship of his poems, Berryman published several volumes of verse, including *Poems* (1942), *The Dispossessed* (1948), and *Berryman's Sonnets* (1967).

Dreiser in *Two Dreisers,* an account of the sources and aims of the novels *Sister Carrie* and *An American Tragedy.* Combining biographical material with critical insight, the study is useful for anyone interested in the work of this neglected major novelist. Another American iconoclast who came to prominence during the 1920's is the subject of Carl Bode's biography, *Mencken.* A more contemporary figure received some needed critical discussion in Don McCall's book *The Example of Richard Wright.*

Other contributions to literary history included *Sherwood Anderson's Memoirs,* edited by Ray Lewis White. It was an attempt to sift fact from fancy in Anderson's numerous autobiographical writings. Robert Fitzgerald edited and also provided an introduction for *The Collected Short Prose of James Agee.* Robert and Sally Fitzgerald were the editors of a compilation of letters, essays, and lectures by Flannery O'Connor entitled *Mystery and Manners.* A little known but important patron of the arts was the subject of B. L. Reid's *The Man from New York: John Quinn and His Friends.*

Collections of critical essays included Allen Tate's *Essays of Four Decades,* A. Alvarez's *Beyond All This Fiddle: Essays 1955–1967,* and Howard Moss' *Writing Against Time.*

History and Biography. The Civil War centennial was over by 1969, but the bicentennial of the American Revolution was fast approaching, and a number of books about the origins and early days of the nation were published in advance of the occasion. One of the most interesting books dealing with colonial times was Chadwick Hansen's *Witchcraft at Salem,* a sound psychological and cultural explanation of one of the dark pages in American history. Hansen effectively uses modern insights into Puritan behavior without distorting facts.

Several new books dealt with the American Revolution and its leaders. Gordon S. Wood, in *The Creation of the American Republic, 1776–1787,* focused on the neglected area of the development of American political thought during the war and its aftermath. Merrill Jensen studied the origins of the nation in *The Founding of a Nation: A History of the American Revolution, 1763–1776,* while John R. Alden surveyed the whole period in *A History of the American Revolution.* George Athan Billias edited an interesting compilation containing essays by a number of scholars in *George Washington's Opponents: British Generals and Admirals in the American Revolution.* Thomas Fleming wrote a sympathetic account of the author of the Declaration of Independence, *The Man from Monticello: An Intimate Life of Thomas Jefferson.*

Works dealing with life in 19th-century America were less numerous. The distinguished historian Samuel Eliot Morison wrote a biography of *Harrison Gray Otis, 1765–1848: The Urbane Federalist.* Walker Lewis compiled and edited the writings of a more famous statesman in *Speak for Yourself, Daniel: A Life of Webster in His Own Words.* Bruce Catton continued his study of the Civil War in *Grant Takes Command,* while post-Civil War politics preoccupied two writers, H. Wayne Morgan in *From Hayes to McKinley: National Party Politics, 1877–1896* and Zane L. Miller in *Boss Cox's Cincinnati: Urban Politics in the Progressive Era.* William L. O'Neill discussed an often ignored subject in *Everyone Was Brave: The Rise and Fall of Feminism in America.*

In the modern era, the 1930's have become an increasingly popular period for historians' studies. T. Harry Williams wrote an impressive biography of a famous populist radical, *Huey Long.* Dan T. Carter examined a famous criminal trial in *Scottsboro: A Tragedy of the American South,* concluding that everyone connected with the case except the convicted men was guilty in some way. Robert Goldston recalled a dark period in *The Great Depression: The United States in the Thirties,* while John Brooks wrote an informal study of the manners and mores of the Stock Exchange, *Once in Golconda: A True Drama of Wall Street, 1920–1938.* An important scholarly collection for students of foreign policy was *Franklin D. Roosevelt and Foreign Affairs,* volumes I through III. The work, edited by Edgar B. Nixon, covers the years 1933–37.

Two very different books discussed the U. S. involvement in World War II. John S. D. Eisenhower, the late President's son, presented a military history of the Battle of the Bulge in *The Bitter Woods.*

Gabriel Kolko tried to pin down the relationship between the nation's diplomatic aims and military objectives in *The Politics of War: The World and United States Foreign Policy, 1943–1945.* He concluded that military decisions were often determined by considerations of America in the postwar world.

Former secretary of state Dean Acheson wrote tartly about his career in the State Department in *Present at the Creation: My Years at the State Department.* The book, beginning before World War II and culminating in Acheson's service as President Truman's secretary of state, aroused controversy because of the author's unflattering treatment of such contemporaries as Gen. Douglas MacArthur and Sen. Robert Taft.

The dramatic events of recent years spawned a number of books in 1969. Theodore H. White wrote the third book in a series, *The Making of the President 1968.* A full and sometimes surprising review of the campaigns of the major parties and their final candidates, the book has been criticized for ignoring or slighting other important aspects of the election, including the meaning of the candidacies of George Wallace, Eugene McCarthy, and the late Robert Kennedy. Joe McGinniss contributed *The Selling of the President 1968,* on the Nixon campaign. The assassination of the second Kennedy brother occasioned several admiring memoirs, including David Halberstam's *The Unfinished Odyssey of Robert Kennedy,* Jules Witcover's *85 Days: The Last Campaign of Robert Kennedy,* and Jack Newfield's *Robert Kennedy: A Memoir.* Kennedy himself had written a book, published posthumously in 1969, about the most famous episode in John Kennedy's administration, *Thirteen Days: A Memoir of the Cuban Missile Crisis.* Late in the year, Sen. Eugene McCarthy published his account of the 1968 presidential race in *The Year of the People.*

Several new historical works dealt with broad subjects and issues. Stefan Lorant described *The Glorious Burden: The American Presidency.* Odie B. Falk made an important contribution to regional history in *Land of Many Frontiers: A History of the American Southwest.* C. Vann Woodward raised questions of historiography in connection with another region in *The Burden of Southern History.*

Other Nonfiction. Many books published in 1969 were concerned with the problems of economics and race in U. S. cities. The man who is President Nixon's adviser in these areas, Daniel Patrick Moynihan, wrote of the failure of earlier programs designed to relieve poverty in *Maximum Feasible Misunderstanding: Community Action in the War on Poverty.* From the other side, two leaders of the Black Power movement attacked the current state of American society: Eldridge Cleaver in *Post-Prison Writings and Speeches* and H. Rap Brown in *Die Nigger Die.*

In a more literary vein, America's foremost man of letters, Edmund Wilson, produced two new books. *The Duke of Palermo and Other Plays* shows his talent for parody, while *The Dead Sea Scrolls: 1947–1969* testifies to his continuing interest in the discovery of Biblical materials in the Middle East. John Dos Passos, a contemporary of Wilson's, wrote a study of the home of his ancestors, *The Portugal Story.* The playwright Lillian Hellman described her life in *An Unfinished Woman.*

(See also PRIZES AND AWARDS.)

JOHN M. M[
The Ohio State Uni[

ANTARCTICA

Research programs in Antarctica during 1969 were generally a continuation of scientific projects already under way at the various stations maintained throughout the continent. Of the 12 member nations of the 10-year-old Antarctic Treaty Organization (an outgrowth of the cooperative effort of the International Geophysical Year begun 13 years ago), the United States conducted by far the most extensive research activities.

Continental Drift Theory. Nearly 200 scientists working on 51 projects during the U. S. Antarctic Research Program (USARP) summer season collected data that further support the widely held theory of continental drift. According to this theory, present-day land masses were once joined together to form two large supercontinents. One of these supercontinents is believed to have comprised what are now South America, Africa, India, Australia, and Antarctica.

Computer analysis of paleobotanical and geological data obtained during a global cruise of the U. S. Coast and Geodetic Survey ship *Oceanographer* concluded that Australia and Antarctica were once united. Also supporting the theory of continental drift was the discovery of a fossil of a Triassic amphibian within 325 miles (520 km) of the South Pole. This amphibian is also known to have inhabited South America and Africa.

Studies of Microorganisms. In Victoria Land, within 80 to 150 miles (128–240 km) of McMurdo Sound, lie unique dry valleys containing yeasts, bacteria, protozoans, and other microorganisms living in a wide range of temperatures and salt concentrations. To help develop instruments for detecting possible life on Mars, the U. S. National Aeronautics and Space Administration (NASA) resumed its studies of the Victoria Land algae and bacteria. These organisms lie dormant during the winter, when temperatures reach as low as $-89°$ F ($-67°$ C), and become active during the summer, when the weather is warmer and water is available from melting glaciers nearby.

Drilling Program. At the South Pole operations were normal, and at Byrd Station the deep drilling program and studies of the electrical properties of ice continued. Prior to the last flight of the season, on Feb. 18, 1969, 700 ice cores were sent via McMurdo station to the Army Terrestrial Science Center at Hanover, N. H.

Ellsworth Land Survey. After its third season, the Ellsworth Land Survey, the largest field party, completed its work in botanical, paleomagnetic, geological, and topographical studies in the coastal regions of western Antarctica. On Jan. 29, 1969, the five scientists and four engineers departed.

Weddell Sea Expedition. The International Weddell Sea Oceanographic Expedition, delayed for more than a month by the U. S. Coast Guard icebreaker *Glacier*'s difficulties with adverse ice conditions in the Ross Sea, finally reached the Weddell \a ice pack on Feb. 18, 1969, only to find even re severe ice conditions. Impenetrable ice 60 s (96 km) thick prevented the recovery of four rged deep-current meters, which had been set h buoys the previous year to record data on waters. However, work continued on ocean-c measurements, bottom photography, and ects. A census showed a predominance of als and Adélie penguins.

Water-Current Studies. Since 1955 considerable information has been obtained on the patterns of water circulation and exchange in Antarctic waters. The general movement of Antarctic water is easterly; transfer out of the area is effected by the northward movement of the very cold bottom water, accompanied by the northward spreading of the subsurface intermediate water. These losses are replaced by southward movement of warmer waters.

Study of Economic Potential. A review of the economic potential of the Antarctica concluded that the greatest assets of the continent are the sea animals, which may eventually become an important source of food; the scenery, which may attract a large tourist trade; and the unique conditions, which are of inestimable value for scientific research.

Palmer Station Activities. At Palmer Station on Anvers Island, winter research continued on the process of photosynthesis in lichen. In December 1968 the Coast Guard ship *Edisto* landed a construction batallion to resume work on the permanent facility there. With the arrival of the new research vessel *Hero,* both ships were used to transport numerous scientific parties to various nearby islands to collect biological and geological specimens. On one trip it was possible to make a four-day reconnaissance of Deception Island, where on Feb. 21, 1969, another volcanic eruption had occurred, causing three large rifts about 250 feet (75 meters) deep. The resulting mudflows destroyed the Chilean station and much of the British station on the island. The Argentine station was unharmed, but researchers from all stations were evacuated.

Japanese Expedition to the South Pole. An 11-man Japanese party reached the South Pole Dec. 19, 1968, 83 days after leaving Showa Base. This group was the eighth expedition to make the overland trek. After a week of rest, the party, led by Masayoshi Murayama, returned, making a stop at the Plateau station where an U. S.-supplied fuel cache awaited them. Much scientific work was done during the 140-day, 3,200-mile (5,120-km) trip.

British-Norwegian Research Program. On Nov. 23, 1968, eight British and six Norwegian scientists left McMurdo station. The Norwegian scientists were placed at Kraul Mountains in Vestfjella, Queen Maud Land, for topographic and geological surveying and for glaciological research. The British party was transported to the Shackleton Range for geological work and ground surveying to provide astronomical fixes for photographic mapping. Both parties of scientists returned in late January 1969.

USSR Programs. At Molodezhnaya, now the headquarters for all Soviet research programs in Antarctica, the first permanent base for launching weather rockets up to 60 miles (96 km) was constructed. On Jan. 15, 1969, the U. S. scientist Michael Maish was transported from McMurdo Station to the USSR's Vostok station, where he continued the studies in upper atmospheric physics as an exchange scientist. A fifth permanent Soviet research station, named Bellingshausen, was established on King George Island in the South Shetland group. Boris Lopatin, a Soviet exchange scientist who participated in the Ellsworth Land Survey, returned to Vostok station along with 5,000 pounds (2,265 kg) of geological specimens to be sent to the Soviet Union.

EDITH M. RONNE
Antarctic Specialist

ANTHROPOLOGY

The most significant trends in anthropology in 1969 were the proliferation of comparative studies of human and primate behavior; heightening anthropological interest in the field of education; the growth of urban anthropology, especially relating to the culture of poverty; and black studies. Significant publications in cultural anthropology included a comparative study of mythology and a cross-cultural survey of song and dance styles.

Annual Meetings. The 68th meeting of the American Anthropological Association was held in November in New Orleans. George M. Foster, Jr., succeeded Cora Du Bois as president of the association. An innovation at these meetings was a series of experimental sessions in which special interests were discussed, with a minimum of formal presentation of papers.

Margaret Mead and Edward Storey organized a session on "Going Hungry"; the participants in the session included poor people, federal, state, and municipal agency representatives, as well as anthropologists and other field researchers. The minority Curriculum Committee held an experimental session on "The Implications of the Current Ethnic Studies Controversy."

Other experimental sessions included "Research in the American South," "Mayan Ethnolinguistics," "Women in the Professions," "Patronage, Clientage and Power Structures in Latin America," and "American Urban Migration" (discussing the migration of American Indians into urban centers).

Sessions that indicated new or expanding interests in anthropology included "The Context of Violence," "Conflict and Warfare," "Modernization of the Great and Little Medical Traditions in Asia," and "Ethnographic Research in Black Communities in the U. S." The Council on Anthropology and Education sponsored symposiums dealing with field methods of anthropologists working in the school and the relationship of minority cultures to the culture of the school.

At the 136th meeting of the American Association for the Advancement of Science, held in December in Boston, the symposiums included "The International Study of the Eskimo," "Field Studies of Nutrition and Behavior," "Land Use, Population and Settlement in Ancient Mexico and Guatemala," and "The City as a Social System."

Human and Primate Behavior. The analysis of human behavior from the perspective of animal studies intensified in 1969. Desmond Morris in his book *The Human Zoo* stressed the parallels between the aberrant behavior of animals confined in cages and that of modern man living in crowded urban conditions. Richard B. Lee and Irven DeVore edited *Man the Hunter,* which presents the results of a symposium at which 67 participants pooled information gathered from archaeological sites and field studies of contemporary hunter-gatherers.

Lionel Tiger in his book *Man in Groups* drew upon man's past as a hunter and suggested that male aggression and male bonding were necessary to produce man the successful predator. According to Tiger, these attributes continue to operate in contemporary cultures.

On the other hand, Ralph L. Holloway, Jr., in the October issue of *Current Anthropology,* questioned the validity of recent studies that tend to blur the line between man and other primates. His article "Culture: A Human Domain" stresses the unique aspects of culture that distinguish man's adaptation from that of all other animals. Through symbolization and tool manufacture, human culture imposes an arbitrary form upon the environment.

INDIAN BURIAL is unearthed by anthropologists at Cahokia Mounds State Park, Illinois. The state of the remains indicated sacrificial death.

UPI

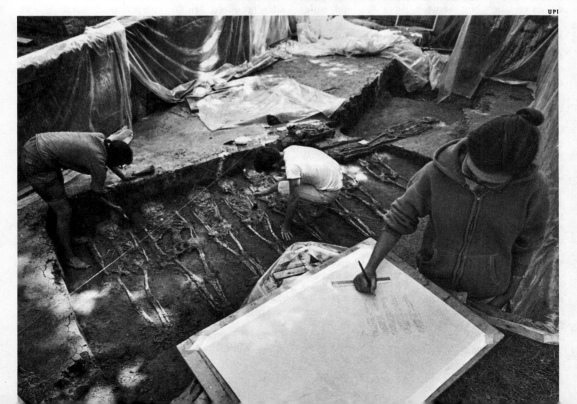

The most unexpected development of 1969 in the field of primate studies was the success of R. Allen Gardner and Beatrice T. Gardner (*Science,* August 15) in their efforts to teach a chimpanzee the American Sign Language, which is used by the deaf in North America. Washoe, a young female chimpanzee, has mastered over 30 of the signs.

The chimpanzee has begun to construct two-word sequences, with "please," "come-gimme," "hurry," and "more" combined as emphasizers, as in "please open hurry" and "gimme drink please." She has also constructed a number of two-word combinations of her own invention, such as "gimme tickle" and "open food drink" (signifying the refrigerator, which had always been signed as "cold box"). The fact that these signs are used to signal information about her environment drastically challenges the belief that the communication potential of primates other than man is limited to gestures and sounds relating only to their feelings.

Cultural Anthropology. The influence of the distinguished French anthropologist Claude Lévi-Strauss continues to grow in the United States and Britain. The translation of *The Raw and The Cooked* has stimulated a great deal of discussion of his method of analyzing mythologies. "The raw" is used metaphorically to represent nature, while "the cooked" represents culture.

Lévi-Strauss's theory is that myths are the key to the thinking processes of the group that possesses them; myth is also the bridge between nature and culture. His method is analogous to the linguist's derivation of the structure of a language from the analysis of speech.

The publication of *Folk Song Style and Culture* by Alan Lomax with the editorial assistance of Edwin E. Erickson is the culmination of years of research. The relationship of song and dance styles to social and cultural contexts, examined with sophisticated statistical methods, shows correlations between song and dance styles and levels of social evolution, modes of subsistence, relationships with deities, relationships between the sexes, and child-rearing practices. Testing Lomax's theories will provide future musicologists with years of research.

Pigs, Pearlshells and Women, edited by R. M. Glass and M. J. Meggitt, is an important addition to the literature on marriage systems in the New Guinea highlands. Many of these highland societies remained relatively uninfluenced by the outside world until the 1930's, and these comparative studies of marriage and exchange systems highlight important theoretical questions in kinship, social structure, and the form and stability of marriages.

The growing interest in the culture of poverty and the study of black ghetto cultures is reflected in Ulf Hannerz' book *Soulside: Inquiries into Ghetto Culture and Community.* This is a study of a black community in Washington, D. C. Hannerz' work goes beyond the descriptive and ethnographic to raise questions that are of theoretical and political importance.

Graduate Schools. The number of graduate schools offering advanced training in anthropology continues to expand. The current *Guide to Departments of Anthropology 1969–1970* lists 127 graduate departments compared with 116 in 1968. For the first time the guide includes exclusively undergraduate departments, listing 44 of them.

GERALD M. HENDERSON
Brooklyn College, City University of New York

ARCHAEOLOGY

Archaeological exploration throughout the world continued to increase in 1969. Africa remained the focus of archaeology's ongoing effort to learn more about man's earliest ancestors and to trace human evolutionary history. Excavations in Europe, the Near East, and Afghanistan brought to light new material related to the development and spread of agriculture in the Neolithic era. The early civilizations of the Near East, the Mediterranean, Mexico, and Peru remained the objects of highly organized archaeological excavation.

EASTERN HEMISPHERE

Archaeological discoveries in 1969 were especially helpful in showing how extensive communications were among prehistoric peoples.

Early Man. An international expedition continued research in the deltaic deposits north of Lake Rudolf in the Omo River basin of southwestern Ethiopia. By the end of 1969, 40 prehistoric teeth and 2 jawbones of early manlike primates were amassed. These mandibles belonged to the rugged *Paranthropus,* an Australopithecine, but were not associated with tools in the volcanic ash deposit dated by the potassium-argon method as two to four million years old. West of Lake Rudolf still older Australopithecine jaw fragments were found in a geological context perhaps 5 million years old.

Another Australopithecine-like cranium was turned up at Olduvai Gorge, where, over the last decade, a number of cranial remains and skeletal fragments have been found in association with the very rudimentary Oldawan stone tool industry. The cranium probably represents the best preserved find of a female skull at Olduvai. This identification is also tentative, until such time as the fossil is extracted from the lime concretion in which it is embedded.

Old Stone Age. On the eastern coast of Taiwan at the small village of Pa-Shian-Tung, the first Palaeolithic remains from the island were found. Cave sites produced Middle Palaeolithic flake tools and choppers, as well as chopping tools older than the Ting-Tsun industry and the same age as some of the materials of the Choukoutienian culture in north China. The most outstanding find was bamboo tools, which usually do not survive the millenia. Palaeolithic men reached Taiwan during the Ice Age when Taiwan had land connections to the mainland.

Considerably later, Pleistocene hunters had begun deliberately to bury their dead. In the cave of Quafzeh, not far from Nazareth in the Holy Land, the burial of a 10-year-old child surrounded by grave goods including tools of Mousterian type was found. While children buried with funeral gifts are known from this time in Europe, usually in the Near East the immature were buried without grave goods. Dating from the later Mousterian—about 40,000 B. C.— the child shows that by this time man had evolved into a relatively modern physical form.

A Carbon-14 date of about 19,000 B. C. for the Uskhi I stone tool industry of Kamchatka, a peninsula in the Bering Sea, sheds light on the crossing of the Bering land bridge by the ancestors of American Indians to populate the Western Hemisphere from the Eastern. This assemblage contains wedge-shaped scrapers and bladelets such as have been found in Alaska and Japan.

Early Farmers. Analysis of materials excavated at Aq Kupruk, located among limestone hills in the

Balkh River province of north-central Afghanistan, has clarified details of a 20,000-year cultural sequence extending from Islamic times and the Iron Age back to the Upper Palaeolithic. Most surprising has been the realization that this region was included in the nuclear Near Eastern area that saw the early domestication of plants and animals. A preceramic Neolithic phase with carbon dating of about 8000 B. C. included domesticated sheep and goats, possibly domesticated cattle, stone hoes and axes, grinding stones, and pounders. Red deer, gazelles, and wild horses were hunted with Upper Palaeolithic-like implements. Nearby rock shelters extended the sequence back almost 20,000 years more to a Mousterian deposit including fragments of a human cranium. The most significant material comes from a late Neolithic assemblage dated by radiocarbon to about 1800 B. C. This culture, with crude black pottery decorated by incised triangles, chevrons, zigzags, and the like, seems to connect with Neolithic complexes similar to those in southern Siberia and Kashmir. Hunting was almost as important as stock raising, but excavators uncovered three pit burials of beheaded domesticated goats, one associated with the remains of three children. These ritual interments have resulted in the name Goat Burial Neolithic for this culture.

At the confluence of the Aisne and Vesle Rivers, in northern Champagne, France, more than 12 villages of the Punctated Linear Ware Culture were detected. Although once characterized as a "Danubian" culture, these finds at Chassemy, Vailly, and Cys-la-Commune represent one of the greatest known concentrations of this widespread European culture of stone age farmers. The villages and burials, dating from about 3500 B. C., represent the first farmers in this part of western Europe.

Early Middle East and India. Cylinder seals from Mesopotamia and stamp seals from the Harappan civilization (3000–1700 B. C.) of northwestern India and West Pakistan were found together in a fortified site in eastern Iran, along with carved steatite bowls similar to those known also from the two areas. These discoveries augment an earlier find from Bahrein Island and evidence trade contacts between the Near East and South Asia at that time.

The ancient script incised on seals and tablets of the Harappan civilization was at last partially deciphered. A team of linguists revealed that the scripts reflect the Proto-Dravidian language. Translation was aided by sifting masses of combinations by computer and by the Harappans' custom of drawing the pictures of concrete objects alongside the signs for abstract concepts when the object and concept were denoted by similarly pronounced words.

Explorations in Saudi Arabia at three habitation sites up to 60 miles (100 km) from the Persian Gulf coast revealed remains of the Ubaid Horizon, not previously known to have extended so far beyond Mesopotamia. Finds included flint tools and the characteristic Ubaidian painted pottery.

Iron Age. Tel Anafa, an ancient city situated by drained Lake Jula near the headwaters of the Jordan River, enjoys a much lusher setting than is usual in that part of the Near East. Although occupied from about 3000 B. C., the site was most important as a Greek center under Alexander and the later Hellenistic Seleucid and Ptolemaic kingdoms. Digging revealed a wide selection of pottery, glass, jewelry, and tools, as well as Greek and Hellenistic trade pottery that is useful for economic analysis and for establishing dating horizons for the Near East. An extensively gilded and painted stucco molding, fundamentally of egg-and-dart design, comes from an elaborate building on the east side of the mound. Of undated origin, the building seems to have been destroyed in the 1st century B. C. when the Seleucid cities were captured by the Hasmonaean Kingdom.

Research teams in the Belgian Ardennes found that during the Iron Age the crest of these mountains formed a vital communication link between the Marne (Champagne) and Hunsrück-Eifel (Rhineland) variants of the La Tene Culture, two important centers of innovation when iron was becoming the basis of the technology for woodland Europe.

IN NEBRASKA archaeologists are uncovering the wreck of a steamboat that sank in the Missouri River in 1865.

Indeed, the Ardennes Crest must have functioned as a sort of information transmittal center, sharing in the advances of both areas, and in some ways enjoying a cultural level more developed than its neighbors. In this region the rate of chariot burial is around 20%, the highest of any European group.

RALPH M. ROWLETT
University of Missouri

WESTERN HEMISPHERE

Archaeologists excavated widely throughout the Americas in 1969. As in previous years, several universities cooperated in conducting summer field work.

Nebraska. One of the most important projects in historic archaeology to be carried out in 1969 was at the DeSoto National Wildlife Refuge. The object was the uncovering of the steamboat *Bertrand*. The vessel sank in 1865 and was soon covered by a mud-bar from which the river has long since moved away. Originally loaded with a cargo for the Montana goldfields, the wreck yielded a variety of materials, ranging from peanuts to cannon balls. Officials plan to preserve the find and build an interpretative museum and a study area near it.

Illinois. Excavations carried on at the south end of Monks Mound, Cahokia Mounds State Park, revealed postholes of an early Indian structure as well as scattered human burials and a crematory basin. Arrangement of the remains in a burial mound excavated to the south of Monks Mound suggests that the mound grew as a result of many mass burials. Skeletal material in this mound was in poor condition due to wet soil and weight of the covering mound, and there were few grave offerings.

New Jersey. Excavations at the probable site of the historic Munsee village of Minisink in northern New Jersey yielded a total of 11,000 ceramic, bone, metal, and chipped stone artifacts, and 120 features were recorded. The finds were assigned to the late Woodland and Historic periods. The end portion of the Owasco sequence seems to represent the earliest occupation, but the heaviest yield was of Iroquoian and Munsee artifacts. Another New Jersey site produced the first recorded house pattern in the state associated with the proto-Iroquois-terminal Owasco period. Pottery and stone artifacts suggest a dating of about 1350 to 1450 A.D.

Michigan. Near Bay City, Mich., archaeologists excavated 35 historic burials of the 1780's and 1790's. The graves contained a spectacular array of trade goods, including silver ornaments, firearms, a complete rum bottle, pikes and spears, brass and iron containers, and medicine bundles. At the Lasanen site, near St. Ignace, 11 burial pits of the early 1700's were excavated. They contained large quantities of French trade items, including glass beads, knives, a variety of iron artifacts, and preserved fabrics and cordage. Items of native manufacture included animal effigies of shell and red clay.

Kansas. During construction of a reservoir north of Topeka, an ancient living site was discovered about 10 feet below the earth's surface. Camp remains were found in an ocher-stained, gray-clay terrace remnant estimated by geologists to date from 3000 B.C. to 8000 B.C. Included in the occupation level were burned-rock hearths and bone deposits composed mostly of bison remains. Artifacts included projectile points, ovate knives, end scrapers, mealing stones, and a stone for grinding maize.

Maryland. In 1969 Maryland recognized the value of archaeology by appointing a state archaeologist. This official's duties are to correlate the activities of amateurs and the two Maryland archaeological societies with his own work. One of the most pressing problems is the salvage of sites threatened by highway construction and urban expansion.

District of Columbia. The anthropology departments of George Washington University, Catholic University, and American University have united in a systematic study of the archaeological problems of the Potomac Basin in the District of Columbia, Virginia, Maryland, and West Virginia. Using 32 students from these schools, the area is being resurveyed, collections in the Smithsonian Institution are being analyzed, and excavation in key sites is underway.

An excavation at the confluence of the Potomac and Monocacy rivers has yielded an estimated 100,000 artifacts. Excavations have been carried to a depth of nine feet, with the lowest levels believed to date to 1600 B.C.

Newfoundland. Excavation of an ancient cemetery on the northern coast of Newfoundland produced a heavy yield of ground and polished stone artifacts. Objects recovered included gouges, stemmed "bayonet" points, and plummets. Chipped stone forms are characteristically leaf-shaped bifaces, and long, stemmed, and side-notched points. Large charcoal samples from ritual fires in the graves yielded radiocarbon dates ranging from 1770 B.C. to 1250 B.C.

Costa Rica. Limited excavations at the foot of the north side of Arenal Volcano in Costa Rica were undertaken to determine if archaeology could help determine the time period of the last eruption previous to that of August 1968. Potsherds were found below an ash layer representing the last unrecorded activity; underground features penetrating the occupational level were identified as impact craters. Study of the data is still in progress, but preliminary studies of the material recovered suggest a date near the beginning of the historic period.

Colombia. The Valley of El Abra contains several rock shelters formed by erosion. One of these, known as El Abra II, was given a radiocarbon date of 10,450 B.C., making it one of the oldest sites in South America. Only one other site of comparable age is known—that of Laguna de Tagua in central Chile. The uppermost levels at the El Abra shelter produced potsherds of Chibcha style, but lower levels were without ceramic remains. The stone artifacts, consisting of scrapers, drills, perforators, and triangular projectile points, were made mainly by percussion flaking. Those from levels 2 to 7 were made from banded chert; those from levels 8 and 9 from cretaceous sandstone. The date was determined from fine charcoal taken from level 7. Undated, but undoubtedly older, stone artifacts were found in level 9.

Venezuela. A survey in the Los Barrancos area located a number of new sites, most of which yielded pottery of a type known as Barrancoid. Stratigraphic excavations were undertaken at Los Barrancos and Delta del Orinoco. On the southern side of the Orinoco River a rock shelter with pictographs was tested. Barrancoid sherds occurred in the upper level, and a number of stone artifacts were obtained from lower levels.

GEORGE S. METCALF
Smithsonian Institution

ARCHERY. See SPORTS.

architecture

ROTATING HOUSE in Wilton, Conn., resembles a hovering spaceship. Designed by Richard T. Foster, it makes one complete turn in 48 minutes.

The deaths of Walter Gropius on July 5 and Ludwig Mies van der Rohe on Aug. 23, 1969, closed an extremely important chapter in the history of modern architecture. Both had been apprenticed in the Berlin office of Peter Behrens, a pioneer force in the formative period of modern architecture in Europe, and both, at different times, had headed the influential Bauhaus school.

Gropius' significant contribution to the development of modern architecture was his recognition of the value of the team process. His long association with Marcel Breuer began at the Bauhaus and continued at Harvard University. His collaboration with Konrad Wachsmann in 1942 produced the sophisticated prefabricated General Panel House system. By forming the Architects Collaborative in 1946, Gropius developed a concern that today has commissions around the world. The wide variety of styles displayed in the current designs of the postwar generation of U. S. architects trained by Gro-

DANIEL REED LIBRARY at State University College, Fredonia, N. Y., rises above monumental steps and platform (*above*), under which ground floor extends (*right*).

pius—Paul Rudolph, I. M. Pei, Ulrich Franzen, John Johansen—attest to his undogmatic influence as an educator.

Mies van der Rohe, the son of a stonemason, developed a singular technological dogma of honest structure achieved by an expert understanding of materials and the constant refinement of detail. The first of modern architects to consider glass, in association with the steel frame, as a significant 20th century material, he developed the glass curtain wall throughout his career. His mastery of spatial manipulation within a single-roofed volume is evident in many of his designs, including the Architecture Building at the Illinois Institute of Technology. His last building to be completed was Westmont Square, Westmont, Ontario, in 1969.

The convergence of Mies van der Rohe's vision and 20th century U. S. technology was a unique coincidence. Mies once said, "I don't want to be interesting—I want to be good." The singlemindedness of his direction made him a difficult architect to emulate. Myron Goldsmith of Skidmore, Owings & Merrill, and Gene Summers of C. F. Murphy Associates are among his few successful followers.

New Housing. The necessity of building 2.6 million housing units a year, in accordance with the Housing and Urban Development Act of 1968, remained, in the face of continuing economic and bureaucratic difficulties in achieving that target. (See also BUILDING AND CONSTRUCTION.)

The City Club of New York gave its first Bard honor award for excellence in civil architecture and urban design to Davis, Brody & Associates for its $12 million cooperative Riverbend Houses. The 624 apartments, connected by sidewalks-in-the-air, enjoy spectacular views of the Harlem River from individual stoops and terraces.

A new type of mass housing unit was employed by Paul Rudolph, who designed trailer units that accommodate a varying number of bedrooms. The units, built in Baltimore, will be transported to New Haven to make 148 units of low-income housing.

In Lancaster, Pa., Neil Mitchell, a Harvard engineer, successfully applied a low-cost concrete framing system that could be assembled by unskilled laborers in a variety of combinations, capable of variation or expansion by the tenant at any time. Extensive application of the system, however, would necessitate revision of outdated building codes and restrictive union procedures.

In Europe, architects have successfully applied the technology of prefabrication to housing. While the USSR's housing developments have been criticized on aesthetic grounds, much is learned from

> *Walter Gropius and Ludwig Mies van der Rohe, two giants of modern architecture, died in 1969. Separate articles focusing on the lives and contributions of these two men, who profoundly influenced the direction of 20th century design, appear under their own headings.*

their advanced techniques, based on the French Coignet system that employs large, prefabricated, concrete apartment-sized boxes. This allows an ultimate capacity of 3 million units per year.

In Britain, the Greater London Council, with architect Hubert Bennett in charge, is constructing a development of some 15,000 units on 1,600 acres of flood-prone land adjoining the Thames River at Thamesmead. Large prefabricated concrete components are hoisted into position by heavy cranes to form a variety of apartments in a pleasing composition that separates cars from pedestrians and offers handsome views of the river.

By contrast, in New York, Co-op City, designed by Herman J. Lessor, accommodates the same number of apartments in 35 mundane 24- to 33-story brick-clad blocks in the Bronx. The largest single housing project in the United States, sponsored by labor unions and underwritten by government funds, the Bronx project conspicuously demonstrates the need for architectural expertise in developments of this size.

Urban Design. Welfare Island, long-neglected island in New York City's East River, has been skillfully planned by architects Philip Johnson and John Burgee as a car-free, high-density residential development surrounding a marina, with large areas of open parkland. The scheme also preserves many forgotten landmarks relating to the early settlement of New York.

The relationship af architect to developer in producing aesthetic construction has, with a few exceptions, been a difficult one. Mies van der Rohe worked successfully with Herbert Greenwald in Chicago, and I. M. Pei collaborated with William Zeckendorf. In Atlanta, architect John Portman has successfully functioned as architect-developer and has shown that good design and sound investment can be compatible in his construction of the six buildings making up Peachtree Center, which is a high-density combined commercial office and hotel development.

University Construction. The need for expanded facilities on many out-dated campuses posed problems in relating new buildings to the often scattered pattern of existing structures. At the State University of Fredonia, New York, I. M. Pei placed five new concrete structures, including an administration building and an art center, along a new pedestrian walk laid out in such a way that it unified all of

SCIENCE CENTER of Ontario, Toronto, is Canada's first permanent science and technology showcase. The $30-million educational complex of three buildings, opened in September, was designed by Raymond Moriyama.

CANADIAN CONSULATE

the campus. Confronted with a similar problem, Kevin Roche and John Dinkeloo proposed a new Art Center at the University of Massachusetts as a raised 600-foot-long block of skylit studios that ties the two sides of the campus together. On the 1874 campus of the University of Guelph, Ontario, John Andrews used a grid of internal elevated pedestrian streets to connect his concrete dormitories.

In England, the firm of Denys Lasdun designed the first stage of the new University of East Anglia at Norwich as an articulated wall in the rolling countryside. Academic and residential structures are connected by an elevated pedestrian walkway system clear of the vehicular movement on the ground. The buildings were constructed rapidly with prefabricated concrete elements that lend the complex an almost medieval quality. The same construction technique will permit an expanded enrollment of 3,000 students within ten years.

Also in England, James Stirling planned the new library for the history faculty at Cambridge University as an extremely functional construction. He placed the faculty offices in a stepped 7-story L-plan that encloses the library and reading room, covered by a pitched double-glazed roof, radiating from the central control point at the intersecting corner of the L.

Stirling also completed an equally rational plan for housing 250 students on a remote site at the University of St. Andrews in Fife, Scotland. Heavy precast concrete elements were first fabricated in Edinburgh and then trucked to the site. At St. Andrews, they were assembled into a radiating finger plan, accommodating the sloping site and affording each room a magnificent view of the mountains and the North Sea.

Boston City Hall. The year 1969 saw the completion of Boston's stunning City Hall. Designed by the firms of Kallman, McKinnell & Knowles and Campbell, Aldrich & Nulty, it is the focal point of the city's redeveloped Government Center. Surrounded by uninspired office buildings, the $26.3 million building, an American Institute of Architects (AIA) Honor Award recipient, employs a painstakingly detailed mixture of cast and precast concrete in a somewhat derivative composition. A thoroughfare allows pedestrians to pass through the heart of the building from the surrounding plaza, designed by the same architects, to experience the monumental open courts within.

Preservation. Symptomatic of the public's growing awareness of the need to preserve old or historic buildings was the rejection of proposals by Marcel Breuer and British developer Morris Saady for building over, and then alternatively demolishing, the Terminal Building at Grand Central Station in New York City in order to construct a 60-story office building. Permission was refused by the New York Zoning Board and the city's Landmarks Preservation Commission.

Similar criticism was leveled by both the press and the public at Architect of the Capitol J. George Stewart's proposal to remove the west facade of the Capitol, the last original section of that historic building. The removal of the facade would permit the construction of 4½ acres of additional offices, auditorium facilities, and dining rooms for the members of Congress. The Fine Arts Commission criticized the proposal in the light of Stewart's capricious destruction of the Washington scene with the visually and economically catastrophic Rayburn Office Building (1965), one of the most expensive public buildings in history.

Awards. William Wurster was awarded the 1969 AIA Gold Medal. Wurster has practiced and taught for many years in San Francisco. Among the winners of AIA Honor Awards in 1969 were the house of Mr. and Mrs. Fred Smith in Darien, Conn., by Richard Meier, a young architect of great promise; and I. M. Pei's Everson Museum of Art and Science in Syracuse, New York.

(See also PRIZES AND AWARDS.)

JOHN FOWLER
Practicing Architect

SLOPING PIERS feature the 60-story First National Bank of Chicago.

UNDERGROUND company cafeteria near St. Louis received AIA design award.

U. S. S. *WHALE* surfaced at the North Pole on April 6, 60 years to the very hour after Robert E. Peary and Matthew Henson reached it in 1909.

ARCTIC REGIONS

The era of polar exploration is not over. In 1969 two remarkable journeys brought to mind the great expeditions of Fridtjof Nansen, Robert E. Peary, Roald Amundsen, and Robert Falcon Scott in the late 19th and early 20th centuries. The men who met the Arctic challenges in 1969 were (1) the four members of a British expedition who, with dog teams, completed the first crossing of the frozen Arctic Ocean on foot, and (2) the crew of the S. S. *Manhattan,* who traversed the ice-covered Northwest Passage in a voyage that may open the way for commercial transportation in the Arctic.

Crossing the Arctic Ocean. The British Trans-Arctic Expedition traveled from Alaska to Svalbard (Spitsbergen)—3,620 miles (5,876 km) across the drifting ice of the Arctic Ocean. The team consisted of Wally Herbert, the leader, Allan Gill, Dr. R. M. Koerner, and Capt. K. H. Hedges.

After leaving Barrow, Alaska, in February 1968, the men spent 477 days traveling with dogs over the broken and treacherous ice pack. The expedition used sleds drawn by 35 huskies to carry their food and equipment. It made two long stops—two months in the summer and five months in the total darkness of winter.

Supplies were dropped to the team by scheduled flights. The journey ended on May 30, 1969, with a landing on a small island north of Spitsbergen. Later the men were picked up by a helicopter from H. M. S. *Endurance* and returned to England on the ship. The expedition's tasks included studying the weather, measuring geomagnetism, and testing survival techniques.

Sailing the Northwest Passage. The S. S. *Manhattan,* a supertanker especially modified to break sea ice, reached Barrow, Alaska, in late September 1969 after completing a successful trip through the Northwest Passage, the sea route across the top of North America. The voyage took the *Manhattan* through Baffin Bay, Lancaster Sound, Viscount Melville Sound, and the Arctic Ocean.

The *Manhattan* was not the first ship to negotiate the ice of the Northwest Passage; it had been done eight times before, first by Amundsen in the *Gjoa* (1903–1906). However, the *Manhattan's* trip indicated that commercial shipping could use the passage on a regular basis. The trip is expected to lead to a tanker route for shipping oil out of the Prudhoe Bay fields of Alaska. It may also open up the other mineral wealth of the north.

The Humble Oil ship was fitted with an icebreaking prow and improved in other ways to make it effective in the pack ice. Because no single shipyard could handle such a large job in the required six months, the ship was cut into four pieces, each of which was fitted out at a separate yard. The ship was reassembled in Chester, Pa., and sailed from there on Aug. 24, 1969. The *Manhattan*—115,000 deadweight tons and 1,005 feet (306 meters) long—is the largest ship of the U. S. merchant fleet. It was accompanied by the Canadian icebreaker *John A. MacDonald* and the U. S. icebreaker *Northwind.*

Polar Visit by Sub. On the 60th anniversary of the arrival of Adm. Robert E. Peary and Matthew Hensen at the North Pole, the U. S. S. *Whale,* a nuclear submarine, surfaced there on April 6, 1969.

KENNETH L. HUNKINS
Lamont-Doherty Geological Observatory

ARGENTINA

For Lt. Gen. Juan Onganía, who had seized the presidency and dissolved the Argentine parliament in 1966, the year 1969 was a troubled one. In May the regime was confronted with a massive, violent protest that threatened its existence. Although the government survived this challenge—as well as another, which coincided with the visit of the Rockefeller mission in late June—Onganía saw fit to dismiss from his cabinet several of the more conservative members of the somewhat divided military establishment that had backed the 1966 coup. As 1969 drew to a close, Onganía remained in control, but his ability to make good on his 1966 promise to stay in power for a full decade appeared more doubtful in the light of the continued discontent of organized labor and the students, the lack of united support from the Roman Catholic Church, and a general dearth of enthusiasm for his regime.

Growth of Unrest. As the year began, the government was addressing itself to such goals as controlling inflation and encouraging moderate economic growth. Hoping to diminish restiveness on the part of organized labor, Onganía in January announced wage increases, though he also made it clear that 1969 would not see a return to free bargaining (suspended since 1966). When it became clear that the increases were to amount to no more than 8% to 11%, labor leaders, who had been arguing for a 40% increase, reacted unfavorably. Another source of trouble was the regime's effort to establish a uniform 48-hour work week, without overtime; some workers had already gained a 44-hour week with a premium for Saturday afternoon work. Grievances were further aggravated by an increase in gasoline prices, causing bus fare rises.

The government also announced early in the year that it would limit the increase in public investment for 1969 to a 10% to 15% advance over the 1968 level. This was a serious blow to the private sector, which had anticipated big government contracts and had purchased much new equipment.

Ranchers and farmers were antagonized by the announcement of a new tax on all landholdings. Some 700 members of the powerful and conservative Rural Society gathered to challenge the tax, threatening to restrict production. Cattle interests were later mollified when restrictions on cattle exports were eased in support of domestic prices.

May Demonstrations. On May 13, a student at the National University in the northern province of Corrientes was shot and killed during a protest against a rise in food prices at that institution. The shooting sparked an explosion of unrest among students, who soon won support in labor ranks and among radical elements of the church.

As student demonstrations spread to the universities of Rosario, Córdoba, Tucumán, La Plata, Santa Fé, Mendoza, and to other cities, the police tried several times to halt the protests. The shooting of a 15-year-old boy by the police in Rosario on May 22 led to an attack by militant students on police headquarters in that city. Federal troops were moved in to restore order. On May 23, the rival factions of the CGT (General Confederation of Labor), which had been quarrelling over whether or not to support the Onganía government, united behind the students and called for a general strike on May 29. On May 28, Onganía imposed a limited state of siege on the entire nation.

The general strike was one of the most effective in Argentine history. Most heavy industry was shut down, much of the nation's rail service was crippled, and public transport was completely stalled in several provincial cities and severely disrupted in Buenos Aires. In defiance of government orders and threats, most Argentine schools were closed through the efforts of the teachers' union.

In Córdoba, the site of the huge Kaiser Industries and many automobile assembly plants, demonstrators set fire to the local officers' club and other buildings. Onganía empowered military commanders to mete out death sentences to civilians, and it was reported that soldiers shot their way into the headquarters of the auto workers' union. Interior Minister Guillermo Borda, in a clear recognition of the breadth of the protest, asserted that the disturbances were caused by leftists.

By May 31, a tense peace had come to the nation. At least 400 persons were under arrest, several union officials had already been sentenced to prison terms, and more than 20 persons were dead.

With calm restored, Onganía moved quickly to combat both his enemies in labor and popular discontent. Raimundo Ongaro, the leader of the radical wing of the CGT, was arrested and held without charges. Onganía then dismissed several of his principal cabinet members, including Interior Minister Borda, whom he replaced with the less conservative Gen. Francisco Imaz. In this and other new appointments, Onganía seemed to be attempting to show a degree of independence of the army, whose most influential officers were identified with the so-called liberal faction, which violently opposed "Peronism" (the pro-labor philosophy associated with the exiled former dictator Juan Perón and his followers) and which stood for conservative economic measures.

ARGENTINA · Information Highlights

Area: 1,072,067 square miles (2,776,656 sq km).
Population: 23,617,000 (1968 est.).
Chief Cities (1960 census): Buenos Aires, the capital, 2,966,-816; Rosario, 671,852; Cordoba, 589,153; La Matanza, 402,642.
Government: *President*—Lt. Gen. Juan Carlos Onganía (took office June 29, 1966); *Parliament*—suspended June 1966.
Religious Faith: Roman Catholics, 88% of population.
Education: *Literacy rate* (1960), 91.4% of population aged 14 and over. *Total school enrollment* (1965)—4,774,172 (primary, 3,124,870; secondary, 795,477; teacher-training, 184,934; vocational, 425,588; higher, 243,303).
Finance (1968 est.): *Revenues,* $2,409,858,000; *expenditures,* $2,734,179,000; *public debt* (1967), $1,269,308,000; *monetary unit,* peso (350 pesos equal U. S.$1).
Gross National Product (1967): $14,848,714,000.
National Income (1967): $14,731,428,000; *average annual income per person,* $623.
Economic Indexes (1967): *Industrial production* (1965), 120 (1958=100); *agricultural production,* 100 (1963=100); *cost of living,* 268 (1963=100).
Manufacturing (metric tons, 1967); Residual fuel oil (1966), 8,191,000; gasoline (1966), 3,594,000; meat, 2,810,000;

wheat flour, 2,161,000.
Crops (metric tons, 1967–68 crop year): Maize, 8,510,000; wheat, 7,320,000; grapes, 2,993,000; potatoes, 1,797,000.
Minerals (metric tons, 1967); Crude petroleum, 15,593,000; natural gas, 4,793,000,000 cubic meters; salt, 817,000; silver (1966), 1,993,352 troy ounces.
Foreign Trade (1968): *Exports,* $1,368,000,000 (chief exports, 1967: meat, $381,000,000; maize, $223,500,000; wheat, $122,100,000; wool, $107,600,000); *imports,* $1,169,000,000 (chief imports, 1967: nonelectrical machinery, $187,300,-000; iron and steel, $134,600,000). *Chief trading partners* (1967): United States (took 8% of exports, supplied 22% of imports); Brazil (took 7% of exports, supplied 11% of imports); West Germany (took 5% of exports, supplied 10% of imports).
Transportation: *Roads* (1965), 84,008 miles (135,194 km); *motor vehicles* (1967), 1,822,500 (automobiles, 1,163,000); *railways* (1965), 27,169 miles (43,470 km); *merchant vessels* (1967), 148 (1,051,000 g.r.t.).
Communications: *Telephones* (1968); 1,583,281; *television stations* (1967), 32; *television sets* (1967), 1,900,000; *radios* (1967), 8,000,000; *newspapers* (1968), 176 (daily circulation, 2,914,000).

Most of the new cabinet members were allied with the more moderate nationalist faction.

Rockefeller Visit. To make matters still more difficult for Onganía, Gov. Nelson Rockefeller and his entourage were due in Argentina on June 29 on their fact-finding mission for U. S. President Nixon. The mission was by now the catalyst for violent anti-U. S. demonstrations throughout Latin America, and Argentina proved to be no exception. On June 26, nine supermarkets in Buenos Aires, all owned by a development enterprise controlled by Rockefeller interests, burned in the aftermath of bomb explosions. The arrival of Rockefeller three days later was marked by nationwide demonstrations.

Some 15,000 plainclothes and uniformed policemen (the army was confined to barracks) kept order and guarded the mission. But at noon on Monday,

TEAR GAS fired by police scatters Buenos Aires demonstrators protesting U. S. envoy Rockefeller's visit.

UPI

June 30, while Rockefeller and Onganía were meeting in downtown Buenos Aires, several well-dressed young men walked into the offices of Augusto Vandor, the leader of the moderate faction of the CGT, and murdered him. The killing was believed to be related to the feud within the ranks of labor, since Vandor had refused to endorse a call for another general strike. A new state of siege was declared, and calm was restored after at least 300 more arrests.

Continuing Labor Troubles. In late July, with Ongaro still in jail and Vandor dead, Onganía appointed Valentín Suárez to manage the CGT. Both wings of the labor organization refused to accept the president's appointee in the absence of major concessions in regard to wage increases and the detention of labor leaders. Labor called another 24-hour general strike for August 27, which was widely observed but elicited only minor concessions from Onganía. Meanwhile, a news magazine was closed for revealing deep divisions within the military.

Economic Affairs. Economically, the Argentine record in 1969 was mixed. Although the gross national product of midyear was reportedly rising at an annual rate of 7%, imports were up sharply, foreign exchange reserves were low, and wage demands were helping to raise again the spectre of serious inflation. The government announced that it hoped for a 10-million-ton wheat harvest, which would include a 4-million-ton surplus for export to finance development programs, but this goal was jeopardized by farmers who were unhappy about trade and credit policies that seemed to favor industrialists. During 1969, Argentina was actually forced to import wheat, owing to earlier overexportation and miscalculation about the size of the harvest. On July 29, a loan of $50 million was arranged with a syndicate of five major U. S. banks.

International Affairs. Argentine foreign relations in 1969 were marked by a sharp conflict with Uruguay over the boundary between the two nations, particularly with respect to islands in the Río de La Plata estuary, where Uruguay intended to drill for oil. Argentina actually moved marines onto one of the disputed islands in early February, but the controversy subsequently cooled.

Relations with the United States were correct if not cordial. Onganía specifically criticized U. S. policy as seeking to achieve an appearance of internationalist aims while remaining protectionist. On May 23, the U. S. Senate confirmed John Davis Lodge as ambassador to Argentina.

JAMES R. LEVY
Pomona College

ARIZONA

Pollution control and conservation measures made news in Arizona during 1969. The state suspended use for one year of the controversial pesticide DDT, the Legislature tightened air pollution control standards, and the Marble Canyon of the Colorado River, in northern Arizona, was set aside for preservation as a national monument.

Suspension of DDT Use. On January 13, the state board of pesticide control suspended for one year the use of DDT in the state. The suspension came as a result of findings of DDT contamination in milk above the prescribed tolerance limits. Since fields on which the cows grazed had not been sprayed with DDT, it is assumed that the pesticide, borne through the air, had contaminated the water used for irrigating the pastures.

Legislation. The Legislature met in regular annual session from January 13 to April 11. The general fund budget of $310 million adopted for the fiscal year 1969–70 included $12.2 million for construction at the state's three universities, as well as funds for planning and initial construction of a state office building and a state institution for delinquent girls. At present female juvenile delinquents are cared for mainly in private institutions on a contract basis. Funds also were provided for combining present computer systems in a new state data-processing center.

The legislators authorized the state health department to establish minimum statewide standards

------- ARIZONA • Information Highlights -------

Area: 113,909 square miles (295,025 sq km).
Population: 1,708,000 (Jan. 1, 1969 est.)
Chief Cities (1965 census): Phoenix, the capital (1968 est.), 520,000; Tucson (1968 est.), 240,000; Mesa, 50,529; Tempe, 45,919; Scottsdale, 54,504.
Government: *Chief Officers*—governor, John R. (Jack) Williams (Republican); secy. of state, Wesley Bolin (Democrat); atty. gen., Gary K. Nelson (R); treas., Morris A. Herring; supt. of pub. instr., Weldon P. Shofstall; chief justice, Lorna E. Lockwood. *Legislature*—Senate, 30 members (17 Democrats, 13 Republicans); House of Representatives, 60 members (34 R, 26 D).
Education: *School enrollment* (1968–69)—public elementary, 292,000 pupils (12,300 teachers); public secondary, 115,000 pupils (4,300 teachers); nonpublic schools, 32,-900 pupils (1,450 teachers); college and university (fall 1967), 78,549 students. *Public school expenditures* (1967–68)—$252,450,000 ($703 per pupil); average teacher's salary, $7,500.
Public Finance (fiscal year 1968): *Revenues,* $660,955,000 (general sales and gross receipt taxes, $107,152,000; motor fuel tax, $52,670,000; federal funds $164,029,000). *Expenditures,* $286,550,000 (education, $136,047,000; health, welfare, and safety, $54,763,000; highways, $116,152,000). *State debt,* $82,969,000.
Personal Income (1968): $5,034,000,000; average annual income per person, $3,027.
Public Assistance (fiscal year 1967–68): $30,646,337 to 54,610 recipients (aged, $9,604,907; dependent children, $14,697,530).
Labor Force (employed persons, July 1969): *Agricultural,* 35,600; *nonagricultural* (wage and salary earners), 576,900 (19% manufacturing, 22% trade, 21% government). *Unemployed persons* (July 1969)—20,300.
Manufacturing (1965): Value added by manufacture, $719,-882,000 (transportation equipment, $13,179,000; primary metals, $84,527,000; nonelectrical machinery, $134,336,-000; electrical machinery, $151,171,000; fabricated metals, $25,664,000; food and products, $71,817,000).
Agriculture (1967): Cash farm income, $574,304,000 (livestock, $239,403,000; crops, $288,116,000; govt. payments, $46,785,000). *Chief crops* (tons)—Citrus fruits, 364,000 (ranks 3d among the states); hay, 1,122,000; sorghum grain, 557,900 (ranks 5th); barley, 288,000.
Mining (1967): Production value $463,858,000. *Chief minerals* (tons)—Copper, 501,741; sand and gravel, 16,580,000; pumice, 1,064,000; lime, 186,000; uranium oxide, 42; silver, 4,588,000 troy ounces; gold, 80,844 troy ounces.
Transportation: *Roads* (1968), 40,843 miles (65,729 km); *motor vehicles* (1968), 1,101,797; *railroads* (1967), 2,492 track miles (4,011 km); *airports* (1969), 11.
Communications (1967): *Telephones* (1968), 742,800; *television stations,* 9; *radio stations,* 64; *newspapers,* 13.

for control of air pollution and to enforce them in counties that fail to set up adequate programs of their own. Counties were authorized to join together in setting and enforcing standards of air pollution control.

A proposed constitutional change in the state criminal code, which would make it more difficult for second offenders to obtain bail, was adopted. This change must be approved by a vote of the people at the next general election. The Legislature also approved the observance of legal holidays on Monday, adopted an implied consent law applicable to motorists suspected of drunken driving, increased the number of judges on the state appeals court from six to nine, and tightened laws against governmental corruption and bribery.

New National Monument. In one of his last official acts, President Lyndon B. Johnson signed on January 20 a proclamation, authorized by the National Antiquities Act of 1906, creating the Marble Canyon National Monument in Arizona. The new national monument preserves a 26,000-acre scenic canyon area, with almost vertical red sandstone and white limestone walls 3,000 feet high. It extends for some 50 miles along the Colorado River, linking Lees Ferry, in the Glen Canyon National Recreation Area near the Arizona-Utah border, with the Grand Canyon National Monument downriver. Marble Canyon includes some of the Colorado River's finest white-water rapids. On its eastern edge the new monument borders the Navajo Indian Reservation. During recent years Marble Canyon had been the subject of national controversy as conservation interests fought to save it from use as a proposed site for a hydroelectric dam.

Phoenix Mayoral Election. In an election on November 11, John Driggs, a savings and loan executive, won the Phoenix mayoralty over incumbent Mayor Milton Graham. Mayor Graham was seeking a fourth term. Driggs was supported by U. S. Sen. Barry Goldwater, as well as the Phoenix Charter Government Committee. The committee has had a record of backing winning mayoral candidates since the late 1940's.

ARKANSAS

The past seemed to reemerge in Arkansas in 1969 when barge navigation on the Arkansas River was extended 153 miles upstream from the Mississippi River and as Little Rock once again became an active river port. At Arkansas Post, the site of the old river port and the state's first settlement and capital, U. S. Rep. Wilbur D. Mills opened Arkansas' Territorial Sesquicentennial Year.

Current issues, however, continued to dominate the news. Headline stories included the partisan feuding between Republican Gov. Winthrop Rockefeller and a Democratic legislature; worsening governmental financial conditions because public employee and welfare clientele demands for more money conflicted with public resistance to tax increases; and mounting racial tensions in schools.

Legislature. In the longest biennial session since 1911, the Arkansas legislature drastically blunted the governor's "era of excellence" plan by cutting his tax-increases program from more than $90 million to about $20 million. The auditing of local governments' fiscal records was transferred from the governor to the legislature. The legislature overrode an executive veto of a bill requiring all can-

--------- **ARKANSAS · Information Highlights** ---------

Area: 53,104 square miles (137,540 sq km).

Population: 1,982,000 (Jan. 1, 1969 est.).

Chief Cities (1968 est.): Little Rock, the capital, 136,000; Fort Smith, 64,000; North Little Rock, 63,000; Pine Bluff, 57,500.

Government: *Chief Officers*—governor, Winthrop Rockefeller (Republican); lt. gov., Maurice Britt (R); secy. of sate, Kelly Bryant (Democrat); atty. gen., Joe Purcell (D); treas., Mrs. Nancy Hall; supt. of pub. instr., Arch Ford; chief justice, Carleton Harris. *General Assembly*—Senate, 35 members (34 Democrats, 1 Republican); House of Representatives, 100 members (96 D, 4 R).

Education: *School enrollment* (1968–69)—public elementary, 250,000 pupils (10,000 teachers); public secondary, 209,000 pupils (9,600 teachers); nonpublic schools, 12,700 pupils (600 teachers); college and university (fall 1967), 48,505 students. *Public school expenditures* (1967–68)—$227,558,000 ($550 per pupil); average teacher's salary, $5,723.

Public Finance (fiscal year 1968): *Revenues,* $552,906,000 (general sales and gross receipts taxes, $92,783,000; motor fuel tax, $65,547,000; federal funds, $188,349,000). *Expenditures,* $556,109,000. *State debt,* $116,772,000 (June 30, 1968).

Personal Income (1968): $4,611,000,000; average annual income per person, $2,322.

Public Assistance (fiscal year 1968–69): $50,306,219 to 100,741 recipients (aged, $40,952,824; dependent children, $9,353,395).

Labor Force (employed persons, calendar year 1968): *Agricultural,* 58,900; *nonagricultural* (wage and salary earners), 610,100 (25.8% manufacturing, 16.7% trade, 15.7% government). *Unemployed* (1968)—30,700.

Manufacturing (1965): Value added by manufacture, $1,216,370,000 (transportation equipment, $21,990,000; primary metals, $56,310,000; nonelectrical machinery, $39,401,000; electrical machinery, $81,599,000; fabricated metals, $46,050,000; food and products, $202,201,000).

Agriculture (1967): Cash farm income, $954,549,000 (livestock, $424,577,000; crops, $426,683,000; govt. payments, $103,289,000). *Chief crops* (tons)—Soybeans, 2,568,900 (ranks 3d among the states); rice, 1,073,300 (ranks 3d); hay, 1,357,000; wheat, 565,140; cottonseed, 214,000; cotton lint, 124,800; corn, 75,260.

Mining (1966): Production value, $190,127,000. *Chief minerals* (tons)—Stone, 19,109,000; petroleum, 23,824,000 barrels; sand and gravel, 16,056,000; bauxite, 1,803,200; clays, 1,097,000; barite, 232,856.

Transportation: *Roads* (1969), 74,468 miles (119,819 km); *motor vehicles* (1968), 1,117,654; *railroads* (1969), 5,950 track miles (9,574 km); airports (1969), 9.

Communications (1969): *Telephones* (1968), 707,500; *television stations,* 6; *radio stations,* 110; *newspapers,* 31 (daily circulation, 735,872).

didates for state and congressional offices to win by a majority vote in the general election. The director of the department of administration, a key figure in Rockefeller's "era of excellence," resigned because of legislative opposition to his projects. But despite the governor's negative evaluation of this regular session, the General Assembly passed a large number of acts including the final merger of the private Little Rock University with the University of Arkansas.

Constitutional Revision. A constitutional convention was assembled; it drafted a tentative document to replace the Constitution of 1874. Public reaction, while acknowledging the need for extensive revision, was sharply critical of the granting of sweeping home rule powers to cities, the altering of the 10% limit on interest rates, and continuance of the existing right-to-work provision. The final draft will be presented to the voters for ratification in 1970.

Politics. State Democratic leaders attempted to rebuild the party. However, efforts to draft a new platform acceptable to all party factions before the gubernatorial nomination met open opposition, and proposals to require loyalty oaths for voting in primary elections from those who supported George Wallace in 1968 sparked threats by the American Independent party to run candidates for local office in 1970.

School Integration. About one half of the Negro public school population was attending unified systems by September. While integration was amicable in many systems, some schools and communities were harassed by court suits, student walkouts, and small-scale riots. Racial turmoil forced the temporary closing of schools in Texarkana and Forrest City. The newly organized Freedom, Inc., the successor to the defunct White Citizens Councils, unsuccessfully challenged total integration, although its candidates won a significant school board election in Pine Bluff.

A suit in a federal court to enjoin the playing of *Dixie* in the Jonesboro school district, although dismissed, illustrated the intensity of the racial controversy over even minor topics.

WILLIAM C. NOLAN
Southern State College

ARMED FORCES. See AIR FORCE; ARMY; DEFENSE FORCES; MARINE CORPS; NATIONAL GUARD; NAVY.

ARMS CONTROL. See DISARMAMENT.

ARMY

While combat in Vietnam leveled off markedly in 1969, the U. S. Army was beset by grave accusations—that a massacre of hundreds of unarmed men, women, and children by U. S. troops had occurred in a South Vietnamese village in 1968; that members of a Special Forces (Green Beret) unit had criminally assassinated a purported South Vietnamese double agent; and that the highest ranking enlisted man and a major general, since retired, had been involved in illegal profiteering on enlisted men's club activities. In combat, a near-mutiny was reported.

Military Operations. Throughout most of the year there were fewer American clashes with the enemy in Vietnam, as the Nixon administration's "Vietnamization" policy called for reductions in U. S. combat forces and increasing assignment of the South Vietnamese army to battle. From a peak of 362,000 in February, U. S. Army strength in Vietnam was reduced to 339,600 in October.

The biggest battle involving U. S. troops took place from May 10 to June 7 at Dong Ap Bia in the A Shau Valley. Units of the 101st Airborne Division (Airmobile), the 3d Marine Division, and the South Vietnamese 1st Division initiated "the Battle of Hill 937," to cut North Vietnamese infiltration and supply routes to Hue and Da Nang. After repeatedly assaulting strong enemy hilltop defenses, a weary U. S. unit refused momentarily to obey a lieutenant's order to carry on. An effective noncom rallied them. The incident created a sensation in the United States.

Only light fighting was reported in the summer and fall, mostly southeast of Saigon, along the Cambodian border and just south of the Demilitarized Zone on the North Vietnamese border. In December there were signs of resumed heavy North Vietnamese infiltration.

War Atrocities. Reports of an alleged massacre by U. S. troops on March 16, 1968, in the South Vietnamese village of Song My were made public in November 1969, with a flurry of press and TV interviews and a formal Army indictment. A group of Song My villagers said U. S. infantrymen had rounded up and killed (according to one estimate) 567 unarmed men, women, and children. At least three discharged U. S. soldiers, one on nationwide TV, said that they personally had taken part in the incident.

MUTINY ACT is read to soldier-prisoners near San Francisco in the Presidio stockade. The prisoners are singing "We Shall Overcome" as a protest against the killing of a prisoner. In 1969 the Army courts-martial sentenced some of the protesters to long prison terms.

UPI

The Army, on November 24, announced a general court martial for 1st Lt. William L. Calley, Jr., 26, of Miami, Fla., on six counts including premeditated murder of at least 109 men, women, and children. The Army said it was investigating the conduct of nine Army men and 15 former Army men in the Song My inquiry. At least one other soldier, a sergeant, was held pending charges.

The Army also said it was investigating the background of an earlier unpublicized inquiry in the case which had concluded no disciplinary action was appropriate. At least two members of Congress said that they had received letters charging other, similar atrocities in Vietnam. The Army said it was investigating these also. The South Vietnamese government had investigated and concluded there had been no massacre, but launched a new inquiry.

Early in 1969, another incident in Vietnam aroused widespread dismay. A suspected South Vietnamese double agent was alleged, in Army charges filed July 31, to have been murdered by a U. S. Special Forces (Green Beret) unit and his body dropped in the China Sea. The Central Intelligence Agency was involved in the case but, in an unusual action, publicly disavowed responsibility. The Army arrested the Green Beret commander in Vietnam, Col. Robert B. Rheault, a West Pointer, and seven of his men. But on September 31 the charges were dropped with the explanation that national security reasons made prosecution undesirable. Rheault resigned from the Army on October 31.

Dissidence. More than ever since the outset of the war in Vietnam, active-duty soldiers openly protested the war. Even in Vietnam, press reports described combat troops wearing black armbands to protest the war. About 200 soldiers in Pleiku signed an open letter of protest to President Nixon and more than 100 ostentatiously fasted on Thanksgiving Day. In Saigon 136 signatures, including those of three West Pointers, were reported on a declaration for the October 15 antiwar moratorium.

Another expression of dissent developed in the opening of several antiwar coffeehouses for GI's in the vicinity of Fort Knox, Ky. The antiwar gatherings became a source of controversy in the civilian community. Another antiwar coffeehouse near Fort Carson, Colo., was operated by two soldiers who openly issued an antiwar newspaper that was promptly banned at the post. An editor of a dissident newspaper was given an undesirable discharge at Fort Gordon, Ga., on April 19.

Scandal. In addition to alleged war crimes, the Army was plagued by charges of scandal. A Senate subcommittee charged that Sgt. Maj. William O. Wooldridge—who in 1968 was lauded and selected as the first sergeant major of the Army, a new and topmost enlisted grade—was involved with a group said to have illegally skimmed hundreds of thousands of dollars from slot-machine profits in enlisted men's clubs throughout the world. Wooldridge's retirement was held up, pending an Army investigation.

Retired Maj. Gen. Carl C. Turner, whose last two posts in the Army were inspector general and provost marshal, in charge of military police, was cited in Congressional testimony—among other charges related to the Wooldridge case—with having sold for his personal profit 400 firearms he received in the line of duty. Following his retirement from the Army, Turner had been named chief United States marshal by the Nixon administration, but he was later asked to resign.

Strength. Authorized uniformed manpower in the Army, 1,550,000 at the beginning of 1969, was scheduled to be reduced to 1,510,000 by June 1970. This was part of a planned overall reduction in the armed forces. The paid drill strength of the Army National Guard was 388,300 on August 31; the Army Reserves was 258,626. The organization of the Army remained unaltered from the previous year—19 active and 8 reserve divisions, including 6 separate active brigades.

Army authorities stressed the so-called "division force," consisting not only of divisions or their equivalent in brigades but initial support increments (ISI's), the units required for sustained combat. These "division forces" are somewhat larger than the old "division slice." A division force totals 48,000 men, compared with 35,000 in the previous divisions and supporting units. The Army was studying means of incorporating reserve units in the divisional table of organization.

In addition to Vietnam deployments, the Army continued to maintain about 200,000 men in Europe, 50,000 in Korea, 10,000 in Hawaii, 5,000 in Japan, 12,000 in the Ryukus, 8,000 in the Caribbean, 12,000 in Alaska, and a total of 50,000 in other scattered overseas posts.

Procurement. In keeping with overall spending cutbacks, the Pentagon requested $5.69 billion for Army equipment and weapons for the fiscal year 1970, compared with $6.7 billion appropriated in 1969 and $6.37 billion appropriated the year before. To counter adverse publicity over defects in some weapons, the Army introduced stringent "hardware" tests as opposed to earlier reliance on blueprints. Cost reductions were sought through management changes. Increasingly in 1969, the armed forces faced the problem of refurbishing and storing equipment brought back from Vietnam.

The first M551 Sheridan armored reconnaissance vehicles were deployed to Vietnam, Korea, and Europe; the first OH-58 Kiowa helicopters entered service in Vietnam. The Army's aircraft inventory rose to a record 9,200 helicopters and 2,300 fixed wing planes, for a total of 11,500.

Training. Based on experience in Vietnam, substantial changes were introduced in basic combat and infantry advanced individual training. Training for mortar crewmen was increased by 19 hours; Vietnam field training exercises increased to three

MAJ. GEN. CARL C. TURNER at Senate hearing admits selling seized guns for his personal profit.

Research and Development. The army canceled the production contract for the heralded Cheyenne helicopter, claiming default by Lockheed Aircraft Corporation. The Army, however, continued research on it.

A new type of helicopter, UTTAS (utility tactical transport aircraft system) was being designed to replace the UH-1 or "Huey" as the workhorse of the helicopter fleet. To replace the CH-54 "flying crane," with its 9-ton lift capability, the Army sought a helicopter with a 23-ton payload.

The main battle tank (MBT-70), a joint project with West Germany, continued in development. A concept for a single replacement for .50 caliber (0.5 inch) and 20-mm (0.79 inch) automatic weapons on armored vehicles was studied. To be called Bushmaster, the proposed weapon could be instantly switched from armor-piercing to antipersonnel ammunition.

Administration. Stanley R. Resor, who was appointed by President Johnson in 1965, was retained by President Nixon as secretary of the Army. Thaddeus R. Beal was appointed as under secretary. Other new civilian officials were Assistant Secretaries Robert L. Johnson, J. Ronald Fox, and John E. Davis.

Gen. William C. Westmoreland continued as chief of staff; Gen. Bruce Palmer as vice chief; and Gen. Creighton W. Abrams as commander in Vietnam.

(See also VIETNAM WAR.)

JACK RAYMOND
President, Thomas J. Deegan Co.
Author, "Power at the Pentagon"

STAYSKAL © 1969, CHICAGO TODAY
"It's my lawyer ... just in case."

instead of two days; and training in mines and booby traps was emphasized.

The year marked the 150th anniversary of military training on college campuses. The Reserve Officers Training Corps, which is the primary source of officers for active duty, commissioned more than 16,000 2d lieutenants from 268 colleges and universities.

When antiwar pressure on some campuses forced either the elimination of or radical changes in ROTC status, the Army then bolstered its junior ROTC program. This program is currently maintained at 570 secondary schools, and the Army expects its junior ROTC division to expand to 650 schools by the fall of 1971.

Lowered standards for induction allowed 350 to 400 men who could not read above fourth-grade level to enter the Army each week. A six-week elementary reading course was established at 12 basic training centers.

GREEN BERETS' commander in South Vietnam, Col. Robert B. Rheault, resigned after officers of the Special Forces were accused of killing a South Vietnamese who was believed to be a double agent.

THE NEW YORK TIMES

ART MUSEUMS with bold new concepts included Everson Museum of Art (*top*), Syracuse, N.Y., and Des Moines Art Center (*below*), Iowa, both of which skillfully blended outer and inner massiveness and grace.

art

Although interest in kinetic and luminist art remained high in 1969, there was a reaction against the technologically elaborate and sensation-rich work of recent years. Many artists turned to projects designed to give subtle aesthetic experiences devoid of sophisticated engineering or aggressive electronics. At its best, the new art gave to spectators a heightened awareness of the power of their own imagination and of the beauty of nature's materials.

NEW DIMENSIONS

Many artists, although not members of a special group and without a common style, shared an interest in such concepts as transience and memory, action and process, and invisibility and destruction. Few of them seemed to care about works of art as such, gallery sales, or museum display.

Anti-Object Art. Critics have called the work of these artists "anti-form" and "anti-object." For example, Keith Sonnier simply pours molten lead on floors and leans lead plates against walls. Bill Bollinger uses dust, while Robert Smithson collects rocky material in bins. Dennis Oppenheim created a 3-mile (5-km) *Time Line* cut into a frozen river. Others, like Douglas Huebler and Joseph Kessuth, are content with merely written proposals, thus creating art that is purely conceptual.

For some, this work was a self-rewarding activity or a reaffirmation of man in nature. For others, it represented a protest against the commercialization of art and an acquisitive society.

An unprecedented number of terms were coined in connection with these new activities. Among them were "thinkpieces," "earthworks," "land art," "nihilart," "abstract geology," "distributional sculpture," and "de-objectified art." Since many projects were extremely large, like Mike Heitzer's mile-long lines painted on the desert, description in art periodicals may displace traditional exhibitions in art galleries as the major method of "display."

Exhibitions. Exhibitions, as numerous and interesting in 1969 as in past years, included showings of various aspects of the new art. New York shows featured Robert Smithson's Non-Sites (Dwan); Robert Morris' presentation of materials like clay, zinc, felt, glass, and asphalt (Castelli); Bill Bollinger's Dust Concepts (Bykert); and group shows such as Anti-Illusion, Procedures Materials (Whitney Museum) and Nine in a Warehouse (Castelli). Outside New York, major group exhibitions of the new art were featured. These included Here and Now, Process Art at the University of Washington galleries, St. Louis; the first exhibit of Earth Art at the Cornell University Museum; Soft Objects at the New Jersey State Museum; Telephone Art at the Museum of Modern Art, Chicago; Other Ideas at the Detroit Institute of Art.

Museums and other institutions cooperated with artists in outdoor displays. New York University presented Les Levine's Process of Elimination in a vacant lot. The Massachusetts Institute of Technology, along with the German Center, sponsored Otto Piene's field of Hot Air Sculpture over snow.

Mass-Produced Art. More and more artists seemed interested in mass-production art, especially in the area of games and toys. In Recklinghausen, West Germany, the entire museum was given over to the exhibit Art as Play—Play as Art. At Christmas, department stores in the United States sold kits of colored, magnetized plastic pieces—"do-it-yourself art-making kits"—designed by the distinguished op artist Victor Vasarely. The kits cost $500, considerably less than the $10,000 to $15,000 charged for the painter's canvases.

SCULPTURE

Developments in sculpture continued to play a major role in the current art scene. Sculptors' work took many forms, from figurative to nonobjective, from "funk" to energy structures. In what was perhaps the first one-man show ever awarded to a living American artist by the Metropolitan Museum of Art in New York, Jules Olitski, a painter, exhibited his sculpture.

New Trends. Television as a medium in sculpture was used by Nam June Paik, Wynn Chamberlain, Frank Gillette, and others at the Wise Gallery. Magnetic works by Takis and light displays by Otto Piene were also featured at the Wise. Les Levine used high-intensity sodium vapor lights and other special light effects to shape and distort space in an exhibit at the Fischbach Gallery. Bruce Nauman displayed experimental work using holograms and video tapes at the Castelli Gallery. Inflatable sculpture on display at the Jewish Museum included work by Andy Warhol, Otto Piene, and Charles Frazier.

Retrospectives. Dan Flavin, America's foremost light sculptor, was honored by a large retrospective at the National Gallery of Canada, Ottawa. The most noted creator of soft sculpture, Claes Oldenburg, was similarly honored at the Museum of

---

BEN SHAHN (1898–1969)

THE NEW YORK TIMES

Ben Shahn, who died in New York City on March 14, 1969, believed that the artist should actively engage in causes serving humanity and, in his paintings and murals, he combined a candid social realism with a type of surrealism that contained elements of poetry and mystery. Among his best known works was the series of paintings *The Passion of Sacco and Vanzetti,* a searing pictorial commentary on the trial and execution of the two Italian-born anarchists. He painted murals for a number of public buildings, including the Social Security (now Federal Security) Building in Washington, D. C., and the Bronx Central Annex Post Office in New York City.

Shahn, the son of a woodcarver, was born in Kaunas, Lithuania, on Sept. 12, 1898, and emigrated to the United States with his family in 1906. He became an apprentice lithographer at the age of 15 and later studied at New York University, at the National Academy of Design, and in Europe. His first one-man show was at the Downtown Gallery in New York in 1930. Shahn gained international recognition with the exhibition of his works at the Venice Biennale in 1954. In his later years he devoted himself largely to book illustration and commercial art. Among the honors he received was the gold medal of the American Institute of Graphic Arts. His book *The Shape of Content* (1957) consists of lectures he delivered as Charles Eliot Norton Professor at Harvard University in 1956.

ROBERT LEHMAN collection, valued at over $100 million, was donated to Metropolitan Museum. El Greco's *St. Jerome (center)*, flanked by Rembrandts, is shown in Lehman mansion.

Modern Art, New York. "Old masters" of modern sculpture who were given retrospectives included David Smith (Guggenheim), Jean Arp (Guggenheim), Julio Gonzales (Saidenberg), Constantin Brancusi (Philadelphia Museum of Art), and Gerhard Marcks (University of California, Los Angeles).

Sculptors receiving important exhibits at New York galleries were Barbara Hepworth (Gimpel), Max Bill (Staemphli), Anthony Caro (Emmerich), José de Rivera (Borgenicht), Louise Nevelson (Pace), Phillip Pavia (Jackson), George Segal (Janis), Paul Suttman (Dintenfass), Carl Andre (Dwan), and Charles Ross (Dwan).

PAINTING

As in 1968, the year 1969 saw a remarkable variety of exhibits devoted to the many diverse aspects of American art. In New York, the first of five major centennial exhibitions at the Metropolitan Museum, New York Painting and Sculpture 1940–1970, included over 400 works by 43 painters and sculptors of the New York school. Other important exhibits were Seven Decades of American Art and American Art in the 1930's (Whitney), American Painting 1750–1950 (Knoedler), American Landscapes (Wildenstein), Black Artists of the 30's (Studio Museum, Harlem), Twelve Afro-American Artists (Nordness), and Pennsylvania German Art (Museum of American Folk Arts).

The Metropolitan Museum's mixed-media exhibit, Harlem on My Mind, stirred an unusual amount of unfavorable reaction. In Philadelphia, the Institute of Contemporary Art presented the first show to survey the comic strip's influence on American art.

Retrospectives. Numerous American painters from an earlier day received exhibits in 1969. At the Whitney Museum, paintings and photographs by

Charles Sheeler and paintings by William Mount were exhibited. Marsden Hartley's work was displayed at Danenberg Galleries, New York, and at the university art museums of the University of Texas, Austin, and the University of Southern California. Other exhibits of older American masters included the works of Childe Hassam, William Merrit Chase, and Philip Evergood.

One-Man Shows. Important one-man shows were given in New York to the painters Roy Lichtenstein (Guggenheim), Robert Motherwell (Marlborough), Willem de Kooning (Museum of Modern Art), Helen Frankenthaler (Whitney), Jackson Pollock (Marlborough), Barnett Newman (Knoedler), Sam Francis (Emmerich), Richard Lindner (Cordier & Ekstrom), Robert Beauchamp (Graham), Larry Poons (Rubin), Lester Johnson (Jackson), Bob Thompson (New School), Morris Louis (Rubin), Allan D'Arcangelo (Fischbach), and Richard Anuszkiewicz (Janis).

New Realism. A growing interest was shown in those trends in representational art which have been called "new realism." Artists grouped under that title at a Milwaukee Art Center exhibition were Jack Beal, Gabriel Laderman, Wayne Thiebaud, Robert Bechtle, Philip Pearlstein, Sidney Tillim, and Alfred Leslie. "New realists" featured in New York galleries were Lowell Nesbit, Philip Pearlstein, Fairfield Porter, Charles Close, and Don Nice.

European Art. Among major exhibitions devoted to European art were, in New York, a scholarly examination of little-known 17th century Florentine art at the Metropolitan Museum; a survey of 20th century German watercolors and drawings at the Frumkin Gallery; and a showing of Viennese fantastic realism at the Austrian Institute. One-man shows were given to Kandinsky (Knoedler and Mu-

We lived on 145th Street near Seventh Avenue. One day we were so hungry we could barely breathe. I started out the door. it was cold as all-hell and I walked from 145th to 133rd down Seventh Avenue, going into every joint trying to find work.

Billie Holiday

UPI

CONTROVERSIAL EXHIBITION entitled "Harlem on My Mind" at the Metropolitan Museum of Art antagonized many Negroes and Jews, but it attracted record crowds.

At the Illinois Institute of Technology in Chicago, tribute was paid to the German Bauhaus, the most influential art school of modern times. Over 2,500 objects were displayed in the show, Fifty Years Bauhaus, which toured Stuttgart, Paris, Toronto, and Pasadena, Calif., and will be shown at the 1970 World's Fair in Osaka.

Rembrandt and His Pupils, one of the most important exhibitions of the season, originated at the Montreal Museum of Fine Arts to commemorate the 300th anniversary of the master's death.

Oriental Art. The Asia House gallery in New York featured the most extensive showing of Tibetan art ever seen in the United States. Twenty-three of the pieces in the exhibit belong to the Dalai Lama, now living in exile in India.

MUSEUMS AND COLLECTIONS

The year saw three major U. S. museums prepare for and celebrate their centennials. The Philadelphia Museum of Art, the Boston Museum of Fine Arts, and the Metropolitan Museum of Art in New York all were founded about 1870. Several magnificent private collections were presented to the nation's museums in 1969.

Gifts. New York's Metropolitan Museum of Art received one of the world's greatest privately owned collections, that of the late Robert Lehman. The gift included almost 3,000 objects of western European art. New York Gov. Nelson Rockefeller made news in the art world by putting on display his remarkable collections of modern art (Museum of Modern Art) and primitive art (Metropolitan Museum of Art). The primitive art will be given to the Metropolitan Museum, where a new wing will be built to house it. Having accepted this gift of Oceanic, African, and Pre-Columbian work, the museum will establish a department for it and thereby recognize primitive art on the level of Oriental and classical, medieval, and other Western art. The 20th century American art holdings of novelist James Michener were presented to the University of Texas, where they will be exhibited in a new building to be constructed for the Humanities Research Center.

Museum of Modern Art. The New York Museum of Modern Art was in the process of reorganizing itself in 1969. William Lieberman was named director of its department of painting and sculpture, and William Rubin was made chief curator of the painting and sculpture collection. The museum revised its exhibition policy. The second-floor exhibition area will feature changing shows dedicated to important themes in modern art. The first of these "collection exhibits" was titled The New American Painting and Sculpture, First Generation, and featured works by Gorky, de Kooning, Hofmann, Newman, Still, Rothko, Reinhardt, Baziotes, and Tomlin.

Appointments. In Washington, D. C., J. Carter Brown succeeded John Walker as director of the National Gallery, and Joshua Taylor of the University of Chicago was named director of the Smithsonian Institution's National Collection of Fine Arts. Agnes Mongan was designated director of Harvard University's Fogg Art Museum. She thus became the only woman to head a major U. S. museum.

New Museums and Additions. The University of Iowa dedicated its new museum and commissioned for it a large kinetic fountain by the Belgian surrealist Pol Bury. Wadsworth Atheneum in Hartford, Conn., reopened after undergoing a 3-year renovation and the construction of a new $4.7

seum of Modern Art), Larionov (Acquavilla), Torres-Garcia (Royal Marks), Horst Antes (Lefebre), Konrad Klapheck (Janis), and Piero Dorazio (Marlborough). Nineteenth century French painting, featuring many forgotten as well as famous names, was exhibited at the Minneapolis Art Institute. The first retrospective show in 20 years for the Hungarian master László Moholy-Nagy was mounted at the Museum of Contemporary Art, Chicago.

ALEXANDER CALDER greets visitors following dedication of his stabile (*background*) in Grand Rapids, Mich.

million wing. The Elvehjem Art Center at the University of Wisconsin, Madison, completed in 1969, ranks among the largest university art museums in the nation. New fine arts buildings were also opened at Northern Illinois University, De Kalb, and the State University at Potsdam, N. Y.

Other Museum Activity. Chicago's newest monumental "art work" was, for a few days, the entire Museum of Contemporary Art, which was "wrapped" by the master of *empaquetage,* Christo. At the Chicago Art Institute, a 2-ton painted wooden tableau of Chicago by Red Grooms was installed.

The Museum of the Rhode Island School of Design commissioned pop artist Andy Warhol to select works which struck his fancy from 45,000 objects in the museum's storage areas. These were then exhibited under the title Raid the Icebox.

Thefts and Damage. Small thefts and minor vandalism continued to plague museums during the year. In Amsterdam, protesting artists and students

NELSON ROCKEFELLER poses with part of his collection of primitive art, donated to Metropolitan Museum.

conducted a sit-in before Rembrandt's *Night Watch.* Fortunately no damage was done. However, several Rembrandts at the Metropolitan Museum, New York, suffered slight damage in what appeared to be a misguided protest gesture. Sixteen paintings, including Bruegel's *Blue Madonna,* valued at $160,000, were stolen from a private collection in Trieste. On the other hand, a small Rembrandt, missing for two months, was recovered by a museum in Geneva.

AWARDS, HONORS, AND GRANTS

Artists were commissioned to paint their reactions to various facets of the nation's space program in a project, Eyewitness to Space, sponsored by the National Aeronautics and Space Administration (NASA) and the National Gallery of Art. Among artists making paintings of the Apollo moon missions were Jamie Wyeth, Lamar Dodd, Tom O'Hara, Peter Hurd, Robert Rauschenberg, and Paul Calle.

Leonard Baskin received a gold medal for his graphic art from the National Institute of Arts and Letters. Painter John Heliker was elected to membership in the institute. John Simon Guggenheim grants were awarded to Larry Bell, Daniel Christensen, Walter de Maria, Herbert Ferber, Joseph Goto, Robert Morris, Slan Saret, and Robert Swain. Guggenheim grants were also given to art critics and historians Dore Ashton, John Coplans, and Edward Maser. Painters Jack Barley of Detroit and Kenneth Lithgow of New York were awarded Rome Prize Fellowships by the American Academy in Rome.

June C. Wayne was honored by the Museum of Modern Art, New York, in an exhibit of lithographs dedicated to the Tamarind workshop. Miss Wayne, with the help of Ford Foundation grants, established the nonprofit Tamarind lithography workshop in Los Angeles in 1959. In the ten years of its existence, Tamarind has played a crucial role in reviving lithography as an art form in the United States.

São Paulo Bienal. The U. S. exhibition that was planned for Brazil's São Paulo Bienal (the largest of the international biennales) was canceled in July because nine of the participating artists withdrew in protest against the policies of Brazil's military regime.

OBITUARIES

Among the important artists and scholars of art who died in 1969 were Paul Burlin (82), one of America's early abstract artists; Thomas Craven (81), a vigorous critic of modern art; Otto Dix (77), one of Germany's leading artists and a founder of the New Objectivity movement; Edmund Forbes (95), who developed Harvard University's Fogg Art Museum into an internationally famous institution; Paul Grigaut (63), a connoisseur and assistant director at the University of Michigan Museum of Art; Martha Jackson (62), a distinguished art dealer and a champion of the abstract expressionists; Robert Lehman (77) a financier and collector; Ludwig Mies van der Rohe (83), a German-born master architect; Alan Priest (70), curator emeritus of Far Eastern art, Metropolitan Museum; Ben Shahn (70), a major American artist best known for his paintings on social justice; William Stevenson Smith (61), curator of Egyptian art, Boston Museum; and Ernest Watson (85), artist, writer, teacher, and cofounder of the *American Artist* magazine.

VICTOR H. MIESEL
University of Michigan

UPI

ASIA

Asia, the largest and most populous of the continents, received a marked degree of world attention in 1969. There was an element of paradox in this, for the chief focus of attention—the war in Vietnam —was taking place in one of the smallest of Asian countries. It has been estimated that there are barely 12 million people in each of the two portions of Vietnam. The entire area is extremely small in size when compared with China, India, the Asiatic part of the Soviet Union, or even with Japan, Indonesia, Pakistan, or Iran, for that matter.

As a theater of war, however, Vietnam possessed a significance that went beyond the question of the area and population of South Vietnam or even of the two Vietnams together. The outcome of the struggle there was likely to have far-reaching repercussions of even worldwide significance.

One of the main issues brought to world attention by the war was whether or not the United States could help its friends and frustrate its enemies in areas of the world remote from its seat of power. The validity and credibility of U. S. commitments were also in question. From the point of view of the Communists, Vietnam was a testing ground for the theory of "wars of national liberation" and of guerrilla actions as opposed to more conventional methods of warfare. If North Vietnam, aided by the USSR and mainland China, should succeed in winning the conflict, few or no non-Communist regimes in Southeast Asia would feel secure. A Communist success in Vietnam would boost the morale of insurgent groups in other Southeast Asian countries and help convince them that they, too, could win similar wars.

Shifts in U. S. Vietnam Policy. The change of administration in Washington brought no substantial changes in the U. S. government's Vietnam policy. However, continuing a process that had begun in 1968, the government was forced to modify its stance somewhat because of the growing antiwar sentiment in the United States.

Opponents of the war covered a broad spectrum of opinion. They ranged from pragmatic critics of

U. S. involvement in land wars on the Asian mainland, such as Professor Hans Morgenthau and Walter Lippman, to members of the extreme left who combined pacifism, sedition, and communism into a heady brew of impassioned denunciation of the United States. All in all, the opposition was too great to be safely ignored by the U. S. government and, as a result, there was a shift in emphasis from the pursuit of "victory" to a search for a "just" or "honorable" peace. In the statements of President Nixon, these two irreconcilable ends were linked to a third demand—the freedom of the South Vietnamese to decide their own form of government.

The Vietnam situation remained remarkably constant throughout 1969. That the goals of the United States in Vietnam began to seem impossible of attainment gave little ground for rejoicing and much reason for reflection on the possible consequences. As the London *Economist* pertinently pointed out:

"It is a struggle to decide which of two radically different systems of government the South Vietnamese, and perhaps the other Southeast Asians as well, will be living under for a very long period to come.... South Vietnam does possess—in its constitution, in its hesitant tolerance of the principle of opposition— .... the means of becoming a democracy. If the war is lost it will pass into the silence that covers the political and economic stagnation of the Communist world.... The Vietnam war, like most great events, is a tragedy in the strict sense of that abused word. It imposes an inescapable choice between one terrible thing and another. Those who find this choice imposed upon them can only weigh the alternatives and decide, as calmly as is possible, which is the worse."

Level of Military Operations. The summer of 1969 witnessed the zenith of U. S. power in the Vietnam War. By the end of the summer, the gradual withdrawal of U. S. troops had begun, and it continued during the rest of the year. Several groups, each numbering 20 to 40 thousand, were withdrawn, but by the end of the year there were still about a half million U. S. troops in Vietnam. However, with the decrease in U. S. forces in Vietnam, it did appear that a significant watershed had been crossed.

The level of military operations throughout the

OSRIN IN THE CLEVELAND PLAIN DEALER

"Sam, you made the pants too long."

could conceivably play a military role they had hitherto proved unable to sustain. Another question was what the United States would do if the South Vietnamese continued to prove incompetent. President Nixon stated that he would not allow the North simply to wreak its will on the South and would continue to use U. S. forces, if necessary, to prevent that. Put pessimistically, it seemed possible that the war might continue indefinitely very much as before. Toward the end of 1969 the infiltration southward of considerable numbers of North Vietnamese reinforcements led many observers to anticipate heavy renewed offensives by the North in 1970.

Laos. One of the more distressing possibilities inherent in the Vietnam situation was the danger that the war might be extended into neighboring Laos. That unhappy country had been a divided and officially neutralized state since 1962, with various factions controlling different areas of the country. Early in December a high government official of Thailand reported that two divisions of Chinese Communist troops had moved into northern Laos, and an official Chinese news agency broadcast, monitored in Tokyo, said that all Communist forces in Laos had been ordered to mobilize for combat.

Despite certain U. S. air activity over Laos, in mid-December the U. S. Senate stated its opposition to the involvement of U. S. ground forces there.

Communist China. Whether Communist China had the surplus strength to become seriously involved in Laos or elsewhere was a difficult question to answer. The 9th Party Congress, held in Peking in April, appeared to Western observers to be a somewhat limited success. The congress was supposed to signal the end of the chaos of the past three years of violent revolutionary agitation and the beginning of an era of reconciliation and steady progress. However, it seemed clear that the tensions between the demands of administrative stability and economic progress, on the one hand, and of revolutionary zeal on the other, had not been resolved. There was still friction between different powerful groups, such as the party bureaucracy, the army, and revolutionary organizations like the Red Guards. Little is known about conditions in the interior of China at present, but it is thought that widespread civil disobedience and passive resistance exist, signs of discontent on the part of a sorely tried people, and that China was becoming genuinely difficult to govern as a centralized political entity. The major outcome of the 9th Party Congress was the formal naming of Defense Minister Lin Piao as successor-designate to Mao Tse-tung.

Throughout the spring and early summer of 1969 there were armed clashes leading to some loss of life along disputed portions of the almost 6,000-mile (9,656-km) frontier that China shares with the Soviet Union. While some experts anticipated an outbreak of serious fighting between the two powers, others doubted whether these two great Communist states would embark upon a suicidal struggle while the capitalist world remained a gleeful bystander. Such skepticism appeared justified when, in the autumn, the Soviet Union and China entered into negotiations about the disputed areas. There can be no doubt that in these border regions China has a legitimate grievance: existing frontiers were fixed to China's disadvantage in the 19th century, at a time when the Chinese Empire was very weak. (See also COMMUNISM.)

There was some speculation in 1969 about

year was somewhat lower than in 1968. There was a very pronounced lull in the fighting from mid-June to mid-August, eventually broken by widespread enemy attacks on cities and bases. All acts of force against North Vietnamese territory had ceased in November 1968, and they were not resumed in 1969. Even air operations over South Vietnam were reduced by about one fifth. The emphasis in U. S. operations shifted from putting maximum pressure on the enemy to holding U. S. combat losses to a minimum while protecting allied troops and the civilian population.

If these reductions in military activity were intended to facilitate significant diplomatic activity, they failed. All U. S. efforts to get serious negotiations under way in Paris were frustrated by North Vietnamese insistence that their own proposals were the only possible basis for negotiation, and by their refusal to negotiate at all with South Vietnam.

Realistically speaking, it was difficult to see any reason why the North Vietnamese should budge from their position. They had been fighting for 24 years with dogged determination, first against France and its Vietnamese allies, and then against the United States and its Vietnamese allies. Since the will of the United States to continue appeared to be ebbing, there was nothing in the situation to induce a conciliatory attitude on the part of the North Vietnamese. Quite the contrary: everything suggested that a further, relatively short period of dogged persistence would bring them complete success and the control of all Vietnam. The death on September 3 of Ho Chi Minh, the symbol of this long-maintained struggle, and his replacement by the aged Ton Duc Thang (reputedly a long-time friend of the Soviet Union) made little difference in policy.

President Nixon's major policy address of November 3 proposed minimizing U. S. involvement by encouraging and training the South Vietnamese to shoulder the greater part of the war's burden. The merits of this plan were obvious. What was less clear was how the Saigon government and its forces

MOULANA BHASHANI, head of Pakistan's National Awami party, led the opposition to President Ayub Khan.

China's seeking a rapprochement with the United States. It was hoped that the resumption in January 1970, in Warsaw, of the ambassadorial talks (suspended early in 1968) between representatives of the United States and China signified a first move in this direction, however modest.

Although mainland China was justifiably reluctant to enter into conventional conflict with a major power, it was still vitally interested in keeping going —sometimes ablaze, sometimes smoldering—a series of guerrilla conflicts against the governments of countries along its southern perimeter of influence. Vietnam is only one of many, although it is the oldest and the best known. All of these struggles are chronic, and they have been maintained with a minimal expenditure of Chinese resources.

On the northeastern border of India, the war of the Naga tribesmen against the Indian government has been supported by the Chinese, who train and indoctrinate selected Nagas and who also provide weapons. In Burma, revolutionary turmoil has been sustained in part by the fact that the Chinese province of Yünnan can be used as a sanctuary and base of operations. Areas of Cambodia are also in the hands of Chinese-sponsored dissidents. Similar fighting has occurred in Thailand since 1965.

These situations all possess a family resemblance and they suggest that, however limited the means at China's disposal at the present time, this most populous of Communist countries is pursuing, with great tactical flexibility but enormous long-range persistence, the goal of eventual hegemony throughout South and Southeast Asia.

Japan. While China struggled to reestablish political unity and coherent domestic and external policies, Japan in 1969 continued its impressive and unprecedented economic growth. It became increasingly clear that inevitably such economic strength must be paralleled by a growing political role, one even likely to exceed China's in the foreseeable future. What is more, it began to seem possible in the 1970's that Japan would emerge as the third most important country in the world, second only to the United States and the Soviet Union.

Although there was speculation about the nature and scope of Japan's emerging political role, there was no doubt whatever about the country's incredible economic progress. The growth rate of the Japanese economy, both in 1968 and 1969, was an amazing 14%–15% a year. This was about five times the current growth rate of the United States.

The gross national product of Japan in the financial year ending March 31, 1969, was approximately $150 billion. It was expected to reach almost $200 billion for the calendar year 1970. The Japanese economy already stood second in the free world (having passed the level of West Germany around the end of 1968) and third in the whole world.

The status of Okinawa, held by the United States since World War II, had been a bone of contention in Japanese-U. S. relations for several years. It was settled amicably in 1969, when the United States agreed to return the island base and the other Ryukyu islands. In Washington in November, U. S. President Nixon and Japanese Prime Minister Eisaku Sato announced that Okinawa would be restored to Japan in 1972, free of nuclear weapons, and that U. S. bases there were to be held under the same conditions as those prevailing in Japan proper.

Sato called an election of the Japanese House of Representatives for December 27 in the hope that his triumph in securing Okinawa's return would increase his party's (Liberal Democrats) parliamentary majority. His strategy proved successful.

Sato indicated that he agreed with those who say that Japan, as a leading industrial nation, must accept responsibility for giving increased aid to poor countries. Another question already looming is that of Japanese rearmament—at present forbidden by the constitution—and even of its acquiring nuclear weapons. In view of Japan's eventually playing a more significant political role, whatever precise form it may take, in East Asia and in the world at large,

PAKISTAN'S students display effigy of President Ayub Khan at Dacca in protest against his government.

it was suggested that a reasonable target for Japanese ambition was the acquisition of a permanent seat in the UN Security Council.

India. The idea, popular in the 1950's of India's becoming the great rival of mainland China for leadership and influence in Asia has seemed less and less plausible with every year that has passed since Nehru's death in 1964. India's downward spiral continued in 1969. The ruling Congress party, holders of a virtual monopoly of power since India gained independence from Britain in 1947, suffered losses in the general election of 1967 and severe setbacks in the state legislature elections of February 1969. Far worse was the complete cleavage of the Congress party in late summer of 1969 into two factions: an old-guard, conservative faction consisting of the traditional bosses of the party (called "The Syndicate"); and a new, radical, and leftist faction led by Prime Minister Indira Gandhi herself. The party split, emerging for some time, became absolute in August, when Mrs. Gandhi refused to support the official Congress candidate, Sanjiva Reddy, in the election for the presidency of India occasioned by the death on May 3 of Zakir Hussain. She supported instead the candidacy of former Vice President V. V. Giri, who won narrowly.

On November 12, Mrs. Gandhi was "expelled" from the party, but she ended up with the bulk of the party behind her in both Parliament and the state organizations. One paradoxical result of the split is that the "old guard" remnant in Parliament, strong enough to satisfy the constitutional requirements for constituting an official opposition party, formed an official opposition for the first time in India's 22 years of independence. If this leads to a genuine two-party system in India, it might in the long run make for more stable and satisfactory politics.

Nevertheless, the immediate future for India seemed dark. Mrs. Gandhi has proved much better at solving the problem of retaining office than at solving any of India's substantive problems. Radical measures that infuriated the right wing of the Congress party, such as the decree on July 19 nationalizing 14 major banks, were populist gestures that will improve nothing.

Pakistan. India's neighbor Pakistan also faced intractable problems. President Ayub Khan, whose career suggests certain remote parallels with that of Charles de Gaulle of France, was forced to give up power in 1969 after 11 years of personal rule. He had taken over in 1958, ending a chaos of feuding party politicians, and in 1969 he was thrust from office by widespread political and economic unrest. Ayub Khan's decision, announced in February, not to run again for the presidency in 1970 was followed on March 25 by his resignation and the assumption of power by Gen. Yahya Khan, army commander in chief. A few days later the general assumed the office of president, and he maintained an uneasy calm in the country for the rest of the year.

Southeast Asia. The racial peace that had hitherto generally prevailed in Malaysia between Chinese and Malays was abruptly and tragically broken by serious rioting in Kuala Lumpur in May.

There was a relaxation of tension in some areas, especially in foreign policy. Malaysia resumed ties with the Philippines. Malaysian-Philippine relations had been suspended for 17 months because of the Philippine claim to Sabah (former British North Borneo). Prime Minister Lee Kuan Yew of Singapore visited Malaysia in a gesture intended to restore good relations. A meeting of representatives of Australia, New Zealand, Britain, Malaysia, and Singapore was held at Canberra in June to consider the problem of regional defense after the announced British withdrawal in 1971.

Cambodia resumed diplomatic relations with the United States in mid-1969. The rupture had occurred in 1965 and had a definite relation to the war in Vietnam.

Regional Groupings. The somewhat ineffectual body, SEATO, held its annual meeting at Bangkok, Thailand, on May 20–21. It is likely that the genuinely indigenous Association of Southeast Asian Nations (ASEAN), which played a part in the Philippine-Malaysian rapprochement, and the larger 9-country Asian and Pacific Council (ASPAC) will play more significant roles in Southeast Asia in the future than SEATO.

ARTHUR C. TURNER
University of California, Riverside

UPI

PHILIPPINE PRESIDENT Ferdinand E. Marcos (*third from left*) raises the hand of Vice President Fernando López in a victory salute after winning his party's nomination to run for reelection. The two victors subsequently won the right to an unprecedented second term. Mrs. Marcos is at left.

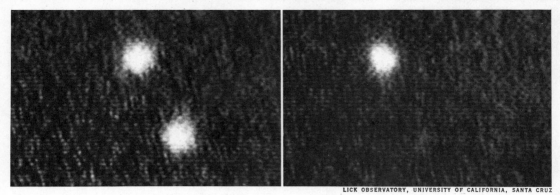

PULSAR (*lower object at left*) in Crab Nebula turns off (*right*) in flashing sequence. An ordinary star (*top, both photos*) glows steadily.

ASTRONOMY

Several especially noteworthy advances were made in 1969 in the study of our home galaxy, the Milky Way. The recently discovered pulsars, all objects within our galaxy, certainly commanded the most attention. However, the discovery of new molecules in interstellar space also is of far-reaching importance and presents astronomers with new clues concerning the properties of matter between the stars. In addition, advances were made in studies of the structure of spiral galaxies and in cosmic ray and radio astronomy. (A special feature accompanying this article presents information derived from the flights of Mars probes Mariners 6 and 7.)

OPTICAL PULSAR IN THE CRAB NEBULA

In the field of galactic astronomy, the most startling discovery of 1969 was the detection, in January, of the first optical pulsar. Of the 40 pulsars, or pulsating radio sources, known thus far, it is the only one to be identified optically.

The object was identified with pulsar NPO532, which is located within the supernova remnant known as the Crab Nebula, and which has the shortest pulsation period—1/30 of a second—of any known pulsar. In January 1969 the object was found to show optical fluctuations of the same period; that is, the pulsar flashes optically at the rate of 30 times per second. The discovery was made with the 36-inch reflecting telescope of Steward Observatory, Arizona, by W. John Cocke, Michael J. Disney, and Donald J. Taylor. Their findings were confirmed with minimum delay, the most striking confirmation coming from Lick Observatory in California, where stroboscopic pictures showed the pulsar at minimum and maximum.

One implication of this discovery is that the pulsar is probably the actual remnant of the famous supernova of 1054 A. D. that produced the Crab Nebula. As for the nature of the present pulsar, the most likely model thus far advanced is that pulsars are stars that have undergone gravitational collapse, resulting in small and extremely dense "neutron" stars. Pulsar NPO532 may have a mass equivalent to the sun's mass, but a diameter of no more than 5 to 10 miles (8 to 16 km). Rotating on its axis, it emits two pulses every 1/30 of a second. This model, suggested by Thomas Gold of Cornell University, is now gaining gradual acceptance.

Two further recent discoveries have been made concerning the Crab Nebula pulsar. The first is that its period of pulsation is gradually slowing down. The observation was made by the Arecibo radio telescope in Puerto Rico and was checked—with startling precision—by four physicists at Princeton University. The second discovery is that X-rays are being emitted by the pulsar, with the same period of 1/30 of a second, and with the X-rays and optical pulses arriving at precisely the same instant. These observations were made by astrophysicists from the U. S. Naval Research Laboratory with the aid of an Aerobee rocket launched from White Sands, N. Mex.; the observation was confirmed by later flights.

STUDIES OF INTERSTELLAR MATTER

From optical data it has long been known that interstellar gas, besides containing hydrogen and helium, has its share of heavier atoms—notably carbon, nitrogen, and oxygen, but also calcium, sodium, potassium, iron, and still heavier elements. Simple molecular compounds, especially of carbon, nitrogen, and hydrogen, also were found from optical spectral evidence.

In radio astronomy, however, after the discovery of the 21-centimeter radio emission line of neutral atomic hydrogen (H) in 1951, no other radio spectral lines were observed for 10 years thereafter. Then, in the 1960's, several significant emission lines (and some absorption features) were discovered. They prove the presence in interstellar space of the hydroxyl radical (OH), ammonia vapor (NH_3), water vapor (H_2O), and formaldehyde (HCHO), all of them in surprisingly high abundance and all generally concentrated in cloudlets. There is as yet no firm evidence for the presence of the hydrogen molecule (H_2) in interstellar space, but it is surmised to exist there.

There are indications that these different molecules often are found in the same cloudlets of interstellar matter, which generally are very small in astronomical terms. Dimensions comparable to the size of the solar system have been found for some OH cloudlets—about 10 astronomical units, the distance between earth and sun being 1 astronomical unit (AU). Ionized hydrogen atoms also are often found in clumps, but the minimum diameters of these cloudlets are found generally to be of the order of 100 to 1,000 AU's; comparable clumpiness is shown by water vapor droplets. (In *(Continued on page 111)*

A CLOSE-UP LOOK AT MARS

Man's knowledge of Mars, earth's mysterious planetary neighbor, was increased greatly in 1969 when U. S. spacecraft Mariner 6 flew past the planet on July 31, followed five days later by Mariner 7. The spacecraft were designed to pass within a few thousand kilometers of Mars and observe its atmosphere and surface; they were not designed to orbit the planet or land on it.

THE MARINER SPACECRAFT

Mariners 6 and 7 were powered by solar panels, which convert sunlight into electricity, and they were oriented during their flight by sensors that kept track of the locations on the earth, the sun, and the star Canopus at all times. Each Mariner communicated its findings by means of a small antenna that radioed messages to the giant, 210-foot (64-meter) radio telescope of the Goldstone Tracking Station in California.

Aboard each Mariner were two vidicon television cameras—one a short focal length camera with color filters of three different kinds and an effective limiting resolution of about 6 miles (10 km), the other a long focal length camera with a single haze filter and a ground resolution of about 0.6 miles (1 km). Each spacecraft also carried two infrared radiometers that measured the heat given off by different locales on Mars both in th daytime and at night, an infrared spectrometer that recorded the Martian spectrum (at wavelengths ranging between 2 and 12 microns) both in reflected sunlight and in thermal emission, and an ultraviolet spectrometer that measured the solar ultraviolet light between 0.19 and 0.43 microns that was scattered by the Martian atmosphere.

Each Mariner mission also incorporated a celestial mechanics experiment whereby such properties as the mass of Mars were determined from the motion of the spacecraft. Each mission also included a radio occultation experiment in which, as the spacecraft passed behind Mars, the rate of fading of its radio communications signal provided data on the Martian atmosphere.

A few highlights of the preliminary analyses of data from Mariners 6 and 7 can be reported here. Not all data is yet in; the computer processing of the television pictures probably will not be completed before the end of 1970.

SURFACE FEATURES OF MARS

The Mariner cameras returned far-encounter pictures of Mars taken several days before closest approach to the planet, and near-encounter pictures taken near the point of closest approach (about 2,100 miles, or 3,400 km). The first far-encounter pictures were comparable to the best photographs obtained by earth-based telescopes, showing recognizable bright and dark markings and the polar caps. As the spacecraft came closer to the planet, fine details—in particular, craters of probable impact origin—were revealed. The combined Mariner 6 and 7 pictures show 10 to 20% of the total Martian surface.

While the Mars revealed by the spacecraft is cratered, it is not very moonlike. That is, a significant fraction of the craters have flat bottoms, as if they had been filled in by windblown dust. In addition, some areas—notably a vast, bright area called Hellas—have no detectable craters at all. The Martian craters are believed to have been formed by the impact of debris from the asteroid belt between Mars and Jupiter. Such debris must fall randomly all over the surface of Mars. Therefore areas like Hellas must have some very efficient and as yet poorly understood process by which large craters with depths as great as several kilometers have been rubbed out or filled in.

One of the two Mariner 7 occultation points occured near the periphery of the Hellas region, where the atmospheric pressure was revealed to be lower than average. This indicated that the periphery is an elevation, which is consistent with the visual impression that Hellas is a depression. Similarly, regions of chaotic terrain, apparently produced by the withdrawal of underlying supporting material (possibly permafrost), appeared to be both brighter and lower than their surroundings. (However, ground-based radar observations of Mars do not support the idea that Martian bright areas tend systematically to be lowlands.) The Mariners noted a remarkable and hitherto unsuspected array of brilliant arcuate features in the bright areas, the significance of which remains a mystery.

Many frostfree areas, including dark-bottomed craters, were apparent in the photographs of the south polar cap. Infrared radiometer temperature measurements near the edge of the polar cap were about —190° F (—120° C), consistent with the idea that the cap is mostly frozen carbon dioxide rather than frozen water. From the way in which the surface temperature varied with time of day on Mars, it is possible to deduce a value for the thermal conductivity of the surface material, a value con-

(Continued on page 110)

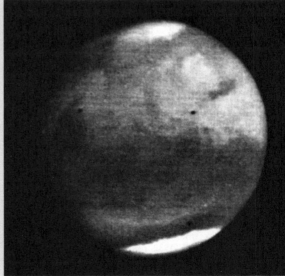

PORTRAIT OF MARS was taken by Mariner 7 in August 1969 at 535,650 miles. Large-scale surface markings can be seen, and the irregular border of the south polar cap is evident.

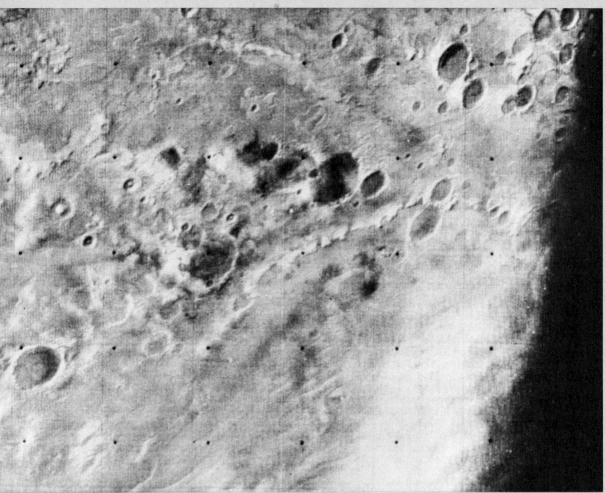

JET PROPULSION LABORATORY, CALIFORNIA INSTITUTE OF TECHNOLOGY, NASA

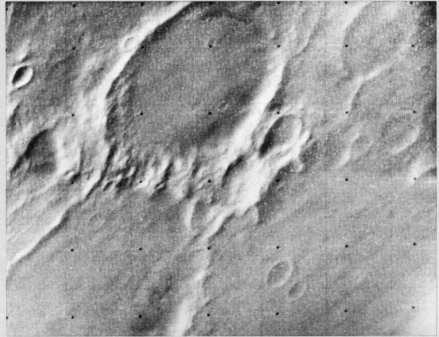

JET PROPULSION LABORATORY, CALIFORNIA INSTITUTE OF TECHNOLOGY, NASA

MARTIAN SOUTH POLAR CAP, as seen by Mariner 7 at about 2,100 miles, reveals a wide variety of craters and other features. A pair of large craters that resemble a footprint in the right center portion of the upper picture are seen in greater detail in the high-resolution lower picture. Snowdrift-like formations are thought to be primarily carbon dioxide ice.

109

(Continued from page 108)
sistent with ground-based measurements and implying that the average surface particles are tens to hundreds of microns in diameter (1 micron equals about 39 millionths of an inch).

THE MARTIAN ATMOSPHERE

The Mariner ultraviolet spectrometers detected emission features from ionized carbon dioxide and carbon monoxide, gases already known to exist in the atmosphere of Mars. They also detected atomic hydrogen and atomic oxygen; these gases are (at least in part) products of the ultraviolet photo-dissociation of water vapor, also known to exist in the Martian atmosphere. In addition, the spectrometers determined that the temperature of the highest part of the atmosphere—the exosphere—is about 630° F (330° C). This temperature, together with the low Martian gravity, suggests that atomic hydrogen can escape efficiently from the planet over geological time but that atoms as heavy as oxygen cannot. Since water vapor is being broken down by ultraviolet light on Mars, and since there is little (if any) oxygen in the atmosphere, it seems very likely that large quantities of oxygen have reacted with the Martian surface during the history of the planet. Indeed, silicates and iron oxides, both of which contain oxygen, have been suggested as surface materials—the iron oxides giving Mars its red color.

No molecular nitrogen was detected in the atmosphere, but it could still be present in some quantity. Photographs taken with a blue filter showed little sign of the enigmatic blue haze observed from earth, suggesting that at least part of the haze actually is an artifact of the earth's own atmosphere (as had previously been suspected on other grounds). The Mariners also observed clouds forming in the Martian afternoon at equatorial latitudes. The clouds do not appear to be either condensed water vapor or condensed carbon dioxide; they constitute another enigma.

Scientists studying infrared spectrometer data initially reported detecting the spectra of methane gas and ammonia gas close to the edge of the south polar cap. Since such gases are associated with biological activity on earth and are chemically unstable in an excess of carbon dioxide (the principal constituent of the Martian atmosphere), this announcement precipitated a range of biological speculations. Subsequently it was discovered that solid carbon dioxide absorbs at precisely the same wavelengths in the near infrared. Part of the responsibility for this contretemps can be laid at the feet of the press, who demand very rapid interpretation of complex space mission data.

THE QUESTION OF LIFE ON MARS

Some of the scientific and much of the popular interest in the exploration of Mars has to do with the possibility that it is a habitat for at least simple life forms. Nothing in the Mariner results provides strong evidence either for or against this possibility. No signs of aqueous erosion were found in the vicinity of very old and cratered terrain; but this does not exclude the possibility that bodies of water persisted for hundreds of millions of years in the early history of Mars, during which time life could have arisen. The fact that the polar cap is largely dry ice says nothing about the abundance of water on the surface of Mars.

While Mars possesses a harsh environment by terrestrial standards, there are in fact terrestrial microorganisms that can survive and grow in simulated Martian environments. To investigate the question of life on Mars further, it will be necessary to make a more detailed scrutiny of its surface and atmosphere.

CARL SAGAN
Cornell University

COMPUTER IMPROVES ON ORIGINAL MARS PHOTO (upper left), *subtracting basket-weave pattern imposed by electronic "pickup"* (upper right) *to produce a cleaner image* (lower left). *Computer then compensates for vidicon tube's limited resolution* (lower right).

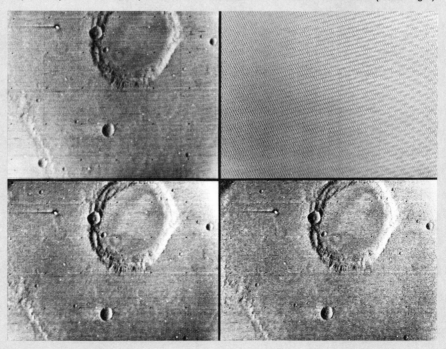

(Continued from page 107)

contrast, the smallest observed cosmic dust concentrations have diameters of the order of 10,000 AU's.) Infrared studies have provided evidence for the existence of small, low-temperature concentrations as well, with diameters of the order of 10 to 100 AU's.

All of these results show that astronomers are rapidly learning new facts about condensations in our galaxy that have diameters comparable to or larger than the solar system. Molecules associated with the phenomena of life (water, hydrogen, and ammonia) are found in these condensations, and the estimated masses of the cloudlets are comparable to the mass of the sun. It can be interpreted that astronomy is reaching a stage in observation —by means of optical, radio, and infrared techniques—in which evidence is being gathered of stars and of solar systems in the process of formation.

SPIRAL STRUCTURE IN GALAXIES

The study of the spiral structure of our own and many other galaxies is assuming increasing importance in galactic research. Young stars—those with ages less than 0.1% of the age of the sun and the earth—and massive concentrations of dust and gas seem to be found mostly in the arms of spiral galaxies. Therefore astronomers must concentrate on the study of the physical conditions in spiral arms if they are to learn the secrets of star formation and evolution.

Optical studies are giving new and useful clues concerning the internal structure of these spiral features. A spiral arm is composed primarily of interstellar gas, most of it being neutral atomic hydrogen. The width of a typical cross section of a spiral arm in neutral hydrogen is about 5,000 light years, and the cosmic dust is concentrated mainly in the insides of the arms.

The most spectacular part of a spiral arm is a ridge near the middle in which young stars and high-temperature interstellar gas are found. The width of this ridge is only half that of the neutral hydrogen concentration—that is, about 2,500 light years. The regions in which star birth is taking place in our own galaxy are all within these narrow bands. Star birth is not taking place uniformly along this ridge, but is confined largely to concentrations in the interstellar gas with densities 10 or more times the average along the ridge. Astronomers are beginning to pinpoint the places of star origin and are gathering increasingly precise information about the physical conditions that prevail at these positions.

Astronomers are still at a loss to know why spiral arms are formed in so many galaxies in the first place, but they now have a good preliminary theory about the mechanisms that maintain the arms once they are formed. This theory, developed by C. C. Lin and associates at the Massachusetts Institute of Technology, advances the concept that spiral arms are maintained by gravitational patterns of density waves in the interstellar gas. These waves steadily redistribute the gas; they move through the gas at a rate less than the general rotational rate of the galaxy, and they provide for ever-present ridges of high gas density in the shapes of spiral arms. It had earlier been supposed that galactic magnetic fields maintained the spiral structure, holding the interstellar gas in magnetic tubes that had the shapes of spiral arms; but this theory was abandoned when it became clear that the observed strengths of the galactic magnetic fields are not sufficiently great to hold together the spiral arms in this manner.

OTHER DEVELOPMENTS

A number of advances made in 1969 in various fields of astronomy may be briefly described.

Cosmic Rays. Increasing evidence suggests that the cosmic rays observed on earth are largely of galactic origin. Cosmic rays are charged atomic nuclei that presumably were ejected into space as by-products of supernova explosions. The presence of some unstable atomic nuclei—He^3, for example— among the cosmic rays suggests that they originate within our own galaxy, since such nuclei could not possibly survive during the long travel times required if they were of extragalactic origin.

Radio Astronomy Techniques. A new technique for the measurement of very precise radio positions of quasars (quasistellar radio sources) has been developed by C. M. Wade of the National Radio Astronomy Observatory at Green Bank, W. Va. Using the three-element radio interferometer, he has succeeded in obtaining declinations for quasars on an absolute basis, accurate to within plus or minus one second of arc, or even better. Relative right ascensions of comparable precision also can be obtained by the same basic techniques.

Intercontinental studies of fine structures of radio sources can now be carried out by simultaneous observations from two widely separated radio observatories. Observatories in the United States and Canada, on the one hand, and in Australia, Sweden, and the Crimea, on the other hand, have performed successful observations. Fine structures a few thousandths of a second of arc in size have been unraveled by this technique.

Ultraviolet Studies. The successful launch of U. S. Orbiting Astronomical Observatory (OAO) 2 in December 1968 has opened new windows for astronomical research in the far-ultraviolet region of the spectrum. (This region lies beyond the wavelength range transmitted by our earth's atmosphere.) As a result of the flight, several new far-ultraviolet absorption lines were discovered in the spectra of the hot B-class stars. New data on the properties of cosmic dust also were obtained; these support the existence of graphite grains in the dust, and possibly the presence of solid grains with mantles of molecular hydrogen. Galaxies were found to be brighter in the ultraviolet region than expected, and the brightest quasar thus far known was observed. A complete catalog of ultraviolet apparent brightnesses of stars is being prepared at the Smithsonian Astrophysical Observatory from OAO 2's data. Stellar astronomy in the far ultraviolet now is a recognized active field of research, having come of age as infrared astronomy did some years ago.

Gravitational Waves. In 1969, Joseph Weber of the University of Maryland detected effects that had been predicted to originate from gravitational waves. According to the theory of relativity, such waves should exist; they may be produced by supernova explosions, pairs of neutron stars, or collapsing stars. (See also PHYSICS.)

BART J. BOK
Director, Steward Observatory
University of Arizona

ATMOSPHERE RESEARCH. See METEOROLOGY.

NUCLEAR TEST, known as Project Milrow, opened cracks in a road near the blast site on Amchitka Island in the Aleutians on Oct. 2, 1969. But the controversial experiment did not set off a feared earthquake. A seismograph at the University of California, Berkeley, recorded the detonation (with a deep, jagged line) as having approximately the force of a major earthquake.

ATOMIC ENERGY

The interaction of man and his environment influenced developments in atomic energy in 1969. Concern was focused on the location of nuclear power plants, the testing of nuclear weapons, and the detonation of nuclear explosives in the U. S. Atomic Energy Commission's Plowshare program.

The pace of building new nuclear electrical generating plants continued to decline in the United States because of opposition to their placement near population centers, as well as sharply increased construction costs for plant components and buildings. Nuclear research remained at a high level in applied and basic areas. Nevertheless 1969 witnessed clear indications that government spending in these areas will be limited in the foreseeable future. These limitations will slow the building of large research facilities, particularly the planned 200 BeV (billion electron volts) particle accelerator in Illinois.

Testing of nuclear weapons underground was continued at a high rate by both the United States and the USSR, and the mainland Chinese continued to test atomic bombs. Scientists expressed continuing concern over the proliferation of nuclear weapons and the development of nuclear-weapon capability by nonnuclear powers. On November 28, Presidents Richard M. Nixon and Nikolai V. Podgorny signed a treaty to prohibit the spread of nuclear weapons, making the United States and the USSR the 23d and 24th nations to do so. (See also DISARMAMENT.)

PEACEFUL USES OF ATOMIC ENERGY

Commercial Power. Plans for four new nuclear commercial power plants with a total capacity of 4,029 megawatts (Mw) were announced in the United States in the first three quarters of 1969. In contrast, 14 plants with a capacity of 14,912 Mw were announced in the same period in 1968. The country has 15 operating plants generating 3,850 Mw; 48 are being built to generate 37,700 Mw; and 41 are planned with a capacity of 36,800 Mw. The country's largest nuclear commercial power plant, built at Oyster Creek, N. J., went critical on May 3, 1969. When operating at capacity it will supply 640 Mw.

Plant Sites. The selection of sites for nuclear power plants continued to be troublesome for the Atomic Energy Commission and advocates of nuclear power. Although low on air pollution, nuclear power plants have a lower efficiency than coal-fired and oil-fired electricity producers, and so they reject more heat to their coolant than do the conventional power plants. The effect of this "thermal pollution" on aquatic life has deeply concerned conservationists. Almost all states have determined their own standards under the Water Quality Control Act of 1965, and most are seeking to apply control procedures for regulating discharges at fossil-fueled and nuclear generating plants.

Safety fears also arise, but AEC-operated plants

have a record of only 1.68 lost-time injuries per million man-hours. According to the National Safety Council, atomic energy has been one of the top three industries in safety.

Nuclear Power Leaders. Britain continues to lead the world in the total amount of electrical power produced from nuclear fuels. Up to August 1969, the accumulated nuclear energy outputs of the non-Communist nations were as follows: Britain, 140 million megawatt hours (10^6Mwh); United States, 55.02 million; Italy, 16.95 million; France, 14.2 million: West Germany, 6.86 million; Japan, 2.42 million; Canada, 2.05 million; Spain, 0.49 million; Belgium, 0.16 million; and the Netherlands, 0.23 million.

Energy Research. Over 84% of all U. S. government funds scheduled for development of energy sources is devoted to atomic energy projects. The Office of Science and Technology said that of $368 million allotted for energy research in fiscal year 1970 some $276 went into fission research. The development of a liquid-metal-cooled fast breeder reactor is the nation's top priority in the nuclear energy program, receiving $122 million in 1970.

The AEC announced that it intends to issue an operating license enabling the Southwest Experimental Fast Oxide Reactor (SEFOR) to run at full power. Situated near Fayetteville, Ark., SEFOR is a fast-spectrum, sodium-cooled reactor. It is a cooperative venture among the AEC, 17 private power utilities in the Southwest and Midwest, and a nonprofit West German corporation, Gesellschaft fur Kernforschung. The experiment is part of the AEC effort to develop a successful fast-breeder reactor—one than can convert the nonfissionable isotope of uranium, U-238, into the fissionable isotope of plutonium, Pu-239. Such a conversion will greatly increase the amount of electrical energy obtainable from uranium fuel and thus lower electrical power costs. The higher efficiencies available in a fast-breeder reactor will also tend to decrease the amount of wasted heat carried off by the coolant.

Full design power of the Advanced Test Reactor (ATR) at the National Reactor Testing Station, Arco, Idaho, was attained on Aug. 16, 1969. Situated in the same complex with the Materials Test Reactor and Engineering Test Reactor, the ATR is designed to test naval reactor cores and advanced fuel systems and materials for the civilian power and space programs. A high flux environment of up to 10^{15} neutrons per square centimeter per second can be provided with power of 250 megawatts.

At France's Cadarache Research Center, the 24-megawatt Rapsodie experimental breeder reactor completed two years of nearly faultless performance. The reactor has been used to study the performance of reactor materials under fast neutron irradiation.

The world's first reactor fueled with the isotope U-233 began operating at Oak Ridge National Laboratory, Tennessee, in 1969 in the Molten Salt Reactor Experiment. In this operation, the fissioning of U-233 is expected to breed additional fuel by neutron capture in the common isotope thorium-232.

Project Rulison. A nuclear device equivalent to 40,000 tons of TNT was exploded 8,430 feet underground in Garfield county, in remote western Colorado, on Sept. 10, 1969. The explosion was designed to fracture a large volume of rock in the Mesa Verde formation to allow natural gas to flow to a well bored after the event. Known as Project Rulison,

this experiment is part of the government-industry "Plowshare" program to study peaceful uses of nuclear explosives. The site of the blast was to remain sealed for six months.

Medical Uses. Significant advances in medical applications of nuclear energy were made again in 1969. Radiation treatment of leukemia by means of extracorporeal irradiation of blood shows promising results. In this procedure, blood is made to flow through a high-intensity radiation field external to the human body, thereby avoiding the deleterious effects of the radiation upon other bodily functions and organs. A commercial irradiator employing a strontium-90 beta-ray source is now being marketed.

Extracorporeal irradiation is also helpful in reducing rejection processes occurring after kidney transplant operations. The neutron emitter, californium-252, is under investigation because of its effectiveness in destroying oxygen-deficient cancer cells. Needles bearing californium-252 are being prepared at the AEC Savannah River Laboratory in South Carolina for internal use in cancer therapy.

Radioactive isotopes are also used to produce electrical power sources for artificial pacemakers, implanted in the body to regulate the rate of heart beats. A nuclear-powered pacemaker was successfully implanted in a dog in May 1969. Powered by an isotopic generator, the pacemaker is expected to have a lifetime of about 10 years as compared with the two-year life of the battery-powered version. Emitting no more radiation than a radium dial wristwatch, the nuclear pacemaker weighs 3.5 ounces and contains 0.5 grams of plutonium-238.

A 40-KILOTON nuclear device is lowered into a hole more than 1.5 miles deep in Project Rulison in Colorado. The 15-foot-long device was detonated in a test for the enhancement of recovery of natural gas.

AUSTRAL OIL COMPANY

The technique of neutron activation has led to the first successful development of a drug, L-Dopa, for treatment of Parkinson's disease. Trace elements, such as manganese, which appear to play a role in such diseases, can be studied by rendering them radioactive through neutron bombardment.

Mining Uses. Production of the heavy artificial isotope californium-252 continued to be emphasized at the AEC's high flux reactors at Savannah River. Californium-252 undergoes spontaneous fission and is an excellent source of neutrons. The isotope has many applications in mineral exploration. It is used to activate the constituent nuclei of ores—for example, gold or silver—whose residual radioactivity can subsequently be detected. Produced in quantities of milligram size in nuclear reactors, californium is sold by the AEC for $100 for one ten-millionth of a gram.

Food Programs. The food irradiation program in the United States has been stalled since 1968, when the Food and Drug Administration requested additional feeding tests before granting clearances for the use of irradiated foods. Only wheat flour and white potatoes now are cleared for unlimited public consumption. Over 50 nations throughout the world, however, have food irradiation programs.

Naval Propulsion. The Japanese have announced their intention of commissioning a 30-knot nuclear-powered container ship by 1975. Interest in large-scale nuclear-powered merchant ships has also been expressed by the U. S. Maritime Administration. There are now three nuclear-powered nonmilitary surface ships in operation—the Soviet ice-breaker *Lenin,* the West German vessel *Otto Hahn,* and the U. S. merchant ship *Savannah.* In 90,000 miles of operation, the *Savannah* consumed only 33 pounds of enriched uranium fuel; to travel the same distance, a conventional ship would have required more than 17,000 tons of fuel oil.

MILITARY AND SPACE APPLICATIONS

Both underground and atmospheric testing of weapons continued unabated in 1969.

Chinese Test. On September 29, an atmospheric test of 3-megaton size was staged by the mainland Chinese in the Lap Nor nuclear test area. In size, the test was comparable to those that China conducted on June 17, 1967, and Dec. 27, 1968.

Aleutian Test. Numerous underground tests, ranging from less than 20 kilotons to about one megaton in TNT equivalents, were staged by the United States and the USSR. The most publicized of these was conducted at Amchitka Island, in the Aleutian Islands, on October 2, and involved a device of about one megaton explosive power. Concern had been expressed that this test might set off an earthquake in the Aleutians, an active seismic region. But the blast, registering 6.5 on the Richter scale, caused no unusual earth tremors.

Rocket Engine. A major step in the AEC-NASA nuclear rocket program was completed in 1969 with the successful testing of the XE engine at the Nuclear Rocket Development Test Station, Jackass Flats, Nev. A full-power thrust of 55,000 pounds was sustained for 3.5 minutes, at simulated high-altitude conditions. The engine is a prototype of the proposed 75,000-pound-thrust NERVA (Nuclear Engine for Rocket Vehicle Applications) rocket. The nuclear rocket engine produces the thrust by exhausting high velocity hydrogen gas which has been heated in a reactor.

OAK RIDGE NATIONAL LABORATORY

FIRST U-233 REACTOR went into operation at Oak Ridge, Tenn., in 1969. This one-sixth scale model shows the setup for the Molten Salt Reactor Experiment.

A-Power on the Moon. The Apollo 11 moon voyage in July 1969 placed a heating system containing the isotope plutonium-238 on the moon. The isotope was contained in a pair of 15-watt heaters engineered to keep a seismometer above a minimum temperature of $-65°$ F during the lunar night. The seismometer was left to record moonquakes.

The Apollo 12 astronauts placed a SNAP 27 nuclear generator—the acronym stands for Systems for Nuclear Auxiliary Power—on the moon's surface on Nov. 19, 1969. The SNAP provides power for a package of scientific instruments expected to operate on the moon's surface for at least a year.

BASIC AND APPLIED RESEARCH

Fusion Research. Significant developments were made in 1969 in the attempt to harness the energy made available by nuclear fusion. In fusion, nuclei of deuterium—the isotope of hydrogen containing one proton and one neutron in its nucleus—would be combined to form nuclei of helium, with a consequent release of energy. The potential of fusion as an energy resource far exceeds that of nuclear fission, and the reaction does not pose any significant problems of radioactive waste disposal.

The key problem in harnessing the power of nuclear fusion has been building a vessel strong enough to hold the thermonuclear reaction. The solution has been sought by constructing a configuration of magnetic fields to hold the intensely heated deuterium plasma. In 1969, British scientists confirmed recent Russian results with the Tokamak system, a doughnut-shaped plasma chamber with an overall diameter of 2 meters utilizing a helically shaped magnetic field. The Russians have obtained temperatures of 900 electron volts and have been able to contain the plasma in the Tokamak for about 0.025 seconds—the best results yet obtained in any plasma program. The Soviets' effort in fusion research remains at a high level. They employ three times as many scientists and spend about twice as much in this field as the United States.

U. S. fusion research is conducted at four laboratories—Oak Ridge, Princeton, Los Alamos, and Lawrence Radiation Laboratory, Livermore, Calif. Funds have been allocated for Tokamaks at Princeton and Oak Ridge, and they should be completed by mid-1970.

In France, research on thermonuclear reactions induced by laser beams on frozen deuterium was reported. This technique represents a new approach.

New Isotope. U. S. researchers discovered a new isotope of element 104 at Berkeley, Calif. To date, five isotopes of the element are known. Russian scientists claim to have discovered the element first, creating a dispute with U. S. scientists.

Hunting the Quark. Physicists continue to search for the elusive "quark," the supposed structural unit of all matter. Some evidence was discovered for the presence of quarks in cloud chamber photographs of cosmic ray showers, taken by an Australian group at the University of Sydney. The evidence, however, was not regarded as conclusive. The scientist who originally proposed the quark, Murray Gell-Mann of the California Institute of Technology, was announced as the winner of the Nobel Prize in physics for 1969. (See also PHYSICS.)

Soviet Physics Research. Basic data in physical research were produced at the USSR's 70 BeV accelerator at Serpukhov. Preliminary results were obtained on the scattering of protons by negative pi-mesons and K-mesons, as well as on proton-proton scattering from 20 to 65 BeV. Scientists from the Serpukhov Institute for High Energy Physics and from the European Organization for Nuclear Research (CERN) collaborated in the experiments.

U. S. ATOMIC ENERGY COMMISSION

New Commissioners. Clarence Larson and Theos J. Thompson were appointed by President Nixon in 1969 to serve 5-year terms as AEC commissioners. Larson, president of the Nuclear Division of Union Carbide and a former director of Oak Ridge National Laboratory, replaced Francesco Costagliola. Thompson, formerly director of the Massachusetts Institute of Technology research reactor, was named to fill the unexpired term of Gerald

Tape. Thompson and Larson join Chairman Glenn T. Seaborg and Commisioners James T. Ramey and Wilfred E. Johnson.

Cutbacks. Severe budgetary restrictions brought about cancellation of the SNAP-29 program, a polonium-210-fueled 400-watt generator for manned and unmanned space applications. In addition, the Materials Test Reactor at the National Reactor Testing Station in Idaho was scheduled for shutdown in 1970 because of budget cuts. The 40-megawatt MTR had been in operation since 1952 and completed more than 19,000 irradiation tests of reactor materials and fuels.

OTHER DEVELOPMENTS

Centrifuge Technique. An international combine was formed in 1969 among Dutch, German, and British concerns to produce enriched uranium by a centrifuge technique. The technique, which separates the fissionable U-235 isotope from its slightly heavier and nonfissioning isotope U-238, may break the monopoly on uranium separation held by government-run diffusion plants.

Return to Bikini. After 22 years of exile, the natives of Bikini atoll are returning to their island home, which in 1946 had been made inhabitable by nuclear weapons tests. Their bodily radioactive intake will be carefully monitored by an AEC research team. The U. S. Department of the Interior estimated the resettlement effort would take about six years.

Awards. The Atoms for Peace Awards of the Ford Foundation were given to six scientists on May 14, 1969. For their work in nuclear structure theory, Professors Aage N. Bohr and Ben R. Mottelson were honored. Bohr is the son of the famed physicist Niels Bohr. For their contributions in nuclear engineering, awards were given to Floyd L. Cutler, Jr., of Oak Ridge and to Compton A. Rennie, a British nuclear engineering consultant. In the medical applications field, Henry S. Kaplan of Stanford was honored. For his contributions to chemical applications of atomic energy, an award was presented to Anthony L. Turkevich of the University of Chicago.

Walter H. Zinn, one of the world's foremost developers of nuclear power reactors, received the $25,000 Enrico Fermi award for 1969 from the AEC. A former director of Argonne National Laboratory, Zinn was a member of the group that, under Fermi's leadership, built the first reactor at Stagg Field, Chicago, on Dec. 2, 1942.

ROBERT E. CHRIEN
Brookhaven National Laboratory

FIRST SEA TRIALS were given in 1969 to a U. S. oceanographic submarine operating on nuclear power.

AUSTRALIA

In 1969, Australia held a national election, moved toward reducing its forces in Vietnam, reached agreement on defense forces in Malaysia and Singapore, and enjoyed increased economic growth.

National Affairs. Prime Minister John Gorton and his Liberal-Country party coalition government emerged from the election of October 25 with a sharply reduced majority in the House of Representatives. The prime minister later won a contest for the leadership of the Liberal party in which he was challenged by his treasurer, William McMahon, and by the minister for national development, David Fairbairn. McMahon, who indicated his willingness to remain as treasurer, was reelected as Liberal deputy leader, but Fairbairn resigned as minister.

When Gorton announced his new government on November 11, there were major changes, including appointment of seven new ministers and removal of three old ones. The former minister for labor and national service, Leslie Bury, became treasurer, while McMahon was appointed minister for external affairs. The previous holder of that position, Gordon Freeth, had been defeated for reelection by a Labor candidate. The former minister for science and education, Malcolm Fraser, became minister for defense in place of Allen Fairhall, who had been deeply involved in a controversy over Australia's purchase of 24 U. S. F-111 jets and who did not seek reelection.

On April 30, Sir Paul Hasluck, who had served as minister for external affairs, was sworn in as governor-general of Australia. The retiring governor-general, Lord Casey, had been appointed in 1966.

International Affairs. Problems of long-range security in Southeast Asia and participation in the Vietnam War remained major foreign policy concerns of the government. Prime Minister Gorton announced in February that Australia would keep land, sea, and air forces in Malaysia and Singapore after the British withdrawal in 1971. Australia would also provide personnel for headquarters, communications, and the jungle warfare training school in Malaysia. Gorton said that Australian forces would not be available to maintain internal law and order but that with specific Australian consent they could be used against infiltration and subversion from abroad.

In June representatives of Australia, New Zealand, Singapore, Malaysia, and the United Kingdom met in Canberra to discuss specific arrangements for cooperative defense. The conference communiqué emphasized that the defense arrangements would be integrated in training and use of facilities and revealed that Britain would continue to participate in defense exercises and training in the area.

Australian policy in Vietnam was to welcome President Nixon's move toward "Vietnamization" of the war but to delay announcement of withdrawal of specific Australian forces. The prime minister talked with Nixon and other U. S. officials in Washington, D. C., in May. Gorton stated after his return that Australia would not withdraw troops "at once" if the United States began to do so. He also emphasized that Nixon had reaffirmed the ANZUS pact and had commended Australia for its decision to keep forces in Southeast Asia.

When Nixon announced in June the first reduc-tion of U. S. forces in Vietnam, Gorton generally supported him but said he would not withdraw Australian troops immediately. In November, Gorton made a special announcement that Australia had discussed with the United States the phasing of Australian troops into future withdrawals. In December he said that Australian troops would be included if future "substantial" reduction of U. S. troops became possible.

Economy. The Australian economy, assisted by a record wheat harvest in contrast to the drought-reduced output of 1968, expanded rapidly during the year. The gross national product increased by 12%, and even with adjustment for inflation and abnormal rural production the real growth rate was 6.5%. Private capital expenditure increased by 16% on housing and by 10% on plant and equipment, described by the government as "boom levels." Average weekly earnings rose 7.25%, consumer spending 6.7%, and the consumer price index 2.9%. Exports increased so substantially that foreign reserves went up by $200 million, and minerals such as iron ore and coal made up 23% of exports as contrasted with 9% in 1968. Unemployment declined, and in September the number of registered unemployed, less than 1% of the work force, was smaller than the number of job vacancies for the first time since 1966.

All of this added up to inflation, and in August the reserve bank required trading banks to increase their deposits with the reserve bank from 9% to 10% and authorized them to increase interest on deposits to 5%. In December the Conciliation and Arbitration Commission granted a pay raise of 3% to more than 2.5 million workers and an increase of nearly 10% in the minimum wage. The worst economic setback was a major drought in inland Queensland that was not relieved until heavy rain fell in most of the state in late December. More than 500,000 cattle and 300,000 sheep died, and despite federal-state emergency transportation for feed and stock, the value of rural production was expected to be cut by at least $134 million.

Government Finance. Social welfare increases, minimal tax concessions, and a small deficit were the main features of the budget introduced by the treasurer in August. Revenue was to be increased by 13.5%, and government spending by 7.2%. The projected deficit of $33.6 million would be nearly $400 million less than that of the year before. Aged and invalid pensioners would receive weekly increases, as would widows and veterans.

A new "tapered" means test projected in the budget provides that income above the allowed limits will reduce pensions by only 56 cents for each $1.12 of income instead of by the full $1.12 as formerly. Increases in both weekly benefits and dependents' allowances for the sick and unemployed were also introduced. The budget also provided for free health insurance benefits for low-income families, for those on unemployment and sickness payments, and for migrants during the first two months

UPI

SYDNEY'S first transit strike was responsible for major traffic jams on Sydney Harbour Bridge and the city's expressways.

PRIME MINISTER John Gorton, accompanied by his wife, arrives in Washington in May for talks with President Richard Nixon.

after their arrival in Australia. Expenditures for education would go up by 38%, and for the first time there would be a government subsidy to private schools.

The few tax concessions in the budget included a small reduction of income tax for pensioners and of inheritance tax to be paid by farmers. Defense expenditures would be down by 5%, mainly because some programs would have their cost spread over several years.

Labor opposition leader Edward Gough Whitlam criticized the budget on grounds it would result in increased taxes and health and housing costs; failed to plan for school needs; did not approach urban development in cooperation with the states; postponed necessary developmental projects; and lacked adequate defense planning, particularly in the lack of cooperative procurement arrangements with regional allies.

Elections. In the national elections in October the Liberal-Country party coalition majority in the House of Representatives dropped from 38 to 7 seats. The government parties lost most heavily in New South Wales, South Australia, and Western Australia.

Labor Leader Whitlam had promised increased subsidization of housing, a health insurance fund with complete coverage, an end of conscription, and canceling Australia's order for the controversial F-111's unless the cancellation cost was too high. Prime Minister Gorton had promised to maintain

JOHN GREY GORTON, prime minister of Australia and leader of the Liberal party since January 1968, announced in February 1969 that Australia would continue to maintain troops in Malaysia and Singapore after the withdrawal of British forces in 1971. In May he visited the United States and reportedly received assurances from President Nixon guaranteeing Australian security under the ANZUS treaty. While pledging continued cooperation in the Vietnam conflict, Gorton indicated that his country might withdraw its 8,000-man force from Vietnam in the event of heavy U. S. withdrawals.

Gorton was born in Melbourne on Sept. 9, 1911. He was educated at Geelong Grammar School and Brasenose College, Oxford, and served as a pilot in World War II. Gorton entered local politics in 1946 and was elected a senator from Victoria in 1950. He became minister of the navy in 1958.

conscription and a mobile navy, reduce the income tax, and improve social welfare.

In state elections in May the Liberal-Country party coalition in Queensland remained in office with a reduced majority. In Tasmania the only remaining Labor government in Australia was eliminated when the election produced equal representation for the Labor and Liberal parties and the one Center party member voted with the Liberals.

RUSSELL H. BARRETT
University of Mississippi

AUSTRALIA • Information Highlights

Area: 2,967,903 square miles (7,686,810 sq km).

Population: 12,031,000 (1968 est.).

Chief Cities (1966 census): Canberra, the capital, 100,938 (1967 census); Sydney, 2,444,735 (met. area); Melbourne, 2,108,499 (met. area); Adelaide, 726,930 (met. area).

Government: *Governor-General*—Sir Paul Hasluck (took office April 30, 1969); *Prime Minister*—John G. Gorton (took office Jan. 10, 1968). *Parliament*—House of Representatives, 125 members (party seating, 1970: Liberal and Country coalition, 66; Labor 59); Senate, 60 members (party seating, 1970: Liberal and Country coalition, 28; Labor 27; Democratic-Labor, 4, Independent, 1).

Religious Faiths: Anglicans, 35% of population; Protestants, 26%; Roman Catholics, 25%; Jews, 1%.

Education: *Literacy rate* (1969), 99% of population (excluding aborigines). *Total school enrollment* (1966)—2,941,130 (primary, 1,703,552; secondary, 946,678; technical/vocational, 145,900; university/higher, 145,000).

Finance (1968): *Revenues,* $6,864,480,000; *expenditures,* $7,-295,680,000; *monetary unit,* Australian dollar (.9005 dollar equal U. S.$1).

Gross National Product (1968): $28,200,000,000.

National Income (1967): $20,406,000,000; *average annual income per person* (1968), $2,300.

Economic Indexes (1967): *Industrial production* (1968), 130 (1963=100); *agricultural production,* 101 (1963=100); *cost of living,* 113 (1963=100).

Manufacturing (metric tons, 1967): Crude steel, 6,288,000; gasoline, 6,214,000; cement, 3,816,000.

Crops (metric tons, 1967–68 crop year): Wool, greasy (1966), 7,979,000 (ranks 1st among world producers); wheat, 7,484,000; barley, 794,000; oats, 762,000.

Minerals (metric tons, 1967): Lead, 381,000 (ranks 1st among world producers); coal, 35,268,000; crude petroleum, 972,-000; silver (1966), 18,278,000 troy ounces; gold (1966), 912,385 troy ounces.

Foreign Trade (1968): *Exports,* $3,402,000,000 (chief exports, 1967: wool, $839,000,000; wheat, $479,670,000; meat and preparations, $300,000,000; dairy products, $121,000,000); *imports:* $3,858,000,000 (chief imports, 1967: nonelectrical machinery, $622,000,000; textiles, $276,800,000; electrical machinery, $222,000,000). *Chief trading partners* (1967): United States (took 12% of exports, supplied 26% of imports); Britain (took 13% of exports, supplied 24% of imports); Japan.

Transportation: *Roads* (1965), 550,000 miles (884,950 km); *motor vehicles* (1967), 4,142,700 (automobiles, 3,241,500); *railways* (1965), 24,933 miles (40,117 km); *merchant vessels* (1967), 102 (637,000 gross registered tons).

Communications: *Telephones* (1968): 3,178,278; *television stations* (1967), 76; *television sets* (1967), 2,700,000; *radios* (1967), 2,538,000; *newspapers* (1966), 60.

AUSTRIA

At the beginning of 1969 the marked economic upswing in Austria during 1968 slackened somewhat, although the overall economic growth continued to be very satisfactory. Real progress was made in the negotiations with Italy over the South Tyrol problem. There was no change in Austria's application for membership in the Common Market.

Politics. The People's party cabinet headed by Chancellor Josef Klaus continued in control of the government. In May a petition bearing 340,000 signatures (6.78% of the electorate) demanded that the introduction of a ninth school year in the primary schools as provided in the law of 1962 should be revoked. When the People's party declared in favor of suspending the law for five years, Education Minister Theodor Piffl-Percevic resigned. He was succeeded by Alois Mock.

General elections were scheduled for March 1, 1970. It will be the first time that 19-year-olds will vote, the voting age having been lowered from 20 years in November 1968. The eligible age for election to office was lowered from 29 to 25 years.

Economic Development. On Jan. 1, 1969, Austria imposed the second series of tariff cuts stipulated by the Kennedy Round of negotiations concluded in 1967 under the General Agreement on Tariffs and Trade (GATT). It was at first predicted that the gross national product, which had increased 5.7% in 1968, would increase by 5% in 1969, but this estimate was raised to over 7% by midyear. The index of industrial production rose from 113.2 in January (1964 = 100) to 137.4 in June, an average increase of 11% over the like period of 1968. Exports constituted the chief factor in economic expansion, rising by 18.4% in the first half of 1969 over the same period in 1968, while imports rose only about 10.4%.

Effective May 30, the Austrian National Bank lowered the minimum cash reserve requirements by 1.5%, thus releasing substantial funds to help finance the economic upswing. The government established a new Development and Renovation Fund, which guarantees credits up to 17 years to finance important projects in industry and tourism. The overall ceiling for such guarantees has been fixed at 2.5 billion schillings ($96 million). On September 11, to compete with higher interest charges abroad, which were leading to the export of Austrian money, the Austrian National Bank raised its bank rate from 3.75% to 4.75%.

Travel. On March 31, 1969, Austrian Airlines (AUA), in cooperation with the Belgian Sabena Airlines, inaugurated a New York-Vienna service with stops at Brussels. From Vienna, AUA flies to 33 cities in 22 countries. Tourism was expected to be up by 6% for the full year 1969. On January 1, the autobahn from Volders, in the Inn Valley, to Brennersee was opened, cutting in half the driving time from Innsbruck to the Brenner Pass.

International Affairs. In June, Austria ratified the nuclear nonproliferation treaty. In August, a new tripartite agreement on atomic control, replacing accords of 1964, was signed by Austria, the United States, and the International Atomic Energy Commission. An atomic power plant is to be built in Tülln, Lower Austria, with U. S. help.

A new agreement with Italy was approved by Austria in December 1969, providing, as it is implemented over the next four years, more autonomy

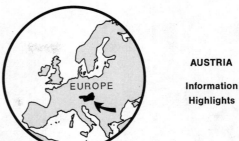

AUSTRIA

Information

Highlights

Area: 32,374 square miles (83,849 sq km).
Population: 7,349,000 (1968 est.).
Chief Cities (1966 census): Vienna, the capital, 1,638,100; Graz, 252,200; Linz, 204,900; Salzburg, 117,400.
Government: *President*—Franz Jonas (took office June 9, 1965); *Chancellor*—Josef Klaus (took office April 2, 1964). *Parliament* (Federal Assembly)—National Council, 165 members (party seating, 1969: People's party, 85; Socialist party, 74; Freedom party, 6); Federal Council, 54 members (party seating, 1969: People's party, 27; Socialist party, 27).
Religious Faiths: Roman Catholics 90% of population; Protestants, 6%; others, 4%.
Education: *Literacy rate* (1969), 100% of population. *Total school enrollment* (1966)—1,392,102 (primary, 812,734; secondary, 332,218; teacher-training, 5,928; technical/vocational, 191,671; university/higher, 49,551).
Finance (1968 est.): *Revenues,* $3,200,000,000; *expenditures,* $3,384,000,000; *public debt,* $1,500,000,000; *monetary unit,* Schilling (25.83 schillings equal U. S.$1).
Gross National Product (1968): $11,420,000,000.
National Income (1968): $8,478,513,000; *average annual income per person,* $1,153.
Economic Indexes (1967): *Industrial production* (1969), 137.4 (1964=100); *agricultural production,* 104 (1963=100); *cost of living,* 116 (1963=100).
Manufacturing (metric tons, 1967): Cement, 4,548,000; crude steel, 3,024,000; beer, 7,628,000 hectoliters.
Crops (metric tons, 1967–68 crop year): Potatoes, 3,049,000; sugar beets, 1,800,000; wheat, 842,000.
Minerals (metric tons, 1967): Crude graphite (1966), 87.677 (ranks 3d among world producers); lignite, 4,604,000; magnesite, 1,535,300; iron ore, 1,099,000.
Foreign Trade (1968): *Exports,* $1,989,000,000 (chief exports, 1967: iron and steel, $22,806,000; nonelectrical machinery, $22,000,000; textile yarn and fabrics, $15,437,000; wood, lumber, and cork, $11,885,000); *imports,* $2,496,000,000 (chief imports, 1967: nonelectrical machinery, $33,276,000; road motor vehicles, $20,662,000; textile yarn and fabrics, $17,800,000). *Chief trading partners* (1967): West Germany (took 22% of exports, supplied 42% of imports); Italy (took 12% of exports, supplied 8% of imports); Switzerland (took 9% of exports, supplied 7% of imports).
Transportation: *Roads* (1966), 20,000 miles (32,200 km); *motor vehicles* (1967), 1,298,200 (automobiles 966,600); *railways* (1965), 4,094 miles (6,587 km); *principal airports,* Vienna (Schwechat), Linz, Salzburg, Graz, Klagenfurt, Innsbruck.
Communications: *Telephones* (1968): 1,163,194; *television stations* (1967), 99; *television sets* (1967), 978,000; *radios* (1967), 2,146,000; *newspapers* (1965), 36.

for the German-speaking people of Italy's Alto Adige province, and officially changing its name to South Tyrol.

At the end of March, Chancellor Kurt Kiesinger of West Germany paid an official visit to Vienna. Britain's Queen Elizabeth II, Prince Philip, and Princess Anne visited Austria on May 5–10. The first British sovereign to visit Vienna since Edward VII was accorded a festive and joyous welcome reminiscent of Austria's monarchical days.

Chancellor Josef Klaus attended the funeral of former U. S. President Dwight Eisenhower on March 31. Ambassador Ernst Lemberger, who had represented Austria in the United States since 1965, was transferred to Paris, and was succeeded by Karl Gruber, who headed the Austrian foreign ministry in 1945–1953.

Austria's seven refugee camps were badly overcrowded. Nearly 1,000 Czechs and Hungarians entered the country each month during 1969.

ERNST C. HELMREICH
Bowdoin College

AUTOMATION. See COMPUTERS.

Some 20,000 new Japanese autos await shipment on a Yokohama warehouse and harbor lot.

UPI

automobiles

Economy cars dominated planning of U. S. automobile producers as they completed a lackluster 1969-model year in which volume declined nearly 100,000 units. A total of 8,309,845 of the 1969 models had been assembled through Oct. 15, 1969, when only a handful of units was still scheduled by year's end from four makes—Chevrolet Camaro and Corvette, Pontiac Firebird, and Checker. In contrast, the 1968-model production lines attained an output of 8,404,976 cars—and this total was reached despite a long strike against Ford Motor Co. No major work stoppage occurred in 1969.

What did highlight the year, however, was introduction of the Detroit-based industry's first direct competitors against the lower-priced imported cars, principally Volkswagen. Ford's Maverick was the first of these subcompact cars to reach the marketplace, arriving in the spring of 1969 as a 1970 model. It was an immediate sales success. U. S. sales of the Volkswagen "beetle" declined through the summer, and two higher-priced compact series, the Chevrolet Corvair and Ford Falcon, were dis-

continued. American Motors brought out its Hornet subcompact in the fall of 1969; Chrysler Corporation and the Chevrolet division of General Motors were preparing comparable 1971 introductions.

1969 MODEL PRODUCTION

Ford. Analysis of the model run discloses that Ford, even without counting the 1970 Maverick, scored the biggest increase in production over the previous year. Ford Motor Company's share of output rose from 23.7% to 25.3%, with the standard-size Ford and Mercury cars registering the greatest numerical gains. The company's three sports entries —Ford Mustang, Mercury Cougar, and Ford Thunderbird—each declined substantially in 1969-model volume.

GM. General Motors finished the 1969-model year with 53.3% of the industry total, off from 54.2% in 1968. The Chevrolet, Pontiac, and Cadillac divisions declined in volume, while Buick and Oldsmobile moved higher. Chevrolet's model run total fell to 2,037,682 through Oct. 15, 1969, from a final

1968 volume of 2,139,426. The standard Chevrolet had the deepest setback among the 1969's, but in keeping with a market swing toward lower-price cars the Chevrolet Nova compact rose to 268,011 units from 201,005 the previous year.

Pontiac entered the personal sports car field in 1969 with the Grand Prix and produced 112,486 of these to lead its sector. However, the standard Pontiac, intermediate Tempest, and sporty Firebird each fell off in volume. Intermediate entries also declined for Buick and Oldsmobile.

Chrysler. Chrysler Corporation's share of model output eased to 18.1% from 18.9% the previous year. Its only models on the upside were the Plymouth intermediate Belvedere and the Dodge compact Dart. Its deepest losses were shown in the standard Plymouth Fury and Dodge Polara.

AMC. American Motors Corporation remained steady at 3.3% of the new-car market. A restyled standard Ambassador and compact Rambler overcame setbacks for the intermediate Rebel and Javelin sportster.

Popularity of Body Sizes. Following is a breakdown of how 1969 models performed in sales in comparison with 1968's by body sizes:

• *Compacts*—764,939, up 19% (Chevrolet Chevy II/Nova, Dodge Dart, Plymouth Valiant, AMC Rambler, Ford Falcon, and 6,000 Chevrolet Corvairs up to discontinuance of the model.)

• *Intermediates*—2,140,877, off 7% (Chevrolet Chevelle, Ford Fairlane, Pontiac Tempest, Plymouth Belvedere, Oldsmobile F-85, Dodge Coronet, Buick Special, Mercury Montego, AMC Rebel).

• *Standards*—2,341,014, down 1% (Chevrolet Impala and Caprice, Ford Galaxie and Custom, Plymouth Fury, AMC Ambassador).

• *Mediums*—1,646,707, unchanged (Buick, Pontiac, Oldsmobile, Chrysler, Mercury, Dodge Polara).

• *Sportsters*—837,901, down 13% (Ford Mustang, Chevrolet Camaro, Mercury Cougar, Pontiac Firebird, AMC Javelin, Plymouth Barracuda, Dodge Charger).

• *Luxury cars*—306,692, up 5% (Cadillac and Eldorado, Lincoln, Mark III, Imperial).

• *Luxury Sportsters*—243,150, up 72% (Pontiac Grand Prix, Buick Riviera, Ford Thunderbird, Oldsmobile Toronado).

• *Two-seaters,* down 3% (Chevrolet Corvette, AMX).

THE 1970 MODELS

A movement to reduce the number of models offered by the U. S. auto industry gained momentum as the 1970 season got under way. Fourteen models were phased out from the 1970 offerings. This included 12 models by General Motors. Ford Motor cut four models and AMC trimmed two, but Chrysler Corporation added four.

As a result, 351 models were being built at the start of the 1970 season, compared to 365 at the end of the 1969 run. GM's 1970 lineup comprised 130 models; Chrysler Corp., 111; Ford Motor, 90; and AMC, 20. Primarily responsible for the year-to-year drop were convertibles and two-door sedans. For 1970, nine fewer convertibles were offered and seven fewer pillar-type two-doors. By market class, 1970 offerings included 169 standards, 119 intermediates, 42 specialty cars, and 21 compacts.

New nameplates for 1970 included the AMC Hornet, which replaced the Rambler and prompted its manufacturer to discontinue the Rambler name in its line; the Chevrolet Monte Carlo, a sportster; the Dodge Challenger, also a sportster; a Plymouth Valiant Duster coupe; the Buick Skylark, replacing the Special; Mercury Montego, replacing Comet; Ford Torino, supplanting Fairlane; and Ford's Maverick. Buick dropped its glass-roof Sportwagon, but Olds kept its version, called the Vista Cruiser.

Scheduled for introduction through the 1970 model year were new versions of the Camaro, Corvette, and Firebird, an AMC junior edition of the Hornet called Gremlin, a Maverick 4-door sedan, and a miniversion of the Maverick called Phoenix.

Styling. The long-hood, short-deck look associated with sports cars made important advances on 1970 models. The 1969 Pontiac Grand Prix coupled this design with a V-shaped grille nose that protruded in front of the bumper. The 1970 Maverick presented a short-hood, short-deck appearance. The 1970 Thunderbird adopted the V-nose, as did 1970 Pontiacs in addition to the Grand Prix.

Front vent windows disappeared from more cars in 1970. Windshield wipers were concealed in recesses on nearly all standard, intermediate, and luxury 1970 models. The late-arriving 1970 Camaro and Firebird went the Cadillac Eldorado one better by eliminating rear side windows—on the Eldorado the rear side window is quite small. However, a

FORD MOTOR CO.

AMERICAN MOTORS CORP.

SUBCOMPACT CARS, such as AMC's Hornet (*left*) and Ford's Maverick (*above*), dominated U. S. auto planning in 1969.

plan to introduce back-sliding front doors on the Camaro and Firebird models was dropped at the last minute, accounting for these models' delay. Concealed headlamps did not spread as predicted on 1970 cars. The slowdown was attributed to a new federal safety standard requiring headlamp covers to open within three seconds.

Safety. Larger lighting on the sides and rear of cars became mandatory by federal safety standards effective Jan. 1, 1970. All 1970 domestic and imported models were required to be equipped with antitheft steering column locks operated by the ignition key. Locking the car with the key also locked the steering column and prevented car thefts by anyone without a key.

U. S. PASSENGER CAR PRODUCTION

Company and make	1968 models	1969 models
AMERICAN MOTORS CORPORATION		
Ambassador	54,681	75,741
Rambler (American)	80,981	96,524
Rebel	73,895	51,669
Javelin	56,444	43,099
AMX	6,725	8,317
Total AMC	272,726	275,350
CHRYSLER CORPORATION		
Fury	285,046	259,917
Belvedere	240,940	246,017
Barracuda	45,412	31,987
Valiant	110,795	107,218
Subtotal Plymouth	685,193	645,139
Chrysler	264,863	260,771
Imperial	15,361	22,077
Dart	191,978	214,751
Charger	96,108	89,199
Coronet	222,559	203,431
Polara	115,510	72,194
Subtotal Dodge	626,155	579,575
Total Chrysler Corporation	1,588,572	1,507,562
FORD MOTOR COMPANY		
Ford	790,670	896,343
Fairlane	372,327	366,911
Falcon	41,650	71,158
Mustang	317,404	299,824
Thunderbird	64,931	49,272
Subtotal Ford	1,586,982	1,683,508[1]
Lincoln	39,134	38,290
Mark III	7,770	23,088
Mercury	117,491	140,516
Montego	123,113	117,421
Cougar	113,726	100,069
Subtotal Mercury	354,330	358,006
Total Ford Motor Company	1,988,216	2,102,892
GENERAL MOTORS CORPORATION		
Buick	375,079	423,937
Riviera	49,284	52,872
Special	227,460	188,613
Subtotal Buick	651,823	665,422
Cadillac	205,475	199,934
Eldorado	24,528	23,333
Subtotal Cadillac	230,003	223,267
Chevrolet	1,236,405	1,108,689
Chevelle	422,893	428,827
Nova (Chevy II)	201,005	268,011
Corvair	15,399	6,000
Camaro	235,151	200,282[2]
Corvette	28,573	25,873[2]
Subtotal Chevrolet	2,139,426	2,037,682[2]
Oldsmobile	315,995	368,870
Toronado	26,521	28,520
F-85	275,128	239,289
Subtotal Oldsmobile	617,644	639,679
Pontiac	457,459	382,419
Grand Prix	...	112,486
Tempest	346,406	284,245
Firebird	107,112	73,441[2]
Subtotal Pontiac	910,977	852,591[2]
Total General Motors Corporation	4,549,873	4,418,641[2]
CHECKER MOTORS CORPORATION	5,589	5,500
Total U. S. production	8,404,976	8,309,945[2]

[1] Excludes Maverick, introduced as 1970 model. [2] 1969 model production through Oct. 15, 1969; totals incomplete for Camaro, Checker, Corvette, and Firebird. Sources: "Ward's Automotive Reports" and "Wall Street Journal."

WORLD MOTOR VEHICLES

	1968 cars produced	1968 trucks produced[1]	1968/69 vehicle registrations
United States	8,848,620	1,971,790	104,702,000[2]
Canada	899,943	276,626	7,099,709
Argentina	127,965	53,011	1,822,500
Australia	314,000	53,000	4,142,701
Austria	600	3,550	1,076,471
Belgium	200,000	15,800	1,766,000
Brazil	192,000	65,000	2,469,100
Czechoslovakia	121,000	21,000	683,981
Finland	...	1,000	651,546
France	1,833,047	242,570	14,181,100
East Germany	115,000	23,000	1,189,677
West Germany	2,535,433	571,525	12,011,076
Hungary	...	9,000	144,601
India	44,640	33,630	888,885
Italy	1,544,933	115,437	8,037,751
Japan	2,055,821	2,030,005	7,140,000
Mexico	102,019	44,529	1,357,500
Netherlands	60,000	10,000	2,000,000
Poland	40,500	39,600	542,226
Portugal	...	350	469,695
Rumania	10,000	15,000	36,813
Spain	313,590	79,500	1,904,400
Sweden	221,000	20,475	2,112,100
Switzerland	...	1,000	1,183,519
United Kingdom	1,699,300	400,700	12,199,900
USSR	300,000	460,000	5,274,000
Yugoslavia	43,000	14,000	451,969
Others	...	...	14,460,341[3]
World total	21,622,411	6,571,098	210,000,000

[1] Includes buses. [2] Excludes Puerto Rico, 403,120; Virgin Islands, 16,063; and Canal Zone, 17,615. [3] Other countries in excess of 1 million: Denmark, 1,141,100; New Zealand, 1,001,000; Republic of South Africa, 1,655,066. Sources: Automobile Manufacturers Association and "Automotive News."

In addition to the continuing federal and state standards on emission of unburned hydrocarbons, California required cars sold there to reduce evaporation from engine exhausts. So concerned was California about its smog problems, especially around Los Angeles, that a bill to outlaw internal combustion engines was passed by the State Senate—only to fail to gain approval in an Assembly committee.

Most 1970 models, as a boon to tire safety, carried newly developed tires with belts made of fiber glass.

Prices. Suggested retail prices of 1970's were increased an average of $125 over prices on 1969 models by General Motors. Higher costs and lower profit margins were given as reasons for the GM move. All other domestic manufacturers also raised prices. The average increase amounted to 3.5% over 1969, the biggest rise in 13 years.

IMPORTS

On Jan. 1, 1969, a total of 5,398,624 foreign-built cars were in operation in the United States, compared with 4,651,091 the year before. Sales of imported new cars for the first eight months of 1969 rose to 658,534, from 605,466 for the same 1968 period. Volkswagen sales fell from 351,036 to 323,211, but other manufacturers reported significant increases: Toyota from 33,617 to 70,860; Opel from 52,947 to 65,341; Datsun from 21,294 to 37,023; and Fiat from 17,456 to 26,374. The imports' share of the U. S. market was about 11%.

MAYNARD M. GORDON
Editor, "Motor News Analysis" and "The Imported Car Reports"

AVIATION. See AIR FORCE; AIR TRANSPORTATION; DEFENSE FORCES.
AWARDS. See PRIZES AND AWARDS.
BACTERIOLOGY. See MICROBIOLOGY.
BADMINTON. See SPORTS.
BAHAMAS. See CARIBBEAN; COMMONWEALTH OF NATIONS.
BALLET. See DANCE.

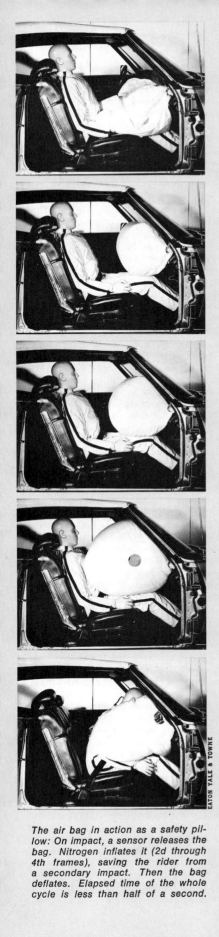

FOR SAFETY

The auto safety movement continued in 1969, propelled by government action and industrial innovation. New federal standards decreed more lighting on sides and rears of cars. Eaton Yale & Towne developed an air bag (left). Inventor John Fitch created a barrier—plastic containers of sand —to protect cars headed for bridge piers, signposts, abutments, and other stationary roadside hazards (tests are shown below).

How sand-filled polyethylene containers soften a 50-mph crash: At Stratford, Conn., a test car rams containers, which burst so that sand flies (second photo), and the driver emerges without injury.

THE NEW YORK TIMES

The air bag in action as a safety pillow: On impact, a sensor releases the bag. Nitrogen inflates it (2d through 4th frames), saving the rider from a secondary impact. Then the bag deflates. Elapsed time of the whole cycle is less than half of a second.

EATON YALE & TOWNE

BALTIMORE

Problems that abrade life in all major U. S. cities —tight city budgets, inadequate public schools, racial tension, the flight of white families to the suburbs, vehicular congestion—continued to affect the city of Baltimore (pop. 907,000) in 1969.

Public Finance. Money, the key to solving most municipal problems, was in short supply in 1969. Mayor Thomas D'Alesandro III failed to win approval of a 10% residential heating tax and a 5% levy on industrial and commercial rentals. Instead, the City Council cut the executive budget and resorted to another property tax increase, bringing the rate to $4.94 per $100. In a special election in May, voters approved lifting the 5% interest ceiling on municipal bonds, permitting the city to borrow a modest $35 million at rates that will require $32 million in interest over the life of the bonds.

Education. The School Board negotiated the first formal contract with Baltimore teachers, covering administrative matters as well as pay scales. School officials cautiously tried some decentralization but stopped short of experiments in community control which, they felt, had produced more problems than solutions in other cities. Integrated teams of black and white teachers moved into most of the schools which remain *de facto* segregated (75 out of a total of 210 in the school system).

Government Agencies. Public faith in official integrity was undermined during 1969 by indictment of two city councilmen for accepting bribes in connection with a poolhall regulation bill and by a newspaper exposé of irregularities in the traffic courts. In addition to disclosing routine parking ticket "fixes," the investigation revealed many cases of changed court records in such serious matters as drunken driving. Later investigations uncovered loose bail-bond practices. The State's Attorney's office began examination of thousands of records and a special grand jury was convened for further investigation.

At year's end the Port Authority, which had enjoyed a large degree of autonomy, was under fire from legislators who sought to curb it. Architects and other professional members of municipal commissions found their status questioned under rigid conflict-of-interest laws that the City Council later sought to make more flexible.

Race Relations. Baltimore experienced no serious violence in 1969, although a badly planned Youth for Decency rally in April was marked by disorders and racial incidents. A survey published a year after the April 1968 riots showed that one third of the damaged or destroyed businesses were still inoperative. A program dedicated to fostering realistic black capitalism had produced 50 transactions for 300 potential buyers.

Transportation. A reconstituted Metropolitan Transit Authority was blocked from starting a planned $2 billion rail rapid transit system by lack of federal funds. However, it began negotiations to buy the existing bus system. Further impetus was provided by Gov. Marvin Mandel's commitment to public purchase of the transit company in 1970.

Sports. Brilliant records for Baltimore's Colts (football), Bullets (basketball), and Orioles (baseball) all ended in post-season disaster at the hands of New York City teams. (See also SPORTS.)

DUDLEY P. DIGGES
Baltimore "Evening Sun"

BANKING

Despite restrictive monetary and fiscal policies aimed at slowing inflation, the U. S. economy passed its 100th month of continuous expansion in 1969. Real economic growth slowed noticeably, however, declining from an annual rate of over 6.5% in the first half of 1968 to only 2% in the first three quarters of 1969.

Inflation continued. The consumer price index rose about ½ of 1% per month throughout the first three quarters. Unemployment rose slowly in the third quarter, reaching a seasonally adjusted rate of 4% of the civilian labor force in September. This rise, coupled with the slowing of the real growth rate, suggested that severely restrictive monetary-fiscal measures might at last be beginning to bite.

Monetary Policy in 1969. To limit the continued expansion in commercial bank lending, the Federal Reserve System, the nation's central bank, raised reserve requirements on deposits in member commercial banks, twice raised its discount rate on member bank borrowings (to a level of 6%, last reached in the 1920's), and sold substantial amounts of government securities through open-market operations, to reduce the banks' nonborrowed reserves. These measures produced a monetary policy of extreme restraint, obviously aimed at permitting no further increase in the money supply.

Mirroring this restraint, member bank borrowings from Federal Reserve banks more than doubled —from an average $600 million in December 1968 to $1.3 billion by mid-1969, for example—as economic expansion continued to generate very high levels of loan demand, especially for business loans. Besides borrowing from the Federal Reserve to meet this demand, larger banks also tapped the Eurodollar market (through foreign branches, correspondents, and brokers) and where possible (that is, through holding-company affiliates) the domestic commercial paper market as well. In both markets, rates rose quite steeply. Three-month Euro-dollars reached 12.5%, while 4-to-6-month commercial paper rates equaled the banks' own prime rate (8.5%) at midyear. The rate on federal funds (one-day loans of reserves by one bank to another) exceeded the prime rate, rising to over 9% in June.

Bank Reserves and the Money Supply. The central bank's restrictive policies led to a decrease in member bank reserves (a key monetary variable providing a base for bank credit and the money supply and including both cash in vault and deposits at Federal Reserve banks). They declined at an annual rate of 3% in the first three quarters of the year. In contrast, they had increased at annual rates of 12% in 1967 and 8% in 1968.

The money supply—redefined in 1969 to include privately owned domestic and foreign demand deposits at American commercial banks, demand deposits of foreign central banks and international organizations at Federal Reserve banks, and currency outside banks—continued to expand in the first half of 1969. But its growth was reduced to zero in the third quarter, providing another suggestion that overall national anti-inflation policies were beginning to produce desired results. For the first three quarters of 1969 as a whole, the annual average growth in money supply was less than 3%, compared with 7% in 1968.

Commercial Bank Loans and Investments. In the face of continued severe Federal Reserve pressure on reserve positions, the banking system was hard put in 1969 even to maintain its existing volume of earning assets. But the composition of these assets changed. The year 1969 saw the most rapid run-off of bank securities portfolios in two decades. Funds released by the sale and maturing of securities, together with funds squeezed out of certain "other loan" categories (loans to purchase or carry securities, loans to finance companies, and real estate loans, for example) were redirected into business lending.

Interest Rates. In five steps, the prime rate (the interest rate that the nation's largest banks charge their biggest and best borrowing customers) was raised from 6.25% in December 1968 to 8.5%, an unprecedented high, in June 1969. Open-market money rates rose commensurately: the yield on prime commercial paper (4–6 months) rose above 8% in June and approached 9% as the year drew to a close; 3-month Treasury bills yielded over 7% from midyear on; intermediate-term (3-to-5 year) Treasury issues were being priced to yield about 8% in October.

High open-market yields drained time and savings deposits from the banks, the more so since interest ceilings on such deposits (set by the Federal Reserve's Regulation Q), ranging from 4% to 6.25%, were not increased. Partly for this reason and partly because of the propensity of individuals and businesses to draw down interest-yielding balances rather than to curtail current expenditure levels in the face of high taxes and prices, bank time and savings deposits declined by over 8% in the first three quarters of 1969. (In contrast, they had increased by 11% in 1968.)

Outlook. Data for the third quarter led some analysts to suggest that a recession in business activity might already have begun, or, if not, that one would develop within 1970. For example: growth in real gross national product in the third quarter was only at the same 2% rate achieved earlier in the year; industrial production, defense spending, and construction contract awards declined; meanwhile, surveys of consumer attitudes at last began to suggest growing uneasiness and caution.

This prospect of recession raised fears in certain quarters that the nation's fiscal and monetary authorities, in their desire to correct inflation, might pursue restrictive policies too long, leading to economic overkill. But as 1969 drew toward its close, the monetary authorities—the Federal Reserve System—showed no inclination to move toward monetary ease. Perhaps they were more concerned about estimates that the inflation rate (6% in 1969) might still be as high as 4% in 1970, even after allowing for a statistically measurable recession.

Banking Structure. The striking growth of "financial congenerics," or one-bank holding companies, which began in 1968, continued into 1969. It appeared to be approaching legislative restrictions, however. These banking conglomerates became possible because the Bank Holding Company Act of 1956 regulates only holding companies with two or more banks. A number of measures were introduced into Congress in 1969 to bring one-bank holding companies under regulation (by the Federal Reserve), and a particularly restrictive bill was passed by the House of Representatives in November 1969. Senate action, if any, was to come in 1970.

CLIFTON H. KREPS, JR.
University of North Carolina at Chapel Hill

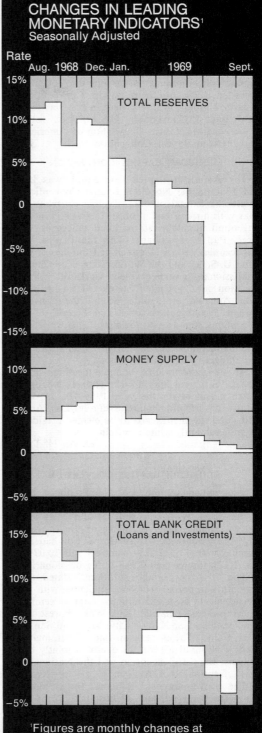

CHANGES IN LEADING
MONETARY INDICATORS[1]
Seasonally Adjusted

Rate

Aug. 1968 Dec. Jan.   1969   Sept.

TOTAL RESERVES

MONEY SUPPLY

TOTAL BANK CREDIT
(Loans and Investments)

[1]Figures are monthly changes at annual rates, smoothed by a centered 3-month moving average. The latest plotting in each series is a 2-month average. Data from Federal Reserve Board.

ADAPTED FROM
"MONTHLY ECONOMIC LETTER,"
FIRST NATIONAL CITY BANK, NEW YORK

BAPTIST CHURCHES

Baptist churches throughout the United States had the largest total membership of any single Protestant denominational group in the country in 1969. The *Yearbook of American Churches* noted 27 autonomous Baptist bodies, whose membership during the past year represented about one third of all U. S. Protestants. The Southern Baptist Convention was the largest group. Ranking next in size was the National Baptist Convention, U.S.A., Inc., followed by the National Baptist Convention of America and the American Baptist Convention.

AMERICAN BAPTIST CONVENTION

The American Baptist Convention was known until 1950 as the Northern Baptist Convention. It represented a total of 6,097 Baptist churches in 44 states with a membership of 1,555,460 in 1969. The convention maintains its national offices at Valley Forge, Pa.; it is affiliated with the Baptist World Alliance, the National Council of Churches of Christ in the U. S. A., and the World Council of Churches.

Missionary and benevolent work and Christian education in the United States, Africa, Asia, and Latin America are conducted by the convention through 5 national societies and boards, 36 state conventions, and 13 city societies. This work is supported by contributions (amounting to $15 million) from Baptist churches to the American Baptist Mission Budget, plus other sources.

At the convention's annual meeting, held in Seattle, Wash., on May 14–18, Thomas Kilgore was elected president for the year 1969–70. He is pastor of the Second Baptist Church, Los Angeles, Calif., and the first Negro to be elected president of the predominantly white denomination.

EDWIN H. TULLER
American Baptist Convention

SOUTHERN BAPTIST CONVENTION

The annual assembly of the Southern Baptist Convention, meeting in New Orleans, La., June 10–14, reelected W. A. Criswell of the First Baptist Church, Dallas, Tex., president of the convention. In 1969 the Southern Baptist Convention had 34,295 churches with 11,332,229 members and 30,079 pastors, 2,371 foreign and 2,385 home missionaries.

The 70 educational institutions related to the convention reported 104,850 students, with 8,017 ministerial students. Southern Baptist seminaries are located in Louisville, Ky.; Wake Forest, N. C.; New Orleans, La.; Kansas City, Mo.; and San Francisco, Calif. The American Baptist Seminary, located in Nashville, Tenn., is operated jointly by the Southern Baptist Convention and the National Baptist Convention, U. S. A., Inc.

The convention has 32 homes for children, 16 homes for the aged, and 34 hospitals, 32 of which are operated by state conventions and 2 by the Southern Baptist Convention. The Executive Committee of the convention is located in Nashville.

PORTER ROUTH
Southern Baptist Convention

BARBADOS

For three months—May, June, and July—in 1969 the small island of Barbados was the center for a comprehensive scientific research program designed to study the sea and its related atmosphere. The

BARBADOS

Information Highlights

Area: 166 square miles (430 sq km).
Population: 253,000 (1968 est.).
Chief Cities (1960 census): Bridgetown, the capital, 11,452.
Government: *Governor-General*—Sir Winston Scott (appointed May 1967); *Prime Minister*—Earl Walton Barrow (took office for 2d 5-year term, Nov. 3, 1966). *Parliament*—Senate, 21 members (appointed); House of Assembly, 24 members (party seating, 1966: Democratic Labor Party, 14; Barbados Labor Party, 8; others, 2).
Religious Faiths: Anglicans, 70% of population.
Education: *Literacy rate* (1965), 91.1% of population aged 15 and over. *Total school enrollment* (1964)—55,011 (primary, 39,173; secondary, 15,431; university, 407).
Monetary Unit: East Caribbean dollar (2.00 equal U. S.$1).
Gross National Product (1966): $107,000,000.
National Income (1966 est.): $92,000,000; average annual income per person, $376.
Cost of Living Index (1967), 103.6 (1966=100).
Manufacturing (metric tons, 1967): Sugar, 209,000; margarine, 1,200.
Crops (metric tons, 1967–68 crop year): Sugarcane, 1,460,000.
Minerals (1967): Natural gas, 3,000,000 cubic meters.
Foreign Trade (1966): Exports, $40,221,000 (chief exports, 1966: Cane sugar, $19,451,000); imports, $76,493,000. *Chief trading partners* (1967): United Kingdom; United States; Canada.
Transportation: *Roads* (1966), 840 miles (13,518 km); *principal airports*, Seawell, Christ Church.
Communications: *Telephones* (1968): 22,159; *television stations* (1966), 1; *television sets* (1967), 9,000; *radios* (1967), 55,000; *newspapers* (1966), 2.

Barbados Oceanographic and Meteorological Experiment (BOMEX) was the first large project under the multi-nation Global Atmospheric Research Program.

The government of Barbados cooperated with the U. S. government, 19 universities, and 7 private industrial laboratories in this $18 million program. Some 1,500 scientists, as well as several satellites, 24 planes, and 10 ships that left from Bridgetown harbor gathered data from a 90,000-square-mile (233,100-sq-km) area just east of the island in the Atlantic Ocean. Readings were taken up to an altitude of 100,000 feet (30,480 meters) above the ocean. Some 80 projects were carried out to examine in detail the exchange of energy between the ocean and its atmosphere and the vertical and horizontal spreading of these energies within each medium. One objective was to learn more about the formation and movement of the frequent tropical hurricanes.

Economy. Drought continued to plague Barbados. Coupled with the uncontrolled burning of the cane fields and other factors, it sharply reduced Barbados sugar production. The 1969 harvest produced about 137,000 tons of sugar, some 25,000 tons less than 1968. As a result, Barbados fell short of its commitments to U. S. and British markets.

This substantial loss to the island's income was partly offset by growth in the tourist industry. In 1969, Barbados received an estimated 191,000 tourists, an increase of about 25% in one year.

Prime Minister Errol W. Barrow also counts on the government's Operation Beehive, an industrial development program, to bolster the island's economy. Since 1962 some 70 firms have been established on the island, creating more than 3,000 new jobs.

THOMAS G. MATHEWS
University of Puerto Rico

BELGIUM

Belgium continued to be harassed in 1969 by the long-standing feud between its two major linguistic groups, the Flemings and the Walloons. The economy boomed, and the government took measures to check inflation.

Fleming-Walloon Disputes. The death on January 21 of Joseph Jean Merlot, the Socialist deputy prime minister and minister for economic affairs, gave rise to uneasiness about the fate of the coalition government of Prime Minister Gaston Eyskens. Merlot was a strong figure in the government and a vigorous champion of Walloon interests, but in the national interest he was able to curb somewhat the extremists of his community. The 1968 election had weakened the position of the major political parties, and it was feared that another election would further strengthen the smaller extremist parties at the expense of the major parties.

However, Eyskens' delicately balanced coalition, formed after a prolonged political crisis, was able to continue. On January 27, Socialist André Cools became deputy prime minister and continued as minister of the budget; Socialist Edmond Leburton became minister for economic affairs.

Under the coalition, a dual Fleming-Walloon administrative organization was inaugurated in certain sensitive ministries in hopes of halting the violent confrontations between the two language communities. But efforts to resolve the 30-year-old dispute have not succeeded. In fact, the dual administrative arrangement seems to have accelerated the drift apart.

The Eyskens government proposed a constitutional revision providing for economic and cultural decentralization. Industrial development and investment planning would be decentralized to relieve the Walloons' anxiety over their declining economic position. Cultural development, including primary and secondary education, the arts, radio, and television would be under the supervision of two councils, one composed of Flemish senators and the other of Walloon senators. However, the Eyskens government does not have the two thirds parliamentary majority necessary to amend the constitution and thus must win support from the opposition parties.

In May, a Walloon-proposed amendment to protect the Walloon position in the largely Fleming Brussels suburban area touched off a bitter debate. Hope for the continuance of Belgium's unitary government is waning, and the creation of a federation seems to be the only way to end the conflict.

Economic Expansion. The year 1969 was one of economic expansion and labor shortages. The rise in exports, which began in the second half of 1967, gained momentum in 1968 and began to accelerate sharply in the second quarter of 1969. The export boom was the most important factor stimulating a strong upswing in economic activity. The overall growth rate increased as consumer and investment demand grew. Belgium was sharing the general expansion of industrial production in the European Economic Community (EEC) countries. Even the stagnating steel industry was enjoying substantially increased prices and expanding demand for its output.

Early in 1969 the government took steps to check inflation, including raises in bank discount rates, a freeze on the hiring of government personnel, additional credit restrictions, and more stringent installment buying regulations.

--------- BELGIUM • Information Highlights ---------

Area: 11,781 square miles (30,513 sq km).
Population: 9,619,000 (1968 est.).
Chief Cities (1966 census): Brussels, the capital, 169,253; Antwerp (1965 est.), 243,426; Ghent, 157,048; Liège, 153,134.
Government: *King*—Baudouin I (acceded July 17, 1951); *Prime Minister*—Gaston Eyskens (took office June 17, 1968). *Parliament*—Senate, 178 members (party seating, 1969: Christian Social party, 64; Belgian Socialist party, 53; Party for Liberty and Progress, 37; Francophone-Walloon Rally, 8; Flemish People's Union, 14; Communist party, 2); Chamber of Representatives, 212 members.
Religious Faiths: Roman Catholics, 95% of population.
Education: *Total school enrollment* (1964)—1,811,625 (primary, 967,124; secondary, 300,406; teacher-training, 24,-840; technical/vocational, 443,766; university/higher, 75,-489).
Finance (1968 est.): *Revenues,* $4,839,190,000; *expenditures,* $5,462,185,000; *public debt,* $10,548,783,000; *monetary unit,* franc (50.14 francs equal U. S.$1).
Gross National Product (1968): $20,662,146,000.
National Income (1968): $16,433,985,000; *average annual income per person,* $1,708.
Economic Indexes (1968): *Industrial production,* 120 (1963= 100); *agricultural production* (including Luxembourg), 100 (1963=100); *cost of living,* 116 (1963=100).
Manufacturing (metric tons, 1967): Crude steel, 9,716,000; cement, 5,820,000; wheat flour, 729,000.
Crops (metric tons, 1967–68 crop year): Sugar beets, 3,615,-000; potatoes, 1,943,000; wheat, 842,000.
Minerals (metric tons, 1968): Coal, 16,435,000; lime (1966), 2,232,000.
Foreign Trade (including Luxembourg, 1968): *Exports,* $8,-150,000,000 (chief exports, 1967: iron and steel, $1,158,-697,000; textiles, $617,949,000; nonelectrical machinery, $456,186,000; passenger cars, $390,780,000; *imports,* $8,195,000,000 (chief imports, 1967: road motor vehicles, $542,782,000; textiles, $292,720,000; nonindustrial diamonds, $274,158,000). *Chief trading partners* (1967): West Germany; Netherlands; France.
Transportation: *Roads* (1964), 58,036 miles (93,397 km); *motor vehicles* (1967), 1,766,000 (automobiles 1,520,000); *railways* (1965), 2,760 miles (4,442 km); *merchant vessels* (1967), 69 (847,000 gross registered tons); *national airline,* Sabena.
Communications: *Telephones* (1968): 1,753,698; *television stations* (1968), 16; *television sets* (1968), 1,700,000; *radios* (1967), 3,190,000; *newspapers* (1968), 54 (daily circulation, 2,701,000).

On September 10 the government announced its decision to postpone until January 1971 the introduction of the added-value tax, which all EEC countries had agreed to institute by January 1970. In view of the economic boom and labor shortages, the government feared the new tax would cause an upsurge in prices and threaten the country's economy.

In August, following the devaluation of the French franc, there was heavy pressure on the Belgian franc. But subsequent revaluation of the German mark eased the pressure. The Belgian and French francs are closely linked, because France now takes nearly 22% of Belgium's exports. Belgian exports to France in the first half of 1969 rose 44% over exports in the corresponding period in 1968.

International Relations. Belgium is looking toward a complete removal of border controls between the Benelux countries (Belgium, the Netherlands, and Luxembourg) by July 1, 1971. In April representatives from the three nations agreed to increase efforts to coordinate their economic, financial, and social policies and to work toward harmonizing their legal systems, transport policies, and policies for the location of industry.

Relations between Belgium and Congo (Kinshasa) were no longer characterized by the violence and suspicion that prevailed for so many years. An economic mission to the Congo in early 1969 received a cordial welcome. An agreement was reached providing for a joint commission to promote trade.

AMRY VANDENBOSCH
University of Kentucky

BERRYMAN, John. See biographical sketch under AMERICAN LITERATURE.

BIOCHEMISTRY

During 1969, biochemists continued to uncover fundamental information about the chemistry of living things. Knowledge of ribosomes, how cells control their activities, enzymes, and inteferon, in particular, increased during the year.

Ribosomes. Since much is already known about the role of messenger RNA and transfer RNA in reading the genetic code and assembling the correct amino acid sequence for the building of proteins in the ribosomes (the sites of protein chain construction in the cell), the major research emphasis turned to the proteins and the RNA found in the ribosomal particles. After separating ribosomes into their two component particles—30S and 50S—Masayasu Nomura and Peter Traub in their research at the University of Wisconsin further subdivided the 30S particles into 16S RNA and some 20 or 21 different proteins. They then reassembled the entire 30S particle, restoring its full biological activity. This technique then enabled them to delete certain proteins, one by one, from the reassembled 30S particle and to identify the proteins involved with certain characteristics of the ribosomes. For example, they determined the protein component concerned with streptomycin resistance in ribosomes.

Control of Cell Activities. Attention also turned to the question of how the cell controls its numerous functions, such as protein synthesis and DNA replication. For example, it is understood that the genetic code contains the information for the amino acid sequence of specific proteins, but a protein must have a beginning and an end. Consequently there must be some control mechanism that informs the protein synthesis machinery to begin to make the protein at one point on the genetic message and to stop when it gets to some other specific point.

Although the way in which protein chain synthesis is initiated in bacteria is known in a general way, very little is understood about how the process stops when a particular protein is completely synthesized. Studying this problem, M. R. Capecchi of Harvard University and C. T. Caskeu of the National Institutes of Health reported that at least three factors are associated with chain termination. Two of these factors, referred to as R1 and R2, recognize specific termination sequences in the genetic code, while the third factor, referred to as S, or T, seems to stimulate the rate of chain termination with either R1 or R2.

DNA (deoxyribonucleic acid) replication, or the copying of the nucleotide sequence of the genetic material so that it can be transfered to subsequent generations of cells, is known to require the enzyme DNA polymerase. Some signal is necessary to initiate replication, and investigators from the University of Pennsylvania reported at a meeting of the American Cancer Society that they had isolated a polypeptodie of low molecular weight that seems to exhibit the properties expected of a DNA replication initiator.

Enzymes. During 1969 a great deal of progress was made toward understanding how enzymes work. Enzymes are protein molecules that regulate the rate of biochemical reactions and provide the kind of precise control of chemical reactions essential to life. A big advance was made by the first laboratory synthesis of an enzyme. The enzyme—ribonuclease—which attacks RNA, was synthesized independently by two different groups of investigators using two different methods. Ribonuclease was the enzyme of choice since its sequence of 124 amino acids had been known since 1960. One of the groups, headed by R. Merrifield and B. Gutte of the Rockefeller University, used a solid-phase method and employed small polystyrene beads as anchors for the growing enzyme chain. The other group, headed by R. G. Denkewalter at Merck Sharp and Dohme, used the fact that ribonuclease can be split into two segments, called S-protein and S-peptide. The S-protein, which contains 104 amino acids, was first built in small pieces, each containing from 6 to 17 amino acids. Later, when combined, these pieces formed a complete S-protein, which, when added to the S-peptide, produced an active enzyme.

The Nobel laureate Arthur Kornberg and his co-workers at Stanford University have studied a larger and more complicated enzyme, DNA polymerase—the enzyme that is most probably responsible for replicating DNA in the cell. In order to function, DNA polymerase must bind itself to the double-stranded DNA molecule that it is copying and also to the four different nucleotides necessary for the synthesis of new DNA strands. It was found that there is only one site for binding nucleotides, not four different sites, and that the template DNA is bound to a single site on the enzyme—a site that in some way includes the last free hydroxyl group on the DNA molecule. Using this and other evidence, these workers then suggested a speculative model for DNA replication. The model calls for two additional enzymes—an endonuclease and a ligase—to explain the sequential and almost simultaneous replication of both strands of the DNA helix.

Enzymes have also been implicated in the process of tooth decay. A team of Massachusetts Institute of Technology investigators, headed by Stephen N. Kreitzman, demonstrated that an enzyme capable of removing the phosphate from the matrix proteins of tooth enamel can cause the rapid loss of mineral from the tooth. Tooth decay was previously thought to be simply the result of bacterial acids, but now this new finding may lead to the development of new ways of controlling tooth decay.

Inteferon. Inteferon, a protein produced by cells as protection from a virus, is the only important defense now known against virus infection. Usually the amount of inteferon produced by a cell is not enough to cure a virus infection. However, during 1969, John Park of the New York Medical College and Samuel Baron of the National Institute of Allergy and Infectious Diseases presented evidence that an animal can be stimulated to produce additional inteferon—enough to cure an infection. They administered a synthetic polymer of inosinic acid and cytidilic acid that resembles RNA to rabbits that had previously been infected with a herpes simplex virus that produced a serious infection of the cornea of the eye. The rabbits recovered by the third day. The investigators attribute the recovery to a sharp increase in the inteferon levels in the rabbits' blood and believe that the synthetic RNA stimulated inteferon production. If this proves true, a valuable new treatment for serious viral infections may be forthcoming.

STEPHEN N. KREITZMAN
Emory University

BIOLOGY. See BIOCHEMISTRY; BOTANY; GENETICS; MARINE BIOLOGY; MICROBIOLOGY; ZOOLOGY.
BIRTHRATES. See POPULATION; VITAL STATISTICS.

BOATING

Dynamic growth with a promise of more to come highlighted the 1969 boating year. Sales of both boats and motors increased over 1968, itself a record-breaking year. A study by the Bureau of Outdoor Recreation projected boating as one of the fastest growing sports in the years ahead. The bureau estimates that in 1969 some 42 million Americans went motor boating, canoeing, or sailing.

Boat Sales. Boat sales continued at high levels with the trend toward larger, more luxurious boats. Shipments ran some 8% above 1968, with dollar values up more than 15%. By the end of 1969 the National Association of Boat and Engine Manufacturers estimated that more than 8.5 million recreational craft were using the nation's waterways.

Houseboats. Despite predictions of a shakeout, houseboat sales posted an astonishing 60% dollar value increase. Cost per boat averages around $10,000. Proliferating all over the United States are houseboat rental agencies where houseboats 30 to 50 feet (9 to 15 meters) in length can be rented for a week or weekend at a cost between $300 and $400, depending on time and size. By the end of 1969 there were some 175 rental agencies, located on almost every important lake, bay, or river.

Outboards. The race for horsepower continued in the outboard motor field. Both Chrysler and Mercury topped 1968's largest outboard, with Chrysler's 135 hp and Mercury's 155 hp limited production models. All manufacturers posted price increases averaging about 8%. Outboard sales by all manufacturers were running some 15% higher than in 1968, with the number of sales actually fewer, but factory values nearly 18% higher. This reflects the demand for large and expensive power packages.

Boat Material. The wooden boat is moving toward obsolescence. In 1969 two of the largest inboard boat manufacturers announced they would no longer offer wooden boats. Fiberglass has long been the dominant material for middle-sized outboard and inboard boats as well as sailboats of all sizes. Only in the smaller fishing boats does aluminum continue in wide use. There was a revival of interest during 1969 in ferrocement for boatbuilding. A framing of iron rods holds wire mesh that is covered with cement. The advantages claimed are strength, durability, and low initial and maintenance costs.

New Waters. The Great Lakes, long devoid of boating, continued to support more recreational boating during the year, thanks to the remarkable restoration of fishing. Coho salmon appeared first in Lake Michigan and since then in most of the other Great Lakes. Hordes of boaters sail forth to fish for them.

Legislation. Laws aimed at curbing water pollution by boaters continued to dominate the legislative scene as most states strengthened their marine police. Access to waters through establishment of new launching points maintained a steady increase during the year, with more than half the states imposing some form of marine tax to finance purchase and construction of new access points.

Sailing. The popularity of sailing and racing continued strong throughout the year as evidenced by a revival of the Canada's Cup, a Great Lakes equivalent of the more famous America's Cup competition. The Canada's Cup was designed to spur international match racing between U. S. and Canadian clubs on the lakes. Although the origins of the cup go back to 1895, it was last contested in 1954 when the Royal Canadian Yacht Club took the prize from the Rochester Yacht Club. In 1969 the Cleveland Yacht Club challenged and various syndicates contested through the summer until the final 3-race series was sailed in September. The Canadian boat, *Manitou,* was the victor.

Oceanic Boating. John Fairfax, a 31-year-old Briton, became the first man to row alone across the Atlantic. He rowed his 24-foot (8-meter) unsinkable rowboat 4,000 miles (6,400 km) from the Canary Islands to Hollywood Beach, Fla., in 180 days, landing July 19.

Tom McClean, a British army survival expert, rowed 2,000 miles (3,200 km), from St. Johns, Nfld., to Blacksod, Ireland, in 72 days, landing July 26.

Mrs. Sharon Sites Adams, 31, an American housewife, sailed a 31-foot ketch alone from Yokohama to San Diego in 74 days, landing July 25.

Capt. Robin Knox-Johnson, an English merchant marine officer, made the first solo voyage around the world without touching land. From Falmouth, England, he sailed his 32-foot ketch for 312 days, returning April 22 to win a prize offered by the London *Sunday Times.*

ZACK TAYLOR
Boats Editor, "Sports Afield"

BOLIVIA

For Bolivia, 1969 proved to be an eventful year. The nation's dynamic president, René Barrientos Ortuño, was killed in a tragic helicopter crash; his constitutional successor was deposed by the military; and the new regime nationalized a number of foreign-owned industrial concerns.

Political Affairs. President Barrientos, a former general who had helped to depose an elected president in 1964 and had won election to the post in 1966, died on April 27, 1969, during the course of one of his numerous flying visits to remote parts of his country. Luis Adolfo Siles Salinas, Barrientos' vice president, assumed the presidency, but Bolivia's military leaders were not pleased with the change and soon were at odds with Siles and his civilian backers. On September 26 a junta led by army chief Alfredo Ovando Candia effected the 185th change of government in the republic's 144-year history and Ovando assumed the presidency.

The professed platform of the new government was "revolutionary." The regime announced that it

BOLIVIAN WOMEN carry signs supporting nationalization of U. S.-owned Gulf Oil holdings in October.

intended to establish diplomatic and trade relations with all countries of the world, whatever their political ideologies, and to defend national resources against the "encroachment of foreign interests." On October 18 the government nationalized the Bolivian Gulf Oil Company, a subsidiary of the Gulf Oil Corporation, and it later seized other foreign-controlled concerns. At year's end there were unofficial reports that Ovando intended to respect the constitution of 1967, which provided for free elections in 1970, but his own public statements on this subject remained evasive.

The guerrilla movement in Bolivia was virtually crushed in September when Ernesto "Che" Guevara's successor, "Inti" Peredo, was shot to death from ambush. Meanwhile, Regis Debray, a French newspaper reporter arrested in 1967 for complicity in Guevara's activities, remained in prison despite continuing pressure upon the government from abroad to grant him his release.

Economic Affairs. The national economy advanced during the year, undeterred by political crises or by the implementation of ambitious and expensive social reforms initiated by Barrientos—one of which was a vigorous program to increase the number of public schools and teachers. The reorganization of the nationalized tin mines that had been carried out in 1968 resulted in increased production and some profit from tin sales, and it was expected that the completion of a new tin refinery in early 1970 would increase such profits. Petroleum sales to foreign consumers increased up to the time of the nationalization of Gulf Oil, after which they dropped sharply. The Gross National Product (GNP) continued to rise at an annual rate of more than 3%, or about 1% more than the rate of population growth.

------- BOLIVIA • Information Highlights -------

Area: 424,162 square miles (1,098,581 sq km).
Population: 4,680,000 (1968 est.).
Chief Cities (1965 census): Sucre, the capital, 58,359; La Paz, 360,329.
Government: *President*—Alfredo Ovando Candia (took office Sept. 26, 1969). *Parliament*—Senate, 27 members (party seating, 1969: Bolivian Revolutionary Front (FRB), 18; Christian Democratic Community (CDC), 8; others, 1); Chamber of Deputies, 102 members (FEB, 82; CDC, 19; others, 1).
Religious Faiths: Roman Catholics, 94% of population.
Education: *Literacy rate* (1964), 37% of population aged 15 and over. *Total school enrollment* (1965)—607,641 (primary, 496,068; secondary, 82,927; teacher-training, 6,605; vocational, 8,615; higher, 13,426).
Finance (1966 est.): *Revenues,* $62,332,000; *expenditures,* $85,513,000; *monetary unit,* peso Boliviano (11.88 pesos equal U. S.$1).
Gross National Product (1968): $803,700,000.
National Income (1968): $687,289,000; *average annual income per person,* $146.
Economic Indexes (1967): *Industrial production* (1965), 139 (1958=100); *agricultural production,* 172 (1952–56=100); *cost of living,* 130 (1963=100).
Manufacturing (metric tons, 1967): Gasoline, 177,000; sugar, 102,000; cement, 65,000.
Crops (metric tons, 1967–68 crop year): Cassava, 170,000; barley, 60,000; dry broad beans, 8,000.
Minerals (metric tons): Tin (1968), 27,721 (ranks 2d among world producers); antimony (exports, 1967), 11,476 (world rank, 3d).
Foreign Trade (1967): *Exports,* $145,000,000 (chief exports, 1967: tin, $90,880,000; wolframite, $7,970,000; silver, $6,670,000; antimony, $6,410,000); *imports,* $151,000,000 (chief imports, 1964: wheat flour, $10,830,000; motor vehicles, $3,810,000). *Chief trading partners* (1967): U. S. (took 41% of exports, supplied 41% of imports); Britain (took 39% of exports, supplied 5% of imports); West Germany (took 5% of exports, supplied 12% of imports).
Transportation: *Roads* (1967), 20,000 miles (32,200 km); *motor vehicles* (1967), 28,000 (automobiles, 21,700); *railways* (1965), 1,734 miles (2,790 km); *national airline,* Lloyd Aéro Boliviano; *principal airport,* La Paz.
Communications: *Telephones* (1968): 29,800; *radios* (1965), 525,000; *newspapers* (1965), 9 (daily circulation, 95,000).

There was marked improvement in the agricultural sector in 1969. Production of meat, coffee, rice, and corn was sufficient not only for domestic consumer needs but for limited export, and the promotion of further gains was a major stated goal of the new government. Under an established program for the "colonization" of eastern Bolivia, involving some financial and technical assistance by the state, Indians were continuing to move from the high plateaus to the lowlands east of the Andean Mountains, and it was hoped that future agricultural gains would result from the settlement of potentially rich farmlands in the Santa Cruz area.

Inter-American Affairs. The nationalization of foreign holdings in Bolivia received only mild support in most other Latin American countries. In the United States the press was generally critical of the moves, and some members of Congress pressed for application of the terms of the "Hickenlooper Amendment," which would stop all technical and other aid funds unless the companies had been properly indemnified within six months. Most of the affected companies were unwilling to accept Bolivia's initial offers to reimburse them out of the future earnings of the nationalized concerns.

Ovando made several overtures to Bolivia's neighbors concerning economic cooperation. He favored a plan of regional development that would allow Bolivia to concentrate on agricultural production.

OLIN E. LEONARD
Ohio State University

BONDS. See STOCKS AND BONDS.

BOOK PUBLISHING

Book sales in the United States remained strong in the face of general market uncertainty during 1969. Some segments of the book industry were worried, especially the publishers of textbooks and scientific materials dependent on government subsidy, which underwent legislative cuts in previous years. However, the overall national retail purchase of books rose about 7% over the $3 billion mark of 1968.

Art books attracted attention once again. Notable publications included a new printing of *The Work of Andrew Wyeth* at a $75 retail price and a magnificent edition of *Alice's Adventures in Wonderland* illustrated by Salvador Dali. The Dali volume carried the record-breaking prices of $375 for the regular edition and $750 for the limited edition.

Paperback titles continued in demand. In recent years the old teacher-prescribed single hardbound textbook has been gradually replaced in many college courses by a lengthy list of paperback books pertinent to the subject of study. This was one factor contributing to the mushrooming paperback book sales of 1969.

International Sales. Overseas sales of U. S. books registered a gain of an estimated 10% over the $200 million reported in 1968. The United States was again well represented in the foreign market through the activities of established agencies and through participation in international book fairs, especially the fair at Frankfurt, West Germany, which was held in the fall.

The United States has followed the lead of Britain in establishing a compatible numbering system, to be completed in 1970, for all of the 250,000 U. S. titles in print.

Bestsellers. A look at 1969's bestseller lists provides an interesting composite of the 10 works of fiction and 10 works of nonfiction which, at some time during the year, were at or near the top. Arranged alphabetically by title, the bestsellers in fiction were: *An Affair of Honor,* by Thornton Wilder; *Airport,* by Arthur Hailey; *The Andromeda Strain,* by Michael Crichton; *The Godfather,* by Mario Puzo; *The Love Machine,* by Jacqueline Susann; *Naked Came the Stranger,* by Penelope Ashe; *Portnoy's Complaint,* by Philip Roth; *The Promise,* by Chaim Potok; *The Salzburg Connection,* by Helen MacInnes; and *A Small Town in Germany,* by John Le Carré. The nonfiction bestsellers were: *The Arms of Krupp,* by William Manchester; *Between Parent and Teenager,* by Haim G. Ginott; *Jennie: The Life of Lady Randolph Churchill,* by Ralph Martin; *The Kingdom And The Power,* by Gay Talese; *The Making of the President 1968,* by Theodore White; *The Money Game,* by "Adam Smith"; *My Life with Jacqueline Kennedy,* by Mary Gallagher; *The 900 Days,* by Harrison E. Salisbury; *The Peter Principle,* by Laurence Peter and Raymond Hull; and *The Selling of the President 1968,* by Joe McGinniss.

Censorship. A unanimous decision of the Supreme Court of the United States ruled for the first time that, constitutionally, it cannot be made a crime to possess obscene film or printed matter in the privacy of one's own home. While there was much talk in many of the nation's state capitols of legislation to parallel the New York State law barring the sale of obscene materials to minors, little action was taken.

A federal circuit court in Atlanta ruled as unconstitutional a section of the law which gives the postmaster general the power to refuse delivery of suspected obscene materials.

Mergers. Mergers were again the order of the year in the book industry. The McGraw-Hill Book Company acquired American Heritage Press. The Macmillan Company absorbed the three leading publishers in the Catholic religious book field: Bruce Publishing Company, P. J. Kenedy & Sons, and Benziger Brothers.

In West Germany a giant merger of German publishing firms took place under the name of Droemer-Knaur.

Among book retailers news was made with the purchase of the Cleveland-based Burrows Brothers, a chain of bookstores, by the Higbee Company, Cleveland's largest department store.

Book Fairs. Crowds of 50,000 to 60,000 attended book fairs in Cleveland, Boston, and Chicago.

JOSEPH A. DUFFY
American Booksellers Association

BOSTON

Many Bostonians voiced their dissatisfaction with the quality of urban life in 1969. While there were no major incidents of racial or other violence during the year, there were many problems moving citizens to protest. Boston is Massachusetts' capital and largest city (1969 est. population: city, 570,000; met. area, 3,600,000).

Issues. The Massachusetts Port Authority met strong resistance in its effort to expand Logan International Airport into the heavily populated East Boston district. Residents of the area picketed to protest new land acquisitions and confronted Authority representatives on the dangers of new flight paths over their neighborhoods.

In the Allston area the attempt of a small number of families to resist an eviction order by the Boston Redevelopment Authority was ended in October. The Redevelopment Authority had been frustrated in its plan to build more than 200 units of low-income housing by eight years of litigation. Work was begun on the project the very day the eviction order was enforced but not before police had to confront demonstrating residents and students.

Several air pollution alerts during August and September dramatized the deterioration of Boston's ecological situation, and Mayor Kevin White was forced to order city installations to burn higher grade, higher priced fuels.

Boston City Hospital, situated on the edge of the Roxbury district and chief medical facility for many of the city's disadvantaged residents, came in for widespread criticism through the year. Clients protested the general level of available services, and medical authorities and staff doctors warned that physical conditions were too crowded to permit good patient care and that equipment was hopelessly inadequate and obsolete.

Continuing efforts to build a modern sports stadium to house the Boston Patriots football team and other major Boston sports teams were unsuccessful. Problems of site acquisition and financing defeated several proposals, and it became increasingly likely that no stadium could be built in time to keep the Patriots from leaving Boston.

Even the renowned Boston Symphony Orchestra fell upon difficulties in 1969. Unable to find a full-time replacement for its retiring conductor, Erich Leinsdorf, the orchestra announced that it would share the services of William Steinberg as music director with the Pittsburgh Symphony.

Schools. Bostonians worried a great deal about their schools in 1969. Four of the city's high schools, including once-famed Boston English High, were threatened with loss of accreditation because of deteriorating buildings and inadequate libraries and equipment. The accreditation problem was one of the largest issues in the November School Committee election.

The opening of the William Trotter Elementary School in September marked a new direction in Boston's attempts to comply with the state's law to combat racial imbalance. The Trotter school was intended to act as a magnet, drawing white students from all parts of the city into the Roxbury ghetto because of the school's educational superiority. White enrollment fell considerably short of the desired 50% however, and black parents protested when school authorities attempted to save seats for white students by holding down black enrollment.

Elections. The November elections for City Council and School Committee were highlighted by the political return of former school committeewoman and narrowly defeated 1967 mayoral candidate Louise Day Hicks. Mrs. Hicks was the largest vote-getter in the election, winning a council seat with more than 76,000 votes. Thomas Atkins, a Negro incumbent, ran second with more than 47,000 votes, despite predictions that he would be defeated. Five other incumbents on the council were reelected. The School Committee ticket was lead by incumbent John J. Kerrigan with 50,000 votes.

BETTY H. ZISK
Boston University

TOMATOES thrive in a greenhouse irrigated by seawater in Sonora, Mexico. Water is desalted by harnessing waste heat from an engine-driven generator.

BOTANY

The 11th International Botanical Congress was held in Seattle, Wash., in August 1969. Three botanical trends were discernible in this Congress: (1) an increasing amount of experimentation involving two or more botanical disciplines and team research; (2) an increasing use of computers for storing, retrieving, and analyzing data; and (3) an increasing involvement of fundamental botanical researchers in problems related to food production, population control, environmental pollution, genetic manipulation, and bioengineering.

Exobotany. Preliminary examinations designed to detect any living or fossil plant material have been made of lunar samples resulting from Apollo 11 explorations. As of September 1969, no evidence of biological material of any type had been detected (*Science,* 165:1211–1238).

Organelles. Histochemical and electron microscopic techniques have enhanced our knowledge of the specialized components, or organelles, of cells in recent years. These discoveries have helped enlarge the important concept of the dissimilarity of cellular components. The most recently described organelle, designated a "cytosome," has been found in several species and is usually pressed against a chloroplast (chlorophyll-containing structure) or pressed between chloroplasts in the leaf cells. S. E. Frederich and E. H. Newcomb (*Science,* 163:1353–1355) indicated that cytosomes are variants of plant microbodies. In green leaf tissue they probably function in the metabolism of glycolate and related compounds (that is, certain plant acids).

Regulation in Plants. Regulation of growth and development in higher plants has been of concern to botanists for nearly 40 years. Recently the following two generalizations have been made: (1) there is a relation between hormones and the genetic control of enzyme formation; and (2) growth and development are regulated by interactions of "inhibitory" and "promoting" hormones. This new information gives an insight into the interactions between plants and the environment that adds to our basic concepts about plant ecology (reported by A. W. Galston and P. J. Davies, *Science,* 163:1288–1297).

Induced enzyme activity has been produced in higher plants in response to changes in such environmental factors as substrates (soil), hormones, light, dark, air, water, and time. In contrast to frequent enzyme *induction* (the activation of enzyme systems already present), only three enzyme systems have been proved to be synthesized *de novo,* that is, to be newly created when required.

Research with higher plants seems to indicate that enzymes undergo a decay, and the important factors controlling such degradation also seem to be significant in the control of metabolic activity. Knowledge about such degradation may prove to be as important as data about enzyme synthesis in helping us to understand higher plant metabolism (reported by P. Filner, J. L. Wray, and J. E. Varner, *Science,* 165:358–367).

Symbiosis. Mycorrhiza are specialized fungi associated with roots of plants. They have been found to be important in the recycling of nutrients —that is, the continuing flow from soil to living organism and back again—in temperate and tropical regions having soils medium to high in organic matter. A. K. Khudairi (*BioScience,* 19:598–599) reported the occurrence of such fungal associations with native and cultivated plants in the Mesopotamian desert region having soils low in organic matter. In desert plants, mycorrhiza are involved in recycling nutrients and possibly moisture. Thus this type of symbiotic association has been an important factor in maintaining the fertility of the valleys of the Tigris and Euphrates rivers for more than 7,000 years.

Thermal Pollution. Since various industries release heated waste waters, heated water is being used in experiments to try to determine the effects of heated soil and heated irrigation water on plant development and growth. Preliminary data have indicated that only certain species—corn (maize), string beans, and others—germinate, grow, and mature faster when subjected to such heated conditions. The use of heated waste water coming from nuclear power plants is being considered. However, various potentially harmful side effects remain to be tested to determine whether these cancel the value of such a venture.

Evolution. The neo-Darwinian, or synthetic, theory of evolution in relation to the differentiation of populations and prevention of gene flow has been evaluated again, this time by P. R. Ehrlich and P. H. Raven (*Science,* 165:1228–1232). The proposition advanced is that the species should not be thought of as the important evolutionary unit, as has been proposed by some biologists. Recent experimentation has shown that it is populations within species that, when subjected to different selective forces, become the differentiating units. Therefore, populations, not species, are the evolutionary units of importance.

DAVID E. FAIRBROTHERS
Rutgers University

BOTSWANA

General elections, the restoration of land formerly held by a South African company, the discovery of an important diamond field, and the appointment of a new ambassador to the United States were among the major events in Botswana in 1969.

General Elections. Voters returned the governing Botswana Democratic party (BDP) to power on October 19 in the first general elections since independence in 1966. The party is led by Oxford-educated Sir Seretse Khama, president of Botswana since 1966. The newly formed Botswana National Front party made some headway in the elections, reducing the BDP assembly lead from 31-3 to 22-13.

During the campaign, left-wing opposition party leader Philip G. Matante urged an aggressive stand against Botswana's powerful white-ruled neighbors, the Republic of South Africa and Rhodesia. President Khama, while opposing apartheid policies, took a moderate position to avoid antagonizing the two neighboring countries.

Land Restoration. In September, President Khama announced that his government had taken control of 338,600 acres (137,000 hectares) in the Francistown area from the South African-owned Tati Company. The company donated one third of the land and the government bought the remainder for a little less than $1.5 million. Control of the area by the South African company had long irritated most Botswana Africans. The land restoration agreement enhanced President Khama's popularity

BOTSWANA

Information Highlights

Area: 231,805 square miles (600,372 sq km).
Population: 543,105 (Jan. 1, 1969 est.).
Chief Cities (1967 est.): Gaberones, the capital, 25,512; Francistown, 39,020; Lobatsi, 22,309.
Government: *President*—Sir Seretse Khama (took office Sept. 30, 1966). *Parliament*—National Assembly, 36 members including 4 members specially elected and the Attorney-General *ex-officio* (party seating, 1969: Democratic Party, 28; People's Party 3); House of Chiefs, 15 members.
Religious Faiths: Roman Catholics, 93% of population.
Education: *Literacy rate* (1967), 20% of population. *Total school enrollment* (1967)—76,087 (primary, 71,577; secondary, 2,255; teacher-training, 310; technical/vocational, 91).
Finance (1968 est.): *Revenues,* $8,100,000; *expenditures,* $20,600,000; *public debt* (1965), $6,220,000; *monetary unit,* rand (.7143 rand equal U.S.$1).
Gross National Product (1967 est.): $58,000,000.
National Income (1966): $49,419,000; average annual income per person, $81.
Manufacturing: Food processing, clothing, soap, tanning.
Crops: Corn, cotton, citrus fruits, grain sorghum, peanuts.
Minerals: Manganese.
Foreign Trade (1967): *Exports,* $9,200,000 (chief exports, 1967: livestock and livestock products, hides and skins, canned meats, beans, sorghum, manganese); *imports,* $20,000,000 (chief imports, 1967: cereals, petroleum products, textiles, sugar). *Chief trading partners* (1966): South Africa; Rhodesia).
Transportation: *Roads* (1968), 5,016 miles (8,071 km); *motor vehicles* (1967), 5,000 (automobiles 2,700); *railways* (1965), 394 miles (634 km); *principal airports,* Gaberones, Maun, Francistown, Ghanzi.
Communications: *Telephones* (1968): 2,543; *radios* (1967), 4,500.

and doubtless won votes for him from among political opponents living in the area.

Diamond Field Discovery. After 13 years of prospecting, De Beers Consolidated Mines, Ltd. confirmed the discovery of a potentially important diamond field near Orapa in northeastern Botswana. De Beers and the Anglo American Corporation are jointly developing the Orapa diamond mine. The capital investment will amount to an estimated $21 million. The Orapa diamond field is believed to be the largest in the world and promises to have a great effect on Botswana's future development.

Ambassador to the United States. Early in 1969 Chief Linchwe II, head of the Bakgatla tribe, was named Botswana's new ambassador to the United States, replacing the late Zachariah K. Matthews.

FRANKLIN PARKER
West Virginia University

BOULEZ, Pierre. See biographical sketch under MUSIC.

BRANDT, Willy. See biographical sketch under GERMANY.

BRAZIL

Developments in Brazil in 1969 were marked by political deterioration and economic improvement. The military, after five years of power, had been unable to bring order and unity to the country. It was succeeding, nevertheless, in curbing inflation and promoting economic progress.

In August, President Artur da Costa e Silva suffered a heart attack, and a military triumvirate temporarily took power. General Emílio Garrastazú Médici became Brazil's new president in October.

Political Repression. In mid-December 1968, "hard line" rightist elements within the military government forced President da Costa e Silva to assume dictatorial powers. By presidential decree, Costa e Silva negated the constitution of 1967, which he had helped to draft. The Congress was dismissed, some state legislatures suspended, and all the communications media were censored.

A 5-man commission was set up to investigate the personal fortunes of prominent figures, who had to prove the legitimacy of recent property acquisitions. The government was authorized to seize "ill-gotten" property.

The president's announcement that a plot to overthrow him had caused termination of civil rights was followed by many arrests. Prominent politicians and public figures, including former presidents Juscelino Kubitschek and Janio Quadros were among those denied political rights for ten years. The loss of political rights meant they could not run for office, vote, or take part in political activities. The number of Brazilians denied these rights continued to mount during 1969. Even the chief justice of the supreme court did not escape the purge.

The press was also a principal target of the government. Prominent newspapers were suppressed, and their publishers were denied politi-

cal rights. The press was effectively restrained from any criticism of the government.

Notwithstanding the worsening of the political situation, most Brazilians continued to acquiesce to military rule. They shared the military's contempt for civilian politicians, and the general atmosphere in the nation appeared to be one of calm.

Terrorist Opposition. However, leftist terrorists mounted a violent, but relatively limited, opposition to the government. The terrorists, some of them Communists but the majority nationalistic and idealistic students, were unified mainly by their dislike of the government. In order to finance their activities and to embarrass the government, the terrorists undertook bank robberies, holdups, bombings, shootings, and kidnappings.

In September, the terrorists scored a dramatic propaganda victory, when they kidnapped U. S. Ambassador C. Burke Elbrick and held him hostage. In return for the ambassador's life, the kidnappers demanded that Brazilian newspapers and radio and TV stations run a lengthy antigovernment manifesto. They also demanded that the government release 15 political prisoners and fly them to sanctuary in Mexico. The government complied with both demands, and the ambassador was released.

Although the price paid for the diplomat's release was a humiliating blow to the government, in the long run the affair reacted against the terrorists. Their action, which violated diplomatic immunity and degraded national dignity, was generally condemned. The government's answer to the kidnapping was to make several hundred arrests and issue new decrees imposing stiff penalties, including capital punishment, for "revolutionary and subversive" activities. It also denied more politicians their political rights.

Presidential Succession. On April 15, President Costa e Silva announced that "the present government will be replaced in 1971 by the government which will be elected in 1970." Despite the opposition of the "hard liners" within the military, who wanted to deal even more stringently with civilian leadership and retain power indefinitely, the President wanted to relinquish power and return to constitutional government. In August it was reported that he planned to announce shortly a revised constitution and the reopening of Congress.

However, this encouraging trend was halted on August 31, when Costa e Silva suffered a stroke that left him partially paralyzed. A military triumvirate (the ministers of the army, navy, and air force) overrode Vice President Pedro Aleixo's rights to the succession and announced its intention of ruling "until the President has recovered."

Due to the slow and uncertain recovery of Costa e Silva, the triumvirate decided to consolidate the leadership in a single military strong man. In October, Gen. Emílio Garrastazú Médici, chief of the National Information Service, or secret police, was drafted into the presidency. Gen. Garrastazú Médici had been linked to the more liberal faction of the armed forces, which had supported Costa e Silva, and he was expected to go along with the political measures that the former president had had in mind. On taking office he pledged to restore democracy before the end of his administration in 1973.

Costa e Silva died on Dec. 17, 1969.

Economic Development. The economic picture in Brazil in 1969 was encouraging. According to a U. S. Department of Commerce analysis of July 14,

---
BRAZIL • Information Highlights

Area: 3,286,470 square miles (8,511,956 sq km).

Population: 88,209,000 (1968 est.).

Chief Cities (1967 census): Brazília, the capital, 348,000; São Paulo, 5,383,000; Rio de Janeiro, 4,031,000; Belo Horizonte, 1,092,000; Recife, 1,056,000.

Government: *President*—Gen. Emílio Garrastazú Médici (took office October 1969); *Vice President*—Adm. Augusto Rademaker Grunewald. *Parliament*—National Congress: Senate, 66 members (party seating, 1969: Aliança Renovadora Nacional (ARENA), 46; Movimento Democrático Brasileiro (MDB), 20); Chamber of Deputies, 409 members (party seating, 1969: ARENA, 269, MDB, 140).

Religious Faiths: Roman Catholic, 93% of population.

Education: *Literacy rate* (1960), 60.7% of population aged 10 and over. *Total school enrollment* (1966)—14,036,677 (primary, 10,695,391; secondary, 2,483,212; teacher-training, 265,626; technical/vocational, 412,339; university/higher, 180,109).

Finance (1968 est.): *Revenues,* $3,066,422,000; *expenditures,* $3,548,511,000; *public debt* (1967), $5,400,000; *monetary unit,* new cruzeiro (3.830 new cruzeiros equal U. S.$1).

Gross National Product (1968 est.): $33,000,000,000.

National Income (1966): $14,944,594,000; est. average annual income per person, $169.

Economic Indexes (1967): *Industrial production,* 117 (1963=100); *agricultural production,* 113 (1963=100); *cost of living,* 576 (1963=100).

Manufacturing (metric tons, 1967): Cement, 6,405,000; residual fuel oil, 5,918,000; gasoline, 4,923,000; sugar, 4,275,-000; steel, 3,696,000.

Crops (metric tons, 1967–68 crop year): cassava, 27,268,000 (ranks 1 among world producers); coffee, 13,979,000 (world rank 1); maize, 12,824,000 (world rank 2); bananas, 5,165,000 (world rank, 1); rice, 6,792,000; sweet potatoes and yams, 2,226,000.

Minerals (metric tons, 1967): Iron ore, 15,163,000 (ranks 7 among world producers); crude petroleum, 6,994,000; lime (1964), 1,438,028; salt, 1,040,000; manganese ore, 597,700; bauxite; 303,000; diamonds exported (1966), 27,-000 carats; natural gas, 875,000,000 cubic meters.

Foreign Trade (1968): Exports, $1,881,000,000 (chief exports, 1967: coffee, $704,730,000; iron ore, $102,780,000; cotton, $92,890,000; cacao, $84,350,000); imports, $2,132,000,000 (chief imports, 1967: nonelectrical machinery, $254,-900,000; grains and grain preparations (1966), $191,660,-000; crude petroleum, $172,410,000). *Chief trading partners* (1967): United States; West Germany; Argentina.

Transportation: *Roads* (1965), 497,902 miles (801,124 km); *motor vehicles* (1967), 2,487,100 (automobiles 1,533,400); *railways* (1965), 20,806 miles (33,477 km); *merchant vessels* (1967), 224 (1,178,000 gross registered tons); *national airline,* Varig, VASP; *principal airports,* Brazília, Rio de Janeiro, São Paulo.

Communications: *Telephones* (1968): 1,472,677; *television stations* (1968), 44; *television sets* (1968), 5,500,000; *radios* (1964), 7,500,000; *newspapers* (1967), 242.

the economy was experiencing its 22d month of steady growth. Brazil was achieving high levels of output and investment; there was a strong demand for goods and services; and the annual growth rate of the gross national product was 7%. Moreover, the government had cut the annual rate of inflation to 24%, and was credited with primary responsibility for stimulating a high level of investment.

The national oil agency, Petrobras, will invest $1 billion in expanded drilling, processing, and handling operations. New fields will be sought and offshore wells drilled.

In 1969, Brazil was the world's fourth-largest sugar producer, surpassed only by the USSR, the United States, and Cuba.

Brazil, which once controlled 75% of the world's coffee market, now has only one third of it. In May, the country held more than 45 million bags of coffee in surplus, in order to stabilize prices. This was 15 million more than the 30 million bags it sells annually. Consequently, Brazil was ordered by the operating agency of the International Coffee Agreement to reduce its stocks to one half of the expected demand in 1972. Thus Brazil has to cut coffee stocks 30 million bags in two years. One of the most severe coffee frosts in years severely af-

BRAZIL'S new president, Emílio Garrastazú Médici (*left*) talks with Vice President Augusto Rademaker.

fected production in the state of Paraná. Export needs were met from the substantial coffee stocks of the Brazilian Coffee Institute.

Brazil has only recently realized the great fishing potential of its territorial waters, which were extended by governmental decree from 6 to 12 miles from the shore. Brazil showed great interest in the success of Peru and Ecuador in extending their sovereignty 200 miles to sea. To encourage the fishing industry, the government has helped to attract foreign private capital and technological aid. Alliance for Progress technical assistance was sought to teach Brazilian fishermen modern techniques. In two years, Brazil has created one of the most rapidly rising fishing industries in the world.

Social Problems. Brazil's impoverished millions did not share in the benefits of the economic boom. The worker's real income was eroded by price increases and a wage policy that held down pay increases, and the government did not seem particularly oriented toward measures of social reform.

The national budget for education dropped from 11% to 7% of total expenditures. Six million of 13 million children 7 to 14 years could not find space in the public schools. With this educational inadequacy the government's claim of 50% adult literacy was no longer valid. Only 181,000 students were enrolled in Brazil's 41 universities and 9 advanced institutes, and in the 1970's Brazil may not be able to produce a sufficient number of engineers and physicians to fill vacancies created by death and retirement.

Many Catholic clergymen agitated in support of socioeconomic reform. Archbishop Helder Câmara of Olinda and Recife called for collaboration with Marxists to better the living conditions of the poor, and some of the priests sounded like Communist militants. Two of them, a Belgian and a German, were deported because of "subversive activities" in fomenting a strike of factory workers in São Paulo. Archbishop Câmara and other members of the Catholic clergy, outspoken in support of church reform, rejected the Pope's edict against contraceptives and insistence on priestly celibacy.

Population Growth. Meanwhile, the population of Brazil, particularly of the cities, was multiplying greatly. The populations of São Paulo and Rio de Janeiro reached over 6 million and 4 million respectively. Belo Horizonte, capital of the state of Minas Gerais, with a population of 1,250,000, passed São Paulo as the fastest-growing large city in the world. Brasília, founded nine years ago as the federal capital city, had a population of 410,000.

Relations with the United States. In May 1969, Brazil imposed a 13 cent tax on every pound of instant coffee exported to the United States, and this seemed to be the end of the long controversy started in 1967. However, the two nations expected to meet in February 1970 to discuss the world coffee situation and seek an accord on Brazil's instant coffee exports. If an agreement is not reached, the United States reserves the right to apply a 30 cent tax on each pound of instant coffee imported from Brazil. The United States argued that Brazil should tax instant coffee in line with taxes placed on raw coffee—about 17 cents—as determined by the International Coffee Agreement. The Brazilian foreign minister, José de Magalhães Pinto, bitterly claimed that the United States was trying to force the Brazilian coffee industry into an unequal competition with the large industrial centers of the world.

President Richard M. Nixon, less worried about relations with the military dictatorship than presidents Kennedy and Johnson, resumed the flow of Alliance for Progress aid, which had been suspended after the December military crackdown on civilian politicians.

Presidential envoy Nelson Rockefeller's fact-finding mission to Latin America, which was marked by violence and anti-U. S. demonstrations in several countries, received a peaceful welcome in Brazil. This circumstance was insured by the government, which placed many of Brazil's militant students and other dissidents under preventive arrest and warned the press to refrain from any unfavorable comments on the Rockefeller visit.

J. LLOYD MECHAM
University of Texas

BREWING INDUSTRY. See ALCOHOLIC BEVERAGES.
BREZHNEV, Leonid Ilyich. See biographical sketch under UNION OF SOVIET SOCIALIST REBUBLICS.

BRIDGES

Two well-known old ferry lines became obsolete in 1969 when new bridges went into operation over coastal waterways on opposite sides of the country —at Narragansett Bay, Rhode Island, and San Diego Bay, California.

Newport Bridge. A high-level span, 2.1 miles (3.4 km) long, opened in June 1969, crossing the East Passage of Narragansett Bay. This $61 million Newport-Jamestown crossing completes the first all-land coastal route between New York and Cape Cod, Mass. The main suspension span is 1,600 feet (488 meters) long, with a vertical clearance of 215 feet (66 meters) at the center. Side spans are 687 feet (209 meters) long.

Supporting the suspension portion are two 15-inch cables, 66 feet apart, to carry four lanes of traffic. Cables consist of 76 shop-fabricated parallel-wire strands, each strand containing 61 wires. Strands were fabricated and cut to exact length in the shop, socketed, and reeled. After delivery to the site, they were anchored at one abutment, carried over the towers, and fixed at the other anchorage. Previously, in the United States, suspension cables were placed by spinning them wire by wire in a slow, expensive operation.

Coronado-San Diego Bridge. The ferry crossing San Diego Bay was replaced in August 1969 by a 2.2-mile (3.4-km), $48 million span connecting San Diego with Coronado. The structure has the longest continuous three-span orthotropic girder in the country, measuring 1,880 feet, or 573 meters. (Orthotropic construction involves an assembly of steel plates welded together.) At its highest point, the deck is 246 feet (75 meters) above the bay, providing a vertical clearance of 200 feet. The bridge carries five traffic lanes.

Lake Pontchartrain Causeway. In May 1969, a parallel, duplicate span was opened only 80 feet (24 meters) away from the world's longest bridge. Like the original, completed in 1956, the newly opened bridge over Lake Pontchartrain in Louisiana is 24 miles (38.4 km) long. The twin structures connect New Orleans with burgeoning St. Tammany Parish to the north. Each bridge carries two lanes of traffic in one direction. Each is built of precast concrete for piles, caps, and decks. Piles and deck sections are also prestressed. Seven crossovers or interconnections serve the pair of 28-foot (8.5-meter) roadways.

Verrazano-Narrows Bridge (Second Level). The six-lane lower deck of the Verrazano-Narrows Bridge in New York City was completed and opened in June 1969. This doubles the traffic capacity of the world's longest suspension span (4,260 feet, or 1,298 meters). The lower deck was designed and built as an integral part of the original structure when it opened in 1964. It was not expected that the lower level would be needed until 1980, but heavier traffic than expected necessitated completion of the second deck 11 years ahead of schedule.

Chester-Bridgeport Bridge. What will be the largest cantilever bridge in the United States and the third largest in the world got under way in 1969 to provide a new crossing of the Delaware River between Chester, Pa., and Bridgeport, N. J. The vehicular project will include a three-span cantilever truss with a 1,644-foot (501-meter) main span and deck truss approach spans. It is scheduled for completion in 1971.

Chesapeake Bay Bridge No. 2. Chesapeake Bay Bridge No. 1, with a 1,600-foot (488-meter) suspension span, built in 1952, is getting a twin, to be completed in 1971. Chesapeake Bay Bridge No. 2, the new, parallel, three-lane vehicular span at Sandy Point, Md., is located 450 feet (137 meters) north of the existing structure. The 4-mile (6 km) crossing will be 186 feet above the channel at the main span.

Girard Point Bridge. A new vehicular bridge over the Schuylkill River at Philadelphia will carry Interstate 95. The Girard Point Bridge, scheduled for completion in 1972, is a double-deck steel truss carrying four traffic lanes on each level. The facility is 1.77 miles (2.8 km) long and rises 135 feet (41 meters) above the river. Five types of high-strength steel totaling 27,834 tons will go into the superstructure. The Girard Point Bridge will cost about $42.5 million.

Japonski Bridge. A cable-stayed steel girder bridge will reach from Sitka to Japonski Island in Alaska. This type of structure has been introduced in Europe, Afric, Australia, and South America,

BETHLEHEM STEEL

but the construction in Alaska will mark its entry into the family of North American bridges.

Nanking-Yangtze River Bridge. In the People's Republic of China, a ferry line crossing the Yangtze River to connect Nanking and Pukow was replaced early in 1969 by a 4.2-mile (6.8-km) double-deck bridge. The lower deck carries a double-track railway; the upper deck accommodates four lanes of vehicular traffic and two sidewalks. This is China's longest bridge, and it is the first span across the lower reaches of the wide, deep, and turbulent Yangtze River. The crossing at Nanking is a junction point in the north-south transportation network of the country. The central portion of the bridge consists of 10 steel cantilever spans supported on masonry piers in the river. Prestressed concrete approach spans on each side make up the rest of the long structure.

Kammon Bridge. Japan is constructing its longest suspension bridge—ninth in length in the world —to link Honshu, the country's main island, with the southern island of Kyushu. Kammon Bridge will cross Shimonoseki Strait with a 2,350-foot (716-

meter) suspension span having a six-lane vehicular deck. On completion in 1973, it is expected to handle 80,000 vehicles daily.

Bosporus Bridge. London consulting engineers have designed a suspension bridge to cross the Bosporus at Istanbul, Turkey, linking Europe and Asia. The 5,118-foot (1,560-meter) bridge will have a main span of 3,523 feet (1,074 meters), making it the fourth largest in the world and the longest in Europe. It will replace 15 car ferries. The new span will have a width of 109 feet (33 meters) to carry six lanes of traffic. The Bosporus Bridge, to be located 4.5 miles (7.2 km) north of the center of the city, is part of a bigger project that includes 12 miles (19 km) of approach highways on both sides of the span, and a 3,117-foot (950-meter) bridge across the waters of the Golden Horn.

Lillebaelt Bridge. Late in 1970, Denmark expects to complete its first suspension bridge—one employing the longest cables ever prefabricated. Lillebaelt (Little Belt) Bridge crosses a sound of the same name, and will connect Funen Island and the Jutland Peninsula. Work on the $30 million, six-

NEWPORT BRIDGE, spanning the East Passage of Rhode Island's Narragansett Bay, incorporates giant, prefabricated cables.

THE NEW YORK TIMES

MOTORCADE of officials opened the lower deck of New York City's Verrazano-Narrows bridge in June 1969.

lane bridge started in 1965. It will replace a two-lane span just south of the new structure. The main span is 1,968 feet (295 meters) long and is flanked by 787-foot (240-meter) side spans. This portion of the superstructure consists of an orthotropic steel box girder. The two 23-inch (58-cm) diameter main cables are 4,920 feet (1,500 meters) long. The two concrete towers are 368 feet high.

Weathering Steel. U. S. steel producers are now marketing a special high-strength, low-alloy steel that will form its own protective coating and can weather naturally without being painted. Initially, lighter shades of rust appear, but this coating changes in time to a deep brown color as the steel ages. The steel develops an adherent protective oxide coating that acts as a barrier to moisture, oxygen, and atmospheric contaminants.

WILLIAM H. QUIRK
"Contractors & Engineers" Magazine

BRITISH COLUMBIA

Voters of British Columbia reelected the Social Credit government of Premier William A. C. Bennett in 1969, surprising many forecasters who had predicted a setback for the party. The economy continued its rapid rate of expansion, with record levels of capital investment and export sales.

Economic Expansion. An $85 million coal mine was to begin shipments in April 1970 from the East Kootenay area to the new Roberts Bank deep-sea terminal near Vancouver. The coal is being exported to Japan under a 15-year contract for up to 55 million tons of coal, valued at nearly $800 million. Near Peachland, production was to start in 1970 at Brenda Mines' $60 million copper-molybdenum property.

Substantial outlays were made by the forest industries in 1969. New pulp mills are under construction at Kitimat and Mackenzie, while a third mill at Skookumchuck reached full production. Large sawmills are being built in eight towns.

In Greater Vancouver, a four-year $32 million railway redevelopment program and a $24 million airlines maintenance base were completed, along with the first phase of the Roberts Bank "superport." Construction began on the $95 million Pacific Centre.

── BRITISH COLUMBIA • Information Highlights ──

Area: 366,255 square miles (948,593 sq km).
Population: 2,056,000 (April 1, 1969 est.).
Chief Cities (June 1, 1968 est.): Victoria, the capital (182,000); Vancouver (955,000); (1966 census): New Westminster (38,013); North Vancouver (26,851).
Government: *Chief Officers*—lt. gov., John Robert Nicholson; premier, William A. C. Bennett (Social Credit Party); prov. secy., Wesley Drewett Black (SC); atty. gen., Leslie Peterson (SC); min. of educ., Donald Brothers (SC); chief justice, Herbert W. Davey. *Legislature*—Legislative Assembly (convened Jan. 23, 1969); 55 members (38 Social Credit, 12 New Democratic Party, 5 Liberal—based on election held Aug. 27, 1969).
Education: *School enrollment* (1968–69)—public elementary and secondary, 477,835 pupils; private schools, 23, 600 pupils; Indian (federal) schools, 4,865 pupils; college and university (fall 1968), 32,960 students. *Public school expenditures* (1967–68)—$160,490,000; median teacher's salary (1966–67) $6,443.
Public Finance (fiscal year 1969–70 est.); *Revenues*, $1,024,-500,000 (general taxes, $200,000,000; natural resources, $131,100,000). *Expenditures*, $1,024,100,000 (education, $325,300,000; health and social welfare, $357,600,000; highways, $143,600,000).
Personal Income (1968 est.): $5,430,000,000; average annual income per person, $2,705.
Public Assistance (fiscal year 1969–70 est.): $99,308,000 (Social Allowances aid to aged, blind and disabled persons, and dependent children, $44,682,000).
Manufacturing (1966): Value added by manufacture, $1,347,-065,000 (wood industries, $354,924,000; paper and allied products, $246,092,000; food and products, $200,999,000; primary metals, $114,314,000).
Agriculture (1968 est.) *Cash farm income,* $207,481,000 (livestock, $133,998,000; crops, $70,320,000; other cash receipts, $3,163,000). *Chief crops* (cash receipts)—Fruits, $31,405,000 (ranks 2d among the provinces); vegetables, $11,595,000 (ranks 3d); wheat, $4,989,000 (ranks 5th); potatoes, $4,879,000 (ranks 7th).
Mining (1968): *Production value,* $405,368,880. *Chief minerals* (short tons)—Copper, 80,497 (ranks 3d by value among the provinces); crude petroleum, 22,151,353 bbl. (ranks 3d); zinc, 149,698 (ranks 3d); lead, 115,814 (ranks 1st); molybdenum, 9,900 (ranks 1st).
Forest Products (1968) Lumber production, 7,846,600,000 board feet; pulp production, 4,289,000 tons; paper production, 1,705,000 tons.
Fisheries (1968): *Total fish landings,* 262,769,000 pounds ($55,694,000). *Leading species*—Salmon, 76,355,000 pounds ($44,887,000). Halibut, 22,507,000 pounds ($5,768,-000).
Transportation: *Roads* (1969), 27,518 miles (44,285 km); *motor vehicles* (1968), 918,612; *railroads* (1969), 4,290 miles of 1st main track (6,903 km).
Communications (1969): *Telephones,* 914,304; *television stations,* 9; *radio stations,* 54.
(All figures given in Canadian dollars equal to U. S. 93¢.)

In northern British Columbia, two additional 227,000-kilowatt generators were installed at the Peace River hydroelectric project. Railway extensions are underway on the Fort St. James-Takla Lake and Fort St. John-Fort Nelson routes.

Provincial Election. In the provincial election held on August 27, the Social Credit party, which has held power since 1952, won 38 of the 55 seats in the Legislative Assembly, a gain of 5 seats from the previous election. The other seats were filled by 12 New Democrats and 5 Liberals.

Legislation. The 1969 session of the legislature approved the Revenue Surplus Appropriations Act. The act invested $130 million of budgetary cash reserve in funds for such purposes as assistance to native Indians, support of amateur athletics, aid to developing countries, encouragement of cultural activities, and protection against major disasters.

The Human Rights Act passed by the legislature guarantees freedom and equality to all citizens.

J. R. MEREDITH
Director, B. C. Bureau of Economics and Statistics

BRITISH COMMONWEALTH. See COMMONWEALTH OF NATIONS.

BROOKS, Angie. See biographical sketch under UNITED NATIONS.

BRUCE, Louis R. See biographical sketch under INDIANS, AMERICAN.

BUDDHISM. See RELIGION—ORIENTAL RELIGIONS.

GUSSET PLATES are installed in sturdy Bell Telephone building, Pittsburgh. As heavy equipment is installed, columns tend to shorten; framework moves into gap at upper end of X-bracing.

BUILDING AND CONSTRUCTION

Governmental activities in the building and construction field in 1969 centered on these major developments:

(1) Establishment of a White House Council for Urban Affairs to coordinate federal programs related to housing and urban development.

(2) Launching of Operation Breakthrough to stimulate industrialization of housing production and to remove institutional barriers to mass production.

(3) Development of another acute shortage of mortgage credit, accompanied by the highest mortgage interest rates in 100 years.

On Jan. 22, 1969, George Romney was sworn in as secretary of housing and urban development. A former president of American Motors Corporation and a former governor of Michigan, Secretary Romney was the most widely known person appointed to the cabinet of the incoming president, Richard M. Nixon.

Council for Urban Affairs. By executive order on January 23, three days after his inauguration, President Nixon created the White House Council for Urban Affairs. Its members are the president, vice president, and seven cabinet members—the attorney general and the secretaries of agriculture; commerce; labor; health, education, and welfare; housing and urban development; and transportation. Nixon named Daniel Patrick Moynihan, assistant to

U.S. PRIVATE HOUSING STARTS
Seasonally Adjusted at Annual Rates

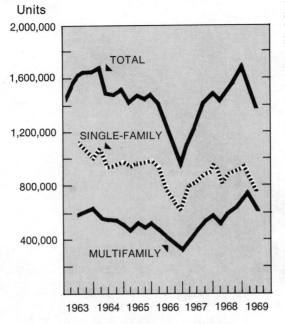

SHELTER COSTS
End of Quarter, Seasonally Adjusted

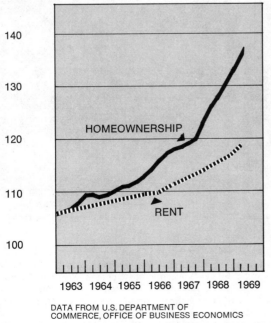

DATA FROM U.S. DEPARTMENT OF
COMMERCE, OFFICE OF BUSINESS ECONOMICS

the president for urban affairs, as executive secretary of the council. The effect of creation of the council was to give to urban problems the same importance in the White House that international affairs has long had through the National Security Council.

Romney, in his early actions, underlined the Nixon administration's emphasis on making existing federal urban programs work effectively rather than on devising new programs.

Through the Council for Urban Affairs, the administration endorsed, with only minor modifications, all the urban programs passed by Congress during the Kennedy and Johnson administrations. These included the model cities program, public housing, and rent supplements and interest-rate subsidies to provide housing for families with low and moderate incomes. The endorsements also included the national goal—established in the Housing and Urban Development Act of 1968—of building 26 million housing units within 10 years, including 6 million subsidized units to replace substandard housing.

Operation Breakthrough. On May 5, Secretary Romney announced the creation of Operation Breakthrough, an ambitious effort at all levels of government to help the private sector break through the constraints that have forced up housing costs and prevented large-scale, assembly-line production of housing. Romney pledged to place all the resources of the U. S. Department of Housing and Urban Development (HUD) behind the Operation Breakthrough effort to stimulate mass production of housing, to develop innovative cost-saving construction systems, and to remove building code and labor restraints that have tended to fractionalize housing production and make it inefficient.

Romney declared: "We are falling behind every day at present rates of production. We need to produce 26 million housing units in the next 10 years. At the rate of the past 10 years, we would wind up with a deficit of more than 11 million homes."

By October 1969, HUD, in response to a request for proposals, had received over 500 proposals for innovative cost-saving housing construction systems. It also had received over 300 proposals from state and local governments to provide sites on which to build prototypes of the mass-production systems selected by HUD as worthy of support.

Funding of Housing Programs. Although faced with the necessity for a sharp cut in federal expenditures to cope with inflation in the national economy, the Nixon administration requested full funding for the rent-supplement and interest-rate subsidy programs. These programs are designed to provide housing within the means of low- and moderate-income families. Late in the year Congress appropriated $90 million of annual contract authority for home ownership interest subsidy payments, $85 million for rental subsidy payments, and $50 million for rent supplements.

On September 23, the Senate passed a housing bill calling for expenditure of $6.3 billion in two years. An innovation was a provision to authorize subsidies to help pay the rents of needy tenants in public housing. Such subsidies in the past have been limited to private housing. On October 23, the House of Representatives passed its $4.9 billion housing bill. Differences between the two versions were to be resolved by a conference committee.

Credit Crunch. When economic activity is high and the supply of money is limited, housing is unable to compete effectively for the limited supply of loan funds available. There is strong demand for installment credit and for loans to finance expansion of industry. So mortgage loan rates rise; the supply of mortgage money dries up. This problem reached crisis proportions in the "credit crunch" of 1966 but then eased somewhat in 1967 and 1968.

The supply of mortgage funds again became gravely inadequate in 1969, and mortgage interest rates climbed to the highest levels since the Civil War. Record highs also were reached in the discounts charged by lenders who were purchasing fixed-interest loans insured by the Federal Housing Administration or guaranteed by the Veterans Administration. The high discounts were imposed even though the regulatory interest-rate ceiling on these loans had risen to a record 7.5%.

FHA reports show that the average interest rate for a conventional mortgage—that is, one not insured by FHA or guaranteed by VA—for new homes ranged between 6.7% and 7.3% during 1968; in January 1969 the average rate was 7.4%, and by August it had jumped to 8.1%.

In August 1969 the average price being paid on FHA new-home mortgages with a 30-year maturity and minimum down payment, and carrying the maximum 7.5% rate, was $93.20 for each $100 of loan amount. This meant that lenders making FHA-insured home loans were requiring, on the average, a yield of 8.36%.

The grim plight of mortgage finance and housing production in a booming economy was forcefully set forth in a report that the Commission on Mortgage Interest Rates made to President Nixon and Congress in August 1969. Late in the year, virtually the only mortgage funds to finance housing construction were being supplied by heavy purchases of FHA and VA mortgages by the Government National Mortgage Association and the Federal National Mortgage Association, the latter in transition from government to private status.

On Sept. 4, 1969, in a move to reduce inflationary pressures, President Nixon ordered that the federal government reduce its own plans for new construction by 75%. (Existing construction projects were to continue.) He urged state and local governments "to follow the example of the federal government by cutting back temporarily on their own construction plans" for undertakings financed jointly by federal and state and local governments. The President noted that the cutback was less than 100%, and said: "This limitation will still permit projects of the highest social priority to be carried forward."

Federal Financing. Federally assisted urban renewal activity in 1969 continued at a high level. Federal funds for this purpose amounted to $947.9 million in 1968 and to $522.4 million in the first half of 1969. By June 1968, total grants made since the beginning of the urban renewal program in 1949 amounted to nearly $8 billion, and 2,585 urban renewal projects and related programs had received federal financial support.

Federally assisted low-rent public housing units completed, under construction, or planned increased from 930,800 at the end of 1968 to 979,535 in June 1969. By June 1969, nearly $86 million in grants had been approved for more than 300 neighborhood facilities; grants of nearly $36 million had gone for 322 urban beautification projects; and nearly $33 million in grants had been made to create 169 urban parks. More than 8,000 direct loans at 3% interest —a $53 million outlay—had been approved by June 1969 for rehabilitation in urban renewal or code enforcement areas. More than 11,000 grants, totaling over $21 million, had been made to low-income homeowners in urban renewal areas to assist them in rehabilitating their houses.

Private groups seeking to build rent supplement projects to house low-income families had received fund reservations for nearly $71 million of annual rent supplement payments. These reservations covered more than 61,000 living units.

Construction Costs. The average cost of building a nonfarm single-family dwelling unit in the United States continued to climb sharply. In 1959 the average was $13,425, but by 1967 it had risen to $17,475, and by June 1969 it was $19,405. The E. H. Boeckh residential construction cost index (1957–59 = 100) stood at 120.2 in 1966, 127.4 in 1967, 136.7 in 1968, and 151.5 in June 1969. The construction cost index of the U. S. Department of Commerce showed a similar increase from 131 in 1968 to 141 in June 1969.

These increases reflect, to some extent, the fact that houses are larger, better constructed, and contain more amenities. Nevertheless, the cost of residential construction in the United States has in recent years risen more sharply than the cost of living generally and more rapidly than family income.

Residential Construction. The number of permanent, nonfarm private housing units started in the United States began to drop in the second quarter of 1969, reflecting high mortgage interest rates and a serious shortage of funds. This signalled the second "credit crunch" since 1966, when housing starts fell to 1,141,500. Housing starts increased only slightly in 1967 to 1,268,400 units. Starts reached 1,483,600 in 1968, and in January 1969 they climbed to a seasonally adjusted rate of 1,845,000. But by June 1969 starts had dropped to a seasonally adjusted figure of 1,441,000. The July rate fell to 1,314,000. Then the rate improved slightly—to 1,369,000 in August and to 1,498,000 in September on a seasonally adjusted basis. But with mortgage credit both scarce and expensive, the expectations were for a further drop in housing activity, perhaps to a level as low as 1,200,000 units by the end of 1969.

Another measure of residential construction volume—the estimated value of construction put in place for private nonfarm housing—showed a similar pattern. This figure dropped from $20.4 billion in 1965 to about $18 billion in 1966 and again in 1967. The revival of residential construction early in 1968 brought the value of new construction put in place to an estimated annual rate of $22.3 billion in May 1968. This figure continued high through 1968 and early 1969, reaching an annual rate of more than $25 billion in March 1969. After that the rate began to decline. In June 1969 a rate was $23.8 billion, and further declines were in prospect.

Nonresidential Construction. All types of new construction other than housing have risen rapidly in the United States in recent years. The value of all new nonhousing construction put in place in 1965 was $51.9 billion, and it jumped to $57.1 billion in 1966, to $58.3 billion in 1967, to $62.3 billion in 1968, and to a seasonally adjusted annual rate of $68.3 billion in June 1969.

Public construction, including highways and streets as well as buildings, showed the most consistent year-to-year increases of any component of construction. It rose from $22.1 billion in 1965 to $24.0 billion in 1966, to $25.6 billion in 1967, to $27.7 billion in 1968, and to $30.6 billion in June 1969.

See also CITIES AND URBAN AFFAIRS.

M. CARTER MCFARLAND
Federal Housing Administration

WIDE WORLD

BULGARIAN OFFICIALS lead a celebration in Sofia honoring the 25th anniversary of the socialist revolution in Bulgaria. Todor Zhivkov, premier and party first secretary, is second from left.

BULGARIA

A tendency toward greater centralization and firmer party control characterized Bulgaria's domestic politics in 1969. In foreign affairs and economic policy, the nation continued to follow the lead of the Soviet Union.

Domestic Politics. Bulgaria's leading party theorist, Cheno Tronkov, condemned "passivity" and "neutralism" in public affairs. In February and March a nationwide campaign was launched by the party to strengthen popular vigilance and mobilize political forces against "bourgeois ideology."

Several ministries were merged. All Politburo members entered the cabinet either as ministers or as deputy prime ministers.

The Czech reform movement and its aftermath kept Bulgaria's leaders on the alert for signs of any internal movement aimed at greater intellectual or artistic freedom. Following the recommendations of the Writers' Conference in May, Georgi Dzhagarov, Writers' Union president, publicly criticized unnamed intellectuals and university professors for supporting "imperialistic ideological subversion." Soon after, Bulgaria's Premier and Party Secretary Todor Zhivkov expressed similar criticisms.

Socialist realism in literature and the arts, long abandoned in Czechoslovakia, Rumania, and Hungary, and discredited even in the Soviet Union, still enjoyed official sponsorship in Bulgaria. "Degenerate influences" by the West in painting, sculpture, theater, and music were frequently condemned by high government and party officials.

Foreign Affairs. Bulgaria seemed to follow Soviet foreign policy more closely than in the past. Moscow's leading role among the Warsaw Pact states and its concept of limited sovereignty continued to receive official Bulgarian support.

In June, at the world conference of Communist leaders in Moscow, Premier Zhivkov denounced nationalism as the root of all deviations from international Communist solidarity. Bulgaria gave unqualified support to Moscow in its conflict with Peking and in its policies toward Bonn and Washington. Improved relations between the USSR and Turkey encouraged the détente between Bulgaria and its traditional enemy and resulted in a new agreement that allowed the remaining Turkish minority in Bulgaria to emigrate. The deterioration of Soviet-Yugoslav relations, caused by the Soviet invasion of Czechoslovakia in August 1968, further complicated the already strained relations between Bulgaria and Yugoslavia. In line with Soviet support of the Arab countries against Israel, Bulgaria agreed to political and economic cooperation with the United Arab Republic, Syria, Algeria, and Kuwait.

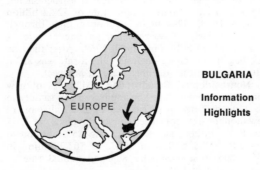

BULGARIA

Information

Highlights

Area: 42,823 square miles (110,912 sq km).
Population: 8,472,000 (Dec. 31, 1969, official est.).
Chief Cities (1966 census): Sofia, the capital, 810,300; Plovdiv, 225,800; Varna, 184,400; Ruse, 131,700.
Government: *President* (Chairman of the Presidium)—Georgi Traikov (took office April 23, 1964); *Premier*—Todor Zhivkov (took office Nov. 19, 1962). *Legislature* (unicameral)—National Assembly, 416 members (party seating, 1969: all members of the Fatherland Front).
Religious Faiths: Majority of believers Eastern Orthodox.
Education: *Literacy rate* (1956), 85% of population aged 15 and over. *Total school enrollment* (1966)—1,857,951 (primary, 1,108,415; secondary, 389,937; teacher-training, 251; technical/vocational, 266,541; university/higher, 92,807).

Finance (1968 est.): *Revenues,* $3,770,085,000; *expenditures,* $3,761,538,000; monetary unit, lev (1.17 leva=U. S.$1).
Net Material Product (1966): $6,213,700,000.
National Income (1968): $7,316,239,000; *average annual income per person,* $874.
Economic Indexes (1968): *Industrial production,* 181 (1963=100); *agricultural production* (1963), 178.3 (1932–38=100); *cost of living* (1966), 100 (1963=100).
Manufacturing (metric tons, 1967): Wheat flour, 1,510,000; crude steel, 1,239,000.
Crops (metric tons, 1967–68 crop year): Wheat, 3,254,000; sugar beets, 2,103,000; maize, 1,919,000; barley, 985,000; grapes, 923,000.
Minerals (metric tons, 1967): Lignite, 26,739,000; lime (1965), 840,000; iron ore, 798,000; crude petroleum, 499,000; coal, 468,000.
Foreign Trade (1967): *Exports,* $1,458,000,000 (chief exports, 1966: foodstuffs, $368,970,000; machinery and equipment, $332,500,000; nonedible organic raw materials, $144,200,000); *imports,* $1,572,000,000 (chief imports, 1966: machinery and equipment, $696,300,000; fuels, minerals, and metals, $376,100,000). *Chief trading partners* (1967): USSR (took 53% of exports, supplied 50% of imports); East Germany (took 8% of exports, supplied 8% of imports); Czechoslovakia (took 6% of exports, supplied 6% of imports).
Transportation: *Roads* (1964), 17,740 miles (28,550 km); *motor vehicles* (1966), 26,900 (automobiles 10,400); *railways* (1965), 2,383 miles (3,834 km); *merchant vessels* (1967), 77 (494,000 gross registered tons); *national airline,* TABSO; *principal airport,* Sofia.
Communications: *Telephones* (1968): 338,446; *television stations* (1967), 39; *television sets* (1967), 420,000; *radios* (1967). 2,218,000; *newspapers* (1967), 12 (daily circulation, 1,545,000).

In June the World Tourism Conference was held in Sofia. Delegations from 65 countries participated. The announced goal was establishment of an international tourism organization, to be part of the United Nations but otherwise autonomous.

On July 10, a new Bulgarian-Hungarian treaty of friendship, cooperation, and mutual assistance was signed in Sofia by Premier Zhivkov and Hungarian Party Secretary János Kádár.

Economy. The new reforms announced in December 1965, and confirmed by the 9th Plenum of the party's Central Committee in July 1968, had provided for liberalization of economic controls and planning. Individual initiative and private enterprises were to be given more encouragement, and economic rationality was to be emphasized. However, no significant changes along these lines took place in 1969.

G. Filipov, first vice chairman of the state planning commission, publicly advocated an extension, rather than a restriction, of central planning. In March, Stanko Todorov, Politburo member and Zhivkov's probable successor, reasserted that control over the national economy was one of the party's most important tasks.

Nevertheless, the economy seemed to grow. Completion of an atomic power plant on the Danube was scheduled for October. The first fiberglass car was manufactured, and a production goal of 400 was set for 1970. Production of heavy trucks also started.

Foreign Trade. Economic ties with the Soviet Union remained as close as ever. Russia accounted for more than 50% of Bulgaria's foreign trade, the highest percentage for any European Communist country. In May six agreements were signed in Moscow. They provided for further coordination of economic plans during the period 1970–75. If implemented, the agreements would increase Bulgaria's dependence on the USSR through a long-range integration of their economies.

As a reward for its compliance, Bulgaria was to receive a credit of $556 million to pay for the Soviet machines needed for its 1971–75 five-year plan. Furthermore, the Soviet Union committed itself during the same period to deliver 1.6 million metric tons of steel as well as 10 million metric tons of petroleum, 3 million cubic meters of natural gas, and 4 billion kilowatt hours of electricity. A similar agreement was concluded between Bulgaria and East Germany.

Trade with non-Communist countries also increased. Bulgaria's two leading western trading partners were Italy and West Germany. As a result of Premier Zhivkov's visit to India, a $56 million trade agreement, covering 1969 alone, was signed in January. Zhivkov's visit to Austria in April led to the signing of an agreement for scientific and technological cooperation.

The industrial and commercial companies that Bulgaria had formed jointly with Japan, Italy, France, and some other countries seemed to be effective. The Foreign Trade Bank increased operations and established contacts with most of the major international money markets and stock exchanges.

On September 22, the 25th International Fair opened in Sofia. About 48 countries and over 500 Western firms participated.

JAN KARSKI
Georgetown University

BURGER, Warren E. See SUPREME COURT.

BURMA

U Nu, the Buddhist former premier ousted by Gen. Ne Win in 1962, managed to get out of Burma in 1969 and launch a campaign from abroad to reestablish representative government in his country.

Politics. Gen. Ne Win, the Burmese premier, established a national Unity Advisory Board late in 1968. The board included Nu and 32 former civilian political leaders. It seemed to suggest the possibility of an early liberalization of Burma's politics, but Nu used his membership on the board to reiterate his claim that he was still the premier of Burma. He proposed the transfer of power to a caretaker government, headed by himself, in preparation for the election of Ne Win as the country's "legal" leader. Opposition developed among the military to this plan and to Nu's "religious speeches" around the country. In April, the former premier claimed

BURMA

Information Highlights

Area: 261,789 square miles (678,033 sq km).
Population: 26,389,000 (1968 est.).
Chief Cities (1964 est.): Rangoon, the capital, 1,530,434; Mandalay, 322,000; Moulmein, 190,000; Bassein (1953), 77,905; Henzada (1953), 61,972.
Government: *Premier*—Gen. Ne Win (took office March 2, 1962). *Parliament*—dissolved on March 3, 1962.
Religious Faiths: Buddhists, 85% of population; Roman Catholics, 1%; others, 14%.
Education: *Literacy rate* (1969), over 60% of population. *Total school enrollment* (1964)—2,417,248 (primary, 1,887,-490; secondary, 503,259; teacher-training, 3,138; technical/vocational, 2,846; university/higher, 20,515).
Finance (1969 est.): *Revenues*, $287,384,000; *expenditures*, $329,212,000; *monetary unit*, Kyat (4.772 kyats equal U. S.$1).
Gross National Product (1967): $1,799,245,000.
National Income (1967): $1,526,194,000; *average annual income per person*, $57.
Economic Indexes (1967): *Agricultural production*, 100 (1963=100); *cost of living* (1964), 102 (1963=100).
Manufacturing (metric tons, 1967): Gasoline, 171,000; cement, 132,000; sugar, 72,000.
Crops (metric tons, 1967–68 crop year): Rice, 7,714,000; peanuts (1966), 278,000; sesame, 83,300; tobacco, 41,300; chick-peas, 41,000; millet and sorghum, 26,000.
Minerals (metric tons, 1967): Crude petroleum, 587,000; salt, 134,000; lead concentrates, 30,000; coal, 15,000; zinc (1966), 11,000; tin concentrates (1966), 376; nickel ore (1966), 350; antimony ore (1966), 200.
Foreign Trade (1967): *Exports*, $123,500,000 (chief exports: rice, $65,800,000; teak, $26,000,000; oilcake, $6,800,000); *imports*, $141,600,000 (chief imports, 1965: woven cotton fabrics, $29,541,000; milk and cream, $14,008,000). *Chief trading partners* (1967): Japan (took 7% of exports, supplied 22% of imports); Communist China (took 8% of exports, supplied 11% of imports); Britain (took 6% of exports, supplied 9% of imports).
Transportation: *Roads* (1969), 16,000 miles (26,000 km); *motor vehicles* (1967), 55,200 (automobiles 27,900); *railways* (1965), 1,925 miles (3,097 km); *merchant vessels* (1967). 8 (45,000 gross registered tons); *national airline*, Union of Burma Airways; *principal airport*, Rangoon.
Communications: *Telephones* (1968): 20,783; *radios* (1966), 367,000; *newspapers* (1966), 27 (daily circulation, 231,000).

he was ill and was therefore allowed to go to India.

In June a majority of the National Unity Advisory Board recommended a return to parliamentary democracy, but it made no reference to Nu's caretaker-government plan. Nu then embarked on a worldwide tour to publicize his campaign to reestablish democracy in Burma. Ne Win rejected the idea of a government headed by Nu, but he neither endorsed nor rejected the board's recommendations. The immediate effect of Nu's efforts may have been to delay liberalization of Burma's politics.

Insurgencies. As many as 20,000 insurgents remained in the field in 1969. The most important faction was a new Communist rebel group in the northeast, headed by Naw Seng, a Chinese-trained Kachin. This group was periodically reinforced by Chinese Communist forces who crossed the Sino-Burmese border and clashed with Burmese troops. The new Communist insurrection in the northeast, however, failed to bolster the badly battered old main wing of Burmese Communists in the south.

The Minority Groups. Kachins not associated with Naw Seng, as well as Karens, Shans, and a smaller number of Chins, also continued to oppose the government by force. They were probably encouraged by U Nu's attempt to return to power. Nu predicted in late 1969 that the minorities would support his bid to unseat Ne Win, and he threatened to resort to force to end military rule.

Foreign Affairs. On eight occasions between January and August, Burmese troops clashed with Chinese forces in major border battles in which 133 Burmese soldiers were killed. These encounters, combined with China's support of the approximately 4,000 minority-group rebels in the northeast, posed the most serious external threat to Burma since the resumption of independence in 1948. Chinese civilians were reported to be administering areas "liberated" by the rebels near the border.

Burmese diplomacy was aimed at encountering this threat and the challenge posed by U Nu's activities abroad. Indian Prime Minister Indira Gandhi and Gen. Ne Win met in March to discuss China's support of rebel elements within their territories. Burma also complained to Britain, the United States, and Thailand about Nu's antigovernment activities on their soil.

Economy. More than 500,000 tons of rice were shipped abroad in 1969, a sizable increase over the previous year but far short of the 2 million tons exported in 1962. Some imports had been cut as much as 40% earlier in the year, but imports were still 50% greater in value than exports. Burma's budget for the fiscal year that began in October 1969 estimated revenues at about $344.5 million and expenditures at about $368 million.

Tourist restrictions were eased in 1969 to permit the ordinary visitor to stay in the country for 72 instead of 24 hours.

RICHARD BUTWELL
The American University

BURNS, Arthur F. See biographical sketch under ECONOMY OF THE U.S.

BURUNDI

Developments in Burundi in 1969 were marked by suspicion, ethnic division, and nationalism. The hopeful but ambivalent character of the country's situation was shown in the circumstances surround-

BURUNDI

Information Highlights

Area: 10,747 square miles (27,834 sq km).
Population: 3,406,000 (1968 est.).
Chief Cities (1965 census): Bujumbura, the capital, 71,000.
Government: *President and Prime Minister*—Michel Micombero (took office Nov. 28, 1966). *Parliament*—dissolved in October 1965.
Religious Faiths: Roman Catholics, 55% of population; others, 45%.
Education: *Total school enrollment* (1966)—163,620 (primary, 152,962; secondary, 6,661; teacher-training, 1,948; technical/vocational, 1,781; university/higher, 268.
Finance (1966 est.): *Revenues*, $15,500,000; *expenditures*, $18,600,000; *monetary unit*, franc (87.50 francs equal U.S.$1).
Gross National Product (1966): $150,000,000.
Economic Indexes (1967): *Cost of living*, 108 (1965=100).
Crops (metric tons, 1967–68 crop year): Coffee, 17,900.
Foreign Trade (1967): *Exports*, $16,891,000 (chief exports, 1967: coffee, $14,400,000; cotton, $1,291,000); *imports*, $19,360,000 (chief imports, 1967: food products, lubricants, metal products). *Chief trading partner* (1966): United States (took 85% of exports, supplied 20% of imports).
Transportation: *Roads* (1967), 3,700 miles (5,953 km); *motor vehicles* (1967), 4,100 (automobiles, 2,900); *principal airport,* Bujumbura.
Communications: *Telephones* (1968): 3,000.

ing an alleged attempt at a coup d'etat in September and the banishment of Belgium's ambassador in October.

Conflict with Belgium. The majority of Burundians apparently took the developments in stride, aware that those arrested in connection with the alleged September plot against the government were Hutu, rather than members of the dominant Tutsi ethnic group. Foreign Minister Lazare Ntawurishira insisted that a foreign power had been involved in the attempted coup, even suggesting that the same unnamed country was also planning to topple the Congo (Kinshasa) government. When, soon after this disclosure, Burundi declared Belgian Ambassador Edouard Henniquiau persona non grata, it became clear which foreign power the government had in mind.

Belgium reacted with barely concealed anger. Testy statements in the Belgian press referred to Burundian ingratitude for Belgian aid, and the Belgian government refused to accept the communication outlining the charges against Henniquiau. The Burundian government soon concluded it had made a mistake. It declared an investigation had cleared Henniquiau of any connection with the plot, apologized, and said the ambassador would be welcomed back.

Foreign Relations. Relations with neighboring Rwanda and Congo (Kinshasa), troubled in the past by angry exchanges over refugees and border problems, continued to improve. The three countries engaged in cordial regular conferences.

EDOUARD BUSTIN
Boston University

BUSINESS. See ECONOMY OF THE U.S.
CABINET, U.S. For a listing and biographies of cabinet officials, see UNITED STATES.
CALDERA RODRIQUEZ, Rafael. See biographical sketch under VENEZUELA.

DEMONSTRATORS urging the creation of a "People's Park" on an empty plot in Berkeley, Calif., are entertained by a blonde who goes topless for the occasion. National Guardsmen patrol disputed park beyond fence (*right*).

UPI

CALIFORNIA

A shift in legislative control, tax relief, a large budget surplus, continued campus disorders, oil-fouled beaches, and severe weather made headlines in California in 1969.

Legislation. The California Legislature operated with a Republican majority in both houses in 1969 for the first time since the Democrats took control in 1958. Long-time Assembly Majority Leader Jesse Unruh and 13-year Senate President Pro Tem Hugh M. Burns, both Democrats, were replaced by Republicans Robert T. Monagan and Howard May. Major tax reform proposals occupied the Legislature most of the year. Major legislation included revision of the state's anti-pornography laws and an overhaul of its divorce law.

Budget and Taxes. The size of the state budget continued to take a back seat in 1969 to controversy over tax relief, with argument over the budget surplus and its use drawing much public attention. California operated without a state budget for several days in July as the Legislature and Gov. Ronald Reagan feuded over demands for tax reform and increased public school aid.

The governor's proposed budget was increased by legislative action only to be trimmed to $6.3 billion

—the largest budget in the state's history—by the governor's item veto. Demands for increased education funds and controversy over tax rebate proposals were heightened by the announcement of a budget surplus of $537 million at the end of the fiscal year in June. Governor Reagan's plan for a 10% income tax rebate in 1970, an election year, provoked charges of political maneuvering from opposition Democrats, but, in a last minute decision, the Legislature agreed to the proposal.

Campus Unrest. Much attention was again focused on disruption on California's college and university campuses in 1969. At the Los Angeles campus of the University of California (UCLA), two members of the Black Panther party were shot and killed in gunplay between rival black groups. Charles E. Young was inaugurated as chancellor in an atmosphere of caution. The Regents refused to allow credit for a course taught by black philosophy professor Angela Davis, an avowed Communist. The ruling was reversed under court order, but, as the year ended, further litigation was expected. On the Berkeley campus, widespread violence broke out in May over use of the so-called "People's Park" owned by the university.

At San Francisco State College, Acting President S. I. Hayakawa was made president in July. Spo-

---
CALIFORNIA • Information Highlights

Area: 158,693 square miles (411,015 sq km).
Population: 19,741,000 (Jan. 1, 1969 est.)
Chief Cities (1968 est.): Sacramento, the capital, 270,000; Los Angeles, 2,810,000; San Francisco, 748,000; San Diego, 680,000; San Jose, 400,000; Long Beach, 380,000; Oakland, 375,000; Fresno, 163,000.
Government: *Chief Officers*—governor, Ronald Reagan (Republican); lt. gov., Ed Reinecke (R); secy. of state, Frank N. Jorden (R); atty. gen., Thomac C. Lynch (Democrat); treas., Ivy Baker Priest; supt. of pub. instr., Max Rafferty; chief justice, Roger J. Traynor. *Legislature*—Senate, 40 members (21 Republicans, 19 Democrats); Assembly, 80 members (41 R, 39 D).
Education: *School enrollment* (1968–69)—public elementary, 2,865,000 pupils (103,300 teachers); public secondary, 1,-681,000 pupils (73,700 teachers); nonpublic schools, 429,-000 pupils (18,040 teachers); college and university (fall 1967), 974,426 students. *Public school expenditures* (1967–68)—$4,008,000,000 ($815 per pupil); average teacher's salary, $9,450.
Public Finance (fiscal year 1969): *Revenues*, $5,453,795,262 (4% sales tax, $1,652,979,449; motor fuel tax, $625,666,-694; federal funds, $2,728,334). *Expenditures*, $5,172,-748,394 (education, $2,137,705,564; health, welfare, and safety, $1,120,989,209; highways, $716,138,338). *State debt*, $4,767,716,000 (June 30, 1969).
Personal Income (1968): $76,581,000,000; average annual income per person, $3,968.
Public Assistance (fiscal year 1966): $1,024,015,726 to 1,085,-

324 recipients (aged, $402,767,740; dependent children, $369,347,458).
Labor Force (employed persons, annual average, 1968); *Agricultural*, 295,000; *nonagricultural* (wage and salary earners), 7,430,000 (22.6% manufacturing, 21.8% trade, 18% government). *Unemployed persons* (annual average, 1968)—366,000.
Manufacturing (1967): Value added by manufacture, $23,123,-000,000 (1966, transportation equipment, $3,213,139,000; nonelectrical machinery, $1,626,148,000; electrical machinery, $2,543,904,000; fabricated metals, $1,355,355,000).
Agriculture (1967): Cash farm income, $3,989,500,000 (livestock, $1,547,457,000; crops, $2,331,754,000; govt. payments, $110,289,000). *Chief crops* (tons)—Hay, 7,579,000 (ranks 2d among the states); sugar beets, 4,080,000 (ranks 1st); citrus fruits, 1,639,700.
Mining (1966): Production value, $1,708,000,000 (ranks 3d among the states). *Chief minerals* (tons)—Crude petroleum, 345,295,000 barrels; sand and gravel, 120,692,000; stone, 43,051,000; gypsum, 1,207,000.
Fisheries (1968): *Commercial catch*, 445,307,370 pounds ($53,-695,507). *Leading species*—Yellowfin tuna, 153,026,509 pounds ($23,812,769); skipjack tuna, 59,234,641 pounds ($7,770,420).
Transportation: *Roads* (1968), 158,159 miles (254,478 km); *motor vehicles* (1969), 12,996,644; *railroads* (1968), 14,497 track miles (23,326 km); *airports* (1969), 34.
Communications (1966): *Telephones* (1968), 11,723,800; *television stations*, 36; *radio stations*, 344; *newspapers*, 128.

145

radic clashes, mainly nonviolent, continued on the troubled campus. Other disturbances occurred at San Jose State College, Stanford University, and the Claremont Colleges.

Oil Spill. Californians' preoccupation with air pollution, especially the control of smog, was overshadowed in 1969 by concern over oil pollution of the ocean and beaches. In late January a leading offshore oil well in the Santa Barbara Channel released crude oil into hundreds of square miles of the Pacific Ocean. The oil endangered ocean life and contaminated about 40 miles of beaches along the Santa Barbara coast. Temporary restraining orders on new oil well development were issued, but litigation and political maneuvering between conservationists, coastal residents, oil interests, and the U. S. government, which is the owner of the Tidelands, promised a lengthy controversy. (See also POLLUTION; ZOOLOGY.)

Rain Storms. Torrential rains fell on California during the first three months of 1969 in what has been called the worst series of storms in a century. Rain-soaked hills collapsed, more than 100 persons lost their lives, hundreds of homes were destroyed by mud slides, and property damage was in the millions of dollars. Late in the year Californians were fearfully awaiting the rainy season when saturated hillsides could still break loose in heavy rains.

Narcotics. Operation Intercept, a federally imposed clampdown on narcotics traffic across the Mexico-U. S. border, disrupted normal traffic and commerce between Mexico and California in September and October. Long delays were experienced by motorists at border stations while federal agents searched for narcotics. In California's border areas, the $100 million spent annually by Mexicans was severely threatened. State officials expressed agreement with the aim of the program to dry up illegal sources of narcotics, but pressure from both U. S. and Mexican interests brought relocation of the drive on October 10.

Judicial Decisions. California's courts redefined two state laws in 1969. The "claim and delivery" law, which allowed law enforcement officers to routinely enter homes and seize articles on which owners were behind on installment payments, was declared unconstitutional since "the home is a place sanctified by the Constitution." The state Supreme Court modified the kidnap law, ruling that a robber who forces his victim to "move" cannot be punished for kidnapping if the movement is incidental to the crime and does not substantially increase the risk of harm. In the Caryl Chessman case of 1951, the court had held the words "kidnaps or carries away" to mean moving one any distance for any purpose.

Special Election. The state's 27th Congressional District voters, in an April 29 special election, sent 30-year-old Barry Goldwater, Jr., son of the Arizona senator and 1964 Republican presidential candidate, to the U. S. House of Representatives.

(See also LOS ANGELES; SAN FRANCISCO.)

GERALD RIGBY
California State Polytechnic College, Pomona

CAMBODIA

The resumption of relations between Cambodia and the United States was one of several indications in 1969 that Prince Norodom Sihanouk, the country's long-time ruler, was preparing safeguards against a Communist victory in South Vietnam.

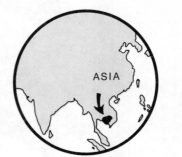

CAMBODIA

Information Highlights

Area: 69,898 square miles (181,035 sq km).
Population: 6,557,000 (1968 est.).
Chief Cities (1962 census): Phnom Penh, the capital, 403,500; Battambang, 38,846; Kompong Cham, 28,534.
Government: *Queen*—Sisowath Kossamak (acceded 1960); *Chief of State*—Prince Norodom Sihanouk (took office June 20, 1960). *President of the Council of Ministers*—Lon Nol (elected Aug. 13, 1969). *Parliament*—National Assembly, 82 members (party seating, 1969: Popular Socialist Community or Sangkum, 82 seats); Council of the Kingdom, 28 members (party seating, 1969: Sangkum, 28 seats).
Religious Faiths: Buddhists, 90% of population.
Education: *Literacy rate* (1962), 41% of population aged 15 and over. *Total school enrollment* (1965)—887,937 (primary, 794,478; secondary, 79,034; teacher-training, 945; technical/vocational, 4,015 university/higher, 9,465).
Finance (1968 budget est.): $196,000,000; monetary unit, riel (35 riels equal U. S.$1).
Gross National Product (1966): $875,000,000.
National Income (1966): $757,142,800; average annual income per person, $115.
Economic Indexes (1967): *cost of living*, 105 (1963=100).
Manufacturing (metric tons, 1967): Tobacco, 3,511,000; cotton yarn, 1,200; sawn wood (1966), 150,000 cubic meters.
Crops (metric tons, 1967–68 crop year): Rice, 2,457,000; corn, 150,000; bananas, 193,000; natural rubber, 51,400; dry beans, 29,000.
Minerals (metric tons, 1967): Phosphate rock (1964), 150,000; salt, 45,000; gold, 4,000 troy ounces.
Foreign Trade (1967): Exports, $83,100,000 (chief exports, 1967: rice, $35,747,900; natural rubber, $20,448,000; textile yarn and fabrics, 1966 , $14,880,000; corn, 1966 , $8,150,000); imports, $96,100,000 (chief imports, 1967: nonelectrical machinery, $12,289,000; textile yarn and fabrics, $8,619,000; iron and steel, $8,089,000). *Chief trading partners* (1967): France (took 10% of exports, supplied 31% of imports); Britain; United States.
Transportation: *Roads* (1967), 3,200 miles (5,150 km); *motor vehicles* (1967), 32,300 (automobiles, 21,700); *railways* (1965), 291 miles (468 km); *national airline*, Royal Air Cambodge; *principal airports*, Phom Penh, Siem Reap, Sihanoukville.
Communications: *Telephones* (1968): 5,900; *television stations* (1968), 2; *television sets* (1968), 7,000; *radios* (1968), 1,000,000; *newspapers* (1966), 18.

Security Conditions. Khmer Rouge (Cambodian Communist) insurgents may have increased their warring bands from 5 or 6 to 50 or 60 in 1969. Bolstered by the defection of three leftist deputies of the National Assembly, the Communist rebels held a road intersection only 20 miles (32 km) north of Phnom Penh, the capital, for 12 hours at midyear. In the first six months of 1969, 300 Cambodian soldiers died fighting the guerrillas, according to the government. Indications were that about the same number died in the second half of the year.

Prince Sihanouk blamed the insurrection on "certain Communist neighbors." He also charged that there were 40,000 North Vietnamese and Vietcong soldiers on Cambodian soil. Communist China, he said, refused to use its influence to end Communist insurrectionary activity.

Politics. Penn Nouth, a close confidant of Sihanouk's, stepped down as premier in mid-1969, ostensibly for reasons of health. Worsening security and economic conditions probably were contributory. Sihanouk himself said the country faced a major financial crisis, occasioned by drought, the alleged American defoliation of 37,000 acres (15,000 hectares) of Cambodian territory, increased smuggling, and deteriorating security conditions.

Sihanouk reorganized the government on July 31, transferring his duties as chief of state to a special council. He remained president of the Sangkum party. He hinted at the possibility of a pro-U. S. military dictatorship if the National Assembly did not quickly name a new premier. In August it unanimously elected Gen. Lon Nol, former deputy premier and defense minister. The change represented a shift to the right, economically and internationally. Premier Lon Nol announced he would discontinue the government's nationalization policies.

Foreign Affairs. United States-Cambodian diplomatic relations were resumed in June, ending a diplomatic break caused by Sihanouk in 1965. U. S. foreign aid to Cambodia, which had contributed $300 million to the country's economic development, had been halted by Sihanouk in 1963. Sihanouk hinted that Cambodia might reaccept U. S. aid.

Irritants persisted, chiefly the hot pursuit of Communist troops into Cambodia by both U. S. and South Vietnamese forces. Typical of Cambodia's reaction was its September 17 "energetic protest" to the newly reestablished U. S. Embassy against "deliberate attacks" by U. S. and South Vietnamese forces on Cambodian villages in August.

The complications of Cambodian diplomacy were reflected in Sihanouk's recognition of the "Provisional Revolutionary Government" (Vietcong) in Vietnam, in June and his rupture of relations with West Germany the same month. The Bonn government had protested as "unfriendly" Cambodia's recognition of East Germany in May.

Economy. Cambodia's very slowly growing economy experienced new problems, partly explaining its modest drift to a more pro-Western posture. The country's gross national product was estimated at $650 million in 1969, an increase of less than 12% since U. S. aid was discontinued in 1963. A severe drought affected the 1969 rice harvest.

Sihanouk's government showed interest in 1969 in foreign aid and investment. Cambodia rejoined the Asian Development Bank and applied for membership in the International Monetary Fund. French aid and technicians remained most numerous and probably most important among sources of foreign aid. The French built a new refinery at Sihanoukville. Soviet and Chinese aid remained important, and Cambodia was seeking foreign private investment.

RICHARD BUTWELL
The American University

CAMEROON

The highlight of 1969 in Cameroon was the annual congress of the country's single political party, the National Cameroonian Union (UNC), in March. The occasion marked the 10th anniversary of the founding of the Cameroonian Union, the UNC's predecessor.

Internal Politics. During the course of the congress at Garoua, the UNC elaborated the main lines of its future policies. In international affairs, the party promised to support the principles of nonalignment and to base its work for the future of Africa on "realistic and effective regional groupings." The party's political bureau, also elected in March, will be headed by Federal President Ahmadou Ahidjo.

The country's three main trade unions merged into the single Union of Cameroonian Workers. In August, the first major incursion by *Union des Populations du Cameroun* (UPC) rebels since 1967 occurred at Djoun, near the Gabon-Congo (Brazzaville) border.

Economic Developments. Government reports described the state of the economy in optimistic terms. However, aluminum production continued to decline and coffee production was expected to be above the quota allotted by international marketing agreements. Cocoa production was up 7% from 1968.

The general condition of the economy was strong enough to permit the government in April to raise salaries in the private sector by 4%. Of significance to the economy in general, and to West Cameroon in particular, was the completion and inauguration of two east-west links: the Douala-Tiko road and the Mbanga-Kumba railway spur.

Foreign Aid. During 1969, Cameroon received $51.3 million in long-term loans, from the World Bank, the International Development Association, the United States, the European Development Fund, and West Germany. Projects funded included extension of the Trans-Cameroon railway, new roads and additional infrastructure, new schools, agricultural development, and the textile industry. A notable private investment was announced in March by Guiness Beer, which will build a $4.1 million brewery in Douala.

VICTOR T. LE VINE
University of Ghana

CAMEROON

Information Highlights

Area: 183,568 square miles (475,442 sq km).
Population: 5,562,000 (1968 est.).
Chief Cities (1965 census): Yaounde, the capital, 101,000; Douala, 200,000; N'kongsamba, 60,000.
Government: *President*—Ahmadou Ahidjo (took office for 2d 5-year term April 1965); *Vice President*—John N. Foncha (same term). *Legislature* (unicameral)—Federal National Assembly, 50 members (party seating, 1969: all members of the Union Nationale Camerounaise, or UNC).
Religious Faiths: Animists, 48% of population; Roman Catholics, 20%; Muslims, 14%; Protestants, 6%.
Education: *Literacy rate* (1969), 15% of population. *Total school enrollment* (1965)—768,301 (primary, 713,557; secondary, 40,853; teacher-training, 2,045; technical/vocational, 10,279; university/higher, 1,567).
Finance (1967 est.): *Revenues,* $128,000,000; *expenditures,* $121,400,000; *monetary unit,* CFA franc (246.85 francs equal U. S.$1).
Gross National Product (1966): $717,000,000.
Economic Indexes (1967): *Cost of living,* 114 (1963=100).
Manufacturing (metric tons, 1968): Aluminum, 45,918.
Crops (metric tons, 1967–68 crop year): Sweet potatoes and yams, 280,000; maize, 217,000; peanuts (1966), 130,000; bananas, 110,000; cacao beans, 94,000; coffee, 66,000; dry beans, 20,000; cotton (lint), 17,000.
Minerals (1966): Gold, 900 troy ounces.
Foreign Trade (1968): *Exports,* $189,000,000 (chief exports, 1967: cacao, $44,958,000; coffee, $43,887,000; aluminum, $20,460,000; cotton, $7,148,000); *Imports,* $188,000,000 (chief imports, 1966: textile yarn and fabrics, $16,558,000; nonelectrical machinery, $15,846,000; road motor vehicles, $10,747,000; cotton (lint), $10,747,000). *Chief trading partners* (1967): France (took 38% of exports, supplied 58% of imports); Netherlands (took 21% of exports, supplied 3% of imports); West Germany (took 13% of exports, supplied 8% of imports).
Transportation: *Roads* (1967), 20,000 miles (32,186 km); *motor vehicles* (1967), 48,200 (automobiles 23,700); *railways* (1965), 330 miles (531 km).
Communications: *Telephones* (1968), 4,800; *newspapers* (1964), 3 (daily circulation, 18,000).

CANADA

Disillusionment and frustration seemed to be the dominant mood of many Canadians during 1969. In many respects the nation appeared to be marking time as a general feeling of uncertainty prevailed about such issues as national unity, inflation, pollution, and violence in the streets. Public attention across Canada was focused on Montreal for much of the year, as terrorist bombings, demonstrations, rioting, the French language question, a crime wave, and a police strike rocked that city. (See also MONTREAL.)

Campus unrest in Canada, previously a pale reflection of the U. S. experience, occurred in several Canadian cities but most notably in Montreal, where demonstrators occupied the computer center of Sir George Williams University for two weeks to protest alleged discrimination against West Indian students. On February 11 the protesters systematically wrecked and burned the center, causing damage estimated at $2 million. The arrest of 97 rioters occasioned an incident in Trinidad two weeks later, when students of the University of the West Indies forcibly prevented a campus tour by Canadian Governor General Michener during a state visit.

A development related to unrest in Montreal and involving the Company of Young Canadians (Canada's domestic "Peace Corps") held nationwide implications as well as national interest. Charges by a senior civic official of Montreal that the CYC contained ex-terrorists and that its Montreal projects involved subversion and participation in riots led to an investigation of the Company in the autumn by a parliamentary committee. The committee found the Company's financial procedures chaotic and its operations dominated by radicals, and it recommended the imposition of a trusteeship and closer financial controls. The latter recommendation was

implemented in December by the appointment of a financial administrator, but no decision was reached by the government on the ultimate fate of the controversial organization.

POLITICAL AFFAIRS

The parliamentary session that resumed on Jan. 14, 1969, after the Christmas recess, was marked by personal clashes between Prime Minister Trudeau and the opposition over such varied issues as Canada's role in Commonwealth affairs, diplomatic recognition of the Vatican, Canada's reduced commitments to the North Atlantic Treaty Organization (NATO), the government's neutrality toward the Nigerian civil war, and lack of government action to combat inflation. Nonetheless, the regular legislative work progressed smoothly toward the anticipated summer recess.

In late June, however, the opposition mounted a filibuster against the government bill to reform House of Commons procedures and especially against those clauses giving the government strong powers to curtail debate. When the date for prorogation passed and the government threatened to use cloture to stop the filibuster, acrimonious exchanges ensued, with the prime minister calling opposition members "nobodies" and Conservative member George Hees retorting that Trudeau was a "self-styled little tin god on wheels." The use of cloture ended the session on July 25 amid opposition shouts of "King Trudeau" and "Sieg heil!"

The second session of the current Parliament opened on October 23 and gave evidence of being a much tamer affair. Both government and opposition appeared to have regained their composure.

The poor press relations that afflicted Trudeau's predecessors overtook him as well in 1969. From the very beginning of the year, Trudeau presented an image different from that of the "swinger" manufactured for him in the election of 1968. He "lost his cool" in London during the January meeting of

TROOPS (*opposite page*) guard public building during Montreal police strike on October 7. Young couple (*right*) looting through a smashed store window were among scores of pillagers.

UPI

Commonwealth prime ministers when reporters dogged his steps in public and showed an insatiable curiosity about his personal life. In May a nationwide poll by the Toronto *Daily Star* reported that only 18% of the people were "very satisfied" with Trudeau as prime minister, compared with 28% in 1968.

Cabinet Changes. Paul Hellyer, who had been minister of defense from 1963 until he was transferred to the department of transport in 1968, resigned from the Trudeau cabinet effective April 30, 1969. At the end of January he had submitted the report of his task force on housing, which had toured Canada from coast to coast in the autumn of 1968 to investigate the housing crisis. The report proposed several remedial steps by the federal government to meet the critical shortage of residential accommodation. But when no action was taken by the cabinet, Hellyer resigned.

Minister Without Portfolio James Richardson was immediately made responsible for housing, but on May 5 this responsibility was transferred to Minister Without Portfolio Robert Andras, and Richardson became minister of supply succeeding Donald Jamieson, who moved to Transport. Andras' previous responsibility for Indian Affairs was left unassigned. On October 15 two new ministers without portfolio were appointed, Robert D. G. Stanbury and Herbert E. Gray. Gray became the first Jew to serve in a federal cabinet.

Federal-Provincial Relations. The three federal-provincial constitutional conferences held during 1969 seemed cursed by the law of diminishing returns. Before the prime minister and provincial premiers actually convened for the first conference, beginning February 10, the premiers of the three prairie provinces met and agreed to present a united front. These three premiers, along with the premiers

---
CANADA • Information Highlights

Area: 3,851,809 square miles (9,976,197 sq km).
Population: 20,772,000 (1968 est.).
Chief Cities (1966 census): Ottawa, the capital, 290,741; Montreal, 1,222,255; Toronto, 664,584; Vancouver, 410,375.
Government: *Governor General*—Roland Michener (took office April 17, 1967); *Prime Minister*—Pierre Elliott Trudeau (took office April 20, 1968). *Parliament*—Senate, 102 members (appointed for life); House of Commons, 264 members (party seating: Liberal, 153; Progressive Conservative, 72; New Democratic, 22; Ralliement Créditiste, 14; independent, 2; vacancy, 1).
Religious Faiths: Roman Catholic, 45.7% of population; United Church of Canada, 20.1%; Anglican, 13.2%; Presbyterian, 4.5%; Lutheran, 3.6%.
Education: *Total school enrollment* (1966)—5,815,442 (primary, 3,768,875; secondary, 1,521,646; technical/vocational, 1,-521,646; university/higher, 372,275).
Finance (1967 est.): *Revenues,* $9,909,580,000; *expenditures,* $10,148,210,000; *public debt,* $28,281,130,000; *monetary unit,* Canadian dollar (1.0728 dollars equal U. S.$1).
Gross National Product (1968): $63,851,600,000.
National Income (1968): $47,073,070,000; *average annual income per person,* $2,266.
Economic Indexes (1967): *Industrial production* (1968), 137 (1963=100); *agricultural production,* 97 (1963=100); *cost of living,* 112 (1963=100).
Manufacturing (metric tons, 1967): Gasoline, 16,700,000; crude steel, 8,794,000; newsprint, 7,582,000; cement,

7,277,000; wheat flour, 1,722,000; meat, 1,372,000; aluminum, 873,900.
Crops (metric tons, 1967–68 crop year): Wheat, 16,137,000 (ranks 3d among world producers); oats, 4,691,000 (world rank, 3d); barley, 5,414,000; potatoes, 2,035,000.
Minerals (metric tons, 1967): Gypsum (1966), 5,982,000 (ranks 2d among world producers); zinc, 1,132,800 (world rank, 1st); titanium slag (1966), 524,773 (world rank, 3d); lead, 308,400 (world rank, 1st); nickel, 225,569 (world rank, 1st); gold (1966), 3,273,905 troy ounces.
Foreign Trade (1968): *Exports,* $12,556,000,000 (chief exports, 1967: manufactured goods, $2,583,140,000; newsprint, $890,470,000; wheat, $691,550,000; wood, $481,260,000); *imports,* $11,431,000,000 (chief imports, 1967: transport equipment, $2,157,060,000; nonelectrical machinery, $2,-023,670,000; electrical machinery, $623,690). *Chief trading partners* (1967): United States (took 64% of exports, supplied 72% of imports); Britain (took 10% of exports, supplied 6% of imports).
Transportation: *Roads* (1966), 440,385 miles (708,712 km); *motor vehicles* (1967), 7,276,900 (automobiles, 5,771,900); *railways* (1966), 43,033.4 miles (69,205 km); *merchant vessels* (1966), 65 (266,000 gross registered tons); *principal airports,* Montreal, Toronto, Vancouver.
Communications: *Telephones* (1968): 8,385,476; *television stations* (1968), 324; *television sets* (1968), 5,900,000; *radios* (1967), 12,050,000; *newspapers* (1966), 113.

149

PRIME MINISTER Trudeau (*right*) and Quebec Premier Bertrand chat at a Federal-Provincial Conference.

THE CANADIAN MINISTRY
(In order of precedence in the Privy Council)

Pierre Elliott Trudeau, Prime Minister
Paul Martin, Government Leader in the Senate
Mitchell Sharp, Secretary of State for External Affairs
George J. McIlraith, Solicitor General
Arthur Laing, Minister of Public Works
Allan J. MacEachen, Minister of Manpower and Immigration
Charles M. Drury, President of the Treasury Board
Edgar J. Benson, Minister of Finance
Léo Cadieux, Minister of National Defense
Jean-Luc Pépin, Minister of Industry, Trade, and Commerce
Jean Marchand, Minister of Regional Economic Expansion
John J. Greene, Minister of Energy, Mines, and Resources
Jean-Pierre Côté, Minister of National Revenue
John N. Turner, Minister of Justice and Attorney General
Jean Chrétien, Minister of Indian Affairs and Northern Development
Bryce S. Mackasey, Minister of Labour
Donald S. Macdonald, President of the Privy Council
John C. Munro, Minister of National Health and Welfare
Gérard Pelletier, Secretary of State
Jack Davis, Minister of Fisheries and Forestry
Horace A. Olson, Minister of Agriculture
Jean-Eudes Dubé, Minister of Veterans Affairs
Ronald Basford, Minister of Consumer Affairs
Donald C. Jamieson, Minister of Transport
Eric W. Kierans, Minister of Communications
Robert K. Andras, Minister without Portfolio
James A. Richardson, Minister of Supply and Services
Otto E. Lang, Minister without Portfolio
Herbert E. Gray, Minister without Portfolio
Robert D. G. Stanbury, Minister without Portfolio

of Ontario and Nova Scotia, asserted in the conference that economic issues were of greater immediate importance than the language question that had dominated discussion at the 1968 conference.

Both Ontario and Quebec were critical of federal invasion of provincial jurisdictions and denounced the federal medicare scheme as the most recent example. The three-day February conference ended with agreement to establish a number of committees to examine various aspects of provincial relations.

A second constitutional conference was held in June, this time behind closed doors. Although agreement was reached that the provinces should receive limited access to the field of indirect taxes, there was a general impression that less progress had been made than hoped for. Premier Ross Thatcher of Saskatchewan warned publicly that the problems of regional economic disparity were not receiving adequate attention at these conferences.

At the third conference, held in early December, the ground gained in June appeared to be lost as even the subjects of equality of access to tax sources and regional economic disparity were referred to committees. Ending with no agreement on any issue, the conference was variously described by the provincial premiers as "little more than a teach-in," "just a rehash of positions," and "an exercise in futility." The first conference in 1970—the fifth in all—was scheduled for February.

Legislation. In March the government's bill to reorganize five departments and to create three crown corporations was passed into law. The post office department became the department of communications, the department of rural development was renamed the department of regional economic expansion, the fisheries and forestry departments were merged, and the departments of industry and of trade and commerce were united, while a new department of supply and services was created. By the same statute the royal Canadian mint, the medical research council, and the science council of Canada became crown corporations.

The bill to amend the criminal code, introduced in December 1967 by Trudeau when he was minister of justice, was approved in May. It resulted in the liberalization of the laws on abortion and homo-sexuality and in the introduction of compulsory breath tests for suspected drunken drivers.

The Official Languages Act, enacted in July and based on the recommendations of the Bilingualism and Biculturalism Commission, established French and English as official languages in federal government operations in all provinces and authorized the establishment of bilingual federal facilities in districts in which 10% of the population speaks the second official language.

Elections. A federal by-election was held on April 8 for the British Columbia riding (electoral district) of Comox-Alberni, in which a court ruling had voided the results of the general election of June 1968 because 12 ballots had been cast illegally. Tom Barnett, New Democratic party (NDP) candidate in both elections, won the by-election, reversing the result of the general election in which he had run second.

In June, E. R. ("Ed") Schreyer, NDP member for Selkirk, resigned his Commons seat to lead the Manitoba NDP to victory at the end of that month in a general provincial election, which saw the incumbent Progressive Conservatives narrowly defeated.

Schreyer's resignation left the standing in the federal House as follows: Liberal, 154; Progressive Conservative, 72; New Democrats, 22; Ralliement Créditiste, 14; independent, 1; and 1 vacancy. On December 3, however, Perry Ryan, Liberal member for one of the Toronto constituencies, left the party to sit as an independent because of what he called government inaction on major national problems.

In a provincial general election for British Columbia held in August, the ruling Social Credit government of W. A. C. Bennett was returned with an increased majority—39 of the 55 seats.

FOREIGN RELATIONS

The major concern of foreign relations during 1969 seemed to be the government's anxiety to protect Canadian sovereignty by implementing policies more than faintly reminiscent of the isolationism of the 1930's.

NATO. At a press conference on April 3, Prime Minister Trudeau announced his new defense policy of "phased reduction" of Canada's military participation in NATO and greater emphasis on the protection of Canadian territory and North America. This policy statement was welcomed by the New Democratic party, which felt that complete withdrawal from NATO was even more desirable, but it was criticized by the Progressive Conservatives as a retreat from responsibilities that would lessen the free world's respect for Canada. Trudeau answered his critics by calling the phasing out of land and air commitments in Europe a redeployment of Canada's limited resources rather than a withdrawal.

The reaction of Canada's NATO allies was guardedly diplomatic at first, although the West German government stated publicly that Canada's decision was "not opportune," and Britain expressed fear that the decision might have a "snowballing" effect. Although it was common knowledge that the policy was opposed within Trudeau's cabinet, no minister resigned; but Liberal Sen. John B. Aird did quit as chairman of the influential Canadian NATO Parliamentary Association because of his strong disagreement with the decision.

U. S. Relations. During Prime Minister Trudeau's visit of March 24–25 to President Nixon—the first visit since they were both elected in 1968—Trudeau refused to comment on the proposed U. S. anti–ballistic missile (ABM) system. Two months later he announced that his government would make no formal representation to the United States on the subject but that unofficially Canada hoped that neither the Soviets nor the Americans would build ABM systems.

In a lighter vein, Trudeau tried in a public address during his Washington visit to explain Canada's attitude toward its southern neighbor. Living next to the United States, he commented, was "in some ways like sleeping with an elephant. No matter how friendly or even-tempered is the beast ... one is affected by every twitch and grunt."

A further commentary on Canadian–U. S. relations came in a report of the Commons committee on defense and external affairs in June, which recommended that Canada remain in the North American Air Defense Command (NORAD) but that in all future defense agreements with the United States the defense of Canada should be the responsibility of Canada's armed forces insofar as possible.

Of political concern to the United States was the announcement in April by External Affairs Minister Mitchell Sharp that Canada would begin talks in May with Red China aimed at diplomatic recognition of the People's Republic. The Nationalist Chinese government on Taiwan stated its opposition to Canada's explicit acceptance of the "one-China" policy, to which Sharp replied that Canada still hoped to maintain *de facto* recognition of Taiwan if the talks with the Chinese Communists succeeded.

Canada's preoccupation with its sovereignty in relation to the United States was further revealed by Canadian interest in the voyage of the giant U. S. tanker S. S. *Manhattan* through the Northwest Passage to Point Barrow, Alaska, in September. Public concern that such trips might endanger Canada's claims in the Arctic region or cause pollution of Canadian waters was rejected by Sharp, who insisted that no threat to Canadian sovereignty was involved. (See also SHIPPING.)

Other Developments. In the first week of January 1969, Prime Minister Trudeau attended the Commonwealth Prime Ministers' Conference in London, where his attempt to steer a middle course on the issue of Rhodesian independence led to a charge by the New Democratic party that Canada's contribution in London had been "one big zero."

From London Trudeau proceeded to Rome, where he opened negotiations with the Vatican for diplomatic recognition. Replying to criticism that recognition of the Vatican could prove divisive within Canada, Trudeau stated that the question of exchanging ambassadors would have to be put to the Canadian people before a decision was made.

PIERRE ELLIOTT TRUDEAU, in the role of politician (*below*), greets small admirer. Also one of world's most eligible bachelors, he squires actress Jennie Hales during a social evening in London (*right*).

CANADIAN CONSULATE

LONDON DAILY EXPRESS

BOMB BLAST in Montreal Stock Exchange on February 13 slightly injured 27 persons. The bomber, admittedly a member of the Quebec Liberation Front, received a sentence of 124 concurrent life terms in prison.

UPI

Nevertheless, such an exchange was completed in October when Canada's first ambassador, John E. Robbins, a Protestant and a noted Canadian educator, was accredited to the Vatican.

Franco-Canadian relations, strained since de Gaulle's espousal of French Canadian nationalism in 1967, were expected to improve with his retirement from the presidency of France in April. But after several months of apparent quiet on this diplomatic front, yet another incident occurred when Jean de Lipkowski, secretary to the French minister of foreign affairs, rejected an invitation to visit Ottawa during his eight-day tour of Quebec in October. Prime Minister Trudeau accused Lipkowski of being both impolite and impertinent, but the latter stated that his actions had been explicitly intended to show that there was no change on France's part from the Gaullist policy of friendship for Quebec.

THE CANADIAN ECONOMY

The national economy continued its upward surge through most of 1969, but the rate of inflation and the weakness of some sectors of the stock markets in the closing months were causes of concern. The gross national product was expected to rise by about 9% during 1969, while the cost of living index by November had advanced to 127.4 (1961 = 100), a 4.5% increase over the same date in 1968.

Major Economic Developments. The continuing rising inflationary spiral was responsible for further restrictions on spending programs at all levels of government but especially at the federal level, where shared-cost programs were largely suspended and a 10% reduction in the civil service rolls instituted.

Canada's exports reached $1.3 billion in the first nine months of 1969, and imports stood at $1.2 billion. This advantageous balance of trade was due in large measure to a 16% increase in Canadian exports to the United States during the first nine months of 1969. Housing starts in the first nine months of 1969 were 161,273, compared with 136,246 for the same period in 1968.

Canada's labor force rose from 7,995,000 in

October 1968 to 8,142,000 in October 1969. Unemployment in October stood at 3.9% of the labor force compared with 3.6% at the same time in 1968. However, a higher Quebec unemployment rate of 5.7% reflected the flight of capital from that province as a result of unstable political conditions and the terrorist activities of small separatist groups.

A milestone in Canada's economic history was the submission to Parliament by Finance Minister Edgar Benson of a White Paper on taxation. Based on the 1967 report of a royal commission, the White Paper proposed a capital gains tax and a variable income tax rate that would fall most heavily on the middle income bracket.

While the general public was skeptical of the practicability of some of the proposals, and industry had a mixed reaction to the reduction of certain existing incentives, the provincial governments were frankly opposed to those features of the plan that would further diminish their already inadequate tax resources.

Finance. The government's spending estimates for 1969–70 presented to Parliament at the beginning of February 1969 called for a record $13.6 billion, a 9.5% increase over the previous fiscal year. The major areas of increased costs were health and welfare, old age pensions, and foreign aid. Before the budget was presented in June, Finance Minister Benson, in a White Paper, forecast a strong upsurge in economic growth during 1969. On the strength of this expectation he announced that the budget deficit for 1968–69 was then estimated at $566 million, or $109 million less than his estimate of October 1968. At the same time the White Paper expressed the government's concern over rising costs and prices.

Introducing his 1969–70 budget on June 3, Benson explained its purpose: "We really mean business in fighting inflation." The budget produced no major tax changes except a user's charge at airports, but the 3% surtax on personal and corporate income was extended to Dec. 31, 1970. As a further anti-inflationary measure, Kennedy Round tariff reductions originally intended for implementation by 1972 were made effective immediately. Revenues were expected to reach $12 billion by March 31, 1970, the end of the fiscal year, and to produce a $250 million surplus, the first since 1956–57. Opposition parties and provincial leaders complained that this budget was not a cure for inflation and that it ignored the problems of the west and the cities.

Further anti-inflationary measures were announced by Prime Minister Trudeau in August when a freeze was imposed on federal government spending and plans were revealed for a 10% reduction in the civil service force. At the end of October, Treasury Board President Charles M. Drury spelled out details of the latter plan—19,000 civil service jobs had already been eliminated and a further 5,000 employees would be laid off in the coming months. Conservative leader Robert Stanfield denounced these layoffs as a "pretty crude instrument" for fighting inflation.

Manufacturing. Most elements of Canadian manufacturing showed increased productivity during 1969. Indexes (1961 = 100) for August 1969, compared with the same month in 1968, showed that total industrial production had risen 4.6 points to 164.2. Manufacturing was up 7.7 to 166.4, with durable goods up 12.4 to 152.7 for the same period.

Agriculture. Canadian agricultural production maintained a high level during 1969, but the national wheat surplus reached crisis proportions that affected both the agricultural industry and politics. The large carry-over of wheat from 1968 caused an estimated 14% reduction in acreage for 1969, but reduced sales left farmers so short of cash that Saskatchewan farmers resorted to bartering grain for goods and services in some instances. In March, Trade Minister Jean-Luc Pépin announced that Canada would sell wheat below the internationally agreed minimum price and that final payments for the 1968 crop would be $1.81 per bushel, the lowest price in more than a decade. By the end of March a record 1,024,000,000 bushels were still in storage,

60% on farms. At the beginning of the summer of 1969 farmers in the western provinces were promised cash advances for their grain.

During Trudeau's visit to the West in July, when he faced personal confrontations and tractor demonstrations by angry farmers, the prime minister admitted that an emergency existed but blamed it on international competition resulting from a world glut of wheat. Statistics released in August showed Canadian wheat sales at their lowest point since 1962–63, and further price cuts were made in addition to reductions of up to 11.5 cents per bushel instituted in July.

As of August 1, the wheat carry-over amounted to 849.8 million bushels, and the 1969 crop was estimated at 684.8 million bushels, an increase of 17% over the same date in 1968 and an increase of 19% in supplies available for export after domestic needs were met. The sale of 128 million bushels to the USSR, announced on December 16, was expected to reduce the surplus by one eighth.

Mining. Mining production generally showed no marked change from the patterns of 1968, but unlike most sectors of the economy, mining was expected to show a considerable decrease in capital investment in 1969. Reduced exports of minerals and metals as a result of strikes caused an estimated loss of $100 million in the third quarter of the year.

Transportation. The announcement by Transport Minister Paul Hellyer at the end of March that the government would build a new international airport for Montreal at St.-Jérôme, north of the city, sparked another sharp exchange between the federal and Quebec governments. Premier Jean Jacques Bertrand criticized the proposed location as unacceptable because it would benefit the city of Ottawa—Quebec's choice of site would be south of Montreal—and Claude Gosselin, provincial minister of lands and forests, charged, "Once again, your government has done everything to push Quebecers into the arms of separatists."

Labor troubles that threatened the Canadian

Computer cards cascaded as students wrecked the computer center at Sir George Williams University.

UPI

National Railways were settled during the winter by agreements that gave 22,000 shop workers and 20,000 trainmen a 13% pay raise over two years. Air Canada, however, had to suspend its services from mid-April to mid-May when 6,300 mechanics and maintenance workers struck. A settlement was reached when the union accepted a 16% wage hike spread over 26 months instead of the 24% raise over two years that it had demanded.

Communications. In January 1969 the province of Quebec signed an agreement with the government of France to study development of a joint satellite project. When the question of Quebec's constitutional power to make such an agreement was raised in the federal House of Commons, Quebec's acting premier, Paul Dozois, denied that the provincial government's representative had such authority. Nevertheless, External Affairs Minister Mitchell Sharp announced that in the future the federal government expected to be informed in advance of any such proposed agreements. The issue was reopened in October during the controversial visit of French aide Jean de Lipkowski, whose statement that the agreement was for joint construction and operation of a satellite caused the Quebec government to reiterate that the agreement involved a feasibility study only.

In June the Canadian government announced an agreement with the United States for the cooperative launching of another satellite in late 1971. Telesat Canada, a joint government-private enterprise company, will supervise the construction and operation of the satellite to be put in orbit by the United States.

(See also TRUDEAU.)

JOHN S. MOIR
University of Toronto

CANADIAN LITERATURE

Canadian writing in 1969 produced many works on public affairs, biographies, autobiographies, histories, books of poetry, and fiction, but there was little scholarship and almost no humor and children's literature.

Public Affairs. Some books on public affairs were light and sensational, but much less soul-searching and searing than usual. Even so, *Canada in Bed* by Michelle Bedard (a pseudonym) did point out that Puritan guilt has won for manly Canadians the coronet for being the world's worst lovers. Three journalists took exceedingly interesting topics for four middling books. Ken Conoley filled *Airlines, Airports and You* with jets, insurance, lore, and safety, but the best material is his history of early airlines. Fred McClement's exposé of airline safety, *It Doesn't Matter Where You Sit,* will, it is hoped, bring about improvements; and his *The Flaming Forests* relates the history and hazards of forest fires and extolls the bush pilots. Robert Reford's *Canada and Three Crises,* dealing with international crises over the Chinese Offshore Islands, Suez, and Cuba, sees a genuine continuity in Canadian foreign policy.

The most serious and most pessimistic prognosis of North American social, economic, and cultural ills is *Technology and Empire* by theologian-scholar George M. Grant, who sees Puritan individualism and liberalism as eventually bringing about an ugly position. More fun, but also thought provoking, is the one-sentence idea elaborated into a thesis by Laurence J. Peter and Raymond Hull, in *The Peter Principle,* or the science of incompetence and "heirarchiology."

Biography and Autobiography. That biography often produces good social history as a by-product is evident from several books. Floyd S. Chalmer's *A Gentleman of the Press* is about stingy John Bayne Maclean's creating "Canada's national magazine." Helen Evans Reid's research problems become the real story in *All Silent, All Damned,* which gives the social background to, and clears the name of, Isaac Barr, who led a group of English colonists to the Canadian West and then abandoned them by disappearing. Collecting some 200 letters of John A. Macdonald (1815–1891), the first prime minister of Canada, and his family, J. K. Johnson reveals social background and history in *Affectionately Yours. Never Sleep Three in a Bed* by Max Braithewaite tells as much of Nokomis as it does of growing up there; and *M.E.: A Portrait of Emily Carr,* by Edythe Hembroff-Schleicher, describes the art milieu as well as the West Coast artist. Farley Mowat's *The Boat Who Wouldn't Float* is egotistical fun, but is not nearly ribald as the dust jacket promises. But the book causing the most comment in the press this year was the wild, seemingly irresponsible, close-to-vulgar *Girl in a Gilded Cage,* Judy LaMarsh's view of herself and her colleagues in parliament.

History. History too brought forth needed background, but not all of it was well written. From a writer of John Swettenham's caliber, the patriotic and nationalistic *Canada and the First World War* is a disappointing book. Also disappointing is Victor Hoar's biased but illuminating account of *The Mackenzie-Papineau Battalion,* the Canadians in the Spanish civil war. Edna Staebler's *Sauerkraut and Enterprise,* though somewhat dull at times, is an affectionate and folksy look at the Ontario Mennonites and their Kitchener market, complete with receipts. Not dull at all is the meticulous scholarship of Gustave Lanctot in *Montreal Under Maisonneuve, 1642–1665.*

Poetry. Poets as usual were strong. Some interesting new people included Charles Barry, obviously a Cohen acolyte, with *You Used to Like My Pies;* Sandra Kilber with didactic but good poems on children and family in *All There Is of Love;* and Elizabeth Gourlay with *Motions, Dreams and Aberrations,* in an exact and pristine language. Rona Murray's second volume, *The Power of the Dog,* again illustrates her ability to bring together inconsequential happenings and to give them meaning, tension, and passion. Elizabeth Brewster's pleasantly old-fashioned and unpretentious *Passage of Summer* is her first volume since 1957. Irving Layton's 22d or 23d volume, *The Whole Bloody Bird,* although repetitious in theme and technique, is a journal of observations, aphorisms, and poems. George Bowering's varied and polished responses to the province of Alberta and its people, *Rocky Mountain Foot,* may possibly be the most important book of poetry this year. Others might say the same of *I've Tasted My Blood* by rough and tough but secretly romantic Milton Acorn. Still others would commend the magic of Gwendolyn MacEwen, surely at her very best in *The Shadow-maker.*

Fiction. In fiction two new writers appear along with older ones, and not all in either group do good work. James Burke's *The Firefly Hunt,* a pleasant fantasy, eventually lags in its story of the born loser. Laurence Earl wrote *Risk,* which is

WILLIAM MORROW & CO.
THOUGHTFUL HUMOR abounds in *The Peter Principle*, by Raymond Hull (*left*) and Laurence J. Peter.

about a coal mine disaster in Nova Scotia. The superficial plot wastes a good theme, though the image of the feudal company town is good. Norman Newton's *The Big Stuffed Hand of Friendship,* a raucous look at hypocrisy and prejudice toward West Coast Indians, bores one by being too diverse in theme and too rambling in its attack on Canadian society. And how any book with as little subtlety could be as successful as Raymond Spence's *Nothing Black But a Cadillac* makes one wonder. Ten short pieces by Mordicai Richler, in *The Street,* again exploit the ghetto. His writing can carry a wallop; however it can also be dull.

But some novels were excellent. Phyllis Gotlieb's well-written first novel, which is about Jews adapting to Canada is called *Why Should I Have All the Grief?* and shows that none of us do. Eric Koch's ironic, witty blending of Napoleon III and the balcony scene as played by de Gaulle in Montreal can be put down, but not easily. Nor can poet Margaret Atwood's gentle story of confused but ordinary people trying to opt into life, *The Edible Woman.* Criticized by male reviewers and praised by female ones, Margaret Laurence's *The Fire-Dwellers* has an unpromising heroine facing the realities of her being a 40-year-old suburban housewife and mother and heroically accepting that she must live with the facts. Perhaps the most important new novelist is Graeme Gibson, with *Five Legs,* a peeling away of the puritanical Canadian's small-town, onionlike soul.

Miscellaneous. Difficult to classify are books like George Case Diltz' interesting and true stories of life around Port Credit at the turn of the century, *Stranger Than Fiction;* or *Newfoundland,* a travel guide or description of the province for inadequate tourists, proving Horwood's writing ability when he bothers, but he bothers only seldom here; or Edith Fowke's very interesting *Sally Go Round the Sun,* an illustrated and musically scored collection of play songs of Canadian children. Two books on Indians are highly successful: Sheila Burnford's *Without Reserve,* about the people of the northern forest and their daily lives, is a joy to read; and in *Potlatch,* George Clutesi's powerful prose brings alive the West Coast Indians and their social rituals.

Scholarship. Perhaps student unrest reduced scholarship and diverted humor; both are rare in the Canadian literature of 1969. Sociologist Lionel Tiger's explanation of the power of men is presented in *Men in Groups.* Literary biographer Philip Akrigg and his geographer wife Helen departed from their vocations to produce a charming collection of anecdotes, history, sociology, science, and fiction in *1001 British Columbia Place Names.*

GORDON R. ELLIOTT
Simon Fraser University

FRENCH CANADIAN LITERATURE

Significant in French Canadian literature in 1969 was the advent of several young novelists for the most part influenced by Réjean Ducharme, who himself published a versified novel, *La Fille de Christophe-Colombe.* Poetry continued in decline.

Fiction. The year 1969 belonged to the storyteller Jacques Ferron, whose collected stories were published—as were two novels (*La Charrette* and *Le ciel de Québec*) and a collection of *Historiettes* (short tales). Several young writers paid him homage, just as others wrote novels under the influence of Ducharme: Jean Nadeau (*Bien vôtre*), Jean-Marie Poupart (*Angoisse-Play* and *Que le diable emporte le titre!*), V.-Lévy Beaulieu (*Mémoires d'outre tonneau* and *Race de monde!*), Paul Villeneuve (*J'ai mon voyage!*), and Louis Provencher (*La Vérence*).

Two other young authors furthered their careers by publishing remarkable works: Roch Carrier (*Floralie, ou es-tu?*) and Claire de Lamirande (*Le Grand Élixir*). There was at least one discovery— Pierre Turgeon, author of *Faire sa mort comme faire l'amour.* Jacques Poulin wrote a very youthful novel, tragic and moving, soberly entitled *Jimmy,* one of the best works of recent years. Older novelists contributed nothing very surprising, except for Claude Jasmin's little book *Rimbaud mon beau salaud.* The prolific Yves Thériault published three novels, of which only one is worth citing: *Tayaout,* sequel to *Agaguk,* his greatest book.

Nonfiction. The Quebec political situation always attracts historians and sociologists. A nationalist historian, Maurice Seguin, described the genesis of nationalist thought in *L'Idée d'indépendance au Québec,* while the sociologist Marcel Rioux published in France *La question du Québec,* an exceptionally clear and intelligent essay on the issue. A young professor, Jean-Cléo Godin, devoted a masterly study, *Une poétique du mystère,* to the novelist Henri Bosco. Literature of revolutionary inspiration is almost unknown; in *L'Esprit révolutionnaire dans la littérature canadienne-française* Joseph Costisella proved once and for all that it exists.

Noteworthy was the publication of the *Correspondance de Charles Gill,* which evokes one of the most productive periods of French Canadian letters. The first Canadian botanist, Brother Marie-Victorin, died 25 years ago; on this anniversary his journal, *Confidence et combat,* and a study of the flora of Anticosti Island were published.

Poetry. Only a few collections sustain interest: *Québec se meurt* and *Ailleurs se tisse* by Guy Robert and *Comme eau retenue,* the collected poems of Jean-Guy Pilon. The review *Barre du Jour* devoted to the Automatistes a special number important for understanding postwar literary evolution.

ANDRÉ MAJOR
Literary Critic, "Le Devoir," Montreal

CANALS

The world's maritime industry, firms engaged in international business, and many other interests are watching progress toward the Atlantic-Pacific Canal, which is intended eventually to link the two oceans somewhere in Central America.

Atlantic-Pacific Canal. While waiting for the final recommendations of the Interoceanic Canal Study Commission due by Dec. 1, 1970, scientists are considering the implications of two proposals made in an interim report: that the canal be at sea-level and that atomic energy be used to dig it.

Recalling the Welland Canal disaster when sea lampreys invaded the Great Lakes to inflict great damage on the fish, concerned scientists point out that the proposed sea-level canal in Central America would have no natural barriers to discourage the migration of organisms from one ocean to the other. An influx of new organisms in one or both oceans could upset the balance of populations and be a serious threat to the ocean food chain. In particular, since a sea-level canal might lead to a mixing of the two oceans, scientists wonder if the interbreeding of species between the Atlantic and the Pacific oceans might lead to:

(1) Sterilization of one or both of the species, and then to eventual extinction.

(2) Upset of the predator-prey relationships, bringing about extinction of a species.

(3) Upset of the balance of marine life through temperature changes, since the Atlantic is warmer than the Pacific.

Other scientists are worried about the proposal to use atomic explosives to dig the canal, thereby contaminating the food chain.

Ecologists at the Smithsonian Institution in Washington would like to learn as much as possible about the existing situation in the Atlantic and Pacific before a massive change such as the linking of the two oceans is introduced as a new element. An environmental research study, they say, might reveal a potential disaster such as that of the Welland Canal which could be forestalled without affecting the usefulness of the canal.

The five-man commission is continuing to gather information. Its final report will recommend a location for the canal, outline the scope of negotiations necessary with the country involved, recommend excavation techniques, assess costs and means of support, and consider the defense system necessary.

Tehama-Colusa Canal. The Bureau of Reclamation has begun work on a dual-use canal that would be employed to irrigate California farmland and to breed salmon as well. The 155-mile-long Tehama-Colusa Canal, scheduled for completion in 1970, will deliver irrigation water to farmland in four Central Valley counties in 1970. Also included in the plans is a spawning nest section that would annually produce 170,000 king salmon, scientifically upgraded into a superior biological strain.

St. Lawrence. Plans to expand the St. Lawrence Seaway were halted after a study done for the U. S. Department of Transportation reported that there was no economic justification now for any new construction to improve the St. Lawrence. The study looked at the possibility of twinning existing locks or conducting a major dredging program, but it concluded that the traffic forecasts for the system do not require such improvements. Even extending the sailing season by six weeks—it is now eight months—would require icebreaking equipment and merely divert traffic from alternative distributive channels that handle it when the seaway is closed.

Chasma-Jhelum Canal. Work is progressing rapidly on the 63-mile Chasma-Jhelum Canal, the last of eight new link canals in a 460-mile system to tie together the Indus and its four major tributaries in West Pakistan. Situated west of Lahore, the canal will run through Chasma Barrage on the Indus southeastward to the Jhelum River, cutting through a swamp area as well as the Tahl Desert on its way.

Chesapeake & Delaware Canal. Contractors have finished dredging the upper Chesapeake Bay part of the Delaware River Basin Inland Waterway. Their goal is to improve a 20-mile section of the Chesapeake & Delaware Canal.

KENNETH E. TROMBLEY
Editor, "Professional Engineer"

TEHAMA-COLUSA CANAL in California has louvers that divert fish to the Sacramento River through a bypass.

U. S. BUREAU OF RECLAMATION

CANCER

Among the various aspects of cancer research studied during 1969 were carcinogens (cancer-inducing agents), medically induced cancers, and methods of detecting breast cancer. Researchers also studied the possible use of interferon in treating cancer.

Carcinogens. There is a growing recognition that many human cancers are probably related to chemical agents in the environment. A causal relationship has long been accepted between lung cancer and the smoking of tobacco as well as between cancer of the mouth and the chewing of betel nuts or tobacco leaves. According to recent research, the high incidence of liver cancer in the Bantu tribes in Africa and in the natives of Guam may be caused by contamination of their food with aflatoxin, a very potent carcinogen produced by some strains of the mold *Aspergillus flavus*. Similarly, a high incidence of gastric cancer in Japan, Iceland, and Chile may be associated with the consumption of fish containing nitrosamines, substances formed during the preservation process.

Cyclamates, the noncaloric sugar substitutes, were found to be potentially carcinogenic and were partially banned by the Food and Drug Administration. Although originally approved only for use in dietetic foods for people whose intake of sugar must be restricted for medical reasons, cyclamates achieved mass distribution in soft drinks, diet desserts, and other food products. Although toxicity tests had been conducted repeatedly, only in 1968 and 1969 did investigators study the effects of high doses over long periods of time. These tests showed that such doses eventually produced cancer of the bladder in rats. (See also NUTRITION.)

Mustard gas was also implicated as a carcinogen during 1969. At the Hiroshima University School of Medicine, S. Wade and his coworkers observed that industrial exposure to mustard gas (in nitrogen mustard factories) more than doubles the incidence of lung cancer and cancer of the upper respiratory tract.

Medically Induced Cancers. Two new examples of medically induced cancers were reported during 1969. In a study by a tuberculosis clinic in Nova Scotia, of the 300 female patients formerly treated with artificial pneumothorax (a treatment for tuberculosis popular between the 1920's and 1950's), 22 developed breast cancer within 15 to 25 years. Among 483 women who did not receive this form of therapy, only four developed breast cancer. Because thousands of women received artificial pneumothorax therapy during the years of its popularity, this finding is of major significance. Artificial pneumothorax requires repeated exposure to X-rays, and radiation has long been known to cause leukemia as well as cancer of the skin, lung, thyroid gland, and bone.

In a study of 400 patients who received kidney transplants, it was found that 15 of them developed lymphomas, cancer of the lymphatic system. Because a person's lymphatic system would normally produce antibodies that would destroy the transplanted organ, patients receiving kidneys are treated with immunosuppressive drugs, drugs that suppress the formation of antibodies. According to John P. Merrill of the Peter Bent Brigham Hospital in Boston, Mass., most of the patients who developed lymphomas had received antilymphatic serum in addition to chemical immunosuppressors. His ob-

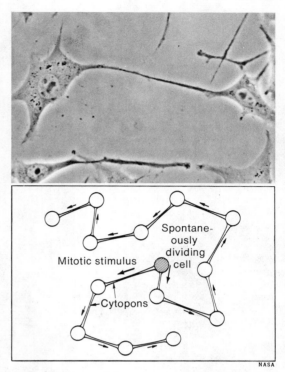

BRIDGES linking mouse cancer cells were found by NASA scientists. One cell (shaded) sends messages to the others so all start dividing almost simultaneously.

servations demonstrate an unforeseen hazard of organ transplantation and also offer support for a hypothesis, most recently advanced by Robert F. Schwartz of Tufts University, that lymphomas arise in a setting of prolonged antigenic stress upon a functionally impaired lymphatic system.

Breast Cancer Detection. Efforts to improve early diagnosis of breast cancer, and thus increase the chance of complete surgical removal of the tumor, continue to center around the use of thermography and mammography. Thermography uses heat sensors to detect breast tumors, which are warmer than the surrounding tissues. Mammography is a special X-ray technique that is adapted for detecting subtle differences in soft tissue densities.

Interferon. Interferon is a protein that is released by virus-infected cells and that protects neighboring cells from infection. Hoping to use interferon therapeutically, M. R. Hilleman and his coworkers at the Merck Institute for Therapeutic Research, developed a synthetic interferon inducer, called polyinosinicpolycytidylic acid (Poly I:C). In laboratory animals it was found to prevent or limit infections with several respiratory and intestinal viruses and to inhibit the induction of cancer by viruses. H. L. Levy and his colleagues at the National Cancer Institute have tested Poly I:C against transplanted tumors in mice and rats, observing a significant inhibition in the growth of certain tumors. Poly I:C is currently being tested against human cancers. (See also BIOCHEMISTRY.)

CHARLES W. YOUNG, M.D.
Sloan-Kettering Institute for Cancer Research

WILLEMSTAD harbor area burns as Curaçao oil refinery workers riot on May 30. Four persons were killed and 150 hurt, and damage was estimated at $30 million.

CARIBBEAN

Economic development of the Caribbean area will be promoted by the Caribbean Regional Development Bank, which was formally chartered and opened for business in 1969. Its parent organization, the Caribbean Free Trade Association, formed in 1968, increased regional trade in 1969, held a regional trade show, and sent a commission to visit and deal with the European Economic Community. Evolving independence in the Caribbean resulted in strained political situations, a peaceful British invasion, and several serious riots.

Caribbean Regional Development Bank. An important step toward further regional cooperation in the Caribbean was taken in 1969 with the setting up of the Caribbean Regional Development Bank, a unit of the Caribbean Free Trade Association. After

many preliminary meetings and extensive studies the charter of the bank was signed by ministerial representatives of the participating governments on October 18 in Kingston, Jamaica. In addition to the former members of the defunct West Indian Federation, participants in the bank include British Honduras, the Bahamas, and Guyana, as well as such dependent areas as the Turks and Caicos Islands, the British Virgin Islands, and Montserrat. The bulk of the financial support for the bank will be contributed by Jamaica, Trinidad and Tobago, Barbados, Guyana, and the Bahamas. Canada and the United Kingdom will contribute $10 million each to the $50 million total capitalization of the bank.

Originally the United States (which sent an observer to the October meetings in Jamaica) and Puerto Rico were to contribute to the bank, but with the defeat of the Popular-Democratic Party in the

1968 Puerto Rico election, a more conservative and less Caribbean-oriented executive came to power. The Dominican Republic also expressed interest in participating.

The bank will make loans to members primarily for infrastructural development and the establishment of new industries. It is expected to make a significant contribution to the economies of the smaller and less developed territories of the region. The bank opened its doors for business in December 1969. The secretariat of the bank is tentatively on Barbados, but Jamaica is trying to have it moved to Kingston. It has a 7-member board of directors, all from Caribbean countries.

Caribbean Free Trade Association. CARIFTA experienced its second successful year of operation. Eleven countries form the trade association, and British Honduras has expressed interest in uniting with the group. Founded in May 1968, CARIFTA has been successful in increasing the flow of trade among member-states. Particularly the larger countries such as Jamaica, Trinidad, and Guyana have found growing nearby markets.

In celebration of the first anniversary of CARIFTA an exposition was held on the island of Grenada. Each cooperating and contributing country set up a pavilion to display local products available through free-trade arrangements. The month-long Expo 69, as it was called, focused public attention upon Caribbean economic cooperation.

The Council of Ministers of CARIFTA, meeting at the secretariat offices in Georgetown, Guyana, demonstrated their concern for the continuing success of the association by naming a top-level commission to visit the seats of government of the countries of the European Economic Community. The possible entrance of the United Kingdom into the EEC caused concern because of the effect this might have on their own trade ties, particularly the sale of sugar to Britain. The ministerial mission was expected to explore the types of protective arrangements that might be open to the Caribbean countries that currently enjoy access to British markets under special conditions. No public statement was made when the commission returned to the Caribbean, but it is understood that the information gathered would serve to orient a regional trade policy in relation to the European Common Market.

U. S. Relations. The visit of Nelson Rockefeller as a special envoy of President Nixon to Jamaica, Haiti, the Dominican Republic, and Trinidad and Tobago was an important event in 1969. Rockefeller's statements while in Port-au-Prince, Haiti, and the subsequent address by President Nixon outlining his Latin American policy clearly indicated that the United States would soon renew its economic aid to Haiti in spite of the dictatorial nature of the regime of François Duvalier, the self-styled life-president of that impoverished nation.

Anguilla. In the pre-dawn invasion of the small island of Anguilla on March 19, 1969, Britain reasserted its control over the island, which had declared its independence in 1967. Some 300 marines and paratroopers with 55 London policemen quietly and without incident or opposition moved into the island, inhabited by about 6,000 people. Anguilla had refused to continue its relationship with St. Kitts, which was charged with the administration of the 11-by-3 mile (18-by-5 km) island. A repeated declaration of independence in January 1969 had prompted the action by the British. Once

loyalty and order were restored, the troops were slowly withdrawn. Those remaining were kept busy repairing the roads, communication system, and port facilities of the neglected island. At the close of 1969 the island's political fate was uncertain.

Associated States. On Oct. 27, 1969, St. Vincent became the sixth island to achieve the status of an "associated state" with Britain. This gave complete local autonomy in internal affairs to St. Vincent, along with Antigua, St. Kitts-Nevis-Anguilla, Dominica, St. Lucia, and Grenada, which had achieved this position in 1968. Britain retains responsibility for defense and foreign policy. The delay of a year in the case of St. Vincent was occasioned by sharply divided political sentiment on the island, which had hampered the formation of a stable government.

Strikes and Riots. Student unrest and labor protests swept many communities of the Caribbean in 1969. Some was stimulated by black-power or racial sentiment, but most of the protests were directed at inattentive governments in which the public had lost faith. In the Netherlands Antilles and Surinam, the governments in power were forced to resign and in subsequent elections lost their majority strength in the parliaments.

Students' strikes in Santo Domingo brought about the death of one teacher and the injury of many students. Student protests against the ROTC program in the University of Puerto Rico closed that institution for two days in October. The Trinidad and Jamaica campuses of the University of the West Indies were both troubled by student protests over the dismissal of professors.

Labor protests against spiraling inflation and alleged government corruption paralyzed Paramaribo, the capital of Surinam, with a general strike and a 3-hour "march of silence" by schoolteachers and government workers. The government of Jopie Pengel, the Negro political leader, resigned and was subsequently replaced after new elections by that of Dr. Jules Sedney.

Automation of the oil refineries of Curaçao and Aruba prompted strikes and labor protests that erupted into violence on the island of Curaçao. The mobs burned several business establishments in the tourist section of downtown Willemstad, Curaçao, and forced the resignation of a government that had been in power for over 15 years. An election produced a parliament evenly split between the parties of the opposition on the one side and the previous majority party. The formation of a government was only possible by assigning three cabinet posts to the leaders of the striking workers. The new government agreed to a number of long overdue social and economic reforms.

Cuban Aid to Trinidad. One final political event that stirred the Caribbean in the closing months of 1969 was the rapprochement initiated by an exploratory letter from the prime minister of Trinidad, Dr. Eric Williams, to Prime Minister Fidel Castro of Cuba. Castro responded favorably, expressing interest in closer relations with Cuba's Caribbean neighbors. One concrete result of this exchange was the expected arrival in Trinidad of a team of Cuban sugar technicians.

THOMAS G. MATHEWS
University of Puerto Rico

CATHOLIC CHURCH. See RELIGION—*Roman Catholicism;* ROMAN CATHOLIC CHURCH.

CENTRAL AFRICAN REPUBLIC

The year 1969 was marked by an attempted coup d'etat organized by Lt. Col. Alexandre Banza. In economic matters, a company that will help to develop the country's uranium resources began operations.

Internal Politics. On April 10, Colonel Banza, a close friend of President Jean Bedel Bokassa and a cabinet minister, allegedly attempted to induce several high ranking officers at the Kassai Military Camp to join him in overthrowing the regime. The officers informed the president, who had Banza arrested and tried by the permanent military tribunal in Bangui. Banza was found guilty and was shot on April 12.

In June the government ordered the trial of ex-President David Dacko, Bokassa's cousin, on charges of having entered into correspondence with foreign states. In July, however, President Bokassa announced that Dacko would not be tried.

Late in September the government was embarrassed when the French revealed that a company of troops had been sent to Bangui in November 1967 at the urgent request of President Bokassa to thwart a feared coup.

Economic Development. In April the Uranium Ores of Bakouma company (URBA) announced that it had begun operations. Production, estimated at about 500 tons of uranium ores per year, will begin in 1972. Total investment by URBA will be about $32.4 million.

Foreign Relations. In February an agreement was concluded with Sudan for the import of 20,000 head of cattle for meat production. The third an-

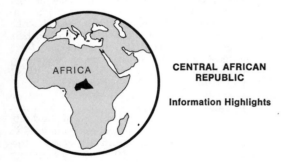

CENTRAL AFRICAN REPUBLIC

Information Highlights

Area: 240,534 square miles (622,984 sq km).
Population: 2,255,536 (1968 census).
Chief Cities (1966 census): Bangui, the capital, 150,000.
Government: *President and Prime Minister*—Jean Bedel Bokassa (seized power Jan. 1, 1966 through a military coup); *Parliament*—National Assembly dissolved on Jan. 4, 1966.
Religious Faiths: Tribal religions, 60% of population; Protestantism, 15%; Roman Catholicism, 14%.
Education: *Literacy rate* (1968 est.), 15% of population. *Total school enrollment* (1966)—165,903 (primary, 148,845; secondary, 6,083; teacher-training, 195; technical/vocational, 1,220).
Finance (1968 est.): *Monetary unit,* CFA franc (246.85 CFA francs equal U. S.$1).
Gross National Product (1966): $70,000,000.
Manufacturing (metric tons, 1967): Meat, 13,000; beer, 8,600.
Crops (metric tons, 1967–68 crop year): Cassava, 1,000,000; peanuts (1966), 59,870; sweet potatoes and yams, 40,000; cottonseed, 25,000.
Minerals (1967–68): Diamonds, 520,628 carats.
Foreign Trade (1967): *Exports,* $29,030,000 (chief exports, 1967: diamonds, $13,579,000; cotton, $6,623,000; coffee, $5,817,000); *imports,* $44,193,000 (chief imports, 1967: nonelectrical machinery, $2,495,000; woven cotton fabrics, $1,949,000). *Chief trading partners* (1967): France (took 42% of exports, supplied 60% of imports); United States (took 30% of exports, supplied 4% of imports); Israel (took 14% of exports).
Transportation: *Roads* (1968), 11,325 miles (18,222 km); *motor vehicles* (1967), 12,100 (automobiles 4,900).
Communications: *Telephones* (1968), 3,500; *radios* (1967), 33,000; *newspapers* (1967), 2 (daily circulation, 800).

nual meeting of the CAR/Cameroon Commission signed four agreements covering culture, technical assistance, nationality, police, and freight. The largest amount of foreign aid, $85,000, came from France.

VICTOR T. LE VINE
University of Ghana

CENTRAL AMERICA. See LATIN AMERICA and the articles on Latin American countries.

CEYLON

Economic problems were the main focus of attention in Ceylon during 1969. The population passed the 12 million mark in May. In September, following a wave of strikes, a national emergency was proclaimed. The end of the year saw increasing interest in the forthcoming general elections, scheduled for the spring of 1970.

Economic Developments. In 1969, Ceylon continued its growth rate of 5%. It had become the first developing country to reach this rate (the goal set by the UN Conference on Trade and Development), in 1968. The position of farmers markedly improved as a result of rising prices for agricultural products, increased yields, a boom in minor crops, and a campaign to increase rice production toward a goal of self-sufficiency by 1971.

Ceylon's unfavorable balance to trade continued to cause anxiety because of the decline in prices of basic exports, notably tea. The government introduced emergency measures to rescue the tea trade. The foreign exchange situation remained critical.

In January the Sino-Ceylonese rice-rubber pact was renewed, and mainland China agreed to lower the price of rice sold to Ceylon and to pay more for Ceylonese rubber. In the same month, India and Ceylon agreed to increase their mutual trade, to continue their program of promoting tea sales, and to propose a new trade and economic grouping that would include all countries affiliated with the UN Economic Commission for Asia and the Far East.

About $150 million in foreign aid was pledged to Ceylon in 1969. A World Bank mission expressed approval of the government's fiscal and development policies and recommended increased aid.

Political Affairs. With the approach of the general elections, spokesmen for the ruling United National party, led by Prime Minister Dudley Senanayake, and those for the main opposition group, the Sri Lanka Freedom party, led by Mrs. Sirimavo Bandaranaike, exchanged sharp charges and countercharges. In early March members of the two parties engaged in fisticuffs in the House of Representatives, and the opposition members walked out.

On April 13 the Tamil Federal party, which had withdrawn its members from the United Front government in September 1968, ended its support of the government completely. This left the government with the support of only 83 of the 157 members of the House of Representatives.

Labor strikes continued to be frequent in 1969. They became so serious in the oil and electricity industries that, on September 15, the government proclaimed a nationwide state of emergency.

Foreign Affairs. Prime Minister Senanayake's scheduled visit to the USSR in May was postponed because the proposed dates were inconvenient for Soviet leaders. Instead, Senanayake visited the United Arab Republic, where he emphasized Ceylon's policy

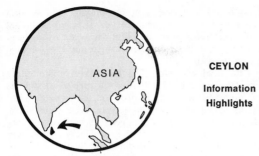

CEYLON

Information Highlights

Area: 25,332 square miles (65,610 sq km).
Population: 11,964,000 (June 1968 est.).
Chief Cities (1963 census): Colombo, the capital, 510,947; Dehiwala-Mount Lavinia, 110,943; Jaffna, 94,248.
Government: *Governor-General:* William Gopallawa (took office March 2, 1962); *Prime Minister*—Dudley Senanayake (took office March 25, 1965). *Parliament*—House of Representatives, 157 members, 6 nominated (party seating, 1969: United National party, 66; Sri Lanka Freedom party, 41; Tamil Federal party, 14; Lanka Sama Samaja party, 10; Sri Lanka Socialist Freedom party, 5; Communist party, 4; Tamil Congress, 3; others, 8); Senate, 30 members.
Religious Faiths: Buddhists, 64% of population; Hindus, 20%; Christians, 9%.
Education: *Literacy rate* (1967), 75.1% of population aged 15 and over. *Total school enrollment* (1968)—2,622,810 (primary, 1,780,559; secondary, 822,810; teacher-training, 5,302; university/higher, 14,139).
Finance (1968 est.): *Revenues,* $298,187,000; *expenditures,* $434,407,000; *monetary unit,* rupee (5.958 rupees equal U.S.$1).
Gross National Product (1967): $1,470,124,000.
National Income (1967): $1,282,000,000; *average annual income per person,* $117.
Economic Indexes (1966): *Industrial production,* 115 (1963= 100); *agricultural production* (1967), 108 (1963=100); *cost of living,* 107 (1963=100).
Manufacturing and Processing (metric tons, 1967): Cement, 189,000; meat, 20,000; beer, 64,000 hectoliters.
Crops (metric tons, 1967–68 crop year): Tea, 220,700 (ranks 2d among world producers); rice, 1,147,000; cassava, 346,000; natural rubber, 143,200; sweet potatoes, 73,000.
Minerals (metric tons, 1967): Salt, 76,000; ilmenite, 49,200; graphite (exports), 8,820.
Foreign Trade (1968): *Exports,* $342,000,000 (chief exports, 1967: tea, $177,950,000; rubber, $47,407,000); *imports,* $365,000,000 (chief imports, 1967: wheatmeal and flour, $38,366,000; rice, $35,332,000; fruit and vegetables, $15,- 235,000). *Chief trading partners* (1967): Britain (took 33% of exports, supplied 20% of imports); Communist China; India.
Transportation: *Roads* (1969), 21,000 miles (33,800 km); *motor vehicles* (1967), 122,200 (automobiles 83,700); *railways* (1966), 922 miles (1,484 km); *national airline,* Air Ceylon Ltd.
Communications: *Telephones* (1968): 55,500; *radios* (1965), 438,000; *newspapers* (1967), 16.

of nonalignment and its interest in restoring peace in the Middle East. A beginning was made in implementing the 5-year-old pact with India for the repatriation, over a 15-year period, of 500,000 Indian immigrants from Ceylon and for the granting of Ceylonese citizenship to more than 300,000 Indians living in Ceylon.

NORMAN D. PALMER
University of Pennsylvania

CHABAN-DELMAS, Jacques. See biographical sketch under FRANCE.

CHAD

Regional dissidence, which had flared up in 1968 with a rebellion of the Toubou people in the Tibesti area, continued to spread in the northern and eastern parts of Chad in 1969. By the end of the year 2,500 French troops had been brought in to help Chadian forces crush the rebellion.

Rebellion. The Chad National Liberation Front (FROLINAT), founded in 1966, was responsible for the outbreaks. It was supported by expatriate Chadians in Libya and Sudan and headed by Dr. Abba Sick, a former Chadian Minister of public education. The express purpose of FROLINAT was to overthrow the regime of President François Tombalbaye. Although Chadian authorities claimed notable successes against the rebels, reliable sources noted that by the end of 1969 vehicles did not move out of Fort Lamy, the capital, except in military convoys. In France the government of President Georges Pompidou was criticized for French involvement in Chad, already described as "France's second Vietnam."

Domestic Affairs. In April President Tombalbaye's 7-year mandate expired. Although he at first declined to run again, the ruling Progressive party of Chad (PPT) persuaded him to become a candidate. He was the only presidential candidate in the June elections and received 93% of the votes counted.

In June the government released 63 political prisoners. In September two decrees reinstated the practice of allowing traditional chiefs to participate in regional administration.

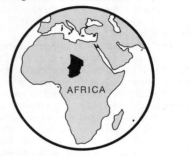

CHAD

Information Highlights

Area: 495,752 square miles (1,284,000 sq km).
Population: 3,460,000 (1968 est.).
Chief Cities (1967 est.): Fort Lamy, the capital, 91,700; Moundou, 25,000; Abéché, 24,000.
Government: *President*—François Tombalbaye (took office Aug. 12, 1960); *Parliament*—National Assembly, 75 members (party seating, 1969: all members of the Progressive Party of Chad, PPT).
Religious Faiths: Muslims, 52% of population; animists, 43%; Roman Catholics, 3%; Protestants, 2%.
Education: *Literacy rate* (1967), 5% of population. *Total school enrollment* (1966)—182,670 (primary, 172,485; secondary, 9,089; teacher-training, 594; technical/vocational, 502).
Finance: *Monetary unit,* CFA franc (246.85 CFA francs equal U.S.$1).
Gross National Product (1966): $220,000,000.
Manufacturing (metric tons, 1967): Meat products, 35,000.
Crops (metric tons, 1967–68 crop year): Peanuts (1966), 118,- 000; cottonseed, 70,000; cotton (lint), 39,000.
Minerals (metric tons, 1966): Natron, 10,000.
Foreign Trade (1968): *Exports,* $28,000,000 (chief export, 1967: cotton, $22,296,900); *imports,* $39,000,000 (chief imports, 1967: petroleum, $5,452,700; textile yarn & fabrics, $3,123,300; road motor vehicles, $3,346,100). *Chief trading partners* (1967): France (took 57% of exports, supplied 46% of imports); Nigeria (took 8% of exports, supplied 6% of imports); United States.
Transportation: *Roads* (1968), 20,000 miles (32,200 km); *motor vehicles* (1967), 8,900 (automobiles 3,100); *principal airport,* Fort Lamy.
Communications: *Telephones* (1968), 3,847; *radios* (1967), 35,000; *newspapers* (1965), 1.

Economic Developments. A revised version of the National Five Year Plan, announced in February, scaled down a number of "overambitious" projections. Crops of cotton, Chad's most important export, reached approximately 140,000 tons for the 1968–69 growing year, 102,000 tons more than the previous year's crop.

Foreign Aid. In April a convention was signed with France for $1.2 million to finance medical installations and teaching equipment.

VICTOR T. LE VINE
University of Ghana

CHARLES, Prince. See biographical sketch under GREAT BRITAIN.

CHEMISTRY

The most important event in chemistry in 1969 was the arrival of rock samples from the moon. Other outstanding achievements include the synthesis by U. S. scientists of element 104 and the synthesis of the enzyme ribonuclease. The existence of an anomalous form of water, called polywater, which had previously been described by Soviet scientists, was confirmed by a group of Americans.

Lunar Chemistry. Rock and fine material were brought back to earth from the moon by Apollo 11 and Apollo 12 astronauts. Some of the material was distributed to scientists for analysis. Preliminary examination of the material revealed the presence of igneous rock, which is rock that was once molten. It is estimated that from 3 to 4 billion years ago the igneous rock was deposited as lava flow and was later fragmented by meteoritic impact and redeposited as debris and breccia (rock composed of fairly large fragments cemented together). This evidence challenges a widely held theory that the moon was always a dead body.

Chemically, these lunar rocks are different from terrestrial rocks or rocks that have been found in meteorites. The metallic iron content of the lunar rocks indicates that when they were formed, practically no oxygen, water, or sulfur were present. On earth little metallic iron occurs in nature because in the presence of oxygen and water it readily forms rust (iron oxide), and with sulfur it forms iron sulfide. Compared with material from the earth, the lunar material contains more of the heavy elements, such as titanium and iron, and less of the lighter elements, such as sodium and potassium. This suggests that the material has been subjected to temperatures as high as 2000° C (3600° F), which could have resulted from volcanic action or impact of meteorites. Some rocks contain small pits lined with glass (melted rock).

Much of the fine material brought from the moon is glass, which is in globular, ragged, spheroidal, ellipsoidal, dumbbell, and teardrop shapes. Some of the glass is colorless, while the rest is dark gray, yellow, orange, red, and shades ranging from green to brown. Unlike glass formed by terrestrial volcanoes, the composition of a single lunar glass particle is not always homogeneous. Large amounts of noble gases (argon, krypton, helium, and xenon) were found in the lunar material. It is believed that these gases have been deposited by solar winds, and therefore can yield information about the isotopic composition of the sun.

Chemical Warfare. The U. S. Army planned to bury at sea some 27,000 tons of surplus chemicals including GB, an organic phosphorus nerve gas, liquid mustard gas, and some nonlethal chemicals. When news of the plan was leaked, public and congressional outcry caused the project to be abandoned. The National Academy of Sciences recommended that the nerve gas be detoxified and the mustard gas be burned.

In March, the Society for Social Responsibility in Science sent G. H. Orians, University of Washington, and E. W. Pfeiffer, University of Montana, to investigate the effects of military use of chemical herbicides on forests and farmlands in Vietnam. They received tacit encouragement from the U. S. Defense Department and the Department of Agriculture. Their reports of extensive ecological damage received considerable publicity.

Chemical Elements. In 1964 the Soviet scientist G. N. Flerov announced the creation of element 104 by the bombardment of plutonium atoms (atomic mass 242) with neon nuclei (atomic mass 22). The Soviets called this element kurchatovium, after a famous Russian physicist. However, there is some dispute as to whether or not the Soviet scientists actually succeeded in producing element 104, and the name "kurchatovium" has not been officially accepted.

The Soviet method of synthesis could not be successfully repeated by U. S. scientists. However, Albert Ghiorso and his associates at the Radiation Laboratory at the University of California, Berkeley, announced the production of element 104 by the bombardment of californium (atomic mass 249) with carbon nuclei (atomic mass 12 or 13). Element 104 is in the same family of metals as titanium, zirconium, and hafnium. The isotopes of element 104 produced in California have atomic weights of 257 and 259. The half-life of the isotope with atomic weight 257 was 4 to 5 seconds; the half-life of the second isotope was 3 to 4 seconds. A third isotope was also synthesized; its atomic weight was 258 and its half-life 100th of a second.

LAWRENCE RADIATION LABORATORY, UNIVERSITY OF CALIFORNIA, BERKELEY

TWO ISOTOPES of element 104 were identified with this device at the Lawrence Radiation Laboratory. Albert Ghiorso, shown here, led a team of five scientists in the identification.

Scientists are now searching for elements 110 and 114, which should resemble platinum and lead, respectively. Unlike the other very heavy elements, elements 110 and 114 may be relatively long-lived. Since element 114 is related to lead, it may occur in very small quantities with lead. With a microscope, Soviet scientists have examined lead supports of very old stained glass. If element 114 is present, the radioactive decay of the element would leave marks on the glass that could be detected. Traces of such decay have been reported by the scientists working on the project.

Polywater. Work by scientists at the University of Maryland confirmed the existence of a new form of water, which had been discovered by the Soviet scientists Boris V. Deryagin and N. N. Fedyakin in 1962. Although there was much skepticism over the original Soviet announcement of polywater, its existence has now been confirmed by several laboratories. The substance has been produced by the distillation of ordinary water into very fine freshly drawn quartz or Pyrex capillary tubes.

The chemical composition of polywater is the same as that of regular water; however, there are several important differences in their chemical and physical properties. One of the most interesting differences is that polywater remains a liquid well below the freezing point of regular water; at about $-40°$ C ($-40°$ F) it solidifies into a glassy (amorphous) mass, while regular water freezes into a crystalline solid at $0°$ C ($32°$ F). Polywater also boils at a far higher temperature than water; it remains a liquid up to about $500°$ C ($900°$ F). Polywater appears to have a density of about 1.4 g/ml compared with 1 g/ml for regular water; this is a difference in density of about 40%.

By using a recent technique involving laser beams, Ellis R. Lippincott and Gerald L. Cessac at the University of Maryland and Robert R. Stromberg and Warren H. Grant at the National Bureau of Standards obtained infrared and Raman spectra of polywater that showed certain structural features not present in water or ice. Infrared data were obtained on the material both within and outside the capillary tubes. The current proposal is that polywater is a true polymer of water molecules. The quartz or Pyrex surface of the capillary tube into which the polywater condenses presumably aids in organizing the water molecules into this pattern.

Scientists are now searching for polywater in nature. It is possible that polywater may be present in certain mineral systems, such as clay, where water with higher-than-usual density can be found.

Biochemistry. Until 1969 the largest protein synthesized in the laboratory was the hormone insulin, which contains 51 amino acid residues. Early in 1969 the first enzyme to be synthesized was produced independently by two groups. The enzyme is ribonuclease (RNase), which speeds the decomposition of ribonucleic acid; this enzyme contains 124 amino acid residues.

Dr. Bruce Merrifield and Dr. Bernd Gutte at the Rockefeller University in New York synthesized RNase by attaching the first amino acid to a solid resin and then lengthening the protein chain one amino acid at a time. The second group, led by Dr. Robert G. Denkewalter at Merck Sharpe & Dohme Research Laboratories prepared segments of the chain and then assembled them. The products showed up to 25% of the activity of natural RNase.

In August a team under the direction of Nobel Prize-winner Dorothy M. Hodgkin (Oxford, England) announced that they had worked out the three-dimensional structure of the hormone insulin. This was achieved by the analysis of photographs obtained by bombarding insulin crystals with X-rays.

New Compounds and Syntheses. N. A. Frigerio at the Argonne National Laboratory succeeded in preparing crystalline permanganic acid, $HMnO_4$, a substance that had been considered too unstable to exist. Another compound that had ben previously unknown, the diflouride of sulfur, SF_2, was trapped long enough to be identified by F. Seel at Saarbruecken using nuclear magnetic resonance and mass spectroscopy. The sulfur difluoride was made from silver fluoride and sulfur.

A silver oxide, AgO, of low silver content, which had long been known only as a powder, was made in crystalline form by L. Nanis at the University of Pennsylvania; this synthesis involved only a simple electrochemical process.

At Hoffman-La Roche, M. Uskovic developed a nine-step synthesis of the antimalarial drug quinine. If this method proves commercially feasible, it could end dependence on supplies of the natural drug.

Ammonia. To combine atmospheric nitrogen with hydrogen to form ammonia, high pressures and temperatures are needed. E. van Tamelen of Stanford University has found a laboratory method for doing this at room temperature. In this process a metal compound, such as titanium tetraisopropoxide, is reduced under nitrogen to its divalent form, which then combines with nitrogen. This product in turn is reduced with sodium naphthalide, and the product reacts with isopropyl alcohol to give ammonia.

Chemical Information. A worldwide network for handling computer-processed chemical information was started in 1969. Five major input centers are envisioned. Agreement for the establishment of two such centers has been reached. The first agreement arranged for an agency in Britain to supply chemical data to the Chemical Abstracts Service, in Columbus, Ohio; this agrement is now in effect. In return, Chemical Abstracts furnishes computer-processed data to a consortium on chemical information, which in turn supplies data to scientists in Britain. A similar agreement was reached with West Germany. This plan will broaden international participation in processing, storing, and distributing chemical information, of which only about 30% originates in the United States.

Textile Chemistry. Despite problems in environmental pollution, production of more throw-away clothing seems inevitable. A fabric of polyethylene fiber was marketed for use in uniforms and work clothing that in terms of cost is competitive with linen service. A cast fabric suitable for work clothing and institutional use was developed. Its advantage is that spinning and weaving, the most costly steps in fabric manufacture, can be eliminated. The starting chemical, a monomer, is mixed with a solvent and frozen in a very thin layer. Tiny crystals of solvent form and become embedded in the monomer, which then becomes a matrix. When the monomer is polymerized by radiation or other methods, and the crystals are melted out, a porous fabric is produced.

THEODOR BENFEY AND EUGENIA KELLER
"Chemistry" Magazine

CHIANG KAI-SHEK. See biographical sketch under CHINA.

CHICAGO

A strike by public school teachers, a sustained drive against racial discrimination in the construction industry, and the conspiracy trial of the "Chicago Eight" occupied the spotlight in Chicago during 1969.

Teachers' Strike. For the first time in history Chicago public school teachers staged a 2-day walkout on May 22–23. The strike was called by the Chicago Teachers Union, which represents approximately 19,000 of the city's 22,458 public school teachers. Some 570,000 pupils were affected. Approximately 76% of the teaching force honored picket lines, but more than 5,000 teachers (primarily black) reported to inner-city schools. Their action underscored a growing schism between many black teachers and the Chicago Teachers Union.

A tentative settlement was reached early, and schools were in full operation on May 26. A key to the settlement was a promise from Mayor Richard J. Daley and Gov. Richard B. Ogilvie to support legislative action to increase the state school aid formula. However, this plan did not yield the school board sufficient revenue to implement fully the terms of the settlement. In late August it was evident that only one third of the proposed salary increase could be met. The school maintenance employees union then threatened to join the teachers in another walkout on September 15. The strike was averted when the City Council agreed to transfer to the school board the city's share of the state income tax for the remainder of 1969.

Black Workers and the Construction Industry. The drive for racial equality in Chicago was focused on the construction industry. Spearheaded by the Coalition for United Community Action (an organization of some 60 religious and civic groups in the black community), a vigorous assault was made on the hiring practices of both the building trades unions and the construction industry. The coalition demanded 10,000 jobs for blacks immediately and proclaimed a long-range goal of obtaining one third of the jobs in the construction industry. In late July and August demonstrators temporarily blocked work on 20 construction projects having an aggregate value of approximately $80 million.

Talks were deadlocked in early September as it became clear that both sides were unrelenting in their positions on key issues. The unions regarded as sacred their control of recruitment and training of apprentices, while the coalition pointed to union discrimination and demanded control of the recruiting and training programs.

On September 22 the coalition held the first of a series of "Black Monday" moratoriums at the Civic Center Plaza. Three days later more than 1,000 white construction workers disrupted a federal hearing investigating charges of discriminatory employment practices in federally financed construction projects. A tentative agreement, reached on November 6, produced a new stalemate and gave little hope for an early resolution of the issues.

"Chicago Eight." The violence that erupted in Chicago's streets during the 1968 Democratic National Convention again took the spotlight during the drawn-out federal district court trial of the "Chicago Eight," who were charged with violating the antiriot provision of the 1968 Civil Rights Act by conspiring to cross state lines to start the riots.

The initial furor occurred when trial judge Julius Hoffman rejected the last-minute request of four defense lawyers to withdraw from the case and cited them for contempt in failing to appear at the start of the trial on September 24. Two of the lawyers were jailed but were released within a few hours on orders from the U. S. court of appeals for the seventh circuit. Judge Hoffman ultimately withdrew the contempt citations and allowed the four attorneys to withdraw from the case.

Controversies reached a new height when defendant Bobby Seale's (national chairman of the Black Panther party) frequent outbursts led Judge Hoffman to have him gagged and shackled. However, two and one-half days of such restraint did not deter Seale, and the judge declared a mistrial in his case, sentencing him to four years imprisonment for criminal contempt of court. The prosecution completed its case on December 5, and the case was not expected to go to the jury until late January 1970.

Other Events. Chicago residents also witnessed moments of civic pride in 1969. The John Hancock Building was completed; the 100-story structure, rising to 1,107 feet (338 meters), is second in height only to New York's Empire State Building. Two rapid transit lines were added to the city's transit system in 1969. They will provide high-speed transportation to Chicago's "Loop."

TWILEY W. BARKER, JR.
University of Illinois at Chicago Circle

CHILD WELFARE. See SOCIAL WELFARE.

CHILDREN'S LITERATURE

Children's book production during 1969 was marked by a sharp drop in the number of individual titles published. Early estimates placed the number at 2,400, down some 400 titles from 1968. The decline was attributed to cutbacks in federal funds available to schools and libraries that are responsible for over 80% of children's books purchases.

The most obvious trend was the proliferation of fiction and nonfiction, for all age groups, dealing with Negroes and other minority groups. While the bulk of these volumes was mediocre to poor in quality, several were singled out for praise: John Steptoe's *Stevie*, Virginia Hamilton's *The Time-Ago Tales of Jahdu*, Walter Goodman's *Black Bondage*, Janet Harris' and Julius W. Hobson's *Black Pride*, and Julius Lester's *Black Folktales*.

The best novel of 1969 was William H. Armstrong's *Sounder*, which *The New York Times* called "an awesome account of childhood pain." It depicts a Negro boy's search for his sharecropper father, who was cruelly punished for stealing to feed his hungry family. *Sounder* was rivaled only by Vera and Bill Cleaver's *Where the Lilies Bloom*, about a 14-year-old white Appalachian girl's determined efforts to keep her fatherless family together.

Awards. The major awards presented in 1969, for children's books published in 1968, were as follows. The American Library Association's John Newbery Medal for the most distinguished contribution to literature for American children went to Lloyd Alexander for *The High King*, the fifth and final volume of a fantasy cycle. The ALA's Randolph Caldecott Medal for the most distinguished picture book was given to Uri Shulevitz, who illustrated *The Fool of the World and the Flying Ship*, a Russian tale retold by Arthur Ransome. Vadim

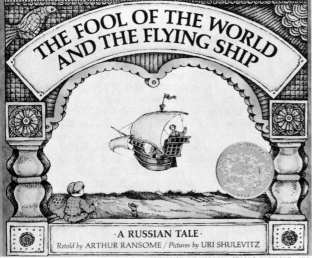

RECIPIENTS of outstanding awards for children's literature in 1969 were *The Fool of the World and the Flying Ship,* winner of the Caldecott Medal for its illustrations, and *The High King,* winner of the John Newbery Medal for distinguished writing.

PERMISSION BY FARRAR, STRAUS & GIROUX, INC.

PERMISSION BY HOLT, RINEHART AND WINSTON, INC.

Frolov, a Russian author, received the award of the Child Study Association of America for dealing realistically and courageously with contemporary problems in *What It's All About.* The National Book Awards added the category of children's books and bestowed the new prize on Meindert DeJong for *Journey From Peppermint Street.*

Fiction. Among picture books for readers 4–7 years old the most noteworthy were William Steig's *Sylvester and the Magic Pebble,* the story of a donkey who learns that having all one's wishes come true is not necessarily happiness; Uri Shulevitz's *Rain Rain Rivers,* showing a downpour over city and country; Harve and Margot Zemach's *The Judge,* a cumulative verse tale about the vagaries of justice; Edna Mitchell Preston's *Pop Corn & Ma Goodness,* illustrated by Robert Andrew Parker, a tale told in alliterative nonsense verse but reflecting the elemental joys and sorrows of life; Eric Carle's *The Very Hungry Caterpillar,* an imaginative presentation of an insect's appetite and metamorphosis; and Seymour Chwast's and Martin Stephen Moskof's *Still Another Alphabet Book.*

Outstanding in the 6-9-year-old category were *Arm in Arm* by Remy Charlip, with puns, riddles, word play, stories, and unique typography, and Bruno Munari's *The Circus in the Mist,* an extraordinarily designed book with translucent pages and cutouts. Also noteworthy were *Broderick* by Edward Ormondroyd, illustrated by John Larrecq with droll drawings of a surfing mouse; M. B. Goffstein's *Goldie the Dollmaker,* the elegant, elusive story of an orphaned woodcarver who breathes a little of her soul into her dolls; and Sandol Stoddard Warburg's *Growing Time,* an account of life, death, and love.

The best books for readers 9–12 years old were Theodore Taylor's *The Cay,* an adventure story containing subtle commentary on racial prejudice; Glendon and Kathryn Swarthout's *The Button Boat,* a comic, suspenseful melodrama set in the Depression; E. L. Konigsburg's *About the B'nai Bagels,* the humorous story of a mother's management of a Little League team; Natalie Babbitt's *The Search for Delicious,* a fantasy adventure; and Paula Fox's *Portrait of Ivan,* about an 11-year-old boy's discovery of his identity, and *The King's Falcon,* a sensitive account of a king imprisoned in his own land and of the falcon that sets him free.

Teenagers' novels increasingly dealt with drugs, sex, and runaways, topics of pertinence to today's youth. The most successful books were *My Darling, My Hamburger* by Paul Zindel, about four high school seniors, one of whom has an abortion; *Escape From Nowhere* by Jeannette Eyerly, a perceptive treatment of the drug theme; John Donovan's *I'll Get There. It Better Be Worth the Trip,* a controversial novel containing an episode of sexual affection between two 13-year-old boys; and John Neufeld's *Lisa, Bright and Dark,* about mental illness.

History and Biography. In the area of history and biography the most distinguished books were Burke Davis' *Yorktown,* a graceful narrative of the Revolutionary campaign; Milton Meltzer's *Brother, Can You Spare a Dime?,* an expert account of the 1929–33 Depression in America; Martha E. Munzer's *Valley of Vision,* the story of the Tennessee Valley Authority, using eyewitness accounts of sharecroppers, hill folk, reporters, and government representatives; and Olivia Coolidge's *Tom Paine, Revolutionary,* in which the man emerges vividly.

Poetry. None of the many volumes of original poetry, published mainly for the very young reader, were particularly distinguished. Anthologies were more satisfactory, but critics complained of the repetitious use of standard poems in such collections. The most successful anthologies were *Some Haystacks Don't Even Have Any Needle,* modern poems compiled by Stephen Dunning, Edward Lueders, and Hugh Smith; *Shrieks at Midnight,* poems macabre, eerie, and humorous, selected by Sara and John E. Brewton; and Walter Lowenfels' collection of 108 poems of protest in *The Writing on the Wall.*

GEORGE A. WOODS
Editor, Children's Books
"The New York Times"

CHILE

The two events of major political significance in Chile during 1969 were the quadrennial congressional election in March and the "Chileanization" of the copper mining operations of the Anaconda Corporation in June. National attention also began to focus upon the presidential election scheduled for October 1970, and strained relations developed between Chile and the United States.

Congressional Election. On March 2 the voters of Chile went to the polls to elect 50 senators and 150 members of the Chamber of Deputies. The results showed a growing public frustration over continuing national problems for which the administration of President Eduardo Frei Montalva had been unable to find effective solutions. Support for the president's Christian Democratic party fell from 42% of the total vote in 1965 to 30% in 1969, and the party lost its majority in the Chamber of Deputies, although it retained pluralities in both houses.

The votes lost by the Christian Democrats went in almost equal proportions to parties of the politi-

cal right and left. The right-of-center National party, a union of the former Conservative and Liberal parties, won 20% of the vote, a gain of 7% over 1965. On the left, the Communist and Socialist parties obtained 16% and 14% respectively—a combined gain of 8%. The centrist Radical party retained the 13% share of the vote that it won in 1965.

With Christian Democratic representation in Congress reduced, the Frei administration could expect less support for its policies during its final year in office. Contributing to the Christian Democrats' decline were the economically disastrous drought of 1968, a resurgent inflation that was again nearing an annual rate of 30%, frequent strikes that disrupted public services and industry, high taxes, and fratricidal quarreling within the party itself.

"Chileanization" of the Copper Industry. For several years, the government had pursued the policy of purchasing 51% of the stock in foreign-owned mining companies, thereby acquiring a controlling voice in their management and a share in profits derived from Chile's natural resources. This so-called "Chileanizing" operation was an alternative to the complete nationalization of extractive industries through direct expropriation of mining companies.

In his annual message to Congress on May 21, President Frei promised to seek majority ownership of the Anaconda Corporation, the largest copper mining company owned by U. S. private interests and the only one not yet "Chileanized." Negotiations with the company were completed in June, and it was agreed that Chile would pay $198 million in government bonds for 51% of the company's shares and would have an option to purchase the remaining shares at a future time. Domestic criticism of this move came from proponents of expropriation.

Presidential Candidacies. Intraparty maneuvering looking to the nomination of candidates for the presidential campaign of 1970 began in earnest early in 1969. A major split in the Christian Democratic party was frankly acknowledged at its national convention in May. President Frei's loss of popularity caused a significant faction to criticize government policy and to advocate faster land reform, complete nationalization of the copper industry, and more open opposition to the U. S. role in Latin America. In August, the Christian Democrats nominated as their presidential candidate Radomiro Tomic, one of the party's founders, who had served as ambassador to the United States and had carefully disassociated himself from recent administration policies. By year's end, other parties had not yet made their nominations, but likely candidates included former President Jorge Alessandri of the National party.

Cancellation of Rockefeller Visit. The announcement of a scheduled visit by Nelson Rockefeller, who was making a survey of Latin American conditions for President Nixon, was met by violent student protests. This and growing anti-U. S. feeling in Chile induced the government, on June 4, to cancel the New York governor's visit.

Army Revolt. On October 21 two army regiments in Santiago rebelled to protest the low pay of military personnel and the poor condition of army equipment. The officers who led the uprising surrendered after one day, but President Frei, fearing an attempt at a coup d'etat, declared a state of siege. This was lifted after four days, and Frei promised to request that Congress raise military pay.

FRANK M. LEWIS
University of Toledo

CHILE · Information Highlights

Area: 292,256 square miles (756,945 sq km).
Population: 9,351,000 (1968 est.).
Chief Cities (1966 census): Santiago, the capital, 2,313,720; Valparaíso, 279,546; Concepción, 178,490.
Government: *President*—Eduardo Frei Montalva (took office Nov. 3, 1964). *Congress*—Chamber of Deputies, 150 members (party seating, 1969: Christian Democrats, 55; Nationalists, 34; Radicals, 24; Communists, 22; Socialists, 15; Senate, 50 members (party seating, 1969: Christian Democrats, 23; Radicals, 9; Communists, 6; Nationalists, 5; Socialists, 4; others, 3).
Religious Faiths: Roman Catholics, 89.5% of population.
Education: *Literacy rate* (1960), 84% of population aged 15 and over. *Total school enrollment* (1965)—1,919,132 (primary, 1,524,979; secondary, 218,305; teacher-training, 6,896; vocational, 125,344; higher, 43,608).
Finance (1968 budget est.): *Revenues,* $1,290,000,000; *public debt* (1966), $851,000,000; *monetary unit,* escudo (7.67 escudos equal U. S.$1).
Gross National Product (1967 est.): $6,200,000,000.
National Income (1967): $3,256,584,000; average annual income per person, $348.
Economic Indexes (1967): *Manufacturing,* 117 (1958=100); *agricultural production,* 99 (1963=100); *cost of living,* 273 (1963=100).
Manufacturing (metric tons, 1967): Gasoline, 1,000,000; cement, 65,000; wheat flour (1966), 18,000.
Crops (metric tons, 1967–68 crop year): Wheat, 1,204,000; sugar beets, 1,164,000; potatoes, 717,000.
Minerals (metric tons, 1967): Iron ore, 10,776,000; limestone (1966), 2,216,000; crude petroleum, 1,608,000; coal, 1,356,000; nitrates (1966), 1,062,000.
Foreign Trade (1968): *Exports,* $933,000,000 (chief exports, 1967: copper, $712,500,000; *imports,* $743,000,000 (chief imports, 1966: electrical machinery and apparatus, $44,-100,000. *Chief trading partner* (1967): United States (took 18% of exports, supplied 30% of imports).
Transportation: *Roads* (1964), 36,425 miles (58,619 km); *motor vehicles* (1967), 232,800 (automobiles 115,500); *railways* (1965), 4,857 miles (7,816 km); *merchant vessels* (1967), 46 (262,000 gross registered tons); *national airline,* Linea Aerea Nacional De Chile (LAN).

CHINA

China, the most populous nation in the world, remains divided into two opposing regimes: Communist China (the People's Republic of China), situated on the mainland; and Nationalist China (the Republic of China), on the island of Taiwan.

COMMUNIST CHINA

The 9th Congress of the Chinese Communist party in 1969 adopted a new party charter designating Lin Piao as Mao Tse-tung's political successor. It elected a new leadership combining leftist supporters of the Cultural Revolution, militarists, and veteran bureaucrats.

Peking's new economic policy, announced in October 1969, stressed the development of light industry and agriculture. It included plans for dispersing industry as a precautionary measure against the possibility of war. In line with this policy, more independence was given to communes to make them self-sufficient units.

Chinese and Soviet troops clashed on the Manchurian border and the Sinkiang frontier. Communist China called for massive war preparations, but agreed to hold border talks with the Soviets at Peking.

The 9th Congress. The 9th Congress of the Chinese Communist party was convened on April 1, 1969. Its purpose was to rebuild the party, which had been practically destroyed during the Cultural Revolution. The 1,512 delegates attending elected Mao Tse-tung chairman, Lin Piao deputy chairman, and Chou En-lai general secretary of its 176-man presidium. The presence of a large number of military men in the presidium indicated the growing influence of the army, but the Cultural Revolution group was also strongly represented; its leader, Chiang Ch'ing ranked 6th in the presidium. The divergent views of the various factions in the congress caused many important issues to be fiercely debated.

To revamp the party machine, the congress adopted a new party charter on April 14. It contained an unusual provision designating Defense Minister Lin Piao as Mao Tse-tung's eventual successor. Lin had already been elevated to second position during the Cultural Revolution and both moves were indicative of the important role played by the army in the purge of Mao's enemies. The charter made it clear that the "Thought of Mao Tse-tung" formed the theoretical basis of the party's guided thinking. It also permitted members to protest and appeal any party decision that might deviate from Mao's policies.

On April 1, on behalf of the party, Lin Piao presented a 24,000-word political report to the 9th Congress. In it he declared that although the Cultural Revolution had won a great victory over China's revisionists, the final victory was yet to come. He called for continued struggle against revisionism both inside and outside the party and placed an extraordinary stress on the role of the army in political affairs.

The defense minister also maintained a hardline policy in international affairs. Condemning "U. S. imperialism" and "Soviet revisionism," he charged that the two countries were working hand-in-glove against Peking. He pledged support for the "revolutionary struggles" of all "oppressed peoples and nations," citing particularly the people of Albania, Vietnam, Southeast Asia, Africa, Latin America, and the black people of the United States. While calling both the United States and the Soviet Union "paper tigers," Lin warned that China must make full preparations against their launching either a large-scale nuclear or a conventional war at an early date.

New Committee Leadership. The new Central Committee elected by the 9th Congress reelected Mao Tse-tung its chairman and named Lin Piao deputy chairman. Larger than the old one, which consisted of 97 members and 99 alternates, the new

EASTFOTO

PEKING DEMONSTRATORS denounce Soviet "renegade revisionists" as long-rumored Sino-Soviet split becomes more pronounced. Russian and Chinese troops confronted each other from April to August on their common border along China's Sinkiang Province, with occasional battles breaking out over disputed borders.

COMMUNIST CHINA • Information Highlights

Area: 3,691,502 square miles (9,561,000 sq km).
Population: 730,000,000 (1968 est.).
Chief Cities (1958 est.): Peking, the capital (1959 est.), 6,800,000; Shanghai, 6,977,000; Tientsin, 3,278,000; Mukden, 2,424,000.
Government: *Premier*—Chou En-lai (took office 1949); *Communist party Chairman*—Mao Tse-tung (took office 1935). *Legislature* (unicameral)—National People's Congress, 3,040 members.
Religious Faiths: Buddhists, 20% of population; Muslims, 5%; Taoists, 4%.
Education: *School enrollment*—primary (1959), 90,000,000; secondary (1958), 8,520,000; teacher-training (1958), 620,-000; technical/vocational (1958), 850,000; university/higher (1962), 820,000.
Finance (1960 est.): *Revenues*, $35,010,000,000; *expenditures*, $35,010,000,000; *monetary unit*, yuan (2 yuan equal U. S.$1).
National Income (1960): $84,500,000,000; *average annual income per person*, $123.
Manufacturing (metric tons, 1967): Crude steel, 11,000,000; cement, 11,000,000; sugar, 2,575,000.
Crops (metric tons, 1967–68 crop year): Rice, 92,000,000 (ranks 1st among world producers); soybeans, 11,200,000 (world rank, 2d).
Minerals (metric tons, 1967): Coal (1966), 325,000,000 (ranks 3d among world producers); magnesite, 800,000 (world rank, 5th); iron ore (1966), 310,000; salt, 13,000,000; crude petroleum (1966), 13,000,000.
Foreign Trade (1964): *Exports*, $1,500,000,000; *Imports*, $1,200,000,000. *Chief trading partners:* Albania (1963) took 28% of exports, supplied 21% of imports); USSR (1964; took 20% of exports, supplied 11% of imports); Hong Kong (1965; took 26% of exports, supplied 1% of imports).
Transportation: *Roads* (1958), 249,000 miles (400,000 km); *motor vehicles* (1965), 246,600 (automobiles, 32,900); *railways* (1965), 19,500 miles (31,381 km); *principal airport*, Peking.
Communications: *Telephones* (1968): 244,028; *television stations* (1967), 30; *television sets* (1967), 100,000; *radios* (1963), 8,000,000; *newspapers* (1955), 392 (daily circulation, 12,000,000).

committee had 170 members and 109 alternates. With the old committee purged of 67% of its members during the Cultural Revolution, the new group was dominated by activists and army men, especially the latter, who composed over 45% of the committee membership.

The Central Committee elected a new Politburo of 21 members and 4 alternate members. Of the 21 full members, seven were trusted followers of Mao Tse-tung and six were close associates of Lin Piao. Chou En-lai remained in third position, but only one of his close associates, Li Hsien-nien, was elected to the Politburo.

A 5-man Standing Committee of the Politburo was also elected by the Central Committee. The reduction of its membership from seven to five reflected the increased concentration of power at the top. In the new Standing Committee were Mao Tse-tung, Lin Piao, Chou En-lai, Ch'en Po-ta and K'ang

Sheng. The last two were leaders of the leftist Cultural Revolution group.

The new group of leaders that emerged from the 9th Congress represented a delicate balance of power. The militarists gained strength in the Central Committee, but the Cultural Revolution group, which had constituted Mao's basic force, was dominant in the Standing Committee, the top echelon of party command. Mao remained the supreme leader and although some resemblance of collective leadership was maintained, it was he who exercised controlling influence in the party. Chou En-lai, who represented the veteran bureaucrats, gained prominence as a pragmatic administrator able to keep the country functioning. A man of great dexterity, he did not, however, have the forceful personality needed to fight for supreme power.

Continuing Disunity. The 9th Congress called for national unity. But unity, badly needed after three years of factional strife, was difficult to attain. Discontent was widespread, and conflict continued in the provinces.

In Shanghai the militant left continued to make bids for greater power in the party committees. In Shansi province the factional struggle became so serious that armed forces had to be dispatched to the provincial capital to enforce a settlement. A document issued by the Central Committee in July revealed that the Shansi dissidents had taken money from state banks and had manufactured weapons in state factories for factional use.

In an intensive campaign launched in August to combat factionalism and anarchy, Peking called for mass criticism to rectify erroneous thoughts and to purge reactionaries. In various provinces "command groups" were formed to go into factories to correct cases of anarchy and apathy. House-to-house visits were made to peasant families to examine their thoughts and to remove their errors.

Economy. On Oct. 14, 1969, Peking issued a lengthy exposition of its economic policy. This was the first such long-range pronouncement since 1966. The statement laid stress on light industry and agriculture as the basis for the development of heavy industry. It also emphasized the importance of self-reliance in economic development and advocated maximum exertion for minimum material reward. To insure greater maneuverability in case of war, Peking called for industry to be dispersed throughout the country.

In the agricultural sector, Peking emphasized the

EASTFOTO

LIN PIAO, defense minister of the People's Republic of China, was formally designated as Chairman Mao Tse-tung's "close comrade-in-arms and successor" in a new constitution adopted by the 9th Communist party Congress in April 1969. In his speech in observance of the 20th anniversary of the People's Republic in October, Lin attacked "United States imperialism" and the "social imperialism" of the Soviet Union.

Lin Piao was born about 1908 in the village of Huilungshan, Huangkang, Hupeh province. He joined the Young Socialist League as a student and later attended Whampoa Military Academy under Chiang Kai-shek, graduating in 1925. Lin joined the Communist party in 1927 and distinguished himself as a strategist of guerrilla warfare. He became one of the major commanders of Communist forces in the civil war.

need for increased mechanization, better electrification, and improved irrigation. It also sought the development of small- and medium-sized industries in the countryside.

Communes would be given more independence so that they could become self-sufficient units equipped to meet their own economic and social needs. They were also expected to generate their own capital to finance local enterprises and services. Communes would be responsible for the operation of factories, mines, and hydroelectric stations in the rural areas and take over the agricultural stations that were formerly managed by state officials.

In spite of the bad weather, floods, and other natural adversities occurring in some areas, Communist China reported excellent grain harvests and high output in cotton, silk cocoons, tea, and tobacco. Peking gave no figures regarding grain yields, but said that they were higher than those of 1968. It attributed the greater rice output to the introduction of new strains developed in China. The new seeds, however, were similar to the "miracle" grain developed in the Philippines.

In September, Peking announced that the discoveries of new oil deposits had made Communist China self-sufficient in that mineral. The statement said that oil output in 1969 had risen several times over that of 1965, which was estimated at 10 million tons by some specialists.

Nuclear Blasts. China detonated two nuclear devices in 1969, on September 23 and 29. The first was an underground nuclear test in the low-intermediate range, but the second was believed to be a 3-megaton hydrogen bomb explosion.

In a speech on September 30, Premier Chou En-lai declared that while China was developing nuclear arms only for defensive purposes, it was prepared for both conventional and nuclear wars against "foreign aggressors."

Soviet Border Clashes. The Sino-Soviet rift, which has lasted over a decade, finally led to serious border clashes in 1969. In March, fighting broke out on Chenpao Island (called Damansky Island by the Soviets) in the Ussuri River, which forms the border between the two countries. A number of Chinese and Soviet soldiers were killed and wounded. Each side charged that troops of the other had crossed into its territory. Since the Ussuri River was frozen at that time of year, fighting largely occurred on the ice.

In a statement issued on March 10, Peking asserted that during boundary negotiations in 1964 the Soviet Union had recognized the island as being within Chinese territory. The Chinese statement traced the Sino-Soviet boundaries to a series of Russian aggressive moves in the 19th century and the resulting treaties of Aigun (1858) and Peking (1860), by which Czarist Russia had annexed large areas of Chinese territory north of the Amur River and east of the Ussuri River. Peking stated that it was willing to accept these treaties as the basis for determining the boundary between the two countries, but made it clear that this should not preclude necessary readjustments at individual places on the boundary.

Anti-Soviet Drive. From March 3 to 14, millions of Chinese took part in anti-Soviet demonstrations throughout the country. In Peking waves of people marched past the Soviet embassy, maintaining a virtual siege in protest over the border clash. Peking proclaimed its determination to smash the Soviets

EASTFOTO

MAO TSE-TUNG, Communist Party Chairman, Lin Piao, Vice Chairman, and Premier Chou En-lai cast their ballots at the ninth congress of China's Communist Party.

"completely, thoroughly and wholly" if they again dared to intrude into Chinese territory.

On August 13 another clash occurred on the western border in Yumin county, where the Soviet republic of Kazakhstan meets the Sinkiang-Uigur Autonomous Region of China. Peking asserted that a Soviet force of several hundred men, supported by helicopters and tanks, penetrated Chinese territory and fired at the Chinese guards, killing and wounding many of them.

War Preparations. Following the border clash in March, both Communist China and the Soviet Union intensified their efforts at a military build-up along their border. It was estimated that the combined total of troops deployed on both sides amounted to at least 1.5 million. Large forces were concentrated in Manchuria, Inner Mongolia, and Sinkiang. They consisted of mobile units and were supported by nuclear weapons.

In August, immediately after the Sinkiang clash, new troop movements were reported in Communist China. Contingents equipped with artillery moved northward from Canton and Wuchang. Militia units were mobilized on the Siberian border and were deployed with border guards.

Negotiations. In spite of intense military preparations, neither side really wanted war. On September 11, Soviet Premier Aleksei N. Kosygin, on his way from Ho Chi Minh's funeral in Hanoi, stopped at the Peking airport to discuss the situation with Premier Chou En-lai. The conference paved the way for the border negotiations, which finally opened at Peking on October 20. The Chinese delegation, headed by Deputy Foreign Minister Ch'iao Kuan-hua, reiterated China's position that while the treaties imposed by Czarist Russia should form the basis of the negotiations, the entire alignment of the boundary must be determined with a view to making necessary adjustments, on the principles of equal footing and mutual accommodation.

No progress in the negotiations was reported at the end of the year. To back up its position at the negotiation table, Peking ordered air-raid shelters built throughout China and people to be trained in guerrilla warfare. (See also COMMUNISM.)

Policy Toward the United States. Peking kept up its attack on the United States after Richard Nixon became president in 1969. Articles in the party organ *Jen Min Jih Pao* described the President as a new "reactionary chieftain" to whom American capitalism, "in deep crisis," had turned.

On February 18, Peking suddenly canceled the ambassadorial-level meeting at Warsaw through which Washington had hoped to discuss the possibility of a détente. The reason given by Peking for barring the meeting was that the United States had granted asylum to a high-ranking Chinese diplomat who had defected in the Netherlands.

The United States took symbolic steps to relax its isolation of Communist China. On July 21, the government announced that U. S. citizens would be permitted to bring home up to $100 worth of goods produced in Communist China. Restrictions against travel to Communist China were also lifted for scholars, students, scientists, physicians, and newsmen. Peking ignored Washington's new policy. Toward the end of the year, however, apparently because of its strained relations with the USSR, Communist China began to show interest in resuming ambassadorial talks with the United States in Warsaw.

Support of North Vietnam. Peking continued its militant policy toward the Vietnam War, urging the Vietnamese Communists to continue fighting until complete victory was won. It expressed displeasure with the Paris peace talks and warned that victory could be attained only on the battlefield.

Premier Chou En-lai flew to Hanoi in the morning of September 4 to offer condolences over the death of President Ho Chi Minh of North Vietnam. He left the same evening, thus avoiding a meeting with Soviet Premier Kosygin, who arrived later. In Hanoi, Chou told the North Vietnamese leaders that Communist China solidly backed the Vietnamese people in their war against the United States.

Other Countries. After the 9th Congress in April, Peking took steps to normalize its diplomatic functions abroad. By August it had appointed 17 ambassadors to replace envoys who had been withdrawn for examination and indoctrination during the

CHOU EN-LAI, Chinese premier, greets Soviet premier Alexei Kosygin at Peking airport on September 11.

UPI

Cultural Revolution. It also relaxed travel restrictions imposed on foreign diplomats since 1967. In June the British chargé d'affaires was permitted to visit Shanghai and Nanking, while ambassadors from other countries were allowed to tour cities away from Peking. Between October ˙and December, Peking released a number of foreign prisoners, including one British reporter, seven Germans, and two Americans.

Peking's normalization efforts should not be interpreted as radical changes in its policy toward the West. Canada and Italy, which had negotiated with Peking on diplomatic recognition since the spring of 1969, reported no agreement at the end of the year.

NATIONALIST CHINA

The Nationalists called for extensive political reforms to invigorate and modernize Taiwan. The fifth 4-year economic plan (1969–1972) aimed at broad industrial and transportation developments. Taipei continued to advocate the establishment of an Asian security system to fight Communism.

National Congress. The 10th National Congress of the Kuomintang (Nationalist party) was convened on March 29. Of the 1,200 persons attending, more than half were delegates and the rest were observers. Chiang Kai-shek was reelected head of the party, and Chang Pao-shu was named secretary general. The congress elected 99 members to the Central Committee and 21 to the Standing Committee, with Defense Minister Chiang Ching-kuo and Vice President Yen Chia-kan heading the respective lists.

The congress called for an acceleration of the political reform needed to make China a wholly modern country. It pledged full support for the early completion of national reconstruction and urged that great efforts be made to bring youth into the party.

Reformation of the party was intended as a prelude to reformation of the government. The Kuomintang leadership wanted an overall political evolution that would match the growth achieved in the economic field. It recognized the need of change and the desirability of an attractive new image.

Cabinet Reshuffle. In a governmental reorganization on June 25, President Chiang Kai-shek named his son, Ching-kuo, vice premier. His son was succeeded as defense minister by Gen. Huang Chieh, who relinquished his post as provincial governor in favor of Gen. Ch'en Tai-ch'ing.

Though theoretically subordinate to Premier Yen Chia-kan, Chiang Ching-kuo was expected to overshadow the premier. The promotion of Ching-kuo to vice premier was regarded as another move by President Chiang Kai-shek, 81 years old, to prepare his son to succeed him eventually.

Local Election. The Kuomintang won 43 out of 48 seats in the election for Taipei's city council on Nov. 15, 1969. It was the first election since the city became a special municipality with the status of a province two years before. Kuomintang candidates were mostly younger men and women, and many of them were native Taiwanese. Five independent candidates were elected, but all minority party members were defeated.

Economic Developments. The fifth 4-year economic plan, which started Jan. 1, 1969, involved a total investment of $4.5 billion. Of this amount $1.7 billion was designated for industrial development. Among the industrial projects were the construction of two petrochemical plants to produce intermediate material for the development of plastics, synthetics,

CHIANG KAI-SHEK, president of the Republic of China, urged his countrymen on the 58th anniversary of the Nationalist Chinese republic to redouble their efforts to recover the Communist-controlled Chinese mainland. Earlier in the year he took steps to make his ruling Kuomintang party more representative of the new economic and political forces on Taiwan and to place greater authority in the hands of his son and probable successor, Chiang Ching-kuo.

Chiang was born on Oct. 30, 1887, at Chikou, in Fenghua, Chekiang province. He joined Sun-Yat-sen's revolutionary forces in 1911, and after becoming commander in chief of republican forces and chairman of the Nanking national government in 1928, he waged intensive warfare against Communist forces, then under Mao Tse-tung. The Communists conquered the mainland in 1949.

and fertilizers; a steel mill to develop metal production; and a large nuclear power plant to be completed by 1975.

The economic plan earmarked $760 million for the improvement of transportation and communications over the 4-year period. Major projects included the completion of a round-the-island rail system, the construction of the Suao-Hualien railway in eastern Taiwan, and the establishment of a deluxe express service between northern and southern Taiwan. Also planned was a new international airport, larger than the one at Taipei, to be built in Taoyuan in northern Taiwan. The new airport would be completed in 1973.

A new international harbor was projected for Wuchi in central Taiwan to cope with the growing volume of shipping. An export processing zone with facilities for 50 factories was also planned for central Taiwan.

Taiwan was confident that economic growth in 1969 would surpass the 7% goal set by the fifth 4-year plan. Industrial growth on the island for the first 10 months of the year was reported at the record high of 19.8%.

Rapid economic growth did not leave Taiwan without problems. Industrialization and booming business brought problems of housing, traffic, and air pollution to urban centers. The shortage of apartments became so serious in Taipei that government subsidies to public housing projects were considered the only solution.

Foreign Relations. Taiwan expressed serious concern in August 1969, after President Nixon's announcement of his new policy of urging Asian nations to be more self-reliant in resisting "Communist aggression" or guerrilla insurrections. Taipei also believed that the U. S. decision to ease trade and travel restrictions against Communist China would have definite ill effects upon the free countries. During his visit to Taipei in August, however, Secretary of State William P. Rogers assured the Nationalist government that the United States would continue to meet its treaty obligations to Taiwan.

Nationalist China was confronted with a serious threat to its diplomatic status in the West when Canada held talks with Communist China on the question of diplomatic recognition. The outcome of Canada's initiative could influence the decisions of Italy, Belgium, Luxembourg, and Portugal, all of which were considering the possible recognition of Peking.

Taipei had long advocated an Asian security organization to fight possible Communist aggression. The theme was given new emphasis during Defense Minister Chiang Ching-kuo's visit to South Korea in February and to Thailand in May. When South Vietnamese President Nguyen Van Thieu visited Taipei in June, President Chiang personally brought up the question of an Asian security organization. South Korea and South Vietnam expressed enthusiasm, but Thailand was cautious. The Nationalists failed to gain support for their security scheme in the meeting of the Asian and Pacific Council that was held in Japan in June.

CHESTER C. TAN
New York University

--- NATIONALIST CHINA • Information Highlights ---

Area: 13,885 square miles (35,961 sq km).
Population: 14,000,000 (1968 est.).
Chief Cities (1968 est.): Taipei, the capital, 1,600,000; Kaohsiung, 713,000; Tainan (1965), 407,714.
Government: *President*—Chiang Kai-shek (reelected for 4th term March 21, 1966); *Premier*—Yen Chia-kan (took office 1963). *Parliament*—Legislative Yüan, 493 members.
Religious Faiths: Buddhists and Taoists, majority of population; Roman Catholics, 2.2%; other Christians, 2%.
Education: *Literacy rate* (1964), 96.7% of population aged 12 and over. *Total school enrollment* (1965)—3,006,819 (primary, 2,257,720; secondary, 543,018; teacher-training, 3,159; technical/vocational, 117,575; university/higher, 85,346).
Finance (1968 est.): *Revenues,* $622,000,000; *expenditures,* $729,000,000; *monetary unit,* new Taiwan dollar (40.10 dollars equal U. S.$1).
Gross National Product (1968): $4,154,613,000.
National Income (1968): $3,314,214,000; *average annual income per person,* $246.
Economic Indexes (1967): *Industrial production* (1968), 228 (1963=100); *agricultural production,* 132 (1963=100); *cost of living,* 105 (1963=100).

Manufacturing (metric tons, 1967): Cement, 3,487,000; sugar, 825,000; crude steel, 443,000.
Crops (metric tons, 1967–68 crop year): Sweet potatoes and yams, 3,720,000 (ranks 3d among world producers); rice, 3,162,000; bananas, 654,000.
Minerals (metric tons, 1967): Bituminous coal, 5,078,000; clays (1965), 1,314,000; salt, 518,000.
Foreign Trade (1968): *Exports,* $843,000,000 (chief exports, 1967: sugar, $37,795,500; rice, $21,000,000; tea, $10,748,-000; petroleum products, $501,000); *imports,* $976,000,000 (chief imports, 1967: nonelectrical machinery, $138,745,-600; transport equipment, $69,471,000; iron and steel, $63,000,000). *Chief trading partners* (1968): Japan (took 18% of exports, supplied 41% of imports); United States (took 32% of exports, supplied 31% of imports); West Germany (took 6% of exports, supplied 4% of imports).
Transportation: *Roads* (1967), 10,421 miles (16,772 km); *motor vehicles* (1967), 211,758 (automobiles 25,108); *railways* (1963), 2,308 miles (3,714 km); *national airlines,* Civil Air Transport; Foshing Airlines; *principal airport,* Sungshan.
Communications: *Telephones* (1968): 230,229; *television stations* (1968), 4; *television sets* (1968), 100,000; *radios* (1967), 1,402,000; *newspapers* (1968) 31.

CHRISTIAN CHURCH (DISCIPLES OF CHRIST)

At its first General Assembly following reorganization as a "church" rather than a convention of congregations and agencies, the Christian Church (Disciples of Christ) took action in 1969 to double the religious body's financial response to the race and poverty crisis. Meeting at Seattle, Wash., August 15–20, the General Assembly, in a voice vote, doubled the goal to $4 million, and lengthened the fund-raising program to four years. In so doing, the General Assembly implicitly endorsed a rejection by the church's General Board the previous May of the "ideology, methodology and language" of the Black Manifesto, the demand by black militants for reparations from churches.

The General Assembly was the first on a biannual basis for the Disciples of Christ. Previously, the Disciples held annual conventions. Until 1967, these were on an everybody-come, everybody-vote basis. The new General Assembly has voting delegates from congregations, regions, and institutions.

Dr. A. Dale Fiers, who had been serving as general minister and president of the church since the restructuring effort in 1968 brought the office into being, was elected to the first full six-year term as chief executive of the church. Dr. James M. Moudy, chancellor of Texas Christian University, was elected moderator.

The Christian Church set these priorities for the period until 1975: leadership; evangelism and renewal; world order, justice, and peace; ecumenical involvement; and reconciliation in the urban crisis.

ROBERT L. FRIEDLY
Director, Office of Interpretation, Christian Church

CHRISTIAN SCIENCE

More than 16,000 Christian Scientists from all parts of the world attended the annual meeting in June and the biennial college organization meeting in August 1969 at the Christian Science denominational headquarters in Boston, Mass. The Christian Science board of directors elected L. Ivimy Gwalter of Boston president of The First Church of Christ, Scientist, for the year ending in June 1970.

David E. Sleeper of Boston was elected to the Christian Science board of directors effective Oct. 24, 1969. He succeeds Thomas E. Hurley, who died in Boston on October 20. Sleeper had served the five-member board of directors as executive administrator since June 1968.

Advertising and sales of the Bible and the Christian Science textbook, *Science and Health with Key to the Scriptures*, by Mary Baker Eddy, increased substantially during the year. With a new Polish edition appearing in 1969, *Science and Health* is published in 11 languages as well as in English braille. More than 75 million pieces of literature were published and distributed by the Christian Science Publishing Society. Christian Science lecturers delivered 4,280 lectures in 56 countries.

The $30 million Church Center on a 16-acre site adjoining the Mother Church and the Christian Science Publishing Society was about 25 percent completed at the end of 1969. The Church Center will provide four new structures including an administration building to replace outdated facilities.

J. BUROUGHS STOKES
The First Church of Christ, Scientist, Boston

CHURCH OF JESUS CHRIST OF LATTER-DAY SAINTS

In 1969 the church had 4,385 wards and independent branches in 473 stakes (territorial units) and 2,112 branches in 83 missions. There were approximately 13,000 full-time missionaries working among nonmembers in missions and about 5,000 part-time missionaries in the stakes. Total church membership was approximately 2,750,000. New stakes were organized in São Paulo, Brazil; Pago Pago, Samoa; Dresden, East Germany; New Zealand; a servicemen's stake in Europe; as well as numerous stakes in the United States. Marvin J. Ashton was sustained as an assistant to the Council of the Twelve. Correlated religious activities have been provided for church students on college campuses by means of institutes, student stakes and councils, and student-led spiritual training.

The Young Women's Mutual Improvement Association, with 370,000 members, commemorated its centennial anniversary. The purpose of this organization as established by Brigham Young is to provide spiritual, cultural, recreational, and social activities for the young women of the church.

Through the Church Indian Placement Program thousands of Indian young people were brought into homes of faithful church members where they are trained in secular subjects with the spiritual enrichment of family and community life.

A world conference on records was held in Salt Lake City in August under the sponsorship of the Genealogical Society of the church.

JOSEPH ANDERSON
Secretary to the First Presidency

CHURCHES OF CHRIST

Radio work continued to hold an important place in the program of Churches of Christ during 1969. Herald of Truth expanded its service on both radio and television. World Radio continued to expand into various countries, preaching in many languages. One outstanding addition was a program on Radio España in Madrid, Spain. Together with Radio Mirimar in Portugal, the stations are able to reach listeners throughout Spain.

Correspondence courses are frequently used in conjunction with radio programs. These courses are tied in with the religious broadcasts on the network in São Paulo State, Brazil. This arrangement reportedly brings in thousands of enrollments.

Emphasis on missionary work continues. The colleges annually promote a World Missions Workshop which was held in 1969 at Northeastern Christian Junior College, Villanova, Pa. Workshops for missionaries themselves are an annual event at Harding College in Arkansas and Abilene Christian College in Texas. Congregations are also holding workshops. One such was held by a Knoxville, Tenn., congregation in 1969 for the fourth time.

Increasing activity in missions took place in Portugal, Liberia, Malaysia, Germany, Ghana, and other countries. Schools of preaching are developing in the mission areas for training workers. The first annual Mediterranean Lectures, held in Athens, Greece, and the first annual Mission Workshop, in Belo Horizonte, Brazil, are typical of efforts for encouraging workers in the field.

ELZA HUFFARD
Northeastern Christian Junior College

BIG-CITY MAYORS, including Chicago's Daley (*foreground*), Cleveland's Stokes, (*left*), and New York's Lindsay (*2d from right*), discuss urban problems with President Nixon and his urban affairs adviser Moynihan (*at President's right*).

WIDE WORLD

cities and urban affairs

The environment of the United States is overwhelmingly an urban one. In 1969 almost two thirds of the American people resided in fairly large cities, and approximately half of the total population was packed into 213 urban areas, occupying less than 1% of the country's land.

Although American social and political values are rooted traditionally in the countryside, the shift from a rural to an urban nation occurred nearly a half century ago, in the early 1920's. This shift developed without plan, prevision, or insight, with the result that American cities have grown uncontrollably, and an urban crisis of monumental proportions exists.

The Urban Crisis. The fate of the cities stands second only to the Vietnam War as an issue in election campaigns, as a topic of popular debate, and as subject matter in the mass media. What is now at stake is literally whether the modern city can exist as a habitable environment—whether the modern city can provide clean air and water, adequate sanitary facilities, satisfactory means of transportation, and relief from noise, congestion, and pollution—not to speak of adequate schools and public services.

The urban crisis is marked by two distinct features: severe deterioration of the city's center and burgeoning suburban sprawl on the perimeter. The drift to the suburbs of relatively well-to-do families tends to diminish the tax base of large cities, reducing their income for public services and urban restoration. In turn, the automobile, linking residential suburbs to central business districts, creates staggering burdens of vehicular congestion on highways and in city streets.

Each feature reinforces the other in a downward spiral of the cities. As the central area declines because of congestion and want of public services, the exodus to the suburbs continues. Congestion from suburban automotive traffic increases, public transit facilities decline, and slum areas around the central business districts proliferate.

Urban Renewal. Renewal plans and new construction have generally served to worsen, rather than improve, the urban environment. Although many ambitious projects have been undertaken, the trend in most cases has been toward gigantism—skyscrapers for business enterprises and high-rise buildings for home dwellers.

Competition to build soaring, often architecturally insipid structures seems to be sweeping leading U. S. cities. The attractive, low-slung cityscape of San Francisco is steadily giving way to skyscrapers. Controversy in the Bay Area in 1969 centered around plans to construct the Transamerica Corporation building, a needle-like structure that will be the largest building in the city. In Dallas, plans were completed in 1969 to erect the world's tallest concrete building, a 913-foot high (278-meter) office building and hotel. Houston has already erected the Shell Building, a 714-foot structure.

173

The tendency toward structural gigantism is not only vertical but also horizontal: during the year Boston completed the first of its "horizontal skyscrapers," the Central Plaza Office Building, a curved, seven-story 900-foot long structure that will provide 75,000 square feet (6,968 sq. meters) of space.

New York City, however, continues to lead the way in urban gigantism. Plans were unfolded in May 1969 to construct Battery Park City, a 90-acre (36-hectare) landfill project of 60-story and 40-story hexagonal structures in lower Manhattan that will provide 19,000 dwelling units for an estimated 55,000 people. The Battery Park City will be linked by pedestrian walkways to the World Trade Center, a complex of skyscrapers that is under construction nearby.

Nearly 61 million square feet (5,667,000 sq. meters) of office space, generally in the form of skyscrapers, have been built in New York City over the past two decades, nearly twice the area devoted to this purpose in the nine next largest U. S. cities combined. An additional 50 million square feet are currently in the planning or construction phases. New York's "Master Plan," released in November 1969, has been the subject of heavy criticism for its lack of proposals to meet needs for adequate housing, schools, and health facilities.

Widespread public resentment and neighborhood resistance are developing against speculators who buy apartment buildings in downgraded sections, expel the underprivileged tenants, and renovate the buildings for occupancy at exorbitant rents.

The shrinking tax-base of large U. S. cities has opened the problem of tax-exempt institutions with large real-estate holdings. In New York City, nearly 35% of potentially taxable property is held by tax-exempt educational institutions, religious bodies, and research groups. In Milwaukee, tax-exempt institutions hold 25% of potentially taxable property; in Pittsburgh and Providence, the figure reaches 33%; and in Boston, the figure soars to 45%.

Transportation. The need to reduce vehicular congestion has focused a great deal of attention on existing and planned public transit facilities. With the number of automobiles in the United States topping the 80-million mark in 1969 and with the prospect of this figure reaching nearly 120 million by 1975, vehicular congestion in city streets threatens to reach unmanageable proportions.

Thus far, San Francisco stands alone among U. S. cities in its effort to provide an adequate public transit system. The Bay Area Rapid Transit System (BART), a 75-mile (120-km) rail complex, will provide the city and its environs with air-conditioned trains operating at an average speed of 50 miles (80

THE NEW YORK TIMES

km) per hour. BART, when it is completed in the early 1970's, will be controlled automatically by scheduling devices, providing trains every two or three minutes during rush hours.

New subway systems are contemplated for Washington, Atlanta, and Los Angeles. In established subway systems, such as those in New York City, Boston, and Chicago, the emphasis has been placed on renovation programs, passenger comfort, and equipment renewal. (See also TRANSPORTATION.)

UPI

DANIEL PATRICK MOYNIHAN, who holds cabinet rank as urban affairs adviser to President Nixon, is credited with being the architect of the President's $4 billion welfare proposals of August 1969 to establish minimum standards of federal aid to families with children.

Moynihan was born on March 16, 1927, in Tulsa, Okla., and grew up in slum neighborhoods of New York City. He graduated from Tufts College (B. A., 1948) and from Tufts' Fletcher School of Law and Diplomacy (M. A., 1949; Ph. D., 1961). An active Democrat, he was on the staff of the governor of New York from 1955 to 1958, and in 1961 he became a special assistant in the Department of Labor. As assistant secretary of labor, from 1963 to 1965, he helped draft the Economic Opportunity Act of 1964 and wrote the controversial *The Negro Family: The Case for National Action* (1965). In 1966 he became director of the Joint Center for Urban Studies of the Massachusetts Institute of Technology and Harvard University.

CO-OP CITY in New York City's Bronx is the world's largest housing development. When completed it will house almost 60,000 persons on 300 acres.

Urban Government. The most serious problem facing U. S. cities is the inadequacy of funds for the maintenance and improvement of urban facilities. Nearly all municipal administrations of large cities have voiced complaints against the enormous outflow of local tax funds to the federal government. Most urban planning programs, in turn, require federal assistance of one kind or another, such as matching funds, grants, and insurance for financially insecure projects.

The federal government has responded by establishing agencies and departments that deal primarily with urban problems. In 1965, a Department of Housing and Urban Development was created on a cabinet level, followed a year later by the formation of a Department of Transportation. Housing and urban development legislation has been passed to provide funds for supplemental rent for underprivileged people, for "model city" demonstration programs, low mortgage rates, and high-speed transportation programs. The funds for these purposes, however, have always been grossly inadequate to meet growing needs.

An indicator of the current trend was the cutback by the Nixon administration of funds for the model cities program. A planned expenditure of some $500 million for 60 cities was reduced in the fall of 1969 to $300 million, presumably to curb inflation. In the meantime, enormous financial resources, direly needed for urban improvement and social welfare programs, were siphoned off to support the war in Vietnam.

The gigantism that marks the modern cityscape in the United States is paralleled by the gigantism that marks urban administration. An integral part of the American political ideal is the concept of local control over community affairs. This ideal has faded steadily in the face of growing federal power, the sweeping bureaucratization of municipal government, and the deterioration of neighborhoods and community life.

The right of the citizen to decide the fate of his community and his neighborhood, and his right to exercise influence in governmental institutions beyond the usual electoral ritual, has become a major issue in urban politics. This is reflected by promises of mayors, such as John V. Lindsay in New York City, to establish neighborhood "city halls" and by demands of ghetto dwellers to have a decisive voice in school boards and the disposition of antipoverty

UPPER INCOME FLIGHT TO SUBURBS

TAX SQUEEZE

CONTINUED DECAY

SCHOOL TROUBLES

CITIES

RACISM

CRIME

GHETTOS

© 1969 BY HERBLOCK IN THE WASHINGTON POST

"Vicious Circle"

funds. Whether in the form of rent strikes, street protests, or demands for "community control," urban Americans are increasingly turning to direct action to assert their sovereignty over centralized bureaucracies.

Outlook. The fate of U. S. cities appears grim. In increasing numbers, city planners believe that the cities are faced with a complete breakdown in the years ahead. The high hopes that "new towns," modeled on the English concept of fairly self-sufficient communities in countrified areas, could provide a solution to congestion, high population densities, and the erosion of public services have collapsed.

Nearly all the U. S. "new towns"—such as Reston near Washington, D. C., Clear Lake City near Houston, and Westlake near Los Angeles—have failed in their essential purposes. They tend to duplicate the suburbs that ring the large cities, developing either into retirement communities for elderly people or residential communities, tied economically and logistically to the large urban entities that are found nearby.

It is becoming evident that the modern U. S. city has expanded to such proportions that only a drastic decentralization of urban life can avert the predicted breakdown. A restoration of the human scale, a proper balance between town and country, a drastic reduction in congestion and pollution, and a recovery of local autonomy are stark preconditions for a stable, satisfying, and viable urban environment. To achieve these goals, however revolutionary their impact may be on existing social and political institutions, has passed from the realm of vision into that of necessity.

LEWIS HERBER
Specialist in City Planning;
Author of "Crisis in Our Cities"

CIVIL RIGHTS AND LIBERTIES

Whether the year 1969 represented the epilogue of a story that began some 15 years before, when Earl Warren was appointed chief justice of the U. S. Supreme Court, or the prologue for a completely new or a revised story was a topic much discussed by analysts of the civil rights movement and students of the political scene. The one thing that was clear was that the 15 years of the "Warren Court" saw the greatest emphasis on legally protected rights that the nation had yet experienced.

But 1969 saw the retirement of Chief Justice Warren and his replacement by Warren E. Burger, and it was the first full year of government under President Nixon, whose election was partially due to antiliberal votes in the South. Many saw his nomination to the Supreme Court of the conservative judge Clement F. Haynsworth as an indication of the era to come. Fear was expressed that the slowdown in desegregation of schools in Mississippi and two other Southern states indicated a dilution of the court's 1954 ruling calling for "all deliberate speed" in the matter.

Nevertheless, in the last months of the Warren Court, that tribunal handed down a few important decisions in favor of civil rights and answered some of the questions left open by its earlier revolutionary judgments on legislative apportionment, freedom of expression, and criminal procedure. Most significantly, a major ruling handed down in October strongly suggested that the Supreme Court under Chief Justice Burger had determined that it would stand by the Warren Court's 1954 landmark decision against school desegregation.

The Mississippi Slowdown. The transition year of 1969 cannot be understood without some emphasis on the "Mississippi slowdown." Under an earlier plan for desegregation that had been ordered by the U. S. Office of Education, Leake County in Mississippi was required to abolish its "attendance centers," or groupings of schools. Two white "centers" were to become integrated high schools, and three Negro groupings and one white one were to become integrated elementary schools. Some 30 school districts were affected in all.

The Nixon administration asked the federal court to delay enforcement of the order for at least a year in order to prevent "chaos, confusion, and a catastrophic educational setback." Similar requests were made in Louisiana and Oklahoma. The basis for the turmoil was the alleged refusal of white families to cooperate by threatening to send their children to private schools or no schools at all.

Almost unanimously, commentators labeled this explanation as a cover for the administration's so-called "Southern strategy." Their opinion was shared by the bi-partisan U. S. Commission on Civil Rights, which labeled the action a "major retreat." Clearly some testimony to the same effect was evidenced in the frenzied welcome given President Nixon when he visited the hurricane-damaged city of Gulfport in early September or by the well-known fact that the Gulfport area remains almost completely segregated in other aspects of life. Critics of the action charged that Southerners would seize on this maneuver as proof that pressure could accomplish further delays.

Supreme Court School Decision. In what could hardly have been a more dramatic initial act, the Burger court, on October 29, handed down a unanimous decision ordering an end to all school desegregation "at once." As a result, several hundred Southern school districts were expected to see a considerable acceleration of the process of ending the dual school system. The Nixon administration, in response to the order, announced its support of the decision but emphasized the difficulties of compliance.

Other Supreme Court Rulings. From a statistical standpoint, 1969 was a banner year for legally protected civil rights. Eighty percent of Supreme Court decisions were in favor of the claimant. Statistics about cases do not of themselves distinguish degrees of importance, however. Although the court entered some previously uncharted areas and decided in favor of new important constitutional protections, most of the decisions were interpretations and applications of previously declared constitutional rights. Few of either type could match in importance the 1954–55 segregation cases, the 1962–64 apportionment rulings, the cases outlawing prayers in public schools, or those that gave federal sanction for the first time to higher standards in state criminal procedure.

Four decisions did create new constitutional guarantees of note, and three of these could affect many individuals. In *Shapiro* v. *Thompson* and companion cases, it was held that a state's denial of welfare benefits to residents of less than a year was discrimination forbidden by the Constitution. The right to travel from state to state is an inherent right of every individual, and any interest of the state in preserving its fiscal integrity must be subsumed to that right.

Stanley v. *Georgia,* quite a different type of decision, held unanimously that the mere possession of obscene material could not be made a crime. Granted that obscenity, however it may be defined, is not entitled to constitutional protection in general, the right to be free and the right to privacy are paramount. Thus, the court, which has unsuccessfully struggled to draw the line between an expanded right of free expression and pure pornography in cases of sale arrived at a decision that many would declare to be obvious.

The third case, *Benton* v. *Maryland,* held, for the first time that the double jeopardy clause of the 5th Amendment was applicable to the states through the due process provision of the 14th Amendment. In the words of the dissent, the court was thus continuing its "march" toward total incorporation of the Bill of Rights into the 14th Amendment. To accomplish this, it was necessary to directly overrule *Palko* v. *Connecticut* (1937). Once again, federalism and the right of a state to determine its own criminal procedure gave way to the activist court's emphasis on a uniform system of protected rights.

A much more melodramatic and newsworthy decision was *Powell* v. *McCormack,* which held that Rep. Adam Clayton Powell of New York had been improperly denied his seat in the 90th Congress. Technically, this decision was based on a narrow interpretation of the constitutional phrase that gives the House power to judge the "elections, returns and qualifications" of its members. This refers to such considerations as age and citizenship and does not include the basis of the House action, namely Powell's misuse of House funds. Many critics argued that the case was moot because the 91st Congress, in which Powell was seated, was already in session. Stripped of all historical and legal arguments, however, the decision stands for its definition of the right of people to choose their own representative. It was a further example of activism by the Warren Court, which took this stand even at the risk of confrontation with another branch of the federal government.

When a court with ultimate power, such as the Supreme Court, makes fundamental and often revolutionary decisions in favor of a civil right, it is necessarily the task of lower tribunals to interpret the meaning of such constitutional freedom. Ultimately, however, much of the interpretation and of the filling-in process is up to the Supreme Court itself. Many of the decisions in 1969 were of this nature. Some of these cases involved interpretations of congressional statutes that recently supplemented judicial decisions.

For example, three Supreme Court opinions broadly interpreted and applied the Voting Rights Act of 1965. State procedures in Mississippi, Alabama, and North Carolina were declared invalid. Racial discrimination was found to exist in a great variety of situations involving housing ordinances, recreation areas, and employment.

Although racially balanced school faculties are not constitutionally or legally required, a unanimous decision of the court required a school board to assign teachers according to racial ratios in order to expedite desegregation of the school system. Two decisions struck down congressional redistricting plans, in Missouri and New York, because they did not meet the basic requirement of "one man, one vote" established in the 1964 decision of *Wesberry* v. *Sanders.*

As in other years, the greatest number of decisions on civil rights, a total of 36, concerned criminal procedure. Included were 8 cases on search and seizure, 5 on wiretapping, 3 on confessions, and 2 on jury trial. The great majority held in favor of the plaintiff.

The Right to Dissent. For various reasons the concept of civil rights and liberties does not ordinarily include riots, racial demonstrations, or student unrest. In particular, the right to dissent, which is at the heart of civil rights, cannot include violent dissent, whether it be a sit-in or a revolution. Rather, civil rights and liberties today encompass all those rights, constitutional or statutory, which are judicially or legislatively protected.

That 1969 may be characterized as the year of dissent is illustrated, however, by such diverse events as the nonviolent antiwar moratorium demonstrations in the fall; the activities involved in the trial of the "Boston 5," who were charged with conspiracy to urge draftees to burn or destroy their draft cards; or the violence at the heart of the case against the "Chicago 8," who were charged with conspiracy to incite a riot during the 1968 Democratic National Convention.

In cases concerning the right to dissent, the issue is usually between individual freedom of expression and some asserted contrary interest of the community. In 1969, Supreme Court decisions held unconstitutional a law banning the teaching of evolution, a school regulation prohibiting the wearing of antiwar arm bands, a vague parade ordinance, and an attempt to prevent distribution of antiwar pamphlets in a bus terminal.

See also SUPREME COURT.

RALPH F. BISCHOFF
New York University

BALLOT POWER

The civil rights movement received a new impetus in 1969 with the appearance of Negroes in positions of political power. In the South, Fayette, Miss., elected Charles Evers, brother of the slain Medgar Evers, as its mayor (above), and five Negroes won seats on the city council. North Carolina's Chapel Hill gained its first Negro mayor, Howard Lee (left, with wife). In the North, Carl Stokes (below) rejoiced with his wife and constituents on winning reelection as mayor of Cleveland in a close race against a white opponent.

CIVIL RIGHTS MOVEMENT

Developments in the civil rights movement in 1969 covered the spectrum from protest to legal and government action. These activities involved both militant and moderate groups and were led by younger as well as older people. The year could not be characterized as one dominated by a particular style of action or locale, as in some previous years. In fact, the movement included exclusivist black organizations as well as those allied with traditional forces (labor, religious, and liberal), in the civil rights struggle.

Protests of Black Students. During the first four months of 1969 black students demanded black studies programs at approximately 140 U. S. colleges and universities, according to a report of the American Council on Education. These protests, which were a continuation of on-campus activity begun a few years earlier, persisted after school opened in September. Dramatic incidents such as the events in April at Cornell University, where black students seized a building and later marched out with guns acquired for self-defense, were widely publicized.

The protests were felt in all parts of the nation, in black as well as in predominantly white colleges. The demands of the students involved such issues as curriculum revision, recruitment of more black students and black faculty, the university's relations with the local black community, and more scholarship funds for black students. As the academic year opened in the fall, many universities were deeply involved in negotiating these demands with students.

Whether the initial action involved the seizure of a building, a boycott of classes, or disruptive tactics, it seemed clear on most campuses that a concensus had been reached by the students and the officials that some major changes should be made and that these changes had to be the result of negotiated settlements. The rhetoric of some protests notwithstanding, it was also quite evident that all parties recognized the ultimate value of keeping the schools open. Many black students recognized the long-term utility of achieving an education. This realization offered the greatest hope for ultimate settlement of differences in the future.

The Black Manifesto and the Churches. In April a new organization, the National Black Economic Development Conference (NBEDC), led by James Forman, was created in Detroit. It passed a resolution known as the Black Manifesto, calling for white churches and Jewish synagogues to pay "reparations" in the amount of $500 million to the NBEDC to atone for what it saw as years of white racism in which the religious organizations took part.

The demand set off months of disruption of church services across the country, endorsements and rejections of the manifesto by white and black clergy and laity, and a general debate on the moral role of the church in U. S. life. Several church organizations agreed with the principle of the manifesto, but rejected the revolutionary language and tactics of the NBEDC. Others rejected the NBEDC as a viable, deserving recipient of funds, but agreed to involve themselves financially in the development of minority communities.

As the year ended, the NBEDC had not received more than $20,000, but many people, black and white, recognized that a very serious national dialogue had been opened on the moral responsibility of the churches in the civil rights struggle. For years, individual leaders of the church had taken an active part in the civil rights movement and individual churches had joined in lobbying activity for civil rights legislation. But, in 1969, the NBEDC was demanding that churches play a more direct and substantial financial role.

Discrimination in the Building Trades. The civil rights movement has a long history of cooperation with organized labor, but that relationship has always been marred by the hiring practices of the unions. In 1969 black activists, joined by white allies, clashed with craft unions over the unions' alleged discriminatory practices in a number of cities. Protesters demanded an end to union apprenticeship programs and to present hiring practices on federally funded construction projects. They demanded that such practices be ended or that the work be stopped. Violence erupted in several cities, including Chicago and Pittsburg.

The U. S. Department of Labor introduced the so-called "Philadelphia plan" to encourage black employment on federally financed construction projects. In December, President Nixon urged the Senate to reverse its vote blocking implementation of the plan. On December 20, the Senate and House approved the President's plan.

MRS. CORETTA KING, widow of Martin Luther King, Jr., speaks at services in St. Paul's, London, March 16—the first woman to preach there at a statutory service.

CENTRAL PRESS, PICTORIAL PARADE

YOUNG MEN—not students —support sit-in of about 50 black women students at Vassar College in October by barring doors to whites.

Protest activity at construction sites was countered in some places with organized and sometimes violent resistance from white workers. This situation developed in part because of the slowness of administrative and judicial processes. Whether protest action in the future will take more militant forms, thereby leading to increased polarization between contentious forces, will depend in large measure on the extent to which the federal government is able to enforce the existing laws against discrimination. In other words, the earlier legal achievements of the civil rights movement must be translated into real benefits, or protest tactics in all likelihood will escalate.

School Desegregation. The U. S. Supreme Court again took the lead in 1969 in desegregating Southern public schools. In October and December the court ordered school districts in Mississippi, Louisiana, Alabama, and Georgia to desegregate— "immediately" in one instance and by Feb. 1, 1970, in other decrees. These decisions effectively superceded the 1954 formula of "all deliberate speed."

Civil rights forces that have waged court battles for about two decades viewed these 1969 decisions as crucial to the desegregation struggle. The court action had added significance in view of the policy adopted in July by the Department of Justice and the Department of Health, Education, and Welfare to delay desegregation in some Southern school districts. Some civil rights groups, most notably the National Association for the Advancement of Colored People (NAACP), saw such a policy as a backward step in the struggle to overcome segregation.

As a result of the Supreme Court rulings, several civil rights groups concluded that their programs for desegregation would receive a much more sympathetic response from the national judiciary than from either the national executive or legislative branches.

(See also SUPREME COURT.)

Civil Rights Coalitions. The forces of the traditional civil rights coalition (labor unions, religious groups, civil liberties organizations, civil rights groups) united twice in 1969—to defeat the nomination of Judge Clement F. Haynsworth to the U. S. Supreme Court, and in the 3-month strike led by the Southern Christian Leadership Conference of black hospital workers in Charleston, S. C.

In both instances, the forces combined in efforts reminiscent of the fight leading to the passage of the 1964 Civil Rights Act and of the protest marches in Birmingham and Selma, Ala. in the early 1960's. In light of recent development of Black Power and "separatist" goals, the coalitions served to point out the continued utility, under certain circumstances, of collective, inter-group action.

Local Pressure Group Activity. As in recent years, a great deal of local civil rights activity centered on the quest for "community control." Local

JAMES FORMAN, chief spokesman of the National Black Economic Development Conference (NBEDC), which he helped form in Detroit in April 1969, confronted the nation's white churches and synagogues during the year with demands for $500 million in reparations for "past injustices" to Negroes. In May he disrupted services at the Riverside Church in New York City and posted his anticapitalist "Black Manifesto" at the door of the Lutheran Church national headquarters in the city.

Forman, 40, is a graduate of Roosevelt University in Chicago and a 4-year veteran of the U. S. Air Force. He did postgraduate work in African studies at Boston University and taught in Chicago schools. In 1961 he became the first executive secretary of the Student Nonviolent Coordinating Committee (SNCC). Forman, who led the organization in sit-ins and other nonviolent actions, became its political theorist. He was replaced in May 1966 when the militant Stokley Carmichael came to power. Forman left another post within SNCC in 1969 to concentrate on the NBEDC.

"SOUL TABLES"—for blacks only—are preferred by black students, members of an Afro-American Society at Wesleyan University.

groups demanded control of local schools and some form of control over the police, a greater voice in antipoverty and Model Cities programs, and more participation in welfare officials' decisions.

At the local level, Black Parent groups, welfare rights organizations, Afro-American patrolmen's leagues, and black social workers worked to gain community control. It was interests such as these that most frequently and enthusiastically continued to work for Black Power, focusing on the fight for local political power and economic sufficiency.

Frequently labeled as separatist by the mass media and opponents, these groups were inaccurately portrayed as seeking to establish a "separate" state or country. Actually, many of them were attempting to increase their power within the existing political system through traditional political means.

Local Electoral Activity. The civil rights movement has focused for the most part on pressure group protest activity and on legal decisions, not on electoral politics. This emphasis is necessarily undergoing a change. Precisely as a result of earlier protest action, which pushed for passage of the Voting Rights Act of 1965, thousands of new black voters have been registered in the South.

Black candidates won and lost, but their presence in the elective process indicated a growing politicization of the civil rights movement. Charles Evers, state director of the NAACP in Mississippi, was elected mayor of Fayette, Miss., and a majority of black candidates were elected to the city council. In July, six black candidates were elected to public office in Greene County, Ala. The Alabama election was ordered by the U. S. Supreme Court after the black candidates were refused places on the ballot.

Black Panthers and the Police. By year end, the frequent clashes between the militant Black Panthers and various local police departments had become a matter of national concern. Throughout the year police raided Panther offices and apartments in Los Angeles, Chicago, and other cities across the country. Often the offices were torn apart; several members of the organization were killed or wounded in shoot-outs.

On December 4, Cook County police raided a Chicago apartment and, in the process, Fred Hampton, chairman of the Illinois Panthers, and another party member were shot to death.

Several civil rights groups and private individuals called for an official investigation of the incidents. These requests represented a broad spectrum of concern not necessarily in support of the revolutionary Marxist ideology or actions of the Black Panther party, but for the protection of civil liberties. In December, former Supreme Court Justice Arthur Goldberg and Roy Wilkins, director of the NAACP, announced the formation of an independent commission to investigate the shootings. The commis-

JESSE LOUIS JACKSON, director of Operation Breadbasket, the economic arm of the Southern Christian Leadership Conference (SCLC), occupies a middle ground between militants and moderates in the civil rights struggle. "Breadbasket," which draws its support mainly from Negro ministers and businessmen, has made substantial gains in providing jobs for low-income Negroes and marketing products of black-owned companies in the ghettos of Chicago and other cities through the power of the economic boycott. In the spring of 1968, Jackson served as manager of Resurrection City, in the capital, to dramatize SCLC's Poor People's Campaign.

Jackson was born in Greenville, S. C., on Oct. 8, 1941. He spent a year at the University of Illinois and then attended North Carolina Agricultural and Technical College in Greensboro, where he became active in civil rights. While attending the Chicago Theological Seminary in 1966, he helped Martin Luther King, Jr., organize Operation Breadbasket, of which he became national director at King's request.

BLACK PANTHERS being arraigned in Los Angeles after a four-hour gun battle with police on December 8.

"But, gee, honey! If you love me so much, why don't you ever take me anywhere?"

sion included Whitney Young, director of the National Urban League, and Julian Bond, the black Georgia state legislator. To end "rumors and speculation" surrounding the incident, the U. S. Justice Department on December 10 ordered a special grand jury to investigate the Chicago raid.

The Outlook. As the year and the decade ended, the civil rights movement gave increasing evidence that it would involve many more groups at the local level and that its goals would be enlarged. Among the new concerns of the civil rights movement were greater awareness of the need for the acquisition of political and economic power, as well as legal and constitutional rights. This would involve more pressure group tactics, increased politicization, and greater demands for a reallocation of national economic resources now tied up in the Vietnam War. Ultimately, much would depend on the nature of the response from official sources at all levels.

CHARLES V. HAMILTON, *Columbia University*

THE BLACK ACADEMY OF ARTS AND LETTERS

The Black Academy of Arts and Letters is dedicated to fostering the arts, letters, and culture of black people and to giving recognition to their achievements. Its members, designated as Fellows, are drawn from those whose contributions to art, literature, and scholarship reflect the richness and vitality of black experience.

Formally established on March 27, 1969, the Black Academy of Arts and Letters was launched with the financial assistance of the Twentieth Century Fund. Conceived by blacks and chartered in New York, the Black Academy is a wholly independent entity whose 50 founding Fellows were black writers, artists, and scholars. Such an academy, said author C. Eric Lincoln, "is a way of affirming the existence of creative excellence in places where we are not accustomed to look for it."

The Black Academy follows in the tradition of an earlier organization pledged to the same mission—the American Negro Academy, founded in 1897. It went out of existence in 1924. Nearly half a century later, when the Black Academy appeared, the number of black notables in arts and letters had multiplied.

The Black Academy proposes to promote exhibits, performances, and showings of the arts and letters of black people and to provide a depository for such works and publications. The Academy proposes to give public recognition and honor to those who exemplify its goals.

It will give fellowships and prizes, including a Black Scholars Award for notable contributions in letters and a Black Artist's Award for notable work in the arts. To encourage young people of promise in these fields, the Academy will also make suitable annual awards. To non-members who make contributions to black culture the Academy will award its Medal of Merit.

The Black Academy operates through a full-time executive director who works under the Academy's officers and board of directors. These officials, along with potential members of the Academy, are elected by the membership. The first board of directors included C. Eric Lincoln, president of the Academy; writer–editor Doris Saunders, its secretary; authors John O. Killens and John A. Williams; psychiatrist Alvin Poussaint; historian Vincent Harding; and artist Charles White.

Additional founding members included such notables as musicians Julian "Cannonball" Adderly and Duke Ellington; actors Ossie Davis, Frederick O'Neal, and Sidney Poitier; choreographers Alvin Ailey and Arthur Mitchell; artists Romare Bearden and Jacob Lawrence; writers Margaret Walker Alexander and Arna Bontemps; and historians John Hope Franklin and Charles H. Wesley.

BENJAMIN QUARLES
Morgan State College, Baltimore
Founding Member, Black Academy of
Arts and Letters

CLEVELAND

Voters in Cleveland (Jan. 1, 1969, est. pop.: 770,000) reelected Mayor Carl B. Stokes in the November election. Business continued to prosper, and major construction remained at a high level.

Election. Stokes, the first Negro mayor of a major U. S. city, defeated Republican Ralph J. Perk, Cuyahoga County auditor, by a margin of 3,451 votes in elections on November 4. The campaign evoked few new issues. Perk's principal charges were that the Stokes administration had been wasteful, increasing city hall employees to 15,000 from 12,000, and that crime in the streets had greatly increased as the city failed to add more policemen to the force until shortly before the election. Voters apparently paid little attention to indictments of two Stokes appointees to the Civil Service Commission for perjury in investigations over the conduct of an examination for new policemen.

Aftermath of Riot. Racial tensions were relatively eased since the July 1968 Glenville rioting in which three policemen and seven other persons were killed. The black nationalist leader in the uprising, Fred (Ahmed) Evans, was found guilty of first degree murder on May 10, 1969, and awaited the results of appeals in death row in Columbus.

Construction. A building weighing 30 million pounds, the University Hospital's Babies and Children's Hospital, was moved 80 feet, July 18–30, to make room on Adelbert Road in University Circle for a $15.2 million child care center to be built by 1971. The moving was one of the largest ever attempted.

New development of downtown East 9th Street as the hub of Cleveland's financial center continued with the opening of an Investment Plaza for brokers and the Central National Bank headquarters. Construction on two other bank headquarters and major Cleveland State University facilities continued.

While construction in the downtown area continued at a healthy pace, the once popular movie theaters on Euclid Avenue—Palace, State, Ohio, and Allen—were dark as plush new film houses were opened in major suburban shopping centers that offered ample free parking.

Economy. Business in the Cleveland area continued at the high levels of 1968, with steel manufacturing, heavy industrial production, consumer goods manufacturing, and commercial business establishments all making gains. The area's business index rose to 170 from a revised figure of 159 in 1968. The city's real estate tax in 1969 was 6.26% of assessed valuation, compared with 6.3% a year earlier. To bring in added operating funds, Cuyahoga County imposed an additional 0.5% sales tax on the Ohio state tax of 4%.

Crime. Lawless elements in Cleveland committed a record number of murders in 1969—averaging almost six a week in the city. The murder that attracted the most attention was that of the wife of a municipal judge, Mrs. Marlene Steele, who was slain in her suburban Euclid home on Jan. 9, 1969. As the year ended the case remained unsolved.

Storm Disaster. Seven persons were killed on Cleveland's near-West Side when a civic program and fireworks display in observance of the 4th of July was swept by converging Lake Erie squalls and tornado-like winds.

JOHN F. HUTH, JR.
"The Plain Dealer," Cleveland

CLOTHING INDUSTRY

Men's and boys' clothing are giving a relatively better account of themselves in production and sales volume than are women's and girls' wear. The gains in men's and boys' wear in the United States reflect the increasingly exciting hold of their fashion revolution—the all-encompassing "youth" market. Conversely, the women's wear industry was suffering the negative effect of a diversity of lengths and silhouettes—the lack of a dominant force. (See also FASHION.)

U. S. APPAREL SHIPMENTS AND PRODUCTION
(In millions)

Kind of apparel	Net value of shipments		Unit output	
	1968	1967	1968	1967
Unit-price dresses	$1,454	$1,479	162.7	175.3
Dozen-price dresses	370	368	104.1	104.6
Coats	485	516	22.5	22.4
Suits	219	212	9.7	10.0
Blouses	431	398	181.1	168.8
Skirts and jackets	437	433	118.2	109.0
Girls' and children's outerwear	...[1]	982	519.2	557.1
Men's suits	...[1]	852[2]	21.7	19.7
Men's overcoats and topcoats	...[1]	101[2]	4.1	4.8
Men's tailored dress and sport coats and jackets	...[1]	317[2]	14.0	13.7
Men's and boys' separate trousers	...[1]	906[2]	158.4	138.6

[1] Not available. [2] 1966 figures.

In 1968, the most recent full year for which statistics are available, production of unit-price and dozen-price dresses, women's suits, and girls' and children's outerwear fell behind 1967 totals. Blouses, skirts and jackets, and women's coats advanced in production to give female attire a nominal rise over 1967.

In contrast, men's suits, tailored dress and sport coats and jackets, and men's and boys' separate trousers moved ahead of year-earlier production. Overcoats and topcoats were the sole men's category to retreat in volume of output.

Largely because of inflation, dollar value of shipments in 1968 showed more annual gains than losses in both women's and men's wear. In the first eight months of 1969, preliminary estimates of dollar volume in women's and children's wear ran 2% above the 1968 level, but physical output slumped appreciably.

The value of clothing imported in the United States in the first seven months of 1969 exceeded that of the same period of 1968 by 22%. The continued rise is expected to be stemmed to some degree through voluntary international agreements or restrictive legislation.

Industry Structure. Through internal expansion and merger, large firms are becoming more prevalent both in men's and women's wear. Nevertheless the clothing industry as a whole remains the province principally of smaller units. New York maintains a substantial national lead in manufacturers' sales of women's, children's, and men's wear.

Canada. The factory value of shipped clothing edged toward $1 billion in Canada in 1967. A summary and comparison with 1966 data:

	1967	1966
Men's clothing	$408,682,000	$409,958,000
Women's clothing	443,540,000	426,484,000
Children's clothing	101,877,000	98,701,000
	$954,099,000	$935,143,000

SAMUEL FEINBERG
"Women's Wear Daily"

COAL. See MINING.

ICEBREAKER *NORTHWIND* breaks thick ice for the tanker S.S. *Manhattan* on its voyage to Alaska through the Northwest Passage in September.

COAST GUARD

The U. S. Coast Guard, a component of the Department of Transportation since 1967, continued in 1969 to promote maritime safety, enforce marine law, and conduct oceanographic research. During the year the 179-year-old agency also continued to serve with the Navy in Vietnam.

Vietnam. Twenty-four 82-foot cutters and five oceangoing cutters were maintained in South Vietnamese waters by the Coast Guard to help bar movement of men and materials from North Vietnam. Five other 82-foot cutters were turned over to South Vietnam; more cutters were to be transferred when South Vietnamese crews became available. The Coast Guard also helped to improve port security and safety, and assist in handling problems resulting from a heavy increase in shipping.

Search and Rescue. The Coast Guard assisted 4,675 persons in peril in 1969. It responded to 48,108 calls for assistance and 19,506 requests for towage. The vessels and aircraft aided were valued (with cargoes included) at more than $2.5 billion.

For rescue work, the Coast Guard retired the 20-year-old Grumman Albatross, a flying boat, and acquired the Sikorsky HH-3F helicopter, which can either land beside or hover over a lifeboat.

Law Enforcement. Coast Guardsmen in 1969 inspected 1,138 foreign vessels, inspected for certification 5,470 U. S. vessels, conducted 5,293 dry dock examinations, and made 6,900 vessel reinspections. There were 30,000 miscellaneous vessel inspections.

Aids to Navigation. The Coast Guard icebreaker *Northwind* accompanied the super tanker-icebreaker *Manhattan* on her historic voyage across the top of North America to the new oil fields at Prudhoe Bay, on the North Slope of Alaska.

Coast Guard icebreakers also conducted oceanographic research in the Arctic and Antarctic. Four ocean stations were maintained in the Atlantic and two in the Pacific to provide search and rescue, communications, and meteorological services. More than 44,648 navigation aids were maintained.

Boating Safety. The Office of Boating Safety was busy promoting higher safety standards for the nation's more than 8 million boatmen. The Auxiliary, a voluntary organization, was active in 1,011 flotillas. It gave instruction in safe boating to 423,-950 persons, examined 161,774 motorboats, patrolled 4,075 regattas, and saved 215 lives.

Budget and Strength. The Coast Guard budget in fiscal 1969 was $585,703,148, compared to $570,-963,261 in fiscal 1968. Military personnel declined from 36,683 to about 34,000; civilian personnel meanwhile dropped from 6,059 to 5,857. The Coast Guard had 330 floating units and 166 fixed-wing and rotating-wing aircraft.

WILLARD J. SMITH, *Admiral, USCG*
Commandant, U. S. Coast Guard

COFFEE

The world's coffee growing nations produced an estimated 65,130,000 bags (each of 60 kilograms, or 132.3 pounds) in the 1969–70 marketing year, an increase of 4,513,000 bags over 1968–69. However, this was 5% less than the large 1967–68 crop.

Coffee for export totaled 47,139,000 bags in 1969–70, 4,088,000 bags more than in 1968–69, but 4,637,000 bags less than in 1967–68.

A substantial increase of production in Brazil, the world's leading coffee producing nation, accounted for most of the world increase. Production in South America totaled 30,582,000 bags in 1969–70, an increase of 3,390,000 bags or 12% over the previous marketing year. Of the total, 19,360,000 bags were for export, 3,090,000 bags more than in 1968–69. North American production totaled 11,-565,000 bags, an increase of 1,008,000 bags or 10% over a year earlier. Coffee for export totaled 8,053,-000 bags, 848,000 bags more than in 1968–69.

African production totaled 18,299,000 bags in 1969–70, an increase of 155,000 bags over the previous year. Of the total 17,248,000 bags were for export, 150,000 bags more than in 1968–69. Production increases in Angola and the Ivory Coast offset declines in Ethiopia and Uganda. Production in Asia and Oceania totaled 4,684,000 bags.

NICHOLAS KOMINUS
Kominus Agri-Info Associates

PRODUCTION OF GREEN COFFEE IN PRINCIPAL COUNTRIES
(Number of bags of 60 kilograms—132.3 pounds—each)

Country	Average 1960–61 to 1964–65	1968–69	1969–70
Brazil	25,840,000	16,500,000	20,000,000
Colombia	7,760,000	7,900,000	7,900,000
Ivory Coast	3,185,000	3,500,000	4,000,000
Angola	2,910,000	3,175,000	3,350,000
Mexico	2,431,000	2,800,000	3,000,000
Uganda	2,429,000	3,150,000	2,750,000
El Salvador	1,812,000	1,900,000	2,300,000
Ethiopia	1,490,000	2,045,000	2,000,000
Indonesia	2,016,000	2,000,000	2,000,000
Guatemala	1,704,000	1,650,000	1,850,000
World total	65,339,000	60,617,000	65,130,000

COIN COLLECTING

The year 1969 was an exciting one for coin collectors. With new proof sets issues, new medals, plus a strong market for older rare coins, the coin hobby continued its strength and popularity.

Apollo Flight. Highlighting the year was the Apollo 11 moon trip reflected in an extensive series of medals and a proposed commemorative coin. In the absence of an official U. S. commemorative coin honoring the flight, the gap was filled by several private mints, which rushed into production with dozens of different medals. One of the largest private mints, the Franklin Mint of Yeadon, Pa., also made news as it announced the construction of a new $10 million minting facility to produce medals and tokens, as well as legal coinage on a contract basis for foreign countries.

New Silver Dollar. In late 1969, the U. S. Treasury announced plans for minting a silver dollar to honor Dwight D. Eisenhower. (The last silver dollars were produced in 1935.) At the end of 1969, many designs for the dollar were proposed, including a reverse design to honor the moon landing.

Federal Reserve Notes. Currency collectors eagerly sought the $1 federal reserve notes bearing the signature of the short-tenured secretary of the Treasury, Joseph W. Barr. Enthusiasm and prices dropped when the Treasury announced a large press run of the bills despite Barr's brief term.

Proof Sets. Early deliveries of 1969-S proof coins began in January and continued throughout the year. During the preceding year, more than 3 million sets were produced, and it is anticipated that the 1969 production figure will be similar.

Each proof set contains five coins: the cent, nickel, dime, quarter, and half dollar. The coins are struck from specially polished dies and sell for $5 at the time of issue. Due to the limited supply, sets from previous years sell at higher prices. For example, a set from 1950 costs $125. At the end of 1969, the 1969-S set was selling for $8. Current sets may be ordered from the Officer in Charge, U. S. Assay Office, San Francisco, Calif.

The concept of issuing proof sets for collectors has spread to many other countries. For many years, only the United States and Canada regularly issued such sets. In recent years, Panama, Liberia, Sudan, India, Jordan, and several new African nations have issued proof coins or announced the intention of doing so.

U. S. Mints. There were three operating U. S. mints at the end of 1969. The San Francisco mint ("S" mintmark) has limited production facilities. The Denver mint ("D" mintmark) established a rec-

CANADIAN DOLLAR of 1970, honoring Manitoba's entry into Confederation, bears the prairie crocus.

CANADIAN CONSULATE

ord on June 11, when it minted 25 million coins, the highest known production of coins in a single day by any mint.

The Philadelphia mint (no mintmark) dedicated its new building on August 14 and opened for business on August 27. Among the innovations introduced at this mint was a new coin-rolling machine. This revolutionary instrument produces coins at high speed from a continuously fed strip, a contrast to the traditional method of striking coins one at a time via single pairs of dies and prepared planchets.

Pre-1965 Silver Coins. The metallic content of pre-1965 U. S. silver coins continued to make news in 1969. The no-melting rule imposed by the Treasury was relaxed, thereby making it legal to melt the coins down for their metal value. Depending on the silver market, the premium paid for bulk unsorted pre-1965 silver coins ranged from 5% to 35% of their face value. This premium caused the withdrawal of virtually all silver coins from circulation. At the end of 1969, a strike in the nickel industry caused a jump in the price of nickel, with the result that a $200-face-value bag of Canadian nickels brought $300 on the U. S. market.

Lilly Collection Displayed. The Josiah K. Lilly collection of gold coins, donated to the Smithsonian Institution in 1968, was placed on public display in 1969. Containing such rarities as the 1822 $5 gold (estimated value nearly $100,000), it elevates the already extensive national coin collection at the Smithsonian to the foremost rank among coin exhibits in the world.

Q. DAVID BOWERS
Author, "Coins and Collectors"
Columnist, "Coin World"

COLLEGES AND UNIVERSITIES

A selected list of accredited junior colleges, senior colleges, and universities in the United States and Canada appears on the following pages.

The information given for each school comprises the following data: its degree-granting status (if it is a senior college or university); the composition of its student body (by sex); the legal controlling agency; and the total enrollment of students of college grade as reported by the registrar (U. S. figures for senior colleges are for fall 1968, for two-year colleges, fall 1967; Canada figures are for 1967–68).

All the U. S. institutions listed are recognized by *Accredited Institutions of Higher Education*, published by the American Council on Education. The Canadian institutions listed are accredited by the provinces in which they are located.

See also EDUCATION.

LINCOLN PENNY bears restyled portrait after new master die replaced old one, worn from usage since 1909.

UPI

MAJOR COLLEGES AND UNIVERSITIES, U.S. AND CANADA

Note: Symbols and abbreviations that follow the name of each school listed are as follows: *Level of Instruction*—(1) 2-year junior college; (2) senior college granting bachelor's and/or first professional degree; (3) senior college granting master's and/or second professional degree; (4) college or university offering a doctoral program. *Student Body*—(M) men only; (W) women only; (Coed) coeducational; (Coord) separate colleges for men and women. *Control*—(Public) district, municipal, state, or federal; (Private) proprietary, corporation, or church. *Enrollment*—For the United States, all students of college grade for the academic year 1968–69, excepting correspondence course students. Canadian figures are for 1967–1968.

Name and Location	Level of Instruction	Student Body	Control	Enrollment
Abilene Christian College, Abilene, Texas	3	Coed	Pvt-Church of Christ	3,103
Abraham Baldwin Agricultural College, Tifton, Ga.	3	Coed	Public	1,559
Acadia University, Wolfville, Nova Scotia	3	Coed	Pvt-Baptist	1,657
Adams State College, Alamosa, Colo.	3	Coed	Public	2,744
Adelphi University, Garden City, N.Y.	4	Coed	Private	8,045
Adrian College, Adrian, Mich.	2	Coed	Pvt-Methodist	1,588
Agnes Scott College, Decatur, Ga.	2	W	Pvt-Presbyterian	739
Air Force Institute of Technology, Wright-Patterson AFB, Ohio	4	Coed	Public	715
Akron, University of, Akron, Ohio	4	Coed	Public	14,469
Alabama, University of, University, Ala.	4	Coed	Public	20,176
Alabama Agricultural and Mechanical College, Normal, Ala.	3	Coed	Public	2,028
Alabama College, Montevallo, Ala.	3	Coed	Public	2,000
Alabama State College, Montgomery, Ala.	3	Coed	Public	2,169
Alaska, University of, College, Alaska (incl. community colleges at Anchorage, Juneau, Kenai, Ketchikan, Palmer, Sitka)	4	Coed	Public	2,240
Alaska Methodist University, Anchorage, Alaska	3	Coed	Pvt-Methodist	736
Albany Junior College, Albany, Ga.	1	Coed	Public	903
Albany State College, Albany, Ga.	2	Coed	Public	1,635
Albemarle, College of the, Elizabeth City, N.C.	1	Coed	Public	663
Alberta, University of, Edmonton & Calgary, Alberta	4	Coed	Public	13,307
Albertus Magnus College, New Haven, Conn.	2	W	Pvt-Roman Catholic	620
Albion College, Albion, Mich.	2	Coed	Pvt-Methodist	1,801
Albright College, Reading, Pa.	2	Coed	Pvt-Methodist	1,283
Albuquerque, University of, Albuquerque, N.M.	2	Coed	Pvt-Roman Catholic	1,436
Alcorn Agricultural & Mechanical College, Lorman, Miss.	2	Coed	Public	2,345
Alderson-Broaddus College, Philippi, W.Va.	2	Coed	Pvt-Baptist	968
Alfred University, Alfred, N.Y.	4	Coed	Public-Private	1,746
Allan Hancock College, Santa Maria, Calif.	1	Coed	Public	3,650
Allegany Community College, Cumberland, Md.	1	Coed	Public	598
Allegheny College, Meadville, Pa.	2	Coed	Pvt-Methodist	1,595
Alliance College, Cambridge Springs, Pa.	2	Coord	Private	625
Alma College, Alma, Mich.	2	Coed	Pvt-Presbyterian	1,218
Alpena Community College, Alpena, Mich.	1	Coed	Public	874
Alverno College, Milwaukee, Wis.	2	W	Pvt-Roman Catholic	985
Amarillo College, Amarillo, Texas	1	Coed	Public	1,394
Alvin Junior College, Alvin, Texas	1	Coed	Public	2,958
American International College, Springfield, Mass.	3	Coed	Private	3,072
American River College, Sacramento, Calif.	1	Coed	Public	8,346
American University, The, Washington, D.C.	4	Coed	Pvt-Methodist	14,891
Amherst College, Amherst, Mass.	3	M	Private	1,230
Anderson College, Anderson, Ind.	3	Coed	Pvt-Church of God	1,591
Anderson College, Anderson, S.C.	1	Coed	Pvt-Baptist	827
Andrew College, Cuthbert, Ga.	1	Coed	Pvt-Methodist	419
Andrews University, Berrien Springs, Mich.	3	Coed	Pvt-Seventh-day Adventist	1,560
Angelo State College, San Angelo, Texas	3	Coed	Public	3,033
Anna Maria College, Paxton, Mass.	3	W	Pvt-Roman Catholic	660
Anne Arundel Community College, Arnold, Md.	1	Coed	Public	1,431
Annhurst College, South Woodstock, Conn.	2	W	Pvt-Roman Catholic	430
Antelope Valley College, Lancaster, Calif.	1	Coed	Public	2,681
Antioch College, Yellow Springs, Ohio	3	Coed	Private	1,901
Appalachian State University, Boone, N.C.	3	Coed	Public	6,209
Aquinas College, Grand Rapids, Mich.	2	Coed	Pvt-Roman Catholic	1,343
Arizona, University of, Tucson, Ariz.	4	Coed	Public	23,617
Arizona State University, Tempe, Ariz.	4	Coed	Public	25,473
Arizona Western College, Yuma, Ariz.	1	Coed	Public	1,889
Arkansas, State College of, Conway, Ark.	3	Coed	Public	4,380
Arkansas, University of, Fayetteville, Ark.	4	Coed	Public	10,965
Arkansas Agricultural, Mechanical, & Normal College, Pine Bluff, Ark.	2	Coed	Public	3,445
Arkansas Agricultural & Mechanical College, College Heights, Ark.	2	Coed	Public	1,192
Arkansas Polytechnic College, Russellville, Ark.	2	Coed	Public	2,530
Arkansas State University, State University, Ark.	3	Coed	Public	7,117
Arlington, University of Texas at, Arlington, Texas	3	Coed	Public	11,873
Armstrong College, Berkeley, Calif.	3	Coed	Private	441
Armstrong State College, Savannah, Ga.	2	Coed	Public	1,721
Aroostook State College, Presque Isle, Me.	2	Coed	Public	499
Art Center College of Design, The, Los Angeles, Calif.	3	Coed	Private	1,189
Art Institute of Chicago, School of the, Chicago, Ill.	3	Coed	Private	1,101
Asbury College, Wilmore, Ky.	2	Coed	Private	960
Asheville-Biltmore College, Asheville, N.C.	2	Coed	Public	691
Ashland College, Ashland, Ohio	2	Coed	Pvt-Brethren	2,607
Assumption College, Worcester, Mass.	3	Coed	Pvt-Roman Catholic	1,464
Athenaeum of Ohio, Norwood, Ohio.	3	M	Pvt-Roman Catholic	416
Athens College, Athens, Ala.	3	Coed	Pvt-Methodist	1,279
Atlanta University, Atlanta, Ga.	4	Coed	Private	1,051
Atlantic Christian College, Wilson, N.C.	2	Coed	Pvt-Disciples of Christ	1,567
Atlantic Union College, South Lancaster, Mass.	2	Coed	Pvt-Seventh-day Adventist	832
Auburn University, Auburn, Ala.	4	Coed	Public	14,422
Augsburg College, Minneapolis, Minn.	2	Coed	Pvt-Lutheran	1,845
Augusta College, Augusta, Ga.	2	Coed	Public	2,491
Augustana College, Rock Island, Ill.	3	Coed	Pvt-Lutheran	1,967
Augustana College, Sioux Falls, S.Dak.	2	Coed	Pvt-Lutheran	2,104
Aurora College, Aurora, Ill.	2	Coed	Pvt-Advent Christian	1,297
Austin, University of Texas at, Austin, Texas	4	Coed	Public	53,468
Austin College, Sherman, Texas	3	Coed	Pvt-Presbyterian	934
Austin Peay State College, Clarksville, Tenn.	3	Coed	Public	3,256
Averett College, Danville, Va.	1	W	Pvt-Baptist	543
Avila College, Kansas City, Mo.	3	W	Pvt-Roman Catholic	401
Azusa Pacific College, Azusa, Calif.	3	Coed	Private	1,009
Babson Institute of Business Administration, Babson Park, Mass.	3	Coed	Private	1,262
Bacone College, Bacone, Okla.	1	Coed	Pvt-Baptist	580
Baker University, Baldwin City, Kans.	2	Coed	Pvt-Methodist	893
Bakersfield College, Bakersfield, Calif.	1	Coed	Public	7,870
Baldwin-Wallace College, Berea, Ohio	2	Coed	Pvt-Methodist	3,002
Ball State University, Muncie, Ind.	4	Coed	Public	15,550
Baltimore, Community College of, Baltimore, Md.	1	Coed	Public	3,569

Name and Location	Level of Instruction	Student Body	Control	Enrollment
Bank Street College of Education, New York, N.Y.	3	Coed	Private	834
Barat College, Lake Forest, Ill.	2	W	Pvt-Roman Catholic	683
Barber-Scotia College, Concord, N.C.	2	Coed	Pvt-Presbyterian	610
Bard College, Annandale-on-Hudson, N.Y.	2	Coed	Private	643
Barnard College (of Columbia University), New York, N.Y.	2	W	Private	1,928
Barrington College, Barrington, R.I.	2	Coed	Private	659
Barry College, Miami, Fla.	3	Coed	Pvt-Roman Catholic	1,224
Barstow College, Barstow, Calif.	1	Coed	Public	1,264
Bates College, Lewiston, Me.	2	Coed	Private	1,001
Bay Path Junior College, Longmeadow, Mass.	1	W	Private	490
Baylor University, Waco, Texas	4	Coed	Pvt-Baptist	6,654
Beaver College, Glenside, Pa.	2	W	Pvt-Presbyterian	817
Belhaven College, Jackson, Miss.	2	Coed	Pvt-Presbyterian	627
Bellarmine-Ursuline College, Louisville, Ky.	2	Coed	Pvt-Roman Catholic	1,870
Belleville Area College, Belleville, Ill.	1	Coed	Public	3,184
Belmont Abbey College, Belmont, N.C.	2	Coed	Pvt-Roman Catholic	799
Belmont College, Nashville, Tenn.	2	Coed	Pvt-Baptist	991
Beloit College, Beloit, Wis.	3	Coed	Private	1,761
Bemidji State College, Bemidji, Minn.	3	Coed	Public	5,097
Benedict College, Columbia, S.C.	2	Coed	Pvt-Baptist	1,254
Bennett College, Greensboro, N.C.	2	W	Pvt-Methodist	684
Bennington College, Bennington, Vt.	3	W	Private	520
Bentley College, Waltham, Mass.	2	Coed	Private	3,989
Berea College, Berea, Ky.	2	Coed	Private	1,392
Berkshire Community College, Pittsfield, Mass.	1	Coed	Public	851
Bernard M. Baruch College (of the City University of New York), New York, N.Y.	3	Coed	Public	10,023
Berry College, Mount Berry, Ga.	2	Coed	Private	1,208
Bethany Bible College, Santa Cruz, Calif.	2	Coed	Pvt-Assemblies of God	496
Bethany College, Lindsborg, Kans.	2	Coed	Pvt-Lutheran	613
Bethany College, Bethany, W.Va.	2	Coed	Pvt-Disciples of Christ	1,140
Bethany-Nazarene College, Bethany, Okla.	3	Coed	Pvt-Nazarene	1,809
Bethel College, North Newton, Kans.	2	Coed	Pvt-Mennonite	581
Bethel College, McKenzie, Tenn.	2	Coed	Pvt-Presbyterian	808
Bethel College, St. Paul, Minn.	3	Coed	Pvt-Baptist	1,006
Bethune-Cookman College, Daytona Beach, Fla.	2	Coed	Pvt-Methodist	962
Big Bend Community College, Moses Lake, Wash.	1	Coed	Public	1,063
Biola College, La Mirada, Calif.	3	Coed	Private	1,360
Birmingham-Southern College, Birmingham, Ala.	2	Coed	Pvt-Methodist	1,101
Bishop College, Dallas, Texas	2	Coed	Pvt-Baptist	1,785
Bishop's University, Lennoxville, Quebec	3	Coed	Pvt-Anglican	951
Bismarck Junior College, Bismarck, N.Dak.	1	Coed	Public	1,125
Black Hawk College, Moline, Ill.	1	Coed	Public	2,502
Black Hills State College, Spearfish, S.Dak.	3	Coed	Public	3,075
Blackburn College, Carlinville, Ill.	2	Coed	Pvt-Presbyterian	606
Blinn College, Brenham, Texas	1	Coed	Public	1,382
Bloomfield College, Bloomfield, N.J.	2	Coed	Pvt-Presbyterian	1,428
Bloomsburg State College, Bloomsburg, Pa.	3	Coed	Public	3,867
Blue Mountain Community College, Pendleton, Oreg.	1	Coed	Public	874
Bluefield College, Bluefield, Va.	1	Coed	Pvt-Baptist	404
Bluefield State College, Bluefield, W.Va.	2	Coed	Public	1,388
Bluffton College, Bluffton, Ohio	2	Coed	Pvt-Mennonite	749
Boise College, Boise, Idaho	3	Coed	Public	4,865
Boston College, Chestnut Hill, Mass.	4	Coed	Pvt-Roman Catholic	9,972
Boston Conservatory of Music, Boston, Mass.	3	Coed	Private	445
Boston University, Boston, Mass.	4	Coed	Private	23,182
Bowdoin College, Brunswick, Me.	2	M	Private	955
Bowie State College, Bowie, Md.	3	Coed	Public	1,328
Bowling Green State University, Bowling Green, Ohio	4	Coed	Public	14,456
Bradford Junior College, Bradford, Mass.	1	W	Private	432
Bradley University, Peoria, Ill.	3	Coed	Private	6,170
Brandeis University, Waltham, Mass.	4	Coed	Private	2,191
Brandon University, Brandon, Manitoba	2	Coed	Private	845
Brenau College, Gainesville, Ga.	2	W	Private	553
Brescia College, Owensboro, Ky.	2	Coed	Pvt-Roman Catholic	1,392

Name and Location	Level of Instruction	Student Body	Control	Enrollment
Brevard College, Brevard, N.C.	1	Coed	Pvt-Methodist	656
Brevard Junior College, Cocoa, Fla.	1	Coed	Public	4,962
Brewton-Parker College, Mount Vernon, Ga.	1	Coed	Pvt-Baptist	614
Briar Cliff College, Sioux City, Iowa	2	Coed	Pvt-Roman Catholic	1,108
Briarcliff College, Briarcliff Manor, N.Y.	2	W	Private	686
Bridgeport, University of, Bridgeport, Conn.	3	Coed	Private	8,657
Bridgewater College, Bridgewater, Va.	2	Coed	Pvt-Brethren	879
Bridgewater State College, Bridgewater, Mass.	3	Coed	Public	2,958
Brigham Young University, Provo, Utah.	4	Coed	Pvt-Latter-day Saints	23,598
British Columbia, University of, Vancouver, B.C.	4	Coed	Public	17,505
Brock University, St. Catharines, Ontario.	3	Coed	Public	703
Bronx Community College (of the City University of New York), Bronx, N.Y.	1	Coed	Public	7,337
Brooklyn, Polytechnic Institute of, Brooklyn, N.Y.	4	Coed	Private	5,054
Brooklyn College (of the City University of New York), Brooklyn, N.Y.	3	Coed	Public	24,422
Brooks Institute, Santa Barbara, Calif.	2	Coed	Public	391
Broome Technical Community College, Binghamton, N.Y.	1	Coed	Public	3,371
Broward Junior College, Fort Lauderdale, Fla.	1	Coed	Public	4,513
Brown University, Providence, R.I. (incl. Pembroke College)	4	Coord	Private	5,164
Brunswick College, Brunswick, Ga.	1	Coed	Private	664
Bryant College, Providence, R.I.	2	Coed	Private	3,036
Bryn Mawr College, Bryn Mawr, Pa.	4	W	Private	1,311
Bucknell University, Lewisburg, Pa.	3	Coed	Private	2,807
Bucks County Community College, Newtown, Pa	1	Coed	Public	2,128
Buena Vista College, Storm Lake, Iowa	2	Coed	Pvt-Presbyterian	1,007
Butler University, Indianapolis, Ind	3	Coed	Private	4,178
Cabrillo College, Aptos, Calif.	1	Coed	Public	3,042
Cabrini College, Radnor, Pa.	2	W	Pvt-Roman Catholic	425
Caldwell College for Women, Caldwell, N.J.	2	W	Pvt-Roman Catholic	984
Calgary, University of, Calgary, Alberta	4	Coed	Public	4,935
California, University of:				
Berkeley.	4	Coed	Public	28,132
Davis.	4	Coed	Public	11,388
Irvine (includes California College of Medicine, Los Angeles).				
Los Angeles.	4	Coed	Public	3,810
Riverside.	4	Coed	Public	28,288
San Diego.	4	Coed	Public	4,565
San Francisco Art Institute.	3	Coed	Public	3,709
Santa Barbara.	4	Coed	Public	12,619
Santa Cruz.	4	Coed	Public	2,638
California Baptist College, Riverside, Calif.	2	Coed	Pvt-Baptist	660
California College of Arts & Crafts, Oakland, Calif.	3	Coed	Private	1,177
California Institute of Technology, Pasadena, Calif.	4	Coed	Private	1,484
California Institute of the Arts, Los Angeles, Calif.	3	Coed	Private	875
California Lutheran College, Thousand Oaks, Calif.	2	Coed	Pvt-Lutheran	1,030
California State College, California, Pa.	3	Coed	Public	5,808
California State College at Dominguez Hills, Calif.	3	Coed	Public	952
California State College at Fullerton, Calif.	3	Coed	Public	11,914
California State College at Hayward, Calif.	3	Coed	Public	11,195
California State College at Long Beach, Calif.	3	Coed	Public	27,176
California State College at Los Angeles, Calif.	3	Coed	Public	24,650
California State College at San Bernardino, Calif.	2	Coed	Public	1,425
California State Polytechnic College, San Luis Obispo & Pomona, Calif.	3	Coed	Public	16,925
Calvin College, Grand Rapids, Mich.	2	Coed	Pvt-Christian Reformed	3,575
Cameron State Agricultural College, Lawton, Okla.	1	Coed	Public	2,950
Campbell College, Buies Creek, N.C.	2	Coed	Pvt-Baptist	2,402
Campbellsville College, Campbellsville, Ky.	1	Coed	Pvt-Baptist	985
Canal Zone College, Balboa Heights, C.Z.	1	Coed	Public	1,284
Canisius College, Buffalo, N.Y.	3	Coed	Pvt-Roman Catholic	3,824
Cape Cod Community College, Hyannis, Mass.	1	Coed	Public	970

Name and Location	Level of Instruction	Student Body	Control	Enrollment
Capital University, Columbus, Ohio	2	Coed	Pvt-Lutheran	1,948
Cardinal Stritch College, Milwaukee, Wis.	3	W	Pvt-Roman Catholic	563
Carleton College, Northfield, Minn.	2	Coed	Private	1,482
Carleton University, Ottawa, Ontario	4	Coed	Private	5,167
Carnegie-Mellon University, Pittsburgh, Pa.	4	Coed	Private	5,203
Carroll College, Helena, Mont.	2	Coed	Pvt-Roman Catholic	1,002
Carroll College, Waukesha, Wis.	2	Coed	Pvt-Presbyterian	1,173
Carson-Newman College, Jefferson City, Tenn.	2	Coed	Pvt-Baptist	1,874
Carthage College, Kenosha, Wis.	2	Coed	Pvt-Lutheran	2,197
Case Western Reserve University, Cleveland, Ohio.	4	Coed	Private	10,337
Casper College, Casper, Wyo.	1	Coed	Public	2,536
Castleton State College, Castleton, Vt.	2	Coed	Public	1,008
Catawba College, Salisbury, N.C.	2	Coed	Pvt-United Church of Christ	1,051
Catherine Spalding College, Louisville, Ky.	3	W	Pvt-Roman Catholic	1,234
Catholic University of America, Washington, D.C.	4	Coord	Pvt-Roman Catholic	6,221
Catholic University of Puerto Rico, Ponce, P.R.	3	Coed	Pvt-Roman Catholic	6,574
Catonsville Community College, Catonsville, Md.	1	Coed	Public	2,009
Cazenovia College, Cazenovia, N.Y.	1	W	Private	587
Cedar Crest College, Allentown, Pa.	2	W	Pvt-Church of Christ	734
Centenary College, Shreveport, La.	2	Coed	Pvt-Methodist	1,310
Centenary College for Women, Hackettstown, N.J.	2	W	Private	663
Central College, Pella, Iowa.	2	Coed	Pvt-Episcopal	1,225
Central Connecticut State College, New Britain, Conn.	3	Coed	Public	8,408
Central Florida Junior College, Ocala, Fla.	1	Coed	Public	1,195
Central Methodist College, Fayette, Mo.	2	Coed	Pvt-Methodist	977
Central Michigan University, Mt. Pleasant, Mich.	3	Coed	Public	13,419
Central Missouri State College, Warrensburg, Mo.	3	Coed	Public	11,944
Central Oregon Community College, Bend, Oreg.	1	Coed	Public	773
Central State University, Wilberforce, Ohio.	2	Coed	Public	2,684
Central State College, Edmond, Okla.	3	Coed	Public	10,239
Central Washington State College, Ellensburg, Wash.	3	Coed	Public	6,490
Centralia College, Centralia, Wash.	1	Coed	Public	1,472
Centre College of Kentucky, Danville, Ky.	2	Coed	Pvt-Presbyterian	739
Cerritos College, Norwalk, Calif.	1	Coed	Public	10,231
Chabot College, Hayward, Calif.	1	Coed	Public	9,488
Chadron State College, Chadron, Nebr.	3	Coed	Public	2,118
Chaffey College, Alta Loma, Calif.	1	Coed	Public	6,317
Chaminade College of Honolulu, Hawaii.	2	Coed	Pvt-Roman Catholic	831
Chapman College, Orange, Calif.	2	Coed	Pvt-Disciples of Christ	3,519
Charleston, College of, Charleston, S.C.	2	Coed	Private	482
Chatham College, Pittsburgh, Pa.	2	W	Private	665
Chattanooga, University of, Chattanooga, Tenn.	3	Coed	Private	2,503
Chattanooga State Technical Institute, Chattanooga, Tenn.	1	Coed	Public	869
Chestnut Hill College, Philadelphia, Pa.	2	W	Pvt-Roman Catholic	1,083
Cheyney State College, Cheyney, Pa.	2	Coed	Public	1,959
Chicago, University of, Chicago, Ill.	4	Coed	Private	10,242
Chicago City College, Chicago, Ill.	1	Coed	Public	35,522
Chicago State College, Chicago, Ill.	3	Coed	Public	5,911
Chico State College, Chico, Calif.	3	Coed	Public	8,875
Chipola Junior College, Marianna, Fla.	1	Coed	Public	1,181
Chowan College, Murfreesboro, N.C.	1	Coed	Pvt-Baptist	1,302
Christian Brothers College, Memphis, Tenn.	2	M	Pvt-Roman Catholic	1,161
Christian College, Columbia, Mo.	1	W	Private	565
Cincinnati, University of, Cincinnati, Ohio.	4	Coed	Public	30,917
Cisco Junior College, Cisco, Texas.	1	Coed	Public	927
Citadel, The, Charleston, S.C.	3	M	Public	2,701
Citrus College, Azusa, Calif.	1	Coed	Public	5,859
City College [of the City University of New York], New York, N.Y.	3	Coed	Public	19,615
City University of New York, N.Y.	4	Coed	Public	157,326
Claflin College, Orangeburg, S.C.	2	Coed	Pvt-Methodist	737
Claremont Graduate School & University Center, Claremont, Calif.	4	Coed	Private	968
Claremont Men's College, Claremont, Calif.	2	M	Private	795
Clarion State College, Clarion, Pa.	3	Coed	Public	3,734
Clark College, Atlanta, Ga.	2	Coed	Pvt-Methodist	1,003
Clark College, Vancouver, Wash.	1	Coed	Public	3,320
Clark University, Worcester, Mass.	4	Coed	Private	2,790
Clarke College, Dubuque, Iowa.	3	W	Pvt-Roman Catholic	1,075
Clarkson College of Technology, Potsdam, N.Y.	3	Coed	Private	2,651
Clatsop Community College, Astoria, Ore.	1	Coed	Public	724
Clemson University, Clemson, S.C.	4	Coed	Public	6,839
Cleveland State University, Cleveland, Ohio.	3	Coed	Public	10,550
Coalinga College, Coalinga, Calif.	1	Coed	Public	685
Coe College, Cedar Rapids, Iowa.	2	Coed	Pvt-Presbyterian	1,418
Colby College, Waterville, Me.	2	Coed	Private	1,602
Colby Junior College, New London, N.H.	2	W	Private	580
Colgate University, Hamilton, N.Y.	3	M	Private	2,002
Colorado, University of, Boulder, Colo.	4	Coed	Public	29,250
Colorado College, Colorado Springs, Colo.	3	Coed	Private	1,703
Colorado School of Mines, Golden, Colo.	4	Coed	Public	1,636
Colorado State College, Greeley, Colo.	4	Coed	Public	10,277
Colorado State University, Fort Collins, Colo.	4	Coed	Public	15,361
Columbia Basin College, Pasco, Wash.	1	Coed	Public	857
Columbia College, Columbia, S.C.	2	W	Pvt-Methodist	2,336
Columbia State Community College, Columbia, Tenn.	1	Coed	Public	1,161
Columbia Union College, Takoma Park, Md.	2	Coed	Pvt-Seventh-day Adventist	971
Columbia University, New York, N.Y. (incl. Columbia University Teachers college, q.v., Columbia College, New York School of Social Work).	4	Coed	Private	16,565
Columbus College, Columbus, Ga.	2	Coed	Public	1,290
Community College of Philadelphia, Pa.	1	Coed	Public	4,059
Compton College, Compton, Calif.	1	Coed	Public	5,233
Concord College, Athens, W. Va.	2	Coed	Public	1,866
Concordia College, Moorhead, Minn.	2	Coed	Pvt-Lutheran	2,340
Concordia College, St. Paul, Minn.	2	Coed	Pvt-Lutheran	742
Concordia Collegiate Institute, Bronxville, N.Y.	1	Coed	Pvt-Lutheran	430
Concordia Lutheran Junior College, Ann Arbor, Mich.	1	Coed	Pvt-Lutheran	506
Concordia Senior College, Fort Wayne, Ind.	2	M	Pvt-Lutheran	478
Concordia Teachers College, River Forest, Ill.	3	Coed	Pvt-Lutheran	1,521
Concordia Teachers College, Seward, Nebr.	3	Coed	Pvt-Lutheran	1,498
Connecticut, University of, Storrs, Conn.	4	Coed	Public	17,130
Connecticut College, New London, Conn.	3	W	Private	1,558
Connors State College, Warner, Okla.	1	Coed	Public	653
Contra Costa College, San Pablo, Calif.	1	Coed	Public	5,361
Converse College, Spartanburg, S.C.	3	W	Private	848
Cooke County Junior College, Gainesville, Texas.	1	Coed	Public	1,198
Cooper Union, New York, N.Y.	4	Coed	Private	1,191
Copiah-Lincoln Junior College, Wesson, Miss.	1	Coed	Public	675
Coppin State College, Baltimore, Md.	2	Coed	Public	1,125
Cornell College, Mount Vernon, Iowa.	2	Coed	Pvt-Methodist	982
Cornell University, Ithaca, N.Y.	4	Coed	Public-Private	15,049
Corning Community College, Corning, N.Y.	1	Coed	Public	2,699
Corpus Christi, University of, Corpus Christi, Texas.	2	Coed	Pvt-Baptist	675
Creighton University, Omaha, Nebr.	3	Coed	Pvt-Roman Catholic	4,181
Cuesta College, San Luis Obispo, Calif.	1	Coed	Public	2,534
Culver-Stockton College, Canton, Mo.	2	Coed	Pvt-Disciples of Christ	865
Cumberland College, Williamsburg, Ky.	2	Coed	Pvt-Baptist	1,771
Cuyahoga Community College—Metropolitan Campus, Cleveland, Ohio.	1	Coed	Public	8,518
Cuyahoga Community College—Western Campus, Parma Heights, Ohio.	1	Coed	Public	4,026
Cypress Junior College, Cypress, Calif.	1	Coed	Public	3,244
Dakota Wesleyan University, Mitchell, S.Dak.	2	Coed	Pvt-Methodist	824
Dalhousie University, Halifax, Nova Scotia (incl. University of King's College).	4	Coed	Private	3,643
Dallas, University of, Dallas, Texas.	4	Coed	Pvt-Roman Catholic	1,272
Dallas Baptist College, Dallas, Texas.	1	Coed	Pvt-Baptist	1,040

Name and Location	Level of Instruction	Student Body	Control	Enrollment
Dana College, Blair, Nebr.	2	Coed	Pvt-Lutheran	989
Danville Junior College, Danville, Ill.	1	Coed	Public	1,254
Dartmouth College, Hanover, N.H.	4	Coed	Private	3,743
David Lipscomb College, Nashville, Tenn.	2	Coed	Pvt-Church of Christ	2,142
Davidson College, Davidson, N.C.	2	M	Pvt-Presbyterian	1,034
Davidson County Community College, Lexington, N.C.	1	Coed	Public	771
Davis and Elkins College, Elkins, W.Va.	1	Coed	Pvt-Presbyterian	844
Dayton, University of, Dayton, Ohio	3	Coed	Pvt-Roman Catholic	10,118
Daytona Beach Junior College, Daytona Beach, Fla.	1	Coed	Public	2,323
Dean Junior College, Franklin, Mass.	1	Coed	Private	946
Defiance College, Defiance, Ohio	2	Coed	Pvt-Church of Christ	1,097
DeKalb College, Clarkston, Ga.	1	Coed	Public	3,462
Delaware, University of, Newark, Del.	4	Coed	Public	13,063
Delaware State College, Dover, Del.	2	Coed	Public	872
Delaware Valley College of Science & Agriculture, Doylestown, Pa.	2	Coed	Private	986
Del Mar College, Corpus Christi, Texas	1	Coed	Public	3,958
Delta College, University Center, Mich.	1	Coed	Public	4,005
Delta State College, Cleveland, Miss.	3	Coed	Public	2,682
Denison University, Granville, Ohio	2	Coed	Public	2,033
Denver, University of, Denver, Colo.	4	Coed	Pvt-Methodist	8,926
DePaul University, Chicago, Ill.	4	Coed	Pvt-Roman Catholic	8,869
DePauw University, Greencastle, Ind.	3	Coed	Pvt-Methodist	2,440
Desert, College of the, Palm Desert, Calif.	1	Coed	Public	1,986
Detroit, University of, Detroit, Mich.	4	Coed	Pvt-Roman Catholic	8,880
Detroit Institute of Technology, Detroit, Mich.	2	Coord	Private	1,452
Diablo Valley College, Pleasant Hill, Calif.	1	Coed	Public	10,093
Dickinson College, Carlisle, Pa.	2	Coed	Pvt-Methodist	1,547
Dickinson State College, Dickinson, N.Dak.	2	Coed	Public	1,627
Dillard University, New Orleans, La.	2	Coed	Private	910
District of Columbia Teachers College, Washington, D.C.	2	Coed	Public	1,678
Dixie College, St. George, Utah	1	Coed	Public	1,026
Doane College, Crete, Nebr.	2	Coed	Pvt-United Church	781
Dodge City Community Junior College, Dodge City, Kans.	1	Coed	Public	596
Dominican College, Houston, Texas	2	Coed	Pvt-Roman Catholic	415
Dominican College, Racine, Wis.	2	W	Pvt-Roman Catholic	697
Dominican College of San Rafael, San Rafael, Calif.	3	Coed	Pvt-Roman Catholic	941
Donnelly College, Kansas City, Kans.	1	Coed	Private	958
Drake University, Des Moines, Iowa	4	Coed	Pvt-Methodist	7,325
Drew University, Madison, N.J.	3	Coed	Pvt-Methodist	1,440
Drexel Institute of Technology, Philadelphia, Pa.	4	Coed	Private	9,366
Drury College, Springfield, Mo.	3	Coed	Pvt-Church of Christ	2,535
Dubuque, University of, Dubuque, Iowa	3	Coed	Pvt-Presbyterian	985
Duke University, Durham, N.C. (incl. Trinity College & Woman's College)	4	Coord		8,041
Dunbarton College of Holy Cross, Washington, D.C.	4	W	Pvt-Roman Catholic	480
DuPage, College of, Naperville, Ill.	1	Coed	Public	2,591
Duquesne University, Pittsburgh, Pa.	4	Coed	Pvt-Roman Catholic	7,414
Dutchess Community College, Poughkeepsie, N.Y.	1	Coed	Public	3,538
D'Youville College, Buffalo, N.Y.	2	W	Pvt-Roman Catholic	1,363
Earlham College, Richmond, Ind.	3	Coed	Pvt-Friends	1,135
East Carolina University, Greenville, N.C.	3	Coed	Public	9,272
East Central Junior College, Decatur, Miss.	1	Coed	Public	3,700
East Central State College, Ada, Okla.	3	Coed	Public	3,058
East Los Angeles College, Los Angeles, Calif.	1	Coed	Public	13,136
East Stroudsburg State College, East Stroudsburg, Pa.	3	Coed	Public	2,336
East Tennessee State University, Johnson City, Tenn.	3	Coed	Public	8,966
East Texas Baptist College, Marshall, Texas	2	Coed	Pvt-Baptist	767
East Texas State University, Commerce, Texas	3	Coed	Public	9,389
Eastern Arizona College, Thatcher, Ariz.	1	Coed	Public	1,034
Eastern Baptist College, St. Davids, Pa.	2	Coed	Pvt-Baptist	531
Eastern Connecticut State College, Willimantic, Conn.	3	Coed	Public	1,491

Name and Location	Level of Instruction	Student Body	Control	Enrollment
Eastern Illinois University, Charleston, Ill.	3	Coed	Public	7,494
Eastern Iowa Community College, Muscatine, Iowa	1	Coed	Public	749
Eastern Kentucky University, Richmond, Ky.	3	Coed	Public	9,180
Eastern Mennonite College, Harrisonburg, Va.	2	Coed	Pvt-Mennonite	883
Eastern Michigan University, Ypsilanti, Mich.	3	Coed	Public	19,235
Eastern Montana College, Billings, Mont.	3	Coed	Public	3,595
Eastern Nazarene College, Quincy, Mass.	3	Coed	Pvt-Nazarene	816
Eastern New Mexico University, Portales, N.Mex.	3	Coed	Public	5,582
Eastern Oklahoma State College, Wilburton, Okla.	1	Coed	Public	1,135
Eastern Oregon College, La Grande, Oreg.	3	Coed	Public	1,694
Eastern Washington State College, Cheney, Wash.	3	Coed	Public	5,494
Edgewood College of the Sacred Heart, Madison, Wis.	2	Coed	Pvt-Roman Catholic	683
Edinboro State College, Edinboro, Pa.	3	Coed	Public	6,064
Edison Junior College, Fort Myers, Fla.	1	Coed	Public	1,211
El Camino College, El Camino College, Calif.	1	Coed	Public	15,413
El Centro College, Dallas, Texas	1	Coed	Public	7,102
El Paso, University of Texas at, El Paso, Texas	3	Coed	Public	9,029
Elizabeth City State College, Elizabeth City, N.C.	2	Coed	Public	963
Elizabethtown College, Elizabethtown, Pa.	2	Coed	Pvt-Brethren	1,896
Elmhurst College, Elmhurst, Ill.	2	Coed	Pvt-Church of Christ	1,665
Elmira College, Elmira, N.Y.	3	W	Private	2,580
Elon College, Elon College, N.C.	2	Coed	Pvt-Church of Christ	1,812
Embry-Riddle Aeronautical Institute, Daytona Beach, Fla.	2	Coed	Private	1,276
Emerson College, Boston, Mass.	3	Coed	Private	1,313
Emmanuel College, Boston, Mass.	2	W	Pvt-Roman Catholic	1,533
Emory & Henry College, Emory, Va.	2	Coed	Pvt-Methodist	870
Emory University, Atlanta, Ga.	4	Coed	Pvt-Methodist	5,419
Emporia, College of, Emporia, Kans.	2	Coed	Pvt-Presbyterian	1,043
Endicott Junior College, Beverly, Mass.	1	W	Private	852
Erskine College, Due West, S.C.	2	Coed	Pvt-Presbyterian	724
Essex Community College, Essex, Md.	1	Coed	Public	1,288
Eureka College, Eureka, Ill.	2	Coed	Pvt-Disciples of Christ	538
Evangel College, Springfield, Mo.	2	Coed	Pvt-Assemblies of God	881
Evansville, University of, Evansville, Ind.	3	Coed	Pvt-Methodist	5,470
Everett Community College, Everett, Wash.	1	Coed	Public	4,295
Fairfield University, Fairfield, Conn.	3	M	Pvt-Roman Catholic	1,666
Fairleigh Dickinson University, Rutherford, Teaneck, Madison, N.J.	4	Coed	Private	19,260
Fairmont State College, Fairmont, W.Va.	3	Coed	Public	2,972
Farmington State College, Farmington, Me.	3	Coed	Public	1,179
Fashion Institute of Technology, New York, N.Y.	2	Coed	Public	5,220
Fayetteville State College, Fayetteville, N.C.	3	Coed	Public	1,243
Fayetteville Technical Institute, Fayetteville, N.C.	1	Coed	Public	600
Ferris State College, Big Rapids, Mich.	3	Coed	Public	8,200
Ferrum Junior College, Ferrum, Va.	1	Coed	Pvt-Methodist	957
Finch College, New York, N.Y.	3	W	Private	404
Findlay College, Findlay, Ohio	2	Coed	Pvt-Church of God	1,413
Fisk University, Nashville, Tenn.	3	Coed	Private	1,161
Fitchburg State College, Fitchburg, Mass.	3	Coed	Public	3,647
Flint Community Junior College, Flint, Mich.	1	Coed	Public	6,558
Florence State College, Florence, Ala.	3	Coed	Public	3,054
Florida, University of, Gainesville, Fla.	4	Coed	Public	19,848
Florida Agricultural & Mechanical University, Tallahassee, Fla.	3	Coed	Public	3,956
Florida Atlantic University, Boca Raton, Fla.	3	Coed	Public	5,413
Florida Institute of Technology, Melbourne, Fla.	3	Coed	Private	1,929
Florida Keys Junior College, Key West, Fla.	1	Coed	Public	561
Florida Memorial College, Miami, Fla.	2	Coed	Pvt-Baptist	756
Florida Presbyterian College, St. Petersburg, Fla.	2	Coed	Pvt-Presbyterian	969
Florida Southern College, Lakeland, Fla.	2	Coed	Pvt-Methodist	1,695
Florida State University, Tallahassee, Fla.	4	Coed	Public	17,496
Fontbonne College, St. Louis, Mo.	2	W	Pvt-Roman Catholic	894
Foothill College, Los Altos Hills, Calif.	1	Coed	Public	8,442
Fordham University, New York, N.Y.	4	Coed	Pvt-Roman Catholic	10,202

Name and Location	Level of Instruction	Student Body	Control	Enrollment
Forsyth Technical Institute, Winston-Salem, N.C.	1	Coed	Public	1,029
Fort Hays Kansas State College, Hays, Kans.	3	Coed	Public	5,459
Fort Lewis College, Durango, Colo.	3	Coed	Public	1,723
Fort Valley State College, Fort Valley, Ga.	3	Coed	Public	2,102
Framingham State College, Framingham, Mass.	3	Coed	Public	2,614
Francis T. Nicholls State College, Thibodaux, La.	3	Coed	Public	4,800
Frank Phillips College, Borger, Texas	1	Coed	Public	704
Franklin & Marshall College, Lancaster, Pa.	3	M	Private	2,417
Franklin College, Franklin, Ind.	3	Coed	Pvt-Baptist	756
Franklin Pierce College, Rindge, N.H.	2	Coed	Private	894
Freed-Hardeman College, Henderson, Tenn.	1	Coed	Pvt-Church of Christ	700
Fresno City College, Fresno, Calif.	1	Coed	Public	9,313
Fresno State College, Fresno, Calif.	3	Coed	Public	19,501
Friends University, Wichita, Kans.	3	Coed	Pvt-Friends	946
Frostburg State College, Frostburg, Md.	3	Coed	Public	2,555
Fullerton Junior College, Fullerton, Calif.	1	Coed	Public	13,064
Furman University, Greenville, S.C.	3	Coed	Pvt-Baptist	1,993
Gadsden State Junior College, Gadsden, Ala.	1	Coed	Public	2,343
Gainesville Junior College, Gainesville, Ga.	1	Coed	Public	720
Gallaudet College, Washington, D.C.	3	Coed	Private	720
Gannon College, Erie, Pa.	3	Coed	Pvt-Roman Catholic	3,413
Gardner-Webb College, Boiling Springs, N.C.	1	Coed	Pvt-Baptist	1,288
Garland College, Boston, Mass.	1	W	Private	390
Gaston College, Gastonia, N.C.	1	Coed	Public	1,320
Gavilan College, Gilroy, Calif.	1	Coed	Public	1,004
General Beadle State College, Madison, S.Dak.	2	Coed	Public	1,220
General Motors Institute, Flint, Mich.	3	Coed	Private	2,892
Geneva College, Beaver Falls, Pa.	3	Coed	Pvt-Presbyterian	1,806
George Fox College, Newberg, Oreg.	2	Coed	Pvt-Friends	391
George Peabody College for Teachers, Nashville, Tenn.	4	Coed	Private	1,806
George Washington University, Washington, D.C.	4	Coed	Private	19,073
George Williams College, Downers Grove, Ill.	3	Coed	Private	850
Georgetown College, Georgetown, Ky.	3	Coed	Pvt-Baptist	1,385
Georgetown University, Washington, D.C.	4	Coed	Pvt-Roman Catholic	7,734
Georgia, University of, Athens, Ga.	4	Coord	Public	21,182
Georgia Institute of Technology, Atlanta, Ga.	3	Coed	Public	7,951
Georgia College at Milledgeville, Milledgeville, Ga.	3	Coed	Public	1,536
Georgia Southern College, Statesboro, Ga.	3	Coed	Public	4,669
Georgia Southwestern College, Americus, Ga.	3	Coed	Public	1,922
Georgia State College, Atlanta, Ga.	4	Coed	Public	10,407
Georgian Court College, Lakewood, N.J.	2	W	Pvt-Roman Catholic	673
Gettysburg College, Gettysburg, Pa.	3	Coed	Pvt-Lutheran	1,883
Glassboro State College, Glassboro, N.J.	3	Coed	Public	8,492
Glendale Community College, Glendale, Calif.	1	Coed	Public	4,909
Glendale College, Glendale, Calif.	1	Coed	Public	4,833
Glenville State College, Glenville, W.Va.	3	Coed	Public	1,587
Goddard College, Plainfield, Vt.	3	Coed	Private	883
Gogebic Community College, Ironwood, Mich.	1	Coed	Public	530
Golden Gate College, San Francisco, Calif.	3	Coed	Private	3,134
Golden West College, Huntington Beach, Calif.	1	Coed	Public	5,155
Gonzaga University, Spokane, Wash.	4	Coed	Pvt-Roman Catholic	2,652
Good Counsel College, White Plains, N.Y.	2	W	Pvt-Roman Catholic	543
Gordon College, Wenham, Mass.	3	Coed	Private	996
Gordon Military College, Barnesville, Ga.	1	Coed	Private	449
Gorham State College, Gorham, Me.	3	Coed	Public	1,998
Goshen College, Goshen, Ind.	3	Coed	Pvt-Mennonite	1,330
Goucher College, Baltimore, Md.	3	W	Private	1,068
Graceland College, Lamoni, Iowa	2	Coed	Pvt-Latter-day Saints	1,236
Graduate Center (of the City University of N.Y.), New York, N.Y.	4	Coed	Public	1,446
Grambling College, Grambling, La.	3	Coed	Public	3,718
Grand Canyon College, Phoenix, Ariz.	2	Coed	Pvt-Baptist	736
Grand Rapids Junior College, Grand Rapids, Mich.	1	Coed	Public	5,041
Grand Valley State College, Allendale, Mich.	2	Coed	Public	2,220
Grand View College, Des Moines, Iowa	1	Coed	Pvt-Lutheran	1,458
Grays Harbor College, Aberdeen, Wash.	1	Coed	Public	1,102
Grayson County Junior College, Sherman-Denison, Texas	1	Coed	Public	1,969
Great Falls, College of, Great Falls, Mont.	2	Coed	Pvt-Roman Catholic	1,264
Green Mountain College, Poultney, Vt.	1	W	Pvt-Methodist	672
Green River Community College, Auburn, Wash.	1	Coed	Public	3,277
Greenfield Community College, Greenfield, Mass.	1	Coed	Public	658
Greensboro College, Greensboro, N.C.	2	Coed	Pvt-Methodist	690
Greenville College, Greenville, Ill.	2	Coed	Pvt-Methodist	790
Greenville Technical Education Center, Greenville, S.C.	1	Coed	Public	6,983
Grinnell College, Grinnell, Iowa	2	Coed	Private	1,166
Grossmont College, El Cajon, Calif.	1	Coed	Public	5,483
Grove City College, Grove City, Pa.	2	Coed	Pvt-Presbyterian	1,990
Guam, University of, Agana, Guam	3	Coed	Public	1,312
Guelph, University of, Guelph, Ont.	4	Coed	Public	4,356
Guilford College, Greensboro, N.C.	3	Coed	Pvt-Friends	1,600
Gulf Coast Junior College, Panama City, Fla.	1	Coed	Public	1,517
Gustavus Adolphus College, St. Peter, Minn.	2	Coed	Pvt-Lutheran	1,835
Gwynedd-Mercy College, Gwynedd Valley, Pa.	2	W	Pvt-Roman Catholic	1,042
Hagerstown Junior College, Hagerstown, Md.	1	Coed	Public	938
Hamilton College, Clinton, N.Y.	3	M	Private	853
Hamline University, St. Paul, Minn.	3	Coed	Pvt-Methodist	1,227
Hampden-Sydney College, Hampden-Sydney, Va.	3	M	Pvt-Presbyterian	633
Hampton Institute, Hampton, Va.	3	Coed	Private	2,377
Hanover College, Hanover, Ind.	3	Coed	Pvt-Presbyterian	1,057
Hardin-Simmons University, Abilene, Texas	3	Coed	Pvt-Baptist	1,723
Harding College, Searcy, Ark.	3	Coed	Pvt-Church of Christ	1,943
Harford Junior College, Bel Air, Md.	1	Coed	Public	1,278
Harris Teachers College, St. Louis, Mo.	3	Coed	Public	1,478
Harrisburg Area Community College, Harrisburg, Pa.	1	Coed	Public	1,981
Hartford, University of, Hartford, Conn.	3	Coed	Private	8,294
Hartnell College, Salinas, Calif.	1	Coed	Public	3,191
Hartwick College, Oneonta, N.Y.	2	Coed	Private	1,558
Harvard University, Cambridge, Mass.	4	Coed	Private	15,198
Hastings College, Hastings, Nebr.	3	Coed	Pvt-Presbyterian	806
Haverford College, Haverford, Pa.	2	M	Pvt-Friends	637
Hawaii, Church College of, Laie, Oahu, Hawaii	3	Coed	Pvt-Latter-day Saints	1,113
Hawaii, University of, Honolulu, Hawaii	4	Coed	Public	19,611
Hebrew Union College-Jewish Institute of Religion, Los Angeles, Calif.	4	Coed	Pvt-Jewish	458
Heidelberg College, Tiffin, Ohio	2	Coed	Pvt-Church of Christ	1,249
Henderson County Junior College, Athens, Texas	1	Coed	Public	1,281
Henderson State College, Arkadelphia, Ark.	3	Coed	Public	3,355
Hendrix College, Conway, Ark.	3	Coed	Pvt-Methodist	918
Henry Ford Community College, Dearborn, Mich.	1	Coed	Public	11,533
Herbert H. Lehman College (of the City University of New York), New York, N.Y.	3	Coed	Public	9,850
Hesston College, Hesston, Kans.	1	Coed	Pvt-Mennonite	448
Hibbing State Junior College, Hibbing, Minn.	1	Coed	Public	748
High Point College, High Point, N.C.	2	Coed	Pvt-Methodist	1,333
Highland Park College, Highland Park, Mich.	1	Coed	Public	3,781
Highline College, Midway, Wash.	1	Coed	Public	4,493
Hill Junior College, Hillsboro, Texas	1	Coed	Public	677
Hillsdale College, Hillsdale, Mich.	3	Coed	Private	1,216
Hinds Junior College, Raymond, Miss.	1	Coed	Public	1,738
Hiram College, Hiram, Ohio	3	Coed	Pvt-Disciples of Christ	1,135
Hiwassee College, Madison, Tenn.	1	Coed	Pvt-Methodist	620
Hobart & William Smith Colleges, Geneva, N.Y.	3	Coord	Private	1,530
Hofstra University, Hempstead, L.I., N.Y.	4	Coed	Private	13,044
Hollins College, Hollins College, Va.	3	W	Private	973
Holmes Junior College, Goodman, Miss.	1	Coed	Public	1,080
Holy Cross, College of the, Worcester, Mass.	3	M	Pvt-Roman Catholic	2,373
Holy Family College, Philadelphia, Pa.	2	W	Pvt-Roman Catholic	628
Holy Family College, Manitowoc, Wis.	2	W	Pvt-Roman Catholic	620

Name and Location	Level of Instruction	Student Body	Control	Enrollment
Holy Names, College of the, Oakland, Calif.	3	W	Pvt-Roman Catholic	979
Hood College, Frederick, Md.	2	W	Private	745
Hope College, Holland, Mich.	2	Coed	Pvt-Reformed	1,950
Houghton College, Houghton, N.Y.	2	Coed	Pvt-Methodist	1,161
Houston, University of, Houston, Texas.	4	Coed	Public	23,713
Houston Baptist College, Houston, Texas.	2	Coed	Pvt-Baptist	769
Howard County Junior College, Big Spring, Texas.	1	Coed	Public	1,013
Howard Payne College, Brownwood, Texas.	3	Coed	Pvt-Baptist	1,278
Howard University, Washington, D.C.	4	Coed	Public-Private	8,740
Humboldt State College, Arcata, Calif.	3	Coed	Public	5,166
Hunter College (of the City University of New York), New York, N.Y.	3	Coed	Public	18,350
Huntingdon College, Montgomery, Ala.	2	Coed	Pvt-Methodist	833
Huntington College, Huntington, Ind.	2	Coed	Pvt-Brethren	520
Huron College (of the University of Western Ontario), London, Ontario.	2	Coed	Pvt-Anglican	497
Huron College, Huron, S.Dak.	2	Coed	Pvt-Presbyterian	732
Huston-Tillotson College, Austin, Texas.	2	Coed	Pvt-Church of Christ and Methodist	832
Hutchinson Community Junior College, Hutchinson, Kans.	1	Coed	Public	1,785
Idaho, College of, Caldwell, Idaho.	3	Coed	Pvt-Presbyterian	1,079
Idaho, University of, Moscow, Idaho.	4	Coed	Public	6,341
Idaho State University, Pocatello, Idaho.	4	Coed	Public	5,830
Illinois, University of, Urbana & Chicago, Ill.	4	Coed	Public	50,983
Illinois College, Jacksonville, Ill.	2	Coed	Pvt-Presbyterian and Church of Christ	895
Illinois Institute of Technology, Chicago, Ill.	4	Coed	Private	7,890
Illinois State University, Normal, Ill.	4	Coed	Public	13,671
Illinois Valley Community College, Oglesby, Ill.	1	Coed	Public	1,705
Illinois Wesleyan University, Bloomington, Ill.	3	Coed	Pvt-Methodist	1,594
Immaculata College, Immaculata, Pa.	2	W	Pvt-Roman Catholic	945
Immaculate Heart College, Los Angeles, Calif.	3	Coed	Pvt-Roman Catholic	1,109
Imperial Valley College, Imperial, Calif.	1	Coed	Public	1,806
Incarnate Word College, San Antonio, Texas.	3	W	Pvt-Roman Catholic	1,226
Independence Community Junior College, Independence, Kans.	1	Coed	Public	520
Indian River Junior College, Fort Pierce, Fla.	1	Coed	Public	1,036
Indiana Central College, Indianapolis, Ind.	3	Coed	Pvt-Methodist	2,373
Indiana Institute of Technology, Fort Wayne, Ind.	2	Coed	Private	926
Indiana State University, Terre Haute, Ind.	4	Coed	Public	16,662
Indiana University of Pennsylvania, Indiana, Pa.	3	Coed	Public	9,132
Indiana University, Bloomington, Ind.	4	Coed	Public	52,101
Insurance, College of, New York, N.Y.	2	Coed	Private	1,419
Inter American University of Puerto Rico, San Germán, P.R.	3	Coed	Pvt-Roman Catholic	6,131
Iona College, New Rochelle, N.Y.	3	M	Pvt-Roman Catholic	3,198
Iowa State University, Ames, Iowa.	4	Coed	Public	18,083
Iowa, University of, Iowa City, Iowa.	4	Coed	Public	19,506
Iowa Wesleyan College, Mt. Pleasant, Iowa.	2	Coed	Pvt-Methodist	930
Itawamba Junior College, Fulton, Miss.	1	Coed	Public	
Ithaca College, Ithaca, N.Y.	3	Coed	Private	3,748
Jackson Community College, Jackson, Mich.	1	Coed	Public	2,960
Jackson State College, Jackson, Miss.	3	Coed	Public	3,686
Jacksonville State University, Jacksonville, Ala.	3	Coed	Public	5,440
Jacksonville University, Jacksonville, Fla.	3	Coed	Private	2,915
James Connally Technical Institute, Waco, Texas.	1	Coed	Public	394
Jamestown College, Jamestown, N. Dak.	2	Coed	Pvt-Presbyterian	612
Jamestown Community College, Jamestown, N.Y.	1	Coed	Public	1,357
Jarvis Christian College, Hawkins, Texas.	2	Coed	Pvt-Disciples of Christ	551
Jean-de-Brébeuf College (of the University of Montreal), Montreal, Quebec.	2	Coed	Pvt-Roman Catholic	625
Jefferson Davis State Junior College, Brewton, Ala.	1	Coed	Public	547
Jefferson State Junior College, Birmingham, Ala.	1	Coed	Public	4,343
Jersey City State College, Jersey City, N.J.	3	Coed	Public	6,938
Jewish Theological Seminary of America, New York, N.Y.	4	Coed	Pvt-Jewish	502
John Brown University, Siloam Springs, Ark.	2	Coed	Private	753
John C. Calhoun State Technical Junior College, Decatur, Ala.	1	Coed	Public	1,612
John Carroll University, Cleveland, Ohio.	3	Coed	Pvt-Roman Catholic	4,302
John Jay College of Criminal Justice (of the University of New York), New York, N.Y.	3	Coed	Public	2,318
Johns Hopkins University, Baltimore, Md.	4	Coord	Private	10,322
Johnson C. Smith University, Charlotte, N.C.	3	Coed	Pvt-Presbyterian	1,339
Johnson State College, Johnson, Vt.	3	Coed	Public	633
Joliet Junior College, Joliet, Ill.	1	Coed	Public	3,206
Jones County Junior College, Ellisville, Miss.	1	Coed	Public	1,871
Judson College, Marion, Ala.	2	Coed	Pvt-Baptist	467
Judaism, University of, Los Angeles, Calif.	4	Coed	Pvt-Jewish	398
Juilliard School of Music, New York, N.Y.	4	Coed	Private	976
Juniata College, Huntington, Pa.	2	Coed	Pvt-Brethren	1,177
Kalamazoo College, Kalamazoo, Mich.	3	Coed	Pvt-Baptist	1,290
Kansas, University of, Lawrence, Kans.	4	Coed	Public	17,790
Kansas City Art Institute, Kansas City, Mo.	2	Coed	Private	693
Kansas City Kansas Community Junior College, Kansas City, Kans.	1	Coed	Public	1,549
Kansas State College of Pittsburg, Kans.	3	Coed	Public	6,309
Kansas State Teachers College, Emporia, Kans.	3	Coed	Public	7,068
Kansas State University, Manhattan, Kans.	4	Coed	Public	12,570
Kansas Wesleyan University, Salina, Kans.	2	Coed	Pvt-Methodist	1,072
Kaskaskia College, Centralia, Ill.	1	Coed	Public	5,488
Kearney State College, Kearney, Nebr.	3	Coed	Public	2,060
Keene State College (of the University of New Hampshire), Keene, N.H.	3	Coed	Public	2,764
Kellogg Community College, Battle Creek, Mich.	1	Coed	Public	608
Kendall College, Evanston, Ill.	1	Coed	Pvt-Methodist	1,278
Kennesaw Junior College, Marietta, Ga.	1	Coed	Public	
Kent State University, Kent, Ohio.	4	Coed	Public	27,125
Kentucky, University of, Lexington, Ky.	4	Coed	Public	15,298
Kentucky State College, Frankfort, Ky.	2	Coed	Public	1,610
Kentucky Wesleyan College, Owensboro, Ky.	2	Coed	Pvt-Methodist	1,183
Kenyon College, Gambier, Ohio.	2	M	Pvt-Episcopal	790
Keuka College, Keuka Park, N.Y.	2	W	Pvt-Baptist	807
Keystone Junior College, La Plume, Pa.	1	Coed	Private	720
Kilgore College, Kilgore, Texas.	1	Coed	Public	2,388
King's College, The, Briarcliff Manor, N.Y.	2	Coed	Private	683
King's College, Wilkes-Barre, Pa.	3	M	Pvt-Roman Catholic	1,964
Kingsborough Community College (of the City University of New York), Brooklyn, N.Y.	1	Coed	Public	2,935
Knox College, Galesburg, Ill.	3	Coed	Private	1,371
Knoxville College, Knoxville, Tenn.	2	Coed	Pvt-Presbyterian	889
Kutztown State College, Kutztown, Pa.	3	Coed	Public	4,441
Ladycliff College, Highland Falls, N.Y.	2	W	Pvt-Roman Catholic	572
Lafayette College, Easton, Pa.	3	M	Pvt-Presbyterian	2,043
La Grange College, La Grange, Ga.	2	Coed	Pvt-Methodist	578
Lake City Junior College and Forest Ranger School, Lake City, Fla.	1	Coed	Public	828
Lake Erie College, Painesville, Ohio.	3	Coed	Private	873
Lake Forest College, Lake Forest, Ill.	3	Coed	Pvt-Presbyterian	1,321
Lake Michigan College, Benton Harbor, Mich.	1	Coed	Public	2,076
Lake-Sumter Junior College, Leesburg, Fla.	1	Coed	Public	909
Lake Superior State College, Marie, Mich.	2	Coed	Public	1,420
Lakehead University, Port Arthur, Ontario.	2	Coed	Private	1,606
Lakeland College, Sheboygan, Wis.	2	Coed	Pvt-Church of Christ	700
Lamar State College of Technology, Beaumont, Texas.	3	Coed	Public	8,111
Lambuth College, Jackson, Tenn.	2	Coed	Pvt-Methodist	833

Name and Location	Level of Instruction	Student Body	Control	Enrollment
Lander College, Greenwood, S.C.	2	Coed	Private	644
Lane College, Jackson, Tenn.	2	Coed	Pvt-Methodist Episcopal	1,102
Lane Community College, Eugene, Oreg.	1	Coed	Public	2,867
Laney College, Oakland, Calif.	1	Coed	Public	4,706
Langston University, Langston, Okla.	2	Coed	Public	1,336
Lansing Community College, Lansing, Mich.	1	Coed	Public	4,582
Laredo Junior College, Laredo, Texas.	1	Coed	Public	1,289
La Salle College, Philadelphia, Pa.	3	M	Pvt-Roman Catholic	6,601
Lasell Junior College, Auburndale, Mass.	1	W	Private	906
Lassen College, Susanville, Calif.	1	Coed	Public	556
Laurentian University of Sudbury, Sudbury, Ontario.		Coed	Public	1,269
Laval University, Quebec, Quebec.	4	Coed	Pvt-Roman Catholic	15,729
La Verne College, La Verne, Calif.	3	Coed	Pvt-Brethren	885
Lawrence Institute of Technology, Southfield, Mich.	3	Coed	Private	4,566
Lawrence University, Appleton, Wis.	4	Coed	Private	1,369
Lebanon Valley College, Annville, Pa.	2	Coed	Pvt-Methodist	1,354
Lee College, Cleveland, Tenn.	2	Coed	Pvt-Church of God	835
Lee College, Baytown, Texas.	1	Coed	Public	1,788
Lees-McRae College, Banner Elk, N.C.	1	Coed	Pvt-Presbyterian	624
Lehigh University, Bethlehem, Pa.	4	Coed	Private	4,954
Le Moyne College, Syracuse, N.Y.	2	Coed	Pvt-Roman Catholic	1,605
Lenoir County Community College, Kingston, N.C.		Coed	Public	695
Lenoir-Rhyne College, Hickory, N.C.	2	Coed	Pvt-Lutheran	1,189
Lesley College, Cambridge, Mass.	3	W	Private	1,309
Lethbridge, University of, Lethbridge, Alberta		Coed	Public	663
Lewis & Clark College, Portland, Oreg.	3	Coed	Pvt-Presbyterian	695
Lewis-Clark Normal School, Lewiston, Idaho.	2	Coed	Public	1,884
Lewis College, Lockport, Ill.	2	Coed	Pvt-Roman Catholic	920
Limestone College, Gaffney, S.C.	2	Coed	Private	2,001
Lincoln College, Lincoln, Ill.	1	Coed	Private	690
Lincoln Memorial University, Harrogate, Tenn.	2	Coed	Private	718
Lincoln University, Jefferson City, Mo.	2	Coed	Public	777
Lincoln University, Lincoln University, Pa.	2	Coed	Public	2,251
Lindenwood College, St. Charles, Mo.	2	W	Pvt-Presbyterian	1,002
Lindsey Wilson Junior College, Columbia, Ky.	1	Coed	Pvt-Methodist	589
Linfield College, McMinnville, Oreg.	3	Coed	Pvt-Baptist	575
Little Rock University, Little Rock, Ark.	3	Coed	Private	1,147
Livingston State College, Livingston, Ala.	3	Coed	Public	3,164
Livingstone College, Salisbury, N.C.	2	Coed	Pvt-Methodist Episcopal	1,651
Lock Haven State College, Lock Haven, Pa.	2	Coed	Public	836
Loma Linda University, Loma Linda, Calif.	4	Coed	Pvt-Seventh-day Adventist	2,179
Long Beach City College, Long Beach, Calif.	1	Coed	Public	3,091
Long Island University, Greenvale, N.Y. (incl. Bklyn. College of Pharmacy; C.W. Post & Southampton campuses, Long Island, N.Y.)		Coed	Private	22,496
Lon Morris College, Jacksonville, Texas.	1	Coed	Pvt-Methodist	21,298
Longwood College, Farmville, Va.	3	W	Public	442
Loras College, Dubuque, Iowa.	3	Coed	Pvt-Roman Catholic	1,771
Loretto Heights College, Denver, Colo.	3	W	Pvt-Roman Catholic	1,757
Los Angeles City College, Los Angeles, Calif.	1	Coed	Public	886
Los Angeles Harbor College, Wilmington, Calif.	1	Coed	Public	18,137
Los Angeles Pierce College, Woodland Hills, Calif.	1	Coed	Public	6,712
Los Angeles Trade-Technical College, Los Angeles, Calif.	1	Coed	Public	12,636
Los Angeles Valley College, Van Nuys, Calif.	1	Coed	Public	14,233
Louisburg College, Louisburg, N.C.	1	Coed	Pvt-Methodist	77,499
Louisiana College, Pineville, La.	2	Coed	Pvt-Baptist	701
Louisiana Polytechnic Institute, Ruston, La.	4	Coed	Public	1,140
Louisiana State University & Agricultural & Mechanical College, Baton Rouge, La.	4	Coed	Public	7,263
Louisville, University of, Louisville, Ky.	4	Coed	Public	31,902
Lowell State College, Lowell, Mass.	3	Coed	Public	8,157
Lowell Technological Institute, Lowell, Mass.	4	Coed	Public	1,811
Lower Columbia College, Longview, Wash.	1	Coed	Public	4,609
Loyola College, Baltimore, Md.	3	Coord	Pvt-Roman Catholic	1,283
				2,945

Name and Location	Level of Instruction	Student Body	Control	Enrollment
Loyola College (of the University of Montreal), Montreal, Quebec.	2	Coed	Pvt-Roman Catholic	3,108
Loyola University, Chicago, Ill.	4	Coed	Pvt-Roman Catholic	13,548
Loyola University, New Orleans, La.	4	Coord	Pvt-Roman Catholic	4,544
Loyola University of Los Angeles, Los Angeles, Calif.	3	Coed	Pvt-Roman Catholic	2,768
Lubbock Christian College, Lubbock, Texas.	1	Coed	Pvt-Church of Christ	715
Luther College, Decorah, Iowa.	2	Coed	Pvt-Lutheran	2,060
Lycoming College, Williamsport, Pa.	2	Coed	Pvt-Methodist	1,562
Lynchburg College, Lynchburg, Va.	3	Coed	Pvt-Disciples of Christ	1,844
Lyndon State College, Lyndonville, Vt.	2	Coed	Public	602
Macalester College, St. Paul, Minn.	3	Coed	Pvt-Presbyterian	1,971
McGill University, Montreal, Quebec.	4	Coed	Public	14,159
McLennan Community College, Waco, Texas.	1	Coed	Public	1,577
McMaster University, Hamilton, Ontario.	4	Coed	Private	5,227
MacMurray College, Jacksonville, Ill.	2	Coord	Pvt-Methodist	1,012
McMurry College, Abilene, Texas.	2	Coed	Pvt-Methodist	1,611
McNeese State College, Lake Charles, La.	3	Coed	Public	4,522
McPherson College, McPherson, Kans.	2	Coed	Pvt-Brethren	805
Madison College, Harrisonburg, Va.	3	W	Public	3,517
Madonna College, Livonia, Mich.	2	W	Pvt-Roman Catholic	727
Maine, University of, Orono, Me.	4	Coed	Public	13,571
Malone College, Canton, Ohio.	2	Coed	Pvt-Friends	1,107
Manatee Junior College, Bradenton, Fla.	1	Coed	Public	2,155
Manchester College, North Manchester, Ind.	2	Coed	Pvt-Brethren	1,469
Manhattan, Borough of, Community College (of the City University of New York), N.Y.	1	Coed	Public	4,747
Manhattan College, New York, N.Y.	3	M	Pvt-Roman Catholic	4,460
Manhattan School of Music, New York, N.Y.	3	Coed	Private	722
Manhattanville College, Purchase, N.Y.	3	W	Pvt-Roman Catholic	1,461
Manitoba, University of, Winnipeg, Man. (incl. St. John's & St. Paul's colleges, qq.v.).	4	Coed	Public	10,405
Mankato State College, Mankato, Minn.	3	Coed	Public	11,699
Mansfield State College, Mansfield, Pa.	3	Coed	Public	2,754
Marian College, Indianapolis, Ind.	2	Coed	Pvt-Roman Catholic	1,074
Marian College of Fond du Lac, Fond du Lac, Wis.	2	W	Pvt-Roman Catholic	519
Marianopolis College (of the University of Montreal), Montreal, Quebec.	2	Coed	Pvt-Roman Catholic	433
Marietta College, Marietta, Ohio.	2	Coed	Private	2,349
Marillac College, St. Louis, Mo.	2	W	Pvt-Roman Catholic	391
Marin, College of, Kentfield, Calif.	1	Coed	Public	5,263
Marion College, Marion, Ind.	2	Coed	Pvt-Methodist	792
Marion Institute, Marion, Ala.	1	M	Private	400
Marist College, Poughkeepsie, N.Y.	2	Coed	Pvt-Roman Catholic	1,790
Marquette University, Milwaukee, Wis.	4	Coed	Pvt-Roman Catholic	10,801
Mars Hill College, Mars Hill, N.C.	2	Coed	Pvt-Baptist	1,324
Marshall University, Huntington, W.Va.	3	Coed	Public	9,255
Martin College, Pulaski, Tenn.	1	W	Pvt-Methodist	441
Mary Baldwin College, Staunton, Va.	3	W	Pvt-Presbyterian	716
Mary Hardin-Baylor College, Belton, Texas.	2	W	Pvt-Baptist	887
Mary Manse College, Toledo, Ohio.	3	W	Pvt-Roman Catholic	1,012
Mary Washington College (of the University of Virginia), Fredericksburg, Va.	2	Coord	Public	2,100
Marycrest College, Davenport, Iowa.	3	W	Pvt-Roman Catholic	1,106
Marygrove College, Detroit, Mich.	3	W	Pvt-Roman Catholic	1,191
Maryland, University of, College Park & Baltimore, Md.	4	Coed	Public	45,802
Maryland Institute, College of Art, Baltimore, Md.	3	Coed	Private	1,292
Maryland State College of the University of Maryland, Princess Anne, Md.	2	Coed	Public	717
Marylhurst College, Marylhurst, Oreg.	2	W	Pvt-Roman Catholic	756
Marymount College, Salina, Kans.	2	Coed	Pvt-Roman Catholic	533
Marymount College, Tarrytown, N.Y.	2	W	Pvt-Roman Catholic	1,060
Marymount College at Loyola University, Los Angeles, Calif.	2	W	Pvt-Roman Catholic	577
Marymount College of Virginia, Arlington, Va.	1	W	Pvt-Roman Catholic	730

Name and Location	Level of Instruction	Student Body	Control	Enrollment
Marymount Manhattan College, New York, N.Y.	2	W	Pvt-Roman Catholic	589
Maryville College, Maryville, Tenn.	2	Coed	Pvt-Presbyterian	757
Maryville College of the Sacred Heart, St. Louis, Mo.	2	W	Pvt-Roman Catholic	490
Marywood College, Scranton, Pa.	3	W	Pvt-Roman Catholic	2,000
Massachusetts, University of, Amherst, Mass.	4	Coed	Public	20,111
Massachusetts Bay Community College, Watertown, Mass.	1	Coed	Public	1,279
Massachusetts College of Art, Boston, Mass.	2	Coed	Public	491
Massachusetts Institute of Technology, Cambridge, Mass.	4	Coed	Private	7,764
Mayville State College, Mayville, N.Dak.	2	Coed	Public	911
Medaille College, Buffalo, N.Y.	3	Coed	Pvt-Roman Catholic	430
Memorial University of Newfoundland, St. John's, Nfld.	4	Coed	Public	4,485
Memphis State University, Memphis, Tenn.	4	Coed	Public	16,637
Menlo College, Menlo Park, Calif.	1	M	Private	518
Menlo College and School of Business Administration, Menlo Park, Calif.	2	M	Private	526
Mercer University, Macon, Ga.	3	Coed	Pvt-Baptist	3,123
Mercy College, Dobbs Ferry, N.Y.	2	Coed	Pvt-Roman Catholic	1,929
Mercy College of Detroit, Detroit, Mich.	2	W	Pvt-Roman Catholic	1,155
Mercyhurst College, Erie, Pa.	2	W	Pvt-Roman Catholic	670
Meredith College, Raleigh, N.C.	2	W	Pvt-Baptist	879
Meridian Junior College, Meridian, Miss.	1	Coed	Public	1,088
Merrimack College, North Andover, Mass.	2	Coed	Pvt-Roman Catholic	2,596
Merritt College, Oakland, Calif.	1	Coed	Public	7,510
Mesa Community College, Mesa, Ariz.	1	Coed	Public	2,717
Mesa Junior College, Grand Junction, Colo.	1	Coed	Public	2,405
Mesabi State Junior College, Virginia, Minn.	1	Coed	Public	679
Messiah College, Grantham, Pa.	2	Coed	Pvt-Brethren	500
Methodist College, Fayetteville, N.C.	2	Coed	Pvt-Methodist	982
Metropolitan Junior College, Kansas City, Mo.	1	Coed	Public	5,689
Miami, University of, Coral Gables, Fla.	4	Coed	Private	14,729
Miami University, Oxford, Ohio	4	Coed	Public	14,451
Miami-Dade Junior College, Miami, Fla.	1	Coed	Public	21,661
Michigan, University of, Ann Arbor, Mich.	4	Coed	Public	38,021
Michigan State University, East Lansing, Mich.	4	Coed	Public	49,515
Michigan Technological University, Houghton, Mich.	4	Coed	Public	4,564
Middle Georgia College, Cochran, Ga.	1	Coed	Public	1,676
Middle Tennessee State University, Murfreesboro, Tenn.	3	Coed	Public	6,779
Middlebury College, Middlebury, Vt.	3	Coed	Private	1,824
Midland Lutheran College, Fremont, Nebr.	2	Coed	Pvt-Lutheran	824
Midwestern University, Wichita Falls, Texas	3	Coed	Public	3,802
Millersville State College, Millersville, Pa.	3	Coed	Public	4,042
Milligan College, Milligan, Tenn.	2	Coed	Private	837
Millikin University, Decatur, Ill.	3	Coed	Pvt-Presbyterian	1,896
Mills College, Oakland, Calif.	3	W	Private	792
Mills College of Education, New York, N.Y.	2	W	Private	485
Millsaps College, Jackson, Miss.	2	Coed	Pvt-Methodist	966
Milton College, Milton, Wis.	2	Coed	Private	638
Milwaukee Technical College, Milwaukee, Wis.	1	Coed	Public	8,856
Minneapolis School of Art, Minneapolis, Minn.	2	Coed	Private	547
Minnesota, University of, Minneapolis, Minn.	4	Coed	Public	66,824
Minot State College, Minot, N.Dak.	3	Coed	Public	2,419
MiraCosta College, Oceanside, Calif.	1	Coed	Public	1,874
Misericordia, College, Dallas, Pa.	2	W	Pvt-Roman Catholic	1,104
Mississippi, University of, University, Miss.	4	Coed	Public	7,738
Mississippi College, Clinton, Miss.	3	Coed	Pvt-Baptist	2,303
Mississippi Delta Junior College, Moorhead, Miss.	1	Coed	Public	795
Mississippi State College for Women, Columbus, Miss.	3	W	Public	2,769
Mississippi State University, State College, Miss.	4	Coed	Public	9,786
Mississippi Valley State College, Itta Bena, Miss.	2	Coed	Public	2,497
Missouri, University of:				
Columbia	4	Coed	Public	20,113
Kansas City	4	Coed	Public	9,003
Rolla	4	Coed	Public	5,919

Name and Location	Level of Instruction	Student Body	Control	Enrollment
St. Louis	3	Coed	Public	8,891
Missouri Baptist College, Hannibal, Mo.	1	Coed	Pvt-Baptist	493
Missouri Southern College, Joplin, Mo.	2	Coed	Public	2,849
Missouri Valley College, Marshall, Mo.	2	Coed	Pvt-Presbyterian	910
Missouri Western Junior College, St. Joseph, Mo.	1	Coed	Public	1,283
Mitchell College, New London, Conn.	1	Coed	Private	1,501
Mitchell College, Statesville, N.C.	1	Coed	Private	543
Modesto Junior College, Modesto, Calif.	1	Coed	Public	4,079
Mohawk Valley Community College, Utica, N.Y.	1	Coed	Public	3,573
Molloy Catholic College for Women, Rockville Center, N.Y.	2	W	Pvt-Roman Catholic	1,083
Moncton, University of, Moncton, New Brunswick	2	Coed	Pvt-Roman Catholic	1,961
Monmouth College, Monmouth, Ill.	2	Coed	Pvt-Presbyterian	1,347
Monmouth College, West Long Branch, N.J.	3	Coed	Private	4,951
Monroe Community College, Rochester, N.Y.	1	Coed	Public	4,838
Montana, University of, Missoula, Mont.	4	Coed	Public	7,508
Montana College of Mineral Science and Technology, Butte, Mont.	3	Coed	Public	734
Montana State University, Bozeman, Mont.	4	Coed	Public	7,312
Montclair State College, Montclair, N.J.	3	Coed	Public	7,527
Monterey Peninsula College, Monterey, Calif.	1	Coed	Public	4,382
Montgomery Junior College, Takoma Park, Md.	1	Coed	Public	5,041
Montreal, University of, Montreal, Quebec (incl. Jean-de-Brébeuf, Loyola, Marianopolis & St. Mary colleges, qq.v.)	4	Coed	Pvt-Roman Catholic	11,353
Montreat-Anderson College, Montreat, N.C.	1	Coed	Pvt-Presbyterian	463
Moore College of Art, Philadelphia, Pa.	2	W	Private	503
Moorhead State College, Moorhead, Minn.	3	Coed	Public	5,018
Moravian College, Bethlehem, Pa.	2	Coed	Pvt-Moravian	1,675
Morehead State University, Morehead, Ky.	3	Coed	Public	6,674
Morehouse College, Atlanta, Ga.	3	M	Private	1,031
Morgan State College, Baltimore, Md.	3	Coed	Public	3,936
Morningside College, Sioux City, Iowa	3	Coed	Pvt-Methodist	1,720
Morris Brown College, Atlanta, Ga.	2	Coed	Pvt-Methodist Episcopal	1,372
Morris Harvey College, Charleston, W.Va.	2	Coed	Private	2,957
Morton College, Cicero, Ill.	1	Coed	Public	2,511
Mount Allison University, Sackville, New Brunswick	3	Coed	Pvt-United Church	1,294
Mount Aloysius Junior College, Cresson, Pa.	1	W	Pvt-Roman Catholic	468
Mount Holyoke College, South Hadley, Mass.	3	W	Private	1,813
Mount Marty College, Yankton, S.Dak.	2	W	Pvt-Roman Catholic	459
Mount Mary College, Milwaukee, Wis.	2	W	Pvt-Roman Catholic	982
Mount Mercy College, Cedar Rapids, Iowa	2	W	Pvt-Roman Catholic	627
Mount Mercy College, Pittsburgh, Pa.	2	W	Pvt-Roman Catholic	1,216
Mount St. Agnes College, Baltimore, Md.	3	W	Pvt-Roman Catholic	486
Mount St. Joseph-on-the-Ohio, College of Mt. St. Joseph, Ohio.	2	W	Pvt-Roman Catholic	929
Mount St. Mary College, Newburgh, N.Y.	2	Coed	Pvt-Roman Catholic	535
Mount St. Mary's College, Los Angeles, Calif.	3	Coord	Pvt-Roman Catholic	1,240
Mount St. Mary's College, Emmitsburg, Md.	3	M	Pvt-Roman Catholic	939
Mount St. Scholastica College, Atchison, Kans.	2	Coed	Pvt-Roman Catholic	917
Mount St. Vincent, College of, New York, N.Y.	2	W	Pvt-Roman Catholic	1,025
Mount St. Vincent College, Halifax, Nova Scotia.	3	W	Pvt-Roman Catholic	627
Mount San Antonio College, Walnut, Calif.	1	Coed	Public	12,599
Mount San Jacinto College, Gilman Hot Springs, Calif	1	Coed	Public	1,076
Mount Union College, Alliance, Ohio.	2	Coed	Pvt-Methodist	1,344
Muhlenberg College, Allentown, Pa.	2	M	Pvt-Lutheran	1,881
Multnomah College, Portland, Oreg.	2	Coed	Private	1,071
Mundelein College, Chicago, Ill.	2	W	Pvt-Roman Catholic	1,243
Murray State College of Agriculture and Applied Science, Tishomingo, Okla.	2	Coed	Public	716
Murray State University, Murray, Ky.	3	Coed	Public	7,334
Muskegon County Community College, Muskegon, Mich.	1	Coed	Public	3,775
Muskingum College, New Concord, Ohio.	2	Coed	Pvt-Presbyterian	1,497
Napa Junior College, Napa, Calif.	1	Coed	Public	2,577

Name and Location	Level of Instruction	Student Body	Control	Enrollment
Nassau Community College, Garden City, N.Y.	1	Coed	Public	10,495
Nasson College, Springvale, Me.	2	Coed	Private	914
National College of Education, Evanston, Ill.	3	Coed	Private	1,398
Naval Postgraduate School, Monterey, Calif.	4	Coed	Public	1,357
Navarro Junior College, Corsicana, Texas.	1	Coed	Public	1,107
Nazareth College, Kalamazoo, Mich.	2	W	Pvt-Roman Catholic	506
Nazareth College of Kentucky, Nazareth, Ky.	2	W	Pvt-Roman Catholic	413
Nazareth College of Rochester, N.Y.	2	W	Pvt-Roman Catholic	1,441
Nebraska, University of, Lincoln and Omaha, Nebr.	4	Coed	Public	20,064
Nebraska Wesleyan University, Lincoln, Nebr.	2	Coed	Pvt-Methodist	1,458
Nevada, University of, Reno, Nev.	4	Coed	Public	6,708
New Brunswick, University of, Fredericton, New Brunswick.	4	Coed	Public	4,188
New England College, Henniker, N.H.	2	Coed	Private	918
New England Conservatory of Music, Boston, Mass.	3	Coed	Private	530
New Hampshire, University of, Durham, N.H.	4	Coed	Public	9,142
New Haven College, West Haven, Conn.	2	Coed	Private	3,834
New Mexico, University of, Albuquerque, N.Mex.	4	Coed	Public	14,440
New Mexico Highlands University, Las Vegas, N.Mex.	3	Coed	Public	2,128
New Mexico Institute of Mining & Technology, Socorro, N.Mex.	4	Coed	Public	717
New Mexico State University, Las Cruces, N.Mex.	4	Coed	Public	7,344
New Orleans Baptist Theological Seminary, New Orleans, La.	4	Coed	Pvt-Baptist	719
New Rochelle, College of, New Rochelle, N.Y.	2	W	Pvt-Roman Catholic	985
New School for Social Research, New York, N.Y.	4	Coed	Private	2,609
New York, State University of, Albany, N.Y.:				225,572
Agricultural & Technical College at Alfred.	1	Coed	Public	1,281
Agricultural & Technical College at Canton.	1	Coed	Public	1,264
Agricultural & Technical College at Cobleskill.	1	Coed	Public	1,619
Agricultural & Technical College at Delhi.	1	Coed	Public	1,398
Agricultural & Technical College at Farmingdale.	1	Coed	Public	8,073
Agricultural & Technical College at Morrisville.	1	Coed	Public	1,526
College of Forestry at Syracuse University, Syracuse.	4	Coed	Public	1,281
Downstate Medical Center, Brooklyn.	4	Coed	Public	884
Maritime College at Fort Schuyler.	4	M	Public	716
State University College at Brockport.	2	Coed	Public	4,574
State University College at Buffalo.	3	Coed	Public	8,180
State University College at Cortland.	3	Coed	Public	4,019
State University College at Fredonia.	3	Coed	Public	3,112
State University College at Geneseo.	3	Coed	Public	3,527
State University College at New Paltz.	3	Coed	Public	4,519
State University College at Oneonta.	3	Coed	Public	4,251
State University College at Oswego.	3	Coed	Public	5,029
State University College at Plattsburgh.	3	Coed	Public	3,496
State University College at Potsdam.	3	Coed	Public	3,009
State University at Albany.	4	Coed	Public	9,018
State University at Binghamton.	4	Coed	Public	4,030
State University at Buffalo.	4	Coed	Public	19,113
State University at Stony Brook.	4	Coed	Public	5,199
Upstate Medical Center, Syracuse.	4	Coed	Public	575
New York City Community College (of the City University of New York), Brooklyn, N.Y.	1	Coed	Public	11,518
New York University, New York, N.Y.	4	Coed	Private	32,495
Newark College of Engineering, Newark, N.J.	4	Coed	Public	4,899
Newark State College, Union, N.J.	3	Coed	Public	10,401
Newberry College, Newberry, S.C.	2	Coed	Pvt-Lutheran	849
Newton College of the Sacred Heart, Newton, Mass.	2	W	Pvt-Roman Catholic	823
Newton Junior College, Newton, Mass.	1	Coed	Public	464
Niagara University, Niagara University, N.Y.	4	Coed	Pvt-Roman Catholic	2,803
Nichols College, Dudley, Mass.	2	M	Private	711
North Adams State College, North Adams, Mass.	3	Coed	Public	1,443
North Carolina Agricultural and Technical State University, Greensboro, N.C.	3	Coed	Public	3,847
North Carolina, University of, at Chapel Hill, N.C.	4	Coed	Public	15,601
North Carolina, University of, at Charlotte, N.C.	2	Coed	Public	2,351
North Carolina, University of, at Greensboro, N.C.	4	Coed	Public	5,889
North Carolina College at Durham, N.C.	3	Coed	Public	3,042
North Carolina State University at Raleigh, N.C.	4	Coed	Public	11,812
North Carolina Wesleyan College, Rocky Mount, N.C.	2	Coed	Pvt-Methodist	643
North Central College, Naperville, Ill.	3	Coed	Pvt-Methodist	1,024
North Dakota, University of, Grand Forks, N.Dak.	4	Coed	Public	7,689
North Dakota State University, Fargo, N.Dak.	4	Coed	Public	6,653
North Florida Junior College, Madison, Fla.	1	Coed	Public	1,065
North Georgia College, Dahlonega, Ga.	2	Coed	Public	1,216
North Greenville College, Tigerville, S.C.	1	Coed	Pvt-Baptist	471
North Idaho Junior College, Coeur d'Alene, Idaho.	1	Coed	Public	889
North Iowa Area Community College, Mason City, Iowa.	1	Coed	Public	1,797
North Park College, Chicago, Ill.	2	Coed	Pvt-Evangelical Covenant	1,792
North Texas State University, Denton, Texas.	4	Coed	Public	14,803
Northeast Louisiana State College, Monroe, La.	3	Coed	Public	7,602
Northeast Mississippi Junior College, Booneville, Miss.	1	Coed	Public	1,079
Northeastern Illinois State College, Chicago, Ill.	3	Coed	Public	5,503
Northeastern Junior College, Sterling, Colo.	1	Coed	Public	7,426
Northeastern Oklahoma Agricultural & Mechanical College, Miami, Okla.	1	Coed	Public	2,241
Northeastern State College, Tahlequah, Okla.	3	Coed	Public	2,089
Northeastern University, Boston, Mass.	3	Coed	Private	35,992
Northern Arizona University, Flagstaff, Ariz.	3	Coed	Public	35,447
Northern Illinois University, De Kalb, Ill.	4	Coed	Public	8,151
Northern Iowa, University of, Cedar Falls, Iowa.	3	Coed	Public	22,728
Northern Michigan University, Marquette, Mich.	3	Coed	Public	9,618
Northern Montana College, Havre, Mont.	2	Coed	Public	7,286
Northern Oklahoma College, Tonkawa, Okla.	1	Coed	Public	1,324
Northern State College, Aberdeen, S.Dak.	3	Coed	Public	1,075
Northern Virginia Community College, Annandale, Va.	1	Coed	Public	3,651
Northland College, Ashland, Wis.	2	Coed	Public	5,271
Northrop Institute of Technology, Inglewood, Calif.	2	Coed	Private	774
Northwest Alabama State Junior College, Phil Campbell, Ala.	1	Coed	Public	1,360
Northwest Christian College, Eugene, Oreg.	2	Coed	Pvt-Disciples of Christ	489
Northwest Community College, Powell, Wyo.	1	Coed	Public	458
Northwest Mississippi Junior College, Senatobia, Miss.	1	Coed	Public	483
Northwest Missouri State College, Maryville, Mo.	3	Coed	Public	4,827
Northwest Nazarene College, Nampa, Idaho.	2	Coed	Pvt-Nazarene	1,182
Northwestern College, Orange City, Iowa.	2	Coed	Pvt-Reformed	734
Northwestern Michigan College, Traverse City, Mich.	1	Coed	Public	1,426
Northwestern State College, Alva, Okla.	3	Coed	Public	2,641
Northwestern State College of Louisiana, Natchitoches, La.	3	Coed	Public	6,555
Northwestern University, Evanston, Ill.	4	Coed	Private	16,734
Norwich University, Northfield, Vt.	2	M	Private	1,215
Notre Dame, College of, Belmont, Calif.	2	W	Pvt-Roman Catholic	568
Notre Dame, University of, Notre Dame, Ind.	4	M	Pvt-Roman Catholic	7,841
Notre Dame College, Cleveland, Ohio.	2	W	Pvt-Roman Catholic	621
Notre Dame College, St. Louis, Mo.	2	W	Pvt-Roman Catholic	417
Notre Dame College of Staten Island, N.Y.	2	W	Pvt-Roman Catholic	1,085
Notre Dame of Maryland, College of, Baltimore, Md.	2	W	Pvt-Roman Catholic	541
Nova Scotia Technical College, Halifax, N.S.	4	Coed	Pvt-Roman Catholic	411
Nyack Missionary College, Nyack, N.Y.	2	Coed	Pvt-Christian Missionary Alliance	587
Oakland University, Rochester, Mich.	3	Coed	Public	5,094
Oakwood College, Huntsville, Ala.	3	Coed	Pvt-Seventh-day Adventist	613
Oberlin College, Oberlin, Ohio.	3	Coed	Private	2,622
Occidental College, Los Angeles, Calif.	3	Coed	Pvt-United Presbyterian	1,779
Odessa Junior College, Odessa, Texas.	1	Coed	Public	2,752

Name and Location	Level of Instruction	Student Body	Control	Enrollment
Oglethorpe College, Atlanta, Ga.	2	Coed	Private	1,100
Ohio Dominican College, Columbus, Ohio	2	Coed	Pvt-Roman Catholic	991
Ohio Northern University, Ada, Ohio	2	Coed	Pvt-Methodist	2,862
Ohio State University, The, Columbus, Ohio	4	Coed	Public	45,262
Ohio University, Athens, Ohio	4	Coed	Public	22,217
Ohio Wesleyan University, Delaware, Ohio	2	Coed	Pvt-Methodist	2,562
Okaloosa-Walton Junior College, Valparaiso, Fla.	1	Coed	Public	1,433
Oklahoma, University of, Norman, Okla.	4	Coed	Public	19,930
Oklahoma Baptist University, Shawnee, Okla.	2	Coed	Pvt-Baptist	1,121
Oklahoma Christian College, Oklahoma City, Okla.	2	Coed	Pvt-Church of Christ	2,521
Oklahoma City University, Oklahoma City, Okla.	3	Coed	Pvt-Methodist	913
Oklahoma College of Liberal Arts, Chickasha, Okla.	2	Coed	Public	1,338
Oklahoma Panhandle State College of Agricultural and Applied Science, Goodwell, Okla.	2	Coed	Public	
Oklahoma State University, Stillwater, Okla.	4	Coed	Public	18,936
Old Dominion College, Norfolk, Va.	4	Coed	Public	9,322
Olivet College, Olivet, Mich.	2	Coed	Private	819
Olivet Nazarene College, Kankakee, Ill.	2	Coed	Pvt-Church of Christ	1,976
Olympic College, Bremerton, Wash.	1	Coed	Pvt-Nazarene	4,155
Orange Coast College, Costa Mesa, Calif.	1	Coed	Public	14,060
Orange County Community College, Middletown, N.Y.	1	Coed	Public	3,135
Oregon, University of, Eugene, Oreg.	4	Coed	Public	14,761
Oregon College of Education, Monmouth, Oreg.	3	Coed	Public	3,215
Oregon State University, Corvallis, Oreg.	4	Coed	Public	14,474
Oregon Technical Institute, Klamath Falls, Oreg.	1	Coed	Public	1,114
Orlando Junior College, Orlando, Fla.	1	Coed	Private	1,771
Otero Junior College, La Junta, Colo.	1	Coed	Public	864
Otis Art Institute of Los Angeles County, Los Angeles, Calif.	3	Coed	Public	406
Ottawa, University of, Ottawa, Ontario	3	Coed	Private	5,523
Ottawa University, Ottawa, Kans.	2	Coed	Pvt-Baptist	1,041
Otterbein College, Westerville, Ohio	2	Coed	Pvt-Methodist	1,380
Ottumwa Heights College, Ottumwa, Iowa	1	Coed	Pvt-Roman Catholic	390
Ouachita Baptist University, Arkadelphia, Ark.	3	Coed	Pvt-Baptist	1,518
Our Lady of the Elms, College of, Chicopee, Mass.	3	W	Pvt-Roman Catholic	660
Our Lady of the Lake College, San Antonio, Texas	3	W	Pvt-Roman Catholic	1,456
Oxford College of Emory University, Oxford, Ga.	1	Coed	Pvt-Methodist	476
Ozarks, College of the, Clarksville, Ark.	2	Coed	Pvt-Presbyterian	579
Ozarks, School of the, Point Lookout, Mo.	2	Coed	Pvt-Presbyterian	887
Pace College, New York, N.Y.	3	Coed	Private	9,265
Pacific, University of the, Stockton, Calif.	3	Coed	Pvt-Methodist	4,160
Pacific Lutheran University, Tacoma, Wash.	3	Coed	Pvt-Lutheran	2,776
Pacific Union College, Angwin, Calif.	3	Coed	Pvt-Seventh-day Adventist	1,611
Pacific University, Forest Grove, Oreg.	3	Coed	Pvt-Church of Christ	1,194
Paine College, Augusta, Ga.	2	Coed	Pvt-Methodist Episcopal & Methodist	713
Palm Beach Junior College, Lake Worth, Fla.	1	Coed	Public	4,664
Palo Verde College, Blythe, Calif.	1	Coed	Public	426
Palomar College, San Marcos, Calif.	1	Coed	Public	4,458
Pan American College, Edinburg, Texas	2	Coed	Public	4,092
Panola Junior College, Carthage, Texas	1	Coed	Public	563
Paris Junior College, Paris, Texas	1	Coed	Public	525
Park College, Parkville, Mo.	2	Coed	Pvt-Presbyterian	
Pasadena City College, Pasadena, Calif.	1	Coed	Public	12,747
Pasadena College, Pasadena, Calif.	3	Coed	Pvt-Nazarene	1,227
Paterson State College, Wayne, N.J.	3	Coed	Public	5,217
Peabody Conservatory of Music, Baltimore, Md.	4	Coed	Private	401
Pearl River Junior College, Poplarville, Miss.	1	Coed	Public	821
Pembroke State College, Pembroke, N.C.	2	Coed	Public	1,564
Peninsula College, Port Angeles, Wash.	1	Coed	Public	882
Pennsylvania, University of, Philadelphia, Pa.	4	Coed	Private	17,707
Pennsylvania College of Optometry, Philadelphia, Pa.	2	Coed	Private	397
Pennsylvania Military College, Chester, Pa.	3	Coed	Private	3,025
Pennsylvania State University, University Park, Abington, Allentown, Altoona, Chester, Dubois, Erie, Hazelton, Hershey, McKeesport, Middletown, Monaca, Mont Alto, New Kensington, Schuylkill, Scranton, Sharon, Uniontown, Wilkes-Barre, Wyomissing and York, Pa.	4	Coed	Private-Public	41,508
Pensacola Junior College, Pensacola, Fla.	1	Coed	Public	4,400
Pepperdine College, Los Angeles, Calif.	3	Coed	Pvt-Church of Christ	1,674
Perkinston College, Perkinston, Miss.	1	Coed	Public	844
Peru State College, Peru, Nebr.	2	Coed	Public	1,242
Pfeiffer College, Misenheimer, N.C.	2	Coed	Pvt-Methodist	957
Philadelphia College of Bible, Philadelphia, Pa.	2	Coed	Private	826
Philadelphia College of Art, Philadelphia, Pa.	2	Coed	Private	1,335
Philadelphia College of Pharmacy & Science, Philadelphia, Pa.	3	Coed	Private	944
Philadelphia College of Textiles & Science, Philadelphia, Pa.	2	Coed	Private	1,696
Philander Smith College, Little Rock, Ark.	2	Coed	Pvt-Methodist	593
Phillips University, Enid, Okla.	3	Coed	Pvt-Disciples of Christ	1,486
Phoenix College, Phoenix, Ariz.	1	Coed	Public	10,386
Piedmont College, Demorest, Ga.	2	Coed	Pvt-Church of Christ	500
Pikeville College, Pikeville, Ky.	2	Coed	Pvt-Presbyterian	1,203
Pine Manor Junior College, Chestnut Hill, Mass.	1	W	Private	402
Pittsburgh, University of, Pittsburgh, Bradford, Greensburg, Johnstown, and Titusville, Pa.	4	Coed	Private	27,259
Pitzer College, Claremont, Calif.	2	W	Private	662
Plymouth State College (of the University of New Hampshire), Plymouth, N.H.	3	Coed	Public	1,977
Pointpark College, Pittsburgh, Pa.	1	Coed	Private	3,190
Polk Junior College, Bartow, Fla.	1	Coed	Public	2,408
Pomona College, Claremont, Calif.	2	Coed	Private	1,313
Porterville College, Porterville, Calif.	1	Coed	Public	988
Portland, University of, Portland, Oreg.	4	Coed	Pvt-Roman Catholic	1,785
Portland State College, Portland, Oreg.	3	Coed	Public	10,206
Potomac State College of West Virginia University, Keyser, W.Va.	1	Coed	Public	821
Prairie State College, Chicago Heights, Ill.	1	Coed	Public	2,097
Prairie View Agricultural & Mechanical College, Prairie View, Texas.	3	Coed	Public	4,030
Pratt Institute, Brooklyn, N.Y.	3	Coed	Private	4,522
Presbyterian College, Clinton, S.C.	2	Coed	Pvt-Presbyterian	718
Princeton Theological Seminary, Princeton, N.J.	4	Coed	Pvt-Presbyterian	640
Princeton University, Princeton, N.J.	4	Coed	Private	4,798
Principia College, Elsah, Ill.	3	Coed	Private	710
Providence College, Providence, R.I.	4	M	Pvt-Roman Catholic	4,043
Puerto Rico, University of, Rio Piedras, P.R.	4	Coed	Public	34,411
Puerto Rico Junior College, Rio Piedras, P.R.	1	Coed	Private	2,700
Puget Sound, University of, Tacoma, Wash.	3	Coed	Pvt-Methodist	3,187
Purdue University, Lafayette, Ind.	4	Coed	Public	36,102
Queens College (of the City University of New York), Flushing, N.Y.	3	Coed	Public	23,135
Queens College, Charlotte, N.C.	2	W	Pvt-Presbyterian	809
Queen's University at Kingston, Ontario.	4	Coed	Private	6,075
Queensborough Community College (of the City University of New York), Bayside, N.Y.	1	Coed	Public	6,460
Quincy College, Quincy, Ill.	2	Coed	Pvt-Roman Catholic	2,024
Quinnipiac College, Hamden, Conn.	2	Coed	Private	2,452
Quinsigamond Community College, Worcester, Mass.	1	Coed	Public	1,251
Radcliffe College (of Harvard University), Cambridge, Mass.	2	W	Private	1,198
Radford College, Radford, Va.	3	Coed	Public	3,633
Randolph-Macon College, Ashland, Va.	2	Coed	Pvt-Methodist	912
Randolph-Macon Woman's College, Lynchburg, Va.	2	W	Pvt-Methodist	835
Ranger Junior College, Ranger, Texas.	1	Coed	Public	394

Name and Location	Level of Instruction	Student Body	Control	Enrollment
Redlands, University of, Redlands, Calif.	3	Coed	Pvt-Baptist	1,715
Redwoods, College of the, Eureka, Calif.	1	Coed	Public	3,400
Reed College, Portland, Oreg.	3	Coed	Private	1,287
Reedley College, Reedley, Calif.	1	Coed	Public	1,863
Regis College, Denver, Colo.	2	Coed	Pvt-Roman Catholic	1,189
Regis College, Weston, Mass.	2	W	Pvt-Roman Catholic	1,153
Rensselaer Polytechnic Institute, Troy, N.Y.	4	Coed	Private	5,891
Rhode Island, University of, Kingston, R.I.	4	Coed	Public	11,961
Rhode Island College, Providence, R.I.	3	Coed	Public	3,010
Rhode Island School of Design, Providence, R.I.	3	Coed	Private	1,078
Rice University, Houston, Texas.	4	Coed	Private	2,974
Richland Technical Education Center, Columbia, S.C.	1	Coed	Public	1,052
Richmond, University of, Richmond, Va.	3	Coord	Pvt-Baptist	4,503
Richmond College (of the City University of New York), Staten Island, N.Y.	3	Coed	Public	1,658
Ricker College, Houlton, Me.	2	Coed	Private	648
Ricks College, Rexburg, Idaho.	1	Coed	Pvt-Latter-day Saints	3,497
Rider College, Trenton, N.J.	3	Coed	Private	5,839
Rio Hondo Junior College, Whittier, Calif.	1	Coed	Public	6,714
Ripon College, Ripon, Wis.	3	Coed	Private	997
Riverside City College, Riverside, Calif.	1	Coed	Public	7,142
Rivier College, Nashua, N.H.	3	W	Pvt-Roman Catholic	783
Roanoke College, Salem, Va.	2	Coed	Pvt-Lutheran	1,572
Robert Morris Junior College, Pittsburgh, Pa.	2	Coed	Private	3,349
Roberts Wesleyan College, North Chili, N.Y.	2	Coed	Pvt-Methodist	728
Rochester, University of, Rochester, N.Y.	4	Coed	Private	8,679
Rochester Institute of Technology, Rochester, N.Y.	3	Coed	Private	10,327
Rochester State Junior College, Rochester, Minn.	1	Coed	Public	2,039
Rockford College, Rockford, Ill.	3	Coed	Private	1,259
Rockhurst College, Kansas City, Mo.	2	Coed	Pvt-Roman Catholic	2,314
Rockingham Community College, Wentworth, N.C.	1	Coed	Public	969
Rockland Community College, Suffern, N.Y.	1	Coed	Public	3,266
Rocky Mountain College, Billings, Mont.	3	Coed	Private	553
Rollins College, Winter Park, Fla.	3	Coed	Private	3,549
Roosevelt University, Chicago, Ill.	3	Coed	Private	6,827
Rosary College, River Forest, Ill.	3	Coed	Pvt-Roman Catholic	1,313
Rosary Hill College, Buffalo, N.Y.	2	M	Pvt-Roman Catholic	1,359
Rose Polytechnic Institute, Terre Haute, Ind.	3	W	Private	971
Rosemont College, Rosemont, Pa.	2	W	Pvt-Roman Catholic	701
Russell Sage College, Troy, N.Y.	3	Coed	Private	4,272
Rutgers—The State University of New Jersey, New Brunswick, N.J. (incl. Douglass College).	4	Coord	Public	26,057
Sacramento City College, Sacramento, Calif.	1	Coed	Public	9,229
Sacramento State College, Sacramento, Calif.	3	Coed	Public	19,312
Sacred Heart, College of the, Santurce, P.R.	2	W	Pvt-Roman Catholic	571
Sacred Heart College, Wichita, Kans.	2	Coed	Pvt-Roman Catholic	762
St. Ambrose College, Davenport, Iowa.	2	Coord	Pvt-Roman Catholic	1,270
St. Andrews Presbyterian College, Laurinburg, N.C.	2	Coed	Pvt-Presbyterian	898
St. Anselm's College, Manchester, N.H.	2	Coord	Pvt-Roman Catholic	1,396
St. Augustine's College, Raleigh, N.C.	2	Coed	Pvt-Episcopal	1,031
St. Benedict, College of, St. Joseph, Minn.	2	W	Pvt-Roman Catholic	619
St. Benedict's College, Atchison, Kans.	2	M	Pvt-Roman Catholic	1,241
St. Bernard College, St. Bernard, Ala.	2	Coed	Pvt-Roman Catholic	832
St. Bonaventure University, St. Bonaventure, N.Y.	4	Coed	Pvt-Roman Catholic	2,551
St. Catherine, College of, St. Paul, Minn.	3	W	Pvt-Roman Catholic	1,303
St. Clair County Community College, Port Huron, Mich.	1	Coed	Public	2,456
St. Cloud State College, St. Cloud, Minn.	3	Coed	Public	9,267
St. Dunstan's University, Charlottetown, P.E.I.	2	Coed	Pvt-Roman Catholic	852
St. Edward's University, Austin, Texas.	2	Coed	Pvt-Roman Catholic	884
St. Elizabeth, College of, Convent Station, N.J.	2	W	Pvt-Roman Catholic	895
St. Francis, College of, Joliet, Ill.	2	Coed	Pvt-Roman Catholic	904
St. Francis College, Fort Wayne, Ind.	3	Coed	Pvt-Roman Catholic	2,017
St. Francis College, Biddeford, Me.	2	Coed	Pvt-Roman Catholic	608
St. Francis College, Brooklyn, N.Y.	2	Coed	Pvt-Roman Catholic	2,353

Name and Location	Level of Instruction	Student Body	Control	Enrollment
St. Francis College, Loretto, Pa.	3	Coed	Pvt-Roman Catholic	1,643
St. Francis Xavier University, Antigonish, Nova Scotia.	3	Coed	Pvt-Roman Catholic	2,531
St. John College of Cleveland, Ohio.	3	W	Pvt-Roman Catholic	1,187
St. John Fisher College, Rochester, N.Y.	2	M	Pvt-Roman Catholic	1,227
St. John's College, Annapolis, Md.	2	Coed	Private	338
St. Johns River Junior College, Palatka, Fla.	1	Coed	Public	2,264
St. John's University, Collegeville, Minn.	4	Coed	Pvt-Roman Catholic	1,521
St. John's University, Jamaica, N.Y.	4	Coed	Pvt-Roman Catholic	12,595
St. Joseph College, West Hartford, Conn.	3	W	Pvt-Roman Catholic	987
St. Joseph College, Emmitsburg, Md.	2	W	Pvt-Roman Catholic	576
St. Joseph's College, Rensselaer, Ind.	2	Coed	Pvt-Roman Catholic	2,665
St. Joseph's College, Philadelphia, Pa.	3	Coed	Pvt-Roman Catholic	6,699
St. Joseph's College for Women, Brooklyn, N.Y.	3	W	Pvt-Roman Catholic	617
St. Lawrence University, Canton, N.Y.	3	Coed	Private	2,173
St. Leo College, St. Leo, Fla.	2	Coed	Pvt-Roman Catholic	1,216
St. Louis, Junior College District of, St. Louis, Mo.	1	Coed	Public	10,019
St. Louis College of Pharmacy, St. Louis, Mo.	2	Coed	Private	447
St. Louis University, St. Louis, Mo. (incl. St. Mary's College, St. Mary's, Kans.).	4	Coed	Pvt-Roman Catholic	10,413
St. Martin's College, Olympia, Wash.	2	Coed	Pvt-Roman Catholic	726
St. Mary, College of, Omaha, Nebr.	2	W	Pvt-Roman Catholic	613
St. Mary College (of the University of Montreal), Montreal, Quebec.	2	Coed	Pvt-Roman Catholic	2,306
St. Mary of the Plains College, Dodge City, Kans.	2	W	Pvt-Roman Catholic	705
St. Mary-of-the-Woods College, St. Mary-of-the-Woods, Ind.	2	W	Pvt-Roman Catholic	561
St. Mary's College, Notre Dame, Ind.	3	W	Pvt-Roman Catholic	1,328
St. Mary's College, Winona, Minn.	3	Coed	Pvt-Roman Catholic	1,119
St. Mary's College, St. Mary's College, Calif.	3	M	Pvt-Roman Catholic	979
St. Mary's College of Maryland, St. Mary's City, Md.	2	Coed	Public	508
St. Mary's Dominican College, New Orleans, La.	2	W	Pvt-Roman Catholic	568
St. Mary's Seminary & University, Baltimore, Md.	3	M	Pvt-Roman Catholic	666
St. Mary's University, Halifax, N.S.	3	Coed	Pvt-Roman Catholic	1,339
St. Mary's University of San Antonio, Texas.	3	Coed	Pvt-Roman Catholic	4,007
St. Michael's College, University of (of the University of Toronto), Toronto, Ontario.	4	W	Pvt-Roman Catholic	1,948
St. Michael's College, Winooski Park, Vt.	2	M	Pvt-Roman Catholic	1,415
St. Norbert College, West De Pere, Wis.	2	Coed	Pvt-Roman Catholic	1,714
St. Olaf College, Northfield, Minn.	2	Coed	Pvt-Lutheran	2,563
St. Paul's College, Lawrenceville, Va.	2	Coed	Pvt-Episcopal	454
St. Paul's College (of the University of Manitoba), Winnipeg, Manitoba.	3	Coed	Pvt-Roman Catholic	607
St. Peter's College, Jersey City, N.J.	2	Coed	Pvt-Roman Catholic	4,716
St. Petersburg Junior College, St. Petersburg, Fla.	1	Coed	Public	8,859
St. Philip's College, San Antonio, Texas.	1	Coed	Public	481
St. Procopius College, Lisle, Ill.	2	Coed	Pvt-Roman Catholic	849
St. Rose, College of, Albany, N.Y.	2	Coord	Pvt-Roman Catholic	1,343
St. Scholastica, College of, Duluth, Minn.	2	Coed	Pvt-Roman Catholic	521
St. Teresa, College of, Winona, Minn.	2	Coord	Pvt-Roman Catholic	1,311
St. Thomas, College of, St. Paul, Minn.	3	W	Pvt-Roman Catholic	2,344
St. Thomas, University of, Houston, Texas.	2	M	Pvt-Roman Catholic	999
St. Vincent College, Latrobe, Pa.	3	Coed	Pvt-Roman Catholic	987
St. Xavier College, Chicago, Ill.	3	W	Pvt-Roman Catholic	872
Salem College, Winston-Salem, N.C.	4	Coed	Pvt-Moravian	552
Salem College, Salem, W.Va.	1	W	Private	1,751
Salem State College, Salem, Mass.	3	Coed	Public	5,971
Salisbury State College, Salisbury, Md.	3	Coed	Public	987
Salve Regina College, Newport, R.I.	2	W	Pvt-Roman Catholic	878
Sam Houston State College, Huntsville, Texas.	3	Coed	Public	7,670
Samford University, Birmingham, Ala.	3	Coed	Pvt-Baptist	11,433
San Antonio College, San Antonio, Texas.	1	Coed	Public	11,328
San Bernardino Valley College, San Bernardino, Calif.	1	Coed	Public	
San Diego, University of, College for Men, San Diego, Calif.	3	M	Pvt-Roman Catholic	615

Name and Location	Level of Instruction	Student Body	Control	Enrollment
San Diego College for Women, San Diego, Calif.	3	W	Pvt-Roman Catholic	534
San Diego Junior Colleges (incl. San Diego City, San Diego Mesa, San Diego Evening College), Calif.	1	Coed	Public	18,068
San Diego State College, San Diego, Calif.	4	Coed	Public	30,077
San Fernando Valley State College, Northridge, Calif.	3	Coed	Public	20,247
San Francisco, City College of, San Francisco, Calif.	1	Coed	Public	12,438
San Francisco, University of, San Francisco, Calif.	3	Coed	Pvt-Roman Catholic	6,302
San Francisco College for Women, San Francisco, Calif.	3	W	Pvt-Roman Catholic	510
San Francisco State College, San Francisco, Calif.	4	Coed	Public	25,585
San Jacinto Junior College, Pasadena, Texas	1	Coed	Public	5,078
San Joaquin Delta College, Stockton, Calif.	1	Coed	Public	7,769
San Jose City College, San Jose, Calif.	1	Coed	Public	11,068
San Jose State College, San Jose, Calif.	4	Coed	Public	32,178
San Mateo, College of, San Mateo, Calif.	1	Coed	Public	17,768
Sandhills Community College, Southern Pines, N.C.	1	Coed	Public	867
Santa Ana College, Santa Ana, Calif.	1	Coed	Public	6,509
Santa Barbara City College, Santa Barbara, Calif.	1	Coed	Public	4,146
Santa Clara, University of, Santa Clara, Calif.	4	Coed	Pvt-Roman Catholic	5,361
Santa Fe, College of, Santa Fe, N.M.	2	Coed	Pvt-Roman Catholic	1,253
Santa Fe Junior College, Gainesville, Fla.	1	Coed	Public	1,866
Santa Monica City College, Santa Monica, Calif.	1	Coed	Public	11,945
Santa Rosa Junior College, Santa Rosa, Calif.	1	Coed	Public	6,644
Sarah Lawrence College, Bronxville, N.Y.	3	Coed	Private	645
Saskatchewan, University of, Saskatoon and Regina, Sask.	4	Coed	Public	12,688
Savannah State College, Savannah, Ga.	2	Coed	Public	1,931
Schoolcraft College, Livonia, Mich.	1	Coed	Public	3,906
Scranton, University of, Scranton, Pa.	3	Coed	Pvt-Roman Catholic	2,963
Scripps College, Claremont, Calif.	2	W	Private	526
Seattle Pacific College, Seattle, Wash.	3	Coed	Pvt-Methodist	1,990
Seattle University, Seattle, Wash.	3	Coed	Pvt-Roman Catholic	3,679
Sequoias, College of the, Visalia, Calif.	1	Coed	Public	4,617
Seton Hall University, South Orange, N.J.	4	Coed	Pvt-Roman Catholic	9,753
Seton Hill College, Greensburg, Pa.	2	Coed	Pvt-Roman Catholic	957
Shasta College, Redding, Calif.	1	Coed	Public	4,798
Shaw University, Raleigh, N.C.	2	Coed	Pvt-Baptist	1,085
Shenandoah College, Winchester, Va.	2	Coed	Pvt-Methodist	532
Shepherd College, Shepherdstown, W.Va.	2	Coed	Public	1,395
Sherbrooke, Université de, Sherbrooke, Quebec	3	Coed	Pvt-Roman Catholic	6,833
Sheridan College, Sheridan, Wyo.	1	Coed	Public	497
Shimer College, Mount Carroll, Ill.	2	Coed	Private	378
Shippensburg State College, Shippensburg, Pa.	3	Coed	Public	3,561
Shoreline Community College, Seattle, Wash.	1	Coed	Public	3,167
Shorter College, Rome, Ga.	2	Coed	Pvt-Baptist	713
Siena College, Loudonville, N.Y.	3	Coed	Pvt-Roman Catholic	1,768
Siena Heights College, Adrian, Mich.	3	Coed	Pvt-Roman Catholic	747
Sierra College, Rocklin, Calif.	1	Coed	Public	2,793
Simmons College, Boston, Mass.	3	W	Private	2,219
Simon Fraser University, Burnaby, B.C.	4	Coed	Public	2,501
Simpson College, Indianola, Iowa	2	Coed	Pvt-Methodist	989
Sioux Falls College, Sioux Falls, S.Dak.	2	Coed	Pvt-Baptist	1,023
Sir George Williams University, Montreal, Quebec	3	Coed	Pvt-YMCA	11,973
Siskiyous, College of the, Weed, Calif.	1	Coed	Public	730
Skagit Valley College, Mount Vernon, Wash.	1	Coed	Public	1,157
Skidmore College, Saratoga Springs, N.Y.	3	W	Private	1,687
Slippery Rock State College, Slippery Rock, Pa.	3	Coord	Public	4,429
Smith College, Northampton, Mass.	3	W	Private	2,383
Snead State Junior College, Boaz, Ala.	1	Coed	Public	405
Solano College, Vallejo, Calif.	1	Coed	Public	4,417
Sonoma State College, Rohnert Park, Calif.	3	Coed	Public	7,078
South Alabama, University of, Mobile, Ala.	3	Coed	Public	802
South Carolina, University of, Columbia, S.C.	4	Coed	Public	14,314
South Carolina State College, Orangeburg, S.C.	3	Coed	Public	3,882
South Dakota, University of, Vermillion, S.Dak.	4	Coed	Public	5,208
South Dakota School of Mines & Technology, Rapid City, S.Dak.	4	Coed	Public	1,780
South Dakota State University, Brookings, S.Dak.	4	Coed	Public	6,214
South Florida, University of, Tampa, Fla.	3	Coed	Public	13,752
South Georgia College, Douglas, Ga.	1	Coed	Public	1,001
South Plains College, Levelland, Texas	1	Coed	Public	1,496
South Texas Junior College, Houston, Texas	1	Coed	Private	4,636
Southeast Missouri State College, Cape Girardeau, Mo.	3	Coed	Public	6,776
Southeastern Community College, Whiteville, N.C.	1	Coed	Public	701
Southeastern Louisiana College, Hammond, La.	3	Coed	Public	5,462
Southeastern Massachusetts Technological Institute, North Dartmouth, Mass.	3	Coed	Public	3,708
Southeastern State College, Durant, Okla.	3	Coed	Public	2,431
Southern Baptist College, Walnut Ridge, Ark.	1	Coed	Pvt-Baptist	687
Southern Baptist Theological Seminary, Louisville, Ky.	4	Coed	Pvt-Baptist	1,077
Southern California, University of, Los Angeles, Calif.	4	Coed	Private	18,972
Southern California College, Costa Mesa, Calif.	2	Coed	Pvt-Assemblies of God	534
Southern Colorado State College, Pueblo, Colo.	3	Coed	Public	5,423
Southern Connecticut State College, New Haven, Conn.	3	Coed	Public	10,269
Southern Idaho, College of, Twin Falls, Idaho	1	Coed	Public	1,517
Southern Illinois University, Carbondale, Ill.	4	Coed	Public	33,386
Southern Methodist University, Dallas, Texas	4	Coed	Pvt-Methodist	
Southern Missionary College, Collegedale, Tenn.	2	Coed	Pvt-Seventh-day Adventist	1,270
Southern Mississippi, University of, Hattiesburg, Miss.	4	Coed	Public	9,403
Southern Oregon College, Ashland, Oreg.	3	Coed	Public	4,045
Southern Oregon Community College, Coos Bay, Oreg.	1	Coed	Public	1,776
Southern State College, Magnolia, Ark.	2	Coed	Public	2,400
Southern State College, Springfield, S.Dak.	2	Coed	Public	1,034
Southern University, Baton Rouge, La.	3	Coed	Public	7,614
Southern Utah, College of, Cedar City, Utah	2	Coed	Public	1,792
Southwest Baptist College, Bolivar, Mo.	2	Coed	Pvt-Baptist	1,308
Southwest Mississippi Junior College, Summit, Miss.	1	Coed	Public	534
Southwest Missouri State College, Springfield, Mo.	3	Coed	Public	7,521
Southwest Texas Junior College, Uvalde, Texas	1	Coed	Public	727
Southwest Texas State College, San Marcos, Texas	3	Coed	Public	8,406
Southwestern Junior College of the Assemblies of God, Waxahachie, Texas	1	Coed	Pvt-Assemblies of God	614
Southwestern at Memphis, Tenn.	3	Coed	Pvt-Presbyterian	996
Southwestern College, Chula Vista, Calif.	1	Coed	Public	4,212
Southwestern College, Winfield, Kans.	3	Coed	Pvt-Methodist	701
Southwestern Louisiana, University of, Lafayette, La.	4	Coed	Public	9,768
Southwestern Oregon Community College, Coos Bay, Oreg.	1	Coed	Public	1,776
Southwestern State College, Weatherford, Okla.	3	Coed	Public	4,861
Southwestern University, Georgetown, Texas	3	Coed	Pvt-Methodist	835
Spartanburg Junior College, Spartanburg, S.C.	1	Coed	Pvt-Methodist	675
Spelman College, Atlanta, Ga.	3	W	Private	945
Spokane Community College, Spokane, Wash.	1	Coed	Public	2,902
Spring Arbor College, Spring Arbor, Mich.	2	Coed	Pvt-Methodist	634
Spring Hill College, Mobile, Ala.	3	Coed	Pvt-Roman Catholic	1,186
Springfield College, Springfield, Mass.	3	Coed	Private	2,373
Springfield Junior College of Illinois, Springfield, Ill.	1	Coed	Pvt-Roman Catholic	974
Stanford University, Stanford, Calif.	4	Coed	Private	11,428
Stanislaus State College, Turlock, Calif.	3	Coed	Public	4,137
Staten Island Community College (of the City University of New York), Staten Island, N.Y.	1	Coed	Public	3,579
Stephen F. Austin State College, Nacogdoches, Texas	3	Coed	Public	8,717
Stephens College, Columbia, Mo.	2	W	Private	1,925
Sterling College, Sterling, Kans.	2	Coed	Pvt-Presbyterian	625
Stetson University, De Land, Fla.	3	Coed	Pvt-Baptist	2,813
Steubenville, College of, Steubenville, Ohio	3	Coed	Pvt-Roman Catholic	1,243
Stevens Institute of Technology, Hoboken, N.J.	4	M	Private	2,755
Stillman College, Tuscaloosa, Ala.	2	Coed	Pvt-Presbyterian	697
Stonehill College, North Easton, Mass.	3	Coed	Pvt-Roman Catholic	1,350
Stout State University, Menomonie, Wis.	3	Coed	Public	4,671
Stratford College, Danville, Va.	2	W	Private	528

Name and Location	Level of Instruction	Student Body	Control	Enrollment
Suffolk County Community College, Selden, N.Y.	1	Coed	Public	6,934
Suffolk University, Boston, Mass.	3	Coed	Private	2,610
Sul Ross State College, Alpine, Texas	3	Coed	Public	2,296
Susquehanna University, Selinsgrove, Pa.	3	Coed	Pvt-Lutheran	1,210
Swarthmore College, Swarthmore, Pa.	3	Coed	Private	1,074
Sweet Briar College, Sweet Briar, Va.	2	W	Private	732
Syracuse University, Syracuse, N.Y.	4	Coed	Private	24,348
Tabor College, Hillsboro, Kans.	2	Coed	Pvt-Mennonite	419
Tacoma Community College, Tacoma, Wash.	1	Coed	Public	2,609
Taft College, Taft, Calif.	1	Coed	Public	721
Talladega College, Talladega, Ala.	2	Coed	Pvt-Church of Christ	579
Tampa, University of, Tampa, Fla.	2	Coed	Private	2,403
Tarkio College, Tarkio, Mo.	2	Coed	Pvt-Presbyterian	784
Tarleton State College, Stephenville, Texas	2	Coed	Public	2,457
Taylor University, Upland, Ind.	2	Coed	Private	1,358
Teachers College (of Columbia University), New York, N.Y.	4	Coed	Private	5,581
Temple Buell College, Denver, Colo.	2	W	Private	1,077
Temple Junior College, Temple, Texas	1	Coed	Public	1,049
Temple University, Philadelphia, Pa.	4	Coed	Public	33,803
Tennessee, University of, Knoxville, Tenn.	4	Coed	Public	30,875
Tennessee Agricultural & Industrial State University, Nashville, Tenn.	3	Coed	Public	4,536
Tennessee Technological University, Cookeville, Tenn.	3	Coed	Public	5,830
Tennessee Wesleyan College, Athens, Tenn.	2	Coed	Pvt-Methodist	808
Texarkana College, Texarkana, Texas.	1	Coed	Public	1,832
Texas Agricultural & Mechanical University, College Station, Texas.	4	Coed	Public	12,867
Texas Arts and Industries University, Kingsville, Texas.	4	Coed	Public	6,404
Texas Christian University, Fort Worth, Texas.	4	Coed	Pvt-Disciples of Christ	6,241
Texas Lutheran College, Seguin, Texas.	2	Coed	Pvt-Lutheran	767
Texas Southmost College, Brownsville, Texas.	1	Coed	Public	1,299
Texas Southern University, Houston, Texas.	3	Coed	Public	4,513
Texas System, University of, Austin, Texas.	4	Coed	Public	58,616
Texas Technological College, Lubbock, Texas.	4	Coed	Public	19,034
Texas Wesleyan College, Fort Worth, Texas.	2	Coed	Pvt-Methodist	2,027
Texas Woman's University, Denton, Texas.	4	W	Public	5,081
Thiel College, Greenville, Pa.	2	Coed	Pvt-Lutheran	1,364
Thomas More College, Covington, Ky.	2	Coed	Pvt-Roman Catholic	2,172
Thornton Junior College, Harvey, Ill.	1	Coed	Public	3,580
Tift College, Forsyth, Ga.	2	W	Pvt-Baptist	650
Toledo, University of, Toledo, Ohio.	4	Coed	Public	13,022
Toronto, University of, Toronto, Ontario (incl. University of St. Michael's College, University of Trinity College, & Victoria University, qq.v.).	4	Coed	Pvt-Anglican	22,123
Tougaloo College, Tougaloo, Miss.	2	Coed	Private	649
Towson State College, Towson, Md.	3	Coed	Public	7,868
Transylvania College, Lexington, Ky.	2	Coed	Pvt-Disciples of Christ	889
Treasure Valley Community College, Ontario, Oreg.	1	Coed	Public	1,093
Trent University, Peterborough, Ontario	3	Coed	Private	754
Trenton Junior College, Trenton, N.J.	1	Coed	Public	2,709
Trenton State College, Trenton, N.J.	3	Coed	Public	8,426
Trinidad State Junior College, Trinidad, Colo.	1	Coed	Public	1,480
Trinity College, Hartford, Conn.	3	Coed	Private	1,793
Trinity College, Washington, D.C.	2	W	Pvt-Roman Catholic	912
Trinity College, Burlington, Vt.	2	W	Pvt-Roman Catholic	450
Trinity College, University of [of the University of Toronto], Toronto, Ont.	4	Coed	Pvt-Anglican	742
Trinity University, San Antonio, Texas.	3	Coed	Pvt-Presbyterian	2,463
Tri-State College, Angola, Ind.	2	Coed	Private	2,022
Troy State University, Troy, Ala.	3	Coed	Public	3,965
Truett McConnell College, Cleveland, Ga.	1	Coed	Pvt-Baptist	469
Tufts University, Medford, Mass.	4	Coed	Private	5,188
Tulane University, New Orleans, La.	4	Coed	Private	8,311
Tulsa, University of, Tulsa, Okla.	4	Coed	Pvt-Presbyterian	6,960
Tusculum College, Greeneville, Tenn.	2	Coed	Pvt-Presbyterian	611
Tuskegee Institute, Tuskegee Institute, Ala.	3	Coed	Private	3,184
Tyler Junior College, Tyler, Texas.	1	Coed	Public	3,271
Union College, Barbourville, Ky.	3	Coed	Pvt-Methodist	888
Union College, Lincoln, Nebr.	3	Coed	Pvt-Seventh-day Adventist	1,037
Union College, Cranford, N.J.	1	Coed	Private	1,537
Union College and University, Schenectady, N.Y.	4	Coed	Private	2,730
Union Theological Seminary, New York, N.Y.	3	Coed	Pvt-Interdenominational	554
Union University, Jackson, Tenn.	2	Coed	Pvt-Baptist	746
United States Air Force Academy, Colorado Springs, Colo.	2	M	Public	3,573
United States Coast Guard Academy, New London, Conn.	2	M	Public	800
United States International University (including California Western University, City Center, and Elliott), San Diego, Calif.	4	Coed	Private	1,831
United States Merchant Marine Academy, King's Point, N.Y.	2	M	Public	1,025
United States Military Academy, West Point, N.Y.	2	M	Public	3,565
United States Naval Academy, Annapolis, Md.	2	M	Public	4,154
Upper Iowa University, Fayette, Iowa.	2	Coed	Private	1,896
Upsala College, East Orange, N.J.	2	Coed	Pvt-Lutheran	2,010
Ursinus College, Collegeville, Pa.	2	Coed	Pvt-Church of Christ	
Ursuline College, Cleveland, Ohio.	2	Coed	Pvt-Roman Catholic	579
Utah, University of, Salt Lake City, Utah (incl. College of Eastern Utah, Price).	4	Coed	Public	19,619
Utah State University of Agriculture & Applied Science, Logan, Utah (incl. Snow College, Ephraim).	4	Coed	Public	8,710
Valdosta State College, Valdosta, Ga.	3	Coed	Public	2,470
Valley City State College, Valley City, N.Dak.	2	Coed	Public	1,264
Valparaiso University, Valparaiso, Ind.	4	Coed	Pvt-Lutheran	4,407
Vanderbilt University, Nashville, Tenn.	3	Coed	Private	5,797
Vassar College, Poughkeepsie, N.Y.	3	W	Private	1,588
Ventura College, Ventura, Calif.	2	Coed	Public	6,980
Vermont, University of, Burlington, Vt.	4	Coed	Public	5,789
Vermont College, Montpelier, Vt.	1	W	Pvt-Methodist	526
Victor Valley College, Victorville, Calif.	1	Coed	Public	1,412
Victoria, University of, Victoria, British Columbia.	1	Coed	Public	4,075
Victoria College, Victoria, Texas.	1	Coed	Public	1,493
Victoria University (of the University of Toronto), Toronto, Ontario.	4	Coed	Pvt-United Church	2,513
Villa Maria College, Erie, Pa.	2	W	Pvt-Roman Catholic	673
Villanova University, Villanova, Pa.	4	Coed	Pvt-Roman Catholic	8,150
Vincennes University, Vincennes, Ind.	1	Coord	Public	2,244
Virginia, University of, Charlottesville, Va.	4	Coord	Public	8,964
Virginia Commonwealth University, Richmond, Va. (includes Medical College of Virginia & Richmond Professional Institute)	4	Coed	Public	11,596
Virginia Intermont College, Bristol, Va.	1	W	Pvt-Baptist	560
Virginia Military Institute, Lexington, Va.	2	M	Public	1,316
Virginia Polytechnic Institute, Blacksburg, Va.	4	Coed	Public	10,283
Virginia State College (including Norfolk Division), Petersburg, Va.	3	Coed	Public	5,544
Virginia Union University, Richmond, Va.	3	Coed	Pvt-Baptist	1,182
Viterbo College, La Crosse, Wis.	2	W	Pvt-Roman Catholic	1,509
Voorhees College, Denmark, S.C.	2	Coed	Pvt-Episcopal	639
Wabash College, Crawfordsville, Ind.	2	M	Private	891
Wagner College, Staten Island, N.Y.	3	Coed	Pvt-Lutheran	2,975
Wake Forest University, Winston-Salem, N.C.	4	Coed	Pvt-Baptist	3,177
Waldorf College, Forest City, Iowa.	1	Coed	Pvt-Lutheran	641
Walker College, Jasper, Ala.	1	Coed	Private	717

Name and Location	Level of Instruction	Student Body	Control	Enrollment
Walla Walla College, College Place, Wash.	3	Coed	Pvt-Seventh-day Adventist	1,533
Wartburg College, Waverly, Iowa	2	Coed	Pvt-Lutheran	1,420
Washburn University of Topeka, Kans.	4	Coed	Public	4,379
Washington, University of, Seattle, Wash.	4	Coed	Public	31,913
Washington and Jefferson College, Washington, Pa.	3	M	Private	861
Washington and Lee University, Lexington, Va.	3	M	Private	1,458
Washington College, Chestertown, Md.	2	Coed	Private	621
Washington State University, Pullman, Wash.	4	Coed	Public	12,263
Washington University, St. Louis, Mo.	4	Coed	Private	11,597
Waterloo, University of (including University of St. Jerome's College), Waterloo, Ontario	4	Coed	Private	7,038
Waterloo Lutheran University, Waterloo, Ontario	3	Coed	Pvt-Lutheran	2,563
Wayland Baptist College, Plainview, Texas	2	Coed	Pvt-Baptist	683
Wayne State College, Wayne, Nebr.	3	Coed	Public	3,068
Wayne State University, Detroit, Mich.	4	Coed	Public	33,177
Waynesburg College, Waynesburg, Pa.	2	Coed	Pvt-Presbyterian	1,108
Weatherford College, Weatherford, Texas	1	Coed	Public	1,001
Weber State College, Ogden, Utah	2	Coed	Public	9,933
Webster College, St. Louis, Mo.	3	W	Private	1,144
Wellesley College, Wellesley, Mass.	3	W	Private	1,773
Wells College, Aurora, N.Y.	3	W	Private	596
Wenatchee Valley College, Wenatchee, Wash.	1	Coed	Public	1,503
Wenonah State Junior College, Birmingham, Ala.	1	Coed	Public	752
Wentworth Institute, Boston, Mass.	1	M	Private	2,186
Wesley College, Dover, Del.	2	Coed	Pvt-Methodist	909
Wesleyan College, Macon, Ga.	3	W	Pvt-Methodist	567
Wesleyan University, Middletown, Conn.	4	Coed	Private	1,645
West Chester State College, West Chester, Pa.	3	Coed	Public	7,751
West Coast University, Los Angeles, Calif.	3	Coed	Private	1,455
West Georgia College, Carrollton, Ga.	3	Coed	Public	3,815
West Liberty State College, West Liberty, W.Va.	3	Coed	Public	3,344
West Texas State University, Canyon, Texas	3	Coed	Public	7,271
West Valley College, Campbell, Calif.	1	Coed	Public	6,699
West Virginia Institute of Technology, Montgomery, W.Va.	2	Coed	Public	2,410
West Virginia State College, Institute, W.Va.	2	Coed	Public	3,074
West Virginia University, Morgantown, W.Va.	4	Coed	Public	16,544
West Virginia Wesleyan College, Buckhannon, W.Va.	2	Coed	Pvt-Methodist	1,754
Westbrook Junior College, Portland, Me.	1	W	Private	462
Western Baptist Bible College, El Cerrito, Calif.	2	Coed	Pvt-Baptist	394
Western Carolina College, Cullowhee, N.C.	3	Coed	Public	4,787
Western College for Women, Oxford, Ohio	3	W	Private	503
Western Connecticut State College, Danbury, Conn.	3	Coed	Public	2,818
Western Illinois University, Macomb, Ill.	3	Coed	Public	9,461
Western Kentucky University, Bowling Green, Ky.	3	Coed	Public	10,570
Western Maryland College, Westminster, Md.	2	Coed	Pvt-Methodist	1,452
Western Michigan University, Kalamazoo, Mich.	4	Coed	Public	16,871
Western Montana College, Dillon, Mont.	3	Coed	Public	988
Western New England College, Springfield, Mass.	3	Coed	Private	2,720
Western New Mexico University, Silver City, N.Mex.	3	Coed	Public	1,439
Western Ontario, University of, London, Ontario (incl. Huron College & King's College, qq.v.)	4	Coed	Private	8,700
Western Piedmont Community College, Morganton, N.C.	1	Coed	Public	763
Western Washington State College, Bellingham, Wash.	3	Coed	Public	8,127
Westfield State College, Westfield, Mass.	2	Coed	Public	3,258
Westmar College, Le Mars, Iowa	2	Coed	Pvt-Methodist	1,169
Westminster College, Fulton, Mo.	2	Coed	Pvt-Presbyterian	757
Westminster College, New Wilmington, Pa.	2	Coed	Pvt-Presbyterian	1,892
Westminster College, Salt Lake City, Utah	2	Coed	Pvt-Methodist	881
Westmont College, Santa Barbara, Calif.	2	Coed	Private	779
Wharton County Junior College, Wharton, Texas	1	Coed	Public	2,043
Wheaton College, Wheaton, Ill.	3	Coed	Private	1,846
Wheaton College, Norton, Mass.	2	Coed	Private	1,132
Wheeling College, Wheeling, W.Va.	2	Coed	Pvt-Roman Catholic	811
Wheelock College, Boston, Mass.	3	W	Private	670
Whitman College, Walla Walla, Wash.	3	Coed	Private	1,103
Whittier College, Whittier, Calif.	3	Coed	Private	1,458
Whitworth College, Spokane, Wash.	3	Coed	Pvt-Presbyterian	1,576
Wichita State University, Wichita, Kans.	4	Coed	Public	11,568
Wilberforce University, Wilberforce, Ohio	2	Coed	Pvt-Methodist Episcopal	1,018
Wiley College, Marshall, Texas	3	Coed	Pvt-Methodist	700
Wilkes College, Wilkes-Barre, Pa.	3	Coed	Private	3,228
Willamette University, Salem, Oreg.	3	Coed	Pvt-Methodist	1,570
William and Mary, College of, Williamsburg, Va.	4	Coed	Public	7,246
William Carey College, Hattiesburg, Miss.	2	Coed	Pvt-Baptist	768
William Jewell College, Liberty, Mo.	2	Coed	Pvt-Baptist	1,072
William Penn College, Oskaloosa, Iowa	2	Coed	Pvt-Friends	950
William Woods College, Fulton, Mo.	2	W	Pvt-Disciples of Christ	815
Williams College, Williamstown, Mass.	3	M	Private	1,311
Wilmington College, Wilmington, N.C.	2	Coed	Public	1,240
Wilmington College, Wilmington, Ohio	2	Coed	Pvt-Friends	963
Wilson College, Chambersburg, Pa.	2	W	Pvt-Presbyterian	690
Windham College, Putney, Vt.	3	Coed	Private	837
Windsor, University of, Windsor, Ont.	4	Coed	Private	8,700
Wingate College, Wingate, N.C.	1	Coed	Pvt-Baptist	1,568
Winnipeg, University of, Winnipeg, Manitoba	3	Coed	Private	1,695
Winona State College, Winona, Minn.	2	Coed	Public	4,102
Winston-Salem State College, Winston-Salem, N.C.	2	Coed	Public	1,301
Winthrop College, Rock Hill, S.C.	4	W	Public	3,336
Wisconsin, University of, Madison & Milwaukee, Wis.	4	Coed	Public	62,206
Wisconsin State University—Eau Claire, Wis.	3	Coed	Public	7,248
Wisconsin State University—La Crosse, Wis.	3	Coed	Public	6,001
Wisconsin State University—Oshkosh, Wis.	3	Coed	Public	11,320
Wisconsin State University—Platteville, Wis.	3	Coed	Public	5,400
Wisconsin State University—River Falls, Wis.	3	Coed	Public	4,052
Wisconsin State University—Stevens Point, Wis.	3	Coed	Public	6,830
Wisconsin State University—Superior, Wis.	3	Coed	Public	3,318
Wisconsin State University—Whitewater, Wis.	3	Coed	Public	9,402
Wittenberg University, Springfield, Ohio	3	Coed	Pvt-Lutheran	3,158
Wofford College, Spartanburg, S.C.	2	M	Pvt-Methodist	1,013
Woodbury College, Los Angeles, Calif.	2	Coed	Private	1,940
Wooster, College of, Wooster, Ohio	3	Coed	Pvt-Presbyterian	1,653
Worcester Junior College, Worcester, Mass.	1	Coed	Private	2,453
Worcester Polytechnic Institute, Worcester, Mass.	4	M	Private	1,847
Worcester State College, Worcester, Mass.	3	Coed	Public	2,834
Wright State University, Dayton, Ohio	3	Coed	Public	7,889
Wyoming, University of, Laramie, Wyo.	4	Coed	Public	8,931
Xavier University of Louisiana, New Orleans, La.	3	Coed	Pvt-Roman Catholic	1,211
Xavier University, Cincinnati, Ohio	3	Coed	Pvt-Roman Catholic	6,003
Yakima Valley Junior College, Yakima, Wash.	1	Coed	Public	3,017
Yale University, New Haven, Conn.	4	Coed	Private	8,722
Yankton College, Yankton, S.Dak.	2	Coed	Pvt-United Church of Christ	676
Yeshiva University, New York, N.Y.	4	Coord	Private	4,772
York College (of the City University of New York), Flushing, N.Y.	2	Coed	Public	994
York College of Pennsylvania, York, Pa.	2	Coed	Private	1,645
York University, Toronto, Ont. (including Osgoode Hall Law School)	4	Coed	Public	2,559
Young Harris College, Young Harris, Ga.	1	Coed	Private	478
Youngstown State University, Youngstown, Ohio	3	Coed	Public	14,115
Yuba College, Marysville, Calif.	1	Coed	Public	4,417

COLOMBIA

In spite of increased guerrilla activity on several fronts, and severe disturbances in the major cities during the year, Colombia ended the 1960's with an enviable record of political and economic development. In a year that saw increasing military control in other Latin American states, the government of President Carlos Lleras Restrepo continued to rule with no serious threat from either the army or guerrillas. President Lleras repeatedly demonstrated his ability to deal with crises without sacrificing democracy or development. Lleras' successor, who will take office on Aug. 1, 1970, will inherit a radically improved economic and political situation.

Politics. Implementation of the constitutional reforms, passed in 1968, began in 1969. As a consequence, the executive was allowed much greater freedom in economic matters, and a minority in Congress could no longer block legislation proposed by the National Front coalition.

In accordance with the alternation provisions of the 1958 agreement establishing the National Front, the 1970 presidential candidate of the Front was to come from the Conservative party. After much jockeying for position within the majority Unionist wing of the party, and between the Unionists and the Liberals, Misael Pastrana Borrero received the official nod. He is a former ambassador to the United States and a supporter of President Lleras. At the end of the year, however, "independent" Conservatives Belisario Betancur and Evaristo Sourdis were receiving considerable support, and ex-dictator Gustavo Rojas Pinilla was running too.

------ **COLOMBIA • Information Highlights** ------

Area: 439,739 square miles (1,138,914 sq km).
Population: 19,825,000 (1968 est.).
Chief Cities (1967 census): Bogotá, the capital, 2,066,131; Medellín, 920,703; Cali, 766,794; Barranquilla, 568,318.
Government: *President*—Dr. Carlos Lleras Restrepo (took office Aug. 7, 1966); *Vice President*—Julio César Turbay Ayala. *Congress*—Senate, 106 members (party seating, 1969: National Front, 69; opposition parties, 37); House, 204 members (party seating, 1969: National Front, 141; opposition parties, 63).
Religious Faiths: Roman Catholics, 97% of population.
Education: *Literacy rate* (1964), 97.9% of population aged 10 and over. *Total school enrollment* (1966)—3,164,928 (primary, 2,408,489; secondary, 513,398; teacher-training, 63,549; technical/vocational, 129,562; university/higher, 49,930).
Finance (1969 est.): *Revenues*, $696,770,000; *expenditures*, $756,755,000; *public debt* (1968) $953,886,000; *monetary unit*, peso (13.50 pesos equal U. S. $1).
Gross National Product (1967): $6,185,185,000.
National Income (1967): $5,096,296,000; average annual income per person, $257.
Economic Indexes (1967): *Industrial production* (1965), 112 (1963=100); *agricultural production*, 112 (1963=100); *cost of living*, 158 (1963=100).
Manufacturing (metric tons, 1967): Cement, 2,900,000; gasoline, 1,648,000; beer, 6,437,000 hectoliters; sugar, 597,000; crude steel, 207,000.
Crops (metric tons, 1967–68 crop year): Coffee, 474,000 (ranks 2d among world producers); bananas, 1,180,000; maize, 1,000,000; potatoes, 800,000.
Minerals (metric tons, 1967): Crude petroleum, 9,603,000; salt, 470,000; gold (1966), 280,837 troy ounces.
Foreign Trade (1968): *Exports*, $558,000,000 (chief exports, 1967: coffee, $322,400,000; petroleum, $61,200,000); *imports*, $643,000,000 (chief imports, 1967: nonelectrical machinery, $141,753,000; transport equipment, $79,682,000; iron and steel, $52,549,000). *Chief trading partners* (1967): United States (took 40% of exports, supplied 47% of imports); West Germany (took 13% of exports, supplied 12% of imports).
Transportation: *Roads* (1967), 22,000 miles (35,398 km); *motor vehicles* (1967), 256,700 (automobiles 140,200); *railways* (1965), 2,164 miles (3,482 km); *merchant vessels* (1967), 25 (145,000 gross registered tons).
Communications: *Telephones* (1968): 515,000; *television stations* (1967), 15; *television sets* (1966), 400,000; *radios* (1967), 2,200,000; *newspapers* (1967), 25.

Domestic Unrest. Antigovernment rioting in Cali in January and March, plus a student riot at the National University in Bogotá in May, were contained fairly easily by the government. The U. S. consulate in Cali was stoned by a mob of 2,000 students on March 27, but no consulate personnel were injured, and property damage was small.

In February, President Lleras asked for and received the resignation of the Army chief of staff, Gen. Guillermo Pinzón Caicedo, who had criticized the government in public. In further reaction to antigovernment activities, Lleras ordered the expulsion from the country of a young Spanish priest, Domingo Lain, in April.

Economy. Much of Colombia's political stability was undoubtedly due to its booming economy. The total gross national product rose by almost 7% in 1969. Industrial activity and consumption of electricity both increased at rates higher than that of the GNP.

During the first six months of the year, exports rose to a record $262 million and imports to $344 million. Coffee continued to provide about 60% of exchange earnings, but other exports produced over $200 million for the first time. The trade deficit was made up through economic assistance from the Colombian Consultative Group, composed of the United States and several European nations. Total aid from this group in 1969 amounted to $328 million, mostly for specific development projects.

Foreign currency reserves continued to grow, and private foreign investment increased to more than $100 million, although half of this amount was for a nickel-processing plant. A pipeline linking the Putumayo oil fields with the Pacific port of Tumaco was opened in March.

The government announced tax reform plans and asked Congress for legislation to provide approximately $68 million more in revenues. In addition to sharp reductions in exemptions for annual incomes over $3,000, a special tax on conspicuous consumption was proposed.

Foreign Affairs. In June, President Lleras became the first Latin American chief of state to be received by the Nixon administration. Colombia continued to be a leader in the Andean common market, although Venezuela's refusal to join dimmed hopes of extending the area of economic cooperation. Discussions were held with Venezuela about ownership of the subterranean shelf extending seaward from the Guajira peninsula, and the status of Colombians illegally present in Venezuela. Discussions were also held with Nicaragua about the disputed ownership of several small islands in the Caribbean. In August, Jack Hood Vaughn, the new U. S. ambassador, arrived in Colombia.

ERNEST A. DUFF
Randolph-Macon Woman's College

COLORADO

Two anti-busing candidates won seats on the Denver school board after a controversial campaign. The Legislature approved the largest budget in history and passed 384 bills. Project Rulison, Colorado's first nuclear explosion, was detonated. Increased funds were allocated for education and highway construction. The economy expanded, and several companies planned new facilities in Colorado.

Elections. On May 20, Republicans Frank K. Southworth and James C. Perrill were elected to the

---- COLORADO · Information Highlights ----

Area: 104,247 square miles (270,000 sq km).
Population: 2,025,000 (1969 est.).
Chief Cities (1969 est.): Denver, the capital, 480,000; Colorado Springs, 103,000; Pueblo, 92,000; Aurora, 70,000; Boulder, 60,000.
Government: *Chief Officers*—governor, John A. Love (Republican); lt. gov., Mark A. Hogan (Democrat); secy. of state, Byron Anderson (R); atty. gen., Duke W. Dunbar (R); treas., Virginia Blue; supt. of pub. instr., Byron W. Hansford; chief justice, Robert McWilliams. *General Assembly*—Senate, 35 members (11 Democrats, 24 Republicans); House of Representatives, 65 members (27 D, 38 R).
Education: *School enrollment* (1968–69)—public elementary, 297,000 pupils (12,500 teachers); public secondary, 223,000 pupils (11,500 teachers); nonpublic schools, 43,100 pupils (2,330 teachers); college and university (fall 1967), 93,309 students. *Public school expenditures* (1967–68)—$361,973,000 ($740 per pupil); average teacher's salary, $7,175.
Public Finance (fiscal year 1968): *Revenues,* $727,156,000 (general sales and gross receipts taxes, $107,473,000; motor fuel tax, $53,136,000; federal funds, $198,236,000). *Expenditures,* $698,014,000 (education, $200,901,000; health, welfare, and safety, $78,670,000; highways, $97,441,000). *State debt,* $149,372,000 (June 30, 1968).
Personal Income (1968): $6,824,000,000; average annual income per person, $3,340.
Public Assistance (fiscal year 1968): $107,683,854.12 to 141,919 recipients (aged, $46,709,661.28; dependent children, $28,555,422.59).
Labor Force (employed persons, 1969): *Agricultural,* 68,000; *nonagricultural* (wage and salary earners), 714,900 (14.2% manufacturing, 21.2% trade, 20.2% government). *Unemployed persons* (August 1969)—25,600.
Manufacturing (1965): Value added by manufacture, $1,225,941,000 (food and products, $277,762,000; nonelectrical machinery, $107,531,000; primary metals, $94,820,000; printing and publishing, $79,441,000; electrical machinery, $64,204,000; fabricated metals, $51,620,000).
Agriculture (1967): Cash farm income, $1,035,407,000 (livestock, $684,984,000; crops, $292,817,000; govt. payments, $57,606,000). *Chief crops* (tons)—Sugar beets, 2,094,000 (ranks 3d among the states); hay, 2,888,000; wheat, 1,149,000; potatoes, 588,800.
Mining (1967): Production value (1968), $376,736,257. *Chief minerals* (tons)—Crude oil, 33,905,248 barrels; coal, 5,426,071; zinc, 31,380; molybdenum, 29,071; vanadium, 7,860.
Transportation: *Roads* (1969), 81,057 miles (130,445 km); *motor vehicles* (1968), 1,457,790; *railroads* (1969), 3,445 track miles (5,442 km); *airports* (1968), 14.
Communications (1969): *Telephones* (1967), 1,078,500; *television stations,* 12; *radio stations,* 100; *newspapers,* 25 (daily circulation, 678,314).

Denver school board by a 2½-to-1 margin over 7 other candidates. The board then rescinded existing integration resolutions involving busing. A suit, filed against the board in district court, went to the 10th Circuit Court of Appeals. That court's decision was appealed to the U. S. Supreme Court, which upheld the district court's preliminary injunction against the board's decision.

Legislation. The General Assembly convened January 8 and recessed May 9. The legislators approved a $338 million budget for the fiscal year 1969–70, including $114 million for elementary and secondary education and $86 million for higher education. Two bills approved the state's takeover of the district and county court systems and created a state public defender's system and a six-member Colorado Court of Appeals. The legislators also adopted a recodification of the state water law which integrates ground and surface water statutes and sets up a system to arbitrate water rights disputes.

Project Rulison. A 40-kiloton nuclear device buried 8,430 feet below the surface near Grand Valley was detonated on September 10 despite protests from the project's opponents who filed a court suit to halt the blast. The purpose of the $6 million project, sponsored by the Atomic Energy Commission, Austral Oil Company of Houston, Texas, and CER Geonuclear Corporation, was to release natural gas trapped in tightly compacted rock formations. (See also ATOMIC ENERGY.)

Economy. The state division of commerce and development estimated that in the first 8 months of the year some 68,300 new jobs were created in business and industry. More than 200 new industries announced construction plans and a $300 million capital outlay was committed for new and expanded facilities by existing companies. Western Electric announced plans to build a $15 million facility 14 miles north of Denver. The facility, expected to be completed in 1972, will employ 3,000 persons. Gates Rubber Company began construction in 1969 on a $5 million tire manufacturing plant near Littleton. CF&I Steel Corporation announced a $45 million expansion program in Pueblo.

Transportation. More than $62 million was paid to contractors for state highway construction in 1969. The Denver and Rio Grande Western Railroad authorized $12 million for improvements.

Tourism. The state division of commerce and development predicted an income of $500 million from 6 million tourists, making tourism the state's second largest industry after agriculture-manufacturing. Visitors to nine of the state's national park reserves increased 7.7% in the first seven months of 1969.

LOIS F. BARR
The Denver "Post"

COMMONWEALTH OF NATIONS

One of the few remaining British colonial territories, St. Vincent, in the Windward Islands group in the Caribbean, became an "associated state" on Oct. 27, 1969, after a delay of some 28 months due to internal political controversies. Under its new status, the island is internally self-governing, with responsibility for its defense and external relations remaining with Britain.

The Commonwealth of Nations is a voluntary association of monarchies, republics, associated states, and colonial territories, linked only by the common recognition of Queen Elizabeth of Britain as its head and the symbol of association.

Commonwealth Relations. The 17th in a series of meetings of Commonwealth heads of government begun in 1944 was held in London from Jan. 7 to 15, 1969. The discussion covered a wide range of world issues, on some of which, notably Rhodesia, differences of opinion were marked.

Informal meetings outside the conference took place on the Nigerian civil war and certain problems of migration between Commonwealth countries. Trade, aid, the monetary situation, and regional cooperation were discussed. The conference emphasized the need for Britain to consult the other Commonwealth members on its application for membership in the European Common Market.

The world economic situation, trade, aid, and the balance of payments position of the sterling area were discussed in greater detail at a meeting of Commonwealth finance ministers in Barbados on September 25 and 26.

Britain introduced greater flexibility into admission procedures for immigrants through the Immigration Appeals Act, which became law on May 16. The act allows immigrants to appeal deportation if already in the country, or, if outside, refusal of entry.

Evidence of the tension in Britain resulting from Commonwealth immigration was manifested in a number of incidents directed mainly against Pakistanis, the most serious of which took place at Leeds in July. Opposition to this immigration continued

"The Commonwealth Conference is under arrest for racial incitement under the terms of the Race Relations Act."

(The cartoon depicts Home Secretary James Gallaghan confronting Prime Minister Harold Wilson at a meeting of Commonwealth heads of government in January.)

CUMMINGS IN THE DAILY EXPRESS, LONDON

to center on Enoch Powell, Conservative member of Parliament, who again advocated its cessation and the repatriation of the immigrants. But a notable contribution to racial understanding was the publication in July of a six-year study, *Colour and Citizenship,* sponsored by the Institute of Race Relations, an independent body.

Rhodesia. Between January and May 1969, a series of messages relating to the October 1968 proposals for a negotiated British-Rhodesian settlement were exchanged between London and Salisbury. These were published in a British white paper on June 3. Meanwhile, the Rhodesian regime formulated its own constitutional proposals, which were entirely unacceptable to both the British government and the Conservative party opposition. In a referendum on June 20, the restricted Rhodesian electorate approved both a republican form of government and the regime's constitutional proposals, designed to prevent African majority rule. As a result, the British-appointed governor, Sir Humphrey Gibbs, resigned, and what British representation there had been in Salisbury was withdrawn.

Nigeria. British Prime Minister Harold Wilson visited Nigeria from March 27 to 31 to investigate the civil war and to talk with the federal government. He followed this with visits to the emperor of Ethiopia and officials of the Organization of African Unity in Addis Ababa in April, but his attempt to meet with the Biafran leader, Col. Odumegwu Ojukwu, failed. British efforts to bring both sides together continued, but were unsuccessful.

Gibraltar. The new constitution for Gibraltar, providing for greater local responsibility for domestic affairs, went into effect on May 30, 1969. Spain then took retaliatory measures, which included the complete closing of the land frontier at La Linea and the barring of all Spanish workers. The consequent labor shortage in Gibraltar was relieved by the use of troops to maintain essential services, by workers taking part-time additional jobs, and by restrictions placed on the freedom to change employment without government permission.

A general election held on July 30 resulted in the formation of a coalition under Maj. Robert Pelizza, composed of his Integration with Britain party (5 seats) and an independent group (3 seats). The Gibraltar Labor party and its allies, under the former chief minister, Sir Joshua Hassan, holds the remaining seven seats.

A Spanish note of June 16 to the UN secretary general claimed that the new constitution disregarded the recommendations of the General Assembly and violated both the Treaty of Utrecht (1713) and the human rights of the Gibraltarians, contentions refuted in a British reply of August 5. In another note, Spain accused Britain of wishing to retain Gibraltar for military reasons.

A mock combat assault on Gibraltar by British forces on August 8 resulted, in addition to a further Spanish note accusing Britain of being interested in Gibraltar only as a military base, in the stationing of Spanish warships in the area and observation flights by the Spanish air force.

Anguilla. Following an announcement by the Anguillan leader, Ronald Webster, early in January 1969 that Anguilla was now an independent republic and no longer part of the associated state of St. Kitts-Nevis-Anguilla, Britain withdrew its representative, Anthony Lee, and suspended development aid. A referendum on February 6 confirmed the republic, of which Webster became president.

The governments of both Britain and St. Kitts-Nevis-Anguilla refused to recognize this status, and William Whitlock, British parliamentary undersecretary of state for foreign and commonwealth affairs, was sent to St. Kitts in the second week of March, after which he went on to Anguilla, arriving on March 11. Having outlined proposals for a settlement, Whitlock hurriedly left the island after a hostile demonstration broke out and shots were fired. A detailed report was given to Michael Stewart, foreign and commonwealth secretary, who later told a press conference he was convinced that Anguilla was dominated by an armed gangster element.

(*Continued on page 204*)

Insults are shouted by an irate Anguillan woman as she and a carload of companions pass a British soldier at a checkpoint. The 2d Battalion of the Parachute Regiment seized the island's airstrip and other strategic locations in bloodless maneuvering.

MINI-INVASION

Shortly before dawn on March 19, 1969, the British troops landed—in a most unlikely spot, the island of Anguilla in the Caribbean. Sixteen miles long and 2 miles wide, Anguilla has only 6,000 residents. It has no central electricity, no telephones, no water mains. But Anguilla had declared its independence of the associated state of St. Kitts-Nevis-Anguilla, and shots had been fired—harmlessly—when a British official called. In the tiny invasion, 300 British paratroops left two frigates in rubber rafts and helicopters, and encountered no opposition. Truce came on March 31.

Britain's Lord Caradon (right) lands at Anguilla on March 28 and confers with local leader Ronald Webster.

Tranquillity prevails, and the paratroops relax on their temporary Caribbean assignment while a few Anguillans look on.

COMMONWEALTH OF NATIONS

Component	Area (sq. mi.)	Pop. (mid-1968)	Status
EUROPE			
Great Britain & islands of British seas[1]	94,522	55,283,000	Sovereign state
Gibraltar	2	25,000	Colony
Malta	122	319,000	Sovereign state
Total in Europe	94,646	55,627,000	
AFRICA			
Botswana	222,000	611,000	Sovereign state
Gambia	4,003	350,000	Sovereign state
Ghana	91,843	8,376,000	Sovereign state
Kenya	224,960	10,209,000	Sovereign state
Lesotho	11,716	910,000	Sovereign state
Malawi	46,066	4,285,000	Sovereign state
Mauritius	809	787,000	Sovereign state
Nigeria[2]	356,668	62,650,000	Sovereign state
Rhodesia[2]	150,333	4,670,000	Internally self-governing colony
St. Helena	47	5,000	Colony
Ascension	34	476	
Tristan da Cunha	81	285	
Seychelles	156	49,000	Colony
Sierra Leone	27,925	2,475,000	Sovereign state
Swaziland	6,704	395,000	Sovereign state
Tanzania	362,820	12,590,000	Sovereign state
Uganda	92,525	8,133,000	Sovereign state
Zambia	288,129	4,080,000	Sovereign state
Total in Africa	1,886,819	120,575,761	
AMERICA			
Antigua	171	62,000	Associated state
Bahamas	4,400	148,000	Internally self-governing colony
Barbados	166	253,000	Sovereign state
Bermuda	20	51,000	Colony
British Honduras	8,867	116,000	Internally self-governing colony
British Virgin Islands	59	9,000	Colony
Canada	3,851,802	20,772,000	Sovereign state
Cayman Islands	100	9,000	Colony
Dominica	305	72,000	Associated state
Falkland Islands[3]	4,618	2,000	Colony
Grenada	133	103,000	Associated state
Guyana	83,000	710,000	Sovereign state
Jamaica	4,232	1,913,000	Sovereign state
Montserrat	32	15,000	Colony
St. Kitts-Nevis-Anguilla	153	56,000	Associated state
St. Lucia	238	108,000	Associated state
St. Vincent	150	93,000	Associated state
Trinidad and Tobago	1,980	1,030,000	Sovereign state
Turks and Caicos	166	6,000	Colony
Total in America	3,960,592	25,528,000	
ASIA			
Bahrain[4]	231	200,000	Protectorate state
British Indian Ocean Territory[5]	30	2,000	Colony
Brunei	2,226	112,000	Protectorate state
Ceylon	25,332	11,964,000	Sovereign state
Cyprus	3,572	622,000	Sovereign state
Hong Kong	398	3,927,000	Colony
India	1,176,150	523,893,000	Sovereign state
Jammu and Kashmir	86,023	3,729,000[6]	In dispute
Malaysia	128,430	10,384,000	Sovereign state
Pakistan	365,528	109,520,000	Sovereign state
Qatar[4]	4,000	80,000	Protected state
Sikkim	2,744	187,000	Protected state
Singapore	224	1,988,000	Sovereign state
Trucial States[4]	32,278	136,000	Protected state
Total in Asia	1,827,166	666,744,000	
OCEANIA			
Australia	2,971,021	12,031,000	Sovereign state
Christmas Island	62	3,000	External territory
Cocos Islands	5	1,000	External territory
New Guinea, Terr	92,996	1,680,000	Trusteeship
Norfolk Island	14	1,000	External territory
Papua	90,540	620,000	External territory
Fiji	7,055	505,000	Colony
Nauru	8	6,000	Sovereign state
New Hebrides	5,700	78,000	Condominium
New Zealand	103,736	2,751,000	Sovereign state
Pitcairn Island	2	92	Colony
Tonga	269	81,000	Protected state
Western Pacific Islands: British Solomon Islands	11,500	147,000	Protectorate
Gilbert and Ellice Islands	349	57,000	Colony
Western Samoa[4]	1,097	137,000	Sovereign state
Total in Oceania	3,284,354	18,098,092	
Grand total	11,053,577	886,572,853	

[1] Includes Northern Ireland, Channel Islands, and Isle of Man.
[2] Rhodesia declared its independence Nov. 11, 1965, but technically retains Commonwealth status. [3] Excludes dependencies. [4] Not an integral part of the Commonwealth. [5] Includes Chagos Archipelago and Aldabra, Farquhar, and Desroches islands; pop. is 1966 est. [6] 1964 est. of India-held portion only.

On March 19, 300 British paratroops landed in Anguilla, and Anthony Lee returned as British commissioner. The prime ministers of both Jamaica and Trinidad immediately protested the use of force. When the UN General Assembly's committee voted to hear Webster's representative, Jeremiah Gumbs, the British delegation walked out.

Coincidentally with demonstrations in Anguilla against the British display of force, Webster proposed a referendum and requested a parliamentary or cabinet delegation to negotiate a settlement. After speaking with Webster in New York, Lord Caradon, chief British representative at the UN, flew to Anguilla on March 28. Later, an agreement with Webster was announced jointly on March 31 under which the British were to withdraw the paratroops and enter into consultations with Anguilla's seven-man council. Lord Caradon then went to St. Kitts to consult its prime minister, Robert Bradshaw.

Following talks in London between Stewart and Bradshaw, it was announced on May 22 that a commission would be appointed later in the year to make recommendations about Anguilla's future. Continued tension in Anguilla and Webster's accusation that the British commissioner was acting in breach of the March 31 agreement had resulted in a further visit by Lord Caradon on April 11. Although he was unable to see Webster or the advisory council, he announced the replacement of Anthony Lee as commissioner by John Cumber.

Defense. Australian Prime Minister John G. Gorton and New Zealand Prime Minister Keith J. Holyoake announced on February 25 that they intended to keep forces in Malaysia and Singapore after the end of the British withdrawal in 1971, with the consent of the local governments. Australia will also provide defense aid.

Aid to the Territories. The 16th annual report of the Colombo Plan consultative committee was published on Feb. 14, 1969. It showed that external assistance to the area (South and Southeast Asia) during 1967–68 totaled $2.8 billion, of which the United States contributed $2.14 billion.

Britain's overseas aid program totaled £210 million in 1968, distributed geographically as follows: Africa, £74 million (all but £1.2 million to Commonwealth countries); Asia, £75 million; Western Hemisphere, £16 million; Europe, £13 million; and the Pacific area, £6 million. Technical assistance totaled £41 million, a 25% increase over 1967. Interest-free loans of £38 million to India and £9.5 million to Pakistan, repayable over 25 years, were announced on June 11, and a development loan to Mauritius of £5 million on similar terms was arranged in July. Loans for Guyana, totaling £4.25 million, of which £3 million will be used for the reconstruction of sea defense works, were announced on July 14. A British government grant of £96,535 toward the construction of a deep-water wharf at Vila, in the New Hebrides, was made in February.

At the beginning of 1969, the nonprofit Commonwealth Development Corporation was operating 156 projects, with £150 million committed.

(See also articles on GREAT BRITAIN and other members of the Commonwealth.)

RICHARD E. WEBB
British Information Services, New York

COMMUNICATIONS. See POST OFFICE; TELEPHONE; TELEVISION AND RADIO.

EAST BERLIN meeting of Communist party chiefs from East Europe, Soviet Union (Leonid Brezhnev, with hand raised), and North Vietnam (Pham Van Dong, far left).

COMMUNISM

For Communists throughout the world, 1969 was a year of greater disunity than ever before. Both the USSR and Communist China began publicizing their border skirmishes, angrily accusing each other of aggression. Although such skirmishes have been commonplace since the early 1960's, both sides in 1969 made the unprecedented move of appealing to world public opinion for support of their conflicting frontier claims.

Meanwhile Czechoslovakia was restive under occupation by a Soviet army that, despite making great efforts at fraternization, acquired few Czechoslovak friends. In the Balkans pro-Chinese Albania, pro-Soviet Bulgaria, and independent Communist Yugoslavia engaged in a three-way battle of mutual recriminations. Such infighting perturbed the Communist parties of the world, which chose sides in awkward disarray. Although most parties were anti-Chinese, many were pro-Czech or pro-Yugoslav. Communism was no longer a unified creed.

World Communist Conference. All this dissension was revealed at the world Communist conference held in Moscow on June 5–17. The USSR had appealed for such a conference for several years before it achieved this meeting. Before the conference convened, the Soviet press listed four main conference tasks: to label China a Communist heretic, to approve the 1968 Soviet invasion of Czechoslovakia, to accept the "Brezhnev doctrine" that the USSR could intervene militarily in Communist countries in which Communist control was threatened, and to create a new worldwide Communist organization like the old Communist International (1919–1943), which Moscow dominated.

To these Soviet requests the 1969 conference was unresponsive. Of the world's 95 Communist parties, only 75 attended the conference, which was boycotted by the parties of China, Burma, Cambodia, Indonesia, Japan, Laos, Malaysia, New Zealand, North Korea, North Vietnam, the Philippines, Singapore, South Vietnam, and Thailand. These Far Eastern parties were either pro-Chinese in the Sino-Soviet dispute or preferred to remain neutral. Five European Communist parties also refused to attend—those of Albania, Iceland, the Netherlands, West Germany, and Yugoslavia.

Soviet and pro-Soviet speakers at the conference criticized China and praised the 1968 USSR invasion of Czechoslovakia. But the Rumanian delegation argued that China should not be criticized. Italian Communist spokesmen insisted that the conference should not be anti-Chinese and that no Communist party should be expelled from the world

WORLD COMMUNIST MEMBERSHIP, 1969

Country	Membership
Africa	
Algeria*	1,000
Morocco*	600
Nigeria*	1,000
Réunion	500
South Africa*	100
Sudan*	7,500
Tunisia*	100
United Arab Republic*	1,000
Asia and Oceania	
Australia	4,750
Burma*	1,500
Cambodia	100
Ceylon	2,300
China, Communist	17,000,000
India	55,000
Indonesia*	5,000
Iran*	1,000
Iraq*	2,000
Israel	1,000
Japan	250,000
Jordan*	700
Korea, North	1,600,000
Laos	40,000
Lebanon*	6,000
Malaysia*	2,000
Mongolia	48,570
Nepal*	8,000
New Zealand	300
Pakistan*	1,450
Philippines*	2,000
Syria*	3,000
Thailand*	2,500
Turkey*	1,250
Vietnam, North	766,000
Vietnam, South*	100,000
Europe	
Albania	66,000
Austria	27,500
Belgium	12,500
Bulgaria	613,000
Cyprus	13,000
Czechoslovakia	1,700,000
Denmark	6,000
Finland	49,000

Country	Membership
France	275,000
Germany, East	1,769,000
Germany, West*	13,000
Greece*	27,000
Hungary	600,000
Iceland	1,000
Ireland	125
Italy	1,500,000
Luxembourg	500
Netherlands	11,500
Norway	2,500
Poland	2,000,000
Portugal*	2,000
Rumania	1,800,000
Spain*	5,000
Sweden	29,000
Switzerland	4,000
United Kingdom	32,500
Yugoslavia	1,700,000
North America	
Canada	2,500
Costa Rica*	600
Cuba	60,000
Dominican Republic*	1,100
El Salvador*	200
Guadeloupe	1,300
Guatemala*	750
Honduras*	300
Mexico	5,250
Nicaragua*	200
Panama*	1,450
United States	15,000
South America	
Argentina*	60,000
Bolivia*	33,000
Brazil*	15,000
Chile	45,000
Colombia	8,000
Ecuador*	750
Guyana	100
Paraguay*	5,000
Peru*	2,000
Uruguay	20,000
Venezuela	5,000
USSR	
USSR	13,500,000

* Countries in which the Communist party is illegal.
Source: U. S. State Department.

World Communist party conference opened on June 5 in St. George's Hall of Great Kremlin Palace, Moscow.

Communist movement for disagreeing with Moscow. Fearful of a rapprochement between the USSR and the United States, the Italian delegates asked Soviet party leaders to consult other Communist parties before making agreements with the United States.

Much to Moscow's displeasure, the 1968 Soviet invasion of Czechoslovakia was openly criticized at the conference by representatives from Australia, Austria, Belgium, Britain, Denmark, France, Italy, Norway, Spain, Sweden, and Switzerland.

The conference concluded by publishing a vague statement of general principles. This statement did not condemn Communist China or justify the Soviet occupation of Czechoslovakia. Every Communist party in the world was declared to be independent (of Moscow) and sovereign. There was no mention of the Brezhnev doctrine or of a new Communist International. Thus the Communist parties at the conference refused to accept the Moscow party line.

Even so, the party representatives of Britain, Cuba, the Dominican Republic, Norway, and Sweden refused to sign the conference statement, preferring not to commit their parties to any specific policy. Rumania criticized the conference statement, but signed it. Only the part of the statement condemning imperialism was accepted by the Communist parties of Australia, Italy, the French island of Réunion, and San Marino. At press conferences, western European Communist leaders interpreted the conference results as granting greater independence from Moscow to other Communist parties.

Sino-Soviet Dispute. Now 11 years old, the Sino-Soviet quarrel continued in 1969 as a cold war of words and a hot war of frontier skirmishes. Each said the other was betraying Marxism-Leninism.

Moscow claimed that China was ruled by an antidemocratic, military-bureaucratic dictatorship that oppressed national minorities, governed by "mass bloody terror," used semislave labor to re-educate youth, helped Britain to keep Hong Kong, encouraged anti-Soviet sentiment in Czechoslovakia, tried to dominate the world Communist movement, and was planning nuclear war against the USSR.

Peking responded that the USSR was ruled by

"mad dogs," "wild animals," and new, aggressive czars who practiced colonialism in eastern Europe, gave foreign aid only to gain political influence, held much territory that was historically Chinese, and threatened China with both nuclear and conventional war. Both China and the USSR expressed the fear that the other might ally itself with the United States to gain support. (For a background discussion of the Sino-Soviet dispute, see pages 208–210.)

Eastern Europe. At a meeting of leaders of the Warsaw Pact alliance (Bulgaria, Czechoslovakia, East Germany, Hungary, Poland, Rumania, and the USSR) in Budapest in March, the USSR proposed a resolution condemning Communist China. Moscow also suggested that the eastern European members of the Warsaw Pact send a small but symbolic number of troops to help Soviet forces guard the Sino-Soviet border. At Rumanian insistence, both the resolution and the troop assignment were rejected. Thus the Warsaw Pact remained a purely European alliance to deal with European crises.

After the Budapest meeting the Czechoslovak press commented that the entire Soviet orbit of nations could not conquer China by war. János Kádár, the first secretary of the Hungarian Communist party, said that war between China and the USSR would be a disaster for both countries, the entire world Communist movement, and all mankind.

Meanwhile, from February to late fall, Warsaw Pact troops conducted international military exercises in Bulgaria, Czechoslovakia, East Germany, Hungary, and Poland. In these war games, Soviet troops maneuvered with forces of various East European satellites. There were even joint USSR-Bulgarian naval exercises in the eastern part of the Mediterranean Sea. In northern East Europe these troop maneuvers were used to intimidate Czechoslovakia into remaining quiet under Soviet occupation. Rumania refused to participate in most Warsaw Pact maneuvers or to allow such maneuvers on Rumanian soil.

Rumania also displayed its independence during 1969 by rejecting the Brezhnev doctrine, by refuting the Soviet argument that inter-Communist quarrels

TASS FROM SOVFOTO

were caused by Western intrigue, and by proposing that all foreign troops withdraw from European countries. Such a troop withdrawal would mean that U. S. forces would quit western Europe, but also that Soviet soldiers would leave East Germany, Hungary, Poland, and Czechoslovakia. In June, Rumania signed a trade pact with Communist China.

In March, Yugoslavia held a congress of its Communist party, inviting foreign Communist parties to send observers. Moscow urged all pro-Soviet parties not to attend; hence of all Communist eastern Europe, only Rumania sent observers to Belgrade. But from western Europe and Scandinavia came observers from the Communist parties of Austria, Belgium, Britain, Finland, France, Italy, Norway, and Spain.

CEMA, or Comecon (the Council for Mutual Economic Assistance, composed of Bulgaria, Czechoslovakia, East Germany, Hungary, Poland, Rumania, the USSR, and Mongolia), held meetings in January and April, with Rumania opposing any proposals giving to CEMA authority over the Rumanian economy. The second meeting decided to establish a CEMA investment bank and to ease currency restrictions among the member states. A problem in eastern Europe was that the differing standards of living among CEMA members hampered the growth of intrabloc trade. Czechoslovakia, Hungary, Bulgaria, and Poland all have higher living standards than the USSR.

Western Europe. Both the Italian Communist party congress of February 1969 and the Swedish party congress of September condemned the Soviet occupation of Czechoslovakia. An April congress of the Finnish Communist party refused to accept control from Moscow. Meanwhile, the French Communist party declared that it was independent and also equal to any Communist party—including that of the USSR.

Despite these expressions of independence, which also occurred at the world party conference, western European and Scandinavian Communist parties echoed Moscow in demanding withdrawal of U. S. troops from Europe, disbandment of the North

Atlantic Treaty Organization (NATO), and continued separation of East and West Germany.

In June the Soviet press asked French Communist voters to boycott the second round of the French national elections. They obeyed, thus ensuring electoral victory for the Gaullist party.

Asia and Oceania. In 1969, as they had before, Far Eastern Communist parties demanded the withdrawal of U. S. troops from Japan, South Korea, Taiwan, Laos, Thailand, and South Vietnam. Near Eastern parties tried to help the Arab countries against Israel.

In the Sino-Soviet dispute, China was supported by the Communist parties of Burma, Cambodia, Indonesia, Laos, Malaysia, New Zealand, Pakistan, Singapore, and Thailand, while the parties of India, Japan, North Korea, North Vietnam, and the Near East remained neutral. The Communists of Ceylon and Mongolia supported the USSR.

In June, Mongolia complained publicly that Communist China had ceased trading with the Mongols and also was sending anti-Soviet Literature and radio broadcasts into Mongolian territory. Stating that China might invade Mongolia, the Mongol leadership declared it was struggling for an anti-Maoist counterrevolution in China.

Africa. In 1969 the small African Communist parties mainly propagandized in favor of freeing Portugal's African possessions. Most parties displayed little interest in the Sino-Soviet dispute or the Soviet occupation of Czechoslovakia. The party leaders of Senegal refused to attend the 1969 world Communist conference in Moscow.

Latin America. In 1969, as they had previously, the Latin American Communist parties propagandized for trade and diplomatic relations with Cuba and against U. S. political and economic influence in Latin America. Most parties approved the Soviet occupation of Czechoslovakia. With regard to the Sino-Soviet dispute, the Latin American parties were deeply divided. Thus the Communists of Peru were pro-Chinese, those of Chile and Paraguay were pro-USSR, and Cuba maintained careful neutrality. Out of respect for independent communism, the parties of Chile and Venezuela sent observers to the 1969 congress of the Yugoslav Communist party.

North America. The small Canadian Communist party, mostly located in the cities of the province of Ontario, urged Canada to withdraw from NATO and to reduce U. S. economic domination of the Canadian economy. The party was anti-Czech, anti-Chinese, and pro-USSR.

In 1969 the small Communist party of the United States celebrated with little fanfare the 50th anniversary of its formation. The party opposed the Vietnam War and the decision of the federal government to construct a defense system of antimissile missiles. Gus Hall, the party secretary-general, attended the world Communist conference in Moscow, where he merely echoed the Soviet speakers. The party approved the USSR occupation of Czechoslovakia and backed the USSR against China.

The U. S. Justice Department stated that Communists were active in inciting antiwar and antiestablishment riots by American students. But the Soviet press in 1969 criticized the "young avantgardism" of radical Western youth as anarchic "rotten goods." (See also separate articles on the Communist countries.)

ELLSWORTH RAYMOND
New York University

THE SINO-SOVIET SPLIT

Relations between Communist China and the Soviet Union hit their lowest point in 1969. The Peking-Moscow split, which had been characterized by rising heights of invective, worsened when sporadic border clashes brought the two countries to the brink of war.

The fighting along the border took place less than two decades after the Russians and the Chinese signed a 30-year Treaty of Friendship, Alliance, and Mutual Assistance on Feb. 14, 1950. The Russians had recognized the new Chinese Communist state the day after it was proclaimed, and the Chinese had publicly proclaimed that they were "leaning to one side"—the side of the Russians—in the East-West confrontation.

The 20th Party Congress. The event that caused the first major cracks to appear in the facade of "unbreakable solidarity" was the 20th Congress of the Communist party of the Soviet Union, held in Moscow in February 1956. At that congress Nikita S. Khrushchev, the party secretary, launched a violent attack on the late Soviet Premier Stalin and denounced the "cult of the individual." Khrushchev also formally outlined the USSR's position on peaceful coexistence, terming it a fundamental principle of Soviet foreign policy, not a tactical move. The only alternative to peaceful coexistence is the most destructive war in history, he said.

Khrushchev's position became a burning issue in the dispute between the Soviet and Chinese parties. In the Chinese view, peaceful coexistence could only be a tactic in the struggle with imperialism, not a principle to be upheld. The Chinese contend that, as long as imperialism exists, there will be wars. While the Russians argue that a nuclear war would destroy both capitalism and communism, the Chinese declare that on the debris of a dead imperialism will be built a new, higher civilization.

The 20th Congress marked a turning point in relations between the Soviet and Chinese parties. No longer did the Chinese meekly follow the Soviet lead. They were increasingly eager to make their voice heard in an attempt to gain a dominant position among the Communist nations. The Chinese elevated Chairman Mao Tse-tung above the Soviet leaders, describing him as an innovator of Marxist thought. Much of the subsequent dispute involved a struggle for supremacy in the Communist world.

Differences stemming from the 20th Congress were not limited to the view on peaceful coexistence. Also included was Khrushchev's drive against the cult of the individual. Chinese reluctance to join in the de-Stalinization campaign was probably due in part to the fact that they were building a cult of the individual around Mao.

A Widening Dispute. Another ideological issue was presented in 1958 with Peking's policy of establishing people's communes. The claim was made that the communes would accelerate socialist construction and complete the building of socialism. The implicit claim—that the Chinese had in 10 years found a shortcut to communism that the Russians had failed to find in 40 years—posed a challenge to Soviet leadership of the Communist world. The Chinese views were firmly rejected by Khrushchev, who declared in January 1959 that no stages could be skipped from capitalism to communism.

While the ideological dispute was widening, differences in national interest became evident and aggravated the strain between China and the USSR. In the summer of 1958, the Chinese Communists launched an intensive campaign to achieve the "liberation" of Taiwan, an objective to which Peking gave the highest priority. The Chinese Communists began an artillery bombardment of the offshore islands of Quemoy and Matsu on August 23, but it was not until after Premier Chou En-lai had offered to negotiate that Khrushchev declared in a letter to President Eisenhower that an attack on China would be regarded as an attack on the USSR.

Relations deteriorated in 1959 with the Chinese-Indian border dispute. The Soviet Union sought to maintain an impartial stand, deploring the resort to arms. China later declared that a Soviet statement of neutrality on the issue had first revealed the existence of a Chinese-Soviet dispute to the outside world. In the Chinese view, the Russian failure to support a fellow Communist nation was a betrayal.

Public signs of the widening rift between the two countries increased in 1960 as the Soviet Union withdrew its army of technical specialists from China. The Chinese later accused the Russians of having unilaterally torn up hundreds of agreements. The sudden withdrawal of Soviet specialists was a serious blow to the Chinese, especially since many of the projects were left uncompleted and the Russians departed with the blueprints.

Together with the withdrawal of specialists, the USSR sharply curtailed its economic aid program to China. Part of the reason for that move was undoubtedly the heavy drain on the Soviet economy imposed by the program, but another reason was that the Chinese had been using Soviet aid funds to support an aid program of their own in an attempt to compete with the USSR for influence among the developing countries. At the same time, the Chinese suggested that the USSR should not press ahead with its own economic development until other Socialist nations had caught up.

Despite attempts to halt the deterioration, relations became more strained. In October 1962 the Chinese-Indian border war caused the Russians even greater embarrassment than in 1959 because the USSR, seeking to establish better relations with neutral India, had promised it military equipment.

The intensification of the war in Vietnam caused further conflict. Charges were traded of collusion with the United States and of hampering the war effort. The USSR hinted that China was obstructing deliveries of Soviet matériel to North Vietnam, and the Chinese declared the assistance deficient both in quantity and quality.

The xenophobic turn that Chinese foreign policy took in the early stages of the "great Proletarian Cultural Revolution," begun in 1966, caused relations with the USSR to fall to a record low. In a tumultuous period, Chinese students battled with the Russian police in Moscow; the Chinese embassy was invaded by Russians and the Soviet embassy in Peking was besieged; Red Guards broke into a Soviet consular office in Peking, smashed furniture, and burned records; Soviet personnel were manhandled and their car set afire; and each country expelled diplomats of the other.

"Rationalize it! If we don't fight them here we'll be fighting them in downtown Moscow—We have to contain Chinese Communism in Asia..."

OLIPHANT IN THE DENVER POST

CONFRONTATION ON THE BORDER

Disunity within the Communist world reached new dimensions in 1969 as the rift widened between the USSR and Communist China. Soviet and Chinese troops clashed sporadically along their common border, and both sides admitted casualties.

(Left) *Soviet frontier guards look out over the Ussuri River to Red China.*

(Below) *Chinese border troops guard the disputed island called Chenpao by China and Damansky by the USSR.*

NOVOSTI FROM SOVFOTO

UPI

Chinese troops, according to Soviet news agency, demonstrate against Soviets at the disputed Ussuri River island.

NOVOSTI FROM SOVFOTO

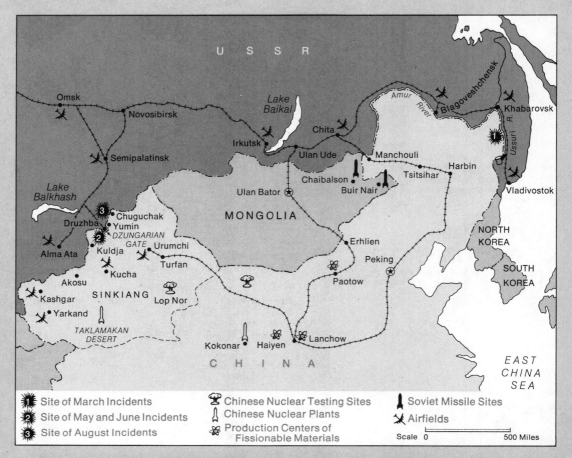

Map locates three principal sites where Sino-Soviet clashes occurred, as well as major strategic installations.

The Soviet invasion of Czechoslovakia in August 1968 was violently condemned by China. The Chinese reported concentrations of Soviet troops along their border, and they began to talk of war preparations. Then, on March 2, 1969, the two antagonists fought an armed skirmish over a disputed island in the frozen Ussuri River.

The Border Question. The roots of the territorial dispute—the issue that triggered the clashes along the 4,500-mile (7,200-km) common border—lie in treaties negotiated in the 19th century between a weakened Manchu dynasty and czarist Russia. In the official Chinese view, expressed in a major statement on May 24, 1969, Russia, through such "unequal treaties," had seized 600,000 square miles (1,500,000 sq km) of Chinese territory.

Despite these long-held grievances, the Chinese are not pressing for renunciation of the treaties. They insist that they are willing to accept the provisions of the treaties but accuse the Russians of encroaching on Chinese territories beyond those lost to the czars.

It is in these disputed areas—which include hundreds of islands in the border rivers—that the clashes of 1969 took place. After the initial skirmish, China staged huge anti-Soviet demonstrations in which 260 million people took part. Smaller anti-Chinese demonstrations were held in the USSR.

The fighting on the Ussuri River marked a new phase in the dispute. Although numerous border incidents had occurred in the past, now for the first time both sides publicized them and also acknowledged casualties.

Fighting over the island—known as Chenpao to China and Damansky to the USSR—was resumed on March 15 and resulted in the death of a Soviet colonel. At the end of the month, the USSR proposed that border talks, which had been broken off in 1964, be held.

The fighting soon spread to the Sinkiang border, and the Chinese accused the Russians of having used tanks and armored cars. Then, in August, fighting broke out on the Amur River while Chinese and Soviet representatives were holding talks at Khabarovsk on navigation problems on border rivers.

Amid Chinese charges that the USSR was mobilizing for war and Soviet warnings that war would involve the use of nuclear weapons, Chou En-lai and Soviet Premier Aleksei N. Kosygin held a surprise meeting in Peking on September 11. After the meeting, the level of polemics was reduced on both sides, and, on October 7, the Chinese announced an agreement to hold border talks with the USSR. On October 20, the talks opened in Peking.

Despite the declared willingness of both sides to solve the border question through negotiations rather than by force of arms, the chances of their reaching and maintaining a long-term border settlement, in the absence of a political reconciliation, do not appear very bright.

FRANK CHING
"The New York Times"

COMPUTERS

In less than 20 years, the electronic computer has evolved from a laboratory device to a major industry. In 1969, sales of electronic digital computers were estimated at $8 billion, up $1 billion from 1968. Since hardware typically constitutes only about one third the cost of a computer installation, a more accurate estimate of computer industry sales for 1969 would exceed $20 billion. Many new products were introduced during the year.

Growing Influence. A survey of hundreds of computer experts by the consulting firm of Parsons & Williams produced forecasts that computers will have far-reaching effects on segments of society that so far have only been lightly touched by this innovation. The developments envisioned include the routine monitoring of hospital patients by computers, automated diagnosis of a patient's illness, the extensive use of computer-aided instruction, the automation of libraries, and the commonplace purchase of computers for use in the home. Beginnings have been made in all of these areas. A Connecticut household, for example, has acquired a small computer for the family's three children.

The growing use of computers in factory operations—the chief trend in industrial automation—is expected to reduce by 50% the labor force necessary to man present industries, some experts said in the survey. They foresaw computer-based industrial unemployment as a serious problem over the next generation. In an installation that typifies the trend, a British firm, Lucas Corp., set up a computerized monitoring system that took over the operation of 250 machine tools. The system even checks maintenance. The company plans to extend the monitoring system to 1,500 more machine tools.

Survey participants also forecast that banking and financial systems would be totally reshaped, with financial transactions consisting largely of electronic records processed by computers. Also predicted was the widespread use of computers to regulate the flow of automobile traffic. On a trial basis, computers already govern the flow of cars on some main arteries in New York City and elsewhere.

New Products. The entry of the computer into everyday affairs is being speeded by a stream of new products. To facilitate remote computing, a number of companies introduced lightweight, portable computer terminals that easily couple to any telephone handset for communicating with a computer that may be thousands of miles away.

International Business Machines Corp. introduced a small business computer, the System/3, featuring a radical departure in punched-card format. The System/3 card is about one third the size of the traditional 80-column card, but it holds 20% more information. It is intended for small businesses that cannot afford larger machines.

At the other end of the scale, IBM announced its most powerful computer ever, the Model 195, to be incorporated in its System/360 line. The Model 195 can process an instruction in 54-billionths of a second. Such speed is valuable in tackling complex problems in science and industry and in some large-scale commercial applications.

MOS Technology. A new company, Viatron Computer Systems Corp., introduced a line of computer products based on a new electronics technology called MOS, for metal oxide semiconductors. MOS technology makes it possible to carry out hundreds and even thousands of electronic functions on miniscule chips in data processing stations, color video displays, and desk-top computers. Viatron announced prices as much as 75% below those charged by manufacturers of similar equipment. Considerable skepticism was accorded the Viatron announcements, but at year's end the company had begun its initial deliveries on schedule and at the prices initially advertised.

Magnetic "Bubbles." In 1969, Bell Telephone Laboratories, where the transistor was invented in 1948, patented a process to make tiny disks of magnetic energy called "bubbles." Also known as basic orthoferrite domains, the bubbles hold out the possibility of another revolution in data processing and storage. They move about on thin

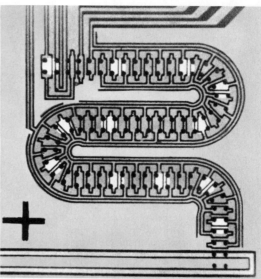

BELL TELEPHONE LABORATORIES

TINY COMPUTERS of the future may count, switch, and perform other functions within one solid magnetic material. This circuit—a photolithographic pattern on a chip of thulium orthoferrite—moves magnetic "bubbles" (large white dots) through a shift register.

chips—magnetized crystals made of rare-earth oxides—to perform such functions as switching, counting, memory, and logic. Bell Lab officials note that so far the achievement is more potential than actual and that the growing of large orthoferrite crystals remains to be perfected.

Pricing and Patents. Virtually all the major computer manufacturers restructured their prices in 1969. IBM led off in announcing a step known as "unbundling"—charging separately for computer-supporting services that were formerly furnished free. These services include programming, customer education, and systems engineering. One after another, the leading companies announced their own unbundling policies.

The U. S. Court of Customs and Patent Appeals ruled on Aug. 14, 1969, that some computer programs—the instructions for the hardware—may be patented. This ruling, along with the separation of prices for supporting services, is expected to spur the growth of the computer software industry.

STANLEY KLEIN
Science Moderator, WEVD Radio

CONGO, Democratic Republic of (Kinshasa)

Congolese relations with other African states did not generally improve in 1969. Quiescence, rather than stability, characterized the country's politics. Prospects for a viable political system other than the existing military regime of President Joseph Mobutu were not good. However, the Congo has undergone a remarkable economic recovery and ranks again as a leading exporter among the independent black African nations.

Foreign Relations. By the beginning of 1969, relations between the Congo and its two western neighbors, Congo (Brazzaville) and the Central African Republic, had rapidly deteriorated. In 1969, both countries boycotted the summit meeting at Kinshasa of the Organisation Commune Africaine et Malgache (OCAM). However, the other members of this French-oriented group went out of their way to appease the Kinshasa government. Although the Congo is a relatively recent and somewhat half-hearted recruit, its economic potential nearly equals that of all the other members put together.

Two conciliation missions headed by the presidents of Upper Volta and Togo failed to achieve anything more than a token normalization of relations between Kinshasa, and Brazzaville and the Central African Republic.

The border between Kinshasa and Brazzaville was closed for the fourth time in five years, following a speech by President Mobutu in November. In his speech, made during celebrations marking his fourth year in office, Mobutu responded to repeated charges from Brazzaville that Kinshasa was plotting against it. He said that the charges were false, but that if ordered to do so his troops would be able to occupy most of Brazzaville's territory within two hours. The speech alarmed the Brazzaville government, which ordered the border closed.

On the other hand, ruptured relations with another OCAM member, Rwanda, were restored, and the border between the two countries was reopened in February.

Despite a state visit by Zambian president Kenneth Kaunda and glowing praise for President Mobutu from Ugandan President Milton Obote, relations with east and central African countries of the Organization of African Unity (OAU) were some-what less cordial than they had been at the height of the Congo's confrontation with Belgian interest groups in 1967. This situation was perhaps due to Mobutu's persistent reluctance to lend assistance to the Angola People's Liberation Movement (MPLA), despite an OAU group's recommendations.

By contrast, Congolese relations with the West were excellent. President Mobutu visited Greece, West Germany, and France in March. In November the spectacular welcome he was given in Belgium put an official end to the period of hostility toward the former colonial power. This development was partly brought about by the Congo's agreement to pay $232 million to the Union Minière in compensation for the 1966 nationalization of the Belgian firm's mining concessions. Sympathy toward the Mobutu regime was shown by the United States when it selected Kinshasa as the only African capital to be visited by the Apollo 11 astronauts during their goodwill tour of the world.

Domestic Politics. After the last embers of the 1964–68 rebellions had finally been smothered, a sort of political torpor descended on the country. The execution of two minor rebel leaders during the early part of 1969 caused no visible stir.

The gradual disappearance of the first generation of Congolese political leaders was emphasized by the quiet death of Joseph Kasavubu, the country's first president, on March 24. On June 29, Moïse Tshombe died in Algeria, where he had been detained for two years. Three of the Congo's most resilient civilian personalities, Justin Bomboko, Victor Nendaka, and Etienne Tshisekedi, were removed from the cabinet on August 1 and given ambassadorial positions. Former Premier Cyrille Adoula, a man with no personal political following, was made foreign minister.

In May the MPR (Popular Revolutionary Movement), the political party established by Mobutu after he had seized power, held its second congress. The event seemed somewhat anticlimactic, especially in view of the regime's consistent refusal to authorize any competing political group. The suggestion that the MPR perhaps did not express "all popular wishes" came dramatically less than two weeks after the congress. A crowd of student demonstrators from Lovanium University clashed violently with the police on June 4. In the ensuing melee, at

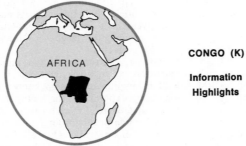

CONGO (K)

Information

Highlights

Area: 905,562 square miles (2,345,409 sq km).
Population: 16,730,000 (1968 est.).
Chief Cities (1969 est.): Kinshasa, the capital, 1,200,000; Lubumbashi, 225,000; Mbuji-Mayi, 200,000.
Government: *President*—Joseph Désiré Mobutu (took office Nov. 25, 1965). *Parliament*—Senate, 132 members; National Chamber of Representatives, 174 members.
Religious Faiths: Animists, 50% of population; Roman Catholics, 35%; Protestants, 7%; others, 8%.
Education: *Literacy rate* (1969), 58% of population. *Total school enrollment* (1964)—1,720,834 (primary, 1,592,225; secondary, 88,891; teacher-training, 19,248; technical/vocational, 17,334; university/higher, 3,136).

Finance (1968 est.): *Revenues,* $205,200,000; *expenditures,* $227,600,000; *monetary unit,* zaire (.50 zaires equal U. S.$1).
Gross National Product (1968 est.): $1,300,000,000.
National Income (1968): $942,000,000; *average annual income per person,* $56.
Economic Indexes (1967): *Cost of living,* 212 (1963=100).
Manufacturing (metric tons, 1966): Beer, 2,240,000 hectoliters; sugar (1967), 35,000; lumber, 150,000 cubic meters.
Crops (metric tons, 1967–68 crop year): Peanuts (1966), 112,000; coffee, 60,000; bananas, 50,000; cottonseed, 17,000; natural rubber, 30,500; tea, 3,000.
Minerals (metric tons, 1967): Cobalt (1966), 11,297 (ranks 1st among world producers); industrial diamonds, 12,890,000 metric carats (world rank, 1st); copper ore, 316,800; manganese ore, 139,600.
Foreign Trade (1967): *Exports,* $443,400,000 (chief exports, 1967: copper, $260,000,000; tin and concentrates, $167,000,000; palm oil, $22,272,000; diamonds, $23,536,000). *Imports,* $265,400,000 (chief imports, 1966: nonelectrical machinery, $45,628,000; road motor vehicles, $31,218,000). *Chief trading partners* (1967): Belgium-Luxembourg (took 30% of exports, supplied 32% of imports); Italy (took 12% of exports, supplied 8% of imports); United States (took 2% of exports, supplied 18% of imports).
Transportation: *Roads* (1964), 90,430 miles (145,529 km); *motor vehicles* (1967), 43,500; *railways* (1969), 3,108 miles (5,002 km); *national airline,* Air Congo; *principal airport,* Kinshasa.
Communications: *Telephones* (1968): 19,695; *television stations* (1968), 1; *television sets* (1968), 7,000; *radios* (1964), 200,000; *newspapers* (1966), 7.

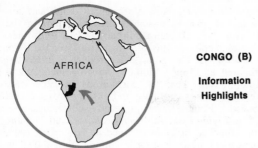

CONGO (B)

Information Highlights

Area: 132,046 square miles (342,000 sq km).
Population: 870,000 (1968 est.).
Chief Cities (1962 census): Brazzaville, the capital, 136,200.
Government: *President*—Maj. Marien Ngouabi (took office Jan. 2, 1969); *Premier*—Maj. Alfred Raoul.
Religious Faiths: Animists, 46% of population; Catholics, 32%.
Education: *Literacy rate* (1969), 25% of population. *Total school enrollment* (1965)—206,674 (primary, 186,544; secondary, 16,049; teacher-training, 516; technical/voca-

tional, 2,755; university/higher, 810).
Finance (1966 est.): *Revenues,* $33,400,000; *expenditures,* $33,400,000; *monetary unit,* CFA franc (246.85 CFA francs equal U. S.$1).
Gross National Product (1968 est.): $203,000,000.
National Income (1968): average annual income per person, $220.
Economic Indexes (1967): *Cost of living,* 116 (1963=100).
Manufacturing (metric tons, 1967): Sugar, 99,000; beer, 58,000 hectoliters; lumber (1966), 32,000 cubic meters.
Minerals (metric tons, 1967): Crude petroleum, 50,000; lead, 1,100; tin, 50; gold, 4,179 troy ounces.
Foreign Trade (1967): *Exports,* $47,519,000 (chief exports, 1967: wood, $20,093,000; diamonds, $15,961,000); *imports,* $81,993,000 (chief imports, 1967: nonelectrical machinery, $11,051,000; road motor vehicles, $6,080,000; petroleum products, $4,808,500). *Chief trading partners* (1967): France (took 15% of exports, supplied 54% of imports); Netherlands (took 21% of exports, supplied 4% of imports); West Germany (took 18% of exports, supplied 13% of imports).
Transportation: *Roads* (1969), 6,737 miles (10,839 km); *motor vehicles* (1966), 11,400 (automobiles 6,500); *railways* (1969), 548 miles (882 km); *national airline,* Lina Congo; *principal airport,* Brazzaville.
Communications: *Telephones* (1969): 9,000; *television stations* (1967), 1; *television sets* (1966), 500; *newspapers* (1966), 3 (daily circulation, 1,100).

least six students were shot and hundreds were arrested. Despite expressions of sympathy in other schools, the regime felt sufficiently secure to pardon the offenders later in the year.

Economy. The success of the 1967 monetary reform, which effectively stabilized the Congolese currency, was confirmed in 1969. Production, which had improved in 1968, continued to rise. Export agriculture returned almost to its 1958 level. The production of most minerals reached unprecedented levels. Copper production headed the list with an estimated 1969 output of 360,000 tons.

The $43.5 million Inga hydroelectric project, under way in 1969, will have an initial capacity of 106 megawatts from two generators by 1972. Development of Katanga's untapped mineral reserves by a Japanese group was also well on its way, with an additional annual production of 53,000 tons of copper expected to start in 1972. Several U. S. firms, including Pan-American Airways, the Union Carbide, General Foods, and Bell Telephone companies, are also involved in projects throughout the country. A rail line projected by a British-Belgian-Japanese consortium would establish a direct link between Katanga and the Congolese ports of Matadi and Banana. Construction of the line would lessen the Congo's reliance on the Portuguese-controlled Benguela railway.

During 1969 the country received financial assistance from the European Development Fund, the World Bank, Belgium, West Germany, and the United States.

The Congo's trade volume for 1969 was again expected to top the $1 billion mark, and the country's gold and foreign exchange reserves rose to about the $200 million level.

EDOUARD BUSTIN
Boston University

CONGO, Republic of the (Brazzaville)

Marien Ngouabi's political primacy was formally recognized on Jan. 2, 1969, when he became president of the republic and president of the National Council of the Revolution (CNR). The Brazzaville government continued to be challenged by factions willing to resort to open violence to overthrow it.

Politics. In early February, the government reported an attempted coup. Former Interior Minister Félix Mouzabakani and one of his aides were ar-

rested, and the army and the police force were purged and reorganized.

During the year, there were changes in the cabinet, the CNR, and the powerful CNR directorate. The CNR's youth organization, the Union Socialiste de la Jeunesse, was also reorganized. A revolutionary court of justice was created and was continuously in operation. Many politicians prominent during the term of former President Alphonse Massamba-Debat were imprisoned.

In November, 37 persons were arrested and charged with planning to assassinate the president and overthrow the government.

A series of strikes involving civil servants and industrial workers resulted in the dismissal of several government secretaries and the disbanding of the central offices of the two Congolese union federations. The trade unions were placed under the watchful eye of the sûreté (police).

Economic Development. The Congo continued to struggle with balance of payments deficits and a growing national debt. However, mineral prospectors submitted encouraging reports, and the newly opened potash complex at Holle was expected to bring in approximately $3.6 million in needed foreign exchange annually.

Foreign Relations. In November, Brazzaville ordered its border with Congo (Kinshasa) closed and put its troops on alert. The measures were taken after the Kinshasa president made an angry speech in response to charges by Brazzaville that Kinshasa was plotting against it.

Relations with France remained close, although somewhat strained. Prime Minister Alfred Raoul was viewed as the government's most effective spokesman in dealing with Paris.

EDOUARD BUSTIN
Boston University

CONGRESS. See UNITED STATES.

CONNECTICUT

A controversial tax program and race riots in Hartford made headlines in Connecticut during 1969.

Legislation. In June 1969 the state fiscal deficit of $154 million presented a tax crisis. After Gov. John Dempsey's veto of a rise in the sales tax from 3.5% to 6% and much bitter quarreling among state Democratic leaders, a $2.6 billion spending and

U.S.S. *FLYING FISH,* a nuclear-powered attack submarine, is launched at Groton, May 17. It was the 34th nuclear sub launched in Connecticut shipyards.

bonding budget was adopted at a special legislative session on July 21. The budget called for a tax increase of $540 million, the largest single increase in Connecticut's history. The sales tax was set at 5% and the cigarette tax was raised from 8¢ to 16¢ per pack, the highest in the nation.

The tax crisis illustrated a widening gulf between the governor and his party's state leaders. The 1969 legislature passed eight bills over the governor's veto. The most far-reaching was a measure that established a Legislative Management Committee providing a permanent staff for operations and research for the legislature. The act will give the legislature, which meets for only one five-month period every two years, fiscal independence from the governor in times when it is not in session. Also proposed was a constitutional amendment calling for annual legislative sessions. This proposal will be voted on in November 1970.

Elections. In the November 1969 municipal elections, Republicans won 97 contests and the Democrats 58. The Democrats were successful in Bridgeport, Waterbury, and New Haven, and Republican mayors were elected in Stamford, New Britain, and Hartford.

Transportation. The Connecticut bureau of highways released a 106-page report in November, entitled *Transportation 2020 in Connecticut.* The study, which divided the coming 50 years into 10-year segments, focused on problems, present and future, in the state's transportation facilities. Highlights of the report included discussions of the use of high-speed transportation and automation.

In November, New York and Connecticut announced a planned bi-state takeover of part of the bankrupt New Haven Railroad's West End lines. Congress approved this agreement on Dec. 15, 1969.

Economy. The gross state product in 1969 was estimated at $16.9 billion. Farm crop income was $165 million. The best cash crops in 1968 were dairy products, greenhouse and nursery produce, and tobacco. Four nuclear-powered submarines, the U. S. S. *Flying Fish, Narwhal, Seahorse,* and *Trepang* were launched or commissioned at Groton in 1969. Connecticut ranked fourth among the states in prime defense contracts awarded in 1969.

Education. A record 653,000 students were enrolled in public schools in 1969. The 1969 General Assembly raised state aid for public schools to $200 per pupil. Despite efforts to increase enrollment of black students, there were only 1,240 black students (2%) among the 56,759 undergraduates in 25 of Connecticut's leading colleges and universities.

Riots. Lagging urban renewal and an article in the *Hartford Times* on August 31 about the Puerto Ricans were blamed in part for disorders in Negro and Puerto Rican sections of Hartford in June and September. The riots in September, considered the worst in the city's history, resulted in a 3-day city-wide curfew. Local police were aided by state troopers in coping with the outbreak of fires, looting, and rioting. Property damage was estimated at $1.3 million.

GEORGE ADAMS
Connecticut State Library

——— **CONNECTICUT • Information Highlights** ———

Area: 5,009 square miles (12,973 sq km).
Population: 2,998,000 (1969 est.).
Chief Cities (Jan., 1969 est.): Hartford, the capital, 159,000; Bridgeport, 150,000; New Haven, 141,000; Stamford, 111,000; Waterbury, 106,000.
Government: *Chief Officers*—governor, John Dempsey (Democrat); lt. gov., Athlio R. Frassinelli (D); secy. of state, Mrs. Ella T. Grasso (D); atty. gen., Robert K. Killian (D); treas., Gerald A. Lamb; supt. of pub. instr., William J. Sandus; chief justice, John Hamilton King. *General Assembly*—Senate, 36 members (24 Democrats, 12 Republicans); House of Representatives, 177 members (110 D, 67 R).
Education: *School enrollment* (1968–69)—public elementary, 402,000 pupils (17,200 teachers); public secondary, 223,000 pupils (12,700 teachers); nonpublic schools, 119,100 pupils (6,010 teachers); college and university (fall 1967), 95,795 students. *Public school expenditures* (1967–68)—$458,350,000 ($809 per pupil); average teacher's salary, $8,400.
Public Finance (fiscal year 1968): *Revenues,* $921,621,000 (general sales and gross receipts taxes, $158,826,000; motor fuel tax, $76,877,000; federal funds, $203,649,000). *Expenditures,* $935,575,000 (education, $125,014,000; health, welfare, and safety, $217,300,000; highways, $168,675,000). *State debt,* $1,444,568,000 (June 30, 1968).
Personal Income (1969): $12,611,000,000; average annual income per person, $4,256.
Public Assistance (fiscal year 1969): $76,582,168 to 86,461 recipients (aged, $8,113,902; dependent children, $57,782,396).
Labor Force (employed persons, August 1969): *Agricultural,* 18,000; *nonagricultural* (wage and salary earners), 1,161,630 (40% manufacturing, 18% trade, 12.2% government). *Unemployed persons* (Aug. 1969)—59,400.
Manufacturing (1966): Value added by manufacture, $6,184,996,000 (transoortation equipment, $1,272,800,000; non-electrical machinery, $951,803,000; electrical machinery, $628,114,000; fabricated metals, $587,478,000; primary metals, $569,227,000; food and products, $219,866,000).
Agriculture (1967): Cash farm income (1969), $165,000,000 (livestock, $93,444,000; crops, $66,400,000; govt. pavments, 887,000). *Chief crops* (tons)—Corn for silage, 752,000; hay, 239,000; tobacco, 4,982.
Fisheries (1967): *Commercial catch,* 5,200,000 pounds ($1,900,000). *Leading species*—Blackback flounder, 831,000 pounds ($58,000); scup or porgy, 519,000 pounds ($85,000).
Transportation: *Roads* (1968), 18,408 miles (29,618 km); *motor vehicles* (1969), 1,734,972; *railroads* (1968), 3,814 track miles (6,137 km); *airports* (1969), 4.
Communications (1968): *Telephones* (1967), 1,772,900; *television stations,* 9; *radio stations,* 37 AM; 15 FM; *newspapers,* 26 (daily circulation, 929,980).

Dump and chemicals (*middle background*) mar view of Mount Greylock, Mass.

conservation

The year 1969 brought changed leadership and reorientation of national policies to the field of conservation as Congress confirmed President Nixon's appointments to the major conservation agencies. Budgetary limitations seriously curtailed conservational actions involving allocation of funds; as a result, few significant proposals were consummated. Records of various hearings and statements by the new administration, however, indicated that strong support for actions to maintain and improve environmental quality ranked as a national policy.

New Leadership. The two U. S. government departments most responsible for conservation of the nation's natural resources received new leadership in 1969. Clifford M. Hardin, chancellor of the University of Nebraska and agricultural economist, was confirmed as secretary of agriculture. Walter J. Hickel, former governor of Alaska, was confirmed as secretary of the interior after withstanding severe attacks by groups and individuals who believed his record revealed inadequate personal dedication to conservation. Other Interior Department appointments were: Russell E. Train, under-secretary; Leslie L. Glasgow, assistant secretary for Fish and Wildlife, Parks, and Marine Resources; Hollis M. Dole, assistant secretary for Mineral Resources; Carl L. Klein, assistant secretary for Water Quality

and Research; and Harrison Loesch, assistant secretary for Public Land Management.

Environmental Quality. In 1969 conservationists saw the fruition of nationwide concern over the deterioration of the environment and a fast growing popular movement for the preservation of environmental quality. The ecological view of the environment as an integrated and interacting totality gained popular appeal. As a result, an "ecological movement" promoting positive action for protecting environmental quality against assaults by bulldozers, pollution by industrial wastes, and population encroachments won support from university students and faculty as well as new and old conservation organizations.

At the federal level, maintenance and improvement of the environment became a national policy in 1969. Outgoing President Johnson, in his January 16 report to Congress, said, "More than ever, American people realize that purposeful action is required to ensure an environment we can all enjoy. Many of our rivers are still open sewers, our atmosphere often unfit to breathe, and much of our land littered with discarded junk." On May 29, President Nixon noted, "We have become victims of our own technological genius. Together we have damaged the environment—and together we can improve it."

215

WAWONA TUNNEL TREE in Yosemite National Park fell during winter of 1968–69. The famous sequoia redwood, 234 feet tall, was estimated to be more than 1,500 years old. (*Below*) Girl climbs from roadway that passed through tree, shown at left in an old photo.

WIDE WORLD

UPI

A cabinet-level Environmental Quality Council composed of six department secretaries (Agriculture; Commerce; Health, Education, and Welfare; Interior; Housing and Urban Development; and Transportation) was created by executive order.

Parks and Other National Areas. At the end of his tenure, President Johnson approved the addition of 384,500 acres to the National Park System. Marble Canyon National Monument of 26,000 acres was established in Arizona. In Utah, 49,000 acres were added to Arches National Monument and 215,000 acres to Capitol Reef National Monument. Katmai National Monument, Alaska, gained 94,500 acres.

Congress approved a bill to designate 508,320 acres in Idaho as the Sawtooth National Recreation Area and authorized $30 million for land purchases. In California, Desolation Wilderness, a 63,469-acre tract, was established in Eldorado National Forest, and Ventana Wilderness of 94,728 acres was established in Los Padres National Forest. The proposed Gateway National Recreation Area in New York-New Jersey, planned to include Breezy Point, Jamaica Bay, and Sandy Hook, was under study for designation as part of the Interior Department's "Parks for People" program to increase facilities near dense populations.

Threat to Everglades National Park. A proposal to build a 38-square-mile international jetport on the north side of Everglades National Park in Florida caused an outcry from conservationists who sought to prevent its construction. A joint study by the departments of the Interior and Transportation focused attention on probable adverse impacts of the jetport on the wilderness park. In September, Secretary of the Interior Hickel announced his opposition and was quoted as saying that "the jetport ... together with resultant commercial development could destroy Everglades National Park and the general ecology of South Florida."

Santa Barbara Oil Spill. The year's worst natural resource disaster began on January 28 when a petroleum drilling operation in a federal lease area of California's Santa Barbara Channel suffered a well "blowout," releasing oil into the sea. The resultant oil slick caused widespread damage to beaches and marine life along 30 miles of the Santa Barbara coastline. On February 7, Secretary Hickel ordered all drilling halted. The Off Shore Outer Continental Shelf Lands Act of 1953 was amended to provide greater protection against such disasters and to make oil companies liable for costs of cleaning oil spills. Twenty-one thousand acres were designated as the Santa Barbara Ecological Preserve.

On June 2, Secretary Hickel authorized the resumption of offshore drilling in the channel although many residents of the coastal area and conservationists continued to seek a complete halt to the operation. (See also ZOOLOGY.)

Alaska Oil Rush. The spectacular 1969 oil rush in Alaska, in which the state leased 175 parcels of land for $900 millions, caused major concern among conservation groups. Fear was expressed that the North Slope wilderness of Alaska would be ruined. Opposition was also directed at a proposed 800-mile pipeline to extend from Prudhoe Bay on the northern

WIDE WORLD

POISON killed millions of fish in the Rhine River in June. A West German official (*right*) inspects the loss.

coast to near Valdez in the south. The Department of the Interior established a task force to prepare guidelines for minimizing damage to the environment both in the North Slope oil area and along the pipeline which would cross federal lands. By October the oil companies planning the pipeline had agreed to strong measures for protection of fish and other wildlife. (See also ALASKA.)

Great Plains Conservation Program. Conservation actions carried out under the Great Plains Program were authorized for extension during the year. In 1969 erosion damage was recorded on 595,000 acres, the lowest figure in 35 years. New land conservation contracts were extended to 5.8 million acres, bringing the total to over 62 million acres. However, the new *Conservation Needs Inventory,* published in 1969, revealed that there remained about 5½ million acres of Great Plains cropland that should be converted to permanent grass or other non-crop usage.

Wild and Scenic Rivers. Twenty-seven rivers were identified for study as possible additions to the Wild and Scenic Rivers System established in 1968. By agreement, 18 of the studies were to be undertaken by the Department of the Interior and 9 by the Department of Agriculture. The system now preserves 700 miles of river shorelines. The additional rivers under study would add 3,800 miles.

Air and Water Quality Control. Conservation of pure air received attention in 1969 as Congress extended the Clean Air Act and provided funds for continued research. The automobile's internal combustion engine as a pollution source came under direct attack when a bill was introduced in the California legislature to ban internal combustion engines. In Congress an amendment was proposed to the Clean Air Act that would have banned internal combustion engines after 1978. In February, Health, Education, and Welfare Secretary Robert H. Finch announced guidelines for control of air quality from sulfur oxides and particulates.

Secretary Hickel reported that all 50 states had submitted water quality standards as required under the Federal Water Pollution Control Act. The Water Quality Improvement Act of 1969, designed to clean the nation's waterways by tightening restrictions on vessel sewage, thermal pollution, and oil spills, received favorable hearings in Congress.

Pesticides. Concern over the accumulative adverse effects of persistent chemicals in pesticides and herbicides increased, especially when excessive DDT residue was found in Great Lakes coho salmon. In July the Department of Agriculture ordered reductions in the use of DDT and other persistent chemicals. On November 12, the Nixon administration announced a far-reaching plan to phase out all nonessential use of DDT within two years. In the meantime, an attempt is being made to develop control chemicals that will be self-destructing.

Proposed Revision of the Mining Law. A bill to revise the basic mining law of 1872 and extend the concept of leasing of mineral lands was introduced in Congress this year. The new bill, the Mining and Minerals Policy Act of 1969, was an outgrowth of a commission established in 1964 to study the need for revision of the nation's mining laws. The new bill is expected to stimulate extensive debate.

Golden Eagle Passport. The Golden Eagle Passport Provision of the Land and Water Conservation Fund Act of 1964, which was repealed by Congress in 1968, apparently was to be restored in 1969. The Senate bill, which gained strong support, would provide for a $10 annual fee and authorize promotion. The passport would admit the purchaser to federal outdoor recreation facilities.

(See also POLLUTION.)

J. GRANVILLE JENSEN
Oregon State University

AMERICAN FALLS in the Niagara River were temporarily stilled in 1969 by a coffer dam as engineers studied means of blocking further erosion.

consumer affairs

A set of proposals hailed as a "consumers' bill of rights" was placed before Congress by President Richard Nixon in 1969, a year marked by increasing emphasis on consumerism, or consumer protection. Inflation and poverty were two other issues dominating news in consumer affairs during the year.

Nixon's message to Congress on October 30 outlined a variety of proposals to protect the buyer against deceptive sales practices and inferior merchandise. He called on Congress to enact a law to enable consumers, as individuals or in groups, to sue in federal court for damages resulting from certain kinds of fraudulent practices. The proposal would cover such practices as making false statements about price reductions, representing old goods as new, making unwarranted claims for products, advertising worthless warranties, and forcing customers to pay for or return unsolicited goods. Nixon also recommended the creation of a new office of consumer affairs in the executive branch and a new division of consumer protection in the Department of Justice.

CONSUMERISM

Calvin Coolidge's dictum that the business of America is business reflected the overwhelmingly producer-oriented society of his time. Since then substantial efforts have been exerted to mitigate the power of producers.

The Rise of Consumerism. At present a "bandwagon" phenomenon is carrying consumer protection to new heights. The Democratic Study Group, an informal alliance of liberal congressmen, in mid-1969 listed 30 pieces of legislation that should be introduced to regulate business in its relations with the public. Shortly thereafter, the U. S. Chamber of Commerce noted that 86 major consumer protection bills had been introduced in Congress and that more were being added daily.

President Nixon also boarded the consumer bandwagon. Not only did he maintain the position of special assistant to the president for consumer affairs created by President Johnson, but he sent his "consumer bill of rights" to Congress aimed at increasing the power of that position.

Reasons for the Rise. The overwhelming cause of rising consumerism seems to be that society finally has solved the "level of production" problem. This could be a "watershed" in U. S. history, as important for the nation's development as the

closing of the frontier about 1890. So long as depression and unemployment were dominant fears, few people wanted to place impediments in the path of business. However, with the advent of "superheated" economic conditions, society suddenly can afford to protect consumers at the expense of business growth. Since the economy must be slowed down anyway, this can be done by increasing consumer protection.

Superheated economic conditions more or less automatically call forth hostile consumer reactions. Workers become careless when they can obtain alternative jobs without effort. Producers become careless when they can sell whatever they turn out. Services become unsatisfactory when the demand for them exceeds their supply. Such conditions of excess demand combined with unfavorable publicity regarding product safety, exaggerated claims made in advertising and sales that lead consumers to expect better products than are delivered—all these factors have caused the influential middle class to demand improvement.

New Legal Climate. A decade ago a power lawnmower manufacturer would have protected himself by providing customers with a warranty expressly limiting his liability to replacing defective

VIRGINIA HARRINGTON WRIGHT KNAUER was appointed by President Nixon to succeed Betty Furness as special assistant to the President for consumer affairs on April 9, 1969. At the time of her appointment she was vice chairman of the Republican party's city committee in Philadelphia and, since early 1968, had been serving as director of the Pennsylvania Bureau of Consumer Protection. In October 1969 she announced government plans to coordinate the activities of federal agencies concerned with consumer protection.

Mrs. Knauer was born in Philadelphia, Pa., on March 28, 1915. After graduating from the University of Pennsylvania, she studied at the Royal Academy of Fine Arts in Florence, Italy. She became active in Republican politics in 1952. From 1960 to 1967 she was a member of the Philadelphia City Council.

parts. He also would have hidden behind the legal doctrine of "privity," which, for liability to exist, requires direct contact between an injured consumer and a negligent manufacturer. (Since purchasers usually buy from stores rather than directly from manufacturers, "privity" shielded producers from consumers.) Finally, an injured buyer would have had to take legal action against the manufacturer on the basis of negligence in tort, whereby the manufacturer must be proved negligent in his production and inspection systems.

All this is now changed. In one series of court decisions the doctrine of "privity" has been eliminated, and producers no longer are shielded merely because customers bought from an intermediary rather than directly. Another series of decisions established the doctrine of "strict liability" in tort, which only requires showing that a specific error of manufacturing or design led to an injury.

The legal meaning of this doctrine is that the burden of proving blame or fault has been removed from the plaintiff. The only question is who should bear the cost of an injury. The social and economic meaning of "strict liability" is implied in a 1963 opinion that indicated that the cost of accidents should be born by customers as a whole in the form of higher prices for safer products rather than by individual victims of lower-priced products. In addition, courts tend to look on certain types of claims in advertising and labels as express warranties. Sweeping claims of high-quality workmanship and trouble-free economical operation provide dissatisfied customers with a basis for compensation for damages and recovery of outlay.

New Legislation. More obvious than the changing court climate are the new legislative and administrative changes favoring consumers. These include the National Traffic and Motor Vehicle Safety Act (1966), the Fair Packaging and Labeling Act (1966), and the Consumer Credit Protection Act (1968). These measures were fought in turn by the automotive, food, and banking and finance industries. In 1968 the tobacco industry was forced to print health hazard warnings on cigarette packages and California passed rather stringent auto pollution emission legislation. New York State experimented in 1969 with a "unit pricing" requirement that put food prices on a per-unit weight basis rather than a per-package basis. Nearly all of these measures have weaknesses and deficiencies; nevertheless, they reflect a willingness to challenge huge vested interests.

The Future of Consumerism. So long as the economy remains "overheated" (meaning that more jobs are available than there are persons to fill them), additional consumer protection can be obtained with little or no reduction of real income (income adjusted for price level changes). In such a situation consumerism probably will grow until real income becomes threatened. Should an economic recession occur, however, concern probably will shift from consumerism to expansion. Then the current trend toward consumer protection would stop and perhaps reverse itself. This concept of "welfare balance" (between real income and consumer protection) suggests that consumerism will grow in the developed nations in the foreseeable future, but will make little headway elsewhere.

Protection "Lag." For short periods of up to about five years, "welfare balance" must be qualified by the problem of lag. Even if a recession should

THE NEW YORK TIMES

THIS CALCULATOR helps shoppers to figure prices. A merchants' association gave away pocket versions.

occur, pressure would continue for increased consumer protection since consumer protection agencies grow less rapidly than the industries they must police. A report submitted in July 1969 by seven senior U. S. Food and Drug Administration officials to the FDA commissioner concluded that the government does a completely inadequate job of protecting consumers from dangerous drugs, tainted foods, and household products that can cause injury or death. It was estimated that 2 to 10 million Americans are made ill each year by eating tainted food. The report also noted that pesticides, flammable fabrics, electrical appliances, and other potentially hazardous products cause an estimated 18,000 deaths and 22 million injuries annually.

These indictments indicate that much additional consumer protection is needed merely to catch up with the backlog of past economic and technological developments. Even if a depression should threaten, consumerism would maintain much momentum until greater protection was achieved.

Business Reaction. Business tends to respond to rising consumerism in several ways. One way is to deny everything charged against it. Others are to blame wrongdoing on small marginal companies, arguing that they are the ones who must cut corners to survive; undertake a public relations campaign to try to modify public opinion; weaken the legislation, as was done with the "truth-in-packaging" law; discredit the critics; or launch a fact-finding committee to discover what really needs to be improved. If all else fails, business must then actually do something to improve the situation.

In November 1969 a study committee of the U. S. Chamber of Commerce outlined a broad program of voluntary business reforms. It advised managers to reexamine their practices, especially in advertising and marketing.

Long-Range Effects. Unfortunately, consumer protection is expensive to implement and risky because of what may go wrong. For these reasons consumerism promises to be an additional force contributing to industrial concentration and the elimination of small firms. It may become one more non-tariff barrier to competitive imports. Its inevitable effect may be to raise prices to consumers.

INFLATION

The inflationary trend continued unabated in 1969. The U. S. consumer price index rose by 4.2% between 1967 and 1968, and by 5.3% between September 1968 and August 1969. The rate of inflation quickened later in 1969, and no end seemed in sight. The rise in interest rates drastically increased the cost of home ownership, which in turn caused a drop in much-needed housing construction.

Effects of Inflation. Inflation reduces the real value of income. In 1969 labor unions fought hard for wage increases only to find their gains wiped out by rising prices. Frustrated, some groups reacted by demanding greater control over producers. Others responded by trying to beat the rate of inflation by raising one's wages as fast as prices went up.

Experiences of inflation-racked foreign countries suggest that those who gain by inflation usually include the skilled, the unionized, and the self-employed, while those hurt by it include the unskilled, the unemployed, the retired, government employees, and non-unionized clerical workers.

Control. There is no inherent reason for inflation in the U. S. economy if politicians have the resolve to stop it. On the other hand, the high interest rates which make housing so expensive may exist for a long time. The rates are caused by the tremendous worldwide demand for capital.

Unfortunately, inflation control is complicated by an inverse relationship between the rates of inflation and of unemployment. For example, in 1961 the annual rate of price rise was a low 1.1%, but the black unemployment rate was 12% and the white unemployment rate was 6%. By the end of 1968 unemployment fell to about half the 1961 levels, but the inflation rate was over 4%. Obviously, national policy is caught between the twin evils of inflation and unemployment, both of which hurt the poor. Humane inflation control needs to be coupled with an attack on unemployment. (See also ECONOMY OF THE U. S.; LABOR.)

POVERTY

The most shocking consumer news during the year concerned the extent of hunger in the United States. Most citizens, complacent about their own prosperity, were unaware of poverty around them.

Widespread Hunger. A 1968 CBS documentary, "Hunger in America," first exposed evidence of the problem to the mass of society. The initial reaction of politicians, government officials, and some citizens was denial and denunciation. However, the Citizens' Board of Inquiry into Hunger and Malnutrition in the United States confirmed the CBS allegations.

Hunger and malnutrition exist in nearly every state, with the greatest incidence in the rural South, among migrant workers, Indians, Eskimos, and, increasingly, among the big-city poor. Research showed that protein deprivation during early youth tends to cause brain damage, which in turn reduces future earning power. Thus, malnutrition instigates a vicious circle of self-perpetuating poverty. Rising unemployment and inflation are likely to worsen the malnutrition problem.

The "Hidden" Poor. The nation's relief rolls have been rising almost 10% a year, and most of the increase is in a single category—aid to families with dependent children. This trend during a period of unprecedented low unemployment, has caused much consternation among economists. One interpretation is that the unsuspected "reservoir" of hidden poverty is emerging faster than national income is growing. This, it is argued, results from increasing awareness by poor persons of their welfare "rights" and from liberalization in the administration of government welfare programs.

Antipoverty programs have promoted welfare applications by the poor, and private groups such as the National Welfare Rights Organization have encouraged poor people to demand their welfare "rights." Many explanations of rising welfare costs have been suggested but all of them seem to contain certain deficiencies. Poverty amidst plenty remains a national enigma. (See also POVERTY.)

Conference. In December, President Nixon's White House Conference on Food, Nutrition, and Health met in Washington, D. C., for three days. The conference, which reflected Nixon's concern with the hunger and nutrition problems of millions of Americans, disappointed some leaders of the poor who had hoped for stronger action than the President proposed.

WARREN J. BILKEY
University of Wisconsin

COPPER. See MINING.
COST OF LIVING. See CONSUMER AFFAIRS.

COSTA RICA

During 1969—a generally encouraging year economically—attention in Costa Rica turned largely to preparations for the 1970 presidential and congressional elections. It was obvious early in the year that at least two former presidents, José Figueres and Mario Echandi, planned to be candidates; but as the year wore on, they encountered opposition within their own political organizations, which caused doubt about their chances of success.

Political Maneuvering. Under Costa Rica's multiparty system, the nation had been governed since 1966 by President José Trejos, who had won election with the backing of a coalition of parties known collectively as the National Unification party. The Legislative Assembly, on the other hand, was in control of the opposition National Liberation party, a situation that led to frequent clashes between the administration and the legislature.

In January, Second Vice President Calvo Sánchez resigned to run for the presidency, seeking the support of the Unification party coalition. The leadership refused to back him, however, and subsequently Rafael Calderón Guardia, leader of the National Republican faction in the coalition, announced his support of Mario Echandi. When the Unification party convention was held in early September, Echandi had the backing of a majority of the delegates, but

Calvo Sánchez was unwilling to accept their decision and withdrew to form a new group called the National Front. The National Union party, another major faction within the coalition, refused to announce immediate support for either candidate.

In the meantime, José Figueres was having serious troubles with his National Liberation party, some of whose members had also quit to form a new faction. Figueres won his party's endorsement as a presidential candidate at a convention in August, but he had to threaten to withdraw from the race to secure party approval of his choices of running mates. On Feb. 1, 1970, however, Figueres made an impressive political comeback, winning the presidential election by a large margin.

Domestic Development. It was announced in July that Costa Rican exports in 1968—a year of economic crises—had actually risen by 20%, making the country's prospects for economic growth appear better than had been thought. Coffee, bananas, livestock, and sugar had all contributed to the rise. Markets for Costa Rican goods continued strong in 1969.

The Instituto Costarricense de Electricidad (ICE)—the government firm controlling power, light, and communications—announced two ambitious new projects calling for an expenditure of

$37.5 million, and the International Bank for Reconstruction and Development announced that it was lending $18.5 million to help finance them. The first project was to involve an addition to the existing Rio Macho power plant and an extension of its transmission lines. The second was to provide for the installation of 26,500 new telephones, 300 long-distance lines, and a telex system of 500 lines.

International Affairs. Some tension arose between Costa Rica and its neighbor Panama, owing to the operations of Panamanian guerrilla forces at or near the Costa Rican border, particularly early in the year. Although the border was occasionally closed by Panama, no serious trouble developed.

Two international conferences of note were held in Costa Rica during the year. In February, the economic ministers of Central America met in San José to attempt to work out the problems facing the Central American Common Market (CACM). In November, the Organization of American States (OAS) held a conference in San José to consider the proposed Inter-American Convention on Human Rights.

ROBERT J. ALEXANDER
Rutgers University

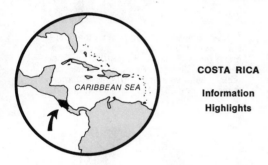

COSTA RICA

Information Highlights

Area: 19,575 square miles (50,700 sq km).
Population: 1,640,000 (1968 est.).
Chief Cities (1966 census): San José, the capital, 182,961; San Sebastián (1963 census), 23,166.
Government: *President*—José Joaquín Trejos Fernández (took office May 8, 1966). *Legislature* (unicameral)—Legislative Assembly, 57 members (party seating, 1969: National Liberation party, 29; National Unification party, 26; others, 2).
Religious Faith: Roman Catholic, 75.9% of population.
Education: *Literacy rate* (1963), 84.3% of population aged 15 and over. *Total school enrollment* (1965)—350,743 (primary, 283,210; secondary, 50,711; teacher-training, 2,108; technical/vocational, 7,485; university/higher, 7,229).
Finance (1967): *Revenues*, $81,737,000; *expenditures*, $102,-537,000; *public debt*, $186,707,000; *monetary unit,* colon (6.62 colones equal U. S.$1).
Gross National Product (1968): $764,955,000.
National Income (1968): $629,607,000; *average annual income per person*, $383.
Cost of Living Index (1967): 104 (1963=100).
Manufacturing and Processing (metric tons, 1967): Sugar, 145,000; cement (1965), 118,900.
Crops (metric tons, 1967–68 crop year): Bananas, 512,000; coffee, 76,800; dry beans, 19,000; cacao beans, 7,400.
Minerals (metric tons, 1966): Salt, 2,000.
Foreign Trade (1968): *Exports,* $172,000,000 (chief exports, 1967: coffee, $54,841,000; bananas, $31,486,000; cacao, $3,400,000); *imports,* $214,000,000 (chief imports, 1967: textile yarn and fabrics, $18,008,000; electrical machinery, $13,323,000; motor vehicles, $11,459,000). *Chief trading partners* (1967): United States (took 48% of exports, supplied 39% of imports); West Germany.
Transportation: *Roads* (1964), 11,931 miles (19,201 km); *motor vehicles* (1967), 45,700 (automobiles, 29,800); *railways* (1965), 437 miles (703 km); *merchant vessels* (1967), 1 (5,000 gross registered tons); *national airline,* LACSA; *principal airport,* El Coco (San José).
Communications: *Telephones* (1968): 27,498; *television stations* (1967), 3; *television sets* (1968), 75,000; *radios* (1965), 130,000; *newspapers* (1966), 4 (daily circulation, 87,000).

COTTON

The United States produced a cotton crop of 10,080,000 bales (each bale weighing about 500 pounds or 225 kg) in 1969. This was 5% smaller than the 1968 crop. Texas retained its position as the leading cotton-producing state. Other major producers were California, Mississippi, and Arkansas.

The 1969 cotton crop was harvested from 11,-094,000 acres (4,437,600 hectares), 10% more than the previous year. The larger acreage was planted because acreage diversion was not required under the federal government's cotton program and payments were not made for voluntary diversion.

The average yield per acre was 436 pounds (198 kg) of lint (unginned cotton), 80 pounds (36 kg) less than the 1968 average. Destruction by insect pests was responsible for the decline in yield.

U. S. Stocks. Cotton stocks carried over into the 1969–1970 marketing year totaled 6,507,600 running bales, an increase of nearly 60,000 bales from the previous year. Stocks were up for the first time in three years.

World Production. World cotton production totaled 52,777,000 bales in 1969, down 245,000 bales from the preceding year but up 2,231,000 bales from the 1963–1967 average. Production increased in all continents except North America and Asia.

In North America cotton production dropped from 14,418,000 bales in 1968 to 13,335,000 bales in 1969. Declines were reported in all the major North American producing nations.

South American production totaled 5,263,000 bales, an increase of 213,000 bales, or 4%, over the preceding year. The crops in Brazil and Columbia were larger than in 1968. The European crop totaled 867,000 bales.

African production totaled 5,601,000 bales, an increase of 381,000 or 7% over 1968. The United Arab Republic accounted for most of this increase. Production in Asia totaled 18,051,000 bales, a drop of 50,000 bales. Declines in China and Turkey offset gains in India, Iran, and Pakistan.

NICHOLAS KOMINUS
Kominus Agri-Info Associates

UPI

Actress Sharon Tate and four other persons were murdered at her Los Angeles home (*above*) August 8. (*Left*) Miss Tate with film director Roman Polanski at their 1968 wedding. (*Right*) Charles Manson, one of the cultists indicted.

WIDE WORLD

UPI

CRIME

Crime continued in 1969 to be a major—perhaps the major—domestic concern in the United States. Public unease about lawlessness, however, remained unfocused in regard to possible cures. Among many people, the solution was seen to lie in increased penalties for offenders and more restricted use of probation and parole. For other persons, the crime problem was viewed as an inevitable consequence of social conditions. For them, housing and welfare reforms, improved race relations, and resolution of the Vietnam conflict were believed necessary before crime rates would decrease.

The crime picture was further complicated by growing concern with the precise manner in which special kinds of criminal behaviors should be handled. Almost a quarter of the state legislatures enacted laws to deal with college campus militancy, although the National Commission on the Causes and Prevention of Violence insisted that this was more likely to aggravate than to ease the problem.

Marihuana. Statutes against marihuana use—violation of which accounts in large measure for the 800% increase in juvenile delinquency arrests in the last decade—came in for much debate in 1969.

Dr. Stanley F. Yolles, director of the National Institute of Mental Health, reported to a congressional committee that at least 8 million Americans had used marihuana one or more times. Opposing an escalation of penalties against marihuana use, Dr. Yolles told the committee: "I know of no clearer instance in which punishment for an infraction of the law is more harmful than the crime." Shortly thereafter, Dr. Margaret Mead, nationally known anthropologist, called for the legalization of marihuana, maintaining that the picture of an adult deploring marihuana use while holding "a cigarette in one hand and a drink in the other" epitomized hypocritical attitudes in the country.

Opponents of these views pointed to the 7 million alcoholics in the United States and insisted that failure to control marihuana use would add an intolerable social burden to U. S. life. Potential dangers of the drug when used by automobile drivers and the absence of research establishing the long-term effects of marihuana were also cited in opposition to relaxation of current laws.

Meanwhile, continuing research on narcotics and hallucinogenics filled in some informational gaps. Dr. Robert Hogan, an assistant professor of psychology at Johns Hopkins University, reported that personality studies of frequent marihuana users showed that they are most typically self-confident, socially poised, and skilled in interpersonal relations. "But they also tend toward narcissism, self-aggrandizement, and overconcern with personal pleasures and diversion," Dr. Hogan noted. In regard to LSD, scientists during the year sharply challenged the accuracy of earlier reports maintaining that the drug produces chromosome breakage, although there was continuing agreement that the erratic behavioral effects produced by LSD made it a dangerous drug.

Efforts by the federal government to deal with marihuana traffic resulted in the midyear inauguration of Operation Intercept, an attempt to scrutinize with great care the contents of vehicles crossing the 2,500-mile border between Mexico and the United States to deter drug smuggling. The deputy attorney general, Richard G. Kleindienst, had indicated the aim of the program: "If we cut off the supply at its sources, we will drive prices sky-high and effectively take the drug out of the hands of 90% of the kids." There had been some fear, however, that drying up of marihuana supplies might turn some youths toward "hard" drugs, including physically addictive substances such as heroin. Protests from the Mexican government about undue interference with tourist trade and other international travel led to revocation of the intercept action within a month. (See also Narcotics and Hallucinogens.)

"Crimes Without Victims." Public interest was being aroused on issues related to so-called "crimes without victims"—offenses such as consensual homosexuality, prostitution, abortion, and gambling. California and Colorado led the way in altering abortion laws to make it easier for a woman to obtain medical aid in eliminating a fetus if its birth would cause serious danger to the mother's health, an item variously defined under the new laws.

A report, "The Right to Abortion: A Psychiatric View," drawn up by the Committee on Psychiatry and Law of the Group for the Advancement of Psychiatry, was issued in October. It recommended that "abortion when performed by a licensed physician should be entirely removed from the domain of criminal law." Opponents of liberalization of abortion laws maintained that destruction of a fetus is equivalent to murder of an innocent person.

Statutes outlawing homosexuality were criticized by a federal study group composed of doctors, lawyers, and behavioral scientists who advocated that the United States follow the lead of Britain and abolish laws forbidding private homosexual relations among consenting adults. The panel estimated that at least 3 to 4 million adults in the United States are predominantly homosexual and insisted that their behavior presents a major problem for the society "largely because of the amount of injustice and suffering entailed in it." However, a Louis Harris public opinion poll indicated that public aversion to nonconforming behavior such as homosexuality has remained rather constant in the United States in the last four years. Thus, 63% of the public feel that homosexual activity is "harmful" to the American way of life. Male homosexual behavior is illegal in all states except Illinois.

Crime Statistics. Official crime statistics continued to show a sharp rise in the amount of serious crime in the United States. The 1968 *Uniform Crime Reports,* issued by the Federal Bureau of Investigation, listed 4.7 million serious crimes during the year. The distribution was as follows: murder, 13,650; forcible rape, 31,060; robbery, 261,730; aggravated assault, 282,400; burglary, 1,828,900; larceny of $50 and over, 1,271,000; auto theft, 777,800. The total of serious crimes rose 17% from 1967.

The *Uniform Crime Reports* also indicated that the risk of becoming a victim of a serious crime in the United States had risen 16% from the previous year and that 2 out of every 100 persons in the population were likely to be victimized in a year. The *Reports* noted that 64 law enforcement officers were killed by felons in the year, most of these in crimes involving the use of firearms.

Guns also figured prominently as weapons employed in perpetrating murders. The breakdown of murder statistics for the year showed the following weapon-use pattern: handguns, 50%; rifles, 6%; shotguns, 9%; cutting or stabbing, 19%; other weapons, such as clubs or poison, 8%; personal weapons, such as hands, fists, or feet, 8%.

The FBI report indicated further that some 63% of the perpetrators of crime were rearrested within five years of release from correctional institutions. This figure rises to 73% of the offenders were under 25 years of age at the time of their release from correctional status.

Early 1969 crime figures, while showing a somewhat less precipitate rise in the crime rate, offered little encouragement that any abrupt reversal in the upward spiral is soon likely. They indicated a further rise of 11% in major crimes in the first nine months of the year.

Examination of criminal offenses during the year by the National Commission on the Causes and Prevention of Violence produced previously unknown information. Looking at the consequences of the possession of weapons by Detroit householders for self-protection, George D. Newton and Franklin E. Zimring found that more persons were killed in household accidents involving firearms in a single year than were murdered by house robbers or house burglars in a five-year period. Similar studies by commission researchers showed that a majority of homicides are committed by persons known to each other, supporting the ironical observation that a person is safer on a dark street than in his own home.

SPECIAL GUARD patrols New York's West Side neighborhood. Hired by a local block association, he is representative of the many special measures that city residents are taking for their own safety.

Also, commission consultants, probing American history, found reason to believe that contemporary times probably are no more violent than earlier periods. Recollections of bygone times tend to be colored, a commission report noted, "by a kind of historical amnesia.... Probably all nations have this tendency to sweeten memories of their past through collective repression."

Technology and Crime. Further advances were made during the year in creating technological barriers to criminal offenses. New model cars now often have locking devices that make "hot wiring," the delinquents' traditional method of auto theft, impossible. More banks are beginning to install photographic equipment to obtain pictures of bank robbers in the attempt to deter an offense that has skyrocketed in recent years. In 1943, for instance, there were only 24 bank robberies; by 1969, the figure had risen to more than 2,000, even though the chances of arrest are higher for bank robbery than for any other major property crime.

In Britain, use of "breathalyser" equipment to detect drinking drivers was said to have contributed during the year to a notable decline in highway deaths and accidents. Mandatory, random road checks correlated with a drop of 1,152 in the number of road deaths and a decline of 11,000—or 11% —in the number of highway accidents in the first year of use of the breathalyser. Later results, however, indicated a slow rise in the number of highway fatalities, indicating, perhaps, that familarity with the new procedure tends to reduce fear and conformity. Failure to pass a breathalyser test leads in Britain to an automatic $240 fine and the possibility of four months to a year in jail.

Corrections. The report of the Joint Commission on Manpower and Training, issued in November after a three-year study period, called for sweeping reforms in the U. S. prison system. Crime would not be reduced, the commission report maintained, so long as "harsh laws, huge, isolated prisons, token program resources, and discriminatory practices" were tolerated. Prison and jail inmates would increase from 1.1 million to 1.6 million by 1975, the commission predicted. To serve such persons adequately, it recommended national legislation to coordinate federal, state, and local prison systems and to provide $25 million annually to finance correctional improvements.

The commission also expressed concern over the number of poorly trained and unqualified correctional workers, as well as the low pay prevailing in the work. It noted: "There are far too many employees in institutions, probation departments, and parole agencies who are there not because they were educated and trained for particular jobs but because their appointments satisfied political ends." (See also PRISONS.)

Capital Punishment. No executions took place in 1969, the third consecutive year without use of the death penalty in the United States. At the end of the year, however, almost 500 persons were being held on death rows in various states, pending the results of the case of *Maxwell* v. *Bishop,* which challenges the constitutionality of capital punishment. In 1969, New Mexico joined the roster of states that have abandoned capital punishment, raising the total to 14.

Crime in the News. The brutal slaying of Sharon Tate, a pregnant, 26-year-old motion picture actress and wife of director Roman Polanski, produced newspaper headlines in August. Four other persons were slaughtered in the same episode. On December 1, Los Angeles police said they had solved the case and identified the suspects as "a roving band of hippies." On December 8, Charles M. Manson, 35-year-old "guru," and four followers were indicted in the murders. They, plus a sixth person, were also indicted in two other murders.

In October, Marine Lance Corp. Rafael Minichiello became the 55th person to hijack a plane during the year by rerouting a Los Angeles-San Francisco TWA flight to Rome. Italian authorities charged Minichiello with nine offenses.

GILBERT GEIS
Coauthor, "Man, Crime, and Society"

CROSS-COUNTRY. See SPORTS.

CUBA

In 1969 the Cuban government directed the efforts of the country toward achieving a record sugar harvest in 1970. Relations with the Soviet Union improved greatly during the year.

Sugar Production. In his speech on Jan. 2, 1969, the tenth anniversary of his coming to power, Premier Fidel Castro announced that all efforts in 1969 would be directed toward achieving the great goal of a 10 million ton sugar harvest in 1970 (in pre-Castro Cuba, sugar harvests had never exceeded 6 million tons). Accordingly, he proclaimed 1969 as the "Year of the Decisive Effort." In the same speech Castro stated that sugar would be rationed, cutting domestic consumption by one third, in order to provide additional foreign exchange for the mechanization of agriculture in preparation for the 1970 harvest.

The results of the 1969 sugar harvest were disappointing. It had been expected to yield 5.5 million tons—high by pre-Castro standards, although still far short of the overly optimistic goal of 9 million tons originally set. Early in May, Castro announced that more than 4 million tons had been harvested. No further figures were given, but unofficially the harvest was stated to have been in the region of 4.5 million tons.

At least in part, the low 1969 yield may have been the result of a deliberate slowdown in cutting in order to increase the volume of the 1970 harvest. When the 1969 harvest was declared closed in May, much cane was still left standing in the fields for the succeeding harvest. The 1970 harvest was begun in July instead of November as in previous years, and is to be prolonged until July 1970. In order to reach the notable goal of 10 million tons, the 1970 harvest is thus being stretched at both ends to last a full year.

Internal Reform. Stringent measures to combat crime, particularly against public property, were announced in April. Common criminals, as well as those accused of political crimes, are now to be judged by "revolutionary tribunals," and the death penalty has been extended to the crime of embezzlement. As in 1968, the authorities expressed concern about the spread of juvenile delinquency, and Castro declared that the juridical practice of milder sentences for minors would have to be reexamined.

The status of the ruling Communist party underwent a significant change. Carlos Rafael Rodriguez, a cabinet minister and member of the Party Secretariat, explained in August that the Communist party was being fused with the state apparatus. The head of each administrative division—ministry, institute, or planning committee—would automatically become the party secretary in that institution. Cuba is the only Communist country in which the party is thus officially subordinated to the state bureaucracy.

Relations with the USSR. Soviet-Cuban relations improved greatly in 1969. Throughout the year Castro and other Cuban spokesmen refrained from the acerbic criticism of Soviet foreign and internal policies that had been practiced in the two preceding years and had even been evident in Castro's speech condoning the Soviet occupation of Czechoslovakia in August 1968. In his speech on Jan. 2, 1969, Castro went out of his way to state that free Soviet arms aid and Soviet food deliveries had been decisive in the most difficult years of the revolutionary regime.

In April a Cuban-Soviet Friendship Association, similar to the friendship societies functioning within the Soviet bloc and in many neutral countries, was at last set up in Havana. Castro and his brother Raul, the Cuban minister of defense, attended the opening ceremonies. In June, Cuba sent an observer to the Soviet-sponsored world conference of Communist parties in Moscow. At the time of U. S. President Nixon's visit to Rumania in July, the Soviet Union ostentatiously sent a naval squadron to Havana on a ceremonial visit. In November, Cuba was honored for the first time by a visit by the Soviet minister of defense, Marshal A. A. Grechko, who thus stressed Moscow's continuing interest in Cuba as a military bastion in the western hemisphere.

Inter-American Affairs. Throughout 1969, Cuba continued its propaganda support of the Castroite guerrillas and urban terrorist bands operating in various Latin American nations. There were several reports of the presence of Cuban nationals among subversive groups in Bolivia, Colombia, and Venezuela. Inti Peredo of Bolivia and Carlos Marighela of Brazil, two important Castroite leaders killed by the police of their own countries in 1969, were acclaimed by Havana as martyrs to the revolutionary cause. But Castro also showed that he was no doctrinaire of guerrilla warfare, and that his criterion for judging a movement or government was not its revolutionary violence but its anti-Americanism. In a speech on July 14 he praised the Peruvian military junta for its confiscation of U. S. oil and sugar holdings and its sweeping land reform.

Cuban relations with Mexico, the only Latin American country still maintaining diplomatic ties with Havana, were strained by two incidents. In August, Havana refused to extradite two Mexican students who had hijacked an airliner. In September, Cuba expelled an official of the Mexican embassy in Havana, charging that he was an agent of the U. S. Central Intelligence Agency (CIA).

CUBA • Information Highlights

Area: 44,218 square miles (114,524 sq km).

Population: 8,074,000 (1968 est.).

Chief Cities (1965 census): Havana, the capital, 982,900; Santiago de Cuba, 240,600; Camagüey, 161,700.

Government: *President*—Osvaldo Dorticos Torrado (took office July 18, 1959); *Prime Minister*—Fidel Castro Ruz (took office Jan. 1, 1959).

Religious Faiths: Roman Catholics, 84% of population.

Education: *Literacy rate* (1968 est.), over 90% of population aged 15 and over. *Total school enrollment* (1966)— 1,600,877 (primary, 1,253,042; secondary, 242,208; teacher-training, 25,547; technical/vocational, 46,376; university/higher, 33,704).

Finance (1965 est.): *Revenues*, $2,535,000,000; *expenditures*, $2,535,000,000; *monetary unit*, peso (1 peso equals U. S.$1).

Gross National Product (1966): $4,039,000,000.

National Income (1966): $3,781,000,000; *average annual income per person*, $468.

Economic Indexes: *Industrial production* (1965), 116 (1963 = 100); *agricultural production* (1967), 133 (1963 = 100).

Manufacturing (metric tons, 1967): Sugar, 6,236,000; cement, 800,000; gasoline (1966), 768,000.

Crops (metric tons, 1967–68 crop year): Citrus fruits (1965), 111,000; tobacco, 51,200.

Minerals (metric tons, 1966): Manganese ore, 31,000; nickel, 25,977; chromium (1967), 10,800.

Foreign Trade (1965): *Exports*, $593,000,000 (chief exports, 1966: sugar, $603,330,000; inorganic chemicals, $25,990,-000; tobacco, $11,960,000); *imports*, $926,000,000 (chief imports, 1966: crude and partly refined petroleum, $62,-310,000; wheat meal and flour, $29,310,000. *Chief trading partners* (1966): USSR (took 46% of exports, supplied 56% of imports); Communist China; Spain.

Transportation: *Roads* (1964), 8,300 miles (13,357 km); *motor vehicles* (1965), 265,700 (automobiles, 162,000); *railways* (1965), 3,562 miles (5,732 km); *merchant vessels* (1967), 40 (223,000 gross registered tons).

Communications: *Telephones* (1968): 238,224; *television stations* (1968), 25; *television sets* (1968), 23,000; *radios* (1964), 1,345,000; *newspapers* (1964), 10.

Apparent moves by the secretary of the Organization of American States (OAS), Galo Plaza, to revive Cuban membership in that organization came to naught, although they were regarded favorably by several Latin American governments.

The Cuban attitude toward the United States and specifically toward the Nixon administration remained uniformly hostile.

The hijacking of U. S. and Latin American planes to Havana continued, although Cuba announced an antihijacking law in September.

Emigration. Emigration from Cuba continued at the rate of more than 4,000 persons per month. Most of those leaving the island were transported to the United States by the daily airlift inaugurated in 1965, which more than 150,000 Cubans have used.

ERNST HALPERIN
Massachusetts Institute of Technology

CYPRUS

During 1969 efforts were made to find a permanent political settlement for Cyprus that would end the long-standing Greek Cypriot-Turkish Cypriot hostility. Intercommunal talks were amicable, but unproductive.

Continued Rivalry. The basic issue was an old one: How should the Turkish minority, 18% of the population, be governed? Previous efforts, including the adoption in 1960 of a constitution giving the Turks substantial rights, had come to naught following the outbreak of communal fighting in December 1963. The civil strife in 1963–64 had resulted in the withdrawal of Turkish Cypriot officials from the government and the creation of Turkish enclaves outside the effective jurisdiction of the Cypriot president, Archbishop Makarios III. With tension persisting, the United Nations continued in 1969 to maintain the peace-keeping force it had installed on the island in 1964. An indication of the depth of the rivalry could be seen in June, when the Turkish Cypriot press severely criticized the departing U. S. ambassador, Taylor Belcher, for making his farewell remarks in Greek.

Intercommunal Talks. Discussions that had started in June 1968 were continued in 1969 by Glavkos Clerides, president of the House of Representatives, and Rauf Denktas, a prominent Turkish Cypriot. While both sides announced that agreement had been reached on minor matters, no decision was made on the political organization of the state. The Turkish Cypriots seemed anxious to transform Cyprus into a federation within which the Turks would have autonomy in areas assigned them. The Greek Cypriots called for the maintenance of a unitary state with minority safeguards for the Turks. This was affirmed as government policy by Foreign Minister Spyros Kyprianou in a speech before the UN General Assembly. Archbishop Makarios emphasized that the previous drive for union (*enosis*) with Greece was not being pressed, and he began to show increasing pessimism over the outcome of the intercommunal talks. UN Secretary General U Thant, however, while noting the lack of progress, praised the talks as the only present hope in the search for a permanent solution.

Foreign Relations. The negotiators Clerides and Denktas traveled to Greece and Turkey, respectively, to keep those governments apprised of the talks. The Cypriot government indicated that the Greek government was backing the Greek Cypriots

fully; and, in turn, the Turkish government affirmed its support of the Turkish Cypriots by granting them substantial economic aid.

The visit of the Turkish president, Gen. Cevdet Sunay, to Moscow in November raised fears among some Greek Cypriots that the Turkish government would come to an accord with the Soviet Union over Cyprus. On the other hand, left-wing elements on the island were denouncing the United States for allegedly trying to engineer a settlement that would bring Cyprus within the framework of the North Atlantic Treaty Organization.

Tourism and the Economy. In an effort to help the economy the Cypriot House of Representatives established a new organization to devise plans and make recommendations for bolstering tourism. Citing advantages of climate, geography, scenery, and historical points of interest for the further development of tourism in Cyprus, Bibiano Osorio-Tafall, the special representative of the UN secretary general on the island, warned the Cypriots to protect their natural resources from destruction.

GEORGE J. MARCOPOULOS
Tufts University

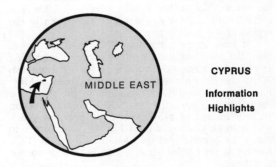

CYPRUS

Information Highlights

Area: 3,572 square miles (9,251 sq km).
Population: 622,000 (1968 est.).
Chief Cities (1966 census): Nicosia, the capital (1964 est.), 106,000; Limassol, 43,593; Famagusta, 34,774; Larnaca, 19,824.
Government: *President*—Archbishop Makarios III (reelected to a 5-year term, Feb. 25, 1968). *Legislature* (unicameral)—House of Representatives, 50 members.
Religious Faiths: Greek Orthodox, 79% of population; Muslims, 18%.
Education: *Literacy rate* (1960), 76% of population aged 15 and over. *Total school enrollment* (1966)—111,645 (primary, 72,933; secondary, 34,297; technical/vocational, 4,107; university/higher, 308).
Finance (1968 est.): *Revenues,* $57,660,000; *expenditures,* $50,050,000; *monetary unit,* pound (0.4167 pound equal U. S.$1).
Gross National Product (1967): $387,569,000.
National Income (1967): $355,891,000; *average annual income per person,* $572.
Economic Indexes (1967): *Industrial production* (1966), 114 (1963=100); *agricultural production,* 139 (1963=100); *cost of living,* 101 (1963=100).
Manufacturing and Processing (metric tons, 1967): Meat, 12,000; olive oil (1966) 3,000; wine (1966), 350,000 hectoliters; beer, 66,000 hectoliters.
Crops (metric tons, 1967–68 crop year): Grapes, 146,000; citrus fruits, 17,000; olives, 17,000; dry broad beans, 2,000.
Minerals (metric tons, 1966): Pyrites, 481,000; gypsum, 65,601; asbestos, 22,180; copper, 17,255.
Foreign Trade (1968): *Exports,* $89,000,000 (chief exports, 1967: copper, $8,470,000; citrus fruits, $7,740,000; iron, $5,940,000; *imports,* $173,000,000 (chief imports, 1967: nonelectrical machinery, $13,890,000; textile yarn and fabrics; $13,000,000; petroleum products, $9,950,000). *Chief trading partners* (1967): Britain (took 41% of exports, supplied 32% of imports); West Germany (took 10% of exports, supplied 9% of imports); Italy (took 5% of exports, supplied 10% of imports).
Transportation: *Roads* (1964), 24,820 miles (39,943 km); *motor vehicles* (1967), 50,100 (automobiles 37,300); *merchant vessels* (1967), 64 (420,000 gross registered tons); *national airline,* Cyprus Airways; *principal airports,* Nicosia.
Communications: *Telephones* (1968): 33,535; *television stations* (1968), 2; *television sets* (1968), 23,000; *radios* (1967), 146,000; *newspapers* (1967), 8.

CZECHOSLOVAKIA

The struggle for democratization and national self-assertion that erupted in Czechoslovakia so dramatically in 1968 continued in 1969. However, under relentless Soviet pressure, the freedoms gained during the "Czechoslovak spring" of 1968 gradually were suppressed, and Soviet-style Communist orthodoxy began to replace the "socialism with a human face" of Alexander Dubček. Dubček himself was replaced as Communist party first secretary by Gustav Husák (see biography with this article). Toward the year's end the Soviet masters had finally obtained a semblance of the "normalization" they had striven for.

Liberal-Dogmatist Tug of War. The struggle to preserve the recently won freedoms gained momentum early in the year with the self-immolation of a student, Jan Palach, in Wenceslas Square, Prague, in protest against the continued Soviet occupation and its consequences. Moved by Palach's sacrifice, on January 16, students, professors, writers, peasants, and youth groups participated in a crescendo of nationwide meetings, petitions, and demonstrations against the endeavors of Soviet-backed dogmatists to reverse the democratization course. Especially significant in this respect was the Czechoslovak Trade Union Congress, held on March 4–7, 1969, which pledged the loyalty of its 5.5 million members to the post-January 1968 reforms. Reaffirming "the right to self-determination and sovereignty of the socialist countries," the Congress rejected in no uncertain terms, the "Brezhnev doctrine" (named for Soviet Communist party chief Leonid I. Brezhnev) of limited sovereignty advanced to justify the Soviet invasion.

The people's bitterness reached a high point at the end of March, when, during celebrations of two Czechoslovak victories over the Soviet team at the world ice hockey championship, anti-Soviet demonstrations occurred in a number of cities, and the Soviet Airline offices in Prague were ransacked. Taking advantage of the incident, the Soviet Union dispatched two officials to Prague with a virtual ultimatum demanding strong measures against "antisocialist" elements. As a result, repression was stepped up: Newspapers with liberal leanings were subjected to censorship, suspension, and confiscation; reformists were dismissed from functions in the party, government agencies, and other organizations; and groups incurring Soviet disfavor were dissolved.

The decisive turning point came on April 17, when Dubček was replaced by Husák, and a number of reformists, including Josef Smrkovský, an outspoken advocate of continued democratization, were dropped from the party's ruling Presidium. Although Husák had been imprisoned at one time as a Slovak "bourgeois nationalist" and had joined the reformist cause in January 1968, his public pronouncements after the Soviet invasion revealed him to be a "realist" willing to do whatever was necessary to accommodate Soviet wishes and thereby, he hoped, earn a measure of Soviet leniency.

The wave of repression reached its peak after the nationwide "Day of Shame." This demonstration was staged Aug. 20–21, 1969, on the first anniversary of the Soviet invasion. Devised by the reformists working underground, the Day of Shame observances featured a boycott of public transportation, stores, and restaurants; decoration of the graves

GAMMA—PIX

TRIBUTES to Jan Palach ring the statue of St. Wenceslas in Prague, the scene of student's self-immolation.

GUSTAV HUSÁK was elected in April 1969 to succeed Alexander Dubček as first secretary of the Communist party of Czechoslovakia. A political moderate, Husák is convinced that "honorable cooperation" with the Soviet Union is essential for Czechoslovakia's survival. At the Moscow summit conference in June 1969 he denounced critics of the August 1968 invasion of Czechoslovakia by the USSR.

Husák was born on Jan. 10, 1913, in Bratislava, Slovakia. During World War II he was one of the leaders of the anti-Nazi Slovak national uprising. After the war he served in various party and government posts until his imprisonment, from 1951 to 1960, for alleged antistate activities. His party membership was restored in 1963, and, in 1968, he was appointed a deputy premier. Following the Soviet invasion, Husák was a member of the negotiating team that went to Moscow.

of national heroes; and a 5-minute halt of all work and traffic.

Angered by the challenge and eager to prove themselves worthy of Soviet trust, Husák and his associates responded with a massive use of the police, which resulted in the death of five demonstrators, injuries to hundreds of civilians and policemen, and the arrest of several thousand people. On the day after the demonstrations, Husák's regime declared a state of emergency and rushed through the Presidium of the Federal Assembly a drastic decree "for the defense of public order." This measure granted the police blanket authority to arrest suspects without court warrants, extended up to three weeks the length of time suspects could be held in police custody for purposes of investigation, increased penalties for even minor infractions of public order, introduced Soviet-style banishment from places of residence, and provided for dismissal of employees and expulsion of students for "loss of trust."

Equipped with these measures, and prodded by the hard-liners, the Husák regime in late summer and early fall moved against the last remnants of

the reformists within the party and government apparatus, ousting them from whatever positions of importance they still held. Included among them were the 29 progressives who were expelled from the party's Central Committee on September 28, as well as Dubček, who lost his membership on the party's Presidium and the chairmanship of the Federal Assembly, to which he had been elected upon his removal from the party's first secretaryship. Finally, in September, the new Czechoslovak leaders ordered that all previous statements protesting and denouncing the Soviet invasion and occupation be rescinded as "incorrect" and "un-Marxist." In a joint Soviet-Czechoslovak declaration signed in Moscow on October 27, they subscribed to the Soviet thesis that the entry of the Warsaw Pact armies was "an act of international solidarity, which helped bar the way to anti-socialist counter-revolutionary forces."

Party and Government. While a massive turnover occurred in 1969 in the personnel of the Czechoslovak Communist party, only two changes were made in the party organization. The 8-man Executive Committee of the party Presidium created in 1968 was abolished in April 1969, when the Pre-

GAMMA—PIX

PRAGUE CITIZENS stand in the rain at the funeral of Jan Palach, Czech student who burned himself to death in January to protest Soviet occupation of country.

Economy. The hectic political developments of 1968–69 adversely affected the country's economy. Slow work became a form of passive resistance. While wages rose 9.3% and the overall money income of the population rose 13.6% in the first half of 1969 over the same period of 1968, industrial production increased only 3.6% and labor productivity in industry a mere 2.9%. Agricultural output, which increased by 3.6% in 1968, was expected to fare worse in 1969. Thus, the discrepancy between purchasing power and available goods widened, especially as a buying fever was generated by a public lack of confidence. Also, the failure of some 50,000 citizens (most of them skilled workers) to return from trips to the West hurt the economy. Private trips to the West were prohibited in October 1969.

Foreign Relations. Retracing the few small steps toward lesser dependence on the Soviet Union undertaken in 1968, Czechoslovakia reverted in 1969 to the status of an obedient Soviet satellite that it had held in the 1950's. The status was sealed by the 8-day visit of the Czechoslovak party and government delegation to the Soviet Union in late October, during which the Czech leaders subscribed unreservedly to the "Brezhnev doctrine" and agreed to a stepped-up integration of the Czechoslovak and Soviet economies as well as to an indefinite stay of the Soviet armed forces in Czechoslovakia.

EDWARD TABORSKY
University of Texas

────── **CZECHOSLOVAKIA • Information Highlights** ──────

Area: 49,370 square miles (127,869 sq km).
Population: 14,362,000 (1968 est.).
Chief Cities (1965 census): Prague, the capital, 1,022,621; Brno, 328,316; Bratislava, 268,422.
Government: *President*—Ludvík Svoboda (elected March 30, 1968); *Premier*—Oldřich Černík (took office April 9, 1968). *Communist party First Secretary*—Gustav Husák (took office April 17, 1969). *Parliament* (Federal Assembly)—Chamber of the People, 200 members; Chamber of Nations, 150 members.
Religious Faiths: Roman Catholics, 64% of population.
Education: *Total school enrollment* (1966)—2,988,848 (primary, 2,164,432; secondary, 398,183; teacher-training, 9,589; vocational, 277,585; higher, 139,059).
Finance (1967 est.): *Revenues,* $19,790,000; *expenditures,* $19,790,000; *monetary unit,* koruna (7.2 korun equal U.S.$1).
Net Material Product (1966): $26,800,000,000.
National Income (1967): $32,500,000,000; *average annual income per person,* $2,262.
Economic Indexes: *Industrial production* (1968), 136 (1963=100); *cost of living* (1967), 104 (1963=100).
Manufacturing and Processing (metric tons, 1967): Crude steel, 10,000,000; cement, 6,460,000; beer, 19,393,000 hectoliters; wheat flour, 1,280,000; meat, 901,000.
Crops (metric tons, 1967–68 crop year): Sugar beets, 7,663,-000; potatoes, 6,037,000; wheat, 2,516,000; barley, 1,936,-000; oats, 968,000.
Minerals (metric tons, 1967): Lignite, 71,363,000; coal, 25,-946,000; lime (1965), 2,488,000; iron ore, 545,000; salt, 202,000; sulfur, 145,000; antimony, 2,000.
Foreign Trade (1967): *Exports,* $3,013,000,000 (chief exports, 1967: machinery and equipment, $1,393,000,000; consumer goods, $525,000,000; fuels, minerals, and metals, $512,-600,000; chemicals, fertilizers, and rubber, $122,300,000); *imports,* $2,680,000,000 (chief imports, 1967: machinery and equipment, $820,000,000; fuels, minerals, and metals, $685,900,000; raw materials of vegetable and animal origin, $342,600,000). *Chief trading partners* (1967): U.S.S.R. (took 34% of exports, supplied 36% of imports); East Germany (took 11% of exports, supplied 12% of imports); Poland.
Transportation: *Highways and first class roads* (1964), 45,256 miles (72,832 km); *motor vehicles* (1967), 686,400 (automobiles 521,200); *railways* (1965), 8,313 miles (13,376 km); *merchant vessels* (1967), 7; *national airlines,* Czechoslovak Airlines; *principal airports,* Bratislava, Brno, Prague.
Communications: *Telephones* (1968): 1,678,717; *television stations* (1968), 28; *television sets* (1968), 2,800,000; *radios* (1966), 3,829,000; *newspapers* (1967), 28.

sidium was reduced from 21 to 11 members; and a new post of deputy first party secretary was filled by Lubomír Štrougal, the diehard Czech Communist, who also heads the Czechoslovak Communist party's Bureau for Czech Communist Party Affairs.

On the other hand, the entire government machinery was reorganized when the constitutional law transforming Czechoslovakia into a federal republic went into effect on Jan. 1, 1969. The new federal organs are: (1) a president of the republic (Ludvík Svoboda, unchanged); (2) a Federal Assembly, consisting of a 200-man Chamber of the People, to be elected directly by the people, and a 150-man Chamber of Nations, half elected by the Czech and half by the Slovak National Council; and (3) a federal cabinet consisting of a premier (Oldřich Černík, unchanged), several vice premiers, seven ministers and seven state secretaries (for the departments of foreign affairs, defense, finance, interior, planning, foreign trade, and labor and social affairs), two ministers without portfolio, and the chairmen of seven coordinating committees. The Czech and Slovak Socialist republics also have their premiers, vice premiers, and ministers.

DAHOMEY

Civil service unrest, long the bane of Dahomey's politics, continued to trouble the state in 1969.

Domestic Affairs. In May, demanding higher family allowances, civil servants launched a 2-week strike. At the same time, high school and university students also went on strike. The strikes collapsed only after Army Chief of Staff Maurice Kouandeté threatened to conscript civil servants who were absent without permission and to expel striking students.

In June, in order to balance the budget, family allowances were cut from $9.00 per month per child to $2.50. The government subsequently decreed that, in the event of future strikes, all civil service workers who refused to return to work could be drafted, jailed, or fined.

Other government actions included the nationalization of major facilities at the port of Cotonou and the establishment of a newspaper.

Two plots against the government were uncovered. In mid-April, 20 persons were arrested, including ex-Mayor Theodore Hessou of Cotonou, former Foreign Minister Gabriel Lozès, and Supreme Court Judge Septime Dadde. In July several officers, including former head of state Alphonse Alley, were jailed, allegedly for plotting to kidnap Kouandeté.

Economy. High payments to government employees, whose salaries accounted for $23 million of the total 1969 budget of $33 million, imperiled

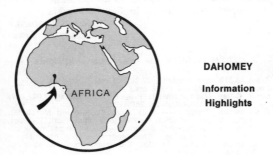

DAHOMEY

Information Highlights

Area: 43,483 square miles (112,622 sq km).
Population: 2,571,000 (1968 est.).
Chief Cities (1969 est.): Porto-Novo, the capital, 70,000; Cotonou, 110,000.
Government: *President*—Émile Derlin Zimsou (took office July 17, 1968).
Religious Faiths: Animists, 68% of population; Muslims, 15%; Roman Catholics, 14%.
Education: *Literacy rate* (1969), 5% of adult population. *Total school enrollment* (1966)—144,223 (primary, 132,690; secondary, 10,425; teacher-training, 322; technical/vocational, 733; university/higher, 53).
Finance (1967 est.): *Revenues,* $30,000,000; *expenditures,* $30,831,000; *monetary unit,* CFA franc (246.85 francs equal U. S.$1).
Gross National Product (1966): $194,450,000.
National Income (1966): $166,900,000; *average annual income per person,* $64.
Manufacturing (metric tons, 1966): Lumber, 8,000 cubic meters; palm oil, 43,000.
Crops (metric tons, 1967–68 crop year): Cassava, 1,120,000; sweet potatoes and yams, 604,000; millet and sorghum, 78,000.
Foreign Trade (1967): Exports, $15,232,000 (chief exports, 1967: palm kernel oil, $3,538,500; oilseed, nuts, and kernels, $2,015,000; palm oil, $1,068,200; raw cotton, $1,342,-500). Imports, $44,318,000 (chief imports, 1967: woven cotton fabrics, $7,387,000; road motor vehicles, $2,915,000; nonelectrical machinery, $2,010,000). *Chief trading partners* (1967): France (took 35% of exports, supplied 50% of imports); United States (took 14% of exports, supplied 4% of imports); Italy (supplied 9% of imports).
Transportation: *Roads* (1968), 8,828 miles (14,207 km); *motor vehicles* (1967), 13,300 (automobiles, 8,000); *railways* (1965), 360 miles (579 km).
Communications: *Telephones* (1968), 4,600; *radios* (1967), 40,000; *newspapers* (1964), 3 (daily circulation, 2,000).

the country's fragile economy. President Émile Derlin Zinsou expressed deep concern over the dangerous state of the country's economy.

Significant foreign assistance included $9.2 million for food from the International Development Agency, and $3.6 million from France for agricultural development in the north, and a West German loan of $500,000 for small and medium industry.

International Relations. Zinsou visited Washington, D. C., early in March and became the first African head of state to call on President Nixon. Dahomey and Togo formed the Benin Electrical Community to purchase power from Ghana. Relations with the Council of the Entente countries (Ivory Coast, Niger, Togo, and Upper Volta) were particularly close. Relations with France, which Zinsou visited in January, remained cordial.

CLAUDE E. WELCH, JR.
State University of New York at Buffalo

DAIRY PRODUCTS. See AGRICULTURE.

DALLAS

Jointly with nearby Fort Worth, Dallas in 1969 began construction of a $400 million, 18,000-acre regional airport. The airport headed a series of major nonresidential construction projects that will cost an estimated $700 million, a record.

Construction. Besides the regional airport, construction projects begun or in process in Dallas in 1969 included a city hall complex, a 16-story federal center, three junior colleges, a regional shopping center, a 58,000-seat professional football stadium, and a science-technical center.

New University. On September 1, the Southwest Center for Advanced Studies, primarily a graduate science-research institution, became the University of Texas at Dallas, a unit of the state university system.

Last Train. Railway passenger service has ceased in Dallas. On May 1, the city's last passenger train —on the Texas and Pacific Railway—left Dallas Union Station, ending service that began on July 17, 1872, on the Houston and Texas Central.

Government. By a narrow margin on June 10, voters approved a $42 million bond issue to air-condition the district's public school buildings. This was in preparation for increased summer use.

The city council sought to increase the ad valorem tax rate by 24 cents per $100 assessed valuation to, meet the rising costs of construction and services, but the plan met such public resistance that the increase was reduced to 11 cents. Dallas, with an estimated population of 860,000, is the largest U. S. city having a council-manager form of government.

Business and Finance. A finance center, Dallas registered a 28% increase in bank debits in 1969, to a record $114 billion. Employment in the six-county Dallas standard metropolitan area averaged 685,000 in 1969, or 4% above 1968; unemployment averaged 2%, unchanged from 1968 and well below the national average. About 25% of employment is in manufacturing, principally clothing, oil-well equipment, aircraft, electronics, and automobile assembling. The city is an insurance center and an international cotton market, and it leads the South in wholesale trade.

ARTHUR A. SMITH
First National Bank in Dallas

INTERNATIONAL BOUNDARY & WATER COMMISSION

AMISTAD DAM on the Rio Grande will serve power and irrigation needs of Mexico (*foreground*) and the United States. Presidents of the two nations dedicated the dam on September 8.

UPI

DAMS

An important aspect of dam construction and planning in 1969 was international cooperation—whether through intergovernmental agreement or the concerted efforts of contractors from different countries. On the national level, major dam projects were continued in Venezuela, Brazil, Egypt, Spain, and the United States.

Amistad Dam. In September 1969 the United States and Mexico dedicated the 254-foot-high (77-meter) Amistad (Friendship) Dam on the Rio Grande. Contractors from both countries constructed the $78 million facility near Del Rio, Texas. The dam, a flood-control and irrigation project with a concrete gravity section and flanking earth embankments, extends 6 miles (9.7 km) across the international boundary. A hydroelectric plant will be added later to furnish power for both the United States and Mexico.

Tarbela Dam. Builders are hoping to complete Tarbela Dam, on the Indus River in West Pakistan, in 1976. To construct the 9,000-foot-long (2,743-meter) by 485-foot-high (148-meter) rock-fill embankment, French and Italian contractors are operating 15 processing plants to produce most of the 180 million cubic yards (138 million cu. meters) of material needed. Tarbela will be the largest dam in the world in total volume of material.

Many nations are involved, as is the World Bank, in the financing of Tarbela Dam. The United States, Britain, West Germany, Canada, Australia, and New Zealand are contributing funds, in addition to Pakistan and India.

Djerdap Dam. In Europe, Yugoslavia and Rumania are proceeding with Djerdap Dam at Iron Gate Gorge on the Danube River, their international boundary. Scheduled for completion in late 1971, the navigation and hydroelectric project will eventually have an annual output of 11.3 billion kilowatt-hours.

Cahora Bassa Dam. Portugal and South Africa are cooperating on the multipurpose Cahora Bassa Dam project in Mozambique. Located on the Zambezi River, the 508-foot-high (155-meter) double curvature concrete arch structure will cost $350 million and have a capacity of 800,000 kilowatts, one of the largest such projects in Africa.

The first phase of the work is scheduled for completion in 1975. Irrigation and navigation are included in the project, which will be built by a consortium of French, German, South African, and Swiss contractors.

Tachien Dam. In Asia, the Republic of China expects to start work in 1970 on Tachien Dam on the Tachia River in Taiwan. An Italian-Japanese combine submitted the low bid to construct the 590-foot-high (180-meter) thin arch concrete structure for use in generating power and storing water for irrigation purposes. The powerhouse will have a capacity of 234,000 kilowatts.

Mekong Project. The United Nations is co-ordinating power and irrigation development in the lower Mekong River basin in Cambodia. Eleven countries have signed an agreement to support the project. Some progress has been made by constructing tributary dams, but to tame the turbulent Mekong River will require big and costly mainstream dams. The cost of such a program, which could

PERINI CORP.

BULLARD'S BAR DAM, on California's Yuba River, is the fourth highest concrete arch dam in the nation.

be patterned after the U. S. Tennessee Valley Authority, has been estimated at from $25 to $50 billion. It would include a series of dams, reservoirs, hydroelectric plants and irrigation and flood-control systems. The project would also benefit Laos, Thailand, and South Vietnam.

Guri Dam. Venezuela is building Guri Dam on the Caroní River in three stages. The 1,579-foot-long (481-meter) concrete gravity structure is now 348 feet (106 meters) high and produces 527,250 kilowatts. In succeeding construction stages, the dam will rise to heights of 442 and 524 feet (135 and 160 meters) to generate eventually 6 million kilowatts.

Ilha Solteira Dam. Another South American nation, Brazil, is building on the Paraná River Ilha Solteira Dam, which will generate 3.2 million kilowatts of hydroelectric power. A concrete gravity section, 5,656 feet (1,724 meters) long will be flanked by rockfill and earth embankments giving the project a length of 4 miles (6.4 km) with a maximum height of 242 feet (74 meters).

Other Brazilian Dams. Another Rio Grande, this one in Brazil, is being exploited for its hydroelectric potential. The largest project in a series of

structures is Furnas Dam, a 12-million-cubic-yard (9.2-million-cu.-meter) rockfill barrier. Downstream 50 miles (80 km) is the Peixoto power station, and 18 miles (29 km) farther, Estreito Dam and power house, which began functioning in 1969. Furnas Dam regulates the water reaching the two downstream plants. Together, the three supply electricity to Rio de Janeiro, São Paulo, and Belo Horizonte.

Aswan High Dam. On the Nile River in Egypt, Aswan High Dam, an earth and rockfill structure, has been under construction for nine years. Its 56-million-cubic-yard (42-million-cu.-meter) embankment is completed, and its power plant is now operating with nine of the 175,000-kilowatt generators. The remaining three units are expected to go on the line in 1970. Aswan is 360 feet (110 meters) high and 2.5 miles (4 km) long.

Almendra Dam. Nearing completion in Spain is the double curvature concrete arch Almendra Dam on the Tormes River. The 646-foot-high (197-meter) structure contains 3.2 million cubic yards (2.4 million cu. meters) of concrete and is being built by a private electric utility company. Costing $114 million, the project has an underground power plant equipped with four 135,000-kilowatt generators.

Bullard's Bar Dam. In the United States in 1969 Bullard's Bar Dam, on California's Yuba River, was completed nine months ahead of schedule. The 635-foot-high (194-meter) double curve concrete arch is the fourth-highest dam in the nation and has a crest length of 2,200 feet (670 meters). The dam for the flood control and hydroelectric project cost $143 million. Two power plants will provide 358,000 kilowatts of energy. The structure contains more than 2.7 million cubic yards (2.1 million cu. meters) of concrete. Construction started in June 1966; concreting was completed in July 1969. For the first year, concrete placing was on a round-the-clock basis, six days a week.

Dworshak Dam. The Army Corps of Engineers is constructing the second-highest U. S. concrete dam on the North Fork of the Clearwater River at Orofino, Idaho. A concrete gravity structure 693 feet (211 meters) high, Dworshak Dam will contain 6.7 million cubic yards (5.1 million cu. meters) of concrete. Nearly 3 million cubic yards (2.3 million cu. meters) were placed in 1969. Completion is scheduled by 1972 at a cost of $131 million.

Carter Dam. Another Corps of Engineers project, Carter Dam on the Coosawattee River in northern Georgia, will be the highest rockfill dam, at 445 feet (136 meters), east of the Mississippi River. The multipurpose project has a 2,050-foot-long (625-meter) embankment and will generate 500,000 kilowatts. First power on the line is expected in 1972.

Grand Coulee Dam. In 1969 the Bureau of Reclamation completed the demolition and removal of a 260-foot (79-meter) section of the existing Grand Coulee Dam on the Columbia River in the state of Washington. The work involved 31,000 cubic yards (23,700 cu. meters) of concrete and 7 million cubic yards (5.4 million cu. meters) of rock and earth at the right abutment of the dam.

The purpose was to make way for a massive third power plant and a new forebay dam. The completed facility will eventually have a total generating capacity of 9.7 million kilowatts—the largest single power complex in the world.

WILLIAM H. QUIRK
"Contractors & Engineers" Magazine

As the decade of the 1960's drew to a close, the United States was established as the world's richest dance power, in range, quantity, and quality. The increase in audiences, particularly young audiences, and the great variety in style in modern dance and ballet left no doubt that in the performing arts in the United States dance was where the action was.

The 1968–69 season, the fullest in the history of New York City, left critics who attempted to cover all major performances gasping for breath, and the beginning of the 1969–70 season was even more strenuous. Although there were active professional companies in Atlanta, Washington, Philadelphia, Boston, San Francisco, and other cities, the capital of the world of dance was clearly New York.

Awards and Grants. Gifts from foundations and grants from government agencies supported many dance activities. Early in the year the National Council on the Arts approved grants totaling $132,760 to cover the costs of creating new works by 15 choreographers: Richard Englund, Eliot Feld, Don Redlich, Anna Sokolow, José Limon, Pauline Koner, Charles Weidman, Richard Kuch, Lucas Hoving, Merce Cunningham, Glen Tetley, Paul Taylor, Alwin Nikolais, Murray Louis, and Ann Halprin.

In October, the Rockefeller Foundation gave the Brooklyn Academy of Music, which had emerged as a major dance center, a grant of $350,000, most of which was to be shared by the Merce Cunningham Dance Company, the Alvin Ailey American Dance Theater, and Eliot Feld's American Ballet Company. In November the National Endowment for the Arts announced an award of matching grants for new productions totaling $612,400, large portions of which were destined for the American Ballet Theater and the New York City Ballet.

Modern American Dance. Two distinguished series, the New York City Center Season of American (*Continued on page 235*)

dance

JOFFREY BALLET members perform *Animus,* an abstract ballet by Gerald Arpino. Reflected within the metallic setting by Ming Cho Lee are dancers Nancy Robinson, Dermot Burke (*center*), and Christian Holder (*bottom*). The score—designed for electronic tape and trombone—was composed by Jacob Druckman.

STUTTGART BALLET

In 1969 the Stuttgart Ballet, in its first visit to New York, was acclaimed by critics and audiences, who hailed the art of prima ballerina Marcia Haydée (above, at Lincoln Center). The group is directed by choreographer John Cranko (lower left). Seen here in "Romeo and Juliet" are (left) Miss Haydée and Richard Cragun in a pas de deux and (below) Egon Madsen.

HANNES KILLIAN, STUTTGART, GERMANY, COURTESY HUROK CONCERTS, INC.

(Continued from page 233)

Dance and the Festival of Dance presented by the Brooklyn Academy and Theater 69, exhibited an unprecedented panorama of modern dance, ranging from the work of such pioneers in the field as José Limón and Martha Graham to the latest activities of the avant-garde. Among the outstanding companies included in these series were those of Alvin Ailey, Paul Taylor, Glen Tetley, Merce Cunningham, Pearl Lang, Donald McKayle, and Alwin Nikolais. Although they are thoroughly American, some of these groups are better known and more highly esteemed in Europe than at home. One of them, the Nikolais company (which had been awarded the Grand Prix at the Paris International Dance Festival in 1968), was having its first season in a major New York theater.

There is a certain amount of controversy over Theater 69's week of avant-garde performances at the Billy Rose Theater in February, presenting the companies of Twyla Tharp, Meredith Monk, Yvonne Rainer, and Don Redlich. Miss Tharp's minimal art was judged to be harmless if rather boring. There was little in the Dada-inspired work of Miss Monk that would fit any conventional definition of dance, and in a New York *Times* interview in November she said, "I don't really call myself a dancer anymore." Most critical wrath was directed at Miss Rainer, whose work often betrayed hostility toward the audience and included films of grim nudes playing ball or engaging in sexual intercourse. Clive Barnes, critic of the *Times*, called the performance "a disgrace to the name of dancing" and accused the Ford Foundation of striking "a ghastly blow at progressive dance." Don Redlich, whose work was more accessible and showed more variety in emotional content and even a sense of humor, fared better. In November his company represented the nation at the Paris International Dance Festival.

At the City Center in April, the Martha Graham company was in excellent form. Although new works, such as *Archaic Hours,* were not regarded as Miss Graham's best, critics hailed the fact that she had begun to train younger dancers in her great roles, which should assure the survival of the best works of this choreographer, now about 75 years old. A Rockefeller grant made possible the documentation on film of Miss Graham's *Cortège of Eagles, Seraphic Dialogue,* and *Acrobats of God.*

Ballet. Some of the best ballet performances of the season were those of the American Ballet Theater, starring permanent guest artists Erik Bruhn and Carla Fracci in *Coppelia* and *Giselle.* (The work of Bruhn and Fracci was preserved in a film of *Giselle,* which was premiered at Lincoln Center in November.) New works presented by the American Ballet Theater in its two engagements at the Brooklyn Academy, in January and December, included two by Michael Smuin—*Gartenfest,* to music of Mozart, and *The Eternal Idol,* to Chopin.

The most important new work unveiled by the New York City Ballet was Jerome Robbins' *Dances at a Gathering,* a plotless ballet to music of Chopin. In May, Suzanne Farrell, the company's principal ballerina, resigned along with her husband, Paul Mejía, in a dispute over Mejía's dancing assignments.

Changes in personnel also affected the City Center Joffrey Ballet, which lost four principal artists long associated closely with the company. Lisa Bradley, Michael Uthoff, and Robert Blankshine resigned, and Maximiliano Zomosa, a leading charac-ter dancer, committed suicide in February. Brunilda Ruiz and Paul Sutherland also left the company to return to the Harkness Ballet. The stability of the Joffrey group was proved by the speed with which their roles were reassigned and learned by other dancers. New works added to the Joffrey repertoire included August Bournonville's *William Tell Variations* and *Konservatoriet* (staged by Hans Brenaa), Frederick Ashton's *Façade,* and Leonide Massine's *Three-Cornered Hat.*

A high point in the year for the National Ballet of Washington was the production of Bournonville's *La Sylphide.* Dame Margot Fonteyn danced the title role with the National Ballet in Washington and elsewhere in the early fall.

A new American ballet company was founded in 1969 by Eliot Feld, generally regarded as the finest choreographer to emerge in the United States since Jerome Robbins. Called the American Ballet Company, Feld's group made its first appearance at the Spoleto Festival in Italy in June. Its New York debut took place in October at the Brooklyn Academy, where the American Ballet Company is among the resident troupes. Its repertoire includes Feld's own works, such as *Harbinger, At Midnight,* and *Meadowlark,* and Herbert Ross' *Caprichos* and *The Maids.*

Visiting Companies. Two major foreign troupes were among those that toured the United States. The Royal British Ballet celebrated the 20th anniversary of its American debut with six weeks of performances at the Metropolitan Opera House in April and May, followed by a national tour. Dame Margot Fonteyn and Rudolph Nureyev were guest stars.

The Stuttgart Ballet from Germany made its American debut at the Metropolitan in June. Composed of dancers from 20 countries, the company is directed by the British choreographer John Cranko. His full-length ballets, such as *Eugene Onegin, Romeo and Juliet,* and *The Taming of the Shrew,* if not great works, are at least flashy and theatrical and are popular with audiences. New York audiences loved the company, particularly the stars Marcia Haydee (from Brazil), Richard Cragun (American), and Egon Madsen (Danish).

Americans in Europe. As befits the world's major dance power, the United States exports many dancers, choreographers, and touring companies. In 1969, European audiences gave particularly enthusiastic receptions to the Glen Tetley Dance Company, the Alwin Nikolais Dance Theater, and the City Center Joffrey Ballet. The French government awarded choreographer Paul Taylor a medal and made him a Chevalier des Arts et des Lettres. Soviet dancers took most of the prizes at the first International Ballet Contest in Moscow in June, but a silver medal was awarded to Helgi Tomasson of the Harkness Ballet. In September, John Taras, balletmaster of the New York City Ballet, took over the direction of the Paris Opera Ballet.

Several Americans were guests at the Grand Théâtre of Geneva, Switzerland, which reorganized its ballet company. Ballerina Patricia Neary was a guest star, Patricia Wilde taught in the company's school, Una Kai supervised rehearsals, and George Balanchine acted as artistic adviser.

WILLIAM LIVINGSTONE
Member of Reviewers Panel, "Ballet Review"
Managing Editor, "Stereo Review"

DEATH RATES. See VITAL STATISTICS.

KEEPING WATCH, U.S. Navy patrol planes fly over a Soviet destroyer off Florida. The vessel was one of six Soviet warships bound for Cuba in July.

DEFENSE FORCES

Dramatic events regarding the levels of defense forces and the policies for their use occurred in the United States and the Soviet Union in 1969. Elsewhere, reflections of the confrontation between the two superpowers, regional rivalries heightened by nationalistic feelings, and internal disputes often exacerbated by external forces fueled efforts by lesser nations—and groups within them—to acquire more and newer weapons.

The hostility in the Middle East between Israel and the majority of Arab states increased. Both sides attempted to improve their military strength by acquiring modern weapons from the more industrial-ized powers. Israel sought equipment from non-Communist states such as the United States, Britain, and France. The Arabs obtained military equipment from various Communist nations, principally the Soviet Union.

Three states with technical capacity to develop nuclear weapons, Israel, India, and Japan, have not signed the nuclear nonproliferation treaty, and at the end of 1969 still kept their option to acquire nuclear weapons. West Germany, after the election of Willy Brandt as chancellor, agreed on Nov. 28, 1969, to sign the treaty.

In Africa, there was civil war in Nigeria, intense hostility in both Rhodesia and the Republic of South Africa between groups of blacks and whites, and guerrilla warfare in Angola and Mozambique which pitted black natives against Portuguese troops attempting to maintain the areas as colonies. Tribal conflict flared here and there on the continent. Such confrontations spurred the various contestants to seek modern arms from any source willing to provide them.

A number of Latin American governments purchased modern weapons abroad for protection against each other and for use against Communist elements seeking their overthrow. Pakistan and India continued to increase the quality of their defense forces because of mutual hostility, and, in the case of India, a fear of mainland China.

UNITED STATES

President Nixon began 1969 with the intention of using defense forces to support "negotiation not confrontation" with the Communist nations. The government claimed, against much dispute, that it pursued this policy during 1969 in several areas.

It appeared that the Nixon administration was returning to the Joint Chiefs of Staff much of the power that had been tightly held by the secretary of defense in the two previous administrations.

The first major "Nixon legislation," passed Nov. 19, 1969, was repeal of the 1967 law prohibiting random selection of men for the draft. Nixon's intention was that all men, on reaching age 19, would be subject to the lottery. Approximately the top third would be called up, either at once or after educational deferment. A group in the middle would not be sure for a while, but the others would know immediately that they were excused from service. The first drawing for the order of calls in 1970, by birthdays, was held in Washington on Dec. 1, 1969. (See also SELECTIVE SERVICE.)

All biological warfare was renounced by President Nixon on Nov. 25, 1969, when he asked the Senate to ratify the Geneva Protocol (Chemical-Biological) of 1925 which prohibits chemical and biological warfare. U. S. stocks of biological warfare agents were to be destroyed, and all research in this field would be moved from the Defense Department to the Department of Health, Education, and Welfare. Nixon reserved the right to use tear gas and

defoliants, and to retaliate with lethal or incapacitating chemical weapons if an enemy used them first against U. S. forces.

Reduction of Cold War Tension. Building upon steps taken by the Johnson administration, Nixon officials reached agreement with their Soviet counterparts to commence discussions of means to retard, or probably halt, the strategic defense and offensive arms competition between the two nations. Known as the Strategic Arms Limitation Talks (SALT), the first sessions began in late November in Helsinki, Finland. The discussions centered on ways to constrain the acquisition of intercontinental ballistic missiles (ICBM's), long range bombers, submarine-launched ballistic missiles (SLBM's), multiple warheads for ballistic missiles, called multiple independently targeted reentry vehicles (MIRV's), and antiballistic-missile missiles (AMB's). (See also DISARMAMENT AND ARMS CONTROL.)

Concerning U. S. defense policy in Asia for the anticipated "post-Vietnam" period, President Nixon offered what he called the Nixon Doctrine. It consisted of three points: (1) The United States would honor its defense commitments with Asian nations with which the United States has formal alliances. These include Japan, South Korea, the Philippines, Australia, New Zealand, Pakistan, Thailand, and Nationalist China (Taiwan). In addition, South Vietnam, Laos, and Cambodia are protocol states of the SEATO treaty, meaning that the provisions of the treaty can be extended to them. (2) The United States would protect nations with which it is allied, and others considered vital to American interests, from nuclear blackmail by the Chinese. (3) The United States would increasingly insist that Asian allies combat internal subversion and external aggression, with the assistance of U. S. supplies and equipment, but not U. S. fighting men. How the Nixon Doctrine would be implemented, and whether it presaged a general reduction of U. S. troops abroad, was widely debated at year's end.

In regard to the Vietnam War, the President sought to disengage the United States by what he termed a policy of "Vietnamization." By this he meant the phased withdrawal of U. S. combat troops and their replacement in the field by South Vietnamese troops largely supplied with U. S. weapons. By end of 1969 the government announced that some

THE F-15 (*shown in drawing*), which the Air Force ordered in 1969, is designed for superiority over any fighter in long-range or close combat.

MCDONNELL DOUGLAS CORPORATION

QUIET observation is conducted by the Army from its new YO-3A, developed from unpowered sail plane.

LOCKHEED

60,000 U. S. troops had been withdrawn, leaving approximately 480,000. In December 1969, Nixon announced an additional 50,000 men would be withdrawn by April 15, 1970. Clamorous groups demanded immediate withdrawal, or at least a speedier return of U. S. forces. Draft calls for January 1970 were cut in half.

U. S. v. Soviet Strategic Forces. In another major development the Nixon administration appeared to have decided, at least temporarily, to accept a new strategic nuclear relationship with the Soviet Union. For the first time in the cold war the Soviet Union possessed greater numbers of certain types of strategic weapons than the United States. The latter claimed, however, to retain the lead in the quality of its weapons.

The comparison was most obvious with regard to land-based ICBM's. By the end of 1969 the Soviet Union had in operation, or under construction, between 1,300 and 1,400. In contrast, the United States possessed 1,000 Minuteman and 54 Titan ICBM's, with no announced plans to increase the number. However, the United States continued to enhance the quality of its ICBM's by replacing older models with newer ones featuring a number of improvements.

In addition to the rapid increase in ICBM's, the USSR continued to construct SLBM-carrying submarines. The number did not approach the 41 SLBM craft operated by the United States (each carrying 16 missiles). However, if the rate of Soviet construction continues unabated for three to five years, and the United States refrains from additional construction, the Soviet SLBM submarine fleet will equal the American one in numbers, if not in quality.

This Soviet activity, in addition to the construction and testing of ABM and medium-range bombers and missiles, and the expansion of conventional naval and air forces, generated heated argument in American defense circles as to Soviet motivations and appropriate U. S. responses. Several schools of thought emerged.

Many concerned with defense planning interpreted the continued Soviet buildup to be the latest phase in the effort to impose Russian-type communism upon the world. Those holding this view expressed the fear that the Soviet Union was seeking to acquire a first-strike capability against the U. S. ICBM's. It was argued that if the USSR knew it

could destroy (1) a high percentage of the U. S. ICBM's before they could be fired, along with the U. S. bomber fleet, and (2) many of the SLBM's after they were fired—then a major constraint against Soviet blackmail and aggression would be removed.

Before the increase in Soviet strategic forces it was generally believed that U. S. strategic forces were relatively invulnerable to destruction either before or after launching. Hence it was argued that their presence and the threat of their use exercised a deterrent effect upon Soviet behavior, particularly regarding any direct threat against the United States. As 1969 wore on, and increasing information became available regarding the magnitude of Soviet arms acquisitions, more officials charged with defense planning voiced their alarm.

Their concern was not based solely on the increased number of Soviet ICBM's, but also on the type of weapon being acquired. The most dangerous missile, in the view of U. S. Defense Secretary Melvin R. Laird, was the SS-9 ICBM. This missile, carrying either a single warhead of 25 megatons (an explosive equivalent to 25 million tons of TNT), or several warheads of 5 megatons, is credited with being accurate to within one-quarter mile (400 meters). It was feared that such a weapon would be able to destroy the U. S. ICBM's which are housed in underground concrete silos with steel doors. In addition to concern over the SS-9 buildup, some strategists increasingly worried that the USSR was developing a military capability in space.

One opposing theory was that the Russians desired merely to obtain a rough strategic parity with the United States as a basis from which to approach arms-control discussions. Another theory was that the Soviet strategic buildup constituted an effort to counter what the Russians may perceive as dramatic increases in U. S. strategic forces looming on the horizon. Still another view is that the USSR is procuring weapons merely as a hedge against an uncertain future, rather than with an intent to attack the United States.

Confidence in the Military. One of the most significant developments in 1969 regarding U. S. defense forces occurred far beyond the Pentagon's offices. This was the diminished public confidence in the military to procure only necessary weapons and to use such weapons and U. S. troops wisely. Frustration with the Vietnam War accounted for much of the disenchantment with the military. But concern over the military was also generated by failures in performance of equipment, greater increases in the cost of expensive weapons, and some scandals involving military personnel.

In addition to huge public demonstrations against the war, the antimilitary mood was evident in the Senate. A sizable minority of senators tried unsuccessfully to reduce the size and influence of the military establishment by cutting the weapons procurement requests of the Department of Defense. The closest the Senate critics came to actually preventing the Pentagon from acquiring a major weapons system was in regard to the Safeguard ABM. An amendment permitting funds to be used for additional research on the system, but prohibiting expenditures for actual deployment, was barely defeated by a 51–49 vote.

Future Strategic-Weapon Options. While Americans debated the size and purpose of their defense forces, possibilities for awesome new weapons continued to be generated by research efforts.

The Seabased Antiballistic Missile Intercept System (SABMIS) is a possible ABM system for the Navy. The Underseas Long-Range Missile System (ULMS) could be developed to replace the current SLBM system. Improvements to help U. S. warheads penetrate defensive systems are collectively called the Advanced Ballistic Reentry System (ABRES). The Airborne Warning and Control System (AWACS) could combine the F-12 interceptor and new radar techniques to provide a defense against enemy bombers. The Subsonic Cruise Armed Decoy (SCAD) could be developed to help U. S. bombers penetrate hostile antiaircraft defenses.

Still other possibilities include a new ICBM, superhard silos for ICBM's, and the Advanced Manned Strategic Aircraft (AMSA), rechristened the B-1 bomber. Such a craft would fly at low level and high speed to avoid enemy defensive systems and could replace the B-52's and B-58's being retired from active service. The F-15 tactical fighter-bomber and the F-14 Navy fighter could in time replace currently operating aircraft.

Military Organization. Several significant changes were made in the operational defense forces of the United States during 1969. The Safeguard ABM replaced the Sentinel ABM as President Nixon decided to protect U. S. ICBM sites, instead of American cities, from enemy missile warheads. The justification was that the sites, because they offered small targets protected by steel and concrete, could be more easily defended, and because their protection was thought less provocative than defense of the U. S. population. Secretary Laird retired the 85 B-58 jet bombers because their age and Soviet antiaircraft defenses combined to reduce their effectiveness. Additional FB-111 swing-wing strategic bombers entered the Strategic Air Command. The fighter version, F-111, was being flown by the Tactical Air Command.

The Strategic Offensive Forces (SOF) were composed of the ICBM's and long-range bombers of the Strategic Air Command and the Polaris and Poseidon SLBM's operated by the Navy. These forces were kept in readiness to retaliate with "assured destruction" against the homeland of any nation attacking the United States, or possibly in reaction to a Soviet invasion of western Europe.

An elaborate network of radars, communications facilities, and fighter planes comprised the bulk of the Strategic Defensive Forces (SDF). "Damage limitation" was the objective of the SDF, should deterrence fail to prevent an attack on the United States. The Civil Defense program was designed to shelter survivors of a nuclear attack while radioactivity remained a hazard.

The General Purpose Forces (GPF) were stationed near danger points about the world, or in the United States whence they could be rapidly deployed overseas. Such forces are maintained, or used, to provide a "flexible response" to aggression ranging from guerrilla war to combat just below general thermonuclear war. Principal forces in the GPF were the 18 Army and 4 Marine combat divisions and their support units, 15 Navy attack carriers and 7 antisubmarine carriers with their associated aircraft, other surface and undersea naval craft, and the several thousand planes of the Tactical Air Command plus lightplanes and helicopters of the Army and Marine Corps. The battleship *New Jersey* returned from Vietnam waters and was retired, along with 75 other warships.

The Airlift and Sealift forces stood ready to transport men and materiel from the United States to overseas zones and then into combat areas. Congress refused the Navy's request for Fast Deployment Logistics (FDL) ships. But the Air Force won approval of its request for 23 more C-5A jet transports (58 were already on order).

The overall strength of the U. S. armed forces stood at 3,155,000 at the end of 1969. Of these approximately 1,150,000 were stationed overseas. The budget for the military establishment, not approved until late in the year, was $69.6 billion.

Administration. The top civilian leadership appointed to Pentagon posts by President Nixon served during 1969 without change. Melvin R. Laird was secretary of defense with David Packard as his deputy. The secretaries of the Navy, Air Force, and Army were, respectively, John H. Chafee, Robert C. Seamans, Jr., and Stanley R. Resor. There was only one change in 1969 among top military commanders. Air Force Chief of Staff Gen. John P. McConnell retired and was replaced by Gen. John D. Ryan, who had headed the Strategic Air Command. Gen. Earle G. Wheeler continued to serve as chairman of the Joint Chiefs of Staff, Gen. William

COMMAND of NATO forces was relinquished in 1969 by Gen. Lyman L. Lemnitzer (*left*), who retired. He is flanked by Gen. Joseph R. Holzapple, U. S. Air Force.

UPI

QUEEN ELIZABETH II, aboard the royal yacht *Britannia* with Prince Philip, reviews 62 NATO ships on the 20th anniversary of the defense alliance.

Westmoreland as Army chief of staff, Adm. Thomas H. Moorer as chief of naval operations, and Gen. Leonard F. Chapman as Marine Corps commandant. Army Gen. Creighton Abrams remained as U. S. commander in Vietnam.

NORTH ATLANTIC TREATY ORGANIZATION

The 20th anniversary of NATO's founding was observed in 1969. Under terms of the treaty, members met again and decided to continue the alliance.

Britain. Reacting to continuing budgetary constraints and a reevaluation of their global responsibilities, the British reduced their defense budget slightly. Plans remain to phase out the three Royal Navy aircraft carriers. In order to reduce expenses the British were developing a new jet plane, the Jaguar, with the French. They also discussed joint development of a new combat aircraft with the West Germans, Dutch, and Italians.

West Germany. Except for the U. S. Army, the 12-division German army of 460,000 men remained the most formidable ground force in western Europe. A major reorganization, shifting from primarily offensive strategy and equipment to a defensive posture, was announced in September. Many tanks and tracked vehicles will be replaced by wheeled ve-

THE MIRAGE 5, a jet fighter upgraded so that it carries 14 bombs, joined the French Air Force in 1969.

hicles. New "Jäger" brigades, similar to the U. S. Green Berets, will defend the hilly one-third of West Germany's eastern border. The German Air Force continued to rely on the U. S.-designed F-104, and ordered some 50 more.

France. The replacement of President Charles de Gaulle by Georges Pompidou had no observable effect on French military policy. France remained in NATO but continued to follow de Gaulle's policy of refusing to integrate French forces with those of the NATO partners. The French moved closer to the early 1970 date when they claim they will have ballistic missiles with hydrogen-bomb warheads, some carried in submarines. The Mirage V jet bomber augmented the French Air Force.

SOVIET UNION

The Soviet Union canceled the role of the military in the annual May Day parade in Moscow. Nevertheless, little doubt existed about the impressive strides the Russians continued to make in strengthening their defense forces.

Forces. The Soviet equivalent to the U. S. Strategic Offensive Forces comprised, or soon would, some 1,000 SS-11 ICBM's with 1-megaton warheads and 300 to 400 of the much larger SS-9 ICBM, which possibly carries a multiple warhead; some 150 long-range bombers; and more than 100 SLBM's carried by nuclear submarines. It was reported in Washington that the Russians were experimenting with a new ICBM, and possibly adding aerial refueling capability to a new medium-range bomber to convert it into a long range bomber.

The USSR maintained an impressive force of medium-range missiles and bombers that have no U. S. counterpart. These weapons were once thought to be primarily targeted on western Europe. With the rapid deterioration of Sino-Soviet relations it is believed that many Russian medium-range weapons have now been assigned targets in China. As is the case with the long-range weapons systems, the USSR is testing new bombers and missiles for the medium-range forces.

The Strategic Defense Forces maintained by the Soviet Union were more extensive than those maintained by the United States. For example, the USSR has already made some deployment of an ABM (the Galosh) that may serve as the base upon which

SS-9 MISSILES (the bottle-shaped pair on the upper right) are paraded in Moscow. These new intercontinental weapons may carry multiple warheads.

to build a more advanced system. In addition, Soviet civil defense is believed better than that of the United States.

The Soviet counterpart to the U. S. General Purpose Forces did not show any dramatic increase in numbers of troops assigned during 1969. However, qualitative improvements were observed in Soviet equipment. Most striking were improvements in and additions to the navy, which ranks second in size to that of the United States. Air force capabilities were increased with the addition of the MIG-23, an improved model in a standard jet fighter series. The AN-22, a large cargo plane roughly comparable to the American C-5A, provides greater capacity to move troops and equipment beyond the borders of Soviet-dominated areas.

Policy. Many Western strategists believe the Soviet defense forces have main purposes similar to those of the United States: to deter nuclear attack, lessen the damage if it comes, and be prepared for a range of combat below the level of general thermonuclear war. A more somber view is that the increasing strength of the Soviet forces suggests a conscious effort to surpass the United States in order to be able to attack the United States in some fashion.

WARSAW PACT NATIONS

In 1955 Poland, East Germany, Albania, Czechoslovakia, Hungary, Rumania, and Bulgaria followed Soviet leadership in signing the Warsaw Pact. It was a defense alliance in reaction to West Germany's entry into NATO.

In 1969 the eastern alliance was less firm than formerly. Albania does not participate in Warsaw Pact deliberations since siding with the Chinese in internal Communist squabbles. The Soviet invasion of Czechoslovakia still reverberates within the alliance. Within recent years Rumania has declined to join Warsaw Pact maneuvers. The 35 to 40 non-Russian divisions of East Germany, Poland, Hungary, and Bulgaria may not be all fully reliable, depending on the circumstances in which they find themselves when called to fight.

TANKS pass in review in Warsaw on June 22 as Poland marks the 25th anniversary of Communist government.

COMMUNIST CHINA

Little change was noted in China's armed forces by Western observers in 1969. It was generally assumed that previously noted efforts to perfect a nuclear missile capability continued during the year. The Chinese apparently developed the ability to test nuclear weapons underground. This had the immediate effect of making it difficult for outsiders to draw conclusions as to the progress of Chinese nuclear programs, since the atmospheric samples from which such inferences are drawn were reduced.

Despite nuclear-weapons advances, China's military strength remained in the People's Liberation Army. This force could be augmented by paramilitary units and conscription from the 800 million population. What China intended to do with her huge army when it was backed by nuclear missiles probably was a mystery to the USSR and the U. S.

(U. S. defense forces are discussed in detail under AIR FORCE; ARMY; COAST GUARD; MARINE CORPS; and NAVY. See also MISSILES; VIETNAM WAR; and separate articles on the major countries.)

ROBERT M. LAWRENCE
University of Arizona

DE GAULLE, Charles. See FRANCE.

DELAWARE MEMORIAL BRIDGE will carry one-way traffic on each of its twin spans as a result of new concrete deck poured in 1969 on the older bridge.

DELAWARE

In January 1969, when Dr. Russell W. Peterson took office as governor of Delaware, Republicans controlled both the executive and legislative branches of the government for the first time in more than a decade. Delaware's U. S. congressional delegation of two senators and one representative was also Republican. Civil rights legislation and changes in governmental structure were among the other highlights of the year.

Civil Rights. The new governor immediately removed National Guard patrols from the streets of Wilmington, where they had been on duty since the riots in April 1968 following the assassination of the Rev. Martin Luther King, Jr. The removal of the National Guard had been urged by leading black citizens. Blacks were pleased when the governor appointed the first Negro, Mrs. Arva Jackson, to the board of trustees of the University of Delaware. Shortly thereafter, the board elected a second Negro to its membership.

The new state legislature enacted a fair housing law in April. A month later a state summer employment program was established in an effort to help keep school-age youths off the streets during the long summer vacation period.

Government Structure. A constitutional revision commission worked throughout 1969 on a complete revision of the 4th state constitution, adopted in 1897. However, the only changes made in governmental structure were as a result of separate legislation. For example, a new department of justice came into existence on January 1 as a result of the previous year's legislation.

A Task Force on Government Reorganization was created in the spring to speed the development of a cabinet form of government to replace the existing system of government by commission or agency. An equitable reapportionment of seats in the New Castle county council was carried out, and is due to go into effect after the 1970 elections.

A constitutional amendment provided for the election of the governor and lieutenant-governor as a unit so that they could not be members of opposite parties. Governor Peterson called for reform of the family court and of the magistrate system. He also sought to organize a Mid-Atlantic governors' conference after he withdrew from the Southern Governors' conference. (It was felt that the problems of Delaware were much more like those of its Middle Atlantic than of its Southern neighbors.)

Population. Rapid population growth continued to be the basis of many problems in Delaware. The U. S. Census Bureau estimated that in 1969 the state's population was 21% greater than in 1960. This estimate ranked Delaware as the 8th most rapidly growing state in the union. Of the states east of the Rocky Mountains, only Florida and Maryland exceed this rate of growth.

Medical Education. Three major Wilmington hospitals, united as the Wilmington Medical Center, chose as their first president Dr. John A. Perkins, formerly president of the University of Delaware and undersecretary of the U. S. Department of Health, Education, and Welfare. A Delaware Institute of Medical Education and Research was established, with equal representation from the state, the University of Delaware, and the Wilmington Medical Center. A program for the education of physicians was worked out in coordination with Jefferson Medical College in Philadelphia, Pa.

JOHN A. MUNROE
University of Delaware

DELAWARE • Information Highlights

Area: 2,057 square miles (5,328 sq km).

Population: 538,000 (1969 est.).

Chief Cities (1969 est.): Dover, the capital, 15,500; Wilmington, 85,000; Newark, 19,400.

Government: Chief Officers—governor, Russell W. Peterson (Republican); lt. gov., Eugene D. Bookhammer (R); secy. of state, Eugene Bunting (R); atty. gen., David P. Buckson (R); treas., Daniel J. Ross; supt. of pub. instr., Kenneth C. Madden; chief justice, Daniel F. Wolcott. General Assembly—Senate, 19 members (13 Republicans, 6 Democrats); House of Representatives, 39 members (25 R, 14 D).

Education: School enrollment (1968)—public elementary, 66,000 pupils (2,700 teachers); public secondary, 53,000 pupils (2,700 teachers); nonpublic schools, 19,600 pupils (850 teachers); college and university (fall 1967), 15,173 students. Public school expenditures (1967–68)—$100,200,000 ($911 per pupil); average teacher's salary, $7,900.

Public Finance (fiscal year 1968): Revenues, $239,073,000 (total sales and gross receipts taxes, $34,829,000; motor fuel tax, $16,429,000; federal funds, $43,584,000). Expenditures, $256,240,000 (education, $50,404,000; health, welfare, and safety, $40,750,000; highways, $40,478,000). State debt, $366,049,000 (June 30, 1968).

Personal Income (1968): $2,026,000,000; average annual income per person, $3,795.

Public Assistance (fiscal year 1967): $7,968,768 to 18,627 recipients (aged, $1,271,621; dependent children, $5,014,801).

Labor Force (employed persons, August 1968): Agricultural, 10,100; nonagricultural (wage and salary earners), 219,000 (1967, 32.4% manufacturing, 17.9% trade, 12.3% government). Unemployed persons—10,200.

Manufacturing (1965): Value added by manufacture, $889,614,000 (primary metals, $22,273,000; nonelectrical machinery, $14,624,000; fabricated metals (1963), $20,768,000; food and products, $130,617,000).

Agriculture (1967): Cash farm income, $133,520,000 (livestock, $87,379,000; crops, $44,574,000; govt. payments, $1,567,000). Chief crops (tons)—Corn for grain, 431,284; soybeans, 106,288.

Mining (1967): Production value, $2,383,000. Chief minerals (tons)—Sand and gravel, 1,966,000; stone, 210,000; clays, 11,000.

Fisheries (1967): Commercial catch, 1,300,000 pounds ($300,000). Leading species—Hard blue crabs, 571,000 pounds ($49,417); clams, 264,100 pounds ($140,280).

Transportation: Roads (1968), 4,351 miles (7,002 km); motor vehicles (1967), 290,033; railroads (1967), 340 track miles (547 km); airports (1968), 1.

Communications (1968): Telephones, 316,100; television stations, 1; radio stations, 12; newspapers, 3 (daily circulation, 150,267).

Students in Copenhagen protest a teachers' strike with a self-teach-in at the Parliament building.

DENMARK

Major attention in Denmark during 1969 centered on controls on the economy, a plebiscite on lowering the voting age, tax and governmental reforms, and moves toward a Nordic economic union.

Domestic Affairs. The center-right coalition government of 1968 remained in power despite continued economic problems. A new tax on value added to goods by transfers was expected to offset losses from abolition of the sales tax. Increased rates for postal, telephone, and telegraph services, higher railroad fares, and an increase in the interest rate were intended to stem inflation. But these efforts were threatened by new wage agreements.

Laws were passed to reform some aspects of Danish government. The number of counties was reduced and their responsibilities were increased. A new law on land utilization and planning standardized land policy, preserved areas for recreation, and established policies regarding urban growth. Areas surrounding cities are to be preserved as rural communities. Another act set new rules for the civil service and required dissemination of information about administrative agencies.

In defense legislation, the government centralized the defense command and reduced involuntary military service to 12 months.

A plebiscite on June 24 about lowering the voting age from 21 to 18 failed by a 4-to-1 margin, even with Social Democratic and some coalition support. Earlier demonstrations and student unrest undoubtedly influenced the vote.

The death of Poul Sørensen, the minister of the interior, forced the redistribution of posts in the cabinet and strengthened its appeal.

Foreign Affairs. The report of the economic planning committee of the Nordic Council raised the choice between a Scandinavian economic union and membership in the European Economic Community. The Danes preferred the latter, but also saw possibilities in the former and gave somewhat grudging consent to its pursuit.

A Nordic meeting in November called for full discussion at Reykjavík, Iceland, in February 1970 and approved further recommendations on agricultural policies. The cabinet announced its intention of supporting the union during Folketing (Parliament) debates in October. At the same time a cautious response was given to a Finnish proposal for a

---

DENMARK · Information Highlights

Area: 16,629 square miles (43,069 sq km).

Population: 4,870,000 (1968 est.).

Chief Cities (1965 census): Copenhagen, the capital, 678,072; Aarhus, 117,748; Frederiksberg, 110,847; Odense, 107,531.

Government: *King*—Frederik IX (b. 1899; acceded 1947); *Prime Minister*—Hilmer Baunsgaard (took office Feb. 1, 1968). *Legislature* (unicameral)—Folketing, 179 members (party seating, 1969: Social Democratic party, 62; Conservative People's party, 37; Liberal party, 34; Radical Liberal party, 27; Socialist People's party, 11; others, 8).

Religious Faith: Lutherans, 96% of population.

Education: *Literacy rate* (1969), 100% of population. *Total school enrollment* (1965)—880,975 (primary, 519,279; secondary, 158,931; teacher-training, 114; technical/vocational, 154,826; university/higher, 47,825).

Finance (1969 est.): *Revenues,* $3,142,247,000; *expenditures,* $3,034,795,000; *public debt* (1967), $465,404,000; *monetary unit,* krone (7.501 kroner equal U. S.$1).

Gross National Product (1968): $12,438,341,000.

National Income (1968): $9,545,393,000; *average annual income per person,* $1,960.

Economic Indexes (1967): *Industrial production,* 126 (1963= 100); *agricultural production,* 105 (1963=100); *cost of living,* 126 (1963=100).

Manufacturing and Processing (metric tons, 1967): Cement, 2,149,000; gasoline, 1,327,000; meat, 956,000; crude steel, 401,000; beer (1966), 5,561,000 hectoliters.

Crops (metric tons, 1967–68 crop year): Barley, 4,382,000 (ranks 6 among world producers); sugar beets, 2,219,000; oats, 904,000; potatoes, 857,000; wheat, 420,000.

Minerals (metric tons, 1967): Lignite, 1,302,000; lime (1966), 425,000; iron ore, 14,000.

Foreign Trade (1968): *Exports,* $2,638,000,000 (chief exports, 1967: manufactured goods, $1,989,000,000; bacon, $234,-648,000; butter, $94,880,000); *imports,* $3,224,000,000 (chief imports, 1967: nonelectrical machinery, $327,000,000; road motor vehicles, $186,481,000; textiles, $185,000,000). *Chief trading partners* (1967): Britain (took 23% of exports, supplied 14% of imports); West Germany (took 13% of exports, supplied 19% of imports); Sweden.

Transportation: *Roads* (1969), 44,850 miles (72,177 km); *motor vehicles* (1967), 1,141,100 (automobiles 887,300); *railways* (1965), 2,476 miles (3,984 km); *merchant vessels* (1967), 342 (2,842,000 gross registered tons); *national airline* (with Norway and Sweden), Scandinavian Airlines System; *principal airport,* Copenhagen.

Communications: *Telephones* (1968): 1,469,195; *television stations* (1968), 18; *television sets* (1968), 1,200,000; *radios* (1967), 1,588,000; *newspapers* (1966), 59.

European security conference, although Danish freedom of action within NATO could not be limited.

Angier Biddle Duke, U. S. ambassador to Denmark, was replaced by the Nixon administration's appointee, Guilford Dudley, Jr., on May 12.

Economy. Inflation and deficits in the balance of trade, together with severe drains on foreign exchange, constituted the major difficulties in 1969. The first was met with increased interest rates. The National Bank raised the rate from 7% to 9%. At the same time, the government increased tax rates, and restricted government expenditures and private investment. A wage agreement for industrial workers seemed to offer little hazard of increasing prices, but a contract for agricultural workers required government subsidies, with consequent expectation of price increases. The severe drain on foreign exchange reserves, caused by speculation in the German mark, stopped to some degree after revaluation by West Germany, but left reserves dangerously low. For a time purchase of foreign exchange was halted. The bright spot was the improved balance of trade during the first part of 1969 and increased production in chemical and engineering enterprises.

Cultural and Social Affairs. Student representation on university councils was expanded, and laws on marriage and divorce were liberalized. Denmark had legalized the sale of unillustrated pornography in 1967 and because sex crimes decreased 34% in the following six months while other crimes were increasing, the Folketing, in 1969, abolished restrictions on erotic pictures and films. The police, however, warned against street display of erotic pictures and against the sale of erotica to those under 17.

Royal Family. Princess Margrethe, heiress to the throne, bore a second son on June 7.

RAYMOND E. LINDGREN
California State College, Long Beach

DENTISTRY

Several advances in dentistry were made during 1969. Dental researchers reported new methods of treating badly diseased teeth and the possibility that periodontal disease may one day be prevented by immunization. In the United States, two more states adopted mandatory fluoridation laws, bringing to seven the number of states having such legislation. The number of dental auxiliary personnel in training rose sharply during 1969, and a new dental school opened with five more scheduled to open in the near future.

New Techniques in Dental Science. Dr. Elena L. Liatukas of Washington, D. C., described a simple method of tooth restoration, using branched pins to support a large amalgam filling. The technique improves reconstructive capabilities for grossly destroyed teeth. Dr. Joseph P. Moffa of San Francisco has also worked on this technique and described the success of pin restorations in a study involving 900 extracted teeth. He found that self-threading pins are most retentive in the tooth structure and the amalgam.

Several other dental scientists have reported on possible ways of preventing or decreasing tooth decay and periodontal disease. Dr. Harald Löe of Denmark suggested that dental science may one day be able to develop a vaccine to prevent periodontal disease, a disease of the tissues supporting and surrounding the teeth that is almost as prevalent as caries and is the greatest factor in adult tooth loss.

Dr. Löe explained that oral bacteria play a role in both the development of caries and of periodontal disease. He said that it may be possible to develop some immunization procedure to prevent bacteria from interacting with foods and oral debris to form caries or calculus, the hard substance that forms on teeth and is an important factor in the development of periodontal disease.

Dr Irving Glickman of Boston has also studied periodontal disease. He placed miniaturized radio transmitters in the teeth and used the transmitters to measure occlusal, or biting, pressures in the mouth. He then reported that the experiments indicated that normal biting pressures are a factor in the beginning of periodontal disease.

There were also reports of possible ways of reducing the incidence of tooth decay. Dr. Harold R. Englander of the National Institute of Dental Research reported that a sodium fluoride gel provided a high concentration of fluoride in the teeth for as long as 23 months. He also found that children so treated experienced about an 80% reduction in tooth decay.

Dr. Ralph H. Stern of Los Angeles reported on studies of extracted teeth treated with laser beams. He found that the lasers appear to fuse beginning carious lesions with the enamel and make the enamel more resistant to dental caries. He suggested that lasers may increase the effectiveness of topically applied fluoride solutions, but he also cautioned that laser beam studies in the field of dentistry are still experimental.

Fluoridation. South Dakota and Ohio joined Connecticut, Minnesota, Illinois, Delaware, and Michigan in adopting mandatory fluoridation laws. In 1969 the number of people served by fluoridated water supplies reached 83 million; of these, some 75 million have artificially fluoridated water, while the remaining 8 million reside in communities with naturally fluoridated water.

During the year, the World Health Organization endorsed fluoridation as a "safe and practicable" method for reducing dental caries. After 40 years of study, fluoridation has now been accepted by virtually the entire scientific community as a safe and highly effective public health program. In 1970 the 25th anniversary of the world's first fluoridation program will be observed in Grand Rapids, Mich.—the first city to add fluoride to its water supply. In the past 25 years, fluoridation has also been adopted by many other nations, including Britain, Ireland, USSR, Australia, Brazil, Japan, and the Netherlands.

Dental Education and Personnel. One new dental school, at the Medical College of Georgia, was established and admitted its first class in 1969. New dental schools are scheduled to open within the next five years at the universities of Colorado, Florida, New York, Oklahoma, and Southern Illinois. At the same time, the nation's private dental schools experienced financial difficulties and two closed during 1969. Other private schools face similar difficulties and Congress has been asked to provide funds to the schools most in need of assistance.

The number of dental auxiliary personnel has almost doubled during the last 10 years. The number of students enrolled in dental hygiene, dental assistant, and dental laboratory technology schools also increased, as did the number of schools training such personnel. In 1967 there were 49 dental hygiene schools, while in 1969 there were 96 such schools. Similarly, there were 60 dental assistant schools in 1967 as compared with 151 in 1969, and 5 dental laboratory technician schools in 1966 as compared with 22 in 1969.

The continued growth in dental auxiliary personnel coupled with a steady increase in the number of dental graduates is expected to make the dental profession better able to meet present and anticipated increased demands for dental care. Dental prepayment, increased wages, and the development of health programs for the needy have already increased the demand for dental care and these demands are expected to rise during the 1970's.

Executive Director for the ADA. After more than 23 years as executive director of the American Dental Association (ADA), Dr. Harold Hillenbrand of Chicago retired on Dec. 31, 1969. During his tenure, Dr. Hillenbrand became a world-famous dental figure as writer, editor, teacher, and administrator. His chosen successor is Dr. C. Gordon Watson of Los Angeles.

LELAND C. HENDERSHOT
Editor-in-Chief, American Dental Association

DETROIT

Detroiters in 1969 elected a new mayor, Roman S. Gribbs, in the closest mayoralty election in the city's history. The school system moved toward decentralization during the year amid the chaos common to big city public schools. The increase in crime was a major concern and an issue in city elections.

Elections. Roman S. Gribbs, the Wayne county sheriff, defeated Wayne county auditor Richard H. Austin for mayor in the nonpartisan November 4 city election by a 6,194 vote margin, less than 1.2% of the votes cast. Austin was the city's first major Negro mayoralty candidate. Gribbs succeeds Jerome P. Cavanagh, who did not seek reelection to a third term. Ernest Browne, Jr., was elected a city councilman, becoming the third Negro on the 9-member council.

Schools. The Detroit Board of Education opened hearings on decentralization of the public school system, which enrolled 290,179 students in 1969. A new state law requires that there be 7 to 10 regional school boards in Detroit by Jan. 1, 1971. Chaotic public hearings reflected the unrest in the schools. Student outbursts forced temporary closing of several junior and senior high schools, parents picketed schools over teacher assignments, and two high school principals resigned. The public schools began a $27 million building program, the first major construction undertaken since 1963. It was financed under a new state law that increased the district's borrowing power by $50 million.

The new Wayne County Community College, primarily serving Detroiters, opened its doors to 7,000 students in 1969. Voters twice had refused tax money for the college, but the state legislature appropriated $998,000 for an initial budget.

Crime and Police. Crime rose 11% during the first 9 months of 1969, compared with the same period of 1968. In October 1969, 56 homicides were reported, the highest total for any month in the city's history. In an effort to cope with increasing crime, the Police Department launched a series of experiments, including the use of motor scooters and massive concentrations of manpower in designated high-crime areas.

WIDE WORLD
ROMAN S. GRIBBS, Wayne County sheriff, claims victory in November election bid for Detroit's mayoralty.

The Detroit police came under heavy criticism following an incident at a Negro church, the New Bethel Baptist, on March 30, 1969. After a patrolman was shot and killed near the church, the police shot their way inside as a meeting of the separatist black Republic of New Africa was dispersing. They arrested 142 persons, including women and children, most of whom were released within hours.

Algiers Motel Case. A former Detroit patrolman, Ronald W. August, charged with first degree murder in the death of 19-year-old Aubrey Pollard, was acquitted by a jury on June 10. Pollard was one of three Negro youths slain in the Algiers Motel annex during the July 1967 riot. The case attracted national attention because of the best-selling book *The Algiers Motel Incident* by John Hersey.

Business. Detroit's J. L. Hudson Company merged with the Dayton Corporation of Minneapolis to form the Dayton-Hudson Corporation. Auto production lagged behind 1968 with 7,607,268 vehicles being produced during the first 11 months of 1969 compared to 8,128,391 for the same period of 1968. Michigan Bell Telephone Company began construction of a new 17-story, $35 million headquarters building in downtown Detroit.

Planning. Massive renewal of the city of Detroit and creation of "metro centers" and "planned communities" in suburban areas as part of a 20-year plan was recommended by the Transportation and Land Use Study. The plan was part of a 4½-year, $5 million study of the area. Also recommended was construction of a $1.1 billion, 81-mile rapid transit system on rails to serve the metropolitan area.

City Government. The city government operated on a 1969–70 budget of $528,683,000, which required a property tax rate of $47.01 per $1,000 of assessed valuation.

CHARLES W. THEISEN
The Detroit "News"

DÍAZ ORDAZ, Gustavo. See biographical sketch under MEXICO.

DIPLOMATIC LIST. See AMBASSADORS AND ENVOYS.

DIRKSEN, Everett McKinley

U. S. senator from Illinois and Republican minority leader of the Senate; b. Pekin, Ill., Jan. 4, 1896; d. Washington, D.C., Sept. 7, 1969.

Everett McKinley Dirksen was unquestionably one of the most effective and colorful senators in the history of the U. S. Senate. A spellbinding orator of the old school, a confidant of and adviser to presidents of the Democratic party as well as those of his own Republican party, he exerted great influence on the national political scene. Although he was a staunch conservative who opposed many liberal programs, he was in large measure responsible for securing passage of the landmark civil rights bills of 1964, 1965, and 1968.

Background and Early Life. Dirksen was born on Jan. 4, 1896, in the farming community of Pekin, Ill. His parents were German immigrants; his father died when Everett was a boy. Supporting himself through part-time jobs, he studied law at the University of Minnesota, but left without a degree in 1917 to enlist in the Army.

Back in Pekin after World War I, Dirksen went into business, eventually buying a wholesale bakery concern with his brothers. In 1927 he was elected to the part-time post of Pekin commissioner of finance, serving until 1931.

National Politics. Dirksen ran for Congress in 1930 but lost to the Republican incumbent in the primary election. He was elected to the U. S. House of Representatives in 1932, however, and served eight consecutive terms. In the House he opposed numerous New Deal measures, including the Tennessee Valley Authority, but—not destined to earn a reputation for constancy—he backed some New Deal programs, including Social Security.

In foreign policy Dirksen was firmly isolationist, casting votes, for example, against reciprocal trade legislation. Although early in 1941 he opposed the lend-lease bill, in October of that year he voted for a supplementary lend-lease bill.

Dirksen had completed his law education at night school in Washington and was admitted to the District of Columbia and Illinois bars in 1936.

Because of failing eyesight Dirksen did not stand for reelection to the House in 1948. He soon recovered his vision, however, and vigorously campaigned for the Senate in 1950. His victory over the incumbent, Scott W. Lucas, who was the Democratic majority leader in the Senate, was an important one for Dirksen and his party. He was to be reelected in 1956, 1962, and 1968.

Rise to Senate Leadership. At the Republican national convention in Chicago in 1952, Dirksen supported Sen. Robert A. Taft of Ohio for the presidential nomination. Pleading for the seating of a pro-Taft delegation from Georgia (instead of the state's pro-Eisenhower delegation), Dirksen made a memorable statement on the convention floor. Pointing to Gov. Thomas E. Dewey, an Eisenhower man, Dirksen exclaimed "We followed you before and you took us down the path to defeat!"

In time Dirksen composed his differences with President Eisenhower, who campaigned for Dirksen's reelection in 1956. In 1954, Dirksen fought unsuccessfully to prevent the censure of fellow Republican Joseph R. McCarthy by the Senate. After Dirksen's election as Senate party leader in 1959 he enthusiastically cooperated with Eisenhower.

EVERETT McKINLEY DIRKSEN (1896–1969)

Despite his innate conservatism and Republican partisanship, Dirksen served as an intimate adviser to Democratic Presidents Kennedy and Johnson and was perhaps more influential in their administrations than in those of Republican Presidents Eisenhower and Nixon. Among his great legislative contributions was his crucial role in mustering Republican support for the civil rights bills of 1964, 1965, and 1968. He also helped secure passage of the United Nations bond proposal (1962) and the nuclear test ban treaty (1963)—both of which were major liberal foreign policy measures.

But he also fought tenaciously against the U. S. Supreme Court's rulings prohibiting prayer in public schools and against the Court's "one man, one vote" ruling on apportionment of state legislatures. He lost these fights, as well as his attempt to get Congress to adopt, as national flower, the marigold.

The "Dirksen Style." Dirksen's performance as minority leader was fascinating to behold. When he was for a measure, he would often start out against it and wind his devious way through the legislative thicket, confusing friend and foe alike and finally reaching his goal by carrying opponents as well as proponents with him. A masterful performer on the lecture platform as well as on the Senate floor and in the cloakroom, the mellifluous-voiced Dirksen was a much-sought-after speaker.

Plagued by numerous illnesses in his last years, Dirksen nevertheless continued to work. He died on Sept. 7, 1969, at Walter Reed Army Hospital in Washington following a lung operation.

Personal Life. Dirksen married Louella Carver of Pekin in 1927. Their daughter, Danice Joy, married Howard H. Baker, Jr., who was elected to the U. S. Senate as a Republican from Tennessee in 1966.

MILTON RAKOVE
University of Illinois at Chicago Circle

DISASTERS. See ACCIDENTS AND DISASTERS.
DISTILLING INDUSTRY. See ALCOHOLIC BEVERAGES.
DISTRICT OF COLUMBIA. See WASHINGTON.
DOG SHOWS. See SPORTS.

DISARMAMENT

The agreement between the United States and the Soviet Union, announced in Helsinki, Finland, on Dec. 22, 1969, to begin full-scale negotiations in early 1970 on limiting strategic nuclear weapons was the most noteworthy event in an unusually active year on the international arms-control front. Reached after five weeks of discussion, this agreement was the culmination of a long, frustrating effort by the United States to start serious talks.

Former President Johnson made the first overture for direct negotiations in 1967. The preliminary Strategic Arms Limitation Talks set for late 1968 were postponed primarily because of the Soviet-led invasion of Czechoslovakia in August 1968. The U. S. delegation at Helsinki was headed by Gerard C. Smith, director of the Arms Control and Disarmament Agency. His Soviet counterpart was Vladimir S. Semyonov, a deputy foreign minister.

Strategic Arms Limitation Talks (SALT). The substantive talks scheduled to open in Vienna, Austria, on April 16, 1970, were expected to cover the whole range of strategic offensive and defensive arms in the arsenals of the two superpowers. The businesslike character of the Helsinki discussions, including the absence of Soviet propaganda, suggested to many observers that the forthcoming negotiations might succeed in formulating agreed limits on the development, manufacture, or deployment of strategic weapons. Both sides accepted the premise of mutual deterrence and the necessity for each to have a nuclear capability sufficient to deter the other from a rational first strike. They agreed that any limitation must be applicable to both sides and that there must be adequate provision for verifying the agreement to detect cheating in time for the other side to take corrective measures.

The SALT talks were to deal with the complex action-reaction cycle in the nuclear equation in which each side develops a weapons system to counter what the other has done or is doing. This was to include offensive arms—intercontinental ballistic missiles (ICBM), manned bombers, and submarine-launched missiles; defensive arms such as the antiballistic missile (ABM); the subtle relationship between offensive and defensive arms; and the means for verifying any agreement to curb future production or deployment or to cut back existing arms.

It was not clear whether the SALT talks would deal directly with the latest technological advance in nuclear weapons, the multiple nuclear warhead known as MIRV (Multiple Independently Targeted Reentry Vehicle). When fitted with MIRVs, land- or submarine-based missiles can carry from three to nine nuclear warheads to widely separated targets. Both Moscow and Washington started testing MIRVs in 1968 and continued the program through 1969.

The substantive SALT talks were expected to last many months, if not years, because they deal with the basic issues of security and survival of the two superpowers. The final result may be formal agreements or tacit understandings based upon mutual restraint. In contrast, the limited arms control agreements of the past few years, including the Nuclear Nonproliferation Treaty, are "peripheral," as President Nixon observed on Dec. 8, 1969. Nevertheless, the movement on these secondary arms-control measures during 1969 tended to reinforce support for the fundamental effort to bring nuclear arms under verifiable control.

In the meantime, Washington and Moscow (as well as Peking) continued to strengthen their nuclear arsenals. Late in 1969 the United States started to deploy its Safeguard ABM system around two Minuteman ICBM bases after a prolonged public debate and a close supporting vote in the Senate. Safeguard was seen by the President and the con-

A TOAST TO SALT is raised at Helsinki prelude to Strategic Arms Limitation Talks. Clockwise from top are Gerard C. Smith (U. S.), President Urho Kekkonen of Finland, Vladimir S. Semyonov (USSR), and interpreter.

gressional majority as a necessary defense measure designed to maintain stability in view of the rapid Soviet buildup in strategic offensive weapons, particularly the massive SS-9 rocket capable of carrying a 30-megaton warhead, and the nuclear submarine fleet. Opponents of Safeguard saw it as a technological and psychological escalation of the arms race that should have been delayed at least long enough to see whether the SALT talks would yield tangible arms-control measures. (See also MISSILES.)

Nuclear Nonproliferation Treaty. As of Dec. 9, 1969, the NPT had been signed by 93 governments, 22 of which had ratified it. The latter included the United States and the Soviet Union, both of which signed the instruments of ratification on November 24. On that occasion President Nixon noted that the Senate had given its consent on March 13, and that his signature culminated a process spanning the "administration of three presidents."

The Soviet Union acted with the full knowledge that the Federal Republic of Germany was on the verge of endorsing it. This occurred on November 28, when Bonn signed the NPT in Washington, London, and Moscow. The United States, the Soviet Union, and other signatories were expected to deposit their instruments of ratification in 1970. The treaty pledges the nuclear powers to refrain from transferring nuclear arms to non-nuclear states and the latter to refrain from acquiring them.

Seabed Treaty. Reminiscent of the Limited Test-Ban Treaty that came into force in 1963 (and which prohibits nuclear explosions in the atmosphere, in outer space, and under water), the United States and the Soviet Union on Oct. 7, 1969, submitted to the 25-nation Disarmament Conference in Geneva a draft treaty prohibiting weapons of mass destruction (nuclear, chemical, and biological) on the ocean floor. Known as the Seabed Treaty (and subsequently revised slightly), the joint draft does not prohibit the use of submarines armed with nuclear weapons or the deployment of any form of military facilities within the territorial waters of states. In response to criticism from several small states that the treaty was too limited, representatives from Washington and Moscow—the only two powers capable of placing nuclear weapons on the seabed— asserted that it was *realistic* and, as U. S. Ambassa-

dor Charles W. Yost said, "Prevention before the fact is far easier than removal after the fact."

The objections to the Seabed pact by certain small powers, particularly neutralist states, reflected a persistent theme of criticism directed against joint Soviet–U. S. efforts to achieve strategic stability through mutual deterrence. This theme was voiced during a UN debate on the draft treaty in November, when Mrs. Alva Myrdal of Sweden accused the two superpowers of attempting to establish "a practical monopoly or, dare I say, a duopoly." This type of criticism reflected a frustration among representatives of many states, including allies of both sides, who have felt cut off from effective participation in the larger decisions of war and peace. But the small states were expected eventually to endorse the Seabed Treaty.

Small States' UN Remonstrance. The United States and the Soviet Union were rebuffed on Dec. 9, 1969, by the small states in a resolution of the UN General Assembly Political Committee calling upon the two superpowers to freeze the arms race immediately without awaiting the SALT outcome.

Biological Warfare Renunciation. Perhaps the most dramatic arms-control development of 1969 was a unilateral act of self-restraint—President Nixon's surprise announcement on November 25, pledging that the United States would not engage in biological warfare and renouncing all but defensive uses of chemical weapons. On chemical warfare, the President said the United States "reaffirms its oft-repeated renunciation of the first use of lethal chemical weapons" and "extends this renunciation to the first use of incapacitating chemicals." To this end, he recommended that the Senate endorse the Geneva Protocol of 1925, which bans the first use of "asphyxiating, poisonous or other gases and of bacteriological methods of warfare." The White House made it clear that tear gas and chemical defoliants, such as those used in Vietnam, were not included in the prohibition.

The President's statement on biological weapons was stronger and did not restrict the ban to the "first use." He said: "The United States shall renounce the use of lethal biological agents and weapons and all other methods of biological warfare" and "will confine its biological research to defensive measures, such as immunization and safety measures," adding that "the Department of Defense has been asked to make recommendations as to the disposal of existing stocks of bacteriological weapons." He also endorsed "the principles and objectives," though not the precise language, of the British draft convention banning "the use of biological methods of warfare" that was submitted to the Geneva Disarmament Conference in August 1969.

President Nixon described his unilateral renunciation as "an initiative toward peace." He said: "Mankind already carries in its own hands too many of the seeds of its own destruction. By the example we set today, we hope to contribute to an atmosphere of peace and understanding."

(See also UNITED NATIONS.)

ERNEST W. LEFEVER
Brookings Institution

"We were bound to meet!"

JAMES J. DOBBINS IN THE BOSTON HERALD-TRAVELER

DISASTERS. See ACCIDENTS AND DISASTERS.
DISTILLING INDUSTRY. See ALCOHOLIC BEVERAGES.
DISTRICT OF COLUMBIA. See WASHINGTON, D. C.
DOG SHOWS. See SPORTS.

DOMINICAN REPUBLIC

Preparations for the presidential and congressional elections scheduled for 1970 overshadowed many other Dominican events during 1969.

Presidential Candidates. Gen. Elías Wessin y Wessin returned to the country on January 12 and announced that he would be a candidate for the presidency. He organized the Quesqueyan Democratic party (PQD) for the purpose of backing his nomination. The general had been the principal military leader opposing the 1965 revolution, and at the end of the civil war that year had been virtually exiled to the United States. More fuel was added to the political fire in February when Héctor García Godoy, ambassador to the United States and provisional president of the republic in 1965–66, announced that he would also run for the office.

President Joaquín Balaguer contributed to political speculation on the occasion of his annual report to Congress on April 5. He indicated that he might run for reelection if he received support from virtually all of the political parties. A change in the constitution would be necessary to permit the president to succeed himself.

In New York City about two dozen Dominicans joined to form the Dominican Action party to support the candidacy of Rafael Trujillo, Jr., son of the late dictator. There was little indication in the Dominican Republic itself that the new party had received any wide support.

Cabinet Change. On April 21, President Balaguer dismissed the police chief, Gen. Braulio Álvarez Sánchez, and the education minister, Luis Alfredo Duvergé Mejía. Col. Joaquín A. Méndez Lara assumed the post of police chief.

The cabinet change came after a resurgence of political terrorism, in which at least seven persons had been killed, including two followers of Wessin y Wessin. León Bosch, son of former President Juan Bosch, had been arrested in connection with the murders. As a result, deputies of Bosch's party, the Partido Revolucionario Dominicano, had boycotted congressional sessions and demanded the removal of Police Chief Álvarez Sánchez. In addition, they had asked for the dismissal of the minister of education. Students criticized Duvergé for the rough handling they had received during demonstrations at the University of Santo Domingo in February, and for his failure to obtain a substantial increase in the university budget.

Opposition Parties. The major opposition party, the Partido Revolucionario Dominicano, adopted a much harder line toward the Balaguer government and the general political situation. In January, the principal leaders of the party met with Juan Bosch, living in self-imposed exile in Spain, to adopt a new declaration of principles. The declaration stated that the party was an alliance of various class groupings in the republic, and sought fundamental social and economic changes. It also said that the party no longer had faith in elections as an effective means of achieving democracy.

The extreme left continued to be active during the year, although not a greatly important factor.

Rockefeller Visit. An important political event was the July visit of U. S. presidential envoy Nelson Rockefeller, on one leg of his extended tour of Latin America. Before and during his visit, there were demonstrations and terrorist attacks, and at least four persons were killed in clashes with the police. All parties except President Balaguer's Reformist party denounced the Rockefeller visit.

Clerical Opposition. The unrest that has recently characterized the Roman Catholic Church throughout Latin America was evident in the Dominican Republic. On March 19, a document signed by 53 priests in Santiago de los Caballeros attacked the government for what it said was a failure to respect the basic rights of the people. A similar document was signed by 12 priests and a bishop in Higüey province in March. In June, two priests were arrested for "provocation of peasants."

Economic Development. The Balaguer government continued its program of economic development. The Dominican Republic joined with the Inter-American Development Bank and the United Nations Development Program in the establishment of a telecommunications network linking all Latin American countries.

ROBERT J. ALEXANDER
Rutgers University

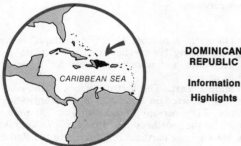

DOMINICAN REPUBLIC

Information Highlights

CARIBBEAN SEA

Area: 18,816 square miles (48,734 sq km).
Population: 4,029,000 (1968 est.).
Chief Cities (1967 census): Santo Domingo, the capital, 577,371; Santiago de los Caballeros, 101,819; San Francisco de Marcoris (1965 est.), 30,824; La Romana, 28,521; San Juan de la Maguana (1965 est.), 24,243.
Government: *President*—Joaquín Balaguer (took office July 1, 1966); *Vice President*—Francisco Augusto Lora (took office July 1, 1966). *Congress*—Senate, 27 members (party seating, 1969: Partido Reformista, 22; Partido Revolucionario Dominicano, 5); Chamber of Deputies, 74 members (party seating, 1969: Partido Reformista, 48; Partido Revolucionario Dominicano, 26).
Religious Faiths: Roman Catholics, 97% of population.

Education: *Literacy rate* (1960), 71.1% of population aged 10 and over. *Total school enrollment* (1966)—680,980 (primary, 585,153; secondary, 63,512; teacher-training, 437; technical/vocational, 25,272; university/higher, 6,606).
Finance (1967 est.): *Revenues,* $178,900,000; *expenditures,* $201,500,000; *monetary unit,* peso (1 peso equals U. S.$1).
Gross National Product (1967): $1,090,000,000.
National Income (1967): $885,000,000; *average annual income per person,* $219.
Economic Indexes (1967): *agricultural production,* 100 (1963=100); *cost of living,* 108 (1963=100).
Manufacturing (metric tons, 1967): Sugar, 819,000; cement, 310,000; beer (hectoliters), 176,000.
Crops (metric tons, 1967–68 crop year): Bananas, 200,000; rice, 147,000; cassava, 160,000; coffee, 38,100; cacao, 29,000.
Minerals (metric tons, 1967): Bauxite, 1,092,000; limestone (1964), 400,000; gypsum (1965), 90,000.
Foreign Trade (1968): *Exports,* $164,000,000 (chief exports, 1966: Sugar, $70,340,000; coffee, $20,950,000; bauxite, $10,350,000; cacao, $10,850,000); *imports,* $197,000,000 (chief imports, 1966: Chemical and pharmaceutical products, $14,300,000; fuel oils, $4,240,000; edible oils, $2,570,000). *Chief trading partners* (1967): United States (took 78% of exports, supplied 55% of imports); West Germany (took 2% of exports, supplied 6% of imports); Japan (supplied 7% of imports).
Transportation: *Roads* (1969), 5,280 miles (8,497 km); *motor vehicles* (1967), 42,600 (automobiles 28,900); *railways* (1965), 137 miles (220 km); *merchant vessels* (1967), 5 (14,000 gross registered tons); *principal airport,* Santo Domingo.
Communications: *Telephones* (1968): 34,234; *television stations* (1968), 7; *television sets* (1968), 75,000; *radios* (1967), 150,000; *newspapers* (1966), 6.

EARTHQUAKE in October devastated the Yugoslavian town of Banja Luka, killing 20 persons and injuring some 400. Rescuers (*above*) seek survivors.

EARTHQUAKES

The most unusual events in seismology in 1969 were the very first recordings from seismometers placed on the moon. On July 22, a seismometer placed by the Apollo 11 astronauts at Tranquility Base recorded a disturbance that may have been of seismic origin. Three days later, further recordings were obtained from the long- and short-period seismometers also placed on the moon by the Apollo 11 astronauts. These recordings, however, were difficult to interpret, and the seismometers went out of operation shortly thereafter.

In mid-November, other seismometers were placed in the Ocean of Storms by the Apollo 12 astronauts. Their first recorded event was the impact of the discarded ascent vehicle. The absence of a sharp impulse on this record seems to indicate cushioning material at the place of impact. But it will take many moon records to determine the nature of the moon's interior.

On earth, a number of major earthquakes were reported during 1969. They occurred in many parts of the world and were responsible for more than 3,800 deaths.

Middle East. The first disastrous earthquake of the year occurred on January 3 on the Iranian-Soviet border. Fifty persons were killed and 300 were injured in the northeastern province of Khurasan. On March 3, an earthquake centered in the Red Sea killed two persons and injured 16 and caused heavy property damage in the United Arab Republic.

Turkey suffered an earthquake on February 23. Although no fatalities were reported, 1,100 houses were destroyed in Demirci and surrounding villages in Anatolia. This same area was hit by an even stronger earthquake on March 28. Heavy damage was reported, and 53 persons were killed at Aleşehir.

Pacific Islands. On February 23 a destructive earthquake occurred off the island of Sulawesi (Celebes) in Indonesia. Twenty persons were killed at Madjine and four villages were destroyed. Six hundred lives were lost when waves generated by the quake hit the western coast of the island.

On August 11 an earthquake occurred between the Kurile Islands and Hokkaido, the northernmost of Japan's main islands. No casualties were reported by Japanese authorities.

Mainland China. On June 18 an earthquake with a magnitude of 7 on the Richter scale hit northeastern China. Heavy damage was reported, but no casualties were announced.

On July 25 eastern China, south of Tientsin, was hit by another earthquake. This one had a magnitude of 6 on the Richter scale, but in terms of loss of life it was by far the most destructive earthquake of the year. An estimated 3,000 people were feared dead.

North Atlantic. The largest earthquake of the year, with a magnitude of 8 on the Richter scale, occurred in the North Atlantic on February 28. Eleven persons were killed in Morocco and two in Portugal, but several deaths due to heart attacks were also attributed to the earthquake. The earthquake was also felt in France, Spain, and the Canary Islands, and by ships at sea.

Africa. On September 29 an earthquake with a magnitude of 6.5 on the Richter scale occurred about 125 miles (201 km) northeast of Capetown, South Africa, an area rarely hit by quakes. This earthquake leveled three villages, and although

only 11 persons were killed, more than 1,000 were left homeless.

Shortly afterward, on October 5, another quake of the same intensity occurred in the same region. This quake gave rise to more landslides and brush fires, but there were no casualties.

Antarctica. On February 21 the South Shetland Islands were hit by an earthquake. Although much damage was done, there were no casualties.

Albania. On April 3 an earthquake occurred in southern Albania. As a result, one person was killed and 65 were injured. Much damage was also done.

Peru. On October 1 an earthquake with a magnitude of 6.4 on the Richter scale struck Huancayo, Peru. The quake destroyed several villages and killed about 80 persons. A farmer reported that northeast of Huancayo a crack about 6.2 miles (10 km) long appeared along the slope of the Huaytapallana Hill. Although some 1,000 aftershocks were reported at the Huancayo station during the next two weeks, no volcanic activity was noticed.

Yugoslavia. On October 27 a major earthquake struck the Bosnian town of Banja Luka, killing 20 persons, injuring 400 others, and destroying about 80% of the buildings. It was the worst quake in the town's history.

J. JOSEPH LYNCH, S. J.
Director, Fordham University Seismic Observatory

TREMORS shook northern California in October. In Santa Rosa, groceries tumbled off market shelves and work crews cleaned up the rubble.

UPI   WIDE WORLD

ECONOMY OF THE U.S.

The production, distribution, and consumption of wealth in the United States in 1969 is examined in this article under the following headings: (1) Economic Review; (2) National Income and Product; (3) Industrial Production; (4) Retail Sales; and (5) Wholesale Sales.

(Other economic developments are reviewed in the articles on BANKING; BUILDING AND CONSTRUCTION; CONSUMER AFFAIRS; INTERNATIONAL FINANCE; INTERNATIONAL TRADE; LABOR; STOCKS AND BONDS; TAXATION; and the UNITED STATES.)

ECONOMIC REVIEW

The year 1969 brought the U. S. economy to the brink of recession while at the same time the rate of inflation accelerated.

Paradoxically, many measures of the economy's overall performance continued to climb upward—often to the dismay of many seasoned observers. Embedded in the glowing dollar gains were persistent price rises that reflected increasing dislocations in the economy and cast the shadow of further difficulties to come. While real output of the economy rose in 1969, gains were less impressive than in earlier years, and some sectors of the economy were experiencing severe strain. It was a year in which the term "recovery" was used by the national administration to hail a slowing in the growth of sales and employment.

Output. Gross national product, the most comprehensive measure of the economy's performance, advanced in 1969 to $932.3 billion, a gain of about 7.7% but lower than the 9.1% rise registered in 1968. The increase in the annual rate of growth was slowing down noticeably toward the end of the year—a development taken by some as a significant one. But the essential point was that at the end of 1969 all of the gain in gross national product was in prices. After accounting for price level advances, real output showed no increase in the last quarter of the year.

Contributing to this result and somewhat clouding the picture, however, was the strike at General Electric, the widespread effect of which was to nullify any real increase that might otherwise have been shown.

Tracing the output performance of the economy in 1969 was the Federal Reserve Board's Index of Industrial Production (1957–59 = 100). The index advanced from January through July from 169.1 to 174.6, and then declined slightly in each of the last five months of the year to 170.9 in December. For the year as a whole there was an average gain almost as high as registered in 1968 over 1967, a little over 7 points, but the last half of 1969 was represented by small but persistent monthly declines. This performance, coupled with the behavior of real GNP data, reinforced the belief that the growth of overall economic activity was at a standstill as the year closed.

Prices. At the center of the difficulty was price increases. Prices advanced on a broad front through the year, and increases appeared to be accelerating as 1969 ended.

The Consumer Price Index (1957–59 = 100) advanced from 124.1% in January to 131.3% in December. Put another way, consumer prices rose 6.4% at an annual rate in the first half of the year and 5.9% in the second half. But, also on an an-nual rate basis, the rise was at a rate of 7.2% as the year closed, a discouraging development in the struggle against inflation and the sharpest advance in nearly two decades.

At the end of 1969 an average worker with three dependents found he had real spendable earnings amounting to $77.69 per week compared with $78.66 a year earlier.

Restraints. The fight against rising prices continued throughout the year and itself had reverberating effects on the economy, particularly in the monetary sector. In December 1968 the Federal Reserve Board had sharply shifted toward monetary restraint, attempting to curb money supply and the frenetic pace of economic activity. Open-market operations were used, discount rates were raised to 6% (the highest level since 1929), bank reserve requirements were increased, and the maximum rates that banks are allowed to pay to attract deposits were checked. As the year progressed, the growth of money supply slowed dramatically.

And with the demand for funds remaining high, and even growing, interest rates skyrocketed, in some cases to heights not reached in a century. Bank prime rates were at a high of 6.75% at the end of 1968; after three raises they reached a record of 8.5% by June 1969.

Housing construction suffered as mortgage money became difficult to obtain under increasingly higher interest rates. New private nonfarm housing units started were actually at a 3-year high of over 1.8 million on an annual rate basis in January 1969 but fell off after that. Except for a brief revival in September, housing starts were down every month and numbered just over 1.2 million units in December. Some housing experts considered the December showing to be less than half the effort needed to meet population expansion and in some cases critical urban housing shortages.

State and local governments, contending with serious urban and environmental problems, found the capital markets tightly restricted or sometimes closed to them in their quest for capital funds. Interest rates advanced to the highest level since the Civil War, and with legal interest rate ceilings on what they could pay, local governments found money often unavailable. Bonds sold by state and local governments declined to a total of $11.4 billion in 1969, some 30% below the level reached in 1968.

Business Spending. Business, however, continued to expand its capital outlays, a development that added to the inflationary fires. Business obtains funds from the capital market, and in many cases it was willing to pay record rates for the money it borrowed as the corporate bond yields rose to around the 9% level. Plant and equipment outlays for the year were more than $71 billion, some $7 billion or 11% higher than in 1968.

Many business firms were willing to pay higher rates for borrowed money to advance capital expansion on the ground that construction costs were rising faster than money costs. In addition, of course, business firms generate a part of their own capital through retained profits and depreciation allowances. During the year a case was made against the 7% investment tax credit business on the grounds it was inflationary, and the credit was repealed as a part of the Tax Reform Act of 1969.

THE U.S. ECONOMIC PICTURE IN 1969

GROSS NATIONAL PRODUCT
(In Current and Constant Dollars)

Billions
of dollars

950
900
850
800
750
700
650
600
550
500
450
400

IN CURRENT DOLLARS ▶

IN 1958 DOLLARS ▼

1958 '59 '60 '61 '62 '63 '64 '65 '66 '67 '68 '69¹

¹Preliminary figure for three quarters, at annual rate.
DATA FROM U.S. DEPARTMENT OF COMMERCE

CONSUMER PRICES

Index, 1957-59=100

150
140
130
120
110

All Services ▶

ALL ITEMS ▶

Food ▶

1966   1967   1968   1969

DATA FROM U.S. DEPARTMENT OF LABOR,
BUREAU OF LABOR STATISTICS

INTEREST RATES

RATE
8%
7%
6%
5%
4%
3%

TREASURY BILLS ▶

LONG-TERM
GOVERNMENT
SECURITIES ▶

FEDERAL RESERVE
DISCOUNT RATE

1966   1967   1968   1969

DATA FROM "FEDERAL RESERVE BULLETIN"
(November 1969)

INDUSTRIAL PRODUCTION
Seasonally Adjusted Index

Index, 1957-59=100

180
160
140
120

1966   1967   1968   1969

DATA FROM FEDERAL RESERVE BOARD

PERSONAL INCOME
Seasonally Adjusted, at Annual Rates

Billions
of dollars

800
700
600
500
400
300

TOTAL ▶

Wage and Salary
Disbursements ▶

1966   1967   1968   1969

DATA FROM U.S. DEPARTMENT OF COMMERCE

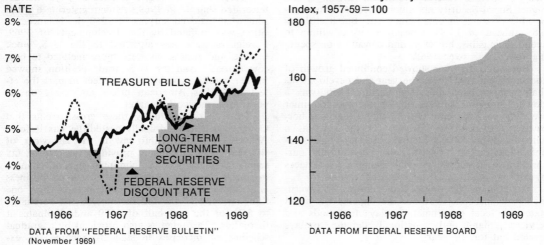
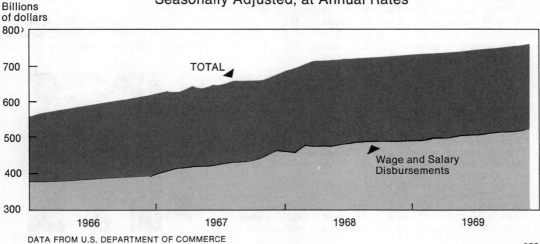

PAUL W(INSTON) McCRACKEN, who became chairman of President Nixon's Council of Economic Advisers in January 1969, is considered an economic pragmatist. Although he has called on business and labor to forego inflationary increases in prices and wages, he has expressed little faith in the effectiveness of federal wage-price guidelines in stemming inflation. In October he asserted that the administration's policies of fiscal and monetary restraint were beginning to cool off the economy.

McCracken, the son of a farmer, was born in Richland, Iowa, on Dec. 29, 1915. He studied at William Penn College (B. A., 1937) and Harvard University (Ph.D., 1948). In 1942–43 he was with the Department of Commerce, and from 1943 to 1948 he was employed by the Federal Reserve Bank of Minneapolis. He joined the faculty of the University of Michigan in 1948 and became Edmund Ezra Day University Professor of Business Administration there in 1966. He was a member of President Eisenhower's Council of Economic Advisers from 1956 to 1959.

UPI

Consumer Spending. Consumers were major contributors to the high level of economic activity during 1969. Unemployment remained low, rising to the level of 4% only in September and generally remaining around 3.5%. As the year ended personal income was running at a seasonally. adjusted annual rate of about $770 billion, although gains were slower than they had been earlier in the year. Even so, personal income was 8.6% over 1968, propelled upward by huge increases in wage and salary rates and in total employment.

Higher taxes at the state and local level, retention of the 10% federal income tax surcharge, and higher Social Security taxes combined to reduce disposable personal income somewhat. But it still ran 6.8% ahead of 1968. Consumers were willing to spend their gains, however, and consumption spending rose 7.5% over 1968.

But while the year showed continued growth of consumer outlays, it was the year-end developments that were perhaps most significant. There was a slowing in growth of personal income and consumer spending near the end of the year. Consumer borrowing slowed in its advance for the year as a whole, and there was a decline in the growth of durable goods outlays by customers. Now durable purchases also slowed down. But spending for services by consumers advanced by 9% for the year.

Government Spending. Expenditures by governments advanced in 1969 but the impetus was from state and local government outlays for goods and services. Significantly, national defense outlays leveled out for the year.

Earnings and the Stock Market. Business generally registered advances for the year on all fronts, in line with the general performance of the economy. But the underlying pervasive rattlings in the price system forecast difficulties. In one area—corporate profits after taxes—a decline began in the second quarter. While the year as a whole showed a gain, the decline in corporate profits coupled with

continued declines in profit margins reflected near full employment of the economy's resources and the difficulty of further real expansion. Cuts in scheduled levels of auto production as the year progressed were symptomatic.

Difficulties in the corporate profit area had been noticed earlier by the stock market. After a booming 1968, when the Standard & Poor's Index of 500 stocks (1941–43 = 10) reached 106.5 in December, the market slipped, regained to 104.6 in May 1969, slipped to 94.7 in July, steadied, and then dropped to 90.4 in December.

Moreover, the nation's balance of payments deteriorated sharply in 1969. After registering a small somewhat artificial surplus in 1968 the balance position was buffeted by the developments of 1969. Foreigners were less attracted to the U. S. stock market, and Americans were more inclined to borrow abroad. And the U. S. trade position showed further erosion, continuing to reflect in part the effect of higher American prices and costs on its position in the world market.

Taxes. It was during these crosscurrents that Congress debated and finally passed the Tax Reform Act of 1969, signed into law in the last week of the year. The act aims at providing tax reform, tax relief, tax incentives, tax continuation, and changes in Social Security benefits. Its effects on business and the economy will be widespread. For one thing, it reduces the federal income tax surcharge to 5% for the first half of 1970 and eliminates it thereafter. Tax relief is also provided by a gradual schedule of increases in standard income tax exemptions. As a whole the act is expected to provide $9.1 billion of tax relief and $6.6 billion of tax increases when fully implemented in 1979. Its immediate effect was expected to be mildly inflationary.

Crossroads. Near the end of 1969, then, the economy stood at a crossroads. Growth in personal income, consumption, and employment was slow, as

UPI

ARTHUR F(RANK) BURNS, who in January 1969 became the first man to serve as counselor to the President with full Cabinet rank, has played an important role in the formulation of the Nixon administration's domestic policies. A fiscal conservative, he is firmly committed to economic restraint and to the battle against inflation. In October he was named by President Nixon to succeed William McChesney Martin, Jr., as chairman of the Federal Reserve Board. He was sworn in on Jan. 31, 1970.

Burns, the son of a house painter, was born in Stanislau, Austria, on April 24, 1904. He worked his way through Columbia University (Ph.D., 1934) and taught economics at Rutgers University from 1927 to 1944. As chairman of President Eisenhower's Council of Economic Advisers from 1953 to 1956 he promoted flexible policies aimed at combating both inflation and recession. Associated with the National Bureau of Economic Research since 1930, he became its president in 1957 and chairman in 1967. His published works include *The Management of Prosperity* (1966).

was industrial production. Price and wage pressures were continuing, however, and price indicators were accelerating. The federal budget promised to be stimulative, as did reduction of the surcharge and increased Social Security benefits. And demand pressures continued strong.

The economy was clearly faced with continued inflationary pressure going into 1970, but it was grasping for whatever hope there was in an indicated pause.

JACKSON PHILLIPS
Dun & Bradstreet, Inc.

NATIONAL INCOME AND PRODUCT

National income rose at a slower pace in the United States in 1969 than it had during the previous year. National income is the total earnings of labor and property that are derived from the current production of goods and services by the nation's economy.

The slowing in the growth of national income in 1969 reflected a marked retardation in the rate at which production increased. The income slowdown was only partly offset by an acceleration in the rate at which prices advanced.

Real output in 1969 increased 3%, a rate only about three fifths as fast as that reported for 1968. The slowing in output growth was noticeable throughout the year, and, by the fourth quarter, output had ceased to expand. The slowing in the growth of output was particularly marked in personal consumption, government purchases, and residential construction. The slowing in these markets was not offset by a considerable speedup in business investment.

Prices rose 4.75% in 1969. This was substantially more than the 4% price rise in 1968 and was the largest increase recorded for any calendar year since 1951. Because of this acceleration in prices, 1969 became the fourth successive year in which overall prices, as measured by the GNP deflator, advanced at a markedly faster pace than in the previous year.

National Income. The national income of the United States totaled $771.5 billion in 1969—8% more than it did in 1968. National income had increased 9.2% in the previous year, when economic growth had been faster.

The slowing in the growth of national income centered in corporate profits and nonfarm proprietor's income, as firms were unable to maintain their profit margins despite the acceleration in price increases. Corporate earnings of $88.7 billion were only 0.9% higher than they had been in 1968; in the earlier year they had risen 11%. Nonfarm proprietors' income, at $50.2 billion in 1969, was up 2% from the previous year; in 1968 such income had increased 4.3%. Net interest rose 9.6% in 1969 to a total of $30.6 billion; in 1968 net interest had increased 13.4%.

The compensation of employees rose moderately faster in 1969 than in 1968. Compensation of employees totaled $564.1 billion in 1969, up 9.9% from the previous year, as compared with a gain of 9.5% in 1968. The rental income of persons rose 1.9% to $21.6 billion in 1969; in the previous year such income had also risen 1.9%.

Farm proprietors' income increased 10.3% to a total of $16.1 billion in 1969. This was a marked turnaround from the 1968 experience, when farm proprietors' income had declined 0.7%.

NATIONAL INCOME BY TYPE OF INCOME
(billions of dollars)[1]

	1966	1967	1968	1969
National income	$620.6	$654.0	$714.4	$771.5
Compensation of employees	435.5	467.4	513.6	564.2
Wages and salaries	394.5	423.5	465.0	509.8
Private	316.8	337.3	369.0	405.3
Government	77.7	86.2	96.0	104.5
Supplements to wages and salaries	41.0	43.9	48.6	54.4
Proprietors' income	61.3	61.9	63.8	66.3
Business and professional	45.2	47.2	49.2	50.2
Farm	16.1	14.7	14.6	16.1
Rental income of persons	20.0	20.8	21.2	21.6
Corporate profits and inventory valuation adjustment	82.4	79.2	87.9	88.7
Profits before tax	84.2	80.3	91.1	94.3
Profits tax liability	34.3	33.0	41.3	43.5
Profits after tax	49.9	47.3	49.8	50.8
Inventory valuation adjustment	−1.8	−1.1	−3.2	−5.6
Net interest	21.4	24.7	28.0	30.6

[1] Detail may not add to total because of rounding. Source: Office of Business Economics, U. S. Department of Agriculture.

Personal Income. The retardation in the growth of national income was not fully matched in personal income, which is the current income received by persons from all sources, inclusive of transfers from government and business. Personal income, at $747.1 billion in 1969, was up 8.6% over the previous year; in 1968 the rate of increase had been 9.2%. The rate of increase in personal income held up better in 1969 than that in national income largely because a major share of the retardation in national income occurred in the share of corporate profits, which is not a component of personal income.

Although personal income grew at a somewhat slower pace in 1969 than it had in 1968, personal tax payments rose at a faster rate—20%—in 1969 than in 1968, when they rose 18.1%. The acceleration of personal tax payments in the face of a slowing in the growth of personal income reflected the fact that the income-tax surtax was in effect for all of 1969 while it was in effect for only nine months of 1968. In addition, there was a marked rise in final settlements in April 1969.

With personal tax payments increasing at a rate more than twice that of personal income, disposable personal income (the income of persons available for spending or saving) increased only 6.7% in 1969 to a total of $629.6 billion, as contrasted with a gain of 8% in 1968.

The slowdown in the growth of disposable personal income was paralleled by a marked slowing in the rate of increase in personal outlays. But since the dollar increase in personal consumption and other outlays was somewhat greater than the dollar

GROSS NATIONAL PRODUCT OR EXPENDITURE
(billions of dollars)[1]

	1966	1967	1968	1969
Gross national product	$749.9	$793.5	$865.7	$932.3
Personal consumption expenditures	466.3	492.3	536.6	576.0
Durable goods	70.8	73.0	83.3	89.6
Nondurable goods	206.9	215.1	230.6	243.8
Services	188.6	204.2	222.8	242.5
Gross private domestic investment	121.4	116.0	126.3	139.6
Fixed investment	106.6	108.6	119.0	131.5
Nonresidential	81.6	83.7	88.8	99.3
Structures	28.5	27.9	29.3	33.4
Producers' durable equipment	53.1	55.7	59.5	65.9
Residential structures	25.0	25.0	30.2	32.2
Change in business inventories	14.8	7.4	7.3	8.0
Net exports of goods and services	5.3	5.2	2.5	2.1
Government purchases of goods and services	156.8	180.1	200.3	214.7
Federal	77.8	90.7	99.5	102.0
State and local	79.0	89.3	100.7	112.7

[1] Detail may not add to total because of rounding. Source: Office of Business Economics, U. S. Department of Commerce.

increase in disposable income, the dollar volume of personal savings in 1969 was down from the 1968 total. Personal saving totaled $37.7 billion in 1969 —$0.7 billion less than in 1968. The fall in personal saving in the face of a rise in disposable personal income brought the saving rate down to 6% of disposable personal income in 1969 from the 6.5% recorded in 1968.

Gross National Product. The slowing in economic activity can be analyzed in terms of the gross national product (GNP), which is the market value of the output of goods and services produced by the nation's economy. The GNP rose 7.7% in 1969 to reach a total of $932.3 billion. In 1968, GNP had increased at a rate of 9.1%.

The retardation in the growth of total GNP in 1969 reflected substantial slowdowns in the pace at which personal consumption expenditures, residential construction, and government purchases increased. Personal consumption expenditures rose 7.3% in 1969 to a total of $576 billion; in 1968 such outlays had increased 9.1%. The slowing was most marked in purchases of consumer durable goods, which increased 7.3% in 1969 as compared with a gain of 14.1% in the previous year. Purchases of nondurable goods and services also rose at a slower rate in 1969 than in 1968.

Residential structures, at $32.2 billion, were up 6.6% in 1969, against 20.8% in 1968.

There was a marked slowing in the rate of advance in federal government purchases of goods and services; at $102 billion in 1969, these purchases were up 2.7% as contrasted with an increase of 9.7% in 1968. The slowing in the growth of state and local government purchases of goods and services was less marked than that in federal purchases; at $112.7 billion in 1969, state and local purchases were up 12% as contrasted with the previous year's gain of 12.8%.

The slowdown in the growth of most GNP components was not shared by business purchases of fixed investment and inventories. Businesses invested $99.3 billion in nonresidential fixed investment in 1969—11.8% more than in 1968; such investment had risen at a rate of 6.1% in 1968. Business inventory accumulation totaled $8 billion in 1969— 9.6% more than it had in 1968. Business inventory accumulation in 1968 was at about the same rate as it had been in the previous year.

JOHN A. GORMAN
National Income Division, Office of Business Economics, U. S. Department of Commerce

INDUSTRIAL PRODUCTION

Industrial production in the United States expanded moderately in 1969, advancing from January through July and then declining without interruption for the last five months. By December, the Federal Reserve seasonally adjusted production index had decreased to 170.9% of the 1957–59 base period—down from the July high of 174.6 but above the December 1968 index of 168.7.

For the full year of 1969, the increase in industrial output amounted to 4.4%—roughly the same as the advance from 1967 to 1968 and also in line with the nation's long-term growth rate of 4%. In contrast, a 7% annual average rate prevailed in the 1961–66 period, which included the expansion from the cyclical low in early 1961 and a sharp spurt in output of defense equipment in the Vietnam War buildup in 1965 and 1966.

All sectors of final demand—consumers, government, and business (the last-named for investment in plant and equipment)—contributed to the increased output in 1969. The slowdown after midsummer reflected easing tendencies in a number of industries as overall demand pressures abated, particularly for producers', military, and consumer hard goods.

Plant Operating Rate. For the third year in a row, most U. S. plants operated in 1969 considerably below the most efficient levels, generally considered to be 90% to 92% of manufacturing capacity. The average rate of capacity operation during 1969, at 83.7%, was only slightly below the average for 1968. New additions to manufacturing capacity about matched the increase in manufacturing output.

Leaders. Dominant features of the production picture in 1969 were the increase in output of machinery, the consistently high and record level of steel production, and the curtailment in output of defense equipment. The combined output of machinery and iron and steel accounted for about three fifths of the advance in total industrial production during the year.

Production of business equipment—largely industrial, commercial, and freight and passenger

U. S. INDUSTRIAL PRODUCTION INDEX
(1957-59 = 100)

	1960	1968	1969
Industrial production, total	108.7	165.5	172.7
Major industry groupings			
Manufacturing, durable and nondurable	108.9	166.9	173.8
Mining	101.6	126.6	130.2
Utilities	115.6	202.5	221.3
Major marketing groupings			
Final products, total	109.9	165.1	170.8
Consumer goods	111.0	156.9	162.4
Equipment including defense	107.6	182.6	188.6
Materials	107.6	165.8	174.6

Source: Board of Governors of the Federal Reserve System.

equipment—advanced 6% from 1968 to 1969. Consumer goods output—passenger cars, household goods, and staple commodities—recorded a respectable gain of 3.5% despite a reduction in new car assemblies. Materials production increased 5%.

New production highs for 1969 were registered for 16 of the 21 major manufacturing industries. Only motor vehicles and parts, aircraft and other transportation equipment, apparel, leather goods, and tobacco products failed to set production records. The reduction in output of transportation equipment held the advance in total durable goods production in 1969 to 4%. Nondurable goods manufacturing accounted for a gain of 4.5%. The advance in output of mining was 3% and in utilities 9%.

Durable Manufactures. The steel industry experienced an exceptionally good year in 1969. Raw steel production reached 141 million tons, up from 131.5 million in 1968 and the high of 134.1 million tons in 1966. During 1969, output rose sharply through June before falling moderately (after seasonal adjustment) in the last half. Higher consumption, some buildup of total steel stocks, and a substantial reduction in net imports of steel contributed to the production advance in iron and steel output.

Booming foreign steel demand, particularly in Europe, reduced exports to the United States by major foreign producers and stimulated exports from the United States. Through October, steel mill products entering U. S. ports totaled 11.9 million tons, a drop of 20% from the record 15 million tons of imports in the like period of 1968. Exports to foreign countries jumped to 3.9 million tons from 1.5 million tons in the same 10-month span of 1968. The reduced import flow of steel in 1969 represented about 14% of domestic steel consumption; this compared with 18% in 1968.

Higher prices and strong demand, both domestic and foreign, greatly stimulated output of the major nonferrous metals. Production increases were quite sizable for copper, aluminum, and lead, reflecting in part the recovery in output from work stoppages in 1968. Because of the high output from domestic sources, imports of nonferrous metals, particularly refined copper, were in considerably reduced volume in 1969.

Strength in the machinery and equipment sector reflected the large increase in business outlays for new capital equipment in 1969. These expenditures increased to $71.3 billion in 1960, or 11% from the 1968 total of $64.1 billion. From 1967 to 1968, the rise was only 4%.

After more than a year of virtually no growth, machinery output registered an advance of 7% in the first nine months of 1969. The uptrend was arrested in the final quarter, however, in part because of a prolonged work stoppage in General Electric plants. For 1969 as a whole, the gain in output of nonelectrical and electrical machinery amounted to 6%, which compared with an increase of less than 1% from 1967 to 1968.

Production of most machinery products in 1969 equaled or exceeded the 1968 volume. Some lines—generating and transmission equipment for the electric utility industry, communication equipment, certain types of industrial machinery, and air conditioning systems—showed continued strong growth trends. In other lines—tractors and construction and farm machinery—moderate decreases were reported.

ANNUAL SURVEY OF MANUFACTURES, 1967

Industry Group	Number of Employees	Payroll (millions)	Value added by manufacture (millions)
All manufacturing establishments, including administrative and auxiliary units, total	19,398,000	$131,876	$259,301
Operating manufacturing establishments	18,570,000	123,256	259,301
Nondurable goods	7,560,000	44,368	107,737
Meat and dairy products	543,000	3,358	6,931
Food crop products	808,000	4,696	13,389
Beverages, candy, and tobacco	378,000	2,335	8,043
Textile and leather products	1,263,000	5,862	10,580
Apparel and related products	1,363,000	5,475	9,693
Paper and allied industries	643,000	4,440	9,676
Printing and publishing	1,064,000	7,295	14,155
Industrial chemicals	429,000	3,424	11,572
Chemical products	425,000	3,094	11,868
Petroleum and coal products	140,000	1,196	5,356
Rubber and plastics products	504,000	3,193	6,474
Durable goods	11,010,000	78,888	151,564
Lumber and wood products	563,000	2,760	4,828
Furniture and miscellaneous	852,000	4,495	8,566
Stone, clay, and glass products	605,000	3,877	8,408
Iron and steel industries	918,000	7,177	14,022
Nonferrous metals industries	365,000	2,660	6,126
Construction metal products	600,000	4,083	7,719
General metal products	707,000	4,926	9,335
Manufacturing machinery	842,000	6,719	12,223
Other nonelectrical machinery	1,030,000	7,581	15,474
Communication products and parts	1,052,000	7,475	13,076
General electric products	832,000	5,461	11,779
Motor vehicles and equipment	781,000	6,236	14,266
Aerospace and transit equipment	1,294,000	11,387	17,507
Instruments and selected ordnance products	569,000	4,051	8,235
Administrative and auxiliary[1]	828,000	8,620	—

[1] Includes storage warehouses, power plants, research laboratories, garages, repair shops, and similar facilities that serve the manufacturing establishments of a company rather than the general public. (Source: U. S. Department of Commerce, Bureau of the Census.)

After four years of continuous expansion, output of defense equipment turned down in the third quarter of 1968 and continued to drift irregularly lower in 1969. The reduction in output reflected the leveling off in military programs under way for more than a year.

Activity in plants turning out commercial aircraft, as measured by deliveries of airframe weight, was maintained at around the 1968 monthly average rate through May, but subsequently declined as order backlogs were trimmed from earlier very high levels.

Production of railroad equipment increased substantially in 1969 after declining in the previous two years. Unfilled orders for new freight cars on November 1 were about half again as large as at the end of December 1968.

The automobile industry was less active in 1969 than in 1968. For most months, assemblies of cars and trucks ran well below the 1968 monthly average. Moreover, monthly assemblies were quite uneven, reflecting in part the lower and irregular pattern of dealers' sales of new cars to consumers and in part the sporadic strikes in some assembly plants. For the full year, the industry turned out about 10.2 million units—8.2 million passenger cars and 2 million trucks.

The passenger car count was about one-half million units below the 1968 volume and approximately 1 million under the peak production year of 1965. Truck assemblies were maintained at the high 1968 rate.

Imports of foreign-produced passenger cars rose to about 1.1 million units in 1969, topping the previous record of 1 million in 1968.

Nondurable Manufactures. Output performances in nondurable goods industries were highlighted by large year-to-year gains in the chemical and the rubber and plastics groups. These fast-growing industries have shown output increases averaging around 10% a year since 1964. The 1969 output gains were less pronounced for paper and products, printing and publishing, and petroleum and coal products.

In textile mills, activity reached a new peak in the summer of 1969 and then receded moderately. For 1969, the 2% increase in output of textile mill products represented only a small fraction of the 6.5% gain from 1967 to 1968. Among textile products, manmade fabrics, knit goods, and floor coverings increased while cotton yarns and fabrics and wool textiles declined. Output of apparel goods averaged a shade lower than in 1968, the third straight year of relatively stable operations. This 3-year level of activity corresponded to the trend of retail sales of these goods, after adjustment for increased prices.

Food and beverage production continued to rise during 1969 about in line with the country's population increase.

Mining. Mining production improved in 1969. There were small gains in output of crude petroleum and gas and somewhat larger advances in metal, stone, and earth minerals. Temporary work stoppages in the spring and again in the fall held bituminous coal output about even with the 1968 volume of 545 million tons.

Utilities. Utility output in 1969 increased 9%, about the same as the advance from 1967 to 1968.

FRANCIS L. HIRT
Office of Business Economics
U. S. Department of Commerce

RETAIL SALES

Retail sales in 1969 rose 4% to a record annual rate of $352.1 billion. By comparison, sales rose 8% in 1968 to $339.3 billion.

Sales at durable goods stores rose 2% to $112.9 billion in contrast to an increase of 10% in 1968. The rate of advance in nondurable goods' store sales also slowed in 1969, rising 4% to $239.2 billion, compared to 7% in 1968.

Increases in sales were reported by all the major kinds of business in durable and nondurable goods, ranging up to 9% for department stores. The smallest gain—1%—was recorded by the furniture and appliance stores.

SALES OF RETAIL STORES
(millions of dollars)

	1967	1968	1969[1]
All retail stores	$313,809	$339,324	$352,081
Durable goods stores[2]	100,173	110,245	112,909
Automotive group	58,273	65,261	67,162
Furniture and appliance group	15,267	16,540	16,663
Lumber, building, hardware group	12,675	14,135	14,586
Nondurable goods stores[2]	213,636	229,079	239,172
Apparel group	18,123	19,265	20,176
Drug and proprietary group	10,721	11,458	11,932
Eating and drinking places	23,473	25,285	25,997
Food group	69,113	72,881	76,121
Gasoline service stations	22,739	24,526	25,111
General merchandise group, with nonstores	49,820	54,493	58,383
Department stores	29,589	33,323	36,315

[1] Preliminary. [2] Includes estimates for other retail stores not shown separately. Source: U.S. Department of Commerce, Bureau of the Census and Office of Business Economics.

Prices. Commodity prices at retail stores rose 5.5% from December 1968 to December 1969, exceeding the 3.8% gain for the preceding 12 months. Price increases were reported both for durable commodities, up 4.5%, and for nondurable commodities, up 5.8%. This acceleration in price increases contrasted strongly with the slower pace in retail sales increases in the same period.

Sales Trends. In 1969 consumers spent about 56% of their income (after taxes) at retail stores— 38% at nondurable goods stores and 18% at durable goods stores. Purchases per capita were equal to $1,733 at a seasonally adjusted rate, up 2% from $1,687 in 1968.

About 29% of all retail sales in 1969 were made in stores with 11 or more outlets.

Sales rose most rapidly from 1968 to 1969 in the South Atlantic states (up 7%) and least rapidly in the West South Central states (1%) and West North Central and Pacific states (2%). Sales in other areas rose from 3% to 5%.

Additional information on retail sales, including data for some large states and cities, is available in the monthly retail trade report of the U.S. Census Bureau.

Inventories. At the end of November 1969, retail inventories totaled $45.5 billion, seasonally adjusted, up $3 billion from November 1968. Durable goods retails added $1.2 billion to their stocks, with about four fifths of this amount—$1 billion—accumulated by auto dealers. Nondurable goods retailers added $1.8 billion to their stocks in the year, including gains for all major kinds of business.

Stocks were equal to 1.54 months of sales in November 1969, up 5% from 1.47 in November 1968.

DOROTHEA S. JONES
Office of Business Economics
U.S. Department of Commerce

WHOLESALE SALES

Merchant wholesalers in the United States attained $113.8 billion in sales in the first half of 1969, an increase of over 7% from the corresponding period of 1968.

Wholesale prices rose about 3.5% between these periods, and the physical volume of goods marketed rose by a similar amount.

Inventories. Merchant wholesalers' inventories increased by $1.5 billion to a total of $20.1 billion in a 12-month period ending June 30, 1969. This accumulation did not fully match the advance in sales, and the stocks fell slightly during the period to equal 1.18 months of sales.

Durable Goods. Sales advanced in every major durable goods line in the first six months of 1969, dealers reported. At $53.3 billion, total durable goods sales were 11% higher than in the first half of 1968.

Lumber and construction materials dealers reported the largest relative sales gain—26%. This gain reflected both higher construction activity and an unusually sharp increase in lumber prices. Larger-than-average sales advances were also reported by dealers in motor vehicles and parts, furniture and appliances, and hardware and heating and plumbing supplies.

MERCHANT WHOLESALERS' SALES, 1967–69
(millions of dollars)

	1967	1968	1968	1969
	Full year		First six months	
Merchant wholesalers, total	$205,187	$219,943	$106,080	$113,828
Durable goods[1]	90,447	100,012	48,052	53,341
Motor vehicles, automotive equipment	14,195	16,696	8,083	9,138
Electrical goods	14,141	14,969	6,980	7,420
Furniture, home furnishings	4,440	4,905	2,239	2,563
Hardware; plumbing and heating equipment and supplies	8,876	9,804	4,649	5,213
Lumber construction materials	8,614	10,427	4,699	5,921
Machinery equipment, supplies	23,836	25,466	12,499	13,903
Metals, metalwork (except scrap)	9,692	10,998	5,488	5,653
Scrap waste material	4,474	4,708	2,504	2,561
Nondurable goods	114,740	119,930	58,026	60,488
Groceries and related products	41,287	44,131	21,537	22,991
Beer, wine, distilled alcoholic beverages	10,427	11,088	5,045	5,455
Drugs, chemicals, allied products	8,074	8,830	4,251	4,566
Tobacco, tobacco products	5,357	5,612	2,710	2,800
Dry goods, apparel	9,772	10,271	4,977	4,909
Paper, paper products (excluding wallpaper)	6,236	6,707	3,229	3,510
Farm products (raw materials)	14,244	13,364	6,607	6,177
Other nondurable goods	18,876	20,203	9,868	10,092

[1] Totals include data for some kinds of business not listed separately. Source: U.S. Department of Commerce.

Nondurable Goods. Sales of nondurable goods by wholesalers totaled $60.5 billion in the first six months of 1969, about 4% above the same period a year earlier.

Sales gains ranging from 1% to 9% were reported in groceries and related products, drugs and chemical products, alcoholic beverages, and paper products. Tobacco products showed a 3% rise. Dry goods and apparel slipped 1% and farm products (raw materials) fell 6% between the first half of 1968 and the first half of 1969. Among food dealers, sales were strong for meats and poultry.

LAWRENCE BRIDGE
Office of Business Economics
U.S. Department of Commerce

ECUADOR

By comparison to the politically troubled years that preceded it, 1969 was relatively calm in Ecuador. The country was being ruled by a coalition headed by José María Velasco Ibarra, who was serving as president for the fifth time, having been deposed on three earlier occasions by military coups. Velasco's position was far from secure, but his opposition was fragmented and seemed reluctant to force his downfall.

Political Events. Several cabinet shakeups reflected the weakness of the coalition government. Elected in June 1968 with a plurality of only 32.7% of the total popular vote, Velasco lacked the support of a congressional majority and even that of his vice president, Jorge Zavala Baquerizo, who belonged to a rival party. Though elected largely on the strength of his reputation as a populist and left-wing nationalist, Velasco moved gradually to a more conservative position as he maneuvered to win greater political backing.

Several severe disorders occurred. Early in the year, radical students disrupted university entrance examinations and forced their cancellation. Later, the students joined radical worker groups in violent protests against economic conditions and social policies in Guayaquil and other major cities. Amid claims by conservatives that Velasco was ineffective in dealing with local disorders, much of the work of peace-keeping in the cities was assumed by unofficial neighborhood citizens' groups.

International Affairs. Contrary to expectations, relations with the United States generally improved. Nelson Rockefeller's visit to Quito on May 28 was accompanied by student-worker riots but was not disrupted by them. In December 1968 the United States had suspended arms sales and aid to Ecuador because of repeated seizures off the Ecuadorian coast of fishing boats owned by U.S. private interests. The United States persisted in disputing Ecuador's claim that its territorial waters extended 200 miles (320 km) out to sea. In July 1969, however, arms sales were renewed when Ecuador agreed to join Peru and Chile (who had made similar claims) in discussing the matter with U.S. representatives. The talks that were subsequently held in Buenos Aires, Argentina, produced no immediate resolution of the issue.

Diplomatic relations with Czechoslovakia, broken off in 1962, were renewed, and the possible renewal of relations with the USSR was seriously debated. Trade with the countries of eastern Europe continued to grow in 1969.

Economic Affairs. The Inter-American Committee of the Alliance for Progress reported that Ecuador's gross national product (GNP) had increased by an average annual rate of 5.3% during the period 1962–67, but that it had dipped sharply in 1968 owing to drought and to the business community's doubt about Velasco's economic policies.

Official Ecuadorian releases gave a contradictory picture of the nation's economic condition in 1969, with evidence of internal stability and business resiliency standing in vivid contrast to reports about growing domestic and foreign indebtedness. Living costs in 1969 were rising at an annual rate of only about 3.5% and the free-market rate of the Ecuadorian *sucre* remained relatively stable after April. On the other hand, there was a steep rise in the national budget deficit. About two fifths of

Ecuador's internal revenues were needed to service the internal government debt, and 15% of all foreign exchange earnings had to be earmarked for servicing the overseas debt. A steady decline in the Central Bank's gold and foreign exchange holdings was only briefly stemmed by an $18,000,000 credit from the International Monetary Fund in April.

Preliminary estimates for 1969 indicated that a sizable foreign trade deficit was likely. Ecuador remained one of the world's leading banana exporters, but nations in the Caribbean area were cutting sharply into this trade, as was Taiwan.

The Texaco-Gulf oil consortium agreement, concluded in March, provided for an eventual U.S. investment of up to $300 million for drilling, pipelines, roads, airports, and other facilities related to Ecuador's petroleum production. As exploration continued, the estimate of petroleum reserves was expected to climb to at least 1.5 billion barrels. Production in the fields at the Putumayo River, east of the Andes, was yielding over 20,000 barrels a day. Several foreign groups, both U.S. and European, were bidding for rights and concessions.

Some economic and social modernization occurred in 1969. Stock exchanges were organized in Guayaquil and Quito, and publicity campaigns in support of public securities issues were launched. In the coastal region, programs were begun to convert surplus banana lands into productive and diversified agricultural acreage. There were major improvements in housing, education, and health and sanitation programs, and a serious attempt was made to increase the efficiency of tax collection procedures.

PHILIP B. TAYLOR, JR.
University of Houston

——— **ECUADOR • Information Highlights** ———

Area: 109,483 square miles (283,561 sq km).
Population: 5,695,000 (1968 est.).
Chief Cities (1965 census): Quito, the capital, 401,811; Guayaquil, 651,542.
Government: *President*—José María Velasco Ibarra (took office Sept. 1, 1968); *Vice President*—Jorge Zavala Baquerizo. *Congress*—Senate, 51 members; Chamber of Deputies, 73 members.
Religious Faiths: Roman Catholics, 94% of population.
Education: *Literacy rate* (1962), 67.3% of population aged 15 and over. *Total school enrollment* (1966)—1,063,140 (primary, 851,117; secondary, 134,307; teacher-training, 15,492; technical/vocational, 46,177; university/higher, 16,047).
Finance (1968 est.): *Revenues*, $152,400,000; *expenditures*, $216,400,000; *monetary unit*, sucre (18.18 sucres equal U.S.$1).
Gross National Product (1968): $1,501,650,000.
National Income (1968): $1,254,125,000; *average annual income per person*, $220.
Economic Indexes: *Agricultural production* (1967), 196 (1952–56=100); *cost of living* (1969), 127 (1963=100).
Manufacturing and Processing (metric tons, 1967): Sugar, 294,000; gasoline, 268,000; wheat flour (1965), 121,000; meat, 80,000; beer, 442,000 hectolitres.
Crops (metric tons, 1967–68 crop year): Bananas, 3,163,000 (ranks 3d among world producers); cassava, 327,000; maize, 231,000; rice, 173,000; coffee, 6,700; citrus fruits, 2,400.
Minerals (metric tons, 1967): Crude petroleum, 290,000; silver (1966), 76,710 troy ounces; gold (1966), 10,901 troy ounces.
Foreign Trade (1968 est.): *Exports*, $210,000,000 (chief exports, 1966: Bananas and plantains, $106,000,000; coffee, $32,144,000; cacao, $17,206,000; sugar, $6.508,000); *imports* (1968), $209,000,000 (chief imports, 1966: transport equipment, $19,928,000; nonelectrical machinery, $18,320,000). *Chief trading partners* (1967): United States (took 49% of exports, supplied 40% of imports); West Germany (took 13% of exports, supplied 15% of imports); Japan (took 3% of exports, supplied 7% of imports).
Transportation: *Roads* (1967), 7,077 miles (11,389 km); *motor vehicles* (1967), 47,900 (automobiles 19,800); *railways* (1967), 727 miles (1,170 km); *merchant vessels* (1967), 5 (26,000 gross registered tons); *principal airports*, Quito, Guayaquil.
Communications: *Telephones* (1968): 45,000; *television stations* (1968), 7; *television sets* (1968), 65,000; *radios* (1967), 801,000; *newspapers* (1967), 23 (daily circulation, 241,000).

RICHARD HENRY, LIFE MAGAZINE © TIME INC.

UPI

GRADUATION DAY, 1969

Symbolic of the changing attitudes that have shaken U.S. college campuses in recent years are these scenes at three commencement exercises in June 1969. Graduates shown are from Wesleyan (above), Brandeis (right), and California, Berkeley (below). Although student radicals captured the headlines, they remained a small part of the total college population.

UPI

REPRINTED FROM THE LOS ANGELES TIMES BY PERMISSION OF THE REGISTER AND TRIBUNE SYNDICATE

"They're to prevent any militant take-over of this office...!"

EDUCATION

Disorders and riots continued in 1969 to plague many colleges and universities in the United States. Confrontations were characterized by a new intensity and violence, and for the first time the National Guard was needed to quell student insurrections.

The integration of Southern schools received a strong push forward in October by the Supreme Court decision requiring an immediate end to segregation. Several other developments in education were significant. The growing trend towards coeducation among major Eastern colleges and universities continued. Catholic schools in the United States faced a growing financial crisis that has forced a number of them to close.

(Continued on page 265)

NUMBER OF U.S. INSTITUTIONS OF HIGHER EDUCATION, BY SIZE OF ENROLLMENT—FALL 1968

Size of enrollment

Size of enrollment	Number
Under 200	302 INSTITUTIONS
200-499	341
500-999	557
1,000-2,499	627
2,500-4,999	266
5,000-9,999	211
10,000-9,999	119
20,000 OR MORE	60

BACHELOR'S AND HIGHER DEGREES CONFERRED BY U.S. INSTITUTIONS OF HIGHER EDUCATION

Number of degrees

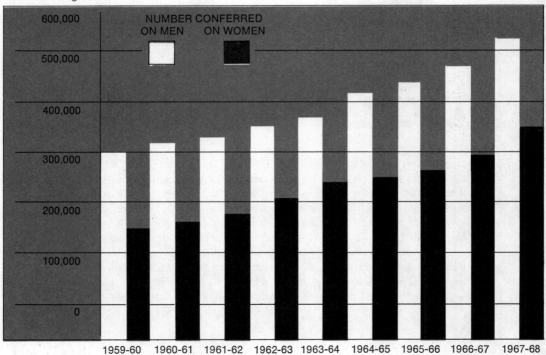

NUMBER CONFERRED ON MEN   ON WOMEN

600,000
500,000
400,000
300,000
200,000
100,000
0

1959-60 1960-61 1961-62 1962-63 1963-64 1964-65 1965-66 1966-67 1967-68

ADAPTED FROM "AMERICAN EDUCATION" MAGAZINE,
U.S. DEPARTMENT OF HEALTH, EDUCATION, AND WELFARE

THE NEW LOOK IN EDUCATION

'NEW MATH' SPEARHEADED WIDE CURRICULUM REFORM IN THE POST-SPUTNIK ERA

Curriculum developments in U. S. elementary and secondary schools continued in 1969 to reflect the curriculum reform movement of the late 1950's and 1960's. This movement probably involved more curriculum change during the past decade than had occurred in the preceding half-century.

The Soviet Union's launching of the first Sputnik in 1957 is generally regarded as the precipitant of the extensive reevaluation and revision of the school curriculum known as the curriculum reform movement. Certainly, Sputnik intensified concern in the United States as to the scientific and national defense position, and it was a major factor in enactment of the National Defense Education Act (1958), which provided federal funds for support of improvement programs in the curriculum areas of mathematics, science, and foreign languages.

By 1969, a large number of national curriculum projects had affected almost all subject areas and levels, and new projects were still in the process of developing programs and materials.

Some characteristics of these projects have been relatively common and thus tend to define the curriculum reform movement: (1) A first aim of most projects is to update curriculum content, and, if possible, to provide a basis for continued updating as knowledge continues to expand and change. (2) The emphasis is most frequently on the discrete academic disciplines, such as biology, rather than on broad fields, such as science, or on curriculum organizations that cut cross subject lines. (3) Curriculum content is organized around the basic principles, processes, and concepts—the structure—of the subject. (4) Curriculum plans and instructional techniques make much provision for the learner to "learn on his own," rather than being confined wholly to content uniformly studied by all students. (5) Many types of teaching-learning aids are used. (6) Traditional notions as to grade placement of many subjects have been greatly modified, with a downward movement especially noticeable.

Mathematics. Reform in mathematics had begun prior to Sputnik with the first national curriculum project in this field initiated in 1951, that of the University of Illinois Committee on School Mathematics. This field has probably produced the first and most interest in curriculum reform, and it has attracted a heavy investment of federal funds.

The new mathematics stresses progression from concrete to symbol to abstract. Various experimental materials and physical models, student discovery approaches, and practical applications are being used in the classroom. Children in the elementary grades are introduced to graphing, geometry, and algebra. High school mathematics may include calculus, computer science, and statistics. Courses utilizing the computer are being offered in many situations.

New topics in the mathematics curriculum include sets, number bases other than 10, vectors, and linear algebra. Emphasis on functions has been increased; trigonometry, for example, is approached through circular functions rather than as the study of the right triangle.

With new textbooks and many other materials, extensive in-service education programs for teachers, and the continuing leadership of various national projects, the mathematics curriculum definitely changed in the 1960's. Some controversy continues as to whether the new math is better and also whether it is changed enough.

Science. The post-Sputnik push to science education was heavily influenced by the aim of developing more scientists, and the early curriculum developments tended to be focused on the more able high school students who might continue study in this field. More recently, the science education reform has also given more attention to the elementary school and to less able students.

The newer science programs stress the scientific method of inquiry. Instead of concentrating on the classification of phenomena and the verification of previously established principles, the new approaches emphasize the processes of science. They are laboratory-centered, with students encouraged to develop their own investigations. The elementary science programs in particular have changed from reading classes to activity-centered ones, with a variety of materials available for classroom use.

The new science at the high school level has consisted primarily of new selections and organizations of content in earth science, biology, chemistry, physics, and physical science. The output of the national projects and the publishers has included textbooks, laboratory programs, audio-visual materials, and various supplementary materials such as teachers' guides and tests. The new texts have not prevented science from still being difficult and unpopular for some students, and efforts are continuing to develop better teacher preparation and methods.

Some science educators now look toward an interdisciplinary approach as a replacement for the separate courses in biology, chemistry, and physics. Priority items as the 1970's approached seemed to be more widespread introduction to science as inquiry, with provisions for laboratory-type activity in the elementary school; better articulation of elementary and secondary school programs; and a continuing supply of teachers better prepared to interest learners of all abilities.

Foreign Languages. Curriculum change in the foreign languages area, which was under way before Sputnik, was given massive support by the National Defense Education Act (1958) and other federal funds thereafter. Our national deficiencies in foreign

LEARNING LANGUAGES: The teacher at his console is connected with students' headsets and microphones.

RAYTHEON

languages had been exposed in World War II; also during that war the new audiolingual methodology had been initiated in the military program. The new funds made possible the acceleration of teacher preparation and the purchase of equipment for the audiolingual approach in schools.

The reformation in foreign languages has had to do both with the scope and extent of foreign language instruction and its focus and method. As to the former, foreign language in the elementary school (FLES) was popularized in the early 1960's, although the movement has been sporadic and uncertain. Another emphasis has been on a longer period of study of a language than the traditional two years in high school. Further, many larger high schools have added additional languages, especially German, Russian, Chinese, and Japanese.

As to focus and methods, the new thrust has been on conversational skills and on the method of oral rather than written communication initially. Electronic language laboratories have been widely installed to facilitate this audiolingual approach.

English Language Art. A "new English" has not developed comparably in singularity of focus and method to the new mathematics, science, and foreign languages. Change has been taking place, much of it generated by continuing projects of the National Council of Teachers of English and by the national curriculum centers supported by the U. S. Office of Education's Project English. The changes include such diverse emphases as these: (1) moving from a standard formal grammar to the study of various linguistic structures; (2) teaching oral English more through informal discussion or talk than formal speeches; (3) relating more closely language, literature, and composition; (4) encouraging creative writing; (5) broadening the choices of literature; (6) relying less on single standards of correctness in oral and written communication; and (7) using a wider variety of materials and media.

Reading has received major attention in recent years, both because of the increased effort to reach students with poor reading backgrounds and skills and the uncertainty from research as to appropriate instructional methods and materials. Thirty concurrent studies funded by the U. S. Office of Education indicated that differences between teachers were more significant than those between methods.

Social Studies. Although social studies was little involved in the beginning years of the curriculum reform movement, by 1969 some 50 national curriculum projects had aimed toward change in this field. These projects varied greatly in breadth, some being concerned with individual courses, some with units of new materials for existing courses, and some with revision of the entire field. Major changes that these projects and some schools were trying with varying success to effect included: (1) more emphasis on current social realities; (2) less emphasis on history and more on other social sciences, especially anthropology, geography, economics, and sociology; (3) more attention to non-Western cultures and world affairs; (4) focus on concepts rather than isolated facts; (5) stress on the student's own investigations and analyses of data; (6) use of varied learning materials such as pamphlets, case studies, selected documents, and various audiovisual materials; and (7) inclusion of more material, including Black studies courses, on the role of the Negro in American history and culture. (See also GEOGRAPHY.)

Fine Arts. Curriculum change in the arts has been attacked with less urgency and less funding, although public and school interest recently has been increasing. The federally supported National Foundation on the Arts and Humanities, Title III of the Elementary and Secondary Education Act (1965), and some philanthropic foundations have recently supported new programs and research projects in the arts. Although high school enrollments have increased, the arts courses are typically on an elective or activity basis and usually overshadowed by requirements of college preparatory courses.

Current trends include major emphasis on aesthetic appreciation and more attention to contemporary music, art, and theater. Creativity is prized, and performance is not neglected.

Practical Arts and Vocational Education. Whether such fields as home economics and industrial arts are general or vocational education, and whether and to what extent vocational education should be provided in high school, continued as issues during the 1960's. Federal legislation through the Vocational Education Act of 1963 and the 1968 Amendments aimed at an expansion and improvement of vocational education at various levels and in various types of programs, including those of junior and senior high schools. National concern for disadvantaged children and youth, for the potential and actual school dropout, and for the unemployed and unemployable have stimulated a great variety of vocationally oriented educational programs for these groups. Earlier occupational orientation, broader work-study program, and training for a wider variety of occupational opportunities are emphasized.

Health and Physical Education. The report of the President's Council on Youth Fitness in 1969 resulted in renewed emphasis on gymnastics and accompanying testing in the physical education program, although interest to the point of preoccupation in interscholastic athletics has continued in some schools. Most noteworthy of recent developments is the increasing attention to leisure activities that can be continued in adult life, and also to corrective and individualized programs.

The inadequate status of health education in the schools was revealed by the School Health Education Study of 1963, and this project developed a curriculum plan for the field that has been widely studied. Problems of drugs, alcohol, tobacco, venereal diseases, and sex behavior have stimulated various types of health education programs.

Interdisciplinary Courses. Several curriculum developments cut across the usual subject fields. Courses in the humanities at the high school level may involve literature, history, art, dramatics, dance, and other subjects. Aesthetic education programs also use such combinations.

Family life and sex education courses became controversial matters in a number of communities in 1969. Many forces emphasized the need for such programs, and many schools instituted cooperative arrangements involving community resources and teachers from such areas as health, home economics, biology, and sociology. Critics questioned the school's responsibility in this area, as well as the competence of teachers to deal with it. As the decade ended both the needs for the programs and the debates about them continued.

WILLIAM M. ALEXANDER
University of Florida

FIREARMS were introduced in the campus protest movement when armed black students barricaded themselves in a Cornell University building. They left, with weapons, after 36 hours.

(*Continued from page 261*)

STUDENT DISORDERS

Perhaps the most disturbing incident of student revolt occurred at Cornell University in April when for six days armed rebellion racked the campus. Some 100 black students held the student union building for 36 hours, emerging with shot guns, rifles, and knives only after the administration had agreed to their demands for amnesty.

The Cornell outbreak aroused national concern, especially over the show of arms and the capitulation of the administration under duress. Both houses of Congress accelerated investigations of campus disorders; there were demands that university officials and local law enforcement agencies apply the law. U. S. Attorney General John N. Mitchell called for "an end to minority tyranny on the nation's campuses."

Harvard's tradition of the right of dissent and discussion exploded in violent action, also in April. As in many other disturbances, the conflict began with a series of "unnegotiable demands," including the abolition of ROTC.

About 250 students, most of them members of Students for a Democratic Society (SDS), invaded the administration building, forcibly evicted the five deans and their assistants, and locked themselves inside the building.

President Nathan M. Pusey decided on forceful eviction. Shortly before dawn, 400 state troopers and local law officers shouted warnings and then forced their way in. By 5:30 A.M. the building was cleared; 184 persons were arrested on charges of criminal trespass; and 45 were injured seriously enough to be treated at hospitals.

A general strike ensued as both faculty and students debated the proper course of action. Mass

meetings were held in Soldiers Field. After several days, students voted to suspend the strike and resume classes. The university agreed to reduce the status of ROTC to an extracurricular activity.

April was also a month of violence in scores of other institutions. At predominately Negro Morehouse College (Atlanta) trustees were locked in as they met. In Virginia, trustees of Hampton Institute announced closing for "an indefinite period" when dissident students occupied the administration building. At Voorhees College in South Carolina, students armed with knives and guns took over the administration building and looted the cafeteria of $5,000 worth of food.

San Francisco State College, the scene of a bloody student strike, was closed down for months, while police raids, arson attempts, and bomb explosions disrupted the institution.

At Dartmouth, in May, state police dragged from the administration building 60 students demanding an end to ROTC. State troopers cleared 300 occupying students from the Purdue administration building. At Brooklyn College militant students clashed with police and firemen responding to a fire in the administration building. The National Guard was required to quell disturbances at Duke and Wisconsin.

City College in New York was closed for two weeks as black and Puerto Rican students, currently numbering 4,500 of the school's 20,000 students, sought a separate school of black and Hispanic studies and an increase in minority group enrollments. Queens College, also in New York City, was closed temporarily after clashes between black and white students.

Commencement at many colleges was a nightmare. Students wore protesting armbands, turned their backs on commencement speakers or rose to

COEDUCATION came suddenly to some Eastern colleges, both men's and women's. New arrivals at Princeton, shown here, received a warm reception.

dispute them, walked out in groups from formal ceremonies, shed their academic robes in the procession, or even organized "counter-commencements."

Reaction. In the midst of the turmoil there were signs of stiffening resistance, mainly through the use of injunctions. At Columbia, SDS members slipped away from two occupied classroom buildings when a bench warrant was issued for their arrest. In Cambridge, 169 defendants were found guilty of criminal trespass during the Harvard riots.

New York State passed strict laws against unauthorized firearms at educational institutions. Five other states enacted similar legislation. California and Wisconsin legislated against disruptive activity on college campuses. In all, more than half the states have reacted with some type of legislation against campus riots.

Causes of Unrest. Student protests, in general, have had a variety of objectives: the war in Vietnam, college ROTC programs. recruiting for the armed services or for the manufacture of napalm, governmental contracts for military-related research, restrictive campus rules, black studies departments or programs, the proportion of minority groups in the student body. Even the naming or design of a building and the operation of the college bookstore have produced mass demonstrations.

There is among some students a disenchantment with society today, especially as the Vietnam in-

volvement continues. Students are impatient, demanding instant gratification of their ideals or purposes. Adult leadership is frequently questioned, especially when it imposes what are regarded as unnecessary restrictions. A role in determining the nature and character of their own education is a frequent cry of youth today.

Student activists, however, represent only a small but vocal minority. It is estimated that less than 2% of the college students are destructive radicals. However, with a current enrollment of 6,700,000, this 2% represents possibly 100,000 individuals scattered among the nation's 2,500 colleges and universities.

SHIFT TO COEDUCATION

With a suddenness that surprised other college administrators as well as old graduates, coeducation came to many of the traditionally one-sex East Coast institutions of higher learning in the fall of 1969.

Princeton, a male stronghold for more than 200 years, admitted 101 women as freshmen and 50 as transfer students from other colleges. Yale accepted 588 women, including 230 freshmen, for fall 1969 enrollment. Vassar registered 91 new male undergraduates. Bennington College enrolled 33 men in coed campus housing.

Through a new 11-college exchange program six Eastern men's colleges (Williams, Amherst, Dartmouth, Trinity, Wesleyan, and Bowdoin) are currently exchanging more than 200 students with five women's colleges (Smith, Mt. Holyoke, Wheaton (Mass.), Connecticut College, and Vassar).

Reasons for the widespread shift to coeducation are somewhat varied. Chief among them is the assertion that coeducation is a more natural environment for young people, as contrasted with the "monastic isolation" of the one-sex school. Students insist that dating practices are more normal and realistic than the frenetic social life of college week ends with members of the other sex.

It is asked frequently if the trend toward coeducation in an age of greater sexual freedom will mean greater promiscuity. On the contrary, college officials and student leaders say that coeducation will encourage healthy relationships between the sexes and discourage promiscuity.

Coeducation is costly, since it involves new facilities and additional faculty. However, many of the remaining one-sex colleges are considering it seriously.

INTEGRATION

In a brief but emphatic decision announced on Oct. 29, 1969, the U. S. Supreme Court flatly and unanimously ruled out any further delay in the desegregation of the nation's schools. The court declared, in its first major decision since the investiture of Chief Justice Warren E. Burger, that "the obligation of every school district is to terminate dual school systems at once and to operate now and hereafter only unitary schools."

The court specifically rejected the "all deliberate speed" standard, emphasizing that such a policy is "no longer constitutionally permissible." It also ruled that the offending school districts must desegregate while they argue over details in the lower courts.

Segregation leaders predicted that the decision would result in chaos in many Southern school systems. NAACP leaders, on the other hand, hailed the ruling as a victory and announced that they would press to have it apply to all pending school litigation.

Some observers regarded the decision as a setback for the Nixon administration. Less than a week before, the Justice Department had argued that delays were permissible in requiring integration in some districts where education programs would be completely disrupted if immediate action was required.

However, on the day following the court's decision the Nixon Administration gave assurances that it would support and enforce the ruling. President Nixon, Attorney General Mitchell, and Robert H. Finch, secretary of Health, Education and Welfare, all issued separate statements to this effect. (See also SUPREME COURT.)

Education of Negroes. While nonwhites still lag in the average number of years of schooling completed as compared with whites, the difference is narrowing. Between 1964 and 1968 the median for whites 25 years and over increased only from 12.0 years to 12.1 years, while the median for nonwhites went from 8.9 years to 9.5 years, according to the Bureau of the Census. In spite of this gain, the median school attainment of nonwhites was still 2.6 years below that for the whites in 1968.

At the college level the enrollment of Negro students increased 85% from 1964 to 1968, while the total enrollment was increasing 46%. However, attendance is still far out of proportion to the ratio of whites to Negroes in the population.

There is no "massive wave of black students." A survey entitled *State Universities and Black Americans* revealed only 23,630 American Negroes, or 1.93%, out of a total undergraduate student body of 1,222,382 in 80 predominantly white state universities in the fall of 1968. Graduate enrollment at the 80 schools was 322,069, of whom 6,149, or 1.91%, were American Negroes.

There is little variation among various sections of the country. Nearly half of the black students at predominantly white schools are freshmen, indicating a trend toward increased enrollment.

Public Negro colleges are growing rapidly. Their 1968–69 enrollment of 93,470 was 7.7% higher than the previous session and more than double the 1956 figure.

CATHOLIC SCHOOL CRISIS

Catholic schools throughout the nation are facing a financial crisis. Not only are educational costs rising constantly but fewer young Catholics are entering religious orders that would train them as classroom teachers.

In Helena, Mont., for example, where rising costs resulted in the sale of the Catholic high school to the public school system, priests and nuns were paid $1,500 a year, while lay teachers began at $6,200. A decade ago there were, nationally, about three times as many nuns, priests, and brothers teaching in Catholic schools as there were lay instructors; the number now is about equal.

Almost all parochial schools have raised tuition rates, with the result that many parents have transferred their children to public schools, especially since taxes for educational purposes have risen sharply.

A survey made by the department of education at the University of Notre Dame revealed that 301 Catholic elementary and secondary schools would close in 1969 and 111 more would begin to eliminate grades and consolidate classes.

Parochial schools educate a sizeable portion of the U. S. children without adding to the burden of taxpayers. In New York State alone it is estimated that transfers into public schools will add $30 million to the cost of public education in 1969.

JAMES EDWARD ALLEN, JR., was appointed by President Nixon on Feb. 3, 1969, as U. S. commissioner of education, with the rank of assistant secretary in the Department of Health, Education, and Welfare. He took office three months later. Since his appointment, Allen has called for massive federal aid to urban education, aimed in particular at meeting the needs of the disadvantaged. On the issue of campus disorders, he has indicated that he favors a positive approach and opposes strict punitive measures.

Allen, son of a college president, was born in Elkins, W. Va., on April 25, 1911, and received his Ph. D. in 1945 from Harvard. After teaching for two years at Syracuse University, he joined the New York State Department of Education in 1947 and served as the state's education commissioner from 1955 until his present appointment. He fought de facto public school segregation, promoted decentralization of schools in New York City, and obtained increased state aid for urban slum schools.

OTHER DEVELOPMENTS

Twelve-month Schooling. Advocates of year-round operation of schools have decried the wasteful practice of allowing costly educational facilities to be idle for three months of the year and pointed out the possibility of providing for one third again as many students if schools were operated for 12 months.

Rising educational costs have led many school systems to consider year-round classes. After a three-year study, Atlanta, Ga., recently adopted a four-quarter plan of operation. The system is flexible, allowing students to choose any quarter they wish for vacation or to attend all year without interruption. Needy students can hold part-time jobs all year if they wish.

Teachers are required to teach only three quarters at their regular salary; they can earn higher pay if they choose to work the whole year.

School officials point to the value of spreading vacations throughout the entire year, of having useful summer activity for disadvantaged children, and of having opportunities for bright students to accelerate and slow learners to receive remedial instruction.

Previous experiments with year-round schooling have revealed opposition to compulsory summer attendance. The voluntary program in Atlanta would seem to overcome this objection.

The New York State Education Department has recommended an 11-month school calendar, for which proposed legislation is being drafted.

Enrollment Trends. For the 25th consecutive year enrollment in the schools and colleges of the nation increased, reaching an all-time high of 58.6 million, according to estimates compiled by the U. S. Office of Education. However, the increase has been at a decelerating rate. This year's increase of 1.2 per cent is the smallest since 1945.

The largest percentage increase—2.9%—occurred at the higher education level. Enrollments in colleges, universities, junior colleges, and professional schools rose from 6,900,000 in fall 1968 to 7,100,000 in fall 1969. The increase was in the public institutions, whose degree-credit student enrollment rose from 4,900,000 to 5,100,000. Enrollment in private institutions remained at 2,000,-000.

These figures do not include approximately 600,-000 undergraduates enrolled in occupational or general studies programs not carrying bachelor's degree credit.

At the high school level, the estimated 1969 fall enrollment of 14,600,000 is an increase of 400,000 or 2.8% over the previous year. At the elementary school level, the enrollment increased only 0.3%, from 36.8 million. This was expected because there has been a gradual decline in the number of children born annually since 1961.

The Office of Education estimates that 61.4 million people, or more than 30% of the population, are directly involved in classroom activities as students and teachers. This does not include superintendents, principals, or school board members.

In fall 1969 there were 1,251,000 elementary and 992,000 secondary classroom teachers, a total of 2,243,000. Slightly more than 2 million of these were in public schools, with 240,000 in nonpublic schools.

The instructional staff in colleges and universities totaled more than 530,000 in fall 1969, an increase of 1.5% over the previous year.

High School Graduates. More than 2.8 million persons graduated from high school in 1969, according to the U. S. Office of Education. The class of 1970 is expected to reach 3 million, a record high.

Projections by statisticians indicate educational attainment as follows for persons now in their middle and late teens: 77% will graduate from high school and 42% will enroll in a degree-credit program. About 21% will earn a bachelor's degree; 6%, a master's; and 1%, a doctorate.

Expenditures for Education. Public and private elementary school expenditures for 1969–70 are expected to total $42 billion, compared with $40.1 billion in 1968–69. Higher education is expected to cost $22.7 billion, an increase of $1.4 billion over the previous year. Total expenditures for education in 1968–69 were 7.1% of the gross national product, according to the U. S. Office of Education.

Federal grants for education have tripled in the past five fiscal years, increasing from $2.4 billion in 1964 to $7.8 billion in fiscal 1969.

Vocational Education. More than 18,000 schools provided vocational education courses to approximately 7.5 million youth and adults during the school year ending June 1968, according to the U. S. Office of Education.

Enrollments increased 7.6% over the previous year, with the greatest increase at the postsecondary education level. State and local governments provided 78% of the $1.2 billion expended in 1968 for vocational education with federal funds making up the remainder.

A relatively new program for persons with special needs (academic, socioeconomic, cultural, or other handicaps) that might prevent them from succeeding in regular vocational courses enrolled 11,019 persons in 1968, an increase of 37.6% in one year.

College Growth. In 1968–69 there were 2,483 colleges, universities, professional schools, and two-year institutions, an increase of more than 500 in a decade. Nearly three fifths of these new institutions were two-year colleges and technical institutes, whose number, in 10 years, increased from 553 to 864. In the fall of 1969, 70 new colleges began admitting students. All but nine were two-year institutions.

Universities are also increasing greatly in size. In the fall of 1958 only four institutions had more than 30,000 students. By fall 1968, there were 25 with an enrollment exceeding 30,000.

The University of California, with 123,275 students (all campuses), was the largest, followed by the University of Minnesota, 66,824, and the University of Wisconsin, 63,370.

Community Colleges. The growth of the two-year college continues at an unprecedented rate. In 1963, there were 700 junior colleges enrolling a million students. Five years later the number had grown to 950 institutions, mainly public, enrolling 1.6 million students. By 1975, it is anticipated that 95% of all first-year students in public institutions will be enrolled in two-year institutions.

The public two-year college is making higher education available to masses of high school graduates throughout the country. Fees are moderate or nominal; institutions are usually within commuting distance; and "open door" admission policies permit enrollment of students regardless of high school achievement records.

SOCIAL RELATIONS CLASS at Franconia College, a small, progressive school in New Hampshire, typifies the relaxation in rules and conduct that has been introduced on a number of campuses in the United States.

THE NEW YORK TIMES

Most two-year colleges offer remedial courses for entering students poorly prepared in the basic learning skills. Testing programs are generally employed to determine areas of weakness, and students are assigned to "basic" or "fundamental" courses, usually without degree credit to overcome deficiencies. However, the drop-out rate among remedial students is high in the freshman year. Current studies are seeking to determine more effective ways of overcoming learning or motivational handicaps.

Degrees Conferred. During 1967–68 institutions of higher learning in the nation awarded 871,832 earned degrees, an increase of 13% over the previous year and an all-time record. Women received 40% of the total, compared with 38% in 1966–67. At the bachelor's degree level 359,747 degrees were awarded to men, and 277,116 to women; at the first professional level (such as law) the proportions were 33,083 and 1,645; master's, 113,749 and 63,401; and doctor's, 20,185 and 2,906.

While men still outnumber women, the number of men receiving degrees in the past decade increased 70%, while in the same period, the number of women increased 125%. The largest percentage increase for women has been at the doctor's level. However, the disproportion is still great, with only about one out of seven doctorates going to women in 1967–68. A decade earlier it was one out of nine.

For the bachelor's and first professional degrees, the most popular fields of study were education, 135,848; social sciences, 121,643; and business and commerce, 80,440. For the master's degree, education again led with 63,664 degrees awarded, followed by social sciences, 20,426, and business and commerce, 17,868. At the doctorate level, education was again the most popular field of study with 4,079 degrees, followed by physical sciences, 3,593, and engineering, 2,932.

"Free University" Courses. An outgrowth of student dissatisfaction with existing higher education has been the development of non-credit courses in whatever subjects may interest students. Usually tuition is not charged, teachers not paid, and grades or credits are not given.

The "free university" movement has spread so rapidly that an estimated 450 institutions now have such courses. The Harvard New College, according to *Time* (June 6, 1969) currently offers 25 courses on "relevant" topics ranging from radical politics to the ethics of middle class suburbia.

Anyone can attend merely by signing up. Classes meet in student rooms or lounges, once or twice a week. Discussion methods predominate, led by teaching fellows or the undergraduates themselves.

The largest operation is the Washington Area Free University, with more than 2,000 students who are also attending formal universities in the area. The quality of teaching is uneven, as might be imagined. Perhaps the best courses are conducted by regular university instructors who voluntarily offer a seminar-type of instruction in subjects that appeal to their special interests but are not taught in the regular academic program.

Rising Costs. Tuition charges at higher institutions continue to rise. A survey made by the Association of State Universities and Land Grant Colleges disclosed a record increase of 16.5% among the 113 member institutions and 14% among the 261 members of the American Association of State Colleges and Universities.

Median tuition and required fees at these public institutions of higher education went from $369 per resident student in 1968–69 to $430 in 1969–70.

College Gifts. The effect of student demonstrations upon voluntary giving by alumni and others has been feared by college officials. However, in 1968 total giving reached an estimated $1,57 billion, according to the Council for Financial Aid to Education. This is the highest figure since the surveys were begun in 1954, and represents an increase of $101.5 million over the amount reported for 1967.

In June, 1969, the University of Richmond announced a gift of $50 million from E. Claiborne Robins, an alumnus who heads a pharmaceutical company in Richmond, Va. It is probably the largest individual contribution in funds ever made to an institution of higher learning.

(See also the listing under Colleges and Universities. Major education developments in other countries appear in the individual country articles.)

EDWARD ALVEY, JR.
Mary Washington College, University of Virginia

EGYPT. See UNITED ARAB REPUBLIC.

WIDE WORLD

DWIGHT DAVID EISENHOWER (1890-1969)

Thirty-fourth President of the United States

EISENHOWER, Dwight David

Thirty-fourth president of the United States: b. Denison, Texas, Oct. 14, 1890; d. Washington, D. C., March 28, 1969.

From humble beginnings, Dwight David Eisenhower rose to the highest positions of power in American and world history. Like Washington and Grant, he was called upon to lead his country on the battlefield in a major war and subsequently to occupy its highest office, the presidency.

Eisenhower excelled as a coordinator of vast, complex enterprises. In World War II he directed a military force of some 3 million men contributed by many nations and operating on several continents. As president, he presided over far-flung alliances of free nations to resist aggression. This task was complicated by the Soviet's mastery of nuclear weapons and their early access to outer space. He adjusted the office of the president to the ponderous demands made upon it by replacing traditional administrative arrangements (which were almost casual) with order and system. Although successors have altered his innovations, their hard core remains.

Eisenhower provides an extraordinarily successful record of working in harness with the most powerful and imperious personalities of his era, including MacArthur, Churchill, Roosevelt, and de Gaulle. Eisenhower, in contrast—and perhaps that is a key to his success—was the acme of modesty, of ability to adapt to the idiosyncracies of others. For all of his responsibilities, he was a man who had no enemies. He shunned deviousness and pettiness—traits not unknown to those in high places.

Eisenhower had his faults. Given heavily to pragmatism, he tended to overvalue the present and undervalue the future. His military decisions were concentrated on the immediate aim of winning the war and reflected little concern for their effect on future international relations. His "Modern Re-

publicanism," potentially a reorientation of his party, was only a scattering of domestic measures, lacking broad conceptions and a long-term program.

EARLY LIFE

Eisenhower was born in Denison, Texas, on Oct. 14, 1890, the third of seven sons of David and Ida Stover Eisenhower. Originally named David Dwight (names that he reversed in early youth), he was always called "Dwight." His forebears, of German and Swiss ancestry, had emigrated to the United States in search of religious freedom. They had settled in Pennsylvania, where they were members of the River Brethren, a Mennonite sect.

In 1885, Eisenhower's parents had migrated to Abilene, Kans., where his father became part-owner of a general merchandise store. A dispute with his partner prompted him to move to Denison, where Eisenhower was born. When he was nearly two years old, the family returned to Abilene, where his father worked in a local creamery. The Eisenhowers were poor but hard-working. The family was religious, holding regular Bible readings and discussions. Although little interested in formal religion, Eisenhower was profoundly respectful of the moral precepts of his parents' faith.

After high school, Eisenhower worked at the creamery and did sundry jobs, but felt that he was drifting, when a friend induced him to apply for admission to the U. S. Naval Academy. Eisenhower also applied for appointment to the U. S. Military Academy. He was accepted at West Point, despite his parents' opposition to a military career.

ARMY CAREER

In June 1911, Eisenhower entered West Point to face a curriculum stressing science and engineering and a life of rigid discipline. He was an outstanding halfback on the football team until he was injured and forced to quit the game. In 1915 he graduated 61st in a class of 164. Eisenhower ranked high in popularity, however. "Everyone was his friend," a classmate said, "but with no loss in dignity or respect."

Commissioned a 2d lieutenant in the U. S. Army, Eisenhower was assigned to Fort Sam Houston, Texas. There he met Mamie Geneva Doud, daughter of a wealthy meat-packer. "Ike" (as Eisenhower was nicknamed) and Mamie were married on July 1, 1916. The Eisenhowers had two sons. The first died at the age of 3; the second, John Sheldon Doud, born in 1922, graduated from West Point and became a career Army officer. In 1969 President Nixon appointed him ambassador to Belgium.

World War I. Upon U. S. entry into World War I, Eisenhower was assigned to posts in the United States. He served as an instructor at an officers' training camp at Fort Oglethorpe, Ga., and was later moved to Camp Colt, near Gettysburg, Pa., to command a training center for tank warfare. In 1918, 28 years old, he was made a lieutenant colonel and awarded the Distinguished Service Medal.

Between the Wars. After the armistice, Eisenhower served briefly at Fort Benning, Ga., and at Fort Meade, Md., where he commanded heavy tank battalions. At Fort Meade, he became friends with Gen. George S. Patton, Jr. In 1922–24, Eisenhower served in the Panama Canal Zone. His commander, Brig. Gen. Fox Connor, helped arrange for his enrollment in 1925 in the Command and General Staff School at Fort Leavenworth, Kans. In a rigorous course, Eisenhower ranked first in a class 275.

In 1928, he graduated from the Army War College. Eisenhower was then assigned to the American Battle Monuments Commission to prepare a guide to World War I battlefields in Europe. His studies gave him intimate knowledge of French battle terrain and tactics. After service in other posts, Eisenhower, in 1933, became an aide to Gen. Douglas MacArthur, Army chief of staff. When MacArthur was appointed military adviser to the Philippines in 1935, Eisenhower followed as his assistant.

World War II. In 1940, Eisenhower was appointed executive officer at Fort Ord, Calif., where he was remembered for his strict discipline. He became Third Army chief of staff in 1941, and, after brilliantly conducting Army maneuvers in Louisiana that fall, was promoted to brigadier general.

Following the Japanese attack on Pearl Harbor in December 1941, Gen. George C. Marshall, Army chief of staff, appointed Eisenhower to the Army's War Plans Division. Eisenhower was to map out a defense of U. S. territories in the Pacific. He was also working on plans for an invasion of Europe when Churchill and his staff arrived in December for conferences with President Roosevelt. Eisenhower met with the two leaders and their staffs. The British were soon urging that he be sent to London.

In March 1942, Eisenhower was promoted to major general and was soon named head of the Operations Division to prepare plans for an invasion across the English Channel. He also developed plans to unify all U. S. forces in Europe under a single commander. In June he was advanced over 366 senior officers, and left for England as commanding general of all U. S. forces in the European Theater of Operations. Observers in London were impressed by his skill at evoking cooperation from Allied military representatives.

Eisenhower planned an invasion of North Africa (Operation Torch) and was promoted to lieutenant general and designated commander of the Allied invasion forces. On Nov. 8, 1942, the Allies landed on the shores of Algeria and Morocco, and by May 1943 they had conquered North Africa. Eisenhower then concentrated on invasions of Sicily and Italy. After an arduous, protracted struggle, the Allies occupied Rome on June 4, 1944. During these campaigns, Eisenhower attended conferences of the Allied leaders at Quebec and Cairo, where plans for a cross-Channel invasion, Operation Over-lord, were made. In December 1943, President Roosevelt, with the unanimous consent of Churchill and the combined staffs, appointed Eisenhower supreme commander of the Allied Expeditionary Forces.

Eisenhower now presided over the most powerful military force in history. He successfully managed the preparations for the final assault to liberate France—a complex cooperative enterprise of stockpiling materials, training men, and arranging for huge forces to be rapidly shifted from England to the Continent. On June 6, 1944, after anxious moments over poor weather, the invasion began. Eisenhower's forces made swift progress into France and he soon moved his headquarters into Normandy. By March 1945, the Allied armies reached the Rhine, and by April, the Elbe. On May 7, 1945, Germany surrendered. Meanwhile, Eisenhower had been promoted to five-star general of the Army.

Eisenhower scrupulously observed the prearranged Soviet zones of operation. He halted Bradley's advance at the Elbe. Deeming Berlin a sec-

---

IMPORTANT DATES IN EISENHOWER'S LIFE

Oct. 14, 1890—Born in Denison, Texas.
June 1915—Commissioned 2d lieutenant in U. S. Army after graduation from West Point.
July 1, 1916—Married Mamie Geneva Doud.
June 1942—Assumed command of the European Theater of Operations.
December 1943—Became supreme commander of the Allied Expeditionary Forces.
June 6, 1944—Directed Allied invasion of Normandy.
December 1944—Promoted to five-star general of the Army.
November 1945—Appointed chief of staff of the Army.
June 1948—Became president of Columbia University; wrote *Crusade in Europe.*
December 1950—Appointed supreme commander of the North Atlantic Treaty Organization.
Nov. 4, 1952—Elected 34th President of the U. S.
December 1953—Presented "Atoms for Peace" proposal to the United Nations.
July 1955—Attended summit conference in Geneva, Switzerland.
September 1955—Suffered first heart attack.
Nov. 6, 1956—Elected to second term of presidency.
January 1957—Announced "Eisenhower Doctrine" against Communist aggression in the Middle East; sent troops to Little Rock, Ark. in school crisis.
September 1959—Met with Soviet Premier Khrushchev at Camp David.
February 1960—Visited Latin America; in June, toured the Far East.
January 1961—Left office and retired to Gettysburg (Pa.) farm.
November 1963—Published first volume of presidential memoirs, *Mandate for Change* (second volume, *Waging Peace: The White House Years, 1956–60,* published in October 1965.)
March 28, 1969—Died in Washington, D. C., at age 78.

---

ondary target, he left it to the Russians and also acceded to the Soviet ambition to capture Prague. Some among the Allies deplored these decisions as indulgences of dangerous political innocence in the face of an evident Soviet appetite for aggrandizement.

After the Victory. In November 1945, Eisenhower replaced General Marshall as Army chief of staff. He then focused on the demobilization of the armed forces, pleading that the rate of discharges from the armed forces be slowed and arguing that a system of universal military training be established to deter surprise attack. Public desire to return to peacetime pursuits thwarted his goals.

In 1948, Eisenhower retired from active military duty and for the next two years served as president of Columbia University. He wrote a book of his wartime experiences, *Crusade in Europe* (1948), which became a best seller and made the author a wealthy man. He continued to advise the Truman administration on the further merger of the armed forces. By 1950, the cold war with Russia was well underway. Eisenhower was appointed supreme commander in Europe of the North Atlantic Treaty Organization (NATO) and served two years.

THE PRESIDENCY

Almost from the hour of his first worldly prominence in World War II, Eisenhower was besought to run for the presidency. In 1948 he rebuffed "drafts" from both the Republican and Democratic parties for his nomination. But in 1952 he yielded to Republican demands and, with Richard M. Nixon as his running mate, easily defeated his Democratic rival, Adlai Stevenson. As a campaigner, Eisenhower promised to "clean up the mess in Washington." Attacking the Truman administration for its conduct of the Korean War, he pledged that "I shall

'FROM THE HEART OF AMERICA'

WIDE WORLD

"And if we in America were proud of Dwight Eisenhower, it was partly because he made us proud of America. He came from the heart of America. And he gave expression to the heart of America and he touched the hearts of the world."

—*From the eulogy by President Nixon at the Rotunda of the Capitol, March 30, 1969.*

Young Lt. Eisenhower and his bride, Mamie Doud, posed for this picture shortly after their marriage on July 1, 1916.

Allied supreme commander gives the order of the day on the fateful June 6, 1944, when the invasion of the continent of Europe began. Ike tells paratroopers preparing to leave England on the first assault: "Full victory—nothing else."

U. S. ARMY

THE NEW YORK TIMES

The President was visited by Soviet Premier Khrushchev in September 1959.

Eisenhower enjoys a round of golf with Arnold Palmer at Gettysburg, Pa., in 1960.

Devoted grandfather gives some advice on fishing to his grandson David in 1955.

WIDE WORLD

AL FRENI

go to Korea" in an effort to end the conflict. "I like Ike" became a national slogan.

First Administration. In his first presidential administration, Eisenhower instituted a staff system, modeled after military practice, for top-level policy making. Experiences in his war years had convinced Eisenhower that the presidency was conducted in an excessively casual fashion, and he was determined to impart more order to presidential administration. Cabinet officers and executives became responsible for discovering problems and taking initiatives in their assigned policy areas. The assistant to the President, Sherman Adams, was the "chief of staff." His job was to coordinate the work of all other executive officials, oversee the preparation of decisions for Eisenhower's action, and relieve the President of routine tasks. The cabinet and National Security Council were used extensively. Early in the administration a new Department of Health, Education and Welfare was created.

Eisenhower's liberal "Modern Republicanism" idea had helped win him the election in 1952, and in his first administration he called for a strengthening of federal social programs; a deemphasis of economic regulation; an increase in state, local, and private responsibility; and a balanced budget. Social security coverage was broadened and the minimum wage increased. The President also reduced federal support of farm prices and launched a huge, badly needed federal highway-building program.

Eisenhower believed in the separation of powers within the federal government, and he was opposed to the strong executive leadership that had marked the Roosevelt era. The new President approached the Republican-dominated Congress that came into office with him with a spirit that was almost deferential. Congress, however, responded with such obstruction that Eisenhower was said to have pondered, in moments of despair, the desirability of founding a new party and even of resigning.

Appropriations that he requested were badly cut, and his appointees were harassed in Senate hearings. With great difficulty he beat off the proposed Bricker Amendment that would have shorn the president of much power in foreign affairs. Sen. Joseph R. McCarthy stirred up controversy with his search for Communists and Communist influence in the executive branch. Eisenhower, who refused to attack McCarthy directly, struck back against "book burners" in a speech at Dartmouth College.

In foreign affairs, Eisenhower moved simultaneously for peace and for the strengthening of defenses against Communist aggression. He brought the Korean War to a close. Although this postelection journey to the war site had no immediate effect, a warning to Communist China that its supply lines would be bombed if peace talks were not held helped start lengthy peace discussions. Finally, a truce was signed on July 27, 1953.

In defense matters, Eisenhower instituted a "new look" policy, emphasizing nuclear weapons over conventional ones. This approach derived from the "massive retaliation" strategy of Secretary of State John Foster Dulles, on whom Eisenhower relied greatly in shaping foreign policy.

Eisenhower actively sought to assure the Soviet Union that the United States wished to displace the cold war with an atmosphere of mutual confidence. He also moved to devise means by which the potential benefits of the new atomic age could further the welfare rather than the destruction of mankind. In

December 1953 his "Atoms for Peace" proposal was presented to the United Nations. The basic idea was for nations to pool their atomic information and materials for mutual advantage and peaceful purposes. By 1957 an International Atomic Energy Agency was formed with 62 nations participating.

In a major effort to bring reason and trust into the relations of Communist and non-Communist nations, Eisenhower journeyed to Geneva, Switzerland, in July 1955 to meet at a summit conference with the leaders of Britain, France, and the Soviet Union. At the conference, he advanced his "open skies" proposal, a plan under which the United States and the Soviet Union would permit inspection of one another's military bases. The Soviet Union, however, rejected the proposal.

Eisenhower suffered two major illnesses during his first term: a heart attack in 1955 and an attack of ileitis. But he recovered rapidly and, after some hesitation, decided to run for a second term. Once again Adlai Stevenson was his opponent, but Eisenhower achieved an even greater landslide victory in 1956 than in 1952. Enforced care for his health prompted Eisenhower to devote more hours to his favorite pastimes, golf and bridge.

Second Administration. Foreign affairs in his second administration (1957–61) represented an area beset by troubles. A series of crises led to the "Eisenhower Doctrine" in 1957. This doctrine pledged U. S. military assistance against Communist aggression to any Middle Eastern nation requesting it. Cyprus, Jordan, and the Suez Canal were among the troubled areas that Eisenhower had to contend with. In the Far East, Communist China shelled the Taiwan-controlled Quemoy Islands. Eisenhower made the U. S. Seventh Fleet available to safeguard shipments from Taiwan to the islands.

Despite a crisis in 1958 over Berlin, relations with the USSR seemed on an upturn when Soviet Premier Khrushchev visited the United States in September 1959. This hopeful mood suddenly vanished in May 1960 when the Soviets shot down an American U-2 reconnaissance plane over its territory. Although the flights had long been made, Khrushchev chose to use the incident to destroy the Paris summit conference in May, and to withdraw his invitation to Eisenhower to visit the Soviet Union. Meanwhile, in Cuba, Fidel Castro, the revolutionary leader who had come to power in 1959, seized U. S. property and accepted financial and economic assistance from the Soviet Union. Eisenhower protested and broke off diplomatic relations with Cuba on Jan. 3, 1961.

President Eisenhower undertook two major goodwill tours in 1960. The first, to Latin America, was a success, and Eisenhower was welcomed with warmth and enthusiasm during his 14-day visit. But during an otherwise friendly trip to the Far East in June, a planned visit to Japan had to be cancelled after student riots posed a threat to his security. By the end of his term he had visited 27 lands.

At home, Eisenhower enjoyed better relations with Congress, which had been under Democratic control since 1954. He became increasingly occupied with the civil rights movement. This movement began to attract nationwide attention in 1954 when the Supreme Court, under Eisenhower's most famous appointee, Chief Justice Earl Warren, banned racial segregation in public schools. In the fall of 1957, the President sent federal troops to Little Rock, Ark., to enforce the court's decision.

Eisenhower was burdened with an economic recession in 1957–58 and the resignation of Sherman Adams because of his acceptance of gifts from a New England industrialist. The President resisted demands from the military for increased spending, and, in his farewell address, the former career Army officer warned of the growth of a "military-industrial complex." In November 1957, Eisenhower suffered a mild stroke; again, he fully recovered.

The President was driven to hasten U. S. entry into the space age when the Soviet Union launched a satellite, Sputnik 1, in 1957. In July, Congress created a National Aeronautics and Space Administration, and on Jan. 31, 1958, the United States placed its first satellite in orbit.

Eisenhower was the first President to be affected by the 22d Amendment, limiting a President to two full elected terms. In January 1961, Eisenhower retired to his Gettysburg farm. By special Congressional order, he was restored his rank as general of the Army in March 1961.

LATER YEARS

The ex-President was never wholly free of the office. President Kennedy consulted him in major foreign affairs problems. Eisenhower also assisted Republicans in the 1962 Congressional elections.

Eisenhower expressed some reservations about Barry Goldwater, the conservative Republican nominee for President in 1964, but said that "after some clarifications" he was satisfied with his candidacy. Eisenhower maintained a pattern of cordiality with President Johnson, and publicly supported the war in Vietnam. In 1968, Eisenhower strongly endorsed Richard Nixon's successful bid for the Presidency.

Among Eisenhower's main interests in his post-White House years were the Eisenhower Library in Abilene and Eisenhower College in New York state. An enthusiastic artist, in 1967 he had a showing of his paintings in New York's Museum of Modern Art. He extended his reputation as a best-selling author by producing two volumes of memoirs of his White House years—*Mandate for Change* (1963) and *Waging Peace: The White House Years, 1956–60* (1965).

Despite the unpromising health record of his presidential years, Eisenhower in his post-presidential years enjoyed relatively good health until he suffered a succession of heart attacks in 1968. Several times he was in critical condition, only to recover. But his vigor finally wore out. Dwight Eisenhower died on March 28, 1969.

General Eisenhower's body lay in state in the Capitol Rotunda, where President Nixon eulogized the former President as a man who "captured the trust and faith and affection of his own people and of the people of the world." Nearly 200 dignitaries from 78 nations journeyed to Washington to pay their respects. These included President de Gaulle of France, Lord Mountbatten of Britain, and former Premier Kishi of Japan.

On March 30, the dignitaries mingled with the thousands of average citizens who filed past the former President's bier in a continuous stream. A brief religious service was held at Washington's National Cathedral the next day, and the casket, accompanied by family and friends, was placed on a special train bound for Abilene. There, in America's heartland, Eisenhower was buried on April 2.

LOUIS W. KOENIG
New York University

REPUBLICAN VICTORS in November gubernatorial races rejoice with President and Mrs. Nixon at White House. (*Left*) New Jersey's William Cahill, with his wife; (*right*) Virginia's Linwood Holton.

ELECTIONS

Local issues and national mood influenced election results in 1969. Almost everywhere in the United States restiveness and division revealed public uneasiness over great issues: inflation, high taxes, and the rising cost of government, the Vietnam conflict and the draft, crime and disorder, dissident youth, and permissiveness in society about dress, drugs, and personal morals.

Congressional Elections. Democrats won five of seven elections to fill vacancies in the U. S. House of Representatives. In three of the victories they captured Republican seats. The winning Democrats:

• Edward Jones, Tennessee, elected March 25, retaining a Democratic seat.

• David Ross Obey, Wisconsin, April 1, replacing Melvin R. Laird (R), who had resigned to become U. S. secretary of defense.

• John Melcher, Montana, June 24, replacing James F. Battin (R), named a federal judge.

• Michael J. Harrington, Massachusetts, September 30, succeeding the late William H. Bates in a long-secure Republican seat. Harrington won 52.4% of the vote to defeat William L. Saltonstall.

• Robert A. Roe, New Jersey, November 4, retaining a Democratic seat.

The winning Republicans:

• Barry Goldwater, Jr., California, April 29, retaining a Republican seat.

• Philip M. Crane, Illinois, November 25, replacing Donald Rumsfeld (R), appointed director of the Office of Economic Opportunity.

State Elections. Virginia and New Jersey voters chose Republican governors on November 4. (The Maryland legislature also named a governor: on January 7, it elected Democrat Marvin Mandel to succeed Republican Spiro T. Agnew, who had resigned before becoming the nation's vice president.)

In Virginia, Linwood Holton gained 52.7% of the votes to defeat William C. Battle, nominated by the Democrats after hotly contested primary and runoff elections. Holton became the state's first Republican governor since Reconstruction. His triumph marked the eclipse of the Democratic political organization of the late Sen. Harry F. Byrd.

In New Jersey, U. S. Representative William T. Cahill became governor by amassing a landslide—60.7% of the votes—to defeat Democrat Robert B. Meyner, a former governor. President Nixon campaigned in both states for the victors.

State constitutional amendments to lower the voting age from 21 to 18 in New Jersey and to 19 in Ohio were defeated. New Jersey voters approved a state lottery.

In state legislative elections Republicans increased their margin of control in New Jersey and enlarged their strength as a minority in Virginia.

City and County Elections. Voters independence of party organization was often apparent in municipal elections in 1969. John V. Lindsay's reelection as mayor of New York ranked as the most dramatic of these contests. In the Republican primary of June 17, the mayor was defeated for renomination by John J. Marchi, a state senator, who got 51% of the vote. But Lindsay, running as the nominee of the Liberal party and the new Independent party, won the general election on November 4. He received 41.8% of the vote, defeating City Controller Mario A. Procaccino, Democratic and Nonpartisan nominee (35%), and Marchi, Republican-Conservative (23.2%). The mayor's support came heavily from black, Puerto Rican, and high-income white voters.

Charles Evers won the Democratic nomination for mayor of Fayette, Miss., on May 13, and then the unopposed election on June 3 to become the first Negro mayor in the state since Reconstruction.

In Greene county, Alabama, on July 29, six Negro

members of the National Democratic Party of Alabama won a special election—ordered by the U. S. Supreme Court because their names had been kept off the ballot earlier. The victory gave them control of the county commission and the school board.

In a Los Angeles runoff election on May 27, Mayor Samuel W. Yorty defeated Councilman Thomas Bradley, who sought to be the first Negro mayor of the city. Yorty received 53% of the vote. He had trailed Bradley in an inconclusive contest with other candidates on April 1. Minneapolis voters on June 10 elected Charles S. Stenvig, a "law and order" candidate for mayor. Both the Minneapolis and the Los Angeles elections were technically nonpartisan.

In Atlanta, Vice Mayor Sam Massell (D), backed by a new coalition of Negroes and white liberals, was elected mayor on October 21. He defeated Rodney Cook (R), a moderate supported by white businessmen.

Cleveland's first Negro mayor, Carl Stokes (D), was reelected on November 4, defeating Ralph J. Perk (R) with 50.5% of the vote. The victory reduced racial polarization by developing a black-white coalition supported by business and the press. Stokes won an estimated 24% of the white vote.

In Detroit, Sheriff Roman S. Gibbs, with 50.5% of the vote, defeated County Auditor Richard H. Austin, a Negro, in a nonpartisan contest for mayor. Racial polarization in voting was more marked in Detroit than in Cleveland.

FRANKLIN L. BURDETTE
University of Maryland

ELECTRICAL INDUSTRIES

Near-blackouts, a strike, rising prices, public opposition, and construction delays marked a new climate for the multi-billion-dollar electrical industries in the United States in 1969.

In many ways, each of these factors adds up to an attitude that could create problems in the future through an aroused public that no longer accepts expansion projects or rate applications without forcing utilities to justify their actions in prolonged hearings.

"Brownouts." The near-blackouts—or brownouts as the utilities refer to them—affected the East Coast, for the most part. For example, New York's Consolidated Edison Company had to curtail service in the summer. Its chairman, Charles F. Luce, placed the blame on opposition of conservationists to all of his company's projects for new nuclear or steam power plants.

A nationwide strike against the General Electric Company, the world's largest electrical manufacturer, was expected to cause further delays in the shipments of gas turbines. This generating equipment was needed to meet the 1970 summer peak demand for electricity in New York City and elsewhere, and lack of it may cause service interruptions. The GE strike began October 27 and continued for the rest of the year. (See also LABOR.)

Rates. The nation's electric utilities filed in 1969 for a record $628 million in rate increases, of which by year-end about $145 million was granted by the various regulatory bodies. In spite of this, the Edison Electric Institute, a trade association, noted that the average price of a kilowatt hour (kwh) consumed in electric service dipped to 2.09 cents in 1969 from 2.12 cents in 1968. This was the 44th annual cut. (In contrast, the rate per kwh in 1925 was 7.3 cents.)

However, the institute warned that "inexorable pressures at work"—notably increased money costs, fuel, wages, taxes, and material costs—may well reverse this trend.

Business Volume. New highs were set by the electric utilities in production, generating capacity, construction outlays, sales and revenues, and research. Production reached 1.443 trillion kwh, up 8.7% in 1969.

Total capability of 334.2 million kw was 8.5% higher, and the industry spent a record $8.3 billion on construction, or 12% of all construction outlays by U. S. industry in 1969. This boosted total investment to $84 billion at year-end.

Sales rose by 8.5% to 1.304 trillion kwh as 1.4 million new customers were added during the year. The average use of electricity in the home rose to a new high of 6,550 kwh a year, a gain of 493 kw, which helped boost gross electric revenues to $17.15 billion, up 8.5%.

The industry's 1969 fuel bill, exclusive of nuclear fuel, came to $3 billion, or 13.2% more than in the preceding year.

The Edison Electric Institute was involved in some 50 research projects valued at a record $42 million, with emphasis on underground transmission and bulk power reliability.

Heavy Equipment and Fuels. The nuclear power boom came to a near-halt in 1969, but this lag was more than offset by an unexpected rise in orders for conventional steam generating equipment that boosted total capacity ordered to a new high. (See also ATOMIC ENERGY.)

Manufacturers of gas turbines and stand-by equipment have benefited from the demand for more reliable power supplies. Allis-Chalmers Manufacturing Company said that it planned to return to the manufacture of turbine-generators, a field it left in 1962, and that it was looking into gas turbines.

The National Coal Association noted that of "at least the next three years" more newly built electric power plants will burn coal than any other fuel.

The National Electrical Manufacturers Association predicted 1970 shipments of $45.9 million to follow the record $44.7 billion of 1969. The expected gain was only 2.7% for 1970 as against 7.6% for 1969 over 1968—an indication of the impact of the slowdown on the economy. Some of this decline could be traced to foreign buying—particularly in power transformers and other heavy equipment—by U. S. utilities. Although domestic manufacturers indicated that they expected prices to continue upward, they also feared price cutting by foreign competitors.

Other Industry Activities. According to statistics collected by the National Electrical Manufacturers Association, sales of consumer products at $10.9 billion in 1969 ran 8% above the 1968 level and were expected to reach $11.2 billion, up 2%, in 1970.

Lighting equipment sales rose 9% to $3.3 billion and should reach $3.34 billion, up 2.5%, in 1970.

The industry's other major category—industrial, electronics, and communications equipment—showed a 3% gain in 1969 to $14 billion. It was expected to rise by approximately a like percentage to $14.4 billion in 1970.

GENE SMITH
Financial Writer, "The New York Times"

ELECTRONICS

The electronics industry in the United States continued to grow during 1969, and total factory sales climbed to nearly $25 billion. The industry's crowning achievement in the year was its contribution to the landing of two teams of astronauts on the moon—highlights of a period filled with change, sometimes spectacular and often controversial.

Communications Policy. The President's Task Force on Communications Policy, a 15-man committee appointed in 1967 by President Lyndon B. Johnson, issued a significant 476-page report in 1969. This highly controversial document called for the creation of a powerful new federal agency in the executive branch: a department of communications that would oversee the nation's telecommunications policy. "The broad goal of public policy on communications," the task force said, "should be to release and encourage potentialities for innovation in technology and in management, both within the public-message telephone network and outside it, where such changes do not affect its basic integrity and viability."

In 1969 the Federal Communications Commission decided to permit cable television (CATV) operators to originate their own programs. The FCC also set technical standards for subscription (pay) TV, authorized the construction of a "for hire" microwave common carrier system, and ordered American Telephone and Telegraph Co. to begin allowing the interconnection of customer-owned equipment to the public telephone network.

AT&T's long-standing practice that nothing but its own equipment could be interconnected with its system was broken by what has become known as the Carterfone decision. The Carterfone is a portable radiotelephone that can be used to dial into the public telephone system. In the short period since the courts and the FCC ruled in favor of Carterfone, there has been a substantial investment in private communications companies and services, aimed at competing for new as well as existing markets.

Domestic Satellite Systems. Interest in establishing a domestic satellite system increased in 1969. An ad hoc committee was formed by the White House to study the development of such a system. In October the three major TV networks, led by Dr. Frank Stanton, president of Columbia Broadcasting System, supported a plan to build their own satellite system in defense against transmission rates set by AT&T. Communications Satellite Corp. immediately announced that it had designed and was ready to build a domestic satellite system with the capacity to handle all major forms of electronic communications—including commercial radio and TV, computer data transmissions, and facsimile—except telephone service. At the end of the year, it was unclear which plan would win government favor.

Electronic Computers. A marriage between the computer and communications industries began to grow during 1969 as it became more apparent that each must provide services essential to the other. The FCC asked the Stanford Research Institute to study the interrelationship of the two technologies and services to aid the commission in its regulatory decision-making process in the computer area.

In its report, the SRI said: "What appears to be most needed in order to avoid serious shortages of personnel, capital, and management during the next decade is careful planning and forecasting. Such planning can be accomplished most effectively by both industries working together with representatives of the commission and state regulatory agencies."

Numerous predictions were made during 1969 that computer installations for solving urban problems can be expected to increase more than 100% in the 1970's. It was estimated that perhaps as many as 700 U. S. cities now use computers for a wide range of tasks. (See also COMPUTERS.)

Divisions of Sales. Each of the industry's major market segments—government products, industrial products, consumer products, and replacement components—made gains in 1969, according to the Electronic Industries Association. The association estimated that:

(1) Government purchases of electronics and related services were only slightly above those of 1968, or just over $12 billion. This was about half of the industry's output. Military expenditures on electronics were essentially unchanged during the year, as spending continued to support the country's military effort in Southeast Asia and research and development on a new generation of weapons systems. Additional government spending went for electronics used in education, pollution control, health, and transportation.

(2) Sales of industrial electronics rose during the year by about 6.8% to nearly $7.2 billion. The demand for industrial electronic equipment remained strong, even though it did not show the relatively high annual growth rate experienced in recent years. Shipments of computing and data processing equipment climbed substantially during 1969, accounting for more than half of the total industrial dollar volume.

(3) Sales of consumer electronics edged upward 4.4% during the year to reach about $4.8 billion. When foreign-label imports sold in the United States are added to factory sales, the total market for consumer electronics surpassed the $5 billion level of 1968. A gain of more than 5% was experienced in the total market during 1969. Growth came primarily from color TV receivers and tape recording-playing equipment.

(4) Replacement component sales rose from $675 million in 1968 to about $690 million in 1969.

Sales Growth. Despite a general leveling off in the defense segment of electronic sales, the Electronic Industries Association has estimated that the $12 billion annual figure will increase 30% over the next decade. A large portion of the government's spending will be aimed at space-oriented and military research.

Semiconductor companies are anticipating a growth rate of 20% a year through the 1970's. Semiconductor monolithic circuits alone showed a sales increase of 37.6% during 1968 to $303 million; 1969 sales advanced 23%, to $374 million.

Sales of other integrated circuit packages in 1969 totaled about $84 million, a substantial increase over $64 million in the previous year.

U. S. exports maintained a favorable balance of trade in 1969, climbing some 10% from the $2.2 billion level of 1968. Imports of electronics increased more than 20% above the $1.4 billion mark established in 1968. The 1969 balance of trade in electronics was estimated at $660 million, about 16% below the 1968 balance of $790 million.

RONALD A. SCHNEIDERMAN
"Electronic News"

EL SALVADOR

The overshadowing event of 1969 for El Salvador was a brief but bitter and destructive border war with Honduras, which left a legacy of hatred and severe economic problems in both nations.

Origins of the War. Relations between El Salvador and Honduras had deteriorated for several years due to the gradual flow to Honduras of some 300,-000 job- and land-seeking Salvadorans. El Salvador's population density (about 400 per square mile) was about 10 times greater than that of less developed Honduras, and only 1% of the landed proprietors of El Salvador possessed more than half of the agricultural land. With the national population growing by more than 3% per year and the conservative land-owning group unwilling to face the need for agrarian reform, many Salvadorans were forced to seek their livelihood abroad, emigrating across the convenient Honduran frontier.

The success of these emigrees in Honduras provoked resentments that finally resulted in the passage of legislation restricting land ownership in that country to Honduran-born citizens. After much delay, this law was implemented in April 1969. In the succeeding two months, some 14,000 Salvadorans are estimated to have re-crossed the border. Truckloads of these refugees, some of them prosperous shopkeepers and farmers, passed through San Salvador, the nation's capital. Their stories of terrorism and murder began to appear in various Salvadoran newspapers.

With the country already facing a decline in economic growth, the small group of dominant wealthy families put pressure on the shaky regime of President Fidel Sánchez Hernández to take action, fearing a full-fledged economic crisis and left-wing agitation among the landless repatriates.

Tension reached the breaking point as a result of several incidents, the most important of which was the violence that accompanied the second of a series of soccer games between teams representing the two nations—scheduled as part of the playoffs in the World Soccer Cup competition. Played in San Salvador on June 15, the game was marred by movement of Salvadoran fans against the Honduran visitors and was followed by a sharp rise of popular bitterness in both countries.

On June 24, the Salvadoran government declared a state of siege and called up reservists. Two days later it broke off relations with Honduras and lodged a charge of genocide against that country with the Inter-American Human Rights Commission of the Organization of American States (OAS). The border, part of which was in dispute, was closed.

Invasion of Honduras. On June 28, both El Salvador and Honduras accepted a mediation offer from Guatemala, Nicaragua, and Costa Rica, but after two weeks of mutual recriminations, El Salvador sent troops and aircraft across the Honduran border (July 14). While Salvadoran ground forces penetrated Honduras up to a distance of 40 miles (65 km), Honduran planes bombed the oil refinery at Acajutla and San Salvador's airport.

A seven-nation peace commission dispatched by the OAS obtained cease-fire and withdrawal agreements from both sides on the night of July 18. But El Salvador balked at removing its troops from Honduran soil until threatened with diplomatic and economic sanctions by the OAS, finally beginning its withdrawal after July 29. (See also HONDURAS.)

Repercussions of the War. Total deaths in the misnamed "Soccer War" were reported to be as high as 2,400, most of the dead being civilians. Tens of thousands in the border area had fled their homes, many of which were destroyed. By December, the exodus of Salvadorans from Honduras was estimated to have exceeded 60,000. While OAS relief units fed the Honduran victims of the war, El Salvador persisted in refusing OAS aid and condemned the organization for failing to force Honduras to lift a road blockade that was effectively stifling Salvadoran commerce with its neighbors.

Trade between El Salvador and Honduras ceased entirely after the war. At year's end the persisting hostility was endangering the future of the Central American Common Market (CACM), hitherto the most successful of Latin America's regional trading blocs.

In late August, the six Roman Catholic bishops of El Salvador sought to attack one of the root causes of the war by calling for agrarian reform and initiating a pilot program for the distribution of some rural church-owned land to landless farmers.

C. ALAN HUTCHINSON
University of Virginia

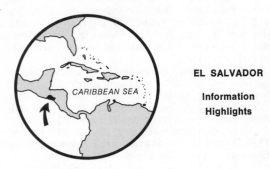

EL SALVADOR

Information

Highlights

Area: 8,260 square miles (21,393 sq km).
Population: 3,266,000 (1968 est.).
Chief Cities (1966 census): San Salvador, the capital, 317,-570; Santa Ana, 152,346; San Miguel (1963 est.), 39,949.
Government: *President*—Fidel Sánchez Hernández (took office July 1, 1967). *Parliament*—Legislative Assembly, 52 members (party seating, 1969: Party of National Conciliation, 27; others, 25).
Religious Faiths: Roman Catholic, 97.7% of population.
Education: *Literacy rate* (1961), 49% of population aged 15 and over. *Total school enrollment* (1965)—456,273 (primary, 397,810; secondary, 38,619; teacher-training, 6,288; technical/vocational, 9,929; university/higher, 3,627).
Finance (1968 est.): *Revenues*, $96,012,000; expenditures, $98,936,000; public debt (1967 est.), $21,932,000; *monetary unit*, Colón (2.5 equal U. S.$1).
Gross National Product (1968): $919,600,000.
National Income (1968): $796,800,000; average annual income per person, $243.
Cost of Living Index (1967): 102 (1963=100).
Manufacturing (metric tons, 1967): Cement, 149,000: sugar, 125,000; gasoline, 93,000.
Crops (metric tons, 1967–68 crop year): Maize, 202,000; coffee, 144,000; rice, 66,000; cottonseed, 59,000.
Minerals (metric tons, 1966): Limestone and sea shells, 213,424; salt, 127,000.
Foreign Trade (1968): *Exports*, $212,000,000 (chief exports, 1967: coffee, $97,092,000; cotton, $16,940,000); *Imports*, 216,000,000 (chief imports, 1967: nonelectrical machinery, $23,092,000; transport equipment, $20,924,000; textile yarn and fabrics, $16,248,000). *Chief trading partners* 1967): United States (took 27% of exports, supplied 31% of imports); West Germany (took 22% of exports, supplied 7% of imports); Guatemala (took 16% of exports, supplied 13% of imports).
Transportation: *Roads* (1969), 7,077 miles (11,389 km); *motor vehicles* (1967), 43,800 (automobiles 30,100); *railways* (1968), 727 miles (1,169 km).
Communications: *Telephones* (1968): 37,796; *television stations* (1968), 4; *television sets* (1968), 35,000; *radios* (1966), 396,000; *newspapers* (1966), 15.

ENGLISH LITERATURE

Publication of *The Complete Poems and Plays of T. S. Eliot* in 1969 prompted numerous critical revaluations of the poet's influence and achievements. While outstanding work in all literary genres was produced in 1969, publishers' lists were dominated by a "safe," conventional literature.

Fiction. The greatest signs of literary vitality were to be found in the novel. A number of English critics published works of fiction. Highest praise went to Barry Cole's *Joseph Winter's Patronage,* the story of an old man's ill-tempered existence in a private "home." Derwent May's *Dear Parson,* commended for the gentle innocence with which it records a young man's progress to maturity, was nonetheless felt to be marred by "a cosiness of tone." Film critic Penelope Mortimer published a volume of short stories, *What's It Like Out?,* which was admired for intelligence and elegance of style. *Clap Hands if You Believe in Fairies,* was widely hailed as a remarkably confident beginning as a novelist for actor John Fraser.

There were other first novels of considerable merit. Richard Wollheim's *A Family Romance* was greeted as a major literary event. The novel takes the form of a diary written by a young man whose life is heavily dependent on fantasy; slowly and painfully, the fantasy is subtracted until he is able to recognize the objective reality around him. Similarly, Jonathan Street's *Rebarbative!* and J. S. Mitchell's *An Abdication* were praised for their construction and intelligence. James Plunkett's first novel, *Strumpet City,* published amid considerable fanfare, deals with Dublin between 1907 and 1914.

The most aggressively experimental novel published in 1969 was B. S. Jonson's *The Unfortunates;* produced in 27 separate, self-contained sections that the reader can shuffle together and read in any sequence, it embodies the author's belief that human experience in its raw form lacks discernible shape or meaning. The novel has a certain crude force, but few readers greeted it with enthusiasm. On the other hand, Dan Greenberg's experimental novel, *Chewsday,* was praised for its Shandian wit and wisdom. *Babel* confirmed Alan Burns' reputation as one of Britain's leading experimental novelists.

The most ambitious and successful experiment in fiction was John Fowles' *The French Lieutenant's Woman.* The novel treats a conventional plot of the 1860's from a distinctly modern point of view; what results is, first, an engaging parody of the Victorian novel, but more significantly a work which questions the role of the author in fiction, standard conceptions of Victorian life, and the intricate turnings of passion and the imagination.

Female novelists continued to play a major role in England. Iris Murdoch's *Bruno's Dream* provoked the same critical disagreement that all her recent work has called forth. Some reviewers found this story of a pathetic, dying man to contain some of the novelist's best observed and most deeply felt passages. Pamela Hansford Johnson published a substantially revised version of *Catherine Carter,* a novel first published in 1952. Miss Johnson was generally admired for the imaginative wit with which she treated the adventures and misadventures of the figures who revolve around a fictionalized Sir Henry Irving in the 1880's in London. There was admiration but little enthusiasm in reviews of Brigid Brophy's *In Transit,* and even less enthusiasm

STEVEN KINBERG

JOHN FOWLES experimented successfully by treating an 1860's plot from a modern standpoint in his ambitious novel *The French Lieutenant's Woman.*

for Elizabeth Bowen's *Eva Trout,* the story of a physical and psychological freak desperate for love, or for Olivia Manning's *The Play Room.* Beautifully written and impeccably structured, Margaret Drabble's *The Waterfall* presents a young woman unable "to reconcile the practical and emotional aspects" of her sexual life. Reviewers also expressed qualified praise for Sarah Gainham's *A Place in the Country,* Barbara Levinge's *Felix,* Maureen Duffy's *Wounds,* Barbara Skelton's *A Love Match,* and Janice Elliot's *Angels Falling.*

A number of new novels dealt with the perennial theme of the young man's approach to maturity. The most interesting of these was a first novel, J. S. Mitchell's *An Abdication,* written when the author was only 20. It records the experiences of a commonplace boy who steadily retreats from reality into a dream kingdom. The novelist's detailing of a threatened adolescent consciousness was described by the *Times Literary Supplement* as "painfully authentic." Garth St. Omer's *Nor Any Country* describes a dislocated young man who comes to realize his own limitations and lost possibilities and to accept the responsibilities of the world. Stanley Middleton's *Wages of Virtues* centers on the adolescence of a boy growing up in the Midlands of the 1930's. The accomplished poet Iain Crichton Smith concentrated on a young boy's final term at school during World War I in *The Last Summer.* Ironically, reviewers criticized the novel's language.

Several complex fictional works were brought to completion in 1969. *The Gale of the World,* the final volume of Henry Williamson's *A Chronicle of Ancient Sunlight,* finds its hero alone in a country cottage, editing a magazine, trying to complete his magnum opus, and struggling with his own emotional needs. Reviewers found little merit in Williamson's work, nor in Alexander Cordell's *Song of Earth,* an old-fashioned, saga-type novel which completed his Welsh trilogy. Doris Lessing's *The Four-Gated City,* the last volume in her series *Children of Violence,* shows its heroine moving rather mechanically through post-war London.

Many established novelists fared less well than the newcomers. L. P. Hartley's *The Love Adept* was slight and insignificant; Paul Gallico's *The Poseidon Adventure* had little distinction; and while Kingsley Amis's *The Green Man* contains passages of admirable novelistic achievement, it has a "ramshackle" quality that prevents its inclusion among his real successes. Robert Shaw's *A Card for Morocco,* however, was praised for the ease and authority with which it explored a wide range of human problems; Colin Wilson's *The Philosopher's Stone* was described by reviewer Barry Cole as "his best novel to date." James Kennaway's posthumously published *The Cost of Living Like This* was admired.

Russell Hoban's *The Mouse and the Child,* while ostensibly a children's book, was praised as "a masterpiece by the standards of any age group." There was also high praise for *Blind Love,* a collection of short stories by V. S. Pritchett.

Other novels of special interest published in 1969 include William Watson's *Better Than One,* Richard Power's *The Hungry Grass,* Julian Moynahan's *Pairing Off,* Philip Callow's *The Bliss Body,* Robin Jenkins' *The Holy Tree,* Rayner Heppenstall's *The Shearers,* Brian Glanville's *The Olympian,* P. G. Wodehouse's *A Pelican for Mr. Blandings,* and Collin MacInnes' *Westward to Laughter.*

Nonfiction. In *The Crane Bag,* Robert Graves collected essays, reviews, and talks on a variety of topics—from the Gettysburg Address to Egypt and old-fashioned Christmases. Sir Compton Mackenzie's *My Life and Times: Octave Eight, 1939–1946* covers the period of World War II and the early months of peace. The literary qualities displayed in the third volume of Bertrand Russel's *Autobiography,* which begins with the dropping of the atomic bomb on Hiroshima and continues through the author's recent and continuing campaign for nuclear disarmament were well noted. The third volume of Harold Macmillan's memoirs, *Tides of Fortune,* is a distinguished work, articulate and informative.

Two "academic" memoirs also claimed special attention. Basil Willey's *Cambridge and Other Memories, 1920–1953* was generally admired, although felt to be lacking in sharpness and immediacy, while D. J. Enright's *Memoirs of a Mendicant Professor* was greeted as a fascinating book.

Malcolm Lowry's wife and his biographer, Douglas Day, carefully edited the manuscript which the author began as a diary in Mexico in 1945, and which grew over the next 11 years to more than 700 pages. Half-memoir, half-novel, *Dark as the Grave Wherein My Friend is Laid* is a record of the author's frustrating Mexican itinerary. Laura Archera Huxley has made a similar contribution to her late husband's work in making available the semi-autobiographical novel which Aldous Huxley began during the final days of his life. *This Time-less Moment* also includes his second wife's own account of their life in California between 1956 and 1963. Another posthumous work provoked literary interest in 1969: *Giacomo Joyce,* edited by Richard Ellman, was the first printing of a short, strongly autobiographical work that James Joyce wrote in Trieste in 1914.

Two memoirs were noteworthy despite the relative obscurity of their authors. A. S. Jasper's *A Hoxton Childhood* describes the author's impoverished childhood before and during World War I. Also admired for its purely literary qualities was Frank Norman's *Banana Boy.*

Although somewhat flawed in the telling, through transcription from recorded conversations with the editor, B. S. Johnson, *The Evacuees* is an intriguing study of the lives of a number of distinguished Britons who were evacuated from London during World War II and sent to live with foster parents. The contributors include Alan Sillitoe, Jonathan Miller, and Barry Cole. Reviewers also took particular note of autobiographies by H. E. Bates, Laurie Lee, Storm Jameson, and Cecil Roberts, and of the second fluently humorous volume of memoirs, *My Father's Son,* by Frank O'Connor.

Poetry. Early in 1969 a collection of essays entitled *The Modern Poet* served as a reminder of the high regard in which the English hold the art of poetry. These essays, taken from England's leading poetry magazine, *The Review,* were edited by Ian Hamilton, whose own skillful verse was generously represented in *Poetry Introduction I,* an anthology containing the work of nine younger poets. Some reviewers, however, found Hamilton's own poetry lacking in creative energy, and many other poets were held to the same charge.

Alan Brownjohn's *Sandgrains on a Tray* was generally dismissed as "poetry of the ordinary"; John Pudney's *Spandrels* criticized for its reliance on "poetikit properties"; and David Harsent's *A Violent Country* judged to be too abstract and literary in approach. Seamus Heaney's *Door into the Dark* was praised for its poetic intelligence and witty technique.

The Lilting House, a collection of Welsh verse edited by John Stuart Williams and Meic Stephens, contained the work of a number of promising younger poets, including Anthony Conran, Bryan Griffiths, Peter Gruffyd, and Sally Roberts. The poetry of Scotland was also well represented in Iain Crichton Smith's *From Bourgeois Land,* David Morrison's *The White Hind,* Charles Senior's *Harbingers,* and Robert Fulton's *Inventories.*

Roy Fisher is often cited as an example of a modernist spirit transforming English verse. One reviewer found that the real strength of his *Collected Poems 1968* rested in their clever use of the traditional. Tom Buchan's *Dolphins at Cochin* helped to further his reputation as a distinguished writer of inventively satirical verse who deserves to be widely read. *A Porter Folio,* by ex-Australian Peter Porter, was praised for its genuine formal sense and its creative uses of European culture.

Laurence Lerner's most recent volume of verse, *Selves,* seemed distinctly uneven to most reviewers. In this respect, Lerner's work is symptomatic of English literature as a whole in 1969: while its actual achievement was disappointing, it offered genuine promise for the 1970's.

DAVID GALLOWAY
Case Western Reserve University

EPISCOPAL CHURCH

In 1969, for the second time in its history (the first having been in 1821), the Episcopal Church held a special General Convention. Recommended by the deputies and formally requested, pursuant to canon law, by the bishops, the special meeting was called by the presiding bishop. It met on the campus of Notre Dame University, South Bend, Ind., from August 31 to September 5.

Relatively unhampered by precedent, and free of many procedural concerns, the convention adopted an agenda combining features of a conference with formal legislative sessions. Most of the more than 100 jurisdictions had already responded to an invitation to send additional representatives—women, young people, and members of minority groups—to join the bishops and the elected clerical and lay deputies, in discussing (in general assemblies and small work groups) the major issues of ministry, mission, and structure that face the church.

It became obvious at the very first general assembly that the mission of the church as it seeks to minister to people deprived of dignity, opportunity, and the power to determine their own destiny, was the overriding concern of those present. Fully half of the time of the convention and the attendant conference sessions was devoted to consideration of this matter. The result was a reaffirmation of the church's "commitment to the principle of self-determination for minority groups ... and ... [of] the role of the Church to support programs which such groups themselves initiate...." To implement this statement, the convention directed the church's Executive Council to allocate funds, from voluntary sources, to be used for black, Indian, and Eskimo community development.

In other actions, the convention adopted legislation to make possible the development of self-supporting ministries, to give certain liturgical functions to women, and to begin a revision of clergy-deployment procedures.

CHARLES M. GUILBERT
Episcopal Church Center

EQUATORIAL GUINEA

Civil unrest broke out in Equatorial Guinea in 1969. It began with a dispute with Spain, and led to the declaration of a state of emergency.

Friction with Spain. In February, President Francisco Macias Nguema objected to the flying of the Spanish flag from Spain's consulate in Bata, the capital of Río Muni province, and Guinean soldiers tore down the flag. It was hoisted again two days later, under the protection of the Spanish civil guard, which also acted to protect Spanish nationals.

Macias charged illegal occupation by Spanish forces and asked the United Nations for a peace-keeping force. A UN representative was sent in March. But by April many of the 7,000 Spanish nationals, terrified, had left the country.

State of Emergency. The dispute seemed to be a result of Spain's disenchantment with Macias' rule and rumors of his imminent replacement by Foreign Minister Atanasio Ndongo, who had opposed Macias for the presidency before independence. Ndongo returned in early March from consultations in Madrid and was arrested on the charge of leading a revolt against the government. President Macias then seized emergency power and made further

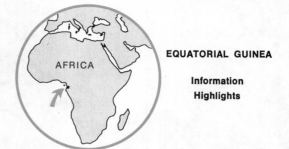

EQUATORIAL GUINEA

Information
Highlights

Area: 10,830 square miles (28,050 sq km).
Population: 281,000 (June 30, 1968 est.).
Chief Cities (1960 census of divisions): Santa Isabel, the capital, 37,237.
Government: *President*—Francisco Macias Nguema (took office Oct. 12, 1968); *Vice President*—Edmundo Bosio Dioco.
Religious Faiths: Roman Catholics, 90% of population.
Monetary Unit: Peseta (70 Guinea pesetas equal U. S.$1).
Crops (metric tons, 1962 crop year): Timber, 400,000.
Foreign Trade (1966): *Exports,* $20,743,000; *imports,* $24,-071,000. *Chief trading partner* (1966): Spain.

arrests. Ndongo and his wife, Saturnino Ibongo (the ambassador to the United Nations) and others were reported to have been killed.

Economy. The dispute with Spain also brought about an economic crisis. However, Spain agreed in August to provide financial aid and to purchase cocoa and timber. A new Spanish-supported currency was introduced on October 12.

FRANKLIN PARKER
West Virginia University

ESHKOL, Levi. See biographical sketch under ISRAEL.

ETHIOPIA

In 1969 the worldwide phenomenon of student protest caught up with Ethiopia, a land where antigovernment demonstrations of any sort had been virtually unknown until recently.

Political Developments. In March, Haile Selassie I University and all secondary schools in Ethiopia were closed because of student agitation. Although couched in terms of educational reform, the students' demands were basically political. The students' unrest appeared to be the result of centuries of resistance to sociopolitical change.

Responding to the arrest and threatened detention without trial of hundreds of students in Addis Ababa, Ethiopian students in Washington and Moscow stormed their embassies, smashed portraits of Emperor Haile Selassie, and denounced his "feudal monarchy." In July they sacked the Ethiopian chancery in Washington just prior to the emperor's arrival on an official visit to the United States.

Antigovernment Muslim separatists, members of the Eritrean Liberation Front, engaged in attacks on Ethiopian airlines refueling in Frankfurt, West Germany, and Karachi, Pakistan. Two were killed while attempting to hijack an Ethiopian flight in December. Separatists continued to harass government troops in Eritrea, to levy road tolls in the province, and to attack rolling stock in Djibouti.

The move initiated in 1968 to improve relations between Somalia and Ethiopia appeared to be succeeding. A state of emergency no longer existed along the border and there was a climate of cooperation between the two countries. Both worked

IN ADDIS ABABA on February 2, U Thant, secretary general of the United Nations, addresses a meeting of the Economic Commission for Africa.

to implement a telecommunications agreement negotiated in 1968 and assisted the U. S. Agency for International Development in a study of the feasibility of a highway linking them to Kenya.

Economy. The Ethiopian government embarked on a third 5-year economic development plan. The total investment under the new plan will amount to $1.25 billion. Most of this amount will come from domestic savings, and the balance will be financed abroad. Particular emphasis will be placed on the development of manufacturing and mining, with transport and communications, housing, and agriculture following in that order.

The foreign sector of Ethiopia's economy fared poorly in the first half of 1969. Falling coffee prices and a rising demand for imports reduced the country's foreign exchange reserves by 10%, compared with the corresponding period in 1968. A small increase in the gold holdings of the national bank only partly offset the erosion. Domestic credit continued to expand; consumer prices held steady.

Foreign Aid. The World Bank continued to support Ethiopian economic development by extending a long-term loan of $23.1 million to help finance construction of a 100-megawatt hydroelectric plant,

the largest in Ethiopia, on the Finchaa River. When completed, the project will more than double the country's present electrical generating capacity. The United States made a $10 million loan for the improvement of airport facilities, and the International Development Association gave $3.5 million to develop agriculture in the Wolamo region.

ERNEST W. LUTHER
Economist; Author of "Ethiopia Today"

──────── **ETHIOPIA · Information Highlights** ────────

Area: 471,776 square miles (1,221,900 sq km).
Population: 24,212,000 (1968 est.).
Chief Cities (1965 est.): Addis Ababa, the capital, 560,000; Asmara (1964 est.), 131,800; Dessie (1963 est.), 56,400; Harar (1963 est.), 42,700.
Government: *Emperor*—Haile Selassie I (proclaimed emperor April 2, 1930); *Prime Minister*—Aklilou Habte Wold (took office April 17, 1961). *Parliament*—Senate, 105 members appointed by the emperor; Chamber of Deputies, 210 members.
Religious Faiths: Ethiopian (Monophysite) Christians, estimated one third of population; Muslim, one third; pagan, one third.
Education: *Literacy rate* (1969), 5% of population. *Total school enrollment* (1965)—441,726 (primary, 378,750; secondary, 55,579; teacher-training, 1,680; technical/vocational, 3,461; university/higher, 2,256).
Finance (1969 est.): *Revenues,* $215,000,000; *expenditures,* $261,000,000; *monetary unit,* Ethiopian dollar (2.5 Ethiopian dollars equal U. S.$1).
Gross National Product (1967): $1,486,000,000.
Economic Indexes (1967): *Agricultural production,* 109 (1963=100).
Manufacturing (metric tons, 1966): Cement, 89,000; sugar (1967), 77,000; wheat flour, 42,000; beer, 185,000 hectoliters; lumber, 56,000 cubic meters; sawn wood (1967), 19,000 cubic meters.
Crops (metric tons, 1967–68 crop year): Millet and sorghum, 3,350,000; barley, 850,000; maize (1966), 750,000; chickpeas, 168,000; dry peas, 120,000; coffee, 150,000.
Minerals (metric tons, 1967): Salt, 202,000; gold, 734 kilograms; platinum (1966), 350 troy ounces.
Foreign Trade (1968): *Exports,* $106,000,000 (chief exports, 1967: coffee, $55,672,800; hides & skins, $11,934,800; fruits and vegetables, $11,280,000; oilseeds, $9,079,600); *imports,* $173,000,000 (chief imports, 1967: transport equipment, $19,888,800; nonelectrical machinery, $16,-942,000; textile yarn and fabrics, $11,181,200). *Chief trading partners* (1967): United States (took 43% of exports, supplied 9% of imports); Italy (took 8% of exports, supplied 19% of imports); West Germany.
Transportation: *Roads* (1967), 14,292 miles (23,000 km); *motor vehicles* (1968), 36,000 (automobiles 27,200); *railways* (1965), 423 miles (681 km); *merchant vessels* (1967), 6 (37,000 gross registered tons); *national airline,* Ethiopian Air Lines.
Communications: *Telephones* (1968), 32,355; *television stations* (1968), 1; *television sets* (1968), 5,000; *radios* (1964), 325,000; *newspapers* (1965), 8.

EMPEROR HAILE SELASSIE was welcomed by President Nixon as a White House visitor on July 8, 1969.

EUROPE

Signs of significant, and perhaps beneficial, changes appeared in Europe in 1969. They had their immediate origin in changes in the men in power in major countries, but there were also deeper causes. The political situation in Europe, particularly in regard to East-West relations and the partition of Germany, had been static for a long time. A new look at some of these problems was certainly due.

Europe continued to enjoy the high prosperity that has been typical of recent years. There was a marked decline everywhere in the incidence of student riots and signs of unrest. The rising tide of prosperity was only slightly stayed by international financial readjustments in the autumn. These financial readjustments affected mostly the two leading continental states, France and West Germany.

FRANCE AND WEST GERMANY

In both France and West Germany there were changes of government; both took place with remarkable smoothness.

Pompidou Replaces de Gaulle. In France, the events of 1969 had the clear character of the end of an era. The rule of President Charles de Gaulle, which had lasted slightly over 10 years, came abruptly to an end. The occasion of the passing from power of this great and extraordinary man was indeed rather trivial—the refusal of the French electorate to approve by plebiscite the creation of novel regional bodies and a reduction in the powers of the Senate—two changes with no logical connection. De Gaulle resigned immediately (April 28), and in the ensuing presidential election the very able Georges Pompidou, once premier under de Gaulle, was an easy winner. The remainder of the year showed strong continuity and comparatively little innovation in French policy. (See also FRANCE.)

Brandt Replaces Kiesinger. The change in Germany followed from the general election of September 28, the sixth general election to be held in West Germany. It registered an increase in the strength of the Social Democratic Party (SPD) and a slight loss of strength by Chancellor Kurt Kiesinger's Christian Democratic Union (CDU), which, however, remained the strongest single party. The election resulted in the breakup of the SPD-CDU "Great Coalition," which had ruled since December 1966. A new coalition of SPD with the small Free Democratic party gave power to Willy Brandt, formerly foreign minister. He was elected chancellor by the Bundestag on October 21.

This change of leadership was no end of an epoch for Germany; that had come earlier, with the resignation (October 1963) and death of Konrad Adenauer. Rather, the significant thing about the German election was its normality: an election produced a modification in party strengths and a peaceful change of government. Democracy in West Germany, 20 years in action, had clearly come of age.

West Germany Overtakes France. In another sense, perhaps a historic turn had been reached. West Germany was coming to dominate developments in western Europe. Under de Gaulle, France had done so, but that period was over. From the beginning, Chancellor Brandt indicated that he would pursue vigorous and innovative policies, and that he would try to end the long frost in East-West relations in Europe. His policies during the last two months of 1969 bore this out. There was more pressure on France to agree to Britain's joining the Common Market and to allow the Market to progress toward its declared goals. The changes of leadership that took place in 1969 at last allowed West Germany's great economic strength to attain its natural corollary of political predominance.

Currency Changes. The direction of events was clearly seen in the fluctuation of value in the mark and the franc during 1969. The French franc had been in a strong position before the 1968 strikes and riots, and subsequent wage increases caused French reserves to sink toward exhaustion. A devaluation of 12.5% was carried through on Aug. 8, 1969—technically, a model of smoothness and secrecy. It caused a minimum of international disturbance, although it did have repercussions on the Common Market.

The West German mark, too strong for its official value, had for long been under the opposite pressure. After the German election its value was allowed to move freely without exchange controls from September 30 to October 26. Then its value was fixed at a new official rate 8.5% higher than the old. (See INTERNATIONAL FINANCE.)

New Initiatives Toward the Eastern Bloc. The striking novelty of Brandt's policy was his immediate attempt to improve trade and cultural relations between East and West Germany, between West Germany and Poland, and in general between the two rigidly demarcated parts of Europe. Brandt created a favorable climate through his government's signing the nuclear nonproliferation treaty on November 28. The Communist states, in a proposal made at Prague in October, suggested an East-West security conference on European issues. Trade talks between Poland and West Germany began in Bonn at the end of October. A West German proposal to East Germany that talks be held in an effort to normalize relations met with a favorable response on December 18.

These and other moves were all auspicious, but it remained to be seen how much concrete result they would have. For example, how pleased would East Germany's Communist party chief Walter Ulbricht be if Polish-West German relations really improved? The attitude of the United States was also something of an enigma. The United States had been deeply involved in peripheral parts of the world for so long that it had almost ceased to have a European policy.

OTHER COUNTRIES

Eastern Bloc. In Czechoslovakia, the sad process already under way in 1968 was intensified and completed in 1969. The country was subjugated to hard-line Communist rulers. Such traces of freedom as had survived from the brief, false dawn of the Dubček experiment were destroyed. Soviet pressure had succeeded, backed by the manifest readiness to use all force necessary. Alexander Dubček was relieved of his post as head of the Czech Communist party on April 17, and deprived of his Presidium seat at the end of September.

Elsewhere, there was much to concern the rulers in the Kremlin. President Nicolae Ceausescu of Rumania persisted in taking an independent line in foreign policy; Yugoslavia, growing prosperous on tourism, resisted Moscow's renewed blandishments. The Soviets, troubled by border disputes with China, were in a mood to consider friendly moves in Europe, perhaps even in the direction of Rome.

Britain. Chronic financial difficulties, typical of British postwar history, began to ease with dramatic suddenness after midyear. An upswing in exports produced balance-of-payments surpluses for the first time in seven years. But the Labour government of Prime Minister Harold Wilson, legally obliged to call a general election before March 1971, was still behind the Conservatives in opinion polls.

In Ireland there was mass violence in Belfast and Londonderry, the greatest violence in Ireland in 50 years. Another British problem was the increasing pressure from Spain—curiously backed up by the United Nations—to relinquish Gibraltar.

Italy. Italy had to sustain a large number of strikes in 1969, and in addition the country had a major political crisis. The political crisis was resolved by the creation in August, by Premier Mariano Rumor, of Italy's 30th postwar government. The South Tyrol problem was eased by concessions that gave more autonomy to the Bolzano province (transferred from Austria at the end of World War I) and its German-speaking majority.

Spain. Signs of political opposition in Spain were growing, but the government of Chief of State Francisco Franco seemed in no serious trouble. In July the aging dictator, then 77, nominated the Bourbon prince Juan Carlos to succeed him as head of state in a revived monarchy when Franco dies or retires. The American-Spanish bases agreement was renewed for two years in June.

SUPRANATIONAL ORGANIZATIONS

Western Europe continued to be divided between two great trading blocs, although there were signs that this unsatisfactory situation might be nearing a change. The most important bloc is the European Economic Community (EEC), or Common Market, comprising France, West Germany, Italy, Belgium, the Netherlands, and Luxembourg. The EEC is linked by a common executive Commission (which completed its second year of office in 1969) with two other 6-nation functional bodies, the European Coal and Steel Community (ECSC) and the European Atomic Energy Community (Euratom). The EEC, ECSC, and Euratom, jointly known as the European Communities, also share a common Council of Ministers, a law court, and a consulative body, the European Parliament. Western Europe's other, looser, trading bloc is the European Free Trade Association, whose members are Austria, Denmark, Norway, Portugal, Sweden, Switzerland, the United Kingdom, and Finland (associate member).

European Economic Community. In its second annual report, released in Brussels on February 18, and in a memorandum of suggestions submitted to the Council of Ministers on February 12, the joint Commission pressed the need for making basic decisions soon. Badly needed were greater coordination of economic policy and the establishment of

P.I.P. PHOTO BY REPORTER ASSOCIÉS

CEREMONIES commemorating 25th anniversary of D-Day (allied invasion of Europe in World War II) were held on June 6 at Sword Beach (*left*) and Pegasus Bridge (*below*) in Normandy.

P.I.P. PHOTO BY REPORTER ASSOCIÉS

HAROLD WILSON (*left*), British prime minister, chats with West German Chancellor Kurt Kiesinger, Foreign Minister Willy Brandt, and the British ambassador Sir Roger Jackling (*left to right*), during a visit to Bonn by Wilson.

KEYSTONE

machinery for monetary cooperation. Events of 1969 showed how necessary and how far from realization these goals still are. Despite its formidable achievements in facilitating economic development among the Six, and despite the great ability of men such as the Community's president, Jean Rey, the Community is still a long way from rivaling the authority of its member governments.

EEC affairs have become extremely complex, with a lore and terminology of their own. Essentially, however, the current problems fall into two main groups. The first concerns the external relations of EEC, the question of bringing in new members, particularly Britain. Most of the second group—the internal problems of the EEC—relate to the intensification of ongoing functions, in particular the common agricultural policy and the financing of EEC's budgets. The two sets of problems are tied together; in both, the policy of France is crucial. In neither problem area was much progress made during 1969.

President Pompidou, at his first press conference, on July 10, spoke of EEC in more favorable terms than had been usual with de Gaulle. "The Community exists," he said; "We feel that the first thing to do is to pursue the construction of this Community." As for the possibility of extending the Community:

"We have no objection in principle to the possible membership of Britain or of any other country. . . . But we think it is right first of all that the Six agree among themselves . . . on the conditions of that membership and the consequences . . . on . . . the very nature of the Community. . . . Britain's membership, which could not fail to be accompanied by the membership of a certain number of other countries, raises some difficult questions and brings about profound changes for the Community."

The question of British membership remained in suspense throughout 1969, as did the question of associate status for Israel. France, in keeping with its current pro-Arab policy, balked at giving membership to Israel. The only positive acts in external policy achieved by EEC in 1969 concerned Africa. They were the signing, on July 29, of the second Yaounde Convention by the EEC and 18 associated states in Africa (mostly former French colonies); and the conclusion at Arusha, Tanzania, on September 24, of a similar association agreement with three former British colonies in East Africa—Kenya, Uganda, and Tanzania. Both of these agreements are to run for five years, until Jan. 31, 1975.

Progress toward solution of EEC's most difficult problem—creation of a common agricultural policy —was rudely interrupted by the French devaluation of the franc, done without prior consultation with its EEC partners. Devaluation altered the relation between the franc and EEC's agricultural unit of account. The Council of Ministers agreed to give France two years in which to achieve adjustment of French prices to the common prices.

Another setback for EEC was related to the introduction of the Community's common turnover tax system—the tax on value added (TVA). As early as April 1967, it had been agreed that the Six would all take steps to introduce a uniform TVA by Jan. 1, 1970. But in response to Belgian and Italian requests, the Commission agreed in October 1969 that the date should be postponed to Jan. 1, 1971.

The EEC summit conference at The Hague, December 1–2, in which both President Pompidou and Chancellor Brandt participated, saw some intense diplomatic bargaining and apparently some progress. France gained a point of crucial importance to its interests—the continuation of farm subsidies. In return, France had to agree that preliminary discussions within the Community on its enlargement should be completed by June 30, 1970, thus permitting the opening of serious negotiations with Britain and other potential members in the second half of the year. Meanwhile, in Britain, as the possibility of EEC membership increased, the complications and disadvantages of membership loomed larger, and enthusiasm waned.

European Coal and Steel Community. The problems of ECSC continued to be what they had been—chiefly a falling demand for coal. ECSC reports noted that in 1968 coal production fell by 4.3% from 189.2 to 181.1 million metric tons. Employment in the mines continued to fall at over 10% per year. In a statement issued in July the Commission also noted that heavy plant investments by Community steel companies held a danger of creating surplus steel capacity in the 1970's.

European Atomic Energy Community. The function of Euratom has become increasingly unclear, and its success more questionable. The original intention, to create a strong European nuclear power industry, has never been achieved. In consequence, the Council of Ministers has turned an increasingly skeptical eye on Euratom. On March 4 the Council reduced Euratom's 1969 budget from the $69 million recommended by the Commission to $48.9 million. Later an interim compromise was agreed on, but the Council failed in 1969 to achieve its intention of framing a 5-year program.

European Free Trade Association. June 1, 1969, marked the 10th anniversary of the meetings at Stockholm that created EFTA. Within its limits, EFTA has been a success, although it will no doubt go out of existence when some or all members join EEC. Intra-EFTA trade in the first half of 1969 was 16% higher than in the same period of 1968. Negotiations took place in 1969 for the admission of Iceland to EFTA. There were also talks concerning the creation of a closer Nordic economic union comprising Norway, Sweden, Denmark, and Finland. At Helsinki, Finland, on December 13, the other three reluctantly agreed to a Finnish request that talks be suspended until after the Finnish election of March 1970.

Council of Europe. This 18-member consultative body continued its normal quasi-parliamentary activities. The third part of the 20th Assembly session was held in Strasbourg, France, January 27–31, and the first part of the 21st session, May 22–27. At the latter meeting, Olivier Reverdin of Switzerland was elected assembly president, and Lujo Toncic of Austria became secretary general. The Scandinavian states campaigned throughout 1969 against the continued membership of Greece, and the Greek government resigned from the Council on December 12.

Western European Union. The 7-member Western European Union (WEU) links Britain with the Six. President de Gaulle suspended French participation in WEU on February 17, on the ground that WEU was being used irregularly to discuss British membership in EEC. In July, President Pompidou indicated that this decision was open to restudy.

Organization for Economic Cooperation and Development (OECD). The chief interest of OECD now lies in the reports that it issues on the economic situation of countries and of the world. A report issued in June by its subordinate body, the European Monetary Agreement (EMA), indicated that world trade had increased enormously in 1968 (by 13%), but that many countries had made little progress toward remedying payments imbalances.

North Atlantic Treaty Organization. The greatest of the Western alliances, now in its 21st year, faced an uncertain future. Support of member governments continued in 1969, perhaps less enthusiastically than in previous years, but popular support certainly declined with the ebb of any feeling of urgency about defense against the Soviet Union.

The spring ministerial meeting of NATO's Council was held in Brussels, May 28, and the Nuclear Planning Group met May 29–30, in London. Gen. Andrew J. Goodpaster of the United States succeeded Gen. Lyman L. Lemnitzer as Supreme Allied Commander, Europe (SACEUR) on July 1. The fall ministerial meeting was also held in Brussels, December 4–5. U. S. Secretary of State William P. Rogers pledged that U. S. troops in Europe would not be reduced for two years, but this promise was difficult to reconcile with other parts of the U. S. government's military and budget policies. Military experts were increasingly disturbed by the deterioration of the situation on the alliance's southern flank, where the Soviet Mediterranean fleet could now inhibit the support of Greece and Turkey.

ARTHUR C. TURNER
University of California, Riverside

EYE DISEASES

Several advances in the diagnosis, understanding, and treatment of eye diseases were made during 1968 and 1969.

New Diagnostic Technique. Scanning with ultrasound proved accurate in localizing pathological conditions of the eye. Such scanning is especially useful in diagnosing intraocular tumors, choroidal melanoma, retinoblastoma, retinal detachment hidden by cataract, cysts, abscesses, and vitreous opacities. It has also proved helpful in recognizing vitreous hemorrhages, monocular cataracts, malignant tumors, subretinal hemorrhages, and several other eye diseases.

Treatment Advances. The use of ultrasound vibrations may soon make cataract removal a minor procedure. In the new technique, a corneoscleral circumference incision of 2 to 3 mm (rather than the 22 mm incision used in standard procedures) and no more than one stitch (instead of 3 to 6) are necessary. A needle that vibrates at an ultrasonic frequency of 40,000 cycles per second is then inserted. The cataract is emulsified by contact with the vibrating needle, and its contents removed by suction through the hollow center of the needle.

Photocoagulation with lasers has improved the treatment of visual loss in central serous retinopathy (any noninflammatory disease of the retina), macular lesions, exudative choroiditis, and some retinal vascular changes due to atrophy of the optic nerve. Minimal laser photocoagulation has also been somewhat effective in treating angiomatosis of the retina and various types of exudative choroiditis.

Since penetrating keratoplasty, or corneal grafting, is not always successful, because of the fragility of the corneal endothelial cell layer, a new technique of using a silicone membrane sutured on the endothelial surface has been found helpful. Plastic corneas have also been implanted in the center of corneas so damaged that they were not suitable for transplant. The use of glue-on plastic contact lens in place of corneal epithelium has also ben useful in patients with scarred corneal epithelium, diseased or perforated corneas, or normal corneas that lack a lens on one side.

Cryosurgery—the destruction of tissue by extreme cold—was further developed in cataract extraction and in the treatment of retinal detachment, glaucoma, and herpes simplex keratitis. The treatment of ocular burns with autochemotherapy, antibiotics, and steroids also improved.

Other Findings. Studies using the electron microscope have revealed herpeslike particles on the iris of patients affected with uveitis, an inflammation of the iris, ciliary body, and choroid. This was the first time that the herpes simplex virus was recognized as the causal agent in inflammations of the iris and ciliary body (iridocyclitis) that are not accompanied by corneal ulcer. Electron microscopy has also furthered knowledge of glaucoma.

Other studies have indicated that genetic factors may play an important role in certain eye diseases, such as cataract and glaucoma. The relationship of oral contraceptives and eye disorders was also investigated, but no evidence that contraceptive pills produce deleterious eye effects has been found.

ROLAND I. PRITIKIN, M. D.
Eye Surgeon and Consulting Ophthalmologist
M. L. DUCHON, M. D.
Ophthalmologist

The year 1969 put the first men on the moon and gave women for the first time a choice of skirt lengths. Influential designers presented a "wardrobe of lengths" for fall that included minis, knee-lengths, mid-knee lengths ("midis"), and ankle-lengths ("maxis"). The fashion press and the big stores supported the revolutionary ideas. Teen-agers and college girls rushed for the maxi coats and shops reported good sales in the style. Mid-calf dresses and coats were adopted by a few sophisticated women. Minis, which ruled city streets all summer, were still applauded in fashion shows. Now the average woman, who liked her skirts at mid-knee or just below, could face the world (and her daughters) and not feel out of style.

The maxi coat, worn over the mini dress, was symbolic of the times. Fashion wound up 1969 in the mood of the decade, with more extremes and exaggerations than middle-of-the-road ideas. However, at the year's very end, in a mood of contradiction, women turned to a nostalgic mood of romance, expressed in full-skirted peasant dresses, rustling antebellum ball gowns, and feminine pompadour hair-do's.

Silhouette. "Long" was the key word for fashion in 1969. There were long coats, long scarves, long jackets, long sweaters, long chemises, long beads, long earrings, longer gloves, long-handled shoulder bags, and conclusively, a long slinky look about the entire silhouette.

The long, lean look had important contributing factors. The return of the lanky chemise, brought about by Yves St. Laurent in Paris, came as a surprise just as everyone was beginning to be conscious

fashion

THE LITTLE BLACK DRESS made its fashion comeback in 1969. This seductive black crepe evening dress by Oscar de la Renta is highlighted by lacing to the waist and a tassle that swings to the hem.

ANTONIO

of the belt. A few of the short chemises were low-belted or low-pocketed, and a popular style had low pleats or flares. The long cardigan jacket suit, featured by U. S. designer Donald Brooks, was worn with a long scarf and a straight short skirt—undeniably a 1920's look. The long jacket with a show of short pleated skirt was the big news at Christian Dior in Paris. This proportion was exaggerated and was reversed in short, waist-length jackets worn with midis. The desirable long-necked look was emphasized by the turtlenecked sweater.

Despite the return of the chemise, the belted look had been established. Many coats were belted, the most popular being the four-pocket "safari" style in versions by Bill Blass, Norman Norell, and Yves St. Laurent. The striped T-shirt dress, carried over from 1968, had a belt for 1969. The ever-popular shirtdress was sashed or belted and worn by day or night.

A short coat with a wide and swingy silhouette had a young and spirited look. Paris' Pierre Cardin showed the full-circle cape. The popular blazer jacket was still on the scene, in black sequins, at Chanel. (The musical "Coco," based on the career of this remarkable Parisian designer, came to Broadway late in the year and was a major fashion event.)

The soft look continued to accentuate the feminine in short, frilly, late-day dresses. The fringe dress became one of the rages of the year. Pleats added style and movement to skirts, flounces, and all-over pleated dresses.

Pants. Pants, which caused such a furor in 1968, were a part of the 1969 scene. They came in well

tailored versions for daytime with a variety of jackets, tunics, and maxi coats, and, for evening in lush fabrics, notably black satin with glitter tops. Some of the airlines put their hostesses in pantsuits. One-piece jumpsuits were worn everywhere from beach to campus, at the office and at home.

Fabrics. The fabric news of the year was patchwork, which appeared in beautiful big skirts, children's clothes, table cloths, bedspreads, and even a bride's dress in Paris. Not only did the most photographed personalities have their originals from New York's Adolfo, but any woman, anywhere, could create her own version at home.

The soft, clingy fabrics in 1968 were still successful in crepe, jersey, chiffon, velvet, panne velvet, and satin. "Art Deco" motifs were seen in elaborately embroidered and printed fabrics. Tweeds reappeared. Leather had contemporary impact in wrapped coats, sashed sleeveless weskits, pants, and, for the daring, bloomers borrowed from the 1920's. Vinyl was used in trimmings, raincoats, and full-length evening coats. The night-time hours brought out the opulent dazzlers: spangled lace, gilded paisleys, jewelled chiffons, and pailletted crepes.

Colors. Navy blue, white, bright green, yellow, and sharp pink were smart choices for spring and summer. Gray became a basic again, and looked new with caramel beige, lilac, and turquoise. In the fall, dark coffee brown, purple, and dark green were popular. Black looked current in velvet and satin at night and in shiny cire fabrics by day in wet-looking raincoats, quilted jackets, and bikinis. Beige saw a big revival in tweeds furred with lynx and

THE NUDE LOOK (*opposite*), so popular in 1969, is seen in these summer fashions. The jeweled breastplate can be worn alone or over a shirt as shown here. The "little nothing" bathing suit is made of lined crocheted cotton. The slinky pants outfit features a bared-down bra with a front tie.

THE LONG LEAN LOOK (*right*) was one of the year's fashion highlights. Victor Joris' casual outfit features a clingy knit sweatercoat and pants, accented by a two-yard-long chiffon scarf and long ropes of pearls.

MAXI COATS (*below*) inspired by those worn by cadets at West Point were popular in 1969. Robert Liberman shows off an authentic uniform while his wife models a coat designed by Bill Blass for Maurice Rentner.

WILLIAM E. SAURO

DAVID GAHR

MIDI COAT worn over long tunic and slightly flared pants by Yves St. Laurent was one of the year's favorites.

FROM VOGUE (C) 1969 FROM CONDE NAST PUBLICATIONS, INC.

badger, influenced by the beautiful collection of Valentino, now hailed as Italy's foremost designer. Reds of the stop-sign variety were also prominent.

Color was perhaps most dramatic in furs. Even the aristocratic chinchilla and mink were dyed in jewel tones. Long fur mufflers in Roman stripes looked well with dark wools. Red fox came in its own natural color. All the long-haired furs and shaggy fakes were favorites. For the more conventional, there was a sleek black sealskin.

The Nude Look. Nudity in fashion took different forms in 1969. The no-bra look was seen under t-shirts and clinging, not necessarily transparent fabrics. Bra manufacturers countered the trend with versions of body stockings and soft supple bras. Open-stitch crocheted minis were the year's new see-through fashions. Plunge necklines plunged lower, bare midriffs were more extensive, and unzippered slit fronts provided further excitement for maxi skirts.

Accessories. The revival of pearls, downgraded in past years for representing the tired chic of the establishment, was one of the big accessory events of 1969. The new pearls, unlike the refined little chokers worn with sweaters and black dresses, were big, bold, and long, dipping to the waist, the finger tips, even to the knees. Caviar-colored pearls were worn with coral tones, while orchid shades came by the yard with gray or white dresses. Black and white crepes were studded with pearls.

The long, narrow scarf, the signature of the fall and winter, was worn with anything, day or night. The long, wide shawl often replaced the sweater on campuses. The fringed shawl belonged to the sophisticate of any age; it was seen in tweed or jersey, or in silk with long fringe—a Spanish dancer's shawl.

Elaborate chains still girdled the waist, but the leather belt was more and more in evidence. Handbags were soft and squashy or hard as a box, many with a luggage look and many with shoulder straps or chains. Body jewelry, another aspect of the bare syndrome, became popular. A gold chain worn just above the bikini line (perhaps the gift of a current love) was the 1960's version of the chastity belt. Leather and wood were used for oversized beads and bracelets.

The shoe silhouette was still heavy, often with tongues, buckles, chains, and big thick heels. Heels were higher but never thin and pointed. Bright patent leathers were favorites in the summer, while fall brought suedes and combinations of leathers and colors. Boots were popular in ankle, knee, and hip heights. There was a craze for zebra boots for both day and evening wear. For evening, shoes in white satin, gold kid, and scarlet crepe were a few of the favored looks. The popularity of textured stockings diminished. Pale sheers took over for the summer, while dark ones were worn for fall.

The year's three favorite hats were the helmet or scarf turban, moulding the sleek small head; the big floppy-brimmed hat, often tied with a scarf; and the "low-brow" knitted or crocheted beret or helmet worn pulled down to the eyebrows.

Children's Fashion. Demands of both parents and children kept adult fashion trends moving in the small world. Little girls wanted (and got) chain belts and little boys craved leather jackets. Bellbottom pants were everywhere, while long sweaters and long scarves also caught on. Jumpers, pantsuits, long sleeved dresses, and turtlenecks were popular and sensible. The crochet idea was used in jumpers and berets. Instead of borrowing their mothers' clothes when they wanted to play grown-up, 6-year-olds had their own maxi skirts. However, conservative mothers and daughters still could find dresses with smocking.

Men's Fashions. Male vanity, submerged for years, began to surface in 1968. In 1969 men's plumage continued to brighten. Jackets had wide lapels and double vents. Trousers were bell-bottom. The bright shirt was the badge of the well-dressed man, and pin-striped shirts were overshadowed by those with wide, bold stripes.

In accessories, wide ties were wider, and shoes had blunt toes, buckled straps, and were cut higher. The scarf, sometimes knotted like a tie with long flowing ends, added great flair.

Men in the creative professions wore blazers, bell-bottoms, and colored shirts to their offices. Suede jackets were worn in town. Corduroy blazers matched the country scene in rust, green, and gold hues. The red jacket was red hot. The conventional suit was for conventional men only—and their numbers seemed to be diminishing.

RUTH MARY (PACKARD) DuBois
Fashion Institute of Technology

FEDERAL BUREAU OF INVESTIGATION. See CRIME.

FINANCE. See BANKING; ECONOMY OF THE UNITED STATES; INTERNATIONAL FINANCE.

FINLAND

Disaffection among the Communists, Nordek economic integration talks, the government's call for a European security conference, and a business upswing were the most important developments in Finland in 1969.

Party Politics. Six of the nine political parties held conventions between April and August. A Stalinist minority (25% of the delegates) left the Communist party congress early in April. The dissidents accused the party leadership of "revisionism" and threatened to run their own candidates in the March 1970 national elections. After the split was patched up in mid-October, a more truculent tone marked the party's speeches. The Communists demanded nationalization of banking, insurance, and medicine, and warned of their possible defection from the coalition cabinet if their views on stabilization were not heeded.

Nordek. The Government took an active part in Nordic economic integration ("Nordek") talks. (Finnish exports to the Scandinavian countries have increased sevenfold between 1959 and 1968.) The initial reaction of the Soviet press to Nordek was hostile, and it was denounced as a stepping-stone to Finnish membership in the European Economic Community, if not in NATO. In February, Prime Minister Mauno Koivisto declared that Finland had not applied, and would not apply, for EEC membership. But as a trade official indicated later, this did not preclude a purely economic association with the six EEC nations. At Leningrad in May, Finnish President Urho Kekkonen reassured Soviet Premier Aleksei Kosygin that "neutrality and the continuance and expansion of trade with the USSR" remained the cornerstones of Finnish policy.

Foreign Affairs. Foreign Minister Ahti Karjalainen said in September that Finland's position in international politics "is as good as it can be for a small nation." The government's offer on May 5 to be host to a general European security meeting received Soviet backing. The President twice visited the USSR and also went to Rumania, Hungary, Czechoslovakia, Senegal, France, Britain, and Sweden.

Soviet journals only rarely revived the specter of right-wing Finnish elements who might be undermining the peaceful ties between the two countries. Instead, *Pravda* spoke glowingly of Finland as an independent and peace-loving state, which followed its own line on world issues.

In November, representatives of the United States and the Soviet Union met in Helsinki to begin preliminary talks on strategic arms limitation. Foreign Minister Karjalainen stressed the importance of the discussions in his speech at the opening session. (See also DISARMAMENT.)

The Economy. The Finnish economy made substantial gains in 1969. Stabilization controls held wages and prices in line and there were few strikes. Two major labor unions voted to merge by 1972.

The gross national product rose 6%, industrial output 9%, and foreign trade (in fair balance) 20%. Credit restrictions were removed from most goods and liberalized for motor vehicles. During the first six months of 1969, 53,000 cars were imported, a 100% increase over the same period in 1968. National unemployment was about 3%, but the figure was higher in northern and eastern Finland.

Finnair's transatlantic service began on May 15, and U. S. and Canadian tourists spent $1.6 million

FINLAND

Information

Highlights

Area: 130,129 square miles (337,032 sq km).
Population: 4,688,000 (1968 est.).
Chief Cities (1969 est.): Helsinki, the capital, 528,000; Tampere, 150,000; Turku, 149,000.
Government: *President*—Urho Kaleva Kekkonen (took office March 1, 1968 for 3d 6-year term); *Prime Minister*—Mauno Koivisto (took office March 21, 1968). *Legislature* (unicameral)—Eduskunta, 200 members (party seating, 1969: Social Democratic party, 55; Center party, 49; People's Democratic League, 41; Conservative party, 26; Swedish People's party, 12; others, 17).
Religious Faiths: Evangelical Lutherans, 92.6% of population.
Education: *Literacy rate* (1961), 99.8% of population. *Total school enrollment* (1966)—1,035,251 (primary, 438,057; secondary, 459,244; teacher-training, 2,403; technical/vocational, 89,258; university/higher, 46,289).
Finance (1969 est.): *Revenues*, $2,051,428,000; *expenditures*, $2,020,476,000; *public debt* (1967), $1,055,000,000; *monetary unit*, markka (4.20 markka equal U. S.$1).
Gross National Product (1968): $8,078,571,000.
National Income (1968): $5,580,952,000; *average annual income per person*, $1,190.
Economic Indexes (1967): *Industrial production* (1968), 132 (1963=100); *agricultural production*, 108 (1963=100); *cost of living*, 127 (1963=100).
Manufacturing and Processing (metric tons, 1967): Newsprint, 1,233,000; steel, 394,000; meat, 182,000; dairy, 138,000; lumber (1966), 6,055,000 cubic meters.
Crops (metric tons, 1967–68 crop year): Oats, 940,000; potatoes, 881,000; barley, 681,000.
Minerals (metric tons, 1966): Limestone and dolomite, 3,553,000; iron ore (1967), 643,200; sulfur pyrite, 264,800; lime, 227,000; zinc (1967), 68,040.
Foreign Trade (1968): *Exports*, $1,637,000,000 (chief exports, 1967: paper, $383,000,000; wood, $205,000,000; wood pulp, $196,000,000; *imports*, $1,598,000,000 (chief imports, 1967: road motor vehicles, $100,576,000. *Chief trading partners* (1967): Britain (took 20% of exports, supplied 13% of imports); USSR (took 17% of exports, supplied 16% of imports); West Germany (took 9% of exports, supplied 16% of imports).
Transportation: *Roads* (1967), 43,391 miles (69,829 km); *motor vehicles* (1967), 651,500 (automobiles 551,200); *railways* (1965), 3,570 miles (5,745 km); *merchant vessels* (1967), 221 (1,012,000 gross registered tons); *national airline*, Finnair.
Communications: *Telephones* (1968), 949,976; *television stations* (1968), 53; *television sets* (1968), 850,000; *radios* (1967), 1,663,000; *newspapers* (1967), 68.

in Finland in 1969. The World Bank made a $22 million loan to Finland in January. Direct foreign investments reached a record $10.5 million in the first half of 1969. Commercial pacts with the USSR included a new 5-year trade treaty for 1971–75 and an agreement for the purchase of nuclear reactor components for the Loviisa atomic power plant, which will be completed in 1976. Laws passed in June dealt with farm incomes, marketing levies on milk and wheat, and reducing the butter surplus.

Financial Affairs. Foreign exchange reserves stood at $250 million on August 29, an 8-month gain of $30 million. The 1970 budget, introduced in September, called for expenditures of $2.4 billion. Expenditures for social services will amount to 25% of the budget, and for education, to 33%. Finland's new chief of staff, Gen. Kaarlo Leinonen, said the $138 million alloted for defense would be inadequate to meet the country's needs.

JOHN I. KOLEHMAINEN
Heidelberg College, Ohio

FIRES

Fires in the United States in 1969 caused 12,000 deaths and $2,415,000,000 in property losses, according to preliminary estimates of the National Fire Protection Association. In comparison with 1968, the number of deaths declined by about 100, but property losses registered an increase of approximately $160 million.

NFPA studies show that substantial progress is being made in controlling life and property losses from fire despite numerical increases over the years. The United States is suffering fewer fire fatalities and less loss of property in relation to increased population and to the growing number of structures, rising value of the gross national product, and depreciated purchasing power of the dollar.

Worst Fires. Two residential fires during 1969 each claimed 12 lives. On June 3, the dozen victims were trapped in an apartment house fire in Kansas City, Mo.; on June 8, both parents and 10 children died in their home in Parkersburg, W. Va., in a fire set by two other children in the family. Eleven persons died in an apartment house fire in Bridgeport, Conn., on April 6. A flash fire on February 25 took the lives of 11 workers in a New York City office building on midtown Fifth Avenue.

The costliest fire of 1969 was the $50 million loss on May 11 at the Rocky Flats, Colo., nuclear weapons plant of the U. S. Atomic Energy Commission. Other major fires occurred on August 5 in the Boston warehouse of a supermarket chain, with loss estimated at $15 million; and on January 1 in Webster, Mass., in an old mill complex being used to manufacture shoes, slippers, and cardboard boxes, with a $10 million loss.

1968 Losses. Final NFPA figures for 1968 show that 2,363,700 fires took 12,100 lives and destroyed property valued at $2,255,000,000. Compared with 1967, the number of fires was down 1.2%, the number of lives lost declined by 100, and dollar losses rose 6.6%. Building fires numbered 974,400 (up 1.4%) and cost $1,786,900,000 (up 10.1%). There were 629,600 fires in houses and apartments, resulting in 6,600 deaths and $583,-400,000 in property losses.

LARGE-LOSS FIRES IN THE UNITED STATES, 1968
(Individual loss of $250,000 or more)

Classification	Number	Loss
Industrial	130	$ 93,810,000
Mercantile	110	56,402,000
Storage and warehousing	100	66,396,000
Schools and colleges	27	21,767,000
Hotels and motels	14	5,624,000
Restaurants and night clubs	13	5,267,000
General business offices	11	6,513,450
Bowling establishments	10	4,695,000
Churches and chapels	8	3,653,000
Apartments	8	3,344,685
Buildings under construction	5	3,048,000
Institutions (hospitals and prisons)	3	2,350,000
Dwellings	3	1,750,000
Banks	3	1,221,000
Miscellaneous occupancies	42	38,521,865
Total	487	$314,363,000

Records maintained by NFPA show that in 1968 U. S. fires in places other than buildings involved aerospace vehicles and aircraft (175); construction and farm equipment (13,100); motor vehicles and forests, brush, and other outdoor areas (1,023,400). A total of 1,389,300 nonbuilding fires cost $486,-100,000 in property destroyed.

CHARLES S. MORGAN
National Fire Protection Association

FISHERIES

Peru continues to lead all nations in commercial fishing. In 1968—the latest year for which worldwide totals are available—the Peruvian industry caught 22.6 billion pounds of fish and shellfish. Japan landed 19 billion pounds, followed by the USSR, 14.8 billion; mainland China, 12.8 billion; Norway, 5.7 billion, and the United States, 4.1 billion. The world catch in 1968 rose to a record 139 billion pounds, up 7 billion pounds in one year.

U. S. 1969 Catch. U. S. fishermen continued hard pressed in 1969 to meet competition from world fleets, and more nations sent more vessels to fish waters off the U. S. coasts. The U. S. catch for 1969 amounted to 4.2 billion pounds, up 100 million pounds from 1968.

New England. Almost all major fisheries suffered declines in New England in 1969. The haddock fishery, for years the mainstay of the New England groundfishery, declined to a mere 45.6 million pounds, down 25.4 million pounds from the previous year and the lowest catch on record. The crisis was the result of the continuous failure of each year class—the group of young produced annually—since 1963. The Soviet fleet fished the 1963 class so intensely that concern has been voiced that the stocks of fish on Georges Bank is in danger of being reduced beyond capability to repopulate.

Whiting (silver hake) was also very scarce. The catch declined from 78 million pounds in 1968 to 33 million pounds in 1969. Scientists were unable to determine whether the cause was a shift in the schools of whiting or the effects of sustained heavy pressure by Soviet and other foreign fleets.

Sea scallop landings were little more than 5 million pounds, the smallest quantity since 1945.

Ocean perch landings continued to decline and reached a low of 56 million pounds, the smallest quantity landed since 1938.

Gulf of Mexico. Fishermen did somewhat better in the Gulf of Mexico. Menhaden fishermen set a record with more than 1.1 billion pounds, all processed into fish meal. The catch was made by about 160 purse siene vessels.

In the shrimp industry, Texas landings were down, but all other Gulf states showed increases. Despite high prices and relatively good catches, problems began to surface in this apparently prosperous industry. The difficulty arose from overcapitalization in the producing fleet—there is a trend toward larger vessels with steel hulls, and owners encounter difficulty in meeting payments.

Other Areas. Dungeness and blue crab fisheries experienced a very good year, but king crab catches declined for the third consecutive year despite increased effort, higher prices, and use of newer vessels.

Salmon landings dropped considerably, mainly because of a 75-million-pound decline in Alaska.

Tuna landings were higher, but this industry also faced serious problems in overcapitalization. Additions to the tuna purse seine fleet in the last few years have increased the catching capacity so much that the entire quota allowed under International Tuna Commission regulations can now be taken in about three months' fishing.

CHARLES H. LYLES
U. S. Fish and Wildlife Service

FLOODS. See ACCIDENTS AND DISASTERS.

FLORIDA

Controversies over government reorganization, higher education, race relations, and a jetport in the Everglades made headlines in Florida in 1969.

Reorganization Struggle. Consolidation of some 200 agencies and boards into no more than 25 departments was required by the state's new constitution, which went into effect on January 7. Gov. Claude Kirk immediately appointed Ray Osborne of St. Petersburg to the position of lieutenant governor (created by the new constitution), but the reshuffling of state agencies proved a formidable task. In its regular session beginning in April, the Legislature was divided between a plan that would put most of the departments under the exclusive control of the governor and one that would leave most of the power in the hands of the seven-member cabinet. Partisan factors were involved, since Governor Kirk was a Republican and the cabinet members were Democrats.

Finally, on June 3, the Legislature adopted a compromise measure which the governor signed into law on June 19. It provided for 23 departments or agencies, with 9 under direct supervision of the governor, 6 under individual cabinet members, and 8 under the collective supervision of the governor and the cabinet.

Legislation. In its regular session the Legislature also granted home-rule power to city and county governments, reformed legislative budget and purchasing practices, funded a state Medicaid program, streamlined welfare administration, centralized state purchasing, set restrictions on the granting of oil and mineral leases by the state, and adopted an annual budget. Although the Legislature claimed that the budget was in balance, Governor Kirk insisted that it would result in a deficit. He let the appropriations bill become law without his signature. Kirk called a special session for December to take up a proposed road bond issue, but the Legislature refused to approve his road bond program.

An emotional furor arose in June when Kirk vetoed an increase in legislative pay to $12,000 a year. With bipartisan support, the Legislature passed the measure over Kirk's veto, charging that he had "played politics" after having consented earlier to an even greater pay increase.

Higher Education. John Champion, who had been involved in a confrontation over censorship of student publications in 1968, resigned as president of Florida State University in Tallahassee in February. J. Stanley Marshall, who became acting president, was named permanent president in June, despite substantial opposition from the faculty and the student body. Student and faculty discontent also forced the resignation of Paul F. Geren as president of Stetson University in DeLand in June.

Also in June, the State Board of Regents named Charles Perry to head the new Florida International University in Miami and selected Thomas G. Carpenter as president of Jacksonville's new University of North Florida. Both institutions were scheduled to open for classes in 1972.

The Board of Regents refused to recognize chapters of Students for a Democratic Society (SDS) on state campuses. It also withheld the granting of tenure to a number of faculty members in a reaction against their expression of allegedly radical opinions. Despite the controversies, Florida voters approved a constitutional amendment to continue earmarking for higher education the revenue from the utilities gross receipts tax, thus providing $35 million in construction funds.

Race Relations. The Legislature approved the creation of a state Human Relations Commission, proposed by Florida's first Negro legislator since Reconstruction, Rep. Joe Lang Kershaw of Dade County. The year also saw an increased number of Negro employees in state government.

The spring brought a rash of school boycotts as Negroes protested the transfer of their children to formerly all-white schools. In the fall there were similar boycotts by the parents of white children assigned to predominantly Negro schools.

In early September, the National Guard was called to Fort Lauderdale after three nights of rioting that resulted in 50 injuries and 160 arrests, and on October 31 police riot squads were needed to quell rioters and looters in East Jacksonville.

Jetport Controversy. The U. S. Interior Department and the Department of Transportation were involved in a dispute in 1969 over a proposed jetport north of Everglades National Park. At the end of the year it appeared that the landing strip, which was already under construction, would be restricted to training flights because of the danger that further development might damage the unique wilderness area.

ROBERT H. AKERMAN
Florida Southern College

FLORIDA • Information Highlights

Area: 52,560 square miles (151,671 sq km).
Population: 6,216,000 (1969 est.).
Chief Cities (1968 est.): Tallahassee, the capital, 64,000; Jacksonville, 490,000; Miami, 320,000; Tampa, 295,000; Saint Petersburg, 205,000; Fort Lauderdale, 122,000.
Government: *Chief Officers*—governor, Claude R. Kirk, Jr. (Republican); lt. gov., Ray Osborne (R); secy. of state, Tom Adams (Democrat); atty. gen., Earl Faircloth (D); treas., Broward Williams; comm. of educ., Floyd T. Christian; chief justice, Richard W. Ervin. *Legislature*—Senate, 48 members (32 Democrats, 16 Republicans); House of Representatives, 119 members (77 D, 42 R).
Education: *School enrollment* (1968–69)—public elementary, 724,000 pupils (28,500 teachers); public secondary, 602,000 pupils (26,000 teachers); nonpublic schools, 89,500 pupils (4,170 teachers); college and university (fall 1967), 179,847 students. *Public school expenditures* (1967–68)—$944,-532,000 ($719 per pupil); average teacher's salary, $7,500.
Public Finance (fiscal year 1968–69): *Revenues*, $3,131,238,-250 (4% sales tax, $573,779,402; motor fuel tax, $196,-675,184; federal funds, $348,542,600). *Expenditures*, $3,-181,141,558 (education, $858,148,232; health, welfare, and safety, $249,393,839; highways, $342,911,612). *State debt*, $823,965,000 (June 30, 1968).
Personal Income (1968): $19,626,000,000; average annual income per person, $3,191.
Public Assistance (fiscal year 1968–69): $123,583,621 to 262,474 recipients (aged, $57,644,426; dependent children, $45,272,822).
Labor Force (employed persons, July 1968): *Agricultural*, 123,300; *nonagricultural* (wage and salary earners), 1,851,-300 (15.7% manufacturing, 26% trade, 18.9% government). *Unemployed persons* (July 1968)—83,200.
Manufacturing (1965): Value added by manufacture, $2,670,-785,000 (transportation equipment, $168,199,000; primary metals, $30,875,000; nonelectrical machinery, $103,914,-000; electrical machinery, $169,855,000; food and products, $511,217,000).
Agriculture (1967): Cash farm income, $1,079,855,000 (livestock, $329,432,000; crops, $732,780,000; govt. payments, $17,643,000). *Chief crops* (tons)—Citrus fruits, 6,093,500 (ranks 1st among the states); sugar cane, 6,320,000 (ranks 3d); corn for grain, 628,600.
Mining (1966): Production value, $295,474,000. *Chief minerals* (tons)—Stone, 35,023,000; phosphate rock (1965), 21,563,-000; clays, 762,000; lime, 135,000.
Fisheries (1967): *Commercial catch*, 196,367,740 pounds ($30,-778,615). *Leading species*—Shrimp, 28,383,664 pounds ($12,975,625); black mullet, 26,179,518 pounds ($1,937,-926); crabs, 23,295,962 pounds ($1,450,794).
Transportation: *Roads* (1968), 82,898 miles (133,383 km); *motor vehicles* (1969), 4,238,928; *railroads* (1968), 4,469 line miles (7,191 km); *airports* (1969), 20.
Communications (1969): *Telephones* (1968), 3,259,700; *television stations*, 26; *radio stations*, 174; *newspapers*, 56 (daily circulation, 1,969,000).

FOOD

World food production kept pace with expanding population in 1969. Food consumption per capita even increased slightly—twice as much in developed as in less developed countries. In rich countries people ate more meat, fruit, and green vegetables; less starch and milk. There were large surpluses of milk and wheat in Europe and North America. U.S. food quality was improving with better packaging and faster freezing, as well as stricter regulation. The U.S. government banned general use of cyclamates.

WORLD FOOD SUPPLY

Food Production. Food production increased in 1969 in most countries at least as much as the population. In the Far East (excluding mainland China), where 30% of the world's people live, the output of food per capita was lifted by record crops of wheat and rice resulting from good weather and the "green revolution." That term has been applied to the results achieved by the proper use of seeds of improved varieties in combination with larger applications of fertilizer, measures for weed and insect control, and, usually, carefully regulated irrigation. The most widely used improved varieties are dwarf wheats developed in Mexico under the leadership of the Rockefeller Foundation, and the IRRI rice varieties developed by the International Rice Research Institute in the Philippines.

The U.S. Department of Agriculture has estimated that in the crop year ending June 30, 1969, new varieties were planted on 7% of the rice land and 16% of the wheat land in the less developed areas of Asia. Under favorable circumstances the new varieties may yield twice as much as local unimproved seeds. However, providing the correct kinds and quantities of fertilizers and other chemicals to all farmers at the appropriate time and giving the farmers expert advice on planting and cultivation practices are also essential to the "revolution."

The good grain harvests of 1968 and 1969 dispelled fears of famine and directed attention to problems in the less developed countries (LDC) associated with abundance—marketing facilities, price stabilization, consumer preferences, and maintenance of farm income. Agricultural analysts wrote little in 1969 about famine (except in war-torn eastern Nigeria) but much about surpluses.

While the LDC have been straining to increase

EXPENDITURES FOR FOOD AS A PERCENTAGE OF TOTAL PRIVATE CONSUMPTION EXPENDITURES

Country	1955	1960	1966
Australia	25.5%[1]	23.7%[1]	22.2%[1]
Austria	38.5	34.1	29.2
Belgium	29.1	27.5	25.6
Canada	23.1	23.0	20.4
Denmark	27.6	23.4	22.2
France	34.0	31.6	29.0
Germany, West	40.7[2]	37.9[2]	34.0[2]
Italy	41.0	39.9	37.9
Japan	51.6[2]	43.9[2]	37.8[2]
Netherlands	33.7	31.0	28.1
Norway	31.6	30.0	28.1
South Africa	30.5	29.5	28.8
Sweden	39.8	27.5	25.5
United Kingdom	31.3[1]	28.3[1]	25.1[1]
United States	22.6[1]	21.3[1]	19.7[1]

[1] Includes nonalcoholic beverages. [2] Includes all beverages and tobacco.

farm output, some of the richer countries have been struggling to restrain agricultural production. Partly because of this, but partly because of mediocre weather conditions the developed areas of the world harvested less grain in 1969 than in 1968.

Consumption. The United Nations has estimated that gross domestic product per capita is increasing nearly 4% a year in the developed countries against less than 2% in the LDC. Consumer expenditures are growing at similar rates. In the rich countries the food share of consumer expenditures is falling, as indicated in the accompanying table.

The declining relative importance of food expenditures in the developed countries reflects the abundance of food. All developed countries either produce or import sufficient food to provide their people with a nutritionally adequate diet. Cases of malnutrition in those countries are not due to food scarcity but to bad food habits or lack of income.

In the poor countries, on the other hand, the national supplies of protein-rich foods are not large enough to meet nutritional requirements of all families, even if those supplies were divided equally. Sometimes, as in parts of West Africa in 1969, supplies of basic foods are reduced by crop failure; prices rise, and poor families are unable to buy enough food, even of the cheapest kind, to meet their calorie requirements.

Consumers in the rich countries are buying less bread, potatoes and similar starchy foods but much more meat, fruit, and green vegetables. In recent years consumption of meat (excluding poultry) per capita has been rising at the following annual rates: Europe, 1.8%; United States, 1.9%; Canada, 2.2%; USSR, 4.1%; and Japan, 7.4%. Per capita consumption of fluid milk, however, has passed its peak

TED SPIEGEL, FROM RAPHO GUILLUMETTE

CORN BREEDING at Kasetsart University, an agricultural institution in Bangkok, Thailand, is supervised by a Rockefeller Foundation agronomist.

and is now declining in the United States, Canada, and most countries in western Europe while still increasing in Australia, the USSR, and Japan.

Surpluses. Production of milk in western Europe has outpaced consumption of fluid milk, and large surplus stocks of butter and dried skim milk have been accumulated. The income-supporting policies which have created these surpluses are popular with farmers, and governments have hesitated to change them. However, the Council of the European Community did take action in October 1969 against the milk surplus by approving two plans. One would pay a farmer with 10 cows or less to slaughter all of them by April 30, 1970. The other plan would pay farmers with more than 10 cows to shift to beef production. Austria and Switzerland also took steps in 1969 to encourage farmers to produce more beef and less milk.

Another commodity in surplus in the rich countries is wheat. During the 1968–69 marketing season stocks rose to record levels in Canada, the European Community, and Australia. Stocks also increased in the United States. While the level in the United States is 16.3 million metric tons less than the record on July 1, 1961, the combined stocks of 61 million tons in the rich countries are only a million tons less than the record level in 1961.

The buildup in European Community stocks occurred in spite of a heavily subsidized gain in exports during the 1968–69 season, while nearly half of the buildup in the other three countries was explained by falling exports. In response to big stocks and shrinking exports, the U. S. Department of agriculture announced on August 11 a reduction in the national wheat allotment, from 51.6 million acres for 1969 to 45.5 million acres for 1970—the lowest allotment ever. Canada and Australia have imposed restrictions on marketing that are likely to reduce the area of wheat for 1970 harvest.

From 1954 to 1969 the United States reduced the area of land used for growing crops by 11%, but other developed countries increased their area of cropland by 9%. These changes have greatly affected trends in output. From 1954 to 1968 the USDA index of agricultural production, population, and agricultural production per capita increased at the following compound rates (percent per year):

	United States	Other Developed Countries*	Less Developed Countries
Agricultural production	1.8%	3.0%	2.8%
Population	1.5	1.1	2.5
Agricultural production per capita	0.3	1.9	0.3

* Canada, Europe, USSR, Japan, South Africa, Australia, New Zealand.

CHARLES A. GIBBONS
Economic Research Division
U. S. Department of Agriculture

U. S. FOOD INDUSTRY

Nutrition became a major concern of the food industry in 1969 when U. S. attention was focused on malnutrition and hunger by hearings of the Senate's Select Committee on Nutrition and Related Needs (see also POVERTY) and the White House Conference on Foods, Nutrition, and Health. One observation was that food laws and regulations, such as those limiting the nutritional enrichment of foods, often are not in the best nutritional interests of the consumer. Technical recommendations of the White House Conference centered on two themes: that new foods and additives be more thoroughly

FREEZING with liquid Freon, a new process for frozen foods, retains size and flavor of such items as shrimp.

tested before marketing, and that consumers be told in detail what they are getting.

Food additives used by the industry also received prominent attention. A furor over whether or not cyclamates—noncaloric sweeteners—were safe for consumption was climaxed when Health, Education, and Welfare Secretary Robert H. Finch removed them from the market. His action was based on the Delaney Clause of the Food Additive Law, which prohibits use of any additive causing cancer in test animals. Laboratory tests had shown bladder tumors occurring in rats fed cyclamates in massive doses (50 times that permitted for humans). All beverages containing cyclamates had to be withdrawn from the market by the end of the year. Dietetic packs of fruits and vegetables could continue to be sold, but after Sept. 1, 1970, they would have to be labeled as "drugs" and the labels would have to state the cyclamate content per average serving. The secretary reasoned that danger of consuming excess quantities of cyclamates from dietetic fruits and vegetables was much less than from dietetic beverages. He considered that medical benefits in weight control and for diabetics outweighed possible harm.

Packaging. New packages and containers for foods have been introduced at an increasing rate during the 1960's. They are usually to improve convenience. Easy-open cans and bottles are one example. Boil-in-bag packaging introduced a wide variety of prepared frozen foods. In 1969, boilable semirigid trays were used for foods that required protection from handling, such as fish fillets in gourmet sauces. Also new were frozen foods wrapped in film that could be baked or roasted without first thawing. The foods included ham and turkey roasts and bakery foods. In France, the shelf life of bread and other bakery foods was extended up to three months by sealing in a nylon film bag and then commercially sterilizing in an infrared oven.

FOOD TESTING for the Food and Drug Administration takes many forms, from tea tasting (*left*) to determining the effects of cyclamates on rats.

Plastic bottles, both returnable and nonreturnable, were being used for milk. Several dairies began using a cheaper plastic envelope or "pitcher-pouch" made of 3 mm film. Cost is less than one cent per quart pouch. To serve, a corner is snipped off after placing in a pitcher. Clear, food-grade vinyl plastic jars, approved in 1968, were widely used in 1969. They are lighter than glass and much less likely to break. Plastic bottles have been used for beer in Germany and Sweden. Intensive development of faster production lines was expected to bring plastic beer and soda bottles to the United States in 1970. One increasingly important objective is to produce a container that can be burned without polluting the air. The same objective is giving renewed impetus to the development of the "flexible can," a plastic pouch that is sterilizable in an autoclave at 250° F. Precooked whole vegetables and main courses were being processed in such plastic pouches in Europe; however, slow production-speeds were preventing widespread use in the United States.

Pollution. Disposals of waste from plants processing foods received more attention as local governments began enforcing stricter pollution requirements. Food plant wastes are not only undesirably high in biologically oxidizable content, but have peak effluent loads at harvest time, when receiving streams are at low flow rates. One method of eliminating liquid wastes resulting from conventional lye peeling of vegetables and fruits was successfully tested on a plant scale for potatoes. After a dip in a strong lye solution, the potatoes are passed through an infrared oven, and then the skins are brushed off. The waste solids are recovered in a dry state and used as animal feed; also, there is less loss of potato. The process, which was developed by the U. S. Department of Agriculture's Western Regional Research Laboratory, is also applicable to peaches.

Faster Freezing. The outstanding processing development of 1969 was the commercialization of direct-immersion Freon freezing. The faster the freezing, the better the fresh-food characteristics are preserved. Liquid nitrogen ultra-fast-freezing is being used, but is too expensive for most applications. Freon freezing costs less than one cent per pound of food frozen. Moreover, even though the freezing temperature is only $-22°$ F ($-30°$ C) compared to $-320°$ F ($-196°$ C) for liquid nitrogen, the rate of freezing is faster because of quicker heat transfer. In Freon freezing, the products are immersed in liquid freon or circulating vapors. There is no shrinkage (as in air-blast freezing), so product quality improves. With more valuable items such as shrimp, elimination of shrinkage more than compensates for the higher processing costs.

Protein for the Hungry. Low-cost high-protein commercial food was being made from a new variety of high-lysine corn developed in the United States. It was being test-marketed in South America. Costing less than two cents each, three daily 8-ounce servings provide 100% of infants' protein requirements. Named Duryea, it is a powder to be mixed with sugar and cooked to a gruel. Duryea's important advantage in this test market is that no change in eating habits is required—usually an impossible hurdle even with a population that is hungry or suffering severe malnutrition.

HOWARD P. MILLEVILLE
Oregon State University

U. S. FOOD INDUSTRY

Group	Employees[1] 1966	Employees[1] 1967	Value added by manufacture[2] (billions) 1966	Value added by manufacture[2] (billions) 1967	Value of shipments[3] (billions) 1966	Value of shipments[3] (billions) 1967
Meat and poultry products	296,000	305,000	$3.2	$3.4	$20.3	$20.8
Dairy products	237,000	238,000	3.3	3.5	12.2	12.9
Canned, preserved, frozen foods	259,000	263,000	3.4	3.6	8.8	9.3
Grain mill products	108,000	109,000	2.5	2.7	9.2	9.6
Bakery products	275,000	269,000	3.4	3.5	6.3	5.3
Sugar (raw and refined)	31,000	30,000	.6	.6	2.1	2.2
Confectionery and related products	82,000	82,000	1.1	1.2	2.4	2.6
Beverages, alcoholic and nonalcoholic	218,000	221,000	4.4	4.8	8.3	9.2
Miscellaneous food products[3]	135,000	137,000	2.9	2.9	9.9	9.9
Total[3]	1,641,000	1,654,000	$24.9	$26.4	$79.8	$81.7

[1] Excludes employees at central administrative offices, distribution warehouses, and other auxiliary establishments. [2] Includes animal and vegetable oils and fats, roasted coffee, macaroni, potato chips, etc. [3] Details may not add to totals because of rounding. Source: U. S. Bureau of the Census; Annual Survey of Manufacturers, 1966 and 1967.

FOOTBALL. See SPORTS.
FOREIGN AFFAIRS. See articles on the continents and countries.

FOREIGN AID

The year 1969 marked the passing of the First Development Decade—the title given by the United Nations to the 1960's effort to aid developing countries—into the Second Development Decade. A survey of the decade gave rise to both disillusionment over past performance and hope for the future. Aid was at a turning point, and major studies took stock of a mixed record in seeking to chart the future.

The 16-nation Development Assistance Committee (DAC), whose members supply some 95% of all foreign economic assistance, reported in 1969 that aid by DAC members to developing countries climbed about 6% a year during the 1960's to reach a record net total of $12.9 billion in 1968. During the decade countries receiving aid averaged an annual gain in gross national product (GNP) of about 5%, the UN's target rate, matching the growth in industrialized nations.

However, the data also showed that soaring populations in the developing countries cut their GNP increases in half, on an average per capita basis, thus widening further the gap in living standards between rich and poor states. The yearly debt repayments required of the nations receiving aid virtually doubled during the decade, and donor states fell farther behind the official target of supplying 1% of their GNP in aid (from an average 0.89% in 1960 to 0.77% in 1968). Furthermore, although private investments were on the rise, thus boosting total aid-flow figures, the easy-term governmental loans and grants most desired by the developing countries began to taper off in the late 1960's.

DAC members continued to extend most of their aid bilaterally, but assistance through multilateral institutions was on the rise. The International Bank for Reconstruction and Development (World Bank), the International Development Association, and the International Finance Corporation committed $1.9 billion in new aid in 1969.

U. S. Aid. The aid policy of the United States, the largest single donor, was of global concern. From its position of leadership in the post-World War II days of the Marshall Plan for Europe's recovery, the United States by 1969 had fallen to 13th place among DAC members in proportion of aid to GNP. The decrease in U. S. aid was attributable to the dwindling public concern with the Cold War, once a major rationale for helping U. S. friends abroad; government deficits and balance of payments difficulties; competition from growing domestic welfare demands; and increasing public disenchantment, abetted by the Vietnam War experience, with U. S. involvement overseas.

The total U. S. flow of aid in 1968 was $5.7 billion including $3.6 billion in public assistance, which

BENEFACTORS OF THE DEVELOPING COUNTRIES[1]

Country	Avg. annual increase (%), 1960–62 to 1968	Total flows as % of GNP 1960–62	Total flows as % of GNP 1968	Avg. annual increase (%) required to reach 1% of GNP in 1975
Norway	22.0	0.30	0.65	11.1
Austria	21.0	0.28	0.66	10.6
Japan	19.3	0.60	0.74	14.0
Sweden	16.1	0.33	0.50	14.7
Australia	15.6	0.42	0.67	13.6
Canada	15.2	0.33	0.49	16.0
Denmark	14.5	0.43	0.55	13.1
Germany	13.1	0.88	1.26	0.8
Italy	8.3	0.63	0.76	10.6
Belgium	6.7	1.27	1.15	1.8
DAC average	**5.9**	**0.89**	**0.77**	**8.8**
Netherlands	5.9	1.48	1.10	2.8
United States	4.3	0.79	0.65	10.9
Switzerland	2.8	1.82	1.26	0.0
Portugal	1.6	1.50	0.94	6.9
France	1.1	0.21	1.24	2.7
United Kingdom	0.1	1.09	0.83	7.5

[1] Total flows of financial resources to developing countries from individual members of the Development Assistance Committee.
Source: Development Assistance Committee.

was down from $3.7 billion in 1967. President Richard Nixon asked Congress in 1969 to continue the program at about the same rate as before while his administration formulated a long-range policy for the 1970's. The President's request met difficulties similar to those that had been encountered by the Johnson administration. The legislators voted a deep slash and failed to pass the appropriations until January 1970, more than half way through the fiscal year. President Nixon named a task force under Bank of America President Rudolph Peterson to conduct a sweeping review of U. S. aid policies.

Other Donors. Although the large aid donors—the United States, Britain, and France—raised their official aid little after the early 1960's, DAC reported that its other members had doubled their flows during the decade. West Germany's aid rose from $625 million in 1960 to $1.7 billion in 1968, making it the second biggest contributor; in 1969 the new government of Chancellor Willy Brandt pledged a further rise of 11% a year in official aid.

Communist states again contributed comparatively small amounts for foreign economic assistance and shunned aid cooperation with non-Communist donors. DAC estimated that annual net aid outlays by Communist states continued at about $325 million.

Reappraisals. In September 1969 a commission headed by Lester B. Pearson, former Canadian prime minister, completed a year's study for the World Bank, producing the most comprehensive report of its kind in aid history. The report found aid at "a turning point" amid "disillusion" among donors and receivers. But commission members agreed that aid was both morally right and in the self-interest of nations in a shrinking world, and an expanded effort could succeed in making most developing lands self-sufficient by the end of the century.

The recommendations of the Pearson report included setting a target of 6% growth in GNP for developing countries, aid amounting to 1% of the donor's GNP to be met by 1975, and doubling the proportion channeled through multilateral institutions to 20% by 1975.

LEWIS GULICK
Diplomatic Affairs Reporter, Associated Press

FOREIGN POLICY OF THE UNITED STATES. See UNITED STATES.
FOREIGN TRADE. See INTERNATIONAL TRADE.

DEBT SERVICE PAYMENTS OF DEVELOPING COUNTRIES
(Millions of U.S. dollars)

	Total	Africa	Southern Europe	East Asia	Middle East	South Asia	Latin America
1961	2,314	172	252	224	170	246	1,250
1962	2,585	225	222	264	210	227	1,437
1963	2,749	494	265	165	188	269	1,368
1964	3,177	433	330	171	212	359	1,672
1965	3,279	445	407	206	182	347	1,692
1966	3,781	463	444	341	200	417	1,916
1967	3,969	535	461	280	168	486	2,039
1968	4,018	443	506	369	162	565	1,973

Source: Pearson Report, 1969.

FORESTRY AND LUMBERING

Forestry highlights in the United States in 1969 included a movement to intensify management of timber on the national forests and a program to increase efforts to control forest fires. National forest grazing fees were increased; timber sales reached a record; and an international union of professional forestry organizations was formed.

Early in 1969, heavy market demand for construction materials brought rapidly escalating prices and temporary shortages of softwood lumber and plywood. Forest industries urged measures to increase the allowable annual cut from the national forests, the country's largest reserve of softwood timber. Following hearings conducted by the Senate and House banking committees, legislation was introduced aimed at giving the U. S. Forest Service long-term funding for intensified timber management.

The measures proposed to make available to the Forest Service for timber management purposes 65% of national forest timber-sale receipts that had been going into general U. S. Treasury funds. Forest Service Chief Edward P. Cliff said that construction of more forest roads, reforestation of the 4.8 million acres of national forest land needing it, and timber stand improvement on 13.4 million acres could increase the allowable cut by 5.8 billion board feet. Conservation groups generally supported the intensified timber management objectives, but they insisted that adequate funding of watershed management, recreation developments, and other multiple-use values and benefits of the national forests should not be jeopardized.

The lumber price escalation was followed by a rapid drop in prices. As a result, the Forest Service lowered its appraised prices for timber-sale offerings in the national forests. The Bureau of Land Management took similar action on timber appraisals on the public domain.

Disaster Fire Program. In line with recommendations of a special task force set up at the urging of the American Forestry Association, legislation was introduced in Congress to implement a program to meet the problem of forest fires that reach disaster proportions. The proposals called for a special $10 million emergency fund in addition to regular fire control appropriations. They also called for the establishment of a Fire Control Board to coordinate the work of existing protection agencies and to develop emergency procedures. Annual appropriation of the full $20 million authorization of federal funds for the federal-state cooperative fire protection program also was sought. The program had been receiving only about $14 million a year from the federal government, although the states were contributing more than $80 million.

Tree Planting. A total of 1,407,690 acres was restocked with trees by planting and seeding in 1968, the Forest Service reported. Most of the planting (984,597 acres) was on private lands, including industrial holdings and farm lands planted under cooperative programs. Reforestation on national forests and other federal lands covered 321,991 acres; on state and local government holdings, 67,327 acres. Wind barrier plantings, mostly on Great Plains farms, covered 33,667 acres. Oregon, Florida, Georgia, and Alabama led in acreage planted.

U. S. Forest Service. President Nixon's budget for fiscal 1970 called for $359,832,000 in regular funds for the Forest Service, U. S. Department of Agriculture. This was an increase of $19,000,000 over the appropriation for the preceding year. The total included $196,518,000 for national forest management, $99,570,000 for forest roads and trails, $41,425,000 for forest research, and $20,529,000 for federal cooperation with states and private forest owners.

The Forest Service put into effect in 1969 a new formula for determining fees for livestock grazing on national forests, calling for gradual increases over a 10-year period. The Interior Department took similar action on grazing fees on the public domain. The increases were designed to bring grazing fees into line with fair market value of the resource, as had long been urged by conservation groups.

Volume of timber harvested on national forests in fiscal 1968 was 12.1 billion board feet, a record, and an increase of 1.3 billion feet over 1967. The timber was cut in accordance with management policies designed to assure sustained yields.

International Meetings. An organization congress of the International Union of Societies of Foresters met in Washington, D. C., in August. The Society of American Foresters was host. The new union is made up of foresters' organizations.

Also meeting in Washington was the Second World Consultation on Forest Tree Breeding. Scientists from 40 nations discussed tree genetics problems and reported accomplishments in developing superior strains of forest trees.

Lumber. Production of lumber in the United States in 1968 was estimated by the National Forest Products Association at 37,094,000,000 board feet, an increase of about 1.8 billion feet over the 1967 figure. Lumber output in the first five months of 1969, amounting to 15.9 billion feet, was running at a seasonally adjusted annual rate about 0.5% below 1968.

U. S. LUMBER PRODUCTION, 1967–68
(In million board feet)

Producing Regions	1967	1968
Southern pine region	6,415	6,870
Douglas fir region	8,046	8,802
Western pine region	10,180	10,851
California redwood region	1,998	2,277
Other softwoods	1,235	1,334
Total softwoods	27,874	30,134
Southern hardwoods	3,774	3,655
Appalachian hardwoods	1,363	1,177
Other hardwoods	2,264	2,128
Total hardwoods	7,401	6,960

In Canada, total lumber production in 1967 was 10,367,000,000 board feet, of which nearly 95% was softwood lumber. The total was down about 85 million feet from 1966.

Estimated world production of sawn wood in 1967, according to the Food and Agriculture Organization of the United Nations, was 370.8 million cubic meters, a drop of about 2 million cubic meters from the revised 1966 figure. (One cubic meter equals 424 board feet.) The decline resulted from a drop in softwood lumber production; the output of hardwood lumber rose slightly. The Soviet Union ranked first in lumber production, followed in order by the United States, Japan, and Canada.

CHARLES E. RANDALL
Forestry Information Specialist

FORMAN, James. See CIVIL RIGHTS MOVEMENT.
FORMOSA. See CHINA—NATIONALIST CHINA.
FOUNDATIONS. See PHILANTHROPY; SOCIETIES AND ORGANIZATIONS.

P.I.P. PHOTO BY REPORTERS ASSOCIÉS

GEORGES POMPIDOU (*left*) addresses audience during his 1969 campaign for the presidency. He was elected on June 15. (*Below*) The retired General and Madame de Gaulle enjoy a quiet walk in the Irish countryside.

J.P. BONNOTTE, FROM GAMMA-PIX

FRANCE

The end of Charles de Gaulle's second period as president of France marked 1969 as an exceptional year. Devaluation of the franc, continued domestic strife, and conflict with France's Common Market partners were all overshadowed by his precipitate resignation following the defeat of his regionalization program in a national referendum. Yet France did not dissolve into chaos. Former Premier Georges Pompidou easily beat off rivals to become de Gaulle's successor, and the nation continued on its way—neither more nor less tranquil than it had been.

DOMESTIC AFFAIRS

Referendum and Resignation. In retrospect it appeared that France had never recovered from the domestic upheaval of May and June 1968. Inflation, rising taxes, and simmering unrest in school and factory characterized the end of 1968, and 1969 opened with signs of malaise. Polls reported public apathy and pessimism. The atmosphere, de Gaulle told his cabinet, was "melancholic." "Oh, you know, the French are never satisfied, sir," Premier Maurice Couve de Murville told a television interviewer. But murmurs of revolt among the loosely allied Gaullist parliamentary majority suggested that the premier might fall when the National Assembly convened in April.

A harbinger of this crisis of confidence was Pompidou's self publicity. After his forced resignation in July 1968, he built up a "secretariat" to keep himself politically alive. As Couve de Murville faltered, Pompidou moved to capture the headlines. In Rome he was received by the Italian president and told reporters, on January 17, that "if General de Gaulle were to retire, I would be a candidate to succeed him." The next day he assured the world that the de Gaulle regime was stable. But since the president's term was not to expire until 1972, the Pompidou candidacy was premature, to say the least. Irked, de Gaulle told his ministers, on Jan. 22, 1969: "It is my duty and my intention to fulfill this mandate to the end." Nevertheless, doubt was sown; thereafter events moved quickly.

During a visit (January 31–February 2) to Brittany, a poor and disaffected region harboring a minority separatist movement, de Gaulle announced plans for submitting constitutional changes—reform

---

FRANCE • Information Highlights

Area: 211,207 square miles (547,026 sq km).

Population: 49,920,000 (1968 est.).

Chief Cities (1962 census): Paris, the capital, 2,790,091; Marseille, 778,071; Lyon, 528,535; Nice, 292,958.

Government: *President*—Georges Pompidou (took office June 20, 1969); *Premier*—Jacques Chaban-Delmas (took office June 24, 1969). *Parliament*—National Assembly, 487 members (party seating, January 1970): Union of Democrats for the Republic, 268 plus 19 affiliates; Independent Republicans, 58 + 4; Socialists, 43 + 13; Communists, 33 + 1; Center for Progress and Modern Democracy, 30 + 3; nonaffiliated, 15).

Religious Faith: Roman Catholics, 82.6% of population.

Education: Literacy rate (1969), 100% of population. *Total school enrollment* (1965)—9,292,867 (primary, 5,523,827; secondary, 2,455,209; teacher-training, 17,442; technical/vocational, 396,743; university/higher, 509,764).

Finance (1967 est.): *Revenues,* $24,474,000,000; *expenditures,* $25,759,000,000; *public debt,* $18,357,000,000; *monetary unit,* franc, (5.54 francs equal U. S.$1, 1970).

Gross National Product (1968): $126,111,560,000.

National Income (1968): $95,998,383,000; *average annual income per person,* $1,923.

Economic Indexes (1967): *Industrial production* (1968), 125 (1963 = 100); *agricultural production,* 114 (1963 = 100); *cost of living,* 112 (1963=100).

Manufacturing and Processing (metric tons, 1967): Cement, 24,768,000; crude steel, 19,656,000; wine, 6,164,000 hectoliters; meat, 2,553,600; sugar, 1,712,000.

Crops (metric tons, 1967–68 crop year): Grapes, 9,513,000 (ranks 2d among world producers); apples, 2,357,000 (world rank, 2d); wheat, 14,383,000; potatoes, 10,632,000.

Minerals (metric tons, 1967): Iron ore, 49,224,000 (ranks 3d among world producers); coal, 47,628,000; salt, 4,875,000; crude petroleum, 2,832,000; bauxite, 2,772,000.

Foreign Trade (1968): *Exports,* $12,675,000,000 (chief exports, 1967: nonelectrical machinery, $1,404,244,000; iron and steel, $949,494,000; textile yarn and fabrics, $703,-536,000; electrical machinery, $589,874,000); *imports,* $13,943,000,000 (chief imports, 1967: nonelectrical machinery, $1,582,437,000; petroleum, $1,303,597,000; iron and steel, $716,147,000). *Chief trading partners* (1967): West Germany (took 17% of exports, supplied 20% of imports); Belgium-Luxembourg; Italy.

Transportation: *Roads* (1964), 888,559 miles (1,429,958 km); *motor vehicles* (1967), 14,181,100 (automobiles, 11,500,-000); *railways* (1966), 24,000 miles (38,623 km); *merchant vessels* (1967), 532, (5,284,000 gross registered tons); *national airline,* Air France; *principal airport,* Orly (Paris).

Communications: *Telephones* (1968): 6,999,621; *television stations* (1968), 91; *television sets* (1968), 7,196,000; *radios* (1967), 15,256,000; *newspapers* (1966), 117.

---

of the Senate and of regional powers—to a referendum. At his press conference on Nov. 27, 1968, he had proposed transforming the Senate, his principal institutional critic, into a half-elected, half-appointed advisory council on social and economic problems, and on Feb. 2, 1969, he announced a plan to divide France into 21 "economic regions," each with an assembly empowered to levy taxes and chart developments. The reconstituted Senate would represent the regional assemblies in Paris. The president of the Senate would cease to be the automatic interim successor to the president of France.

The regionalization plan met with opposition, and many politicians urged a "no" vote in the referendum scheduled for April 27. Foreign Minister Michel Debré was among the more prominent opponents. Centralist Jacques Duhamel condemned the device of tying regional reform in with de Gaulle's determination to eliminate the old Senate. Socialist leader Guy Mollet called the plan "fake regionalization."

De Gaulle threatened resignation should he meet "reckless" opposition. "What sort of man would I be," he asked on April 10, "if I failed to draw at once the conclusions from such a profound rift—and tried foolishly to retain my present functions?" The gamble was risky. Street graffiti proclaimed "Ten years is enough." Many doubted that the regionalization plan would, as de Gaulle claimed "repel the threats hanging over France."

The government mobilized its resources to achieve a favorable vote, promising no new taxes in 1969 and predicting that a negative vote was a vote for communism—for sabotaging the currency and the economy. *Le Monde* accused the president of blackmail; the polls indicated coming defeat; the franc slipped. An apparent majority no longer considered de Gaulle indispensable—especially as an acceptable alternative, Pompidou, was in the wings.

More than 23 million voted on April 27, almost 80% of the registered voters, and of these more than 52% voted "no." The feminine vote had dropped, and youth had come out in force against de Gaulle. Generalized discontent among underpaid workers, small businessmen shy of new taxes, big business fearing worker "participation," and those disliking the Gaullist foreign policy had turned the tide. The shift was not enormous, but it was decisive.

On April 28, de Gaulle ordered release of a previously prepared, terse statement: "I am ceasing to exercise my functions as President of the Republic. This takes effect at noon today." Thereafter he said nothing. The immense silence, a last theatrical gesture, recalled his departure of 1946. Now after ten years and four months as president of the Fifth Republic, de Gaulle had vanished from the Elysee Palace. No one doubted that it was final.

Couve de Murville told the nation "with profound sadness" that the political consequences would be severe, and Alain Poher, the centrist president of the Senate, who automatically became interim president of France, appealed for unity. Interest focused on the presidential race.

Campaign and Election. Pompidou was the first to announce his candidacy, appealing to his record as premier from 1962 to 1968. He was quickly endorsed by the majority Gaullist party. No other candidate was conceivable, despite the jealousies of the older Gaullists. The conservative Independents, after former Premier Antoine Pinay declined to run, also backed Pompidou.

(*Continued on page 304*)

JACQUES PIERRE MICHEL CHABAN-DELMAS was appointed premier of France by President Georges Pompidou on June 20, 1969. Upon taking office he pledged his efforts to safeguard the purchasing power of the worker, to work toward greater humanization of government administration, and to continue France's independent foreign policy while cooperating with the Atlantic Alliance and seeking friendly relations with the United States. After the devaluation of the franc in August, he announced austerity measures to restore balance to the economy.

Chaban-Delmas was born in Paris on March 7, 1915, and earned degrees in law and political science at the University of Paris. A Resistance hero during World War II, he became a deputy in the National Assembly in 1946. He was still holding this post at the time of his appointment to the premiership. In the interim he had held three ministries, and had been serving as president of the National Assembly since 1958.

THE DE GAULLE YEARS

An era in French history ended abruptly on April 28, 1969, with the resignation of Charles de Gaulle, more than three years before the expiration of his second 7-year term as president of the Fifth Republic. The end of the Gaullist era was as undramatic as its origins had been extraordinary. How profoundly France, Europe—indeed the entire Western world—had been marked by de Gaulle's 10-year presidency historians may one day be able to judge. But a tentative evaluation suggests that this exceptional regime will be well remembered.

DE GAULLE IN POWER

The First Period. De Gaulle's first political career had ended in the spring of 1953. It had carried him from a brief undersecretaryship in 1940, through the heroic years as leader of the Free French during World War II, to become provisional president of liberated France in 1944. Unhappy with the subordinate role of the executive, he made a calculated resignation in January 1946. He then organized the RPF (Rally of the French People) movement, which was designed to bring about his return as master of the nation. The RPF could not prevail against the political orthodoxy of the Fourth Republic, however, and for five years (1953–58) de Gaulle waited in retirement.

De Gaulle's Return. In the spring of 1958 that crisis occurred. France seemed to be on the brink of civil and military upheaval. Having shed so much empire so painfully since 1945, many Frenchmen, led by the Army, were determined not to lose rebellious Algeria. As parliament and the government were not so convinced, the specter of a military coup d'etat was evoked.

Amid the complex interplay of men and events de Gaulle engineered a national mandate for himself. As the crisis deepened in Paris and Algiers, he maneuvered much of political France into waiting on him and won the acceptance of the Army. Making only the most formal concessions to parliamentary conventions, he took office as premier on June 1. He was granted exceptional powers for six months and had a new constitution drafted and approved by referendum. In January 1959 he was inaugurated as the first president of the Fifth Republic.

Thus began his second political career, the Gaullist era (1959–69). Built upon popular support independent of the old political parties, it was authoritarian without being tyrannical. The program was both traditional and modern. In scope it had no rival since Napoleonic times.

PROGRAM FOR THE FIFTH REPUBLIC

Three massive problems confronted the Fifth Republic: (1) liquidation of the burdensome imperial heritage; (2) restoration of France's great power status; and (3) reform of domestic institutions.

Algeria and the End of Empire. The Fourth Republic had already begun the withdrawal from empire, but Algeria was a special case, having a large European population and being legally a part of metropolitan France. De Gaulle managed to bring most of France, including the Army, to accept the inevitability of "abandoning" Algeria and granting it independence, but this took four years.

GEN. CHARLES DE GAULLE stands at attention in his most familiar role as France's soldier-statesman.

GILLES CARON, FROM GAMMA-PIX

De Gaulle's Algerian policy was pragmatic, searching, Machiavellian. Repeatedly his own life was threatened by would-be assassins sworn to avenge the "sell-out." The gravest threat to his regime came in April 1961 when four generals at Algiers proclaimed a military government. It was feared that sympathetic officers in France would rally to this rebellion and that Paris might be seized by parachute troops. Appealing to the population to help him, de Gaulle savagely denounced the generals, chastised his panicky ministers, and waited for invasion. However, the Algiers movement collapsed for lack of support among the troops.

By the spring of 1962 agreement was reached, and in April the French people ratified the settlement ending, after eight years, one of the last and most merciless of colonial wars. France saved little in North Africa, yielding even the oil-rich Sahara. By this time most of the former French colonies had gained independence, but the enormous personal authority of de Gaulle made loss of empire possible with minimal loss of prestige.

French Prestige and European Unity. Algeria had been the graveyard of the Fourth Republic, but part of the crisis precipitating de Gaulle's return in 1958 resulted from the steady decline of France among the great nations. Cabinet upsets, economic failures, costly imperial wars, and hesitations about European unity had led the United States and Britain to treat France harshly in the world forum. This changed when the general took office; overnight the nation was invested with a new authority. De Gaulle's course in world affairs was tortured, but the goals never changed: restoration of French primacy in Europe and creation of a European grouping independent of the United States and the Soviet Union.

The first approach to renewed great-power

301

status was a secret proposal to Washington and London, in September 1958, of a three-power directorate of the Western world. The negative reply served to increase de Gaulle's hostility toward U. S. dominance and British subservience. Thereafter, he began withdrawal of France from more than token membership in the North Atlantic Treaty Organization, and in 1967 he expelled NATO forces from French soil.

President de Gaulle also battled against the concept of a supranational European community, which was inherent in the Treaty of Rome establishing the European Economic Community (EEC) in 1957. Instead, he strove to make France the leader of a loose association of European states—a "third force" as he called it. Rejected as an equal by Britain and the United States, he cultivated the West German republic, trying to wean West Germany and western Europe away from dependence upon the United States. His efforts reached a high point early in 1963 with the conclusion of a Franco-German treaty and the veto of Britain's application for membership in EEC. He raised France's stock by his forceful style, his stinging rebuffs to the United States, Britain, and the Soviet Union, and the clarity of much of his analysis, and he obtained the nuclear trappings of a great state. However, Europe resisted his design, and thus his attempt to achieve the primacy of France in Europe fell short of the mark.

Restructuring the Nation. The general argued that France had fallen so low in 1958 because of its feeble governmental institutions. From the outset he launched an assault upon parliamentarism, and year after year he struck out at the traditional political parties—their divisions and their incompetence. The Constitution of 1958 provided for a strong presidency and a cabinet largely dependent on it, and de Gaulle made full use of his powers.

In his battle for constitutional reform and adoption of his policies, de Gaulle repeatedly made use of the popular referendum. Backed by his success in decolonization, his prestige in the world, and the coincident rise of French prosperity, he wielded this weapon effectively despite the Council of State's declaring it unconstitutional. His familiar tactic was to threaten immediate resignation—and predict resultant chaos—should the nation not support him against the opposition parties. By the referendum of October 1962 he succeeded in strengthening the presidency by making it popularly elected. This, plus the disarray of the parties and the growth of an opportunist Gaullist party, created a situation in which the general had little to fear from his cabinet or the Assembly.

Thus France's institutions seemed immensely stable. But the conditions of this imposing personal power depended not only upon constitutional arrangements but upon presidential personality and the continuing general failure of the political parties. These conditions could not be guaranteed forever. As the spring of 1969 showed, even the exceptional politician might miscalculate and find that the indispensable popular support had slipped away.

AN APPRAISAL

As the years pass and the record becomes fuller, de Gaulle's handling of the three major problems he faced may be differently appraised. But certainly no contemporary estimate could underrate the magnitude of his achievement in Africa. However he had seen the problem at the outset, whatever the enormities of the four years of struggle, undeniably he had resurrected French strength by leading the nation out of the colonial labyrinth. And, for the most part, he managed to retain the esteem of the former colonies.

Equally, de Gaulle handed on to his successor a state that had been restored to the front rank in Europe and the world. As for the domestic political arrangements, he gave them a clarification unknown for nearly 100 years. Here, however, his faults were glaring, for he battered the political process destructively. He was slow to respond to crises in housing, education, social services, local government, and national economy, and his approach to democracy was authoritarian.

The catalog of faults attributed to de Gaulle might be continued at length. Supporters of European unity insisted that he had set that cause back many years, if not forever. Foreigners complained about the proliferation of nuclear weapons, and domestic critics attacked the expenditures on military hardware when a whole class of Frenchmen had only subsistence wages. But good might be said of him, too.

At a time when the role of Britain was far from clear, and when West Germany was still recovering from post-World War II eclipse, de Gaulle had dramatically spotlighted both France and continental Europe. His claim to the historic primacy of Europeans was scoffed at, and his fundamental weakness in representing only 50 million people in a country by no means industrially imposing limited the impact of what he did. But Frenchmen would recall the enthusiastic, respectful attention he had received in Germany, Poland, Rumania, and the Soviet Union. It had made them all stand taller.

De Gaulle's overtures to Communist China were largely without issue. His comments on Vietnam and the U. S. role there were lost in the rush of events. His 1967 escapade in support of Quebec separatism was a vulgar miscalculation. Highhanded with French miners in 1963, he was forced to back down. Neglectful of social issues, he was brought to the brink of domestic chaos in 1968. Condoning violence and terrorism by the Army, he subverted justice at home. De Gaulle used men coldly; he was brutal, rude, and remote. Intensely jealous of power, he forgave no untoward ambition. But he had rescued the country in 1958, put through some fundamental reforms, envisioned a worldwide French-speaking community centered in France, and, more than any contemporary statesman, more than any French ruler in nearly 150 years, he had been a bit larger than life.

Finally, in 1969, miscalculating or perhaps falling into a political trap, at nearly 79 years of age, he appeared to accept the conclusion of his career. On his desk was a quote from Nietzsche: "Everything is emptiness, everything is one, everything that is and will be has been." Isolated at his home in Colombey, he worked on his memoirs, raged at the mediocrity of men and events, and prepared for a modest funeral, knowing that his life, his actions, his writings, and the things that time would lend to his memory would make him one of the most monumental figures of France and of the whole 20th century.

JOHN C. CAIRNS
University of Toronto

De Gaulle, with his predecessor René Coty (at right), at the Arc de Triomphe immediately after he was installed as president of the Fifth Republic on Jan. 8, 1959. The new president shakes hands with veterans of two World Wars.

(Below) De Gaulle and Soviet Premier Nikita Khrushchev exchange gifts during latter's state visit to France in 1960.

DELMAS-PIX

DELMAS-PIX

LE GRAND CHARLES

Charles de Gaulle, architect of France's modern rebirth, left his imprint on history from the moment he marched into liberated Paris in 1944. He made France a leader in Europe and a nuclear power; freed its colonies; and widened its influence. Throughout, he stoutly championed the glory of France.

(Below) Western allies confer at 1959 Paris meeting: UK Prime Minister Macmillan, U.S. President Eisenhower, de Gaulle, German Chancellor Adenauer, and French Premier Debré.

(Below) In Algeria, on one of a number of visits he made between 1959 and 1962 while the Algerian War was in progress, de Gaulle greets crowd.

ROBERT COHEN, FROM BLACK STAR

P.I.P.

(*Continued from page 300*)

The Left, its fragile 1965 alliance (Communists, Socialists, and Radicals) shattered during 1968, displayed only division. François Mitterrand, de Gaulle's strongest challenger in 1965, declined to run. Gaston Defferre, the anti-Communist mayor of Marseille, backed by former premier Pierre Mendès-France, became the Socialist candidate, but he was opposed by Guy Mollet, secretary general of the Socialist party, who promised support for Poher or for a Communist. The Communists put up Jacques Duclos. The tiny Unified Socialist party ran Michel Rocard. The Center finally found a candidate in Poher. A Trotskyite, Alain Krivine, and an "individualist," Louis Ducatel, completed the field.

The campaign quickly demonstrated that the essential contest, on June 1, would be between Pompidou and Poher, the latter hitherto all but unknown. Poher's surprising following caused Pompidou to play down his own past and sell himself as "a Frenchman like so many others," promising close relations with parliament and hinting at a softened attitude toward British entry into the Common Market. "The future President will not be able to govern the way General de Gaulle did," he remarked. He himself would not be "a distant chief of state locked in a palace among officials, military men and ambassadors."

As interim president, Poher took steps that increased his popularity. He freed television and radio of government control, reduced security measures—thereby ridiculing Gaullist predictions of chaos when the General stepped down—and fired the head of the secret police network. The spectacle of this "average" man colliding with the prominent Gaullist ministers had wide appeal. Support of Poher, however, waxed and waned. In the end, the experience and the ultimate plausibility of the Gaullist party and its candidate won out.

Pompidou whirled across France, concealing the poet, banker, bon vivant, and repressor of the 1968 riots, and presenting himself as "the grandson of a peasant." Poher, in a low key, promised reform, abandonment of costly "prestige" projects, European unity, and something suggestive of a "new deal." Defferre, Duclos, and the others trailed, involved in internecine left-wing warfare.

There was no majority winner on June 1. Pompidou received 44% of the vote; Poher, 23%; Duclos, 21%; Defferre, 5%; Rocard, less than 4%; Ducatel more than 1%; and Krivine, 1%. Poher rejected invitations from all sides to quit and permit a polarized race between Pompidou and Duclos in the June 15 runoff. The result in the contest between Pompidou and Poher was predictable. Pompidou captured 58% of the votes cast. From Ireland, where he had gone on leaving office, de Gaulle cabled him cryptically, "For all national and personal reasons, I offer you my most cordial congratulations."

The New Regime. On June 20, Pompidou was installed as the second president of the Fifth Republic. He chose as his premier the Assembly president, mayor of Bordeaux, and longtime Gaullist, Jacques Chaban-Delmas. General de Gaulle then ended his self-imposed exile, but the bitterness among some followers over the referendum affair lingered on. One former Gaullist minister suggested that the new president was about to betray de Gaulle, and diehard Gaullists resisted giving ministries to men, such as Valéry Giscard d'Estaing, who had earlier opposed de Gaulle only to rally to Pompidou. Pompidou, however, continued to praise his predecessor.

Chaban-Delmas was not a strong politician, and the large cabinet announced June 12 (18 ministers, 20 secretaries of state) was clearly Pompidou's choice. To the dismay of orthodox Gaullists, Debré lost the foreign ministry to Maurice Schumann, a wartime Gaullist turned centrist and Europeanist, but a man unlikely to challenge Pompidou. Debré received the defense portfolio, and Giscard d'Estaing took the ministry of finance. Three centrists received major portfolios: René Pleven, justice; Jacques Duhamel, agriculture; and Joseph Fontanet, labor. The greatly criticized ministry of information was eliminated.

Despite speeches to the contrary, this was not a government in the image of its predecessors. Significantly, Edgar Faure was replaced as minister of education by Olivier Guichard, and André Malraux, de Gaulle's cultural affairs minister, retired. With a flexible prime minister and a parliamentary majority, Pompidou could airily salute de Gaulle as "the greatest of Frenchmen" and promise reforms in "this old and illustrious house which is France." However, on June 25, he put before the Assembly a bill to annul most punishments imposed under de Gaulle for offenses during the 1968 troubles.

The Political Future. Ahead stretched an immense number of problems—economic, social, and political. The regime was in no danger, but the civic life of France, after more than a decade of strong paternal rule, remained largely inert. The ordinary functioning of the constitution had yet to be tested. The crucial moment would come politically when the Left pulled itself together and the essentially opportunist Gaullist party sorted itself out.

There were indications of strife within the cabinet and many were skeptical of Pompidou. In the

ALAIN POHER, interim president after de Gaulle resigned in 1969, honors Tomb of the Unknown Soldier.

Assembly sat five of the six former ministers dropped by the new president and elected to seats on October 19. (Couve de Murville alone was defeated.) From them might come an opposition of consequence. The governmental changes had brought no fresh vigor to politics, but Chaban-Delmas claimed the new regime would initiate a "New Society."

Labor Troubles. Apart from disturbances connected with Breton separatism, demonstrations were largely confined to labor unions and shopkeepers' organizations during 1969. Strikes were frequent, involving, among others, miners, garbage collectors, printers, bus drivers, postmen, and utility workers. Sporadic stoppages in February were followed by a 24-hour general strike on March 10–11, backed partly by the Communist-led General Confederation of Labor (CGT), the Socialist Workers Force, and the Catholic Democratic Confederation of Labor, and pressing what Couve de Murville called "absurd" demands for wage increases up to 12%, a 40-hour workweek, and the tying of wages to price increases. Huge parades in Paris and other cities heard shouts of "Down with capitalism!" and "Down with de Gaulle!" Extremists were attacked by riot police. De Gaulle assailed strike leaders in a television address on March 11 as "the same assailants, backed by the same accomplices, using the same means and threatening again to sink the currency, the economy and the Republic." The government stood by its 4% offer; the unions yielded.

President Poher's brief term was marked by newspaper shutdowns. President Pompidou inherited the policies and liabilities of the de Gaulle regime. The austerity program following devaluation on August 8 produced more strikes. Railway workers walked out for a week, September 11–18, without giving the mandatory five days notice, and got a settlement breaching the government's own guidelines. CGT secretary-general Georges Séguy called for action to "wear out an already anemic government" and replace it with a "democratic alternative," provoking Pompidou to warn that he would maintain order "in any circumstances." An increase in the minimum wage granted October 1 did little to damp down discontent. Electricity and gas workers struck on November 25–26.

Shopkeepers had shut down on March 5 and April 11, protesting sales taxes and general economic policy. Throughout the autumn small businessmen demonstrated. Militants among them fought police after a big protest rally in Paris on October 13, which drew grocers, plumbers, and hotelkeepers from the provinces. Led by cafe-owner Gérard Nicoud, "The Movement" reminded France again that this tough class of independent and inefficient small proprietors would continue fighting rationalization of the economy.

Devaluation and the Economy. With high employment, pressures for higher wages and lower taxes, and with a widening trade gap and outflow of capital, the government struggled on with the "battle of the franc." Early in January new consumer taxes to slow inflation were introduced, but union damands were steady. Economists predicted that de Gaulle could not indefinitely refuse devaluation. His successor, equally adamant and equally plagued by balance of payment troubles and steadily draining reserves, sought vainly to cut spending and stiffen credit restrictions and exchange controls before capitulating to the inevitable and announcing an 11.1% devaluation on August 8. The Communist party and the unions denounced the measure for cutting workers' purchasing power. But it was the 15% wage increase, following the strikes of 1968, that had accelerated the inflationary crisis. "Our franc," Pompidou said on September 22, "was doped."

This deft devaluation was followed by a 5-week retail and wholesale price freeze while the government worked out its austerity program. On September 16 the Assembly accepted government measures to reduce spending, encourage exports, and balance the budget. French society, Chaban-Delmas claimed, was "archaic": there was too little industry, too much class prejudice and too little social mobility, too much verbal and too little practical revolution; and state control was "tentacular and ineffective." He promised improvements, including greater autonomy in nationalized sectors, more spending on education, reorganization of the bureaucracy, and freedom for television and radio.

The opposition quickly underlined the criticism of de Gaulle's policies implied in all this, but the Pompidou regime took this in its stride. The budget for 1970, approved Oct. 8, 1969, generated optimism. The first balanced budget in five years, it provided for expenditures of $28.4 billion, a $17.2 million surplus, cutbacks in outlays for nationalized industry, agriculture, and social services, and a 4.7% increase in military spending. Overall revenue was to be increased 12%, domestic production 9%, and expenditure 6.2%. But fundamental reform lay far ahead, "a herculean task," as *Le Monde* noted, requiring "the unblocking of French society."

Education. Strains in the education system that had unleashed the 1968 domestic crisis remained far from remedied. The Faure reforms were not fully instituted in 1969. Collisions occurred between police and university and lycée students on January 23–25 in Paris, Vincennes, Caen, and Besançon, and there was a militant teacher occupation of the Sorbonne on February 12.

Defense. The new president made no great changes in defense policy. He planned to continue the buildup of nuclear weaponry (France's first nuclear submarine went to sea June 25), refused to sign the international nuclear test-ban treaty, and announced resumption of thermonuclear testing in the Pacific in 1970. He gave no sign of tightening relations with the North Atlantic Treaty Organization, but the armed forces chief of staff, Gen. Michel Fourquet, proposed closer cooperation with NATO and adoption of U. S.-style "flexible response" to Soviet attack to replace the former "all azimuths" defense of instant nuclear retaliation.

FOREIGN AFFAIRS

Common Market. The new government did not depart dramatically from the Gaullist policy toward the European Economic Community (EEC), but slight progress toward a "united Europe" was noticeable by the close of 1969. Early in the year a storm blew up when Britain informed France's Common Market partners of proposals put to the British ambassador to France, Christopher Soames, by de Gaulle on February 4, allegedly envisioning replacement of EEC by a broader free-trade area in which France, Germany, Italy, and Britain would form a 4-power directorate. Furious about this disclosure, de Gaulle staged a series of boycotts of Western European Union meetings and charged that Britain was using WEU as a back door to the Common Market. This mood changed slightly under Pompidou,

SUPERTANKER *Frimaire* (141,000 tons), the largest ever built at Marseille, is towed to pier after launching.

when Foreign Minister Schumann, on July 22, proposed an EEC summit conference to discuss possible British entry. The price France demanded was the continuance of subsidies to French farmers (derived from levies paid by the Market partners on imported food) beyond the Dec. 31, 1969, deadline when uniform support levels were to take effect. The EEC council agreed to this at an emergency meeting in August, and France pledged to bring its prices into line by the end of the 1970–71 agricultural year. At the summit conference held at The Hague on December 1–2, Pompidou insisted that agreement on the farm problem must be reached before preparatory talks on British entry could begin, in the summer of 1970. Thus, though de Gaulle had suggested replacing the Market with a 4-power directorate, his successor reluctantly agreed to open negotiations on Britain within EEC.

Relations with West Germany. Agreements for Franco-German development of the Saar and of Lorraine, for German purchases of French-produced Algerian oil, and for joint development of a European air bus were reached at the March 13–14 meeting of de Gaulle and Chancellor Kurt Georg Kiesinger in Paris. The second semiannual meeting at Bonn on September 8–9, between Pompidou and Kiesinger, was less strained. But Pompidou's rigidity on the British problem reassured Gaullist "purists" that foreign policy had not changed.

Relations with Britain. Franco-British relations took a turn for the worse after the "Soames Affair" in February. They were not improved after the British refused to help build the 250-passenger short-haul air bus, which France predicted would draw 800 orders around the world. At the end of 1969, the EEC summit decisions had done nothing to clarify French relations with Britain. If Pompidou seemed more positive in his attitude, the British themselves had no clear policy toward joining the Market.

Relations with the Soviet Union. France remained on generally good terms with the Soviet Union. Talks in Paris early in January and in Moscow in February and May provided for a 5-year agreement to double trade between the two countries. France would provide equipment for Soviet refineries and factories. A plan to orbit a French satellite with a Soviet rocket in 1971 was canceled, but the two nations agreed to a joint effort to put a laser reflector on the moon in 1970.

Relations with the United States. The Franco-American climate improved when President Richard M. Nixon visited Paris February 28–March 2. De Gaulle was unusually cordial, and Nixon lavished praise on his host. Congratulating Pompidou on June 16, Nixon said he looked forward to working with him, and in August it was agreed that the new French president would visit Washington in 1970.

Relations with Canada. By contrast, the cold war between Canada and France continued, with the Gaullist party's likening the Canadian province of Quebec to Vietnam and Czechoslovakia, as an area seeking "national emancipation." In January, de Gaulle feted visiting Quebec cabinet ministers and snubbed the Canadian ambassador. In October, Pompidou sent two secretaries of state to Quebec and forbade their visiting Ottawa. Canadian Prime Minister Pierre Elliott Trudeau denounced the attitude and remarks of one of the secretaries as "impertinent" and "grossly misinformed."

Middle East Policy. France remained critical of Israel, and stressed good relations with the Arab states. In January, de Gaulle placed an embargo on arms deliveries to Israel, including an order of 50 Mirage jets already paid for. The grand rabbi of France expressed sadness, and even some Gaullists called the embargo unjust. On June 28, Premier Chaban-Delmas said that the government might reconsider the embargo if other nations failed to follow France's "example," but at his first news conference on July 10, Pompidou maintained the embargo on offensive weapons and envisaged only possible delivery of "defensive" weapons. By contrast, in August, France decided to deliver 28 combat aircraft to Algeria, pledged aid to Lebanon, and joined in the UN Security Council resolution of September 15, demanding that Israel rescind all measures altering the status of Jerusalem.

African Policy. France continued military assistance to the government of Chad, believing that President Tombalbaye's struggle with rebels affected French interests in Central and West Africa. De Gaulle and Pompidou refused to join in Security Council condemnations of the Republic of South Africa (March 20) and Portugal (July 28). On May 2 it was announced that France was helping South Africa develop a ground-to-air missile. The French role in Biafra, the secessionist region of Nigeria, was unclear. De Gaulle sent a fact-finding mission there in February and was reported to be purchasing Bulgarian ammunition for Biafra. But by May, Pompidou was said to have agreed, under British and U. S. pressure, not to recognize the Biafran regime (which came to an end in January 1970) nor to send further arms.

The esteem France still enjoyed among its 14 former colonies in Africa was reflected in their aligning their currencies with the franc after August 8. And the vitality of the idea of a worldwide Francophone community was reaffirmed on February 17–20 at the 30-nation conference in Niamey, Niger.

Asian Policy. The French presence in Asia was manifest in agreements to sell wheat to both Communist China and Japan. France sent an official delegation to the funeral of President Ho Chi Minh of North Vietnam on September 9.

(See also POMPIDOU, GEORGES.)

JOHN C. CAIRNS
University of Toronto

FRENCH LITERATURE

The celebration of the bicentenary of Napoleon Bonaparte's birth flooded the market with a large number of books on Napoleon and his times. Among them were two volumes by the well-known popularizer André Castelot, *Bonaparte* and *Napoléon*. The iconoclastic Henri Guillemin, in his *Napoléon tel quel*, debunked the myths and legends that have grown up about Napoleon. He portrayed the Emperor as a man without a country, a kind of gangster in the service of capitalism.

The best answer to Guillemin's book may be found in the writings of Napoleon himself. Historian Octave Aubry published *Ecrits de Napoléon*, excerpts from the letters, tales, essays, dissertations, and philosophical aphorisms of Napoleon. These reveal one of Napoleon's least-known aspects—his great talent as a writer.

Nonfiction. Generally speaking, the year was more favorable to history books, essays, and memoirs than to fiction. The most successful book in 1969 (more than 350,000 copies were sold in eight weeks) was *Papillon*, by Henri Charrier, a long autobiography by a former convict who escaped from the prisons of Cayenne and Devil's Island in French Guiana, and settled in Caracas, Venezuela, where he began a new life and became a prosperous restaurant owner. The book is remarkable for its frankness, its humor, and its story of suffering and horror, and of a man's indomitable will to live.

Piaf, a book of memoirs written by Simone Berteaut, Edith Piaf's sister, is a straightforward, unpolished account of the singer's life, and her rise from poverty to fame.

Novels. Several works by already recognized authors must be mentioned. Henri de Montherlant, in his novel *Les garçons,* presents the same theme as in his earlier play, *La ville dont le prince est un enfant,* but develops it more completely, adds several characters, and ties the novel to two others already published (*Les bestiaires* and *Le songe*) to form a trilogy. It is an interesting and often well-written book, but the situations it portrays seem somewhat anachronistic and foreign today.

Other established authors who published this year were Vercors, whose *Le radeau de la Méduse* is a study of rebellion—good and bad; Jacques Perret, who wrote a meandering novel, *La compagnie des eaux;* Romain Gary, whose *L'adieu à Gary Cooper* treats of youth's malaise; and Jorge Semprun, who wrote a political and ideological book, *La deuxième mort de Ramon Mercader.* Robert Sabatier's *Les allumettes suédoises* is a populist account of life along the streets of Montmartre. Michel Mohrt set the action of his technically fascinating dialogue-novel about purity, truth, disillusion, and comic irony, *L'ours des Adirondacks,* in the United States, a country he knows well. J. L. Curtis brought out an excellent collection of short stories under the title of *Le thé sous les cypres.* Francoise Sagan's novel, *Un peu de soleil dans l'eau froide* is a new variation on the themes of love, boredom, and the search for something else.

Younger Authors. Among the offerings of the younger authors, mention should be made of *Passacaille* by Robert Pinget, a *nouveau roman* of theme and variations in several voices, and Claude Simon's *La bataille de Pharsale.* Jean-Marie Le Clezio wrote an obscure and verbose book called *Le livre des fuites,* which leads one to think that this undeniably talented and lyrical author has become somewhat bogged down.

Literary Prizes. Prizes in 1969 did not reveal any extraordinary new talents, except perhaps for the Grand Prix de l'Académie Française, which went to *Belle du Seigneur* by Albert Cohen, a writer more than 70 years old. His book deals with two separate subjects: a beautiful, lyrical love story and the world of the League of Nations between World Wars I and II, described with devastating satirical wit.

Poetry. The humorous and iconoclastic Raymond Queneau's latest collection of poems, *Fendre les flots,* does not, as might be supposed, sing of the sea, or far-off lands, but continues the derisive odyssey of everyday happenings and things that was the subject of *Courir les rues* and *Battre la campagne. L'inespéré,* by Jean-Philippe Salabreuil, is a "defense and illustration" of love poetry, which celebrates nature's complicity and sings of bliss and illuminating passion. Guy Thomas' *Vers boiteux pour un aveugle* is a series of slightly anarchistic poems, of populist leanings, whose facetious puns and playful use of words are worthy of Queneau's writings. Two collections by established poets were Jean Grosjean's *La gloire* and André du Bouchet's *Où le soleil.*

Theater. Two popular comedies attracted favorable attention: *La facture,* by Françoise Dorin, and *Quatre pièces sur jardin* by Barillet and Gredy.

PIERRE BRODIN
Lycée Français de New York

FRIENDS, RELIGIOUS SOCIETY OF

The American Friends Service Committee (AFSC) sent medical supplies to North Vietnam, despite legal restrictions, and continued medical relief projects in South Vietnam in 1969. It placed major emphasis on relief and reconstruction programs in Nigeria and Biafra. The board of directors of AFSC, supported by 1,300 other Quakers, held a silent vigil in front of the White House on May 7, and issued a "white paper" against the war in Vietnam. Henry C. Beerits, a Philadelphia attorney, was named as chairman of the board, replacing Gilbert F. White, the internationally known geographer.

One half of the 600 Quakers attending the Friends General Conference at Wilmington, Ohio, in June were of college age or younger. C. Lloyd Bailey, a New York social agency executive, was named chairman of the conference.

Participants in the Friends United Meeting (FUM) sessions at Richmond, Ind., included Joseph D. Otiende, Minister for Health in Kenya, a member of the East Africa Yearly Meeting of Friends. FUM urged its members to pledge an additional 1% of their income to overseas development, and 1% to meeting domestic problems, beyond what is now given. Howard C. Mills, of Indianapolis, Ind., was chosen as the new presiding clerk.

The Associated Executive Committee of Friends on Indian Affairs commemorated its centennial in meetings at Wyandotte, Okla., in May. It was formed during President Grant's administration to undertake work with the Indians.

EDWIN B. BRONNER
Haverford College

FRUITS. See AGRICULTURE.
FUELS. See ATOMIC ENERGY; GAS; MINING; PETROLEUM.

GABON

Gabon in 1969 expanded its role as France's "dutiful friend" by acting as a conciliator in intra-African disputes. Although it annoyed most African governments by recognizing Biafra, Gabon took advantage of its position as a "humanitarian outcast."

Foreign Affairs. In early June, President Albert-Bernard Bongo played a prominent role in securing the release of 18 condemned European technicians imprisoned in Biafra. In September, Nigeria's President Yakubu Gowan approached Bongo to have him arrange meetings with Biafra's leader, Lt. Col. Odummegwu Ojukwu. Bongo also acted as an intermediary in attempts to ease tensions between Congo (Brazzaville) and Congo (Kinshasa) and tried to better relations between the countries in the Central African Economic and Customs Union (UDEAC).

Domestic Politics. National and communal elections, the first since Gabon became a one-party state in March 1968, were held early in 1969.

The first of two cabinet changes took place on January 9. The second, in February, introduced military officers into the government for the first time in the history of independent Gabon.

A month later, on the first anniversary of the founding of the Gabonese Democratic party, the country's only political party, Bongo announced the release of some members of the group accused of plotting the February 1964 coup d'etat.

Economic Development. Prospecting continued to indicate additional mineral wealth. Rail links are being developed between the port under construction at Owendo (near Libreville) and the rich mineral deposits in the interior.

Exports of forest products continued to provide the largest amount of Gabon's foreign exchange, with crude oil and petroleum products second, followed by manganese and uranium. Gabon was one of the few underdeveloped countries maintaining a favorable balance of payments position (with a $52,128,000 surplus in 1968).

EDOUARD BUSTIN
Boston University

GAMBIA

Relations between Gambia (officially, The Gambia) and Senegal did not improve in 1969. Gambia's ruling political party submitted plans for changing the government from a monarchy to a republic. The state budget was balanced without British aid.

Political Developments. Prime Minister Dauda Jawara officially protested strong statements by Senegalese President Léopold Senghor on Gambian smuggling. At a February meeting of heads of state in Bathurst there were minor disturbances directed against Senegal, and 20 Gambians were arrested.

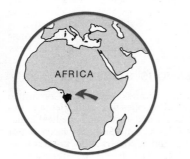

GABON

Information
Highlights

Area: 103,346 square miles (267,667 sq km).
Population: 480,000 (1968 est.).
Chief Cities (1967 census): Libreville, the capital, 57,000; Port Gentil (1969 est.), 30,000.
Government: *President*—Albert-Bernard Bongo (took office Dec. 4, 1967); *Vice President*—Leon Mebiame. *Legislature* (unicameral)—National Assembly, 47 members (party seating, 1969: all members of the Parti Démocratique Gabonais).
Religious Faiths: Roman Catholics, 44% of population; animists, 42%; Protestants, 8%; others, 6%.
Education: *Literacy rate* (1961), 12.4% of population aged 15 and over. *Total school enrollment* (1965)—85,811 (primary, 79,162; secondary, 4,750; teacher-training, 418; technical/vocational, 1,427; university/higher, 54).
Finance (1967 est.): *Revenues*, $58,900,000; *expenditures*, $58,900,000; *monetary unit*, CFA franc (246.85 francs equal U. S.$1).
Gross National Product (1969 est): $240,000,000.
National Income (1963): $152,319,000; *average annual income per person*, $334.
Cost Of Living Index (1967): 112 (1963=100).
Manufacturing: Sawn wood (1967), 36,000 cubic meters; lumber (1965), 31,000 cubic meters.
Crops (metric tons, 1967–68 crop year): Cassava, 125,000; cocoa beans, 4,500.
Minerals (metric tons, 1967): Crude petroleum, 3,444,000; manganese ore, 585,600; uranium (1966), 1,599; natural gas, 17,000,000 cubic meters; gold (1966), 34,466 troy ounces.
Foreign Trade (1968): *Exports*, $124,000,000 (chief exports, 1967: petroleum, $35,973,000; manganese, $32,530,000; wood, $26,575,000; uranium, $7,981,000); *imports*, $65,000,-000 (chief imports, 1967: nonelectrical machinery, $11,918,-000; electrical machinery, $4,439,900; railway vehicles, $3,240,000). *Chief trading partners* (1967): France (took 36% of exports, supplied 60% of imports); United States (took 20% of exports, supplied 10% of imports); West Germany (took 11% of exports, supplied 7% of imports).
Transportation: *Roads* (1967), 3,635 miles (5,849 km); *motor vehicles* (1967), 9,700 (automobiles 5,200); *national airlines*, Air Gabon, Transgabon; *principal airport*, Libreville.
Communications: Telephones (1968), 4,100; television stations (1968), 2; television sets (1968), 1,000; radios (1967), 50,000.

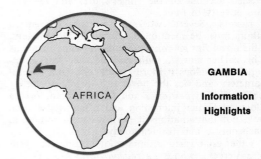

GAMBIA

Information
Highlights

Area: 4,361 square miles (11,295 sq km).
Population: 350,000 (1968 est.).
Chief Cities (1966 census): Bathurst, the capital, 30,865.
Government: *Governor-General*—Farimang M. Singhateh (took office Feb. 9, 1966); *Prime Minister*—Dauda Kairaba Jawara (took office for 2d term May 27, 1966). *Legislature* (unicameral)—National Assembly, 40 members (party seating, 1969: People's Progressive party, 21; United party, 7; People's Progressive Alliance, 4; 4 members elected by chiefs in Assembly; 4 members appointed by the government).
Religious Faiths: Muslims, 73% of population; others, 27%.
Education: *Literacy rate* (1969), 25% of population aged 10 and over. *Total school enrollment* (1965)—18,220 (primary, 14,218; secondary, 3,689; teacher-training, 129; technical/vocational, 184).
Finance (1967 est.): *Revenues*, $6,000,000; *expenditures*, $5,500,000; *public debt* (1964), $1,120,000; *monetary unit*, pound (.4167 pound equals U. S.$1).
Gross National Product (1967): $33,000,000.
Crops (metric tons, 1967–68 crop year): Peanuts, 152,000; groundnuts (in shell), 120,000; rice, 20,000.
Foreign Trade (1966): *Exports*, $21,000,000 (chief exports, 1966: vegetable oils and fats, $6,518,000; peanuts, $6,342,-000; fodder, $3,489,000; palm kernels, $358,000); *imports*, $20,100,000 (chief imports, 1966: cotton fabrics, $3,184,000; rice, $1,019,000; electrical machinery, $974,000). *Chief trading partners* (1966): Britain (took 61% of exports, supplied 36% of imports); Portugal (took 32% of exports); Japan (supplied 32% of imports).
Transportation: *Roads* (1967), 845 miles (1,360 km); *motor vehicles* (1967), 3,800 (automobiles 1,700); *principal airport*, Yundum.
Communications: Telephones (1968), 1,370; radios (1966), 60,000; newspapers (1969), 1 (daily circulation, 1,500).

Little was done in 1969 to implement Senghor's suggestions for a closer economic union between the two states.

The Executive Committee of the ruling People's Progressive party decided to submit the question of changing to a republican form of government to the electorate. A similar scheme was rejected by only 700 votes at a plebiscite in 1965. The United party of Pierre N'jie opposed the plan, but the proposal will probably be accepted unless the other major party, the People's Progressive Alliance led by former Finance Minister Sherif Sisay, joins in opposition.

Economic Development. Gambia's economic future, despite an increase in rice production, is still tied to the export of peanuts. In the 1968–69 season the marketing board purchased a total of 123,-827 tons of peanuts, a modest increase over the previous year. The position of the farmers, however, was undercut by the effects of the severe drought, which meant that food supplies had to be imported under the World Food Program.

Finance Minister S. M. Dibba announced that for the third consecutive year British aid would not be needed to balance the budget. Gambia achieved this solvency through stringent economies in operation and increased taxes on cigarettes and beer. The 1968–69 development budget of approximately $3 million was devoted largely to road improvements.

HARRY A. GAILEY
San Jose State College

GANDHI, Indira. See sketch under INDIA.

GARDENING AND HORTICULTURE

Near-revolutionary changes occurred in commercial horticulture in the United States in 1969 as the result of multiple labor problems.

Horticulture meanwhile continued to be one of the leading hobbies in the nation. Homeowners and other amateur horticulturists spent millions of dollars for plants, seed, pesticides, and other supplies and services. For the development and care of lawns, the U. S. homeowner spent in excess of $4 billion in the year.

Professional horticulturists experienced an increase in demand for their services. In part the demand came from expansion of the nation's highway network, giving rise to highway beautification programs and the development of roadside parks and recreation areas.

Commercial Horticulture. Some production and marketing patterns in commercial horticulture changed significantly because of restrictions placed by the federal government on the use of foreign labor, the inability of growers to get sufficient domestic labor to meet their needs, and problems arising from efforts to unionize farm labor. U. S. acreages of tomatoes, strawberries, and mushrooms were reduced so greatly as to cause concern. There was a notable migration of commercial production of tomatoes and strawberries to Mexico.

Because of manpower problems, research on mechanized production and harvesting systems is now being given high priority by public and private agencies. Tomatoes, cucumbers, pecans, and other crops are being successfully harvested mechanically. Prototype machines for harvest of peaches, strawberries, okra, brambles, and other difficult-to-harvest crops are being tested and show promise. Much

SCIENTISTS (*above*) at Institute of Paper Chemistry, Appleton, Wis., hold an aspen tree believed to be the first tree produced by tissue culture processes. (*Below, from left*) stem segment from which growth starts; stem with callus of new cells; callus on nutrients; new tree.

effort is being expended by plant breeders in an effort to develop varieties that possess good horticultural characters, have resistance to a multitude of diseases and insects, and can mature a sufficiently large number of fruits so that a high yield can be obtained from "once over" mechanical harvesting.

The use of chemicals that affect plant growth and development is being widely studied. Ethrel, a growth-regulating chemical, appears to bring about virtually simultaneous maturity of hot peppers and may prove helpful in developing a system by which this crop and others can be mechanically harvested.

The use of gamma and fast neutron irradiation in development of new varieties of flowers shows particular promise. New carnation and chrysanthemum varieties have been developed by the use of gamma irradiation. One commercial producer of poinsettias recently included this technique in his variety improvement program.

Increasing emphasis is being placed on the development of varieties of fruits and vegetables that are resistant to insects. This is necessary because restrictions continue to be placed on use of many insecticides that are effective in controlling insects. Some insects have developed resistance to insecticides that once were effective in controlling them. Resistance to certain kinds of insects has been incorporated into tomatoes and sweet potatoes.

All-America Winners. For the first time since 1956, only one All-America rose selection winner was named for 1970. First Prize, a hybrid tea rose

UPI

UPI

JUDY GARLAND, one of the world's most beloved stars, died on June 22. (*Left*) She captured audiences' hearts as Dorothy in the *Wizard of Oz*. (*Above*) Her live concerts won a new generation of fans.

developed by the late Eugene S. Boerner, was the only winner. Its blossoms have 20 to 30 large, deep pink petals of a satiny texture. The inside of the petals is light pink; the outside is dark pink to light red.

Four other flowers were selected as All-America winners for 1970. One was Bolero, a dwarf double bicolored bright red and gold marigold, an early, free-flowering type that produces a profusion of flowers over a long season. Another selection was the hybrid snapdragon Madame Butterfly, which produces spikes up to 30 inches long with florets ranging from scarlet through crimson, orange yellow, and bronze to magenta red. *Dianthus chinensis,* China Doll, was the third winner. It produces double flowers almost an inch in diameter in red, red and white, and salmon. The fourth winner was the morning glory Early Call Rose, an early-flowering type that produces large, deep rose blossoms with a contrasting white throat.

The tomato Small Fry, a hybrid cherry type that produces cherry-sized bright red fruit and is resistant to Fusarium and Veriticillium wilts, and the winter squash Waltham Butternut, which produces greater yields of high quality fruit than Butternut, were the only two All-America vegetable winners.

Horticultural Societies. Several hundred thousand Americans are members of the 50 federated state garden clubs. Special interest groups, such as the American Rose Society and the American Camellia Society, attract increasing numbers.

Professional horticulturists, who create and disseminate information on production of horticultural plants, are members of state, regional, national, and international societies. The American Society for Horticultural Science has 3,000 members, some from other countries. The International Society for Horticultural Science has 1,500 members in 33 countries and is affiliated with 130 organizations.

Sources of Information. Many garden centers and nurseries provide information on gardening and horticulture; however, the most accurate, up-to-date information can be obtained from the county agent's office or from the state extension horticulturist. Bulletins on production of fruits, nuts, vegetables, and ornamental plants are available from these

sources, as well as from horticulturists and landscape architects in private practice. Research by the agricultural experiment stations provides information on new varieties of fruits, vegetables, and ornamental plants, and on the production practices.

New Books. Rose fanciers will be interested in *The Pocket Encyclopedia of Roses,* by Henry Edland. Other books published in 1969 of interest to gardeners and homeowners include *Informal Gardening,* by B. Cory Kilvert, Jr.; *Anyone Can Have a Green Thumb,* by Alice DeWolf Pardee; and *Do's and Don't's of Home Landscape Design,* by Robert J. Stoffel.

DONALD W. NEWSOM
Louisiana State University

GARLAND, JUDY

U. S. singer and film star: b. Grand Rapids, Minn., June 10, 1922; d. London, England, June 22, 1969.

"There was always an underlying tragic feeling about Judy," said Sen. George Murphy, who had once co-starred with her in films. Perhaps it was for this reason that no other movie star's death in the past quarter-century was so mourned as was that of Judy Garland. The crowds lined up to pay their last respects were greater than any collected for a movie personality since the death of Rudolph Valentino. And in the newspapers, radio, and television, there were an unprecedented number of eulogies for the star who had died suddenly at the age of 47 from an overdose of sleeping pills.

The Legend. The "Garland legend" was born in films. Judy Garland probably introduced or revived more popular songs than any other singer in motion pictures. Yet at her death, she had not sung on the screen for more than six years, and had been forced to focus her energies on live performances, at which she developed a large and enthusiastic following.

She was not the prettiest of actresses, nor was her singing technically always the best. But her style and her radiant personality animated her work and more than compensated for any of her human deficiencies. Of the more than 30 films in which Judy Garland sang, her portrayal of the little girl Dorothy in *The Wizard of Oz* (1938) continues to remain memorable. The film earned her a special Oscar. Judy sang "Somewhere Over the Rainbow," and the song became her professional and personal theme.

Career. Judy was born Frances Gumm, the daughter of two vaudeville performers. In 1936, when she was 13, Judy made her film debut with Deanna Durbin in the MGM short, *Every Sunday*.

Miss Garland's movie career paralleled the hit songs of the day. Judy introduced "You Made Me Love You" in *Broadway Melody of 1938,* and in the same year she sang "Zing Went the Strings of My Heart" in *Listen Darling.* She costarred with Mickey Rooney in three Andy Hardy films and in *Babes in Arms* (1939), singing "I Cried for You." In 1942, Judy Garland's name was being billed before the title of the film *For Me and My Gal,* in which she sang the title song. Judy teamed with Mickey Rooney in *Girl Crazy* (1943), singing "I Got Rhythm" and "Embraceable You." One of her most memorable performances was as Esther Smith, the girl next door, in *Meet Me in St. Louis* (1944), in which she sang "The Trolley Song."

The Harvey Girls (1946) introduced "On the Atchison, Topeka and the Santa Fe," and *Till the Clouds Roll By* (1946) revived "Look for the Silver Lining." *Easter Parade* (1948) teamed Judy with Fred Astaire for the famous title song and the notable "We're a Couple of Swells" routine. In 1948, Judy rejoined Mickey Rooney in *Words and Music,* singing "Johnny One Note." In 1949 she sang "Meet Me Tonight in Dreamland" in the film *In The Good Old Summertime.* In *Summer Stock* (1950), Judy sang "Get Happy," and in *A Star is Born* (1954), she did her last big production number in films, the 18-minute "Born in a Trunk."

Misfortunes. Despite the many high points in her career, Judy Garland's personal life was plagued by misfortune. Her constant fight against overweight and psychological problems led her to an increasing dependency on drugs. Judy's marriages to composer-conductor David Rose, director Vincente Minnelli, producer Sidney Luft, and actor Mark Herron all ended in divorce. She was hospitalized several times for exhaustion or nervous breakdowns.

Her increasing unreliability led to her suspension from MGM in 1949. In June 1950, after unsuccessful tries at working on other films, Judy attempted suicide. She was released from her contract with MGM. Other Hollywood studios were reluctant to employ her.

Comeback. Judy Garland made a brilliant comeback to films in *A Star is Born* (1954), and appeared in two dramas, *Judgment at Nuremburg* (1961) and *A Child Is Waiting* (1963). Her last screen role was that of a lonely and sick singer in *I Could Go On Singing* (1962). From 1951, Judy had several successful singing engagements in London and New York, but she was tormented by illness and voice problems. Her last public appearance was a concert in London in early 1969.

Death. At her death, Judy Garland had been married to singer Mickey Deans for only three months. She left three children: Liza, born of her marriage to Vincente Minnelli, and Lorna and Joseph, born of her marriage to Sidney. Luft.

HOWARD SUBER
University of California, Los Angeles

GAS

The threat of coming shortages of natural gas supplies clouded an otherwise record-breaking year for the industry in the United States in 1969. New highs were reported in most operations.

Business Volume. Just over 900,000 new customers were added during the year, boosting the total to 41.5 million. Sales rose by 10.9 billion therms to 155.6 billion therms, while revenues increased from $8.8 billion in 1968 to $9.4 billion. The only apparent slowdown came in construction as the $3 billion outlay just about equalled the amount spent in 1968. Such expenditures added 32,000 miles to the pipelines, which now total 893,000 miles. Plant investment stood at $38 billion, up $2.4 billion.

Pricing. The gas industry long has blamed "area pricing"—by which the prevailing price in a given area became the fixed rate for all gas in that area—for the lack of drilling incentives and thus for

LEADING PRODUCERS OF NATURAL GAS
(Marketed production in cubic feet[1])

Country or state	1967
United States	18,171,360,000
Texas	7,189,000,000
Louisiana	5,717,000,000
Oklahoma	1,413,000,000
New Mexico	1,068,000,000
Kansas	872,000,000
USSR	5,560,090,000
Canada	1,697,960,000
Rumania	724,020,000
Mexico	572,910,000[2]
Italy	330,330,000
Venezuela	265,210,000
Netherlands	248,900,000
France	196,450,000
West Germany	172,050,000
Argentina	169,260,000
Hungary	86,340,000
Algeria	76,210,000
Japan	75,820,000[2]

[1] Excluding gas used for repressuring, as well as gas flared, vented, or otherwise wasted. [2] Estimate. Source: U. S. Department of the Interior, U. S. Bureau of Mines.

the growing shortness of supplies. In 1969 the industry received some relief as the Federal Power Commission recognized slightly higher prices for "new" gas as it is found.

Sources. The American Gas Association described threatened gas shortages as "short-term and localized in nature" and said that they "should not affect the long-range demand" through 1990 projections. It based its optimism on "the availability of natural gas, synthetic gas, or imports, including liquefied natural gas (LNG)."

Two major contracts for importing LNG from Libya were announced during 1969 as was a plan for bringing LNG from Venezuela to Philadelphia. However, economists doubted that the quoted low prices could be met, because of the need for building supertankers, liquefaction plants, and deepwater ports near markets.

Another possibility was the importing of natural gas from the North Slope of Alaska either by tanker or by a pipeline built to the upper Midwest.

Outlook. Stiffer air pollution controls are expected to increase the demand for natural gas. Other favorable factors include the rising popularity of total energy systems (on-site generators providing electricity and heating and cooling from natural gas) and also chilled/heated water service fueled by gas.

GENE SMITH
"The New York Times"

GENETICS

Advances in genetics during 1969 included the mapping of mammalian genes, the discovery of factors that regulate gene activity, the isolation of a single gene, and new analyses of the type of mutations involved in evolution. Three geneticists—Max Delbruck, Alfred D. Hershey, and Salvador E. Luria—were awarded the 1969 Nobel Prize in physiology or medicine (see NOBEL PRIZES).

Genetic Mapping. The discovery of segregation of chromosomes from somatic cell hybrids provides a new method for mapping the genes of humans and other mammals. One successful example of this method, developed by Howard Green and his colleagues at New York University, uses hybrid cells made by fusing a strain of human cells with a strain of mouse cells that lack a gene known as the TK gene. Unlike normal cells, cells lacking this gene are killed by a certain chemical. The first hybrid cells contained a full set of mouse chromosomes and variable numbers of human chromosomes. During the growth of the hybrid cells in cell culture, most of the human chromosomes were gradually lost, yielding cells that contained mostly mouse chromosomes. When these cells were allowed to grow in the presence of the toxic chemical that kills cells without the TK gene, the only cells that survived were those that retained that particular gene. When a hybrid cell line that contained only one human chromosome was obtained, this chromosome had to be the one carrying the TK gene.

E. Engle and B. J. McGee of Vanderbilt University and Henry Harris of Oxford University have extended studies of somatic cell hybrid genetics to include genetic recombination. Two mouse cell lines with different genetically-caused enzymatic defects were fused and the resulting hybrids contained all their chromosomes. If the defective genes are called *a* and *b*, and the normal genes are called *A* and *B*, the hybrids contained *a, b, A,* and *B* genes and, therefore, were not enzymatically defective. After prolonged growth and division in culture, the scientists isolated segregants that contained the single parental number of chromosomes. Some of these cells were recombinant for the *A* and *B* genes, each derived from a different parental line. The application of this method to many mutant cells lines will eventually permit the detailed genetic mapping of other mammalian cells.

Regulation of Gene Activity. Different genes are active at different times in the life cycles of many types of cells. For example, when a virulent bacterial virus infects its host, a strictly timed program of events is initiated. The genes determining the synthesis of special enzymes for viral reproduction become active in the first few minutes ("early genes"), while genes directing the synthesis of viral protein components are active later ("late genes"). This control is exerted directly on gene transcription into messenger RNA molecules.

Geneticists at Harvard and Rutgers universities have now shown that this selectivity resides partly in the enzyme RNA polymerase, which is responsible for messenger RNA synthesis on the DNA template. This enzyme can be fractioned into two protein parts: the core enzyme and the sigma factor. While the core enzyme itself is not active in transcribing viral genes, in combination with the sigma factor it is active on early viral genes but not on late ones. The late genes are probably transcribed only after the synthesis of a second factor.

Gene Isolation. In November, James Shapiro, Jonathan R. Beckwith, and their associates at Harvard Medical School reported the isolation of a single gene from the common intestinal bacterium *Escherichia coli.* The availability of this homogeneous DNA preparation will greatly facilitate the study of the biochemistry of gene regulation.

Mutations and Evolution. The Darwinian theory of evolution proposes the selection of organisms containing advantageous mutations and the elimination of organisms containing harmful ones. The extent to which a mutation confers a selective advantage depends on the organism's environment; it was predicted that the rates of evolution of various species evolving at different times and in different places would be unequal. But, the rates of evolution of the genes specifying the hemoglobins of many vertebrate species have been calculated and found to be nearly equal. This suggests that many mutations are selectively neutral since the rate of fixation of a neutral mutation into a population occurs by chance, independently of environmental conditions.

FRANK G. ROTHMAN
Brown University

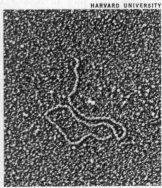

ISOLATION of a single gene was accomplished by Harvard University researchers Jonathan Beckwith (*seated*), James Shapiro (*left*), and Lawrence Eron. Gene is shown in micrograph below.

GEOGRAPHY

The changes that have characterized the teaching of geography and the work of geographers in recent years continued in 1969. Improved curricula and teaching methods in elementary and high schools made geography more popular and meaningful to pupils. At undergraduate and graduate schools, students and professors alike enjoyed broader study and research experiences. As a field of employment, geography offered growing opportunities in federal, state, and local agencies as well as in teaching and in private industry.

Geography in Education. In keeping with the spirit of the new geography, teachers of the subject continued to emphasize the "why's and wherefore's" of city locations, crop production, and world trade, as opposed to memorization of city names, crop production figures, or national and international commerce data. The High School Geography Project, begun by the Association of American Geographers in 1964, reflects the modern trends in geography. Conceived as a program to create new teaching techniques as well as textbooks and map materials, the project will provide a one-year course for 10th graders. The curriculum will permit pupils to play-act the roles of farmers, merchants, and others in textbook situations that simulate real-life conditions. Called *Geography in an Urban Age,* the project made substantial progress in 1969, publishing two text units during the year. The four remaining units, were scheduled for release in early 1970. The association also sponsors a commission on college geography.

The National Council for Geographic Education (NCGE), comprised chiefly of elementary and high school geography teachers, continued to be active in its various programs to upgrade curriculum content and instructional skills. Late in 1969 it sponsored the Media Institute in Geography with support from the U. S. Office of Education. The Media Institute, which met in Mexico, was designed to acquaint teachers with methods of field study and the concepts of communications that utilize newer media. This meeting was followed by the NCGE annual convention, whose theme was "Geographic Learning for the Future."

Geographers at Work. Geographers continued to study environmental sciences—such as geology, climatology, soils, and botany—in an attempt to relate these fields to man's welfare by gaining a better understanding of his relationship to the physical environment. New space-age techniques provided the geographer with data that led him to new concepts for analyzing crop productivity, adequacy of rainfall, and air and water pollution.

The success of programs developed by geographers to utilize geographic research data gathered by various means has given new impetus to geography studies. With support from the U. S. Department of the Interior and the National Aeronautics and Space Administration (NASA), and leadership provided by geography departments in several universities, new projects were initiated in 1969 to carry out experiments using remote sensing techniques and data as they apply to the analysis of spatial patterns of cities, urban growth, and transportation networks.

Federal agencies such as the State Department, the Department of the Interior, the Census Bureau, and various offices within the Department of Defense continued to seek geographers to assist in analyzing the impact of geographic factors on a variety of problems. Regional, state, and municipal planning agencies and publishing firms were among organizations offering positions in geography.

Activities of Organizations. Research and publishing activities were increased by geography organizations during 1969 as part of an effort to increase the contribution of geography to society.

The Association of American Geographers issued four papers—*Perspectives on Geomorphic Processes, Perception of Environment, Spatial Diffusion,* and *Computer-Assisted Instruction in Geography*—on themes designed to familiarize teachers of geography with the substance of various research fields. Financed by National Science Foundation funds, these monographs supplemented other periodic publications.

The National Council for Geographic Education began a newsletter, *Perspective,* for distribution to members. In addition, the council published the first of a planned series of yearbooks late in 1969.

The American Geographical Society carried on several long-term research projects, including studies in environmental perception, glaciology, theoretical cartography, and Antarctic mapping and research. Its monthly newsletter *Focus* continued to provide up-to-date and factual discussions of newly emerging nations and analyses of regions and subjects of current interest. Other publications of the society covered such wide-ranging topics as minority populations of New York City, shellfish of the North Sea, and natural resource potential of the Antarctic.

The National Geographic Society maintained its support of various programs of research and exploration and initiated projects on underwater life, astronomy, and archaeology. In addition to publishing the popular *National Geographic,* the society added five books, four television programs, and several maps to its program of activities. Its map depicting the floor of the Pacific Ocean was of special interest.

International Conference. The Pan American Institute of Geography and History held its quadrennial meeting in Washington, D. C., in June, 1969. An agency of the Organization of American States, with representatives from all the American republics, the institute includes among its members outstanding geographers and cartographers who, acting through several commissions, maintain continuing programs of research and study into problems that concern nations of the Americas.

Cartography. The complexities of modern life in civil and military areas continued to dictate a need for better cartographic products. Plans for new cities and highways require new maps; congestion of the airways requires improved charts for aircraft; and military operations of all kinds require a variety of both maps and charts.

The development of a technology to prepare maps and charts by automated methods, a project which promises to revolutionize cartography, continued to receive support. Part of the new technology of map-making incorporates visual displays on cathode ray tubes, with cartographic elements shown from data stored on magnetic tape and arranged by a computer. Despite such radical improvements, most map-making still relies on the geographer for background research and initial compilation.

J. WARREN NYSTROM
Association of American Geographers

GEOLOGY

Rocks as documents of geologic history were very much in the news in 1969. Astronauts of the Apollo missions returned with lunar rock and fine material said to be the most expensive substances ever gathered by man. (See also the special report on the Apollo flights, beginning on page 14.)

Moon Landing Sites. The landing site of Apollo 11 in Mare Tranquillitatis lies between rays of material ejected from the large but distant craters of Theophilus, Afraganus, and Tycho. A crater 200 feet (60 meters) from the landing site is about 14 feet (4.2 meters) deep and seems to reach solid bedrock; it is inferred that bedrock at the site is overlain by several feet of looser material. Lunar soil is cohesive enough to retain clear footprints. It has a specific gravity of 3.1, compared with about 2.7 for earth soil. While the Apollo 12 landing site in the Ocean of Storms appeared to be similar to the landing site of Apollo 11, the rocks gathered from the two sites are significantly different.

Lunar Sample. Rock fragments over one-half inch (1.3 cm) in diameter make up half of the Apollo 11 sample. Included are fine- and medium-grained crystalline, igneous rocks and consolidated breccias of complex history and composition. The most common minerals are clinopyroxene, olivine, plagioclase, ilmenite, and crystabolite. The major constituents are silicon, aluminum, titanium, iron, calcium and magnesium. By comparison with earth rocks there is a high concentration of titanium, zirconium, and yttrium. No hydrated minerals were found, indicating that water was not significant in the mineral- and rock-making processes. The Apollo 12 rocks contain less titanium and have more iron and nickel than the Apollo 11 rocks.

Much of the Apollo 11 sample resembles terrestrial olivine-bearing basalt, and could have solidified in the cooling phases of lava flows or lakes. The lava may have originated from earth-like volcanoes or by surface melting from massive impacts.

Glassy material, especially in small spheres, is surprisingly abundant in the Apollo 11 sample. The glassy spheres make up relatively large proportions of some breccias and are thought to have formed as molten material was ejected and cooled. The breccias appear to have formed from igneous rocks by successive shocks from falling meteorites. The Apollo 12 sample is almost completely void of breccias. That there are erosive processes at work on the moon is shown by the pitting and rounding of exposed surfaces of specimens. Impacts by fine particles are chiefly responsible for the pitting.

Several preliminary age determinations of the Apollo 11 sample indicate that the rocks are 3.8 billion to 4.6 billion years old. Other tests suggest that the material has been within a few feet of the surface for 20 to 60 million years. Preliminary tests on the Apollo 12 rocks indicate that they are a half-billion to a billion years younger than the Apollo 11 rocks. All indications are that lunar topography and rocks are very old and that much of the surface material may be much older than the oldest rocks known on earth.

Moonquakes. A special seismometer was left on the moon by Apollo 11 in hope of detecting disturbances such as "moonquakes," meteoritic impacts, and landslides. Only a number of minor vibrations —mostly thought to have been caused by sliding of loose material from crater walls—were recorded until a manmade moonquake was created during the Apollo 12 mission.

Mars. New information on the geology of Mars came with the signals from Mariner 6 and 7 spacecraft. The photographs show the "ice cap" with a sharp but irregular edge, numerous craters of all sizes, and areas of jumbled topography unlike anything on the earth or moon. The polar cap is thought to be composed of carbon dioxide crystals, and there is evidence that these are being drifted by atmospheric currents. (See also ASTRONOMY.)

Terrestrial Research. Meanwhile, important discoveries continued to be made on earth with respect to ocean basins, global tectonics, and continental drift. Expeditions sponsored by the JOIDES Deep Sea Drilling Project obtained information on sea-bottom geology. A project in the North Atlantic completed 12 holes and found that the sediments immediately above the basement rock show ages that increase linearly with increasing distance from the Mid-Atlantic Ridge. Another project completed 12 drilling sites between San Diego and Honolulu. Calcareous and siliceous sediments ranging from early Eocene to Pleistocene were found almost everywhere. Six sites were penetrated to sample the basaltic basement. Comparison of fossil ages and ages based on magnetic anomalies showed agreement.

Thirty-four holes at 17 sites were completed in a wide area of the western Pacific between Honolulu and Guam; one site was in water 19,622 feet (5,981 meters) deep. As expected, the age of sediments increased westward from the Pacific Rise, and samples as old as 140 million years (Jurassic Period of the Mesozoic) were found east of the Mariana-Bonin Islands and north of the Caroline Islands. Oceanic sediments this old are known from only one other spot, along the western Atlantic. Not expected was the finding of a large area of much younger sea bottom 20 to 50 million years old beneath the Phillipine Sea and near the Caroline Islands, indicating that the basaltic sea floor may form at places and by processes not associated with the oceanic ridges.

LUNAR ROCK specimen collected by crew of Apollo 11 went on display at Smithsonian Institution in September.

THE SMITHSONIAN INSTITUTION

GEORGIA'S GOVERNOR, Lester Maddox, unorthodoxly opened a 63-mile section of Interstate 285 in December. The road will bypass downtown Atlanta, allowing motorists to travel to Miami, Fla., unhindered by stoplights.

UPI

The jig-saw pieces of the ancient continent of Gondwanaland, broken apart and dispersed by continental drift, continued to be assembled. A good fit of Australia and Antarctica was achieved by computer analyses, placing the toe of Tasmania in the Ross Sea and the southwestern corner of Australia against Knox Coast. New fossil evidence establishing the former lining of the southern continents was found in Antarctica. (See also PALEONTOLOGY.)

W. LEE STOKES
University of Utah

GEORGIA

Taxes and schools were the major concerns in Georgia during 1969. Attention also was focused on the Atlanta mayoralty race and conservation issues.

Taxes and Legislation. Gov. Lester Maddox started the year by proposing a record $1.15 billion budget for fiscal 1970 and asking the 1969 General Assembly to pass $214 million in new taxes to support it. However, the lawmakers, most of whom were convinced a taxpayers' revolt was brewing, turned down the proposed personal income tax and sales tax hikes and passed their own $933 million budget. The governor called the legislators back into special session in June, but the Assembly promptly voted down his new tax proposals.

The legislature passed a model law providing a "Bill of Rights" for mental patients and a medical, rather than legal, commitment procedure.

Commissions were set up to revise Georgia's constitution and tax structure in time for action by the 1970 General Assembly.

Schools. Racial integration of schools continued to be a major issue in Georgia as the U. S. Justice Department selected the state for a first-in-the-nation suit to force state school officials to be responsible for total integration of schools. Some state officials welcomed the suit because it would take the matter out of the hands of the U. S. Department of Health, Education, and Welfare and would mean a resumption of federal funds cut off earlier for violations of HEW desegregation guidelines.

Governor Maddox and others, however, urged defiance of any "federal control" of schools. Maddox urged communities to build private schools and even contributed money towards construction of one. The federal suit against the state board of education did not come to court in 1969, but the decision on October 29 of the U. S. Supreme Court requiring immediate desegregation of Mississippi school districts was expected to be applicable to Georgia.

Sen. Herman Talmage toured Georgia schools in April and announced that he found hunger in them.

GEORGIA · Information Highlights

Area: 58,876 square miles (152,489 sq km).

Population: 4,548,000 (1968 est.).

Chief Cities (1968 est.): Atlanta, the capital, 515,000; Savannah, 134,000; Macon, 128,000; Columbus, 125,000.

Government: *Chief Officers*—governor, Lester G. Maddox (Democrat); lt. gov., George T. Smith (D); secy. of state, Ben W. Fortson, Jr. (D); atty. gen., Arthur K. Bolton (D); treas., Jack B. Ray; supt. of schools, Jack P. Nix; chief justice, William Henry Duckworth. *General Assembly*—Senate, 56 members (48 Democrats, 7 Republicans, 1 independent); House of Representatives, 195 members (171 D, 23 R, 1 independent).

Education: *School enrollment* (1968–69)—public elementary, 713,000 pupils (26,000 teachers); public secondary, 393,-000 pupils (16,800 teachers); nonpublic schools, 28,000 pupils (1,570 teachers); college and university (fall 1967), 98,476 students. *Public school expenditures* (1967–68)—$592,047,000 ($583 per pupil); average teacher's salary, $6,775.

Public Finance (fiscal year 1968): *Revenues*, $1,322,560,000 (general sales and gross receipts taxes, $271,227,000; motor fuel tax, $131,330,000; federal funds, $360,865,000). *Expenditures*, $1,298,891,000 (education, $270,749,000; health, welfare, and safety, $247,502,000; highways, $173,-470,000). *State debt*, $849,000,000 (Dec. 2, 1968).

Personal Income (1968): $12,705,000,000; average annual income per person, $2,781.

Public Assistance (fiscal year 1968–69): $120,728,191 to 263,109 recipients (aged, $55,022,202; dependent children, $41,469,389).

Labor Force (employed persons, August 1969): *Agricultural*, 95,600; *nonagricultural* (wage and salary earners), 1,506,-300 (31.6% manufacturing, 20.6% trade, 18.4% government). *Unemployed persons* (August 1969)—58,100.

Manufacturing (1965): *Value added by manufacture*, $4,060,-703,000 (transportation equipment, $700,417,000; food and products, $493,310,000; machinery, $212,903,000).

Agriculture (1967): *Cash farm income*, $1,110,938,000 (livestock, $576,209,000; crops, $456,904,000; govt. payments, $77,825,000). *Chief crops* (tons)—Peanuts, 487,560 (ranks 1st among the states); peaches, 72,000 (ranks 3d); pecans, 24,000 (ranks 2d).

Mining: *Production value*, $153,458,000. *Chief minerals* (tons) —Clays, 4,953,000; iron ore, 267,000.

Fisheries (1967): *Commercial catch*, 16,400,000 pounds ($3,700,000). *Leading species* (1966)—Hard blue crabs, 8,555,820 pounds ($324,767).

Transportation: *Roads* (1968), 97,427 miles (156,760 km); *motor vehicles* (1968), 2,488,918; *railroads* (1966), 5,519 track miles (8,882 km); *airports* (1968), 14.

Communications (1968): *Telephones*, 1,922,300; *television stations*, 23; *radio stations*, 224; *newspapers*, 33 (daily circulation, 1,005,599).

He introduced legislation in Congress to provide free food stamps and other measures to curb hunger.

Atlanta Election. A white Jewish mayor, Sam Massell, and a Negro vice mayor, Maynard Jackson, both considered liberal Democrats, were elected in Atlanta. Jackson, a lawyer, won a clear-cut majority in the regular October 2 balloting, but a run-off election was held on October 21 between Massell, the incumbent vice mayor, and his closest rival, Republican state legislator Rodney Cook.

The campaign was marked by charges that Massell used improper fund-raising techniques, and incumbent mayor Ivan Allen, himself a Democrat, asked Massell to withdraw from the race. Massell countered with charges of anti-semitism and claimed that his opponents were members of a business "power structure" trying to keep control of Atlanta.

Conservation. Plans to use a 700-acre site in rural Georgia as a dumping ground for nuclear waste were abandoned because of public protest. Conservationists also showed concern over watershed projects, stream and air pollution, proposed coastal mining and destruction of salt marshes. Tobacco heiress Mrs. R. J. Reynolds sold Sapelo Island to the state to be maintained in its natural condition.

Kidnapping. Gary Steven Krist and Ruth Eisemann-Schier were convicted in May in Decatur, Ga., of the 1968 kidnapping of Emory University coed Barbara Jane Mackle, buried alive for 80 hours while the kidnappers collected a $500,000 ransom.

GENE STEPHENS
The Atlanta "Constitution"

GERMAN LITERATURE

Most of the German literary works of 1969 were in the field of either prose fiction or literary scholarship and biographical studies.

Prose Fiction. The texts of Wolf Wondratschek's *Früher begann der Tag mit einer Schussewunde* are in a sense merely sketches or miniatures, each of which is not a representation of an action but a reflection of a situation or concept. Using questions, statements, and idiomatic expressions, the author concentrates on the power of single sentences to mirror a "world within itself." Manfred von Conta's *Der Totmacher* is in the form of the diary of a murderer relegated to a mental hospital. The central point of the novel is that in the story of this one mentally sick man the living conditions and personal relationships of a whole society are reflected.

An der Baumgrenze by Thomas Bernhard is a collection of three tales in which the psychic difficulties of each protagonist are projected into the external world creating an astonishing, confusing mixture of allegory and reality. In his epic novel *Murmeljagd,* Ulrich Becher describes an exile of only four weeks in Switzerland, but in doing so he outlines four centuries of Austrian life mirrored in a typically Austrian form of fiction combining the mystical with the wholly concrete realities of daily life. The basic characteristic of Günter Herburger's novel *Die Messe* might be described as an attempt to unite the German past with the still vivid "Auschwitz complex" in the lives of the Germans today.

In kaleidoscopic fashion G. F. Jonke portrays the life within a small village in his novel *Geometrischer Heimatsroman. Die Schattengrenze* by Dieter Wellershoff is the story of a man who becomes a criminal through the pressure and influences of the society in which he lives. Joachim Burkhardt's *Der Komödiant* is a simple and yet complicated story of a comedian whose real personality remains hidden behind his stage transformations.

Poetry. Rudolf Hagelstange's little volume *Der Krak in Prag—Ein Frühlingsmärchen* is basically a ballad, divided into 10 chapters, that bitterly censures totalitarianism in any form and wherever found. *Sensible Wege* is a collection of poems by Reiner Kunze in which conscious use of the dialectic of Bertolt Brecht is employed to explore in the form of decorative images a wholly "new land of poetry."

Theater. *Die Nachtwächter* by the Austrian writer Oskar Zemme is the drama of an embittered man who seeks revenge against his employer for having stolen his wife. *Kurzschluss,* by the Swiss dramatist Peter Zeindler, is a political-social critique of a society that could countenance the "misuse" of a murderer (by keeping alive within him the hope of escaping execution) only because his talents are useful to that very society. Artur Joseph's *Theater unter vier Augen: Gespräche mit Prominenten* is a collection of interviews with leading actors, dramatists, and producers from five countries.

Biography. *Wallenstein,* by Hellmut Diwald, is a sweeping depiction of the rise of Albrecht Wallenstein (1582–1684) to the position of one of Germany's leading military strategists and statesmen, his powerful influence on German history, and his tragic death. Eckart von Naso's *Caroline Schlegel—Dame Lucifer* is an artistic narrative of the heroine's life that not only relates facts but understandingly analyzes the subtle range of feelings of the heroine's soul. The special edition of the 5-volume collection *Genius der Deutschen: Die Grossen Dichter, Philosophen, Historiker,* edited by Hermann Heimpel, Theodor Heuss, and Benno Reifenberg (1966) is a work devoted to short biographies of the poets, philosophers, and historians who have decisively influenced the development of modern society. Karl Ludwig Schneider and Gerhard Burckhardt's documentary *Georg Heym—Dokumente zu seinem Leben und Werk* is the first comprehensive portrayal of the author's life and personality, a research effort based on his works and papers.

The value of Elisabeth Mangold's *Ottilie von Goethe* lies primarily in the information provided indirectly on the aged Goethe, much less so on Ottilie herself. The established myth of Goethe as the Olympian figure, aloof and difficult to live with, is here replaced by a more appealing characterization of a man very fond of his son August and his daughter-in-law Ottilie, and a genius who dearly loves his grandchildren and plays with them as any doting grandfather would.

Miscellany: Das Problem des Realismus bei Thomas Mann by Klaus-Jürgen Rothenberg is a study treating Thomas Mann's concepts of "reality" as depicted mainly in his novel *Die Buddenbrooks.* Rainer Gruenter's *Abschiede—16 Essays* is a volume of portraits, impressions and literary memoirs collected by the author on his travels through Europe. *Deutsch-Französische Vignetten* by Otto Rombach is a collection of short historical sketches on seemingly insignificant events which in the final analysis have proved more interesting than some world-shaking catastrophes. Among them are Marie Antoinette's journey from Vienna to Paris to marry the future Louis XVI, and Napoleon's murder of the Duke d'Enghien, who never did conspire against him.

RANDOLPH J. KLAWITER
University of Notre Dame

Willy Brandt, installed in 1969 as the first Socialist chancellor of West Germany, takes his seat in the Bundestag.

GAMMA-PIX

GERMANY

Throughout 1969 the two parts of divided Germany continued on their separate courses. The Federal Republic of Germany (West Germany) is a democratic, parliamentary republic and a member of such Western organizations as the North Atlantic Treaty Organization (NATO), the European Coal and Steel Community, and the European Economic Community (Common Market). The German Democratic Republic (East Germany) is for all practical purposes a Communist one-party dictatorship. It is affiliated with the Warsaw Pact and the Council for Mutual Economic Assistance (COMECON), the East European counterparts of NATO and the Common Market respectively.

Between these two states, West Berlin, a Western outpost within East Germany, maintains its precarious existence. Economically it is fully integrated into the Federal Republic, but politically it is a semiseparate entity. Militarily West Berlin remains under U. S., British, and French protection.

FEDERAL REPUBLIC OF GERMANY
(West Germany)

Until the parliamentary elections of September 28, West Germany was governed by a "grand coalition" government composed of members of the Christian Democratic Union (CDU) and the Social Democratic party (SPD). The CDU chairman Kurt Georg Kiesinger was its chancellor, and Willy Brandt, the SPD's chairman, its vice chancellor and foreign minister. Formed in December 1966 to fight a sharp economic recession, the government had accomplished this task so effectively that in 1969 its main concern was to check inflationary trends.

Presidential Election. President Heinrich Lübke, whose growing incapacity had been a matter of na-

WILLY BRANDT, the fourth chancellor of the Federal Republic of Germany, was sworn in on Oct. 21, 1969. He named a coalition cabinet of Social Democrats and Free Democrats, which excluded the Christian Democrats from power for the first time in the 20-year history of the Federal Republic. Since 1966, Brandt had been vice-chancellor and foreign minister in the coalition government.

Brandt was born in Lübeck on Dec. 18, 1913, became an active Socialist in high school. After Hitler's rise to power in 1933, he went to Norway, where he became a journalist. He moved to Sweden when the Germans occupied Norway in 1940. Returning to Germany after the war, he helped rebuild the Social Democratic party and held various political offices. As mayor of West Berlin from 1957 to 1966 he dealt effectively with crises and attained considerable popularity.

tional embarrassment for some time, agreed to resign his office a few months before the end of his second term. On March 5, the Federal Assembly, a special body, elected the Social Democrat Gustav Heinemann, minister of justice in the Kiesinger government, president by a narrow majority, 512 to 506.

Heinemann owed his victory over his Christian Democratic opponent, Defense Minister Gerhard Schröder, to the support of the Free Democratic party (FDP). The FDP, a small party in which staunch conservatives and old-line liberals predominated, had lost ground steadily for many years. Under a new chairman, Walter Scheel, a one-time small-business man, and with the counsel of Professor Ralf Dahrendorf, a leading sociologist, the party sought to attract new voters by assuming a more progressive stance. The backing of Heinemann was an application of this new strategy.

Parliamentary Elections. On September 28, at the end of the four-year term of the Bundestag, the

317

WEST GERMANY • Information Highlights

Area: 95,937 square miles (248,541 sq km).
Population: 58,015,000 (1968 est., excluding West Berlin).
Chief Cities (1966 census): Bonn, the capital, 140,482; Hamburg, 1,851,327; Munich, 1,231,458; Cologne, 861,027.
Government: *President*—Gustav Heinemann (took office July 1, 1969); *Chancellor*—Willy Brandt (took office Oct. 21, 1969). *Parliament*—Bundesrat (upper house), 45 members. Bundestag (lower house), 496 members (party seating, 1969: Christian Democratic Union, 242, Social Democratic party, 224; Free Democratic party, 30).
Religious Faiths: Evangelical Lutherans, 51% of population, Roman Catholics, 47.6%; others, 1.4%.
Education: *Literacy rate* (1969), 100% of population. *Total school enrollment* (1966)—11,982,610 (primary, 5,671,876; secondary, 3,781,436; technical/vocational, 2,122,467; university/higher, 406,831).
Finance (1967 est.): *Revenues*, $16,656,000,000; *expenditures*, $18,725,000,000; *public debt*, $10,872,500,000; *monetary unit*, Deutsche mark (3.6 Deutsche marks equal U. S.$1).
Gross National Product (1968): $132,250,000,000.
National Income (1968): $100,500,000,000.
Economic Indexes (1967): *Industrial production* (1968), 128 (1963=100); *agricultural production*, 105 (1963=100); *cost of living*, 111 (1963=100).
Manufacturing (metric tons, 1967): Crude steel, 36,744,000; gasoline, 11,555,000; beer, 71,342 hectoliters.

Crops (metric tons, 1967–68 crop year): Potatoes, 20,856,000 (ranks 3d among world producers); rye, 3,159,000 (world rank, 3d); sugar beets, 13,700,000.
Minerals (metric tons, 1967): Lignite, 96,768,000 (ranks 3d among world producers); potash (1966), 2,535,000 (world rank, 2d); barite (1968), 455,900 (world rank, 2d); feldspar, 314,642 (world rank, 1st); coal, 112,296,000 (world rank, 5th); iron ore, 6,780,000; crude petroleum, 7,932,000.
Foreign Trade (1968): *Exports*, $24,842,000,000 (chief exports, 1967: nonelectrical machinery, $4,952,200,000; transport equipment, $3,069,900,000; iron and steel, $1,758,700,000; textile yarn and fabrics, $832,200,000); *imports*, $20,-150,000,000 (chief imports, 1967: crude and partly refined petroleum, $1,164,000,000; fruit and vegetables, $1,160,500,000; nonelectrical machinery, $1,151,400,000). *Chief trading partners* (1967): France (took 12% of exports, supplied 12% of imports); United States (took 9% of exports, supplied 12% of imports); Netherlands.
Transportation: *Roads* (1966), 209,495 miles (337,140 km); *motor vehicles* (1967), 11,656,400 (automobiles, 10,764,-500); *railways* (1969), 22,022 miles (35,433 km); *merchant vessels* (1967), 886; *national airline*, The Deutsche Lufthansa AG; *principal airport*, Cologne.
Communications: .*Telephones* (1968): 10,321,281; *television stations* (1968), 143; *television sets* (1967), 13,806,000; *radios* (1967), 27,800,000; *newspapers* (1967), 423.

lower house of parliament, new elections were held. The SPD could point to an impressive record in the government. The Social Democrat Karl Schiller, as economics minister, had led the country out of the recession of 1966–67 into a period of renewed prosperity. The Social Democratic ministers of justice Gustav Heinemann and Horst Ehmke, Heinemann's successor, had initiated long-overdue legal reforms. Another Social Democrat, Transportation Minister George Leber, had improved badly snarled traffic conditions. And although Willy Brandt's foreign policy had run into impasses in both East and West, this was attributed to causes beyond his control. The party also was confident it had proven its "respectability" to middle-class voters traditionally suspicious of it.

Looking to the future, the SPD proposed tax reforms raising inheritance taxes and easing the tax burden of the low-income groups, profit sharing for workers and employees, improved city planning, and educational reforms providing better facilities and equal opportunities for all social strata. In foreign policy the SPD called for a more active policy in the East, and specifically for a rapprochement with East Germany and Poland. Pointing to its government record, the SPD proclaimed proudly that it had the right men to solve these issues.

The CDU tried to counter this strategy by maintaining that it was not individual ministers, but the chancellor who "counted." It sought to pit the handsome, patrician Kiesinger against plodding, colorless Willy Brandt. To the dismay of the CDU, however, the Kiesinger-Brandt confrontation quickly turned into one between Kiesinger and Schiller, the father of the nation's "second economic miracle."

Substantively, the CDU promised continued stability both at home and in foreign relations, and warned against any "experiments." Opposing the revaluation of the West German mark, CDU speakers stressed that they placed the national interest in a stable currency above rescue actions on behalf of foreign countries with "sickly currencies." The CDU too declared itself ready to seek an accommodation with eastern Europe but urged caution in view of the risks involved. It also called for a continuation of the policy of long-range economic planning and proposed "participatory wages" for workers.

The FDP advocated far-reaching political reforms, among them party primaries, referenda, and public sessions of parliamentary committees. It too came out for equality of opportunity in education and other liberalizing reforms. In foreign policy it was the most outspoken supporter of a more flexible attitude toward East Germany as well as eastern Europe.

The program of the rightist National Democratic party (NDP) was the only one to call for reunification, without saying, however, how this could be achieved. Catering to the expellees, it demanded the return of the lost territory east of the Oder-Neisse Line. The party supported the Common Market but opposed "international economic entanglements and foreign influences." While approving of NATO, it rejected the stationing of foreign troops on German soil. Farmers were to be aided but not subsidized. Apart from these ambiguities the NDP demanded popular presidential elections, greater powers for the federal government, and financial and educational reforms. But the main thrust of its propaganda was directed at the country's prosperity. It warned that

GUSTAV (WALTER) HEINEMANN succeeded Heinrich Lübke on July 1, 1969, as president of the Federal Republic of Germany. In his inaugural address he called for concerted efforts toward world peace. Heinemann, a Social Democrat, had been elected on March 5 with the aid of Free Democratic party votes over Christian Democratic candidate Gerhard Schröder. As minister of justice in Chancellor Kurt Kiesinger's "grand coalition" cabinet since 1966, he had promoted liberalization of the penal code, expansion of civil liberties, and continued prosecution of Nazi war criminals.

Heinemann was born in Schwelm, Westphalia, on July 23, 1899. After obtaining degrees in law and political science, he served as legal counsel and later as an executive of a steel company. During the Nazi era he was a leader of the anti-Hitler opposition in the German Protestant church. He was minister of the interior in Konrad Adenauer's first cabinet but resigned in 1950 in oppositon to the chancellor's rearmament policies.

this was a facade behind which German society was disintegrating, and it untiringly called for the restoration of discipline and authority.

Though there were few serious clashes, the campaign was not peaceful. Youthful leftist elements, known as the Extraparliamentary Opposition, staged numerous protest demonstrations against NPD meetings. There was also some interference with CDU and SPD gatherings; on two occasions Kiesinger was prevented from speaking. On the right, the Bavarian affiliate of the CDU and its chairman, federal Finance Minister Franz Josef Strauss, attracted attention by their inflammatory attacks on the SPD and the Extraparliamentary Opposition.

As is customary in West Germany, the great majority of the voters—86.8%—participated in the elections. Each voter cast two votes, one for a specific candidate in his electoral district (of which there were 248), and one for the party of his choice on a state list (each of the 10 states compiled such a list). The CDU obtained 242 seats, 121 in the direct district elections (as against 154 in 1965) and 121 seats on the state lists (91 in 1965). The SPD won a total of 224 seats, 127 direct mandates (94 in 1965) and 97 on state lists (108 in 1965). The FDP won no direct seats, but got 30 seats on the state lists (49 in 1965). It received 5.8% of the total state list vote (9.5% in 1965). This was barely enough to meet the minimum requirement of 5% for representation in the Bundestag. The NDP elected no direct candidates either and got only 4.3% of the state list vote.

The Brandt-Scheel Government. The SPD and FDP entered into a coalition, and a new government was formed in October with Willy Brandt as chancellor and Walter Scheel as vice chancellor and foreign minister. Karl Schiller remained minister of economics. The first major step taken by the new government was the revaluation of the currency. A few weeks later the government signed the nuclear nonproliferation treaty, after having received assurances from both the United States and the Soviet Union that it would be free to produce atomic energy for peaceful use. At year's end, however, the Bundestag had not ratified the treaty.

Economic Policy. Economics Minister Karl Schiller (SPD) tried to control price rises in 1969 by a policy of "concerted action" on the part of employers, workers, and government. Price and wage rises were to be kept to a minimum and correlated with each other. The policy, only partly successful, led Schiller to call for an upward revaluation of the currency. His expectation was that an increase in the price of the mark would lead to an increase of imports and a reduction of exports, making it easier to meet domestic demand.

The seriousness of the need for revaluation was debatable. The question became an issue in the election campaign in September: the Social Democrats supported Schiller's proposal, while the Christian Democrats pledged themselves not to "tamper" with the currency. At the height of the campaign wildcat strikes broke out among coal and steel workers who demanded wage increases in view of the increased profits of their industries. The strikes spread to textile plants and shipbuilding yards. They led to substantial wage increases, adding to the fears of imminent major inflation.

Once a new government led by the Social Democrats had been formed after the Bundestag elections, one of its first acts was to raise the price of the

NATIONAL DEMOCRATIC PARTY delegates gather at Schwabach for party day. The neo-Nazis made gains in early 1969 but fell below 5 percent in election vote.

mark by 9.3%, making one mark worth 27.3 U.S. cents, as against the previous 25 cents.

West Germany's farmers sharply attacked the measure. Under the monetary rules of the Common Market they would now receive less for their produce because Common Market farm prices are based on the dollar. The Bonn government hoped to provide some compensation for them, after obtaining the required approval of the other Market members.

Social Policy. Economic prosperity facilitated the enactment of several social reforms during 1969. Among them was a law providing for continued wage payments to blue-collar workers in case of sickness. A work furtherance law aimed at the prevention of unemployment by special training and retraining programs. Old age insurance was put on a sounder and less burdensome financial basis. These measures were taken within the framework of a "social budget" that was drawn up in accordance with the government's financial and economic projections for the next 15 years.

Federalism. The relationship between the federal government and the states, long a sensitive issue, was a source of new friction in 1969. In December 1968 the Bundestag had passed a bill that would give the federal government an increased share of tax revenues (the states receive 65% of all income and corporation taxes as well as the entire turnover tax). The bill also granted the federal authorities greater influence on regional planning and agricultural reforms. The Federal Council, the upper house of parliament, representing the states, rejected these proposals. Only a limited financial reform was carried out.

The Armed Forces. The status of the army within the nation was a matter of recurring concern. As one public opinion poll found, less than half of the population accepts the necessity of an army. Many doubted its military value, and others opposed it for political or ideological reasons. The most serious threat to the army resulted from the material attractions of civilian life. Compared to civilian comforts, the low pay, discipline, and physical hardships of military service had little appeal.

Industrial enterprises, moreover, hired away large numbers of technicians trained by the services as soon as they had fulfilled their military obligations. Some firms even paid stipends to trainees to keep them from reenlisting. For the armed forces this raised the problem of retaining an adequate number of skilled technical specialists.

Conscientious objectors increased in numbers. In West Germany refusal of military service on grounds of conscience is a constitutional right. It may be invoked not only before an individual is drafted but also while he is on active duty. In 1968, 3,500 soldiers out of 451,000 were certified as conscientious objectors. Although this was less than 1%, it was 1,000 more than during the entire preceding decade. Of those to be drafted, 1.09% claimed the right of conscientious objection.

Neo-Nazism. The National Democratic party (NDP), whose ideology bears some striking similarities to that of the Nazi party, appeared to be gaining further ground in the early part of the year, especially among younger people. One opinion poll claimed that 20 to 25% of the armed forces might be susceptible to NDP propaganda. In the parliamentary elections 11 of its candidates were servicemen, among them a naval captain.

The government considered asking the Federal Constitutional Court for a determination that the NDP was antidemocratic and hence unconstitutional, but in the end did not act. It never made clear whether it lacked adequate evidence to support such a charge or whether it thought it wiser to fight the party in the political rather than the legal arena. In the elections the NDP failed to gain the 5% vote required to make it eligible for representation in parliament. The defeat was ascribed to the country's prosperity, since the bulk of the NDP's followers, according to the opinion polls, supported the party primarily for economic reasons.

The Defregger Case. The issue of the Nazi past was revived in the case of Matthias Defregger, auxiliary bishop of Munich. In July the weekly *Der Spiegel* disclosed that Defregger, then a captain in the army, had, in 1944, passed on an order for the execution of 17 unarmed Italian civilians. The case had been investigated by the public prosecutor in Frankfurt but had been dropped on the grounds that no punishable crime had been committed.

Adding to the concern of many was the fact that Defregger had been promoted to his high ecclesias-

tical position although his involvement in the mass killings had been known to his superior, Julius Cardinal Döpfner. Defregger was relieved of his spiritual duties and his case reopened by the public prosecutor in Munich.

Foreign Affairs. With the possible exception of the West German-Soviet talks initiated in December, West German foreign policy could claim no major accomplishments during 1969. Differences with France were not notably eased by the resignation of French President Charles de Gaulle. Contrary to Bonn's hopes, Paris still was reluctant to invite Britain into the Common Market.

But West Germany remained eager to preserve its ties with the West. Among other measures, it resorted to revaluation—rather than increased taxation or other anti-inflationary measures—to ease the economic plight of Britain and France, both of which were badly in need of increased exports. The revaluation of the currency at a higher rate than expected was apparently also a measure taken in the interest of Bonn's Western allies.

During most of 1969 the hoped-for détente with the East was still blocked by the aftermath of the 1968 Czech crisis. For a time tension also increased over the holding of West Germany's presidential elections in West Berlin. Despite the political stalemate, however, the economic relations between the Federal Republic and both Soviet Russia and the East European countries kept expanding. Even so, they amounted only to 6% of West Germany's foreign trade.

On Dec. 7, 1969, the USSR suddenly announced that the following day it would begin negotiating with West Germany a pact renouncing the use or threat of force in mutual relations. The talks opened in Moscow between Soviet Foreign Minister Andrei A. Gromyko and the West German ambassador. Although West Germany had proposed renunciation-of-force pacts with East European countries in 1966, Moscow's acceptance followed a specific proposal made by the new Brandt government in November and was considered a promising step toward Brandt's goal of establishing better relations with the USSR and other Warsaw Pact nations.

RADIO TELESCOPE being built in Bad Münster/Eifel, near Euskirchen, is largest in the world. It will be used for observing quasars and radio galaxies.

WALTER ULBRICHT (*center*) and his wife, with party officials, respond to greeting of crowds celebrating May Day.

GERMAN DEMOCRATIC REPUBLIC
(East Germany)

In internal politics 1969 was an uneventful year for the German Democratic Republic (or, from the initials of its name in German, DDR). Walter Ulbricht continued as chairman of the Council of State and as first secretary of the Socialist Unity (Communist) party. Willi Stoph, a member of the party's Politburo, remained as minister president. The main event of the year was the 20th anniversary of the DDR on October 7. The day was the occasion of self-confident stock-taking and extensive statewide celebrations.

Economic Policy. Economic progress continued throughout the year. The DDR ranked as the second-largest producer in the Communist bloc and the eighth in the world. East Germany's living standard was the highest of all the Communist nations, including the Soviet Union. With continued emphasis on the production of capital goods, however, this standard still lay one third below that of West Germany.

The growth in productivity was due to many reasons, including the decentralization of economic decision-making; strong emphasis on efficiency, competitiveness, and profitability; and a more realistic assessment of capital assets and their depreciation. New investments were financed out of profits or through bank loans rather than by state subsidies. Similarly, bonuses and other incentives were correlated with plant turnover and profits. Later on, cooperation between universities and industrial enterprises was closely coordinated. Students were to work in the plants to get practical training, while the universities were asked to place greater emphasis on applied research.

The reforms led to a reformulation of Marxist-Leninist theory. The new profit-oriented socialist system that was being developed was no longer viewed as the first phase of communism that Marx and Engels had foreseen, but as a separate "socio-

WALTER (ERNST KARL) ULBRICHT, chairman of the Council of State and first secretary of the Socialist Unity (Communist) party of the German Democratic Republic, celebrated the 20th anniversary of the East German state in October by reaffirming its solidarity with the USSR. To West Germany's new Brandt government, he guardedly offered "good-neighborly relations."

Ulbricht was born in Leipzig on June 30, 1893. While still in his teens he became active in the Social Democratic party and the trade union movement. He helped found the German Communist party in 1919 and later served as a Communist member of the Reichstag. After Hitler's rise to power he went abroad and spent a number of years in the Soviet Union. Returning to Germany at the end of World War II, he helped establish the Socialist Unity party in the Soviet zone.

economic formation." It was defined as the "comprehensive development of socialism," intervening between the capitalist phase and communism. The advent of the Communist society, in which everyone would work according to his ability and receive according to his needs, with profits and special incentives no longer a consideration, thus was put off officially into the remote future.

Religious Developments. One of the few remaining links between East and West Germany, the United Evangelical Church, was dissolved in September. Yielding to increasing government pressure, a synod of the East German Protestant churches seceded from the all-German body. A new union, encompassing all East German Protestant churches, was formed. However, in a statute drawn up for the new organization, the synod reaffirmed the existence of "a special community of all Evangelical Christianity in Germany."

Foreign Policy. The DDR used many occasions in the course of the year to stress its cordial relations with the Soviet Union. Possibly it was eager

EAST GERMAN soldiers guard autobahn to Berlin. It was closed during West German presidential elections.

to counter rumors of friction between Moscow and East Berlin. There were indications of disagreement over policies to be adopted toward West Germany, with Moscow assuming a more flexible position. In the course of the year, East Germany was granted diplomatic recognition by several states, among them Iraq, Cambodia, Syria, and the United Arab Republic. In late September the government signed the nuclear nonproliferation pact.

EAST-WEST GERMAN RELATIONS

Trade between East and West Germany continued to grow in 1969. During the first half of the year the total volume amounted to $417 million, or a 26% increase over the first half of 1968. It

---

—— EAST GERMANY • Information Highlights ——

Area: 41,814 square miles (108,299 sq km).

Population: 16,002,000 (1968 est.).

Chief Cities (1966 census): East Berlin, the capital (1965 est.), 1,073,647; Leipzig, 595,712; Dresden, 507,470.

Government: *Chairman of the Council of State*—Walter Ulbricht (took office Sept. 12, 1960); *Minister President*—Willi Stoph (took office Sept. 24, 1964). *Parliament*—Volkskammer (People's Chamber), 500 members.

Religious Faiths: Protestants, 80% of population; Roman Catholics, 11%; others, 9%.

Education: *Literacy rate* (1969), 100% of population. *Total school enrollment* (1966)—3,501,256.

Finance (1965 est.): *Revenues,* $15,000,000,000; *expenditures,* $14,900,000,000; *monetary unit,* Ostmark (2.22 Ostmarks equal U. S.$1).

Gross National Product (1967): $45,585,585,500.

National Income (1967): $41,531,531,500; *average annual income per person,* $260.

Economic Indexes (1967): *Industrial production* (1968), 136 (1963=100); *cost of living* (1966), 100 (1963=100).

Manufacturing (metric tons, 1967): Cement, 7,188,000; crude steel, 4,644,000; gasoline, 1,852,000.

Crops (metric tons, 1967–68 crop year): Potatoes, 14,065,000; sugar beets, 6,948,000; wheat, 2,012,000; rye, 1,986,000.

Minerals (metric tons, 1967): Lignite, 242,028,000 (ranks 1st among world producers); lime (1966), 3,500,000; potash (1966), 2,000,000; coal, 1,788,000.

Foreign Trade (1967): *Exports,* $3,456,000,000 (chief exports, 1966: nonelectrical machinery, $159,000,000; transport equipment, $67,500,000; electrical machinery, $55,000,000; *imports,* $3,279,000,000. *Chief trading partners* (1967): USSR (took 41% of exports, supplied 43% of imports); Czechoslovakia (took 9% of exports, supplied 10% of imports); West Berlin.

Transportation: *Classified Roads* (1964), 28,291 miles (45,530 km); *motor vehicles* (1967), 1,157,800 (automobiles, 827,000); *railways* (1965), 9,232 miles (14,856 km).

Communications: *Telephones* (1968): 1,780,319; *television stations* (1968), 22; *television sets* (1968), 3,600,000; *radios* (1967), 5,874,000.

---

was expected to amount to $1 billion for the entire year, as against $725 million in 1968. One of the beneficiaries of this expansion was West Berlin, which got milk and other food deliveries from the surrounding East German countryside. Negotiations also got under way between the two German states on problems of improving postal services, road maintenance, and water transport.

There was as yet no similar political rapprochement between the Federal Republic and the DDR. Some small signs suggested, however, that a political détente might follow. Speaking of the East German state, West Germans now called it the DDR rather than the "so-called DDR." Similarly most of them referred to it geographically as "East Germany" rather than "Middle Germany," as they used to. The implication here was that the land east of the Oder-Neisse line was irretrievably lost. In fact, West Berlin's mayor, Klaus Schütz, called publicly for the recognition of the Oder-Neisse line as the boundary between Poland and the DDR.

On the other hand, the Bonn government disapproved formally of East Germany's diplomatic recognition by Iraq and Cambodia. Keisinger and other CDU spokesmen also denied any intention of recognizing the East German state or accepting the Oder-Neisse line. Yet in the West German election campaign all parties except the NDP proposed that the Bonn government take a more flexible attitude toward East Germany—the CDU less determinedly, though, than the SPD and FDP.

On taking over the government, Chancellor Brandt did not call for reunification. Nor did he claim the right for his government, as the only genuinely representative one, to speak for all Germans, East and West, as all of his predecessors had done. The post of "Minister for All-German Questions" in the Bonn government was renamed "Minister of Intra-German Relations." In his first address to the Bundestag, Brandt accepted the fact that two German states did exist. He added, however, that since both states were parts of one nation, an international recognition of the DDR was "out of the question." Instead, he proposed the establishment of relations "of a special nature."

The East German government, too, reiterated its interest in a normalization of relations with Bonn. Yet it insisted that there could be no such improvement until the DDR had been recognized as a sovereign state in accordance with international law. Ulbricht maintained that "international relations are entirely possible between sovereign states of the same nationality."

East Germany's reception of the Brandt government was notably friendlier than that accorded all earlier West German governments. The hope was expressed that the new government would act "realistically" and recognize the DDR, thus paving the way for better relations. In mid-December Ulbricht dispatched to Bonn a draft treaty providing for mutual international recognition and accepting the existing state borders. International recognition was considered imperative because of West German laws claiming jurisdiction over East German citizens (as "Germans"). These laws, East Berlin felt, would be invalidated only by the recognition of the DDR as a wholly separate state. In reply, Brandt proposed talks on all matters of common concern but also continued to oppose international recognition.

ANDREAS DORPALEN
The Ohio State University

GHANA

In 1969 a Constituent Assembly established a new constitution that returned Ghana to civilian government on October 1. The Progress party won a landslide victory in the August elections for the National Assembly. The party's leader, Kofi Busia, became Ghana's new prime minister.

Lt. Gen. Joseph A. Ankrah had resigned as Ghana's head of state in April 1969, after admitting that he had accepted money from a private company for political purposes. The National Liberation Council (NLC), which ruled Ghana until October 1, was then headed by Brigadier Akwasi A. Afrifa.

Constitutional Reform. In November 1968 an NLC decree established a Constituent Assembly to make recommendations for the new constitution. Of the Assembly's 150 members, 10 were appointed by the NLC and 140 were indirectly elected by district assemblies and occupational and student groups.

In meetings held from January 6 to August 22, the assembly approved the constitution and discussed the problems of promulgation, freedom of the press, and legal immunity for those who had participated in the 1966 NLC coup. Instead of a single president, a three-man presidential commission, to serve for three years, was established. The members of the commission are Brigadier Afrifa, Police Inspector General John W. K. Harlley, and Maj. Gen. A. K. Ocran, chief of the defense staff. The constitution was promulgated on August 22.

Election Results. With the convening of the Constituent Assembly, there was a renewal of political party activity, prohibited earlier by the NLC. Campaigning for the August 29 elections began officially on August 1. The election was generally seen as honest and efficient.

Four political parties emerged. The Progress party (PP), with its center of support in Ashanti, Brong-Ahafo, and the Central region, won a landslide victory of 105 out of 140 seats. The party was led by an opponent of former President Kwame Nkrumah, Kofi Busia, who became Ghana's new prime minister. The National Alliance of Liberals (NAL), with its strength in the Volta region, won 29 seats. Its leader was Komla Gbedemah, finance minister under Nkrumah. The People's Action party (PAP) won two seats, as did the United Nationalist party (UNP). A single seat was won by the All People's Republican party (APRP), and another by an independent.

After it assumed power on October 1, the National Assembly proceeded to set up committees and investigate the functioning of the various ministries. Busia's cabinet included many members carried over from the NLC government.

Labor Unrest. On March 3, four men died in riots in a strike against the Ashanti Goldfields Corporation. This was followed by a strike of 2,000 workers at the Ghana Rubber Estate in Abura. The Mills-Odoi Commission criticized the government in April for holding down wages in the "production sector" to avoid increasing public service pay.

Economy. Ghana's major creditors, including the United States, Britain, and West Germany, had agreed at a London meeting in October 1968 to let Ghana postpone payments on $360 million of medium- and long-term loans. Ghana will repay only 20% of the total due between 1969 and 1973, less than $24 million annually. Original payments would have exceeded 50% of annual export earnings.

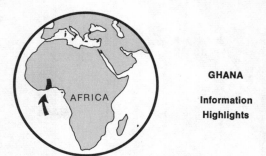

GHANA

Information Highlights

Area: 92,100 square miles (238,537 sq km).
Population: 8,376,000 (1968 est.).
Chief Cities (1966 census): Accra, the capital, 521,000; Kumasi, 249,200; Sekondi-Takoradi, 110,800.
Government: *Presidential Commission*—Akwasi A. Afrifa, John W. K. Harlley, A. K. Ocran (took office Aug. 22, 1969); *Prime Minister*—Kofi Busia (took office Oct. 1, 1969). *Legislature* (unicameral)—National Assembly, 140 members (party seating, 1969: Progress party, 105; National Alliance of Liberals, 29; People's Action party, 2; United Nationalist party, 2; All People's Republican party, 1; independent, 1).
Religious Faiths: Animists, 62% of population; Christians, 24%; Muslims, 14%.
Education: *Literacy rate* (1969), 25% of population. *Total school enrollment* (1965)—1,496,046 (primary, 1,145,488; secondary, 316,197; teacher-training, 15,144; vocational, 14,950; higher, 4,267).
Finance (1969 est.): *Revenues,* $340,000,000; *expenditures,* $285,000,000; *monetary unit,* new cedi (1.0204 new cedis equal U. S.$1).
Gross National Product (1968): $2,032,500,000.
National Income (1968): $1,799,294,000; *average annual income per person,* $214.
Economic Indexes: *Industrial production* (1968), 130 (1963= 100); *cost of living* (1967), 140 (1963=100).
Manufacturing (metric tons, 1967): Gasoline, 140,000; beer, 284,000 hectoliters; lumber, 346,000 cubic meters.
Crops (metric tons, 1967–68 crop year): Cacao beans, 421,200 (ranks 1st among world producers); cassava, 1,174,000; sorghum, 84,000; millet, 80,000.
Minerals (metric tons, 1967): Bauxite, 351,000; manganese ore, 239,200; salt, 36,000; diamonds, 2,537,000 carats; gold, 684,395 troy ounces.
Foreign Trade (1968): *Exports,* $307,000,000 (chief exports, 1967: cacao, $128,000,000; wood, $22,266,000); *imports,* $308,000,000 (chief imports, 1967: textile yarn and fabrics, $28,710,000; nonelectrical machinery, $28,050,000). *Chief trading partners* (1967): Britain (took 21% of exports, supplied 30% of imports); United States; West Germany.
Transportation (1967): *Roads,* 20,629 miles (33,198 km); *motor vehicles,* 48,000 (automobiles 29,200); *railways,* 790 miles (1,271 km); *merchant vessels,* 14; *national airline,* Ghana Airways Corporation; *principal airport,* Accra.
Communications: *Telephones* (1968): 37,225; *television stations* (1967), 4; *television sets* (1968), 5,000; *radios* (1966), 555,000; *newspapers* (1966), 4.

On January 24 Lonrho, a London-based holding company, signed a 50-year lease on the Obuasi goldmine and took over operations from the Ashanti Goldfields Corporation. It issued to the government 20% of the Ashanti shares it had purchased, with an option to buy a further 20%.

Plans were made for a high-tension transmission line from the Akosombo power station to Togo and Dahomey. In the future, the station may expand its capacity to become the center of a wide-ranging West African power network.

Foreign Relations. On February 26 the captains of two Soviet trawlers seized in October 1968 were charged with violation of Ghana's territorial waters. Trey were fined $190 each, and their crews and ships were released.

C. DIANE CHRISTENSEN
Columbia University

GIBRALTAR. See COMMONWEALTH OF NATIONS.
GORTON, John. See biographical sketch under AUSTRALIA.
GOLD. See INTERNATIONAL FINANCE.
GOLF. See SPORTS.
GRAINS. See AGRICULTURE.

GREAT BRITAIN

PRINCE CHARLES (*right*) was invested as Prince of Wales on July 1 by his mother, Queen Elizabeth, at Caernarvon Castle (*facing page*).

CENTRAL PRESS, FROM PICTORIAL PARADE

Britons made history in a modest way in 1969 by reversing throughout the latter half of the year the deficit in their balance of payments. In some other respects, however, history returned to haunt them. In Northern Ireland ancient enmities between Protestants and Roman Catholics, which had provoked minor disturbances in 1968, led to more serious fighting and, ultimately, to British military intervention in the province. In Wales renascent Welsh nationalism briefly threatened to upset Prince Charles' investiture as Prince of Wales, and in Nigeria secessionist Biafra's continued armed resistance to central government control posed agonizing choices for Britain, which as colonial overseer had designed the Nigerian federal state.

ECONOMY AND LABOR

Throughout 1969 the government continued its policy of maximizing the benefits of the 1967 devaluation of the pound by attempting to limit consumption—and thus imports—and by supporting an export drive. Chancellor of the Exchequer Roy Jenkins' intention of achieving a permanent, substantial balance of payments surplus was repeatedly defended as the only means of facilitating economic growth and thereby making possible significant long-term increases in expenditure on the social services.

Balance of Payments. Britain began the year with an inherited balance of payments deficit for the last quarter of 1968 of £80 million a month on current account (all goods and services) and a monthly trade gap (excess of imports over exports) of £55 million. By April the quarterly payments deficit had been reduced to a monthly average of £20 million, and by July the monthly trade gap was down to £28 million. The July-September

PRINCE CHARLES (PHILIP ARTHUR GEORGE WINDSOR), oldest son of Queen Elizabeth II of Britain and of Prince Philip, Duke of Edinburgh, was formally invested as Prince of Wales at Caernarvon Castle on July 1, 1969. Charles, who became heir apparent to the British crown when his mother ascended the throne in 1952, has been prime regent-designate and head of the six councillors of state since his 18th birthday in 1966. He was installed as a Knight of the Garter on June 17, 1968.

Charles was born on November 14, 1948, at Buckingham Palace in London. He received his early schooling at the palace, at the Cheam School, and at Gordonstoun, an austere preparatary school in Scotland. Since 1967 he has been a student at Trinity College, Cambridge, where he studied anthropology in his first year and changed to a history major in the second year.

figures revealed a trade surplus of £26 million a month and also the fact that Britain had had a payments surplus since May—the first time since the formation of the Labour government in 1964 that a payments surplus had been maintained for four consecutive months. By November some analysts at home and abroad were predicting that the government would achieve its goal of a £270 million net payments surplus for the year ending March 31, 1970.

The government regarded these trends as a vindication of its economic policies but emphasized that it will still too early to relax economic restrictions. It noted that imports had not fallen to the level expected after devaluation, and that exports could be increased further. It showed its unwillingness to be content with current progress in several ways.

Area: 93,605 square miles (242,437 sq km).

Population: 55,283,000 (1968 est.).

Chief Cities (1966 census); London, the capital (metropolitan area) 7,913,600; Manchester, 2,453,450; Birmingham, 2,437,060; Liverpool, 1,373,120.

Government: *Queen*—Elizabeth II (acceded Feb. 6, 1952); *Prime Minister*—Harold Wilson (took office Oct. 16, 1964). *Parliament*—House of Commons, 630 members (party seating, 1970: Labour, 347; Conservative, 262; Liberal, 13; others, 6; vacancies, 2). House of Lords, 975 members.

Religious Faiths: Anglicans, 55% of population; Roman Catholics, 8%; Presbyterians, 3%; Methodists, 2%.

Education: *Total school enrollment* (1965)—9,519,919 (primary, 4,620,262; secondary, 3,146,349; technical/vocational, 1,531,667; university/higher, 231,641).

Finance (1967 est.): *Revenues,* $30,566,000,000; *expenditures,* $29,345,000,000; *public debt* (1965) $85,235,000,000; *monetary unit,* pound (.4194 pound equal U. S.$1).

Gross National Product (1968): $100,143,000,000.

National Income (1968): $78,922,260,000; *average annual income per person,* $1,427.

Economic Indexes (1967): *Industrial production* (1968), 120 (1963=100); *agricultural production,* 113 (1963=100); *cost of living,* 115 (1963=100).

Manufacturing (metric tons, 1967): Crude steel, 24,276,000; cement, 17,892,000; gasoline, 9,034,000; wheat flour, 3,708,000; meat, 2,170,800; plastics and resins, 1,108,800; sugar, 974,000.

Crops (metric tons, 1967–68 crop year): Barley, 9,391,000 (ranks 2d among world producers); potatoes, 7,201,000; sugar beets, 6,880,000; wheat, 3,898,000; oats, 1,362,000; apples, 308,000.

Minerals (metric tons, 1967): Coal, 174,898,000 (ranks 2d among world producers); salt, 7,095,000; gypsum and anhydrite (1966), 4,358,000; iron ore, 3,624,000; fluorspar (1966), 185,000; barite (1966), 31,000.

Foreign Trade (1968): *Exports,* $14,838,000,000 (chief exports, 1967: nonelectrical machinery, $2,469,500,000; motor vehicles, $1,246,440,000; electrical machinery, $822,240,000; textile yarn and fabrics, $596,850,000); *Imports,* $18,410,000,000 (chief imports, 1967: nonelectrical machinery, $1,220,520,000; crude and partly refined petroleum, $1,165,850,000; nonferrous metals, $907,000,000). *Chief trading partners* (1967): United States (took 12% of exports, supplied 13% of imports); Canada (took 4% of exports, supplied 7% of imports); West Germany (took 5% of exports, supplied 5% of imports).

Transportation: *Roads* (1969), 201,023 miles (323,506 km); *motor vehicles* (1967), 12,199,900 (automobiles, 10,426,100); *railways* (1969), 15,319 miles (24,648 km); *merchant vessels* (1967), 1,903 (20,005,000 gross registered tons); *national airlines,* BOAC, BEA; *principal airport,* London.

Communications: *Telephones* (1968): 12,099,000; *television stations* (1968), 137; *television sets* (1968), 15,200,000; *radios* (1967), 17,493,000; *newspapers* (1966), 106 (daily circulation, 26,700,000).

In February the government's concern over the high level of personal consumption led to an increase from 7% to 8% in the bank rate, the basic lending rate to established financial institutions. In June, £417 million of credit was negotiated on a standby basis with the International Monetary Fund; and in his "letter of intent" to the fund, Jenkins

PRIME MINISTER WILSON, in May 5 speech, announced his determination to stay in office despite rumors of a revolt against his leadership within the Labour party.

reiterated his long-range goal of a regular payments surplus of £300 million a year and his determination to continue domestic restrictions to that end.

In his April budget the chancellor announced increases in the selective employment levy and in taxes on estate duties, corporation income, gasoline, wines, and betting. On the other hand, old age pensions and income tax allowances were increased. The chancellor expected economic growth in 1969–70 to be about 3.5%.

The attitude of cautious optimism about the long run and determination to pursue restraint in the short run was reinforced during the summer, when devaluation of the French franc had no serious repercussions on sterling. Nevertheless, the government announced increased charges for state provision of dentures and eye glasses.

Labor Reform. As it had previously, the government's policy of restraint encountered serious opposition, especially from the labor unions. Since 1964 the government has regarded the frequency of strikes—particularly of wildcat strikes—as a major obstacle to its aims. Furthermore, insofar as strikes are successful in winning wage increases, the government sees them as having inflationary consequences. It regards the number of man-hours lost by strikes as a serious brake on productivity and, therefore, on increases in exports.

The conflict between the government's restrictions and the unions' opposition came to a head over government proposals to tackle the strike problem. In January the government published *In Place of Strife,* a White Paper that recommended the creation of an industrial relations commission and the vesting of new powers in the secretary of state for employment and productivity (Barbara Castle). It proposed that the secretary be empowered to order a 28-day "conciliation pause" before strike action, and in some circumstances, to order a ballot of union members before strikes could occur. Proposed penalties for breach of the secretary's rulings included levying fines and attaching workers' earnings.

The commission was duly established, but the unions opposed the suggested power to fine strikers. In June the unions proposed their own machinery for dealing with strikes. Notwithstanding repeated assurances that it would proceed with a bill to create the regulatory powers proposed in the White Paper,

QUEEN ELIZABETH and Prince Philip chat with President Nixon before luncheon for the President at Buckingham Palace on February 25.

the government ultimately gave way and accepted the union's own machinery as a substitute.

In December the unions' opposition to legal restrictions on wage bargaining was rekindled by Mrs. Castle's announcement that she proposed to reactivate her powers to order delays in wage and price increases, as provided by the prices and incomes act of 1965. Although the government stated that its ultimate aim was the replacement of legal by voluntary controls, it emphasized that it had no intention of allowing a "wages and prices free-for-all" to destroy the gains of recent years.

Postal and Other Reforms. In July the post office was transformed from a government department into a public corporation designed to increase the flexibility and efficiency of postal and wire communications. The queen's speech at the opening of Parliament in October promised legislation on industrial relations, equal pay for women, the reorganization of seaports, and the merging of the prices and incomes board with the monopolies commission. The last proposal is part of a program to rationalize the government machinery that deals with the related problems of prices and incomes and the structure of industry.

CIVIL RIGHTS AND SOCIAL WELFARE

In the area of social affairs the conflict between Protestants and Roman Catholics in Northern Ireland dominated the headlines. However, important steps were taken by the government to protect the rights of colored minorities, and it advanced proposals for changing the structure of Britain's welfare state.

Northern Ireland. The unrest in Northern Ireland that began in 1968 was accompanied by allegations that the Unionist (Protestant) government there practiced discrimination against Roman Catholics—mainly in the fields of housing and civil rights. In January violent clashes between Protestant extremists and militant civil rights supporters were renewed. Prime Minister Terrence O'Neill repeated his intention of introducing reforms while maintaining law and order.

A general election held in Northern Ireland in February confirmed the Unionists in office but revealed deep rifts in the governing party. O'Neill won a vote of confidence after the election but suf-

fered a serious reversal in March when violence again was renewed. In April, following the sharp clashes between Protestants and civil rights supporters, Bernadette Devlin, a 21-year-old Irish Catholic, was returned as a pro-civil rights member of Parliament for the former Conservative-Unionist seat of Mid-Ulster. At the same time the British government made troops available to guard public installations in Northern Ireland.

At the end of April, O'Neill resigned as prime minister after his Unionist colleagues had refused him the support necessary to implement the reforms on which the party had agreed. He was succeeded by James D. Chichester-Clark, who was regarded as more likely than O'Neill to unite the Unionists behind a policy of reform.

In August rioting was renewed in Londonderry and Belfast, and the British government sent in more troops to preserve order. The tendency was for the British government to take over ultimate responsibility for security and for domestic policy in Northern Ireland to be determined in close consultation with the British government. Britain thus was acting to ensure the basis of financial and military stability on which social and constitutional reforms could be built in an orderly way.

Minority Rights and Income Maintenance. In immigration policy the government continued its established practices of tightening controls on further immigration while extending the rights of immigrant Britons and ensuring that existing controls on discrimination are fairly administered. In January the government announced that males from the Commonwealth no longer would be allowed to enter Britain solely in order to marry and settle there, regardless of the place of origin of the woman concerned. On the other hand, in May it passed the immigration appeals act, extending the facilities open to Commonwealth citizens to appeal immigration and deportation rulings.

Early in the year the government also publicly reconsidered its position on social security. In January it published a White Paper outlining its proposals for the future of national insurance. The proposals, accepted in principle by the Commons in March, represent an extension of Labour's policy of relating state pension benefits more closely to individual earnings, in order to lessen the likelihood

BRITISH TROOPS patrol riot-torn streets of Belfast (*left*). Bernadette Devlin (*above*), youngest member of Parliament, addresses crowd at Bogside, Londonderry.

of a sharp drop in income when an individual retires from work. Because contributions, as well as benefits, are to be related to earnings, the scheme is another example of the extent to which Britain is moving away from the idea of a welfare state based on flat-rate contributions and benefits.

Education. In May the Open University, first proposed in 1966, received its royal charter. The university is designed to extend the facilities for university-level education beyond the institutions and clientele already served. Courses at the Open University will be based on television tuition, supplemented by correspondence courses and teaching centers in various localities.

That the government's plans to introduce the comprehensive principle into British secondary edu-

cation are coming to meet with resistance from a number of local authorities was evident in the queen's speech in October. The government announced its intention to introduce legislation to enable it to compel all local authorities to introduce schemes for comprehensive education.

POLITICS AND GOVERNMENT

In November 1968 the government had announced its intention of reforming the composition of the House of Lords by a bill designed in the long run to deprive hereditary peers of their voting rights. A long campaign against the bill by an unusual combination of Labour left-wingers and Conservative right-wingers had resulted in the government's dropping the bill in April. Ironically, the government had withdrawn the bill in order to allow time for debate on the industrial relations bill, which was dropped, in turn, as a result of opposition from elements in the Labour party and the labor unions.

In April a representation of the people act lowered the voting age from 21 to 18. The new law will be in effect at the next general election.

Local Government and Districting. In June the Redcliffe-Maud report on local government was published and received favorably by the government. The report recommended amalgamating and rationalizing local authorities in England and Wales—reforms that already have been implemented in some large urban areas, including London. Specifically, it recommended a new structure comprising (for all areas except London) eight "provincial councils" and, under them, 61 new local government areas.

The Redcliffe-Maud proposals also had implications for the boundaries of parliamentary constituencies, the revision of which has brought the government a good deal of political trouble. The home secretary, James Callaghan, announced in June that the independent boundary commissioners, who study electoral districting, would propose sweeping changes in existing constituency boundaries. The home secretary urged that, because the Redcliffe-Maud report involved changes in existing local boundaries, the government would prefer to postpone action on parliamentary boundaries until it had introduced its legislation to implement local government reform. Both parliamentary and local changes could then be introduced at the same time, he said.

The home secretary's attempt thereby to release the government from its obligations to act on the boundary commission's recommendations was opposed by the House of Lords. The government was accused by its opponents of trying to postpone boundary changes of parliamentary districts until after the next general election, since changes proposed by the commission would work to the advantage of the Conservatives. In November the home secretary announced his intention of submitting the recommended changes to the Commons (as required by law) but of invoking the Labour party machinery so as to ensure their defeat. This maneuver clearly was designed to achieve the result that the next general election would be fought on the constituency boundaries in force at the last one.

The Cabinet. In October, Prime Minister Wilson continued regrouping the government departments into a small number of "super ministers." The ministry of technology, under Anthony Wedgwood Benn, extended its functions to cover public power, some of the functions formerly exercised by the board of trade, and most of the functions formerly exercised by the department of economic affairs. A new ministry of local government and regional planning was created, covering the ministries of housing and transport. As a result, some ministries, such as transport, were effectively demoted to the status of subministries, while others, such as the department of economic affairs, ceased to exist.

The changes reflect Wilson's determination to introduce a two-tier system of administration, with a small number of "general" ministers presiding over a large number of small departments, the former organized along such general functional lines as technology, regional planning, and social services.

Party Politics and Elections. Although the government received less criticism on some issues—most notably on immigration—in 1969 than it had in 1968, and although the balance of payments surplus appeared to vindicate its economic policies, its political and electoral difficulties tended to increase. Criticism by the labor unions and the Labour party's left wing of the restrictions involved in the government's economic policies continued unabated and resulted in the government's dropping the industrial relations bill. Its subsequent failure to enact its proposals to reform the Lords combined with its difficulties over electoral boundary changes to produce a year in which back-bench members of Parliament were unusually successful in thwarting the leadership.

Any new hopes of entering the Common Market that the resignation of French President Charles de Gaulle had raised were limited in impact by a perceptible swing in political and public opinion in both major parties against joining. Both Labour and Conservative elements also heatedly opposed the government's policy of supplying arms to federal

Nigeria, and the Mylai massacre revived opposition to British support of U. S. policies in Vietnam.

Within the Labour party, the increasing discontent of labor union elements and the left-wing was accompanied by a consolidation of the position of importance held by the party's "intellectual right." Former "Gaitskellites," such as Denis Healey, Roy Jenkins, and Anthony Crosland, increased their influence, while left-wing leaders, such as Mrs. Castle, suffered from their identification with anti-union policies. Wilson's position tended to vary in relation to the condition of the party as a whole.

The Conservative party, meanwhile, devoted itself increasingly to maintaining unity, on the assumption that the next general election would be held in 1970 and that the Conservatives would win it. Their leads in the opinion polls, however, were substantially reduced.

Labour suffered severe losses in the municipal elections in May. It also sustained considerable damage, and adverse voting swings averaging almost 10%, in the 13 by-elections held during the year. Much of this pattern, however, seems to have been due to Labour abstentions rather than positive conversions of votes to the Conservatives, and Edward Heath, the Conservative leader, failed to keep up with his party in the popularity ratings.

Royal Family. Queen Elizabeth and Prince Philip made only one state visit abroad in 1969—to Vienna, Austria, in May. However, while traveling unofficially in the United States, the prince stirred up a mild controversy by stating that Parliament's financial grant toward royal expenses had failed to keep pace with increases in the cost of living. The government indicated its intention to review the machinery of the royal grant.

In April, Prince Charles began a 9-week term at the University College of Wales in Aberystwyth preparatory to his investiture as Prince of Wales. The investiture took place in Caernarvon on July 1, after several incidents. In one, two Welshmen accidentally killed themselves with their own bomb.

FOREIGN AFFAIRS

In the field of foreign affairs, Britain continued to play a moderating role in the politics of the major powers. It played a more forceful role, including, in one case, direct military intervention, in Commonwealth areas.

Mutual Defense. In February, Denis Healey, the secretary of state for defense, presented a White Paper in which he revealed that since coming into office in 1964 the Labour government had cut annual defense expenditures by $2 million. In the ensuing Parliamentary debate, Healey reiterated his view that Britain's mutual defense commitments were primarily in NATO and announced increased contributions to that organization. The potential weaknesses of NATO clearly were worrying the government, however, and were among the topics discussed with President Nixon during his visit in February and, again, during Wilson's visit to Bonn in the same month.

Some of the economies stressed by Healey have resulted from Britain's decision to withdraw from military positions east of Suez by 1971. In June, Britain met with representatives from Australia, Malaysia, Singapore, and New Zealand to discuss the issues raised by the withdrawal. The British refused to reconsider either the decision or the projected date for withdrawal but offered assistance in increasing the ability of the countries affected to make their own defense arrangements.

Europe. Franco-British relations were strained in February as a result of the "Soames affair." Christopher Soames, the British ambassador in Paris, was called for talks with President de Gaulle, at which, the British alleged, de Gaulle envisaged a looser European organization than the European Economic Community (EEC). It would be controlled by Italy, France, Britain, and West Germany and would act independently of NATO and the United States, they said. The government appears to have suspected a trap and, in order to prevent the French from using British interest in such a proposal as evidence of a basic lack of sympathy with the existing EEC, leaked the content of the talks to France's Common Market partners. The French government denied the British interpretation.

De Gaulle's resignation in April revived hopes that Britain's entry into the "Six" might be possible, especially as the new West German chancellor, Willy Brandt, appeared very favorably inclined. New initiatives were made by the West Germans and others at a meeting of the "Six" in November. The French appeared accommodating but cautious. The British government reaffirmed its desire to join the EEC but denied that there was either serious urgency or any need to appear in the role of supplicant.

Communist Countries. The Soviet Union's determination to use Gerald Brooke—a Briton imprisoned in Russia in July 1965 for "subversive activi-

ties"—as a lever to gain concessions for pro-Soviet spies imprisoned in Britain reached a crisis in the late spring. Rumors that Brooke was to be tried on even more serious charges led to British agreement, in July, that he be exchanged for Peter and Helen Kroger, two agents arrested in Britain for passing British naval secrets to the Soviets in 1961. Brooke arrived home in July, and the Krogers flew east in October. Also in October the Chinese People's Republic released Anthony Grey, a British newsman arrested in Peking in July 1967 in retaliation for Britain's seizure of Chinese nationals during disturbances in Hong Kong.

Africa. The Commonwealth prime ministers' conference met in London in January against a background of failure to settle outstanding differences with Rhodesia and continuing civil war in Nigeria. The communiqué at the end of the conference admitted that the Afro-Asian prime ministers had failed to reach any substantive agreement with Britain over Rhodesia.

In May, Ian Smith, the Rhodesian prime minister, announced that he had given up hope of reaching a settlement with Britain and that a referendum would be held in June on a new constitution to convert Rhodesia into a republic. The referendum resulted in an 81% majority in favor of a republic, and the British government, while maintaining its view that the Smith government's declaration of independence was illegal, recalled the British governor of Rhodesia, Sir Humphrey Gibbs.

Britain meanwhile continued its policy of supplying arms to the Nigerian federal forces for use against secessionist Biafra. The government argued that its arms policy increased the likelihood of Britain's being able to guide the Nigerian government toward a peaceful settlement, and in the short run, of its being able to influence both sides to facilitate international efforts to fly food and medicine into Biafra. Wilson visited Lagos in March.

Gibraltar. The government continued to resist Spanish attempts to force Britain to cede Gibraltar to Spain. In May it granted Gibraltar a new constitution, which conferred dominion status. The former colony was given an assurance that Britain would make no change in the sovereignty of Gibraltar except by act of Parliament—in effect, an assurance that Britain had no intention of altering the position of Gibraltar by executive agreements.

The Spanish government regarded the new constitution as inconsistent with both the Treaty of Utrecht (1713) and recent UN resolutions. It continued its efforts to isolate Gibraltar from the Spanish mainland.

Anguilla. In March the British foreign secretary, Michael Stewart, announced that British troops had taken control of Anguilla, a former British colony in the Caribbean that had broken away from the St. Kitts-Nevis-Anguilla Federation. The government took the position that intervention was necessary to prevent Anguilla from falling under the control of a small armed minority. Ronald Webster, the selfstyled president of Anguilla, demanded the removal of the British troops. The troops were withdrawn in September, after talks between the British government and the Anguillans on such questions as economic development and internal security.

(See also COMMONWEALTH OF NATIONS; WILSON, HAROLD.)

A. J. BEATTIE
London School of Economics

NEW LUXURY LINER, *Queen Elizabeth 2*, returns to Southampton after three days of successful sea trials.

UPI

EXPATRIATE KING Constantine of Greece, his wife, Anne-Marie, and their two children pose with Danish Queen Ingrid, Queen Anne-Marie's mother, during visit to Denmark.

WIDE WORLD

GREECE

During 1969 Greece continued to be ruled by the same leaders who had seized power in the military coup of April 21, 1967. Even though Premier George Papadopoulos maintained that his ultimate goal was democracy, his regime remained absolutist. Relations between the government and King Constantine II, living in Rome, continued to be uneasy.

Government Controls. Purges removed persons who did not seem loyal from military and civil posi-

----------- GREECE • Information Highlights -----------

Area: 50,996 square miles (131,944 sq km).
Population: 8,803,000 (1968 est.).
Chief Cities (1961 census): Athens, the capital, 627,564; Salonika (Thessaloniki), 250,920; Piraeus, 183,957.
Government: *King*—Constantine II (acceded March 6, 1964; in exile since December 1967); *Premier*—George Papadopoulos (took office Dec. 13, 1967). *Parliament*—dissolved in February 1967.
Religious Faiths: Greek Orthodox Christians, 97%.
Education: *Literacy rate* (1969), 83% of population. *Total school enrollment* (1964)—1,521,322 (primary, 965,782; secondary, 430,318; technical/vocational, 71,917; university/higher, 53,305).
Finance (1969 est.): *Revenues,* $1,700,000,000; *expenditures,* $1,621,000,000; *public debt* (1965), $1,142,000,000; *monetary unit,* drachma (30 drachmas equal U. S.$1).
Gross National Product (1967): $7,093,000,000.
National Income (1967): $5,727,000,000; *average annual income per person,* $656.
Economic Indexes (1967): *Industrial production* (1968), 158 (1963=100); *agricultural production,* 117 (1963=100); *cost of living,* 111 (1963=100).
Manufacturing (metric tons, 1967): Wheat flour (1963), 1,010,-000; wine (1966), 3,844,000 hectoliters; gasoline, 381,000; olive oil, 195,000; cheese, 146,000.
Crops (metric tons, 1967–68 crop year): Wheat, 1,848,000; grapes, 1,406,000; sugar beets, 930,000; barley, 839,000; citrus fruit (1966), 516,000.
Minerals (metric tons, 1967): Lignite, 5,162,000; bauxite, 1,687,000; pozzolan, 350,000; magnesite (1966), 337,800; pumice, 300,000.
Foreign Trade (1968): *Exports,* $468,000,000 (chief exports, 1967: tobacco, $137,333,000; currants, other raisins, and grapes, $39,833,000); *imports,* $1,393,000,000 (chief imports, 1967: nonelectrical machinery, $179,987,000; transport equipment, $148,274,000; iron and steel, $64,432,000). *Chief trading partners* (1967): West Germany (took 16% of exports, supplied 19% of imports); Italy (took 10% of exports, supplied 10% of imports); United States (took 13% of exports, supplied 8% of imports).
Transportation: *Roads* (1966), 27,440 miles (44,151 km); *motor vehicles* (1967), 236,200 (automobiles 145,500); *railways* (1965), 1,616 miles (2,601 km); *merchant vessels* (1969), 1,943 (9,200,000 gross registered tons); *national airline,* Olympic Airways; *principal airport,* Athens.
Communications: *Telephones* (1968), 660,129; *television stations* (1968), 1; *television sets* (1968), 7,000; *radios* (1967), 994,000; *newspapers* (1966), 113.

tions. Political trials were held, and individuals were banished to outlying areas.

In June the council of state, the highest Greek court, voided the government's dismissal in 1968 of 21 high judges. The government then announced that it had accepted the resignation of the council's president, Michael Stasinopoulos. Stasinopoulos, however, maintained that he had not tendered his resignation.

The government announced in April that three basic rights—the inviolability of homes, the right of assembly, and the right of association—were being restored. But the effects of the decree were actually limited by the continuance of martial law.

On October 3, Premier Papadopoulos announced further liberalization measures. These included freedom of the press, but so many restrictions remained in effect that newspapers continued to be stringently controlled. The government in November issued a new, highly restrictive press code of 101 articles to take effect on Jan. 1, 1970.

Opposition to the Government. Among influential Greeks who spoke out against the regime was the distinguished poet-diplomat Georgios S. Seferiades, who won the 1963 Nobel Prize for literature under the pen-name "George Seferis." Constantine Caramanlis, founder of the conservative National Radical Union and premier of Greece from 1955 to 1963, denounced the Greek government in September. He called on the military to oust the country's current leaders, if they would not resign their offices voluntarily.

Within Greece there were a number of bomb explosions, apparently set off by Greeks to harass the government and to discourage tourists, whose spending is important to the Greek economy. One blast, apparently not connected with the others, was set off by Jordanians on November 27 at the Athens office of El Al, Israel's national airline.

Church-State Relations. In February the government issued a new charter for the Greek Orthodox state church. The charter gave the church greater autonomy and arranged for more participation by laymen in the administration of church affairs, but it still maintained overall government control. Some church hierarchs criticized the charter, but opposition was quelled by Archbishop Ieronymos of Athens, the primate of Greece since May 1967. He tendered his resignation to the assembly of bishops and then withdrew it when he secured a vote of confidence.

The monks at Mount Athos, a center of Greek Orthodox monasticism, condemned the government for taking away the privileges they had secured in 1926, when Mount Athos was recognized as a self-governing entity with its own ruling council.

Crown-Government Relations. Relations between King Constantine II and the government remained uneasy. However, the government continued to recognize Constantine as king of the Hellenes and to send a stipend to him in Rome. Although Constantine attended the funeral of former U. S. President Dwight D. Eisenhower in Washington, D. C. on March 31, Deputy Premier Stylianos Patakos served as the official representative of the Greek government. The rigorously censored Greek press and radio were not initially allowed to mention the presence of the king at the funeral.

In June, Premier Papadopoulos announced that a pro-royalist plot to overthrow the government had been crushed. As rumors of an imminent open clash between king and government spread, Constantine flew to Switzerland on August 28 for a conference with the ailing Greek foreign minister, Panayiotis Pipinelis. It was said that the king demanded free elections, a free press, and the release of political prisoners before he would consider returning to Greece.

Shortly afterward, Greek newspapers carried articles strongly criticizing the king's mother, Queen Frederika, for her alleged interference in political and military matters during the reign of her husband, King Paul I. Conversely, in October, the government had disparaging references to Constantine removed from a new history textbook.

On October 1 in Rome, Constantine's wife, Queen Anne-Marie, bore a son, Prince Nicholas, the couple's third child.

During a visit to London with Queen Anne-Marie in November, Constantine met privately with British Prime Minister Harold Wilson. This appeared to raise the ire of the Greek government, because the British foreign office was known at the time to be working for the expulsion of Greece from the Council of Europe.

The Economy. Minister of Coordination Nicholas Makarezos issued figures that showed the Greek economy to be growing, strong, and stable. But former Premier Caramanlis claimed that the Papadopoulos regime was covering up serious deficiencies in the economy.

The government in October canceled a multi-million dollar contract with Litton Industries for the development of the western Peloponnesus and Crete. The agreement was canceled because Litton was unable to attract the required foreign capital.

Foreign Affairs. Criticism of the Papadopoulos regime increased among Greece's allies in the North Atlantic Treaty Organization and among other countries.

In May the Council of Europe warned Greece that it was in danger of expulsion. The European Commission for Human Rights, an agency of the council, in November issued a report charging that torture was allowed in Greek prisons. The report also stated that there had been no danger of a Communist revolt in Greece in April 1967. At that time leaders of the coup had used the threat of such a revolt to justify their overthrow of constitutional government. Greece withdrew from the Council of Europe on December 12, before a resolution could be passed suspending it for not observing principles of human rights and democracy.

After a delay of almost eight months from his inauguration, President Nixon in August announced the nomination of a new ambassador to Greece, Henry J. Tasca. The delay was thought to imply that the U. S. government was putting pressure on Greece to restore democratic rule. The Senate confirmed the appointment on December 19.

Death of Princess Andrew. Princess Andrew of Greece, mother of Britain's Prince Philip, died at Buckingham Palace on December 5. Born Princess Alice of Battenberg in 1885, she was a great-grand-daughter of Queen Victoria, a niece of the last Russian empress, and a sister of Earl Mountbatten of Burma. Her husband, Prince Andrew, whom she had married in 1903, died in 1944. In the latter part of her life she had been a Greek Orthodox nun.

GEORGE J. MARCOPOULOS
Tufts University

GREEK ORTHODOX CHURCH. See RELIGION.

GREEK PREMIER George Papadopoulos announces cessation of prepublication press censorship on October 3.

THE MUSEUM OF MODERN ART, NEW YORK

WALTER GROPIUS, German architect who died in Boston on July 5, founded and designed the Bauhaus, cradle of avant-garde art and architecture.

DPA-PICTORIAL PARADE

GROPIUS, Walter Adolf

German architect: b. Berlin, Germany, May 18, 1883; d. Boston, Mass., July 5, 1969.

Walter Gropius was one of the founders of that form of modern architecture later named the International Style. Furthermore, through the Bauhaus School of Design his impact on architectural education was revolutionary. No single individual can claim sole responsibility for any major style in architecture. But when all allowances to others have been made, it remains true that Gropius' earlier designs are probably the first complete statements of the International Style.

Early Career. Gropius was trained at the universities of Charlottenburg and Munich. From 1907 to 1910, he worked for Peter Behrens, an important forerunner of modern architecture. Behrens was then building the AEG Turbine Factory in Berlin, a project remarkable for its complete rejection of historic styles of architecture and for its functional use of materials.

From 1910 to 1914, Gropius had an independent practice. In 1911 he designed the Fagus Shoe Last Factory at Alfeld an der Leine in collaboration with Adolf Meyer. This was perhaps the first building with glass walls and an interior frame. The design consists of horizontal rectangles defined by narrow brick piers and thin spandrel walls between the floors. The glass is flush with the wall plane, like a skin drawn over a frame. Traditional materials required strength at the corners of buildings, but steel and reinforced concrete permit cantilevered floors. Gropius therefore eliminated the corner column, which was no longer necessary. Although most of these innovations in the Faguswerk can find precedent in various earlier buildings, their coherent combination in a single structure may mark it as the first example of the International Style. Gropius' design of the Machine Hall for the Werkbund Exposition at Cologne (1914) was equally radical; the steel bents of the interior are fully expressed on its exterior.

The Bauhaus School. After service in World War I, Gropius became head of the Bauhaus School of Design. It was then located at Weimar, but moved in 1925 to its new quarters at Dessau, which were designed by Gropius. The school trained students in architecture, art, and applied design. It emphasized the union of craftsman and artist, of head and hand.

Instead of relying completely on drawings, the students were compelled to design in actual materials, learning thereby the possibilities of materials and their own limitations. Recognizing the machine as basic in modern life, the students were urged to adapt their designs to mass production and to give order to architecture, to the community, and to industrial design. Furthermore, they collaborated in their projects, guided by such teachers as Ludwig Mies van der Rohe, the architect who later succeeded Gropius in the Bauhaus, the painters Paul Klee and Wassily Kandinsky, and the sculptor Laszlo Moholy-Nagy. (See MIES VAN DER ROHE.)

The workshop that Gropius designed for the Bauhaus is a glass box. Through the unbroken plane of glass the reinforced concrete floors and the supporting columns can be seen. The glass simply hangs from the edge of the cantilevered roof and in turn overhangs the ground floor by several feet. No decoration or moldings are tolerated. The result is severe, but impressive.

Although Gropius had been forbidden any kind of political activity at the Bauhaus, its aesthetic philosophy was radical. This brought it progressively under fire as Nazism began its rise to power. Gropius tried to avert criticism of the school by resigning in 1928. A few years later, in 1934, he escaped from Germany to England where, in collaboration with Maxwell Fry, he designed Impington College, Cambridge, with its glass-walled classrooms.

Harvard and Later Career. From 1938 to 1952, Gropius took charge of the department of architecture in Harvard's Graduate School of Design. His architectural personality set the tone of the school. While there he built the graduate center (1949) with its dormitories and ample social rooms.

After his retirement, Gropius formed TAC, The Architects' Collaborative. Throughout his life, he emphasized collaboration, at first with Meyer, and later with such architects as Fry, Marcel Breuer, and Pietro Belluschi. With the last he designed the Pan Am Building (1963) in New York City. Among his other later commissions were the U. S. embassy in Athens and the University of Baghdad.

EVERARD M. UPJOHN
Columbia University

GUATEMALA

The year 1969 was marked by an early launching of the 1970 presidential campaign and a consequent renewal of terrorism in Guatemala City after a lull of several months. The economy was shaken by a tropical storm that caused widespread death and destruction. Leftist attacks on potential foreign investment countered Guatemalan government efforts to entice development capital from abroad.

Presidential Campaign. Electioneering started in January, after the rightist National Liberation Movement (MLN) and the Institutional Democratic party (PID) jointly endorsed Col. Carlos Arana for president. He is a 50-year-old hero of the 1967–68 antiguerrilla campaign. On February 3, the left-of-center Christian Democrats announced that Col. Jorge Lucas Caballero, a 40-year-old former treasury minister who supports "civilian" government, would be their standard-bearer. On March 31, the moderate Revolutionary party (PR) chose Treasury Minister Mario Fuentes Pieruccini, a 47-year-old lawyer. By the end of 1969, Fuentes Pieruccini appeared to be leading the race.

Terrorism. The assassinations in May and June of MLN public relations director Mario López Villatoro and two other MLN officials were attributed to the Revolutionary Armed Forces (FAR). The renewal of violence in Guatemala City, after months of relative calm, appeared to be an attempt by terrorist groups to bring about a military coup and block the upcoming elections.

Economic Affairs. A catastrophic economic setback resulted from severe storms in September and October. Hurricane Francella flooded densely populated highland areas, killing at least 75 persons and leaving thousands homeless. An estimated 60% of all crops and livestock were lost. These reverses in agriculture, combined with losses in sales to the paralyzed Central American Common Market, affected an already serious imbalance of payments.

A million-ton silver ore deposit was discovered in eastern Guatemala by the Minnesota Mining and Manufacturing Corporation. A subsidiary, Minas de Oriente, S. A., indicated that it could be in full-scale production within two years.

An International Nickel Company subsidiary, Explotaciones Mineras Izabal (EXMIBAL), reached an agreement with the Guatemalan government. The company foresaw a 25,000-ton annual production of nickel at its mine in eastern Guatemala, requiring an investment of $180 million and a work force of 1,200 men. EXMIBAL agreed to pay Guatemala 35% of its net income before taxes. This operation in Guatemala would be the first major mining activity in Central America. But the contract with the nickel company was attacked by leftists, who called for its cancellation and a full congressional debate on any later agreement.

Construction. The National Housing Institute (INVI) launched a $15 million urban development and housing program, which would benefit 33,000 people from different income groups. Although a $5 million loan was obtained from the Inter-American Development Bank (IABD), private resources will cover 30% of the cost of the 6,000 units.

An IABD loan of $9.5 million was approved for three universities in the capital city, two of them private. The funds will be used for constructing laboratories, libraries, and residence halls. The bank loan covered part of a $15.7 million program for university education. Meanwhile, the education ministry claimed that it was opening elementary schools at the rate of one every 36 hours.

A $4.8 million international air terminal was opened outside of Guatemala City. It can handle 14 passenger and three cargo jets in one hour.

Guatemala completed its 300-mile (480-km) portion of the Inter-American Highway, which has been under construction for 24 years. The total cost of the Guatemalan highway was $64 million.

International Relations. Guatemala took an active role in achieving a withdrawal of Salvadorean troops from Honduran territory after the July invasion. The Guatemalan government said it would reject any changes in Honduras' borders as a result of force. As Hondurans fled across the border, it also blamed the Salvadorean government for creating a refugee problem in Guatemala.

LARRY L. PIPPIN
Elbert Covell College,
University of the Pacific

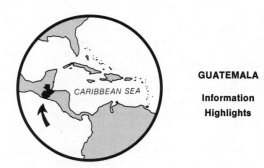

GUATEMALA

Information Highlights

Area: 42,042 square miles (108,889 sq km).
Population: 4,864,000 (1968 est.).
Chief Cities (1964 prelim. census): Guatemala City, the capital, 572,937; Quezaltenango, 45,195; Escuintla, 24,832.
Government: *President*—Julio César Méndez Montenegro (took office July 1, 1966); *Vice-President*—Clemente Marroquín Rojas. *Legislature* (unicameral)—Congreso Nacional, 55 members (party seating, 1969: Partido Revolucionario, 31; Partido Institucional Democrático, 19; Movimiento de Liberación Nacional, 5).
Religious Faiths: Roman Catholics, 92% of population.
Education: *Literacy rate* (1964), 37.9% of population aged 15 and over. *Total school enrollment* (1965)—478,252 (primary, 421,446; secondary, 35,541; teacher-training, 6,798.

Finance (1967 est.): *Revenues*, $124,300,000; *expenditures*, $151,400,000; *public debt*, $162,400,000; *monetary unit*, quetzal (1 quetzal equals U. S.$1).
Gross National Product (1967): $1,454,000,000.
National Income (1967): $1,246,000,000; *average annual income per person*, $256.
Economic Indexes (1967): *Industrial production* (1968), 125 (1963=100); *agricultural production*, 110 (1963=100); *cost of living*, 100 (1963=100).
Manufacturing and Processing (metric tons, 1967): Cement, 206,000; sugar, 171,000; gasoline, 139,000; wheat flour, 71,000; meat, 41,000.
Crops (metric tons, 1967–68 crop year): Maize, 690,000; cottonseed, 120,000; coffee, 111,000; bananas, 76,000; cotton (lint) 76,000.
Minerals (metric tons, 1966): Limestone, 371,000; quartz, 26,000; silver, 3,000 troy ounces.
Foreign Trade (1967): *Exports*, $199,000,000 (chief exports, 1967: coffee, $68,000,000; cotton, $31,600,000); *imports*, $247,000,000 (chief imports, 1967: nonelectrical machinery, $29,579,000; transport equipment, $22,767,000). *Chief trading partners:* United States (took 31% of exports, supplied 41% of imports); El Salvador (took 15% of exports, supplied 12% of imports); West Germany (took 12% of exports, supplied 10% of imports).
Transportation: *Roads* (1964), 7,575 miles (12,190 km); *motor vehicles* (1967), 52,800 (automobiles 33,400); *railways* (1967), 510 miles (821 km); *merchant vessels* (1967), 2 (4,000 gross registered tons); *national airline*, Aviateca; *principal airports*, Guatemala City.
Communications: *Telephones* (1968): 35,103; *television stations* (1968), 2; *television sets* (1968), 60,000; *radios* (1961), 210,000; *newspapers* (1966), 6 (daily circulation, 180,000).

GUINEA

Information Highlights

Area: 94,925 square miles (245,857 sq km).
Population: 3,795,000 (1968 est.).
Chief Cities (1967 census): Conakry, the capital, 197,26..
Government: *President*—Sékou Touré. *Legislature* (unicameral)—National Assembly, 75 members (party seating, 1969: all members of the Parti Démocratique de Guinée).
Religious Faiths: Muslims, 61% of population; animists, 37%.
Education: *Literacy rate* (1969), 10% of population. *Total*

school enrollment (1965)—187,900 (primary, 164,119; secondary, 16,698; teacher-training, 822; technical/vocational, 5,018; university/higher, 1,243).
Finance (1967 budget est.): $167,600,000; *monetary unit,* franc (246.85 francs equal U. S.$1).
Gross National Product (1969): $310,000,000.
Cost of Living Index (1960): 108 (1958 = 100).
Manufacturing (1965): Lumber, 40,000 cubic meters.
Crops (metric tons, 1967–68 crop year): Cassava, 446,000; bananas, 92,000; peanuts (1966), 16,000; coffee, 10,200.
Minerals (metric tons, 1966): Bauxite, 1,609,000; iron ore, 1,600,000; diamonds, 72,000 carats.
Foreign Trade (1966): *Exports,* $46,000,000 (chief exports, 1962: alumina, $26,800,000; bananas, $4,500,000; palm nuts and kernels, $3,000,000; raw coffee, $2,900,000); *Imports,* $55,000,000 (chief imports, 1962: printed cotton fabrics, $7,200,000; rice, $6,300,000; nonelectrical machinery, $4,800,000). *Chief trading partners* (1966): Communist bloc (took 17% of exports, supplied 39% of imports); United States (took 26% of exports, supplied 22% of imports); France.
Transportation: *Roads* (1969), 4,725 miles (7,604 km); *motor vehicles* (1967), 19,100 (automobiles 7,600); *railways* (1967), 511 miles (822 km); *merchant vessels* (1967), 1 (11,000 gross registered tons); *national airline,* Air Guinée; *principal airports,* Conakry, Kankan.
Communications: *Telephones* (1968), 6,500; *radios* (1967), 80,000; *newspapers* (1966), 1.

GUINEA

Both domestic and foreign policy in Guinea in 1969 were strongly influenced by the government's efforts to prevent a coup.

Internal Affairs. The November 1968 revolution in neighboring Mali caused the ruling Parti Démocratique de Guinée (PDG) to speed up various reforms announced earlier. In December 1968 the PDG had stated its intention of integrating the 4,800-man army into the civil service. In January, President Sékou Touré elaborated on the plan, which gave the army a specific role in economic development. Comités de Base, local units for political indoctrination, were established at each army post. To make the chance of an army coup even less likely, a militia of 30,000 men was also established. In January and February there was a major restructuring of executive positions in the government and a reshuffling of personnel, including the appointment of a second military man to the cabinet.

President Touré's concern over subversion was proved correct, when the details of a major plot against the government were learned in March. The key to the plot was to have been the assassination of President Touré when he visited Labe. A large number of officials and highly placed civilians were immediately arrested. Among these were Fodeba Keita, the organizer of the internationally renowned Guinean dance troupe Ballets Africains and former minister of defense, and Colonel Kaman Diaby, army chief of staff. On May 1 the government announced more arrests. Thirteen men, including Diaby and Keita, were tried and condemned to death, and 27 others were given long prison sentences. The higher officials in the government were again reshuffled, and Touré assumed direct control of the army. Following more arrests at Labe, Touré announced a purge of the army.

The government's actions apparently postponed further immediate attempts to overthrow Touré.

Foreign Affairs. In January, Guinea appeared to be following a policy of rapprochement with other West African states. However, Guinea's foreign policy became increasingly tied to Touré's fears of a coup. In January there were major changes in Guinea's diplomatic missions to Senegal, Algeria, the Congo (Brazzaville), the United Arab Republic, and the United Nations. After February, Touré criticized the new government of President Moussa Traoré in Mali and linked it with "French imperial-

ism." He also accused France, Ivory Coast, and Mali of giving aid to subversive elements in Guinea, and attacked the Busia government of Ghana as a dictatorship. By the end of 1969, Guinea was once more in its self-imposed political isolation.

Economic Developments. Although handicapped by government controls, the economy slowly continued to improve. Grängesberg, a Swedish firm, showed an interest in developing Guinea's iron resources. A $7.5 million surplus food agreement was signed with the United States in February. Work on the $160 million bauxite project at Boké began on October 2.

HARRY A. GAILEY
San Jose State College

GUYANA

In Guyana the year 1969 was marked by economic progress and by troubles in border areas that involved the country in disputes with its neighbors.

Border Incidents. On January 2 rebels seized the village of Lethem in the Rupununi district, near the boundary with Brazil and Venezuela. The group was led by local ranchers and miners (among them a pair of Guyana-born U. S. citizens) and included a number of the American Indians who made up most of the population of the district. Within four days, Guyanese troops had crushed the rebellion.

Prime Minister Forbes Burnham accused the Venezuelan government, which had long claimed the region as its own, of instigating the revolt in a bid to set up an independent state in that territory. This charge was denied by Venezuela. The Burnham government then sought to deal with some of the many grievances of the Amerindians of the district and in March announced that it would grant the Indians full title to the lands on which their villages stood. Early in June security exercises were held throughout Guyana because of reports of "renewed activities" on the Venezuelan border.

In August there was a brief clash with Surinam's troops on the southeastern border in the New River Triangle, an area claimed by both countries.

Political Affairs. Taking advantage of the clear parliamentary majority won by his party (the People's National Congress) in the election of Dec. 16, 1968, Prime Minister Burnham reorganized his cabinet on Feb. 1, 1969, naming PNC members to all posts. The United Force, the nation's third party, thus lost its role as a participant in a coalition gov-

GUYANA

Information Highlights

Area: 83,086 square miles (214,969 sq km).
Population: 710,000 (1968 est.).
Chief Cities (1960 census): Georgetown, the capital, 72,964; New Amsterdam, 14,053.
Government: *Prime Minister*—Linden Forbes Burnham (took office Dec. 15, 1964). *Parliament*—National Assembly, 53 members (party seating, 1969: People's National Congress, 30; People's Progressive party, 19; United Force, 4).
Religious Faiths: Hindus, 33% of population; Anglicans, 20%; Roman Catholics, 15%; Muslims, 9%; others, 23%.
Education: *Literacy rate* (1961), 72% of population aged 15 and over. *Total school enrollment* (1965)—183,479 (primary, 163,344; secondary, 17,683; vocational, 2,197; higher, 255).
Finance (1967 est.): *Revenues,* $49,650,000; *expenditures,* $59,700,000; *public debt,* $87,950,000; *monetary unit,* Guyana dollar (2 Guyana dollars equal U.S.$1).
Gross National Product (1967): $198,250,000.
National Income (1967): $162,500,000; average annual income per person, $238.
Cost of Living Index (1967): 108 (1963=100).
Manufacturing (metric tons, 1967): Sugar, 367,000; margarine, 1,100; beer, 66,000 hectoliters.
Crops (metric tons, 1967–68 crop year): Rice, 198,000.
Minerals (metric tons, 1966): Bauxite, 2,865,000 (ranks 4th among world producers); manganese ore, 182,889.
Foreign Trade (1967): *Exports,* $96,950,000 (chief exports, 1967: sugar, $27,285,000; bauxite, $38,542,500; rice, $12,-624,000; *imports,* $113,850,000 (chief imports, 1967: petroleum products, $8,931,500; textile yarn and fabrics, $7,-153,000; motor vehicles, $5,520,000). *Chief trading partners* (1967): United States (took 23% of exports, supplied 28% of imports); Britain (took 24% of exports, supplied 26% of imports); Canada (took 18% of exports, supplied 11% of imports).
Transportation: *Roads* (1964), 879 miles (1,415 km); *motor vehicles* (1967), 18,400 (automobiles 13,200); *railways* (1965), 79 miles (127 km).
Communications: *Telephones* (1968): 12,070; *radio stations* (1968), 2; *radios* (1966), 90,000; *newspapers* (1967), 2 (daily circulation, 130,000).

ernment. Later it was further weakened by the defection of some of its most distinguished members.

In June, Cheddi Jagan, leader of the People's Progressive party (the major opposition to the ruling PNC), attended a meeting of pro-Soviet Communist parties in Moscow, where he declared the PPP to be a full-fledged Communist party. The PPP was reorganized to conform to that model.

In February the Prime Minister announced that Guyana would become a republic early in 1970.

Economic Affairs. Burnham pressed his economic program throughout the year. Settlement of the vast interior was encouraged, incentives were granted to foreign investors, and studies were begun looking to a complete reform of the tax structure. In July the United Kingdom granted loans totaling more than $10 million to assist in the fulfillment of Guyana's 1966–72 Development Program. Production of sugar, the country's principal export, reached record levels in 1969—a year when production in other Caribbean areas generally declined.

ROBERT J. ALEXANDER
Rutgers University

HAITI

President François Duvalier continued to rule Haiti with a firm hand in 1969, and outwardly, at least, the country appeared calm. The major disturbances were tensions within the president's family and circle of advisers and an inconsequential air raid by exiles on Port-au-Prince. With conditions peaceful, tourism expanded but other aspects of the economy lagged. Duvalier's repeated attempts to revive U.S. economic assistance were unsuccessful.

Political Affairs. On June 4 a plane dropped several bombs near the presidential palace. Damage and casualties were light, and the crewmen were arrested when they landed in the Bahamas to refuel.

Recent attacks by exiles have been launched from the Bahamas, but the center of Haitian exile

UPI

GUYANA'S DEFENSE FORCE parades through Georgetown, February 14, in ceremonies marking the opening of the National Assembly.

HAITI

Information Highlights

CARIBBEAN SEA

Area: 10,714 square miles (27,750 sq km).
Population: 4,674,000 (1968 est.).
Chief Cities (1961 est.): Port-au-Prince, the capital, 151,200; Cap-Haïtien, 27,538; Gonaïves, 15,373; Les Cayes, 13,088; Jérémie, 12,456.
Government: *President*—François Duvalier (took office 1957; assumed presidency for life, June 22, 1964). *Legislature* (unicameral)—National Assembly, 58 members (all members of the Parti Unique de l'Action Révolutionnaire et Gouvernementale).

Religious Faiths: Roman Catholics, 90% of population.
Education: *Literacy rate* (1950), 10.5% of population aged 15 and over. *Total school enrollment* (1965)—314,306 (primary, 283,799; secondary, 24,514; teacher-training, 213; vocational, 4,173; higher, 1,607).
Finance (1967 est.): *Revenues,* $280,400,000; *expenditures,* $280,400,000; *public debt,* $747,400,000; *monetary unit,* gourde (5 gourdes equal U. S.$1).
Gross National Product (1968 est.): $345,500,000.
Cost of Living Index (1967): 117 (1963=100).
Manufacturing (metric tons, 1967): Sugar, 65,000; wheat flour, 42,000; cement, 35,000.
Crops (metric tons, 1967–68 crop year): Bananas, 220,000; coffee, 30,000; sisal (1966), 19,026; cacao beans, 2,700.
Minerals (metric tons, 1966): Limestone, 370,000; bauxite (1967), 370,000; salt, 10,000; copper (1967), 2,400; silver, 50,690 troy ounces; gold, 5,071 troy ounces.
Foreign Trade (1967): *Exports,* $33,360,000 (chief exports: coffee, $12,400,000; sugar, $3,500,000; bauxite, $3,260,000; sisal, $1,480,000); *imports,* $41,400,000 (chief imports: foodstuffs, cotton fabrics, motor vehicles, industrial machinery). *Chief trading partner* (1965): United States.
Transportation: *Roads* (1964), 2,024 miles (3,257 km); *motor vehicles* (1967), 6,900; *railways* (1965), 187 miles (301 km); *merchant vessels* (1967), 1 (7,000 gross registered tons); *principal airport,* Port-au-Prince.
Communications: *Telephones* (1968): 4,335; *television stations* (1968), 1; *television sets* (1968), 10,000; *radios* (1967), 75,000; *newspapers* (1965), 6.

politics remains New York City. Early in the year a secret Haitian military training base was uncovered in the Florida Everglades.

More serious problems faced the Duvalier government internally. Following previous practice, the president shuffled about his close aides. In the spring he arrested his economic adviser and his former private secretary. He also dismissed the chief of the Tonton Macoutes, or security police, and transferred the commander of his elite presidential guard.

Early in May Duvalier suffered a heart attack, and during his 2-month illness his son-in-law and daughter, Col. and Mme. Max Dominique, virtually ran the country. When Duvalier recovered in July, however, Colonel Dominique was named ambassador to France, and the Dominiques departed for Paris along with Duvalier's only son and youngest daughter. In early August members of the once-powerful Fucard family, including another daughter of the president, arrived in Miami, apparently in exile. These moves seemed to confirm the impression that Duvalier trusted no one in power.

Responding to the February merger of two radical political organizations into the United Party of Haitian Communists, a self-styled "national liberation movement," the government decreed the death penalty for all Communist activities. In April government forces attacked Communist headquarters outside the capital, killing some 30 people, and in June some 20 alleged Communists found hiding in a house in Port-au-Prince were also killed. In August nine Catholic priests were exiled for distributing "Communist articles harmful to the Government and to the person of the Chief Executive."

Economic Affairs. The economy was largely stagnant. Tourism prospered, but did not reach the level of the mid-1950's. Public services were lagging, and the government was behind schedule in paying public employees. The unfinished model village of Duvalierville was deteriorating. Agricultural production of Haiti's three main crops—cacao beans, sugar, and coffee—remained stationary.

Foreign Affairs. The government concentrated its major foreign policy efforts on seeking restoration of U. S. aid. Duvalier cited his stand against communism and argued that his government was trying to promote responsible economic development. No aid was forthcoming, but the U. S. attitude toward Haiti warmed slightly, and U. S. presidential envoy Nelson Rockefeller visited Haiti in July.

Relations with the Bahamas improved. In January four Haitians were sentenced to death in Nassau for the assassination of the Haitian consul in 1968. They were later acquitted on appeal, but in the meantime the Bahamian prime minister was warmly received on a February visit to Haiti. In March, Haiti recognized Biafra, the secessionist eastern region of Nigeria, and in September, Haiti boycotted the United Nations to protest its rule that states behind in contributions lose their votes.

KARL M. SCHMITT
University of Texas

HALLUCINOGENIC DRUGS. See NARCOTICS AND HALLUCINOGENS.

HANDBALL. See SPORTS.

HARNESS RACING. See SPORTS.

HARRIS, Fred. See biographical sketch under POLITICAL PARTIES.

HARRIS, Julie. See biographical sketch under THEATER.

HAWAII

In 1969 the highly politicized Hawaiian Islands were the stage for a series of small confrontations that seemed to set the mood for coming political and social struggles. Democratic and Republican politicians prepared for the 1970 elections, and labor unrest seemed likely to continue because of Hawaii's high taxes and rising cost of living.

Political Battles. Gov. John Burns and Lt. Gov. Thomas Gill, both powerful leaders within the Democratic party, conducted undisguised war against each other in what seemed to be the prelude to an open confrontation, since both are expected to enter the race for governor in 1970. U. S. Representatives Patsy Mink and Spark Matsunaga, and Honolulu Mayor Frank Fasi, all Democrats, continued to build bases of support independent of the party in preparation for possible entry into the U. S. Senate race. The Democratic leader in the state Senate, David McClung, continued to try to play a broker's role in the hopes that Gill would seek the U. S. Senate seat of incumbent Republican Hiram Fong, instead of opposing Governor Burns. McClung's hopes, however, depended on agreement from Gill, Mink, Matsunaga, and Fasi, and such agreement was unlikely.

The Republicans were somehow unable to make any obvious headway in the face of Democratic

HAWAII'S new state capitol in Honolulu, Oahu, with its roof shaped to resemble a volcanic cone.

splits. State Senator Nelson Doi, frequent foe of the governor and Senate Democratic leaders, was elevated to Hawaii's Third Circuit Court. The elimination of Doi from the political struggle strengthened McClung's ability to lead the Democratic majority. State Senator James Clark's shift from the Republican to the Democratic party increased McClung's power, and Republican disarray, even more.

University Affairs. Trouble at the University of Hawaii subsided when former U. S. ambassador to NATO Harlan Cleveland was named as the university's new president. The fight over tenure for Professor Oliver Lee led to the resignation of qualified administrators and lowered the university's prestige. President Cleveland still faces a reconsideration of Lee's case in 1970.

HAWAII • Information Highlights

Area: 6,424 square miles (16,638 sq km).
Population: 775,000 (1969 est.)
Chief Cities (1969 est.): Honolulu, the capital, 335,000; Kailua, 34,000; Kaneohe, 28,000; Hilo, 26,000.
Government: *Chief Officers*—governor, John A. Burns (Democrat); lt. gov., Thomas P. Gill (D); atty. gen., Bertram T. Kanbara; comptroller, Ke Nam Kim; supt. of pub. instr., Ralph H. Kiyosaki; chief justice, William S. Richardson. *Legislature*—Senate, 25 members (17 Democrats, 8 Republicans); House of Representatives, 51 members (39 D, 12 R).
Education: *School enrollment* (1968–69)—public elementary, 99,000 pupils (4,000 teachers); public secondary, 74,000 pupils (2,800 teachers); nonpublic schools, 28,800 pupils (1,420 teachers); college and university (fall 1967), 27,847 students. *Public school expenditures* (1967–68)—$133,808,000 ($784 per pupil); average teacher's salary, $8,100.
Public Finance (fiscal year 1969): *Revenues,* $629,504,140 (4% sales tax, $61,712,434; motor fuel tax, $23,916,990; federal funds, $123,607,859). *Expenditures,* $575,254,124 (education, $221,262,352; health, welfare, and safety, $88,976,629; highways, $56,011,883). State debt, $343,406,000 (June 30, 1968).
Personal Income (1968): $2,705,000,000; average annual income per person, $3,513.
Public Assistance (fiscal year 1968–69): $32,726,000 to 34,-

558 recipients (aged, $3,595,000; dependent children, $15,985,000).
Labor Force (employed persons, fiscal year 1969): *Agricultural,* 15,800; *nonagricultural* (wage and salary earners), 287,300 (8.4% manufacturing, 21.2% trade, 24.6% government). *Unemployed persons* (fiscal year 1969)—8,400.
Manufacturing (1966): Value added by manufacture, $310,763,000 (food and products, $180,287,000; printing and publishing, $25,422,000; stone, clay, and glass products, $20,759,000; fabricated metals, $10,551,000; nonelectrical machinery, $10,131,000).
Agriculture (1967): *Cash farm income,* $207,514,000 (livestock, $37,349,000; crops, $161,611,000; govt. payments, $8,554,000). *Chief crops* (tons)—Sugarcane, 11,228,000 (ranks 1st among states); pineapple, 29,714,443 cases canned fruit; papayas, 11,823; macadamia nuts, 4,400.
Mining (1966): *Production value,* $21,253,000. *Chief minerals* (tons)—Stone, 5,079,000.
Fisheries (1967): *Commercial catch,* 12,000,000 pounds ($2,-800,000). *Leading species* (1966)—Skipjack tuna, 9,385,-000 pounds ($1,404,000); marlin, 494,000 pounds ($87,-000); red snapper, 89,000 pounds ($84,000).
Transportation: *Roads* (1967) 3,402 miles (5,474 km); *motor vehicles* (1969), 244,078; *railroads* (1968) 9,765 track miles (15,715 km); *airports* (1969), 11.
Communications (1968): *Telephones* (1967), 343,400; *television stations,* 16; *radio stations,* 21; *newspapers,* 7.

Economy. Economic indicators for the state were mixed. Even with the large increase in the number of tourists, not enough use was made of all the hotel space that had been created in previous overbuilding. Hawaii's state and local tax burden, the highest in the nation, acted as a possible deterrent to industrial growth and as a certain cause of demands for increased wages. U. S. Bureau of Labor statistics reported Honolulu to be the most expensive U. S. city to live in—even a can of pineapple, grown and canned in Hawaii, was cheaper on the U. S. mainland.

Labor Unrest. Labor unrest in the islands centered around a 2½-day newspaper strike that started in January, and a 30-day all-island sugar strike of 9,000 workers from 23 plantations. The sugar strike was settled with the help of a federal mediator on March 18. On April 18 approximately 2,000 members of the Hawaii Government Employees Association staged a mass demonstration, unprecedented in Hawaii's history, in front of the newly dedicated $28 million state capitol.

Land Problem. Controversy about the future of Diamond Head (whether the landmark should become a building site or a public park) continued, with pleas from the military, naturalists, and recreation-oriented citizens. The problem was closely related to Hawaii's continuing search for a solution to the problem of its limited amount of usable land.

ALLAN A. SPITZ
Michigan State University

HEALTH, Public. See PUBLIC HEALTH.

HEART DISEASE

Research on the causes and treatment of heart disease continued at a rapid pace during 1969. Some of the more important developments were concerned with artificial heart devices, cardiac pacemakers, ultrasonics in diagnosis, and the relationships of diet and oral contraceptives to heart disease.

The area of heart transplants received less attention than in previous years. On Aug. 17, 1969, Philip Blaiberg, the world's second heart transplant patient, died after living 19 months and 15 days with his new heart. Blaiberg had been the longest transplant survivor. At the time of Blaiberg's death 38 of the world's 143 transplant patients were still alive. Although the surgical techniques for transplanting human hearts have been fairly well perfected, the key to patient survival lies in preventing the recipient's body from rejecting the donor's heart. It is generally felt that this type of rejection can be delayed by a close matching of the donor's and recipient's tissues.

Artificial Heart Devices. On Apr. 4, 1969, Denton A. Cooley of Baylor University, Houston, Texas, implanted an artificial heart device into the chest of Haskell Karp, a 47-year-old patient considered to be near death. After living 63 hours with the implanted device, Karp was given a human heart. He died 38 hours later.

Under the sponsorship of the National Heart Institute, studies of implantable artificial hearts in animals continued. One type of device uses a tiny steam engine powered by heat stored in an insulated container of lithium salts. This engine may be refueled by electric power from an outside source. Another experimental device is powered by changing heat energy into pressurized gas.

Cardiac Pacemakers. Cardiac pacemakers control the rate of heartbeat by electronically stimulating the heart muscle. Conventional pacemakers are powered by mercury batteries and have a life of 2 to 3 years. A pacemaker currently being tested by the National Institutes of Health is powered by nuclear energy and is designed to perform for as long as 10 years.

Cardiac pacing with a catheter passed through a vein in the arm or neck to the heart is now being used to treat rapid heartbeat as well as to treat hearts that beat too slowly. Stimulation is applied to the lining of the heart through electrodes at the catheter tip. Since the catheterization procedure is performed easily, this method may eventually be used to treat many serious heart irregularities. The presence of the pacing catheter may also permit the use of drugs in doses required to suppress the rapid heart rate without the fear of excessively slowing the heart rate.

Ultrasonics in Diagnosis. The use of ultrasonic (radar-like) methods for diagnosing cardiac tumors, valve diseases, and accumulation of fluid surrounding the heart have been of increasing value. The principle underlying this technique is the graphic recording of high frequency sound waves as they bounce back to the recorder after striking an unusual structure within or outside the heart. This technique is also known as echo cardiography.

Diet and Heart Disease. An 8-year clinical trial of a diet high in unsaturated fats (vegetable oils) and low in cholesterol was reported by a group of investigators in California. Those taking part in this study were 424 middle-aged and elderly men who volunteered to follow such a diet. A similar group continued to eat the typical American diet, which is high in saturated fats (animal fats) as well as cholesterol. The experimental diet induced a prompt drop of 12.7% in the level of cholesterol in the blood, and during the study, 96 of the men eating conventional diets but only 66 of those eating the experimental diet suffered heart attacks or strokes. The prophylactic effect of the experimental diet was most apparent for those under the age of 65, particularly in those whose cholesterol levels were originally above average for their age.

Heart Disease and The Pill. After a 4-year study a committee of U. S. doctors advised the Food and Drug Administration that women using birth control pills face more than four times the risk of serious blood clotting diseases than women not using the pills. However, the incidence of thrombophlebitis (blood clots) and pulmonary embolism in women using oral contraceptives is decidedly less than in pregnant women, and the benefits of the pills were considered important enough for the committee to deem them safe.

Heart Surgery. A 3-year study by the American College of Chest Physicians revealed encouraging statistics on surgery to relieve advanced coronary artery disease by transplanting the patient's internal mammary artery into the heart muscle. The transplant increases the flow of blood to the heart muscle.

JOHNSON McGUIRE, M. D.
ARNOLD IGLAUER, M. D.
University of Cincinnati

HEINEMANN, Gustav. See biographical sketch under GERMANY.
HERSHEY, Lewis B. See biographical sketch under SELECTIVE SERVICE.

HIGHWAYS

More than $16.7 billion was available to federal, state, and local governments for highway construction in 1969. The amount included $16.8 billion from highway receipts and $1.8 billion from bond sales, but it was reduced by $1.7 billion needed for redemption of and interest on bonds issued in prior years. Highway Trust Fund receipts were expected to reach $4.6 billion, and various state fees, $8.4 billion, with the balance provided largely by local governments from general fund appropriations.

Maintenance and traffic service used 24% of the available funds. Of the balance, highway construction expenditures accounted for 78% of the capital outlay. Of the total, 39% was earmarked for the National System of Interstate and Defense Highways, with 36% for other federal aid systems.

Interstate System. When completed, the 42,500-mile Interstate system will link 90% of the nation's cities having a population of 50,000 or more. In the 12-month period ending Sept. 30, 1969, 2,239 miles of new Interstate highways were opened, making 28,750 miles of the system available to the public. An additional 5,259 miles were under construction, and engineering work was under way on another 6,615 miles so that only 4% of the system had not advanced beyond the preliminary stage.

Since 1956, the cost of the program has been $38.16 billion, of which $27.33 billion is for work already completed, including $22.38 billion for construction, and $4.95 billion for engineering and right-of-way acquisition. At the end of September, $7.37 billion of construction and $3.46 billion of engineering and acquisition was under way.

Federal Aid Program. Under the federal aid program to primary, secondary, and urban highways, 233,855 miles of highway have been opened since 1956 at a cost of $20.49 billion. On June 30, work on 15,351 miles was under way, involving expenditures of $3.92 billion. An additional $1.43 billion was apportioned for 1970.

Appalachia. The Appalachian Regional Commission (ARC) is developing a highway system to link communities in this region with national markets so that they can be more attractive to industry. As of 1969, 2,981 miles of primary roads and 465.9 miles of feeder roads were authorized, in addition to the 3,700 miles of Interstate highways also authorized for this region. In 1969, 720 miles of primary roads were open or under construction, 1,112 miles were in the design stage, and location studies were underway for another 716 miles. With 70% federal and 30% state funding, the ARC has obligated $429.6 million since the program began in 1965, including $131.3 million in 1969. An additional $175 million will be obligated by June 30, 1970. Further, 235.1 miles of feeder roads were open, 136.8 miles were being designed and 94 more miles were approved. When completed, the feeder road system will have cost $47.5 million and the primary roads $3.85 billion.

Highway Debt. Total debt outstanding for highways reached $18.2 billion at the end of 1969, including $13.3 billion at the state level, $1.5 billion at the county and township level, and $3.4 billion at the municipality level. Of the total, $10 billion was used for toll-free facilities.

Vehicle Registration. At the end of 1969, 104,-702,000 motor vehicles were registered in the United States, an increase of 3,662,887 over 1968. (All of Europe was estimated to have 62.8 million vehicles in 1968.) U. S. passenger car registration increased by 3.4% to 86,560,000 and truck/bus registrations increased by 4.6% to 18,142,000. More than 3 million vehicles were registered in each of 9 states, and 14 additional states each had more than 1 million registrations. California led in registrations with 11.4 million, followed by New York with 6.5 million, and Texas with 6.4 million. Pennsylvania, Ohio, and Illinois each had more than 5 million registrations. Motorcycle registrations increased by 154,923 to a total of 2,255,470.

Safety. With such an increase in the number of vehicles, and with highway deaths for the first 8 months of 1969 amounting to 36,330 and an estimated total of 56,310 for the entire year, safety was an important subject. President Nixon created a presidential task force on highway safety. In 1969, 13 more states enacted "implied consent" legislation, bringing to 45 the number of states that have such laws. Such legislation means that any operator, when he signs his license, implies his consent to submit to a chemical test to determine the alcoholic content in his blood. In 31 states, the District of Columbia, and Puerto Rico, laws require periodic vehicle inspection.

Two thirds of the fatal accidents in the United States involved only a single vehicle, including 53.1% of the fatal accidents that were caused by vehicles leaving the road. Most of the single-vehicle accidents occurred between 2 and 3 A.M., and 53% of the fatalities occurred from Friday to Sunday.

Truck Size. Efforts were continued by trucking concerns during 1969 to increase size and weight limits for truck and bus operations on the Interstate Highway System. The current standards were adopted when lane widths were typically 10 feet, compared with 12 feet in 1969. While there were various bills, in general the proposals would permit individual states to increase length from 65 to 70 feet and width from 96 to 102 inches. Weight limits would increase from 18,000 to 20,000 pounds for single-axle vehicles, and from 32,000 to 34,000 or 36,000 pounds for tandem-axle vehicles.

Beautification Failure. The Highway Beautification Act, passed in October 1965, "appears to stack up as a failure," according to a New York Times survey published on Aug. 31, 1969. The Federal Bureau of Public Roads had reported that: (1) only 21 states had taken steps to comply with the program; (2) of 139,000 signs invalidated by the Act, only 750 had been removed; (3) of 17,000 eyesore junkyards, only 121 had been liquidated and 1,427 screened; (4) of $325 million in federal beautification aid authorized since 1965, only $167 million had been appropriated or allocated, and only 10% of this went for removal of signs and junkyards; and (5) the 1965 Act prescribed a 10% penalty deduction in federal highway subsidies to noncomplying states, and this had not been applied at all.

In July, Secretary of Transportation John A. Volpe denied federal funds, and thereby in effect canceled, a proposed section of the Interstate Highway System that would have damaged New Orleans' charming French Quarter.

JAMES R. ROMAN, JR.
The George Washington University

HOCKEY. See SPORTS.
HOLLAND. See NETHERLANDS.
HOME ECONOMICS. See CONSUMER AFFAIRS.

CAMERA PRESS—PIX

HO CHI MINH (1890–1969)

HO CHI MINH

Communist revolutionary; b. Kim-Lien village, Nghe An province, Annam (now part of North Vietnam), May 19, 1890; d. Hanoi, Sept. 3, 1969.

Ho Chi Minh was one of the outstanding political activists of the contemporary period. As the acknowledged leader of the Vietnamese struggle for independence, he served as the first president of the Democratic Republic of Vietnam and presided over his country's conversion to a Communist state. His notable achievement was to adapt Marxism-Leninism to the Vietnamese mentality and environment by drawing on nationalism and revolutionary tradition. A small, ascetic man, he was widely revered in both North and South Vietnam as a patriot and liberator. Abroad he was recognized as an elder statesman of the international Communist movement.

Early Years. His name at birth was Nguyen Sinh Cung, but this was later changed by his father to Nguyen That Thanh. His boyhood was profoundly influenced by his family's involvement in the nationalist movement against the French. Following a secondary school education, he left Indochina in 1911 to serve as a kitchen helper aboard a French passenger liner. During the next several years he visited Europe, North Africa, and North America. In 1917 he settled in Paris as a photographer's assistant and adopted the name Nguyen Ai Quoc (Nguyen the Patriot). He joined the French Socialist party and became an anticolonial agitator.

Communist Activist. In 1920, Nguyen Ai Quoc broke with the Socialists over the question of rapid independence for colonial areas and became a founding member of the French Communist party. He attended the Fourth Comintern Congress in Moscow in 1922 and left France permanently the following year to study in Moscow at the University of the Toilers of the East.

In December 1924 he was sent to Canton to serve as an interpreter for the Soviet advisory mission under Michael Borodin. Here he organized the Vietnam Revolutionary Youth Association and trained political refugees for infiltration into Indochina. Chiang Kai-shek's rupture with the Communists forced him to return to Moscow in 1927. Two years later he was back in Asia, this time in Siam (Thailand), where, disguised as a Buddhist monk, he promoted Communism in the Vietnamese community.

In late 1929 he was ordered to Hong Kong by the Comintern to settle dissention among three Communist factions in Vietnam. His efforts brought into being a unified movement that became the Indochinese Communist party. The arrest and interrogation of another agent, however, led to Nguyen Ai Quoc's exposure and arrest by Hong Kong authorities in June 1931. A French demand for his extradition to Indochina, where he had been sentenced to death in absentia, was denied by the British, and he was released in early 1932. He went to China and in 1934 returned to Moscow.

In 1939 he was again back in southern China. In 1941 he settled on the Tonkin frontier and created a front organization known as the League for the Independence of Vietnam, commonly designated Vietminh. This was composed mainly of anti-French nationalist exiles residing in China and remnants of the Indochinese Communist party. The Communists' ascendancy, however, aroused Chinese suspicions, and in August 1942 Nguyen Ai Quoc was imprisoned. He secured his release a year later and took the name Ho Chi Minh (He Who Enlightens).

By the spring of 1945 the Vietminh controlled wide areas of northern Tonkin (all of Indochina had been occupied by the Japanese). After the military collapse of Japan, Ho Chi Minh moved swiftly to fill the political vacuum. The Vietminh occupied Hanoi, and on Sept. 2, 1945, promulgated the Democratic Republic of Vietnam with Ho Chi Minh as president.

Ho's Presidency. The new government was immediately confronted by the Chinese, who briefly occupied northern Indochina in accordance with the Potsdam Agreement, and by the returning French. Internally the Communist-dominated Vietminh faced nationalist groups contesting its leadership, but within a year these had been either neutralized or ruthlessly exterminated.

In March 1946, Ho Chi Minh signed with France a preliminary accord recognizing the Democratic Republic as a free state within the French Union. But the unresolved status of Cochin China satisfied neither party. Relations deteriorated rapidly, and in December a general uprising in Hanoi marked the beginning of the Indochina War. This was to result in a Vietminh victory in 1954 and the division of Vietnam into a Communist north and non-Communist south. In the early 1960's northern efforts to take over the South brought a new conflict, this time involving the United States.

During his later years Ho Chi Minh became a paternalistic national symbol. He steered a careful course between Moscow and Peking in an effort to preserve independence. Ho died of a heart attack on Sept. 3, 1969, at a time when the outcome of the war in South Vietnam was still unknown.

LEONARD C. OVERTON
Yale University

HOCKEY. See SPORTS.
HOLLAND. See NETHERLANDS.
HOME ECONOMICS. See CONSUMER AFFAIRS.

HONDURAS

The presence of a large Salvadoran minority population became a prime concern in Honduras in 1969, overshadowing issues as important as agrarian reform, economic development, and even presidential politics. In July, a border war occurred between Honduras and El Salvador, causing disruptions whose damaging effects were long felt.

Salvadoran Conflict. The spring months saw the first vigorous effort by the Honduran regime to deal with the problem of some 300,000 Salvadorans who had occupied farm lands and had established businesses in Honduras after emigrating from their overpopulated country. The application of a law that limited land ownership in Honduras to citizens of Honduran birth caused several thousands of Salvadorans, most of them illegal entrants, to flee to El Salvador, where they reported many stories of persecution and violence at Honduran hands.

On June 15, Honduran soccer fans attending a World Cup elimination playoff in San Salvador, were attacked by angry crowds. After this, relations between the two countries degenerated rapidly. Diplomatic ties were severed by El Salvador on June 26, and attempted mediation by the foreign ministers of Guatemala, Nicaragua, and Costa Rica failed to prevent an armed invasion of Honduras on July 14. The invaders occupied some 15 border towns before a truce in the so-called "Soccer War" could be arranged by the Organization of American States (OAS) on July 18. (See also EL SALVADOR.)

Estimates of the dead and missing among the military and the civilian populations exceeded 2,000, and there were great property losses in the towns captured by Salvadoran forces. The "hot" war was followed by a "cold" one that continued for the rest of the year. The OAS, resisting both El Salvador's charge of "genocide" against Hondurans and Honduran attempts to brand the Salvadorans as aggressors, sought to normalize relations between the two countries, but Honduras held up the reestablishment of commercial and diplomatic ties while an adamant El Salvador refused to agree to a definitive mapping of the long-disputed Honduran boundary. However, both countries participated in an OAS-arranged exchange of prisoners, and Honduras ordered its troops out of the war zone. Additional thousands of Salvadorans left Honduras after the war.

Agrarian Reform. The National Agrarian Institute (INA) became an object of wrath to both landowners and squatters as the government embarked upon a $15 million agrarian reform project. In April, the Institute initiated an eviction program to clear squatters from certain public properties that were to be incorporated into a forthcoming INA land distribution. Not surprisingly, many of the first victims of the program were Salvadorans, displaced from government holdings in Yoro Department and legally ineligible to receive new land parcels.

Economic Affairs. Vigorous business activity was noted early in 1969, with exports expanding, construction booming, and the government mobilizing domestic and foreign development capital, but the economy was hard hit by the July hostilities and by storms in September. Hurricane Francella and its attendant floods left export-crop and property damage of about $50 million in Cortes and Yoro departments. All shipments of Honduran products to El Salvador—a trade that had climbed to the $14 million level in 1968—were cut off at midyear.

Economic losses were partially offset by relief funds and supplies provided by the United States, Venezuela, Mexico, and other countries. A $7.5 million war bond issue was sold to reequip the national army, which had proved ill-prepared for war.

Presidential Politics. Although a presidential election was scheduled for 1971, it became evident that its fate would depend on the plans of the incumbent president, Gen. Oswaldo López Arellano. Before the Salvadoran war, his statement admitting that the constitution as written would not permit his reelection evoked a few declarations of presidential candidacy. However, all partisan activity ceased during the summer as a result of the invasion, and López Arellano emerged from the crisis with more popular support than he had enjoyed at any time since his seizure of power in 1963. This encouraged his backers to call for a postponement of the 1971 election and his continuance in office.

LARRY L. PIPPIN
Elbert Covell College, University of the Pacific

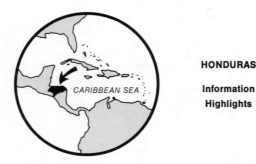

HONDURAS

Information Highlights

CARIBBEAN SEA

Area: 43,277 square miles (112,088 sq km).
Population: 2,535,000 (1968 est.).
Chief Cities (1965 census): Tegucigalpa, the capital, 170,535; San Pedro Sula, 58,632; La Ceiba (1961 census), 24,861.
Government: *President*—Oswaldo López Arellano (took office June 6, 1965). *Parliament*—National Congress, 64 members (party seating, 1969: Nationalist party, 35; Liberal party, 29).
Religious Faiths: Roman Catholics, 97% of population.
Education: *Literacy rate* (1961), 45% of population aged 15 and over. *Total school enrollment* (1965)—310,168 (primary, 283,606; secondary, 17,980; teacher-training, 3,554; technical/vocational, 2,450.
Finance (1968 est.): *Revenues,* $68,850,000; *expenditures,* $90,100,000; *public debts,* $92,500,000; *monetary unit,* Lempira (2 lempiras equal U. S.$1).
Gross National Product (1967): $598,000,000.
National Income (1967): $510,000,000; *average annual income per person,* $201.
Economic Indexes (1967): *Agricultural production,* 115 (1963=100); *cost of living,* 113 (1963=100).
Manufacturing (metric tons, 1967): Cement, 111,000; sugar, 44,000; wheat flour, 23,000; beer, 186,000 hectoliters (1966).
Crops (metric tons, 1967–68 crop year): Bananas, 1,100,000 (ranks 6th among world producers); maize, 355,000; millet and sorghum, 48,000; dry beans, 51,000; coffee, 28,800.
Minerals (metric tons, 1966): Limestone, 153,530; zinc, 12,393; gypsum, 11,780; lead, 11,704; salt, 10,000; gold, 4,274 troy ounces; silver, 3,734 troy ounces.
Foreign Trade (1968): *Exports,* $180,000,000 (chief exports, 1967: bananas, $78,831,000; coffee, $17,735,000; wood, $7,255,000; silver, $4,460,000); *imports,* $185,000,000 (chief imports, 1967: nonelectric machinery, $22,874,000; transport equipment, $16,800,000; paper and paper board, $12,460,000). *Chief trading partners* (1967): United States (took 46% of exports, supplied 48% of imports); West Germany (took 2% of exports, supplied 5% of imports).
Transportation: *Roads* (1969), 3,000 miles (4,800 km); *motor vehicles* (1967), 22,700 (automobiles 11,200); *railways* (1967), 752 miles (12,102 km); *merchant vessels* (1967), 13 (51,000 gross registered tons); *principal airports,* Tegucigalpa, La Mesa, San Pedro Sula.
Communications: *Telephones* (1968): 10,161; *television stations* (1968), 5; *television sets* (1968), 10,500; *radios* (1967), 135,000; *newspapers* (1964), 7 (daily circulation, 41,000).

HONG KONG

Hong Kong entered a new phase of prosperity in 1969. Trade and industry thrived, tourism flourished, and the political situation was stabilized.

Economic Conditions. Hong Kong enjoyed an acceleration of economic growth in 1969. The export value of products in the first eight months of the year was 25% more than in the corresponding period of 1968. Manufacturing industries still played a vital part in the economy, constituting 40% of Hong Kong's income. Textiles and plastics remained the most important light industries, but new industries, particularly electronics, have been developing at a rapid rate. The ship-breaking and steel-milling industries, which had declined since 1961, were booming again because of a rise in world demand for steel bars. Tourism, another large source of revenue, accounted for 5.5% of Hong Kong's income. In 1968, visitors to Hong Kong spent more than $215 million. This amount was exceeded in 1969, when the number of tourists was well above 700,000.

Population Growth. Population growth has paralleled Hong Kong's economic expansion. It was estimated that the new census to be conducted in 1971 would show a population 30% greater than that of the 1961 census.

To meet future demand for water, the government considered building another reservoir, which would be formed by damming both ends of the sea passage between High Island and the southern coast of the Sai Kung Peninsula. A preliminary investigation for the reservoir scheme was begun. Also, an experimental desalting plant will be built to test the quality of sea water at various parts of the colony.

Transportation. In the summer of 1969 a bill was passed making mini-buses, an important means of land transport, legal public transportation.

The Cross-Harbor Tunnel Bill was passed in June. The tunnel, which will connect Hong Kong Island with Kowloon peninsula, is to be completed by 1972 at a cost of about $48 million.

Because of the expansion in passenger travel and the possible scheduling of commercial Boeing 747 jet flights to Hong Kong, the government is planning to expand the airport. The project, which includes the lengthening of the runway, will cost about $14.9 million, and when completed in 1971 will give Hong Kong one of the most modern airports in the world.

—————— **HONG KONG** • **Information Highlights** ——————

Area (including ocean area): 1,126 square miles (2,916 sq km).
Population: 3,927,000 (1968 est.).
Chief Cities (1961 census): Victoria, the capital, 633,138.
Government: *Governor*—Sir David Trench (took office 1965); *Colonial Secretary*—Sir Michael Gass (took office 1965).
Religious Faiths: Buddhists and Taoists, majority of population; Roman Catholics, 5.8%.
Education: *Literacy rate* (1968), 75% of population. *Total school enrollment* (1966)—902,691.
Finance (1969–70 est.): *Revenues,* $360,000,000; *expenditures,* $350,000,000; *monetary unit,* Hong Kong dollar (6.06 Hong Kong dollars equal U. S.$1).
Gross National Product (1969): $2,400,000,000.
Cost of Living Index (1967): 111 (1963=100).
Manufacturing (metric tons, 1967): Cement, 215,000; cotton yarn, 137,300; beer, 186,000 hectoliters.
Crops (metric tons, 1967–68 crop year): Rice, 12,000.
Minerals (metric tons, 1967): Iron ore, 80,000.
Foreign Trade (1968): *Exports,* $1,744,000,000 (chief exports, 1967: clothing, $360,369,000; textile yarn and fabrics, $222,829,000; electrical machinery, $88,687,000; toys and games, $82,451,000); *Imports,* $2,058,000,000 (chief imports, 1967: textile yarn and fabrics, $257,854,000; electrical machinery, $124,818,000; live animals, $60,300,000). *Chief trading partners* (1967): United States (took 30% of exports, supplied 14% of imports); Communist China; Japan.
Transportation: *Roads* (1966), 575 miles (925 km); *motor vehicles* (1967), 85,100 (automobiles 64,600); *railways* (1967), 29 miles (47 km); *principal airport,* Kai Tak.
Communications: *Telephones* (1968), 353,912; *television stations* (1968), 2; *television sets* (1968), 85,000; *radios* (1967), 623,000; *newspapers* (1967), 50.

Political Situation. Hong Kong is ruled by a British-appointed governor, who is assisted by a Legislative Council and an Executive Council. As the members of these two councils are nominated by the governor, Hong Kong has very limited autonomy. Suggestions were made in 1969 that some elected members of the Urban Council should be appointed to serve on the Legislative and Executive councils, and that Hong Kong should aim at self-government or independence. However, these suggestions were rejected because of Britain's carefully maintained nonprovocative policy designed to improve Sino-British relations. Both Communist China and Britain recognize the advantage of Hong Kong's continuing stability and security, well aware that the introduction of self-government might upset this acceptable situation.

DAVID CHUEN-YAN LAI
University of Victoria

HORSE RACING. See SPORTS.
HORSE SHOWS. See SPORTS.
HORTICULTURE. See GARDENING AND HORTICULTURE.

UPI

RELEASED DETAINEES from Communist China arrive in Hong Kong in April after being held for 46 days. Three women from among 15 persons on yachts seized by the Communists savor the pleasure of freedom. They are (*from left*) Christine von Sydow and her mother, Joan, and Jocelyn Budge.

HOSPITALS

The American consumer's consciousness of hospitals developed in 1969 to an extent never before reached. There was an increased acceptance of the hospital as a focal point in daily lives. Approximately one of every seven U. S. citizens spent some time during the year in a hospital as an in-patient. When hospital visitors, hospital staff members, and hospital supply personnel are added to the number of patients, it becomes clear that a large proportion of the population was affected—physically, emotionally, or financially, directly or indirectly—by the hospital.

Services. The character of the hospital is undergoing changes, in part because of advances in medical sciences but to a greater degree because of the rapidly rising influence of engineering, automation, and marketing on hospital care. There was an increased awareness in 1969 of the necessity for furnishing a higher standard of patient care, and new evaluation techniques were utilized. Hospital services—prevention, diagnosis, treatment, rehabilitation, education, and research—were being developed and offered in a broader spectrum to provide more efficient and more effective care of patients.

More and more the hospital was influencing the community at large. Greater emphasis was placed on making the hospital the center of community health activities. The general pattern called for co-operative association with public health, welfare, and other agencies concerned with community health, resulting in integration of all community health services.

There was continued heavy emphasis on building new facilities to provide new beds and services for the increasing numbers of patients. But there also was a trend toward providing other types of services —extended care, nursing homes, and ambulatory care. The increased use of hospitals has in large part resulted from the addition of Medicare and Medicaid to the nation's Social Security system, starting in 1966.

Costs. The cost of providing hospital care continued to rise dramatically in 1969 as the average price for one day of in-patient care moved toward the $80 mark. This contrasted to an average cost of $32 a day only a decade earlier. The average cost of a single hospital stay in 1969 was about $500 —more than double the average cost of a stay a decade earlier. In all, hospital care costs in 1969 rose by 11% over the previous year, and total hospital bills alone exceeded $19 billion.

THE RISING COST OF MEDICAL CARE IN THE UNITED STATES
(1957–59 = 100)

Year	Index number	Year	Index number
1960	108.1	1965	122.3
1961	111.3	1966	127.7
1962	114.2	1967	136.7
1963	117.0	1968	145.0
1964	119.4	1969 (Nov.)	157.4

Source: U. S. Bureau of Labor Statistics, "Consumer Price Index."

Trouble spots developed in the handling of both Medicare and Medicaid. In the latter case, costs to the federal government were double the original estimates.

The hospitals' share of the health dollar keeps rising. In the mid-1950's it was less than 30 cents, but by 1969 it had climbed to about 35 cents.

Trends. As was the case in the preceding year, the almost-out-of-hand increases in hospital expenses in 1969 led to growing concern over the total health system. Consumers made greater demands for a larger participating role in hospital management. Unrest developed in professional staffs and personnel groups within the hospitals, and there was an increase in union activity among these groups.

Federal and local government agencies began instituting corrective measures to reduce hospital costs and to achieve more efficient operations. Steps included the reevaluating of the disbursement of funds from Medicare and Medicaid programs, and new legislation resulted in a closer auditing of bills under these programs. Greater emphasis was placed on making studies to provide new means for paying for Medicare and Medicaid.

Reviewing groups were established to evaluate drug use, both for price and for efficacy. Other groups reviewed the cost of hospital equipment, or sought to establish tighter controls on the type and amount of hospital care provided to patients.

Another important development was a shift of federal and local funds from new hospital construction to the building of other, less-costly preventive and continuing-care facilities that are now closely associated with the modern hospital.

The trend toward making the hospital a true center for delivering comprehensive health services has created a dual responsibility for hospital administrators and for other health personnel concerned with planning and managing the delivery of such services. Their dual responsibility at the start of the 1970's in the United States involved (1) making available national health resources that are organized and utilized within a dynamic structure, and (2) paying increased attention to the basic elements of sound administrative practices.

LEON GINTZIG
George Washington University

HOTELS AND MOTELS. See TOURISM.
HOUSING. See BUILDING AND CONSTRUCTION.

HOUSTON

Houston, largest city in Texas and the nation's third-ranking port, maintained in 1969 the high rate of growth that has characterized it during the 1960's. The 1969 estimated population of the city—1,187,-000—represents an increase of more than 25% over the 1960 census. The five-county metropolitan area, with an estimated population of 1,839,000, has shown a 30% increase during the decade.

Events of the year that attracted wide attention were the opening of the Houston Intercontinental Airport, the mayoral election, and two Apollo lunar landings, which were planned and directed by the National Aeronautics and Space Administration's Manned Spacecraft Center near Houston.

New Airport. The Houston Intercontinental Airport, situated 20 miles north of downtown Houston, was opened on June 8 after a 2-year delay that boosted the cost of the two terminals from $17 million to more than $19 million and brought the total cost of the project to $110 million. The airport, designed specifically for jet planes, occupies a 7,300-acre site between the Eastex Freeway and the North Freeway. It includes twin terminal buildings, with concourses 300 feet long extending from the four corners of each building to circular flight stations, from which passengers board and leave planes. Each building provides parking spaces for 750 automobiles, and electronically run trains carry passengers within the area of the terminals.

Although most major facilities are complete, the city plans to extend the east-west runway to make it entirely adequate for the Boeing 747. A $10 million, 350-room hotel is scheduled for completion early in 1971. It is estimated that the airport will handle 4.5 million passengers during its first year of operation and that the annual figure will double by the mid-1970's.

Mayoral Election. Mayor Louie Welch won a fourth consecutive term in the Houston mayoral election on November 15. His chief opponent was Curtis M. Graves, a member of the state House of Representatives and the city's first Negro mayoral candidate. Welch polled about 52% of the votes cast, as against 32% for Graves.

The campaign was relatively quiet, the main issue being the record of the incumbent in dealing with such problems as crime, air and water pollution, and housing conditions in predominantly Negro areas. (Currently the population of the city is estimated to be about 20% Negro.) Graves, expressing concern over the high crime rate, stressed "law and justice." After the election he indicated his possible interest in entering the next mayoral race. Mayor Welch promised to urge adoption of a minimum housing code to improve housing.

Space Achievements. The manned Spacecraft Center attracted worldwide attention during the flights of Apollo 11 and Apollo 12 and the subsequent quarantine of the astronauts and the initial examination of the lunar samples (see SPACE EXPLORATION). On August 16 the city provided a day-long homecoming celebration for the Apollo 11 astronauts.

HUNGARY

In 1969 the Hungarian government permitted more freedom in both economic and cultural fields. Hungary endorsed the foreign policies of the Soviet Union, and Soviet aid continued to be the key to the country's economic development.

Economic Development. As a result of economic reforms initiated in 1967, the standard of living continued to rise in 1969. The country's industry expanded. According to government sources the most important weaknesses of the national economy were in the areas of employment, energy, machine building, raw materials, and agriculture. To offset economic difficulties, government and party leaders advocated expansion and further liberalization of foreign trade, currency convertibility within COMECON (the eastern European trade bloc), and increases in domestic productivity, which still lagged.

In order to ease unemployment and expose young and unskilled workers to more advanced technology, Hungary took advantage of industrial labor shortages in East Germany. Some 10,000 Hungarian workers were placed in East German centers such as Erfurt, Arnstadt, Dresden, and Ebersbach. The program will include 16,000 persons by 1972.

In June, Premier Jenö Fock opened a 600-megawatt thermal power plant on the Danube River. It furnishes one quarter of the country's electric power. The Szazhalombatta oil refinery, opened in the same ceremony, produces 1.5 million metric tons of fuel

a year. Fock publicly praised Soviet aid, as well as the cooperation of other countries.

Politics. Essentially, the political pattern in Hungary did not change in 1969. The Communist party preserved its monopoly of power as effectively as before. On the other hand, both the party and the government tried to liberalize the system as much as possible, within safe limits. On August 20, Constitution Day, the chairman of the National Assembly, Gyula Kallai, emphasized that resurgence of the "cult of the leader" would represent the most serious threat to Communist theory and practice.

As the result of an apparent truce between Budapest and the Vatican, two new archbishops and eight new bishops received government investiture. In January Jozsef Prantner, head of the state office for church affairs, publicly indicated that the government was ready and willing to negotiate a solution to the "problem" of Cardinal Mindszenty, who has lived in the U. S. embassy in Budapest since 1956.

Relations with the USSR. In 1969 about 80,000 Soviet troops were still stationed in Hungary, and there were no indications of their early withdrawal.

Despite cultural and economic liberalization at home, Hungary followed the policies set by the Soviet Union in international affairs. The Hungarian government denounced Communist China's "adventurist policy" on numerous occasions. It officially and repeatedly recognized Moscow as a guarantor of socialism in eastern Europe. Officials in Budapest approved the support of Soviet policies expressed by the June international party conference held in Moscow.

HUNGARY · Information Highlights

Area: 35,919 square miles (93,030 sq km).
Population: 10,255,000 (1968 est.).
Chief Cities (1966 census): Budapest, the capital, 1,960,000; Miskolc, 173,000; Debrecen, 150,000.
Government: Chairman of the Presidential Council—Pál Losonczi (took office April 14, 1967); Prime Minister—Jenö Fock (took office April 14, 1967); First Secretary of the Hungarian Socialist Workers' party—János Kádár (took office Oct. 25, 1956). Parliament—National Assembly (unicameral), 349 members.
Religious Faiths: Roman Catholics, 59% of population; Protestants, 30%; other, 11%.
Education: Literacy rate (1963), 97.4% of population aged 15 and over. Total school enrollment (1966)—1,757,057 (primary, 1,380,286; secondary, 230,299; technical/vocational, 94,145; university/higher, 52,327).
Finance (1968 est.): Revenues, $11,693,000,000; expenditures, $11,812,000,000; monetary unit, forint (11.74 forints equal U. S.$1).
Gross National Product (1966): $15,843,000,000.
National Income (1968): $18,824,532,000; average annual income per person, $1,835.
Economic Indexes (1968): Industrial production, 131 (1963= 100); agricultural production (1964), 148 (1949=100); cost of living (1967), 106 (1963=100).
Manufacturing (metric tons, 1967): Crude steel, 2,739,000; cement, 2,656,000; wheat flour, 1,301,000; sugar, 469,000; wine, 4,789,000 hectoliters; meat, 407,000.
Crops (metric tons, 1967–68 crop year): Maize, 3,580,000; sugar beets, 3,356,000; potatoes, 1,855,000.
Minerals (metric tons, 1967): Lignite, 22,976,000; bituminous coal, 4,053,000; crude petroleum, 1,686,000; bauxite, 1,-649,000; lime (1966), 773,000; dolomite, 580,000; iron ore, 176,000.
Foreign Trade (1967): Exports, $1,702,000,000 (chief exports, 1967: transport equipment, $208,475,000; nonelectrical machinery, $182,938,000; electrical machinery, $130,638,-000; fruit and vegetables, $111,465,000); imports, $1,776,-000,000 (chief imports, 1967: nonelectrical machinery; $327,660,000; transport equipment, $176,524,000; iron and steel, $102,708,000). Chief trading partners (1967): USSR (took 36% of exports, supplied 33% of imports); East Germany (took 10% of exports, supplied 11% of imports); Czechoslovakia.
Transportation: Roads (1964), 18,169 miles (29,240 km); motor vehicles (1966), 144,600; railways (1965), 5,036 miles (8,103 km); merchant vessels (1967), 17 (21,000 gross registered tons); national airline, Hungarian Airlines (Malev); principal airport, Ferihegy.
Communications: Telephones (1968), 634,527; television stations (1968), 11; television sets (1968), 1,200,000; radios (1967), 2,479,000; newspapers (1967), 25.

Soviet Aid. Hungary continued to be dependent on the Soviet Union for both exports and imports. Without Soviet raw materials, industrial equipment, and spare parts Hungarian industry, and to a lesser degree agriculture, could hardly have functioned. Hungary imported 68% of all its raw materials, including iron ore, pig iron, coke, crude oil, fertilizers, timber, and cotton, from the USSR. Almost 30% of all imports from the USSR was equipment for industry, mining, and agriculture.

Almost 80% of all Hungarian exports, including land and maritime transportation equipment, food, and pharmaceutical products, went to the Soviet Union. A special agreement increased planned Soviet deliveries of complete plants and equipment for 1971–75, the period of Hungary's fourth 5-year plan. Nine new plants for the chemical, housing, and crude oil industries were to be built with Soviet aid. On August 19, Hungary and the USSR signed an agreement in Moscow providing for construction of the "Friendship II," a crude oil pipeline linking the Transcarpathian Oblast of the Ukraine with Hungary.

Other Economic Agreements. Hungarian authorities made considerable efforts to improve trade with the non-Communist countries. In April the Hungarian Central Bank, acting for the Hungarian Aluminum Corporation, concluded arrangements with a consortium of eight Western banks for a 5-year loan of 15 million Eurodollars. It was the first time since 1945 that the Hungarians had allowed foreign non-Communist scrutiny of their industry.

Hungary concluded new economic agreements with Japan, Sweden, West Germany, and Italy, and progress was being made on agreements with Britain, France, and Austria. By the end of 1969, Hungary had exported about 1,500 metric tons of canned ham to the United States. In addition, it sent over 21,000 tons of wheat to Britain and Czechoslovakia and 1,700 tons of rye to Austria. Also, the Hungarians approached Brazil to see if Brazilian markets would be available for the remaining grain surplus.

Relations with the United States. In August a significant breakthrough in relations with the United States took place. The United States and Hungary signed four agreements concerning conditions for payment of Hungary's debt, U. S. social security payments to some 300 beneficiaries from Hungary who had returned to their homeland, mutual expansion of embassy staffs, and establishment of a Hungarian commercial office in New York.

JAN KARSKI
Georgetown Universtiy

HUSAK, Gustav. See biographical sketch under CZECHOSLOVAKIA.

ICELAND

Iceland faced severe economic problems in 1969, with strikes, losses in income because of low prices for fish, and unemployment.

Labor Disputes. In January 1969, workers, refusing to bear the costs of the 1968 currency devaluation alone, went on strike. A fishermen's strike, lasting four weeks, ended in February after owners agreed to wage increases. A two-day general strike began on April 10 to protest the government's decision to stop tying wages to the price index.

The strikes were eventually settled through government intervention. Special legislation was re-

---

──────── **ICELAND** • Information Highlights ────────

Area: 39,758 square miles (102,972 sq km).
Population: 200,000 (1968 est.).
Chief Cities (1966 est.): Reykjavík, the capital, 79,202.
Government: *President*—Kristján Eldjárn (took office June 1968); *Prime Minister*—Bjarni Benediktsson (took office November 1963). *Parliament*—Althing, Lower House, 40 members; Upper House, 20 members (party seating, 1969: Independence party, 23; Progressive party, 18; People's Alliance, 10; People's party, 9).
Religious Faiths: Evangelical Lutherans, 96% of population; others, 4%.
Education: *Literacy rate* (1969), 99% of population. *Total school enrollment* (1965)—50,257 (primary, 25,380; secondary, 18,437; teacher-training, 423; technical/vocational, 4,901; university/higher, 1,116).
Finance (1968 est.): *Revenues*, $109,200,000; *expenditures*, $107,400,000; *monetary unit*, króna (88 krónur equal U. S.$1).
Gross National Product (1968): $447,000,000.
National Income (1967): $197,784,000; *average annual income per person*, $988.
Economic Indexes (1967): *Fish production*, 116 (1963=100); *cost of living*, 146 (1963=100).
Manufacturing (metric tons, 1967): Fish meal, 178,000; cement, 116,000; salted herring (1966), 43,500.
Agriculture (metric tons, 1967–68 crop year): Milk, 121,000; potatoes, 8,000; cattle, 55,000 head.
Minerals: Shell sand, liparite, perlite, pumice, peat.
Foreign Trade (1968): *Exports*, $82,000,000 (chief exports, 1967: frozen fish, $14,839,886; herring meal, $8,347,000; herring oil, $4,871,363; undressed hides and skins, $1,352,000); *Imports*, $138,000,000 (chief imports, 1967: transport equipment, $13,800,000; electrical machinery, $6,000,000; petroleum products, $6,000,000). *Chief trading partners* (1967): United States (took 15% of exports, supplied 15% of imports); Britain (took 21% of exports, supplied 13% of imports); West Germany (took 6% of exports, supplied 13% of imports).
Transportation: *Roads* (1966), 8,626 miles (13,879 km); *motor vehicles* (1967), 42,100 (automobiles 35,500); *merchant vessels* (1967), 23 (51,000 gross registered tons); *airlines*, Iceland Air, Icelandic Airlines.
Communications: *Telephones* (1968), 62,698; *radios* (1967), 59,000; *newspapers* (1965), 5 (daily circulation, 83,000).

---

quired, and almost the entire session of the Althing (parliament) was devoted to solving labor problems.

Once they had been granted special powers, government leaders moved to settle the disputes by promising higher wages and fringe benefits. In the end, wages for low-income groups were increased, a cost of living index was established, pensions were improved, and overtime pay provisions were added. It was a significant wage agreement for Iceland, because of its far-reaching provisions and the government's role in negotiating the settlement.

Other Legislation. The Althing also approved a provisional law that imposed uniform regulations for the preparation of frozen or salted fish on the fishing fleets. Another law, which claimed national rights to gas and all other minerals and properties on the continental shelf, sought to help the economy by exploiting these resources.

Economy. Low prices for fish products and three years of unusually poor catches left Iceland's economy in dire straits. A slight note of optimism came during the later part of 1969, with increased fishing catches and better world prices for fish products. International loans aided the government in assisting the shaky Icelandic economy.

Foreign Policy. The main interest of the government was in new trade agreements that would help solve economic problems. The Althing approved Icelandic membership in the European Free Trade Association, and application was made for entry. Proposals for Iceland's withdrawal from NATO were debated, but the government continued to favor the alliance.

University Reforms. Reforms in the universities created new institutes, expanded fields of study, and provided for increased student participation in university administration.

RAYMOND E. LINDGREN
California State College, Long Beach

IDAHO

An active legislative year, marked by major controversy over the state budget, and important developments in conservation and agriculture were among the highlights of 1969 in Idaho.

Legislature. Although Gov. Don Samuelson strongly opposed a budget larger than $202 million, the Legislature refused to accept that low a figure and the governor eventually signed bills totaling $220.8 million. Both public and higher education received about 35% more than in 1967. Of the general budget, 71% is now spent for education.

The Legislature increased expense allowances for its members to $35 a day during sessions and $200 a month between sessions. However, a petition was circulated to reduce this allowance to $25 a day. Although the Legislature increased state spending by 22%, it limited local governments to a 4% increase in their budgets each year. Because the lawmakers failed to designate an enforcing agency, district courts were not enforcing the 4% limitation.

A revision commission created by the Legislature to draft a new constitution held public hearings for reactions to its proposals.

A court reform bill, which will take effect in 1971, merged probate, police, and justice courts into one division, and provided a system for appointing judges. Other new laws provided for open housing, established a Human Rights Commission, and raised maximum interest rates to 10%.

Agriculture and Conservation. A newly created state tax commission ordered the assessor of Nez

--- **IDAHO · Information Highlights** ---

Area: 83,557 square miles (216,413 sq km).
Population: 702,000 (1969 est.).
Chief Cities (1969 est.): Boise, the capital, 73,000; Pocatello, 41,000; Idaho Falls, 36,500; Twin Falls, 20,900.
Government: *Chief Officers*—governor, Don Samuelson (Republican); lt. gov., Jack M. Murphy (R); secy. of state, Pete T. Cenarrusa (R); atty. gen., Robert Robson (R); treas., Marjorie Ruth Moon; supt. of pub. instr., D. F. Engleking; chief justice, Joseph J. McFadden. *Legislature*—Senate, 35 members (21 Republicans, 14 Democrats); House of Representatives, 70 members (38 R, 32 D).
Education: *School enrollment* (1968–69)—public elementary, 91,000 pupils (3,700 teachers); public secondary, 88,000 pupils (4,200 teachers); nonpublic schools, 8,800 pupils (340 teachers); college and university (fall 1967), 26,372 students. *Public school expenditures* (1967–68)—$101,-409,000 ($600 per pupil); average teacher's salary $6,200.
Public Finance (fiscal year 1968): *Revenues,* $271,953,000 (general sales and gross receipts taxes, $35,127,000; motor fuel tax, $21,714,000; federal funds, $66,477,000). *Expenditures,* $236,446,000 (education, $33,789,000; health, welfare, and safety, $30,646,000; highways, $46,820,000). *State debt,* $18,515,000 (June 30, 1968).
Personal Income (1968): $1,876,000,000; average annual income per person, $2,668.
Public Assistance (fiscal year 1968): $19,370,925 to 20,197 recipients (aged, $2,557,671; dependent children $7,-078,065).
Labor Force (employed persons, annual average 1968): *Agricultural,* 48,100; *nonagricultural* (wage and salary earners), 227,000 (19.6% manufacturing, 23.9% trade, 18.4% government). *Unemployed persons* (annual average 1968)—12,300.
Manufacturing (1968): *Value added by manufacture,* $610,-000,000 (transportation equipment, $6,850,000; lumber and wood products, $101,698,000; nonelectrical machinery, $5,437,000; chemicals and allied products, $95,046,000; fabricated metals, $3,916,000; food and products, $129,-441,000).
Agriculture (1967): *Cash farm income,* $335,740,000 (livestock, $227,081,000; crops, $71,589,000; govt. payments, $37,070,000). *Chief crops* (tons)—Potatoes, 3,195,000 (ranks 1st among the states); sugar beets, 2,946,000 (ranks 2d); hay, 3,714,000; wheat, 1,707,150.
Mining (1968): *Production value,* $114,253,000. *Chief minerals* (tons)—Zinc, 57,248; lead, 54,790; copper, 3,525; silver, 15,958,715 troy ounces; gold, 3,227 troy ounces.
Transportation: *Roads* (1968), 54,758 miles (88,122 km); *motor vehicles* (1968), 515,285; *railroads* (1968), 3,073 track miles (4,945 km); *airports* (1967), 111.
Communications (1968): *Telephones,* 300,100; *television stations,* 6; *radio stations,* 41; *newspapers,* 13.

Perce County to restore valuations on farmland that had been reduced by county commissioners. Farmers contended that farmland be taxed at the income-producing value rather than at the sale price.

Lower farm prices and average crops did not improve the farm economy. Early in 1969 the lumber industry enjoyed excessively high prices, but severe price decreases left operations below normal by the year's end. Heavy snowfalls gave southern Idaho adequate irrigation water, but made transportation difficult in the north. Record low temperatures killed many trees and shrubs, and reduced winter wheat yields in the north. The summer was extremely dry, but large forest fires were avoided.

The American Smelting and Refining Company asked permission to build a road into the White Cloud Mountains to develop its molybdenum claims. The Forest Service held public hearings, and while conservation groups reacted strongly Governor Samuelson supported the mining firms, contending that the project would help the economy of the area.

U. S. Senators Frank Church and Len Jordan introduced an amendment to their pending Sawtooth National Recreation Area bill that would add the adjoining White Cloud area. The Senate failed to pass a bill declaring a 10-year moratorium on dam building, but the Department of the Interior asked for a 5-year moratorium. Federal fund cutbacks will delay construction of Lower Granite Dam on the Snake River.

Court Decision. The validity of Idaho's bonding laws were placed in doubt when the U. S. Supreme Court held that states could not require property ownership as a prerequisite to voting in revenue bond elections.

CLIFFORD DOBLER
University of Idaho

ILLINOIS

The adoption of a state income tax, the convening of a constitutional convention, a major crisis in the state supreme court, and the death on September 7 of Everett M. Dirksen, Illinois' senior U. S. senator (see DIRKSEN), shared the spotlight in Illinois during 1969.

Legislation. Under a measure enacted by the General Assembly on June 30, Illinois became the 39th state to adopt an income tax. Sponsored by the new Republican administration of Gov. Richard B. Ogilvie as a solution to the state's revenue crisis, the measure came under vigorous attack early in the session by Democrats and some downstate Republicans because the proposed 4% flat rate made no distinction between corporations and individuals. In addition, many legislators were apprehensive about supporting any income tax with the 1970 general elections just a short time away.

Late in the session the administration lowered its request to a 3% flat-rate tax, and when this was defeated the governor abandoned the flat-rate formula to save the tax. Although expressing doubts about its constitutionality, he accepted a compromise plan introduced by the Democrats, fixing the rate at 4% on net income of corporations and 2½% on gross income (less $1,000 per dependent) of individuals. An immediate challenge to the tax was rejected by the state supreme court.

Other legislation included provisions for a bureau of the budget and a change from a biennial to an annual budget, a department of local governmental affairs, a department of law enforcement (patterned after the FBI), an office of human resources, and increased aid to local governments and schools. The legislators also set up the machinery for the constitutional convention.

Constitutional Convention. The opening of a constitutional convention in Springfield on December 8 marked Illinois' second effort during this century to update its 100-year-old constitution. (The constitution drafted by the 1920–22 convention was rejected by the voters.) Despite the nonpartisan election of the 116 delegates, most of those elected were regular Democrats and Republicans. But a generous sprinkling of independents could serve as a catalyst to some urgently needed constitutional reform. The many issues confronting the convention may make it difficult for the delegates to complete their work in the 8-month period alloted by law.

The State Supreme Court Crisis. Confidence in the Illinois judiciary was shaken during the summer when the chief justice and one associate justice of the seven-member supreme court resigned under a cloud of suspicion. The crisis was precipitated by an independent legal researcher who charged that Chief Justice Roy J. Solfisburg, Jr., and Justice Ray I. Klingbiel were guilty of "undue influence and the appearance of impropriety" in their actions in the court's dismissal in 1967 of a criminal indictment against Theodore J. Isaacs, a former state director of internal revenue. A subsequent investigation by a special commission appointed by the court itself disclosed that there was no actual proof

of impropriety, but the commission suggested that the justices resign as a necessary step to restore public confidence in the state judiciary. Steadfastly maintaining their innocence of any wrongdoing, the justices resigned early in August.

A month later the functioning membership of the court dropped to four when one of the remaining justices died of a stroke. Under the constitution no case can be decided without the concurrence of four justices. Consequently, unanimity would be necessary to decide a case, and no action could be taken if any one justice were to disqualify himself. Adding to the dilemma was a decision by the court itself, earlier in the year, declaring gubernatorial appointment to fill judicial vacancies to be unconstitutional. The court itself finally provided temporary relief by invoking its constitutional authority to recall three retired lower court judges to sit with the supreme court until the vacancies are filled in the 1970 general election.

New U. S. Senator. Republican Ralph T. Smith of Alton, speaker of the Illinois House of Representatives, was appointed by Governor Ogilvie on September 17 to the vacancy caused by the death of Senator Dirksen. He must stand for election in 1970 for the remaining four years of the term.

Racial Unrest. The major trouble spot during the year was the river town of Cairo, where about 42% of the population of some 8,000 is black. Early in the year groups in the black community were organized into the United Front, which presented city officials with demands, including the naming of black city officials and the disbanding of an all-white vigilante group known as the "White Hats." Sniping and firebombing incidents resulted in the governor's sending National Guardsmen to the scene in April and state policemen in June. Marches on police headquarters and city hall and the boycotting of white businesses by blacks brought on ordinances restricting assembly and picketing.

As the situation worsened, Lt. Gov. Paul Simon, the state's ombudsman, attempted to reestablish communication between blacks and whites. The governor promised immediate aid for community projects; the mayor and the police chief resigned in a move to lessen tensions; and a black man was named to the city council. At year's end, however, these efforts had fallen short of establishing racial harmony.

TWILEY W. BARKER
University of Illinois at Chicago Circle

IMMIGRATION

More than 231 million entries were made across the land borders of the United States and at seaports and airports during the year ending June 30, 1969, exceeding the number for 1968 by 6%. Multiple crossings of Canadian and Mexican borders and multiple entries of crewmen accounted for 96% of the total. Alien admissions totaled nearly 135 million, while U. S. citizen admissions totaled 96 million.

Immigration Regulation. The Immigration and Nationality Act of Oct. 3, 1965, set a numerical limitation of 170,000 immigrants from countries outside the Western Hemisphere. Preference is given to relatives of citizens and resident aliens, aliens with talents and skills needed in the United States, and refugees. Also beginning in July 1968, an annual ceiling of 120,000 was put on immigration from countries of the Western Hemisphere. Western Hemisphere visa numbers are allocated on a first-come, first-served basis. Parents, spouses, and children of U. S. citizens are designated "immediate relatives," and are not subject to the numerical limitations.

Section 212(a)(14) of the Immigration and Nationality Act of 1952, as amended in 1965, provides that aliens entering the United States to be gainfully employed must have certification from the secretary of labor that the alien's employment will not adversely affect wages and working conditions in the United States.

Public Law 89–732, which became effective Nov. 2, 1966, enabled Cuban refugees who met other legal requirements to become permanent residents after two years' residence in the United States.

Immigrants. In the fiscal year ending June 30, 1969, 358,579 aliens became permanent residents of the United States. Of this total, 319,791 obtained visas abroad and 38,788 were in the U. S.

Immigrants subject to numerical limitations numbered 290,995 or 81% of the total. Of the 67,584 immigrants not subject to these limitations, 60,016 were "immediate relatives" of U. S. citizens. There were 120,086 immigrants of European birth, 132,426 North American, 73,621 Asian, and 23,928 South American. By June 30, 1969, the status of 123,615 Cuban refugees had been adjusted to that of permanent residents under Public Law 89–732.

Table 1—PRINCIPAL COUNTRIES OF FORMER ALLEGIANCE OF PERSONS NATURALIZED IN THE UNITED STATES
(Years ended June 30, 1966–69)

Country or region of former allegiance	1966	1967	1968	1969
All countries	103,059	104,902	102,726	98,709
Europe	62,410	61,534	58,267	51,847
Albania	110	110	109	103
Austria	1,012	973	825	688
Belgium	334	337	330	291
Bulgaria	69	75	92	74
Czechoslovakia	551	458	438	340
Denmark	408	442	428	316
Estonia	127	95	96	94
Finland	265	265	251	236
France	1,446	1,472	1,424	1,416
Germany	13,706	13,204	12,692	10,618
Greece	3,373	3,438	3,256	3,029
Hungary	2,971	2,376	2,139	1,725
Iceland	41	41	26	45
Ireland	2,885	3,083	2,959	2,620
Italy	10,981	10,572	9,379	8,773
Latvia	388	353	403	331
Lithuania	393	397	360	345
Luxembourg	63	55	56	56
Malta	111	131	122	112
Netherlands	2,762	2,698	2,555	1,930
Norway	497	506	488	461
Poland	3,833	4,072	3,893	3,643
Portugal	2,179	2,156	1,694	1,543
Rumania	299	367	717	434
Spain	731	796	713	721
Sweden	327	367	359	325
Switzerland	587	578	521	514
Turkey	347	406	452	444
United Kingdom	8,930	8,777	8,466	7,979
USSR	848	874	887	767
Yugoslavia	1,764	1,976	2,067	1,808
Other Europe	72	84	70	66
Asia	14,369	14,259	14,980	15,362
China (Including Taiwan)	3,111	2,924	3,186	3,399
India	224	262	303	384
Israel	2,814	2,276	2,271	1,836
Japan	2,673	2,553	2,476	2,067
Philippines	2,384	2,958	2,807	3,877
Other Asia	3,163	3,286	3,937	3,799
North America	20,899	22,597	23,167	24,831
Canada	8,579	8,120	6,984	6,387
Mexico	5,677	6,044	6,134	5,111
Cuba	3,829	5,485	6,784	9,654
Other North America	9,457	11,381	13,314	17,012
South America	2,538	3,065	3,081	3,758
Africa	562	576	905	671
Oceania	422	429	461	384

Source: U. S. Department of Justice, Immigration and Naturalization Service.

Table 2—IMMIGRANT ALIENS ADMITTED TO THE UNITED STATES
(Year ended June 30, 1969)

	Total admitted	Quota immigrants	Nonquota immigrants
All countries	358,579	290,995	67,584
Europe	120,086	94,813	25,273
Czechoslovakia	3,307	3,028	279
France	2,024	1,252	772
Germany	9,289	3,919	5,370
Greece	17,724	15,534	2,190
Hungary	1,795	1,322	473
Iceland	1,989	1,579	410
Italy	23,617	18,494	5,123
Netherlands	1,303	882	421
Poland	4,052	3,253	799
Portugal	16,528	15,490	1,038
Rumania	1,435	1,082	353
Spain	3,916	2,869	1,047
Sweden	722	520	202
Switzerland	691	528	163
Turkey (Europe and Asia)	2,058	1,576	482
United Kingdom	15,014	11,327	3,687
USSR (Europe and Asia)	931	709	222
Yugoslavia	8,868	7,850	1,018
Other Europe	4,823	3,599	1,224
North America	132,426	111,948	20,478
Canada	18,582	14,954	3,628
Mexico	44,623	31,951	12,672
Cuba	13,751	13,286	465
Other West Indies	45,644	43,153	2,491
Central America	9,692	8,524	1,168
Other North America	134	80	54
South America	23,928	22,295	1,633
Asia	73,621	55,322	16,299
Africa	5,876	4,925	951
Oceania	2,639	1,691	948
Australia	1,384	854	530
New Zealand	494	285	209
Other Oceania	761	552	209
Other countries	3	1	2

Nonimmigrants. Nonimmigrants are aliens admitted to the United States for temporary periods of time, or alien residents of the United States who have been abroad temporarily. Exclusive of the multiple entries at land borders and of alien crewmen, 3,645,328 nonimmigrants arrived in the United States as tourists, students, exchange visitors, aliens in transit, and representatives of foreign governments. Tourists, mostly from Canada, Mexico, the United Kingdom, and Germany, numbered 2,382,198. Students totaled 90,486; exchange visitors, 47,175; temporary workers and trainees, 62,952; aliens in transit; 210,543; visitors admitted on a temporary basis to conduct business with U. S. firms, 299,810; foreign government officials, 48,095; and returning resident aliens, 441,082.

Deportable Aliens. The number of deportable aliens located was 283,557, a 34% increase over 1968. Of the total, 41% were aliens who became deportable by violating the status for which they were admitted. The remainder were aliens who entered the United States illegally. Mexican aliens accounted for 71% of all deportable aliens located. Aliens formally deported numbered 10,505, and 240,958 were required to depart without formal proceedings.

Naturalizations. A total of 98,709 permanent resident aliens became U. S. citizens in 1969. This was a small decrease from 1968. Included were 73,489 who were naturalized under the general provisions of the law; 19,617 spouses and children of U. S. citizens, 5,458 under military provisions, and 145 others. Certificates of citizenship were awarded to 16,606 children born abroad to U. S. citizens, as well as 13,133 persons who acquired citizenship through the naturalization of parents or through marriage.

RAYMOND F. FARRELL
Commissioner of Immigration and Naturalization
U. S. Department of Justice

INCOME. See ECONOMY OF THE UNITED STATES.

V. V. Giri, elected president of India with the help of Prime Minister Indira Gandhi, salutes crowds after swearing-in ceremonies in New Delhi, August 24.

INDIA

In 1969, India celebrated the centenary of the birth of Mohandas K. Gandhi, the great apostle of nonviolence, but the celebrations were muted because of the worst Hindu-Muslim riots since partition and independence 22 years before. The economic situation improved, but the political situation bcame more unstable, largely as a result of midterm elections in five Indian states and of the split in the ruling Congress party, a development of great significance and unknown consequences.

DOMESTIC AFFAIRS

Midterm Elections. In February legislative elections were held in four states—Bihar, the Punjab, Uttar Pradesh, and West Bengal—and in the Union Territory of Pondicherry, all of which had been under direct rule by the central government, and in Nagaland, which had held elections five years before. The results seemed to confirm the political changes dramatized by the fourth general elections in 1967, featuring the decline of the Congress party and a confused political situation in many states.

New ministries were formed in all the states in which elections were held. In Bihar the Congress party, for the first time, headed a coalition government, but it lasted only four months and another period of instability ensued. In the Punjab the Sikh Akali Dal party formed a government with the unlikely support of the right-wing, primarily Hindu, Jana Sangh. Although the Congress gained 10 seats in Uttar Pradesh, for a time a grouping composed mainly of dissident Congressmen, known as the Bhartiya Kranti Dal, headed a coalition government. However, in a few weeks this ministry fell, and C. B. Gupta, a former chief minister, returned at the head of a Congress government. In Nagaland the Nata National Organization remained in power.

In West Bengal the Congress suffered a real rout, losing more than half its seats while the Left Communists nearly doubled their strength. Significant gains also were made by the Right Communists and the Forward Bloc. These three parties, together with the Bangla Congress, a group of dissident Congressmen, were the main elements of the United Front of 14 parties whose coalition tactics overwhelmed the Congress. After the elections the UF formed a government with a Bangla Congress chief minister and a Left Communist deputy chief minister.

Mrs. Gandhi and the "Syndicate." Immediately after the midterm elections Prime Minister Indira Gandhi reshuffled her cabinet, appointing new ministers of external affairs, education, health, steel, foreign trade, petrochemicals, and railways. The most controversial appointee was Dinesh Singh, minister for external affairs. This reshuffle seemed to proclaim Mrs. Gandhi's independence of the old-guard Congress party bosses known as the Syndicate.

The struggle between Mrs. Gandhi and the Syndicate became more apparent after the death of Dr. Zakir Husain, president of India, on May 3. V. V. Giri, the vice president, became acting president, and even though he was 75 years old, it was thought that he would be the Congress party choice for president, especially since Mrs. Gandhi favored him. Instead, in mid-July the Syndicate-dominated Congress Parliamentary Board, over Mrs. Gandhi's objections, chose N. Sanjiva Reddy, speaker of the Lok Sabha (House of the People) as the candidate.

Mrs. Gandhi defied the Syndicate by announcing a decision to nationalize the 14 largest banks in India, and on July 16 she dismissed Morarji Desai as finance minister. Desai thereupon resigned as deputy prime minister and became more openly associated with the Syndicate.

Area: 1,178,995 square miles (3,053,597 sq km).

Population: 523,893,000 (1968 est.).

Chief Cities (1967 census): New Delhi, the capital, 324,283; Bombay (1968), 5,368,484; Calcutta, 3,072,196.

Government: *President*—V. V. Giri (took office Aug. 24, 1969); *Vice President*—G. S. Pathak (took office Aug. 24, 1969); *Prime Minister*—Mrs. Indira Gandhi (took office Jan. 24, 1966). *Parliament*—Rajya Sabha (Council of the States), 240 members; Lok Sabha (House of the People), 520 members (party seating, 1967: Congress, 282; Swatantra, 44; Communists, 41; Jana Sangh, 35; others, 118).

Religious Faiths: Hindus, 84% of population; Muslims, 11%.

Education: *Literacy rate* (1969), 28% of population. *Total school enrollment* (1965)—66,314,554 (primary, 49,639,-000; secondary, 15,050,000; teacher-training, 140,000; vocational, 340,000; higher, 1,145,554).

Finance (1968 est.): *Revenues*, $4,481,100,000; *expenditures*, $6,191,100,000; *monetary unit*, rupee (7.57 equal U. S.$1).

Gross National Product (1968): $46,000,000,000.

National Income (1967): $36,856,000,000; *average annual income per person*, $70.

Economic Indexes (1968): *Industrial production*, 127 (1963 = 100); *agricultural production*, 104 (1963 = 100); *cost of living*, 156, (1963 = 100).

Manufacturing (metric tons, 1967): Cement, 11,309,000; crude steel, 6,380,000; sugar, 2,357,000; gasoline, 2,531,000; wheat flour, 1,309,000.

Crops (metric tons, 1967–68 crop year): Rice, 56,787,000 (ranks 2d among world producers); sorghum, 10,107,000 (world rank, 2d); millet, 9,075,000 (world rank, 1st); peanuts, 6,000,000 (world rank, 1st); rapeseed, 1,228,000.

Minerals (metric tons, 1967): Manganese ore (1966), 1,678,-000 (ranks 3d among world producers); coal, 68,220,000; iron ore, 25,704,000.

Foreign Trade (1968): *Exports*, $1,754,000,000 (chief exports, 1967: textile yarn and fabrics, $462,932,000; tea, $238,000,-000); *imports*, $2,510,000,000 (chief imports, 1967: non-electrical machinery, $443,804,000; unmilled wheat and meslin, $499,960,000). *Chief trading partners* (1967): United States (took 17% of exports, supplied 39% of imports); Britain (took 19% of exports, supplied 8% of imports); Japan.

Transportation: *Roads* (1966), 513,000 miles (825,571 km); *motor vehicles* (1967), 888,800 (automobiles 477,200); *railways* (1966), 36,126 miles (58,138 km); *national airlines*, Air India; Indian Airlines Corporation; *principal airports*, Bombay, Calcutta, Delhi.

Communications: *Telephones* (1968): 993,590; *television stations* (1967), 1; *television sets* (1967), 6,000; *radios* (1967), 7,579,000; *newspapers* (1967), 588.

Refusing to support Reddy, the Congress nominee, in the presidential election held August 16, Mrs. Gandhi backed Giri, who ran as an independent. In a close contest the electoral college chose Giri, thanks to support of some Congress electors.

Congress Party Split. On August 25 the Congress party Working Committee (executive board) adopted a "unity" resolution, but events that followed soon led to the official breakup of the 84-year-old party. In late August, S. Nijalingappa, president of the party, removed two of Mrs. Gandhi's supporters from the Working Committee. Mrs. Gandhi retaliated by refusing to attend a meeting of the Committee on November 1 and called a rival meeting of her own. Eleven members of the Committee attended the regular meeting, and 10 went to Mrs. Gandhi's meeting. On November 12 the Syndicate and its followers in the truncated Working Committee voted to expel Mrs. Gandhi from the party for "grave acts of indiscipline." Mrs. Gandhi rejected this action as "illegal and of no validity," and the following day about three fourths of the members of the Congress Parliamentary party reaffirmed their confidence in her leadership.

When the winter session of Parliament opened on November 17 the Syndicate supporters took seats on opposition benches and were officially recognized as an opposition party, the "Congress Party in Parliament (Opposition)," with Dr. Ram Subhag Singh as leader. An adjournment motion was defeated by a vote of 306 to 140, thus giving Mrs. Gandhi an impressive victory and seemingly ensuring her continuance in office for some time, in spite of the opposition of the Syndicate. On November 22 and 23 more than half of the members of the All-India Congress Committee, meeting at the call of Mrs. Gandhi, voted to remove Nijalingappa as party president and selected C. Subramaniam as interim president. In December the two party factions met separately in plenary sessions.

State Politics. The contest between the two factions of the divided Congress party affected the party and its members at every level and in every state. The divisive effects were first seen in Bihar, where a former chief minister, Harihar Singh, failed to form another Congress-led coalition, and in Uttar Pradesh, where Deputy Chief Minister Kamalapati Tripathi and seven other members of the state cabinet resigned on November 21. Tripathi openly supported Mrs. Gandhi and headed the opposition to Chief Minister Gupta, who sided with the Syndicate.

In March the Congress regained control of Madhya Pradesh, 20 months after it had been ousted from power by an opposition coalition. On October 24, after the resignation of seven ministers and a vote of no-confidence in the assembly, the United Front government in Kerala, which had been dominated by the Left Communists, fell, and on November 1 it was succeeded by a four-party coalition ministry headed by a Right Communist.

Internal Disorders. Recurrent agitation, riots, acts of violence, and occasional bloodshed marked the scene in several Indian states in 1969. In

UPI

INDIRA GANDHI, prime minister of India, was confronted in 1969 by a split within her ruling Congress party. Under attack from the party's old-guard, she won a personal triumph in August, when V. V. Giri, running as an independent, defeated the party's right-wing candidate for president of India. But Mrs. Gandhi's hold on the premiership was tenuous. In November the party's executive board "expelled" her, but the Congress Parliamentary party gave its support, and she withstood a vote of no-confidence.

Mrs. Gandhi, the daughter of the late Prime Minister Jawaharlal Nehru and the widow of a lawyer, Feroze Gandhi, was born in Allahabad on Nov. 19, 1917. She was educated at Visva-Bharati University and at Oxford. A member of the Congress party since 1938, she was its president in 1959–60. She was minister of information from 1964 until becoming prime minister in 1966.

POLITICAL VICTORS: Mrs. Gandhi (*above*) overcame a party split on November 17 that threatened to topple her government. Communist supporters (*below*) celebrated a victory in West Bengal elections, February 10.

Andhra Pradesh rioting accompanied demands for greater concessions—perhaps even statehood—for Telengana, a region comprising much of the former Hyderabad state. In West Bengal extreme leftists, especially the so-called "Naxalites," seemed to be attempting to erode all respect for authority, and on April 10 a general strike was organized in Calcutta by the United Front government itself. In December the chief minister went on a fast in protest against the breakdown of law and order.

In Gujarat, in late September, a seven-day orgy of communal violence—the worst since 1947—led to hundreds (perhaps thousands) of deaths of Hindus and Muslims. It was particularly ironic that this tragedy occurred in the very part of India where Gandhi was born, immediately before the centenary of his birth (October 2). The Punjab witnessed frequent demonstrations over the failure of the national government to accede to demands to merge the city of Chandigarh with it. The greatest crisis there came after an aged Sikh leader died on October 27, on the 74th day of a fast on this Chandigarh issue.

Visit of Ghaffar Khan. On October 1, just before the Gandhi centenary, Khan Abdul Ghaffar Khan, an 80-year-old former associate and disciple of Gandhi and a leader of the Pathans of the former Northwest Frontier province, arrived in India for his first visit since independence. In the intervening years he had been living first in Pakistan and then in Afghanistan campaigning for a separate Pathan state. Although he was outspoken in his criticism of many things he observed in India, Khan was received with great deference by Prime Minister Gandhi and other political leaders.

Economy. In contrast to the political scene, the economic situation in 1969 continued to improve in many important aspects. Speaking before Parliament on February 17, President Zakir Husain referred to the following "milestones passed on the road to our economic recovery": "A decisive upward turn in agriculture, a recovery in a large segment of industry, relative price stability and a striking improvement in the balance of payments."

Production of foodgrains was about 95 million tons in 1968–69 and was expected to exceed 100 million tons in 1969–70. Industrial output increased by some 6%. The upward trend of prices was largely checked, and the prices of foodgrains actually declined in 1968–69 by nearly 10%. Exports in 1968–69 reached record levels, increasing some 13%, and imports were substantially reduced.

In April the fourth 5-year plan, originally scheduled to enter into effect three years previously, officially commenced. The final version of the plan was considerably more realistic and less ambitious than the draft outline released in 1966. It called for a modest expenditure over the period 1969–74 of $32.5 billion—$19.2 billion in the public and $13.3 billion in the private sector—and it envisaged annual increases of about 5% in agriculture, 8 to 10% in industry, 7% in exports, and an overall growth rate of 5.5%. The emphasis of the plan was on "stability and self-reliance." It held out the prospect that inequalities in income would be reduced, living standards raised, food aid eliminated, and dependence on foreign aid substantially reduced.

FOREIGN AFFAIRS

Absorbed with domestic problems, Prime Minister Gandhi and other government leaders gave relatively little attention to foreign affairs in 1969.

There were signs that India was gearing its foreign policy to its new economic policies, with an emphasis on increased trade. In general India seemed to be seeking more flexibility and a new independence of both the United States and the Soviet Union.

Relations with China and Pakistan. On New Year's Day, 1969, Mrs. Gandhi hinted at some modifications in India's policy toward Communist China, but there was no response from Peking. Relations with Pakistan remained frozen in molds of hostility and distrust. India renewed its offer to reopen trade and resume communications interrupted since the 1965 war, but Pakistan continued to demand concessions on Kashmir and on the allocation of the waters of the Ganges. An Indian protest to Pakistan over the alleged presence in the Pakistan-held portion of northern Kashmir of some 12,000 Chinese working on a new road was sharply rejected.

Diplomacy. In March, Marshal Andrei Grechko, the Soviet minister of defense, visited India, and in October his Indian counterpart, Swaran Singh, visited the Soviet Union. In late May and early June, Mrs. Gandhi visited Indonesia, and in June she went to Japan and Afghanistan on official visits. Foreign Minister Dinesh Singh visited the United States twice, in June and in September-October, and the Soviet Union and Yugoslavia in September.

U. S. President Richard M. Nixon stopped briefly in New Delhi in early June. India welcomed President Ceauşescu of Rumania in October and President Losonczi of Hungary in November.

Islamic Summit Conference. India's most traumatic experience in foreign policy in 1969 came in connection with the Islamic "summit" conference in Rabat, Morocco, in late September, which was convened mainly to protest the burning of the Al Aksa mosque in Jerusalem. Although India originally was not invited, Indian government leaders felt that as the country with the third largest Muslim population in the world it should be included. India was invited at the last moment, and a temporary delegation attended one session. But because of the vigorous opposition of Pakistan's President Yahya Khan to the seating of India, the regular Indian delegation was not permitted to participate. The Indian government officially protested, and on October 13 it recalled its senior envoys from Morocco and Jordan in retaliation against the attitude of these countries.

This episode, which coincided with the outbreak of Hindu-Muslim violence in Gujarat, was highly embarrassing to India, and was generally interpreted as a blow to its international prestige. Indian opposition parties severely criticized the government for the Rabat venture, and the Syndicate supporters in the Congress party Working Committee officially censured Prime Minister Gandhi and the government over it.

And it was on this issue that Mrs. Gandhi's opponents initiated an adjournment motion—in effect a motion of no-confidence—in Parliament on November 17. While the motion was decisively defeated, there could be no doubt that India had experienced a grave reversal, which would have repercussions in domestic and foreign affairs.

NORMAN D. PALMER
University of Pennsylvania

CENTENNIAL of Mohandas Gandhi's birth is observed by these women bowing before the shrine of the great spiritual leader in New Delhi.

UPI

WRECKAGE of Allegheny Airlines jet covers field near Indianapolis. Carrying 82 persons, the jet collided with a small plane on September 9, killing all aboard.

INDIANA

Although there was no general election in Indiana in 1969, politics remained in the spotlight. Economic problems also attracted attention in the state during the year.

Finance and Economy. The Republican-dominated General Assembly began its 61-day biennial session in January and adjourned in March. Much bipartisan support existed for revamping the state tax structure to reduce the levy on property by shifting the load to income and sales taxes. Many proponents of this effort wanted a more productive tax base, but Gov. Edgar D. Whitcomb steadfastly promised to veto any general tax increase. Although the new $2.6 billion biennial budget increased various expenditures, a general tax rise was averted. The tax on gasoline, however, was raised from 6 to 8 cents per gallon to speed highway construction. The budget increase, modest in comparison to previous ones, was achieved without revising the state tax structure, but demand for the revision has continued.

Following the legislative session, fiscal economy continued to be emphasized by the governor. His insistence that the number of state employees (excluding teachers) be reduced by 10% produced substantial results. Having made such progress, the chief executive obtained significant salary increases for key state administrators. Fiscal gains were also achieved by following the recommendations of Governor Whitcomb's task force on economy in government, but the governor rejected a recommendation urging much reduction in partisan patronage in an effort to induce increased, improved services from state employees. The general stability of Indiana's economy and its continued high level of productivity sustained state revenues at a favorable level.

Educational Unrest. The new biennial budget had a strong impact on state universities. Budgets were especially tight for main campuses, and large fee increases were required. Regional campuses suffered less. Student demonstrations and demands flared into a boycott of classes at Indiana and Purdue universities, with some students occupying build-

ings to press their cause. As a result of this, certain students were suspended or arrested. Promises of financial aid and other considerations diminished some student discontent, but various issues remained unresolved. A variety of student demonstrations and protests on behalf of such movements as peace in Vietnam, relaxed dormitory rules, and educational programs for blacks occurred at private and church colleges as well as at state universities.

Reapportionment. A political bombshell was set off in July when a panel of federal judges ordered reapportionment of Indiana's legislative districts into single-member units. Governor Whitcomb vainly sought from the U. S. Supreme Court a reversal of this mandate and then declined to call the General Assembly into session to comply with it. Consequently, late in 1969 the federal panel itself made the necessary changes, breaking precedent by creating only single-member districts and by splitting various counties into two or more units.

Other Events. Indiana experienced both unusual tragedy and unique success in the field of travel. Highway deaths exceeded 1,600, and in September the collision of two planes near Shelbyville resulted in the death of 83 persons. On July 20, however, Indiana contributed significantly to space travel when Purdue University graduate Neil A. Armstrong became the first man to set foot on the moon.

DONALD F. CARMONY
Indiana University
Editor, "Indiana Magazine of History"

─────── **INDIANA • Information Highlights** ───────

Area: 36,291 square miles (93,994 sq km).
Population: 5,084,000 (1969 est.).
Chief Cities (1969 est.): Indianapolis, the capital, 510,000; Fort Wayne, 176,000; Gary, 175,000; Evansville, 145,000; South Bend, 128,000; Hammond, 109,000.
Government: *Chief Officers*—governor, Edgar D. Whitcomb (Republican); lt. gov., Richard E. Folz (R); secy. of state, William N. Salin (R); atty. gen., Theodore L. Sendak (R); treas., John K. Snyder; supt. of pub. instr., Richard D. Wells; chief justice, Roger O. De Bruler, *General Assembly*—Senate, 50 members (35 Republicans, 15 Democrats); House of Representatives, 100 members (73 R, 27 D).
Education: *School enrollment* (1968)—public elementary, 724,000 pupils (27,100 teachers); public secondary, 479,000 pupils (22,700 teachers); nonpublic schools, 134,500 pupils (4,990 teachers); college and university (fall 1967), 163,393 students. *Public school expenditures* (1967–68)—$860,200,000 ($780 per pupil); average teacher's salary, $8,200.
Public Finance (fiscal year 1968–69): *Revenues,* $1,162,334,908 (2% sales tax, $199,433,722; motor fuel tax, $153,726,987; federal funds, $251,168,374). *Expenditures,* $1,160,925,554 (education, $469,189,529; health, welfare, and safety, $194,726,518; highways, $312,480,724). *State debt,* $561,287,000 (June 30, 1968).
Personal Income (1968): $17,270,000,000; average annual income per person, $3,412.
Public Assistance (fiscal year 1968–69): $73,088,448 to 84,600 recipients (aged, $27,098,619; dependent children, $27,922,955).
Labor Force (employed persons, Mid-August 1968): *Agricultural,* 64,500; *nonagricultural* (wage and salary earners), 1,812,200 (36.4% manufacturing, 17.6% trade, 13.6% government). *Unemployed persons* (Mid-August 1968)—64,300.
Manufacturing (1966): Value added by manufacture, $10,116,658,000 (transportation equipment, $1,455,965,000; primary metals, $1,821,319,000; nonelectrical machinery, $1,005,112,000; electrical machinery, $1,650,824,000; fabricated metals, $569,989,000).
Agriculture (1967): Cash farm income, $1,468,907,000 (livestock, $752,091,000; crops, $639,499,000; govt. payments, $77,317,000). *Chief crops* (tons)—Corn for grain, 12,538,512 (ranks 3d among the states); soybeans, 1,968,820 (ranks 5th); hay, 1,894,000; wheat, 1,451,880.
Mining (1967): Production value, $293,218,511. *Chief minerals* (tons)—Crushed limestone, 262,298,817; sand and gravel, 25,627,542; coal, 18,418,660; crude petroleum, 10,081,152 barrels.
Transportation: *Roads* (1968), 90,950 miles (146,366 km); *motor vehicles* (1968), 3,120,442; *railroads* (1969), 12,123 track miles (19,510 km); airports (1969), 10.
Communications (1969): *Telephones* (1968), 2,493,200; *television stations,* 18; *radio stations,* 153; *newspapers,* 84 (daily circulation, 1,712,826).

INDIANS, AMERICAN

In recent years, the American Indians have become a vocal and even radical minority. Although rarely acknowledged, the success of radical black reformist groups has impressed Indian leaders, who have begun to overcome the apathy and resignation with which their forefathers often met the demands of white power.

The Indian and the Executive Branch. All branches of the federal government—executive, legislative, and judicial—are concerned with the Indian, but his closest link is with the executive branch. During the 1968 presidential campaign, candidate Richard M. Nixon promised the Indian a greater voice in his own affairs. He promised to appoint an Indian to the Indian Claims Commission, a judicial body set up in 1946 to hear and determine claims against the government by Indian groups. He also disavowed the policy of "termination" of Indian tribal identity and the breakup of reservations, which was enunciated by Congress during the period of his vice presidency under Dwight D. Eisenhower.

The president's agent for Indian affairs is the secretary of the interior, within whose department the Bureau of Indian Affairs is located. The appointment as secretary of the interior of Walter Hickel, former governor of Alaska, the state with the largest proportion of Indian inhabitants (20%), was greeted by some with alarm. Many Indians and conservationists feared his reported "hard line" attitude toward both the natural and human resources of the nation. Extensive hearings in January modified the opposition of both groups and Hickel's appointment was confirmed by the Senate.

Secretary Hickel let it be known that he did not wish to retain the incumbent commissioner of Indian affairs, Robert L. Bennett, an Indian. The latter resigned, and was replaced in August by Louis R. Bruce, Jr., a Mohawk-Sioux advertising executive of New York City. Bruce took over a bureau that many regard as incapable of reform, despite the best intentions of each succeeding administration.

The Indian and the Legislative Branch. The traditional legislative determinants of Indian policy, the Interior and Insular Affairs committees of the Senate and House of Representatives, continued their work on matters of concern to the Indian people. These committees were overshadowed, however, by the special subcommittee on education of the Senate Labor and Public Welfare Committee.

The chairman of that subcommittee, Sen. Edward Kennedy of Massachusetts, was fulfilling a commitment made by his late brother, Robert F. Kennedy, in the previous Congress. Nine volumes of hearings, two issued in 1969, documented the subcommittee's investigation into the nation's alleged failure to provide a viable educational system for the Indians. On November 12 the subcommittee issued its final report, entitled "Indian Education: A National Tragedy—A National Challenge." It made 60 recommendations for improving the education available to the nation's 600,000 Indians.

Alaskan Settlement. The biggest news of 1969 concerning the American Indian was the attempt by Congress to settle the claims of Alaska's native inhabitants. Unlike the natives of the lower 48 states, the Alaskan Indians, Eskimos, and Aleuts have never entered into treaties with the United States, been pushed off their lands, or (with certain minor exceptions) been given reservation status. In the treaty of cession from Russia and in the Alaskan Statehood Act of 1958, the rights of the natives were reserved, their precise definition being left to later determination by Congress or by the courts.

The snail's pace of court proceedings—both of the Court of Claims and of the Indian Claims Commission—caused the Department of the Interior in 1968 to recommend that the U. S. Congress determine how much land and money should be provided to the natives in settlement of their aboriginal right to the 90% of Alaska's territory they could claim.

Once the Indian claims have been settled, the state can select from the federal lands the remainder of the 103 million acres authorized it under the Alaskan Statehood Act. The acquisition of such lands by the state was stopped in 1966 by Secretary of the Interior Stewart Udall (after 4 million acres had been formally transferred and 13 million acres tentatively approved for transfer) until the rights of the native inhabitants could be determined. The then governor of Alaska, Hickel, filed suit against Secretary Udall to force him to lift the "freeze." Prior to his confirmation as secretary of the interior, Mr. Hickel assured the Senate Interior and Insular Affairs committee that he would continue the land freeze for two years, by which time Congress will presumably have acted in the matter.

Various bills introduced in the Congress have proposed land settlements ranging from 4 to 40 mil-

N. SCOTT MOMADAY, a Kiowa Indian, was awarded the Pulitzer Prize in fiction in May 1969 for his first novel, *House Made of Dawn* (1968). The book deals with the trials and frustrations faced by a young American Indian war veteran who returns to his reservation at the end of World War II. His second book, *The Way to Rainy Mountain* (1969), is a collection of Kiowa folk tales.

Momaday was born in Lawton, Okla., in 1934. His father, Al Momaday, is a noted artist, and his mother, Natachee Scott Momaday, is an artist and writer. He grew up on various Indian reservations in the Southwest and attended Indian schools. He graduated from the University of New Mexico in 1958 and received his master's degree there in 1960. Stanford University awarded him a doctorate in 1963. Momaday teaches English at the University of California, Santa Barbara.

STEPHEN SHAMES/PHOTON WEST

Demonstrators calmly fish from barge backed by painted signs proclaiming Alcatraz Island to be Indian property.

INDIANS TAKE 'THE ROCK'

American Indians—78 strong—invaded Alcatraz Island, in San Francisco Bay, on November 20, demanding that it be made available for an Indian cultural center. They refused to leave Alcatraz—"the Rock," site of a former federal penitentiary but barren since 1963—offering to purchase it for $24 in beads and cloth.

UPI

UPI

Indian girl contributes her share to invasion of Alcatraz in letters large enough for both foe and friend to read.

Young invaders inspect prison galleries in the main cell block on Alcatraz in a survey of their island "conquest."

lion acres and a monetary settlement of $100 million to $500 million for Alaska's 54,000 native inhabitants. Most of the bills proposed by the government deny the Indians any long-term royalty on the subsurface mineral wealth of the land turned over to the state. The potential value of the land is indicated by the amount of money, nearly a billion dollars, offered in bids by oil companies in 1969 for the right to exploit the oil under a small portion of the land already selected by the state.

The Indians, Eskimos, and Aleuts have presented a united front, operating through their combined organization, the Alaska Federation of Natives. Representing the federation at the congressional hearings on the Alaskan problem were Arthur Goldberg, former justice of the Supreme Court, and Ramsey Clark, former attorney general of the United States.

The bill recommended by the native federation —brilliantly espoused by Goldberg and Clark— would allocate 40 million acres (10% of Alaska's land) to the 20% of the population who are natives, and a $500 million cash settlement. More importantly, the federation's proposed bill calls for a continuing 2% overriding gross royalty from the proceeds of the lands to be yielded by the settlement. As the year ended, determination of the settlement had not been made, but a bill was expected to emerge from committee deliberation in both houses of Congress in 1970.

The Indian and the Judiciary. On February 28, the U. S. District Court for the District of Arizona found that the Navajo Tribal Council had illegally expelled from the reservation a white man, Theodore Mitchell, the director of a nonprofit organization operating on the reservation. The decision was the first rendered under the Indian Constitutional Rights Act of 1968. That act extends the traditional protection of the Bill of Rights of the Constitution to individuals involved in disputes with tribal governments. The possibility that the act, while enhancing the rights of the individual Indian, would diminish the autonomy of Indian tribal governments became somewhat apparent.

Pursuant to his campaign promise, President Nixon appointed an Indian—Brantley Blue, a Lumbee of North Carolina—to the Indian Claims Commission.

Industrial Development on the Reservation. Although the policy of bringing industry to the reservation is often mistakenly seen as an instant solution to the high Indian unemployment rate (40%), the policy has benefited several Indian communities. Perhaps the most successful example is the Fairchild semiconductor plant on the Navajo Reservation at Shiprock, N. Mex., which manufactures transistors and other electronic devices. The plant, which started in 1965 with 50 workers, in 1969 employed 1,200 people, of whom only 24 were non-Indian.

Higher Education and the Indian. Several universities, including the University of Minnesota and the University of Montana, initiated "Red Studies" programs. Foundations moved to support Indian studies in numerous ways, including the support of Indian students in the nation's universities.

The emergence of a dedicated group of Indian intellectuals became more apparent. In literature, that emergence was signaled by the award of the 1969 Pulitzer Prize for fiction to N. Scott Momaday, associate professor of English at the University of California, for his novel *House Made of Dawn.*

The continued success of the American Indian Historical Society (founded in 1964) and of its journal, *The Indian Historian,* is similarly suggestive of the growing strength of the community of Indian intellectuals. The society issued a call in the fall of 1969 for the first Convocation of American Indian Scholars. The meeting is to be held at Princeton University in the spring of 1970.

Who Speaks for the Indian? The greatest threat to the American Indian movement is the persistent problem of factionalism. The Indian "establishment" is represented by the National Congress of American Indians, with headquarters in Washington, D. C. Competing for the right to represent the Indian are numerous more militant and more specialized organizations. Among these organizations are American Indians United and the American Indian Movement, both promoting the interests of urban Indians.

The leaders of these new organizations claim to speak in behalf of Indians in general rather than for any specific tribe. Sometimes they work against existing tribal leaders, particularly when they feel that the latter are too ready to make an accommodation to the power of the white world.

Complicating the problem of Indian leadership is the existence of non-Indian organizations devoted to furthering the cause of the Indian. One such white-organized Indian-help organization is the Citizens Advocate Center, supported by the Ford Foundation and other white philanthropic groups, and directed by a white lawyer, Edgar Cahn. The Citizens Advocate Center issued on November 1 a report entitled *Our Brother's Keeper,* a narrative of the discrimination to which the Indian is subjected by white society and by state and federal governments.

No one group or individual has yet achieved the authority to speak for the Indian. The voice of the Indian is still confused and often strident, but his message is coming through more effectively than it ever has in the past.

WILCOMB E. WASHBURN
Smithsonian Institution

LOUIS ROOKS BRUCE, JR. was nominated by President Nixon on Aug. 7, 1969, to succeed Robert L. Bennett as commissioner of the Bureau of Indian Affairs. He is the second American Indian to be named to this office in almost a century. A dairy farmer from upstate New York, and a lifelong Republican, Bruce has been a champion of Indian rights for many years. He has spoken out strongly for greater Indian self-determination, and he is expected to institute far-reaching reforms in the Bureau of Indian Affairs.

Bruce, whose Mohawk name is Agwelius, was born on the Onondaga reservation in New York on Dec. 30, 1906. His father, a Mohawk, was a professional baseball player, dentist, and Methodist minister. His mother was an Oglala Sioux from South Dakota. He grew up on the St. Regis Mohawk reservation and graduated from Syracuse University in 1930. Over the years he has served in various posts, including director for Indian projects with the National Youth Administration in New York State.

JAVANESE DANCERS entertain President Suharto (*center*) and his guest, U. S. President Richard M. Nixon, in Djakarta on July 27.

UPI

INDONESIA

In 1969 the Indonesian government grappled with overwhelming economic problems. President Suharto strengthened his control over the military, and parliament finally set a date for national elections in 1971. By a complex and controversial "consultative" process, West Irian voted to remain with Indonesia. Foreign policy remained unaligned, but warmed somewhat toward the United States.

Foreign Policy. U. S. President Richard M. Nixon received a warm welcome on his arrival in Djakarta, July 27, 1969. Indonesia leaders had pinned great hopes on this visit, the first of its kind by a U. S. president. The United States had been providing the largest share of the multilateral aid by means of which the Suharto government had begun to rebuild the shattered economy after the downfall of Sukarno in 1967. Without continued massive assistance, economic chaos would again engulf Indonesia. In addition to increased economic aid, Suharto's government wanted armaments and aircraft to replace the worn-out equipment Sukarno had received from the Soviet Union.

Indonesia is distinctly more friendly toward the United States than it was when Nixon visited Djakarta as U. S. vice president in 1953, but forces favoring nonalignment are still dominant in the government. U. S. relations with Indonesia are handicapped by the fact that the latter, as a Muslim country, is sympathetic with the Arab countries in their quarrel with Israel, while the United States generally supports Israel. Most Indonesian government officials view communism merely as an internal threat. They would welcome a promise of defense from the United States, but they insist upon maintaining Indonesia's position as a nonaligned country. Others, notably the military, fear mainland Chinese aggression and favor participation in a U. S.-sponsored Asian anti-Communist defense system.

Economy. Indonesia has succeeded in halting its runaway inflation, but the economy is virtually stagnant. There is little new investment in business, and small growth in consumer demand. Enormous problems confront the government: roads, ports, and communications facilities need improvement; unemployment and underemployment are staggering; capital is short; and skilled technical, organizational, and managerial forces are lacking.

Getting the economy moving is Indonesia's most pressing matter. It is immensely difficult because all the while the population is expanding enormously. No progress has been made in paying off the astronomical foreign debt, but one hopeful sign is the flurry of foreign investment in the exploitation of oil in Indonesia, particularly in offshore areas.

A modest 5-year development plan was launched on April 1, 1969, but implementation has proceeded very slowly. The plan's chief emphasis is on the development of agriculture, particularly rice production, which is a major factor in the country's economy and a strong influence on the cost of living.

Government. President Suharto has scrupulously observed constitutional forms, but he has done little to strengthen the role of political parties. The multiplicity of parties, many of which have ethnic or religious bases, makes it difficult to develop an alternative to control of the country by the military.

Several steps have been taken that serve to strengthen the hold of the military while centralizing Suharto's control over the military. On November 7 an agreement was reached giving the military establishment the right to appoint one fifth of the members of the provincial district assemblies, nearly one fourth of the members of parliament, and one third of the members of the Peoples' Consultative Congress. On November 10, President Suharto ordered unification of the armed forces and appointed a deputy chief of staff to head the unified services. Suharto remained chief of all the armed forces and defense minister.

Earlier, various reforms had been instituted to curb the inefficiency and poor discipline in the armed forces. Some 100 senior officers were demoted, and a new army training program was initiated. As lack of occupation had aggravated the situation, the army was put to work building schools, roads, and bridges, and harvesting crops.

The government proposed holding a national election, already once postponed, and finally, on November 22, the parliament passed a national electoral law setting the date for July 5, 1971.

The cost of feeding and guarding some 80,000 political prisoners, the result of the abortive Communist coup of 1965, has become a financial burden as well as a political issue. Suharto announced on August 10 that some 2,500 Communists were being shipped to the Island of Buru for rehabilitation. It is anticipated that 10,000 in all will be sent there, where they will be expected to support themselves. Some 4,000 prisoners will be brought to trial, and the remainder will be allowed to return to their native villages.

West Irian Plebescite. According to the 1962 agreement whereby the Dutch gave up West Irian, Indonesia was to grant self-government to the West Irianese and to permit them in 1969 freely to make a choice of whether they would continue as a part of Indonesia or become independent. The "act of free choice" was to be conducted under the supervision of the United Nations. Fernando Ortiz-Sanz of Bolivia was named to head an 18-member UN team. The team was to "advise, assist and participate in the arrangements" for ascertaining the wishes of the West Irianese.

In the years immediately preceding transfer of the territory, the Dutch had poured some $30 million annually into West Irian and instituted preparations for self-government. Engrossed in the Malaysian confrontation after the takeover, Sukarno ignored the remote island territory, and the Djakarta government continued to neglect West Irian after the end of the Malaysian episode. It is alleged that the civil administrators and military people assigned to West Irian stripped the island of whatever could be taken away.

The West Irianese in the more developed coastal areas became increasingly restless under Indonesian rule. A Free Papuan Movement developed, and as the time for the act of free choice drew near, violence broke out. Early in May 1969, after five air-fields had been put out of commission, Indonesia sent in 500 paratroopers to quell the disorders. The Indonesian government on May 6 voiced the suspicion that foreign elements "in the Netherlands, Australia and other places were supporting" the insurgent movement in West Irian. Alleging a terrorist campaign in West Irian, Djakarta banned journalists and foreign diplomats from the area.

It was reported that Ortiz-Sanz, the UN representative, appealed to the Indonesian government for amnesty for West Irian political dissidents, but the appeal was rejected. On June 27, the Papua-New Guinea House of Assembly in East New Guinea, which is under an Australian mandate, voted to condemn the "act of free choice" as conducted by Indonesia and requested Australia to convey its protest to the United Nations.

During the preparations for the consultations on West Irian's future, Ortiz-Sanz suggested that the process be on a "one-man-one-vote" basis in the developed coastal areas and by "collective consultation" in the jungle and mountain areas. This suggestion was rejected because of geographic considerations and the primitive state of development of many West Irianese.

Instead, government-appointed committees chose 1,025 delegates. The delegates then gathered in 8 councils, sometimes traveling great distances over rugged country. These councils, through consultation with Indonesian government officials, without a dissenting vote chose to remain within the Indonesian republic. The consultative process continued from July 1 through August 2.

When UN Secretary-General U Thant reported the result of the referendum to the UN General Assembly on November 13, a group of African countries succeeded in postponing action on the report in order to permit further investigation of the manner in which the consensus of the West Irianese had been obtained. Even Indonesian officials admitted in the General Assembly that there had been criticism of the methods used.

AMRY VANDENBOSCH
University of Kentucky

INDUSTRIAL PRODUCTION. See ECONOMY OF THE UNITED STATES.

INDONESIA

Information Highlights

Area: 575,892 square miles (1,491,564 sq km).
Population: 112,825,000 (1968 est.).
Chief Cities (1961 census): Djakarta, the capital, 2,906,533; Surabaja, 1,007,945; Bandung, 972,566; Semerang, 503,153.
Government: *President*—Suharto (took office March 27, 1968). *Supreme Organ of State*—People's Consultative Congress (about 650 members, including all members of parliament, plus representatives of regions and of functional groups). *Parliament* (House of Representatives)—about 360 elective members.
Religious Faiths: Muslims, 85% of population.
Education: *Literacy rate* (1961), 43% of population aged 15 and over. *Total school enrollment* (1967)—14,751,619 (primary, 12,574,820; *secondary*, 1,607,312; teacher-training, 106,575; technical/vocational, 352,235; university/higher, 110,677).
Finance (1969 est.): *Revenues,* $3,847,058,823; *expenditures,* $3,847,058,823; *monetary unit,* rupiah (85 rupiahs equal U.S.$1).
Gross National Product (1967): $10,844,705,882.
National Income (1967): $9,840,000,000; *average annual income per person,* $87.
Economic Indexes (1967): *Industrial production* (1966), 110 1963=100); *agricultural production,* 114 (1963=100); *cost of living,* 25,612 (1963=100).
Manufacturing (1967): Gasoline (1967), 1,325,000 metric tons; lumber (1963), 1,781,000 cubic meters.
Crops (metric tons, 1967–68 crop year): Cassava, 1,291,000 (ranks 2d among world producers); sweet potatoes and yams, 2,023,000 (world rank, 2d); natural rubber, 7,157,000 (world rank, 2d); rice, 13,932,000.
Minerals (metric tons, 1967): Crude petroleum, 25,310,000; tin, 13,819.
Foreign Trade (1968): *Exports,* $868,000,000 (chief exports, 1966: natural gums and rubbers, $223,280,000; crude petroleum, $203,430,000; palm oil, $34,400,000; unroasted coffee, $32,650,000); *imports,* $830,000,000 (chief imports, 1965: rice, $79,200,000; power generating machinery, $21,830,000; railway vehicles, $13,190,000). *Chief trading partners* (1965): Japan (took 16% of exports, supplied 41% of imports); United States (took 22% of exports, supplied 9% of imports); West Germany.
Transportation: *Roads* (1964), 6,146 miles (9,891 km); *motor vehicles* (1967), 298,700 (automobiles 185,000); *railways* (1967), 3,788 miles (6,100 km).
Communications: *Telephones* (1968): 169,142; *television stations* (1967), 3; *television sets* (1967), 54,000.

INSURANCE

The insurance industry in the United States continues to experience growth. Premium income and assets have reached all-time highs in property and liability and life and health insurance. News developments reflect the industry's continuing adjustment to a changing social and economic environment.

PROPERTY AND LIABILITY INSURANCE

Progress was achieved in 1969 toward solution of some of the more acute problems in the business through cooperation between private insurance and government. Federal riot and flood reinsurance programs enacted by Congress are being implemented on a state-by-state basis. The antitrust and monopoly subcommittee of the Senate Judiciary Committee continued its hearings on auto insurance, and the U. S. Department of Transportation pursued a major study of the present system of indemnifying victims of automobile accidents.

Unprofitable Operations. Record losses from fires and auto accidents, an unprecedented increase in the incidence of crimes, and rapid proliferation of natural and man-made catastrophes, including riots and civil disorders, contributed to making underwriting operations unprofitable in the property and liability insurance business in 1968. The cumulative $175 million underwriting loss for the year followed two years in which small underwriting profits were realized. Before that, losses in consecutive years—1963, 1964, and 1965—reached a total of $1 billion.

In 1969, indications at midyear were that results were mixed, with some companies showing an improvement and others a continuation of the underwriting losses of 1968.

Although property and liability insurance is a business that handles many billions of dollars a year, it has failed over the years to match the profitability of most other types of business enterprises. A study by the research firm of Arthur D. Little, Inc., of Cambridge, Mass., made public in 1968, showed that the average rate of return for property and liability insurers was 4.4% for the 1955-to-1965 period—lower than that of any of 59 other major manufacturing and financial industries in the study. The rate of return was less than half that of other industries having about the same degree of risk on invested funds.

Volume. An expanding economy and inflationary conditions kept premium volumes on property and liability insurance rising, passing $28.8 billion by the end of 1969, up about 10% from the previous year. This growing volume of insurance activity provided more than 570,000 persons with employment.

LIFE INSURANCE

The latest national consumer survey shows that 71% of all Americans have some type of life insurance protection. With $1.3 trillion of the protection in force with life insurance companies, the average U. S. family with insurance at the end of 1969 was insured for $24,600 of life insurance.

Purchases and Benefit Payments. Purchases of new life insurance protection amounted to $158 billion in 1969. Of this sum, $113 billion represented individually bought, ordinary insurance; new purchases of group life insurance totaled $38 billion. During 1969 life insurance companies paid more than $15 billion in benefits to policyholders and in death payments to beneficiaries in the United States.

Investments. Assets of the more than 1,800 legal reserve life insurance companies totaled $198 billion in 1969. Corporate securities accounted for $86 billion of investment holdings of the companies, and mortgages accounted for $72 billion. The net earning rate on life insurance company investments before federal taxes was 5.07%, the highest yield since 1926.

Funds for Cities. In April 1969, the life insurance business pledged to divert $1 billion from the normal channels of its investments for the second time in a special effort to help alleviate "inner-city" problems in the nation's larger cities.

The first such pledge, 90% complete at the time the second commitment was made, led to the creation of 65,000 housing units and more than 30,000 permanent jobs.

In receiving word of the pledge from the insurance industry, President Nixon commented that it "demonstrates again the depth of their concern about the problems of our cities, and it will provide an effective way to bring more jobs and better housing to many Americans who need them."

Trend Toward Equity Products. The insurance business is increasingly interested in equity products. Companies have looked more closely into the merits of mutual fund programs and individual variable annuities for their policyholders. A trend now appears in the making toward the formation by life companies of wholly owned mutual funds, or the acquisition or establishment of a selling relationship with existing funds. Perhaps even more significant is a serious interest in and a beginning trend toward combining equity investments and life insurance protection in the same contract, tentatively labeled "variable life insurance."

Holding Companies. Another significant development is the utilization of the holding company device to acquire subsidiaries, both insurance companies themselves and organizations involved in related activity, such as mutual funds, investment advisory companies, and computer software companies. This development reflects the trend, in a number of companies, toward providing a broad range of financial services.

HEALTH INSURANCE

A record 176 million persons were insured through private organizations at the end of 1969. Private health insurance policyholders received $14 billion in benefit payments in 1969. This coverage was provided by insurance companies, Blue Cross-Blue Shield organizations and medical society-approved plans, and independent plans.

Of those Americans with hospitalization insurance, 91% also had surgical expense insurance and 77% had regular medical (nonsurgical) protection. In addition, insurers provided major medical expense insurance to 72 million persons, a growth of 50 million since 1959. This insurance provides benefits that commonly have a maximum of $10,000 but can range to $20,000 or more per illness or per lifetime, depending on the policy.

In 1969 almost 60 million persons had short-term disability protection with insurance companies; long-term disability protection with insurance companies covered 9 million persons.

KENNETH BLACK, JR.
Georgia State University

Ornate Victorian vestibule by J. B. Maurer for the Steer Palace restaurant, New York City.

Interior Design

Atmosphere and a pleasing quality of fantasy through use of a special decorative theme are evident in most of the work completed by interior designers during 1969.

Restaurants and Clubs. A theme of the "Gay Nineties" was utilized by John B. Maurer in the Steer Palace, a restaurant in New York City. Everett Brown created the effect of a classic French restaurant for the new La Seine, also in New York. Alan L. Ferry used wide plank floors, beams and mantels from old homes, and antique fixtures and furniture to recapture successfully an atmosphere of ante-bellum Southern hospitality for Pittypat's Porch restaurant, in Atlanta, Ga. In the Chatham Club, a men's luncheon club located in the DeSoto Hilton Hotel in Savannah, Ga., a traditional character was achieved by the use of old barn wood. The furnishing were selected by Alan L. Ferry.

Perhaps the most spectacular example of distinctive atmosphere in interior design is the Circus Circus casino in Las Vegas. In a masterpiece of design coordination, a circus-carnival effect was created inside, while the building itself is shaped like a huge tent. One of the largest inns in Florida, the new Manager Motor Inn in Tampa was designed by Ellen Lehman McCluskey in a jungle motif. Pine-

apples, bamboo, jungle foliage, and exotic birds provide a lush appearance.

A popular restaurant on Cape Cod, the Christopher Ryder House, was enlarged to seat 500 patrons in several dining rooms. The interior, designed by Lloyd Bell, preserves the atmosphere of the 19th century seaside house.

Hotels. The largest and most luxurious hotel to be completed during the year was the El Conquistador, in Puerto Rico. A giant complex with hundreds of guest rooms, 73 of which face the ocean, the hotel required 2½ years to complete. Designer Alan Jonathan Lanigan successfully blended modern design into the basically Spanish motif.

The DeSoto Hilton, largest hotel in Savannah, Ga., was designed by David T. Williams. Its interiors reflect the traditional interior design of Savannah and the hospitality of the old South.

A fresh and original approach to hotel interiors was taken by John Fitler-Ellis for architect George Bennett's modern Cherry Hill Lodge at Cherry Hill, N. J. The large complex of lodge and inn, modern in design, stresses spaciousness. Its impressive lobby, 22 feet high, with a copper-hooded fireplace and balcony at one end, is outstanding.

Proximity to campus surroundings inspired the

contemporary decor of the 14-story, 200-room Fenway Motor Hotel in Cambridge, Mass. The interiors are by Roland Wm. Jutras Associates. The project uses red brick both inside and out, establishing an empathy with the neighboring campus buildings.

Colleges. Marc T. Nielsen was the interior designer for the new center and the women's dormitory at Principia College, Elsah, Ill. Red brick predominates in both the exterior and interior of the buildings. As part of the Haverford (Pa.) College expansion program, a new building was constructed around the existing James P. Magill library. The new structure is in traditional style, but has updated reading facilities. Interior designer Herbert W. Kramer derived the color scheme from the structural materials.

Other new student centers of notable size and modern design include those at the University of Houston, with interiors by Sally S. Walsh, and at Illinois College, Jacksonville, Ill., with interiors by Thomas F. Ogilvie. The Illinois College center is characterized by brick walls, a see-through fireplace, and an overall spaciousness.

Industry. The administration building of Clairol, Inc., in Stamford, Conn., is a masterpiece of coordination between interior design and architecture. The interiors were created by Designs for Business, Inc. The building is characterized by a completely revised lighting system and economical use of space that achieves a flexibility with private offices of various sizes.

Joseph Whited designed the new 8-floor administration building of Hoffman-La Roche, a large pharmeceutical firm in Nutley, N. J. The building is the first of three to be erected around a great central plaza. Whited developed a concept of modern design coordinated with meticulous detailing for an effect of openness. This is enhanced by low custom space dividers throughout. Luxurious hand-woven fabrics, leather upholstery, and live plants are a part of the decor.

A complex of three massive precast concrete buildings surrounding twin gardens make up the offices of the Employers Insurance of Wausau, in Wisconsin. The buildings are set on a 250-acre site, eventually to be landscaped with trees and shrubs.

The interiors, which are dominated by earth colors, mixed with a variety of pastel tones to avoid monotony, were designed by Louis Forrer and David Klumb. Furnishings are simple in form and a variety of woods are used for the furniture and sheathing of walls.

Another outstanding example of commercial interior design is the home of the Corinthian Broadcasting Corp. in Sacramento, Calif. Architects Starks, Jozens, Nacht & Lewis designed the building of old and new brick, in a style reminiscent of early California. Interiors by Doree Kerr complement the exterior paneling and brickwork, and 17th century Spanish and modern design blend for a completely contemporary effect.

Residences. Perhaps the most novel residence built during the year was a rotating house by architect Richard Foster. Resting on a great central pedestal with a ball-bearing assembly underneath, it resembles a large mushroom. The entire house rotates, and it makes a complete turn in 48 minutes. One is aware that it is turning only because the scenery changes. The outer walls are glazed and fitted for draw curtains for privacy, and the rooms are wedge-shaped.

More drama in the round is expressed in the curve-swept, glass-walled house owned and decorated by Arthur Elrod. The house, by architect John Lautner, is a monolithic structure that appears quarried from its geological site in the southern California desert.

Race Tracks. The clubhouse of Belmont Park, in Elmont, N. Y., was completely rebuilt from plans by architect Arthur Forelich. The interiors, designed by Ellen Gordon Needles and by Gilman Arnold of the Bramlett Co., lack nothing in imagination and color. The vast oval track offers a magnificent panorama of playing fountains, swans, and lakes.

Conferences. The 6th annual conference of the National Society of Interior Designers (NSID) was held in Chicago on June 9–14, 1969. The 38th annual conference of the American Institute of Interior Designers (AID) was held in Atlanta, Ga., on September 6–11.

LEE CANNON
Managing Editor, "Interior Design" Magazine

TRANSPARENT BALL of acrylic plastic by Danilo Silvestri opens into a two-seated rocker (*right*). It is an example of the adaptation of design to new media and of the growing use of plastics for home furnishings.

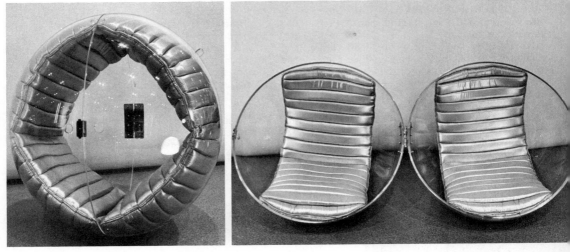

INTERNATIONAL FINANCE

Adjustment and accommodation dominated international finance in 1969. The year saw changes in the rates of the French franc and the German mark, the creation of man-made international reserves for the first time, the highest interest rates in over a century, and an unprecedented growth in international trade.

PAYMENTS ADJUSTMENTS

The effects of an unresolved foreign exchange crisis that developed in November 1968 lingered on at the start of 1969. There had been strong speculation on the upward revaluation of the West German mark, and over $2 billion flowed into Germany in anticipation of short-term gains. Much of this money came from France, where economic and social conditions were still unsettled following the student-worker riots of the summer of 1968. At first, President Charles de Gaulle of France refused to devalue the French franc, and the German government of Chancellor Kurt Kiesinger similarly refused to revalue the German mark, although it did adjust border taxes by 4% and take other measures to stem the inflow of funds.

Financial markets remained relatively quiet in the following months, until de Gaulle's resignation on April 28 and certain public statements in Germany in May revived speculation on a French devaluation and a German revaluation. At this time $4 billion flowed into Germany in a few weeks. The impact of these flows on the foreign exchange reserves of a number of European countries was aggravated by the extremely tight conditions prevailing in international money markets, largely in response to very tight U. S. monetary conditions.

France. For several years France faced a dilemma in the management of its economy—a dilemma aggravated by the 1968 student-worker riots. The government wanted to achieve a moderate expansion of the domestic economy. Unemployment, while still low by the standards of many countries, was at a postwar high for France. However, internal economic expansion would have worsened the country's balance-of-payments position, resulted in

PAR VALUE OF CURRENCIES OF MEMBER COUNTRIES OF THE INTERNATIONAL MONETARY FUND

Member	Currency unit	U. S. cents per unit Nov. 15, 1969	Member	Currency unit	U. S. cents per unit Nov. 15, 1969
Afghanistan[1]	afghani	2.22222	Lebanon[2]	pound	45.6313
Algeria	dinar	...[3]	Lesotho	S. African rand	140.0
Argentina[2]	peso	...	Liberia	dollar	100.0
Australia	dollar	112.0	Libya	pound	280.0
Austria	schilling	3.84615	Luxembourg	franc	2.0
Belgium	franc	2.0	Malagasy Republic	franc	...[3]
Bolivia[2]	peso Boliviano	...	Malawi	pound	240.0
Botswana	S. African rand	140.0	Malaysia[2]	dollar	32.6667
Brazil[2]	new cruzeiro	...	Mali	franc	...[3]
Burma	kyat	21.0	Malta	pound	240.00
Burundi	franc	1.14286	Mauritania	CFA[4] franc	...[3]
Cameroon	CFA[4] franc	...[3]	Mauritius	rupee	...
Canada	dollar	92.5	Mexico	peso	8.0
Central African Republic	CFA[4] franc	...[3]	Morocco	dirham	19.7609
Ceylon	rupee	16.8	Nepal	rupee	9.87654
Chad	CFA[4] franc	...[3]	Netherlands	guilder	27.6243
Chile[2]	escudo	...	New Zealand	dollar	112.0
China (Nationalist)	yuan	...[3]	Nicaragua	córdoba	14.2857
Colombia[2]	peso	...	Niger	CFA[4] franc	...[3]
Congo (Brazzaville)	CFA[4] franc	...	Nigeria	pound	280.0
Congo, Democratic Republic of	zaire	...	Norway	krone	14.0
Costa Rica	colón	15.0943	Pakistan[1]	rupee	21.0
Cyprus	pound	240.0	Panama	balboa	100.0
Dahomey	CFA[4] franc	...[3]	Paraguay[2]	guaraní	...
Denmark	krone	13.3333	Peru[2]	sol	...
Dominican Republic	peso	100.0	Philippines	peso	25.641
Ecuador[1]	sucre	5.55556	Portugal	escudo	3.47826
El Salvador	colón	40.0	Rwanda	franc	1.00
Ethiopia	dollar	40.0	Saudi Arabia	riyal	22.2222
Finland	markka	23.8097	Senegal	CFA[4] franc	...[3]
France	franc	18.0044	Sierra Leone	leone	120.0
Gabon	CFA[4] franc	...[3]	Singapore	dollar	32.6667
Gambia	pound	240.0	Somalia	Somali shilling	14.0
Germany, West	Deutsche mark	27.3224	South Africa	rand	140.0
Ghana	new cedi	98.0	Southern Yemen	dinar	...[3]
Greece	drachma	3.33333	Spain	peseta	1.42857
Guatemala	quetzal	100.0	Sudan	pound	287.156
Guinea	franc	...[3]	Swaziland	S. African rand	
Guyana	dollar	50.0	Sweden	krona	19.3304
Haiti	gourde	20.0	Syrian Arab Republic[2]	pound	45.6313
Honduras	lempira	50.0	Tanzania	shilling	14.0
Iceland	króna	1.13636	Thailand	baht	4.80769
India	rupee	13.3333	Togo	CFA[4] franc	...[3]
Indonesia	rupiah	...[3]	Trinidad and Tobago	TT dollar	50.0
Iran	rial	1.32013	Tunisia	dinar	190.476
Iraq	dinar	280.00	Turkey	lira	11.1111
Ireland	pound	240.00	Uganda	shilling	14.0
Israel	pound	28.5714	United Arab Republic[2]	pound	287.156
Italy	lira	0.16	United Kingdom	pound	240.0
Ivory Coast	CFA[4] franc	...[3]	United States	dollar	100.0
Jamaica	dollar	120.00	Upper Volta	CFA[4] franc	...[3]
Japan	yen	0.277778	Uruguay[2]	peso	13.5135
Jordan	dinar	280.00	Venezuela[2]	bolívar	...
Kenya	shilling	14.0	Vietnam, South	piastre	...[3]
Korea, South	won	...[3]	Yugoslavia	dinar	8.0
Kuwait	dinar	280.00	Zambia	kwacha	140.00
Laos	kip	...[3]			

[1] Not all transactions in the exchange market take place at rates governed by the par value. [2] No transactions in the exchange market take place at rates governed by the par value last agreed with the IMF. [3] Par value not yet established. [4] African Financial Community (Communauté Financière Africaine).

U.S. BALANCE OF INTERNATIONAL PAYMENTS

Quarterly data, seasonally adjusted

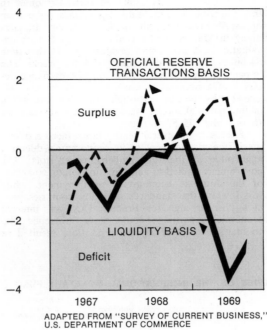

Billions of dollars

OFFICIAL RESERVE TRANSACTIONS BASIS

Surplus

LIQUIDITY BASIS

Deficit

1967 1968 1969

ADAPTED FROM "SURVEY OF CURRENT BUSINESS,"
U.S. DEPARTMENT OF COMMERCE

an outflow of reserves, revived traditional French reservations about the value of their national currency, and perhaps forced a devaluation of the franc. The French government briefly pursued an expansionary policy in the latter half of 1968 but reversed course following the exchange crisis of November. The dilemma was known to be a source of disagreement within the French government.

Following the sudden resignation of de Gaulle when the French public failed to endorse his proposals for reorganizing regional government, the new government of Georges Pompidou embarked upon an expansionary policy. He surprised the financial world by devaluing the French franc—by 11.1% (to 18.0044 U. S. cents, from 20.255 cents) —on August 8, during the European vacation period when exchange markets were generally quiet. The devaluation was expected to provide the franc with enough external strength to permit successful expansion of the French economy. The government took measures, technically in violation of the common agricultural policy of the European Economic Community, to prevent the devaluation from driving up the prices of French food products.

West Germany. Like France, West Germany also faced a dilemma in timing its economic policies, but it was of an opposite kind. Germany's balance-of-payments position was exceptionally strong, and Germany had been made conscious of the pressure it was exerting on the rest of the world. At the same time, the German economy was gradually moving into an overheated condition. Consumer prices rose by 3%—small by international standards but large for the inflation-conscious German public.

On domestic grounds, the German government wanted to pursue somewhat more restrictionist economic policy. But this would have increased the already large trade surplus. This dilemma became an issue in the election campaign of 1969, in which

the Social Democratic party (SPD) endorsed an upward revaluation of the mark as a way to reduce inflationary pressures on the economy. The governing Christian Democratic party (CDU) opposed revaluation, largely on grounds that it would hurt profits of German business and under the common agricultural policy of the European Common Market would reduce the earnings of German farmers.

As the September 29 election approached, funds began to move into Germany in increasing amounts. The exchange markets were closed immediately before the election. The SPD won, and the mark was allowed to float freely for over three weeks while a government was being formed. On October 24, a new exchange rate was set at 27.3 U. S. cents per German mark—9.3% above the 25 cents prevailing before the election.

Britain. As a financial center, Britain experienced strong pressures in each period of financial crisis. The British pound remained under a cloud at the beginning of the year. Britain adopted a tight budget in April, and in June it agreed to impose a ceiling on domestic credit creation as a condition for a loan from the International Monetary Fund.

A tight reign on domestic policies and the devaluation of late 1967 at last produced a payments surplus—the first since 1963—in the first half of 1969. Britain's trade position improved further in

U.S. MONETARY RESERVES AND LIABILITIES TO FOREIGN GOVERNMENTS AND CENTRAL BANKS

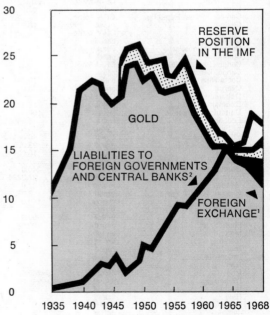

BILLIONS OF DOLLARS

RESERVE POSITION IN THE IMF

GOLD

LIABILITIES TO FOREIGN GOVERNMENTS AND CENTRAL BANKS[2]

FOREIGN EXCHANGE[1]

1935 1940 1945 1950 1955 1960 1965 1968

1. Largely assets acquired as a result of general support in foreign exchange markets for other currencies such as sterling. The United States can, therefore, use such holdings only for bilateral settlements.

2. Deposits, short-term money market instruments, and U.S. government notes and bonds, including special nonmarketable Treasury securities.

364

the second half of the year. The retirement of de Gaulle opened the way for possible British entry in the European Common Market, and Britain prepared to renew discussions of the economic adjustments that would be necessary for entry.

United States. The U. S. balance-of-payments position is complicated by the use of the U. S. dollar as a major international currency. This complication was dramatically illustrated during the year: on one official measure of payments (official reserve transactions), the United States ran a surplus of $2 billion in the first nine months; in contrast, on a second measure (so-called liquidity), the United States ran an unprecedentedly large deficit of more than $10 billion in the same period (both at annual rates). The principal explanation: U. S. banks were borrowing heavily in foreign markets, especially the Eurodollar market, to meet the demands of their customers for funds at home. By autumn such borrowings exceeded $14 billion.

The U. S. trade position remained weak because of the domestic economic boom but improved somewhat near the end of the year. The new Nixon administration in 1969 relaxed modestly some controls that had been placed on U. S. business investment abroad for balance-of-payments reasons in early 1968, but it also announced that the program of restraint would continue at least through 1970.

New Proposals. While devaluation of the French franc and revaluation of the German mark could be expected to move the world economy toward payments equilibrium, these steps left unresolved the basic question of how smooth balance-of-payments adjustment was to be assured in the future. During the year, official sentiment grew for exploring possible improvements in the international rules and conventions governing relationships among exchange rates. Sympathetic hearing was given to a number of proposals introducing greater flexibility into exchange rates, including those calling for a band of flexibility wider than the prevailing 2% around parity and those calling for modest but frequent changes in exchange rate parities—the so-called gliding parity. But governments remained hesitant about making basic changes in the international payments system and agreed merely to examine such possible changes seriously under International Monetary Fund auspices.

INTERNATIONAL LIQUIDITY

SDR's. Governments did agree collectively to take a major step in creating for the first time manmade international reserves, called Special Drawing Rights (SDR's), at the International Monetary Fund. A plan for creating SDR's had been agreed upon in 1968, and on Oct. 3, 1969, in Washington, D. C., IMF member nations voted that SDR's should be created for the first time on Jan. 1, 1970, in the amount of $3.5 billion, equal to roughly 5% of total world reserves. The agreement included subsequent creation of $3 billion of SDR's in 1971 and again in 1972. These SDR's, to be allocated among the 113 nations belonging to the IMF in proportion to their IMF quotas, were expected to supplement gold, dollars, and sterling as international reserves to be used for settling temporary payments imbalances among nations.

IMF Quotas. The IMF also began discussions for an increase by about one third in the normal IMF quotas, permitting countries to borrow more when they were in balance-of-payments difficulties,

GOLD AND U.S. DOLLAR RESERVES OF GOVERNMENTS AND CENTRAL BANKS OTHER THAN THE U.S.[1]

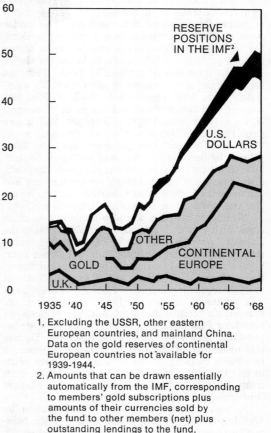

BILLIONS OF DOLLARS

RESERVE POSITIONS IN THE IMF[2]

U.S. DOLLARS

OTHER CONTINENTAL EUROPE

GOLD

U.K.

1935 '40 '45 '50 '55 '60 '65 '68

1. Excluding the USSR, other eastern European countries, and mainland China. Data on the gold reserves of continental European countries not available for 1939-1944.
2. Amounts that can be drawn essentially automatically from the IMF, corresponding to members' gold subscriptions plus amounts of their currencies sold by the fund to other members (net) plus outstanding lendings to the fund.

provided they met criteria laid down by the IMF. Such an increase, to take place in 1970, would bring total IMF quotas to over $28 billion.

Gold. The private demand for gold receded in 1969. Revaluation of the German mark and the decision to create SDR's reduced the prospect of an increase in the official price of gold, set by the U. S. Treasury at $35 per ounce. This reassessment was reinforced by the absence of serious defections from the two-price gold system, established in early 1968, whereby private demands for gold were to be satisfied at a market-determined price in private gold markets, while official transactions in gold between central banks and governments were to take place at the official price. The private price of gold dropped from a high of $44 an ounce to around $35 in December.

INTERNATIONAL FINANCIAL CONDITIONS

Extraordinarily high interest rates prevailed throughout the year. All major countries except Japan raised their discount rates, and by autumn the U. S. and German discount rates stood at 6%, the French rate at 7%, and the British rate at 8%. Market interest rates were similarly high, with U. S. Treasury bill rates remaining about 7% in the second half of the year.

RICHARD N. COOPER, *Yale University*
Author of "The Economics of Interdependence"

INTERNATIONAL LAW

The year 1969 was marked by significant developments in three important areas of international law: arms control and disarmament, law development, and settlement of disputes.

Arms Control and Disarmament. The major event of 1969 was the agreement reached in October between the United States and the Soviet Union to open preliminary talks at Helsinki on November 17 on the limitation of strategic weapons. The plan for strategic arms limitation talks (SALT) originated at the 1967 meeting between U. S. President Johnson and Soviet Premier Kosygin at Glassboro, N. J. At that time, Defense Secretary McNamara gave Premier Kosygin a dramatic presentation of the dangers of continuing the arms race. The talks, delayed by the Vietnam War and the Soviet occupation of Czechoslovakia, were expected to deal with a wide range of issues relating to development and deployment of offensive and defensive nuclear weapons and could be of unparalleled importance.

Significant progress was also made in two other areas during 1969. First came the submission to the Geneva Conference of drafts of a treaty banning nuclear weapons on the seabed and the ocean floor. Separate U. S. and Soviet drafts were submitted to the conference in March, and a joint U. S.-Soviet draft incorporating proposals from the former drafts was submitted on Oct. 7, 1969. The draft treaty banned the emplacement of nuclear weapons or launching facilities on the seabed or ocean floor beyond the limits of national jurisdiction. Despite this unanimity of the two big powers, however, a two-thirds majority of the General Assembly voted in mid-December to send the Soviet-American draft treaty back to the 26-nation Geneva disarmament conference for further discussion.

A second major event was the ratification by Washington and Moscow of the Treaty on the Nonproliferation of Nuclear Weapons on November 24, when it was signed by President Nixon and President Nicolai V. Podgorny (with copies to be filed for formal completion). The treaty was to go into force after ratification by 43 nations, of which the United States and the USSR were 23d and 24th. (See also DISARMAMENT AND ARMS CONTROL.)

Law Development. The United Nations has become increasingly active in the codification and progressive development of international law. During 1969, significant advances were achieved by the legal work of eight specialized UN bodies. The UN Commission on International Trade Law discussed uniform laws on the international sale of goods and international legislation on shipping. The UN International Law Commission met at Geneva to adopt draft articles for a convention on the relations between states and international organizations for transmission to the UN Specialized Agencies. It continued work on state responsibility and the most-favored-nation clause commonly found in bilateral establishment and trade treaties.

The Special Committee on Principles of International Law Concerning Friendly Relations and Cooperation among States also tried to draft agreed texts on the principle that states should refrain from the threat or use of force, and on equal rights and self-determination of peoples. The Committee on the Peaceful Uses of the Sea-Bed and the Ocean Floor established a Legal Sub-Committee, which met in March and August to study legal principles.

The Legal Sub-Committee of the Committee on Peaceful Uses of Outer Space considered principles of compensation for damage caused by objects launched into outer space. The Legal Sub-Committee also decided to continue its study of the definition of outer space and to study technical aspects of the registration of objects launched for the exploration and use of outer space.

The General Assembly's Sixth Committee made a detailed study of draft articles for a convention on special missions adopted by the International Law Commission in 1967. The Assembly was expected to finish this work in December 1969 and adopt the convention for signature and ratification.

Concluding 20 years of development through the UN International Law Commission and the General Assembly's Sixth Committee, the UN Conference on the Law of Treaties adopted the Vienna Convention on the Law of Treaties on May 23, 1969. The Convention broke important new ground in providing that a party seeking to avoid the obligations of a treaty must normally give three months notice and must seek to settle disputes through the means specified in Article 33 of the UN Charter and through a special conciliation procedure. The Convention was to enter into force when ratified by 35 states.

Settlement of Disputes. The major event in this area in 1969 was the decision by the International Court of Justice in two cases concerning delimitation of the North Sea continental shelf submitted to the court in 1967 by Denmark and the Netherlands, on the one hand, and by the Federal Republic of Germany on the other. The parties asked the court to state the principles and rules of international law applicable to delimitation of the continental shelf.

The court considered that each party had a right to those areas of the continental shelf that "constitute a natural prolongation of its land territory into and under the sea" and that any areas of overlap "are to be divided between them in agreed proportions or, failing agreement, equally, unless they [the parties] decide on a regime of joint jurisdiction." The court specified the following factors to be taken into account: (1) the general configuration of the coasts of the parties; (2) the physical and geological structure, and the natural resources, of the continental shelf areas involved; and (3) a "reasonable degree of proportionality, which a delimitation carried out in accordance with equitable principles ought to bring about," taking into account the extent of the continental shelf areas of each party.

Another dispute in 1969 concerned exports of soluble or "instant" coffee to the United States from Brazil. Acting under provisions of the International Coffee Agreement of 1968, the United States complained that Brazil discriminated in favor of exports of processed coffee over green coffee beans, in violation of the agreement and to the detriment of U. S. coffee processors. The dispute was submitted to an arbitration panel, which found that discriminatory treatment existed and that the United States could take counter measures. The arbitration resulted in an agreement between the United States and Brazil under which Brazil would tax exports of soluble coffee to the United States at the rate of 13 cents per pound, and both parties would meet in January 1970 to seek further agreement.

ARTHUR LARSON
Duke University

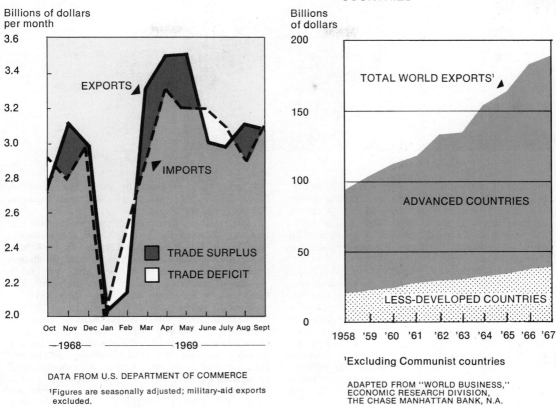

FOREIGN TRADE OF THE UNITED STATES[1]

Billions of dollars per month

EXPORTS
IMPORTS

TRADE SURPLUS
TRADE DEFICIT

Oct Nov Dec Jan Feb Mar Apr May June July Aug Sept
—1968— 1969

DATA FROM U.S. DEPARTMENT OF COMMERCE

[1]Figures are seasonally adjusted; military-aid exports excluded.

SMALLER SHARE OF EXPORTS FOR LESS-DEVELOPED COUNTRIES

Billions of dollars

TOTAL WORLD EXPORTS[1]

ADVANCED COUNTRIES

LESS-DEVELOPED COUNTRIES

1958 '59 '60 '61 '62 '63 '64 '65 '66 '67

[1]Excluding Communist countries

ADAPTED FROM "WORLD BUSINESS," ECONOMIC RESEARCH DIVISION, THE CHASE MANHATTAN BANK, N.A.

INTERNATIONAL TRADE

International trade expanded in 1969 more buoyantly than for many years. This lively growth occurred despite a major strike that closed most key ports in the United States, the world's largest trader, at the beginning of the year and despite some months of uncertainty about the valuation of the currencies of France and West Germany.

TRADE DEVELOPMENTS

Moving at a faster pace than in any recent period, exports in the non-Communist world grew by 15% in the first half of 1969. This boom in trade, led by western Europe and Japan, brought world exports close to a yearly rate of $250 billion by midyear.

A part of this unusually strong advance represented higher prices for goods traded internationally, as the costs of both primary commodities and manufactured goods resumed their upward movement. By far the major part of the increase, however, stemmed from sizable gains in the volume of goods moving throughout the world.

U. S. trade, and that of overseas countries whose exchange of goods with the United States is substantial, was affected by a longshoremen's strike in all East and Gulf Coast ports. The strike began on Dec. 20, 1968, and lasted in some places as late as April 13, 1969. A limited amount of cargo was diverted to air and to West Coast or Canadian ports

not affected by the strike. Most outgoing and incoming shipments, however, were immobilized. Even after the ports reopened, on various dates after February 15, congestion delayed the movement of goods for weeks.

Trade Bill. On November 18, President Nixon sent to Congress a message on trade and a proposed Trade Act of 1969. This proposal, characterized by Nixon as "modest," would, if enacted, provide: (1) authority for limited tariff reductions; (2) steps toward lowering nontariff barriers to trade, including elimination of the American selling price system of customs valuation for a few products, principally benzenoid chemicals; (3) readier relief for industries, companies, and workers faced with import competition; and (4) strengthening of U. S. funding of the General Agreement on Tariffs and Trade.

No action was taken on the proposed legislation by the end of 1969.

Currency Changes. The devaluation of the French franc on August 8 and the upward revaluation of the German mark on October 27 were designed to correct imbalances in those countries' trade and to restore monetary equilibrium. Changes in trade patterns normally take months to develop, and thus few effects were discernible in 1969. (See also INTERNATIONAL FINANCE.)

At the annual autumn meetings of the International Monetary Fund, a momentous innovation in

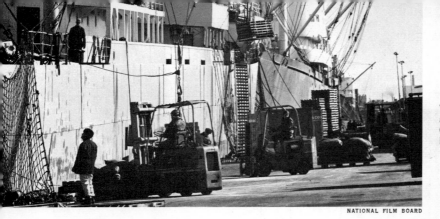

VESSELS load cargo for export at Hamilton, Canada's steel city. Canada boosted exports by 17% in the first nine months of 1969.

the field of international liquidity was set in motion. Beginning Jan. 1, 1970, special drawing rights, known as SDR's, were allocated to the 74 nations agreeing to participate as of October 3. The resultant easing in financial reserves was expected to assist materially in the flow of goods and services throughout the world.

United States. U. S. imports slowed abruptly in 1969 after their exceptional pace the previous year, but exports continued to advance somewhat above their recent trend rate. Foreign goods arriving in the United States rose in the first nine months by about 7%, less than one third as fast as in 1968 when they had been swelled by a booming economy and certain exceptional factors. Exports expanded through September by about 8%, little different from 1968. These diverse developments resulted in a small increase in the trade surplus over the 1968 level to a total of about $1 billion.

Although U. S. agricultural sales dropped for the third year in a row, demand for U. S. manufactured and other nonagricultural products abroad remained strong. About one third of the 1969 advance was in machinery exports, including electronic computers, automotive engines, and materials handling equipment. The movement of automotive equipment to Canada continued to be spurred by the 1965 agreement for duty-free trade in these products, but the rate of expansion slowed considerably.

Following a year when steel shipments were limited by a threatened strike in the industry, exports of these products soared by over 50% to a record level. Aluminum sales, which had dropped in value in 1968 because of a strike, also showed a large rise.

An especially buoyant factor in exports was deliveries of military aircraft and other military equipment to foreign governments. The value of military planes shipped abroad more than doubled to a total of half a billion dollars in January-September 1969 over the same months of 1968.

Agricultural shipments were 11% lower in this period. The dock strike lasted longest in Gulf ports, through which large quantities of grain and cotton move, and caused permanent losses in food shipments. Foreign demand was also reduced in 1969 because of larger supplies in importing countries.

The expansion in purchases of U. S. products in foreign markets was largely in industrialized areas. Sales to Canada continued strong, as they have been in recent years. Large gains were likewise registered in two other major markets, Japan and West Germany. Sales to the latter have been sluggish for several years, but in 1969 they climbed by 20%.

The developing countries as a group took only 2% more U. S. products, by value, than in 1968. Sharp declines were recorded in shipments to India, Pakistan, and the Philippines.

The relatively slow rate of gain in imports was due to a drop in the level of food and industrial supplies arriving in the United States. In 1968 those imports were exceptionally high because of hedge-buying in anticipation of strikes at the ports and in the metal industries. In 1969, not only was this factor absent, but stocks were drawn on.

Coffee imports were 30% lower through September than in 1968, while copper arrivals were less than half the previous year's rate. Steel-mill products purchased abroad were limited by voluntary quotas negotiated with the Common Market and Japan, as well as by large supplies imported in 1968 in anticipation of a strike that was averted.

Imports of capital equipment and consumer goods both climbed by about a fourth in value over 1968. Automobiles and parts from Canada remained strong, although the rate of import gain also slowed somewhat. Clothing imports topped a billion dollars in 1969, about a third higher than in 1968. Japan, Hong Kong, and other East Asian sources accounted for the major part of the increase. Footwear—especially from Italy and Spain—climbed sharply. These imports now account for about one quarter of U. S. supplies, compared with one sixth three years earlier. Radios, TV sets, and gem diamonds were other consumer products imported in vastly increased quantities in 1969.

Stimulated by continued domestic business expansion in the United States, arrivals of machinery and other types of capital equipment climbed to an annual rate of almost $4 billion through September. That value compared with a level of $1 billion only five years earlier.

Canada expanded her position as the largest source of U. S. imports in 1969. Purchases from Japan, Australia, and the developing countries of the Far East also jumped sharply. From Latin America and western Europe, however, imports dropped below their 1968 level.

U. S. Payments Balance. The U. S. balance of international payments moved into a heavy deficit through the first nine months of 1969, following a year when a small surplus was recorded for the first time since 1957. Through September, the deficit totalled $8.1 billion on a seasonally adjusted basis, the largest ever recorded.

Contributing to the deficit were sizable private net capital outflows resulting from a withdrawal of foreign funds invested in the United States and a relaxation in January of the mandatory government controls over direct investment.

Foreign payments on military account totalled over $3 billion in annual rate, and government grants and credits to foreigners were nearly $4 billion. Investment income remained at about the same level as in 1968.

The Export-Import Bank of the United States authorized $2.5 billion of loans, guarantees, and credits to support U. S. export sales in the fiscal year ending June 30, 1969. The nearly $1 billion in long-term loans helped finance capital equipment and defense articles and services. The former included extensive financing of commercial jet aircraft, atomic power projects, mining machinery, and telecommunications equipment.

Canada. In concert with most other major countries, Canada reported strong growth in its external trade in 1969. Through September, imports climbed by 17% and exports by 10.5%. In June, Canada announced that it would immediately implement all remaining tariff reductions agreed in the Kennedy Round of negotiations instead of spacing them out over the next 2½ years as originally planned. This step, made in an effort to expose Canadian producers to more foreign competition, was taken as a step in that country's war against inflation. It no doubt helped stimulate the high level of 1969 imports.

Although purchases of goods from Britain and other Commonwealth countries were particularly buoyant, the level of imports from the United States, which accounted for almost three fourths of the total, largely determined the rate of expansion. Greater purchases of automotive parts and engines, trucks, aircraft, and computers contributed to the growth in purchases from this country.

Exports to the United States included more petroleum, iron ore, newsprint, lumber, wood pulp, and especially much greater amounts of motor cars than in the preceding year. Canada's sales of wheat, though still a major export item, fell by a third in value. Copper sales, stimulated in 1968 by a long strike of U. S. refineries, fell back to more normal levels.

Canadian sales—except to the United States where shipments gained by 16%—were sluggish. Those to Britain and other Commonwealth countries were less than in 1968, as were exports to mainland China, Venezuela, and several other major markets.

The current account deficit of Canada's international payments deteriorated in the first half of 1969 compared with the same period of 1968. Transactions in goods and services with foreign countries resulted in an outflow of $635 million, 2½ times that in the preceding year. A decrease in the surplus on merchandise trade, augmented by a growing deficit in nonmerchandise items, was responsible for the larger deficit. Net capital movements into Canada were over half a billion dollars, five times the amount in the first half of 1968. The balance of both current and capital account transactions led to a fall of $96 million in official monetary assets in the first half of 1969.

Latin America. Spurred by booming demand and rising prices for some of their major export products, shipments from the 19 Latin American republics to foreign markets in the first half of 1969 showed a record increase for the decade. Coffee, sugar, hides, cocoa, and nonferrous metals were all bringing higher prices on world markets at midyear. Three countries—Mexico, Brazil, and Argentina—made major contributions to the export growth of

the area, and these same nations accounted for most of the considerable rise in imports as well.

Mexico, traditionally running a sizable trade deficit that is met by tourist receipts and capital inflows, reduced its import surplus in 1969 as a result of strong growth in sales and a minimal advance in foreign purchases. Through July, exports climbed by 20% over the first seven months of 1968 while imports rose by only 4%. The exceptional increase in exports resulted from a large improvement in agricultural sales and from a 37% rise in shipments of manufactured products. The latter, which signified progress in Mexico's efforts to make these goods competitive in world markets, included textiles, processed food, chemicals, petroleum products, and machinery. The limited import rise reflected successful steps toward restraint initiated by the government.

Brazil's strong export performance resulted from four major factors: favorable internal monetary policies, high foreign demand, good crops, and new government incentives. A flexible exchange rate system, adopted in September 1968, resulted in nine "mini" devaluations through the autumn of 1969, which cut the cruzeiro by 14% in terms of the dollar. These reductions, designed so that none was large enough to call for big domestic price increases, acted as a spur to exports. In the first seven months of 1969, shipments totalled 18% over the same period of 1968. Additional incentives for the export of manufactures were introduced in July through provision of a tax credit of 15% of the value of shipments. Brazil's success in pushing such sales is illustrated from the growth in its share of total exports from 3.8% in 1962 to 11.2% in 1969.

Argentina's trade showed the most spectacular growth of any of the Latin American republics. After stagnating for half a dozen years, imports rose by over 40% in the first half of 1969 while exports—which had declined in value in 1967 and 1968—rose by half that rate. The high level of imports reflected surging economic activity and extensive development programs in the nation. Substantially greater sales of agricultural products contributed to boosting exports.

U. S. TRADING PARTNERS, 1968–69
(Millions of dollars)

Country	Exports and reexports		Imports	
	1968	Jan.–Sept. 1969	1968	Jan.–Sept. 1969
TOTAL	$34,129	$27,305	$32,456	$25,887
Argentina	281	270	207	118
Australia	872	612	485	437
Belgium-Luxembourg	796	670	766	511
Brazil	709	502	670	439
Canada	8,058	6,700	8,925	7,467
Chile	307	229	203	119
Colombia	319	215	264	169
France	1,078	878	842	628
Germany, West	1,712	1,520	2,720	1,895
Hong Kong	304	269	637	600
India[1]	718	422	312	266
Israel	278	296	117	98
Italy	1,120	909	1,102	908
Japan	2,950	2,456	4,057	3,599
Korea, South	510	531	199	227
Mexico	1,365	1,030	893	755
Netherlands	1,370	1,026	456	334
Philippines	436	287	435	319
South Africa	455	364	253	178
Spain	519	402	308	221
Sweden	439	352	390	264
Switzerland	558	426	438	322
Taiwan	388	285	270	288
United Kingdom	2,180	1,706	2,048	1,562
Venezuela	655	531	950	700
Other countries	5,752	4,417	4,509	3,463

[1] Exports exclude "special category" shipments for which information is withheld for security reasons. Source: U. S. Department of Commerce.

Western Europe. The fastest growth for any year in the decade was recorded for western European trade through the first nine months of 1969. Total exports and imports jumped by 18% over the corresponding period of the previous year. Intra-European trade was even more expansive than that with other areas.

Throughout 1969 western Europe experienced a boom both in external and internal demand, though there was some slackening in the rate of expansion after midsummer. Industrial output in this area rose substantially, stimulating imports of many materials. The utilization of plant and labor pushed nearer capacity levels, bringing new demands for capital equipment and labor-saving machinery. Vigorous expansion in consumer expenditures also stimulated larger imports of consumer products.

The countries of the European Economic Community (Common Market) continued their strong trade growth, both with nonmembers and with one another. The thrust of the expansionary export demand outside the EEC in 1969 came from continental European Free Trade Association (EFTA) countries, Canada, and Japan, rather than from the United States as in 1968. Imports from nonmembers rose exceptionally fast so that the balance of trade with those countries dropped sharply, compared with the previous year, although it remained in small surplus.

Within the Common Market, trade also contin-

CHIEF U. S. EXPORTS AND IMPORTS, 1968–69
(Millions of dollars)

Commodity	1968	Jan.-Sept. 1969
TOTAL EXPORTS AND REEXPORTS	$34,413	$27,498
Wheat and flour	1,101	604
Coarse grains	929	590
Other food	1,860	1,458
Tobacco	524	326
Soybeans	810	446
Other crude materials	2,685	2,027
Coal	524	452
Petroleum and products	460	324
Chemical elements and compounds	1,241	999
Plastic materials	590	437
Other chemicals	1,458	1,058
Paper and manufactures	545	424
Textiles and clothing	698	570
Iron and steel mill products	582	614
Nonferrous metals and alloys	601	511
Metal manufactures	641	522
Power generating machinery and parts	1,162	926
Agricultural machinery and tractors	627	494
Office machinery	749	731
Construction, excavating, and mining machinery	1,099	905
Other nonelectrical machinery	2,683	2,202
Electric power apparatus	531	422
Other electric apparatus	1,755	1,558
Automotive vehicles and parts	3,372	2,754
Aircraft and parts	2,312	1,813
Scientific and photographic instruments	665	587
Firearms and ammunition	572	556
All other domestic exports	3,206	2,791
Reexports	431	397
TOTAL IMPORTS	$33,114	$26,402
Meat	746	653
Fish	631	506
Fruits, nuts, and vegetables	653	513
Coffee	1,140	606
Other food	1,407	999
Alcoholic beverages	626	431
Ores and metal scrap	958	704
Lumber	558	501
Other crude materials	1,781	1,345
Petroleum and products	2,345	1,892
Chemicals	1,135	912
Newsprint	863	687
Textiles	963	781
Clothing	855	829
Iron and steel mill products	1,962	1,349
Copper	855	360
Other nonferrous metals	1,078	808
Nonelectrical machinery	2,198	1,894
Electrical apparatus	1,495	1,386
Automotive vehicles and parts	3,712	3,260
All other imports	7,153	5,986

Source: U. S. Department of Commerce.

ued to be lively. The overheated French economy generated heavy demands for consumer goods.

The eight EFTA countries continued to run a large deficit with the world in the first half of 1969, but it was well below that in the previous year. Total exports of the area grew by nearly 15% while imports were only 9% higher. All member countries shared in the export expansion. The United Kingdom, by far the largest trader in the group, recorded only a 12.5% rise, largely because shipments to the United States barely changed in the first six months. This dampened the overall rate of EFTA export growth. Trade among the member countries expanded to represent a quarter of their total exports.

Imports into these countries also would have been much greater except for the relatively modest 6% advance in Britain's foreign purchases and a rise of less than 1% in Norwegian imports.

In early December, the Common Market countries reached agreement on discussions looking toward admission of Britain and possibly several other EFTA countries. (See also EUROPE.)

FRANCES L. HALL
Director, International Trade Analysis Division
U. S. Department of Commerce

TARIFFS

The U. S. trade surplus, an influence in world trade since 1950, had virtually disappeared by 1968–69. The commercial policies of U. S. trading partners, especially those belonging to regional economic organizations, are an increasing challenge to U. S. foreign trade. Tariff and other commercial discrimination against third countries is a common feature of such regional groupings. Although the second phase of duty reductions negotiated under the Kennedy Round became effective in 1969, this incentive to trade was partly offset by increased resort to nontariff barriers.

U. S. Developments. The second stage of duty reductions under the Kennedy Round of tariff negotiations became effective in 1969. Concessions had been granted on U. S. imports totaling $19 billion and U. S. exports totaling $26 billion in 1964. Legislative authority for further tariff negotiations expired in 1967, but provision for adjustment assistance remained in effect. The Tariff Commission received petitions from industries producing canned sardines, glass, carpets, and pianos, and from workers producing steel pipe and transmission towers, who asked relief from alleged injury due to import competition resulting from U. S. tariff concessions.

In response to a request from President Nixon, the Tariff Commission instituted an investigation in August 1969 to determine the economic factors affecting the use by U. S. manufacturers of certain tariff items. Under these provisions, American-made components may be exported for assembly abroad; when the assembled products are returned to the United States, customs duties do not apply against the value of the American components. These provisions have assisted some developing countries to begin manufacturing operations and thus made them less dependent on foreign aid, but American labor alleges that they also result in loss of American jobs to lower paid workers abroad.

U. S. customs receipts in fiscal 1969 were about $2.1 billion, or 1.2% of federal budget receipts. Such receipts were once the largest source of federal revenue, until exceeded by internal revenue taxes in 1914. Customs receipts are still the major source of government revenue for many countries.

Individual members of Congress introduced many bills in 1969 for tariff and quota protection of various industries. Several of these took the form of proposed "orderly marketing" arrangements. However, the only tariff bills enacted in 1969 were those continuing the suspension of duties on certain raw materials.

In 1969 the Philippines and the United States discussed a trade and tariff agreement to replace the present preferences due to be phased out by 1974. The Philippine negotiators asked for non-reciprocal tariff preference, which would grant U. S. preference on Philippine articles but no Philippine preference on U. S. articles.

The president's third annual report on the Automotive Products Trade Act, issued in 1969, showed an increase in U. S. imports of cars and parts from Canada—from $76 million in 1964 to $2.58 billion in 1968. There was a corresponding increase in U. S. exports of cars and parts to Canada—from $654 million to $2.42 billion. The Canadian manufacturers, chiefly subsidiaries of U. S. companies, were able to economize by making longer production runs of fewer models and importing other models duty-free from the United States.

Border-tax Adjustments. In recent years the value-added tax has gained popularity in European countries. It has been introduced in France (1954), Denmark (1967), West Germany (1968), the Netherlands (1969), Sweden (1969), and Norway (effective in 1970). It is to be adopted uniformly in all countries of the European Economic Community during 1970. When goods are exported from a country that imposes this tax or other indirect taxes, the exporter receives a rebate; in contrast, imported goods are taxed at the border at rates calculated to correspond to the indirect taxes that would have been charged against them if they had been produced in the importing country. Thus, this levy as applied to imports has become known as a "border tax."

In the view of the U. S. government, the border tax is similar to an additional import duty and discriminates against countries that employ direct taxes. Therefore, in 1969, at the request of the United States, nations held discussions that might lead to some changes in these practices.

Preferences. The 130 countries that attended the second United Nations Conference on Trade and Development in 1968 unanimously proposed that developed countries should extend tariff preferences to all developing countries without requiring a reciprocal preference from them. The proposed general preferences would aid poorer countries but would modify the most-favored-nation policy historically adhered to by the United States and most developed countries. In the negotiations for joining the Commonwealth preference area to that of the European Economic Community (embracing most of the former colonies of France, Belgium, the Netherlands, and Italy), Britain offered to broaden its tariff preferences so they would apply to products of all developing countries. In 1969, these proposals were under study in the Organization for Economic Cooperation and Development and in the United States.

Regional Arrangements. In recent years the principal free trade areas and customs unions have experienced faster growth in their regional trade than in their trade with nonmembers. With greater specialization and freer competition, the member countries have turned their attention increasingly to economic problems that are affected by tariff policy, such as internal taxation and wage and monetary policies.

European Economic Community. In the first 10 years of the EEC, trade between the six member countries quadrupled while their trade with third countries doubled. Free trade among members and a common external tariff became fully effective in 1968. The common agricultural policy was also implemented after a series of transitional measures. A system of variable levies insures that the prices of agricultural products imported from outside the community will not be less than internally supported prices. During 1969 the common market arrangements were strained by the relative weakness of the franc and strength of the mark. Even after currency values were adjusted, difficulties persisted in administering the community's farm price controls.

The EEC Council in 1968 considered proposals by Benelux, Italy, and West Germany to arrange interim tariff preferences for Britain, Denmark, Norway, and Ireland. The alternative of full membership for these countries was still under consideration in 1969. The United States has consistently opposed anything short of full membership and eventual free trade among all parties.

EFTA. A 1969 report shows that exports to one another among the countries that make up the European Free Trade Association—Austria, Denmark, Finland, Norway, Portugal, Sweden, Switzerland, and Britain—increased 145% between 1959 and 1968 while their total exports increased 86%. Trade between the United States and the EFTA has expanded more than the total trade of either, though less rapidly than intra-EFTA trade.

Britain, which was incurring a larger than usual trade deficit in 1968–69, adopted an import deposit requirement in 1969 in an effort to retard imports without changing tariffs. Meanwhile, the Nordic countries discussed plans to intensify their economic cooperation within the association.

LAFTA. Several regional complementation agreements were ratified by the Latin American Free Trade Association in 1969. These permitted free trade among certain Latin American republics in designated products, chiefly of new industries requiring a multinational market for their operations.

The republics of the Plata Basin (Cuenca del Plata) met at Brasilia in April 1969 to plan regional economic integration. Its efforts are to be coordinated within the LAFTA.

Intra-LAFTA trade increased 143% from 1961 to 1968, while the members' trade with the United States increased 27%.

CACM. The presidents of Costa Rica, Guatemala, Honduras, Nicaragua, and El Salvador—the Central American Common Market—met with President Nixon in July 1969 to discuss trade and other affairs. The trade among the five increased from $37 million in 1961 to $260 million in 1968, facilitated by the partial but progressive removal of duties. By Jan. 1, 1969, a common external tariff had been applied to 95% of the tariff items. The temporary import surcharge imposed in 1968 was removed on most "intra" trade.

GLENN W. SUTTON
Chairman, United States Tariff Commission

IOWA

In 1969, Iowa enjoyed a relatively strong economy. An active legislative year and controversy with the federal government over water pollution were other important developments.

Economy. Iowa's farmers harvested a record 94 bushels of corn per acre. The new harvest broke the previous high yield of 1968 by an average of one bushel per acre. Total production of corn, however, was only 884,070,000 bushels, the 4th largest crop in the state's history. The higher average yield and lower total harvest were due to the fact that farmers had taken out of production 3.9 million acres normally planted with corn. Iowa's soybean crop for 1969 was 171,675,000 bushels, about 6 million fewer than the record 1968 crop. The average yield was 31.5 bushels per acre—a half bushel below 1968.

The employment picture in Iowa continued good, with the number of jobless remaining below the national average.

Legislation. The first session of the 63d Iowa General Assembly passed the record biennial budget proposed by Republican Gov. Robert Ray. In spite of the new high in appropriations, however, the General Assembly refused to legislate new taxes, in keeping with the Republican party's promises during the campaign.

A tax on advertising imposed by the 1967 session was repealed by the 1969 legislature. Among the bills passed into law was an annual salary for the

---
IOWA • Information Highlights

Area: 56,290 square miles (145,791 sq km).
Population: 2,745,000 (1969 est.).
Chief Cities (1969 est.): Des Moines, the capital, 207,000; Cedar Rapids, 107,000; Davenport, 98,500; Sioux City, 86,000; Waterloo, 78,500; Dubuque, 65,000.
Government: *Chief Officers*—governor, Robert D. Ray (Rep.); lt. gov., Roger W. Jepsen (R); secy. of state, Melvin D. Synhorst (R); atty. gen., Richard C. Turner (R); treas., Maurice E. Baringer; chief justice, Theodore G. Garfield. *General Assembly*—Senate, 60 members (44 Republicans, 16 Democrats); House of Representatives, 124 members (86 R, 38 D).
Education: *School enrollment* (1968)—public elementary, 361,000 pupils (17,600 teachers); public secondary, 295,000 pupils (14,400 teachers); nonpublic schools, 95,400 pupils (4,130 teachers); college and university (fall 1967), 99,072 students. *Public school expenditures* (1967–68)—$419,-000,000 ($678 per pupil); average teacher's salary, $7,382.
Public Finance (fiscal year 1969): *Revenues*, $1,117,897,032 (3% sales tax, $173,698,969; motor fuel tax, $134,800,817; federal funds, $180,881,476). *Expenditures*, $1,090,708,726 (education, $244,368,392; health, welfare, and safety, $307,589,354; highways, $314,667,344). *State debt*, $99,-677,000 (June 1969).
Personal Income (1968): $9,057,000,000; average annual income per person, $3,265.
Public Assistance (fiscal year 1968): $96,162,027 to 90,941 recipients (aged, $29,161,464; dependent children, $33,-425,944).
Labor Force (employed persons, July 1969): *Agricultural*, 401,700; *nonagricultural* (wage and salary earners), 877,-900 (16.8% manufacturing, 15.7% trade, 12.4% government). *Unemployed persons* (July 1969)—39,500.
Manufacturing (1966): Value added by manufacture, $3,030,-559,000 (transportation equipment, $42,325,000; primary metals, $107,632,000; nonelectrical machinery, $731,839,-000; electrical machinery, $368,781,000; fabricated metals, $155,175,000; food and products, $742,126,000).
Agriculture (1967): Cash farm income, $3,580,331,000 (livestock, $2,546,951,000; crops, $890,541,000; govt. payments, $142,839,000). *Chief crops* (1969)—Corn for grain, 884,-070,000 bushels (ranks 2d among the states); hay, 7,132,-000 tons (ranks 1st); (1969), soybeans, 171,675,000 bushels (ranks 2d); oats, 1,427,722 tons (ranks 3d); popcorn, 47,500 tons (ranks 2d).
Mining (1966): Production value, $119,313,000. *Chief minerals* (tons)—Stone, 40,081,000; sand and gravel, 18,213,000; gypsum, 5,577,000; coal, 5,577,000.
Transportation: *Roads* (1969), 112,342 miles (180,792 km); *motor vehicles* (1968), 1,696,000; *railroads* (1967), 12,325 track miles (19,835 km); *airports* (1969), 15.
Communications (1968): *Telephones*, 1,439,600; *television stations*, 11; *radio stations*, 107; *newspapers*, 45.

members of the General Assembly of $5,500 per year with per diem expenses of $15.00 while the legislature is in session. The new pay plan will become effective with the first session of the General Assembly in 1971.

Reapportionment. In accordance with a constitutional amendment on reapportionment approved by the voters in 1968, the 1969 session of the General Assembly redrafted the 50 senatorial districts and 100 single-member house districts to comply with the "one man, one vote" mandate. The new districts are to be used in the 1970 elections, but the Democratic State General Committee has filed a case with the Iowa supreme court declaring them unconstitutional.

Education. The activation of five Regional Service units, each serving a number of counties, reduced the number of county school superintendents.

The General Assembly appropriated funds for the purchase of land in the city of Atlantic for the site of the new Western Iowa University. The Board of Regents, the agency directed to proceed with the purchase of land, was reluctant to execute any contracts, asserting that the legislature's appropriations were inadequate to finance even the existing institutions of higher learning.

The three Board of Regents institutions—the University of Iowa, Iowa State University, and Northern Iowa University—all increased both resident and out-of-state tuitions to a record high. In spite of this, increased enrollment was noted at all three universities.

Water Pollution. A controversy with the federal government over discharges of municipal and agricultural wastes into the Mississippi and Missouri Rivers continued through most of 1969. Iowa claimed that the pollution standard of the rivers was not affected by their sewage. This defense was not accepted by the federal government, which invoked its power to set quality standards for a state and insisted that Iowa provide secondary treatment of all wastes flowing into the rivers by December 1973.

RUSSELL M. ROSS
University of Iowa

IRAN

During 1969, Iran continued to enjoy the general prosperity that had marked the previous four years. Faced with the danger of inflation, however, the government of Premier Amir Abbas Hoveida took steps to cool the overheating economy. On August 7 the Central Bank increased the deposit requirements of commercial banks and raised the rediscount rate from 7% to 8%.

In January, Iran, which had been one of the world's largest producers of opium until the growing of opium poppies was prohibited in 1955, decided to resume limited production of the drug. The government claimed that the failure of Turkey and Afghanistan to control production had rendered Iran's efforts at prohibition ineffective.

Economic Development. The nation's economic growth in both the public and the private sector was encouraged by the government under the provisions of the fourth 5-year development plan, inaugurated in March 1968, which was designed to raise the gross national product to $12 billion by 1973. In the first year of this plan (1968–69) the GNP rose 10%.

————— **IRAN • Information Highlights** —————

Area: 636,363 square miles (1,648,182 sq km).
Population: 26,985,000 (1968 est.).
Chief Cities (1966 census): Teheran, the capital, 2,695,283; Isfahan, 423,777; Meshed, 409,281; Tabriz, 404,855.
Government: *King*—Shah Mohammed Reza Pahlavi (acceded 1941); *Premier*—Amir Abbas Hoveida (took office Jan. 27, 1965). *Parliament*—Senate, 60 members; Majlis (National Assembly), 200 members.
Religious Faiths: Muslims, 98% of population, of whom majority are Shiites.
Education: *Literacy rate* (1966), 23% of population aged 15 and over. *Total school enrollment* (1966)—3,015,567 (primary, 2,378,082; secondary, 579,716; teacher-training, 5,679; technical/vocational, 15,840; university/higher, 36,250).
Finance (1968 est.): *Revenues,* $1,498,300,000; *expenditures,* $1,858,700,000; *public debt* (1966), $975,200,000; *monetary unit,* rial (75.75 rials equal U. S.$1).
Gross National Product (1968): $6,900,000.
National Income (1967): $6,389,000,000; *average annual income per person,* $242.
Economic Indexes (1967): *Industrial production* (1968), 124 (1963=100); *agricultural production,* 104 (1963=100); *cost of living,* 156 (1963=100).
Manufacturing (metric tons, 1967): Gasoline, 2,319,000; cement, 1,538,000; wheat flour, 1,309,000.
Crops (metric tons, 1968 crop year): Wheat, 4,000,000; barley, 1,020,000; rice, 954,000; grapes, 260,000; cottonseed, 260,000; citrus fruit, 65,000.
Minerals (metric tons, 1967): Crude petroleum, 128,761,000 (ranks 3d among world producers); coal, 300,000; salt (1966), 245,000; chromite (1966), 175,000; sulfur (1966), 4,000; natural gas, 1,466,000,000 cubic meters.
Foreign Trade (1968): *Exports,* $1,879,000,000 (chief export, 1967: petroleum, $1,506,000,000); *imports,* $1,386,000,000 (chief import, 1967: nonelectrical machinery, $531,392,-000). *Chief trading partners* (1967): Japan (took 28% of exports, supplied 8% of imports); Britain (took 22% of exports, supplied 12% of imports); West Germany (took 3% of exports, supplied 22% of imports).
Transportation: *Roads* (1969), 22,195 miles (35,718 km); *motor vehicles* (1967), 223,900 (automobiles 164,200); *railways* (1969), 2,500 miles (4,023 km); *merchant vessels* (1967), 5 (58,000 gross registered tons); *principal airport,* Teheran.
Communications: *Telephones* (1968): 77,500; *television stations* (1967), 4; *television sets* (1967), 131,000; *radios* (1967), 1,790,000; *newspapers* (1961), 27.

Construction continued on the country's first large steel complex, at Isfahan, financed by Soviet credits arranged in 1966 and 1968. It was expected to go into production in 1970. On February 10 the International Finance Corporation announced that, with the help of private investors in Europe and the United States, it would provide $3.9 million in share and loan capital for an $18.1 million rolling and pipe mill to be constructed near Ahwaz in southwestern Iran. On May 7 the World Bank granted a loan of $40 million to the Industrial and Mining Development Bank of Iran to enable it to step up its already extensive lending program to private industry. Later in the year a syndicate of 19 international banks granted a 5-year $80 million credit in Eurodollars to the Central Bank of Iran for furthering development projects.

In the agricultural sector, where production was to be increased by 28% during the period of the fourth development plan, the Parliament approved legislation described as "the final blow to feudalism," under which over a million tenant farmers were expected to become landowners. In March the World Bank announced a $30 million loan for additional irrigation works and the introduction of modern agricultural techniques in the Dez area of Khuzistan province.

Petroleum Production. Domestic and foreign investment and foreign loans notwithstanding, the development program is financed principally from oil revenues. Following the pattern set in 1968, the government again urged the international consortium that produces about 90% of Iran's crude petroleum to step up production in order to increase its contribution to the development plan. After four days of intensive discussions at Teheran, the government

and the consortium announced agreement on May 14. Shah Mohammed Reza Pahlavi said that Iran would receive $1.01 billion from the consortium in 1969–70 through a 10% increase in oil production, a 12% increase in payments, and loans to the government sufficient to cover any deficit.

At the same time the government sought a further increase in its oil revenues by encouraging production outside the areas reserved for exploitation by the consortium. On March 3 the government-owned National Iranian Oil Company entered into an agreement with a group of European oil companies for exploration and production in a 10,400 square mile (27,000-sq km) area in southern Iran between the Zagros Mountains and the Persian Gulf. Production at the Sassan field in the waters of the Gulf, in which four American oil companies have a half interest, was expanded toward the target of 10 million tons annually by late 1969 or early 1970.

Foreign Relations. Iran continued its membership in the Central Treaty Organization (CENTO), with Turkey, Pakistan, Britain, and the United States, and on May 26 and 27 the 16th annual Ministerial Council of CENTO met in Teheran. Through their Regional Cooperation for Development organization, Iran, Turkey, and Pakistan made progress toward linking their transportation and communication networks. Plans were under consideration for construction of a 1,000-mile (1,600-km) pipeline from the oil fields of southwestern Iran to the Turkish Mediterranean port of İskenderun. Trade and cultural contacts with India were fostered early in January when the shah visited New Delhi.

Relations with Saudi Arabia and Kuwait, cemented late in 1968, remained cordial, but those with other Arab states deteriorated. On April 2, Iran broke off diplomatic relations with Lebanon when that country refused to extradite a former Iranian interior minister accused of embezzlement and misuse of power. The long-smoldering quarrel with Iraq over definition of the frontier and navigational rights in the Shatt-al-Arab, the confluence of the Tigris and Euphrates rivers, resulted on April 19 in Iranian denunciation of the Iranian-Iraqi treaty of 1937. Tension remained high for months, with Baghdad charging Iran with spy activity in Iraq and aid to the Kurdish rebels, and Iran providing naval escorts for its shipping in the Shatt-al-Arab.

Iran also continued to protest the inclusion of Bahrain, to which it had a territorial claim, in the emerging Federation of Arab Amirates and sought to lay foundations for establishing a secure position in the Persian Gulf after the British withdrawal scheduled for 1971. Although the Iranian government continued to support the November 1967 United Nations resolution on the settlement of the Israeli-Arab war, and the shah attended the meeting of representatives of Muslim states in Rabat, Morocco, in September, for the most part Iran avoided direct involvement in the Palestine problem.

Good relations were maintained with both the Soviet Union and the United States. A joint Iranian-Soviet transportation committee, meeting in Moscow early in January 1969, agreed to introduce direct travel by rail between the two countries in the spring of 1970. In late October the shah paid an official visit to Washington, where he conferred with President Richard Nixon, Secretary of State William Rogers, and Secretary of Defense Melvin Laird.

PAUL L. HANNA
University of Florida

IRAQ

The execution of more than 50 alleged spies drew world attention to Iraq during 1969 and highlighted the insecurity of the Baath party government of President Ahmed Hassan al-Bakr that had seized power in July 1968. Despite political instability and a resurgence of the Kurdish revolt, the long-stagnant economy showed signs of revival.

The Spy Furor. On January 27, 14 Iraqi citizens, including 9 Jews, were executed in Baghdad and Basra for allegedly plotting to overthrow the regime and install a new government conciliatory to Israel. The public display of their corpses and the celebration that followed evoked widespread foreign condemnation. Paul T. Bail, a U. S. employee of the Iraq Petroleum Company, who was arrested in December 1968 on charges of espionage for the United States, was released in February 1969, although the Iraqi government claimed it had sufficient evidence to convict him.

On February 20, Iraq executed 8 more Iraqis as Israeli spies. Four persons charged with being U. S. spies were executed on April 13, and 10 others were executed on May 15 as agents of the United States, Israel, and Iran. Fifteen persons (including 2 Jews) were executed on August 25 and 3 on September 8, having been convicted of spying on behalf of the United States and Israel.

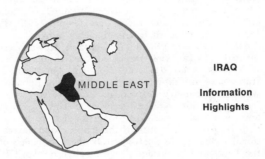

IRAQ

Information Highlights

Area: 167,847 square miles (434,724 sq km).
Population: 8,634,000 (1968 est.).
Chief Cities (1965 census): Baghdad, the capital, 1,745,328; Basra, 313,327; Mosul, 243,311; Kirkuk, 167,413.
Government: *President and Premier*—Ahmed Hassan al-Bakr (took office July 1968). *Parliament*—legislative power is exercised by the Revolutionary Command Council.
Religious Faiths: Muslims, 96% of population.
Education: *Literacy rate* (1957), 15% of population aged 15 and over. *Total school enrollment* (1965)—1,247,188 (primary, 964,327; secondary, 241,065; teacher-training, 5,760; vocational, 7,626; higher, 28,410).
Finance (1969 est.): *Revenues*, $1,467,000,000; *expenditures*, $1,708,000,000; *monetary unit*, dinar (0.3571 dinar equals U. S.$1).
Gross National Product (1966): $1,800,000,000.
National Income (1965): $1,769,600,000; *average annual income per person*, $216.
Economic Indexes (1967): *Industrial (petroleum) production*, 106 (1963=100); *agricultural production*, 133 (1963=100); *cost of living*, 101 (1963=100).
Manufacturing (metric tons, 1967): Residual fuel oil, 1,294,000; cement (1966), 1,279,000; gasoline, 343,000.
Crops (metric tons, 1967–68 crop year): Wheat, 866,000; barley, 860,000; rice, 308,000; dates, 265,000; onions, 155,000; cottonseed, 22,000.
Minerals (metric tons, 1967): Crude petroleum, 60,168,000.
Foreign Trade (1968): *Exports*, $1,028,000,000 (chief export, 1967: petroleum, $768,410,000); *imports*, $404,000,000 (chief imports, 1967: sugar, $21,450,000; motor vehicles, $23,630,000). *Chief trading partners* (1967): France (took 24% of exports, supplied 4% of imports); Italy (took 16% of exports, supplied 5% of imports); Britain.
Transportation: *Roads* (1966), 12,950 miles (20,840 km); *motor vehicles* (1967), 99,900 (automobiles 60,700); *railways* (1966), 1,050 miles (1,690 km); *principal airports*, Baghdad, Basra.
Communications: *Telephones* (1968): 77,500; *television stations* (1967), 1; *television sets* (1967), 175,000; *radios* (1965), 2,500,000; *newspapers* (1963), 8.

Domestic Affairs. Little progress was made toward reestablishing constitutional government, and power remained with the self-appointed Revolutionary Command Council. However, domestic opposition grew, and late in March the government curbed activities of Palestine commando groups, accusing them of collaboration with domestic enemies of the regime. In the summer there were reports of increasing antigovernment sentiment within the Shiite community in southern Iraq.

The failure of the government to implement the local autonomy that had been promised the Kurds prompted renewed violence in the north. On March 1, Kurdish dissidents launched a mortar attack on installations of the Iraq Petroleum Company at Kirkuk. In late September, following clashes between Kurdish rebels and security forces, the government resumed military operations against the forces of Gen. Mustafa al-Barzani, the Kurdish rebel leader.

Economic Developments. Unpredictably, economic conditions improved. While relations between the government and the internationally controlled Iraq Petroleum Company, which produces most of the nation's crude oil, remained strained, oil production and revenues increased significantly. Even though military expenditures siphoned off funds, greater investment in the badly starved 1965–70 development plan became possible.

Substantial loans for mineral and industrial development were granted by the Soviet Union, Poland, and East Germany. Encouraged, the government announced a new 5-year plan for 1970–75, calling for an investment of $2.7 billion and an annual increase in the gross national product of 7.1%.

Efforts to increase oil production still further by developing fields outside the concession area of the Iraq Petroleum Company continued to be made. Early in 1969 the government-owned Iraq National Oil Company invited 13 western European and Soviet bloc enterprises to bid on preparing the rich North Rumaila oil field for production. In July, however, plans were altered when the Soviet Union agreed to lend Iraq $70 million to make possible direct development of the field by the national oil company.

Foreign Affairs. During 1969 the Iraqi government strengthened its military posture against Israel. Some 12,000 troops were maintained in northern Jordan and 6,000 in southern Syria. Iraq joined Syria and Jordan in establishing a joint military command along the Israeli frontier.

Though President al-Bakr did not attend the Arab summit meeting at Rabat, Morocco, on December 21–23 that sought unsuccessfully to forge a united Arab policy on the Palestine problem, Iraq was represented at the sessions by the deputy premier, Lt. Gen. Hardan Takriti.

The long-standing quarrel with Iran over territorial and navigational rights in the Shatt-al-Arab, the common mouth of the Tigris and Euphrates rivers, flared in 1969. Iraq rejected an Iranian demand to renegotiate the 1937 treaty, which established the river frontier, and charged Iran with breaching the pact and aiding the Kurdish rebels.

Contacts with states within the Soviet sphere of influence grew more cordial, and on April 30, Iraq became the first Arab nation to recognize East Germany.

PAUL L. HANNA
University of Florida

IRELAND

The bitter civil and sectarian strife in Northern Ireland in 1969 had many repercussions in the Irish Republic, where sympathy for their Roman Catholic co-religionists in the north was widespread and intense. Repeated clashes between militant Protestants and Catholic civil rights demonstrators in the northern cities, leading to riots, barricades, arson, and sabotage, forced Irish politicians to steer a perilous course between too much and too little interference in the affairs of the northern state, the existence of which they have objected to since partition in 1922.

Elections in May strengthened the position of the government of Irish Prime Minister Jack Lynch.

Problems in the North. The problems in Northern Ireland in 1969 reopened many of the old wounds in Anglo-Irish relations. After the outbreak of severe rioting in Londonderry on April 19–20, Prime Minister Lynch met with British Prime Minister Harold Wilson to discuss ways of guaranteeing the civil rights of the Catholic minority in the north. On April 23 Frank Aiken, the Irish minister for external affairs, conferred with UN Secretary General U Thant about the disorders in Northern Ireland.

Elections. On May 21, Prime Minister Lynch formally dissolved the 18th Dáil (parliament) and appealed to the electorate for a new mandate. The results of the general election, held on June 18, strengthened the position of his government. Lynch's Fianna Fáil party won 75 seats in the new Dáil. The Fine Gael party won 4 new seats and returned with a total of 50. The Labour party held on to 18 seats, and one independent was returned. Among the newly elected members was Dr. Conor Cruise O'Brien, the author, playwright, and former UN representative in Katanga.

Prime Minister Lynch in July appointed Patrick Hillery the new minister for external affairs following the resignation of Frank Aiken. Erskine Childers, the new minister for health, was appointed deputy prime minister.

Request for UN Intervention. Renewed fighting and sabotage by Protestants and Catholics in the north forced the British government to send troops to guard public utilities there in July and August. On August 13, while the people of Bogside in Londonderry were fighting to defend their homes, Prime Minister Lynch made a public appeal to the British government to request intervention by a UN peacekeeping force. The prime minister also announced that field hospitals had been set up by the Irish army in Donegal to treat riot casualties from across the border in Londonderry. On August 15, some 2,000 members of Ireland's First Line Reserve were mobilized for possible use as a peace-keeping force in the north.

After unsuccessful talks with government officials in London, Patrick Hillery flew to New York, where he tried to persuade the UN Security Council to intervene in the north. However, Britain's UN representative, Lord Caradon, insisted, that the UN had no right to interfere in what Britain regarded as a domestic affair. The Security Council did not approve Hillery's request, but it did listen to his version of the origins and consequences of the crisis.

Prime Minister Lynch on August 28 proposed negotiations for the merger of Northern Ireland and the Irish Republic. His unexpected and unwelcome proposal was rejected by the government of Northern Ireland.

Economy. The economic position of Ireland in 1969 was generally healthy, following a 5½% growth rate in the previous year. Sunny weather helped to produce a bountiful harvest. Increases in industrial output were offset to some extent by rising wages and, more important, by a jump in imports from the United Kingdom. Trade returns for September showed imports exceeding exports by a value of more than $33.6 millions. The government stepped up its industrial development program and continued its efforts to gain entrance to the European Economic Community at the earliest opportunity.

Franco-Irish relations were improved in 1969 by the arrival of General and Madame de Gaulle in County Kerry on May 10. The former French president spent almost a month on private vacation near Sneem.

L. PERRY CURTIS JR.
University of California, Berkeley

IRELAND

Information Highlights

Area: 27,163 square miles (70,280 sq km).
Population: 2,910,000 (1968 est.).
Chief Cities (1966 census): Dublin, the capital, 568,271; Cork, 122,066; Limerick, 55,885.
Government: *President*—Éamon de Valéra (took office for 2d 7-year term June 25, 1966); *Prime Minister*—John (Jack) Lynch (took office Nov. 10, 1966). *Parliament*—Dáil Éireann (House of Representatives), 144 members (party seating, 1969: Fianna Fáil, 75; Fine Gael, 50; Labour, 18; independent, 1); Seanad Éireann (Senate), 60 members.
Religious Faiths: Roman Catholics, 95% of population.
Education: *Total school enrollment* (1965)—915,021 (primary, 498,396; secondary, 250,314; technical/vocational, 144,500; university/higher, 21,811).
Finance (1968 est.): *Revenues,* $791,770,000; *expenditures,* $908,000,000; *public debt* (1967), $1,887,000,000; *monetary unit,* pound (.4194 pound equals U. S.$1).
Gross National Product (1968): $2,889,842,000.
National Income (1968): $2,339,000,000; average annual income per person, $803.
Economic Indexes (1967): *Industrial production* (1968), 143 (1963=100); *agricultural production,* 102 (1963=100); *cost of living,* 119 (1963=100).
Manufacturing (metric tons, 1967): Cement, 1,299,000; beer, 3,481,000 hectoliters; gasoline, 475,000.
Crops (metric tons, 1967–68 crop year): Potatoes, 1,748,000; sugar beets, 956,000; barley, 677,000; oats, 294,000.
Minerals (metric tons, 1966): Peat, 4,671,000 (ranks 2d among world producers); limestone, 4,359,000; sand and gravel, 2,358,000; gypsum, 218,000.
Foreign Trade (1968): *Exports,* $799,000,000 (chief exports, 1967: cattle, $116,990,000; meat, $115,330,000; dairy products and eggs, $45,960,000); *imports,* $1,175,000,000 (chief imports, 1967: nonelectrical machinery, $106,260,000; textile yarn and fabrics, $58,960,000). *Chief trading partners* (1967): Britain (took 73% of exports, supplied 50% of imports); United States (took 9% of exports, supplied 8% of imports); West Germany (supplied 6% of imports).
Transportation: *Roads* (1969), 51,473 miles (82,841 km); *motor vehicles* (1967), 367,700 (automobiles 318,600); *railways* (1966), 1,455 miles (2,341 km); *national airline,* Air Lingus-Irish International Airlines; *principal airport,* Dublin.
Communications: *Telephones* (1968), 249,473; *television stations* (1968), 20; *television sets* (1968), 395,000; *radios* (1966), 816,000; *newspapers* (1967), 7 (daily circulation, 703,000).

OIL FIRE burned for 5 hours when pipeline was blown up at Haifa. Arab sabotage was suspected. Pipe carries oil more than 200 miles from refineries to Elath, which is located on the Gulf of Aqaba.

PIX

ISRAEL

The year 1969 saw the death in late February of the prime minister of Israel, Levi Eshkol, and the selection of Mrs. Golda Meir as his successor (see biographies with this article). In elections held in October the Labor party retained its dominant position in the coalition government, but suffered a loss of seats in the legislature (Knesset).

Arab sabotage and terrorism directed against Israel continued both in Israel and abroad, and unrest and guerrilla activities increased in the areas occupied by Israel since the Israeli-Arab war of 1967. Despite international efforts, no real progress was made toward formulating acceptable terms of peace. Observance of the 1967 cease-fire agreements virtually broke down.

Domestic Politics. The death of Premier Eshkol on Feb. 26, 1969, appeared likely to precipitate a struggle for succession within the Labor party, which is the dominant member of the coalition that had governed Israel since the 1967 war. The major contenders for leadership were Yigal Allon, the deputy prime minister, and Moshe Dayan, the minister of defense. Allon served briefly as interim premier but on March 7 the Central Committee of the Labor party, in a move to avoid a party split, nominated for the premiership Golda Meir, 70, a former foreign minister and a long-time party leader. Mrs. Meir reconstituted the Eshkol cabinet and was sworn in as premier on March 17.

On October 28 elections were held for the seventh Knesset with 16 parties vying for seats in the 120-member body. The Labor party and the United Workers party (Mapam), which had signed a "covenant of alliance" in January and which together held 63 seats in the outgoing Knesset, entered a single list of candidates. The alignment won only 56 seats, but Mrs. Meir was able to reestablish a broadly based coalition controlling 98 seats. On December 11 she presented a new 24-member cabinet.

Economic Conditions. The government endeavored to maintain a growth rate of about 12% while preserving price and wage stability in an economy that was essentially on a war footing. A wage freeze continued in effect, and expenditures for social services were curtailed. The budget estimates for 1969–70 projected expenditures of $2.24 billion, with defense spending accounting for $714 million. The foreign trade gap was expected to widen to $695 million in 1969.

Arab Guerrilla Activity. The activities of the various Palestine Arab commando organizations dedicated to the restoration, through violence and force, of what they regard as Arab rights in Palestine were significantly stepped up. Positions in Israel and Israeli-held territory were subjected to attacks from across the cease-fire lines. Raiders penetrated deep into Israel to lay mines and engage in sabotage, and Israelis and Israeli property were attacked outside of Israel.

The activities of al-Fatah, the largest of the commando organizations, were concentrated primarily along the cease-fire lines and in the occupied areas.

UPI

GOLDA MEIR became premier of Israel on March 17, 1969, succeeding Levi Eshkol. Although her Mapai party lost strength in the national elections of October 28, she salvaged sufficient support to continue in office. In Israel's conflict with the Arab states, Mrs. Meir has indicated willingness to negotiate, but insists on firm guarantees for national security.

A native of Kiev, the Ukraine, Golda Meir (Mrs. Morris Myerson) was born Golda Mabovitch on May 3, 1898, and went to the United States in 1906. She became a schoolteacher in Milwaukee and was active in Zionist causes. Emigrating to Palestine in 1921, she worked on a communal settlement and helped organize Histadruth, the confederation of labor, serving in an executive capacity from 1946 to 1948. She headed the political department of the Jewish Agency from 1946 to 1948 and was a signer of Israel's declaration of independence. Thereafter, she served as minister to the Soviet Union (1948–49), minister of labor (1949–56), foreign minister (1956–66), and secretary-general of the Mapai (1966–68).

The smaller, more radical Popular Front for the Liberation of Palestine engaged in dramatic acts of terrorism in Israel and abroad that caught the attention of the world press.

On February 18, four members of the Popular Front attacked an Israeli El Al commercial airliner with submachine guns as it prepared for takeoff at Zurich, Switzerland. On May 30, Arab guerrillas blew up a section of the Trans-Arabian oil pipeline in the occupied Golan Heights area. On June 24 and again on August 15, pipelines in Haifa were blown up. On August 29, two representatives of the Popular Front hijacked a Trans-World Airlines jet bound from Rome to Tel Aviv and diverted it to Damascus, Syria, where two Israeli passengers were held until exchanged for Syrian prisoners on December 5.

As the year progressed, the Israeli government increased the severity of its responses to terrorist and guerrilla activities. Commando bases in Jordan, Syria, and Lebanon were attacked by artillery fire, air bombing and strafing, and raids across the frontiers. On March 22, Israel announced its intention to seek out and destroy commando bases rather than to await raids and retaliate.

Al Aksa Mosque Fire. On August 21 a fire damaged Al Aksa mosque within the Old City of Jerusalem. The arrest of Michael Rohan, an Australian Christian religious fanatic, on charges of arson, failed to still the Arab outcry that Israel had been responsible for burning the Islamic shrine. Rohan was later found guilty and judged insane.

On September 15, the UN Security Council, called to consider the Aksa fire, adopted a resolution demanding that Israel rescind all measures aimed at altering the status of Jerusalem. A meeting of representatives of Islamic states, held in Rabat, Morocco, on September 22–25, called for the

---

LEVI ESHKOL (1895–1969)

BLACK STAR

Levi Eshkol, premier of Israel, who died in Jerusalem on Feb. 26, 1969, was a political moderate and conciliator. Among his achievements were the establishment of diplomatic relations with West Germany and the creation of a parliamentary majority through unification of the dominant Mapai party with other labor factions. His six years in office were marked by the continuing Israeli-Arab conflict, culminating in Israel's victory in the six-day war of 1967. A close associate of David Ben-Gurion, whom he succeeded as premier in June 1963, Eshkol later broke with him, and in 1965 he withstood Ben-Gurion's efforts to unseat him.

Eshkol, who was descended from a long line of rabbis, was born Levi Shkolnik in Oratova (Oratov), Kiev province, in the Ukraine, on Oct. 25, 1895 and received a traditional Jewish education. In 1914 he went to Palestine, where he helped found an agricultural settlement. In the 1920's he was active in the leadership of the labor movement and party and in the 1930's he directed immigration of German Jews to Palestine. During the years preceding the Israeli independence he helped organize Haganah, the Jewish defense army, and served as its treasurer. In 1948 he became director-general of the Israeli defense ministry and in 1952 minister of finance.

---

speedy withdrawal of Israel from occupied Arab territory.

Frontier Clashes. In spite of increasing guerrilla activity in southern Lebanon that resulted in late October in a major confrontation between the guerrillas and the Lebanese government, there were only relatively minor clashes of Israeli and Lebanese forces during 1969. Syria, too, though offering strong support to guerrilla activity, in general tended to avoid direct involvement of its forces with the Israelis. Air encounters, however, took place over Syria and the Golan Heights on February 12 and 24 and on July 31.

Extensive guerrilla activities along the cease-fire line with Jordan aroused heavy Israeli reprisals and often evoked action by the Jordanian military forces. Included in these almost daily clashes were a rocket attack by Arab guerrillas on the city of Elath on April 8 and Israeli action that several times knocked out of operation Jordan's East Ghor irrigation canal.

The most complete breakdown in the 1967 cease-fire agreements, however, came along the Suez Canal, where the United Arab Republic attempted to prevent Israel from establishing impregnable defense positions. In March and April a series of artillery duels was fought across the waterway. In April, UAR commandos attacked Israeli positions on the east bank. Israel retaliated in a series of helicopter-borne commando raids deep inside the United Arab Republic, and on July 20 began air strikes against UAR military installations on the west bank of the canal. An Israeli amphibious force crossed the Gulf of Suez on September 9 and conducted a military sweep along 50 miles (80 km) of the UAR coast. On November 9 the UAR shelled Israeli positions on the Mediterranean coast of the Sinai Peninsula.

Efforts at Peacemaking. Hopes for peace in the Middle East centered on the possibility of common action by the United States, the Soviet Union, Britain, and France (or at least by the first two) in formulating and urging upon the Arabs and Israelis some plan of settlement. A series of meetings of representatives of the Big Four, held in New York between April 3 and July 1, resulted in no agreement, and U. S.-Soviet discussions held later in the year were inconclusive.

Israel rejected the idea of an imposed settlement and remained firm in its demand for direct negotiations with the Arabs. President Nasser of the UAR, continued to reject direct negotiations and to talk of renewed military action for the recovery of the occupied Arab territories.

Foreign Relations. Israel found itself increasingly isolated in its relations with foreign countries. The Communist bloc remained hostile, except for Rumania, which on August 16 raised its legation in Israel to the status of an embassy. France continued its arms embargo, but the Israelis managed to purchase five French gunboats through the ruse of a dummy Norwegian company.

Relations with the United States were strained late in the year. On September 6 the United States announced that it had begun delivering to Israel 50 F-4 Phantom jets that had been contracted for in 1968. On September 25 and 26, Prime Minister Meir visited Washington and conferred with President Nixon, reputedly about purchasing aircraft and missiles. However, in December, Israel expressed disapproval over U. S. proposals for a Middle East settlement, claiming it amounted to appeasement of Arabs. (See also MIDDLE EAST.)

PAUL L. HANNA
University of Florida

ITALIAN LITERATURE

In 1969 many lively discussions on the decline of fiction erupted in Italian periodicals, and many critics claimed that the interest of readers was being shifted from novels to informative literature. But even if it is admitted that there was a slight drop in fictional sales in 1969, the number of novels and short stories on the Italian market still remained quite large.

Literary Prizes. The Strega Prize was awarded in 1969 to Lalla Romano, who narrates the relationship between a mother and her only child, a strange and difficult boy in *Le parole da noi leggere.* The boy grows into an unworldly youth and defies conventions, making a virtue of his laziness and refusing to take part in the competition for money, status, and power. In a fresh, direct manner, enlivened by humor, Lalla Romano succeeds in drawing an excellent portrait of a "hippie," Italian style.

The Viareggio Prize went to Giorgio Bassani for his novel *l'Airone.*

A Viareggio prize for a first work in fiction was awarded to *Genus,* written by Franco Cordero, a professor of philosophy at the Catholic University. It depicts an ambitious member of the Christian Democratic party who struggles for an influential political position but changes completely after a heart attack reveals to him all the human values he has missed during his life. It is interesting to compare *Genus* with *I numeri* by Rodolfo Doni, a skillful novelist. Doni's hero, a senator, is forced by the Christian Democrat machine to abandon politics. In retiring to his family circle he finds warm human beings who do not wish to be reduced to the status of numbers and anonymous voters.

Other Fiction. Several contenders who failed to win one of the coveted prizes were compensated by the success they obtained with readers. *Il buio e il miele* by the well-known Giovanni Arpino, climbed to the top of the best-seller list. This novel unfolds the story of an army captain blinded by an accident during artillery tests. He displays bitter cynicism and misanthropy but finally undergoes a regeneration through love. Less melodramatic is *La zona mimobile* by Giorgio Chiesura, a tale in verse of World War II and the German occupation.

L'albero dei sogni by Fulvio Tomizza attracted a large readership by its flow of fantasy and imaginative power. *Il mondo salvato dai ragazzi* by Elsa Morante, former wife of Alberto Moravia and a prominent author in her own right, received full appreciation (including a Sicilian prize) in 1969, after having been published at the end of 1968. Composed both in verse and rhythmic prose, this unusual and often fascinating work presents allegorical and political scenes, and deals in a poetic and surrealistic fashion with the issues of contemporary civilization.

Great interest was aroused in literary circles by the posthumous *Citta del mondo* by Elio Vittorini (who died in 1966), a novel of symbolic design encompassing travelers and vagabonds who roam about a beautiful island (obviously Sicily) in search of an ideal city of mankind. *Le radiose giornate* by Carlo Bernari, a subtle story of strange adventures against the background of Naples at the end of World War II, is one of the best creations of a writer known as a veteran of neo-realism. *Verbale d'amore,* the second novel by Alcide Paolini, is a love story lived and seen by a man confined to a sick bed. Its twisting plot and psychological exploration of complex characters attest to the author's art. Mention must be made of *Memorie di Stefano* by Antonio Barolini; *Aprire il fuoco,* by Luciano Bianciardi, who combines archaic language with popular idiom; and *L'uovo al cianura,* a collection of stories in Boccaccio vein by Piero Chiari. *l'Afrodite* by Riccardo Baccheilli, is a *romanzo d'amore* that will not add new laurels to the well-established reputation of this old master.

Nonfiction. Lydia Storoni Mazzolani, who won the Viareggio prize for essays in 1967, published in 1969 a brilliant work *Sul mare della vita,* in which she explores the idea of death among the ancient Romans, taking as a departure the epitaphs from 4th- and 5th-century tombs. Academic circles gave high praise to Franco Venturi's *Settecento riformatore,* an exhaustive interpretation of ideas and economic and social conditions in the 18th century.

Another important historical work was the first two volumes of *Storia di Napoli,* edited by Ernesto Pontieri and planned as a 10-volume series (covering the period from the Greek origins of the city through World War II). The Viareggio prize for literary criticism was awarded to *Barocco in poesia e prosa* by Giovanni Getto.

Obituary. Giovanni Commisso, an author renowned for his poetic short stories, novels, and travelogues, died in January 1969. The reviews of his recently published *Diaries 1951–1964* were reminders of his remarkable literary career.

MARC SLONIM
Sarah Lawrence College Foreign Studies

ITALY

Italian construction and metal workers demonstrating before Coliseum in Rome, September 18, were part of widespread turmoil that plagued the nation in 1969.

UPI

In his first full year as premier of Italy, Mariano Rumor presided over a country beset by class conflict, political polarization, and violence. The year 1969 began with workers and students in turmoil and ended, after widespread strikes, in the violent death of 14 Milanese from anarchists' bombs—a senseless outrage that cast doubt on the nation's political stability. In July, Rumor's center-left coalition collapsed. He replaced it with a minority Christian Democratic government that survived at the year's end only at the pleasure of other parties.

POLITICS AND GOVERNMENT

In an unexpectedly blunt New Year's message to the nation, President Giuseppe Saragat warned that Italy was in crisis because politicians were unable to keep up with social changes and because intelligent members of the poorer classes had too little chance to break into the "establishment." The timeliness of Saragat's analysis was underscored by mounting unrest among urban and rural workers as well as university students. Although the center-left government was enacting some reforms in the fields of education, taxation, and regional administra-

tion, its reluctance to act in other sectors was making it vulnerable to widespread political criticism.

Warning of growing Communist efforts to foment strikes and violence, Premier Mariano Rumor, a moderately conservative Christian Democrat, announced on January 17 his resignation as secretary of his party in order to devote full time to his government office. The party's national council thereupon elected a centrist, Flaminio Piccoli, secretary.

Communist Party Affairs. Italy's Communist party, 1.5 million strong and the biggest in western Europe, held its 12th congress in the "Red citadel" of Bologna on February 8–15. Amid general applause, party Secretary Luigi Longo reaffirmed the party's strong opposition to Soviet intervention in Czechoslovakia. On the domestic front he urged the party to seek contact with new upsurges of "confrontation" by students and others, but to fight anarchist factions. In closed session, the party followed Longo's moderate majority in removing members of the "new left" from positions of power and rejecting their strategy of total confrontation.

The congress ended with endorsements of Longo's leadership, the "reformist" road to revolution,

---

ITALY • Information Highlights

Area: 116,303 square miles (301,225 sq km).
Population: 57,750,000 (1968 est.).
Chief Cities (1965 census): Rome, the capital, 2,484,737; Milan, 1,669,536; Naples, 1,228,092; Turin, 1,111,669.
Government: *President*—Giuseppe Saragat (took office Dec. 28, 1964); *Premier*—Mariano Rumor (took office Dec. 13, 1968). *Parliament*—Senate, 315 members (party seating, 1969: Christian Democratic, 135; Communist, 87; Socialist, 46; Liberal, 16; others, 31. Chamber of Deputies, 630 members (party seating, 1969: Christian Democratic, 266, Communist, 177; Socialist, 91; Liberal, 31; others, 65).
Religious Faith: Roman Catholics, 99.4% of population.
Education: *Literacy rate* (1966), 93% of population. *Total school enrollment* (1969)—9,122,473 (primary, 4,525,111; secondary, 3,198,892; teacher-training, 246,489; technical/vocational, 809,503; university/higher, 342,478).
Finance (1968 est.): *Revenues*, $13,941,619,800; *expenditures*, $14,954,611,000; *public debt*, $11,182,518,000; *monetary unit*, lira (623.50 lire equal U. S.$1).
Gross National Product (1968): $74,482,758,000.
National Income (1968): $60,760,224,000; *average annual income per person*, $1,052.
Economic Indexes (1967): *Industrial production* (1968), 136 (1958=100); *agricultural production*, 123 (1963=100); *cost of living*, 118 (1963=100).
Manufacturing (metric tons, 1967): Cement, 26,271,000; crude steel, 15,890,000; gasoline, 11,693,000; wine, 75,025,000 hectoliters; sugar, 1,680,000.

Crops (metric tons, 1967–68 crop year): Grapes, 11,740,000 (ranks 1st among world producers); tomatoes, 3,459,000 (world rank, 2d); olives, 2,450,000 (world rank, 2d); citrus fruit, 2,110,000 (world rank, 4th).
Minerals (metric tons, 1967): Mercury, 1,657 (ranks 2d among world producers); gypsum (1966), 3,300,000; lignite, 2,201,000.
Foreign Trade (1968): *Exports*, $10,183,000,000 (chief exports, 1967: nonelectrical machinery, $1,520,102,600; transport equipment, $845,711,300; textile yarn and fabrics, $628,-748,900; fresh fruits and nuts, $387,197,500); *imports*, $10,253,000,000 (chief imports, 1967: petroleum, $1,331,-255,800; cereal and preparations, $381,018,400; electrical machinery, $368,205,200). *Chief trading partners* (1967): West Germany (took 18% of exports, supplied 17% of imports); France (took 12% of exports, supplied 11% of imports); United States (took 10% of exports, supplied 11% of imports); United Kingdom (took 5% of exports, supplied 4% of imports).
Transportation: *Roads* (1964), 120,918 miles (194,593 km); *motor vehicles* (1967), 8,037,800 (automobiles, 7,311,400); *railways* (1965), 10,313 miles (16,594 km); *merchant vessels* (1967), 613 (5,943 gross registered tons); *national air line*, Alitalia.
Communications: *Telephones* (1968): 7,057,187; *television stations* (1968), 64; *television sets* (1968), 7,605,000; *radios* (1967), 11,621,000; *newspapers* (1966) 88 (daily circulation, 5,973,000).

friendly "autonomy" in dealing with the USSR, and neutralism for Italy. Enrico Berlinger, a 46-year-old Sardinian deputy, was elected vice secretary. Observers predicted he would be Longo's heir.

Student and Labor Unrest. A new political crisis occurred in the wake of disorders that marred President Richard M. Nixon's visit to Rome in February. At dawn on March 1 some 3,000 police, acting on government orders, raided the student-occupied campus of the University of Rome, seized seven youths, and forced the others to flee. The police contended that extremist student minorities, some of which had participated in the anti-Nixon demonstrations, were seeking to turn the university reform movement into a revolutionary force. University buildings had been extremely damaged.

While the leftist press denounced the raid, the minister of education, Fiorentino Sullo, resigned and was replaced by Mario Ferrari-Aggradi. On March 26 the Rumor government won a vote of confidence in the Chamber of Deputies (327 to 230) over its handling of the affair. In the next few days, however, the Palace of Justice and another building in Rome were damaged by bomb explosions.

A clash between unemployed workers and police in the small southern town of Battipaglia on April 9 left two dead, 200 injured, and the city hall in flames. The clash precipitated a 3-hour nationwide strike and rioting in Rome and Milan and elsewhere in which 150 more were injured.

Breakup of Governing Coalition. On June 15, regional parliamentary elections in Sardinia returned the island's center-left government of Christian Democrats and Socialists. This pattern was not to be upheld in the nation at large, however. Instead, the center-left coalition in the national government was breaking up over the question of how to deal with the Communists, who control 27% of the electorate and 25% of the seats in Parliament and who seem (at least in the judgment of some leftwing Socialists and Catholics) to be moving in the direction of democratic respectability.

The conflicts of opinion among the Christian Democrats surfaced early in June at that party's national congress. Ex-Premier Aldo Moro labored to displace Rumor's center-right forces with leftist-oriented ones, who favored cooperation with the Communists.

The Socialist party was even more seriously divided. Left-wing leaders, such as Deputy Premier Francesco De Martino and Riccardo Lombardi,

brought their party to schism by advocating a virtual popular front with the Communists. On July 4 the party split. Next day the government (Italy's 29th since the war) collapsed as the nation entered what was generally regarded as its most serious political crisis of the decade. Efforts by 78-year-old Pietro Nenni to arrange a compromise within the Socialist party failed. Defeated by 67 to 52 in the central committee, he resigned as party president.

De Martino became the new leader, thereby placing the left-wing Socialists in a position to seek an accommodation with the Communists. This caused the right-wing to secede on July 5 and organize the new Socialist Unity party (PSU), led by Mario Tanassi, who had been minister of industry.

Delighted by the Socialist split, the Communists announced their readiness to share in a new governing coalition. The nub of the political crisis in the ensuing month was whether Italy would veer sharply left or follow the swing to the right that was in progress in most other western European nations. Ugo La Malfa, whose small Republican party had been in the center-left coalition, denounced leftist leaders in both the Christian Democratic and Socialist camps for bringing on a crisis.

Minority Cabinet Rule. President Saragat consulted urgently with leaders of all parties and tried to bring about a renewal of the center-left coalition. But this was vetoed by the right wing of the Christian Democratic party. After a month in which Italy had no government, Rumor tried another strategy—creating a temporary, minority cabinet of only Christian Democrats (who receive about 40% of Italy's vote). He previously had obtained assurances of support from De Martino's Socialists.

Such a *monocolore* government was announced on August 6, the new cabinet being considerably farther to the right than the old. The Socialists tacitly supported the arrangement because they doubted that the probable alternative—new parliamentary elections—would help them. Rumor's new government won a vote of confidence in the Chamber (346 to 245) on August 10 and in the Senate (179 to 115) two days later. Both Socialist parties supported it; the Republicans abstained. An epilogue to the story was written in November when the Christian Democrats chose as their new party secretary Arnaldo Forlani, a 43-year-old journalist who hopes to revive the center-left formula in 1970.

Renewed Violence. As the protracted cabinet crisis came to an end, Italy entered a "long hot

MARIANO RUMOR, premier of Italy, whose center-left coalition cabinet, composed of Christian Democrats, Socialists, and Republicans, collapsed on July 5, 1969, because of a split in Socialist ranks, was sworn in on August 6 as head of a minority cabinet composed only of Christian Democrats.

Rumor, the son of a newspaper publisher, was born in Vicenza, Italy, on June 6, 1915. He graduated in 1939 from the University of Padua. After World War II he helped organize the Christian Democratic party and became identified with its centrist faction. He was elected to parliament in 1948 and was minister of agriculture from 1959 to 1963. Rumor was elected political secretary of the Christian Democratic party in 1964 but resigned in January 1969 to devote himself to the premiership, to which he had been appointed in December 1968.

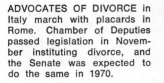

ADVOCATES OF DIVORCE in Italy march with placards in Rome. Chamber of Deputies passed legislation in November instituting divorce, and the Senate was expected to do the same in 1970.

autumn" of wage disputes. For the rest of 1969 the country was embroiled in an endless series of wildcat strikes, punctuated by frequent disorders on the part of neo-Fascists and Maoists.

In Pisa, for example, 1,000 policemen had to patrol the city on October 28 (anniversary of the Fascist march on Rome) after a night of violence left one dead and 100 injured. Milan and Turin became centers of unrest in the next two months. The death of a policeman in Milan on November 19 led to rioting by Fascist toughs. The government hastily appropriated $480 million for urgently needed low-rent housing for workers.

The high point in Italy's growing wave of violence occurred on December 12, when anarchistic extremists exploded bombs in a Milan bank, killing 14 and injuring 90. Simultaneously three explosions in Rome hurt 17 others. Shocked by the outrages, millions of Italians voiced serious concern over the country's future.

Divorce and Adultery Reforms. As 1969 drew to a close and Italy prepared to commemorate the 100th anniversary of the overthrow of papal political rule in Rome, advocates of civil divorce won a signal victory in Parliament. Despite bitter opposition from the Vatican, their bill to enact the country's first divorce legislation was approved by the Chamber of Deputies (325 to 283) on November 29 and sent to the Senate. Favorable action by that body was expected in 1970.

On December 4, Italy's Constitutional Court invalidated two Fascist-era penal code provisions for adultery that had treated men and women unequally. (A woman could be jailed up to two years for an "adulterous relationship," whereas a man could be jailed only if he kept a "concubine in the conjugal home or notoriously elsewhere.") The court's decision removed all criminal penalties for marital infidelity, leaving it a civil offense constituting grounds for legal separation.

ECONOMY

Until September it seemed that 1969 would be marked by a harmonious relationship of prices, wages, and productivity in Italy, for all three were rising gradually along parallel lines. This pattern changed radically with the advent of the "hot autumn" of wage disputes. Some 60 major industrial contracts covering more than 5 million workers were up for renegotiation, most of them for a 3-year period.

Strikes and Higher Wages. Numerous strikes were called before the new contracts were signed. At one point the minister of labor, Carlo Donati-Cattin, was compelled to take an unprecedented step and act as mediator, thereby achieving considerable public acclaim. By December 9 the government was ready to agree to inflationary settlements. A strike involving 180,000 state-employed metalworkers was ended that day on the basis of an average wage increase of 65 lire (about 10 cents) per hour and a reduction in the work week from 43 to 40 hours. On December 21, unions representing 1.2 million privately employed metalworkers obtained a similar contract.

Altogether, the strikes cost the nation more than 300 million working hours and about $2 billion in production. The country's anticipated 6% to 7% growth rate was cut to about 5.4%. Wage increases jumped ahead of the growth of gross national product for the first time since 1963. Whereas wages had risen only 8.7% through September, the settlements in December brought the year's average up to about 16%. Thus Italy entered 1970 confronted by the threat of inflation and increased unemployment.

Problems and Prospects. If Italian industry tries to pass on its higher labor costs to consumers, it will accelerate the inflationary cycle and thereby reduce Italy's ability to compete in foreign markets. If it tries to counteract the higher costs by technological improvements, it may displace workers at a time when a predicted decline in construction already threatens large layoffs. New investment, therefore, is needed. To reduce the likelihood of a serious recession in 1970, Italy must check the flight of Italian capital to other countries. This outflow, primarily the result of higher interest rates abroad, drained $3.92 billion from the country in 1969, despite a June increase in the discount rate from 3.5% to 5%.

The status of Italy's economy in 1970 may well determine whether a new center-left political coali-

STRIKING METAL WORKERS with steel drums were among 50,000 persons in Italy's biggest labor march of year, in Rome on November 28.

tion is possible. If there is a serious recession, the Socialists may be reluctant to associate themselves with the Christian Democrats in an austerity program. (They remember a similar unpleasant experience in 1963.)

Trade and Economic Growth. Italy's imports in 1969 rose to $9.1 billion, exceeding those of 1968 by 22.5%. Exports, at $8.9 billion, increased 20.9%. This left a trade gap of about $200 million, but tourism and other "invisible" items produced a balance of payments surplus of $2.6 million.

Treasury Minister Emilio Colombi predicted that 1970 would see an 11% increase in gross national product at current prices. How much of the increase will be real growth and how much price inflation will depend on his success in controlling the economy.

FOREIGN RELATIONS

While continuing to honor its allegiance to the North Atlantic Treaty Organization and to pursue a closer West European economic and political union, Italy sought détente and increased trade with Communist countries in 1969.

Communist Countries. In January, Foreign Minister Pietro Nenni announced to Parliament that the government had decided to take steps to recognize Communist China. Peking's response, however, was cool, and at the year's end nothing more had happened.

On December 10, Italy's National Hydrocarbons Trust (ENI) signed a $3 billion, 2-year agreement with the Soviet Union to pipe natural gas from the Ukraine to Trieste. The agreement marks another important economic link between Italy and the USSR, Fiat having previously opened a giant automobile plant in Toliyatti (formerly Stavropol.)

United States and Western Europe. On his visit to Rome at the end of February, President Nixon was greeted warmly by President Saragat and other high Italian officials. Notwithstanding demonstrations by thousands of students and Communists and,

later, the Italian authorities' apparent refusal to extradite Raffaele Minichiello, an Italian-born U.S. marine who hijacked a U.S. commercial jet to Italy in November, relations between the two governments remained cordial throughout the year.

From April 22 to 30, President Saragat and Foreign Minister Nenni paid a state visit to Britain. Following talks that both sides described as unusually friendly, the Italian government reaffirmed its support of British entry into the Common Market.

The Italian delegation to the European Parliament, the representative assembly of the European (economic) Communities, included for the first time members of the Communist party. Mario Scelba, a Christian Democrat and former premier, was elected president of the parliament in March.

Central Europe. In December the foreign ministers of Italy and Austria announced a significant breakthrough in the resolution of a protracted, violence-filled dispute over the status of 230,000 German-speaking and 130,000 Italian-speaking residents of South Tyrol (Alto Adige). The two countries agreed to sign a 1946 Italo-Austrian accord requiring all disputes to be referred to the World Court.

The accord, when ratified, will give the province increased self-government and a wider scope for use of the German language. Moreover, the postwar merger of Trentino (where Italians predominate) and Alto Adige will be reversed, and the label "South Tyrol" will replace that of "Alto Adige."

Memories of the German occupation of Italy in World War II were stirred in midsummer when the German magazine *Der Spiegel* identified Matthias Defregger, Roman Catholic auxiliary bishop of Munich, as a former German army officer who in 1944 passed on the order to execute 17 unarmed Italian hostages in the village of Filetto di Camarda in the Abruzzi. At year's end an Italian judiciary police inquiry was still in progress.

CHARLES F. DELZELL
Vanderbilt University

382

IVORY COAST

The only notable unrest in the Ivory Coast in 1969 occurred within the university and was quickly brought under control. The country's economy continued prosperous, although there was a drop in the production of coffee, the major export crop.

Student Unrest. Following the dissolution of the national student organization by the government in 1968, students formed a new union, the Movement of Students and Pupils of the Ivory Coast (MEECI). On March 21, 1969, demonstrating students at the University of Abidjan were surrounded and dispersed by troops. The university was closed down until the government decided to reopen it on May 31, after MEECI became part of the ruling party.

Economy. Coffee production for the season ending July 15, 1969, fell to 202,923 tons, compared with 285,700 tons for 1968. The general outlook of the economy, however, was good.

On February 17 the Vridi electricity generating station, the largest thermal unit in French-speaking black Africa, was inaugurated.

A World Bank loan of $17 million was earmarked for development of palm and coconut oil production, and in early January a second palm oil works began production near Abidjan.

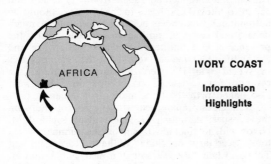

IVORY COAST

Information Highlights

Area: 124,503 square miles (322,463 sq km).
Population: 4,100,000 (1968 est.).
Chief Cities (1969 est.): Abidjan, the capital, 400,000; Bouaké, 100,000.
Government: *President*—Félix Houphouët-Boigny (took office Nov. 27, 1960). *Legislature* (unicameral)—National Assembly, 85 members (party seating, 1969: all members of the Parti Démocratique de la Côte d'Ivoire).
Religious Faiths: Animists, 65% of population; Muslims, 23%; Roman Catholics, 8.3%; others, 3.7%.
Education: *Literacy rate* (1969), 20% of population. *Total school enrollment* (1966)—422,086 (primary, 381,452; secondary, 35,829; teacher-training, 717; technical/vocational, 2,522; university/higher, 1,566).
Finance (1969): *Budget* (est.), $180,000,000; *monetary unit,* CFA franc (246.85 CFA francs equal U. S.$1).
Gross National Product (1967): $1,118,000,000.
National Income (1967): $834,514,000; *average annual income per person,* $208.
Cost of Living Index (1967): 111 (1963=100).
Manufacturing (1967): Lumber, 306,000 cubic meters.
Crops (metric tons, 1967–68 crop year): Sweet potatoes and yams, 1,920,000; cassava, 1,100,000; maize, 205,000; coffee (1968–69), 202,293; cocoa, 146,600; bananas, 143,000.
Minerals (metric tons, 1967): Manganese ore, 67,200; aluminum (1965), 221; diamonds, 176,000 carats.
Foreign Trade (1968): *Exports,* $425,000,000 (chief exports, 1967: coffee, $103,500,000; wood, $88,640,000; cocoa, $56,490,000); *imports,* $315,000,000 (chief imports, 1967: textile yarn and fabrics, $36,483,000; nonelectrical machinery, $30,350,000; transport equipment, $29,957,000). *Chief trading partners* (1967): France (took 37% of exports, supplied 55% of imports); United States (took 14% of exports, supplied 6% of imports); West Germany (took 8% of exports, supplied 7% of imports).
Transportation: *Roads* (1966), 20,701 miles (33,314 km); *motor vehicles* (1967), 71,700 (automobiles 41,900); *railways* (1966), 375 miles (603 km); *merchant vessels* (1967), 4 (20,000 gross registered tons); *civil airline,* Air Afrique; *principal airport,* Abidjan-Port Buet.
Communications: *Telephones* (1968), 21,300; *television stations* (1967), 1; *television sets* (1967), 2,000; *radios* (1967), 65,000; *newspapers* (1966), 1.

Foreign Relations. The government emphasized friendly relations with the Arab world, especially since the United Arab Republic was eager to offset growing Israeli influence in the Ivory Coast.

On May 30 the Ivory Coast broke off diplomatic relations with the USSR.

C. DIANE CHRISTENSEN
Columbia University

JACKSON, Jesse. See biographical sketch under CIVIL RIGHTS MOVEMENT.

JAMAICA

Jamaican politics remained relatively stable during 1969. Economically, the year was mixed.

Domestic Politics. The Jamaica Labour party of Prime Minister Hugh Shearer made some gains in the municipal elections held in March. Norman Manley, leader of the opposition People's National party for 30 years, retired and was succeeded by his son Michael. The death of Norman Manley on September 2 was widely mourned.

Foreign Affairs. Jamaica joined the Organization of American States in August. There had been opposition from some OAS members, because Jamaica maintained consular relations with Cuba, and in January had announced that it was considering extending diplomatic recognition to the Castro regime.

The Economy. Sugar production continued to decline. The situation became so serious that the island had to import between 15,000 and 20,000 tons of refined sugar during the last months of 1969. However, bauxite production continued to expand. In May, a new $165 million aluminum refinery was opened.

The government-owned Jamaica Development Bank opened in September. It is equipped to provide more than twice as much financial aid to economic projects as the agency that preceded it.

ROBERT J. ALEXANDER
Rutgers University

──────── **JAMAICA • Information Highlights** ────────

Area: 4,232 square miles (10,962 sq km).
Population: 1,913,000 (1968 est.).
Chief Cities (1960 census): Kingston, the capital, 123,403; Montego Bay, 23,610; Spanish Town, 14,706.
Government: *Governor-General*—Clifford Campbell; *Prime Minister*—Hugh Shearer (took office April 11, 1967). *Parliament*—Senate, 21 members (13 nominated by the prime minister, 8 by the leader of the opposition); House of Representatives, 53 members.
Religious Faiths: Protestants, 55% of population.
Education: *Literacy rate* (1969), 85% of population. *Total school enrollment* (1965)—376,968.
Finance (1969 est.): *Revenues,* $218,000,000; *expenditures,* $282,000,000; *monetary unit,* pound (.4167 pound equals U. S.$1).
Gross National Product (1968): $988,720,000.
National Income (1968): $787,137,000; *average annual income per person,* $411.
Cost of Living Index (1967): 110 (1963=100).
Manufacturing (metric tons, 1967): Sugar, 465,000; cement, 335,000; gasoline, 192,000.
Crops (metric tons, 1967–68 crop year): Bananas, 300,000; sweet potatoes and yams, 205,000.
Minerals (metric tons, 1967): Bauxite, 9,396,000 (ranks 1st among world producers); glass sand (1964), 8,636,000.
Foreign Trade (1968): *Exports,* $224,000,000 (chief exports, 1967: alumina, $50,136,000; bauxite, $45,000,000; sugar, $39,740,000; bananas, $15,740,000); *imports,* $383,000,000 (chief imports, 1967: nonelectrical machinery, $38,320,000; cereals and preparations, $22,320,000). *Chief trading partners* (1967): United States (took 40% of exports, supplied 39% of imports); Britain; Canada.
Transportation: *Roads* (1969), 9,581 miles (15,416 km); *motor vehicles* (1967), 68,600 (automobiles, 54,200); *railways* (1965), 205 miles (330 km); *merchant vessels* (1967), 3 (15,000 gross registered tons).
Communications: *Telephones* (1968), 56,709; *television stations* (1968), 9; *television sets* (1968), 40,000; *radios* (1967), 423,000; *newspapers* (1965), 2.

JAPAN

EXPO '70 site at Osaka, Japan, is shown under construction. From left to right are the pavilions of the Soviet Union, Hitachi, Miderinkan, Furukawa, and Electric Power.

In 1969, after having achieved the second-highest gross national product in the non-Communist world, Japan looked forward eagerly to the future. For fiscal 1968 the gross national product totaled $146,960 million. Economic strength was reflected in plans for Expo '70, scheduled to open at Osaka in March, with 50 million visitors expected.

The year was not without problems, however. During 1969, Japan had to deal with serious foreign policy issues and the need to form a national consensus amid rapid economic growth.

INTERNATIONAL AFFAIRS

Japan's revived international status was reflected in its playing host to the fourth annual meeting of the Asian and Pacific Council (ASPAC), at Ito, in June. Prime Minister Eisaku Sato stressed the need for regional cooperation "transcending national borders" and proposed that the region be called "Pacific Asia." The concept fitted U. S. plans for gradual withdrawal from Southeast Asia and modest retrenchment in East Asia.

Relations with the United States. Although day-to-day contacts over complex trade issues were typical of those between two developed powers, U. S.-Japanese diplomatic relations were dominated by

problems of security. The question of whether the U. S.-Japan Security Treaty, which obligates the United States to defend Japan from aggression and Japan to allow U. S. bases in the country, should be automatically extended beyond 1970, caused much debate and some turmoil in Japan. The treaty, the presence of U. S. military bases in Japan proper, and the status of Okinawa (seized by the United States in World War II) were, in Japanese minds, the residue of war, defeat, and occupation. They were also linked with the U. S. agony in Vietnam.

Both sides prepared carefully for negotiations on these issues. Although U. S. President Richard M. Nixon did not include Japan on his summer world tour, Secretary of State William Rogers visited Tokyo in late July. Washington also sent Armin H. Meyer, an experienced ambassador—if unfamiliar to Japan—to fill the post vacated by U. Alexis Johnson, who became U. S. deputy undersecretary of state. Foreign Minister Kiichi Aichi of Japan was in Washington in June, prior to Prime Minister Sato's visit in November.

In December 1968 the Japanese government had welcomed a U. S. plan for reversion, relocation, or joint use of some 50 military bases or areas in Japan. On May 3, however, Foreign Minister Aichi

--- JAPAN • Information Highlights ---

Area: 142,726 square miles (369,661 sq km).
Population: 101,090,000 (1968 est.).
Chief Cities (1966 census): Tokyo, the capital, 8,907,000; Osaka, 3,133,000; Nagoya, 1,954,000; Yokohoma, 1,860,000.
Government: *Emperor*—Hirohito (acceded Dec. 25, 1926); *Prime Minister*—Eisaku Sato (took office Nov. 9, 1964). *Parliament* (Diet)—House of Representatives, 486 members (party seating, 1969: Liberal Democratic party, or LDP, 288; Japan Socialist party, or JSP, 90; Komeito, or KMT, 47; Japan Democratic Socialist party, or DSP, 31; Japan Communist party, or JCP, 14; independents, 16); House of Councillors, 250 members (party seating, 1969: LDP, 137; JSP, 65; KMT, 24; DSP, 10; JCP, 7; ind., 7).
Education: *Literacy rate* (1969), 98% of population. *Total school enrollment* (1965)—21,916,474 (primary, 9,775,532; secondary, 8,964,354; technical/vocational, 2,060,158; university/higher, 1,116,430).
Finance (1969 est.): *Revenues,* $19,220,000,000; *expenditures,* $20,000,000,000; *public debt* (1967), $4,126,000,000; *monetary unit,* yen (357.7 yen equal U. S.$1).
Gross National Product (1968): $146,960,000,000.
National Income (1968): $112,924,000,000; *average annual income per person,* $1,117.
Economic Indexes (1967): *Industrial production* (1968), 190 (1963=100); *agricultural production,* 120 (1963=100); *cost of living,* 121 (1963=100).

Manufacturing (metric tons, 1967): Crude steel, 62,148,000; cement, 42,492,000; beer, 24,319,000 hectoliters.
Crops (metric tons, 1967–68 crop year): Rice, 18,770,000 (ranks 3d among world producers); sweet potatoes and yams, 4,031,000 (world rank, 1st).
Minerals (metric tons, 1966): Limestone, 71,477,000; phosphates, 1,191,000; crude petroleum, 788,000; silver, 18,327,000 troy ounces.
Foreign Trade (1968): *Exports,* $12,972,000,000 (chief exports, 1967: transport equipment, $1,933,590,000; iron and steel, $1,272,530,000; electrical machinery, $1,155,850,000; nonelectrical machinery, $927,830,000); *imports,* $12,987,000,000 (chief imports, 1967: petroleum, $1,457,240,000; cereals and preparations, $885,090,000; nonelectrical machinery, $619,470,000). *Chief trading partners* (1967): United States (took 29% of exports, supplied 28% of imports); Australia (took 3% of exports, supplied 7% of imports); Canada.
Transportation: *Roads* (1969), 612,000 miles (984,892 km); *motor vehicles* (1967), 10,050,000 (automobiles 3,836,000); *railways* (1969), 29,200 miles (46,992 km); *merchant vessels* (1967), 1,582 (23,987,000 gross registered tons, 1968); *national airline,* Japan Airlines.
Communications: *Telephones* (1968): 18,216,767; *television stations* (1968), 153; *television sets* (1968), 20,000,000; *radios* (1966), 24,787,000; *newspapers* (1966), 174.

stated that Japan could deny the request for the use of a Japanese port for U. S. Navy Task Force 71, if asked in one of the "prior consultation" sessions provided by the security treaty. The ships had been operating in the Sea of Japan since April, when North Korea downed a U. S. intelligence aircraft.

After extensive consultations in Washington, Ambassador Meyer arrived in Tokyo on July 1. As he bade Secretary Rogers farewell at Haneda International Airport on July 31, Meyer was suddenly attacked by an enraged youth armed with a knife, but he was not seriously injured.

Japan's ruling Liberal-Democratic party decided in October that the security treaty should be continued beyond 1970 "indefinitely." The decision was in accord with Article 10, which states that the pact will remain in force "until in the opinion of the Governments of Japan and the United States there shall have come into force such UN arrangements as will satisfactorily provide for the maintenance of international peace and security in the Japanese area." This decision came under fire from some party members, who contended that the treaty should be reexamined with a view to a new pact and that Japan should step up efforts for its own defense. A Kyodo News Service public opinion poll demonstrated that less than half of those questioned placed full confidence in the U. S. pledge to defend Japan under the treaty. Also, the treaty's fate seemed to be tied to the status of Okinawa.

In December 1968 the popularly elected, Socialist-backed chief executive of Okinawa, Chobyo Yara, had met with Prime Minister Sato in Tokyo and appealed for "unconditional and total reversion of Okinawa." By March 22, Sato seemed to have adopted the so-called *hondo-nami* ("same-as-mainland") formula suggested by his advisers. He promised to enter into negotiations with the United States, demanding: (1) administrative control to revert to Japan by 1972; (2) Japanese self-defense forces to assume responsibility for the defense of Okinawa; (3) the security treaty, including the "prior consultation" clause, to apply; and (4) the Status of Forces Agreement to place restrictions (including nonnuclear status) on island bases similar to those applied to facilities in Japan.

In his June visit to the United States, Foreign Minister Aichi reported to President Nixon that a majority of Japanese supported the position of the Sato government on Okinawa. According to his data (from survey research conducted by the office of the prime minister), about 80% of a sample wanted Okinawa returned and half of those questioned supported continuation of the security treaty.

During the summer Okinawa itself was disturbed by demonstrations and a strike by the military employees union. When on June 5, U. S. military policemen forcibly removed pickets at bayonet point, loud protests were heard in the Diet in Tokyo. The U. S. position worsened in late July, when leaking nerve gases stored on Okinawa hospitalized U. S. personnel. Japan welcomed a U. S. Department of

NEW HIGHWAY in Tokyo is jammed with holiday traffic as motorists head for resort areas outlying the city.

ARMORED vehicle of Japan's Self-Defense Force practices maneuvers in a peaceful setting near Mt. Fuji.

of nontariff barriers was being debated in the GATT meetings at Geneva).

After temporary suspension, aviation talks resumed in Tokyo on September 16. The United States and Japan agreed to allow Japan Air Lines (JAL) to fly from Tokyo to New York via Anchorage. JAL was also licensed to operate a new Tokyo-Saipan-Guam service.

Relations with the USSR. Similarly, on November 5, Japan and the USSR signed an agreement providing air service by JAL and Aeroflot over Siberian routes, beginning in March 1970. Initial flights will be over the routes Tokyo-Moscow-Paris and Tokyo-Moscow-London.

Negotiations for reversion of a group of islands off eastern Hokkaido and at the southern tip of the Kuriles, however, were less successful. Shikotan, Habomai, Etorofu, and Kunashiri, which have been under Soviet occupation since the end of World War II, will not be returned. In September in Moscow, Premier Kosygin told Aichi that the Soviet Union had no intention of altering boundaries defined at the end of the war. Foreign Minister Gromyko did agree to consider the Japanese plan to allow fishermen to operate up to 3 miles (4.8 km) off Soviet-held islands. He also indicated that the USSR would release some 100 Japanese detained in Russia.

Aichi announced that Soviet President Podgorny planned to visit Expo '70 in April 1970. If he did, it would be the first visit to Japan by a head of state of the Soviet Union.

Relations with Other Asian States. Japan's tightening bonds with nations in "Pacific Asia" necessarily restricted contact with mainland China. At the United Nations, Japan sided with those who regarded the Chinese representation issue as "an important question," that is, one requiring a two-thirds majority vote. On November 11 it joined the majority in refusing a seat to the Chinese Communist regime. Upon his return to Japan on November 26, however, Prime Minister Sato stressed the fact that Japan would not permit reintroduction of nuclear arms on Okinawa, thus, it was hoped, reducing tension with China.

The Asian and Pacific Council (ASPAC) nations, which opened a meeting in Japan on June 9, are states with which Japan had regular formal contact: Australia, the Republic of China (Taiwan), South Korea, Malaysia, New Zealand, the Philippines, Thailand, and South Vietnam.

Japan in the United Nations. When the General Assembly opened in New York on September 19, Senjin Tsuruoka, the Japanese ambassador to the United Nations, expressed his country's desire for revision of the UN Charter in 1970, the 25th anniversary of the organization. In November, Japan's

Defense announcement on August 2 that chemical weapons would be removed from the island.

In the face of violent "Okinawa Day" demonstrations on April 28, "Security Treaty" rallies on October 10, "Antiwar Day" strikes on October 21, and "hit-and-run" battles with riot police on the eve of his departure on November 17, Prime Minister Sato left Tokyo on schedule for his talks with President Nixon in Washington on November 19–21.

The Sato-Nixon communiqué was released on November 21 and contained only one surprise, but a major one. As expected, the United States agreed to return Okinawa by 1972. The security treaty, which was to continue indefinitely, would apply to Okinawa after reversion. Like bases in Japan proper, Okinawan bases would be subject to "prior consultation" before major military maneuvers and especially before any deployment of nuclear weapons (otherwise to be removed).

Unexpectedly, the United States apparently won relatively flexible stipulations for the use of forces on Okinawa and in Japan (previously restricted to defense of that country). Two needs were recognized: (1) U.S. security commitments to South Korea (essential to Japanese security as well), Taiwan, and other Asian countries; and (2) a Japanese national consensus in support of a more positive political, economic, and security role in Asia.

In the communiqué, President Nixon reaffirmed a U.S. commitment to "the principles of free trade," and Prime Minister Sato pledged an acceleration in "reduction of Japan's trade and capital restrictions." This agreement had been prepared in October, during negotiations on decontrol of imports (relaxation

EISAKU SATO, prime minister of Japan, called repeatedly in 1969 for the return of Okinawa to Japanese control. He indicated that Japan would eventually play the leading role in guaranteeing Asian security, and he expressed the hope that relations with Communist China could be normalized. In August, Sato's Liberal Democratic party, responding to radical student demonstrators protesting Japan's cooperation with the United States, obtained passage of a law aimed at coping with campus disorders. Sato visited the United States in November, and with President Nixon announced Okinawa would be returned to Japan in 1972.

A native of Tabuse in southern Honshu, Sato was born on March 27, 1901. He graduated from Tokyo Imperial University with a law degree in 1924, after which he went to work for the ministry of railways. In 1947 he was appointed vice minister of transportation. Elected a representative in the national Diet in 1949, Sato served in several cabinet posts before being chosen as premier, on Nov. 9, 1964.

foreign ministry revealed a plan for the reorganization of the UN Security Council to permit Japan's admission as a permanent member and to abolish the veto. Japan also called for review of wartime articles referring to "enemy states," and of those regarding the Trusteeship Council, which had completed its task.

Although Japan's delegation at Geneva announced on November 1 that the government would sign the nuclear nonproliferation treaty in January 1970, the mass media at home doubted that signature would occur "at an early date" and criticized the treaty for underwriting the nuclear powers' "monopoly."

DOMESTIC AFFAIRS

During 1969, Japan's domestic politics were closely linked to foreign affairs, especially the issue of reversion of Okinawa and the status of the security treaty. In addition, the Diet was faced with campus unrest and rising commodity prices.

When the 61st regular session of the Diet was reconvened on January 27, the Liberal Democratic party (LDP) enjoyed a majority in both houses, followed by the Japan Socialist party (JSP). In the House of Representatives, the Japan Democratic Socialist party (DSP) held third place ahead of the Komeito (KMT), but in the House of Councillors this order was reversed. The strength of the LDP was increased by the December elections.

Elections. On July 13 the LDP, despite declines in popularity ratings, made a strong showing in elections for assemblymen for the Tokyo metropolis. The LDP elected 54 members; the JSP dropped from 45 to 24, placing it behind the KMT, which had 25.

Following his reelection as president of the LDP in December 1968, Prime Minister Sato reshuffled his cabinet. Shigeru Hori became chief cabinet secretary, Takeo Fukuda the minister of finance, Kiichi Aichi the foreign minister, and Michita Sakata the minister of education. As predicted, Sato, upon his return from Washington, dissolved the Diet on December 2 and called for general elections.

Prime Minister Sato interpreted the results of the December 27 elections as a mandate for his policies. The LDP increased its membership in the House of Representatives from 272 to 288 seats, while the JSP dropped from 134 to 90. The KMT won 47 seats and the DSP retained its 31 seats.

Economic Developments. In November the economic planning agency estimated that Japan's actual annual growth rate was 13% (the nominal rate was 18%). The gross national product (GNP) for fiscal 1969 (March 31, 1969–April 1, 1970) was projected at about 62,400 billion yen ($173,300 million, compared with $146,960 million for 1968).

By the end of March 1969 a favorable balance of payments created a total surplus of $1,630 million for fiscal 1968. By November, the growth of exports was expected to produce a surplus of about $3,850 million for fiscal 1969. At the end of September, Japan's gold and foreign exchange reserves reached an all-time high of $3,226 million.

During 1968, Japan's production of over 4 million automobiles ranked it second to the United States in value of automotive exports. Japan also produced about 13% of the world's total steel output, ranking it third, after the United States and the USSR.

Steel also provided the most important business news of the year. After the Fair Trade Commission

BLACK STAR

POLICE helicopters over Tokyo University spray tear gas on students hurling fire bombs from a rooftop.

had blocked a merger of Yawata Steel and Fuji Iron & Steel scheduled for June 1, the companies moved to reduce excessive market control in several product lines. On November 1 the commission conditionally approved the merger, scheduled for March 31, 1970. The new firm was to be called the Shin Nihon Steel Corporation and would be the second largest steel maker in the world, after U. S. Steel.

Social Unrest. Student and left-wing dissent continued throughout 1969. It was aimed mainly at obtaining the immediate return of Okinawa, abrogation of the security treaty, and university reforms.

Symptomatic of university unrest was the critical situation at Tokyo University. In January, student battles with riot police left 35 persons (30 of them police) injured and 400 students arrested. The university's president had resigned in 1968 and his position was not filled until April 5, 1969, when Ichiro Kato, after being chosen in a secret election held off campus, became the 19th president of the university. He set about reorganizing the institution, which had been closed for over a year.

Because of the unrest in the universities, the government stated clearly that "universities are not outside the scope of Japanese laws." By mid-1969 the cabinet took stern action. In May the education ministry unveiled the draft of its bill to restore order to the 34 national, 4 municipal, and 8 private universities. Its provisions called for greater concentration of power in administrative hands; severe penalties for disruptive students, staff, and faculty (including a 30% pay cut for personnel); and, in the case of protracted trouble in a suspended institution, outright dissolution of the university.

(*Continued on page 389*)

SPOTLIGHT ON
OKINAWA

A pre-World War II Japanese prefecture, Okinawa is the largest island in a chain (*Ryukyu* or *Nansei shoto* in Japanese; *Liu Ch'iu* in Chinese) stretching more than 400 miles (644 km) from Japan southwestward toward Taiwan. It is 454 square miles (1,176 sq km) in area, and in 1968 its 845,640 people accounted for 87% of the archipelago's population.

History. Originally founded in the 14th century by the lord of Chuzan at Shuri and maintained without arms for 450 years, Okinawa's tiny kingdom was made up of officials, farmers, fishermen, and traders handling goods sent from Southeast Asia to the ports of China, Korea, and Japan. Fearing the approach of Europeans, Japanese from the Satsuma domain on Kyushu invaded the Ryukyus in 1609. Thereafter, Okinawa served as a buffer between China and Japan and paid tribute to both countries.

In June 1853, on his way to Japan, Commodore Matthew Perry landed a token force on Okinawa and requested permission to establish a base at Naha. The "Compact between the United States and the Kingdom of Lewchew" ended the first U. S. occupation in 1854.

Soon after the Meiji Restoration in 1868, a Japanese force landed at Naha, deposed the king, and in 1872 created Okinawa Prefecture. From then until 1945, Tokyo endeavored to integrate Okinawa's economy with that of Japan, but because of the distance from Japan and the collapse of old trade patterns, Okinawa became the poorest of the empire's prefectures.

Although Okinawans had little to do with starting the Pacific war in World War II, they were the chief sufferers in the battle for Okinawa, which began on April 1, 1945 and took 93 days for U. S. forces to win. No family remained untouched by the "Iron Typhoon"; about 100,000 civilians were killed and another 100,000 wounded.

Okinawa, devastated, was neglected by the United States until 1949, when the highly critical Vickery Report appeared. Then, in 1950, the Korean conflict brought a vast base-expansion program. Article 3 of the peace treaty with Japan, signed Sept. 8, 1951, provided the United States with "the right to exercise all and any powers of administration, legislation, and jurisdiction," pending a proposal to place the islands under a UN trusteeship. With the Korean truce in 1953, Japan expected reversion. Instead, the United States allowed the northern Ryukyus (including Amami Oshima) to revert, assigned "residual sovereignty" over Okinawa to Japan, and continued to control the island.

With the deepening U. S. involvement in the Vietnam conflict, Okinawa was developed rapidly as a staging base. U. S. forces leased about one fourth of the land area. In addition to 40,000 troops (including one third of the Marines in the Pacific), there were about 40,000 dependents and U. S. workers, plus 50,000 Okinawans employed by U. S. forces. A 550-bed hospital was one of the largest in Asia. At Kadena Air Base, a gigantic complex with two 12,000-foot (3,658-meter) run-

ways, the 313th Air Division was responsible for a large area of the western Pacific. In 1969 the U. S. military presence accounted for 40% of a $734 million annual economy.

Reversion. Meanwhile, sentiment for reversion continued to build up in both Okinawa and Japan. As Prime Minister Sato put it, "So long as Okinawa is 'occupied' by the Americans the postwar period goes on." By 1969 it became clear that the reversion of Okinawa was one of Japan's requirements for its extension of the U. S.-Japan security treaty.

After careful preparations had been made by both governments during 1969, Prime Minister Sato visited Washington to discuss Okinawa with President Nixon November 19–21. Their joint communiqué closely followed the *"hondo-nami"* ("same as mainland") formula, worked out earlier by Sato's advisers. Administrative control over Okinawa would revert to Japan no later than 1972. The security treaty, including the "prior consultation" clause, and status of forces agreement would continue and would extend the same restrictions applicable to facilities in Japan proper to Okinawa.

In 1970 Japan will have serious problems that must be solved prior to reversion. Both Prime Minister Sato and the Socialist-backed, popularly elected chief executive of Okinawa, Chobyo Yara, announced their determination not to allow the island to become again the poorest prefecture in Japan. An estimated disbursement of 50,000 million yen will be needed to extend health and welfare insurance, to integrate the educational system with Japan's, and to pay for U. S. fixed assets.

To close the gap between Okinawa and Japan, the Tokyo government in October 1969 began to draft a basic plan for shifting the island's U. S. base-oriented economy to an integrated Okinawan one. Japan planned to establish an Okinawan Affairs Agency in Tokyo. In addition, observer status was to be given to elected Okinawan representatives on the floor of the Diet in Tokyo.

ARDATH W. BURKS

The ruling LDP, in a surprise tactic on the floor of the upper house on August 3, rammed the "university normalization" bill through the Diet. The opposition parties reacted by boycotting legislative proceedings, and numerous college presidents offered their resignations. Tokyo University's President Kato denounced the action as an affront to parliamentary democracy and predicted that the bill would make solutions more difficult. Events at Kyoto University on September 21 fulfilled the prediction. More than 2,000 riot police were used to clear campus barricades, enter the buildings, and arrest revolutionary students. Classes, which had been suspended since January, were finally resumed under police guard.

Street *"demo,"* or demonstrations, rose to a crescendo during the year in efforts to defeat the government's policies. Train service in Tokyo virtually came to a halt on "Okinawa Day" (April 28) as students stormed key passenger stations. By August 1 national police officials estimated that some 6,000 persons had been arrested in the first half of 1969. In rallies across the nation on October 10, about 100,000 people staged protests against the security treaty, U. S. involvement in Vietnam, and U. S. occupation of Okinawa. In Tokyo's Meiji Park radical students of the Antiwar Youth Committee (AYC), the Peace-for-Vietnam Committee (*Beheiren*), and the Federation of All-Campus Struggle Committees (*Zenkoku Zenkyoto*) held meetings ringed by riot police. On October 21, "International Antiwar Day," students employed guerrilla tactics against their "enemy," the 25,000-man riot police corps. In an all-time high for a single day, police arrested more than 1,400 persons (1,221 in Tokyo alone).

Despite radical and student attempts to prevent Prime Minister Sato from departing for Washington, he was able to leave on November 17. He was encouraged upon his return on November 26 by an opinion survey conducted by the newspaper *Sankei* indicating that 73.7% of those polled supported the Sato-Nixon settlement. Despite the prime minister's success (or possibly because of it), opposition, dissent, and disorder, especially student confrontations, threatened to continue challenging the LDP leadership indefinitely.

At the opposite extreme from left-of-center dissent, voices were heard urging the Sato government and LDP to seek a mandate on three issues: reversion of Okinawa and review of the security treaty; comprehensive reform of the educational system; and revision of the Diet law to ensure normal parliamentary proceedings.

The Japan Federation of Employers (*Nikkeiren*) argued that while the nation had achieved rapid economic growth, its system of parliamentary democracy had weakened. The federation further urged that Japan's Constitution needed revision. It felt that with the reversion of Okinawa, Japan will find it necessary "truly to stand on its own feet" and seriously to consider defense requirements independently of the United States. Article 9 of the Constitution, which foreswears all but defensive forces, will prove to be an obstacle to Japan's efforts to form a collective security system for East Asia.

Expo '70. Many Japanese preferred to ignore political issues and to look forward eagerly to the Japan World Exposition, Expo '70, the first world's fair to be held in Asia. It is scheduled to open precisely at 11:34 A. M., March 15, 1970. It was estimated that from then until September 13, 50 million guests would visit the 4,000,000-square-yard (3,060,000-sq-meter) site in the rolling forest land of the Senri Hills between Osaka and Kyoto. The government of Japan and those of the city and prefecture of Osaka had already pledged over $2 billion to develop the tract and to provide adequate mass transportation facilities to the fair.

Buildings were designed for more countries than have ever before participated in an international fair, as well as for several international organizations, numerous states, provinces, cities, and a number of Japanese and international corporations. The largest exhibits were expected to be those of the United States, the Soviet Union, and Japan. The fair will also feature the largest exhibition hall in the world, actually an outdoor plaza covered with a roof 1,000 feet (305 meters) in length and weighing 5,000 tons. The central theme of Expo '70 will be "Progress and Harmony for Mankind."

ARDATH W. BURKS
Rutgers University

JAPANESE STUDENTS, with helmets and long poles, mass at Tokyo's railroad station to demand reversion of Okinawa.

JAPANESE LITERATURE

In Japan the year 1969 opened in an atmosphere of celebration for Yasunari Kawabata, the 1968 Nobel Prize winner in literature. For the most part, the aesthetic tradition of Japan, which is the core of Kawabata's writing, is not a popular theme in current Japanese literature. Many contemporary authors prefer to view Japanese culture as a part of world history rather than in isolation. Expressive of this trend were the several books in comparative literature and culture that appeared in 1969. They included *Kaigai-ni-okeru Nihon Kindai Bungaku Kenkyu (Report on Studies of Modern Japanese Literature Done by Non-Japanese)* by Sadataka Muramatsu and Katsuhiko Takeda, *Uchi-to Soto-kara-no Bungaku (Literature from Inside and Outside)* by Shoichi Saeki, and *Nihon Bunka Ron (Study of Japanese Culture)* by Eiichiro Ishida.

Fiction. One of the year's major works of historical fiction was Yasushi Inoue's *Orosha Koku Suimu Tan (Russian Odyssey of Daikokuya-Kodayuu)*, a saga reflecting the Tokugawa government's attitude in the late 18th century toward Japanese who visited forbidden places. The writing style is fresh and clean. Another topic, the problem of old age, was dealt with in *Henyo (Transfiguration)* by Sei (Hitoshi) Ito; *Kitsune-bi (Fox-fire)* by Enchi Fumiko; and *Toshi-no Nokori (The Remaining Years of Life)* by Saiichi Maruya.

The widespread unrest on Japanese campuses during 1969 was reflected in the works of younger writers, especially of writer-professors who had resigned because of the tension. Shumon Miura, writing energetically since leaving Nihon University, produced *Oshie-no Niwa (Garden of Teaching)*, *Daigaku Funso (Campus Unrest)*, *Niju-nen (Twenty Years)*, all involving campus situations. *Waga Kaitai (My Disintegration)* by Kazumi Takahashi is another example. Many books in this category reflect the writers' uncertainty about their opinions on the current upheaval and the role they should play in it. By contrast, Yukio Mishima, whose new books *Haru-no Yuki (Spring Snow)* and *Hon-ba (Running Horse)* are best-sellers, makes his position very clear. His discussions with Zengakuren students show the writer participating in events.

Shusaku Endo, author of *Chinmoku (The Silence of God)*, holds a unique place in Japanese literature. In the past he had raised the question of what a transplanted Christianity could do to the Japanese mind. A tentative answer emerged in his latest works, *Haha-narumono (Mother-Natured)*, *Chiisana Machi-nite (At a Small Town)*, and in a play *Bara-no Yakata (House of Roses)*, which deal with the transformation of a judgmental and father-oriented Christianity into a forgiving, mother-oriented religion. Buddhist themes were explored by Fumio Niwa in his novel, *Shinran*.

Poetry. Publications of books of poetry averaged more than one a day in 1969. Many collections of non-traditional poetry from the Meiji period to the present were completed. In the approximately 200 poetry magazines in Japan, however, little space was given to the works of contemporary poets. The reason may be in the quality of the poetry, sometimes no more than a mosaic of nonsense words that catch the eye of the reader but lack the sensitivity to reach the depth of the human heart. Among the year's major poems were *Waga Izumo Waga Chinkon (My Izumo, Repose of my Soul)* by

Yasuo Irisawa, *Murano Shiro Zenshishu (Entire Collection of Works of Shiro Murano)*, and *Kowareta Orugan (A Broken Organ)* by Shinpei Kusano.

As part of the revival of ancient poetic forms, new ways of writing *tanka* were discussed and published in magazines, such as *Shin Tanka (New Tanka)*, *Gendai Tanka (Modern Tanka)*, and *Geijutsu-to Jiyu (Art and Freedom)*. Though efforts still faltered, there were some notable works, namely *Kuro-Hyo (Black Leopard)* by Yoshimi Kondo, *Kisaragi Yayoi (February March)* by Eiichi Fukada, and *Fuyu-no-Kazoku (Family in Winter)* by Hirohiko Okano. A reevaluation of Haiku was also underway in the magazine *Haiku Kenkyu (Study on Haiku)*. Among the best of the genre were *Shuchuka (Blossom in Wine)* by Hakyo Ishida and *Bo-on (Sound Forgotten)* by Ryota Iida.

Drama. Yukio Mishima published two plays in 1969, *Waga Tomo Hitler (My Friend Hitler)* and *Raiono Terasu (Terrace of a Leprous King)*. Expressive of the growing trend toward allegory were Kimifusa Abe's three separate plays—*Kaban (The Brief Case)*, *Toki-no Gake (The Cliff of Time)*, and *Bo-ni Natta Otoko (The Man Who Became a Stick)*—to be performed together under the last title.

Buristoviru-no Gogo (Afternoon of Bristolville) by Shotaro Yasuoka deals with unhappy Japanese students who are studying in the United States, a theme that in the past few years has appeared often in fiction, essays, and discussions of critics. One reason for its frequent occurrence may be the tendency for modern Japanese to regard Tokyo as the center of culture, and that to be away from it is to be in exile. Other plays published during the year were *Shijin Torokkii (Trotsky the Poet)* by Isamu Kurita and *Kasabuta-Shikibuko (A New Religion by Kasabuta-Shikibu)* by Matsuyo Akimoto.

KASHIHI TANAKA
University of California, Santa Barbara

JEHOVAH'S WITNESSES

Jehovah's Witnesses were active in 203 countries during 1969, operating 25,694 congregations under the direction of 94 branch offices. During the year 120,905 new ministers (members) were baptized, increasing the total ministers to 1,336,112.

The "Peace on Earth" international assemblies were held in 13 major cities of the United States, Canada, and Europe. More than 840,000 heard the main talk, "The Approaching Peace of a Thousand Years." Additional assemblies of the same series were held in Japan, Korea, Australia, and·New Zealand, and in Mexico and Latin America later in the year. A Bible textbook, *Is the Bible Really the Word of God?*, was released to provide scientific evidence that confirms the Bible's truthfulness.

The Brooklyn, N. Y., headquarters printing plant produced 24,038,531 bound books and Bibles and more than 194 million copies of magazines during the year. Circulation of *The Watchtower*, the official journal of Jehovah's Witnesses, rose to 5,850,-000 in 72 languages, and its companion, *Awake!*, attained a circulation of 5,700,000 in 26 languages. A new office and residence building was completed and put into use during the year.

N. H. KNORR
Watch Tower Bible & Tract Society

JONES, James Earl. See biographical sketch under THEATER.

JORDANIANS PROTEST the burning of the Al Aksa Mosque in Jerusalem, August 22. Thousands, including armed Palestinian guerillas, march through center of Amman.

JORDAN

The unresolved Arab-Israeli conflict in the Middle East dominated domestic and foreign affairs in Jordan during 1969. Increased Arab guerrilla activities and intensified Israeli preventive and retaliatory actions kept western Jordan in constant turmoil. In the face of opposing pressures to support or to curb the guerrillas, King Hussein twice reshuffled his cabinet. The Jordanian economy continued to be supported by extensive foreign aid.

Border Conditions. Throughout 1969 a number of Palestine Arab guerrilla groups, especially al-

---

JORDAN • Information Highlights

Area: 37,737 square miles (97,740 sq km).

Population: 2,102,000 (1968 est.).

Chief Cities (1967 census): Amman, the capital, 330,396; Zarqa, 119,744; Nablus (1961 census), 45,768.

Government: *King*—Hussein (acceded Aug. 11, 1952); *Prime Minister*—Bahjat al-Talhouni (held office Oct. 7, 1967– March 24, 1969; took office again Aug. 12, 1969). *Parliament*—Council of Representatives, 60 members; Council of Notables, 30 members.

Religious Faiths: Muslims, 94% of population; Roman Catholics, 2.6%; others, 3.4%.

Education: *Literacy rate* (1969), 35%–40% of population. *Total school enrollment* (1965)—592,377 (primary, 295,177; secondary, 99,076; teacher-training, 98; technical/vocational, 3,267; university/higher, 2,023).

Finance (1969 est.): *Revenues*, $210,800,000; *expenditures*, $250,000,000; *monetary unit*, dinar (.3571 dinar equals U. S.$1).

Gross National Product (1967): $543,000,000.

National Income (1967): $506,860,820; *average annual income per person*, $241.

Manufacturing (metric tons, 1967): Cement, 321,000; wheat flour (1965), 101,000; gasoline, 72,000; olive oil, 20,000; beer, 11,000 hectoliters.

Crops (metric tons, 1967–68 crop year): Wheat, 226,000; tomatoes, 150,000; olives, 103,000; lentils, 22,000; figs, 3,000; dry broad beans, 2,000.

Minerals (metric tons, 1967): Phosphate rock, 1,082,000; salt, 12,000; marble (1966), 200 square meters.

Foreign Trade (1968): *Exports*, $40,000,000 (chief exports, 1967: natural phosphates, $9,730,000; tomatoes, $4,929,-000; tobacco, $1,890,000; dry pulses, $1,270,000); *imports*, $1,061,000,000 (chief imports, 1967: automotive parts, $7,750,000; petroleum, $6,020,000; wheat or meslin flour, $5,770,000). *Chief trading partners* (1967): United States (supplied 12% of imports); Britain (supplied 12% of imports); West Germany.

Transportation: *Roads* (1969), 3,480 miles (5,599 km); *motor vehicles* (1967), 23,100 (automobiles 16,400); *railways* (1965), 227 miles (365 km).

Communications: *Telephones* (1968): 33,000; *television sets* (1968), 10,000; *radios* (1965), 269,000; *newspapers* (1965), 7 (daily circulation, 17,000).

Fatah and the Popular Front for the Liberation of Palestine, were active in Jordan, training commandos, launching attacks across the 1967 cease-fire lines with Israel, and using Jordanian territory as a base for disruption and sabotage in Israel and the Israeli-occupied areas. Israel retaliated with artillery fire across the cease-fire lines, air attacks on guerrilla bases and other objectives in Jordan, and raids into Jordanian territory.

On March 26, Israeli jets bombed a guerrilla base near Salt, an action for which Israel was censured by the UN Security Council on April 1. On June 23, as a reprisal for guerrilla actions, an Israeli commando group rendered inoperable the East Ghor Canal, which irrigates more than 36,000 acres (14,600 hectares) of agricultural land on the east bank of the Jordan River. Israeli artillery fire prevented repairs from being made until June 30, when the Jordanian government agreed, through the good offices of the United States, to curb guerrilla activity. There followed some reduction in Arab commando attacks, but when repairs to the canal were completed in July, guerrilla activities resumed. On August 10 and on December 31, Israel again attacked the canal, disrupting its operation.

Domestic Affairs. During 1969 the Jordanian government wavered between support for the guerrillas and preparation for renewed war on the one hand, and acceptance of some sort of political settlement with Israel on the other. Early in the year King Hussein seemed hopeful that the United States, the Soviet Union, Britain, and France might propose a settlement acceptable to the Arabs. On March 24 he apparently solicited the resignation of his prime minister, Bahjat al-Talhouni, who had grown pessimistic about any accommodation with Israel, and appointed in his place Abdel Monem Rifai, the former foreign minister. While Rifai hoped to avoid confrontation with the guerrillas and rejected direct negotiations with Israel, he favored a political settlement. As time passed without agreement between the United States and the Soviet Union or among the Big Four powers, however, King Hussein adopted a more militant stance. On August 12, Rifai resigned, and Talhouni returned to the premiership.

Economic Conditions. The Jordanian economy continued to reveal the effects of the dislocations caused by the 1967 war and the ongoing guerrilla campaign. Agricultural production on the east bank of the Jordan was curtailed by recurrent military activities and by damage to the East Ghor Canal. The government was forced to abandon construction of the long-projected Arab Potash Works on the east side of the Dead Sea because of the area's proximity to the battle lines. The budget for 1969 revealed a reduction in spending for economic development from $87.5 million in 1968 to $73.5 million.

Phosphate production, however, showed a healthy increase, and building construction boomed, especially in the vicinity of Amman. Large sums of money flowed into the country in the form of local expenditures of the UN Relief and Works Agency for Palestine Refugees; expenditures in Jordan of the various guerrilla groups that raised funds throughout the Arab world; economic aid and development loans from the United States, Britain, West Germany, and some of the other Arab states; and $105.6 million in special grants from Saudi Arabia, Kuwait, and Libya, which had been arranged in 1967 to compensate Jordan for its losses in the Israeli-Arab war. Inflationary pressures became a matter of concern to the government in the second half of 1969.

Foreign Relations. During the year, Jordan entered into closer relations with the other Arab states most deeply involved in the struggle with Israel. Iraq continued to maintain some 12,000 troops in Jordan, and in July Syria sent a military brigade to bolster Jordan's northern front. King Hussein held cordial meetings with President Nasser of the United Arab Republic in Cairo on March 16–17 and again on August 30, on the eve of a "little summit" meeting of the top leaders of Jordan, the UAR, Syria, Iraq, and Sudan that sought to coordinate Arab military policy against Israel.

Jordan also moved cautiously toward closer relations with the Soviet Union. On January 20, at the end of an 11-day visit to Moscow by the Jordanian minister of national economy, the Soviet Union and Jordan signed their first agreement for technical and economic cooperation. In general, however, Jordan maintained its traditional ties with the United States and Britain. In the spring, King Hussein visited the United States, where he conferred with President Richard M. Nixon and other U. S. officials.

PAUL L. HANNA
University of Florida

JUAN CARLOS. See biographical sketch under SPAIN.

JUDAISM. See RELIGION—*Judaism*.

JUVENILE DELINQUENCY. See CRIME.

KANSAS

The body of Dwight David Eisenhower, 34th President of the United States, was returned to his hometown, Abilene, on April 2, 1969, for burial. The ceremonies at the Eisenhower Center in Abilene were witnessed by Mrs. Mamie Eisenhower, President and Mrs. Nixon, and former President Lyndon B. Johnson.

Eisenhower Honors. On Eisenhower's 79th birthday anniversary, October 14, ceremonies for the first-day issuance of a commemorative stamp in his honor were held on the Eisenhower Library steps in Abilene. The number of visitors to the Eisenhower

--- KANSAS • Information Highlights ---

Area: 82,264 square miles (213,064 sq km).
Population: 2,323,000 (1969, est.).
Chief Cities (1969 est.): Topeka, the capital, 127,000; Wichita, 292,000; Kansas City, 172,000; Overland Park, 74,000.
Government: *Chief Officers*—governor, Robert B. Docking (Dem.); lt. gov., James H. Decoursey (D); secy. of state, Elwill M. Shanahan (Rep.); atty. gen., Kent Frizzell (R); treas., Walter H. Peery; comm. of ed., Whittier C. Taylor; chief justice, Robert T. Price. *Legislature*—Senate, 40 members (8 Democrats, 32 Republicans); House of Representatives, 125 members (38 D, 87 R).
Education: *School enrollment* (1968–69)—public elementary, 374,000 pupils (14,300 teachers); public secondary, 156,-000 pupils (11,200 teachers); nonpublic schools, 48,800 pupils (2,010 teachers); college and university (fall 1967), 89,069 students. *Public school expenditures* (1967–68)—$326,000,000 ($684 per pupil); average teacher's salary, $6,723.
Public Finance (fiscal year 1969): *Revenues,* $677,633,412 (3% sales tax, $137,322,620; motor fuel tax, $57,272,850; federal funds, $172,555,545). *Expenditures,* $645,273,415 (education, $299,382,102; health, welfare, and safety, $154,422,135; highways, $136,953,519). *State debt,* none (June 30, 1969).
Personal Income (1968): $7,574,000,000; average annual income per person, $3,303.
Public Assistance (fiscal year 1968): $98,815,000 to 73,682 recipients (aged, $21,718,000; dependent children, $34,-305,000).
Labor Force (employed persons, 1968): *Agricultural,* 82,100; *nonagricultural* (wage and salary earners), 767,200 (21.6% manufacturing, 22.3% trade, 23.3% government). *Unemployed persons* (calendar 1968)—23,200.
Manufacturing (1966): *Value added by manufacture,* $1,955,-000,000 (transportation equipment, $606,650,000; food and products, $249,047,000; chemicals, $246,895,000; petroleum and coal, $158,315,000; nonelectrical machinery, $153,488,000; fabricated metals, $92,001,000).
Agriculture (1967): *Cash farm income,* $1,692,636,000 (livestock, $951,919,000; crops, $528,338,000; govt. payments, $212,379,000). *Chief crops* (tons)—Wheat, 6,648,600 (ranks 1st among the states); sorghum grain, 4,183,424 (ranks 2d); hay, 5,282,000; corn for grain, 2,018,240.
Mining (1968): *Production value,* $577,360,000. *Chief minerals* (tons)—Stone, 14,402,000; sand and gravel, 12,427,000; coal, 1,268,000; salt, 1,128,000; clays, 879,000; crude oil, 94,505,000 bbls.
Transportation: *Roads* (1968), 123,327 miles (198,470 km); *motor vehicles* (1968), 1,459,121; *railroads* (1965), 12,065 track miles (19,402 km); *airports* (1968), 13.
Communications (1968): *Telephones,* 1,140,800; *television stations,* 13; *radio stations,* 93; *newspapers* (1969), 52 (daily circulation, 673,291).

Center, which includes the Eisenhower family home, a museum, the Eisenhower Library and the Meditation Chapel where he is buried, increased greatly during 1969. Congress approved plans that will nearly double the size of the museum. (See also EISENHOWER, DWIGHT D.)

Legislature. A record $740 million was appropriated by the Kansas Legislature during its annual session which ended in April. That total was $29.7 million more than Gov. Robert Docking's recommendations, with much of the increase—$27 million—earmarked for additional state aid for local school districts. The appropriations also provide for increased spending at Kansas universities, at mental hospitals, and for various welfare programs.

Other bills passed by the Legislature provided for a revised criminal code that will liberalize Kansas abortion laws, and for the establishment of a statewide plan of development for Kansas junior colleges. A statewide meat inspection plan, to be administered by the state board of agriculture, was also adopted, and the issuance of 24-hour, $1 fishing permits for non-residents was approved.

The Kansas gasoline tax was increased from 5¢ to 7¢ per gallon, and the diesel fuels tax from 7¢ to 8¢. These taxes will raise more than $25 million a year, of which half will go to new state freeway construction, and the remainder to cities and counties for improvement of local streets and roads.

Another act passed by the Legislature would have provided a tax on non-cigarette tobacco products in an amount equal to the current levy on cigarettes. But this act was subsequently declared invalid by a district court because of a defective title.

The Legislature proposed a constitutional amendment to permit the sale of liquor by the drink. It will be submitted to the voters in the November 1970 general election.

Agricultural Production. Kansas produced 305 million bushels of wheat in 1969, the second largest crop in history. The soybean and hay crops also were the second largest on record. Sorghum grain production (183 million bushels) was an all-time record, as was the sugar beet crop. The corn crop (91 million bushels) was the best in 25 years. The index of 1969 all-crop production was 169% of the 1947–1949 base, making 1969 the state's best crop year in history. The 745,000 cattle and calves on grain feed for the slaughter market in Kansas feedlots on October 1 was a record for the date.

Industry and Recreation. The mobile housing industry continued to expand in Kansas. The state became the 4th largest manufacturer of mobile homes and recreation campers in the United States. The annual payroll of mobile unit manufacturers, suppliers to the industry, dealers, and park operators topped $100 million for approximately 15,000 employees. There were more than 50 plants manufacturing mobile homes and travel trailers in Kansas at the end of 1970. Their construction was second only to aircraft in manufacturing importance to the state.

NYLE H. MILLER
Kansas State Historical Society

KARLOFF, Boris. See biographical sketch under MOTION PICTURES.

KENNEDY, Edward Moore

During a brief six months in 1969, Edward Moore Kennedy rose higher and faster only to fall further and harder than any national political figure in recent memory. Even before Richard Nixon's inauguration the last of the four Kennedy sons seemed ready to accept the apparent inevitability that he would be Nixon's opponent in the 1972 presidential race. In his own words he had picked up "the fallen standard" of his brothers. By the end of June, Massachusetts' 37-year-old senior senator was recognized as the dominant personality in the Democratic party, but by the end of July his future had dimmed to such an extent that many were calling it ended.

Misadventure on Chappaquiddick. Senator Kennedy's course was reversed with melodramatic suddenness on the night of July 18 when he drove a black sedan off a narrow wooden bridge on Chappaquiddick Island, an isolated resort adjacent to Martha's Vineyard. Riding in the car with him was Mary Jo Kopechne, a 28-year-old former campaign worker of Robert Kennedy. Apparently she never had a chance to fight clear of the car, which overturned in a shallow saltwater pond. Senator Kennedy said later that he had experienced the sensation of drowning when the car went into the water and could not remember his struggle to free himself. He made repeated dives for the young woman, he said, but failed to reach her. The next morning, before he identified himself as the driver of the car and even before the body had been identified, the young woman was pronounced dead by drowning.

Aftermath and Explanations. The tragic circumstances of Miss Kopechne's death were enough to place the young senator in an exceedingly awkward position, but it was his reaction to the accident, rather than the accident itself, that finally rendered him vulnerable to criticism. By Kennedy's own reckoning, about 10 hours elapsed between the accident and his appearance to report it the next morning at the Edgartown police station on Martha's Vineyard. His first two accounts of what transpired during these hours—a statement to the police on July 19 and a televised address to Massachusetts voters nearly a week later—were less than consistent and less than complete. Kennedy, who could not spell Miss Kopechne's name when he dictated his statement for the police, called his actions "indefensible" in the televised statement. The morning before he went on television he had pleaded guilty to a charge of leaving the scene of an accident that resulted in personal injuries. He received a 2-month suspended sentence.

Inquest Ordered. The case was pronounced closed but constant cataloging of its "unanswered questions" by newspapers and periodicals kept the matter before the public. Then, in early August, the case was suddenly reopened with the ordering of an inquest into Miss Kopechne's death by District Attorney Edmund Dinis of New Bedford, Mass. The inquest was then postponed on an appeal from Senator Kennedy, whose lawyers contended that the heavy publicity it would inevitably receive would compromise his constitutional rights. This argument was upheld on September 2 by the Superior Judicial Court of Massachusetts, which ruled that the inquest had to be held behind closed doors. By this time Kennedy's supporters and friends were saying he was ready to tell the whole story at the earliest opportunity. They also acknowledged that he might never recover from the damage done by the delay. The inquest, closed to the public and the press, began on Jan. 5, 1970.

Emergence of a Leader. In the wake of the accident it was difficult to recall Senator Kennedy's vivid and confident emergence in a position of national leadership in the early part of the year. The assassination of Robert Kennedy had placed on him the terrible burden of a legacy that virtually dictated a decision to seek the presidency. Yet Edward Kennedy had not displayed the depth and capabilities of his older brothers, and even those who looked to him for leadership frankly wondered if he would be able to provide it.

Ending his period of private mourning, Senator Kennedy returned to Congress in January 1969 and immediately laid claim to the position of majority whip—an audacious challenge to the Senate establishment for any backbencher. His victory by five votes over Sen. Russell Long of Louisiana, the incumbent, indicated how strongly the Democratic party felt the need for fresh leadership.

Soon Kennedy was speaking out on a wide range of issues, challenging expenditures on the space program in a time of domestic crisis, military strategy in Vietnam, and the new president's support of a ballistic missile defense system. He seemed driven to take a stand on as many questions as possible, especially those issues involving social justice that had mattered most to Robert Kennedy in his last months, but he was usually well prepared and complaints that he was spreading himself thin were few. The youngest Kennedy son, it was acknowledged, was gaining in stature and establishing an identity of his own. Only after the July accident did some analysts profess to see in him a hidden wish to slough off the role that had been thrust on him.

Accident on Martha's Vineyard, Mass., bridge (*top*) brought injury to Sen. Edward Kennedy and death to Mary Jo Kopechne (*below*) as their car swerved into the water in the dark. The accident caused pundits to share the cartoonist's view (*right*) of Kennedy's 1972 presidential hopes.

UPI

REPRINTED FROM LOS ANGELES TIMES BY PERMISSION OF REGISTER AND TRIBUNE SYNDICATE

The Outlook. Chappaquiddick changed the picture. It crippled Kennedy's ability to influence political life outside the Senate, and a personal display of resilience was not enough to restore him to the place he had inherited and begun to earn. Kennedy seemed to recognize this and to accept his lot. Yet even while the Kopechne case hung over him, there were those who recalled that he would be as young in 1992 as Hubert H. Humphrey, the former vice president, would be in 1972. If it only took the passage of years, there could be time for a comeback.

JOSEPH LELYVELD
"The New York Times"

KENTUCKY

Kentucky experienced a relatively quiet year in 1969. Manifestations of racial tension and student unrest were moderate; tobacco farmers became somewhat apprehensive of possible future price declines; and the general election yielded some interesting results.

Civil Rights. Negroes continued to make slow progress in various fields. Under the state's 1968 open-housing law, at least 151 black families had moved by the late summer of 1969 into formerly all-white neighborhoods in 10 cities.

------ **KENTUCKY** • Information Highlights ------

Area: 40,395 square miles (104,623 sq km).
Population: 3,205,000 (1969 est.).
Chief Cities (1969 est.): Frankfort, the capital, 23,000; Louisville, 380,000; Lexington, 90,000; Covington, 55,000; Owensboro, 47,500.
Government: *Chief Officers*—governor, Louie B. Nunn (Republican); lt. gov., Wendell H. Ford (Democrat); secy. of state, Elmer Begley (R); atty. gen., John B. Breckinridge (D); treas., Mrs. Thelma L. Stovall; supt. of pub. instr., Wendell P. Butler; chief justice, Edward P. Hill. *General Assembly*—Senate, 38 members (24 Democrats, 14 Republicans); House of Representatives, 100 members (56 D, 41 R).
Education: *School enrollment* (1968–69)—public elementary, 449,000 pupils (17,600 teachers); public secondary, 249,-000 pupils (11,400 teachers); nonpublic schools, 89,000 pupils (3,600 teachers); college and university (fall 1967), 90,211 students. *Public school expenditures* (1967–68)—$350,975,000 ($546 per pupil); average teacher's salary, $6,500.
Public Finance (fiscal year 1968): *Revenues,* $989,044,065 (3% sales tax, $155,429,247; motor fuel tax, $91,772,326; federal funds, $299,518,533). *Expenditures,* $1,090,818,000 (education, $346,782,686; health, welfare, and safety, $211,355,221; highways, $312,846,192). *State debt,* $5,266,-942 (June 30, 1968).
Personal Income (1968): $8,516,000,000; average annual income per person, $2,645.
Public Assistance (fiscal year 1968–69): $146,572,604 to 289,-400 recipients (aged, $40,177,976; dependent children, $40,461,686).
Labor Force (employed persons, June 30, 1969): *Agricultural,* 118,600; *nonagricultural* (wage and salary earners), 1,022,-700 (23.9% manufacturing, 17.9% trade, 16.1% government). *Unemployed persons* (June 30, 1969): 50,800.
Manufacturing (1965): *Value added by manufacture,* $3,135,-372,000 (food and products, $484,688,000; electrical machinery, $441,544,000; nonelectrical machinery, $340,-095,000; transportation equipment, $277,351,000; fabricated metals, $169,504,000).
Agriculture (1967): *Cash farm income,* $862,388,000 (livestock, $380,812,000; crops, $440,049,000; govt. payments, $41,527,000). *Chief crops* (tons)—Tobacco, 209,480 (ranks 2d among the states); hay, 2,947,000; corn for grain, 2,616,320; soybeans, 304,192.
Mining (1966): *Production value,* $498,364,000. *Chief minerals* (tons)—Coal, 93,156,000; clays, 1,152,000; fluorspar, 28,-704; zinc, 6,586; petroleum, 18,066,000 barrels; natural gas, 76,536,000,000 cubic feet.
Transportation: *Roads* (1969) 69,505 miles (111,855 km); *motor vehicles* (1968) 1,698,433; *railroads* (1966) 3,503 track miles (4,636 km); *airports* (1969), 7.
Communications (1969): *Telephones* (1968), 1,219,300; *television stations,* 9; *radio stations,* 100; *newspapers,* 27 (daily circulation, 756,800).

The number of Negroes holding elective offices across the state rose from about 20 to 35 in November. Luska J. Twyman, already serving by appointment as mayor of Glasgow, won a 4-year term in that office to become the first of his race ever elected to head the government of a Kentucky city.

Politics. Democrats showed unexpected strength in the fall election, retaining control of the General Assembly and ousting Republican administrations in Louisville and in the counties of Fayette and Jefferson. The sole statewide race—to fill an unexpired term as state auditor—was won by Mary Louise Foust, an independent Democrat. Republican Gov. Louie B. Nunn's tax program came under increasing attack as the opening of the 1970 biennial session of the Assembly drew near.

The Council of State Governments moved its headquarters in April from Chicago to Lexington. At about the same time the Republican Governors' Conference met in Lexington.

Education. Colleges and universities faced increasing enrollments and comparatively mild student rebellion. Blacks at the University of Louisville occupied a campus building. They were removed by police, and eight of the protesters were dismissed from the university. Brief rioting followed in the city, but confrontation ended with a "moratorium," and the appointment of Negro Hanford D. Stafford as the university's Director of Black Affairs helped ease tension.

Financial stress closed Kentucky Southern College, a private institution in Louisville. The University of Kentucky's Northern Community College, at Covington, was scheduled to be transformed into a new 4-year state school. It was agreed that the University of Louisville would join the state system in 1970, but the exact relationship of that school to the University of Kentucky was not fully clarified.

Consolidation of elementary schools in Ohio County led to a boycott at the beginning of the fall term. Concessions were made by the state Department of Education after two weeks of negotiations.

Conservation. A long fight to prevent flooding of the scenic Red River gorge in eastern Kentucky ended in victory for conservationists. The U. S. Senate's appropriations committee specified relocation of a dam, downstream from the site chosen earlier by the Army Corps of Engineers.

In August, the state purchased 550 acres of virgin woodland in eastern Kentucky. They will be preserved as a forest museum and laboratory.

Agriculture. Burley tobacco brought, during the 1968–69 sales, a record high average price of $73.71 per 100 pounds. The 1969 crop appeared to be good, but average prices offered during early sales in the new season were lower than those paid in 1968. Meat prices continued to rise, and law enforcement officers reported increased cattle rustling as a consequence.

JAMES F. HOPKINS
University of Kentucky

KENYA

In 1969, Kenya experienced increased political and tribal tensions. National unity was seriously threatened by the assassination of Kenyan leader Tom Mboya in July. The results of the elections held in December represented a defeat for the government of President Jomo Kenyatta.

Political Rivalry. Issues of academic freedom, local political autonomy, Africanization, and economic development challenged the ruling Kenya African National Union (KANU) party and its leader, Jomo Kenyatta. In January the government refused to permit Oginga Odinga, the leader of the opposition Kenya Peoples Union (KPU), to speak at University College, Nairobi, and was forced to close the school temporarily following a student strike. Between January and April struggles for power within local KANU chapters in the Western and Coast provinces severely weakened the party structure and challenged the central leadership. The KPU continued to attack the capitalist policies of the government and in February demanded the nationalization of large businesses, an end to government harassment of the KPU, and the removal of the civil service and police from politics.

Mboya Assassination. Tom Mboya, the minister of economic planning and development and a member of KANU and of the Luo tribe, was assassinated in Nairobi on July 5. Despite repeated requests for calm by both government and opposition leaders, Mboya's death produced a series of confrontations between police and predominantly Luo crowds, who believed that the Kikuyu, who dominate KANU and the government, were responsible for the assassination. The belief appeared confirmed when a Kikuyu, N. Ngoroje, was convicted of the murder on September 10. Thereafter, Kenya politics were charged with the bitterness created by Mboya's death, and

---

TOM MBOYA (1930–1969)

Tom Mboya, Kenya's minister of economic planning and development and secretary general of the Kenya African National Union (KANU), was killed by an assassin in Nairobi on July 5, 1969. A protégé of President Jomo Kenyatta, Mboya was one of the most influential leaders among Africa's newly independent nations. He favored economic cooperation among African nations and maintained a conciliatory attitude toward the former colonial powers. On his many visits to the United States he promoted the establishment of scholarships for African students.

Thomas Joseph Mboya, a member of the Luo tribe, was born on Aug. 15, 1930, on a sisal plantation in Kenya's White Highlands. He received his early education at Roman Catholic mission schools and later studied at Oxford University. In the early 1950's he helped organize African government workers and became the general secretary of the Kenya Federation of Labor. Mboya was elected to the Kenya Legislative Council in 1957 and served as chairman of the All-African People's Conference at Accra, Ghana, in December 1958. He was minister of labor and minister of justice and constitutional affairs in the early 1960's. When Kenya became a republic in 1964, Mboya was appointed minister of economic planning and development.

---

fear and rivalry between the Kikuyu and Luo tribes increased tensions between the KANU and the KPU.

On October 25 the situation was further embittered when a speech given by President Kenyatta in Kisumu was followed by a riot in which 11 people died. As a result of the riot the government banned the KPU on October 30 and arrested Oginga Odinga and other KPU leaders on charges of conspiring with foreign powers to overthrow the government.

Elections. The proscription of the KPU temporarily restored peace within Kenya but made the KANU primaries (in effect, general elections) in early December a test of the government's policy. The elections represented a defeat for the government, as a number of incumbents were turned out of office in all parts of the country. Although Kenyatta's position was not jeopardized, the election proved the political vulnerability of the leaders who had led Kenya to independence.

Foreign Affairs. Kenya continued to follow a moderate foreign policy and to work toward greater unity in East Africa. The agreement between Kenya and Somalia to end their border problems was sealed by the visit of Prime Minister Mohammed Ibrahim Egal of Somalia to Kenya in February. Both countries agreed to increase cooperation along the frontier, repatriate refugees, release political prisoners, and end the state of emergency in their border provinces.

The ambitious but often hesitant move toward greater unity in East and Central Africa continued as Ethiopia, Zambia, Somalia, and Burundi carried on negotiations for associate membership in the East African Economic Community. Relations with states outside Africa remained cordial, although the question of immigration to Britain of Kenya Indians with British passports continued to strain relations between the two countries. In April relations with the Soviet Union were compromised when the first secretary of the Soviet embassy and a *Pravda* correspondent were expelled from Kenya.

Economy. In 1969, Kenya was faced with problems caused by falling world prices for its agricultural products, dislocation resulting from the emigration of Indian merchants, and the rapid Africanization of many businesses. A decline in the availability of foreign loans also contributed to the economic problems. Generally, however, Kenya's economic position remained relatively strong. Gains in agricultural and industrial production and tourism offset internal and external economic problems. An agreement with the European Economic Community in July opened the large European market to Kenyan products. This, combined with an agreement with Communist China for the sale of cotton and the movement toward the enlargement of the East African free trade area, suggested that Kenya would be able to maintain its steady growth rate.

ROBERT O. COLLINS
University of California, Santa Barbara

KNAUER, Virginia H. See biographical sketch under CONSUMER AFFAIRS.

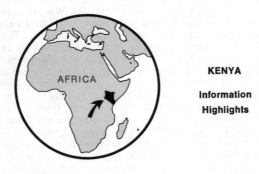

KENYA

Information Highlights

Area: 224,959 square miles (582,644 sq km).
Population: 10,209,000 (1968 est.).
Chief Cities (1962 census): Nairobi, the capital, 266,794; Mombasa, 179,575; Nakuru, 38,181.
Government: *President*—Jomo Kenyatta (took office June 1, 1963). *Parliament* (unicameral)—National Assembly, 158 elected members, 12 appointed (party seating, 1969: all members of the Kenya African National Union).
Religious Faiths: Anglicans and Protestants, 47% of population; Roman Catholics, 10.5%; Muslims, 4%; others, 38.5%.
Education: *Literacy rate* (1969), 25% of population. *Total school enrollment* (1965)—1,068,022.
Finance (1968 est.): *Revenues,* $212,000,000; *expenditures,* $247,800,000; *monetary unit,* East African shilling (7.143 shillings equal U. S.$1).
Gross National Product (1968): $1,235,000,000.
Economic Indexes: *Industrial production* (1966), 127 (1963= 100); *cost of living* (1967), 110 (1963=100).
Manufacturing (metric tons, 1967): Cement, 494,000; gasoline, 269,000; sugar, 60,000.
Crops (metric tons, 1967–68 crop year): Coffee, 493,000; wheat, 128,000; sisal (1965), 64,000.
Minerals (metric tons, 1966): Soda ash, 112,400; gypsum, 33,743; salt, 25,000; limestone, 16,734.
Foreign Trade (1968): *Exports,* $175,000,000 (chief exports, 1967: coffee, $43,959,000; tea, $20,720,000; sisal, $5,740,-000); *imports,* $321,000,000 (chief imports, 1967: crude and partly refined petroleum, $25,463,000; road motor vehicles, $16,680,000; iron and steel, $13,927,000). *Chief trading partners* (1967): Britain (took 24% of exports, supplied 33% of imports); Uganda (took 14% of exports, supplied 7% of imports).
Transportation: *Roads* (1969), 26,354 miles (42,411 km); *motor vehicles* (1967), 92,400 (automobiles, 78,600); *principal airport,* Nairobi.
Communications: *Telephones* (1968), 60,691; *television stations* (1968), 3; *television sets* (1967), 14,000; *radios* (1965), 350,000; *newspapers* (1966), 3.

KOREAN STUDENTS demonstrate against constitutional amendment allowing President Park Chung Hee a third term.

KOREA

The tragic effects of Korea's national division loomed larger in 1969 and aggravated the atmosphere of international conflict in East Asia. The year began with a sigh of relief following the release of the crew of the U. S. S. *Pueblo* in December 1968, but a number of subsequent critical events dashed any hopes for relaxation of tensions over Korea.

As the possibility of another major war remained, the governments of both South and North Korea expedited defense preparations, intensified internal regimentation, and strengthened military relations with their respective allies. This process further contributed to the persistence of two extremely hostile political entities in the small peninsula.

SOUTH KOREA

The domestic political scene was almost completely dominated in 1969 by the heated controversies over a constitutional amendment that would enable President Park Chung Hee to run for his third 4-year term in 1971.

Internal Affairs. President Park finally broke his public silence on July 25 and announced his clear endorsement of such an amendment. His opponents, led by the New Democratic party and supported by students, denounced the "anti-democratic" amendment and organized massive protest demonstrations. But the government, equipped with the slogan "stability or chaos," closed down many colleges and high schools and effectively suppressed the opposition forces. When the National Assembly chamber was occupied by anti-Park members on September 14, the ruling Democratic-Republican party secretly assembled its supporters in an adjacent building and promptly adopted the constitutional amendment bill.

In the national referendum held on October 17, the amendment was approved by an overwhelming majority of 67.5% of the total valid votes. Shortly thereafter, President Park made a major reshuffle of his cabinet and dismissed two powerful lieutenants—the presidential secretary and the director of the Central Intelligence Agency. The National Assembly failed to resume its normal functions.

Internal security was frequently disturbed by the infiltration of North Korean guerrillas and spies along the Demilitarized Zone and off the coast of South Korea. The size of each succeeding infiltration unit became smaller, but the number of units rose in 1969.

In spite of this external harassment, South Korea continued to show remarkable progress toward the early fulfillment of the second 5-year economic plan (1967–71), after having already registered a real

---

SOUTH KOREA • Information Highlights

Area: 38,004 square miles (98,431 sq km).

Population: 30,470,000 (1968 est.).

Chief Cities (1966 census): Seoul, the capital, 3,794,959; Pusan, 1,425,703; Taegu, 845,073; Inchon, 525,072.

Government: *President*—Park Chung Hee (took office Dec. 17, 1963); *Legislature* (unicameral)—National Assembly, 175 members.

Religious Faiths: Buddhists, 27% of population; Roman Catholics, 21%; other Christians, 22%; Confucians, 17%; others, 13%.

Education: *Literacy rate* (1969), 90% of population. *Total school enrollment* (1966)—7,115,981 (primary, 5,382,500; secondary, 1,369,221; technical/vocational, 198,199; university/higher, 166,061).

Finance (1968 est.): *Revenues,* $790,604,982; *expenditures,* $928,683,274; *monetary unit,* won (281 won equal U. S.$1).

Gross National Product (1968): $5,523,131,672.

National Income (1968): $4,729,537,366; *average annual income per person,* $155.

Economic Indexes (1967): *Industrial production* (1968), 258 (1963=100); *agricultural production,* 123 (1963=100); *cost of living,* 123 (1963=100).

Manufacturing (metric tons, 1967): Cement, 2,436,000; wheat flour, 566,400; crude steel, 320,400.

Crops (metric tons, 1967–68 crop year): Rice, 4,869,000; sweet potatoes and yams, 1,671,000; barley, 1,916,000.

Minerals (metric tons, 1967): Graphite (1966), 144,338 (ranks 1st among world producers); coal, 12,432,000.

Foreign Trade (1968): *Exports,* $455,000,000 (chief exports, 1967: textile yarn and fabrics, $49,039,000; plywood, $36,-447,000; metalliferous ores, $21,568,000; fresh fish, $13,-495,000); *imports,* $1,468,000,000 (chief imports, 1967: nonelectrical machinery, $141,187,000; transport equipment, $121,401,000; textile yarn and fabrics, $69,-636,000). *Chief trading partners* (1967): United States (took 43% of exports, supplied 31% of imports); Japan (took 26% of exports, supplied 44% of imports); West Germany (took 2% of exports, supplied 3% of imports).

Transportation: *Roads* (1964), 17,434 miles (28,057 km); *motor vehicles* (1967), 60,700 (automobiles 23,200); *railways* (1965), 1,897 miles (3,053 km); *principal airport,* Seoul.

Communications: *Telephones* (1968): 421,091; *television stations* (1966), 8; *television sets* (1967), 78,000; *radios* (1966), 2,632,000; *newspapers* (1966), 41 (daily circulation, 1,490,000).

growth rate of 13.1% in 1968. But the national economy was faced with some potentially serious problems, such as heavy defense obligations (almost 25% of the national budget), the urban-rural gap, trade deficits, and the inflationary trend.

Foreign Affairs. President Richard M. Nixon reaffirmed U. S. commitments to respect the security pact with South Korea, bolster its military and economic capabilities, and maintain close cooperation in Vietnam and elsewhere. These commitments were manifested in the joint U. S.-Korean airborne exercise in March called Focus Retina, the delivery of F-4 Phantom fighters, and the visits of Deputy Defense Secretary David Packard (June), Secretary of State William Rogers (August), and Gen. Earle G. Wheeler (October). When Presidents Park and Nixon met in San Francisco in August they agreed that the South Korean Army and U. S. forces stationed in Korea "must remain strong and alert" against North Korea's "continuing acts of aggression." President Nixon pledged to assist the Homeland Reserve Defense Force and to continue to provide annual military aid of $160 million.

South Korea improved its relations with Japan by holding a series of cabinet-level meetings in August. In order to enhance its diplomatic position, the South Korean government sent five delegations to about 40 countries during the summer.

The government was pleased with a diplomatic victory won at the 24th UN General Assembly. The Political Committee rejected a Soviet-sponsored resolution that would have simultaneously and unconditionally invited both South and North Korea to take part in the discussion of the Korean question; by a vote of 65 to 31, with 27 abstentions, it decided to invite a South Korean delegation. The United Nations also turned down a resolution calling for the withdrawal from South Korea of all foreign forces serving under UN auspices. This served to justify the continuing presence of U. S. forces—about 53,000 men and 100 combat planes—in Korea.

NORTH KOREA

Premier Kim Il Sung further consolidated his absolute one-man rule in 1969, after another round of political purges in November 1968.

Internal Affairs. Premier Kim's personal cult was extensively fostered both at home and abroad; he was depicted not only as the beloved father of all 40 million Koreans, but also as the most distinguished leader of contemporary international Communist movements. The crescendo of internal indoctrination efforts was used to stimulate military modernization and economic construction.

However, there appeared no visible sign in 1969 of any successful progress in the extended 7-year economic plan (1961–70). Although Finance Minister Yoon claimed in April that the growth rate was 15% in industry and 11% in agriculture for 1968, he readily admitted the existence of economic difficulties due to unprecedented natural calamities, the electrical power shortage, and the defense burden. To convert the entire country into an "ironwall fortress," North Korea earmarked 30% of its national budget for military expenditures—an 11% increase over 1968. The government emphasized an austerity program at the Korean Workers' party Central Committee meeting in June and attached a top priority to heavy industries and the military.

Foreign Affairs. During 1969, North Korea stepped up its determined challenge to U. S. military and intelligence operations in Korea. It shot down a U. S. Navy reconnaissance plane with 31 men aboard over the Sea of Japan in April. (All aboard were presumed to have died in the crash.) A U. S. Army helicopter with three crewmen was shot down over North Korea in August. The crewmen were held prisoner until December 3, when they were released after the United States signed a statement of apology. U. S. soldiers and facilities along the Demilitarized Zone were attacked on numerous occasions.

Although upholding his professed independent line in Communist affairs, Premier Kim also attempted to readjust his complicated relations with the Soviet Union and Communist China. When Soviet vessels aided in U. S. search efforts for the destroyed reconnaissance plane, Kim expressed signs of displeasure toward Moscow. In May, Chairman Nikolai Podgorny of the Presidium of the Supreme Soviet of the USSR and First Deputy Foreign Minister Vasili Kuznetsov paid a 6-day visit to North Korea to woo Kim. But Kim, like Ho Chi Minh of North Vietnam and Mao Tse-tung of Communist China, refused to send a representative to the conference of Communist and Workers' parties that took place in Moscow during June.

In the first half of 1969 there were various reports of persistent conflict between Pyongyang and Peking, such as scattered armed clashes along the Yalu River, territorial disputes, and the Chinese Red Guards' condemnation of Kim's "revisionism." Indeed, Premier Kim failed to send even a fraternal greeting to the 9th National Congress of the Chinese Communist party in April. At the end of September, however, Chairman Choi Yong Kun of the Presidium of North Korea's Supreme People's Assembly led a delegation to attend the 20th anniversary of the Chinese People's Republic. He held long discussions with Chinese Premier Chou En-lai, who stressed the "continuous growth and consolidation of the militant friendship between the peoples of China and Korea." This new development was suggestive of a possible thaw in the strained Pyongyang-Peking relations, which had gradually deteriorated since 1965.

The North Koreans also made deep diplomatic and economic penetration into Africa, Southeast Asia, and the Middle East.

CHAE-JIN LEE
University of Kansas

NORTH KOREA • Information Highlights ————

Area: 46,540 square miles (120,538 sq km).
Population: 13,000,000 (1968 est.).
Chief City (1960 est.): Pyongyang, the capital, 653,100.
Government: *Chairman of Presidium of the Supreme People's Assembly*—Choi Yong Kun (took office 1957); *Premier*—Marshal Kim Il Sung (took office 1948). *Legislature* (unicameral)—Supreme People's Assembly, 383 members.
Education: *Total school enrollment* (1963–64)—2,570,000.
Finance (1965 est.): *Revenues,* $3,080,000,000; *expenditures,* $3,080,000,000; *monetary unit,* won (1.20 won equal U. S.$1).
Manufacturing (metric tons, 1967): Cement, 2,500,000; metallurgical coke (1966), 1,800,000; pig iron and ferroalloys (1966), 1,535,000.
Crops (metric tons, 1967–68 crop year): Rice (1965), 2,500,-000; barley, 250,000.
Minerals (metric tons, 1967): Graphite (1966), 75,000; coal, 17,000,000; iron ore, 3,250,000; magnesite, 1,000,000; salt, 550,000; pyrites (1966), 450,000; apatite (1966), 200,000; silver (1966), 640,000 troy ounces; gold (1966), 160,000 troy ounces.
Foreign Trade (1962): *Chief exports,* metals, 48.5% of total export value; farm products, 12%; *chief import,* machines, 34.1% of total import value. *Chief trading partners:* USSR, 60%; Communist China, 3%.
Transportation: *Railways* (1964), 6,500 miles (10,460 km); *principal airport,* Pyongyang.
Communications: *Radios* (1961), 600,000.

KOSYGIN, Aleksei Nikolayevich

Premier of the Union of Soviet Socialist Republics: b. St. Petersburg (now Leningrad), Russia, Feb. 20, 1904.

In 1969, Soviet Premier Kosygin achieved the diplomatic feat of inducing Communist China to negotiate its boundary disputes with the USSR. At home, however, he appeared to be losing some of his authority.

Diplomacy. During the spring and summer of 1969, small-scale battles along the common frontiers of the Chinese region of Sinkiang and the Soviet Republic of Kazakhstan and on the Amur and Ussuri rivers brought both China and the USSR to the point of announcing the possibility of full-scale war. But in September, Premier Kosygin, en route home from the funeral of North Vietnamese President Ho Chi Minh, requested and received Chinese permission to visit Peking. Arriving there on September 11, he was not permitted to enter the city itself but had to talk with Chinese Premier Chou En-lai at the Peking airport. Although the conversation lasted only a few hours, it ended the border incidents, and Kosygin convinced the Chinese government to commence formal negotiations with the USSR to solve border disputes and revive mutual trade.

Other diplomatic tours in 1969 took Kosygin to India, Afghanistan, and Pakistan, where he investigated the progress of economic projects supported by Soviet technical aid. In May, Kosygin attended the funeral of Indian President Zakir Husain.

Domestic Position. Despite Kosygin's success in Asian diplomacy, at home he appeared to become increasingly less powerful than his coruler, party Secretary-General Leonid I. Brezhnev. A new official history of the Soviet Communist party quoted Brezhnev 21 times, while Kosygin was quoted once. In the autumn a state decree ordered a drastic reduction of the Soviet governmental and industrial bureaucracy, which Kosygin heads as premier. The decree left intact Brezhnev's huge party bureaucracy. Yet Kosygin remained the second most important person in the Soviet ruling elite. Many Soviets have said that they prefer Kosygin, the industrialist, to Brezhnev, the politician.

Background. Aleksei Kosygin's background is mainly industrial. After graduating from a trade high school in 1924, he worked for 10 years in Siberian consumer cooperatives, joining the Communist party in 1927. Returning to his native Leningrad, he completed his education in the Leningrad Textile Institute in 1935. Meanwhile his career progressed rapidly: 1935—shop superintendent, Zhelyabov factory; 1937—director, October Cloth Weaving Plant; 1938—mayor of Leningrad; 1939—minister of the textile industry of the USSR; 1940—vice premier of the USSR; 1946—candidate member of the Communist party Politburo; 1948—full Politburo member.

After Stalin's death in 1953, Kosygin lost his vice premiership and Politburo membership but held various economic ministerships. He again became a Politburo candidate member in 1957, Politburo member and vice premier in 1960, and finally in 1964, after Nikita Khrushchev's resignation, he became premier of the USSR. He is the first trained economist to become premier.

ELLSWORTH RAYMOND
New York University

KUWAIT

In 1969 leaders of Kuwait voiced concern at many world forums over the plight of the Palestinian Arabs. Kuwait supported various commando organizations in their activities against Israel.

Foreign Affairs. In September, Amir Sabah al-Salim al-Sabah attended the Muslim summit meeting in Rabat, Morocco, where he urged a unified stand against the incorporation of all Jerusalem into Israel. At the fifth Arab summit meeting in Rabat in December he supported the Palestinian movement but would not agree to increase his country's aid to Jordan and the United Arab Republic. He did agree to continue placing Kuwaiti troops in the UAR to support the fighting around the Suez Canal.

Economy. Oil, the basis of the economy of Kuwait, contributes an overwhelming part of the income of the state. The 1969–70 budget estimated an income of $847 million and expenditures of $657 million. The surplus is invested for future contingencies or put into the Kuwait Fund for Arab Economic Development (KFAED). By the end of its 7th fiscal year in March, KFAED had made loans of more than $192 million to other Arab governments or Arab public organizations. Kuwait contributes $130 million annually to Jordan and the United Arab Republic to offset the loss of revenue from the closing of the Suez Canal.

In June contracts were signed with a French firm for a 5-unit distillation plant which will double the country's water supply by 1973.

State Development. A $4 million industrial training center that will aid 300 workers a year was started, and a low income housing development for over 300 families was under construction. Plans were announced for establishing a medical school.

SYDNEY NETTLETON FISHER
The Ohio State University

KUWAIT

Information Highlights

Area: 6,178 square miles (16,000 sq km).
Population: 540,000 (1968 est.).
Chief City (1965 census): Kuwait City, the capital, 99,609.
Government: *Head of State* (Amir)—Sabah al-Salim al-Sabah (acceded Nov. 27, 1965); *Prime Minister*—Jabir al-Ahmad al-Jabir (took office Nov. 30, 1965). *Parliament*—National Assembly, 50 members.
Religious Faiths: Muslims, 94% of population.
Education: *Literacy rate* (1969), 50% of population. *Total school enrollment* (1966)—92,988.
Finance (1969 est.): *Revenues,* $724,400,000; monetary unit, dinar (0.3571 dinar equals U. S.$1).
Gross National Product (1967): $2,542,000,000.
National Income (1967): $1,800,000,000; *average annual income per person,* $3,333.
Manufacturing (metric tons, 1967): Residual fuel oil, 314,000; fertilizer, 123,500.
Minerals (metric tons, 1967): Crude petroleum, 115,175,000; natural gas, 1,982,000,000 cubic meters.
Foreign Trade (1968): *Exports,* $1,391,000,000 (chief export, 1967: crude petroleum); *Imports,* $611,000,000.
Transportation: *Roads* (1969), 750 miles (1,200 km); *motor vehicles* (1967), 106,600 (automobiles 73,000).
Communications: *Telephones* (1968), 43,012; *television stations* (1968), 2; *television sets* (1968), 80,000.

The biggest U. S. strike of the year, beginning on October 27, involved nearly 150,000 General Electric workers. At year's end, 90% of GE's production and maintenance workers were still on strike. (*Above*) Workers at GE's plant in Lynn, Mass., scuffle with police as massive walkout begins.

LABOR

A marked increase in unemployment, particularly Negro unemployment, in the wake of the U. S. government's anti-inflation policies was feared but did not materialize in 1969. Unemployment has remained generally at or below 4% since December 1965. It fell to 3.3% in December 1968 and stayed there in January and February 1969, the lowest level in 16 years. Although unemployment rose in the second and third quarters, it fell to 3.4% by year's end, averaging 3.5% for the year, slightly lower than in 1968.

The Nixon administration's deflationary fiscal policy and the Federal Reserve Board's tight monetary policy did not slow the economy as much as had been expected. Consequently, gross national product (GNP) was expected to grow about $65 billion—very similar to 1968's growth—to about $930 billion by year's end. In October 1969, consumer prices stood at 5.6% above the level of October 1968 and accounted for most of the increase in GNP over the first three quarters.

STRIKES AND SETTLEMENTS

Workers included under major collective bargaining agreements (affecting 1,000 workers or more) totaled about 2.7 million in 1969, compared with 4.6 million in 1968 and 4.4 million in 1967. In 1969, the workers included were divided about equally between manufacturing and nonmanufacturing. Over 300,000 more workers were represented in bargaining under wage-reopening clauses. By contrast, over 7 million workers received wage increases deferred in agreements concluded in previous years, the largest number during the 1960's.

The median increase in wages and benefits in key settlements (affecting 5,000 workers or more) reached in 1969 was 8.2%, compared with 6.6% in 1968. Median first-year wage boosts in major settlements reached in 1969 amounted to 8.2%, compared with 7.2% in 1968. Typically, deferred wage increases are smaller than currently bargained increases. Thus, the large number of workers receiving deferred increases will tend to lower the size of the median increase for all workers getting raises in 1969.

More work stoppages (5,600) took place in the twelve months of 1969 than in any other year in the 1960's. However, less work time was lost (about 45 million man-days) than in 1968 (about 49 million man-days). Notable stoppages occurred in the East Coast longshore industry, railroads, construction, coal mining, the airlines industry, and the electrical industry. Except for a four-month strike at two public hospitals in Charleston, S. C., public employee bargaining was much quieter than it had been in 1968.

Dock Strike. Unlike its West Coast counterpart, the East Coast dock industry has been strikeprone since World War II. In October 1968, the federal government secured the seventh Taft-Hartly Act injunction affecting the East Coast docks to halt a two-day walkout. No agreement was concluded during the 80-day cooling-off period, which served mainly to delay the walkout until Dec. 20, 1968.

The International Longshoremen's Association sought a substantial wage boost, improved fringe benefits, a guarantee of annual employment, and some control over containerized cargo. The economic issues were not the only obstacles in the bargaining, however, since the longshoremen also sought contracts at the North Atlantic, South Atlantic, and Gulf ports that were as uniform as local conditions permitted. During the 80-day cooling-off period, a tentative settlement had been reached for New York longshoremen, but it collapsed when the parties were unable to agree on its applicability to other North Atlantic ports.

The first agreement was reached at the New York port. However, it took National Labor Relations Board action and a federal court order to get the longshoremen to vote on the tentative settlement as they tried to wait until other settlements were reached. In February, by a 3–1 margin, the longshoremen approved the agreement, which provided a $1.60 an hour wage and fringe benefits boost over the contract's life, improvement in pensions, guaranteed employment for a year, and repacking rights on containers packed within a 50-mile (80-km) radius of New York. The New York settlement keyed later settlements at other Atlantic and Gulf ports.

Railroads. Four nonoperating brotherhoods—the Boilermakers, Electricians, Machinists, and Sheet

NONFARM PAYROLL EMPLOYMENT IN THE UNITED STATES

Division and industry group	1968 Annual Average	October 1969
Total	68,146,000	71,222,000
Manufacturing	19,740,000	20,376,000
Durable goods	11,578,000	12,013,000
Ordnance and accessories	342,100	311,500
Lumber and wood products	601,600	596,400
Furniture and fixtures	473,600	496,000
Stone, clay, and glass products	638,200	668,200
Primary metal industries	1,300,900	1,357,600
Fabricated metal products	1,389,100	1,472,500
Machinery, except electrical	1,957,600	2,012,700
Electrical equipment	1,963,100	2,097,200
Transportation equipment	2,025,600	2,066,700
Instruments and related products	450,600	469,400
Miscellaneous manufacturing	436,100	464,300
Nondurable goods	8,162,000	8,363,000
Food and kindred products	1,780,100	1,881,700
Tobacco manufactures	85,600	91,600
Textile-mill products	984,900	981,100
Apparel and other textile products	1,416,800	1,429,700
Paper and allied products	698,100	722,200
Printing and publishing	1,063,400	1,098,400
Chemicals and allied products	1,031,900	1,045,400
Petroleum and coal products	186,700	192,300
Rubber and plastic products	557,600	586,900
Leather and leather products	356,900	333,600
Wholesale and retail trade	14,111,000	14,849,000
Wholesale trade	3,669,000	3,832,000
Retail trade	10,442,000	11,017,000
Government	12,202,000	12,396,000
Federal	2,737,000	2,727,000
State and local	9,465,000	9,669,000
Services	10,504,000	11,262,000
Hotels and other lodging places	720,300	716,300
Personal services	1,020,700	1,024,400
Medical and other health services	2,653,300	2,914,600
Educational services	1,043,600	1,162,600
Transportation and public utilities	4,348,000	4,498,000
Contract construction	3,259,000	3,610,000
Finance, insurance, and real estate	3,357,000	3,597,000
Mining	625,000	634,000

Note: Figures include all full-time and part-time employees in nonagricultural establishments. Proprietors, self-employed persons, unpaid volunteers, family workers, and private household workers are excluded. Source: Bureau of Labor Statistics, U.S. Department of Labor, except federal government, which is prepared by the U.S. Civil Service Commission.

EMPLOYMENT STATUS OF THE U. S. POPULATION

	Annual Average 1968	October 1969
Total labor force	82,272,000	85,014,000
Civilian labor force	78,737,000	81,486,000
Employed persons	75,920,000	78,325,000
Agriculture	3,817,000	3,332,000
Nonagricultural industries	72,103,000	74,993,000
Unemployed persons	2,817,000	3,161,000

Metal Workers—engaged in a year-long dispute with Class I railroads. The four unions sought a 10% general wage boost, additional boosts for skilled workers, an escalator clause, and other improvements. The carriers insisted that they could not grant the demands because of the danger of upsetting earlier settlements with 13 unions covering about three fourths of the industry's workers. These settlements, reached after President Johnson had impaneled a series of emergency boards, provided wage boosts of 2% effective on Jan. 1, 1969, and an additional 3% increase effective July 1.

The unions planned a selective strike against six railroads, and the railroads threatened to lock out all striking unions to prevent pitting of struck lines against those that were not struck. In early October, President Nixon impaneled an emergency board under the Railway Labor Act, forestalling action by either side at least until December 3.

In late October, the emergency board recommended acceptance of the carriers' offer, primarily because the other rail unions had accepted the terms in "good faith." They also recommended that the carriers accept the union proposal for uniform minimum wage rates and that the parties negotiate a new class I mechanic's rate. An agreement reached on December 4, granting the four unions a larger increase (about 11%) than other railroad workers, was rejected by the Sheet Metal Workers.

Construction. Major settlements concluded in construction during the first nine months of 1969 provided a median wage increase of 14%, considerably higher than the median increase in other industries. But the scheduled bargaining, involving over 400,000 workers, was overshadowed by impromptu bargaining between civil rights organizations and contractors and unions over more and better-paying jobs for Negroes.

Black demonstrations in Pittsburgh and Chicago in midsummer temporarily shut down over $300 million in construction. In both cities, white workers demonstrated against the work stoppages and the protesters, and in Chicago, picketed and disrupted a federal hearing on minority group employment in construction. Mediation by the American Federation of Labor-Congress of Industrial Organizations (AFL-CIO) civil rights department and some intervention by local officials helped the disputants reach agreements in both cities to provide more jobs and training for Negroes and other minority group workers.

In June, the federal government introduced its controversial "Philadelphia plan," which set "goals" for employment of minority group workers in federal or federally assisted construction contracts valued at $500,000 or more. The goals were set for six craft categories—electricians, elevator constructors, ironworkers, plumbers and pipefitters, roofing and waterproofing workers, and sheet metal workers —that had very low minority group membership. The U. S. comptroller general and some congressmen denounced the plan as a violation of the Civil Rights Act of 1964. The comptroller general also threatened not to pay contracts let under the plan. But the U. S. Justice Department issued an opinion stating that the plan did not violate the act. The U. S. Labor Department revised the plan and promulgated it in August. The first contract under the plan was let in November, and the U. S. Departments of Labor and Health, Education, and Welfare announced jointly that all bidders had submitted bids containing acceptable "goals" for employment of minority group workers.

Coal Mining. The growing furor over "black lung" disease came to a head in 1969 when West Virginia coal miners shut down mines in support of pending state legislation to provide compensation to miners disabled by the disease. A West Virginia compensation law was enacted in March, and in October the U. S. House of Representatives and Senate passed separate versions of legislation covering mine inspection and safety, permissible coal dust levels, and interim compensation payments under a federal-state plan. On December 30 President Nixon signed the landmark federal coal mine health and safety measure.

Airlines Industry. In January, National Airlines was struck by the Machinists Union in a dispute over reduction in the size of plane-taxiing crews and suspension of union members. The airline retaliated by locking out about 1,000 unionists. Many of the strikers refused to return to work in spite of two court injunctions and urging by the union.

The dispute was referred to the National Mediation Board under the Railway Labor Act. The union filed court actions for reinstatement of the strikers and to move the dispute along the steps provided in the act. In September, the fifth federal circuit court ruled that the airline had to take back all strikers for whom replacements had not been hired because the mass discharge was illegal under the act. Bargaining in the dispute, however, remained deadlocked as 1970 began.

Electrical Industry. Bargaining between the General Electric Co. and a 13-union coordinated bargaining team, led by the Electrical Workers (IUE), deadlocked, resulting in a strike by 147,000 workers as contracts expired October 26. The company offered a 6% (about 20 cents) hourly wage increase in the contract's first year with wage-reopening provisions for the second and third years.

The union sought about a 90-cent increase over three years, an additional 50 cents an hour for skilled workers, and an improved cost of living escalator. The AFL-CIO mobilized the entire federation to support the striking unions and launched a boycott of all General Electric Co. products just after Thanksgiving.

Public Employment. In March, subprofessional workers, mostly black, at the South Carolina Medical College Hospital and the Charleston County Hospital walked out in support of wage, union recognition, and other demands. Most of them returned to work in July, having won wage increases of 30 to 70 cents hourly, a grievance procedure, ultimate reinstatement of strikers, and other improvements.

During the four-month strike, the strikers received financial and other aid from New York's local 1199 of the Retail, Wholesale and Department Store Union, the AFL-CIO, the South Carolina labor movement, and the Alliance for Labor Action (ALA). The Southern Christian Leadership Conference led day and night protest marches in support of the strikers.

In contrast to the New York teachers' strikes and other teacher walkouts in 1968, teachers con-

WALTER REUTHER (*third from left*) and Ralph Abernathy (*right*) join hospital workers in Charleston, S. C., who struck on March 20 demanding right to join a union.

BLACK WORKERS, protesting discrimination in construction industry, stage marches in several cities, like this one September 15 in Pittsburgh.

fined self-help tactics to very brief stoppages, such as the two-day walkout in Chicago, the one-day boycott in Los Angeles, and the one-day stoppage by half of Indiana's teachers. State and local employees received sizable wage increases and improvements in benefits, partly because of inflationary losses. Federal employees received the last step of a three-stage pay increase intended to make their pay comparable with that in private employment.

TRADE UNION DEVELOPMENTS

Membership in North American national and international trade unions increased to 20.2 million in 1968, according to a Bureau of Labor Statistics survey. Over 18.8 million were U. S. members and the remainder were Canadian. The increase represented a 5% gain since 1966 or just over 900,000 members in the two-year period. AFL-CIO membership was 15.6 million in 1968, a fall from the 16.2 million reported in 1966, but a gain of 880,000 if the disaffiliated United Automobile Workers are dropped from the totals. Over 4.6 million U. S. workers were in national unions not affiliated with the AFL-CIO, including the nation's two largest unions, the Teamsters and the Automobile Workers.

The split in labor's ranks was accented at the eighth biennial AFL-CIO convention in October, when the delegates voted by a 50–1 margin to expel the International Chemical Workers Union for affiliating with the Alliance for Labor Action, organized in 1968 by the Automobile Workers and the Teamsters. The expulsion followed the federation's warning to affiliates that joining the ALA would be a violation of the AFL-CIO's constitution, subjecting the union to suspension or expulsion.

In April, the AFL-CIO issued a 40,000-word report on the dispute with the Automobile Workers. The report branded UAW officials with having figured prominently in the decisions that they later turned around and criticized. The document scored the UAW's "two-year campaign of public vilifica-

tion" and the UAW's failure to agree to resolve the issues within the "forums of the trade union movement." It stressed that the federation had been and would continue to be in the forefront of organizing the unorganized, striving for social justice, promoting minority job opportunities and civil rights, and forging stable international trade union relations. The UAW leadership promised to respond to the federation's charges at a later time.

The AFL-CIO convention voted to increase each member's monthly assessments from 7 to 10 cents per worker to finance organizing, bargaining, and voter registration initiatives in the 1970's. The loss of about $1 million in annual assessments due to the disaffiliation of the Automobile Workers probably also figured in the dues increase.

Alliance for Labor Action. The new alliance of the Automobile Workers and the Teamsters held its first convention in May 1969 in Washington, D. C. Walter Reuther and Frank Fitzsimmons became cochairmen of the organization, and the International Chemical Workers Union was accepted as an affiliate. The alliance turned down the affiliation bid of an independent telephone union and gave loans to two breakaway locals of the Retail, Wholesale and Department Store Union. In September, the alliance named Atlanta as the site of its first concerted organizing campaign.

Leadership Changes. The AFL-CIO convention elected Joseph Lane Kirkland, former executive assistant to President George Meany as the AFL-CIO secretary-treasurer, succeeding William Schnitzler, who retired in June, ending 35 years of trade union activity. At its May meeting, the federation's executive council had appointed Kirkland to the post and recommended expansion of the council from 29 to 35 seats. The October convention elected Peter Bommarito (United Rubber Workers), Peter Fosco (Laborers' International Union), Thomas Gleason (Longshoremen's Association), John Griner (Federal Government Employees), Frederick O'Neal

(Actors' Equity), and Jerry Wurf (State, County and Municipal Employees) to the new posts. In addition, Louis Stulberg (Ladies' Garment Workers' Union), Floyd Smith (Association of Machinists), and Charles Luna (United Transportation Union) were elevated to vacant seats on the executive body.

In significant union elections, the Steelworkers' president, I. W. Abel, had an unexpectedly difficult time defeating Emil Narick, a lawyer for the union, in February. The United Mine Workers' president, W. A. Boyle, after a tough reelection campaign, defeated Joseph Yablonski in December. (Yablonski was murdered, along with his wife and daughter, at the end of the month.) President Joseph Curran of the Maritime Union was certified as properly reelected by the U. S. Department of Labor and a New York federal judge. The union's 1966 election had to be held again in 1968 after a Labor Department suit invalidated the 1966 contest.

John L. Lewis, a key figure in modern labor history, died in June at the age of 89. He had helped to found the industrial union movement and was a fiery representative of the United Mine Workers and the labor movement for 40 years. The UMW closed down the mines in his honor. (See LEWIS, JOHN L.)

COURT DECISIONS AND LEGISLATION

In the *Wyman-Gordon Co.* decision, a 7–2 Supreme Court majority ruled on April 23 that the National Labor Relations Board could require an employer to furnish lists of workers eligible to vote in a representation election to the interested union. The majority, however, disagreed over whether the Board could promulgate "rules" (as it had done in the famous 1966 *Excelsior* case) in the course of deciding a case.

Four justices who supported the Board's order in *Wyman-Gordon* held that the Board had to use the Administrative Procedure Act to promulgate "rules" having the standing of administrative "legislation." The other three justices supporting the decision held that the Board could make rules either in hearing a case or in formal APA proceedings. The two dissenting justices held that the Board could only "legislate" in the APA process and since it had not done this in the *Excelsior* case, it could not apply the

"rule" promulgated in that case in *Wyman-Gordon*.

A company may be ordered to bargain with a union on the basis of authorization cards, even though the union loses the representation election, if the employer commits unfair labor practices that affect the outcome. This was in essence the holding of the Supreme Court in *NLRB* v. *Gissel Packing Co.,* and others, and *Sinclair Co.* v. *NLRB.* The high court agreed with the Board that where an employer commits widespread, "atrocious" unfair labor practices leading up to a representation election, a bargaining order is called for even if the union had never achieved a majority on authorization cards. Where the practices are serious enough to cause a majority on authorization cards to evaporate by election time, the court held that a bargaining order was also proper.

Issues of racial and other invidious discrimination and their relationship to labor-management relations have been raised from time to time, particularly with regard to union discrimination. In 1969, a decision respecting the effect of employer discrimination on labor-management relations was rendered by the District of Columbia Court of Appeals in *United Packinghouse Workers* v. *NLRB.*

The Packinghouse Workers union charged an employer with unfair labor practices and refusal to bargain about elimination of the company's alleged discrimination. The board found the employer violated the National Labor Relations Act with respect to refusal to bargain but did not rule that discrimination violated the act. The appeals court ruled that invidious discrimination violated the NLRA and remanded the case to the board to determine whether discrimination had occurred. In November, the Supreme Court left the appeals court decision standing.

Federal Legislation. The Nixon administration proposed extension of the unemployment insurance system to about 4.8 million workers, a farm labor relations act, coal mine and construction safety bills, and legislation to enable the Equal Employment Opportunity Commission to go into federal court in cases of discrimination.

In August, the President signed the construction safety bill. At the end of the year he signed the coal mine safety bill, which also contained a compensation program for disabled miners. Although Nixon called the new law "an historic advance in industrial practices," he stressed that the compensation provisions were temporary and would not set a precedent for future federal legislation.

It also appeared that some form of the unemployment insurance extension would become law. Under 1966 amendments to the Fair Labor Standards Act, coverage was extended to employees of smaller retail and service concerns on Feb. 1, 1969.

State Legislation. Forty-seven states, Puerto Rico, and Guam enacted some form of labor legislation in 1969. Texas passed a new minimum wage act to replace one repealed 50 years earlier, bringing to 37 the number of states with such laws. Eight states also enacted laws curtailing discharge for wage garnishment. States with laws requiring payment of prevailing wage rates on public construction contracts totaled 39 at the end of 1969. Florida, Idaho, and Minnesota passed "equal pay for equal work" laws. Legislatures continued to deal with public employee bargaining, bringing to 12 the states with such laws. Several states changed their laws affecting minority employment opportunities.

UNION COUNCIL met at White House in May. (*Seated*) AFL-CIO's Meany with President. (*Standing*) AFL-CIO's Schindler between Secretaries Rogers (*left*) and Laird.

The main thrust in unemployment insurance was to improve benefits rather than extend coverage, with considerable examination of financing and review of eligibility provisions. In workmen's compensation, over 200 amendments were adopted by 47 states, including some providing "flexible maximum" benefits (first introduced in 1959) and extension of coverage to "black lung" disease.

THE LABOR FORCE

The civilian labor force averaged about 80.6 million a month in 1969. About 77.8 million people were employed on average, up about 1.9 million from the 1968 level. Unemployed persons averaged 2.8 million a month. About 2.6 million were out of work in January; by October, with unemployment at 3.9% of the labor force, the unemployed had risen to 2.8 million. The unemployment rate then dropped to 3.4%.

The structure of unemployment that has persisted since the 1950's continued in 1969. Roughly twice as many nonwhites, proportionately, as whites were out of work. Women's rates were higher than men's. Teenagers' rates were from 3 to 6 times as high as those for adult men. Blue collar and service workers' rates were twice as high as those for white collar workers and farm workers.

Earnings. In October 1969, average hourly earnings in the nonfarm private economy stood at $3.11, up 20 cents from the October 1968 level. Weekly earnings averaged $116.94 that month, up $6.65 from the level in October 1968, and ranged from $91.52 in wholesale and retail trade to $189.20 in construction.

Although weekly money earnings were up again in 1969, real earnings had hardly changed since mid-1965. In October 1969, a worker with three dependents had spendable average weekly earnings—after deduction of federal taxes—of $101.78, up less than $5 from a year earlier. Real earnings were actually down a few cents over the year. Workers with no dependents were in a comparable situation. A fall in the work week contributed to the fall in money earnings.

Jobs for the Disadvantaged. The U. S. Department of Labor reported that the National Alliance of Businessmen, which was launched during the Johnson administration in the wake of the 1968 urban riots, had placed almost 269,000 disadvantaged unemployed workers in jobs between May 1968, when the program started, and September 1969.

The Nixon administration reorganized the manpower programs with the intent of providing clear lines of authority and more state and local control. Manpower training programs were placed under a new training and employment service.

The administration also sought a $2.3 billion manpower budget—the largest ever—with the lion's share going to states and localities. The administration took the Job Corps out of the Office of Economic Opportunity, cut 59 of its training centers, and placed it in the U. S. Labor Department. All of these changes were made with the intention of moving people more efficiently from school, underemployment, or the depths of unemployment into solid, well-paying jobs.

ROBERT W. FISHER
Bureau of Labor Statistics
U. S. Department of Labor

LABRADOR. See NEWFOUNDLAND.

LAIRD, Melvin Robert

U. S. Secretary of Defense: b. Omaha, Nebr., Sept. 1, 1922.

Secretary Laird's first year in the Pentagon was marked by the elaboration of a changing U. S. defense policy and by a new method of management inside the Department of Defense.

Defense Policy. Laird began to implement a new national defense policy based on a national security memorandum which called for the mainte-  nance of U. S. strategic forces at existing levels but ordered sharp reductions in levels of conventional forces. Laird began to put the new policy in effect by cutting $4.1 billion from the annual defense budget. Future budgets will also be lower, with a $72 billion budget planned for fiscal 1971. The planned reduction in conventional forces was predicated on the success of the "Vietnamization" program for the gradual withdrawal of U. S. forces from Vietnam and their replacement by South Vietnamese troops. In December, Secretary Laird visited South Vietnam.

Internal Management. Under the slogan "people not paper," Laird instituted a policy of participatory management in the Defense Department which contrasted with Robert McNamara and Clark Clifford's emphasis on systems analysis and computers. To implement the new policy, Laird placed major responsibility on Deputy Secretary David Packard and Assistant Secretary for Administration Robert F. Froehlke. Froehlke was also named as coordinator of all intelligence activities inside the Department of Defense. Laird also instituted a "Human Goals" program to stress the role of the individual in the defense establishment.

Programs. Laird gave vigorous support to the Safeguard program for the deployment of a limited antiballistic missile defense system. His testimony before Congress helped the program gain a one-vote victory in August. The secretary of defense also gave attention to improved antisubmarine warfare programs, to an advanced manned strategic aircraft, and to multiple independently targeted reentry vehicles (MIRV's). He advised the President on his decision, announced in December, to renounce U. S. use of chemical and bacteriological weapons.

Career. Laird grew up in Marshfield, Wis., and graduated from Carleton College with a political science degree in 1942. He served in the Navy during World War II, earning five battle stars. He was elected to the Wisconsin Senate in 1946 and to the U. S. House of Representatives in 1952. He served continuously in the House until his appointment as secretary of defense. (He was sworn in on Jan. 22, 1969.)

Laird was a national leader of the Republican party and was chairman of the Platform Committee of the 1964 Republican National Convention. In 1962 he published *A House Divided: America's Strategy Gap*, a book on defense policy.

WALTER DARNELL JACOBS
University of Maryland

LAOS

In 1969 the "forgotten" war in Laos became, in the words of U. S. Sen. J. William Fulbright, a "well-fleshed-out war." The first confirmed U. S. battle death occurred during the year. U. S. air attacks—possibly surpassing the level of onetime U. S. assaults against adjacent North Vietnam—and logistic support of the Royal Laotian forces escalated dramatically in 1969.

The United States and Laos. President Richard Nixon, in response to congressional and press prodding, stated in September that there were no U. S. military forces in Laos "at the present time on a combat basis." According to the U. S. State Department there were 830 U. S. personnel officially in the country, only 75 of whom were military, attached either to the embassy in the capital, Vientiane, or to the country's six military regions.

Persisting press reports, however, claimed that there were approximately 300 U. S. Central Intelligence Agency (CIA) personnel in Laos, mainly attached to local Lao commanders and taking part in combat activity. The State Department figure, moreover, did not include private citizens of the United States, including personnel flying and servicing the CIA-contracted support activity of civilian Continental Airlines and Air America.

U. S. air attacks against the Communist Pathet Lao and North Vietnamese elements increased 5-fold in 1969. U. S. air assaults took mainly two forms: attacks by Thai-based U. S. planes against the Ho Chi Minh Trail, used by North Vietnam to bring supplies to the South; and tactical air support of Royal Laotian forces against both their indigenous Communist and North Vietnamese foes, particularly in the northeastern corner of the country. From May to October, in the wet-season assault against these two types of targets, U. S. planes prob-

ably averaged 200 sorties a day against the Ho Chi Minh Trail and as many as 300 daily sorties against antigovernment forces inside Laos.

Senator Fulbright claimed that the United States was spending $150 million a year for the supply, training, and transport of a 36,000-man "clandestine army" led by General Vang Pao, a progovernment tribesman.

Premier Souvanna Phouma visited Washington in October and indicated that he had received assurances of continued U. S. support from President Nixon. Senate concern over the mounting U.S. involvement in Laos was reflected in the amendment introduced by Sen. John Sherman Cooper to a $20-billion military authorization bill, which stated that none of the funds authorized by the bill could be used for U. S. combat support of "local forces" in Laos or Thailand.

The "Semi-Secret War." The "semi-secret war," as the struggle for Laos came to be called by the press, went from bad to worse for Laotian government forces in the first half of 1969 and then improved dramatically in the late months of the annual wet season (August–October). The government-held town of Muong Soui, northwest of the strategic Plain of Jars, fell to Communist forces in late June despite intense American bombing.

By September, however, not only had Muong Soui been regained, but Lao forces, aided by both the Americans and Thai soldiers (the latter in Laotian uniforms), had taken over the Plain of Jars itself. The successful September assault was the first time government forces had made a major effort to reclaim the key plain since it was lost to the Communists in 1964 in the first major battle of the revived Lao civil war after the failure of the 1962 Geneva agreement to neutralize Laos.

The September assaults seemed to take the Communists by surprise, resulting in little resistance and much destruction of supply caches and disruption of enemy communications. The cost was high for government forces, however—an average of 400 dead a month in fighting throughout the year.

An estimated 50,000 North Vietnamese remained in Laos, augmented by the movement of as many as 4,000 additional Communist Vietnamese forces across the frontier following the Laotian government's September successes. The advent of the dry season in November and the resumption of Communist offensive activity raised the question of whether the government could hold its newly won gains.

Economy. Premier Souvanna Phouma stated in the May budget debate in the National Assembly that the civil war had greatly retarded the government's development program. More than half of the $32 million national budget went to the support of the armed forces. U. S. aid to Laos, in excess of $250 million in 1969 (four fifths of which was for military assistance and training), was the highest per capita U. S. aid to any country in the world.

Rice, once the country's main export, continued to be imported despite U. S. AID efforts to encourage cultivation of "miracle rice." Taxes on imported (and re-exported) gold, which once provided one third of the government's revenue, continued to decline. The United States continued to provide support for the stabilization of the kip, the Laotian currency, and to provide much of the financial support for the country's 200,000 war refugees.

RICHARD BUTWELL
The American University

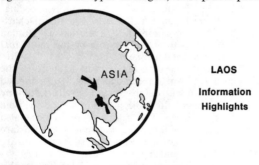

LAOS

Information Highlights

Area: 91,428 square miles (236,800 sq km).
Population: 2,825,000 (1968 est.).
Chief City (1962 census): Vientiane, the capital, 162,297.
Government: *King*—Savang Vatthana (acceded Nov. 4, 1959); *Premier*—Prince Souvanna Phouma (took office June 23, 1966). *Parliament*—National Assembly, 59 members.
State Religion: Buddhism.
Education: *Literacy rate* (1969), 15% of population. *Total school enrollment* (1966)—191,411 (primary, 177,288; secondary, 10,417; teacher-training, 2,171; technical/vocational, 1,300; university/higher, 235).
Monetary unit: Kip (240 kips equal U. S.$1).
Gross National Product (1967): $194,000,000.
Average Annual Income per Person (1967): $70.
Cost of Living Index (1967): 274 (1963=100).
Chief Crop (metric tons, 1967): Rice, 623,000.
Minerals (metric tons, 1967): Tin concentrate, 305.
Foreign Trade (1968 est.): *Exports*, $12,000,000 (chief exports, 1967: tin ore, coffee, spices, forest products); *Imports*, $36,000,000 (chief imports, 1967: machinery, petroleum products, textiles, foodstuffs). *Chief trading partners* (1967): United States (supplied 30% of imports); Britain, France, Japan, Malaysia, Thailand.
Transportation: *Roads* (1969), 2,734 miles (4,400 km); *motor vehicles* (1966), 9,000 (automobiles 6,800).
Communications: *Telephones* (1968): 1,076; *radios* (1964), 50,000; *newspapers* (1967), 7.

Honduran troops view the bodies of Salvadoran soldiers slain in the brief but destructive "Soccer War" in July.

UPI

LATIN AMERICA

Throughout Latin America, the year 1969 was one of rampant nationalism. One more country (Bolivia) saw its democratically elected government replaced by a military junta, raising the number of Latin Americans under the rule of military dictatorships to over 130 million—substantially more than half of the area's total population. Anti-U. S. feeling was evidenced in the expropriation of many privately-owned U. S. business concerns and in the hostile demonstrations that greeted Gov. Nelson Rockefeller during his fact-finding tour for President Richard M. Nixon. After studying the governor's recommendations, President Nixon formulated an "Action for Progress" policy designed to eliminate some of the most glaring inadequacies of the Alliance for Progress program. In Central America, hostility between El Salvador and Honduras escalated in July into a brief but tragically destructive war.

MILITARY RULE AND NATIONALIZATION

Despite repression of democratic institutions and civil liberties, several military regimes won local support through attempts to reduce corruption, check inflation, and foster economic development. The year seemed to bring fresh evidence of the emergence of a new breed of Latin military leader, dedicated to efficiency, growth, and social reform. Military men of this type, coming from the lower or middle classes and equipped with technical skills, appeared to be more deeply loyal to their countries than to the oligarchic class. They soon learned that development policies that included the expropriation of foreign-owned companies could bring them an extra measure of acclaim from a xenophobic public.

Military Dictatorship. In a coup d'etat on Sept. 26, 1969, Bolivia became the ninth Latin American country to succumb to military rule since the inauguration of the Alliance for Progress in 1961. Gen. Alfredo Ovando Candia deposed Luis Adolfo Siles Salinas. The conservative Salinas, as vice president, had succeeded President René Barrientos Ortuño after the latter's death in a helicopter crash (April 27).

When Brazil's President Arthur da Costa e Silva was stricken with a paralyzing stroke on August 29 (he died on December 17), the country's military leaders chose Gen. Emilio Garrastazú Médici to succeed him. Although more in tune with younger, reform-minded military officers than his predecessor had been, the new chief executive inherited a government that had censored the press and the mass media, had stripped hundreds of politicians of all political rights, had purged 70 professors from the two leading universities in April, 1969, and had jailed dozens of Brazilians on unspecified charges. Deeply shaken by massive student and labor riots
(Continued on page 409)

407

In the Dominican Republic, fact-finder Rockefeller (left) confers with President Joaquin Balaguer.

FACT-FINDING TOUR

Nelson Rockefeller, a recognized authority on Latin American affairs before becoming governor of New York State, toured 20 Latin American countries in the summer of 1969 on a fact-finding mission for President Richard M. Nixon. Rockefeller's flying travels led not only to the expected talks with government heads but also to hostile demonstrations by the public in many countries, indicating the existence of widespread Latin resentment of U.S. policies.

OLIPHANT IN THE DENVER POST

"Orders are that we check with the local dictator and ask what we can do for the people."

In Haiti, President François Duvalier (left) and Rockefeller wave from the National Palace.

President Nixon received Rockefeller's reports on his mission and used them to draft an "Action for Progress" program.

and effective general strikes, the conservatively inclined military regime of General Juan Carlos Onganía in Argentina was forced to upgrade education and make concessions to labor groups.

The reform orientation of the military regime of Brig. Gen. Omar Torrijos in Panama was dramatized by an abortive coup d'etat on December 15, led by two self-seeking military aides and supported by conservative businessmen. Restored on the following day as commander of the National Guard, his only official post, the strongman proceeded with a program looking to eventual agrarian reform, economic diversification, and the reduction of the power of Panama's entrenched aristocracy.

Military groups were also restive in such democracies as Chile, where a brief revolt by two regiments caused President Eduardo Frei Montalva to impose a state of emergency, and Uruguay, where the vigor of the military response to guerrilla activity raised the specter of a possible coup.

Nationalization. Much of the thrust for the resurgence of political activism by military groups came from the example of the regime of Maj. Gen. Juan Velasco Alvarado, which had deposed the civilian government of Fernando Belaúnde Terry in Peru on Oct. 3, 1968. On June 24, 1969, the Velasco administration decreed a drastic land reform program, expropriating all rural holdings of more than 390 acres (155 hectares), including two W. R. Grace & Company sugar plantations valued at $20 million and which produced 17% of Peru's sugar. The government had already taken over 18 cattle ranches of the Cerro de Pasco Company. The sugar estates were to be run as cooperatives. Farm land was to be distributed in small plots to landless peasants, and the land owners were reimbursed by the government with government bonds and cash.

In Chile, the popularity of Peru's expropriation policy and the flagging political support for the ruling Christian Democratic party prompted President Frei to "Chileanize" the Anaconda Corporation, a U. S. copper mining concern. The June 1969 agreement provided for the immediate acquisition by Chile of 51% of the stock of the company for $200 million, to be paid over a 12-year period, with the remaining stock to be sold by Jan. 1, 1973. Anaconda officials were to continue managing the mines.

Late in 1969 the new Ovando military regime in Bolivia nationalized the $140-million facilities of the Bolivian Gulf Oil Company, a subsidiary of Gulf Oil Corp. Although the action resulted in the suspension of U. S. aid and the termination of Gulf's annual $6.5 million payment to Bolivia, it brought political support both at home and from the country's neighbors. In December, Argentina announced that it would guarantee a World Bank loan of $23 million for the construction of a pipeline from Santa Cruz, Bolivia, to the Argentine border, assuming a guarantee abandoned by Gulf after the seizure.

Fishing Controversy. An exaggerated nationalism was also reflected in claims by Ecuador, Peru, and Chile that their territorial waters extended 200 miles (320 km) into the Pacific. The United States recognized only a 12-mile (19-km) limit. Between 1961 and 1970, navy vessels from Ecuador and Peru had captured and fined 78 U. S. tuna boats fishing less than 200 miles from their shores. A meeting in Buenos Aires in August between representatives of Chile, Peru, Ecuador, and the United States failed to resolve the dispute.

CUBA, COMMUNISM, AND GUERRILLAS

The 10th anniversary of Fidel Castro's revolution found Cuba with a per capita gross national product (GNP) below that of 1958, despite the Soviet Union's transfusion of aid amounting to $400 million annually. More cordial relations had developed between the Soviets and their querulous ally after Castro threw his support behind the USSR during the Czechoslovakian invasion in 1968. Meanwhile, in Uruguay, Brazil, and Argentina, urban guerrillas, becoming self-sufficient through robbery and kidnapping, increased their terrorism.

Ten Years of Castroism. The first decade of Castro rule in Cuba had succeeded in benefiting rural groups at the expense of urban dwellers and professional and business groups. Medical and educational facilities, extended for the first time to small farmers, reduced child mortality and accounted for a sharp drop in illiteracy. However, per capita income declined from $422 in 1958 to $415 in 1968, and food (including sugar) was rationed.

Meanwhile, urban centers had been neglected, an estimated 500,000 Cubans (or 6% of the population) had fled the country, and the rural housing program had all but been abandoned. The economic blockade of Cuba by the Organization of American States (OAS) had retarded economic development but, more importantly, had given the Cuban government a ready-made excuse for economic failures and had sponsored a siege mentality among the people, reducing resistance to militarism.

The USSR in Latin America. As cold war suspicions receded, an increasing number of Latin countries exchanged diplomatic recognition and approved trade agreements with the Soviet Union. Peru's military regime renewed relations with the USSR in February. Bolivia followed suit in September. Both Venezuela and Ecuador were at the point of renewing Soviet relations, leaving only Paraguay in South America without prospective representation in Moscow. Trade and diplomatic agreements were also being concluded with many eastern European countries.

While Soviet trade represented only 7.2% of the Latin trade total in 1968 (as compared to 43% for the United States), it had increased to $260 million from a 1965 level of $157 million. Soviet influence was the more welcome for the restraint exercised by local Moscow-oriented Communist parties as compared with the activist and guerrilla groups that looked to Castro or Mao for inspiration.

Urban Guerrillas. Whereas rural guerrilla movements appeared to be in general decline, urban guerrillas seriously challenged the public order in several countries. In Uruguay, a movement calling itself *Tupamaros* won considerable popular support by cultivating a Robin Hood image. In Brazil, leftist guerrilla groups, located mainly in São Paulo and Rio de Janeiro, engaged in almost daily bombings and bank robberies. Their most flamboyant act was the kidnapping of the U. S. ambassador to Brazil, C. Burke Elbrick, on September 4. They agreed to release him 72 hours later, after 15 Brazilian political prisoners went to Mexican exile.

INTER-AMERICAN RELATIONS

A year of relative international harmony among the Latin American nations was shattered in July by a short but bloody war between El Salvador and Honduras. The ending of the military phase of the war after only a few days of fighting represented a significant victory for the Organization of American States (OAS) and its new secretary general, Galo Plaza Lasso, but in the months that followed the OAS made little progress in improving relations between the two Central American neighbors.

President Nixon's "Action for Progress" policy for Latin America was finally detailed on October 31, several weeks after he had received the reports of Gov. Nelson Rockefeller of New York, who had made an intensive fact-finding tour of the region on his behalf. The announced new policy of the president incorporated many of the recommendations made by Rockefeller, which in turn had reflected some of the suggestions made to the governor by Latin leaders.

The "Soccer War." The first major military conflict between American republics since the Chaco War of 1928–1935 between Bolivia and Paraguay broke out between El Salvador and Honduras on July 14, 1969. A root cause was the alleged mistreatment of some 300,000 Salvadoran citizens who had moved to Honduras during the preceding two decades, leaving an overcrowded country in which a conservative family oligarchy known as *las catorce* (the 14 families) held a tight grip on 95% of the land. (See EL SALVADOR.)

Increasingly, Hondurans had come to resent the loss of land and jobs to the typically more aggressive Salvadoran newcomers. New legislation denying to non-Hondurans the right to own land began to be applied in 1969, and Honduran bullies started to terrorize the Salvadoran expatriates. By mid-1969 reports of arson, murder, and rape had been carried back to El Salvador by thousands of refugees.

In June, a series of three soccer games, held to determine which country would represent Central America in the World Cup competition, escalated the tension. Crowds in the Salvadoran capital attacked Honduran visitors during the second of these games on June 15, and this was followed by a wave of vandalism against Salvadoran stores in Honduras. El Salvador accused Honduras of genocide and severed diplomatic relations on June 26, and both

PANAMANIAN LEADER Omar Torrijos addresses nation after abortive coup by military aides on December 15.

UPI

governments appealed to the OAS' Inter-American Commission on Human Rights. Full-scale hostilities erupted on July 14, when 10,000 Salvadoran troops invaded Honduras, advancing many miles into that country at several points along their common border.

On July 15, the Council of the OAS called upon the belligerent parties to suspend hostilities. The call was heeded on July 18, but an order to withdraw troops within four days was resisted. Meanwhile, more than 100 OAS staff members were selected to man observation posts in both countries.

The OAS Council summoned a full dress meeting of Consultation of Foreign Ministers for July 26, but El Salvador continued to demand that certain measures be taken to guarantee the rights of Salvadorans in Honduras. By July 28, the foreign ministers were prepared to condemn El Salvador as an aggressor and to impose economic sanctions that would have wrecked its economy. Before the crucial vote, however, Secretary General Plaza met privately in a night-long session with the Salvadoran delegates and secured a troop-withdrawal agreement, whereupon he locked the entire delegation in his office to prevent them from changing their minds before the foreign ministers' meeting could be reconvened (July 29). The troops were withdrawn by August 3.

More than 2,000 soldiers and civilians had been killed and the war had cost both nations many millions in military expenses and economic losses. During succeeding months, Honduras blockaded its section of the Inter-American Highway, depriving El Salvador of this access to other countries of the Central American Common Market (CACM). The exodus of Salvadorans from Honduras under pressure continued, reaching more than 60,000 by the end of 1969. Honduras also continued to boycott Salvadoran products. A piqued Salvador refused to accept $100,000 offered by the OAS for refugee relief. However, diplomatic talks under a moderator from the OAS secretary general were approved by both nations and scheduled for January 1970.

Developments Within the OAS. During his first year in office, Secretary General Galo Plaza Lasso, a respected former president of Ecuador, modernized the structure of the Organization of American States. The developmental role of the organization was strengthened and a major portion of OAS efforts were reoriented to field programs and to projects undertaken in direct response to requests from member governments. Developmental programs were reduced from 31 to 16 to promote more effective use of available funds. New chiefs were appointed to man the major services, new systems of finance control were instituted, and five regional offices were established.

On October 30, Jamaica became the 24th member of OAS.

Evolution of a Nixon Policy. President Nixon's Latin American policy was slow in developing. Soon after his inauguration he requested Nelson Rockefeller, an authority on the area, to make a fact-finding trip through Latin America. The president indicated that the New York governor's report would be closely studied before a new U. S. policy was announced.

The new administration was also slow in making appointments to critical decision-making posts, delaying the selection of an assistant secretary of state for inter-American affairs for two months and a U. S. representative to the OAS for four months.

GUAYAQUIL police officer (*right*) attempts to retrieve slain policeman's gun from civilian during student demonstrations in Ecuadoran port on June 13.

UPI

The former post finally went to Charles A. Meyer, who brought to the position an extensive knowledge of Latin America, where, as vice president of Sears Roebuck, he had extended Sears stores through the area. A career diplomat, Joseph J. Jova, was appointed as U. S. Ambassador to the OAS.

The Nelson Rockefeller Report. Governor Rockefeller arranged his visits to 20 Latin American countries in four separate missions between May 11 and July 7. His entourage included a staff of 25 specialists and a covey of reporters (whose expenses were partly paid by the governor and whose presence guaranteed more publicity than such a fact-finding tour might otherwise have garnered).

In virtually every capital, Rockefeller's arrival catalyzed longstanding Latin resentments and frustrations. There were anti-U. S. demonstrations, some riots, and at least seven deaths. Visits had to be cancelled to Peru because of government hostility and to Venezuela and Chile because of threats of violence. Fear of bloodshed also caused the Bolivian

visit to be reduced to a three-hour airport meeting. Thus, the mission served, among other things, to dramatize the depth and breadth of anti-U. S. feeling in the area.

Rockefeller submitted two reports to the president on September 3. One dealt with sensitive security matters and Rockefeller's estimate of U. S. diplomatic personnel. The other was a 40-page document carrying 20 general and 71 specific recommendations. The Nixon administration was urged to transform U. S. paternalism into a partnership. The report emphasized the danger of Castroism and communism and recommended the creation of a Western Hemisphere Security Council to combat subversion.

The report also recommended that Latin military regimes be accepted—the more so because many of the new soldier-politicians were attuned to popular aspirations. There was a plea that U. S. quotas and tariffs on sugar, coffee, and meat be revised to permit a doubling of U. S. trade with the area by 1976.

SOVIET SUBMARINE passing Morro Castle at entrance to Havana Harbor was part of fleet of seven Soviet warships visiting Cuba in July.

KEYSTONE

Nixon's Action for Progress Policy. President Nixon's long-awaited Latin American policy declaration was presented before the Inter-American Press Association on October 31 and was entitled "Action for Progress for the Americas." Its mood signaled a lower profile for the United States in Latin America and a disenchantment with the moralistic rhetoric and unworkable assumptions of the Alliance for Progress. It reflected a move away from open support for major economic and social change in Latin America and toward a new kind of partnership in which the United States would lecture less and listen more.

Specifically, Nixon recommended that U. S. aid funds be channeled into a multilateral Inter-American agency in order to strengthen Latin participation. He indicated U. S. willingness to deal with any established government, even a military dictatorship. (He provided proof of this on November 27, when he ended the unofficial U. S. embargo against Peru by endorsing a proposed $100-million loan to it by the Inter-American Development Bank.)

President Nixon proposed to upgrade the office of assistant secretary of state for inter-American affairs to the rank of under secretary. He also promised a reduction of non-tariff restrictions on Latin purchases.

Latin Consensus on Inter-American Policy. On May 17, long before President Nixon had announced the Action for Progress program, representatives of 20 countries convened at Viña del Mar, Chile, to formulate their own position on inter-American policies. Their report, called the "Concensus of Viña del Mar," embraced some 46 proposals and was a catalogue of Latin American complaints and recommendations. It demanded the removal of U. S. and European trade barriers to Latin exports, more adequate economic assistance, and hemispheric development of technology, science, and education.

At the 6th meeting of the Inter-American Economic and Social Council (IA-ECOSOC), held in Port of Spain, Trinidad, in June, the United States, in a partial response to the Latin consensus, announced the termination of the much disliked "additionality clause." This rule, invoked in 1964 to slow the dollar drain, had, in effect, required that the Latin nations spend most of their aid funds in the United States, even though the goods that they desired might be purchased elsewhere for less.

SOCIAL AND ECONOMIC DEVELOPMENT

Despite a 2.5% per capita economic growth rate for Latin America in 1969, the decade-old Alliance for Progress was besieged by the same problems that it had confronted in 1961. The region was plunged more deeply into foreign debt, it had lost ground in world trade, and unemployment levels were continuing to rise. Spiraling population, declining per capita farm production, and the failures of experiments in regional economic cooperation remained troublesome.

Trade. Latin American export earnings in 1969 climbed to $12.9 billion, 3% above the 1968 total and substantially above the levels of the early 1960's. However, recent trends in world trade had been unfavorable to Latin America, which was competing with Africa and Asia in exports of basic commodities, and which had been slow in developing manufactures. An average 3% annual increase in Latin exports had been maintained from 1950 to 1969, but world exports had increased at a rate of

7% a year. As a result, the area's share of world trade shrank from 11% in 1950 to about 5% in 1969.

Japanese trade with the area registered phenomenal growth in the late 1960's, having doubled in 1967 and again in 1968, when Japan absorbed $855 million of Latin American exports. Higher coffee prices brought significantly increased foreign exchange revenues to coffee exporting states.

Although the "Soccer War" had seriously disrupted the Central American Common Market (CACM) and negotiations for further tariff reductions within the Latin American Free Trade Association (LAFTA) had come to a standstill, five Andean nations (Bolivia, Chile, Peru, Ecuador, and Colombia) signed the Andean Common Market pact in Bogotá, Colombia, on May 27. The treaty called for the abolition of all tariff barriers among these states in 11 years. The new regional market included 60 million people in an area about half the size of the United States.

Elsewhere, the Caribbean Free Trade Association (CFTA), formed in 1968 by 10 former British colonies and Montserrat, was in full operation. With few exceptions, the treaty had provided for the immediate removal of all tariffs on trade.

Finance. Repatriated profits from U. S. investments in Latin America and the servicing of a mounting public foreign debt for the area made heavy demands on supplies of foreign exchange. The external private and public debt had doubled during the 1960's, reaching $20 billion in 1968. The resulting outflow of profits and interest rose to 36% of Latin America's export income in 1968, as compared to 25% in the 1955–59 period.

During 1968, private U. S. firms had repatriated $812 million in Latin American profits—more than the amount that they had reinvested in the area. The tremendous influence of U. S. business in Latin America was evidenced by the fact that it employed 2 million Latins, that it payed 20% of the area's taxes, and that it produced 12% of the value of Latin America's total output.

U. S. government aid to Latin America, channeled mainly through the Agency for International Development (AID) and the Export-Import Bank, declined from $1,050 million in 1967 to less than $890 million in 1968.

Population Growth and Unemployment. The population explosion not only inhibited the per capita economic growth rate but was also largely responsible for increasing problems in housing, food and water resources, education, and health. Only five of the Latin countries (Argentina, Bolivia, Chile, Haiti, and Uruguay) had population growth rates of less than 3% per year. Because of the rapid rate of increase, public school facilities, which had received major attention under the Alliance for Progress, were lacking for 750,000 more children in 1968 than in 1961.

Population growth, together with sluggish economic development, accounted for an increase in the known unemployed from 18 million in 1960 to 23 million in 1969. Moreover, at current economic growth rates, only 5 million additional jobs could be expected to materialize by 1975, when 25 million more people would need employment. The problem was particularly acute in rural areas, where the annual per capita income of some 70 million people averaged only $90.

MARTIN B. TRAVIS
State University of New York at Stony Brook

LATIN AMERICAN LITERATURE

Two well-known novelists of Latin America died in 1969. Rómulo Gallegos of Venezuela, one of the giants of the Latin American novel, died on April 5, at the age of 85. Best known for *Doña Bárbara* (1929), a study of the struggle between savagery and civilizing forces in the Venezuelan backlands, Gallegos was often mentioned as a candidate for the Nobel Prize. One of the last surviving members of the group responsible for the flourishing of the Latin American novel 40 years ago, Gallegos was also one of the few whose best work withstood the double test of time and greater literary sophistication. Also dead is Bruno Traven (Mexico), widely known for *The Treasure of Sierra Madre,* and identified at last as U. S.-born (1890) Traven Torsvan Groves.

Prose Fiction. Julio Cortázar of Argentina published *62. Modelo para armar,* a collection of tales in which diverse story lines are interwoven and ordinary chronology and structure thoroughly violated, as Cortázar continues his search for hidden meanings behind the commonplace and his defiance of orthodox literary canons. Another Argentine, Eduardo Mallea, published *La red,* a collection of short narratives that present Buenos Aires as an organic being, a development from Mallea's theories of the visible and invisible Argentina.

Younger novelists dominated the Mexican scene. Jorge Ibargüengoitia, who seems to have abandoned the theater, continued his characteristically witty satire of the vagaries of the political scene in *Maten al león.* Orlando Ortiz won a special contest aimed at discovering young talent with his *En caso de duda* and René Avilés Fabila attracted attention with *Hacia el fin del mundo,* a collection of short stories.

Important prizes for the novel went to Alberto Duque López (Colombia), Adrián González León (Venezuela), and Renato Prada Oropeza (Bolivia). González León won the Biblioteca Breve award for *País portátil,* an imaginative account of a trip through Caracas as analogy to Venezuela's recent history. Prada Oropeza was awarded the Casa de las Américas prize for *Los fundadores del alba,* a realistic presentation of Bolivian guerrilla life. A reversion to a simpler technique, mixed with irreverent humor, was used by Antonio Skarmenta (Chile), recipient of the short story award of the Casa in *Desnudo en el tejado.* Other notable collections were *Los días de suerte* by Amalia Jamilis (Argentina), in the vein of Cortázar, and *Nuevo diario de Noé* by Germán Arciniegas (Colombia), celebrating the joy of life and recreating the personal past of a distinguished man of letters.

Poetry. José Emilio Pacheco (Mexico) showed further development in his search for the purification of poetry and the rejection of verbalism in *No me preguntes cómo pasa el tiempo,* recipient of the National Poetry Prize. Marco Antonio Montes de Oca (Mexico) again displayed the baroque richness of his verse in *Pedir el fuego,* but with the addition of a social dimension. Octavio Paz (Mexico) anticipated new trends in *Discos visuales* (1968), an interesting concept which is here reduced to a sort of dial-a-poem. In a more traditional vein was *Immensa soledad del Orinoco,* by Rafael Pineda (Venezuela), winner of the Caracas Premio Municipal.

Drama. Several novelists have successfully cultivated a new genre. The Mexican Vicente Leñero's *Los albañiles,* a widely acclaimed novel, is now a successful drama, and Miguel Angel Asturias staged in Paris his *Torotumbo,* a further recreation of the world of Maya myth which is so important in his novels. Griselda Gambaro of Argentina, who has been highly successful within a contemporary dramatic idiom, received the Argentores Prize for *El campo,* an examination of the concentration camp. Alonso Alegría (Peru), son of the distinguished novelist Ciro Alegría, won the Casa de las Américas award for *El cruce sobre el Niágara,* a dramatic analysis of the nature of human courage and dependence based on the life of the French aerialist Blonden. Ricardo Talesnick's *La fiaca,* a witty assault on urban dehumanization of man, which was a considerable hit in Buenos Aires in 1968, has also had the same success in Mexico.

Essays. *El río de mi sangre,* a posthumous personal memoir by Genaro Fernández (Mexico; died 1959), man of letters and public figure, was of par-

JERRY BAUER

JULIO CORTÁZAR, Argentine writer, continued to defy orthodox literary canons in his *62. Modelo para armar.*

ticular interest. The Casa de las Américas prize went to a left-wing piece, *Peru 1965,* a treatment of the 1965 insurrection by one of its leaders, Hector Béjar Rivera. Long-needed fundamental works in scholarship areas included Walter Rela's *Fuentes para el estudio de la literatura uruguaya* and *Historia del teatro uruguayo.* One of the most interesting works on the Argentine writer Ernesto Sábato is Angela Dellepiane's study *Ernesto Sábato* (1968). Important works of criticism included Emir Rodríguez Monegal's *El arte de narrar* (1968), a study of the contemporary short story. Two important editions are the *Epistolario y archivo* of Mariano Azuela (Mexico) and the *Obras completas* of the Colombian poet Madre Castillo (1671–1742), edited by Darío Achury Valenzuela.

Translations. Important translations include Miguel Angel Asturias' *Strong Wind,* tr. by Gregory Rabassa; Julio Cortázar's *Blowup and Other Stories* and *Cronopios and Famas,* tr. by Paul Blackburn; Emilio Carballido's *The Norther,* tr. by Margaret Peden; César Vallejo's *Poemas humanos;* Nicanor Parra's *Poems and Antipoems;* Juan Carlos Onetti's *The Shipyard;* José Gorostiza's *Death Without End,* tr. by Laura Villasenor; Sergio Galindo's *The Precipice,* tr. by John and Caroline Brushwood; Agustín Yañez's *The Lean Lands,* tr. by Ethel Brinton; Miguel Leon Portilla's *Precolumbian Literatures of Mexico,* tr. by Grace Lobanov and Miguel Portilla; Mario Vargas Llosa's *The Green House,* tr. by Gregory Rabassa; Nestor Rodriguez Escudero's *Litoral,* tr. by Louise Sweetman; an anthology, *Nine Latin American Poets,* tr. by Rachel Benson.

FRANK N. DAUSTER
Rutgers University

LAW

Legal developments in the United States during 1969 reflected a continuing concern with such problems as environmental pollution, campus unrest, civil rights, selective service, constitutional changes, torts, and administration of justice.

Legislation. Amid general dissatisfaction with the Selective Service System, the 91st Congress passed a Draft Reform Law, repealing a provision of the 1967 Military Selective Service Act. It authorizes a random selection system in a prime age group (19–26), with the youngest eligibles to be selected first. Undergraduate students at colleges and universities will continue to be deferred until they obtain degrees or reach age 24.

Congress enacted two laws to reduce environmental pollution. A Clean Air Act authorizes $45 million for research on fuels and vehicles in relation to air pollution, and a National Environmental Policy Act of 1969 creates a permanent council on environmental quality with an annual appropriation of $1 million to pay its members and staff.

Two highly important constitutional changes were under consideration at the end of 1969. With the present electoral college system, a president and vice president can be elected with a minority of the popular vote, provided they obtain a majority vote in the electoral college. The risk, when three candidates run for these offices, is that no one would receive a majority in the electoral college, and in that case, the U. S. Constitution provides that the final vote be decided in the House of Representatives, with only one vote for each state delegation. Following the close 1969 presidential election, Congress proposed a constitutional amendment (H. J. Res. 681), abolishing the electoral college and calling for the election of the president and vice president by popular vote in the nation as a whole. The proposed amendment also provides that if none of the candidates receives more than 40%, then a run-off election will be held between the two candidates receiving the highest number of popular votes. It was adopted by the House of Representatives with 66 more than the necessary two-thirds vote. If passed by a two-thirds vote of the Senate and ratified by the legislatures of three fourths of the states, it would become the 26th Amendment.

A highly controversial constitutional conflict was narrowly avoided during 1969. This involved an application for a constitutional convention to consider depriving the federal courts of jurisdiction over the apportionment of state legislatures. This proposed application was adopted by 33 state legislatures, and lacked only one of the necessary two-thirds Congressional vote required by the U. S. Constitution. However, two of the 33 applications submitted were declared invalid on the ground that the state legislatures making the application were themselves malapportioned. The issue did not come to the fore, because Wisconsin, as the 34th state legislature to consider such an application, voted against it. In the event, however, that another state legislature should apply to Congress for such a constitutional convention, there is little doubt that a bitter political storm would ensue.

An equal employment opportunity (popularly known as the Philadelphia Plan) was devised by the U. S. Labor Department to crack exclusionary racial practices of some construction unions by requiring bidders on federal and federally assisted construction projects exceeding $500,000 to submit specific programs for using minority workers. This was construed as a "quota system" by the U. S. comptroller general, in violation of the Civil Rights Act of 1964. But the U. S. attorney general, in a written opinion, held that it met the provisions of the act.

Case Law. Since the landmark 1961 case of *Dixon* v. *Alabama State Board of Education,* the courts have spelled out the requirements of constitutional "due process" for students violating academic disciplinary rules. The student must be advised of the charges, he must be advised of the actual evidence, and he must be allowed to defend himself; also, he must not be punished unless the charges are substantially proven. As reinforced in *Stricklin* v. *University of Wisconsin Regents,* students have a constitutional right to a hearing before being penalized for infraction of campus rules.

In the civil rights field, a federal government agency was ordered by the U. S. Court of Appeals for the District of Columbia, not to dismiss one of its employees because he was an active homosexual. In *Norton* v. *Macy,* the court held that for dismissal, an agency would have to show (1) possibility of blackmail jeopardizing the security of classified communications or (2) evidence of an unstable personality, or (3) that the individual's contact with the public would be impaired by notorious conduct.

The right to privacy arose in a landmark District of Columbia case involving abortion. The law prohibited all abortions unless "necessary for the preservation of the mother's life or health and under the direction of a competent licensed practitioner of medicine." But a U. S. District Court for the District of Columbia, in *U. S.* v. *Vuitch,* ruled the statute unconstitutional because the word "health" is impermissibly vague, requiring the physician to make a decision at his own peril; and the phrase "necessary for the preservation of the mother's life or health" encroaches on such constitutional rights as personal privacy. Also important is a 1969 California case, *People* v. *Belous,* which declared unconstitutionally vague an 1850 California statute prohibiting all abortions not "necessary to preserve (the mother's) life." This ruling may set a trend in 40 other states with similar abortion statutes.

In the field of torts (civil wrongs), only three states—Massachusetts, Rhode Island, and South Carolina—now allow immunity from tort liability to charitable institutions, particularly hospitals. With the 1969 decision in *Abernathy* v. *Sisters of St. Mary's,* Missouri joined the 46 other states on the now-established theory that charity is a big business, and should be able to pay its own way and also protect itself by liability insurance.

Courts in many state jurisdictions are now allowing "innocent bystanders" to hold both the manufacturer and retailer of an automobile responsible for injuries occurring as a result of defective production. In the past, only the consumer or user of the product could bring such an action. But now, under the doctrine of strict liability, a California Court in *Elmore* v. *American Motors Corp.* held that "if anything, bystanders should be entitled to greater protection than the consumer or user where injury to bystander from the defect is reasonably foreseeable." Courts in Texas (*Daryl* v. *Ford Motor Co.*) and the state of Washington (*Ulmer* v. *Ford Motor Co.*) also followed this trend in 1969.

(See also INTERNATIONAL LAW.)

JULIUS J. MARKE, *New York University*

LEBANON

The fragile national consensus between the Muslims and Christians and among the numerous political parties in Lebanon was subjected to serious strains during 1969. Guerrilla activity against Israel increased following the devastating Israeli reprisal raid on Beirut airport in December 1968. Disagreement over preparations for national defense and over policy toward the guerrillas led to a series of cabinet crises and left the country with only a caretaker government for much of the year. Clashes between the guerrillas and Lebanese security forces were halted only by tenuous compromises.

Guerrilla Activity. Though sympathetic with the objectives of the Palestine Arab guerrillas, the Lebanese government, concerned for national security, attempted to prevent the commando organizations from using Lebanon as a base for attacks on Israel. In April clashes occurred between the Lebanese Army and the guerrillas, and anti-government riots flared throughout the country. Early in May, Yasir Arafat, leader of al-Fatah, the largest guerrilla group, and head of the Palestine Liberation Organization, and Hassan Sabry al-Kholy, a representative of President Nasser of the United Arab Republic, met with Lebanese officials and arranged what proved to be a temporary and unsatisfactory settlement.

By late summer commando activity in Lebanon was again on the rise, and on August 11, Israel retaliated with an air strike against 7 alleged guerrilla bases. Though the UN Security Council, on August 26, condemned this action, Israel again directed air attacks against guerrilla concentrations in Lebanon on September 3 and 5, and carried out commando raids into Lebanon on September 4 and October 3.

The Lebanese armed forces, on October 20, commenced a new crackdown on the guerrillas that came close to involving the country in civil war. The guerrillas seized control of most of the Palestine refugee camps in Lebanon, occupied several areas along the Syrian border, and on October 24 and 25 instigated pro-commando riots in Tripoli, Beirut, and other cities. Again President Nasser intervened

as mediator. Not until November 2, however, was a cease-fire agreed upon in Cairo between Arafat and Maj. Gen. Emile Bustani, commander of the Lebanese Army. A compromise settlement, announced on November 3, reportedly involved government concessions to the guerrillas and agreement by the commandos to respect Lebanese sovereignty and to "coordinate" their activities with the authorities.

Governmental Crises. Faced with dissension in his cabinet and subjected to increasingly bitter public criticism in the wake of the Israeli raid on the Beirut airport, Premier Abdullah Yaffi submitted his resignation to President Charles Helou on January 7. Rashid Karami, the relatively moderate leader of the leftward-leaning Democratic Bloc, managed to assemble a widely representative coalition government on January 15, but members from the conservative Christian parties soon withdrew. On April 24, facing mounting criticism of the government's handling of the guerrilla problem, Karami submitted his resignation. Since no alternative government could be formed, however, he remained in office in a caretaker capacity. After another attempt to resign, Karami, on November 25, was able to form a' new, broadly based coalition government.

Foreign Affairs. Lebanon continued its generally pro-Western stance in world affairs but was drawn into closer relations of either conflict or cooperation with the other Arab states as guerrilla activities increased and as Israel's actual or threatened reprisals posed a rising danger to Lebanese security. The long-standing friction with Syria was intensified by strong Syrian support for the guerrillas, especially for Saiqah, the commando group affiliated with the ruling Syrian Baath party. For 23 days in October and November the Damascus government kept its borders with Lebanon closed, thereby disrupting Lebanon's trade with several Arab states, and Syria threatened even more drastic action to halt Lebanese efforts to curb the guerrillas. On the other hand, Lebanese relations with the United Arab Republic became more cordial as President Nasser twice acted to mediate the Lebanese-guerrilla clashes.

PAUL L. HANNA
University of Florida

LEBANON • Information Highlights

Area: 4,015 square miles (10,400 sq km).
Population: 2,580,000 (1968 est.).
Chief City (1964 census): Beirut, the capital, 700,000.
Government: *President*—Charles Helou (took office Sept. 23, 1964); *Premier*—Rashid Karami (took office Jan. 15, 1969). *Legislature* (unicameral)—Chamber of Deputies, 99 members (party seating, 1968: right-wing alliance, 30; Democratic Bloc, 24; independents and leftists, 45).
Religious Faiths: Christians, 50% of population; Muslims, 34%.
Education: *Literacy rate* (1969), 85% of population. *Total school enrollment* (1966)—492,196.
Finance (1968 est.): *Revenues,* $179,654,000; *expenditures,* $203,930,800; *monetary unit,* pound (3.18 pounds equal U. S.$1 at the free market rates).
Gross National Product (1968 est.): $1,260,000,000.
Manufacturing (metric tons, 1967): Meat, 35,000; olive oil, 8,000.
Crops (metric tons, 1967–68 crop year): Citrus fruit (1966), 250,000; apples, 157,000; grapes, 88,000.
Minerals (metric tons): Lime (1966), 65,000; salt (1967), 25,000.
Foreign Trade (1967): *Exports,* $119,000,000 (chief exports: apples, pears, and quinces, $11,374,200; eggs, $6,254,700; dried beans, $5,748,400; oranges and tangerines, $5,179,-200); *imports,* $471,000,000 (chief imports: live animals, $30,000,000; wheat and meslin, $15,779,800; paper and cardboard, $11,795,500). *Chief trading partner:* Britain.
Transportation: *Roads,* 4,660 miles (7,498 km); *motor vehicles* (1967), 129,100 (automobiles 114,200); *railways* (1965), 208 miles (335 km); merchant vessels (1967), 105.
Communications: *Telephones* (1968): 130,000; *television stations* (1968), 9; *television sets* (1968), 165,000; *radios* (1967), 451,000; *newspapers* (1965), 37.

LESOTHO

The main concerns in Lesotho in 1969 were voter registration, denial of a political refugee's appeal for asylum, a bus accident, and economic development plans.

Voter Registration. Voter registration began on January 13 for the 1970 National Assembly by-elections, which will be held in three constituencies. The registration was announced partly in reaction to opposition party charges that Prime Minister Leabua Jonathan was ruling as a dictator.

Refugee Appeal. On May 30 the Privy Council in London denied the appeal of South African political refugee Joseph Molefi to forestall his deportation from Lesotho. The Supreme Court of Lesotho had ruled in August 1968 that Molefi and 70 other political refugees from the Republic of South Africa did not qualify for asylum under the Geneva Convention. Molefi's appeal was regarded as a test case for other refugees.

Bus Tragedy. On August 5 a bus crashed on a mountainous road in southern Lesotho and plunged down an embankment along the Orange River. More

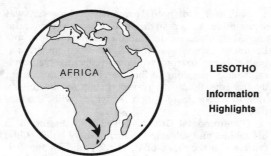

LESOTHO

Information
Highlights

Area: 11,716 square miles (30,344 sq km).
Population: 910,000 (1968 est.).
Chief Cities (1966 census): Maseru, the capital, 14,000.
Government: *King*—Moshoeshoe II (installed March 12, 1960); *Prime Minister*—Chief Leabua Jonathan (took office April 1965). *Parliament*—National Assembly, 60 members; Senate, 33 members.
Religious Faiths: Roman Catholics, 41% of population; other Christians, 30%; others, 29%.
Education: *Literacy rate* (1969), 40% of population. *Total school enrollment* (1966)—171,744.
Finance (1969–70 est.): *Revenues,* $9,500,000; *expenditures,* $9,500,000; *monetary unit,* rand (7.143 rands equal U. S. $1).
Gross National Product (1967): $80,000,000.
Crops (metric tons, 1967–68 crop year): Maize, 110,000; wheat, 50,000; dry peas, 12,000; barley, 4,000.
Minerals (metric tons, 1967): Diamonds, 22,000 carats.
Foreign Trade (1966): *Exports,* $6,100,000 (chief exports, 1966: wool, mohair, diamonds, livestock, foodstuffs; *imports,* $32,100,000 (chief imports, 1966: foodstuffs, manufactured goods, textiles and clothing, transport equipment, chemicals). *Chief trading partners* (1966): South Africa; United States.
Transportation: *Roads* (1969), 1,240 miles (1,996 km); *motor vehicles* (1964), 2,100 (automobiles 1,800).
Communications: *Telephones* (1968): 1,775; *radios* (1965), 25,000.

than 40 persons were killed and about 30 injured.

Economic Development. It was announced in June that Lesotho would receive $151,200 from the United Nations Food and Agriculture Organization. The assistance is part of the Freedom From Hunger campaign organized by Sweden to improve crops.

The World Bank set aside $900,000 to study the feasibility of a project to divert water from Lesotho's mountains into the Hendrik Verwoerd Dam, part of the Republic of South Africa's Orange River Hydroelectric Project. The industrial potential anticipated for Lesotho could free it from economic dependence on surrounding South Africa.

FRANKLIN PARKER
West Virginia University

LEWIS, John Llewellyn

U. S. labor leader; b. Lucas, Iowa, Feb. 12, 1880; d. Washington, D. C., June 11, 1969.

As president of the Congress of Industrial Organization from 1935 to 1940, the height of his career, John L. Lewis was one of the most powerful men in the United States. As president of the United Mine Workers of America for 40 years, until his retirement in 1960, he was one of the two or three most important labor leaders in American history.

His own words to the UMWA described his career well: "I have pleaded your case not in the tones of a feeble mendicant asking alms but in the thundering voice of the captain of a mighty host, demanding the rights to which free men are entitled."

Early Career. The son of an immigrant miner from Wales, Lewis went to work at 12 and was mining coal in Colorado before he was 15.

Lewis' career as a trade union leader began in 1909 when he was appointed legislative agent of the mine workers' union. Two years later he became an organizer for the American Federation of Labor, then headed by Samuel Gompers. In 1917 he was elected a vice president; two years later he became acting president; in 1920 he was elected UMWA president in his own right.

He first attracted national attention in 1919 during a coal strike against which the U. S. attorney general obtained an injunction. Lewis announced, "We can not fight the government." But no miner returned to work. The settlement that followed was regarded as a Lewis victory. But it was his last for more than a decade.

During the 1920's—a period of economic decline for the coal industry—Lewis, as UMWA leader, found himself whipsawed between operators, who knew they could produce all the coal the nation needed on a part-time basis, and unhappy district mine leaders, made querulous and rebellious by the hard times that befell the union. He began a "witch hunt" for Communists within the UMWA; it is suspected that he did so in order to salvage his leadership. Membership dwindled from 400,000 to 150,000. In 1930, Lewis was an unsuccessful leader.

The CIO. Early in the New Deal period Lewis' fortune changed. Using Section 7(a) of the National Industrial Recovery Act, which guaranteed labor's right to organize and bargain collectively, he launched an organizing campaign in the coal fields. But he soon found his success threatened by the AFL's failure to exploit the upsurge of unionism that developed simultaneously in other industries. Angered, Lewis—and seven other labor leaders—organized the CIO in 1935.

Fierce campaigns followed in the steel, automobile, coal, rubber, electrical equipment, textile, garment, and packinghouse industries, and among longshoremen. By the end of 1937 the CIO boasted 3,700,000 members against the AFL's 3,400,000. The UMWA had 600,000.

It was during these and the next few years that

JOHN L. LEWIS, who died on June 11, 1969, is shown in 1961 emerging from a West Frankfort, Ill., mine after investigating a blast that killed 119 men.

UPI

Lewis, as president of the CIO, reached the peak of his fame. They were years of bitter jurisdictional warfare between the CIO and AFL. Employers and editors almost unanimously denounced him as the ruthless enemy of free enterprise; workingmen, also almost unanimously, hailed him as the two-fisted champion of labor's welfare.

Break with Roosevelt. Through most of this period Lewis appeared to be a firm supporter of President Roosevelt. But in 1940, in the midst of Roosevelt's bid for a third term, he announced his opposition. The rift between the two men probably began during the Little Steel Strike of 1937 when Roosevelt called down "a plague on both your houses." Lewis denounced the statement in the pseudo-Shakespearean idiom for which he had become famous: "It ill behooves one who has supped at labor's table and who has been sheltered in labor's house [a reference to labor support in the 1936 presidential campaign] to curse with equal fervor and fine impartiality both labor and its adversaries when they become locked in deadly embrace." In 1940, Lewis informed the CIO that if Roosevelt were reelected against his advice, he would retire as president. He kept his promise.

Later Career. Lewis nevertheless remained in the forefront of the labor movement. As president of the UMWA he led three dramatic strikes: one for union recognition in the captive coal mines of the steel industry in 1941; a second for "portal to portal" wages in 1943; and a third for the establishment of health, welfare, and retirement funds in 1946 (at two different times). These strikes alienated the public. They were a reason for enactment of the Smith-Connolly Act of 1943 and the Taft-Hartley Act of 1947. But for Lewis and the mine workers the strikes were victories.

Lewis engaged in no dramatic struggles with the coal operators after 1946. He worked for federal legislation to assure safer mine conditions and with mine operators to modernize mining methods by introduction of machinery. Although mechanization cost some miners their jobs and reduced union membership to 350,000, it enlarged the miners' health, welfare, and retirement funds.

Joseph G. Rayback, *Temple University*
Author of "A History of American Labor"

LIBERIA

The former chief of staff of the Liberian Army, Gen. Albert White, was arrested, and there continued to be muted dissatisfaction in 1969 over the Fahnbulleh trial of 1968. Otherwise, the situation in Liberia remained relatively quiet.

Internal Politics. During 1969, President William V. S. Tubman celebrated the 25th anniversary of his accession to the presidency. Gen. J. A. Ankrah, Ghana's chief of state, visited Liberia for the celebration and was decorated by the president.

In February, the Liberian Supreme Court dismissed the appeal of former Ambassador to Kenya and Tanzania Henry Fahnbulleh, who had been convicted of treason and sedition in 1968.

The government announced in October the arrest of General Albert White on charges of sedition. General White, in retirement at Tchien, about 350 miles (560 km) from Monrovia, was alleged to have encouraged dissension among the local population.

In November, 75 Negroes who had emigrated to Liberia from the United States in 1967 were asked

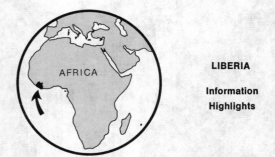

LIBERIA

Information Highlights

Area: 43,000 square miles (111,369 sq km).
Population: 1,130,000 (1968 est.).
Chief City (1962 census): Monrovia, the capital, 80,992.
Government: *President*—William V. S. Tubman (took office Jan. 7, 1944); *Vice President*—William Richard Tolbert. *Congress*—Senate, 18 members; House of Representatives, 52 members (all members of the True Whig party).
Religious Faiths: Protestants, 70% of population.
Education: *Literacy rate* (1969), 5%–10% of population. *Total school enrollment* (1966)—125,642.
Finance (1968 est.): *Revenues,* $55,900,000; *expenditures,* $55,900,000; *monetary unit,* Liberian dollar (1 Liberian dollar equals U. S.$1).
Gross National Product (1967): $240,000,000.
National Income (1966): $168,300,000; *average annual income per person,* $154.
Cost of Living Index (1966): 103 (1963=100).
Crops: Cassava; rubber; cacao beans; palm kernels.
Minerals: Iron ore; diamonds; gold.
Foreign Trade (1967): *Exports,* $159,000,000 (chief exports, 1967: iron ore and concentrates, $115,146,000; natural rubber, $26,573,000; industrial diamonds, $5,356,000; coffee, $2,500,000); *imports* $125,000,000 (chief imports, 1967: nonelectrical machinery, $18,236,000; transport equipment, $10,626,000; road motor vehicles, $9,496,000). *Chief trading partners* (1967): United States (took 30% of exports, supplied 44% of imports); West Germany; Britain.
Transportation: *Roads* (1969), 2,226 miles (3,582 km); *motor vehicles* (1967), 13,400 (automobiles 8,300); *railways* (1969), 300 miles (483 km); *merchant vessels* (1967), 1,496 (23,881,000 gross registered tons); *national airline,* Liberian National Airlines.
Communications: *Telephones* (1968), 3,500; *television stations* (1968), 1; *television sets* (1968), 4,000; *radios* (1966), 152,000; *newspapers* (1966), 3.

to leave the country within seven days. Liberian Attorney General James Pierre said the group had not shown any interest in working or "becoming useful to the country." However, the government apparently reversed its decision a week later and said it would allow the immigrants to take the first steps toward becoming Liberian citizens.

Economic Development. Plans were announced in May for a survey of the iron ore deposits at Wologisi. The deposits are estimated at about 500 million tons and could be made to produce about 10 million tons a year. Liberia is already the largest iron ore producer in Africa.

The Liberian American Mining Company (LAMCO), the largest iron ore concern in Liberia, announced in September that its net earnings for the first six months of 1969 came to $2,391,000; earnings for the same period in 1968 had been $1,399,-000. Between January and June, LAMCO shipped 4,037,000 tons of iron ore and pellets. Total shipments for 1969 were projected at 8 million tons.

Foreign Relations. During 1969, the Liberian government became increasingly involved in attempts by the Organization of African States to end the conflict between Nigeria and the secessionist state of Biafra. The OAU Consultative Committee on Nigeria, of which Liberia is a charter member, met in Monrovia in April. The meeting was not successful in developing any new approach to help resolve the conflict.

Victor T. Le Vine
University of Ghana

MILL VALLEY (Calif.) Library received award from the American Institute of Architects for design that blends with near- by redwoods. Below is an interior view.

libraries

A black-on-yellow button reading "Libraries to the People" was symbolic in 1969 of efforts to bring the library profession into closer conformity with national ideals. The "new" librarians called for the abandonment of professional convenience as a norm of library education and practice and for the advent of less rigidly organized libraries offering services that satisfy community needs. They also asserted that libraries should assume some responsibilities in connection with the major issues of the times —war and peace, race, inequality of opportunity, civil rights, violence, and censorship.

Two new organizations sought to make the li- brary more responsive to its environment. The So- cial Responsibilities Round Table was established in late January to effect internal reform of the Ameri- can Library Association (ALA). The Congress for Change, a coalition of young librarians and library school students, convened in Washington, D. C., in late June to formulate a philosophy of library in- volvement in the issues of the day. Stimulated by a mixed-media presentation showing the gap between social realities and the rhetoric of the "establish- ment," the congress adopted statements calling for greater relevance and flexibility in professional or- ganization, more activity in the area of intellectual freedom, the reform of graduate library school ac- creditation, and improved library service to the urban poor. The group also expressed its opposi- tion to the war in Vietnam.

National Planning. The report of the National Advisory Commission on Libraries (*Library Services for the Nation's Needs: Toward Fulfillment of a National Policy*) urged the creation of a permanent National Commission on Libraries and Information Science. The need for such a commission was underscored during the year when it was determined that the number of libraries in the United States had doubled since 1960. Legislation introduced in Congress in the spring proposed a 15-member National Commission to be appointed by the President; 10 persons with an interest in the informational requirements of society and 5 representatives of professional librarianship and information service would each serve 5-year terms. The issues of the commission's function (planning or political advocacy) and its placement in the government (the White House, or the Library of Congress) were unresolved.

Plans moved ahead for a conference on interlibrary communications and networks to help promote the reconciliation of divergent points of view on network organization. This important conference will be held in 1970 and will be sponsored by the Division of Information Technology and Dissemination of the Bureau of Research of the U. S. Office of Education. The interaction between libraries was reinforced by the approval in January 1969 of a final version of the new Model Interlibrary Loan Code for Regional, States, Local, or Other Special Groups of Libraries.

Federal Legislation. For the fiscal year 1970, Congress had originally authorized appropriations of up to $670.1 million for library programs under the Elementary and Secondary Education Act, the Library Services and Construction Act, the Higher Education Act, and the National Defense Education Act. The fiscal 1970 budget prepared by outgoing President Johnson had requested $134.5 million for library activities, or 20% of the amount authorized.

In its supplementary budget proposals for fiscal 1970, the Nixon administration recommended only $46.2 million for libraries, or 7% of the original authorization. The Nixon budget of $46.2 million, to be divided among 201 million Americans, averaged about 25 cents per person. The $88.3 million difference between the Johnson and Nixon library budgets for fiscal 1970 constituted one fourth of the budget reduction imposed by the Nixon administration on the entire appropriation request for the U. S. Office of Education.

The Johnson budget had proposed $42 million for school library resources, textbooks, and other instructional materials. The Nixon recommendation was for no funds. In the Johnson budget, $49.9 million was asked for public library services and construction, while in the Nixon budget the amount was $23.2 million. The Johnson proposal allowed $42.6 million for academic and research libraries and for education for librarianship. The Nixon budget suggested an appropriation of $23 million.

Because of the apparent low priority given to the funding of library programs, a National Citizens Committee to Save Education and Library Funds was former in 1969. Detlev Bronk, committee chairman, had formerly served as chairman of the National Science Foundation and president of the Rockefeller University.

Library of Congress. The final report on the Machine-Readable Cataloging (MARC) Pilot Project appeared in 1969. As a result of MARC experimentation, nearly 50 institutional subscribers now receive, on a weekly basis, magnetic tapes containing the cataloging records for 1,000 Library of Congress acquisitions. The fundamental contribution of Project MARC at the Library of Congress was recognized when the chairman of the United States of America Standards Institute, Sectional Committee Z39, Library Work and Documentation, approved publication of the draft *USA Standard for a Format for Bibliographic Information Interchange on Magnetic Tape*. Committee Z39 also published two important implementations based on the MARC pilot report: (1) *Preliminary Guidelines for the Library of Congress, National Library of Medicine, and National Agricultural Library Implementation of the Proposed American Standard for a Format for Bibliographic Information Exchange on Magnetic Tape as Applied to Records Representing Monographic Materials in Textual Printed Form (Books)* and (2) *Preliminary Committee on Scientific and Technical Information (COSATI) Guidelines for Implementation of the USA Standard.*

In early 1969, Mansell Information/Publishing Ltd. published the first five volumes of the *National Union Catalog*'s pre-1956 imprints series. The completed book catalog will cover 610 volumes of 704 pages each and will provide the location of 10 million books in about 700 American and Canadian libraries.

The Architect of the Capitol requested $18.4 million during fiscal 1970 for preliminary excavation and foundation work on the James Madison Memorial Building of the Library of Congress.

Other Federal Library Activity. The Department of the Interior held discussions in 1969 regarding the possible establishment of a National Library of Natural Resources. Such a library, which would rank with the National Library of Medicine and the National Agricultural Library as an information source, would collect material in the areas of environmental and ecological science.

Academic Libraries. Student unrest affected several academic libraries during the year. Protesters sometimes focused their anger on the library's card catalog and the shelf list, perhaps the most vulnerable of library files. On the University of California campus at Berkeley, members of the Third World Movement destroyed a portion of the main library's card catalog. At the University of Illinois, some 16,000 cards were removed at random from the public catalog, and 20 black students dumped catalog cards at Queens College in New York shortly after the beginning of the new year.

In a more positive but related development, the United Board for College Development, an extension of the National Council of Churches of Christ, received $233,000 from the Carnegie Corporation to support a center for the cooperative development of libraries in predominantly Negro colleges. The center, to begin by centralizing acquisition and processing of books, will ultimately provide library services to 30 public and private institutions.

Recognizing the breadth and complexity of academic librarianship and the need for firsthand observation of what is occurring elsewhere in the library profession, the Council on Library Resources initiated a fellowship program during 1969 that permits study and travel by a small number of academic librarians who have demonstrated potential for leadership. Fifteen librarians were selected as fellows from a list of candidates prepared by prominent librarians. The council's 12th annual report, which appeared in 1969, indicated a decline of $235,389 in disbursements for 1967–68 as compared with 1966–67. While reaffirming its faith in the application of the new technology to librarianship, the council's report noted that the continuing support of existing projects suggests the need for massive research and automation expenditures, far beyond what the council can afford, in the future.

Public Libraries. A number of experiments in community-controlled library service were under way in 1969 in the predominantly black, and invariably impoverished, urban ghettos of the nation.

The Langston Hughes Cultural and Information Center is a joint effort of the Queensborough Public Library of New York City and leaders in the Corona-East Elmhurst community. In the Midwest, a combination branch public library and cultural center is being developed through the joint effort of the St. Louis Public Library and the Mid-City Community Congress. Containing both a performing arts area and a library emphasizing Afro-Americana, the new center is designed to meet the needs of a poor, inner-city community with approximately 10,000 residents. In Terre Haute, Ind., however, the Vigo county public library met defeat in its attempt to create a railroad-car library in the mainly black Hyte section of the city. Hoping to capitalize on youth's fascination with the railroad, the library worked with the Hyte Section Community Center in the development of the library. A failure in grass-roots communication resulted, however, in interpretation of the railroad-car library as a substitute for new library extension service in the area and in the general belief that no legitimate authority had authorized the placement of the railroad car on Hyte Center property.

In September, the U. S. Office of Education announced that researchers would study library projects in 15 inner cities to discover the most effective ways for public libraries in the nation to reach the urban poor, uneducated, or disadvantaged. Projects in Chicago; Milwaukee; New Haven, Conn.; New York; Oakland; and Philadelphia will be the first to be surveyed in the 9-month study.

Elsewhere, the public libraries of Newark, N. J., and of New York City were beset by financial crises. In February, the Newark City Council voted to cut off all public funds to the Newark Public Library and its offspring, the Newark Museum. When the National Association for the Advancement of Colored People (NAACP), the Congress of Racial Equality (CORE), the Urban Coalition, and the New Jersey Library Association lined up on the side of the library, the city council decided to rescind its action. Because many users of the library and the museum come from outside Newark, it is commonly held that these and other urban cultural and informational services will require more financial support from the state and federal governments. After weathering a crisis over funds to support its public services in branch libraries, the New York Public Library received its first public support for the research libraries in mid-Manhattan. Of the $1 million made available in state and city funds, about half will be employed in support of the library's role in the graduate program of the City University.

Library Response to Urban Change, a study of the Chicago Public Library by Lowell Martin, was published in 1969. This report recommended the expansion of service outlets and bookmobile service and the development of people- rather than goal-oriented programs of acquiring services and materials. It also suggested the creation of neighborhood storefront libraries with locally controlled staffing and planning.

School Libraries. After two years of study by a committee of the American Association of School Libraries and the Department of Audiovisual Instruction of the National Education Association, *Standards for School Media Programs* was published in 1969. These standards apply both to multimedia information centers with print and audiovisual materials and to schools with separate libraries and audiovisual centers. Replacing the 1960 School Library Standards and the 1966 Audiovisual Standards, the new standards connect quality education with the development of unified media programs.

National Library Week. National Library Week, April 20–26, 1969, again had as its theme "Be all you can be. Read." The 12th annual observance of this week was sponsored by the National Book Committee in collaboration with the American Library Association. Support for this activity has waned in recent years, in part because of its emphasis on print and its neglect of other library media.

Library Education. The number of graduate library schools accredited by the American Library Association increased to 48 in 1969 with the approval of the master's degree programs offered by the School of Library and Information Science of the University of Western Ontario, the School of Library and Informational Science of the University of Missouri, the École de Bibliothéconomie of the University of Montreal, and the Department of Librarianship of San Jose State College in California.

In the Office for Library Education of the American Library Association, studies were underway during the year concerning revision of accreditation standards and the education required for different levels of library service. *Criteria for Programs to Prepare Library Technical Assistants* appeared as an outgrowth of these studies and as a result of the demand by community colleges for guidance in the preparation of library technicians.

Awards. The 1969 Beta Phi Mu Award for Good Teaching went to Esther Stallmann of the Graduate School of Library Science, University of Texas. The Beta Phi Mu Award for Distinguished Service to Education for librarianship was received by Ethel M. Fair, director of the Library School, New Jersey College for Women, from 1930 to 1950.

The Melvil Dewey Award for recent creative professional achievement in librarianship was given to William Dix, librarian of Princeton University. The Lippincott Award for distinguished service to the library profession was received by Germaine Krettek, associate executive director and director of the Washington office of the American Library Association. The Mann Citation for cataloging was awarded to Katharine Ball of the Library School, University of Toronto. To Richard Dougherty, associate director of Libraries at the University of Colorado, went the Piercy Award for contributions to librarianship in the field of technical services.

International Library Activity. In 1969, the United Nations Educational, Scientific and Cultural Organization (UNESCO) provided funds to help support the administrative and publishing activities of the International Federation of Library Associations (IFLA) and the International Federation for Documentation (FID). IFLA held its 1969 convention in Copenhagen, Denmark, in late summer; FID held its 35th conference in Buenos Aires, Argentina, in the fall.

DAN BERGEN
The University of Mississippi

LIBYA

A military coup that replaced King Idris I in September dominated the news in Libya in 1969.

Military Coup. On September 1, 1969, King Idris I was overthrown in a bloodless coup led by Col. Muammar al-Qaddafi, president of the Revolutionary Command Council (RCC). A Socialist Libyan Arab Republic was proclaimed. The RCC replaced Premier Wanis al-Quaddafi with Mahmoud Soliman al-Maghrebi.

The coup was conducted by a youthful group of some 60 Arab nationalist army officers with the avowed purpose of ending corruption, reaction, and imperialism in Libya, and of heading off an expected coup by the powerful Shalhis clan of Cyrenaica.

Foreign Relations. The new regime stated that U. S. and British air base agreements would not be renewed. On November 7, Lt. Col. Adam al-Hawaz, the new defense minister, disclosed that Libya had canceled a British agreement for a $312 million antiaircraft missile defense system. Britain agreed to remove all its forces by March 31, 1970. Libya and the United States held talks in mid-December on U. S. withdrawal from Wheelus Air Force Base.

In contrast to the mild anti-Israel stand of King Idris, Colonel Qaddafi declared that "all of our resources will be placed in the service of the battle and the Palestinian cause." The RCC donated $250,000 to the Palestinian Liberation Organization. In late December, after the failure of the Arab

WIDE WORLD

OVERTURNED KING: Libyan students remove portrait of their King Idris, deposed by junta on September 1.

Summit Conference in Rabat, Morocco, it was announced that Libya, the United Arab Republic, and Sudan would meet every four months to coordinate action against Israel.

Domestic Affairs. Arabization of Libyan life and politics was ordered by the RCC. A general amnesty for all political prisoners was declared. The suppression of foreign languages in schools and on public signs was decreed. In mid-November all foreign banks were nationalized.

The new regime guaranteed the security of foreign nationals and properties, and in early October it was stated that foreign oil concessions would be respected as long as the companies respected the interests of the Libyan people. The premier noted that posted oil prices, on which a major share of the government's income were based, were too low. Annual oil revenue was expected to surpass $1 billion in 1969.

On December 10 the government charged that a group of officers in the defense ministry was plotting the overthrow of the RCC. Colonel Qaddafi disclosed that Defense Minister Adam al-Hawaz had confessed his complicity in the plot and had tried to kill himself.

JOHN NORMAN
Pace College Westchester

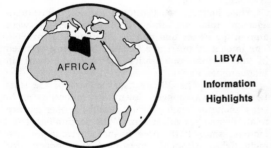

LIBYA

Information

Highlights

Area: 679,358 square miles (1,759,540 sq km).
Population: 1,803,000 (1968 est.).
Chief Cities (1964 census): Tripoli, joint capital, 213,506; Benghazi, joint capital, 137,295.
Government: *Chairman of the Revolutionary Command Council*—Col. Muammur al-Qaddafi (took office following a military coup on Sept. 1, 1969). *Premier*—Mahmoud Soliman al-Maghrebi. *Parliament*—dissolved on Sept. 1, 1969.
Religious Faiths: Muslims, 95% (est.) of population; Roman Catholics, 2.5%; other, 2.5%.
Education: *Literacy rate* (1969), 35% of population. *Total school enrollment* (1966)—256,392.
Finance (1967–68 est.): *Revenues,* $632,800,000; *expenditures,* $632,800,000; *monetary unit,* Libyan pound (.3571 pound equals U. S $1).
Gross National Product (1968 est.): $2,338,000,000.
Average Annual Income per Person (1968): $1,250.
Economic Indexes (1967): *Agricultural production,* 157 (1963=100); *cost of living,* 118 (1963=100).
Manufacturing (metric tons, 1967): Residual fuel oil, 107,000; gasoline, 46,000; olive oil, 27,000; beer, 43,000 hectoliters; tobacco, 145,000,000.
Crops (metric tons, 1967–68 crop year): Barley, 110,000; olives, 134,000; dates, 55,000.
Minerals (metric tons, 1967): Crude petroleum, 82,540,000; natural gas (1966), 361,247,000,000 cubic feet.
Foreign Trade (1968): *Exports,* $1,872,000,000 (chief exports, 1967: crude petroleum, $1,166,130,000; hides and skins, undressed, $71,000; groundnuts, $69,000; fruit and vegetables, $32,000); *imports,* $645,000,000 (chief imports, 1967: nonelectrical machinery, $82.600,000; motor vehicles, $42,110,000; e'ectrical machinerv, $37.910,000). *Chief trading partners* (1967): Italy (took 20% of exports, supplied 29% of imports); West Germany; Britain.
Transportation: *Roads* (1964), 11,577 miles (18.631 km); *motor vehicles* (1967), 92,800 (automobiles 63,200); *railways* (1965), 220 miles (354 km).
Communications: *Telephones* (1968): 25,395; *radios* (1967), 75,000; *newspapers* (1966), 4 (daily circulation, 8,000).

LIN PAIO. See biographical sketch under CHINA.
LINDSAY, John V. See biographical sketch under NEW YORK CITY.
LIQUOR INDUSTRY. See ALCOHOLIC BEVERAGES.
LITERATURE. See AMERICAN LITERATURE; CANADIAN LITERATURE; CHILDREN'S LITERATURE; ENGLISH LITERATURE; FRENCH LITERATURE; GERMAN LITERATURE; ITALIAN LITERATURE; JAPANESE LITERATURE; LATIN AMERICAN LITERATURE; SOVIET LITERATURE; SPANISH LITERATURE.
LOPEZ MATEOS, Adolfo. See biographical sketch under MEXICO.

LOS ANGELES

The mayoralty election, problems in the city schools, and increasing budgets were the big events of 1969 in the nation's third-largest city (metropolitan area, est. pop. Jan. 1, 1969, 7,070,000).

Elections. Two-term Mayor Sam Yorty lost the April primary to Councilman Thomas Bradley, a Negro, who won 46% of the vote to Yorty's 26% in an election in which there were 14 candidates. But when the votes were counted in the May run-off election, Yorty had won his third term with 53% to 47% for Bradley. Public opinion pollsters had picked Bradley to win by margins of from 5% to 18%. An unusually large number—80%—of the eligible voters—turned out for the election.

California's 27th congressional district in Los Angeles elected Barry Goldwater, Jr., son of the 1964 presidential candidate, to Congress.

City Councilman Douglas F. Dollarhide was elected mayor of Compton. This inner suburb of Los Angeles became the largest city west of the Mississippi to have a Negro mayor. Blacks make up 61.5% of Compton's 78,000 people.

Weather. In rains that began in January, and continued intermittently through March, southern California suffered the worst storm damage in over 100 years. Rain-soaked hills collapsed in many areas, hundreds of homes were destroyed, and millions of dollars worth of damage was done. Particularly hard-hit were the hillside developments in some of the affluent metropolitan areas. As late as November, an entire cliff, possibly weakened by the storms, began slipping into the Pacific, destroying a dozen expensive homes. A series of small earthquakes that rolled through the Los Angeles area in late October also may have contributed to the collapse of the rain-soaked hills.

Education. The city's board of education adopted a $690 million budget, which required a 56-cent rise in the property tax rate. School Superintendent Jack Crowther had indicated the need for another $26 million to take care of the additional 22,500 students expected in the 1969–70 school year. The final budget was $41 million higher than that of the previous year. The tax rate increase will be the largest in the district's history.

Los Angeles residents continued to be concerned about reading-test scores indicating that, compared with national norms, students of the city's schools had subnormal reading skills. There was some improvement toward national norms at the year's end.

A one-day teachers' strike in mid-September closed 279 of the 565 Los Angeles city schools. Teacher's demands included increased pay, more money for supplies, limitation of the size of classes, an end to double sessions, and arbitration of teacher grievances.

A Los Angeles county superior court convicted 20 of the 21 San Fernando Valley State College students involved in a 1968 student take-over of the administration building. UCLA, in West Los Angeles, received national attention in a controversy over the hiring of a black professor of philosophy who admitted she was a Communist. (See also CALIFORNIA.)

Sirhan Trial. Sirhan B. Sirhan, who was accused of assassinating Sen. Robert F. Kennedy, was convicted of the crime on April 17 after a lengthy trial. At the year's end he was finishing his eighth month in San Quentin's death row.

Budgets. The Los Angeles City Council adopted a $467 million budget, $20.2 million higher than that of the previous year. Nevertheless, the Council was able to reduce the record high tax rate by 6.43 cents. The county's budget rose to a record $1.46 billion, and the county's tax rate was increased by 28.73 cents, the biggest increase since 1950–51.

Tate Murder. The city was shocked by the bizarre slaying of five people, including actress Sharon Tate and heiress Abigail Folger, on August 9 in Beverly Hills. Months of police investigation resulted in the arrest in December of members of a nomadic hippie band. Long legal battles were expected before trials. (See also CRIME.)

New Police Chief. The city got a new police chief, Edward M. Davis, the 52-year-old deputy chief who previously had headed the planning and control section of the department. Davis had been on the force for 29 years. Chief Tom Reddin, who had served since February 1967, resigned early in 1969 to become a newscaster.

Coroner Reinstated. County Coroner Thomas T. Noguchi, fired in 1968 by the board of supervisors for alleged misconduct, was reinstated by the county civil service commission after a 3-week hearing that cleared him of all charges.

GERALD RIGBY
California State Polytechnic College, Pomona

LOUISIANA

State finance, constitutional revision, labor-management relations, and school desegregation were among the issues that concerned Louisiana in 1969. The impact of hurricane Camille in August resulted in the virtual obliteration of several towns in Plaquemines Parish.

Finance. The 30-day fiscal session of the state Legislature was bogged down with numerous problems, including such patently non-fiscal ones as race relations and sex education. With no significant tax increase since 1948, state finances became increasingly tight. Although investment requirements for idle state funds were made more flexible and cash flow procedures were improved, these gains were offset by more revenue dedications, increased retirement benefits, and increased salaries and expense allowances for all elective state officials. Local governments complained that the salary and fee increases and other mandatory appropriations imposed on them by the Legislature were impossible to meet without state aid or authorization to increase their revenues.

The general fund, which had a $7 million deficit at the beginning of the 1968–69 fiscal year, had a net deficit of $21 million by July 1969, the end of the fiscal year. Gov. John J. McKeithen proposed "freezes" and other measures, but the Legislature adopted a budget that increased the deficit to $26 million. The governor sought and obtained an authorization to reduce budgets and determine spending levels in order to balance the budget.

Other Legislation. Spurred by the U. S. Supreme Court decision overturning Missouri's and New York's congressional redistricting plans, and by a local suit, the Legislature passed a new apportionment act more nearly conforming to the court's guidelines. However, the new act applies to the 1970 elections only.

Several proposals for complete constitutional revision, including a plan for a convention and another for revision committees, were introduced but failed to win legislative approval. The Louisiana Law Institute, a professional organization, proceeded with its revision-by-article plan, but the original proponent of this idea, an organization representing business and industrial groups, abandoned it to support a revision-by-subject plan.

Several task forces charged by the Louisiana Council on Governmental Reorganization with making recommendations for both statutory and constitutional changes reported during 1969.

School Desegregation. Efforts to perpetuate the "freedom of choice" plan in local school districts were frustrated by the Supreme Court decision in October invalidating such plans. Private school plans continued to grow, and a number of boycotts took place when schools opened.

Economy. The economy of the state showed a 5% increase in real growth during the year. Construction was slightly higher than in 1968, but industrial growth slowed somewhat, partly because of labor-management difficulties.

Hurricane Camille. Damage from hurricane Camille, which hit the Louisiana coast on August 18, was fortunately confined to the lower delta area. President Nixon declared several parishes major disaster areas, and immediately allocated $1 million in federal disaster funds to the state.

――――― **LOUISIANA • Information Highlights** ―――――

Area: 48,523 square miles (125,675 sq km).
Population: 3,738,000 (1969 est.).
Chief Cities (1969 est.): Baton Rouge, the capital, 174,000; New Orleans, 660,000; Shreveport, 159,000; Metairie, 127,000.
Government: *Chief officers*—governor, John J. McKeithen (Democrat); lt. gov., C. C. "Taddy" Aycock (D); secy. of state, Wade O. Martin, Jr. (D); atty. gen., Jack P. F. Gremillion (D); treas., Mrs. Mary Evelyn Parker; supt. of pub. instr., William Joseph Dodd; chief justice, John B. Fournet. *Legislature*—Senate, 39 members (39 Democrats); House of Representatives, 105 members (105 Democrats).
Education: *School enrollment* (1968)—public elementary, 515,-000 pupils (20,200 teachers); public secondary, 341,000 pupils (15,300 teachers); nonpublic schools, 135,800 pupils (5,580 teachers); college and university (fall 1967), 104,171 students. *Public school expenditures* (1967–68)— $589,400,000 ($754 per pupil); average teacher's salary, $7,448.
Public Finance (fiscal year 1968): *Revenues,* $1,442,978,000 (general sales and gross receipts taxes, $152,229,000; motor fuel tax, $85,269,000; federal funds, $346,547,000). *Expenditures,* $1,449,964,000 (education, $224,741,000; health, welfare, and safety, $332,145,000; highways, $219,-484,000). *State debt,* $737,110,000 (June 30, 1968).
Personal Income (1968): $9,814,000,000; average annual income per person, $2,634.
Public Assistance (fiscal year 1968): $227,164,410 to 322,208 recipients (aged, $101,459,767; dependent children, $46,-299,629).
Labor Force (employed persons, annual average 1968): *Agricultural,* 92,500; *nonagricultural* (wage and salary earners) 1,037,300 (17.1% manufacturing, 21.8% trade, 19.5% government). *Unemployed persons* (Annual average 1968)—65,600.
Manufacturing (1965): *Value added by manufacture,* $2,255,-262,000 (food and products, $350,944,000; transportation equipment, $255,800,000; fabricated metals, $101,534,000; primary metals, $90,746,000).
Agriculture (1967): *Cash farm income,* $649,537,000 (livestock, $216,044,000; crops, $378,030,000; govt. payments, $55,-463,000). *Chief crops* (tons)—Rice, 1,101.750 (ranks 2d among the states); sweet potatoes, 220,000 (ranks 4th); soybeans, 841.064; hay, 644.000.
Mining (1966): *Production value,* $3,430,140,000 (ranks 2d among the states). *Chief minerals* (tons)—Sand and gravel, 18,216,000; salt, 8,736,000; stone, 8,091,000; sulfur, 4,018,000; crude petroleum, 674,318,000 bbls.
Fisheries (1967): *Commercial catch,* 643.300,000 pounds ($37,-300,000). *Leading species* (1966)—Menhaden, 555,852,100 pounds ($9,557,646); saltwater shrimp, 62,269,400 pounds ($24,387,589).
Transportation: *Roads* (1968), 51,742 miles (83,268 km); *motor vehicles* (1968), 1,535,017; *railroads* (1966), 3,809 track miles (6,130 km); *airports* (1968), 8.
Communications (1966): *Telephones* (1969), 1,621,900; *television stations,* 12; *radio stations,* 104; *newspapers,* 22.

Attorney General Indicted. The state's attorney general, Jack P. F. Gremillion, was indicted on March 1 on charges of fraud and conspiracy in the bankruptcy of a New Orleans financial corporation. The federal grand jury charged that Gremillion helped the Louisiana Loan and Thrift Corporation bypass regulation by the Securities and Exchange Commission.

LOUIS E. NEWMAN
Louisiana State University

LUMBER. See FORESTRY AND LUMBERING.

LUTHERAN CHURCHES

Lutheran churches moved closer together in 1969 when a declaration of pulpit and altar fellowship by the American Lutheran Church (ALC) was accepted by the three bodies to which it was offered— the Lutheran Church in America (LCA), the Lutheran Church-Missouri Synod (LC-MS), and the Synod of Evangelical Lutheran Churches (SELC). The latter's action was a token gesture as the SELC voted to become a district of the LC-MS as a prelude to full merger in 1977. (Churches in fellowship are free to practice intercommunion and their pastors to exchange pulpits.)

Affirmative action by the LC-MS had appeared doubtful when its presidency passed from a staunch advocate to an avowed opponent of fellowship. Unseated was Dr. Oliver R. Harms, 67, after seven years in office. Named in his stead was Dr. Jacob A. O. Preus, 49, a conservative theologian and head of the Concordia Seminary at Springfield, Ill.

While approving suffrage for women and their election to boards and commissions of the church, the LC-MS stressed that women must neither hold the pastoral office nor exercise authority over men. Ordination of women is currently under study, and both the LCA and the ALC seem likely to deal with the controversial issue at conventions in 1970. The LC-MC also reversed itself by endorsing selective conscientious objection to a particular war.

Formation of the Lutheran Student Movement marked another step toward closer unity in 1969. The new organization merged the Lutheran Student Association of America, comprising ALC and LCA students, and International Gamma Delta, serving LC-MS students. Lutheran and Roman Catholic students who met for the first time in a joint conference at Boulder, Colo., in August, joined in an unofficial celebration of the Eucharist as a symbol of their quest for Christian unity.

Lutheran and Catholic theologians held the 8th and 9th sessions in a series of doctrinal discussions begun in 1965. The Lutherans met for the second time with the Eastern Orthodox and also initiated talks with both American Judaism and the Episcopal Church.

The Wisconsin Evangelical Lutheran Synod elected Dr. Oscar J. Naumann of Milwaukee to his ninth 2-year term as president. With 370,000 members, it is the nation's fourth largest Lutheran body.

In 1970, Lutheran World Relief passed $200 million in the value of supplies shipped to 46 countries since the material aid agency began in 1946.

A gain of 12,651 members was recorded by Lutheran church bodies in the United States and Canada for a total membership of 9,239,274.

ERIK W. MODEAN
Lutheran Council in the U. S. A.

Area: 998 square miles (2,586 sq km).
Population: 336,000 (1968 est.).
Chief Cities (1965 census): Luxembourg-ville, the capital, 78,721.
Government: *Grand Duke*—Jean (acceded Nov. 12, 1964); *Premier*—Pierre Werner (took office Feb. 26, 1959). *Parliament*—Chamber of Deputies, 56 members (party seating, 1969: Christian Social, 21; Socialist, 18; Democratic (Liberal), 11; Communist, 6).
Religious Faiths: Roman Catholics, 97% of population.
Education: *Literacy rate* (1969), 99% of population. *Total school enrollment* (1965)—55,663 (primary, 36,546; secondary, 12,959; technical/vocational, 5,542; university/ higher, 616).
Finance (1966 est.): *Revenues,* $173,720,000; *expenditures,* $173,967,000; *monetary unit,* franc (50 francs equal U. S.$1).
Gross National Product (1967): $732,120,000.
National Income (1967): $554,000,000; average annual income per person, $1,653.
Economic Indexes (1967): *Industrial production* (1968), 114 (1963=100); *agricultural production* (Belgium-Luxembourg), 102 (1963=100); *cost of living,* 112 (1963=100).
Manufacturing (metric tons, 1967): Crude steel, 4,481,000; cement, 183,000; beer, 528,000 hectoliters.
Crops (metric tons, 1967–68 crop year): Wheat, 49,000; oats, 45,000; barley, 46,000; grapes, 17,000.
Minerals (metric tons, 1967): Iron ore, 6,300,000.
Transportation: *Roads* (1964), 2,759 miles (4,440 km); *motor vehicles* (1967), 84,200; *railways* (1965), 210 miles (338 km); *national airline,* Luxair.
Communications: *Telephones* (1968), 93,767; *television stations* (1968), 1; *television sets* (1968), 42,000; *radios* (1967), 133,000; *newspapers* (1965), 7.

LUXEMBOURG

A coalition of Christian Socialists and Liberals (Democrats) began to govern Luxembourg early in 1969. The economy of the country benefited from overall improvements in the steel industry.

New Coalition. Luxembourg was in the throes of a political crisis at the beginning of 1969. The ministry of Pierre Werner had resigned late in 1968 after the Christian Socialist—Socialist coalition had broken up over the issue of financing social welfare services. Efforts to reform the coalition had failed, and in the general election of Nov. 15, 1968, the Liberals made the greatest gains.

On Jan. 27, 1969, the Christian Socialists and the Liberals reached an agreement on measures to stimulate the economy through creation of new employment facilities, establishment of new industries, restriction of the growth of the national debt, and participation of workers in the management of state enterprises. Christian Socialist Pierre Werner, as premier and minister of finance, announced on January 29 his new cabinet, which took office two days later.

Steel Industry. Luxembourg's economy is heavily dependent on steel. The end of 1968 and the beginning of 1969 saw a reversal of trends in the steel market. For the first time in four years expansion in demand was accompanied by substantial price increases. There was a general increase in demand for durable consumer goods and equipment in Europe, and there were slight increases in overseas demands as well.

Benelux Relations. As a member of the Benelux economic union Luxembourg worked with Belgium and the Netherlands to further economic collaboration among the three countries. At a meeting in The Hague on April 28–29 representatives of the three countries agreed to seek removal of all border controls among their nations by July 1, 1971.

AMRY VANDENBOSCH
University of Kentucky

McCRACKEN, Paul W. See biographical sketch under ECONOMY.

MAGAZINES

The year 1969 brought major changes in two empires that have dominated magazine publishing in this century. One, the once-prosperous Curtis Publishing Company, saw the dismantling of its holdings continue unchecked. The other, Time Inc., moved to forestall trouble.

With the issue dated Feb. 8, 1969, the *Saturday Evening Post,* published continuously for 148 years (with 72 years under Curtis), ceased publication after a 1968 deficit of $5 million. Once the country's most widely read and profitable magazine, the *Post* fell into serious financial trouble in the 1960's, and neither editorial nor management reorganization saved it.

In its final months, the *Post* was published by a new entity called the Saturday Evening Post Company, half-owned by Curtis but controlled by the Perfect Film & Chemical Company, which had advanced Curtis money. Perfect's president, Martin S. Ackerman, was serving as president of Curtis and of the Post Company, but he resigned in March as head of Curtis under pressure of stockholders' lawsuits. One stockholder group, representing the founding Curtis family, won control of Curtis Publishing at the annual meeting, but Ackerman had left Curtis control only of its printing plant and paper mill. Perfect still held the remaining Curtis magazines, *Status, Holiday,* and *Jack & Jill.* Moreover, the printing plant lost the bulk of its business when major printing contracts expired at midyear. Late in 1969 the Curtis interests reacquired *Jack & Jill* and *Holiday.*

Time Inc. continued the reorganizations that began after the death of its cofounder, Henry R. Luce, in 1967. For the first time since Luce's death, the post of chief executive officer was filled; the new occupant was Andrew Heiskell, who was already chairman of the board. Meanwhile, the company's biggest magazine, *Life,* underwent staff and content changes under a new managing editor, Ralph A. Graves, following two years of declining advertising revenue. Time Inc. also moved into the suburban newspaper field with the purchase of two groups of newspapers in the Chicago area.

Awards. The leading award winner was a McGraw-Hill magazine, the *American Machinist,* which won the National Magazine Award and a Jesse H. Neal Award (given to business periodicals) for a special issue on employment training. The Society of Publication Designers gave its 1969 grand award for consumer magazines to *Avant Garde; Architectural Forum* won the award for business magazines.

New Publications. Leisure activities provided the focus of many of the general-interest magazines started in 1969. Among the new periodicals were: *Change* (education), *Family Health, Fly Fisherman, Gap* (for parents of college students), *Girl Talk* (distributed through beauty salons), *His and Hers, Hollywood Now, Jock* (sports), *Living Health, New Lady* (for Negro women), *Pro Sports Weekly, Quarterback, Sapphire* (also for Negro women), *Singles,* and *The Washington Monthly* (political).

New business and professional magazines included *The Analyst* (marketing), *Casting/Engineering, Computer Decision, Computer Services, Electro-Optical Systems Design, Information Science, Medical Insight, Medical Laboratory Observer, Men's Week* (clothing), *Physicians' Portfolio, Pollution Engineering, Priests' Forum, Remote Sensing of Environment, Top Operator* (farming), and *Western Outfitter.*

Discontinued Publications. Besides the *Saturday Evening Post,* the following ceased publication in 1969: *This Week,* the Sunday newspaper supplement published since 1935; *Eye,* a monthly for youth; *American Builder;* and *Careers Today,* which began publication in January and closed in March.

Business Trends. In 1969 the trend toward consolidation and diversification among magazine properties continued. Crowell Collier & Macmillan's purchased Standard Rate & Data Service, the media statistical service, for $17 million; McGraw-Hill, Inc., acquired the American Heritage Publishing Co., publishers of *American Heritage* and *Horizon,* for $9.8 million; and *The New York Times* purchased *Golf Digest* for more than $3 million.

The magazine industry gained in total advertising revenue. Magazine Publishers Association figures for the first nine months of 1969 showed that general and farm magazines received $869,989,024, a gain of 5% over the same 1968 period. The nine-month total of advertising pages was 59,289, up 1% over the same 1968 period. Circulation of 287 general and farm magazines and groups in the Audit Bureau of Circulation totaled 237,101,335 at the end of 1968, a slight increase over mid-1968.

Business publications also gained. The American Business Press, Inc., forecast a rise of $30.5 million in advertising revenue, for a projected 1969 total of $811.8 million. Advertising pages were expected to increase slightly to 1,213,000. The total number of business publications rose by 60 to 2,335, but circulation was off, decreasing by more than 2 million to 57,003,530.

JAMES BOYLAN
Columbia University

MAINE

Maine in 1969 became the 36th state to adopt a personal income tax. Gov. Kenneth M. Curtis was faced with the delicate task of mediating between the claims of the state's growing oil industry, on the one hand, and the claims of conservationist groups and the tourist industry on the other hand.

Legislative Session. From the work of the 104th Maine Legislature there emerged a number of historic actions, including the levying of the state's first personal and corporate income taxes. The personal income tax was graduated from 1% to 6%, and the corporate tax was fixed at 4%. A record $320 million state budget was passed.

The Legislature handed the voters nine bond issues and four constitutional amendments for their action on November 4. The voters approved $85 million in bonds, including a $50 million pollution-abatement measure. Rejected bond issues included $7.5 million for the University of Maine and $21 million for state highway construction. Also rejected was an amendment that would have placed the state's credit behind private college construction.

Education. The new University of the State of Maine, created in 1968 from eight state-supported schools, was the center of much interest. A Comission on Higher Education Policy, headed by Judge Frank Coffin, reported to the chancellor in November. Among the Commission's recommendations were (1) the conversion of Fort Kent and Washington State colleges to two-year institutions, (2) the merger of Gorham State College and the University of Maine, Portland, and (3) the merger of Maine's four vocational-technical institutes with the University of Maine.

Dr. Stanley F. Salwak was named president of Aroostook State College. The establishment of a new college at Bar Harbor, The College of the Atlantic, was announced.

Economy. Maine's economy continued its modest growth. Some of the major activity was fostered by out-of-state oil companies. The Portland city council rezoned Long Island in Casco Bay to permit a Colorado company to build an oil storage and transfer terminal. Conservationists expressed concern about the possible future threat of such industrial development to Maine's natural beauty. Still awaiting favorable action by the U. S. Congress was the Lincoln-Dickey hydroelectric project on the St. John River, and a controversial oil refinery project at Machiasport.

Rising national demands were pressing the mining industry to increase its reserves of raw materials, and Maine began to feel the surge of "hard" mineral exploration, especially for sulfides in combination with copper, zinc, molybdenum, and nickel.

Recreation and Tourism. Tourists flocked to Maine as the state continued to develop a four-season recreational industry. Tourism in 1969 reached an all-time high, 15% above the level of 1968. Over 200,000 people fished Maine waters—about one third of them from out-of-state, and more than 190,000 hunting licenses were sold in 1969.

RONALD F. BANKS
University of Maine

──────── **MAINE • Information Highlights** ────────

Area: 33,215 square miles (86,027 sq km).
Population: 975,000 (1969 est.).
Chief Cities (1969 est.): Augusta, the capital, 21,200; Portland, 67,000; Lewiston, 40,500; Bangor, 37,000; Auburn, 23,500; South Portland, 22,500.
Government: *Chief Officers*—governor, Kenneth M. Curtis (Democrat); secy. of state, Joseph T. Edgar (Republican); atty. gen., James S. Erwin (R); treas., Norman K. Ferguson; Comm. of educ., William T. Logan; chief justice, Robert B. Williamson. *Legislature*—Senate, 32 members (18 Republicans, 14 Democrats); House of Representatives, 151 members (85 R, 66 D).
Education: *School enrollment* (1968–69)—public elementary, 171,000 pupils (7,300 teachers); public secondary, 62,000 pupils (3,900 teachers); nonpublic schools, 30,100 pupils (1,510 teachers); colleges (fall 1967), 25,519 students. *Public school expenditures* (1967–68)—$128,500,000 ($578 per pupil); average teacher's salary, $6,300.
Public Finance (fiscal year 1968): *Revenues,* $313,210,000 (general sales and gross receipts taxes, $62,304,000; motor fuel tax, $29,457,000; federal funds, $64,904,000). *Expenditures,* $311,171,000 (education, $56,327,000; health, welfare, and safety, $54,283,000; highways, $61,904,000). *State debt,* $175,272,000 (June 30, 1968).
Personal Income (1968): $2,757,000,000; average annual income per person, $2,824.
Public Assistance (fiscal year 1968): $25,015,727 to 38,758 recipients (aged, $15,675,705; dependent children, $9,340,022).
Labor Force (employed persons, 413,000, 1969): *Agricultural,* 19,500; *nonagricultural* (wage and salary earners), 375,300 (35.4% manufacturing, 19.2% government). *Unemployed persons* (August 1969)—18,100.
Manufacturing (1965): *Value added by manufacture,* $899,178,000 (transportation equipment, $38,537,000; food and products, $123,488,000).
Agriculture (1967): *Cash farm income,* $214,542,000 (livestock, $133,041,000; crops, $79,356,000; govt. payments, $2,145,000). *Chief crops* (tons)—Potatoes, 1,908,000 (ranks 2d among the states).
Mining (1967): *Production value,* $14,882,000. *Chief minerals* (tons)—Sand and gravel, 11,627,000; stone, 1,159,000; clays, 42,000; peat (1966), 1,600.
Fisheries (1967): *Commercial catch,* 197,437,735 pounds ($22,973,039). *Leading species*—Maine lobsters, 16,489,196 pounds ($13,597,869).
Transportation: *Roads* (1969), 21,309 miles (34,280 km); *motor vehicles* (1968), 479,568; *railroads* (1968), 2,490 track miles (4,007 km); *airports* (1969), 8.
Communications (1968): *Telephones,* 423,400; *television stations,* 11; *radio stations,* 51; *newspapers,* 9.

MALAGASY REPUBLIC

In 1969 the government of the Malagasy Republic sought to encourage the development of trade and diplomatic relations with South Africa.

Foreign Relations. President Philibert Tsiranana continued efforts begun in 1968 to increase trade with South Africa and to encourage South African tourists. Some 1,000 tourists from South Africa were anticipated in 1969; there had been approximately 300 in 1968. The Malagasy Republic joined Mauritius and the French islands of Comoro and Réunion to form the Indian Ocean Tourist Alliance.

Despite criticism from the opposition press, President Tsiranana offered to exchange ambassadors with South Africa and was host to visiting South African business executives. The president believes that the presence in South Africa of diplomats from independent African countries can help produce a conciliatory attitude toward black Africans in the segregated republic. In part, his policy toward South Africa was also a reaction to the post-Gaullist government in France, which has given only uncertain economic support to the French African community.

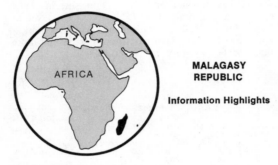

**MALAGASY
REPUBLIC**

Information Highlights

Area: 226,657 square miles (587,041 sq km).
Population: 6,500,000 (1968 est.).
Chief Cities (1966 census): Tananarive, the capital, 335,149; Tamatave (1969 est.), 49,400.
Government: *President*—Philibert Tsiranana (reelected for 2d term, March 30, 1965); *Vice President*—Calvin Tsiebo. *Parliament*—Senate, 54 members (party seating, 1969: Parti Social Démocrate, 52; nominated members, 2); National Assembly, 107 members (party seating, 1969: Parti Social Démocrate, 104; Parti du Congrès de L'Indépendance, 3).
Religious Faiths: Animists, 50% of population; Roman Catholics, 20%; other Christians, 18%.
Education: *Literacy rate* (1969), 30–35% of population. *Total school enrollment* (1965)—740,415 (primary, 672,100; secondary, 55,439; teacher-training, 2,079; technical/vocational, 7,715; university/higher, 3,082).
Finance (1968 est.): *Revenues*, $122,500,000; *expenditures*, $175,100,000; *monetary unit*, Malagasy franc (246.85 francs equal U. S.$1).
Gross National Product (1967): $730,000,000.
Average Annual Income per Person (1967): $115.
Cost of Living Index (1968): 108 (1963 = 100).
Manufacturing (metric tons, 1966): Sugar, 110,000; cement, 60,000; beer, 50,000 hectoliters; tobacco, 1,296.
Crops (metric tons, 1967–68 crop year): Rice, 1,700,000; cassava, 900,000; sweet potatoes and yams, 320,000; bananas, 170,000; maize, 97,000.
Minerals (metric tons, 1966): Graphite, 16,366; titanium concentrate, 6,188; chromite (1965), 2,384; coal (1965), 2,000; monazite, 850; mica, 717.
Foreign Trade (1968): *Exports*, $116,000,000 (chief exports, 1967: coffee, $32,894,000; sugar, $8,669,000); *imports*, $170,000,000 (chief imports, 1966: nonelectrical machinery, $15,487,000; transport equipment, $14,418,000). *Chief trading partners* (1967): France (took 37% of exports, supplied 65% of imports); United States (took 25% of exports, supplied 7% of imports); West Germany (took 3% of exports, supplied 5% of imports).
Transportation: *Roads* (1969), 24,855 miles (40,000 km); *motor vehicles* (1967), 64,100 (automobiles 38,100); *railways* (1969), 532 miles (856 km); *national airline*, Air Madagascar; *principal airports*, Tananarive, Majunga.
Communications: *Telephones* (1968), 22,701; *radios* (1967), 350,000; *newspapers* (1964), 20 (daily circulation, 80,000).

French Devaluation. The Malagasy Republic was represented at the meeting (August 10–13) in Paris of finance ministers of the 14 former French African colonies, whose currencies are tied to the French franc. They discussed the impact of the devaluation of the franc and agreed to devalue their own currencies. It was expected that an adjustment of French export and import payments would leave the Malagasy Republic in essentially the same financial position as before the devaluation of the franc.

Agricultural Loan. In April the International Bank for Reconstruction and Development announced a loan of $2.8 million to Malagasy to finance a pilot project to put livestock production on a marketing, rather than a subsistence, basis.

Cabinet Reshuffle. On December 2 the 12-member cabinet was dismissed; all members but one were soon reappointed. Alleged reasons for the unusual move were to reassert Tsiranana's authority (he was reportedly in ill health) and to offset political opposition in Tananarive and Tamatave.

FRANKLIN PARKER
West Virginia University

MALAWI

Malawi continued in 1969 as the leading independent African nation trying to improve diplomatic and trade relations with the remaining white-ruled African states. Executions for treason, new legislation dealing with the courts, and a request for the departure of U. S. Peace Corps volunteers were other major developments in Malawi during 1969.

Relations with White-Ruled Africa. The presence of a Negro diplomat from Malawi in Pretoria, Republic of South Africa, seemed to indicate a change in that segregated country's attitude toward diplomats from independent African countries. Frank Ntonya, the first secretary of the Malawi legation, arrived in South Africa in February 1968, and during the temporary absence in 1969 of the head of the legation, Philip Richardson, Ntonya acted as chargé d'affaires. The nondiscriminatory acceptance of the 32-year-old Malawian, his wife, and two children was seen as a test case of South African Prime Minister John Vorster's new policy of rapprochement with black Africa. The move was in line with Malawian President Hastings Kamuzu Banda's expanded diplomatic and trade ties with white-ruled Africa.

Malawi's imports from South Africa rose to 15% of its total imports in 1969 as against 7% three years ago. Current South African aid includes $12 million to build a new capital at Lilongwe and $11 million for a rail link to the Mozambique port of Nacala. Banda has also encouraged Portuguese aid, which includes the training of Malawian seamen on the northwest shore of Lake Malawi and plans for a Portuguese-sponsored harbor in Malawi.

Executions for Treason. It was announced on April 21 that eight men had been hanged for their attempt two years earlier to assassinate Banda and overthrow the government. They had been found guilty in a trial held in June 1968. The plot had been uncovered in October 1967, when security forces killed two guerrilla infiltrators allegedly trained by Chinese Communists. Others in the plot were thought to have escaped to Tanzania.

New Court Legislation. On November 18 the Malawi National Assembly passed a bill giving local

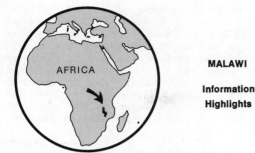

MALAWI

**Information
Highlights**

Area: 45,828 square miles (117,800 sq km).
Population: 4,285,000 (1968 est.).
Chief Cities (1966 census): Zomba, the capital, 19,000; Blantyre, 109,795.
Government: *President*—Hastings Kamuzu Banda (took office July 6, 1966). *Legislature*—National Assembly, 55 members (party seating, 1969: all members of the Malawi Congress party, or MCP).
Religious Faiths: Muslims, Animists, and others, 81% of population; Christians, 19%.
Education: *Literacy rate* (1969), 5%–10% of population. *Total school enrollment* (1966)—296,033 (primary, 286,753; secondary, 6,718; teacher-training, 1,350; technical/vocational, 886; university/higher, 326).
Finance (1969 est.): *Revenues*, $35,500,000; *expenditures*, $42,200,000; *monetary unit*, pound (.4167 pound equals U. S.$1).
Gross National Product (1968): $205,000,000.
Average Annual Income Per Person, $47.40.
Cost of Living Index (1964): 102 (1963=100).
Manufacturing (metric tons, 1967): Cement, 41,000; lumber, 11,000 cu. meters.
Crops (metric tons, 1967–68 crop year): Maize, 1,300,000; cassava, 140,000.
Foreign Trade (1968): *Exports*, $48,500,000 (chief exports, 1967: tea, $10,778,000; tobacco, $10,156,000; peanuts, $8,242,000); *Imports*, $71,000,000 (chief imports, 1966: machinery and transport equipment, $20,028,000). *Chief trading partners* (1967): Britain (took 55% of exports, supplied 28% of imports); Southern Rhodesia (took 4% of exports, supplied 21% of imports); Japan (supplied 8% of imports).
Transportation: *Roads* (1969), 6,411 miles (10,315 km); *motor vehicles* (1967), 14,300 (automobiles 8,400); *railways* (1965), 316 miles (509 km); *national airline*, Air Malawi.
Communications: *Telephones* (1968): 9,127; *radios* (1966), 85,000.

courts the right to try serious civil and criminal cases and to impose the death penalty. Capital cases hitherto had been tried by British-trained judges of the high court, and it was charged that guilty individuals had been acquitted on technical grounds. The new legislation prevents appeals from reaching beyond the district appeals court.

Peace Corps. In a resolution adopted on September 6, the Malawi Congress party asked that the 168 U. S. Peace Corps volunteers leave the country within 18 months. The resolution charged "complaints by our people about the influence that Peace Corps volunteers have over our children because of their bad conduct and behavior and slovenliness."

FRANKLIN PARKER
West Virginia University

MALAYSIA

Malaysia was torn by racial strife in 1969. The worst riots in the nation's history broke out between bands of Malays and Chinese in the federal capital of Kuala Lumpur on May 13, in the aftermath of West Malaysia's parliamentary election. The rioting led to the suspension of the constitution and the imposition of emergency rule.

Elections. In a bitterly fought campaign, the long tenure of the Alliance party, headed by Prime Minister Tunku (Prince) Abdul Rahman, was challenged by a number of opposition parties. The Alliance party, which is comprised of three parties, each representing one of Malaysia's principal ethnic

groups—Malay, Chinese, and Indian—has ruled the country since Malaya achieved independence from Britain in 1957.

Three of the opposition parties drew their major support from Chinese urban electorates—the Gerakan Rakyat Malaysia, the Democratic Action party (DAP), and the People's Progressive party (PPP). The right-wing Pan-Malayan Islamic party (PMIP), militant champion of Malay rights, attracted Malay support in Kelantan and east coast electorates. The opposition parties were united in their desire to cut Alliance margins in the House of Representatives in order to prevent the government from easily amending the federal constitution, which required a two-thirds votes.

In the May 10 elections the Alliance party retained a parliamentary majority but lost 23 of its 89 seats. It registered 49% of the vote, 9% less than its 1964 vote. The PMIP, DAP, and Gerakan all scored impressive gains. The Gerakan won control of Penang state, and opposition coalitions appeared likely in Selangor and Perak. Dissolution of the Alliance party appeared imminent when Finance Minister Tan Siew Sin, leader of the Malayan Chinese Association (MCA), which had lost heavily to opposition candidates, announced that his party could no longer represent Chinese interests in the Alliance nor continue to hold cabinet posts.

Post-Election Riots. When the Gerakan and DAP staged victory celebrations in Kuala Lumpur, Malay activists in Rahman's United Malays National Organization (UMNO) organized counterdemonstrations, and in this heated atmosphere rioting erupted. By conservative government estimates nearly 200 persons were killed and many more injured. Sections of the city were in flames and more than 5,000 persons were left homeless. The Chinese suffered disproportionately heavy casualties.

Emergency Rule. The government quickly proclaimed a national emergency and suspended the constitution on May 14. Two days later the prime minister set up a National Operations Council (NOC), a small executive body headed by Deputy Prime Minister Tun Abdul Razak, to restore law and order and govern the country for an indefinite period until parliamentary government was restored. A prolonged curfew was instituted in critical areas, and large-scale arrests of suspected troublemakers were made. Pending elections in the eastern Malaysian states of Sarawak and Sabah were suspended, and a decree was issued prohibiting customary political party activities, including a ban on all public meetings.

The government initially blamed "Communist terrorists" for instigating the riots, but foreign press representatives on the scene demurred. The official view was later modified to include widespread unrest among unemployed Malay youth as an important contributory factor. Although racial tensions subsided after a second outbreak of violence in June, few informed observers expected an early return to parliamentary government. There was considerable speculation concerning an eventual take-over by a military junta.

Relatively few policy innovations were made by the NOC, which set up an elaborate structure of goodwill committees to allay racial tensions. NOC member Ghazali Shaffie was entrusted with a newly created department of national unity, with the ambitious task of devising a national ideology based on the federal constitution. The primary goal of this effort was ostensibly to perpetuate the constitutionally entrenched position of the Malays. The department's initial assignment was to devise a code of political conduct that would prevent the recurrence of racial excesses in future political campaigns.

Attacks on Rahman. Prime Minister Rahman's long ascendancy as leader of the UMNO and head of the Alliance government was under heavy attack both from within the top UMNO leadership and from a sizable number of Malay students at the University of Malaya and the Mara Institute of Technology. Charging the prime minister with an excessively placatory policy toward the Chinese and with having failed to adopt policies that would significantly improve the economically disadvantageous position of the Malays, these critics demanded that Rahman immediately step down as prime minister. They argued that the recent election results merely confirmed the declining position of the Malays and the growing political assertiveness of the Chinese.

In July, Rahman struck back. Two of his important UMNO critics—Dr. Mahathir bin Mohammed and Musa Hitam—were expelled from their positions on the party's executive council. In August, when students in serious disturbances at the University of Malaya voiced a demand for Rahman's ouster, the NOC ordered police action and four student protest leaders were briefly detained.

MALAYSIA

Information Highlights

Area: 128,430 square miles (332,633 sq km).
Population: 10,384,000 (1968 est.).
Chief Cities (1963 est.): Kuala Lumpur, the capital, 316,230; Kuching (1960 census), 50,579; Jesselton (1960 census) 21,719.
Government: *Paramount Ruler*—Sultan Ismail Nasiruddin Shah (took office Sept. 16, 1963); *Prime Minister*—Tunku Abdul Rahman (took office Sept. 16, 1963). *Parliament* —House of Representatives (suspended May 14, 1969).
Religious Faiths: Muslims, over 50% of population; Roman Catholics, 1.7%.
Education: *Literacy rate* (1960), 22.3% of population aged 15 and over. *Total school enrollment* (1966)—1,987,691.
Finance (1968 est.): *Revenues,* $594,805,000; *expenditures,* $871,720,000; *public debt* (1966), $984,000,000; *monetary unit,* Malaysian dollar (3.08 dollars equal U. S.$1).
Gross National Product (1968): $3,483,000,000.
Average Annual Income per Person (1968): $335.
Cost of Living Index (1969): 105 (1963=100).
Manufacturing (metric tons, 1966): Cement, 784,000; gasoline, 530,000.
Crops (metric tons, 1967–68 crop year): Natural rubber, 1,-933,800 (ranks 1st among world producers); rice, 887,000.
Minerals (metric tons, 1967): Tin, 73,272,000 (ranks 1st among world producers); iron ore, 5,436,000.
Foreign Trade (1967): *Exports,* $1,216,300,000 (chief exports: rubber, $416,500,000; tin, $246,700,000); *imports,* $1,086,-900,000 (chief imports, 1966: nonelectrical machinery, $319,000,000; transport equipment, $148,000,000). *Chief trading partners* (West Malaysia, 1967): Singapore (took 21% of exports, supplied 8% of imports); Japan (took 14% of exports, supplied 14% of imports); Britain (took 7% of exports, supplied 16% of imports).
Transportation: *Roads* (1965), 11,027 miles (17,746 km); *motor vehicles* (1967), 269,900 (automobiles 212,800); *railways* (1965), 1,124 miles (1,809 km); *principal airport,* Kuala Lumpur.
Communications: *Telephones* (1968): 145,425; *television stations* (1966), 10; *television sets* (1968), 100,000; *radios* (1967), 530,000; *newspapers* (1966), 35 (daily circulation, 620,000).

Foreign Affairs. Malaysia's search for a new regional arrangement to replace the British forces expected to be withdrawn in 1971 continued without marked success. Only marginal agreements were completed at the five-power Canberra Conference held in June with Britain, Australia, New Zealand, and Singapore. Australia's Prime Minister John Gorton indicated that only West Malaysia warranted a defense commitment and that his country would not get involved in the Malaysian-Philippine dispute over Sabah.

C. PAUL BRADLEY
Flint College, University of Michigan

MALDIVE ISLANDS

The Maldive Islands, long considered one of the most remote regions in the world, seemed to be starting to move out of isolation in 1969. Modern airstrips made it possible for planes from Colombo, Ceylon, to fly to Malé, the capital island, and to the island of Gan.

The government invited a pop music group from Colombo to perform at Republic Day celebrations in March. The group's appearance was unusual because the majority of Maldivians are Muslims who have traditionally rejected the influences of other cultures. For centuries they have been proud of their isolation and strict adherence to their religion.

The Maldive Islands, with an area of about 115 square miles (298 sq km), are located about 417 miles (671 km) southwest of Ceylon. The population (106,969 in 1968) is scattered over some 215 islands. Malé, with a population of 12,000, is the only one that does not have ample room for expansion.

The islands were formerly ruled by a sultan and became a republic on Nov. 11, 1968. The young president, Amir Ibrahim Nasir, prime minister under the sultanate, is considered a modernist. He is interested in improving the islands' education, public health, and fisheries industry. The basis of the Maldivian economy is dried bonito.

MALI

The new military government of Mali increasingly took on a rational and technical outlook in 1969, as it learned the business of government. Lt. Moussa Traoré, leader of the army junta that had ousted Modibo Keita in 1968, assumed the presidency on Sept. 19, 1969. He replaced Yoro Diakhité, head of the provisional government.

Political Affairs. After releasing "political" prisoners and lifting the curfew, the government announced it would stay in office until economic recovery and national reconciliation were achieved. Military leaders sought a power base by encouraging democratization of the political system, abolishing the hated para-military militia, and keeping an unassuming public style.

Nevertheless, Mali continued to be faced with discontent. There were student demonstrations, and in August an alleged plot, involving military officers, suggested that there was disunity in the armed forces.

Economy. Mali's persistent economic problems caused the government to adopt an economic policy that was both pragmatic and liberal. During 1969, French, U. S., and Soviet aid dwindled. Private enterprise was encouraged to contribute its share to

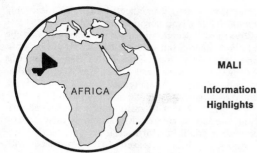

MALI

Information Highlights

Area: 478,766 square miles (1,240,000 sq km).
Population: 4,900,000 (1968 est.).
Chief Cities (1965 census): Bamako, the capital, 165,000 (city and suburbs); Kayes (1969 est.), 32,000; Segou (1969 est.), 32,000.
Government: *President*—Moussa Traoré (took office Sept. 19, 1969).
Religious Faiths: Muslims, 62% of population; Animists, 37%; Roman Catholics, 0.5%; others, 0.5%.
Education: *Literacy rate* (1969), 5–10% of population. *Total school enrollment* (1965)—167,168 (primary, 161,605; secondary, 3,176; teacher-training, 748; technical/vocational, 1,417; university/higher, 222).
Finance (1968 est.): *Revenues*, $33,300,000; *expenditures*, $40,400,000; *monetary unit*, Mali franc (555.41 francs equal U. S.$1 after currency devaluation in August).
Gross National Product (1967): $333,000,000.
Average Annual Income per Person: $70.
Crops (metric tons, 1967–68 crop year): Millet and sorghum, 920,000; rice, 140,000; peanuts (1966), 127,000.
Foreign Trade (1967): *Exports*, $17,000,000 (chief exports, 1967: cotton, $2,448,800; fish, $1,130,200; peanuts, $893,200; fruit and vegetables, $204,500); *imports*, $51,000,000 (chief imports, 1967: textile yarn and fabrics, $3,649,900; transport equipment, $3,028,000; nonelectrical machinery, $1,776,300). *Chief trading partners* (1967): France (took 9% of exports, supplied 30% of imports); Ivory Coast (took 28% of exports, supplied 7% of imports); Communist China.
Transportation: *Roads* (1969), 7,507 miles (12,081 km); *motor vehicles* (1967), 9,400 (automobiles 4,500); *railways* (1969), 416 miles (669 km).
Communications: *Telephones* (1968): 6,670; *radios* (1967), 30,000; *newspapers* (1966), 2 (daily circulation, 3,000).

national development, but the investment outlook remained dismal. A drought and relaxed controls led to lower food production and higher prices, and malnutrition and smuggling continued to be widespread.

Foreign Affairs. The new government reverted to the nonalignment stance that had been abandoned by its predecessor. Relations with the United States, Britain, and Israel were renewed, while those with the USSR and Communist China were maintained. In keeping with its neutrality, Mali saw that editorials on international events were restrained, replaced ideological tirades with low-keyed speeches, and condemned the Soviet Union's intervention in Czechoslovakia.

Mali's neighbor, Guinea, was angered when about 200 Chinese visited Conakry, its capital, after being asked to leave Mali. Guinea charged Mali leaders with complicity in an assassination attempt on Guinean President Touré. It also alleged that armed conflict had broken out between military units of the two countries. Mali denied all allegations and reiterated its desire to cooperate, especially with the development of the Senegal River basin and the building of a Communist Chinese-sponsored railroad between Bamako and Kouroussa, Guinea.

W. A. E. SKURNIK
University of Colorado

MALTA

Britain's 170-year naval link with Malta ended on March 31, 1969, when the last five Malta-based British warships left the island.

British Aid. In late July the British and Maltese governments reached a deadlock over the issue of future economic aid to Malta. Under the agreement on financial assistance that had accompanied independence in 1964, Britain pledged to provide $54.5 million in assistance from 1969 to 1974. The Maltese government took the position that 75% of this money should be an outright grant and that 25% should be in loans, as in the preceding 5-year period. Britain proposed a 50–50 split, with the grant element also including $9.6 million for the dry docks and historic buildings pledged to Malta in 1968. The Maltese prime minister, Giorgio Borg Olivier, categorically rejected the British offer and gave a thinly veiled warning that the 1964 defense agreement might have to be revoked if his demands were not met.

Economy. Malta's economic situation was improved to some extent by a significant rise in the number of tourists—from 40,000 a year in 1964 to 137,000 in 1968—and an influx of new residents seeking a tax haven. The result was a sharp rise in real estate prices and prosperity for builders.

In November the government was reported to be drafting two acts designed to attract foreign capital by giving tax benefits to foreign companies.

Domestic Politics. The opposition Malta Labour party in April strengthened its political position by ending its 10-year rift with the Catholic Church.

RICHARD E. WEBB
British Information Service, New York City

MALTA

Information Highlights

Area: 122 square miles (316 sq km).
Population: 319,000 (1968 est.).
Chief Cities (1967 est.): Valletta, the capital, 17,810; Sliema, 24,500.
Government: *High Commissioner*—Geoffrey Tory (took office Feb. 6, 1967); *Prime Minister*—Giorgio Borg Olivier (took office March 3, 1962). *Parliament*—House of Representatives, 50 members (party seating, 1969: Nationalist party, 28; Malta Labour party, 22).
Religious Faiths: Roman Catholics, 97% of population.
Education: *Literacy rate* (1960), 22.3% of population aged 15 and over. *Total school enrollment* (1964)—58,769 (primary, 55,364; technical/vocational, 2,055; university/higher, 1,350).
Finance (1965–66 est.): *Revenues*, $60,460,000; *expenditures*, $60,000,000; *monetary unit*, pound (.4167 pound equals U. S.$1).
Gross National Product (1967): $152,867,770.
National Income (1967): $138,708,900; *average annual income per person*, $434.
Cost of Living Index (1967): 105 (1963=100).
Crops (metric tons, 1967–68 crop year): Potatoes, 17,000; onions, 4,000; grapes, 4,000; barley, 2,000; dry broad beans, 1,000.
Foreign Trade (1966): *Exports*, $21,406,000 (chief exports, 1967: textile yarn and fabrics, $5,720,000; clothing, $3,530,000); *imports*, $108,400,000 (chief imports, 1967: textile yarn and fabrics, $7,450,000; cereals and preparations, $6,900,000; nonelectrical machinery, $6,500,000). *Chief trading partners* (1967): Britain (took 32% of exports, supplied 39% of imports); Italy (took 9% of exports, supplied 16% of imports); United States.
Transportation: *Roads* (1967), 565 miles (909 km); *motor vehicles* (1967), 35,900 (automobiles 27,400); *Principal airport*, Luqa.
Communications: *Telephones* (1968), 28,100; *television stations* (1966), 1; *television sets* (1968), 38,000; *radios* (1966), 82,000; *newspapers* (1967), 7.

MANITOBA

A political upset placed Manitoba in Canadian headlines in 1969. In July, Edward R. Schreyer took office as Manitoba's new premier. The province became the first in Canada to have a New Democratic party government.

Politics. On May 22, Progressive Conservative Premier Walter Weir suddenly called a general election for June 25 and dissolved the legislature. Premier Weir, encouraged by his party's victory in three of the four by-elections in February, hoped for a decisive endorsement. The principal issues in a generally dull campaign were Medicare premiums and northern development policies, particularly a controversial proposal to flood the Indian community of South Indian Lake to create a hydroelectric reservoir.

In the June 25 elections the New Democratic party won an upset victory under its newly elected leader, 33-year-old Edward R. Schreyer. The NDP increased its seats in the 57-member legislature from 12 to 28, while the Progressive Conservatives fell from 31 seats to 22. The number of seats held by the Liberal party, the former official opposition, fell from 13 to 5. The Weir government resigned on July 15, and Schreyer formed the first NDP government in Canada.

Legislation. The NDP government held its first legislative session between August 14 and October 10. Medicare premiums were reduced by 88%, the decision of the previous government to flood the South Indian Lake village was reversed, the voting age was reduced to 18 from 21, and the office of ombudsman was established. Finance Minister Saul

─────── MANITOBA • Information Highlights ───────

Area: 251,000 square miles (650,091 sq km).
Population: 976,000 (Jan. 1, 1969, est.).
Chief Cities (1966 census): Winnipeg, the capital (257,005); St. Boniface (43,214); St. James (35,685).
Government: *Chief Officers*—lt. gov., Richard S. Bowles; premier, Edward Richard Schreyer (New Democratic Party); atty. gen., A. H. Mackling (NDP); min. of finance, Saul Mark Cherniak (NDP); min. of youth and educ. Saul A. Miller (NDP); chief justice, Charles Rhodes Smith. *Legislature*—Legislative Assembly (elections of June 25, 1969); 57 members (28 New Democratic Party, 22 Progressive Conservative, 5 Liberal, 1 Social Credit, 1 independent).
Education: *School enrollment* (1966–67)—public elementary and secondary, 224,532 pupils (9,430 teachers); private schools, 10,244 pupils (557 teachers); Indian (federal) schools, 6,683 pupils (260 teachers); college and university (fall 1966), 12,389 students. *Public school expenditures* (1963)—$71,885,000 ($376 per pupil).
Public Finance (fiscal year 1968 est.): *Revenues,* $319,480,-000 (sales tax, $106,780,000; income tax, $88,189,000; federal funds, $56,193,000). *Expenditures,* $315,490,000 (education, $122,750,000; health and social welfare, $73,-450,000).
Personal Income (1967 est.): $2,231,000,000; *average annual income per person,* $2,317.
Social Welfare (fiscal year 1968): $12,220,000 (aged and blind, $510,000; dependents and unemployed, $9,030,000).
Manufacturing (1966): Value added by manufacture, $402,-954,000 (food and beverages, $103,823,000; fabricated metals, $38,782,000; clothing industries, $33,392,000; primary metals, $27,795,000; nonelectrical machinery, $25,-899,000.
Agriculture (1968 est.): *Cash farm income,* $368,341,000 (livestock, $172,252,000; crops, $186,971,000). *Chief crops* (cash receipts)—Wheat, $77,540,000 (ranks 3d among the provinces); barley, $12,403,000 (ranks 3d); flaxseed, $15,-399,000 (ranks 1st).
Mining (1967 est.): *Production value,* $182,865,972. *Chief minerals* (tons)—nickel, 55,542 (ranks 2d among the provinces); copper, 29,959 (ranks 4th); crude petroleum, 5,567,000 barrels (ranks 4th).
Transportation: *Roads* (1966), 43,512 miles (70,024 km); *motor vehicles* (1966), 356,693; *railroads* (1966), 4,735 track miles (7,620 km); *licensed airports* (1966) 17.
Communications (1967): *Telephones* (1966), 366,652; *television stations,* 4; *radio stations,* 13; *daily newspapers* (1966), 7. All figures given in Canadian dollars equal to U. S.93¢.

Cherniak presented a balanced budget by increasing personal income and corporation taxes.

Economy. Economic activity appeared to be sound and steady, but unspectacular. Manitoba's unemployment rate from January to September was 2.9%, while the national average was 4.8%. Wages and salaries in 1969 increased 11.9% over 1968, compared with the national average of 9.3%.

The glut of world grain markets seriously affected the prosperity of Manitoba farmers. Crop yields were good, but farm cash receipts from January to September decreased 14% compared with the same period in 1968.

JOHN A. BOVEY
Provincial Archivist of Manitoba

MANUFACTURING. See ECONOMY OF THE UNITED STATES.

MAO TSE-TUNG

Chairman of the Chinese Communist party: b. Hsiangtan, Hunan, Dec. 26, 1893.

In 1969, Mao Tse-tung's attempt at political reconstruction led to the convening of the 9th National Congress of the Chinese Communist party, the reorganization of the party leadership, and the official designation of Lin Piao as Mao's successor. Mao's paramount position was reaffirmed and the "Thought of Mao Tse-tung" enshrined as the nation's supreme doctrine. He called for continuing revolution, but directed his attention to orderly economic development. While maintaining a hard-line policy toward the United States and the USSR, he took steps to normalize China's diplomatic operations.

The 9th Congress. After vanquishing his political enemies through the Cultural Revolution, Mao began to rebuild the party, which had been shattered in the process. The 9th Congress was convened in April 1969 to provide a new leadership. By skillful political manipulation Mao succeeded in uniting the three powerful factions within his party: the army headed by Lin Piao, the Red Guards led by Mao's wife Chiang Ch'ing, and the veteran bureaucrats represented by Premier Chou En-lai.

Mao presided over the opening session of the congress and delivered a key speech. He stressed the unity of the nation and the need for continued struggle against deviation. To achieve unity he advised "educating all that can be educated, sparing all that can be spared," but granting no lenience to incorrigible enemies.

Personality Cult. As Mao mounted the rostrum at the opening session of the 9th Congress, he was received with prolonged, thunderous applause. Newspapers throughout the nation reiterated the theme that all the party's achievements were due to Chairman Mao's "wise leadership." His theory of continuing revolution was regarded as the fundamental principle for consolidating the dictatorship of the proletariat in China.

Immense efforts were made throughout China to instill absolute loyalty to Mao. Some professions of loyalty closely resembled idolatry. Peasants, workers, and military men often began and ended their work by standing before a portrait of Mao, and some groups "reported" to the portrait on their work.

Public Appearances. Mao made several public appearances during the first months of 1969. In September, after he had failed to appear in public for four months, rumors spread that he was seriously ill or even dead. The rumor ended by his appearance at the 20th anniversary of Communist China on October 1, looking healthy and cheerful.

Background. Mao took part in the formation of the Chinese Communist party in 1921, and soon distinguished himself as a leader of guerrilla warfare and of the peasant movement. In 1935 he assumed leadership of the party, and 14 years later, when the Communists defeated the Nationalists, he became the ruler of mainland China.

Party opposition to Mao's policies grew as a result of the failure of the Great Leap Forward in 1958, peasant discontent, and Peking's growing isolation in world politics. Mao launched the Cultural Revolution in 1966 to eliminate opposition and to ensure the continuation of his policies.

CHESTER C. TAN
New York University

MARCIANO, Rocky. See SPORTS.

MARINE BIOLOGY

The year 1969 may be remembered as the year that the public finally caught up with the ecologists in recognizing the imminent peril that mankind's activities pose to his environment. Several of the events that contributed to this awareness involved aspects of marine biology. On the U.S. Atlantic coast, Howard L. Sanders of the Wood's Hole Oceanographic Institution remarked, "Mankind is rapidly ... progressing toward a world environment which won't support life," and on the Pacific coast, the staff of the Hopkins Marine Station opened a campaign against pesticides in the ocean.

Santa Barbara Oil Seepage. The most spectacular event of 1969 was the oil seepage from the shallow submarine field at Santa Barbara, Calif. Crude oil from a vast suppurating wound in the earth polluted hundreds of square miles of the ocean, from the shore to beyond the Channel Islands. The leakage became severe in late January and caused the death of many birds and possibly some marine mammals. The effect on marine life was less spectacular than that caused by the *Torrey Canyon* spill of 1967, when detergents were used to clean up the oil that polluted the coast of Britain. Although the heavy use of detergents was avoided in the Santa Barbara episode, the damage was considerable and it still continued at the end of 1969. (See also ZOOLOGY.)

Sea-Level Panama Canal. Much discussion during 1969 was concerned with the possible effects of a sea-level canal across Panama. A series of preliminary reports on many aspects of the project appeared in the magazine *BioScience*. The most provocative paper was written by John C. Briggs, who suggested that there would be a biological catastrophe from the intermixing of the marine faunas of the Atlantic and Pacific oceans. According to Briggs, the Atlantic fauna is more diverse and has greater "apparent competitive dominance" and would therefore replace the Pacific fauna: "The fact that a large-scale extinction would take place is inescapable." However, little solid data have been presented to support this prediction. It would seem that there are greater dangers to the life of the sea. Extermination by pollution is a more serious threat.

Explosion of Starfish Population. Pollution by pesticides or mining operations is one of the possible causes suggested for the apparent population explosion of the crown of thorns starfish (*Acanthaster planci*). Although depredation by this starfish on the corals of the Great Barrier Reef of Australia had been noticed some years ago, it became apparent in 1969 that more than 100 square miles (260 sq km) of the reef were affected. Outbreaks were also noted in Guam, Saipan, Fiji, and the Solomon Islands. If this starfish is relentlessly eating the corals of the Pacific, as claimed in various newspaper and magazine accounts, it may set in motion a sequence of events that would change the character of the Pacific islands since the action of waves will break down the dead corals.

Causes for the increase of the starfish population are unknown, but excessive harvesting of its principal predator, the triton *Charonia tritonis,* or the initial destruction by pollution of the corals themselves (which may consume larval stages of the starfish) have been suggested. Little light has been shed on the matter, but there was extensive publicity during the year about a crash program that enlisted teams of divers using injections of formaldehyde to kill many of the starfish. The circumstances are of considerable theoretical interest, since if it can be demonstrated that extensive changes in a diverse system can be induced by the removal of a single predator (the tritons in this case), the relation between diversity and community stability will have to be reexamined.

New Laboratory. In the summer of 1969, the Catalina Island Marine Laboratory of the University of Southern California held its first formal session, inaugurating year-round activities of this newest marine biology laboratory.

Symposium. A noteworthy symposium on intertidal biology was held at the Dallas AAAS meetings in 1968 and published in the May 1969 issue of the *American Zoologist*.

JOEL W. HEDGPETH
Oregon State University

STARFISH that attack coral are injected with formalin by divers in effort to save Pacific coral islands.

DIANE DICKERSON FROM BLACK STAR

UPI PHOTO BY S. AKATSUKA

UPI

MARINES were part of troops withdrawn from Vietnam. Men of 9th Battalion (*above*) were among the first, on July 14. (*Left*) Men of Third Division left in October.

MARINE CORPS

Problems of racial tension plagued the U. S. Marine Corps in 1969. There were also widely publicized charges of maltreatment of recruits. In Vietnam, where in 1965 Marines were the first U. S. ground combat troops to join the war against communist insurgency, Marine units were among the first withdrawals in the Nixon administration's plan to restore the combat burden to the government of South Vietnam. By the end of 1969, 60,000 Marines remained in Vietnam, compared with a peak of 84,000 the year before.

Racial Tension. On July 20, after an enlisted men's dance at Camp Lejeune, N. C., a group of 30 Negro and Puerto Rican Marines fought 14 whites. A 20-year-old white corporal died of a fractured skull. Three Negroes and two Puerto Ricans were charged with murder, rioting, and assault, and faced general courts-martial. On August 10, at the Kaneohe Marine Corps Air Station in Hawaii, 16 Negro and white Marines had to be treated for injuries following a 20-minute melee. According to press reports, relations between Negroes and whites had been strained for months.

On September 3, Marine Corps headquarters conceded anti-Negro discrimination and ordered corrective measures. Commanders were directed to assure Negroes the right of redress for grievances. Afro-style haircuts were permitted as were "Black Power" clenched-fist salutes if they constituted a greeting rather than defiance of authority. "Soul music" was permitted in servicemen's clubs.

Maltreatment. Officials at Camp Pendleton, California, acknowledged on September 14, after press disclosure, that recruits had been handcuffed in front of a mirror and forced to look at themselves "for self-appraisal and to stimulate an attitude change." This form of discipline was ordered ended. An 18-year-old enlistee died at the Marine Corps Recruit Depot at Parris Island, S. C., on September 21. His mother had received a letter from him claiming he had been beaten by a drill instructor. The incident drew wide attention and a demand by at least one congressman for an investigation.

War in Vietnam. March 8, 1969, marked the beginning of the fifth year of fighting by Leathernecks in Vietnam. Most of the small but bloody clashes that marked fighting in Vietnam in 1969 occurred in the Marine Corps' sector along the demilitarized zone.

In Operations Meade River and Taylor Common, south of Danang, Marine air/ground teamwork reportedly destroyed 2,700 enemy personnel, captured 600, and made the biggest haul of the war in enemy arms and munitions. In May, June, and July, Marines of Special Landing Forces Alpha twice invaded Barrier Island, near Danang, killing nearly 400 of the enemy and detaining 1,000 suspected Vietcong. (See also VIETNAM WAR.)

Strength. Deployments, economy-motivated reduction, and phased withdrawals from Vietnam reduced the Marine Corps strength to 295,000, still above the Korean peak of 261,000 but less than the 307,000 of 1968.

The 8,000-man Regimental Landing Team 9, which led the Marines into Vietnam in March 1965, was among the first units withdrawn in 1969. By December 15 the entire Third Marine Division was united in Okinawa. A squadron of the First Marine Aircraft Wing was relocated from Vietnam to Iwakuni Air Base, Japan.

Command. Gen. Leonard F. Chapman, Jr., continued in his post as Marine Corps commandant. Gen. Lewis W. Walt, assistant commandant, was promoted to four-star rank in May. In August, Sgt. Major Joseph Daily became the fifth sergeant major of the Marine Corps.

JACK RAYMOND
Author of "Power at the Pentagon"

MARRIAGE AND DIVORCE. See VITAL STATISTICS.

MARYLAND

Former speaker of the House of Delegates, Marvin Mandel, elected by the legislature to complete the term of former Gov. Spiro T. Agnew, assumed office in January 1969. Among his early appointments was Blair Lee III, former state legislator, as secretary of state.

Revenue. Inability to sell state bonds led Governor Mandel in November to call upon leading state banks for short-term loans. The funds were needed for construction projects already underway. The state, which has the highest possible bond rating, has a legal bond interest rate limit of 5%. By mid-1969, bond rates had soared to over 6%. In December, Governor Mandel called for a special session of the General Assembly to remove the 5% limit and to approve the transfer of surplus operating funds to capital construction projects. This surplus, the first in three years, is partly the result of a 1% sales tax increase approved in 1969. Alternative proposals for use of these funds include bonuses for programs held to austerity levels for 3 years.

Wetlands Controversy. The state Board of Public Works imposed a moratorium on the controversial transfer of state marshlands to developers for token fees pending 1970 action by the General Assembly. Stricter procedural guidelines, including requirements for local hearings and prior approval of state and local conservation boards is being considered by the Assembly.

Nuclear Power Plants. Public concern over the impact of a nuclear power plant recently constructed on Chesapeake Bay prompted the legislative council in November to approve a five-year ban on power plant construction on the bay or its tributaries. During that time an exhaustive study will be made of the impact of thermal pollution on marine life.

School Integration. In late spring, one secondary and two higher education systems of the state were ordered by the federal Department of Health, Education, and Welfare to submit plans for prompt integration. In September, two of these systems—the University of Maryland and the state college system—submitted plans that were approved.

The third order involved secondary schools in Prince Georges County, adjacent to the District of Columbia. The county's plan, submitted and approved in November, will negate the previous "neighborhood system" adopted in 1966 and will redraw school districts to achieve the full integration of several predominately black high schools.

Drugs. Maryland became the first state to permit indigent narcotic addicts to use Medicaid funds to buy methadone, a synthetic drug found useful in addict rehabilitation. The program now operates in two centers in the city of Baltimore. Other efforts to crack down on drug traffic and abuse include planned legislation to permit parents to seek help for children suspected of drug use without running the risk of criminal prosecution.

Drunken Drivers. Maryland's legislature adopted a unique "express consent" law that requires all persons applying for driver permits or renewals to sign a pledge to submit to sobriety tests if accused of drunken driving. This system differs from "implied consent" laws of other states, which assume consent is given at the time of application for a license.

JEAN E. SPENCER
University of Maryland

——————— MARYLAND · Information Highlights ———————

Area: 10,577 square miles (27,394 sq km).
Population: 3,789,000 (1969 est.).
Chief Cities (1969 est.): Annapolis, the capital, 30,000; Baltimore, 905,000; Dundalk, 87,500; Silver Spring, 84,500; Bethesda, 76,000.
Government: *Chief Officers*—governor, Marvin Mandel (Democrat); secy. of state, Blair Lee III (D); atty. gen., Francis B. Burch (D); treas., John A. Luetkemeyer; supt. of pub. instr., James A. Sensenbaugh; chief justice, Hon. Hall Hammond. *General Assembly*—Senate, 43 members (35 Democrats, 8 Republicans); House of Representatives, 142 members (117 D, 25 R).
Education: *School enrollment* (1968)—public elementary, 482,000 pupils (19,700 teachers); public secondary, 360,000 pupils (17,500 teachers); nonpublic schools, 131,800 pupils (5,670 teachers); college and university (fall 1967), 115,510 students. *Public school expenditures* (1967–68)—$721,970,000 ($921 per pupil); average annual teacher's salary, $8,316.
Public Finance (fiscal year 1968): *Revenues,* $2,720,467,982 (3% sales tax, $162,405,033; motor fuel tax, $104,273,557; federal funds, $175,270,418). *Expenditures,* $1,200,095,000 (education, $464,710,296; health, welfare, and safety, $118,515,241; highways, $414,611,939). *State debt,* $926,660,000 (June 30, 1968).
Personal Income (1968): $14,048,000,000; average annual income per person, $3,742.
Public Assistance (fiscal year 1968): $118,483,565 to 152,323 recipients (aged, $6,604,907; dependent children, $55,380,739).
Labor Force (employed persons, 1,500,500, 1969): *Agricultural* 30,400; *nonagricultural* (wage and salary earners), 1,480,500 (19.2% manufacturing, 19.9% trade, 20.4% government). *Unemployed persons* (July 1969)—53,400.
Manufacturing (1965): *Value added by manufacture,* $3,342,878,000 (transportation equipment, $327,747,000; primary metals, $542,679,000; nonelectrical machinery, $172,961,000; electrical machinery, $290,861,000; fabricated metals, $175,912,000; food and products, $475,676,000).
Agriculture (1967): *Cash farm income,* $333,404,000 (livestock, $219,523,000; crops, $108,564,000; govt. payments, $5,317,000). *Chief crops* (tons)—Corn for grain, 1,207,696; hay, 710,000; wheat, 179,010.
Mining (1967): *Production value,* $71,232,000. *Chief minerals* (tons)—Stone, 28,581,000; coal, 4,548,000.
Fisheries (1967): *Commercial catch,* 73,400,000 pounds ($16,900,000). *Leading species* (1966)—Blue crabs, 31,850,032 pounds ($2,933,362); oyster meat, 12,068,785 pounds ($7,861,846).
Transportation: *Roads* (1966), 23,360 miles (37,593 km); *motor vehicles* (1967), 1,583,000; *railroads* (1966), 2,000 track miles (3,219 km); *airports* (1966), 120.
Communications (1966): *Telephones* (1968), 2,070,800; *television stations,* 4; *radio stations,* 78; *newspapers,* 13 (daily circulation, 1,272,334).

MASSACHUSETTS

For the residents of Massachusetts, 1969 was a year of challenge and change. A number of important issues affecting the political, social, and economic life of the state arose during the year, and although there were no statewide elections, a great deal of political activity was evident.

Politics. Republican Gov. Francis W. Sargent, in his first full year in office, faced a series of uphill battles with the legislature and the Governor's Council, both strongly controlled by Democrats. The governor's attempt to appoint Walter J. Skinner, former counsel for the now-defunct Massachusetts Crime Commission, to the state superior court provoked furious opposition from the council. The nomination was submitted three times and rejected on each occasion.

On the legislative front, a number of important bills championed by the governor met with little success. Automobile insurance reform, a goal of several governors over many years, was again defeated amidst charges and countercharges as to the probable effects of reform proposals on insurance rates and congestion in the courts. A proposal to reduce the size of the state House of Representatives, overwhelmingly approved by the voters in a 1968 referendum, met with no success. The new speaker of the house, David M. Bartley, argued that his administration should be given an opportunity to prove that the present 240-member body could function efficiently. He promised that the issue would be heard again early in 1970.

The governor's relations with citizenry were highlighted by his support of the so-called "taxpayers' revolt" early in the year. The revolt mushroomed into prominence after several citizens' groups had formed to protest the steady rise in state taxes. But neither the pleas of the public nor the support of the governor sufficed to bring about tax reform in 1969.

Welfare. The Massachusetts welfare system, which the state took over from cities and towns on July 1, 1968, produced a long string of conflicts and controversies. Throughout 1969, state officials were confronted by angry protests from members of two groups—the Mothers for Adequate Welfare (MAW) and the National Welfare Rights Organization. In December, Governor Sargent announced a program to raise basic welfare stipends and eliminate "special purpose" grants. Speaking to the Massachusetts Conference on Social Welfare, he argued that his program would distribute funds more equitably, but many welfare recipients interpreted the program to imply a net decrease in welfare services.

State Government Reorganization. Governor Sargent's major victory with the legislature in 1969 was the passage of the organization program initiated by Gov. John A. Volpe in 1968. The plan reorganizes much of the state executive branch along lines similar to the federal cabinet system. Passage of the proposal climaxed a struggle of more than a decade on the part of political leaders and various citizens' groups.

Metropolitan Reorganization. In June a regional conference was held to establish task forces for the study of metropolitan area problems in taxation, transportation, education, and environment. In November, Mayor Kevin White of Boston used the conference report as the basis of a proposed regional government plan. It called for the establishment of a 200-member Eastern Massachusetts Council of Governments, composed of representatives of 100 cities and towns in the greater Boston metropolitan area. The council would have control over such existing metropolitan agencies as the Massachusetts Port Authority, the Massachusetts Bay Transportation Authority, and the Metropolitan District Commission, and it would serve as a forum for discussion and solution of major common problems.

Special Election. On November 4 a special election was held in the 6th Congressional District to fill the seat left vacant by the death on June 22 of Republican U. S. Rep. William H. Bates. The Republican candidate was state Sen. William L. Saltonstall, son of former U. S. Sen. Leverett Saltonstall. The Democratic nominee was state Rep. Michael J. Harrington of Salem. Saltonstall campaigned on a platform of complete support for President Nixon's Vietnam policy. Harrington, who spoke out strongly for withdrawal of U. S. troops by the end of 1970, was the winner, with 72,029 votes to Saltonstall's 65,452. His victory gave the seat to a Democrat for the first time in almost a century.

Kennedy Accident. U. S. Sen. Edward M. Kennedy escaped serious injury but Mary Jo Kopechne, a passenger in an automobile driven by him, was found dead in the vehicle after it plunged off a bridge on Chappaquiddick Island on July 18 (see KENNEDY, EDWARD M.).

BETTY H. ZISK
Boston University

WIDE WORLD

MICHAEL J. HARRINGTON is cheered by aides after winning a special October election as the first Democrat to represent Massachusetts' 6th Congressional District.

─── **MASSACHUSETTS • Information Highlights** ───

Area: 8,257 square miles (21,386 sq km).
Population: 5,508,000 (1969 est.).
Chief Cities (1969 est.): Boston, the capital, 570,000; Worcester, 176,000; Springfield, 158,000; Cambridge, 100,000.
Government: *Chief Officers*—governor, Francis W. Sargent (Republican); lt. gov., vacancy; secy. of state, John F. X. Davoren (Democrat); atty. gen., Robert H. Quinn (D); treas., Robert Q. Crane; supt. of pub. instr., Neil V. Sullivan; chief justice, Raymond S. Wilkins. *General Court* —Senate, 40 members (27 Democrats, 13 Republicans); House of Representatives, 240 members (170 D, 69 R, 1 vacancy).
Education: *School enrollment* (1968–69)—public elementary, 616,000 pupils (26,000 teachers); public secondary, 484,-000 pupils (22,900 teachers); nonpublic schools, 245,500 pupils (10,570 teachers); college and university (fall 1967), 252,638 students. *Public school expenditures* (1967–68)— $761,640,000 ($816 per pupil); average teacher's salary, $8,383.
Public Finance (fiscal year 1969): *Revenues*, $1,825,655,044 (3% sales tax, $153,275,573; motor fuel tax, $127,443,633; federal funds, $447,986,263). *Expenditures*, $1,874,245,679 (education, $429,541,552; health, welfare, and safety, $727,152,621; highways, $252,318,749). *State debt*, $1,800,-603,000 (June 30, 1968).
Personal Income (1968): $20,974,000,000; average annual income per person, $3,835.
Public Assistance (fiscal year 1969): $452,498,633 to 409,661 recipients (aged, $56,406,818; dependent children, $128,-096,621).
Labor Force (employed persons, July 1969): *Agricultural,* 20,100; *nonagricultural* (wage and salary earners), 2,259,-900 (30.0% manufacturing, 21.0% trade, 13.3% government). *Unemployed persons* (July 1969)—115,500.
Manufacturing (1966): *Value added by manufacture,* $7,750,-329,116 (1965: electrical machinery, $1,087,516,000; nonelectrical machinery, $832,873,000; fabricated metals, $529,388,000; food and products, $520,680,000).
Agriculture (1967): *Cash farm income,* $156,704,000 (livestock, $87,453,000; crops, $68,595,000; govt. payments, $656,-000). *Chief crops* (tons)—Cranberries, 28,000 (ranks 1st among the states); corn, 455,000.
Mining (1967): *Production value,* $40,612,000. *Chief minerals* (tons)—Sand and gravel, 17,881,000; stone, 6,203,000; clays, (1966), 202,000; lime, 195,000.
Fisheries (1967): *Commercial catch,* 316,026,874 pounds ($33,-244,717). *Leading species*—Scrod haddock, 54,167,643 pounds ($6,492,723); yellowtail flounder, 46,436,430 pounds ($4,959,796).
Transportation (1968): *Roads,* 27,805 miles (44,745 km); *motor vehicles,* 2,365,517; *railroads,* 3,022 track miles (4,863 km); *airports* (1969), 9.
Communications (1969): *Telephones* (1967), 3,131,700; *television stations,* 11; *radio stations,* 121; *newspapers,* 43 (daily circulation, 1966, 3,887,907).

MATERIALS

In 1969 there was a large increase in the use of many composite materials and plastics. Also, a ceramic material with three times the strength of regular glass has been developed.

Composites. Composite materials are produced by combining two or more dissimilar materials, such as fiber glass and plastic, to make a stronger, stiffer product. The greatest interest in new composite materials centers on the use of boron and graphite continuous fibers for the reinforcement of plastics and metals. These fibers have extremely high strengths and are much stiffer than glass fibers. Their high cost (over $200 a pound), however, limits their use to highly technical, high-cost products, such as jet engines and high-performance airplanes. A boron-reinforced aluminum component has been successfully operated in the fan section of a turbofan engine. This first stage of the fan is 40 inches in diameter and is 40% lighter when made of the composite rather than the usual titanium metal. A graphite fiber reinforced plastic is being used in various components of the jet engine of Lockheed's airbus. A boron-polymide (plastic) structural wing beam has been delivered for use in the supersonic transport airplane. The beam, which is 10 feet long, is the first attempt to use boron composite in a large structural part.

The use of glass fiber reinforced plastic parts in automobiles and trucks will double during the period from 1968 to 1970. However, reinforced plastics are still not replacing steel for large, high-production automobile stampings because of the high production rates possible with steel stampings and the high cost of finishing plastic surfaces.

Fiber glass-plastic boats can be built that are up to 200 feet in length. It is estimated that the cost of such boats would be 10% to 15% higher than boats built of wood and about the same as those built of steel; however, the fiber glass-plastic boats are one third lighter in weight.

Plastics. There was approximately a 15% increase in the consumption of plastics during 1969; 18.5 billion pounds were used, which was an increase of 2.5 billion pounds over 1968. Plastic pipe can now be produced in diameters up to 15 inches; 260 million pounds of plastics were used for pipe in 1969. The "instant destruct" tapes seen on tele-vision in *Mission Impossible* are now in production. A new kind of plastic called pyrrone polymer has been developed; it is stable at 260° C (500° F) and is usable for short periods at a temperature of 538° C (1000° F). World War II ships can be converted to practically unsinkable mine-sweepers by using plastic foam below decks.

Ceramics. Glass windows that have been chemically strengthened are being used experimentally in some trains. These windows have been strengthened by putting their surfaces in compression; they have three times the strength of ordinary window glass. Because of their strength, thinner panes can be used. A new laminated window for automobiles has been developed that is capable of bending without breaking when a passenger's head strikes it. The outer layer of glass is ordinary, and a blow from inside causes it (the outside layer) to break immediately. The inside layer is thin and strong and capable of bending extensively after the outside glass has shattered. A glass-ceramic range top has been developed that is capable of withstanding temperatures up to 705° C (1300° F). Former glass-ceramic tops could only be used to about 260° C (500° F).

Metals. Beryllium metal disk brakes are to be used on the huge Lockheed C-5A airplane. The beryllium brakes are 35% lighter than those made with steel; about 742 pounds of beryllium is used in the brakes for each aircraft.

J. R. TINKLEPAUGH
Alfred University

MAURITANIA

Domestic politics in Mauritania remained relatively quiet during 1969, and prospects for economic growth improved greatly.

Political Affairs. The relative calm in Mauritania's domestic affairs reflected the government's policy of national reconciliation. The single Parti du Peuple Mauritanien was democratized somewhat in 1969, and the government was able to weather opposition from students and union leaders who had defected from the country's only national trade union.

Economy. Mineral exploitation and the encouragement of foreign trade boosted Mauritania's economy. Its gross national product (GNP) was projected as growing at an annual rate of 10%, and doubling in 20 years. Also, the scheduled exporta-

LETTERFLEX, a new system developed for use in the printing industry, produces flexible plastic relief plates from photographic negatives. The new plate permits the printing industry to take advantage of photocomposition while retaining its letterpresses. Here, the unexposed portion of the plate is removed from etching bath.

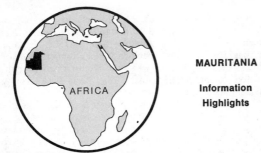

MAURITANIA

Information

Highlights

Area: 397,850 square miles (1,030,700 sq km).
Population: 1,120,000 (1968 est.).
Chief Cities (1965 census): Nouakchott, the capital, 15,000.
Government: *President*—Mokhtar Ould Daddah (took office Aug. 7, 1966, for 2d 5-year term); *Legislature* (unicameral) —National Assembly, 40 members (all members of the Parti du Peuple Mauritanien).
Religious Faiths: Muslims, 99% of population; Roman Catholics, 0.3%; others, 0.7%.
Education: *Literacy rate* (1969), 5% of population. *Total school enrollment* (1967)—21,091 (primary, 19,103; secondary, 1,684; teacher-training, 107; technical, 197).
Finance (1969 budget est.): $27,100,000; *monetary unit,* CFA Franc (277.70 francs equal U.S.$1 after the currency devaluation in August 1969).
Gross National Product (1966 est.): $167,000,000.
Cost of Living Index (1966): 112 (1963=100).
Crops (metric tons, 1967–68 crop year): Dates, 15,000.
Foreign Trade (1967): *Exports,* $72,000,000 (chief export, 1967: Iron ore, $62,300,000); *imports,* $35,800,000 (chief imports, 1967: nonelectrical machinery, $5,720,000; railway vehicles, $2,130,000; motor vehicles, $1,570,000). *Chief trading partners* (1966): France (took 31% of exports, supplied 55% of imports); Britain (took 20% of exports, supplied 1% of imports); West Germany.
Transportation: *Roads* (1969), 3,700 miles (5,954 km); *motor vehicles* (1967), 6,000 (automobiles 3,000); *railways* (1964), 419 miles (674 km); *national airline,* Air-Mauritanie; *principal airport,* Nouakchott.
Communications: *Telephones* (1968): 1,200; *radios* (1964), 31,000.

tion of 8 million tons of iron ore in 1969 was expected to provide one third of the national revenue.

Trade relations began to be diversified, although France retained its "privileged" position. Trade with the USSR continued to expand, and a new agreement with Liberia followed Liberian President Tubman's visit to Nouakchott in late February. As part of this agreement, Mauritania hopes to exchange meat for timber.

Foreign Affairs. A reconciliation occurred between Mauritanian President Mokhtar Ould Daddah and King Hassan II of Morocco during the Islamic Summit Conference in Morocco, September 22–25. The only indication of the rapprochement was the fact that the president had been invited to Morocco, especially over opposition of Morocco's Istiqlal party.

On August 2 it was announced that Mauritania had recognized the South Vietnamese NLF provisional government. Mauritania's "radical" stance is based largely on national interest. The presence of Chinese Communists on the north bank of the Senegal River, for example, helps keep Senegal at arm's length. At the same time, Mauritania tries to offset leftist elements in the party by forming Western ties. The government resumed relations with the United States and welcomed Western aid.

W. A. E. SKURNIK
University of Colorado

MAURITIUS

Consolidation was the main objective in 1969 for the island nation of Mauritius, which had become independent on March 12, 1968. On the first anniversary of independence, five cabinet members resigned. Sir Seewoosagur Ramegoolam remained prime min-

ister, but his Independence party, a loose alliance of smaller parties, broke apart. A new coalition of parties was forming at the end of 1969.

Agriculture. The island is dependent on cane sugar, which accounts for more than 95% of exports. Mauritius joined the International Sugar Agreement, intended to stabilize prices. Remaining a party to the Commonwealth Sugar Agreement, Mauritius also can sell to British at preferential prices.

The aloe plant is grown for its fiber, from which sacks are made. Tea and tobacco production are expanding. Most food is imported, but vegetable production is increasing. There is research on growing rice, the staple food.

Industry. New industries developed since independence are iron and steel rolling, metal door and window fabrication, manufacture of car batteries, and refining of edible oil. The number of tourists rose from 4,000 in 1961 to 15,000 in 1967. Mauritius Hotels, Ltd., in which the government has an interest, is planning more hotels.

Development Loan. Britain promised a £5 million ($12 million), 25-year interest-free development credit, as of April 1, 1970. Construction projects under way at the end of 1969 included a hospital, the University of Mauritius, and a government center.

Population. Overpopulation and consequent unemployment remained the worst problem in 1969, and the Family Planning Movement had government support. Estimated population on Jan. 1, 1969, was 794,746.

BURTON BENEDICT
University of California, Berkeley

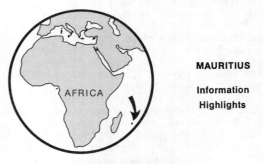

MAURITIUS

Information

Highlights

Area: 809 square miles (1,865 sq km).
Population: 794,746 (1969 est.).
Chief Cities (1966 census): Port Louis, the capital, 132,700.
Government: *Governor-General*—Sir Leonard Williams (took office Sept. 1968); *Prime Minister*—Sir Seewoosagur Ramegoolam (took office Sept. 1968). *Parliament*—Legislative Assembly, 70 members (party seating, 1969: Independence Party, 43; Parti Mauricien Social Démocrate, 27).
Religious Faiths: Hindus, 48% of population; Roman Catholics, 28%; Muslims, 16%; others, 8%.
Education: *Literacy rate* (1969), 60% of population. *Total school enrollment* (1967)—181,701.
Finance (1967–68 est.): *Revenues,* $38,700,000; *expenditures,* $41,800,000; *monetary unit,* rupee (5.555 rupees equal U.S.$1).
Gross National Product (1967): $175,157,515.
National Income (1967): $151,215,121; average annual income per person, $192.
Economic Index (1967): *Cost of living,* 108 (1963=100).
Manufacturing (metric tons, 1967): Sugar, 674,000.
Crops (metric tons, 1967–68 crop year): Sugarcane, 5,814,000.
Foreign Trade (1968): *Exports,* $64,000,000 (chief export, 1967: unrefined sugar cane, $64,340,000); *imports,* $76,000,000 (chief import, 1967: rice, $7,956,000). *Chief trading partners* (1967): Britain (took 88% of exports, supplied 21% of imports); South Africa.
Transportation: *Roads* (1969), 824 miles (881 km); *motor vehicles*
Communications: *Telephones* (1968): 15,328; *radios* (1967), 70,000; *newspapers* (1967), 11.

MBOYA, Tom. See biographical sketch under KENYA.

MEDICARE. See SOCIAL SECURITY.

MEDICINE

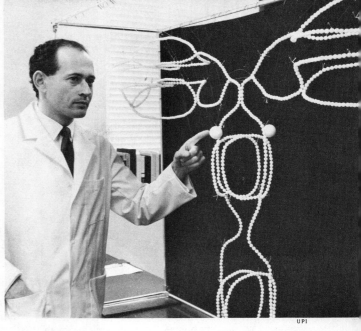

Antibody structure was deciphered by Gerald M. Edelman and colleagues at Rockefeller University. This model, made with golf balls and plastic beads, shows how the many amino acids and other chemical components are arranged to form a single molecule of gamma globulin.

In the field of medical research, many of the events of 1969 continued to demonstrate man's growing understanding of the basic biological processes of the human body. Among the most important achievements of the year were the isolation of a single gene and the discovery of the structure of antibodies. However, just at a time when much of the scientific knowledge acquired in recent decades seemed about to become fruitful, President Nixon's new administration seemed less than eager to support the research needed for medical progress.

EVENTS AND ACHIEVEMENTS

Solid progress was made in a number of areas of medical research, including genetics, immunity, organ transplantation, and tropical medicine. Also, several new drugs and vaccines were developed, and public attention focused on oral contraceptives and two widely used food additives—cyclamates and monosodium glutamate (MSG).

Genetics. The award of the 1969 Nobel Prize in physiology or medicine served to throw light on the significant advances reported during the year. The three laureates—Max Delbruck, Alfred Hershey, and Salvatore Luria—played a central role in providing the groundwork for the modern study of bacterial genetics. In describing how a bacterial virus reproduces itself inside the host cell, the 1969 Nobelists had set in motion the investigations that led to the unraveling of the structure of deoxyribonucleic acid (DNA) and the eventual deciphering of the genetic code. Their work, which was done during the late 1950's, resulted in the successful development of the branch of science known as molecular biology, and it has now put man in the position of approaching the cure of many virus diseases, hereditary diseases, and perhaps, before the century is out, of controlling life itself.

Probably the single most outstanding event in the field of genetics in 1969 was the isolation of a single gene. Using the bacterium *Escherichia coli,* which normally inhabits the digestive system, a group of Harvard University scientists succeeded in isolating from it a single unit of pure genetic material, in particular the gene that enables the bacterium to break down lactose into glucose. The group, headed by Jonathan Beckwith, now hopes to find out how genes are repressed and derepressed—turned off and on—so that genes can be made to operate when required. This concept, known as the operon concept, was first formulated by the French scientists François Jacob, André Lwoff, and Jacques Monod, who won the 1965 Nobel Prize. "Now the tool is at hand to demonstrate how it works," said Beckwith. "We can now ask: what factors make a gene express itself?" The answer, he indicated, may lead to finding the means of preventing hereditary diseases and perhaps even cancer. Presumably concerned about the uses to which the group's work might be put, Beckwith added: "The techniques do not yet exist for purifying human genes, but it is not inconceivable that they could be purified by methods similar to ours and I think it is obvious that this work could lead to genetic manipulation."

Also during 1969, at Stanford University, California, another Nobel Prize-winner, Arthur Kornberg, outlined the steps by which a living cell repairs the defects in its genetic machinery. And at the University of California in San Francisco, James Cleaver identified the cause of a fatal skin disease by finding that patients with the disease lack a certain enzyme. His next step is to try to supply this enzyme by using a harmless virus that makes it.

Immunity. In 1969 man unraveled the chemical structure of another vital biological material—antibodies. These are the body's defenders, the agents that disarm viruses, bacteria, and other foreign invaders. Although they protect the body by attacking harmful agents, they may be harmful themselves by attacking transplanted organs and tissues. Because of this dual role, the deciphering of the chemical structure of antibodies was hailed as a great medical advance.

The work on antibody structure was done by Gerald M. Edelman of Rockefeller University in New York. He described his work as one of the necessary steps toward understanding the complete mechanism of immunity. "When we have succeeded in understanding this mechanism we will be able to control the immune process," he said.

Viruses and Cancer. For over 50 years some scientists have believed that viruses play a role in

CIGARETTES
KILL
WITH
CONGRESSIONAL
OK

COMMITTEE
APPROVES
RETROACTIVE
BIRTH CONTROL
NO HEALTH
WARNING
IN
CIGARETTE

CAUTION!
SOME
CONGRESSMEN
ARE
HAZARDOUS
TO YOUR
HEALTH

UPI

ANTISMOKING GROUP demonstrates outside U. S. Capitol in May for strong action against cigarettes.

causing cancer. Although they could identify some animal cancers caused by viruses, they were never able to find virus-caused cancers in man.

Apart from the impossibility of direct experimentation on healthy humans, one research problem is that if viruses are involved in human cancers, their role is more subtle than in other virus diseases. Either the cancer virus is so common that it is present in all humans and animals or it does its infecting in a roundabout way.

During the past year, Robert J. Huebner of the National Cancer Institute offered a theory based on observations. According to this theory, the cancer-producing villain is a ribonucleic acid (RNA) virus particle, and the genome (genetic information) for making this virus is passed from a mother to her child. Later it may be activated by agents such as radiation or tobacco smoke. Huebner also believes that the virus can also be activated by the normal aging process.

Research on cancer and viruses through 1969 gave new impetus to the hope of ultimately controlling the disease. A form of anticancer vaccine may shortly be available for preventing a form of leukemia that attacks chickens. The results, however, will not be restricted to poultry, for the virus that causes chicken leukemia is similar to the EB virus.

This virus has been found to be associated with human cancers, particularly African lymphoma. It is also seen in chronic leukemia and in cancers of the back of the nose and the throat—conditions common in Africa, China, and Hong Kong. The EB virus has also been found to be involved in the fairly common disease infectious mononucleosis, a blood disease that can produce symptoms similar to those of leukemia.

"The appearance of mononucleosis leads scientists to speculate that it may be a benign reversible form of leukemia," according to James T. Grace of the Roswell Park Memorial Institute in Buffalo, N. Y. "Most people have antibodies against mononucleosis, indicating that they have been infected with the disease in the past." Grace is now at work on developing an experimental vaccine against EB virus infections. If this vaccine works against mononucleosis, it should then be possible to find out if it has an effect on EB-associated cancers.

Leukemia Research. Progress also continued in the management of leukemia with chemicals. A promising new drug, cytosine arabinoside (Cytosar),

was licensed by the Food and Drug Administration in 1969. This drug selectively prevents leukemia cells from multiplying, and although it is not a cure, it has kept patients with certain forms of leukemia free of the disease for over a year and a half. An advantage of Cytosar is that, unlike many other anticancer drugs, it has no unpredictable side effects, but the FDA has ruled that it can only be used by experienced physicians. Cytosar was first synthesized early in the 1950's, but it was extremely expensive to produce. The price has since dropped, but had it not been for a testing program undertaken by the National Cancer Institute, the drug might have remained a laboratory curiosity.

Doctors in the United States, France, and the Soviet Union continued a program of exchanging the blood of leukemia patients in an attempt to trigger an immunity response in patients and thus possibly control the disease. The technique has worked with mice, and George Mathé of the Institut Gustave Roussy in France is now trying it with humans. According to Mathé, the results have been promising.

Heart Transplants. On August 17, one of the world's most famous patients—Philip Blaiberg—died. The death of this Cape Town dentist who had lived for 19½ months with a transplanted heart focused new attention on heart transplantation.

During 1968, 101 heart transplant operations were performed in the world, but during 1969 there were only 47. When queried on why the number had dropped so sharply, Christiaan Barnard, the surgeon who had performed the first human heart transplant, answered that heart transplant surgeons are like generals in an army that has suffered severe losses. They are regrouping, he said, and considering whether and where they should attack again. Barnard believes that heart transplants can achieve better results, and his opinion is supported by C. Walton Lillehei of the New York Hospital-Cornell Medical Center in New York. "If you can keep someone going for 19 months," he said, "you can do it for 38, or even 72. We've learned much about the management of these cases."

Other transplant surgeons, however, are not so sure about the future of such operations. At the Montreal Institute of Cardiology, Pierre Grondin suspended all heart transplant operations to study such factors as tissue matching between donors and recipients and ways to suppress the body's rejection of the grafted organ. It was this natural rejection reaction that led to the death of Blaiberg.

Artificial Heart Aids. On April 4, another major step in treating severely damaged hearts was taken by Denton Cooley of St. Luke's Episcopal Hospital in Houston, Texas. A surgeon with 18 heart transplant operations to his credit, Cooley stitched a completely artificial heart device onto the chest of a 47-year-old patient, Haskell Karp. Although the artificial device kept Karp alive for more than 60 hours, he was then given a human heart and died 38 hours after the transplant operation.

Cooley's operation quickly set off a storm of controversy, partly because the device he had used was only in the early stages of development and also because public funds had been used to develop it. At issue was whether or not Cooley had violated the guidlines set by the National Heart and Lung Institute on clinical trials of devices made with their financial support. Cooley denied these charges and maintained that as a surgeon he had the right, indeed the duty, to do what he considered right and proper for his patient. Nevertheless, three months later he resigned as professor of surgery at Baylor College of Medicine, thereby side-stepping the issue. As a private practitioner, he would be exempt from the rules on human experimentation.

Many surgeons thought that the controversy over Cooley's use of the heart device was unfortunate because it obscured the fact that a perfected artificial heart offers greater hope than transplantation in treating irreversible heart disease. The famous Houston heart surgeon Michael E. DeBakey commented, "In the long run, I feel that heart transplantation will have a rather limited application. Even when the immunological difficulties are overcome, there will never be enough heart donors to meet the demand." He foresaw greater reliance upon mechanical devices to aid and replace hearts.

At the end of the year, a committee reporting on both types of heart replacement for the National Heart and Lung Institute concluded that it makes better sense to try to prevent heart disease in the first place. This approach may be less spectacular but could probably save more lives, maintained Theodore Cooper, the Institute's head. Nearly half of the 200,000 Americans who die from heart disease below the age of 65 do so without warning, Cooper argued. These people would not benefit from transplants or artificial hearts. However, Cooper suggested, if research could identify individuals who are liable to suffer heart attacks, the disease, it was hoped, could be slowed down by early treatment—dieting, exercise, or possibly the use of certain drugs.

One problem with any artificial heart device is that the surfaces over which the blood flows tend to make the blood form clots. To solve this problem, William F. Bernard of the Children's Hospital Medical Center in Boston developed a mechanical heart pump lined with living tissue. The pump's inner surface is seeded with living cells from embryos, and according to Bernard, it has been used successfully in calves for as long as four months.

Pacemakers, special devices that are used to regularize the beating of hearts with abnormal rhythms, have benefited many hundreds of patients. Usually, they are powered by batteries, but during 1969 the Atomic Energy Commission unveiled a pacemaker that is powered by radioactive isotopes. This pacemaker is designed to last for 10 years, considerably longer than the battery-powered pacemakers which must be replaced every two or three years through a surgical operation.

Pancreas, Kidney, and Larynx Transplants. Eight young people with diabetes were given transplanted pancreases during 1969 by surgeon Richard D. Lillehei of the University of Minnesota. Although six of them later died, none of the deaths were attributed to rejection reactions. The two other patients are now out of the hospital. Pancreas transplantation in diabetes is an attempt to prevent secondary complications involving the kidneys, eyes, and blood vessels. Young diabetics are especially prone to such complications. The transplantation procedure may also help to indicate whether it is a lack of insulin that causes these problems.

In the years between 1954, when the world's first successful kidney transplant was performed, and 1968 there were only 2,000 kidney transplant operations performed in the world. In 1969 alone, however, there were 1,000 such operations. At a meeting at the end of 1969, transplantation experts predicted that within five years there would be 2,000 to 3,000 kidney transplants a year. Improved surgical techniques and better patient management have given both doctors and patients more confidence in this type of operation.

The world's first larynx transplant was performed in 1969. Following surgery, the patient was able to speak and swallow well although he died of cancer 10 months later. The operation was performed at the University of Ghent in Belgium, the same hospital where a lung transplant patient lived

UPI

INOCULATION against German measles is given to 6th grade pupils in a New Hampshire school. The first mass immunization program in the United States, covering children up to the 6th grade in the city of Laconia and 5 nearby communities, was carried out with a new vaccine.

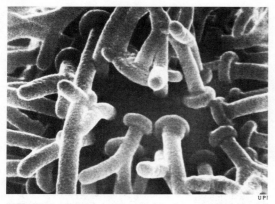

SYNAPTIC KNOBS at the ends of nerve fibers were photographed for the first time by bioengineers at the University of California. These structures are seen magnified 5,000 times through an electron microscope.

for 10 months. The previous record of survival was only 28 days.

Tropical Medicine. In the field of tropical medicine there was much progress in both treatment and prevention of disease. At the Johns Hopkins Medical School in Baltimore scientists developed a new vaccine against cholera. This vaccine was found to be effective in 90% of the cases and affords protection against the disease for up to a year. Previous anticholera vaccines were only effective in 70% of the cases and protection lasted only four to six months. Field trials of the vaccine are now under way and it is hoped that the vaccine soon will be available for use in Asian countries where cholera is still a scourge.

Also in the field of tropical medicine, world health authorities warn that 6 million Egyptians may become victims of schistosomiasis when the Aswan High Dam irrigation project begins. Schistosomiasis is caused by infestation with certain blood flukes. These flukes spend part of their life cycle inside certain snails so that one way of controlling the disease involves eradicating the host snails. Through intensive research, scientists have already found one promising chemical—Bayluscide—which destroys the snails. One advantage of this chemical is that it does not harm other forms of life, only the snails. Another development in the control of schistosomiasis was the introduction of a new drug, hycanthone, which has been effective in curing 80% of the patients treated. This drug is effective through a single injection.

Malaria, a menace even more devastating than schistosomiasis, is now presenting a cruel dilemma to many developing countries: to use more DDT, which is now known to be a health hazard, or to experience soaring rates of malaria incidence. One complication is that mosquitoes, the carriers of the disease, are showing a growing resistance to DDT. This problem was discussed at the World Health Assembly in Boston and their conclusion was that until a new method of fighting the disease is developed, the use of DDT is essential in malaria-stricken areas.

Israeli scientists, in collaboration with Burmese scientists, have come up with a new approach to the world's most crippling eye disease—trachoma. The infectious agent that causes trachoma is similar to a virus, and a drug called rifomycin, which is used in Europe to treat tuberculosis, has been found to be effective against the organism, at least in laboratory studies.

New Vaccines and Other Drugs. An approved vaccine against rubella (German measles) went into mass production in the United States in 1969, and it is now being administered to children in hopes of eradicating the disease. Although German measles is only a mild disease in children, it may be disastrous to fetuses if pregnant women become infected.

A new, more effective and less toxic antirabies vaccine was also developed in 1969. Only one injection of this vaccine is required, and it is many times more potent in building immunity to the disease than previous vaccines. A U. S. Army scientist, Malcolm Artenstein, also made notable progress in developing a vaccine against the most common types of meningitis, and two Florida scientists also reported a new drug for this disease. Other researchers are currently working on the early steps in the development of a vaccine against hepatitis.

Two antibiotics—aureomycin and tetracycline—were made artificially in the laboratory for the first time, promising the production of less expensive and more effective drugs. The three-dimensional structure of insulin, a hormone that has been used for more than 40 years to treat diabetes, was deciphered by the British Nobelist (1964) Dorothy Hodgkin. This discovery may have far-reaching implications for the treatment of this disease. Also during the year, scientists succeeded in synthesizing one of the largest biological molecules, an enzyme called ribonuclease. This enzyme is important in countless reactions that occur in the body, and it is likely that these reactions can now be studied more successfully.

Food Additives. The artificial sweetening agents cyclamates were banned by the Food and Drug Administration when bladder cancers developed in mice that were fed large quantities of these noncaloric sugar substitutes over long periods of time. However, since cyclamates are also used by patients who cannot use ordinary sugar, the FDA's ban was partially rescinded to allow cyclamates to be sold as long as a warning is printed on the label. This warning must state that careful medical supervision is necessary for safe use.

Also during 1969 there was much public concern over monosodium glutamate (MSG), a flavor enhancer that is widely used in Chinese cooking. A St. Louis psychiatrist reported that MSG caused brain damage in newborn mice, and although the amounts of MSG used in his experiments were far higher than any amount likely to be consumed during an average meal, the finding was enough to make manufacturers of baby foods halt the use of MSG in these products. Also, an FDA panel is looking into the safety of MSG.

Oral Contraceptives. Oral contraceptives—female hormones that prevent ovulation—have for some time been implicated as a cause of blood clots in some women. Last year, a new possible hazard of the Pill—cancer—was cited. One study showed that cancer of the cervix (the neck of the uterus) is twice as high in users of the Pill as in women who use mechanical methods of contraception. The FDA's Advisory Committee on Obstetrics and Gynecology reported in late summer that whether the Pill causes cancer is still an open question.

Early in 1970, the safety of oral contraceptives was the subject of a Senate inquiry.

Ban on DDT. Mounting concern over the use of DDT resulted in the governments calling for a ban on the pesticide within two years. This decision was based partly on evidence linking DDT with cancer and diseases of the liver, but it also high-lighted the increasing concern over harmful chemicals and the pollution of the environment.

APPOINTMENTS

One of the most controversial nominations of the year was that of John Knowles as health adviser to the Department of Health, Education, and Welfare. In January, as soon as he was confirmed as Secretary of HEW, Robert Finch announced that he wanted the Massachusetts General Hospital administrator as his health adviser.

Although he is a Republican, Knowles is regarded as being highly controversial by some of the more conservative members of the American medical profession, and these forces found an ally in the late Sen. Everett Dirksen, who, in one of his last acts before his death later in the year, publicly announced that he was against the Knowles appointment. Finally, late in June, Secretary Finch acknowledged the defeat of his nominee and chose instead another equally outspoken medical man, Roger O. Egeberg, the dean of the medical school at the University of Southern California. Although many people predicted from his past record that Egeberg would enlarge and improve the federal government's role in providing health services, by the end of the year he had done very little except fulfill a large number of speaking engagements.

Toward the end of 1969, the commissioner of the Food and Drug Administration, Herbert L. Ley, Jr., was replaced by Charles C. Edwards. Edwards had once been an official of the American Medical Association and was working for a management consultant firm before he became commissioner.

FEDERAL POLICIES TOWARD MEDICAL CARE

A month after the appointment of Egeberg, he, Secretary Finch, and President Nixon held a conference at which they announced that the nation's medical system was heading toward a "massive crisis." They also charged that the Johnson administration's Medicaid program was "badly conceived and badly organized," and that it attempted to provide medical services for the poor by using the nation's already over-burdened health care system without developing the capacity to serve these people.

With increasing public demands for health services in the face of severely limited resources, the Department of Health, Education and Welfare maintains that it is working on the most feasible short-term solution to the problem—improving the efficiency of the health services delivery system. Because a monolithic health care system may not be the most effective solution of the numerous problems of health services delivery, HEW is looking into a flexible, pluralistic approach. It is weighing the relative advantages of group versus solo practice; prepaid group practice versus health insurance plans; and comprehensive types of health care versus episodic health care.

Controlling medical care costs is intimately related to the organization and delivery of health services, HEW spokesmen maintained, pointing out that the department is exploring methods of eliminating financial barriers to good medical care while also controlling costs and preventing the system's collapse. Certainly Congress had been concerned about physicians' profiteering from the Medicaid program, and HEW indicated that it would take action, such as holding back payments and suspending doctors from the program, even taking them to court should criminal fraud be involved. In actuality, however, little was done about medical costs, mainly because a task force, headed by Blue Cross Association President Walter McNerney, is studying ways to overhaul Medicaid health programs, and it was decided that no action would be taken until this study has been completed.

While HEW was discussing the control of medical care costs, compulsory national health insurance was supported as an answer to the problem by various groups, including one headed by Walter Reuther, the president of the United Auto Workers. These groups were joined by some congressional leaders, including Sen. Jacob K. Javits and Rep. John Dingell, a long-time supporter of such a plan.

Although well over three quarters of the population of the United States is already covered by health insurance of one form or another, Reuther maintained that a national plan could catch on because two thirds of health care costs are not being met by private health insurance.

The first hint of the new administration's policies toward the control of medical care costs appeared in August, when a confidential memorandum outlining the administration's 5-year plan in health began circulating around Washington. "Health dollars will grow only moderately over the next five years," this memo predicted.

Although Health, Education, and Welfare officials protested that the memo was undergoing extensive revision, the outline of their overall policy was clear—HEW's budget was to be used in the fight against inflation. This policy had begun to be evident by the end of 1969, and it was drawing protests from many medical authorities.

Testifying before sympathetic congressmen, a number of doctors and scientists pointed out the fallacy of saving money by cutting support for health care, medical education, and research. "What amazes me," declared one witness, Abraham B. Bergman, professor of pediatrics and preventive medicine at the University of Washington, Seattle, "is that administration spokesmen can say that increased aid for health education is inflationary. What on earth do they think is going to happen to medical care costs if these shortages continue to get worse?"

Much the same note was struck by research-oriented scientists faced with cutbacks in their programs. They pointed out that without the necessary knowledge to alleviate, if not cure, disease, health services would be strained to provide custodial care for those who might otherwise have been rehabilitated.

At the end of the year, the Senate was considering a $19.7 billion bill that would provide $1.26 billion more than requested by the administration for health and education. Although the Senate passed the bill in January 1970, it was vetoed by President Nixon.

(See also the Index entry, *Medicine.*)

CHARLES S. MARWICK
Washington Bureau Science Correspondent
"Medical World News"

MEIR, Golda. See biographical sketch under ISRAEL.

MENTAL HEALTH

The year 1969 was not marked by major breakthroughs in the field of mental health, although some current research was more promising than any in several decades. Mental health programs throughout the nation continued to stagnate, primarily for economic reasons. In the last years of the Johnson administration, federal funding for mental health activities began to show only meager increases, which, in certain crucial areas such as research, were so slight as to constitute a major cutback when taken together with the higher cost of living. This trend continued under the Nixon administration. Many states followed the lead of the federal government in similar retrenchment.

Legislation and Legal Matters. It was not a strikingly innovative year for legislation in mental health. There were growing demands that treatment of the mentally ill be more fully included under the Medicare and Medicaid programs. Increased attention was focused on inclusion of care for the mentally ill under the relatively new concept of regional medical care. There was an increased tendency at the national level to see mental illness as a group of conditions to be subsumed under the general health systems.

The federal government, however, has spent much of its energy and money, since the early 1960's, in devising a different system—the Community Mental Health Center program. This system, providing for relatively small, community-based, all-purpose mental health establishments, was initiated in 1963 and came up for refunding in 1969. There is little doubt that Congress will continue the program, but it is likely that cuts will be made. Nevertheless, new laws will probably embody several new concepts, including preferential treatment for rural and urban poverty areas and for children's services to encourage and stimulate development of mental health services in these neglected areas.

A considerable and long overdue emphasis was placed on malnutrition and its relation to human behavior in 1969. Evidence that inadequate nutrition in the fetus or young child can lead to difficulties in later learning is strong. The evidence that inadequate nutrition is widespread in U.S. society is also strong, but it attracted little public concern until various senators, notably Sen. Ernest F. Hollings of South Carolina, and a CBS documentary on hunger called the nation's attention to it. The White House Conference on Food, Nutrition and Health met in December. How far its recommendations will be carried out in the austere economic climate remains to be seen.

Several states had completed, or were about to complete, the laborious task of recodifying their laws relating to the mentally ill by the end of 1969. Most of these proposed codes were considerably more "liberal" than older legislation. However, the code of New York state, which proposed to do away with many restrictions on patients' liberties, was being attacked by civil liberties groups for being too conservative. These groups contend that the mentally ill constitute no major threat to society and do not need to be dealt with by involuntary commitments.

Institutions and Manpower. Community mental health centers continued to appear, rather slowly, across the country, but considerable dissatisfaction with these medically-oriented institutions was voiced by other professional groups, notably psychologists. Difficulties in obtaining the manpower to staff them continued and there was extensive discussion of the need to train more professionals and to create new professions within the mental health field. Information compiled by the National Association for Mental Health indicated that there were over 700 training programs for mental health workers of various kinds in the United States. A few of these appear to be markedly innovative undertakings. The junior college, especially, seems to be a pioneer in training mental health workers of different types.

There was growing impatience with the slowness of many states in implementing adequate financial and career benefits. This grievance was fed by the general dissatisfaction of blacks and other minority groups with the status quo and has led to a needed reexamination of job opportunities and conditions in the mental health field.

New Approaches. A considerable flurry was caused by the apparent linking of a chromosomal anomaly (the XYY syndrome) with violent behavior. Males carrying two Y chromosomes (the usual male carries only one) were said to be taller, more aggressive, and less intelligent than the average male. Some of these conclusions probably arose from biased sampling, since the first cases described were already institutionalized individuals. The importance of studies in this area lies in the possibility of linking a specific chromosomal anomaly with fairly specific patterns of behavior.

The study of the relationship of biological processes to human behavior seems somewhat more promising than it has been in several decades. The general acceptance of the chemical lithium as a highly specific treatment for mania illustrates one reason for optimism. There appears to be growing agreement that some type of diffuse mid-brain damage may be highly associated with such major illnesses as schizophrenia. Further evidence has been reported of the importance of the genetic factor in this condition.

These possibilities do not imply therapeutic pessimism, however. Considerable progress has been made in demonstrating that people with supposedly chronic mental disabilities can function fairly well if a hospital milieu is adjusted along rational lines or if community support, when indicated, is readily available. The increasing use of therapeutic maneuvers derived from learning theory is also extremely promising.

Some of the most powerful new concepts appear to be derived from biological and sociological approaches. With the important exception of techniques derived from learning theories, psychology-based techniques appear to be showing a smaller increment of growth than procedures that are derived from conceptual frameworks based on both sociology and biology.

Although psychoanalysis remains the major theoretical system of most older U.S. psychiatrists, it has not shown any advance in theory since the publications of E. H. Erikson in the late 1950's. A study by Erikson of Mahatma Gandhi, published in 1969, was a brilliant work but did not demonstrate any striking conceptual advance over his previous positions.

DONALD P. KENFICK, M. D.
National Association for Mental Health

MERCHANT MARINE. See SHIPPING.

BLIZZARD of February 1969 immobilized New York City. The heavy snowfall brought most vehicular traffic in the city to a standstill.

UPI

METEOROLOGY

In Project BOMEX, a large-scale air-and-sea experiment in the Atlantic Ocean east of Barbados, lasting for three months in 1969, the United States contributed the first major research project to the ambitious Global Atmospheric Research Program. Sponsored by the World Meteorological Association, GARP is directed toward development of the World Weather Watch.

Project BOMEX. Attempts at a better understanding of what happens when air and sea meet in tropical oceans were made by meteorologists in Project BOMEX in May, June, and July. BOMEX (Barbados Oceanographic and Meteorological Experiment) was a joint venture of 7 U. S. government agencies, 19 universities, and 7 research institutions, in cooperation with the government of Barbados. There were 1,500 scientists participating, along with 24 aircraft, 10 ships, several weather satellites, and 12 oceanographic and weather buoys.

A main objective was to determine how much heat and moisture left the experimental area—90,000 square miles (about 233,000 sq km) of the Atlantic, from the sea floor to an altitude of 100,000 feet (130,480 meters). Meteorologists will need several years to study the information that was collected in more than 80 studies. A surprising discovery was the finding of small atmospheric fronts in the tropical oceanic atmosphere. These fronts are 3 to 4 miles (about 5 to 6.5 km) long. Sudden temperature and humidity increases are followed by a rapid drop in temperature while the humidity decreases slowly.

Numerical Forecasting. Experiments in numerical forecasts through the use of computers were extended to a worldwide scale in 1969. For the first time, a 24-hour weather map of the whole earth was made in this way. But it required 30 computing hours—too long for use in regular service.

For the experiment, the National Center for Atmospheric Research, Boulder, Colo., selected 11 levels of the atmosphere and used 10,000 items of information on temperature, pressure, and wind distribution from the day chosen—March 1, 1965. The test was extended to a 24-day forecast, and the computer calculations compared well with the events that took place in the atmosphere. As soon as faster computers become available, the mathematical system of forecasting can be used operationally. World data coverage, however, is still not sufficient to permit the perfection of this forecasting method.

A statistical approach has also produced rather useful extended-range forecasts for some localities, including California's central agricultural region. Rainfall in that area has been successfully forecast from two observed elements. The best combined indicators are the pressure pattern at 40,000 feet (about 12,000 meters) over north-central Canada and that at 5,000 feet over the southwestern United States. The procedure now works satisfactorily only where there are distinct wet and dry seasons.

A SUMMARY OF WEATHER IN 1969

Weather inflicted a variety of disasters in 1969. A summary of the year's weather follows.

Winter. The winter of 1968–69 was one of the coldest on record in the Northern Hemisphere. Arctic air extended southward from the polar regions into the moderate latitudes. The Asian parts of the USSR suffered worst. Northern Montana had its coldest winter. The extent of the cold area was without precedent, embracing all North America, Europe except Spain, Asia, the Arctic Ocean, and the eastern North Atlantic.

The semipermanent low-pressure zones near the Aleutians and Iceland were displaced far southward, leading to strong precipitation in the south and causing floods in southern California that took 91 lives and did $35 million damage. Rare snows fell in the hills of Israel, and the Jordan River flooded.

In the USSR, extremely strong winds in the farm regions of Kazakhstan created a situation reminiscent of the U. S. dust bowl of the 1930's. Virgin lands had been plowed without providing shelter belts, and so hundreds of thousands of acres of wheat were ruined, and farm machinery was clogged by dust.

In the United States, record snowfalls occurred in Oregon, Washington, Idaho, California, and Montana. Two February storms caused havoc in metropolitan areas from Pennsylvania to Maine. A February 24–28 storm set snowfall records for a single storm in Maine, Vermont, New Hampshire, and Massachusetts. It paralyzed Boston and New York. Early tornadoes in January killed 29 in Mississippi.

In Brazil, drought prevailed in São Paulo, where a heat wave caused 113 deaths and sent 10,000 to hospitals for treatment for dehydration. Floods destroyed a shanty town near Rio de Janeiro and made thousands homeless in northern Minas Gerais state. In Africa, Ghana's cocoa crop was severely damaged by excessive rainfall. South Africa had one of its worst droughts, necessitating water rationing in the Witwatersrand.

Spring. March floods in the state of Alagoas in Brazil killed 400 persons and made 40,000 homeless. In Iraq a rare Tigris flood south of Baghdad drove 8,000 persons from their homes. Zambia suffered from heavy rains. In the USSR a massive ice jam on the Dniester River caused inundation of hundreds of homes in the Moldavian S.S.R.

A cyclone that was accompanied by 22 inches of rain killed over 1,000 in the Dacca region of East Pakistan and injured 5,000 on April 14. A similar death toll was exacted on May 23 by the worst cyclone in 20

years to hit the Indian state of Andhra Pradesh, where it caused severe floods in the Guntur district. In mainland China's Shantung province, on the northern coast, tidal waves whipped by 200-mph winds surged inland for 13 miles on April 23 and affected more than 100,000 people. China, however, announced no casualty figures.

The United States had close to average spring temperatures. However, exceptional cold lingered in the Arctic and killed winter crops in the eastern USSR. The Tokyo region had its latest heavy snowfalls since 1893. The Mississippi and Des Moines rivers overflowed in April and forced thousands from their homes, but warnings by the weather bureau and hasty sandbagging prevented deaths and reduced damage. Major New England rivers also had bad floods. In the Denver, Colo., area more than half of the annual average precipitation fell in one week and caused flash floods. A rash of tornadoes hit the Midwest from May 8 to 10, injuring scores and making hundreds homeless.

Summer. Persistent, severe drought plagued northern and central Mexico. Wheat losses alone mounted to $30 million. In contrast, heavy rains in southern Mexico flooded lowlands, and thousands had to be evacuated from their homes in the state of Oaxaca.

In Asia storms and floods took a fearful toll. June floods in Suruya Bay, Japan, swept scores to their death, sank eight ships, and washed out 37 bridges. Rain-induced landslides killed many on Japan's Kyushu Island. The Yangtze River reportedly rose to its highest peak in history in Anhwei province, China. In August, 15,000 Laotians had to flee their houses along the Mekong River. Torrential downpours made more than 10,000 homeless near Seoul, Korea.

In the United States, a flash thunderstorm along Lake Erie in Ohio on July 4 took at least 41 lives, injured several hundred persons, and caused about $70 million property damage.

Hurricane Camille—the strongest storm to strike the country in recorded history, registering 200 mph winds —devastated the coast of Mississippi between Gulfport and Biloxi, as well as parts of the Louisiana lowlands, on August 17. Moving northward in its deteriorating phases, the hurricane dumped up to 11 inches of rain on Virginia, creating flash floods and an unpredicted rise of the upper James River that brought death and destruction. Hurricane Camille killed at least 300 persons, made 200,000 temporarily homeless, and did $1 billion worth of property damage, including the loss of 94 vessels sunk or stranded.

A later storm, Hurricane Francelia, did extensive damage in Honduras and El Salvador.

Fall. Exceptional storminess developed over the Northern Hemisphere. By the last week of November, when few tropical storms occur, Martha became the 13th of the year, bringing heavy rains and floods to Costa Rica, Nicaragua, and Panama.

In September, New York City had its heaviest 2-day rainfall in 25 years, and Hurricane Gerda skirted New England, producing copious rains. October rains caused floods in the central Great Plains and Texas. (Meanwhile, continued drought drove many people from their farms in the Mexican state of Durango.)

Severe September floods occurred in Pakistan and in South Korea, where 300 died and 400,000 became homeless. Typhoon Elsie killed scores in Taiwan and destroyed 5,000 homes.

Unusual North African rainfalls led to unprecedented floods in Tunisia, leaving hundreds of thousands homeless. Kairouan in that country had 20 inches of rain— its normal 3-year total—in one month. The rains also reached into the northern sector of the Sahara. In southern Spain, the rains were the heaviest since 1930.

The Red Cross had to shelter 100,000 Nigerians as a result of floods. Southern England and Sydney, Australia, also were hit by floods.

"Frankly, I don't like the look of the weather . . ."

NORRIS IN THE ''VANCOUVER SUN''

444

Precipitation Studies. Many attempts at a better understanding of the ways precipitation is naturally formed are in progress. In England, corner reflectors were dropped by parachute into warm-front systems. These were tracked by radar to measure the horizontal convergence of wind flow. From this were calculated the speeds of updrafts, which attained up to 20 cm (8 inches) per second. The magnitude of the updrafts corresponded well with rainfall amounts measured at the ground. Precipitation cells extended about 50 to 100 km (30 to 60 miles).

A mass spectrometer analysis of oxygen isotope ratios in various layers of large hailstones yielded their thermal history and showed that they were cycled up and down in the clouds several times before falling to earth. For 5-cm (2-inch) hailstones, updrafts of 50 meters (about 160 feet) per second were indicated.

Laser beams have been used to produce holograms of cloud elements in a quart volume. This permits better sampling of drop concentrations.

Airborne studies of the electrical properties of large convective clouds of the type leading to thunderstorms have shown that charges are highest on rimed (frosted) aggregates of ice crystals. These are usually found at levels where both frozen and liquid droplets are present. The electrification structure of mature clouds was found to be very complex, but it appears that inductive processes cause the separation of electric charges. When lightning occurs, coalescence of droplets is often initiated, leading to heavy gushes of rain at the surface.

Weather Modification. Several systems for dispersing fog at airports passed operational tests. For eliminating subcooled fog droplets, liquid propane dispersal from the ground or the use of silver iodide fusees showed favorable results. For warm fog a number of other techniques have been introduced. The U. S. Air Force showed that the heat from the 16 jet engines of four parked aircraft, carried on winds up to 6 mph, can improve visibilities to more than one half mile. Inversion ground fogs have been cleared by mixing the lower cold air with higher-level warm, dry air through a downward-directed draft from a helicopter rotor. Among the chemical methods of warm fog dispersal is the spreading of finely ground common salt.

An attempt to modify Hurricane Debbie by cloud seeding was conducted in the Atlantic Ocean 600 miles (960 km) east of Puerto Rico as planes dropped silver iodide into the storm on August 18 and 20.

On December 4, after extensive analysis of results, Commerce Secretary Maurice H. Stans and Navy Secretary John H. Chafee said jointly: "We report an extremely encouraging development.... We believe that the force of Debbie was weakened by seeding." Maximum winds dropped from 98 to 68 knots, or 30%, on August 18, and 15% on August 20, studies showed.

The results of a long-term study by the USSR, released in 1969, showed that forest areas increase precipitation by 10% to 15%. This confirms an Indian reforestation experiment, conducted in the 19th century, showing about the same effect.

Concern is growing about man's inadvertent influence on weather and climate. For 15 years London, England, has had more rainfall on Thursdays than on other days. This rainfall has been attributed to cloud seeding by air pollutants accumulating in the first three days of the work week.

UPI

HURRICANE CAMILLE swept the Mississippi Gulf coast in August, wrecking these homes in Biloxi, Miss.

Jet aircraft often leave condensation trails in the substratosphere. Under suitable temperature and humidity conditions, these spread to cover the entire sky in an area. The interception of solar radiation can be significant enough to cause temperature changes near the surface. Natural contamination has shown that suspensions cause strong effects. In 1968 the atmospheric dust content—a leftover from a volcano eruption in 1963—was still above normal.

Satellite Meteorology. U. S. weather satellites send cloud-cover pictures to receivers in 50 nations. The country's 21st weather satellite, ESSA 9, was launched on Feb. 2, 1969, to make an 887-mile-high (1,427-km) polar orbit every 115 minutes.

Nimbus 3, launched April 14, made a major advance with a satellite infrared spectrometer, capable of scanning into the atmosphere to obtain vertical temperature profiles. These profiles reach at least to the cloud tops and in clear areas to the surfaces. The information compares favorably with data obtained by conventional radiosondes. During a scan, the satellite obtained 5,000 vertical temperature profiles, compared with only 70 from balloon ascents from the ground. Excellent upper-air weather maps above the cloud layers—valuable for jet flights—have been constructed from the data.

Great promise is attached to a Nimbus Interrogation, Recording and Locating System that collects weather information from remote stations and weather buoys anchored at sea. On each orbit the satellite interrogates the automatic stations and stores the data received on magnetic tape. When it passes over a ground data-collection center, the satellite transmits what is stored in its memory.

H. E. Landsberg
University of Maryland

METHODIST CHURCH. See United Methodist Church.

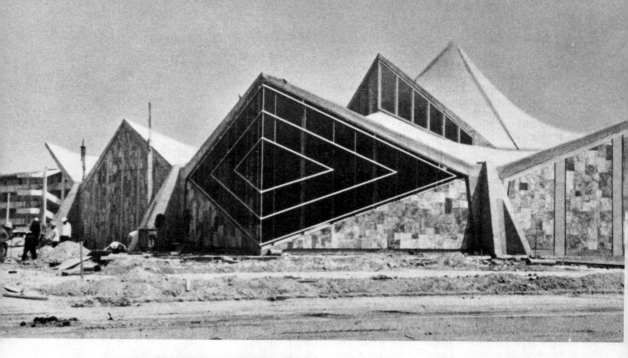

MEXICO

The year 1969 in Mexico was marked by continued economic growth at a rapid rate and by the opening of the political campaign for the presidential election of July 1970. Despite some problems and much grumbling about the repressive effects of one-party rule, the outlook appeared to be good for long-term prosperity and relative political stability.

The Economy. All signs pointed to a continuation of the economic boom that had seen Mexico rise to first place among Latin American nations in value of total production. Real growth since 1950 had averaged over 6% per year, and in the 6-year period 1963–68 it had averaged more than 7% annually, one of the highest rates in the world.

This rate apparently would be maintained in 1969. The slow pace of price advances continued, while savings and investment increased at fairly high rates. Although the income of a sizable minority of the population remained low, real wages and average annual income continued to increase slowly despite the rapid growth of population, which has made Mexico the 14th most populous nation.

In the first half of 1969, Mexico's international commodity trade gap narrowed by $60 million from the level of the first six months of 1968. There were notable increases in exports of cotton, fresh fruits, and manufactured products (up 32.4%), and lesser increases in corn, petroleum and derivatives, and fresh meats. Much of the gap in commodity exchange again was compensated for by large inflows from a continuously expanding tourist business.

Exports to the nations of the Latin American Free Trade Association (LAFTA) continued to grow more rapidly than did imports from the other member nations. Observers again were impressed by Mexican skill in adjusting export lines to changes in international demand. Mexicans were especially gratified by the continuing gains in their drive toward industrial maturity, as indicated particularly by the large rise in exports of manufactured goods.

MEXICO • Information Highlights

Area: 761,895 square miles (1,972,546 sq km).
Population: 47,267,000 (1968 est.).
Chief Cities (1967 census): Mexico City, the capital—Federal District (1966), 5,990,000, metropolitan area (1969 est.), 7,500,000; Guadalajara, 1,182,558; Monterrey, 900,630; Ciudad Juárez, 448,405.
Government: *President*—Gustavo Díaz Ordaz (took office Dec. 1, 1964). *Congress*—Chamber of Senators, 60 members (party seating, 1969: Institutional Revolutionary party, or PRI, 60); Chamber of Deputies, 210 members (party seating, 1969: PRI, 178; others, 32).
Religious Faith: Roman Catholics, 94% of population.
Education: *Literacy rate* (1969), over 79% of population aged 15 and over. *Total school enrollment* (1967)—10,170,036 (primary, 7,772,257; secondary, 1,121,745; teacher-training, 57,845; vocational, 1,063,900; higher, 154,289).
Finance (1967 est.): *Revenues,* $1,720,700,000; *expenditures,* $1,721,600,000; *public debt* (1968), $6,788,893,000; *monetary unit,* peso (12.49 pesos equal U. S.$1).
Gross National Product (1968): $27,301,841,400.
National Income (1968): $24,179,343,400; *average annual income per person,* $511.
Economic Indexes (1967): *Industrial production* (1968), 154 (1963=100); *agricultural production,* 119 (1963=100); *cost of living,* 114 (1963=100).
Manufacturing (metric tons, 1967): Cement, 5,597,000; gasoline, 4,919,000; crude steel, 3,060,000; sugar, 2,411,000; beer, 10,983,000 hectoliters.
Crops (metric tons, 1967–68 crop year): Sugar, 23,500,000 (ranks 6th among world producers); wheat, 2,400,000; sorghum, 1,150,000; citrus fruit (1966), 1,034,000.
Minerals (metric tons, 1967): Silver (1966), 41,983,529 troy ounces (ranks 2d among world producers); fluorspar, 799,602 (world rank, 1st); barite, 223,300 (1966) (world rank, 4th); crude petroleum, 19,020,000; iron ore, 2,988,000.
Foreign Trade (1968): *Exports,* $1,254,000,000 (chief exports, 1967: cotton, $143,749,300; sugar, $67,293,800; *imports,* $1,960,000,000 (chief imports, 1967: nonelectrical machinery, $478,831,800; transport equipment, $247,931,100; electrical machinery, $174,776,600).
Transportation: *Roads* (1966), 39,071 miles (62,877 km); *motor vehicles* (1967), 1,357,500 (automobiles, 917,300); *railways* (1965), 14,179 miles (22,818 km); *merchant vessels* (1967), 47 (326,000 gross registered tons).
Communications: *Telephones* (1968): 1,044,415; *television stations* (1968), 33; *television sets* (1968), 2,200,000; *radios* (1967), 10,932,000; *newspapers* (1965), 220 (daily circulation, 4,763,000).

STRIKING DESIGNS enhance Mexico City's new subway system. Highlights include the Sanlazaro station (*left*) and the decorated columns in the Insurgentes station (*right*). The first of three lines began operations in September.

Government. No news was good news for the government as the year elapsed without a repetition of the serious student unrest of 1968. However, the aftermath of those events remained to embitter political debate. President Gustavo Díaz Ordaz, in his annual message of September 1, called for national unity and condemned the violence of the preceding year. The message also contained detailed data on economic and social progress. It called for improvement in the lives of the poor, especially in the rural sector, and spoke of the need of sharing wealth more equitably.

Intermittently throughout the year, the projected new Federal Labor Law was discussed by Congress, interest groups, and the press. Controversial sections of the bill included a proposal for the financing of workers' housing by private enterprise, a new profit-sharing provision, and a provision restricting the allowable number of nonunion employees in any firm. Organized labor supported the bill, but business spokesmen declared that it would slow economic growth. The business community was not reassured by a July presidential decree that increased government control of the private radio and television industry. These and other developments stimulated fear that the government contemplated large new interventions in the economy.

The National Subsistence Commodity Company (CONASUPO), a government corporation, continued to expand its huge operation designed to provide low-priced necessities to the poor; it bought entire crops and sold commodities through more than 1,000 stores. Education—the most ambitious of the government's social services—continued to enjoy strong support, as more than 10 million students were enrolled in all types of institutions. The long-awaited opening of Mexico City's first subway line occurred in September; work continued at a rapid pace on other lines.

Political Affairs. In March, the dominant Institutional Revolutionary party (PRI) celebrated its 40th anniversary, marking four decades of uninterrupted control of the national presidency and almost all other important elective offices in the country. In February, the National Action party (PAN), the most important opposition group, elected a new party president, Manuel González Hinojosa. PAN continued its efforts to build a larger following, claiming to be to the left of PRI and calling for an end to the PRI monopoly of office.

GUSTAVO DÍAZ ORDAZ, president of Mexico, called for "equitable commerce with the United States" in May 1969, during the visit of U. S. presidential envoy Nelson A. Rockefeller. Díaz Ordaz met with President Nixon in September at ceremonies dedicating the new Amistad Dam between Del Rio, Texas, and Ciudad Acuña, Mexico. In October he criticized "Operation Intercept," instituted by U. S. authorities to halt the flow of narcotics from Mexico, as a "bureaucratic error" that was raising a "wall of suspicion" between the two countries.

Díaz Ordaz was born on March 12, 1911, in the state of Puebla, in what is now Ciudad Serdán. He graduated from the University of Puebla with a law degree in 1937 and served in judicial posts before joining the university law faculty. Elected to the Chamber of Deputes in 1946, he later became a senator and was appointed director general of judicial affairs in 1952. He served as minister of government from 1958 until his inauguration as president in December 1964.

A war of words was waged, notably in March and July, between *El Nacional,* the government newspaper, and *Excélsior,* the largest private daily in Mexico. *El Nacional* charged that *Excélsior* was distorting statements by PRI leaders and asserted that the big private paper was politically conservative and opposed to reform. PAN and various independent leftists characterized this controversy as a charade, claiming that the government and the PRI consistently supported the conservative interest groups favored by *Excélsior.*

In the various state elections held during the year, PRI won its usual sweeping victories. PAN continued to have trouble finding willing candidates. In the gubernatorial race in the state of Mexico, the PAN candidate was declared unqualified. The PRI candidate, Carlos Hank González, a recent director of CONASUPO, easily defeated his only remaining opponent, who ran as an independent.

By all odds the most notable electoral contest was that for the governorship of Yucatán. There was tension in that state because of economic depression and because of long-standing Yucatecán distrust of Mexico City and the PRI. In 1967, PAN had scored one of its few great triumphs in electing Víctor Correa Rachó as mayor of Mérida, the state capital. Throughout 1969, dispute was incessant between Correa Racho and Governor Luís Torres Mesías, a PRI man. The governor attempted to take control of the police in Mérida, and there were a number of incidents of violence involving PRI and PAN members. A general strike called by PAN

ADOLFO LOPEZ MATEOS

Adolfo López Mateos, president of Mexico from 1958 to 1964, who died in Mexico City on Sept. 22, 1969, was a leading representative of the moderate, anti-Communist left in Latin America and one of the most respected statesmen in Mexican history. During his presidential term he promoted economic prosperity and maintained WIDE WORLD friendly relations with the United States, while adhering to an independent foreign policy. He fostered diversification of industry and encouraged foreign investments. He began negotiations for the return of the El Chamizal strip to Mexico and sided with the United States in the 1962 Cuban missile crisis.

López Mateos was born in Atizapan de Zaragoza on May 26, 1910, and received a law degree from the Universidad Nacional Autónoma de Mexico in 1934. After beginning his public service career as district attorney of the state of Mexico in 1930 he worked in various posts with the government and the Institutional Revolutionary party. As federal senator from the state of Mexico from 1946 to 1952 he served as chairman of the Senate foreign relations committee and helped write the 1951 treaty regulating the entry of Mexican laborers into the United States. During his term as minister of labor, from 1952 to 1958, he helped settle more than 13,000 labor disputes.

DROUGHT seared the state of Puebla, destroying crops. A machete-carrying farmer walks the parched earth.

UPI

closed down most business and other activity in Mérida on June 13 and seemed to indicate wide support for the party. The state government arrested some PAN officials in July.

The approach of the gubernatorial election of November 23 undoubtedly increased the tensions in Yucatán. PAN nominated Mayor Correa Rachó for governor; PRI, after a prolonged canvass, nominated a federal senator, Carlos Loret de Mola. As usual, the PRI candidate won, but there were widespread charges of fraud, supported by vigorous claims that a majority of the Yucatecán populace clearly preferred the PAN candidate.

Presidential Campaign. Speculation began early over who would be the PRI candidate for president of Mexico in the election scheduled for July 1970. By late July of 1969, the press was quoting influential PRI members on leading "pre-candidates." One of the prominent names was that of Luís Echeverría Alvarez, minister of government in the Díaz Ordaz administration. In mid-August two former presidents, Adolfo Ruíz Cortines and Emilio Portes Gil, in separate statements, called for national unity behind Díaz Ordaz and asserted that all former presidents of the nation should support the PRI nominee for the presidency.

At this time, it was generally believed that the PRI directorate would announce the candidate just before the party convention, scheduled for November 17–20. In fact, the selection of Echeverría was announced late in October and was merely formalized at the convention. Echeverría, aged 47, had been active in PRI since his university days. He had held several appointive federal offices before becoming minister of government, a post of great influence that brought him into contact with a host of important PRI officials and politicians. His nomination appeared to guarantee the continuation of the pragmatic orientation of recent administrations. Resigning his office, Echeverría immediately began an energetic campaign throughout Mexico, reported on voluminously by a press that generally favored PRI.

PAN also held its nominating convention in November and selected as its presidential candidate Efraín González Morfín, the son of one of the founders of the party. Not even the PAN expected anything but a PRI victory, yet the minority party was determined to seek a record number of votes for its candidate, hoping that the size of the vote might indicate support for the PAN position on the issue of reducing the PRI monopoly of office.

Inter-American Relations. The international development that generated the most heat in 1969 was a September step-up in the campaign by the United States to control the flow of drugs from Mexico. Labeled "Operation Intercept," the campaign entailed time-consuming searches of large numbers of Mexican and U. S. citizens as they crossed the border. Intense Mexican objections to the operation, which was launched without consultation with Mexico, led to joint discussions and, in October, to a modification of U. S. inspection rules and the adoption of new cooperative procedures.

Mexico continued in 1969 to protest U. S. restrictions on the importation of Mexican tomatoes. In July, in a move affecting some U. S. fishing interests, Mexico announced that the northern third of the Gulf of California had been nationalized and was no longer open to international fishing. In September, on a friendlier note, Presidents Nixon and Díaz Ordaz met at Ciudad Acuña on the Texas-Mexican border for the dedication of the giant Amistad Dam.

ROBERT JONES SHAFER
Syracuse University

MICHIGAN

For Michigan, 1969 was a year of relative peace and prosperity. Welfare controversies, college and high school unrest, educational reform, and urban affairs in the Detroit area (see DETROIT) provided most of the news. Lt. Gov. William G. Milliken assumed the governorship in January, when Gov. George Romney resigned to become secretary of housing and urban development in the Nixon administration.

Legislation. Governor Milliken inherited a legislature almost evenly divided between Democrats and Republicans. One of his main requests was for an appropriation measure that would not require new taxes, and the first legislative session, beginning in January, was devoted largely to this problem. The lawmakers, resisting pressures for increased expenditures, managed to fit a budget only slightly larger than that of the preceding year into the "no new taxes" principle. There was much discussion both in the Legislature and in the state of the propriety of public support of private schools. A measure to provide token funds for this purpose was defeated, and the governor promised attention to the problem in a later session.

Funds provided by a $100 million bond issue for recreational purposes, approved by the people in 1968, were allocated under a formula that gave 30% to communities on a population basis and 70% to

state projects, with $25 million of the state's share being earmarked for state-initiated projects in or near urban areas.

Educational Reform Program. After a summer recess the Legislature reconvened in October to consider a program for far-reaching reform of the public school system, which had been prepared by a select commission under Governor Milliken's leadership. The commission's recommendations were prompted by a number of factors. Financing of local schools had become a continuing problem throughout the state. In many local elections the voters had refused to provide increased funds to meet rising costs. School boards were caught between lack of funds and teachers' demands for salary improvements and in some instances were compelled to use capital funds for operating purposes. In September a number of schools had to delay opening because of unresolved salary disputes. A few parochial schools had to be closed or operated on reduced programs.

The provisions of the program included: (1) a state property tax for school purposes to replace, wholly or in part, local school taxes; (2) an appointed director of education to replace the elected 8-member state board of education; (3) increased taxes on cigarettes and a probable increase in the state income tax to finance educational improvement; and (4) $25 million in public aid to private schools. Although the governor pressed vigorously for his program, there was much opposition to its

────── **MICHIGAN • Information Highlights** ──────

Area: 58,216 square miles (150,780 sq km).
Population: 8,790,000 (1969 est.).
Chief Cities (1969 est.): Lansing, the capital, 134,000; Detroit, 1,570,000; Grand Rapids, 205,000; Flint, 200,000; Warren, 180,000; Dearborn, 110,000.
Government: *Chief Officers*—governor, William G. Milliken (Republican); lt. gov., vacancy; secy of state, James M. Hare (Democrat); atty. gen., Frank J. Kelley (D); treas., Allison Green; supt. of pub. instr., Ira Polley; chief justice, John R. Dethmers. *Legislature*—Senate, 38 members (18 Democrats, 20 Republicans); House of Representatives, 110 members (57 D, 53 R).
Education: *School enrollment* (1968)—public elementary, 1,194,000 pupils (43,000 teachers); public secondary, 889,000 pupils (41,800 teachers); nonpublic schools, 336,600 pupils (11,690 teachers); college and university (fall 1967), 317,466 students. *Public school expenditures* (1967–68)—$1,510,000,000 ($782 per pupil); average teacher's salary, $8,000.
Public Finance (fiscal year 1968–69): *Revenues,* $2,874,624,353 (4% sales tax, $713,261,570; motor fuel tax, $257,854,219; federal funds, $474,215,101). *Expenditures,* $2,765,053,234 (education, $1,188,761,761; health, welfare, and safety, $741,285,182; highways, $423,398,095). *State debt,* $17,200,000 (June 30, 1969).
Personal Income (1968): $32,119,000,000; average annual income per person, $3,675.
Public Assistance (fiscal year 1968–69): $171,500,867 to 110,687 recipients (aged $31,649,889; dependent children, $115,172,027).
Labor Force (employed persons, fiscal year 1968–69): *Agricultural,* 61,900; *nonagricultural* (wage and salary earners), 3,328,900 (34.9% manufacturing, 17.3% trade, 15.3% government). *Unemployed persons* (fiscal year 1968–69)—147,700.
Manufacturing (1966): *Value added by manufacture,* $17,629,228,000 (transportation equipment, $6,729,740,000; primary metals, $1,619,686,000; nonelectrical machinery, $2,751,731,000; electrical machinery, $582,390,000; fabricated metals, $1,499,328,000; food and products, $835,151,000).
Agriculture (1967): *Cash farm income,* $911,370,000 (livestock, $455,642,000; crops, $399,689,000; govt. payments, $56,039,000). *Chief crops* (tons)—Apples, 276,000 (ranks 3d among the states); dry edible beans, 269,100 (ranks 1st); cherries, 59,000 (ranks 1st).
Fisheries (1967): *Commercial catch,* 27,800,000 pounds ($2,700,000). *Leading species* (1965)—Chubs, 5,296,373 pounds ($934,825); lake herring, 3,698,932 pounds ($306,285).
Transportation: *Roads* (1968), 114,168 miles (183,731 km); *motor vehicles* (1969), 5,100,684; *railroads* (1967), 6,511 track miles (10,476 km); *airports* (1969), 23.
Communications (1969): *Telephones,* 4,711,400; *television stations,* 22; *radio stations,* 194; *newspapers,* 55.

various provisions, and the legislators could not agree to the whole package. After two key votes failed, the session adjourned without taking any action, but educational reform seemed certain to become an important item for the 1970 Legislature.

Economy. Automobile production, the gauge of state industry, was somewhat below that of 1968, particularly in the latter part of the year, but there was no significant unemployment. Construction of individual dwellings was slowed, perhaps by high interest rates, but multiple housing and other construction continued at a satisfactory rate.

People in the News. Semon E. Knudsen was dismissed on September 2 as president of the Ford Motor Company, 19 months after he had resigned from General Motors and accepted the post with Ford. With the appointment of Dr. Clifton R. Wharton, Jr., to the presidency of Michigan State University on October 17, that university became the first major educational institution in the state to be headed by a Negro. Pamela Anne Eldred of Birmingham was named Miss America for 1970. (See PRIZES AND AWARDS.)

Other Events. Michigan became the first of the 50 states to take action toward banning the sale of DDT when the state department of agriculture voted on April 16 to cancel licenses under which the controversial pesticide is sold in the state. The order banning sales (with only a few minor exceptions) became effective in June.

A series of brutal murders, covering a 2-year period and involving seven young women in the Ann Arbor–Ypsilanti area, culminated in the indictment on August 1 of a college student on first-degree murder charges.

The University of Michigan football team played in the Rose Bowl on Jan. 1, 1970, but lost, 10–3, to the University of Southern California.

CHARLES M. DAVIS
University of Michigan

MICROBIOLOGY

The field of microbiology expanded rapidly in 1969. Important advances were made in the areas of general microbiology, food microbiology, and applied microbiology. There were also important discoveries about various pathogenic (disease-producing) microorganisms.

In the field of microbial genetics, one of the outstanding events of the year was the awarding of the Nobel Prize in physiology or medicine to three Americans—Max Delbruck, Alfred Hershey, and Salvador E. Luria—for their research on the genetic structure and function of bacterial viruses. (See also NOBEL PRIZES.)

General Microbiology. In the field of general microbiology, numerous research reports appeared on the taxonomy, ecology, morphology, and biochemical activities of microorganisms. One important study was concerned with the synthesis of vitamin K by microorganisms. The pathways for the synthesis of some vitamins by microorganisms are understood, but it was not until 1969 that scientists began to discover what compounds are required by organisms to synthesize vitamin K. Researchers found that a colony variant of *Staphylococcus aureus* requires certain intermediates to synthesize vitamin K_2. When either menadione or shikimic acid is added to their growth medium, these bacteria are able to synthesize the vitamin.

Food Microbiology. Because of the shortage of many foods (particularly those containing high-quality protein) in many parts of the world, efforts are being made to use microorganisms as a supplementary source of proteins and fats. One bacterium, *Hydrogenomonas eutropha,* is known to contain 12% to 14% protein and 9% fat. The protein has been shown to be of high quality, but the fat is not well utilized by the body.

Researchers are also continuing to study the use of hydrocarbons and oil gases as substrates for the large-scale cultivation of bacteria, fungi, and algae. These organisms are grown not only for protein, but also for vitamins and organic acids.

Applied Microbiology. The use of microorganisms in industry is continuing to grow. Rennin, the milk-clotting enzyme usually obtained from the stomachs of calves, is in short supply and may greatly limit cheese production. A rennin produced from certain molds (*Mucor* and *Rhizopus*) has the same properties as the rennin from calves' stomachs, and may be used for making various cheeses.

Several bacteria, including *Thiobacillus ferroxidans,* are playing a role in mining and metallurgy. They are especially useful in leaching copper, uranium, and other economically valuable metals from low-grade ores, slags, and other wastes. In one operation, 1,500 pounds (675 kg) of uranium oxide is being removed every month through microbially assisted leaching.

For several years the enzyme L-asparaginase has been used experimentally for inhibiting the growth of certain forms of cancer. It is now being produced commercially from various bacteria, including *Erwinia cartovora.*

The larvae (caterpillars) of the cotton bollworm, corn earworm, and soybean podworm damage an estimated $300 million of crops in the United States every year. The bacterium *Bacillus thuringiensis* is being used as a form of biological control to combat these pests. Once inside the larva, the microorganism produces a crystalline protein that stops the larva's digestive process.

Animal Pathogens. Streptococcal sore throat, influenza, and infectious hepatitis continue to rank among the most common microbial diseases reported in the United States. The first two diseases are being brought under control, and researchers are investigating the cause and prevention of infectious hepatitis.

A vaccine against German measels (rubella) has proved to be 93% to 95% effective in preventing the disease among children. This vaccine will soon be available for widespread use. A new drug, calcium elenolate, has been found to inactivate a number of viruses, including the polio virus, the influenza virus, and the herpes virus. This finding was made by Harold E. Renis of the Upjohn Company, who reported it in October.

In some areas of the world the incidence of trachoma, an infectious eye disease, is 60% to 90%. The antibiotic rifampicin has been found to inhibit the trachoma virus, and this drug may become the most useful agent for treating the disease.

A virus that causes leukemia in cats has been cultivated for the first time in human tissue cultures as well as in cultures prepared from other animal tissues. This discovery strengthens the theory that leukemia in man may be caused by a virus.

J. R. PORTER
University of Iowa

MIDDLE EAST

Political conditions in the Middle East, crossroads of Asia, Africa, and Europe, worsened alarmingly in 1969. The crux of the situation was the chronic Arab-Israeli conflict. Not only did the fabric of order and peace crumble locally, but implicit in the situation were manifest possibilities of involvement of the greater interested parties outside the area—the United States and the Soviet Union—in mutually antagonistic actions in the Middle East more direct than any that had yet occurred. These possibilities appeared to be more vividly present in the minds of policy-makers in the United States than in the awareness of their opposite numbers in the Soviet Union.

At any rate, the Soviet Union in 1969 pursued a policy of wholehearted and unrestrained support and encouragement for its protégé Arab states. There was little parallelism in the U. S. policy toward Israel, which was one of cautious and equivocal support. Meanwhile, the success of the Soviet Union in its fishing in troubled Middle Eastern waters was evident in the general trend toward radical policies on the part of the Arab states.

Between War and Peace. The basic situation in the Middle East had remained unchanged in its major outlines since the end of the Six-Day War of June 1967. But in nearly all aspects concerning the attitudes, techniques, and armaments of the parties concerned, it had become worse. The situation in Israel and the surrounding states was one of neither war nor peace. Extremely embittered foes, who had already fought each other in actual war three times (1948, 1956, and 1967), faced each other across frontiers that were continually being violated by raids and crossed by combat planes. No part of Lebanon, Syria, Jordan, or the United Arab Republic that was adjacent to Israel was physically secure from the threat or actuality of Israeli action. As for Israel, no part whatever of its territory could be regarded as entirely secure from enemy action of some kind.

The twilight struggle of air raids and commando forays, infiltration and sabotage was continually being exacerbated by fresh incidents of various kinds. One such incident was the hanging by Iraq on January 27 of 14 Iraqi citizens, 9 of them Jews, accused of spying for Israel. Another was the August 21 fire at the Al Aksa mosque in Jerusalem. The Arab nations charged Israel authorities with having set the fire—an irrational charge inasmuch as the Israelis would hardly wish to commit a pointless act that would make the Arab populations under their control harder to rule. An Australian Christian fanatic was put on trial as the arsonist, found guilty, and judged insane.

UN Secretary General U Thant commented on October 28 that the world might be "witnessing in the Middle East something like the early stages of a new hundred years' war." Indeed, the warfare had already been going on for 22 years, since the end of the British mandate over Palestine.

Acts of War. The cease-fire achieved in 1967 became more and more nominal in 1969 as acts of war across the disputed frontiers increased in tempo and scale. New precedents of violence were continually being set. The Israeli-Syrian air battle over the Golan Heights on July 8 was said to be the fiercest

air battle since June 1967. On July 31, for the first time, Israeli planes hit Arab guerrilla bases on the Syrian-Lebanese border. On the next day, Syrian pilots flew into Israel for the first time. On August 11, Israeli jets made their first attack on military positions inside Lebanese territory.

On August 10, Israeli planes bombed the Ghor Canal in Jordan out of service. The reason for this was that Arab armed forces in Jordan had breached a secret Israeli-Jordanian agreement whereby both sides undertook to exercise certain restraints in their actions. The difficulty was that Jordan's King Hussein, one of the more moderate Arab leaders, no longer had much control over anti-Israel commando activities launched from his territory. The breach of this agreement exposed the curious fact —at least it was reported as a fact in the press— that several bilateral secret pacts had been concluded between Israel and Jordan and between Israel and Lebanon, and it was reported that the United States had participated in these negotiations.

An escalation of military activity also took place during 1969 on Israel's front with the United Arab Republic. Commando raids in one or the other direction across the disused Suez Canal became relatively common. On August 27, Israeli commandos struck 160 miles (257 km) inside UAR territory and attacked an army post on the Nile. On September 8, Israel conducted a combined land, sea, and air operation lasting 10 hours, which sent weapons across the Gulf of Suez to destroy a number of UAR posts and a considerable amount of materiel. Several UAR counter-raids across the canal took place later in the year.

In this endless series of violent incidents there was a continual attrition of lives and property. Israel, engaged in a desperate struggle for survival, was in a much poorer position to sustain these losses than were the surrounding Arab states. Israel's population is one-twentieth of theirs, and Israel has no certain source for military hardware such as the Arab states have in the Soviet Union. It appeared that the United States was Israel's only arms supplier—and a reluctant one at that. At attempt by Israel in 1969 to buy arms from Britain failed, and the French government continued to renege on the agreement to supply 50 Mirage jet fighters already contracted for and paid for by Israel. The Israelis managed, however to purchase five French gunboats in late December, using a nonexistent Norwegian company as a front.

Arab Guerrilla Activity. Probably the most ominous development in the whole Middle Eastern situation in 1969 was the growing strength, organization, and daring of the Arab commando terrorist groups operating out of some of Israel's neighbors. Within the year these groups became a third force in the Middle East alongside the official state structures of the Arab world—and with comparable prestige. Since the terrorist groups are uncompromisingly extreme in their political views and dedicated to the destruction of Israel, they make the achievement of peace in the area even more remote than it would otherwise be.

Activity in Jordan. Originally the Arab terrorist organizations were based mainly in Syria. Early in

(Continued on page 454)

Israeli gunner attacks radar installation of the United Arab Republic along the strife-torn Gulf of Suez.

"I still say you launched your revenge before we commenced our retaliation."

BETWEEN WAR AND PEACE

Al Aksa Mosque in Jerusalem, badly damaged by fire in August, became another source of Arab-Israeli vituperation.

Young Arab guerrillas being trained in Jordan to pursue the battle against Israel. The trainees were recruited from the Arab refugee camps.

The existing cease-fire, which ended the six-day Arab-Israeli War of 1967, did not prevent the conflict in the Middle East from assuming warlike dimension in 1969. Several of the Arab governments became increasingly radical in their attitudes toward Israel, and the more moderate regimes either would not or could not prevent guerrillas from operating from their territories. For its part, Israel took strong measures in retaliation. Prospects for permanent peace were dim.

Al-Fatah chief Yasir Arafat (left) directs the guerrilla war against Israel.

Israeli girls must all serve in the nation's army and receive weapons training. They are an important part of Israel's forces.

(Continued from page 451)
1969, however, it became very clear that King Hussein was lacking the strength to prevent their using Jordanian soil as a base of operations for raiding across the Jordan River. The guerrilla groups operated virtually as a state within a state in Jordan. They competed with and usurped the legitimate authority of the monarchy.

For this reason, the question of what policy the royal government of Jordan wished to pursue toward the neighboring Jewish state became irrelevant to the real situation pertaining on the Israeli-Jordanian border.

Lebanon Under Pressure. In the second half of 1969 somewhat parallel developments were in process in Israel's northern neighbor, Lebanon. Half-Christian Lebanon, a banking center known as "the Switzerland of the Middle East," had hitherto, as far as possible, been neutral in the Arab-Israeli struggles. But Lebanon is small and has a small army; so when terrorist groups began to act boldly on its soil in the fall, it was difficult for the government to move effectively against them. Furthermore, such action would be a very unpopular policy throughout the Arab world and would confirm suspicions that Lebanese zeal for the Palestinian cause was lukewarm.

By the beginning of December, Arab commandos had taken control of all 15 refugee camps in Lebanon and were turning them into training and staging areas for terrorist raids into Israel. These camps are supported mainly by the United States, which now found itself in the interesting position of financing the organizing of terrorist attacks on Israeli civilians. A cabinet reshuffle in Lebanon in December appeared to have produced a government more friendly to the commandos.

The terrorist groups' activities expanded during the year to affect other than Israeli civilians. About a dozen acts of terrorism were committed in various parts of Europe—including Athens, Zurich, and London—against Israeli shipping and airline offices and planes.

Changes of Regime. Apart from the terrorist groups, Arab radicalism also scored some striking successes in gaining control of governments. In Sudan the revolution of May 25 placed in power a revolutionary council that proclaimed a policy of "Arab socialism," anti-Western and anti-Israeli. More serious in its implications was the coup in Libya on September 1, which deposed the octogenarian King Idris (then on a visit to Greece) and replaced him by a "National Revolutionary Council" of young officers who proclaimed a change-over to an "Arab-oriented" foreign policy.

The Libyan coup was a disaster for Western interests, the scope and consequences of which it would be difficult to exaggerate. Libya's rich oilfields were operated by British and U. S. oil companies, and both Britain and the United States had defense agreements with Libya and military bases there. As soon as the new regime was in power, U. S. utilization of its air base at Wheelus, the one remaining base available to the United States in the whole Middle East, was throttled down virtually to nothing. In December, Britain was forced to make an agreement to evacuate all British forces from Libya by March 31, 1970; U. S, forces, similarly, are to leave by June 30, 1970. The enormous installations of Wheelus are to be abandoned, with no compensation.

Frustrated Diplomacy. Diplomatic efforts to end, or even moderate, the chronic hostilities in the Middle East made no measurable progress during the year. Such efforts, in any case, were being made only by outsiders—the United States, the Soviet Union, and, more peripherally, by Britain, France, and the UN. Israel's objective of entering into direct negotiations with the Arab states was consistently rejected by the Arab states. In the fall, U. S.-Soviet talks, which had seemed promising in the spring, were resumed in a considerably worsened atmosphere. In a major initiative revealed on December 9, the United States proposed that Israel withdraw from occupied territory in exchange for "binding commitments" from the United Arab Republic. This proposal was rejected emphatically by all the interested parties and served to strain relations between the United States and Israel.

Loss of Western Influence. In general throughout the Middle East, there was a striking degeneration in the position of the United States and its allies, and in their capacity to influence events, and a corresponding increase in the influence of the Soviet Union. The more moderate and somewhat Western-oriented Arab states, such as Jordan, Saudi Arabia, Kuwait, and Lebanon, were losing ground *vis-a-vis* the more radical states and the commando groups. On the Mediterranean Sea the aging U. S. Sixth Fleet was rivaled by an up-to-date Soviet fleet of some 40 to 60 vessels. Even old and staunch Western allies, such as Turkey, had moved far toward economic cooperation and friendly relations with the Soviet Union.

Arab Conferences. On the other hand, the states of the Arab world had little ground for complacency. There regional meetings were far from harmonious and failed to demonstrate Arab solidarity. The Islamic conference held at Rabat, Morocco, September 22–24, was chiefly notable as the occasion of a bitter quarrel between Pakistan and India. Participants in the Arab summit conference at Rabat on December 21–23 were likewise contentious. The guerrilla leader Yasir Arafat was present as an official conference member, but both he and UAR President Nasser were disappointed in the amount of military and monetary support promised by the wealthier Arab states, most of which, as it happens, do not have common borders with Israel.

Crucial Steps for Trucial States. The nine minor Persian Gulf states, seven of which are known as the Trucial States, are faced with an uncertain future after the withdrawal of British power from the area announced for 1971. Talks aimed at creating a federation of the states began at Abu Dhabi in October. It is uncertain how successful the federation, if created, will be or whether it can prevent these amirates, some now oil-rich, from becoming a prize of Iranian or Saudi Arabian, or perhaps Soviet, ambitions.

CENTO. The 16th ministerial conference of the Central Treaty Organization was held at Teheran, Iran, on May 26, 1969, and was addressed by U. S. Secretary of State William P. Rogers. The conference paid little attention to the question of the military security of the region—which is CENTO's reason for being—but concentrated on questions of economic and technical cooperation.

(See also UNITED NATIONS and separate articles on the Middle Eastern countries.)

ARTHUR C. TURNER
University of California, Riverside

MIES VAN DER ROHE, LUDWIG

German-American architect: b. Aachen, Germany, March 27, 1886; d. Chicago, Aug. 18, 1969.

Ludwig Mies van der Rohe transformed the traditional masonry-clad skyscraper into a tower of metal and glass. His earliest training in construction came from his father, who was a stone mason. His formal architectural education came from apprenticeship to and contacts with such men as Bruno Paul, Peter Behrens, and H. P. Berlage, and from the work of Frank Lloyd Wright shown at the Berlin exhibition of 1910. Mies began his own architectural practice in 1913. He continued his practice, after World War I, with such prophetic projects as a glass walled skyscraper in 1919 and a concrete and glass office building in 1922.

Earlier Career. One of the most famous of his early designs was for the German Pavilion at the Barcelona exhibition of 1929. This was a long, low building whose simple plan seemed akin to cubist painting in its subtle proportions of solids and voids. Mies used a rich palette of materials: Roman travertine, green Tinian marble, onyx, various kinds of glass, and chrome-plated steel columns. For this building he designed the Barcelona chair in chrome-steel and natural leather, a design now regarded as a modern classic and still in production.

Another famous early design was the Tugenhardt house in Brno, Czechoslovakia (1930). These designs helped to make Mies one of the pioneers of modern architecture and one of the leading exponents of the "International style," characterized by an absence of applied ornament, dynamic and asymmetrical compositions, as well as volumes of space rather than of mass.

In 1930, Mies became the third director of the Bauhaus School of Design in Dessau, Germany—the major 20th century center of reform in architectural education. He moved the school to Berlin because of the local pressure of the Nazis and finally disbanded the center in 1933 to avoid further political interference. Mies remained in Germany until 1937–38, when he went to Chicago, Ill., as the director of architecture at the Armour Institute, now the Illinois Institute of Technology (IIT). He retired from this position in 1958.

Later Work. Among the best examples of Mies' later work are the Farnsworth House, Plano, Ill.

(1950); the apartments at 860 Lakeshore Drive, Chicago (1951); Crown Hall on the IIT campus, Chicago (1955); the Seagram building, New York City (1958); Colonnade Park, Newark, N. J. (1960); the Bacardi office building, Mexico City (1961); and the National Gallery, Berlin, Germany (1969). These superbly disciplined, minutely ordered, and extraordinarily simple designs make Mies, together with Le Corbusier and Frank Lloyd Wright, one of the best and most influential designers of the 20th century.

Mies' special contribution, and one widely imitated, was the skyscraper sheathed in glass and metal, such as his Chicago Federal Center (1964).

Concepts of Architecture. Mies once said that "Architecture is the will of an epoch translated into space...." But it was Mies who willed that architecture reflect today's advanced technology by exposing the beauty of the working structures of the building. He refined modern architecture with designs that were both simple and elegant. He showed the beauty of discipline in his scrupulous regard for consistency in the design of the large and small elements of structure.

Although Mies wrote little, his phrase that "less is more" became the famous aesthetic defense of his work. By this phrase he meant the difficult task of reducing and refining the various elements of structure and function to what is fundamental and essential; and then, by giving these factors honest expression, the designer may produce a work of art.

Ironically, in an age when the lifespan of buildings is decreasing, Mies tried to give his buildings an immortality by accounting for only such basic patterns of use as would make the structure adaptable to any time, any place, and any circumstance. He added to these impressions of immortality by the use of such monumental materials as marbles and bronze.

Unlike many creative architects, Mies did not object to his many followers and copiers, for he sought a style so simple and understandable that it could be copied and endlessly multiplied by modern technology.

Two colleagues and friends have published excellent accounts of his art: Philip C. Johnson, *Mies van der Rohe* (1953), and Ludwig Hilbersheimer, *Mies van der Rohe* (1956).

ALEXANDER R. BUTLER
Michigan State University

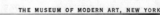

MIES VAN DER ROHE regarded the German Pavilion (*below*) at the 1929 International Exposition in Barcelona, Spain, as among his most important buildings.

THE MUSEUM OF MODERN ART, NEW YORK

WIDE WORLD

THE PERFORMING ARTS CENTER, opened in downtown Milwaukee on September 17, is surrounded by a tree grove, fountain, and sculpture.

MILWAUKEE

The opening of a $12 million Performing Arts Center and increasing urban problems dominated the news in 1969 in Milwaukee (1969 est. pop., 780,000).

Arts Center. The Performing Arts Center, built with public donations, opened in September with a gala season of concerts, operas, plays, and recitals. The center, located on the Milwaukee River, attracted capacity crowds to its 2,300-seat concert hall. In the same building is a smaller recital hall as well as a theater for Milwaukee's repertory company.

Housing. The newly organized Milwaukee Tenant's Union dramatized the need for low-rent housing by occupying the empty officers quarters of the Army's disciplinary barracks in Milwaukee. The squatters, 17 large families unable to find housing, were allowed to remain while an antipoverty agency attempted to arrange a lease with the Army.

The threatened loss of housing resulted in strong opposition to a proposed freeway on the far north side of the city. As a result, the County Expressway Commission began considering alternative plans.

A major food store chain announced plans to build an entire new community of homes, apartments, stores, schools, and community facilities in a one-square-mile area on the city's northwest side.

In 1968, Milwaukee had been granted $262,000 to plan a model cities program by the Department of Housing and Urban Development. Plans for the program were hotly disputed between those supporting Mayor Henry Maier's views and those opposed.

Transportation. City and county officials opened talks on mass transportation after the Transport Company, operator of the area's privately owned bus system, asked for new fare increases for the second time within a year. Transport Company officials said that the bus system would need to be subsidized or service would deteriorate. The City Council began study of a proposal to set up a local transit authority to help out.

Refuse Disposal. After nearly two years of study the County Board approved a countywide refuse disposal plan. Under the agreement, the county will enter into a 20-year contract with a private disposal firm to compress and bury refuse collected from all 19 municipalities in the county. It is hoped that the plan will eliminate the need for new incinerators in Milwaukee.

Economy. The city's economy was good and unemployment was low. Employment of nonwhites increased in companies affiliated with the Milwaukee Voluntary Equal Opportunity council.

Budgets and taxes soared to record highs in 1969. The City Council approved a 1970 budget of $229 million, while the county's budget was set at $218 million. Although the tax rate dropped slightly, tax payments were up because of the city's recent reassessment.

Some of the county budget increase resulted from action by the state legislature that forced higher welfare costs on county governments.

The state legislature also rejected forms of the state tax system which would have benefitted a majority of the state's towns, villages, and cities by providing them with more state tax money. A package of bills aimed at relieving Milwaukee's financial problems was also turned down by the rural-dominated legislature.

LAWRENCE C. LOHMANN
The Milwaukee "Journal"

MINING

Activities and trends in mining are reviewed in this article under two headings: (1) U.S. Mining Technology and (2) World Mineral Production.

U.S. MINING TECHNOLOGY

Some 144,000 Americans put on hard hats each day to earn their livelihood working at one of the nation's most hazardous jobs: mining from underground seams the massive amounts of coal that Americans require for heat and power. On Nov. 20, 1968, the nation was reminded of the miner's dangerous working environment when powerful explosions ripped through a large West Virginia mine, trapping 78 men underground. Rescue efforts at the Consolidation Coal Company No. 9 mine near Mannington were futile because continued explosions and uncontrollable fires wracked the mine workings. Nine days after the first explosion, the mine had to be sealed.

The West Virginia disaster, like past coal mining tragedies, triggered new public demands for improved safety conditions in coal mines. At the same time concern was voiced for more effective control of the coal dust inhaled by miners on the job. Inhalation of fine coal dust has been linked to the disease pneumoconiosis, which can severely damage a miner's lungs and ultimately stop his breathing.

Federal response to widespread public interest in safe and healthful coal mine working conditions was immediate. President Nixon's first message to Congress after he assumed office urged adoption of strong coal mine health and safety legislation adequate to meet the problems inherent in contemporary mining practices. Before Senate hearings on the proposed legislation, Secretary of the Interior Walter Hickel underscored the twin approach that the administration thought would improve conditions.

"We are committed to a strengthening of research and development to solve the technologic problems that underlie many of these hazards," Hickel said. "We are intensifying our efforts to understand and more effectively cope with the human failures that result in death or injury. At the same time we realize that, while improved technology and better knowledge can do much to make coal mining safer and more healthful, strong and sensible regulation will be absolutely essential for the foreseeable future. The need for this legislation is unmistakable—there has been no improvement in the overall fatality trend since 1947. On the other hand, since passage of the Federal Coal Mine Safety Act with its antidisaster provisions in 1952, the fatality rate from disasters has been cut by about 50%. This should provide some idea of the potential inherent in enforceable laws."

Legislation. The Federal Coal Mine Health and Safety Act of 1969 was passed by the senate, 73–0, on October 2, and by the House, 389–4, on October 29. President Nixon signed the act on December 30. The legislation:

(1) Made retired miners eligible for a new category of federal disability benefits.

(2) Provided federal authority needed to assure greater protection against all hazards, at surface as well as underground mines. (Earlier law permitted federal enforcement only under circumstances that could result in a major disaster and only at underground coal mines.)

(3) Empowered the secretary of the interior to

AMERICAN METAL CLIMAX, INC.

ORE TRAIN being loaded at Mount Newman in western Australia, where in 1969 an international group of companies began one of the largest mining ventures in history. The mile-long train carries 12,000 long tons of high-grade iron ore to Port Hedland on the coast.

establish and enforce new safety and health standards as the need for them develops. Standards previously were changed only by amending the law.

(4) Provided authority to levy substantial penalties for violations of mandatory standards. Under previous law, a penalty could be imposed only if a mine operator refused to obey a federal inspector's order.

(5) Established a minimum standard for inhalable coal dust and provided for protection of any miner showing evidence of pneumoconiosis. (Previous dust standards related only to explosion hazards; the new provision is the first federal health standard aimed at protecting coal miners' health.)

Bureau Activities. Action was taken by the Interior Department's Bureau of Mines in 1969 to assure that existing federal authority is fully and consistently utilized. The entire coal mine health and safety program of the Bureau of Mines was closely reviewed.

The bureau's health and safety activity was reorganized to operate more efficiently in carrying out research, training, and mine inspection. Also, the reorganization made the bureau ready to extend its inspection activities to noncoal mines under legislation enacted in 1966. Through expanded programs for mineral industry health, coal mine safety, metal and nonmetal mine safety, accident prevention and education, and research and testing, the bureau prepared to assume far broader responsibilities than it has ever had.

New research efforts were begun and work on others was intensified. Additional emphasis was placed on development of mining systems specifically designed to provide the miner with a safe and healthful working environment. The bureau continued investigating improved recovery and processing on minerals and fuels.

JOHN F. O'LEARY
Director, U. S. Bureau of Mines
(Continued on page 460)

WORLD PRODUCTION OF MAJOR MINERALS[1]

Aluminum (Thousands of metric tons)

	1967	1968
Australia	92.4	97.3
Austria	78.7	85.9
Cameroon	48.5	45.4
Canada	874.0	893.6
China	80.0.(?)	90.0.(?)
Czechoslovakia	65.0(?)	65.0(?)
France	361.2	365.6
Germany, East	50.0(?)	80.0(?)
Germany, West	252.9	257.0
Ghana	39.7	108.9
Hungary	61.8	63.1
India	96.4	120.1
Italy	127.8	142.3
Japan	355.5	482.9
Norway[2]	362.2	470.1
Poland[2]	92.3	93.5
Rumania	50.0(?)	76.3
Spain	69.8	89.0
Switzerland	72.3	76.9
USSR	965.0(?)	1,000.0(?)
United Kingdom	39.1	38.2
United States	2,965.8	2,952.9
Yugoslavia	48.5	48.1
Total (est.)	7,451.0	8,061.0

Antimony (metric tons)

	1967	1968
Austria	192.	161.
Bolivia	11,268.	11,055.
Canada	564.	510.
China	12,000.(?)	12,000.(?)
Czechoslovakia	2,000.(?)	1,100.
Italy	440.(?)	785.
Japan	58.	19.
Mexico	3,738.	3,464.
Morocco	1,590.	1,212.
Peru	635.	816.
South Africa	12,335.	16,793.
Thailand	1,026.	189.(?)
Turkey	965.	3,126.
USSR	6,400.(?)	6,400.(?)
United States	809.	777.
Yugoslavia[5]	2,297.	1,755.
Total (est.)	58,000.	61,800.

Asbestos (Thousands of metric tons)

	1967	1968
Canada[6]	1,309.1	1,447.9
China	150.0(?)	150.0(?)
Italy	100.7	104.0
Rhodesia	150.0(?)	120.0(?)
South Africa	243.6	236.4
USSR	769.0(?)	800.0(?)
United States	111.8	109.5
Total (est.)	2,992.0	3,098.0

Barite (Thousands of metric tons)

	1967	1968
Brazil	54.5	43.1
Canada	181.1	124.9
China	100.0(?)	120.0(?)
France	95.0	100.0(?)
Germany, West[7]	428.2	455.9
Greece	150.0	65.0
India	46.6	51.7
Ireland	76.0	143.0
Italy	154.1	204.0
Japan	37.6	55.4
Korea, North	100.0(?)	110.0(?)
Mexico	223.3	246.5
Morocco	90.5	78.2
Peru	110.0	66.6
Poland	47.0(?)	47.0(?)
Spain	55.0(?)	55.0(?)
USSR	260.0(?)	260.0(?)
United Kingdom	37.0	40.0(?)
United States	856.5	840.7
Yugoslavia	90.0(?)	86.0(?)
Total (est.)	3,508.0	3,502.0

Bauxite (Thousands of metric tons)

	1967	1968
Australia	4,236.1	4,958.1
China	350.0(?)	380.0(?)
Dominican Rep.	983.0	994.3
France	2,812.6	2,800.0
Ghana	351.0	284.7
Greece	1,692.0	1,750.0(?)
Guinea	1,617.0	2,118.0
Guyana	3,381.2	2,800.0(?)
Haiti[8]	359.2	445.7
Hungary	1,649.0	1,959.0
India	759.0	936.3
Indonesia	912.3	879.3
Italy	242.0	216.2
Jamaica[8]	9,392.0	8,525.5
Malaysia	899.6	798.7
Sierra Leone	341.6	350.0
Surinam	5,300.0(?)	5,572.0
USSR	5,000.0(?)	5,000.0(?)
United States	1,680.3	1,691.4
Yugoslavia	2,131.0	2,072.0
Total (est.)	44,608.0	44,863.0

Cement (Millions of metric tons)

	1967	1968
Argentina	3.55	4.21
Australia	3.82	3.94
Austria	4.55	4.55
Belgium	5.82	6.00
Brazil	6.41	7.28
Canada[6]	7.16	7.51
China	8.00(?)	9.00(?)
Czechoslovakia	6.20(?)	6.42
France	24.60	25.30(?)
Germany, East	7.19	7.55
Germany, West	31.51	33.44
Greece	3.45	4.00
India	11.70	11.94
Italy	26.27	29.54
Japan	42.99	48.01
Mexico	6.26(?)	6.13
Netherlands	3.35	3.44
Poland	11.14	11.60
Rumania	6.34	7.03
South Africa	3.81	4.10(?)
Spain	13.10	15.10(?)
Sweden	3.84	3.91
Switzerland	4.18	4.32
Turkey	4.25	4.73
USSR	84.80	87.50
United Kingdom	17.58	17.82
United States	65.81	67.81
Yugoslavia	3.31	3.77
Total (est.)	479.91	510.10

Chromite (Thousands of metric tons)

	1967	1968
Albania	317.0(?)	327.0(?)
Cuba	30.0(?)	(?)
Greece	50.0(?)	13.0(?)
India	104.0	205.7
Iran	180.0(?)	160.0(?)
Japan	45.2	27.9
Pakistan	30.0(?)	26.0
Philippines	419.7	439.2
Rhodesia	400.0(?)	275.0(?)
South Africa	1,149.1	1,152.9
Turkey	615.4	603.1
USSR	1,570.0(?)	1,650.0
Yugoslavia	47.2	47.0(?)
Total (est.)	5,094.0	5,025.0

Coal (Millions of metric tons)

	1967	1968
Australia	59.03	64.4
Belgium	16.44	14.8
Bulgaria	29.27(?)	29.5(?)
China	225.00(?)	300.0(?)
Czechoslovakia	90.80(?)	95.8(?)
France	50.56	45.1
Germany, East	251.80(?)	248.9
Germany, West	209.70	214.4
Hungary	27.03	27.2
India	73.40	73.4
Japan	47.41	46.9
Netherlands	8.07	6.7
Poland	147.80	155.5
South Africa[7]	49.30	51.7
USSR	595.00(?)	594.0(?)
United Kingdom	174.93	166.7
United States	510.98	509.4
Yugoslavia	26.46	26.7
Total (est.)	2,721.52	2,783.96

Copper (mine) (Thousands of metric tons)

	1967	1968
Australia	89.1	106.8
Bulgaria	31.0(?)	32.0(?)
Canada[9]	546.7	551.9
Chile	663.8	661.8
China	80.0(?)	90.0(?)
Congo (Kinshana)[5]	320.5	320.6
Cyprus[3]	15.2	17.0
Finland	28.8	29.8(?)
Germany, East	20.0(?)	20.0(?)
Japan	117.7	119.7
Mexico	56.0	61.1
Peru	181.1	213.5
Philippines	83.8	113.9
Rhodesia	17.4(?)	18.1(?)
South Africa[5]	127.5	128.2
S. West Africa	33.8	37.0(?)
Sweden	15.0	18.2
Turkey	31.0	28.8
USSR[5]	800.0(?)	800.0(?)
United States[9]	865.5	1,092.8
Yugoslavia	61.1	64.0(?)
Zambia	662.2	665.1
Total (est.)	4,986.3	5,362.0

Diamonds (Thousands of carats)

	1967	1968
Angola	1,300.(?)	1,667.
Brazil	320.(?)	320.
Central African Republic	520.	609.(?)
Congo (Kinshana)	18,453.(?)	11,904.

Diamonds (cont'd) (Thousands of carats)

	1967	1968
Ghana	2,537.	2,447.(?)
Liberia[3]	550.	750.
Sierra Leone	1,400.(?)	1,410.(?)
South Africa	7,000.(?)	7,433.
S. West Africa	1,900.(?)	1,722.
Tanzania	988.	702.
USSR	7,000.(?)	7,000.(?)
Total (est.)	42,388.	36,387.

Gold (Millions of ounces)

	1967	1968
Australia	0.63	0.80
Canada	2.96	2.69
Colombia	0.26	0.24
Congo (Kinshana)	0.15	0.17
Ghana	0.76	0.73
Japan	0.25	0.24
Mexico	0.18	0.18
Nicaragua	0.18	0.19
Philippines	0.50	0.53
Rhodesia[4]	0.55(?)	0.50(?)
South Africa	30.53	31.09
USSR	5.70(?)	6.04
United States	1.58	1.48
Total (est.)	45.61	46.19

Graphite (Thousands of metric tons)

	1967	1968
Austria	32.5	25.5
Brazil	2.9	2.3
Ceylon[3]	10.4	10.8
China	30.0(?)	30.0(?)
Germany, West	11.9	12.0(?)
Japan	1.7	1.5
Korea, South	63.9	129.8
Malagasy	16.4	16.4
Mexico	40.7	53.0
Norway	8.0(?)	8.2
USSR	65.0(?)	70.0(?)
United States[10]		
Total (est.)	378.0	437.0

Gypsum (Thousands of metric tons)

	1967	1968
Australia	787.0	833.0
Austria	738.0	698.0
Canada	4,465.6	5,575.0
France	5,300.0(?)	5,000.0
Germany, West[7]	1,116.0	1,100.0
India	1,148.0	1,321.0
Iran	1,810.0(?)	982.0
Italy	3,300.0(?)	3,300.0(?)
Japan	587.0	562.0
Mexico	976.4	1,235.0
Poland	760.0(?)	780.0
South Africa	207.6	316.0
Spain	3,000.0(?)	3,350.0(?)
UAR (Egypt)	250.0(?)	406.0
USSR	4,500.0(?)	4,850.0(?)
United Kingdom	4,593.0	4,798.0
United States	8,521.0	9,088.0
Total (est.)	46,626.0	48,925.0

Iron (pig) including ferroalloys (Millions of metric tons)

	1967	1968
Australia	5.12(?)	5.58
Austria	2.14	2.48
Belgium	8.99	10.37
Brazil	3.03(?)	3.41
Canada	6.45	7.76
China	14.00(?)	19.00(?)
Czechoslovakia	6.40(?)	6.90
France	15.68	16.70
Germany, East	2.52	2.33
Germany, West	27.37	30.31
Hungary	1.65	1.64
India	6.95	7.32(?)
Italy	7.46	7.99
Japan	41.04	47.50
Luxembourg	3.96	4.00(?)
Netherlands	2.58(?)	2.82
Poland	6.58	6.84
Rumania	2.20(?)	3.00
South Africa	3.42	4.12
Spain	2.73(?)	2.88
Sweden	2.51	2.72
USSR	74.80	78.80
United Kingdom	15.40	16.69
United States	81.17	82.87
Yugoslavia	1.18	1.29
Total (est.)	355.56	386.10

Lead (smelter) (Thousands of metric tons)

	1967	1968
Argentina	22.0	25.0
Australia[11]	291.1	286.3
Belgium[2]	107.8	95.5
Bulgaria	92.0(?)	97.0
Burma	13.0(?)	8.5
Canada	172.6	183.3
China	90.0(?)	100.0(?)

WORLD PRODUCTION OF MAJOR MINERALS, Cont'd.

Lead (smelter) (cont'd)

(Thousands of metric tons)

	1967	1968
France	115.9(?)	99.9
Germany, East[2]	25.0(?)	25.0(?)
Germany, West	136.3	120.0
Italy	60.5	57.6
Japan	150.0	164.6
Korea, North	55.0(?)	55.0(?)
Mexico	161.7	172.3
Morocco	21.4	24.2
Peru	81.8	83.4
Poland	44.3	42.0
Rumania[5]	39.9(?)	40.0(?)
S. West Africa	70.4	61.2
Spain	52.1	63.7
Sweden	42.0	41.9
Tunisia	13.2	14.0
USSR[2]	400.0(?)	400.0(?)
United Kingdom	26.8	31.9
United States	344.6	423.9
Yugoslavia	93.9	94.8
Zambia	19.1	21.0
Total (est.)	2,768.6	2,919.9

Magnesium

(Thousands of metric tons)

	1967	1968
Canada	7.88	8.96
China	1.00(?)	1.00(?)
France	4.17	4.50
Italy	6.60(?)	6.59
Japan	6.40(?)	5.66
Norway	28.50(?)	31.34(?)
USSR	40.00(?)	40.00(?)
United States	88.37	89.24
Total (est.)	183.10	187.30

Manganese Ore

(Thousands of metric tons)

	1967	1968
Australia	550.0(?)	749.4
Brazil	1,145.0	1,426.0
Bulgaria	43.0(?)	30.0(?)
China	700.0(?)	900.0(?)
Congo (Kinshana)	271.6	321.8
Gabon[8]	1,124.6	1,220.9
Ghana[8]	498.4	413.3
Guyana	178.6	130.8
Hungary	215.0(?)	209.0
India (incl. Goa)	1,599.0	1,602.0
Ivory Coast	149.4	116.7
Japan	340.2	323.0
Malaysia	85.1	45.1
Mexico	111.0	86.1
Morocco	286.1	160.2
New Hebrides	71.4	55.0(?)
Philippines	86.4	66.0
Rumania	112.0(?)	80.0(?)
South Africa	1,817.0	1,971.7
USSR	7,200.0(?)	7,500.0(?)
United States	11.4	10.3
Total (est.)	17,073.0	17,730.0

Mercury

(Thousands of flasks)

	1967	1968
Canada	...	5.00
China	20.00(?)	20.00(?)
Czechoslovakia	0.90(?)	0.90(?)
Italy	48.07	53.32
Japan	4.61	5.05
Mexico	23.87	17.20
Peru	2.98	3.12
Philippines	2.61	3.54
Spain	50.00(?)	57.26
Turkey	3.50(?)	4.32
USSR	45.00(?)	45.00(?)
United States	23.78	28.87
Yugoslavia	15.89	14.79
Total (est.)	242.00	259.80

Nickel (mine)

(Thousands of metric tons)

	1967	1968
Australia	2.1	4.6
Canada	224.0	239.1
Cuba	26.6(?)	27.2(?)
Finland	3.2(?)	3.5
Indonesia	6.0	7.9
New Caledonia[9]	61.6	79.8
South Africa	5.4(?)	5.5(?)
USSR	95.0(?)	95.0(?)
United States	13.3	13.7
Total (est.)	439.0	483.0

Petroleum

(Millions of barrels)

	1967	1968
Algeria	282.2(?)	325.1
Argentina	114.7	125.5
Canada	352.5	435.9
Colombia	68.9	63.4
Germany, West	57.3	57.7
Indonesia[12]	185.0	219.9
Iran	952.4(?)	1,039.4

Petroleum (cont'd)

(Millions of barrels)

	1967	1968
Iraq	445.8	550.1
Kuwait	836.7	886.1
Kuwait—Neutral Zone	152.9	156.7
Libya	636.5	948.5
Mexico	133.0	160.5
Nigeria	116.5	52.9
Qatar	118.1	124.2
Rumania	98.4	99.0
Saudi Arabia	948.1	1,035.8
Trinidad	65.0	66.9
Trucial States	139.5	181.8
USSR	2,116.0	2,252.0
United States	3,215.7	3,329.0
Venezuela	1,292.9	1,319.3
Total (est.)	12,889.7	14,168.0

Phosphates

(Thousands of metric tons)

	1967	1968
Brazil	390.0(?)	147.0
China	1,000.0(?)	1,000.0(?)
Christmas Is.[3]	910.0(?)	1,131.0
Israel	600.0(?)	777.0
Jordan	1,000.0(?)	1,162.0
Morocco	10,545.0	10,512.0
Nauru Island[3]	2,000.0(?)	2,254.0
Ocean Island[3]	450.0(?)	528.0
Senegal	1,266.3	1,145.0(?)
South Africa	1,300.0(?)	1,565.0
Togo	1,123.0	1,374.0
Tunisia	2,810.0	3,444.0
UAR (Egypt)	610.0(?)	1,441.0(?)
USSR[13]	16,350.0(?)	17,700.0
United States	36,079.0	37,422.0
Total (est.)	78,703.0	83,743.0

Potash[14]

(Thousands of metric tons)

	1967	1968
Canada	2,207.2	2,623.0
France	1,780.2	1,719.0
Germany, East	2,200.0(?)	2,200.0(?)
Germany, West	2,300.0(?)	2,220.0
Israel	380.0(?)	310.0
Spain	468.0	592.0(?)
USSR	2,760.0(?)	3,150.0(?)
United States	2,992.8	2,469.0
Total (est.)	15,400.0	15,549.0

Pyrite

(Thousands of metric tons)

	1967	1968
Australia	270.0(?)	170.0(?)
Canada[6]	340.5	290.0
China	1,500.0(?)	1,500.0(?)
Cyprus	1,200.0(?)	874.0
Finland	516.0(?)	774.0
Germany, West	556.0	615.0
Italy	1,411.0	1,406.0
Japan	4,527.0	4,475.0
Norway	633.7	688.0
Portugal	528.0	553.0
South Africa	552.7	704.0
Spain	2,291.0	2,403.0
Sweden	440.0(?)	474.0
Turkey	125.0	137.0
USSR	3,500.0(?)	3,500.0(?)
United States	874.7	886.0
Yugoslavia	425.0(?)	274.0(?)
Total (est.)	22,410.0	22,104.0

Salt

(Millions of metric tons)

	1967	1968
Brazil	1.04	1.54
Canada	4.86	4.43
China	13.00(?)	15.00(?)
France	4.50(?)	4.12
Germany, East	2.00(?)	2.00(?)
Germany, West[7]	6.47(?)	7.54
India	5.63	5.04
Italy	4.08(?)	3.93
Japan	0.97	0.97
Mexico	3.33	3.50
Netherlands	1.93	2.41
Poland	2.50(?)	2.63
Rumania	2.10(?)	2.10(?)
Spain	1.80(?)	1.80(?)
UAR (Egypt)	0.63(?)	0.62
USSR	9.50(?)	11.00(?)
United Kingdom	7.10	7.68
United States	35.34	37.47
Total (est.)	118.26	125.98

Silver

(Millions of ounces)

	1967	1968
Argentina	2.20(?)	2.42
Australia	19.77	21.61
Bolivia[3]	4.28	5.18
Burma	0.92	0.78
Canada	36.43	45.62
Chile	3.07	3.76

Silver (cont'd)

(Millions of ounces)

	1967	1968
Congo (Kinshana)	1.84	2.14
Germany, West	2.00(?)	2.00(?)
Honduras	4.01	4.40
Italy	1.38	1.16
Japan	10.83	10.71
Mexico	37.94	40.03
Peru[9]	35.87	36.02
Philippines	1.40	1.58
South Africa	3.06	3.34
S.W. Africa[9]	1.45	1.35
Spain	2.00(?)	2.40(?)
Sweden	4.00(?)	3.52
USSR	35.00(?)	35.00(?)
United States	32.12	32.73
Yugoslavia	3.08	2.58
Total (est.)	260.92	274.93

Sulfur

(elemental) (Millions of metric tons)

	1967	1968
Canada[6]	2.11	2.35
France	1.65	1.62
Mexico	1.89	1.69
Poland	0.48(?)	1.31
USSR	1.50(?)	1.50(?)
United States	8.42	8.96
Total (est.)	17.44	18.94

Tin (mine)

(Thousands of long tons)

	1967	1968
Bolivia	26.9	28.6
China[5]	20.0(?)	20.0(?)
Congo (Kinshana)	7.0	6.9
Indonesia	13.6	16.6
Malaysia	72.1	75.1
Nigeria	9.3	9.6
Thailand	22.5	23.7
USSR[5]	25.0(?)	26.0(?)
Total (est.)	216.1	227.6

Titanium

(ilmenite) (Thousands of metric tons)

	1967	1968
Australia	547.7	558.9
Canada	546.5	610.4
Ceylon	53.1	74.6
Finland	125.0	140.0
India	38.0	58.7
Malaysia[3]	90.8	125.8
Norway	400.0(?)	427.4
Spain	37.9	39.5
United States	848.3	887.7
Total (est.)[16]	2,710.3	2,945.7

Tungsten[15]

(Metric tons)

	1967	1968
Australia	956.0	1,148.0
Bolivia	1,585.0	1,811.0
Burma	90.0(?)	160.0(?)
Canada	(?)	1,295.0
China	8,000.0(?)	8,000.0(?)
Japan	391.0	529.0
Korea, South	2,025.0	2,092.0
Peru	256.0	509.0
Portugal	1,107.0	1,313.0
USSR	6,200.0(?)	6,200.0(?)
United States	3,765.0	4,621.0
Total (est.)	28,100.0	32,019.0

Uranium Oxide

U_3O_8 (Metric tons)

	1967	1968
Australia	300.0(?)	300.0(?)
Canada	3,405.0	3,360.0
France	(?)	1,311.0
Gabon	450.0(?)	528.0
South Africa	3,048.0	3,514.0
United States	8,278.0	11,193.0
Total (est.)[16]	16,900.0	20,474.0

Zinc (smelter)

(Thousands of metric tons)

	1967	1968
Australia	197.6	208.8
Belgium[2]	227.3	254.2
Bulgaria	80.0(?)	73.0(?)
Canada	359.4	387.3
China	80.0(?)	90.0(?)
France	185.7	207.3
Germany, West	102.7	122.0
Italy	89.0	112.3
Japan	516.2	605.6
Mexico	75.7	80.0
Peru	63.0	68.0
Poland	196.0	202.5
Spain	69.7	75.4
USSR	540.0(?)	540.0(?)
United Kingdom	104.3	142.9
United States	851.7	926.1
Total (est.)	4,128.8	4,551.5

[1] Output of minor countries not listed are included in totals. In general, listing includes countries that have produced more than 1 % of the total. [2] Includes secondary. [3] Exports. [4] 1966 data. [5] Smelter output. [6] Sales. [7] Marketable. [8] Dry weight. [9] Recoverable. [10] Withheld to avoid disclosing individual company confidential data. [11] Includes lead content of lead bullion (for export). [12] Includes West Irian. [13] Includes sedimentary rock. [14] Marketable in equivalent K_2O. [15] Contained tungsten (W basis). [16] Excludes estimate for USSR. A question (?) means an estimate or not available. Source: U.S. Bureau of Mines.

(Continued from page 457)

WORLD MINERAL PRODUCTION

New financial and institutional patterns were emerging in the world's mineral industries as they headed into the 1970's.

Although price behavior varied from commodity to commodity, the general trend of mineral prices was resolutely upward in 1969. Factors contributing to the higher prices included not only inflation but also an accelerating rate of growth in mineral demand, a rising cost of finance, and an increasing capital investment required for mineral development.

The changing financial elements led to a trend toward vertical integration of companies and a second trend toward the signing of long-term sales contracts to reduce stop-and-go production.

Vertical integration moved in both directions. Mineral processors and fabricators were integrating backward to ensure their raw material supplies. (For example, a firm with Midwestern plants opened a mine—its first—in Utah to end its dependence on imported ore.) At the same time, mineral producers were integrating forward into advanced processing and fabricating (that is, not only extracting a commodity but also making products from it).

The trend toward long-term sales contracts arises primarily from the larger capital needs of new mineral projects. Such contracts serve as investment capital by providing a steady flow of funds with which to finance uninterrupted future production.

Production Leaders. In 1968, the most recent year for which reasonably complete statistics are available, new highs were achieved in mineral production around the world. Only four metals, five nonmetals, and two fuels declined below 1967 production levels.

The United States continued to lead in output of 24 minerals. The USSR led in 11, Canada in six, and South Africa in four. U. S. leadership included aluminum, copper, crude oil, natural gas, molybdenum, phosphate, and elemental sulfur. The USSR predominated in production of lead, cement, chromite, coal, iron ore, and potash, among others. Canada is the leading source of nickel, asbestos, and silver. South Africa is preeminent in gold, platinum, and gem diamonds.

The great expansion of worldwide mineral activity is exemplified by Australia's emergence as a major mineral producer. Since 1960, Australia has risen from 22d to 9th place as a bauxite producer, from 24th to 13th in aluminum, from 18th to 8th in iron ore, and from no production to 7th place in nickel. Canada, particularly British Columbia, and Ireland are also experiencing a mining boom.

Precious Metals. In 1968 world production increased for gold (by 1.1%), silver (by 6.2%), and platinum-group metals (by 5.4%). U. S. gold production, largely a by-product of copper and base metal mining, was reduced by strikes. Probably the most spectacular event was the near-loss of about 8% of South African gold production when the West Driefonten Mine flooded in October. The influx of over 85 million gallons of water per day was brought under control in the following month, but just in time to save the whole mine from flooding.

In 1968, for the first time, there were no controls on silver prices in the United States. The prices fluctuated markedly, but the effect of demonetization upon silver production will not be apparent for some time yet.

Ferrous Metals and Ferro-Alloys. World iron ore production increased 9.2% for a record. The shift away from direct-shipping (high-grade) ore to the production of pellets continued. In the United States, pellet capacity has risen from about 1 million metric tons in 1955 to nearly 80 million tons in 1968. Because of the looming shortage of metallurgical coking coal, efforts continue to find and implement iron- and steel-making processes that bypass the conventional blast furnace.

Manganese ore production rose 6.3% in 1968. The manganese market remained depressed because of aggressive sales competition among producers.

World nickel output rose 9% despite the failure of Canadian production to reach expected levels— the result of serious skilled-labor shortages. Demand continued to outstrip supplies, no new sales were made from the U. S. government stockpile, and prices rose a bit in anticipation of a shortage.

The dependence of the free world upon the Soviet Union as a source of metallurgical grade chromite increased as the United Nations sanctions against Rhodesia reduced that country's output and barred its production from the market.

Tungsten prices remained strong, around $43 per short ton unit, the price at which surplus material is sold from the U. S. stockpile. Mainland China, with its vast reserves, remains the world's leading producer and the ultimate power in the market, but in recent years the U. S. stockpile has been the more immediate influence.

Major Nonferrous Metals. World bauxite production increased only 0.8%, although aluminum output rose by 6.4%. Declines in bauxite output in some of the leading countries was offset by the increasingly important output from Australia, where no deposits were known in the mid-1950's. Biggest news was the successful financing for development of the Boke deposit in Guinea to a planned initial annual capacity of 4.7 million metric tons by 1972. The developing countries in which most of the bauxite is produced are beginning to require that their bauxite be processed to alumina before being exported, and there are signs that this insistence upon local processing may extend to aluminum. The United States, USSR, Canada, Japan, Norway, and France together account for 77% of aluminum metal production.

Despite continuation of the U. S. base metal strike, until April 1968, world copper production increased 6.9%. Continued strong demand resulted in significant price increases.

Lead output, 4.9% above 1967, set a record. The USSR captured first place from Australia. The United States might have edged out Canada for third place had it not been for losses occasioned by the prolonged base metal strike and start-up difficulties in several new mines in Missouri.

Zinc production increased by 2.7% over 1967 and prices held stable except for an end-of-the-year increase of a half-cent on the London Metal Exchange. In West Germany, the Rammelsberg lead, zinc, and copper mine celebrated its 1,000th year of continuous operations in 1968.

Tin production increased 5.8% and outstripped demand for the second consecutive year, resulting in the imposition of mild export quotas by the International Tin Council upon producers.

Miscellaneous Metals. World antimony output increased 6.9%. However, unexpectedly reduced supplies from the largest producer, mainland China, resulted in higher European prices by year's end.

Mercury supply and demand remained pretty well in balance in 1968 as reflected by the high but unusually stable price that prevailed (New York average $535.36 per flask). Mercury output, up 11.6%, increased for the first time in two years, but output does not appear to be responding as expected to the continued high prices.

Beryllium production in 1968 increased 31% in response largely to U. S. missile and space program demands. Bertrandite deposits of Utah are being developed to end U. S. dependence upon imports.

Uranium production in the non-Communist world increased 18.9% as a result of the expanding use of nuclear energy for generating electricity.

Fertilizer Minerals. World production of the three major fertilizer minerals increased—phosphate by 7.2%, potash by 1.7%, and sulfur by 5.7%. Consumption, however, did not grow at the expected rate, and the industries showed signs of over capacity.

Fuel Minerals. World production of coal increased slightly in 1968, but production continued to decline throughout western Europe. U. S. production fell slightly because of labor difficulties. There was a stronger demand for coal for the generation of electricity in steam plants.

Crude petroleum production continued to increase. (For details, see PETROLEUM.)

FRANK H. SKELDING
President, AMDEC Corporation
Mineral Industry Consultants

MINNESOTA

For Minnesota, 1969 was a year of increasing fiscal crisis in city government. Residents of the Twin Cities (St. Paul-Minneapolis) and Duluth, as well as smaller communities, were faced with new taxes or sharply curtailed municipal services. During the year public attention was also focused on problems of law enforcement and pollution control.

Urban Developments. In its biennial session, the state legislature did not attempt to deal comprehensively with city problems. Laws were passed in response to some specific needs: a seven-county sewer authority was established for the Twin Cities and suburbs; provision was made for public acquisition of "open spaces" in metropolitan areas; penalties for certain crimes were stiffened. But financial relief was not forthcoming for the hard-pressed cities, which had to resort to patchwork expedients. In September, Duluth voters approved a 1% city sales tax. A city income tax was rejected by St. Paul voters on December 9. Meanwhile, civic leaders continued to plead for statewide tax reform to meet the needs of city governments.

Widespread concern over law and order seemed to be reflected in the election on June 10 of former policeman Charles Stenvig as mayor of Minneapolis. Stenvig's election drew national attention because he had run on a platform advocating strict law enforcement. He received 62% of the vote in an abnormally heavy turnout.

The feasibility of an integrated mass transit system for the Twin City area was under intensive study by the Metropolitan Transit Authority. Interest in public purchase of the privately owned Twin City Lines, largest of the metropolitan bus companies, increased after suspension of service during a strike from November 17 to December 12. Opposition

─────── **MINNESOTA** • Information Highlights ───────

Area: 84,086 square miles (217,736 sq km).
Population: 3,632,000 (1969 est.).
Chief Cities (1969 est.): St. Paul, the capital, 300,000; Minneapolis, 440,000; Duluth, 101,000.
Government: *Chief Officers*—governor, Harold LeVander (Republican); lt. gov., James B. Goetz (R); secy. of state, Joseph L. Donovan (Democratic-Farmer-Labor); atty. gen., Douglas M. Head (R); treas., Val Bjornson; supt. of pub. instr., Duane J. Mattheis; chief justice, Oscar R. Knutson. *Legislature*—Senate, 67 members (nonpartisan); House of Representatives, 135 members (nonpartisan).
Education: *School enrollment* (1968)—public elementary, 479,000 pupils (19,000 teachers); public secondary, 403,000 pupils (20,500 teachers); nonpublic schools, 154,900 pupils (6,390 teachers); college and university (fall 1967), 138,239 students. *Public school expenditures* (1967–68)—$726,033,000 ($894 per pupil); average teacher's salary, $7,859.
Public Finance (fiscal year 1968): *Revenues,* $1,472,194,000 (sales and gross receipts taxes, $113,078,000; motor fuel tax, $108,114,000; federal funds, $349,474,000). *Expenditures,* $1,357,616,000 (education, $272,766,000; health, welfare, and safety, $96,813,000; highways, $208,876,000). *State debt,* $356,641,000 (Dec. 31, 1968).
Personal Income (1968): $12,185,000,000; average annual income per person, $3,341.
Public Assistance (fiscal year 1968): $157,986,600 to 139,775 recipients.
Labor Force (employed persons, Aug. 12, 1967): *Agricultural,* 243,000; *nonagricultural* (wage and salary earners), 1,381,900. *Unemployed persons* (Aug. 20, 1967)—44,000.
Manufacturing (1967 est.): Value added by manufacture, $3,850,000,000 (1965, transportation equipment, $153,060,000; nonelectrical machinery, $670,004,000; electrical machinery, $269,008,000; fabricated metals, $165,969,000; food and products, $637,082,000).
Agriculture (1967): Cash farm income, $1,925,995,000 (livestock, $1,236,728,000; crops, $594,016,000; govt. payments, $95,251,000). *Chief crops* (tons)—Hay, 7,583,000 (ranks 1st among the states); oats, 2,515,712 (ranks 1st); flaxseed, 105,924 (ranks 3d).
Mining (1966): Production value, $550,277,000. *Chief mineral* (tons)—Iron ore, 55,133,000.
Fisheries (1966): *Commercial catch,* 13,092,000 pounds ($995,000).
Transportation: *Roads* (1968), 127,099 miles (204,539 km); *motor vehicles* (1968), 2,267,111; *railroads* (1968), 12,066 track miles (19,418 km); *airports* (1969), 11.
Communications (1967): *Telephones* (1968), 1,906,200; *television stations,* 17; *radio stations,* 107.

from residents near projected sites delayed selection of a location for a critically needed second airport.

Anti-Pollution Issue. The legislature extended the powers of the Minnesota Pollution Control Agency and authorized state payment of interest on bonds sold by communities to finance pollution abatement facilities. A dispute developed between state authorities and the Northern States Power Company over regulation of waste disposal from nuclear generating plants. Gov. Harold LeVander vigorously upheld the right of the state to establish higher standards than those approved by the federal Atomic Energy Commission. Challenging this, Northern States Power sued the state.

Legislative Action. Appropriations by the legislature for the 1969–71 biennium included $850.8 million for education (an increase of $191.9 million over 1967–69) and $270.5 million for welfare and corrections (an increase of $62.3 million). A reorganization of the state's administration was authorized, significantly increasing the power of the governor. The most controversial of the legislature's actions was the adoption of a statute requiring school districts providing free busing for public school students to give the same service to students of private schools.

Natural Disasters. Record snowfalls in the state during the 1968–69 winter were followed by damaging spring floods in communities along the Mississippi and Minnesota rivers. A series of tornadoes struck the lake resort area of north-central Minnesota on August 6, killing 15 persons.

JEANNE SINNEN
University of Minnesota Press

ABM ISSUE was hotly debated before the Senate Armed Services Committee in March. Committee is in foreground, military heads at table.

MISSILES

Although in 1969 the United States maintained superiority in missile forces by virtue of its combined submarine, bomber, and intercontinental ballistic missile assets, the Soviet Union for the first time surpassed it in one aspect. Instead of leveling off production of ICBM's, the USSR continued to produce and deploy SS-9 missiles.

In early spring, the Soviets had more than 1,000 operational ICBM's on launchers, achieving parity with the United States for the first time. By midsummer, the number surpassed 1,200, and by the end of 1969 the total was expected to reach 1,400.

SALT. A significant event was the beginning of Strategic Arms Limitation Talks (SALT) between the United States and the Soviet Union. The meeting opened on November 17 in Helsinki, Finland, with discussions of broad areas of development and deployment of nuclear arms that might be curtailed through agreement. (See also DISARMAMENT.)

U. S. ICBM Force. The United States maintained its force of 1,000 Minuteman I's and II's, and 54 Titan II missiles, improving the ability of these weapons to survive attack rather than increasing their numbers. At the end of 1969, replacement of I's and II's had resulted in a total of about 550 I's and 450 II's. Plans called for replacing the remaining I's with the newer Minuteman III missile, for a force of about 500 II's and 500 III's.

The conversion of the Polaris submarines to enable them to carry the multiwarhead Poseidon missile continued, with 31 out of 41 Polaris submarines to be fitted for the larger, improved missile. The United States had 656 Polaris missiles deployed in nuclear submarines, with some of the later A-3 models carrying clusters of three warheads for "shotgun" effect.

MIRV. Development of the true multiple, independently targeted reentry vehicle (MIRV) payloads for both Minuteman III and the Poseidon missile continued. Some 14 Minuteman and 13 Poseidon missile test launches had been conducted by the end of 1969. The Minuteman III will carry three Mark 12 reentry vehicles with a warhead yield of about

170 kilotons each, while Poseidon is to carry up to 10 Mark III reentry vehicles with a yield of 40 kilotons each. Development was expected to be complete by mid-1970.

MIRV deployment, along with the anti-ballistic missile (ABM) system, became one of the most controversial subjects of the year. A unilateral moratorium on MIRV testing was opposed by the Defense Department, on the grounds that the United States needed MIRV as long as the USSR had an ABM system. By separating the reentry vehicles carried by one missile, a number of targets could be attacked, and the chances of penetrating an ABM defense would be much greater. Although there were arguments that MIRV intensified the arms race by multiplying the number of warheads, the Defense Department claimed that because of the weight of the "bus," or vehicle that carried the reentry vehicles, and its guidance system, each warhead would be so much smaller that MIRV could not be used by the United States for a first strike. The enemy would have no doubt that it was for deterrent use only.

The USSR also conducted MIRV tests in the Pacific, and the Pentagon estimated it could deploy the SS-9 missile with a MIRV triplet in late 1970. Defense Secretary Melvil R. Laird said the pattern in which the Soviet dummy warheads landed coincided with the spacing of U. S. Minuteman silos (underground launch sites). Laird estimated that, because of the greater boost of Soviet missiles, three reentry vehicles of five megatons each could be mounted on the SS-9. Each could knock out a Minuteman silo.

Silos. The search went on for sites for construction of new ICBM silos in areas with extremely hard rock, which would withstand a close hit by a missile. Although some that appeared suitable at first were found to have internal fissures and cracks, the Air Force reported it could find enough areas to carry on the project.

Airborne Missiles. The Air Force continued to upgrade its strategic intercontinental bomber force, with development of the Short Range Attack Missile (SRAM). SRAM was expected to go into production in 1970, after experiencing engine difficulties late in development. The Air Force also initiated a new Subsonic Cruise Armed Decoy (SCAD) missile program. SCAD, the same size of SRAM, also would be carried by the B-52, the FB-111, and later by the new B-1 bombers. SCAD would both act as a decoy for the bomber and carry a nuclear warhead. The warhead, Air Force strategists thought, would make it necessary for enemy defenses to counter the decoys, exhausting their interceptor defenses and diverting attention from the bomber.

U. S. Tactical Missiles. The United States continued advanced development of the Navy's long-range air-to-ground Condor standoff missile and the Army's extended-range surface-to-surface Lance, both of which developed propulsion problems.

A major Navy development was the initiation of the NATO Sea Sparrow missile system with Italy, Norway, and Denmark. The NATO Sea Sparrow system will have a completely new fire-control system for launching the Sparrow missile. The United States has a particular interest in the program as part of its plan for integrating defenses against the Soviet Styx and other cruise missiles. Other portions of the U. S. Ship Anti-Missile Integrated Defense (SAMID) program included upgrading the ability of the Terrier, Tartar, and Talos missiles to attack incoming missiles, and new electronic warfare techniques. Improvements were made in a number of U. S. warships under the SAMID program.

The Army also initiated production of an improved Hawk surface-to-air missile system, incorporating a computer to automate the Hawk battery.

Both the Air Force and Navy started work on short-range air-to-air "dogfight" missiles for new fighters. The Defense Department cut out some of the duplicating missile programs—the Air Force's AGMX-3 long-range standoff missile was canceled.

U. S. Missiles in Vietnam. The most important U. S. missile development in the Vietnam War was the introduction of laser guidance for bombs and missiles. The Air Force used a laser on its F-4 aircraft to focus a beam on the target. The missile or bomb, fitted with a special seeker, would home in on the reflected light. The Pentagon's research chief, John Foster, said the increased accuracy would reduce by 90% the number of bombs that must be dropped on a target. It would also cut down aircraft losses, because of the reduced number of flights necessary.

Such air-to-air missiles as Sparrow and Sidewinder, and air-to-ground missiles as Walleye, Standard ABM, and Shrike, continued in use in Vietnam.

Soviet Union. More than 275 of the Soviet Union's estimated 1,400 intercontinental ballistic missiles were believed to be SS-9's, a missile with a warhead yield of up to 25 megatons. U. S. intelligence believed that the SS-9, even when carrying several warheads with a lower yield each, would be capable of destroying a Minuteman ICBM in its silo.

Defense Secretary Laird said that by the mid-1970's, the USSR would have about 400 operational SS-9's, including a new version with considerably greater accuracy. If the Soviet Union increased its force to 420 SS-9's, and improved their accuracy to within 0.25 mile (400 meters) from the target, they could destroy 95% of the U. S. Minuteman force, leaving only 50 surviving, Laird told Congress.

More than two thirds of the Soviet missile force still consisted of SS-11's, a small liquid-fuel missile about the size of the U. S. Minuteman. With its currently estimated warhead size and accuracy, the Defense Department said, it did not pose a threat to the Minuteman force at the present time. The USSR also started deployment of a new solid-fuel ICBM, designated the SS-13, which had an even smaller warhead and was considered even less of a threat than the SS-11.

Soviet intentions regarding deployment of the Fractional Orbital Bombardment System (FOBS) were unclear after the initial test program was completed. FOBS would be launched into partial orbit, traveling at a lower altitude than other ICBM's and thus approaching the United States below the traditional defense screens of the Ballistic Missile Early Warning System (BMEWS) and other radars.

The United States continued its deployment of over-the-horizon radar to provide radar coverage in case of a FOBS attack. Because the FOBS weapons used the same launchers as the SS-9 missile, U. S.

(*Continued on page 465*)

DIRECTORY OF MAJOR U. S. MISSILES

Missile	Status[1]	Service	Range[2] (nautical miles)	Propulsion
Surface-to-Surface				
Asroc[3]	O	Navy	5	Solid
Dragon[4]	P	Army	500–1500 yards	Solid
Extended Range Lance	D	Army	60	Storable liquid
Honest John	O	Army	12	Solid
Little John	O	Army	10	Solid
Mace B	O	AF	1200+	Solid or turbojet
Minuteman I, II	O	AF	6300 and 7000	Solid
Minuteman III	D	AF	. . .	Solid
Pershing	O	Army	500	Solid
Polaris A-2, A-3	O	Navy	1200 and 2500	Solid
Poseidon	D	Navy	2800+	Solid
Sergeant	O	Army	75+	Solid
Shillelagh	P	Army	short	Solid
STAM[3]	S	Navy	. . .	. . .
Subroc[3]	O	Navy	25–30	Solid
Titan II	O	AF	6300+	Storable liquid
Tow[4]	P	Army	. . .	Solid
ULMS and SLMS	S	Navy	5000+	Solid
WS-140A or Minuteman IV	S	AF	8000+	Solid
Surface-to-Air				
Antisatellite Weapon	O	AF	. . .	. . .
APDMS	S	Navy	. . .	. . .
Bomarc B	O	AF	400	Solid or ramjet
Chaparral	P	Army	. . .	Solid
Hawk	O	Army	22	Solid
Improved Hawk	P	Army	. . .	Solid
Nike Hercules	O	Army	75	Solid
Redeye	O	Army	. . .	Solid
Sam-D	D	Army	. . .	Solid
Sea Sparrow	O	Navy	. . .	Solid
Sea Sparrow, NATO	D	Navy, NATO	. . .	Solid
Spartan	P	Army	300–400	Solid
Sprint	P	Army	20–30	Solid
Standard	O	Navy	10–30+	Solid
Talos	O	Navy	65+	Solid or ramjet
Tartar	O	Navy	10+	Solid
Terrier	O	Navy	10+	Solid
Air-to-Air				
Dogfight, AF	S	AF	. . .	. . .
Dogfight, Navy	S	Navy	. . .	. . .
Falcon	O	AF	2+	Solid
Genie	O	AF	6+	Solid
Phoenix	D	Navy	50+	Solid
Sidewinder	O	AF–Navy	2+	Solid
Sparrow	O	AF–Navy	5–8	Solid
Sparrow (Advanced)	D	AF–Navy	. . .	Solid
Air-to-Surface				
Bullpup	O	AF–Navy	3–6	Storable liquid
Condor	D	Navy	40+	Storable liquid
Hound Dog	O	AF	600+	Turbojet
Maverick	P	AF	. . .	Solid
SCAD	D	AF	1000	Solid
Shrike	O	AF–Navy	. . .	Solid
SRAM	D	AF	50+	Solid
Standard ARM	O	AF–Navy	. . .	Solid
Walleye	O	AF–Navy	3–6	None
Zuni	O	Navy	5	Solid

[1] Status code: D, under development; O, operational; P, production; S, study. [2] One nautical mile equals 1.15 statute miles or 1.85 km. [3] Antisubmarine missile. [4] Antitank missile.

THE GREAT ABM DEBATE

The Nixon administration made significant changes in the planned U. S. anti-ballistic missile system in 1969, shifting the emphasis from protection of the cities to protection of the Minuteman ICBM sites. Work on the Sentinel system was halted on February 6, and the new Safeguard modified system was announced early in March.

Defense Secretary Melvin R. Laird said the decision was made because the Sentinel system offered little, if any, protection against a massive attack. The Safeguard system, by contrast, should prevent an attack by the USSR or Communist China by protecting the deterrent ICBM force so it could survive a first strike and retaliate.

The Safeguard system would use the same components as the Sentinel but arranged differently. Included would be Perimeter Acquisition Radars (PAR) along the northern boundary and in the two southern corners of the United States. These phased-array radars, with computer complexes, could sight incoming missiles more than 1,000 miles away, discriminate between missiles and decoys to some extent, and track up to 100 incoming objects at the same time. Short-range Missile Site Radars would take over as the incoming objects approached, relaying information to the interceptor missile guidance systems. The Spartan missile, with a range of from 300 to 400 miles, would be launched against targets at a distance, and the Sprint, with a 30-mile range, used for terminal defense of the Minuteman sites.

The administration proposed to start construction at the two Minuteman bases at Malmstrom AFB, Mont., and Grand Forks, N. Dak. The cost of ringing two Minuteman bases with ABM protection was estimated at $2.1 billion. The next step, the administration said, would be based on the enemy threat. If the USSR increased its ICBM force in a way that appeared to threaten the Minuteman force, two more ABM sites would be constructed at other Minuteman bases. If the Soviet submarine ballistic missile threat to the U. S. bomber force, or the Chinese missile threat should increase, the Pentagon proposed bringing the number of ABM sites to 12. Additional sites might also be added in Hawaii and Alaska, bringing the total cost to $10.8 billion, including nuclear warheads furnished by the Atomic Energy Commission.

In Congress the proposal triggered an almost unprecedented debate, cutting across party lines and lasting most of the summer. In the Senate, the attack on the ABM was led initially by Senators Mike Mansfield, Edward Kennedy, George McGovern, John Sherman Cooper, and J. William Fulbright. Their arguments included the disbelief that the system would work; fear that it might provoke the Soviet Union into putting multiple warheads on its missiles in the same way that the United States had reacted to the Soviet ABM system several years earlier; and suspicion that the system would commit the United States to a "thick" system of city protection.

Scientists reinforced the arguments with technical data. Hans Bethe, professor of physics at Cornell University, raised doubts about the ability of the system to counter penetration aids and decoys, and suggested that the radars could be "blacked out" by the first nuclear burst.

A report commissioned by Sen. Edward Kennedy and written by Abram Chayes of Harvard and Jerome B. Wiesner, former scientific adviser to President Kennedy, was distributed to senators on May 6. Entitled *An Evaluation of the Decision to Employ an Antiballistic Missile System,* it summarized many of the views critical of the ABM. The basic technical objection was that Safeguard's radars and computers could not be fully tested before an enemy attack, and would probably fail.

Proponents of the system immediately counterattacked. The American Security Council, an independent Washington-based organization, published a report, also on May 6, calling the ABM the "soundest insurance for peace and against war that the United States can buy." It was written by a committee headed by Nobel Prize winner Willard F. Libby, William J. Thaler of Georgetown University, and Gen. Nathan F. Twining, USAF, retired, former chairman of the Joint Chiefs of Staff. They rejected arguments that the system would not work, and that it would accelerate the arms race. Another book, *Why ABM?,* was published by the Hudson Institute, which had done research for the Defense Department. The book claimed that the system would provide protection against the Communist Chinese or an accidental Soviet launch.

The Senate Armed Services Committee recommended Safeguard for approval by the Senate. Senators John Sherman Cooper and Philip Hart presented an amendment to preclude use of budget funds for deployment. Senators Clinton Anderson and John Williams were uncommitted and considered to have the key votes. Sen. Margaret Chase Smith of Maine forced the issue by offering an amendment to bar funds for any aspect of development or construction. This was defeated, 51 to 50. The Cooper and Hart amendment was defeated, 51–49, with Senator Smith voting against the amendment. The vote paved the way for quick House passage, and the Defense Department started selection of sites in North Dakota.

HEATHER M. DAVID

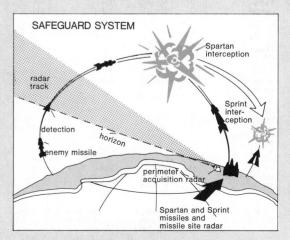

SAFEGUARD SYSTEM

Spartan interception

radar track

Sprint interception

detection

horizon

enemy missile

perimeter acquisition radar

Spartan and Sprint missiles and missile site radar

"Tut Tut—A Mere Sliver Of Ice"

SANE, a pacifist group, sponsored the ad below.

From the people who brought you Vietnam:

The anti ballistic missile system.

(*Continued from page 463*)
intelligence was unable to give an accurate account of their deployment.

There was evidence that the USSR intended to try to match the United States in numbers of submarine-launched ballistic missiles. The Soviets put into production its "Y" class submarine, which closely resembles the U. S. Polaris submarine. At least eight or nine Y-class submarines were launched. Each of these carried 16 new, storable liquid-fuel missiles that were believed to have a range of up to 1,500 miles. U. S. intelligence reported that the two Soviet submarine shipyards could produce as many as eight vessels a year. Even at a rate of only six Y-class submarines a year, the Soviet SLBM force would equal the U. S. fleet by 1975.

The Soviet Union also had a number of "H" class nuclear-powered submarines with three to six shorter-range missiles each. Neither missile was considered a threat to the Minuteman force because of their low warhead yield and lack of accuracy, but they did cause concern for the U. S. bomber bases.

The Soviet cruise missile was also a matter of great concern to the U. S. Navy, particularly since the USSR had furnished it to many allies, including North Korea, North Vietnam, Cuba, and the United Arab Republic. The USSR was believed to have at least three types of cruise missiles, with ranges up to 400 miles. The missiles are carried on aircraft, submarines, warships, and small boats. Of particular concern to the United States was the Styx missile, carried on small patrol boats such as the *Osa* and *Komar*. Because these boats have appeared in increasing numbers in crowded areas such as the Mediterranean, the United States began an intensive program to counter this threat. Although the cruise missile was considered much slower than a rocket-propelled missile, it could travel at low altitude and evade radar detection until close to the target.

Communist China. The People's Republic of China failed to launch an expected ICBM or satellite in 1969, but the Defense Department still believed it had a potential missile threat.

China tested a medium-range ballistic missile (MRBM) system up to ranges of about 1,000 miles, and the intelligence community believed it was ready to start deploying an MRBM. By the mid-1970's, the Communist Chinese would have from 80 to 100 operational missiles, the Pentagon predicted. These would not threaten the United States, but could be used for nuclear blackmail in Asia.

The Communist Chinese had constructed a large ballistic-missile launch facility, which led the intelligence community to conclude that an ICBM shot was imminent. A large ballistic-missile production facility also was detected, leading to the conclusion that MRBM's probably were being produced there, and possibly even ICBM's.

Some of the other prerequisites of an operational ICBM force also appeared to be present. The Communist Chinese were producing both U-235 and plutonium, and had conducted tests of nuclear devices.

Because of internal political and economic factors in China, U. S. intelligence predicted that although the earliest operational ICBM capability could be achieved by 1972, it probably would lag two or three years later. By 1975, the Pentagon predicted, China would have from 10 to 25 ICBM's.

(See also AIR FORCE; DEFENSE FORCES.)

HEATHER M. DAVID
Pentagon Correspondent, Fairchild Publications

MISSISSIPPI

Hurricane Camille, one of the most powerful storms ever to strike the United States, ravaged the Mississippi coastal area in mid-August. In other events of 1969, Mississippi schools were the subject of a landmark decision in which the U. S. Supreme Court declared that "all deliberate speed" is no longer a permissible standard for desegregation; the Legislature approved Gov. John Bell Williams' programs for highway improvements and Medicaid; and both Republican and Negro candidates achieved some success in municipal elections.

Storm Disasters. With winds nearing 200 miles per hour and tides up to 25 feet above normal, hurricane Camille swept head-on into the populous Gulf coast of Mississippi on August 17. The storm left 127 persons known dead, 5 others missing, and property damage estimated at about $1 billion. Nearly 4,000 dwellings were destroyed, and 42,000 others were damaged. Both President Nixon and Vice President Agnew visited the stricken area.

On January 23 several tornadoes moved across southern Mississippi, killing more than 25 persons.

School Desegregation. Although in May a federal district court had upheld the continued use of "freedom of choice" as a method for disestablishing dual school systems in certain Mississippi school districts, the U. S. Court of Appeals for the Fifth Circuit overruled the lower court in July and ordered the school boards to submit new desegregation plans to go into effect at the beginning of the 1969–70 school year. This order was overturned on August 28, when the U. S. Department of Justice —in a historic break with civil rights forces and in support of the contention that local authorities needed additional time to overcome "logistical" problems—obtained an order from the circuit court postponing the filing of desegregation plans until December 1. Meanwhile, however, in a decision on October 29 the U. S. Supreme Court unanimously ordered the termination of dual public school systems in Mississippi, and the circuit court promptly began the task of implementing the Supreme Court's decision. Immediately affected were 33 of the state's 149 school districts. (See SUPREME COURT.)

Despite scattered boycotts by both Negroes and whites in protest of certain court-ordered desegregation plans, the beginning of the 1969–1970 school year was marked by increased integration.

Legislation. In a 77-day special session, the Legislature approved a $300 million bond issue for highway improvements and increased the gasoline tax by 1 cent to retire the bonds. Other measures gaining approval included a limited Medicaid program, minimal funds for short-term educational television, and state loans for pupils attending nonpublic schools. A suit charging the student-loan act with a segregation intent was filed in U. S. district court, and the state was enjoined from making loans pending a decision.

Elections. The U. S. Supreme Court ruled in March that several recent Mississippi election statutes were required by the 1965 Voting Rights Act to be submitted to the U. S. attorney general for approval prior to becoming effective.

In May and June elections held in nearly 260 of 273 municipalities, 7 Republicans were chosen as mayors and 20 others as members of governing bodies. Negroes won 17 places on governing boards in 8 racially mixed towns, and Charles Evers, field director of the NAACP, was elected mayor of Fayette. His election marked the first time since Reconstruction that a Negro had gained such office in a biracial Mississippi town.

Colleges and Universities. A speaker-clearance policy that the state college board had been applying since 1955 was declared unconstitutional on December 4 by a three-judge federal panel, which set forth new court-drawn guidelines. In October the U. S. Court of Appeals for the Fifth Circuit ruled that a University of Mississippi policy prohibiting members of the law faculty from accepting part-time employment with an antipoverty legal services program was unconstitutional, since other part-time employment was not denied. The U. S. Department of Health, Education, and Welfare in March directed the state college board to prepare a plan of action for desegregation in the eight institutions under its control or face loss of federal funds.

Student Protests. During the spring semester Negro students at several Mississippi colleges and universities staged demonstrations protesting the way in which officials were responding to their grievances. In the spring, compulsory ROTC became the target of nonracial protest. A small proportion of students on scattered campuses participated in antiwar demonstrations as part of the nationwide Vietnam moratorium observances.

DANA B. BRAMMER
University of Mississippi

--------- **MISSISSIPPI • Information Highlights** ---------

Area: 47,716 square miles (123,585 sq km).

Population: 2,367,000 (1969 est.).

Chief Cities (1969 est.): Jackson, the capital, 165,000; Biloxi, 54,000; Meridian, 53,000; Gulfport, 47,000.

Government: *Chief Officers*—governor, John Bell Williams (Dem.); lt. gov., Charles Sullivan (Dem.); secy. of state, Heber Ladner (Dem.); atty gen., A. F. Summer (Dem.); treas., Evelyn Gandy; supt. of pub. instr., Garvin Johnston; chief justice, W. N. Ethridge, Jr. *Legislature*—Senate, 52 members (49 Democrats, 3 Republicans); House Representatives, 122 members (120 D, 2 R).

Education: *School enrollment* (1968)—public elementary, 350,000 pupils (11,900 teachers); public secondary, 245,000 pupils (9,800 teachers); nonpublic schools, 20,600 pupils (1,070 teachers); college and university (fall 1967), 64,716 students. *Public school expenditures* (1967–68)—$236,900,000 ($413 per pupil); average teacher's salary, $4,735.

Public Finance (fiscal year 1968): *Revenues*, $668,900,000 (general sales and gross receipts taxes, $135,957,000; motor fuel tax, $69,513,000; federal funds, $203,189,000). *Expenditures*, $681,809,000 (education, $100,096,000; Health, welfare, and safety, $111,517,000; highways, $108,466,000). *State debt*, $445,259,000.

Personal Income (1968): $4,878,000,000; average annual income per person, $2,081.

Public Assistance (fiscal year 1969): $55,900,603 to 180,215 recipients (aged, $31,511,581; dependent children, $11,336,594).

Labor Force (employed persons, 818,900, Aug. 1969): *Agricultural* 106,400; *nonagricultural* (wage and salary earners), 564,200 (31.85% manufacturing, 18.23% trade, 22.31% government). *Unemployed persons* (Aug. 1969)—35,200.

Manufacturing (1966): *Value added by manufacture*, $1,488,483,000 (transportation equipment, $148,834,000; nonelectrical machinery, $90,772,000; electrical machinery, $74,873,000; fabricated metals, $84,814,000; food and products, $165,103,000).

Agriculture (1967): *Cash farm income*, $927,790,000 (livestock, $384,246,000; crops, $396,630,000; govt. payments, $146,914,000). *Chief crops* (tons)—cottonseed, 450,000 (ranks 2d among the states); cotton lint, 264,000 (ranks 2d); soybeans, 1,394,960.

Mining (1967): *Production value*, $217,257,000. *Chief minerals* (tons)—Stone, 1,879,000; sand and gravel, 14,039,000; coal (1966), 3,582,000; clays, 1,654,000; iron ore (1966), 2,113,440; crude petroleum, 57,147,000 bbls.

Fisheries (1967): *Commercial catch*, 262,058,881 pounds ($8,986,487). *Leading species*—Menhaden, 166,527,400 pounds ($2,144,868); shrimp, 9,624,611 pounds ($3,121,871).

Transportation (1968): *Roads*, 66,104 miles (106,381 km); *motor vehicles*, 1,077,947; *railroads*, 3,667 track miles (5,900 km); *airports* (1969), 13.

Communications (1969): *Telephones*, 781,300; *television stations*, 9; *radio stations*, 129; *newspapers*, 20.

MISSOURI

A legislative session marked by a split within the Democratic party and disastrous storms and floods were among the significant events of 1969 in Missouri.

Legislature. From the time it convened in January 1969 through the end of its second session, the Missouri General Assembly was torn by a split in the Democratic party. The rift centered around party factions led respectively by Gov. Warren E. Hearnes and the newly elected president pro tem of the Senate, Earl R. Blackwell. At the outset of the regular session, through the efforts of Blackwell, the Senate deprived Lt. Gov. William S. Morris, a Hearnes ally, of most of his powers as presiding officer of that body. The most intense conflict centered around Hearnes' efforts to increase taxes.

In contrast to preceding sessions the governor's program suffered a number of legislative defeats. Only 16 of the 27 measures sought by Hearnes were enacted into law. Among programs supported by the governor that the legislature failed to enact were the establishment of a public defender system, open and binding state-wide party primaries and legislation specifying that congressional reapportionment would be carried out by a bipartisan commission instead of by the state legislature.

Among the significant enactments of the 1969 session were bills authorizing cities of more than 500 inhabitants to impose a local sales tax through voter approval, a proposed constitutional amendment to authorize state toll roads, and an increase in the state cigarette tax.

────── **MISSOURI • Information Highlights** ──────

Area: 69,686 square miles (180,487 sq km).
Population: 4,665,000 (1969 est.).
Chief Cities (1969 est.): Jefferson City, the capital, 29,500; Saint Louis, 665,000; Kansas City, 555,000; Springfield, 113,000; Independence, 112,000.
Government: *Chief Officers*—governor, Warren E. Hearnes (Democrat); lt. gov., William S. Morris (D); secy of state, James C. Kirkpatrick (D); atty. gen., John C. Danforth (Republican); treas., William E. Robinson; chief justice, Fred L. Henley. *General Assembly*—Senate, 34 members (23 D, 11 R); House of Representatives, 163 members (108 D, 55 R).
Education: *School enrollment* (1968)—public elementary, 746,000 pupils (26,900 teachers); public secondary, 271,-000 pupils (14,400 teachers); nonpublic schools, 167,600 pupils (6,870 teachers); college and university (fall 1967), 153,281 students. *Public school expenditures* (1967–68)—$585,650,000 ($627 per pupil); average teacher's salary, $6,807.
Public Finance (fiscal year 1968): *Revenues*, $1,169,165,000 (general sales and gross receipts taxes, $268,689,000; motor fuel tax, $101,126,000; federal funds, $319,025,000). *Expenditures*, $1,111,382,000 (education, $189,389,000; health, welfare, and safety, $251,084,000; highways, $207,-782,000). *State debt*, $145,849,000 (June 30, 1968).
Personal Income (1968): $15,065,000,000; average annual income per person, $3,257.
Public Assistance (fiscal year 1968): $157,961,700 to 226,866 recipients (aged, $79,869,300; dependent children, $34,-008,600).
Labor Force (employed persons, annual average 1968): *Agricultural*, 155,400; *nonagricultural* (wage and salary earners), 1,623,100 (28.2% manufacturing, 22.1% trade, 16.6% government). *Unemployed persons* (annual average 1968) —68,400.
Manufacturing (1967): *Value added by manufacture*, $6,600,-000,000 (transportation equipment, $1,234,690,000; primary metals, $187,515,000; nonelectrical machinery, $368,141,-000).
Agriculture (1967): *Cash farm income*, $1,458,270,000 (livestock, $895,350,000; crops, $447,802,000; govt. payments, $115,838,000). *Chief crops* (tons)—Hay, 5,642,000; corn for grain, 5,548,704; soybeans, 2,067,296; wheat, 1,614,720.
Mining (1967): *Production value*, $234,642,000. *Chief minerals* (tons)—Limestone, 35,496,000; sand and gravel, 9,716,000.
Transportation: *Roads* (1969), 33,000 miles (53,107 km); *motor vehicles* (1967), 2,211,000; *railroads* (1968), 7,004 track miles (11,272 km); *airports* (1969), 10.
Communications (1969): *Telephones* (1968), 2,405,600; *television stations*, 14; *radio stations*, 96; *newspapers*, 53.

State Income Tax. The regular session of the legislature adjourned at the end of June without enacting the governor's proposed increase in the state income tax. In the early fall, with the lower house's approval, the governor called a special session of the legislature. The tax increase, scheduled to go into effect Jan. 1, 1970, will provide an estimated additional $106 million in revenue for the state. Blackwell, however, has initiated a petition drive to force a voter referendum on the increase. If enough signatures are obtained, the measure will not become effective and the issue will be submitted to the voters in November 1970.

Congressional Reapportionment. For the fourth time since 1960 the legislature was confronted with reapportioning the state's 10 national congressional districts. Reapportionment plans passed in 1961, 1965, and 1967 have been successively ruled invalid by the federal courts. In April the U. S. Supreme Court upheld a lower court ruling that the 1967 reapportionment did not meet the "one man-one vote" criteria. At the end of its regular session the legislature enacted a new plan which decreased still further the population discrepancies between districts. It is generally believed that the major impact of the new districting will be to ensure the safety of seats held by current incumbents. The legislature is heavily Democratic, and Democrats now hold 9 out of 10 congressional seats.

Storms and Floods. The year 1969 proved an unusually wet one for Missouri. On three separate occasions heavy rains brought severe floods in various parts of the state. On June 23, tornadoes and severe thunderstorms swept through the "leadbelt" area south of St. Louis, killing six persons and injuring many more. The following week heavy winds hit St. Louis causing heavy property loss. A series of extensive rain storms caused the Mississippi River to flood the lowlands along the eastern side of the state in mid-July. Coming in the middle of the growing season, this flooding caused extensive damage to crops. It was estimated that 800,000 acres were water-logged because of heavy rains.

RICHARD E. DAWSON
Washington University, St. Louis, Mo.

MOMADAY, N. Scott. See biographical sketch under INDIANS, AMERICAN.

MONGOLIA

The Mongolian People's Republic continued in 1969 to support the Soviet Union in all aspects of the Sino-Soviet dispute. Mongolian press and propaganda attacks on Communist China went so far as to call for the overthrow of Mao Tse-tung. China in turn claimed that the Mongolian people were being ruthlessly exploited by the colonialist Soviet Union. Prime Minister and Party First Secretary Yumzhagiyn Tsedenbal continued as the leading political figure in Mongolia, and Soviet-inspired defense and military activity took precedence over all other concerns.

Military and Economic Development. With the increasingly bitter words against China came a marked militarization. Many Soviet troops entered Mongolia and took up positions on the border with China. The Mongolian Army itself has substantially increased in size, although the small population of the country makes it unlikely that the army will attain a strength of as much as 100,000 men.

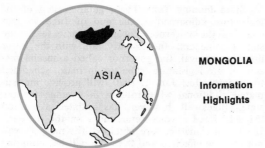

MONGOLIA

Information Highlights

Area: 604,246 square miles (1,565,000 sq km).
Population: 1,174,000 (1967 est.).
Chief Cities (1967 est.): Ulan Bator, the capital, 250,000; Darkhan, 35,000.
Government: *Chief of State*—Zhamsarangin Sambu (took office July 1954); *Premier and Communist Party First Secretary*—Yumzhagiyn Tsedenbal (took office January 1952). *Legislature* (unicameral)—Great People's Khural, 287 members (all members of the Mongolian People's Revolutionary party).
Principal Religious Faiths: Buddhism and Islam.
Education: *Literacy rate* (1966), 99% of population aged 9–50. *Total school enrollment* (1966)—188,300 (primary/secondary, 170,000; technical/vocational, 9,700; university/higher, 8,600).
Finance (1966 est.): *Revenues,* $386,000,000; *expenditures,* $384,000,000; *monetary unit,* tugrik (4 tugriks equal U. S.$1).
Manufacturing (metric tons, 1965): Gasoline, 17,000; distillate fuel oils, 7,000.
Chief crop (metric tons, 1965): Grains, 354,400.
Minerals (metric tons, 1966): Coal, 1,000,000; fluorspar, 75,000; lime, 35,000; gypsum, 20,000; crude oil, 20,000; salt (1967), 8,000.
Foreign Trade (1965): *Exports,* $75,000,000; *imports,* $150,000,000. *Chief trading partner:* USSR.
Transportation (1961): *Roads,* 46,700 miles (75,154 km); *railways* (1965), 887 miles (1,427 km); *national airline,* Mongolair; *principal airport,* Ulan Bator.
Communications: *Telephones* (1968): 14,720; *television stations* (1967), 1; *radios* (1966), 61,000; *newspapers* (1963), 2 (daily circulation, 92,000).

The USSR continued to pursue its strategy of building up the Mongolian People's Republic in manpower and fostering economic development along the line from the Soviet border in eastern Siberia directly southward to the Mongolian capital of Ulan Bator. The recently developed city of Darkhan provides the best evidence of this policy. Another location marked for Soviet-supported development is at Choibalsan in eastern Mongolia, and the press and other indicators have forecast a third area for concentrated development in the southeastern Gobi near the Chinese border. These are all primarily military-strategic ventures with economic development aimed at supporting maximum defense strength.

Role of the Soviet Union. Persistent reports indicate that the Soviet Union has already established missile installations on Mongolian territory and in essence has moved its own strategic frontier directly to the Mongolian-Chinese border. Thus, the Mongolian People's Republic has become an intimate part of Sino-Soviet relations.

ROBERT A. RUPEN
University of North Carolina

MONTANA

An active legislature and a program of economic growth were among the highlights of 1969 in Montana.

Legislature. The year opened with a generally harmonious 41st legislative session, although a Republican House faced a Senate and governor's office controlled by Democrats. Important enactments included referendum measures providing for constitu-

tional revision, legislation on water conservation, and increased revenue for cities. The legislature refused to increase minimum wage levels, to expand collective bargaining legislation, or to enlarge the coverage of the state merit system.

A 10-day special session of the legislature adopted revenue bills that balanced the budget at about $161,666,072 for the 1969–71 biennium. A general sales tax was rejected, but individual income taxes were raised about 18% and corporation license taxes by about the same amount. In September, Gov. Forrest Anderson instituted a two-year study on consolidating some 125 state agencies into 20 functional departments. He hoped that a referendum allowing such consolidation would be approved.

Elections. A political upset occurred in the special election on June 24 when Democrat John Melcher was elected congressman from the 2d District, usually considered safely Republican. Melcher replaced veteran Republican James F. Battin, who had been named to a federal judgeship. The election gave Democrats complete control of Montana's congressional delegation.

Economic Development. Montana's biggest industrial firm, the Anaconda Company, whose mammoth copper holdings in Chile were nationalized in June, announced in October that it would further enlarge its open pit copper operations in Butte and construct a second large ore treatment plant.

Concern over increasing absentee ownership of Montana's business enterprises was heightened when, in January, the state's major flour producer, the Montana Flour Mills Company, was sold to the Ne-

---
MONTANA • Information Highlights

Area: 147,138 square miles (381,088 sq km).
Population: 700,000 (1969 est.).
Chief Cities (1969 est.): Helena, the capital, 22,500; Great Falls, 61,000; Billings, 55,000; Missoula, 33,500; Butte, 26,000.
Government: *Chief Officers*—governor, Forrest H. Anderson (Dem.); lt. gov., Thomas L. Judge (Dem.); secy. of state, Frank Murray (Dem.); atty. gen., Robert L. Woodahl (Rep.); treas., Alex B. Stephenson; supt. of pub. instr., Dolores Colburg; chief justice, James T. Harrison. *Legislative Assembly*—Senate, 55 members (30 Democrats, 25 Republicans); House of Representatives, 104 members (58 R, 46 D).
Education: *School enrollment* (1968)—public elementary, 110,000 pupils (5,400 teachers); public secondary, 63,000 pupils (2,900 teachers); nonpublic schools, 18,200 pupils (770 teachers); college and university (fall 1967), 23,175 students. *Public school expenditures* (1967–68)—$120,350,000 ($734 per pupil); average teacher's salary, $6,650.
Public Finance (fiscal year 1968): *Revenues,* $279,938,000 (motor fuel tax, $24,781,000; federal funds, $83,746,000). *Expenditures,* $268,976,000 (education, $52,274,000; health, welfare, and safety, $31,663,000; highways, $71,168,000). *State debt,* $84,776,000 (1968).
Personal Income (1968): $2,039,000,000; average annual income per person, $2,942.
Public Assistance (fiscal year 1968): $18,254,295 to 21,180 recipients (aged, $2,761,002; dependent children, $4,738,405).
Labor Force (employed persons, Aug. 1969): *Agricultural,* 485,000: *nonagricultural* (wage and salary earners), 239,000 (10.6% manufacturing, 20.5% trade, 23.1% government). *Unemployed persons* (Aug. 1969)—11,600.
Manufacturing (1965): *Value added by manufacture.* $284,809,000 (lumber and wood products, $75,376,000; primary metals, $72,443,000; printing and publishing, $17,256,000; stone, clay, and glass products, $12,009,000).
Agriculture (1968): *Cash farm income,* $549,894,000 (livestock. $281,310,000; crops, $195,563,000; govt. payments, $73,021,000). *Chief crops* (bushels)—Wheat, 125,869,000; barley, 42,735,000; sugar beets (tons), 1,051,000; hay (tons), 3,585,000.
Mining (1968): *Production value,* $228,131,000. *Chief minerals* (tons)—copper, 69,480; zinc, 3,778; lead, 1,870; silver, 2,132,571 troy ounces: gold, 13,385 troy ounces.
Transportation: *Roads* (1968). 76,437 miles (123,010 km); *motor vehicles* (1968), 538,690; *railroads* (1968), 6,711 track miles (10,801 km); *airports* (1969), 15.
Communications (1968): *Telephones,* 318,900; *television stations,* 8; *radio stations,* 46; *newspapers,* 17 (daily circulation, 234,646).

braska Consolidated Mills Company of Omaha.

The Avco Corporation, which leased the huge deactivated Strategic Air Command base at Glasgow, relieved locally depressed conditions by employing some 600 men.

The recently enlarged state Board of Planning and Economic Development launched a vigorous program of active contact with industrial and governmental agencies in order to project economic growth. The board received a substantial budget increase.

Missile Controversy. President Nixon's announcement in February of the Safeguard antiballistic missile program and the proposed installation of one of the sites at Malmstrom Air Force Base in Montana, touched off a continuing statewide controversy as to whether such missile installations would strengthen or endanger a major area of the state.

Culture and Recreation. Expansion of cultural activities in the state included the opening of a major exhibit at the Montana Historical Society Museum, the dedication of a large addition to the Charles M. Russell Gallery in Great Falls, and the opening of the Hockaday Memorial Art Center in Kalispell. A record snowfall increased tourism and made all of western Montana a winter sports area for a full four-month period.

MERRILL G. BURLINGAME
Montana State University

MONTREAL

Montreal, Canada's largest city (1968 est. pop., 1,438,000), is the second largest French-speaking city in the world. The Parti civique, or Civic party (the only purely municipal political party in Canada), let by Mayor Jean Drapeau, held 44 of the 48 council seats in 1969.

Municipal Finance. Montreal's financial position improved in 1969. In July the city was able to retire over $20 million of debt, a feat not equaled since 1961. At the same time, small reductions were made in water and business taxes from the high levels in which they were placed in the budget.

The city budget stood at $280 million. An additional $132 million (in round figures) was collected in school property taxes, thus bringing the total budget to over $400 million. The failure of the sales tax and the voluntary tax—the euphemism for the city-run lottery—to produce anticipated returns caused general taxation to remain high. In spite of rigorous economy, Montreal's current spending was up about 13% from 1968. Substantial improvement in financing would clearly require closer integration with other Montreal Island municipalities and a widening of taxation powers.

Supra-Government. This term was employed to describe various schemes of unification for the municipalities of Montreal Island. In 1969, initiative came from the Quebec government, whose minister of municipal affairs made three important pronouncements advocating the fusion of certain municipal services. Failing to receive support either from Montreal or from the surrounding towns, the government laid aside its plans "for a year at least."

Important local mergers took place, however, in the metropolitan area. The suburb of Saraguay joined Montreal and, on the South Shore, Jacques Cartier and Longueuil united. This merger produced a city—to be called Longueuil—of over 100,000 people, the fourth largest in Quebec.

"Man and His World." The decision to continue the international exhibition "Man and His World" was reached only after a great deal of discussion. Mayor Drapeau made a personal issue of it, and in January he considered retiring from office should the show not go on. By the end of February, with aid promised by both Quebec and Ottawa, it was resolved that "the son of Expo" should be revived.

"Man and His World" opened on June 12 and closed on September 7. Attendance stood at 6,387,-000, or approximately half of the 1968 figure. The amusement center, La Ronde, continued on weekends until October 13 and raised the total for 1969 to 6,575,317. It was expected that "Man and His World" will be repeated in 1970. A connection with the great Expo 67 was broken in May 1969 with the death of Pierre Dupuy, the commissioner general of the 1967 world's fair.

Urban Development. Montreal registered a satisfactory although reduced rate of growth in 1969. There was no construction of really large buildings, such as characterized the early 1960's. Preliminary work on the southeast extension of the Decarie expressway was undertaken, and plans were drawn for an expansion of the subway system, for which ground is to be broken in 1970.

Considerable progress was made in the construction of low-cost housing. Where possible, renovation was employed. In the area of Richmond Square, existing houses were rebuilt and modernized. In this way, much of their original appearance was retained along with the general character of the neighborhood. A total of some 2,000 low-cost units was constructed. Unfortunately, the nonprofit cooperative organizations that were to have supplemented the city's construction were not able to act; hence, the total for the year was about 1,000 short of the goal of 3,000 units.

Civil Disturbances. Montreal witnessed more than its share of violence in 1969. The most destructive incident occurred in February when $2 million of damage was done at Sir George Williams University. The most dangerous event took place during a wildcat strike of Montreal police and firemen on the night of October 7, when the central section of the city was ravaged by looters. Damage amounted to about $1 million, and two persons were killed. An order-in-council forced the police back to duty, and they were supplemented by provincial police and troops. Vandalism attended a French-language protest march on McGill University.

Another display of violence occurred on the French Canadian national holiday, St. Jean Baptiste Day (June 24), when the traditional parade was attacked by hoodlums, who were themselves French Canadians.

JOHN I. COOPER
McGill University

MORMONS. See CHURCH OF JESUS CHRIST OF LATTER-DAY SAINTS.

MOROCCO

For the second consecutive year, bumper crops in 1969 heralded what appeared to be the start of an agrarian revolution in Morocco. Royalists won most of the seats contested in the two elections held in the country in 1969. The Islamic Summit Conference at Rabat in September seemed to show the success of foreign policy of King Hassan II.

Agricultural Development. New government sponsored seeding programs, the introduction of improved strains of wheat, regional irrigation projects, and excellent rainfall helped to produce an estimated 4 million metric tons of cereals in 1969, about double the normal yearly harvest. There were more than enough cereal grains to feed the population, now growing at a rate of 3.2% annually. Morocco has earmarked 46% of the budget of the 1968–72 economic plan for agricultural development. The government will try to add 2.75 million acres of irrigated land to productivity during the next five years. It will also begin to modernize the livestock industry and will attempt to transform some of the subsistence farmers (about 60–65% of the population) into producers for export markets. A new inheritance code introduced in January 1969, if enforced, will prevent heirs from dividing land holdings into small plots. Local authorities will choose one son to inherit all of the family lands. The government hopes that larger farms will prove more efficient than smaller ones, and it has assumed the right to confiscate properties of owners who benefit by the new code but do not increase production.

The government's gravest agricultural problems have been in finding storage space and export outlets for the last two harvests and in obtaining funds for farm credit. With an increase of 13% in worldwide wheat production and a decrease of 14% in international wheat exports in 1968–69, it has been impossible for Morocco to dispose of its stocks. But increased farm yields will stir consumer demand and stimulate investment in local industries.

Political Developments. The announcement of higher taxes on tobacco and fuel at the end of 1968 touched off a series of strikes by urban shopkeepers. Except for these brief protests at the beginning of 1969, the country remained calm throughout the year.

On October 3, Morocco's third elections for 11,116 communal and municipal council representatives were held. "Neutral" or promonarchical candidates, selected by local administrators, won 82.8% of the seats. The Popular Movement, a Berber-based rural party, was second, with 12.7%. The Istiqlal party, which criticized the government for "electoral rigging," won only 4%. The National Union of Popular Forces (UNFP), the other opposition party, boycotted the election completely. Interior Minister Mohamed Oufkir interpreted the election results as a victory for "independents." Some commentators, however, viewed the results as a sign of the end of the multiparty system in Morocco. This conclusion was reinforced by the October 24 elections for provincial and prefectorial assemblies, in which "neutral" candidates won 289 out of 359 seats.

The results of the two elections showed the ineffectiveness of the reconciliation between UNFP and the Istiqlal party. The Communist party, which attempted to regroup its forces under the banner of the Party of Liberation and Socialism, was banned again in September.

Two of King Hassan's advisers, Director of the Royal Cabinet Driss M'Hammedi and M'hamed Zeghari, governor of the Moroccan National Bank, died in March. In February the king named former Minister of Justice Driss Slaoui to replace M'Hammedi. He also brought former Minister of Interior and Economy Ahmed Rheda Guedira back into the government. Guedira had helped to formulate the agreement of association with the European Economic Community signed in March.

In other cabinet changes in October the king raised former Foreign Minister Ahmed Laraki to the post of prime minister, as his reward for successfully arranging the September Islamic Summit Conference in Rabat. At the same time, former Prime Minister Mohammed Benhima took over the agriculture portfolio. The appointment of Abdelhadi Boutaleb, the only Arabist scholar in the government, to the office of minister of foreign affairs indicated the king's concern with arranging a negotiated settlement in the dispute between Israel and the Arab states.

Foreign Affairs. The Islamic conferences at Rabat could be viewed as a major success for King Hassan's foreign policy. For several years, Hassan, King Faisal of Saudi Arabia, and the shah of Iran had planned to gather together the heads of Muslim states in order to counteract more radical Arab leaders. The September meeting confirmed the moderates' position. The presence of Mauritanian President Mukhtar Ould Daddah at the Rabat Conference signaled the reconciliation between Morocco and its Saharan neighbor. In the same way the presence of Algerian President Houari Boumedienne symbolized Algerian-Moroccan friendship.

An alliance of convenience between Morocco, Mauritania, and Algeria could weaken Spain's control of the Spanish Sahara. Joint African pressure might dislodge Spain and open the area's rich phosphate reserves to exploitation by the three African states. In July Spain returned to Morocco the southern enclave of Ifni, having ruled it 35 years.

STUART SCHAAR
Brooklyn College, City University of New York

MORTON, Rogers. See biographical sketch under POLITICAL PARTIES.

——— **MOROCCO • Information Highlights** ———

Area: 171,834 square miles (445,050 sq km).
Population: 14,580,000 (1968 est.).
Chief Cities (1966 urban census): Rabat-Sale, the capital, 370,000; Casablanca, 1,120,000; Marrakech, 275,000; Fés, 255,000.
Government: *King*—Hassan II (acceded Feb. 26, 1961); *Prime Minister*—Ahmed Laraki (took office October 1969). *Parliament*—suspended in June 1965.
Religious Faiths: Muslims, 95% of population.
Education: *Literacy rate* (1969), 10–15% of population. *Total school enrollment* (1965)—1,351,334 (primary, 1,115,645; secondary, 210,931; teacher-training, 1,057; technical/vocational, 14,705; university/higher, 8,996).
Finance (1968 est.): *Revenues,* $467,000,000; *expenditures,* $492,000,000; *monetary unit,* dirham (5.06 dirhams equal U.S.$1).
Gross National Product (1968): $3,000,000,000.
National Income (1968): $2,697,000,000; *average annual income per person,* $184.
Economic Indexes (1967): *Industrial production,* 109 (1963=100); *agricultural production,* 99 (1963=100); *cost of living,* 106 (1963=100).
Manufacturing (metric tons, 1967): Cement, 868,000; gasoline, 252,000; wine, 1,300,000 hectoliters.
Crops (metric tons, 1967–68 crop year): Barley, 1,100,000; wheat, 1,090,000; citrus fruit, 631,000; grapes, 256,000.
Minerals (metric tons, 1969): Phosphate rock, 12,200,000; iron ore, 648,000; coal (1967), 482,000; manganese ore, 291,000; pyrrhotite, 500,000.
Foreign Trade (1968): *Exports,* $450,000,000 (chief exports, 1967: phosphates, $107,890,000; citrus fruit, $68,400,000); *imports,* $551,000,000 (chief imports, 1967: nonelectrical machinery, $75,745,000; cereals and preparations, $66,541,000). *Chief trading partners* (1967): France (took 41% of exports, supplied 37% of imports); West Germany (took 8% of exports, supplied 9% of imports); United States (took 2% of exports, supplied 10% of imports).
Transportation: *Roads* (1969), 32,180 miles (51,787 km); *motor vehicles* (1967), 249,300 (automobiles 178,400); *railways* (1965), 1,110 miles (1,786 km); *national airline,* Royal Air Maroc; *principal airports,* Casablanca-Anfa; Casablanca Novaceur.
Communications: *Telephones* (1968), 145,000; *television stations* (1968), 7; *television sets* (1968), 51,000; *radios* (1967), 800,000; *newspapers* (1966), 9 (daily circulation, 197,000).

Easy Rider earned acclaim for its stars and coproducers Dennis Hopper (*left*) and Peter Fonda (with hitchhiker).

MOTION PICTURES

The most timely—although by no means the best —motion pictures of 1969 were those that focused on some aspect of youthful revolt. The Hollywood studios, despite grave financial problems, continued to turn out giant musicals and canned versions of Broadway plays.

The Youth Revolt. Arthur Penn's *Alice's Restaurant* took as its point of departure the real-life, role-playing, long-haired noncomformism of the folk singer Arlo Guthrie. Lindsay Anderson's *If . . .* in-troduced surrealist submachine guns into a British public school reminiscent of the anarchic institution immortalized by the late Jean Vigo in *Zero de Conduite* in 1934, when anarchy was less fashionable and hence more heroic than it was in 1969. Barbet Schroeder's *More* limited the fatal revolt of its young characters to the realms of drugs and sex; Vilgot Sjoman's *I Am Curious (Yellow)* exploited softcore pornography to expound relatively conventional socialist arguments.

Dennis Hopper's *Easy Rider* took the mythic motorcyclist of the past two decades and transformed him, at the close of the 1960's, into a metaphor of youthful paranaoia and establishment persecution. Robert Downey's *Putney Swope* reversed the roles of the races in an irreverent satire on Madison Avenue suddenly infused with "soul." Haskel Wexler's *Medium Cool,* which professed to examine the traumatic effects of the 1968 Democratic convention in Chicago, was a muddled mixture of

(*Above*) SWEDISH FILM *I Am Curious (Yellow)* follows youth's search for identity. Shown here are its stars, Lena Nyman and Borje Ahlstedt.

conscience and contrivance. Larry Kent's *High,* Martin Scorsese's *Who's That Knocking at My Door,* and Francis Ford Coppola's *The Rain People* were more lyrical than lucid as they probed the paradoxes of the youthful revolt against convention.

Most successful of the "now" pictures (at least at the box office) was perhaps John Schlesinger's *Midnight Cowboy,* a saga of the romantic friendship of two Times Square hustlers played by Jon Voight and Dustin Hoffman. The homosexuality was treated with relative candor, although not without a trace of sentimental coyness. The same subject was treated as wild farce in Bruce Kessler's *The Gay Deceivers,* and, in a more latent form, as a malignantly feminist subplot in Alan Pakula's *The Sterile Cuckoo.*

Foreign Films. The strident contemporaneity of the most prominent U.S. movies made the better foreign entries seem classical and reflective. The reputation of the late Max Ophuls was restored with uncut versions of his two 1950's classics: *Lola Montes* and *La Ronde.* The late Japanese master Kenji Mizoguchi was honored for *The Bailiff.* Also outstanding were Claude Chabrol's *La femme infidele;* François Truffaut's *Stolen Kisses;* Jean-Luc Godard's *Pierrot le Fou;* Luis Buñuel's *Simon of the Desert;* Ivan Passer's *Intimate Lighting;* Bo Widerberg's *Adalen 31;* Ousmane Sembene's *Black Girl;* Miklós Jancsó's *The Round-Up* and *The Red and the White;* and Vatroslav Mimica's *Kaya, I'll Kill You.*

Other notable foreign films included Robert Enrico's *The Last Adventure;* Jean-Daniel Simon's *Adelaide;* Jean Eustace's *Bad Company;* Jean-Marie Straub's *The Chronicle of Anna Magdalena Bach;* Alain Cavalier's *La Chamade;* Claude Lelouch's *Life, Love, Death;* Claude Berri's *Marry Me! Marry*

CINEMA V

(Above) Z, a French film, starring Yves Montand and Irene Papas, is based on political assassination in Greece.

(Opposite) MIDNIGHT COWBOY stars Dustin Hoffman *(left)* and Jon Voight seek shelter from the cold in New York City.

(Below) BARBRA STREISAND, as Dolly Levi, offers money to Horace Vandergelder, played by Walter Matthau, in *Hello Dolly!*

20TH CENTURY FOX

Me!; Zbynek Brynych's *Signs of the Virgin;* and Jean-Gabriel Albicocco's *The Wanderer.*

The *nouveau roman* was represented on the screen by the bewildering and beguiling ambiguities of Susan Sontag's *Duet for Cannibals,* made in Sweden, and Alain Robbe-Grillet's *L'Immortelle.* Less intense but equally whimsical were Agnes Varda's *Lions Love* (stylistically more-Warholian-than-Warhol) and Jacques Demy's *The Model Shop.*

Classics, Old and New. American films released in 1969 showed that filmmakers and audiences had not completely renounced the classical styles of the past. A revival of Charles Chaplin's *The Circus,* made in 1928, was the comic triumph of 1969. And the return of Walt Disney's 1941 *Fantasia* began a rush of the avant-garde and underground film public to this extraordinarily ambiguous work.

Also in the classical mold were such films as Alfred Hitchcock's *Topaz,* Orson Welles's *The Immortal Story,* John Huston's *A Walk With Love and Death,* John Frankenheimer's *Gypsy Moths,* Elia Kazan's *The Arrangement,* George Cukor's *Justine,* and Otto Preminger's *Skidoo.* These films, dismissed by most critics as old-fashioned, more than made up in beauty and feeling what they lacked in "relevance."

Political Commentary. The critical consensus converged overwhelmingly on *Z,* a French film shot in Algeria, and based on an actual political assassination in Greece. The end titles clearly linked
(Continued on page 476)

20TH CENTURY FOX

(Above) HISTORY of Old West lives in *Butch Cassidy and the Sundance Kid,* with *(from left)* Robert Redford, Katharine Ross, and Paul Newman.

NOTABLE MOTION PICTURES OF 1969

The following list of films released in 1969 presents a cross section of the most popular, most typical, or most widely discussed motion pictures of the year.

Adalen 31 (Swedish). Director-scenarist, Bo Widerberg. With Peter Schildt, Kerstin Tidelius, Anita Bjork, Marie De Geer.

Adelaide (French). Director, Jean-Daniel Simon; producer, Franco Riganti; writer Jean-Pierre Petrolacci. With Jean Sorel, Ingrid Thulin, Sylvie Fennec.

Alfred the Great (MGM). Director, Clive Donner; screenplay, Ken Taylor and James R. Webb from story by Webb based on novel by Elenor Shipley Duckett; producer, Bernard Smith. With David Hemmings, Michael York, Prunella Ransome, Vivien Merchant.

Alice's Restaurant (Warners). Director, Arthur Penn; producer, Hillard Elkins; screenplay, Arthur Penn and Venable Herndon. With Arlo Guthrie, Pat Quinn, James Broderick.

The Arrangement (Warners). Director-producer-scenarist, Elia Kazan from his novel. With Kirk Douglas, Faye Dunaway, Deborah Kerr, Richard Boone, Hume Cronyn.

Baby Love (English). Director, Alistair Reed; producer, Guido Coen; screenplay, Reed and Coen. With Linda Hayden, Keith Barron, Ann Lynn.

The Bailiff (Japanese). Director, Kenji Mizoguchi; screenplay, Juli Yahiro and Yoshikata Yoda from the novel by Ogai Mori. With Kinuyo Tanayaka, Yoshiaki Hanayagi, Kyoko Kagawe, Eitaro Shindo.

The Bed Sitting Room (United Artists). Director-producer, Richard Lester; screenplay, John Antrobus; adaptation, Charles Wood from stage play by Spike Milligan and Antrobus. With Rita Tushingham, Ralph Richardson, Michael Hordern, Peter Cook, Dudley Moore.

The Big Bounce (Warners). Director, Alex March; producer, William Dozier; writer, Dozier. With Ryan O'Neal, Leigh Taylor-Young, Lee Grant, Robert Webber, Van Heflin.

Black Girl (Senegalese). Director, Ousmane Sembene; writer, Sembene. With Mbissini Therese Diop, Anne-Marie, Robert Fontaine.

Bob & Carol & Ted & Alice (Columbia). Director, Paul Mazursky; producers, M. J. Frankovich and Larry Tucker; screenplay, Mazursky and Tucker. With Natalie Wood, Robert Culp, Elliott Gould, Dyan Cannon, Horst Ebersberg, Donald F. Muhich.

A Boy Named Charlie Brown (National General). Director, Bill Melendez; producers, Lee Mendelson and Melendez; writer, Charles M. Schulz. Voices: Peter Robbins (Charlie Brown), Pamelyn Ferdin (Lucy Van Pelt), Glenn Gilger (Linus Van Pelt), Andy Pforsich (Schroeder), Erin Sullivan (Sally), Bill Melendez (Snoopy).

Butch Cassidy and the Sundance Kid (Fox). Director, George Roy Hill; producers, Paul Monash and John Foreman; screenplay, William Goldman. With Paul Newman, Robert Redford, Katharine Ross, Strother Martin.

Castle Keep (United Artists). Director, Sydney Pollack; producer, Martin Ransahoff; screenplay, Daniel Taradash. With Burt Lancaster, Patrick O'Neal, Jean-Pierre Aumont.

The Chronicle of Anna Magdalena Bach (German). Director, Jean-Marie Straub; producer, Gian Vittorio Baldi; screenplay, Straub and Daniele Huillet. With Gustav Leonhardt, Christiane Lang.

Coming Apart (Kaleidoscope). Director-scenarist, Milton Moses Ginsberg; producers, Israel Davis and Andrew J. Kuehn. With Rip Torn, Megan McCormick, Lois Markle, Lynn Swann, Viveca Lindfors, Sally Kirkland.

The Damned (Warners). Director, Luchino Visconti; producers, Alfredo Levy and Ever Haggiag; screenplay, Nicola Badalucco, Enrice Medioli, and Visconti. With Dirk Bogarde, Ingrid Thulin, Helmut Grien, Helmut Berger, Charlotte Rampling, Rene Kolldehoff, Umberto Orsini.

Death of a Gunfighter (Universal). Director, Allen Smithee; producer, Richard Lyons; writer, Joseph Calvelli. With Richard Widmark, Lena Horne, John Saxon.

Downhill Racer (Paramount). Director, Michael Ritchie; producer, Richard Gregson; screenplay, James Salter from novel *The Downhill Racers* by Oakley Hall. With Robert Redford, Gene Hackman, Camilla Sparv, Carole Carle.

A Dream of Kings (National General). Director, Daniel Mann; producer, Jules Schermer; screenplay, Harry Mark Petrakis and Ian Hunter from novel by Petrakis. With Anthony Quinn, Irene Papas, Inger Stevens.

Duet for Cannibals (Swedish). Director-scenarist, Susan Sontag; producer, Goran Lindgren. With Adriana Asti, Lars Ekborg, Gosta Ekman, Agneta Ekmanner.

Easy Rider (Columbia). Director, Dennis Hopper; producer, Peter Fonda; screenplay, Fonda, Hopper and Terry Southern. With Fonda, Hopper, Jack Nicholson.

The Gay Deceivers (Commonwealth United). Director, Bruce Kessler; producer, Joe Solomon; screenplay, Jerry Wish. With Kevin Coughlin, Larry Casey, Brooke Bundy, Michael Greer.

Goodbye Columbus (Paramount). Director, Larry Peerce; producer, Stanley Jaffe; screenplay, Arnold Schulman from novel by Philip Roth. With Richard Benjamin, Ali McGraw, Jack Klugman.

Goodbye, Mr. Chips (MGM). Director, Herbert Ross; producer, Arthur P. Jacobs; screenplay, Terence Rattigan from novel by James Hilton. With Peter O'Toole, Petula Clark, Sir Michael Redgrave, George Baker.

The Gypsy Moths (MGM). Director, John Frankenheimer; producer, Edward Lewis; screenplay, William Hanley from novel by James Drought. With Burt Lancaster, Deborah Kerr, Gene Hackman, Scott Wilson.

Hamlet (Columbia). Director, Nicol Williamson; producer, Neil Hartley. With Williamson, Gordon Jackson, Anthony Hopkins, Judy Parfitt, Mark Dignam, Marianne Faithfull.

The Happy Ending (United Artists). Director-producer-scenarist, Richard Brooks. With Jean Simmons, John Forsythe, Shirley Jones, Lloyd Bridges, Teresa Wright, Nanette Fabray.

Hell in the Pacific (Cinema Center). Director, John Boorman; producer, Eric Berkovich; screenplay, Berkovich and Alexander Jacobs. With Lee Marvin, Toshiro Mifune.

Hello, Dolly! (Fox). Director, Gene Kelly; screenplay, Ernest Lehman from stage play by Michael Stewart based on play *The Matchmaker* by Thornton Wilder. With Barbra Streisand, Walter Matthau, Michael Crawford, Louis Armstrong.

High (Joseph Brenner). Director-producer-scenarist, Larry Kent. With Astri Thorvik and Lanny Beckman.

I Am Curious (Yellow) (Swedish). Director, Vilgot Sjoman; producers, Goran Lindgren and Lena Malmsjo. With Lena Nyman, Peter Lindgren, Borje Ahlstedt, Magnus Nilsson.

If... (Paramount). Director, Lindsay Anderson; producers, Michael Medwin and Anderson; screenplay, Robert Swann and David Sherwin. With Malcolm McDowell, Christine Noonan, Richard Warwick, David Wood.

The Immortal Story (Altura). Director-scenarist, Orson Welles; producer, Micheline Rozan; author, Isak Dinesen. With Orson Welles, Jeanne Moreau, Roger Coggio, Norman Ashley.

In the Year of the Pig (Pathe Contemporary). Director-producer, Emile de Antonio.

Intimate Lighting (Czechoslovakian). Director, Ivan Passer; screenplay, Vaclav Sasek, Jaroslav Paposek, and Passer. With Vera Kresadlova, Zdenek Bezusek, Jan Vostrcil, Vlastimila Vikova.

Justine (Fox). Director, George Cukor; producers, Pandro S. Berman and Cukor; screenplay, Lawrence B. Marcus from *Alexandria Quartet*, novels written by Lawrence Durrell. With Anouk Aimée, Dirk Bogarde, Robert Forster, Anna Karina, Philippe Noiret, Michael York.

Kaya, I'll Kill You (Yugoslavian). Director, Vatroslav Mimica; screenplay, Kruno Quien and Mimica. With Zaim Muzaferila, Ugliesa Koiadinović, Antun Nalis, Jolanda Dačić, Izet Haidarhodzić.

La Chamade (French). Director, Alain Cavalier; screenplay, Françoise Sagan and Cavalier from novel by Sagan. With Catherine Deneuve, Michel Piccoli, Roger Van Hool.

Le femme infidele (French). Director-scenarist, Claude Chabrol; producer, André Genoves. With Stephane Audran, Michel Bouquet, Maurice Ronet.

La Prisonnière (French). Director, Henri-Georges Clouzot; producer, Robert Dorfmann; screenplay, Clouzot, Monique Lange, Marcel Moussy. With Laurent Terzieff, Bernard Fresson, Elizabeth Wiener, Dany Carrel.

The Last Adventure (French). Director, Robert Enrico; screenplay, José Giovanni, Enrico, and Pierre Pelegri from novel by Giovanni. With Alain Delon, Lino Ventura, Joanna Shimkus.

Last Summer (Allied Artists). Director, Frank Perry; producers, Sidney Beckerman, Alfred Crown and Frank Perry; screenplay, Eleanor Perry from novel by Evan Hunter. With Barbara Hershey, Richard Thomas, Bruce Davison, Cathy Burns.

Laughter in the Dark (Lopert). Director, Tony Richardson; producer, Neil Hartley; screenplay by Edward Bond from novel by Vladimir Nabokov. With Nicol Williamson, Anna Karina, Jean-Claude Drouot.

The Learning Tree (Warners). Director, Gordon Parks; producers, Parks and James Lydon; screenplay, Parks from his novel. With Kyle Johnson, Alex Clarke, Estelle Evans, Dana Elcar.

Life, Love, Death (French). Director, Claude Lelouch. With Amidou, Caroline Cellier, Janine Magnan, Marcel Bozzuffi.

L'Immortelle (French). Director-scenarist, Alain Robbe-Grillet; producers, Michel Fano and Samy Halfon. With Françoise Brion and Jacques Doniol-Valcroze.

Lions Love (Max L. Raab). Director-scenarist, Agnes Varda. With Viva, Jerome Ragni, James Rado, Shirley Clarke, Carlos Clarens, Eddie Constantine.

Lola Montes (French). Director, Max Ophuls; screenplay, Ophuls, Annette Wademant, Franz Geiger from book by Cecil de Laurent. With Martine Carol, Peter Ustinov, Oskar Werner, Anton Walbrook, Ivan Desny.

The Loves of Isadora (Universal). Director, Karel Reisz; producers, Robert and Raymond Hakim; screenplay, Melvin Bragg and Clive Exton. With Vanessa Redgrave, James Fox, Ivan Tchenko, and Jason Robards.

Marlowe (MGM). Director, Paul Bogart; producers, Gabriel Katzka and Sidney Beckerman; screenplay, Stirling Silliphant from novel *The Little Sister* by Raymond Chandler. With James Garner, Gayle Hunnicutt, Carroll O'Connor, Rita Moreno, Sharon Farrell, William Daniels.

Marry Me! Marry Me! (French). Director-scenarist, Claude Berri; producer, Emmanuel Wolf. With Claude Berri, Elizabeth Weiner, Prudence Harrington.

Me, Natalie (National General). Director, Fred Coe; producer, Stanley Shapiro; screenplay, A. Martin Zwieback. With Patty Duke, James Farrentino, Salome Jens, Elsa Lanchaster, Martin Balsam.

Medium Cool (Warners). Director-producer-scenarist, Haskell Wexler. With Robert Forster, Verna Bloom, Harold Blankenship.

Midnight Cowboy (United Artists). Director, John Schlesinger; producer, Jerome Hellman; screenplay, Waldo Salt from novel by James Leo Herlihy. With Dustin Hoffman, Jon Voight, Brenda Vacarro, John McGiver, Ruth White, Sylvia Miles, Barnard Hughes.

The Model Shop (Columbia). Director-producer-scenarist, Jacques Demy. With Anouk Aimée, Gary Lockwood, Alexandra Hay, Carol Cole.

Monterey Pop (Leacock-Pennebaker). Director, D. A. Pennebaker; producers, John Phillips and Lou Adler. With Janis Joplin, Otis Redding, Jimmy Hendrix and other rock stars.

More (Cinema V). Director, Barbet Schroeder; screenplay, Schroeder and Paul Gegauff. With Mimsy Farmer, Klaus Grunberg.

More Dead Than Alive (United Artists). Director, Robert Sparr; producer, Hal Klein; screenplay, George Schenck. With Clint Walker, Vincent Price, Anne Francis, Paul Hampton, Mike Henry, Craig Littler.

The Night of the Following Day (Universal). Director-producer-scenarist, Hubert Cornfield. From novel *The Snatchers* by Lionel White. With Marlon Brando, Richard Boone, Rita Moreno, Pamela Franklin, Jess Hahn.

Oh! What a Lovely War (Paramount). Director, Richard Attenborough; producers, Brian Duffy and Attenborough. With Maggie Smith, Vanessa Redgrave, John Gielgud, Ralph Richardson, Laurence Olivier, Michael Redgrave, John Mills.

Once Upon a Time in the West (Paramount). Director, Sergio Leone; producers, Fulvio Marcella and Bino Cicogna; screenplay, Leone, Sergio Donati, from story by Dario Argento, Bernardo Bertolucci, and Leone. With Claudia Cardinale, Jason Robards, Henry Fonda, Charles Bronson, Gabriele Ferzetti.

On Her Majesty's Secret Service (United Artists). Director, Peter Hunt; producers, Albert R. Broccoli and Harry Saltzmann; screenplay, Richard Maibaum from novel by Ian Fleming. With George Lazenby, Diana Rigg, Telly Savalas, Ilse Steppat, Gabriele Ferzetti.

Paint Your Wagon (Paramount). Director, Joshua Logan; producer, Alan Jay Lerner; screenplay and lyrics, Lerner; adaptation, Paddy Chayefsky from the Lerner and Loewe Broadway musical. With Lee Marvin, Clint Eastwood, Jean Seberg. Ray Walston, Harve Presnell.

Pendulum (Columbia). Director, George Schaefer; producer-scenarist, Stanley Niss. With George Peppard, Jean Seberg, Richard Kiley.

Pierrot le Fou (French). Director, Jean-Luc Godard; producer, Georges de Beauregard; screenplay, Godard, based on novel *Obsession* by Lionel White. With Jean-Paul Belmondo, Anna Karina, Dirk Sanders.

Play Dirty (United Artists). Director, Andre de Toth; producer, Harry Saltzmann; screenplay, Lotte Colin and Melvin Bragg from story by George Marton. With Michael Caine, Nigel Davenport, Nigel Green, Harry Andrews, Ay Ben Ayed, Vivian Pickles, Bernard Achard.

Popcorn (Sherpix). Director, Peter Clifton; producer, Peter Ryan. With The Rolling Stones, Otis Redding.

Popi (United Artists). Director, Arthur Hiller; producer, Herbert B. Leonard; screenplay, Tina and Lester Pine. With Alan Arkin, Rita Moreno, Miguel Alejandro.

The Prime of Miss Jean Brodie (Fox). Director, Ronald Neame; screenplay, Jay Presson Allen from her play adapted from the novel by Muriel Spark. With Maggie Smith, Robert Stephens, Pamela Franklin, Gloria Jackson, Celia Johnson.

Putney Swope (Cinema V). Director-scenarist, Robert Downey. With Arnold Johnson, Laura Greene, Antonio Fargas, Elzbieta Czyzewska.

The Rain People (Warners). Director-scenarist, Francis Ford Coppola; producer, Bart Patton. With Shirley Knight, James Caan, Robert Duvall.

The Red and the White (Hungarian). Director, Miklós Jancsó; screenplay, George Mdivami, Gyula Hernadi, and Jancsó. With Tatyana Kanukova, Krystyna Mikolaiewska. Mikhail Kozakov, Victor Avddushko.

The Reivers (National General). Director, Mark Rydell; producers, Irving Ravetch and Robert E. Reiyea; screenplay, Ravetch and Harriet Frank, Jr. With Steve McQueen, Sharon Farrell, Will Geer, Michael Constantine, Rupert Crosse.

The Round-Up (Hungarian). Director, Miklós Jancsó; screenplay, Gyula Hernadi. With Jarios Gorbe, Tibor Molnar, Andreas Kozak.

Royal Hunt of the Sun (National General). Director, Irving Lerner; producers, Eugene Frenke and Philip Yordan; screenplay, Yordan from Peter Shaffer play. With Robert Shaw, Christopher Plummer, Nigel Davenport, Michael Craig.

Salesman (Maysles). Directors-producers, David and Albert Maysles. With Paul Brennan, Charles McDevitt, James Baker.

Sign of the Virgin (Czechoslovakian). Director, Zbynek Brynych; screenplay, Milan Unde and Brynych from the story by Unde. With Josef Cap, Jaroslava Obermaierova.

Simon of the Desert (Spanish). Director, Luis Buñel; producer, Gustavo Alatriste; screenplay, Buñel and Julio Alejandro. With Claudio Brook, Sylvia Pinal.

Skidoo (Paramount). Director-producer, Otto Preminger; screenplay, Doran William Cannon. With Jackie Gleason, Carol Channing, Alexandra Hay, John Philip Law, Frankie Avalon, Austin Pendleton, Luna.

Spirits of the Dead (Paramount). Three short films: "Metzengerstein"; writer-director, Roger Vadim. With Jane Fonda, Peter Fonda. "William Wilson"; director-writer, Louis Malle. With Alain Delon and Brigitte Bardot. "Never Bet the Devil Your Head," or "Toby Damit"; director-writer, Federico Fellini. With Terence Stamp, Fabrizio Angeli.

The Sterile Cuckoo (Paramount). Director-producer, Alan Pakula; screenplay, Alvin Sargent from novel by John Nichols. With Liza Minnelli, Wendell Burton, Tim McIntire, Elizabeth Harrower.

Stolen Kisses (French). Director, François Truffaut; screenplay, Truffaut and Claude de Givray. With Jean-Pierre Leaud, Delphine Seyrig, Michel Lonsdale, Claude Jade.

Sweet Charity (Universal). Director, Bob Fosse; producer, Robert Arthur; screenplay, Peter Stone from Fellini's *Cabiria*. With Shirley MacLaine, John McMartin, Ricardo Montalban, Chita Rivera, Paula Kelly.

Take the Money and Run (Cinerama). Director, Woody Allen; producer, Charles H. Joffe; screenplay, Allen and Mickey Rose. With Allen, Janet Margolin, Marcel Hillaire, Jacquelyn Hyde.

Tell Them Willie Boy Is Here (Universal). Director-scenarist, Abraham Polonsky from book *Willie Boy* by Harry Lawton. With Robert Redford, Katharine Ross, Robert Blake, Susan Clark, Barry Sullivan, John Vernon.

Thank You All Very Much (Universal). Director, Waris Hussein; producer, Max Rosenberg; writer, Margaret Drabble. With Sandy Dennis, Ian McKellen, Eleanor Bron.

That Cold Day in the Park (Cinerama). Director, Robert Altman; producer, Donald Factor; writer, Gillian Freeman. With Sandy Dennis, Michael Burns, Susanne Benton.

They Shoot Horses, Don't They? (Cinerama). Director, Sydney Pollack; producers, Irwin Winkler and Robert Chartoff; screenplay, James Poe and Robert Thompson from novel by Horace McCoy. With Jane Fonda, Michael Sarrazin, Susannah York, Gig Young, Red Buttons, Bonnie Bedelia, Michael Conrad, Bruce Dern.

Topaz (Universal). Director, Alfred Hitchcock; screenplay, Samuel Taylor from novel by Leon Uris. With Frederick Stafford, Dany Robin, John Vernon, Karin Dor, Michel Piccoli, Phillipe Noiret, Roscoe Lee Browne, Per-Axel Arosenius, John Forsythe.

Trilogy (Allied Artists). Director-producer, Frank Perry; screenplay, Truman Capote and Eleanor Perry from Capote short stories "Miriam," "Among the Paths to Eden," and "A Christmas Memory." With Geraldine Page, Donnie Melvin, Maureen Stapleton, Martin Balsam, Mildred Natwick.

True Grit (Paramount). Director, Henry Hathaway; producer, Hal Wallis; screenplay, Marguerite Roberts, based on novel by Charles Portis. With John Wayne, Glen Campbell, Kim Darby.

A Walk With Love and Death (Fox). Director, John Huston; producer, Carter De Haven; screenplay, Dale Wasserman from novel by Hans Konigsberger. With Anjelica Huston, Assaf Dayan, Anthony Corlan, John Hallam.

The Wanderer (French). Director-scenarist, Jean-Gabriel Albinocco. With Brigitte Fossey, Jean Blaise, Alain Libolt.

Where Eagles Dare (MGM). Director, Brian G. Hutton; producer, Elliot Kastner; screenplay, Alistair MacLean. With Richard Burton, Clint Eastwood, Mary Ure.

Who's That Knocking at My Door (Brenner). Director-scenarist, Martin Scorsese; producer, Joseph Weill. With Harvey Keitel, Zina Bethune.

The Wild Bunch (Warners). Director, Sam Peckinpah; producer, Phil Feldman; screenplay, Peckinpah and Walon Green. With William Holden, Ernest Borgnine, Robert Ryan.

Z (French). Director, Costa-Gavras; producers, Jacques Perrin and Hamed Rachedi; screenplay, Jorge Semprun and Costa-Gavras from novel by Vassil Vassilikos. With Yves Montand, Charles Denner, Georges Geret, Jean-Louis Trintignant, Renato Salvatori, Jacques Perrin, Irene Papas.

UNITED ARTISTS

RICHARD THOMAS (*left*), Barbara Hershey, and Bruce Davison pass time on a rainy day in *Last Summer*.

(*Continued from page 473*)
the film to the current political situation in Greece, ruled since 1967 by a junta of army colonels. A minority of critics, while acknowledging the merits of the film as a conventional thriller, questioned its claims as a political statement.

Another controversial film on an explosive political subject—the birth in fire of Nazi Germany—was Luchino Visconti's *The Damned*. Its flamboyant treatment of a German commercial family reminiscent of the Krupps was in the thematic vein of Shakespeare's *Macbeth*.

Less effective on any level were such strained antiwar satires as Richard Lester's *The Bed Sitting Room* (against World War II) and Richard Attenborough's *Oh! What a Lovely War* (against World War I). The Vietnam War remained a screen issue (although just barely) in some marginally commercial enterprises including Emile de Antonio's *In the Year of the Pig*, as well as *Terry Whitmore, For Example,* and *Deserter, U. S. A.* More interesting as cinematic art, and more effective as antiwar allegory, were such sardonic World War II movie yarns as Andre De Toth's *Play Dirty,* John Boorman's *Hell in the Pacific,* and Sydney Pollack's *Castle Keep.*

The Studio System. The disintegration of the studio system proceeded at an accelerated pace in 1969. Warners, Metro-Goldwyn-Mayer, and Paramount announced cancellations of many multimillion dollar projects. Perhaps the most spectacular

and controversial action was Metro's repudiation of its commitments to Fred Zinnemann for a $6 million production of André Malraux's *Man's Fate*. Zinnemann was within one week of beginning production when the blow fell. The demise of his project struck many insiders as an example of the insensitivity of the new breed of conglomerate carpetbaggers.

Musicals. Despite the waning of the studio system a succession of high-priced musical extravaganzas lumbered off the studio assembly lines like lethargic dinosaurs from another era. Most were flops: *Sweet Charity* (Universal), *Paint Your Wagon* (Paramount), *Goodbye, Mr. Chips* (Metro). Returns were not yet in on *Hello, Dolly!* but at a cost of $22 million, it would have to gross $40 million merely to break even. Even a nonmusical project such as *Catch 22* had run up a production cost of $22 million, and rumor had it that Paramount was offering the entire project for sale merely to obtain some working capital.

Westerns. It was a banner year for westerns even in cultural sectors not normally attuned to the genre. The most striking departures from the old formulas were represented by Sergio Leone's *Once Upon a Time in the West,* Sam Peckinpah's *The Wild Bunch,* Abraham Polonsky's *Tell Them Willie Boy Is Here,* Henry Hathaway's *True Grit,* Robert Sparr's *More Dead Than Alive,* George Roy Hill's *Butch Cassidy and the Sundance Kid,* Allen Smithee's *Death of a Gunfighter,* and Burt Kennedy's *Support Your Local Sheriff.*

UPI

CLIFF ROBERTSON received the best actor award of the Academy of Motion Picture Arts and Sciences for 1968 for his sensitive portrayal of a mentally retarded adult in *Charly*, a role he had created on television in the 1960–61 season in the network production of *The Two Worlds of Charly Gordon*. Previously he had been best known for his portrayal of John F. Kennedy as a young naval officer in the film *PT-109* (1963).

Clifford Parker Robertson, 3d, was born in La Jolla, Calif., on Sept. 9, 1925. He began to act in high school and studied at Antioch College and at the Actors Studio. After appearing in summer stock and in the national company of *Mister Roberts,* he made his New York stage debut in *Late Love* (1953). His first motion picture role was in *Picnic* (1955). Other films in which he appeared include *Autumn Leaves* (1956), *The Naked and the Dead* (1958), *Battle of the Coral Sea* (1959), *The Big Show* (1961), *The Interns* (1962), *Sunday in New York* (1964), *The Best Man* (1964), *The Honey Pot* (1967), and *The Devil's Brigade* (1968).

Other U. S. Films. Espionage and crime melodramas were paced by Peter Hunt's *On Her Majesty's Secret Service,* Paul Bogart's *Marlowe,* Alex March's *The Big Bounce,* Hubert Cornfield's *The Night of the Following Day,* Brian Hutton's *Where Eagles Dare,* and George Schaefer's *Pendulum.* Gordon Parks mixed melodrama and nostalgia in *The Learning Tree,* his autobiographical account of a black childhood in Kansas.

The increasing frankness and permissiveness of the cinema was reflected in the fact that the most popular comedy of the year, *Bob & Carol & Ted & Alice* dealt with wife-swapping—more theoretically than practically, however.

Other noteworthy comedies and romances were Alistair Reed's *Baby Love,* Larry Peerce's *Goodbye Columbus* (from the Philip Roth novel), Richard Brooks' *The Happy Ending,* Peter Yates' *John and Mary,* Frank Perry's *Last Summer,* Karel Reisz's *The Loves of Isadora,* Fred Coe's *Me, Natalie,* Arthur Hiller's *Popi,* Daniel Mann's *A Dream of Kings,* Ronald Neame's *The Prime of Miss Jean Brodie,* Mark Rydell's *The Reivers,* Alan Pakula's *The Sterile Cuckoo,* Woody Allen's *Take the Money and Run,* Waris Husein's *Thank You All Very Much* and Robert Altman's *That Cold Day in the Park,* Sydney Pollack's *They Shoot Horses, Don't They?,* Norman Jewison's *Gaily Gaily,* Tony Richardson's *Laughter in the Dark* (from the Vladimir Nabokov novel), Michael Ritchie's *Downhill Racer* and the Frank and Eleanor Perry/Truman Capote collaboration, *Trilogy.* Tony Richardson and Nicol Williamson presented a controversially concise but intellectually stimulating *Hamlet.* Canned plays such as *Cactus Flower* and *Generation* were still very much part of the film scene.

The thin line between exploitation of sex and psychological analysis was crossed time and again by Milton Moses Ginsberg's *Coming Apart,* Russ Meyer's *Vixen,* and Mack Bing's *All the Loving Couples.* Despite public protestations of boredom the number of films exploiting nudity on the screen seemed to increase in geometric progression.

The Maysles' Brothers *Salesman,* and *Monterey Pop* and *Popcorn* (the latter two pop music festival compilations) topped a lean year for documentaries.

Deaths. Many who had contributed to the golden days of Hollywood died in 1969. One of Hollywood's youngest stars, Sharon Tate, wife of the director Roman Polanski, was murdered

Among other prominent persons related to the film world who died in 1969 were Iris Barry, John Boles, Whitney Bolton, Fortunio Bonanova, Charles Brackett, Sir Lewis Casson, Irene Castle, Eduardo Ciannelli, Ivy Compton-Burnett, Vicki Cummings, Henri Decoin, Constance Dowling, Ian Fleming,

---

━━ BORIS KARLOFF (1887–1969) ━━

Boris Karloff, popular character actor of the theater and motion pictures, who died in Midhurst, Sussex, England, on Feb. 2, 1969, was best known for his roles in horror films, a genre he helped originate. He won almost instant stardom with his portrayal, in 1931, of the man-made monster in *Frankenstein,* the first major horror film produced in Hollywood. As a stage actor, Karloff won acclaim with his Broadway debut, in 1941, as the sinister Jonathan Brewster in the long-running *Arsenic and Old Lace.*

Karloff was born William Henry Pratt in London on Nov. 23, 1887. Headed for the diplomatic service, he attended King's College in London for a time. In 1909 he emigrated to Canada, where he made his debut in Molnar's *The Devil.* From 1910 to 1916 he toured western Canada and the United States as a member of stock companies. He began his motion picture career as a Hollywood extra in 1917. Among the 130 films in which he appeared were: *The Lost Patrol, The Tower of London, The Walking Dead, The Man They Could Not Hang, The Mummy, You'll Find Out, The Body Snatcher, Bedlam, The Raven, The Mask of Fu Manchu, Isle of the Dead, The House of Rothschild,* and three sequels to *Frankenstein.* His last motion picture role was in *Targets* (1968).

Stage plays in which he was featured included *Peter Pan* and *On Borrowed Time.*

Judy Garland, Leo Gorcey, Mitzi Green, Sigrid Gurie, George (Gabby) Hayes, Sonja Henie, Martita Hunt, Jeffrey Hunter, Rex Ingram, Boris Karloff, Jack Kerouac, Jack Kirkland, Rod La Rocque, Frank Lawton, Frank Loesser, Ella Logan, Barton MacLane, Allan Mowbray, Van Nest Polglase, Eric Portman, Stephen Potter, Thelma Ritter, Robert Sparr, Gladys Swarthout, Natalie Talmadge, Robert Taylor, B. Traven, Frank Tuttle, Josef von Sternberg, Raymond Walburn, Josh White, Ruth White, Hugh Williams, Rhys Williams, and Charles Winninger.

Awards. The New York Film Critics Circle selected *Z* as the best picture of 1969. Its other choices: best actress, Jane Fonda, for *They Shoot Horses, Don't They?;* best actor, Jon Voight for *Midnight Cowboy;* best supporting actress, Dyan Cannon, for *Bob & Carol & Ted & Alice;* best supporting actor, Jack Nicholson, for *Easy Rider;* best director, Costa-Gavras for *Z;* best screenplay, Paul Mazursky and Larry Tucker, for *Bob & Carol & Ted & Alice.*

BARBRA STREISAND was co-recipient, with Katharine Hepburn, of the 1968 best actress award of the Academy of Motion Picture Arts and Sciences. She received the award for her portrayal of Fanny Brice in the film version of the musical *Funny Girl,* a role in which she had previously starred on the Broadway stage in 1964–65. Miss Streisand also appeared in the title role of the motion picture version of the Broadway musical hit *Hello, Dolly!*

A native of Brooklyn, N. Y., Barbara Joan Streisand was born on April 24, 1942. After briefly studying acting, she began her show business career as a singer in Greenwich Village nightclubs. Her Broadway debut, as Miss Marmelstein in the musical *I Can Get It for You Wholesale,* won her critical acclaim as a comedienne. It was as a singer that she first attained great success. She has made many television appearances, and most of her record albums are best-sellers. In 1966 she won a Peabody Award for the 1965 television special *My Name is Barbra.*

The National Society of Film Critics also selected *Z* as the best picture. Its other choices: Vanessa Redgrave, best actress, for *Isadora;* Jon Voight, best actor, for *Midnight Cowboy;* Peter O'Toole's wife, Sian Phillips, best supporting actress, for *Goodbye, Mr. Chips;* Jack Nicholson, best supporting actor, for *Easy Rider;* Mazursky and Tucker, best screenplay, for *Bob & Carol & Ted & Alice;* Lucien Ballard, best photography, for *The Wild Bunch.* Special awards went to the directors Ivan Passer (*Intimate Lighting*) and Dennis Hopper (*Easy Rider*).

(See also PRIZES AND AWARDS.)

ANDREW SARRIS
Columbia University

MOTOR TRANSPORTATION

Truck transportation in the United States continued to increase in 1969 over the levels attained a year earlier. Bus travel increased slightly, between 1968 and 1969, in intercity and local-transit operations, and school bus transportation.

Trucking. The U. S. motor truck fleet in 1969 increased by more than 700,000 vehicles above the previous year. Registrations, excluding government-owned trucks, reached an all-time high of about 16.8 million, compared with 16.1 million in 1968. The industry carried about 400 billion ton-miles of freight in 1969.

Total operating revenues for some 15,000 for-hire truck lines engaged in U. S. interstate commerce rose to about $13 billion from $12 billion in 1968. The new high was more than $2 billion above the annual freight revenues of all U. S. railroads. Private and for-hire trucking operators not regulated by the Interstate Commerce Commission earned additional billions of shipping dollars.

The trucking industry's impact on the economy was felt in several areas. Trucks used nearly 22.3 billion gallons of motor fuel in 1969 costing more than $5 billion exclusive of taxes.

The industry also provided employment for more than 8 million persons, and had a payroll totaling approximately $55 billion. In 1969, motor trucks paid an estimated $5 billion in federal and state highway use taxes, including taxes levied for construction of the Interstate Defense Highway System.

Bus Operations. Intercity bus travel, according to the National Association of Motor Bus Owners, totaled approximately 24.75 billion passenger miles in 1969. This represents an increase of about 1% from the total for 1968, a result primarily of continuing increases in charter-party and special-service travel. Travel on regular-route bus schedules declined slightly—probably about 0.5%. Transportation of express packages in regular bus service continued to expand in 1969.

Travel on local and suburban bus systems continued the trend of the past few years with a very slight decline between 1968 and 1969, but the number of revenue passengers carried during 1969 again totaled more than 4.33 billion, according to data from the American Transit Association.

Several bills to increase the size and duration of the federal transit aid program were introduced in Congress, including the Nixon administration's Public Transportation Assistance Act of 1969, which recognized a need for at least $10 billion in federal aid over the next 12 years.

The school bus fleet totaled about 262,000 vehicles in 1968, an increase of about 6% over 1967, according to the Bureau of Public Roads of the U. S. Department of Transportation. The number of pupils transported at public expense is reported by the National Education Association to have been about 17.3 million for the 1967–68 school year.

There were more than 352,000 buses of all kinds in the United States in 1968. This total has been increasing during recent years at 2% to 5% annually, largely as a result of steady expansion in the number of school buses.

WILLIAM A. BRESNAHAN
American Trucking Associations, Inc.

MOTORBOAT RACING. See SPORTS.
MOYNIHAN, Daniel P. See biographical sketch under CITIES AND URBAN AFFAIRS.

MUSCAT AND OMAN

The sultanate of Muscat and Oman occupies almost the entire Arabian coast of the Gulf of Oman, the peninsula of Rus al-Jibal at the entrance to the Persian Gulf, the eastern half of the Arabian coast (mainly in the Dhufar region) on the Arabian Sea, and a territory of undetermined extent in the interior, to which the name "Oman" is properly applied.

Oil Production and Exploration. The production of oil, begun in 1967, soared in September 1969 to an average of 360,000 barrels a day, an increase of about 50% over the average for 1968. The only producing company was Petroleum Development (Oman) Ltd. (PDO), 85% of which is owned by Royal Dutch Shell. The search for oil in Dhufar by U. S. concerns was abandoned.

Other Developments. Sultan Said ibn Taymur elaborated a program for improving the living conditions of his people, but he moved cautiously to avoid disrupting the old fabric of society.

Plans called for the construction of a modern harbor at Matrah near Muscat to make it the chief trading center of the country.

The sultanate's disputes with Saudi Arabia and the exiled imam of Oman, Ghalib ibn Ali, remained unresolved, and dissidents backed by neighboring Southern Yemen caused some trouble in Dhufar.

GEORGE RENTZ
Hoover Institution, Stanford University

MUSCAT AND OMAN

Information Highlights

MIDDLE EAST

Area: 82,000 square miles (212,379 sq km).
Population: 565,000 (1968 est.).
Chief Cities (1968 est.): Muscat, the capital, 7,000; Matrah, 14,000
Government: *Sultan*—Said ibn Taymur (acceded 1932).
Principal Religious Faith: Islam.
Finance (1969 est.): *Revenues,* $90–100,000,000; *monetary unit,* Saidi Riyal.
Crops: Cereals, dates, pomegranates, limes.
Major Mineral: Petroleum.
Foreign Trade: *Major export,* petroleum, *Chief trading partner:* Britain.

Music

Money, always a principal motive in the fabric of musical life in the United States, seemed to rise to the level of an *idée fixe* in 1969. While managements of orchestras and opera houses were bemoaning rising costs and dwindling resources, musicians from San Francisco to New York were pressing for higher salaries and benefits to meet inflation. But musical life went on as usual. In the United States, openings of new facilities and appointments created excitement; abroad, interest centered on cen-

LEONARD BERNSTEIN conducted his final concert as director of the New York Philharmonic on May 19, 1969.

tennial celebrations and the successful appearances of several American artists.

CLASSICAL MUSIC

Financial Problems. In September the board of directors of the John F. Kennedy Center for the Performing Arts, still under construction in Washington, D. C., announced that because of steadily rising construction costs the opening date had been set back to the spring of 1971.

In New York, the Metropolitan Opera remained closed throughout the fall as a result of a contract dispute with its orchestra members, principals, chorus, and corps de ballet. A settlement finally made possible a December 29 opening, but the Metropolitan management said the terms would add considerably to the strains on its budget.

A study commissioned by the "Big Five" symphony orchestras—New York, Boston, Chicago, Cleveland, and Philadelphia—showed that their annual aggregate operating deficit had risen from $2.9 million in 1963–64 to $5.7 million in 1967–68. As a result they arranged a meeting of the presidents of 77 major U. S. symphony orchestras, under the auspices of the American Symphony Orchestra League. At this meeting, held in New York in November, plans were made to request increased federal appropriations.

In Kansas City, a strike for higher wages by the Philharmonic's musicians forced cancellation of the orchestra's fall programs. One proposed method for cutting expenses, the merger of symphony orchestras into regional organizations—Buffalo with Rochester and Indianapolis with Cincinnati were the two most widely discussed—stirred controversy and was largely responsible for the resignation of Lukas Foss as music director of the Buffalo Philharmonic. Lincoln Center for the Performing Arts in New York City closed its capital fund drive but was undergoing a period of cost-cutting under its new chief of staff, John W. Mazzola.

New Facilities. The most widely heralded of the new facilities to be formally opened in the United States in 1969 was the Juilliard School's new home at Lincoln Center in New York. The building, raised at a cost of $29,500,000, was ready for classes in early October and was dedicated in nationally televised ceremonies on October 26. The new structure has three times as much room as the old building at 120 Claremont Avenue in New York, which was taken over by the Manhattan School of Music.

Dedication ceremonies for the new Juilliard building included a concert in Alice Tully Hall, a 1,096-seat public recital hall on the school's street level. The $4.5 million facility had itself been formally inaugurated earlier, on September 11, with a concert by the new Chamber Music Society of Lincoln Center.

After 25 years of planning, the $12 million Milwaukee County Performing Arts Center was inaugurated on September 17 with a program in Uihlein Hall, a multipurpose theater for ballet, opera, and orchestra performances with a capacity of 2,329. The center also has a 482-seat recital hall.

In Canada, a 2-week festival of music and drama featuring Canadians launched the new National Arts Centre in Ottawa, opened on May 31. A 2,300-seat combination opera house and concert hall is one of three auditoriums in the $46.4 million complex.

In Manila, the Cultural Center of the Philippines inaugurated a 2,000-seat multipurpose theater on September 10 with a "dularawan"—a distinctively Philippine mixed-media work that combines drama, dance, song, and music employing native gongs, conches, bamboo flutes, xylophones, and trumpets. An international festival of music, drama, and dance followed.

Orchestras. In June the French-born conductor and composer Pierre Boulez was named music director of the New York Philharmonic for three years beginning with the 1971–72 season. During the period between his accession and Leonard Bernstein's retirement in May 1969, the orchestra is in the hands of George Szell, music director of the Cleveland Orchestra, who is serving as music adviser and senior guest conductor. In January, Boulez had also been named chief conductor of the BBC Orchestra in London for three seasons beginning 1971–72. He replaces Colin Davis, who will take command of the Royal Opera, Covent Garden, in the same season.

Seiji Ozawa and Gunther Schuller were appointed codirectors of the Tanglewood (Mass.) musical organization beginning in 1970. They succeed Erich Leinsdorf. Ozawa will be in charge of the Boston Symphony Orchestra's summer season and the other concerts that make up the Berkshire Festival; Schuller will be in charge of educational activities, including the Berkshire Music Center.

After the Houston Symphony dropped its music director, André Previn, it was announced in May that the American conductor Antonio de Almeida was to be principal guest conductor for the 1969–70 season. Antal Dorati was named to succeed the retiring Howard Mitchell as conductor of the Washington, D. C., National Symphony Orchestra; he will start there in the 1970–71 season, but will keep his post as conductor of the Stockholm Philharmonic in Sweden. Thomas Schippers was appointed successor to Max Rudolf as music director of the Cincinnati Symphony Orchestra beginning in the 1970–71 season, and the Hungarian-born conductor of the Cologne Opera, István Kertész, was appointed principal conductor of the Ravinia Festival in Chicago, replacing Ozawa.

In January, Erich Leinsdorf and the Boston Symphony Orchestra offered Boston a concert version of Richard Strauss' opera *Ariadne auf Naxos* in the seldom-heard version of 1912. Beverly Sills of the New York City Opera was spectacular in the role of Zerbinetta. In the Philadelphia Academy of Music, Eugene Ormandy led two premieres with that city's orchestra: the American premiere of the Polish composer Krzysztof Penderecki's *Threnody to the Victims of Hiroshima*, and the world premiere of American composer William Schuman's Symphony No. 9.

At the Cincinnati May Festival, Max Rudolf led the Cincinnati Symphony in the world premiere of a secular cantata, *The Pied Piper of Hamelin* by Peter Mennin. Two works commissioned by the New York Philharmonic for its 125th anniversary season (1967–68) were given their world premieres by the orchestra in 1969: Milton Babbitt's *Relata II* and Leon Kirchner's *Music for Orchestra*. Leopold Stokowski opened his American Symphony Orchestra's fall season with the first New York performance of the *Montevideo Symphony* by the 19th century U. S. composer Louis Moreau Gottschalk.

In the fall, patrons at New York's Philharmonic Hall heard the results of the final acoustical alterations begun in the hall the summer after its opening in September 1962, and most agreed that there had been much improvement. With Leonard Bernstein now serving as laureate conductor, a series of guest conductors led the New York Philharmonic. In California, the first season of the new Los Angeles Chamber Orchestra began in the Mark Taper Forum of Los Angeles' Music Center with a concert led by the group's musical director, Neville Marriner.

Among distinguished foreign ensembles visiting the United States in 1969 were the Hague Philharmonic, under its conductor Willem van Otterloo; the Moscow State Symphony, under Yevgeny Svetlanov; the Prague Symphony, under Václav Smetáček; and the Israel Chamber Orchestra.

Opera. In January the Metropolitan Opera unveiled its lavish new production of Richard Strauss' *Der Rosenkavalier,* directed by Nathaniel Merrill and designed by Robert O'Hearn. Leonie Rysanek, Régine Crespin, and Christa Ludwig were heard in the role of the Marschallin in the performances that

THE NEW YORK TIMES

JUILLIARD Theater (*above*), in New York's Lincoln Center, has complex adjustable ceiling.

METROPOLITAN OPERA orchestra and chorus members (*opposite page*) demonstrate with signs and music during contract dispute.

followed the opening; Karl Böhm conducted. Other high points of the spring season were revivals of Britten's *Peter Grimes* and Berg's *Wozzeck,* both led by Colin Davis.

The 50th season of the New York City Opera was particularly noteworthy for two new productions, Boïto's *Mefistofele* and Donizetti's *Lucia di Lammermoor.* Tito Capobianco was responsible for both productions.

Two American premieres marked the Santa Fe Opera's summer season: Penderecki's first opera, *The Devils of Loudun,* and Gian Carlo Menotti's *Help! Help! The Globolinks,* a spoof of electronic music. In New York, students of the Juilliard School presented the American premiere of Honegger's one-act opera *Antigone.* Britten's third parable for church performance, *The Prodigal Son,* had its American premiere at the Caramoor Festival in Katonah, N. Y.

The San Francisco Opera's fall season opened with *La Traviata* directed by August Everding. Also heard were *Ariadne auf Naxos,* led by Gunther Schuller; a new production of *Die Götterdämmerung* directed by Paul Hager; and a revival of *Fidelio* with Gwyneth Jones as Leonore. Mussorgsky's *Khovanshchina* was the Chicago Lyric Opera's first fall offering. Conducted by Bruno Bartoletti, the opera was sung in Russian by Nicolai Ghiaurov, Boris Shtokolov, and Ruza Pospinov-Baldani in leading roles. A new production of *Der fliegende Holländer,* directed by Wieland Wagner's son Wolf Siegfried, followed.

In Washington, D. C., the Opera Society of Washington bowed on October 17 with Rossini's *Comte Ory;* in November it offered Britten's *Turn of the Screw.* The soprano Magda Olivero appeared in the Connecticut Opera Association's production of Cilea's *Adriana Lécouvreur* in Hartford on October 18.

Festivals. On August 24, Erich Leinsdorf capped his final season as head of the Berkshire Festival with a performance of Beethoven's Ninth Symphony before an audience of 14,120. Another outstanding event was the Berkshire Music Center's fine student production of Berg's *Wozzeck.*

The Newport Music Festival in Rhode Island offered rare music by minor composers of the Romantic era. At the Blossom Music Center, in Ohio, Pierre Boulez led the resident Cleveland Orchestra as guest conductor and taught at the Blossom Festival School at Kent University. The 1969 Congregation of the Arts at the Hopkins Center of Dartmouth College, Hanover, N. H., had Luigi Dallapiccola and Roger Sessions as composers in residence. Walter Piston was a visiting composer, and master classes were held by Barry Tuckwell, horn; Siegfried Palm, cello; and Noel Lee, piano.

The London Symphony again participated in the Florida International Festival at Daytona Beach, and the Zagreb Philharmonic was in residence at Temple University's summer Music Festival and Institute. The second International Choral Festival was held in New York City in March and April.

Contemporary Music. Experimentation with "mixed media" continued. A major festival, "Cross Talk Intermedia," was held in Tokyo in February, under the auspices of the American Cultural Center. In the United States a notable premiere in mixed-media form was the UCLA Committee on Fine Arts Production's offering, January 9, in McGowan Hall, of Harry Partch's ritual music drama *Delusion of the Fury.* Based on African and Japanese stories, it was performed by a large ensemble playing instruments made by Partch. The program featured vocalists and dancers, as well as scenic and lighting effects.

Modern-music societies continued to flourish in New York. "The Continuing Avant-Garde," a series sponsored by the League of Composers-International Society for Contemporary Music, celebrated the 60th birthday of the American composer Elliott Carter with a concert of his works in February. The 1969 Laurel Leaf award of the American Composers Alliance went to the Group for Contemporary Music at Columbia University, under the codirection of Charles Wuorinen and Harvey Sollberger.

Mixing of media in another sense was the result of a rare attempt to bridge the gap between "classical" and "popular" music. The young American pianist Lorin Hollander played a program largely made up of traditional "classical" pieces at the pop-music auditorium Fillmore East in New York in February, using a Baldwin electronic concert grand.

Prizes and Competitions. The Lauritz Melchior Heldentenor Foundation made its first awards in 1969. They went to two Americans, William Cochran and John Russell. The Pulitzer Prize for Music went to Karel Husa for his String Quartet No. 3. The Sang Prize for Critics of the Fine Arts, awarded by Knox College in Galesburg, Ill., went to the music critics Eric Salzman of *Stereo Review* magazine and Michael Steinberg of the Boston *Globe.*

European Events. The centennial of the death of Hector Berlioz (1803–1869) was celebrated in Britain, France, and Austria. In London, the Royal
(Continued on page 485)

WOODSTOCK

Wearing dungarees, love beads, and sandals, they arrived in brightly decorated campers, in VW buses, on foot. They tied up the roads leading to Bethel, 70 miles northwest of New York City, for several days and captured front-page attention across the country. It was the weekend of Aug. 17–19, 1969, and "they" were somewhere between 300,000 and 400,000 young people, generally ranging in age from 15 to 25. They came from all corners of the United States, descending on the small dairy farming-summer bungalow community of Bethel (pop. 2,366) on White Lake, New York, for the Woodstock Music and Art Fair.

The pretext for this mass gathering was an outdoor music festival advertised as "three days of peace and music" and subtitled "An Aquarian Exposition," in reference to the newly dawning Age of Aquarius on the astrology charts. The festival promised the biggest group of pop performers ever assembled—32 top rock and folk musicians including Janis Joplin; Blood, Sweat and Tears; Jimi Hendrix; Joan Baez; Arlo Guthrie; and the Jefferson Airplane. As it turned out, however, the music was secondary.

The Planning. The festival was organized by four young promoters: Mike Lang, 24; Artie Kornfield, 26; John Roberts, 24; and Joel Rosenman, 26. Roberts, heir to a drug-company fortune, was the principal financial backer. The festival was originally planned for Woodstock, N.Y. But the promoters quickly abandoned Woodstock as impractical and settled on nearby Wallkill.

One month before the festival, a group of Wallkill residents obtained an injunction prohibiting the promoters from holding the festival in their town.

A few days later, Max Yasgur, a dairy farmer in Bethel, offered to rent 600 acres of his land for the festival. The promoters thus had only three weeks in which to transform Yasgur's alfalfa field into an outdoor rock-concert hall and camping ground.

Despite intensive, round-the-clock work, the stage was never completed. The hastily constructed toilets and showers proved inadequate to handle the crowds, which were six times the 50,-000 per-day originally anticipated. Food and drinking water were stockpiled, but the supplies ran out. Trucks could not bring in additional supplies because roads leading to the site were impassable for a 20-mile radius. On Thursday, the day before the festival was to begin, the promoters learned that they would have to replace their 350-man security force of off-duty New York City policemen, who had been warned by their commissioner that Woodstock employment would be in violation of departmental regulations.

The Festival. Perhaps the most devastating blow to the festival came in the form of the torrential rains that began Friday night after the concert opened. The storm knocked down tents and homemade shacks, and drenched sleeping bags, camp supplies, food, and clothing. The festival site became one vast ankle-deep, fertilizer-enriched mud puddle.

By Saturday morning, the situation was critical. People roamed the grounds with injuries and adverse drug reactions. The medical facilities broke down trying to handle the more than 4,000 people needing aid. Helicopters landed at 10-minute intervals all day Saturday, airlifting medical supplies,
(Continued on page 484)

A vast sea of the young descended on a pasture in Bethel, N. Y., in August for a "pop" music festival, clogging access roads for miles. Despite shortages in facilities and food, they achieved a rapport and peace that awed their elders, although the open use of drugs by festival-goers aroused concern.

484

TUCKER RANSON, FROM PICTORIAL PARADE

JANIS JOPLIN

TUCKER RANSON, FROM PICTORIAL PARADE

(*Above*) JOHN SEBASTIAN
(*Below*) Two members of Santana group

TUCKER RANSON, FROM PICTORIAL PARADE

doctors, and food. Radio stations throughout New York broadcast pleas to people en route to the fair to turn back. Festival officials, unable to cope with the crowds, stopped collecting tickets (at $7 a performance) at the gate. There were rumors that the entire festival would be declared a disaster area.

Yet the music, and the peace, continued. Thousands of wet enthusiasts slept in the open to keep their places near the stage. Then on Sunday afternoon it began to rain again. Some of the audience left, but most stayed to enjoy the high point of the festival—a 19-hour marathon of music lasting from 3 o'clock Sunday afternoon until 10 o'clock the next morning.

The Significance. Reflections on the meaning of Woodstock went on for weeks after the festival. Observers noted the absence of any violence despite the huge size of the crowd and the conditions under which it had lived. Photographs of nude young men and women bathing together in nearby ponds, along with the generous sharing of food, shelter, and drugs, gave to the Woodstock experience an almost pastoral quality. There was a unique spirit of togetherness among the young, and the crowds got along well with the police. As the local county sheriff said, "This is the nicest bunch of kids I've ever dealt with."

Critics of the fair pointed out that most of the young people present smoked marihuana. Every type of drug was available for the asking, and pushers openly advertised their wares. Observers saw the definite existence of a drug culture among young people and noted that although the youth at Woodstock had many hippie values, they were mainly college and high school students from middle-class homes. The thousands of drug users and the absence of arrests raised questions about the present drug laws.

Three persons died (one from an overdose of drugs) and two babies were born. The festival became a public forum for the new ideas and mores in the United States, and whether one liked it or not, the rock festival had become a part of American social history.

The partnership of Woodstock Ventures, Inc., later split up into Lang and Kornfeld, and Roberts and Rosenman. Both sides maintained they were planning a 1970 successor to Woodstock despite a $1.3 million loss incurred by the 1969 festival. Because of the unexpectedly large turnout, tickets could not be sold at the gate and the promoters had been forced to obtain loans to pay for the additional food, medical supplies and police needed.

Other Rock Festivals. Woodstock was not the only rock festival in 1969. Music festivals were held earlier in the summer in Atlanta, Ga., Atlantic City, N. J., and Newport, R. I.

An important festival was held on August 30 on the Isle of Wight, in the English Channel. This fair attracted 130,000 people and starred Bob Dylan, making his first concert appearance in three years. That same weekend, newspapers reported a number of festivals across the United States. They all received a great deal of attention in the aftermath of Woodstock, but no other festival approached Woodstock in terms of sheer size. And it was Woodstock that was to come to represent an entire generation.

ABIGAIL L. KUFLIK
Music Reporter, "Newsweek" Magazine

PIERRE BOULEZ, noted French composer and conductor, and one of the foremost representatives of avant-garde music, was appointed music director of the New York Philharmonic Orchestra on June 10, 1969. In contrast to conductors of the Romantic school, Boulez is considered primarily a logician, who is more concerned with the structure of musical compositions than with their emotional content. Since 1960 he had been chief conductor with the Southwest German radio in Baden-Baden.

Boulez was born in Montbrison, France, on March 26, 1925. He graduated in 1945 from the Paris Conservatory, where he became interested in the 12-tone music of Arnold Schoenberg. Boulez soon established himself as France's leading composer of 12-tone music. In 1948 he became music bardirector of the Jean-Louis Barrault–Madeleine Renaud company at the Théâtre Marigny in Paris. To promote avant-garde music he instituted in 1954 a series of concerts known as the "Domaine Musicale." His works include the *Symphonie Concertante* for piano and orchestra (1950).

CAMERA PRESS-PIX

(Continued from page 481)
Opera, Covent Garden, revived his opera *Benvenuto Cellini*. Colin Davis led the London Symphony Orchestra and massed choirs in performances of the *Requiem* and the *Te Deum* in St. Paul's Cathedral. *The Damnation of Faust* was staged by Sadler's Wells Opera in London and by the Volksoper in Vienna.

The greatest interest was stimulated by several productions of Berlioz's two-part epic Vergilian drama *Les Troyens*. The Scottish Opera presented it uncut in English at the Kings Theatre, Glasgow, in May. The Royal Opera, Covent Garden, opening its 1969–70 season in September, presented what was said to be the first complete production of the opera in French. Colin Davis conducted and the principal singers were Josephine Veasey and Jon Vickers. The Paris Opéra's production in November had many cuts in the score and was the object of vocal audience disapproval.

The Vienna State Opera celebrated the 100th birthday of its home in May with a performance of Beethoven's *Missa solemnis,* led by Leonard Bernstein. The centennial was the theme of the 1969 Vienna Festival Weeks, which included performances of Berg's *Wozzeck* and *Lulu* and Janáček's *Jenufa,* as well as appearances by the Joffrey Ballet of New York City and Leningrad's Kirov Ballet.

At La Scala in Milan, the high point of the spring season was the appearance of four Americans —soprano Beverly Sills, mezzo-soprano Marilyn Horne, bass Justino Diaz, and conductor Thomas Schippers—who cooperated in presenting Rossini's *Siege of Corinth*.

Europe's many festivals in 1969 generated little excitement. Bayreuth offered a new production of *Der fliegende Holländer,* directed by August Everding and designed by Josef Svoboda. The opera was performed without intermission, as the composer intended, and there was general praise for Leonie Rysanek's passionately sung Senta.

At the Salzburg Easter festival, Herbert von Karajan led his production of *Siegfried,* the third of the *Ring* operas that was to have been seen at the Metropolitan Opera in the fall. The summer festival at Salzburg saw a new production of Mozart's *Cosi fan tutte* by Jean-Pierre Ponnelle, *Fidelio* with Ingrid Bjoner and James King, and *Der Rosenkavalier* under Karl Böhm.

At Benjamin Britten's Aldeburgh Festival, the chief concert hall, the Maltings at Snape, was damaged by fire shortly before the first performance, but the festival went on. Mozart's *Idomeneo* was given in a local church three nights after the fire. The Edinburgh Festival featured works of Italian composers; a highlight was Tito Gobbi's production of Puccini's *Gianni Schicchi* starring himself.

POPULAR MUSIC

Rock is king—or so it would seem on the basis of the generous amount of attention it received in 1969 from the media, recording companies, and critics. Many continue to believe that the rock phenomenon is more significant for its sociological implications than for its musical value. Others disagree, and the Music Educators' National Conference, in late 1969, endorsed the teaching of rock in schools and universities.

DELUSION OF THE FURY, a ritual music drama by Harry Partch and a notable example of mixed-media experimentation, was premiered by UCLA Committee on Fine Arts Production, January 9.

Perhaps rock is king, but the Duke is still a member of the royal family. President Nixon held a White House dinner honoring Duke Ellington on his 70th birthday, April 29. After Nixon presented Ellington with the Presidential Medal of Freedom, guests heard 100 minutes of the Duke's compositions played by such jazz musicians as Dave Brubeck, Gerry Mulligan, and Paul Desmond.

But rock fans served notice that the summer was theirs. Deprived of seats for the appearance at the Newport Jazz Festival of Sly and the Family Stone—one of the few rock groups invited to perform at the event—several hundred drove paying customers from their seats. Thereafter it was just a matter of making the scene: 100,000 at Atlanta, 150,000 at Dallas, and at Woodstock (actually Bethel, N. Y.), upwards of 300,000. There were also rock festivals in such spots as Lewisville, Texas; Prairieville, La.; and Tenino, Wash.

At year's end, the Rolling Stones filled Madison Square Garden in New York City, and The Who, a British rock foursome, staged a "rock opera," *Tommy,* at the Fillmore East, also in New York. If rock was not here to stay, its practitioners seemed to be making sure that its fleeting moment would be memorable.

ROBERT S. CLARK
Associate Editor, "Stereo Review"

NABOKOV, Vladimir. See biographical sketch under AMERICAN LITERATURE.

NARCOTICS AND HALLUCINOGENS

The national and international pattern of drug abuse during 1969 reflected a continuing increase in the use of most psychochemicals. The U. S. Bureau of Narcotics and Dangerous Drugs reported that more than 68,000 narcotics addicts were known to it as of Dec. 31, 1968, representing a 10% increase over the previous year. The actual number of people addicted to heroin, morphine, and other opiates is estimated to be more than double that figure.

NARCOTICS

Narcotics addiction, at least for the past few decades, has been considered a psychosocial disorder most prevalent in urban slums. While this is still true, a new trend has been developing over the past several years. Middle and upper class urban and suburban young people are becoming more and more involved in the use of heroin, using it for subcutaneous ("joypopping") and intravenous ("mainlining") injections.

Heroin. The quality of illicit heroin is highly variable, ranging from 0% to 80% heroin. A typical bag of heroin purchased on the street ordinarily contains only from 0% to 5% heroin. This low quality of much illicit heroin partially explains why some people can take a few shots and not become physically addicted to it. It is also, in part, the reason for many fatalities among heroin addicts. In most instances, death following a heroin injection is due to an overdose, and it occurs when the addict is deliberately or accidentally sold high-quality heroin. The physical tolerance that he has built up to the ordinary weak heroin is not sufficient to protect him against 50% or 80% heroin.

Treatment of Addicts. The treatment of narcotics addicts can be divided into two phases: detoxification and aftercare. During detoxification, a heroin substitute is administered, if necessary. The dosage of this substitute is gradually reduced each day, and within a week it is discontinued completely. This phase of treatment is relatively easy to accomplish. Much more difficult is the long-term aftercare phase. The person who has been a narcotics addict for many years has made a career of his drug use, and rehabilitation requires a whole new structuring of his life. The relapse rate during this phase of treatment is very high.

There are many paths leading to the cure of addiction. One is the civil commitment process that a few states and the federal government have established. Another is represented by the wide variety of self-help groups of former addicts who have established therapeutic communities. Such operations as Synanon, Daytop, Phoenix House, and Odyssey House have been successful for some addicts.

Another alternative is the use of a heroin-like drug to eliminate the addict's cravings and develop sufficient tolerance so that an injection of heroin will have no euphoric effects. The drug most commonly used for this purpose is methadone. It is a long-acting drug that can be taken by mouth, and it serves to block the effects of heroin, morphine, or other opiates. Close supervision of the patient is a basic requirement in methadone therapy.

HALLUCINOGENS

The hallucinogens, or psychedelics, are a group of natural plant substances and synthetic chemicals that evoke alterations of awareness, thought content, emotional states, and sensation. Their potency ranges enormously from the weak domestic marihuana to pure lysergic acid diethylamide (LSD).

LSD. The current wave of hallucinogen abuse began in 1961 with the popularity of LSD. The use of LSD spread among urban college groups until the summer of 1967. Over the past two years a decline in the use of LSD has been observed. This decline has been due, in part, to the bad "trips" that terrified many users, the frequency of disturbing "flashbacks," and the prolonged anxiety states and psychotic reactions that were experienced. Another contributing factor to the decline in popularity of LSD is the still-unanswered question of its role in causing chromosomal changes in people taking the drug. However, the reports of congenital abnormalities in the children of parents who used LSD, especially of mothers who took the drug during their pregnancy, require further confirmation.

Another reason for the reversal of the trend in LSD use was the recognition by many who experimented with the drug that the enlightenments accompanying the LSD experiences were all too often illusory. Many of those who originally advocated the use of LSD have turned to nonchemical forms of meditation and contemplation, finding them to be more sustaining.

The question of possible changes in the brain cells of people who have taken large amounts of LSD frequently for years is currently being studied by many researchers. A number of investigators are hoping that their findings will show that the carefully controlled administration of LSD may be helpful in altering the drinking patterns of chronic alcoholics. However, this therapeutic use of LSD has not yet been confirmed.

The apparent decline in LSD use among college-age people has not been reflected in the use of the drug by junior and senior high school students. At

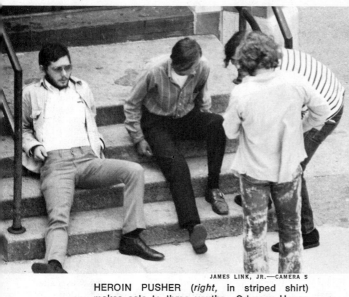

JAMES LINK, JR.—CAMERA 5

HEROIN PUSHER (*right,* in striped shirt) makes sale to three youths. Odyssey House (*right*) in New York City is among organizations helping former addicts to abstain from drug use through self-help programs.

THE NEW YORK TIMES

present, these adolescents are showing an increase in LSD use. This increase is particularly unfortunate because the brain cells of these youngsters are more sensitive to psychochemicals.

Marihuana. Marihuana is the mild hallucinogen obtained from the leaves and flowering tops of the female hemp plant (*Cannabis indica*). Although the overall use of marihuana is increasing rapidly, the majority of marihuana users are considered to be only occasional users and experimenters. It is estimated that more than half of all marihuana users have tried it less than 10 times. In a Roper survey published in May 1969, 22% of a sample of students from 50 colleges responded "yes" to the question, "Have you ever tried marihuana?" In metropolitan areas, the same results are found among high school students.

The severe legal penalties—2 to 10 years for a first offense—for the possession of marihuana are no deterrent to substantial numbers of people. Current legislation to alter the penalty structure gives little comfort to those advocating the legalization of marihuana. The recently introduced administration bill continues the felony level for marihuana offenses, but other bills call for a reduction of marihuana possession to a misdemeanor.

The active ingredient in marihuana, tetrahydrocannabinol (THC), was first synthesized in 1966 and has been used by scientists to study the drug more precisely. However, variations in the potency of marihuana, ranging from 0% to 2% THC, have impeded exact research. Furthermore, THC deteriorates with age, and the amount of it that reaches the user's bloodstream varies according to how the marihuana is smoked.

Hashish, the resin collected from the leaves and tops of the female hemp plant, usually contains from 4% to 12% THC. Red oil, a distillate of the same parts of the hemp plant, has about 20% THC. Although a substance called THC is sold on the street, analyzed samples have been found to contain no traces of this chemical but a variety of other substances. The manufacture and storage of THC are difficult and require unusual techniques.

Laboratory studies of the effects of THC on humans and animals have shown that it is a quite potent chemical. With certain exceptions, it produces symptoms similar to those of LSD. The exceptions include a more rapid heart rate and an increased reddening of the eyeballs. THC is more potent when smoked, rather than swallowed, and researchers are currently investigating what changes occur when it is smoked and when it is taken orally.

Extensive research on every aspect of marihuana is either under way or in the planning stages. Answers to questions about its long-term use, its effect on all the body's organ systems, and its psychological effects are urgently needed.

Other Drugs. In addition to LSD and marihuana, other hallucinogenic substances, such as mescaline and the seeds of certain varieties of the common morning glory, are also consumed. Some synthesized chemicals are also popular hallucinogens. These include dimethoxy-methylamphetamine (DOM or STP), dimethylated triptamine (DMT), and trimethoxy-amphetamine (TMA).

SIDNEY COHEN, M. D., *Director,*
Division of Narcotics Addiction and Drug Abuse,
National Institute for Mental Health

NASSAR, Gamal Abdel. See biographical sketch under UNITED ARAB REPUBLIC.

NATIONAL DEFENSE. See DEFENSE FORCES.

NATIONAL GUARD defends University of California gate on Berkeley campus against a group of girl students. Masks protect guardsmen against gas used to disperse some 1,500 dissident students who started an illegal rally on campus.

UPI

NATIONAL GUARD

All Air National Guard units, mobilized in January, April, and May 1968, were restored to state control by June 1969; and all Army Guard units, mobilized in May 1968 were restored to state control by the end of 1969. The National Guard thus completed the 115th federal mobilization in its 301-year history after the tension of early 1968 when North Korea captured the U. S. Navy intelligence ship *Pueblo* and fighting intensified in Vietnam.

Of 10,511 Air Guardsmen who saw active duty, more than 2,000 were deployed to the combat zone in Vietnam and 4,000 to other overseas missions, primarily in Korea and Japan. Of 12,234 mobilized Army Guardsmen, 7,040 served in Vietnam. At home, National Guardsmen were called repeatedly to cope with civil disturbances.

Combat Duty. Air Guardsmen saw combat for the first time in the 16 years since the Korean War. Five of the 13 F-100 tactical fighter squadrons in Vietnam were Air Guard. Four were the 120th of Colorado; 174th of Iowa; 188th of New Mexico; and 136th of New York, while the fifth, the 355th, an active Air Force unit, was 85% manned by Air Guard volunteers from the 121st Tactical Fighter Squadron of Washington, D. C., and the 119th Tactical Fighter Squadron of Atlantic City, N. J.

Seven of 34 major Army National Guard units mobilized saw service in Vietnam. They were Alabama's 650th Medical Detachment (Dental), whose 32 men took up duties throughout the country; 116th Engineer Battalion of Idaho, at Boa Loc; 2d Battalion, 138th Artillery, of Kentucky, at Phu Bai; 107th Signal Company, Support, of Rhode Island, at Long Binh; Company D (Ranger), 151st Infantry of Indiana; 131st Engineer Company of Vermont; and the 3d battalion, 197th Artillery of New Hampshire.

Civil Disorders. By November 1969, 43,511 Guardsmen had been summoned in at least 55 instances of civil disturbance to help maintain order, often on university campuses. Student disorders at the Berkeley campus of the University of California from May 15 to June 3 prompted declaration of a state of emergency by Gov. Ronald Reagan. In one incident, Guardsmen in helicopters sprayed skin-stinging powder on student demonstrators.

In Chicago on April 3, Gov. Richard B. Ogilvie mobilized Guardsmen to put down shooting, stoning, looting, and street fighting in Negro neighborhoods on the eve of the first anniversary of the assassination of the Rev. Martin Luther King, Jr.; in the same city, on October 9, the Guard was called to quell the Weatherman faction of the Students for a Democratic Society (SDS) after a wild night of window-breaking and fighting.

Gov. James A. Rhodes called out the Guard on July 22 in Columbus, Ohio, to quell looting, arson, and sniper fire that followed the fatal shooting of a Negro by a white store owner. In York, Pa., Gov. Raymond P. Shafer called out the Guard in July after sniping, rioting, and "shoot-outs" developed between whites and Negroes.

During the massive antiwar demonstration in Washington, D. C., on Nov. 13–15, 1969, Army and Air National Guardsmen were held in reserve but not called upon as police effectively quelled demonstrations led by Yippies (Youth International Party), who rioted around the Justice Department and the Dupont Circle area.

Force Structure. Army National Guard strength at the end of the fiscal year 1969 was 388,954—barely below authorized strength of 398,419. For the Air Guard, actual strength was 83,414, and authorized strength, 100,670. The below-strength level was due to the mobilization of Guardsmen for active duty. "Selected Reserve Force" designation for units capable of mobilization within seven days after alert with a minimum of 93% strength was discontinued on September 30.

Recruiting. Guard officials renewed attention to recruiting in late 1969 as terms of service expired for mobilized veterans. There was continued evidence of lagging Negro enlistment, especially in the South.

With the object of raising the Guard's Negro membership from about 1% to 12% within 5 years, as urged by several advisory commissions since 1967, Congress authorized extra funds and voted permission to exceed strength limits of 0.8% in fiscal 1970, the overage to be reserved for Negroes. Congress, however, did not appropriate the additional money. Each year the overage for Negroes was to be increased. The Department of Defense said that the number of black Guardsmen rose only from 1.24% to 1.26% from the end of 1967 to the end of 1968.

JACK RAYMOND
Author of "Power at the Pentagon"

NATIONAL PARKS. See CONSERVATION.

U. S. S. *Enterprise* is assisted by the destroyer *Rogers* during a fire that swept the carrier's flight deck, killing 25 men and injuring 85.

NAVY

The major U. S. naval event of 1969, in terms of national interest, was the court of inquiry regarding surrender of the electronic surveillance ship U. S. S. *Pueblo* to North Korean naval units and the intense public reaction that accompanied it.

The ship's crew, captured Jan. 23, 1968, was released exactly 11 months later and the men rejoined their families in San Diego under a spotlight of heavy press and television coverage and with the sympathy of their countrymen for their harsh treatment in North Korea. This was followed in early January 1969 by the customary fact-finding naval court of inquiry into the circumstances of the capture and the crew's conduct in prison.

Early in his testimony before this court, Comdr. Lloyd M. Bucher, *Pueblo*'s commanding officer, was informed that he was possibly liable for court-martial in violating Article 0703, U. S. Navy Regulations: "The commanding officer shall not permit his command to be searched by any person representing a foreign state, nor permit any of the personnel under his command to be removed from the command by any such persons, so long as he has the power to resist." The substance of this article has been in Navy Regulations since the *Chesapeake-Leopard* affair of 1807 but was obviously intended for a different kind of ship.

This normal legal warning, to protect Bucher from giving evidence against himself, however, was interpreted by the public as an attempt to place on him the blame for a national disgrace in which higher officials were obviously involved. An outburst of indignation against the Navy followed.

The court, composed of five admirals, sat from January to March, hearing 104 witnesses and taking over 4,000 pages of testimony. It eventually recommended courts-martial for Comdr. Bucher and Lt. Stephen R. Harris, the ship's intelligence officer; letters of reprimand for Rear Adm. Frank L. Johnson, commander of Naval Forces Japan, under

U.S.S. *Frank E. Evans,* cut in half by an Australian aircraft carrier, lost 74 men. The vessel's stern was towed (*above*) to Subic Bay, where the flag was lowered for the last time (*left*) on July 1.

whose control *Pueblo* was operating, and Capt. Everett B. Gladding, director of Naval Security Group Pacific, responsible for readiness of the ship's intelligence unit; and a letter of admonition to Lt. Edward R. Murphy, Jr., executive officer.

The commander of the Pacific Fleet, Adm. John S. Hyland, reviewed the results and recommended letters of reprimand only for Bucher and Harris.

The final authority, Secretary of the Navy John H. Chaffee, in office only a short time, largely settled the affair to public satisfaction by dropping all charges. "They have suffered enough and further punishment would not be justified," he declared. Two sister ships of the *Pueblo* were subsequently decommissioned.

Accidents. Serious mishaps continued to plague the Navy in 1969. Another carrier fire occurred on January 14 aboard the nuclear-powered *Enterprise,* off Hawaii, killing 25 and injuring 85 men. On February 17 a Sealab III civilian diver lost his life and the project, already delayed by several accidents, was postponed indefinitely. On May 15, the uncompleted nuclear-powered submarine *Guitarro* sank at its dock in the Mare Island Naval Shipyard on San Francisco Bay, due to "inexcusable carelessness," a House Armed Services subcommittee said. The year's worst naval disaster came on June 3 when a faulty maneuver by the U.S. destroyer *Frank E. Evans* caused a collision with the Australian carrier *Melbourne* during a SEATO exercise in the South China Sea. A total of 74 Americans died.

Ships. In August, Senators Walter F. Mondale (D.-Minn.) and Clifford P. Case (R.-N.J.) introduced an amendment to the military procurement bill to withhold $377 million authorized for a *Nimitz* class nuclear carrier pending a review of the usefulness of such vessels. The amendment was defeated, but its introduction implied that the Navy might have to fight for future carrier appropriations.

A seapower subcommittee of the House Armed Services Committee, headed by Charles E. Bennett (D.-Fla.), submitted a report March 19 on the unsatisfactory condition of naval ships. It included numerous photographs to document the findings that

the overall condition of readiness of the Atlantic Fleet was close to a critical level, with 53% of its ships over 20 years old, and that many ships of the Pacific fleet did not meet combat standards.

Budget Cut. Military spending was fiercely attacked by Sen. William Proxmire, head of the Joint Economic Subcommittee on Economy in Government. Secretary of Defense Melvin Laird announced defense spending cuts totaling $4.1 billion, of which $148 million was in the Navy budget. The Navy was ordered to retire 98 ships, reduce its force by 72,000 men, and to deactivate 11 aviation units. The battleship *New Jersey,* after a single tour of artillery-support duty in Vietnam that cost $45 million, returned to mothballs in Bremerton, Wash.

Accomplishments. Navy achievements during 1969 were mainly unspectacular and so received little public notice. The Military Sea Transportation Service (MSTS) found itself able to cut back on its monumental task of supporting Vietnam forces with its run-down merchant fleet.

Construction battalions (Sea Bees) in South Vietnam were transferring their efforts from construction of ports and shore facilities to civil action programs rehabilitating devastated areas. The Army-Navy Mobile Riverine Force had so effectively accomplished its job of clearing the enemy from the extensive inland waters of South Vietnam that the 1,200 Navymen and their Army counterparts of the 9th Division were able to turn over this task in June to South Vietnamese forces. This joint U.S. unit was credited with saving the Mekong Delta during the Tet offensive early in 1968.

A new type of vessel was tested—the DSRV, or Deep Submergence Rescue Vessel. It can rescue crews of disabled submarines down to a depth of 5,000 feet (1,524 meters).

Aircraft. Congress canceled the Navy's F111B program, the overweight carrier version of the fighter-bomber that the Air Force was beginning to use. The Navy initiated its F-14 program, developing an 1,800-mph Grumman fighter to enter the fleet in 1973. In the meantime, carriers will retain the outstanding McDonnell F-4 Phantom.

More significant perhaps and certainly cheaper will be the incorporation of A-NEW, an advanced antisubmarine data processing system, into an existing aircraft, the reliable P3 Orion patrol plane, a naval modification of the Lockheed Electra.

Soviet Navy Visit. Ironically, the best friend of the U. S. Navy in 1969 was perhaps the Soviet navy itself. The American press had been reporting the Soviet navy's new missile-armed surface ships and helicopter carriers, its harassing tactics against the U. S. Sixth Fleet in the Mediterranean, and its increasing presence in the Indian Ocean. But the vulnerability of U. S. maritime geography and the need for an adequate well-maintained navy was highlighted for Americans by a visit of a Russian squadron to Havana, Cuba, in July. This squadron consisted of three large missile-carrying destroyers, two submarines, a submarine tender and an oil tanker. The Havana visit was well covered in the press.

Virtually ignored, however, was the more significant replenishment of the squadron in shallow waters 40 miles (74 km) from the Dry Tortugas keys, Florida, before entering Havana; the subsequent antisubmarine exercises deep within the Gulf of Mexico about 300 miles (556 km) from the Mississippi delta; and the visit of detached ships to Fort-de-France, Martinique and Bridgetown, Barbados on the return voyage. A 5,200 ton *Kynda* type (Soviet admiral class) destroyer—mounting eight launchers capable of firing Shaddock surface-to-surface 200-mile (370-km) missiles—spent August 5–8 at the French Caribbean port. A smaller Kildin-type destroyer and the oiler were at the former British Leeward Island colony on August 10–12. This Soviet squadron was the first European naval force with less than friendly intensions to enter Gulf waters since the French-British invasion of Mexico during the American Civil War.

Perhaps the most salutary effect of the rise of Soviet sea power has been the U. S. Navy's own self-examination. This has been evidenced in the monthly *Proceedings* and the annual *Naval Review*, both published by the 96-year-old, quasi-official U. S. Naval Institute, whose board of control consists of Navy officers on active duty. One article in *Naval Review* 1969 includes this succinct appraisal: "Whatever its technical capability in ASW [antisub-marine warfare], the U. S. Navy has paid little attention to the problems of wartime protection of trade. It is a navy largely dominated by aviation officers with little experience in ships other than carriers. A major portion of its naval capital is invested in nuclear deterrence."

JOHN D. HAYES
Rear Admiral, U. S. Navy, Retired

NEBRASKA

A long, productive legislative session, stresses in education, bumper crops, and racial disturbances characterized the year 1969 in Nebraska.

Legislature. The 1969 unicameral Nebraska Legislature met longer (165 days), considered more bills (1,440), enacted more laws (869), and appropriated more money ($385.7 million) than any previous legislature in the state's history. Important legislation provided for an accelerated highway program, collective bargaining for public employees, homestead tax exemption, a professional parole board, and a series of state aid programs for the mentally retarded and for mental patient care, vocational-technical schools, and nursing education. Other major bills were passed in areas of open housing, riot control, and the citizen's right to defend himself. The legislature also referred to the electorate 15 amendments ranging from lowering the voting age to 20 to providing state funds to students of non-public schools.

Education. Enrollment increases at Kearney State College and the University of Nebraska at Omaha brought pressures to bear on campus facili-

─────── **NEBRASKA · Information Highlights** ───────

Area: 77,227 square miles (200,018 sq km).
Population: 1,477,000 (1969 est.).
Chief Cities (1969 est.): Lincoln, the capital, 155,000; Omaha, 362,000; Grand Island, 30,000; Fremont, 22,600.
Government: *Chief Officers*—governor, Norbert T. Tieman (Rep.); lt. gov., John E. Everroad (Rep.); secy. of state, Frank Marsh (Rep.); atty. gen., Clarence Meyer (Rep.); treas., Wayne Swanson; chief justice, Paul W. White. *Legislature* (unicameral)—49 members (nonpartisan).
Education: *School enrollment* (1968–69)—public elementary, 195,000; pupils (9,000 teachers); public secondary, 137,000 pupils (7,500 teachers); nonpublic schools, 56,400 pupils (2,430 teachers); college and university (fall 1967), 54,955 students. *Public school expenditures* (1967–68)—$198,-096,000 ($611 per pupil); average teacher's salary, $6,250.
Public Finance (fiscal year 1969): *Revenues,* $465,142,886 (2% sales tax, $72,417,269; motor fuel tax, $60,945,801; federal funds, $106,020,161). *Expenditures,* $441,637,398 (education, $179,728,512; health, welfare, and safety, $87,982,495; highways, $67,246,433). *State debt,* none (June 30, 1969).
Personal Income (1968): $4,661,000,000; average annual income per person, $3,239.
Public Assistance (fiscal year 1968): $44,660,946 to 43,835 recipients (aged, $5,575,025; dependent children, $11,-496,658).
Labor Force (employed persons, 647,400, Dec. 1968): *Agricultural,* 110,000; *nonagricultural* (wage and salary earners), 521,700 (16% manufacturing, 21.8% trade, 18.6% government). *Unemployed persons* (Dec. 31, 1968)—15,500.
Manufacturing (1965): *Value added by manufacture,* $870,155,-000 (transportation equipment, $35,739,000; primary metals, $43,513,000; nonelectrical machinery, $68,128,000; electrical machinery, $73,821,000; fabricated metals, $54,-151,000; food and products, $338,303,000).
Agriculture (1967): *Cash farm income,* $1,869,935,000 (livestock, $1,162,431,000; crops, $572,990,000; govt. payments, $134,514,000). *Chief crops* (tons)—Sorghum grain, 3,-667,608 (ranks 3d among the states); corn for grain, 9,218,440; hay, 6,604,000; wheat, 2,643,000.
Mining (1967): *Production value,* $70,868,000. *Chief minerals*—Crude petroleum, 13,373,000 barrels; natural gas, 8,-463,000,000 cubic feet.
Transportation: *Roads* (1969), 103,463 miles (166,472 km); *motor vehicles* (1968), 986,398; *railroads* (1967), 3,908 track miles (6,290 km); *airports* (1969), 12.
Communications (1969): *Telephones* (1967), 735,600; *television stations,* 21; *radio stations,* 54; *newspapers,* 21 (daily circulation, 540,000).

COMDR. LLOYD M. BUCHER (*left*) was freed of all charges concerning his surrender of the U. S. S. *Pueblo.*

UPI

ties. The University of Nebraska budget for 1969–70 was increased over the 1968–69 budget, rising from $8.8 million to $57.5 million. New facilities permitted Creighton University to locate all its schools on the central campus.

Rural school redistricting was stalled when a sharply divided state board of education fired Education Commissioner Floyd Miller and the legislature refused to place mandatory redistricting on the 1970 general election ballot. State aid to local schools was increased.

Agriculture. Total crop production in 1969 exceeded the previous record high set in 1966. Yields per acre of corn, sorghum grain, and soybeans reached new highs. Beef continued to provide about half the state's agricultural income.

Clifford M. Hardin, former University of Nebraska Chancellor, became U. S. secretary of agriculture.

Industry. Swift's Omaha meat packing plant closed in 1969 just as the Armour plant had closed in 1968. Violence accompanied a long strike at the Dakota City Iowa Beef Packers' plant. Briefly, in February, the state's manufacturing force outnumbered its agricultural force for the first time.

Race Relations. In June racial violence hit a predominantly black section of Omaha for several consecutive nights after a policeman shot and killed a Negro girl. More than 60 arrests were made.

Transportation. Both the Burlington and the Union Pacific railroads drastically reduced passenger service. The legislature substantially increased the size of trucks permitted on state highways.

Excavation. The excavation of the steamboat *Bertrand,* sunk at DeSoto Bend in the Missouri River in 1865, provided Nebraska with an historical treasure of national significance.

Taxes. Increased legislative appropriations required increased taxes. In 1970 the sales tax will be raised from 2% to 2½%, the income tax from 10% to 13%, the corporation income tax from 2% to 2.6%, and the gasoline tax from 7½ cents to 8½ cents a gallon. Cities were authorized to levy sales taxes. Lincoln and Omaha adopted a 0.5% tax.

ORVILLE H. ZABEL
Creighton University, Omaha

NECROLOGY, 1969. See the selected listing of prominent persons who died in 1969 on pages 761–772. Separate biographies of certain prominent persons appear under their own headings in this volume.

NEPAL

The most significant political development in Nepal in 1969 was the failure to achieve a reconciliation between King Mahendra and Bishweshwar Prasad Koirala, prime minister in the government formed by the Nepali Congress party that the king had forced out of power in 1960.

Internal Politics. The king had released Koirala and other Nepali Congress party leaders from jail in late 1968, in the hope that they would agree to work within the framework of his "partyless panchayat (assembly) democracy." Koirala, however, made a series of strongly worded speeches in February and March 1969 criticizing the lack of social and economic progress in Nepal since the king had begun to assert direct authority over affairs in 1960.

Koirala's hard line precipitated the king's dismissal of Prime Minister Surya Bahadur Thapa, an advocate of reconciliation between the king and Koirala. Thapa was replaced by Kirtinidhi Bista, former deputy prime minister and an opponent of reconciliation. Since then, Koirala has lived in self-imposed exile in Varanasi, India. Several other cabinet ministers were replaced in April.

Clashes between student supporters of the banned Communist and Nepali Congress parties took place in several towns. The most serious dispute occurred in Katmandu in July and resulted in the arrest of many students and the temporary banning of three newspapers.

Government Plans. The Bista administration promised to organize an effective campaign against corruption at all levels of government and pledged to settle the 1.9 million land disputes that have impeded the land reform program. It also promised to repay with interest all the compulsory savings collected from the villagers since 1964.

Nepal's development plan for 1970–75 (the fourth) emphasized agriculture, and the new administration publicized a variety of agricultural input schemes to be implemented in 1970.

Relations with India. In late June, Bista demanded that India withdraw its 23-man military mission from Katmandu and its technical personnel from their posts along Nepal's rugged Tibetan frontier, where they were observing Chinese military activities. India acceded "in principle" to this demand in early September. The dispute involved the critical issues of Nepal's independence and India's national security. Although tension subsided after the negotiations in September, a boundary dispute, smuggling, and other problems continued to prevent a cordial relationship between the two neighbors.

FREDERICK H. GAIGE
Davidson College

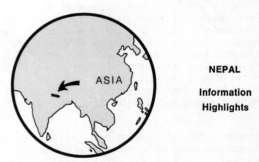

NEPAL

Information Highlights

Area: 54,362 square miles (140,797 sq km).
Population: 10,700,000 (1968 est.).
Chief Cities (1961 census): Katmandu, the capital, 122,507; Lalitpur, 48,776; Bhaktapur, 37,075.
Government: *King*—Mahendra Bir Bikram Shah Deva (acceded 1955); *Prime Minister*—Kirtinidhi Bista (took office April 7, 1969). *Legislature* (unicameral)—National Panchayat, 125 members.
Religious Faiths: Hinduism and Buddhism.
Education: *Literacy rate* (1969), 12% of population. *Total school enrollment* (1965)—452,068 (primary, 386,100; secondary, 57,440; teacher-training, 428; university/higher, 8,100).
Finance (1969 est.): *Revenues,* $63,300,000; *expenditures,* $63,300,000; *monetary unit,* rupee (10.125 rupees equal U. S.$1).
Gross National Product (1968 est.): $831,000,000.
Average Annual Income per Person (1968): $77.
Crops (metric tons, 1967–68 crop year): Rice, 2,217,000; jute, 38,000.
Foreign Trade (1967): *Exports,* $82,000,000 (chief exports, 1967: clarified butter, herbs, jute and jute products, oil seeds, rice, and timber); *Imports,* $107,000,000 (chief imports, 1967: foodstuffs, machinery and equipment, petroleum products, textiles).
Transportation: *Roads* (1968), 1,050 miles (1,689 km); *motor vehicles* (1967), 5,100 (automobiles 3,600); *railways* (1965), 63 miles (101 km).

NETHERLANDS

A runaway economy was brought under control in 1969 with price freezes, credit restrictions, and successive increases in the bank rate. Planning began for large uranium and steel plants. Riots in Curacao were quelled by Dutch Marines. Queen Juliana promised further democratization of policies regarding education and cultural affairs.

Economy. Early in 1969 a very rapid rise in economic activity confronted the Netherlands government with the problem of how to keep the boom within limits. Foreign exports were rising, investments in public and private sectors had gone up sharply, and a 10% increase in labor productivity in 1968 had about offset wage increases.

But from Dec. 15, 1968, to April 15, 1969, prices increased more than 6%. The price spiral was due in part to increases in some indirect taxes and the introduction on Jan. 1, 1969 of the tax-on-value levy agreed to by members of the European Common Market. Wages, rising steadily for years, spurted upward. The government, fearing labor unrest in a tight labor market, was unwilling to invalidate wage agreements. Since 1959 there has been a steady erosion of the profit margin. Anticipating more wage increases, producers and tradesmen saw a chance to even up matters at a time when prices were going up due to the new tax. By February there were loud complaints of exorbitant price increases; on April 9 the government rolled back and froze prices at the March 14 level.

Credit restrictions imposed in late 1968 were followed in early 1969 by suspension of tax incentives for private industry. The general price freeze, which halted the climb of prices, was replaced on September 4 by the "calculation rule," allowing merchants and manufacturers to add certain costs to their prices. The bank rate was raised twice in 1969, reaching 6% on August 4.

Industry. On March 11 the Netherlands announced an agreement with West Germany and Britain to build plants in Britain and the Netherlands to produce enriched uranium and to manufacture centrifuges.

Plans to build a $400 million steel plant in the Netherlands were announced on March 21 by West German and Dutch steel interests. Initial capacity will be 2.4 million tons annually.

Vereinigte Flugtechnische Werke of West Germany and Fokker of the Netherlands announced on May 2 a merger of the two aircraft manufacturers with headquarters in Dusseldorf.

Foreign Trade. The gains made in 1967 and 1968 in the Netherlands' competitive position in foreign trade were threatened by an estimated 10% wage increase in 1969 and an estimated 4% productivity rate increase. Thus unit labor costs will rise some 6%, twice the rise of competing nations.

Rotterdam claimed first place among the ports of the world. In 1968 the port handled 156.9 million metric tons of foreign ocean-borne cargo.

Benelux. The Benelux economic union continued to move forward. By July 1, 1971, all border controls among Belgium, the Netherlands, and Luxembourg will be removed. Meeting in The Hague, April 28–29, representatives of the three countries agreed to intensify steps to coordinate their economic, financial, and social policies and to work toward harmonizing legal systems, transport policies, and policies with regard to location of industry.

Netherlands Antilles. On May 30, at the request of the Netherlands Antilles government, Dutch Marines and riot troops were flown into Willemstad, Curaçao, to assist police in quelling riots. The government alleged that Communist agitators were responsible for disorders flaring up in Willemstad over labor troubles. Communist aggression is one of the causes specified by law as requisite for calling in military aid from the Netherlands. On June 1 some 500 protesters from Curaçao marched in The Hague and called for independence for the Antilles.

As a part of the kingdom of the Netherlands, the Antilles enjoys self-government except in matters of defense and foreign affairs. In recent years there has been sentiment in the Dutch Parliament for granting complete independence to the Antilles.

Students and Artists. Unrest among students and artists won concessions from Queen Juliana. In her speech from the throne on September 16 at the opening of Parliament she stated that legislation would be submitted to reform the governing bodies of universities and colleges. Students had been agitating for democratic reforms in education. The queen also announced that the government in consultation with artists would consider their proposals for revision of government policy in cultural affairs.

Defector. At his request on January 24, Liao Ho-shu, chargé d'affaires of the People's Republic of China in The Hague, was granted asylum. His wife and two children were in China. Later he was flown to the United States.

New Prince. On October 11, 1969, Crown Princess Beatrix bore her third son, Prince Constantine.

AMRY VANDENBOSCH
University of Kentucky

──────── **NETHERLANDS · Information Highlights** ────────

Area: 12,978 square miles (33,612 sq km).
Population: 12,743,000 (1968 est.).
Chief Cities (1966 census): Amsterdam, the capital, 861,034; Rotterdam, 727,207; The Hague, 589,862.
Government: *Queen*—Juliana (b. 1909; acceded 1948); *Premier*—Petrus J. S. de Jong (took office April 4, 1967). *Parliament* (Staaten-Generaal)—First Chamber, 75 members (party seating, 1967: Catholic People's party, 25; Labor party, 22; People's Party for Freedom and Democracy, 8; Protestant Revolutionary party, 7; Christian Historical Union, 7; others, 6); Second Chamber, 150 deputies (party seating, 1967: Catholic People's party, 42; Labor party, 37; People's Party for Freedom and Democracy, 17; others, 54).
Religious Faiths: Protestants, 43% of population; Roman Catholics, 38.5%; Jews, 0.1%; other, 18.4%.
Education: *Literacy rate* (1969), 100% of population. *Total school enrollment* (1966)—3,269,470 (primary, 1,418,665; secondary, 1,112,449; teacher-training, 12,780; vocational, 562,363; higher, 163,213).
Finance (1968 est.): *Revenues*, $5,843,000,000; *expenditures*, $6,147,000,000; *public debt* (1967), $6,980,000,000; *monetary unit*, guilder (3.606 equal U. S.$1).
Gross National Product (1968): $25,207,986,000.
National Income (1968): $20,521,353,000; average annual income per person, $1,610.
Economic Indexes (1968): *Industrial production*, 143 (1963=100); *agricultural production* (1967), 107 (1963=100); *cost of living* (1967), 121 (1963=100).
Manufacturing (metric tons, 1967): Crude steel, 3,407,000; gasoline, 2,370,000; wheat flour, 680,000.
Crops (metric tons, 1967–68 crop year): Sugar beets, 5,074,-000; potatoes, 4,840,000; wheat, 739,000; barley, 447,000.
Minerals (metric tons, 1967): Coal, 8,065,000; crude petroleum, 2,265,000; salt, 1,926,000.
Foreign Trade (1968): *Exports*, $8,341,000,000 (chief exports, 1967: Electrical machinery, $665,806,000; textiles, $932,-600,000); *imports*, $9,293,000,000 (chief imports, 1967: Nonelectrical machinery, $806,738,000. *Chief trading partner* (1967): West Germany.
Transportation: *Roads* (1964), 54,400 miles (87,546 km); *motor vehicles* (1967), 31,300 (automobiles 26,300); *railways* (1965), 2,023 miles (3,256 km); *merchant vessels* (1967), 456; *national airline*, KLM Royal Dutch Airlines.
Communications: *Telephones* (1968): 24,610; *television stations* (1967), 3; *television sets* (1966), 25,000; *radios* (1966), 121,000; *newspapers* (1967), 91.

NEVADA

The most important political development in Nevada in 1969 was Gov. Paul Laxalt's announcement that he would retire from public life after completing his first term of office in January 1971. The news was welcomed by Democratic Sen. Howard W. Cannon, who had considered Laxalt a likely opponent in his reelection campaign. Cannon defeated Laxalt by 84 votes in the 1964 election.

Legislation. The governor's programs fared very well in the longest legislative session (95 days) in Nevada history. His only major defeat came on the Fair Housing bill which was killed in the Senate Finance Committee. The Legislature passed a 10.4% increase for the state's classified employees, provided for collective bargaining for civil service employees, revamped the judicial system to provide for stronger lower-level courts, approved a revision of the corporate gambling license law, increased cigarette, liquor, and gasoline taxes, provided for an optional half-cent county sales tax, and set up an interim finance committee to handle emergency money matters between legislative sessions.

Constitutional amendments to provide for annual legislative sessions and to allow the Legislature to set its own salary were approved by the 1969 Legislature and will be voted on in the 1970 election. Another amendment, to allow 18-year-olds to vote, was approved, but it must be passed by the 1971 Legislature before going to a popular vote.

A controversial abortion reform bill was defeated by one vote in the lower house of the Legislature by a coalition of Catholic and Mormon assemblymen.

The Legislature earmarked 61% of the general fund expenditures for education, including $15 million more in state aid to the school districts than the governor had recommended. An extra $6 million for teachers' salaries was added after a two-day strike sponsored by the teachers' association.

NEVADA · Information Highlights

Area: 110,540 square miles (286,299 sq km).
Population: 465,000 (1969 est.).
Chief Cities (1969 est.): Carson City, the capital, 9,500; Las Vegas, 120,000; Reno, 73,000.
Government: *Chief Officers*—governor, Paul Laxalt (Republican); lt. gov., Ed Fike (R); secy. of state, John Koontz (D); atty. gen., Harvey Dickerson (D); treas., Michael Mirabelli; supt. of pub. instr., Burnell Larson; chief justice, Jon Collins. *Legislature*—Senate, 20 members (11 D, 9 R); Assembly, 40 members (22 R, 18 D).
Education: *School enrollment* (1968)—public elementary, 69,000 pupils (2,800 teachers); public secondary, 45,000 pupils (2,100 teachers); nonpublic schools, 4,500 pupils (200 teachers); college and university (fall 1967), 8,575 students. *Public school expenditures* (1967–68)—$87,-138,000 ($815 per pupil); average teacher's salary, $8,200.
Public Finance (fiscal year 1968): *Revenues*, $213,967,000 (general sales and gross receipts taxes, $34,527,000; motor fuel tax, $16,829,000; federal funds, $52,802,000). *Expenditures*, $210,901,000 (education, $26,056,000; health, welfare, and safety, $22,593,000; highways, $45,644,000).
Personal Income (1968): $1,777,000,000; average annual income per person, $3,957.
Public Assistance (fiscal year 1969): $12,950,413.
Labor Force (employed persons, calendar year 1968): *Agricultural*, 4,600; *nonagricultural* (wage and salary earners), 177,300 (4.0% manufacturing, 19% trade, 19.2% government). *Unemployed persons*—10,500.
Manufacturing (1965): *Value added by manufacture*, $106,-897,000 (chemical and allied products, $21,672,000; stone, clay, and glass products, $16,178,000).
Agriculture (1967): *Cash farm income*, $59,070,000. *Chief crops* (tons)—Hay, 809,000; wheat, 37,200.
Mining (1967): *Production value* (1968), $120,041,000. *Chief minerals* (tons)—Iron ore, 1,061,760; copper, 79,825; silver, 819,000 troy oz.; gold, 364,000 troy oz.
Transportation: *Roads* (1969), 47,562 miles (75,642 km); *motor vehicles* (1968), 305,484; *railroads* (1969), 2,047 track miles (3,294 km); *airports* (1969), 4.
Communications (1969): *Telephones* (1967), 236,700; *television stations*, 5; *radio stations*, 25; *newspapers*, 7.

The unexpected windfall in gambling revenue from Clark County, largely attributed to the accurate reporting of winnings by the Howard Hughes gaming operations, was used for necessary construction on the Reno and Las Vegas campuses of the University of Nevada.

Racial Unrest. Racial problems began to surface in Nevada in 1969. In October large-scale rioting and looting broke out in a predominantly black west side section of Las Vegas.

Charges of discrimination often voiced by the black community were later reinforced by the Nevada Equal Rights Commission. The Commission claimed that the unfair hiring practices in nonservice positions of Las Vegas strip hotels constituted a definite threat to the well-being of the state.

Minerals. Total mineral production in Nevada for 1968 rose to $120,041,000, exceeding the excellent 1966 record.

DON W. DRIGGS
University of Nevada

NEW BRUNSWICK

New Brunswick was more deeply affected than other provinces by Canada's sense of impending financial difficulty and new austerity. After eight years of steady economic growth, which had been accompanied by heavy government spending and higher costs of living, retrenchment became a watchword.

Financial Problems. After announcing a total government deficit of $273.8 million on March 18, Finance Minister L. G. DesBrisay declared a 10% surcharge on personal income tax and increased taxes on liquor, tobacco, and gasoline. In addition, he announced a 2% increase in the sales tax, raising it to 8%, the highest in Canada.

Public distress over the new taxes was vociferously expressed by the Save New Brunswick Committee, an independent organization of citizens. Premier Louis J. Robichaud defended the tax measures by showing the need for finances for the Plan for Equal Opportunity, introduced in 1967. He also pointed to improved services on winter roads, new school construction, and provisions for technical and trade schools. The financial straits of the province were reflected in the year's moratorium on hospital construction and the government's inability to introduce the national Medicare plan.

New Brunswick, the Canadian province with the largest proportion of French-speaking people (38%), received attention when the provincial legislature passed the Official Languages Act, designed to give equality to the two national founding groups. The law required the use of the French language in addition to English, in law courts and in the printing of provincial statutes. It aroused a sensational, although temporary, backlash of English-speaking opinion, concentrated in Westmorland county, where the Canadian Loyalist Association has its headquarters.

Economic Development. In spite of the prevailing high interest rates, the economy was buoyant. In St. John there was massive new construction, broad implementation of urban renewal, the opening of university buildings at Tucker Park, and completion of the port at Mispec for large oil cargoes. The federal government gave Charlotte county, a neglected area, a $16 million paper mill. Development of the tourist industry was encouraged by the federal government's provision for Kent National

—— NEW BRUNSWICK • Information Highlights ——

Area: 28,354 square miles (73,437 sq km).
Population: 626,000 (Jan. 1, 1969 est.).
Chief Cities (1966 census): Fredericton, the capital, 22,460; St. John, 51,567; Moncton, 45,847.
Government: *Chief Officers*—Lt. gov., Wallace Samuel Bird; premier, Louis J. Robichaud (Liberal); prov. secy., Joseph E. LeBlanc (L); min. of justice, Bernard A. Jean (L); min. of finance, L. G. DesBrisay (L); min. of educ., W. W. Meldrum (L); chief justice, G. F. G. Bridges. *House of Assembly*—(convened March 4, 1969) 58 members (31 Liberal, 27 Progressive Conservative).
Education: *School enrollment* (1966–67 est.)—public elementary and secondary, 166,750 pupils (7,000 teachers); private schools, 1,389 pupils (104 teachers); Indian (federal) schools, 638 pupils (25 teachers); college and university (fall 1966), 6,862 students. *Public school expenditures* (1963)—$35,996,000.
Public Finance (fiscal year 1968 est.): *Revenues*, $221,000,000 (sales tax, $68,910,000; income tax, $28,972,000; federal funds, $79,833,000). *Expenditures*, $231,000,000 (education, $92,120,000; health and social welfare, $50,310,000; transport and communications, $40,930,000).
Personal Income (1967 est.): $1,028,000,000; average annual income per person, $1,658.
Social Welfare (fiscal year 1968 est.): $10,840,000 (aged and blind, $3,510,000; dependents and unemployed, $3,670,-000).
Manufacturing (1966): *Value added by manufacture*, $211,295,-000 (paper and allied industries, $61,542,000; food and products, $61,391,000).
Agriculture (1968): *Cash farm income*, $49,368,000. *Chief crop* (cash receipts)—Potatoes, $12,543,000 (ranks 2d among the provinces).
Mining (1967 est.): *Production value*, $89,863,348. *Chief minerals* (tons)—Stone, 3,573,497 (ranks 3d among the provinces); zinc, 153,721 (ranks 4th); sand and gravel, 8,390,000; silver, 2,785,198 troy ounces.
Fisheries (1968): *Commercial catch*, 534,801,000 pounds ($14,624,000). *Leading species*—Herring, 425,371,000 pounds ($4,899,000); cod, 21,042,000 pounds ($914,000); lobster, 5,965,000 pounds ($3,991,000).
Transportation: *Roads* (1966), 13,171 miles (21,196 km); *motor vehicles* (1966), 183,676; *railroads* (1966), 1,671 track miles (2,689 km); *licensed airports* (1966), 10.
Communications (1966): *Telephones*, 184,150; *television stations*, 3; *radio stations*, 13; *daily newspapers*, 6.
All figures given in Canadian dollars equal to U. S.93¢.

Park, 96 square miles (249 sq km) on the shore of Northumberland Strait.

Capital investment for the year amounted to $499 million, an increase of $55 million over 1968. The average weekly wage rose to $96. Housing starts easily broke all records.

Politics. The political scene was comparatively quiet. In June Richard Hatfield, a Woodstock lawyer, was chosen leader of the Progressive Conservative party. At the end of the year public concern was aroused by the charges of New Brunswick Sen. Charles McElman against St. John industrialist K. C. Irving, who allegedly had secured a monopoly of all daily English-language newspapers.

W. S. MacNutt
The University of New Brunswick

NEW HAMPSHIRE

A major goal of first-term Republican Gov. Walter R. Peterson, Jr., was achieved in 1969 with the creation of a 300-member Citizens' Task Force to conduct a sweeping review of all major aspects of policy-making in New Hampshire. The legislature, meeting in regular biennial session, refused to levy new statewide taxes but passed an important drug-control act.

Task Force. The Citizens' Task Force was mandated to explore a wide range of problems, including environmental control, economic development, education, and the adequacy of state and local government units. The last such study, limited to state administrative reorganization, was completed in 1950 under Gov. Sherman Adams.

Preliminary findings of Governor Peterson's task force have already generated considerable controversy, and it is expected that the final report, parts

of which will be submitted to a special legislative session in 1970, will spark a debate that will carry over into the 1970 party primaries. Final recommendations are expected to include such controversial proposals as a 4-year gubernatorial term instead of the present 2-year term, annual legislative sessions, and an expanded tax base. Similar proposals have been consistently rejected in the past, either by the legislature or by the voters.

Legislation. The critical need for new sources of state revenue was highlighted again in 1969 by a growing state deficit and mounting evidence of financial crisis in New Hampshire's large parochial school system. Proposals to subsidize the nonpublic schools were introduced in the legislature, but immediate action was postponed by referring the measures to an interim study group. As in previous sessions, the legislature decisively rejected all efforts to enact a statewide sales or income tax.

The negative mood of the legislature was further reflected in the defeat of two key proposals by the Peterson administration—a teachers' negotiation law and the creation of a special fund for the financing of public education. Also defeated were bills to abolish capital punishment, create an office of consumer counsel in the governor's office, legalize greyhound racing, add a student trustee to the governing board of the University of New Hampshire, and lower the voting age to 18. Proponents of a liberalized abortion law met success in the House but were defeated in the Senate.

Perhaps the most notable accomplishments of the legislature were passage of new laws on drug control and the regulation of highway billboards. Under the new drug-control act, penalties for the use and

—— NEW HAMPSHIRE • Information Highlights ——

Area: 9,304 square miles (24,097 sq km).
Population: 701,000 (1969 est.).
Chief Cities (1969 est.): Concord, the capital, 29,200; Manchester, 87,000; Nashua, 47,500; Dover, 23,500.
Government: *Chief Officers*—governor, Walter R. Peterson, Jr. (Republican); secy. of state, Robert L. Stark (R); atty. gen., George S. Pappagianis (R); treas., Robert W. Flanders; comm. of educ., Newell J. Paire; chief justice, Frank R. Kenison. *General Court*—Senate, 24 members (15 Republicans, 9 Democrats); House of Representatives, 400 members (255 R, 145 D).
Education: *School enrollment* (1968)—public elementary, 85,000 pupils (3,700 teachers); public secondary, 57,000 pupils (2,900 teachers); nonpublic schools, 34,100 pupils (1,670 teachers); college and university (fall 1967), 25,793 students. *Public school expenditures* (1967–68)—$96,519,-000 ($743 per pupil); average teacher's salary, $6,450.
Public Finance fiscal year 1968–69): *Revenues*, $294,339,709 (state tax sources, $77,733,825; motor fuel tax, $21,704,-222; federal funds, $44,401,216). *Expenditures*, $298,361,-436 (education, $46,971,000; health, welfare, and safety, $28,171,000; highways, $52,249,000). *State debt*, $111,039,-000 (June 30, 1969).
Personal Income (1968): $2,288,000,000; average annual income per person, $3,259.
Public Assistance (fiscal year 1968): $10,261,892 to 11,934 recipients.
Labor Force (employed persons, 313,300, Aug. 1969): *Agricultural*, 5,100; *nonagricultural* (wage and salary earners), 272,550 (36.4% manufacturing, 18.2% trade, 13.0% government). *Unemployed persons* (Aug. 1969)—6,100.
Manufacturing (1965): *Value added by manufacture*, $770,940,-000 (electrical machinery, $132,535,000; nonelectrical machinery, $113,458,000).
Agriculture (1967): *Cash farm income*, $56,765,000 (livestock, $44,185,000; crops, $11,905,000; govt. payments, $675,000). *Chief crops* (tons)—Hay, 234,000; apples, 34,560; potatoes, 12,600.
Mining (1966): *Production value*, $7,000,000. *Chief mineral* (tons)—Stone, 206,454.
Fisheries (1967): *Commercial catch*, 1,200,000 pounds ($800,-000). *Leading species* (1966)—Northern lobsters, 807,000 pounds ($585,000).
Transportation (1969): *Roads*, 14,677 miles (23,623 km); *motor vehicles*, 345,564; *railroads*, 1,015 track miles (1,633 km); *airports*, 4.
Communications (1969): *Telephones*, 336,200; *television stations*, 2; *radio stations*, 27; *newspapers*, 9.

possession of certain drugs have been made more flexible and humane, with a clear distinction being drawn between "hard" narcotics, such as heroin, and "lesser" drugs, such as marihuana. It will now be possible, for example, for judges to define the use and possession of marihuana as a misdemeanor rather than a felony.

The new billboard legislation is designed to impose comprehensive controls over outdoor advertising along the state's interstate and federally aided primary highways. Under the new law, all billboards must be licensed by the state and must conform to certain minimum requirements.

Municipal Elections. In the November municipal elections Republican mayoralty candidates retained control of two traditionally Democratic cities—Manchester and Somersworth—and ousted a Democratic incumbent in Rochester.

JOSEPH P. FORD
University of New Hampshire

NEW JERSEY

Charges that organized crime had infiltrated all levels of government and the election of a new governor dominated headlines in New Jersey in 1969.

Crime Investigation. As the year began, a legislative committee was conducting an investigation of allegations made by William J. Brennan, Jr., a deputy state attorney general, that members of the legislature were friendly with known criminals. During the hearings, the names of two assemblymen and one state senator were revealed. The committee concluded that some improprieties had occurred, and censured two of the legislators. The committee also was critical of Brennan for making his charges in a manner that implicated all legislators.

In June, the FBI released voluminous transcripts of taped conversations involving alleged Mafia leaders and public officials. Following the disclosures, several investigations of organized crime were conducted, including one by a newly created state investigation commission and others by grand juries at the federal, state, and county levels.

Early in December, public attention was concentrated on the city of Newark, where Mayor Hugh J.

WILLIAM T. CAHILL celebrates big victory for New Jersey governorship over Democrat Robert B. Meyner.

Addonizio, all nine councilmen, and various other city officials were subpoenaed. Addonizio refused to answer questions, pleading the Fifth Amendment. Corporation Counsel Philip Gordon resigned after appearing before the grand jury, and Mayor Addonizio reported that Gordon had admitted to accepting a bribe while serving as a city councilman. Almost concurrently, the chief city magistrate was removed from office by the state supreme court, and a Union County judge was indicted for offering a bribe to a prosecutor in Somerset County.

On December 17, Mayor Addonizio and nine city officials or former officials were indicted on charges of extortion totaling $253,000, and on conspiracy and income tax evasion. Following the grand jury action, the New Jersey Chamber of Commerce urged the removal of Mayor Addonizio from office.

Elections. Both parties in the 1969 gubernatorial campaign chose candidates in hotly contested primaries. The Republicans selected William T. Cahill, an experienced congressman and former FBI agent and county prosecutor, while the Democrats nominated former two-term Gov. Robert B. Meyner. In the campaign, Cahill emphasized his law enforcement experience, while Meyner stressed his eight years of experience as governor during the 1950's.

The contest quickly deteriorated into a morass of charges and countercharges, prolonged by an extensive series of debates. What had been rated as a very close race became a landslide for Cahill, who

-------- **NEW JERSEY · Information Highlights** --------

Area: 7,836 square miles (20,295 sq km).
Population: 7,106,000 (1969 est.).
Chief Cities (1969 est.): Trenton, the capital, 103,000; Newark, 390,000; Jersey City, 269,000; Paterson, 144,000; Elizabeth, 118,000; Camden, 109,000.
Government: *Chief Officers*—governor, Richard J. Hughes (Democrat); secy. of state, Robert J. Burkhardt (D); atty. gen., Arthur J. Sills (D); treas., John A. Kervick; supt. of pub. instr., Carl L. Marburger; chief justice, Joseph Weintraub. *Legislature*—Senate, 40 members (31 Republicans, 9 Democrats); House of Representatives, 80 members (58 D, 22 R).
Education: *School enrollment* (1968)—public elementary, 911,000 pupils (37,200 teachers); public secondary, 491,000 pupils (27,100 teachers); nonpublic schools, 860,200 pupils (11,530 teachers); college and university (fall 1967), 152,548 students. *Public school expenditures* (1967–68)—$1,207,000,000 ($943 per pupil); average teacher's salary, $8,167.
Public Finance (fiscal year 1968): *Revenues,* $1,943,783,000 (general sales and gross receipts taxes, $238,292,000; motor fuel tax, $156,073,000; federal funds, $355,185,000). *Expenditures,* $1,661,131,000 (education, $203,516,000; health, welfare, and safety, $138,284,000; highways, $317,883,000). *State debt* $337,307,000 (June 30, 1969).
Personal Income (1968): $28,047,000,000; average annual income per person, $3,954.
Public Assistance (fiscal year 1968): $230,589,465 to 259,447 recipients (aged, $15,240,451; dependent children, $144,507,080).
Labor Force (employed persons, July 1969): *Agricultural,* 42,700; *nonagricultural* (wage and salary earners), 2,557,300 (31% manufacturing, 18.1% trade, 12.5% government). *Unemployed persons* (July 1969)—149,500.
Manufacturing (1966): *Value added by manufacture,* $12,246,302,000 (electrical machinery, $1,671,922,000; food and products, $1,106,223,000; nonelectrical machinery, $974,011,000; fabricated metals, $828,827,000; transportation equipment, $670,102,000; primary metals, $828,827,000).
Agriculture (1967): *Cash farm income,* $256,117,000 (livestock, $101,807,000; crops, $150,169,000; govt. payments, $4,201,000). *Chief crops* (tons)—Hay, 383,000; corn for grain, 177,408; cranberries, 8,150 (ranks 3d among the states).
Mining (1967): *Production value,* $72,747,000. *Chief mineral* (tons)—Sand and gravel, 18,626,000.
Fisheries (1967): *Commercial catch,* 123,022,309 pounds ($10,580,873). *Leading species*—Menhaden, 45,813,744 pounds ($642,155); surf clams, 41,584,487 pounds ($4,050,608).
Transportation: *Roads* (1968), 31,522 miles (50,728 km); *motor vehicles* (1968), 3,102,910; *railroads* (1968), 4,346 track miles (6,989 km); *airports* (1968), 3.
Communications (1969): *Telephones* (1968), 4,144,000; *television stations,* 3; *radio stations,* 55; *newspapers,* 30 (daily circulation, 1968, 1,732,149).

won by 475,000 votes, the largest plurality ever gained by a New Jersey gubernatorial candidate. A major factor in Cahill's victory was his gaining the support of Hudson County Democratic leader John V. Kenny. Normally a Democratic county, Hudson went to the Republican candidate by 30,000 votes.

Elections for the General Assembly followed a similar pattern, with Republican candidates winning 59 of the 80 seats, one more than they held in the previous Assembly. A number of incumbents were not returned to office, however, since a new computer-designed reapportionment plan had changed the boundaries of many districts.

The voters approved a bond issue of $271 million for water pollution control and authorized a state lottery. They soundly defeated a proposal to lower the voting age to 18.

Student Unrest. Following campus unrest at Rutgers, the university announced an open enrollment policy for disadvantaged students from Newark, New Brunswick, and Camden, where the university maintains major campuses. Since no funds were immediately available, the program evoked considerable criticism. The university's board of trustees diverted enough money from capital funds to start the program in September, but its continuation depended on quick legislative action.

White students also took part in disruptive action. Students occupied buildings at Paterson State College in the fall. At Trenton State College, a substantial portion of the faculty sought the ouster of President Robert Heussler. At issue were Heussler's efforts to reorient the college from a teacher-training institution to a liberal arts college, and his alleged unresponsiveness to the faculty and students.

ERNEST C. REOCK, JR.
Rutgers University

NEW MEXICO

A struggle with change marked the year 1969 for New Mexicans. An unsuccessful attempt to adopt a new state constitution, controversies over air pollution and academic freedom, and the passage of one of the nation's most liberal abortion laws were the highlights.

Constitutional Revision. Seventy delegates convened in Santa Fe in August and September to update the state constitution. The original document, dating from 1910, had been revised with numerous amendments and counteramendments that adversely affected its clarity and coherence. The updated version proposed by the convention recommended a streamlined administration, and greater authority in the office of the governor. Such offices as secretary of state, state treasurer, attorney general, and members of the state board of education, all formerly elected, would become gubernatorial appointments. Some slight recognition was given to the growing interest of youth in public affairs with the lowering of the voting age to 20. In a special election held December 9, New Mexico voters rejected the proposed constitution.

Air Pollution. One of the innovations of the constitution was a section on the protection of the environment, indicative of an increasing awareness of the pollution which often accompanies development. Threats to clean air attracted particular attention. Citizen groups were organized to battle against the location of a pulp and paper mill near Albuquerque. Although the firm proposing the plant went to great trouble to prove that pollution would be negligible, the controversy continued until the company decided to locate elsewhere.

Although unsuccessful, strong efforts were made in the 1969 session of the legislature to strengthen pollution control laws and to increase the appropriations of the state enforcement agency. Witnesses at hearings on air quality control standards clamored for more stringent pollution regulations. The increasing degradation of the air in the Rio Grande Valley resulting from coal-fueled power plants was marked as a warning for the future.

Education. Heated arguments arose in the areas of education and academic freedom. A legislative investigating committee was appointed to study supervision of state supported institutions following the highly publicized disclosure of an allegedly obscene poem read by a freshman English class at the University of New Mexico. The argument was carried over into the following fall when the state Board of Regents suppressed an issue of a literary magazine published by the university.

Abortion Reform. In March a liberal abortion law was adopted by the New Mexican legislature, despite strong opposition from the Roman Catholic Church and the refusal of Gov. David F. Cargo to sign it. The law will permit abortions in licensed hospitals when two staff physicians agree that pregnancy would have grave effect on the physical or mental health of the mother or child, or when the pregnancy resulted from rape or incest.

HELEN M. INGRAM
University of New Mexico

——— NEW MEXICO • Information Highlights ———

Area: 121,666 square miles (315,115 sq km).
Population: 1,008,000 (1969 est.).
Chief Cities (1969 est.): Santa Fe, the capital, 42,000; Albuquerque, 225,000; Las Cruces, 40,000.
Government: *Chief Officers*—governor, David F. Cargo (Rep.); lt. gov., E. Lee Francis (R); secy. of state, Ernestine D. Evans (Dem.); atty. gen., James A. Maloney (D); treas., Jesse D. Kornegay; supt. of pub. instr., Leonard J. De-Layo; chief justice, M. E. Noble. *Legislature—Senate*, 42 members (25 Democrats, 17 Republicans); House of Representatives, 70 members (44 D, 26 R).
Education: *School enrollment* (1968–69)—public elementary, 151,000 pupils (6,200 teachers); public secondary, 124,-000 pupils (5,500 teachers); nonpublic schools, 23,400 pupils (1,120 teachers); college and university (fall 1968), 33,767 students. *Public school expenditures* (1967–68)—$200,338,000 ($766 per pupil); average teacher's salary, $7,299.
Public Finance (fiscal year 1968): *Revenues,* $489,287,000 (general sales and gross receipts taxes, $71,647,000; motor fuel tax, $29,288,000; federal funds, $148,884,000). *Expenditures,* $454,401,000 (education, $103,550,000; health, welfare, and safety, $62,893,000; highways, $5,-780,000). *State debt,* $135,104,000 (June 30, 1968).
Personal Income (1968): $2,667,000,000; average annual income per person, $2,651.
Public Assistance (fiscal year 1969): $28,279,205 to 61,948 recipients (aged, $6,197,530; dependent children, 16,028,-233).
Labor Force (employed persons, Dec. 31, 1968): *Nonagricultural* (wage and salary earners), 179,580 (10.7% manufacturing, 33.8% trade). *Unemployed persons* (Dec. 13, 1968)—4,914.
Manufacturing (1965): *Value added by manufacture,* $141,-627,000 (food and products, $38,744,000; stone, clay, and glass products, $19,966,000; printing and publishing, $14,-775,000; lumber and wood products, $11,012,000).
Agriculture (1967): *Cash farm income,* $350,734,000 (livestock, $221,041,000; crops, $96,378,000; govt. payments, $33,315,000). *Chief crops* (tons)—Hay, 963,000; sorghum grain, 536,312; wheat, 118,440.
Mining (1967): *Production value,* $876,106,000. *Chief minerals* (tons)—Sand and gravel, 14,672,000; bituminous coal, 3,463,000; potassium salts, 2,883,000; crude petroleum, 126,144,000 bbl.; silver, 157,000 troy ounces.
Transportation: *Roads* (1969), 66,450 miles (106,938 km); *motor vehicles* (1969), 599,021; railroads (1969), 2,225 track miles (3,580 km); airports (1969), 13.
Communications (1969): *Telephones* (1968), 426,500; *television stations,* 7; *radio stations,* 52; *newspapers,* 19.

NEW ORLEANS

The problems of New Orleans in 1969 were primarily fiscal planning and intergovernmental relations. The population estimate for 1969 was 700,163.

Finances. For some time one of the most under-financed metropolitan areas of the United States, New Orleans did very little to improve its fiscal position in 1969. Mayor Victor H. Schiro's threatened suit for property tax equalization was not pushed, capital and operating budgets continued at low levels, and tentative proposals for a municipal income tax to be shared with adjacent metropolitan parishes met with strong opposition.

Planning. The Regional Planning Commission, concerned with the problem of airport obsolescence, proposed to apply to the U. S. Department of Transportation for a regional transportation plan. A state agency, the Orleans Parish Levee Board, asked the city to take over the management of its general aviation facility, the New Orleans Airport.

The planned Riverfront Expressway was canceled by the Department of Transporation in order to preserve the historic French Quarter, but certain groups still contended the road was necessary.

Intergovernmental Relations. The Sewerage and Water Board engaged in a controversy with the City Civil Service Commission regarding wage rates for its employees. A proposed new Mississippi River bridge continued to cause city-state controversy in the planning and site-location stage. The proposed downtown domed stadium ran into trouble with protesters, who filed suit to halt construction and the sale of bonds.

Race Relations. The Human Relations Committee continued its work in the city, and no racial conflict of consequence was apparent. There was black participation in neighborhood planning for urban renewal and housing upgrading. Most of the public swimming pools, closed since 1963, were reopened on an integrated basis without incident.

Politics. New Orleans in 1968 sent the first Negro to the Louisiana Legislature since 1898, and in 1969 chose a black Democratic nominee who was expected to be elected to the Legislature in 1970.

The mayoralty race marked a significant change from the tradition of highly centralized factional politics. A total of 12 candidates vied for the office being vacated by retiring Mayor Schiro, and there was considerable cross endorsement of candidates for other city and parish posts. After the November 8 Democratic primary and the December 13 runoff, the nominee was Moon Landrieu. As a Democrat, he was virtually assured of election in April 1970.

The parish district attorney, Jim Garrison, of the Kennedy assassination investigation and subsequent trial of Clay Shaw, won nomination in the first primary.

Economics. After a high first quarter, the economy of the city tapered off to a level that remained constant, with a possible drop in sales volume by year's end. The major components of the economy continued to be port activity, shipbuilding, and tourism, in that order.

Public Employees. The American Federation of Teachers threatened a strike among school teachers for union recognition. The police and fire departments staged a work slowdown in an effort to increase their starting salary to $900 per month.

LOUIS E. NEWMAN
Louisiana State University

NEW YORK

Fiscal difficulties arising from the growing need for social services and the mounting cost of state government continued to be the major concern for citizens of New York state in 1969.

Legislation. The record $5.4 billion budget for the fiscal year 1969 was increased by 16% for fiscal 1970 to an "austerity" budget of $6.4 billion. Despite the increase in spending, New York City and other urban localities were faced with cutbacks in services.

Among the budget bills passed by the Legislature after bitter debate were measures reducing welfare payments, raising the eligibility requirements for Medicaid, and limiting nursing home care for the elderly to 100 days. Opponents of these cuts saw them as inspired by anti-Negro and anti-Puerto Rican interests.

Voter protests over cuts in school aid led to the restoration of $24 million of a $104 million cut proposed by Gov. Nelson A. Rockefeller. Mounting pressures and demonstrations by welfare recipients were partly responsible for the announcement in September of a $1.3 million program of temporary additional payments to the aged, blind, and disabled on welfare rolls. The Legislature increased the state sales tax from 2% to 3%, bringing the total sales tax to 6% in some communities such as New York City, which have a local 3% tax.

Despite criticism voiced over the cuts in social services, the Legislature passed bills at the end of the session to increase the pay for top appointed state officials and to raise substantially the expense allowance of legislative committee chairmen and senior minority members.

Public Health. The much-debated legislation to liberalize New York's 86-year-old abortion law was narrowly defeated in the Assembly after an emotional speech by Republican Assemblyman Martin Ginsburg. It had appeared certain that the three-year effort would succeed.

Two strong narcotics laws providing for sentences of 25 years to life for those who peddle specific amounts of heroin and other drugs were passed after Governor Rockefeller warned that such legislation was needed to combat the "alarming rise in the incidence of the use of narcotics, particularly among young people."

Early in the year the first of 15 mental rehabilitation centers planned with state financing was completed and opened in Middletown.

Education. On April 21, Governor Rockefeller signed a bill requiring colleges and universities in the state to adopt rules and regulations for the "maintenance of public order" or risk the loss of state financial aid. The measure was one of several bills passed to control disorders that occurred during the year at many campuses in New York. It was inspired particularly by events in April at Cornell University where armed black students seized a building.

Just before the Legislature adjourned, Governor Rockefeller unexpectedly signed into law a measure that banned the use of bussing by appointed school boards and the state commissioner of education as a means of integrating public schools.

Labor. After sharp debate and close vote, the Legislature approved amendments strengthening penalties for breach of the Taylor Law, which forbids strikes by public employees. These measures resulted

———— **NEW YORK** • Information Highlights ————

Area: 49,576 square miles (128,402 sq km).
Population: 18,210,000 (1969 est.).
Chief Cities (1969, est.): Albany, the capital, 122,000; New York, 7,975,000; Buffalo, 450,000; Rochester, 295,000; Syracuse, 210,000.
Government: *Chief Officers*—governor, Nelson A. Rockefeller (Rep.); lt. gov., Malcolm Wilson (R); secy. of state, John P. Lomenzo (R); atty. gen., Louis J. Lefkowitz (R); treas., Arthur Levitt; supt. of pub. instr., James A. Allen, Jr.; chief justice, Stanley H. Fuld. *Legislature*—Senate, 57 members (24 Democrats, 33 Republicans); House of Representatives, 150 members (72 D, 77 R).
Education: *School enrollment* (1968)—public elementary, 1,913,000 pupils (84,700 teachers); public secondary, 1,474,000 pupils (82,300 teachers); nonpublic schools 860,200 pupils (33,880 teachers); college and university (fall 1967), 677,251 students. *Public school expenditures* (1967–68)—$3,494,000,000 ($1,125 per pupil); average teacher's salary, $8,600.
Public Finance (fiscal year 1968): *Revenues,* $7,604,454,000 (general sales and gross receipts taxes, $630,912,000; motor fuel tax, $291,848,000; federal funds, $1,204,160,000). *Expenditures,* $7,595,930,000 (education, $780,585,000; health, welfare, and safety, $723,078,000; highways, $631,073,000). *State debt,* $5,663,618,000 (June 30, 1968).
Personal Income (1969): $75,049,000,000; average annual income per person, $4,151.
Public Assistance (fiscal year 1968): $1,098,019,000 to 1,265,526 recipients (aged, $92,176,000; dependent children, $772,539,000).
Labor Force (employed persons, 1969, 8,360,000): *Agricultural,* 121,000; *nonagricultural* (wage and salary earners), 7,207,000 (26.3% manufacturing, 19.7% trade, 15.9% government). *Unemployed persons* (August 1969)—275,000.
Manufacturing (1966): *Value added by manufacture,* $24,588,259,000 (transportation equipment, $1,982,019,000; primary metals, $1,126,194,000; nonelectrical machinery, $2,695,362,000; electrical machinery, $2,533,403,000).
Agriculture (1967): *Cash farm income,* $1,014,318,000 (livestock, $698,517,000; crops, $295,586,000; govt. payments, $20,215,000). *Chief crops* (tons)—Apples, 540,000 (ranks 2d among the states); hay, 5,845,000.
Mining (1966): *Production value,* $301,264,000. *Chief minerals* (tons)—Sand and gravel, 41,903,000; stone, 34,130,000.
Fisheries (1967): *Commercial catch,* 37,800,000 pounds ($12,700,000).
Transportation: *Roads* (1967), 102,292 miles (164,619 km); *motor vehicles* (1968), 6,721,049; *railroads* (1968), 7,650 track miles (12,311 km); *airports* (1969), 22.
Communication (1969): *Telephones,* 11,706,400; *television stations,* 35; *radio stations,* 202; *newspapers,* 81 (daily circulation, 7,742,000).

principally from reactions to strikes in 1968 by teachers and other governmental employees, including New York City sanitation men.

The Senate passed a bill, effective in 1971, which will give New York state residents four more 3-day weekends by shifting to Monday four legal holidays that sometimes fall in mid-week. The holidays are Washington's Birthday, Memorial Day, Columbus Day, and Veterans Day.

State farm workers were guaranteed a minimum wage of $1.40 an hour, to be increased by February 1971 to $1.50 an hour.

Reapportionment. The involved problem of redistricting was further complicated in 1969 when the U. S. Supreme Court ruled that the state's 1968 redistricting law violated the "one-man, one-vote" doctrine established by the court. A 3-judge federal court ordered the state Legislature to enact a new apportionment law for the 1970 congressional elections. It was given until Jan. 30, 1970, to prepare a revised plan with a more equal distribution between congressional districts.

Politics. In January the Supreme Court upheld the seating in the U. S. Senate of Charles E. Goodell until December 1970. Goodell, appointed by the governor to fill the seat of Sen. Robert F. Kennedy in September 1968, has become one of the Senate's leading opponents of the Vietnam War.

No statewide elections were held during the year, but four amendments to the state constitution were all approved by the voters. The amendments involved apportionment, loans to hospitals and related facilities, bonds issued by the Job Development

Authority, and conservation and historical preserves.

Erosion Control at Niagara Falls. Waters flowing to the 1,000-foot-wide American Falls, a section of Niagara Falls, were diverted on June 12, baring the rock beneath for the first time. The cut-off was part of a $1.5 million project by the U. S. Army Corps of Engineers to find a means of preventing the serious rockfalls and erosion that threaten the area. The falls was reactivated in December.

Rock Festival. The Woodstock Music and Art Fair held at Bethel in August attracted at least 300,000 young rock music lovers from all over the United States. For three days massive traffic tie-ups and other inconveniences were overlooked as the well-behaved crowd enjoyed itself. Drugs were freely used, and some 4,000 persons required medical aid before the crowd left the 600-acre farm rented for the event. (See special report in MUSIC.)

LEO HERSHKOWITZ
Queens College, City University of New York

NEW YORK CITY

Social tensions and racial and labor unrest, so much a part of the New York City scene in recent years, were not as evident in 1969. Instead, attention was focused on the hard-fought mayoralty campaign, which incumbent Mayor John V. Lindsay won without the support of a major party.

Elections. In the mayoralty election on November 4 three candidates—Mayor Lindsay, Liberal-Independent; Controller Mario A. Procaccino, Democrat; and State Sen. John J. Marchi, Republican-Conservative—were pitted against each other for what has been called the second most important elective office in the country. The election marked a personal triumph for Lindsay, who had been vilified by many before and during the campaign.

The mayor received Liberal party endorsement but was denied Republican backing when he lost that party's primary to Senator Marchi on June 18. Controller Procaccino won the Democratic primary, defeating former Mayor Robert F. Wagner, Bronx Borough President Herman Badillo, Rep. James Scheuer, and novelist Norman Mailer.

With the Democrats badly split between liberal and moderate factions, the mayor had an opportunity to create an "urban party," which by late summer became known as the Independent party. The party was formed to attract liberal Republicans and Democrats, many of whom broke party loyalties to support Lindsay. The mayor received the endorsements of Republican Senators Jacob K. Javits and Charles E. Goodell and Democrats Badillo, Scheuer, Arthur J. Goldberg, and Paul O'Dwyer, as well as the New Democratic Coalition.

In the bitter campaign the principal issues were "law and order" and the administrative capabilities of the candidates. Mayor Lindsay brought national issues to the contest when he strongly supported the October 15 Moratorium Day and voiced his opposition to the Vietnam War. Although an underdog early in the campaign the mayor was well ahead by November and won the election easily, receiving 981,810 votes to 821,824 for Procaccino and 544,758 for Marchi.

In other contests, Lindsay's running mate, former Chief Inspector Sanford D. Garelik (Rep.-Lib.), defeated the incumbent Francis X. Smith (Dem.) for city council president. However, in the race for controller, Abraham D. Beame (Dem.) defeated Fioravante G. Perrotta (Rep.-Lib), former executive assistant to Mayor Lindsay, and Vito Battista (Cons.). The Liberal party, hitherto unrepresented on the City Council, elected 4 candidates to the legislative body which has, in addition, 30 Democrats and 2 Republicans.

Rents and Housing. In New York City's growing housing problem, Puerto Rican and black residents were especially affected as new low-income housing failed to keep pace with their needs. In stark contrast was the booming construction rate in office building and high-cost apartments. Faced with rising rents and living costs and fewer vacancies, many middle-class citizens moved to the suburbs.

Under pressure from city officials who sought to ease the rent crisis for tenants in apartments without rent control, the real estate industry on March 12 accepted a 15% ceiling to be imposed on rent increases on new 2-year leases. On April 24 the City Council reduced the increase to 10% for such leases and permitted a 15% rise on 3-year leases affecting 400,000 units. The law was signed by the mayor on May 6.

Education. An attempt was made to solve the problems of school decentralization in April when the state Legislature passed a bill creating 30 to 33 local districts and a 5-member interim school board to replace the 13-member board. The permanent board was to be elected in 1970, but the system of electing one member from each borough was declared unconstitutional by a federal district court. At year end, three controversial demonstration districts, including Ocean Hill-Brownsville, were ordered incorporated into three large districts, but threats of noncompliance were voiced.

The City University of New York set September 1970 as the target date for offering admission to the university to all high school graduates. The plan could mean a substantial increase in the number of Negro and Puerto Rican students attending the municipal university. Such an increased enrollment was a major demand of student protesters on many campuses of the university in the spring. One protest forced the shutdown of City College for a few weeks.

Economy. The city continued to see rising costs of municipal services, a growing welfare burden, and a growing budget, while the middle-class population declined and a poorer nonwhite population grew. The expense budget for fiscal 1968–69 was approved at $6.6 billion, a new record high, while the capital budget totaled $1.1 billion. To meet its obligations, the city was forced to pay ever-rising interest rates, which in July stood at 6.2%, the highest rate since 1932.

Welfare. A large item in the city budget is welfare, which in 1968–69 was $1.6 billion. An average of $71 per month is paid to dependent children, compared with $41 nationally. The welfare picture was clouded during the year by charges of corruption and inefficiency within the city's Human Resources Administration.

Police. The city's war on crime featured the institution of a fourth platoon of police to patrol dangerous areas during high crime hours and the use of a $5-million computer to improve the police department's communications system. Department personnel received salary increases. However, despite modernization of department equipment and

WIDE WORLD

TRIUMPHANT in 3-way race, New York's Mayor John V. Lindsay flashes victory sign early on November 5.

JOHN V(LIET) LINDSAY was elected on Nov. 4, 1969, to a second 4-year term as mayor of New York City, emerging as the nation's leading City Hall spokesman on urban problems. The mayor, running as a Liberal-Independent, won with a plurality of 41.7% of the vote. Criticized for his alleged neglect of middle-class interests and his handling of several strikes, Lindsay promised a "government of reconciliation . . . between this city and its neighborhoods."

Lindsay was born in New York City on Nov. 24, 1921. He studied at Yale University (B. A., 1944; LL.B, 1948). In 1955 he was appointed executive assistant to the U. S. attorney general. Elected in 1958 as representative of New York's 17th Congressional District, he served on the House Judiciary Committee and compiled a liberal voting record. He first became mayor in January 1966.

an increase in its manpower, crime in New York City continued to rise.

Pollution. Concern over air pollution helped bring about a reduction of 28% of the sulfur dioxide in the air, due to reduced low sulfur used by the Consolidated Edison Company. A $5.2 million budget was allocated for controlling air pollution in 1969–70.

Heavy Snow. On February 10 a sudden 15-inch snow fell on New York and, for almost a week, parts of the city were snowbound and traffic was clogged. The death toll attributed to the snow was set at 25. Queens residents, perhaps hardest hit, shouted insults at the mayor as he toured the borough.

Baseball. The city's beloved Mets had all New Yorkers cheering as they won the National League pennant and went on to defeat the Baltimore Orioles in the World Series. Earlier, the Jets upset the Baltimore Colts in professional football's Super Bowl. (See SPORTS.)

Population. U. S. Census Bureau estimates seem to indicate that the population of New York City is declining. There were 7,964,200 persons in July 1968, compared with 8,019,100 in July 1966.

LEO HERSHKOWITZ
Queens College, City University of New York

NEW ZEALAND

In 1969, New Zealand's economy continued to develop buoyancy as it recovered from the 1967 recession. For the first time in its history the value of New Zealand's exports topped $1 billion (New Zealand dollars).

In the November general election the National party of Prime Minister Keith J. Holyoake, which has held power since 1960, won a fourth successive 3-year term.

Among the highlights of 1969 were celebrations to mark the bicentenary anniversary of the voyage of the *Endeavour* under the British navigator Capt. James Cook and the first landing of a European in New Zealand.

Economy. In April, in a major review of the economy, Prime Minister Holyoake noted that, although recovery had continued, the government would curb any excessive increase in state expenditure. The budget, described as heralding a "back to normal" situation, concentrated on savings and incentives as a means to encourage development in the farming and export areas. Spending for education was up an estimated 13%, compared with 6% for defense.

In May the second plenary session of the National Development Conference (NDC) was attended by 500 experts. The aim of the NDC is to evolve a comprehensive program of development. A target annual growth rate of 4½% of the gross national product was adopted, and the government undertook to appoint a commission to inquire into the workings of the social security system.

Major developments in the fields of energy and transport were presaged with the discovery of crude black oil and natural gas condensate off the Taranaki coast and the decision that Auckland and Wellington would be the first two ports converted for container shipping.

General Election. At the general election on November 29, 20-year-olds, who had been given both the franchise and the right to drink in hotels, voted for the first time. The National party, which has held office for 17 of the past 20 years, retained its 1966 majority of six seats in Parliament. It emerged with 45 seats while the Labour party won 39 and the Social Credit party was eliminated from Parliament. The campaign was marked by disorders at the prime minister's meetings.

Defense. Prime Minister Holyoake announced in Parliament on February 25 that government policy is to maintain military forces in Malaysia and Singapore at their present strength after the projected British withdrawal in 1971. New Zealand participated in 5-power talks in June in Canberra, Australia, on future defense arrangements for Southeast Asia.

During the visit of U. S. Secretary of State William Rogers in August, it was announced that New Zealand would not make a unilateral reduction of its troops in Vietnam.

Holyoake's Visits. In January Prime Minister Holyoake attended the Commonwealth Conference in London and subsequently held talks in various European capitals. While in the United States for the United Nations General Assembly session in September, he discussed the Vietnam War and New Zealand export prospects with President Nixon.

Security Intelligence Act. After agitation for the Security Service to be placed under constitutional surveillance, Parliament passed an act making the service responsible to a cabinet minister and ultimately to the legislature.

Papal Honor. In March, Roman Catholic Archbishop Peter Thomas McKeefry became the first New Zealander to be elevated to the College of Cardinals.

GRAHAM BUSH
University of Auckland

NEW ZEALAND • Information Highlights

Area: 103,740 square miles (268,676 sq km).
Population: 2,786,123 (September 1969 est.).
Chief Cities (metropolitan areas, Dec. 1968 est.): Wellington, the capital, 291,600; Auckland, 577,300.
Government: *Sovereign*—Queen Elizabeth II of Britain; *Governor-General*—Sir Arthur Porritt (appointed Dec. 17, 1966; *Prime Minister*—Keith J. Holyoake (took office for 3d term Dec. 12, 1966). *Parliament*—House of Representatives, 84 members (party seating, 1969: National party, 45; Labour party, 39).
Religious Faiths: Anglicans, 35% of population; Presbyterians, 22%; Roman Catholics, 14.4%; others, 28.6%.
Education: *Literacy rate* (1969), 99% of population. *Total school enrollment* (1965)—849,338.
Finance (1967 est.): *Revenues*, $1,241,860,000; *expenditures*, $1,439,090,000; *public debt*, $2,682,000,000; *monetary unit*, New Zealand dollar (0.8992 N.Z. dollar equal U. S.$1).
Gross National Product (1969 est.): $4,500,000,000.
National Income (1967): $3,838,967,000; *average annual income per person*, $1,400.
Economic Indexes (1967): *Manufacturing production*, 125

(1963=100); *agricultural production*, 116 (1963=100; *cost of living*, 117 (1963=100).
Manufacturing (metric tons, 1967): Gasoline, 1,057,000; meat, 860,000; cement, 814,000.
Crops (metric tons, 1967–68 crop year): Wheat, 348,000; wool (1966), 321,600; potatoes, 250,000; barley, 135,000.
Minerals (metric tons, 1967): Limestone (1966), 2,856,000; lignite, 1,813,000; coal, 595,000; salt, 56,000.
Foreign Trade (1968): *Exports*, $1,010,000,000 (chief exports, 1967: wool, $157,024,000; lamb and mutton, $140,000,000; butter, $130,000,000; fruits and vegetables, $1,261,000); *imports*, $895,000,000 (chief imports, 1967: nonelectrical machinery, $107,520,000; transport equipment, $92,550,000; electrical machinery, $57,320,000). *Chief trading partners* (1967): Britain (took 45% of exports, supplied 31% of imports); United States; Australia.
Transportation: *Roads* (1969), 57,439 miles (92,437 km); *motor vehicles* (1967), 979,600 (automobiles 807,700); *railways* (1969), 3,300 miles (5,311 km).
Communications: *Telephones* (1968): 1,119,422; *television stations* (1966), 15; *television sets* (1966), 515,000.

NEWFOUNDLAND

The year 1969 marked the 20th anniversary of confederation between Canada and Newfoundland. Late in the year, the Liberal party confirmed the architect of confederation, Premier Joseph R. Smallwood, as its leader, in spite of mounting criticism.

Natural Resources. Industrial pollution, which had killed fish and threatened the livelihood of 200 fishermen, caused the closing of Placentia Bay, west of St. John's, in May. Waste from a phosphorus plant owned by the Electrolytic Reduction Company was blamed for the trouble. After the company installed new equipment, the bay was reopened on July 16. The federal minister of transport, Donald Jamieson, announced that the federal government would sponsor a test case against ERCO. Some fishermen accepted an offer of $300,000 in compensation, but others filed writs for damages.

Legislature. The third session of the seventh parliament since confederation met on February 24 and adjourned on May 13. The April budget was one of restraint in government spending, and called for an increase in taxation and ceilings on student enrollment at trade and technical colleges and the university. Tuition payments and student salaries were cut by nearly $575,000. The legislature approved a new education act, which curbed the influence of religious denominations in education.

Politics. During 1969 the electoral districts prepared for the leadership convention of the Liberal party. In July, the premier stated that his work was not yet done and announced that he would be a candidate. The other leading contender was John C. Crosbie, who had resigned from the cabinet in May 1968 because of a dispute over financial policies. A

------ **NEWFOUNDLAND • Information Highlights** ------

Area: 156,185 square miles (404,520 sq km).
Population: 512,000 (Jan. 1, 1969 est.).
Chief Cities (1966 census): St. John's, the capital (79,884); Corner Brook (27,116).
Government: *Chief Officers*—lt. gov., Ewart John Arlington Harnum; premier, Joseph R. Smallwood (Liberal); min. of justice, T. A. Hickman (L); min. of finance, H. R. V. Earle (L); min. of educ., Frederick W. Rowe (L); chief justice, Robert Stafford Furlong. *Legislature*—Legislative Assembly (convened Feb. 24, 1969); 42 members (36 Liberal, 4 Progressive Conservative, 1 Independent).
Education: *School enrollment* (1966–67 est.)—public elementary and secondary, 147,760 pupils (5,645 teachers); private schools, 466 pupils (38 teachers); college and university (fall 1966), 3,893 students. *Public school expenditures* (1963)—$23,597,000 ($188 per pupil); median teacher's salary (1966–67), $3,529.
Public Finance (fiscal year 1968 est.): *Revenues,* $194,670,-000 (sales tax, $61,300,000; income tax, $22,954,000; federal funds, $86,092,000). *Expenditures,* $224,560,000 (education, $69,280,000; health and social welfare, $55,-490,000; transport and communications, $37,980,000).
Personal Income (1967 est.): $712,000,000; *average annual income per person,* $1,424.
Social Welfare (fiscal year 1968 est.): $20,380,000 (aged and blind, $660,000; dependents and unemployed, $16,990,000).
Manufacturing (1966): Value added by manufacture, $93,043,-000 (food and beverages, $32,605,000; paper and allied industries (1965), $37,680,000; nonmetallic mineral products, $4,878,000).
Mining (1967 est.): *Production value,* $259,838,940. *Chief minerals* (tons)—iron ore, 16,270,000 (ranks 1st among the provinces); asbestos, 63,000 (ranks 3d); lead, 23,500 (ranks 4th); copper, 19,689 (ranks 6th).
Fisheries (1968): *Commercial catch,* 941,504,000 pounds ($28,531,000). *Leading species*—cod, 366,169,000 pounds ($14,258,000); herring, 321,144,000 pounds ($3,284,000); flounder and sole, 127,567,000 pounds ($4,113,000); redfish, 64,300,000 pounds ($1,535,000); lobster, 4,009,000 pounds ($2,500,000).
Transportation: *Roads* (1966) 5,427 miles (8,734 km); *motor vehicles* (1966), 95,704; *railroads* (1966), 936 track miles (1,506 km).
Communications (1966): *Telephones,* 94,035; *television stations,* 2; *daily newspapers,* 3.
All figures given in Canadian dollars equal to U. S.93¢.

third serious candidate, former Minister of Justice T. Alex Hickman, entered the race late in the campaign. The result on November 1 was an overwhelming victory for Smallwood.

Resettlement. The federal-provincial resettlement program continued to assist Newfoundlanders in moving from isolated hamlets to larger settlements. About 8,000 people from 100 communities have already moved, and 10,000 more are expected to move in the next two years.

SUSAN McCORQUODALE
Memorial University of Newfoundland

NEWSPAPERS

North American newspapers enjoyed unprecedented prosperity in 1969. Almost without exception newspapers that make public their earnings showed a record year, as the industry as a whole took in $5.24 billion in advertising and added a million new subscribers. The reasons were partly the inflated dollar, partly the decline of major tieups, mostly the basic soundness of the industry. A U. S. Department of Commerce list of 55 "pacesetter" industries included newspapers among them.

The New York Times, for example, posted record earnings that were up 26% over the previous year. The only cloud on the otherwise bright horizon concerned Cowles Communications, Inc., whose 3-year-old Suffolk (Long Island) *Sun* failed to make the grade and was closed in October to cut the company's losses. It was 1969's only major closing.

Acquisitions. The most striking evidence of the health of the industry was the rush to buy up newspapers. In large part the acquisitions consisted of the expansion of chains. A wave of transactions was set off when John H. Perry, Jr., decided to sell his Florida newspaper properties—10 weeklies and 18 dailies from Palm Beach to Pensacola. Cox Newspapers, owner of the Miami *News,* annexed some. The Gannett chain, already with holdings in the Cape Kennedy area, took the Pensacola *Journal* and *News.* Cowles Communications, with holdings in central Florida, added to its group from the Perry auction. Freedom Newspapers, a coast-to-coast chain of smaller dailies, took five Perry properties. A combination of brokers took the rest.

Some others in the acquisition stampede: The San Bernardino (Calif.) *Sun-Telegram,* which had been purchased by the Times-Mirror Company of Los Angeles in a deal that was subsequently negated by the courts for antitrust reasons, was snapped up by Gannett. The Lee chain (16 Midwest and Montana dailies) bought the Racine (Wis.) *Journal-Times* and the Corvallis (Oreg.) *Gazette-Times.* The Scripps League Newspapers (total 31) moved into Beloit, Wis., and DeKalb, Ill. Multimedia, Inc., bought the Montgomery (Ala.) *Advertiser* and *Alabama Journal.* Knight Newspapers, Inc., acquired the Macon (Ga.) *Telegraph* and *News.* Lord Thomson of Fleet enlarged his newspaper empire with the New Glasgow (Nova Scotia) *News,* the *Valley Independent,* published in Monessen, Pa., and the Ansonia (Conn.) *Sentinel.*

Time, Inc., moved into the newspaper field, taking the Hollister group of weeklies in suburban Chicago with the expectation of converting some or all to daily publication. The Pontiac (Mich.) *Press* went to Capital Cities Broadcasting Co. The Frankfort (Ind.) *Times* joined the Nixon Newspaper Associates, a Midwest chain of six. Media General, a growing group with roots in Richmond, Va., moved to buy the two Winston-Salem, N. C., dailies. The Kenosha (Wis.) *News* bought the Attleboro (Mass.) *Sun.* Southam Press, Ltd., added its 11th daily with acquisition of the Prince George (B. C.) *Citizen.* The Copley chain sold its Culver City (Nev.) *Star-News-Vanguard* to a local publisher. The Moline (Ill.) *Daily Dispatch* was bought by Len Small, publisher of other Illinois papers. The Ridder group acquired the Boulder (Colo.) *Camera.*

The Los Angeles *Times* announced in September an agreement to buy the Dallas *Times Herald* and its broadcasting interests for $91.5 million, the highest newspaper transaction in history. For $55 million, Knight Newspapers bought the Philadelphia *Inquirer* and the Philadelphia *Daily News* in October. After 50 years of family ownership, the Roanoke *Times* and *World-News* were sold to the corporation that owns the Norfolk newspapers.

New Dailies. A number of new dailies came into being during the year: the *Pennsylvania Mirror* in State College, the *Northwest Day*—a Field Enterprises project—in suburban Chicago, the Anderson (S. C.) *News-Leader,* and the Osceola (Fla.) *Sun.* Two weeklies in Toronto and Wallaceburg, Ont., converted to dailies, as did four weeklies owned by Paddock Publications in suburban Chicago. The Chicago *American* took on a new format and name, *Chicago Today.* There were 1,752 dailies, three more than the year before, with a total circulation of 62,535,394.

Anxieties. One aspect of newspaper prosperity caused considerable worry in management circles. This was their ownership of lucrative broadcasting properties, and the worry stemmed from federal moves against monopoly. In the United States, 155 publishers own 260 television stations and many more own radio stations. The Justice Department and the Federal Communications Commission were showing increasing concern over single-market ownership of the media. A license in Beaumont, Texas, was canceled. Gannett had to divest itself of its stations in Rockford, Ill. The *Herald Traveler* in Boston lost its station WHDH-TV. Newspapermen expected more actions of this kind in the years ahead.

There were other developments that brought twinges of anxiety to newspaperdom:
- The dropping of cigarette advertising in many papers would decrease their earnings.
- A wave of parajournalistic publications, the so-called underground press, was mounting a serious challenge to established dailies. Estimates were that there were 627 of these new papers, circulating perhaps 3 million copies, and apparently satisfying a need not answered by the regular press.
- The U. S. Supreme Court ruled against the joint operation of the *Arizona Daily Star* and Tucson *Daily Citizen* for "price fixing, profit pooling and market control." All other papers involved in joint operations read the ruling with concern.
- The credibility of the press issue continued to trouble the profession. "The (credibility) gap exists; there is no question about it," read a report to the Associated Press Managing Editors Association. Inaccuracies, sensationalism, editorial bias, refusals to correct—these were major readers' complaints.

The year was singularly free of strikes. Short stoppages afflicted the Associated Press and all three dailies in Washington, D. C. Longer ones occurred in Erie, Pa., and Dayton, Ohio.

Awards. The gold medallion of the World Press Achievement Award went to *El Norte* of Monterrey, Mexico. The Pulitzer gold medal for meritorious public service went to the Los Angeles *Times* for its investigation of malfeasance in city government.

RICHARD T. BAKER
Columbia University

NICARAGUA

Economic problems continued to preoccupy the Nicaraguan government in 1969.

Economic Developments. In March, President Anastasio Somoza Debayle, Jr., imposed tariffs on manufactured goods from Guatemala, El Salvador, Honduras, and Costa Rica. The action was taken to strengthen Nicaragua's unfavorable balance of trade with these countries, its partners in the Central American Common Market (CACM). His action was opposed both by those nations and by Nicaraguan business interests, who feared the loss of outlets within the CACM and possible difficulty in obtaining capital from outside sources. At an emergency meeting, the finance ministers of the other

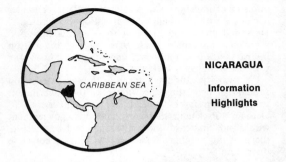

NICARAGUA

Information Highlights

CARIBBEAN SEA

Area: 57,143 square miles (148,000 sq km).
Population: 1,842,000 (1968 est.).
Chief Cities (1965 census): Managua, the capital, 262,047 (1965 est.); Leon, 44,053; Granada, 28,507.
Government: *President*—Gen. Anastasio Somoza Debayle, Jr. (took office May 1, 1967); *Vice Presidents*—Francisco Urcuyo Maliaños, Alfonso Callejas Deshón. *Congress*—Senate, 16 elected members (party seating, 1969: National Liberal party (PLN), 12; Conservative party (PCT), 4); Chamber of Deputies, 42 elected members (party seating, 1969: PLN, 28; PCT, 14).
Religious Faiths: Roman Catholics, 94% of population.
Education: *Literacy rate* (1963), 50% of population aged 15 and over. *Total school enrollment* (1965)—236,269 (primary, 206,349; secondary, 18,754; teacher-training, 4,822; technical/vocational, 3,001; university/higher, 3,343).
Finance (1967 est): *Revenues,* $65,285,000; *expenditures,* $74,785,000; *monetary unit,* córdoba (7.026 córdobas equal U. S.$1).
Gross National Product (1968): $714,062,000.
National Income (1968): $614,289,000; average annual income per person, $333.
Economic Indexes (1967): *Cost of living,* 114 (1963=100).
Manufacturing (metric tons, 1967): Sugar, 108,000; gasoline, 94,000; cement (1966), 79,000.
Crops (metric tons, 1967–68 crop year): Cottonseed, 173,000; maize, 174,000; cotton (lint), 102,000; dry beans, 38,000; rice, 60,000; coffee, 33,000.
Minerals (metric tons, 1967): Lime (1966), 24,000; salt, 19,000; copper, 9,300; gypsum (1965), 5,400; silver, 446,886 troy ounces; gold, 150,079 troy ounces.
Foreign Trade (1968): *Exports,* $157,000,000 (chief exports, 1967: cotton, $56,000,000; coffee, $21,100,000; meat, $12,520,000; sugar, $5,950,000); *imports,* $185,000,000 (chief imports, 1967: nonelectrical machinery, $42,900,000; transport, $24,500,000; textile yarn and fabrics, $20,000,000). *Chief trading partners* (1967): United States (took 28% of exports, supplied 43% of imports); Japan (took 31% of exports, supplied 7% of imports); West Germany.
Transportation: *Roads* (1964), 3,813 miles (6,136 km); *motor vehicles* (1966), 30,055 (automobiles 23,547); *railways* (1967), 270 miles (435 km); *merchant vessels* (1967), 5, (14,000 gross registered tons); *national airline,* Lanica; *principal airport,* Managua.
Communications: *Telephones* (1968): 13,200; *television stations* (1966), 2; *television sets* (1968), 25,000; *radios* (1966), 105,000; *newspapers* (1965), 6.

CACM member-states voted to remove the duty-free privileges of Nicaraguan exports to their countries.

Nicaragua then rescinded its tariff on imports but substituted a compensatory consumer tax. Nicaragua's CACM neighbors opposed this measure. The tax also had adverse effects on Nicaragua's own domestic economy, and the nation's cost of living rose sharply during the first half of 1969. However, on October 17, Dr. Tapia Mercado, vice minister of economic integration, announced that Nicaragua would have a favorable balance of trade with the CACM countries in 1969, in part as a result of the replacement of the tariff by consumer taxes, which hindered imports but did not restrict Nicaraguan exports. Another factor was the development of new chemical industries using Nicaraguan raw materials.

On February 6 the Managua Cotton Cooperative announced the sale of 25,000 bales of cotton to Czechoslovakia, Nicaragua's first commercial transaction with a Communist country since the late 1940's.

Political Affairs. President Somoza made major changes in his cabinet on January 13. He appointed Juan José Martínez minister of economy, Antonio Mora minister of education, and Mariano Buitrago minister of interior. The president made the changes because he was "unhappy about national conditions." He stated that school construction was a year behind schedule, the tourist trade was lagging, the cotton industry was in a recession, and major public works projects were being delayed.

University students staged a hunger strike on January 2, protesting the failure of the government to provide a larger budget for the university. In October, President Somoza said his government would not increase the university budget, despite the growing number of students wishing to continue their studies.

In May the Sandinista Front of National Liberation (FSLN), an anti-Somoza rebel organization, kidnapped two wealthy plantation owners. The men were released after large ransoms were paid.

Foreign Affairs. A dispute between Nicaragua and Colombia developed over Quitasueño, a sandbar off the Caribbean coast of Nicaragua, when Nicaragua granted exploration rights to Western Caribbean Oil, an American company. On September 17, Colombia affirmed its sovereignty over Quitasueño and nearby Roncador and Serrana banks, but the government stated on October 1 that these areas were provably part of its own continental platform.

On April 17 the Nicaraguan government announced the seizure of two U. S. fishing boats within its territorial waters, which according to Nicaraguan claims extend for 200 miles (320 km) from its coastline. The boats were released on April 22.

C. ALAN HUTCHINSON
University of Virginia

NIGER

Political developments in Niger during 1969 continued to be dominated by the activities of President Hamani Diori. With his domestic power base assured, the president devoted most of his efforts to improving foreign relations.

International Affairs. Diori sought closer ties between the European Economic Community (EEC) and its associated African states. At the end of 1968, he spent six weeks touring European capitals to obtain support for the increased economic aid requested by the African EEC associates. In mid-1969, a 6-year pact provided slightly more than $1 billion in aid, although the associates had demanded more than $1.5 billion. Special price supports for tropical products were abolished, a move that particularly affected Niger's peanut crop. Diori criticized a special "disaster fund" of $74 million as insufficient, noting that prices of tropical products had dropped as much as 30% since 1958.

The President encouraged greater cooperation among French-language states (La Francophonie). Representatives of 26 French-speaking countries met in Niamey from February 17 to 20 and agreed to establish an agency for cultural and technical cooperation, with Diori as its provisional head. France will pay 45% and Canada 30% of the initial costs. Diori also promoted OCAM, a 14-member organization of primarily French-speaking African states.

Economic Development. Peanuts continued to be the mainstay of Niger's economy. Food production lagged, with a fall in per capita output.

Uranium mining began in the north, and the United Nations Development Program agreed to underwrite costs for a 3-year mineralogical survey.

France contributed $1.2 million for a variety of projects, including executive training, road construction, and architectural assistance. The European Development Fund provided an additional $640,000 in aid. The Chad Basin Commission, formed by Niger, Cameroon, Chad, and Nigeria, agreed to launch a $3.5 million development program.

CLAUDE E. WELCH, JR.
State University of New York, Buffalo

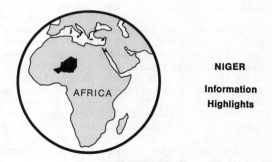

NIGER

Information Highlights

Area: 489,378 square miles (1,267,000 sq km).
Population: 3,806,000 (1968 est.).
Chief Cities (1967 census): Niamey, the capital, 60,000.
Government: *President*—Hamani Diori (took office Feb. 25, 1959); *Parliament*—Legislative Assembly, 60 members (all belonging to the Niger Progressive party).
Religious Faiths: Muslims, 70% of population; animists, 27%.
Education: *Literacy rate* (1969), 5% of population. *Total school enrollment* (1966)—76,535 (primary, 70,657; secondary, 4,473; teacher-training, 557; technical/vocational, 848).
Finance (1967 budget): *Revenues,* $37,000,000; *expenditures,* $37,000,000; *monetary unit,* CFA franc (246.85 CFA francs equal U. S.$1).
Gross National Product (1967 est.): $320,000,000.
Average Annual Income (per person, 1967): $90.
Cost of Living (1967) 116 (1963=100).
Manufacturing (metric tons, 1967): Meat, 34,000.
Crops (metric tons, 1967–68 crop year): Millet, 1,000,000; sorghum, 342,000; peanuts, 292,000; cassava, 169,000.
Minerals (cubic meters, 1964): Tin (1967), 60 metric tons; gravel, 4,822; sand, 4,207; building stone, 455.
Foreign Trade (1967): *Exports,* $25,526,000 (chief export, 1966: peanuts, $21,592,000); *imports,* $45,987,000 (chief imports, 1966: textile yarn and fabrics, $10,456,000; petroleum products, $3,783,000; nonelectrical machinery, $3,-751,000). *Chief trading partners* (1967): France (took 77% of exports, supplied 48% of imports); Nigeria (took 16% of exports, supplied 2% of imports); Communist China.
Transportation: *Roads* (1969), 4,482 miles (7,213 km); *motor vehicles* (1967), 7,100 (automobiles 2,600); *principal airport,* Niamey.
Communications: *Telephones* (1968), 2,900; *radios* (1967), 75,000; *newspapers* (1965), 1.

NIGERIA

In 1969 the government of Maj. Gen. Yakubu Gowon continued the war to regain control of Biafra, the former Eastern Region of Nigeria. Serious difficulties arose in providing relief to refugees in the recaptured areas and in Biafra. The war ended with the capitulation of Biafra on Jan. 12, 1970.

The federal government also faced major disorders in the Western State, where members of the Yoruba tribe rebelled against an increase in taxes.

Biafra and the War. The Nigerian civil war entered its third year, with Biafra only one tenth its size at the beginning of the conflict. Biafra was surrounded on three sides and cut off from aid, except through the Uli airstrip. On April 15 the town of Bende fell to federal forces, and the capital city of Umuahia was captured seven days later. Many of the 7 million Biafrans suffered from malnutrition; thousands were starving to death.

Despite these circumstances, the Biafran leader, Col. Odumegwu Ojukwu, remained confident of victory. Biafra received more guns and supplies flown in from Gabon and the Ivory Coast. As a result, it was able to take the offensive on the southern front and capture Owerri on April 25. On the western front, Biafran irregulars crossed the Niger River at will, forcing a concentration of federal forces in the Mid-West. Biafra attacked on this front in July and August, and there was heavy fighting near Onitsha. In May, Biafra started using planes to raid federal airports and refineries. By July its airforce had grown to 13 planes, and the attacks were having an effect on oil production.

On Jan. 11, 1970 it was reported that federal forces had recaptured Owerri and that the Uli airstrip, Biafra's last link to the outside world, had been put out of action. Gen. Ojukwu fled the country. Brig. Philip Effiong, the Biafran chief of staff who had been placed in charge by Ojukwu, delivered the speech of capitulation on January 12.

Foreign Affairs. Despite Biafra's efforts in 1969, it was recognized by only one more state—Haiti. Premier Siaka Stevens of Sierra Leone, however, said in August that he was considering recognizing Biafra. But there were indications that exports of war goods from France, which supported Biafra, have declined since Georges Pompidou took office.

At the meeting of Commonwealth prime ministers in London in January, Nigeria kept the Biafran issue off the agenda. British Prime Minister Harold Wilson stated Britain's opinion that the conflict was a civil war. His lengthy visit to Nigeria in March again showed Britain's support of the federal government. The United States continued to recognize Nigeria but refused to send arms. The Soviet Union continued to give Nigeria low-level direct support.

In February the Organization of African Unity (OAU) called for a cease fire and asked both sides to make another attempt to end the war. The appeal was repeated in June and September. However, the OAU call was for negotiations to preserve Nigeria's unity and was not acceptable to Biafra.

In July, before his visit to Uganda, Pope Paul VI announced his intention of trying to end the conflict. His two meetings with representatives of both sides had no positive effects because of the inflexible positions of the protagonists.

Refugee and Relief Problems. Since the beginning of the war Nigeria has recognized the International Red Cross (ICRC) as the coordinating

UPI

STARVING CHILDREN, like this little one left behind while others rush to a UNICEF relief truck, became common on both sides of the Nigerian conflict.

agency for relief. By April the ICRC was feeding almost one million people in federal areas. It operated two ships, four aircraft from Fernando Po in Equatorial Guinea, and six from Cotonou, Dahomey. The airplanes were used to fly supplies into Biafra at night and by May were supporting more than 900,000 people. In addition, UNICEF spent over $10 million on Biafran relief. The Joint

Church Aid airlift operating from the Portuguese island of São Tomé was carrying more tonnage into Uli than the Red Cross. August Lindt, chief Red Cross official in Nigeria, reported in May that famine in Biafra was under control.

After the Nigerian government charged that the mercy flights were masking arms shipments, Equatorial Guinea stopped Red Cross flights from Fernando Po. On June 5 a Red Cross DC-7 was shot down by federal jets, and two Joint Church Aid aircraft were damaged. Relief flights were temporarily suspended. Flights from São Tomé were soon resumed, but those of the Red Cross were not.

After two months of negotiations the ICRC agreed to new arrangements with Nigeria, but Biafra refused to agree to these terms and the flights did not resume. The results of the restrictions on supplies were noticeable in Biafra by late August. Observers noted the decreasing supply of food and the higher incidence of kwashiorkor disease in children.

On October 2 the Nigerian Red Cross took over control of all relief operations from the ICRC, but a lack of funds soon led to a cutback in relief. The first change removed 350,000 persons in the occupied areas from the relief rolls. It appeared likely that many more thousands of Biafrans would die of starvation if the war continued. After the Biafran capitulation General Gowon condemned foreign relief agencies that had sent aid to the rebels.

State Governments. Reorganization of the governmental structure continued, and General Gowon announced his satisfaction with the speed of devolution of power to the 12 new federal states, established in 1968.

The new state governments had major administrative and financial problems. Northern states had the most difficulty. Before the 1966 coup it had been difficult to staff a single administration in the north, and competent personnel had now to be found for six. Because of the war, the three eastern states have not been able to establish more than a framework for activity except in handling refugee and relief problems.

Western Disorders. The Western State, with a population composed mostly of Yoruba, has been racked by disorders since late 1968, when new taxes were announced. A government investigation of the early disturbances reported bad cacao harvests, low prices, and dishonest local officials as the underlying causes of the resistance to the higher taxes. Many of the Yoruba were also dissatisfied with the government of Brig. Gen. R. A. Adebayo.

The federal government made concessions, including a 50% reduction of the announced tax rates, but riots occurred at Ishara, Ijebu-Igbo, and Ogbomosho in May. At Illa-Orangun, 55 people were arrested. On July 1 a series of demonstrations occurred in the Ibadan area. Dissidents set up road blocks at Ogbomosho and held the city against police for more than a day, killing the supreme chief and five subordinate chiefs. Hundreds of persons were arrested and sent to prison, but the government did not move swiftly enough to placate the dissident elements and there were new outbreaks in October. General Adebayo imposed a dawn-to-dusk curfew in certain places, and police and army units were deployed throughout the disaffected areas.

Economy. Most sectors of the Nigerian economy showed improvement over previous years. By the end of January 1969, 198,000 tons of peanuts from the 1968 crop had been exported from the north. By May, 764,000 tons of peanuts had been purchased, 100,000 tons more than in 1968.

Cacao production was affected by the black pod disease, but the amount exported was not substantially less than in the previous year. Petroleum was Nigeria's greatest money earner, with almost one half of government revenue coming from this source. New oil fields were discovered in the Mid-West near the Forcados estuary and in the James Creek area. In April a record average of 594,000 barrels a day was produced. Increased Biafran air and land attacks lowered this to 470,000 barrels a day in August.

Despite production levels, Nigeria had an adverse trade balance of $72 million, compared with the previous year. To keep the reserves of the central banks near the safe level of $89 million, it was necessary to make some foreign creditors wait months for payment. The reason for Nigeria's precarious finances was the war, which had cost the country more than $120 million by the beginning of 1969. By August the conflict was costing $800,000 per day.

HARRY A. GAILEY
San Jose State College

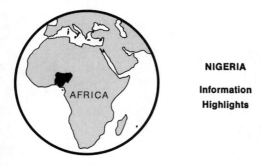

NIGERIA

Information

Highlights

Area: 356,667 square miles (923,768 sq km).
Population: 62,650,000 (1968 est.).
Chief Cities (1963 census): Lagos, the capital, 665,246; Ibadan, 627,379; Ogbomosho, 343,279; Mushin, 312,063.
Government: President—Maj. Gen. Yakubu Gowon (assumed power Aug. 1, 1966).
Religious Faiths: Muslims, 42% of population; animists, 27%.
Education: Literacy rate (1969), 30%–35% of population. Total school enrollment (1966)—3,349,125 (primary, 3,-025,981; secondary, 257,403; teacher training, 28,673; technical 26,092; higher, 10,976).

Finance (1968–69 est.): Revenues, $425,600,000; expenditures, $420,000,000; monetary unit, pound (.3571 pound equals U. S.$1).
Gross National Product (1967): $5,400,000,000.
Cost of Living Index (1967): 111 (1963=100).
Manufacturing (metric tons, 1967): Cement, 750,000; beer, 606,000 hectoliters, sawn wood (1966), 320,000 cu. meters.
Crops (metric tons, 1967–68 crop year): Sweet potatoes and yams, 13,000,000 (ranks 1st among world producers); cassava, 7,300,000 (world rank, 3d); peanuts, 1,719,000 (world rank, 3d); cacao beans, 234,000 (world rank, 2d).
Minerals (metric tons, 1967): Columbite (1966), 2,262 (ranks 3d among world producers); crude petroleum, 15,588,000; limestone (1966), 1,098,000; coal, 97,200.
Foreign Trade (1968): Exports, $575,000,000 (chief exports, 1967: crude and partly refined petroleum, $201,920,000; cacao beans, $153,140,000; peanuts, $99,160,000; tin and alloys, $36,620,000); imports, $540,000,000 (chief imports, 1967: textile yarn and fabrics, $92,530,000; nonelectrical machinery, $82,090,000; road motor vehicles, $56,030,000). Chief trading partners (1967): Britain (took 30% of exports, supplied 29% of imports); West Germany (took 11% of exports, supplied 11% of imports); United States.
Transportation: Roads (1969), 56,000 miles (90,120 km); motor vehicles (1967), 104,000 (automobiles 73,000); railways (1969), 2,356 miles (3,769 km); national airline, Nigerian Airways; principal airports, Lagos, Kano.
Communications: Telephones (1968), 74,425; television stations (1968), 8; television sets (1968), 38,000; radios (1964), 600,000; newspapers (1966), 24.

NIXON, Richard Milhous

Thirty-seventh president of the United States: b. Yorba Linda, Calif., Jan. 9, 1913.

In his inaugural address on January 20, President Nixon offered a sobering appraisal of the national condition. "We find ourselves rich in goods but ragged in spirit," he said. "We are caught in war, wanting peace. We are torn by division, wanting unity." Setting the tone for his administration, the President urged his countrymen to lower their voices: "We cannot learn from one another until we stop shouting at one another—until we speak quietly enough so that our words can be heard as well as our voices."

Style. In keeping with his inaugural message, Nixon and his advisers set out to lead in a somewhat subdued manner. Rather than bold innovation, they stressed better management. Nixon himself, in his statements and actions, appeared to be striving for a contrast with the often flamboyant and abrasive style of his predecessor, Lyndon Johnson.

This understated concept of the presidency was evidenced on Nixon's first trip abroad in late February. In an eight-day tour of six European capitals and the Vatican, he kept his pledge not to indulge in "showboat diplomacy."

Relations with Critics. Inevitably, the early good will the President accumulated at home and abroad could not be sustained solely by modesty and calm. Critics contended that the grave problems Nixon had inherited demanded faster action than his administration seemed prepared to take. Democrats in Congress took the President to task for not moving swiftly enough on poverty and the urban crisis. Members of both parties challenged the wisdom of the administration's first major policy decision—to deploy an antiballistic missile system. Not only on Capitol Hill but elsewhere across the nation passionate voices were raised demanding that the President move more vigorously to end the war in Vietnam.

The stridency of his critics naturally strained Nixon's resolve to remain above partisan battle. On June 3 he raised his own voice and answered back. Speaking on the tranquil campus of General Beadle State College in Madison, S. Dak., he strongly condemned violence by campus demonstrators and warned that if the violence continued, "We have the power to strike back, if need be, and to prevail."

The next day, addressing Air Force Academy cadets in Colorado Springs, the President counterattacked administration critics who had focused their fire on the "military-industrial complex." Nixon declared, "It is open season on the armed forces," and he denounced "new isolationists" who, he charged, were preaching "unilateral disarmament." But if Nixon was not always able to keep debate on national policy as temperate as he wished, he still retained the prestige inherent in the presidency, and he demonstrated that he knew how to use it to good advantage.

Foreign Policy. In June, Nixon met with President Nguyen Van Thieu of South Vietnam on Midway Island in the Pacific, where he announced the withdrawal of 25,000 U. S. troops as a start toward deescalation of the Vietnam War. In July the President was able to benefit from the surge of national pride and satisfaction when two astronauts of the spacecraft Apollo 11 successfully landed on the moon.

Nixon had no sooner welcomed the space heroes back to earth than he embarked on his second major overseas tour. He traveled to five Asian capitals where he outlined a new U. S. policy for the Far East. While the United States would stand by its treaty obligations, it would be reluctant, Nixon said, to become directly involved in another Asian war unless one of its allies was attacked by an outside aggressor. Nixon's 12-day trip was climaxed by a wildly enthusiastic reception in Bucharest, the capital of Communist Rumania. The visit helped dramatize the administration's interest in maintaining peaceful relations with the countries of eastern Europe.

Domestic Policy. In August, the President was able to celebrate his administration's first important legislative victory. After a long and bitter debate the Senate by a hairbreadth margin approved the funds for the Safeguard ABM system. On August 8 the President unveiled a widely praised proposal to revamp the nation's welfare system by establishing a national minimum level of support and more than doubling the number of persons eligible for aid.

However, these achievements could not shield the President from mounting criticism in the vital area of civil rights. Liberals accused the President and Attorney General John N. Mitchell of following a "Southern strategy,"—by sacrificing Negro rights in the South in order to keep promises made to Southern politicians in the 1968 campaign and to assure their support in 1972. The liberals cited efforts by the Justice Department to delay desegregation of 33 Mississippi school districts.

Charges that the administration was displaying undue favoritism toward the South also figured in

INDONESIAN WELLWISHERS with American flags surround President Nixon as he arrives at the Jakarta Fair Grounds during his visit to their country, on July 27.

UPI

the Senate's rejection of Nixon's nomination of Judge Clement F. Haynsworth, Jr., to the Supreme Court on November 21. Although most of the opposition to Judge Haynsworth stemmed from allegations of ethical impropriety, his cause also was hurt by charges that some of his decisions supported segregation.

Nixon and Dissent. In the economic sphere, the country was plagued by persistent inflation throughout the year, despite the administration's determined efforts to curb public and private spending. As the year progressed, Nixon faced continuing opposition to his Vietnam policies. On October 15 advocates of a speedy end to the war staged a nationwide "moratorium," involving hundreds of thousands of citizens in peaceful demonstrations. On November 15 there was another huge public protest.

Nixon insisted that he would not be swayed by the public clamor. Instead, he said, he would continue on his course of gradually diminishing U. S. military involvement in Vietnam. In a nationwide telecast on November 3 he promised that his approach would end the war and bring a "just and lasting peace." The President appealed in his speech for the support of what he called "the great silent majority" of Americans, and a flood of favorable mail to the White House indicated that he had received it. Moreover, a Gallup poll taken in the midst of the November anti-war demonstrations gave the President a popularity rating of 68%, a new high for him.

Achievements. To justify the public's endorsement, the President and his advisers could point to some substantial achievements. The trend toward escalation of the Vietnam War had been reversed with the withdrawal of more than 50,000 U. S. troops by year's end. The President also had signed the nuclear nonproliferation treaty, announced a ban on the use of biological weapons, and begun arms limitation talks with the Soviet Union. To eliminate some of the inequities of the selective service system he had instituted a draft lottery. In domestic affairs, in addition to his proposed welfare reforms, Nixon could take credit for extending the income tax surcharge designed to curb inflation.

Of course a host of problems remained unresolved, and critics still contended that Nixon displayed too much caution and too little imagination in dealing with them. But the administration had seen a tapering off of the violence that had seriously threatened American society in recent years.

Background. Nixon, after serving in the Navy in World War II, won election to Congress from California in 1946 and soon became a controversial figure for his role in the investigation of Alger Hiss. He was elected to the Senate in 1950 and chosen as Dwight Eisenhower's running mate in 1952. After eight years as vice president, Nixon was the Republican candidate for president in 1960. His narrow defeat by John F. Kennedy in that election was followed by another setback in 1962 when he lost the race for governor of California. When Nixon moved to New York and entered private law practice in 1963, his career as a public official appeared to be ended, but he remained active in the Republican party, campaigning and raising funds for other candidates. In 1968 he again won his party's presidential nomination.

(See also UNITED STATES.)

ROBERT SHOGAN
Washington Bureau, "Newsweek" Magazine

NOBEL PRIZES

Nobel prizes were awarded in 1959 for peace, literature, physics, chemistry, and physiology or medicine—the full set of areas covered under the will of Swedish inventor Alfred Bernhard Nobel. For the first time, prizes also were awarded in economics, under an award established by the Bank of Sweden in memory of Nobel. The 1969 awards included $73,000 certificates. The peace prize was presented on December 10 in Oslo, Norway; the others were presented in Stockholm by King Gustaf VI Adolf of Sweden.

Peace. The International Labor Organization (ILO) was awarded the Nobel Peace Prize for 1969 by vote of a committee appointed by the Norwegian parliament. The committee's chairman, Mrs. Aase Lionaus, said that the ILO "has become a global institution in the work of peace" since World War II and "is now deeply engaged in the enormous problem of solving unemployment." The Red Cross (1944), UN High Commission for Refugees (1954), and UN Children's Fund (1955) also have won this award.

The ILO. Chartered by the 1919 Treaty of Versailles, the ILO was originally an affiliate of the League of Nations. It became the first specialized agency of the United Nations in 1946, with responsibilities for social and labor questions. Now the organization represents 118 countries. Its operations are directed by three-part bodies consisting of representatives of government, employers, and workers. The permanent secretariat, called the International Labor Office, has more than 1,500 officials, most of them serving in Geneva, Switzerland. "Poverty anywhere," the ILO proclaimed, "constitutes a danger to everywhere." Acting on this motto, the ILO devotes more than half of its efforts to technical assistance to member countries.

Literature. The 1969 Nobel Prize for literature went to Samuel Beckett, the Irish-born writer of enigmatic novels and plays of human degradation and despair. Although he is best known for the play *Waiting for Godot* (1952), the award covered all his work. The selection committee cited Beckett "for his writing, which—in new forms for the novel and drama—in the destitution of modern man acquires its elevation." He expressed gratitude but did not go to Stockholm to receive the award.

Samuel Barclay Beckett, who writes in both French and English and has lived in France since 1937, was born in Dublin on April 13, 1906. After graduation from Trinity College, Dublin, in 1927, he spent the next several years in Paris, Dublin, and London and began to contribute poems and stories to avant-garde magazines. His first major works were novels—*Murphy* and *Watt* (written in English, 1938 and 1942–44, respectively) and the trilogy *Molloy, Malone Dies,* and *The Unnameable* (written in French during the late 1940's and early 1950's, with his own later English translations). Following the international success of *Waiting for Godot,* he emerged as one of the leading figures in contemporary literature and has continued to write both plays and novels.

Physics. The 1969 Nobel Prize in physics was won by Murray Gell-Mann of the California Institute of Technology "for his contributions and discoveries concerning the classification of elementary particles and their interactions." The 40-year-old theorist first explained "strange" particles by describing their energy states (1953) and later proposed the quark—any one of three types of particles—as the fundamental unit of all matter.

Murray Gell-Mann was born in New York City on Sept. 15, 1929. In high school, he found that physics was "terribly boring," and in college he studied physics because he was not sure of any other field of specialization. Becoming a physicist, he has said, "just happened." Gell-Mann graduated from Yale University in 1948 and received his

NOBEL PRIZE WINNERS displaying their awards are (*from left*): Max Delbruck, U. S., medicine; Murray Geil-Mann, U. S., physics; Derek H. R. Barton, England, and Odd Hassel, Norway, chemistry; Alfred D. Hershey and Salvador E. Luria, U. S., medicine; and Jan Tinbergen, Netherlands, economics.

Ph.D from the Massachusetts Institute of Technology in 1951. At the University of Chicago from 1952 to 1955, he rose from instructor to associate professor. He became an associate professor at the California Institute of Technology in 1955 and was promoted to professor in 1956. Besides teaching, he has made contributions to elementary particle physics, nuclear physics, and quantum field theory.

Chemistry. The 1969 Nobel Prize in chemistry was shared by the Norwegian physical chemist Odd Hassel and the English organic chemist Derek H. R. Barton for their work on the three-dimensional orientation of molecules. The study of spatial orientation is known as corformational analysis. In the late 1930's, Hassel did the first such studies by determining the structure of cyclohexane, a six-carbon ring compound. Barton has worked on the spatial orientation of a number of types of organic compounds, including terpenes and steroids.

Odd Hassel was born in Oslo, Norway. He studied in Norway and in Germany, and received his Ph.D from Berlin University in 1924. In 1934 he became a professor of physical chemistry at the University of Oslo, remaining there until 1964. In his studies of cyclohexane, Hassel found that hydrogen atoms attached to the carbon ring can adopt positions either parallel with or perpendicular to the axis of the molecule.

Derek H. R. Barton was born in Gravesend, Kent, England, on Sept. 8, 1918. He studied at the Imperial College of Science and Technology, London, where he received his B.S. in 1940 and Ph.D. in 1942. In 1953 he was made professor at Birbeck College of London University, and two years later he went to the University of Glasgow. In 1957, he returned to the Imperial College as professor of organic chemistry.

He has served as a visiting professor at Harvard and Massachusetts Institute of Technology.

Physiology or Medicine. The 1969 Nobel Prize in physiology or medicine was awarded to three Americans: Max Delbruck of the California Institute of Technology, Alfred D. Hershey of the Carnegie Institution at Cold Spring Harbor, N. Y., and Salvador E. Luria of the Massachusetts Institute of Technology "for their discoveries concerning the replication mechanism and genetic structure of viruses." The men were selected for having "set the foundation on which modern molecular biology rests."

Max Delbruck was born in Berlin, Germany, on Sept. 4, 1906. He received his Ph.D in physics from the University of Gottingen in 1930, and was a Rockefeller fellow in biology at the California Institute of Technology. He taught at Vanderbilt University (1939–47) and then returned to Cal Tech as professor of biology. Delbruck found that genetic recombination occurs in replicating bacterial viruses.

Alfred D. Hershey was born in Owosso, Mich., on Dec. 4, 1908. He received his Ph.D in chemistry from Michigan State College in 1934. After teaching at Washington University's School of Medicine, he went to the Carnegie Institution genetics research unit in Cold Springs Harbor, N.Y., in 1950. Hershey found that when a bacterial virus infects a bacterium, only the viral nucleic acid enters the bacterium, indicating that hereditary material is in the nucelic acid.

Salvador E. Luria was born in Turin, Italy, on Aug. 13, 1912. He studied medicine, physics, and radiology in Italy. He taught in several universities in the United States before joining the faculty of the Massachusetts Institute of Technology in 1958. Luria has done much research on growth, replication, and mutation in bacterial viruses.

Economics. Ragnar Frisch, Norwegian economist, and Jan Tinbergen, Dutch economist, were joint winners of the first Nobel Prize in economic science "for having developed and applied dynamic models for the analysis of economic processes." They were pioneers in econometrics—the endeavor to express in mathematical terms the shifting relationships among various forms of economic activity.

Econometrics can, for example, measure the effects of reduced government spending on an economy, and so it has opened the way to greater precision in formulating economic policy.

Ragnar Frisch was born in Oslo, Norway, on March 3, 1895, and was educated at the University of Oslo. From 1931 to 1965 he was professor of social economy and statistics at Oslo and director of research at the university's Economic Institute. He was a founder (1931) of the Econometric Society and was chief editor of its journal, *Econometrica*, from 1933 to 1955. He frequently advised governments of the less-developed countries.

Jan Tinbergen was born in The Hague on April 12, 1903, and was educated at Leiden University. He was on the staff of the Netherlands' central bureau of statistics from 1929 to 1945, except in 1936–38 when he was a business-cycle expert with the League of Nations. For 10 years after 1945 he was director of the Netherlands' central planning bureau at The Hague. From 1933 he was also professor of development planning at the Rotterdam School of Economics. In the late 1960's he was chairman of the UN committee for development planning.

NORTH ATLANTIC TREATY ORGANIZATION. See Europe.

NORTH CAROLINA

North Carolina took significant steps in legislation and education in 1969.

General Legislation. The General Assembly of 1969 was the longest legislative session in the state's history. It set a modern record for the number of bills introduced—2,347 (of which 1,427 were enacted into law). It adopted a biennial budget of $3.5 billion, by far the largest in North Carolina's history. For the first time taxes were placed on cigarettes (2 cents a package), on soft drinks (1 cent a bottle), and on syrup for soft drinks ($1 a gallon). Taxes on beer and liquor were increased. Gasoline tax went up 2 cents, to 9 cents a gallon.

The 1969 legislature built a substantial record of conservation legislation. Heading the list were laws protecting coastal estuaries and navigable waters, strengthening local air pollution control powers, and regulating mining activities.

Seven constitutional amendments were approved by the legislature. One authorized a general revision of the state and local government provisions of the Constitution. Another provides for reassigning escheats among all the states' institutions of higher learning.

Education. The 1969 General Assembly voted more money for public schools and for higher education than any previous legislature. It voted pay increases of 12% for public school teachers and 8% for teachers in institutions of higher learning. Two

------ NORTH CAROLINA • Information Highlights ------

Area: 52,712 square miles (136,524 sq km).
Population: 5,114,000 (1969 est.).
Chief Cities (1969 est.): Raleigh, the capital, 115,000; Charlotte, 264,000; Winston-Salem, 141,000; Greensboro, 138,-000; Durham, 98,000.
Government: *Chief Officers*—governor, Robert W. Scott (Democrat); lt. gov., H. Patrick Tayloe, Jr. (D); secy. of state, Thad Eure (D); atty. gen., Robert Morgan (D); treas., Edwin Gill; supt. of pub. instr., Craig Phillips; chief justice, R. Hunt Parker. *General Assembly*—Senate, 38 Democrats, 12 Republicans; House of Representatives, 91 D, 29 R.
Education: *School enrollment* (1968)—public elementary, 867,244 pupils (33,986 teachers); public secondary, 353,-382 pupils (16,410 teachers); nonpublic schools, 21,500 pupils (1,280 teachers); college and university (fall 1968), 126,839 students. *Public school expenditures* (1967–68)—$628,997,000 ($541 per pupil); average teacher's salary, $6,443.
Public Finance (fiscal year 1968): *Revenues,* $895,557,982 (3% sales tax, $216,173,811; motor fuel tax, $153,258,381; federal funds, $311,192,821). *Expenditures,* $1,432,222,000 (education, $469,794,269; health, welfare, and safety, $106,947,988; highways, $216,260,004). *State debt,* $493,-781,000.
Personal Income (1968): $13,642,000,000; average annual income per person, $2,664.
Public Assistance (fiscal year 1967): $96,879,400 to 174,708 recipients.
Labor Force (employed persons, July 1969): *Agricultural,* 436,000; *nonagricultural* (wage and salary earners), 1,679,500 (41.2% manufacturing, 18.0% trade, 13.1% government). *Unemployed persons* (July 1969)—86,000.
Manufacturing (1969): Value added by manufacture, $7,726,-000,000 (transportation equipment, $39,026,000; primary metals, $40,993,000; nonelectrical machinery, $117,206,-000; electrical machinery, $279,179,000; food and products, $322,861,000).
Agriculture (1967): *Cash farm income,* $1,341,430,000 (livestock, $463,141,000; crops, $816,593,000; govt. payments, $61,696,000). *Chief crops* (tons)—Tobacco, 421,300 (ranks 1st among the states); peanuts, 181,500 (ranks 2d); sweet potatoes, 109,250 (ranks 2d); corn for grain, 3,000,500.
Mining (1966): *Production value,* $71,878,000. *Chief minerals* (tons)—Stone, 22,377,000; sand and gravel, 11,601,000; clays, 3,381,000; feldspar, 338,240.
Fisheries (1967): *Commercial catch,* 225,000,000 pounds ($8,400,000). *Leading species* (1966)—Menhaden, 182,-288,821 pounds ($2,537,808); shrimp, 5,697,297 pounds ($2,565,981).
Transportation: *Roads* (1969), 85,029 miles (136,837 km); *motor vehicles* (1968), 2,898,420; *railroads* (1968), 6,261 track miles (10,076 km); *airports* (1967), 49.
Communications (1969): *Telephones* (1968), 1,877,200; *television stations,* 27; *radio stations,* 262; *newspapers,* 48.

colleges, Asheville-Biltmore and Wilmington, were made branches of the University of North Carolina.

Perhaps the most significant educational legislation was the creation of an enlarged system of regional universities out of the state's system of four-year senior colleges. Pembroke College received university status. North Carolina College at Durham became North Carolina Central University. Elizabeth City State College, Fayetteville State College, and Winston-Salem State College were also designated regional universities.

The legislature voted $375,000 for "study and development of a two-year medical school curriculum" at East Carolina University. It granted $350,000 to provide state aid for education of North Carolina residents at Duke and Bowman Gray medical schools.

The General Assembly voted $250,000 as the first step in the establishment of a state zoo.

More than 20 bills dealing with riots, civil disorders, and campus unrest were introduced. (During the year more than a score of persons were hurt at Duke University on February 14; one student was killed by gunfire at North Carolina Agricultural and Technical University at Greensboro on May 22.)

One new law prohibits outsiders on campus during university-declared curfews; another revokes state scholarships of students on state-supported campuses who are convicted of serious crimes in campus disorders; a third law authorizes the governor to order public buildings evacuated in public emergencies. Other laws increase the punishment for sit-ins in public buildings and make an assault on a policeman or fireman a felony.

The Economy. In general, North Carolina had a good year. Cash farm income amounted to almost $1 billion. The value added by manufactures was estimated at $7,726,000,000.

Obituary. North Carolina in 1969 mourned the loss of one of its most distinguished novelists, Inglis (Mrs. John) Fletcher, who died at Edenton on May 30. Between 1942 and 1962, she published a dozen novels relating to early North Carolina history.

HUGH T. LEFLER
University of North Carolina

NORTH DAKOTA

Disastrous spring floods, controversy over the location of antiballistic missile sites, and an active legislative season dominated the news in North Dakota in 1969.

Floods. In March the worst spring floods of this century cost North Dakota an estimated $54.5 million. Especially hard hit by the overflowing Souris and Red River North rivers were the areas around Minot, in the north, and the Red River Valley in the northeast. Six dams in the Forest River Watershed Program held back billions of gallons of water, preventing even greater destruction. In April, President Nixon declared North Dakota, South Dakota, and Minnesota disaster areas.

ABM Missile Sites. Opinion was divided as to the wisdom of locating a Safeguard antiballistic missile site at Grand Forks Air Force Base in North Dakota, the first of two in the United States. Although there was some opposition to the plan, small towns near the prospective sites welcomed the proposals.

Legislation. To replace the loss of funds created by the ending of the personal property tax in Jan-

—— **NORTH DAKOTA · Information Highlights** ——

Area: 70,665 square miles (183,023 sq km).
Population: 633,000 (1969 est.).
Chief Cities (Jan. 1, 1969 est.): Bismarck, the capital, 33,-700; Fargo, 52,000; Grand Forks, 41,000; Minot, 34,000.
Government: *Chief Officers*—governor, William Guy (Dem.); lt. gov., Richard Larsen (Rep.); secy. of state, Ben Meier (Rep.); atty. gen., Helgi Johanneson (Rep.); treas., Bernice Asbridge; supt. of pub. instr., M. F. Peterson; chief justice, Obert C. Teigen. *Legislative Assembly*—Senate, 49 members (6 Democrats, 43 Republicans); House of Representatives, 98 members (17 D, 81 R).
Education: *School enrollment* (1968)—public elementary, 94,000 pupils (4,400 teachers); public secondary, 57,000 pupils (3,300 teachers); nonpublic schools, 18,500 pupils (910 teachers); college and university (fall 1967), 26,501 students. *Public school expenditures* (1967–68—$98,115 ($689 per pupil); average teacher's salary, $5,750.
Public Finance (fiscal year 1968): *Revenues,* $263,298,000 (3% sales tax, $61,073,000; motor fuel tax, $15,575,000; federal funds, $68,235,000). *Expenditures,* $264,542,000 (education, $56,657,000; health, welfare, and safety, $33,-485,000; highways, $54,409,000). *State debt,* $31,767,000 (June 30, 1968).
Personal Income (1968): $1,712,000,000; average annual income per person, $2,730.
Public Assistance (fiscal year 1969): $22,037,419 to 20,166 recipients (aged, $3,772,902; dependent children, $5,528,-217).
Labor Force (employed persons, 1969): *Agricultural,* 92,000; *nonagricultural* (wage and salary earners), 180,220 (4.9% manufacturing, 24.3% trade, 24.6% government). *Unemployed persons* (July 15, 1969)—8,950.
Manufacturing (1965): Value added by manufacture, $94,138,-000 (transportation equipment (1963), $13,400,000; printing and publishing, $13,267,000; nonelectrical machinery, $8,884,000).
Agriculture (1967): Cash farm income, $848,238,000 (livestock, $281,773,000; crops, $435,615,000; govt. payments, $130,850,000). *Chief crops* (tons)—Wheat, 5,304,840 (ranks 2d among the states); barley, 2,059,780 (ranks 1st); flaxseed, 259,620 (ranks 1st); rye, 112,780 (ranks 2d); hay, 4,145,000; oats, 980,350.
Mining (1968): Production value, $97,704,000. *Chief minerals* (tons, 1967)—Sand and gravel, 8,822,000; lignite, 4,413,-458; stone, 596,000; clays (1966), 78,000; crude petroleum, 25,210,000 barrels.
Transportation: *Roads* (1967), 107,163 miles (172,457 km); *motor vehicles* (1968), 407,067; *railroads* (1968), 6,286 track miles (10,116 km); *airports* (1968), 70.
Communications (1969): *Telephones* (1968), 283,900; *television stations,* 12; *radio stations,* 37; *newspapers,* 10 (daily circulation, 187,542).

uary 1970, the legislature increased sales and use taxes from 3 to 4%. On July 1 increased taxes were established for gasoline, alcoholic beverages, tobacco, and oleomargarine. Income from business, farming, ranching, trades, and professions will pay either a 1% net income tax or $20, whichever is larger. Assessments on public utilities, however, were reduced. Cities received increased funds from state revenues. Hunting laws for deer and fox were liberalized, while pheasant hunting was prohibited.

North Dakota's federal representatives raised hopes for the development of a "water bank," from which owners might obtain federal payments similar to those paid for cropland retirement. The state's wetlands produce 80% of the nation's waterfowl.

Other Events. On May 10 the town of Zap, in central North Dakota, was invaded by hundreds of students and other young people from neighboring parts of the United States and Canada. What began as a joke ended with National Guardsmen clearing the "Zap-in" of nearly 3,000 young people. Damage amounting to nearly $3,000 was partially compensated by a statewide relief fund of $1,350.

The Great Northern and Northern Pacific Railroads, each losing $8 million a year in passenger service in the state, discontinued certain trains and closed 20 depots. An additional 35 producing oil wells in the state brought the total to 2,018 wells. Secretary of the Interior Walter J. Hickel stated that the trans-Alaska Pipeline System might be extended across North Dakota.

FELIX J. VONDRACEK
University of North Dakota

NORTHWEST TERRITORIES

On April 1, 1969, the government of the Northwest Territories assumed responsibility for government services in the Mackenzie District, formerly administered by the Federal Department of Indian Affairs and Northern Development. The federal government retained responsibility for the development of the area's resources. Plans were progressing for the transfer of responsibilities in the Eastern Arctic scheduled for April 1, 1970.

The territorial government now has 10 departments, all located in Yellowknife, the capital.

Council Affairs. In 1969 the Council of the Northwest Territories held two sessions in Yellowknife and one at Baker Lake in the Central Arctic. It approved a record budget of more than $40 million for 1969–70. The Council received a report from a Liquor Inquiry Board, which recommended extensive changes in liquor legislation, including lowering the drinking age from 21 to 19 years and establishing a Liquor Control Board. Legislation based on the report is expected in January 1970. The council also passed a hamlet ordinance to establish a new level of local government. Fort Simpson and Pine Point became hamlets in 1969.

Economic Development. A major development was the introduction of jet service from Edmonton, Alberta, to Fort Smith, Hay River, Yellowknife, Norman Wells, and Inuvik in the west, and from Montreal, Quebec, to Frobisher Bay and Resolute in the east. A lateral air route was also initiated from Yellowknife to Churchill, Manitoba. Oil exploration continued in the Arctic islands and on the northern coast, spurred on by the oil discovery on Alaska's North Slope. Northerners welcomed the successful voyage of the S. S. *Manhattan* through the Northwest Passage.

Centennial Plans. Preparations advanced for the 1970 centennial of the Northwest Territories. Plans range from a marathon 1,200-mile (1,930-km) canoe race down the Mackenzie River to building recreation centers in several Arctic villages.

STUART M. HODGSON
Commissioner, Northwest Territories

—**NORTHWEST TERRITORIES · Information Highlights**—

Area: 1,304,903 square miles (3,379,000 sq km).
Population: 32,000 (Oct. 1, 1969 est.).
Chief Town (1969 est.): Yellowknife, the capital (6,000).
Government: *Chief Officers*—commissioner, Stuart M. Hodgson; deputy commissioner, John H. Parker; assistant commissioner, C. W. Gilchrist; judge of the territorial court, W. G. Morrow. *Legislature*—Territorial Council, 12 members (7 elected locally, 5 appointed).
Education: School enrollment (1968–1969)—public elementary and secondary, 8,474 pupils (456 teachers), including 3,342 Eskimos, 1,512 Indians, 3,620 others. *Public school expenditures* (1962)—$1,038,000.
Public Finance (fiscal year 1968–69): *Revenues,* $20,218,000 (liquor profits, $1,908,000). *Expenditures,* $20,218,000 (education, $3,078,000; health $2,963,000; social development $1,427,000; capital projects, $4,556,000).
Personal Income (1966 est. including Yukon): $64,000,000.
Public Assistance (fiscal year 1966 est.): $220,080 (aged and blind, $106,032; dependents and unemployed, $116,-043).
Manufacturing (1966): Value added by manufacture, $914,000.
Mining (1968 est.): *Production value,* $121,317,002. *Chief minerals* (tons)—Zinc, 210,500; lead, 130,000 (ranks 1st among the provinces); gold, 347,012 troy ounces; silver, 3,855,967 troy ounces. *Fur Production* (1968–69 est.): $1,180,000 value. *Forest Products* (1966): Lumber, 3,501,-600 board feet. *Fisheries* (1964): *Commercial catch,* 5,960,000 pounds ($808,000).
Transportation: *Roads* (1969), 783 miles (1260 km); *motor vehicles* (1968), 6,756; *railroads* (1969) 339 track miles (546 km); *licensed airports,* 35.
Communications (1969 est.): *Telephones,* 5,500; *television stations,* 3; *radio stations,* 3; *newspapers,* 4.
(All figures given in Canadian dollars equal to U. S.93¢.)

NORWAY

Norway's coalition government won a narrow victory over the Labor opposition in the parliamentary elections. The economy prospered in 1969.

Elections. In the elections held on September 7 and 8, the four parties of the ruling coalition (Conservative, Center, Liberal, and Christian) won only 76 seats in the 150-member Storting (Parliament). The coalition had previously held 80 seats. The Labor party increased its share from 68 to 74 seats, taking votes from the left as well as the right. The radical, anti-NATO Socialist People's party lost its two seats.

Tax Reform. The coalition's victory meant it could press ahead with the tax reform program announced in January 1969 and approved by the Storting in June. The program, which will go into effect on Jan. 1, 1970, will lighten the burden of direct taxes and increase the role of indirect taxation. An added value tax of 20% will replace the present sales tax of 13.64%. The changeover will raise prices. To cushion the effect on low-income groups, social service payments will also be increased at the beginning of the year.

The Storting. King Olav V opened the 114th session of the Storting on October 9. In the Speech from the Throne, the king presented the government's program, which included increased aid to developing countries. The Labor opposition in the Storting said it would work for the introduction of a 40-hour week for workers.

The Economy. There was a very marked rise in domestic demand, compared with 1968, and export demand also rose. Industrial output increased sharp-

ly, with the biggest rises recorded in the wood products, base metals, and electrotechnical industries. The gross national product for 1969 was expected to be 4.5% higher than in 1968.

For the second year in a row, a substantial balance of payments surplus was expected. However, the surplus was mainly the result of temporary factors, such as a rise in sales of second-hand ships and a brief decline in imports of new merchant vessels. A balance of payments deficit is expected again in 1970, as ship imports rise and sales of second-hand tonnage fall.

The government raised the Bank of Norway's interest rate from 3.5% to 4.5% on September 27, the first change in nearly 15 years. At the same time, it announced a price freeze and moves to control the credit supply. The measures were chiefly designed to meet problems connected with the transition to the new tax system in January 1970. They were partly forced, however, by the steady rise in interest rates outside Norway.

The fruit harvest was abundant, after one of the warmest summers in more than 20 years. But the dry summer resulted in below-average grain and potato crops. Water shortages cut hydroelectric power production, and in some districts electricity for industrial users had to be rationed.

Oil Exploration. Several groups of oil companies continued test drilling for undersea oil and gas off Norway's west coast, but no significant find was announced. Early in the year, Minister of Industry Sverre W. Rostoft said the government would hire more petroleum geologists of its own to help it make independent decisions about the extent of oil or gas deposits in Norwegian waters. The government is studying a recommendation for a state-financed oil and gas search in the part of the con-

YOUNG NORWEGIAN DEMONSTRATORS in Oslo burn flag of the USSR as they commemorate first anniversary of the Soviet invasion of Czechoslovakia, August 21.

NTB PHOTO

----------- NORWAY • Information Highlights -----------

Area: 125,181 square miles (324,219 sq km).
Population: 3,819,000 (1968 est.).
Chief Cities (1966 est.): Oslo, the capital, 484,479; Trondheim, 117,417; Bergen, 117,353.
Government: *King*—Olav V (acceded Sept. 21, 1957); *Prime Minister*—Per Borten (took office Oct. 12, 1965). *Parliament*—Storting, 150 members (party seating, 1969: Labor, 74; Conservative, 29; Center, 20; Christian People's, 14; Liberal, 13).
Religious Faiths: Evangelical Lutheran, 96% of population.
Education: *Literacy rate* (1962), 99% of population. *Total school enrollment* (1966)—780,891 (primary, 407,055; secondary, 277,172; teacher-training, 7,908; technical/vocational, 67,755; university/higher, 21,001).
Finance (1969 est.): *Revenues,* $2,124,943,000; *expenditures,* $2,339,649,000; *public debt* (1967), $1,970,084,000; *monetary unit,* krone (7.14 kroner equal U.S.$1).
Gross National Product (1968): $9,145,658,000.
National Income (1968): $6,904,761,000; average annual income per person, $1,808.
Economic Indexes (1968): *Industrial production,* 132 (1963 = 100); *agricultural production* (1967), 97 (1963=100); *cost of living* (1967), 119 (1963=100).
Manufacturing (metric tons, 1967): Wood pulp, 955,000; cement, 2,066,000; steel, 790,000; newsprint, 389,000.
Crops (metric tons, 1967–68 crop year): Potatoes, 807,000; barley, 485,000; oats, 123,000; apples, 49,000.
Minerals (metric tons, 1967): Magnesium (1966), 30,300 (ranks 3d among world producers); limestone, 4,000,000; iron ore, 2,000,000; pyrites, 673,458.
Foreign Trade (1968): *Exports,* $1,938,000,000 (chief exports, 1967: manufactured goods, $421,100,000; ships, $213,100,000; aluminum, $159,700,000; fish, $141,400,000); *imports,* $2,706,000,000 (chief imports, 1967: ships, $521,-400,000). *Chief trading partners* (1967): Sweden (took 16% of exports, supplied 19% of imports); Britain (took 19% of exports, supplied 14% of imports); West Germany (took 12% of exports, supplied 14% of imports).
Transportation: *Roads* (1967), 31,825 miles (51,216 km); *motor vehicles* (1967), 706,900 (automobiles, 569,200); *railways* (1965), 2,702 miles (4,348 km); *merchant vessels* (1967), 1,368 (18,666 gross registered tons).
Communications: *Telephones* (1968), 987,292; *television stations* (1968), 34; *television sets* (1968), 670,000; *radios* (1967), 1,135,000; *newspapers* (1967), 81.

tinental shelf north of the 62d parallel, an area not yet opened up for private exploration.

Foreign Affairs. Work continued on the "Nordek" plan, which would provide for a customs union and closer economic cooperation between Norway and its Nordic neighbors Finland, Sweden, and Denmark. A draft treaty of economic union, worked out by government officials, was published in July, and debate continued at a meeting of the Nordic prime ministers in Stockholm in November. But the December meeting of the European Economic Community (EEC) prime ministers seemed to improve Norwegian and Dutch chances of early EEC membership. Finland expressed doubts about the Nordek scheme, and its whole future appeared in jeopardy.

The government continued its strong support of the United Nations and the North Atlantic Treaty Organization. It explicitly dissociated Norway from the Swedish pledge of economic aid to North Vietnam. Foreign Minister John Lyng said Sweden had not informed Norway in advance about the pledge, although the three Scandinavian countries often coordinate their aid to developing nations.

King Olav V paid state visits to Tunisia in May and Yugoslavia in October.

Overseas Investment. The Borregaard concern, producers of paper, pulp, and chemicals, and one of Norway's largest industrial companies, started work in 1969 on a $42 million cellulose plant in Brazil. The plant will use cheap, fast-growing Brazilian timber as raw material. This is the biggest foreign investment project ever undertaken by a Norwegian company.

THOR GJESTER
"Norwegian Journal of Commerce and Shipping,"
Oslo

NOVA SCOTIA

In September, Nova Scotia's Progressive Conservative Premier George I. Smith announced his second cabinet shuffle since he became premier in 1967. New ministers in the cabinet are John Buchanan, minister of fisheries and of public works; Gordon Tidman, minister of public welfare; and Gerald Ritcey, minister of trade and industry. James M. Harding left the cabinet, W. S. K. Jones moved from trade and industry to municipal affairs, and Thomas J. McKeough retained labour and also became minister of finance and economics.

Legislation. During the 1969 session of the Nova Scotia Legislature 146 acts were passed. One major new bill was the Direct Sellers Act, which governs house-to-house selling and the sale or soliciting of orders for the sale of goods and services. The law set requirements for the contents of a direct sales contract and for delivery of a copy to the purchaser, who is given a right of breaking the contract. In addition, there are restrictions on repossession when two thirds of the price has been paid. The Law Reform Act established the Nova Scotia Law Reform Advisory Commission, which will review legislation and other matters referred to it.

Economy. The provincial economy was strong in 1969. Housing construction was up considerably. Farm cash receipts and the value of fish landings and manufacturing shipments showed moderately strong gains. Total investment was up, reflecting investment gains in housing, utilities, and services, although investment declined in the primary industries, construction, manufacturing, and social capital.

---NOVA SCOTIA · Information Highlights---

Area: 21,425 square miles (55,491 sq km).
Population: 763,000 (June 1, 1969 est.).
Chief Cities (1966 census): Halifax, the capital, 86,792; Dartmouth, 58,745; Sydney, 32,767.
Government: *Chief Officers*—lt. gov., Victor Oland; premier, George Isaac Smith (Progressive Conservative); prov. secy., Edward D. Haliburton (PC); atty. gen., Richard A. Donahoe (PC); minister of finance and economics, Thomas James McKeough (PC); chief justice, Alexander Hugh McKinnon. *Legislature*—Legislative Assembly (convened Feb. 13, 1969); 46 members (41 Progressive Conservative, 5 Liberal).
Education: School enrollment (1966–67 est.)—public elementary and secondary, 200,681 pupils (8,080 teachers); private schools, 4,508 pupils (243 teachers); Indian (federal) schools, 750 pupils (27 teachers); college and university (fall 1966), 9,806 students. *Public school expenditures* (1963)—$52,970,000 ($303 per pupil); median teacher's salary (1966–67), $4,303.
Public Finance (fiscal year 1968 est.): *Revenues*, $236,400,-000 (sales tax, $59,800,000; income tax, $39,612,000; federal funds, $99,580,000). *Expenditures*, $283,280,000 (education, $99,290,000; health and social welfare, $67,-090,000).
Personal Income (1967 est.): $1,355,000,000; average annual income per person, $1,790.
Social Welfare (fiscal year 1968 est.): $19,000,000 (aged and blind, $1,240,000; dependents and unemployed, $8,190,-000).
Manufacturing (1967): Value added by manufacture, $240,-783,000 (food and beverages, $66,206,000; transportation equipment, $35,070,000; paper and allied industries, $24,-770,000).
Agriculture (1968 est.): *Cash farm income,* $54,786,000 (livestock, $43,996,000; crops, $8,856,000). *Chief crops* (cash receipts)—Fruits, $4,170,000 (ranks 4th among the provinces); vegetables, $1,807,000.
Mining (1968 est.): *Production value,* $58,399,179. *Chief minerals* (tons)—coal, 3,119,692 (ranks 2d among the provinces); gypsum, 4,451,500 (ranks 1st).
Fisheries (1968): *Commercial catch,* 795,188,000 pounds ($54,600,000). *Leading species*—Herring, 351,801,000 pounds ($3,545,000); cod, 143,231,000 pounds ($7,364,-000); lobster, 15,810,000 pounds ($10,944,000); scallops, 13,413,000 pounds ($11,861,000).
Transportation: *Roads* (1969), 15,478 miles (24,909 km); *motor vehicles* (1966), 234,532; *railroads* (1966), 1,313 track miles (2,113 km); *licensed airports* (1966), 60.
Communications (1966): *Telephones,* 232,428; *television stations,* 3; *radio stations,* 16; *daily newspapers,* 6 (daily circulation, 159,525).
(All figures given in Canadian dollars equal to U. S.93¢.)

Industrial Development. In June, a report prepared for Deuterium of Canada, a provincial Crown corporation, was presented to Premier Smith. It indicated that $30 million and two years would be required before the company's heavy water plant, officially opened at Glace Bay in 1967, could be put into operation. The plant has been plagued with difficulties and, after expenditures in excess of $100 million, had not begun production. The Nova Scotia government had assumed full control of the plant in January and is currently considering its future.

In April, Nova Scotia Pulp Ltd., of Point Tupper, announced plans for a $60 million expansion program, scheduled for completion in March 1971. In July, Scott Maritime Pulp Ltd., of Abercrombie, said that it would spend $3,350,000 for expansion scheduled for completion in the fall of 1970. Michelin Tire Co. announced in July that it would invest $75 to $100 million in two tire plants, which will employ about 1,300 workers. A plant in Bridgewater will make steel core components, while another plant at Granton, near New Glasgow, will produce finished tires.

Canada Summer Games. Canada's first Summer Games were held in Halifax from August 16 to 25, with 2,344 athletes from all ten provinces, the Yukon, and the Northwest Territories competing in 15 events. (See also SPORTS.)

ANDREW S. HARVEY
Dalhousie University

NUCLEAR ENERGY. See ATOMIC ENERGY.

NURSES remain in short supply despite a rising need for their services, as in operating a patient-care monitor.

HEWLETT-PACKARD

NURSING

Salaries of registered nurses rose significantly in the United States in 1969. The shortage of RN's continued, and expectations are that the rate of growth of nurse manpower over the next several years will leave a serious gap between need and the number of nurses in practice.

Salaries. Pay increases appeared to average about 10% in new settlements during the year. Most voluntary hospitals in the San Francisco area were starting nurses at $7,800 for new graduates and $8,160 for experienced persons in staff-nurse positions. In 1970, new graduates were to start at $8,250 and staff nurses at $8,600. Leading private hospitals in New York City were starting nurses in 1969 at $8,600. In collective bargaining, state nurses' associations serve as the nurses' representatives.

In mid-1966, general-duty nurses averaged $100.50 for a 40-hour week; in January 1969, according to a study of nonfederal short-term general hospitals having at least 200 beds, the average starting salary for staff nurses was $6,900 per year.

Nurse Population. An estimated 680,000 RN's were actively practicing their profession in the United States at the beginning of 1969, but more than 27% of this total were working on a part-time basis. Although the registered nurse population has been growing at an estimated 3% annually from 1967 through 1969, the U. S. Department of Health, Education, and Welfare has forecast a continuing shortage. If adequate nursing care is to be provided, says HEW, the country will need 850,000 RN's in 1970 and one million by 1975.

The American Nurses' Association, the professional association of RN's, with headquarters in New York City, has worked to recruit more young people—especially minority group members—into nursing, and it has sought to bring inactive registered nurses back into employment. A recent study found that more than 295,000 nurses who held current licenses to practice were not employed in nursing. Many of these were mothers under 40 years of age. It appeared likely that a large proportion will return to practice when their children are grown.

Places of Employment. Hospitals and related institutions of course are the largest employers of nurses—66.9% of the total. A study shows that, in 1966, the rest of the employed nurses worked in the following areas: private duty, 9.9%; office nurses, 8.2%; public health, 4.5%; schools of nursing, 3.6%; school nurses, 3.5%; industrial nurses, 3.1%, and other, 0.3%.

Education. There appears to be an increasing tendency among today's students to obtain their nursing education in a collegiate setting. During the last few years there has been a large growth in nursing programs, particularly in junior and community colleges. There are three basic routes to becoming an RN: the hospital diploma, associate, and baccalaureate degree programs.

Trends. Through the American Nurses' Association, the nursing profession has begun to deal with the need to devise better systems for the delivery of health care. Nursing services and nursing education are being reevaluated in the light of current health problems. Closer liaison with other health occupations and with federal and state officials appear likely to increase in the near future.

AMERICAN NURSES' ASSOCIATION

NUTRITION

The field of nutrition gained a great deal of attention during 1969. Investigations of two well-known food additives—cyclamates and monosodium glutamate (MSG)—received wide publicity and both of them were removed from certain foods. Also during the year, the White House Conference on Food, Nutrition, and Health heard reports on the consequences of nutritional deficiencies in infants.

Cyclamates. The cyclamates—calcium and sodium cyclohexysulfamate—are very sweet, noncaloric chemicals that have been widely used as substitutes for sugar. The first cyclamate was introduced to the public in 1950, and since then these chemicals have been extensively used, often in conjunction with saccharin, to make many diet foods, particularly low-calorie carbonated beverages. The ratio of cyclamates to saccharin in these diet drinks was generally ten to one.

Saccharin, a sugar substitute first discovered in 1879, has been used for many years by diabetics and other people restricting their sugar intake. The major disadvantage of saccharin is that many people experience a slightly bitter aftertaste and when foods containing saccharin are heated, this unpleasant flavor becomes stronger. Cyclamates do not have this characteristic, and after their introduction they were in great demand for diet foods as well as for foods for diabetics. By 1969, the yearly production of cyclamates in the United States was more than 20 million pounds.

As the cyclamates became more popular, an increasing number of studies of their safety were carried out on human subjects as well as animals. One study showed that the consumption of large amounts of cyclamates produces loose stools. In humans, this occurred when the subjects consumed 5 grams of cyclamates a day. Since some bottles of diet soft drinks contained almost 1 gram of cyclamates, a person drinking five or more bottles of these beverages a day might develop the same symptom.

Other studies indicated that certain compounds closely related to cyclamates produce chromosome fragmentation in free-growing cells in a liquid medium. It was found that one in every ten persons metabolizes these compounds from a small portion of the cyclamates they ingest. Still other studies showed that when large amounts of cyclamates are fed to rats over long periods of time, they can cause cancer of the bladder.

These various studies led to the Department of Health, Education, and Welfare's prohibition of the sale of certain products containing cyclamates after Feb. 1, 1970. After Sept. 1, 1970, this prohibition will include all foods containing cyclamates. By the end of 1969 many food companies had already introduced new diet foods without cyclamates.

Monosodium Glutamate. MSG is the sodium salt of glutamic acid, an amino acid found in the proteins of meat, milk, beans, and other common foods. The Chinese and Japanese were perhaps the first to use MSG in their cooking, but during the past several years it has been widely used by U. S. food manufacturers and housewives for flavoring.

The first report of adverse effects from eating foods with MSG came in 1968. Dr. Robert H. Kwok of Silver Springs, Md., after eating in a restaurant serving northern Chinese cooking, felt a numbness at the back of his neck, general weakness, and palpitations. This syndrome, labeled the "Chinese restaurant syndrome," was confirmed by Dr. Herbert H. Schaumberg and his coworkers at the Albert Einstein College of Medicine, New York City, who traced it to foods containing MSG.

Shortly afterward, Dr. John W. Olney of Washington University School of Medicine, St. Louis, Mo., reported that newborn mice, after being injected with MSG, became obese, presumably as a result of lesions in the brain. Whether the obesity was due to an increased accumulation of fat or other substances was not reported. Olney's findings, publicized through television and other media, resulted in baby food manufacturers volunarily removing MSG from their products. (Since MSG is only a flavoring agent and has no nutritive value, its use in baby foods had been open to question.)

At the time of the announcement by the baby food manufacturers, on Oct. 25, 1969, many nutrition scientists felt that there was not enough information available to determine whether the amounts of MSG generally used in foods is harmful. Undoubtedly, Olney's technique of using MSG to produce obesity will be studied by others interested in the problem. As in studying any aspect of health and disease, a major problem is to translate the results of animal studies in terms of human reactions. Certainly as long as any animal species shows an adverse reaction to a substance, the use of the substance should be carefully evaluated and, if possible, restricted.

White House Conference. The White House Conference on Food, Nutrition, and Health, held in early December 1969, was charged by President Nixon to formulate a national nutrition program. Impetus for this conference came from reports suggesting that large segments of the lower income groups in the United States consume diets not only inadequate in quantity but inadequate in quality. These reports especially emphasized the consequences of nutritional deficiencies in infants.

Both clinical and laboratory studies have suggested that a deficiency of protein early in life permanently stunts intellectual development. At birth, an infant's brain is approximately 50% to 60% of its maximum adult weight. During the next four years, the brain grows disproportionately faster than the rest of the body. By the child's fourth year, the brain reaches 90% of its maximum size. Dietary deprivation during infancy and early childhood presumably inhibits the normal rapid increase in brain size, causing mental retardation.

Experiments with animals support to this belief. Such studies suggest that the retardation of growth in rats from birth to weaning (the first 21 days of life) results in consistently smaller size throughout life despite an adequate diet after weaning. In addition to physical retardation, the rats in these studies suffered mental retardation.

Further evidence was provided by studies conducted by scientists at the Hospital Infantil de Mexico. In these studies, it was shown that at birth an infant's grasping reflex, grip strength, and ability to follow a finger moving close to his face may be normal, but if the child later develops kwashiorkor (a severe protein deficiency disease) his "intellective" performance deteriorates. Even two to three years after recovering from the disease such children had IQ's below those of their siblings who had never had kwashiorkor. A few scientists have suggested that this relationship might be not as clear as it initially appeared to be. They pointed out that children with cystic fibrosis and congenital heart disease are often retarded in growth during their first year or two, but that many pediatricians saw nothing in them to suggest any mental disturbance resulting from their slow start in life.

MODESTO G. YANG and OLAF MICKELSEN
Michigan State University

OBITUARIES. For a list of prominent persons who died in 1969, see the NECROLOGY on pages 761–772.

BEN FRANKLIN, submerged for 31 days, drifted from Florida to Nova Scotia. The research vessel is shown arriving in New York City after the voyage.

UPI

OCEANOGRAPHY

Drilling of the ocean bottom to retrieve samples of material from the earth's crust was continued in the Atlantic and extended into the Pacific in 1969. The deep submersible *Ben Franklin* drifted the length of the Gulf Stream submerged. Important hydrographic studies of currents and of mixing processes were carried out in Drake's Passage and in the Mediterranean Sea. A major study of the air-sea interaction was conducted near Barbados.

Deep-Sea Drilling Project. Deep-sea drilling of the ocean floor in the Atlantic was concluded by the Joint Oceanographic Institutions for Deep Earth Sampling (JOIDES) project in late March 1969. Major findings in the Atlantic included determination of the ages of the oldest sediments at each drilling site and establishment of very close agreement between these ages and those derived from the theory of sea floor spreading, according to which oceanic crust spreads horizontally away from the axis of major mid-ocean ridges (such as the Mid-Atlantic Ridge). The permanent magnetization of crustal material retains the direction that the earth's magnetic field had when the crustal material cooled as it was extruded from the ridge. So a set of crustal samples gathered along a line at right angles to the ridge axis may be dated by correlating their directions of magnetization with an independently obtained record of the geological times of reversal of the earth's magnetic field. In this way, rates of sea floor spreading and ages of ocean basins may be inferred. The Atlantic data suggest that the North Atlantic began to form about 150 million years ago, the South Atlantic about 200 million years ago.

Drilling in the east Pacific was begun in mid-April. Cores taken in the northeast Pacific show an agreement between paleontological and paleomagnetic ages similar to that found in the Atlantic, although with less close correspondence. Drilling across the central and west Pacific brought up crustal material that was progressively older as the line of drilling sites was extended westward. The earliest sediments, about 140 million years old, were recovered east of the Mariana-Bonin Islands. This progression of ages is in accord with the idea that crustal material has spread westward from the East Pacific Rise.

All drilling has been done from the *Glomar Challenger*, designed by Global Marine, Inc. A system of dynamic stabilization involving computer-controlled thrusters and sea-floor acoustic beacons enables the ship to remain over the drill hole even in severe weather.

Drifting Up the Gulf Stream. The 50-foot-long submersible *Ben Franklin*, designed by its captain Jacques Piccard, drifted with Piccard and five crewmen from Florida to Nova Scotia. With the exception of one ascent, the entire 31-day drift—which ended on Aug. 14, 1969—was accomplished submerged. (The vehicle ascended once for repositioning in the axis of the stream after having been cast out entirely by strong eddying.) The major portion of the drift was at depths near 600 feet (about 180 meters), although descents as deep as 1,800 feet were made for bottom photography and acoustic experimentation. The rate of drift was unexpectedly high (at times, nearly 4 knots) and the commonly observed deep scattering layer of small marine organisms was not present.

Recovery of the Alvin. The submersible *Alvin,* operated by Woods Hole Oceanographic Institution in conjunction with the Office of Naval Research and lost on Oct. 16, 1968, when a holding cable parted during launching operations, was relocated on June 9, 1969, by the naval research vessel *Mizar* in almost 5,000 feet (about 1,500 meters) of water 120 miles south of Cape Cod. On Aug. 29, 1969, the *Alvin* was recovered with the help of the submersible *Aluminaut,* which descended to the sunken *Alvin* and placed a spring-loaded toggle bar (attached with a 7,000-foot lift line to a surface vessel) through the *Alvin's* open hatch.

Undersea Habitat. Four scientists from the U. S. Department of the Interior spent two months in a four-room habitat, Tektite I, nearly 50 feet below the surface of the sea in the Virgin Islands National Park. They surfaced on April 15, 1969. Their oxygen-nitrogen breathing mixture was maintained at the outside (water) pressure of over two atmospheres; study of the effects on the aquanauts of the resulting nitrogen saturation of body tissues for 60 days was a prime objective of the project. Because internal and external pressures were identical, a floor hatch in the habitat's wet lab could be kept open permanently for ready access to the water.

The four participants served as subjects in an extensive set of physiological and psychological investigations by the Navy and by NASA and pursued their research interests.

Death of an Aquanaut. An accident resulted in the death of Barry L. Cannon, 33, a civilian electronics engineer, while he was opening the hatch of Sealab 3 at a depth of 600 feet (180 meters) near San Clemente, Calif., on Feb. 17, 1969. It caused the U. S. Navy to postpone the projected experiment in ocean-bottom living.

New Hydrographic Work. As the result of a study carried out between Antarctica and South America, the total transport of water through Drake's Passage (about 300 miles or 480 km wide) is estimated at 270 million tons per second—a value nearly double the previous estimate and roughly three times the transport of the Gulf Stream. A series of five near-bottom current meter measurements, which yielded average speeds ranging from 1/20 to 1/3 mph, were combined with conventional measurements of temperature and salinity at many depths to obtain the estimate. The study was part of a cruise by the research vessel *Argo,* operated by the Scripps Institution of Oceanography.

Aircraft and ships from the United States, Britain, France, and Italy collaborated in a study of vertical mixing in the Mediterranean Sea during the winter of 1968–69. Initially, the location of the most dense surface water was ascertained. With the onset of winter storms and the accompanying flow of cold air from the north, the water at this location was observed to become so much more dense that overturning occurred. The results of this study are expected to shed light on similar processes that are thought to occur in the Atlantic at high latitudes.

Project BOMEX. During May, June, and July 1969, a massive investigation of the exchange of energy between the ocean and the atmosphere took place east of Barbados in an area of 90,000 square miles (233,000 sq km). This Barbados Oceanographic and Meteorological Expedition—Project BOMEX—involved seven U. S. federal departments and agencies led by the Environmental Sciences Services Administration, together with the government of Barbados and many academic and industrial institutions.

Tour Around the Americas. The CSS *Hudson,* a Canadian research vessel, departed on Nov. 19, 1969 on an expedition that, if completed, would constitute the first circumnavigation of the Americas. Investigations to be conducted during the outward leg of this cruise, from Halifax, Nova Scotia, to Vancouver, British Columbia, were to include an attempt to measure directly the tilt of the sea surface associated with the flow of the Antarctic Circumpolar Current. The rest of the expedition was to involve primarily marine geophysical studies.

Marine Pollution. Public awareness that human activity could result in the serious contamination of large ocean areas was heightened when an offshore oil well being drilled in the Santa Barbara Channel off southern California began to spill crude oil directly into the water on Jan. 28, 1969. The flow was brought under control after 11 days, but spilling continued at a reduced rate until early March. The resulting surface slick had spread over several hundred square miles by the eighth day. Estimates of the degree of contamination of the nearby coastline and of damage to marine life in the area vary widely. (See also CONSERVATION; POLLUTION; ZOOLOGY.)

Northwest Passage. The 1,065-foot-long (about 325 meters) tanker-icebreaker *Manhattan,* specially reconstructed for operation under severe conditions of sea ice by the Humble Oil and Refining Co., traversed the Northwest Passage around the North American continent, arriving at Point Barrow in late September. (For details, see ARCTIC REGIONS; SHIPPING.)

Sea Observation from Satellites. The high-precision infrared radiometer data from the Nimbus 1 and Nimbus 2 satellites have been used to construct charts of sea-surface temperature for regions of limited geographical extent.

Satellite TV pictures of the earth's surface suggest that regions of upwelling and major ocean currents are sometimes associated with characteristic cloud-cover configurations and may thus be indirectly delineated from satellite altitude.

Color photographs of the sea taken aboard manned space flights show a surprising amount of detail, most of which may now be interpreted only provisionally. The bottom is sometimes visible in certain regions of shallow and clear water.

In spite of the limitations inherent in only looking at the surface of the sea, satellite observations of the sea—either directly or by relay of radio signals from ocean buoys—offer the only hope of observing large areas simultaneously. They will certainly be more extensively pursued.

MYRL C. HENDERSHOTT
Scripps Institution of Oceanography

STORMSWEPT BOAT on Lake Erie reflects violence of the wind and rain storm that buffeted northeastern Ohio on July 4. At least 36 persons died in the storm.

OHIO

Ohioans had cause to be proud in 1969 when astronaut Neil Armstrong, a native son, became the first man to set foot on the moon. Racial disturbances, severe summer storms, and legislative action also made headlines.

Legislature. On February 5, Gov. James A. Rhodes outlined an extensive "solutions for the Seventies" program before the annual session of the Ohio General Assembly, which met from January 6 until August 8, returning on August 18 and September 11 to conclude business. During the session, increased support for education was provided at all levels. More than $2 billion was authorized for schools and universities for the 1969–71 biennium. Augmented costs were to be met by increased taxes on cigarettes, liquor, corporate franchises, and public utilities.

In February several hundred welfare marchers descended on the state capitol with demands that included payment of all established welfare benefits. An 8-hour vigil was maintained in the capitol rotunda until many participants were arrested for trespassing on state property. The legislature finally increased welfare appropriations for the biennium from $250 million to $879 million.

Authorization was also made for capital improvement provided for by the passage of a 1968 bond issue. The expenditures were to be made primarily in areas of mental hygiene and correction, natural resources, state buildings, airports, and urban transportation bottlenecks. Provision was made for the nation's largest highway and transportation research center, to be situated between Bellefontaine and Marysville.

The Assembly also provided for workmen's compensation for miners who contract "black lung" disease from coal dust; extended the Ohio open housing law to cover one-family dwelling units in accord with federal law; changed state election laws to provide easier qualifications for independent and third-party candidates; reduced residency requirements for voting from one year to six months; and authorized a 32-member commission to study possible changes in the state constitution.

Racial Violence. Racial disturbances were less extensive in Ohio's cities in 1969 than in recent years. In July, however, the National Guard was called to Youngstown after snipers opened fire on police following the alleged mistreatment of a black customer in a white-owned dairy store. A few days later, Columbus, which had previously escaped major racial disorders, was the scene of sniper fire and rioting that followed the killing of a Negro by a white man, climaxing a long-standing neighborhood feud. The National Guard was summoned, and calm was gradually restored.

Elections. In the off-year elections on November 4, Carl B. Stokes narrowly won reelection as mayor of Cleveland. He thus became the first Negro mayor of a major U. S. city to secure reelection over a white opponent. Dr. John Rosemond became the first Negro elected to the Columbus city council in this century.

Two proposed amendments to the state constitution were submitted to the voters in 1969. One, providing for changing the legal age for voting from 21 to 19, was defeated. The second, which was approved, removed the necessity for a special election for certain state officials when a vacancy occurred, if the remainder of the term was for less than a year. Hundreds of communities sought approval for

---

OHIO • Information Highlights

Area: 41,222 square miles (106,765 sq km).

Population: 10,614,000 (1969 est.).

Chief Cities (1969 est.): Columbus, the capital, 535,000; Cleveland, 770,000; Cincinnati, 495,000; Toledo, 385,000; Akron, 285,000; Dayton, 255,000.

Government (1969): *Chief Officers*—governor, James A. Rhodes (Republican); lt. gov., John W. Brown (R); secy. of state, Ted W. Brown (R); atty. gen., Paul W. Brown (R); treas., John D. Herbert (R); supt. of pub. instr., Martin W. Essex; chief justice, Kingsley A. Taft. *General Assembly*—Senate, 33 members (21 Republicans, 12 Democrats); House of Representatives, 99 members (64 R, 35 D).

Education: *School enrollment* (1968–69)—public elementary, 1,715,000 pupils (54,500 teachers); public secondary, 678,000 pupils (40,400 teachers); nonpublic schools, 363,200 pupils (12,990 teachers); college and university (fall 1967), 313,956 students. *Public school expenditures* (1967–68)—$1,540,000,000 ($691 per pupil); average teacher's salary, $7,600.

Public Finance (fiscal year 1968): *Revenues,* $3,149,451,000 (general sales and gross receipts taxes, $508,598,000; motor fuel tax, $285,170,000; federal funds, $312,276,000). *Expenditures,* $2,907,693,000 (education, $440,718,000; health, welfare, and safety, $402,152,000; highways, $481,-112,000). *State debt,* $1,282,622,000 (June 30, 1968).

Personal Income (1968): $37,151,000,000; average annual income per person, $3,509.

Public Assistance (fiscal year 1969): $320,306,158 to 386,943 recipients (aged, $92,613,642; dependent children, $136,-548,066).

Labor Force (employed persons, August 1966): *Agricultural,* 127,300; *nonagricultural* (wage and salary earners), 3,516,-000. *Unemployed persons* (August 1966)—123,900.

Manufacturing (1966): *Value added by manufacture,* $20,132,-127,000 (transportation equipment, $3,059,396,000; primary metals, $2,855,628,000; nonelectrical machinery, $3,008,-458,000; electrical machinery, $2,003,955,000).

Agriculture (1967): *Cash farm income,* $1,304,652,000 (livestock, $696,266,000; crops, $538,031,000; govt. payments, $70,355,000). *Chief crops* (tons)—Corn for grain, 7,166,-880; hay, 2,936,000.

Mining (1967): Production value (1968), $424,994,000. *Chief minerals* (tons)—Bituminous coal, 45,891,615; limestone, 44,658,513; crude petroleum, 9,891,325 barrels.

Transportation: *Roads* (1969), 107,783 miles (173,456 km); *motor vehicles* (1968), 6,064,961; *railroads* (1966), 8,084 track miles (13,010 km); *airports* (1969), 11.

Communications (1968): *Telephones,* 5,481,400; *television stations,* 35; *radio stations,* 178; *newspapers,* 103 (daily circulation, 3,490,331).

school-operating levies. In spite of strong resistance to increased taxes, over half of the levies were passed.

Judicial Decision. In June the U. S. Supreme Court, on appeal from the Ohio supreme court, unanimously declared unconstitutional Ohio's Criminal Syndicalism Act of 1955. The court ruled that the act was an infringement of free speech guaranteed by the First Amendment. The decision reversed the conviction of Clarence Brandenburg, a Ku Klux Klansman from Columbus who had filmed and televised denunciations of Negroes, Jews, and the Supreme Court.

Astronaut's Welcome. In August, Neil Armstrong of Wapakoneta received a hero's welcome when the Apollo 11 astronaut who voyaged to the moon returned to his home town. Public and private funds were contributed for a Neil Armstrong Astronaut Museum in the town.

Storms. On July 4 severe winds and rains in northeastern Ohio caused at least 36 deaths and property damage estimated at $70 million. The storm centered on Toledo, Sandusky, Cleveland, and Wooster. A tornado on August 9 resulted in 4 deaths and more than 200 injuries, with damage or destruction to at least 615 homes and businesses along the northern border of Cincinnati.

FRANCIS P. WEISENBURGER
The Ohio State University

OIL. See PETROLEUM.

OKLAHOMA

The state's two principal cities, Tulsa and Oklahoma City, the capital, moved ahead of schedule on urban renewal programs in 1969, and both began programs to integrate their public high schools. The capital city experienced a prolonged strike by sanitation workers.

Downtown Tulsa. Tulsa, an initial selection in the model cities program, pushed toward completion of its downtown beautification program. Widened sidewalks, rest benches, raised shrubbery beds, and trees increased its attractiveness to visitors and shoppers. A new junior college, the first new state college authorized in 50 years, was being built on 40 acres in the downtown area and was scheduled to open in 1970.

Integration Of High Schools. Under separate federal district court orders, Tulsa and Oklahoma City began integration of their public high schools with the fall 1969 term. The Tulsa system submitted a plan for integration that was approved by the court. The Oklahoma City system began operation under a compulsory court order that required 11 bus routes to carry students to their schools.

Sanitation Workers' Strike. Some 200 sanitation workers in Oklahoma City struck for higher wages and shorter hours from August 19 to November 7. A citizens' fact-finding committee recommended wage increases but City Manager Robert Oldland and the majority of the city council wanted to include the wage demands in a general review of adjustments for all city personnel. Oldland was also adamant against rehiring 11 leaders of the strike. For 80 days, Oklahoma City witnessed marches and assemblies in support of the strikers. The strike was ended when civic leaders promised jobs for the 11 men denied employment by the city. Other demands of the strikers were met.

College President Dismissed. In October in Stillwater the board of regents for Oklahoma Agricultural and Mechanical Colleges dismissed, on grounds of personal misconduct, William H. Hale, president of the predominantly black Langston University in Langston. Langston students demonstrated in protest of the dismissal at the state house the following day, but the tension at the university gradually decreased under Hale's skillful handling of the situation.

State House Politics. In January, Gov. Dewey Bartlett dismissed two members of the state highway commission for what he deemed had been unethical solicitation of campaign funds in behalf of Richard Nixon. He also dismissed William M. Dane, director of the highway department. State Treasurer Leo Winters won a court decision that gave him the right to designate the amount of state money for deposit in banks, a right that had been challenged by the other two members of the state depository board—the governor and the attorney general.

Town Evacuated. On April 3, a freight train was derailed near the outskirts of Wetumka in Hughes County. Because one car contained hydrochloric acid, all 2,300 residents of the town and surrounding area had to be evacuated for about 24 hours until crews repaired the railway track and moved the cars.

J. STANLEY CLARK
Oklahoma City University

───── **OKLAHOMA • Information Highlights** ─────

Area: 69,919 square miles (181,090 sq km).
Population: 2,539,000 (1969 est.).
Chief Cities (1969 est.): Oklahoma City, the capital, 385,000; Tulsa, 325,000; Lawton, 76,000; Norman, 50,000; Midwest City, 47,000.
Government (1969): *Chief Officers*—governor, Dewey F. Bartlett (Republican); lt. gov., George Nigh (Democrat); secy. of state, John Rogers (D); atty. gen., G. T. Blankenship (R); treas., Leo Winters; supt. of pub. instr., D. D. Creech; chief justice, Pat Irwin. *Legislature*—Senate, 48 members (38 Democrats, 10 Republicans); House of Representatives, 99 members (77 D, 22 R).
Education: *School enrollment* (1968–69)—public elementary, 341,000 pupils (13,700 teachers); public secondary, 254,000 pupils (12,900 teachers); nonpublic schools, 17,600 pupils (890 teachers); college and university (fall 1967), 100,352 students. *Public school expenditures* (1967–68)—$347,800,000 ($622 per pupil); average teacher's salary, $6,203.
Public Finance (fiscal year 1968): *Revenues*, $929,953,000 (general sales and gross receipts taxes, $79,541,000; motor fuel tax, $80,729,000; federal funds, $312,267,000). *Expenditures*, $949,299,000 (education, $182,830,000; health, welfare, and safety, $274,688,000; highways, $151,628,000). *State debt*, $665,734,000 (June 30, 1968).
Personal Income (1968): $7,259,000,000; average annual income per person, $2,880.
Public Assistance (fiscal year 1968): $134,156,322 to 195,503 recipients (aged, $69,093,206; dependent children, $46,731,986).
Labor Force (employed persons, annual average 1968): *Agricultural*, 119,900; *nonagricultural* (wage and salary earners), 726,500 (16.6% manufacturing, 22.0% trade, 24.8% government). *Unemployed persons* (annual average 1968)—35,200.
Manufacturing (1965): *Value added by manufacture*, $1,096,262,000 (transportation equipment, $113,833,000; primary metals, $46,413,000; nonelectrical machinery, $139,155,000; electrical machinery, $87,710,000; fabricated metals, $112,121,000; food and products, $156,993,000).
Agriculture (1967): *Cash farm income*, $918,819,000 (livestock, $543,691,000; crops, $263,031,000; govt. payments, $112,097,000). *Chief crops* (tons)—Wheat, 266,067 (ranks 5th among the states); hay, 3,065,000; sorghum, 722,456; soybeans, 101,024; barley, 92,184; cottonseed, 82,000; oats, 53,760.
Mining (1966): *Production value*, $979,737,000. *Chief minerals* (tons)—Stone, 17,178,000; sand and gravel, 5,400,000; bituminous coal, 850,000; gypsum, 816,000; clays, 754,000; crude petroleum, 224,000,000 barrels.
Transportation: *Roads* (1969), 107,321 miles (172,712 km); *motor vehicles* (1968), 1,714,371; *railroads* (1969), 5,561 track miles (8,949 km); *airports* (1969), 10.
Communications (1969): *Telephones* (1968), 1,249,600; *television stations*, 11; *radio stations*, 88; *newspapers*, 55 (daily circulation, 929,959).

THE NEW YORK TIMES

"SENIOR POWER" buttons abounded as elderly persons (*above*), some 4,000 strong, rallied in New York City on October 22 to protest the squeeze on their incomes. Retired persons are caught "between a fixed income and rising prices," one speaker asserted.

(*Right*) Elderly woman in need eats a lonely meal at a New York shelter.

THE NEW YORK TIMES

OLDER POPULATION

Inflation, restricted appropriations, and assignment of national priorities to children and youth operated in 1969 to level off progress in improving the circumstances of the elderly. Yet, several developments during the year indicated that American society had not lost concern for its older people.

Appointment and Legislation. The stature of the Administration on Aging, the government's focal point for advocacy on behalf of older people, was enhanced by President Nixon's appointment of John B. Martin of Grand Rapids as commissioner of aging. Martin was given the additional title of special assistant to the President for aging.

One of the initiatives taken by the new commissioner of aging led to a joint agreement between the departments of Health, Education, and Welfare (HEW) and Housing and Urban Development (HUD) to assure that the special needs of older people are recognized in implementation of programs and services in model city neighborhoods, a matter hitherto largely overlooked in model city planning. Immediate action resulted in development of guides and special grants.

Bipartisan support led to almost unanimous passage of the Older Americans Act Amendments of 1969, increasing financial authorization (but not im-

mediate appropriations) for programs conducted under the act, and broadening responsibilities of the states for planning and initiating services for their older populations. The Administration on Aging was awarded full responsibility for the Foster Grandparent Program (shared formerly with the Office of Economic Opportunity) and directed to plan for a nationwide Retired Senior Volunteer Program.

Conferences and Hearings. Various meetings were held during the year to report progress in research on aging and to chart directions. Employing the theme, "The Aging Consumer," the 22d annual University of Michigan Conference on Aging attracted more than 1,000 persons. Conferees expressed concern over the increasing victimization of older people, and recommended stepping up consumer education and legislative controls. In October, the White House Conference on Food, Nutrition, and Health gave its attention to eating habits and dietary deficiencies of the elderly.

The U. S. Senate Special Committee on Aging conducted a year-long inquiry into "The Economics of Aging: Toward a Full Share in Abundance." Hearings were held in Washington and elsewhere on the income situation of older people, and on such related topics as financial aspects of medical care, consumer protection, nutrition, and retirement.

A committee paper warned that present middle-aged Americans face a more severe retirement income pinch than today's elderly, unless society becomes aware of the problem and decides to allocate a larger share of resources to support them during the post-work years.

The 8th International Congress of Gerontology brought 1,850 research and professional workers in aging from 35 countries to Washington for five days of interchange of new knowledge and experience. Subject matter ranged from molecular biology of aging to special planning for the elderly. One of the world's most distinguished geronotologists, Dr. Alex Comfort of London, stated that man is now in a position, given the necessary resources, to exercise a large amount of control over his life span and postpone the onset of physical and mental deterioration, and he advised actuaries who estimate annuities to take heed.

Pursuant to 1968 legislation, the President issued a proclamation for a White House Conference on Aging to be held in November 1971. It is expected that thousands of older people, younger persons, and professionals will become involved in formulating comprehensive goals and politics with respect to the older population.

An International Center for Social Gerontology, with its headquarters in Paris, was created for promoting research and training and disseminating information.

Income Problems. Figures reported in 1969 revealed that the median income of older couples increased from $3,928 in 1967 to $4,592 in 1968 and for older unattached individuals from $1,480 to $1,734, largely as a result of increased Social Security benefits awarded early in 1968. Before the end of 1969, however, inflation had eroded much of the increases; the median income of older families had fallen to less than one half that of younger families; and 20 percent of the older population was still below the poverty level.

Taking note of these circumstances, President Nixon proposed legislation for a 10 percent increase in Social Security benefits for retired workers, widows' benefits equal to those of primary beneficiaries, an increase in the amount of earnings permitted without a benefit loss, and an automatic cost-of-living escalator. Increased costs would be covered by raising the Social Security tax base from the first $7,800 to the first $9,000 of earnings, and by increased revenue from growth in general economic activity. The Congress enacted legislation providing for a 15 percent increase, effective Jan. 1, 1970. President Nixon signed the bill.

Strongly supported by a study revealing that the majority of present and retired federal workers are in favor of it, the U. S. Civil Service Commission undertook a program to encourage all federal agencies to provide retirement preparation for their employees.

Rising Medical Costs. Continued rise in medical service charges (27 percent since the inception of Medicare-Medicaid in July 1966) forced retrenchment of services in some states. Effective Jan. 1, 1970, Medicare required the older patient to bear the first $52 instead of the first $44 of hospital charges. The $4 per month in the premium payment for supplementary insurance under Medicare's Plan B will be raised to $5.30 per month on July 1, 1970. The secretary of HEW announced that measures would be proposed for holding service charges and expenditures within reasonable limits.

Growth of Older Population. The older population maintained its annual net increase of approximately 300,000 during 1969. Its rate of increase, for many years half again as great as that for the total population, appeared to have leveled off at the rate for total population, about 2 percent per year. Thus persons 65 and over will continue to account for about 10 percent of the population, and the present ratio of one older person for five and one-half persons in the 20–64 year working ages will be sustained.

CLARK TIBBITTS
Administration on Aging
U. S. Department of Health, Education and Welfare

MORLEY BAER

TASTEFUL architecture and pleasing distances mark this retirement home—Carmel Valley Manor, Carmel Valley, Calif. It was designed by Skidmore, Owings & Merrill.

ONTARIO

During 1969, Ontario took the lead among Canadian provinces in adopting strict air pollution curbs and in banning the general use of the insecticide DDT. Other forward-looking measures included the appointment of a special commission to make a 2-year study of all areas of the provincial government and the signing of two pacts with neighboring Quebec—one for the purchase of hydroelectric power and another for an educational and cultural exchange. See also OTTAWA; TORONTO.

Legislation. The budget presented to the legislature on March 4 forecast revenues of $2,998,400,-000 for the fiscal year 1969–70 and expenditures of $2,996,500,000. This forecast would have given Ontario its second surplus in 16 years, but on December 1, Premier John P. Robarts announced supplementary estimates of about $55 million for expenditures that had been unforseen earlier. Tax changes included increases in cigarette and liquor taxes and in the tax on mining profits.

Under legislation approved in June, Ontario entered the federal medical care insurance plan, effective October 1. About 350 members of the Ontario Tenants Association marched on the legislature on October 4, demanding the adoption of measures recommended in a 1968 interim report of the Ontario Law Reform Committee. These included the aboli-

--------- **ONTARIO · Information Highlights** ---------

Area: 412,582 square miles (1,068,589 sq km).
Population: 7,392,000 (Jan. 1, 1969 est.).
Chief Cities (1966 census): Toronto, the provincial capital (1969 est., 689,304); Hamilton (298,121); Ottawa, the federal capital (1968 est., 299,466); London (194,416); Windsor (192,544).
Government: *Chief Officers*—lt. gov., W. Ross MacDonald; premier, John P. Robarts (Progressive Conservative); prov. secy., Robert S. Welch (PC); min. of justice and atty. gen., Arthur A. Wishart (PC); prov. treas., Charles S. MacNaughton (PC); min. of educ., William G. Davis (PC); chief justice, G. A. Gale. *Legislature*—House of Assembly, 117 members (standings as of Sept. 30, 1969—68 Progressive Conservative, 27 Liberal, 21 New Democratic Party, 1 Independent).
Education: *School enrollment* (1966–67 est.)—public elementary and secondary, 1,800,897 pupils (71,889 teachers); private schools, 46,072 pupils (3,240 teachers); Indian (federal) schools, 6,495 pupils (277 teachers); college and university (fall 1966), 68,589 students. *Public school expenditures* (1963)—$697,707,000 ($496 per pupil); median teacher's salary (est.) $5,732.
Public Finance (fiscal year 1968–69 est.): *Revenues*, $2,821,-450,000 (sales tax, $928,030,000; income tax, $930,003,000; federal funds, $143,393,000). *Expenditures*, $3,101,690,000 (education, $1,162,190,000; health and social welfare, $734,270,000; transport and communications, $455,080,000).
Personal Income (1967 est.): $18,758,000,000; *average annual income per person*, $2,624.
Social Welfare (fiscal year 1968–69 est.): $123,380,000 (aged and blind, $29,840,000; dependents and unemployed, $38,220,000).
Manufacturing (1966): *Value added by manufacture*, $8,648,-180,000 (transportation equipment, $1,188,482,000; food and beverages, $1,059,079,000; primary metals, $849,488,-000; fabricated metals, $820,672,000; electrical machinery, $761,099,000; chemicals and chemical products, $668,898,-000).
Agriculture (1968 est.): *Cash farm income*, $1,327,247,000 (livestock, $916,298,000; crops, $370,042,000). *Chief crops (cash receipts)*—Tobacco, $136,365,000 (ranks 1st among the provinces); vegetables, $63,078,000 (ranks 1st); fruits, $35,330,000 (ranks 1st); corn, $26,158,000 (ranks 1st); wheat, $22,710,000 (ranks 4th); soybeans, $22,363,000 (ranks 1st).
Mining (1967 est.): *Production value*, $992,788,746. *Chief minerals* (tons)—sand and gravel, 98,760,000 (ranks 1st among the provinces); copper, 269,855 (ranks 1st); nickel, 190,684 (ranks 1st); gold, 1,492,620 troy ounces (ranks 1st).
Transportation (1966): *Roads*, 88,448 miles (142,339 km); *motor vehicles*, 2,643,474; *railroads*, 9,965 track miles (16,036 km); *licensed airports*, 82.
Communications: *Telephones* (1966), 3,099,574; *television stations* (1967), 19; *radio stations* (1967), 78; *daily newspapers* (1966), 50 (daily circulation, 1,843,127).
(All figures given in Canadian dollars equal to U. S. 93¢)

tion of security deposits, the right of collective bargaining, and rent controls. A landlord-tenant bill, incorporating most of the desired measures except rent control, was presented to the legislature late in November.

Atty. Gen. Arthur A. Wishart became Ontario's first minister of justice under a bill of March 26, which changed the name of the attorney general's department to the department of justice. Wishart assumed the dual title of minister of justice and attorney general. In November, Premier Robarts announced increases in legislators' salaries to $18,000 from $12,000 annually. Cabinet members received increases to $34,000–$35,000 (depending on their portfolios) from $25,000–$26,000; and the premier, an increase to $40,000 from $30,000.

Pollution Control and DDT Ban. Stringent regulations governing air pollution from highway vehicles, iron foundries, and oil refineries and water pollution from the dumping of human waste from pleasure craft went into effect in Ontario in July. Regulations controlling pollution from other kinds of industrial plants were to be announced later.

A ban on the general use in Ontario of the insecticide DDT was announced by Thomas Wells, minister of health, on September 24, to become effective on Jan. 1, 1970. Use of the controversial product will be allowed only in a few special cases, such as by licensed exterminators for the control of bats and in certain kinds of plant bug infestations. No vendor will be allowed to sell DDT in the province without a permit from the health department.

Ontario-Quebec Pacts. The Hydro-Electric Power Commission of Ontario announced in May plans to purchase $95.5 million worth of power from the Quebec Hydro-Electric Commission during the 1970's. It was anticipated that the power-purchase agreement would lead to negotiation of a pact providing for mutual assistance in emergencies.

On June 4, the premiers of Ontario and Quebec signed an agreement for an educational and cultural exchange between the two provinces. The agreement will be implemented by a body known as the Permanent Commission for Ontario and Quebec Cooperation. Each government will name at least five representatives to the commission and will allocate a minimum of $150,000 annually to the project.

Labor Problems. A work stoppage that began on July 10 at Ontario mines of the International Nickel Co. of Canada Ltd. resulted in worldwide shortages of nickel before wage and benefit disputes were settled on November 14. Workers at the Hamilton plant of the Steel Co. of Canada Ltd., along with workers in the company's fabricating plants elsewhere in Ontario and in Quebec, were on strike from August 1 to October 19.

Higher Education. The appointment of Lester B. Pearson, a former prime minister of Canada, as chancellor of Carleton University, in Ottawa, was announced on January 16. He succeeded Dr. C. J. Mackenzie, who retired.

A degree course in Indian studies, the first such course in Canada, was started in the autumn at Trent University, Peterborough. On September 19 the Committee of Presidents of Universities of Ontario announced that students found guilty of violence or obstruction on provincially assisted university campuses would be subject to expulsion. The decision was part of a working paper on campus order formulated by the university presidents at a meeting on September 16.

OREGON

The 1969 session of the Oregon legislature, the shortest in recent years, was relatively harmonious and productive. Major steps were taken toward governmental reorganization, and toward the redirection of the corrections program. An attempt to reduce property taxes by means of a state sales tax was overwhelmingly defeated by the voters.

Governmental Reorganization. The most dramatic change in executive reorganization was the elimination of the board of control, composed of the governor, secretary of state, and state treasurer, which had supervised state institutions since 1913. These institutions have been placed under division heads who are responsible to the governor. This change, together with the transfer of other duties from the secretary of state and treasurer, is expected to reduce the political influence of these offices.

Three new departments were created. The department of transportation unites several existing agencies and has new administrative divisions for ports and mass transit. The department of revenue combines separate tax authorities under a single director. The executive department, under the governor's executive assistant, coordinates such functions as finance and economic planning.

Taxes. On June 3, Oregon voters rejected by an 8 to 1 margin a proposed constitutional amendment providing for a 3% sales tax. The measure, which exempted food, drugs, and farm supplies, would also have updated the tax bases of all school districts. Proceeds from the tax, estimated to yield $100 million annually, would have been applied to property tax relief. Rising property taxes had led to recurring defeats of school budgets. Opponents of the measure contended, however, that the primary beneficiaries would be owners of farms and businesses rather than homeowners, and that the proposal did not adequately meet the problems of the schools.

Corrections. Creation of a new full-time parole board, which is expected to permit the release of more men on parole, is part of the state correction system's new emphasis on rehabilitation rather than on custody. More attention is to be paid to education and job training, and provision has been made for the expansion of a work release program.

Court Decision. On April 16, 1969, the Oregon supreme court unanimously overturned a circuit court action in December 1968, which had denied office to the duly elected candidate for attorney general, Republican Lee Johnson. The lower court claimed that Johnson had violated the Corrupt Practices Act, and had allowed incumbent Robert Y. Thornton to retain the office. The supreme court held that Johnson's overspending of personal funds was not a deliberate or material violation, and that his filing of an erroneous expense report was not willful or relevant to the outcome of the election.

Pollution. During the summer of 1969, air pollution caused by agricultural field burning became acute in the Willamette Valley, especially in the area of Eugene. Protests to Gov. Tom McCall prompted him to suspend field-burning for seven days in early August, and to initiate new burning controls. Research was directed toward finding alternate solutions to such pollution problems.

SAMUEL K. ANDERSON
Oregon College of Education

ORGANIZATIONS, American. See SOCIETIES AND ORGANIZATIONS.

ORTHODOX CHURCHES. See RELIGION—*Eastern Orthodoxy.*

OTTAWA

Ottawa is Canada's national capital and fourth-largest metropolitan area (1968 est. pop.: city, 299,466; met. area, 518,000). On Jan. 1, 1969, a new form of regional municipal government encompassing the city of Ottawa, Vanier City (formerly Eastview), and the townships and villages of Carleton County became operative as Ottawa-Carleton.

Government. Dennis Coolican, appointed in 1968, continued in 1969 as chairman of the Regional Council, which consists of 31 members appointed by the local councils of the region. Representing Ottawa on the Council are the mayor (Kenneth Fogarty, who was elected to a 3-year term in December 1969; the incumbent, Donald B. Reid, did not seek reelection), the four members of the Board of Control, and those aldermen who headed the poll in each of the city's 11 wards.

Ottawa-Carleton has responsibility for assessment, water supply, sewage, regional roads, public health and welfare, capital financing, and planning throughout the regional area. Local councils have retained their powers over and responsibilities for local services. In the city itself and the suburban parts of the region a broad extension of the regional government's powers is being advocated with a cor-

---

————— OREGON • Information Highlights —————

Area: 96,981 square miles (251,181 sq km).
Population: 2,043,000 (1969 est.).
Chief Cities (1969 est.): Salem, the capital, 68,000; Portland, 375,000; Eugene, 78,000; Corvallis, 30,500.
Government: *Chief Officers*—governor, Tom McCall (Republican); secy. of state, Clay Myers (R); atty. gen., Lee Johnson (R); treas., Robert W. Straub; supt. of pub. instr., Dale Parnell; chief justice, William C. Perry. *Legislature*—Senate, 30 members (16 Democrats, 14 Republicans); House of Representatives, 60 members (38 R, 22 D).
Education: *School enrollment* (1968)—public elementary, 278,000 pupils (12,800 teachers); public secondary, 194,000 pupils (10,300 teachers); nonpublic schools, 33,600 pupils (1,520 teachers); college and university (fall 1967), 90,305 students. *Public school expenditures* (1967–68)—$344,000,000 ($794 per pupil).
Public Finance (fiscal year 1968–69): *Revenues,* $1,999,245,003 (motor fuel tax, $124,231,577; federal funds, $455,987,342). *Expenditures,* $1,760,443,836 (education, $538,657,825; health, welfare, and safety, $180,837,193; highways, $264,415,228). *State debt,* $540,928,000 (Nov. 10, 1968).
Personal Income (1968): $6,660,000,000; *average annual income per person,* $3,317.
Public Assistance (fiscal year 1968): $39,463,619 to 76,736 recipients (aged, $6,047,247; dependent children, $22,223,063).
Labor Force (employed persons, 1968): *Agricultural,* 57,500; *nonagricultural* (wage and salary earners), 782,900 (22% manufacturing, 19.3% trade, 17.3% government). *Unemployed persons* (1968)—38,600.
Manufacturing (1966): *Value added by manufacture,* $1,992,308,000 (transportation equipment, $102,520,000; nonelectrical machinery, $102,526,000; electrical machinery, $97,546,000; fabricated metals, $67,280,000; food and products, $281,411,000).
Agriculture (1967): *Cash farm income,* $546,270,000 (livestock, $229,077,000; crops, $294,566,000; govt. payments, $22,627,000). *Chief crops* (tons)—Pears, 151,000 (ranks 1st among the states); hay, 2,325,000.
Mining (1967): *Production value* (1968), $64,449,000. *Chief minerals* (tons)—Stone, 21,000,000; sand and gravel, 20,000,000; pumice, 660,000.
Fisheries (1968): *Commercial catch* (1967), 89,000,000 pounds ($15,300,000). *Leading species*—Tuna, 37,751,599 pounds ($7,556,320); shellfish, 22,969,181 pounds ($3,320,157); bottomfish, 22,402,709 pounds ($1,400,000); salmon, 9,990,626 pounds ($4,045,697).
Transportation: *Roads* (1969), 90,810 miles (146,141 km); *motor vehicles* (1969), 1,378,715; *railroads* (1969), 4,998 track miles (8,045 km); *airports* (1969), 13.
Communications (1969): *Telephones,* 1,075,600; *television stations,* 14; *radio stations,* 115; *newspapers,* 21.

CROMBIE MCNEILL FROM THE CANADIAN CONSULATE

NATIONAL ARTS CENTRE (*above*) in Ottawa was built at cost of $44 million.

OPERA HOUSE-concert hall in Ottawa's arts complex seats 2,300.

NATIONAL FILM BOARD

$56,542,333 is to be raised by taxation and $95,755,394 by provincial and federal government grants, fees, and miscellaneous sources.

The regional municipality of Ottawa-Carleton estimated an expenditure of $34,319,000 in 1969, of which $13,320,000 is to be financed by levies on the regional municipalities (the city of Ottawa's portion approximating $10,000,000) and the balance largely by provincial grants and water sales.

Education. A new area school board responsible for public elementary and high schools in Ottawa, Vanier, and Rockcliffe becomes effective in 1970; a similar board for the remainder of the region is already operative.

School enrollment for 1969 was: in Ottawa, public primary schools, 25,994; Roman Catholic primary schools, 27,437 (14,149 in the English-speaking section, 13,288 in the French); and collegiate high schools, 24,099; in the remainder of the region, public schools, 27,901 (20,058 in primary and 7,843 in high schools) and separate schools, 10,005 (5,513 in English and 4,492 in French).

The Arts. The National Arts Centre was opened in 1969. Built by the federal government at a cost of over $44 million to mark the 1967 Centennial of Confederation, it contains an opera house, a theater, a studio (for experimental theater and chamber works), and various restaurants and stores. It has a resident orchestra and two theater companies, one playing in French, the other in English.

PETER J. KING
Carleton University

responding reduction in the authority and size of the local councils. The ultimate amalgamation of all area governmental bodies into one single-tier government is being urged. Municipal candidates supporting such policies won impressive victories in the 1969 elections.

Municipal Budget. Total estimated expenditures in the city budget for 1969, including school and hospital expenditures, were $152,297,727 (an increase of about 17% over the previous year). Of the total,

TWO PRESIDENTS—Richard M. Nixon of the United States and Nguyen Van Thieu of South Vietnam—review troops in June 8 conference at Midway Island.

PACIFIC ISLANDS

Representatives of Pacific island territories and member nations of the South Pacific Commission attended an annual South Pacific Conference at the commission headquarters in Noumea, New Caledonia, on October 8–18, 1969, to discuss economic, social, and political problems of the islands. Prime Minister Albert R. Henry of the Cook Islands was the conference chairman. Delegates from 14 dependent territories questioned the dominance of the region by Western powers.

Trust Territory of the Pacific Islands. At ceremonies on Saipan in May, U. S. Secretary of the Interior Walter J. Hickel installed Edward J. Johnston, a Honolulu insurance executive, as high commissioner of the Trust Territory of the Pacific Islands. Johnston replaced William R. Norwood, who had served as high commissioner since 1966. During his visit to the territory, Secretary Hickel pledged accelerated economic development and increased participation by Micronesians in local government.

Eleven Bikinians assisted engineers in 1969 in the first phase of operations to restore the habitability of Bikini Atoll in the northwestern Marshall Islands. Under the direction of the U. S. Atomic Support Agency they removed debris left by nuclear tests from 1946 to 1958 and cleared tropical growth to provide crop land. Some of the structures once used in connection with nuclear testing are being converted to community facilities. A landing strip on Enyu Island will accommodate propeller aircraft. Tropical crops and fish from Bikini lagoon are expected to meet local needs for food by 1972, when many of the Bikini people will have returned from present homes on Kili in the southern Marshalls.

British Solomon Islands. Sir Michael Gass became British high commissioner of the Western Pacific at the end of 1968. Western Pacific Commission headquarters are at Honiara on Guadalcanal, in the British Solomon Islands Protectorate.

Construction begun on Henderson Field near Honiara in 1968 has resulted in a resurfaced and extended runway accommodating large propeller aircraft. The site was a strategic airfield in the decisive battle of Guadalcanal in World War II.

Fiji. Sir Derek Jakeway, retiring governor of Fiji, departed from Suva in November 1968 to return to Britain. The new governor of the British crown colony is Sir Robert Foster, former high commissioner of the Western Pacific, who arrived at the end of 1968 from Honiara.

The Fijian government reported a decline in the birth rate from 40 per 1,000 in 1962 to 30 per 1,000 during the 2-year period ending in 1968. The medical department and the Family Planning Association have set 25 per 1,000 as a target for 1980. Even if the birth rate continues to decline, Fiji's population of 512,000 is expected to double in about 35 years.

A fiberglass factory, which began operations at Walu Bay, Suva, will manufacture fishing boats,

PACIFIC ISLANDS OF THE UNITED STATES

Island or Group	Area (sq mi)	(km)	Population (mid-1968 est.)	Capital (1960 census)
American Samoa[1].	76	197	31,000	Pago Pago (1,251)
Baker[2].	1	2.59	. . .	. . .
Canton and Enderbury[3].	27	70	320[4]	. . .
Guam[1].	212	549	100,000	Agana (1,642)
Howland[2].	0.6	1.6	. . .	. . .
Jarvis[2].	2.2	5.7	. . .	. . .
Johnston and Sand Islands[5].	. . .[6]	. . .	156[4]	. . .
Kingman Reef[5]. . .	. . .[6]	. . .	. . .	. . .
Midway[5].	2	5	2,356[4]	. . .
Palmyra[2].	4	10	. . .	. . .
Ryukyu Islands[7]. .	848	2,196	965,000	Naha (266,000)
Trust Territory of the Pacific Islands (including Carolines, Marianas, Marshalls)[2]	687	1,779	96,000	Saipan (7,464)
Wake[2].	3	8	1,097[4]	. . .

[1] Unincorporated territory of the United States. [2] Administered by U. S. Department of the Interior. [3] Jointly administered by United Kingdom and United States. [4] 1960 census. [5] Under U. S. Navy control. [6] Less than 0.5 square miles. [7] Administered under military government by United States.

food containers, storage tanks, and floor coverings. The new industry was developed as a partnership between a Fijian company and a New Zealand fiberglass molding firm.

Australian investments in Fiji during 1969 will provide for development of a logging operation on Vanua Levu and exports of high-grade manganese ore from a mine near Lautoka on Viti Levu.

Tonga. During 1969, continued progress was made toward independence for the kingdom of Tonga. This was marked by the establishment of a Tongan consulate in London in September. Complete independence may come as early as 1970.

The Tongan government announced in April a change of policy regarding foreign investments and called for outside capital to initiate a wide range of new businesses and industries. Laws and regulations are to be revised to encourage economic development by foreign companies.

Cook Islands. Rarotonga, which normally has heavy rains and floods during the November to April hurricane season, experienced drought and high temperatures in early 1969. Water for agricultural use was prohibited, and domestic use was restricted.

French Polynesia. Pierre Angeli, former director of the French Department of Overseas Departments and Overseas Territories, arrived in Tahiti on March 11 to assume duties as governor of French Polynesia. Jean Sicurani, governor for the previous four years, left in January to become president of the National Assembly of France.

American Samoa. John M. Haydon, former president of the Seattle Port Commission, became the 46th governor of American Samoa on August 1. He was appointed by President Nixon to succeed Owen Aspinall, who had held the post for two years.

Guam. Dr. Carlos Camacho, a Guamanian dentist, was appointed governor of Guam by President Nixon in June. Beginning in 1971, governors of Guam will be elected by popular vote.

Spending by tourists in Guam during 1969 was more than double that of 1968, lessening the island's dependence on government and military spending. Japanese visitors accounted for a large share of the growth, and Japanese investors have led in the development of new tourist facilities.

Papua and New Guinea. More than 1,000 athletes from 12 Pacific island territories competed in the Third South Pacific Games at Port Moresby, New Guinea, August 13–23. The large teams from New Caledonia, Papua-New Guinea, and Fiji led in number of medals won, but a 13-member Tongan team took a total of 12 medals. The Fourth South Pacific Games will be held at Papeete, Tahiti, in 1971, a year earlier than usual to avoid conflict with the 1972 Olympics in Munich, West Germany.

HOWARD J. CRITCHFIELD
Western Washington State College

PAINTING AND SCULPTURE. See ART.

PAKISTAN

The 11-year regime of Field Marshal Mohammed Ayub Khan fell in March 1969 following months of rioting and unrest. Ayub was replaced as chief of state by Gen. Agha Mohammed Yahya Khan, commander in chief of the army. By year's end Yahya, too, had endured political disturbances. He promised a new constitution, elections, and more representation for East Pakistan.

Pakistan continued to be friendly with the Communist countries, especially mainland China, but its attitude toward the United States improved. However, enmity toward India remained the rule. Pakistan's economy developed steadily during 1969, and West Pakistan achieved self-sufficiency in grains.

Fall of Ayub Khan. A chapter in Pakistani history closed in 1969 with the fall of Ayub Khan. The previous year had ended with a number of opposition leaders in jail and others challenging Ayub to hold elections. Rioting in the major cities, which had begun in October 1968, claimed more than 20 lives in one week in January 1969 alone.

Ayub responded with concessions and with increased security measures. In February he reiterated his promise for 1970 presidential elections and exempted himself as a candidate. Ayub then met with opposition leaders (some of whom he had just released from jail) and announced that agreement had been reached over Pakistan's future. Yet violence persisted. The situation was particularly acute in East Pakistan, where government control broke down completely. In March the army was called in to quell rioting in Karachi.

Finally, on March 25, Ayub dissolved the national and provincial assemblies, established martial law, and announced his resignation. He named as martial law administrator—in effect strong man of Pakistan—Agha Mohammed Yahya Khan, the army commander in chief. Six days later General Yahya announced his assumption of the presidency as of March 25. The country was to be run by a man who was Ayub's protégé in the army and who, like Ayub, is a West Pakistani and a Pathan.

The New Regime. At first the country returned to a restive calm. Although the army was in control opposition leaders were permitted to continue polit-

---

PAKISTAN · Information Highlights

Area: 365,542 square miles (946,716 sq km).
Population: 109,520,000 (1968 est.).
Chief Cities (1967 census): Islamabad, the capital (under construction; population not available); Karachi, 2,721,000; Lahore, 1,674,100; Dacca, 740,600.
Government: *President*—Gen. Agha Mohammed Yahya Khan (took office March 25, 1969); *Parliament*—suspended under temporary martial law.
Religious Faiths: Muslims, 88% of population; Hindus, 11%.
Education: *Literacy rate* (1969), 20% of population. *Total school enrollment* (1965)—9,600,090 (primary, 6,813,622; secondary, 2,484,743; teacher-training, 15,989; technical/vocational, 20,148; university/higher, 265,588).
Finance (1969 est.): *Revenues*, $1,990,000,000; *expenditures*, $916,000,000; *monetary unit*, rupee (4.787 rupees equal U. S.$1).
Gross National Product (1968): $14,550,000,000.
National Income (1968): $13,181,533,000; *average annual income per person*, $120.
Economic Indexes: *Industrial production* (1968), 150 (1963=100); *agricultural production* (1967), 109 (1963=100); *cost of living* (1967), 126 (1963=100).
Manufacturing (metric tons, 1967): Cement, 2,038,000; residual fuel oil, 1,492,000; sugar, 555,000.
Crops (metric tons, 1967–68 crop year): Jute, 1,264,000 (ranks 1st among world producers); chick peas, 578,000 (world rank, 2d); rice, 19,005,000.
Minerals (metric tons, 1967): Coal, 1,400,000; salt, 696,000; chromium ore, 12,900.
Foreign Trade (1968): *Exports*, $720,000,000 (chief exports, 1967: jute, $179,000,000; cotton, $73,114,000; nonelectrical machinery, $34,000,000; cereals and preparations, $33,-600,000); *imports*, $996,000,000 (chief imports, 1967: nonelectrical machinery, $228,932,000; unmilled wheat and meslin, $146,187,000; iron and steel, $110,779,000). *Chief trading partners* (1967): United States (took 13% of exports, supplied 33% of imports); Britain (took 13% of exports, supplied 13% of imports); Japan.
Transportation: *Roads* (1966), 25,600 miles (41,198 km); *motor vehicles* (1966), 169,200 (automobiles 113,200); *railways* (1965), 7,039 miles (11,328 km); *merchant vessels* (1967), 61 (467,000 gross registered tons); *national airline*, Pakistan International Airlines.
Communications: *Telephones* (1968): 162,642; *television stations* (1968), 3; *television sets* (1968), 30,000; *radios* (1966), 1,014,000; *newspapers* (1965), 95.

ical activity. In July, Yahya pledged the ultimate return to democracy and established the machinery for creating a new constitution and holding elections "in a year or 18 months." In August he appointed civilian ministers to all posts except those for planning, defense, and foreign affairs.

The opposition was not placated, however. Student demonstrations and labor unrest prevailed. Zulfikar Ali Bhutto, a former foreign minister, had earlier called for a breakup of West Pakistan into its former provinces and a federal system for East and West Pakistan, and Sheik Mujibur Rahman, leader of the Awami league, continued to demand autonomy for East Pakistan.

By the end of 1969, President Yahya had virtually accepted both of these demands. He also promised broad-scale political reforms. Elections for a national assembly were scheduled for Oct. 5, 1970, on the basis of a "provisional legal framework," and the assembly was to be charged with drawing up a permanent constitution. Yahya indicated his own intention to retire from political life.

Other Domestic Affairs. During 1969, Pakistan's last autonomous principality, Swat, in the northwest, was being absorbed into the regular governmental system. In November, Maj. Gen. Iskander Mirza, Pakistan's first president, died at the age of 70.

Economy. Economically, Pakistan remained on a course of solid achievement. Growth of gross national product was down somewhat from the steady 6% rate of previous years, but social and welfare services were increased out of funds that had previously gone for development. The most remarkable achievement was the attainment by West Pakistan of self-sufficiency in food grains. This was announced in May, and in the same month the United Nations gave "high marks" for Pakistan's birth control program. Although the goal of the program, to reduce births by 6 million over the period 1965–70, is not likely to be attained, efforts were considered "well organized and imaginatively promoted."

East Pakistan remains underdeveloped compared with West Pakistan—adding to the political tensions of the nation. Although the current budget calls for 53% of developmental spending to be in the eastern sector, the East Pakistanis complain that it is too little. The usual floods and tornadoes in East Pakistan destroyed many lives and property during 1969.

Relations with India. Sullen, but quiet, animosity characterized Indian-Pakistani relations during 1969. None of the big issues between the two

RELEASED after house arrest, Zulfikar Ali Bhutto, opponent of Ayub Khan, symbolically "breaks chains."

nations was settled, and Pakistan declined negotiation on most small issues in order to exert pressure for action on the larger ones. In July, Pakistan refused to normalize its non-existent trade with India and to resume air traffic. Virtually the only agreement between the two countries during the year was the delineation of their border in the Rann of Kutch, over which they had fought in 1965.

Relations with Other Nations. U. S. President Richard M. Nixon visited Pakistan briefly in August and discerned a friendlier feeling toward the United States, reflecting Pakistani approval of some features of current U. S. policy. In late 1969 the United States was reconsidering its ban on military equipment to India and Pakistan.

Pakistan maintained good relations with the Soviet Union and Communist China. A Chinese caravan inaugurated trade over a new road linking China with northwest Pakistan (and Pakistani Kashmir). A Pakistani delegation headed by Air Marshal Malik Nur Khan visited China in July. Partly as a gesture to the Soviet Union and China, Pakistan persuaded the United States to begin dismantling its "electronic surveillance" base at Peshawar.

CARL LEIDEN
University of Texas

WIDE WORLD

GEN. AGHA MOHAMMED YAHYA KHAN, commander in chief of the Pakistani army, became head of the government of Pakistan on March 25, 1969, and assumed the presidency amid political turmoil and popular unrest. He succeeded Mohammed Ayub Khan, who resigned as president, abrogating the constitution and instituting martial law. After restoring a measure of stability, Yahya Khan announced in November that full political activity would be restored in 1970.

Yahya Khan, a member of an aristocratic family, was born in Peshawar, British India, in 1917. He attended Punjab University and the Indian Military Academy and served in World War II. After independence in 1947 he established the Pakistani Staff College. He took part in the coup that brought Ayub Khan to power in 1958. In 1966 he became commander in chief of the army.

LYSTROSAURUS, an extinct reptile found in Antarctica, is an important clue to the movements of continents.

SKULL of *Dromaeosaurus*, a small carnivorous dinosaur recently described from Canada.

FROM "THE AGE OF REPTILES," BY E. H. COLBERT, THE NORTON CO., 1965

PALEONTOLOGY

A number of significant contributions to paleontological knowledge were made in 1969. Topics ranged from the identity of the tiny, puzzling conodonts to the Antarctic discovery of a reptilian skull that strongly supports the theory of continental drift.

Conodonts. One of the exciting paleontological discoveries of the year was the disclosure of what conodonts really are. These tiny (often less than 1/16 inch, or 1.5 mm, in length), amber-brown, serrated or toothlike structures, composed of calcium phosphate, have been found in deposits ranging from Cambrian through Cretaceous in age (600 million to 70 million years old). Conodonts have been intensively studied for many years, but their true identity remained unknown. They have been variously considered teeth, scales, or other objects originating from fishes, worms, mollusks, or other animals.

It now appears that conodonts are structures that were set in a ring of tissue at the upper end of an as yet unidentified coelenterate (a member of the phylum that includes corals, jellyfishes, and sea anemones). Collection and study of conodonts are being vigorously carried out by Robert Fields and his staff at the University of Montana.

Reptiles. In early December 1969, Dr. Edwin H. Colbert of the American Museum of Natural History, New York City, and other members of an Antarctic field team discovered part of a skull of *Lystrosaurus,* a mammal-like reptile that is known to have lived in South Africa and Asia during the Triassic period, some 225 million years ago. *Lystrosaurus,* a reptile about 3 feet (1 meter) long, is believed to have been semi-aquatic in habit.

The find is extremely significant to the theory of "continental drift." The theory states that the continents were once united—with Antarctica much closer to the equator than it is now—and then slowly moved apart to their present positions. The presence of *Lystrosaurus* in the now widely separated continents of Africa and frigid Antarctica strongly corroborates other paleontological and geological evidence of continental movement.

Colbert also joined Dale A. Russell of the National Museum, Ottawa, in publishing a detailed description of the skull, footbones, and other remains of the small carnivorous dinosaur *Dromaeosaurus,* found in late Cretaceous (about 90-million-year-old) deposits in Alberta, Canada. *Dromaeosaurus* is considered highly important because it belongs to the infraorder Deinonychosauria, which places it between the infraorders Coelurosauria (mostly small, lightly built dinosaurs) and Carnosauria (massive and powerful animals, including *Tyrannosaurus*).

AMERICAN MUSEUM OF NATURAL HISTORY

Mammals. The description of a lower jaw of *Hyracotherium* ("Eohippus," the dawn horse) from the Polecat Bench Formation of Wyoming has extended the record of horses from the Eocene (about 60 million years ago) into the Paleocene (about 65 million years ago), and consequently suggests that the Perissodactyla (horses, rhinos, tapirs, and related forms) originated earlier than assumed.

A survey by Michael R. Voorhies of the University of Georgia on the taphonomy (sequence and arrangement of fossil deposition) and population dynamics of an early Pliocene (about 10-million-year-old) vertebrate fauna in Nebraska provided a valuable model analysis for paleontologists.

W. E. SWINTON
Massey College, University of Toronto

PALME, Olof. See SWEDEN.

PANAMA

During 1969, Panama witnessed a consolidation of power in the hands of Brig. Gen. Omar Torrijos Herrera, the National Guard commander who had been a leader of the coup that deposed President Arnulfo Arias shortly after his inauguration in October 1968. In December 1969 an unsuccessful attempt by military subordinates to oust Torrijos left the strongman even more solidly entrenched.

The Aborted Coup. On December 15, while Torrijos was visiting Mexico City, his two chief aides in the Guard, Col. Ramiro Silvera and Col. Amado Sanjur, announced that Torrijos had been removed as commander, charging, in effect, that he had become the center of a personality cult. Torrijos apparently had little difficulty lining up support for a counter-coup among other elements of the National Guard. On December 16, he returned to Panama City, where he was greeted by a large, emotional crowd of loyal guardsmen and civilians. Silvera and Sanjur were jailed, and Demetrio Lakas

Bahas, a civilian supporter of Torrijos, was named to the post of president, replacing Col. José M. Pinilla, a tacit supporter of the revolt.

Political Affairs. Although the attempted takeover was the most dramatic of the year's developments, the earlier months of 1969 were not altogether calm. In February, a schism within the military hierarchy brought about a purge by Torrijos of disaffected elements, an early victim being his articulate chief-of-staff, Col. Boris Martínez. There were also a pair of cabinet crises. Five of eight civilians in the cabinet resigned in January, citing "military dictatorship" and lack of progress in returning to "institutional normality." At midyear, the new minister of justice, Modesto Justinian, was removed after a dispute having to do with the assignment of television channels.

In a sweeping "anticorruption" campaign, 200 persons were arrested and jailed early in the year. Most were released by November, when constitutional rights were restored. The University of Panama reopened in July, after being purged of hundreds of activist students and 40 professors.

Antigovernment activity was also evident near the Costa Rican border, where some 200 guerrillas sporadically engaged the counterinsurgency unit of the National Guard. Guardsmen occasionally pursued the irregulars into Costa Rica, causing uneasiness in Panama's relations with that country.

Economic Conditions. Government economists forecast a 7% rise in the gross national product (GNP) in 1969. The value of exports was rising, and zealous enforcement of tax laws was producing greater revenues. A decline in private investment was partly offset by a $45-million public works program that included projects in both urban and rural areas. The World Bank granted a $34 million loan for a 150,000-kilowatt hydroelectric project.

Some 50 companies expressed interest in the copper deposits discovered in 1968. Test borings

------------ **PANAMA · Information Highlights** ------------

Area: 29,208 square miles (75,650 sq km).
Population: 1,372,000 (1968 est.).
Chief City (1967 census): Panamá, the capital, 358,200.
Government: Military junta led by Brig. Gen. Omar Torrijos Herrera (took power Oct. 11, 1968).
Major Religious Faith: Roman Catholic, 73% of population.
Education: *Literacy rate* (1969), 78% of population. *Total school enrollment* (1966)—300,699 (primary, 210,628; secondary, 60,238; teacher-training, 1,313; technical, 21,278; higher, 7,247).
Finance (1968 est.): *Revenues,* $130,000,000; *expenditures,* $130,000,000; *public debt* (1967), $154,800,000; *monetary unit,* balboa (1 balboa equals U. S.$1).
Gross National Product (1967): $697,800,000.
National Income (1967): $581,000,000; average annual income per person, $453.
Economic Indexes (1967): *Industrial production* (1966), 123 (1963=100); *agricultural production,* 127 (1963=100); *cost of living,* 104 (1963=100).
Manufacturing (metric tons, 1967): Gasoline, 327,000; cement, 150,000; sugar, 63,000.
Crops (metric tons, 1967–68 crop year): Bananas, 600,000; rice, 151,000; coffee, 5,100.
Minerals (metric tons): Limestone and siltstone (1966), 124,696; clay and shale (1966), 40,844; salt (1967), 11,000.
Foreign Trade: *Exports* (1968 est.): $120,000,000 (chief exports, 1967: bananas, $48,620,000; petroleum products, $22,824,000); *imports* (1968 est.), $234,000,000 (chief imports, 1967: crude petroleum, $48,145,000; nonelectrical machinery, $25,710,000; transport equipment, $19,266,000). *Chief trading partner* (1967): United States (took 77% of exports, supplied 40% of imports).
Transportation: *Roads* (1964), 3,845 miles (6,188 km); *motor vehicles* (1967), 46,600 (automobiles 35,000); *merchant vessels* (1967), 585 (4,691,000 gross registered tons); *national airline,* Compañía Panameña de Auiación; *principal airport,* Panama City.
Communications: *Telephones* (1968): 57,759; *television stations* (1968), 8; *television sets* (1968), 83,000; *radios* (1965), 500,000; *newspapers* (1966), 12 (daily circulation, 101,000).

showed that copper content was suitable for commercial mining. Whether reserves were sufficiently extensive was not known.

Possible New Canal Projects. The Office of Inter-Oceanic Canal Studies studied proposals for a canal along the Chorrera-Lagarto route, just to the west of the Canal Zone. The project called for the use of conventional excavation techniques rather than for the nuclear devices so often discussed in the 1960's. Another plan called for a 100-mile (160-km) canal through Panama and Columbia to supplement the present canal. It was suggested that the earth excavated during its construction could be used in building the road that was needed to fill in the "Darien Gap" in the Inter-American Highway.

LARRY L. PIPPIN
Elbert Covell College, University of the Pacific

PANAMA CANAL AND CANAL ZONE

The Panama Canal, which crosses the Isthmus of Panama, connects the Atlantic and Pacific oceans. Its length is 51.2 miles (82.4 km) from deep water to deep water, and 42.1 miles (67.8 km) from shore to shore. It is located in a 10-mile-wide (6 km) strip of land, the Canal Zone, granted "in perpetuity" to the United States by the Republic of Panama in 1903. Including tidal water, the Canal Zone covers 647.29 square miles. By the treaty of 1900 the United States was given jurisdiction in the area in exchange for $10 million and an annuity of $250,000, later increased to $1,930,000.

Population. The 51,780 residents of the Canal Zone in 1969 consisted almost entirely of employees of the U. S. government and their families, of whom 43,474 were U. S. citizens.

Administration and Government. The Canal Zone government, with headquarters at Balboa Heights, was created by Congress. The governor of the Canal Zone, appointed by the president of the United States, is automatically president of the U. S. government-owned Panama Canal Company. The Panama Canal Company operates the canal and repays the net operating costs of the government (about $22 million annually) to the U. S. Treasury. Interest of about $12 million a year on the interest-bearing U. S. investment in the Zone (almost $332 million) must also be paid.

In addition to the annuity, an estimated $130 million annually reaches the Panamanian economy through the Panama Canal Company expenditures and spending by the U. S. armed forces and other U. S. agencies in Panama.

Education. The school system in the Canal Zone is modeled after U. S. programs, taught in English, with Spanish as a language course. The Latin American schools, for non-U. S. citizens, conducted in Spanish, are comparable to schools in Panama.

Canal Traffic. In the fiscal year ending June 30, 1969, records were set for tonnage and tolls. A total of 13,150 oceangoing commercial ships passed through the canal, carrying 101,391,132 long tons of cargo. Commercial ships paid $87,457,895.

Gaillard Cut. Work on the widening of the Gaillard Cut to a width of 500 feet (150 meters) was expected to be completed by late 1969.

Colon Free Zone. The 120-acre duty-free zone, where goods may be assembled, combined, specially packaged, or stored, handled a record $333 million worth of shipments in 1968—more shipped by air than by sea. Japan is the main user.

PARAGUAY

A weak trend toward greater democracy was reversed in 1969—Paraguay's 15th year under the rule of its strongman president, Gen. Alfredo Stroessner. Despite increasing opposition from the Roman Catholic Church, the regime grew more dictatorial.

Political Repression. In the February 1968 election, several opposition parties had been permitted to mount token campaigns. In late 1968 and early 1969, opponents of the administration, encouraged by liberalized censorship laws, began to demand the release of political prisoners and criticized the government on several points.

Stung by public criticism, the president reimposed restrictions on the news media. Opposition broadcasts were prohibited altogether. The president also asked Congress—controlled by his Colorado party— to pass a law "in defense of democracy and the political and social order." Under the law, anyone caught reading antigovernment literature could be imprisoned for up to three years. To some it appeared that the bill empowered the police to dispose quietly of anyone hostile to the regime.

As 1969 ended, the political environment was more repressive than it had been at any time in 14 years. A state of seige, in force off and on for many years, was extended into 1970 in the capital and in three other departments.

Church-State Relations. For years the Roman Catholic Church in Paraguay had been an acquiescent and passive institution. By 1969, those days seemed to be over, for the church had developed into the government's most outspoken and vehement critic.

The 12 bishops of Paraguay denounced the "defense of democracy" law as a form of the "totalitarian absolutism" repeatedly condemned by the Vatican. In May, they refused a presidential demand that four Jesuit faculty members of the Catholic University be dismissed for subversion. In October, a Jesuit broadcaster was deported to Argentina for making inflammatory statements. To protest this incident, faculty and students of the university marched, with the result that several demonstrators, including a 73-year-old Jesuit priest, were beaten. The archbishop of Asunción promptly excommunicated all of those responsible. He also suspended Sunday masses—the first time such a thing had happened in Asunción's history.

For its part, the government closed the Catholic weekly, *Communidad,* and its editor fled to Argentina. Stroessner warned the church that he would tolerate no opposition to his regime from religious institutions. As a result of the year's developments, church and state became almost totally estranged.

Inter-American Affairs. Among the most prominent of foreign dignitaries to visit Paraguay in 1969 was Gov. Nelson Rockefeller of New York, who was conducting a fact-finding mission for President Nixon. His meeting with President Stroessner in June was cordial. Protests were held to a minimum, although one U. S. flag was burned by students.

Relations with neighboring states were placid. Economic disputes between Paraguay and Argentina, relating especially to Paraguay's restrictions on the export of its lumber to Argentina and Argentine import restrictions on Paraguayan citrus fruit, were being negotiated in 1969.

Economic Conditions. The political stability enforced by Stroessner over a 15-year period had encouraged foreign capital and loans for Paraguayan domestic development. As a result, a heavy debt service was plaguing the government. In addition, Paraguay expected to end 1969 with a trade deficit. The meat-packing industry, long a major source of earnings, was in recession throughout the year, but this condition was partially offset by a rise in exports of cotton, coffee, and tobacco.

Tourism, which had taken its place beside meat and lumber as a major producer of foreign exchange, also brought in sizeable sums. More than 100,000 persons visited Paraguay in 1969, straining existing facilities to the limit. The government was pressing forward with a major construction plan for motels, hotels, and swimming pools, and the Asunción airport was being expanded to accommodate large jet planes.

With the government encouraging wheat production to reduce expensive wheat imports from Argentina, a harvest of 50,000 tons—half of Paraguay's needs—was anticipated from the 1969 crop. A new state cement factory was expected in the near future to begin producing 100,000 tons of cement per year.

LEO B. LOTT
University of Montana

Area: 157,047 square miles (406,752 sq km).
Population: 2,231,000 (1968 est.).
Chief Cities (1962 census): Asunción, the capital, 305,160; Encarnación, 18,504.
Government: *President*—Gen. Alfredo Stroessner (took office in 1954). *Congress*—Senate, 30 members (party seating, 1969: Colorado party, 20; others, 10); Chamber of Deputies, 60 members (party seating, 1969: Colorado party, 40; others, 20).
Religious Faiths: Roman Catholics, 92% of population.
Education: *Literacy rate* (1969), 68% of population. *Total school enrollment* (1964–65), 397,253 (primary, 356,728;

secondary, 30,404; teacher-training, 3,285; technical, 3,054; higher, 3,782).
Finance (1968 est.): *Revenues,* $58,900,000; *expenditures,* $60,500,000; *monetary unit,* guaraní (126 guaraníes equal U. S.$1).
Gross National Product (1968): $519,047,619.
National Income (1968): $434,920,634; average annual income per person, $194.
Economic Indexes (1967): *Manufacturing production,* 124 (1963=100); *agricultural production,* 137 (1963=100); *cost of living,* 108 (1963=100).
Manufacturing (metric tons, 1967): wheat flour, 61,000; sugar, 39,000; cotton yarn (1965), 14,300; cement, 14,000.
Crops (metric tons, 1967–68 crop year): Cassava, 1,460,000; bananas, 259,000; citrus fruits (1966), 236,000; maize, 225,000; sweet potatoes, 90,000; dry beans, 23,000; peanuts, 21,000.
Minerals (metric tons, 1966): Limestone, 67,000.
Foreign Trade (1968): *Exports,* $48,000,000 (chief exports, 1967: meat, $17,170,000; wood, $7,700,000; tobacco, $3,370,000; tung oil, $2,930,000); *imports,* $62,000,000 (chief imports, 1967: machinery, $12,570,000; iron and steel products, $5,910,000; wheat and preparations, $5,620,000). *Chief trading partners* (1967): Argentina (took 24% of exports, supplied 20% of imports); United States (took 25% of exports, supplied 18% of imports); Britain (took 16% of exports, supplied 5% of imports).
Transportation: *Roads* (1964), 7,786 miles (12,530 km); *motor vehicles* (1967), 12,900 (automobiles 6,400); *railways* (1969), 808 miles (1,300 km); *principal airport,* Asunción.
Communications: *Telephones* (1968): 16,048; *radios* (1964), 160,000; *newspapers* (1966), 8.

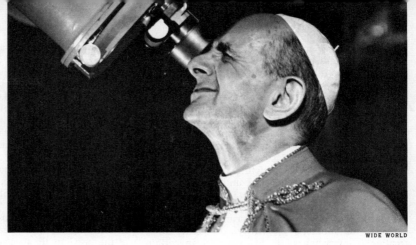

POPE Paul views through telescope the Apollo 11 landing site on the moon. The pontiff hailed the feat by saying it "spreads to the heavens the wise dominion and courage of man."

PAUL VI, Pope

During the year 1969, Pope Paul VI continued his policy of being a "traveling pope."

He also maintained his views regarding birth control and celibacy, despite widespread criticism of his stands both from Catholics and others. His approach on these and other issues may be considered critical and cautionary rather than "progressive."

Papal Travels. The pope's trip to Kampala, Uganda (July 31–August 2), was perhaps the first visit ever of a Roman pontiff to the African continent. There he met civil and ecclesiastical African leaders. The pope stressed the fact that Christianity is not a European thing, urging "indigenization"— the use of native clergy and adaptation to local culture.

The pope's other important trip in 1969 was to Geneva (June 10) on the occasion of the International Labor Organization's anniversary. There he addressed the ILO and used the opportunity to visit leaders of the World Council of Churches.

Synod of Bishops. The major event of the year in the pope's life was the Roman Synod (October 11–28). Despite the pessimism of many who felt that nothing would be accomplished in the meeting of leading bishops, the synod proved more active and satisfactory than had been anticipated. For one thing, instead of remaining at a distance from the bishops, Pope Paul personally attended most of the sessions. This was of considerable symbolic significance, indicating that while head of the bishops he recognized that he was within their body.

This development is very much a consequence of a new stress at Vatican Council II, where the bishops were quite concerned with the principle of "collegiality"—the corporate responsibility of pope and bishops together, in a "college."

Internationalization of the Curia. During 1969, the pope did a great deal toward internationalizing the Curia. For a long time, most of the important posts at the Vatican had been held by Italians. Following Vatican Council II, widespread dislike was expressed of this practice. In 1969 more non-Italians were put into high positions, and at the end of the year they outnumbered the Italians, although most of the lesser functionaries continued to be Italian.

New Cardinals. Pope Paul created 33 new cardinals in April. They included four U. S. prelates (Archbishop Terence J. Cooke of New York; Archbishop John E. Dearden of Detroit; Archbishop John J. Carberry of St. Louis; and Bishop John J. Wright of Pittsburgh).

Liturgical Changes. On another matter, Pope Paul made several gestures in a "liberal direction" —the further changes in the church's official worship, or liturgy. For the first time in centuries a revised Mass structure was presented to the Catholic world by Rome, after considerable research and planning by liturgical experts. Other important changes authorized by Vatican Council II had to do with revised funeral ceremonies and the rites of several sacraments. The changes met with a certain amount of resistance on the part of conservative Catholics. Pope Paul made some gestures of conciliation toward these conservatives, by allowing use of the new rites to be postponed briefly.

C. J. McNaspy, S. J.
Associate Editor, "America" Magazine

PEDIATRICS

The field of pediatrics saw a number of scientific advances during 1969. There was also an increased awareness of the inadequacy of medical care provided many children in the United States, and new experimental programs were designed to correct some of the inequities in child health care.

U. S. Infant Mortality. The U. S. infant mortality rate of about 26 deaths before the age of 1 for every 1,000 infants born is still much higher than that of most European countries and twice that of Sweden. In addition, some Southern states have a non-white infant mortality rate more than twice the national average. Comparable non-white mortality rates were found to exist in northern urban slum areas.

Improving Medical Care. During 1969, many pediatricians were active in establishing a number of programs to provide medical care to the rural and urban poor. Pilot projects staffed by university pediatrics departments were initiated in many Southern states as well as in Northern urban slums. The initial results of these Neighborhood Health centers were encouraging.

It has become apparent that the demand for pediatric care will continue to exceed the supply of available physicians, and several university pediatrics departments are currently training nurses and other pediatric assistants to supplement the efforts of the physician. As pediatric assistants graduate from these programs, they will assume the responsibility for child health care in many regions, referring to physicians only those children needing expert medical consultation. Initial studies indicate that pediatric assistants can provide satisfactory health care for 75% of the children currently being treated by pediatricians. It is likely that during the next decade these health workers will provide medical care to large numbers of children for whom health care would not otherwise be available.

Diagnosing Hereditary Diseases. There is a large group of inherited diseases characterized by metabolic or enzymatic defects, and many of these disorders can now be diagnosed during the first three months after conception. To make this diagnosis, amniotic fluid (the fluid surrounding the embryo) is obtained by a needle puncture and the cells of the fluid are grown in cultures until enough tissue is available for chemical analyses. When an abnormality is suspected because of a known disease in a parent or sibling, the diagnosis can be made very early in the mother's pregnancy. In some cases, treatment, consisting of a diet deficient in certain amino acids, can be instituted as soon as the baby is born.

Bone Marrow Transplants. A rare group of diseases is characterized by a partial or total inability of the infant to manufacture antibodies, substances that help the body fight infection. Using new techniques, investigators at the University of Minnesota have experimented with transplanting bone marrow cells (including those that manufacture antibodies) from a sibling or parent into the affected child. Since the child's body does not make any antibodies, the foreign marrow cells are not rejected. In initial trials, donor bone marrow cells appeared to survive indefinitely while providing the recipient with adequate antibody protection. However, a major problem encountered in these studies is that the donor cells, unless carefully selected from a compatible donor, may attack and destroy the cells of the recipient.

Dawson's Encephalitis. Dawson's encephalitis is a disease characterized by chonic inflammation of the brain, gradual loss of cerebral function, and death. The cause of the disease has not been known, but· in 1969 several research groups recovered a virus from the brains of affected children. Initial reports indicate that this virus is the same virus that causes measles. If this finding is correct, the measles virus will be classified as a "slow virus" because it can be harbored in the patient's body for months or even years after the initial infection and then become reactivated. Kuru, a disease that exists in man only in isolated areas of New Guinea, is one of the few diseases already known to be caused by a "slow virus."

WILLIAM E. SEGAR, M. D.
Mayo Clinic, Rochester, Minn.

PENNSYLVANIA

Gov. Raymond P. Shafer began 1969 by proposing considerably increased expenditures in education, welfare, and industrial development. To fund his program, the governor recommended a $500 million increase in appropriations with a 3% personal income tax to carry most of the new tax burden. At the year's end the governor had neither the full increase in appropriations nor the personal income tax.

In September 1969, Sen. Hugh Scott of Pennsylvania was elected the Republican leader of the U. S. Senate to succeed the late Sen. Everett Dirksen of Illinois. Scott defeated Sen. Howard Baker, Jr. of Tennessee, 24–19 for the post. Scott's victory marked the first time a Pennsylvanian has become the Senate leader of either party.

Elections. A proposal that judges of the state's supreme, superior, and other courts be appointed from a list of persons selected by a 7-man commission, later subject to retention by the voters, was defeated 643,970 to 624,453 in the May 1969 primary. The current system of partisan election was retained.

In the November general election, Thomas W. Pomeroy, Republican incumbent on the state supreme court, who was appointed at the death of Judge Michael Musmanno, won election over Democrat Louis B. Manderino, 1,720,030 to 1,422,699.

Budget. Governor Shafer proposed a $2.5 billion budget at a joint session of the legislature early in 1969 and proposed a personal income tax to make up for the increase in the budget over that of the previous fiscal year. After several months of legislative deadlock over a possible tax package, due to differences in views between the Democrat-controlled House and the Republican-controlled Senate, the Shafer administration borrowed $200 million to head off state government backruptcy. State operations were financed on an interim basis by a $2.1 billion general appropriations bill committing all existing taxes, and $200 million in tax anticipation notes.

Late in December the Pennsylvania legislature finally passed a tax bill providing for a $251 million increase in business levies retroactive to Jan. 1, 1969. Governor Shafer signed the measure into law but asked the legislature to provide for more than $225 million in additional taxes needed to be collected in the 1969–70 fiscal year.

------ **PENNSYLVANIA · Information Highlights** ------

Area: 45,333 square miles (117,413 sq km).
Population: 11,675,000 (1969 est.).
Chief Cities (1969 est.): Harrisburg, the capital, 73,000; Philadelphia, 2,015,000; Pittsburgh, 530,000; Erie, 134,000; Allentown, 109,000.
Government: *Chief Officers*—governor, Raymond P. Shafer (Republican); lt. gov., Raymond J. Broderick (R); secy. of state, Joseph J. Kelley, Jr. (R); atty. gen., William C. Sennett (R); treas., Grace M. Sloan; supt. of pub. instr., David H. Kurtzman; chief justice, John C. Bell, Jr., *General Assembly*—Senate, 50 members (23 Democrats, 26 Republicans, 1 vacancy); House of Representatives, 203 members (106 D; 96 R, 1 vacancy).
Education: *School enrollment* (1968)—public elementary, 1,249,000 pupils (49,300 teachers); public secondary, 1,055,000 pupils (51,200 teachers); nonpublic schools, 572,700 pupils (19,970 teachers); college and university (fall 1967), 347,894 students. *Public school expenditures* (1967–68)—$1,792,870,000 ($809 per pupil); average teacher's salary, $7,450.
Public Finance (fiscal year 1968–69): *Revenues,* $4,188,249,-556 (6% sales tax, $891,222,944; motor fuel tax, $284,-409,626; federal funds, $852,085,824). *Expenditures,* $3,-971,721,349 (education, $1,123,788,523; health, welfare, and safety, $756,523,061; highways, $678,341,306). *State debt,* $491,430,000 (June 30, 1969).
Personal Income (1968): $40,102,000,000; average annual income per person, $3,419.
Public Assistance (fiscal year 1968–69): $476,219,070 to 532,476 recipients (aged, 1967–68, $39,868,938; dependent children, 1967–68, $184,016,477).
Labor Force (employed persons, June 1969): *Agricultural,* 95,200; *nonagricultural* (wage and salary earners), 4,791,-200 (33% manufacturing, 17% trade, 12.7% government). *Unemployed persons* (June 1969)—164,000.
Manufacturing (1966): *Value added by manufacture,* $18,-752,302,000 (transportation equipment, $1,158,607,000; primary metals, $3,758,875,000; nonelectrical machinery, $1,-832,812,000; electrical machinery, $1,856,971).
Agriculture (1967): *Cash farm income,* $909,476,000 (livestock, $657,441,000; crops, $230,844,000; govt. payments, $21,191,000). *Chief crops* (tons)—Hay, 4,035,000; corn for grain, 2,269,372; wheat, 518,400.
Mining (1966): *Production value,* $903,408,000 (ranks 4th among the states). *Chief minerals* (tons)—Bituminous coal (1967), 79,101,385; anthracite coal (1967), 11,552,-441; clays, 3,293,114.
Transportation: *Roads* (1969), 114,006 miles (183,486 km); *motor vehicles* (1969), 6,073,900; *railroads* (1966), 8,585 track miles (13,816 km); *airports* (1966), 61.
Communications (1966): *Telephones* (1969), 6,873,500; *television stations,* 20; *radio stations,* 250; newspapers, 116.

The new taxes include a 4.5% increase in the corporate net income tax; a one-mill increase in the tax on shares of banks, title insurance, and trust companies; and a 3.5% increase each in taxes on mutual thrift institutions and the excise tax on property of out-of-state corporations.

Welfare. The year was marked by concern over an increase in the number of persons on public welfare in Pennsylvania. The upward trend began in July 1968 with 428,282 persons and continued through July 1969 when 532,476 persons received public assistance. This represented an increase of 104,194 persons, or 24% during one year.

Attention to the Department of Public Welfare was increased in 1969 when it authorized the newly organized Welfare Rights Organization (WRO), an agency composed of welfare recipients and others, to set up its activities in state and county public assistance offices. WRO's purpose is to initiate programs to inform and advise citizens of the eligibility criteria for public dependency.

Dr. Thomas Georges, Jr., head of the state Department of Public Welfare, resigned the post late in 1969 when some legislators demanded reasons for the increases and after Governor Shafer ordered sharp cutbacks in public relief spending.

Total public assistance expenditures for the state in the fiscal year ending June 30, 1969, amounted to $476,219,070. Of this amount, $285,374,986 was from federal funds. Expenditures from state funds totaled $277,612,305. The remainder, $13,231,779, was from county funds.

Legislation. Little major legislation was enacted in 1969. Minimum starting salaries for public school teachers in Pennsylvania were increased from $5,400 to $6,000 a year. Voters were granted the right, through judicial district referendum, to replace justices of the peace and aldermen with legally trained community court judges to be elected for 10-year terms. Local governments and state authorities were authorized for one year to increase the maximum bond interest rate from 6% to 7%.

Philadelphia Plan. After demonstrations by blacks against all-white construction unions in Pittsburgh and elsewhere, the U. S. Department of Labor ruled that contractors on federally assisted jobs must raise the proportion of minority-group workmen, from 4% in 1969 to 26% by 1973. Called the "Philadelphia Plan," it was applied there first, then in other cities.

HARRY A. BAILEY, JR.
Temple University

PERSIAN GULF STATES

The Persian Gulf States consist of nine small amirates in eastern Arabia. Eight lie on the coast of the Persian Gulf (which the Arabs call the Arabian Gulf), and the ninth, or easternmost, state lies on the Gulf of Oman. From west to east the amirates are Bahrain, Qatar, and the Trucial states of Abu Dhabi, Dubai, Sharja, Ajman, Umm al-Qaiwain, Ras al-Khaima, and Fujaira.

All nine amirates have special treaty ties with Britain, dating back, except in the case of Qatar, to the 19th century, when Britain became militarily and politically dominant in the Persian Gulf. The treaties accord Britain priority rights in the exploitation of natural resources and control over the foreign affairs of the amirates in return for protection of the little states from aggression by sea.

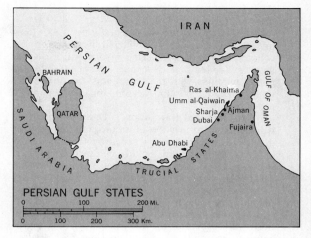

British Withdrawal. In 1968 the British government announced that its garrisons would be withdrawn from the Persian Gulf by the end of 1971. Since then the nine amirates have been trying to draw together in an independent federation that would take the place of British military and political power on their side of the gulf.

But disparities between the states constitute obstacles to the formation of a federation. Populations range from Bahrain's 200,000 to Ajman's 5,000. Abu Dhabi's annual income from oil is about $200 million, but no oil has been found in five of the other six Trucial states. The wholly Arab character of the proposed Federation of Arab Amirates is challenged by Iran's claim to Bahrain.

In 1968 the rulers of the nine amirates formed a supreme council for the federation. Meeting in Abu Dhabi in October 1969, the council tried hard to solve outstanding problems and bring the federation itself into being. Agreement appeared to have been reached on the choice of the ruler of Abu Dhabi as president of the federation and the heir apparent of Qatar as prime minister, as well as on an equal apportionment of seats in the future national assembly; but at the last moment the meeting broke up without any decisions being announced.

The ruler of Ras al-Khaima blamed British interference for the council's disruption, but it may also have been due to internal rivalries and the statement by Iran that the federation would be unacceptable as long as the status of Bahrain was not legally clarified. Late in 1969 attempts were being made to arrange another meeting of the nine rulers.

If the federation is not established before the British withdraw, Bahrain may go its own way as an independent state, Qatar may draw closer to Saudi Arabia, and the Trucial states may try to unite.

Economy. The increase in oil production in 1969 was substantial in Abu Dhabi, where two new fields were discovered, but only modest in Qatar and Bahrain. Dubai became the fourth producer among the amirates. These four states continued to move ahead with programs for economic and social improvement. Abu Dhabi inaugurated a 5–year plan that calls for the expenditure of more than $600 million. Dubai was undertaking to build the biggest deep-water port in the Middle East and an airport for jumbo jets. The four richer states gave aid to the other five.

GEORGE RENTZ
Hoover Institution, Stanford University

PERU

The year 1969 was turbulent for Peru as a new military government consolidated its hold on the country. The regime became involved in a dispute with the United States, opened diplomatic and economic relations with the Communist countries, and nationalized important sectors of the country's economy.

The "National Revolution." Despite continuous demands for the election of a constitutional government, the military group headed by Gen. Juan Velasco Alvarado became solidly entrenched in office. By seizing all International Petroleum Company holdings in Peru and by introducing an agrarian reform law that expropriated all large land-holdings, the military government won wide public support. Although no legislature met and although local elections were canceled, the government did not try to enforce unanimity, allowing considerable freedom of press, speech, and assembly. A few persons were arrested and one editor was exiled for three months, but, generally speaking, people were free to do as they pleased.

On Peru's Independence Day (July 28), General Velasco described the kind of revolution he and the army hoped to bring about. It was to be nationalistic and progressive, but not communistic. Reforms of the land-tenure system, public administration, the fishing industry, and the tax and credit systems were to be introduced.

In January, the government had ordered that all banks reconstitute themselves in such a way that at least 80% of their directors would be Peruvians and that 75% of their stock would be owned by Peruvians. A one-year deadline was set.

PERU • Information Highlights

Area: 496,222 square miles (1,285,216 sq km).
Population: 12,772,000 (1968 est.).
Chief Cities (1966 census): Lima, the capital, 1,833,700 (city and suburbs); Callao, 279,500; Arequipa, 167,080.
Government: *President*—Gen. Juan Velasco Alvarado (took office Oct. 3, 1968). *Congress*—Senate, 45 members; Chamber of Deputies, 132 members (both houses suspended on Oct. 3, 1968).
Religious Faith: Roman Catholics, 95% of population.
Education: *Literacy rate* (1969), 60% of population. *Total school enrollment* (1964)—2,267,159 (primary, 1,876,825; secondary, 325,535; technical, 64,799.
Finance (1968 est.): *Revenues,* $766,873,300; *expenditures,* $707,209,300; *monetary unit,* sol (38.70 soles equal U. S.$1).
Gross National Product (1967): $3,913,500,000.
National Income (1966): $2,870,000,000; *average annual income per person,* $231.
Economic Indexes (1967): *Manufacturing production,* 134 (1963=100); *agricultural production,* 99 (1963=100); *cost of living,* 110 (1963=100).
Manufacturing (metric tons, 1967): Gasoline, 881,000; sugar, 731,000.
Crops (metric tons, 1967–68 crop year): Potatoes, 1,712,000; maize, 591,000; cassava, 507,000; rice, 461,000; cottonseed, 163,000; wheat, 152,000.
Minerals (metric tons, 1967): Silver (1966), 32,841,243 troy ounces (ranks 3d among world producers); iron ore, 4,809,000; crude petroleum, 3,453,000.
Foreign Trade (1968): *Exports,* $865,000,000 (chief exports, 1967: copper, $157,810,000; fish meal, $135,420,000; iron ore, $48,600,000; cotton, $43,160,000); *imports,* $630,000,-000 (chief imports, 1966: nonelectrical machinery, $85,-994,800; electrical machinery, $37,723,500; transport equipment, $21,751,900. *Chief trading partners* (1967): United States (took 42% of exports, supplied 37% of imports); West Germany (took 11% of exports, supplied 12% of imports); Japan.
Transportation: *Roads* (1966), 25,700 miles (41,359 km); *motor vehicles* (1967), 306,900 (automobiles, 195,100); *railways* (1965), 1,509 miles (2,428 km); *merchant vessels* (1967), 30 (165,000 gross registered tons); *national airlines,* Aerolíneas Peruanas SA; Expreso Aéreo Peruana SA; *principal airport,* Lima.
Communications: *Telephones* (1968): 152,136; *television stations* (1966), 17; *television sets* (1966), 275,000; *newspapers* (1959). 53 (daily circulation, 492,000).

International Relations. Peru's relations with the United States were very tense until about July, because U. S. law (the so-called Hickenlooper Amendment) required a stoppage of foreign aid to any country that expropriated U. S.-owned property without adequate compensation. The law required U. S. action by April 9. President Nixon sent a special envoy, John N. Irwin, a New York lawyer, to Peru to try to negotiate the differences between the two countries. Months of talks took place, but no settlement was reached. Meanwhile, President Nixon announced that the April 9 deadline would not be observed since negotiations were in progress.

U. S. opinion was also inflamed because, in February, a Peruvian war vessel fired at two U. S.-flag fishing boats, hitting and capturing one of them. The vessel was released after payment of a $2,000 fine. This was the 28th U. S.-flag fishing vessel seized by Peru since 1961 and the 75th seized by a South American country due to disagreement over the extent of a nation's territorial waters. In March, two more U. S. fishing vessels were seized and released only after fines of $17,000 and $8,000 were paid.

Relations between the United States and Peru became so strained that the U. S. Senate Committee on Foreign Relations held hearings to try to find ways of improving them. At various times during the year bombs were exploded at the U. S. Embassy, the U. S. Cultural Institute, and the Peruvian plants of the General Motors Corporation.

Meanwhile, the military government signed agreements to open diplomatic and commercial relations with the USSR, Hungary, Bulgaria, Poland, Yugoslavia, Rumania, and Czechoslovakia.

Expropriations. On January 4, Peru's Supreme Court dismissed a habeus corpus injunction submitted by the U. S.-owned International Petroleum Company protesting the seizure of its property. The Peruvian government continued to insist that I.P.C. owed Peru $690,524,283 for its activities since 1924, a debt denied by the oil company. In March the government deposited $71,015,314 in a Lima bank to the credit of the I.P.C., stating that the company could have the money as compensation for its property if it paid the alleged $690 million debt.

On January 14, the government expropriated 18 cattle ranches owned by the Cerro de Pasco Copper Company, which was to receive 20-year bonds for $3,620,000 as compensation for the land, installations, and cattle. On May 16, the regime announced that it would gradually expropriate the country's telecommunications industry. In June, the government occupied the offices of all large land-owners and took over their bank accounts. On July 27, it nationalized the country's water resources, including all ocean water within 200 miles of the coast.

Economy. The Peruvian economy remained stagnant in 1969. During 1968, the rate of increase in the gross national product had dipped to 3.5%. Since the population was growing by about 3% per year, the economy could be said to be standing still. Peru was one of only four Latin American nations to show a drop in its economic growth rate in 1968. In June 1969 the importation of luxury and nonessential items was prohibited for the rest of the year.

On a more hopeful note, Peru in 1969 joined with Bolivia, Colombia, Chile, and Ecuador in the formation of an Andean Common Market.

HARRY KANTOR
Marquette University

PETROLEUM

Despite a healthy volume growth in 1969, the international petroleum industry achieved only modest financial gains. An important factor concerning the future financial status of U. S. oil companies was the reduction (from 27.5% to 22%) in the oil depletion allowance. (See also TAXATION.)

The intensified search for more oil in Arctic regions was dramatized by the successful voyage through the Northwest Passage of a specially designed ice-breaking tanker, the *Manhattan* (see also ALASKA; SHIPPING). Bidding by major oil companies for lease rights in Alaska's rich North Slope region reached a total of nearly $1 billion. Another major event of the year was the leakage of oil from a drilling site off the coast of southern California. The oil polluted hundreds of square miles of water. (See CONSERVATION; MARINE BIOLOGY; ZOOLOGY.)

Production. The world output of crude oil in 1969 was 40,836,700 barrels per day (b/d), 6% higher than in 1968. In the Middle East, output rose 8%; in the Far East it went up 14%; and in Africa it rose 24%, due largely to the resumed flow of oil from Nigeria and a big rise in Libya, the fifth-largest producer in the world. Other states with good increases were Indonesia, India, Abu Dhabi, Egypt, and Cabinda (Angola). All these increases were somewhat offset by a decline in western Europe, a slight rise in the United States, and a leveling off in South America.

Exploration. After many years, the decline in drilling leveled off. The number of wells drilled in the non-Communist nations was about 39,000, a 1.1% increase over 1968. The United States, which accounts for almost 80% of all drilling activity, again decreased, but only slightly. In virtually all other parts of the world drilling increased, most strongly in the Far East, Asia, Africa, and the Middle East.

Reserves. Improvements in technology and measuring methods have led to an upward adjustment in estimates of proved reserves of crude oil. The total, at the end of 1968, was said to be about 420 billion barrels, a 4.3% increase over the adjusted level for the end of 1967.

Consumption. The world's consumption of crude oil and liquid hydrocarbons derived from natural gas increased 6.5% in 1969 to an average of 40,-824,000 b/d. The eight countries with a consumption of more than 1 million b/d are, in descending order: the United States, the Soviet Union, Japan, West Germany, Britain, Italy, France, and Canada.

Tankers. As of the middle of 1969, oil tankers of 10,000 deadweight tons (dwt) or more totaled 3,136 vessels, a net increase of 48 ships over the previous year. More and more of the new tankers are reaching mammoth sizes. Half of the new ships being built (192 tankers) are 200,000 dwt or more.

Pipelines. Construction under way at the end of 1969 will add 22,000 miles (35,200 km) of lines to the more than 500,000 miles (800,000 km) in operation throughout the world. Of the new work, about 57% is for natural gas—mainly in the United States, Canada, Algeria, and Iran. Crude oil lines account for 4,176 miles (6,680 km), primarily in northern Africa, Europe, Canada, and the United States. The number of underwater pipelines, for offshore facilities, is also substantial. More than $600 million will be spent on such construction.

WORLD CRUDE OIL PRODUCTION
(Thousands of barrels daily)

	1966[1]	1967[1]	1968[2]	1969[2]
North America:				
Canada	878.0	962.0	1,039.2	1,106.7
Mexico	331.9	368.0	387.7	405.1
United States	8,295.2	8,812.0	9,110.0	9,185.9
Total	9,505.1	10,142.0	10,536.9	10,697.7
South America and West Indies:				
Argentina	287.0	294.0	340.6	338.9
Bolivia	16.7	40.0	37.0	45.3
Brazil	116.3	147.0	160.5	179.6
Chile	34.1	34.0	37.6	37.4
Colombia	196.0	189.0	180.0	208.1
Cuba	0.7	0.7	.07	0.7
Ecuador	7.3	6.0	5.4	4.9
Peru	63.1	71.0	76.0	70.8
Trinidad & Tobago	152.3	178.0	182.9	163.6
Venezuela	3,371.2	3,542.1	3,604.8	3,570.4
Total	4,244.7	4,501.8	4,625.5	4,619.7
Total, Western Hemisphere	13,749.8	14,643.8	15,162.4	15,317.4
Europe (excluding USSR and other Communist countries):				
Austria	52.7	55.8	51.5	51.2
France	58.5	56.5	54.7	50.6
Germany, West	156.4	157.0	157.5	155.1
Italy	35.2	31.8	29.1	29.0
Netherlands	44.2	43.3	40.9	38.8
Spain	0.6	1.9	4.7	3.7
United Kingdom	1.5	1.7	2.0	2.0
Yugoslavia	45.1	48.4	51.7	52.9
Total	393.2	396.4	392.1	383.3
USSR and other Communist countries:				
Albania	16.0	21.0	20.0	22.5
Bulgaria	6.0	10.0	9.5	7.2
Czechoslovakia	4.0	4.0	4.0	4.0
Germany, East	1.0	2.0	1.0	1.0
Hungary	34.0	34.0	36.0	38.0
Poland	8.0	9.0	9.5	9.6
Romania	259.0	261.0	268.0	264.0
USSR	5,400.0	5,733.0	6,180.0	6,300.0
Total[3]	5,728.0	6,074.0	6,528.0	6,646.3
Africa:				
Algeria	718.8	815.0	901.7	935.1
Angola	12.5	11.0	10.7	10.1
Cabinda	0	0	8.4	37.3
Gabon[4]	29.9	70.3	90.1	94.5
Libya	1,507.4	1,744.0	2,600.0	3,050.9
Morocco	2.1	2.0	2.0	1.4
Nigeria	417.6	319.0	137.8	538.7
Tunisia	12.1	47.0	61.6	79.6
Total	2,700.4	3,007.3	3,812.3	4,747.6
Middle East:				
Abu Dhabi[5]	359.7	384.0	498.5	615.3
Bahrain	61.7	69.2	75.3	76.0
Iran	2,113.0	2,595.7	2,841.1	3,289.8
Iraq	1,384.7	1,227.8	1,505.9	1,527.6
Israel	3.7	23.8[6]	53.0[6]	52.5[6]
Kuwait	2,275.4	2,292.4	2,421.1	2,514.5
Neutral Zone	420.4	416.0	428.0	451.9
Oman[5]	5	57.2	240.0	313.9
Qatar	290.3	322.3	338.4	352.7
Saudi Arabia	2,392.7	2,598.0	2,830.1	2,867.9
Syria	0	0	27.2	61.0
Turkey	36.4	44.0	58.4	68.6
United Arab Republic	120.7	107.0	183.2	234.9
Total	9,458.7	10,137.4	11,500.2	12,426.6
Far East and Oceania:				
Australia	9.3	22.0	36.6	41.1
Brunei and Sarawak	94.9	112.0	122.3	121.0
Burma	11.6	11.8	15.6	16.0
Communist China	180.0	180.0	196.0	240.0
India	97.6	126.0	133.4	150.1
Indonesia	463.5	508.0	600.4	721.7
Japan	14.9	16.0	15.9	15.8
Pakistan	9.4	9.8	9.8	9.8
Total	881.2	995.6	1,130.0	1,315.5
Total, Eastern Hemisphere	19,161.5	20,610.7	23,362.6	25,519.3
World total	32,911.3	35,254.5	38,525.0	40,836.7

[1] Final. [2] Preliminary (Sources U.S. Bureau of Mines and "World Petroleum"). [3] Because of the use of several sources of data for the USSR and its satellites, the figures given for the individual countries do not always add up to the total shown for the group. [4] Starting with 1966, Congo is included with Gabon. [5] Oman included with Abu Dhabi up to 1967. [6] Includes production from Sinai fields, which were in Egypt (UAR) prior to mid-1967.

Refining. The world total capacity for crude oil distillation in 1969 was 45,271,300 b/d, or 10.6% over the previous year. Much of the growth continued in western Europe and Japan, although there was an upswing in the United States. At the

PETROLEUM STORAGE TANK is towed to position near Dubai, in the Arabian Gulf, where it was submerged. The 15,000-ton steel tank is the first of its kind.

end of 1969 there were 10 countries with a capacity of 1 million b/d or more. Accounting for 74% of the world total, they were, in descending order: the United States, the Soviet Union, Japan, Italy, West Germany, France, Britain, Venezuela, Netherlands, and Canada.

Hydrogen processing continued to be the fastest growing downstream process. It rose 18% during 1969, to 8,951,500 b/d, while catalytic reforming increased 10%, to 5,341,300 b/d, and catalytic cracking increased 3%, to 6,339,900 b/d.

In the manufacture of petrochemicals, there were 1,294 operating plants throughout the world, a 5.6% increase over 1968. The largest volume was in the production of synthetic fertilizers and basic materials for textiles and plastic materials.

(See also GAS.)

WILLIAM C. UHL
Editorial Director, "World Petroleum"

PHILADELPHIA

The year 1969 in Philadelphia was marked by 42 teen-age gang killings, resulting in expansion of the gang control unit to 64 policemen.

Long debate over city and school budgets continued but resulted in no new taxes for the 1968–69 fiscal year. Early in the year the state supreme court threw out all but a tiny portion of the city's $44.5 million emergency interim tax package on the grounds that the General Assembly had not conferred interim taxing power upon the city. Later the city finance director said collection of wage and real estate taxes would provide enough revenue to meet obligations through the fiscal year.

Elections. In the municipal election the Republicans made a comeback after only two minor successes since 1947. Arlen Spector won a second

term as district attorney over Democrat David Berger, and State Representative Thomas Gola became city controller in a contest with Democrat A. Charles Peruto. Four Republican candidates for common pleas judgeships also won office.

Budget. The city's 12-month budget for the period from July 1, 1969, to June 30, 1970, came to $535.3 million, a decrease of $58.9 million from the city's irregular 18-month budget for the period January 1968 to July 1969. The new budget necessitated tax increases on corporate net income, general business, and wages.

Education. Considerable debate continued within and around the public schools. Early in 1969 the Principals Association of Philadelphia, representing more than 300 principals and vice principals, voted overwhelmingly to seek affiliation with the International Brotherhood of Teamsters. The ostensible reason for joining the union was inability of the principals to open up lines of communication with the administration.

A teacher strike was averted in March by an agreement between the teachers' union and the school board, limiting nonteaching duties.

For the first time in recent history, Philadelphia voters, in the May primary, defeated a bond issue for public school construction. The defeat of the $90 million issue was attributed to the busing controversy, racial disorders in the schools, a feeling that the schools wanted too much money, and political conflict between the school board and city hall. The school board scaled down the bond issue to $65 million, and, after a summer of extensive civic campaigning, both political parties supported the issue. It carried 246,623 to 150,813 in the November general election.

Public school enrollment in September 1969, up about 5,000 in a year, was about 290,000, with 174,000 or 60% nonwhite and 116,000 or 40% white. (Philadelphia's October 1969 estimated population was 2,032,400 of which about 586,000 or 30% were black.)

Police. Efforts to revive the Philadelphia Police Advisory Board became futile when Mayor James H. J. Tate issued an executive order finally dissolving it. The 8-member civilian board was created in 1958 to hear complaints against police and to recommend appropriate action.

Transportation. The Philadelphia Transport Workers Union went on strike Jan. 14, 1969, when negotiations with the Southeastern Pennsylvania Transportation Authority (SEPTA) failed to produce new contract terms. The strike ended after two days. Union wages were increased and the basic fare for the riding public was raised to 30 cents. In July, SEPTA concluded purchase of Suburban Transportation Company (Red Arrow) for $13.5 million, effective early in 1970. SEPTA also awarded Red Arrow $600,000 to establish three new suburban routes.

Employment. In October 1969 unemployment in the metropolitan area totaled 54,100 or 2.6% of a work force of 2,084,300. For nonwhites the rate of unemployment was about 2.3% higher than for whites. The total work force grew 61,900 in 1969.

New Mint. The new $39.4 million U. S. Mint was opened in August. Capacity is 8 billion coins per year. Visitors see the process, from hot metal to finished coins. It is a major tourist attraction.

HARRY A. BAILEY, JR.
Temple University

PHILANTHROPY

The year 1969 probably witnessed more uncertainty about the future of private giving in the United States than any year since flows of philanthropic money became an important factor in society. Much of the uncertainty was caused by congressional activity, which produced a number of legislative proposals. Many of these proposals would require radical changes in the regulation and tax treatment of private giving.

Proposals in Congress. Of all the types of givers, those most profoundly affected by the congressional proposals would be the philanthropic foundations. Some versions of the bills would tax their investment incomes, limit their duration, and require them to make philanthropic outlays by formulas that, in most cases, would result in a significant increase in their spending. Going beyond their economic operations, some proposals would more directly regulate the kinds of philanthropic programs that have been developed. Specifically, some bills would ban foundation support of voter registration drives and other activities that might be regarded as indirectly influencing legislation. Some observers are concerned lest this attack on the foundations, whether or not formalized in legislation, would make them more cautious and less effective in dealing with social problems.

Individual giving may be significantly affected by a congressional proposal to increase the standard deduction option allowed in the personal income tax. In 1966, the latest year for which data are available, three fifths of the $9.1 billion contributions itemized on tax returns was reported by taxpayers with incomes over $10,000 for whom the standard deduction usually represents little alternative to itemizing. Were the standard deduction offered to large numbers of those people, many of them might not continue to contribute to charity because they would no longer use the argument that such contributions are tax deductible.

State Actions. Private philanthropic organizations may also be affected by developments occurring in several states. In Pennsylvania, legislation was introduced to tax land owned by educational, religious, medical, and governmental organizations. The New York Supreme Court has agreed to hear an appeal on the constitutionality of state laws that exempt churches from paying real estate taxes.

In August 1969 the California legislature repealed the current exemption on church-owned, nonreligious business, making it subject to the states 7% tax on gross income. This bill was not opposed by any church group.

Statistical Data. Total private giving in the United States probably exceeds $16 billion a year. Noteworthy among recent philanthropic actions was the $1.5 million grant given by the National Broadcasting Company for the support of educational television stations and to the nonprofit Corporation for Public Broadcasting. Mrs. Ailsa Mellon Bruce, who died in 1969, left the greater part of a $500 million estate to the Avalon Foundation. During 1968, colleges and universities in the United States received a record total of $1.57 billion, up $101 million from the previous year.

RALPH L. NELSON
Queens College, The City University of New York

PHILATELY. See STAMP COLLECTING.

PHILIPPINES

The presidential election held on November 11 was the main preoccupation of the Philippine nation during most of 1969. Intensive campaigning created tensions that remained even after President Ferdinand E. Marcos and Vice President Fernando López were confirmed in office for their second 4-year terms. Marcos, standard bearer of the Nationalist party, defeated Liberal party candidate Sen. Sergio Osmeña, Jr., by a vote of 5,017,343 to 3,043,122. Marcos was the first Philippine president to be reelected. The Nationalists also won a large congressional victory.

Less spectacular but important events also took place in matters of congressional legislation, foreign relations, and economic developments. Despite public instances of anti-Americanism, relations with the United States remained warm.

Elections. The political campaign was marked by defections from both parties. Former Senate minority leader Ambrosio Padilla left the Liberal party and won reelection as a "guest candidate" on the Nationalist ticket. On the other hand, Sen. Rodolfo Ganzón switched affiliation and failed of reelection as a Liberal "guest candidate." Perhaps most significant, Sen. Genaro Magsaysay, a former Nationalist leader and brother of the late President Ramón Magsaysay, was the Liberal party vice-presidential candidate.

President Marcos campaigned on the record of his administration. He claimed credit for the construction of an unprecedented number of infrastructure projects; for solving the perennial rice shortage problem; for a campaign against graft, corruption, and criminality; for launching a program to meet industry's need for skilled workers; and for taking

────── **PHILIPPINES · Information Highlights** ──────

Area: 115,830 square miles (300,000 sq km).
Population: 35,993,000 (1968 est.).
Chief Cities (1966 census): Quezon City, the capital, 501,800; Manila, 1,402,000; Cebu, 310,100.
Government: *President*—Ferdinand E. Marcos (took office for 2d term Dec. 30, 1969); *Vice President*—Fernando López (took office for 2d term Dec. 30, 1969); *Congress*—House of Representatives, 104 members; Senate, 24 members.
Religious Faiths: Roman Catholics, 86% of population.
Education: *Literacy rate* (1960), 71.9% of population aged 15 and over. *Total school enrollment* (1964)—8,769,641 (primary, 5,527,986; secondary, 1,644,945; teacher-training, 68,667; technical/vocational, 1,253,572; university/higher, 274,471).
Finance (1968 est.): *Revenues*, $660,800,000; *expenditures*, $689,300,000; *public debt*, $1,221,600,000; *monetary unit*, peso (3.9 pesos equal U. S.$1).
Gross National Product (1967): $6,392,300,000.
National Income (1967): $5,233,000,000; *average annual income per person*, $151.
Economic Indexes (1969): *Industrial production*, 125 (1963= 100); *agricultural production*, 113 (1967=100); *cost of living*, 125 (1963=100).
Manufacturing (metric tons, 1967): Cement, 1,713,000; sugar, 1,599,000; gasoline, 1,370,000.
Crops (metric tons, 1967–68 crop year): Abaca fibers, 80,900 (ranks 1st among world producers); rice, 4,561,000.
Minerals (metric tons): Iron ore (1967), 929,000; chromite (1966), 560,000; salt, 116,000.
Foreign Trade (1968): *Exports*, $848,000,000 (chief exports, 1967: wood, $213,590,000; metal ores and scrap, $114,- 430,000; sugar, $143,080,000); *imports*, $1,280,000,000 (chief imports, 1967: nonelectrical machinery, $216,160,- 000; transport equipment, $110,400,000; iron and steel, $83,620,000). *Chief trading partners* (1967): United States (took 44% of exports, supplied 36% of imports); Japan (took 33% of exports, supplied 26% of imports); Netherlands.
Transportation: *Roads* (1969), 35,000 miles (56,326 km); *motor vehicles* (1967), 332,600 (automobiles, 182,900); *railways* (1969), 1,150 miles (1,851 km); *merchant vessels* (1967), 133 (707,000 gross registered tons); *national airline*, Philippine Airlines; *principal airport*, Manila.
Communications: *Telephones* (1968): 207,593; *television stations* (1968), 14; *television sets* (1968), 190,000; *radios* (1966), 639,000; *newspapers* (1966), 23.

other bold steps to promote economic progress. Osmeña charged the Marcos administration with harboring graft and corruption in high levels, with erratic handling of the national economy, and with imposing burdensome taxes that resulted in a high cost of living. He also claimed that there was a serious breakdown in law and order.

In foreign policy Marcos took a nationalistic line, favoring a reevaluation of the traditional defense and economic ties with the United States. Osmeña, on the other hand, stood for continuation of the traditional policy.

Three private organizations helped the Commission on Elections bring about free, peaceful, and orderly elections: the ACT Foundation, which made nationwide arrangements for rapid reporting of election results; the Advertising Council of the Philippines, which launched an extensive mass-media campaign to encourage registration of new voters and active participation of the electorate; and the Citizens National Electoral Assembly, representing some 45 civic, religious, professional, youth, women's, and veterans' groups.

Legislation. In its 1969 session Congress approved the following significant measures: (1) the so-called Magna Carta of Social Justice and Economic Freedom, which established guidelines for endeavors toward economic development and social justice; (2) the Manpower Development Act, aimed at meeting industry's urgent need for skilled workers; (3) the Omnibus Tax Code, which modernized the national tax system; (4) the Total Electrification Bill, designed to provide cheap power to underdeveloped communities; (5) the Upper Pampanga River Multi-Purpose Project Bill, designed to develop Central Luzon; and (6) the Civil Service Reform Bill, which decentralized the Civil Service Commission for greater efficiency and enhancement of the merit system.

Foreign Affairs. Probably the most significant event of 1969 in foreign relations was U. S. President Richard Nixon's enunciation of a new U. S. attitude toward the Philippines. Speaking at Manila International Airport upon his arrival for a 24-hour visit to the Philippines (July 26–27), Nixon said that the "old ties have been swept away by the winds of change" and that a new era in Philippine-U. S. relationships was beginning "based on mutual trust, mutual respect, mutual confidence, mutual cooperation."

The U. S. government approved a Philippine proposal to channel U. S. dollar expenditures in the Philippines to Philippine banks as a means of boosting Philippine dollar reserves. Japan granted a $30 million loan for construction of the Philippine-Japan Friendship Highway in the Philippines. The Philippine coconut industry was expected to benefit from the Philippine's joining the Asian Coconut Community.

Economic Developments. Three events of much significance to the economy took place during 1969: (1) the inauguration (January 17) of the Iligan Integrated Steel Mills; (2) the inauguration (October 2) of the Elizalde Steel Rolling Mills plant; and (3) the inauguration (October 19) of the Marcopper Mining Plant, a project that President Marcos called "a testament of the wisdom of a nationalist-oriented economic policy as it applies to foreign investments."

NICOLAS ZAFRA
University of the Philippines

PHILOSOPHY

A strong wave of interest in practical issues is now apparent in philosophy. A considerable amount of this new interest has been stimulated by concern about the Vietnam War. For a good part of the postwar period U. S. philosophers by and large had withdrawn from the consideration of social and political philosophy or normative ethics. Of the new breed of philosophers who are turning to social questions, Noam Chomsky can be considered typical.

Philosophy and Current Issues. In 1969 a new Society for Philosophy and Public Policy was formed, whose announced intention is to encourage concern with public issues among professional philosophers. In an international meeting held in May 1969, John Rawls and John M. Dolan participated in a symposium on "Conscription," and Ronald Dworkin and Alasdair McIntyre took part in a symposium on "Equal Protection and Compensatory Justice." The American Philosophical Association, Eastern Division, discussed the problem of "Violence" at its annual meeting in December. *The Monist* scheduled a special issue on "Legal Obligation and Civil Disobedience" (July 1970), and *The Humanist*, the journal of normative ethics with the largest circulation in the United States, continued to welcome to its pages philosophers who deal with practical moral and social issues.

There has also been a noticeable surge of interest in Marxism, particularly among younger faculty members and graduate students. This ferment is not confined to philosophy and has pervaded many other social science and humanities departments. What is remarkable is the continuity of this development with the historic pragmatism of U. S. thought. Although many students of philosophy have attacked pragmatism, the demand for "relevance" is in accord with their native pragmatism.

U. S. Philosophy. The kind of philosophy practiced during the so-called "Golden Age" of philosophy in the United States (1870–1940) seems to have waned during the past 25 years, and most philosophers have turned to analytic philosophy or existentialist phenomenology. Yet in the past two or three years there has been a revival of interest in the roots of U. S. philosophy, as illustrated by the great number of books published in this area.

Publications. Among the most significant books published in 1969 were H. S. Thayer's *Meaning and Action: A History of Pragmatism,* A. J. Ayer's *The Origins of Pragmatism,* Darnell Rucker's *The Chicago Pragmatists,* and John Wild's *The Radical Empiricism of William James.*

Other important books were published during the year. In the philosophy of language, Max Black brought out *The Labyrinth of Language* and Sidney Hook edited *Language and Philosophy.* In the philosophy of art, Nelson Goodman published *Language and Art: An Approach To a Theory of Symbols* and Mortimer R. Kadish, *Reason and Controversy in the Arts.* John H. Randall, Jr., the outstanding U. S. historian of philosophy, published *Plato: Dramatist of the Life of Reason;* P. A. Schilip edited *The Philosophy of C. I. Lewis.*

International Conferences. There were two significant international conferences in the United States in honor of the philosophers, Edmund Husserl (in April) and Martin Heidegger (in September).

PAUL KURTZ
State University of New York at Buffalo

photography

The important role that photography plays in extending human senses was demonstrated by a number of events in 1969. Thus, the major data-collecting instruments used by the astronauts of the Apollo 11 and 12 lunar landing missions were their cameras. Back on earth, researchers from many disciplines met on several occasions to consider the application of photography to air and water pollution studies, the detection of crop and forest diseases, biomedical research, underwater exploration, geology, and climatology. In many of these fields photography is combined with airborne and satellite instruments, both optical and electronic, for what is broadly called remote sensing of the environment.

Several groups of photographers and workers in the business of photographic supply met in New York City in the summer of 1969, concurrent with the Photo-Expo '69 exhibition being held there in June. Meetings of societies for professional photographers, photographic dealers, and manufacturers, and technical seminars on pattern recognition and color aerial photography, brought together thousands of people to see the vast equipment exhibits. Photo-Expo '69 displayed the wares of 350 manufacturers and distributors from the United States, West Germany, the United Kingdom, and Japan. A few weeks later the first conference of the Society of Photographic Collectors of North America met at the Ohio State University, giving evidence of the growing interest in the history of photography.

PROCESSES AND EQUIPMENT

Processing. A new and completely dry photosensitive process was presented by DuPont. The Dylux process provides grainless, continuous-tone images without using liquids or heat. Depending upon the order in which light and ultraviolet exposures are made, either positive or negative images may be produced. Another new method, the 3M Dry Color process, uses light exposure and heat development to produce a high-contrast, positive-color image on paper, its three dyes yielding a wide color range.

Unicolor chemicals, marketed by KMS Industries, may be combined in different proportions to process all of the common color negative films and papers available in the United States. Process times range from 7 to 11 minutes. Color printing also is simplified by two devices made by the same company: an additive filter wheel for mounting on the enlarger lens, and an exposure gauge.

Films. Agfa-Gevaert offered its new Contour film to researchers studying the brightness distribution of objects; applications are seen in astronomy, interferometry, and photometry. Successive exposures on this unusual film record areas of equal brightness in the same way that contour lines on a map show areas of equal elevation.

Eastman Kodak introduced new materials in several fields. Kodak Electron Microscope Film 4489 can be used in the high vacuum chamber of an electron microscope without emitting volatile components. A new Kodak color film improves identification-card photography, providing a pleasing portrait and crisp reproduction of printed matter. Another new Kodak film, for infrared aerial photography, has a dimensionally stable base to provide high accuracy in mapping cameras and mechanical strength in reconnaissance cameras. Kodak Ektapan

Film 4162 is intended for use in commercial and professional photography, and provides good highlight separation.

Lenses. Of the many fine lenses introduced in 1969, only a few that have very special properties can be mentioned. For high-precision mapping, the 85-mm, f/4 Zeiss S-Pleogon lens covers a frame 9 inches (23 cm) square; the 125° field of view has no distortion greater than 7 microns. The same company also introduced the 105-mm, f/4.3 UV-Sonnar lens, in a Hasselblad mount, for scientific ultraviolet photography.

The 180-mm, f/1.3 Zoomitar lens offers extreme speed for its focal length, and is available in mounts for several formats. In the series of Fisheye Nikkor lenses, the most recent encompasses a field of view of 220°, has a 6.2-mm focal length, and is mounted for the Nikon F camera; the image is circular, as it has to be to present its field of view on a flat film surface.

The Zeiss-Ikon Hologon Ultrawide 35-mm camera came into being to fit an unusual lens, the 15-mm, f/8 Hologon, which presents an undistorted view of 110°. It renders straight lines correctly, not curving them as do extreme wide-angle lenses. A spirit level, visible in the viewfinder, helps to align the camera for architectural views.

Light Meters. The Calumet flash meter, a hand-sized instrument, measures the intensity of continuous illumination such as flood lamps and daylight, as well as electronic flash exposures. The ratio of continuous to flash exposure may be measured in both incident and reflected modes.

The Gossen Multibeam cadmium sulfide (CdS) meter contains no delicate, jewelled movement to indicate correct exposure. Instead it uses completely electronic means. The user adjusts a dial until two indicator lamps show equal brightness; the correct setting has then been made. The angle of view can be varied to include 10, 20, or 30°.

Other Equipment. Tiffen announced two special filters for better tone rendering on color films exposed under fluorescent lamps. Ilex introduced an electronically-controlled shutter having accurate speeds from 1/125 of a second to 4 seconds.

STILL AND MOTION PICTURE CAMERAS

New still cameras shown at Photo-Expo '69 ranged from the simplest of snapshot cameras to complex professional instruments. Cameras for making super-8 movies appeared in wide variety.

Still Cameras. Only a few cameras with new or unusual features can be described (although it might be mentioned that new models of the Rollei 35 appeared, indicating a revived consumer interest in pocket-sized, good-quality cameras for tourism). For example, the Bell and Howell Focus-Matic system adjusts the camera for sharp focus when the photographer aims the viewfinder at the foot of the subject and presses a button; the pull of gravity determines the distance, through trigonometric means. A number of new Agfa cameras have a Sensor shutter release, designed to minimize camera vibration at the instant of exposure.

Among new developments in flash units, Revere instant-loading cameras have a capacitor-discharge circuit to provide more positive flash operation. The flashcube on the Keystone 125 camera rotates

(Continued on page 544)

BRUCE DAVIDSON-MAGNUM

'America in Crisis'

A SELECTION OF PHOTOGRAPHS

CHARLES HARBUTT-MAGNUM

CHARLES HARBUTT-MAGNUM

Some aspects of life in the United States during the turbulent decade of the Sixties appear on these and the following pages. The pictures, by Magnum photographers, are among those published in America in Crisis (Ridge Press—Holt, Rinehart and Winston: 1969) and were included in a show at the Riverside Museum, New York City.

BRUCE DAVIDSON-MAGNUM

BRUCE DAVIDSON-MAGNUM

ELLIOTT ERWITT-MAGNUM

543

CHARLES HARBUTT-MAGNUM

CONSTANTINE MANOS-MAGNUM

(Continued from page 539)

slightly during exposure; this is said to minimize the "red eye" effect often found in flash pictures. The Polaroid Model 360 camera has an electronic flash unit, the intensity of which is adjusted by louvers coupled to the focussing mechanism to provide correct exposure for flash pictures.

The Warner 6 by 6 camera is a single lens reflex (SLR) that makes square-format pictures on 120 and 220 roll films. It is styled like a typical 35-mm SLR and has similar features, with only slightly more bulk. The Koni-Omegaflex "M" camera is a twin lens reflex for 120 and 220 roll films; four interchangeable lens panels are offered for it, covering the range of focal lengths from 58 to 180 mm. The first 35-mm rangefinder camera to incorporate a leaf shutter capable of timing 1/1,000 of a second is the Zeiss-Ikon Vitessa 1000 camera; its new shutter is made by Prontor.

Several special-purpose still cameras were announced. The Nikonos II underwater camera is watertight down to 160 feet (50 meters); accessory lenses and focal frames make close-ups easier, with prime lenses in focal lengths of 28, 35, and 80 mm now available. The Gowland aerial camera is simple, small, and lightweight; its 150-mm, Symmar lens is used with several picture formats, up to 4 by 5 inches.

When the exact date and time of a photograph needs to be known, this is easily done with the Konica Autoreflex-W camera, which incorporates a calendar watch; a second internal lens exposes an image of the watch on the film at the instant of exposure. The ultra-miniature Minox camera is available in a new model containing a sensitive CdS light meter for automatic exposure control, ranging from 1/1,000 of a second to 7 seconds.

Motion Picture Cameras and Projectors. Of the many new models of super-8 cameras, two that offer special features can be described. The Beaulieu 4008ZM camera has an f/1.8, Angenieux lens covering a zoom focal length range of 8 to 64 mm; it can focus as close as one mm from its front surface, and its frame rate can be varied from 2 to 70 frames per second with automatic exposure control. The Bauer C-Royal camera is the first super-8 to provide backwinding, thus permitting double exposures and lap-dissolves to be made.

For news and documentary photographers, the Mitchellmatic 16 camera offers the features and ruggedness that is demanded by such work. The fully-enclosed camera is able to operate under adverse weather conditions, and its efficient shutter and f/2.2 zoom lens permit filming in dim light.

Among the new super-8 projectors with unusual features is the Eumig Mark S-712, with sound-on-sound recording and a 600-foot (180-meter) film capacity. The Sankyo Sonavic 8 projector shows one reel of film while rewinding the previous one, reducing the awkward wait between reels. The Noris Sonomat projector may be coupled mechanically to a portable cassette tape recorder to present synchronized tape and film programs. Finally, a new technique for projecting any conventional motion picture stereoscopically was introduced by Ingenuics. Two consecutive frames are projected at once through polarizing filters onto an ordinary screen; viewers must also use polarizing glasses. The slight displacement of moving objects from one frame to the next provides the image difference necessary to produce an illusion of depth.

AUDIO-VISUAL EDUCATION

The growing importance of photography's place in education is indicated by the many materials designed specifically for this market. Among them is the Kalivox slide-tape machine made by Kalart. Special holders contain a standard 2-by-2 inch slide and a short magnetic tape for commentary purposes. The Kalivox device fits atop Kodak Carousel projectors. The versatility of these Kodak Carousel and of Ektagraphic slide projectors was increased to include filmstrip projection as well. The Kodak Ektagraphic filmstrip adapter, consisting of a transport mechanism and a 3-inch lens, replaces the conventional projection lens of these machines. Strips as short as two frames can be projected.

The Astoria Stereo Black projection screen from Japan is said to have special reflectance properties allowing color pictures to be projected in lighted classrooms without sacrificing image brightness and color saturation. Its surface consists of a multitude of transparent layers on a dark support.

Super-8 Systems. The compact size and economy of super-8 films and projection equipment, in particular, make that format of increasing importance as a teaching tool. The potential effectiveness of the super-8 format was increased by the recent announcement by Kodak of two new films. Kodak Ektachrome Commercial film 7252, a camera-original film of high sharpness, and Eastman color print film 7381, with high printing speed and sharpness, should make possible the economical mass publication of high-quality prints of teaching films.

Reliable automatic projection systems for such films will help to remove the disinclination on the part of some students and teachers to use these new tools. Cartridge loading and fully-automatic threading and projection are desirable features for super-8 systems in the teaching field. Although there is as yet no industry standard to permit the ready use of films from any source in any projector, several manufacturers have brought out automatic cartridge machines. The Bolex system is limited to 50-foot (15-meter) cartridges of a little more than three minutes viewing time. The Bolex projector handles stacks of cartridges in sequence, with instantaneous changing to the next cartridge. The Bell and Howell system uses cartridges in sizes that range up to 400 feet (120 meters). The Kodak system, which is also used by Fairchild-Eumig, handles 50- to 100-foot film cartridges.

Literature. In the year of the Apollo missions that placed men on the moon's surface, it is appropriate to have two books on aerial and space photography appear. *Airborne Camera, the World from the Air and Outer Space,* by Beaumont Newhall (Hastings House), covers its subject from the earliest balloon photographs to present astronautical achievements. In *Overview, a Lifelong Adventure in Aerial Photography* (Doubleday), U. S. Air Force Brig. Gen. George W. Goddard, one of the men responsible for building the nation's military aerial reconnaissance capabilities, presents his memoirs. *Seventy Years of Cinema,* by Peter Cowie (Barnes), is illustrated with stills from films of 1895 to 1967. *Perspective World Report 1966–1969 of the Photographic Industries, Technologies, and Science,* edited by L. A. Mannheim (Focal Press), is a collective work that does justice to its broad title.

MARTIN L. SCOTT
Eastman Kodak Company

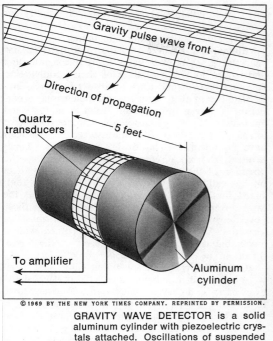

GRAVITY WAVE DETECTOR is a solid aluminum cylinder with piezoelectric crystals attached. Oscillations of suspended cylinder caused by gravity waves are converted into electric signals by crystals. (*Right*) Joseph Weber adjusts the device.

PHYSICS

The year 1969 was an exciting one in physics. An experiment conducted in Australia, if verified, may be one of the 20th century's major achievements: a proof that quarks actually exist. The existence of gravity waves was fairly firmly established, and the discovery of element 104 was definitely confirmed.

Quarks. A few years ago, American physicists Murray Gell-Mann and Georg Zweig independently proposed a new elementary particle that Gell-Mann named the quark (a word he derived from the works of James Joyce). Quarks were suggested as ultimate elementary particles out of which all other elementary particles could be constructed. Most physicists did not take this proposal very seriously, because one of the properties of a quark would be a fractional charge (either $\frac{1}{3}$ or $\frac{2}{3}$ of the charge on an electron), whereas unity of charge is a basic tenet of modern physics.

Nevertheless experimenters began to search for quarks. Because the particles, in theory, would be relatively massive, a great deal of energy would be needed to create or release them. No man-made accelerator presently has enough energy for this purpose, but nature provides extremely high-energy particles in the form of cosmic rays.

Accordingly Charles McCusker, a physicist at the University of Sydney, Australia, decided to hunt for possible quarks produced when cosmic rays strike the atmosphere. Whenever a burst of particles was recorded in his detectors (indicating the entrance of a very high energy cosmic ray into the atmosphere), a set of cloud chambers was triggered. Among many thousands of tracks of known particles, McCusker found several that were consistent with a particle having a charge two thirds that of an electron. That is, the special tracks had about $(\frac{2}{3})^2$,

or $\frac{4}{9}$, as many droplets as did the standard tracks, the number of condensed droplets along the trail of a charged particle being proportional to the square of the charge of the particle.

Most physicists are still very skeptical about the existence of quarks. Around the world, they are setting out to prove or disprove McCusker's contentions.

Gravity Waves. Half a century after the first publication of his theory of general relativity, Albert Einstein still represents the "new physics" to the public at large. His theory of special relativity has been thoroughly tested and proven experimentally, and is accepted by modern physics. However, the status of general relativity—Einstein's theory of gravitation—is quite different. One fundamental test of the theory is the study of gravity waves, which general relativity predicts will be emitted when mass is accelerated. Yet the gravity waves would have such an extremely low energy that, until recently, their measurement seemed hopelessly difficult. It was not until 1969 that a University of Maryland physicist, Joseph Weber, who had been working on the problem for some time, claimed to have observed such waves from outer space.

Weber's detectors are a pair of massive aluminum cylinders suspended by wire in a vacuum chamber. Piezoelectric crystals are bonded to the surfaces of the cylinders, and when the cylinders move—theoretically in response to gravity waves—the crystals convert the motion into an electric signal. One of the detectors is located in Maryland and the other at Argonne National Laboratory, about 600 miles (about 1,000 km) away. A telephone line carries signals from the second cylinder back to Maryland. If both detectors register a response to a disturbance within less than a second, the event is counted. In the first three months of 1969, Weber observed 17 significant events—a number that was far higher than had been expected.

The basic question now concerns the number and origin of the gravity waves. The exploding stars called supernovae may be intense emitters of such waves. (It is predicted that a star undergoing gravitational collapse would emit a very intense gravitational radiation pulse.) However, Weber observed as many as two events in one week, whereas astronomers think only one supernova occurs in our galaxy every 200 years. Therefore, although the existence of gravity waves is now close to being established as more and more physicists accept them, questions raised by the discovery are still extremely puzzling.

Nuclear Physics. Element 104 was produced at the Lawrence Radiation Laboratory in Berkeley, Calif., by physicist Albert Ghiorso and his co-workers. Three isotopes of the element have been identified, with mass numbers 257, 258, and 259. (Russian scientists claimed to have produced this element back in 1964, but this was not verified.)

According to the periodic table of the elements, element 104 should be similar to hafnium in its properties. Therefore it is temporarily known as eka-hafnium (meaning "beyond hafnium"). Glenn Seaborg, chairman of the U. S. Atomic Energy Commission since 1961, predicts that succeeding elements would show normal chemical behavior until element 121 is reached. However, since production of very heavy man-made elements has been increasingly difficult to accomplish, it might appear that element 104 marks the end of the line, more or less, for such efforts.

Even if very heavy elements could be created, it might be expected that the lifetimes of these elements would be extremely short. This is not necessarily true. Recent calculations based on the shell model of the nucleus indicate certain "magic numbers"—mass numbers that would correspond to very stable heavy nuclei. The next "magic number" beyond element 104 is the isotope of element 114 that would have a mass number of 294. Detailed calculations indicate that this isotope might last for many millions of years.

With a half-life of such duration, very heavy elements that were created during the formation of the solar system might still be present on the earth. There is no strong evidence as yet for the existence of these superheavy elements, but the possibility has so excited nuclear physicists that there are now a number of proposals to build accelerators for creating superheavy elements artificially. Many of the plans involve a special Van de Graaff accelerator to generate beams of heavy ions. The output of the accelerator would be injected into a cyclotron in order to increase the energy of the particles to approximately 8 million electron volts per nucleon. At these energies it should be possible to bombard a uranium target with a beam of uranium ions and still expect some nuclear processes to take place.

There is speculation about "islands" of stability for atoms with nuclei that are hundreds of mass units larger than those now found in nature.

Elementary Particle Physics. For the past few years there has been a major effort to examine and understand possible violations of charge conjugation (C), parity (P), and time reversal (T), three fundamental symmetry properties of elementary particles. (Charge conjugation relates matter and antimatter. Parity relates a reaction to its mirror image, that is, the parity rule asserts that particles have no intrinsic right- or left-handedness. Time-reversal invariance refers to the principle that the direction of the flow of time should have no effect on the validity of physical laws.) These are combined in the CPT theorem, which states that the laws governing antimatter are the same as those governing matter, except that antimatter must be viewed as if in a mirror and as if timed with a clock that runs backwards—in terms of the "time-direction" of ordinary matter.

Originally it was believed that C, P, and T all were conserved in subatomic events. In 1957, however, parity and charge conjugation were overthrown in the case of weak interactions between particles, in which intrinsic right- or left-handedness was displayed. In addition, in 1964 a group of experimentalists at Princeton University discovered that CP is not conserved in the decay of the K_2^0 meson. The conclusion to be drawn was either that T is not conserved in these instances, and that CPT still holds, or that T is conserved whereas CPT is not. It was assumed that time reversal in fact was violated and that the CPT theorem holds true, but the first proof of this assumption was not carried out until recently.

In 1969, Russell Casella of the U. S. National Bureau of Standards collected all available experimental data and, with calculations, showed that time reversal was indeed violated. At the moment the CPT theorem still seems valid—a relief to physicists, since the very foundation of quantum mechanics and relativity rests on the CPT theorem.

Polywater. Recent work on the properties of water indicated that there is a different form of this very familiar compound. Anomalous water, as this different form is called, was discovered by a Soviet physical chemist, Boris Deryagin, a few years ago. Deryagin reported that he had observed a form of water that displayed unusual properties, including lower vapor pressure, higher density, stability at temperatures up to about 930° F (500° C), and solidification to a glassy form rather different from ordinary ice.

Scientists in general were extremely skeptical, but in 1969 a group from the National Bureau of Standards and the University of Maryland performed a careful study of the spectra of a sample of possible anomalous water. These spectra were quite different from those obtained with ordinary water, yet they showed no trace of likely contaminants. Recent work suggests that anomalous water does exist, and that it is a polymer of the water molecule H_2O. The formula of this so-called *polywater* is $(H_2O)_n$. Its possible structure is actively being investigated. However, the fundamental question is still whether the polymer actually exists. Scientific opinion is quite mixed, ranging from extreme skepticism to enthusiastic support.

GARY MITCHELL
North Carolina State University at Raleigh

BISHOP James A. Pike died in the desert of Judea under circumstances that befitted the drama and color of his life. His wife, Diane *(2d from left)*, is among the small group of mourners at the Protestant cemetery in Jaffa, Israel.

UPI

PIKE, James Albert

Former Episcopal bishop of the Diocese of California; b. Oklahoma City, Okla., Feb. 14, 1913; d. Israeli-occupied Jordan, probably Sept. 3 or 4, 1969.

James A. Pike's death in the Judean wilderness was in keeping with his whole career; it was dramatic, rich in symbolism, and well reported. Concerned in his later years with the study of Christian origins and particularly with the meaning of Jesus of Nazareth in today's world, he was writing a book on the subject. In order to have the feeling of identification with Jesus, he immersed himself in the Palestinian environment. With his third wife, the former Diane Kennedy, he had driven out into the wilderness where Jesus was pictured as having undergone his temptations. The Pikes became lost, their rented automobile failed them, and they parted in quest of help. Mrs. Pike found her way out of the desert areas, but for days the search continued for her husband. Eventually he was found dead, a victim of the desert's heat.

Career. Pike's spiritual odyssey took him from childhood Catholicism through agnosticism, across the spectrum of Anglican approaches to faith, and beyond this to what he called "alumni" status, as he left the conventional church but continued to pursue spiritual themes. Similarly, his vocation had moved from his early aspiration to the Catholic priesthood, through law and military service, then in 1952 to prominent churchly position as dean of New York's Cathedral of St. John the Divine, to its ecclesiastical climax when he headed the Episcopal diocese of California. When he left this position (though he remained a bishop), he took secular employment as a fellow at the Center for the Study of Democratic Institutions at Santa Barbara, Calif., although he was no longer on its staff at the time of his death.

Controversial Appeal. Pike was widely loved or deeply hated, depending upon where his observers stood in relation to controversial matters in their time. His gift of candor, his ability to locate the issues of the moment, his quick mind, his phrase-making ability—all these served to bring him to public attention during those first years in New York. The cathedral was near Columbia University, and he found particular success at communicating the Christian faith to collegians. At the same time, located in the mass media center that is New York, he learned to use television to spread his views.

During these years Pike was known not so much for innovation as he was for his ability to rephrase the Christian faith and make it meaningful to people with personal problems. *Beyond Anxiety* was a typical title among his books in the 1950's.

When the subject of mixed marriages between Protestants and Catholics, birth control, "new morality," or the question of a Roman Catholic president exercised the public, Pike was on hand with speeches and writings on the subject. Never afraid to take unpopular positions, he involved himself with the civil rights movement before that kind of activity became widespread. Later he took a lead in opposing America's part in the Vietnam War.

If This Be Heresy. A surprisingly effective administrator and leader of his diocese, Pike also took to the campus and lecture circuit. Appealing to the anti-institutional mood of students, he attacked the forms and moral posture of the church. But he was also increasingly ill at ease with its theology, and in a sequence of books published between 1964 and 1967—*Time for Christian Candor, What Is This Treasure,* and *If This Be Heresy*—he attacked such teachings as the doctrine of the Trinity.

Efforts by a few Episcopal clergymen to bring Pike to trial for heresy were encouraged by the bishop, who wanted a showdown, but were discouraged by most other of his church's leaders. *The Bishop Pike Affair* (1967) by William Stringfellow recounts events that led up to a kind of compromise or revision of procedures having to do with heresy matters, all of which Pike saw as a vindication.

Personal tragedy marked Pike's career. He had struggled with alcoholism, seen the annulment of one marriage and divorce after a second, and weathered the suicide of a son, James, in 1966. In 1968 he wrote *The Other Side,* telling of seances in which he believed he may have spoken to his dead son.

Pike's works on theology presented virtually no fresh ideas with which other professional theologians had to reckon. But the way he spoke and lived attracted to him many others, particularly the young, who shared his quest for life's meaning and who admired his courage and his gift of expression.

MARTIN E. MARTY
University of Chicago
Associate Editor, "The Christian Century"

PLASTICS. See MATERIALS.
POETRY. See appropriate sections in the various articles on national literatures.

POLAND

The year 1969 was one of relative calm in Poland, in the aftermath of the political turbulence of 1968.

Domestic Politics. Party leader Władysław Gomułka moved to consolidate his victory over Gen. Mieczysław Moczar at the November 1968 Communist (United Workers') party congress. Although Moczar himself did not lose his official positions, a number of officials allied with him were removed from the party's propaganda and secret police units.

Parliamentary elections in June produced only minor changes in the government. Józef Cyrankiewicz of the ruling Communist party continued as premier. Three new deputy premiers were added to the cabinet—two of these, Marian Olewinski and Stanisław Majewski, represented the Communists; one, Zdzislaw Tomal, represented the United Peasant party (ZSL), a reliable Communist ally.

Some 20 million persons, 97.6% of those eligible, were reported to have voted for representatives to the unicameral, 460-member parliament (Sejm). Polish voters could choose only from among names of the Communist-led National Unity Front (FJN). Premier Cyrankiewicz, Foreign Minister Stefan Jedrychowski, and President Marian Spychalski reportedly ranked at the bottom of the poll in their respective districts. The 1969 election did not change the distribution of seats in the Sejm.

In July the leaders of several Soviet bloc nations, led by the USSR's party chief Leonid Brezhnev and President Nikolai Podgorny, visited Warsaw. They participated in ceremonies marking the 25th anniversary of the establishment of Poland's Communist regime. The Soviet leaders apparently showed satisfaction with the reliably orthodox policies of Gomułka.

The "anti-Zionist" campaign of the party press continued, although it was somewhat more moderate than in 1968. In January two teaching assistants at Warsaw University, Jacek Kuron and Karol Modzelewski, charged with Zionist sympathies, drew 3½ year jail sentences for instigating the student uprisings of March 1968. In February the government prosecuted the son of Roman Zambrowski, a Jewish former member of the Politburo, allegedly for disseminating false accounts of life in Poland.

The government announced in June that stringent restrictions would be placed, beginning in September, on further Jewish emigration to Israel. The announcement was generally attributed to the government's concern over the loss of valuable skilled manpower and objections from the Arab states that these workers were strengthening Israel. The announcement coincided with a disclosure by the official Polish press agency (PAP) that 5,264 Jews had emigrated between mid-1967 and mid-1968. This represented more than 20% of the approximately 25,000 Jews believed to be still living in Poland in 1968.

Foreign Relations. During 1969 there were significant Polish initiatives for improving relations with West Germany. Following talks with Soviet and East German leaders earlier in the spring, Gomułka offered in May to negotiate a separate Polish-West German agreement recognizing the Oder-Neisse boundary as Poland's permanent frontier in the west. As conditions for the settlement, he called on West Germany to recognize the independence and territorial integrity of East Germany and to adhere to the nuclear nonproliferation treaty.

In June Klaus Schütz, mayor of West Berlin, was invited to visit the Polish trade fair in Poznán. He was the highest ranking West German official to visit Poland since World War II. For the first time Gomułka and the Polish press noted that West Germany was showing some "healthy and positive" signs of a reconciliation with Poland. However, Warsaw did not respond to the appeal of West German Chancellor Willy Brandt for an exchange of declarations renouncing the use of force, and the two leaders did not begin direct diplomatic talks.

The government's most daring move in foreign affairs in 1969 was the establishment of consular relations with Spain. Poland became the second Communist state, after Rumania, to deal directly with Spanish Chief of State Franco.

The Church. In church-state relations 1969 was a year of relative calm. However, Stefan Cardinal Wyszyński, head of the Polish Roman Catholic Church, called upon the government to ease restrictions on permits and materials for the construction of new churches, criticizing its past record.

Economic Policy. There were indications of cautious reforms within Poland's rigid, centralized planning system. In June the deputy chairman of the State Planning Commission, Jan Pajestka, announced that an effort would be made to invest funds more "selectively." Inefficient industrial enterprises requiring heavy capital outlays would be sacrificed for the benefit of more easily maintained and productive enterprises.

ALEXANDER J. GROTH
University of California, Davis

POLAND · Information Highlights

Area: 120,664 square miles (312,520 sq km).
Population: 32,207,000 (1968 est.).
Chief Cities (1966 census): Warsaw, the capital, 1,261,300; Łódz, 745,400; Kraków, 525,000; Wrocław, 477,300.
Government: *President of the Council of State*—Marian Spychalski (took office April 11, 1968); *Premier*—Józef Cyrankiewicz (reelected June 1969); *First Secretary, United Workers' Party*—Władyslaw Gomułka (took office 1956). *Parliament*—Sejm (unicameral), 460 members (party seating, 1969: United Workers' party, 255; United Peasant party, 117; Democratic party, 39; independents, 49).
Religious Faiths: Roman Catholics, 91.7% of population.
Education: *Literacy rate* (1960), 95% of population aged 14 and over. *Total school enrollment* (1966)—8,769,641 (primary, 5,527,986; secondary, 1,644,945; teacher-training, 68,667; technical/vocational, 1,253,572; university/higher, 274,471).
Finance (1967 est.): *Revenues,* $79,200,000; *expenditures,* $79,025,000; *monetary unit,* zloty (4 zlotys equal U. S.$1).
Net Material Product (1966): $141,800,000,000.
National Income (1968): $166,250,000,000.
Economic Indexes (1968): *Industrial production,* 152 (1963= 100); *agricultural production* (1964), 152 (1949=100); *cost of living* (1966), 103 (1963=100).
Manufacturing (metric tons, 1967): Cement, 11,138,000; crude steel, 10,454,000; beet sugar, 1,786,000; wheat flour, 1,774,000; meat products, 1,807,000.
Crops (metric tons, 1967–68 crop year): Potatoes, 48,620,000 (ranks 2d among world producers); rye, 7,691,000 (world rank, 2d); sugar beets, 15,521,000; wheat, 3,934,000.
Minerals (metric tons, 1967): Coal, 123,881,000 (ranks 4th among world producers); lignite, 23,922,000; iron ore, 838,000; copper ore, 16,000; salt, 2,488,000; crude petroleum, 450,000; zinc ore, 218,000.
Foreign Trade (1967): *Exports,* $2,527,000,000 (chief exports, 1967: coal, $276,950,000; meat and products, $154,000,000; ships and boats, $132,000,000; freight wagons, $47,000,- 000); *imports,* $2,645,000,000 (chief imports, 1967: cotton, $918,000,000; iron ore, $257,000,000; wheat, $97,000,000). *Chief trading partners* (1967): USSR (took 36% of exports, supplied 35% of imports); East Germany; Czechoslovakia.
Transportation: *Roads* (1964), 196,520 miles (316,260 km); *motor vehicles* (1967), 542,200 (automobiles 331,900); *railways* (1965), 16,728 miles (26,915 km); *merchant vessels* (1967), 197 (1,178,000 gross registered tons); *national airline,* Polish State Air Service (LOT); *principal airport,* Warsaw.
Communications: *Telephones* (1968), 1,530,479; *television stations* (1968), 19; *television sets* (1968), 2,710,000; *radios* (1967), 5,539,000; *newspapers* (1967), 43.

ELECTRONIC COMMAND POST at New York City police headquarters enables police to monitor events anywhere in the city. A companion data system on patrol assignments speeds help where needed.

POLICE

"Pigs is beautiful," proclaimed a sign held by a young man during a 1969 street demonstration in Los Angeles. "Pigs" had by now become the familiar epithet attached by many dissidents to law enforcement officers. The ambiguity of the sign, however, might be taken to symbolize the uncertain image of the police prevailing in the United States today.

On the one side, there appears to be a strong conviction that law enforcement personnel are being

POLICEMEN'S UNION was formed in November for the first time. Leading organizers were (from left) Robert Bragg, Omaha; John Cassese, New York; and Bill Bloom, Nebraska.

castigated unfairly and unreasonably and that they are being made to bear the burden for social ills that they neither caused nor can control. Efforts to quell unruly demonstrations and to keep protests within bounds inevitably come to be centered upon the use of the police to maintain order. As one officer noted: "Society must be protected, and the policeman is not paid to be a theoretical psychologist or a social reformer." In the same vein, a police chief remarked: "People expect a policeman to be a demigod on the salary of an upstairs maid."

Among persons unsympathetic to the police, however, there is a strong belief that police officers personally tend to share in the scorn of militants and dissidents and to perform their duties at times with a good deal more enthusiasm than operational manuals demand. This behavior was said to stem in considerable measure from the fact that law enforcement officers are most often recruited from working-class families and that policemen feel especially threatened by the casual manner in which middle-class and well-to-do youngsters treat the very things that the officers themselves are striving to attain—things such as status, financial well-being, and social respectability.

Police and Politics. Widespread public sympathy for strenuous law enforcement action was clearly visible during 1969 in voters' responses to political candidates who ran on platforms calling for stepped-up police efforts. In June police detective Charles S. Stenvig captured 62% of the vote to become the new mayor of Minneapolis. Stenvig's support came from throughout the city, with majorities supplied by 11 of Minneapolis' 13 precincts. In Detroit in November, Sheriff Roman S. Gribbs emerged victorious in a mayoralty contest in which he had campaigned for stricter law enforcement procedures.

Emergence of individual police officers as political candidates was being accompanied, according to a report from a consultant group to the National

Commission on the Causes and Prevention of Violence, by a "dangerous tendency" of police forces themselves to enter the political arena to achieve their ends. In many cities, the Violence Commission consultants maintained, the police have become an "independent political entity" that often "rivals even duly elected officials in influence." Challenges to civilian authority were being made by police groups because officers were "increasingly frustrated, alienated, and angry," the report noted, adding: "We find that the policeman in America is overworked, undertrained, underpaid, and undereducated."

These difficulties, the report said, are compounded by a gross insensitivity among the police to the importance and legitimacy of social factors, such as poverty and discrimination, in producing discontent and by a lack of understanding of the proper role of protest in a democracy.

Critics of the Commission-sponsored study remained unimpressed with its allegations, finding them largely a restatement of dissidents' clichés with little support in fact.

Community Relations. Partly in response to the criticism of their work with minorities that appeared in the 1968 report of the National Advisory Commission on Civil Disorders (the Kerner Commission), many police departments inaugurated community relations programs during the course of the year.

In Houston, for instance, 1,500 officers participated in planned "confrontation" sessions with persons from minority groups in an attempt to air mutual grievances. During the period of the program's operation, complaints about police behavior from the minority community were reported to have decreased by 70%. In St. Louis, the police department established storefront centers in slum areas where persons could seek assistance or register their complaints.

In October, the New York City Police Department, responding to the need for improved community relations, established an all-volunteer 23-man Preventive Enforcement Patrol designed, in the words of its commander, "to talk to the kids in their own language." The commander noted that "We're not a goon squad or a cooling squad [special police units sometimes used to move forefully against residents of an area or special units used to keep the peace by placating antagonists]. We are visible policemen, riding in patrol cars and making arrests. But we want to show the people that we're sensitive to their problems and that we understand the community."

Such efforts have been accompanied by stepped-up campaigns to hire persons from minority groups for police work. Reluctance to accept law enforcement jobs and, on occasion, an inability to meet recruitment standards have, however, kept down the number of minority group persons in police work.

In addition, increased race awareness among black policemen was reported during the year to be leading to growing tension within many metropolitan police departments between black and white officers. In earlier years, it was believed that minority group policemen tended to be more punitive toward minority group persons, partly to establish their own distinctiveness and partly as an overcompensation against what might otherwise be thought to be a show of favoritism. But today evidence indicates that minority group policemen are becoming more protective of the rights and welfare of persons sharing their ethnic and racial affiliations.

Montreal Police Strike. The year's most vivid demonstration of the importance of police in maintaining public safety took place in Montreal, Canada's largest city, on October 7. For 17 hours, 3,700 law enforcement officers and 2,400 firemen staged a wildcat strike in a dispute over wages. During this period there was a wave of bank robberies and burglaries, some 1,000 plate-glass store windows were smashed in downtown Montreal, and hundreds of stores were looted.

Although the editor of the Montreal *Star* noted that there was "a carnival atmosphere," he also reported that for many people the major lesson of those 17 hours without police protection was "the discovery of their vulnerability."

GILBERT GEIS
State University of New York, Albany
Coauthor, "Man, Crime, and Society"

UPI

WISCONSIN POLICE with riot equipment move into a crowd of youthful protesters on the capitol grounds in Madison, October 3. Special training to control disorders is now a requirement in most big city police departments.

POLITICAL LEADERS gather for President Nixon's inaugural: *left,* Senator Muskie, Democratic nominee for vice president in 1968; *right foreground,* Senator Goldwater, 1964 Republican presidential candidate.

POLITICAL PARTIES

Uncertainty about the political future disturbed most party leaders in 1969, whether they contemplated 1970 or the more distant future. Discontent and frustration among the voters, evident in opinion polls and scattered election results, gave pause to politicians who had been counting on a return to party stability and old alignments.

The Republican party, clearly led by President Richard M. Nixon, showed strains among its liberal, moderate, and conservative supporters. Democrats, divided even before the defeat of their presidential candidate Hubert H. Humphrey, failed to find unifying national leadership in 1969.

Despite continuing public debate over the Vietnam conflict and ways of ending it—and controversy over the handling of crime, inflation, taxation, housing, welfare, education, and other problems—President Nixon's level of approval in opinion polls was high, rising to 68% in November.

CONGRESS

When the 91st Congress convened on Jan. 3, 1969, Democrats controlled both houses—243 to 192 in the House and 57 to 43 in the Senate.

House. John W. McCormack of Massachusetts was reelected speaker of the House, surviving a challenge in the Democratic caucus from younger liberals who supported Morris K. Udall of Arizona. Carl Albert, Oklahoma, and Gerald R. Ford, Michigan, remained as majority and minority leaders.

Senate. In the Senate, Mike Mansfield, Democrat of Montana, and Everett M. Dirksen, Republican of Illinois, continued as party leaders. In a party-bruising challenge, Edward M. Kennedy of Massachusetts ousted the more conservative Russell B. Long, Louisiana, as majority whip. For the vacant position of minority whip, Hugh Scott of Pennsylvania, regarded as a moderate, defeated conservative-supported Roman L. Hruska of Nebraska. Gordon Allott, Colorado, defeated Robert P. Griffin, Michigan, for chairman of the Republican policy committee.

Senator Kennedy, involved on July 18 in an automobile accident in which a female passenger died, announced on July 30 that he would remain in the Senate and seek reelection in 1970. He added on July 31 that he would not run for president in 1972. (See also KENNEDY, EDWARD M.)

The death of Sen. Everett M. Dirksen on September 7 led to a significant contest for Republican leader, won by Senator Scott on September 24. He received 24 votes to 19 for Howard H. Baker, Jr., of Tennessee, who drew conservative support. Robert P. Griffin, Michigan, was then elected minority whip, 23–20, over Baker. (See also DIRKSEN, EVERETT M.)

Relations With the President. In response to complaints from the press and other sources about legislative inactivity, House Democrats in caucus on September 17 accused the administration of providing "rhetoric" instead of "meaningful programs." Rep. Ford replied two days later that President Nixon was disappointed with the slow pace of congressional action on some of his programs.

The President received his most publicized rebuff when the Senate on November 21 rejected, 55–45, his nominee, Judge Clement F. Haynsworth, Jr., of South Carolina, for associate justice of the Supreme Court. Haynsworth was opposed by labor and civil

FRED R(OY) HARRIS, junior U. S. senator from Oklahoma, succeeded Lawrence F. O'Brien in January 1969 as chairman of the Democratic National Committee. A proponent of liberal policies and a leading critic of the Nixon administration, he opposed the antiballistic missile program, the cutbacks in the job corps program, the President's tax reform bill, and the nomination of Clement F. Haynsworth, Jr., to the Supreme Court. He called for U. S. withdrawal from Vietnam. An expert on urban affairs, Harris served in 1968 on the Kerner commission on civil disorders.

Harris, the son of a sharecropper, was born on a farm at Walters, Okla., on Nov. 13, 1930. After graduating from the University of Oklahoma in 1954, he practiced law. He served in the Oklahoma state senate from 1956 until 1964, when he was elected to the U. S. Senate seat vacated by the death of Robert S. Kerr. In 1966 he was reelected for a 6-year term. He serves on Senate committees on government operations, public works, and small business, and on the permanent subcommittee on investigations.

ROGERS C(LARK) B(ALLARD) MORTON, U. S. congressman from Maryland, was unanimously elected to succeed Ray C. Bliss as chairman of the Republican National Committee on April 14, 1969. Although his voting record in Congress has been generally conservative, he has occasionally supported civil rights legislation and other liberal measures. He believes that in order to regain control of Congress the Republican party must take into consideration the needs of labor, youth, and ethnic minorities and should not make undue concessions to Southern conservatives. In November he spoke in support of Vice President Spiro Agnew's criticisms of the news media.

A member of a prominent Kentucky family, Morton was born in Louisville on Sept. 19, 1914. He graduated from Yale University (B. A., 1937) and was a captain in the army in World War II. From 1947 to 1951 he was president of the family flour-milling firm, Ballard and Ballard, which later merged with the Pillsbury Company.

WIDE WORLD

rights leaders and by others who charged him with insensitivity to conflict-of-interest problems arising from investments he held during his service on the federal bench. Seventeen Republican senators, including Scott and Griffin, joined 38 Democrats in rejecting the nomination. (See also SUPREME COURT.)

The House approved on September 18 a proposed constitutional amendment, subject to Senate action before submission to the states, which would abolish the electoral college and provide direct popular election of the president.

PARTY ORGANIZATION

A mood of critical self-appraisal and a desire to improve party organization gripped Democrats and Republicans during 1969. Both parties had an eye on the great prizes that would become available in the 1970 elections—35 governorships, 35 Senate seats, and all seats in the House of Representatives.

Former Gov. George C. Wallace of Alabama endorsed the organization of the American party at Cincinnati in May. He said he would run for president in 1972 unless the Nixon administration could honorably end the war in Vietnam, cut spending, and end federal control of local institutions such as schools.

Republican Party. After a meeting with the President-elect, Ray C. Bliss said in January that he had agreed to remain indefinitely as chairman of the Republican national committee. But in February, the White House announced that Bliss had resigned, and that Rep. Rogers C. B. Morton of Maryland would be the new chairman, serving without salary and remaining in the House. He was unani-

mously elected by the committee on April 14. With no deficit, and a budget of $3.2 million for the year, the reorganized staff of 190 set to work creating a new party image under the operational direction of deputy chairman James Allison, Jr., of Texas.

Democratic Party. Lawrence F. O'Brien resigned as chairman of the Democratic national committee in January. Sen. Fred R. Harris of Oklahoma was elected to replace him. To its debt of $6.1 million, the committee added the pre-convention debts (about $1 million each) of Democratic presidential candidates Humphrey and the late Robert F. Kennedy.

Operating with less than half the staff of its Republican counterpart, the Democratic national committee turned its attention to party reform and to issues of public policy. Chairman Harris announced on February 8 the appointment of two commissions—one on party structure and delegate selection (headed by Sen. George McGovern, South Dakota) and the other (under the chairmanship of Rep. James G. O'Hara, Michigan) to propose reform of party rules. Guidelines made public on September 23 by McGovern's commission would abolish the unit voting rule at all levels of the party; apportion national convention delegates to favor those areas in each state that have the heaviest concentration of Democratic voters; and assign convention delegates to candidates, in presidential primary election states, in proportion to votes received.

Chairman Harris announced in September the formation of a new Democratic policy council to be headed by Humphrey. The council, like the commissions, generated opposition from conservatives.

FRANKLIN L. BURDETTE
University of Maryland

DEMOCRATIC FRIENDS, Senator Kennedy and former Vice President Humphrey, meet at a fund-raising dinner.

WIDE WORLD

SEN. HUGH SCOTT embraces his wife after being elected Republican leader of the Senate on September 24.

UPI

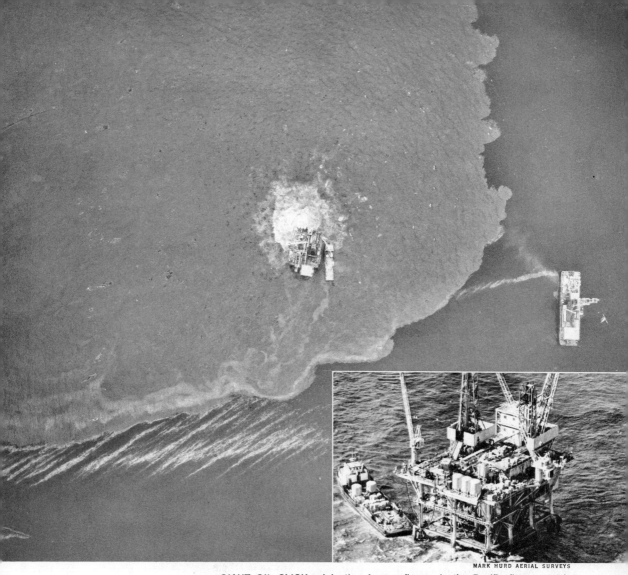

GIANT OIL SLICK originating from a fissure in the Pacific floor spreads toward prime California resort beaches along the Santa Barbara Channel.

POLLUTION

Great national concern over the deterioration in environmental quality in the United States was reflected in 1969 in a presidential executive order establishing a Council on Environmental Quality. This council is composed of members of the cabinet, with the President serving as chairman. Independently, Congress moved to set up special bodies to evaluate the nation's needs and to advise the president on desirable policies and programs.

WATER POLLUTION

Oil Seepage. One of the most spectacular cases of water pollution during the year was the oil pollution episode in Santa Barbara (Calif.) harbor. In January, a mishap in offshore drilling resulted in the seepage of hundreds of thousands of gallons of oil to the overlying waters. (See CONSERVATION; ZOOLOGY.)

Insecticide Contamination. Almost equally dramatic was the pollution of the Rhine River with the insecticide endosulfan in June. The source of the insecticide was traced to West Germany. In the Netherlands, the use of the Rhine for drinking purposes had to be temporarily discontinued in many communities. The only sign of this poison in the water was the death of millions of fish.

In the United States, concern was expressed over the use of DDT and other chlorinated hydrocarbon insecticides. In November, Robert Finch, the Secretary of Health, Education, and Welfare, announced plans to ban all but essential uses of DDT during the next two years. Earlier, Arizona had declared a 1-year ban on DDT, and California and Michigan had imposed rigorous restrictions on the use of this insecticide. These restrictions would effectively reduce the quantity of DDT by more than 90%.

Proposed Federal Legislation. A major development in water pollution during 1969 was the proposal of a federal Water Quality Act by Sen. Edmund Muskie. The act would provide that activities carried on under federal permit or lease must comply with state water quality standards. This provision is aimed primarily at controlling thermal pollution associated with nuclear power plants. The act would also control any pollution resulting from the disposal of dredging by Corps of Engineers contractors.

In another provision, heavy penalties—up to $14 million for vessels and $8 million for onshore and offshore drilling facilities—would be imposed on dischargers who willfully or negligently permit oil to pollute coastal waters. It would be the discharger's responsibility to prove that willfullness or negligence was not involved. A similar provision would control hazardous materials other than oil carried by vessels or handled in onshore or offshore facilities. In addition, the proposed legislation calls for the control of sewage discharges by vessels, the expansion of research to control acid mine drainage, and the support of projects that would demonstrate ways to eliminate pollution in the Great Lakes.

Sewage Treatment. The demand for a high level of federal financial support for the construction of municipal sewage treatment plants came in conflict during the year with an almost equally strong demand for budget retrenchment. Proponents of water pollution control called for an appropriation of $1 billion, the full amount authorized under the Clean Water Restoration Act of 1966 to assist the municipalities in the construction of sewage works. The administration put a ceiling of $214 million on this program, but it appeared that a compromise of $800 million would be reached.

Federal Enforcement. During 1969, the federal government stepped up its antipollution enforcement activity. The vigor of this approach was reflected in proceedings initiated against the city of Toledo and four major steel companies which, it was alleged, had failed to submit their pollution abatement plans to implement the water quality standards established for tributaries of Lake Erie.

In an unprecedented step, the Department of the Interior intervened in Iowa by requiring secondary treatment for communities discharging their waste effluents into the Mississippi and Missouri rivers. The state itself refused to take this step on the basis that primary treatment was adequate to meet the standards set for these waterways.

The issue at hand in the Iowa intervention concerned the general requirement by the Department of the Interior that secondary treatment or its equivalent be applied to all municipal and industrial wastes. This policy was also attacked as uneconomical in many locations. The comptroller general of the United States supported this view in a special report issued to Congress. But, in order to dispel any notion that the federal government would weaken this requirement, the government's policy was reaffirmed by the Commissioner of the Federal Water Pollution Control Administration.

Eutrophication. Eutrophication is the increase in the growth of aquatic plants due to the addition of plant nutrients to the water. Continuing concern over eutrophication in Lake Erie and Lake Ontario was expressed by the International Joint Commission, which called for effective measures to reduce the quantities of phosphates in wastes reaching these bodies of water. The IJC recommended that detergent manufacturers reduce the amounts of phosphate-based detergents in use, and it called for complete replacement of phosphates in detergent formulations by the year 1972. The IJC also recommended that waste treatment plants provide at least an 80% reduction of phosphates in municipal and industrial effluents discharged into Lake Erie and the Detroit River by 1972 and into Lake Ontario by 1975.

Dredgings. The possible pollutional impact of sediment was a matter of increasing concern to the Federal Water Pollution Control Administration because of the Corps of Engineers' traditional practice of disposing of dredgings from tributaries of the Great Lakes into offshore waters. A study sponsored by the Corps to determine the nature and degree of ecological impairment resulting from this practice indicated that no immediate hazard could be discerned. However, uncertainty regarding the long-term effect led the administration to request the Corps to discontinue such practices in selected areas and to dispose of dredgings by other means, presumably dikes.

AIR POLLUTION

According to the National Atmospheric Pollution Control Administration (NAPCA), New York City led all other U. S. cities in the severity of air pollution. Following close behind were Chicago, Philadelphia, Los Angeles, and Pittsburgh. NAPCA also estimated that combined state, regional, county, and local expenditures for air pollution control averaged less than 25 cents per capita per year, half representing federal grant funds. For comparison purposes, it was reported that the per capita expenditures for solid waste disposal was $15 per year.

Automobile Exhausts. Automobiles continued to be the worst air pollutors during 1969. Frustration with efforts to control this source of pollution was expressed in the California Assembly, in which a bill was introduced to ban the use of all vehicles driven by internal combustion engines by 1972. Frustration was also reflected in the growing realization that the deterioration of devices installed on new cars to reduce the emission of hydrocarbons and carbon monoxide is seldom corrected because of generally inadequate inspection facilities. A federal charge against major automobile manufacturers alleging a conspiracy to delay development and use of pollution control devices was settled by a consent decree, which the Justice Department said would insure desirable competition in the development of efficient anti-pollution devices.

There was also much emphasis on research to improve automobile propulsion systems. The National Liquid Petroleum Gas Association predicted that within a few years, gas derived from liquid petroleum would be widely used as engine fuel because it produces emissions containing less than half as much hydrocarbon as conventional systems. The use of natural gas for fueling internal combustion engines was put to a large-scale test in California, where more than 1,100 state-owned service vehicles were equipped with such systems. An experiment with steamdriven buses was begun in the San Francisco Bay area. Evaluations of electrically powered vehicles continued during the year, although it seems likely that large-scale battery recharging could place a significant strain on regional power sources.

Aircraft Exhausts. Major emphasis was placed on the automobile as the major source of air pollution, but jet aircraft also began to attract attention as important sources of pollution. The airplane industry generally took a dim view of demands that it provide aircraft with smokeless engines. The industry indicated that it would provide clean combustors only when present engines have to be replaced.

Quality Control Regions. Of the 57 metropolitan areas designated as potential air quality control regions by NAPCA, 24 had been proposed by the end of October. Illinois was the first state to approve final air quality standards for such regions, which include that state's portions of metropolitan Chicago and St. Louis. It is expected that both Indiana and Missouri will adopt standards consistent with those of Illinois.

SOLID WASTES

The disposal of garbage and refuse both efficiently and without nuisance became increasingly irksome during 1969. Impatience and frustration grew as incinerators continued to pollute the atmosphere and as burning dumps produced widespread palls of smog.

Three broad categories of projects were described by the Office of Science and Technology as meriting high priority for research and development: new and improved methods of waste storage, collection, and transportation; improvement in the aesthetics and efficiency of existing disposal systems; and the reclamation from solid wastes of marketable resources or usable energy.

A proposed Resource Recovery Act of 1969 was introduced aimed at strengthening federal and state activities in solid wastes management. If it is enacted, the bill would authorize an expenditure of $833 million over a 5-year period to provide grants for the construction of solid wastes disposal systems and materials recovery systems; the development of standards for collection and disposal; and the development of model legislation and codes. While the objectives of this bill are generally considered to be sound, the administration opposed it on the basis that waste producers, and not the federal government, should pay for the cost of waste disposal.

NOISE POLLUTION

A valuable report, "Noise—Sound Without Value," was issued by the Federal Council for Science and Technology. Acording to this report, the public is becoming more aware of the noise problem. Evidence of this concern is exemplified by public protests about jet aircraft noise, particularly sonic booms; complaints of apartment dwellers about the lack of effective sound insulation; articles about noise appearing in newspapers, magazines, and journals throughout the country, and complaints from civic associations about aircraft, expressway, and industrial noise. The report also cited the emergence of such organizations as Citizens for a Quieter City and the Citizens League Against the Sonic Boom as examples of the increased public concern.

The report called for an expanded program in research, development of governmental standards, coordination of inter-governmental actions, and education programs.

BERNARD B. BERGER
University of Massachusetts

POMPIDOU, Georges

President of France: b. Montboudif, France, July 5, 1911.

Displaced as premier after colliding with President Charles de Gaulle in 1968, Pompidou, early in 1969, reminded France that he would be a candidate for the presidency whenever de Gaulle stepped down. That event seemed remote at the time, but shortly afterward the president chose to risk his office by submitting constitutional reforms to a referendum held on April 27. Pompidou campaigned on behalf of the government, but after the decision against de Gaulle, he was quick to enter the presidential race. The fact that Pompidou had been de

FRENCH EMBASSY PRESS & INFORMATION DIVISION

Gaulle's premier for six years did not diminish the view of him as a strong personality. Capturing 58% of the vote in the second round of the June 1–15 election, he defeated interim president Alain Poher.

Pompidou relaxed the political atmosphere by choosing both followers of de Gaulle and Gaullist critics as cabinet ministers. Presidential news conferences became less formal; ministers were freer to express their views; TV and radio control was relaxed; and a sustained effort was made to establish contact with trade unions, farmers, and merchants' organizations. President Pompidou carried through devaluation of the currency on August 8 and mounted an austerity program to restore a balanced budget. Still unresolved, however, were profound difficulties arising from inflation, labor dissatisfaction, and other domestic problems.

On the international scene, Pompidou made no clear break with de Gaulle's policies. During the campaign he had proposed making France into "something like Sweden with a little more sunshine," but it was evident that he intended to maintain France's recently acquired international prestige. France's Common Market partners hoped the new president would welcome Britain, but Pompidou agreed only to preliminary talks. No immediate changes in NATO (North Atlantic Treaty Organization) policy were seen, and independent nuclear strength was maintained.

Background. The son of a schoolmaster, Pompidou left his native village to attain high distinction at the École Normale Supérieure. A schoolmaster in Albi, Marseilles, and Paris, Pompidou joined General de Gaulle's staff after the liberation of France in 1944. Close association with de Gaulle followed, lasting through the general's retirement. From 1946 to 1954 Pompidou served on the council of state, and then he joined the Rothschild Bank, advancing to director-general in 1956. On de Gaulle's return to power in 1958, Pompidou became head of his personal staff. He returned to the bank in 1959, but was called to the premiership by President de Gaulle in 1962. The de Gaulle-Pompidou partnership endured a variety of domestic and foreign trials.

JOHN C. CAIRNS
University of Toronto

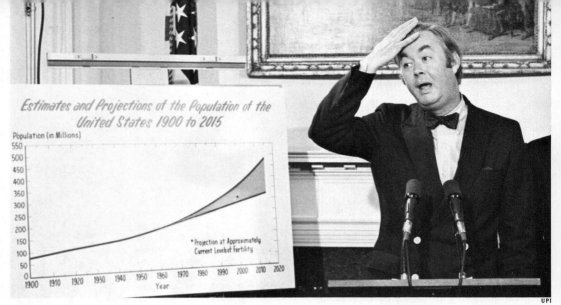

An expanded U. S. birth control program was requested by President Nixon on July 10. Daniel P. Moynihan (*above*), his urban affairs assistant, discusses the problems.

POPULATION

No important changes occurred in the determinants of population growth during 1969. The continuation of past trends, however, proved again that policies adopted to control the increase were often ineffective. A number of official bodies, both national and international, expressed greater concern about the increasing numbers of people and their deleterious effects on human welfare.

WORLD POPULATION

Since any estimate of the world's population must include guesses about some of the largest components, none can be more than an approximation. However, growth trends must be taken seriously. According to UN figures, the world's population increased from 3.479 billion in mid-1968 to 3.551 billion in mid-1969—almost 2.1% in one year compared with 1.4% during the previous year.

With the probable continuing decline in mortality and no change in the present level of fertility, the world's population will more than double by the year 2000, according to UN projections. If there is a moderate decline in fertility, it will increase by almost three fourths. In either case, the greatest jump will be in the populations of underdeveloped areas (Latin America, Africa, Asia), which will constitute a far larger proportion of the world's total than at present.

Successes in controlling the fertility of peasant countries during 1969 were limited, as before, to a few small, politically stable nations, some of which are transitional to modernization rather than truly underdeveloped. Such relatively successful campaigns included those, for instance, in Taiwan, South Korea, Hong Kong, and Thailand. In the major underdeveloped countries, however, efforts to limit family size have typically been instituted too recently to appraise their results. Where a judgment is possible, it generally must be negative.

UAR. A good example is the United Arab Republic. In mid-1969 its population was estimated at 32.5 million, increasing at 2.9% per year. According to the National Charter of the UAR (May 21, 1962), "This increase constitutes the most dangerous obstacle that faces the Egyptian people in their drive to raise the standard of production in their country." At the end of 1965 there was established a Supreme Council for Family Planning, which was to distribute oral contraceptives and intra-uterine devices (IUD's) throughout the country. For the year 1968–69 the program had a budget of more than $1.8 million. But in July 1969, President Nasser notified his countrymen that the number of births in Egypt exceeded a million annually—considerably more than in previous years. The seeming consequence of a birth-control program in effect for half a decade was a considerable rise in fertility. To reduce population pressure, the UAR for the first time began encouraging emigration.

India. A more striking case is India, which of all the important countries of the underdeveloped world has tried most consistently to reduce its birthrate. The means first used was the Lippes loop, an intra-uterine device. But in 1969 the number of women willing to use the device declined for the third year in a row. In part because of the failure of the campaign based on IUD's, the Indian government shifted to advocacy of male sterilization. But

U. N. ESTIMATES AND PROJECTIONS OF WORLD POPULATION
(in millions)

Region	Mid-1969 Population	"Constant Fertility" Population in 2000	"Constant Fertility" Increase 1969–2000	"Moderate Fall" in Fertility Population in 2000	"Moderate Fall" in Fertility Increase 1969–2000
World	3,551	7,522	112%	6,130	73%
Asia (without USSR)	1,990	4,513	127%	3,458	74%
Africa	344	860	150%	768	123%
Latin America	276	756	174%	638	131%
USSR	241	402	67%	353	46%
Europe (without USSR)	456	571	25%	527	16%
U. S. and Canada	225	388	72%	354	57%
Oceania	19	33	74%	32	68%

in the first quarter of 1969 the number of men willing to undergo the operation fell by almost a fifth.

The initial phase of the sterilization program, it is thought in India, depended on a backlog of acquiescent patients, whose number may have become exhausted. Little progress was expected in reducing the country's birthrate by this method.

EFFECTS OF POPULATION INCREASE

The major harmful effect of population increase is that it impedes economic development. When most of a nation's inadequate resources must go to feeding nonproductive infants and children, little is left with which to industrialize. This means that improvement in human welfare is slow or, at worst, nil. But that was extended to even more pessimistic conclusions. Several public bodies recently faced up to the fact that the consequences of population growth may be social and economic retrogression.

After a survey of illiteracy in more than 90 countries, UNESCO issued a report on its findings in the fall of 1969. The number of illiterates in the world increased over the prior decade by almost 60 million, to a total of about 800 million. In many nations this deterioration occurred in spite of literacy projects subsidized by the UN.

Mortality Rates. For a full generation now, the mortality rate in underdeveloped nations has been declining, and the numbers that survive because of this improved death control overwhelm efforts to establish even so important an element of modernization as basic schooling. The decline of the death rate in underdeveloped areas was usually brought about through international agencies using modern scientific techniques administered by Western specialists. In short, the death control did not depend, as it did earlier in the West, on prior improvements in the country's culture.

With a static culture, however, an ever-growing congestion is dangerous. The point was stressed in a report by the World Health Organization, according to which the all-time low incidence of cholera in the early 1960's may be at an end. In 1968 the reported cases, mostly in India and Pakistan, increased by 25% over the year earlier. This datum suggests that if means are not found to reduce the frightening rate of population increase by controlling fertility, the consequence will be a rise in the death rate. For the control of such diseases as cholera depends less on medical facilities than on modern sanitation or, lacking this, the wide dispersion of the population.

Family Planning. The general failure of family-planning projects in underdeveloped countries has stimulated a number of U. S. demographers to rethink current policies. In several issues during 1968–69, the journal *Science* published critical articles (especially by Professors Kingsley and Judith Davis, both of the University of California at Berkeley) and responses by administrators of the foundations that have funded present projects.

The Davises make several points. From all that we know about the psychological determinants of family size, prospective parents do not decide lightly that they will not have a child. Current birth-control policies depend mainly on ready access to contraceptives, along with advertising to publicize their availability. But according to a wide array of public opinion polls, parents in underdeveloped countries want about four children on the average. If facilities were available so that they could realize

© PUNCH, FROM THE BEN ROTH AGENCY

"Are you kidding?"

their desires completely, the resultant fertility would still be disastrously high. The sum of parents' decisions need not make good social policy, which must be based on new means of shaping those decisions so that smaller families become more attractive.

POPULATION OF THE UNITED STATES

The estimated population of the United States at mid-1969 was 203.1 million, growing at 1.0% per year. Neither the size of the population nor its rate of increase has impeded a steady growth in the U. S. economy. According to estimates by the Bureau of the Census (*Current Population Reports,* Series P-20, No. 189, Aug. 18, 1969), median family income reached a new high of $8,600 in 1968, up 8.3% from the previous year (or 3.9% in constant dollars). The income of Negro families relative to white has improved steadily, in part because the gap in education has been reduced. In 1960 only 36% of nonwhite males aged 25–29 had completed high school (compared with 63% of whites); in 1969 the comparable figures were 60% of Negroes compared with 78% of whites.

Population and Pollution. The ability of the United States both to absorb the increasing population and to raise its level of living has depended on its powerful industrial economy. During 1969 more citizens and public officials became aware that, apart from its great benefits, this economy is exacting sizable costs. A modern society not only rapidly uses up irreplaceable raw materials, but without proper safeguards it damages the human environment more than any nonindustrial society.

Pollution has been in part the consequence of public indifference. The same technical skill that creates it can largely correct the poisoning of the environment. But the problem is aggravated by population growth, especially since internal migration continues to be toward metropolitan areas. On Dec. 24, 1969, according to the guess of local demog-

(*Continued on page 559*)

VITAL STATISTICS OF SELECTED COUNTRIES

	Estimated population mid-1969	Birth rate per 1,000 population	Death rate per 1,000 population	Current rate of population growth	Population under 15 years (Percent)	Population projections to 1980 (millions)	Per capita gross national product (U.S. $)
World..................	3,551,000,000	34	15	1.9	37	4,368	589
North America							
Canada.................	21,300,000	18	7.3	2.0	33	22.3	2,240
Cuba..................	8,200,000	27	8	2.0	37	10.1	320
Dominican Republic......	4,200,000	49	15	3.4	47	6.2	250
El Salvador............	3,300,000	47	13	3.3	45	4.9	270
Guatemala..............	5,000,000	43	15	2.8	46	6.9	320
Haiti.................	5,100,000	44	20	2.4	38	6.8	70
Honduras..............	2,500,000	49	17	3.4	51	3.7	220
Mexico................	49,000,000	43	9	3.4	46	71.4	470
Nicaragua.............	2,000,000	46	16	3.0	48	2.8	330
Puerto Rico...........	2,700,000	26	6	1.1	39	3.1	1,090
United States.........	203,100,000	17.4	9.6	1.0	30	240.1	3,520
South America							
Argentina.............	24,000,000	23	9	1.5	29	28.2	780
Bolivia..............	4,500,000	44	19	2.4	44	6.0	160
Brazil...............	90,600,000	38	10	2.8	43	124.0	240
Chile................	9,600,000	33	10	2.3	40	12.2	510
Columbia.............	21,400,000	45	11	3.4	47	31.4	280
Ecuador..............	5,800,000	45	11	3.4	48	8.4	190
Paraguay.............	2,300,000	45	11	3.4	45	3.5	200
Peru.................	13,200,000	42	11	3.1	45	18.5	320
Uruguay..............	2,900,000	21	9	1.2	28	3.3	570
Venezuela.............	10,400,000	41	8	3.3	46	15.0	850
Europe							
Austria...............	7,400,000	17.4	13.0	0.5	24	7.7	1,150
Belgium...............	9,700,000	15.2	12.2	0.1	24	10.2	1,630
Bulgaria.............	8,400,000	15.0	9.0	0.6	24	9.2	620
Czechoslovakia.........	14,400,000	15.1	10.1	0.5	25	15.8	1,010
Denmark..............	4,900,000	18.4	10.3	0.9	24	5.3	1,830
Finland..............	4,700,000	16.5	9.4	0.6	27	5.2	1,600
France...............	50,000,000	16.9	10.9	1.0	25	53.8	1,730
Germany, East..........	16,000,000	14.8	13.2	0.1	22	17.7	1,220
Germany, West..........	58,100,000	17.3	11.2	0.4	23	61.0	1,700
Greece...............	8,900,000	18.5	8.3	1.2	25	9.3	660
Hungary..............	10,300,000	14.6	10.7	0.3	23	10.7	800
Ireland..............	2,900,000	21.1	10.7	0.5	31	3.5	850
Italy................	53,100,000	18.1	9.7	0.7	24	58.8	1,030
Netherlands..........	12,900,000	18.9	7.9	1.1	28	15.3	1,420
Norway...............	3,800,000	18.0	9.2	0.8	25	4.3	1,710
Poland...............	32,500,000	16.3	7.7	0.8	30	36.6	730
Portugal.............	9,600,000	21.1	10.0	1.1	29	10.9	380
Rumania..............	20,000,000	27.1	9.3	1.8	26	22.4	650
Spain................	32,700,000	21.1	8.7	0.8	27	34.8	640
Sweden...............	8,000,000	15.4	10.1	0.8	21	8.6	2,270
Switzerland..........	6,200,000	17.7	9.0	0.9	23	5.9	2,250
United Kingdom........	55,700,000	17.5	11.2	0.6	23	60.2	1,620
USSR................	241,000,000	18	8	1.0	32	277.8	890
Yugoslavia............	20,400,000	19.5	8.7	1.1	30	22.8	510
Africa							
Algeria...............	13,300,000	44	11–14	2.9	47	19.5	220
Congo (Kinshasa).........	17,100,000	43	20	2.3	39	...	60
Ethiopia..............	24,400,000	...	...	2.0	..	30.1	60
Kenya................	10,600,000	50	20	3.0	46	14.6	90
Morocco..............	15,000,000	46	15–19	3.0	46	22.4	170
Nigeria..............	53,700,000	50	25	2.5	43	...	80
South Africa..........	19,600,000	46	...	2.4	40	26.8	550
Sudan................	15,200,000	52	18–22	3.0	47	21.0	100
Tanzania.............	12,900,000	45	23	2.9	42	...	80
United Arab Republic......	32,500,000	43	15	2.9	43	46.7	160
Asia							
Afghanistan...........	16,500,000	...	...	2.3	..	22.1	70
Burma................	27,000,000	50	25–31	2.2	40	35.0	60
Ceylon...............	12,300,000	32	8	2.4	41	16.3	150
China, Mainland........	740,300,000	34	11	1.4	..	843.0	...
China, Nationalist........	13,800,000	29	6	2.6	44	17.6	230
India................	536,900,000	43	18	2.5	41	...	90
Indonesia............	115,400,000	43	21	2.4	42	152.8	100
Iran.................	27,900,000	50	20	3.1	46	38.0	250
Japan................	102,100,000	19	6.8	1.1	25	112.9	860
Korea, North..........	13,300,000	38	10–14	2.4	..	17.5	...
Korea, South..........	31,200,000	41	10–14	2.8	42	43.4	150
Malaysia.............	10,700,000	36	7	3.1	44	14.9	280
Nepal................	10,900,000	41	21	2.0	40	14.1	70
Pakistan.............	131,600,000	52	19	3.3	45	183.0	90
Philippines...........	37,100,000	50	10–15	3.5	47	55.8	160
Thailand.............	34,700,000	46	13	3.1	43	47.5	130
Turkey...............	34,400,000	46	18	2.5	44	48.5	280
Vietnam, North.........	21,400,000	...	...	3.1	38	...	...
Vietnam, South.........	17,900,000	...	...	2.6	..	...	120
Oceania							
Australia.............	12,200,000	19.4	8.7	1.8	29	15.2	1,840
New Zealand...........	2,800,000	22.4	8.4	1.9	33	3.6	1,930

[1] Population totals take into account smaller areas not listed on table. [2] Mid-1969 population estimates for this group are taken from figures of the Latin American Demographic Center of the United Nations; these figures are more recent than those of the 1967 U.N. Demographic Yearbook on which most of this table is based. [3] U.N. estimate; other estimates range from 800 million to 950 million. [4] Foreigners with resident permits not taken into account.

Source: Information Service, Population Reference Bureau, Washington, D. C.

(Continued)

raphers, the population of California passed 20 million. With its massive growth during the past generation, California became the most populous state and the wealthiest, but much of its grand natural beauty was destroyed in the process.

During 1969 the pollution of the biosphere—the poisoning of plants, wildlife, and man himself—became an important political issue. An oil drill off the shore of California at Santa Barbara twice poured oil into the sea and along the shoreline. Earlier, wrecked tankers had fouled beaches of England, France, and Puerto Rico.

The U. S. government, in an effort to stem pollution of the biosphere, took steps to substitute for DDT a pesticide that would not harm fish or birds. New York State enacted the nation's first "conservation bill of rights." (See POLLUTION.)

Population and Politics. During 1969, population growth also became a political issue on a new scale. A commission appointed by President Johnson had recommended that the federal government adopt more effective measures to facilitate birth control throughout the nation. For the first time in a presidential message to Congress, President Nixon designated overpopulation as a national problem.

Several bills were offered in Congress that would, with minor differences, set up a National Center for Population and Family Planning in the Department of Health, Education, and Welfare. In an address to Planned Parenthood-World Population, Dr. Roger O. Egeberg, assistant secretary for health and scientific affairs, said the threat of U. S. overpopulation by 2000 is so great that government should teach Americans now to have fewer children.

Side Effects of "The Pill." More than 7 million U. S. women and 14 million elsewhere were using the oral contraceptive pill in 1969. Concern was caused by British and U. S. studies suggesting that thromboembolic (blood-clotting) side effects cause death to three women of each 100,000 taking the pill, the risk being twice as great for women over 35 as for those under 35. According to Dr. Louis M. Hellman, chairman of the U. S. Food and Drug Administration's advisory committee on obstetrics and gynecology, this risk is about the same as with a pessary: of each 100,000 women using a diaphragm, 10,000 have unwanted babies, and three or four of the women die in the process.

Even so, on Jan. 19, 1970, the Food and Drug Administration sent letters to 381,000 doctors and hospital administrators, urging them to advise women of the potential hazard of the pill. The FDA also ordered that labels note the risk of blood clots.

Birth-Control Research. The U. S. government's Center for Population Research spent $15 million for research on the physiology of conception and contraception in 1969. Many private laboratories around the nation were also studying these problems.

The Population Council's Bio-Medical Division, at Rockefeller University in New York City, was trying a new contraceptive on monkeys. This is a tiny pellet of progestin in artificial rubber to be inserted in the skin of the female's abdomen, whence it would release a minuscule amount of progestin daily for three years or more.

WILLIAM PETERSEN
The Ohio State University
Author of "Population"

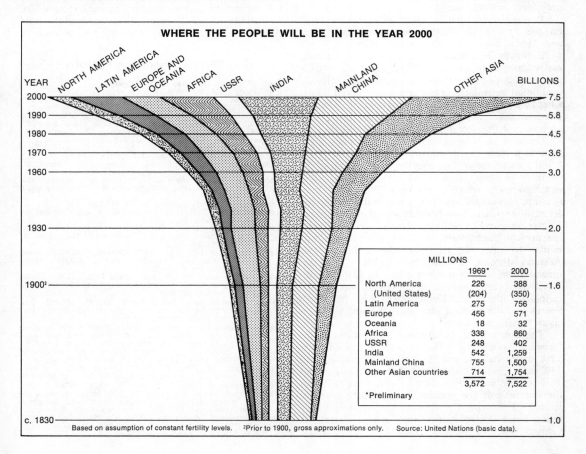

WHERE THE PEOPLE WILL BE IN THE YEAR 2000

MILLIONS		
	1969*	2000
North America	226	388
(United States)	(204)	(350)
Latin America	275	756
Europe	456	571
Oceania	18	32
Africa	338	860
USSR	248	402
India	542	1,259
Mainland China	755	1,500
Other Asian countries	714	1,754
	3,572	7,522

*Preliminary

Based on assumption of constant fertility levels.   [2]Prior to 1900, gross approximations only.   Source: United Nations (basic data).

BALLOT is cast by Prime Minister Marcello Caetano as National Union party sweeps Portugal's elections.

PORTUGAL

In 1969, Premier Marcello Caetano moved warily to find a policy that would resolve Portuguese national problems and gain him political support. The all-absorbing political event was the election of the National Assembly in October. As expected, all seats were won by the National Union, the country's only legal political party.

Portugal continued to divert resources to carry on the fight against nationalist forces in Angola and Mozambique, its African territories.

Domestic Politics. In March, Premier Caetano made changes in the cabinet, primarily to provide new solutions for economic problems. Despite traditional restraints, censorship was relaxed somewhat to permit some electoral campaigning. Greater freedom was extended to professional and labor groups, and the secret police were restrained.

On May 16, a republican congress was permitted to hold a three-day demonstration at Aveiro, where 1,300 foes of the regime cheered a succession of 56 speakers in their criticism of national defects. A new movement, which called itself "Portuguese Renovation," demanded the restoration of the monarchy. Its manifesto issued on May 24 was signed by some former monarchist leaders closely identified with the present government. In June priests were forbidden to enter the elections, and a month later Adriano Moreira, Caetano's principal rival, was dismissed from his government post. In Lisbon a divided democratic opposition presented two lists of candidates, the Social Democrats headed by Mario Soares and the Radical Democrats headed by Francisco Pereira de Moura.

The outcome of the October 26 elections was a foregone conclusion. The opposition polled only 12% of the ballots, and the National Union won all 130 seats in the National Assembly. Only about 10% of the population cast ballots, since 40% of the one fifth of the population entitled to vote abstained. Following the election the ministry of interior again declared opposition groups illegal. A General Office of Security replaced the secret police.

Protests. Some 5,000 students and many professors at the usually conservative University of Coimbra boycotted classes to hold a rally on April 23, after students had been denied participation in the dedication of the new mathematics building. Fifteen students were suspended because of the incident. Two months later, 4,000 students boycotted examinations to protest the suspension of eight of their leaders, who were later reinstated. On October 5, Republic Day, 3,000 people gathered to pay homage to the founders of the republic. The police did not interrupt the ceremony but cleared a nearby plaza of a few students and struck some people placing a wreath at the statue of an early hero.

Economy. Portugal had an unfavorable balance of trade and dwindling gold and foreign exchange reserves in 1969. The gross national product (GNP) increased to $5.1 billion in 1968, from $4.6 billion in 1967. Portugal is slowly becoming industrialized, but its industry is not efficient enough to expand under the government's rigid policy of protection. One third of the labor force was employed in agriculture, which also suffered from the protectionist policy.

Portugal's sardine industry has been threatened because the sardines have left their usual haunts and the trawling fleet, without refrigeration, is unable to follow them. To meet the crisis a national organization for the development of the fishing industry was established. Some fishermen have found employment in construction in France and West Germany, while others have turned to the tourist industry for work in hotels and restaurants.

Tourism has become increasingly important to the Portuguese economy. In 1968 there were 2.5 million visitors, and the industry earned $155 million.

African Wars. Portugal is determined to hold Angola and Mozambique, although the defense of

─────── **PORTUGAL · Information Highlights** ───────

Area: 35,510 square miles (91,971 sq km).
Population: 9,505,000 (1968 est.).
Chief Cities (1966 census): Lisbon, the capital, 825,800; Oporto, 321,900.
Government: President—Américo Thomaz (took office June 8, 1958); Premier—Marcello Caetano (took office Sept. 27, 1968). Parliament—National Assembly, 130 members.
Religious Faith: Roman Catholics, 91% of population.
Education: Literacy rate (1969), 80% of population. Total school enrollment (1966)—1,431,013 (primary, 891,082; secondary, 333,080; teacher-training, 2,867; technical/vocational, 167,652; university/higher, 36,332).
Finance (1969 est.): Revenues, $881,000,000; expenditures, $881,000,000; monetary unit, escudo (28.77 escudos equal U.S.$1).
Gross National Product (1968): $4,994,786,200.
National Income (1968): $4,337,851,900; average annual income per person, $456.
Economic Indexes (1967): Industrial production, 134 (1963= 100); agricultural production, 103 (1963=100); cost of living, 119 (1963=100).
Manufacturing (metric tons, 1967): Cement, 1,824,000; wine, 742,000; wheat flour, 436,800; gasoline, 407,000; crude steel, 315,600; meat, 103,200.
Crops (metric tons, 1967–68 crop year): Figs, 350,000 (ranks 1st among world producers); grapes, 1,359,000; potatoes, 1,296,000; wheat, 637,000.
Minerals (metric tons, 1967): Pyrites (1966), 557,856; iron ore, 196,800; lignite, 38,400; silver (1966), 53,000 troy ounces; gold (1966), 18,000 troy ounces.
Foreign Trade (1968): Exports, $761,000,000 (chief exports, 1967: wine, $51,650,600; fish, $50,058,300; fruit and vegetables, $44,652,000; cork, $20,852,900); imports, $1,178,-000,000 (chief imports, 1967: nonelectrical machinery, $144,708,000; transport equipment, $95,498,000; electrical machinery, $62,925,200). Chief trading partner (1967): Britain (took 21% of exports, supplied 14% of imports).
Transportation: National roads (1964), 10,952 miles (17,625 km); motor vehicles (1966), 370,000 (automobiles, 280,-000); railways (1965), 2,238 miles (3,602 km); merchant vessels (1967), 92 (605,000 gross registered tons).
Communications: Telephones (1968), 615,965; television stations (1968), 6; television sets (1968), 277,000; radios (1967), 1,345,000; newspapers (1966), 29.

"If We Can Get Men to the Moon . . . Who Knows? We May Even Learn to Get the Mail Across Town"

HAYNIE IN THE LOUISVILLE COURIER-JOURNAL

these African provinces consumed 8% of the GNP and 40% of the national budget in 1969 and has cost the lives of 1,868 soldiers since March 1961. This determination was symbolized by the conclusion of contracts between Portugal and South Africa for the $350 million Cahora Bassa hydroelectric project on the Zambezi River, in the heart of guerrilla activity.

To combat nationalist guerrillas the government has adopted the policy of concentrating the black population in controlled villages, defended by troops. In Mozambique the Portuguese tried to win the support of the fierce Makonde tribesmen, formerly members of the liberation front.

Angola and Mozambique are Africa's richest territories, with fertile farmlands, valuable fishing grounds, and vast mineral reserves. Oil strikes, offshore in the Angolan enclave of Cabinda, are expected to produce 150,000 barrels a day by 1970.

There was some Catholic opposition in Lisbon to the war, and Premier Caetano made a 9-day tour of the provinces in mid-April to restore public confidence in official policy.

The African wars also led to international complications for Portugal. On July 28 the UN Security Council voted 11–0 to censure Portugal for a bombing attack on a Zambian village in June. On August 7, Portugal warned Zambia against continued assistance to nationalists in their attacks on the frontiers of Angola and Mozambique.

RHEA MARSH SMITH
Rollins College

POST OFFICE

The Nixon administration proposed legislation in 1969 to reform the postal system by creating a self-supporting postal corporation wholly owned by the federal government, but the proposal was stalled by a tie vote in the House Post Office Committee. Postmaster General Winston M. Blount removed politics as a consideration in appointments to postmaster and rural carrier positions. He also began decentralizing the department by delegating additional authority to regional offices and local postmasters.

Training. An ultramodern postal training center was established on the campus of the University of Oklahoma, as an arm of the Postal Service Institute. At the Washington, D. C., headquarters of the Institute, management training and guidance were provided to postmasters of large cities in a series of one-week sessions.

In the summer of 1969, more than 8,000 underprivileged youths were hired in big-city post offices in a program designed to provide a meaningful work experience for the educationally disadvantaged; 1,660 postal employees voluntarily acted as counselors, providing training and guidance to groups of five or less of these summer aides, 94% of whom stayed on the job all summer.

Postal Experiments. The department began a Model Post Office program during 1969, initially testing new programs in nine post offices around the country. Also initiated was a joint experiment with Western Union for a combination letter-telegram that would be faster than a letter but cheaper than a telegram. The department also contracted for a "state of the art" study of electronic communication techniques, such as microwave and laser beam, that could possibly transmit the mails.

Operations. Gross revenues and reimbursements in the fiscal year ending June 30, 1969, totaled $6,264,870,000. Net revenue was $6,114,397,000. Mail volume processed during the year increased 3.1% to a total of 82 billion pieces. As of June 30, 1969, there were 32,064 post offices and an additional 11,156 branches and stations in the United States, with more than 742,000 workers. Convictions for violations of all postal statutes in fiscal year 1969 totaled 11,472.

Special services such as money orders, registered and certified mail, insurance, special delivery, and COD, numbered 576 million. Railway post offices covered over 10 million miles, and U. S. flag carriers moved 1.25 billion tons of mail by air.

JAMES R. HOLLAND
Special Assistant to the Postmaster General

THE NEW YORK TIMES

CHRONIC HUNGER and severe malnutrition among poor black families in the rural South was brought to the country's attention by Dr. Donald Gatch.

POVERTY

The year 1969 saw several major and a number of minor but significant efforts to improve the lot of the poor in the United States. Contrary to the expectations of many, the Nixon administration continued to support the so-called War on Poverty initiated by former President Johnson, proposed a sweeping plan for reforming the welfare system, and recommended substantial increases in federal expenditures for feeding the poor.

The Poor. Based on an annual income of $3,550 for a family of four as the poverty dividing line, the nation's poor were estimated to number about 25 million persons in 1969, or about 13% of the total population. About 15 million of these were children, two thirds of whom were currently ineligible for public assistance. From 12 to 15 million persons lived in families earning under $2,200 a year and 5.2 million of these had annual incomes of less than $1,000. Thirteen million persons living in poverty had a working parent; over a million families had full-time working fathers who earned less than welfare provides.

Welfare Reforms. For many years proposals have come from various positions in the political spectrum recommending a "negative income tax" or a guaranteed annual income. In August, President Nixon surprised critics and supporters alike by calling for a "family assistance program" guaranteeing each family of four a minimum annual income of $1,600. The first $720 per year earned by each eligible family would bring no reduction

of guaranteed income, but each dollar beyond this figure would produce a 50-cent reduction in the welfare grant. When family earnings reached $3,920, all aid would cease.

In order to qualify for these benefits, however, employable members of a family must either accept a job or engage in a job training program. Failure to comply with this requirement would lead to the forfeiture of welfare payments for the violator but not for other members of the family. If jobless heads of families take part in a training program, they are granted a bonus of $30 a month. Job training programs, now largely in federal hands, would gradually be turned over to state and local governments as long as these authorities demonstrated a capacity to handle the programs efficiently.

The welfare program, scheduled to begin operations in January 1971, would cost an estimated $4 billion. It would replace Aid to Families with Dependent Children (AFDC), an antipoverty program now costing $2.5 billion a year.

Reaction to Nixon's Program. President Nixon's recommendations, largely authored by presidential aide Daniel Moynihan, were widely praised in the press. Polls also showed a heavy majority of Americans favoring the program. Dissatisfaction with welfare payments running as low as $9.50 per person each month in Mississippi and with AFDC in general contributed to this support.

Others regarded the program's payment levels as inadequate. The requirement of compulsory work training also came in for criticism, especially as it applied to mothers of young children. George Meany, president of the AFL-CIO, said the program would "subsidize employers who pay less than a living wage." Instead of granting cash benefits to working poor, he preferred to raise the minimum wage to $2 an hour. Those favoring the program pointed out that a $2-an-hour minimum wage could deprive the unskilled, the blacks, and the young of thousands of marginal jobs. Nixon's proposals faced prolonged hearings, but affirmative congressional action on a plan like the President's is expected.

Developments in Welfare Policy. Many states have adopted rules declaring persons newly arrived from other states ineligible for welfare payments until they have resided for at least one year. The rules were designed to discourage jobless persons from moving to states that offer more liberal welfare benefits than other states. However, in April the U. S. Supreme Court declared such laws were a violation of the "equal protection of the laws" provision of the 14th Amendment. As a result, an estimated 100,000 to 200,000 persons became eligible for welfare payments.

An important innovation in welfare policy was initiated on July 1 when Robert Finch, secretary of health, education, and welfare ruled that, in certain areas and for trial purposes, persons applying for welfare benefits would not be subjected to intensive investigations prior to the granting of benefits. Applicants would be required to submit only an income affidavit subject to subsequent spot check audits. This policy would enable needy persons to qualify much more rapidly for benefits and would relieve trained social workers of a great burden of paper work. If the experiment is successful, it will be applied to old age assistance on Jan. 1, 1970, and to AFDC cases on April 1, 1970.

Welfare beneficiaries, under a new regulation, are also entitled to demand hearings before benefit payments can be terminated. During the period of investigation, welfare payments continue and the state is obliged to provide free legal services to the complainant.

Income Maintenance Commission Report. A commission on income maintenance programs established by former President Johnson issued a report in November, which, while hailing Nixon's welfare program as "courageous and pioneering," suggested a "universal income supplement" that would guarantee a four-member family an income of $2,400 a year. The commission proposals would directly benefit 36 million persons, compared with an estimated 22.4 million aided under Nixon's plan.

The commission concluded that almost all poverty is caused by the absence of work opportunities or by other factors beyond the control of the poor. Noting that there are about 4.5 million heads of poor families below 65 years of age, the commission declared that only 3% of these could be regarded as "shiftless."

Changes in the OEO. President Nixon proposed the retention of the Office of Economic Opportunity (OEO), which administers antipoverty programs, and even recommended slightly higher appropriations for it. However, the OEO was slated to become less an action agency than a laboratory agency to experiment with methods of dealing with poverty.

On November 6 the House Education and Labor Committee approved a $2.3 billion, 2-year extension of the antipoverty program. The sum was $295 million more than the amount requested by President Nixon and OEO director Donald Rumsfeld. Republicans were expected to offer amendments for stronger state control over OEO's programs. Unsuccessful efforts were made to grant veto power to governors over the agency's legal assistance program. Such a veto would have halted OEO efforts to give legal aid to the poor in some states.

Job Training. In July, President Nixon closed down over half of OEO's Job Corps centers, which attempt to give remedial education and job skills to school dropouts. About two thirds of the young men and women served by these camps would be diverted to other training programs, thereby allowing a $100 million cut in the Job Corps budget. A lesser reduction would be made in the total $2 billion spent to administer job training programs.

CHILDREN of a poverty-stricken family in the Mississippi Delta huddle together in bed for warmth.

NAVAHO FAMILY shelters in its hogan during blizzard that shut off the normally limited food supply.

One of the programs scheduled for enlargement under President Nixon was Job Opportunities in the Business Sector (JOBS), administered by the National Alliance of Businessmen (NAB). This group actively seeks out the hard-core unemployed, waives many normal job qualifications, and makes intensive efforts to help the jobless adjust to the demands of on-the-job training for a reasonably well paying job. The federal government pays cooperating businessmen an average of $3,000 per apprentice worker over an 18-month period. By the end of 1969, NAB had hired about 250,000 high-risk jobless and had managed to keep about half of them on the job. The government had spent about $500 million on the program, and Nixon hoped to subsidize another 150,000 trainees.

Secretary of Labor George Shultz proposed the establishment of computer "job banks" to match persons with jobs. He made it clear, however, that the administration did not plan to become an "employer of last resort" by providing or subsidizing the local creation of jobs for those who are unable to find employment with private enterprise or existing public agencies.

Tax Relief. In another development affecting the poor in 1969, the Nixon administration in April recommended a tax reform bill with a provision which would take about 2 million poor off the federal tax rolls. A family of four, now paying no federal taxes on its first $3,000 of annual income, would pay no taxes on its first $3,500 under the bill.

Housing. With 11 million U.S. families still living in substandard homes in 1969, the problem of adequate low-cost housing remained unsolved. Secretary of Housing and Urban Development George Romney advocated "Operation Breakthrough," a program designed to encourage private enterprise to adopt mass production techniques for home construction.

Hunger. Throughout the year there was public concern about the prevalence of hunger and malnutrition in the United States. Sen. Charles E. Goodell of New York declared that over 10 million Americans were living on diets which supplied less than two thirds of the nutritional requirements for good health. Federal food programs, he said, helped less than 20% of the poor, while federal school lunch programs fed fewer than a third of poor children.

A series of four reports prepared for the White House Conference on Food, Nutrition and Health stressed the need for immediate action. The reports declared hunger to be so widespread that the President should declare an immediate state of national emergency. One of the reports stated that 25 million Americans lived on incomes that prevented them from getting enough to eat. All four reports also favored cash rather than food assistance but argued for expanded food programs until adequate income maintenance legislation can be passed. (See also NUTRITION.)

Federal Food Programs. The administration currently spends about $1.3 billion annually on two specific food programs, one that enables the poor to buy food stamps at heavy discounts and redeem them at grocery stores, and one that makes available surplus government commodities to needy families and institutions caring for the needy. Again, contrary to expectation, President Nixon proposed a $1 billion increase in the food stamp program for the 1970–71 fiscal year. No increase was authorized for fiscal 1969–70.

Considerable differences of opinion existed in Congress over the food stamp program. While some thought the stamps should be entirely free for persons in low-income brackets, others felt a small payment should be required to avoid the development of a "handout" psychology.

Interest in an enlarged federal food program was enhanced by a study which showed that 3.5% of children aged 1–3 in low-income families suffered retarded bone growth because of malnutrition. According to the study, a third of poor children had anemia and 12% to 16% had vitamin C deficiency.

Education. In the area of education for the poor, no striking advances were made during the year. With so-called "compensatory education" programs achieving little or no results, many educators were at a loss as to how to improve the educational environment for those who come from impoverished physical and cultural backgrounds.

The Head Start program continued to have strong support, and efforts were underway to extend preschooling to 3- and 4-year-olds. Some educational psychologists believe that enrichment of a child's range of experiences and stimuli during the earliest years may be of critical importance to the development of his intellectual capacities. Except for small experiments, however, this theory has not been converted into effective public policy.

The Outlook. With termination of the Vietnam War, many anticipated the release of funds to strengthen the War on Poverty. However, with $4 billion sought for Nixon's welfare program and with a host of demands for federal funds for other causes, it was unclear how great the acceleration would be. The national mood during 1969 was increasingly conservative and may have an adverse effect on efforts to intensify antipoverty efforts.

Inflation presents another threat to the funding of poverty programs. The Nixon administration is determined to halt the rate of inflation which has

(Continued on page 566)

An unemployed migrant lives in an abandoned bus in "The Quarters," a migrant labor camp in Immokalee, Fla.

THE NEW YORK TIMES

Senators George McGovern (right) and Allen Ellender (left) investigated hunger in Florida labor camps.

WIDE WORLD

MIGRANT LABOR

A Senate committee investigating hunger in America focused attention in 1969 on conditions in migrant labor camps. These scenes are of camps near Immokalee, Florida, where many migrants work each winter on the vegetable crops.

A migrant worker and her two young children live in a trailer that rents for over half her weekly earnings.

THE NEW YORK TIMES

reached the level of 5% to 6% a year. Many economists are convinced that inflation can be halted only if cutbacks in public and private spending reach levels which reduce the demand for labor. If they are correct, the price to be paid for cutting the annual rate of inflation to an acceptable level of 2% or 2½% may be unemployment rising from 3.6% of early 1969 to a level of 5% or more.

The impact of greater joblessness would fall primarily on the unskilled and the poor. It could cripple the JOBS program. Welfare rolls, which have been rising at a rate of about 10% a year, might rise much higher. Since a disproportionate number of the poor are black, this development could certainly have a serious impact on domestic tranquility. But the effects of continuing high-level inflation also would be serious. Public debate over the balance to be struck between inflation and unemployment is expected to be very intense.

(See also CONSUMER AFFAIRS; SOCIAL WELFARE.)

REO M. CHRISTENSON
Miami University, Oxford, Ohio

PRESBYTERIAN CHURCHES

The number of Presbyterian denominations in the United States decreased by one in 1969, when the Associate Presbyterian Church of North America and the Reformed Presbyterian Church of North America merged on June 7, becoming the Associate Reformed Presbyterian Church. The other churches were: the United Presbyterian Church in the U. S. A.; the Presbyterian Church in the U. S.; the Cumberland Presbyterian Church; the Associate Reformed Presbyterian Church; the Orthodox Presbyterian Church; the Reformed Presbyterian Church, Evangelical Synod; the Bible Presbyterian Church; and the Second Cumberland Presbyterian Church.

In 1969 church union continued to be an important topic at many of the Presbyterian national meetings. Merger discussions were under way between the Orthodox Presbyterian Church and the Reformed Presbyterian Church, Evangelical Synod. The Cumberland Presbyterian Church also increased its ecumenical participation. Following the defeat of union negotiations between the Presbyterian Church in the U. S. and the Reformed Church in America by the latter church, the Presbyterian Church in the U. S. voted to invite the United Presbyterian Church to discuss merger.

The 181st General Assembly of the United Presbyterian Church, meeting in San Antonio, Texas, May 14–21, 1969, elected Dr. George E. Sweazey, of St. Louis, Mo., as moderator. The Assembly voted funds for minority peoples in the United States and authorized the establishment of a Council on Church Support.

The Rev. Matthew Lynn, Midland, Texas, was elected moderator of the 109th General Assembly of the Presbyterian Church in the U. S., meeting in Mobile, Ala., on April 24–29. Several committees were created by the Assembly to study internal problems of the church and the restructuring of the denomination's programs.

GERALD W. GILLETTE
The Presbyterian Historical Society

PRINCE EDWARD ISLAND

In 1969 the government of Prince Edward Island signed an agreement with the Canadian federal government for a $725 million economic development plan.

New Plan. The plan, announced in March, is designed to encourage the province's economic growth and improve its public services. Ottawa will provide $225 million for the 15-year program. A department of development has been established to supervise the overall program.

Agriculture. Greatly increased agricultural production, with fewer farms and larger acreage, is one goal of the multi-million dollar economic plan. But early acceptance of the plan by farmers is unlikely, because of the reluctance of many to accept the advice of technical experts.

Tobacco production is rapidly becoming an important feature of agriculture on Prince Edward Island and could become a major cash crop in the next decade. Tobacco farming in the province started less than 10 years ago but has proved so profitable that the number of growers was expected to double in 1969.

Potatoes have long been the main cash crop, but recurring low-price years have threatened the exis-

PRESBYTERIAN CHURCH STATISTICS, 1969

Church	Ministers	Churches	Members
Associate Reformed Presbyterian Church	144	148	28,312
Bible Presbyterian Church[1]	150	70	10,800
Cumberland Presbyterian Church	728	914	88,669
Orthodox Presbyterian Church	170	130	14,038
Presbyterian Church in the U. S.	4,337	3,960	957,430
Reformed Presbyterian Church, Evangelical Synod	274	115	11,835
Reformed Presbyterian Church of North America	92	70	5,550
Second Cumberland Presbyterian Church[2]	120	141	7,500
United Presbyterian Church in the U. S. A.	12,939	8,768	3,229,724

[1] 1968 data. [2] 1966 data.

YOUTHFUL OFFENDERS receive rehabilitative training to reshape their behavior at the new Robert F. Kennedy Youth Center in West Virginia.

tence of all but the most efficient farmers. Dairy farming, too, is steadily losing ground.

Government Change. J. George MacKay, former minister of highways and a member of the legislature for 17 years, took office as the new lieutenant-governor of Prince Edward Island on October 1.

NEIL A. MATHESON
"The Guardian," Charlottetown

PRISONS

The U. S. correctional systems were given much needed help in 1969 through funds authorized under the 1968 Omnibus Crime Control and Safe Streets Act. The Law Enforcement Assistance Administration, an agency of the Department of Justice established to administer programs under the act, provided the states with $44 million in grants to plan and carry out improvements in their criminal justice systems.

Prison Population. For the second consecutive year, the increasing crime rate across the nation was reflected in an increase in prison population. On June 30, 1969, there was a total of 20,555 inmates in custody, an increase of 304 over June 30, 1968.

The character of the federal institutional population reflected the national upsurge in serious crime. Of those inmates in custody, nearly 3,500 were convicted of assaultive offenses such as robbery and homicide. An additional 1,400 offenders were convicted for violation of narcotic laws. There was also a steady increase in the number of younger offenders. In 1969, the median age of convicts dropped to 28.3, the lowest in recent history.

Rehabilitation Programs. Correctional agencies searched for new ways to stop the habitual criminal: more than half of all offenders in prison are repeaters. The greatest effort was directed toward youthful offenders, who have the best potential for rehabilitation. In January, the Bureau of Prisons

opened the Robert F. Kennedy Youth Center, Morgantown, West Va., where 15- to 19-year-olds undergo training to reshape their behavior. Treatment programs and staff are matched to the different personality types and behavior problems presented by the young men. Life in the cottage-type institution parallels that on the "outside" as much as possible, and an integrated curriculum combines school and vocational training so that as a boy learns a work skill, he also progresses toward a high school diploma.

Work and Study Release. Community resources were increasingly used in the rehabilitation of prisoners. Work-release programs, authorized in more than half the states, permitted inmates to leave the prison and work in the community during the day. In 1969 over 2,000 federal inmates were assigned to work-release. They paid taxes and supported dependents with the money they earned.

A companion program, study-release, permitted inmates to attend daytime classes in the community, and a furlough program allowed them to make unescorted trips, such as emergency home visits, for employment interviews, or other approved reasons. Many offenders nearing the end of their sentences were assigned to transitional residential centers in an effort to help their adjustment to community life. The federal Bureau of Prisons' eight community treatment centers rendered assistance to 1,200 inmates during 1969.

Drug Program. The Federal Prisons System's fourth treatment unit for narcotic addicts was established at the Federal Correctional Institution, Milan, Mich. Authorized under the Narcotic Addict Rehabilitation Act of 1966, the unit provided intensive treatment of addict offenders. Three other units are located in federal institutions in Danbury, Conn., Alderson, W. Va., and Terminal Island, Calif.

MYRL E. ALEXANDER
Director, U. S. Bureau of Prisons

PRIZE-WINNING beauties crowned in 1969: (upper left) Miss America—Pamela Eldred, Michigan; (upper right) Miss Black America—Gloria Smith, New York; (lower left) Miss Universe—Gloria Diaz, Philippines; (lower right) Miss World—Eva Rueber-Staier, Austria.

PRIZES AND AWARDS

Prize committees in many fields of endeavor focused attention on achievements in aeronautics and astronautics in 1969 and hastened to honor members of the U. S. space program as the National Aeronautics and Space Administration (NASA) placed the first men on the moon. Among the many prizes awarded Apollo astronauts was a special trustees' prize of the Academy of Television Arts and Sciences honoring the astronauts of Apollo flights 7, 8, 9, and 10 for "bringing television to earth from outer space."

New awards were announced and some long-established awards were discontinued. Columbia University announced in December that a Pulitzer Prize for "distinguished criticism or commentary" would be awarded in 1970. The $1,000 prize will replace a fellowship in critical writing. The Atoms for Peace Award, established in 1955, was given for the last time in 1969 because the original $1 million appropriation has run out. At the 1969 Venice Film Festival all awards except the Critics' Prize were discontinued in response to student charges that the festival was too commercial.

Norman Mailer, winner of the National Book Award in arts and letters for *The Armies of the Night*, also shared the Pulitzer Prize for general nonfiction with Rene Dubos, the microbiologist.

A selected list of the most important and newsworthy prizes and awards announced in 1969 follows.

PULITZER PRIZES

Winners of the Pulitzer Prizes were announced by the trustees of Columbia University on May 5, 1969. No award was made in the category of international reporting. Each prize was worth $1,000 except the public service gold medal.

Journalism. Local general reporting—John Fetterman of the Louisville *Courier-Journal*, for his story on the burial in rural Kentucky of a soldier killed in Vietnam. Local investigative reporting—Albert L. Delugach and Denny Walsh of the St. Louis *Globe-Democrat*, for a series of articles exposing fraud and abuse of power in Local 562 of the St. Louis Steamfitters union. Editorial writing—Paul Greenberg of the Pine Bluff (Ark.) *Commercial*. Editorial cartooning—John Fischetti of the Chicago *Daily News*. National reporting—Robert Cahn of the *Christian Science Monitor*, for his series of articles on the need for saving the national parks. Spot news photography—Edward T. Adams of the Associated Press. Feature photography—Moneta Sleet, Jr., of *Ebony* magazine. Meritorious public service—the *Los Angeles Times*, for exposing "wrongdoing within the Los Angeles city government commissions."

Letters. History—Leonard W. Levy, for *Origins of the Fifth Amendment*. Biography—B. L. Reid, for *The Man from New York*. Poetry—George Oppen, for *Of Being Numerous*. Drama—Howard Sackler, for *The Great White Hope*. Fiction—N. Scott Momaday, for *House Made of Dawn*. General nonfiction—Norman Mailer, for *The Armies of the Night* and Dr. Rene Jules Dubos, for *So Human an Animal*.

Music. Karel Husa, for his String Quartet No. 3.

ARTS

American Composers Alliance Laurel Leaf Award for "distinguished service to contemporary music"—The Group for Contemporary Music at Columbia University.

American Institute of Architects awards: gold medal—William Wilson Wurster; fine arts medal—Jacques Lipchitz; critic medal—Ada Louise Huxtable of the New York *Times*.

American Institute of Graphic Arts Gold Medal—Robert L. Leslie.

Brandeis University Creative Arts Awards ($1,000 each): Ernst Krenek, composer; Leonie Adams, poet; José Di Rivera, sculptor; Boris Aronson, stage designer; special medal for notable creative achievement—Lewis Mumford, author and architecture critic.

Capezio Dance Award ($1,000)—John Martin, critic.

Van Cliburn International Piano Competition Award ($10,000)—Christina Ortiz of Brazil.

Kirsten Flagstad Awards: ($1,000) Patricia Guthrie, soprano; ($500) Donna Roll, soprano, and David Stone, pianist.

Leventritt International Piano Competition Award ($1,000)—Joseph Kalichstein of Israel.

Dimitri Mitropoulos International Music Competition Awards ($5,000 each)—Michael Zearott, Uri Segal, Alfredo Bonavera, and Mesru Mehmedov.

National Academy of Arts and Sciences Grammy Awards for excellence in phonograph records: record of the year—*Mrs. Robinson*, sung by Simon and Garfunkel; album—*By the Time I get to Phoenix*, Glen Campbell; classical album—*Boulez Conducts Debussy*, conducted by Pierre Boulez; opera recording—Mozart's *Cosi fan tutte*, conducted by Erich Leinsdorf; new artist—José Feliciano; song of the year—*Little Green Apples* by Bobby Russell; contemporary-pop vocal performance by a male—José Feliciano for *Light My Fire*; contemporary-pop vocal performance by a female—Dionne Warwick for *Do You Know the Way to San Jose;* contemporary-pop performance by a vocal duo or group—Simon and Garfunkel for *Mrs. Robinson;* original score for a motion picture—Paul Simon for *The Graduate;* score from an original cast show album—*Hair.*

National Academy of Design, Benjamin Altman Awards ($2,500 each)—Paul W. Zimmerman, Burton Silverman; ($1,250 each)—William Thon, Leon Kroll.

National Institute of Arts and Letters awards; art—Lennart Anderson, William Christopher, Frank Gallo, Leonel Gongora, Red Grooms, Sidney Hurwitz, Ben Kamihira, and Alice Neel; music—Michael Brozen, Jacob Druckman, Nicolas Roussakis, and Claudio Spies; distinguished service to the arts award—Leopold Stokowski; Arnold W. Brunner Memorial Prize in architecture—Noel Michael McKinnell; Marjorie Peabody Waite Award ($1,500)—Herbert Elwell; Richard and Hinda Rosenthal Foundation Awards ($2,000)—Frederick Exley and Nicholas Sperakis.

New York Architectural League Award—Mayor John Lindsay for his "special concern for the quality of the urban environment."

Elsie and Philip Sang Prize for critics of the fine arts, sponsored by Knox College ($2,500 each)—Michael Steinberg and Eric Salzman, music critics.

JOURNALISM

American Newspaper Guild Heywood Broun Memorial Award ($1,000)—Mike Royko of the Chicago *Daily News.*

Maria Moors Cabot Gold Medals for "distinguished journalistic contributions to the advancement of inter-American understanding" ($1,000)—Alceu Amoroso Lima, Brazilian author, essayist, and critic; Elsa Arana Freire, Sunday magazine editor of *La Prensa* of Lima, Peru; Edward W. Barrett, director of the Communications Institute of the Academy for Educational Development; George H. Beebe, senior managing editor of the Miami (Fla.) *Herald;* and Luis Gabriel Cano, general manager of *El Espectador* of Bogotá, Colombia.

Sidney Hillman Foundation Awards for achievement in the communications field ($500): George R. Stewart, Charles and Bonnie Remsberg, James K. Batten, Dwayne E. Walls, William E. Osterhaus, and Dick Hubert.

Albert Lasker Medical Journalism Awards ($2,500): NBC News and Len Giovannitti, producer-director; C. P. Gilmore, free-lance magazine writer; and Barbara Yuncker of the New York *Post.*

Long Island University, George Polk Memorial Awards: international reporting—David Kraslow and Stuart H. Loory of the Los Angeles *Times;* magazine reporting—Norman Mailer, for articles in *Harper's* magazine; national reporting—Bernard D. Nossiter of the Washington *Post;* regional reporting—James K. Batten and Dwayne E. Walls of the Charlotte (N. C.) *Observer;* news photography—Edward T. Adams of the Associated Press; criticism—John Simon of the *New Leader;* television reporting—news departments of NBC, CBS, and ABC; book—Charles Rembar for *The End of Obscenity;* political reporting—Martin Arnold of the New York *Times;* community service—David Burnham of the New York *Times.*

Society of Magazine Writers awards: Maya Pines of the New York *Times Magazine;* Daniel Lang of *The New Yorker;* Ronnie Dugger of the *Atlantic Monthly;* Gilbert Voyat of the *Saturday Review;* Lawrence Lader of *Look* magazine; and Shirley Streshinsky of *Redbook* magazine.

National Cartoonist Society Award, Cartoonist of the Year (Reuben Award)—John Hart and Pat Oliphant.

Newspaper Guild of New York Page One Awards: local reporting—Marvin Smilon of the New York *Post;* foreign reporting—Thomas A. Johnson of the New York *Times.*

Overseas Press Club awards: George Polk Memorial Award for the best reporting requiring exceptional courage and enterprise abroad—Peter Rehak of the Associated Press; Robert Capa Gold Medal for photography—John Olson of *Life* magazine; Asia Magazine award—Bernard Kalb of CBS; F. W. Fairchild Award for business news reporting from abroad—Clyde Farnsworth of the New York *Times; Vision* Magazine Ed Stout Award for reporting on Latin America—Henry Giniger of the New York *Times;* book on foreign affairs—*The Discipline of Power* by George Ball; magazine reporting from abroad—J. Robert Moskin of *Look* magazine; magazine interpretation of foreign affairs—James Thomson of the *Atlantic Monthly;* television reporting from abroad—Liz Trotta of NBC; television interpretation of foreign affairs—Charles Collingwood of CBS; radio reporting from abroad—Bernard Redmont of the Westinghouse Broadcasting Company; radio interpretation of foreign affairs—Elie Abel of NBC; best cartoon on foreign affairs—Don Wright of the Miami (Fla.) *News;* photographic reporting from abroad in a magazine or book—Romano Cagnoni and David Robison of *Life* magazine; newspaper or wire service photographic reporting from abroad—Edward T. Adams of the Associated Press; newspaper or wire service interpretation of foreign affairs—Robert S. Elegant of the Los Angeles *Times;* daily newspaper or wire service reporting from abroad—Peter Rehak of the Associated Press; Special President's Award—the newsmen of Czechoslovakia in all media for "their defense of tradition of a free press before and during the Soviet invasion of their homeland."

LITERATURE

Academy of American Poets Fellowship Award ($5,000)—Richard Eberhart.

American Library Association awards: Newbery Medal—Lloyd Alexander for *The High King;* Caldecott Medal—Uri Shulevitz, illustrator, for *The Fool of the World and the Flying Ship;* Beta Phi Mu Award ($50)—Ethel M. Fair, director of the Library School, New Jersey College for Women; Francis Joseph Campbell Award—Alexander Skrzypek, regional librarian for the Blind and Physically Handicapped, Chicago Public Library; Joseph W. Lippincott Award ($1,000)—Germaine Krettek, associate executive director and director of the Washington office of the American Library Association; Melvil Dewey Award—William S. Dix, librarian at Princeton University; Margaret Mann Citation—Katherine L. Ball, professor in the University of Toronto Library School, Ontario; Clarence Day Award—Clifton Fadiman, essayist.

Bancroft Prize of Columbia University for distinguished writing in American history—Winthrop D. Jordan for *White Over Black; American Attitudes toward the Negro, 1550–1812;* N. Gordon Levin, Jr., for *Woodrow Wilson and World Politics: America's Response to War and Revolution;* Rexford Guy Tugwell for *The Brains Trust.*

Carey-Thomas Award for a distinguished project of creative book publishing—the W. W. Norton Company for *The Norton Facsimile: The First Folio of Shakespeare.*

William Faulkner Foundation First Novel Award—Frederick Exley for *A Fan's Notes.*

George Freedley Memorial Award of the Theatre Library Association—Louis Sheaffer for *O'Neill, Son and Playwright.*

Goncourt Prize in literature—Félicien Marceau for *Creezy.*

Governor General's Awards (Canadian): French fiction—Marie-Clare Blais, Hubert Aquin; French nonfiction—Ferand Dumont; English fiction—Mordecai Richler; English poetry—Margaret Atwood; English nonfiction—Robert Furfords.

Lamont Poetry Prize, sponsored by the Academy of American Poets—Marvin Bell for *A Probable Volume of Dreams.*

Mystery Writers of America, Edgar Allen Poe ("Edgar") Awards for 1968: mystery novel—Jeffrey Hudson for *A Case of Need;* first mystery novel—Dorothy Uhnak for *The Bait* and E. Richard Johnson for *Silver Street;* mystery short story—Warner Law for *The Man who Fooled the World*, which appeared in the *Saturday Evening Post;* true-crime book—John Walsh for *Poe the Detective.*

National Book Awards ($1,000 each): fiction—Jerzy Kosinski for *Steps;* arts and letters—Norman Mailer for *The Armies of the Night;* science, philosophy, and religion—Robert Jay Lifton for *Death in Life;* history and biography—Winthrop D. Jordan for *White Over Black: American Attitudes toward the Negro, 1550–1812;* poetry—John Berryman for *His Toy, His Dream, His Rest;* translation—William Weaver for his translation of *Cosmocomics* by Italo Calvino; children's literature—Meindert DeJong for *Journey from Peppermint Street.*

National Book Committee, National Medal for Literature ($5,000)—Conrad Aiken.

National Council on the Arts awards for "lifelong contribution to American letters" ($7,000)—Kenneth Burke, critic, and Reed Whittemore, poet, critic, and editor.

National Institute of Arts and Letters Gold Medal for drama—Tennesseee Williams.

National Institute of Arts and Letters Award of Merit for the Novel ($1,000)—Vladimir Nabokov.

National Insitute of Arts and Letters awards ($5,000): writing—John Ashbery, George P. Elliott, Allen Ginsberg, Hugh Kenner, and L. E. Sissman; traveling fellowship in literature ($9,000)—Robert Stone, novelist.

Nebula Awards of the Science Fiction Writers of America: Alexei Panshin for *Rites of Passage,* Anne McCaffrey for *Dragonrider,* and Richard Wilson for *Mother of the World.*

P. E. N. American Center Translation Award ($1,000)—W. S. Merwin for *Selected Translations, 1948–1968.*

Phi Beta Kappa Society awards for outstanding books: Peter Gay for *Weimar Culture: the Outsider as Insider;* Louis Crompton for *Shaw the Dramatist;* G. J. V. Nossal for *Antibodies and Immunity.*

Poetry Society of America Awards: Alice Fay di Castagnola Award for a work in progress ($3,500)—Wade Van Doren; Shelley Award ($1,700)—Ann Stanford; Melville Cane Award ($500)—Ruth Miller; Christopher Morley Award ($500)—David Ross; John Masefield Award ($1,000)—Siv Cedering Fox.

PUBLIC SERVICE

American Friends of the Hebrew University, Scopus Award —Charles C. Bassing, industrialist.

Anti-Defamation League of B'nai B'rith, Human Rights Award—Sen. Edmund S. Muskie.

Max Berg Award ($10,000)—George Wald for his "outstanding leadership in the peace movement."

Brotherhood-in-Action Awards—George Romney, Kenneth B. Clark, Ed Sullivan, Howard A. Rusk, Samuel Hausman, and John MacCrate.

Albert Einstein Commemorative Awards for outstanding contributions to man's betterment: John W. Gardner, chairman of the Urban Coalition; Marshall W. Nirenberg, chief of the biochemical genetics laboratory of the National Heart Institute; Joseph I. Lubin, real estate investor and philanthropist; and Jacques Lipschitz, sculptor.

Antonio Feltrinelli Prize for humanitarian work of Italy's Accademia del Lincei ($16,000)—Mrs. Martin Luther King, Jr.

Freedom Foundation awards: George Washington Award ($5,000)—Gen. Harold K. Johnson; American Exemplar Award —Leon H. Sullivan; Free Enterprise Exemplar Medal—J. Howard Wood.

Freedom House, Freedom Award for 1969—Earl Warren.

Robert F. Kennedy Humanitarian Award—W. Averell Harriman.

National Conference of Christians and Jews, Brotherhood Award—Leo Jaffe, president of Columbia Pictures.

National Urban League Awards—Earl Warren and Maurice Lee, Sr.

New York Civil Liberties Union, Florina Lasker Civil Liberties Award ($1,000)—Cesar Chavez.

Rockefeller Public Service Awards for outstanding longterm service to the federal government, administered by Princeton University's Woodrow Wilson School of Public and International Affairs: ($10,000) Robert R. Gilruth, Arthur E. Hess, William T. Pecora, Ashley Foard, and John W. Evans; ($5,000) Philip C. Habib and John F. Thomas.

Margaret Sanger Award in World Leadership—Lord Caradon, British ambassador to the United Nations.

SCIENCE AND TECHNOLOGY

American Chemical Society, Priestley Medal—Kenneth S. Pitzer.

American Geographical Society Awards: Charles P. Daly Medal—Paul B. Sears and William O. Field; Cullum Geographical Medal—the Apollo 11 astronauts: Neil A. Armstrong, Edwin E. Aldrin, Jr., Michael Collins.

American Institute of Aeronautics and Astronautics awards: Goddard Award ($10,000)—Perry W. Pratt and Stanley G. Hooker; Haley Astronautics Award ($500)—astronauts Donn F. Eisele, R. Walter Cunningham, and Walter M. Schirra, Jr.; Hill Space Transportation Award ($5,000)—William H. Pickering.

American Institute of Physics, U. S. Steel Foundation Award in Physics and Astronomy ($1,500)—Walter Sullivan, science editor of the New York *Times.*

American Physical Society awards: Oliver E. Buckley Solid-State Physics Prize ($1,000)—J. J. Hopfield and D. G. Thomas; High Polymer-Physics Prize ($1,000)—Charles W. Bunn; Irving Langmuir Prize in Chemical Physics ($5,000)—Charles P. Slichter; Bonner Prize in Nuclear Physics ($1,000)—Gregory Breit.

Arches of Science Award of the Pacific Science Center,

for outstanding contributions to the public understanding of science ($25,000)—Gerard Piel, publisher of *Scientific American* magazine.

Astronomical Society of the Pacific, Catherine Wolfe Bruce Gold Medal—Horace W. Babcock.

Atoms for Peace Award: ($15,000 each) Agae N. Bohr, Ben R. Mottelson, Floyd L. Culler, Jr., Henry S. Kaplan, Anthony L. Yurkevich, M. S. Ioffe, Compton A. Rennie; ($50,000) Dwight D. Eisenhower (posthumously) for his contribution to efforts for the peaceful use of atomic energy.

Dreyfus Medical Foundation Award ($75,000)—Tracy Jackson Putnam, senior consultant in neurosurgery at Cedars of Lebanon Hospital in Los Angeles.

Franklin Medal in biochemistry of the Franklin Institute—Marshall W. Nirenberg.

Galabert International Astronautics Prize ($4,000)—the Apollo 11 astronauts: Neil A. Armstrong, Edwin E. Aldrin, Jr., Michael Collins.

Geological Society Penrose Medal in pure geology: John Tuzo Wilson of the University of Toronto.

Guggenheim International Astronautics Award ($1,000)—Zdeněk Svestka of the Astronomical Institute of the Czechoslovak Academy of Sciences.

Harmon International Aviation Trophy—Maj. Jerauld R. Gentry; Astronaut's Trophy—Apollo 8 astronauts: Frank Borman, James A. Lovell, Jr., William A. Anders.

Louisa Gross Horowitz Prize for outstanding research in biology ($25,000)—Max Delbruck of the California Institute of Technology and Salvador Luria of the Massachusetts Institute of Technology.

International Feltrinelli Prize for medicine ($32,000)—Rita Levi Montalcin.

Albert Lasker Medical Research Awards ($10,000 each): clinical research—George C. Cotzias of Brookhaven National Laboratory; basic research—Bruce Merrifield of Rockefeller University.

National Academy of Engineering, Founders Medal—Harry Nyquist.

National Academy of Sciences awards: U. S. Steel Foundation Award for research in molecular biology ($5,000) —William B. Wood III; Henry Arctowsky Medal for studies of solar activity—Eugene N. Parker and J. Paul Wild; James K. Watson Medal—Jürgen K. Moser; Alexander Agassiz Medal —Frederick C. Fuglister.

National Aeronautics Association, Robert J. Collier Trophy —the Apollo 8 astronauts: Frank Borman, James A. Lovell, Jr., William A. Anders.

National Medals of Science for 1968: H. Albert Barker, professor of biochemistry, University of California at Berkeley; Bernard B. Brodie, chief of the Laboratory of Chemical Pharmacology, National Institute of Health; Detlev W. Bronk, president emeritus of Rockefeller University; B. Frederic Skinner, professor of psychology at Harvard University; J. L. Lush, professor of animal breeding at Iowa State University; J. Presper Eckert, vice president of the Remington Rand Univac Division, Sperry Rand Corp.; Mason M. Newmark, professor of civil engineering at the University of Illinois; Jerzy Neyman, professor of mathematics at the University of California at Berkeley; Paul D. Bartlett, professor of chemistry at Harvard University; Herbert Friedman, superintendent of the Atmosphere and Astrophysics Division, Naval Research Laboratory; Lars Onsager, professor of chemistry at Yale University; Eugene P. Wigner, professor of mathematical physics at Princeton University.

Research Corporation Award ($10,000)—Murray Gell-Mann of the California Institute of Technology.

Alfred P. Sloan Memorial Award for dedication to the cause of cancer control—Laurance S. Rockefeller.

Stouffer Prize for contribution to the understanding of blood pressure ($13,500 each)—John H. Laragh, Jerome W. Conn, Jacques Genest, and Franz Gross.

TELEVISION AND RADIO

Academy of Television Arts and Sciences ("Emmy") Awards: dramatic program—*Teacher, Teacher* (NBC); musical or variety program—*The Bill Cosby Special* (NBC); comedy series—*Get Smart* (NBC); dramatic series—*N.E.T. Playhouse* (National Educational Television); musical or variety series—*Rowan and Martin's Laugh-In* (NBC); leading actor in a comedy series—Don Adams in *Get Smart;* best single performances in a drama—Paul Scofield in *Male of the Species* (NBC) and Geraldine Page in *A Thanksgiving Visitor* (ABC); actor in a leading role in a dramatic series—Carl Betz in *Judd for the Defense* (CBS); actress in a leading role in a dramatic series—Barbara Bain in *Mission Impossible* (CBS); actress in a comedy series—Hope Lange for *The Ghost and Mrs. Muir* (ABC); supporting actor in a comedy series—Werner Klemperer in *Hogan's Heroes* (CBS); supporting actress in a drama series—Susan Saint James in *The Name of the Game* (NBC); writing achievement in drama—J. P. Miller for *The People Next Door* (CBS); writing achievement in comedy or variety—Dick and Tom Smothers for *The Smothers Brothers Comedy Hour* (CBS); directorial achievement in drama—David Greene for *The People Next Door;* news documentary—*CBS Reports: Hunger in America;* cultural documentary—*Don't Count the Candles* (NBC); cinematography—Lord Snowdon for *Don't Count the Candles;* board of trustees award—the astronauts of Apollo 7, 8, 9, and 10 for "bringing television to earth from outer space"; special plaque—Billy Schulman for his role in *Teacher, Teacher.*

George Foster Peabody Awards for distinguished achievement in television and radio: special television award—*CBS Reports: Hunger in America* (CBS); television public service—Westinghouse Broadcasting Company for *One Nation Indivisible;* television documentary—*Book Beat* on WTTW in Chicago and *How Life Begins, Hemingway's Spain, The Secret of Michelangelo,* and *The Road to Gettysburg* (all ABC); television news—Charles Kuralt of *CBS News* (CBS); children's television—National Educational Television for *Misterogers Neighborhood;* radio entertainment—WQXR for *Steinway Hall;* radio news—*Second Sunday* (NBC); radio public service—*Kaleidoscope* and station WJR in Detroit; radio educational program—*The World Tomorrow* of station WEEI in Boston.

THEATER AND MOTION PICTURES

Academy of Motion Picture Arts and Sciences ("Oscar") Awards for 1969: best film—*Oliver!;* best foreign-language film—*War and Peace* (USSR); best actress—Barbara Streisand for *Funny Girl* and Katherine Hepburn for *The Lion in Winter;* best actor—Cliff Robertson for *Charly;* supporting actress—Ruth Gordon for *Rosemary's Baby;* supporting actor—Jack Albertson for *The Subject was Roses;* director—Sir Carol Reed for *Oliver!;* screenplay based on material from another medium—James Goldman for *The Lion in Winter;* original screenplay—Mel Brooks for *The Producers;* musical score (original)—John Barry for *The Lion in Winter;* musical score (adaptation)—John Green for *Oliver!;* original song—*The Windmills of Your Mind* from *The Thomas Crown Affair,* by Michel Legrand; art direction—John Box and Terence Marsh for *Oliver!;* cinematography—Pasqualino De Santis for *Romeo and Juliet;* set decoration—Ken Muggleston and Vernon Dixon for *Oliver!;* costume design—Danilo Donati for *Romeo and Juliet;* sound—Shepperton Studio sound department for *Oliver!;* special visual effects—Stanley Kubrick for *2001: A Space Odyssey;* short subject (live action)—Charles Guggenheim, producer, for *Robert Kennedy Remembered;* short subject (cartoon)—Walt Disney, prcducers, for *Winnie the Pooh and the Blustery Day;* documentary feature film—Alex Grasshoff, producer, for *Journey into Self;* short subject documentary film—Saul Bass, producer, for *Why Man Creates;* film editing—Frank P. Keller for *Bullitt.*

America Theater Wing, Antoinette Perry ("Tony") Awards: best drama—*The Great White Hope* by Howard Sackler; best musical—*1776* by Peter Stone; best actor (musical)—Jerry Orbach for *Promises, Promises;* best actor (drama)—James Earl Jones for *The Great White Hope;* best actress (musical)—Angela Lansbury for *Dear World;* best actress (drama)—Julie Harris for *Forty Carats;* dramatic supporting actor—Al Pacino for *Does a Tiger Wear a Necktie?;* dramatic supporting actress—Jane Alexander for *The Great White Hope;* musical supporting actor—Ronald Holgate in *1776;* musical supporting actress—Marian Mercer for *Promises, Promises;* director (drama)—Peter Dews for *Hadrian VII;* director (musical)—Peter Hunt for *1776;* costume design—Louden Sainthill for *Canterbury Tales;* set design—Boris Anderson for *Zorba;* choreography—Joe Layton for *George MI;* special awards—Sir Laurence Olivier, Carol Burnett, Leonard Bernstein, Rex Harrison, and the Negro Ensemble Company.

Cannes International Film Festival Awards: Gold Palm Grand Prix—*If...* (British); special jury prizes—*Adalen 31* (Swedish) and *Z* (French); actress—Vanessa Redgrave for *The Loves of Isadora;* actor—Jean Louis Trintignant for *Z;* directorial debut—Dennis Hopper for *Easy Rider.*

Drama Desk-Vernon Rice Awards for outstanding achievements in the on- and off-Broadway theater; director—Edwin Sherin for *The Great White Hope;* performance—James Earl Jones for *The Great White Hope;* set design—Ming Cho Lee for *Invitation to a Beheading;* costume design—Tanya Moiseiwitsch for *The House of Atreus;* composer—Al Carmines for *Peace;* cheorography—George Dale for *Billy;* musical writer—Peter Stone for *1776.*

New York Drama Critics' Circle Theater Awards: drama—*The Great White Hope;* musical—*1776.*

New York Film Critics Awards: best film: *Z;* actor—Jon Voight in *Midnight Cowboy;* actress—Jane Fonda in *They Shoot Horses, Don't They?;* director—Costa-Gavras for *Z.*

PROTESTANTISM. See RELIGION—*Protestantism.*

PSYCHIATRY. See MENTAL HEALTH.

PSYCHOLOGY

The major activities and concerns of psychologists were thrust into public view as the American Psychological Association held its 1969 convention in Washington, D. C., on Aug. 31–Sept. 4. For the first time the convention had a theme: "Psychology and the Problems of Society."

Dissent and Observations. Some convention meetings were disrupted by activists who, dissatisfied with the pace of scholarly deliberations, made demands for rapid change. The APA responded by creating a committee to consider the demands and make recommendations for the Council of Representatives, its ruling body, to consider further.

The association's president, George A. Miller of Rockefeller University, spoke on "Psychology as a Means of Promoting Human Welfare" and pointed out that the goals of scientific research are not always those of social action and "relevance."

The incoming president, George W. Albee of Case Western Reserve University, interpreted concern with application of research to social issues as evidence of psychology's coming of age.

The president-elect for 1970, Kenneth B. Clark of the City College of New York, is noted for his studies of Negroes in the United States and for demonstrating the effects of segregation and other social pressures on such aspects of behavior as intelligence test scores and achievement patterns.

Awards. The APA's awards for Distinguished Scientific Contributions are, along with its choice of presidents, the best indication of where most psychologists think most major advances are being made. The 1969 awards went to:

(1) Jean Piaget of the University of Geneva, whose sensitive and elegant inquiries into children's thoughts and behavior made him first an innovator and now an elder statesman for developmental psychology.

(2) Herbert A. Simon of Carnegie-Mellon University, who has studied organizational behavior and decision making and has recently specialized in constructing and testing computer programs as models of human perception, learning, and thinking.

(3) Stanley Schachter of Columbia University, whose work is in the provocative border area between personality and social psychology, such as the relation of birth order (and thus status in the family group) to affiliative needs and to behavior under stress.

The 1968 award winners addressed the society: James E. Birren, "Toward an Experimental Psychology of Aging"; Eleanor J. Gibson, "The Experimental Analysis of Reading Skill"; and Muzafer Sherif, "On the Relevance of Social Psychology."

Henry Murray of Harvard University, a pioneer in experimental tests of psychoanalytic theories, received the APA's Gold Medal Award.

Organization. About 29,000 of the 35,000 psychologists in the United States are members of the APA. Its membership grew by 6.3% in 1969. The APA's two new divisions, Psychological Hypnosis and State Psychological Affairs, show its increasing concern with research on therapeutic techniques and with professionalization. Special societies are proliferating for points of view such as the humanistic one or for important techniques such as physiological feedback.

GERTRUDE R. SCHMEIDLER
City College, The City University of New York

PUBLIC HEALTH

An eight-page report on the state of public health in the United States was released on July 10, 1969, by Secretary of Health, Education, and Welfare Robert Finch and Dr. Roger O. Egeberg, newly appointed assistant secretary of health and scientific affairs. The report warned of a crisis in health care. "This nation," the report began, "is faced with a breakdown in the delivery of health care unless immediate concerted action is taken by Government and the private sector." The report cited inflation of medical costs as one of the immediate problems. The Medicaid program also came under attack.

The Nixon administration pledged full cooperation in implementing recommendations of the report, which included a reevaluation of the Medicaid program and increased studies of drug use, drug prices, and hospital costs. Finally, the report, and President Nixon, stressed the need for full cooperation between government and private institutions for an effective public health program.

Measles Control. In the control of communicable disease, the year was notable for progress against rubella (German measles). A live-virus rubella vaccine was licensed by the federal government on June 10. The drug is being used primarily to immunize school-age children. Plans were also made for a mass immunization program throughout the United States. The Public Health Service awarded 70 grants to immunization programs.

Government Programs. To strengthen health services for children, Secretary Finch in September transferred the health programs of the Children's Bureau to the Health Services and Mental Health Administration. A National Center for Family Planning has been established as part of HSMHA; one function of the center is to serve as a clearinghouse for information on family planning.

The National Center for Health Services Research and Development focused much of its energy in 1969 on the problems of health care for the disadvantaged and on containment of the rising cost of health services. The National Institute of Mental Health established a Center for Studies of Schizophrenia, and provided financial assistance to 16 community-based diagnostic and treatment programs for narcotic addicts. The National Institute also aided in the development of community mental health centers. By July 1969, a total of 376 mental health centers had been funded throughout the country, and 160 new centers had been opened.

The 10,000th grant was awarded in the Hill-Burton program of hospital and health facility construction and modernization. The grant helped to build a comprehensive rehabilitation pavilion as part of a rehabilitation center in San Antonio, Texas.

New Surgeon General. On Dec. 22, 1969, Dr. Jesse L. Steinfeld was sworn in as surgeon general of the Public Health Service, replacing Dr. William H. Stewart, who had retired in July. Dr. Steinfeld had been serving as deputy assistant secretary for health and scientific affairs under Dr. Egeberg and continues to hold that post as well. Dr. Steinfeld was professor of medicine at the University of Southern California when he took the HEW assignment, but he had previously served as deputy director of the National Cancer Institute.

JOSEPH T. ENGLISH, M. D.
Administrator, Health Services
and Mental Health Administration

PUBLIC OPINION RESEARCH

Opinion polls in 1969 documented the public's growing disillusionment with the war in Vietnam. In September, the Gallup Poll reported that 58% of U. S. adults—a new high—believe the United States made a mistake in sending troops to fight in Vietnam. During the previous two years, according to the same source, the proportion who describe themselves as "hawks" on the war issue declined from 52% to 31%, while those who consider themselves "doves" increased from 35% to 55%. Nevertheless, only 21% of the public favored withdrawing all troops immediately; 74% rejected this proposal.

President Richard M. Nixon's popularity, as measured by the proportion of the public who approve of his performance in office fluctuated between a low of 56% and a high of 68%. The higher figure was reached in mid-November, following the President's November 3 address to the nation on Vietnam and during antiwar demonstrations.

Surveys recorded a sharp decline in the popularity of Sen. Edward M. Kennedy after his involvement in a car accident in July in which a young political aide was killed. The 71% holding a favorable opinion of him in February dropped to 48% in August. (See also KENNEDY, EDWARD M.)

Racial Divisions. Harris and Gallup surveys reported racial divisions in the United States. Gallup found that almost half the white population, but only 20% of the black, believe that integration of schools is proceeding too fast. Harris reported that only 46% of whites, as compared with 84% of Negroes, feel that black people are discriminated against in the United States. Three years earlier 61% of the white public had recognized discrimination. The college-educated and persons under 30, however, share views that differ sharply from those held by the rest of the population. Indeed, one Harris survey showed that white teenagers are much closer to the black public than to white adults in their attitudes toward such issues as the draft, civil rights, student protests, and government authority.

Other Opinion Surveys. The two major polls represent only a small fraction of the public opinion surveys mounted each year. Business, government agencies, foundations, universities, the mass media, and other groups serving public or private interests, take numerous opinion surveys, many of them never published. Some are reported in the popular press in such articles as "American Youth: What They Believe" (January 1969 issue of *Fortune*), and others are published in book form, as scholarly papers, or in official and other reports.

The increasing salience of race and poverty as social problems in the U. S. has led to a great increase in surveys among the black poor to determine their needs and attitudes, and to evaluate the effectiveness of remedial programs. Similarly, increasing concern with the attitudes of youth has resulted in more surveys of teenagers and college students.

National Council on Public Polls. A nonprofit organization called the National Council on Public Polls was incorporated in 1969, with Richard M. Scammon, former director of the Bureau of the Census, as president. The Council reflects the desire of established polltakers to develop a common code of practice with respect to disclosure of methods, and their desire to educate the news media and the public to recognize properly conducted surveys.

Sales and Mergers. The year 1969 was marked by the sale of several formerly independent research companies to larger corporations, and the merger of other research organizations. Opinion Research Corporation, one of the oldest market and opinion research agencies, was purchased by McGraw-Hill, Inc. Daniel Yankelovich, Inc. was bought by Leasco Data Processing Equipment Corporation. And Oliver Quayle and Company, which had served numerous political figures (including Hubert H. Humphrey in 1968), was acquired by Harper's Magazine, Inc. Late in 1969 it was announced that Louis Harris & Associates, whose Harris Survey is probably second only to the Gallup Poll in influence, had been purchased by the financial firm of Donaldson, Lufkin & Jenrette, Inc. In all cases the research firms will continue to operate as autonomous subsidiaries.

Daniel Starch & Staff, Inc., a pioneer in the field of magazine readership surveys, acquired the firm of C. E. Hooper, Inc., known for its measures of the radio audience. Starch & Staff also agreed to purchase Roper Research Associates, descendant of the firm first started by Elmo Roper in 1933.

"The Analyst." A monthly magazine, *The Analyst,* was started in March; it covered new developments in academic and commercial use of survey research. The publication reached a wide audience and was favorably received, but after seven issues economic factors forced it to suspend publication.

Death of Hadley Cantril. Polling lost one of its most influential figures in the death of psychologist Hadley Cantril on May 29, 1969. Cantril was one of the first academicians to recognize the importance of survey techniques in the social sciences.

PAUL B. SHEATSLEY
National Opinion Research Center
University of Chicago

PUBLIC UTILITIES. See ELECTRICAL INDUSTRIES; GAS; TELEPHONE.

PUBLISHING. See BOOK PUBLISHING; MAGAZINES; NEWSPAPERS.

PUERTO RICO

Luis A. Ferré, Puerto Rico's leading industrialist, became governor on Jan. 2, 1969. In the 1968 elections, his New Progressive party also won control of the commonwealth's House of Representatives, while the Popular Democratic party, which had controlled the island's politics since 1941, retained the Senate.

Puerto Rico's Status. In Washington, D. C., on September 19, Ferré conferred with President Nixon, urging a larger role for Puerto Rico in the Caribbean and a study of the possibility of Puerto Ricans' voting for the U. S. president. Urged by his opposition to implement the 1967 referendum that favored permanent commonwealth status with certain improvements, Ferré said he intended to hold a new referendum, but only after a few years of promoting statehood.

Ferré's desire for statehood brought intensification of activity for independence. Many advocates are students or faculty at the University of Puerto Rico. On September 26 they demonstrated against the Reserve Officers Training Corps, breaking into and damaging the ROTC building. Despite much agitation, the university decided to keep the ROTC.

Industrial Growth. Puerto Rico's economic and industrial growth rates continued at a strong pace. By June 30, 1969, the total number of new factories

———— PUERTO RICO · Information Highlights ————

Area: 3,435 square miles (8,897 sq km).
Population: 2,781,000 (July 1, 1969 est.).
Chief Cities (1968 est.): San Juan, the capital (metropolitan area), 794,000; Ponce, 161,900.
Government: *Chief Officers*—governor, Luis A. Ferré (New Progressive Party); secy. of state, Fernando Chardon (NPP); atty. gen., Gilberto Gierbolini (NPP); treas., Angel Martín (NPP); chief justice, Luis Negron Fernandez. *Legislature*—Senate, 27 members (15 Popular Democrats, 12 New Progressive party; House of Representatives, 51 members (25 PDP, 26 NPP).
Education: *School enrollment* (May 1969)—public elementary, 419,000; public secondary, 231,880 (total teachers, 21,838; nonpublic schools, 79,300 pupils; college and university (Jan. 1969), 46,030 students. *Public school expenditures* (1968–69, incl. univ.), $256,688,976.
Public Finance (fiscal year 1968–69): *Revenues*, $754,815,000 (motor fuel tax, $20,074,000; federal funds, $246,700,000). *Expenditures*, $677,100,000 (education, 30.2%; health, welfare and safety, 31%; transportation and communications, 5.4%). Commonwealth gross debt, $476,000,000 (June 30, 1969).
Personal Income (1969): $3,420,630,000; average annual income per person, $1,230.
Public Assistance (fiscal year 1968): $18,399,932 to 115,816 recipients (aged, $3,527,800; dependent children, $10,-815,178).
Labor Force (employed persons, fiscal 1969): 722,000. *Agricultural*, 85,000; *industrial, service, government and others*, 637,000. *Unemployed persons*, 86,000; 11% of the labor force.
Manufacturing (1969): net income from manufacturing, $753,-000,000. (1968, apparel and related products, $136,300,-000; chemicals and allied products, $59,000,000; metal products and machinery, $134,300,000; wood products and furniture, $22,700,000.)
Agriculture (1969): Net income from agriculture, $175,900,000. *Chief crops* (tons)—sugarcane, 5,890,869; coffee, 13,000; tobacco, 4,000. Total value of agricultural production dropped from $269 million in fiscal 1968 to $259 million in 1969.
Mining (1968 est.): *Production value*, $62,169,000. *Chief minerals* (tons)—sand and gravel, 14,920,000; stone, 7,355,000; cement, 1,666,432; clays, 411,000.
Fisheries (1969): Commercial catch, 10,000,000 pounds.
External Trade (fiscal 1969): *Exports*, $1,606,000,000 (chiefly manufactured goods); *Imports*, $2,263,000,000.
Transportation: *Paved roads* (June 1969), 5,830 miles (9,386 km); *motor vehicles* (1969), 530,000; *airports* (1969), 6.
Communications (1969): *Telephones*, 282,373; *television stations*, 11; *radio stations*, 71; *newspapers*, 4.

in Puerto Rico promoted by the Economic Development Administration had risen to 1,785, with investment above $1.3 billion. This compared with 1,694 plants and $1.25 billion in investment during "Operation Bootstrap" in the period from 1950 to the end of fiscal 1968.

Southwestern Development. Governor Ferré, who is from Ponce, began an ambitious development of the southwestern third of the island. Under construction were the Ponce-Mayaguez highway and a large reservoir. The $18 million Lajas airport, which will accommodate jumbo jets, was planned for use in 1972. Development of copper mining, petrochemicals, and tourism were also being planned.

Agriculture. The sugar industry was in severe decline. Governor Ferré supported the industry's 5-year modernization plan, requiring a government subsidy of $80 million.

Tourism. Visitors in the year ending June 30, 1969, totaled 1,100,000—up 170,000 from 1968— and spent an estimated $242 million.

Culture. The first Pan American Congress of Lexicography met in Puerto Rico from November 26 to December 4. It was organized under the auspices of the Puerto Rican Academy of Language. The 8 delegates from Spain and 30 from Latin American countries discussed a possible dictionary of Latin American Spanish.

EARL PARKER HANSON
Former Consultant, Department of State
Commonwealth of Puerto Rico

PULITZER PRIZES. See PRIZES AND AWARDS.
QUAKERS. See FRIENDS, RELIGIOUS SOCIETY OF.

QUEBEC

In 1969, Premier Jean-Jacques Bertrand, who came into office following the death of Premier Daniel Johnson in September 1968, gained power in the Union Nationale party by winning the leadership in his own right. He also promoted his personal policies in regard to Quebec's international relations (particularly its relations with France), cooperation in the formulation of a new federal constitution, and the problem of French cultural supremacy in Quebec. These policies materialized while the province was restless with acts of violence and was struggling with the same economic and financial problems as in 1968.

Leadership Convention. At a Union Nationale party leadership convention in June, which he had initiated, Premier Bertrand won over his main opponent, Education Minister Jean-Guy Cardinal. Considered by many the protégé of former Premier Johnson, Cardinal carried on a hard and close fight. His defeat created deep uneasiness within the party and forced the premier to act vigorously in pursuit of his personal policies, such as the passage in November of a bill (the highly controversial language rights bill) that obviously displeased Cardinal. Although unrest has remained in the party, Premier Bertrand seems to have become its undisputed leader.

Paris-Ottawa-Quebec Relations. While supporting the need for Quebec's links with France and other countries in matters within its jurisdiction, Premier Bertrand decided to maintain those links on a friendly basis and tried to normalize them. Such events as the joint visit to Paris in January of Education Minister Cardinal and Industry and Commerce Minister Beaudry and the visit to Quebec in October of Jean de Lipkowski, secretary to the French minister for foreign affairs, aroused the anger of the Canadian government. Lipkowski declined invitations to visit Ottawa during his stay. But Premier Bertrand, Canadian Prime Minister Pierre Trudeau, and the French government stated repeatedly their firm intention of establishing a normalized framework for tripartite relations.

Constitutional Conferences. Federal-provincial conferences on the federal constitution held in February, June, and December pointed up continuing frictions in regard to Quebec's position in the confederation: Quebec still claimed full jurisdiction over its social, cultural, and fiscal affairs; Prime Minister Trudeau became more fully resolved to use the federal government as a center for initiating and controlling regional development; and the other provinces became increasingly uninterested in and annoyed at Quebec's demands. However, Premier Bertrand overtly declared himself for Canadian federation and specified that his party shared that stand. Such a step was a significant deviation from the traditionally nationalistic stand of his party. It followed the Quebec Liberal party's similar stand, thus simplifying the political situation in Quebec. Those two parties now openly favor federalism; only the Parti Québecois promotes independence.

Legislation. The legislature passed important bills, such as those setting up the University of Quebec and abolishing the Legislative Council. Yet the project that best suited Premier Bertrand's personal views and the one that brought the most criticism was undoubtedly the language rights bill, known as Bill 63.

The premier had repeatedly stated his intention to establish the primacy of the French language and culture in Quebec while protecting the rights of minority English-speaking groups. Bill 63 aimed at compelling—under the education minister's control—all English-speaking students to have a working knowledge of the French language. It also outlined the government's intention to promote to the utmost the integration of immigrants into the French-speaking community. Finally, it acknowledged the right of parents to choose the language in which their children are to be taught. The bill aroused protests from the French-speaking population, but neither the wide demonstration campaign nor the filibustering of some political leaders shook the premier's determination or deterred the adoption of the bill, which many serious observers felt was inadequate and deficient.

Political Parties. The resignation in August of former premier Jean Lesage as head of the Liberal party and the calling of a leadership convention in January 1970 were great challenges for the Liberals on the eve of general elections, which have been announced for 1970. Jacques Parizeau—a leading Canadian economist and a former adviser to Premiers Lesage, Johnson, and Bertrand—announced in September that he had joined the Parti Québecois and will run for the next elections.

ROBERT BOILY
Université de Montréal

--------- **QUEBEC · Information Highlights** ---------

Area: 594,860 square miles (1,540,669 sq km).
Population: 5,962,000 (Jan. 1, 1969 est.).
Chief Cities (1966 census): Quebec, the capital (166,984); Montreal (1,222,255); Laval (196,088).
Government: *Chief Officers*—lt. gov., Hugues Lapointe; premier, Jean-Jacques Bertrand (Union Nationale); prov. secy. and min. of justice, Rémi Paul (U. N.); min. of finance, Mario Beaulieu (U. N.); min. of educ., Jean-Guy Cardinal (U. N.) *Legislature* (convened Feb. 25, 1969)—National Assembly, 108 members (standing of the parties as of Oct. 8, 1969—56 Union Nationale, 46 Liberal, 5 independent, 1 vacancy).
Education: *School enrollment* (1966–67 est.)—public elementary and secondary, 1,415,800 pupils (68,200 teachers); private schools, 94,500 pupils (6,300 teachers); college and university (fall 1966), 75,070 students. *Public school expenditures* (1967–68)—$617,030,000.
Public Finance (fiscal year 1968 est.): *Revenues,* $2,696,500,-000 (sales tax, $915,560,000; income tax, $860,679,000; federal funds, $474,902,000). *Expenditures,* $2,747,430,000 (education, $751,560,000; transport and communications, $291,260,000).
Personal Income (1967 est.): $12,141,000,000; *average annual income per person,* $2,069.
Social Welfare (fiscal year 1968 est.): $401,750,000 (aged and blind, $32,800,000; dependents and unemployed, $178,400,000).
Manufacturing (1966): *Value added by manufacture,* $4,704,-799,000 (food and beverages, $648,138,000; paper and allied industries, $521,122,000; fabricated metals, $353,-595,000; clothing industries, $338,640,000; primary metals, $322,277,000).
Agriculture (1968 est.): *Cash farm income,* $634,602,000 (livestock, $515,487,000; crops, $56,723,000). *Chief crops* (cash receipts)—Vegetables, $17,632,000 (ranks 2d among the provinces); potatoes, $13,243,000 (ranks 1st); fruits, $9,170,000 (ranks 3d); tobacco, $6,018,000 (ranks 2d).
Mining (1967 est.): *Production value,* $715,900,973. *Chief minerals* (tons)—Zinc, 485,881,925 (ranks 2d among the the provinces); stone, 48,849,204 (ranks 1st); iron ore, 14,518,000 (ranks 2d); asbestos, 1,260,468 (ranks 1st).
Fisheries (1967): *Commercial catch,* 192,236,000 pounds ($7,-961,000). *Leading species*—Cod, 50,647,000 pounds ($2,-067,000); redfish, 70,445,000 pounds ($1,898,000); lobster, 2,807,000 pounds ($1,751,000).
Transportation (1966): *Roads,* 55,747 miles (89,714 km); *motor vehicles* (1967), 1,872,585; *railroads,* 5,138 track miles (8,269 km); *licensed airports,* 61.
Communications (1967): *Telephones* (1966) 2,163,049; *television stations,* 16; *radio stations,* 55; *daily newspapers* (1966), 14 (daily circulation, 1,032,102).
(All figures given in Canadian dollars equal to U. S.$0.93.)

RADIO. See TELEVISION AND RADIO.

FLOATING on an air cushion, a new French experimental train can attain a speed of 186 mph (300 km/hr) in its 70-mile run between Paris and Orléans.

RAILROADS

Freight operations continued to be the mainstay of U. S. railroads in 1969. The Association of American Railroads estimated that 10,000 freight trains a day moved over the railroads' 209,000-mile network, accounting for 40% of all U. S. freight ton-miles and bringing in 95% of all railroad operating revenues. (A ton-mile is one ton of freight hauled one mile.) But it was the passenger train, apparently rolling toward extinction, that caught the eye of an aroused public and made the big railroad news of the year.

Passenger Operations. By 1969 railroads were handling only 1% of all intercity travel, and the number of intercity passenger trains had shrunk to 480. The Interstate Commerce Commission's own cost study, involving eight railroads that in 1968 provided 40% of all noncommuter passenger service, showed that these carriers could have saved $118 million had they abandoned these trains. But as train-discontinuance petitions mounted at the ICC, public protests also rose, and the ICC, apparently responding to increasing pressures from Congress, stiffened its stance. In the period 1958–1968, the ICC permitted abandonment of 745 trains. In 12 cases in 1969 involving 24 trains, the ICC refused to permit discontinuance.

Against this background, the railroads broke with long-standing tradition and asked federal subsidies for those trains whose operation was ruled to be "in the public convenience and necessity" but which could not pay their way. Late in 1969, a bill emerged in Congress that would authorize the secretary of transportation to designate certain trains as part of a National Passenger Railroad System, eligible for federal aid to the extent of 75% of their operating losses.

Metroliners and TurboTrains. A bright spot was provided by the spectacular success of the highspeed Metroliners that went into service between New York and Washington in January 1969 on the lines of the Penn Central Railroad. Traveling at speeds up to 120 mph and cutting travel time between New York and Washington from 3 hours and 45 minutes to 2 hours 30 minutes, the Metroliners brought about a 72% increase in train travel in their territory. By December 1969, 12 Metroliners were operating in this experiment, funded jointly by the railroad and the federal government, and more were to be added in 1970.

Both the railroads and their critics took comfort from the success of the Metroliners. The railroads said that it supported their contentions that the future of train travel lies in medium-distance runs in highly congested areas. Railroad critics contended that the Metroliners had demonstrated that the public would ride trains as long as these trains were fast, frequent, and modern.

Another set of "new breed" trains, the Turbo-Trains, went into service between Boston and New York in April, with more modest success.

Commuters. The year 1969 also saw new action on the part of local governments to assume responsibility for commuter-train losses. The Penn Central, which took over the bankrupt New Haven Railroad under terms of an ICC order that permitted merger of the Pennsylvania and the New York Central in 1968, reached an agreement late in 1969 with the states of New York and Connecticut. Under the agreement, the two states would provide new equipment for commuter service on the New Haven line and subsidize its operations.

Freight Operations. While passenger trains were the smudgy showcase through which most Americans viewed the railroad industry, freight trains continued to pay the bills. Railroads in 1969 hauled an estimated 28,290,000 carloads of freight, an increase of about 1/10th of 1% over 1968. They performed 767 billion ton-miles of service, an increase of about 3% over 1968. Because of bigger cars and longer hauls, the ton-mile increase was higher than the carloading increase.

Piggyback traffic leveled off in 1969, and loadings were only slightly above the 1,337,000 cars and 2,175,000 trailers handled in 1968.

Freight Rates. For the third time in two years, the railroads won a rate increase. A 6% emergency increase granted by the ICC in November was estimated to yield $600 million annually. The earlier increases—5% in 1968 and 3% in 1967—yielded $860 million. Even with the third rate hike, railroads said there would remain a gap of $400 million between increased costs and increased revenues.

Finances. Total railroad operating revenues peaked at close to $11 billion in 1969, but rising labor and operating costs kept net income below $600 million. The rate of return on depreciated net investment of $27 billion was 2.6%.

Labor. Average labor costs rose 6% during 1969. About 500,000 employees settled for wage increases averaging 5%, but four shopcraft unions representing 48,000 employees held out. After twice bringing the railroads to the brink of a nationwide shutdown, the shopcrafts early in December negotiated an 11% increase retroactive to January 1969 and an additional 7% in 1970. On December 17, however, the sheet metal workers—one of the four unions involved—declined to ratify the agreement, and negotiations were scheduled for 1970.

A crew-consist dispute, involving trainmen, was settled early in 1969 after a brief strike shut down the Illinois Central Railroad. Another, involving the presence of firemen on diesel locomotives, was scheduled to go into third-party mediation in 1970.

Equipment. Railroads placed orders in 1969 for 80,000 new freight cars, compared to 63,500 in 1968. The American Railway Car Institute predicted that new-car orders would drop to 63,100 in 1970, because of loss of the 7% investment tax credit. To help compensate for the loss of this investment incentive, the Congress agreed to permit railroads to depreciate new equipment over the relatively short period of five years. On Dec. 31, 1969, an estimated 1.8 million freight cars were in service throughout the nation. There were 27,000 locomotives in service, with acquisitions continuing at the rate of about 1,000 annually.

Mergers. In March an ICC examiner recommended merger of the Chesapeake & Ohio and the Norfolk & Western into a new 27,000-mile railroad with annual revenues of $1.9 billion.

The complex case involving opposing bids for the Chicago, Rock Island & Pacific was reopened by the ICC.

The so-called Northern Lines merger, involving consolidation of the Burlington Lines, the Northern Pacific, and the Great Northern into the proposed Burlington Northern remained stalled at the U. S. Supreme Court.

Safety. A rising number of derailments led to congressional action aimed at tightening safety procedures. Late in the year Congress was offered a bill that would empower the secretary of transportation to prescribe broad safety standards. Since 1963, the railroad accident rate has increased 66% to a monthly average of 700 train accidents. During this period, 45 communities were evacuated when an explosion or fire resulting from a derailment threatened the town. A major section of the new legislation would permit the Department of Transportation to deal with hazardous movements.

At the same time, the railroads maintained their position as the safest mode of personal travel. Only 13 railroad passengers met accidental death in 1968, with a resulting fatality rate of .10 per 100 million passenger miles. In the same year, the highway fatality rate was 2.4 per 100 million passenger miles, and the airline fatality rate was .30.

Technology. The 15.5-mile, $45-million Muskingum Electric mining railroad, opened in Ohio in 1969, was widely viewed as a "test tube" for possible future electrification of U. S. main lines.

Both the Santa Fe and Southern Pacific railroads acquired simulators for teaching locomotive and train operation to new engineers. The Santa Fe also unveiled the model of a caterpillar-like "coaxial train," designed to operate over existing roadbeds at high speeds.

The Chesapeake & Ohio and Bethlehem Steel Corp. jointly developed a 125-ton articulated hopper car with a flexible joint at midsection permitting it to bend around curves.

Golden Spike. On May 10, 1969, the Golden Spike Centennial was observed at Promontory, Utah, with a reenactment of the ceremony that 100 years ago linked the Union Pacific and the Central Pacific (now Southern Pacific) and thus created the nation's first transcontinental railroad. Secretary of Transportation John A. Volpe took the occasion to declare that, despite present and well-publicized problems, "The railroads are just beginning to roll."

LUTHER S. MILLER
Editor, "Railway Age"

SPEEDS up to 250 mph are envisioned for a Garrett-built air-cushion vehicle. This prototype has a linear induction motor, free of moving parts.

THE GARRETT CORPORATION

Recordings

WALTER CARLOS brought a new dimension to the record industry in 1969 with his recording of Bach and other composers on the Moog synthesizer, a five-octave electric action keyboard.

COLUMBIA RECORDS

Columbia Stereo MS 7286 MASTERWORKS

Trans-Electronic Music Productions, Inc. Presents

Walter Carlos

and

The Well-Tempered Synthesizer

More virtuoso electronic performances of Bach, Monteverdi, Scarlatti, Handel

COLUMBIA RECORDS

The year 1969 in the recording industry witnessed the unusual situation in which followers of popular music became enamored of Bach, through the electronic sound synthesizer. Avant-garde jazz did not continue the notable impact that it had made on recorded music in 1968. Country-rock and folk-rock grew in public favor, and performing groups multiplied. In the classical field, the industry noted that 1969 was the 100th anniversary of the death of French composer Hector Berlioz.

CLASSICAL RECORDS

For the record industry, 1969 was the year of the Moog synthesizer. This electronic sound generator (developed by engineer Robert Moog) offers an extraordinary range of sonic possibilities, limited only by human perception itself. Previously the exclusive toy of the serious electronic composer, the Moog became big business in 1969 after the release of Columbia's *Switched-on Bach,* unquestionably the runaway best-selling classical album of the season.

Switched-on Bach, released at the end of 1968, consists essentially of electronically pitched presentations of favorite Bach compositions, painstakingly executed by avant-garde composer Walter Carlos and his assistant, Benjamin Folkman. The public, entranced by the novelty of baroque music offered in this space-age guise, bought over a million copies. RCA countered with *The Moog Strikes Bach ... to Say Nothing of Chopin, Mozart, Rachmaninoff, Paganini and Prokofiev,* which extended the electronic treatment to other classical composers. Probably for the first time in history, classical records influenced the pop market, for the triumph of *Switched-on Bach* and Carlos' 1969 release, *The Well-Tempered Synthesizer,* inspired a deluge of albums in the popular field, all utilizing the Moog synthesizer with varying degrees of success.

Meanwhile, Columbia continued its exploration of the off-beat—one might even say the lunatic fringe—with many records promoting the far-far-out classical avant-garde. Included in this category were discs devoted to Harry Partch, who writes music for instruments of his own invention; Conlon Nancarrow, who composes directly onto piano rolls; Moondog, a blind musician-composer who spends most of his time standing on the corner of New York's Sixth Avenue and 56th Street clad in full Viking regalia; and Terry Riley, whose *In C* consists of a 40-minute repetition of the chord of C major.

More sober representatives of the classical establishment convened once again in Montreux, Switzerland, to award their second annual prizes to the best records of the year. The Gold Award went to Bach's B-minor Mass performed on authentic (and unsynthesized) baroque instruments by Nikolaus Harnoncourt and the Concentus Musicus (Telefunken). Second and third prizes were awarded to Monteverdi's *Selva Morale e Spirituale* (Erato) and Berio's *Sinfonia* (Columbia).

Unfamiliar operatic fare included such rare items as Catalani's *La Wally* (London), Donizetti's *Roberto Devereux* (Westminster), Mascagni's *L'Amico Fritz* (Angel), and Giordano's *Fedora* (London). Pianists, too, were also rediscovering the past: Raymond Lewenthal (Columbia) and Earl Wild (RCA) recorded two once-popular romantic concertos by Adolph von Henselt and Xaver Scharwenka, and Ivan Davis (London) released an entire disc of neglected virtuoso showpieces of yesteryear.

The year's centenary composer was Hector Berlioz—1969 was the 100th anniversary of his death. To mark the occasion, Philips embarked upon an ambitious project to record all of the composer's works under the direction of the British conductor Colin Davis. The two performances so far released, the dramatic symphony *Roméo et Juliette* and the massive *Te Deum,* indicate that this may well turn out to be a major phonographic enterprise.

Outstanding Releases. Following is a selected list of notable classical releases in 1969.

BACH, *Mass in B Minor:* Rotraud Hansmann, Emiko Iiyama, and other singers; Concentus Musicus, Nikolaus Harnoncourt, director (Telefunken, 3 discs)
BACH. *Sonatas and Partitas for Unaccompanied Violin:* Henryk Szeryng, violin (Deutsche Grammaphon, 3 discs)
BERG, *Violin Concerto:* Arthur Grumiaux, violin; Concertgebouw Orchestra, Igor Markevitch, conductor (Philips)
BERIO, *Sinfonia:* Swingle Singers; New York Philharmonic, Luciano Berio, conductor (Columbia)
BERLIOZ, *Roméo et Juliette:* Soloists, John Alldis Choir; London Symphony Chorus and Orchestra, Colin Davis, conductor (Philips, 2 discs)
BILLINGS, *The Continental Harmony:* Gregg Smith Singers, Gregg Smith, conductor (Columbia)
CARLOS, WALTER, *The Well-Tempered Synthesizer;* the Moog synthesizer (Columbia)
CAVALLI, *L'Ormindo:* Hanneke van Bork, Isabel Garcisanz, and other singers; London Philharmonic Orchestra, Raymond Leppard, conductor (Argo, 3 discs)
HANDEL, *Samson:* Martina Arroyo, Helen Donath, and other singers; Munich Bach Chorus and Orchestra, Karl Richter, conductor (Archive, 4 discs)
HAYDN, *The Seasons:* Soloists; BBC Chorus and Orchestra, Colin Davis, conductor (Philips, 3 discs)
KODALY, *Háry János:* Erszébet Komlóssy, Margit László, and other singers; London Symphony Orchestra, Istvan Kertesz, conductor (London, 2 discs)
MASCAGNI, *L'Amico Fritz:* Mirella Freni, Luciano Pavarotti, and other singers; Chorus and Orchestra of Covent Garden, Gianandrea Gavazzeni, conductor (Angel, 3 discs)
MENDELSSOHN, *Elijah:* Gwyneth Jones, Janet Baker, and other singers; New Philharmonia Chorus and Orchestra, Rafael Frühbeck de Burgos, conductor (Angel, 3 discs)
MOZART, *Symphonies Nos. 36 and 39:* Boston Symphony Orchestra, Erich Leinsdorf, conductor (RCA)
MOZART, *Symphony No. 40; Serenata Notturna:* English Chamber Orchestra, Benjamin Britten, conductor (London)
PARTCH, *Daphne of the Dunes; Barstow; Castor and Pollux:*

Vocal and Instrumental Ensemble, Danlee Mitchell, conductor (Columbia)
SCHUBERT, *Lieder Recital:* Werner Krenn, tenor; Gerald Moore, piano (London)
SCRIABIN, *Sonata No. 3;* PROKOFIEV, *Sonata No. 7:* Glenn Gould, piano (Columbia)
SESSIONS, *Symphony No. 3;* LEES, *Concerto for String Quartet and Orchestra:* Royal Philharmonic Orchestra, Igor Buketoff, conductor (RCA)
SILLS, BEVERLY, *Scenes and Arias from French Operas:* Beverly Sills, soprano (Westminster)
STRAUSS, RICHARD, *Salome:* Montserrat Caballé, Regina Resnick, and other singers; London Symphony Orchestra, Erich Leinsdorf, conductor (RCA)
VAUGHAN WILLIAMS, *Symphony No. 1; The Wasps:* London Philharmonic Chorus and Orchestra, Sir Adrian Boult, conductor (Angel, 2 discs)
VERDI, *La Traviata:* Pilar Lorengar, Giacomo Aragall, and other singers; Chorus and Orchestra of the Berlin State Opera, Lorin Maazel, conductor (London, 2 discs)
VERDI, *Otello:* Gwyneth Jones, James McCracken; Ambrosian Opera Chorus and Orchestra, Sir Adrian Boult, conductor (Angel, 2 discs)
WAGNER, *Siegfried:* Helga Dernesch, and other singers; Berlin Philharmonic Orchestra, Herbert von Karajan, conductor (Deutsche Grammophon, 5 discs)
WUORINEN, *Time's Encomium:* Synthesized and processed synthesized sound (Nonesuch)

PETER G. DAVIS
Music Editor, "High Fidelity" Magazine

POPULAR RECORDS

Synthesis was the password for popular music in 1969. In an appropriate conclusion to the most eclectic decade in American popular music, the year was flooded with such new combinations as jazz-rock, folk-rock, and country-rock.

Jazz-Rock. By far the most influential group was Blood, Sweat & Tears, a 9-piece ensemble that was reorganized after the release of a moderately successful first recording in 1968. Blood, Sweat & Tears mixed jazz improvisations, rock rhythms, and blues vocals in a highly disciplined "big band" sound that reached across a still-prominent generation gap. By the end of the year, such relative old-timers as Frank Sinatra, Peggy Lee, and Andy Williams were singing arrangements and songs that were directly inspired by the Blood, Sweat & Tears sound.

Supergroups. Group personnel showed an extraordinary mobility. The remnants of Cream and Traffic re-formed to become Blind Faith, and Crosby, Stills, Nash & Young left Buffalo Springfield and other groups to form their own unit. Listeners fol-

(*Left*) BEATLES retained their popularity in 1969 with a new album, *Abbey Road.* (*Below*) JAZZ-ROCK nine, Blood, Sweat & Tears, with their "big band" sound had a major influence on record styles.

COLUMBIA RECORDS

Among the year's most successful LP's were the original cast album of *Hair* (RCA); *In A Gadda Da Vida,* Iron Butterfly (Atlantic); *Blood, Sweat & Tears* (Columbia); *The Beatles* (Apple); *Donovan's Greatest Hits* (Epic); *Led Zepplin* (Atlantic); the sound track from *Romeo and Juliet* (Capitol); *Wichita Lineman,* Glenn Campbell (Capitol); *Bayou Country,* Creedence Clearwater Revival (Fantasy); and the sound track from *Funny Girl* (Columbia).

Some of the best-selling singles were: *Sugar, Sugar,* The Archies (Kirshner); *Honky Tonk Woman,* Rolling Stones (London); *Aquarius/Let the Sun Shine In,* Fifth Dimension (Soul City); *I Heard It Through The Grapevine,* Marvin Gaye (Tamla); and *Everyday People,* Sly and the Family Stone (Epic).

DON HECKMAN
Contributing Editor, "Stereo Review"

JAZZ RECORDS

After 25 years of almost constant emphasis on newness and innovation—from bebop in the Forties, cool jazz and "third stream" music in the Fifties, to the "new thing" of the avant-garde jazzmen of the Sixties—jazz in the year 1969 seemed to be taking a breather. This was not the result of any strong movement toward the past such as occurred right after World War II, when the traditional jazz revival ran parallel with the arrival of bebop.

Some of the older jazz forms did receive a little more attention than usual, but this was less a consequence of anything comparable to the traditional jazz revival than of a quiescence in the jazz vanguard, which created a performing and listening vacuum partially filled by older jazz forms.

Popular Favorites. The lists of best-selling jazz records were dominated during most of 1969 by middle-ground performers whose primary appeal lay beyond the jazz audience. Their work fitted into

lowed the games of musical chairs with fascination; the Blind Faith recording, for example, was released before the group had performed in public and quickly hit the magic million level.

Established Names. The Beatles retained their popularity with widespread sales of the double-disc *The Beatles* collection issued in late 1968 and a new album, *Abbey Road,* released in late 1969. Persistent rumors of the death of Beatle Paul McCartney kept the group in the limelight during the summer. The Rolling Stones toured the United States in a highly publicized series of concerts late in the year. Bob Dylan surprised his fans with *Nashville Skyline,* a collection of mellow, country music–style love songs. His voice was smooth and sweet, in marked contrast to the raspy, singsong sound of his earlier work. Jefferson Airplane, Simon & Garfunkel, Sly and the Family Stone, the Fifth Dimension, the Doors, the Grateful Dead, the Band, and the Union Gap were a few of the many established groups who released best-selling recordings.

The Power of Television. The best-selling single record of the year, *Sugar, Sugar,* was recorded by studio musicians serving as anonymous musical alter egos for an animated television cartoon rock group called The Archies. Glenn Campbell and John Hartford also came to prominence through television. Johnny Cash, long a favorite with followers of country and Western music, had several hit recordings and was featured in a television show.

Heavy Rock. The blues revival of 1968 dissipated itself somewhat, but groups that combined simple traditional blues songs with electronic distortion effects, high-intensity volume, and thunderous bass rhythms more than filled the gap. Iron Butterfly's first recording hit the charts in late 1968 and continued in the top listings throughout most of 1969. Similarly, first releases by Three Dog Night, Creedence Clearwater Revival, Led Zepplin, and Santana won immediate popularity.

GARY BURTON plays the vibraharp in the Gary Burton Quartet, a jazz group whose 1969 record *Throb* won praise.

ATLANTIC RECORDS

(*Above*) JAZZ VETERANS Yank Lawson and Bob Haggart, who bill their group as the World's Greatest Jazz Band, in 1969 offered *Extra!*, a jazz-pop blend. (*Right*) Pharoah Sanders' *Karma* brought him a following among avant-garde audiences.

such categories as "Easy Listening" and "Rhythm and Blues." Ramsey Lewis, Charlie Byrd, and Sergio Mendes were among the artists in the first category, and Lou Donaldson, Eddie Harris, and Young-Holt, Ltd., in the second.

Miles Davis, among the long-established jazz stars, continued to have a strong following, as evidenced by the sale of his album *In a Silent Way* (Columbia CS 9857), while the response to Pharoah Sanders' *Karma* (Impulse 981) indicated that he was attracting the avant-garde audience.

Major Releases. The jazz group that moved most positively to the forefront of the field in 1969 was the Gary Burton Quartet, which had been developing rapidly for several years. In 1969, Burton, a vibra-harpist, put together a combination of musicians and material that blended in a more provocative fashion than his earlier efforts. On *Throb* (Atlantic 1531), a recording that epitomizes this blend, he added to his regular instrumentation (vibraharp, electric guitar, bass, and drums) a violinist, Richard Green, whose unusually varied background spanned Bill Monroe's Bluegrass Boys, Jim Kweskin's Jug Band, and Sea Train, a rock group. Green's presence added a dimension to Burton's quartet that broadened its appeal even while it moved toward new, but not radical, musical ground.

The formation of the World's Greatest Jazz Band exerted a stimulating force on the older styles of jazz during 1969. Led by Yank Lawson and Bob Haggart, two one-time members of Bob Crosby's band of the Thirties, the band featured such established jazz stars as Bud Freeman, Lou McGarity, Bob Wilber, and Ralph Sutton.

On *The World's Greatest Jazz Band* (Project 3 5033) and *Extra!* (Project 3 5039), the group played a mixture of old jazz standards and current pop material done in Swing Era fashion. Wilber also paired with Maxine Sullivan, another artist of the Thirties, on two LPs, *The Music of Hoagy Carmichael* (Monmouth-Evergreen 6917) and *Close As Pages in a Book* (Monmouth-Evergreen 6919).

An even more distant generation of jazz was evoked by pianist Eubie Blake, a veteran of the ragtime days, on *The 86 Years of Eubie Blake* (Columbia C2S 847). On this 2-disc set, he recalls his early ragtime playing as well as his music for Broadway musicals.

Other jazz releases of special interest included:

Illinois Jacquet, *The Soul Explosion* (Prestige 7629)
Gary McFarland, *America the Beautiful* (Skye 8)
Modern Jazz Quartet, *Space* (Apple 3360)
James Moody, *The Blues and Other Colors* (Milestone 9023)
Max Roach, *Members Don't Get Weary* (Atlantic 1510)
Chuck Slate and his Traditional Jazz Band (Dee Bess 1729)
Joe Turner, *The Real Boss of the Blues* (Bluestime 9002)

JOHN S. WILSON
"The New York Times"
and "High Fidelity" Magazine

AUDIO EQUIPMENT AND TECHNIQUES

The year 1969 saw the first appearance of four-channel prerecorded tapes and playback equipment on the consumer market, as well as the first commercial four-channel stereo broadcasts. The initial broadcasts took place in Boston through the cooperation of FM stations WGBH and WCRB, the Boston Pops Orchestra, and Acoustic Research. There followed similar experiments in New York City, mutually undertaken by the FM stereo facilities of WNYC and WKCR.

Four-Channel Stereo. In theory, four-channel stereo is capable of forming a stereo image that encompasses the listener on all sides. In a typical configuration, the four speakers are placed two in front of the listener in the normal stereo positions, and two behind, similarly spaced. Each speaker is driven by its own amplifier, which gets audio information from one channel of a four-channel playback tape machine or from one channel of one of the two stereo FM tuners needed to receive the broadcasts. The stereo image presented by the four speakers will depend on how the performance was recorded. A common practice for orchestral recordings is to place two microphones at the front of the concert hall and two more toward the rear. When the recording is played back, the listener experiences the orchestra arrayed before him as in a conventional two-channel stereo recording, but also hears the sound reflected from the structural surfaces of the concert hall realistically reproduced with respect to direction and time delay. Some of the four-channel tapes produced in this way have not been entirely successful in presenting this effect convincingly, but it is felt that better results will be forthcoming.

Four-channel stereo has also been used for special effects. An example would be the *Tuba mirum* section of the Berlioz Requiem, the score of which suggests that the four brass choirs called for be placed in the concert hall at the four points of the compass. In the Vanguard recording of this work, each choir is heard through a different speaker.

At present four-channel recordings are exclusively a tape medium, although some promising experimental work has been done with phonograph discs. Among the manufacturers who have made four-channel tape decks available are Crown International, Teac, and Telex, while Nortronics offers kits for replacing playback heads on existing tape machines with four-channel simultaneous-playback heads. Scott's 499 "Quadrant" amplifier incorporates the equivalent of four integrated amplifiers (two integrated stereo amplifiers) on a single chassis, with special control facilities for four-channel reproduction.

Frequency Compensators. Several multiple tone-control devices to provide selective control of narrow bands of the audio frequency range were introduced in 1969. They are intended to compensate for room acoustics and frequency imbalance in recordings and equipment. Frazier's Environmental Equalizer and Altec Lansing's Acousta-Voicette are among the most complex; professional installation with instruments is recommended. The Altec Lansing unit has 24 controls for each channel, permitting a continuously variable boost or cut of any ⅓-octave band of the audio spectrum. Less critical devices such as Advent's Frequency Balance Control (1-octave bands) are intended to be adjusted by the user. JVC's 5003 receiver has five 2-octave controls in place of conventional tone controls.

High-Fi Equipment. Many receivers introduced in 1969 made use of crystal or ceramic i.f. filters, field-effect transistors, and integrated circuits. While amplifier sections of receivers did not grow in power, Marantz's Model 16 stereo power amplifier (80 watts per channel) set a standard for high-power, low-distortion performance. Moderately priced tape recorders approached professional standards with Teac's A-1200U ($299.50) and Concord's Mark III ($260). Cassette players and recorders gained in the audiophile market, with cassette decks contained in receivers and compact systems manufactured by Scott, Harman-Kardon, and several others. TDK introduced a cassette with a denser, finer oxide formula said to improve frequency response and signal-to-noise ratio.

Several new loudspeakers experimented with reflected or multidirectional sound propagation, among them the Scott Q-100, Epicure's Models 1000 and 201, and the speakers used in Electro Voice's Landmark 100 system. In record players, Dual's automatic turntable has a control to lower its tone arm parallel to the platter for a single-play operation. Rabco's SL-8 tone arm is driven radially across the surface of a record by a battery-powered servomotor.

RALPH W. HODGES
Assistant Technical Editor, "Stereo Review"

REFUGEES

The world's refugee population was estimated on Oct. 1, 1969, to be 17,318,000, down from 19.6 million 10 months earlier. The problem continued to be extremely serious, because refugees always remain a threat to peace. They pose very serious problems for the 80 countries in which they have found asylum. Refugee populations were estimated to be 7,162,435 in Asia, 1,819,527 in the Middle East, 5,206,213 in Africa, 869,619 in Europe and the United Kingdom, and 2,260,526 in the Americas.

Asia. The homeless civilian population in Vietnam was expected to remain the most serious problem in Asia as long as hostilities continue. In one year, over 300,000 persons returned to their home villages or were otherwise permanently resettled, although at the end of June 1969, 1,997,143 people were listed as active refugees in South Vietnam.

Hong Kong's refugee population of over 2 million was increasing, by immigration from Communist China, at the rate of approximately 20,000 per year. The 55,000 Tibetans who found asylum in India were receiving significant and well-coordinated assistance from the government of India and the intergovernmental community, and were expected to be resettled in the foreseeable future.

The Middle East. In addition to the registered refugees in the Middle East, there were some 300,000 homeless people who were unregistered but for whom housing and basic emergency care had to be provided. Most of them had been refugees since the formation of the state of Israel in 1948, although the June 1967 war had made many of them refugees a second time and created a new problem for homeless persons who fled the areas where military activity took place.

Africa. The problem of some 3 million refugees in Nigeria/Biafra continued to worsen. No practical or military solution for the fighting in Nigeria was found in 1969, and this tragedy continued until the collapse of Biafra in January 1970. Starvation was the major problem. Joint Church Aid, an international interfaith organization, was providing the only succor for these millions of hungry people in 1969.

Europe and the United Kingdom. The flow of refugees from Eastern Europe, particularly from Czechoslovakia, but also from Poland, Rumania, Yugoslavia, Bulgaria, and Hungary, increased during 1969. The numbers involved were relatively small compared to those elsewhere; however, the congestion of the refugee population in key centers such as Vienna was very serious at the end of 1969. Major countries of asylum for these people are the United States, Canada, South Africa, and Israel, as well as nations of Western Europe.

Western Hemisphere. The major inflow of refugees into the United States continued to come from Cuba. Cuban refugees were entering Miami, Fla., at a rate of 4,000 per month. They were also arriving in New York from Spain. Other movements to the United States were the Chinese from Hong Kong and the Czechs.

Reference Sources. Information about refugees may be obtained from the United Nations, the U. S. Department of State, or the U. S. Committee for Refugees, 20 West 40th Street, New York, N. Y. 10018.

R. NORRIS WILSON
United States Committee for Refugees

RELIGION

Criticism of organizational structures and a search for more relevant modes of operation were evident in the world's religions in 1969. These developments are treated in this article under the following headings: (1) A General Survey; (2) Protestantism; (3) Roman Catholicism; (4) Judaism; (5) Eastern Orthodoxy; (6) Islam; and (7) Oriental Religions. The article is supplemented by a table listing membership of all major U.S. churches. (Leading U.S. and Canadian church groups are treated in separate articles; for example, BAPTIST CHURCHES.)

A GENERAL SURVEY

The life of the world's religious bodies was marked by considerable unrest in 1969. There was mounting criticism of organizational structures; demand for more radical involvement of religious bodies in economic and political action on behalf of minority and underprivileged groups; and insistence on a free search for intellectual formulations of faith more in accord with modern thought.

Synod of Bishops. In October, 144 representatives of 92 national conferences of bishops met in Rome to explore the implementation of the principle of collegiality in governing the Roman Catholic Church, as it had been enunciated by Vatican Council II. The bishops advocated a more significant and continuing voice in formulating and carrying out church policy and teaching, and the decentralization of many church activities. Pope Paul VI responded cautiously but sympathetically.

National Council of Churches. In December the triennial meeting of the General Assembly of the National Council of Churches of Christ in America —which embraces 33 major church bodies—was faced with demands for complete restructuring of the NCCC to make it more responsive to new factors of social change, and for the election of blacks to the top administrative posts in the Assembly and in the Council. Mrs. Cynthia Wedel was elected the first woman president of the Assembly, and the Council will undertake major organizational reform.

Black Manifesto. In April, James Forman, on behalf of a conference on black capitalism held in Detroit, issued a "Black Manifesto," calling upon the churches and synagogues of the United States to provide $3 billion for a black economic development program to be administered by a black organization, the Black Economic Development Conference, as reparation for injustices suffered by black Americans. In the following months local congregations, national conventions, and national headquarters of churches and synagogues were scenes of dramatic confrontations in behalf of these demands. Few religious groups responded with direct contributions to the organization with which Forman is associated, and many criticized the rhetoric of the appeal to the principle of reparations. However, many religious bodies have substantially increased their support of programs designed to aid minority groups to achieve self-determination.

Anglican Methodist Unity. In July the Convocations of Canterbury and York of the Church of England rejected a proposal for union with British Methodists, who had earlier approved a plan of union.

Other Developments. In the United States there was growing interest, especially among college and university students, in mystical experience and its relation to drug-culture, and in the teachings of the historic Eastern religions. A U.S. branch of the militant Japanese Buddhist Soka Gokkai sect, which possesses considerable political power in Japan, reported that it was undergoing dramatic growth among non-Japanese Americans.

In India there were new outbreaks of Hindu-Muslim conflict in some areas, and militantly conservative Hindu groups threatened established political arrangements in others.

Buddhist groups in South Vietnam were permitted greater freedom by the government there, though some continued to experience difficulties. Major religious groups throughout the world continued to call for an early end of the Vietnam War. Burmese Buddhist leaders abroad sought to stimulate modification of Burmese policy. Muslim and Jewish groups continued to reflect concern over the Middle East crisis and to call on their coreligionists for support of their members in the Middle East.

J. A. MARTIN, JR.
Columbia University

ECUMENICAL SERVICE at New York's Greek Orthodox Cathedral of the Holy Trinity, Jan. 26, 1969, unites Protestant, Roman Catholic, and Orthodox leaders. The Rev. R. H. Edwin Espy, general secretary of the National Council of Churches, speaks at left. Others included Archbishop Iakovos, Greek primate (*right*, under canopy), and Roman Catholic Archbishop (later Cardinal) Terence Cooke.

U.S. CHURCH MEMBERSHIP

Religious Body	Members
Adventists, Seventh-day	384,878
American Carpatho-Russian Orthodox Greek Catholic Church	104,500
Apostolic Overcoming Holy Church of God	75,000[1]
Armenian Church, Diocese of America	136,000
Assemblies of God	595,231
Baptist Association, American	745,620
Baptist Association, North American	275,000
Baptist Association of America, Conservative	300,000
Baptist Church, United Free Will	100,000[8]
Baptist Churches, General Association of Regular	170,299[16]
Baptist Convention, American	1,454,965
Baptist Convention, Inc., National Primitive	1,235,000
Baptist Convention, Inc., Progressive National	521,692
Baptist Convention, Southern	11,140,486
Baptist Convention, U. S. A., Inc., National	5,500,000[3]
Baptist Convention of America, National	2,668,799
Baptist Evangelical Life and Soul Saving Assembly of U. S. A., National	57,674[5]
Baptist General Conference	96,416
Baptist General Conference, North American National Association	54,358
Baptists, Free Will	250,000
Baptists, Primitive	72,000[6]
Baptists, The General	65,000
Baptists, United	63,641[7]
Brethren, Church of the	191,402
Buddhist Churches of America	92,000[2]
Bulgarian Eastern Orthodox Church	86,000[9]
Christian and Missionary Alliance, The	68,679
Christian Churches (Disciples of Christ), International Convention	1,875,400
Christian Congregation, The One	45,767
Church of Christ, Scientist	268,915[10]
Church of God, The	74,101
Church of God (Anderson, Ind.)	144,243
Church of God (Cleveland, Tenn.)	220,405[16]
Church of God in Christ	425,500[2]
Church of the Nazarene	358,346
Churches of Christ	2,350,000[2]
Congregational Christian Churches, National Association of	110,000
Episcopal Church, The	3,420,297
Evangelical Covenant Church of America	65,496
Evangelical United Brethren Church	737,762
Friends, United Meeting	69,353

Religious Body	Members
Greek Orthodox Archdiocese of North and South America	1,770,000[2]
Independent Fundamental Churches of America	119,970
Int'l Church of the Foursquare Gospel	89,215[12]
Jehovah's Witnesses	330,358[2]
Jewish Congregations	5,725,000
Latter-day Saints, Church of Jesus Christ of	1,891,965
Latter Day Saints, Reorganized Church of Jesus Christ of	169,248
Lutheran Church, The American	2,575,506
Lutheran Church in America	3,157,543
Lutheran Church-Missouri Synod	2,759,308
Lutheran Synod, Wisconsin Evangelical	358,466
Mennonite Church	83,627
Methodist Church	10,289,214
Methodist Church of North America, Free	62,090
Methodist Episcopal Church, African	1,166,301[5]
Methodist Episcopal Church, Christian	466,718[2]
Methodist Episcopal Zion Church, African	1,100,000[2]
Moravian Church in America	60,574
North American Old Roman Catholic Church	18,500[2]
Pentecostal Church, Inc., United	225,000
Pentecostal Church of God of America, Inc.	115,000
Pentecostal Holiness Church, Inc.	67,027
Polish National Catholic Church of America	282,411[14]
Presbyterian Church, Cumberland	88,540
Presbyterian Church in the U. S.	960,776
Presbyterian Church in the U.S.A., The United	3,268,761
Reformed Church, Christian	278,869
Reformed Church in America	384,751
Roman Catholic Church	47,468,333
Romanian Orthodox Episcopate of America	50,000
Russian Orthdox Catholic Church in America Patriarchal Exarchate	152,973
Russian Orthodox Church Outside Russia	55,000[7]
Russian Orthodox Greek Catholic Church of America	56,549[16]
Salvation Army	324,911
Serbian Orthodox Church in the U. S. A. and Canada	65,000
Spiritualists, International General Assembly of	164,072[4]
Syrian Antiochian Orthodox Church	120,000
Triumph the Church and Kingdom of God in Christ	45,000
Ukrainian Orthodox Church of U. S. A.	87,475
Unitarian Universalist Association	283,000
United Church of Christ	2,052,857

Figures are mainly for the calendar year 1967 or a fiscal year ending in 1967. [1] 1956. [2] 1965. [3] 1958. [4] 1956. [5] 1951. [6] 1950. [7] 1955. [8] 1952. [9] 1962. [10] Data not reported; figure given here from U. S. Census of Religious Bodies, 1936. [11] 1964. [12] 1963. [13] Worldwide statistics. [14] 1960. [15] Includes members of Congregational Christian and Evangelical and Reformed churches. [16] 1966. (Source: National Council of Churches of Christ in the U. S. A., Yearbook of American Churches for 1969.)

PROTESTANTISM

A popular book written by Jeffrey K. Hadden, *The Gathering Storm in the Churches,* was an apt prediction for the state of Protestantism in 1969. It was a year of confrontations and conflict, but also a year of creative witness and attempts at reconciliation.

The Black Revolution and the Churches. The revolution of black people focused upon all the churches with explosive intensity. The most controversial event was the so-called Black Manifesto, issued by the newly formed Black Economic Development Conference (BEDC), which demanded an initial payment of $500 million in "reparations"

from white churches and synagogues for their complicity in Western structures that have denied opportunity and equality to black people. James Forman (the dominant figure in the controversy) and others caused confrontations with local congregations (the first was in Riverside Church, New York City, in May) and denominational assemblies alike. Their activities included the temporary seizure of national church offices located in New York City.

Black militants issued a "Black Manifesto" to U. S. churches in 1969, demanding reparations for the injustices black people have suffered. While generally rejecting the demand, most faiths were sympathetic to the needs of the black community and set up action programs to deal with its problems.

WIDE WORLD

(*Above*) Black militant James Forman debates "reparations" with Dr. Ernest Campbell of Riverside Church, New York.

(*Below*) Dr. Campbell and associates pass Forman as they leave altar on his arrival to read militants' demands for "reparations."

OLIPHANT, IN THE DENVER POST

THE NEW YORK TIMES

In London, a World Council of Churches–sponsored Consultation on Racism described racism as a worldwide phenomenon that affects people of all races. The National Committee of Black Churchmen was host to a convocation at Oakland, Calif., that coordinated the goals and strategies of major black church groups, such as BEDC and the Interreligious Foundation for Community Organization. An overwhelming number of books and articles were issued during 1969 about the black perspective on the Christian faith. An important example was James Cone's *Black Theology and Black Power*.

Ecumenism. At Canterbury, England, the World Council of Churches Central Committee received into membership seven churches, including the Kimbanguist Church of Christ on Earth, a 3-million-member indigenous Congolese church. In September, 72 churches met at Abidjan, Ivory Coast, for the Second General Assembly of the All-Africa Conference of Churches.

In December the 8th triennial General Assembly of the U. S. National Council of Churches met in stormy session, and elected an Episcopal laywoman, Mrs. Cynthia Wedel, its first woman president.

The Anglican-Methodist negotiations in England for church union were temporarily delayed when only 69% of the Anglicans (short of the 75% agreed upon by both churches) approved the first stage of a two-step plan of union. In northern India all seven negotiating churches voted affirmatively on their plan and assured the second united church in India. In the United States the Consultation on Church Union met at Atlanta, Ga., in March for its 8th plenary session; "Guidelines for Local Interchurch Action" were recommended. In New Zealand the Congregational Churches voted to unite with the Presbyterian Church, while both continue to engage in wider conversations with Disciples of Christ, Methodists, and Anglicans.

Many new forms of local ecumenism took shape during the year. The Texas Conference of Churches and the Arizona Ecumenical Council brought Protestant, Roman Catholic, and Orthodox churches into interdenominational relationships. In another direction, the Massachusetts Black Ecumenical Commission was formed.

Theological Education. After several years of decline, theological seminaries experienced a slight (0.5%) increase in enrollment. Like the universities, some seminaries, such as Union Theological Seminary in New York, devised ways for stronger student participation and voice in all phases of seminary life. Others developed special institutes for black studies, as did the Graduate Theological Union in Berkeley and Colgate-Rochester Theological Seminary. The necessary trend toward consolidation among theological schools slowly continued as six institutions in the vicinity of Toronto, Canada, formed the Toronto School of Theology.

Other Developments. Church groups participated in the nationwide moratorium in Washington, D. C., November 15, as a peaceful demonstration against the Vietnam War. The first U. S. Congress on Evangelism, held at Minneapolis, Minn., called upon 4,700 evangelical Protestants and their churches to become involved in the social problems of American society. The ultrafundamentalist Carl McIntire was removed from leadership in his anti-ecumenical American Council of Churches.

Prominent Protestants who died in 1969 included Harry Emerson Fosdick, the eminent American preacher; Josef Hromadka, the Czech theologian who sparked the Christian-Marxist dialogue; Clarence Jordan, a Georgia prophet of interracial justice; and James A. Pike, the controversial former Episcopal bishop (see PIKE, JAMES A.)

PAUL A. CROW, JR.
General Secretary, Consultation on Church Union

ROMAN CATHOLICISM

The principal event in the Roman Catholic Church in 1969 was the summoning and the success of the Roman Synod (Oct. 11–28). The Synod was a meeting of bishops representing national hierarchies from all over the world together with the Pope. It was preceded by many expressions of pessimism from those who felt that the church was changing too slowly. In Rome there had been rather open disapproval of criticism, notably from high officials in the Vatican Curia, who were especially dismayed at the open criticisms uttered by Cardinal Suenens of Belgium. However, the Synod came off peacefully and to the relative satisfaction of "progressives" in the church.

A Year of Stress. At the same time, 1969 was a year of continued stress among Catholics. Disaffection for the Pope's stand on birth control continued to be shown, without the Pope's offering any change. In fact, the year saw more open confrontation between lower and higher clergy than at any time in recent history. For example, when a group of European bishops met in Chur, Switzerland, in July they were confronted by a fairly large group of priests from several countries, insisting on changes in ecclesiastical life-style and celibacy.

Within religious orders, especially of nuns, tensions between "progressives" and conservatives continued to grow, or at least not to diminish. A number of orders of women, in their efforts to up-date their life-styles, found reconciliation between the two poles increasingly difficult. This led to a great number of members leaving their orders, or forming splinter groups.

Among Catholics, as among other religious communities, the challenge from the young remained serious, perhaps more serious than ever. Many youths, while personally religious, became increasingly dissatisfied with institutional forms used in the church. A decline in the number of candidates for seminaries and religious life was still noted, though there were signs that this trend had begun to level off.

Growing Nationalism. Another continued development in 1969 was in the direction of national self-consciousness among Roman Catholics in different parts of the world. Especially since Pope Paul's encyclical on birth control, different national groups of bishops have published their own response, some of them considerably less strict than the Pope's own position.

Bishops in countries or large areas have had more frequent meetings, notably in the Netherlands. The Indian bishops held an important meeting in 1969 at Bangalore in which they attempted to come to grips with national problems. During his visit to Uganda, Africa (July 31–August 2), Pope Paul stressed the church's need to embrace indigenous values, thus to be more African in Africa.

The Church in Latin America. A phenomenon that was increasingly prominent in 1969 was the growing identification of the Roman Catholic Church in Latin America with social issues and social change. Bishops of most countries endorsed the decisions of the Medellín (Colombia) Conference, which was held in 1968, and strongly advocated social reform. The archbishop of Lima put his prestige behind the sweeping socioeconomic reforms of the new Peruvian government. Several bishops in Brazil and Paraguay were outspoken critics of repressive policies of the governments in those countries. Broadly speaking, one may say that this marks a great change in the image of the church in Latin America, an institution that was often previously identified with the status quo.

Theological Commission. A positive development in Roman Catholic theology was the appointment by the Pope of a theological commission. It included a number of the most respected theologians of the world, some of them men who just a few years ago were considered suspect, if not heretical. Among them are Karl Rahner, S. J.; Yves Congar, O. P.; Joseph Ratzinger, S. J.; and others. This suggests a phenomenon that has been observed often in the life of the church: one generation's radical is the next generation's norm or even conservative. It also shows that Pope Paul, though considered a conservative by many "progressives," has made a number of moves in the other direction.

Reform of the Liturgy. One of the Pope's liberal moves was in the direction of liturgical reform. Vatican Council II had insisted on the need for reform in the public worship (liturgy) of the church, updating it in the direction of contemporary religious thought and in line with historical research. After some years of preparation, the new *Ordo Missae* (Ordinary of the Mass) was released on April 3. It provided a simpler, more intelligible structure for the Eucharist. Despite protests from conservative quarters, Pope Paul insisted that this and other liturgical changes be implemented.

C. J. McNaspy, S. J.
Associate Editor, "America" Magazine

JUDAISM

Developments in Judaism during 1969 reflected the general trends of contemporary society as well as specifically Jewish concerns.

A survey of Jewish theology, which was conducted by Edward B. Fiske and published in the New York *Times* on Nov. 23, 1969, found that among many Jewish leaders there is "a renewed interest in the recovery of traditional Jewish religious customs and teachings." Little propensity is shown to adopt the radical positions characteristic in contemporary Christianity. The published survey also noted that "for the first time since the Enlightenment the major trends in Jewish thinking are in opposition to those of Christian thinkers. Christians are moving away from religious law to the new morality while Jews are returning to it. Christian theologians are questioning whether God exists, while we [the Jews] are becoming more conservative."

Closer cooperation between the various groups of Jews and renewed interest in Jewish traditions even by some Jewish radicals has been the result of this emphasis. The consciousness of ethnic identity, which has been spurred in large measure by the black renaissance, has been reflected in the interest shown in Judaism by various groups of youths who have organized themselves on campuses and in large cities, in an attempt to find their way back to Judaism.

Jewish religious leadership, however, has begun to show increased concern about the nihilistic tendencies of New Left groups (a large number of whose members are Jews). This concern has also been extended to the more subtle attacks on traditional Jewish values exhibited by such bestselling books as *Portnoy's Complaint* by Philip Roth. More attention and more funds are being directed toward working with Jewish college youth.

Militant Negroes. Increasing disquiet was evi-

POPE PAUL VI (*upper left*) concelebrates mass at St. Peter's with the 33 new cardinals whom he nominated during 1969. Their number brings the College of Cardinals to 134—the largest membership in its history.

KEYSTONE

dent concerning some of the militant positions taken by black spokesmen. The official Jewish organizations rejected demands of the "Black Manifesto" for reparations to blacks and were generally not in sympathy with such extremist groups as the Black Panthers.

Jews, in large part, continued their traditional sympathy for the black struggle for justice and equality. However, by and large, the feeling was that progress could be better attained through the traditional modes of legislation, government programs, and self-help.

Antisemitism. There was considerable concern over the resurgence of antisemitism in the Communist countries, especially in Poland, and the continued suppression of the remaining Jewish communities in the Arab countries, such as Iraq where several Jews were executed together with others for alleged espionage. Notwithstanding the continued suppression, there were increasing signs of a Jewish renaissance in the Soviet Union. Several statements and declarations emanated from groups of Jews in that country declaring their commitment to Judaism. These statements are the more remarkable when it is recalled that religious instruction has not been available to Soviet Jews since the revolution in 1917.

Israel and Judaism. Israel continued to play an important role in the religious life of world Jewry. American Jews were delighted by the reception afforded Mrs. Golda Meir, the prime minister of Israel, during her visit to the United States in September.

The complicated question "Who is a Jew?" was brought before the supreme court of Israel in 1969. The question was whether Jewish traditional law, which recognizes a child of a Jewish mother or a convert as a Jew, should be retained or whether more secular considerations such as national identity should be recognized. The court effectively favored more secular considerations as the criteria, and the decision caused a government crisis in Israel. Compromise legislation, however, was introduced in the Israeli parliament by the government.

Increasing Interest in Jewish Studies. A world congress of Jewish scholars, which included hundreds of intellectuals from all over the world, was held in Jerusalem in 1969, indicating the increased interest in Jewish scholarship. This is also reflected in the increasing numbers of universities and colleges that are instituting departments of Jewish studies.

SEYMOUR SIEGEL
Jewish Theological Seminary, New York

EASTERN ORTHODOXY

The relations of the Orthodox churches with the Church of Rome, the Protestant world, and other Christian bodies, as well as among themselves, continued to progress in 1969.

Orthodoxy Around the World. A meeting of Orthodox patriarchs took place in 1969 at the Bulgarian Orthodox patriarchate in Sofia, Bulgaria, on the occasion of the 1100th anniversary of the death of St. Cyril, the Greek missionary, who, together with his brother, St. Methodius, had brought Christianity to the Bulgarian people. The Ecumenical Patriarch Athenagoras, Patriarch Nicholas of Alexandria, Archbishop Ieronymos of Greece, and representatives of other Orthodox churches attended the commemorative services and programs at the invitation of Patriarch Cyril of Bulgaria.

A historic meeting of Orthodox and Roman Catholic theologians, which was organized by a special commission of the Holy See, was held in Bari, Italy, on April 30.

On July 4, the second European Ecumenical Symposium was held in Athens. Patriarch Athenagoras forwarded a message urging the designation of a common date (the second Sunday of April) for the celebration of Easter by Eastern and Western Christians. Pope Paul VI and the Second Vatican Council had already expressed themselves in favor of such an idea, providing that all other Christian churches agree.

The Orthodox churches are preparing for a Pan-Orthodox Conference whose agenda was prepared, but not finalized, by the first Pan-Orthodox Conference which met in Rhodes in 1961.

Orthodoxy in America. Representing all of the canonical Orthodox jurisdictions, Archbishp Iakovos, of the Greek orthodox archdiocese of North and South America, delivered one of the prayers at the inauguration of President Richard M. Nixon, on January 20.

At its meeting on April 17 the Standing Conference of Orthodox Bishops of America considered a comment on the revision of the Guidelines for the Orthodox in Ecumenical Relations. It also decided to ask the Ecumenical Patriarchate to include in the agenda of the forthcoming Pan-Orthodox Conference the issue of the jurisdictional situation in America. The unity and cooperation of the various Orthodox jurisdictions in North America will be advanced if and when the mother churches in Europe and Asia approve the proposed creation of a local Orthodox Synod in America under the spiritual jurisdiction of the Ecumenical Patriarchate of Constantinople.

On January 26 an Ecumenical Doxology was conducted at the Holy Trinity Greek Orthodox Cathedral in New York. Participating were Orthodox and Roman Catholic leaders and representatives of the World Council of Churches and the National Council of Churches, who delivered addresses on the 20th anniversary of the enthronement of Patriarch Athenagoras.

In an ecumenical service on January 19 in St. Patrick's Cathedral in New York, Archbishop Iakovos of the Greek Orthodox Church became the first prelate of Eastern Orthodoxy to preach in this Roman Catholic cathedral. Archbishop Iakovos was marking the opening in New York of the worldwide week of Prayer for Christian Unity.

BASIL G. VASILIADIS
*Greek Orthodox Archdiocese
of North and South America*

ISLAM

In 1969 an important world Islamic conference was held in Malaysia to reexamine Islamic law in the light of modern conditions. After Al Aksa mosque in Jerusalem was damaged by fire, another conference of Muslim leaders met in Rabat, Morocco, to consider concerted Muslim action against Israel. Communal violence in India revealed that Hindu-Muslim tensions there are still explosive.

Muslim Scholars Meet. Muslim scholars from 23 countries met in Kuala Lampur in May, 1969, at the request of Malaysia's Prime Minister Abdul Rahman. Rahman sponsored the conference to find ways to rid the Muslim world of "illogical beliefs" that hamper Muslim social and economic progress.

The conference focused entirely on "non-political" matters. In the medical field, organ transplants were deemed acceptable under Islamic law. The conference also endorsed birth control in special hardship cases. Following the traditional interpretation of the Koranic condemnation of usury, the scholars declared "interest-oriented" economic systems to be un-Islamic. A resolution was passed calling for the establishment of an international Islamic bank for interest-free loans. Plans were also laid for the development of a world Islamic research center.

Jerusalem. Jerusalem's famous Al Aksa mosque was heavily damaged by fire on August 20. Israeli authorities arrested an Australian visitor, Dennis Rohan, and charged him with arson. Nevertheless, Jerusalem Arabs staged street demonstrations, and various Muslim leaders—Arab and non-Arab—blamed the fire on Israeli occupation of Old Jerusalem.

Arab Summit Meeting. In September a summit meeting of leaders from 24 Muslim countries was sponsored by the United Arab Republic, Saudi Arabia and Morocco. It was occasioned by the fire in Al Aksa mosque. The announced aims of the conference were to show a united Islamic front in condemning Israel's annexation of Jerusalem and to consider other concerted action against Israel.

The conference leaders demanded that Israel withdraw from all occupied Arab territory and pledged the "full backing of the Islamic peoples to the Palestine struggle for national liberation."

Riots in India. Communal riots erupted in Gujarat in October. Over 1,000 Hindus and Muslims were dead after a week of violence in Ahamadabad alone, and more than 30,000 were homeless. According to some reports, the immediate cause of the

THICH THIEN MINH, Buddhist opposition leader in South Vietnam, enters his pagoda after serving sentence on variety of charges.

violence was Muslim mistreatment of a group of Hindu holy men who drove their herd of sacred cows into the path of a Muslim religious procession. Not since the partition of India and Pakistan have communal riots been so costly in lives and property. "Secular" government in India has not solved the problem of Hindu-Muslim antagonism.

W. PAUL MCLEAN
Southern Methodist University

ORIENTAL RELIGIONS

Tension among various religious groups in Asia mounted in 1969, increased by ethnic and economic factors, particularly in India and Vietnam.

Hinduism. Deep antagonism exists between many of the 460 million Hindus and the 60 million Muslims of India. Riots between them occurred in every month of 1969, the worst being the 7-day September rampage that engulfed Ahmadabad, theretofor free of disturbances. The explosion came shortly after 100,000 Muslims paraded to protest the burning of the Al Aksa mosque in Jerusalem. When 1,000 Muslims in procession were impeded by sacred cows herded by Hindu holy men, they chased the holy men from their cows into a nearby temple and stoned it. Frenzied mobs destroyed buildings, dragged people outdoors to cut their throats or truss them up, doused them with gasoline, and set them afire. By the end of the week 1,000 Indians lay dead, most of them Muslims.

Although the conservative Jan Sangh party did not gain in the Indian elections, other dissatisfied groups sought to improve their positions by breaking with the established political parties, thus causing further fragmentation. This process was quickened when Jagadguru Shankaracharya, a conservative Hindu, stirred up discord by urging that untouchability be strictly enforced according to the ancient dharmashastras. Prime Minister Indira Gandhi reacted sharply, urging that the guru be prosecuted under the law that makes advocating untouchability a penal offense. Later, Mrs. Gandhi hailed modern science and scored superstition, the caste system, and ethnic and religious antagonisms.

Buddhism. In Ceylon, Tamil-dominated, Hindu-oriented political groups are turning against Prime Minister Senanayake, and have reduced his support to 83 out of 157 members of parliament.

In June the exiled Dalai Lama of Tibet, seeking to strengthen his position, gathered monks and supporters from India and other countries to hear a sermon lasting 60 hours and spread over 11 days.

In South Vietnam, in May, a 24-hour cease-fire was observed to mark Gautama Buddha's birthday. President Thieu took the occasion to reduce the sentence of the Buddhist leader Thich Thien Minh from 10 to 3 years. Thien Minh had been sentenced in March by a military court for harboring draft dodgers and deserters, illegally possessing arms, and having Communist documents in his possession. He had denied the charges. His arrest and sentencing brought a strong protest from leaders of the militant An Quang faction of the United Buddhist Church, who charged that Thieu, a Roman Catholic, was using foreign support to destroy Buddhism. On Vietnam's National Day, November 1, Thien Minh was pardoned and released.

JOHN B. NOSS
Author's of "Man's Religions"

REPUBLICAN PARTY. See POLITICAL PARTIES.

RESPIRATORY DISEASES

Respiratory diseases, especially the acute viral diseases, continued to rank among the most common of the infectious diseases during 1969. This was underscored by the worldwide pandemic of Hong Kong influenza, which started in 1968 and was widespread throughout the United States in 1969.

Hong Kong Influenza. Although it is not definitely certain, the Hong Kong strain of the A2 influenza virus probably originated on the mainland of China. The occurence of half a million cases in Hong Kong in the middle of July 1968 heralded a pandemic of worldwide proportions. From Hong Kong, the virus spread rapidly to Singapore, the Philippines, Vietnam, Taiwan, Malaysia, Thailand, India, and the northern territories of Australia. Except in the United States, the spread of the disease slowed down and only little spread was noted until the beginning of 1969.

The first reports of the Hong Kong influenza virus in the United States occurred in November 1968. Unlike other countries, the United States reported a large number of "excess deaths" associated with the disease. These "excess deaths" occurred mostly among the elderly and the very young. Several large epidemics of the Hong Kong flu were also noted in Europe during the winter of 1968–69, but unlike the United States, school/work absenteeism was relatively low and there were no reports of "excess deaths." In general, the Hong Kong influenza pandemic was considered to be mild, especially in comparison with the influenza pandemic of 1957, the first year that the Asian strain of the virus appeared.

Lest it be thought that the Hong Kong influenza pandemic has ended, recent reports indicate that outbreaks of the disease have occurred in Australia, Europe, New Zealand, South Africa, and several countries in South America. However, the United States would certainly not expect an epidemic of the Hong Kong flu during the winter of 1969–70. If outbreaks do occur, the fact that the Hong Kong virus has been included in influenza vaccines should help to modify the severity of any outbreaks.

Prevention of Respiratory Disease. Although prevention continues to be the only rational approach to the control of viral respiratory diseases, there is increased optimism that antiviral agents may eventually play a role in both the prevention and treatment of virus diseases as antibacterial agents are effective against bacterial diseases. One of these antiviral substances, interferon, is a protein that is produced by cells after they have been infected by a virus. Once interferon is produced, it helps protect neighboring cells by inhibiting the reproduction of the virus.

Interferon has been known to exist for many years, but the production of this substance in quantities sufficient to control or treat virus infections has been technically infeasible. However, recent experiments using a synthetic nucleic acid substance similar to that found in viruses are promising. When this substance is injected into animals with different types of virus infections, including virus-caused cancer, it stimulates the production of interferon within the animal. The amount of interferon thus produced is sufficient to modify the course of the infection. This interferon-inducing substance, called poly I:C, has not yet been tried in the treatment of virus infections in humans.

So far, the only vaccine that has been definitely shown to be of value in preventing respiratory disease in civilians is influenza vaccine. It contains several viral strains and is thus effective against several types of influenza. There is still no vaccine available against the common cold. This is largely because there are at least 100 known virus strains that are capable of producing the disease. At present, scientists are expending a great deal of effort toward the production of mutated respiratory viruses in an attempt to provide a vaccine for acute respiratory viral diseases. This type of vaccine is most needed for infants and children.

Viruses and Chronic Lung Disease. The role of viruses in the initiation of chronic lung diseases, such as emphysema, continues to be an enigma. What is definitely known is that intercurrent viral infections occurring in individuals with chronic respiratory disease do produce relapses. The importance of studying chronic lung diseases has been emphasized by the findings that in some areas the number of deaths associated with emphysema has increased by 1200%. In a recent study conducted in Los Angeles county, 15% of the 45,000 adults tested were found to be suffering from early or late stages of chronic lung disease.

BERNARD PORTNOY, M. D.
University of Southern California

RETAIL SELLING. See ECONOMY OF THE UNITED STATES.

RHODE ISLAND

Unified government returned to Rhode Island in 1969 as Democratic Gov. Frank Licht took over the executive office, introduced a far-reaching program, and saw most of it enacted by a General Assembly in which members of his own party had an overwhelming predominance. During 1969 Rhode Island also concerned itself with improvements in its educational system.

Politics. Governmental changes included a recasting of the judicial branch under the uniform administration of the chief justice of the supreme court, and a reduction in the number of district courts, to be headed by full-time rather than part-time judges. In the executive branch, the governor was empowered to reorganize specified departments of state government at his discretion.

One successful innovation was the administration's plan to set up "little state houses" throughout the state. People will then be able to bring their problems more directly to the attention of the executive office. Also enacted were such varied measures as the liberalization of workman's conpensation laws; enlargement of the lending power of the State Recreational Building Authority; and a revision of the corporate laws. In a bow to more participatory democracy, the state established a primary to determine candidates for the U. S. presidency.

Education. Perhaps no single piece of legislation had greater long-term import than the restructuring of the state's educational system. This restructuring was accomplished by the creation of a Board of Regents to supplant both the state Board of Education and the Board of Trustees of the state colleges. The new board is charged with making policy for all public education.

Another law, which touched off much contro-

———RHODE ISLAND • Information Highlights ———

Area: 1,214 square miles (3,144 sq km).
Population: 908,000 (1969 est.).
Chief Cities (1969 est.): Providence, the capital, 177,000; Warwick, 81,500; Cranston, 76,000; Pawtucket, 76,000.
Government (1969): *Chief Officers*—governor, Frank Licht (Democrat); lt. gov., J. Joseph Garrahy (Democrat); secy. of state, August P. LaFrance (Democrat); atty. gen., Herbert F. DeSimone (Republican); treas., Raymond H. Hawksley; commissioner of education, William P. Robinson; chief justice, Thomas H. Roberts. *General Assembly*—Senate, 50 members (37 Democrats, 13 Republicans); House of Representatives, 100 members (76 D, 24 R).
Education: *School enrollment* (1968)—public elementary, 96,000 pupils (3,700 teachers); public secondary, 74,000 pupils (3,800 teachers); nonpublic schools, 48,400 pupils (2,000 teachers); college and university (fall 1967), 36,909 students. *Public school expenditures* (1967–68)—$124,-862,000 ($839 per pupil); average teacher's salary, $7,650.
Public Finance (fiscal year 1968–69): *Revenues,* $265,542,822 (5% sales tax, $71,699,386; motor fuel tax, $25,867,493; federal funds, $49,521,410). *Expenditures,* $261,459,096 (education, $88,699,192; health, welfare, and safety, $120,-400,306; highways, $21,738,638). *State debt,* $217,893,000 (June 30, 1969).
Personal Income (1968): $3,244,000,000; average annual income per person, $3,549.
Public Assistance (fiscal year 1968): $66,448,287 to 51,419 recipients (aged, $7,631,617; dependent children, $18,-937,153).
Labor Force (monthly average, 1969): *Agricultural,* 3,000; *nonagricultural* (wage and salary earners), 356,200 (40.5% manufacturing, 18.6% trade, 13.5% government). *Unemployed persons* (May 1969)—13,500.
Manufacturing (1965): *Value added by manufacture,* $1,193,-646,000 (textile mill products, $167,913,000; nonelectrical machinery, $134,681,000; primary metals, $129,735,000; fabricated metals, $80,561,000).
Agriculture (1967): *Cash farm income,* $19,613,000 (livestock, $10,361,000; crops, $9,176,000; govt. payments, $76,000). *Chief crops* (tons)—Hay, apples, potatoes.
Mining (1967): *Production value,* $4,035,000. *Chief minerals*—Sand and gravel; stone.
Fisheries (1967): *Commercial catch,* 75,960,436 pounds ($5,055,275). *Leading species*—Northern lobster, 1,928,975 pounds ($1,579,149); scup, 6,415,987 pounds ($1,303,627).
Transportation: *Roads* (1969), 5,203 miles (8,373 km); *motor vehicles* (1967), 467,386; *railroads* (1968), 326 track miles (525 km); *airports* (1969), 4.
Communications (1968): *Telephones* (1967), 471,800; *television stations,* 3; *radio stations,* 18; *newspapers* (1966), 7 (daily circulation, 316,118).

versy, provided for salary subsidies for teachers of secular subjects in parochial and other private elementary schools. But perhaps the most newsworthy event in education in 1969 occurred in November when the teachers of Providence staged a strike, demanding a higher salary scale. Mayor Joseph Doorley was compelled to seek and obtain an injunction calling upon the teachers to return to their classrooms.

Economy. The problem of financing the rising cost of government loomed large, as it had during the gubernatorial campaign in 1968. In that year, Governor Licht had campaigned in opposition to a personal income tax as a solution to the problem of government expenses, offering instead a tax program based mainly on profits from investments and savings. The yield from this tax program appeared to be running short of expectations by the end of 1969.

Meanwhile, budgetary requests of the various state agencies, concerned with programs and projects they deemed necessary, mounted.

The dilemma facing Governor Licht and the state legislators was how to meet these needs and yet not alienate an electorate already opposed to spiraling expenditures. Voters had demonstrated this opposition at the special election in June, when they rejected all five referenda authorizing bond issues for state road construction, the expansion of a junior college, and improvement of certain institutional facilities.

DAVID D. WARREN
University of Rhode Island

RHODESIA

During 1969, Rhodesian voters approved a new constitution perpetuating white minority rule and endorsed the establishment of a republic that would sever remaining ties with Britain. The vote brought wide criticism in Rhodesia itself, Britain, the United Nations, and elsewhere around the world.

New Constitution Debated. On February 15 the ruling Rhodesian Front party announced details of the complex proposals later incorporated into the draft constitution aimed at retaining power in white hands. The publication of the draft constitution on May 21 evoked wide discussion and some protests.

Some African and white students of the University College of Rhodesia protested in Salisbury, carrying placards reading "Stand firm against apartheid" and "Abandon hope, all ye who vote yes." British Foreign Secretary Michael Stewart called the draft constitution "disastrous." Roy Welensky, formerly prime minister of the now defunct Federation of Rhodesia and Nyasaland, said the plan was "a complete break with the tradition of Cecil Rhodes and Winston Churchill."

Constitutional Referendum. The small, white-dominated Rhodesian electorate overwhelmingly supported Prime Minister Ian Douglas Smith in the constitutional referendum vote on June 20. They approved both a new constitution and the establishment of a republic. Those qualified to vote under the existing constitution number 81,583 whites out of a total white population of 280,000, and 6,634

RHODESIA

Information

Highlights

Area: 150,332 square miles (389,361 sq km).
Population: 4,670,000 (1968 est.).
Chief City (1966 census): Salisbury, the capital, 172,000.
Government: *Prime Minister*—Ian D. Smith (took office April 1964). *Parliament*—Legislative Assembly, 65 members.
Education: *Total school enrollment* (1965)—643,811 (primary, 627,806; secondary, 11,495; teacher-training, 2,819; technical, 832; higher, 859).
Finance (1968 est.): *Revenues,* $241,900,000; *expenditures,* $264,900,000; *monetary unit,* pound (0.3571 pound equals U. S.$1).
Gross National Product (1968): $1,176,141,130.
National Income (1968): $1,058,527,020; *average annual income per person,* $226.
Economic Indexes: *Industrial production* (1967), 118 (1963=100); *cost of living* (1965), 107 (1963=100).
Manufacturing (metric tons, 1967): Sugar, 150,000; cement, 250,000; crude steel (1966), 130,000.
Crops (metric tons, 1967–68 crop year): Maize, 600,000; tobacco, 93,700; citrus fruit (1965), 22,000.
Minerals (metric tons, 1967): Lithium (1965), 62,900 (ranks 1st among world producers); coal, 2,739,000.
Foreign Trade (1968): *Exports,* $257,000,000 (chief exports, 1965: unmanufactured tobacco, $131,500,000; asbestos, $30,130,000; iron and steel, $18,140,000); *imports,* $290,-000,000 (chief imports, 1965: transport equipment, $45,-390,000; nonelectrical machinery, $44,610,000; textile yarn and fabrics, $34,970,000). *Chief trading partner* (1967): South Africa.
Transportation: *Roads* (1969), 47,754 miles (76,851 km); *motor vehicles* (1967), 153,200 (automobiles 111,000); *railways* (1969), 2,655 miles (4,272 km); *national airline,* Central African Airways Corp.; *principal airports,* Salisbury, Bulawayo, Fort Victoria, Kariba.
Communications: *Telephones* (1968): 112,086; *television stations* (1967), 2; *television sets* (1967), 45,000; *radios* (1965), 240,000; *newspapers* (1965), 4.

Africans out of a grand total of 4,818,000 Africans.

The vote on the new constitution was 54,724 "yes" and 20,776 "no" or 72% approval. Some who voted "no" were believed to represent white extremists who did not think the new constitution went far enough in guaranteeing permanent white supremacy. The vote on proclaiming Rhodesia a republic was 61,130 "yes" and 14,327 "no," or 82% approval.

New Constitutional Provisions. When the new constitution, signed by the government on November 29, goes into effect, it will provide for two racially separate electoral rolls, one for whites, Asians, and coloreds, and the other for Africans. The head of state will be chosen by the executive council.

In the 2-chamber parliament a 23-member Senate will contain 10 African chiefs (5 each from Matabeleland and Mashonaland), 10 whites elected by the lower house, and 3 members of any race appointed by the head of state. The 66-member House of Assembly will contain 50 whites elected from the white electoral role and 16 Africans, of whom 8 will be elected by four constituencies each in Matabeleland and Mashonaland and 8 by four tribal electoral colleges in each of the two areas.

African representation in the lower house will eventually increase proportionally as African income tax payments reach parity with those of whites, until a balance is achieved of 50 Africans and 50 whites. Africans now pay a small fraction of Rhodesia's total income taxes, and their present average annual income is $403 as against $3,959 for whites.

A declaration of rights in the new constitution promises freedom of expression and assembly and protection from inhuman treatment. It also gives the government powers over dissent with preventive detention, search, and regulation of the press.

Prime Minister Smith declared that the new constitution "virtually enshrines white supremacy, but it does it on merit, which no one can undermine." Welensky contended that "it will lead to eventual confrontation" and "is a departure from representation based on merit to straight racial representation." Secretary General U Thant of the United Nations declared on June 21 that the new constitution posed a threat to peace that must not be ignored.

U. S. Policy. Policy on Rhodesia was debated before the U. S. House Foreign Affairs Africa Subcommittee. On October 17, Assistant Secretary of State for African Affairs David D. Newsom supported more stringent sanctions against Rhodesia, saying "we have continued to recognize British sovereignty in Rhodesia and regard the Smith regime as illegal." He justified keeping open the U. S. consulate in Salisbury as a listening post and as protection for the 1,100 U. S. residents in Rhodesia. Under UN economic sanctions, U. S. trade with Rhodesia dropped from nearly $33 million in 1965 to $3.7 million in 1968, all in exempted medical supplies and book materials. Before the same subcommittee on November 19, former Secretary of State Dean Acheson urged the United States to give up sanctions against Rhodesia as impractical. Opposing testimony, given by former Secretary of State for African Affairs G. Mennen Williams, pressed for continued sanctions and the closing of the U. S. consulate in Salisbury.

FRANKLIN PARKER
West Virginia University

ROBERTSON, Cliff. See biographical sketch under MOTION PICTURES.

ROGERS, William Pierce

U. S. Secretary of State: b. Norfolk, N. Y., June 23, 1913.

A longtime confidant and personal friend of President Nixon, Rogers was sworn in as secretary of state on Jan. 22, 1969. His previous experience in foreign affairs was limited, but Rogers' appointment met with general approval because of his demonstrated skill as a negotiator and his successful earlier career in international law and in government.

Negotiator. The theme of Rogers's administration was set by President Nixon as "negotiation, not confrontation." In accord with this theme, Rogers supported the nuclear nonproliferation treaty and began Strategic Arms Limitation Talks (SALT) with the Soviet Union in October at Helsinki. Rogers also made extensive tours, visiting leaders of the nations of the world. He accompanied the President to Europe in February and made trips of his own to the Pacific area and to Asia.

Foreign Policy. Rogers early established good relations with the Senate Foreign Relations Committee, an accomplishment that had eluded Dean Rusk. He made frequent public statements on U. S. policy. He condemned the mistreatment of U. S. prisoners of war by the North Vietnamese, stressed the need for stronger U. S.-Latin American relations (while calling Gov. Nelson Rockefeller's visit to South America "helpful"), supported Nixon's "Vietnamization" program, gave West Germany assurance on the nonproliferation treaty, and restated policies of support for the United Nations.

Style. In his first months in office, Rogers demonstrated a coolness of character and a quiet competence. He displayed vigor and imagination in his activities. Some observers had suspected that Rogers might be sensitive about the major foreign policy role assigned to Henry A. Kissinger. (Kissinger was named the White House assistant on foreign affairs and, in December, became the chairman of the Defense Programs Review Committee.) Rogers, who gave no public indication of resenting Kissinger, seemed content with President Nixon's statement that Rogers would be his "principal foreign policy adviser."

Career. Rogers graduated from Colgate University in 1934 and from Cornell University's law school in 1937. He was assistant district attorney of New York county under Gov. Thomas E. Dewey from 1938 to 1942. After World War II service in the Navy, he acted as counsel to Senate committees. President Eisenhower appointed him deputy attorney general in 1953 and attorney general in 1957. While in the Department of Justice, Rogers strongly supported civil rights legislation and antitrust activity. He was a member of the U. S. delegation to the United Nations in 1965 and served on the ad hoc Committee on South West Africa. Secretary Rogers has been a close adviser to Nixon since World War II.

WALTER DARNELL JACOBS
University of Maryland

FOUR AMERICANS were designated cardinals by Pope Paul VI in 1969. From left, with St. Peter's cupola in Vatican City in the background, are Terence Cardinal Cooke, New York; John Cardinal Dearden, Detroit; John J. Cardinal Carberry, St. Louis; and John Joseph Cardinal Wright, Pittsburgh.

UPI

ROMAN CATHOLIC CHURCH

The Roman Catholic Church in the United States underwent a number of significant developments in 1969, including a continuing crisis over authority and its exercise in the Church.

Bishop Shannon. The most startling event was the departure of Bishop James Shannon, auxiliary bishop of St. Paul, Minn., from the active ministry. Having expressed his distress over present structures, within which he found it impossible to function, Bishop Shannon retired to private life and married (August 2). At the same time, he steadfastly refused to be associated with a small but vocal group of former priests called "Priests for a Free Ministry." Nonetheless, his resignation as bishop was a great blow to liberal Catholics in the United States.

A Liberal Leader. As chairman of the U.S. bishops' conference, John Cardinal Dearden, archbishop of Detroit, helped make that conference more effective, addressing itself to national moral problems. A clear statement on conscientious objection, quite unpopular in military circles, recognized the morality of selective objection. Cardinal Dearden showed great leadership, too, in his own diocese by setting up a representative synod that may prove a model for other dioceses. .

Meeting of Bishops. The National Conference of Catholic Bishops, meeting in Washington in November, somewhat surprisingly agreed to hear Father Patrick O'Malley, president of the National Federation of Priests' Councils. He stated with some vigor the complaints and desires of American priests, and was listened to with serious attention. Black priests, now associated and more vocal than in the past, were listened to as well, and were allowed to set up a Central Office of Black Catholicism. A new group of Spanish-American priests (called PADRES) also presented their case to the American bishops and were heard sympathetically.

Relocation of Theological Schools. Another change on the U.S. scene was the move of several important theological faculties away from rural areas to urban and ecumenical centers. Most significant of these were the transfer of Alma College to the General Theological Union in Berkeley, Calif., and of Woodstock College to Cambridge, Mass., where it shares library and other facilities with Protestant divinity schools.

Crisis of Catholic Schools. At the parish level, the situation of Catholic schools has become increasingly acute. Costs have doubled in recent years, as the number of teaching sisters has dropped. At the college and university level, too, it has become more and more necessary to acquire some civic aid. Catholic colleges and universities have shared, too, in the general malaise affecting U.S. campuses.

Priests' Associations. Priests' associations and diocesan synods, both official and unofficial, increased in number and importance during 1969. Almost every diocese now has some such group, and the general mood of confrontation throughout the country has been sensed in their relationship to bishops. Meantime, many bishops have shown themselves progressively more open to their priests, while others have retired into a fortresslike attitude of resistance. The general attitude of the hierarchy, however, has been one of increased involvement in civic and social needs. One development has been the frequency of retirement of bishops over the age of 75.

Reform Among Nuns. Religious orders of women (especially those involved in teaching and other activities) continued to feel the stresses of change and resistance to change. The most publicized of these were the Immaculate Heart nuns (largely of Los Angeles). After endless disagreements with the archbishop of Los Angeles, Cardinal MacIntyre, they finally agreed to become disestablished as a religious order and to pursue much of their work as a lay group.

Another development in 1969 was the establishment of a National Association of Contemplatives (nuns whose principal work is prayer). These women have been working on the Americanization of a style of life that originated some years ago in Europe. With the counsel of professional theologians, and drawing upon their own experience and inner resources, they have taken a number of vigorous steps toward this end.

Pentecostalism. A phenomenon that has been developing over the past few years in the Roman Catholic Church in the United States is one previously associated with Protestantism—that of Pentecostalism. On most Catholic college campuses, sometimes in connection with small, freewheeling liturgical groups, informal meetings for spontaneous prayer have become common.

C. J. McNaspy, S. J.
Associate Editor, "America" Magazine

ROWING. See Sports.

RUBBER

U. S. rubber industry sales reached $16.5 billion in 1969, a 6.5% increase over the 1968 total of $15.5 billion. For 1970, the rate of growth was expected to be even higher: about 7%. Most of this dollar growth has been caused by the industry's fast shift from bias ply tires to the more expensive, but longer lasting, belted bias tire.

Approximately $4 billion of the industry's income in 1969 came from the sale of tires to both the replacement and original-equipment markets. Some $6.3 billion was accounted for by the non-tire sector; while the remaining $6.2 billion was brought into the industry through the sale of plastic materials and products.

Of the 5.8 billion pounds of natural and synthetic rubber consumed in 1969 by the U. S. rubber industry, 67% went into the manufacture of 220 million tires for automobiles, trucks, buses, farm equipment, aircraft, industrial vehicles, and motorcycles. Passenger tires accounted for the greater part with over 178 million units; truck and bus tire shipments ranked second with 27 million units.

The remaining 33% of 1969 rubber consumption was used to make hundreds of different products—belting, hose, footwear, medical goods, balloons, and a host of other molded and extruded products.

New Technology. The U. S. rubber industry expected that between 1970 and 1975 it would concentrate much of its resources on the development and manufacture of radial ply tires and on automation. Research and development will continue on polymers, chemicals, textiles, adhesives, plastics, and rubber products.

Safety. The Federal Highway Administration began enforcing the National Traffic and Motor Vehicle Safety Act of 1966 by fining certain manufacturers of tires that did not meet federal standards.

World Consumption and Production. Worldwide consumption of new rubber reached 7.02 million long tons in 1969, an 8.84% increase over 1968. Synthetics represented 4.18 million long tons (59.5%); natural rubber, 2.84 million long tons (40.5%). The continuing trend in nearly all countries—particularly the USSR—was toward self-sufficiency in synthetics by establishing domestic production facilities. However, natural rubber's many outstanding properties combined with the industry's ongoing programs to improve the quality of natural rubber were expected to insure this tree-derived material a continually expanding worldwide market.

JOSEPH V. DEL GATTO
Executive Editor, "Rubber World"

WORLD RUBBER CONSUMPTION—1969[1]
(in long tons of 2,240 pounds or 1,016 kg)

Country	Natural Rubber	Synthetic Rubber	Total
United States	585,000	1,980,000	2,565,000
Japan	260,000	393,000	653,000
West Germany	184,000	279,000	463,000
United Kingdom	185,000	244,000	429,000
France	157,000	235,000	392,000
China[2]	263,000	10,000	273,000
Italy	100,000	170,000	270,000
USSR[2]	258,000	6,000	264,000
Canada	48,000	123,000	171,000
India	86,000	30,000	116,000
Brazil	34,000	68,000	102,000
Australia	39,000	41,000	80,000
Netherlands	19,000	27,000	46,000
Other countries	622,000	574,000	1,196,000
Total	2,840,000	4,180,000	7,020,000

[1] Estimated   [2] Refers to imports

RUMANIA

The most celebrated event in Rumania in 1969 was the 27-hour official visit of U. S. President Richard M. Nixon to Bucharest on August 2–3. Rumania became the first Communist country to be visited by a U. S. president since World War II.

Nixon's visit bolstered the position of Rumania's president and party chief, Nicolae Ceauşescu. In 1969, Ceauşescu seemed to be the most prudent and courageous Communist leader to appear in decades. He proved his ability by soothing Soviet sensitivies when he could do so without sacrificing Rumanian principles. But ceremonial gestures to Moscow could not conceal Rumania's genuine insistence upon real sovereign independence within the Communist bloc. Orthodoxy in domestic affairs and Rumania's geographical position accounted for the success of Ceauşescu's balancing act. His policies, admired in Eastern Europe, also led to economic progress.

Nixon's Visit. Nixon was welcomed by Ceauşescu at unfinished Otopeni airport. The two had met before when Nixon, as vice president, visited Rumania. Nixon, long a fighter against the spread of communism in the United States, received a great welcome.

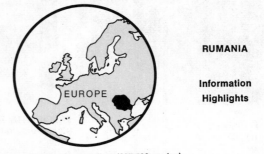

RUMANIA

Information Highlights

Area: 91,699 square miles (237,500 sq km).
Population: 19,721,000 (1968 est.).
Chief Cities (1966 census): Bucharest, the capital, 1,372,937; Cluj, 186,483; Timisoara, 175,421.
Government: *President of the State Council and General Secretary of the Communist party*—Nicolae Ceauşescu (took office July 25, 1965); *Chairman of the Council of Ministers*—Ion Gheorghe Maurer (took office 1960). *Parliament*—Grand National Assembly, 465 members.
Religious Faiths: Rumanian Orthodox Christians, 90% of population.
Education: *Literacy rate* (1956), 89% of population. *Total school enrollment* (1966)—3,874,755 (primary, 2,907,943; secondary, 523,305; teacher-training, 10,723; vocational, 295,836; higher, 136,948).
Finance (1966 est.): *Revenues,* $17,900,000,000; *expenditures,* $17,700,000,000; *monetary unit,* leu (6 lei equal U. S.$1).
Industrial Production Index (1968), 182 (1963=100).
Manufacturing (metric tons, 1967): Cement, 6,336,000; crude steel, 4,092,000; wheat flour, 2,388,000.
Crops (metric tons, 1967–68 crop year): Sunflower seed (1966), 671,000 (ranks 3d among world producers); maize, 6,800,000.
Minerals (metric tons, 1967): Petroleum, 13,200,000; lignite, 7,848,000; coal, 5,112,000; iron ore, 2,796,000.
Foreign Trade (1968): *Exports,* $1,469,000,000 (chief exports, 1967: fuels, minerals, and metals, $285,916,666; machinery and equipment, $264,800,000; foodstuffs, $210,700,000; inedible organic raw materials, $179,300,000); *imports,* $1,609,000,000 (chief imports, 1967: machinery and equipment, $754,733,333; fuels, minerals and metals, $384,533,-333; inedible organic raw materials, $138,050,000). *Chief trading partners* (1967): U.S.S.R. (took 31% of exports, supplied 26% of imports); West Germany (took 7% of exports, supplied 17% of imports); Italy.
Transportation: *Roads* (1964), 7,155 miles (11,515 km); *motor vehicles* (1967), 36,800; *railways* (1965), 6,838 miles (11,004 km); *national airline,* TAROM (Rumanian Air Transport); *principal airport,* Bucharest.
Communications: *Telephones* (1968), 550,000; *television stations* (1967), 9; *television sets* (1967), 570,000; *radios* (1967), 3,019,000; *newspapers* (1967), 33.

UPI

PRESIDENTS Richard Nixon of the United States and Nicolae Ceauşescu (*right, foreground*) of Rumania dance the hora with folk dancers during Nixon's enthusiastically hailed official visit to Rumania, August 2–3.

An estimated half million persons lined the 12 miles traveled by the motorcade into the capital, and thousands waved American flags furnished by the police. Nixon thrilled the crowds by shouting in Rumanian, "Long live American-Rumanian friendship!" Bystanders tossed flowers into his car and shouted greetings. Nixon later ate grapes at a farmers' market, joined Ceauşescu in a hora with a folk dance troupe, and was a guest at a lavish dinner in a former royal palace.

The two leaders discussed improved economic relations, establishment of information libraries in their countries, a consular convention, and a civil air accord (U. S. planes do not yet fly into Rumania). They also considered the acquisition of a new U. S. embassy building in Bucharest for the new ambassador, Leonard C. Meeker. An official communiqué stated that both Ceauşescu and Nixon supported a policy of respect for the sovereignty and equal rights of all states, large and small, as well as the right of all states to preserve their own national institutions and unique national character.

According to unconfirmed reports, Nixon wished to assure Communist China, friendly toward Rumania, that he did not intend to join Moscow in an anti-Peking alliance. By defending Rumania's independence of Moscow, Nixon thus indirectly denounced the "Brezhnev Doctrine," which authorizes Soviet interference in the internal affairs of other Communist-bloc nations. During his visit to Rumania, Nixon seemed to be following a new U. S.

policy, replacing the atmosphere of East-West confrontation with a mood of negotiation.

Relations with the United States. Nixon's visit was also the culmination of considerably improved U. S.-Rumanian relations. A nuclear cooperation agreement between the two countries, signed in 1968, was the first such agreement concluded by Washington with a Communist-bloc nation. The accord envisaged research grants, exchanges of scholars, and information centers. Trade between the two nations totals about $23 million annually, of which about two thirds consists of Rumanian imports from the U. S.

Nixon also asked the U. S. Congress to grant Rumania most-favored-nation status (enjoyed only by Yugoslavia and Poland within the Communist bloc), in order to increase Rumania's foreign exchange earnings, which are urgently needed to modernize its economy and industry. The United States apparently wished to reward Rumania for its independent behavior within the bloc.

Soviet Displeasure. The Soviet Union expressed its hostility toward the Nixon visit by canceling the planned July visit to Bucharest of Soviet leaders Leonid Brezhnev, Aleksei Kosygin, and Nikolai Podgorny. The purpose of the visit had been to renew the expired Soviet-Rumanian friendship treaty. The three leaders refused to attend the 10th Congress of the Rumanian Communist party, which began three days after Nixon's departure. Moscow was represented instead by Konstantin Katushev, a party functionary, who criticized Nixon's visit as "perfidious bridge-building to undermine socialist cohesion."

Ceauşescu's Foreign Policy. During the party congress held in August, Ceauşescu defended Rumania's independent line. He had earlier irked Moscow by repudiating the "Brezhnev Doctrine," by refusing to join in a denunciation of Peking at the June international Communist conference in Moscow, and by rejecting Soviet plans for economic integration within COMECON (Council of Mutual Economic Assistance) in April. Rumania also opposed the Soviet Union's condemnation of Israel as an aggressor and declined to renew its friendship treaty with Moscow. In December, Ceauşescu urged other Communist nations to open diplomatic relations with West Germany.

During 1969 Rumania persistently demanded the withdrawal of troops and the closing of bases on the territories of all foreign nations. This policy was aimed at bringing about a pullout of Soviet troops from Czechoslovakia, as well as NATO forces from western Europe.

By deft maneuvering Ceauşescu showed that Rumania could stand up to the Soviet Union. He served notice that any violation of Rumania's territory would constitute an act of war. The militia, called up during the Czech crisis in 1968, remained on active duty.

Yet, despite Soviet impatience, Ceauşescu apparently wished to sustain, not wreck, the Communist bloc. By 1969, he had succeeded in establishing relations with dissident Communists from Peking to Belgrade. Rumania apparently arranged the unusual meeting between Chinese Premier Chou En-lai and Soviet Premier Kosygin in Peking in November, after the funeral of North Vietnamese leader Ho Chi Minh. A Soviet-Rumanian trade agreement was signed in the same month.

Domestic Affairs. Ceauşescu emerged with considerably greater power than any of his predecessors. His methods were a blend of orthodoxy, revisionism, and opportunism. He introduced some reforms, including eased passport regulations, accelerated housing construction, and improved medical services, to increase his popularity. Nevertheless, he removed all his potential rivals from office and emerged virtually supreme in Rumanian affairs.

National elections in March confirmed his policies. He added to his office the posts of president of the council of national defense and commander in chief of the armed forces. In August the party congress reelected him secretary-general.

Economy and Trade. Judging by the state of Rumania's economy, Ceauşescu's popularity could only increase. Rumania's industrial production grew by 12% in 1969, the greatest increase for any Communist-bloc nation. This expansion was more than twice as rapid as that of Czechoslovakia and Hungary; it exceeded Soviet growth by one third.

In 1969, Rumania negotiated new trade agreements with Turkey, Iran (visited by Ceauşescu in September), Yugoslavia, Britain, Belgium, Luxembourg, Austria, Norway, the United Arab Republic, Jordan, and Israel. Rumania and West Germany had excellent trade relations.

SHERMAN D. SPECTOR
Russell Sage College

RUSSIA. See UNION OF SOVIET SOCIALIST REPUBLICS.

RUSSIAN LITERATURE. See SOVIET LITERATURE.

RWANDA

For Rwanda the year 1969 was, by African standards, a reasonably tranquil one. According to official reports, President Grégoire Kayibanda received 99.6% of the popular vote in the September national elections. His government continued its efforts to solve the country's economic and social ills without excessive fanfare, but with some meaningful participation by the representative National Assembly.

Foreign Relations. Aid agreements with Belgium were renegotiated in 1969, as they have been each fall since independence. In addition, in mid-November, France's Secretary of State for Foreign Affairs M. Bourges made his first visit to Kigali since agreements with France were signed in 1962.

Besides negotiating bilateral and multilateral aid agreements, Rwanda made interinstitutional arrangements. It renewed an agreement between its university and Belgian universities. The University of Ghent has been cooperating in the development of an indigenous medical corps. Nine medical doctors received diplomas under this program in 1968, and six more graduated in 1969.

Relations with Burundi and Congo (Kinshasa) have remained stable since early 1968, despite tensions between the Tutsi and Hutu ethnic groups in Burundi. Representatives of the three countries met regularly to discuss common problems of education, electrical power, and communications.

EDOUARD BUSTIN
Boston University

RWANDA

Information Highlights

Area: 10,169 square miles (26,338 sq km).
Population: 3,405,000 (1968 est.).
Chief Cities (1969 est.): Kigali, the capital, 15,000.
Government: *President and Prime Minister*—Grégoire Kayibanda (took office for 2d term Oct. 3, 1965); *Parliament*—National Assembly, 47 members.
Religious Faiths: Roman Catholics, 26% of population.
Education: *Total school enrollment* (1963)—367,246 (primary, 359,542; secondary, 2,268; teacher-training, 2,016; vocational, 3,370; university/higher, 50).
Finance (1969 est.): *Revenues,* $15,000,000; *expenditures,* $16,500,000; *monetary unit,* franc (100 francs equal U. S.$1).
Gross National Product (1967): $165,000,000.
Average Annual Income per Person, $40.
Cost of Living Index (1967): 119 (1964–66 = 100).
Crops (metric tons, 1967–68 crop year): Cassava, 190,000; sweet potatoes and yams, 300,000; coffee, 11,400.
Minerals (metric tons, 1967): Tin concentrates, 1,343; tungsten, 377; lithium (1965), 295.
Foreign Trade (1967): *Exports,* $14,039,000 (chief exports, 1967: coffee, $7,743,500; tin, $4,164,600); *imports,* $20,-222,000 (chief imports, 1967: textile yarn and fabrics, $3,601,900; transport equipment, $2,708,300; motor vehicles, $2,169,100). *Chief trading partners* (1967): Belgium-Luxembourg.
Transportation: *Roads* (1969), 3,534 miles (5,686 km); *motor vehicles* (1967), 3,600 (automobiles 2,400).

SAILING. See SPORTS—*Yachting.*

ST. LOUIS

Democrats remained in control of St. Louis in 1969, despite the surprise victory of a Republican as president of the Board of Aldermen. A ruling that the 28 aldermanic districts would have to be reapportioned and a nine-month public housing rent strike were among other significant events.

City Government. In April's municipal elections, incumbent Democrats Mayor Alfonso J. Cervantes and Comptroller John Poelker were reelected. In an upset victory Joseph Badaraco, a Republican, won the race for president of the Board of Aldermen. He was the first Republican to win a citywide election in 18 years. Although the Republicans gained additional seats in the city's legislature, the Democrats remain in firm control, having won 14 of the 16 seats contested in the 1969 election.

On June 30 the U.S. Federal District Court ordered the reapportionment of the city's 28 wards or aldermanic districts. The court pointed out that the wards, as presently constituted, vary greatly in population, and are therefore not in keeping with the "one man-one vote" requirement. The court further ruled that the ward boundaries were to be based on actual population rather than on number of registered voters.

Rent Strike. A nine-month organized rent strike by tenants in several public housing projects led to major alteration in rent structures and management of public housing. The strike began in February, when a group of tenants agreed not to turn rent money over to the housing authority, and it was not settled until the end of October. During the strike the proportion of tenants not paying rent increased to 35%. The settlement of the strike resulted in significant concessions by the city. These included new and lower rent schedules and a provision that no tenant will have to spend more than 25% of his income for rent. In addition, the tenants will be granted more control over the governing of the projects, and the housing authority pledged to improve living conditions and to seek improvements in security measures in the projects.

Culture and Recreation. The Spanish Pavilion, built for the 1964–65 New York World's Fair, was formally dedicated in St. Louis on May 25. The ceremony was attended by the mayor of Seville and the Spanish minister of information. The building has been reerected on a spot adjacent to the new stadium in downtown St. Louis. The structure holds three restaurants, a theater, and exhibition space, as well as the St. Louis Visitors' center.

Another Spanish-built structure, a replica of Columbus's flagship the Santa Maria, was acquired for St. Louis. The replica was towed down the East coast and up the Mississippi River to serve as a tourist attraction on the St. Louis riverfront. The ship was rechristened and opened to the public on May 15. In late June, however, a severe storm ripped the ship from its moorings, and sank it.

Musical offerings were expanded in the summer of 1969 with the inauguration of the Mississippi River Festival. Jointly sponsored by the St. Louis Symphony and Southern Illinois University at Edwardsville, the festival included performances by the St. Louis symphony as well as a variety of popular artists. The concerts were held on the Southern Illinois University campus.

RICHARD E. DAWSON
Washington University, St. Louis, Mo.

SALVATION ARMY

Commissioner Erik Wickberg was elected ninth general of the Salvation Army in the summer of 1969, succeeding Gen. Frederick Coutts, who retired Sept. 17 upon reaching the mandatory retirement age of 70. General Wickberg was born in Sweden. Prior to his election as general, he was chief of the staff, the second in command at the Army's international headquarters in London.

The title of "general" designates the Salvation Army's top administrator, who is responsible for the worldwide ecclesiastical and humanitarian activities of the 2 million member organization that serves in 70 countries.

The new general was elected by the High Council, a group of 45 Salvation Army officers from all parts of the world, who hold the rank of commissioner or command a territory.

Life-long concern for human welfare, particularly that of young people, and most especially that of urban young people; and commitment to the principles of freedom, equality and justice for all Americans—these were some of the reasons cited for presenting Dr. Jerome H. Holland, a leading Negro educator, with the Annual Award of The Salvation Army Association of New York. Dr. Holland was subsequently appointed U.S. ambassador to Sweden.

A highlight of Salvation Army participation in the National Conference on Social Welfare was its own reexamination of the relationships between Christian ethics, human rights, and the Army.

The Salvation Army's newest and largest residence for senior citizens—a 15-story structure in midtown Manhattan, in New York City, offering comfortable, safe, yet independent living quarters to 400 older men and women—was opened in 1969.

During countless emergencies—fires, floods, snowstorms, airplane crashes, and power failures—Salvationists served around-the-clock to bring practical help and spiritual comfort to the victims. An example of the Salvation Army's work occurred in Stamford, Conn., during the winter of 1969, when, in one of the worst snowstorms ever to hit the eastern United States, over 1,000 persons, including 800 stranded in a train without heat or food, were fed and sheltered by the Salvation Army.

JOHN GRACE
The Salvation Army

SAMOA. See PACIFIC ISLANDS; WESTERN SAMOA.

SAN FRANCISCO

The announcement of a comprehensive new redevelopment project, a sharp increase in the local tax rate, and the rejection by the voters of a new city charter were among the noteworthy events of 1969 in San Francisco (1969 est. pop., 705,000).

Finances. At the November 4 election voters expressed their dissatisfaction at the steady rise in municipal spending by rejecting all but one measure likely to increase the cost of city government. The sole exception was Proposition F, which provided for a larger police force. Proposition E, asking approval of a new charter giving broader powers to the mayor, was decisively rejected. Of the five members of the Board of Supervisors up for reelection, three were returned to office.

The budget for the 1969–70 fiscal year was fixed at $598 million, the highest in the city's history. To

SAN FRANCISCO'S new 52-story world headquarters of the Bank of America was one of three major office buildings completed in the city in 1969.

BANK OF AMERICA

help finance it the tax rate was raised to $12.29 per $100 assessed valuation, an increase of $2.06 over that of the previous year.

Bay Tunnel. During the year, financial problems besetting the Bay Area Rapid Transit System (BART), which will provide high-speed transportation between the city and eastbay communities, were alleviated by the imposition of an additional half cent to the sales tax in the three counties the system will serve. Meanwhile, progress on the $1.3 billion project continued. The 3.6-mile tunnel beneath the bay was broken through on April 22, and by the end of 1969 subway construction on Market Street had progressed enough so that normal surface traffic can be resumed in the fall of 1970. The system is to go into full operation in 1972.

New Construction. The year 1969 saw the completion of three major office buildings, including the 52-story world headquarters of the Bank of America, and the beginning of a number of others. Among the latter were the 45-story Security Pacific National Bank Building (the first unit of the $200 million Embarcadero Center Project), the Chinese Cultural Center opposite Portsmouth Square, and, further uptown, a block-long, 32-story annex to the St. Francis Hotel. Prominent among buildings in the planning stage was the new headquarters of the Transamerica Corporation at Montgomery and Washington streets, to be a pyramid-shaped structure of 48 stories.

In June the San Francisco Redevelopment Agency announced plans for the first unit of the Yerba Buena Center, which, when completed, will replace six blocks of outmoded buildings south of Market Street with a badly needed convention hall and a sports arena. The Center will also include an 800-room hotel, office buildings, theater, and shops. The complex will be drawn together by landscaped plazas and pedestrian malls. The work of clearing the site has been delayed pending the provision of satisfactory low-cost housing for several thousand persons now living in the area.

Crime. Efforts to suppress crime and to control the sale of dangerous drugs remained a major concern of the city law enforcement agencies. The sta-

tistics for 1968 (the latest available) reveal that more than 106,000 crimes, ranging from murder, robbery, and rape to shoplifting, drunkenness, and other minor offenses, were reported to the police. Of the nearly 38,000 persons arrested, 27,000 were brought to trial and some 9,000 received jail sentences. During the first 10 months of 1969, 130 murders were reported, as compared with 83 for the same period in the previous year.

Allegations Against Mayor. Joseph L. Alioto, serving his first term as mayor, hotly denied allegations published in *Look* magazine linking him with the Mafia, and filed suit for $12.5 million damages against the magazine's publishers. In January 1970 he announced that he would not seek Democratic nomination for governor in 1970.

OSCAR LEWIS
Author, "San Francisco: Mission to Metropolis"

MAYOR Joseph Alioto hotly denied *Look* magazine story linking him with the Mafia.

UPI

SASKATCHEWAN

The political and economic concerns of Saskatchewan in 1969 revolved around Canada's growing wheat surplus, the pressure of inflation, and the possibility of a recession. Farm equipment, automobile, and retail sales all showed declines. The provincial government, anticipating a drop in revenue, cut expenses by $11 million in September. The situation eased, at least psychologically, in late September with significant wheat sales to Communist China and Poland.

Farm Discontent. When Prime Minister Pierre Trudeau visited Saskatchewan in July, he was met by angry farmers protesting the lack of cash income caused by lagging grain sales. Tractors patrolled the highways carrying signs and slowing traffic to publicize farm discontent. Demonstrators in Regina and Saskatoon called for a significant injection of cash into the agricultural economy.

Agriculture. Grain crops in 1969 were above average. Late spring frosts delayed growth at first, but timely rains followed by good weather produced excellent crops through most of the province. Good fall weather permitted completion of most harvesting without difficulty. Much grain was stored outside because of inadequate granary space.

Demand for beef exceeded supply through most of 1969, forcing prices sharply upward. The resulting demand for feeder cattle forced that market upward as well. The time required to raise cattle to market age makes it likely that this situation will continue for some time.

Potash. New supplies of potash from Saskatchewan's vast reserves have upset markets and interfered with production from U. S. deposits in New

Mexico. After meetings with the state government of New Mexico, Saskatchewan decided to establish a floor price and export licensing system designed to force a reduction of Saskatchewan production by about 40%. This was balanced by a promise from New Mexico that the move would not lead to increased production from the Carlsbad deposits. If the agreement is confirmed it will permit orderly closure of the nearly exhausted Carlsbad operations without doing permanent damage to the expanding Saskatchewan companies. Growing world markets should take up the slack in the Saskatchewan industry quickly.

Water Resources. Research by the Saskatchewan-Nelson Basin Board led to signing of an interprovincial water agreement among the prairie provinces (Saskatchewan, Manitoba, and Alberta) in October. The agreement covers waters flowing from west to east over interprovincial boundaries, primarily the North and South Saskatchewan Rivers, which begin in Alberta and flow through Saskatchewan to join the Nelson River in Manitoba. The agreement is a pioneer attempt to increase the efficiency of water usage in the system by intergovernmental cooperation.

The Coteau Creek hydroelectric plant at Gardiner Dam was officially opened on June 7. The three generators will put 800 million kilowatt hours a year into the provincial power grid.

Floods. High snowfall and a sudden thaw in April caused widespread flooding in the prairie provinces and the northern United States. Weyburn, Estevan, Moose Jaw, and many other centers in Saskatchewan suffered extensive property damage. Lumsden was saved from inundation only after a tense battle lasting several days. Losses were estimated at $1.5 million.

Communications. Full Canadian Broadcasting Corporation (CBC) television service became available in Saskatchewan for the first time in September. CHAB/CHRE-TV was purchased by the CBC and became CBKMT/CBKRT, a part of the national network. The new station serves the Moose Jaw and Regina areas. CKCK-TV, a former affiliated station, joined the CTV network.

GARTH BLUE
*Librarian, Western Region, Canada
Department of Regional Economic Expansion*

─────── SASKATCHEWAN • Information Highlights ───────

Area: 251,700 square miles (651,904 sq km).
Population: 961,000 (Jan. 1, 1969).
Chief Cities (1966 census): Regina, the capital (131,127); Saskatoon (115,892); Moose Jaw (33,417); Prince Albert (26,269); Swift Current (14,485).
Government: *Chief Officers*—lt. gov., Robert L. Hanbidge; premier and prov. treas., W. Ross Thatcher (Liberal); prov. secy. and atty. gen., D. V. Heald (L); min. of educ., J. C. McIsaac (L); chief justice, E. M. Culliton. *Legislature*—Legislative Assembly (convened Jan. 30, 1969); 59 members (34 Liberal, 24 New Democratic party, 1 vacant).
Education: *School enrollment* (1966–67 est.)—public elementary and secondary, 242,137 pupils (10,900 teachers); Indian (federal) schools, 2,227 pupils (166 teachers); college and university (fall 1966), 11,577 students. *Public school expenditures* (1963)—$85,796,000 ($422 per pupil); median teacher's salary (1966–67) $5,723.
Public Finance (fiscal year 1968 est.): *Revenues,* $355,860,000 (sales tax, $119,570,000; income tax, $73,466,000; federal funds, $35,231,000). *Expenditures,* $349,760,000 (education, $110,660,000; health and social welfare, $100,910,000; transport and communications, $71,670,000).
Personal Income (1967 est.): $2,091,000,000; *average annual income per person,* $2,183.
Social Welfare (fiscal year 1968 est.): $18,780,000 (aged and blind, $880,000; dependents and unemployed, $9,970,000).
Manufacturing (1966): Value added by manufacture, $154,-534,000 (food and beverages, $62,140,000; petroleum and coal products, $17,113,000; non-metallic mineral products, $14,394,000; fabricated metals, $11,194,000).
Agriculture (1968 est.): *Cash farm income,* $900,486,000 (livestock, $235,330,000; crops, $660,197,000). *Chief crops* (cash receipts)—Wheat, $349,175,000 (ranks 1st among the provinces); barley, $18,776,000 (ranks 2d); rapeseed, $14,-740,000 (ranks 2d); flaxseed, $5,666,000 (ranks 2d).
Mining (1967 est.): *Production value,* $328,167,375. *Chief minerals* (tons)—potash, 2,578,000 (ranks 1st among the provinces); sodium sulphate, 425,033 (ranks 1st); copper, 22,738 (ranks 5th); uranium, 1,000 (ranks 2d); crude petroleum, 92,915,500 bbl. (ranks 2d).
Transportation: *Roads* (1966), 124,615 miles (200,543 km); *motor vehicles* (1966), 438,558; *railroads* (1966), 8,567 track miles (13,787 km); *licensed airports,* 29.
Communications: *Telephones* (1966), 320,841; *television stations,* 6; *radio stations,* 17; *daily newspapers* (1966), 4 (daily circulation, 125,920).
All figures given in Canadian dollars equal to U. S. 93¢.

SATO, Eisaku. See biographical sketch under JAPAN.

SAUDI ARABIA

Throughout 1969, Saudi Arabia remained involved in the Arab struggle against Israel and in the political affairs of the Persian Gulf and southern Arabia.

The Arab World. Saudi Arabia occupied a pivotal position among the four member states of the Arab League still under dynastic rule. Not to be outdone in enmity towards Israel, King Faisal issued a call for a holy war after the burning of the Al Aksa Mosque in Jerusalem in August. He played a leading role in the Islamic summit conference held in Morocco in September to consider the consequences of the fire. Despite some misgivings over closer collaboration with the Arab republics, Faisal attended the Arab summit conference in Rabat, Morocco, in December, which attempted to work out a new strategy based on the growing Arab belief that a political settlement with Israel was impossible.

Saudi Arabia continued to make an annual grant of $140 million to the United Arab Republic and Jordan, states in the front line in the struggle against Israel.

The Persian Gulf. As the scheduled 1971 withdrawal of British military forces from the Persian Gulf drew nearer, Saudi Arabia showed great interest in the efforts being made to devise new arrangements to replace the old British dominance. Although Iran still insisted that the status of Bahrain, which it has long been claiming, should be clarified, Saudi Arabia encouraged Bahrain to join Qatar and the seven Trucial states in the proposed Federation of Arab Amirates. Saudi Arabia's strongest ties in this part of the gulf are with Qatar and two of the Trucial states, Dubai and Ras al-Khaima. Saudi Arabia still has an unresolved boundary dispute with Abu Dhabi, the largest and richest of the Trucial states, relating to the Buraimi Oasis and other territory in the interior where oil companies working for Abu Dhabi have been active in recent years.

Southern Arabia. The hopes engendered in 1968 for better relations between Saudi Arabia and the Yemen Arab Republic were not realized. In November 1969 the republic accused Saudi Arabia of giving aid to adherents of the old royalist regime, which had been driven out by republican forces in 1962. Relations between Saudi Arabia and Southern Yemen were even worse, as bitter land and air fighting broke out in November along the undefined border between the two countries.

Attempted Coups. Two abortive uprisings against the Saudi Arabian government during 1969 were reported. In September the government denied that it had executed any armed forces officers suspected of taking part in the coups.

Economy. During the first eight months of 1969, Saudi Arabia's oil production remained at almost the same level as its production for the first eight months of 1968, the average being slightly over three million barrels a day. Production was held back by the sabotage in May of the Trans-Arabian pipeline, which carries oil from the Persian Gulf basin to the Mediterranean coast of Lebanon. The sabotage was perpetrated by Palestinian guerrillas on the section of the line running through Israeli-occupied Syrian territory as a protest against U. S. support for Israel. The break was not repaired until 112 days later. The shutdown cost the Saudi Arabian government many millions of dollars, and the U. S. company that owns the pipeline had to pay Israel $2 million against damage caused by oil spillage. In September, Saudi Arabia's production moved up to nearly 3.5 million barrels a day. The country's estimated oil reserves rose by more than 8 billion barrels to a total of over 90 billion, the highest in the world.

The government's budget for the fiscal year beginning in September 1969 was balanced at $1.33 billion, or nearly 8% more than the previous year's budget. A large share of the budget was allotted to development projects, and better than one fourth of it went to the ministry of defense.

In September the council of ministers approved a 5-year development plan prepared by the Central Planning Organization. Implementation of the plan will begin in 1970. The goal is an annual growth of 9.3% in the gross national product, in contrast to the recent rate of 8.5%. The plan emphasizes the maximum development of the talents of the citizens and the diversification of the sources of the national income.

Revenue from the pilgrimage to Mecca was particularly good in 1969, with 375,000 foreign Muslims coming from 80 countries, 17% more than in the previous year. The largest delegations hailed from Yemen and Turkey. The pilgrimage provides the kingdom with its best source of foreign exchange after the oil industry.

The Saudi Arabian government is seeking to lessen the excessive dependence of its economy on oil. The government hopes to do this by producing other minerals. In March 1969 the government's General Petroleum and Mineral Organization concluded an agreement with a local concern, National Saudi Minerals, and U. S. interests, the Arabian Shield Companies, to promote the exploitation of minerals such as iron, copper, gold, and silver. Arabian Shield will do prospecting and drilling until minerals are discovered in commercial quantities.

GEORGE RENTZ
Hoover Institution, Stanford University

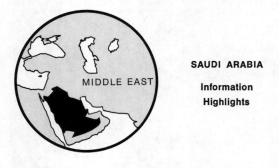

SAUDI ARABIA

Information
Highlights

Area: 800,000 square miles (2,149,690 sq km).
Population: 6,990,000 (July 1, 1967 est).
Chief Cities (1965 census): Riyadh, the capital, 225,000; Jidda, 194,000; Mecca, 186,000.
Government: *King*—Faisal ibn Abd al-Aziz (acceded 1964).
Major Religious Faith: Muslims, 99% of population.
Education: *Total school enrollment* (1965)—305,084 (primary, 260,586; secondary, 33,548; teacher-training, 6,406; technical/vocational, 2,713; university/higher, 1,831).
Finance (1968/69 budget est.): $1,230,000,000; *monetary unit,* riyal (4.5 riyals equal U. S.$1).
Gross National Product (1968): $2,000,000,000.
National Income (1966): $1,978,222,222; *average annual income per person,* $283.
Manufacturing (metric tons, 1967): Residual fuel oil, 9,765,-000; gasoline, 2,416,000; distillate fuel oil, 1,215,000; jet fuel, 1,215,000.
Major Crops (metric tons, 1967–68 crop year): dates, 380,000 (ranks 1st among world producers).
Major Mineral (metric tons, 1967): crude petroleum, 129,-304,000 (ranks 4th among world producers).
Foreign Trade (1967–68): *Exports,* $1,760,000,000 (chief exports, 1966: crude petroleum, $1,163,000,000; petroleum products, $209,000,000); *imports,* $491,500,000 (chief imports, 1966: motor vehicles, $78,210,000; rice, $22,700,000; wood, $12,890,000). *Chief trading partners* (1967): Japan (took 17% of exports, supplied 7% of imports); Italy (took 13% of exports, supplied 8% of imports); United States (took 6% of exports, supplied 22% of imports).
Transportation: *Roads* (1969), 11,000 miles (17,702 km); *motor vehicles* (1966), 88,800 (automobiles 65,800); *railways* (1969), 356 miles (573 km); *merchant vessels* (1967), 13; *national airline,* Saudi Arabian Airlines; *principal airports,* Dhahran, Jidda, Riyadh.
Communications: *Telephones* (1968): 29,000; *television stations* (1967), 4; *television sets* (1967), 40,000; *radios* (1964), 1,000,000; *newspapers* (1966), 7 (daily circulation, 55,000).

SCHOOLS. See COLLEGES AND UNIVERSITIES; EDUCATION; and the *Information Highlights* tables of articles on countries, states, and provinces.
SCIENCE. See articles on the various sciences; ASTRONOMY, CHEMISTRY, PHYSICS, etc.
SEISMOLOGY. See EARTHQUAKES.

'Draft lottery drawing begins on December 1 as Rep. Alexander Pirnie of New York picks the first capsule.

SELECTIVE SERVICE

The year 1969 was a time of great change for the Selective Service. It remains to be seen whether these changes have been far-reaching enough to quiet the controversy over the draft, which became entwined with the domestic strife over the Vietnam War and conduct of foreign policy. In October, President Nixon announced that Lt. Gen. Lewis B. Hershey would be relieved as Selective Service director in February 1970. Congress approved a draft lottery to determine the order of consideration for selection into the military with 19-year-olds first.

The Need for Draft Reform. President Nixon entered office having made a promise to end the draft and develop a volunteer army, although he indicated on several occasions that the change would have to await the end of the Vietnam War. But the draft seemed to be caught in the growing unpopularity of the war. Polls even showed that public support was lagging for the general principle of conscription, which had always enjoyed high support despite disagreement over the fairness of the system. Thus the Nixon administration had to set aside for the moment its concern with a volunteer force and seek a reform formula that would mute dissent.

Perhaps in an effort to upstage President Nixon or to prod him into action, both Republicans and Democrats introduced bills in Congress to abolish the draft and set up a volunteer force. The President ordered a Pentagon feasibility study of a volunteer force "when Vietnam expenditures had been substantially reduced."

In February, L. Mendel Rivers, chairman of the House Armed Services Committee and principal congressional obstacle to draft reform, announced that his committee might revise the draft law and institute a lottery. Representative Rivers may have wished to seize the initiative from the President or from fellow Democrat, Sen. Edward Kennedy, who was once again preparing draft reform legislation. This move by Rivers, and the growing awareness of the administration that an early shift to a volunteer force was unlikely, may have led to the announcement that the President would seek draft reform as a first priority. The task of developing plans for a volunteer force was assigned to a commission headed by former Secretary of Defense Thomas Gates.

Draft resistance and protests continued. Concern deepened that resistance would grow because of the increasing unpopularity of the Vietnam War, the general negative reaction to the military, and, finally, the growing surplus of manpower, which made more evident the inequities of the draft system. The surplus problem led to an emphasis on a lottery and a minimizing of changes in the structure and processes of the Selective Service. Each year 1.9 million young men reach draft age. Of these 1.3 million are physically and mentally qualified, but at most only 600,000 are needed (the annual average needed throughout the Vietnam War has been 260,000). When so few are needed some equitable means of deferring the remainder must be found. The existing policies have proven incapable of providing an equitable basis for deferring such large numbers of men. A lottery would select only the amount of men needed and free the rest for all but a national emergency. Those selected would then be processed by local boards and deferred or inducted in the same manner as in the past.

In May, President Nixon sent a special message to Congress proposing a lottery to determine the

GENERAL HERSHEY, Selective Service director slated for retirement, is jeered by draft protesters as he leaves his headquarters, December 1.

UPI

LEWIS B(LAINE) HERSHEY, director of the Selective Service System for 28 years, was relieved of his post on Feb. 16, 1970. Announcing Hershey's retirement on Oct. 10, 1969, President Nixon said that Hershey would be promoted to four-star rank and become a presidential adviser on manpower mobilization. A controversial figure, Hershey had in recent years come under fire for his virtual one-man rule over a draft system that many consider oppressive and for advocating harshness toward student antiwar demonstrators.

Hershey was born in Steuben County, Ind., on Sept. 12, 1893. He joined the army in 1911. Appointed secretary and executive officer of the joint Army-Navy Selective Service Committee in 1936, he helped lay the groundwork for the World War II military draft. In July 1941 he was named director of the Selective Service.

order for consideration of selection (or, who would not be considered) and reversing induction from the oldest first to 19-year-olds. He also ordered the National Security Council to review all guidelines, standards, and procedures and to report their recommendations by the year's end. Notably absent in his proposal were changes considered crucial by many draft critics, including elimination of student and occupational deferments, easing of the narrow, religious-based definition of conscientious objection, and changes in the structure of the system or powers of local boards to determine eligibility for deferment.

Congress was generally receptive to the President's proposals. General Hershey, who had previously derided a lottery announced his support. However, months followed without any action being taken; 42 proposals piled up before the House Armed Services Committee and 81 House members petitioned for action before Congressman Rivers announced in October that he would hold hearings "as soon as committee business permits."

During the many months of delay the Selective Service made one change of its own, establishing advisory committees of youths to advise state and regional directors. But this had no discernible effect on the worsening situation. Voluntary enlistments dropped and even the national conventions of Young

Republicans and the conservative Young Americans for Freedom called for reform. The Chairman of the Selective Service National Appeals Board resigned in August after accusing General Hershey of trying to control the board's decisions. Draft cases doubled over fiscal 1968 and constituted 15% of the federal criminal cases.

While congressional leaders continued to speak pessimistically about the prospects of reform, polls showed that Negro opposition to the draft had risen 22% since 1966, and a Louis Harris poll showed that national support for conscription had fallen to 44%, while 43% were opposed and the majority of those between the ages of 16 and 20 were opposed. Harassment and bombings of Selective Service offices continued and General Hershey admitted that he was being seriously impeded in meeting draft quotas. University presidents predicted mass disorder in the fall unless reforms were made.

At the start of the school year tension mounted with announcement of plans for antiwar moratorium days in October and November. The administration, feeling that dissent at home was seriously hampering negotiations with the North Vietnamese, urged congressional action and threatened to act through executive order if no law was passed. The leadership of the Democratic congressional majority pointed out the President's delay in submitting a bill; although he sent a special message to Congress in May it was August before he actually sent a bill and secured sponsors. The Democrats also claimed that the President could effect virtually all reforms himself, possibly even a system resembling a lottery in its results. In fact the administration had announced that if no law was forthcoming it would institute a "moving calendar" system in which the dates of liability within a month were altered.

After conferences with congressional leaders, the administration announced it would seek to change only one sentence in the 1967 draft law so as to permit a lottery. Other changes, it was admitted, could be made administratively.

In October the President initiated several moves in an effort to undercut campus protests. He ordered sharp cuts in draft quotas, and it was stated that total suspension was under consideration. The cuts were said to be based primarily on the "winding down" of the war, but there was also a desire

INDUCTION CENTER in New York City was heavily damaged on October 8 when a bomb exploded in the personnel and psychological testing offices.

to minimize the inequities of the existing draft system. The President ordered that graduate students due to be inducted be allowed to finish the school year, rather than only the semester. Just days before the October 15 moratorium the President sought to ease dissent by removing General Hershey from his post as director of the Selective Service, effective in February 1970. Hershey will be made a full general and serve as a special adviser on manpower mobilization.

Approval of the Lottery. Two days after the massive moratorium and a general effort by the President to prod Congress, the House Armed Services Committee unexpectedly recommended the initiation of a lottery. The full House soon concurred. In the Senate a struggle developed between those like Senator Kennedy, who sought comprehensive reform, and those like Sen. John Stennis, who would reluctantly accept a lottery. Finally, it was agreed to pass a lottery bill but to consider broader measures early in 1970.

The first lottery was held on December 1. Normally the young men in the lottery would all be 19-year-olds and those who had been previously deferred but were now graduating or completing a first year of graduate study. In this first lottery, however, all 1-A's under 26 were included so that no one escaped vulnerability in the transition to a lottery of the youngest. Days of the year (treated as birthdates of registrants) were scrambled and drawn randomly. Thus each person had a number indicating his vulnerability for selection consideration. The Defense Department estimated that those drawing numbers higher than 200 were unlikely to be reached by their boards in the coming year; their vulnerability would cease after that. To establish priorities for men with the same birthdates, the letters of the alphabet (treated as the first letters of

last names) were scrambled and drawn. Men who drew a number in the lottery but held college deferments were placed back into a current pool; they will hold their same number after graduating or dropping out. A local board could defer a man on the same grounds that had always been used.

Court Decisions. Dr. Benjamin Spock, Rev. William Sloane Coffin, Michael Ferber, and Mitchell Goodman, who in 1968 were found guilty of conspiring to hamper the draft, appealed their conviction in 1969. Former Supreme Court Justice and UN Ambassador Arthur Goldberg, acting as their defense counsel, charged the government with "inability to distinguish between political association and criminal conspiracy." On July 11 a U. S. Circuit Court of Appeals reversed the original conviction of Dr. Spock and Ferber on grounds of insufficient evidence, and the cases of Rev. Coffin and Goodman were remanded for retrial because of errors by the judge.

In April, Massachusetts federal district Judge Charles Wyzanski declared unconstitutional the 1967 draft law that limited conscientious objector status to those whose objections to war were religious. He found that it discriminated against atheists and agnostics and thus failed to meet the test of separation of church and state. The Justice Department appealed the decision to the Supreme Court.

A U. S. Court of Appeals ruled on June 6 that local draft boards had no right to reclassify registrants for antiwar or antidraft activities. The court severely criticized General Hershey's 1968 memo to local boards suggesting reclassification for protest activities without distinguishing between legal and illegal acts.

Prospects. It remains to be seen whether the struggle over the Selective Service is at an end and if the present level of reform will suppress dissent.

While some observers predict the lottery will split draft critics and war dissenters into those numbed by low numbers and those who forget about reform and dissent because of a high number, others doubted it would have any measurable effect. The lottery's major result was to reduce the visibility of the inequities and inadequacies of the Selective Service System, which remain unchanged.

The heart of any real reform would be a change in the basic structure of the system along the lines urged by the National Advisory Commission in 1967. Its recommendations included a change in status of the 4,000 plus local boards from decision-makers to boards of first appeal; the establishment of districts larger than local boards staffed by trained civil servants who would make uniform decisions based on national guidelines; establishment of a computerized national pool of eligible men; and the elimination of local board quotas.

It is in local boards and their quotas that the real inequities lie. As New York Congressman Otis Pike said of the Nixon draft reform proposal, "This bill deals with how people get pulled out of the hat for the draft. It doesn't deal in any manner with who gets put in the hat in the first place." Whether the lottery will pass for reform and undercut criticism and war dissent remains to be seen in the year ahead.

GARY L. WAMSLEY
Vanderbilt University

SENATE, U. S. See UNITED STATES.

SENEGAL

Senegal continued to experience economic difficulties in 1969. Despite the efforts of the ruling Senegal Progressive Union to prevent unrest, students and workers staged a series of strikes.

Economy. Peanuts are the country's only major export crop, and their world price has been constantly falling. Removal of the French subsidy caused a 25% drop in peanut farmers' incomes.

The cost of all products and services has been steadily rising. Senegal has a larger civil service than other African states, and over 50% of its budget is devoted to salaries. In the past five years the government's operating expenses have risen 26%, while the revenues of the state have increased only 3%. Despite increased taxes, President Leopold Senghor's government could not afford to raise salaries, and workers repeatedly went on strike.

Despite these problems, certain sectors of the economy improved in 1969. The third 4-year economic plan, adopted on July 1, stressed diversification of the agricultural sector, the improvement of fisheries, and support for tourism.

Student and Labor Strikes. Political unrest in Senegal throughout 1969 reflected the nation's economic difficulties. To promote a reconciliation between the government and dissident students and workers the National Council of the Senegal Progressive Union (UPS) in January established a series of action committees to increase party unity. A coordinating commission to work with the powerful National Union of Senegalese Workers (UNTS) was also created.

However, the creation of these new structures and the president's resolve to achieve national unity did not prevent a series of worker and student strikes from beginning in March. First, students in *lycées* in the vicinity of Dakar went on strike for educational reforms. They were joined by students from the University of Dakar. As late as September many students were still on strike.

In May and June petroleum, bank, and post and telegraph employees all struck for higher wages and better working conditions. In mid-June the UNTS called for a 48-hour general strike throughout the country. The government proclaimed a state of emergency, but the strike collapsed almost immediately. Some union leaders, publicly denouncing the political overtones of the strike, formed a rival union, the National Confederation of Senegalese Workers (CNTS).

The government survived the strike challenge because of the weakness of its opponents. However, the undercurrents of unrest caused the UPS leadership to announce that it intended to restructure the constitution of the state. Specifically, it proposed to reestablish the office of premier.

Foreign Affairs. President Senghor remained the main African advocate for a French-speaking commonwealth. Good relations with Mali were maintained after the overthrow of the Keita regime. Senghor's statements concerning smuggling from Gambia caused hostility in Gambia. However, normal relations were restored after a meeting of officials of the two countries at Bathurst in February.

HARRY A. GAILEY
San Jose State College

SHAHN, Ben. See biographical sketch under ART.

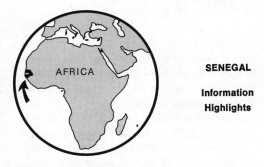

SENEGAL

Information Highlights

Area: 75,750 square miles (196,192 sq km).
Population: 3,685,000 (1968 est.).
Chief City (1963 est.): Dakar, the capital, 382,980.
Government: *President*—Leopold-Sedar Senghor (took office Dec. 1, 1963). *Parliament*—National Assembly, 80 members (party seating, 1969: all members of the Union Progressiste Sénégalaise).

Religious Faiths: Muslims, 90% of population.
Education: *Literacy rate* (1969), 10% of population. *Total school enrollment* (1965)—251,664 (primary, 218,795; secondary, 25,574; vocational and higher, 7,295).
Finance: *Budget* (1969 est.): $150,000,000; *monetary unit,* CFA franc (246.85 francs equal U. S.$1).
Gross National Product (1967 est.): $790,000,000.
Average Annual Income per Person (1967): $215.
Economic Indexes (1967): *Industrial production* (1968), 122 (1963=100); *cost of living,* 108 (1963=100).
Manufacturing, (metric tons, 1967): Cement, 172,000; gasoline, 99,000; wheat flour, 79,000; meat, 30,000; beer, 74,000 hectoliters; lumber, 14,000 cu. meters.
Crops (metric tons, 1967–68 crop year): Peanuts, 1,114,000; millet and sorghum, 616,000.
Minerals (metric tons, 1967): Calcium phosphate (1966), 990,000; salt, 71,000; zirconium concentrate (1964), 554.
Foreign Trade (1968): *Exports,* $151,000,000 (chief exports, 1967: peanut oil, $58,363,300; oil-seeds, nuts, and kernels, $31,958,600; peanuts, $31,484,700); *imports,* $180,-000,000 (chief imports, 1967: cereals, $30,277,400; rice, $22,329,300; textiles and fabrics, $20,980,300).
Transportation: *Roads* (1969), 9,107 miles (14,653 km); *motor vehicles* (1967), 51,600 (automobiles 32,000); *railways* (1969), 645 miles (1,032 km); *national airline,* Air Sénégal.
Communications: *Telephones* (1968), 25,700; *radios* (1967), 262,000; newspapers (1966), 1.

NORTHWEST PASSAGE

Triumphing over formidable ice, the U.S. tanker *Manhattan* in 1969 sailed from the eastern United States through the Northwest Passage to the new oil fields of the North Slope of Alaska and back again. *(Left)* The Canadian icebreaker *John A. MacDonald*, trailed by the U.S. Coast Guard icebreaker *Staten Island*, accompanied the *Manhattan*. *(Top)* A view of the *Manhattan's* special icebreaking prow. Map shows strategic location of the passage in relation to major world trade centers on three continents.

SHIPPING

The expansion in shipping services and the revolution in ship size and design, which have been going on for more than a decade, continued in 1969. In addition, there were two major shipping events: the passage of the U. S. tanker *Manhattan* through the Northwest Passage and the initial voyage of the first ship of the LASH (Lighter Aboard SHip) type.

Two basic types of transport are provided by ocean shipping: raw materials and processed goods. Each requires its own type of ship. The vessels carrying raw materials are divided into tankers, which are used for transporting liquids, and bulk carriers, which are used for carrying dry materials. Processed goods are carried by the conventional types or by the new container ships. Both types are called liners because they generally follow a definite route and schedule.

Petroleum products make up 50% of all overseas trade. Another 25% is made up of such commodities as iron ore, coal, and grain. Carried in lesser amounts are phosphates, bauxite, manganese ore, lumber, and sugar.

Expansion of Shipping. Since 1950, overseas transport has increased at an average annual rate of 7.5%, while that for petroleum has been 9.5%. These increases were brought about by the economic growth of western Europe and Japan; the changeover in these countries from coal to oil as a major energy source; the exploitation of Middle East petroleum; and the depletion of resources in the United States and discovery of new resources in Canada, South America, Africa, and Australia. Food shortages, especially in India and China, necessitated huge shipments of food from the food-producing areas of the United States, Canada, Australia, and Argentina. Coal for western Europe and Japan now comes largely from the United States.

Changes in Design. More spectacular than the increase in shipping has been the revolution in ship design. Tankers have increased in size from 20,000 tons (18,000 metric tons) in World War II, to 60,000 tons (54,000 metric tons) in 1961, and 300,000 tons (270,000 metric tons) in 1969. Ships transporting dry raw materials have also increased in size—from 9,000-ton (8,100-metric-ton) tramps to 100,000-ton (90,000-metric-ton) bulk carriers, many of which are equipped to handle their own cargo. The trend now is toward a combination type of ship that is able to carry liquid or dry cargo in the same hold, thus reducing unprofitable voyages in ballast.

The most radical changes have taken place in the liners, with ships now designed to carry stacked containers or to handle trucks that drive aboard and drive off. Both concepts are basically extensions of land transport methods to sea transport. Automation has been adopted within the ship, particularly in the bridge control of engines and cargo hatches. Such improvements have reduced the need for manpower, a situation that the maritime unions are loath to accept without compensatory shares in the profits.

Manhattan Voyage. The S. S. *Manhattan* project was a $40 million gamble by the Humble Oil (90% of the cost), Atlantic-Richfield, and British Petroleum companies to test the feasibility of bringing crude oil east by sea from the potentially rich oil fields near Prudhoe Bay in Alaska. A seven-month alteration job was necessary to prepare the 115,000-ton (103,500-metric-ton) ship, which was cut into four parts by the Sun Shipbuilding Company, the prime contractor. Bath Ironworks built a special icebreaking bow designed by Comdr. Roderick White of the U. S. Coast Guard. This bow first has an 18° slope to enter the ice and then the 30° slope of a conventional icebreaker, thus putting more of the ship's weight on the ice.

On Aug. 24, 1969, the S. S. *Manhattan* departed from Chester, Pa. During the voyage it reportedly attained a speed of 12 knots in ice 15 feet (4.5 meters) thick. Although the ship failed to negotiate the McClure Strait, it made the passage through the Prince of Wales Strait and arrived on Sept. 21, 1969, at Point Barrow in Alaska. The ship returned to New York City on Nov. 12, 1969, with a hole ripped by ice in its non-reenforced section. Months of studying the accumulated data will be necessary to determine if the route taken by the *Manhattan* is actually practicable. If so, oil can be brought out at about 90 cents per barrel, compared with $1.45 by pipeline.

The voyage of the *Manhattan* raised questions in Canada about that nation's rights and duties in the Northwest Passage, especially in the matter of pollution. Canada has asserted rights over the islands, but has not taken a position on the surrounding waters, which the United States views as international. The success of the *Manhattan's* voyage was partly due to Canadian help, especially Canadian studies of northern geology, topography, and ice. The Canadian icebreaker *John A. MacDonald* accompanied the *Manhattan,* and retired Capt. Thomas C. Pullen, Canada's foremost ice navigator, was aboard the tanker.

LASH. LASH, a much publicized U. S. shipbuilding concept, became a reality in October 1969 with the construction of the *Acadia Forest,* a trim, 860-foot (260-meter), 43,000-ton (38,700-metric-ton) ocean-going barge carrier. The ship was built in Japan and flies Norway's flag. The first U. S. ship of this type will not be ready for another year.

The *Acadia Forest* is designed to pick up, carry, and lower loaded barges, thus eliminating the time the ship would have to spend loading and discharging cargo. Seventy-three barges, each with a capacity of almost 400 tons (360 metric tons), are lifted over the stern and stacked in five holds by a 510-ton (460-metric-ton) crane. A barge can be loaded aboard every 15 minutes. Chartered to a U. S. company, the *Acadia Forest* departed from New Orleans for Europe on Nov. 14, 1969, after having been delayed for two weeks by labor difficulties. It was loaded with paper products.

JOHN D. HAYES
Rear Admiral, U. S. Navy, Retired

MERCHANT FLEETS OF THE WORLD
(1,000 gross tons and over)

	Jan. 1, 1969		Jan. 1, 1968	
	Ships	Gross tons	Ships	Gross tons
World total	19,361	184,242,000	18,800	171,522,000
United States	2,071	18,675,000	2,162	19,179,000
Privately owned	967	10,649,000	974	10,480,000
Government-owned	1,104	8,026,000	1,188	8,699,000
Liberia	1,613	26,984,000	1,496	23,881,000
United Kingdom	1,840	20,845,000	1,903	20,005,000
Norway	1,308	19,231,000	1,368	18,666,000
Japan	1,766	18,797,000	1,582	16,101,000
USSR*	1,634	9,457,000	1,449	8,562,000
Greece	1,006	7,890,000	975	7,275,000
West Germany	909	6,399,000	886	5,870,000
Italy	620	6,266,000	613	5,943,000
France	485	5,414,000	532	5,284,000
Other countries	6,109	44,284,000	5,834	40,756,000

* Source material limited. Source: Maritime Administration, U.S. Department of Commerce.

SIERRA LEONE

The government of Prime Minister Siaka Stevens, restored to power by a counter-coup in April 1968, consolidated its support in by-elections and moved toward constitutional reforms in 1969.

Draft Constitution. On January 6, Prime Minister Stevens, leader of the ruling All People's Congress (APC), promised a republican constitution for Sierra Leone by the end of 1969. The document is to be based on the draft produced by the government of former Prime Minister Albert Margai. Included in the document will be amendments curbing the president's power so that he can act only on the advice of the prime minister or parliament. A 28-member Committee on the Republican Constitution then began work on the proposed draft.

Political Affairs. The nationwide state of emergency, imposed on Nov. 20, 1968, when eight by-elections were postponed because of unrest, was suspended in February. Elections were held in April 1969 in the Bo and Kanema districts, previously strongholds of the opposition Sierra Leone People's party (SLPP). The results consolidated the power of the APC, which was left firmly in control of the House of Representatives and the government. The APC now holds 48 seats in the 78-seat legislature, with 12 seats held by the SLPP, 6 by independents, and 12 by paramount chiefs backing the government.

A sweeping cabinet shuffle resulted in the withdrawal of the minister of education, the last SLPP member in the cabinet. On June 10 the SLPP announced that it was withdrawing from the government to form an opposition under the leadership of Salia Jusu-Sheriff, who was released from detention on February 26.

Foreign Affairs. The expulsion of 104 Ghanaian fishermen in December 1968 had raised the question of the revision of entry permit requirements for Commonwealth citizens. The Sierra Leone government was concerned with the large numbers of Ghanaians resident in Sierra Leone and with the recent tightening of immigration laws in Ghana.

In May, Prime Minister Stevens traveled around the world on a good-will tour, visiting the president of the World Bank, the head of the U. S. Peace Corps, and students from Sierra Leone in the United States.

Economy. The outlook for the economy was viewed as heartening in 1969. Foreign exchange reserves were at a record 29 million leones (0.8333 leone equals U. S. $1), twice the 1967 level, and total revenue during the first six months of 1969 rose to 25.62 million leones, compared with 19.27 million leones for early 1968. On March 28 the International Monetary Fund presented Sierra Leone with $2.5 million in a 12-month "stand-by credit" to help consolidate recent economic gains.

A 13-man committee was formed on July 19 to advise on the Africanization of trade and industry. On August 1 a bill was passed restricting foreigners from engaging in certain branches of retail trade.

C. DIANE CHRISTENSEN
Columbia University

SIERRA LEONE

Information

Highlights

SILK. See TEXTILE INDUSTRY.
SILVER. See MINING.

SINGAPORE

In 1969, Singapore marked the 150th anniversary of its founding by Sir Stamford Raffles. Special observances on National Day, August 9, included an official visit by Princess Alexandra of Britain and a performance by Moscow's Bolshoi Ballet.

Major attention during the celebration was focused on an impressive public display of the city-state's new military equipment. These included some of the 50 second-hand French AMX tanks recently purchased from Israel, armored personnel carriers with 122-mm mortars, and recoilless antitank weapons in jeeps. It was announced that key personnel for the new armored battalion would be trained in Israel, which has provided a special advisory team on defense matters since 1967.

Defense. The government sought to strengthen the country's defenses before the scheduled British withdrawal in 1971. Sixty surface-to-air missiles and a number of Hawker Hunter fighter planes will be acquired from Britain as the basis of an interceptor system. The 5-power Canberra Conference held in June with Australia, New Zealand, Britain, and Malaysia failed to produce a firm commitment from Australia and New Zealand for Singapore-Malaysian defense after 1971, and the command structure for a joint air defense system with Malaysia remained unsettled. Reflecting a pessimistic attitude toward lagging regional defense arrangements, Foreign Minister S. Rajaratnam, in October, invited the major powers to take a "vested interest" in Singapore's stability and "use its facilities."

Area: 27,699 square miles (71,740 sq km).
Population: 2,475,000 (1968 est.).
Chief City (1966 census): Freetown, the capital, 148,000.
Government: *Prime Minister*—Siaka P. Stevens (took office April 26, 1968). *Legislature*—House of Representatives, 78 members, 12 paramount chiefs, 66 elected (party seating, 1969: All People's Congress, 48; Sierra Leone People's party, 12; independents, 6).
Education: *Literacy rate* (1969), 10% of population; *Total school enrollment* (1965)—145,017 (primary, 125,943; secondary, 15,972; teacher training, 948; technical/vocational, 1,435; university/higher, 719).
Finance (1969 budget est.): $46,100,000; *monetary unit,* leone (0.8333 leone equals U. S.$1).
Gross National Product (1967): $380,000,000.
National Income (1965): $299,600,000; *average annual income per person* (1967), $156.
Cost of Living Index (1967): 128 (1963=100).
Crops (metric tons, 1967–68 crop year): Rice, 400,000; sweet potatoes and yams, 9,000.
Minerals (metric tons, 1967): Diamonds, 1,400,000 carats; iron ore, 1,259,000.
Foreign Trade (1968): *Exports,* $96,000,000 (chief exports, 1967: diamonds, $35,690,000; iron ore, $10,830,000; cacao beans, $1,740,000; palm kernels, $1,310,000); *imports,* $91,000,000 (chief imports, 1967: textile yarn and fibers, $9,140,000; cereals and preparations, $6,270,000; petroleum products, $5,620,000). *Chief trading partners* (1967): Britain (took 71% of exports, supplied 28% of imports); Netherlands (took 12% of exports, supplied 5% of imports); United States (took 2% of exports, supplied 10% of imports).
Transportation: *Roads* (1969), 4,950 miles (7,965 km); *motor vehicles* (1967), 21,000 (automobiles 15,000); *railways* (1969), 371 miles (597 km); *national airline,* Sierra Leone Airways; *principal airport,* Lungi.
Communications: *Telephones* (1968): 6,500; *television stations* (1966), 1; *television sets* (1967), 2,500; *radios* (1965), 105,000; *newspapers* (1966), 2 (daily circulation, 25,000).

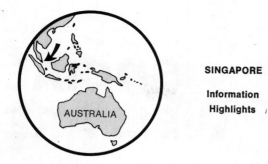

SINGAPORE

Information Highlights /

Area: 224 square miles (581 sq km).
Population: 1,988,000 (1968 est.).
Chief City (1967 census): Singapore, the capital, 1,955,600.
Government: *President*—Inche Yusaf bin Ishak (took office Dec. 3, 1959); *Prime Minister*—Lee Kuan Yew (took office May 1959); *Parliament*—Legislative Assembly, 58 members (all members of the People's Action party).
Education: *Literacy rate* (1967), 60% of population aged 15 and over. *Total school enrollment* (1966)—528,068 (primary, 364,846; secondary, 133,497; technical/vocational, 16,541; university/higher, 13,184).
Finance (1969/70 est.): *Revenues,* $331,000,000; *expenditures,* $335,000,000; *monetary unit,* Singapore dollar (3.08 dollars equal U. S. $1).
Gross National Product (1968): $1,334,000,000.
Average Annual Income per Person (1968): $667.
Cost of Living Index (1967): 107 (1963 = 100).
Major Crop (metric tons, 1967–68 crop year): Natural rubber, 1,500.
Foreign Trade (1968): *Exports,* $1,271,000,000 (chief exports, 1967: crude rubber, $248,379,800; petroleum products, $219,308,400; textile yarn and fabrics, $40,292,200; transport equipment, $32,662,300); *imports,* $1,661,000,000 (chief imports, 1967: crude rubber, $148,522,700; petroleum products, $73,564,900; electrical machinery, $54,500,000). *Chief trading partners* (1967): West Malaysia (took 24% of exports, supplied 19% of imports); Japan (took 4% of exports, supplied 12% of imports); Britain (took 6% of exports, supplied 8% of imports).
Transportation: *Roads* (1964), 520 miles (837 km); *motor vehicles* (1967), 148,300 (automobiles 121,500); *merchant vessels* (1967), 13 (55,000 gross registered tons).
Communications: *Telephones* (1968): 106,124; *television stations* (1967), 2; *television sets* (1967), 94,000; *radios* (1964), 389,000; *newspapers* (1967), 13 (daily circulation, 635,000).

Relations with Malaysia. Political relations with Malaysia remained troubled. In May, Malaysia's Alliance party leaders charged that Singapore's governing People's Action party was interfering in the West Malaysian election campaign. In an official note the Singapore government sternly rejected the accusation. At the end of May, several weeks after the severe racial riots in Kuala Lumpur, racial disturbances of a lesser degree broke out in Singapore. Some observers reported that members of Chinese secret societies had come from Malaysia to avenge themselves against the Malay minority in Singapore. Because of the prompt action taken by the multiracial security forces, there were only four fatalities during a tense week. The government claimed that "outsiders" were responsible for the disturbances, a contention that was not well received in Malaysia.

Economy. The economy remained buoyant. Total foreign trade increased by 13.6% in 1968 and the important entrepôt trade by 20.3%. In May, Singapore was chosen as headquarters of the new Asia dollar project, initiated by the Bank of America. The purpose of the project is to attract United States and European investment in Asian economic development.

C. PAUL BRADLEY
Flint College, University of Michigan

SKATING. See SPORTS.
SKIING. See SPORTS.
SOCCER. See SPORTS.

SOCIAL SECURITY

On Dec. 30, 1969, President Nixon signed the Tax Reform Act of 1969, which included amendments to the Social Security Act that raised benefits 15%, beginning with payments for January 1970. The increase was actually first included in the March payment (mailed in April), and a separate retroactive payment covered the January and February raises. (Bills to amend other Social Security Act provisions were being considered by Congress early in 1970.)

Also on Dec. 30, 1969, President Nixon signed the Federal Coal Mine Health and Safety Act, which sets up certain standards for the coal-mining industry and provides for monthly cash benefits for coal miners suffering from black-lung disease. For claims filed by Dec. 31, 1972, for these benefits, payment will be handled by the Social Security Administration; for claims filed after that date, the Department of Labor will be responsible.

Operations and Financing. During 1969 employers and employees paid contributions of 4.8% on their earnings up to $7,800, including 0.6% for hospital insurance. The self-employed also paid 0.6% for hospital insurance, and their contributions for old-age, survivors, and disability insurance were 6.3% of their earnings.

Monthly cash benefits and lump-sum payments totaled $26,176,000,000 in the fiscal year ending June 30, 1969. In September 1969 monthly benefits were being paid to 25,187,000 persons at a rate of $2,141,533,000 a month. For a retired worker, the average check was $100 a month. Disabled workers averaged $112.50. The average payment for retired workers just coming on the rolls was about $106.

Medicare. At the beginning of Medicare's third year 19.8 million individuals aged 65 and over were eligible for hospital benefits and 18.8 million had enrolled for medical benefits. From July 1968 through June 1969 about 5.8 million hospital claims were approved.

The average hospital stay per claim was 13.4 days, and the average amount reimbursed to the individual was $638. Bills recorded under medical insurance numbered 36 million, and the average charge per bill was $62 for all services. The total amount paid for both types of Medicare benefits from July 1968 through June 1969 was $6.3 billion.

As a result of the annual review of hospital costs under Medicare required by law, the deductible amount—the amount to be paid by the patient before reimbursement—was raised with respect to hospital benefits from $44 to $52, beginning Jan. 1, 1970. Also starting on that date, the Medicare beneficiary pays $13 instead of $11 for the 61st through the 90th days of a hospital stay; $6.50 instead of $5.50 for days over 20 in an extended-care facility; and if after 90 days of care, he must draw on his "lifetime reserve," he pays $26 instead of $22 for each additional day. Those hospitalized before 1970 were to pay toward the costs at the previous rates.

The monthly premium paid for medical insurance by those persons enrolled for medical benefits under Medicare (and matched by the federal government) was $4 during 1969 and the first 6 months of 1970. On Dec. 28, 1969, the secretary of Health, Education, and Welfare announced that the rate for the 12 months beginning July 1, 1970, would be $5.30 a month.

ROBERT M. BALL
Commissioner of Social Security

SOCIAL WELFARE

THE NEW YORK TIMES

WELFARE CUTBACKS in New York City cost one man (*left*), blind at 72, his 24-cents-a-day allowance for dog food. Another (*right*), ill and trying to raise a large family, had monthly payments cut by $127.

Important modifications of the income maintenance programs in the United States occurred or were proposed during 1969. A Supreme Court decision added to the already great pressures for revision of the federal-state system of public assistance by ruling out residency requirements for eligibility, thus making it easier for persons to move to states with higher assistance grants. (See SUPREME COURT.)

Family Assistance Plan. A welter of proposals have been put forward, including child allowances, a reverse income tax, a guaranteed minimum income, and a completely federalized public assistance system. Attention was centered on an administration proposal, announced by President Nixon on August 8, for a federally financed and administered "Family Assistance Plan." Under this plan any family with dependent children but without income would receive payments of $500 each annually for the first two family members and $300 for each additional member ($1,600 for a family of four). Such families would receive state supplements in varying amounts so that they would receive no less, and in most cases more, than under Aid to Families with Dependent Children (AFDC). For other families most income (after the first $720) would result in reductions of one dollar of benefits for each two dollars earned. A family of four might earn at least $3,920 before family assistance payments would be terminated. Competing proposals would provide benefits higher than those proposed under the administration plan.

The family assistance proposal requires work or work training on the part of those capable of such activities and hence calls for effective training and placement services. Proliferation of manpower training programs under various auspices in recent years has resulted at times in confusion and friction. The administration has moved to consolidate programs and center authority in the states. However, three decades of experience with state administration of public assistance and unemployment insurance leads some people to doubt the states' ability to achieve reasonable uniformity and quality of program across the country. At the same time, city officials

and others who have been associated with local employment and training programs under the Office of Economic Opportunity (OEO) fear that the values of local and participant concern and initiative will be lost when a statewide bureaucracy takes over control.

In June 1969, over 1.6 million families, including 6.5 million persons, received AFDC benefits. The administration estimates that under its proposal an additional 2 million families would be eligible for family assistance at an increased cost to the federal government of $2.5 billion annually.

In spite of the traditional authority of the states with respect to public welfare, the Nixon proposal would transfer the largest public assistance program (which increased 20% from 1968 to 1969) to federal administration; it would set a national minimum level of family income; it would abolish the widely observed practice of refusing help to families in which the father is present, and the traditional rigid division between self-support and dependency; and it would establish a formula to encourage marginal workers to participate as far as possible in the economy.

Resistance to this and to related proposals may be expected, due on the one hand to the relatively low level of benefits proposed, and on the other to ingrained political and social values. However, a number of factors support the changes. Heavy financial burdens make governors and state legislators receptive to the transfer of part of the load to the federal government. Since inadequate state assistance grants are thought to have contributed to social unrest, improved levels of assistance might help ease the national crisis. More or less similar measures have been advocated by people as diverse as business executives and conservative, as well as radical economists. And a commission appointed by President Johnson has come out strongly in favor of the idea.

Less controversial is a proposal to require consolidation of Old Age Assistance, Aid to the Blind, and Aid to the Disabled. States have been permitted to consolidate these programs since 1962.

Social Security and Health Care. On December 19, Congress passed, and the President subsequently signed, a tax reform bill that also contained a Social Security payment rise of 15 percent for all recipients, effective Jan. 1, 1970. Action on financing this increase was postponed until the 1970 session of Congress.

Widespread concern over unexpectedly high costs of Medicare and Medicaid led the administration to introduce legislation to establish tighter fiscal controls. These programs were added to the Social Security Act in 1965. Political pressure for health care legislation had been building for three decades before Congress acted. Title XVIII established health insurance (Medicare) for persons over 65 covered by social security. Title XIX established a program of payment for medical care (Medicaid) for aged, blind, or disabled persons and for families with dependent children where income was not sufficient to provide adequate medical care. Medicare is federally administered by the Social Security Administration. Medicaid is administered by the states with federal grants-in-aid.

These two programs accounted for three fourths of a 28% increase in national expenditures for personal health care between 1966 and 1968. Total expenditures under public programs nearly doubled from $7.9 billion to $15.7 billion. Of this increase, two thirds ($5.1 billion) was in Medicare while another one fourth ($1.8 billion) was in Medicaid, mostly for persons under 65.

Many reasons have been advanced for the large increase in health care spending: the availability of paid care to millions of persons who previously could not secure anything but gratuitous service from physicians and hospitals; increases in hospital charges to meet rising costs, especially wages of hospital personnel (many of whom had been at the lowest rung of the economic ladder); and allegations of overcharging and irregular practices on the part of some physicians and other suppliers of goods and services.

Many persons have thought of Medicare and Medicaid as steps toward a universal health care program. The proposed nomination of Dr. John Knowles as assistant secretary of Health, Education, and Welfare was blocked in 1969 by the American Medical Association on the ground that he was an advocate of expanded health care programs. This episode has not quieted the controversy, and many groups, including prestigious physicians and vocal medical students, are pushing for the extension of health care programs.

Administrative Changes. Considerable restructuring of federal administration relating to social welfare has occurred. Some programs of the Office of Economic Opportunity (OEO), such as manpower training and the educational program Head Start, have been transferred to "old line" agencies with resultant readjustment and reorganization.

Within HEW rearrangements of function are being worked out to separate the administration of financial payments from the host of other programs and services for which the department is responsible. An example of particular interest is the virtual elimination of the U. S. Children's Bureau. The creation of the bureau in 1912 has been widely regarded as a landmark in federal social welfare activities. Under the leadership of such chiefs as Julia Lathrop, Edith Abbot, Katherine Lenroot, and Dr. Martha Eliot, it gained responsibility for most federal child and maternal health and welfare programs, including research, training, and grants-in-aid to the states. Now assigned as part of the newly created Child Development Administration, the Children's Bureau is stripped of all except its original responsibilities for research and reporting. To some, continuation of its unifying force in social administration is not readily identifiable, and for these persons this transformation symbolizes the end of an era.

Congress repealed the "freeze" on Aid to Families with Dependent Children (AFDC), which was enacted in 1967 in an effort to put a limit to this burgeoning assistance program. The freeze had never been put into effect due to the protests of the states over the financial burden on them that would result.

Reassessment in Britain. Among the economic-ally developed nations, particularly significant re-evaluation of welfare programs is taking place in Britain. There, National Insurance benefits for all retired persons have been identical ("the dole") and have frequently required supplementation from the National Assistance funds. It is now proposed to change to a sliding scale of benefits related to the individuals' earning records.

UN Conference. An international Conference of Ministers Responsible for Social Welfare was held at the United Nations in September 1968. Eighty-nine countries were represented by official delegations. Wide differences in social and eco-nomic conditions, aspirations, and programs pre-cluded agreement on many details, but a series of 29 recommendations was adopted.

Many countries represented at the conference had not previously affirmed governmental responsi-bility for social welfare or for the well-being of all people within their jurisdictions. Adoption of reso-

REV. JAMES GROPPI quiets demonstrating welfare mothers facing National Guardsmen in Madison, Wis.

lutions asserting and supporting that policy, there-fore, may be expected to lend importance and recognition to social welfare in the development plans of the various nations involved. An inte-grated view of national activities was emphasized, with social welfare as part of a team working for total development. The leadership role of govern-ment as well as the crucial part to be played by qualified social welfare personnel were also empha-sized.

The importance assigned to social welfare man-power needs led to agreement on a regional ap-proach on the part of developing countries. During 1969 plans were being developed for regional meet-ings in the Far East, the Middle East, Africa, and Latin America, where further steps toward estab-lishment of regional training centers could be taken.

(See also POVERTY; SOCIAL SECURITY.)

RALPH E. PUMPHREY
Washington University, St. Louis

SOCIALISM

The Socialist International, at its 11th confer-ence at Eastbourne, England, in June 1969, favored Britain's entrance into the European Common Mar-ket, denounced the military regime in Greece, and advocated greater economic and cultural cooperation with the Communists of central and eastern Europe.

The British Labour party remained in power with Harold Wilson as prime minister and with a ma-jority of 66 in Parliament.

In West Germany, Gustav Heinemann, Social Democrat, was elected president of the federal re-public on March 5. Following the October 21 na-tional election, Willy Brandt, former foreign min-ister and head of the Socialist Democratic party, was elected chancellor by a vote of 251 to 235. The Social Democrats united with the Free Demo-crats to form the government.

In France a new Socialist party was formed con-sisting of the French Socialist party, a number of Socialist clubs, and the Convention of Socialist In-stitutions. The party continued as an opposition party to President Georges Pompidou, successor to Charles de Gaulle.

In Italy, Mariano Rumor's coalition government dissolved after the resignation on July 4 of Socialist members who had split with the Socialist party over the majority's decision to cooperate more closely with the Communists and to organize a moderate Unitary Socialist party. Socialists later renewed ef-forts to form a coalition government under Rumor after he promised to clear up a backlog of legisla-tion dealing with students and workers.

The Swedish Social Democrats continued in con-trol of the government and as a majority party in the Parliament. Social Democratic Premier Tage Erlander resigned on September 28 and was suc-ceeded by Education Minister Olof Palme. In 1969, Sweden recognized the North Vietnamese govern-ment. The Norwegian Labor party was closely de-feated in September by coalition government forces.

The Social Democrats of Austria won 63 out of 100 seats in the Vienna city council, a gain of 3. They achieved passage, by a large margin, of their referendum favoring the 40-hour week.

Israeli Socialists lost by death (February 26) Premier Levi Eshkol, who was succeeded on March 6 by Mrs. Golda Meir, a former Milwaukee, Wis., school teacher. Three Israeli labor parties united in 1969 to form the United Labor party.

The Japanese Socialists, the government's chief opposition party, agitated during the year for the end of the U. S.-Japanese Security Treaty and for the Parliament. Social Democratic Premier Tage

The Australian Labour party was defeated on October 25 in a close election (61 to 58 seats) by Prime Minister John Gorton's conservative coalition. In New Zealand the Labour party ran a close second to the National party in the November 29 elections.

The Kenya Socialist movement suffered a serious loss in the assassination on July 5 of Tom Mboya, former minister of economic affairs.

The labor-socialist New Democratic party of Canada elected 28 out of 57 members of the Mani-toba legislature—an increase of 16 seats. Thomas Douglas, the party leader, was returned to Parlia-ment in a by-election. In the United States, the Socialist party advocated ending the Vietnam War.

HARRY W. LAIDLER
Author of "History of Socialism"

SOCIETIES AND ORGANIZATIONS

This article lists a selection of some of the most noteworthy associations, societies, foundations, and trusts of the United States and Canada. The information for each listing has been furnished by the organization concerned, and includes membership figures, dates of annual meetings, officers, and headquarters location or address.

Alcoholics Anonymous (The General Service Board of A. A., Inc.). Membership: approximately 425,000 in more than 15,000 affiliated groups. Annual conference: New York, N. Y., April 20–25, 1970. 35th Anniversary International Convention, Miami Beach, Fla., July 3–5, 1970. Chairman John L. Norris, M. D. Headquarters: 305 East 45th St., New York, N. Y. 10017.

American Academy of Arts and Letters. Membership: 50. Annual meeting: New York, N. Y., December 1969. President, George F. Kennan; secretary, John Hersey. Headquarters: 633 West 155th St., New York, N. Y. 10032.

American Academy of Arts and Sciences. Membership: approx. 2,300. Annual meeting: Boston, Mass., May 14, 1969. President, Talcott Parsons; secretary, Raymond A. Bauer. Headquarters: 280 Newton St., Brookline Station, Boston, Mass. 02146.

American Academy of Political and Social Science. Membership: 24,787, including 6,452 libraries. Annual meeting: Philadelphia, Pa., April 10–11, 1970. President, James C. Charlesworth; business mgr., Ingeborg Hessler. Headquarters: 3937 Chestnut St., Philadelphia, Pa. 19104.

American Anthropological Association. Membership: 6,100. Annual meeting: San Diego, Calif., Nov. 19–22, 1970. President: George Foster; secretary, Conrad C. Reining; executive director: Edward J. Lehman. Headquarters: 1703 New Hampshire Ave. NW, Washington, D. C. 20009.

American Association for the Advancement of Science. Membership: 125,000 and 293 affiliated groups. Annual meeting: Chicago, Ill., Dec. 26–31, 1970. President, Athelstan Spilhaus; secretary, Dael Wolfle. Headquarters: 1515 Massachusetts Ave. NW, Washington, D. C. 20005.

American Association of University Professors. Membership: 95,000. Annual meeting: Los Angeles, Calif., April 24–25, 1970. President, Ralph S. Brown, Jr.; general secretary, Bertram H. Davis. Headquarters: One Dupont Circle, NW, Washington, D. C. 20036.

American Association of University Women. Membership: 174,000. President, Anne Gary Pannell; general director, Alice L. Beeman. Headquarters: 2401 Virginia Ave. NW, Washington, D. C. 20037.

American Astronomical Society. Membership: 2,500. Meeting: University of Colorado, Boulder, Colo., June 9–12, 1970. President, A. E. Whitford; acting secretary, L. W. Fredrick; exec. officer, H. M. Gurin. Address: 211 Fitz-Randolph Rd., Princeton, N. J. 08540.

American Automobile Association. Membership: 12 million in 846 affiliated groups. Annual meeting: Los Angeles, Calif., Oct. 12–14, 1970. President, Harry D. Holt; secretary, William B. Spencer. Headquarters: 1712 G St. NW, Washington, D. C. 20006.

American Bankers Association. Membership: 18,503 banks and branches. Annual meeting: Miami Beach, Fla., Oct. 10–14, 1970. President, Nat S. Rogers; secretary, George H. Gustafson. Headquarters: 90 Park Ave., New York, N. Y., 10016.

American Bar Association. Membership: 143,000. Annual meeting: St. Louis, Mo., Aug. 10–14, 1970. President, Bernard G. Segal; secretary, Wm. Reece Smith, Jr., Headquarters: 1155 East 60th St., Chicago, Ill. 60637.

American Bible Society. 1968 Scripture distribution: 77,950,979 copies. Annual meeting: New York, N. Y., May 14, 1970. President, Edmund F. Wagner; general secretary, Laton E. Holmgren; treas., Charles W. Baas. Headquarters: 1865 Broadway, New York, N. Y. 10023.

American Book Publishers Council. Membership: approx. 187. Annual meeting: Pocono Manor, Pa., May 11–13, 1970. President, Edward E. Booher; managing director, Richard H. Sullivan; senior assoc. manag. dir. and economist, Robert W. Frase; assoc. manag. dir., Kyrill Schabert, Headquarters: One Park Ave., New York, N. Y. 10016.

American Booksellers Association, Inc. Membership: 3,000. National convention: Washington, D. C., June 7–10, 1970. President, Arnold H. Swenson; exec. dir., Joseph A. Duffy. Headquarters: 175 Fifth Ave., New York, N. Y. 10010.

American Cancer Society, Inc. Membership: 182 voting members; 58 chartered divisions. Annual meeting: New York, N. Y., Nov. 4–6, 1970. President, Jonathan E. Rhoads, M. D.; secretary, Joseph S. Silber. Headquarters: 219 East 42nd St., New York, N. Y. 10017.

American Chemical Society. Membership: 115,000. National meetings, 1970: Houston, Texas, Feb. 22–27; Toronto, Ont., May 24–29 (with Chemical Institute of Canada); Chicago, Ill., Sept. 13–18. President, Byron Riegel; exec. director, F. T. Wall. Headquarters: 1155 16th St. NW, Washington, D. C. 20036.

American Civil Liberties Union. Membership: 130,000. Exec. dir., John de J. Pemberton, Jr.; board chairman, Edward Ennis. Headquarters: 156 Fifth Ave., New York, N. Y. 10010.

American College of Physicians. Membership: 15,600. Annual meeting: Philadelphia, Pa., April 12–17, 1970. President, Samuel P. Asper, M. D.; exec. director, Edward C. Rosenow, Jr., M. D. Headquarters: 4200 Pine St., Philadelphia, Pa. 19104.

American College of Surgeons. Membership: 31,000. Annual meeting: Chicago, Ill., Oct. 12–16, 1970. President, Joel W. Baker, M. D.; director, C. Rollins Hanlon, M. D. Headquarters: 55 E. Erie St., Chicago, Ill. 60611.

American Council of Learned Societies. Membership: 33 professional societies concerned with the humanities and the humanistic aspects of the social sciences. Annual meeting: Washington, D. C., Jan. 22–24, 1970. President, Frederick Burkhardt; admin. secy., Charlotte Bowman. Headquarters: 345 East 46th St., New York, N. Y. 10017.

American Council on Education. Membership: 1,345 colleges and universities, and 212 educational organizations plus 80 affiliate organizations. Annual meeting: St. Louis, Mo., Oct. 7–9, 1970. President, Logan Wilson; exec. secretary, Charles G. Dobbins. Headquarters: One Dupont Circle, NW, Washington, D. C. 20036.

American Dental Association. Membership: 112,078. Annual session: Las Vegas, Nev., Nov. 8–12, 1970. President, Harry M. Klenda, D. D. S.; exec. director, C. Gordon Watson, D. D. S. Headquarters: 211 E. Chicago Ave., Chicago, Ill. 60611.

American Economic Association. Membership: 18,026 and 6,745 subscribers. Annual meeting: New York, N. Y., Dec. 28–30, 1969. President, William J. Fellner; secretary, Harold F. Williamson. Headquarters: 629 Noyes St., Evanston, Ill. 60201.

American Farm Bureau Federation. Membership: 1,865,854 families. Annual meeting: December of each year. President, Charles B. Shuman; secretary-treasurer, Roger Fleming. Headquarters: Merchandise Mart, Chicago, Ill. 60654.

American Geographical Society. Membership: 5,000. Annual dinner: New York, N. Y., Nov. 21, 1969. President, Serge A. Korff; acting director, Mrs. Wilma B. Fairchild. Headquarters: Broadway at 156th St., New York, N. Y. 10032.

American Geophysical Union. Membership: 9,700 and 63 organizations. National Fall Meeting: San Francisco, Calif., Dec. 15–18, 1969 (Golden Anniversary). Annual Meeting: Washington, D. C., April 20–24, 1970. President, Helmut E. Landsberg; gen. secy., Charles A. Whitten; exec. director, Waldo E. Smith. Headquarters: 2100 Pennsylvania Ave. NW, Washington, D. C. 20037.

American Heart Association. Membership: 72,000 in 55 affiliates, 139 chapters, and 1,000 local subdivisions. Annual meeting: Atlantic City, N. J., Nov. 12–17, 1970. President, W. Proctor Harvey, M. D.; secretary, Elwood Ennis. Headquarters: 44 East 23rd St., New York, N. Y., 10010.

American Historical Association. Membership: 16,000. Annual meeting: Washington, D. C., Dec. 28–30, 1969. President, C. Vann Woodward; exec. secretary, Paul L. Ward. Headquarters: 400 A St. SE, Washington, D. C. 20003.

American Home Economics Association. Membership: 35,000 professionals, 15,000 students in 52 affiliated state organizations. Annual meeting: Cleveland, Ohio, June 22–26, 1970. President, Dr. Lela O'Toole; secretary, Dr. Marjorie East. Headquarters: 1600 20th St. N. W., Washington, D. C. 20009.

American Horticultural Society, Inc. Membership: 4,250 individual; 250 organizational, institutional, and commercial. National congress: Miami Beach, Fla., Nov. 1–4, 1970.

American Hospital Association. Membership: 14,475 personal; 9,525 institutional. Annual meeting: Washington, D. C., Feb. 16–19, 1970; Annual convention: Houston, Texas, Sept. 14–17, 1970. President, Mark Berke, exec. vice pres. Edwin L. Crosby, M. D.; secretary, James E. Hague. Headquarters: 840 N. Lake Shore Dr., Chicago, Ill. 60611.

American Institute of Aeronautics and Astronautics. Membership: 33,000. Annual meeting: Houston, Texas, Oct. 19–22, 1970. Exec. secretary, James J. Hartford. Headquarters: 1290 Avenue of the Americas, New York, N. Y. 10019.

American Institute of Architects. Membership: 23,300. National convention: Boston, Mass., June 21–25, 1970. President, Rex W. Allen; first vice president, Robert F. Hastings; secretary, Preston M. Bolton. Headquarters: 1735 New York Ave. NW, Washington, D. C. 20006.

American Institute of Biological Sciences. Membership: 14,500, with 46 adherent societies and 18 industrial member groups. Annual meeting: Indiana University, Bloomington, Ind., Aug. 23–29, 1970; first national biological congress, Detroit, Mich., Nov. 6–10, 1970. President; Dr. George L. McNew; vice president, Dr. David E. Davis; secretary-treas. Dr. Richard S. Cowan; director, Dr. John R. Olive. Headquarters: 3900 Wisconsin Ave. NW, Washington, D. C. 20016.

American Institute of Certified Public Accountants. Membership: 71,000. Annual meeting: New York, N. Y., Sept. 20–23, 1970. President, Louis M. Kessler; exec. vice pres., Leonard M. Savoie; admin. vice pres. and secretary, John Lawler. Headquarters: 666 Fifth Ave., New York, N. Y. 10019.

American Institute of Chemical Engineers. Membership: 36,511. Annual meetings: Chicago Ill., Nov. 29–Dec. 3, 1969; San Francisco, Calif., Nov. 28–Dec. 2, 1970. President, A. L. Conn; secretary, F. J. Van Antwerpen. Headquarters: 345 East 47th St., New York, N. Y. 10017.

American Institute of Graphic Arts. Membership: 1,900. President, Allen F. Hurlburt; executive director, Edward Gottschall. Headquarters: 1059 Third Ave., New York, N. Y. 10021.

American Institute of Mining, Metallurgical, and Petroleum Engineers, Inc. Membership: 47,332. Annual meeting: Denver, Colo., Feb. 15–19, 1970. President, John C. Kinnear, Jr., exec. director, Joe B. Alford. Headquarters: 345 East 47th St., New York, N. Y. 10017.

American Legion, The. Membership: 2,664,388. National convention: Atlanta, Ga., Aug. 22–28, 1969. National Commander, J. Milton Patrick; national adjutant, William F. Hauck. Headquarters: 700 N. Pennsylvania St., Indianapolis, Ind. 46206.

American Management Association. Membership: 61,000. Annual meeting: New York City, Sept. 24, 1969. Chairman of the Board, Lawrence A. Appley; President, A. B. Trowbridge; secretary, Fred E. Lee. Headquarters: 135 West 50th St., New York, N. Y., 10020.

American Mathematical Society. Membership: 13,300. Annual meeting: San Antonio, Texas, Jan. 22–26, 1970. President, Oscar Zariski; secretary, E. Pitcher. Headquarters: P. O. Box 6248, Providence, R. I. 02904.

American Medical Association. Membership: 217,212. Annual meeting: Chicago Ill., June 21–25, 1970. President, Gerald D. Dorman, M. D.; treas., Alvin J. Ingram, M. D. Headquarters: 535 N. Dearborn St., Chicago, Ill. 60610.

American Meteorological Society. Membership: 9,000 inc. 130 corp. members. Annual meeting: Boston, Mass., Dec. 30, 1969. President, Eugene Bollay; exec. director, Dr. Kenneth C. Spengler; secretary-treas., David F. Landrigan. Headquarters: 45 Beacon St., Boston, Mass. 02108.

American National Red Cross. Adult membership: 33,-396,300 in 3,300 chapters. National convention: Chicago, Ill., May 17–20, 1970. Chairman, E. Roland Harriman; president, James F. Collins. Headquarters: 17th and D Sts., Washington, D. C. 20006.

American Newspaper Publishers Association. Membership: 1,056. Annual convention: New York, N. Y., April 21–24, 1969. President, William F. Schmick; gen. manager, Stanford Smith. Headquarters: 750 Third Ave., New York, N. Y. 10017.

American Nurses Association. Membership: 200,000 in 54 states and territorial associations. National convention: Miami, Fla., May 4–8, 1970. President, Dorothy A. Cornelius; exec. dir., Hildegard E. Peplau. Headquarters: 10 Columbus Circle, New York, N. Y., 10019.

American Personnel and Guidance Association. Membership: 29,200. National convention: New Orleans, La., March 22–26, 1970. President, Dr. Merle M. Ohlsen, exec. director, Willis E. Dugan. Headquarters: 1607 New Hampshire Ave. NW, Washington, D C. 20009.

American Philological Association. Membership: 2,400. Annual meeting: New York, N. Y., Dec. 28–30, 1970. President, Malcolm F. McGregor; secretary-treas., John J. Bateman. Headquarters: University of Illinois, 361 Lincoln Hall, Urbana, Ill. 61801.

American Philosophical Association. Membership: 3,000. Annual meetings (1970): Berkeley, Calif., March 26–28; St. Louis, Mo., May 7–9; Philadelphia, Pa., Dec. 27–29. Chairman, Maurice Mandelbaum; exec. secy., Alan Pasch. Headquarters: 117 Lehigh Rd., College Park, Md. 20742.

American Physical Society. Membership: 26,000 American and foreign members. Annual meeting: Chicago, Ill., Jan. 26–29, 1970. President, Dr. E. M. Purcell; exec. secretary, W. W. Havens, Jr. Headquarters: 335 East 45th St., New York, N. Y. 10017.

American Political Science Association. Membership: 17,500. Annual meeting: Los Angeles, Calif., Sept. 8–12, 1970. President, Karl W. Deutsch; exec. dir., Evron M. Kirkpatrick. Headquarters: 1527 New Hampshire Ave. NW, Washington, D. C. 20036.

American Psychiatric Association. Membership: 17,129; 63 district branches. Annual meeting: San Francisco, Calif., May 11–15, 1970. President, Raymond W. Waggoner, M. D.; secretary, George Tarjan, M. D.; medical dir., Walter E. Barton, M. D. Headquarters: 1700 18th St. NW, Washington, D. C. 20009.

American Psychological Association. Membership: 30,300. Annual meeting: Miami, Fla., Sept. 3–8, 1970. President, George W. Albee; exec. officer, Kenneth B. Little. Headquarters: 1200 17th St., NW. Washington, D. C. 20036.

American Society of Civil Engineers. Membership: 62,757. Annual meeting: Chicago, Ill., Oct. 13–17, 1969. President, Thomas M. Niles; director, William H. Wisely. Headquarters: 345 East 47th St., New York, N. Y. 10017.

American Society of Composers, Authors, and Publishers. Membership: 11,251 composers and authors; 3,768 publishers. Annual meeting: New York, N. Y., March 1970. President, Stanley Adams; secretary, Morton Gould. Headquarters: 575 Madison Ave., New York, N. Y. 10022.

American Society of International Law. Membership: 4,800. Annual meeting: New York, N. Y., April 24–26, 1970. President, Oscar Schachter; exec. director, Stephen M. Schwebel. Headquarters: 2223 Massachusetts Ave. NW, Washington, D. C. 20008.

American Society of Mechanical Engineers. Membership: 62,636. President, Donald E. Marlowe; exec. director and secretary, O. B. Schier, II. Headquarters: 345 East 47th St., New York, N. Y. 10017.

American Society of Newspaper Editors. Membership: 710. National convention: San Francisco, Calif., May 11–14, 1970. President, Norman E. Isaacs; secretary, J. Edward Murray. Headquarters: 750 Third Ave., New York, N. Y. 10017.

American Sociological Association. Membership: 13,000. Annual meeting: Washington, D. C., Aug. 31–Sept. 3, 1970. President, Reinhard Bendix; secretary, Peter H. Rossi. Headquarters: 1001 Connecticut Ave. NW, Washington, D. C. 20036.

American Statistical Association. Membership: 10,000. Annual meeting: Detroit, Mich., Dec. 27–30, 1970. President, Dr. T. A. Bancroft; secretary, John W. Lehman. Headquarters: 810 18th St. NW, Washington, D. C. 20006.

American Veterans Committee. Membership: 25,000 in 60 regional groups. Annual meeting: Washington, D. C., June 26–28, 1970. National chairman: Samuel Byer; exec. director, June A. Willenz. Headquarters: 1333 Connecticut Ave. NW, Washington, D. C. 20036.

American Veterinary Medical Association. Membership: 20,110 in 50 states. Annual meeting: Las Vegas, Nev., June 22–26, 1970. President, John B. Herrick, D. V. M.; exec. vice pres., M. R. Clarkson, D. V. M. Headquarters: 600 S. Michigan Ave., Chicago, Ill. 60605.

American Youth Hostels, Inc. Membership: 41,000 in 25 AYH Councils. Annual meeting: San Francisco, Calif., Dec. 1969. President, Lyman Moore; Chairman of the Board, Stephens Dietz; exec. director, Frank D. Cosgrove. Headquarters: 20 West 17th St., New York, N. Y. 10011.

Archaeological Institute of America. Membership: 6,000; subscribers, 12,000. Annual meeting: San Francisco, Calif., Dec. 27–30, 1969. President, Rodney S. Young; gen. secretary, Jane Sammis Ord. Headquarters: 260 W. Broadway, New York, N. Y. 10013.

Arthritis Foundation, The. Membership: 77 chapters. Annual meeting: Detroit, Mich., June 20, 1970. President, William S. Clark, M. D.; secretary, Edward S. Hand. Headquarters: 1212 Avenue of the Americas, New York, N. Y. 10036.

Association of Better Business Bureaus, International. Membership: 146 bureaus in U. S., Canada, Israel, Mexico, Puerto Rico, and Venezuela. Annual meeting: Detroit, Mich., June 8–11, 1970. President, Victor H. Nyborg. Headquarters: 1 Greenwich Plaza, Greenwich, Conn. 06830.

Association of the Junior Leagues of America, Inc. Membership: more than 216 member Leagues in U. S., Canada, and Mexico. Annual conference: Boca Raton, Fla., May 10–14, 1969. President, Mrs. Milo Yalich. Headquarters: 825 Third Ave., New York, N. Y. 10022.

Benevolent and Protective Order of Elks. Membership: 1,480,412 in 2,124 Lodges. National convention: San Francisco, Calif., July 12–16, 1970. Grand Exalted Ruler, Frank Hise; grand secretary, Franklin J. Fitzpatrick. Headquarters: 2750 Lake View Ave., Chicago, Ill. 60614.

B'nai B'rith. Membership: 500,000 in 4,000 local groups. President, William A. Wexler; exec. vice president, Rabbi Jay Kaufman. Headquarters: 1640 Rhode Island Ave. NW, Washington, D. C. 20036.

Boy Scouts of America. Membership: 6,247,160 boys and leaders in 508 Boy Scout councils. Annual meeting: Denver, Colo., May 20–22, 1970. President, Irving Feist; Chief Scout Executive, Alden G. Barber. Headquarters: New Brunswick, N. J. 08903.

Boys' Clubs of America. Membership: 850,000 in 850 clubs. National convention: Boston, Mass., April 19–23, 1970. President, John L. Burns; national director, A. Boyd Hinds. Headquarters: 771 First Ave., New York, N. Y. 10017.

Camp Fire Girls, Inc. Membership: 630,000 in over 9,000 communities. National council meeting: Des Moines, Iowa, Nov. 7–10, 1970. President, Mrs. Mortimer Fleishhacker, Jr.; exec. vice pres., national exec. dir., and secretary, Dr. Hester Turner. Headquarters: 65 Worth St., New York, N. Y. 10013.

Canadian Library Association (Association Canadienne des Bibliothèques). Membership: 2,600 persons and 900 organizations. Annual conference: Hamilton, Ont., June 20–25, 1970. President, Bruce Peel; exec. director, Clifford Currie. Headquarters: 63 Sparks St., Ottawa 4, Ont.

Canadian Medical Association. Membership: 21,421. Annual meeting: Winnipeg, Man., June 15–18, 1970. President, R. M. Matthews, M. D.; gen. secretary, A. F. W. Peart, M. D. Headquarters: 1867 Alta Vista Dr., Ottawa 8, Ont.

Catholic Library Association. Membership: 4,050. National convention: Boston, Mass., March 30–April 3, 1970. President, Sister Helen Sheehan, S. N. D.; exec. dir., M. Richard Wilt. Headquarters: 461 W. Lancaster Ave., Haverford, Pa. 19041.

Chamber of Commerce of the United States of America. Membership: about 4,000 trade associations and local chambers, 32,000 business members, and 4,600,000 underlying membership. Annual meeting: Washington, D. C., April 26–28, 1970. President, Jenkins Lloyd Jones; exec. vice president, Arch N. Booth. Headquarters: 1615 H St. NW, Washington, D. C. 20006.

Council on Foreign Relations, Inc. Membership: 1,500. Annual meeting: New York, N. Y., Oct. 8, 1969. President, Grayson Kirk; executive director, George S. Franklin, Jr. Headquarters: 58 East 68th St., New York, N. Y. 10021.

Daughters of the American Revolution (National Society). Membership: 189,000 members in 2,894 chapters. Continental congress: Washington, D. C., April 20–24, 1970. President General, Mrs. Erwin Frees Seimes. Headquarters: 1776 D St. NW, Washington, D. C. 20006.

4-H Clubs. Membership: 3.5 million participating members. National conference: Washington, D. C., April 19–24, 1970. Director, Dr. E. Dean Vaughan. Address: Federal Extension Service, U. S. Dept. of Agriculture, Washington, D. C. 20250.

Freemasonry, Ancient Accepted Scottish Rite of (Northern Masonic Jurisdiction): Supreme Council, 33°. Membership: 510,857 in 387 affiliated groups. Annual meeting: Milwaukee, Wis., Sept. 22–24, 1970. Sovereign grand commander, George A. Newbury; grand secy. gen., Laurence E. Eaton; exec. secy., Stanley F. Maxwell. Headquarters: 39 Marrett Road, Lexington, Mass. 02173.

Freemasonry, Ancient and Accepted Scottish Rite of (Southern Jurisdiction): Supreme Council, 33°. Membership: 563,000 in 209 affiliated groups. National convention: Washington, D. C., Oct. 20–23, 1969. Sovereign grand commander, Henry C. Clausen; secy. gen., C. Fred Kleinknecht, Jr. Headquarters: 1733 16th St. NW, Washington, D. C. 20009.

Future Farmers of America. Membership: 448,091 in 50 state associations. National convention: Kansas City, Mo., Oct. 13–16, 1970. National adviser, H. N. Hunsicker; secretary, William Paul Gray. Headquarters: U. S. Office of Education, Washington, D. C. 20202.

Garden Club of America, The. Membership: about 12,000 in 175 member clubs. Annual meeting: Boston, Mass., May 11–14, 1970. President, Mrs. Jerome K. Doolan; secretary, Mrs. Frederick N. Blodgett. Headquarters: 598 Madison Ave., New York, N. Y. 10022.

General Federation of Women's Clubs. Membership: 11,000,000 in 16,000 clubs and organizations. National convention: San Antonio, Texas, 1970. President, Mrs. Walter Varney Magee; exec. secretary, Mrs. Wilson Y. Christian. Headquarters: 1734 N St. NW, Washington, D. C. 20036.

Geological Society of America. Membership: 7,800. Annual meeting: Milwaukee, Wis., Nov. 11–13, 1970. President, John Rodgers; acting exec. secretary, Edwin B. Eckel. Headquarters: P. O. Box 1719, Colorado Building, Boulder, Colo. 80302.

Girl Scouts of the U. S. A. Membership: 3,922,000. National president, Mrs. Douglas H. MacNeil; exec. director, Louise A. Wood. Headquarters: 830 Third Ave., New York, N. Y. 10022.

Holy Name, Confraternity of the. Membership: 5,000,000 in 19,000 affiliated groups. National director, Brendan Larnen. Headquarters: 141 E. 65th St., New York, N. Y.

Institute of Electrical and Electronics Engineers, Inc. Membership: 166,000. International convention: New York, N. Y., March 23–26, 1970. President, John V. N. Granger; secretary, R. H. Tanner. Address: 345 East 47th St., New York, N. Y. 10017.

International Council of Scientific Unions (Conseil International des Unions Scientifiques). Membership: 16 international scientific unions and 60 national societies. General assembly: 1970. President, V. A. Ambartsumian; Secretary-general, K. Chandrasekharan. Headquarters: 7 Via C. Celso, Rome, Italy 00161.

Jewish War Veterans of the U. S. A. Membership: 100,000 in 750 organizations. Annual convention: Los Angeles, Calif., Aug. 1969. National Commander, Bernard B. Direnfeld; national exec. director, Felix M. Putterman. Headquarters: 1712 New Hampshire Ave. NW, Washington, D. C. 20009.

Kiwanis International. Membership: 275,000 in 5,700 clubs in U. S., Canada, Mexico, Western Europe, the Far East, the Caribbean, South and Central America, New Zealand, and Australia. Annual convention: Detroit, Mich., June 21–24, 1970. President, Robert F. Weber; secretary, R. P. Merridew. Headquarters: 101 E. Erie St., Chicago, Ill. 60611.

Knights of Columbus. Membership: 1,200,000. Annual meeting: Houston, Texas, Aug. 18–20, 1970. Supreme knight, John W. McDevitt; supreme secretary, Virgil C. Dechant. Headquarters: Columbus Plaza, New Haven, Conn. 06507.

Knights of Pythias, Supreme Lodge. Membership: 190,-000 in 1,917 subordinate lodges. Biennial meeting: Raleigh, N. C., Aug. 11–15, 1969. Supreme chancellor, Otto Shuman; supreme secretary, Jule O. Pritchard. Office: 47 N. Grant St., Stockton, Calif. 95202.

League of Women Voters of the United States. Membership: 157,000. National convention: Washington, D. C., May 4–8, 1970. President, Mrs. Bruce B. Benson; first vice-pres., Mrs. William M. Christopherson. Headquarters: 1730 M St. NW, Washington, D. C. 20036.

Lions International. Membership: 910,000 in 23,900 clubs in 145 countries. President (1970–71), Dr. Robert D. McCullough. Headquarters: 209 N. Michigan Ave., Chicago, Ill. 60601.

Loyal Order of Moose. Membership: 1,116,215 in 3,902 units. National convention: Mooseheart and Chicago, Ill., June 14–18, 1970. Director general, Paul P. Schmitz; supreme secretary, Carl A. Weis. Headquarters: Mooseheart, Ill. 60539.

Modern Language Association of America. Membership: 27,000. Annual meeting: New York, N. Y., Dec. 27–30, 1970. President, Maynard Mack; exec. secretary, John Hurt Fisher. Headquarters: 62 Fifth Ave., New York, N. Y. 10011.

National Academy of Sciences. Membership: 850. Annual meeting: Washington, D. C., April 27–29, 1970. President, Philip Handler; exec. officer, John S. Coleman. Headquarters: 2101 Constitution Ave. NW, Washington, D. C. 20418.

National Association for Mental Health, Inc. Membership: 1,000 state and local organizations. Annual meeting: Los Angeles, Calif., Nov. 16–21, 1970. President, James E. Chapman; exec. dir., Brian O'Connell. Headquarters: 10 Columbus Circle, New York, N. Y. 10019.

National Association for the Advancement of Colored People. Membership: 450,000 in 1,800 units. National convention: Cincinnati, Ohio, June 29–July 4, 1970. President, Kivie Kaplan; exec. director, Roy Wilkins. Headquarters: 1790 Broadway, New York N. Y., 10019.

National Association of Manufacturers. Membership: 14,000. Annual meeting: New York, N. Y., Dec. 2–4, 1970. President, W. P. Gullander; secretary, John McGraw. Headquarters: 277 Park Ave., New York, N. Y. 10017.

National Audubon Society. Membership: 81,000. Annual meeting: Seattle, Wash., May 15–19, 1970. President, Dr. Elvis J. Stahr; exec. vice pres., Charles H. Callison; secretary, John W. Hanes, Jr. Headquarters: 1130 Fifth Ave., New York, N. Y. 10028.

National Conference of Christians and Jews, Inc. Membership: 75 regional offices. Annual meeting: Washington, D. C., Nov. 16–17, 1969. President, Dr. Sterling W. Brown; secretary, Oscar M. Lazrus. Headquarters: 43 West 57th St., New York, N. Y. 10019.

National Congress of Parents and Teachers. Membership: 10,249,740 in 43,390 PTA's. National convention: New Orleans, La., May 31–June 3, 1969. President, Mrs. Leon S. Price; secretary, Mrs. J. M. Herndon. Headquarters: 700 N. Rush St., Chicago, Ill. 60611.

National Council of the Churches of Christ in the U. S. A. Membership: 33 Protestant, Anglican, and Orthodox denominations. Triennial general assembly: Dallas, Texas, Dec. 3–9, 1972. President, Dr. Cynthia Wedel; general secretary, R. H. Edwin Espy. Headquarters: 475 Riverside Dr., New York, N. Y. 10027.

National Council of the Young Men's Christian Association. Membership: 5,650,610 in 1,748 organizations. National board chairman, W. M. McFeely; exec. director, James F. Bunting. Headquarters: 291 Broadway, New York, N. Y.

National Easter Seal Society for Crippled Children and Adults. Membership: 52 state and territorial societies. National golden anniversary convention: Columbus, Ohio, Nov. 19–23, 1969. President, George A. Haas; exec. director, Sumner G. Whittier. Headquarters: 2023 W. Ogden Ave., Chicago, Ill. 60612.

National Education Association of the U. S. Membership: 1,014,414, with units in every state and 8,827 local affiliates. Annual meeting: San Francisco, Calif., June 30–July 6, 1970. President, George D. Fischer; exec. secretary, Sam M. Lambert. Headquarters: 1201 16th St. NW, Washington, D. C. 20036.

National Federation of Business and Professional Women's Clubs, Inc. Membership: 178,500 in 3,800 clubs. National convention: Honolulu, Hawaii, July 19–23, 1970. President, Mrs. Myra Ruth Harmon; fed. director, Lucille H. Shriver. Headquarters: 2012 Massachusetts Ave. NW, Washington, D. C. 20036.

National Federation of Music Clubs. Membership: 600,-000 in 4,300 clubs and 13 national affiliates. Annual meeting: Detroit, Mich., Aug. 20–24, 1970; biennial convention, New Orleans, La., April 19–25, 1971. President, Mrs. Maurice Honigman; office manager, Mrs. John McDonald. Headquarters: 600 S. Michigan Ave., Chicago, Ill. 60605.

National Foundation—March of Dimes, The. Membership: 3,000 chapters. President, Basil O'Connor; senior vice president, Joseph F. Nee. Headquarters: 800 Second Ave., New York, N. Y. 10017.

National Recreation and Park Association. Membership of 30,000 includes professional park and recreation administrators and citizens concerned with conservation of natural resources. Annual congress: Philadelphia, Pa., Sept. 27–Oct. 1, 1970. Chairman of the Board, Endicott P. Davison; president, Dr. Sal J. Prezioso. Headquarters: 1700 Pennsylvania Ave. NW, Washington, D. C. 20006.

National Research Council of Canada. Membership: council 21; laboratory staff, 3,039. Annual meeting: Ottawa, Ont., March 1970. President, Dr. W. G. Schneider; secretary, B. D. Leddy. Headquarters: Montreal Rd., Ottawa 7, Ont.

National Safety Council. Membership: 11,000. National Safety Congress and Exposition: Chicago, Ill., Oct. 26–29, 1970. President, Howard Pyle; secretary, H. W. Champlin. Headquarters: 425 N. Michigan Ave., Chicago, Ill. 60611.

National Tuberculosis and Respiratory Disease Association. Membership: 1,310 affiliated groups. Annual meeting: Cleveland, Ohio, May 24–27, 1970. President, Judge Ernest E. Mason; managing dir., James E. Perkins, M. D. Headquarters: 1740 Broadway, New York, N. Y. 10019.

National Urban League, Inc. President, James A. Linen; board of trustees secretary, Mrs. Ersa H. Poston; exec. director, Whitney M. Young, Jr. Headquarters: 55 East 52nd St., New York, N. Y. 10022.

National Woman's Christian Temperance Union. Membership: 265,000 in 6,000 local unions. National convention: Los Angeles, Calif., Sept. 6–13, 1970. President, Mrs. Fred J. Tooze; secretary, Mrs. Herman Stanley. Headquarters: 1730 Chicago Ave., Evanston, Ill. 60201.

Phi Beta Kappa. Membership: 225,000 in 184 chapters and 58 associations. President, H. Bentley Glass; secretary, Carl Billman. Headquarters: 1811 Q St. NW, Washington, D. C. 20009.

Planned Parenthood-World Population (Planned Parenthood Federation of America, Inc.). Membership: 188 affiliates. Annual meeting: October 1970. President, Alan F. Guttmacher, M. D.; chairman of board, Jerome H. Holland; secretary, Mrs. Charles F. Whitten. Headquarters: 515 Madison Ave., New York, N. Y. 10022.

Rotary International. Membership: 660,500 in 14,000 clubs functioning in 148 countries. International convention: Atlanta, Ga., May 31–June 4, 1970. President, James F. Conway; gen. secretary, George R. Means. Headquarters: 1600 Ridge Ave., Evanston, Ill. 60201.

Special Libraries Association. Membership: 7,000. Annual conference: Detroit, Mich., June 7–11, 1970. President, Robert W. Gibson, Jr.; president-elect, Florine A. Oltman; exec. dir., George H. Ginader. Headquarters: 235 Park Ave. South, New York, N. Y. 10003.

Travelers Aid Association of America. Membership: 81 local societies. Biennial convention: New Orleans, La., April 19–22, 1970. President, Alfred D. Bell, Jr.; exec. dir., Paul W. Guyler. Headquarters: 44 East 23d St., New York, N. Y. 10010.

United Community Funds and Councils of America, Inc. Membership: local United Funds, Community Chests, and Community Health and Welfare Councils in 1,367 North American communities. President, Bayard Ewing; secretary, Helen Alvord. Headquarters: 345 East 46th St., New York, N. Y. 10017.

United States Jaycees, The. Membership: 325,000 in 6,400 affiliated groups. Annual meeting: St. Louis, Mo., June 23–25, 1970. President, André E. LeTendre; exec. vice-pres., Thomas R. Donnelly, Jr. Headquarters: Box 7, Tulsa, Okla. 74102.

Veterans of Foreign Wars of the United States. Membership, V. F. W. and Auxiliary: 2,050,000. National convention: Miami Beach, Florida, Aug. 14–21, 1970. Commander-in-Chief, Ray Gallagher; Adjutant General, Julian Dickenson. Headquarters: V. F. W. Building, Broadway at 34th St., Kansas City, Mo. 64111.

World Council of Churches (United States Conference). Membership: 28 churches or denominations in U. S. Annual meeting: Buck Hill Falls, Pa., April 29–May 1, 1970. Chairman, John Coventry Smith; exec. secretary, Eugene L. Smith. Headquarters: 475 Riverside Dr., New York, N. Y. 10027.

Young Women's Christian Association of the U. S. A. Membership: approx. 2,000,000. President, Mrs. Robert W. Claytor; exec. director, Edith M. Lerrigo. Headquarters: 600 Lexington Ave., New York, N. Y. 10022.

Zionist Organization of America. Membership: 100,000 in 600 districts. National convention: New York, N. Y., Sept. 3–6, 1970. President, Jacques Torczyner; national secretary and exec. director, Leon Ilutovich. Headquarters: 145 East 32d St., New York, N. Y. 10016.

SOCIOLOGY

Sociologists in 1969 were giving increasing attention to the scope of their research programs, particularly with reference to the social problems involved in current public protest movements.

A Design for Sociology. The results of a special conference held by 20 invited sociologists, was given in a monograph entitled, *A Design for Sociology: Scope, Objectives, and Methods,* published by the American Academy of Political and Social Science, April 1969. In describing "The Optimum Scope of Sociology," Neil J. Smelser, of the University of California, Berkeley, outlined the distinctive conceptual frameworks to which sociologists refer empirical data for assessment: demography and ecology; social psychology; the group roles; and cultural phenomena that regulate social interaction.

Robert M. Williams, Jr., of Cornell University, summarized the subject matter of sociology in terms of social interaction, collectivities, and institutions as systems of statuses defined by norms. Robert A. Nisbet, of the University of California, Riverside, noted five conceptual frameworks of sociology in the following terms: personality; groups; social structures; social roles; and values or norms. In a general summary, Robert Bierstadt, of New York University, indicated that sociology is better equipped with methods for dealing with an orderly society than with "a shattered society" that is being torn apart with problems "of race tension, poverty amid affluence, pollutions of the air, wars, and threats of nuclear destruction."

Basic Conflicts in Sociology. Sociologists are increasingly confronted with a basic dilemma that is described by Ernest Q. Campbell, of Vanderbilt University, in *Social Forces,* March 1969 ("Negroes, Education, and the Southern States"). The dilemma was related in terms of the following conflicts: (1) between analysis of data and advocacy of a social policy; (2) between keeping detached from the aspects of social life that are being studied, and taking part in them while studying them; (3) between maintaining simultaneously the professional role and the citizen role regarding a given social problem; (4) between maintaining professional competence in research and being personally relevant and involved; (5) between centering inquiry on the intellectual needs of the discipline and attending to the reform needs, or the stability needs, of the social system; and (6) between the roles of scientific inquiry and advocacy of a given social action.

The American Sociological Association. The 64th annual meeting of the American Sociological

Association (ASA) was held Sept. 1–4, 1969, in San Francisco, with a total of 117 section and general meetings, under the direction of President Ralph H. Turner, University of California, Los Angeles. The presidential address was entitled, "The Public Perception of Protest." It discussed several theoretical vantage points "as bases for formulating hypotheses under which disturbances by one social group will be defined by another group as social protest."

President Turner conducted a plenary session on the theme, "The American Sociological Association and Questions of Public Policy." An unusual feature of the annual meeting was the presentation of two presidential addresses. Arnold M. Rose, University of Minnesota, who had been elected president for 1969, died in 1968 at the age of 49. The address that he had prepared, "Varieties of Sociological Imagination," was read by his wife, Caroline M. Rose. The general theme for the 1969 annual meeting was, "Group Conflict and Mutual Acceptance."

The 65th Annual Meeting of the ASA is scheduled to be held in Washington, D. C., Aug. 31–Sept. 3, 1970, under the general direction of President Reinhard Bendix of the University of California, Berkeley. The 19th Annual Meeting of the Society for the Study of Social Problems was held in San Francisco, Aug. 30–Sept. 3, 1969.

Dictionary of Sociology. A *Dictionary of Modern Sociology* (Littlefield, Adams & Co., 1969) was prepared by Thomas F. Hoult, of Arizona State University, with the assistance of Kimball Young, Talcott Parsons, and Wilbert E. Moore. An emphasis is given to terms in current usage. Of a total of 1,700 terms that are defined, about 450 relate to methodology, 325 to sociocultural concepts, 250 to social psychology, 240 to social organization and social institutions, 185 to social problems and social disorganization, and 100 to demography and population. In defining many of the concepts, the authors give brief and explanatory quotations from the works of various sociologists and related writers, totaling about 600 different referents.

EMORY S. BOGARDUS
University of Southern California

SOMALIA

Events in the Somali Democratic Republic during 1969 were overshadowed by a presidential assassination and a military coup in October. The coup came as a surprise to many who viewed Somalia as one of the most democratic African states.

Elections. In the elections held on March 26 the governing Somali Youth League (SYL) gained only 40% of the votes but won 73 out of the 123 seats in the National Assembly. The elections showed a deep fragmentation in Somali politics; there were more than 2,000 candidates and 63 political parties. By June most of the opposition parliamentarians had shifted to the SYL and Prime Minister Mohammed Ibrahim Egal received a substantial vote of confidence (116 for and 1 against). But it took three months to form the new government.

Coup d'etat. President Abdirashid Ali Shermarke was assassinated on October 15, and six days later the army and police overthrew the government of Prime Minister Egal and seized power in a bloodless coup. The military established a Supreme Revolutionary Council (SRC), with army head Maj. Gen.

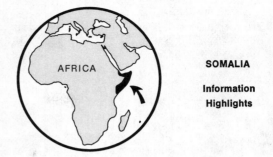

SOMALIA

Information
Highlights

Area: 246,202 square miles (637,657 sq km).
Population: 2,745,000 (1968 est.).
Chief Cities (1966 census): Mogadishu, the capital, 170,000; Merca (1968 est.) 56,000.
Government: *President of the Supreme Revolutionary Council* —Maj. Gen. Mohammed Siad Barre (assumed power Oct. 21, 1969).
Religious Faiths: Sunni Muslims, 99% of population.
Education: *Literacy rate* (1969), 5% of population. *Total school enrollment* (1965)—42,834 (primary, 28,890; secondary, 10,494; teacher-training, 763; technical/vocational, 2,627; university/higher, 60).
Finance (1968 est.): *Revenues,* $36,300,000; *expenditures,* 39,400,000; *monetary unit,* Somali shilling (7.143 shillings equal U. S.$1).
Gross National Product (1967): $132,000,000.
Average Annual Income Per Person (1967): $50.
Manufacturing (metric tons, 1967): Sugar, 38,000.
Chief Crop (metric tons, 1967–68 crop year): Bananas, 184,000.
Chief mineral (metric tons, 1965): Salt, 5,442.
Foreign Trade (1968): *Exports,* $30,500,000 (chief exports, 1967: bananas, $9,571,000; wood charcoal, $1,595,000; hides and skins, $1,161,000); *Imports,* 47,600,000 (chief imports, 1967: textile yarn and fabrics, $4,823,000; rice, 2,877,000; road motor vehicles, $2,610,000). *Chief trading partners* (1967): Italy (took 38% of exports, supplied 29% of imports); Southern Yemen (took 57% of exports, supplied 5% of imports); Japan (supplied 9% of imports).
Transportation: *Roads* (1969), 8,016 miles (12,900 km); *motor vehicles* (1967), 14,500 (automobiles, 6,700); *national airline,* Somali Airlines.
Communications: *Telephones* (1968): 4,500; *radios* (1967), 40,000; *newspapers* (1964), 2 (daily circulation, 5,000).

Mohammed Siad Barre as president. The SRC explained that the nearly "anarchic" political situation was the main cause of the coup. It renamed the country the Somali Democratic Republic.

The goal of the Supreme Revolutionary Council is to "root out corruption," eliminate tribalism, and establish a solid foundation for a "true democratic" government. The regime declared that it will nationalize industries only if necessary. It is also intent on bringing about a reinvigorated Muslim order.

Foreign Affairs. The civilian government of Prime Minister Egal had succeeded in bringing about a detente between Somalia and its neighbors, Kenya and Ethiopia. The actions of the SRC suggest that it will not seek substantially to reverse this policy. It defines its objective as self-determination (or Pan Somali unity) through peaceful means. It seemed likely that the new government would alter its predecessor's pro-West policy by moving closer to the East; but it insists on maintaining absolute neutrality.

Economy. The failure of civilian governments to get the Somali economy off the ground was another reason for the coup. Deficits in the national budget and the balance of payments persisted. The SRC had no rational plan for bringing about a more rapid pace of development but it pledged to do so. Although it does not intend to discourage foreign assistance, the SRC insists that stress should be placed on self-reliance.

A. A. CASTAGNO
Boston University

CAMERA PRESS-PIX

CAPE TOWN, as viewed by night from nearby Signal Hill, is an attractive, modern metropolis with extensive suburbs stretching out in the distance. The docks serving its busy port are seen at left.

SOUTH AFRICA

South Africa's political, social, and economic development remained essentially unchanged in 1969. Under the leadership of Prime Minister Balthazar J. Vorster and the Nationalist party, South Africa maintained its rigorous commitment to apartheid policies and the further expansion of the Bantustan program. The country continued to show strong economic growth, and the crowded harbors of Durban and Cape Town reflected the boom conditions resulting from the closing of the Suez canal and the revolution in bulk oil transportation.

Politics. The *verkrampte* (narrow-minded) opposition within the ranks of the Nationalist party to the *verligte* (enlightened) policies of its leadership continued a split that posed a threat to the 21-year-old supremacy of the governing party. The political importance of the schism will soon be known. In September, Prime Minister Vorster announced plans to move the date of the general election ahead from 1971 to April 22, 1970. The earlier date appeared to be aimed at eliminating the *verkrampte* extremists. Headed by Albert Hertzog, the influential former minister of posts and telegraphs, the *verkrampte* faction launched a new political party in October. The new party, the Reformed National party, has as its aim an even stricter enforcement of apartheid.

Apartheid. A major issue between the Nationalist party and the opposition United party in the forthcoming elections—which will of course be all white—will be the future of the Bantustans (African reserves). In Parliament on February 3 the

leader of the United party, Sir de Villiers Graaff, condemned the government policy and called for the repudiation of a policy of total territorial separation in favor of a representative federal system for all South Africa under white leadership. In September, Prime Minister Vorster reiterated his government's commitment to separate development, which, he declared, will lead to politically independent and economically interdependent nations. The United party believes that the Bantustans can neither support the majority of Africans nor become economically viable; and it is hardly more hopeful about the feasibility of the border industries plan.

The year 1968 closed with the number of "self-governing" Bantustans at four—the Transkei, Ovamboland, the Ciskei, and Tswanaland—but with the promise of more to follow soon. Since then at least three more—the Basotho, Vendaland, and Matshangana—have been added. In spite of the government's continued expansion of its Bantustan program in 1969, the number of Africans leaving their homelands for work in the cities was increasing.

In 1968, South Africa's 1.8 million Cape Coloured (racially mixed) people had lost their four seats in Parliament. They will instead be represented in the newly established Coloured Persons' Representative Council, which will regulate matters "of specifically Coloured interest." The Council consists of 40 elected members and 20 members nominated by the government; of the 40 electoral divisions 28 are in Cape Province, 6 in the Transvaal, and 3 each in Natal and the Orange Free State.

In the first elections, held on Sept. 24, 1969, 26 seats were won by the Labour party, which is opposed to the government's policy of apartheid. But the government's use of the nominated seats enabled the defeated Federal party, which accepts apartheid, to reverse the results of the polls and command a majority; the leader of the Federal party was designated by the government as chairman of the Council's executive.

The Trade Union Council of South Africa (TUCSA) at its 15th annual conference voted 87 to 2 to amend its constitution to exclude Africans from membership. The general secretary stated that this was necessary to ensure the continued existence of TUCSA, which had been under considerable pressure from the government to drop its multiracial membership. Its action followed warnings by cabinet members and the withdrawal of important white unions from the council.

In September the South African Council of Churches issued a message rejecting apartheid on moral and theological grounds. The Council stated that the existing social order in South Africa was an ideology opposed to Christianity, which demands love and association between people and groups. In July the Council and the interdenominational Christian Institute of South Africa announced the establishment of a 2-year joint study project on "Christianity in apartheid society." The project will attempt to find a practical and morally acceptable alternative to apartheid.

Relations in Southern Africa. The government continued to stress the importance of sound diplomatic relations with African states. The term *uitwaartse beweging* (outward movement) was nearly as much in use as *verkrampte-verligte* and just as divisive; it is an important element in the Nationalist party split. Despite the emphasis on *uitwaartse beweging,* the idea is neither new nor out of line with the vital interests of the states concerned. South Africa needs a buffer zone of friendly states and their good will; they in turn are economically dependent on South Africa.

On December 11, South Africa, Botswana, Lesotho, and Swaziland signed a new agreement continuing the 1910 customs union between them that would have terminated in 1970. Speaking at an official luncheon for the ministerial delegations in Pretoria, South Africa's minister of economic affairs, J. E. W. Haak, stressed the importance of cooperation based on mutual respect, recognition of sovereign independence, and noninterference in the affairs of other countries. He added that it was South Africa's "wish to live in harmony with our neighbours, despite differences which may exist in political systems and ideologies and domestic policies."

An agreement signed with Swaziland provides for South Africa upon request to recruit, pay, and equip South Africans to serve in Swaziland's local administration. South African engineers have been assisting in plans for the development of Swaziland's broadcasting services.

In October a South African parliamentary delegation visited Malawi, the first such delegation to visit an independent African state. In addition to the loan toward the building of Malawi's new capital at Lilongwe, South African assistance is involved in a new railway line, which will join the Portuguese line in Mozambique, thus providing Malawi with another outlet to the sea. The new line will be built by a South African consortium and financed by the South African Industrial Corporation in the form of a loan to Malawi.

Considerable medical assistance has been offered and given to Malawi, Lesotho, and other neighboring states. This aid will shortly be coordinated by a committee representing government departments and the South African Medical Association.

Relations with the United Nations. On March 20 the UN Security Council voted 13 to 0 to condemn South Africa's continued control of Namibia (the new official name for South West Africa) and called on South Africa to withdraw immediately from the territory. On August 12 the Security Council once more called for immediate withdrawal from Namibia and set October 4 as the deadline; it also resolved that it would meet immediately to consider effective measures to be taken against South Africa if it refused to comply. In October, Foreign Minister Hilgard Muller handed UN Secretary General U Thant South Africa's refusal to comply and a comprehensive legal and factual review of the dispute as seen by South Africa. (See also UNITED NATIONS.)

The UN General Assembly on December 13 considered an Afro-Asian resolution to suspend South Africa from the UN Conference on Trade and Development. The UN's legal counsel described the resolution as not being in accordance with the provisions of the Charter, and it failed to obtain the necessary two-thirds majority.

Economy. South Africa's economy continued its rapid growth in 1969. Gold production in the country, which is the largest producer of gold in the world, reached a record high of 31.168 million ounces worth $1.09 billion in 1968.

RONALD B. BALLINGER
Rhode Island College

SOUTH AFRICA • Information Highlights

Area: 471,446 square miles (1,221,037 sq km).
Population: 19,167,000 (1968 est.).
Chief Cities (metropolitan areas, 1960 census): Pretoria, the administrative capital, 422,590; Cape Town, the legislative capital, 807,211; Johannesburg, 1,152,525; Durban, 681,492.
Government: *President*—Jacobus Johannes Fouche (took office April 10, 1968); *Prime Minister*—Balthazar J. Vorster (took office Sept. 13, 1966). *Parliament*—House of Assembly, 170 members (party seating, 1968: Nationalist party, 126; United party, 40; Progressive party, 1; independents, 3); Senate, 54 members (party seating, 1968: Nationalist party, 41; United party, 13).
Religious Faith: Protestants, 57% of population.
Education: *Literacy rate* (1969), 100% of white population. *Total school enrollment* (1963–65)—3,231,202.
Finance (1970 est.): *Revenues,* $2,300,000,000; *expenditures,* $2,300,000,000; *monetary unit,* rand (0.7196 rand equals U. S.$1).
Gross National Product (1968): $14,289,883,200.
National Income (1968): $11,648,438,020; *average annual income per person,* $609.
Economic Indexes (1967): *Industrial production* (1968), 143 (1963=100); *agricultural production,* 127 (1963=100); *cost of living,* 114 (1963=100).
Manufacturing (metric tons, 1967): Cement, 4,008,000; crude steel, 3,648,000.
Crops (metric tons, 1967–68 crop year): Maize, 9,299,000 (ranks 3d among world producers); wheat 1,023,000; citrus fruit (1966), 510,000.
Minerals (metric tons, 1967): Gold (1968), 31,168,000 troy ounces (ranks 1st among world producers); chromite (1966), 1,060,941 (world rank, 2d); manganese, 828,100 (world rank, 2d); diamonds, 6,668,000 carats (world rank, 2d); asbestos (1966), 250,924 (world rank, 3d).
Foreign Trade (1967): *Exports,* $1,884,000,000 (chief exports: diamonds, $216,320,000; wool, $148,080,000; fruit and vegetables, $147,590,000; cereals and preparations, $126,-840,000); *imports,* $2,677,000,000 (chief imports: transport equipment, $388,240,000; textile yarn and fabrics, $201,-440,000; electrical machinery, $199,240,000). *Chief trading partners* (1967): Britain (took 30% of exports, supplied 26% of imports); United States (took 8% of exports, supplied 17% of imports).
Transportation: *Roads* (1969), 220,000 miles (354,000 km); *motor vehicles* (1967), 1,655,100 (automobiles, 1,312,900); *railways* (1969), 13,621 miles (21,916 km); *national airline,* South African Airways; *principal airports,* Johannesburg, Pretoria, Cape Town.
Communications: *Telephones* (1968): 1,322,101; *radios* (1967), 2,700,000; *newspapers* (1961), 21.

SOUTH CAROLINA

Although no loss of life occurred, the year 1969 was marked by racial strife, especially the strike of workers at hospitals in Charleston and of garbage and waterworks employees of that city. The General Assembly, meeting in one of the longest sessions in its history, passed a record budget and major tax increases. Plans were in full swing at the end of the year for the celebration in 1970 of South Carolina's 300th anniversary.

Racial Relations. Some 400 hourly workers, predominantly Negro women, at the state-supported Medical University Hospital in Charleston walked off their jobs on March 20 in protest against the dismissal of 12 workers, allegedly for union activities. A short time later about 100 workers at the Charleston County Hospital joined the strike, which soon attracted national attention and the support of prominent civil rights leaders. The disputes were settled but only after disturbances and negotiations that lasted until mid-July. Unions were not recognized, since the state has no legislation enabling state and local agencies to negotiate union contracts, but workers received substantial salary increases, shorter hours, and better grievance procedures.

National attention also was drawn to the needs of poverty-stricken residents of South Carolina's predominantly Negro counties, and state and local authorities acted to improve nutritional and sanitary

conditions. Plans were developed, under black leadership, to expand home ownership by Negroes.

Legislation. The General Assembly, in a session lasting from January 14 to July 17, enacted a variety of significant legislation. The sales tax was increased from 3 cents to 4 cents and the cigarette tax from 5 cents to 6 cents a package. An average salary increase of $800 was provided for teachers, an overall classification and compensation plan was drawn up for state employees, and the juvenile correctional system was reorganized.

Among other major laws were those making three years' separation a legal ground for divorce, creating a system for the legal defense of indigents, and granting larger shares of state-collected revenues to local government.

Education. The Assembly approved a new four-year college, Marion State College at Florence, and established a board to govern two- and four-year institutions. During the year facilities and programs at the many state technical schools were greatly expanded. A pilot program to establish a public kindergarten system was started in 67 schools under a $500,000 appropriation.

There was a 15% increase in the integration of all-white schools, and several districts with dual school systems came under the U. S. Supreme Court's "integration now" ruling of October 29.

Economic Developments. Industrial expansion continued at a record rate, with significant investment of foreign capital in chemicals. Pollution problems were attacked, union activity increased, and real gains were made in Negro employment.

Tricentennial Plans. Although most communities plan festivities, the highlights of the Tricentennial will be the opening of exposition centers in the three geographic regions of the state. The Low Country center, at Charleston, opens on April 4, 1970, marking the 300th anniversary of the first permanent Carolina settlement. The Midlands center, at Columbia, opens on April 18, and the Piedmont center, near Greenville, on May 2.

ROBERT H. STOUDEMIRE
University of South Carolina

SOUTH DAKOTA

In 1969, South Dakotans suffered from harsh natural conditions, from disappointment in the lack of legislative reforms, and from racial tensions. They enjoyed satisfactory economic conditions, however, and improvement in their educational system.

Natural Conditions. Between Dec. 15, 1968 and March 1, 1969 approximately 7½ feet of snow fell across eastern South Dakota. With the spring thaw came floods, and 26 counties were declared "disaster areas." Thousands fled from their homes, and public and private property losses probably exceeded $20 million. The agrarian outlook was bleak, as water covered the fields far into the planting season.

Economy. Favorable weather conditions followed the floods, and agriculture—the state's economic mainstay—exceeded earlier expectations. Crops matured normally. Livestock and poultry inventory values rose 8% above those of 1968. Annual cash farm income for 1968 reached $1,049,285,-000, 6% above 1967.

Legislation. The 1969 "problem-solving" legislature failed to discover satisfactory solutions for the state's major problems. It struggled with the need for enlarged educational appropriations, and

SOUTH DAKOTA • Information Highlights

Area: 77,047 square miles (199,552 sq km).
Population: 670,000 (1969 est.).
Chief Cities (1966 est.): Pierre, the capital, 11,200; Sioux Falls, 70,500; Rapid City, 49,000; Aberdeen, 24,500; Huron, 14,800; Watertown, 14,300; Mitchell, 12,700.
Government: *Chief Officers*—governor, Frank L. Farrar (Republican); lt. gov., James Abdnor (R); secy. of state, Alma Larson (R); atty. gen., Gordon Mydland (R); treas., Neal Strand; supt. of pub. instr., Gordon A. Diedtrich; chief justice, Frank Biegelmier, *Legislature*—Senate, 35 members (27 Republicans, 8 Democrats); House of Representatives, 75 members (59 R, 16 D).
Education: *School enrollment* (1969)—public elementary, 115,944 pupils (5,783 teachers); public secondary, 50,720 pupils (3,281 teachers); nonpublic schools, 17,561 pupils (984 teachers); college and university (fall 1969), 25,750 students. *Public school expenditures* (1967–68)—$105,-225,000 ($685 per pupil); average teacher's salary, $5,425.
Public Finance (fiscal year 1968): *Revenues,* $212,192,000 (general sales and gross receipts taxes, $32,743,000; motor fuel tax, $19,560,000; federal funds, $79,681,000). *Expenditures,* $215,364,000 (education, $53,841,000; health, welfare, and safety, $31,198,000; highways, $68,140,000). *State debt,* $28,250,000 (1968).
Personal Income (1968): $1,887,000,000; average annual income per person, $2,876.
Public Assistance (fiscal year 1968–69): $15,025,964 to 23,-033 recipients (aged, $3,950,809; dependent children, $9,097,579).
Labor Force (employed persons, December 1968): *Agricultural,* 80,900; *nonagricultural* (wage and salary earners), 166,900 (9.5% manufacturing, 26.4% trade). *Unemployed persons* (Dec. 1968)—7,800.
Manufacturing (1965): *Value added by manufacture,* $157,-449,000 (food and products, $93,746,000; printing and publishing, $13,380,000).
Agriculture (1968): *Cash farm income,* $1,049,285,000 (1967; livestock, $705,795,000; crops, $218,265,000; govt. payments, $65,944,000). *Chief crops* (tons)—Oats, 1,753,600 (ranks 2d among the states); flaxseed, 184,548 (ranks 2d).
Mining (1967): *Production value,* $52,618,000. *Chief minerals* (tons)—Sand and gravel, 13,463,000; stone, 1,866,-000; clays, 199,000; feldspar, 68,780; gold, 601,785 troy ounces; crude petroleum, 211,000 barrels.
Transportation: *Roads* (1968), 84,333 miles (135,717 km); *motor vehicles* (1969), 444,915; *railroads* (1969), 4,370 track miles (7,426 km); *airports* (1969), 9.
Communications (1969): *Telephones,* 306,100; *television stations,* 11; *radio stations,* 42; *newspapers,* 12.

for new tax levies to support them; but it increased educational spending only slightly, and provided the revenue with a controversial 1% increase in the sales tax. Legislators studied repeal of a long-standing restriction on out-of-state waterfowl hunters, urged by the U. S. Congress before it would finance the Oahe Irrigation Project. The restriction, however, was modified so little as to leave the project in jeopardy. The legislators considered, but failed to repeal, capital punishment. It was a disappointing session for all who expected reforms.

Indian Affairs. Racial tension developed over double standards before the law. White rancher Baxter Berry was acquitted in his trial for killing an Indian, but Indian student Thomas White Hawk failed to have his death sentence repealed, which he had received for killing a Caucasian. Many of the state's 40,000 Indians accused the courts of racial discrimination. The resentment grew so strong that commutation of Hawk's sentence to life imprisonment did not stop the allegations.

Education. Public school district reorganization advanced rapidly. The number of districts was reduced to only 967; a cut of nearly 600 districts.

Meanwhile, Richard Gibb, the commissioner of higher education, developed a plan for reorganization of state-supported colleges and universities which would diminish duplication of programs, coordinate extension services, enhance curriculum quality, and increase faculty benefits.

HERBERT T. HOOVER
University of South Dakota

SOUTH WEST AFRICA. See SOUTH AFRICA; UNITED NATIONS.

SOUTHERN YEMEN

The People's Republic of Southern Yemen was established in November 1967, when the British withdrew from Aden and its hinterland. The anti-British National Liberation Front (NLF) gained the upper hand over the Front for the Liberation of Southern Yemen (FLOSY). Qahtan al-Shaabi, the head of the NLF, became the first president of the republic, with the NLF as the only party.

Internal Affairs. In 1969 the port of Aden suffered from the continued closing of the Suez Canal. In August a high government official spoke of "the suffocating economic crisis." The Anglophobe stance of the government kept Southern Yemen from receiving British aid, and a Soviet loan of 2 million rubles proved disappointingly small. Southern Yemen and Algeria formed a joint oil company, but oil was yet to be found.

In June young leftists of the NLF forced Qahtan al-Shaabi out of office, replacing him with a presidency council under Salim Rubai as chairman. Muhammad Ali Haitham became prime minister.

Foreign Affairs. The new regime developed even closer ties with Soviet Union. In October, Southern Yemen broke off diplomatic relations with the United States because of purported U. S. backing of the Lebanese government against the Palestinian guerrillas.

Although an ultimate union is the announced goal of both Southern Yemen and the Yemen Arab Republic (YAR), the two states remain far from friendly. In 1969, FLOSY, barred by the NLF from Southern Yemen, operated openly in the YAR in an effort to regain a foothold in the south.

Southern Yemen's relations with Saudi Arabia were even worse. Armed clashes along their undefined border took place in November, although an uneasy peace was restored in December. Saudi Arabia accused Southern Yemen of being an avenue

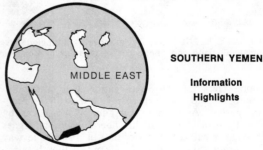

MIDDLE EAST

SOUTHERN YEMEN

Information Highlights

Area: 111,075 square miles (287,682 sq km).
Population: 1,195,000 (1968 est.).
Chief Cities (1964 census): Madinat al-Shaab, the capital, 29,897; Aden, 150,000.
Government: *Chairman of Presidency Council*—Salim Rubai (took office June 1969); *Prime Minister*—Muhammad Ali Haitham (took office June 1969).
Education: *Total school enrollment* (1967)—50,909.
Finance: *Monetary unit,* South Arabian dinar (0.4167 dinar equal U. S.$1).
Economic Indexes (1967): *Cost of living,* 109 (1963 = 100).
Manufacturing (metric tons, 1967): Residual fuel oil, 3,154,-000; distillate fuel oil, 1,179,000; gasoline, 335,000.
Minerals (metric tons, 1967): Salt, 72,000.
Foreign Trade (1968): *Exports,* $110,000,000 (chief exports, 1966: Distillate fuel and residual fuel oils, $35,450,000); *imports,* $203,000,000 (chief imports, 1966: Crude and partly refined petroleum, $92,480,000). *Chief trading partners* (1966): Britain (took 22% of exports, supplied 11% of imports); Japan; Iraq.
Transportation: *Motor vehicles* (1967), 16,800 (automobiles, 13,600); *national airline,* Yemen Airlines.
Communications: *Telephones* (1968): 9,440; *television stations* (1966), 4; *television sets* (1967), 30,000; *radios* (1965), 300,000.

for communism to penetrate the Arabian Peninsula. Southern Yemen's sponsorship of the Popular Front for the Liberation of the Arabian (Persian) Gulf caused concern in Saudi Arabia and among the conservative Arab amirates on the gulf.

In December, Salim Rubai attended the Arab summit conference in Rabat, the final session of which was boycotted by Southern Yemen and three other states favoring stronger measures against Israel.

GEORGE RENTZ
Hoover Institution, Stanford University

SOVIET LITERATURE

Two completely different works attracted the attention of Soviet readers and critics in 1969: *The Poor Avrosimov*, by the popular 45-year-old poet Bulat Okudzhava, and *What Do You Finally Want?* by Vsevolod Kochetov, a 57-year-old novelist and a spokesman of Stalinism in the Communist party.

In his historical narrative, Okudzhava places Colonel Pestel, a leading figure in the noblemen's uprising of 1825, in opposition to Avrosimov, a

KEYSTONE
ANATOLY KUZNETSOV, Soviet novelist, obtained asylum in England and denounced sham trials in Moscow.

young clerk of the Investigation Committee appointed by the czar to prepare the trial of the revolutionaries. Avrosimov is gradually won over by Pestel's personality and his liberal ideas, and goes through a painful moral crisis. In an oblique way the author suggests disturbing comparisons between the past and the present. Despite its inflated and sophisticated style, this is the most interesting novel of 1969, and its original tonality and texture make it unique in current Soviet fiction.

Kochetov, on the other hand, conceives his long novel as a political pamphlet. He denounces the conspiracy by the United States and former Nazis seeking to undermine the Communist regime, and he tells how they try to corrupt Russian youth by exporting "decadent avant-garde art," luscious Negro songstresses, jazz musicians, and spies disguised as students of history and promoters of culture. Kochetov copies many of his protagonists from recognizable models, and does not veil his attacks against living Soviet and Western writers and artists.

Other Fiction. In the spring of 1969 the monthly *Youth* published *Fire*, a novel by Anatoly Kuz-

netsov about the inauguration of a smelting furnace in a provincial town, where the narrator meets his disillusioned and defeated schoolmates. In July, Kuznetsov obtained asylum in England and disclosed in articles and interviews the difficulties created for writers in the USSR by censorship, secret police, and administrative persecution.

At the beginning of November, Alexander Solzhenitsyn, author of *The Cancer Ward* and *The First Circle* (banned in the USSR but best-sellers in the United States and Europe), and probably the most important living Soviet novelist, was expelled from the Union of Russian Writers.

With the exception of *Kubik*, a novelette by the septuagenarian Valentin Katayev, who lately has begun to write psychological tales in an almost surrealistic style, and *The School Show*, an analytical story by Veniamin Kaverin, current fiction continues to be conventional, following the tenets of socialist realism. Critics attacked *Youth in Zheleznodolsk* by Nikolay Voronov since it rejected the stereotype of optimism and described the gloomy conditions of want and misery in a metallurgical center during World War II. *Relatives* by Yuri Bondarev is the story of a history professor who served as an informer against his own sister (accused of "deviations" and sent to a prison camp). The truth is reached after her death.

The first volume of *Their Own Load* by Alexander Putko, gives a light, rather superficial image of life in Moscow in the 1930's, and provides some curious insights into the customs and activities of Soviet journalists. *The Expropriated Zone* by Anatoly Bezuglov and Yuri Klarov, is a typical specimen of the Soviet detective story, vividly told by an inspector of the CID who traces bandits, speculators, and members of a monarchist intrigue. *The Third Circle* by Mark Gorchakov is an unaffected, perhaps naive but refreshing story of love projected against the exotic background of Central Asia.

The Underground Press. As a result of censorship and political pressure, the underground press, mostly mimeographed and called *samizdat* (or "self-publication") assumed large proportions in the Soviet Union. Some of the copies were smuggled over the border and published abroad, usually without the knowledge or consent of the authors. This was the case with Alexander Twardovsky's poem on Stalin, *Kolyma Tales* about prison camps by Varlam Shalamov, and *My Testimony*, also about prison camps, by Anatoly Marchenko (recently rearrested). A separate niche should be reserved for *Only a Year* by Svetlana Alliluyeva, Stalin's daughter, in which she tells of her escape from Russia by way of India.

Nonfiction. Among the many reminiscences of Red Army marshals, the *Memoirs* of Georgy Zhukov is particularly important as an obvious attempt to rehabilitate Stalin. *Biological Science and the Cult of Personality* by Jaures Medvedev reveals how Trofim Lysenko damaged the science of genetics in the USSR and provoked tragic purges of scholars in the late 1930's.

Obituary. Korney Chukovsky, translator of Walt Whitman and other U. S. and English poets, beloved author of poems and stories for children, critic and essayist, died in November at the age of 88.

MARC SLONIM
Sarah Lawrence College Foreign Studies

SOVIET UNION. See UNION OF SOVIET SOCIALIST REPUBLICS.

David Scott, standing in Apollo 9 command module hatch, is viewed from the craft's lunar module.

SPACE EXPLORATION

By far the most spectacular event of 1969 in the exploration of space was the landing of men on the moon—the first time that men had ever set foot on an alien world. As Neil A. Armstrong, commander of the Apollo 11 mission, said as he stepped down onto the lunar surface on July 20, at 10:56 P. M. (Eastern Daylight Time), "That's one small step for a man, one giant leap for mankind." A second successful lunar landing mission was made and a number of other manned flights took place during the year. Meanwhile a program for developing a "space shuttle" was under way. Men again took a close look at the neighboring planets of Venus and Mars, and the United States and the USSR launched important scientific and technological satellites.

MANNED SPACE FLIGHT

Four U. S. astronauts walked on the surface of the moon in 1969: Neil Armstrong and Edwin Aldrin of Apollo 11, and Charles Conrad and Alan Bean of Apollo 12. (For detailed descriptions of these flights, see THE YEAR OF THE MOON, beginning on page 14.) In addition, several other astronauts voyaged to the moon without landing there. The Soviet Union orbited a total of five manned spacecraft in the Soyuz series during the year.

U. S. Apollo Flights. As part of the preparation for the Apollo 11 lunar landing mission, Apollo 9 was launched on March 3 with astronauts James McDivitt, David Scott, and Russell Schweickart aboard. Their earth-orbital mission included exten-

sive performance tests of the lunar module (LM), a rendezvous of the LM with the command and service modules of the Apollo craft, and two hours of extravehicular activity by the LM pilot. To the maximum achievable extent, the rendezvous in earth orbit was made to resemble the kind of rendezvous that would take place in lunar orbit following a lunar landing.

The first five days of the 10-day mission were the busiest. They included LM engine tests and system checkouts, firings of the service module's engine while the command/service module and LM were docked, the hand-over-hand transfer of the LM pilot from his module to the command module and back again, and rendezvous. The major activities during the sixth through the tenth day included landmark-tracking exercises, spacecraft systems exercises, and a multispectral terrain photography experiment for studying earth resources. On March 13 the spacecraft splashed down in the Atlantic Ocean.

The second of the 1969 readiness flights, Apollo 10, was launched on May 18. Astronauts Thomas Stafford, John Young, and Eugene Cernan undertook the eight-day lunar orbital mission. Apollo 10 marked the second manned flight of the LM and the first time that the complete Apollo spacecraft operated in orbit around the moon. The mission closely followed the schedule and trajectory to be used in the Apollo 11 mission, including an eight-hour sequence of LM undocked activity during which the two astronauts in the LM descended to within 9.7

UPI

APOLLO 10 PILOTS Eugene Cernan, Thomas Stafford, and John Young made a lunar-orbital flight in May 1969.

miles (15.6 km) of the lunar surface and later rejoined the command/service module in a circular orbit 60 miles (97 km) above the moon. All other aspects of the mission also duplicated conditions of the lunar landing mission as closely as possible, except that no actual attempt was made to land on the moon's surface.

The Apollo 10 flight was designed simply to provide additional operational experience for the astronauts in their space vehicle, and for the mission support facilities back on earth. Space navigation experience around the moon was another benefit gained from flying a rehearsal mission before making a lunar landing. More knowledge of the lunar potential, or gravitational effect, provided additional refinements of tracking techniques, and the broad landmark-tracking exercises bolstered this knowledge. Apollo 10 returned safely to earth on May 26, splashing down in the Pacific Ocean.

The readiness missions did their job well; the Apollo 11 and 12 lunar landing missions were almost flawless. Years will pass before all the scientific dividends are realized. The 55 pounds (25 kg) of rocks returned by Apollo 11, plus the data

PREPARING TO ENTER SOYUZ 7, cosmonauts Vladislav Volkov and Anatoly Filipchenko pose for cameramen.

TASS FROM SOVFOTO

from the solar wind, laser, and seismometer experiments it established on the moon, are yielding vital information on the sun, earth, moon, and, indeed, the universe as a whole.

Apollo 12, which was launched on November 14, continued the lunar exploration begun in July by the Apollo 11 crew. The Apollo 12 mission expanded on the efforts of the first landing party. Thus, the time spent on the surface of the moon was approximately 10 hours longer than in the previous flight, with the LM crew leaving their spacecraft twice to set up scientific experiments and make geological investigations on the Ocean of Storms. One of the first jobs of the Apollo 12 astronauts on the moon was to deploy the Apollo lunar surface experiments package (ALSEP 1). The instruments of ALSEP 1 are now gathering and relaying long-term scientific and engineering data to earth on the moon's physical and environmental properties. A second objective also was carried out successfully—to retrieve portions of the Surveyor 3 spacecraft that had been exposed to the lunar environment since the unmanned craft soft-landed on the inner slope of a lunar crater on April 20, 1967.

USSR Manned Space Flights. On January 14, cosmonaut Vladimir Shatalov rode his Soyuz 4 spacecraft into orbit, to be followed the next day by Boris Volynov, Alexei Yeliseyev, and Yevgeny Khrunov in Soyuz 5. After the two large spacecraft docked, Khrunov eased out of Soyuz 5 to become, himself, a weightless artificial earth satellite. He was then joined in space by Yeliseyev. The two men spent an hour outside their spacecraft before working their way over to Soyuz 4 and crawling through the hatch to greet Shatalov. The spacecraft then separated and returned to earth with this new deployment of crew members. Soviet officials heralded their achievement as a prerequisite for carrying out such future space operations as the replacement of crews of long-term space stations and the rescue of cosmonauts in distress.

The tests of the Soyuz spacecraft were continued with the launching of Soyuzes 6, 7, and 8 during a 48-hour period starting October 11. The mission of Soyuz 6 was to test the various systems on board the spacecraft, conduct a number of scientific observations, photograph geological features on the earth, explore the physical characteristics of outer space near the earth, carry out medical and biological investigations into the effect of space flight on human organisms, and test various methods of welding metals under the conditions of weightlessness and hard vacuum.

While cosmonauts Georgi Shonin and Valeri Kubasov were conducting these tests in Soyuz 6, Anatoly Filipchenko, Vladislav Volkov, and Viktor Gorbatko in Soyuz 7 were performing maneuvering tests and staging joint navigation observations of the Soyuz 6 and Soyuz 7 spacecraft, observing celestial bodies and the horizon of the earth, determining the luminosity of various stars, and observing the changes in illumination created by the sun as they moved around the earth.

Soyuz 8, which was manned by veteran cosmonauts Vladimir Shatalov and Aleksei Yeliseyev, tested the complex system of simultaneously controlling a group of three maneuvering spacecraft in orbit, with the aim of solving a number of problems associated with future orbital space stations. At no time during their missions did the three spacecraft physically dock.

EARTH SATELLITES AND SPACE PROBES

The United States successfully launched 14 non-military automated earth satellites or space probes in 1969, while the USSR launched 31 satellites or space probes that are believed to be of a nonmilitary nature. The European Space Research Organization (ESRO) continued its flight operations that were begun in 1968 with the launch of the ESRO 1B satellite. In addition, the first satellite of the Federal Republic of Germany, AZUR, was launched.

Planetary Exploration. Four space probes were sent to two different planets in 1969: the Soviet Union launched Veneras 5 and 6 toward Venus, and the United States sent Mariners 6 and 7 on trajectories past Mars.

The Veneras 5 and 6, launched on January 5 and January 10, respectively, were identical spacecraft, each weighing 2,486 pounds (1,227 kg). They entered the atmosphere of Venus on May 16 and 17 and measured its characteristics during their slow descent to the surface. Each descent package was almost spherical, with a diameter of about 3 feet (1 meter) and a weight of 890 pounds (403 kg). The packages carried gas analyzers, a system of temperature and pressure sensors designed for different ranges of measurements, a densitometer for measuring atmospheric density, and photo-elements for measuring light intensities.

The results indicated that the atmosphere of Venus is composed of 93 to 94% carbon dioxide, with the amount of oxygen being less than 0.4%. The amount of nitrogen, together with the inert gases, is between 2 and 5%; the remaining constituents are unidentified. Although the descent packages probably stopped functioning before they reached the surface, the estimated ground-level conditions of 760° F (nearly 405° C) and 60 atmospheres (60 times the air pressure on earth at sea level) should be a reasonable approximation.

On February 24 and March 27, Mariners 6 and 7 were launched from Cape Kennedy, Fla., to pass within about 2,100 miles (3,400 km) of the surface of Mars in late July and early August. The two 900-pound (408-kg) spacecraft were identical, although they performed different missions at the time of the Mars encounters. Mariner 6 examined the equatorial region of Mars, whereas Mariner 7 covered some of the same area but concentrated on the southern hemisphere and a portion of the south polar cap. Two television cameras aboard each spacecraft photographed the disk of Mars during the approach to the planet and the surface during the flyby. Two instruments, an infrared spectrometer and an ultraviolet spectrometer, probed the Martian atmosphere to determine its composition. An infrared radiometer measured surface temperatures on both the light and the dark side of the planet. These experiments were activated at the time of planetary encounter. The mapping cameras took slightly overlapping pictures covering (in total) about 10% of the Martian surface in the two indicated bands of latitude—equatorial and south polar.

The television experiment revealed an extensively cratered surface. Most of the Martian craters were in the range of 30 to 50 miles (50 to 80 km) wide, but some were up to 300 miles (500 km) wide. Sharp surface demarcations observed from earth were found, under higher resolution, to be diffused and discontinuous. The kinds and distribution of the craters showed distinct differences from the craters on the moon, indicating that there are different surface materials or modifying processes on the moon and Mars. The infrared radiometer equipment reported light-side surface temperatures ranging from $-63°$ to $+63°$ F ($-53°$ to $+17°$ C), and dark-side temperatures from $-153°$ to $-63°$ F ($-103°$ to $-53°$ C). Other instruments detected solid carbon dioxide in the atmosphere; small amounts of water ice, atmosphere fog, and carbon monoxide also were observed at all latitudes. No nitrogen and little molecular oxygen was found. (See also ASTRONOMY.)

USSR Lunar Probes. The Soviet Union continued to explore the moon and test its lunar spacecraft systems with the launch of Luna 15 on July 13 and Zond 7 on August 8. Lunar 15 remained in lunar orbit for two days and then, on July 21, probably failed in an attempt to land softly on the surface. It was a new kind of spacecraft, designed to land on many areas of the moon's surface to study its composition and take photographs. Zond 7 was programmed to study the lunar space environment, photograph the moon's surface, and test improved rocket and spacecraft systems. After completing a circumlunar flight, Zond 7 returned to earth and was recovered successfully near the city of Kustanai in northern Kazakhstan.

Space Physics and Environment Studies. The U. S. Orbiting Solar Observatories (OSO's) 5 and 6 were launched on January 22 and August 11 to continue to study the physics of the sun. Understanding the mechanics of the sun is of vital importance not only to science but to all mankind as well, since the sun sustains life on earth. The instruments carried by the OSO satellites were designed to study evolutionary changes in various features of the sun, with special emphasis on solar active regions (such as sunspots and prominences). The primary objective of the eight experiments placed on OSO 5 was to obtain high spectral resolution data (within the range of about 1 angstrom to 1,250 angstroms) during solar rotation, including scans of the sun's disk in selected wavelengths. A new feature of OSO 6 was that, for the first time in the program, an OSO was given the capability of studying in detail the ultraviolet and X-ray spectrum at any point on the solar disk.

The Canadian-built ISIS 1 was launched on January 30 to continue the joint Canadian-United States program of ionospheric research. ISIS 1 was the third Canadian ionospheric satellite and the second of five satellites in the cooperative effort. The 532-pound (239-kg) satellite carries five Canadian and five U. S. experiments. These satellites are providing the information on the nature and behavior of the ionosphere that is needed to improve long-range radio transmissions.

The last of the U. S. Orbiting Geophysical Observatories, OGO 6, was launched on June 5. The 25 experiments aboard OGO 6 are investigating latitude-dependent atmospheric phenomena during a period of maximum solar activity. They study atmospheric and neutron densities; electron density and temperatures; electrons trapped in the Van Allen belts; neutral atmospheric composition; ion concentration and mass; auroral particles and auroral and airglow emissions; magnetic and electric fields; very low frequency radio emissions; solar ultraviolet, solar cosmic, and solar X-rays; and galactic cosmic rays.

The seventh spacecraft in the U. S. Interplanetary Monitory Platform (IMP) series was launched

SUCCESSFUL NONMILITARY EARTH SATELLITES AND SPACE PROBES, 1969

Name	Launch site and date[1]	Launch vehicle[2]	Spacecraft weight at lift-off (pounds)[3]	Apsides of orbit (miles)[4]	Initial period (minutes)	Inclination of orbit (degrees)	Remarks[5]
Venera 5	T, Jan. 5	N.A.	2,486	Trajectory to Venus			Reached Venus May 16
Venera 6	T, Jan. 10	N.A.	2,486	Trajectory to Venus			Reached Venus May 17
Cosmos 263	P, Jan. 12	N.A.	N.A.[6]	127-215	89.8	64.4	Unannounced payload
Soyuz 4	T, Jan. 14	N.A.	14,000	107-140	88.25	51.4	Manned space flight
Soyuz 5	T, Jan. 15	N.A.	14,000	124-143	88.7	51.4	Manned space flight
OSO 5	K, Jan. 22	T-D	641	333-349	95.6	32.9	Solar radiation monitor
Cosmos 264	T, Jan. 23	N.A.	N.A.	136-205	89.7	70.0	Unannounced payload
ISIS 1	V, Jan. 30	T-D	532	356-2,184	128.3	88.5	Ionospheric studies
INTELSAT 3 F-3	K, Feb. 5	LT-D	642	22,215-22,235	1435.8	1.29	Communications satellite
Cosmos 265	P, Feb. 7	N.A.	N.A.	176-301	91.9	71.0	Unannounced payload
Mariner 6	K, Feb. 24	A-C	910	Trajectory to Mars			Flew past Mars July 31
Cosmos 266	P, Feb. 25	N.A.	N.A.	129-222	89.9	72.9	Unannounced payload
ESSA 9	K, Feb. 26	T-D	320	883-943	115	102.0	Meteorological satellite
Cosmos 267	T, Feb. 26	N.A.	N.A.	130-215	89.9	65.0	Unannounced payload
Apollo 9	K, Mar. 3	Sn 5	291,500	118-120	89.4	33.6	Manned space flight
Cosmos 268	KY, Mar. 5	N.A.	N.A.	136-1,358	109.2	48.4	Unannounced payload
Cosmos 269	P, Mar. 5	N.A.	N.A.	327-347	95.3	74.0	Unannounced payload
Cosmos 270	P, Mar. 6	N.A.	N.A.	127-217	89.8	65.4	Unannounced payload
Cosmos 271	P, Mar. 15	N.A.	N.A.	124-213	89.7	65.4	Unannounced payload
Cosmos 272	P, Mar. 18	N.A.	N.A.	743-758	109.4	74.0	Navigation and geodetic satellite
Cosmos 273	P, Mar. 22	N.A.	N.A.	127-221	89.9	65.4	Unannounced payload
Cosmos 274	B, Mar. 24	N.A.	N.A.	132-200	89.6	65.0	Unannounced payload
Meteor 1	P, Mar. 26	N.A.	N.A.	400-443	97.9	81.2	Meteorological payload
Mariner 7	K, Mar. 27	A.C.	910	Trajectory to Mars			Flew past Mars August 5
Cosmos 275	P, Mar. 28	N.A.	N.A.	177-500	95.2	71.0	Solar radiation monitor
Cosmos 276	P, Apr. 4	N.A.	N.A.	133-255	90.4	81.4	Unannounced payload
Cosmos 277	P, Apr. 4	N.A.	N.A.	174-307	92.0	71.0	Solar radiation monitor
Cosmos 278	B, Apr. 9	N.A.	N.A.	126-210	89.7	65.0	Unannounced payload
Molinya 1K	B, Apr. 9	N.A.	N.A.	292-24,669	713	65.0	Communications satellite
Nimbus 3	V, Apr. 14	T-G	1,260	676-703	107.4	99.9	Meteorological satellite
Cosmos 279	P, Apr. 15	N.A.	N.A.	121-174	89.1	51.8	Unannounced payload
Cosmos 280	B, Apr. 23	N.A.	N.A.	128-147	89.1	51.6	Spacecraft test
Cosmos 281	P, May 13	N.A.	N.A.	121-147	89.4	65.4	Unannounced payload
Apollo 10	K, May 18	Sn 5	139,369[7]	Trajectory to moon			Manned lunar orbital mission
Cosmos 282	P, May 20	N.A.	N.A.	130-213	89.8	65.4	Unannounced payload
INTELSAT 3 F-4	K, May 22	LT-D	642	173-22,787	265.0	28.5	Communications satellite
Cosmos 283	P, May 27	N.A.	N.A.	131-956	102.1	82.0	Solar radiation monitor
Cosmos 284	B, May 29	N.A.	N.A.	129-191	89.5	51.8	Unannounced payload
Cosmos 285	P, June 3	N.A.	N.A.	173-322	92.2	71.0	Solar radiation monitor
OGO G	V, June 5	T-G	1,400	248-683	100.0	82.0	Particle and field studies
Cosmos 286	P, June 15	N.A.	N.A.	128-217	89.8	65.4	Unannounced payload
Explorer 41	V, June 21	T-D	174	241-132,800	4840.0	83.7	Particles and fields monitor
Cosmos 287	B, June 24	N.A.	N.A.	118-166	89.0	51.8	Unannounced payload
Cosmos 288	B, June 27/28	N.A.	N.A.	125-175	89.2	51.8	Unannounced payload
Biosat 3	K, June 29	LT-D	1485	221-241	92.0	33.5	Biological satellite
Cosmos 289	P, July 10	N.A.	N.A.	124-217	89.8	65.4	Unannounced payload
Luna 15	K, July 13	N.A.	N.A.	Trajectory to moon			Lunar probe
Apollo 11	K, July 16	Sn 5	139,369[7]	Trajectory to moon			Manned lunar landing
Cosmos 290	P, July 22	N.A.	N.A.	124-218	89.8	65.4	Unannounced payload
Molinya 1L	B, July 22	N.A.	N.A.	323-24,570	711.0	64.9	Communications satellite
Cosmos 291	B, Aug. 6	N.A.	N.A.	95-357	91.5	62.3	Spacecraft test
Zond 7	B, Aug. 8	N.A.	N.A.	Trajectory to moon			Lunar probe
OSO 6	K, Aug. 11	LT-D	640	305-344	95.1	32.9	Solar radiation monitor
Cosmos 292	P, Aug. 14	N.A.	N.A.	464-488	99.9	74.0	Navigation and geodetic satellite
Cosmos 293	B, Aug. 16	N.A.	N.A.	130-167	89.1	51.8	Unannounced payload
Cosmos 294	P, Aug. 19	N.A.	N.A.	125-216	89.8	65.4	Unannounced payload
Cosmos 295	P, Aug. 22	N.A.	N.A.	175-310	92.0	71.0	Solar radiation monitor
Cosmos 296	B, Aug. 29	N.A.	N.A.	131-200	89.6	65.0	Unannounced payload
Cosmos 297	P, Sept. 2	N.A.	N.A.	131-208	89.7	72.9	Unannounced payload
Cosmos 298	B, Sept. 15	N.A.	N.A.	87-131	87.3	50.0	Reentry test
Cosmos 299	B, Sept. 18	N.A.	N.A.	132-193	89.5	65.0	Unannounced payload
Cosmos 300	B, Sept. 23	N.A.	N.A.	118-129	88.2	51.5	Spacecraft tests
Cosmos 301	P, Sept. 24	N.A.	N.A.	122-190	89.4	65.4	Unannounced payload
ESRO 1B	V, Oct. 1	S	176	181-237	91.2	85.1	Ionospheric studies
Meteor 2	P, Oct. 6	N.A.	N.A.	391-428	97.7	81.2	Meteorological satellite
Soyuz 6	B, Oct. 11	N.A.	14,000	115-139	88.4	51.7	Manned space flight
Soyuz 7	B, Oct. 12	N.A.	14,000	128-140	88.6	51.7	Manned space flight
Soyuz 8	B, Oct. 13	N.A.	14,000	128-139	88.6	51.9	Manned space flight
Intercosmos 1	KY, Oct. 14	N.A.	N.A.	161-397	93.3	48.4	Radiation studies
Cosmos 302	P, Oct. 17	N.A.	N.A.	125-211	89.7	65.4	Unannounced payload
Cosmos 303	P, Oct. 18	N.A.	N.A.	175-305	92.0	71.0	Solar radiation monitor
Cosmos 304	P, Oct. 21	N.A.	N.A.	465-478	99.9	74.0	Navigation and geodetic satellite
Cosmos 305	B, Oct. 22	N.A.	N.A.	119-127	88.4	51.5	Spacecraft test
Cosmos 306	B, Oct. 24	N.A.	N.A.	129-206	98.7	65.0	Unannounced payload
Cosmos 307	KY, Oct. 24	N.A.	N.A.	136-1353	103	48.4	Geo-astrophysical studies
Cosmos 308	P, Nov. 4	N.A.	N.A.	174-262	91	71.0	Unannounced payload
Azur	V, Nov. 8	S	157	248-1923	122	103.0	Radiation belt & aurorae studies
Cosmos 309	P, Nov. 11	N.A.	N.A.	126-238	90.1	65.4	Unannounced payload
Apollo 12	K, Nov. 14	Sn 5	139,369[7]	Trajectory to Moon			Manned lunar landing
Cosmos 310	B, Nov. 15	N.A.	N.A.	129-216	89.8	65.0	Unannounced payload
Cosmos 311	P, Nov. 24	N.A.	N.A.	177-308	92	71.0	Solar radiation monitor
Cosmos 312	P, Nov. 24	N.A.	N.A.	712-738	108.6	74.0	Navigation and geodetic satellite
Cosmos 313	P, Dec. 3	N.A.	N.A.	128-172	89.1	65.4	Unannounced payload
Cosmos 314	P, Dec. 11	N.A.	N.A.	175-305	91.9	71.0	Unannounced payload
Cosmos 315	P, Dec. 20	N.A.	N.A.	323-345	95.3	74.0	Unannounced payload
Cosmos 316	B, Dec. 23	N.A.	N.A.	96-1025	102.7	49.5	Unannounced payload
Cosmos 317	P, Dec. 23	N.A.	N.A.	130-188	89.4	65.4	Unannounced payload
Intercosmos 2	KY, Dec. 25	N.A.	N.A.	128-746	98.5	48.4	Radiation studies

[1] Code for launch sites: K—Cape Kennedy, Fla.; V—Vandenberg AFB (Western Test Range), Calif.; W—Wallops Island, Va.; B—Baikonur, USSR; KY—Kapustin Yar, USSR; P—Plesetsk, USSR; T—Tyuratam, USSR. [2] Launch vehicles: A-A, Atlas-Agena; A-C, Atlas-Centaur; T-D, Thrust Augmented Thor-Delta; LT-D, Long Tank Thrust Augmented Thor–Delta; S, Scout; Sn 5, Saturn 5; T-G, Thorad–Agena. [3] 1 pound equals 0.45 kg. [4] 1 mile equals 1.61 km. [5] Purpose of USSR spacecraft in many cases is unknown. [6] N.A.—Not available. [7] At translunar injection.

as Explorer 41 on June 21. The 174-pound (78.9-kg) spacecraft is in a highly elliptical orbit reaching about halfway to the orbit of the moon. It carries 12 individual experiments designed to study solar plasma, magnetic fields, and cosmic rays. The IMP series has provided the first accurate measurements of the interplanetary magnetic field, the magnetosphere boundary, and the so-called collisionless magnetohydrodynamic shock wave associated with the interaction of the solar wind and the earth's magnetic field.

On October 1, the ESRO 1B satellite was launched to study the polar ionosphere, the auroral displays, and related phenomena. The 176-pound (79.8-kg) satellite, designed and built in Europe, is the fourth in a cooperative program between the European Space Research Organization and the United States.

AZUR, the first satellite in a cooperative space program between the Federal Republic of Germany and the United States, was launched on November 8. The 157-pound (71.2-kg), German-built satellite carries seven scientific experiments designed to study the earth's radiation belt, the aurorae, and solar particle events in the atmosphere. Special emphasis is being placed on measuring the intensity and distribution of protons and electrons in terms of time and location.

The Soviet Union launched several satellites, under the general Cosmos designation, that were designed to study the radiation environment of the earth. They also orbited their second and third spacecraft—Intercosmos 1 and 2—in the "Intercosmos" series. These satellites contained instruments built by the Soviet Union, Czechoslovakia, and East Germany for the study of solar radiation, and the program was directed by a group of specialists from these three countries. Other countries participating in the scientific effort include Bulgaria, Hungary, and Rumania.

Space Biology. The U. S. Biosatellite 3, carrying a pig-tailed monkey, was launched on June 28. Its mission was to orbit the earth for a month at an altitude of about 230 miles (370 km). Three areas of investigation were planned: a study of the interrelationship of several factors bearing on central nervous system function, a study of the effects of weightlessness on the mechanical functioning of the circulatory system, and a study of the effects of weightlessness on body chemistry. After eight and a half days in orbit, however, the monkey's condition deteriorated and the satellite was returned to earth. Twelve hours after the recovery of Biosatellite 3, the monkey died of heart failure. Its death was linked to the effects of weightlessness.

Applications Satellites. Three communications satellites, each capable of supplying 1,200 two-way voice channels, were launched for the Communications Satellite Corporation, Comsat, on behalf of the 68 countries of the International Telecommunications Satellite Consortium, of which Comsat is the U. S. representative. INTELSATS 3 F-3, F-4, and F-5 were orbited on February 5, May 22, and August 25. However, because of a launch vehicle malfunction, F-5 failed to achieve a useful orbit.

Environmental Survey Satellite (ESSA) 9 was launched on February 26 for the Environmental Science Services Administration, to provide global cloud pictures for use in weather prediction through the ESSA ground stations at Gilmore Creek, Alaska,

and Wallops Island, Va. As with ESSA's 3, 5, and 7, it also contains an array of atmospheric radiation sensors to gather information for research on the earth's heat balance.

The Nimbus 3 experimental weather satellite was orbited on April 14, carrying advanced experiments that scientists hope ultimately will lead to reliable long-range weather forecasting. The 1,200-pound (540-kg) observatory—the heaviest weather satellite launched to date by the United States—carries seven meteorological experiments. It is the first weather satellite to provide radiometric data for determination of the vertical profiles of temperature and water vapor, needed for numerical weather prediction. The temperature data obtained compared favorably with that supplied by local radiosondes. Other instruments on Nimbus 3 provided information on the worldwide distribution of water vapor, carbon dioxide, and stratospheric temperatures.

On August 12, Applications Technology Satellite (ATS) 5 was launched to conduct gravity-gradient stabilization tests, L-band communications tests, and air traffic control experiments. However, because of a malfunction in the spacecraft, only a few of the planned experiments could be conducted.

The Soviet Union launched two communications satellites, Molniyas 1K and 1L, on April 11 and July 22, as part of its orbital communications network. Two meteorological satellites, Meteors 1 and 2, were launched on March 26 and October 6, marking the first time that the Soviet Union did not give a Cosmos designation to their meteorological satellites. The Soviet Union also launched what are believed to be several navigation/geodetic satellites under the Cosmos designation.

PITT G. THOME
National Aeronautics and Space Administration

ADVANCES IN SPACE TECHNOLOGY

Remarkable evidence of the capabilities of U. S. rocket technology was provided in 1969, when two successive Apollo flights landed men on the moon. The Saturn 5 vehicle of the Apollo program demonstrated its high efficiency and reliability, its operational behavior falling within 0.5% of that predicted. New programs in the areas of military and civilian rocketry also were begun or improved in 1969, and work continued on the development of advanced propulsion systems.

U. S. Military Programs. The cancellation of the Air Force's Manned Orbiting Laboratory (MOL) program represented a setback to the further development of the Titan 3 rocket system. However, the Air Force continued improvement studies of the rocket and its variants. A better guidance system was devised to permit precision injection into synchronous and polar orbits, with a view to the future launching of advanced communications and meteorological satellites weighing several tons.

Development, on a low level, also continued on recoverable rockets—that is, on rocket stages that can be returned to earth using wings or parachutes. In this area the Air Force is collaborating with the National Aeronautics and Space Administration (NASA), at least in research and development.

The Department of Defense (DOD) has suggested, in occasional news releases, that an advanced intercontinental ballistic missile (ICBM) system is being considered for development, and that a concurrent improvement in the technology of rocket motors using solid propellants is being supported.

Another development—that of an antiballistic missile (ABM) system—would mean a major step forward in this area of technology, since such rockets are capable of the quick ignition and immediate launch needed in an ABM system.

Continued Navy tests of the Poseidon solid-propellant, submarine-launched rocket showed that it is ready for operational use, and the submarine fleet is being outfitted with the missile. The Navy also continued to develop rockets powered by storable liquid propellants, for shipboard use. Such rockets have a greater efficiency than solid-propellant rockets, are more compact, and in many cases can withstand a wider variety of temperature, humidity, and vibration conditions. (See also AIR FORCE; DEFENSE FORCES; MISSILES.)

NASA Programs. NASA is strenuously planning new programs for the 1970's, along with six or eight more Apollo lunar missions. The most important new concept is that of the "space shuttle," capable of being launched into orbit and making a controlled return to the earth's surface. NASA has considered this concept for a long time. Now, since Vice President Spiro T. Agnew has stated that a manned landing on Mars might be a desirable goal for the United States, and since the special task force on space technology has concluded that a manned Mars landing is feasible—it did not say desirable—NASA has accelerated its studies of the techniques needed to construct a space shuttle.

Although many configurations for a shuttle have been proposed, present plans call for a vehicle with perhaps two F-1 Apollo-type kerosine/oxygen engines (or six Apollo-type J-2 hydrogen/oxygen engines) in its aft end. Several prototype models have already been built and exhibited by NASA. The body shape looks much like that of a supersonic transport (SST), and the vehicle would be made of titanium or stainless steel; at present there is no plan to add air-breathing engines such as jet engines. The shuttle would carry its payload into space and then remain in a suborbital mode for about an hour before returning to an appropriate landing site on earth, its power being kept off except during the final approach to an airfield. If NASA obtains the necessary funds, the design of a space shuttle vehicle could begin in 1970 and construction of a prototype by 1972 or 1973.

Smaller NASA launch vehicles continue to produce reasonably good results in orbiting foreign satellites. The workhorse of these vehicles is the Thor-Delta, whose upper two stages are derived from the original Vanguard rocket and whose lower stage is a modified Thor kerosine/oxygen booster. Unfortunately, the Delta malfunctioned twice in 1969; a communications and a scientific satellite were lost as a result. However, an intensive improvement effort apparently has solved these structural and engine difficulties, and the Delta improvement program continues. The rocket's structure has been made lighter and stronger, the main-stage thrust has been increased by 10%, and the guidance system has been modified.

Solid- and Liquid-Propellant Systems. Interest in the air-breathing rocket has been revived at NASA. This propulsion device is essentially a rocket thrust chamber with a ring-shaped duct. As the rocket moves through the atmosphere, it heats the air rammed through the duct, adding energy that otherwise would be lost in the exhaust system. An augmentation of the thrust and hence of propulsion efficiency is achieved thereby. NASA at one time had planned such a rocket system for suborbital or low-orbit launch vehicles, and the air-breathing rocket has also been proposed for the shuttle system described above. However, at present there is no firm plan for using such specialized rocket devices; if they are to be applied at all, it would probably be with some special system of the Defense Department.

Considerable improvements were made in 1969 in the use of lithium, beryllium, and boron additives in solid propellants. The advanced solid-propellant grains now available—although not yet operationally ready—can achieve total propulsion efficiency comparable to the best liquid-propellant systems. Beryllium, especially, has remarkable potential for increasing combustion efficiency, even though its poisonous nature and the relative difficulty of dispersing it among the solid grains have prevented its operational use thus far.

The Aerojet Corporation has closed its Florida facility for the production of large, solid booster units, 260 inches (660 cm) in diameter. However, the company continues to do scale testing and evaluation of such units, with some support from NASA. (If a manned Mars landing is decided on, such giant solid boosters may prove to be a relatively inexpensive means for achieving this goal.) In addition, other companies are evaluating new materials for producing booster units, including such ceramics as beryllia (an oxide of beryllium). When properly sintered—a difficult task—this remarkable ceramic material has proven to be one of the most promising materials for lining high-temperature combustion chambers, such as occur in a rocket, or in certain kinds of jet engines.

Nuclear Rockets. Beryllia also may prove to be a mainstay for applications in the nuclear rocket program, whose funding, despite setbacks and threats of cancellation, has been continued. This program must draw on all available technical advances if the great propulsion potential of the scheme is to be realized.

Static firings of the thrust chamber of the hydrogen-fueled nuclear rocket in Nevada have continued almost on a routine basis. One possible use of such a rocket is in a major mission to Mars; calculations show that unless an impossibly large earth-based launch vehicle for a Mars mission were contemplated, a nuclear upper stage (or stages) would be required for the mission. There is little doubt that an operational turbopump nuclear rocket system could be ready by the early 1970's This is a more optimistic view than has been held in the past by NASA, and it has resulted from the encouraging progress made in the past year.

Electric Propulsion Systems. At NASA's Lewis Research Center, progress was made toward building an electric propulsion package prototype that could be coupled with a deep-space vehicle for interplanetary flights even beyond Jupiter. Several thousand hours of test time have been achieved with ion-electric thrusters using ionized vapors of cesium or mercury as the working fluids. The electric propulsor is approaching operational readiness; within a year or so NASA will have to decide where such propulsors can be applied, if the technology is not to languish.

KURT R. STEHLING
Aerospace Consultant
Executive Office of the President

SPAIN

Student disorders in Spain in the winter of 1968–69 caused the government of Chief of State Francisco Franco to declare a "state of exception" that lasted from January until March. In July, Franco named Prince Juan Carlos, son of the pretender to the Spanish throne, to be his legal successor. Cabinet changes in October gave control of the government to members of the Opus Dei, a Roman Catholic organization.

In foreign policy, the Spanish government attempted to strengthen relations with the United States and Western Europe.

State of Exception. Demonstrations occurred in which classrooms were occupied, the Spanish flag was burned, and threats were made to throw the rector of the University of Barcelona out the window. During the state of exception, which began on January 24, the government suspended five articles of the constitution, to enable it to meet opposition. The police were endowed with almost unlimited power, and censorship of the press was restored. On January 25 the police began to arrest students, workers, and others suspected of illegal activity. The emergency powers remained in force until the latter part of March, when some cabinet ministers expressed fear that the strong measure would endanger foreign policy objectives.

The only sustained resistance to the state of exception occurred in Bilbao, where strikes closed three plants and 19,000 workers were involved.

Carlist Demonstration. On May 4, 10,000 persons in the Carlist stronghold of Estella staged an annual demonstration of hostility to the regime. The Carlists support the claims of 79-year-old Prince Xavier of Bourbon-Parma and his 38-year-old son, Prince Carlos Hugo, to the Spanish throne. The two princes were expelled from Spain in December 1968 for their "excessive" political activity.

Succession. The Spanish Cortes (parliament), on July 23, approved the law proclaiming Prince Juan Carlos as Franco's heir. The designation of Juan Carlos reportedly embittered his father, Don Juan, Count of Barcelona, who was passed over in favor of his son because his views are unacceptable to Franco. Juan Carlos has been trained and educated under the generalissimo's supervision.

In announcing the selection of the prince, Franco did not indicate when he would retire, but guaranteed the "unity and permanence of the National Movement's principles." At his formal investiture as the future king of Spain, the prince took an oath of loyalty to the principles of the Franco regime.

Franco, who celebrated his 77th birthday on December 4, seemed gradually to be relinquishing the burdens of his office to Prince Juan Carlos and Vice President Luis Carrero Blanco. The vice president presided at regular cabinet meetings each Wednesday and submitted decisions for the official approval of the chief of state.

Opus Dei Cabinet. Franco further clarified the lines of succession with a major cabinet change on October 28. The cabinet change showed that Franco has apparently abandoned his policy of exerting power through shifting coalitions, since it gave virtually complete control of the government to the Opus Dei faction.

The Opus Dei is an association of Roman Catholic laymen and priests whose purpose is to bring religious practice into the daily life of its members. Opus Dei members have gradually occupied a growing number of key political, economic, and educational positions in Spain.

In the cabinet shift, Franco retained his position as president of the government. Vice President Luis Carrero Blanco and Laureano López Rodó, minister of planning, kept their positions but with added prestige. The principal advocate of the change was López Rodó, a member of the Opus Dei. Associates of López Rodó received key cabinet posts, while his opponents were ousted. Three of the ministers were members of the Opus Dei, a fourth was an auxiliary member, and all but six of the 15 others were close associates of López Rodó.

The Opus Dei faction has been especially antagonistic toward the Falangists, who formerly dominated the Spanish government under Franco. Several hundred young Falangists protested the cabinet change because they believed it showed Franco's betrayal of the ideas of the National Movement.

New Laws. The government on July 3 approved regulations which permitted political associations in Spain for the first time since the civil war in 1936–39. The assocations, however, will be strictly controlled within the National Movement. In October the government issued a new law which allowed it to continue to control labor union activities.

Details of a law to change the Spanish educational system for the first time since 1857 were announced on October 11. The law guaranteed free primary education and scholarships for those quali-

---

SPAIN • Information Highlights

Area: 194,883 square miles (504,750 sq km).
Population: 32,411,000 (1968 est.).
Chief Cities (1965 census): Madrid, the capital, 2,599,330; Barcelona, 1,696,756; Valencia, 501,795; Seville, 474,082.
Government: *President*—Gen. Francisco Franco (officially assumed power Aug. 4, 1939); *Vice President*—Luis Carrero Blanco (took office Sept. 22, 1967). *Parliament* (unicameral)—Cortes, 564 members.
Religious Faiths: Roman Catholics, 75% of population; others, 25%.
Education: *Literacy rate* (1969), 91% of population. *Total school enrollment* (1965)—4,634,905 (primary, 3,357,813; secondary, 800,380; teacher-training, 64,316; vocational, 292,071; higher, 120,325).
Finance: *Budget* (1968 est.), $3,396,000,000; *public debt* (1966), $2,952,000,000; *monetary unit*, peseta (69.83 pesetas equal U. S.$1).
Gross National Product (1968): $25,375,912,900.
National Income (1968): $21,666,905,300; *average income per person*, $668.
Economic Indexes (1967): *Industrial production* (1968), 163 (1963=100); *agricultural production*, 102 (1963=100); *cost of living*, 137 (1963=100).
Manufacturing (metric tons, 1967): Cement, 13,117,000; crude steel, 4,335,000; wheat flour, 3,400,000; gasoline, 2,236,000; wine, 23,578,000 hectoliters.
Crops (metric tons, 1967–68 crop year): Grapes, 3,630,000 (ranks 3d among world producers); citrus fruit (1966), 2,267,000 (world rank, 3d); tomatoes, 1,216,000 (world rank, 6th) wheat, 5,654,000; potatoes, 4,490,000; sugar beets, 4,287,000.
Minerals (metric tons, 1967): Mercury (1966), 78,002 76-lb flasks (ranks 1st among world producers); coal, 12,648,000; iron ore, 5,196,000; lignite, 2,652,000; fluorspar (1966), 239,501.
Foreign Trade (1968): *Exports*, $1,589,000,000 (chief exports, 1967: citrus fruit, $121,500,700; olive oil, $53,091,700; textile yarn and fabrics, $32,145,200); *imports*, $3,502,000,000 (chief imports, 1967: nonelectrical machinery, $565,931,500; crude petroleum, $312,927,100; iron and steel, $163,101,800). *Chief trading partners* (1967): United States (took 17.6% of exports, supplied 16.8% of imports); West Germany; France.
Transportation: *Roads* (1967), 82,025 miles (132,003 km); *motor vehicles* (1967), 1,863,800 (automobiles 1,301,900); *railways* (1966), 11,395 miles (18,335 km); *merchant vessels* (1967), 361; *national airline*, Iberia; *principal airports*, Barcelona, Madrid.
Communications: *Telephones* (1968), 3,378,865; *television stations* (1966), 271; *television sets* (1968), 2,350,000; *radios* (1967), 7,150,000; *newspapers* (1967), 118 (daily circulation, 5,100,000).

fied for higher education. The universities, often centers of disorder, were given greater autonomy.

Export Credit Scandal. A major political scandal was revealed on September 26, when Juan Vila Reyes resigned as president of Matesa, a Barcelona textile-machinery export company. Matesa held the patent to a shuttleless loom and received $140 million in export credits, largely for loom sales that had never been made. The scandal was not only unfavorable to the Spanish export credit program but also raised grave questions about the honesty and efficiency of the official financial administration. The affair provoked new attacks on the Opus Dei faction in the government.

PRINCE JUAN CARLOS, named by Francisco Franco (seated) on July 22 as the future ruler of Spain, affirms loyalty to Franco in his acceptance speech.

KEYSTONE

Economy. Foreign trade flourished, although Spain had an unfavorable balance of trade in 1969. The United States supplied 16.8% of the $3.5 billion imports in 1968 and bought 17.6% of the $1.5 billion exports. About $700 million of the total foreign investment of $1.7 billion came from the United States.

Industry developed rapidly, and the gross national product increased from $23.1 billion in 1967 to more than $25 billion in 1968. Agriculture employed 25% of the labor force and supplied 40% of Spain's exports. It was still hampered, however, by a lack of modern equipment and limited application of modern farming methods.

Spain attracted 19.2 million visitors in 1968, and tourism brought the country $1.2 billion.

Foreign Relations. In 1969 the Spanish government took steps to maintain closer relations with the United States and the countries of Western Europe. Foreign Minister Gregorio López Bravo had long been an advocate of closer economic cooperation with these nations.

Spain and the United States in June signed an agreement allowing the United States to continue using its military bases in Spain for another two years. The United States will keep control of a Polaris nuclear submarine base at Rota, near Cadiz; three air bases; a fuel oil pipeline; and communications facilities. In return, the United States granted Spain $50 million in arms, including F-104 fighter interceptors for the "common defense" of the Western Mediterranean. Credits of $35 million were granted Spain for additional arms purchases. On June 25, under a second agreement, the United States was given a 10-year extension for use of a space-tracking station near Madrid.

Prince Juan Carlos on December 6 made a semi-official visit to Brussels, Belgium. He sought to emphasize the desire of the Spanish government for closer links with other nations on the continent. At the same time, Spain inaugurated consular relations with Poland, to strengthen its ties to eastern Europe. Spain had previously established relations with Rumania.

International Problems. The extensive and heated dispute over Gibraltar continued to plague relations between Spain and Britain. The British issued a new constitution for Gibraltar on May 30. In retaliation the Spanish government closed the frontier with Gibraltar at midnight on June 8, thereby barring the passage of some 4,800 Spanish

JUAN CARLOS DE BORBÓN Y BORBÓN was formally invested as prince of Spain on July 23, 1969, the day after Generalissimo Francisco Franco named him as his legal successor. Juan Carlos pledged his loyalty to Franco but also declared sympathy with the young in their hope for "a better and more genuine world." His claim to the throne is contested by his father, Don Juan de Borbón y Battenberg, Count of Barcelona.

Juan Carlos is the grandson of Alfonso XIII, the last king of Spain, who abdicated in 1931. Juan Carlos was born on Jan. 5, 1938, in Rome, where his family was living in exile. In 1947, at the urging of Franco, he was brought to Spain for his education. As part of his apprenticeship, Juan Carlos has served in various departments of the Spanish government. In 1962 he married Princess Sophia of Greece, and they have three children.

laborers to Gibraltar. The Spaniards contended that the British had defied a United Nations resolution providing for the return of Gibraltar to Spain by October 1. When the deadline expired without the colony being restored, the Spanish government applied additional pressure on Britain by terminating telephone and cable service with Gibraltar.

Some 2,500 members of a Portuguese group known as "The Friends of Olivenza" exerted pressure on the Spanish government for the return of Olivenza, a frontier town in the province of Badajor, which had belonged to Portugal until 1801. The Portuguese government, however, did not press the issue.

On May 13, Spain and Morocco ratified a treaty returning the Spanish enclave of Ifni to Morocco. Spain had occupied the 760 square mile (1,968 sq km) tract of desert since 1860. Ifni was formally returned to Morocco on June 30. But this still left unsettled the problem of Moroccan claims to Ceuta and Melilla, occupied as garrison towns by Spain since the 15th century.

Tensions also arose in 1969 between Spain and Equatorial Guinea, a former Spanish colony that was granted independence on Oct. 12, 1968. Both Equatorial Guinea and Spain appealed to U. N. Secretary General U Thant for assistance in ending the dispute. But the Spanish interest was primarily restricted to assuring the safety of the 8,000 Europeans in the country. (See EQUATORIAL GUINEA.)

RHEA MARSH SMITH
Rollins College

SPANISH LITERATURE

The promise of unrestricted expression for Spanish writers has yet to materialize fully (witness the publication of Francisco Ayala's *Obras narrativas completas* in Mexico rather than Spain), a fact that undoubtedly retards the full impact of contemporary Spanish literature within the Western world. In effect, despite some works of exceptional quality in 1969, Spanish literature remained below previous standards and present potential. Again, as could be predicted under the circumstances, lyrical poetry made up the outstanding contribution to Spanish literature.

Fiction. No major novel appeared in 1969, but an impressive list of quality works expressed the measure of Spain's literary potential. Among them were the winners of the major prizes. The Nadal prize was awarded to Alvaro Cunqueiro for *Un hombre que se parecía a Orestes,* a work reflecting the contemporary vogue of the classical world in novelistic fiction, but otherwise quite conservative in stylistic and thematic development. The Alfaguara prize went to Daniel Sueiro for *Corte de corteza,* realistically drawn from the present but actually set 15 years hence (when brain transplants may be a working possibility) in the United States.

Other novelists receiving special awards were Juan Benet, awarded the Biblioteca Breve prize for *Una meditación;* Raul Torres, awarded the Café Gijón prize for his *Equipaje de sol y vino;* and veteran novelist Ana María Matute, whom the Spanish Royal Academy distinguished with its Fastenrath prize for her *Los soldados lloran de noche.*

Alfonso Martinez Mena's *Conozco tu vida, John,* all interior monologue, Manuel Pombo Angulo's *La sombra de las banderas,* which touches on the Spanish Civil War, and Carlos Puente's *El nuevo*

silencio, on the theme of infidelity, are typical of other novels published during 1969.

Surprisingly, short-story collections surpassed novelistic production in quality. This new importance—which reflects the reading needs of a rapidly modernized Spain—was evident in such publications as Miguel Delibes' *Viejas historias de Castilla la Vieja,* on the author's favorite subjects, hunting and Castile; Ignacio Aldecoa's *Santa Olaja de acero y otras historias,* and especially Juan Antonio Gaya Nuño's *Los gatos salvajes,* which focuses on the loyalist side of the Spanish Civil War. Other important collections were Luis Olmo's *Golfos de bien* and Baltasar Porcel's *Las sombras chinescas.*

Nonfiction. Some important scholarly publications during 1969 were Francisco Márquez Villanueva's *Espiritualidad y literatura en el siglo XVI,* Olga Costa's *Pedro Salinas frente a la realidad,* J. F. Montesinos' *Galdós,* Solita Salinas de Marichal's *El mundo poético de Rafael Alberti,* A. Zamora Vicente's *La realidad esperpéntica,* Antonio Iglesias Laguna's *Treinta años de novela española, 1938–1968,* and Charles V. Aubrun's *La comedia española, 1600–1680.*

In the general area of the essay, 1969 saw the appearance of the fourth volumes of both Gregorio Maranón's and Manuel Azaña's *Obras completas.*

Poetry. The coveted Adonais prize was awarded to the Hondurian poet Roberto Sosa for *Los pobres,* a collection of short poems in a surrealistic vein; and the Leopoldo Panero prize went to Fernando Gutiérrez for *Las puertas del tiempo.*

Foremost among contributions of older poets was Vincente Aleixandre's *Poemas de consumación,* the aging master's projection of quiet despair, which was awarded the 1969 Critic's prize for poetry. The year also witnessed the publication of Luis Rosales' *El contenido del corazón,* Rafael Alberti's *Roma, peligro para caminantes,* Dámaso Alonso's *Poemas escogidos,* and Aleixandre's own *Obras completas.*

Important contributions by established younger poets were Luis Jiménez Martos' *Encuentro con Ulises,* an evocation of the Mediterranean; Leopoldo de Luis' *Poesía, 1946–1968,* Gloria Fuertes' *Poeta de guardia,* Jose Angel Valente's *Breve son,* and Concha Zardoya's *Hondo sur,* which reflects her years in the U. S. South.

Noteworthy newcomers in the area of lyrical poetry included Francisco Salgueiro (*Solo con mis palabras*) and A. Carvajal (*Tigres en el jardín*).

Theater. This literary medium was the greatest disappointment in 1969. The promise of a younger generation of playwrights, to both stimulate and extend the powerful creativity of such as Buero Vallejo and Miguel Mihura, again failed to materialize.

The Lope de Vega prize was awarded to Diego Salvador Blanes for *Los niños,* but this award itself has lost considerable prestige in recent years. Two new openings were not altogether lacking in interest: Victor Ruiz Iriarte's *Historia de un adulterio* and Jose Luis Martin Descalzo's *La hoguera feliz,* the latter reworking the Joan of Arc theme.

Translations. Important translations into English during 1969 included José María Gironella's *Peace after War,* tr. by Joan Maclean; Juan Goytisolo's *Marks of Identity,* tr. by Gregory Rabassa; Juan Ruiz's *Book of Good Love,* tr. by Elisha Kent Kane; and J. Vicens Vives' *Economic History of Spain,* tr. by Frances M. López-Morillas.

ALFRED RODRIGUEZ
University of Wisconsin—Milwaukee

SPORTS

JUBILATION follows the last out in the 1969 World Series as the New York Mets become world champions. (*Left*) Ed Charles, Jerry Grote, and Jerry Koosman go into victory dance on the pitcher's mound. (*Below*) Massive ticker-tape parade up Broadway honors the Amazing Ones.

CONTENTS

Shortly after man landed on the moon, the New York Mets took off on a flight that carried them, their frenzied fans, and nearly all sports followers right out of this world. The team that was mocked for its inability to play the game and that was in last place on April 28, after 18 games, won the world baseball championship amid delirium that brought dancing in the streets in New York and wild exultations of victory among the downtrodden everywhere. The splendid drive to the top by the team with the youngest players in baseball was hailed as the Impossible Dream—like the landing on the moon—and revived with unbelievable reality the adage that hope springs eternal.

The great surge of the Mets, traditionally a last-place club, overtook the Chicago Cubs for the division title, swept past the Atlanta Braves for the National League pennant, and engulfed the strong Baltimore Orioles in five games in the World Series. The heavily favored Orioles had routed the Minnesota Twins for the American League championship.

It seemed possible that the success bug that bit the Mets might have been left in the Shea Stadium dressing rooms that they shared with the New York Jets. That football team, under the guidance of Weeb Ewbank and the field direction of Joe Namath, had stunned the sports world in January by trouncing the Baltimore Colts, 16–7, in the Super Bowl. It was the first major victory for an American League club over the older National League. However, the bug did not stay around for the winter of 1969. The Jets, shaky all season, were eliminated in the play-offs by Kansas City. The Chiefs then blasted past the Oakland Raiders to the American League championship and proved their power by trouncing the Minnesota Vikings, the National League titleholder, 23–7, in the second straight Super Bowl upset. To get to the Super Bowl, the Vikings had subdued the Los Angeles Rams, 23–20, and then romped, 27–7, over the Cleveland Browns, who had defeated Dallas in the playoffs, 38–14.

Another club got the contagious New York victory fever at the start of the 1969–70 pro basketball season. The Knicks broke the National Basketball Association's record for consecutive victories with a string of 18 straight. They had finished the 1968–69 season strongly but lost in the play-offs to the Boston Celtics, who outlasted the Los Angeles Lakers and won the NBA championship again.

A victory bug seemed to operate in the Boston Garden, too, for the Bruins, long an underdog in National Hockey League play, became a powerful team. They were led by Bobby Orr, a young defense star, and Phil Esposito, who set a record for total points for the season with 126. However, neither the Bruins nor any other team could hold off the Montreal Canadiens, who won the title for the second season in a row and the Stanley Cup for the 16th time.

One of the strange phenomena of the season was that of quickly ending "retirements." This had happened occasionally with hockey players, but in 1969 it spread to many fields. The foremost "un-retirer" was Namath. Told by pro football commissioner Pete Rozelle that he must divest himself of part ownership in a restaurant alleged to be a gathering place for gamblers, Joe tearfully quit the game in June. In July he disassociated himself from the café and rejoined the Jets. Bobby Hull retired again from hockey until his contract with the Black Hawks was adjusted. Maury Wills and Donn Clendenon quit baseball as members of the Montreal Expos. Two days later Wills returned to his old team, the Dodgers. Clendenon joined the Mets, where he picked up $18,338 as his share and a car as the outstanding player in the World Series.

Pancho Gonzales quit tennis a couple of times, but reconsidered after he got some rest. Mrs. Margaret Smith Court also had hung up her racket after winning the Australian championship for the eighth time. However, she ventured back onto the court and won all the top tournaments except Wimbledon.

There were those who retired and made it stick. Chief of these were Mickey Mantle, the hero of kids of all ages; Don Drysdale, who had to quit in midseason; Roger Maris, Ed Mathews, and Rocky Colavito, also in baseball; Bill Russell, the playing coach of the Boston Celtics in basketball; and Don Meredith, the Dallas Cowboys quarterback. Jim Ryun, the distance runner, displeased with himself, quit for the season in July.

Among others who achieved fame and fortune were Lew Alcindor, the lanky center of the UCLA basketball team. After he had led the Bruins to their third straight national title, he was signed by the Milwaukee Bucks and successfully began his pro career, already a wealthy man. Frank Beard led a group of 11 golfers who earned over $100,000, but the Golfer of the Year was Orville Moody, the U. S. Open champion. Rod Laver won about as much in capturing the grand slam of tennis and other honors. In auto racing, purse money was revved up, and Mario Andretti set a record for drivers by winning $363,283. Pele, the soccer star, scored his 1,000th goal after refusing big offers to leave Santos of Brazil.

Outstanding amateurs who attained fame but not fortune included Mike Burton, who lowered the 1,500-meter swim record to 16:04.5, and the world track record-breakers Curtis Mills in the 440, John Pennel in the pole vault, and Bill Toomey in the decathlon. Liz Allan, a statuesque 18-year-old water-skier from Winter Haven, Fla., overwhelmed all opposition in the World, U. S., and Masters championships, taking all three events in each meet with the maximum point total of 3,000 overall.

In Alpine skiing, two Austrians, Karl Schranz and Gertrud Gabl won World Cup honors. The

Cochran family of Richmond, Vt., took three of the U. S. titles. Barbara won two slalom events and Bobby, one.

Among changes made in the search for better things were new arrivals in Washington. Ted Williams came out of retirement to manage the Senators; Vince Lombardi became head coach of the Redskins; and Richard Milhaus Nixon, a former squad member at Whittier College, presented a plaque to his choice (Texas) as the Number 1 college football team.

ARCHERY

World Championships
(Valley Forge, Pa., Aug. 13–20)

Men—Hardy Ward, Mt. Pleasant, Texas (2,423) points)
Women—Dorothy Lidstone, Vancouver, B. C. (2,361)
Team—Men: United States (7,194); Denmark (6,955), Britain (6,898); women: USSR (6,897), Canada (6,779), Poland (6,756)

Field Archery
Men—Freestyle: Richard Branstetter, Creve Coeur, Ill. (1,031); instinctive: Warren Cowles, Herndon, Va. (910)
Women—Freestyle: Irma Danielson, Sweden (904); instinctive: Mrs. Rae Dabelow, Galveston, Ind. (642)

National Field Archery Association Championships
(Watkins Glen, N. Y., July 28–Aug. 1)

Barebow
Men—Open: David Hughes, Irving, Texas (2,693); amateur: Emil Lehan, Pittsburgh (2,500)
Women—Open: Nancy Schultz, Norwell, Mass. (2,125); amateur: Eunice Schewe, Roscoe, Ill. (2,169)

Freestyle
Men—Open: Wendell Davis, Johnson, Tenn. (2,656); amateur: Jamie Selkirk, Canton, Ill. (2,651)
Women—Open: Peg Southern, Cockeysville, Md. (2,489); amateur: Diane Vetrecin, Chula Vista, Calif. (2,295)

Bowhunter
Men—Open: Tom Frye, Leesburg, Va. (2,272); amateur: Bob Souder, Front Royal, Va. (1,277)
Women—Open: Ida Revis, Guthrie, Okla. (1,003)

National Archery Association Championships
(Valley Forge, Pa., Aug. 21–24)

Men—Ray Rogers, Muskogee, Okla. (2,768); professional: Earl Hoyt, Bridgeton, Mo. (2,501); crossbow: George Gerick, Moline, Ill. (2,866)
Women—Mrs. Doreen Wilber, Jefferson, Iowa (2,768); professional: Nancy Brown, Ledyard, Conn. (2,093); crossbow: Ann Neill, Cape May Court House, N. J. (2,040)

Field Archery
(York, Pa., June 14–15)

Men—Freestyle: John C. Lamb, Cincinnati (1,033); barebow: Larry Forester, Oxford, Pa. (982)
Women—Freestyle: Barbara Brown, Ledyard, Conn. (855); barebow: June Baeckel, Oxford, Pa. (683)

AUTO RACING

World Championship Grand Prix Races

South Africa (Johannesburg, March 1)—Jackie Stewart, Scotland (driving a Matra-Ford; distance 204 miles; time: 1:50:39.1; average 110.62 mph)

JACK SHANKLIN emerged unhurt after this flip in a 300-mile stock car race at Daytona Beach in February.

UPI

Spain (Barcelona, May 4)—Stewart (212.4 mi; 2:16:56; 93.45 mph)
Monaco (Monte Carlo, May 18)—Graham Hill; Britain (Lotus-Ford; 156.8 mi; 1:56:59.4; 80.16 mph)
Netherlands (Zandvoort, June 21)—Stewart (235.5 mi; 2:06:42.-08; 111.041 mph)
France (Clermont-Ferrand, July 6)—Stewart (189.9 mi; 1:56:47.4; 97.7 mph)
England (Silverstone, July 19)—Stewart (246.1 mi; 1:55:55.6; 127.25 mph)
Germany (Adenau, Aug. 3)—Jackie Ickx, Belgium (Brabham-Ford; 198.8 mi; 1:49:55.4; 108.43 mph)
Italy (Monza, Sept. 7)—Stewart (242.95 mi; 1:39:11.26; 146.97 mph)
Canada (Bowmanville, Ont., Sept. 20)—Ickx (221 mi; 1:59:25.7; 112.76 mph)
United States (Watkins Glen, N. Y., Oct. 5)—Jochen Rindt, Austria (Lotus-Ford; 248 mi; 1:57:56.8; 126.36 mph)
Mexico (Mexico City, Oct. 19)—Denis Hulme, New Zealand (McLaren-Ford; 208 mi; 1:54:08.8; 106.157 mph)

Other Races

Indianapolis 500 (May 30)—Mario Andretti, Nazareth, Pa. (Granatelli STP Oil Treatment Special Hawk-Ford; 3:11:-14.71; 156.867 mph; purse, $206,727)
24 hours of Daytona (Daytona Beach, Fla., Feb. 1–2)—Mark Donohue, Media, Pa., and Chuck Parsons, Deerfield, Ill. (Lola-Chevrolet; 2,385.06 miles; 99.268 mph)
12-Hour Endurance (Sebring, Fla., March 22)—Jackie Ickx, Belgium, and Jackie Oliver, Britain (Ford GT-40; 1,242.8 miles; 103.363 mph)
Riverside 500 (Riverside, Calif., Feb. 1)—Richard Petty, Randleman, N. C. (Ford).
Daytona 500 (Daytona Beach, Fla., Feb. 23)—Lee Roy Yarbrough, Columbia, S. C. (Ford; 157.95 mph)
Carolina 500 (Rockingham, N. C., March 9)—David Pearson, Spartanburg, S. C. (Ford).
Atlanta 500 (Atlanta, Ga., March 30)—Cale Yarborough, Timmonsville, S. C. (Mercury; 132.759 mph)
World 600 (Charlotte, N. C., May 25)—Lee Roy Yarbrough (Mercury; 134 mph)
Motor State 500 (Cambridge Junction, Mich., June 15)—Cale Yarborough (Mercury; 139.323 mph)
Firecracker 400 (Daytona Beach, July 4)—Lee Roy Yarbrough (Ford; 160.875 mph)
Northern 300 (Trenton, N. J., July 13)—David Pearson, Spartanburg, S. C. (Ford; 121.005 mph)
Volunteer 500 (Bristol, Tenn., July 20)—Pearson (Ford; 79.737 mph)
Southern 500 (Darlington, S. C., Sept. 1)—Lee Roy Yarbrough (race cut to 316 miles by rain, 2:59.40; 105.612 mph)
Talladega 500 (Talladega, Ala., Sept. 14)—Richard Brickhouse, Rocky Point, S. C. (Dodge; 153.778 mph)
Trenton 300 (Sept. 21)—Mario Andretti, Nazareth, Pa. (Hawk-Ford; 134.81 mph)
National 500 (Charlotte, N. C., Oct. 12)—Donnie Allison, Hueytown, Ala. (Ford; 131.262 mph)
American 500 (Rockingham, N. C., Oct. 26)—Lee Roy Yarbrough (Ford; 111.938 mph)
Texas 500 (College Station, Dec. 7)—Bobby Isaac (Dodge; 144.265 mph)
Rex Mays 300 (Riverside, Calif., Dec. 7)—Mario Andretti (Hawk-Ford; 109.44 mph)

Foreign

Monza 1,000-kilometer (Monza, Italy, April 25)—Jo Siffert, Switzerland, and Brian Redman, Britain (Porsche 908; 123.8 mph)
Targa Florida (Palermo, Sicily, May 4)—Gerhard Mitter and Udo Schutz, West Germany (Porsche 908; 73.106 mph)
Francorchamps 1,000 kilometers (Belgium, May 11)—Siffert and Redman (Porsche 908; 138.405 mph)
24-Hour Endurance (Le Mans, France, June 15)—Jackie Ickx, Belgium, and Jackie Oliver, Britain (Ford GT-40; 3,098.76 miles; 129.923 mph)
Francorhamps 24-Hours (July 27; touring cars)—Guy Chasseuil and Claude Ballotena, France (Porsche; 2,572.21 miles; 111.3 mph)
World Challenge Cup (Fuji Speedway, Japan, 200 miles, Nov. 23)—Minoru Kawai, Japan (Toyota 7; 118.607 mph)

Individual Champions

World Grand Prix—Jackie Stewart, Scotland
U. S. Auto Club—big car: Mario Andretti, Nazareth, Pa. (5,025 pts); stock car: Roger McCluskey, Tucson, Ariz. (4,184); sprint car: Gary Bettenhausen, Tinley Park, Ill. (779.6); midgets: Bob Tattersall, Streator, Ill. (499.12)
NASCAR—Grand National: David Pearson, Spartanburg, S. C. (4,170 pts); grand touring: Ken Rush, High Point, N. C. (1,769); late model sportsman: Red Farmer, Hueytown, Ala. (8,276); modified: Bugs Stevens, Rehobeth, Mass. (1,769); rookie: Wayne Andrews Siler City, N. C.

Sports Car Club of America

Trans-American Sedan Series (12 races)—Mark Donohue, Media, Pa. (78 pts). Manufacturer: over 2 liters: Chevrolet; under 2 liters: Porsche
Canadian-American Challenge Cup Series (11 races)—Bruce McLaren, New Zealand (165 pts)
Continental Championship (13 races)—Tony Adamowicz, Wilton, Conn. (Eagle-Chevrolet)

American Road Race of Champions
(Daytona Beach, Fla., Nov. 25–30)

A Production—Gerald Clawson, Clawson, Mich. (Corvette; average speed, 106.2 mph)
B Production—Allan Barker, Jeffersonville, Ind. (Sting Ray; 102.385 mph)

GIL HODGES suffered a mild heart attack in September 1968, and it was feared that the former Brooklyn Dodger star would have to give up his post as manager of the New York Mets. But Hodges recovered and devoted himself to making a baseball team out of the young squad. His reward was the 1969 world championship.

Gilbert Ray Hodges was a soft-spoken catcher and first baseman who hit a ball hard. He was born in Princeton, Ind., on April 4, 1924, and attended St. Joseph's College in Indiana. He reported to the Dodgers in 1943 and to the U. S. Marines in 1944, where he served for three years. Back in Brooklyn as a catcher in 1947, he shifted to first base in 1948 and, batting cleanup, helped Brooklyn win six pennants and Los Angeles one. He hit 370 home runs in his 16-year career, four in one game in 1950. Hodges became manager of the Senators in May 1963, and went to the Mets as their manager in 1968. After his team won the pennant, the Mets gave Hodges a bonus and a new 3-year contract at $70,000 a year.

UPI

METS' MANAGERS, past and present, celebrate a world championship as Casey Stengel hugs Gil Hodges.

C Production—Milton Minter, Santa Susana, Calif. (Porsche; 97.212 mph)
D Production—Jack Scoville, Corvallis, Oreg. (Datsun; 95.384 mph)
E Production—Mike Downs, Falls Church, Va. (Triumph; 97.043 mph)
F Production—Lee Mueller, Lynwood, Calif. (Triumph; 93.781 mph)
G Production—Paul Spruell, Atlanta, Ga. (Alfa Romeo; 85.121 mph)
H Production—Randall Canfield, Chevy Chase, Md. (Sprite; 83.152 mph)
A Sedan—Bill Petree, Riverview, Mich. (Camaro; 103.333 mph)
B Sedan—Peter Gregg, Jacksonville, Fla. (Porsche; 95.221 mph)
C Sedan—Harry Theodoracopulos, New York (Alfa Romeo; 88.291 mph)
D Sedan—Bill Allen, Chino, Calif. (NSU-TTS; 83.90 mph)
Formula A—Peter Rehl, Easton, Conn. (Cooper; 11.023 mph)
Formula B—William Monson, Kent, Wash. (Brabham; 107.307 mph)
Formula C—Bill Rutan, Essex, Conn. (Tecno; 102.305 mph)
Formula F—Skip Barber, Carlisle, Mass. (Caldwell; 95.711 mph)
Formula V—James Killion, Ashland, Ohio (Zink; 83.408 mph)
A Sports Racing—Jerry Hansen, Minneapolis (Lola-Chevrolet; 113.414 mph)
B Sports Racing—Scooter Patrick, Manhattan Beach, Calif. (Alfa Romeo; 104.494 mph)
C Sports Racing—Dan Carmichael, Columbus, Ohio (Lotus-Ford; 95.711 mph)
D Sports Racing—Eric Kerman, Merrick, N. Y. (Arachnid-Honda, 88.151 mph)
President's Cup (outstanding competitor and sportsman)—Paul Spruell, Atlanta, Ga.

BADMINTON

All-England Championship (Wembley, England, March 19–22) —Men's Singles: Rudy Hartono, Indonesia; women's singles: Hiroe Yuki, Japan; men's doubles: Henning Borch and Erland Kops, Denmark; women's doubles: Sue Boxall and Margaret Whetnall, England; mixed doubles: Roger Mills and Gillian Perrin, England
U.S. Championship (Natchitoches, La., April 2–5)—Men's singles: Rudy Hartono, Indonesia; women's singles: Miss Minarni, Indonesia; men's doubles: Ng Boon Bee and Gunalan, Malaysia; women's doubles: Miss Minarni and Retno Koestijah, Indonesia; mixed doubles: Erland Kops and P. M. Hansen, Denmark; senior men's singles: John Lieb, San Diego, Calif.; senior men's doubles: Wynn Rogers, Arcadia, Calif., and Bob Cerzine, Torrance, Calif.; senior women's doubles: Ethel Marshall and Bea Massman, Buffalo, N. Y.; senior mixed doubles: Rogers and Ethel Marshall
Canadian Open (Toronto, March 28–30)—Men's singles: Rudy Hartono, Indonesia; women's singles: Eva Twedburg, Sweden; men's doubles: Bob McCoig, Scotland, and Tony Jordan, England; women's doubles: Miss Minarni and Retno Koestijah, Indonesia; mixed doubles: Darmadi and Miss Minarni, Indonesia
Uber Cup (women's team championship, Tokyo, June 8–14)—semi-finals: England defeated Thailand, 7–0; Indonesia defeated United States, 7–0; final: Indonesia defeated England, 4–3.

BASEBALL

Major league baseball began the 1969 season under a new format that gave it renewed vigor, and finished with a new champion who rekindled the enthusiasm of the world's fans. The new format, brought about by the addition of two clubs to both the National and the American leagues, divided each league into two divisions of six teams and provided four champions. The division leaders played off for the league title and a World Series role. When the long season ended, the champion of them all was the New York Mets, who discarded all aspects of a ragtag, tail-end club and marched through the play-offs and the Series in the manner of baseball's legendary champions.

There were two other events of importance during the year. First, the players refused to report to training camps until the owners adjusted their contributions to the pension fund. Agreement was reached on February 25 with a 3-year pact that also reduced the minimum playing time required for eligibility for a limited pension to four years. Second, the batters caught up with the pitchers and, therefore, hitting increased somewhat from its 1968 low. The year's activities were watched over by Bowie Kuhn, an attorney who went to bat as commissioner in a pinch-hitting role in February and made such a hit that he won a permanent position in August with a 7-year contract.

Expansion had carried the American League back into Kansas City and into the Northwest at Seattle. The National League established another base on the Pacific Coast at San Diego and gave the majors an international ranking with a club at Montreal, which unfortunately lost 20 games in a row.

The Mets did not adopt championship ways until the second half of the season. The early leader in the Eastern Division of the National League was the Chicago Cubs, which held a lead of 7½ games by Memorial Day and 4½ games at the All-Star break. Early in June the Mets, who had finished either last or next to last in their seven previous seasons, soared over .500 in the standings and moved into second place; and baseball was on its way toward one of its most exciting seasons and exhilarating episodes.

Mostly a team of young men, the Mets got strong pitching from Tom Seaver, a 24-year-old right-hander, and Jerry Koosman, 25, a left-hander.

Back of them were Gary Gentry, 25; Nolan Ryan, 22, with a blazing fast ball; Tug McGraw, 25; Jim McAndrew, 25; Don Cardwell, 36; and Ron Taylor, 31. The leading batters were outfielders: Cleon Jones, 27, who hit .340; Tommie Agee, 27, his teammate in high school football at Mobile, Ala.; and Art Shamsky and Ron Swoboda. The infield was sparked by Bud Harrelson, 25, at shortstop. Gil Hodges, a former Brooklyn Dodger star, was their quiet, efficient manager.

By July 9, the Mets had cut the Cubs' margin to three games. Then they faded and dropped back of the resurgent St. Louis Cardinals, the 1968 champions, into third place, 9½ games out of first. That was on August 13.

But the young team had begun to believe in itself and started upward again, and on September 10 the Mets moved into first place for the first time in their history. They never slowed down. They clinched the Eastern Division championship on September 23, although suffering in one week the ignominies that had been their lot as cellar-dwellers. First, 19 Mets struck out as Steve Carlton of the Cards made a modern record for strikeouts in a game (the Mets won, 4–3, on Swoboda's two home runs). Then they lost a double-header to the crippled Pittsburgh team; and finally Bob Moose of the Pirates set them down without a hit on September 20. Meanwhile, the Cubs were losing steadily.

The Western Division of the league had an exciting four-way battle under way. At one point in mid-September, only 9 percentage points and 1½ games separated Atlanta, San Francisco, Los Angeles, and Cincinnati. However, in the American league, Baltimore in the Eastern Division and Minnesota in the Western had jumped out in front. The Detroit Tigers, the 1968 World Series winners, were struggling and never regained their form.

In the division play-offs, the Mets swept the Atlanta Braves, who had outlasted the San Francisco Giants, in three games, 9–5, 11–6, and 7–4. In the American, Baltimore administered the same treatment to Minnesota, which had shaken off a serious Oakland bid in the West. The Orioles won 4–3 in 12 innings; 1–0 in 11; and 11–2.

The World Series began in Baltimore with the favored Orioles winning the opener, 4–1, behind the 6-hit pitching of Mike Cuellar. But that was the end for the heavy-hitting Orioles. The Mets took turns at heroics—unbelievable catches in the outfield, great infield play, and timely hitting and slugging by weak batters. Koosman beat Baltimore's Dave McNally, 2–1, in the second game. Then the teams moved to Shea Stadium in New York. Gentry, with the aid of Ryan and Agee, who made two incredible catches that cut off five runs, beat Jim Palmer, 5–0. Next, Seaver in a return against Cuellar won in 10 innings, 2–1, with Swoboda making a miraculous catch. For a finale, the Mets let the Orioles take a 3-run lead, then Koosman limited them to a single in the last six innings. Donn Clendenon hit a 2-run homer (his third of the Series) and Al Weis also hit a homer, having hit only two all year, and tied the score. A 2-run flurry in the 8th inning won the game, 5–3, the World Series, and everlasting fame for the Mets as the underdogs who would not be beaten.

Seaver was voted the Cy Young Award as the outstanding pitcher in the National league; Cuellar and Dennis McLain of Detroit shared the award in the American league. The two leading home run hitters, Willie McCovey of the Giants and Harmon Killebrew of the Twins were named the most valuable players.

Willie Mays, at 38, hit 13 homers and reached the 600 plateau. Moving up on him was Henry Aaron, who hit 44 for a total of 554. Aaron moved into third place in the all-time records, passing Mickey Mantle, who retired before the start of the season with 536 in his 18-year career. Another great star who retired, in mid-season, was Don Drysdale, the Dodgers' big right-handed pitcher, because of an ailing shoulder. He had won 209 games and lost 166 in his 15 years. Warren Giles, who had been the president of the National league since 1951, retired in December and was succeeded by Charles S. (Chub) Feeney, a vice president of the Giants.

Professional—Major Leagues

AMERICAN LEAGUE (Final Standings, 1969) EASTERN DIVISION				NATIONAL LEAGUE (Final Standings, 1969) EASTERN DIVISION			
	Won	Lost	Pct.		Won	Lost	Pct.
Baltimore	109	53	.673	New York	100	62	.617
Detroit	90	72	.556	Chicago	92	70	.568
Boston	87	75	.537	Pittsburgh	88	74	.543
Washington	86	76	.531	St. Louis	87	75	.537
New York	80	81	.497	Philadelphia	63	99	.389
Cleveland	62	99	.385	Montreal	52	110	.321
WESTERN DIVISION				**WESTERN DIVISION**			
Minnesota	97	65	.599	Atlanta	93	69	.574
Oakland	88	74	.543	San Francisco	90	72	.556
California	71	91	.438	Cincinnati	89	73	.549
Kansas City	69	93	.426	Los Angeles	85	77	.525
Chicago	68	94	.420	Houston	81	81	.500
Seattle	64	98	.395	San Diego	52	110	.321

Play-offs—American League: Baltimore Orioles defeated Minnesota Twins, 3 games to 0; National League: New York Mets defeated Atlanta Braves, 3 games to 0

World Series—Won by New York Mets; paid attendance, 5 games, 272,378; total receipts, $2,857,782.78; commissioner's share, $428,667.41; players' share, $1,142,200.93, including full shares of $18,338.18 for each Met and $14,904.21 for each Oriole; each club's share and each league's share, $321,728.61

Standings: New York (NL) won 4, lost 1, pct. .800; Baltimore (AL) won 1, lost 4, pct. .200

First game (Memorial Stadium, Baltimore, Oct. 11): Baltimore 4, New York 1; Second game (Memorial Stadium, Oct. 12): New York 2, Baltimore 1; Third game (Shea Stadium, New York, Oct. 14): New York 5, Baltimore 0; Fourth game (Shea Stadium, Oct. 15): New York 2, Baltimore 1; Fifth game (Shea Stadium, Oct. 16): New York 5, Baltimore 3.

All-Star Game (Washington, D. C., July 23) National 9, American 3. (Game postponed one day because of rain)

Most Valuable Players—American: Harmon Killebrew, Minnesota 3d baseman; National: Willie McCovey, San Francisco 1st baseman

Cy Young Memorial Award (outstanding pitcher)—American: Mike Cuellar, Baltimore, and Dennis McLain, Detroit; National: Tom Seaver, New York

Rookies of the Year—American: Lou Piniella, Kansas City outfielder; National: Ted Sizemore, Los Angeles infielder

Leading Batters: Percentage—American: Rod Carew, Minnesota, .332; National: Pete Rose, Cincinnati, .348. Home Runs—American: Harmon Killebrew, Minnesota, 49; National: Willie McCovey, San Francisco, 45. Runs Batted In—American: Killibrew, 143; National: McCovey, 126

Leading Pitchers: best percentage (10 or more victories)—American: Jim Palmer, Baltimore (16–4), .800; National: Bob Moose, Pittsburgh (14–3), .824. Most Victories—American: Dennis McLain, Detroit, 24; National: Tom Seaver, New York, 25. Earned run average—American: Palmer, 2.34; National: Juan Marichal, San Francisco, 2.10

No-Hit Games pitched—Bill Stoneman, Montreal, vs. Philadelphia, 7–0; Jim Maloney, Cincinnati, vs. Houston, 10–0; Don Wilson, Houston, vs. Cincinnati, 4–0; Jim Palmer, Baltimore, vs. Oakland, 8–0; Ken Holtzman, Chicago Cubs, vs. Atlanta, 3–0; Bob Moose, Pittsburgh, vs. New York Mets, 4–0

Hall of Fame Inductees—Roy Campanella, Brooklyn Dodgers, catcher; Stanley Coveleski, Cleveland Indians, pitcher; Stanley Musial, St. Louis Cardinals, outfielder and first baseman; and Waite Hoyt, pitcher with New York Yankees and other clubs

Professional—Minor Leagues

(When two teams are named, the first team won the regular season championship and the second won the play-off; otherwise, the team named won both.)

American Association (AAA)—Omaha (no play-off)
International (AAA)—Tidewater, Syracuse
Pacific Coast (AAA)—Tacoma (Northern Division and play-off), Eugene (Southern Division)

Mexican (AAA)—Reynosa (no play-off)
Eastern (AA)—York (play-off canceled, rain)
Southern (AA)—Charlotte (no play-off)
Texas (AA)—Memphis (Eastern Division and play-off), Amarillo (Western Division)
California (A)—Stockton (first half and play-off), Visalia (second half)
Carolina (A)—Rocky Mount (Eastern Division), Salem (Western Division), Raleigh-Durham (play-off)
Florida State (A)—Miami (Southern Division and play-off), Orlando (Central Division)
Midwest (A)—Appleton
New York-Pennsylvania (A)—Oneonta
Northern (A)—Duluth-Superior
Northwest (A)—Rogue Valley
Western Carolina (A)—Greenwood (first half and play-off), Shelby (second half)
Appalachian (Rookie)—Pulaski (Northern), Marion (Southern)
Gulf Coast (Rookie)—Expos (no play-off)
Pioneer (Rookie)—Ogden (no play-off)

Other Champions

All-American Amateur—Adray Appliance, Detroit
American Legion—Portland, Oreg.
Babe Ruth World Series—El Segundo, Calif.
Babe Ruth (16–18)—San Antonio, Texas
Big Little League—Mojave Desert, Calif.
Colt League—Santa Clara, Calif.
Connie Mack League—Bellflower-Compton (Calif.) Giants
Little League World Series—Taiwan (Nationalist China) Red Leafs
Mickey Mantle League—Dallas Giants
National Amateur Federation Sophomores—Eastside Sports, Detroit
National Baseball Congress—Anchorage (Alaska) Glacier Pilots
Pony League—Honolulu
Stan Musial League—Taber Chevrolet, Atlanta
World Amateur—Cuba

Intercollegiate Champions

NCAA—Arizona State (defeated Tulsa, in final, 10–1); College division: Illinois State University (defeated Southwest Missouri in final, 12–0)
NAIA—William Carey (Hattiesburg, Miss.) defeated La Verne (Calif.) in final, 5–3

BASKETBALL
Professional

The National Basketball Association's 1968–69 season began in October, and after 574 regular-season games and 38 play-off contests its championship was decided in a single game on May 5. In a mad scramble, the Boston Celtics won the seventh game of the final series from the Los Angeles Lakers, 108–106, and the title 4 games to 3.

This championship, the 10th in 11 years for the Celtics, was the one they definitely were not supposed to be in contention for. They finished fourth in the Eastern Division, getting the final play-off berth. Injuries to their opponents helped them to get through the division play-offs. In the championship play-off, the Lakers' Jerry West, who was named the most valuable player of the post-season competition, was hampered by a leg injury, and Wilt Chamberlain twisted a knee in the final hectic game and had to retire with five minutes left to play. The Celtics' outstanding players were John Havlicek and Bill Russell, the 6-foot-10-inch playing coach who afterward announced his retirement.

Westley Unseld of the Baltimore Bullets was named the NBA's most valuable player as well as rookie of the year. Scoring honors went to another rookie, Elvin Hayes of the San Diego Rockets, who scored 2,327 points, an average of 28.4 a game.

In the American Basketball Association the Oakland Oaks, the Western Division champions, defeated the Indiana Pacers, Eastern Division leaders, 4 games to 1, for the title. After the season, Earl Foreman bought the Oaks and moved the club to Washington, D. C., renaming the team the Capitols. The Minneapolis team returned to Pittsburgh, and the Houston franchise was moved to a base at Greensboro, N. C., and called Carolina. George Mikan resigned as commissioner in July; the post went to Jack Dolph, who had been director of sports for CBS.

NATIONAL BASKETBALL ASSOCIATION
(Final Standings, 1969)

EASTERN DIVISION				WESTERN DIVISION			
Team	Won	Lost	Pct.	Team	Won	Lost	Pct.
Baltimore	57	25	.695	Los Angeles	55	27	.671
Philadelphia	55	27	.671	Atlanta	48	34	.585
New York	54	28	.659	San Francisco	41	41	.500
Boston	48	34	.585	San Diego	37	45	.451
Cincinnati	41	41	.500	Chicago	33	49	.402
Detroit	32	50	.390	Seattle	30	52	.366
Milwaukee	27	55	.329	Phoenix	16	66	.195

Eastern Division play-offs: Boston defeated New York, 4 games to 3; *Western Division play-offs:* Los Angeles defeated Atlanta, 4 games to 1; *NBA Championship:* Boston defeated Los Angeles, 4 games to 3. Most valuable player in play-offs: Jerry West, Los Angeles Lakers
Most Valuable Player Award—Westley Unseld, Baltimore
Rookie of the Year—Unseld
Leading Scorer—Elvin Hayes, San Diego, 2,327 points; 28.4 average per game

AMERICAN BASKETBALL ASSOCIATION
(Final Standings, 1969)

EASTERN DIVISION				WESTERN DIVISION			
Team	Won	Lost	Pct.	Team	Won	Lost	Pct.
Indiana	44	34	.564	Oakland	60	18	.769
Miami	43	35	.551	New Orleans	46	32	.590
Kentucky	42	36	.538	Denver	44	34	.564
Minnesota	36	42	.462	Dallas	41	37	.526
New York	17	61	.218	Los Angeles	33	45	.423
				Houston	23	55	.295

Eastern Division play-offs: Indiana defeated Miami, 4 games to 1; *Western Division play-offs:* Oakland defeated New Orleans, 4 games to 0; *ABA Championship:* Oakland defeated Indiana, 4 games to 1
Most Valuable Player—Mel Daniels, Indiana Pacers
Rookie of the Year—Warren Armstrong, Oakland Oaks
Leading Scorer—Rick Barry, Oakland Oaks, 1,190 points; 34 average per game

College

As had been predicted, the University of California at Los Angeles won its third consecutive National Collegiate Athletic Association championship in 1968–69. With the formal completion of the crowning—a Bruin victory over Purdue, 92–72, in the tournament final—UCLA bid adieu to its star center, Lew Alcindor, and the pro clubs made their final frantic bids for his services.

A flip of the coin with the Phoenix Suns gave the Milwaukee Bucks the right to draft Alcindor in the National Basketball Association. The American Basketball Association tried to land him for any club, but ostensibly for the New York Nets. Alcindor wearied of the frenzy and decided to accept the Bucks' offer, which was a package deal said to be for $1.4 million for five years.

The Bruins' rush to a third straight national championship, the first ever, had little interruption. They were frustrated, however, in a bid for an undefeated season by their crosstown rivals, the University of Southern California, who defeated them in the final Pacific Eight Conference game. This setback also ended a 41-game winning streak. UCLA beat Santa Clara in the regional eliminations and Drake in the semifinals.

In the other championships, Kentucky Wesleyan defeated Southwest Missouri, 75–71, for the NCAA small college title; and Eastern New Mexico beat Maryland State, 99–76, for the National Association of Intercollegiate Athletics crown. The National Invitation Tournament in New York was won by Temple, 89–76, over Boston College.

Amateur
Major Tournaments

NCAA—University of California at Los Angeles (defeated Purdue, 92–72); *College division:* Kentucky Wesleyan (defeated Southwest Missouri, 75–71)
National Invitation (New York)—Temple (defeated Boston College, 89–76)
National Intercollegiate (NAIA)—Eastern New Mexico (defeated Maryland State, 99–76)
Men's AAU—Armed Forces All-Stars (defeated Akron, Ohio, Goodyear Wingfoots, 62–45)
Women's AAU—Nashville (Tenn.) Business College

College Conference Champions

(Figures in parentheses represent victories and losses in conference games only.)

Athletic Association of Western Universities—University of California at Los Angeles (13–1)

Atlantic Coast—North Carolina (12–2); won championship tournament

Big Eight—Colorado (10–4)

Big Sky—Weber State (15–0)

Big Ten—Purdue (13–1)

Central Intercollegiate A. A.—Elizabeth City (N. C.) State (18–2)

Ivy League—Princeton (14–0)

Mid-American—Miami (10–2)

Middle Atlantic—*University division:* St. Joseph's (17–10); *Northern college division:* Scranton (11–3); *Southern college division:* Muhlenberg (12–3)

Missouri Valley—Drake and Louisville (13–3); Drake won play-off for NCAA tournament berth

Ohio Valley—Murray State and Morehead State (11–3); Murray State won play-off for NCAA berth

Southeastern—Kentucky (16–2)

Southern—Davidson (9–0); won championship tournament

Southwest—Texas A&M (12–2)

Western Athletic—Brigham Young and Wyoming (6–4); Brigham Young won play-off for NCAA berth

West Coast Athletic—Santa Clara (13–1)

Leading College Independents

East—Boston College (24–4); Rutgers (21–4); Duquesne (21–5); Villanova (21–5); Temple (22–8); St. John's (23–6); Scranton (20–5)

South—Jacksonville (17–7); Florida State (18–8)

Middle West—Marquette (24–5); Dayton (20–7); Notre Dame (20–7)

Southwest—West Texas State (18–7); Oklahoma City (18–9); Houston (16–10)

Far West—New Mexico State (24–5); Puget Sound (20–2); Azusa Pacific (26–7); University of Nevada, Las Vegas (21–7); Seattle (19–8)

BOBSLEDDING

World Championships (Lake Placid, N. Y., Feb. 15–16, 22–23)—2-man: Nevio DeZordo (driver) and Adriano Frassinelli (brake), Italy (4-heat total, 4:31:73); 4-man: Wolfgang

LEW ALCINDOR, leading UCLA to national honors for 3d straight year, scores against Purdue in title game.

WIDE WORLD

Zimmerer (driver), Stephen Geisreiter, Walter Steinbauer, Peter Utzschneider (brake), West Germany (4-heat total, 4:20:75)

North American Championships (Lake Placid, N. Y., Feb. 7)—2-man: Paul Lamey (driver) and Robert Huscher (brake), U. S. Navy (4-heat total, 4:38:42); 4-man: races canceled, bad track

AAU Championships (Lake Placid, N. Y., Feb. 5–6)—2-man: Lamey and Huscher (4-heat total, 4:41:65); 4-man: Fred Fortune (driver), Andy Kanaby, Robert Goodspeed, James Lord (brake), Cleveland Bobsled Club (2-heat total, 2:16:52)

BOWLING

American Bowling Congress Tournament (Madison, Wis., Feb. 22–May 11)—*Regular Division: singles,* Greg Campbell, Florissant, Mo. (751 pins); *doubles,* Charles Guedel and Robert Maschmeyer, Indianapolis (1,379); *all-events,* Eddie Jackson, Cincinnati (1,988); *team,* PAC Advertising Co., Lansing, Mich. (3,165). *Classic Division: singles,* Nelson Burton, Jr., St. Louis (732); *doubles,* Don McCune, Munster, Ind., and Jim Stefanich, Joliet, Ill. (1,355); *all-events,* Larry Lichstein, Hartford, Conn. (2,060); *team,* Weber Wrist Masters, Santa Ana, Calif. (6,413). *Booster Division: team,* Colman Florist, Rock Island, Ill. (2,842). *Masters:* Jim Chestney, Denver, Colo.

Woman's International Bowling Congress Tournament (San Diego, Calif., April 3–May 26)—*Open Division: singles,* Joan Bender, Denver, Colo. (690 pins); *doubles,* Gloria Bouvia, Portland, Oreg., and Judy Cook, Grand View, Mo. (1,315); *all-events,* Helen Duval, Berkeley, Calif. (1,927); *team,* Fitzpatrick Chevrolet, Concord, Calif. (2,986). *Division I: singles,* Ann Keerbs, Churdan, Iowa (649); *doubles,* Bertha Keeney and Joyce Georgeson, Wheatridge, Colo. (1,205); *all-events,* Janice Pickle, Tucson, Ariz. (1,743); *team,* Bolorado Lanes, Fort Collins, Colo. (2,719). *Division II: singles,* Marcia White, Rowland Heights, Calif. (607); *doubles,* Patricia Rose and Mary Redman, Sierra Madre, Calif. (1,047); *all-events,* Beverly Pluhowsky, Phoenix, Ariz. (1,668); *team,* Five Pins, Fullerton, Calif. (2,416). *Queens Tournament:* Ann Feigel, Tucson

Bowling Proprietors' Association of America All-Star Champions (Hialeah, Fla., May 3–9)—Men: Billy Hardwick, Louisville, Ky. (12,585); women: Dotty Fothergill, North Attleboro, Mass. (8,284)

Professional Bowlers Association Championship (Garden City, N. Y., Dec. 6, final)—Mike McGrath, El Cerrito, Calif. (13,670)

National Duckpin Bowling Congress Tournament (Bethesda, Md.)—Men: singles, William Wall, Washington, D. C. (485); doubles, Al Grandy and Jerry Rosen, Plainfield, Conn. (885); all-events, Sterling Fritz, Baltimore (1,333); team, Snelling and Snelling, Baltimore, Md. (2,057). Women: singles, Gertha Wilson, Washington, D. C. (438); doubles, Mary Ann Mitchell and Cathy Dyak, Manchester, Conn. (803); all-events, Minerva Weisenhorn, Baltimore, Md. (1,248); team: Eudowood Gardens, Baltimore (1,871). Mixed doubles, Fran Haas, Morris, Conn., and Dan Lopardo, Torrington, Conn. (867)

BOXING

World Professional Champions

Flyweight—Efran Torres, Mexico; WBA champion: Bernabe Villacampo, Philippines

Bantamweight—Rubén Olivares, Mexico

Featherweight—Johnny Famechon, Australia; WBA champion: Sho Saijo, Japan

Junior Lightweight—Rene Barrientos, Philippines; WBA champion: Hiroshi Kobayashi, Japan

Lightweight—Mando Ramos, Long Beach, Calif.

Junior Welterweight—Nicoline Loche, Argentina

Welterweight—José Napoles, Mexico

Junior Middleweight—Freddie Little, Las Vegas, Nev.

Middleweight—Nino Benvenuti, Italy

Light Heavyweight—Bob Foster, Washington

Heavyweight—WBA champion: Jimmy Ellis, Louisville, Ky.; New York champion (recognized in Maine, Mass., Pa., and Ill.): Joe Frazier, Philadelphia

National AAU Championships
(San Diego, Calif., April 18–20)

106 Pounds—Dennis Mince, Kenner, La.

112 Pounds—Caleb Long, U. S. Army

119 Pounds—Terry Pullen, Metairie, La.

125 Pounds—Joe Bennett, Joliet, Ill.

132 Pounds—Juan Ruis, U. S. Air Force

139 Pounds—Rudy Bolds, Braddock, Pa.

147 Pounds—Armando Muniz, U. S. Army

156 Pounds—Larry Carlisle, U. S. Marines

165 Pounds—Larry Ward, Milwaukee

178 Pounds—Dave Matthews, Akron, Ohio

Heavyweight—Ernie Shaver, Warren, Ohio

BRIDGE, CONTRACT

World Team (Rio de Janeiro, final May 17)—Italy (Giorgio Belladonna, Walter Avarelli, Massimo D'Alelio, Benito Garozzo, Pietro Forquet, Camillo Pabis-Ticci, and Angelo Tracanella, nonplaying captain) defeated China in final

ROCKY MARCIANO (1923–1969)

WIDE WORLD

Rocky Marciano, a former world heavyweight boxing champion, was killed in an airplane crash near Newton, Iowa, on August 31, a few hours before his 46th birthday. Marciano, who had retired undefeated on April 27, 1956, was buried in Fort Lauderdale, Fla., where he had been engaged in public relations work. The bruising fighter won the heavyweight title by knocking out Jersey Joe Walcott on Sept. 23, 1952, at Philadelphia. In his professional career, Rocky won all of his 49 bouts, 43 of them by knockouts, and grossed about $1.7 million in purses.

The son of an emigrant Italian shoemaker, Rocco Marchegiano was born in Brockton, Mass., on Sept. 1, 1923. A star high school football and baseball player, he started boxing while in the U. S. Army at Fort Lewis, Wash. Rocky turned pro in 1947 and knocked out his first 10 opponents. In his first major test he outpointed Roland LaStarza on March 24, 1950, in 10 rounds. Matched with Joe Louis, who was making a comeback, Marciano knocked out the former champion in the 8th round on Oct. 26, 1951. After four more winning bouts he got his chance with Walcott. During his 3½-year reign as champion, the "Brockton Blockbuster" defended six times and won five of the bouts by knockouts. He was knocked down only twice, one by Walcott and once by Archie Moore in Marciano's last bout, Sept. 21, 1955.

Spring Nationals
(Cleveland, March 14–23)
Harold S. Vanderbilt Cup Team—Richard Walsh, John Swanson, Paul Soloway, Jerry Hallee, Los Angeles
Men's Pairs—Michael Martino and Frank Vine, Hamilton, Ont.
Women's Pairs—Gale Clark, McLean, Va., and Gloria Noszka, Pittsburgh, Pa.
Men's Team—Alvin Roth, Paul Trent, and Jim Cayne, New York; Chuck Burger, Detroit
Women's Team—Karen Allison and Jan Stone, New York; Edith Kemp, Miami Beach, Fla.; Virginia Heckel, Chicago; Alicia Kempner and Helen Portugal, Los Angeles
Mixed Pairs—Peter Rank, Walnut Creek, Calif., and Marilyn Johnson, Oakland, Calif.
Open Pairs—Robert Freedman and James Mathis, Buffalo

Summer Nationals
(Los Angeles, August 8–19)
Master Mixed Teams—Ivar and Alice Stakgold, Evanston, Ill.; Janice Cohn, Northbrook, Ill.; Charles Peres, Flo Orner, and Dan Rotman, Chicago
Master Knockout Team (Spingold)—Dallas Aces (Jim Jacoby, Robert Hamman, Robert Wolff, Bill Eisenberg, Michael Lawrence, and Bob Goldman)
Life Master Pairs—Eric Murray and Sam Kehela, Toronto
Mixed Pairs—Roger Stern and Sandra Roark, New York
Women's Pairs—Bertha Epstein and Muriel Donner, Los Angeles
Men's Pairs—Monroe Ingberman, New Paltz, N. Y., and Charles Peres, Chicago

Fall Nationals
(Miami Beach, Nov. 21–30)
Reisinger Board-a-Match Teams—Ira Rubin, Paramus, N. J.; Philip Feldesman, William Grieve, and Jeff Westheimer, New York
Blue Ribbon Pairs—Alex Tschekaloff, Erik Paulsen, Los Angeles
Life Master Men's Pairs—Jim Gayne, New York, and Chuck Burger, Detroit
Life Master Women's Pairs—Sylvia Stein, Southfield, Mich., and Gratian Goldstein, Miami Beach
Mixed Pairs—Steve and Peggy Parker, Greenbelt, Md.
Open Pairs—Barbara Birnholz, Livingston, N. J., and Robert Ryder, West Caldwell, N. J.
Men's Teams—Tie: Mike Lawrence and Bob Goldman, Dallas, Texas, teamed with Gaylor Kasle, Tucson, Ariz., and Mike King, Springfield, Mo.; Jessel Rothfield and Wally Scott, Melbourne, Australia, teamed with Gene Prosnitz and Ken Lebensold, New York
Women's Teams—Bee Schenken and Gail Moss, New York, Marietta Passell, Hartsdale, N. Y., and Sallie Johnson, Westport, Conn.

CANADA GAMES

Athletes from Ontario won the overall championship of the Jeux Canada Games held in Halifax and Dartmouth, Nova Scotia, August 16–24. Ontario finished first in 8 of the 15 events for a total of 180 points. This was only 11 more than British Columbia, which won five events. Quebec, the victor in the other two sports, was third in points with 136. The competition drew about 2,400 athletes from the 10 provinces and two territories.

Canada Games are held in a two-year cycle, alternating between winter and summer competitions. The first was the Winter Games in Quebec City in 1967. The 1971 Winter Games will be held in Saskatoon, Saskatchewan.

Final Point Standings

Ontario	180	Saskatchewan	87.5
British Columbia	169	New Brunswick	85.5
Quebec	136	Newfoundland	58
Nova Scotia	129	Prince Edward Island	42
Alberta	127.5	Northwest Territories	8
Manitoba	125.5	Yukon	8

Final Medal Standings
(Gold for 1st place, silver for 2d, and bronze for 3d)

	1st	2d	3d	Tota
Ontario	51	24	29	104
British Columbia	36	43	21	100
Alberta	10	9	20	39
Quebec	9	14	17	40
Nova Scotia	3	8	7	18
Manitoba	1	7	10	18
Saskatchewan	1	5	6	12
New Brunswick	1	1	1	3
Prince Edward Island	1	0	0	1
Newfoundland	0	0	1	1

Because of a tie for 1st place in the women's 200-meter breaststroke, two gold medals were awarded, and no silver medal.

Team Leaders in Events
(First five places—points awarded on a 12-11-10-9-8-7-6-5-4-3-2-1 basis for first through 12th place)
Baseball—Ontario, Quebec, Nova Scotia, New Brunswick, Saskatchewan
Canoeing—Ontario, Nova Scotia, Quebec, British Columbia, New Brunswick
Cycling—Quebec, Ontario, British Columbia, Alberta, Manitoba
Field Hockey—British Columbia, New Brunswick, Ontario, Nova Scotia, Alberta
Lacrosse, Box—British Columbia, Ontario, Quebec, Manitoba, Alberta
Lawn Bowling—Ontario, British Columbia, New Brunswick, Nova Scotia, Manitoba
Rowing—Ontario, British Columbia, Manitoba, Nova Scotia, Quebec
Sailing—British Columbia, Ontario, Nova Scotia, Alberta, Quebec
Soccer—British Columbia, Ontario, Newfoundland, Nova Scotia, Manitoba
Softball—Ontario, British Columbia, Alberta, Manitoba, Nova Scotia
Swimming and Diving—British Columbia, 24; Alberta, 20.5; Ontario, 19; Saskatchewan, 17.5; Manitoba, 17 (team points awarded separately for each sport)
Tennis—Ontario, British Columbia, Quebec, Nova Scotia, Manitoba
Track and Field—Quebec, Ontario, Alberta, Manitoba, British Columbia
Water Polo—Quebec, Ontario, Alberta, Manitoba, British Columbia
Water Skiing—Ontario, Quebec, Manitoba, British Columbia, Alberta

CHESS

World Champions
Men—Boris V. Spassky, USSR (defeated Tigran Petrosian, USSR champion since 1963, in 23-game challenge match that ended June 17, 12½–10½)
Women—Nona Gaprindashvili, USSR

United States Champions
Men—Sammy Reshevsky, Spring Valley, N. Y.
Women—Mrs. Gisela K. Gresser, New York
Open—Arthur Bisguier, Hartsdale, N. Y., Pal Benko, New York, and Milan Vukcevich, Cleveland Heights, Ohio
Junior—Kenneth Rogoff, Rochester, N. Y.

CROSS COUNTRY

AAU (Bloomfield Hills, Mich., Nov. 29, 10,000 meters)—Jack Bacheler, Florida Track Club, Gainesville, Fla. (30:49.8); team: Pacific Coast Club (42 pts)

NCAA—*University Division* (New York, Nov. 24, 6 miles): Gerry Lindgren, Washington State (28:59.2); *team:* University of Texas, El Paso (74 pts). *College Division* (Wheaton, Ill., Nov. 15, 5 miles): Ron Stonitsch, C.W. Post College (24:53); *team:* Eastern Illinois (84 pts)

NAIA (Oklahoma City, Nov. 22, 5 miles)—Ralph Foote, Taylor (Ind.) University (24:53); *team:* Fort Hayes (Kans.) State (102 pts)

IC4-A (New York, Nov. 17, 5 miles)—*University Division:* Arthur Dulong, Holy Cross (24:06.8); *team:* Villanova (60 pts). *College Division:* Ron Stonitsch, C.W. Post (25:03.3); *team:* Lehigh (36 pts). *Freshmen* (3 miles)—*University Division:* Phil Banning, Villanova (14:52.4); *team:* William and Mary (76 pts). *College Division:* Dan Moynihan, Wesleyan (15:04.7); *team:* West Chester State (54 pts)

U. S. Track and Field Federation (University Park, Pa., Nov. 26, 6 miles)—Jack Bacheler, Florida Track Club (29:35); *team:* University of Texas, El Paso (44 pts)

Women's AAU (Inglewood, Calif., Nov. 29, 2 miles)—Doris Brown, Falcon (Seattle) Track Club (10:56.2); *team:* Wolverine Parkettes (35 pts)

CURLING

World Cup (Perth, Scotland)—Canada (Ron Northcott, skip)

U. S. Men (Grand Forks, N. Dak.)—Superior, Wis. (Bud Somerville)

U. S. Women (Milwaukee, Wis.)—Pardeeville (Wis.) Pipers (Mrs. Al Miller)

Canadian—Calgary Curling Club (Northcott)

Gordon International Medal (Montreal)—United States 367, Canada 362

Gordon Champion Rink (Schenectady, N. Y.)—Albany Curling Club (J. C. Lisuzzo)

DOG SHOWS

Westminster Kennel Club (New York, Feb. 10–11)—Group winners (2,589 dogs shown): *sporting:* Wayne D. Magill's English springer spaniel Ch. Magill's Patrick, Renton, Wash.; *hound:* Mrs. Charles C. Stalter's smooth dachshund Ch. Crosswynd's Crackerjack, Woodcliff Lake, N. J.; *working:* Mr. and Mrs. Howard Sherline's Old English sheepdog Ch. Prince Andrew of Sherline, Detroit; *nonsporting:* Donald L. Brennan's and Mrs. Valetta E. Gotschall's chow chow Ch. Gotschall's Van Van, Getzville, N. Y.; *toy:* Marie Elizabeth and Charles A. T. O'Neill's Manchester toy terrier Ch. Renreh Lorelei of Charmaron, Philadelphia; *terrier and best in show:* Walter F. Goodman's and Mrs. Adele F. Goodman's Skye terrier Ch. Glamoor Good News, Center Island, N. Y.

International Kennel Club (Chicago, April 5–6)—Group winners (3,402 dogs shown): *sporting:* Joyce Scott-Paine's English cocker spaniel Ch. Ancram's Simon, Ancramdale, N. Y.; *nonsporting:* Round Table Kennels' miniature poodle Ch. Round Table Loramar Yeoman, Middletown, Del.; *working and best in show:* Dr. and Mrs. P. J. Pagano's and Dr. Teodore S. Fickes' boxer Ch. Arriba's Prima Donna, Pelham Manor, N. Y. and Marblehead, Mass.; *hound:* Estate of Fred A. Vaught's American foxhound Ch. Vaught's John Paul, Hartsville, Tenn.; *terrier:* Walter F. Goodman's and Mrs. Adele F. Goodman's Skye Ch. Glamoor Go Go Go, Oyster Bay, N. Y.; *toy:* Mrs. L. S. Gordon Jr.'s and Janet Bennett's Yorkshire terrier Ch. Continuation of Gleno, Glenville, Ill.

FENCING

United States Championships
(Van Nuys, Calif., June 28–July 5)

Individual—*Foil:* Carl Borack, Salle du Nord, Santa Monica, Calif.; *épée:* Steve Netburn, Salle Csiszar, Philadelphia; *saber:* Alex Orban, New York A. C.; *women's foil:* Ruth White, Baltimore Fencers Club

Team—*Foil:* Salle Csiszar *épée:* Salle Mori, Beverley Hills, Calif.; *saber:* New York A. C.; *women's foil:* Salle Santelli, New York; *overall:* New York A. C.

National Collegiate (NCAA) Championships
(Raleigh, N. C., March 27–29)

Individual—*Foil:* Anthony Kestler, Columbia; *épée:* James Wetzler, Pennsylvania; *saber:* Norman Braslow, Pennsylvania

Team (3-weapon)—Pennsylvania (54 pts)

World Championships
(Havana, October 3–11)

Individual—*Foil:* Friederich Wessel, West Germany; *épée:* Bohdan Andrzejewski, Poland; *saber:* Viktor Sidiak, USSR; *women's foil:* Yelena Novikova, USSR

Team—*Foil, épée, and saber:* USSR; *women's foil:* Rumania

Women's Collegiate

Women's Intercollegiate Fencing Association (Brooklyn, N. Y., March 28–29)—*Individual:* Sally Pechinsky, New York University; *team:* Cornell

FOOTBALL
Professional

There were too many Chiefs and not enough Vikings in the right places at the right time in the Super Bowl on Jan. 11, 1970, and Kansas City routed Minneapolis, 23–7, for the championship of pro football. The Vikings were 13-point and 7–2 favorites to emphasize National League superiority, but, for the second straight year the American League shattered that illusion.

Nonetheless, the result would not affect the merger of the two leagues scheduled three weeks later in February 1970. Then the American League would be absorbed into the National, retaining its identity as a group only in the designation "American Conference." In order to have two equal divisions of 13 teams, three clubs from the National League—Baltimore, Cleveland, and Pittsburgh—were to be aligned with the 10 AL clubs. The other division would be the National Conference. Each division would have groupings of 4, 4, and 4 teams.

The Chiefs, who had entered the league as the Dallas Texans, were coached by Hank Stram, the only coach who was with the AL from its inception in 1960 to the merger. For Stram and his quarterback, Len Dawson, the victory carried extra pleasure, for they had guided the Kansas City eleven that lost to Green Bay in the first Super Bowl. The Chiefs' running attack was sparked by three 5-foot 9-inch backs—Mike Garrett, Robert Holmes, and Warren McVea. Their main receiver was Otis Taylor; and Curly Culp, Aaron Brown, and Jerry Mays led the defensive unit.

UPI

PRESIDENT NIXON moved into the football spotlight—and controversy—by presenting Texas with a plaque calling it the nation's No. 1 team. (*Left*) Nixon shakes hands with quarterback James Street after Texas topped Arkansas to close the season undefeated. But Penn State also was unbeaten (in 30 games in three years).

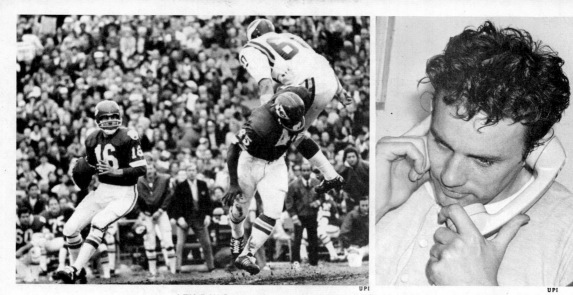

LEN DAWSON gets off a pass (*left*) and later receives a telephone call from President Nixon as Kansas City Chiefs subdue Minnesota in the 1970 Super Bowl.

LEN DAWSON, the 34-year-old quarterback for Kansas City, went into the 1970 Super Bowl game with problems. His weak left knee, which had kept him out of six games, was vulnerable, and he had been mentioned as a player who would be questioned in a gambling investigation. Against Minnesota, however, Dawson directed the Chiefs to a 23–7 victory, completing 12 of 17 passes, one for a touchdown; and he was voted the most valuable player.

The Super Bowl performance capped a 13-year pro career for Leonard Ray Dawson, who was born in Alliance, Ohio, June 20, 1935. At Purdue, he led the Big Ten in offense and, after graduation in 1957, spent five years in the NFL, three at Pittsburgh and two at Cleveland. Acquired by Dallas (which moved to Kansas City the following season) in 1962, he led the Texans to the AFL title. He led the league in passing again in 1964, 1966, and 1968. He threw six touchdown passes in a game in 1964, and set a record of 15 straight pass completions in 1967.

Kansas City finished second to Oakland in season play in the Western Division but got another chance in the inter-division play-offs. First they stopped the Jets (13–6), who had jolted the National League in the 1969 Super Bowl. Then the Chiefs, two-time losers to the Raiders, gained the Super Bowl by beating Oakland, 17–7. The Vikings, beaten in their opening game, had run off a record 12 victories in a row, and their defense had allowed only 133 points and 16 touchdowns in the 14-game season. Their coach was Bud Grant, who had been successful at Winnipeg in the Canadian League. The quarterback was rugged Joe Kapp, who equaled the pro record by throwing seven touchdown passes against Baltimore on September 28.

The Vikings squelched the strong Los Angeles Rams in their Western Conference, 23–20, and routed the Cleveland Browns, 27–7, for the league championship.

Jan Stenerud, a Norwegian who set a record with 16 field goals in 16 attempts, led the Chief's scoring with 119 points. The Vikings' Fred Cox booted the ball for 121 points.

Steve O'Neal, the Jets' punter, set a record in Denver, September 21, with a 98-yard kick, booting from the one-yard line to the one-yard line.

NATIONAL FOOTBALL LEAGUE
(Final Standings, 1969)
Eastern Conference
Capital Division

	Won	Lost	Tied	Pct.	Pts.	OP
Dallas	11	2	1	.846	369	223
Washington	7	5	2	.583	307	319
New Orleans	5	9	0	.357	311	393
Philadelphia	4	9	1	.308	279	377

Century Division

	Won	Lost	Tied	Pct.	Pts.	OP
Cleveland	10	3	1	.769	351	300
New York	6	8	0	.429	264	298
St. Louis	4	9	1	.308	314	389
Pittsburgh	1	13	0	.071	218	404

Conference champion—Cleveland (defeated Dallas, 38–14, at Dallas, Dec. 28)

Western Conference
Coastal Division

	Won	Lost	Tied	Pct.	Pts.	OP
Los Angeles	11	3	0	.785	320	243
Baltimore	8	5	1	.615	279	268
Atlanta	6	8	0	.429	276	268
San Francisco	4	8	2	.333	277	319

Central Division

	Won	Lost	Tied	Pct.	Pts.	OP
Minnesota	12	2	0	.857	379	133
Detroit	9	4	1	.692	259	188
Green Bay	8	6	0	.571	269	221
Chicago	1	13	0	.071	210	339

Conference champion—Minnesota (defeated Los Angeles, 23–20, at Bloomington, Minn., Dec. 27)
League champion—Minnesota (defeated Cleveland, 27–7, at Bloomington, Minn., Jan. 4)

AMERICAN FOOTBALL LEAGUE
(Final Standings, 1969)
Eastern Division

	Won	Lost	Tied	Pct.	Pts.	OP
New York	10	4	0	.714	353	269
Houston	6	6	2	.500	278	279
Boston	4	10	0	.286	266	316
Buffalo	4	10	0	.286	230	359
Miami	3	10	1	.231	233	332

Western Division

	Won	Lost	Tied	Pct.	Pts.	OP
Oakland	12	1	1	.923	377	242
Kansas City	11	3	0	.786	359	177
San Diego	8	6	0	.571	288	276
Denver	5	8	1	.385	297	344
Cincinnati	4	9	1	.308	280	367

Inter-Divisional Play-offs
Kansas City (defeated New York, 13–6, at New York, Dec. 20)
Oakland (defeated Houston, 56–7, at Oakland, Dec. 21)
League champion—Kansas City (defeated Oakland, 17–7, at Oakland, Jan. 4, 1970)

Bowl and All-Star Games in 1970
Play-off Bowl (Miami, Jan. 4)—Los Angeles defeated Dallas, 31–0

AFL All-Star (Houston, Jan. 17)—West defeated East, 26–3
NFL Pro (Los Angeles, Jan. 18)—West defeated East, 16–13
Super Bowl (New Orleans, Jan. 11)—Kansas City (AL) 23, Minnesota (NL) 7

CANADIAN FOOTBALL LEAGUE

Grey Cup (Montreal, Nov. 30)—Ottawa Rough Riders defeated Saskatchewan Roughriders, 29–11

College

The President of the United States became involved in college football for the first time since 1905 and probably made Democrats out of numerous fans in the Nittany Mountains of Pennsylvania in December. Theodore Roosevelt had been concerned about the integrity and roughness of the game, but President Richard M. Nixon elected to attend the Texas-Arkansas game on December 6 and present a plaque to the winner as the nation's No. 1 team. Each team was undefeated, but so was Penn State, and protests from the governor of Pennsylvania failed to halt Nixon in his mission.

Texas then showed real championship qualities by coming from behind, gambling on fourth-down passes, and winning, 15–14. To maintain the right to the plaque received from the President after the game, the Longhorns again rallied in the closing minutes on New Year's Day in the Cotton Bowl and defeated Notre Dame, 21–17. Meanwhile, Penn State bolstered its claim to the top-ranking honor by defeating Missouri, 10–3, in the Orange Bowl for its 22d straight victory, extending its undefeated streak to 30 games over a three-year span. The Nittany Lions won 10 regular-season games, all by good margins except for a 15–14 squeaker over Syracuse. Texas also won 10 games, 7 from Southwest Conference foes, being hard-pressed only by Oklahoma and Arkansas.

Oddly enough, none of these had been considered the top team until the last week of the season. Ohio State, the 1968 champion, had been proclaimed the best in the land and trounced all of its foes by at least three touchdowns in running its winning streak to 22 games. Then, before a record crowd of 103,588 at Ann Arbor, the Buckeyes had their one bad day; an inspired Michigan eleven knocked them off the throne, 24–12. The pollsters, in their odd way, then forgot about the team they had hailed for a year as supreme.

Individual honors went to Steve Owens, an Oklahoma running back who led the nation in rushing. He won the Heisman Trophy as the outstanding player, receiving 151 more points than Mike Phipps, the Purdue quarterback.

The most notable achievement of the season, however, was that of Chester Marcol of Hillsdale (Mich.) College, who kicked a 62-yard field goal on October 18 against Fairmount State. It broke all records, college and professional, and came only one week after Cloyce Hinton of Mississippi had set the mark with a 59-yard kick, 3 yards longer than the pro record held by Bert Rechichar.

Intercollegiate and Conference Champions

National (AP and UPI polls)—Texas
National Football Foundation Award (MacArthur Bowl)—Texas
Eastern (Lambert Trophy)—Penn State
Eastern Small College—*Lambert Cup:* Delaware and Wesleyan; *Lambert Bowl:* Kings Point
Athletic Association of Western Universities (Pacific Eight)—Southern California (6–0)
Atlantic Coast—South Carolina (6–0)
Big Eight—Missouri and Nebraska (6–1)
Big Ten—Michigan and Ohio State (6–1)
Ivy League—Dartmouth, Princeton, Yale (6–1)
Mid-American—Toledo (5–0)
Middle Atlantic—*University Division:* Delaware (6–0); *College Division: north:* Wilkes (5–0); *south:* Johns Hopkins and Lebanon Valley (5–2)

Missouri Valley—Memphis State (4–0)
Ohio Valley—East Tennessee State (6–0–1)
Southeastern—Tennessee (5–1)
Southern—Davidson and Richmond (5–1)
Southwest—Texas (7–0)
Western Athletic—Arizona State (6–1)
NAIA Championship Bowl (Kingsville, Texas, Dec. 13)—Texas A & I 32, Concordia (Minn.) 7

Leading Independents

East—Penn State (10–0), Boston University (9–1), West Virginia (9–1)
Midwest—Notre Dame (8–1–1)
Southwest—Houston (7–2), West Texas State (6–3)
South—Florida State (6–2–1)
Far West—Air Force Academy (6–4)

NCAA Regional Bowls
(All games played Dec. 13)

Boardwalk (Atlantic Coast at Atlantic City)—Delaware 31, North Carolina Central 13
Grantland Rice (Mideast at Baton Rouge, La.)—East Tennessee 34, Louisiana Tech 14
Pecan (Midwest at Arlington, Texas)—Arkansas State 29, Drake 21
Camelia (Pacific Coast at Sacramento, Calif.)—North Dakota State 30, Montana 3

Major Bowl and All-Star Games
(Nov.–Dec. 1969)

Silver (Sterling, Kans., Nov. 27)—Hutchinson (Kans.) Junior College 32, Nassau (N.Y.) Community College 7
National Junior College Championship (Savannah, Ga., Nov. 28)—Northeast Oklahoma A & M 20, Arizona Western 6
Mineral Water (Excelsior Springs, Mo., Nov. 29)—St. John's (Minn.) 21, Simpson 0
Knute Rockne (Bridgeport, Conn., Nov. 29)—Randolph-Macon 47, Bridgeport 28
Amos Alonzo Stagg (Springfield, Ohio, Nov. 29)—Wittenberg 27, William Jewell 21
Orange Blossom Classic (Miami, Dec. 6)—Florida A & M 23, Grambling 19
Pasadena (Pasadena, Calif., Dec. 6)—San Diego State 28, Boston University 7
Liberty (Memphis, Tenn., Dec. 13)—Colorado 47, Alabama 33
Sun (El Paso, Texas, Dec. 20)—Nebraska 45, Georgia 6
North-South Shrine All-Star (Miami, Dec. 25)—North 31, South 10
Tangerine (Orlando, Fla., Dec. 26)—Toledo 56, Davidson 33
Gator (Jacksonville, Fla., Dec. 27)—Florida 14, Tennessee 13
Blue-Gray All-Star (Montgomery, Ala., Dec. 27)—North 6, South 6
East-West Shrine All-Star (San Francisco, Dec. 27)—West 15, East 0
Peach (Atlanta, Dec. 30)—West Virginia 14, South Carolina 3
Astro-Bluebonnet (Houston, Dec. 31)—Houston 36, Auburn 7
(January 1970)
Cotton (Dallas, Jan. 1)—Texas 21, Notre Dame 17
Orange (Miami, Jan. 1)—Penn State 10, Missouri 3
Rose (Pasadena, Calif., Jan. 1)—Southern California 10, Michigan 3
Sugar (New Orleans, Jan. 1)—Mississippi 27, Arkansas 22
American (Tampa, Fla., Jan. 3)—South 24, North 23
Hula (Honolulu, Jan. 10)—South 35, North 13
Senior (Mobile, Ala., Jan. 10)—North 37, South 37

GOLF

The Professional Golfers' Association chose Orville Moody, a former Army sergeant, as Golfer of the Year in 1969, emphasizing the fact that the game is no longer dominated by the "top-name" players. Moody, of course, earned the award, mainly by winning the U. S. Open championship at Houston by a stroke, with 281, and the World Series of Golf at Akron by 2 strokes.

The other three players in the World Series, which is a 36-hole competition among the winners of the top four world tournaments, were about as little-known as Moody. They were George Archer of Gilroy, Calif., the Masters champion; Tony Jacklin, a young Briton who won the British Open; and Ray Floyd of Chicago, the PGA winner, who spends his spare time working out with the Chicago Cubs.

The top-name players—Jack Nicklaus, Billy Casper, Arnold Palmer, and Gary Player—were around, but, possibly because of other interests they seldom won, although they piled up prize money. Palmer finished in a tie for sixth in the U. S. Open, but had to withdraw during the tour because of hip trouble. However, he returned in the late fall and won the last two tournaments, raising his earnings for the year to $105,128 and his career total to $1,121,556. Nicklaus won the Williams–San Diego, the Sahara, and the fall Kaiser International and a total of $140,167. Casper was low in the Hope Desert Classic, Western Open, and Alcan, and picked up $104,689. Player earned $123,897, although his only victory was in the Tournament of Champions.

The leading money-winner was Frank Beard of Louisville, with $175,223. Second was Dave Hill of Jackson, Mich., with 156,423.

Carol Mann of Buffalo took top honors among the women pros, winning eight of the Ladies Professional Golf Association (LPGA) tournaments and $49,448. Kathy Whitworth was runner-up with seven victories and $48,971. However, she moved into the all-time earnings lead with 268,974 in 11 years, $807 more than Mickey Wright, the previous top winner. Betsy Rawls returned to competition briefly and won the LPGA. However, a comparative unknown, Donna Caponi of Burbank, Calif., won the U. S. Open.

U. S. Amateur championships went to Steve Melnyk of Brunswick, Ga., and to Catherine Lacoste, the daughter of the former tennis star of France, René Lacoste.

In team play, U. S. amateurs defeated the British 10–8 for the Walker Cup; the American and British pros played to a 16–16 tie in the Ryder Cup; and the U. S. team won the World Cup at Singapore. Lee Trevino took high individual honors and Moody, the other American, finished third, a stroke back of Roberto de Vicenzo of Argentina.

UPI

ORVILLE J. MOODY, on his way to victory in the U. S. Open, shows elation as he sinks a 15-foot putt.

Leading Money Winners 1969

Men's PGA

Frank Beard	$175,223
Dave Hill	$156,423
Jack Nicklaus	$140,167
Gary Player	$123,897
Bruce Crampton	$118,955
Gene Littler	$112,737
Lee Trevino	$112,417
Ray Floyd	$109,956
Arnold Palmer	$105,128
Billy Casper	$104,689
George Archer	$102,707

Ladies PGA

Carol Mann	$ 49,448
Kathy Whitworth	$ 48,971
Donna Caponi	$ 30,725
Shirley Englehorn	$ 24,832
Sandra Haynie	$ 24,605
Sandra Spuzich	$ 20,550
Susie M. Berning	$ 20,333
Murle Lindstrom	$ 19,914
Sandra Palmer	$ 18,806
Mickey Wright	$ 18,309

10 Top Lifetime

Arnold Palmer	$1,121,556
Jack Nicklaus	$ 996,524
Billy Casper	$ 981,924
Julius Boros	$ 761,732
Gene Littler	$ 637,159
Gary Player	$ 592,623
Doug Sanders	$ 549,087
Frank Beard	$ 514,402
Dan Sikes	$ 453,775
Sam Snead	$ 442,241

10 Top Lifetime

Kathy Whitworth	$ 268,974
Mickey Wright	$ 268,167
Betsy Rawls	$ 237,474
Marlene Hagge	$ 197,403
Marilynn Smith	$ 189,942
Carol Mann	$ 184,239
Patty Berg	$ 181,611
Louis Suggs	$ 180,980
Sandra Haynie	$ 165,754
Ruth Jessen	$ 119,287

Men's Individual Champions

U. S. Open–Orville Moody, Killeen, Texas
U. S. Amateur–Steve Melnyk, Brunswick, Ga.
Masters–George Archer, Gilroy, Calif.
Professional Golfers' Association–Ray Floyd, Chicago
Vardon Trophy–Dave Hill, Jackson, Mich.
U. S. Public Links–John Jackson, Jr., Tempe, Ariz.
British Open–Tony Jacklin, England
British Amateur–Michael Bonallack, England
Canadian Open–Tommy Aaron, Callaway Gardens, Ga.
Canadian Amateur–Wayne McDonald, Hornby, Ont.
Canadian PGA–Bobby Cox, Richmond, B. C.
French Open–Jean Garialde, France
French Amateur–Alexis Godillot, France
World Senior Pro–Tommy Bolt, Sarasota, Fla.
World Senior Amateur–Dave Goldman, Dallas, Texas
World Series of Golf–Orville Moody
Los Angeles Open–Charles Sifford, Los Angeles
Crosby Pro-Am–George Archer
Williams–San Diego Open–Jack Nicklaus, Columbus, Ohio
Hope Desert Classic–Billy Casper, Bonita, Calif.
Phoenix Open–Gene Littler, La Jolla, Calif.
Tucson Open–Lee Trevino, Horizon City, Texas
Doral Open–Tom Shaw, Golf, Ill.
Florida Citrus Open–Ken Still, Tacoma, Wash.
National Airlines Open–Bunky Henry, Peachtree City, Ga.
Greensboro Open–Gene Littler
Tournament of Champions–Gary Player, South Africa
New Orleans Open–Larry Hinson, Douglas, Ga.
Texas Open–Deane Beman, Bethesda, Md.
Memphis Open–Dave Hill
Western Open–Billy Casper
Kemper Open–Dale Douglass, Denver, Colo.

Cleveland Open–Charles Coody, Abilene, Texas
Buick Open–Dave Hill
Philadelphia Classic–Dave Hill
American Classic–Ray Floyd
Avco Classic–Tom Shaw
Greater Hartford Open–Bob Lunn, Sacramento, Calif.
Westchester Classic–Frank Beard, Louisville, Ky.
Alcan–Billy Casper
San Francisco Open–Steve Spray, Cedar Rapids, Iowa
Hawaii Open–Bruce Crampton, Australia
Heritage–Arnold Palmer, Latrobe, Pa.
Kaiser International–Jack Nicklaus
Thomas-Diplomat–Arnold Palmer
Eastern Amateur–Lanny Wadkins, Richmond, Va.
Trans-Mississippi Amateur–Allen Miller, Pensacola, Fla.
Pacific Coast Amateur–Mike Davis, Portland, Oreg.
Southern Amateur–Hubert Green, Birmingham, Ala.
Northeast Amateur–Jerry Courville, East Norwalk, Conn.
Southeastern Amateur–Bob Barbarossa, Ft. Lauderdale, Fla.
Lefthanders–Gary Terry, Shawnee, Okla.
USGA Junior–Aly Trompas, San Diego, Calif.
USGA Senior–Curtis Person, Memphis, Tenn.
U. S. Senior–William Scott Jr., San Francisco
U. S. Senior Pro–Tommy Bolt
National Intercollegiate (NAIA)–Ken Hyland, Malone College, Canton, Ohio
National Collegiate (NCAA)–University Division: Bob Clark, California State at Los Angeles; College Division: Mike Spang, Portland State

Women's Individual Champions

U. S. Open–Donna Caponi, Burbank, Calif.
U. S. Amateur–Catherine Lacoste, France
Ladies PGA–Betsy Rawls, Spartanburg, S. C.
Vare Trophy–Kathy Whitworth, San Antonio, Texas
British Amateur–Catherine Lacoste
Canadian Supertest Open–Sandra Haynie, Fort Worth, Texas
Canadian Open Amateur–Marlene Streit, Fonthill, Ont.
Tournament of Champions–Carol Mann, Baltimore
Lady Carling (Atlanta)–Kathy Whitworth
Lady Carling (Baltimore)–Susie M. Berning, Lake Tahoe, Nev.
Lady Carling (Danbury, Conn.)–Carol Mann
Burdine–JoAnne G. Carner (amateur), Seekonk, Mass.
Dallas Civitan–Carol Mann
St. Louis Open–Sandra Haynie
Patty Berg Classic–Kathy Whitworth
Pabst Classic–Susie M. Berning
Buckeye Savings–Sandra Spuzich, Indianapolis
Molson Open–Carol Mann
Wendell-West Open–Kathy Whitworth
USGA Junior–Hollis Stacy, Savannah, Ga.
USGA Senior–Mrs. Philip Cudone, Myrtle Beach, S. C.
U. S. Senior–Mrs. Allison Choate, Rye, N. Y.
Trans-Mississippi–Jane Bastanchury, Whittier, Calif.
Western Amateur–Jane Bastanchury
Intercollegiate–Jane Bastanchury

Team Champions

World Cup (professional, at Singapore, Oct. 2–5)—United States (Lee Trevino and Orville Moody) 552, Japan 560, Argentina 561. *High individual:* Lee Trevino 275; Roberto de Vicenzo, Argentina, 276; Orville Moody 277; Hsieh Yung Yu, Taiwan, 277, Sukree Onchum, Thailand, 277
Ryder Cup (professional, Southport, England, Sept. 18–20)—United States 16, Britain 16
Walker Cup (amateur, Milwaukee, Aug. 22–23)—United States 10, Britain 8
NCAA (Colorado Springs)—*University Division:* Houston; *College Division:* San Fernando Valley State
NAIA—Texas Wesleyan Seniors (St. Andrews, Scotland)—United States 908, Canada 929, Britain-Ireland 931
U. S. Senior Women's G. A.—Mrs. Allison Choate, Rye, N. Y., and Mrs. Joseph Nesbitt, Greenwich, Conn.

GYMNASTICS

National AAU Championships
(Atlanta, May 8–10)

Men

All-Around—Mauno Nissinen, Husky Gym Club, Seattle
Side Horse—Dave Thor, Michigan State
Horizontal Bar—John Ellas, Northwestern (Louisiana) State
Floor Exercise—Toby Towson, Michigan State
Parallel Bars—Yoshi Hayasaki, Husky Gym Club, Seattle
Long Horse—Paul Tickenoff, Northwestern (Louisiana) State
Rings—Bob Emery, Penn State
Tumbling—John Crosby, New York Athletic Club
Trampoline—George Huntzicker, U. of Michigan
Team—Husky Gym Club

Women

All-Around—Joyce Tanac, Seattle Downtown YMCA
Floor Exercise—Joyce Tanac
Uneven Bars—Joyce Tanac
Side Horse—Joyce Tanac
Balance Beam—Joyce Tanac
Tumbling—Sherry Almy, East Lansing, Mich.
Trampoline—Vicki Bolinger, Springfield, Ill.
Team—Seattle Downtown YMCA

National Collegiate (NCAA) Championships
(Seattle, Wash., April 3–5)

All-Around—Mauno Nissinen, Washington (108.2 pts)
Floor Exercise—Toby Towson, Michigan State (18.95)
Side Horse—Keith McCanless, Iowa (19.05)
Rings—Tie between Paul Vexler, Penn State, and Ward Maythaler, Iowa (18.65)
Long Horse—Tie between Dan Bowles, California, and Jack McCarthy, Illinois (18.40)
Parallel Bars—Ron Rapper, Michigan (18.70)
Horizontal Bar—Bob Manna, New Mexico (18.85)
Team—Iowa (161.74 pts), Penn State (160.45), Iowa State (159.77)
College Division (at Northridge, Calif., March 27–29)—San Fernando Valley State (151.8 pts), Southern Connecticut (145.575), Springfield (145.475)

HANDBALL

U. S. Handball Association Champions

4-Wall—*Singles:* Paul Haber, Milwaukee; *doubles:* Lou Kramberg and Lou Russo, New York; *masters singles:* Dr. John Scopis, Detroit; *masters doubles:* Ken Schneider and Gus Lewis, Chicago; *collegiate singles:* Fred Lewis, University of Miami; *collegiate doubles:* Joel Galpern and Jackie Lewis, Miami; *collegiate team:* Miami
National Contenders—*Singles:* Pat Kirby, Toronto; *doubles:* Mel Sandland and Matt Kelly, Long Beach, Calif.; *masters singles:* Ralph Kaufman, Miami; *masters doubles:* Joe Ardito and Ben Costello, Chicago

National AAU Champions

1-Wall—*Singles:* Steve Sandler, New York; *doubles:* Sandler and Marty Decatur, New York; *masters doubles:* Al Goldstein and Nat Schifter, Brooklyn

National YMCA Championships

4-Wall—*Singles:* Gordon Pfeiffer, Tacoma, Wash.; *doubles:* Paul Schulz and Gary Rohrer, St. Paul

HARNESS RACING

In racing to his third consecutive award as Harness Horse of the Year, Nevele Pride obliterated one of the sport's more hallowed records—Greyhound's 1:55¼ for one mile, established in 1938. Nevele Pride trotted the distance on a one-mile track in 1:54⅘ at Indianapolis, August 31, in a time trial. The pacing record of 1:53⅗ is held by Bret Hanover, the first horse to win three consecutive Horse of the Year awards, 1964–66.

The mile record was only one of three major ones that Nevele Pride, who competed with a hairline crack of the left front ankle, set during the year. The trotter did the mile in 1:56⅘ on a half-mile track and 1:58 on a ⅝-mile oval. The 4-year-old stallion was sold to a syndicate for $3 million and retired to stud in October after earning $871,738. Nevele Pride was driven through most of his career, in which he won 57 of 67 races, by Stanley Dancer.

U. S. Trotting Association Champions

Trotters

2-Year-Old—Victory Star
3-Year-Old—Lindy's Pride
4-Year-Old—Nevele Pride
Aged—Fresh Yankee

Pacers

2-Year-Old—Truluck
3-Year-Old—Laverne Hanover
4-Year-Old—Miss Conna Adios
Aged—Overcall

Harness Horse of the Year

Nevele Pride (133 votes); Overcall (56); Lindy's Pride (15); Laverne Hanover (4); Truluck (2)

Major Stakes Winners

Trotting

American Championship (Roosevelt)—Nevele Pride
American-National (Sportman's)—Snow Speed
Challenge Cup (Roosevelt)—Fresh Yankee
Colonial (Liberty Bell)—Lindy's Pride
Dexter (Roosevelt)—Lindy's Pride
Hambletonian (Du Quoin, Ill.)—Lindy's Pride
Harriman (Yonkers)—Victory Star
Kentucky Futurity (Lexington)—Lindy's Pride
Realization (Roosevelt)—Nevele Pride
Roosevelt International—Une de Mai (France)
United Nations (Yonkers)—Snow Speed
Volomite (Yonkers)—Lady B. Fast
Westbury Futurity (Roosevelt)—Gunner
Yonkers Futurity—Lindy's Pride

Pacing

Adios (Meadows)—Laverne Hanover
American Classic (Hollywood)—Overcall
Cane Futurity (Yonkers)—Kat Byrd
Fox (Indianapolis)—Truluck
Good Time (Yonkers)—Overcall
Hoosier Futurity (Indianapolis)—Andover Rainbow
Horseman Futurity (Indianapolis)—Laverne Hanover
Lady Suffolk (Roosevelt)—Flowing Speed
Little Brown Jug (Delaware, Ohio)—Laverne Hanover

UPI

NEVELE PRIDE (*right*) driven by Stanley Dancer, heads for a world trotting record of 1:54.8 in the mile at the Indiana State Fair on August 31. The horse at the left assists by serving as a prompter during the time trial.

HOCKEY

In winning their second straight National Hockey League championship in 1969 the Montreal Canadiens were extended slightly more than they were in the previous year. They lost two games in three series in the Stanley Cup play-offs. The preceding season, they had lost but one while winning 12 against three clubs.

The team that gave them some trouble was the Boston Bruins, who had finished only 3 points behind the Canadians in the East Division. The Bruins, with a surge on their home ice, even had the semifinal cup series deadlocked at two games each, before the Canadiens skated away. Montreal had eliminated the New York Rangers, 4 games to 0. They completed the victory over Boston, 4 games to 2, and then swept past the St. Louis Blues, the West Division champion, 4 games to 0.

Boston, led by Bobby Orr, the young defenseman, and Phil Esposito, a rangy forward obtained in a trade with the Chicago Black Hawks, became a dynamic team. Esposito broke the league scoring record for total points (goals and assists) by getting 126. His 49 goals set a record for a center, and his 77 assists were the most ever registered in the league. Orr, who at the age of 20 won the Norris Trophy as the outstanding defenseman and who was voted to the All-Star team for the second time, also set scoring records. His 29 goals and 64 total points were the most ever scored by a defenseman.

The Black Hawks were the big surprise, slumping to last place in the East and failing to make the play-offs for the first time in 10 years. However, their star wing, Bobby Hull, raised his own record for goals in a season from 54 to 58.

The NHL voted in November to add Buffalo and Vancouver, B. C., to its East Division roster in the fall of 1970. The Chicago Black Hawks will move into the West Division to balance the league and keep all of the Canadian clubs in one division.

NATIONAL HOCKEY LEAGUE
(Final Standings, 1969)

East Division

Team	Won	Lost	Tied	Goals For	Goals Against	Pts.
Montreal	46	19	11	271	202	103
Boston	42	18	16	303	221	100
New York	41	26	9	231	196	91
Toronto	35	26	15	234	217	85
Detroit	33	31	12	239	221	78
Chicago	34	33	9	280	246	77

West Division

	Won	Lost	Tied	Goals For	Goals Against	Pts.
St. Louis	37	25	14	204	157	88
Oakland	29	36	11	219	251	69
Philadelphia	20	35	21	174	225	61
Los Angeles	24	42	10	185	260	58
Pittsburgh	20	45	11	189	252	51
Minnesota	18	43	15	189	270	51

Stanley Cup Play-offs

Preliminary Series—*East Division:* Montreal defeated New York, 4 games to 0; Boston defeated Toronto, 4 games to 0. *West Division:* St. Louis defeated Philadelphia, 4 games to 0; Los Angeles defeated Oakland, 4 games to 3 *Semifinals—East:* Montreal defeated Boston, 4 games to 2. *West:* St. Louis defeated Los Angeles, 4 games to 0 *Final—*Montreal defeated St. Louis, 4 games to 0

Individual National Hockey League Awards

Hart Trophy (most valuable player)—Phil Esposito, Boston
Ross Trophy (leading scorer)—Esposito
Norris Trophy (leading defenseman)—Bobby Orr, Boston
Lady Byng Trophy (sportsmanship)—Alex Delvecchio, Detroit

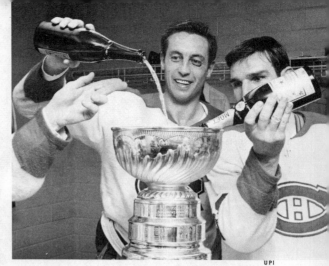

UPI

TWO CANADIENS, Jean Beliveau and John Ferguson, pour champagne into Montreal's newly won Stanley Cup.

Calder Trophy (outstanding rookie)—Danny Grant, Minnesota
Vezina Trophy (fewest goals scored against)—Glenn Hall and Jacques Plante, St. Louis
Conn Smythe Trophy (most valuable in play-offs)—Serge Savard, Montreal

NHL All-Star Teams

(Players are selected by writers and broadcasters in NHL cities. NHL pays $1,000 to each final first-team member and $500 to each second-team one.)

Position	First Team	Second Team
Goal	Glenn Hall, St. Louis	Ed Giacomin, New York
Defense	Bobby Orr, Boston	Ted Green, Boston
Defense	Tim Horton, Toronto	Ted Harris, Montreal
Center	Phil Esposito, Boston	Jean Beliveau, Montreal
R. Wing	Gordie Howe, Detroit	Yvan Cournoyer, Montreal
L. Wing	Bobby Hull, Chicago	Frank Mahovlich, Detroit

Other Professional Champions

American League—*Eastern Division and Calder Cup play-off:* Hershey Bears; *Western Division:* Buffalo Bisons
Western League—*Regular season:* Portland Buckaroos; *play-off:* Vancouver Canucks
Central League—*Northern Division:* Tulsa Oilers; *Southern Division:* Oklahoma City Blazers; *play-off:* Dallas Black Hawks

Amateur Champions

Eastern League—*Northern division and play-offs:* Clinton Comets; *Southern division:* Greensboro Generals
International League—*Regular season and play-offs:* Dayton Gems

United States Intercollegiate

NCAA—Denver University (defeated Cornell in final, 4–3)
ECAC—Cornell (defeated Harvard in final, 4–2)
NAIA—Bemidji (Minn.) State (defeated Lake Superior (Mich.) State, in final, 6–2
Ivy League—Cornell
American Hockey Association of the US—*International USA:* Taconite of Minneapolis; *junior:* St. Clair Shores, Mich.; *midget:* Detroit; *bantam:* St. Clair Shores; *Pee Wee:* St. Clair Shores

HORSE RACING

Arts and Letters missed winning the Triple Crown by a neck and a head in 1969 but took the Horse of the Year honors by a wide margin. The chestnut son of Ribot, owned by Paul Mellon of the Rokeby Stables, won the Belmont Stakes, the Woodward, Travers, Jockey Club Gold Cup, and four other races in 14 starts in which he did not finish worse than third. The horse earned $555,064 during the year.

Actually, Majestic Prince, a big chestnut colt from California, came closest to winning the Triple Crown. The colt, owned by Frank McMahon and trained by Johnny Longden, a former jockey, won the Kentucky Derby by a neck from Arts and Let-

MAJESTIC PRINCE (*left*), with Bill Hartack aboard, thunders to a close victory over Arts and Letters in the Kentucky Derby. But Horse of the Year honors for 1969 went to Arts and Letters.

ters. He then took the Preakness by a head over the Rokeby colt, whose rider, Braulio Baeza, filed an objection; Baeza claimed that the Prince had bumped Arts and Letters during the early running.

Longden was reluctant to run Majestic Prince in the Belmont, the last of the Triple Crown races, saying the horse was overworked. He should have stuck with the decision, for Arts and Letters beat the Prince by five lengths as Willie Hartack, the jockey, apparently misjudged the slow pace and Baeza did not.

The jockeys as a group, however, underwent a radical change in their ranks. Women were added to their membership at U. S. pari-mutuel betting tracks. The change came only after stern opposition and, in some cases, with resentment. After several attempts, 20-year-old Diane Crump of Woodmount, Conn., was the first girl to race. Her mount was Bridle n' Bit, a long shot, at Hialeah, February 7, and she finished 10th in the 12-horse field. A fortnight later, 19-year-old Barbara Jo Rubin piloted Cohesian to victory in a 6½-furlong race at Charles Town track in West Virginia for a woman jockey's first triumph at a U. S. thoroughbred track.

Thoroughbred Racing Association Champions

American Champion—Arts and Letters
Older Horse—Nodouble
Older Filly or Mare—Gamely
2-Year-Old Colt—Silent Screen
2-Year-Old Filly—Fast Attack and Tudor Queen
3-Year-Old Colt—Arts and Letters
3-Year-Old Filly—Gallant Bloom
Steeplechase—L'Escargot
Turf—Hawaii

Stakes Winners

American Derby (Arlington)—Fast Hilarious
Amory L. Haskell Handicap (Monmouth)—Verbatim
Arlington Classic—Ack Ack
Arlington-Washington Lassie—Clover Lane
Arlington-Washington Park Futurity—Silent Screen
Benjamin Lindheimer Handicap (Arlington)—Tampa Trouble
Belmont Stakes—Arts and Letters
Brook Steeplechase Handicap (Belmont)—Curator
Brooklyn Handicap (Aqueduct)—Nodouble
California Derby (Golden Gate)—Jay Ray
Californian (Hollywood)—Nodouble
Campbell Handicap (Bowie)—Juvenile John
Champagne Stakes (Belmont)—Silent Screen
Coaching Club American Oaks (Belmont)—Shuvee
Delaware Handicap—Obeah
Flamingo (Hialeah)—Top Knight
Florida Derby (Gulfstream)—Top Knight
Frizette (Belmont)—Tudor Queen
Futurity (Belmont)—High Echelon
Garden State Stakes—Forum
Gardenia (Garden State)—Fast Attack
Governor Nicolls (Belmont)—Verbatim
Gulfstream Park Handicap—Court Recess
Hawthorne Gold Cup—Nodouble
Hialeah Turf Cup—Blanquette II
Hollywood Derby—Tell
Hollywood Gold Cup—Figonero

Hollywood Juvenile—Insubordination
Hollywood Turf Handicap—Fort Marcy
Hopeful (Saratoga)—Irish Castle
Jersey Derby (Garden State)—Al Hattab
Jockey Club Gold Cup (Aqueduct)—Arts and Letters
Kentucky Derby (Churchill Downs)—Majestic Prince
Man o' War Handicap (Belmont)—Hawaii
Matron (Belmont)—Cold Comfort
Metropolitan Handicap (Belmont)—Arts and Letters
Michigan Handicap (Detroit)—Calandrito
Monmouth Handicap—Al Hattab
Mother Goose Stakes (Belmont)—Shuvee
Oak Tree Stakes (Santa Anita)—Czar Alexander
Oak Leaf Stakes (Santa Anita)—Opening Bid
Penn Handicap (Liberty Bell)—Tropic King II
Pimlico-Laurel Futurity—High Echelon
Preakness (Pimlico)—Majestic Prince
San Antonio Stakes (Santa Anita)—Praise Joy
San Juan Capistrano (Santa Anita)—Petrone
Santa Anita Derby—Majestic Prince
Santa Anita Handicap—Nodouble
Santa Margarita (Santa Anita)—Princessnesian
Sapling (Monmouth)—Ring For Nurse
Selima (Laurel)—Predictable
Sorority (Monmouth)—Box the Compass
Strub (Santa Anita)—Dignitas
Suburban Handicap (Aqueduct)—Mr. Right
Sunset Handicap (Hollywood Park)—Petrone
Temple Gwathmey Steeplechase (Belmont)—Somaten
Travers (Saratoga)—Arts and Letters
United Nations Handicap (Atlantic City)—Hawaii
Washington D.C. International (Laurel)—Karabas
Washington Park Handicap (Arlington)—Night Invader
Whitney (Saratoga)—Verbatim
Widener (Hialeah)—Yumbel
Wood Memorial (Aqueduct)—Dike
Woodward Stakes (Belmont)—Arts and Letters
Yankee Gold Cup Handicap (Suffolk Downs)—Jean-Pierre

Foreign Races

Ascot Gold Cup—Levmoss
Epsom Derby (England)—Blakeney
Epsom Oaks (England)—Sleeping Partner
Grand National Steeplechase (England)—Highland Wedding
Grand Prix de Paris (Longchamps)—Chaparral
Irish Sweeps Derby (The Curragh, Ireland)—Prince Regent
Irish Oaks (Dublin)—Gaia
King George VI and Queen Elizabeth (England)—Park Top
Melbourne Derby (Australia)—Rain Lover
1,000 Guineas (England)—Full Dress II
Prix de l'Arc de Triomphe (France)—Levmoss
Queens Plate (Canada)—Jumpin Joseph
St. Leger (England)—Intermezzo
2,000 Guineas (England)—Right Tack
Canadian Champion—Jumpin Joseph

HORSE SHOWS

American Horse Shows Association
High-Score Winners

Green Conformation Hunter—Mr. and Mrs. J. Eliott Cottrelle's Boyne Valley
Regular Conformation Hunter—Marvin Van Rapoport's Spindletop Showdown
Green Working Hunter—Holly Fuller's Cashe Walk
Regular Working Hunter—Mr. Charles R. McGinnes' Beau Mac
Amateur Owner Hunter—Jane E. Womble's Sign the Card
Junior Hunter—Valerie Peck's Chance Step
Small Pony Hunter—Nancy Baroody's Midget
Large Pony Hunter—Cynthia Weiner's Chimney Sweep
Amateur Owner Jumper—Brooke Hodgson's Advance Ticket
Junior Jumper—Muffie Mauger's Little Advice
Hackney Pony—Springhaven Stable's King's Fanfare of Dawn Acres

Harness Pony—Mrs. Victoria Armstrong's Fashion's Miss Alice
Open Fine Harness Horse—Mr. and Mrs. Kenneth Wheeler's Tashi Ling
Amateur Fine Harness Horse—Dr. Read Holland's Look at Me
Open 3-Gaited Saddle Horse—Mrs. John R. B. Byres' Vanity's Jewel
Amateur 3-Gaited Saddle Horse—Mrs. Read Holland's Precious
Junior Exhibitor's 3-Gaited Saddle Horse—Mrs. Robert O'Connor's The Legend
Open 5-Gaited Saddle Horse—Mr. A. C. Huffman's Wings Fair Lady
Amateur 5-Gaited Saddle Horse—Mr. Huffman's Dream Lover
Junior Exhibitor's 5-Gaited Saddle Horse—Mr. and Mrs. John Ehrlich's Gallent Barrymore
American Saddlebred 3-Gaited Pleasure Horse—Mrs. Alan R. Robson's Social Butterfly
Western Pleasure Horse—Mrs. Shirley C. Ewing's Seatac
Morgan Pleasure Horse—Mrs. Mary H. DeWitt's Orcland Donlendon
Welsh Pleasure Pony—Mrs. J. Austin duPont's Liseter Twinkle
Morgan Park Horse—Mrs. DeWitt's A-Okay
Roadster—R. W. Kuhne's Miss Dean Key
Shetland Roadster—F. E. Birtcher's Mounds Merc Stardust
Shetland Harness—Arthur B. Birtcher's The Patrolman
Stock Horse—Mrs. Katherine H. Haley's Shirley Chex
Tennessee Walking Horse—Mr. and Mrs. Cebern L. Lee's Society Souvenir
Trail Horse—Herbert Aptel's Little Nebraska
Arabian Horse—Leslie Connor's Que Hama
Half Arabian—Invictus Farm's Karate

Equestrian Championships

Hunter Seat (at Harrisburg, Pa.)—Fred Bauer, South Norwalk, Conn.
Saddle Seat (at Kansas City)—Barbara Hoffman, Highland, Ill.
Stock Seat (at Santa Barbara, Calif.)—Libbie Rudnick, Bakersfield, Calif.
Dressage (at Pebble Beach, Calif.)—Inez Fischer-Credo, Canada
3-Day (at Pebble Beach, Calif.)—Hilda Gurney, Woodland Hills, Calif.
National Junior 3-Day (at Woodstock, Vt.)—Lee Thibodeau, Presque Isle, Me.

National Horse Show Awards

NHS Saddle Seat Trophy (Good Hands)—Janet Henry, Tulsa, Okla.
ASPCA Maclay Trophy (Hunter Seat)—Katie Monahan, Orchard Lake, Mich.
AHSA Dressage Medal Class—Coco Wendling, Westlake Village, Calif.
International Jumping—Team: United States (William Steinkraus, Kathy Kusner, Frank Chapot, Jared Brinsmade); individual: Steinkraus; leading foreign rider: Lt. Roberto Pistarini, Argentina

Special Awards

Horseman of the Year—Frank D. Chapot
Horsewoman of the Year—Jolie Richardson
High Score Amateur Saddle Horse—Mr. and Mrs. A. C. Huffman's Dream Lover
High Score Hunter—Charles R. McGinnes' Beau Mac
High Score Arabian Gelding—Mrs. Lucille C. Betts' Zarwi
AHSA Jumper Course Designers' Contest—Jane Thayer and Judith Greelish

ICE SKATING

Figure Skating

World Championships
(Colorado Springs, Feb. 25–March 2)

Men—Tim Wood, Detroit
Ladies—Gabriele Seyfert, East Germany
Pairs—Aleksei Ulanov and Irina Rodnina, USSR
Dance—Diane Towler and Bernard Ford, Britain

North American Championships
(Oakland, Calif., Feb. 7–9)

Men—Tim Wood
Ladies—Janet Lynn, Rockford, Ill.
Pairs—Ronald and Cynthia Kauffman, Seattle
Dance—Donna Taylor and Bruce Lennie, Toronto

United States Championships
(Seattle, Jan. 29–Feb. 1)

Men—Tim Wood
Ladies—Janet Lynn
Pairs—Ronald and Cynthia Kauffman
Gold Dance—Judy Schwomeyer, Indianapolis, and James Sladky, Rochester, N. Y.

Speed Skating

World Championships

Men
(Deventer, Netherlands, Feb. 15–16)

All-Around—Dag Fornaess, Norway (177.368 pts)

Women
(Grenoble, France, Feb. 1–2)

All-Around—Lasma Kauniste, USSR (189.556)

United States National Outdoor
(St. Paul, Minn., Feb. 1–2)

Men's All-Around—Pete Cefalu, West Allis, Wis. (26 pts)
Women's All-Around—Sally Blatchford, Northbrook, Ill. (13)

United States National Indoor
(St. Louis, March 8–9)

Men's All-Around—Bill Lanigan, New York (23)
Women's All-Around—Mary Blair, West Allis, Wis. (12)

United States Open Outdoor
(Binghamton, N. Y., Feb. 15–16)

Men's All-Around—Richard Wurster, Ballston Spa, N. Y. (29)
Women's All-Around—Sue Bradle, Peekskill, N. Y. (19)

United States Open Indoor
(Utica, N. Y., March 1–2)

Men's All-Around—Bill Lanigan, New York (22)
Women's All-Around—Cathy Crowe, St. Louis (17)

LACROSSE

National Intercollegiate Champion (Wingate Trophy)—Army and Johns Hopkins (tie)
National Open—Long Island Athletic Club
All-Star Game—South 12, North 11
Division Champions—Mideastern (Miller): Army and Johns Hopkins (tie); Ivy League: Brown, Cornell, and Yale (tie); South Atlantic (Strobhar): Washington College; Central Atlantic (Moore): Bucknell; New York Metropolitan (Lydecker): Hofstra, Fairleigh Dickinson at Madison, and C. W. Post (tie); Central New York (Cox)—Cortland State; Northern New York (Morrill)—Ithaca and St. Lawrence (tie); Northeast (Taylor): Massachusetts; Colonial (Bacharach Rasin): Plymouth State; Midwest (Hixson): Denison; Rocky Mountain (Cooper): Air Force Academy

MOTORBOATING

Major Trophy Winners

Atomic Cup (Tri-Cities, Wash.)—Myr's Special (driver, Dean Chenoweth)
Dixie Cup (Guntersville, Ala.)—Miss Budweiser (Bill Sterett)
Gold Cup (San Diego)—Miss Budweiser (Sterett)
Indiana Governor's Cup (Madison)—Myr's Special (Chenoweth)
Kentucky Governor's Cup (Owensboro)—Miss Budweiser (Sterett)
Seafair Trophy (Seattle)—Miss Budweiser (Sterett)
World Championship (Detroit)—Miss U. S. (Bill Muncey)
Unlimited High-Point Champion—Miss Budweiser (6,775 pts)
Champion Driver—Bill Sterett (6,275 pts)

Distance Races

Bahamas 500 (512 mi)—Don Aronow, Miami (8:24:15; 64.5 mph)
California Y. C. Offshore (182 mi)—Peter Rothschild (2:55:32; 62.5 mph)
Cowes-Torquay, England (236 mi)—Aronow (3:33; 66 mph)
Long Beach-Ensenada (180 mi)—Aronow (64.1 mph)
Long Beach Hennessy (206 mi)—Aronow (4:12:16; 48.6 mph)
New York Hennessy (22.6 mi)—Peter Rittmaster-Bob Schiffenhaus, Miami (4:38)
Sam Griffith Memorial (216.6 miles)—Bill Wishnick, New York (3:05; 70 mph)
Viareggio-Bastia, Italy (214 mi)—Aronow (2:51:45; 73.1 mph)
World Championship (Lake Havasu, Ariz., 8 hours over two days)—Cesare Scotti, Italy (584 miles; 73 mph)

Predicted Log Trophies

APBA National Championship—Milton Horwitz, Chicago (5,044 pts)
APBA High-Point Award—Horwitz
George W. Codrington Trophy—Fred Woodward, Whittier, Calif. (3,167)
Herbert L. Stone Trophy—Horwitz
Martini & Rossi Trophy—Woodward

Individual Champions

World—Don Aronow, Miami
United States—Aronow

PARACHUTING

National Championships
(Marana, Ariz., June 28–July 4)

Men—Overall: Jim Lowe, Portland, Oreg; accuracy: William Hayes, Florissant, Mo.; style: Douglas Metcalfe, Kent, Ohio
Women—Overall: Martha Huddleston, Stephenville, Texas; accuracy: Martha Huddleston; style: Bonnie Hickey, Dallas, Texas

National Collegiate Championships
(Phoenix, Ariz., Nov. 27–30)

Individual—Accuracy: Edwin Yost, Stout State (Menomonie, Wis.); style: Gregory O'Kelly, U. S. Air Force Academy; overall: Gregory Martin, Air Force Academy.
Team—Accuracy: Air Force Academy; overall: Air Force Academy

POLO

International

Cup of the Americas (Buenos Aires, Oct. 25 and Nov. 2)—First game: Argentina 12, U. S. 6; second game: Argentina 18, U. S. 6

U. S. Polo Association Champions

Open—Tulsa Green Hills 11 (Hap Sharp, Tommy Wayman, Gaston Dorignac, Ray Harrington, Bill Atkinson), Milwaukee 10

20-Goal—Oak Brook (Ill.) **7**, Milwaukee 6
16-Goal—Tulsa 10, Meadow Brook (N. Y.) 4
12-Goal—Midland (Texas) High Sky 11, Wilson Ranch, Midland, Texas, 6
8-Goal—Brandywine (Pa.) 8, Mallet Hill (Pa.) 3
12-Goal Intercircuit—Menlo Park (Calif.) 10, Tulsa 6
8-Goal Intercircuit—Fairfield County 9, Brandywine 5
Intercollegiate (Indoor)—Yale 17, Cornell 16

RODEO

Rodeo Cowboy Association Champions
All-Around—Larry Mahan, Brooks, Oreg.
Saddle Bronc Riding—Bill Smith, Cody, Wyo.
Bareback Bronc Riding—Gary Tucker, Carlsbad, N. Mex.
Steer Wrestling—Roy Duvall, Boynton, Okla.
Bull Riding—Doug Brown, Silverton, Oreg.
Calf Roping—Dean Oliver, Boise, Idaho
Team Roping—Jerold Camarillo, Oakdale, Calif., and John Miller, Pawhuska, Okla.

Girls Rodeo Association
Barrel Racing—Missy Long, Duncan, Okla.

ROWING

United States Championships
(Philadelphia, Aug. 15–17; all events except dashes at 2,000 meters)
150-Pound Quarter-Mile—Larry Klecatsky, New York Athletic Club (1:23.2)
150-Pound Singles—Klecatsky (7:25.7)
150-Pound Doubles—Klecatsky and Tom Quinn, New York A. C. (7:12)
150-Pound Quads—New York A. C. (7:22)
150-Pound Fours with Coxswain—Potomac Boat Club, Washington, D. C. (7:42.2)
150-Pound Eights—Potomac B. C. (6:29.8)
Intermediate Fours with Coxswain—Argonaut Rowing Club, Toronto (7:16.6)
Intermediate—Penn A.C., Philadelphia (6:59.5)
Quarter-Mile Dash—James Dietz, New York A. C. (1:19.4)
Singles—William Maher, Detroit (8:02.1)
Association Singles—Dietz (8:22)
Doubles—John Van Blom and Tom McKibbin, Long Beach (Calif.) Rowing Association (6:47.2)
Pairs—Tony Johnson and Larry Hough, Potomac B. C. (7:07.2)
Pairs with Coxswain—Johnson, Hough, and Jim Stone (7:58.9)
Fours—Vesper B. C., Philadelphia (6:45.7)
Fours with Coxswain—Union B. C., Boston (7:19.9)
Quads—Vesper B. C. (6:32.6)
Eights—Ecorse (Mich.) B. C.—Union B. C. combination crew (6:11.9)
Team (Barnes Trophy)—Potomac B. C., Washington, D. C. (139.5 pts)

Intercollegiate Team Champions
(2,000 meters except where noted)
IRA Regatta (Syracuse, N. Y., June 12–14)—*Varsity:* Pennsylvania (6:30.4); *junior varsity:* Cornell (6:26.6); *freshmen:* dead heat between Pennsylvania and Washington (6:27.4); *fours with coxswain:* Rutgers (7:24.3); *Ten Eyck Trophy (team)*—Pennsylvania (17½ pts)
Eastern Sprints (Worcester, Mass., May 9–10)—*Heavyweight: varsity:* Harvard (6:01.3); *junior varsity:* Harvard (6:17); *freshmen:* Pennsylvania (6:15); *Rowe Cup (team):* Harvard (40 pts). *Lightweight: varsity:* Harvard (6:24.8); *junior varsity:* Harvard (6:30.8); *freshmen:* Harvard (6:31.5); *Jope Cup (team):* Harvard (38 pts)
Harvard-Yale (4 mi)—Harvard (19:37.2)
Oxford-Cambridge (4½ mi)—Cambridge (18:04)
Southern Regatta (Charleston, S. C., April 26)—*Varsity:* Rollins (6:26.6); *junior varsity:* Rollins (6:46.6); *freshmen:* Virginia (6:43.5)
Western Sprints (San Diego, May 15–16)—*Varsity:* Washington (6:18.7); *junior varsity:* UCLA (6:27.5); *freshmen:* Washington (6:40); *fours:* Santa Clara (7:21); *lightweight:* Long Beach State (6:38.2)
Cups and Trophies (all races at 2,000 meters)—*Adams Cup:* Pennsylvania (6:30); *Bill Cup:* Dartmouth (6:58.6); *Blackwell Cup:* Pennsylvania (5:26.8); *Callow Cup:* Trinity (6:20.7); *Carnegie Cup:* Princeton (6:35); *Childs Cup:* Pennsylvania (6:24); *Compton Cup:* Harvard (5:55.3); *Dad Vail Trophy:* Georgetown (6:19.4); *Goes Trophy:* Cornell (6:12.8); *Grimaldi Cup:* Villanova (6:58.2); *Hughes Trophy:* New York A. C. (6:24.2); *Logg Cup:* Princeton (6:01.4); *Madeira Cup:* Pennsylvania (6:38); *Mason-Downs Cup:* Trinity (6:24.3); *O'Hare Cup:* Ithaca (7:04.3); *President's Cup (Marist College):* St. Joseph's at Philadelphia (5:22); *Stein Cup:* Harvard (5:42.7); *Sulger Trophy:* Iona (7:24)
Interscholastic Championships (Washington, May 24; one mile)—*Singles:* Alfred Medioli, Syosset, N. Y. (6:35.2); *doubles:* LaSalle High School, Philadelphia (6:01); *fours:* Lower Merion (Pa.) High School (5:54); *eights:* Ridley College School, St. Catharines, Ont. (5.14)

British Henley
(Henley-on-Thames, July 2–5; all races at one mile, 550 yards)
Diamond Sculls (singles)—Hans Joachim Bohmer, East Germany (8:06)
Double Sculls—Denis Oswald and Melchoer Burgin, Switzerland (7:35)
Silver Goblets (pairs)—Urs Bitterli and Urs Frankhauser, Switzerland (7:56)
Wyfold Cup (fours)—London R. C. (7:16)

WIDE WORLD

KARL SCHRANZ, World Cup winner, shows his style in winning downhill race at Megève, France, in January.

Thames Challenge Cup (eights)—Leander Club, England (6:43)
Prince Philip Cup (fours with coxswain)—Laga Dieft, Netherlands (7:19)
Ladies Plate (eights)—Nereus, Netherlands (6:55)
Princess Elizabeth Cup (schoolboy eights)—Washington-Lee High, Alexandria, Va. (7.00)
Grand Challenge Cup (eights)—Einheit Sports Club, Dresden, East Germany (6:28)

Canadian Henley
(St. Catharines, Ont., July 31–Aug. 3)
Open Dash—James Dietz, New York A. C. (1:34)
Lightweight Dash—Larry Klecatsky, New York A. C. (1:36.3)
Singles—Dietz (7:04.1)
Association Singles—Rick Stehlik, Malta B. C., Philadelphia (7:22.9)
Pairs—Tony Johnson and Larry Hough, Potomac B. C., Washington, D. C. (6:45.1)
Pairs with Coxswain—Johnson, Hough and Jim Stone, Potomac B. C. (7:12)
Doubles—Bob Montgomery and Tom Ward, Vesper B. C., Philadelphia (6:48.5)
Fours—Vesper B. C. (6:34.6)
Fours with Coxswain—Union B. C., Boston (6:20.6)
Eight-oared dash—St. Catharines R. C. (1:18.6)
Eights—Vesper B. C. (5:48.5)
Junior Eights—Argonaut R. C., Toronto (6:01.9)
Team—St. Catharines R. C. (245½ pts)

SHOOTING

Trap
Grand American Championships
(Vandalia, Ohio, Aug. 13–23)
Grand American Handicap—*Men:* Bernard Bonn, Jr., Dayton, Ohio (99 at 19 yards); *women:* JoAnn Nelson, Lone Tree, Iowa (94 at 19½ won shoot-off); *juniors:* Danny Miller, Beardstown, Ill. (97 at 23); *veterans:* M. M. Matson, Rock Island, Ill. (96 at 23½); *industry:* Bob Oxsen, Livermore, Calif. (93 at 27)
Champion of Champions—*Men:* John Imbt, Denver (200x200); *women:* Loral I. Delaney, Anoka, Minn. (196x200); *junior:* Garth Henley, Bexley, Ohio (199x200)
High Overall—*Men:* Frank Little, Endicott, N. Y. (963x1,000); *women:* Loral I. Delaney (931x1,000); *juniors:* Mike Scarbrough, Sarasota, Fla. (951x1,000); *veterans:* Henry Bullock, Milmay, N. J. (918x1,000); *industry:* Bob Oxsen (960x1,000).
Clay Target—*Men:* Dean Stoy, Tulsa (200x200); *women:* Ruby Jenner, Waupaca, Wis. (198x200)
Doubles—*Men:* Hugh Driggs, Palmyra, Mich. (99x100); *women:* Gail Pierson, Natchitoches, La. (93x100)

Skeet
National Skeet Shooting Association Championships
(Rush, N. Y., Aug. 2–9)
All-Around—*Open:* Robert F. Shuley, Roselle, Ill. (546x550); *women:* Sgt. Margaret Burdett, RCAF, Angus, Ont.

MANCHETE FROM PICTORIAL PARADE

PÉLÉ, ace of Brazil's Santos team, set a modern soccer mark by kicking his 1,000th goal on November 19.

(530x550); *veterans:* Carl B. Stutzman, Peoria, Ill. (524x550); *senior:* Ted V. Hannaford, Warren, Mich. (540x550); *sub-senior:* Clayton Kenworthy, Buffalo, N.Y. (542x550); *junior:* Guy DiTommaso, Brooklyn, N. Y. (540x-550); *industry:* Barney C. Hartman, St. Lambert, Que. (546x550)
Other Individual Champions—*12-gauge:* Walter Badorek, Klamath Falls, Oreg. (250x250); *20-gauge:* Richard Bienapfl, Minneapolis (100x100); *28-gauge:* Kenny Barnes, Jr., Bakersfield, Calif. (100x100); *.410-gauge:* Donald Johnson, Mount Royal, Que. (100x100)

SKIING

World Cup—Individual Championships
(Points awarded for performances in a series of selected international Alpine-type events)
Men—Karl Schranz, Austria (182 pts)
Women—Gertrude Gabl, Austria (131)

United States Championships
Alpine (Bear Valley, Calif., Feb. 21–23)—*Men: slalom:* Bobby Cochran, Richmond, Vt. (1:39.18); *giant slalom:* Hank Kashiwa, Old Forge, N.Y. (3:11.71); *downhill:* Vladimir Sabich, Kyburz, Calif. (1:42.82); *combined:* Malcolm Milne, Australia. *Women: slalom* (at Norden, Calif., April 12): Barbara Cochran, Richmond, Vt. (1:30.12); *giant slalom:* Barbara Cochran (1:33.85); *downhill:* Ann Black, Seattle (1:51.98); *combined:* no champion.
Nordic (Durango, Colo., March 4–9)—*Jumping:* Jay Rand, Colorado (217 pts); *15-kilometer cross-country:* Clark Matis, Colo. (51:53); *30-kilometer cross-country:* Matis (1:50.26); *combined:* Jim Miller, Fort Lewis College (439.356 pts). *Women: 5-kilometer cross-country:* Martha Rockwell, Putney, Vt. (30:49); *8-kilometer cross-country:* Martha Rockwell (41:43). *Relays: men's 10-kilometer:* U. S. Eastern Amateur Ski Association (Peter Davis, Bob Gray, Jon Chaffee; 1:49:30); *women's 5-kilometer:* Rocky Mountain Division (Twila Hinkle, Mary Atkins, Kris Zdechlich; 1:15:11).
Jumping (Brattleboro, Vt., Feb. 22–23)—*Senior:* Adrian Watt, Duluth, Minn. (195 pts); *veterans:* Don Hurst, Ishpeming, Mich. (142.6); *junior:* Greg Swor, Duluth (173.1)

National Collegiate (NCAA) Championships
(Steamboat Springs, Colo., March 27–29)
Alpine—*Slalom:* Paul Rachetto, Denver (1:31.43); *downhill:* Mike Lafferty, Colorado (1:31.41); *combined:* Rachetto (185.3 pts)
Nordic—*Cross-country:* Clark Matis, Colorado (52:22); *jumping:* Odd Hammerness, Denver (220 pts); *combined:* Georg Krog, Denver (442.2 pts)
Skimeister (all-events award)—Ed Damon, Dartmouth (347.6 pts)
Team champion—Denver (388.6 pts); Dartmouth (372)

Canadian Championships
Alpine (Garibaldi, B. C., Feb. 21–24)—*Men: downhill:* Keith Shepherd, Waskesiu, Sask. (2:52.78); *slalom:* Peter Duncan, Mont Tremblant, Que. (1:56.97); *giant slalom:* Duncan

(2:24.63); *combined:* Duncan. *Women: downhill:* Laurie Kreiner (2:20.90); *slalom:* Judi Leinweber, Kimberley, B. C. (2:08.18); *giant slalom:* Sue Graves, Ottawa (1:55.09); *combined:* Judi Leimweber

SOCCER

United States Amateur Champions
National Challenge Cup—New York Greek Americans
National Amateur Cup—British Lions, Washington
National Junior Cup—St. Philip Neri, St. Louis
Intercollegiate (NCAA)—St. Louis University defeated San Francisco U., 4–0, in final.

Foreign Champions
English Division 1—Leeds United
English League Cup—Swindon Town
English Football Association Cup—Manchester City
Scottish Division 1—Celtic
Scottish League Cup—Celtic
Scottish Football Association Cup—Celtic
European Cup of Champions—Athletic Club of Milan
European Cup-Winners Cup—Slovan Bratislava, Czechoslovakia
English Amateur Cup—North Shields

World Cup
(Groupings for final competition that begins in Mexico, May 31, 1970)
Group I (to play in Aztec Stadium, Mexico City)—Belgium, El Salvador, Mexico, USSR
Group II (to play in Pueblo and León)—Israel, Italy, Sweden, Uruguay
Group III (to play in Guadalajara)—Brazil, Czechoslovakia, England, Rumania
Group IV (to play in León)—Bulgaria, Morocco, Peru, West Germany

SOFTBALL

Amateur Softball Association Champions
Men—Raybestos Cardinals, Stratford, Conn.
Women—Lionettes, Orange, Calif.
Slow Pitch (open)—Copper Hearth, Milwaukee
Slow Pitch (women)—Converse Dots, Hialeah, Fla.
Slow Pitch (industrial)—Avco Lycoming, Stratford, Conn.
Slow Pitch (16-inch)—Dr. Carlucci Boosters, Fox Lake, Ill.

SQUASH RACQUETS

National Champions

Men
Singles—Anil Nayar, Bombay, India, and Harvard
Doubles—Sam Howe, Philadelphia, and Ralph Howe, New York
Veterans—Henri Salaun, Boston
North American Open—Sharif Khan, Detroit
Senior—Ed Hahn, New York
Senior doubles—William T. Ketcham Jr., New York, and James M. Ethridge 3rd, Greenwich, Conn.
Team—Ontario
Intercollegiate—Anil Nayar
Intercollegiate team—Harvard
Lapham Cup (singles)—United States
Grant Trophy (doubles)—United States
Junior Singles—Farooq Mir, Greenville, S. C.

Women
Singles—Joyce Davenport, Ardmore, Pa.
Doubles—Joyce Davenport and Carol Thesieres, Cynwyd, Pa.
Senior Singles—Baba Lewis, Boston
Senior Doubles—Louisa Manly-Powers and Barbara Newlin, Philadelphia

SURFING

United States Championships
(Huntington Beach, Calif.)
Men—Corky Carroll, Dana Point, Calif.
Women—Sharon Weber, Hawaii
Senior—Dewey Weber, Venice, Calif.
Mixed Tandems—Hal Sachs, Capistrano Beach, Calif., and Patti Young, Glendale, Calif.
Junior—Niles Osborne, Los Alamitos, Calif.
Duke Kahanamoku Trophy—Corky Carroll

SWIMMING

After their hectic Olympic year, the world's women swimmers slowed down a bit, but the men continued to churn the pool waters. They added a couple of young stars and broke records in all categories and at all distances in meets in the United States and East Germany. The men set nine world records and the women only three.

Actually the men's records were accounted for by only five swimmers. Mike Burton of Carmichael,

MIKE BURTON shattered world records for the 800-meter and 1,500-meter freestyle in AAU championships.

Calif., Nikolai Pankin of the Soviet Union, Roland Matthes of East Germany, and Gary Hall of Garden Grove, Calif., broke two records each. The single performance was achieved by Hans Fassnacht of West Germany, a student at Long Beach (Calif.) State College. He swam 400 meters freestyle in 4 minutes 4 seconds at the National AAU meet in Louisville, August 14.

Hall, a 17-year-old high school senior, was the most outstanding of the newcomers, setting world records of 2:09.6 in the 200-meter individual medley at Louisville and 4:33.9 in the 400-meter event two days later. On the intervening day he stroked to a world record of 2:06.6 in the 200-meter backstroke. This record was short-lived, however, for Matthes lowered it to 2:06.4 two weeks later in East Berlin. Matthes had set a mark of 57.8 seconds for the 100-meter backstroke six days previously in Wurzburg.

Burton, too, set his records in the AAU meet, in the 1,500-meter freestyle event, which he did in 16:04.5. En route, he was clocked at 8:28.5 for 800 meters. Pankin's two records were achieved at Magdeburg, East Germany, where he swam the 100-meter breaststroke in 1:06.2, and the 200-meter breaststroke in 2:25.4.

Well-known swimmers chalked up two new standards in women's competition. Debbie Meyer, the winner of the Sullivan Award as the leading U. S. amateur athlete of 1968 for her season's record-breaking feats and three individual Olympic championships, lowered her own record in the 1,500-meter freestyle at the AAU championships to 17:-19.9. Karen Muir of South Africa broke the 100-meter backstroke record in the Netherlands, doing 1:05.6. But it was another youngster, 16-year-old Susie Atwood of the Lakewood (Calif.) Swim Club, who took the third record. She swam the 200-meter backstroke in 2:21.5 at Louisville.

Men's National AAU Outdoor Championships
(Louisville, Ky., Aug. 14–17)

100-Meter Freestyle—Don Havens, Los Angeles A.C. (0:52.5)
200-Meter Freestyle—Hans Fassnacht, Phillips 66, Long Beach, Calif. (1:56.5)
400-Meter Freestyle—Fassnacht (4:04)
1,500-Meter Freestyle—Mike Burton, Arden Hills Swimming Club, Sacramento, Calif (16:04.5)
100-Meter Backstroke—Mitch Ivey, Santa Clara (Calif.) S.C. (1:00.2)
200-Meter Backstroke—Gary Hall, Phillips 66 (2:06.6)
100-Meter Breaststroke—José Fiolo, Phillips 66 (1:06.9)
200-Meter Breaststroke—Mike Dirksen, David Douglas S.C., Portland, Oreg. (2:26.9)

100-Meter Butterfly—Doug Russell, Burford S.C., Arlington, Texas (0:56)
200-Meter Butterfly—Burton (2:06.5)
200-Meter Medley—Hall (2:09.6)
400-Meter Medley—Hall (4:33.9)
400-Meter Freestyle Relay—Los Angeles A.C. (Dan Frawley, Henry DeWitt, Stephen Frieken, Havens; 3:32.8)
800-Meter Freestyle Relay—Phillips 66 (Juan Bello, Andrew Strenk, Hall, Fassnacht; 7:52.7)
400-Meter Medley Relay—Phillips 66 (Charles Campbell, Fiolo, Hall, Bello; 3:57.5)
1-Meter Dive—Jim Henry, Bloomington (Ind.) S.C. (510.69 pts)
3-Meter Dive—Henry (515.88 pts)
Platform Dive—Dick Rydze, Ann Arbor, Mich. (552.96 pts)
Team—Phillips 66

Women's National AAU Outdoor Championships
(Louisville, Ky., Aug. 14–17)

100-Meter Freestyle—Sue Pedersen, Arden Hills S.C., Sacramento, Calif. (0:59.7)
200-Meter Freestyle—Sue Pedersen (2:07.8)
400-Meter Freestyle—Debbie Meyer, Arden Hills (4:26.4)
1,500-Meter Freestyle—Debbie Meyer (17:19.9)
100-Meter Backstroke—Susie Atwood, Lakewood (Calif.) A.C. (1:06)
200-Meter Backstroke—Susie Atwood (2:21.5)
100-Meter Breaststroke—Kim Brecht, Lakewood A.C. (1:15.7)
200-Meter Breaststroke—Kim Brecht (2:45.4)
100-Meter Butterfly—Virginia Durkin, St. Petersburg (Fla.) Recreation (1:05.9)
200-Meter Butterfly—Lynn Colella, Cascade S.C., Seattle (2:21.6)
200-Meter Medley—Lynn Vidali, Santa Clara (Calif.) S.C. (2:26.2)
400-Meter Medley—Debbie Meyer (5:08.6)
400-Meter Freestyle Relay—Santa Clara S.C. (Jan Henne, Laura Fritz, Lynn Vidali, Linda Gustavson; 4:02.9)
800-Meter Freestyle Relay—Arden Hills (Evie Kossner, Vicki King, Debbie Meyer, Sue Pedersen; 8:42.3)
400-Meter Medley Relay—Lakewood A.C. (Susie Atwood, Kim Brecht, Pam Lines, Bonnie Adair; 4:31.4)
1-Meter Dive—Cynthia Potter, Houston, Texas (463.95 pts)
3-Meter Dive—Micki King, U.S. Air Force (472.86 pts)
Platform Dive—Micki King (411.57 pts)
Team—Arden Hills S.C.

Men's National AAU Indoor Championships
(Long Beach, Calif., April 10–13)

100-Yard Freestyle—Don Havens, University of Southern California (0:45.92)
200-Yard Freestyle—Frank Heckl, USC (1:42.29)
500-Yard Freestyle—Hans Fassnacht, Phillips 66, Long Beach, Calif. (4:32.99)
1,650-Yard Freestyle—Mike Burton, Arden Hills S.C. Sacramento, Calif. (15:40.1)
100-Yard Backstroke—Fred Haywood, Santa Clara (Calif.) S.C. (0:52.26)
200-Yard Backstroke—Gary Hall, Garden Grove, Calif. (1:52)
100-Yard Breaststroke—Brian Job, Santa Clara (0:58.11)
200-Yard Breaststroke—Job (2:07.34)
100-Yard Butterfly—Ross Wales, Princeton (0:50.54)
200-Yard Butterfly—Burton (1:52.63)
200-Yard Medley—David Johnson, Yale (1:56.22)
400-Yard Medley—Hall (4:00.85)
400-Yard Freestyle Relay—Southern California (Heckl, Dan Frawley, Russell Kidder, Havens; 3:05)
800-Yard Freestyle Relay—USC (Mark Mader, Kidder, Greg Charlton, Heckl; 6:53.47)
400-Yard Medley Relay—Yale (Ed Bettendorf, Phil Long, Paul Katz, Steve Job, 3:30.4)
1-Meter Dive—Jim Henry, Bloomington, Ind. (506.25 pts)
3-Meter Dive—Win Young, Bloomington (559.68 pts)
Platform Dive—Dick Rydze, Ann Arbor, Mich. (549.39 pts)
Team—USC (400 pts)

Women's National AAU Indoor Championships
(Long Beach, Calif., April 10–13)

100-Yard Freestyle—Wendy Fordyce, Miami Springs (Fla.) Recreation (0:52.8)
200-Yard Freestyle—Linda Gustavson, Santa Clara (Calif.) S.C. (1:54.48)
500-Yard Freestyle—Vicki King, Arden Hills S.C., Sacramento, Calif. (5:00.65)
1,650-Yard Freestyle—Debbie Meyer, Arden Hills (17:04.4)
100-Yard Backstroke—Susie Atwood, Lakewood (Calif.) Aquatic Club (0:58.8)
200-Yard Backstroke—Susie Atwood (2:07.51)
100-Yard Breaststroke—Sharon Wichman, Club Olympia, Fort Wayne, Ind. (1:07.6)
200-Yard Breaststroke—Kim Brecht, Lakewood A.C. (2:24.44)
100-Yard Butterfly—Ellie Daniel, Vesper B.C., Philadelphia (0:58.39)
200-Yard Butterfly—Ellie Daniel (2:06.65)
200-Yard Medley—Lynn Vidali, Santa Clara S.C. (2:09.21)
400-Yard Medley—Lynn Vidali (4:36.78)
400-Yard Freestyle Relay—Santa Clara S.C. (Jan Henne, Pam Carpinelli, Pokey Watson, Linda Gustavson; 3:35.41)
800-Yard Freestyle Relay—Arden Hills (Evelyn Kossner, Vicki King, Sue Pedersen, Debbie Meyer; 7:44.34)
400-Yard Medley Relay—Santa Clara S.C. (Jane Swagerty, Jan Henne, Lynn Vidali, Linda Gustavson; 4:00.67)
1-Meter Dive—Cynthia Potter, Bloomington, Ind. (442.62 pts)
3-Meter Dive—Cynthia Potter (447.51 pts)
Platform Dive—Beverly Boys, Oshawa A.C., Pickering, Ont. (361.11 pts)
Team—Santa Clara S.C. (320.5 pts)

National Collegiate (NCAA) Indoor Championships
(Bloomington, Ind., March 27–29)

50-Yard Freestyle—Dan Frawley, University of Southern California (0:21.04)
100-Yard Freestyle—Francis Heath, UCLA (0:46.24)
200-Yard Freestyle—Mark Spitz, Indiana (1:39.53)
500-Yard Freestyle—Spitz (4:33.48)
1,650-Yard Freestyle—Hans Fassnacht, Long Beach State (15:54.21)
100-Yard Backstroke—Fred Haywood, Stanford (0:52.44)
200-Yard Backstroke—Charles Hickcox, Indiana (1:53.67)
100-Yard Breaststroke—Don McKenzie, Indiana (0:58.36)
200-Yard Breaststroke—Mike Dirksen, Oregon (2:08.62)
100-Yard Butterfly—Spitz (0:49.69)
200-Yard Butterfly—John Ferris, Stanford (1:49.61)
200-Yard Medley—Hickcox (1:54.43)
400-Yard Medley—Fassnacht (4:07.77)
400-Yard Freestyle Relay—Southern California (Frawley, Russell Kidder, Frank Heckl, Don Havens; 3:02.77)
800-Yard Freestyle Relay—USC (George Watson, Mark Mader, Greg Charlton, Heckl; 6:49.50)
400-Yard Medley Relay—Indiana (Hickcox, McKenzie, Steve Borowski, Bryan Bateman; 3:25.89)
1-Meter Dive—Jim Henry, Indiana (531.06 pts)
3-Meter Dive—Henry (574.68 pts)
Team—Indiana (427 pts)

TABLE TENNIS

United States Championships
(San Francisco, May 9–11)

Singles—Men: Dal Joon Lee, Cleveland, Ohio; women: Patty Martinez, San Diego, Calif.

ROD LAVER, who won the grand slam of tennis for the second time in 1969, found his latest triumph the more satisfying because the victories in the Australian, French, Wimbledon, and United States Opens were scored in competition with the world's best players. (His grand slam in 1962 was against amateurs only.) The left-handed Australian, who was born on a farm near Rockhampton, Aug. 9, 1938, also became the first player to win over $123,000 prize money in a single tennis season. In addition to the big four tournaments, Laver won many other major and minor events, establishing himself as the best player in the world.

Laver, who is 5 feet 9½ inches tall, began playing in big tournaments in 1956, and scored his first major triumph in 1960 by winning the Australian title. The next year he won at Wimbledon, where he had been the runner-up the preceding two years. Then came the grand slam in 1962, the first sweep of its kind since Donald Budge achieved it in 1938, the year Laver was born. Laver turned pro in 1963.

Doubles: Men: Lee and Glen Cowan, Los Angeles; women: Patty Martinez and Wendy Hicks, Santa Barbara, Calif.; mixed: Martinez and Lee
Senior Singles—Men: William Cross, New Brunswick, N. J.
Senior Doubles—Ruben Gomez, Los Angeles, and Helmuth Vorherr, Albuquerque, N. Mex.

World Championships
(Munich, April 17–27)

Singles—Men: Shigeo Ito, Japan; women: Toshiko Kowada, Japan.
Doubles—Men: Hans Alser and Kjell Johansson, Sweden; women: Svetlana Grinberg and Zoya Rudnova, USSR; mixed: Nobuhiko Hasegawa and Yasunko Konno, Japan
Team—Men (Swaythling Cup): Japan; women (Corbillon Cup): USSR

TENNIS

Open tennis tournaments, in their second year, grew in number and favor in 1969. In some of them Rod Laver did not win the men's singles championship. But these were few and not of major importance. The 31-year-old Australian left-hander completed the grand slam of tennis by winning the Australian, French, Wimbledon, and U. S. titles. It was the first such sweep of the opens but the second such performance for Laver, who had taken them all in 1962 when he and the tournaments were strictly amateur. The only other grand slam winner was Don Budge, in 1938.

Mrs. Margaret Smith Court, also of Australia, returning to full-time competition, just missed the grand slam. She lost at Wimbledon as Mrs. Ann Haydon Jones became the first Englishwoman to win there since Angela Mortimer in 1961 and only the second since 1937. Mrs. Jones ended Mrs. Billie Jean King's string of three straight in the final.

However, Australian players did not take all of the world honors. The United States retained the Davis Cup, which it had won at Adelaide in December 1968, by turning back Rumania, 5 matches to 0, in the Challenge Round at Cleveland Heights, Ohio. The U. S. players were Arthur Ashe of Richmond, Va., and Stan Smith of Pasadena, Calif., in the singles, and Smith and Bob Lutz of Los Angeles in the doubles.

Early in the year the United States Lawn Tennis Association accepted a reclassification of players establishing three categories: amateur, registered (or independent pros), and professionals (touring,

UPI

ROD LAVER hoists high the U. S. Lawn Tennis Association Trophy after scoring a 4-set victory over Tony Roche in the finals of the U. S. Open championship. The triumph enabled the Australian to complete his second grand slam of tennis.

or contract, pros). The amateurs receive only expense money; the registered players, who must be over 19 years of age, may receive cash prizes as well as expense money, as do the pros. The registered players, however, remain under the jurisdiction of the USLTA. Ashe, Smith, Lutz, and Clark Graebner were the leading independent pros and were eligible for Davis Cup play, which is not open to the touring pros.

The USLTA also set up a tourney strictly for amateurs, and the singles honors were won by George (Butch) Seewagen, Jr., of New York, and Linda Tuero of Metairie, La. Its previous amateur tourney, now the National grass court, was played at Brookline, Mass., with Stan Smith and Mrs. Court taking the titles.

Major Tournaments

Davis Cup—United States (defeated Rumania, 5–0, at Cleveland Heights, Ohio, Sept. 19–21)
Wightman Cup (women)—United States (defeated Britain, 5–2, at Cleveland Heights, Ohio, Aug. 9–11)
Federation Cup (women)—United States (defeated Australia, 2–1, in final at Athens, May 25)
Stevens Cup (seniors)—United States (defeated Canada, 5–2, at Forest Hills, N.Y., Aug. 21–23)
U. S. Open (Forest Hills, Aug. 27–Sept. 9)—men's singles: Rod Laver, Australia, pro; women's singles: Margaret Smith Court, Australia; men's doubles: Fred Stolle, Australia, pro, and Ken Rosewall, Australia, pro; women's doubles: Darlene Hard, Long Beach, Calif., and Françoise Durr, France, pro; mixed doubles: Mrs. Court, Australia, and Marty Riessen, Evanston, Ill., pro; senior doubles: Bobby Riggs, Plandome, N.Y., and Emery Neale, Portland, Oreg.
U. S. Nationals (Brookline, Mass., Aug. 16–23)—men's singles: Stan Smith, Pasadena, Calif.; women's singles: Mrs. Court, Australia; men's doubles: Richard Crealy and Allan Stone, both Australia; women's doubles: Mrs. Court, Australia, and Virginia Wade, England; mixed doubles: Patti Hogan, La Jolla, Calif., and Paul Sullivan, Boston
U. S. Amateur (Rochester, N.Y., July 13, final)—men's singles: George Seewagen Jr., New York; women's singles: Linda Tuero, Metairie, La.; men's doubles: Erik Van Dillen, San Mateo, Calif., and Tom Leonard, Los Angeles; women's doubles: Emilie Burrer, San Antonio, Texas, and Pat Richmond, Shawnee, Kans.
U. S. Men's Indoor (Salisbury, Md., Feb. 11–16)—singles: Stan Smith, Pasadena, Calif.; doubles: Smith and Bob Lutz, Los Angeles
U. S. Women's Indoor (Winchester, Mass., Feb. 18–23)—singles: Mary Ann Eisel (Mrs. Peter Curtis), St. Louis; doubles: Mary Ann Eisel and Valerie Ziegenfuss, San Diego, Calif.
U. S. Clay Court (Indianapolis, July 22–27)—men's singles: Zeljko Franulović, Yugoslavia; women's singles: Gail Sherriff Chanfreau, France; men's doubles: Clark Graebner, New York, and Bill Bowrey, Australia; women's doubles: Mrs. Chanfreau, France, and Lesley Bowrey, Australia
U. S. Senior Women (Narragansett, R.I., Aug. 22)—singles: Betty Rosenquest Pratt, Maitland, Fla.; doubles: Dorothy Cheney, Santa Monica, Calif., and June Gay, Piedmont, Calif.
U. S. Senior (Philadelphia, Aug. 31)—singles: Bobby Riggs, Plandome, N.Y.; doubles: Riggs and Gardnar Mulloy, Coral Gables, Fla.
Australian Open (Brisbane; Jan. 27, final))—men's singles: Rod Laver, Australia, pro; women's singles: Mrs. Court, Australia; men's doubles: Roy Emerson, Australia, pro, and Laver, pro; women's doubles: Mrs. Court and Judy Tegart, both Australia, pro
French Open (Paris; June 8, final)—men's singles: Rod Laver, Australia, pro; women's singles: Mrs. Court, Australia; men's doubles: John Newcombe and Tony Roche, Australia, pros; women's doubles: Mrs. Ann Haydon Jones, England, pro, and Françoise Durr, France, pro; mixed doubles: Mrs. Court, Australia, and Marty Riessen, Evanston, Ill., pro
Wimbledon Open (England, June 20–July 5)—men's singles: Rod Laver, Australia, pro; women's singles: Mrs. Jones, England, pro; men's doubles: John Newcombe, Australia, pro, and Tony Roche, pro; women's doubles: Mrs. Court and Judy Tegart, both Australia; mixed doubles: Mrs. Jones, England, and Fred Stolle, Australia, pro
Canadian Open (Toronto; Aug. 10, final)—men's singles: Cliff Richey, San Angelo, Tex.; women's singles: Faye Urban, Windsor, Ont.; men's doubles: John Newcombe, Australia, pro; women's doubles: Miss Urban, Ont., and Vicki Berner, Vancouver, B.C.; mixed doubles: Bill Higgins, Bahamas, and Harry Fauquier, Toronto

Other U. S. Champions

National Collegiate (NCAA)—Singles: Joaquin Loyo-Mayo, University of Southern California; doubles: Loyo-Mayo and Marcello Lara, USC. College division: singles: Steve Messmer, San Fernando Valley; doubles: Messmer and Doug Barrow, Hope
National Association of Intercollegiate Athletics—Singles: Doug Verdieck, Redlands; doubles: co-champions (rain washed out final): Doug and Randy Verdieck, Redlands, and George and Jim Amaya, Presbyterian
Junior singles—Erik Van Dillen, San Mateo, Calif.
Junior doubles—Dick Stockton, Garden City, N.Y., and Van Dillen
Interscholastic singles—Freddie McNair, Landon School, Bethesda, Md.
Interscholastic doubles—Roscoe Tanner and David Dick, Baylor School, Chattanooga
Women's Collegiate Championships—Singles: Emilie Burrer, Trinity (Texas); doubles: Miss Burrer and Becky Vest, Trinity
Girls' singles—Sharon Walsh, San Raphael, Calif.
Girls' doubles—Gail Hansen, Palo Alto, Calif., and Patty Ann Reese, St. Petersburg, Fla.
Girls Interscholastic—Connie Capozzi, Hillsdale, Middletown, Ohio
Girls Interscholastic doubles—Alice DeRochemont and Karen Cotter, Capt. Shreve High, Shreveport, La.

TRACK AND FIELD

Among several track and field marks that were broken in 1969, during a relatively uneventful season, were another step toward the zenith in pole-vaulting and a sizzling time in the quarter-mile dash.

John Pennel, who had been the first to vault 16 feet, got the record back June 21 when he cleared 17 feet 10½ inches in a night meet at Sacramento. Pennel's vault bettered the mark of 17′ 9″ that Bob Seagren had made in 1968. Curtis Mills, a student at Texas A. & M., outsped Lee Evans and Larry James in the 440 in the National Collegiate championships at Knoxville, Tenn., in 44.7 seconds, breaking Tommie Smith's 1967 record.

Another determined athlete finally succeeded in getting the world record he wanted before he retired. He was Bill Toomey, the Olympic decathlon champion, who piled up 8,417 points on December 10–11 in Los Angeles, bettering the record of 8,319 held by Kurt Bendlin of West Germany. Toomey won the James E. Sullivan Memorial Award as the outstanding amateur athlete of 1969.

Jim Ryun, the world record holder, ran the fastest mile of the year—3:55.9 at Los Angeles, June 9, but was beaten by 10 yards in the NCAA

BILL TOOMEY set a world decathlon mark and won the Sullivan Award as the top amateur athlete of 1969.

WIDE WORLD

mile by Marty Liquori of Cedar Grove, N. J., and Villanova on June 21. Liquori's time of 3:57.7 set a record for the meet and put the 19-year-old star even, for Ryun had beaten him by inches for the title in the indoor meet in March in Detroit. When they competed eight days later in the AAU meet in Miami, Ryun dropped out of the race before the halfway mark, and Liquori raced on to the national title. Ryun, who had been running under pressure for eight years and had married a few months previously, quit for the season the next day, uncertain as to whether his retirement was permanent or not. It was the fourth time that he had withdrawn from a race during the season. The 22-year-old athlete said his trouble was mental, not physical. However, during the year no runner seriously challenged his three world records—the half-mile, the mile, and 1,500 meters—even though Liquori had now become America's premier miler.

Men's AAU Outdoor Championships
(Miami, Fla., June 28–29)

100 Yards—Ivory Crockett, Southern Illinois (0:09.3)
220 Yards—John Carlos, Piney Point, Md. (0:20.2)
440 Yards—Lee Evans, San Jose State (0:45.6)
880 Yards—Byron Dyce, United Athletic Association, New York (1:46.6)
Mile—Marty Liquori, Cedar Grove, N. J. (3:59.5)
3 Miles—Tracy Smith, Southern California Striders and U. S. Army (13:18.4)
6 Miles—Jack Bachelor, Florida Track Club (28:12.2)
2-Mile Walk—Ron Laird, New York A.C. (13:31.6)
3,000-Meter Steeplechase—Mike Manley, S. Calif. Striders (8:36.6)
120-Yard High Hurdles—Tie: Willie Davenport, Houston Striders, and Leon Coleman, S. Calif. Striders (0:13.3)
440-Yard Hurdles—Ralph Mann, S. Calif. Striders (0:50.1)
Long Jump—Bob Beamon, Piney Point, Md. (26 ft 11 in)
Triple Jump—John Craft, Eastern Illinois (52 ft 9¼ in)
High Jump—Otis Burrell, S. Calif. Striders (7 ft 1 in)
Pole Vault—Bob Seagren, S. Calif. Striders (17 ft 6 in)
Shot Put—Neal Steinhauer, Pacific Coast Club, Long Beach, Calif. (67 ft 4 in)
Discus—Jon Cole, Pacific Coast Club (208 ft 10 in)
Hammer Throw—Tom Gage, New York A.C. (228 ft 5 in)
Javelin—Mark Murro, Newark, N. J. (284 ft 3 in)
Team—Southern California Striders (129 pts)

Women's AAU Outdoor Championships
(Dayton, Ohio, July 5–6)

100 Yards—Barbara Ferrell, Los Angeles Mercurettes (0:10.7)
220 Yards—Barbara Ferrell (0:23.8)
440 Yards—Kathy Hammond, Sacramento, Calif. (0:54.4)
880 Yards—Madeline Manning, Tennessee State (2:11.1)
1,500-Meters—Doris Brown, Falcon Track Club (4:27.3)
100-Meter High Hurdles—Chi Cheng, Crown Tri-Cities T. C., Claremont, Calif. (0:13.7)
200-Meter Hurdles—Pat Hawkins, Atoms T. C., Brooklyn (0:27.4)
440-Yard Relay—Mayor Daley Youth Foundation, Chicago (0:46.4)
880-Yard Medley Relay—Tennessee State (1:42.4)
Mile Relay—Angels T. C., Seattle, Wash. (4:07.8)
Long Jump—Willye White, Mayor Daley Y. F. (19 ft 8¾ in)
High Jump—Eleanor Montgomery, Tennessee State (5 ft 11 in)
Shot Put—Lynn Graham, Millbrae (Calif.) Lions (48 ft 11¾ in)
Discus—Carol Frost, Nebraska T. C., Lincoln (167 ft 3 in)
Javelin—Kathy Schmidt, Long Beach (Calif.) Comets (177 ft 4 in)
Team—Tennessee State (55 pts)

Men's AAU Indoor Championships
(Philadelphia, March 1)

60 Yards—Charlie Greene, Huskers T. C., Lincoln, Nebr. (0:06)
600 Yards—Martin McGrady, unattached (1:12.3)
1,000 Yards—Herb Germann, New York A. C. (2:08)
Mile—Henryk Szordykowski, Poland (4:05)
3 Miles—George Young, Casa Grande, Ariz. (13:09.8)
Mile Walk—Dave Romansky, Penns Grove, N. J. (6:21.9)
60-Yard Hurdles—Willie Davenport, Houston Striders (0:07)
1,060-Yard Medley Relay—Grand Street Boys, New York (Carl Richardson, John Davis, Russ Rogers, Charlie Mays; 1:55.7)
Mile Relay—Sports International Club, Washington (John Collins, Mark Young, Andy Bell, Ed Roberts; 3:18.1)
2-Mile Relay—Chicago U. Track Club (Bob O'Connor, Ken Sparks, John Kenton, Lowell Paul; 7:35)
Long Jump—Norman Tate, East Orange, N. J. (25 ft 8 in)
Triple Jump—Tate (53 ft 1 in)
High Jump—John Rambo, Pacific Coast Club (6 ft 10 in)
Pole Vault—Peter Chen, Sports International (16 ft 6 in)
Shot Put—George Woods, Pacific Coast Club (63 ft 11½ in)
35-Pound Weight—Al Hall, unattached (70 ft 9 in)
Team—Pacific Coast Club

Women's AAU Indoor Championships
(Philadelphia, March 1)

60 Yards—Barbara Ferrell, Los Angeles Mercurettes (0:06.7)
220 Yards—Barbara Ferrell (0:27.5)

440 Yards—Jarvis Scott, L. A. Mercurettes (0:56.4)
880 Yards—Madeline Manning, Tennessee State (2:07.9)
Mile—Abby Hoffman, Toronto Outdoor Club (4:59.3)
60-Yard Hurdles—Mamie Rallins, Mayor Daley Y. F. Chicago (0:07.7)
640-Yard Relay—Tennessee State (Matteline Render, Iris Davis, Martha Watson, Una Morris; 1:12.4)
Sprint Medley Relay—Tennessee State (Madeline Manning, Matteline Render, Iris Davis, Una Morris; 1:46.6)
Long Jump—Irene K. Szewinska, Poland (20 ft 3¼ in)
High Jump—Eleanor Montgomery, Tennessee State (5 ft 10 in)
Shot Put—Maren Seidler, Mayor Daley Y. F. (48 ft 2 in)
Basketball Throw—Mary Boron, Canton T. C. (108 ft 7 in)
Team—Tennessee State (26 pts)

U. S. Track and Field Federation Outdoor Championships
(Lexington, Ky., June 13–14)

100 Yards—Ivory Crockett, Southern Illinois (0:09.5)
220 Yards—Tom Randolph, Western Michigan (0:20.8)
440 Yards—Curtis Mills, Texas A & M (0:46.1)
880 Yards—Mark Winzenried, Wisconsin (1:48.5)
Mile—Al Robinson, Southern Illinois (4:04.4)
3 Miles—Dave Ellis, Eastern Michigan (13:47.2)
6 Miles—Jerry Jobski, Arizona State (28:58.6)
3,000-Meter Steeplechase—Ken Silvious, Eastern Kentucky (9:02.4)
120-Yard Hurdles—Richmond Flowers, Tennessee (0.13.7)
440-Yard Hurdles—Carl Wood, Richmond (0:50.8)
440-Yard Relay—Western Michigan (Stan Tucker, Warren Coleman, Rick Manuszak, Randolph; 0:41.5)
Mile Relay—Abilene Christian (Hubert Jones, Roger Colglazier, Mark Fry, Ron Crawford; 3:11.9)
Long Jump—Henry Hines, Sacramento C. C. (25 ft 4¼ in)
Triple Jump—Pertti Pousi, Brigham Young (51 ft 4¾ in)
High Jump—Chri Celion, Brigham Young (6 ft 8 in)
Pole Vault—Peter Chen, Sports International Club, Washington (16 ft 2 in)
Shot Put—John Birkelbach, Texas-El Paso (55 ft 11 in)
Discus—Bob Stoltman, Western Kentucky (117 ft 9 in)
Hammer Throw—Dewitt Davies, Dartmouth (189 ft 9 in)
Javelin—Mark Murro, Arizona State (280 ft 2 in)

National Collegiate (NCAA) Outdoor Championships
(Knoxville, Tenn., June 19–21)

100 Yards—John Carlos, San Jose State (0:09.2)
220 Yards—Carlos (0:20.2)
440 Yards—Curtis Mills, Texas A & M (0:44.7)
880 Yards—Byron Dyce, New York U. (1:45.9)
Mile—Marty Liquori, Villanova (3:57.7)
3 Miles—Ole Oleson, Southern California (13:41.9)
6 Miles—Frank Shorter, Yale (29:00.2)
3,000-Meter Steeplechase—Jim Barkley, Oregon State (8:44.4)
120-Yard Hurdles—Erv Hall, Villanova (0:13.3)
440-Yard Hurdles—Ralph Mann, Brigham Young (0:49.6)
440-Yard Relay—San Jose State (Sam Davis, Kirk Clayton, Ronnie Ray Smith, Carlos; 0:39.1)
Mile Relay—UCLA (John Smith, Len Van Hofwegen, Andy Young, Wayne Collett; 3:03.4)
Long Jump—Jerry Proctor, Redlands (26 ft 11¾ in)
Triple Jump—Pertti Pousi, Brigham Young (52 ft 1½ in)
High Jump—Dick Fosbury, Oregon State (7 ft 2½ in)
Pole Vault—Bob Seagren, Southern California (17 ft 7½ in)
Shot Put—Karl Salb, Kansas (64 ft 9 in)
Discus—John Van Reenen, Washington State (200 ft 8 in)
Hammer Throw—Steve DeAutremont, Oregon State (190 ft 5 in)
Javelin—Mark Murro, Arizona State (265 ft 9 in)
Team—San Jose State (48 pts)

National Collegiate (NCAA) Indoor Championships
(Detroit, March 14–15)

60 Yards—John Carlos, San Jose State (0:06)
60-Yard Hurdles—Erv Hall, Villanova (0:07)
440 Yards—Larry James, Villanova (0:47.3)
600 Yards—Bill Wehrwein, Michigan State (1:09.8)
880 Yards—Frank Murphy, Villanova (1:51.1)
1,000 Yards—Ray Arrington, Wisconsin (2:08)
Mile—Jim Ryun, Kansas (4:02.6)
2 Miles—Ole Oleson, Southern California (8:45.2)
Mile Relay—Tennessee (Gary Womble, Larry Kelly, Audry Hardy, Hardee McAlhaney; 3:14.6)
2-Mile Relay—Kansas State (Dave Peterson, Jerome Howe, Bob Barratti, Ken Swenson; 7:32.2)
2½-Mile Medley Relay—Villanova (Andy O'Reilly, Ernie Bradshaw, Chris Mason, Frank Murphy; 9:45.8)
Long Jump—Ron Jessie, Kansas (25 ft 2½ in)
Triple Jump—Lennox Burgher, Nebraska (52 ft ½ in)
High Jump—Ron Jourdan, Florida (7 ft ¾ in)
Pole Vault—Lester Smith, Miami of Ohio (16 ft 6 in)
Shot Put—Karl Salb, Kansas (66 ft 8¾ in)
35-Pound Weight—Charles Ajootian, Harvard (61 ft 8½ in)
Team—Kansas (41½ pts)

AAU Long-Distance Events

15,000 Meters—Garry Bjorklund, Proctor, Minn. (49:53.9)
50-Mile Run—Jim McDonough, Millrose A. A., New York (5:50:34)
One-Hour Run—Fred Ritcherson, S. Calif. Striders (12 mi 23 yds)
10,000-Meter Walk—Ron Laird, New York A. C. (46:42)
15,000-Meter Walk—Laird (66:44.1)
40,000-Meter Walk—Laird (3:33:56)
50,000-Meter Walk—Bryon Overton, S. Calif. Striders (4:56:07)

Intercollegiate Champions

NCAA—College Division: California Poly at San Luis Obispo (76 pts)

NAIA—*indoor:* Eastern Michigan (96⅓); *outdoor:* Prairie View (69½)

Other Events

Boston Marathon—Yoshiaki Unetani, Japan (2:13:49)
USTFF Marathon—Jay Dirksen, Brookings, S. Dak. (2:35:17.6)
World Cross Country (Glasgow)—Gaston Roelants, Belgium 36:25)
AAU 56-Pound Weight Throw—George Frenn, Long Beach, Calif. (49 ft 7 in)
AAU Decathlon—Bill Toomey, Santa Barbara, Calif. (7,818)
USTFF Decathlon—Tie: Jeff Bennett, Oklahoma Christian, and Norm Johnston, unattached (7,438 pts)
NAIA Decathlon—Bennett (7,551)

WATER SKIING

World Championships
(Copenhagen, Aug. 4–10)

Men

Overall—Mike Suyderhound, San Anselmo, Calif. (2,888.8 pts)
Slalom—Victor Palomo, Spain (49 buoys)
Jumping—Wayne Grimditch, Pompano Beach, Fla. (141 ft)
Tricks—Bruce Cockburn, Australia (4,516 pts)

Women

Overall—Liz Allan, Winter Park, Fla. (3,000 pts)
Slalom—Liz Allan (47 buoys)
Jumping—Liz Allan (100 ft)
Tricks—Liz Allan (3,599 pts)

United States Championships
(Berkeley, Calif., Aug. 21–24)

Men

Overall—Mike Suyderhoud, San Anselmo, Calif. (2,982 pts)
Slalom—Bruce Martin, San Lorenzo, Calif. (53 buoys)
Jumping—Suyderhoud (158 ft)
Tricks—Alan Kempton, Tampa, Fla. (4,853 pts)

Women

Overall—Liz Allan, Winter Park, Fla. (3,000 pts)
Slalom—Liz Allan (54½ buoys)
Jumping—Liz Allan (108 ft)
Tricks—Liz Allan (3,962 pts)

Masters Championships
(Callaway Gardens, Ga., July 11–13)

Men

Overall—Alan Kempton, Tampa, Fla. (2,899 pts)
Slalom—Frankie Dees, Cypress Gardens, Fla. (40 buoys)
Jumping—Mike Suyderhoud, San Anselmo, Calif. (157 ft)
Tricks—Ricky McCormick, Independence, Mo. (4,967 pts)

Women

Overall—Liz Allan, Winter Park, Fla. (3,000 pts)
Slalom—Liz Allan (39½ buoys)
Jumping—Liz Allan (109 ft)
Tricks—Liz Allan (3,680 pts)

WEIGHT LIFTING

World Championships
(Warsaw, Sept. 22–28)

Flyweight—Vladislaw Krischishin, USSR (743¾ lbs)
Bantamweight—Mohamed Nassiri, Iran (793¼ lbs)
Featherweight—Yoshiyuki Miyake, Japan (848½ lbs)
Lightweight—Waldemar Baozanowski, Poland (981)
Middleweight—Viktor Kurentzov, USSR (1,031¾)
Light Heavyweight—Masushi Ouchi, Japan (1,074)
Middle Heavyweight—Kaarlo Kangasniemi, Finland (1,135¼)
Heavyweight—Jan Talts, USSR (1,206½)
Super-Heavyweight—Joseph Dube, York, Pa. (1,272½)

National AAU Championships
(Chicago, June 14–15)

123 Pounds—Fernando Baez, Puerto Rico (745 lbs)
132 Pounds—Gary Hanson, York (Pa.) Bar Bell Club (770)
148 Pounds—Steve Mansour, Highland Park, Mich. (860)
165 Pounds—Fred Lowe, York BBC (950)
181 Pounds—Mike Karchut, Duncan Y, Chicago (1,035)
198 Pounds—Frank Capsouras, York BBC (1,080)
242 Pounds—Bob Bednarski, York BBC (1,210)
Super-Heavyweight—Ken Patera, Multnomah A. C., Portland, Oreg. (1,195)
Team—York BBC

WRESTLING

World Championships
(Mar del Plata, Argentina, March 3–10)

105.5 Pounds—Javadie Ebrahim, Iran
114.5 Pounds—Rich Sanders, Portland, Oreg.
125.5 Pounds—Tanaka Tadamichi, Japan
136.5 Pounds—Marita Takeo, Japan
149.5 Pounds—Abdullah Mohaved, Iran
163 Pounds—Zarbeg Beriashvili, USSR
180.5 Pounds—Fred Fozzard, Stillwater, Okla.
198 Pounds—Boris Gurevich, USSR
220 Pounds—Chota Lomidse, USSR

Unlimited—Aleksandr Medved, USSR
Team—USSR

National AAU Championships
(Waterloo, Iowa, April 10–12)

Freestyle

105.5 Pounds—Dale Kestel, Michigan Wrestling Club
114.5 Pounds—Yasou Katsumura, Nebraska Olympic Club
125.5 Pounds—Tashio Nakano, Japan
136.7 Pounds—Dan Gable, Iowa State
149.5 Pounds—Fumiaki Nakamura, New York A. C.
163 Pounds—Lee Detrick, Michigan W. C.
180.5 Pounds—Len Kaufman, U. S. Army
198 Pounds—Buck Deadrich, Mayor Daley Youth Foundation, Chicago
220 Pounds—Jess Lewis, Oregon State
Unlimited—Dale Stearns, Iowa
Team—Michigan W. C.

Greco-Roman

105.5 Pounds—Bill Davids, Michigan W. C.
114.5 Pounds—Yasou Katsumura, Nebraska O. C.
125.5 Pounds—David Hazewinkel, U. S. Army
136.5 Pounds—James Hazewinkel, U. S. Army
149.5 Pounds—Kenshiro Matsunami, New York A. C.
163 Pounds—James Tanniehill, Minnesota A. C.
180.5 Pounds—Rudy Williams, Michigan W. C.
220 Pounds—Robert Roop, Mayor Daley Youth Foundation, Chicago
198 Pounds—Wayne Baughman, U. S. Air Force

National Collegiate (NCAA) Championships
(Provo, Utah, March 27–29)

115 Pounds—John Miller, Oregon
123 Pounds—Wayne Boyd, Temple
130 Pounds—David McGuire, Oklahoma
137 Pounds—Dan Gable, Iowa State
145 Pounds—Mike Grant, Oklahoma
152 Pounds—Gobel Kline, Maryland
160 Pounds—Cleo McGlory, Oklahoma
167 Pounds—Jason Smith, Iowa State
177 Pounds—Chuck Jean, Iowa State
191 Pounds—Tom Kline, California Poly at San Luis Obispo
Unlimited—Jess Lewis, Oregon State
Team—Iowa State (104 pts)
Outstanding Wrestler—Gable

YACHTING

North American Yacht Racing Union Champions

Men (Mallory Cup)—Graham Hall, Larchmont, N. Y.
Women (Adams Cup)—Mrs. Jan O'Malley, Mantoloking, N. J.
Single-Handed (O'Day Trophy)—Gordon Bowers, Wayzata, Minn.
Junior (Sears Cup)—Manton Scott, Noroton, Conn.
Interclub (Prince of Wales Bowl)—Quissett (Mass.) Y. C. (Edward Burt, skipper)

Ocean and Distance Racing

Annapolis-Newport (473 miles)—*Overall, Class I and first to finish:* Ted Turner's *American Eagle,* Atlanta (69.4340 elapsed time, 61.4473 corrected). *Class II:* Walter S. Frank's *Salty Tiger,* Bombay Hook, Del. (90.4497; 74.4534). *Class III:* A. Justin's *Windquest* (99.5548; 79.4768). *Class IV:* Charles L. Shumway's *Arete* (100.2273; 79.5008). *Class V:* Raymond M. Brown's *Fleetwind* (109.3788; 84.5982)
Chicago-Mackinac (333 mi)—Pat Haggerty's *Bay Bea,* Houston
Marblehead-Halifax (330 mi)—Irwin S. Tyson's *Summertime,* White Plains, N. Y.
Miami-Montego Bay (811 mi)—Ogden R. Reid's *Flyway,* Harrison, N. Y. (sailed by Ted Turner)
Port Huron-Mackinac (235 mi)—Peter Stern's *Diavolo,* Chicago
Trans-Atlantic, Newport, R. I.-Cork, Ireland (2,750 mi)—James B. Kilroy's *Kioloa II,* Los Angeles (elapsed time: 13 days, 5 hours, 43 minutes; corrected time: 12:21:06:35). *First to finish:* S. A. Long's *Ondine,* Larchmont, N. Y. (12:21:54:55)
Trans-Pacific, San Pedro, Calif.-Honolulu (2,225 mi)—Jon Andron's *Argonaut,* Santa Barbara, Calif. (elapsed time: 11 days, 16 hours, 35 minutes, 23 seconds; corrected time: 6:20:44:07). *First to finish:* Ken DeMeuse's *Blackfin,* San Francisco (9:09:24:54, record)
Fastnet, Cowes-Plymouth, England (605 miles)—R. E. Carter's *Red Rooster,* U. S.
Skaw, Denmark (290 miles)—A. Nordenskjöld's *Barracuda,* Sweden
Sydney, Australia-Hobart, Tasmania (630 mi)—Edward Heath's *Morning Cloud,* England

Other Trophies

Canada's Cup (Toronto, Sept. 7–10)—*Manitou,* Canada (Perry Connolly, skipper) defeated *Niagara,* United States (John Lovett), 3 races to none.
Southern Ocean Racing Conference—*Salty Tiger,* owned by Jack Powell, Madeira Beach, Fla., and Wally Frank, Darien, Conn.
Morss Trophy (College)—San Diego State (Edward Butler and Thomas McLaughlin)
John F. Kennedy Regatta (College)—Cornell (Dave McFaull)
Women's Intercollegiate—Radcliffe (Jane Chalmers)
Interscholastic (Mallory Trophy)—St. Andrew's, Middletown, Del. (Wally Greene)
Congressional Cup—Henry Sprague 3d, Long Beach, Calif.

BILL BRADDOCK
"The New York Times"

PRIZE STAMP of 1969 was that showing Neil Armstrong stepping onto the lunar surface. The astronauts cancelled this copy in space. An accompanying die was later plated and first covers released on September 9.

STAMP COLLECTING

The stamp world's major activity in 1969 revolved around the Apollo 11 moon flight. Countries all over the globe issued commemorative stamps to honor the moon walk on July 20. In the United States, the Post Office announced in November that demands for first-day covers of its commemorative stamp had been so great that it had already processed 7½ million and "the end was not yet in sight."

Apollo 11 Stamp. The Apollo 11 spacecraft carried the original steel die of a 10-cent commemorative stamp, an unaddressed envelope to which a multicolor die proof impression had been affixed, and a cancellation device to postmark the cover while on the lunar surface. The "July 20" cancellation, however, was actually applied two days after the space walk, with all three astronauts gripping the handstamp to make the imprint.

U. S. COMMEMORATIVE STAMPS OF 1969

Subject	Denomination	Date of Issue
Beautify America	6¢	January 16
American Legion	6¢	March 15
Grandma Moses	6¢	May 1
Apollo 8	6¢	May 5
W. C. Handy	6¢	May 17
Flag stamp coil	6¢	May 30
California Settlement	6¢	July 16
John W. Powell	6¢	August 1
Alabama Statehood	6¢	August 2
International Botanical Congress	6¢	August 23
Apollo 11	10¢	September 9
Daniel Webster	6¢	September 22
Professional Baseball	6¢	September 24
Intercollegiate Football	6¢	September 26
Dwight D. Eisenhower	6¢	October 14
Christmas	6¢	November 3
Rehabilitation of Crippled Children and Adults	6¢	November 20

After the splashdown, the die was flown to Houston for decontamination. It was then sent to Washington where the Bureau of Engraving and Printing made plates and began the press run. The stamps were officially issued on September 9. Postmaster General Winton Blount presented panes of the new stamp—the largest commemorative in Post Office history—to the Apollo 11 astronauts and NASA chief Thomas O. Paine at a ceremony attended by more than 4,000 foreign and U. S. dignitaries and philatelic leaders.

Stamp Design. Domestic philatelists had one major disappointment in 1969. During his campaign President Nixon promised that if elected, he would drastically revise policies that had caused U. S. stamps to become some of the world's most mediocre in design and popularity. Instead, Blount decided to retain his predecessors' practices.

Exhibitions. The year witnessed many important international stamp shows. The Royal Philatelic Society marked its centenary with a show in London in April. Switzerland, Germany, and Columbia held exhibitions celebrating the 50th anniversary of their air mail service. A show in Japan honored the 95th anniversary of the Universal Postal Union.

Miscellaneous. The Philatelic Press Club's annual award was won by the Netherlands for its active role in promoting stamp collecting. In April, the American Academy of Philately was formed with the aim of eventually including in it every organized stamp collector group in the United States.

Britain announced that it will issue a commemorative for Mohandas K. Gandhi. This will be the first British stamp to honor a foreign statesman.

ERNEST A. KEHR
Stamp News Bureau

STEEL

Production of steel increased in 1969 due to a world boom in steel demand that materialized unexpectedly in the early spring. This strong demand was the result of buoyant economic activity in Europe and the Far East that had not been fully anticipated by the steel industry. The American Iron and Steel Institute estimated U. S. raw steel production for 1969 at a record 141 million net tons, 5.1% higher than the 1966 record of 134.1 million tons and 7.2% above 1968's 131.5 million tons. The International Iron and Steel Institute forecast world raw steel production in 1969 at around 625 million net tons, an increase of 7.7% over the 1968 total of 580.5 million tons.

U. S. Developments. Record domestic steel production in 1969 can be traced largely to sharp improvement in the industry's foreign-trade balance in steel shipments. In recent years, imports had exceeded exports by a wide margin. In 1968, only 2.2 million tons of steel were exported against an inflow of more than 18 million tons. During 1969 the boom abroad soaked up foreign surplus steel. U. S. exports rose to more than 5 million tons while imports declined to around 14 million tons, a reflection, in part, of a dock strike earlier in the year. On balance, this added 7 million tons to apparent domestic consumption.

The industry's large capital investment program continued, with about $2.3 billion spent during 1969 for new and improved facilities and machinery. Strand casting, which is the direct casting of molten steel into slabs, blooms or billets, took on more importance as various firms announced the completed installation or planned construction of strand-casting facilities.

In 1969 the basic oxygen process for steelmaking came within 1% of outproducing the open hearths that have been the main steel producers since they surpassed the Bessemer furnaces in 1908. Of the 141 million tons produced in the United States, 61 million tons, or 43.3%, were poured by open hearths and 60 million tons, or 42.5%, by basic oxygen furnaces. In 1968 the figures were 65.8 million tons (50.1%) and 48.8 million tons (37.1%), respectively. Electric furnaces, once used primarily for the manufacture of stainless and alloy steel but now producing carbon steel also, poured 20 million tons in 1969 for a 14.2% share of the total. The 1968 output was 16.8 million tons, or 12.8% of all steel poured.

World Developments. During 1968, the leading steel-producing nations were the United States in first place, followed by the USSR, Japan, West Germany, and the United Kingdom. The USSR was expected to remain in second place during 1969, producing about 123 million tons.

The Japanese steel industry continued to flourish in 1969, with an estimated production of 83 million tons, compared with 74 million tons in 1968. Japan's more than 70 basic oxygen furnaces accounted for approximately 80% of this total. The pending merger between Yawata Iron and Steel Company and Fuji Iron and Steel Company was approved by the government for March 1970. Japan also announced that the world's largest blast furnace, with a daily capacity of 7,000 tons, was "blown in" at Nippon Kokan's Fukuyama Works.

The British Steel Corporation, nationalized in 1967, was granted a 5.3% price increase in 1969 by the government's Price and Income Board. Although this would bring some $96 million in revenue, the company continued to be plagued with financial difficulties.

In the European Coal and Steel Community, merger plans were announced by firms in Belgium, France, and Germany.

GEORGE N. STOUMPAS
American Iron and Steel Institute

PRODUCTION OF IRON ORE, PIG IRON AND FERROALLOYS, AND RAW STEEL[1]

Country	1968 Iron ore, concentrates and agglomerates (long tons of 2,240 lb)	1968 Pig iron and ferroalloys (short tons of 2,000 lb)	1968 Raw steel[1] (short tons of 2,000 lb)
Algeria	3,037,000	...	...
Angola	1,181,000	...	...
Argentina	217,000	617,000	1,711,000
Australia	22,932,000	6,184,000	7,160,000
Austria	3,420,000	2,727,000	3,825,000
Belgium	81,000	11,511,000	18,079,000[2]
Brazil	24,605,000	3,505,000	4,887,000
Bulgaria	2,461,000	1,190,000	1,578,000
Burma	4,000	...	...
Canada	42,321,000	8,004,000	11,251,000
Chile	11,466,000	474,000	678,000
China, Communist	31,494,000	17,086,000	15,000,000
China, Nationalist	...	88,000	275,000
Colombia	886,000	220,000	277,000
Cuba	2,000	...	55,000
Czechoslovakia	1,516,000	7,661,000	11,676,000
Denmark	30,000	205,000	513,000
Finland	1,004,000	1,058,000	684,000
France	54,902,000	18,117,000	22,491,000
Germany, East	1,476,000	2,590,000	4,586,000
Germany, West	7,592,000	33,405,000	45,366,000
Greece	98,000	...	300,000
Guinea	591,000	...	...
Hong Kong	157,000	...	...
Hungary	679,000	1,830,000	3,189,000
India	27,243,000	7,716,000	6,953,000
Iran	59,000	...	...
Ireland	...	...	55,000
Israel	...	...	93,000
Italy	1,191,000	8,644,000	18,694,000
Japan	2,096,000	50,651,000	73,730,000
Korea, North	5,905,000	1,736,000	1,500,000
Korea, South	...	28,000	400,000
Lebanon	2,000	...	20,000
Liberia	17,913,000	...	...
Luxembourg	6,297,000	4,749,000	...[3]
Malaysia	5,275,000	...	...
Mauritania	7,382,000	...	...
Mexico	3,445,000	1,775,000	3,591,000
Morocco	837,000	...	...
Netherlands	...	3,111,000	4,081,000
New Caledonia	217,000	...	...
New Zealand	3,000	...	75,000
Norway	4,065,000	1,488,000	898,000
Pakistan	5,000	...	120,000
Peru	7,382,000	33,000	96,000
Philippines	1,181,000	...	95,000
Poland	3,051,000	7,330,000	12,133,000
Portugal	212,000	309,000	342,000
Rhodesia	1,279,000	287,000	154,000
Rumania	2,638,000	3,131,000	5,237,000
Sierra Leone	2,559,000	...	...
South Africa	7,972,000	4,134,000	4,328,000
Spain	5,561,000	3,164,000	5,566,000
Sudan	39,000	...	...
Swaziland	1,968,000	...	...
Sweden	31,822,000	2,750,000	5,580,000
Switzerland	...	28,000	490,000
Thailand	492,000	6,000	...
Tunisia	1,004,000	...	...
Turkey	1,476,000	551,000	1,143,000
USSR	174,205,000	86,861,000	117,064,000
United Arab Republic	492,000	220,000	300,000
United Kingdom	13,779,000	18,405,000	28,965,000
United States	85,860,000	91,362,000	131,462,000[4]
Venezuela	16,732,000	595,000	949,000
Yugoslavia	2,775,000	1,334,000	2,178,000
Other countries	...	...	653,000
Total (estimate)[5]	656,000,000	416,870,000	580,526,000

[1] Steel in the first solid state after melting, suitable for further processing or sale. [2] Figure includes data for Luxembourg. [3] Included under Belgium. [4] United States data exclude 1,557,000 net tons of steel produced by foundries that reported their output to the Bureau of Census but did not report to American Iron and Steel Institute. [5] Details do not necessarily add to total because of rounded figures. (Sources: Statistical Quarterly Report for Iron and Steel Industry; West Germany Iron and Steel Federation, Dusseldorf; American Iron and Steel Institute, New York; Bureau of Mines of the U. S. Department of the Interior.

STOCKS AND BONDS

After moving gradually higher for two years, stock prices declined sharply in 1969. The widely followed stock market indicators ended the year with 10% to 18% declines, and many individual issues were off by much greater amounts. The bond market, which had been depressed for more than three years, continued under pressure. Yields on many issues again reached all-time highs.

Stock Prices. A decline in stock prices began in December 1968 and continued into early 1969. There was some strength in January as the new Nixon administration took steps toward slowing business and checking inflation, but the downturn was resumed in February. Stock prices then moved in a narrow range through early May, when peace rumors and news of President Nixon's intention to withdraw troops from Vietnam sent prices up sharply.

Before long, prices began to move lower again as concern about inflation set in, worries of a recession arose, and the peace negotiations dragged on endlessly. The market hit bottom in July, and in the following months investor opinion was about evenly divided between those who expected a further drop and those who felt that a rally was in store. Talk of major troop withdrawals and some evidence indicating a lesser degree of credit restraint led to a small rally in October. However, the decline set in once again in November, and by late December prices were near the lows for the year.

For 1969 as a whole, prices fell 10.3% on the Standard & Poor's index of 425 industrial stocks.

Market action in 1969, in terms of the Standard & Poor's stock price indexes (1941–43 = 10), is shown in the accompanying table.

Questions relating to the government's ability to halt inflation and to resolve the conflict in Vietnam were uppermost in investors' minds in 1969, and the uncertainty relating to these two continuing problems was a prime cause of the market decline. As the year wore on, there was also increasing concern that the economy would suffer a recession some time in 1970 and that corporate profits would suffer as a result.

Earnings and Dividends. The earnings performance of most companies was favorable in 1969, but the increases were generally less than those of the preceding several years. In terms of the industrial stock price index, net income (partly estimated) was $6.31 a share. This was about 2.5% above the $6.16 net income of 1968.

Dividends increased again in 1969, reaching the equivalent of $3.28 a share on the Standard & Poor's index, compared with $3.18 in 1968.

At year's end, stocks sold at an average price of 16 times earnings, with an average dividend return of 3.2%.

Bond Prices. The bond market continued to be under pressure, as it had been since 1965. The declines in individual issues were sometimes substan-

STOCKS AND BONDS
(Standard & Poor's Index)

Date[1]	425 Industrials	20 Rails	55 Utilities	500 Stocks
1968 low.......Mar. 5	95.05	40.82	61.06	87.72
1968 high......Nov. 29	118.03	56.08	72.30	108.37
1969 high......May 14	116.24	50.58	70.74	106.74
1969 low.......July 29	97.75	35.26	54.33	88.04
1969 close.....Dec. 31	101.49	37.16	56.09	92.06

[1] Dates are for industrials. Rail and utility highs and lows in some instances occurred on other dates.

MOST ACTIVE STOCKS IN 1969—
NEW YORK STOCK EXCHANGE

Stock	Sales	Close	Net Change
Occidental Petroleum	30,427,700	24⅜	−23
Benguet	24,537,900	12⅜	− 4⅞
American Tel & Tel	23,930,400	48⅝	− 4⅜
Natomas	21,395,400	63⅜	+28⅛
Gulf Oil	15,014,000	31	−12⅛
Atlantic Richfield	14,382,500	86⅛	−31⅞
City Investing	14,198,500	28⅛	− 8⅜
General Motors	13,081,900	69⅛	−10
Brunswick	12,672,600	17¾	− ½
Chrysler	12,552,400	34⅜	−21⅝
Sperry Rand	12,147,900	37⅛	− 9¼
Pan American World Airways	11,649,300	11⅝	−17⅝
Great Western Financial	11,598,800	20½	− 3⅝
Polaroid	11,574,200	125	+ 7⅞
International Tel & Tel	11,496,800	59¼	+ 1

MOST ACTIVE STOCKS IN 1969—
AMERICAN STOCK EXCHANGE

Stock	Sales	Close	Net Change
Asamera Oil	24,511,800	18¼	− 5⅝
British Petroleum	17,020,100	12⅜	− 7⅞
AMK Warrants	14,462,900	8⅞	..
National General Warrants	12,450,400	6⅛	−12⅜
Leasco Warrants	9,716,900	14½	−13
Canadian Homestead	9,676,300	13⅜	+ 2
AO Industries	9,659,400	3⅞	− 5⅜
Four Seasons Nursing	9,169,500	65⅞	+20
North Canadian Oils	9,163,900	6½	− 2¾
Siboney	8,943,000	3⅛	− 2½
Syntex	8,823,500	65⅛	− 2⅛
Airlift	8,308,600	2	− 5⅛
Loews Warrants	7,929,300	16¾	−16
Equity Funding	7,625,800	54⅝	− 1⅞
Home Oil A	7,317,800	29¼	−17⅝

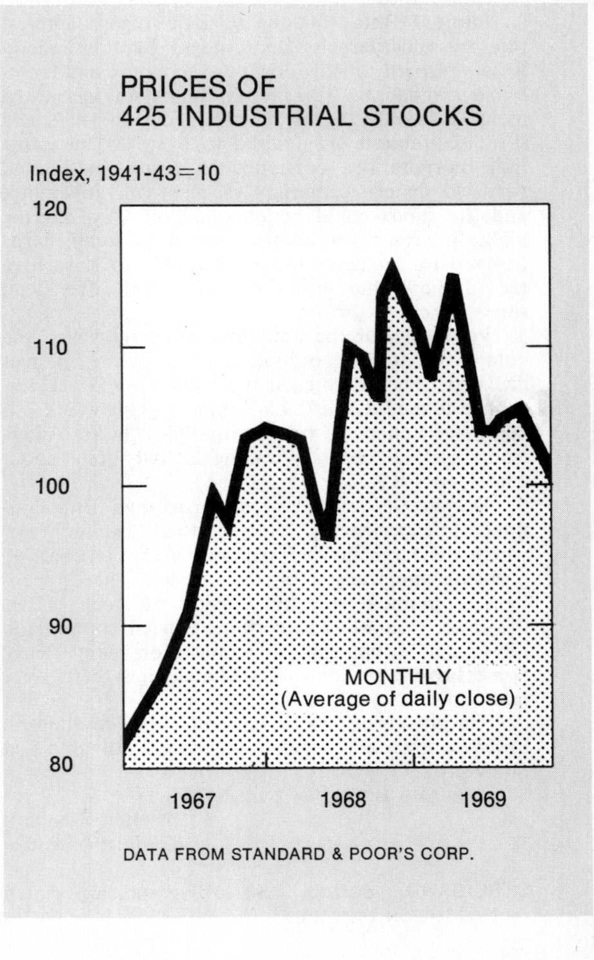
PRICES OF
425 INDUSTRIAL STOCKS
Index, 1941-43=10
120
110
100
90
80
MONTHLY
(Average of daily close)
1967
1968
1969
DATA FROM STANDARD & POOR'S CORP.

MOUNTAINS of paper traditionally clutter the back offices of Wall Street brokerage firms, but this Control Data automation center eliminates that tangle by processing stock transactions as they occur. The firm of Hornblower & Weeks—Hemphill, Noyes said its new system cost about $6 million and required 2 years' planning.

HORNBLOWER & WEEKS—HEMPHILL, NOYES

tial, and the percentage losses were often greater than the drop in stock prices. Long-term government bonds, for example, moved from an average yield of about 5.95% early in 1969 to a high of 6.88% in December. During the same time, yields on high-grade utility bonds rose from 6.75% to 7.95%. In December a milestone was reached when yields on highest-quality corporate bonds topped 9% for the first time in U. S. financial history.

Interest Rate Influences. The record interest rates resulted largely from moves by the Federal Reserve Board to slow down the economy and thereby stem inflation. The money supply was permitted to increase only slightly, if at all, during 1969, and the discount rate was raised to 6%. At the same time, corporations continued to require additional funds to finance expansion of plant and inventory, and the funds could be obtained only by offering higher interest rates. Because of the unusually large demand for funds, banks were forced to raise to a record 8.5% the prime rate at which they lend funds.

Volume. For the first time in recent years, the volume of trading on the major stock exchanges declined. The volume on the New York Stock Exchange totaled 2,850,784,841 shares. This was 2.7% below the volume of trading in 1968. On the American Stock Exchange, trading activity fell about 13.5% in 1969.

Despite the lower volume, brokerage firms continued to experience problems in their "back offices," where the large flow of paperwork created massive problems in transferring securities. These problems, combined with the erosion of stock prices, the lower volume, and certain reduced commission rates, caused financial difficulties for many firms. Some brokerage houses liquidated, and there were many mergers.

Sharply rising operating costs also resulted in lower compensation and bonuses for individuals at many brokerage firms.

(See also ECONOMY OF THE U.S.).

STEPHEN SANBORN
Kohlmeyer & Co.

STREISAND, Barbra. See biographical sketch under MOTION PICTURES.

SUDAN

The problems of political instability and southern separatism which have plagued Sudan since independence again dominated events in 1969. On May 25, young army officers led by Col. Jaafar Mohammad al-Nimeiry successfully deposed the 5-year-old civilian government of President Ismail al-Azhari and established a Revolutionary Command Council (RCC) and a 21-man cabinet to rule the country. The situation in southern Sudan (where non-Muslims have been in rebellion for 15 years) changed little.

Revolutionary Government. The new government was composed primarily of Nasserite socialists, who said they were determined to set Sudan on the road to "freedom and socialism" and to find a solution to the southern problem. The government was led by Nimeiry, the head of the RCC, and by a leftist former supreme court judge, Abu Bakr Awadallah, who became the new prime minister.

In late May and June the new government began a reevaluation of all old laws and sought a settlement with southern leaders. In July a law was promulgated to cover the offenses committed by political leaders between 1956 and 1969, and people's military courts were established to try the offenders.

On August 26, former President Ismail al-Azhari, one of Sudan's most important nationalist leaders, died of a heart attack while in detention.

Throughout the later months of 1969 the government worked to solidify its position. On October 1 complete press censorship was reestablished. The RCC and the cabinet were reorganized on October 28 to make Nimeiry prime minister as well as head of the RCC, and Awadallah foreign minister and minister of justice. Four men, including two Communists, were dropped, leaving 8 military men and 18 civilians in control of the government.

Southern Sudan. The leadership of southern Sudan both inside and outside the country remained divided on basic policy issues. In March, Mourtat Mayen, vice president in Aggrey Jaden's Southern Sudan provisional government, broke with Jaden and formed the Nile provisional government.

Nimeiry announced his government's southern policy on June 10. He said that the government

SUDAN

Information Highlights

Area: 967,494 square miles (2,505,813 sq km).
Population: 14,770,000 (1968 est.).
Chief Cities (1966 census): Khartoum, the capital, 185,000; Omdurman, 198,000.
Government: *President of the Revolutionary Council*—Col. Jaafar Mohammad al-Nimeiry (took office following a military coup in May 1969).
Religious Faiths: Muslims, 65% of population; Animists, 25%; Roman Catholics, 4%; others, 6%.
Education: *Literacy rate* (1969), 10%–15% of population. *Total school enrollment* (1965)—600,264 (primary, 492,-085; secondary, 92,407; teacher-training, 1,680; technical/vocational, 6,391; university/higher, 7,701).
Finance (1968–69 est.): *Revenues,* $324,000,000; *expenditures,* $287,000,000; *monetary unit,* Sudanese pound (.3482 pound equals U. S.$1).
Gross National Product (1968): $1,567,000,000.
Average Annual Income per Person (1968): $97.
Cost of Living Index (1967): 114 (1963=100).
Manufacturing (metric tons, 1967): Cement, 133,000; sugar, 77,000.
Crops (metric tons, 1967–68 crop year): Sesame, 168,000 (ranks 4th among world producers); sorghum, 1,850,000; cottonseed, 358,000; peanuts, 307,000.
Minerals (metric tons, 1967): Salt, 58,000; chromite (1966), 17,000; iron ore, 7,000.
Foreign Trade (1968): *Exports,* $223,000,000 (chief exports, 1967: cotton, $117,540,000; gum arabic, $23,940,000; peanuts, $18,690,000; oilseed cake, $11,570,000); *imports,* $258,000,000 (chief imports, 1967: Textile yarn and fabrics, $33,020,000; transport equipment, $20,450,000; nonelectrical equipment, $19,800,000). *Chief trading partners* (1967): Britain (took 8% of exports, supplied 22% of imports); India (took 9% of exports, supplied 11% of imports); West Germany (took 12% of exports, supplied 6% of imports).
Transportation: *Roads* (1969), 6,562 miles (10,560 km); *motor vehicles* (1966), 41,300 (automobiles 23,700); *railways* (1969), 2,945 miles (4,739 km); *national airline,* Sudan Airways; *principal airport,* Khartoum.
Communications: *Telephones* (1968), 42,524; *television stations* (1967), 1; *television sets* (1966), 11,000; *radios* (1964), 225,000; *newspapers* (1962), 7 (daily circulation, 64,000).

would extend the amnesty introduced in 1968; initiate an intensive program of social, economic, and cultural development; appoint a minister of southern affairs and a special committee for southern development; and establish a program to train southerners for positions of leadership. The reaction of the south was mixed. In September, as an indication of the trend of events, Nimeiry's government announced the death of 79 southern guerrillas in a battle in the Upper Nile province.

Foreign Affairs. The revolutionary government seemed to align itself more closely with the United Arab Republic. In February the government of President al-Azhari announced that it would not resume diplomatic relations with the United States or West Germany until the two countries changed their policies toward Israel. In May, Nimeiry reaffirmed this policy and in June he established relations with East Germany. In September his government requested a new summit meeting of Arab leaders to plan a unified strategy against Israel.

Economy. The most important economic change resulting from the May coup was the acceleration of the movement toward greater cooperation with the UAR and the Communist bloc countries. In

September the government signed an agreement strengthening its economic ties with the UAR and realigned its import policy to give more trade to eastern European countries. It was announced in November that the Sudanese, UAR, and Libyan governments had agreed to integrate their economies more closely.

ROBERT O. COLLINS
University of California, Santa Barbara

SUGAR

The world produced a record 79,362,000 tons of sugar in 1969–70, an increase of 3,916,000 tons or 5% over 1968–69. Favorable weather led to increases on all continents, but not in Oceania.

North American production totaled 19,982,000 tons—3,129,000 tons or 19% above 1968–69. There was a large gain in Cuba, the world's leading cane producer. U. S. production improved slightly. Increases in Hawaii and Puerto Rico offset declines in beet sugar and mainland cane sugar production. Beet sugar production totaled 3.5 million tons, slightly less than in 1968–69. Florida and Louisiana cane production totaled 1 million tons, a drop of 114,000 tons or 9% from 1968–69. Hawaiian production was 1,235,000 tons, a gain of 55,000 tons or 5% over 1968–69. Puerto Rico produced 575,000 tons—92,000 tons or 19% more than in 1968–69.

South American production was 9,414,000 tons in 1969–70, up 600,000 tons or 7% from a year earlier. There were large gains in Brazil and Peru.

European production was 17,318,000 tons, an increase of 811,000 tons or 5%. Production totaled 11,367,000 tons in Western Europe, and 5,951,000 tons in Eastern Europe. The USSR remained the world's leading sugar producer.

African production totaled 4,980,000 tons, a slight increase over 1968–69.

Production in Asia totaled 13,956,000 tons, a gain of 683,000 tons or 5% over 1968–69. Production in Oceania dropped from 3,503,000 tons in 1968–69 to 2,712,000 tons in 1969–70.

NICHOLAS KOMINUS
U. S. Cane Sugar Refiners Association

CENTRIFUGAL SUGAR PRODUCTION BY MAJOR COUNTRIES[1]
(In tons, raw value)

	Average 1961–65	1968–69	Preliminary 1969–70
USSR[2]	7,623,000	11,651,000	11,000,000
Cuba	5,596,000	5,200,000	8,000,000
United States[3]	5,862,000	6,387,000	6,410,000
Brazil	3,815,000	4,804,000	5,048,000
India	3,694,000	4,640,000	4,978,000
France[2]	2,309,000	2,623,000	2,741,000
Australia	1,806,000	3,055,000	2,365,000
Mexico	1,899,000	2,220,000	2,300,000
China (Communist)[3]	1,022,000	2,200,000	2,200,000
Germany, West[2]	1,980,000	2,174,000	2,193,000
Philippines	1,681,000	1,755,000	1,903,000
South Africa	1,216,000	1,659,000	1,740,000
Poland[2]	1,693,000	1,881,000	1,700,000
Italy[2]	1,082,000	1,422,000	1,498,000
Czechoslovakia[2]	1,160,000	1,005,000	1,100,000
United Kingdom[2]	988,000	1,075,000	1,073,000
Argentina	949,000	1,019,000	1,068,000
Germany, East[2]	838,000	815,000	1,000,000
Spain[3]	554,000	815,000	952,000
Dominican Republic	852,000	920,000	950,000
Peru	873,000	678,000	827,000
Colombia	421,000	784,000	818,000
Indonesia	700,000	750,000	800,000
Netherlands[2]	620,000	792,000	797,000
China (Taiwan)	992,000	834,000	788,000
World total	61,035,000	75,446,000	79,362,000

[1] Centrifugal sugar includes cane and beet sugar produced by the centrifugal processes, and is the principal kind used in international trade. Years shown are crop-harvesting years. Cane sugar unless otherwise noted. [2] Beet sugar. [3] Cane and beet sugar. (Source: U. S. Cane Sugar Refiners Association.)

(*Left*) Judge Clement Haynsworth, Jr. (*right*), awaits Senate hearing on his appointment to Supreme Court. With him is his state's senator, Strom Thurmond of South Carolina.

(*Below*) Justice Abe Fortas resigned from the Supreme Court as a result of controversy involving charges of unethical conduct.

SUPREME COURT

The 1968–69 term of the U. S. Supreme Court opened on October 7 with Chief Justice Earl Warren still presiding, contrary to expectations. His effort to retire had been frustrated when President Johnson's nominee to succeed him, Justice Abe Fortas, had withdrawn his name after strong opposition developed in the Senate. Warren then agreed to remain on the court, and at the request of incoming President Nixon he continued to the end of the term. Immediately after adjourning the 1968–69 term, Warren administered the oath of office to the new chief justice, Warren Earl Burger.

The term saw an event unprecedented in Supreme Court history, as Justice Fortas was forced by public pressure to resign from the court because of charges of unethical conduct. Fortas had agreed to accept an annual fee of $20,000 for services to a private foundation headed by Louis E. Wolfson, who was then under prosecution in federal court. The Fortas debacle led to renewed concern about the off-the-court activities of Justice William O. Douglas, and he subsequently resigned his salaried connection with an educational program financed by the Parvin Foundation, whose principal assets were Las Vegas gambling establishments.

These events led Congress to consider legislation defining judicial ethics, and on June 10 the Judicial Conference of the United States, headed by Chief Justice Warren, adopted resolutions including a request that federal judges decline fees for extra-judicial activities. (This was rescinded on November 1, under Chief Justice Burger, with judges merely being required to report that income to a national council of judges.)

In the midst of this heightened concern about judicial ethics, President Nixon on Aug. 18, 1969, nominated Clement F. Haynsworth, Jr., to fill the Fortas vacancy. Haynsworth was from South Carolina and, like Burger, a federal appeals court judge, having served on the Fourth Circuit since 1957. Some liberals charged that the President was paying a political debt to Sen. Strom Thurmond of South Carolina, and labor and civil rights groups protested certain of Haynsworth's decisions. Serious questions were raised when Haynsworth's stock investments were made public.

Charges that as a judge he had not been sufficiently sensitive to possible conflicts of interest resulting from his active financial operations led many Democrats and a substantial number of Republicans in the Senate to oppose the nomination, and the 1969 term of the Supreme Court opened in October with Haynsworth unconfirmed. The Fortas seat remained vacant when the Senate on November 21 voted against the Haynsworth nomination, 55 to 45.

The composition of the court for the 1968 term was as follows: Chief Justice Warren and, in order of seniority, Associate Justices Hugo L. Black, Douglas, John M. Harlan, William J. Brennan, Jr., Potter Stewart, Byron R. White, Fortas (until his resignation on May 14, 1969), and Thurgood Marshall. The Warren Court was controversial to the end, overruling precedents in several cases and strongly defending the constitutional rights of Negroes, voters, demonstrators, students, the poor, and defendants in criminal prosecutions.

THE POWELL CASE

Chief Justice Warren's last opinion for the court held in *Powell* v. *McCormack* (395 U. S. 285) that the House of Representatives had acted unconstitutionally when it excluded New York Rep. Adam Clayton Powell from his seat in 1967 on grounds of alleged misuse of House funds. In a 7-to-1 decision, the court ruled that the House had no authority to exclude a duly elected member who met constitutional requirements of age, citizenship, and residence. If the House should find such a member lacking in integrity, the proper constitutional procedure was expulsion by two-thirds vote.

REAPPORTIONMENT AND ELECTIONS

On the occasion of his retirement, Chief Justice Warren expressed the view that the most important achievement of the Warren Court was the one-man, one-vote decision guaranteeing equal representation in state legislatures. Implementation of this rule continued in the 1968–69 term as the court decided reapportionment cases from Missouri and New York, laying down even more rigorous standards of mathematical equality between districts in *Kirkpatrick* v. *Preisler* (394 U. S. 527) and *Wells* v. *Rockefeller* (394 U. S. 542).

The court also went further than ever before in establishing judicial supervision of the American election system. The laws of many states make it very difficult for third parties to get onto the ballot. Supporters of George Wallace's American Independent Party succeeded in surmounting these hurdles in every state except Ohio, where they secured the huge number of 450,000 signatures but failed to meet the time deadline. The court in *Williams* v. *Rhodes* (393 U. S. 23) ruled that such unreasonable restrictions on the right to associate for political purposes violated the equal protection clause of the Fourteenth Amendment, and that the Wallace party must be placed on the Ohio ballot.

In *Kramer* v. *Union Free School District No. 15* (395 U. S. 621) and *Cipriano* v. *City of Houma* (395 U. S. 701), the court invalidated restrictions on the franchise imposed by laws in two states. One was a New York law limiting the right to vote in school board elections to property owners, lessees, and parents or guardians of school children. The other was a Louisiana law permitting only property taxpayers to vote on issuance of municipal bonds.

CIVIL RIGHTS

Ever since the Warren Court declared racial segregation in the public schools unconstitutional in 1954 and ordered the federal courts to proceed toward desegregation "with all deliberate speed," federal judges have been reviewing various enforcement plans. An unusual tactic came before the court in *United States* v. *Montgomery County Board of Education* (395 U. S. 225), where the district court required that a specific ratio of black to white teachers be achieved. Although classifications based on race are usually invalid, the court upheld this plan as a reasonable step toward desegregation, and stressed possible experimentation in this field.

The Voting Rights Act of 1965, intended to guarantee the franchise to Negroes, was strictly enforced against Mississippi and Virginia in *Allen* v. *State Board of Elections* (393 U. S. 544). The court ordered new elections in an Alabama county where state laws had been applied unequally to disqualify Negro candidates in *Hadnott* v. *Amos* (393 U. S. 996). In *Gaston County* v. *United States* (395 U. S. 285), the court ruled that previously segregated and inferior schools for Negroes in a North Carolina county so affected educational opportunity that current use of a literacy test for voters abridged the right to vote on the basis of race.

The voters of Akron, Ohio, by popular referendum adopted a charter amendment suspending the city's fair housing ordinance and requiring the approval of the voters before any future fair housing law could go into effect. In *Hunter* v. *Erickson* (393 U. S. 385), the court held that this requirement, which did not apply to ordinances on any other subject, was invalid.

The public accommodations provisions of the 1964 Civil Rights Act were given an interesting interpretation when the court held in *Daniel* v. *Paul* (395 U. S. 298) that a recreational facility which purported to be a private club, but which sold "memberships" for 25 cents, was a public accommodation and could not exclude Negroes.

FREEDOM OF EXPRESSION AND ASSEMBLY

The court continued to take a strong line on protecting the freedom of expression and assembly. In two cases campus demonstrations were at issue. *Tinker* v. *Des Moines Independent Community School District* (393 U. S. 503) arose when three public school students wore black armbands to school to express their opposition to the Vietnam War. The school district had banned such insignia as likely to cause disruption in the school, and the students were suspended. The court held this action was an unconstitutional denial of the students' right to expression of opinion. "In our system, state-operated schools may not be enclaves of totalitarianism," wrote Justice Fortas. However, campus violence was a different matter. In *Barker* v. *Hardway* (394 U. S. 905), the court declined to review the expulsion of students from a West Virginia college who had physically assaulted school administrators.

The court protected the rights of assembly for demonstrators on both sides of current civil rights conflicts. In *Gregory* v. *Chicago* (394 U. S. 111), peaceful picketing by blacks around the home of Chicago's Mayor Daley incited white residents of the area, and the police, fearing violence, ordered the marchers to disperse and arrested them for disorderly conduct when they failed to do so. The court unanimously voided the conviction since there was no evidence of actual disorderly conduct. Then, with even-handed justice, the court in *Carroll* v. *Princess Anne County* (393 U. S. 175), struck down an injunction forbidding a rally by the right-wing National States' Rights Party. The injunction had been secured by local officials fearing that inflammatory speeches against Negroes and Jews would endanger the peace.

In the 1967–68 term the court had decided that burning a draft card to express opposition to the war in Vietnam was not "symbolic speech" protected by the First Amendment. However, a case settled in the subsequent term had a different outcome. *Street* v. *New York* (394 U. S. 576) involved a Brooklyn Negro who, angered by the shooting of James Meredith in Mississippi, burned an American flag in the street, at the same time saying that if such a thing could happen, "We don't need no damn flag." The court reversed his conviction but without discussing the status of flag-burning as symbolic speech. The reasoning was that the conviction might have been based on the spoken words, which were clearly protected by the First Amendment.

In terms of constitutional doctrine one of the most important decisions of the 1968–69 term was *Brandenburg* v. *Ohio* (395 U. S. 444), which reversed the conviction of a Ku Klux Klan leader for violating Ohio's criminal syndicalism act. The court, following the logic of recent decisions, held that the states cannot treat as a crime abstract advocacy of the use of force or violence. Only incitement to imminent lawless action can be criminally punished.

Defining obscenity has been one of the Warren Court's most frustrating problems. However, the 1968–69 term's obscenity case, *Stanley* v. *Georgia* (394 U. S. 557), was not a difficult one. Georgia police were making a legal search of the house of a suspected bookmaker when they came upon some reels of film. Using the owner's projector, they viewed the films, determined they were obscene, and arrested the householder. The court voided the conviction, holding that, whatever the case for regulating obscenity, it does not apply in the privacy of a home. Said Justice Marshall, "a State has no business telling a man, sitting alone in his own house, what books he may read or what films he may watch."

Echoes of the famous 1925 "monkey trial" in Tennessee were heard in *Epperson* v. *Arkansas* (393 U. S. 97), in which a high school biology teacher had been convicted of violating the state law forbidding the teaching of evolution. The court held that the statute had a religious motivation to outlaw anything except the Bible story of creation, and so violated the neutrality that religion clauses of the First Amendment require the states to observe.

A protest by radio and television broadcasters against the FCC fairness doctrine, which requires stations to provide time for response to personal attacks, failed in *Red Lion Broadcasting Co.* v. *Federal Communications Commission* (395 U. S. 367). The court denied that this rule was a violation of the freedoms of speech and press, saying that the public's First Amendment right to hear different sides of public issues was superior to the broadcasters' right to be free of government regulation.

LAW OF THE POOR

The Warren Court continued to manifest its interest in providing judicial remedies for the woes of the poor. Many states have statutes denying welfare assistance to persons who have not resided in the state for one year. In *Shapiro* v. *Thompson* (394 U. S. 618) the court held this was a denial of equal protection and an unreasonable burden on the right to travel from state to state. The court tightened garnishment procedures in *Sniadach* v. *Family Finance Corp.* (393 U. S. 1078), holding that creditors cannot attach salaries until there has been a court hearing to establish the validity of the debt.

CRIMINAL PROSECUTIONS

The Warren Court continued to the end to shatter precedents by reinterpreting the rights of defendants in criminal proceedings. The famous 1937 decision in *Palko* v. *Connecticut* was overruled in *Benton* v. *Maryland* (395 U. S. 784). The new rule is that the double jeopardy provision of the Fifth Amendment, applicable in federal prosecutions, is now also effective against the states.

Chimel v. *California* (395 U. S. 752) was an important decision tightening up the rules against unreasonable search and seizure. Police, lacking evidence to secure a search warrant, arrested a burglary suspect in his home and then, as an incident to the arrest, searched the entire house. The court, overruling two of its earlier decisions, held that an arrest justifies a search only of the person arrested and the area immediately around him, but not in other rooms or in closed drawers.

In *Alderman* v. *United States* (394 U. S. 165) the court heavily penalized illegal government eavesdropping by requiring all material obtained in this manner to be turned over to defendants for examination to see whether their rights had been violated, even in national security cases. The court remanded to lower courts a number of cases, including the draft evasion conviction of boxer Cassius Clay and the jury-tampering conviction of union leader James Hoffa, for determination on illegal surveillance.

Davis v. *Mississippi* (394 U. S. 721) held that police could not, without a warrant, detain a suspect for the purpose of obtaining his fingerprints. *Overton* v. *New York* (393 U. S. 85) reversed a high school student's conviction for possession of marihuana found in a school locker by a police officer permitted by school officials to search the locker without the student's consent.

Timothy Leary's conviction under the federal marihuana act was reversed in *Leary* v. *United States* (395 U. S. 6). The court ruled that the statutory requirement that the names of all who pay the tax must be turned over to law enforcement officers amounts to compulsory self-incrimination. State prison rules that forbid inmates to help other prisoners prepare petitions for post-conviction relief were declared in violation of the federal right of habeas corpus in *Johnson* v. *Avery* (393 U. S. 483).

SELECTIVE SERVICE AND MILITARY JUSTICE

The Supreme Court has been reluctant to involve itself in review of the validity or operation of the Selective Service system. In general, the only way a draftee can challenge an induction order is to refuse to submit to induction and defend his position in the subsequent criminal proceeding. *Oestereich* v. *Selective Service* (393 U. S. 233) was noteworthy because here for the first time the court agreed than an injunction would issue against induction in certain restricted areas. The case arose after Lt. Gen. Lewis B. Hershey, Selective Service director, issued a memorandum to all local draft boards encouraging them to induct war protesters. Oestereich, who had a ministerial student exemption, was reclassified 1-A after he returned his draft card in protest against the war. The court enjoined his induction, holding that the ministerial student exemption had been conferred by statute and that a draft board could not lawfully withdraw it.

In the field of military justice, the court in *O'Callahan* v. *Parker* (395 U. S. 258) ruled that members of the armed forces can be tried by military courts only for "service-connected" offenses. This case involved a soldier who had committed rape in a Honolulu hotel room while on an overnight pass. In a 5-to-3 ruling the court held that a court-martial's basic purpose is to ensure military discipline, not to dispense justice, and pointed to the differences between civil and military courts that increase the probability of court-martial convictions.

C. HERMAN PRITCHETT
University of California, Santa Barbara

Warren Earl Burger

15th chief justice of the U. S. Supreme Court; b. St. Paul, Minn., Sept. 17, 1907.

Warren E. Burger was nominated by President Nixon to be chief justice of the United States on May 21, 1969, following the retirement of Earl Warren. His parents, Charles and Katharine Burger, were of Swiss-German descent. He graduated from the St. Paul College of Law in 1931. In 1933 he married Elvera Stromberg, and they have a son, Wade Allan, and daughter, Margaret Elizabeth.

Career. Burger, a former St. Paul lawyer and a Republican, had served in the Eisenhower administration as assistant attorney general in charge of the Civil Division of the Justice Department (1953–56), and since then had been a judge of the Court of Appeals for the District of Columbia. In contrast to President Johnson's earlier nomination of Abe Fortas, withdrawn because of Senate opposition, the Burger appointment was promptly confirmed by the Senate on June 9 by a vote of 74 to 3.

In choosing the 61-year-old Burger, President Nixon departed from past practice that nominees for the chief justiceship should be men of considerable public reputation. A comparison of Burger—who was unknown to the general public before his appointment—with some of his predecessors points up this contrast. Earl Warren had been governor of California, candidate for president, and Republican nominee for vice president in 1948; Fred M. Vinson had been an influential congressman and secretary of the Treasury; Charles Evans Hughes had been governor of New York, Republican candidate for president in 1916, and secretary of state.

Special Choice. President Nixon's selection of a chief justice without political experience or a public reputation was clearly intended to move the court away from the controversies that had marred the latter years of the Warren Court. Justice Fortas, who had been criticized for continuing to advise President Johnson while on the bench, had resigned under the cloud of a questionable financial arrangment only a week before the Burger appointment. In an unusual interview on May 22, President Nixon explained that the Fortas affair had led him to avoid any charge of "cronyism" by excluding from consideration personal or political associates, such as Atty. Gen. John N. Mitchell or former Att. Gen. Herbert Brownell. Associate Justice Potter Stewart, prominently mentioned in speculation on the post, had requested that he not be considered, since he did not believe a sitting judge would be the best choice for chief justice.

President Nixon told reporters that he chose Judge Burger largely because he felt that Burger shared his view that the Constitution should be rigorously interpreted, and because Burger, in his decisions as an appeals court judge, had shown that he believed the Supreme Court had gone too far in broadening some rights of suspects in criminal cases. Burger's reputation as a man opposed to judicial activism appeared to qualify him to lead a more conservative court.

Philosophy. Past experience has shown that it is risky to predict the performance of a man appointed to the Supreme Court on the basis of his previously expressed opinions. Burger was best known for his views on the handling of criminal

WARREN E. BURGER, preparing on June 23 to take oath of office as 15th chief justice of the United States, pauses as his wife, Elvera, adjusts his judicial robe.

prosecutions, which had often caused him to be classified as a "law and order" judge. He frequently disagreed with his more liberal colleagues on the Court of Appeals, and he had also not hesitated to criticize certain rulings of the Warren Court, both on and off the bench. He had particularly opposed the restrictions imposed by the Supreme Court in 1957, 1964, and 1966 (in the *Mallory, Escobedo,* and *Miranda* decisions) on police interrogation and the use of confessions as evidence in court. In a 1969 dissent (*Frazier* v. *U. S.*) Judge Burger condemned "the seeming anxiety of judges to protect every accused person from every consequence of his voluntary utterances. . . . Guilt or innocence becomes irrelevant in the criminal trial as we flounder in a morass of artificial rules poorly conceived and often impossible of application."

In public speeches and comments, Burger had suggested that the European system of justice, based on trial by a panel of three judges instead of before a jury, had some advantages over the American practice. Following his appointment, the new chief justice stated that he would take an active role in reforming the administration of justice, emphasizing the need to eliminate delays and to provide for more efficient court management through the use of trained administrators. He also stressed the need to reform the penal system for more effective rehabilitation of prisoners.

In several opinions on the Court of Appeals, Burger had warned his colleagues against usurping the policy making powers of the president and Congress, and he was one of the judges who held that Adam Clayton Powell's expulsion by the House of Representatives was not judicially reviewable—a position which the Warren Court subsequently overruled. His position on civil liberties appeared rather liberal, and in one opinion he rebuked the Federal Communications Commission for failing to withdraw the license of a Mississippi television station accused of racially discriminatory programming.

C. HERMAN PRITCHETT

SURGERY

Notable developments in surgery during 1969 were largely confined to problems of organ transplantation and diseases of the heart and major blood vessels. Surgeons also studied cancer vaccines and a new approach in treating multiple polyposis, a rare inherited disease.

Heart Transplants. For about a year after Christiaan Barnard's historic operation in December 1967, the number of heart transplants progressively increased, with a total of 26 recorded in November, 1968. Since then, however, the frequency of such operations declined as surgeons paused to study the results of these initial trials.

Probably the most famous heart transplant patient, Philip Blaiberg, died on August 17, after living 19½ months with his new heart. According to C. Walton Lillehei of the New York Hospital-Cornell Medical Center, "... if you can keep someone going for 19 months, you can do it for 38, or for 72. We've learned so much about the management of these cases." Among this information the surgeons learned was the surprising cause of Blaiberg's death—severe atherosclerosis of the new heart's arteries. Barnard attributed the rapid development of atherosclerosis to damage of the arterial walls by the rejection reaction, with resulting excessive deposition of cholesterol in the arteries.

Other Organ Transplants. Kidney transplantation has enjoyed continued success, with 75% of the patients surviving at least one year in cases where the donor was a relative. Trials in transplanting the human liver were continued by Thomas E. Starzl in Denver, Colo., but there were only sporadic reports of transplants of the pancreas, lung, and spleen.

Surgical Treatment of Heart Attack. Most heart attacks are caused by atherosclerosis of the coronary arteries. When these tiny arteries become obstructed, the portion of heart muscle they supply cannot function properly. Several operations, each designed to establish communications between the coronary arteries and tissues near the heart, have been used in an attempt to compensate for the decreased flow of blood through the coronary arteries. Recent reports by Rene G. Favaloro of the Cleveland Clinic Foundation suggest one of these procedures to be especially promising. In this operation, one end of a segment of vein removed from the patient's thigh is attached to the aorta and the other end is sutured to the diseased coronary artery beyond the point of obstruction.

Although this operation is not suitable for all patients with disease of the coronary arteries, there has been an increase in the percentage of patients in whom the operation is technically feasible. The death rate of only one patient in every 20 undergoing the operation is remarkably low considering the seriousness of the disease being treated.

Mechanical Aids. Two examples of mechanical devices produced through cooperative research between engineers and surgeons attracted considerable attention in 1969. On April 4, Denton A. Cooley, chief of surgery at St. Luke's-Texas Children's Hospital, replaced the heart of Haskell Karp of Skokie, Ill., with an artificial heart. After the device had sustained the patient for 65 hours, it was removed and a human heart was transplanted. (Karp died 32 hours later.)

Controversy concerning the operation centered around whether suitable testing of the device in animals was done before it was used in a human. An additional concern was whether monies from the National Institutes of Health were utilized in its development, thereby requiring permission for its use from an on-site committee of surgeons as stipulated by National Heart Institute guidelines. Although the feasibility of a totally artificial heart was demonstrated, it is likely that the resulting controversy has discouraged further trials in the near future.

A second mechanical device developed during 1969 was a small metal umbrella-like structure that is used to prevent blood clots formed in the veins of the legs from travelling through the heart and finally obstructing the vital arteries carrying blood to the lungs. Devised by Kazi Mobin-Uddin, Hooshang Bolook, and James R. Jude of the University of Miami School of Medicine, the "umbrella" is fixed on the end of a tube, passed into a vein in the neck, and positioned in the inferior vena cava, the large vein carrying blood from the legs to the heart. The "umbrella" is then opened, allowing its six metallic spokes to penetrate the wall of the vein and fix its position. Since the "umbrella" has many holes in it, blood continues to flow through the vein but large clots are stopped. Before the development of this device, the migration of blood clots from the legs to the lungs could only be prevented by operations through the patient's side or abdomen.

Cancer Vaccines. One of the more exciting developments in the treatment of cancer by vaccines was reported at the 1969 Clinical Congress of the American College of Surgeons in San Francisco. Loren J. Humphrey, associate professor of surgery at Emory University in Atlanta, Ga., prepared a vaccine consisting of an acellular homogenate of tumor tissue obtained from a cancer patient. This material was injected into a second cancer patient, resulting in active immunization of the second patient by the formation of antibodies to the tissue homogenate. These antibodies act to interfere with the growth of the cancer in the patient. In addition, blood may be withdrawn from the second patient and, after the cells of the blood have been discarded, the remaining serum, containing the tumor antibodies, can be injected into the first patient, thereby confering passive immunity against his cancer.

In a series of 38 patients, each one played the role of both the first and second patient so that each was actively and passively immunized. In 8 of these 38 terminal or inoperable patients, the treatment either halted the growth of the tumor, reduced it in size, or eliminated it completely for periods ranging from a few months to 2½ years. Humphrey's vaccine is distinctly different from other vaccines in use in that it contains no tumor cells. Also, there is no attempt to match the patients with respect to the type of tumor present.

Multiple Polyposis. Another development in the field of malignant disease concerns patients with inherited multiple polyposis of the large intestine (colon and rectum). This disease is distinctly different from the problem of one, two, or even several polyps of the large intestine, a relatively common finding in men and women over the age of 40. Multiple polyposis is a rare disease. The polyps usually appear before the age of 20, and the entire lining of the colon is covered with myriads of polyps. Without treatment, more than 50% of these patients may be expected to develop cancer of the large intestine.

Until recently, the majority of surgeons have recommended removal of the colon and joining the end of the small intestine directly to the rectum. This operation preserves normal bowel function. In addition, the only remaining polyps are those of the rectum, the lining of which may be easily seen through an instrument (proctoscope) inserted into the anus. Thus, the rectum can be examined periodically and the polyps can be destroyed with electrocautery, hopefully preventing the development of cancer of the rectum.

However, a report from Charles Moertel, Martin Adson, John Hill, and Edgar Harrison, Jr., of the Mayo Clinic suggests that this method of managing the disease is hazardous. Despite careful periodic examination of the rectum, more than 50% of the patients followed for 20 years did develop cancer of the rectum. This finding suggests that the rectum must be removed together with the colon to avoid the hazard of cancer of the rectum. After the removal of the colon and rectum, the open end of the small intestine is fixed to the skin surface of the abdomen and body wastes are collected in a plastic bag. Although this procedure is inconvenient and at times unpleasant, it is safe and allows the patient to continue his normal activities. More important for patients with multiple polyposis, it reduces the risk of developing cancer from 50% to nil.

NEIL R. THOMFORD
Ohio State University

SWAZILAND

King Sobhuza II led the celebration of the first anniversary of Swaziland's independence on Sept. 6, 1969. He had high hopes for continued political stability and economic improvement in Swaziland.

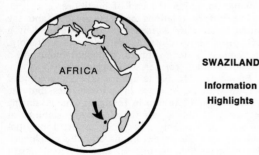

SWAZILAND

Information

Highlights

Area: 6,705 square miles (17,365 sq km).
Population: 395,000 (1968 est.).
Chief City (1962 census): Mbabane, the capital, 8,390.
Government: *King*—Sobhuza II (acceded 1921); *Prime Minister*—Prince Makhosini (took office April 1967). *Parliament*—Senate, 12 members (6 appointed by the king, 6 elected by members of the House of Assembly); House of Assembly, 31 members.
Education: *Literacy rate* (1969), 35% of population. *Total school enrollment* (1968)—59,662.
Finance (1969–70 est.): *Revenues,* $15,700,000; *expenditures,* $20,400,000; *monetary unit,* South African rand (0.7143 rand equals U. S.$1).
Gross National Product (1967): $73,000,000.
National Income (1966): $57,958,840.
Manufacturing (metric tons, 1967): Sugar, 173,000.
Crops (metric tons, 1967–68 crop year): Maize, 60,000.
Minerals (metric tons, 1967): Iron ore, 1,098,000; bituminous coal, 78,000; asbestos (1966), 32,787.
Foreign Trade (1967): *Exports,* $58,200,000; *imports,* $49,-700,000. *Chief trading partners* (1966): Britain (took 33% of exports); South Africa.
Transportation: *Roads* (1969), 1,400 miles (2,240 km); *motor vehicles* (1966), 6,586 (automobiles 3,910); *railways* (1969), 140 miles (225 km); *principal airport,* Matsapa.

British Aid. Swaziland continued to rely on economic aid from Britain, which had granted it independence after 66 years as a British protectorate. British aid to Swaziland's budget and economy amounted to $7.1 million in 1969, and $5.8 million in development aid is contemplated for the 1970–72 period. In 1969 negotiations continued between Britain and Swaziland over compensation claimed by Swaziland for land granted to white settlers during the protectorate period.

Economy. Swaziland's hopes for an improved economy rest on development of its iron, asbestos (Swaziland is the world's fifth largest producer of asbestos), and forest resources. Swaziland also grows choice citrus fruit, pineapples, and papayas. It was reported in the capital of Mbabane in September that a U. S. packing company, Libby, McNeill and Libby, was planning to establish a canning plant.

Income from gambling has increased since independence. Gambling is concentrated in a hotel and casino in the Ezulwin Valley, a few miles south of Mbabane. Between $50,000 and $120,000 is wagered each week, netting the Swaziland government more than $700,000 a year in income tax.

Relations with South Africa. Swaziland is almost entirely surrounded by the Republic of South Africa. It has been in a customs union with South Africa, Lesotho, and Botswana since 1911. New terms for the union were being negotiated in 1969, in order to increase the tariff revenues of the three black African countries.

FRANKLIN PARKER
West Virginia University

SWEDEN

The retirement of Tage Erlander, who had held the office of premier for 23 years, was the major political event in Sweden in 1969. He was replaced by Olof Palme, the minister of education.

Discussions of the formation of a Nordic economic union continued. Sweden kept up its fight against economic inflation.

New Government. Premier Erlander's retirement had been expected, since he had stated in 1968 that he intended to leave office before the 1970 general elections. The selection of Palme to succeed him as premier and leader of the Social Democratic party had also been clearly indicated, and took place at the party's congress in October. Palme formally took office on October 14. The 42-year-old new premier has been a severe critic of U. S. policy in Vietnam.

Necessary changes in the cabinet took place without an alteration of policy. Ingvar Carlsson was appointed minister of education to succeed Palme. A new minister of justice, Lennart Geijer, succeeded Herman Kling, who became Sweden's ambassador to Denmark. Premier Palme outlined the new government's policies, which included provisions for using technological advances for social purposes, a widening of democracy, tax reforms, full employment, and a 40-hour week by 1973.

Riksdag Sessions. The Riksdag (parliament) voted in February to change from the present bicameral legislative system to a unicameral one. The plan will go into effect on Jan. 1, 1971.

In its fall and spring sessions the Riksdag discussed lowering the voting age to 20, and finally passed a bill to make the change. The Riksdag also

OLOF PALME, named in October to succeed Tage Erlander as Sweden's premier, is seen here with his wife, Lisbet, and children. A Social Democrat whose ideas have stirred controversy, Palme has been outspokenly critical of U. S. involvement in Vietnam.

UPI

voted for measures to provide for more autonomy and responsibility at local levels of government.

Gunnar Sträng, the minister of finance, brought forward proposals for restructuring the tax administration system. He called for a merger of the three tax agencies into one.

The Riksdag voted to provide financial support to the local Swedish press. It also lowered taxes on newsprint, helped pay postal charges, and provided some direct payments to newspapers.

University reforms continued but would require time for full implementation. Student opposition to these reforms led to some modifications, and students were given a greater role in university administration and in determining curriculums. The reforms were aimed at expanding student democracy in all areas of the university, and eventually in secondary schools.

Economic Union. Discussion of a Nordic economic union took place in the Riksdag, in the press, and at party congresses. Most Swedes approved of the union, but wanted some modifications in the proposals submitted by experts of the five Nordic countries in July. The plan for an economic union seemed likely to be approved because of Sweden's experience with the European Free Trade Association. The matter will be fully discussed in 1970 by the Nordic Council and the five Nordic premiers.

--- **SWEDEN • Information Highlights** ---

Area: 173,665 square miles (449,793 sq km).
Population: 7,912,000 (1968 est.).
Chief Cities (1966 census): Stockholm, the capital, 777,115; Göteborg, 443,292; Malmö, 253,502; Västeras, 107,048.
Government: King—Gustav VI Adolf (acceded Oct. 29, 1950); Premier—Olof Palme (took office Oct. 14, 1969). Parliament (Riksdag)—First Chamber, 151 members (party seating, 1969: Social Democratic Labor party, 79; Liberal party, 25; Conservative party, 25; Center party, 21; Communist party, 1); Second Chamber, 233 members (party seating, 1969: Social Democratic Labor party, 125; Center party, 39; Liberal party, 34; Conservative party, 32; Communist party, 3).
Religious Faiths: Evangelical Lutherans, 94% of population.
Education: Literacy rate (1969), 99% of population. Total school enrollment (1966)—1,531,007.
Finance (1968 est.): Revenues, $6,696,000,000; expenditures, $6,955,000,000; monetary unit, krona (5.180 kronor equal U. S.$1).
Gross National Product (1968): $25,521,235,000.
National Income (1968): $22,316,602,000; average annual income per person, $2,820.
Economic Indexes (1967): Industrial production (1968), 133 (1963=100); agricultural production, 112 (1963=100); cost of living, 120 (1963=100).
Minerals (metric tons, 1967): Iron ore, 28,332,000; lime (1965), 995,000; white arsenic (1966), 16,510.
Foreign Trade (1968): Exports, $4,941,000,000 (chief exports, 1967: wood pulp, $438,000,000; paper, $412,000,000; wood, $293,000,000); imports, $5,126,000,000 (chief imports, 1967: nonelectrical machinery, $615,579,000; transport equipment, $406,467,000; petroleum products, $363,629,000). Chief trading partners (1967): West Germany; Britain.
Transportation: Roads (1964), 59,869 miles (96,347 km); motor vehicles (1967), 2,115,900; railways (1969), 9,000 miles (14,484 km); merchant vessels (1967), 422.

Foreign Affairs. In October, Sweden announced a $40 million grant to North Vietnam. This led to considerable debate, even after Foreign Minister Torsten Nilsson stated that the grant would be available only after the end of hostilities.

The uneasy relations between Sweden and the United States were worsened by the grant and by a U. S. proposal to close its consulate at Göteborg. The United States withheld its appointment of a new ambassador, further straining relations.

Economy. The battle against inflation continued in 1969 with an increase in interest rates, but the loss of almost $2 billion in foreign exchange during the past year and a half threatened the stability of the Swedish economy. The long contract negotiations between the trade unions and the employers' associations added to unease, and the final agreement contributed to the inflationary trend.

Agricultural price controls and supports were again voted by the Riksdag to assist farmers in a steadily deteriorating situation. However, foreign trade improved in 1969, and the balance of trade for 1969 was expected to be favorable.

Swedish industrial production improved, and there were lower unemployment and even some labor shortages. Engineering industries showed the greatest improvement, and iron and steel production increased. The forest products industry also gained because of the improved price structure. Agricultural harvests were good, although autumnal storms in southern Sweden caused much damage.

RAYMOND E. LINDGREN
California State College, Long Beach

SWIMMING. See SPORTS.

SWITZERLAND · Information Highlights

Area: 15,941 square miles (41,288 sq km).
Population: 6,147,000 (1968 est.).
Chief Cities (1967 census): Bern, the capital, 166,000; Zürich, 433,200; Basel, 212,800; Geneva, 169,700.
Government: *President*—Ludwig von Moos (took office Jan. 1, 1969). *Parliament* (Federal Assembly)—Council of States, 44 members (party seating, 1968: Conservative Christian Social party, 18; Radical Democratic party, 13; others, 13); National Council, 200 members (party seating, 1968: Social Democratic party, 51; Radical Democratic party, 49; Conservative Christian Social party, 45; others, 55).
Religious Faiths: Protestants, 58% of population; Roman Catholics, 40%; others, 2%.
Education: *Literacy rate* (1969), 100% of population. *Total school enrollment* (1965–66)—804,312 (primary, 468,664; secondary, 272,159; teacher-training, 10,410; technical/vocational, 19,500; university/higher, 33,579).
Finance (1968 est.): *Revenues,* $1,468,735,000; *expenditures,* $1,510,553,000; *public debt* (1967), $1,125,000,000; *monetary unit,* Swiss franc (4.302 francs equal U.S.$1).
Gross National Product (1968): $16,852,626,000.
National Income (1968): $14,342,166,000; *average annual income per person,* $2,333.
Economic Indexes (1967): *Industrial production* (1968), 123

(1963=100); *agricultural production,* 113 (1963=100); *cost of living,* 116 (1963=100).
Manufacturing (metric tons, 1967): Cement, 4,176,000; paper, 515,000; crude steel, 445,000; wheat flour, 350,000; beer, 4,685,000 hectoliters.
Crops (metric tons, 1967–68 crop year): Potatoes, 1,125,000; wheat, 424,000; sugar beets, 423,000; apples, 355,000; pears, 196,000.
Minerals (metric tons, 1967): Salt, 216,000; lime (1966), 166,717; iron ore, 2,000.
Foreign Trade (1968): *Exports,* $3,966,000,000 (chief exports, 1967: timepieces, $504,672,000; textiles, $252,208,000; machinery, $250,534,000); *imports,* $4,513,000,000 (chief imports, 1967: nonelectrical machinery, $412,389,000; transport equipment, $340,655,000; electrical machinery, $255,648,000). *Chief trading partners* (1967): West Germany (took 13% of exports, supplied 29% of imports); France (took 9% of exports, supplied 14% of imports); Italy.
Transportation: *Roads* (1964), 31,300 miles (50,371 km); *motor vehicles* (1967), 1,183,500 (automobiles, 1,081,400); *railways* (1969), 3,300 miles (5,311 km); *national airline,* Swissair.
Communications: *Telephones* (1968): 2,533,684; *television stations* (1966), 88; *television sets* (1968), 850,000; *radios* (1967), 1,734,000; *newspapers* (1966), 126.

SWITZERLAND

Women's suffrage, student activism, and economic inflation dominated the domestic scene in Switzerland during 1969, while unintentional involvement in Middle East tensions preempted attention in foreign affairs.

Domestic Issues. Recent progress toward women's suffrage was reflected in a government announcement on March 5 that it was studying the possibility of amending the constitution to allow women the right to vote and seek public office at the federal level. As present only men who have completed their basic military service may vote in federal elections. On October 19 the Italian speaking canton of Ticino became the sixth canton to grant women voting rights in both cantonal and municipal elections.

Upset by the government's failure to grant them a role in their school's administration, Zürich engineering students led a successful campaign to repeal by referendum a law regulating the administration of the state's engineering schools.

Economic Affairs. Economic growth, which continued at a rapid pace in 1969, was partially offset by a rapid rise in domestic prices. On September 1, Swiss domestic banks voluntarily agreed to impose a limit of 9% on annual expansion of domestic credit. On September 15 the national bank raised its discount rate from 3% to 3¾%.

Under the provisions of the Kennedy Round agreements, Switzerland reduced its tariffs and duties approximately 7% on January 1. On March 29 the government ordered all firms employing three or more foreign workers to reduce their foreign staff by 4%, bringing the total reduction of foreign labor since 1965 to 17%.

Exports for the first three quarters of 1969 totaled $3,289 million, an increase of 16.2% over the first three quarters of 1968. Imports rose 15.4% to $3,786 million. Despite the more rapid percentage growth in exports, the total value of imports over exports increased by approximately $47 million.

Foreign Affairs. On February 18 an Israeli El Al airliner was attacked at Zürich International Airport by four members of an anti-Israeli Arab terrorist organization. The Swiss government protested officially to the Syrian, Lebanese, and Jordanian governments on the grounds that they openly supported the terrorist organization. The protests were rejected. On December 22 the three surviving terror-

ists were sentenced by a Swiss court to 12 years in prison for the murder of the plane's copilot.

The government released a study on June 30 indicating little popular support for Swiss membership in the United Nations, and Foreign Minister Willy Spühler formally announced that Switzerland was not ready to join. However, he emphasized Switzerland's willingness to develop its relations with the United Nations through continued participation in the World Bank and International Monetary Fund, and promised an increase in Switzerland's contribution to the support of UN peace-keeping forces and to technological assistance for underdeveloped nations through UN agencies.

Papal Visit. On June 10, Pope Paul VI became the first Roman Catholic pontiff to visit Switzerland since the 16th century. The highlight of his visit was a speech to the World Council of Churches. Popular reception to the Pope in Geneva was described as cool in comparison to that in other areas visited by the Pope in recent years.

PAUL C. HELMREICH
Wheaton College, Mass.

SYRIA

In the early months of 1969, continuing factionalism within the dominant Baath party threatened the provisional government of the Syrian Arab Republic with overthrow by military coup. The unresolved conflict with Israel was marked by guerrilla activity and scattered military actions.

Domestic Politics. In January and February friction increased between the "progressive" faction of the Syrian Baath party, led by Salah Jadid, who was then regarded as the strong man behind the president-premier, Nureddin el-Atassi, and the "nationalist" faction, led by the defense minister, Lt. Gen. Hafez el-Assad. At the end of February, Assad redeployed units of the army in what appeared to be preparations for a military coup and confronted Atassi and Jadid with a series of demands, including closer cooperation with Iraq and the United Arab Republic, stepped up preparations for war with Israel, and a more independent stance in dealing with the Soviet Union. After several days of high tension, during which the United Arab Republic and Algeria sent special envoys to Syria to mediate the dispute, Assad agreed on March 7 to submit his demands to a Baath party congress. The outcome was a compromise favorable to Assad.

GAMMA—PIX

SYRIAN women's army, a volunteer corps, was organized to counter the threat posed by Israel's female soldiers.

On May 1, in response to a resolution of the party congress, the Atassi government issued an interim constitution, which defined Syria as a democratic, popular, and socialist republic and provided for the election of a People's Assembly that would select the chief of state and ratify all laws. On May 30, President el-Atassi formed a new, predominantly Baathist cabinet. General el-Assad, who was increasingly regarded as the real power in the government, remained minister of defense.

SYRIA • Information Highlights

Area: 71,665 square miles (185,180 sq km).
Population: 5,738,000 (1968 est.).
Chief Cities (1966 census): Damascus, the capital, 618,457; Aleppo, 578,861; Hama, 198,852; Homs, 142,968.
Government: *President-Premier*—Nureddin el-Atassi (took office as president Feb. 23, 1966; assumed premiership Oct. 29, 1968).
Religious Faiths: Muslims, 82% of population; Christians, 12%; others, 6%.
Education: *Literacy rate* (1969), 35% of population. *Total school enrollment* (1965)—912,400 (primary, 688,165; secondary, 177,174; teacher-training, 7,038; vocational, 8,030; higher, 31,993).
Finance (1968 est.): *Revenues,* $299,141,300; *expenditures,* $299,141,300; *monetary unit,* pound (3.82 pounds equal U. S.$1).
Gross National Product (1965): $1,125,000,000.
National Income (1965): $841,623,036; *average annual income per person,* $146.
Economic Indexes (1967): *Industrial production* (1966), 129 (1963=100); *agricultural production,* 102 (1963=100); *cost of living,* 113 (1963=100).
Manufacturing (metric tons, 1967): Cement, 688,000; residual fuel oil, 456,000; kerosine, 172,000; gasoline, 168,000; cheese, 30,000.
Crops (metric tons, 1967–68 crop year): Wheat, 1,049,000; barley, 590,000; cottonseed, 207,000; sugar beets, 154,000; tomatoes, 162,000; cotton lint, 127,000.
Minerals (metric tons, 1966): Natural asphalt, 60,000; salt (1967), 20,000; gypsum, 15,000; glass sand, 10,000.
Foreign Trade (1968): *Exports,* $168,000,000 (chief exports, 1967: cotton, $68,089,000; wool, $56,335,000); *imports,* $330,000,000 (chief imports, 1967: iron and steel, $36,-298,400; cereals and preparations, $16,827,200; petroleum products, $11,264,300). *Chief trading partners* (1967): USSR (took 12% of exports, supplied 10% of imports); Lebanon; Italy.
Transportation: *Roads* (1969), 7,430 miles (11,957 km); *motor vehicles* (1967), 44,400 (automobiles 30,000); *railways* (1969), 850 miles (909 km); *principal airports,* Damascus, Aleppo.
Communications: *Telephones* (1968): 91,383; *television stations* (1967), 5; *television sets* (1967), 70,000; *radios* (1965), 1,745,000; *newspapers* (1966), 8.

The Conflict with Israel. Although the Syrian government rejected a political settlement with Israel and favored Palestinian guerrilla action, it had, during 1968, discouraged commando activities launched directly from Syria and had kept the ceasefire line with Israel reasonably quiet. On Feb. 12, 1969, however, Syrian and Israeli aircraft clashed above the cease-fire line. On February 24, Israeli jets bombed several sites on the Damascus-Beirut road, allegedly used as bases for commando raids into Israeli-occupied territory. On May 30, Arab guerrillas blew up a section of the Arabian-American Oil Company's petroleum pipeline in the Golan Heights. On July 30, Israeli planes attacked guerrilla bases along the Syrian-Lebanese frontier, and on the following day the Syrians mounted an air attack on Israeli positions in the occupied area.

On August 29, agents of the Popular Front for the Liberation of Palestine hijacked to Damascus a TWA airliner bound from Rome to Tel Aviv. The hijackers were released by the Syrian authorities on October 13, but two Israeli passengers were detained until December 5, when they were exchanged for 13 Syrians held by the Israelis. When the Lebanese government attempted to curb guerrilla activities in Lebanon, the Syrian government offered the commandos moral and material support. On October 21, Syria closed its frontier with Lebanon for 23 days and threatened more drastic actions.

Economic Conditions. Efforts to develop the largely nationalized, but still agricultural, economy continued under the 5-year plan for 1966–70. Work on the Euphrates dam and irrigation scheme in northeast Syria proceeded with the help of Soviet loans and technical advice. A $36 million international airport was formally opened in Damascus on September 15. The trade deficit shrank as cotton exports increased and petroleum production from the new Karachuk fields rose toward 3.9 million tons.

International Relations. Syria followed a somewhat erratic course in its foreign relations during 1969. Although the Soviet Union continued to be a major source of economic and military aid, there was dissatisfaction in Syria with Moscow's efforts to promote a political settlement of the Palestine problem and with Soviet delay in providing Syria with modern weapons. In May, President el-Atassi cancelled a trip to Moscow, and a Syrian military mission visited Communist China. Early in July, however, the president made an extended visit to the Soviet Union. Contacts with the eastern European states of the Soviet bloc were, in general, strengthened. On June 5, Syria gave formal recognition to the East German government. Relations with the Western powers showed little improvement except that the 2-year ban on the entry of West German, British, and U. S. citizens was ended in hopes of encouraging use of the new Damascus airport.

The Syrian government had its closest relations with the leftist members of the Arab League—Algeria, the United Arab Republic, and Iraq. Even here, the split between the Syrian and Iraqi wings of the Baath party caused friction between Damascus and Baghdad, especially before the rising power of General el-Assad in the Syrian government brought about a rapprochement. On March 15, a detachment of Iraqi troops moved into southern Syria, and a joint Syrian-Iraqi-Jordanian military command was established.

PAUL L. HANNA
University of Florida

TANZANIA

Politics in Tanzania remained almost completely free of the attempts at coups, political arrests, assassinations, and scandals that upset the politics of many other African states in 1969. In foreign affairs, Tanzania continued to follow its policies of nonalignment in international relations and regional unity in Africa.

Political Arrests. In September the former vice president of Zanzibar, Abdullah Hanga, and the former Tanzanian ambassador to the United States, Othman Shariff, were secretly arrested and sent to Zanzibar for trial. In October, President Julius Nyerere and Vice President Abeid Karume of Zanzibar announced that these two men and two others had been executed for plotting to overthrow the government, and that 16 others had been imprisoned or would be tried on the same charges. These cases, however, were the exceptions to the generally peaceful rule of government.

Integration. On April 26 the fifth anniversary of the union of Tanganyika and Zanzibar was celebrated in Dar es Salaam, the capital. President Nyerere said on this occasion that the union "is being firmly cemented and will remain cemented forever." As part of the continuing integration of the country, the Zanzibari government has given up its control of foreign affairs, emigration, police, taxes, and citizenship. Vice President Karume still has considerable autonomy but, as Nyerere said, the union "is going on as well as anyone could expect."

Foreign Affairs. In February the government was host to a conference of foreign ministers of the 14 East and Central African states. The meeting was held as a preliminary to the April summit conference of heads of state, which was convened in Lusaka, Zambia. The ministers discussed the need for greater economic cooperation and established committees to prepare a practical 10-year approach to economic planning and integration. In September and October, President Nyerere made a 28-day tour of Canada, Sweden, the USSR, Hungary, and Yugoslavia, during which he stressed Tanzania's determination to follow an independent path in international politics.

African Economic Relations. Tanzania, a member state in the East African Community (EAC), has realized that its future depends on economic coordination with its neighbors. Throughout 1968 and 1969, Tanzania and its partners in the EAC, Kenya and Uganda, negotiated to facilitate the entrance of Burundi, Ethiopia, Zambia, and Somalia into the community. The tie with Zambia, at present hampered by poor communications, will become especially important when a road and railroad now being surveyed and built are completed. The high priority being given these projects, and the politically diverse character of the nations assisting in their construction, show clearly that Tanzania remains firmly committed to the policies of anti-colonialism, regional integration, and neutralism that have been the keystones of its foreign policy since independence.

Economy. On May 28, President Nyerere presented Tanzania's new 5-year development plan to the 14th conference of the Tanganyika African National Union (TANU) in Dar es Salaam. This plan, which, it is hoped, will be funded by investments of more than $1.1 billion, is aimed at generating a growth rate of 6.5% and anticipates

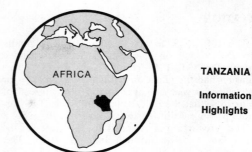

TANZANIA

Information Highlights

Area: 362,819 square miles (939,701 sq km).
Population: 12,590,000 (1968 est.).
Chief City (1967 census): Dar es Salaam, the capital, 272,515.
Government: President—Julius K. Nyerere (first took office April 26, 1964); First Vice President—Abeid Karume. Legislative Parliament (unicameral)—National Assembly, 189 members (party seating, 1969: all members of the Tanganyika African National Union or its affiliate in Zanzibar, the Afro-Shirazi party).
Religious Faiths: Animists, 55% of population; Christians, 22%; Muslims, 22%; others, 1%.
Education: Literacy rate (1969), 15–20% of population. Total school enrollment (1966)—775,211.
Finance (1969 est.): Revenues, $174,000,000; expenditures, $207,000,000; monetary unit, Tanzania shilling (7.143 shillings equal U. S.$1).
Gross National Product (1968 est.): $915,000,000.
National Income (1967): $565,320,000; average annual income per person, $46.
Cost of Living Index (1967): 117 (1963=100).
Manufacturing and Processing (metric tons, 1967): Meat, 94,000; sugar, 72,000; wheat flour (1966), 40,000; beer, 206,000 hectoliters.
Crops (metric tons, 1967–68 crop year): Cassava, 1,120,000; maize, 800,000; sisal (1966), 224,800.
Minerals (metric tons): Salt (1967), 40,000; lime (1966), 8,906.
Foreign Trade (1968): Exports, $227,000,000 (chief exports, Tanganyika only, 1967: cotton, $17,590,000; coffee, $16,-720,000; diamonds, $15,590,000; cloves, $3,410,000); imports, $214,000,000 (chief imports, Tanganyika only, 1967: transport equipment, $14,750,000; nonelectrical machinery, $13,620,000; iron and steel, $9,270,000). Chief trading partners (1967): Britain (took 30% of exports, supplied 29% of imports); Italy; United States.
Transportation: Roads (1969), 20,464 miles (32,933 km); motor vehicles (1966), 47,500 (automobiles, 36,000); railways (1969), 3,670 miles (5,872 km); merchant vessels (1967), 2; national airline, East African Airways.
Communications: Telephones (1968), 29,282; radios (1967), 138,000; newspapers (1962), 7.

making the government-controlled sector the backbone of the economy. The new plan is ideologically based on Nyerere's 1967 Arusha Declaration, which stressed social equality and African economic integration as being necessary for the desired economic and social transformation. Much of the investment will be directed toward rural development, improvement of the transport infrastructure, and greater socialization of the economy.

In June the 1969–70 budget was presented to the National Assembly. It called for expenditures of about $212 million, a 15% increase over 1968–69. To raise the necessary revenue, the government increased the sales tax on all luxury goods by 10%-20%. These tax and expenditure adjustments, which placed more stress on rural development, shifted most of the tax burden from the rural farmers to the urban population.

Compensation Agreements. In June it was announced that the government had signed compensation agreements with most of the companies and banks whose property had been nationalized in 1967, when the government took its initial steps in building the socialist state first outlined in the Arusha Declaration.

ROBERT O. COLLINS
University of California, Santa Barbara

TARIFFS. See INTERNATIONAL TRADE.

TAXATION

The 10% U. S. income tax surcharge originally scheduled to end on June 30, 1969, was extended through Dec. 31, 1969 (Public Law 91–53). This extension had the effect of making the surcharge for 1969 calendar-year taxpayers a full 10% instead of the net 5% that it would have been if the 10% surcharge had been allowed to end on June 30, 1969.

The surcharge was extended at a 5% rate for the period Jan. 1, 1970, through June 30, 1970. This action means that the effective surcharge rate for a 1970 calendar-year taxpayer will be 2.5%.

Tax Reform. The Tax Reform Act of 1969 was signed into law by President Nixon on Dec. 30, 1969 (Public Law 91–172). It is the most widespread tax reform measure in the history of tax legislation in the United States.

The chief purpose of this legislation when it started through Congress was to remove or minimize various tax benefits and advantages in the Internal Revenue Code. Before the bill was finally enacted into law, Congress also incorporated a very substantial amount of tax relief along with the tax reform. Here are some of the reform highlights:

(1) The rules covering the creation and operation of private charitable foundations were tightened so that it is now more difficult or impossible for the creators of foundations to use them primarily or substantially for their personal tax benefit rather than for charitable purposes.

(2) Charitable contributions of appreciated property such as inventory or securities on which there are short-term capital gains can no longer enable the donor to avoid ordinary income tax on the appreciation while giving him a charitable deduction for the full appreciated value of the property.

(3) Capital gains in excess of $50,000 a year have lost the benefit of the long-standing 25% ceiling on long-term capital gains.

(4) Percentage depletion for oil and gas production was reduced from 27.5% to 22%.

(5) The use of various accelerated depreciation methods for real property was sharply restricted.

(6) Bad-debt deductions by commercial banks, mutual savings banks, and savings and loan institutions were reduced.

(7) A "minimum tax" of 10% is imposed on "tax preferences" in excess of $30,000 a year. The tax preferences include a variety of specified deductions that enable a taxpayer to shield otherwise taxable income from regular tax.

Many other reforms were made, including those covering deductions for farm expenses, use of multiple corporations to save taxes, and use of certain types of trusts to save taxes.

Tax Relief. Under the Tax Reform Act of 1969 tax relief consists primarily of these changes:

(1) The $600 deduction for personal dependency exemptions has been raised to $625 for 1970 and will rise in annual stages to $750 by 1973.

(2) A new $1,100 low-income allowance combined with the higher exemption deductions will help take many individuals off the tax rolls altogether.

(3) The standard deduction will rise from the present 10%, subject to a $1,000 maximum, to 13% and a $1,500 maximum in 1971, and then ultimately to 15% and $2,000.

(4) The tax rate schedule for single taxpayers was adjusted so that they will not pay a rate that is higher than 20% of the comparable income bracket rate for a married taxpayer.

(5) For higher-bracket taxpayers, the ceiling rate on "earned income" will ultimately become 50%. This is intended to encourage executives, professional men, and others to focus on their business operations rather than on tax devices for shielding their income from the top-rate bracket of 70%.

Extension. The interest equalization tax originally scheduled to terminate on July 31, 1969, was extended several times on a one-month basis, then finally extended to March 31, 1971 (Public Law 91–128).

U. S. Court Decisions. When an individual travels to another area for medical treatment, his expenses for meals and lodging while in transit are deductible as medical expenses.

An investor's cab fares to and from his broker's office are deductible if he goes there to seek investment advice but are not deductible if he goes merely to watch the ticker.

Even though an employee must live far from his job for reasons beyond his control, such as geographical remoteness of the job area or security rules against living in that area, he may not deduct the cost of commuting to and from the job by car.

Group life insurance provided by an employer may be effectively assigned away by a covered employee even though the assignment does not meet all Treasury requirements for a valid transfer.

Christmas gifts by business or professional men to elevator operators, doormen, or delivery boys are not deductible business expenses unless the donor can prove they are "appropriate and helpful, or even proximately related to" his business.

A scholarship given to an employee by his firm to use during a leave of absence in exchange for his promise to return and work for a specified period of time is taxable income to the employee.

The penalty tax on corporations that unreasonably accumulate their income applies if one of the reasons for accumulation is to save taxes for its shareholders, regardless of any other reasons for the accumulations and the weight of these other reasons.

U. S. Treasury Rulings. The Internal Revenue Service completely revised its individual income tax returns for 1969. Instead of providing a card Form 1040A and the larger Form 1040, the IRS now furnishes a one-page Form 1040 for all individual taxpayers, plus a series of separate schedules that a taxpayer will select and fill out as they pertain to his items of income and deductions.

"Points" paid by home buyers in addition to regular interest on their mortgage may be deducted as interest if paid as an additional charge for the mortgage loan rather than for services performed by the lender.

Damage resulting from common household accidents can constitute a deductible casualty loss if it qualifies for deduction in all other respects.

Lottery winnings are not eligible for "income averaging" computation, which may otherwise enable an individual to pay less taxes where his income in one year rises substantially higher than the average of his income for the four previous years.

"Professional corporations" consisting of lawyers, doctors, and others were finally recognized as valid corporations for tax purposes after years of Treasury refusal to do so.

Revenue Collection. U. S. federal internal revenue collections skyrocketed from $153,671,000,000 for fiscal year 1968 to a record $187,843,000,000 for fiscal 1969.

Local government tax collections rose to a new high of $31,171,000,000 for fiscal 1968. Property taxes produced $26,835,000,000 of the total.

OTHER COUNTRIES

Albania abolished personal income taxes.

Britain raised its corporate tax rate from 42.5% to 45%, increased payroll taxes by 28%, and boosted taxes on gasoline, gambling and wine.

Canada announced a sweeping revision of its entire tax system, which was expected to become law in 1971. A key feature of the new program is the first Canadian tax on capital gains, including a method of taxing certain unrealized capital gains at 5-year intervals. Canada also extended the 3% surtax on personal and corporate income for a year beyond its scheduled expiration on Dec. 31, 1969.

France supported its devaluation of the franc with various tax measures, including a speedup of corporation tax payments, tightening of depreciation and investment tax credits, extension of the 1969 temporary income tax surcharge through 1970 at half the 1969 rate, and a special levy on bank profits.

India raised tax rates on personal incomes over 10,000 rupees and reduced the amount of corporate income exemption from tax from 24,000 to 10,000 rupees.

Ireland raised its wholesale tax from 10% to 15% on a wide range of items, including motor vehicles, radios, and television sets.

Norway enacted a value-added tax at the general rate of 20%.

South Africa raised its company tax from 26.66% to 40% and imposed a selective sales tax at the manufacturer's level, with rates ranging from 5% to 20%.

Spain increased its luxury tax rates from 15% to 20% on radios and television sets, from 25% to 40% on wines, liquors, and brandies, and up to 49% on various cigars and cigarettes.

LEON GOLD
Tax Research Institute of America, Inc.

TAYLOR, ROBERT

U. S. film star: b. Filley, Nebr., Aug. 5, 1911; d. Santa Monica, Calif., June 8, 1969.

He appeared in 75 films and had one of the longest-running exclusive contracts of any star in Hollywood's history, but Robert Taylor never elicited much critical acclaim for his performances during his more than 30 years in motion pictures. Candid and unassuming, Taylor perhaps best summed up his career when he said: "I've never been terribly ambitious—simply wanted to do a good job at whatever I did. The reviews usually said I gave an adequate or good performance. I never got raves, but neither did I get pans. I've never had an Oscar and probably never will. I'm content to try to do as well as I can."

Youth. Robert Taylor was born Spangler Arlington Brugh. He received his elementary and secondary education in Beatrice, Nebr., where he played

BETTMANN ARCHIVE
ROBERT TAYLOR, Hollywood film star, shown here with Greta Garbo in the 1936 film *Camille,* died on June 8.

the cello and participated in public speaking. Taylor entered Doane College, Crete, Nebr., but soon transferred to Pomona College, Claremont, Calif.

Career. Taylor was seen by a casting director from Metro-Goldwyn-Mayer in one of the student dramatic productions at Pomona. He was offered free acting lessons at the studio, but turned the offer down. After graduation in 1933, however, Taylor changed his mind about acting as a career. He was soon signed by MGM. The studio changed his name to the one with which he became famous and then immediately loaned him to 20th Century Fox, where he made his film debut in *Handy Andy* (1934).

Taylor played a variety of roles in the next few years, and even sang and danced in *Broadway Melody of 1936,* for the first and last time. He rose to stardom with his performance as the playboy in *Magnificent Obsession* (1935), and in 1936 he appeared opposite Greta Garbo in *Camille,* playing his most memorable role, Camille's lover Armand.

Taylor became a major movie idol of the 1930's and 1940's. It was in the 1940 production of *Waterloo Bridge* that Taylor himself felt he gave his best performance. His appearance "came at a time when I didn't think I was a good actor," he said. "When I saw the picture, I was surprised—along with everybody else."

During World War II, Taylor, an amateur pilot, enlisted in the Navy Air Corps. He directed numerous training films and in 1944 narrated the award-winning documentary *The Fighting Lady.* After the war, Taylor changed from the romantic lead in "ladies' pictures" to more serious roles. He was a Secret Service man in *The Bribe* (1949), and played the lead in the historical spectacle *Quo Vadis* (1951). In the 1960's Taylor appeared in many Westerns. On television, he played Captain Mat Hobrook in *The Detectives,* and in 1966 he became host-narrator of the series *Death Valley Days.*

Personal Life. Taylor was married to Barbara Stanwyck from 1939 to 1951. In 1954 he married Ursula Thiess. They had two children. He died of lung cancer in St. John's Hospital, Santa Monica.

HOWARD SUBER
University of California, Los Angeles

TEA

The 1969 tea crop of the world (excluding mainland China) totaled a record 2,321,000,000 pounds, up 50.2 million pounds from 1968 and 412.4 million pounds from the 1960–64 average.

Asia. Asian production totaled 2,026,100,000 pounds, an increase of 19.1 million pounds, or 1%, from 1968. Asia accounts for nearly 90% of the world's tea production, but it is facing increased competition from Africa and South America. India, the leader among the nations, reported another record crop in 1969, as did second-ranked Ceylon.

TEA PRODUCTION IN PRINCIPAL COUNTRIES
(In pounds)

	Average 1960–64	1968	Forecast 1969
India	767,700,000	885,800,000	886,000,000
Ceylon	464,700,000	495,600,000	503,000,000
Japan	176,700,000	187,300,000	190,000,000
USSR	92,700,000	118,800,000	120,000,000
Indonesia	97,100,000	88,000,000	88,000,000
Kenya	35,800,000	65,600,000	78,000,000
Pakistan	53,700,000	62,600,000	66,000,000
Taiwan	41,700,000	53,800,000	55,000,000
Turkey	17,500,000	53,000,000	55,000,000
Iran	24,400,000	44,000,000	45,000,000
Argentina	20,700,000	37,500,000	40,000,000
Uganda	13,200,000	33,400,000	40,000,000
World total	1,908,600,000	2,270,800,000	2,321,000,000

Africa and South America. African production, which has nearly doubled in the last few years, totaled 236.9 million pounds in 1969, up 28.6 million pounds, or 14% from 1968. Kenya, Malawi, Mozambique, Tanzania, and Uganda reported large increases. South America produced 58 million pounds, an increase of 2.5 million pounds, or 5%, from 1968.

Consumption and Sales. The United Kingdom ranks first worldwide in the consumption of tea, and India is second. Ceylon is the largest exporter.

Retail sales of tea in the United States in 1968 reached an all-time high of 111 million pounds, valued at $263 million. Commercial use added another 30 million pounds, bringing total consumption to a record 141 million pounds.

NICHOLAS KOMINUS
Kominus Agri-Info Associates

TELEPHONE

The longest long-distance call ever made highlighted telephone events in 1969. On July 21, President Nixon picked up his desk phone in the White House and within seconds was talking to astronauts Neil Armstrong and Edwin Aldrin on the moon.

The call, by Bell System calculation, traveled 290,000 miles, part of the distance by land lines of the national telecommunications network and the remainder by radio to the moon. The call was seen, as well as heard, on live television carried to homes through the same telecommunications network used to make the historic call.

Service. The lunar conversation was one of the 115 billion calls handled by Bell System facilities during 1969, an increase of 10 billion over the total for 1968. Long distance calling was up 12%, totaling 6.6 billion calls for the year.

As 1970 began, there were 115.3 million telephones in service in the United States, and almost the same number of instruments serving the entire rest of the world. The Bell System's 23 operating companies listed 96 million phones; the remaining 19.3 million phones are served by the nearly 1,900 independent (non-Bell) companies in the country.

In August, hurricane Camille, one of the worst natural disasters in the United States in recent years, badly damaged Gulf Coast telecommunications facilities. More than 200,000 telephones were out of service. Restoration required the efforts of 1,000 workmen flown into the stricken area from telephone companies all over the country.

During 1969 work continued on the development of Picturephone service with plans for introducing the see-as-you-talk service by the middle of 1970. The first two cities to be so linked are New York and Pittsburgh.

Sharply increased telephone use and the difficulty of forecasting this demand caused overloading in some metropolitan exchanges. To speed the installation of new equipment and improve service, New York City's telephone company borrowed 1,500 technicians from other telephone companies while accelerating its own programs for training and recruiting employees.

Telephone Cables. The Bell System completed the last link of its high capacity Boston-to-Miami cable in September. The 20-tube coaxial cable carries 32,400 simultaneous conversations, twice as many as any existing cable system.

The summer of 1969 saw a fifth transatlantic telephone cable begin to snake its way across the ocean floor. The 720-channel facility will eventually link Green Hill, R. I., and San Fernando, Spain, and will be extended by radio relay to Portugal and Italy. Service is expected to begin early in 1970.

Rate Reduction. In December 1969, following a review by the Federal Communications Commission, the Bell System announced long distance rate reductions amounting to $150 million, which took effect on Jan. 1, 1970. Significant savings were listed for persons not requiring an operator's assistance. An innovation was the establishment of a one-minute time period for certain calls.

Scientific Discovery. Bell Telephone laboratories generated excitement in the scientific world with their discoveries in magnetic domains. They hold the possibility for low-power, high-capacity information storage. (See also COMPUTERS.)

JOHN T. GEOGHEGAN
American Telephone and Telegraph Company

TELEPHONES IN MAJOR COUNTRIES

Country	Telephones Jan. 1, 1969	% increase over 1968	No. per 100 population
Argentina	1,599,861	3.0	6.72
Australia	3,392,436	6.7	28.20
Austria	1,242,785	6.8	16.88
Belgium	1,847,363	5.3	19.18
Brazil	1,560,701	6.0	1.74
Canada	8,820,770	5.2	42.12
Colombia	574,700 (est.)	9.5	2.85
Czechoslovakia	1,789,373	6.6	12.44
Denmark	1,516,802	3.2	30.88
Finland	1,009,336	6.2	21.50
France	7,503,491	7.2	14.98
Germany, East	1,896,151	6.5	11.10
Germany, West	11,248,979	9.0	18.65
Greece	761,550	15.4	8.63
Hungary	684,389	7.9	6.66
India	1,057,193	6.4	0.20
Italy	7,752,042	9.8	14.37
Japan	20,525,211	12.7	20.12
Mexico	1,174,943	12.5	2.44
Netherlands	2,917,384	7.4	22.80
New Zealand	1,155,465	3.2	41.56
Norway	1,036,027	4.9	27.02
Poland	1,650,896	7.9	5.08
Portugal	653,407	6.1	6.87
Rumania	596,000 (est.)	8.0	2.99
South Africa	1,397,725	5.7	7.29
Spain	3,723,239	10.2	11.44
Sweden	4,110,579	4.5	51.76
Switzerland	2,685,800	6.0	43.42
United Kingdom	12,901,000	6.6	23.26
USSR	9,900,000 (est.)	8.8	4.14
United States	109,256,000	5.3	54.02
Yugoslavia	549,019	8.5	2.70

television and radio

DOOR

SESAME STREET, a bright new television program for children, helps them learn "D" for Door, Duck, and Dog (*upper right*) and numbers (*left*). A puppet, Kermit the Frog, gives a short, humorous lecture on the letter "W".

News broadcasts, rather than entertainment programs, captured most of the interest—enthusiastic praise as well as criticism—on television during 1969. And the spectacular TV broadcasts by U. S. spacemen from the moon were the most impressive engineering achievement of the year. Radio, after having enjoyed a record revenue year in 1968, felt a slight drop in advertising during 1969.

TELEVISION BROADCASTING

It was news broadcasting that created the most excitement on television during 1969. The news divisions of the three major networks were hailed for their virtually flawless coverage of Apollo 11 and for their simulations of the Apollo 12 moonwalk when the astronauts' color television camera blanked out. On July 1, TV brought the public moments of high splendor in the broadcast of the investiture of Britain's Prince Charles as Prince of Wales. The networks were absolved by the Federal Communications Commission (FCC), in February, of the charge of being "unfair" in their coverage of the Democratic National Convention in the summer of 1968. And they made a nationally visible figure of Vice President Spiro T. Agnew by giving full coverage to his November 13 speech blasting the networks as biased in their reporting of the Nixon administration. Some critics of the media said that Agnew overstated and television overreacted. What-

ever the case, CBS's response on *60 Minutes* (November 25) was a fine piece of broadcast journalism.

Two polls—the Roper survey for the Television Information Office (in March) and the Harris poll for *Time* magazine (in September)—showed that television had become the public's major source of news and that, by as high as 2 to 1 over newspapers, the public found it "the most believable news source." The Roper poll showed the public strongly opposed (about 7 to 1) to any government control of TV news and in favor of editorializing by stations.

Commercial Programs. The year 1969 produced little in the way of fresh new programing, although there were a number of changes at the start of "the second season" in January, and, of course, in September's "new season." Winter and spring were enlivened by a one-night disaster for ABC entitled *Turn-On* and by the demise of the *Smothers Brothers Comedy Hour* at CBS. *Turn-On,* a spinoff from *Laugh-In,* was an ABC "second season" offering on February 5. The immediate outcry, from audience and affiliates alike, against its vulgarity was so great that ABC canceled the series after the first broadcast.

The trade press had for months carried stories about a feud between the Smothers brothers and CBS over the question of censorship or, perhaps, taste. The issue came to a head on April 3, when CBS notified the Smothers brothers that they had breached their contract by failing to submit the following Sunday's tape in time for prescreening by the network and affiliates. After gaining widespread publicity for their side of the story, the Smothers brothers filed suit against CBS, challenging the right of a television network to censor the programs it puts on the air and to monopolize the prime time of its affiliates. All told, there were three separate suits; total damages sought amounted to $31,110,000.

To replace the Smothers brothers in the all-important time—Sunday evening at 9—CBS chose a variety program starring Leslie Uggams. Miss Uggams was not able to maintain the share of audience (against NBC's *Bonanza*) that the Smothers brothers had, and so was replaced in December by the *Glen Campbell Goodtime Hour,* itself a spin-off from the *Smothers Brothers Comedy Hour.* The Glen Campbell Wednesday night time was given to *Hee Haw!*

Of the new shows presented in September few turned out to be real hits—only Bill Cosby (NBC), Jim Nabors (CBS), *Room 222* (ABC), and *Marcus Welby, M. D.* (ABC). *Then Came Bronson* (NBC) and *Love American Style* (ABC) were also worth more than one look. ABC's *The Survivors,* perhaps as costly a regular series as any network has ever offered, was a total disaster and was dropped in January.

As has so often been the case in recent years, specials were the highlights of 1969: *Hallmark Hall of Fame's* "Teacher, Teacher"; *On Stage's* "Male of the Species" and "Mirror, Mirror, Off the Wall"; Rod Sterling's "Night Gallery"; the CBS Playhouse "Appalachian Autumn"; and variety specials starring Julie Andrews, Petula Clark (both with Harry Belafonte), Woody Allen, Mitzi Gaynor, Dick Van Dyke, Bill Cosby, and others. And certainly the Mets' unexpected drive to capture baseball's National League pennant and then the World Series was a superspecial and a reminder that television is at its best when it covers actuality.

It is noteworthy that, when the prestigious George Foster Peabody Awards for distinguished achievement by television and radio were announced in April, for the second time in four years there was no award made in the TV entertainment category.

Public Television. Public television, the now-accepted term for what used to be called educational television, scored successes and became more visible to the American public during the year. *The Forsyte Saga,* the British Broadcasting Corporation's superbly produced dramatization of the John Galsworthy novels, was presented in the fall by NET and promptly won, from those discerning enough to hunt out the series, the same enthusiastic acceptance that it has had from viewers in 80 countries, including the Soviet Union. Also in the fall came *Sesame Street,* a daily hour for preschoolers that had been in the planning for two years, supported by foundations and by the Department of Health, Education, and Welfare. *Sesame Street* was considered an unqualified success.

The Corporation for Public Broadcasting found itself a new president in February, after a lengthy search. He is John W. Macy, Jr., former chairman of the U. S. Civil Service Commission.

The Industry. Television faced many troublesome problems quite apart from those connected with providing high-rated programs. During 1969 it concluded lengthy negotiations with the American Society of Composers, Authors, and Publishers

VICE PRESIDENT AGNEW, "loaded for bear," criticized the networks in a speech on November 13.

KEN ALEXANDER, FROM SAN FRANCISCO EXAMINER

(ASCAP) over the use of ASCAP music on television. Yielding to attacks by members of Congress and to the recommendations of the National Commission on the Causes and Prevention of Violence, the networks began to downgrade violence in their action and adventure series. Long-established westerns such as *Gunsmoke, Bonanza,* and *The Virginian,* for example, were forced into quieter story patterns with less "shoot-em-up" action and more emphasis on character.

In March, Sen. John O. Pastore, chairman of the Senate Communications Subcommittee, initiated a study by the surgeon general of the effects of televised violence. He began to put pressure on the networks to submit their programs for clearance by the National Association of Broadcasters' Code Authority. NBC and ABC went along with the senator's recommendation; CBS refused, essentially on the ground that a single, centralized authority would inevitably be exposed to government pressures and therefore to a kind of control of program content that is forbidden under the First Amendment. Senator Pastore, incensed by the "take it all off" shaving cream commercial, also began to demand less sexual overtones in television.

Two months earlier, in January, the television board of directors of the NAB had adopted new rules governing an area of advertising that has been in controversy for a long time, the area of personal products. The new rules opened the way for television advertising of personal products, notably in feminine hygiene. Shortly afterward, Westinghouse withdrew its five television stations from the NAB code in protest. National audiences have yet to see the results of the change in the code, but it is noteworthy that the Avco group of stations announced its decision to accept commercials for lingerie using live models, a practice still barred by the NAB code.

TV's advertising of cigarettes—a traffic that earns the TV industry well in excess of $200 million annually—was one of the most controversial issues of the year. In February the FCC announced that (if Congress approved) it planned to ban all cigarette advertising on television and radio, unless the broadcasters voluntarily gave up the business. The move brought the issue to a head; it seemed to be resolved with the announcement in July by the tobacco industry itself that it would withdraw all cigarette advertising from television by September 1970, provided it was guaranteed freedom from antitrust action if it were to do so. At the end of 1969 the problem was before Congress.

The industry also found itself bombarded with congressional bills and plans for reducing the cost of television time to political candidates. Perhaps the most radical suggestion came from the Twentieth Century Fund's Commission on Campaign Costs. It recommended a series of prime-time half-hours on all networks and stations at half price, the charges to be paid by the government. The half-hours would supersede all regular programing; in other words, the public would have no choice.

Federal Communications Commission. In January the Justice Department urged the FCC to give more of its attention to breaking up monopolies in mass media, as in those communities where the one TV station, the newspapers, the radio station, and CATV (community antenna television, or cable TV) are owned by one company. Specifically, the Justice Department was questioning the advisability of renewing the license of KFBC-TV, Cheyenne, Wyo. As license renewal time came up, there was a spate of challenges to license renewals. A bill offering broadcasters some protection against challenges at license renewal time was introduced in Congress by Sen. John Pastore.

The FCC's "fairness doctrine" and its rules on personal attacks were upheld by the Supreme Court in June, in a landmark decision that held that it is the public's right of access "to social, political, esthetic, moral, and other ideas ... which is crucial." The court further stated that "it is the right of the viewers and listeners, not the right of the broadcasters, which is paramount." The case is generally referred to as the Red Lion case.

In October the FCC adopted rules developing still further the obligations of community antenna television operators. CATV systems with more than 3,500 subscribers were ordered to begin providing original programing "to a significant extent" by

---

OUTSTANDING U.S. TELEVISION PROGRAMS OF 1969

THE ABM (CBS Reports)—A comprehensive analysis and discussion of President Nixon's proposed limited anti-ballistic missile system. CBS, April 29.

APOLLO 11—The spectacular walk on the moon by astronauts Neil A. Armstrong and Edwin E. Aldrin. Live on all networks, July 20–21.

ADVENTURES AT THE JADE SEA—A view of the primitive tribes and wildlife that struggle to survive in the brutal environment surrounding Lake Rudolf in Kenya, narrated by William Holden. CBS, March 26.

AN EVENING WITH JULIE ANDREWS AND HARRY BELAFONTE—An hour-long musical show produced, directed, and choreographed by Gower Champion and with musical direction by Michael Legrand. NBC, Nov. 9.

APPALACHIAN SPRING (CBS Playhouse)—A drama, set in Appalachia, about the conflict between a father and his artist son, starring Arthur Kennedy, Teresa Wright, and Estelle Winwood. CBS, Oct. 7.

CHARLIE BROWN AND CHARLES SCHULZ—A tribute to the "Peanuts" characters and their creator, narrated by Don Sherwood and featuring Rod McKuen, Robert Short, and others. CBS, May 24.

CHINA TODAY AND TOMORROW—A panel discussion of Communist China by a group of specialists, moderated by Edwin Newman. NBC, March 23.

ELECTIONS '69—A live debate on public safety, education, city services, and human relations, among the three major New York mayoral candidates: Mayor John V. Lindsay, Mario Procaccino, and John Marchi. ABC, Oct. 19.

ETHICS IN GOVERNMENT—A discussion of the various aspects of ethics in Congress, with Henry Steele Commager, Wright Patman, Willis Alexander, and Sen. Robert Packwood. ABC, Sept. 19.

THE FIRST AMERICANS—The story of the first human inhabitants of the North American continent. NBC, March 21.

FELICIANO-VERY SPECIAL—A musical show with singer-guitarist José Feliciano and such guest artists as Andy Williams, Dionne Warwick, and Burt Bacharach. NBC, April 27.

FOUL! (New York Television Theater)—Ten young playwrights offer brief dramatic sketches on the universal, contemporary problem of pollution. Nine actors participate. NET, Nov. 25.

FROM HERE TO THE SEVENTIES—An evaluation of the present condition of the United States, in terms of such issues as national politics, poverty, the race situation, space, and pollution, and forecasts of what may lie ahead in the new decade, led by Paul Newman, and featuring Chet Huntley, Frank McGee, Sandor Vanocur, and others. NBC, Oct. 7.

GIVE US BARABBAS (Hallmark Hall of Fame)—The dramatic search of Barabbas, who was freed instead of Jesus, to discover the real identity of his fellow Prisoner. Actors include James Daly and Kim Hunter. NBC, March 28.

HARLEM FESTIVAL—A program exploring the role of the black artist in the world of entertainment, with Max Roach, George Kirby, the Chamber Brothers, the Fifth Dimension, and others. CBS, July 28.

JUILLIARD SCHOOL DEDICATORY CONCERT AT LINCOLN CENTER—Concert honoring the opening of the Juilliard School with pianist Van Cliburn, violinist Itzhak Perlman, mezzo-soprano Shirley Verrett, and conductors Leopold Stokowski and Jean Morel. CBS, Oct. 26.

THE LIGHT IN THE WILDERNESS—The name of an oratorio composed by jazz-pianist Dave Brubeck and performed by him, along with his combo, organist Norman Scribner, baritone William Justus, and a choir of some 300 voices at the Washington Cathedral in Washington, D.C. CBS, April 6.

THE MAKING OF THE PRESIDENT: 1968—A special program based on Theodore H. White's best seller about the 1968 Presidential campaign, narrated by Joseph Campanella. CBS, Sept. 9.

MALE OF THE SPECIES (Prudential's On Stage)—A comedy drama in three parts about a girl's relationship with her father, a charming young Irishman, and a shrewd, middle-aged Welsh barrister, featuring Sean Connery, Michael Caine, Paul Scofield, and Anna Calder-Marshall, with Sir Laurence Olivier as host. NBC, Jan. 3.

MEET GEORGE WASHINGTON—A program featuring highlights of the life of the first President of the United States, narrated by Melvyn Douglas. NBC, April 24.

A MIDSUMMER NIGHT'S DREAM—A new production by The Royal Shakespeare Company, with a cast including Diana Rigg, Ian Richardson, and Bill Travers, and directed by Peter Hall. CBS, Feb. 9.

PORTRAIT OF PETULA—A musical program, starring singer Petula Clark and featuring Andy Williams, Sacha Distel, and Ron Moody. NBC, April 7.

RIDDLE OF THE MAYAN CAVE—The efforts of a team of 10 men and a woman to discover the secrets of the once-thriving Mayan civilization by examining the network of caves in the Guatemalan highlands, thought to have been used by the Mayans from 300 to 900 A.D. ABC, May 9.

ROYAL FAMILY—A program devoted to the depiction of the public and private lives of the chief members of Great Britain's royal family. CBS, Sept. 21.

S. HUROK PRESENTS—A special offering performances by pianist Emil Gilels and cellist Mstislav Rostropovich. CBS, Dec. 21.

THE SAVAGE HEART—A CONVERSATION WITH ERIC HOFFER (CBS News Special)—An interview with the longshoreman-philosopher by Eric Sevareid. CBS, Jan. 28.

THE WONDERFUL WORLD OF PIZZAZZ—A salute to self-expression in music and fashion, featuring Pat Paulsen, The Cowsills, and Harpers Bizarre, and co-hosted by Carl Reiner and Michele Lee. NBC, March 18.

TINY TIM and his bride, Miss Vicki—with host Johnny Carson (*right*)—
after wedding on the *Tonight* show before a record television audience.

Jan. 1, 1971. They were also given permission to carry commercials "during natural breaks" in programs.

With the retirement of Rosel Hyde as chairman of the FCC and the appointment of Commissioner James J. Wadsworth to a diplomatic post, the FCC lost two familiar faces. President Nixon appointed Dean Burch, chairman of the Republican National Committee for a brief period in 1964–65, to be the new chairman of the FCC, and Robert Wells, an officer in a newspaper-broadcasting group of Garden City, Kans., to be the new commission member.

RADIO BROADCASTING

Statistics compiled in 1969 confirmed what radio broadcasters had surmised—that 1968 was a banner year for radio. In that year radio made its biggest annual sales gain since the advent of television (it had the largest rate of increase of all the major media) and enjoyed the first billion-dollar year in its history. The Radio Advertising Bureau figured the rate of increase at about 12%, against approximately 9% for television, 5% for newspapers, and 3% for magazines. The figures for 1969 are expected to be far less spectacular.

Commercial FM stations, of which there are now more than 2,000, continued to lag behind AM outlets in revenue. Hope for some improvement in this situation was raised in the spring, when Sen. Frank Moss and Rep. Alvin O'Konsky reintroduced in Congress the all-channel radio receiver bill, which would require that all new radios be capable of receiving both AM and FM signals. The bill is aimed particularly at new automobile radios. In September the FCC proposed rules that also would force the growth of radio services into FM, largely by tightening application requirements for new AM stations.

Noncommercial FM stations, numbering more than 400, got a shot in the arm from the Corporation for Public Broadcasting (CPB) in the form of small grants and a study jointly underwritten by CPB and the Ford Foundation. The study called for the establishment in CPB of a radio bureau to advance noncommercial radio; the strengthening of both the National Educational Radio division of the National Association of Educational Broadcasters (NAEB) and the National Educational Radio Network; the establishment of a new production center for informational programing; and the beginning of live networking.

The FCC in May denied the petition of the Mutual Broadcasting System to halt ABC's four-network radio service. CBS radio, in order to meet the competition, strengthened its *Dimension* series by dropping "soft" features in favor of "hard" news features.

JOHN M. GUNN
State University of New York at Albany

TELEVISION AND RADIO ENGINEERING

The principal engineering developments in television and radio during 1969 were the increasing rate of expansion of cable television systems and distribution, and the diminishing rate of growth of television and radio broadcasting.

Cable TV Expansion. The most spectacular growth in television during 1969 was in the area of cable television. CATV moved increasingly into the large cities, with the number of systems in operation increasing from 2,260 to 2,385 during 1969. The number of homes served by cable systems increased from 3.6 million to 4.5 million. CATV systems increasingly featured programs from distant stations. Cable TV expansion also continued in Canada, although slowed somewhat by an action of the Canadian Radio Television Commission (CRTC) limiting the importation on cable systems of U. S. programs.

Expansion. The pace of television broadcasting expansion in the United States slackened during 1969, with only 25 new stations going on the air. Of these, 10 were educational and 15 were commercial. Only 4 of the 25 broadcast on the very high frequency, or VHF (channels 2–13); the rest broadcast on ultra high frequency, UHF (channels 14–83).

The number of AM radio stations in the nation increased from 4,265 to 4,292 during 1969, and

SUMMARY OF WORLD TELEVISION, JAN. 1, 1970

Country	Stations	Number of TV Sets	Country	Stations	Number of TV Sets	Country	Stations	Number of TV Sets
Albania	1	2,500	Haiti	1	10,500	Okinawa	2	170,000
Algeria	6	150,000	Honduras	5	17,000	Pakistan	5	80,000
Argentina	30	3,000,000	Hong Kong	3	220,000	Panama	9	125,000
Australia	85	2,951,000	Hungary	11	1,500,000	Paraguay	1	25,000
Austria	25	1,134,500	Iceland	7	31,000	Peru	18	325,000
Barbados	1	16,000	India	1	8,000	Philippines	14	355,000
Belgium	19	1,875,000	Indonesia	4	75,000	Poland	19	3,500,000
Bermuda	2	18,000	Iran	7	250,000	Portugal	7	360,000
Bolivia	1	7,500	Iraq	2	180,000	Rhodesia	2	50,000
Brazil	43	6,500,000	Ireland	20	460,000	Rumania	9	900,000
Bulgaria	4	190,000	Israel	8	200,000	Saudi Arabia	8	300,000
Cambodia	2	18,000	Italy	68	8,950,000	Senegal	1	750
Canada	355	7,140,000	Ivory Coast	4	11,000	Sierra Leone	1	3,500
Chile	3	400,000	Jamaica	9	56,000	Singapore	2	123,000
China (Mainland)	30	300,000	Japan	157	22,000,000	Southern Yemen	6	22,000
Colombia	14	600,000	Jordan	1	20,000	Spain	28	3,600,000
Congo (Brazzaville)	1	1,500	Kenya	3	16,000	Sudan	1	65,000
Congo (Kinshasna)	1	6,500	Korea	5	300,000	Sweden	115	2,375,000
Costa Rica	3	100,000	Kuwait	2	100,000	Switzerland	51	1,145,000
Cuba	25	555,000	Lebanon	9	250,000	Syria	5	130,000
Cyprus	2	38,000	Liberia	1	6,500	Taiwan	4	420,000
Czechoslovakia	28	2,870,000	Libya	1	500	Tanzania	1	4,000
Denmark	26	1,255,300	Luxembourg	1	57,000	Thailand	5	225,000
Dominican Republic	6	77,000	Malagasy Republic	1	1,000	Trinidad and Tobago	2	45,000
Ecuador	10	65,000	Malaysia	8	150,000	Tunisia	6	38,000
El Salvador	4	75,000	Malta	1	53,000	Turkey	3	25,000
Equatorial Guinea	1	500	Mauritius	1	15,000	Uganda	6	12,000
Ethiopia	1	6,500	Mexico	49	2,525,000	United Arab Republic	23	500,000
Finland	53	985,000	Mongolia	1	600	United Kingdom	221	16,360,000
France	93	9,580,000	Morocco	8	105,000	United States	862	88,941,000●
Gabon	2	2,400	Netherlands	13	2,910,000	Upper Volta	—	3,000
Germany (East)	15	5,310,000	Netherlands Antilles	2	32,000	Uruguay	9	225,000
Germany (West)	169	16,350,000	New Zealand	20	625,000	USSR	167	27,000,000
Ghana	4	10,000	Nicaragua	2	45,000	Venezuela	29	700,000
Greece	1	80,000	Niger	1	100	Vietnam (South)	1	14,000
Guatemala	2	61,000	Nigeria	8	53,000	Yugoslavia	33	1,480,000
Guyana	—	3,500	Norway	58	801,200	Zambia	3	18,500

●Includes Guam, Puerto Rico, and Virgin Islands. (Source: Television Factbook).

the number of FM stations increased from 2,330 to 2,468. Future expansion of AM broadcasting was made unlikely by FCC action prohibiting the construction of new AM radio stations except under very special circumstances.

Sales of radios capable of receiving both FM and AM stations continued to increase with FM saturation passing the 50% mark during the year. Successful tests were conducted of FM "translator" and "booster" stations, intended to relay FM service into remote and shadowed areas.

Diversion of TV Channels. The land mobile radio services, with users ranging from fire and police dispatchers to sand and gravel delivery operators, have experienced a phenomenal growth in recent years. Current estimates place the number of these stations now on the air at 3.5 million, and the industry predicts a growth in the number of transmitters to 5.2 million by 1975.

Engineering studies in 1969 investigated simultaneous land mobile operation on television channels, or the outright diversion of some television channels to land mobile service. Government action on the problem was expected in early 1970.

Space Uses of TV Broadcasting. Television served and was served by satellites and space exploration in 1969. The two manned moon flights—Apollo 11 and Apollo 12—demonstrated both black-and-white and color television transmission to earth stations. The failure of a color television camera on the moon deprived millions of home viewers of color pictures from the moon during the landing of Apollo 12.

The use of earth-orbiting satellites for tele-

(Below) *Male of the Species,* with Michael Caine and Anna Calder-Marshall. (*Right*) *Teacher, Teacher,* an Emmy Award winner with Billy Schulman (*left*) as a mentally retarded boy and David McCallum as his mentor.

NBC

vision relaying between countries increased during 1969, and proposals for the use of satellites for domestic television relaying received White House approval in January 1970.

Home TV Sets. The production of both monochrome and color television receivers continued at a slackened pace during 1969. Of the estimated 10 million new television receivers sold during the year, more than half were color receivers. These new receivers featured automatic frequency control (AFC) to provide automatic fine tuning and better flesh tones.

Charges made by consumer groups that some television receivers were unsafe because of X-ray emission or fire hazards proved on careful study to have been greatly exaggerated. Manufacturers moved to eliminate both hazards and federal regulations were drawn up to control X-ray emission.

A new home video reproducer—PREVS (Pre-Recorded Video System)—was demonstrated by RCA in 1969 as a competitor of CBS's Electronic Video Recorder and various other models of home video tape recorders. However, these systems will not be available for home use for some time.

HOWARD T. HEAD
A. D. Ring & Associates

TENNESSEE

At his trial in Memphis, James Earl Ray pleaded guilty in the assassination of Dr. Martin Luther King, Jr., and was sentenced on March 10 to 99 years in prison. His later efforts to obtain a new trial and to sue his lawyers were ineffectual.

Memphis, the scene of the assassination on April 4, 1968, experienced racial tensions throughout most of 1969. In other developments, the University of Tennessee liberalized some of its policies in response to student demands, and for the first time in the 20th century a Republican became speaker of the Tennessee House of Representatives.

Legislation. At the organization session of the Legislature, which convened on January 7, Republican William L. Jenkins was elected speaker of the lower house. The Democrats, still in control of the Senate, reelected Frank C. Gorrell as speaker—an office including that of lieutenant governor.

At its legislative session, beginning on February 25, the lawmakers approved Gov. Buford Ellington's record budget of $1.2 billion for the fiscal year 1969–1970. The appropriations included provisions for a statewide system of kindergartens, increased aid to elementary and secondary education, and a Medicaid program. Other legislation increased the cigarette tax from 8 cents to 13 cents a package, restricted political activities of state employees, and made it a felony for a nonstudent to incite or participate in a riot at any public school.

Education and Civil Rights. Controversy over an "open speaker" policy—which arose in 1968 at the University of Tennessee in Knoxville because of the administration's refusal to permit the civil rights activist Dick Gregory to speak on campus—was taken to a federal district court, which ruled in 1969 that the university policy violated the constitutional right of free speech. The university not only accepted the decision but also adopted a more lenient policy regarding dormitory hours for women students and, under pressure, agreed to permit students (under the leadership of James Baxter, the first Negro president of the student body) to participate in an advisory capacity in the selection of a new president of the university. A neighboring private institution, Maryville College, went further and gave students equal representation with faculty and administration on an All-College Council, with an equal voice in decision-making.

Memphis experienced a series of "Black Mondays," involving boycotts of classes by Negro students in support of demands for Negro representation on the city board of education and for improved conditions for Negro hospital workers. Ralph D. Abernathy, the successor of Dr. King as head of the Southern Christian Leadership Conference, went to Memphis in November and led 2,000 Negroes in a march in support of the demands. The school boycotts were ended as a result of a $10 million damage suit by the board of education against the sponsoring United Black Coalition. Meanwhile, in an election in Knoxville, Negroes won representation not only on the board of education but also on the city council.

Deaths of State Leaders. Three prominent Tennesseeans died during 1969: Prentice Cooper, governor of Tennessee from 1939 to 1945, died on May 18; Frank G. Clement, governor from 1963 to 1967, on November 4; and Robert A. Everett, Democratic member of the U. S. House of Representatives since 1958, on January 26. Edward Jones, a Democrat and a former state commissioner of agriculture, won Everett's seat in a special election on March 25.

STANLEY J. FOLMSBEE
University of Tennessee

TENNESSEE • Information Highlights

Area: 42,244 square miles (109,412 sq km).
Population: 3,933,000 (1969 est.).
Chief Cities (1969 est.): Nashville, the capital, 270,000; Memphis, 545,000; Knoxville, 187,000; Chattanooga, 122,000.
Government: *Chief Officers*—governor, Buford Ellington (Democrat); lt. gov., Frank C. Gorrell (D); secy. of state, Joe C. Carr (D); atty. gen., George M. Pack (D); treas., Charles Worley; comr. of educ., J. Howard Warf; chief justice, Ross W. Dyer. *General Assembly*—Senate, 33 members (20 Democrats, 13 Republicans); House of Representatives, 99 members (49 D, 49 R, 1 independent).
Education: *School enrollment* (1968)—public elementary, 567,000 pupils (20,000 teachers); public secondary, 323,000 pupils (13,200 teachers); nonpublic schools, 33,800 pupils (1,960 teachers); college and university (fall 1967), 112,583 students. *Public school expenditures* (1968)—$461,200,000 ($541 per pupil); average teacher's salary, $6,170.
Public Finance (fiscal year 1968–69): *Revenues*, $1,034,971,000 (general sales and gross receipts taxes, $205,325,000; motor fuel tax, $22,176,000; federal funds, $289,002,000). *Expenditures*, $993,351,000 (education, $192,928,000; health, welfare, and safety, $167,247,000; highways, $167,842,000). *State debt*, $363,119,000 (June 30, 1968).
Personal Income (1968): $10,252,000,000; average annual income per person, $2,579.
Public Assistance (fiscal year 1968–69): $98,048,368 to 180,910 recipients (aged, $44,720,097; dependent children, $35,032,560).
Labor Force (employed persons, annual avg. 1968): *Agricultural*, 129,900; *nonagricultural* (wage and salary earners), 1,270,400 (35.8% manufacturing, 19.1% trade, 17.1% government). *Unemployed persons* (annual avg. 1968)—59,600.
Manufacturing (1966): *Value added by manufacture*, $4,652,099,000 (transportation equipment, $156,911,000; primary metals, $213,755,000; nonelectrical machinery, $166,713,000; electrical machinery, $449,860,000).
Agriculture (1967): *Cash farm income*, $675,091,000 (livestock, $358,696,000; crops, $242,612,000; govt. payments, $73,783,000). *Chief crops* (tons)—Hay, 1,951,000; corn for grain, 1,249,668; soybeans, 780,500; wheat, 255,780.
Mining (1968): *Production value*, $198,435,000. *Chief minerals* (tons)—Coal, 7,500,000; phosphates, 3,119,000; zinc ore, 120,000; copper, 14,000.
Transportation: *Roads* (1968), 77,617 miles (131,235 km); *motor vehicles* (1968), 2,319,438; *railroads* (1969), 3,400 track miles (5,472 km); *airports* (1967), 71.
Communications (1968): *Telephones*, 1,631,600; *television stations*, 19; *radio stations*, 157; *newspapers*, 29.

TENNIS. See SPORTS.

TEXAS

Like most other U. S. citizens, Texans in 1969 reacted to their troubled times, dividing over the war in Vietnam, complaining about inflation and high taxes, and agonizing over the behavior of dissidents and militants.

Yet life, business, and politics went on. The state's best-known political figure, former President Lyndon Johnson, retired to his ranch on the Pedernales where he seemed content to leave politics to others. The Apollo flights to the moon were successfully directed from the Manned Spacecraft Center at Houston, and the football team of the University of Texas was ranked first in the nation.

New Governor. Gov. Preston Smith's new administration got off to a rocky start, with appointments a particular headache. His predecessor, Gov. John Connally, made a number of midnight appointments that could not be undone despite their doubtful legality, and the state Senate delayed or denied confirmation of several key Smith appointees. The new governor's partiality to old friends and to West Texans led to charges of "cronyism."

Legislature. Governor Smith also found the 61st biennial session of the Legislature troublesome. His relationship with Lt. Gov. Ben Barnes was not the best, and a strong liberal element in the Senate often forced the modification or abandonment of legislation. Speaker of the House Gus Mutscher controlled but could not lead his chamber.

─────── **TEXAS • Information Highlights** ───────

Area: 267,338 square miles (692,406 sq km).
Population: 11,064,000 (1967 est.).
Chief Cities (1969, est.): Austin, the capital, 234,000; Houston, 1,187,000; Dallas, 815,000; San Antonio, 695,000; Fort Worth, 355,000; El Paso, 315,000.
Government: *Chief Officers*—governor, Preston Smith (Dem.): lt. gov., Ben Barnes (D); secy of state, Martin Dies, Jr. (D); atty. gen., Crawford Martin (D); treas., Jesse James; comm. of educ., J. W. Edgar; chief justice, Robert W. Calvert. *Legislature*—Senate, 31 members (29 Democrats, 2 Republicans); House of Representatives, 150 members (141 D, 8 R, 1 independent).
Education: *School enrollment* (1968)—public elementary, 1,929,000 pupils (60,600 teachers); public secondary, 745,000 pupils (49,600 teachers); nonpublic schools, 152,700 pupils (7,320 teachers); college and university (fall 1967), 348,481 students. *Public school expenditures* (1967–68)—$1,414,991,000 ($612 per pupil); average teacher's salary, $6,675.
Public Finance (fiscal year 1969): *Revenues,* $3,890,017,186. (3% sales tax, $438,524,669; motor fuel tax, $293,998,234; federal funds, $511,431,497). *Expenditures,* $3,835,151,229 (education, $1,149,021,557; health, welfare, and safety, $465,188,379; highways, $557,196,920).
Personal Income (1968): $33,254,000,000; average annual income per person, $3,029.
Public Assistance (fiscal year 1969): $216,578,758 to 416,208 recipients (aged, $163,238,842; dependent children, $35,- 303,781).
Labor Force (employed persons, August 1969): *Agricultural,* 317,300; *nonagricultural* (wage and salary earners), 4,198,- 700 (18.3% manufacturing, 24.9% trade, 15.4% government). *Unemployed persons* (August 1969)—124,000.
Manufacturing (1967): *Value added by manufacture,* $10,- 861,000,000 (transportation equipment, $1,046,496,000; primary metals, $605,180,000; nonelectrical machinery, $686,982,000; food and products, $1,137,371,000).
Agriculture (1967): *Cash farm income,* $2,984,146,000 (livestock, $1,368,976,000; crops, $1,153,007,000; govt. payments, $462,163,000). Chief crops (tons)—Sorghum grain, 9,617,580 (ranks 1st among the states); rice, 1,295,400 (ranks 1st); cottonseed, 1,182,000 (ranks 1st); cotton lint, 679,200 (ranks 1st).
Mining (1966): *Production value,* $5,019,750,000 (ranks 1st among the states). *Chief minerals*—Crude petroleum, 1,057,706,000 bbls; natural gas, 6,953,790,000,000 cubic feet; salt, 7,724,000 tons; sulfur, 4,147,360 tons.
Fisheries (1967): *Commercial catch,* 139,200,000 pounds ($49,800,000). *Leading species*—Shrimp, oysters, menhaden, blue crabs.
Transportation: *Roads* (1969), 203,080 miles (326,817 km); *motor vehicles* (1969), 7,016,159; *railroads* (1968), 19,830 track miles (31,912 km); *airports* (1967), 27.
Communications (1969): *Telephones* (1968), 5,168,100; *television stations,* 51; *radio stations,* 370; *newspapers,* 111.

GRIFFIN SQUARE, LTD.

CIRCULAR OFFICE-HOTEL in Dallas (pictured in artist's sketch) will rise 913 feet and cost $30 million.

When, at the end of the regular session, the Legislature provided—for the third straight year— a one-year rather than a two-year appropriation bill, the governor vetoed it and called a special session for late summer. To provide the additional financing needed, the governor, lieutenant governor, and the speaker of the House agreed to press for an extension of the state's general sales tax to food purchases. The proposal squeaked past filibustering senators by one vote, but the public reacted with one of the most spontaneous outpourings of anger ever seen in Texas politics. This impressed enough members of the House to prevent passage of the measure. The Legislature then went into a second special session. In this session, agreement was finally reached on a tax package more evenly balanced between business and consumers.

In other areas the legislative record was, as usual, mixed. Major enactments included the state's first minimum wage law, a pay raise for teachers, improvements in workmen's compensation benefits, a tort claims act partially removing governmental immunity to lawsuits, and an "implied consent" law to facilitate testing for alleged drunken driving. The lawmakers also chipped away at drug abuse, family law, and liquor control but failed to make a comprehensive assault on such problems as educational reform, state constitutional revision, pollution, highway safety, welfare and poverty, and civil rights. Comic relief was supplied by an acrimonious dispute between certain representatives and the commissioner of the general land office, Jerry Sadler, involving the disposition of treasure from a 16th century Spanish galleon recovered in the Gulf of Mexico. The commissioner's conduct finally provoked the House to a rare vote of censure.

Texans voted on nine constitutional amendments on August 5. Five of the amendments were disapproved, including proposals for annual legislative sessions, a pay raise for legislators, and a massive $3.5 billion water development program. Among the four approved was an amendment increasing the ceiling on welfare payments.

Education. In addition to passing a bill to curb campus unrest, the Legislature created three new medical schools and three new senior colleges. They also reorganized the governing boards of several institutions and transformed several state colleges into universities. In general, the Legislature demonstrated that higher education is too good a thing politically to leave to the Coordinating Board of the Texas College and University System. There were signs of increasing student militancy at several institutions including the University of Texas at Austin.

Civil Rights. For Mexican-Americans and Negroes the year 1969 brought little in the way of immediate improvement. Desegregation of schools and other public facilities moved along slowly, as did the development of employment and housing opportunities for minorities. The legislature did authorize bilingual educational programs, and the creation of a 50-member Committee on Human Relations to be appointed by Governor Smith (who had initiated the proposal). Militants were active among both minority groups, but there was relatively little open conflict with the larger community.

CLIFTON McCLESKEY
University of Texas

TEXTILE INDUSTRY

For the first time, U. S. consumption of man-made fibers exceeded that of natural fibers in 1968. The nation consumed 5,102,000,000 pounds of man-made fibers, as against 4,436,000,000 pounds of the three natural fibers—cotton, previously the textile leader for more than a century (4,104,000,000 pounds); wool (330 million pounds); and silk, 2 million pounds. Man-made fibers led in value at $3.6 billion, followed by raw cotton at $1 billion, raw wool at $400 million, and silk at $9 million.

During 1968 each U. S. resident used an average of 26.6 pounds of man-made fiber, 22 pounds of cotton, and 2.3 pounds of wool. The total consumed per person was 8.5% more than in 1967.

Fiber Consumption. The annual rate of total

SELECTED U. S. TEXTILE INDUSTRY DATA

	1966	1967	1968	First Half 1969
Fiber Consumption		(Millions of pounds)		
Raw cotton................	4,621	4,414	4,104	2,011
Raw wool, total[1]...........	370	313	330	166
Apparel class...........	267	229	238	119
Carpet class............	103	84	92	47
Raw silk.................	4	3	2	1
Man-made fibers[2].........	3,879	4,096	5,102	2,691
Rayon+acetate yarn......	781	740	795	380
Rayon+acetate staple.....	810	760	893	463
Noncellulosic yarn[3]......	1,082	1,183	1,543	808
Noncellulosic staple[4].....	892	1,110	1,487	820
Textile glass fiber........	314	303	384	220
Total fiber consumption....	8,874	8,826	9,538	4,869
Tire cord and tire fabric output[5]				
Total cotton..............	8	4	5	2
Total man-made...........	518	468	569	311
Tire cord and cord fabric.....	502	459	555	294
Rayon.................	187	126	155	65
Nylon and polyester......	315	333	400	229
Chafer and other.........	16	9	14	17
Total tire cord and fabric...	526	472	574	313
Broad woven fabric output[6]		(Millions of linear yards)		
Cotton fabrics.............	8,840	8,278	7,460	...
Man-made fiber fabrics......	4,208	4,246	5,262	...
Woolen and worsted fabrics....	265	238	243	135
Silk fabrics...............	18	17	13	...
Paper and other fabrics......	6	6	5	...
Total broad woven goods...	13,337	12,785	12,983	...

[1] Clean basis. [2] U. S. producers' domestic shipments plus imports for consumption. [3] Includes acrylic, nylon (polyamide), olefin (polyethylene and polypropylene), saran, spandex, vinyon, (polyvinyl chloride) and TFE-fluorocarbon fiber. [4] Includes acrylic and modacrylic, nylon, olefin, polyester and vinyon. [5] Cotton chafer excluded. [6] Except tire fabrics and carpets, rugs, and felts. (Source: Textile Economics Bureau, Inc.).

mill consumption of fiber in 1969, based on data for the first nine months, was 9.6 billion pounds. The 1969 annual rate of mill consumption included a 5% increase for man-made fibers. Raw cotton decreased 5% and raw wool 3%, while raw silk consumption remained the same. At these 1969 rates, man-made fibers accounted for 56% of the total and cotton 41%.

Broad Woven Fabric Output. U. S. production of broad woven fabric, based on actual data for the first half of 1969, will total 13.1 billion linear yards for the year, 1% more than in 1968.

Prices. The average price of 1-inch middling raw cotton for the first nine months of 1969 was 21.9 cents per pound, and raw wool (clean basis, at Boston) was $1.22. Prices remained unchanged for rayon staple (28 cents), 150 denier rayon yarn (93 cents), and 150 denier acetate yarn (74 cents).

Employment and Earnings. Employment in domestic knitting and weaving mills and in finished textile products averaged 2,130,000 in the first half of 1969. Mill workers averaged $93.28 in weekly earnings; workers in the apparel cutting and related trades averaged $82.07.

Imports and Exports. The U. S. textile import balance in 1968 was $782 million, 28% more than the previous high of $610 million in 1966. Imports of all textile fibers and products were valued at $2,078,000,000 and exports at $1,296,000,000.

Imports of raw flax and linen yarns totaled 10.6 million pounds in 1968; imports of linen and chiefly linen fabrics totaled 30.6 million pounds.

Canadian Developments. Canadian fabric shipments in 1968 totaled 597 million square yards—315 million square yards of cotton, 36 million square yards of wool, and 246 million square yards of man-made fiber fabrics. Production of rayon and acetate yarn and staple in 1968 totaled 101.4 million pounds. Noncellulosic fiber production was 137.6 million pounds.

STANLEY B. HUNT
President, Textile Economics Bureau, Inc.

THAILAND

Events in Thailand in 1969 were highlighted by the return of constitutional and civilian government and the resumption of normal political activity after a long period of martial law. Relations with the United States largely centered on whether U. S. armed forces would continue to be stationed in Thailand and in what numbers, and whether, in the event of attack, U. S. combat troops would be committed to Thai defense.

General Election. Thailand's first general election since 1958 was held on February 10, ending 11 years of martial law. Although the ruling United Thai People's party, headed by the premier, Field Marshal Thanom Kittikachorn, failed to win a majority of the 219 seats in the House of Representatives, it captured 75 seats and had no difficulty in forming a government. There were no major changes in the cabinet reshuffle.

Thai Insurgency. Although the Thai struggle against insurgency did not seem as intense during 1969, there was little evidence that it was ended. In April the revolt among Meo tribesmen in northeastern Thailand was still considered grave. The government continued to blame Communist infiltration for the revolt.

In December the Thai army announced the imposition of a nighttime curfew in the provinces along the Malaysian border, beset by terrorist attacks.

Relations with the United States. Debate about the U. S. role in Thailand and the size of its military forces there continued in both Thailand and in the United States throughout 1969. In February, Foreign Minister Thanat Khoman said that the Thai people "were not too happy about the presence of foreign troops on Thai soil" and that these troops would have to leave at the end of the Vietnam War "unless there was some compelling reason for them to stay." But by September, Thanat indicated that Thailand would be happy to have U. S. forces remain in the country.

In the United States, critics demanded an explanation for a hitherto unrevealed contingency agreement (apparently signed with Thailand in 1964), which stated that U. S. combat troops would be utilized under Thai command if Thailand was threatened by Communist forces. In August 1969, Secretary of Defense Melvin Laird said that this plan had not yet won the approval of the Nixon administration, and in September, Vice President Spiro Agnew supported limitations on the use of U. S. troops in Thailand.

In September formal talks were opened between the two countries on the "gradual reduction" of the approximately 50,000 men stationed in Thailand. Agreement was reached on the reduction of U. S. forces by some 6,000 men by July 1970. Green Beret units were among those slated to be withdrawn.

During a brief visit to Bangkok in July, President Richard Nixon said that "the United States will stand proudly with Thailand against those who might threaten it from abroad or from within." Despite this remark the Thais seemed concerned over increasing U. S. insistence that Asian countries take a greater responsibility for their own defense. In

QUEEN SIRIKIT (*left*) of Thailand entertains Mrs. Richard Nixon, who accompanied her husband on a state visit.

UPI

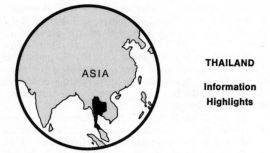

THAILAND

Information Highlights

Area: 198,455 square miles (514,000 sq km).
Population: 33,693,000 (1968 est.).
Chief Cities (1963 census): Bangkok, the capital, 1,608,305; Thonburi, 459,555.
Government: *King*—Bhumibol Adulyadej (acceded June 9, 1946); *Premier*—Thanom Kittikachorn (took office Dec. 8, 1963). *Parliament* (National Assembly)—House of Representatives, 219 members (party seating, 1969: United Thai People's party, 75; Democratic party, 57; others, 87); Senate, 164 members appointed by the king.
Major Religious Faith: Buddhists, 93% of population.
Education: *Literacy rate* (1969), 70% of population aged 10 and over. *Total school enrollment* (1965)—5,104,364 (pri-

mary, 4,630,424; secondary, 369,977; teacher-training, 14,-727; technical/vocational, 38,514; university/higher, 50,-722).
Finance (1969 est.): *Revenues,* $860,000,000; *expenditures,* $1,200,000,000; *monetary unit,* baht (20.85 bahts equal U. S.$1).
Gross National Product (1968): $5,600,000,000.
Average annual income per person (1968): $160.
Cost of Living Index (1967): 111 (1963=100).
Manufacturing (metric tons, 1967): Cement, 1,736,000;. sugar, 232,000; cotton yarn (1966), 23,900.
Crops (metric tons, 1967–68 crop year): Rice, 9,595,000; cassava, 1,800,000; bananas, 1,200,000.
Minerals (metric tons, 1967): Iron ore, 332,000; lignite, 335,000; salt, 110,000.
Foreign Trade (1968): *Exports,* $660,000,000 (chief exports, 1967: rice, $223,172,400; tin, $87,305,000; jute, $41,540,500; fresh fish, $13,736,000); *imports,* $1,188,000,000 (chief imports, 1967: nonelectrical machinery, $170,899,000; road motor vehicles, $117,330,900; petroleum products, $40,-983,600). *Chief trading partners* (1967): Japan (took 21% of exports, supplied 37% of imports); United States (took 14% of exports, supplied 17% of imports); Britain (took 3% of exports, supplied 7% of imports).
Transportation: *Roads* (1969), 8,000 miles (12,874 km); *motor vehicles* (1967), 242,500 (automobiles, 110,000); *railways* (1969), 2,235 miles (3,597 km); *merchant vessels* (1967), 13 (43,000 gross registered tons); *national airline,* Thai Airways Co. Ltd. (TAC); *principal airport,* Bangkok.
Communications: *Telephones* (1968): 98,390; *television stations* (1966), 10; *television sets* (1967), 210,000; *radios* (1966), 2,765,000; *newspapers* (1962), 7 (daily circulation, 32,000).

late August, Secretary of State William Rogers reassured the Thais that the United States would stand by its SEATO treaty commitments. Nevertheless, in late December, President Nixon endorsed a Senate amendment to the defense appropriations bill (adopted 73–17), prohibiting "the commitment of ground combat troops to Laos and Thailand."

In late November it was revealed in Congress that the United States had spent about $1 billion to obtain "the deployment of a Thai division to fight in South Vietnam."

Economy. The $1.3 billion budget announced in August represented a 14% increase over 1968 and was the largest Thai budget on record. The gross national product in 1968 increased some 8% over 1967, but 1969 opened with much concern over the stability and strength of the economy.

In April, Thailand was represented in the Ministerial Conference for Economic Development of Southeast Asia, which ended on a note of cooperation by the member states.

CARL LEIDEN
University of Texas

THANT, U

Burmese statesman and secretary-general of the United Nations: b. Pantanaw, Burma, Jan. 22, 1909.

U Thant, secretary-general of the United Nations since 1961, repeatedly stressed the urgency of the military and environmental problems facing the world in 1969. He also continued to play an active role in mediating international conflicts.

Speeches. Secretary-General Thant emphasized the problems of environmental pollution, the explosion of world population, and the growing inequality in living standards between the rich and poor nations. In a speech delivered before the Institute of Man and Science in New York on May 9, he said that, from the information available to him, the members of the United Nations had perhaps 10 years to end their quarrels and begin to work together on these problems. He expressed the fear that the dangers present would grow beyond man's capacity to control if a global partnership were not forged within the next decade.

Reports. Official reports issued in his name in 1969 indicated the magnitude of two of the problems which Secretary-General Thant emphasized. In May he submitted a report on the "Problems of the Human Environment" to the 47th session of the Economic and Social Council. The report provided a basis for planning for the Conference on the Human Environment to be held in 1972. On July 1, the secretary-general released a report to the UN General Assembly on "chemical and bacteriological (biological) weapons and the effects of their possible use." It stressed the need for international action in the control of such weapons.

International Mediation. U Thant repeatedly attempted to simmer down events in the Middle East and tried through agents to mitigate the conflict between Nigeria and Biafra. He provided UN observers to facilitate the final resolution of the West Irian dispute between Indonesia and the Netherlands. He offered to help mediate the soccer war between El Salvador and Honduras, sent a representative to Equatorial Guinea to try to end its dispute with Spain, spoke out against the hanging of alleged spies in Iraq, and attempted to mobilize states to control the hijacking of planes. The secretary-general also made two trips to Europe, two to Africa, and one to Mexico.

Background. U Thant was educated at the University College in Rangoon. He became a teacher of English and modern history and later headmaster of the National School at Pantanaw. With the British grant of independence to Burma in 1948, he became the principal adviser to the first prime minister, U Nu. In 1949, Thant became the head of the ministry of information and broadcasting. He was a member of his country's delegation to the United Nations in 1952–53 and in 1957 became Burma's permanent representative. After the death of UN Secretary-General Dag Hammarskjöld in September 1961, Thant was elected acting secretary-general on Nov. 3, 1961. His selection ended a dispute between the United States and the Soviet Union over the role of the Secretariat. U Thant was confirmed in the post on Nov. 3, 1962 and was reelected for a 5-year term on Dec. 2, 1966.

THOMAS HOVET, JR.
University of Oregon

THEATER

Quality is always scarce on Broadway; in 1969 quantity was as great a problem. Only a dozen new shows opened in the first half of the 1969–70 season, and by November the New York *Times* ran an article inquiring whether Broadway was dead. Some writers, including Paddy Chayefsky and John Osborne, responded with an unequivocal yes.

With the stock market plummeting and interest rates jumping, the Broadway angels grew tightfisted. The few plays that did reach the boards were largely undistinguished or worse. Anyone who had to assess the Broadway season professionally was likely to turn into a Jeremiah, lamenting the wasteland, perhaps overpraising any play with a wriggle of life. It was the most depressing season in recent years.

Broadway Plays. Symptomatic of the poverty of imagination in 1969 is the fact that the longest running play has been comedian Woody Allen's *Play It Again, Sam,* a slight, whimsical fantasy. Allen plays his familiar timid "shnook" trying to convince himself that he is a torrid lover. The twist of this situation comedy is original: Humphrey Bogart, worshiped as the ideal lover, materializes to coach the hero in the subtlest of human arts.

The one play evidencing artistic ambition, Arthur Kopit's *Indians,* reached Broadway after runs in England and at Washington, D. C.'s Arena Stage. It is an epic treatment of the plight of the American Indian, with clear thematic reference to contemporary social turmoil. The play's form alternates between Buffalo Bill's rousing Wild West show and the hearings of a U. S. Commission on Indian Problems. Kopit makes wily use of a folk hero, superbly played by Stacy Keach, to illustrate the damage that can be done by a well-meaning liberalism that shades imperceptibly into exploitation.

A sentimental ending marred the powerful naturalism of Don Peterson's *Does a Tiger Wear a Necktie?* The play, set in a rehabilitation center for hardened youthful narcotics addicts, was notable mainly for Al Pacino's brilliant performance as a hopeless and embittered junkie.

Revivals of representative American plays were among the few highlights of 1969. The brash Hecht-MacArthur vehicle of 45 years ago, *The Front Page,* was offered in the spring. Robert Ryan acted the ruthless editor in this, to speak kindly, dated "classic"; but hit-hungry Broadway was delighted with the nostalgic corn. It was still running at the end of 1969 and had managed to coax Helen Hayes out of her short-lived retirement for a bit part.

At Lincoln Center there was a fine revival of Saroyan's *The Time of Your Life,* wherein the good-of-heart triumph, even if victory involves the killing of the bad-of-heart. But it is one of our theater's fantasies, not to be taken realistically or called to account for its moral message. The Broadway scene was littered with such resuscitated wishfulfillments at the end of 1969. Playing simultaneously were *Our Town, Three Men on a Horse,* and *The Front Page,* with *Harvey* soon to come.

MARTHA SWOPE

1776 portrays the founding fathers composing the Declaration of Independence. William Daniels (*foreground*) is John Adams; Howard da Silva is Ben Franklin.

Foreign imports ranked high among the more interesting efforts. John Osborne's study of homosexuality in military intelligence circles, *A Patriot for Me,* was disappointing, despite its celebrated drag party. The brilliant actor Nicol Williamson, who had achieved stardom in Osborne's *Inadmissible Evidence,* appeared in the title role of *Hamlet.* From Ireland came Brian Friel's *The Mundy Scheme,* a political comedy about an ingenious solu-

681

tion to that country's economic distress. Rejected by the Abbey Theatre, this satire, which proposes that the West of Ireland be turned into an international graveyard, seemed mild enough, too thinly drawn for a full-length play on a single point.

One play set an unenviable record. Comedian Jackie Mason's *A Teaspoon Every Four Hours* ran for an unprecedented 97 previews and then closed after one performance.

Broadway Musicals. Near the close of 1969 two heralded debuts sparked interest in an otherwise tepid season for musicals. Muhammed Ali (Cassius Clay) and Katharine Hepburn were making their first appearances in musicals. Clay opened in *Buck White,* a watered-down version of 1968's off-Broadway success, *Big Time Buck White,* about a controversial and flamboyant heavyweight champion. The off-Broadway work had been a powerful confrontation of racial issues and the original audience participation play. However, it lost its immediacy and outspokenness in an expensive uptown version. Clay sang pleasantly, but the critical consensus declared him the innocent victim of an unfortunate promotional idea. The play ran a week.

Miss Hepburn, on the other hand, added a new dimension to one of the most flexible talents and distinguished careers in show business. As Gabrielle Chanel, the French designer, the Divine Katie assured a long run to the otherwise pallid Alan Jay Lerner-André Previn effort, *Coco.*

As *Coco* opened, there were only two musicals running on Broadway that had opened in 1969: *Jimmy,* a bland show based on the life of Mayor Jimmy Walker; and *1776,* the charming Peter Stone-Sherman Edwards show that deals with the personages who signed the Declaration of Independence.

Hello, Dolly! became the second-longest-run musical in the history of the Broadway theater, replacing *Oklahoma!* in June, behind *My Fair Lady.*

Off-Broadway. The American theater was graced in 1969 by the visit of Jerzy Grotowski's versatile, disciplined, and innovative Polish Laboratory Theater company. The three productions offered from this awesome company's repertory provided the theatrical event of the season. Avant-garde theater in the West has for several years been influenced by Grotowski's work: Peter Brook in England, and the Living Theater, the Performance Group, and the Open Theater in the United States have introduced their variations of Grotowski-inspired techniques.

Grotowski and his actors utilize dance, music, and chant, and spare scenic trappings to an expressive minimum. In *The Constant Prince* of Calderón and Wyspianski's *Akropolis,* they reshape classical works in contemporary terms. Their concern is the human spirit; their art is reflective of a nation that has lived with death and terror, faced oblivion, and survived. Grotowski unites a Catholic existentialism and Marxist politics to create a high theatrical art capable of marshaling a vast range of creative responses from the audience, whose number is not allowed to exceed 100 at each performance.

Black theater continued to burgeon off-Broadway, offering some of today's best plays. The excellent Negro Ensemble Company produced Lonne Elder III's *Ceremonies in Dark Old Men,* a moving and realistic portrait of ghetto life. The loosely autobiographical story details the tribulations of a decent ex-dancer turned barber trying to raise a family and run a shop in Harlem. The play is in the best tradition of American urban realism.

FRIEDMAN-ABELES

KATHARINE HEPBURN, in her first stage musical, *Coco,* brought vibrant gaiety to the role of designer Gabrielle Chanel.

Charles Gordone's *No Place to be Somebody,* presented by the New York Shakespeare Festival Public Theater, is reminiscent of *The Time of Your Life* and O'Neill's *The Iceman Cometh.* Set in a Greenwich Village bar, the episodic play parades a sequence of off-beat characters.

A few other off-Broadway productions may be singled out for merit. Elaine May made her debut as a playwright with the hit satire *Adaptation,* coupled with *Next,* a short play by one of the more interesting younger dramatists, Terence MacNally. Miss May directed both plays. Thomas Murphy's *A Whistle in the Dark,* originally produced in London, recounts the tragic attempt of a young Irishman to escape the effects of the violence of Irish country life.

Nudity had held the center stage of sensationalism in 1968. In 1969 off-Broadway moved into simulated intercourse. Perhaps the most talked-about and financially successful off-Broadway show of the season was the "entertainment with music" *Oh! Calcutta!,* which featured dance, music, nudity,

(Continued on page 685)

BUTTERFLIES ARE FREE, a light comedy, had Keir Dullea as a well-adjusted blind youth and Blythe Danner as his friend.

(Below) REPERTORY PLAYERS from Polish Laboratory Theater portray Auschwitz prisoners in Akropolis. The director, Jerzy Grotowski, is famed for his avant-gardism.

MARTHA SWOPE

DOUGLAS H. JEFFERY

DAMES AT SEA, an off-Broadway production, was a hit musical spoof on the song and dance films of the 1930's.

SAUL RICHMOND

BROADWAY OPENINGS IN 1969

PLAYS

But, Seriously, by Julius J. Epstein; directed by John Allen; with Tom Poston and Bethel Leslie; February 27-March 1.

Butterflies Are Free, by Leonard Gershe; directed by Milton Katselas; with Keir Dullea and Blythe Danner; October 21—.

Cock-A-Doodle Dandy, by Sean O'Casey; directed by Jack O'Brien and Donald Moffat; with Barry Bostwick, Sydney Walker, Donald Moffat, and Ellis Rabb; January 22-April 26 (in repertory).

Cop-Out and **Home Fires,** two comedies by John Guare; directed by Melvin Bernhardt, with Ron Leibman, Linda Lavin, George Bartenieff, and Carrie Nye; April 7-April 13.

Does A Tiger Wear A Necktie?, by Don Petersen; directed by Michael A. Schultz; with Hal Holbrook, and Al Pacino; February 25-March 29.

The Dozens, by Laird Koenig; directed by Edward Parone; with Paula Kelly, Al Freeman, Jr., and Morgan Freeman; March 13-March 15.

Fire!, by John Roc; directed by Charles Werner Moore; with Peter Maclean and Rene Auberjonois; January 28-February 1.

A Flea in Her Ear, by Georges Feydeau; directed by Gower Champion; with Michael O'Sullivan; October 3-October 25 (in repertory).

The Front Page, by Ben Hecht and Charles MacArthur; directed by Harold J. Kennedy; with Peggy Cass, Robert Ryan, and Bert Convy; May 10-July 5; October 18—.

The Gingham Dog, by Lanford Wilson; directed by Alan Schneider, with Diana Sands and George Grizzard; April 23-April 26.

Hadrian VII, by Peter Luke; directed by Peter Dews; with Alec McCowen; January 8-November 15.

Hamlet, by William Shakespeare; directed by Ellis Rabb; with Ellis Rabb; March 3-April 26 (in repertory).

Hamlet, by William Shakespeare; directed by Tony Richardson; with Nicol Williamson; May 1-June 14.

Henry V, by William Shakespeare; directed by Michael Kahn; with Len Cariou; November 10-November 22.

In the Matter of J. Robert Oppenheimer, by Heinar Kipphardt; directed by Gordon Davidson; with Joseph Wiseman; March 6-September 27.

Indians, by Arthur Kopit; directed by Gene Frankel; with Stacy Keach; October 13—.

Last of the Red Hot Lovers, by Neil Simon; directed by Robert Moore; with James Coco; December 28—.

Love Is A Time of Day, by John Patrick; directed by Bernard Thomas; with Sandy Duncan and John Ligon; December 22-27.

The Miser, by Moliere; directed by Carl Weber; with Robert Symonds; May 8-June 21.

The Mother Lover, by Jerome Weidman; directed by Larry Blyden; with Eileen Heckart, Larry Blyden, and Valerie French; February 1 (1 performance).

The Mundy Scheme, by Brian Friel; directed by Donal Donelly; with Godfrey Quigley, Jack Cassidy, Patrick Bedford, and Dorothy Stickney; December 11.

My Daughter, Your Son, by Phoebe and Henry Ephron; directed by Larry Arrick; with Robert Alda, Lee Lawson, and Vivian Vance; May 13-June 21.

Our Town, by Thornton Wilder; directed by Donald Driver; with Henry Fonda; November 27-December 27.

A Patriot For Me, by John Osborne; directed by Peter Glenville; with Maximillian Schell; October 5-November 15.

The Penny Wars, by Elliot Baker; directed by Barbara Harris; with Kim Hunter; October 15-October 18.

Play It Again, Sam, by Woody Allen; directed by Joseph Hardy; with Woody Allen; February 12—.

Private Lives, by Noel Coward; with Brian Bedford and Tammy Grimes; directed by Stephen Porter; December 14—.

A Teaspoon Every Four Hours, by Jackie Mason and Mike Mortman; directed by Roger Girard; with Jackie Mason; June 14 (1 performance).

Three Men On A Horse, by John Cecil Holm and George Abbott; directed by George Abbott; with Jack Gilford and Sam Levene; October 16—.

Three Sisters, by Anton Chekov; directed by Eugene Barcone; with Angela Paton, Michael Learned, and Kitty Winn; October 9-October 25.

The Time of Your Life, by William Saroyan; directed by John Hirsch; with James Broderick; November 6—.

Tiny Alice, by Edward Albee; directed by William Ball; with Paul Shenar; September 29-October 25.

Trumpets of the Lord, adapted by Vinnette Carroll from J. W. Johnson's *God's Trombones;* directed by Theodore Mann; with Cicely Tyson, Bernard Ward, and Lex Monson; April 29-May 3.

The Watering Place, by Lyle Kessler; directed by Alan Schneider; with Shirley Knight; March 12 (1 performance).

The Wrong Way Light Bulb, by Leonard Spigelgass; directed by Stephen Porter; with James Patterson and Claudia McNeil; March 4-March 8.

Zelda, by Sylvia Regan; directed by Delbert Mann; with Ed Begley; March 5-March 8.

MUSICALS

Angela, by Sumner Arthur Long; directed by Jack Ragotzy; with Geraldine Page; October 30-November 1.

Billy, book by Stephen Glassman; music and lyrics by Ron Dante and Gene Allen; directed by Arthur A. Seidelman; with Robert Salvio; March 22.

Buck White, book, music, and lyrics by Oscar Brown, Jr.; directed by Oscar Brown, Jr. and Jean Pace; with Muhammed Ali (Cassius Clay); December 2-6.

Canterbury Tales, book by Martin Starkie and Nevill Coghill; music by Richard Hill and John Hawkins; lyrics by Nevill Coghill; directed by Martin Starkie; with George Rose, Hermione Baddeley, and Martyn Green; February 3-May 18.

Celebration, words by Tom Jones; music by Harvey Schmidt; directed by Tom Jones; with Keith Charles, Susan Watson, and Ted Thurston; January 22-April 26.

Coco, book and lyrics by Alan Jay Lerner; music by André Previn; directed by Michael Benthall; with Katharine Hepburn; December 18—.

Come Summer, book and lyrics by Will Holt; music by David Baker; directed by Agnes DeMille; with Ray Bolger; March 18-March 22.

Dear World, book by Jerome Lawrence and Robert E. Lee; music and lyrics by Jerry Herman; directed by Joe Layton; with Angela Lansbury; February 6-May 31.

The Fig Leaves Are Falling, book and lyrics by Allan Sherman; music by Albert Hague; directed by George Abbott; with Barry Nelson and Dorothy Loudon; January 2-January 4.

Jimmy, book by Melville Shavelson; music and lyrics by Bill and Patti Jacob; directed by Josephy Anthony; with Frank Gorshin; October 23—.

La Strada, book by Charles K. Peck; music and lyrics by Lionel Bart; directed by Alan Schneider; with Bernadette Peters and Stephen Pearlman; December 14.

Oklahoma! (revival), music by Richard Rodgers; lyrics by Oscar Hammerstein II; directed by John Kennedy; with Margaret Hamilton; Bruce Yarnell; and Lee Beery; June 23-September 6.

Red, White and Maddox, by Don Tucker and Jay Broad; directed by Jay Broad and Don Tucker; with Jay Garner; January 26-March 2.

1776, book by Peter Stone; music and lyrics by Sherman Edwards; directed by Peter Hunt; with Howard da Silva and William Daniels; March 16—.

JULIE HARRIS won a Tony award as the best dramatic actress of the 1968–69 Broadway season for her performance in the comedy, *Forty Carats.* The work was adapted by Jay Allen from a play by Pierre Barillet and Jean–Pierre Gredy. Miss Harris was born in Grosse Pointe, Mich., on Dec. 2, 1925. She studied in New York and at the Yale Drama School and made her Broadway debut in *It's a Gift* in 1945. She became famous in 1950 as the tomboy in *The Member of the Wedding.* Her performance in *I Am a Camera* earned her the 1952 Drama Critics Circle award as best actress, and in 1956 she won a Tony for her portrayal of Joan of Arc in *The Lark.* Other Broadway plays in which she has appeared are *Montserrat* (1949) and *Mlle. Colombe* (1954). From 1952 she acted in films, including *The Member of the Wedding* (1952), *East of Eden* (1955), and *I Am a Camera* (1955). She has also acted on television, and in 1962 won an Emmy award for her interpretation of the title role in *Victoria Regina.*

(Continued from page 682)

obscenity, and simulated sexual activity. Devised by Kenneth Tynan, the show consists of a series of skits by such authors as Samuel Beckett and John Lennon. Other less successful shows that followed the current vogue for nudity, obscenity, and simulated sex were *Che!,* a tedious piece about late mastermind of the Cuban revolution, and a trifling concoction called *DeSade Illustrated.* The chief claim to fame of *Che!* was that its entire cast and production personnel were arrested after opening night.

The nudity situation, however, seemed so threatening that in May, Actors' Equity Association formed a corpus of rules to protect its members. The rules include a guarantee of bail, payment of fines, and legal counsel in case of arrest.

Outside New York. The overall achievement of regional theater in 1969 was not as groundbreaking as in recent years. A few established companies, notably Washington, D. C.'s, eminent Arena Stage, continued to foster new plays, the best of which were snatched up by desperate Broadway. In 1968, *The Great White Hope* went from the Arena to Broadway with great acclaim. In 1969, Kopit's *Indians* made the journey; it was one of the few meritorious new plays. Elsewhere, the rule was mostly the standard fare of revivals of proven classics, French bedroom farces, and rehashed Broadway hits. For example, the Alliance Resident Theater premiered in Atlanta and included *You Can't Take It With You* as a typical offering on its maiden program. Another case in point is the American Conservatory Theater of San Francisco, perpetually on the brink of financial disaster and always dramatically rescued by the Ford Foundation and civic contributions. Of high artistic quality, the troupe presents many first-rate productions of the same tired summer stock repertory, but new plays are rare.

Broadway is fallow, and decentralization is urgently needed, yet our most lavishly supported regional theaters are not finding or nurturing new playwrights. A few years ago regional theater companies like the Minnesota Firehouse were discovering young dramatists such as Megan Terry, and joining them in a forceful artistic collaboration; but this vibrancy now seems to be dying. Perhaps campus rebellion and virulent antiwar protest were prime sources in creating a climate favorable to a momentary resurgence of aliveness in regional theater. The dubious aesthetic durability of much of the youthful and politically motivated theater in recent years seemed beside the point next to a new excitement in the theatrical enterprise. For all too brief a spell there was a sense of true union between our theater and our national life.

The general picture outside New York is not all bleak, however. The Cleveland Play House risked atypical material with Heinar Kipphardt's *In the Matter of J. Robert Oppenheimer,* which was running concurrently in New York. More explosive, although artistically inferior, was Donald Freed's *The U. S. vs. Julius and Ethel Rosenberg.* Both plays recalled a period of political repressiveness, with the nostalgic dominating current applicability.

Among university theaters, Yale still reigns supreme. It seems at times that any kind of controversy, even the arrest of naked actors for indecent exposure, is a measure of value in our theater. Yale was spared that kind of value and publicity in 1969, after the visit of the rambunctious Living Theater in 1968. But internal squabbles were plentiful. The student editor of *Yale Theater* resigned, charging "psychological censorship." A group of black students forced the second consecutive cancellation of a play, claiming that Sam Sheppard's *Operation Sidewinder* was racist.

International Theater. While *Hair* was rocking to full houses in Tokyo and Belgrade, the Royal Shakespeare Company in England was using sensitive rock scores in superb productions of Shakespeare's *Pericles* and *The Winter's Tale.* The brilliance of

JAMES EARL JONES received a Tony award as the best dramatic actor of the 1968–69 Broadway season for his performance in Howard Sackler's play, *The Great White Hope,* based on the career of the Negro heavyweight boxing champion Jack Johnson. Jones is also scheduled to star in the forthcoming motion picture version of the play. He was born in Arkabutla, Miss., on Jan. 17, 1931. Jones graduated from the University of Michigan, where he had studied drama, in 1953. In 1957 he received a diploma from the American Theatre Wing. He obtained his first major part in the off-Broadway production of Genet's *The Blacks* (1961). In 1962 he won the Obie award of the *Village Voice* for his work in such off-Broadway plays as *Moon on a Rainbow Shawl.* He has appeared with the New York Shakespeare Festival in the title roles of *Othello* and *Macbeth* and in 1967 toured Europe in O'Neill's *Emperor Jones.* In 1965 he received an Emmy award for his part in the CBS-TV documentary *Beyond the Blues.*

MICHAEL CHILDERS, FROM CAMERA 5

OH! CALCUTTA! is a pastiche of sketches by noted authors. This dance is one of the acts played in the nude.

the Stratford season was typical of the strength of English theater in 1969, as imaginative revivals overshadowed new work. At the Chichester Festival, Margaret Leighton created a memorable Cleopatra in *Antony and Cleopatra,* and Maggie Smith performed outstandingly in the title role of Wycherly's *The Country Wife.* The National Theater offered the most sophisticated of all English comedies, Congreve's *The Way of the World,* as well as that monster "metaphysical Pentateuch," Bernard Shaw's *Back to Methusaleh,* in two parts. This company came as close as possible to making viable theater of this perhaps ultimately unstageable play.

Tony Richardson opened the Free Theater in London with an electric portrayal of Hamlet by Nicol Williamson, widely regarded as the finest actor in England under the age of 40. Among new plays the most interesting were *Landscape* and *Silence,* a double bill, the latest works of Harold Pinter.

Awards. Howard Sackler's *The Great White Hope* was the fifth play to win Broadway's triple crown: the Antoinette Perry (Tony) and New York Drama Critics Circle awards and the Pulitzer Prize for best play of the season. Other Tonies went to: James Earl Jones, best actor (*The Great White Hope*); Julie Harris, best actress (*Forty Carats*); Peter Dews, best director (*Hadrian VII*); for musicals: Angela Lansbury, best actress (*Dear World*); Jerry Ohrbach, best actor (*Promises, Promises*); Peter Hunt, best director (*1776*); and *1776,* best musical and also the Drama Critics Circle choice.

The coveted Clarence Derwent Acting Awards for nonfeatured performers were extended for the first time to include off-Broadway as well as Broadway plays. Winners were Marlene Warfield (*The Great White Hope*) and Ron O'Neal (*No Place to Be Somebody*).

The Drama Desk group reversed the procedure of the Derwent awards and extended its nominees, originally chosen exclusively from off-Broadway plays, to include Broadway and repertory. James Earl Jones again captured top honors for a male actor; Linda Lavin (*Little Murders*) was named best actress; Peter Stone (*1776*) was again awarded a prize for the best musical book.

HAROLD FERRAR
Columbia University

TITO, Josip. See YUGOSLAVIA.

TOBACCO

World production of tobacco totaled 9,893,515,-000 pounds in 1969, a decrease of 52,147,000 pounds over the preceding year. Production increased in North and South America, and especially in Oceania, but declined in Europe, Asia, and Africa.

North and South America. Production in North America totaled 2,337,383,000 pounds, an increase of 7% from a year earlier. Large crops in the United States and Canada, and a record crop in Mexico, accounted for the increase. South American production totaled 708,308,000 pounds, an increase of 8%.

Around 570 billion cigarettes were produced in the United States in 1969, a decline of nearly 2% from the record production of 1968. Per capita consumption of cigarettes declined for the third straight year. Production of cigars and cigarillos totaled 6 billion.

Europe. Tobacco production in Europe declined to 1,211,928,000 pounds in 1969. The smaller crop was attributed to reduced yields and acreage in France and Italy, and poor weather in Eastern Europe.

Africa and Asia. African production totaled 426,394,000 pounds, a drop of less than 1% from 1968. Increases in Rhodesia and Angola were offset

TOBACCO PRODUCTION IN MAJOR COUNTRIES
(In pounds)

	Average 1960–64	1968	1969
United States	2,178,400,000	1,712,299,000	1,799,447,000
India	736,399,000	812,836,000	765,437,000
USSR	368,206,000	562,200,000	570,000,000
Brazil	336,211,000	334,793,000	409,202,000
Pakistan	212,912,000	410,000,000	400,000,000
Japan	333,382,000	426,365,000	389,328,000
Turkey	278,771,000	356,325,000	321,100,000
Canada	196,295,000	218,807,000	237,340,000
Indonesia	159,569,000	231,500,000	220,500,000
Greece	218,741,000	194,368,000	178,919,000
South Korea	76,291,000	153,654,000	176,368,000
Philippines	152,708,000	194,159,000	171,606,000
Italy	125,595,000	163,425,000	167,285,000
Rhodesia	226,233,000	132,180,000	137,300,000
Mexico	96,364,000	101,412,000	136,906,000
France	92,090,000	117,018,000	110,230,000
Argentina	106,262,000	135,834,000	107,454,000
Colombia	76,950,000	91,490,000	96,980,000
World total	8,902,925,000	9,945,662,000	9,893,515,000

by declines in Nigeria, Malawi, and Zambia. Tobacco production declined in most of the Asian countries by a drop of 4% from 1968 and 1967, giving a total of 4,599,022,000 pounds.

NICHOLAS KOMINUS
Kominus Afri-Info Associates

TOBAGO. See TRINIDAD AND TOBAGO.

TOGO

The government of Togo vacillated during 1969 between restoration of civilian rule and continued army control. By the end of the year Brigadier Étienne Eyadema had made clear his intention of remaining as president for an extended period. In December, Togo was faced with thousands of refugees when a deportation of aliens without work permits began in Ghana.

Politics. On January 13, two years after his seizure of power, Eyadema announced that banned political activities could resume. The decision was reversed four days later, purportedly because of strong resistance in the north. In September Eyadema proposed the formation of a single political party "uniting all the sons of Togo in a vast regrouping." A meeting of 200 chiefs and traditional rulers unanimously supported his suggestion.

Regional tensions remained strong. A 20-member commission of civil servants was established to resolve north-south antagonisms in March. Former political leader Nicholas Grunitzky, who had served as president in 1963–67 and as prime minister in 1956–58, died in Paris in September.

Economic Development. The 1969 budget, 7% above that for 1968, set aside $1.6 million for capital investment and $21.6 million for regular government expenses. The 5-year plan was reviewed, with experts calling for better coordination of rural planning, the creation of a government transport service, the drafting of a commercial code, increased Africanization in private business, and the construction of a new fishing port. Investments under the plan topped $5.4 million, including $1.9 million for oil palm development and $1.7 million for a phosphate factory. Phosphate production rose 20% to 1.4 million tons.

International Relations. Togo and Upper Volta jointly established an economic commission. To show its close ties with the other countries of the Council of the Entente (Dahomey, Ivory Coast, Niger, and Upper Volta), Togo started construction of a $1 million "Entente Village" in Lomé. Major economic assistance continued to come from France, including $785,000 for a hospital at Atakpamé and $375,000 for airport and telecommunications improvement. Import controls were imposed on Japanese textiles to protect a Togolese factory operating at only 30% of capacity.

CLAUDE E. WELCH, JR.
State University of New York at Buffalo

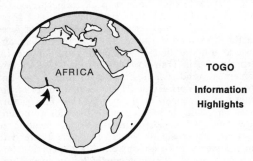

TOGO

Information Highlights

Area: 21,853 square miles (56,000 sq km).
Population: 1,772,000 (1968 est.).
Chief Cities (1968 est.): Lomé, the capital, 126,000.
Government: *President*—Brigadier Étienne Eyadema (took office April 14, 1967).
Religious Faiths: Animists, 70% of population; Roman Catholics, 17%; Muslims, 5%; others, 8%.
Education: *Literacy rate* (1969), 10% of population. *Total school enrollment* (1966)—172,942 (primary, 157,548; secondary, 13,949; teacher-training, 57; technical/vocational, 1,303; university/higher, 85).
Finance (1968 est.): *Revenues*, $23,873,200; *expenditures*, $25,084,400; *monetary unit*, CFA franc (246.85 francs equal U. S.$1).
Gross National Product (1967): $205,000,000.
Average Annual Income per Person (1967): $119.
Crops (metric tons, 1967–68 crop year): Sweet potatoes and yams, 1,149,000; cassava, 1,118,000.
Minerals (metric tons, 1967): Phosphate rock, 1,139,000.
Foreign Trade (1968): *Exports*, $39,000,000 (chief exports, 1967: phosphates, $12,340,000; cacao, $9,560,000); *imports*, $47,000,000 (chief imports, 1966: woven cotton, $8,351,000; nonelectrical machinery, $4,842,000). *Chief trading partners* (1967): France (took 38% of exports, supplied 29% of imports); West Germany (took 11% of exports, supplied 11% of imports); Japan (took 4% of exports, supplied 13% of imports).
Transportation: *Roads* (1968), 2,933 miles (4,720 km); *motor vehicles* (1967), 8,800 (automobiles 4,800); *railways* (1966), 305 miles (326 km); *principal airport*, Lomé.
Communications: *Telephones* (1968): 2,768; *radios* (1967), 31,000; *newspapers* (1967), 2.

TORONTO

Situated on Lake Ontario, Toronto is the capital of Ontario and Canada's second-largest city (1969 est. pop., city, 689,304; metropolitan area, 1,947,207). Major events in 1969 were the entrance of political parties in the traditionally nonpartisan municipal election, new development projects, and the opposition of the Ontario government to the expansion of metropolitan Toronto's 720-square-mile (1,815-sq km) area.

Politics. William R. Allen, Metropolitan Council chairman since 1961, retired in September and the Council elected Scarboro Mayor Albert M. Campbell to succeed him. In the December 1 municipal election, Mayor William Dennison was given a second term, and the entrance of political parties into formerly nonpartisan municipal politics resulted in the election of 3 New Democrats, 1 Liberal, and 5 members of the local CIVAC (Civic Action) party. In the Council, reformers captured 3 of the 4 seats on the new executive committee. Toronto city voters approved, by a 5–to–1 majority, total amalgamation of the 5 boroughs with the city. They also approved a municipal sweepstakes.

Development. In January the Canadian National-Canadian Pacific Railways announced plans for a 190-acre (77-hectare), billion dollar complex, the Metro Centre. Robert Campeau projected a $250 million waterfront development. Manufacturers Life Association announced the 51-story, $48-million Bay-Bloor Centre.

Education. Toronto's first French-language high school, Étienne Brûlé, opened in September. Rochdale College, a student-operated, nonstructured educational center, collapsed after 14 months because the residents would not pay their rent. Scandals broke out over several trustees' attending a music conference in Hawaii, and a $74,000 retirement party for the director of education of North York.

The $30 million Ontario Science Center opened in September in Toronto. The Center features hundreds of "participational" exhibits that are operated by push buttons.

Recreation. The Ontario government unveiled its design for the $13 million Ontario Showcase. This is a pavilion that will be built on stilts in Lake Ontario at the Canadian National Exposition. J. Grant Glassco bequeathed 480 acres (194 hectares) near Kleinberg for a new metropolitan park, and plans proceeded for the 1,250-acre (506-hectare) Rouge River Zoo.

Transportation. The federal government promised a $69 million expansion of the Malton Airport and a second airport for the city, while Ontario established noise zones for development in an 80 square-mile (207 sq km) area around the present airport. Metro Council approved a second extension of the Yonge Street subway to Finch Avenue. The construction of the controversial Spadina expressway ran into increasing opposition.

Government. A number of changes in city government occurred in 1969. These included the abolition of the city Board of Control in favor of a 4-man executive committee elected by the Metropolitan Council, and an increase in the number of wards from 9 to 11. On orders from the Ontario Municipal Board, the new wards are arranged in blocks instead of the traditional strips.

FREDERICK H. ARMSTRONG
University of Western Ontario

TOURISM

In a year that saw a Republican succeed a Democrat as president, it was not surprising that one of the new chief executive's first acts after inauguration was to stay implementation of his predecessor's allocation of hotly contested new air routes in the Pacific. Then President Nixon let it be known that he would not ask Congress to levy a tax on overseas tourism, as the Johnson administration had recommended. Nixon made his own route awards, plus several other major air-travel decisions.

Air travel made the big news in 1969. The first jumbo jet was delivered to an airline, supersonic transports began flight testing, and air fares on the lucrative transatlantic routes were thrown into a chaotic jumble. Hijackings reached a new record, and the world was treated to the strangest air race yet.

While the airlines were carrying record numbers of tourists, cruising also expanded. North Atlantic passenger-ship business continued to decline; hence steamship lines vied for rich new territories in the Caribbean and Pacific.

Devaluation of the franc, and the defeat at the polls of President Charles de Gaulle, helped France in 1969 to regain its position as the chief destination for U. S. travelers. But perhaps that would not matter as much as it once had—a survey showed that while Americans undoubtedly traveled most, they were no longer the biggest spenders. Little Denmark and the citizens of eight other nations all spent more per capita on foreign travel.

Certainly there was a great deal of traveling in 1969. The year 1968 had recorded the first drop in U. S. travel expenditures in more than 20 years, with a resultant sizable decrease in the travel balance-of-payments deficit. But in 1969 Americans returned to their old pattern. In December, U. S. travel officials were forecasting a 12% increase in American travel abroad in 1969 and a moderate rise in the payments-balance deficit.

Air Travel. Newspapers dated Jan. 1, 1969, carried the important news: the USSR had made the first flight of a supersonic transport, its Tu-144, beating the British and French. The latter were not far behind with their joint venture, the Concorde, 10 miles per hour slower at 1,400 miles (3,250 km) per hour than the Soviet plane, but capable of carrying 132 passengers—12 more than the Tu-144. On March 2, the sleek Concorde gracefully lifted off a Toulouse runway. The French testing program continued at such speed that observers said the Concorde had overtaken the Tu-144 in development late in the year and would be delivered to airlines in 1973 or 1974.

Meanwhile, after many months of indecision spanning two administrations, President Nixon on September 23 told the Boeing Company to build an SST designed to travel at 1,800 miles (2,900 km) per hour and carry 300 passengers. The American SST, however, was not planned for commercial service until 1976–78.

The United States was ahead, meanwhile, with another new passenger aircraft, the jumbo jet. Late in 1969, Pan American accepted delivery of the first Boeing 747. The jet is so big that it has 10 doors and carries 14 stewardesses to tend its 362 passengers. The first passenger flight was made in January 1970.

One of President Nixon's early acts after taking office was to suspend the route awards made by President Johnson late in his term. After a good bit of political maneuvering over these airline plums, Nixon made his own awards. Chief among the casualties were Continental Airlines, to which the Johnson Administration had awarded a new California–South Pacific route. Instead, American Airlines got Nixon's nod. Other major route awards in 1969 included new nonstop and one-stop routes to Hawaii given to several lines, a Miami-London nonstop route awarded to National, and several southern transcontinental routes to Northeast, Eastern, and Delta.

Air travel also experienced major problems in 1969. One, the stack-up of flights over major airports at busy periods of the day, had been nagging since 1968, when flight controllers had staged a slowdown to dramatize the problem. On March 27, agreement was finally reached among 60 airlines to shift flights and reduce the loads at peak hours. The number of flights per hour was curtailed at five big airports serving New York City, Washington, and Chicago. At New York's Kennedy Airport, for instance, a maximum of 70 airline take-offs and landings per hour was set, except between 5 and 8 P. M., when 80 per hour were allowed. This compared with 130 to 135 per hour in peak traffic periods of 1968, when delays reached six hours.

Increasingly annoyed by the multiplicity of fares on the transatlantic routes, Alitalia, the Italian airline, announced that it was pulling out of the International Air Transport Association (IATA) fare agreements and would set its own rates. The line cut the New York-Rome 21-day excursion fare from $409 to $299, throwing the transatlantic fare picture into confusion. In an attempt to forestall a budding rate war, IATA called an emergency meeting in Caracas, Venezuela, at which 43 airlines agreed to cut the New York-London round-trip excursion fare to a record low $250 in winter, $265 in spring, and $295 in summer. Group minimums went as low as $170 in winter. As the year ended, the question remained whether a rate war really had been stopped, or merely blunted.

A third problem, hijacking, acquired greater urgency in 1969 and still defied solution. By mid-December, the number of hijackings averaged well over one a week for the year, despite a $25,000 reward offered by the airline industry for information leading to the conviction of anyone hijacking a U. S. airliner. A record distance was set when a Marine named Raphael Minichiello escaped on the way to his court-martial for robbery. He hijacked a TWA jet in California and took it on an 18-hour, 6,900-mile (11,100-km), 5-stop journey to Rome.

The year also saw what may have been the strangest air race in history. For a week in May, the world was treated to the spectacle of almost 400 contestants seeking $144,000 in prizes for the fastest trip from the top of the Post Office Tower, London's tallest structure, to the top of the Empire State

EXPENDITURES OF U. S. TOURISTS ABROAD

Area	1966	1967	1968
Canada	$ 678,000,000	$1,070,000,000	$ 829,000,000
Mexico	575,000,000	590,000,000	620,000,000
Europe and Mediterranean	920,000,000	1,018,000,000	955,000,000
West Indies and Central America	259,000,000	295,000,000	325,000,000
South America	65,000,000	70,000,000	87,000,000
Other	160,000,000	152,000,000	267,000,000
Total	$2,657,000,000	$3,195,000,000	$3,083,000,000

Source: 1969 Statistical Abstract of the United States

GIANT 747 dwarfs its sister ship, the Boeing 707. The 747's first commercial flight on Jan. 22, 1970, took 332 passengers from New York to London.

Building in New York City. Among the contestants was a chimpanzee named Tina who had to ride as baggage in a jetliner, a prince who tore his trousers while hurrying to a helicopter, and several Americans, two of whom crashed without injury. The winner was British Navy Lt. Cmdr. Peter Goddard, who made it in 5 hours, 11 minutes, 22 seconds. (See also AIR TRANSPORTATION.)

Passenger Ships. The warm waters of the Caribbean began to look more and more inviting to passenger lines. The *Queen Elizabeth 2* made her delayed maiden voyage and went mostly into transatlantic service, but other new ships were being built mainly for cruising in tropical and subtropical waters. The airlines also set up new air-sea vacation packages. Eastern Airlines alone went from one air-sea package in 1968 to 125 in 1969.

With the passenger ship becoming more a floating resort and less a means of transportation, Miami and Port Everglades in Florida were becoming important in the cruise picture. Miami, in fact, topped New York City for the first time in cruise passengers in the fiscal year 1969, but it still lagged substantially behind in berth-days. The trend to modernity was not confined to ships; Miami completed a luxurious, radically modern cruise terminal.

Railroads. Passenger train service was further reduced. In mid–1968 there had been 590 regular intercity passenger trains in service; by late 1969 there were fewer than 500. Among the casualties were the famed California Zephyr between Denver and Salt Lake City, and the Hummingbird between Cincinnati and New Orleans.

One bright spot stood out, however. In the first major advance in railroading in years, a brand new train—the Metroliner—began high-speed service between Washington, D. C., and New York City. An instant success, it made the 226-mile run in 179 minutes, cutting more than a half hour from the previous schedule. (See also RAILROADS.)

Visas for Red China. After an adverse court decision, the U. S. State Department announced it was easing trade and travel restrictions with Communist China, lifting the ban on travel for U. S. scholars, students, scientists, physicians, and newsmen. China treated the U. S. announcement coolly,

and entry permits remained difficult to obtain. U. S. travelers were given permission to bring home up to $100 worth of goods made in Communist China.

Travel Spending. A survey by the International Union of Official Travel Organizations, in Geneva, found that while the United States was by far the biggest spender on foreign travel (see table), its citizens ranked only 10th in per capita foreign spending ($16.20). Denmark ranked first at $46.90, followed by Switzerland, Belgium and Luxembourg, Sweden, Canada, the Netherlands, Austria, West Germany, and France. In total expenditures, the United States spent twice as much as its nearest rival, West Germany ($1.53 billion). Next came France, the United Kingdom, Canada, the Netherlands, Belgium and Luxembourg, Italy, Sweden, and Switzerland.

Airport Tax. Late in 1969 the New Jersey Legislature passed, over Gov. Richard J. Hughes' veto, a tax on all passengers departing by airplane or helicopter from Newark Airport. The 16 airlines using Newark refused to collect it and in December 1969 obtained a temporary injunction against the tax, charging that it infringed the citizen's right to travel freely. The travel industry was expected to put up a strong fight against all such travel taxes at a hearing in early 1970.

United States Travel Service (USTS). President Nixon's appointee as director of the USTS, C. Langhorne Washburne outlined an aggressive program to encourage travel within the United States in an address to the Society of American Travel Writers in Las Vegas in October. Salient points included: increased international advertising tailored to individual countries and stressing activities at U. S. destinations; traveling trailer vans abroad showing U. S. travel displays; host centers in U. S. liners at foreign ports; recruiting of multilingual receptionists at ports of entry; offices in Europe to bring European conventions and businessmen to America; a bureau for easy rental of campers by foreigners; an "Amerailpass" for discounts on railroads; and use of Pullman cars as low-cost hotel space at the Grand Canyon, on Indian reserves, and at Cape Kennedy.

JAY CLARKE
The Miami "Herald"

EL CONQUISTADOR, a luxury hotel in Puerto Rico, opened in 1969. Ocean-fronted guest rooms (*foreground*) have private terraces overlooking Olympic-sized pool.

HOTELS AND MOTELS

Chains of hotels and motels, operating both in the United States and in other countries, continued to account for much of the growth in the lodging industry in 1969. A study at midyear showed that 172 U. S. chains had 4,563 hotels and motels with 687,532 rooms. These totals represented an increase of 177 properties and 26,846 rooms over the figures of the previous year. During the same period, 57 hotels with a total of 10,185 rooms were completed outside the United States by U. S. systems. The chief new development in the U. S. lodging industry was the computerization of reservation systems, making it possible for prospective guests to get immediately confirmed bookings at chain or independent hotels or motels by calling toll-free telephone numbers.

New Hotels. The title of largest hotel in the world passed from the 2,500-room Conrad Hilton in Chicago to the finally completed 6,000-guest Hotel Russia in Moscow. Other large hotels completed outside the United States in 1969 were the newly enlarged 850-room Maria Isabel-Sheraton in Mexico City; the 440-room Acapulco Marriott in Mexico; the 422-room Caracas Hilton in Venezuela; the 280-room Camino Real in Puerto Vallarta, Mexico; the 276-room Nairobi Hilton in Kenya; the 268-room Marbella Hilton in Spain; the 251-room Mainz Hilton in Germany; the 250-room Addis Ababa Hilton in Ethiopia; the 235-room Kuwait Hilton in Kuwait; and the 142-room Camino Real-Guatemala in Guatemala City.

For both of America's largest hotel chains, the word seemed to be "Go south!" Both Sheraton and Hilton, eyeing the sleeping giant of tourism, South America, announced plans for building large hotels in Buenos Aires. Both were also planning to build, or negotiating to buy, other hotels in South America.

The largest new U. S. hotel was the International in Las Vegas, whose 1,519 rooms, 8½-acre swim-tennis-lounge roof, legitimate theater, 2,000-seat showroom, golf course, casino, and five restaurants are said to have cost financier Kirk Kerkorian $60 million. Publicity blanketed the country for both the opening of the International on July 2 and the opening on July 1 of the Landmark, across the street from it. The Landmark's claim to fame is a 31-story mushroom-shaped tower with a large casino on the 30th floor. Howard Hughes is the owner.

Other large new hotels in the United States were the $20 million, 715-room Washington Plaza in Seattle; the $15 million, 500-room Sheraton-Universal in North Hollywood, Calif.; the 500-room Royal Sonesta in New Orleans; the $10 million, 450-room Surfrider in Honolulu; and the 430-room Boston Marriott.

New Motels. Holiday Inns of America opened 127 inns with 20,259 rooms in 1969. The largest was the $12 million, 499-room Holiday Inn-Philadelphia City Line in Philadelphia. Other new motels included 34 Howard Johnson's Motor Lodges with a total of 2,500 rooms, 24 Sheraton Inns with 3,509 rooms, and 3 Hilton Inns with 381 rooms.

Inkeeping Statistics. Total sales for the 65,500 U. S. hotels and motels rose to $6.35 billion in 1969, up from $5.9 billion in 1968. Average occupancy in 1969 was 65%, up from 63% in 1968.

ALBERT E. KUDRLE
American Hotel & Motel Association

TRADE. See INTERNATIONAL TRADE.

TRANSPORTATION

Dramatic new vehicles such as the Boeing 747 superjet and the icebreaker-tanker S. S. *Manhattan* won the major attention of the public in 1969, but meanwhile government and various segments of the transportation industry were taking steps toward future programs. President Nixon's administration proposed vast new undertakings in metropolitan mass transit and in airport building. The costs of carrying passengers and freight rose rapidly, and all major modes of transportation in the United States increased rates in 1969 to pay for existing services.

Mass Transit Proposal. Pointing out that 25% of the people of the United States lack access to a car and need public transportation, President Nixon recommended to Congress on Aug. 8, 1969, that the federal government spend $10 billion in 12 years to help cities with a mass transit program. Federal expenditures of $9.5 billion for capital investment and $500 million for research and development would cover two thirds of the cost, and local governments would pay for the rest. The President recommended general revenue financing, which requires annual appropriations by Congress. Some congressmen, however, favor a trust fund supported by automobile excise levies.

Federal Transportation Aid. Proposals for federal financial aid for aviation facilities, highways, and waterways were offered during 1969.

Aviation. Air congestion became so severe that the Federal Aviation Agency imposed restrictions on the number of flight operations per hour at airports in New York, Chicago, and Washington. The FAA estimated that 900 new airports would be needed by 1980. To pay for these airports and related airway control facilities, President Nixon proposed a comprehensive program including federal aid, matching local aid, and increased user charges. Tax increases proposed included a domestic ticket tax of 8% rather than the present 5%, a new flat-rate tax of $3 on international passenger tickets, a new 5% levy on air-freight waybills, and a new 9 cents per gallon tax on all fuel used by general aviation. The user taxes would provide about $569 million during the fiscal year 1970, compared with the $295 million that would be generated under the present tax structure. Over a 10-year period the taxes would generate about $9.1 billion.

Highways. To promote equitable distribution of construction costs and to maintain the existing level of highway construction, the administration proposed that diesel fuel taxes paid by motor carriers be increased 2 cents per gallon and that vehicles over 26,000 pounds pay a graduated weight tax from $3.50 to $9.50 per 100 pounds rather than a flat fee of $3.

Waterways. Expenditures of $280 million for waterways in fiscal 1969 were made entirely by the federal government. But the administration proposed that barge lines pay a tax of 2 cents per gallon on all fuel, including diesel fuel. The tax, estimated to yield revenues of only $7 million annually, would not be a full-cost user charge but would only establish a precedent. The U. S. Army Corps of Engineers was conducting a study of other possible waterway user charges.

Higher Fares. All modes of transportation applied for rate increases in 1969. In April the intercity bus operators were allowed to increase fares up to 10%.

The railroads asked to be granted an emergency rate increase of 6% in October without the normal 30-day notification. Even though the rails would lose $11.5 million a week, the Interstate Commerce Commission insisted on the normal procedures.

The airlines received an emergency increase of 3.8% in February and a second increase of 6.35% in October, after a detailed investigation. The fare increases were structured to recognize the higher costs of operation in congested terminal areas.

AIR TRAFFIC congestion at Kennedy (*below*) and other airports resulted in U. S. restrictions on number of flights.

"PLANE-MATE," a lounge to carry passengers from terminal to aircraft, can be raised to plane-door height (as shown here) or lowered to run as a bus.

THE BUDD COMPANY

Youth fare discounts of from 33.3% to 50%, for those between 12 and 22, will be continued, since the Civil Aeronautics Board found that overall public benefits outweighed any discriminatory factors.

International air fares, as worked out by International Air Transport Association members, are binding only so long as all members adhere to the schedule. An open rate situation developed when Alitalia cut the lowest-price individual New York-Rome round trip fare to $299 from $409. Most of the 20 other airlines flying the North Atlantic announced fare reductions, but the rate war did not immediately spread to first class and regular coach tickets.

Air Transportation Trends. The Boeing 747 jumbo jet or superjet, with an average capacity of 362 passengers or more than 100 tons of cargo, first flew in tests in 1969 but was delayed in starting commercial service until early 1970.

In January 1969 the Soviet Union became the first nation to fly a commercial supersonic aircraft. Its Tu-144, which can carry 120 to 130 passengers at possibly up to 1,550 mph, will enter commercial service late in 1970. The British-French Concorde, a 136-passenger, 1,450-mph aircraft, had its first flight in April and will enter commercial service possibly late in 1971. In September, President Nixon authorized construction of prototypes of the U. S. SST, able to carry 300 passengers at 1,800 mph, but it will not be ready for commercial use until 1978.

After final awards in the trans-Pacific route investigation, all but 4 of the 12 major U. S. domestic airlines have authority to serve Hawaii. Australia will be served from the East Coast of the United States, and scheduled all-cargo service will be provided to the Far East.

Sea Transportation Trends. A Northwest Passage became a reality in September when the S. S. *Manhattan* reached Point Barrow, Alaska. Use of this route for transporting oil to the U. S. East Coast from Alaska's North Slope could reduce transportation costs by 50% over alternate routes. Although the *Manhattan* had 43,000 shaft hp, 50% more than conventional ships twice its size, it was stuck in the ice eight times. It operated at from 3 to 6 knots in the ice and 12 to 14 knots in open water.

Noting that 75% of the U. S. merchant marine fleet is more than 20 years old (only 25% of the world's fleet is that old) and that it carries only 5% of U. S. import-export tonnage, President Nixon in October offered Congress a new program for constructing 300 ships, including three with nuclear power, in 10 years. Operating differential subsidies would be continued to offset wage and insurance costs, which are higher for U. S. operators than foreign operators, but maintenance, repair, and subsistence subsidies would be eliminated. The "recapture" provision, which requires subsidized operators to return a portion of their profits, is to be eliminated. To encourage improved construction techniques, the construction differential subsidies would be reduced from 55% to 45% in 1970–71, and then by 2% a year until they reach 35%.

The worldwide container ship fleet expanded by 93 vessels in 1969, and 24 more such vessels were ordered for 1970. After these deliveries 258 vessels will have container capability, including 110 full container ships and 52 of the roll-on roll-off (RO-RO) type. The RO-RO ships are becoming relatively more popular because the required port in-

TURN-AROUND TIME in port is speeded by this new type of freighter that carries a dozen pre-loaded barges.

INTERNATIONAL PAPER COMPANY

vestment is less than for full container ships.

The land-bridge concept, which would provide a 23% mileage reduction between Hamburg and Yokohama, took steps toward reality when both the Union Pacific-Norfolk & Western and the Santa Fe-Penn Central developed plans to move international container traffic from coast to coast in the United States in expedited movements. Under this plan, traffic from Europe to the Far East moves in container ships from Europe to the U. S. East Coast, is off-loaded onto trains for the transcontinental journey, and is again loaded on ships on the U. S. West Coast.

Rail Transportation Trends. Installation of Kar-Trak (automatic car identification) equipment continued during 1969 so that the system—which optically scans identification cards on freight cars and reports this location to a central computer—could begin operations on Jan. 1, 1970. KarTrak should increase the utilization of cars by 10%, providing the equivalent of an additional 180,000 cars.

After 18 months of debate within the Interstate Commerce Commission, the agency ruled in a 7-to-2 vote that it does not have the power to regulate the quality of passenger train service. It has asked Congress to give it that power.

In the Northwest Corridor the Metroliner, capable of speeds to 170 mph, began running in January 1969. Operating with a top speed of 120 mph on the New York-Washington run, the Metroliner reduced travel time to 3 hours when several stops are made and to 2.5 hours without stops. The trains operated with full loads all year.

Late in the year, the French began service with a turboprop-propelled train that glides on a cushion of air on an 11-mile (18-km) track near Orléans. The track will be extended to Paris, and the Aerotrain will make the trip at speeds to 185 mph.

Pipeline. Construction of the longest and largest slurry pipeline began in April 1969, and it is expected to be in operation by 1971. The $35 million, 18-inch-diameter line will transport liquefied coal 273 miles from strip mines in Arizona to an electric generating station in Nevada. Fully automatic pumping stations will be situated about 30 to 60 miles apart, and 1,700-hp pumps will force the coal to flow at 4 mph.

(See also AIR TRANSPORTATION; ARCTIC; MOTOR TRANSPORTATION; RAILROADS; SHIPPING; TOURISM: TUNNELS.)

JAMES R. ROMAN, JR.
George Washington University

TRINIDAD AND TOBAGO

The most significant economic event in Trinidad and Tobago was the announcement by the government of the third 5-year development plan (1969–73). The plan's three major purposes are to build up the country's economic structure, diversify the economy, and increase local control over economic activity.

To strengthen the infrastructure, the plan assigns $71.6 million to transport and communications. Plans were being rushed in 1969 to enlarge Piarco International Airport for the new jumbo jets.

Diversification. The year 1969 was designated as "agriculture year" by the government. Every effort was being made to diversify agriculture, which until recently had concentrated on sugar. With the possible entrance of Britain into the European Common Market, Trinidad and Tobago could lose a protected sugar market. Thus, specifically, the 5-year plan proposed continuing acquisition of sugar land by the government for, in the case of Trinidad Sugar Estates, corn and soybean production. Increased agricultural exports to the neighboring island members of the Caribbean Free Trade Association will be sought.

The plan also envisions intensified production of traditional crops through higher yield techniques. In line with this some sugar technicians from Cuba were invited to visit Trinidad. Prime Minister Eric Williams advocated restoring trade with Cuba.

Two large oil companies announced a sizable investment in fishing facilities at Chaguaramas, the former U. S. naval base. With help from the United Nations, construction of a fish-processing plant will be undertaken.

Local Control. A third major aim of the 5-year plan was to shift decision-making in investment, production, employment, management, and marketing from overseas control to local control. It was suggested that the country embark on "a protective but creative program of economic nationalism" to achieve this end.

A major step in 1969 was the purchase of all holdings of the British Petroleum Company. This was in part prompted by the company's announced policy of cutting back its Trinidad operations. The newly formed National Petroleum Company will also control extensive deposits of natural gas discovered in 1968 and explored in 1969. Major oil strikes were made off the east coast in May and September 1968.

THOMAS G. MATHEWS
University of Puerto Rico

— TRINIDAD AND TOBAGO • Information Highlights —

Area: 1,980 square miles (5,128 sq km).
Population: 1,030,000 (1968 est.).
Chief Cities (1960 census): Port of Spain, the capital, 93,954; San Fernando, 39,830.
Government: *Governor-General*—Sir Salomon Hochoy (took office Aug. 1962); *Prime Minister*—Dr. Eric Williams (took office Nov. 1966). *Parliament*—Senate, 24 members (party seating, 1967: People's National Movement, 13; Democratic Labour party, 4; others appointed by governor-general); House of Representatives, 36 members (party seating, 1969: People's National Movement, 24; Democratic Labour party, 11; People's Democratic party, 1).
Religious Faiths: Roman Catholics, 35% of population; Hindus, 23%; Anglicans, 21%; others, 21%.
Education: *Literacy rate* (1969), 80% of population. *Total school enrollment* (1963–65)—243,918 (primary, 207,265; secondary, 34,692; technical/vocational, 1,051; university/higher, 910).
Finance (1969 est.): *Revenues,* $173,400,000; *expenditures,* $173,300,000; *monetary unit,* Trinidad and Tobago dollar (2 dollars equal U. S.$1).
Gross National Product (1968): $600,000,000.
National Income (1968) $740,000,000; *average annual income per person,* $615.
Economic Indexes (1967): *cost of living,* 109 (1963=100).
Manufacturing (metric tons, 1967): Gasoline, 2,497,000; sugar, 205,000; cement, 190,000.
Crops (metric tons, 1967–68 crop year): citrus fruit (1966), 39,000; cacao beans, 5,300; coffee, 3,500.
Minerals (metric tons, 1967): ·Crude petroleum, 9,192,000; sand and gravel (1966), 291,000.
Foreign Trade (1968): *Exports,* $465,000,000 (chief exports, 1967: petroleum, $265,760,000; sugar, $189,150,000); *imports,* $419,000,000 (chief import, 1967: crude petroleum, $174,480,000). *Chief trading partners* (1967): United States (took 39% of exports, supplied 15% of imports); Britain (took 13% of exports, supplied 15% of imports); Venezuela (took 2% of exports, supplied 40% of imports).
Transportation: *Roads* (1964), 4,000 miles (6,400 km); *motor vehicles* (1967), 80,300 (automobiles 62,900); *railways* (1969), 109 miles (175 km); *national airline,* British West Indian Airways; *principal airport,* Piarco (near Port of Spain).
Communications: *Telephones* (1968): 46,089; *television stations* (1967), 2; *television sets* (1967), 32,000; *radios* (1966), 200,000; *newspapers* (1965), 3 (daily circulation, 97,000).

TRUDEAU, Pierre Elliott

Prime Minister of Canada: b. Montreal, Quebec, Canada, Oct. 18, 1919.

"Trudeaumania"—the popular enthusiasm that swept Pierre Trudeau to the Liberal leadership, the office of prime minister, and a decisive election victory in 1968—was replaced in 1969 by disturbing evidences of "Trudeauphobia." While visiting the prairie provinces in July, Trudeau was accosted by hecklers throwing grain and waving placards inscribed "Trudeau is a pig" and "Hustle wheat, not women." Visibly angered by these outbursts against his government's failure to sell Canada's huge wheat surplus, he vowed he would not tolerate such insults from the west again.

In August, in Vancouver, Trudeau lost his traditional "cool" when abused by anti-Vietnam War demonstrators and responded by ripping an offensive sign from a young woman and striking a youth who called him a "creep." Another demonstration against him at a Liberal party picnic in Toronto was averted by the arrest of three men who seemed to be threatening physical violence. Even in his home province of Quebec, Trudeau's popularity had waned to the point that a plot against his life was discovered prior to his attending the Quebec City winter carnival.

This antipathy toward Trudeau in Quebec stemmed largely from the extremists and separatists who see him as a "vendu"—a French Canadian who has sold out to English-speaking Canada and federalism. In the West the basic cause of "Trudeauphobia" was the economic distress of the wheat farmers. Nevertheless, many Canadians who were distressed by the violence directed against the prime minister were themselves feeling disillusioned with Trudeau, the "swinging" leader they had hailed just one year earlier.

Causes of Criticism. Anti-Trudeau feeling can be traced to at least four factors: a natural letdown in popular support after the high political excitement of 1968; the discovery by Canadians that the Trudeau who had won hearts and votes in 1968 was the product of professional "image makers"; Trudeau's poor relations with the press; and his "sins" of both commission and omission in terms of government policies.

Trudeau first appeared in Canadian politics as the dedicated, reforming intellectual; but in 1968 his campaign managers created a new image of him as the youthful, debonaire, "with-it" man of the jet-set age. One year of power revealed yet another Trudeau—the politically hard technocrat whose actions and policies seemed to deny his stated intention to "plug people into the decision-making process" in his promised "just society" for Canada.

Poor relations with the press have plagued most modern prime ministers of Canada, but Trudeau's relations have deteriorated more rapidly than those of his predecessors, and almost entirely because of his own hostility toward the fourth estate. He resents the all but pathological interest of the press in his private life, an interest that was encouraged largely by his own image makers. His angry statement, "I'm not public property," is more an expression of desire than fact.

Throughout 1969, Trudeau's policies were widely criticized, and his practice of announcing decisions personally, often at press conferences, rather than through his ministers in Parliament, has concen-

WIDE WORLD

PRIME MINISTER TRUDEAU strolls with U.S. President Nixon outside White House after March conference.

trated that criticism on himself. Typical of such controversial policies was his statement to the press in April that Canada's land and air commitments to the North Atlantic Treaty Organization in Europe would be phased out. Cuts in defense spending and reductions in the size of Canada's active and reserve armed forces have disturbed a substantial minority of Canadians who fear such developments indicate a deliberate drift to isolationism.

The failure of his government to grapple with a national housing shortage, with the western wheat surplus, and with Canada's serious inflationary trend has alienated many more Canadians and has caused defections from his cabinet and his parliamentary majority, as well as grumbling among Liberal party supporters.

Career. A 1943 graduate of the University of Montreal law school, Trudeau did postgraduate studies in economics, political science, and law at Harvard and in Paris and London. In the 1950's he was a leader of the reform movement in Quebec. Elected to Parliament in 1965, Trudeau was chosen by Liberal Prime Minister Lester B. Pearson as his parliamentary secretary (1966) and minister of justice (1967). The Liberal party in 1968 chose Trudeau to be Pearson's successor as party leader and Prime Minister.

JOHN S. MOIR
University of Toronto

TUNISIA

Seven weeks of heavy rainstorms (September 22–October 28) devastated four fifths of Tunisia, killing more than 525 persons and leaving more than 160,000 homeless. In September, President Habib Bourguiba removed Ahmed Ben Salah, a socialist-oriented cabinet member and one of Tunisia's most powerful politicians, from his economic ministries.

Floods. Ten of the 13 provinces of Tunisia were designated disaster areas as floods caused losses amounting to an estimated $200 million. River courses changed, many bridges collapsed, and four villages vanished. Four fifths of the livestock perished, and the date and olive harvests were destroyed. Hundreds of miles of roads and railroads were demolished, five major dams were damaged, the vital phosphate industry was severely crippled, and a score of factories were flooded. Foreign Minister Habib Bourguiba, Jr., declared that "something like eight or nine years of development have been wiped out."

The first country to send aid was Libya. The United States sent the first rescue helicopter from Wheelus Air Force Base in Libya, and helicopters were also flown in from Morocco, France, and West Germany. The United States allotted about $1 million for reconstruction and $200,000 for tents, blankets, and wheat. Similar assistance came from Switzerland, Belgium, the Netherlands, France, and West Germany. Quick aid was also supplied by CARE, the American Red Cross, Project Hope, the Joint Distribution Committee, and Catholic Relief Services. Tunisia had already been receiving more foreign aid per person than almost any other Arab or African nation because it has no heavy industry nor any known sizable oil reserves.

Domestic Politics. On Dec. 6, 1968, President Bourguiba ousted Tahar Belkhodja, director general of public security, on the ground of "abuses of power." His dismissal was reported to have been connected with the split between supporters and opponents of the economic policy of Ahmed Ben Salah, the socialist-oriented minister of economic planning, finance, industry, agriculture, and education. Under his policy much farm land was expropriated by law and organized into cooperatives. But the peasants opposed this move, the cooperatives failed, and Ben Salah himself was dismissed from all his ministries except education by President Bourguiba on Sept. 8, 1969. Another reason advanced for Ben Salah's demotion, which was generally taken as a sign that the government was moving to the right, was the September 1 coup in Libya. The coup placed moderate Tunisia between two now more radical neighbors, Libya and Algeria.

Ben Salah had been groomed as a possible successor to Bourguiba, who was said to be suffering from persistent hepatitis. Besides Ben Salah, there were two other major aspirants to leadership. One was Bahi Ladgham, the president's chief secretary of state and acting chief of government during Bourguiba's illness. The other was Ahmed Mestiri, former secretary of defense, who was openly critical of the president.

In the presidential and legislative elections on November 2, Bourguiba won 99.7% of the vote for a third term as president. The election results not only reaffirmed confidence in his leadership, but reflected the national determination to rebuild Tunisia. Ben Salah received only 8,000 votes for parliament compared with 51,000, 48,000, and 34,000 respectively for the three other candidates on the single party list.

On November 7, Bourguiba created the office of premier, responsible to the president, and named Bahi Ladgham to the new post.

Foreign Aid. On Nov. 27, 1968, the International Bank for Reconstruction and Development (IBRD) announced a loan of $8.5 million for port improvements. On Jan. 17, 1969, the IBRD and Sweden announced loans totaling $20 million to aid in developing the country's water supply. The IBRD and its affiliate, the International Development Association, also pledged loans of $17 million in June to help modernize Tunisia's railways. The IBRD disclosed on November 26 that it had approved a $10 million loan to the Société Nationale d'Investissement of Tunisia to finance investments in tourist and industrial ventures.

On Dec. 24, 1968, the U. S. Agriculture Department reported the signing of a Food for Freedom agreement to supply Tunisia with $15.4 million in farm items. It was estimated that the U. S. was furnishing 58% of all foreign aid to Tunisia.

Foreign Affairs. Tunisia's relations with France, Italy, Rumania, and East Africa became closer as a result of good-will visits by Tunisian officials in late 1968 and in 1969. In December 1968, Tunisia indicated that it would establish diplomatic relations with Kenya, Tanzania, and Uganda.

Tunisia reiterated its basic opposition to the Arab League's operations, but in October 1969 Foreign Minister Bourguiba expressed support for the Palestine Liberation Organization and its struggle against Israel. However, recruitment of non-Palestinian Arabs was not permitted in Tunisia.

JOHN NORMAN
Pace College Westchester

--------- **TUNISIA • Information Highlights** ---------

Area: 63,378 square miles (164,150 sq km).
Population: 4,660,000 (1968 est.).
Chief Cities (1963 est.): Tunis, the capital (1964 census), 662,000; Sfax, 65,635; Sousse, 48,172.
Government: *President*—Habib Bourguiba (took office July 25, 1957). *Legislature* (unicameral)—National Assembly, 90 members (party seating, 1969: all members of the Destourian Socialist party).
Religious Faiths: Muslims, 92% of population.
Education: *Literacy rate* (1969), 25%–35% of population. *Total school enrollment* (1965)—854,924 (primary, 734,216; secondary, 103,339; teacher-training, 4,745; vocational, 6,394; higher, 6,230).
Finance (1967 est.): *Revenues,* $205,400,000; *expenditures,* $186,400,000; *monetary unit,* dinar (.525 dinars equals U. S.$1).
Gross National Product (1968): $1,089,523,809.
National Income (1968): $845,714,285; *average annual income per person,* $181.
Economic Indexes (1967): *Industrial production* (1968), 113 (1963=100); *agricultural production,* 76 (1963=100); *cost of living,* 119 (1963=100).
Manufacturing (metric tons, 1967): Cement, 472,000; gasoline, 74,000; wine, 900,000 hectoliters.
Crops (metric tons, 1967–68 crop year): Wheat, 330,000; olives, 245,000; grapes, 140,000.
Minerals (metric tons, 1967): Phosphate rock, 2,810,000 (ranks 4th among world producers); iron ore, 501,000; salt, 257,000; lime (1966), 172,000.
Foreign Trade (1968): *Exports,* $158,000,000 (chief exports, 1967: phosphates, $23,907,000; olive oil, $15,157,000; wine, $10,084,000; iron and steel, $4,121,000); *imports,* $217,-000,000 (chief imports, 1967: nonelectrical machinery, $32,421,000; textile yarn and fabrics, $18,279,000; iron and steel, $16,652,000). *Chief trading partners* (1967): France (took 28% of exports, supplied 31% of imports); United States; Italy.
Transportation: *Roads* (1969), 9,662 miles (15,546 km); *motor vehicles* (1967), 88,900 (automobiles 56,600); *railways* (1969), 1,488 miles (2,394 km); *merchant vessels* (1967), 19,000 gross registered tons; *national airline,* Tunis Air.
Communications: *Telephones* (1968), 64,875; *television stations* (1967), 2; *television sets* (1967), 5,500; *radios* (1967), 375,000; *newspapers* (1966), 5.

TUNNELS

Tunnel construction is active in many parts of the world to satisfy the needs for rapid transit rail lines, vehicular travel, and water supply. Some are driven through rock by drilling, blasting, and excavating. Mechanical moles bore out others. Many underwater tunnels are built by fabricating tubes on shore, floating them into position, and then sinking and connecting the sections in a trench dug into the bed of the waterway.

Rapid Transit Lines. In 1969 the San Francisco Bay Area Rapid Transit District completed its 3.6-mile (5.8-km) Trans-Bay Tube. The sunken-tube structure, with 57 sections, is the longest in the world, and is a key link in the first new rapid transit system to be built in the United States in half a century. The double-track tunnel is part of the 75-mile (121-km) line scheduled for completion in 1971. In addition to the underwater tube, the project includes 36 other tunnels under San Francisco, Oakland, and Berkeley.

New York City expected to start work in 1970 on a 4-track, 3,140-foot (957-meter) tunnel under the East River. Consisting of precast tubes sunk to 100 feet (30 meters) below water level, the project will take about seven years to complete.

Although the new 22-mile (35-km) Metro subway system in Mexico City will not be completed until 1971, an 8-mile (13-km) section opened in 1969. This initial line runs between Chapultepec Park and International Airport.

Vienna, Austria, will get a 4-line, 24-mile (39-km) subway system, to be built over 11 years, at a cost of about $195 million.

A 24-mile underground line will be constructed to give Helsinki, Finland, its first subway. The initial stage will link the Kamppi city center with the suburb Puotinharju.

London expects to complete its new 14-mile (23-km) Victoria Underground section early in 1971.

Water Supply. After four years of work, the 4.7-mile (8-km) Carley Porter Tunnel holed through in 1969. The 23-foot (7-meter) diameter bore is a major link in the California Water Project, a multibillion dollar plan to carry water from northern to southern California. It will carry up to 110 million gallons of water per hour.

The U. S. Bureau of Reclamation will complete in 1970 a 3.9-mile (6-km) tunnel bored through the hard rock of Nevada's River Mountains as part of the Southern Nevada Water Project. A mechanical mole handled the excavation for the 12-foot (4-meter) diameter tunnel.

Vehicular Tunnels. To meet future traffic demands, Virginia is planning to construct a second Hampton Roads Bridge-tunnel crossing between Norfolk and Hampton. The new project will parallel the existing 4-mile bridge-tunnel crossing, opened in 1957. It will consist of a 7,500-foot (2,286-meter) tunnel flanked by concrete trestle bridges. The portals of the tunnel emerge on manmade islands in the middle of the waterway.

A new tunnel carrying Interstate 77 will be bored through East River Mountain to connect Virginia and West Virginia. Twin tubes, 5,661 feet long (1,725 meters), each carrying two lanes of traffic, will have a 16.5-foot (5-meter) vertical clearance. The project is to be completed in 1973.

Under the Mobile River at Mobile, Ala., a new 3,000-foot (914-meter) tunnel will parallel Bank-head Tunnel, completed in 1941. The sunken tubes will carry Interstate 10 in two tubes of two lanes each. Completion is scheduled for 1972.

Heinenoord Tunnel under the Oude Maas River at Rotterdam, the Netherlands, went into service in 1969. Replacing an 80-year-old narrow lift bridge, the 3,491-foot (1,064-meter) tunnel consists of two tubes, each with a 2-lane roadway.

In Antwerp, Belgium, the John F. Kennedy Tunnel under the Schelde River was opened to traffic in 1969. The tube carries two railroad tracks in a single duct 34 feet (10 meters) wide, and has two 3-lane vehicular ducts each 47 feet (14 meters) wide. These are the largest precast concrete tunnel elements ever built. The tunnel is 2,260 feet (689 meters) long and carries the E-3 highway.

Work got under way in 1969 on Hong Kong's $53-million, mile-long (1.6 km) cross-harbor tunnel. The 4-lane project will consist of 15 sunken tubes, each 357 feet (109 meters) long by 34 feet (10 meters) wide. Construction will take three years. The tunnel will connect Hong Kong and Kowloon.

Railroad Tunnel. The second longest railroad tunnel in North America—a 7-mile (11.3-km) bore through Montana's Flathead Mountains—was completed in 1967. It is part of a relocation of the Great Northern Railway.

WILLIAM H. QUIRK
"Contractors & Engineers" Magazine

TURKEY

Despite internal problems and an election in October 1969, in which Premier Süleyman Demirel was returned to power, Turkey continued to be preoccupied with economic development under the second 5-year-plan. There were no basic changes in foreign policy.

Politics. Turkish politics in 1969 illustrated the essential conservatism of the people, especially the peasants, who transferred their political loyalty to the Justice party, following the demise of the Democratic party after the 1960 coup. The Republican People's party, now primarily an opposition party, with little likelihood of returning to power, followed a moderate reform policy, while more extreme groups, including students, campaigned for socialism, withdrawal from the North Atlantic Treaty Organization (NATO), and the abolition of U. S. bases.

A series of anti-U.S. riots occurred between November 1968 and February 1969—a period that saw the arrival of a new U. S. ambassador, Robert W. Komer, and a visit of the U. S. Sixth Fleet—and for a time universities in Istanbul and Ankara were closed. A new crisis occurred in May 1969, when the Justice party sought to restore the rights of leaders of the former Democratic party, and the Army indicated its opposition, with implications of a possible military coup. Orderly elections were held on October 12, and the Justice party was returned to power with 252 of the 450 seats in the National Assembly. Premier Süleyman was re-elected to his second 4-year term.

Economic Development. Under a "planned development with Western measures," the Turkish gross national product showed a 6.6% increase during 1968, with a 12.4% increase in industrial output; a growth of 6.8% was forecast for 1969. Of a total of some $12.4 billion during the second 5-year plan (1968–72), $2.5 billion were to be spent during

1969 to promote industrial and agricultural development and various public services. Estimated total expenditures during 1968–69 reached a new record of $2,401,333,000 as did revenues at $2,345,777,-000. The 1970 budget, submitted in November 1969, estimated expenditures at $3.2 billion, including $528 million for defense.

Although industrial development slowed somewhat during 1969, the economy appeared healthy. Grain production was estimated at 19 million tons, with wheat (Sonora) approximately 13.5 million tons. Imports were estimated at $790 million for 1969, with exports at some $496 million. Although West Germany stood first in Turkish trade, exports to the United States reached a level of some $121 million, slightly above that of 1968, and U. S. trade had shifted from cargoes financed by the Agency for Industrial Development (AID) to commercial sales and shipments of food grains.

The Turkish government entered into significant trade agreements with Rumania, Poland, Yugoslavia, Iraq, Libya, and Jordan. It also undertook further discussions concerning a more formal association with the European Economic Community. Among important elements in Turkey's favor was the fact that about 200,000 Turkish workers were abroad, remitting some $120 million in 1969.

With AID assistance sharply reduced since 1967, Turkey sought assistance elsewhere. The government estimated that it would seek external credits of about $147 million—$140 million from the Aid-to-Turkey Consortium. It entered into an agreement with the European Investment Bank for $7.6 million for construction of the Gokchkaya-İzmir power line, and with the World Food Program for $22 million of food aid for economic and social development projects. In November the Soviet Economic Aid Mission in Turkey announced that 600 Soviet technicians would arrive in Turkey in 1970 to help construct Turkey's third iron and steel plant at İskenderun. Under a Turco-Soviet economic agreement, the Soviet Union was to lend Turkey $360 million to finance a refinery at İzmir, an aluminum plant at Seydisehir, and other long-term industrial projects. The loan was to be repaid over 15 years, at 2.5% interest, with agricultural and industrial products.

Education. Turkey continued to make significant progress in the field of education, although the literacy rate in the countryside was only 30% (65% in the towns and cities). By 1968 there were about 31,900 primary schools, with 93,400 teachers and 4,274,000 pupils; 1,357 secondary schools with 23,460 teachers and 655,250 students; 829 technical or vocational schools, with 11,500 teachers and 194,325 students; and 110 institutions of collegiate or university rank, with 6,200 teachers and 113,000 students. Special stress continued to be given to the development of technical and university education as a prerequisite to the modernization of the country. An eighth university, Selcuk University, was to be established in 1970, and there were plans for 10 more over the country.

Foreign Policy. The problem of Cyprus continued as a constant theme in Turkish foreign relations, especially with Greece, although there were indications that a *modus vivendi* might be worked out by the local Greek and Turkish Cypriot communities. Turkey continued to normalize its relations with its Balkan and Arab neighbors, pursued a cautious policy relative to Israel, and based its policy in the Arab-Israeli conflict on the resolution

——— TURKEY • Information Highlights ———

Area: 301,380 square miles (780,576 sq km).
Population: 33,539,000 (1968 est.).
Chief Cities (1965 census): Ankara, the capital, 902,216; Istanbul, 1,750,642; İzmir, 417,411; Adana, 290,515.
Government: *President*—Gen. Cevdet Sunay (took office Oct. 27, 1965); *Premier*—Süleyman Demirel (took office for second 4-year term October 1969). *Parliament* (Grand National Assembly)—Senate, 183 members (party seating, 1968: Justice, 101; Republican People's, 34; Reliance, 11; others, elective and appointive, 37); National Assembly, 450 members (party seating, 1970: Justice, 252; Republican People's 143; Reliance, 15; National, 6; New Turkish, 6; other parties, 15; independents, 13).
Religious Faith: Muslims, 99% of population.
Education: *Literacy rate* (1969), 47% of population. *Total school enrollment* (1964)—4,446,862 (primary, 3,735,512; secondary, 478,595; teacher-training, 42,276; technical/vocational, 99,281; university/higher, 91,198).
Finance (1967 est.): *Revenues*, $1,985,000,000; *expenditures*, $2,090,000,000; *public debt*, $2,233,000,000; *monetary unit*, lira (9.08 liras equal U. S.$1).
Gross National Product (1968): $12,411,894,200.
National Income (1968): $10,539,647,500; *average annual income per person*, $314.
Economic Indexes (1967): *Industrial production* (1966), 170 (1963=100); *agricultural production*, 116 (1963=100); *cost of living*, 133 (1963=100).
Manufacturing (metric tons, 1967): Cement, 4,236,000; crude steel, 996,000; gasoline, 797,000; sugar, 723,000; meat, 194,000.
Crops (metric tons, 1967–68 crop year): Wheat, 10,110,000; barley, 3,800,000; sugar beets, 5,253,000; grapes, 3,500,-000; potatoes, 1,760,000.
Minerals (metric tons, 1967): Chromite (1966), 511,645 (ranks 3d among world producers); coal, 5,031,000; lignite, 3,416,000; crude petroleum, 2,728,000.
Foreign Trade (1968): *Exports*, $496,000,000 (chief exports: cotton, $130,295,000; tobacco, $116,922,900; hazelnuts, $86,273,100; dried fruit, $31,362,300); *imports*, $770,000,000 (chief imports: road motor vehicles, $54,046,200; electrical machinery, $50,179,500; iron and steel, $36,725,700). *Chief trading partners* (1967): West Germany (took 16% of exports, supplied 20% of imports); United States (took 18% of exports, supplied 18% of imports); Britain.
Transportation: *Roads* (1966), 36,000 miles (57,935 km); *motor vehicles* (1967), 325,100 (automobiles, 105,900); *railways* (1965), 4,907 miles (7,897 km); *merchant vessels* (1967), 101 (575,000 gross registered tons); *national airline*, Turkish Airlines.
Communications: *Telephones* (1968): 427,770; *television stations* (1967), 1; *television sets* (1967), 2,000; *radios* (1967), 2,789,000; *newspapers* (1961), 472.

of Nov. 22, 1967, of the UN Security Council. It remained faithful to the NATO and CENTO (Central Treaty Organization) alliances, as being in the national interest. Turco-U. S. relations remained normal and realistic, and a new Defense Cooperative Agreement was signed in 1969. President Cevdet Sunay's visit of November 12–22 to the Soviet Union marked a peak in Turco-Soviet relations, although it was noted that the more friendly atmosphere had not led the USSR to renounce its claims to Kars, Ardahan, and Artvin, in eastern Anatolia.

HARRY N. HOWARD
The American University

UGANDA

The difficulty of uniting disparate groups continued to be the major problem for Uganda in 1969. President Milton Obote spoke of a new "movement to the left" which would join "nationalism with socialism" in an attempt to unite the country. But while this new program made the government appear progressive, its effort to suppress division made it seem antiliberal.

Domestic Politics. In January a member of the National Assembly, Abubaker Majanja, and the well-known editor of *Transition* magazine, Rajat Neogy, were brought to trial. The judge upheld the right of the two men to freedom of expression, as guaranteed by the Ugandan constitution. Although acquitted, both remained in detention.

In the same month a White Paper that outlined a moderate scheme for the Africanization of business

POPE PAUL VI met with African Roman Catholic prelates during his historic visit to Uganda, July 31–August 2.

was published. The government announced it would initiate a licensing and work permits system to insure the rapid "Ugandanization" of the economy. The plan called for the placement of black Ugandans in jobs, both public and private, which are currently held by non-Ugandans. All companies will be required to have operating licenses, and some specific business lines will be reserved for Ugandans. All non-Ugandans will have to obtain work permits.

In September the leader of the opposition Democratic party, former Prime Minister Benedicto Kiwanuku, was brought to trial by the government on charges of sedition and libel.

A month later President Obote announced the "Common Man's Charter," which dedicated the government to an economic plan designed to give assistance to the majority of the people of Uganda. He also proposed a national service scheme which would mobilize all able-bodied men to upgrade rural life and promote national unity.

The National Assembly on October 1 extended the state of emergency in the area of the former kingdom of Buganda, in effect since 1966, for six more months. In November, Sir Edward Mutesa,

the deposed kabaka (king) of Buganda, died in London. His death left the Buganda nationalists without traditional leadership and added to tensions.

On December 18, after he had addressed a meeting of the Uganda People's Congress, President Obote was seriously wounded in an assassination attempt. A state of emergency was then declared.

Economy. In June the 1969–70 budget of about $42 million, an increase of $2.1 million from 1968–69, was announced. About $59 million of the proposed expenditures was for development projects, a decrease of almost $3.1 million from 1968. Increases in spending for the police, army, and prisons reflected Uganda's political problems.

A new ministry of marketing and cooperatives was established.

Pope's Visit. On July 31, Pope Paul VI arrived in Uganda, the first trip by a pontiff to Africa.

ROBERT O. COLLINS
University of California, Santa Barbara

ULBRICHT, Walter. See biographical sketch under GERMANY.

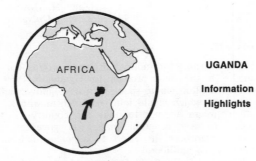

UGANDA

Information

Highlights

Area: 91,133 square miles (236,036 sq km).
Population: 8,133,000 (1968 est.).
Chief Cities (1959 census): Kampala, the capital, 46,735; Jinja, 29,741; Mbale, 13,569; Entebbe, 10,941.
Government: *President*—(Apollo) Milton Obote (took office April 15, 1966); *Vice President*—John K. Babiiha. *Parliament* (unicameral)—National Assembly, 92 members, 82 elected (party seating, 1969: Uganda People's Congress, 70; Democratic party, 6; Kabakka Yekka, 1; vacant, 15).
Religious Faiths: Roman Catholics, 32% of population; Anglicans and Protestants, 27%; Muslims, 5%.
Education: *Literacy rate* (1969), 25% of population. Total

school enrollment (1965–66)—670,784 (primary, 564,190; secondary, 98,129; teacher-training, 4,097; technical/vocational, 3,128; university/higher, 1,240).
Finance (1968 est.): *Revenues,* $136,200,000; *expenditures,* $162,700,000; *monetary unit,* Uganda shilling (7.143 shillings equal U. S.$1).
Gross National Product (1968): $756,000,000.
Cost of Living Index (1967): 128 (1963=100).
Manufacturing (metric tons, 1967): Meat, 145,000; sugar, 137,-000; cement, 140,000; beer, 221,000 hectoliters; copper, 14,400; sawn wood, 59,000 cubic meters.
Crops (metric tons, 1967–68 crop year): Peanuts, 200,000; cottonseed, 167,000; coffee, 157,500; cotton lint, 73,000; sesame, 20,000; tea, 11,200.
Minerals (metric tons, 1967): Apatite (1966), 15,798; salt, 5,000; lime (1966), 4,000.
Foreign Trade (1968): *Exports,* $186,000,000 (chief exports, 1967: coffee, $48,430,000; cotton, $21,420,000; copper, $7,-650,000); *imports,* $123,000,000 (chief imports, 1967: non-electrical machinery, $11,040,000; transport equipment, $9,980,000; electrical machinery, $2,970,000). *Chief trading partners* (1967): Britain (took 24% of exports, supplied 34% of imports); United States (took 22% of exports, supplied 7% of imports); Japan (took 9% of exports, supplied 6% of imports).
Transportation: *Roads* (1964), 31,332 miles (50,423 km); *motor vehicles* (1967), 38,900 (automobiles, 32,800); *railways* (1969), 3,670 miles (5,906 km); *principal airport,* Entebbe.
Communications: *Telephones* (1968), 23,368; *television stations* (1967), 6; *television sets* (1967), 8,500; *radios* (1965), 200,000; *newspapers* (1965), 5.

UPI

Soviet sportsmen march through Moscow's Red Square in May Day parade. The 1969 ceremonies eschewed the usual display of military might.

USSR

Grave difficulties beset the Kremlin in 1969. Border battles along the Chinese-Soviet frontier threatened to erupt into full-scale war. Within the USSR, industrial reforms yielded mediocre results, while the grain harvest slumped because of bad weather. Many Soviet intellectuals continued to criticize government policy through underground publications, which the police were unable to suppress. One of the régime's favorite authors defected to the West, exposing how his writings had been almost rewritten by Soviet editorial censorship.

Perhaps more important than intellectual unrest was evidence of some opposition to the ruling Politburo from the Communist party itself. Preparations were delayed for a new party congress, where such party dissatisfaction could burst into the open.

Even space activities went awry. While Americans made the first moon-walk in history, an unmanned Soviet rocket went out of control and crashed into the lunar surface. News media of the East European countries embarrassed the USSR by giving tremendous publicity to the United States' space success.

All of these troubles probably explained the strenuous efforts Soviet leaders made to negotiate with Communist China, and to achieve better relations with West Germany and the United States. As the year ended these efforts lessened tensions with both East and West, although no outstanding disputes had been settled.

FOREIGN AFFAIRS

Asia. Sino-Soviet tension rose to new heights during the spring and summer of 1969 when a series of border battles received widespread publicity in both countries. Each side accused the other of starting the conflicts, and both sides claimed victory in the fighting.

The first clash ocurred on March 2 over the ownership of Damanski Island in the Ussuri River, which is the boundary between Manchuria and Siberia's Maritime Province. The Soviet press claimed that 200 Chinese soldiers attacked and were repulsed. On March 14 and 15 a second Damanski battle was fought, and according to Soviet sources, the Chinese attacked in 100-man groups supported by fire from machine guns, mortars, and light artillery.

Following these fights, in April and May, the USSR proposed resumption of Sino-Soviet border negotiations, which had been broken off five years before. In reply, China accused Soviet frontier troops of intruding into Sinkiang on June 11 from Soviet Central Asia.

Again the USSR proposed a Sino-Soviet conference, and China agreed to negotiations concerning boat traffic on the navigable Amur, Ussuri, and Argun rivers, which separate Manchuria from eastern Siberia. These negotiations, lasting from June 18 to August 8, resulted in a pact regulating 1969 river traffic. However, in July, while the conference was in session, the USSR claimed that Chinese soldiers had attacked Soviet river sailors. On August 13, shortly after the talks had ended, Soviet and Chinese troops battled to control a mountain on the Sinkiang border. According to Soviet accounts, the mountain clash was a small-scale infantry engagement with some casualties.

In September the USSR proposed that Soviet and Chinese leaders meet at Hanoi while attending the funeral of President Ho Chi Minh of North Vietnam. The Chinese refused but did permit Premier Kosygin to land at Peking airport en route home. There on September 11 he talked with the Chinese premier, Chou En-lai, and this fateful meeting resulted in an agreement to open Sino-Soviet boundary and trade negotiations. A delegation from the Soviet foreign ministry was then sent to Peking, where the negotiations began on October 20.

Meanwhile, the USSR continued to support the Communist side in the Vietnam War. On June 13 the Soviet government formally recognized the Viet Cong rebels as the "Provisional Revolutionary Gov-

ernment of South Vietnam." In October a new aid agreement was concluded with North Vietnam, which in 1969 received fewer Soviet supplies than in 1968 because the United States forces were no longer bombing North Vietnamese cities.

A Soviet foreign aid fiasco was evident in Indonesia, where the USSR had granted credits worth $850 million to the government of President Sukarno, who was overthrown in 1965. In 1969 the USSR tried unsuccessfully to collect this debt from Sukarno's successors, who supported the Thieu régime in South Vietnam.

Regarding the Near East, Soviet spokesmen continued to demand Israeli withdrawal from United Arab Republic, Jordanian, and Syrian territories conquered by Israel two years before. To help Nasser, the USSR in 1969 supplied one third of the grain needs of the United Arab Republic. Also in the year, new agreements providing more Soviet technical aid to Iraq and Syria were concluded.

In June, Soviet party leader Brezhnev launched the idea of an Asian collective security pact that could include the USSR. As the year ended, this proposal remained vague, evidently still being in the planning stage.

Africa. On May 30 the Ivory Coast, which the Soviet press often had described as pro-Western, severed diplomatic relations with Moscow. In June the USSR established diplomatic relations with Equatorial Guinea, which became an independent nation late in 1968.

In March a new Soviet technical assistance agreement was concluded with Algeria, which at the time was receiving more Soviet technical aid than any other African country except the UAR. Some 2,000 Soviet technicians were at work in Algeria on 82 projects. The USSR purchases half of Algeria's production of wine.

Europe. Soviet-West German relations took a bad turn in February, when the USSR warned the West German government not to stage the election of its president in West Berlin. When West Germany ignored the warning, Soviet and East German troops maneuvered around Berlin in March during the election. By May the Soviet press described the West German embassy in Moscow as a "nest of spies."

After the Social Democratic party won the West German national elections in October, the Soviet attitude changed. While visiting East Germany that month, Brezhnev stated that the Soviet Union was willing to negotiate its disputes with West Germany. On December 5, a Soviet-inspired announcement by the Warsaw Pact nations (Bulgaria, Czechoslovakia, East Germany, Hungary, Poland, Rumania, and the USSR) made similar friendly overtures toward the West German government. Finally, on December 7, the Soviet Union announced that it had accepted a West German proposal to start bilateral negotiations on a nonaggressive pact. Preliminary talks began the next day.

France concluded an economic cooperation agreement with the USSR in January and a new trade pact in October. The two countries thus returned to friendly relations, which had been impaired by the 1968 Soviet occupation of Czechoslovakia.

None of the Kremlin's kindness toward western Europe found its way to Czechoslovakia, which fell increasingly under Soviet control. In Moscow both the press and government leaders harped on the so-called "Brezhnev doctrine"—that the USSR has

---

USSR • Information Highlights

Area: 8,647,489 square miles (22,402,200 sq km).

Population: 239,000,000 (1969 est.).

Chief Cities (1967 est.): Moscow, the capital, 6,500,000; Leningrad, 3,706,000; Kiev, 1,413,000; Tashkent, 1,239,000.

Government: *President*—Nikolai V. Podgorny (took office 1965); *Premier*—Aleksei N. Kosygin (took office 1964); *Communist party Secretary-General*—Leonid I. Brezhnev. *Parliament* (Supreme Soviet)—Soviet of the Union, 767 members; Soviet of Nationalities, 750 members.

Religious Faiths: Russian Orthodox, 50% of population; Muslims, 10%; Protestants, 5%; Roman Catholics, 4%; Jews, 1%.

Education: *Literacy Rate* (1968), 97% of adult population. *Total school enrollment* (1969)—57,800,000.

Finance (1969 est.): *Revenues,* $147,510,000,000; *expenditures,* $147,290,000,000; *public debt,* $28,700,000,000; *monetary unit,* ruble (0.9 ruble equals U. S.$1).

National Income (1968): $230,000,000,000; *average annual income per person,* $970.

Economic Indexes (1968): *Industrial production,* 240 (1958 = 100); *agricultural production,* 138 (1958 = 100); *taxation,* 187 (1958 = 100).

Manufacturing (metric tons, 1968): Crude steel, 107,000,000; cement, 88,000,000; chemical fertilizer, 43,000,000.

Crops (metric tons, 1968): Grain, 169,200,000 (ranks 3d among world producers); potatoes, 101,600,000 (world rank, 1st); sugar beets, 93,600,000 (world rank, 1st); sunflower seed, 6,640,000 (world rank, 1st).

Minerals (metric tons, 1968): Coal, 594,000,000 (ranks 1st among world producers); crude petroleum, 309,000,000 (world rank, 2nd); iron ore, 177,000,000 (world rank, 1st); natural gas, 171,000,000,000 cubic meters (world rank, 2nd).

Foreign Trade (1968): *Exports,* $10,527,990,000 (chief exports: machinery and equipment, $2,274,000,000, fuels, $1,632,000,000; metals, $1,168,600,000); *Imports,* $9,315,900,000 (chief imports: machinery and equipment, $3,437,-000,000; textiles, clothing and shoes, $1,145,900,000; foodstuffs, $988,500,000). *Chief trading partners* (1968): East Germany (took 13% of exports, supplied 12% of imports); Czechoslovakia (took 9% of exports, supplied 8% of imports); Poland.

Transportation: *Roads* (1968), 266,000 miles (430,600 km); *motor vehicles* (1968), 4,713,000 (automobiles, 1,200,000); *railways* (1968), 82,500 miles (133,000 km); *merchant vessels* (1968), 1,449 (8,562,000 gross registered tons).

Communications: *Telephones* (1968 est.), 9,100,000; *TV stations* (1969), 167; *TV Sets* (1969), 20,000,000; *radios* (1966), 39,800,000; *newspapers* (1967), 7,700.

the right to interfere in the affairs of other Communist countries in defense of communism.

In May a series of unusual Soviet-Bulgarian economic agreements provided that Bulgarian engineers, technicians, and workers will help build a steel plant, a cellulose and paper factory, and a gas pipeline within the USSR. In return, Bulgaria will receive part of the steel, cellulose, paper, and gas from these projects when they are completed.

Latin America. On Feb. 1, 1969, the USSR and Peru established diplomatic relations. Thus the USSR had diplomatic ties with eight Latin American countries. During the year, Soviet trade pacts were concluded with Cuba, Ecuador, Peru, and Uruguay. Cuban economic dependence on the USSR was highlighted by the fact that Soviet petroleum filled 90% of Cuba's needs for oil.

United States. Soviet-U. S. relations generally improved in 1969. In April, when the North Koreans shot down a United States reconnaissance plane over the Sea of Japan, the Soviet Navy helped the U. S. Navy search for the plane's survivors.

In July the Soviet press praised the first moonwalk by U. S. astronauts, who received personal congratulations from President Podgorny when they visited Moscow later in the year. More important, a speech on July 10 by Soviet Foreign Minister Andrei Gromyko appealed for "good relations" with the United States.

On October 25 the United States and the USSR simultaneously announced that they would start strategic arms limitation talks (SALT) on November 17 in the Finnish capital city of Helsinki. The negotiations began on schedule, with expressions of hope from both delegations. (See also DISARMAMENT.)

But Soviet official goodwill toward the United States did not include approval of the U. S. way of life. In September, when the dean of Soviet nuclear scientists Peter Kapitsa was visiting the United States, he was asked if he believed in the "convergence theory," that the Soviet and U. S. civilizations were becoming similar. Kapitsa approved the theory. The Soviet press immediately responded that there was no convergence, and that "bridge-building," rapprochement, and cultural exchange are capitalist attempts to weaken Soviet Communist morality.

DEFENSE AND SPACE

Probably because of the danger of war with China, the Soviet military and civilian press in 1969 contained many belligerent statements, such as: war may break out unexpectedly; Soviet armament must be strengthened; and the USSR must be ready to fight for its independence. In the summer Col.-Gen. V. F. Tolubko, former deputy commander of Soviet

HERBLOCK IN THE WASHINGTON POST

"Don't Just Stand There—Help Me"

missile forces, was appointed commander of the Far Eastern Military District, which borders Communist China.

Land and Naval Forces. The Soviet armed forces in 1969 comprised about 3.2 million men and an additional 250,000 police troops. Their armament included some 50,000 tanks, 10,000 combat planes, 350 conventional submarines, 55 nuclear-powered submarines, 120 destroyers, 14 cruisers, and two helicopter carriers. As a result of great efforts, the number of land-based intercontinental missiles had risen to 1,200, a few more than the number possessed by the United States. The USSR still lagged behind the United States in long-range bombing planes and submarine-based intermediate-range missiles.

During 1969 the Soviet proved that it could operate far from its home ports. Soviet naval flotillas made goodwill visits to Iran, Iraq, South Yemen, and Yemen in the Near East; Guinea, Mauritius, Nigeria, Tanzania, and Zanzibar in Africa; Finland and Yugoslavia in Europe; and Cuba, Martinique, and Barbados in the Caribbean Sea. The Soviet Mediterranean naval fleet was reduced to about 20

SOVFOTO

LEONID ILICH BREZHNEV, first secretary of the Communist party of the Soviet Union, emphasized his nation's desire for peaceful negotiations with Western countries in his May Day speech of 1969. Although he had denounced the Chinese Communist leaders in June, he expressed a conciliatory attitude toward both China and the new West German coalition government headed by Willy Brandt in October, following a U. S.-Soviet agreement to commence strategic arms limitation talks.

Brezhnev was born in Dneprodzerzhinsk in the Ukraine on Dec. 19, 1906. He joined the Communist party in 1931 and rose through its ranks as a protégé of Nikita S. Khrushchev. During World War II he served as a political commissar with the Red Army. In 1952 he was elected to the party's Central Committee, and from 1960 to 1964 he was chairman of the Presidium of the Supreme Soviet of the USSR. Since October 1964, when he took over the party leadership from Khrushchev, he has been governing the USSR jointly with Premier Aleksei N. Kosygin.

ships early in 1969, then quickly increased to some 50 vessels (the same strength as in mid-1968). In March the Soviet Union's Arctic and Baltic naval fleets held training maneuvers in the mid-Atlantic Ocean. (See also DEFENSE FORCES; MISSILES.)

A distinguished Soviet military man, Kliment Y. Voroshilov, died on December 3 in Moscow at the age of 88. He had been Soviet war minister from 1925 to 1940, a Politburo member from 1926 to 1960, and president of the USSR from 1953 to 1960. He was buried with full honors near the Kremlin wall.

Space and Aircraft. Of the many Soviet space achievements of 1969, two successful probes of the planet Venus by unmanned rockets were perhaps the most important. In January, Soviet space scientists accomplished another "first" when two cosmonauts transferred from one spaceship to another while in earth orbit. Three manned Soviet rockets orbited the earth simultaneously in October, when welding experiments in space were conducted for the first time. (See also SPACE EXPLORATION.)

In March a Soviet V-12 helicopter set a world record by lifting 30 tons of cargo to a height of 2,950 meters (9,680 feet). Just before the year began, on Dec. 31, 1968, the USSR conducted its first test flight of the Tu-144, the world's first operational supersonic passenger plane. Although designed and built in the USSR, the Tu-144 contains some British electrical and electronic equipment.

GOVERNMENT AND POLITICS

The Communist party Politburo (Policy Bureau), the ruling group of the USSR, underwent no change in membership in 1969. A provincial party leader stated publicly that Brezhnev was "head" of the Politburo, meaning the most powerful leader in the USSR.

On January 23 a Leningrad army officer dressed as a policeman fired several shots at an automobile carrying Soviet cosmonauts in a Moscow parade. It is believed that he was trying to assassinate top Soviet leaders, who were riding in the automobile just behind the cosmonauts. Neither the cosmonauts nor the leaders were hurt, and the would-be assassin was arrested on the spot. His fate was never announced.

Statistics released in 1969 show that the Communist party in the Soviet Union had 14 million full and candidate members, the largest membership in Soviet history. By family origin 16% of the members were peasants, 39% laborers, and 45% white-collar workers and employees. The party was predominantly male, only 21% of the membership being women.

Penal Reform. In July the supreme court of the Soviet Union issued a list of "basic principles for corrective labor colonies" (prison camps) as a guide to camp administrators. According to the list, only a court can sentence a criminal to a prison camp; the camp cash pay should be 10% of the salary for similar work performed by free labor; in the less rigorous camps, where short-term prisoners are housed, relatives or friends may visit each prisoner five times a year; prisoners violating the camp rules may be punished, and the punishment may include a cut in food rations; and dangerous criminals can be sent to camps outside their native Soviet republic.

The court's declaration is the first case in Soviet history of prison camp regulations having been published in detail. In announcing the principles, a supreme court spokesman said that 99% of Soviet prisoners are in prison camps, rather than prison.

Communist Party Affairs. An unusual political aspect of 1969 was the official publication of two pamphlets and a lengthy magazine article indirectly attacking Politburo rule over the Soviet Communist party. All three publications were written by party spokesmen who previously were considered staunch Stalinists. Among their assertions were the follow-

SOYUZ 5, poised for a mission from Baikonur in January 1969, docked in orbit with Soyuz 4. Two of its three cosmonauts transferred to the second craft.

TASS FROM SOVFOTO

SOVFOTO

WIDE WORLD

U. S. ASTRONAUT Frank Borman, who commanded Apollo 8 in the first manned orbiting of the moon, visited the USSR in July. The first astronaut to travel to the Soviet Union, he cited the desirability of U. S.-Soviet cooperation in space programs. Borman (*above, in light suit*) visited the cosmonaut community near Moscow and posed with Soviet cosmonauts. (*Left*) On a tour of Leningrad, Borman signs autographs.

ing: Only the Communist party congress can determine the party line; the party central committee, not the Politburo, should be the collective leadership; all party members should be kept informed of party business; party leaders must accept public criticism, must openly admit their errors, and after admitting errors must correct them; every Communist party and every Communist country is equal and sovereign; and one Communist country may not interfere in another Communist state's internal affairs.

Although the authors safeguarded themselves by quoting Lenin, they obviously appealed for party democracy. The last two statements cited above are also an attack on the Brezhnev doctrine. Such writings could not be published without support from persons high in the party hierarchy. Thus, there appears to be an intra-party struggle.

A party congress is preceded by local party elections, which choose the delegates to the congress. These elections normally occur several months before the congress convenes. The Politburo announced that a congress would meet early in 1970. But 1969 ended with no further word about the congress, and no local party elections being held.

CULTURE

Intellectual Unrest. Outside the Communist party criticism of the Soviet rulers continued unabated through the year. Illegal underground newssheets circulated widely, despite police efforts to suppress them. Some underground editors and reporters were arrested, but others carried on their work. The underground press appealed for civil rights justice for all Soviet citizens—Russians, Tatars, Jews, and others—regardless of race, religion, or nationality. It also carefully reported on the circumstances of political prisoners and on the arrest, trial, and imprisonment of political offenders.

Among the illegal documents circulated was one by Pyotr Yakir, an historian and the son of a general executed by Stalin. Yakir's tract demanded that Stalin be tried posthumously for his crimes and sentenced posthumously to death.

In July, Anatoly V. Kuznetsov, a supposed Stalinist Soviet novelist, defected to the West while on a visit to England. He stated that his novels had been virtually rewritten by Soviet editors to fit the Communist party line and that he had been under constant watch by the Soviet secret police. In the West he hoped to republish his novels in their original forms.

Another Soviet author, Aleksandr I. Solzhenitsyn, was expelled from the Soviet Writers' Union in November and officially invited to leave the USSR forever. His recent works had not been published in the USSR (because they criticized the Soviet régime), but they were smuggled abroad and published in the West, where they won wide popularity.

Izvestia, the chief newspaper of the Soviet government, conducted a poll of its readers during the year asking whether they believed the news *Izvestia* printed. Of the respondents, 56% did not believe the economic news, 55% the internal political news, and 36% the foreign news.

Nationality Unrest. Evidence of unrest among the USSR's non-Russian minorities also mounted in 1969. National party headquarters warned Tadzhik party leaders in Central Asia not to defend Tadzhik cultural nationalism. In June the radio station in Kiev, capital of the Ukrainian Soviet Republic, began a series of programs on the struggle of the Communist party against Ukrainian nationalism in the western Ukraine.

In the spring, Uzbek publications in Central Asia contradicted the Communist party line by praising Uzbekistan's struggle against colonial conquest by Czarist Russia. (According to the Communist party, Czarist Russian conquest was beneficial to the Uzbeks.) An Uzbek writer also quoted Lenin as saying that minority nationalities should not be forced to learn the Russian language.

Religion. Because of the atheist Soviet government's harassment of churches and religious believers, some religious unrest has always existed in the USSR. In 1969, however, it was compounded by resentment toward the Moscow patriarch of the Russian Orthodox Church, Aleksei, who seemed merely to be a pawn of the government. In June a teacher named Talantov was arrested, and later sentenced to two years' imprisonment, for writing letters to Aleksei and the government protesting the latter's closure of churches. In September,

HUBERT HUMPHREY, former U.S. vice president, joins sightseers in Moscow's Red Square, July 17.

WIDE WORLD

Anatoli E. Levitin-Krasnov, a church secretary and well-known church historian, was arrested because he criticized the Moscow patriarchate for not resisting either the government's closures or police persecution of religious believers. Krasnov, who was imprisoned for seven years by Stalin, considers himself a Christian Marxist completely loyal to communism.

In July, Aleksei convened an international conference of Christian, Muslim, Buddhist, and Hebrew clergymen from Asia, Africa, Europe, and the Americas. The theme of the conference was "religious responsibility for peace on earth and cooperation of nations," but its real purpose was to provide a means of countering "terrible anti-Soviet propaganda" overseas. The conferees did not discuss religion at all. Instead they passed resolutions (on which foreign guests could not vote) calling for withdrawal of United States troops from Vietnam, diplomatic recognition of East Germany by the West, a prohibition against nuclear weapons for West Germany, and an end to Western intrigue to break up the Soviet orbit of nations.

Two days after the conference ended, *Pravda* demanded improvement of atheist propaganda throughout the USSR.

Education. Perhaps because intellectuals tended to be the spokesmen for literary, minority, and religious unrest, the government decreed in September that the colleges and universities should admit more workers, peasants, and ex-servicemen as students. (Most students have come from white-collar families.) The government also decreed that a preparatory school be established at each college and university to train the new recruits for admission.

During the year the Soviet press complained that three fourths of Soviet high schools and other upper-grade schools had no music teachers. The press noted that music teachers' colleges had a student dropout rate varying from 20% to 60% of freshman enrollment.

ECONOMY

Industry. Some 80% of Soviet industrial production in 1969 came from factories and mines operating under a new system whereby plant efficiency is judged by profits rather than overall physical production. Notwithstanding the encouragement of the profit motive, Soviet industrial growth was very slow, especially early in the year. The inertia was due partly to resistance from the industrial bureaucracy, which continued to give detailed orders to plant directors, who under the new system were supposed to have more authority in making plant decisions. Part of the trouble also was a severe winter, which hampered the transportation of raw materials and fuel to industrial establishments.

Nevertheless, in 1969 the USSR was operating an industry second in size only to that of the United States. The USSR outproduced the United States in coal, iron ore, cement, and nonferrous metals, such as antimony, bauxite, copper, gold, lead, mercury, silver, and tin. Soviet armament output increased during the year, probably because of fear of war with Communist China. Perhaps because of this increase, the original plans for the 1970 production of coal, oil, and natural gas were all reduced.

Data referring to 1968 but released in 1969 seemed to indicate how slowly the Soviet Union has introduced computers into its economy. In 1968 the USSR had only 4,000 computers, compared

MODERN skyscraper in Moscow serves as the headquarters of COMECON (Council for Mutual Economic Assistance). The building is part of a new complex in the center of the capital.

UPI

with some 70,000 in operation in the United States.

Agriculture. Nature was unkind to Soviet agriculture in 1969. At the year's start, violent dust storms struck the northern Caucasus, lower Volga valley, and southern Ukraine, all of which are important Soviet granaries. Much of the winter grain was killed by these unusual storms. Meanwhile, heavy snows, accompanied by violent winds and bitter cold, trapped many large herds of livestock in Central Asia. As a result, the total grain crop decreased from 169.2 million metric tons in 1968 to 155 million tons in 1969. Total herds of cows, sheep, and goats also decreased. However, most field crops other than grain were near the normal harvest level.

Data released in 1969 indicated how little of Soviet collective and state farming is actually mechanized. Only 2% of cattle feeding and 2.5% of cow milking are done by machine. Of the 18.2 million collective farmers, a minority of 2 million operate farm machinery. The remainder are all engaged in hand labor.

A 1966–69 plan to put much grain acreage under irrigation was far behind schedule, probably because during those years state funds spent on agriculture fell far short of planned assistance. A Soviet financial magazine complained that state investment to aid agriculture in 1969 was lagging because budgeted funds had been diverted to increased armament.

Transport. In 1969, as before, railways were the backbone of Soviet internal transport, hauling about 70% of total freight. Little was heard about a crash road-building program that was supposed to start during the year.

Sea and air transport, however, advanced in several ways. The Leningrad shipyards launched a 62,000-ton tanker, while the Gorki yards completed the world's fastest hydrofoil, carrying 150 passengers at a speed of 55 miles (88 km) per hour. Testing continued on the Tu-144 supersonic transport, and in December the USSR announced that in 1970, British, French, and Japanese passenger planes will be permitted to fly between Japan and western Europe via the USSR.

Foreign Trade. At a February meeting of the United Nations Conference on Trade and Development, the USSR announced that it would not greatly increase its foreign aid and that it was not responsible for economic difficulties in underdeveloped nations. From 1954 through 1968, $6.3 billion of Soviet foreign aid had been pledged to non-Communist nations, of which $2.9 billion was allotted to South Asia, $2.3 billion to the Near East, $900 million to Africa, and $200 million to Latin America.

Standard of Living. The Soviet standard of living remained lower than that in many industrialized countries. The press reported retail shortages of such items as vegetables, white bread, milk, butter, sugar, cheese, fruit, meat, shoes, medicines, kitchen equipment, and children's clothes. The average city wage was 118 rubles ($129.80) per month. State farm pay was 30% below the urban level, and collective farm pay 50% below. In February higher wages were decreed for workers in the construction industry.

(See also COMMUNISM; KOSYGIN, ALEKSEI.)

ELLSWORTH RAYMOND
New York University

OIL TANK at Suez was set afire on March 8 during 5-hour artillery duel along the Suez Canal between Israeli and Egyptian forces.

WIDE WORLD

UNITED ARAB REPUBLIC

Events in the United Arab Republic in 1969 were dominated by the continued conflict with Israel. Desultory fighting, punctuated by sharp encounters, characterized the entire year. Israel continued to occupy the Sinai Peninsula, and the Suez Canal remained closed. The Egyptian economy, aided by spectacular oil exploitation, made significant strides in its recovery from the 1967 war.

Relations with Israel. The year was characterized by constant fighting across the 1967 cease-fire lines, with little substantive advantage being gained by either the UAR or Israel. Both countries instigated numerous border incidents. These included an Egyptian commando raid across the canal in early December, when some 250 Egyptian commandos occupied Israeli positions for about 24 hours and then withdrew, and an Israeli tank raid across the Gulf of Suez in September, labeled the most extensive since the 1967 war.

On March 9 the Egyptian chief of staff, Lt. Gen. Abdel Moneim Riad, was killed by an Israeli shell while touring the front at Ismailia. He was replaced by Maj. Gen. Ahmed Ismail Ali, who was replaced in turn by Lt. Gen. Mohammed Sadek in a shakeup in September.

In April the Egyptian government claimed that the 1967 cease-fire agreement was no longer to be considered in force. President Gamal Abdel Nasser claimed in July that the "liberation stage" in the war was now at hand. In the aftermath of the fire in the Al Aksa mosque in Jerusalem in August, Nasser declared that it was a "sacred duty" for Arabs (and not only Egyptian Arabs) to go to war against Israel, and he promised the liberation of Jerusalem. In November the UAR leader responded to various attempts to suggest an Israeli-Arab settlement by stating that a solution would come only by "fire and blood."

In February, Nasser had proposed a plan for peace, and in October he declared his support of a "Rhodes-type formula" of indirect discussions through an intermediary for negotiation of a settlement. In general Nasser has argued that if Israel accepts all of the UN resolutions (including withdrawal from all occupied territory) there will be no impediment to peace. But the war continues and an early settlement is not likely.

Relations with the Arab World. Compared with former·years the UAR's relations with its fellow Arab states have been reasonably harmonious. The core of this harmony has been the continuing struggle against Israel. However, Nasser walked out of the conference of Arab leaders in Morocco in December because of the unwillingness of Saudi Arabia

─────────── UNITED ARAB REPUBLIC • Information Highlights ───────────

Area: 386,663 square miles (1,001,449 sq km).
Population: 33,000,000 (1969 est.).
Chief Cities (1966 census): Cairo, the capital, 4,219,853; Alexandria, 1,801,056; Giza, 571,249: Port Said, 282,977.
Government: *President and Premier*—Gamal Abdel Nasser (took office as president for new 6-year term March 25, 1965; took office as premier June 19, 1967). *Parliament*—National Assembly, 350 members.
Religious Faiths: Muslims, 93% of population; Christians, 6%; others, 1%.
Education: *Literacy rate* (1960), 26% of population aged 15 and over. *Total school enrollment* (1965)—4,514,016 (primary, 3,450,338; secondary, 819,373; teacher-training, 49,-448; technical/vocational, 127,734; university/higher, 177,123).
Finance (1968 est.): *Revenues*, $1,275,060,000; *expenditures*, $2,560,250,000; *monetary unit*, Egyptian pound (0.4348 equals U. S.$1).
Gross National Product (1966): $5,735,970,560.
National Income (1966): $5,002,299,900; *average annual income per person*, $157.
Economic Indexes (1967): *Industrial production*, 111 (1963= 100); *agricultural production*, 105 (1963=100); *cost of living*, 131 (1963=100).

Manufacturing (metric tons, 1967): Residual fuel oil, 3,227,-000; cement (1966) 2,629,000; gasoline, 763,000; sugar, 364,000; meat, 231,000; crude steel (1966), 195,000; cotton yarn (1966), 147,800.
Crops (metric tons, 1967–68 crop year): Dates, 319,000 (ranks 2d among world producers); rice, 2,316,000; maize, 2,169,000; wheat, 1,293,000.
Minerals (metric tons, 1967): Crude petroleum, 5,716,000; phosphate rock, 683,000; salt, 584,000; gypsum (1966), 459,000; iron ore, 211,000.
Foreign Trade (1967): *Exports*, $566,030,000 (chief exports: cotton, $281,020,000; rice, $68,530,000); *imports*, $792,120,-000 (chief imports: cereals and preparations, $194,310,000; unmilled wheat and meslin, $126,560,000; nonelectrical machinery, $83,210,000). *Chief trading partner* (1967): USSR (took 25% of exports, supplied 21% of imports).
Transportation: *Roads* (1964), 26,627 miles (42,851 km); *motor vehicles* (1967), 135,100 (automobiles, 108,000); *railways* (1969), 4,200 miles (6,759 km); *merchant vessels* (1967), 44 (194,000 gross registered tons).
Communications: *Telephones* (1968): 335,000; *television stations* (1967), 19; *television sets* (1967), 475,000; *radios* (1965), 1,613,000; *newspapers* (1965), 14.

and Kuwait to increase their financial support of the war against Israel.

Syria's president, Nureddin el-Atassi, visited Cairo in August for talks with President Nasser, and among other things pressed for a reunion of Egypt and Syria (there was such a union between 1958 and 1961).

Nasser strongly supported the Libyan army overthrow of King Idris in September; but he offered Idris asylum in the UAR. Heavy arms sales to Libya by the French were thought to be destined for the UAR.

The UAR has fairly consistently (although perhaps reluctantly) supported the various Palestinian guerrilla groups, notably al-Fatah and its leader, Yasir Arafat. The virtually open warfare in Lebanon between these guerrillas and the government was mediated by the UAR. Nasser referred to Arafat's followers as "the noblest and most honest element of the Arab struggle." Arafat himself has acquired the virtual status of a head of government.

In September the UAR conceded that should the Arabs gain victory over Israel the Jews should be permitted to remain in Palestine, but that Zionism would be uprooted.

Relations with the Soviet Union. The UAR's attitude toward the USSR might be called reluctantly warm. In spite of heavy Soviet aid and considerable influence the Egyptians prefer ties with the West. At the year's end the UAR was definitely pro-French.

In January the USSR published its Middle East peace proposals, which included an evacuation by Israel in stages of occupied territories, a new UN peace force, and a declaration by the Arabs and Israelis alike of nonbelligerency. During the year the USSR and the United States continued their thus far abortive efforts to effect a resolution of the Palestine embroglio. In the meantime Soviet arms shipments continued.

Soviet Foreign Minister Andrei Gromyko visited Cairo in June and a Soviet nuclear submarine went to Alexandria in March. In December an Egyptian delegation visited Moscow.

In July the UAR opened diplomatic relations with East Germany, to the dismay of the West German government.

Relations with the United States. It was generally expected that diplomatic relations (broken by the UAR during the 1967 war) would be resumed after the new U.S. president, Richard Nixon, took office. In February the UAR indicated that it did not blame President Nixon for the actions of the administration of President Lyndon Johnson in the Middle East. Early statements of the Nixon administration were interpreted as being friendly to the Arab world. In February the U.S. government viewed Nasser's peace proposals as "positive and encouraging." But by the year's end little had changed.

In April the United States backed the Arab stand that its Palestinian refugees be given the option of repatriation to Israel in lieu of compensation. But in October, U.S. citizens were given permission to serve in the Israeli armed forces without losing their citizenship; the UAR reaction was one of anger.

The United States continued to participate in Big Four talks on a Middle East settlement. In late December, UN Secretary General U Thant predicted a breakthrough before February 1970.

Domestic Affairs. In 1969 the UAR celebrated the 1,000th anniversary of the founding of Cairo. The atmosphere was once again "normal" but the city remained on a war footing, with the constant possibility of Israeli air raids. President Nasser retained power during the year, although there was a considerable undercurrent of complaint and disaffection. In July the government restricted the travel of foreigners to Cairo, Giza, Alexandria, Luxor, and Aswan.

The UAR was concerned over its rising birth rate. Its population was estimated at 33 million in 1969, and it was generally acknowledged that the government's birth control program was a failure. As a result the government reversed its policy and began to encourage emigration; about 50,000 Egyptians seek entry into the United States each year.

Economy. Oil strikes during the year and increased production from existing fields have at last given the UAR the beginnings of an economic base. Tourism, down since the 1967 war, revived somewhat in 1969. Altogether the economy made significant strides in 1969. The 1970 budget was announced in June, with no new taxes; it amounts to $5.5 billion, with $563 million for defense.

(See also MIDDLE EAST.)

CARL LEIDEN
University of Texas

GAMAL ABDEL NASSER, president of the United Arab Republic, tried during 1969 to mobilize the Arab nations for a "battle of liberation" aimed at wresting from Israel control over Arab territory gained in the 6-day war of June 1967. A summit conference of heads of Arab states, called by Nasser in December at Rabat, Morocco, broke down when he walked out in protest over the refusal of some Arab states to pledge increased financial aid for the anti-Israel struggle.

Nasser was born in Beni Mar, Egypt, on Jan. 15, 1918. A leader in the coup that overthrew King Farouk in 1952, he gradually attained absolute power in Egypt and was elected president in 1956. When Egypt was united with Syria in 1958, Nasser became president of the UAR, from which Syria withdrew in 1961. In recent years, Nasser has moved closer to the Soviet bloc while trying to maintain avenues open to the West.

UAR's NASSER (*center*), Jordan's Hussein (*right*), and Syria's Nureddin al-Atassi met in Cairo in September.

KEYSTONE

UNITED CHURCH OF CANADA

Founded in 1925 by a historic union of the Congregational, Methodist, and most of the Presbyterian churches in Canada, the United Church of Canada has grown from 600,000 members at the time of union to nearly 1,090,000 by 1969. On Jan. 1, 1968, the Canada Conference of the Evangelical United Brethren Church became part of the United Church of Canada.

In 1968 the Church's Board of World Mission had a force of 278 missionaries serving in 24 countries around the world. The United Church contributed over $1 million for overseas relief and inter-church aid and development and approximately $12,000,000 for all purposes beyond local support.

The United Church also maintains 4 universities, several residential colleges and secondary schools, 24 homes for senior citizens, several homes for unmarried mothers, an increasing number of clinics and counseling centers, and 4 lay training centers.

ERNEST E. LONG
Secretary of the General Council

UNITED CHURCH OF CHRIST

The United Church of Christ was formed in 1957 through the union of the Congregational Christian Churches and the Evangelical and Reformed Church. As of Dec. 31, 1968, the United Church of Christ reported 2,032,048 members in 6,866 congregations.

The United Church of Christ, at its 7th General Synod, in Boston, June 25–July 2, responded to the current crisis in the nation by changing the status of the Committee for Racial Justice to a Commission for Racial Justice. The commission, which will be appointed by the president of the Church, will have 15 members, 8 of whom must be black. The Synod guaranteed funding for the commission of $500,000 in 1970 and $600,000 in 1971, and its inclusion in the annual budget in 1972. It also asked the Board for Homeland Ministries to study the feasibility of establishing a black university in the South, of organizing black printing and publishing enterprises, and of having the United Church of Christ participate in the establishment of a southern land bank.

The General Synod also called for the "drastic revision" of the Selective Service Law to protect both individual freedom and national security. It said "We challenge the use of the draft as normal public policy. We ask for a return to the American tradition which regarded conscription as an emergency service." It also called for an end to deferments for clergy and theological students.

The Synod called for the elimination of tax loopholes and tax exemptions for businesses owned by churches and other nonprofit organizations.

The Synod voted that persons under 30 years of age should constitute at least 20% of the membership of the next Synod and should have a 20% representation on its major committees.

The General Synod elected the Rev. Robert V. Moss, former president of Lancaster Theological Seminary, to the presidency of the United Church of Christ, succeeding the Rev. Ben Mohr Herbster.

ROBERT V. MOSS
United Church of Christ

UNITED KINGDOM. See GREAT BRITAIN.

UNITED METHODIST CHURCH

Reconciliation, particularly among races, generations, and economic groups, was the major focus of the United Methodist Church at all levels during 1969 as the denomination embarked on a four-year program called "A New Church for a New World." The year 1969 was the first full year for the denomination formed in April 1968 by the union of the Methodist and Evangelical United Brethren churches. The church has more than 11,000,000 members in the United States and approximately 1,000,000 members in the more than 50 other countries.

Progress of Reconciliation Program. Major attention was given to two phases of the quadrennial program: a $20 million Fund for Reconciliation and a Voluntary Service Program patterned somewhat after the U. S. Peace Corps. Unofficial estimates by the Council of Bishops indicated that most, if not all, of the $20 million goal had been pledged during the year. Half of the money is to stay within the contributing annual (regional) conferences and half is to be spent nationally. Of the latter half, $1,500,000 is being spent on the Voluntary Service Program, which had recruited more than 130 volunteers by the close of the summer. The volunteers, mostly young adults, will serve in community organization, day-care centers, employment services, education, and family counseling. More than 30 projects in seven states were also approved for national funding. Most of these were related to racial reconciliation, especially in poverty areas, involving social services, voter registration, and job training.

A new Commission on Religion and Race, also financed by the Fund for Reconciliation, opened headquarters in Washington, D. C., with the Rev. Woodie W. White as its general secretary.

Ecumenical and Merger Efforts. Another relatively new agency, the United Methodist Commission on Ecumenical Affairs, moved its offices from Evanston, Ill., to the Church Center for the United Nations in New York. General Secretary is the Rev. Dr. Robert W. Huston.

United Methodists continued to have dialogue with Roman Catholic leaders and to participate with nine Protestant denominations in the Consultation on Church Union. Vatican and World Methodist Council leaders met at Valetta, Malta, in September. The sixth national dialogue to study official documents on ecumenism issued by both churches was held in Delaware, Ohio, in October.

Plans for the first step toward union between British Methodists and the Church of England failed when the Anglicans received only 69% of a required 75% affirmative vote. British Methodists approved the plan by a 77.4% majority.

Three predominantly Negro Methodist denominations moved toward a projected merger in 1974 by announcing plans to publish jointly church school literature, a hymnal, and an official organ. The African Methodist Episcopal, the African Methodist Episcopal Zion, and the Christian Methodist Episcopal churches have a combined membership of more than 2,750,000.

Higher Education. A United Methodist Foundation for Christian Higher Education named a director, elected a board of trustees, and launched a drive to raise $100 million to aid colleges and universities related to the denomination.

THOMAS S. MCANALLY
United Methodist Information, Nashville, Tenn.

Liberian delegate Angie E. Brooks receives gavel as newly elected president of the UN General Assembly's 24th regular session from Guatemala's Alberto Fuentes Mohr, on September 16.

UNITED NATIONS

The 24th year of the United Nations, beginning Oct. 24, 1969, was characterized by continued deterioration of the international system.

Despite the concern of the UN, tension between Israel and the Arab states increased under the eyes of UN observers. Although the UN Peace-Keeping Force in Cyprus prevented outbreaks of violence, progress toward a reconciliation of the Greek and the Turkish Cypriote communities was no nearer than in 1968. Conflict among the major powers—and other elements of power politics—continued to prevent the UN from even becoming involved in any role in Vietnam and in the tragic war in Nigeria.

Although concern with chemical and bacteriological weapons indicated some hope in disarmament efforts, the frightening possibility of a further escalation of nuclear weapons, involving antimissile defense systems and missiles with multiple warheads, increased. On the more hopeful side of the arms race were resolutions directed toward ensuring that the seabed be used only for peaceful purposes.

Although the United Nations continued to be concerned with the problems of colonialism and apartheid in southern Africa, those problems have persisted in defiance of the organization. The states that could facilitate the solving of the problems have not done so, and the situation in the Portuguese colonies and South Africa, as well as Rhodesia and Namibia has continued.

In the economic and social area, most efforts in 1969 were concentrated on the formulation of goals of the Second United Nations Development Decade. Increasingly, too, the concern of the various organs of the UN was focusing on the problems of the human environment. Steps were taken in preparation for the United Nations Conference on the Human Environment in 1972.

Although efforts to solve the multitude of problems continued, the year 1969 in some senses was one of foreboding at the United Nations. It was a year, culminating the decade of the 1960's, in which almost suddenly all of the problems facing the world became clear in their immensity. In the introduction to his annual report, Secretary-General U Thant seemed to reflect this mood. Thant said he had a strong feeling that time was running out—that the problems were so deep that they were beginning to determine events and it was almost beyond a time when man or the states could even hope to alter the situations. The problems he stressed included those of man and his environment and disarmament and the arms race. Thant also focused on the increasing disparity between the developed and the developing states.

The principal activities of the United Nations in its 24th year are discussed below under the headings (1) General Assembly; (2) Security Council; (3) Economic and Social Council; (4) Trusteeship

Council; (5) International Court of Justice; and (6) Specialized Agencies.

GENERAL ASSEMBLY

The 24th session of the General Assembly was held in New York, Sept. 16–Dec. 17, 1969. In evaluating this session, Secretary-General U Thant remarked on the final day, "We are now witnessing in many parts of the world the revolt of the young, the weak, and the poor.... This has been an Assembly of the poor against the rich, the weak against the strong, and the young against the old." It was a session in which the small states—for almost the first time in the history of the UN—demonstrated their frustrations with the major powers by using their numerical majority to pass a great many resolutions opposed by the big states. Traditionally, the small states have shown deference toward the major powers, recognizing that, in the final analysis, resolutions will be implemented only if they are supported by the major powers, who have the ability to implement them.

Political and Security Affairs. The Assembly adopted numerous resolutions on political and security questions, including arms control, the peaceful uses of outer space and the seabed, and political situations.

Arms Control. The resolutions were adopted on December 16 regarding various aspects of disarmament efforts. By a vote of 82 to 0, with 37 abstentions, the Assembly urged the United States and the Soviet Union to agree to a moratorium on further testing and deployment of new offensive and defensive strategic nuclear weapons systems. The Assembly decided to enlarge the Committee on Disarmament from 18 to 26 states and to call it the Conference of the Committee on Disarmament. The Assembly then requested the enlarged body to (1) continue work on a draft treaty prohibiting weapons of mass destruction on the seabed, (2) consider effective control measures against radiological warfare, and (3) study the implications of the possible military applications of laser technology. The Assembly also declared the 1970's as a Disarmament Decade and requested the committee to proceed with its work on complete and total disarmament.

Having declared the use of any chemical or biological agents of warfare to be contrary to rules of international law, the Assembly invited all states to accede to, or ratify, the Geneva Protocol of 1925 on the use of such weapons. It also called on all states to suspend nuclear weapons tests and invited states to take steps to establish an exchange of seismic information to help achieve a comprehensive nuclear test ban. Finally, the Assembly invited the nuclear powers to make available to the International Atomic Energy Agency information on the peaceful uses of nuclear explosions and made certain recommendations with regard to the financing of major nuclear projects for peaceful purposes.

Space. On December 16 the Assembly unanimously requested that the Committee on the Peaceful Uses of Outer Space continue study of the definition and utilization of outer space, and approved the appointment of a UN official to promote practical applications of space technology. At the same time the Assembly urged the committee to complete a draft convention on the liability for damage caused by objects launched into outer space. It also invited states to make available to other states their experience in the surveying of remote earth resources.

Seabed. The Committee on the Peaceful Uses of the Sea-Bed and Ocean Floor beyond the Limits of National Jurisdiction was requested on December 15 to expedite a statement of principles regarding international cooperation in exploration and exploitation of seabed resources. It was asked also to formulate recommendations regarding the economic and technical conditions, as well as rules, for the exploitation of such resources. At the same time the Assembly asked the secretary-general to (1) survey states to determine whether they wanted a conference on defining the international principles involved, together with an international regime for the seabed, (2) prepare a study on the various types of international machinery that might be devised to assure international control and supervision over the seabed, and (3) declare that, pending the establishment of an international regime, no claims to the area would be recognized and states and individuals would be bound to refrain from activities that would exploit seabed resources.

The China Question. On November 11 the Assembly once again decided to continue to recognize the Chinese government on Taiwan as the representative of China. The resolution was adopted by a vote of 71 to 48, with 4 abstentions—a slightly smaller majority than in the previous year.

Other Political Questions. The report of the secretary-general on the successful conclusion of the West Irian (West New Guinea) situation was endorsed on November 19. Under a 1962 agreement between Indonesia and the Netherlands, the people of West Irian were to be consulted in 1969 to determine the future disposition of their territory. They decided to remain with Indonesia.

On November 20 the Assembly endorsed the Manifesto on Southern Africa, which had been adopted in September by the Organization of African Unity. Also in November, the Assembly again urged steps toward unification of Korea. Continuation of the work of the Committee on Peace-Keeping Operations was authorized on December 15.

"...*World Peace ... World Peace ...*
... World Peace ... World Peace...."

REPRINTED FROM THE LOS ANGELES TIMES
BY PERMISSION OF REGISTER AND TRIBUNE SYNDICATE

ANGIE ELIZABETH BROOKS, assistant secretary of state of Liberia, was elected president of the UN General Assembly, with 113 of 118 votes, at the opening of the 24th session on Sept. 16, 1969. She is the second woman and the third African to hold this post. In her acceptance speech she urged the delegates to concentrate on essential world needs rather than peripheral problems.

Miss Brooks was born in Liberia on Aug. 24, 1928, and was educated in the United States and England. She attended Shaw University in Raleigh, N. C., and obtained a law degree at the University of Wisconsin. She joined the Liberian delegation in 1954 and was assigned to the Assembly Committee on Trusteeship. In 1966 she was president of the Trusteeship Council. In Liberia she has served as assistant attorney general and since 1958 as assistant secretary of state.

Finally, the Assembly asked all states to make special efforts toward strengthening international security during the 25th year of the United Nations in 1970.

Economic and Financial Affairs. The 24th session of the Assembly adopted a wide variety of resolutions bearing on economic programs and issues in preparation for the Second United Nations Development Decade. Among resolutions of a general nature were those directed toward mobilizing public interest, evolving agreement on an international development strategy for the 1970's, and exploring the possibility of establishing an intergovernmental tourism organization and a UN-sponsored international university. Resolutions pertaining to the needs of the developing countries included those calling for preferential or free entry of manufactures and semimanufactures exported by developing countries to the developed countries, technical assistance for industrial development, the training of national technical personnel for accelerated industrialization, and special measures in favor both of those countries that are the least developed and of those that are landlocked.

Resolutions also were adopted with respect to the UN Institute for Training and Research, membership on the UN Industrial Development Board, pledges for the World Food Program in 1971–72, and preparations for the UN Conference on Human Environment in 1972 and for a UN role in the International Education Year of 1970.

UN Development Program. At its 7th session, held in New York, Jan. 9–23, 1969, the Governing Council of the United Nations Development Program (UNDP) decided upon substantial increases in assistance to developing countries. It approved a record 104 new large-scale preinvestment projects, as well as supplementary financial assistance for 19 projects already in progress. These projects, which benefit 84 different countries, will cost $340.7 million, of which $179.9 million will be furnished by the UNDP and the remainder by the recipient governments. The Governing Council also decided to initiate the operations of the UN Capital Development Fund, which had received pledges totaling $2.7 million as of the end of 1968.

The 8th session of the Governing Council, held in Geneva, June 16–July 3, approved $102 million for 52 new preinvestment projects and for supplemental financing of 5 existing ones. The projects were to benefit 78 different countries. With these decisions the total number of projects so far approved by the Governing Council stood at 1,075, which on completion will have cost the UNDP and the recipient countries a total of $2.5 billion, with the UNDP contributing some $1 billion.

At a one-day pledging conference of the UNDP, held in New York on October 9, pledges amounting to $131.6 million were announced by 98 governments. The pledges, some of which were subject to final parliamentary approval, will be used in the 1970 program of the UNDP.

Assessment of the Development System. On December 1 the UNDP issued a report entitled *A Study of the Capacity of the United Nations Development System.* It had been commissioned by the UNDP and prepared by Sir Robert Jackson of Australia. The aim of the report was to assess the capacity of UN system to deliver an effective program of aid to developing countries at a level of resources that now total $200 million per year and can be expected to double within five years. The report concluded that despite its present limitations the UN is the ideal instrument for the task.

Noting that the machinery of the system is under the control of more than 30 separate governing bodies, the report recommended that, as an immediate remedial step, the UNDP be restructured into a "strong, central coordinating organization" between the various agencies of the UN and the governing bodies of the Specialized Agencies. Two chief criticisms were made of the UNDP itself— that it is slow and that it is not making the best use of its resources. The report also argued that about 20% of the UNDP projects would not meet the test of being essential to the development of the state.

Two major innovations were proposed: (1) an integrated Development Cooperation Cycle covering programming, project formulation, implementation, evaluation, and follow-up on a country-centered approach, and (2) a comprehensive information system. Suggestions for a phased implementation of the plan over the next five years was proposed.

Social and Humanitarian Affairs. On December 11 the Assembly adopted a draft Declaration on Social Progress and Development. This declaration is the first international instrument to provide clear guidelines not only for social policies but for the improvement of the social environment and the well-being of the individual. The president of the Assembly, Miss Angie E. Brooks, characterized this declaration as "a truly significant step in pursuance of the objective of promoting social progress and better standards of life in larger freedom as set out in the United Nations Charter."

Human rights were the subject of resolutions in regard to the implementation of the recommendations of the 1968 International Conference on Human Rights, the creation of a post of UN commissioner of human rights, and a program for the observance of 1971 as an International Year for Action to Combat Racism and Racial Discrimination. Other human rights resolutions pertained to measures against nazism and racial intolerance and against violation of human rights and fundamental freedoms. Specifically, the Assembly called for implementation of human rights in territories occupied by Israel and for measures to combat racial discrimination and policies of apartheid and segregation in southern Africa.

Resolutions on a variety of other subjects included those pertaining to the possibility of the adoption of an international convention for the control of psychotropic substances (drugs that affect the mind) not yet under international control, problems of the elderly, and the question of youth and its participation in national development.

Decolonization. The Special Committee of 24 on the implementation of the 1960 declaration on the elimination of colonialism maintained in 1969 its active role in prodding governments to continue efforts at decolonization. The activities of this committee were reflected in a wide variety of resolutions on decolonization adopted by the 24th General Assembly. On October 31 the Assembly again condemned South Africa for its persistent refusal to withdraw its administration from Namibia (South West Africa). The Assembly also, on November 21, condemned the policies of Portugal in preventing the self-determination of the peoples in its African colonies. At the same time the Assembly urged action by the Security Council against the racist minority government of Rhodesia and condemned the intervention of South African armed forces in support of Rhodesia.

On December 1 the Assembly called for Security Council action against South Africa over Namibia and passed a resolution on activities of foreign economic and other interests that are impeding the elimination of colonialism in the Portuguese colonies, Rhodesia, and Namibia. The Assembly also passed resolutions on study and training facilities for inhabitants of non-self-governing territories, UN educational and training programs for southern Africa, and questions relating to Muscat and Oman, Papua and the UN Trust Territory of New Guinea, Spanish Sahara, French Somaliland, and Gibraltar, as well as the decolonization problems of a multitude of island territories.

Administrative and Budgetary Affairs. On December 16 the Assembly approved a supplementary budget for 1969 of $2,052,050, raising the total 1969 budget to $156,967,300. The next day a budget of $168,420,000 was authorized for 1970, and the Working Capital Fund was continued at $40,000,000. The Assembly also authorized the secretary-general to proceed with plans for a $73.4 million building project at the UN headquarters to provide space for the expanding staff, with $25 million to come from the UN budget and the rest largely from United States sources.

The financial situation of the UN continued to be precarious during 1969. At the end of the fiscal year (June), the obligations of the UN exceeded its assets by $5.8 million with respect to the regular budget. Delays in appropriations by national governments meant that by the year-end $103.3 million still remained as assessments due to be paid for the 1969 regular budget. Furthermore, $22.3 million of this balance was unlikely to be paid because some members were refusing to pay parts of the regular budget that they argued were illegally included.

Beyond this, the special budgets for the UN Emergency Force and for the UN operations in the Congo had unpaid assessments of $50.6 million and $82.1 million, respectively, which are considered virtually uncollectible. The deficit in the separate budget for the UN Peace-Keeping Force in Cyprus was about $10.8 million. Thus at the end of 1969, member states owed about $246.8 million in assessments from the regular and special budgets of the UN, and questions about the alleged illegality of certain items made it appear that $155 million of the total amount due was virtually uncollectible.

Legal Issues. The International Convention on the Elimination of All Forms of Racial Discrimination, adopted by the Assembly in 1966, became effective on January 4—30 days after the 27th ratification was deposited. The 2d session of the UN Conference on the Law of Treaties met in Vienna April 9–May 22, and adopted a new Convention on the Law of Treaties and a Final Act of the Conference. The Convention on the Law of Treaties was the culmination of efforts of some 20 years.

On December 8 the General Assembly adopted and opened for ratification a Convention on Special Missions and an optional protocol concerning the compulsory settlement of disputes arising from applications of this convention. The Assembly also adopted resolutions on the settlement of civil claims, reports of the International Commission on International Trade Law and the International Law Commission, and the question of defining aggression.

A resolution on the forcible diversion of civil aircraft in flight was adopted on December 12. It urged states to prosecute persons who perpetrate such acts, called on the International Civil Aviation Organization to take steps toward an international convention for measures with respect to the unlawful seizure of civil aircraft, and invited all states to ratify the Convention on Offenses and Certain Other Acts Committed on Board Aircraft, which was signed in September 1963.

SECURITY COUNCIL

The Security Council in 1969 was concerned primarily with the gradual escalation of the conflict in the Middle East and with continued problems of decolonization in Africa.

Middle East. Conversations between UN representatives of the "Big Four" states—France, the USSR, the United Kingdom, and the United States—continued behind the scenes during 1969, with no success, in efforts to find a solution to the situation in the Middle East. On February 8, Jordan requested a meeting of the Security Council to consider "continued Israeli defiance" of the May 1968 security resolution calling on Israel to desist from further actions toward altering the legal status of Jerusalem. The president of the Security Council announced on February 10 the postponement of this meeting because Israel had decided to defer the legislation that Jordan was protesting.

Complaints by Jordan and Israel were considered by the Security Council in eight meetings between

March 27 and April 1. On April 1 (by a vote of 11 to 0, with 4 abstentions) the Council condemned "the recent premeditated air attacks launched by Israel on Jordanian villages and populated areas in flagrant violation of the United Nations Charter and the cease-fire resolutions." The Council deplored the loss of civilian life and damage to property and warned Israel that if such attacks were repeated, "further more effective steps as envisaged in the Charter" would have to be considered.

After three meetings on the issue, the Security Council on July 3 voted unanimously to censure in the strongest terms all measures taken to change the status of Jerusalem. The Council also deplored Israel's failure to show any regard for resolutions on that city made by the General Assembly and the Security Council. The Security Council had begun consideration of the question on June 30, following a complaint lodged by Jordan against Israel for the measures taken in Jerusalem.

On August 12, Lebanon requested an urgent meeting of the Security Council "in view of the situation endangering the peace and security of Lebanon." The request detailed Israeli air attacks on civilian villages in southern Lebanon on August 11. Israel, in a letter on August 12, complained that Lebanon was harboring terrorists and said Israel had been forced to take measures in self-defense.

The Council considered the matter in five meetings, beginning on August 13, and on August 26 adopted unanimously a resolution condemning the premeditated air attack by Israel on villages in southern Lebanon and deploring all violent incidents in violation of the cease-fire. The Council also deplored "the extension of the area of the fighting" and declared that "such actions of military reprisal

ORGANIZATION OF THE UNITED NATIONS

THE SECRETARIAT

Secretary-General: U Thant

THE GENERAL ASSEMBLY

President: Angie E. Brooks (Liberia), 24th session. The 126 member nations are as follows:

Afghanistan	Ghana	Nigeria
Albania	Greece	Norway
Algeria	Guatemala	Pakistan
Argentina	Guinea	Panama
Australia	Guyana	Paraguay
Austria	Haiti	Peru
Barbados	Honduras	Philippines
Belgium	Hungary	Poland
Belorussia	Iceland	Portugal
Bolivia	India	Rumania
Botswana	Indonesia	Rwanda
Brazil	Iran	Saudi Arabia
Bulgaria	Iraq	Senegal
Burma	Ireland	Sierra Leone
Burundi	Israel	Singapore
Cambodia	Italy	Somalia
Cameroon	Ivory Coast	South Africa
Canada	Jamaica	Southern Yemen
Central African	Japan	Spain
Republic	Jordan	Sudan
Ceylon	Kenya	Swaziland
Chad	Kuwait	Sweden
Chile	Laos	Syria
China	Lebanon	Tanzania
Colombia	Lesotho	Thailand
Congo (Brazzaville)	Liberia	Togo
Congo (Kinshasa)	Libya	Trinidad and
Costa Rica	Luxembourg	Tobago
Cuba	Malagasy Republic	Tunisia
Cyprus	Malawi	Turkey
Czechoslovakia	Malaysia	Uganda
Dahomey	Maldive Islands	Ukraine
Denmark	Mali	USSR
Dominican	Malta	United Arab
Republic	Mauritania	Republic
Ecuador	Mauritius	United Kingdom
El Salvador	Mexico	United States
Equatorial Guinea	Mongolia	Upper Volta
Ethiopia	Morocco	Uruguay
Finland	Nepal	Venezuela
France	Netherlands	Yemen
Gabon	New Zealand	Yugoslavia
Gambia	Nicaragua	Zambia
	Niger	

COMMITTEES

General: Composed of 25 members as follows: the General Assembly president; the 17 General Assembly vice presidents (heads of delegations, or their deputies, of Barbados, Chile, China, Denmark, France, Ghana, Indonesia, Jordan, Luxembourg, Malawi, Mongolia, Nigeria, Panama, USSR, United Kingdom, United States, and Yugoslavia); and the chairmen of the following 7 main committees, which are composed of representatives of all 126 member countries:

First (Political and Security): Agha Shahi (Pakistan)
Special Political: Eugeniusz Kulaga (Poland)
Second (Economic and Financial): Costa P. Caranicas (Greece)
Third (Social, Humanitarian and Cultural): Mrs. Abdallahi Ould Daddah Turkia (Mauritania)
Fourth (Trust and Non-Self-Governing Territories): Theodore Idzumbuir (Congo—Kinshasa)
Fifth (Administrative and Budgetary): David Silveira da Mota, Jr. (Brazil)
Sixth (Legal): Gonzalo Alcivar (Ecuador)

THE SECURITY COUNCIL

(Membership ends on December 31 of the year noted; asterisks indicate permanent membership.)

Burundi (1971)	Nepal (1970)	Syria (1971)
China*	Nicaragua (1971)	USSR*
Colombia (1970)	Poland (1971)	United Kingdom*
Finland (1970)	Sierra Leone (1971)	United States*
France*	Spain (1970)	Zambia (1970)

Military Staff Committee: Representatives of chiefs of staffs of China, France, USSR, United Kingdom, and United States.
Disarmament Commission: Representatives of all 126 members.

THE ECONOMIC AND SOCIAL COUNCIL

President: Raymond Scheyven (Belgium), 46th and 47th sessions. (Membership ends on December 31 of the year noted.)

Argentina (1970)	India (1970)	Sudan (1971)
Brazil (1972)	Indonesia (1971)	Tunisia (1972)
Bulgaria (1970)	Ireland (1970)	USSR (1971)
Ceylon (1972)	Italy (1972)	United Kingdom
Chad (1970)	Jamaica (1971)	(1971)
Congo (Brazzaville)	Japan (1970)	United States
(1970)	Kenya (1972)	(1970)
France (1972)	Norway (1971)	Upper Volta (1970)
Ghana (1972)	Pakistan (1971)	Uruguay (1971)
Greece (1972)	Peru (1972)	Yugoslavia (1971)

THE TRUSTEESHIP COUNCIL

President: Paul Gaschignard (France), 36th session.

Australia[1]	France[2]	United Kingdom[2]
China[2]	USSR[2]	United States[1]

[1] Administers trust territory. [2] Permanent member of Security Council not administering trust territory.

THE INTERNATIONAL COURT OF JUSTICE

President: Muhammad Zafrullah Khan (Pakistan).
Vice President: Fouad Ammoun (Lebanon).

(Judges listed in order of precedence)

Sir Gerald Fitzmaurice (UK)	Charles D. Onyeama
Luis Padilla Nervo	(Nigeria)
(Mexico)	Federico de Castro (Spain)
Isaac Forster (Senegal)	Hardy C. Dillard (USA)
André Gros (France)	Louis Ignacio-Pinto
César Bengzon (Philippines)	(Dahomey)
Sture Petrén (Sweden)	Eduardo Jiménez de Aréchaga
Manfred Lachs (Poland)	(Uruguay)
	Platon D. Morozov (USSR)

SPECIALIZED AGENCIES

Food and Agriculture Organization of the United Nations (FAO); Intergovernmental Maritime Consultative Organization (IMCO); International Bank for Reconstruction and Development (World Bank; IBRD); International Civil Aviation Organization (ICAO); International Development Association (IDA); International Finance Corporation (IFC); International Labor Organization (ILO); International Monetary Fund (IMF); International Telecommunication Union (ITU); United Nations Educational, Scientific and Cultural Organization (UNESCO); Universal Postal Union (UPU); World Health Organization (WHO); World Meteorological Organization (WMO).

and other grave violations of the cease-fire cannot be tolerated."

Following a fire on August 21 in the Al Aksa (Aqsa) Mosque in Jerusalem, 25 states requested an urgent meeting "to consider the grievous situation resulting from the extensive damage caused by arson to the Holy Al Aqsa Mosque." At the same time the states again questioned the "legitimacy of Israeli authority over the Holy City." The Security Council considered the matters in four meetings and on September 15 adopted a resolution determining that the "execrable act of desecration and profanation" emphasized the immediate necessity of Israel's desisting from violation of UN resolutions on Jerusalem and rescinding all measures designed to alter the status of the city.

Between mid-September and the end of 1969, outbreaks along the cease-fire lines between Israel and her Arab neighbors occurred almost daily. By December, daily air attacks across the borders were commonplace, and the extent of deterioration of the situation was reflected in the fact that none of the parties bothered to make formal requests for Security Council meetings. But the Council continued to be informed on the incidents by the UN observer missions along the cease-fire lines.

Rhodesia. The Security Council committee concerning Rhodesia, created in May 1968, reported in January that Rhodesia's trade remained substantial, despite the Council's sanction resolutions, because only certain commodities were involved and because some states continued to trade with the area in contravention of the embargo. Late in May, 60 governments requested an urgent meeting of the Council to attempt to take steps to enforce sanctions against the regime in Rhodesia. After seven meetings, beginning on June 13, the Security Council on June 24 failed in its attempt to adopt a resolution asking all states to sever all relations with Rhodesia.

Namibia. Following a request from 46 states, the Security Council on March 20 called on South Africa to withdraw its administration from the territory of Namibia. After meetings held between July 30 and August 12 at the request of the 11 states comprising the UN Council for Namibia, the Security Council on August 12 again called on South Africa to withdraw "immediately and, in any case, before October 4," or the Council would take additional steps. On October 24 the UN Council for Namibia reported to the Security Council on South Africa's continued presence and expressed its grave concern, but no action followed.

Cyprus. The Security Council decided on June 10 to extend the mandate of the UN Peace-Keeping Force in Cyprus until Dec. 15, 1969. On December 11 the Council extended the force until June 15, 1970, "in the expectation that by then sufficient progress towards a final solution will make possible a withdrawal or substantial reduction of the force."

Zambia. Following a protest by Zambia and the states in the Organization of African Unity, the Council on July 28 censured the Portuguese attacks on a village in Zambia on June 30 and called on Portugal to desist from violating Zambia's territorial integrity and carrying out unprovoked raids against that country.

Senegal. On November 27, Senegal complained to the Security Council that Portugal had shelled a village in Senegal. The Council considered the matter and on December 9 "strongly" condemned the Portuguese authorities for the shelling.

Northern Ireland. The Security Council met on August 20 to consider a request by Ireland that "a UN peace-keeping force be sent to the Six Counties of Northern Ireland." But after hearing various spokesmen, the meeting adjourned without adopting the agenda.

Micro-States. At the request of the United States, the Security Council held meetings and on August 29 decided to establish a committee of experts to consider the relationship of the very small emerging states with the United Nations.

ECONOMIC AND SOCIAL COUNCIL

The 46th session of the Economic and Social Council was held in New York, May 12–June 6, 1969. The session endorsed new measures to strengthen respect for human rights, combat more effectively the policies of apartheid, prevent infringements of trade union rights in southern Africa, protect the rights of women, and ensure the effective control of narcotic drugs. The Council also took action to promote progress as an integral part of development and to intensify activities in science and technology. Plans were approved to facilitate the conclusion of tax treaties between developed and developing countries, and resolutions were passed on land reform, the role of cooperative movements in economic development, and the granting of consultative status to a number of nongovernmental organizations.

The 47th session of the Council was held in Geneva, July 14–August 8. Recommendations were adopted on measures to improve UN activities in promoting tourism, private foreign investment and exports in the developing countries, study of mineral resources of the sea, applications of science and technology to development, and regional technical cooperation. Work was also done in preparation for the UN Conference on Human Environment in 1972, and resolutions were adopted on an international volunteer corps, preparations for the Second Development Decade and the International Education Year, and international action relating to youth.

The 47th session was resumed in meetings in New York in October, during which the Council considered a report on progress in preparing an international development strategy for the 1970's. Reports from a variety of UN bodies also were considered. The session resumed again on November 18 and adopted a resolution recommending the transformation of the International Union of Official Travel Organizations—a nongovernmental organization—into an intergovernmental tourism body.

TRUSTEESHIP COUNCIL

The Trusteeship Council held its 36th session in New York, May 29–June 19. It adopted conclusions and recommendations concerning the political, social, economic, and educational advancement of the two remaining Trust Territories—New Guinea, administered by Australia, and the Pacific Islands (Micronesia), administered by the United States.

INTERNATIONAL COURT OF JUSTICE

On February 20 the court delivered its judgment, by 11 votes to 6, in the North Sea Continental Shelf cases (Federal Republic of Germany v. Denmark; Federal Republic of Germany v. Netherlands). The cases, which had been brought to the Court in 1967, pertained to the delimitation of the continental shelf between the parties involved in each case.

The parties asked the court to state the principles and rules of international law applicable.

The court rejected the contentions of Denmark and the Netherlands that the delimitations had to be carried out according to the principles of equidistance as defined by Article 6 of the 1958 Geneva Convention on the Continental Shelf, holding that the Federal Republic of Germany was not bound by the article because it had not ratified the treaty. The court also rejected the German argument that sought acceptance of the principle of apportionment of the continental shelf into equitable shares. It held that each party had an original right to those areas of the shelf that constitute the natural prolongation of its land territory into and under the sea and that the question was one of delimiting those areas, not of apportioning them. The parties agreed thereafter to carry out the delimitation on the basis of the principles stated by the court.

The court continued its hearings of the Barcelona Traction, Light and Power Company Limited case (Belgium v. Spain). The case involves compensation being sought for damages alleged to have been caused to Belgium nationals (shareholders in the traction company) by the conduct of various Spanish government organs.

(See also INTERNATIONAL LAW.)

SPECIALIZED AGENCIES

Although the specialized agencies are international agencies totally separate technically from the UN, they are in a unique relationship to it in the implementation of its recommended economic and social programs. The activities of these agencies during 1969 involved hundreds of programs. The following are some of the highlights of their work.

Food and Agriculture Organization. The biennial conference of the FAO, held in November in Rome, adopted the Indicative World Plan for agricultural development. This plan, which has been in preparation for four years, sets goals aimed at meeting the food and agricultural needs of an additional 1 billion people by 1985.

Intergovernmental Maritime Consultative Organization. In November and December the IMCO sponsored an International Legal Conference on Marine Pollution to proceed with the drafting of an international convention concerning both joint actions and liabilities that might be involved in the threat of pollution resulting from an accident on the high seas, such as the disastrous oil spill from the tanker *Torrey Canyon* off the coast of Cornwall, England, in 1967.

International Bank for Reconstruction and Development. The annual report of the IBRD (World Bank), issued in September, indicated that the bank, the International Development Association, and the International Finance Corporation had made a record level of commitments to developing countries totaling $1,877,000,000. This was almost double the level of 1968 and 67% above the average for the previous five years.

Also reported was the belief of the World Bank that for the first time the development effort was beginning to show results. (See also FOREIGN AID.)

International Civil Aviation Organization. The Council of the ICAO established in May a special committee to develop preventive measures and procedures aimed at effectively discouraging the illegal seizure of civil aircraft. The 1963 Convention on Offenses and Certain Other Acts Committed on

UNITED NATIONS

NEW U. S. DELEGATE to the UN in 1969 was Mrs. Shirley Temple Black, former child star of motion pictures.

Board Aircraft came into effect on December 4, following by 90 days the required 12th ratification of the treaty.

International Labor Organization. As a testimony to the 40-year effort of the ILO to promote social justice, the ILO was awarded the Nobel Peace Prize in Oslo on December 10. (See NOBEL PRIZES.)

International Telecommunication Union. May 17 was celebrated as World Telecommunication Day, marking the 104th anniversary of the international organization that is now the ITU. The ITU's major efforts during 1969 were in promoting international cooperation and the development of new technical facilities in telecommunications.

United Nations Educational, Scientific and Cultural Organization. The Executive Board of UNESCO adopted resolutions in October 1969 aimed at preserving cultural properties caught in the areas of the Middle East crisis. In December, 50 countries met in Paris under the auspices of UNESCO to discuss international conventions designed to ensure the fullest use of space communication for education, science, culture, and information.

World Health Organization. World Health Day, sponsored by WHO, was observed on April 7. The theme of the 1969 observance, "Health, Labor, and Productivity," was aimed at focusing attention on the reciprocal relationship between health and economic productivity. The World Health Assembly met in Boston, July 8–24, and adopted a working budget of $67,650,000 to carry out its health programs in 1970.

World Meteorological Organization. The Typhoon Committee of ECAFE (Economic Commission for Asia and the Far East) held a six-day conference in Manila in December. The conference was sponsored by the World Meteorological Organization in the interest of redoubling efforts to control typhoon damage in Southeast Asia.

THOMAS HOVET, JR.
University of Oregon

In a shining display of national scientific and technological competence, the United States sent astronauts to the moon's surface in 1969. (*Left*) Applause resounded as Neil Armstrong, the first man to set foot on the moon, addressed a joint session of Congress on September 16. In the background are Vice President Spiro T. Agnew (*left*) and House Speaker John McCormack. (*Opposite page*) New York City gave the Apollo 11 crew its acclaim in a jubilant parade on August 13.

UPI

UNITED STATES

"We have found ourselves rich in goods, but ragged in spirit; reaching with magnificent precision for the moon, but falling into raucous discord on earth. We are caught in war, wanting peace. We are torn by division, wanting unity. We see around us empty lives, wanting fulfillment. We see tasks that need doing, waiting for hands to do them...."
—From the Inaugural Address of Richard M. Nixon, 37th President of the United States (Jan. 20, 1969)

DOMESTIC AFFAIRS

The divisions and disunity that President Nixon described in his Inaugural Address had been an abrasive fact of life in the United States during much of the 1960's. Between January 1967 and August 1968, more than 40% of the central cities in the United States had experienced civil disorders—a chain "reaction of racial violence" that the National Advisory Commission on Civil Disorders attributed primarily to "white racism." College and university campuses were also centers of deep unrest, related both to the war in Vietnam and to dissatisfactions with university life and policies.

These problems remained at the beginning of 1969 and were complicated by other divisions in American life. The disparities between the poor and the nonpoor persisted. Although median family income had risen to $8,632, the Census Bureau still counted 25 million people living in poverty in 1969. There were continuing tensions and hostilities between black and white and between educational and economic classes. The "Generation Gap"—between old and new values, old and new life styles—was a continuing preoccupation in families and forums.

In a political and intellectual sense, the lines of a class struggle had also been drawn. It was defined by the political historian, Theodore H. White, who observed that "never have America's leading cultural media, its university thinkers, its influence makers been more intrigued by experiment and change; but in no election [1968] have the mute masses more completely separated themselves from such leadership and thinking. Mr. Nixon's problem [in 1969] is to interpret what the silent people think, and govern the country against the grain of what its more important thinkers think."

There was more to 1969, however, than conflict and disunity. In the most triumphant voyages in the history of man, the United States twice landed men on the moon while the world watched in enchantment, by television. The U. S. economy produced new heights of prosperity. It was a year for underdogs, as the New York Jets won the professional football championship and the New York Mets became the baseball champions against heavy odds. For the first time, American involvement in the war in Vietnam began to diminish. U. S. battle deaths declined 36% from 1968.

These positive developments failed to still entirely the "raucous discord" that had been the leitmotiv of life in the United States in the 1960's. But 1969 saw a dramatic decrease in the levels of social violence and unrest and a cooling of passions. At year's end there was a sense—perhaps false—that the country was regaining its moorings.

Politics. It was popular to describe 1969 as the year of the "Middle Americans." *Time* magazine named them "Man and Woman of the Year" and described them thus:

"Their car windows were plastered with American-flag decals, their ideological totems. In the bumper-sticker dialogue of the freeways, they answered 'Make Love Not War' with 'Honor America' or 'Spiro Is My Hero.' They sent Richard Nixon to the White House and two teams of astronauts to the moon. They were both exalted and afraid. The mysteries of space were nothing, after all, compared with the menacing confusions of their own society."

President Nixon appealed to them as the "Forgot-

HUNDREDS OF THOUSANDS of war protesters staged a peaceful rally in Washington, D.C., November 15.

TELEGRAMS OF SUPPORT piled up on Nixon's desk after he spoke, November 3, on plans to end the war.

'CAUGHT IN WAR, WANTING PEACE'

The United States found itself entangled throughout 1969 in a position that President Nixon summed up as "caught in war, wanting peace." Massive peace rallies, some with roll calls of the dead, developed as a new American phenomenon. But many citizens—Nixon viewed them as the "silent majority"—opposed a quick, complete pullout from combat in Vietnam.

ABOUT 100,000 persons jammed the Boston Common in the October 15 Moratorium Day.

ten Americans" who had "become angry . . . because they love America and they don't like what has been happening to America for the last four years."

They were angered, the opinion polls revealed, by the behavior of campus radicals, by urban rioting, by demonstrations against the war in Vietnam, by the problems of crime and inflation, by the repudiation of their moral values by the avant-garde, and by their sense of powerlessness. Their frustrations brought forth in 1969 "law and order" candidates in major cities across the country and palpable support for President Nixon's cautious efforts

to extricate the United States from the war in Vietnam.

The White House and Congress responded to their mood with proposals to combat "crime in the streets," with legislation to relieve the tax burden on the "average man," and with a consensual decision to forego large new programs of social experimentation and reform. The result, at year's end, was a high popularity rating for the President in the polls and a sense of frustration for the Democrats, who appeared leaderless and groping for issues.

It had been assumed, at the beginning of the

BY CANDLELIGHT, peace demonstrators in New York mass outside St. Patrick's Cathedral.

WASHINGTON ARCH provides the background as young New Yorkers stage a peace ceremony.

GOLD STAR MOTHERS gather at Arlington National Cemetery to back Nixon's policies.

year, that Sen. Edward Kennedy of Massachusetts— the last surviving brother in the Kennedy "dynasty" —would emerge as the Democratic party's leader and as its probable candidate for president in 1972. But in July he was involved in an automobile accident on Chappaquiddick Island off the Massachusetts coast. A young secretary in the car, Mary Jo Kopechne, was killed.

Kennedy's failure to report the accident for hours, along with his incomplete public explanation, ballooned into a national scandal. His political future was left in doubt, although he announced that he would seek reelection to the Senate in 1970. (See also KENNEDY, EDWARD M.)

There were other political casualties during the year. Sen. Eugene McCarthy, who had led the Democratic uprising against President Lyndon Johnson in 1968, announced that he would not seek reelection in 1970. Abe Fortas, who had been denied elevation to chief justice in 1968, resigned from the Supreme Court on May 14 after revelations that he had tentatively accepted a lifetime fee from a foundation headed by a convicted financier, Louis Wolfson. On September 7, Sen. Everett Dirksen of Illinois, long-

UNITED STATES • Information Highlights

Area: 3,615,123 square miles (9,363,096 sq km).

Population: 202,748,000 (1969 est.).

Chief Cities (1968 est.): Washington, D. C., the capital, 815,-000; New York City, 8,020,000; Chicago, 3,460,000; Los Angeles, 2,810,000; Philadelphia, 2,040,000.

Government (1969): *President,* Richard M. Nixon; *Vice President,* Spiro T. Agnew. *Congress*—Senate, 100 members (57 Democrats, 43 Republicans); House of Representatives, 435 members (245 Democrats, 188 Republicans; 2 vacancies).

Religious Faiths: Protestants and Episcopalians, 55% of population; Roman Catholics, 23%; Jews, 5%; Eastern Orthodox, 3%.

Education: *Literacy rate* (1960), 98% of population aged 14 and over. *Total school enrollment* (1966–67)—56,929,872 (elementary, 32,527,000; secondary, 17,328,000; university and higher, 6,389,872).

Finance (1970 est.): *Revenues,* $198,686,000,000; *expenditures,* $195,272,000,000; *public debt,* $371,500,000,000.

Gross National Product (1969): $932,300,000,000.

National Income (1969): $771,200,000,000; *average annual income per person,* $3,803.

Economic Indexes: *Industrial production* (1969) 172.7 (1957–59=100); *agricultural "all-crop" production* (1969), 121 (1957–59=100); *consumer prices* (December 1969), 131.3 (1957–59=100).

Manufacturing (metric tons, 1967): Crude steel, (1969) 141,-000,000 short tons; cement, 64,452,000; meat, 15,517,400; wheat flour, 11,124,000; plastics and resins, 5,736,000.

Crops (metric tons): Corn or maize (1969), 111,121,000 (ranks 1st among world producers); wheat (1969) 42,471,000 (ranks 2d); soybeans (1968), 26,473,000 (ranks 1st); sorghum (1968), 19,447,000 (ranks 1st); cottonseed (1968), 2,842,000 (ranks 2d); citrus fruits, 7,349,000 (ranks 1st).

Minerals (metric tons, 1967): Coal, 510,980,000 (ranks 2d among world producers); crude petroleum, 434,568,000 (ranks 1st); iron ore, 85,332,000 (ranks 2d); phosphate rock, 36,079,000 (ranks 1st); gypsum (1966), 8,749,000 (ranks 1st); copper, 865,500 (ranks 1st); silver (1966), 43,-668,988 troy ounces (ranks 1st).

Foreign Trade (1968): *Exports,* $34,199,000,000 (chief exports, 1967: nonelectrical machinery, $5,950,900,000; transport equipment, $4,525,200,000; cereals and preparations, $2,-681,400,000; electrical machinery, $2,096,900,000); *imports,* $33,066,000,000 (chief imports, 1967: transport equipment, $2,762,400,000; nonelectrical machinery, $1,889,000,000; nonferrous metals, $1,562,300,000). *Chief trading partners:* Canada (took 23% of exports, supplied 26% of imports); Japan (took 9% of exports, supplied 11% of imports); Britain (took 6% of exports, supplied 6% of imports).

Transportation: *Roads* (1966), 3,698,000 miles (5,951,400 km); *motor vehicles* (1967), 95,582,200 (automobiles 80,059,-300); *railways* (1967), 209,292 miles (336,960 km); *merchant vessels* (1967), 2,162 (19,179,000 gross registered tons); *principal airports* (1967), 10,126.

Communications: *Telephones* (1968) 103,385,000; *television stations* (1969), 862; *television sets* (1969), 88,941,000; *radios* (1967), 285,000,000; *daily newspapers* (1968), 1,752.

time leader of Republicans in the Senate, died. A few weks later, House Speaker John McCormack was damaged by allegations that members of his staff had permitted lobbyists to use his congressional office and trade on his name.

The "peace movement," as a political force, also had its setbacks. It mounted in Washington on November 15 the largest political demonstration in the city's history. Perhaps 250,000 people assembled at the Washington Monument to demand an immediate end to the war. But the White House and most members of Congress ignored the demonstration, and by December the peace movement seemed disorganized and uncertain of its future course.

Social Unrest. The Negro ghettos of the central cities became increasingly crowded in 1969, and the conditions of ghetto life showed no dramatic change. At the end of the year, Negroes were more urbanized than whites and accounted for 20% of the

DWIGHT D. EISENHOWER, the 34th U. S. President, died on March 28. His body lay in state at the Capitol.

UPI

total population of the central cities, compared with only 12% in 1950.

Urban disorders, primarily in black neighborhoods, continued in 1969. But there were declines in both the level and incidence of violence. The most serious outbreaks were in moderately large cities—Jacksonville, Hartford, Omaha, Sacramento, Fort Lauderdale. The largest cities escaped serious rioting altogether, but they experienced numerous small-scale confrontations between policemen and bands of black militants. These clashes, said the National Commission on the Causes and Prevention of Violence, "may have marked the beginning of a new pattern" of urban violence: guerrilla fighting.

In Detroit, Chicago, and Los Angeles, there were gun battles between Black Panthers or other militant Negroes and police. The deaths of militants in these battles led to the charge—denied by authorities—that the federal government and local police were engaged in a concerted effort to destroy the Panthers and their allies through repressive tactics. (See also CIVIL RIGHTS MOVEMENT.)

Overall, however, there were 50% fewer incidents of urban disorder than in 1968, according to the Justice Department. But there was no progress in reversing the upward spiral of urban crime. A national study commission reported in 1969 a "significant and disturbing increase" since 1960 in crimes of violence—homicide, robbery, and assault—primarily in the 26 cities with populations of 500,000 or more. They were the result, the commission said, of "conditions of life in the ghetto slum"; if remedial steps were not taken the outlook was for suburbs resembling armed camps and central city neighborhoods so unsafe that they might become "entirely out of police control during nighttime hours."

Compared with those of the central cities, the problems and unrest on the university campuses were of little consequence, although disorders were a common occurrence in the first half of 1969. They involved, according to the American Council of Education, roughly one fifth of the nation's 2,500 institutions of higher learning and about 28% of the 7 million students enrolled in the 1968–69 academic year. Half of the disruptions were protests against the war in Vietnam.

The last half of the year brought a period of campus pacification. The winding down of the war

TEAR GAS and shotguns were fired by police at rock-throwing demonstrators protesting closure of a "people's park" near the University of California, Berkeley, on May 15.

was thought to be a factor, along with the university reforms and a sterner attitude toward disruptions by administrators, who have been encouraged by President Nixon to "have the backbone to stand up against" campus violence. Another factor may have been the declining campus influence of radical groups such as Students for a Democratic Society, which split up into warring, minuscule factions in 1969. At year's end it was estimated that fewer than 3% of college and university students subscribed to "radical" philosophies. (See also EDUCATION.)

The Nixon Administration. President Nixon assumed office in 1969 with the theoretical handicaps that he was a minority president (elected with 43.4% of the vote) and that he faced a Congress controlled at the beginning of his term by the opposition party—the first president to do so since Zachary Taylor in 1849. He was also faced with unrest and disunity.

His first concern was to cool the public passions and to demonstrate that he could govern. "In these difficult years," he said, "America has suffered from a fever of words; from inflated rhetoric that promises more than it can deliver; from angry rhetoric that fans discontents into hatreds; from bombastic rhetoric that postures instead of persuading. We cannot learn from one another until we stop shouting at one another—until we speak quietly enough so that our words can be heard as well as our voices."

In domestic affairs, there were two overriding Nixon priorities, and they were interrelated. He aimed at checking the inflationary tendencies in the economy, which had become severe in 1969 and continued throughout the year. And he aimed at making the federal government "workable"—at finding out which government social programs were effective and at improving "the delivery of federal services." The anti-inflation and workability goals were complementary because both called for a check on increased government spending.

"We do not seek more and more of the same," the President said. "We were not elected to pile new resources and manpower on the top of old programs. We were elected to initiate an era of change. We intend to begin a decade of government reform such as this nation has not witnessed in half a century."

He quickly ordered a cut in the budget for fiscal 1970 proposed by his predecessor: from $195.3 billion to $192 billion. This was followed by a proposal for a drastic reform in the nation's welfare system. Instead of the hodgepodge of existing welfare programs, he asked Congress to enact a "family assistance plan" that would provide every needy family of four with a minimum of $1,600 a year. It was, in effect, a proposal for a guaranteed annual income for all families and was well received.

Late in 1969, the President secured a major reform in the selective service system—a change to induction by lottery—and announced: "We shall not be satisfied until we finally can have the system which I advocated during the campaign of a completely volunteer armed force."

In general, the Nixon administration in its first year sought no major changes in the Great
(*Continued on Page 725*)

IN GOD WE TRUST

91ST CONGRESS OF THE U.S.

(SECOND SESSION)

UPI

SENATE

OFFICERS

President of the Senate: Spiro T. Agnew
President Pro Tempore: Richard B. Russell (D-Ga.)
Majority Leader: Mike Mansfield (D-Mont.)
Majority Whip. Edward M. Kennedy (D-Mass.)
Minority Leader: Hugh Scott (R-Pa.)
Minority Whip: Robert P. Griffin (R-Mich.)

COMMITTEE CHAIRMEN

Aeronautical and Space Sciences: Clinton P. Anderson (D-N. Mex.)
Agriculture and Forestry: Allen J. Ellender (D-La.)
Appropriations: Richard B. Russell (D-Ga.)
Armed Services: John Stennis (D-Miss.)
Banking and Currency: John J. Sparkman (D-Ala.)
Commerce: Warren G. Magnuson (D-Wash.)
District of Columbia: Joseph D. Tydings (D-Md.)
Finance: Russell B. Long (D-La.)
Foreign Relations: J. William Fulbright (D-Ark.)
Government Operations: John L. McClellan (D-Ark.)
Interior and Insular Affairs: Henry M. Jackson (D-Wash.)
Judiciary: James O. Eastland (D-Miss.)
Labor and Public Welfare: Ralph W. Yarborough (D-Texas)
Post Office and Civil Service: Gale W. McGee (D-Wyo.)
Public Works: Jennings Randolph (D-W. Va.)
Rules and Administration: B. Everett Jordan (D-N. C.)

HOUSE

OFFICERS

Speaker of the House: John W. McCormack (D-Mass.)
Majority Leader: Carl Albert (D-Okla.)
Majority Whip: Hale Boggs (D-La.)
Minority Leader: Gerald R. Ford (R-Mich.)
Minority Whip: Leslie C. Arends (R-Ill.)

COMMITTEE CHAIRMEN

Agriculture: W. R. Poage (D-Texas)
Appropriations: George H. Mahon (D-Texas)
Armed Services: L. Mendel Rivers (D-S. C.)
Banking and Currency: Wright Patman (D-Texas)
District of Columbia: John L. McMillan (D-S. C.)
Education and Labor: Carl D. Perkins (D-Ky.)
Foreign Affairs: Thomas E. Morgan (D-Pa.)

Government Operations: William L. Dawson (D-Ill.)
House Administration: Samuel N. Friedel (D-Md.)
Interior and Insular Affairs: Wayne N. Aspinall (D-Colo.)
Interstate and Foreign Commerce: Harley O. Staggers (D-W. Va.)
Judiciary: Emanuel Cellar (D-N. Y.)
Merchant Marine and Fisheries: Edward A. Garmatz (D-Md.)
Post Office and Civil Service: Thaddeus J. Dulski (D-N. Y.)
Public Works: George H. Fallon (D-Md.)
Rules: William M. Colmer (D-Miss.)
Science and Astronautics: George P. Miller (D-Calif.)
Standards of Official Conduct: Melvin Price (D-Ill.)
Un-American Activities: Edwin E. Willis (R-La.)
Veterans' Affairs: Olin E. Teague (D-Texas)
Ways and Means: Wilbur D. Mills (D-Ark.)

SENATE MEMBERSHIP

(As of Jan. 21, 1970: 57 Democrats, 43 Republicans)

Letters after senators' names refer to party affiliation—D for Democrat, R for Republican. Single asterisk (*) denotes term expiring in January 1971; double asterisk (**), term expiring in January 1973; triple asterisk (***) term expiring in January 1975.

ALABAMA
**J. Sparkman, D
***J. B. Allen, D

ALASKA
**T. F. Stevens, R
***M. Gravel, D

ARIZONA
*P. J. Fannin, R
***B. Goldwater, R

ARKANSAS
**J. L. McClellan, D
***J. W. Fulbright, D

CALIFORNIA
*G. Murphy, R
***A. Cranston, D

COLORADO
**G. Allott, R
**P. H. Dominick, R

CONNECTICUT
*T. J. Dodd, D
***A. A. Ribicoff, D

DELAWARE
*J. J. Williams, R
**J. C. Boggs, R

FLORIDA
*S. L. Holland, D
***E. J. Gurney, R

GEORGIA
**R. B. Russell, D
***H. E. Talmadge, D

HAWAII
*H. L. Fong, R
***D. K. Inouye, D

IDAHO
***F. Church, D
**L. B. Jordan, R

ILLINOIS
**C. H. Percy, R
***R. T. Smith, R

INDIANA
*V. Hartke, D
***B. E. Bayh, D

IOWA
**J. Miller, R
***H. E. Hughes, D

KANSAS
**J. B. Pearson, R
***R. Dole, R

KENTUCKY
**J. S. Cooper, R
***M. W. Cook, R

LOUISIANA
**A. J. Ellender, D
***R. B. Long, D

MAINE
**M. Chase Smith, R
*E. S. Muskie, D

MARYLAND
*J. D. Tydings, D
***C. McC. Mathias, Jr., R

MASSACHUSETTS
*E. M. Kennedy, D
**E. W. Brooke, R

MICHIGAN
*P. A. Hart, D
**R. P. Griffin, R

MINNESOTA
*E. J. McCarthy, D
**W. F. Mondale, D

MISSISSIPPI
**J. O. Eastland, D
*J. Stennis, D

MISSOURI
*S. Symington, D
***T. F. Eagleton, D

MONTANA
*M. Mansfield, D
**L. Metcalf, D

NEBRASKA
*R. L. Hruska, R
**C. T. Curtis, R

NEVADA
***A. Bible, D
*H. W. Cannon, D

NEW HAMPSHIRE
***N. Cotton, R
**T. J. McIntyre, D

NEW JERSEY
**C. P. Case, R
*H. A. Williams, Jr., D

NEW MEXICO
**C. P. Anderson, D
*J. M. Montoya, D

NEW YORK
***J. K. Javits, R
*C. E. Goodell, R

NORTH CAROLINA
***S. J. Ervin, Jr., D
**B. E. Jordan, D

NORTH DAKOTA
***M. R. Young, R
*Q. Burdick, D

OHIO
*S. M. Young, D
***W. B. Saxbe, R

OKLAHOMA
*F. R. Harris, D
***H. Bellmon, R

OREGON
**M. Hatfield, R
***R. W. Packwood, R

PENNSYLVANIA
*H. Scott, R
***R. S. Schweiker, R

RHODE ISLAND
*J. O. Pastore, D
**C. Pell, D

SOUTH CAROLINA
**S. Thurmond, R
***E. F. Hollings, D

SOUTH DAKOTA
**K. E. Mundt, R
***G. S. McGovern, D

TENNESSEE
*A. Gore, D
**H. H. Baker, Jr., R

TEXAS
*R. W. Yarborough, D
**J. G. Tower, R

UTAH
***W. F. Bennett, R
*F. E. Moss, D

VERMONT
***G. D. Aiken, R
*W. L. Prouty, R

VIRGINIA
*H. Flood Byrd, Jr., D
**W. B. Spong, Jr., D

WASHINGTON
***W. G. Magnuson, D
*H. M. Jackson, D

WEST VIRGINIA
**J. Randolph, D
*R. C. Byrd, D

WISCONSIN
*W. Proxmire, D
***G. Nelson, D

WYOMING
*G. W. McGee, D
**C. P. Hansen, R

HOUSE MEMBERSHIP

(As of Jan. 21, 1970: 245 Democrats, 188 Republicans, 2 vacancies)

Letters after representatives' names refer to party affiliation—D for Democrat, R for Republican. The abbreviation "At-L." in place of congressional district number means "representative at large." Asterisk (*) before member's name indicates incumbent reelected in 1968 (had served in 90th Congress); double asterisk (**) before name indicates nonincumbent elected in 1968; triple asterisk (***) before name indicates elected in 1969.

ALABAMA
1. *J. Edwards, R
2. *W. L. Dickinson, R
3. *G. W. Andrews, D
4. *W. Nichols, D
5. **W. Flowers, D
6. *J. Buchanan, R
7. *T. Bevill, D
8. *R. E. Jones, D

ALASKA
At-L. *H. W. Pollock, R

ARIZONA
1. *J. J. Rhodes, R
2. *M. K. Udall, D
3. *S. Steiger, R

ARKANSAS
1. **B. Alexander, Jr., D
2. *W. D. Mills, D
3. *J. P. Hammerschmidt, R
4. *D. Pryor, D

CALIFORNIA
1. *D. H. Clausen, R
2. *H. T. Johnson, D
3. *J. E. Moss, D
4. *R. L. Leggett, D
5. *P. Burton, D
6. *W. S. Mailliard, R
7. *J. Cohelan, D

8. *G. P. Miller, D
9. *D. Edwards, D
10. *C. S. Gubser, R
11. *P. N. McCloskey, Jr., R
12. *B. L. Talcott, R
13. *C. M. Teague, R
14. *J. R. Waldie, D
15. *J. J. McFall, D
16. *B. F. Sisk, D
17. **G. M. Anderson, D
18. *R. B. (Bob) Mathias, R
19. *C. Holifield, D
20. *H. A. Smith, R
21. *A. F. Hawkins, D
22. *J. C. Corman, D
23. *D. Clawson, R
24. *G. P. Lipscomb, R
25. *C. E. Wiggins, R
26. *T. M. Rees, D
27. ***B. M. Goldwater, Jr., R
28. *A. Bell, D
29. *G. E. Brown, Jr., D
30. *E. R. Roybal, D
31. *C. H. Wilson, D
32. *C. Hosmer, R
33. *J. L. Pettis, R
34. *R. T. Hanna, D
35. *J. B. Utt, R
36. *Bob Wilson, R
37. *L. Van Deerlin, D
38. *J. V. Tunney, D

COLORADO
1. *B. G. Rogers, D
2. *D. G. Brotzman, R
3. *F. E. Evans, D
4. *W. N. Aspinall, D

CONNECTICUT
1. *E. Q. Daddario, D
2. *W. L. St. Onge, D
3. *R. N. Giaimo, D
4. **L. P. Weicker, Jr., R
5. *J. S. Monagan, D
6. *T. J. Meskill, R

DELAWARE
At-L. *W. V. Roth, Jr., R

FLORIDA
1. *R. L. F. Sikes, D
2. *D. Fuqua, D
3. *C. E. Bennett, D
4. *W. V. Chappell, Jr., D
5. **L. Frey, Jr., R
6. *S. M. Gibbons, D
7. *J. A. Haley, D
8. *W. C. Cramer, R
9. *P. G. Rogers, D
10. *J. H. Burke, R
11. *C. D. Pepper, D
12. *D. B. Fascell, D

GEORGIA
1. *G. E. Hagan, D
2. *M. E. O'Neal, Jr., D

3. *J. T. Brinkley, D
4. *B. B. Blackburn, R
5. *F. Thompson, R
6. *J. J. Flynt, Jr., D
7. *J. W. Davis, D
8. *W. S. Stuckey, Jr., D
9. *P.M. Landrum, D
10. *R. G. Stephens, Jr., D

HAWAII
At-L. *S. M. Matsunaga, D
At-L. *P. T. Mink, D

IDAHO
1. *J. A. McClure, R
2. **O. Hansen, R

ILLLINOIS
1. *W. L. Dawson, D
2. **A. J. Mikva, D
3. *W. T. Murphy, D
4. *E. J. Derwinski, R
5. *J. C. Kluczynski, D
6. Vacancy
7. *F. Annunzio, D
8. *D. Rostenkowski, D
9. *S. R. Yates, D
10. *H. R. Collier, R
11. *R. C. Pucinski, D
12. *R. McClory, R
13. Vacancy
14. *J. N. Erlenborn, R
15. *C. T. Reid, R

16. *J. B. Anderson, R
17. *L. C. Arends, R
18. *R. H. Michel, R
19. *T. F. Railsback, R
20. *P. Findley, R
21. *K. J. Gray, D
22. *W. L. Springer, R
23. *G. E. Shipley, D
24. *C. M. Price, D

INDIANA
1. *R. J. Madden, D
2. **E. F. Landgrebe, R
3. *J. Brademas, D
4. *E. R. Adair, R
5. *R. L. Roudebush, R
6. *W. G. Bray, R
7. *J. T. Myers, R
8. *R. H. Zion, R
9. *L. H. Hamilton, D
10. **D. W. Dennis, R
11. *A. Jacobs, Jr., D

IOWA
1. *F. Schwengel, R
2. *J. C. Culver, D
3. *H. R. Gross, R
4. *J. H. Kyl, R
5. *N. Smith, D
6. *W. Mayne, R
7. *W. J. Scherle, R

KANSAS
1. **K. G. Sebelius, R
2. *C. L. Mize, R
3. *L. Winn, Jr., R
4. *G. E. Shriver, R
5. *J. Skubitz, R

KENTUCKY
1. *F. A. Stubblefield, D
2. *W. H. Natcher, D
3. *W. O. Cowger, R
4. *M. G. (Gene) Snyder, R
5. *T. L. Carter, R
6. *J. C. Watts, D
7. *C. D. Perkins, D

LOUISIANA
1. *F. E. Hébert, D
2. *H. Boggs, D
3. **P. T. Caffery, D
4. *J. D. Waggonner, Jr., D
5. *O. E. Passman, D
6. *J. R. Rarick, D
7. *E. W. Edwards, D
8. *S. O. Long, D

MAINE
1. *P. N. Kyros, D
2. *W. D. Hathaway, D

MARYLAND
1. *R. C. B. Morton, R
2. *C. D. Long, D
3. *E. A. Garmatz, D
4. *G. H. Fallon, D
5. **L. J. Hogan, R
6. **J. G. Beall, Jr., R
7. *S. N. Friedel, D
8. *G. Gude, R

MASSACHUSETTS
1. *S. O. Conte, R
2. *E.P. Boland, D
3. *P. J. Philbin, D
4. *H. D. Donohue, D
5. *F. B. Morse, R
6. ***M. J. Harrington, D
7. *T. H. Macdonald, D
8. *T. P. O'Neill, Jr., D
9. *J. W. McCormack, D
10. *M. M. Heckler, R
11. *J. A. Burke, D
12. *H. Keith, R

MICHIGAN
1. *J. Conyers, Jr., D
2. *M. L. Esch, R
3. *G. Brown, R
4. *E. Hutchinson, R
5. *G. R. Ford, R
6. *C. E. Chamberlain, R
7. *D. W. Riegle, Jr., R
8. *J. Harvey, R
9. *G. A. Vander Jagt, R
10. *E. A. Cederberg, R
11. *P. E. Ruppe, R
12. *J. G. O'Hara, D
13. *C. C. Diggs, Jr., D
14. *L. N. Nedzi, D
15. *W. D. Ford, D

16. *J. D. Dingell, D
17. *M. W. Griffiths, D
18. *W. S. Broomfield, R
19. *J. H. McDonald, R

MINNESOTA
1. *A. H. Quie, R
2. *A. Nelsen, R
3. *C. MacGregor, R
4. *J. E. Karth, D
5. *D. M. Fraser, D
6. *J. M. Zwach, R
7. *O. Langen, R
8. *J. A. Blatnik, D

MISSISSIPPI
1. *T. G. Abernethy, D
2. *J. L. Whitten, D
3. *C. H. Griffin, D
4. *G. V. Montgomery, D
5. *W. M. Colmer, D

MISSOURI
1. **W. L. Clay, D
2. **J. W. Symington, D
3. *L. K. Sullivan, D
4. *W. J. Randall, D
5. *R. Bolling, D
6. *W. R. Hull, Jr., D
7. *D. G. Hall, D
8. *R. H. Ichord, D
9. *W. L. Hungate, D
10. **B. D. Burlison, D

MONTANA
1. *A. Olsen, D
2. ***J. Melcher, D

NEBRASKA
1. *R. V. Denney, R
2. *G. C. Cunningham, R
3. *D. T. Martin, R

NEVADA
At-L. *W. S. Baring, D

NEW HAMPSHIRE
1. *L. C. Wyman, R
2. *J. C. Cleveland, R

NEW JERSEY
1. *J. E. Hunt, R
2. *C. W. Sandman, Jr., R
3. *J. J. Howard, D
4. *F. Thompson, Jr., D
5. *P. H. B. Frelinghuysen, R
6. *W. T. Cahill, R
7. *W. B. Widnall, R
8. ***R. A. Roe, D
9. *H. Helstoski, D
10. *P. W. Rodino, Jr., D
11. *J. G. Minish, D
12. *F. P. Dwyer, D
13. *C. E. Gallagher, D
14. *D. V. Daniels, D
15. *E. J. Patten, D

NEW MEXICO
1. **M. Lujan, Jr., R
2. **Ed Foreman, R

NEW YORK
1. *O. G. Pike, D
2. *J. R. Grover, Jr., R
3. *L. L. Wolff,, D
4. *J. W. Wydler, R
5. *A. K. Lowenstein, D
6. *S. Halpern, R
7. *J. P. Addabbo, D
8. *B. S. Rosenthal, D
9. *J. J. Delaney, D
10. *E. Celler, D
11. *F. J. Brasco, D
12. **S. Chisholm, D
13. *B. L. Podell, D
14. *J. J. Rooney, D
15. *H. L. Carey, D
16. *J. M. Murphy, D
17. *E. I. Koch, D
18. *A. C. Powell, D†
19. *L. Farbstein, D
20. *W. F. Ryan, D
21. *J. H. Scheuer, D
22. *J. H. Gilbert, D
23. *J. B. Bingham, D
24. **M. Biaggi, D
25. *R. L. Ottinger, D
26. *O. R. Reid, R
27. **M. B. McKneally, R
28. **H. Fish, Jr., R
29. *D. E. Button, R
30. *C. J. King, R

31. *R. C. McEwen, R
32. *A. Pirnie, R
33. *H. W. Robison, R
34. *J. M. Hanley, D
35. *S. S. Stratton, D
36. *F. Horton, R
37. *B. B. Conable, Jr., R
38. **J. F. Hastings, R
39. *R. D. McCarthy, D
40. *H. P. Smith III, R
41. *T. J. Dulski, D

NORTH CAROLINA
1. *W. B. Jones, D
2. *L. H. Fountain, D
3. *D. N. Henderson, D
4. *N. Galifianakis, D
5. **W. (Vinegar Bend) Mizell, R
6. **L. R. Preyer, D
7. *A. A. Lennon, D
8. **E. B. Ruth, R
9. *C. Raper Jonas, R
10. *J. T. Broyhill, R
11. *R. A. Taylor, D

NORTH DAKOTA
1. *M. Andrews, R
2. *T. S. Kleppe, R

OHIO
1. *R. Taft, Jr., R
2. *D. D. Clancy, R
3. *C. W. Whalen, Jr., R
4. *W. M. McCulloch, R
5. *D. L. Latta, R
6. *W. H. Harsha, R
7. *C. J. Brown, Jr., R
8. *J. E. Betts, R
9. *T. L. Ashley, D
10. *C. E. Miller, R
11. *J. W. Stanton, R
12. *S. L. Devine, R
13. *C. A. Mosher, R
14. *W. H. Ayres, R
15. *C. P. Wylie, R
16. *F. T. Bow, R
17. *J. M. Ashbrook, R
18. *W. L. Hays, D
19. *M. J. Kirwan, D
20. *M. A. Feighan, D
21. **L. Stokes, D
22. *C. A. Vanik, D
23. *W. E. Minshall, R
24. *D. E. Lukens, R

OKLAHOMA
1. *P. Belcher, R
2. *Ed Edmondson, D
3. *C. B. Albert, D
4. *T. Steed, D
5. *J. Jarman, D
6. **J. N. (Happy) Camp, R

OREGON
1. *W. Wyatt, R
2. *Al Ullman, D
3. *E. Green, D
4. *J. Dellenback, R

PENNSYLVANIA
1. *W. A. Barrett, D
2. *R. N. C. Nix, D
3. *J. A. Byrne, D
4. *J. Eilberg, D
5. *W. J. Green III, D
6. **G. Yatron, D
7. *L. G. Williams, R
8. *E. G. Biester, Jr., R
9. *G. R. Watkins, R
10. *J. M. McDade, R
11. *D. J. Flood, D
12. *J. I. Whalley, R
13. **R. L. Coughlin, R
14. *W. S. Moorhead, D
15. *F. B. Rooney, D
16. *E. D. Eshleman, R
17. *H. T. Schneebeli, R
18. *R. J. Corbett, R
19. *G. A. Goodling, R
20. *J. M. Gaydos, D††
21. *J. H. Dent, D
22. *J. P. Saylor, R
23. *A. W. Johnson, R
24. *J. P. Vigorito, D
25. *F. M. Clark, D
26. *T. E. Morgan, D
27. *J. G. Fulton, R

RHODE ISLAND
1. *F. J. St. Germain, D
2. *R. O. Tiernan, D

SOUTH CAROLINA
1. *L. M. Rivers, D
2. *A. W. Watson, R
3. *Wm. J. B. Dorn, D
4. **J. R. Mann, D
5. *T. S. Gettys, D
6. *J. L. McMillan, D

SOUTH DAKOTA
1. *B. Reifel, R
2. *E. Y. Berry, R

TENNESSEE
1. *J. H. Quillen, R
2. *J. J. Duncan, R
3. *W. E. Brock III, R
4. *J. L. Evins, D
5. *R. H. Fulton, D
6. *W. R. Anderson, D
7. *L. R. Blanton, D
8. ***Ed Jones, D
9. *D. H. Kuykendall, R

TEXAS
1. *W. Patman, D
2. *J. Dowdy, D
3. *J. M. Collins, R
4. *R. Roberts, D
5. *E. Cabell, D
6. *O. E. Teague, D
7. *G. H. W. Bush, R
8. *B. Eckhardt, D
9. *J. Brooks, D
10. *J. J. Pickle, D
11. *W. R. Poage, D
12. *J. C. Wright, D
13. *G. Purcell, D
14. *J. Young, D
15. *E. de la Garza, D
16. *R. C. White, D
17. *O. Burleson, D
18. *R. D. Price, R
19. *G. H. Mahon, D
20. *H. B. Gonzalez, D
21. *O. C. Fisher, D
22. *Bob Casey, D
23. *A. Kazen, Jr., D

UTAH
1. *L. J. Burton, R
2. *S. P. Lloyd, D

VERMONT
At-L. *R. T. Stafford, R

VIRGINIA
1. *T. N. Downing, D
2. **G. W. Whitehurst, R
3. *D. E. Satterfield III, D
4. *W. M. Abbitt, D
5. **W. C. (Dan) Daniel, D
6. *R. H. Poff, R
7. *J. O. Marsh, Jr., D
8. *W. L. Scott, R
9. *W. C. Wampler, R
10. *J. T. Broyhill, R

WASHINGTON
1. *T. M. Pelly, R
2. *L. Meeds, D
3. *J. B. Hansen, D
4. *C. May, R
5. *T. S. Foley, D
6. *F. V. Hicks, D
7. *B. Adams, D

WEST VIRGINIA
1. **R. H. (Bob) Mollohan, D
2. *H. O. Staggers, D
3. *J. M. Slack, Jr., D
4. *K. Hechler, D
5. *J. Kee, D

WISCONSIN
1. *H. C. Schadeberg, R
2. *R. W. Kastenmeier, D
3. *V. W. Thomson, R
4. *C. J. Zablocki, D
5. *H. S. Reuss, D
6. *W. A. Steiger, R
7. ***D. R. Obey, D
8. *J. W. Byrnes, R
9. *G. W. Davis, R
10. *A. E. O'Konski, R

WYOMING
At-L. **J. Wold, R

PUERTO RICO
Resident Commissioner
**J. L. Córdova-Díaz

† Elected to 90th Congress, but barred from seat by vote of the House.
†† Elected to 91st Congress, but sat in 90th to fill unexpired term of deceased incumbent.

(*Continued from Page 721*)
Society programs it had inherited from the Johnson administration. But it sought no expansion in most of these programs, pending cabinet and commission studies to determine the workability of the federal apparatus. As a result, political analysis and commentators found it difficult to pigeonhole the President as either a "liberal" or "conservative" in his first year. His cabinet also was difficult to characterize. It contained a mixture of academicians, businessmen, "liberals," and "conservatives"—the last led by Attorney General John Mitchell and Vice President Spiro Agnew, whose "law and order" postures won wide favor with Middle America.

The President made it clear even before he took office that he intended to bring "balance" to the Supreme Court by the appointment of "strict Constitutional constructionists" as vacancies occurred. For chief justice he chose Warren Earl Burger, who met the President's standards but nevertheless joined a unanimous court in declaring that school desegregation in the South could no longer be delayed. The President's second Supreme Court nominee— Appellate Judge Clement Haynsworth of South Carolina—was rejected by the Senate, 55–45, on November 21, on grounds of ethical "insensitivity" and because of dissatisfaction with his rulings in labor and civil rights cases. (See also SUPREME COURT.)

The civil rights issue caused Nixon other difficulties. His administration's sympathetic attitude toward school desegregation problems in the South was condemned by liberals, while its efforts to open up Negro employment opportunities in labor unions were condemned by the AFL-CIO.

Congress. For Congress 1969 was a year for sorting out national priorities. A principal target in this process was the Defense Department. Its $70 billion defense budget was subjected to the most intense scrutiny in history as congressional committees turned up case after case of waste and duplication in the Pentagon's procurement of weaponry. The highwater mark in this revolt against military waste came when defense critics failed by only one vote in their effort to deny the President funds to begin construction of the Safeguard system of defense against nuclear missiles. (See also MISSILES.) Despite this defeat, military requests were reduced by $5 billion.

The major legislative act was a tax reform bill that lowered individual income tax rates by an average of 5%, exempted 9 million low-income people from the tax rolls, increased Social Security benefits by 15%, and closed or modified many tax loopholes. It reduced the oil depletion allowance from 27.5% to 22%. (See also TAXATION.)

Few other major domestic laws were passed, in keeping with the administration's desire to examine existing federal programs before embarking on new ones. But the shape of future legislative issues emerged. One of these is the new political phenomenon of "consumerism," the effort to make economic and political institutions responsive to popular demands for safety and quality in the products they consume and the environment they inhabit. The phenomenon was also called "Naderism," because of the successful crusades of a young lawyer, Ralph Nader, against unsafe automobiles, industrial hazards, and environmental pollution. Broad public support for these efforts was reflected in numerous legislative proposals for a massive federal attack on consumer problems. (See also CONSUMER AFFAIRS.)

Another emergent issue involved the future role of Congress in U. S. foreign policy commitments. The Senate passed two resolutions on the subject, demanding prior consultation from the executive branch before commitments are made and specifically prohibiting the introduction of U. S. ground combat troops into Laos or Thailand. To some, this reflected the "New Isolationism" in the country, a view that was reinforced by congressional insistence in 1969 on the smallest foreign aid appropriation ($1.8 billion) in the history of the program.

Otherwise, there was general congressional approval of President Nixon's foreign policy initiatives —the deescalation in Vietnam, his moves to improve relations with mainland China, and his efforts to secure a halt to the arms race through negotiations with the Soviet Union on the limitation of strategic weapons.

The 1969 congressional debates over national priorities were certain to continue in the 1970's, centering on the shift of defense funds to domestic purposes. The President expressed agreement in principle to this shift and announced near the end of the year that the Pentagon's share of the federal budget in 1970 would be the smallest since World War II.

Still another unresolved issue raised in Congress was the continuing inflation in the U. S. economy. The President's position was that federal spending must be held in check. Many Democrats, however, insisted on increased federal expenditures, coupled with more vigorous efforts by the White House to hold down the wage-price spiral by persuasion and executive actions.

The Economy. The great horn of plenty, which the U. S. economy had been throughout the 1960's, continued to pour out its goods in 1969. The gross national product (in current dollars) grew from $865.7 billion in 1968 to $932.3 billion in 1969. There was an abundance of jobs for trained workers, and the unemployment rate remained at the low level of between 3% and 4% throughout the year. Affluence was pervasive but far from universal, and there were serious problems that would have to be dealt with in the 1970's.

The median income of white families in the United States was $166 a week, but that for Negro families was only $103. Roughly 12% of the population lived in poverty, as defined by the government. There were at least 11 million substandard and overcrowded dwelling units in the country— 16% of the total housing inventory. Environmental pollution, a product of economic growth, was a matter of increasing national concern.

The most immediate problem of the economy in 1969, however, was inflation. The consumer price index rose by more than 5% in the year—the greatest increase since 1951. Between 1964 and 1969, the cost of living rose 20%. Between January and October 1969, the price of a dozen eggs in Pittsburgh rose from 43 cents to 83 cents. The average cost of a new home rose from $24,200 in 1968 to $25,900 in 1969.

The Nixon administration attempted in 1969 to halt the inflationary spiral with monetary controls and curbs in federal spending. By the end of the year, there were indications of an economic slowdown and even some predictions of a recession in 1970. (See also ECONOMY OF THE UNITED STATES.)

RICHARD HARWOOD
National Editor, "The Washington Post"

UNITED STATES CABINET MEMBERS

President Nixon's cabinet is drawn from the campus and the business world. Ten members are sketched here; biographies of Melvin R. Laird and William P. Rogers appear under their own headings.

DAVID MATTHEW KENNEDY, secretary of the treasury, called in 1969 for moderate tax reform, monetary restraint, and a budgetary surplus. He gave priority to the administration's inflation control measures, which, he conceded, might lead to some increased unemployment. Kennedy is a former board chairman of the Continental Illinois Bank, Chicago, where he led programs to aid the urban poor.

JOHN N(EWTON) MITCHELL, attorney general, tried in 1969 to enhance the administration's image in the South by proposing conservative candidates for federal judgeships and by advocating a slowdown in federal school desegregation efforts. He urged harsh measures against student rioters and narcotics violators. A New York lawyer, he had specialized in bond financing.

WINTON MALCOLM BLOUNT, postmaster general, unsuccessfully proposed in 1969 the elimination of the Post Office Department and the transfer of postal service to a public corporation. He took steps to place postmaster appointments under a merit system. Formerly, he helped found Blount Brothers Corporation, a successful Alabama contracting firm, and was president of the U. S. Chamber of Commerce.

WALTER JOSEPH HICKEL, secretary of the interior, sought to allay the fears of conservationists in 1969 by promoting measures to combat air and water pollution, to restrict offshore oil drilling, to preserve such wilderness areas as the Everglades, and to ensure mine safety. In his earlier career in Alaska, he worked at various trades, built a construction firm in Anchorage, and served as governor.

CLIFFORD MORRIS HARDIN, secretary of agriculture, was concerned in 1969 with alleviating rural poverty and improving the lot of the marginal farmer. A farmer's son, he holds a Ph.D. degree in agricultural economics from Purdue and is an authority on agricultural problems of developing nations. He taught at the University of Wisconsin and Michigan State and was University of Nebraska chancellor.

MAURICE HUBERT STANS, secretary of commerce, concentrated his efforts in 1969 on stimulating trade, building up the maritime industry, and aiding the establishment of business enterprises in the slums. Previously, as a partner in Alexander Grant & Co., a Chicago accounting firm, he helped build it into one of the largest in its field. In 1958–60 he served as director of the U. S. Bureau of the Budget.

GEORGE PRATT SHULTZ, secretary of labor, in 1969 made important contributions to the administration's welfare-reform and job-training programs and took steps to expand employment opportunities for blacks and other minorities. He also promoted improvement in the unemployment insurance program. Formerly, he was a professor at MIT and dean of the University of Chicago graduate school of business.

ROBERT HUTCHINSON FINCH, secretary of health, education, and welfare, in 1969 centered his efforts and those of his staff on reform in welfare and education and improvement of opportunities for slum dwellers. He came in conflict with conservatives on issues such as school desegregation. A California lawyer, he managed Nixon's 1960 campaign and later became lieutenant governor of California.

GEORGE WILCKEN ROMNEY, secretary of housing and urban development, fought an uphill battle in 1969 in efforts to overcome the shortage of capital and other obstacles to mass construction of housing. He was president of American Motors Corp. from 1954 to 1962. As governor of Michigan (1963–68), Romney came into direct confrontation with the urban crisis during the Detroit riots of 1967.

JOHN ANTHONY VOLPE, secretary of transportation, overcame strong opposition in 1969 to his plan to continue development of a supersonic transport plane, but failed to gain enough support to establish a mass transit trust fund. Once a hod carrier, he built his John A. Volpe Construction Co. into a multi-million-dollar firm. He has been federal highway administrator and governor of Massachusetts.

FOREIGN AFFAIRS

The irony of President Nixon's conduct of foreign policy during his first year in office was that what he had to do ran deeply contrary to past expressions of his attitudes and beliefs.

First, the mood of the nation and the political premises of liberal and moderate Democrats and Republicans alike was to pull out of Vietnam. Yet Nixon believed South Vietnam was vital to American security. He had advocated U. S. intervention in 1954 and criticized President Johnson only for not adopting a harder-hitting military policy.

Second, the President found himself presiding over the changing role of the United States from "world policeman" to a more limited role, especially in Asia, in shoring up the international balance of power. As a product of the most intense days of the Cold War, a militant anti-Communist at home and abroad, Nixon must have found this reassessment of America's postwar policy difficult, if not distasteful. This was probably particularly true with regard to U. S.–Soviet relations.

When Nixon was vice president, the Soviet Union was the undisputed leader of a cohesive Communist bloc; any advance by any Communist nation anywhere tended to be viewed as an advance of Soviet power that, because it might upset the balance of power, had to be prevented. But by 1969 the Soviet Union had lost much of its ideological fervor; some of its former satellites wanted greater independence (such as Czechoslovakia, which Moscow crushed in 1968, and Rumania, which President Nixon visited in July); and the Sino-Soviet schism had erupted into a number of border clashes and produced rumors of a preventive Soviet strike. Above all, Moscow had become a nuclear giant. These combined changes all suggested alterations of past U. S.–Soviet behavior. The United States was still in conflict with the Soviets and needed to preserve its deterrent capacity, but it also shared a common interest in maintaining peace, and therefore it needed to cooperate.

Finally and fundamentally, the President, whose primary interest lay in foreign policy, had to face the whole issue of the balance between foreign and domestic affairs. Ending the war in Vietnam, limiting America's overseas commitments, stabilizing political and strategic relationships with the Soviet Union—these were all part of the reexamination of priorities that disillusionment over Vietnam, plus the major urban and racial crisis at home, had brought to the fore of America's political consciousness and conscience.

Vietnam. Concluding the war was the President's prerequisite for dealing with America's domestic problems and restoring a measure of unity and tranquility among its people; failure to end the conflict would drive him from the presidency as it had his predecessor. Among other things, he proposed in May an 8-point program for a mutual withdrawal of North Vietnamese and U. S. troops. (The Communists had earlier suggested a 10-point program demanding a unilateral and unconditional U. S. withdrawal). He also changed American battlefield orders from "maximum pressure" to "protective reaction" to reduce casualties; announced three successive withdrawals amounting to a total of 110,000 troops; speeded up the "Vietnamization" of the war; and exerted pressure on South Vietnamese President Nguyen Van Thieu to offer direct private

negotiations to the Vietcong and establish a commission, including the Vietcong, to arrange internationally supervised elections.

But Hanoi and the Vietcong, which in June established itself as a "provisional government," failed to respond. They apparently felt that if they waited long enough, U. S. public opinion would weary of the war and they could collect the chips. The President was well aware of this purported strategy. By such measures as withdrawing troops and cutting draft calls, he hoped to win time at home and convince the enemy that the United States could maintain a military presence in Vietnam for a long period. By Vietnamizing the hostilities, he expected to entice the Communists into settling now rather than continuing to fight against an increasingly powerful Saigon regime and army.

Nixon's gamble thus depended on continued domestic support and an improvement of South Vietnam's leadership. Domestic criticisms and pressure, however, intensified. In Congress, calls for faster troop withdrawals and the abandonment of the Thieu regime multiplied. On the campuses, resistance grew, spreading to the nation as a whole. Resistance was expressed through moratoriums in October and November—perhaps the most spontaneous and extensive demonstrations for peace in the nation's history. Furthermore, in Saigon, Thieu, instead of broadening his government to attract popular support, narrowed it by replacing a civilian premier with a general, and he took increasingly adamant positions against free elections and a coalition government.

Thus the Communists, before and after Ho Chi Minh's death on September 3, remained adamant, as every move seemed to confirm their belief that the pressure in the United States to quit Vietnam was becoming overwhelming and that the South Vietnamese regime, deprived of American support, would collapse. By year's end, President Nixon's time to extricate the country from Vietnam with an "honorable settlement"—and from Laos, where U. S. air power was apparently increasingly involved in helping the neutralist government fight the Pathet Lao and North Vietnamese forces—was therefore running out.

Overseas Commitments. Until Vietnam, the great fear was of appeasing aggression; since Vietnam, the fear has been of further military involvement. Consequently, the war sparked a reexamination of the global commitments undertaken in the late 1940's and throughout the 1950's, when different international conditions had prevailed. This was particularly true for Asia, as the President explained on his quick global tour following the successful July moon-landing. In the "Guam Doctrine," he declared that the United States would remain a Pacific power and play its role in safeguarding Asia's peace.

It would do so by fulfilling present commitments, plus informal commitments to such nations as India whose importance required U. S. help in case of nuclear threats to them. But existing commitments would not be interpreted in a manner justifying the use of force to repress domestic rebellion. The best defense against insurgency was preventive political and economic reforms; nevertheless, if internal revolts occurred, the United States would provide material and technical assistance and training for governments it deemed worthy of help—but it would provide no ground forces. Asian nations would get economic help to modernize themselves—although no large contributions were promised—and encouraged toward greater regional collective security

UPI

TOGETHER on Midway Island, June 8, Presidents Thieu and Nixon view a military ceremony before conferring about the course of the war in South Vietnam.

arrangements. In short, the principal responsibility for Asian development and security would be on the Asians themselves.

The nature of the more modest U. S. role was best expressed by the President in announcing a new Latin American policy involving a shift away from the Alliance for Progress under U. S. leadership. "For years we in the United States have pursued the illusion that we could remake continents," he said. "Conscious of our wealth and technology, seized by the force of our good intentions, driven by our habitual impatience ... we have sometimes imagined that we knew what was best for everybody else and that we could and should make it happen. But experience has taught us better ...." The United States would continue to assist with funds, but as toward Asia, no dramatic increases were suggested; as a partner rather than a leader, the United States would primarily help through giving the Southern Hemisphere tariff preferences (if Congress agreed).

If Asians and Latin Americans were to rely more upon themselves, so might Europeans. Clearly, U. S. relations with Europe were considered primary. Within a few weeks of assuming office, President Nixon visited Europe to emphasize this point. He first visited NATO headquarters in Belgium, thereby symbolizing the importance with which the United States viewed its most important alliance on the 20th anniversary of that alliance. Then he visited the U. S. allies: West Germany, France (where he established cordial relations with President Charles de Gaulle just before the latter quit office), and Britain.

Everywhere, Nixon expressed his desire to place American-European relations on a more equitable basis; he clearly recognized that the days of U. S. hegemony had passed. While the formulation of a concrete policy toward Europe seemed to await the end of the Vietnam War, the application of the partnership principle to NATO foreshadowed a greater U. S. emphasis upon European responsibility in the alliance's functioning.

U. S.–Soviet Relations. Despite the continued hostility of the United States and the USSR to one another, the danger of nuclear war had increasingly provided both superpowers with a common interest in avoiding total war—and also in avoiding even lesser clashes that might escalate. The symptoms of this mutual recognition of their lot were their increasingly cautious behavior and a number of "arms control" agreement, of which the nuclear antiproliferation treaty was the latest.

The complexity of the new U. S.–Soviet adversary relations was particularly evident in the antiballistic missile (ABM) controversy. On the one hand, their persistent conflict meant that both powers needed to protect themselves: as one acquired a particular weapons system the other felt compelled to follow. On the other hand, their perception of their common interest in preserving peace—strengthened by a tacit understanding that both wanted to contain mainland China—demanded a stabilization of the arms race.

The central issue for each was that of maintaining its deterrent capacity, which depends upon preserving an offensive edge. The opponent must never doubt that he can be destroyed should he attack. Meanwhile, each superpower also was continually trying to devise new defensive weapons to improve protective ability. Since both nations were highly industrialized and scientifically sophisticated, the possibility of a technological breakthrough was seen as a very real threat by each antagonist. Thus the rivalry became a series of offensive and defensive arms spirals as technology constantly devised new arms.

It was in this context that the ABM issue arose. Secretary of Defense Melvin R. Laird contended that the Soviets had attained parity in land-based missiles and were continuing their buildup, particularly of the powerful SS-9 missile. The SS-9 was said to be extremely accurate and capable of carrying a 25-megaton warhead or three 5-megaton warheads that might destroy U. S. Minutemen in their silos in a first strike. The United States had therefore to protect enough of its missiles to ensure their survival to retaliate. Hence the administration proposed a Safeguard system, which, starting with two bases, could be expanded to 12 bases if needed.

The administration's assertion that the nation needed an ABM defense was, however, widely questioned. Among the arguments advanced against the system were: (1) that Safeguard was so technologically complex that it could not be expected to work reliably; (2) that even if it did, it could be overcome by decoys and by saturating the defense with incoming missiles; (3) that the country already had all the strategic hardware it needed to deter a Soviet attack; and (4) that Safeguard would undermine future efforts at arms control and spur a new arms race, as demonstrated by the administration's testing of missiles with multiple, independently targeted vehicles (MIRV's) that could overwhelm any expansion of the Soviet ABM system around Moscow.

The resulting fantastic cost and possible destabilization of the "balance of terror," therefore, made it imperative to halt the arms race at the current technological plateau and missile strengths. The administration, in fact, began exploring this possibility with the Soviets at Helsinki in the Strategic

Arms Limitation Talks (SALT) during November. (See also DEFENSE FORCES; DISARMAMENT.)

The ABM fight in Congress, especially in the Senate, was thus an argument over whether ABM's and MIRV's would contribute to or detract from the strategic balance in the 1970's—a difficult question to assess in an era when the test of weapons is their nonuse rather than their employment. More basically, however, the issue was the balance between foreign and domestic affairs. (See also MISSILES.)

Priorities. ABM and MIRV were in the final analysis symbolic issues. Since the end of World War II, presidents have been preoccupied with foreign policy. Even the presidents whose primary interests were domestic saw their programs overwhelmed by foreign policy. Thus Harry Truman's Fair Deal gave way to containment of communism, and Lyndon Johnson's Great Society was overcome by Vietnam. But the price for this concentration of attention and intellectual and economic resources on the conduct of external policy was the neglect of major domestic problems such as urban blight, race relations, poverty, and pollution. By 1969 these could no longer be neglected or papered over. Therefore, the struggle over priorities confronted the Nixon administration from the outset.

This basic issue aroused intense emotion and led to vigorous denunciations of the "military-industrial complex," which presumably had a stake in a high level of international tension to justify more arms for soldiers, greater profits for businessmen, and reelection of congressmen who brought jobs and money to their constituents. The widely held assumption that the military-industrial complex was a powerful monolith and that it "made" hard-line foreign policy decisions was the reverse side of the desire to reduce external commitments and to divert extensive financial resources to domestic purposes. (The administration sought to discourage hopes of a massive "peace dividend" by saying that existing nondefense expenditures would absorb most of the funds that would be released from defense spending when the Vietnam fighting should end.)

Although the Safeguard ABM system scraped through by one vote in the Senate on August 6, a bipartisan bloc of senators immediately afterward voted that all major weapons contracts be subject to regular cost reporting and independent auditing. The lawmakers also agreed unanimously to control the development and use of chemical and biological weapons; they questioned the development of a number of weapons systems; and they pushed for a reduction in the size of the armed forces.

Most of these matters were omitted or watered down in the final Senate-House authorization bill for military procurement, but the fight was a sign that the Senate at least was no longer willing to let any program labeled "defense" pass unchallenged. Indeed, in June it put the President on notice that it would not continue merely to approve executive foreign policy. In the National Commitment Resolution, stating that U. S. commitments could stem only from affirmative action by the executive and legislative branches, it told the President to seek its advice if he wished its consent. In December, it warned him not to involve the country in another Vietnam type of action in Laos or Cambodia.

While these expressions of the Senate's sentiment could not tie the President's hands, they did inform him that he must act with restraint. For Richard Nixon, this must have awakened a memory. During the Eisenhower administration, in the (Joseph) McCarthy period, it had been the conservatives of both parties in the Senate who wanted to restrain the President "because he might be too soft" on communism and appease the Kremlin. Now it was a bipartisan coalition of liberals who urged the restraint of the President because he might be too "hard" on communism and involve the nation in more military adventures.

JOHN W. SPANIER
University of Florida

UPI

THREE WITHDRAWALS of U. S. troops, calling for a total reduction of 110,000 men, were announced in 1969. These men of the Third Marine Division, leaving a combat area near the demilitarized zone to prepare for the journey home, display their feelings.

UPPER VOLTA

The major political event in Upper Volta in 1969 was the trial of former president Maurice Yaméogo and his principal secretary, André Compaoré, slightly more than three years after the overthrow of Yaméogo's government by the current president, Gen. Sangoulé Lamizana. Government-sponsored austerity measures initiated in 1967 began to show results in 1969.

Internal Politics. Yaméogo and Compaoré were charged with embezzling $3 million in funds and properties. On May 8 both defendants were found guilty. Yaméogo was sentenced to five years at hard labor and fined $213,000, and Compaoré was sentenced to three years in prison and given a fine of $27,000. In June, President Lamizana ordered Yaméogo's sentence reduced to two years, and that of Compaoré reduced to 18 months. Yaméogo's son Herman and others involved in a 1967 plot to restore Yaméogo to power were released from detention in June.

In a New Year speech, President Lamizana said that political activity might resume in Upper Volta by the end of 1969. He indicated that this would be in preparation for a return to civilian rule at an unspecified time in the future.

In May, Nazi Boni, a politician long in exile and once prominent in Upper Volta politics, was killed in an automobile accident.

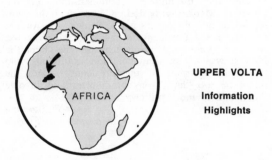

UPPER VOLTA

Information Highlights

Area: 105,869 square miles (274,200 sq km).
Population: 5,175,000 (1968 est.).
Chief Cities (1962): Ouagadougou, the capital, 63,000.
Government: *President*—Sangoulé Lamizana (took office Jan. 3, 1966). *Parliament*—National Assembly dissolved on Jan. 5, 1966.
Religious Faiths: Muslims, 26% of population; Roman Catholics, 3.5%; others, 70.5%.
Education: *Literacy rate* (1969), 5–10% of population. *Total school enrollment* (1965)—115,258 (primary, 107,588; secondary, 5,468; teacher-training, 1,164; technical/vocational, 1,010; university/higher, 28).
Finance (1969): *Revenues,* $36,860,000; *expenditures,* $36,-860,000; *monetary unit,* CFA franc (246.85 francs equal U. S.$1).
Gross National Product (1967): $253,000,000.
Average Annual Income per Person (1967): $50.
Cost of Living Index (1967): 98 (1963 = 100).
Manufacturing (metric tons, 1967): Meat, 11,000.
Crops (metric tons, 1967–68 crop year): Sorghum, 744,000; millet, 350,000; maize, 110,000; peanuts, 94,000; sweet potatoes and yams, 33,000.
Minerals (metric tons, 1966): Gold, 16,075 troy ounces.
Foreign Trade (1967): *Exports,* $18,030,000 (chief exports, 1967: live animals, $9,199,900; raw cotton, $3,410,900; oil-seeds, oil nuts, and oil-kernels, $2,313,100; peanuts, $1,146,400); *imports,* $36,508,000 (chief imports, 1967: textile yarn and fabrics, $4,938,200; transport equipment, $3,435,200; petroleum products, $2,349,600). *Chief trading partners* (1967): France (took 14% of exports, supplied 45% of imports); Ivory Coast (took 49% of exports, supplied 21% of imports); Ghana (took 14% of exports, supplied 16% of imports).
Transportation: *Roads* (1965), 10,380 miles (16,705 km); *motor vehicles* (1967), 10,400 (automobiles 4,800); *railways* (1969), 341 miles (489 km); *principal airport,* Ouagadougou.
Communications: *Telephones* (1968), 2,800; *television stations* (1967), 1; *television sets* (1967), 250; *radios* (1967), 70,000.

Economic Development. At least 60% of the country's outstanding debts in the private sector had been repaid by the end of 1969. Foreign investment was being resumed, and French aid was coming in again. The upturn had been accomplished by severe cuts (30%–50%) in civil servants' and ministers' pay and emoluments. The minister of finance, Maj. Tiemoko Garango, also claimed that most public foreign debts had either been paid or rescheduled. There was still a large trade deficit, though the country's foreign exchange holdings were at their highest levels since 1960.

Foreign Aid. Upper Volta and the United Nations Development Program made an agreement for financing and exploiting the manganese deposits at Tambao. The government will supply about one third of the estimated $1.7 million needed.

The International Development Agency granted $800,000 for development and repair of telecommunications networks and promised more by 1971. Approximately $1.3 million in aid was given by the World Food Program to assist in settling and feeding some 1,800 persons in the Kou River Valley.

VICTOR T. LE VINE
University of Ghana

URBAN AFFAIRS. See BUILDING AND CONSTRUCTION; CITIES AND URBAN AFFAIRS.

URUGUAY

In 1969, Uraguay remained in the state of economic and political crisis that had begun in 1960, although there were mixed signs of improvement. By the end of the year there was confidence that some slackening of austerity and discipline was possible. Living costs rose only 15% in 1969, compared with 66% in 1968 and 136% in 1967.

The government seemed generally to be in political control. But the "Tupamaros," a guerrilla movement that also calls itself the National Liberation Front, attacked property and people openly and almost with impunity during most of the year. Overt extremists in labor unions retained their disruptive capacity, although the members tended to be calm.

Crisis and Response. Crisis has affected the tone of Uruguayan life. President Jorge Pacheco Areco fought for dominance over the General Assembly during much of 1969 and apparently won a victory. However, many observers felt he had breached the constitution; clearly he had reversed a 40-year trend toward an ineffective presidency.

The army was used to threaten strikers and their bank owner employers; the soldiers were uncomfortable in a quasi-political role not played before in this century. Unions were forced to accept governmental discipline and employers used the crisis to gain advantages. The government developed a program of severe social austerity and cut benefits to welfare and retirement beneficiaries.

President Pacheco maintained special security measures throughout most of 1969. They were lifted on March 15 but were reimposed on June 24 following two months of rapidly rising violence and chaos in Montevideo. The disorder was provoked by leftist agitators and students who rejected economic controls, austerity, and rising unemployment.

On July 26 the government ordered all striking bank employees mobilized into the army. The National Assembly declared the move unconstitutional, but in August it backed down on its demand that

URUGUAY

Information Highlights

Area: 72,173 square miles (186,926 sq km).
Population: 2,818,000 (1968 est.).
Chief Cities (1963 census): Montevideo, the capital, 1,158,632; Salto, 57,714; Paysandú, 51,645.
Government: *President*—Jorge Pacheco Areco (took office Dec. 6, 1967). *Parliament* (National Assembly)—Senate, 31 members (party seating, 1968: Colorado party, 16; Blanco party, 13; others, 2); Chamber of Deputies, 99 members (party seating, 1968: Colorado party, 50; Blanco party, 41; others, 8).
Religious Faiths: Roman Catholics, 66.6% of population.
Education: *Literacy rate* (1969), over 91% of population. *Total school enrollment* (1965)—474,792 (primary, 335,089; secondary, 91,371; teacher-training, 4,947; technical/vocational, 26,298; university/higher, 17,087).
Finance (1968 est.): *Revenues,* $390,700,000; *expenditures,* $454,200,000; *monetary unit,* peso (free rate: 249.50 pesos equal U.S.$1).
Gross National Product (1968): $1,558,000,000.
National Income (1966): $446,200,000; *average annual income per person,* $552.
Economic Indexes (1967): *Industrial production* (1966), 109 (1963=100); *agricultural production,* 87 (1963=100); *cost of living,* 736 (1963=100).
Manufacturing (metric tons, 1967): Cement (1966), 465,000; gasoline, 290,000; wine (1966), 850,000 hectoliters.
Crops (metric tons, 1967–68 crop year): Sugar beets, 250,-000; wheat, 147,000; grapes, 100,000.
Minerals (metric tons, 1966): Limestone, 770,669; sand and gravel, 745,372; lime, 60,000.
Foreign Trade (1968): *Exports,* $179,000,000 (chief exports: wool, $53,077,000; meat, 40,430,000; hides, $14,420,000; linseed oil, $1,880,000); *Imports,* $165,000,000 (chief imports, 1967: crude petroleum, $24,040,000; road motor vehicles, $19,170,000; chemicals, drugs, and pharmaceutical products, $6,460,000). *Chief trading partners* (1967): Britain (took 22% of exports, supplied 8% of imports); U.S. (took 7% of exports, supplied 14% of imports); Brazil (took 3% of exports, supplied 12% of imports).
Transportation: *Roads* (1969), 23,488 miles (37,800 km); *motor vehicles* (1967), 236,000 (automobiles 144,000); *railways* (1964), 1,866 miles (3,003 km); *merchant vessels* (1967), 18 (123,000 gross registered tons); *national airline,* Pluna; *principal airport,* Carrasco.
Communications: *Telephones* (1968): 195,000; *television stations* (1967), 6; *television sets* (1967), 200,000; *radios* (1967), 1,000,000; *newspapers* (1965), 35 (daily circulation, 800,000).

President Pacheco rescind the decree. Defense Minister Antonio Francese had told an assembly committee rebellious at presidential rule by decree, "I am here not as a minister but as a general" supporting the president.

The political effects of austerity were severe. Decisive executive leadership had been unknown for half a century and interest groups inevitably have forced concessions. President Pacheco's intimidation of the assembly caused partisan tension. Conflict continued as the assembly and the political parties remained recalcitrant. The conservative Pacheco tended to favor private sector groups; business won concessions and large ranchers forced the resignation of several cabinet members. Working class groups felt they had paid an unfair share of the austerity program.

Economy. In December the National Assembly approved the establishment of a tripartite Committee on Productivity, Prices, and Income, which was effective in limiting cost factors and price rises. The Central Bank acquired much control over private banks, including the right to regulate lending and interest rate policies, numbers of branch offices, and labor policies. The Central Bank may order a bank out of business for failure to comply with its regulations.

In October 1969, President Pacheco began to seek funds to stabilize the economy and begin development plans. Old and new products, including iron ore, rice, and fruits, would be developed for export. Tourism, highways, housing, electric power, and irrigation especially were needed, and many private jobs were required to absorb discharged government and bank employees. Although national funds were not yet available, Pacheco's policies seem to have encouraged the return of some capital.

The International Monetary Fund demanded devaluation of the overvalued peso from the current exchange rate of 250 pesos to U.S.$1 as the price for approving new credits from international or private lending agencies. Pacheco feared devaluation would bring renewed inflation, which would be untenable in internal political terms. The stalemate continued at the end of 1969, as the economy suffered.

Foreign Relations. U.S. envoy Nelson Rockefeller, on a fact finding mission to Latin America for President Nixon, met with President Pacheco at Punta del Este in June. The meeting was shifted from Montevideo following riots and bombings.

In May the government announced its decision to extend its territorial waters from 6 to 12 miles (10–19 km), primarily for fishing rights. In December it increased its claim to 200 miles (320 km). This change is believed to result from a cooling of relations with Brazil and a warming with Argentina. Brazil is actively expanding its fishing industry, and Argentina, trying to protect what it has, urged Uruguay to join it in claiming the further limit.

PHILIP B. TAYLOR, JR.
University of Houston

UTAH

An active legislative year, highlighted by the development of a new state board of higher education, and significant increases in mining marked the year 1969 in Utah.

Legislature and Politics. The 38th state Legislature convened in regular session on Jan. 13, 1969, and adjourned on March 13. During that time it passed 266 laws and 46 resolutions. One of its most significant actions was the creation of the new state board of higher education, which became operative on July 1, 1969. The new board was vested with all the powers and responsibilities formerly held by the governing boards of the individual institutions.

Two significant proposals for amending the state constitution were passed by the legislature and will be submitted to a referendum in the 1970 general election. One of these proposed changing the residence requirement for voting from one year to six months. The other provided for adopting U.S. income tax laws by reference to the federal tax code instead of copying the code in full.

The municipal elections held in 1969 returned to office a majority of the incumbents who chose to run. While Utah's elections are not usually party oriented (the winner's victory is usually attributable to his personal popularity rather than to party label), a trend toward the emergence of local parties has been noted. Among the proposals appearing on the ballot was the creation of a transit authority in the Salt Lake City area. The city of Maeser voted to disincorporate, and the state's two home-rule cities amended their charters. Ogden made the mayoralty an elective, rather than appointive, office. An amendment in Tooele provided for primary elections for municipal officials.

Mining. A hydroelectric site in the bituminous coal fields of the Kaiparowitz Plateau, long a subject of discussion, at last became a reality in 1969. The U. S. Department of the Interior approved the project and the allocation of adequate water for the generation of electricity. The process has been slow while further studies are made on the use of the electricity to be distributed, but as finally developed it promises to be one of the most important industries in the southern part of the state.

Utah's newly functioning beryllium mines in the center of the state are expected to become the non-Communist world's largest source of the metal. When completed, the mines will free the nation of its dependence on overseas sources of beryllium.

These mines, and the recently renewed search for gold in the area around Ophir and Mercur, about 40 miles southwest of Salt Lake City, have greatly eased the state's employment problems.

Minority Groups. The problem of dropouts and juvenile delinquents led to the creation of Women Alert for the Salt Lake Area. This effort was based on the successful action by the women of Indianapolis, Ind.

Life on the Indian reservations of Utah is changing. For several years the Navajo Indians have required little outside help. Recently the Ute Indians on the Duchesne and Ouray reservations initiated self-help programs that are making them much more independent and able to compete in the American market with merchandise and skills.

ELLSWORTH E. WEAVER
University of Utah

UTAH • Information Highlights

Area: 84,916 square miles (219,933 sq km).
Population: 1,048,000 (1969 est.).
Chief Cities (Jan. 1, 1969): Salt Lake City, the capital, 188,000; Ogden, 72,000; Provo, 45,000; Holladay, 25,000.
Government: *Chief Officers*—governor, Calvin L. Rampton (Democrat); Auditor, Sherman J. Preece (Republican); secy. of state, Clyde L. Miller (D); atty. gen., Vernon B. Romney (R); treas., Golden L. Allen; supt. of pub. instr., T. H. Bell; chief justice, J. Allan Crockett. *Legislature*—Senate, 28 members (20 R, 8 D); House of Representatives, 69 members (48 R, 21 D).
Education: *School enrollment* (1968)—public elementary, 171,000 pupils (5,900 teachers); public secondary, 132,000 pupils (5,400 teachers); nonpublic schools, 6,000 pupils (310 teachers); college and university (fall 1967), 75,773 students. *Public school expenditures* (1967–68)—$195,100,000 ($677 per pupil); *average teacher's salary,* $7,050.
Public Finance (fiscal year 1968): *Revenues,* $435,335,000 (general sales and gross receipts taxes, $58,386,000; motor fuel tax, $28,514,000; federal funds, $130,757,000). *Expenditures,* $423,714,000 (education, $113,924,000; health, welfare, and safety, $53,485,000; highways, $76,715,000). *State debt,* $110,638,000 (June 30, 1968).
Personal Income (1968): $2,885,000,000; *average annual income per person,* $2,790.
Public Assistance (fiscal year 1968): $34,118,671 to 42,973 recipients (aged, $6,675,138; dependent children, $17,562,876).
Labor Force (employed persons, Sept. 1966): *Agricultural,* 19,500; *nonagricultural* (wage and salary earners), 326,000 (16% manufacturing, 22% trade, 28% government). *Unemployed persons* (Sept. 1966)—12,000.
Manufacturing (1965): *Value added by manufacture,* $683,163,000 (food and products, $95,984,000; nonelectrical machinery, $40,900,000; petroleum and coal products, $39,085,000).
Agriculture (1967): *Cash farm income,* $199,545,000 (livestock, $145,371,000; crops, $45,220,000; govt. payments, $8,954,000). *Chief crops* (tons)—Hay, 1,665,000; sugar beets, 460,000; wheat, 259,470; barley, 180,000; potatoes, 73,150.
Mining (1968): *Production value,* $423,593,000. *Chief minerals*—Bituminous coal, 4,100,000 tons; copper, 228,300 tons; crude petroleum, 23,050,000 bbls.; gold, 346,750 troy oz.
Transportation: *Roads* (1968), 39,040 miles (57,827 km); *motor vehicles* (1969), 633,110; *railroads* (1968), 3,057 track miles (4,920 km); *airports* (1969), 4.
Communications (1969): *Telephones* (1968), 510,800; *television stations,* 8; *radio stations,* 44; *newspapers,* 5 (daily circulation, 259,057).

VANCOUVER

Vancouver, the largest city and economic capital of British Columbia and Canada's third-largest city, was troubled by labor disputes throughout 1969, but it continued to be one of the nation's fastest growing cities (1969 est. city pop., 500,000; metropolitan area, 955,000).

Labor Disputes. Many of Vancouver's supermarkets were closed during the summer (May 26–August 24), when locked-out meatcutters placed picket lines around them. Also locked out were 3,000 supermarket clerks, but their 2-month dispute ended in July.

The port of Vancouver and five other British Columbian ports were closed for 7 weeks by a longshoremen's strike. It ended in November with a 90-day truce, under which the dockers returned to work to allow their union to solve internal problems.

Oil workers struck for 5½ months in a dispute that ended in November. Union picket lines closed the Vancouver International Airport and halted city buses for a few hours during the strike until court injunctions banned the pickets.

In December, city teachers banned all extracurricular activities, such as sports, to protest the board's refusal to resume direct salary talks. The board submitted the dispute to compulsory arbitration.

Higher Education. The University of British Columbia, in Vancouver, enrolled 21,018 students in the 1969 fall session, nearly 1,000 more than in 1968. But at Simon Fraser University, in suburban Burnaby, the undergraduate enrollment of 4,820 was 280 below the 1968 figure. The decrease may have been due to strife on the campus, which culminated in a 7-week strike (September 24–November 5) by some students and faculty members. It began as a protest over the imposition of trusteeship on the department of political science, sociology, and anthropology and ended when 8 suspended department professors voted to resume their classes.

Both universities acquired new presidents. Dr. Walter H. Gage, former dean of interfaculty and student affairs, became president of the University of British Columbia, succeeding Dr. F. Kenneth Hare, who resigned in January. In September, Dr. Kenneth Strand, a U. S.-born economist, became the first permanent head of Simon Fraser University since 1968.

Other Events. During a visit in October, Prince Philip opened a $2 million addition to the city hall. Another new project, the $1.65 million Bloedel Conservatory of tropical plants, opened in December. Vancouver made national headlines when Prime Minister Pierre Trudeau became involved in an incident accompanying a Vietnam war protest on August 8. A 17-year-old youth, alleging that Trudeau had struck him, charged the prime minister with common assault, but the complaint was later set aside.

MOIRA FARROW
The Vancouver "Sun"

RESCUERS sift wreckage of VIASA DC-9 that fell in a Maracaibo suburb on March 16, killing 83 aboard the plane and about 70 on the ground.

VENEZUELA

A new administration took office in Venezuela in March 1969. President Rafael Caldera entered office with substantially less popular and legislative support than had been enjoyed by his predecessor, Raúl Leoni, and encountered considerable difficulties during the first few months of his term.

Political Affairs. Caldera, a lawyer and professor and the leader of the Social Christian party (COPEI), had won less than 30% of the vote on Dec. 1, 1968, in an election in which six presidential candidates and no less than 18 political parties had participated. Caldera's party elected only 59 of the 213 deputies and 16 of the 52 senators. Although badly split, Acción Democrática (AD)—the dominant partner in Leoni's coalition government—seated the largest number of legislators.

AD spurned the efforts of COPEI to draw it into a new coalition and embarked upon a policy of vigorous opposition and even obstruction. It secured passage of a measure that took away from the executive the power to appoint inferior judges and vested this power in a committee over which AD expected to have a dominant influence. The president suffered his most serious early defeat when the Supreme Court upheld the validity of this law. Disagreement over the makeup of the new committee delayed the opening of the fall session of Congress, but when faced with total congressional paralysis and the possibility of severe damage to Venezuela's democratic system, both sides finally compromised, allow-

---

VENEZUELA · Information Highlights

Area: 352,143 square miles (912,050 sq km).

Population: 9,686,000 (1968 est.).

Chief Cities (1966 census): Caracas, the capital (metropolitan area), 1,764,274; Maracaibo, 558,953.

Government: *President*—Rafael Caldera (took office March 11, 1969). *National Congress*—Senate, 52 members (party seating, 1969: Democratic Action party, or AD, 19; Social Christian party, or COPEI, 16; People's Electoral Movement, or MEP, 5; others, 12); Chamber of Deputies, 214 members (party seating, 1969: AD, 66; COPEI, 59; MEP, 26; others, 62).

Religious Faith: Roman Catholics, 92.5% of population.

Education: *Literacy rate* (1969), 90% of population. *Total school enrollment* (1965)—1,795,669 (primary, 1,453,310; secondary, 189,583; teacher-training, 12,831; vocational, 93,120; higher, 46,825).

Finance (1969 est.): *Revenues,* $2,018,000,000; *expenditures,* $2,027,333,330; *public debt,* $825,111,110; *monetary unit,* bolívar (4.5 bolívares equal U. S.$1).

Gross National Product (1968): $9,933,333,330.

National Income (1968): $7,755,555,550; *average annual income per person,* $800.

Economic Indexes (1967): *Industrial production,* 120 (1963= 100); *agricultural production,* 131 (1963=100); *cost of living,* 102 (1963=100).

Manufacturing (metric tons, 1967): Residual fuel oil, 38,963,-000; gasoline, 6,018,000; cement, 2,278,000; sugar, 413,000.

Crops (metric tons, 1967–68 crop year): Bananas, 1,276,000; maize, 604,000; cassava, 328,000.

Minerals (metric tons, 1967): Crude petroleum, 185,409,000 (ranks 3d among world producers); iron ore, 10,959,000; limestone (1966), 2,750,000; diamonds, 70,000 carats; gold (1966), 18,872 troy ounces.

Foreign Trade (1968): *Exports,* $2,857,000,000 (chief exports, 1967: Petroleum, $1,827,800,000; iron ore, $134,311,110); *imports,* $1,450,000,000 (chief imports, 1967: nonelectrical machinery, $251,355,550; motor vehicles, $144,977,770; iron and steel, $74,000,000). *Chief trading partners* (1967): United States (took 34% of exports, supplied 50% of imports); Netherlands Antilles (took 21% of exports, supplied 7% of imports); Canada (took 9% of exports, supplied 5% of imports).

Transportation: *Roads* (1969), 22,506 miles (36,219 km); *motor vehicles* (1967), 641,400 (automobiles, 450,000); *railways* (1965), 220 miles (354 km); *merchant vessels* (1967), 34 (293,000 gross registered tons); *national airlines,* LAV; AVENSA; *principal airport,* Caracas.

Communications: *Telephones* (1968), 327,038; *television stations* (1967), 30; *television sets* (1967), 650,000; *radios* (1967), 1,676,000; *newspapers* (1966), 35 (daily circulation, 617,000).

RAFAEL CALDERA (RODRIGUEZ), leader of the moderately leftist Christian Democratic party (COPEI), succeeded Raúl Leoni as president of Venezuela on March 11, 1969, becoming the first opposition leader to attain power peacefully in that country's history. He was elected in his fourth bid for the presidency in December 1968 by a narrow plurality, receiving 29.1 percent of the vote. After his inauguration, he announced plans for furthering the oil industry and improving housing and education.

Caldera, the son of a lawyer, was born in San Felipe, Yaracuy, on Jan. 24, 1916. He obtained a law degree and a doctorate in political science at the Central University of Venezuela. In 1947 he helped found COPEI, originally a right-of-center Roman Catholic party. During the 1950's he was arrested several times for his opposition to the dictatorial regime of Marcos Pérez Jiménez. After the overthrow of the dictatorship he collaborated with rival political leader Rómulo Betancourt and others in establishing democratic rule in Venezuela.

WIDE WORLD

ing the legislators to take up such pressing business as the national budget and a controversial bill dealing with new oil service contracts.

By the end of 1969, Caldera had not been able to put together a stable parliamentary majority and was leaning on disparate splinter groups of the left and center and even on the rightist supporters of former dictator Marcos Pérez Jiménez, whose Crusada Cívica Nacionalista (CCN) had seated 21 deputies and three senators. (Pérez Jiménez himself had won a fourth CCN Senate seat, but was barred from taking it by a ruling of the Supreme Court.)

In dealing with his many problems, Caldera exhibited a judicious mixture of conciliation and firmness. By negotiating with guerrilla leaders, he was able to reduce the scale of their activities in the interior. When faced with trouble from the army, on the other hand, he ordered the arrest of several high-ranking officers on charges of insubordination.

In late October the president sent armed forces into the Central University in Caracas to suppress student unrest and subsequently closed all schools for an indefinite period. Caldera also had to cope with a strike late in the year by 30,000 teachers who had been disappointed by the failure of the government to grant their ambitious wage demands.

International Affairs. The president was prevented in 1969 from signing a treaty that would have taken Venezuela into the new Andean Common Market formed by five other nations. Opponents in Congress and industry argued that the treaty would give inadequate protection to the country's developing economy. The deadline for Venezuelan entry into the regional association is Dec. 31, 1970.

Venezuelan representatives began negotiations in Washington looking to a revision of U.S. oil policy and to the establishment of free access to U.S. markets for Venezuelan petroleum. A scheduled visit to Caracas by President Nixon's emissary, Gov. Nelson Rockefeller, was canceled at the request of the Venezuelan government, which feared violent protest.

Venezuela and Argentina exchanged ambassadors for the first time since 1966, but the scheduled resumption of diplomatic relations with the USSR was delayed by a dispute over personnel.

Economic Growth. Venezuela's petroleum-based economy continued to expand. The rate of growth of the gross national product (GNP) was estimated at about 4.5% per year during the late 1960's. The end of a decade of AD government in March 1969 provided an occasion for much self-congratulation by the outgoing administration, which pointed with pride to a Venezuelan per capita income of more than $800, by far the highest enjoyed by any of the nations of Latin America.

Death of Gallegos. Venezuela mourned the loss, on April 4, 1969, of one of its most famous citizens, Rómulo Gallegos. The distinguished novelist, educator, and statesman, who had become this country's first popularly elected president in 1947, died in Caracas at the age of 84.

LEO B. LOTT
University of Montana

VERMONT

For Vermont, 1969 was an active political year, marked by increased polarization between liberals and conservatives.

Economy. Many Vermonters felt that Republican Gov. Deane C. Davis would bring a return to the "good old days," a prospect pleasing to conservatives. Disillusionment came quickly. Davis' first message proclaimed the need for an austerity program and a long-rejected and distasteful sales tax. Democrats were united in opposition to the plan. The 3% sales tax gave rise to additional complaints from all sides when early returns exceeded estimates by about 50%, and a surplus of $6 million to $10 million was seen. Rejoicing ceased when officials pointed out that requests for essential services valued at nearly $20 million remained unfilled.

The largest state budget in history failed to please anyone. Complaints about wasteful welfare expenditures brought about creation of a governor's investigating committee. Its report criticized the department of social welfare for spending too much on recipients and not enough on administration and staff. An auxiliary investigation costing $8,000 found only six cases of possible welfare abuse.

Legislature. Conservative foot-dragging caused the legislature's failure to act on many bills, which were then assigned to committees for study. Reports must be submitted to the General Assembly in January 1970. Full publicity has been given to the committees and their work.

A referendum was held in June to determine whether or not to convene a constitutional convention for the first time in 100 years. The referendum, designed to decide which of seven issues would be placed on the limited agenda, resulted in a decisive rejection of the constitutional plan. The short pre-election campaign was marked by questionable statements by conservatives opposed to the changes.

In December a special governor's committee on administrative coordination turned in a report calling for a new cabinet system for state administration. Bills implementing the proposals will be presented to the legislature in January 1970.

Other Events. Rural Vermont received a major blow during the year. Unregulated development projects threatened to pollute streams and soil in many areas of southern Vermont, and had to be stopped by gubernatorial action. Several murders in the Montpelier and Windham areas caused widespread fear.

Many Vermont residents took part in Vietnam Moratorium demonstrations in October and November. The lieutenant governor's participation in these activities provoked criticism and may result in a political split within the Republican party.

ANDREW E. NUQUIST
University of Vermont

VETERINARY MEDICINE

One of the most widely publicized events in the field of veterinary medicine during 1968–69 was the poisoning of more than 6,000 sheep in Utah following the release of a nerve gas in a nearby area. Attention was also focused on brucellosis in dogs, a new method of controlling mastitis in cows, the "soring" of horses, eye defects in collies, and the hog cholera eradication program.

Sheep Poisoning. In March 1968, in the area of Skull Valley, Utah, about 6,300 sheep became ill after eating forage contaminated with an organophosphate compound. Of the affected sheep, about 4,500 died or had to be killed. The organophosphate was traced to a nerve gas being tested by the U. S. Army at the Dugway Proving Ground near Skull Valley. It had been released from a low-flying aircraft, and about 1½ hours after the spraying test a meteorological front passed through the area, accompanied by a shift in the wind direction. Later there were light rain and snow showers. These conditions

were responsible for the organophosphate being carried 40 miles (64 km) to where the sheep were grazing.

Six months later the area was declared free of contamination, and livestock were permitted to graze there. Livestock owners who filed claims for losses of sheep were reimbursed by the U. S. government.

Brucellosis in Dogs. Since June 1966, when brucellosis was diagnosed in a colony of beagles in Ithaca, N. Y., the disease has been attracting much attention from veterinarians and researchers. This disease causes abortions in pregnant females, usually in the last third of pregnancy. Caused by a bacterium tentatively called *Brucella canis,* it is highly contagious.

The control of canine brucellosis depends on identifying infected dogs and isolating them from others. The ultimate danger is that infected dogs will come in contact with dogs in the general pet population and cause the disease to become widely disseminated.

Soring of Horses. Soring is an abusive training practice performed on Tennessee walking horses to produce a high, skipping gait. In 1969, bills to ban soring were introduced into Congress by Sen. Joseph B. Tydings of Maryland, Rep. William Whitehurst of Virginia, and others. On Dec. 18, 1969, the Senate passed the Horse Protection Act that bans soring.

Soring involves application of a caustic agent, such as oil of mustard, to the pastern area of the horse's legs and wrapping the area with chains or metal rollers. The intense pain that the horse feels makes him lift his feet quickly and thrust them forward, producing the desired gait. This same gait can be achieved through patient and careful training.

The American Veterinary Medical Association, in a statement before the Senate's Committee on Commerce, condemned soring as inhumane and unnecessary, being nothing more than an objectionable shortcut to selective breeding and competent training.

Mastitis Control. A method to control mastitis in cows, a disease of the udder that drastically affects milk production, was extensively field-tested by a team of veterinarians at the New York State Veterinary College in Ithaca, N. Y., during 1968–69. The program's success generated new hope among dairymen whose herds are plagued with this disease, which is responsible for an estimated loss of $1 billion a year in the United States.

Eye Defects in Collies. Since it was first described in 1953, a peculiar eye disorder, principally in the form of chorioretinal dysplasia, has been observed in thousands of collies. Recent investigations show that more than 75% of purebred collies are affected in degrees ranging from mild disturbance of the ocular fundus to total blindness. The condition is inherited, probably as a simple autosomal (not sex-linked) gene.

Ideally, collies with eye defects should not be bred. However, because so many collies are affected, some veterinarians and breeders believe that a drastic culling of affected dogs would seriously discourage organized attempts to eliminate the defect.

Hog Cholera Eradication Program. By October 1969 only six states, none of which is a main hog-producing state, were not yet in the eradication phases of the state-federal hog cholera eradication program. Twelve states, at that time, were completely free of hog cholera.

ARTHUR FREEMAN
Editor, American Veterinary Medical Association

PRESIDENT THIEU of South Vietnam bids farewell to the first U.S. troops being withdrawn from country.

VIETNAM

An era ended in 1969 with the death on September 3 of North Vietnam's 79-year-old President Ho Chi Minh, leader of the 1946–54 revolt that ended French colonial rule in Vietnam, and titular head for the next 15 years of the government that ruled the Communist northern half of divided Vietnam. The death of the long-time North Vietnamese leader was not followed by any apparent succession struggle north of the 17th parallel. In South Vietnam, on the other hand, the struggle for political ascendency heightened as the year ended. At stake was the leadership of the non-Communist side in the inevitable political confrontation that would follow a settlement, or reduction, of the Vietnam War.

SOUTH VIETNAM

The Saigon government displayed new strength in 1969 in extending its influence in the rural parts of the country, especially the Mekong Delta, despite the Communists' creation of a rival "government" to rule the south. It was still seriously challenged, however, by both Communists and non-Communists.

Politics. South Vietnamese President Nguyen Van Thieu, responding to pressure from the United States, seemed to be trying to broaden the base of support for his government with the formation in May of a 6-party National Social Democratic Front (including his own People's Alliance for Social Revolution). The effort was short lived, however, because Thieu in August engineered the resignation of his popular civilian premier, Tran Van Huong, and replaced him with an old associate, 4-star general Tran Thien Khiem. The new cabinet was composed of other military officers, obscure technocrats, and associates of former President Ngo Dinh Diem (overthrown and murdered in 1963).

The leader of the 1963 coup against Diem, Gen. Duong Van Minh ("Big Minh"), emerged in November 1969 as a major challenger to Thieu's leadership. Minh, a former chief of state who had returned from exile in Thailand in 1968, called in early November for a "people's convention" to judge the Thieu government and its policies. The action was generally interpreted as a move by Minh and his backers, such as the senator and former general Tran Van Don, to oust Thieu by extra-constitutional methods before the 1971 elections.

President Thieu was also the object of continuing opposition from the militant An Quang Buddhist faction, which seemed to be moving to form a "third force"—possibly in concert with Minh—to force an early termination of Thieu's rule. One aim of such a third force would be to end the war and create a neutralist South Vietnam. The Thieu government sought at the end of 1969 to label its opponents as allies of the Communists.

"Provisional Revolutionary Government." The Communist political opposition to Thieu also sharpened in 1969, with the announcement on June 10 of the formation of a "provisional revolutionary government" to try to rival the legitimacy of the Saigon regime. According to the Communists, the new "government" had taken over responsibility from the National Liberation Front for "steering the fight" against the U.S. "aggressors." Huynh Tan Phat was named president of the provisional revolutionary government, which was immediately recognized by Cambodia, Communist China, the Soviet Union, and North Vietnam (among other states).

Pacification. Establishment of the Communist provisional revolutionary government did not hinder pursuit of the Saigon government's pacification program, which seemed to be achieving unparalleled success in 1969. The main reason was the dramatically improved security conditions, as well as the government's ability to pump large sums of money into the countryside. According to the Thieu government, the rural population under "relatively secure" control increased from 50% to 84% in the year that ended August 31.

The Thieu government was successful in decentralizing government functions by employing a

---

SOUTH VIETNAM • Information Highlights

Area: 65,987 square miles (170,906 sq km).
Population: 17,414,000 (1968 est.).
Chief Cities (1965 census): Saigon, the capital, 1,485,300; Da Nang, 228,040; Hue, 114,485.
Government: *President*—Nguyen Van Thieu (elected Sept. 3, 1967); *Premier*—Tran Thien Khiem (took office Aug. 23, 1969); *Parliament* (National Assembly)—Senate, 60 members; House of Representatives, 137 members.
Religious Faiths: Buddhists, 65% of population; Roman Catholics, 9%; others, 26%.
Education: *Literacy rate* (1969), 40%–50% of population. *Total school enrollment* (1965)—2,068,803 (primary, 1,660,-968; secondary, 370,668; teacher-training, 2,497; vocational, 7,565; higher, 27,105).
Monetary Unit: Piastre (117.5 piastres equal U.S.$1).
Gross National Product (1967): $3,000,000,000.
Average Annual Income per Person (1967): $178.
Cost of Living Index (1967): 279 (1963=100).
Manufacturing (metric tons, 1967): Cement, 181,000; beer, 1,300,000 hectoliters.
Crops (metric tons, 1967–68 crop year): Rice, 4,688,000; cassava, 262,000; sweet potatoes and yams, 253,000.
Minerals (metric tons): Salt (1966), 87,000; coal (1964), 72,-000.
Foreign Trade (1968): *Exports*, $12,000,000 (chief export, 1967: rubber, $8,994,890); *imports*, $466,000,000 (chief imports, 1966: iron and steel, $20,105,000; textile yarn and fabrics, $14,750,000; nonelectrical machinery, $14,580,000). *Chief trading partners* (1967): United States (took 2% of exports, supplied 32% of imports); Japan; Nationalist China.
Transportation: *Roads* (1969), 12,850 miles (20,680 km); *motor vehicles* (1967), 73,800 (automobiles 31,300); *railways* (1969), 875 miles (1,408 km); *national airline*, Air Vietnam; *principal airport*, Saigon.
Communications: *Telephones* (1968): 27,082; *radios* (1967), 1,300,000; *newspapers* (1967), 43 (daily circulation, 950,-000).

combination of military forces and rural development teams to secure villages and hamlets and then to prepare them for greater autonomy than the countryside had known since the power consolidation moves of the late President Diem. The government's "open arms" policy for Vietcong defectors registered a monthly record of 5,615 surrendering Communists in October.

Enlarged and improved regional and local popular militia elements played a major role in the successful pacification efforts, in which some 7,800 U.S. civilian advisers also took part.

Economy. Inflationary pressures persisted in 1969, the cost of living rising about 30% during the year. U.S. prodding resulted in the imposition of new import duties in June, which had the unexpected and undesired result of providing an opportunity for speculators to further increase the cost of several commodities, particularly foodstuffs.

Despite a fall in rice reserves in July to the lowest level in more than a year, the rice crop being harvested at the year's end was expected to be the highest in four years. South Vietnam still had a deficit of 220,000 tons of the grain in 1969, made up by U.S.–financed imports worth $35 million, but self-sufficiency was predicted by 1971. The improved output was the result of increasing the use of so-called "miracle rice" and fertilizers as well as improved security conditions.

NORTH VIETNAM

Ho Chi Minh's death in September had no demonstrable effect in North or South Vietnam, largely because Ho's role had been that of a figurehead for several years despite his legendary appeal to many of his countrymen. (See Ho Chi Minh.)

Politics. The death of Ho was followed by the elevation of the 81-year-old Vice President Ton Duc Thang to the presidency, a move designed to forestall a succession struggle among Ho's four longtime chief aides: Le Duan, first secretary of the ruling Lao Dong (Communist) party and founder of the Vietcong in the south; Truong Chinh, Maoist former party first secretary; Defense Minister Gen. Vo Nguyen Giap; and Premier Pham Van Dong. The naming of Le Duan to head the committee for Ho's state funeral probably indicated his political paramountcy.

The creation in late 1969 of several new ministries was probably more the consequence of worsening economic problems in the country than of political rivalries among Ho's heirs. The four months that followed his death saw no apparent change in Hanoi's conduct of the war, the North Vietnamese position at the Paris peace talks, or relations with China or the USSR.

Relations With China. Communist China pulled out two thirds of the 40,000 noncombatant troops it reportedly had in North Vietnam at the start of 1969. Relations between Hanoi and Peking improved steadily throughout the year after signs of strain in 1968, as indicated in part by the nonrefundable aid agreement reached by the two countries in September. Chinese Premier Chou En-lai paid a dramatically quick visit to Hanoi in the immediate wake of Ho Chi Minh's death in September. China's continued support of the war against the Saigon government was also displayed in October, when Peking pledged renewed backing for the Vietcong on the occasion of the visit of Nguyen Huu Tho, president of the National Liberation Front.

──── **NORTH VIETNAM • Information Highlights** ────

Area: 61,293 square miles (158,750 sq km).
Population: 20,700,000 (1968 est.).
Chief City (1960 census): Hanoi, the capital, 414,620.
Government: *President*—Ton Duc Thang (took office September 1969); *Premier*—Pham Van Dong (took office July 1954). *Parliament*—National Assembly, 366 members.
Education: *Literacy rate* (1960), 65% of population aged 12 and over. *Total school enrollment* (1964–65)—2,728,600.
Monetary Unit: Dong (2.94 dong equal U.S.$1).
Manufacturing (metric tons, 1967): Cement, 750,000.
Crops (metric tons, 1967–68 crop year): Rice, 4,700,000; sweet potatoes and yams, 800,000; cassava, 720,000.
Minerals (metric tons, 1967): Coal, 2,800,000; phosphate rock, 1,050,000; apatite (1966), 1,000,000; salt (1966), 150,000; chromite (1966), 30,000.
Transportation: *Roads* (1963), 4,076 miles (6,560 km); *railways* (1960), 485 miles (780 km); *principal airport,* Hanoi.
Communications: *Newspapers* (1965), 4.

Soviet Aid. The Soviet Union and North Vietnam signed a new aid agreement for 1970. It was believed to exceed $1 billion. The Soviets offered the Hanoi government nonrefundable and military aid as well as long-term economic loans for the rehabilitation of the country's war-devastated economy after the termination of the fighting.

Economy. Food shortages and industrial troubles plagued North Vietnam at the end of 1969. The burden of continued prosecution of the war as well as bad management played a part in the country's mounting economic difficulties. There were also indications of policy differences between advocates of increased farm collectivization and those who urged greater incentives for peasants. The farm problem, however, probably derived, as much as anything else, from the manpower shortage caused by the war and a shortage of farm implements resulting from the emphasis on the production of war goods.

RICHARD BUTWELL
The American University

BODY OF HO CHI MINH, who died on September 3, lies in state as North Vietnamese leaders pay respects.

UPI

Vietnam War is over for these men of the U. S. Third Marine Division, preparing to board ship at Da Nang on October 2 under President Nixon's troop cutback plan.

VIETNAM WAR

De-escalation of the Vietnam War commenced in 1969, following a decade of continuous growth of the complicated civil-international conflict. President Nixon began the process of disengagement of U. S. combat forces in June, and by the end of the year U. S. service personnel in South Vietnam totaled fewer than 484,000. But the year was still a very costly one for the United States. U. S. casualties in the first six months of the Nixon administration were appreciably higher than in the last half year of the Johnson presidency. And the $25.4 billion Vietnam War outlay in the 1970 defense budget brought the known costs of the conflict to the United States to more than $100 billion.

During the middle and late months of 1969 the level of fighting was the lowest in two years. Direct encounters between U. S. forces and Communist Vietnamese units were down dramatically, with a resulting drop in U. S. casualties in the latter part of the year. The de facto diminution of the conflict was not paralleled by progress in the Paris peace talks, which seemed stalemated at year-end. But the U. S. disengagement was clearly proceeding despite this failure on the diplomatic front.

THE FIGHTING

Exceptions to the generally diminished fighting in 1969 were the Communists' February-March offensive and subsequent isolated outbreaks, such as the intensive mortar attacks of mid-August. The toll suffered by U. S. forces in February and March, however, was high, and it seemed designed to intensify antiwar feeling in the United States. U. S. battle deaths in the week ending March 1 totaled

453, the highest in nearly a year and greater than in the first week of the Tet (lunar new year) offensive of January–February 1968. Enemy casualties in attacks early in 1969 were strikingly lower than in the previous year's "winter offensive."

Strategy. Subsequently—particularly after June —the Vietnamese Communists seemed to seek to keep the fighting at a reduced level. This was partly a conscious strategic decision and partly the consequence of losses sustained by both the Vietcong guerrillas and regular North Vietnamese units, which were driven back to the borders (and across them into such sanctuaries as Cambodia) and into jungle hideaways. Small-unit activity, instigated by Communist insurgents and terrorists, increased during the same period, however—a reflection of the adversary's change in strategy.

By the end of 1969, the Vietnam War had become, even more than previously, a conflict of attrition. The Communists' strategy was to minimize their own losses while continuing to undermine the efforts of the South Vietnamese government and its U. S. ally to stabilize the political-military situation, the increase in guerrilla-style incidents being part of this strategy.

The United States responded by consciously letting its foe determine both the scale and the frequency of direct encounters. As a result, clashes between U. S. forces and Communist Vietnamese declined dramatically in the second half of 1969. South Vietnamese forces, on the other hand, continued to seek out the enemy at about the same level as they—and the U. S. forces—had previously done, regardless of the scale of Communist-instigated activity.

Communist emphasis during the second half of 1969 was on fighting those South Vietnamese units that had replaced U.S. forces in the "Vietnamization" of the war. The Communists also scaled down the level of their infiltration and supply of their forces in the south, especially in mid-1969.

North Vietnamese infiltration was "negligible," according to U.S. sources, in the period May through October, falling far short of making up for Communist battlefield losses. During this period the previously 100,000-man North Vietnamese military force may have been reduced by as many as "tens of thousands," U.S. officials stated. By mid-October through mid-November, however, Communist infiltration seemed to be increasing again— possibly to the 1968 level of 17,000 a month. North Vietnamese infiltration during this period by way of the Ho Chi Minh Trail (in Laos) reportedly quadrupled above the rate of the previous months. But such infiltration from North Vietnam to South Vietnam tapered off again in December.

Communist Casualties. The high level of Communist casualties persisted throughout 1969, reaching 568,989 dead (North Vietnamese and Vietcong combined) for the period Jan. 1, 1961, through Nov. 8, 1969. This compared with a reported 97,708 South Vietnamese combat deaths during the same period. As of early November, approximately 65,000 Communist soldiers had lost their lives in the Vietnam fighting in 1969. The continuing high number of deaths, which took a particularly heavy toll of the Vietcong, probably accounted for the appearance for the first time of two North Vietnamese regiments in the Mekong Delta in late 1969.

Communist defections reached a high for a single year in 1969, totaling 40,466 through November 8. This compared with 18,171 for all of 1968.

U.S. Casualties and Costs. From Jan. 1, 1961, to Dec. 20, 1969, a total of 39,893 U.S. servicemen had lost their lives in combat in Vietnam. In addition, more than 250,000 U.S. military personnel had been wounded, nearly 1,400 were listed as missing or captured, and another 7,000 or more died in Vietnam in noncombat circumstances. The fact that the first half of 1969 was one of the costliest periods of the war from the standpoint of U.S. casualties was probably an important factor in President Nixon's decision to begin disengagement. The 6,358 U.S. deaths during the first six months of 1969 represented a 30% increase over the 4,894 combat fatalities during the last six months of 1968.

But U.S. fatalities dropped sharply in the second half of 1969, the 64 men killed in combat during the first week in October being the lowest casualty figure since October 1966. The last months of 1969 were marked by weekly casualties of fewer than 100 men, and the 66 U.S. combat deaths during the week ending December 20 represented the second-lowest weekly total of the year. South Vietnamese combat deaths rose as those of the U.S. forces dropped, the consequence of the Vietnamization of the war. In October, for example, 83% of all non-Communist combat deaths were South Vietnamese.

The 1970 U.S. defense budget added $25.4 billion to the officially admitted U.S. costs in fighting the Vietnam War. This pushed the total for the conflict (since 1965) to $108.2 billion. In comparison, the cost of waging the Korean War of the early 1950's was $18 billion. Another measure of the cost of the war to the United States was the number of aircraft lost in Vietnam between 1961 and mid-1969—more than 5,500 aircraft worth at least $3 billion.

THE NEGOTIATIONS

The Paris peace talks seemed to be stalemated at year-end. Partly for this reason President Nixon's chief negotiator, former Ambassador to Saigon Henry Cabot Lodge, resigned his position, effective December 8, and returned to the United States, as did Lodge's deputy, Lawrence E. Walsh. From all outward appearances, nothing was accomplished in 1969 at the Paris talks, which had been enlarged on the eve of Nixon's ascendancy to the presidency as part of the bargain by which President Johnson had ended the bombing of North Vietnam in November

WILLIAM CALLEY, JR. (*right*), Army 1st lieutenant, prepares to enter hearing on alleged civilian massacre at Song My village in Vietnam. (*Below*) Capt. Ernest L. Medina, commander of infantry company involved, appears at a press conference with his attorney, F. Lee Bailey.

1968. The fact that Hanoi's position seemed to harden even before the death of North Vietnamese President Ho Chi Minh on September 3 suggested that the lack of progress was not the result of indecisiveness, or a different posture, on the part of Ho's successors.

Earlier, in April and May, there had been indications of some possible progress in the talks. The Soviet Union approached the United States privately to encourage the South Vietnamese to negotiate directly with Hanoi. There were also signs that the North Vietnamese might desire to have secret talks with the United States on the periphery of the formal four-party Paris discussions. But neither of these situations developed into the hoped-for diplomatic breakthrough. By June, the Vietnamese Communists had hardened their position, and their subsequent behavior suggested no likelihood that they would move from their negotiating posture that an unconditional withdrawal of all U. S. and other foreign forces must precede any discussion of a political settlement in Vietnam.

Clearly both the United States and South Vietnam modified some of their positions in the hope of a political, or diplomatic, settlement, especially in the first half of the year. South Vietnamese President Nguyen Van Thieu seemed to modify his position in various ways. At the meeting of President Thieu and President Nixon at Midway Island on June 8, the two leaders discussed an "election strategy" for inducing a political settlement. Thereafter, in July, Thieu proposed the establishment of a commission—in which the National Liberation Front (the Vietcong's political arm) would participate—to arrange for free elections to decide the question of who should govern in South Vietnam. The Vietcong categorically rejected this proposal, just as it had earlier turned down Thieu's offer of secret talks in Paris—which once seemed imminent.

Thieu, for his part, adamantly opposed the demand of the National Liberation Front for a provisional coalition government. He also stated that this was the only question on which he would not negotiate. U. S. Secretary of State William P. Rogers, reflecting a growing U. S. flexibility, stated in June that the United States was "not wedded to any government in Saigon" but was committed to the free choice of their government by the people of South Vietnam.

TROOP WITHDRAWAL

The U. S. military presence in Vietnam reached its peak in February 1969, when there were 543,054 U. S. servicemen in the country. The process of troop withdrawal began with President Nixon's announcement of an initial reduction of 25,000 men on June 8, following his Midway Island conference with President Thieu. A second and larger withdrawal of 35,000 was announced on September 16 and completed by early December. In a third withdrawal announcement on December 15, President Nixon indicated a still bigger reduction of 50,000 military personnel—to be completed by April 15, 1970—which would reduce the U. S. service presence in Vietnam to 434,000 by that date.

Even so, President Nixon failed to fulfill his earlier declared intention to recall U. S. troops faster than suggested by the former Johnson administration defense secretary, Clark M. Clifford, in a widely cited article in the July issue of *Foreign Affairs*. Clifford urged a recall of 100,000 ground combat soldiers by the end of 1969, whereas the announced Nixon timetable set April 15, 1970, as the date by which 110,000 would be withdrawn. Clifford had also advocated the recall of all U. S. ground combat forces by the end of 1970, thereby reducing the U. S. military presence to 270,000 by that time. The Nixon timetable seemed to be seeking to achieve a level of 250,000 men in Vietnam by early or mid-1971, 150,000 by the end of 1971, and a residual contingent of approximately the Korea level of 50,000 by mid-1972.

In announcing the third troop withdrawal, President Nixon noted that the move was being made despite reports of increased North Vietnamese infiltration. Nixon's objective had been a negotiated settlement, which would permit a fairly fast U. S. troop withdrawal, with the ultimate political settlement to be determined by the Saigon government and the Vietcong (through elections, a negotiated sharing of the seats in the legislature, or other means). But U. S. troops would be withdrawn in any event, according to the Nixon strategy, with the process being slowed down and the South Vietnamese forces assuming an increasingly larger combat role if a negotiated settlement proved elusive.

The United States clearly had decided to get out of Vietnam—at least in terms of bearing responsi-

UPI

CHILDREN of South Vietnam watch U. S. tanks pass down a road near village of Duc Pho. Such armored squadrons are a common sight.

WOUNDED U. S. PARATROOPER is rushed to evacuation helicopter on "Hamburger Hill" during fierce battle against North Vietnamese, May 18.

bility for ground combat operations. The aim of the United States was to withdraw its ground troops and then other supporting elements at such a pace as to avoid the appearance of defeat, maintain its image in the world as a reliable ally, and not undercut the anti-Communist political cause in the south.

"Vietnamization." Failing to obtain a diplomatic conclusion of the conflict, the United States in 1969 began in earnest the process of "Vietnamization," or "de-Americanization," of the war. As the year progressed, South Vietnamese increasingly relieved U. S. forces of combat responsibility, but the change was a costly one for South Vietnam. The trend toward higher South Vietnamese—and lower U. S.—battlefield deaths began the week of May 11–17. The tendency was to be strongly accelerated as a result of the departure of the first U. S. fighting units.

The size of South Vietnam's armed forces grew in 1969. An increase of 88,000 men, reported for the last six months of 1969, was an important factor in the third Nixon troop withdrawal. Men under arms for the Saigon government totaled 1,090,-000 at year-end, contrasted with 1,002,000 in mid-1969. The regular armed services increased by 32,000 men, the popular forces by 8,000, and the paramilitary units by 35,000. The desertion rate was 2%.

The performance of the South Vietnamese soldier improved during the year, but the country's armed forces continued to suffer from a shortage of quality officer personnel, inadequate logistics support, and not enough of the right kind of equipment. The highest percentage of population control claimed during the Vietnam War—92.5% of South Vietnam's inhabitants living in areas under government control—was announced in mid-December.

RANGERS of South Vietnam rush enemy-occupied building in Bien Hoa. In 1969 the South Vietnamese took on more of the fighting.

"Try it!"

and November unquestionably encouraged him to persist with the withdrawal of U. S. troops from Vietnam. His appeal to what he called "the silent majority" was a bid to mobilize public opinion behind his policy and buy time for disengagement.

The President feared the effect on his Vietnam policies of the public disclosure in November of the alleged massacre of innocent civilians by U. S. troops at My Lai (one of several hamlets in the village of Song My) in March 1968. An earlier field investigation apparently dismissed the incident as having been caused by "artillery fire," and the Nixon administration reportedly did not learn about it until April 1969. Earlier in the year the alleged murder of a suspected South Vietnamese double agent by a U. S. Special Forces (Green Beret) unit had caused widespread discussion (see ARMY).

RICHARD BUTWELL
The American University

VIRGIN ISLANDS

Three persons served as governor of the Virgin Islands in 1969. In February, Gov. Ralph M. Paiewonsky, who had been appointed by both Presidents Kennedy and Johnson, resigned and became chairman of the powerful V. I. Port Authority, which he had just helped to create. Government Secretary Cyril E. King was acting governor until President Nixon on July 1 appointed Dr. Melvin H. Evans of St. Croix, who had been a Democrat until shortly before the 1968 election. Governor Evans would serve only until November 1970 when the islanders will elect their own governor.

The population was estimated at close to 55,000 (not including aliens) and the Virgin Islands continued to be the fastest growing area under the U. S. flag. Fortunately the booming tourist industry kept pace with the growth of population. Over a million tourists spent well over $100 million in 1969.

Airport. A near-tragic accident to an incoming airplane emphasized the need for prompt relocation of the Harry S. Truman Airport on St. Thomas. A site at the eastern end of St. Thomas, recommended by a consulting firm, was opposed by some on the island because certain individuals were profiting by it.

Corruption. Governor Evans stated over nationwide television from Washington that many charges of corruption were being investigated.

Aliens. During the peak tourist season the number of "down island" alien workers may be 30,000 to 40,000, many working illegally. A study in 1969 pointed out possible remedies for the problems related to the aliens. Schooling was provided for the children of many aliens in 1969 for the first time.

THOMAS G. MATHEWS
University of Puerto Rico

Vietnamization of the war, it was openly admitted in Saigon, would probably lower this figure in the immediate future. The announced positioning of South Vietnamese units, as the U. S. withdrawal proceeded, suggested that the Thieu government had no illusions about its ability to control as much territory as the U. S. forces had recently been controlling.

Diplomacy of Disengagement. The U. S. troop withdrawals from Vietnam could not help having an effect on the other countries fighting against the Communists there. By the end of 1969, all the 2,000 Filipino military personnel in the country—none of them ever involved in combat—had been recalled, the Philippines becoming the first of the allies to withdraw any of its forces. In the Philippines, as in the United States, Australia, and New Zealand (but not, apparently, in Thailand and South Korea), the Vietnam conflict had gained in unpopularity during the second half of the 1960's, and the withdrawal was largely in response to domestic pressures.

Australia announced that it would be removing its forces at about the same pace as the United States, but none of the other allies had indicated a similar intention by the year-end. The Thai government declared in late December that it had no immediate plans for withdrawing any of its 12,000 troops in Vietnam. The United States, however, was withdrawing some of its forces from Thailand, largely Air Force personnel employed in support of air action against the Communists in both Vietnam and Laos. By December, 2,400 U. S. servicemen, of 49,000 stationed in that country, had departed.

The purpose of President Nixon's July-August trip to the Philippines, Thailand, and Indonesia was to encourage Southeast Asian leaders to carry the main burden against internal insurgencies and to assure those friendly states that the United States was not disengaging altogether from Southeast Asia.

U. S. PUBLIC OPINION

President Nixon sought to keep ahead of U. S. opinion on the war, if only by a step. He said that he would not be influenced by mass demonstrations, but the Moratorium demonstrations in October

—— VIRGIN ISLANDS • Information Highlights ——

Area: 133 square miles (344 sq km)—St. Croix, 82 sq mi; St. Thomas, 32 sq mi; St. John, 19 sq mi.
Population: 55,000 (1968 est.).
Capital: Charlotte Amalie (St. Thomas).
Government (1969): *Governor*—Melvin Evans (presidential appointee). *Territorial Legislature,* 15 members.
Education (1968–69): *School enrollment*—public elementary, 8,613 pupils (435 teachers); public secondary, 4,050 pupils (235 teachers). *Public school expenditures,* $12,200,000.
Finance (fiscal year 1968): *Revenues,* $71,894,766; *expenditures,* $80,856,031.
Foreign Trade: *Imports* (1967), $172,100,000; *exports* (1967), $74,500,000.
Transportation and Communication: *Motor vehicles* (1966), 15,000; *telephones* (1968), 12,625.

VIRGINIA

Elections in Virginia during 1969 inaugurated a new age in the politics of the state. In the Democratic gubernatorial primaries, moderate William C. Battle won a surprisingly difficult victory over a liberal challenger. More important, in the general election on November 4 the Republican candidate, Linwood Holton, defeated Battle to become Virginia's first Republican governor in the 20th century.

Democratic Primaries. In 1969 Democratic primaries clearly spelled the demise of the old conservative organization of the late U.S. Sen. Harry F. Byrd as a dominant force in the party. Three candidates contended for the gubernatorial nomination: Lt. Gov. Fred G. Pollard, William C. Battle (the son of former Gov. John S. Battle), and state Sen. Henry E. Howell, Jr.

Pollard obtained support chiefly from old-line conservatives. Battle attempted to project an image of youth and progress; his support came mainly from a moderate group identified with U.S. Sen. William Spong. Howell proved to be the major phenomenon of the election. With an evangelical style rare in Virginia politics, he mounted an aggressive, emotional, and frankly class-oriented attack against the Democratic "establishment." Appealing to the frustrations of the consumer and the "little man" generally, he coined the slogan "Keep the big boys honest," which rallied his supporters and produced charges of demaguery from his opponents. His backing came heavily from labor and Negro groups.

In the July 15 balloting, Battle barely led Howell, while Pollard trailed a poor third. In a runoff primary on August 19, Battle won the nomination by a narrow margin. The primaries also produced victories for two other moderate candidates: state Sen. J. Sargeant Reynolds for lieutenant governor and Andrew P. Miller for attorney general.

General Election. Linwood Holton, a 46-year-old Roanoke lawyer unopposed for the Republican nomination in a March convention, had also carried the Republican gubernatorial banner four years earlier against Mills E. Godwin, Jr. In his 1969 campaign against Battle, Holton adopted a middle-of-the-road strategy. Appealing to conservatives, he emphasized his close connections with President Nixon and spoke of the need for a rationally aligned two-party system. Appealing also to Howell's liberal supporters, he played upon Howell's demand for repeal of the sales tax on food by advocating state income tax rebate of $9 for each dependent. Battle rejected this proposal, and partly as a result Holton inherited some of Howell's labor and Negro support.

In general, both Battle and Holton championed moderate programs of progress for Virginia in education, mental health, and highways. But Holton made the bolder promises, labeling Battle a "no-can-do" candidate for his fiscal caution.

The November 4 election produced a split-ticket result. Holton defeated Battle, 466,648 votes to 400,021. But Democrats Reynolds and Miller defeated their Republican opponents. In the races for for the 100 seats in the state House of Delegates, Republicans increased their minority from 14 to 24.

Constitutional Amendments. Surprisingly little attention was paid during the campaign to proposed amendments to the state constitution. The Commission on Constitutional Revision, established in 1968, submitted its lengthy recommendations in January, and Governor Godwin called a special session of the General Assembly in late February. It adopted numerous amendments, which must also be approved by the 1970 regular legislative session and then by the people in a referendum.

In an effort to avoid jeopardizing passage of the revisions because of controversy surrounding specific proposals, the Assembly separated five potentially controversial items for separate votes. These are proposals to (1) permit lotteries, (2) allow state aid to handicapped children in private schools, sectarian or nonsectarian, (3) permit the Assembly to alter the boundaries of Richmond, the capital city, (4) place the credit of the state behind revenue-producing capital bonds, and (5) enlarge the state's capacity to incur general obligation debt for capital projects.

Among the amendments rejected by the Assembly were proposals to lower the voting age to 18 and eliminate the 1-term tenure limit of governors.

Hurricane Disaster. In the morning of August 20, Hurricane Camille left a bizarre path of destruction across Virginia as it veered eastward to the Atlantic from the Gulf coast of Mississippi. Parts of Virginia's west central mountain areas, between Lynchburg and Waynesboro, were heavily damaged by landslides and flooding resulting from devasting downpours. At one Nelson county locality 31 inches of rain fell in 12 hours. The number of known dead reached 113, and 39 persons were missing.

WILLIAM LARSEN
Radford College

VIRGINIA · Information Highlights

Area: 40,815 square miles (105,711 sq km).
Population: 4,648,000 (1969 est.).
Chief Cities (1969 est.): Richmond, the capital, 221,000; Norfolk, 300,000; Arlington, 185,000; Virginia Beach, 149,000.
Government (1969): *Chief Officers*—governor, Mills E. Godwin, Jr. (Democrat); lt. gov., Fred G. Pollard (D); secy. of state, Martha Bell Conway (D); atty. gen., Robert Y. Button (D); treas., Lewis H. Vaden; supt. of pub. instr., Woodrow W. Wilkerson; chief justice, Harold F. Snead. *General Assembly*—Senate, 40 members (33 Democrats, 7 Republicans); House of Delegates, 100 members (85 D, 14 R, 1 independent).
Education: *School enrollment* (1968)—public elementary, 633,000 pupils (24,000 teachers); public secondary, 408,-000 pupils (19,800 teachers); nonpublic schools, 60,200 pupils (3,370 teachers); college and university (fall 1967), 117,531 students. *Public school expenditures* (1967–68)—$665,000,000 ($686 per pupil); average teacher's salary, $6,900.
Public Finance (fiscal year 1968): *Revenues,* $1,378,883,000 (general sales and gross receipts taxes, $115,950,000; motor fuel tax, $130,573,000; federal funds, $270,127,000). *Expenditures,* $1,340,235,000 (education, $228,377,000; health, welfare, and safety, $113,123,000; highways, $307,-111,000). *State debt,* $258,878,000 (June 30, 1968).
Personal Income (1968): $14,100,000,000; average annual income per person, $3,068.
Public Assistance (fiscal year 1969): $57,267,398 to 95,039 recipients (aged, $14,842,788; dependent children, $27,-584,910).
Labor Force (employed persons, annual avg. 1967): *Agricultural,* 90,200; *nonagricultural* (wage and salary earners), 1,547,200 (26% manufacturing, 20.2% trade, 20.2% government). *Unemployed persons*—47,800.
Manufacturing (1967): *Value added by manufacture,* $3,992,-446,000 (food and products, $377,999,000; electrical machinery, $281,871,000; lumber and wood products, $143,-148,000).
Agriculture (1967): *Cash farm income,* $530,068,000 (livestock, $272,924,000; crops, $239,562,000; govt. payments, $17,582,000). *Chief crops* (tons)—Hay, 1,532,000; corn for grain, 982,296; soybeans, 230,552; potatoes, 202,300; apples, 192,000.
Mining (1968): *Production value,* $298,609,000. *Chief minerals* (tons)—Bituminous coal, 38,100,000; stone, 31,857,000; sand and gravel, 10,147,000.
Fisheries (1967): *Commercial catch,* 347,599,774 pounds ($18,090,365). *Leading species*—Menhaden, 220,265,872 pounds ($2,993,441); hard blue crabs, 54,803,332 pounds ($2,949,863); oysters, 9,058,146 pounds ($5,958,915).
Transportation (1967): *Roads,* 56,877 miles (91,515 km); *motor vehicles,* 1,934,000; *railroads,* 4,435 track miles (7,136 km); *airports,* 12.
Communications (1967): *Telephones,* 1,914,500; *television stations,* 27; *radio stations,* 184; *newspapers,* 32.

VITAL STATISTICS

Marriages passed the 2 million mark in the United States in 1968 for the second time in history. (The other time was in 1946, the first full year in which military personnel returned from World War II). Births, meanwhile, continued to decline in 1968, reaching the lowest rate in U. S. history and the lowest total since 1946.

Nevertheless the excess of births over deaths added about 1,547,000 to the nation's population. In 1968 there were 3,470,000 births (about 1% below the 1967 total) and 1,923,000 deaths (up about 4%, primarily because two major outbreaks of influenza occurred in 1968). The rate of natural increase was 7.8 per 1,000 population.

For the first seven months of 1969, births and deaths both rose slightly in total numbers in comparison with the same period of 1968. Provisional data announced by the National Center for Health Statistics, a U. S. Public Health Service unit at Washington, were as follows:

Period	Births	Deaths
Jan.–July 1968	1,955,000	1,127,000
Jan.–July 1969	2,022,000	1,134,000

Births. The birthrate for 1968 dropped to 17.4 births per 1,000 population—"the lowest rate ever observed for the United States when underreporting of earlier years is considered," the National Center for Health Statistics commented. The rate had been 17.8 a year earlier and 21.7 five years earlier.

The fertility rate also continued a decline that was uninterrupted throughout the 1960's. In 1968 the fertility rate dropped to 84.8 births per 1,000 women 15 through 44 years of age. This was in contrast to a rate of 87.6 only one year earlier and 108.5 five years earlier. However, the fertility rate still remained well above the low levels of 76 and 79 that prevailed in the depressed years of 1933 through 1939.

The number of women of childbearing age in the United States is beginning to increase rapidly. In mid-1968 there were 14.3 million women in the 20-through-29-year age range, where fertility rates are highest. This category was expected to reach 15.5 million by 1970 and to 18.3 million by 1975.

Two changes in the timing of childbirth account for much of the decline in fertility. The National Center for Health Statistics explained:

(1) "Women at the older childbearing ages—30 and over—have been having lower birthrates because most of them married early, and had their children in the younger reproductive years, and are now no longer having children."

(2) "Women at the younger childbearing ages have also been having relatively low birthrates because of a tendency to delay some births until later ages."

SELECTED DATA ON U. S. BIRTHS

Year	Live births	Birthrate per 1,000 population	Fertility rate per 1,000 women aged 15–44
1960	4,257,850	23.7	118.0
1961	4,268,326	23.3	117.2
1962	4,167,362	22.4	112.2
1963	4,098,020	21.7	108.5
1964	4,027,490	21.0	105.0
1965	3,760,358	19.4	96.6
1966	3,606,274	18.4	91.3
1967	3,520,959	17.8	87.6
1968	3,470,000	17.4	84.8

(Source: National Center for Health Statistics, Public Health Service, U. S. Department of Health, Education, and Welfare.)

Deaths. The U. S. death rate, which declined steadily throughout the 20th century until 1955, has leveled off since then and stays on a plateau that varies from about 9.3 to 9.6 deaths per year per 1,000 population. (In contrast, deaths per 1,000 population ran 14.7 in 1910 and 10.6 as recently as 1945.) In 1968 the rate rose to 9.62 per 1,000—as against 9.36 a year earlier—largely because there was a major influenza outbreak early in the year and another near the end.

Diseases of the heart again paced the causes of death, accounting for 38.8% of the year's total, as against 39.1% a year earlier. There was no significant change in the relative percentages of the other main causes of death—cancer, 16.6%; strokes, 10.9%; and accidents, 5.8%.

LEADING CAUSES OF DEATH IN U. S., 1968

Cause of death	Death rate per 100,000 population[1]	Percent of total deaths
Diseases of heart	372.9	38.8
Cancer (malignant neoplasms, including neoplasms of lymphatic and hematopoietic tissues	159.6	16.6
Strokes (cerebrovascular disease)	104.8	10.9
Accidents	55.8	5.8
Influenza and pneumonia	34.9	3.6
Certain causes of mortality in early infancy	21.2	2.2
Diabetes mellitus	19.2	2.0
Arteriosclerosis	16.7	1.7
Bronchitis, emphysema, and asthma	16.6	1.7
Cirrhosis of liver	14.5	1.5
All other causes	146.0	15.2
All causes	962.2	100.0

[1] Based on a 10% sample of deaths. (Source: National Center for Health Statistics, Public Health Service, U. S. Department of Health, Education, and Welfare.)

Marriages and Divorces. The U. S. marriage boom has moved along without letup in numbers since 1958 and in rate since 1962. The 1968 total of 2,059,000 marriages was exceeded only by the 1946 total of 2,291,000. The 1968 rate—10.3 marriages per 1,000 population—was the highest since 1951. For the first seven months of 1969, marriages totaled 1,134,000, up 7,000 from the same period of 1968.

Contributing to the marriage boom was the fast-growing 18-to-24-year age class. It numbered 16 million in 1960 and 22 million only eight years later.

Divorces and annulments in 1968 were estimated at 582,000, an increase of about 9% over 1967. The divorce rate per 1,000 population increased to 2.9 in 1969—up from 2.7 in 1967 and 2.5 in the two years before that. The 1968 divorce rate was surpassed only at the close of World War II, in the years 1945, 1946, and 1947.

Expectation of Life. An American child born in 1968 had an estimated expectation of 70.2 years of life. In four years—1961, 1964, 1965, and 1967—the estimated expectation of life at birth was a record 70.5 years. (This figure indicates the average number of years that an infant could be expected to live if the age-specific death rates observed during the year of his birth were to continue unchanged throughout his lifetime.)

Canada. There were 370,894 births and 150,283 deaths in Canada in 1967, resulting in a natural increase of 220,611. Per 1,000 population there were 18.2 births (compared with a 1961–65 average of 24.2) and 7.4 deaths (compared with a 1961–65 average of 7.7).

Marriages numbered 165,879 in 1967, for a rate of 8.1 per 1,000 population. Divorces granted in the same year totaled 11,165, at a rate of 0.55 per 1,000 population.

WASHINGTON

An active Legislature, which devoted considerable attention to tax reform, and aircraft developments involving Seattle's Boeing Aircraft Corporation were key events in Washington in 1969.

Legislature. The 1969 Legislature, in its longest session of the 20th century, once again avoided action on constitutional reform. But it did enact a wide-ranging tax reform measure that had as its principal feature a provision to establish a single-rate state income tax. An income tax is specifically prohibited by the state constitution, and the voters have rejected previous attempts to remove the prohibition. Sponsors of the tax reform bill hope to obtain voter approval by making the income tax only one part of the general tax reform. The sponsors had hoped to enact an annual elections measure so that the tax bill could be placed before the voters in 1969. However, the measure failed to pass, and voter consideration of the tax reform bill must wait until the November 1970 elections.

Several bills were passed that were obviously in response to school disturbances and the increase in crime. One of the strongest was a measure providing mandatory prison sentences for persons committing certain "inherently dangerous" misdemeanors

--------- **WASHINGTON · Information Highlights** ---------

Area: 68,192 square miles (176,617 sq km).
Population: 3,190,000 (1969 est.).
Chief Cities (1969 est.): Olympia, the capital, 21,500; Seattle, 550,000; Spokane, 160,000; Tacoma, 145,000.
Government: *Chief Officers*—governor, Daniel J. Evans (Rep.); lt. gov., John A. Cherberg (Dem.); secy. of state, A. Ludlow Kramer (R); atty. gen., Slade Gorton (R); treas., Robert S. O'Brien; supt. of pub. instr., Louis J. Bruno; chief justice, Robert T. Hunter. *Legislature*—Senate, 49 members (27 D, 22 R); House of Representatives, 99 members (56 R, 43 D).
Education: *School enrollment* (1968–69)—public elementary, 440,000 pupils (17,100 teachers); public secondary, 359,-000 pupils (14,900 teachers); nonpublic schools, 56,500 pupils (2,350 teachers); college and university (fall 1967), 144,496 students. *Public school expenditures* (1967–68)—$561,000,000 ($727 per pupil); average teacher's salary, $8,100.
Public Finance (fiscal year 1968): *Revenues,* $1,681,842,000 (general sales and gross receipts taxes, $473,184,000; motor fuel tax, $125,980,000; federal funds, $302,804,000). *Expenditures,* $1,497,172,000 (education, $307,549,000; health, welfare, and safety, $213,180,000; highways, $218,-069,000). *State debt,* $636,911,000 (June 30, 1968).
Personal Income (1968): $12,081,000,000; *average annual income per person,* $3,688.
Public Assistance (fiscal year 1969): $181,657,600 to 2,160,147 recipients (aged, $17,617,605; dependent children, $42,-853,838).
Labor Force (employed persons, August 1969): *Agricultural,* 81,300; *nonagricultural* (wage and salary earners), 1,280,-300 (25.3% manufacturing, 21.8% trade, 20.3% government). *Unemployed persons* (August 1969)—67,600.
Manufacturing (1966): *Value added by manufacture,* $3,289,-275,000 (transportation equipment, $942,900,000; primary metals, $275,566,000; nonelectrical machinery, $120,888,-000).
Agriculture (1967): *Cash farm income,* $837,000,000 (livestock, $253,431,000; crops, $528,248,000; govt. payments, $55,-321,000). *Chief crops* (tons)—Wheat, 3,553,920; apples, 650,400 (ranks 1st among the states); pears, 139,500 (ranks 2d).
Fisheries (1968): *Commercial catch,* 127,792,262 pounds ($20,773,737). *Leading species*—Bottomfish, 44,298,866 pounds ($2,756,485); salmon, 25,753,392 pounds ($9,677,-533); halibut, 12,359,856 pounds ($3,064,317); oysters, 6,474,966 pounds ($1,989,955).
Transportation: *Roads* (1969), 73,955 miles (119,015 km); *motor vehicles* (1968), 2,284,276; *railroads* (1968), 5,836 track miles (9,390 km); *airports* (1969), 12.
Communications (1969): *Telephones,* 1,816,800; *television stations,* 13; *radio stations,* 147; *newspapers,* 24.

while carrying a gun. The Legislature also made it unlawful to wield a weapon in a manner calculated to intimidate, or to occupy a public building after having been ordered to leave.

Largely because Seattle voters had rejected a previous bond proposal to finance urban rapid transit, the Legislature in 1969 passed a bill permitting diversion of half the state's 2% motor vehicle excise tax to help pay the cost of public transportation. The state money would have to be matched by local tax dollars. The bill does not take effect until 1971.

Boeing Aircraft. A new era of air travel moved closer when, on February 9, the Boeing Company first tested its Boeing 747 in flight. The 335-ton jumbo jet, designed to carry up to 490 passengers at subsonic speed, entered airline service in 1970.

The Boeing 2707—an 1,800-mph, supersonic transport (SST)—also moved a step closer to reality. The SST program had been plagued with design problems that forced the company to abandon its earlier design of a movable wing plane in favor of a fixed delta wing. Following the resolution of these problems, the program ran into difficulty in obtaining funds from Congress. Late in the year the Boeing Company received Congressional approval for the construction of two prototypes.

Other Events. On June 29, at 3:30 A. M., a dynamite blast tore open the front of the administration building at the University of Washington, causing $300,000 in damage and shattering windows in houses more than a block away. At the end of 1969 there were still no clues to the identity of the bombers or to the motive.

In late September and early October the Seattle Central Area Contractors Association protested the lack of work opportunities on public projects for minority groups. Picketing and demonstrations stopped work for almost two weeks on several large construction projects at the University of Washington and at the Seattle-Tacoma International Airport.

WARREN W. ETCHESON
University of Washington

WASHINGTON (DISTRICT OF COLUMBIA)

In January 1969, President Nixon reappointed Walter E. Washington as mayor and Thomas W. Fletcher as deputy mayor of the District of Columbia. Fletcher, who resigned in late fall, was succeeded by Graham W. Watt. Nixon's other appointments to city posts were Gilbert Hahn, Jr., chairman of the city council; Sterling Tucker, vice chairman; and the Rev. Jerry A. Moore, Jr., council member.

Self-government. On April 28, President Nixon proposed a series of steps to improve the District's government, including the creation of a special commission to recommend procedures and plans for "meaningful self-government." He also proposed a constitutional amendment providing the District with one or more voting members in the U. S. House of Representatives and the possibility of two senators. The President suggested the immediate authorization of one non-voting representative until the amendment was passed.

Other proposals would increase the number of supergrade civil service positions in the city government and transfer additional powers from Congress to the mayor and council.

Transit. The District's single major breakthrough in 1969 was the authorization of a rapid

WASHINGTON, D. C., broke ground on December 10 for a rapid transit rail system. This sketch shows a station to be built at 12th and G Streets, N. W.

rail transit system. Formal groundbreaking on December 9 marked the end of almost two decades of controversy over public transportation for the city. A week earlier Congress had approved $1.1 billion in federal funds to build a 98-mile system for the city and its Maryland and Virginia suburbs. Congress also authorized $150,000 to study the feasibility of extending a transit line to nearby Dulles Airport in Virginia.

In 1965, Congress had authorized a basic 25-mile system and approved $100 million in federal funds and $50 million in district funds to begin construction. However, the program became enmeshed in the dispute over the city's highway program. The problem arose when congressional support for the North Central freeway and Inner Loop programs conflicted sharply with the view of the city government and civil rights groups that the roads were not needed and would destroy the homes and neighborhoods of Negro residents who would have difficulty finding new homes in the largely white suburbs. Federal funds were withheld until 1969 when the conflict was resolved largely through a compromise which would allow the parallel development of the transit and road systems.

Crime. Figures released in late fall showed a continuous increase in crimes committed in the city, particularly juvenile crimes which accounted for over 40% of all violent crimes. Among the proposals under consideration in Congress is the administration's "model anticrime package," which would revise Washington's criminal laws and procedures, reorganize its court structure, and provide improved legal services. Existing legal aid services would be converted into a full city department authorized to represent up to 60% of those unable to obtain adequate representation. Private attorneys would be paid to represent the remaining 40%.

The more controversial proposals would permit trial of juveniles as adults, the use of wiretapping in specified cases, indeterminate sentencing of 3-time felony offenders, and bail reform. Increased police recruitment, modernization of court procedures to ease chronic backlogs, and major changes in correction programs and facilities were also proposed.

Education. A disappointingly small number of Washington voters turned out in November to elect 5 new members of the 11-member school board. Raleigh C. Hobson, an outspoken critic of the city's education system was ousted by election of a new member. Facing the board is the task of appointing a successor to William R. Manning, school superintendent, who resigned in mid-year.

Budget. In the second budget prepared under budget powers authorized in 1967, the mayor and council requested $751 million for the fiscal year 1970, a substantial increase for teachers, police, and firemen, and larger appropriations for crime prevention, education, and health care and facilities. However, by December no final congressional action had been taken. A Senate committee authorization of $645 million was $37.7 million less than the total allowed by the House. Hardest hit by cuts were requests for construction funds.

Revenue. To increase city revenues, Congress approved five new taxes and five tax increases, effective in November, which were expected to raise at least $21 million in additional revenue.

Peace March. On November 15 over 250,000 persons paraded down Pennsylvania Avenue in a massive, peaceful appeal for a speedy withdrawal of U. S. troops from Vietnam. Late in the day some demonstrators clashed with police at the Justice Department.

JEAN E. SPENCER
University of Maryland

NEW BRIDGE over the Ohio River was opened at Henderson, W. Va., December 15. It replaces the Silver Bridge, which collapsed in 1968.

ALLIED STRUCTURAL STEEL COMPANY

WEST VIRGINIA

Gov. Arch A. Moore, Jr., West Virginia's second Republican chief executive in 36 years, began his four-year term in January with a strongly Democratic legislature and an all-Democratic Board of Public Works. The lawmakers enacted two thirds of the governor's program in one of the most productive legislative sessions in recent years. But Gov. Moore's relations with the Board and with many minor officials were for the most part a year-long running battle. In March, the governor fired 3,600 striking State Road Commission workers who refused to return to work in the face of a severe snowstorm. At year's end he was in conflict with Attorney General Chauncey Browning, Jr., over the sale of road bonds.

Legislature. Among the 59th Legislature's more significant accomplishments were a $1,000 across-the-board salary increase for teachers and lesser raises for non-teaching personnel; the establishment of a board of regents for all public higher education; and the suspension of certain consumer sales tax exemptions for one year, primarily affecting manufacturers, contractors, and the mining industry. Increased revenue from the sales tax changes was primarily intended for the teachers' pay raise.

The Legislature also authorized further road bond sales; raised salaries of state department heads and Supreme Court judges; completely rewrote the state's municipal code; revised workmens' compensation laws to cover pneumoconiosis (miners' "black lung"); updated banking, divorce, and election regulations; and strengthened water pollution laws where oil or gas drilling is involved. They also placed on the 1970 general election ballot a proposal that would extend all legislative sessions to 60 days (instead of the 30-day sessions now held in even-numbered years), and another that would allow special elections for constitutional amendments.

Economy. A blue ribbon task force examined management procedures of the state government and recommended changes that it said would save $50 million annually. A special one-week session of the Legislature in July provided tax incentives for new industry, aimed at creating 15,000 new jobs. Unemployment had substantially decreased at the end of October, down 15.1% from the previous year. Sixteen of the standard business indicators were up at the end of October; one of the more significant—

consumer sales tax receipts—was up almost 15%.

Referendum Procedure Ruling. The state Supreme Court in July handed down a decision that was expected to trigger similar tests in other states; it held that a simple majority should rule in bond issue and excess levy elections. West Virginia's constitution—like those of several other states—currently provides for a 60% affirmative vote in such referendums. The court held that this violates the federal "one man, one vote" principle. An appeal was pending in federal courts at the end of the year.

─────── **WEST VIRGINIA · Information Highlights** ───────

Area: 24,181 square miles (62,629 sq km).
Population: 1,791,000 (1969 est.).
Chief Cities (1969 est.): Charleston, the capital, 82,000; Huntington, 80,000; Wheeling, 48,000; Parkersburg, 47,000; Weirton, 29,000; Morgantown, 28,500.
Government: *Chief Officers*—governor, Arch A. Moore, Jr. (Rep.); secy. of state, John D. Rockefeller IV (Dem.); atty. gen., Chauncey H. Browning, Jr. (Dem.); treas., John H. Kelly; supt. of pub. instr., Rex M. Smith; chief justice, Frank C. Haymond. *Legislature*—Senate, 34 members (25 Democrats, 9 Republicans); House of Representatives, 100 members (64 D, 36 R).
Education: *School enrollment* (1968)—public elementary, 234,000 pupils (8,700 teachers); public secondary, 190,000 pupils (7,300 teachers); nonpublic schools, 14,000 pupils (650 teachers); college and university (fall 1967), 52,688 students. *Public school expenditures* (1968)—$218,800 ($540 per pupil); average teacher's salary, $6,300.
Public Finance (fiscal year 1968): *Revenues,* $682,976,448 (3% sales tax, $65,260,453; motor fuel tax, $47,262,992; federal funds, $223,393,487). *Expenditures,* $687,706,000 (education, $287,207,869; health, welfare, and safety, $124,368,712; highways, $199,139,695). *State debt,* $439,126,000 (1968).
Personal Income (1968): $4,451,000,000; average annual income per person, $2,470.
Public Assistance (fiscal year 1968): $40,866,836.38 to 108,892 recipients (aged, $8,740,712.70; dependent children, $27,380,128.03).
Labor Force (employed persons, annual monthly 1968): *Agricultural,* 628,400; *nonagricultural* (wage and salary earners), 507,800 (26.1% manufacturing, 17.8% trade, 18.7% government). *Unemployed persons* (annual monthly 1968)—40,300.
Manufacturing (1965): *Value added by manufacture,* $2,033,122,000 (chemicals and allied products, $865,025,000; primary metals, $431,489,000; electrical machinery, $98,524,000; fabricated metals, $78,930,000; food and products, $72,397,000).
Agriculture (1967): *Cash farm income,* $97,563,000 (livestock, $72,978,000; crops, $20,701,000; govt. payments, $3,884,000). *Chief crops* (tons)—Hay, 912,000; apples, 110,400; corn for grain, 100,352; wheat, 19,800; potatoes, 17,750.
Mining (1968): *Production value,* $921,778,000. Chief minerals (tons)—Bituminous coal, 148,500,000; stone, 8,815,000; sand and gravel, 6,050,000; salt, 1,290,000; clays, 225,000; crude petroleum, 3,500,000 bbls.
Transportation: *Roads* (1968), 31,686 miles (50,992 km); *motor vehicles* (1967), 765,000; *railroads* (1967), 3,799 track miles (6,114 km); *airports* (1967), 10.
Communications (1967): *Telephones* (1968), 683,700; *television stations,* 9; *radio stations,* 77; *newspapers,* 31 (daily circulation, 498,000).

Disasters. West Virginia, normally protected from tropical storms by its mountains, was hit hard by hurricane Camille in August. Parts of West Virginia and Virginia were proclaimed disaster areas.

With the fire finally out in the Farmington mine where 78 perished in November 1968, recovery operations began on Sept. 15, 1969. Two bodies had been brought to the surface by late October, but officials predicted that it would be many months before the tragic work was completed.

DONOVAN H. BOND
West Virginia University

WESTERN SAMOA

Improved agricultural production, new construction activity, and progress in economic planning gave Western Samoa one of its most promising years since it gained independence in 1962.

Economic Development. Increased production of the three leading exports, copra, cacao, and bananas, marked a recovery from the severe damage caused by the hurricanes of 1966 and 1968.

Potlatch Forests Inc. leased a total of 23,000 acres (9,000 hectares) of forest land to provide timber for its first five years of logging.

—— **WESTERN SAMOA · Information Highlights** ——

Area: 1,097 square miles (2,842 sq km).
Population: 137,000 (1968 est.).
Chief City (1966 census): Apia, the capital, 25,480 (urban area).
Government: *King*—Malietoa Tanumafili II (acceded Jan. 1, 1962); *Prime Minister*—Fiame Mata'afa Faumuina Mulinu'u II (took office 1962). *Parliament*—Legislative Assembly, 47 members.
Religious Faiths: Christians, 99.7% of population.
Education: *Literacy rate* (1951), 86% of population aged 15 and over. *Total school enrollment* (1966)—42,950.
Finance (1964 est.): *Revenues,* $5,589,000; *expenditures,* $5,808,000; *monetary unit,* tala (0.8929 tala equals U. S.$1).
Crops (metric tons, 1967–68 crop year): Bananas, 3,000; cacao beans, 4,000.
Foreign Trade (1967): *Exports,* $4,365,000 (chief exports, 1967: cacao beans, $1,610,000; copra, $1,030,000; bananas and plantains, $290,000); *imports,* $7,701,000 (chief imports, 1967: canned meat, $360,000; wheat meal and flour, $230,000). *Chief trading partners* (1967): New Zealand (took 46% of exports, supplied 27% of imports); Australia; Britain.
Transportation: *Roads* (1964), 450 miles (724 km); *motor vehicles* (1964), 1,473 (automobiles 829).
Communications: *Telephones* (1968), 1,739; *radios* (1966), 15,000.

Completion of blasting and dredging to deepen the channel entrance to Asau Harbor on Savaii Island is expected in 1970. Waste from the project will be used to create a 4000-foot (1220 meter) airstrip on a nearby reef. The government is planning modernization of Faleolo Airport and improvement of the road between Apia and Faleolo.

To continue its policy of expanding tourism, the government has begun negotiations with an Australian company for development of a modern tourist facility on the Casino Hotel site near Apia.

Government. On March 27 the Western Samoan Legislative Assembly voted by a majority of 37 to 6 to retain the traditional *matai* system of representative government. Under the system, 8,500 *matais* (chiefs) represent more than 30,000 adult Western Samoans in parliamentary elections.

HOWARD J. CRITCHFIELD
Western Washington State College

WHOLESALE SALES. See ECONOMY OF THE UNITED STATES.

WILSON, (James) Harold

Prime Minister of Britain: b. Huddersfield, Yorkshire, England, March 11, 1916.

Prime Minister Wilson's fifth full year in office began with his popularity at a low ebb—mainly because of his government's continued apparent failure to solve Britain's balance of payments problems. By the end of September 1969, however, Britain had maintained a balance of payments surplus for four consecutive months, and support for Wilson, and for his Labour party, grew. The public opinion polls recorded a continuous improvement in Labour's fortunes in the second half of the year, although at the year's end the party still lagged significantly behind the Conservatives, and the prime minister still was subject to distrust among the nation's voters.

Domestic Affairs. Unfortunately, the party's improved position with the voters did not solve Wilson's difficulties in managing the party. Left-wing and trade union opposition to his deflationary policies continued, forcing the government in June to drop its proposal to introduce legal penalties for certain kinds of strike action. In April the government had dropped plans to reform the House of Lords. Because both the strike and Lords reform bills had been underwritten personally by Wilson, their miscarriage considerably undermined his standing in Parliament and the Labour party.

In his most characteristic undertaking of 1969, the prime minister in October made further changes in the machinery of government. His expansion of the ministry of technology into the chief instrument of government control over the economy, and his creation of a new ministry of local government and regional planning, continued a process of rationalization in which he has been engaged since becoming prime minister in 1964. Ultimately he aims to create a two-tier system of administration, with a few "super ministries" exercising overall control of a larger number of specialized departments.

Foreign Affairs. Wilson's prestige suffered another of its periodic setbacks in June when Rhodesia voted overwhelmingly in favor of a republican constitution that embodies *apartheid* features. The prime minister had identified himself personally with attempts to negotiate a settlement with Rhodesia that would safeguard the rights of the African majority there. Other aspects of his foreign policy were criticized as well. The My Lai massacre reactivated left wing opposition to his support of U. S. policies in Vietnam, and elements in both major parties voiced increasing opposition to his policy of supplying arms to the Nigerian federal government for use against secessionist Biafra.

How Wilson's personal popularity was affected by the departure from office of French President Charles de Gaulle and the consequent improvement of Britain's hopes for entering the Common Market was not clear. By the end of 1969, British opinion was moving against entry, and the government's statements were correspondingly cautious.

Career. After graduating from Oxford in 1937, Wilson taught economics there until 1940. In World War II he worked as a civil servant. He entered Parliament in 1945 and the cabinet in 1947 and was elected Labour party leader in 1963.

A. J. BEATTIE
The London School of Economics

WISCONSIN

Against the backdrop of a simmering taxpayers' revolt, Wisconsin in 1969 witnessed the growth of conservative forces and the drama of a welfare crisis.

Conservative Strength. Evidence of the public's growing dissatisfaction with rising taxes was evident in the spring elections. Mayors of several cities—including Kenosha, the state's fifth largest— were turned out of office by candidates who stressed the need for holding the line. But there was even greater evidence of the unrest in the Legislature.

The state could have expected harmony, since Gov. Warren P. Knowles' Republican party was in control of both houses. But while Governor Knowles and most state senators were moderates, conservatives gained power in the Assembly. Assembly Speaker Harold Froehlich of Appleton led this group, and Assemblyman Kenneth Merkel, an active John Birch Society member from Brookfield, was one of its most articulate spokesmen.

The conservatives were largely responsible for the Legislature's rejection of the governor's budget. The $1.56 billion budget that was finally adopted, while higher than the previous biennium's, sharply reduced welfare programs and ignored Knowles' pleas for aid to the cities, especially Milwaukee.

Rejecting proposals to increase income or corporate taxes, the Legislature approved a 1% increase in the 3% sales tax and extended it to include clothing and drugs. The governor then proposed a special

---

WISCONSIN • Information Highlights

Area: 56,154 square miles (145,439 sq km).

Population: 4,269,000 (1969 est.).

Chief Cities (1969 est.): Madison, the capital, 172,000; Milwaukee, 750,000; Racine, 98,000; Green Bay, 86,000.

Government: *Chief Officers*—governor, Warren P. Knowles (Rep.); lt. gov., Jack B. Olson (Rep.); secy. of state, Robert C. Zimmerman (Rep.); atty. gen., Robert W. Warren (Rep.); treas., Harold W. Clemens; supt. of pub. instr., William C. Kahl; chief justice, E. Harold Hallows. *Legislature*—Senate, 33 members (10 Democrats, 21 Republicans); House of Representatives, 100 members (47 D, 51 R).

Education: *School enrollment* (1968)—public elementary, 550,000 pupils (23,000 teachers); public secondary, 388,000 pupils (21,400 teachers); nonpublic schools, 257,900 pupils (9,630 teachers); college and university (fall 1967), 156,533 students. *Public school expenditures* (1967–68)— $706,133,000 ($834 per pupil); *average teacher's salary*, $7,537.

Public Finance (fiscal year 1968): *Revenues*, $1,644,232,000 (3% sales tax, $112,402,986; motor fuel tax, $115,396,000; federal funds, $292,721,000). *Expenditures*, $1,637,403,000 (education, $384,502,000; health, welfare, and safety, $192,581,000; highways, $133,405,000). *State debt*, $445,280,000 (June 30, 1968).

Personal Income (1968): $14,197,000,000; *average annual income per person*, $3,363.

Public Assistance (fiscal year 1968): $44,175,942 to 78,732 recipients (aged, $12,550,169; dependent children, $31,625,773).

Labor Force (employed persons, annual average): *Agricultural*, 170,400; *nonagricultural* (wage and salary earners), 1,609,000 (31.5% manufacturing, 19.2% trade, 15.1% government). *Unemployed persons* (annual average 1968) —63,900.

Manufacturing (1966): *Value added by manufacture*, $6,831,674,000 (transportation equipment, $569,334,000; primary metals, $453,838,000; nonelectrical machinery, $1,549,316,000; electrical machinery, $761,973,000; fabricated metals, $497,833,000; food and products, $877,211,000).

Agriculture (1967): *Cash farm income*, $1,461,336,000 (livestock, $1,212,178,000; crops, $207,931,000; govt. payments, $41,227,000). *Chief crops* (tons)—Hay, 10,268,000 (ranks 1st among the states); oats, 1,714,832 (ranks 3d); cranberries, 25,000 (ranks 2d).

Mining (1966): *Production value*, $76,010,000.

Fisheries (1967): *Commercial catch*, 50,300,000 pounds ($2,800,000).

Transportation: *Roads* (1968), 101,727 miles (163,709 km); *motor vehicles* (1969), 2,153,407; *railroads* (1968), 9,631 track miles (15,499 km); *airports* (1969), 23.

Communications (1969): *Telephones* (1968) 2,070,300; *television stations*, 19; *radio stations*, 181; *newspapers*, 38 (daily circulation, 1,212,000).

$33 million welfare and urban-aid package, and called a special session of the Legislature to enact it.

Welfare Crisis. Any hope for passage of a welfare and urban-aid bill was apparently wrecked on the opening day of the special session. On that day, September 29, welfare demonstrators broke open a door to the Assembly and took over the chamber. They remained there for 11 hours, demanding restoration of welfare funds, including money for the program to aid families with dependent children.

The 1,000 protesters, including University of Wisconsin students and welfare mothers, were led by the Rev. James E. Groppi, the militant Roman Catholic priest who was already widely known for his civil rights campaigns. The welfare and urban-aid package was shunted aside and the Assembly invoked an 1848 law to cite Father Groppi for contempt. He was first jailed on this charge and then on charges of violation of an earlier probation. Few major bills were passed in the rest of the seven-week session.

Legislative Action. Bills passed by the Legislature during its regular nine-month session imposed more severe penalties on students convicted of disorders, gave the attorney general more power against organized crime, and created a pesticide review board to consider objections to DDT. The Legislature also approved $3.2 million for the private, financially troubled Marquette School of Medicine, Inc., in Milwaukee. The money was obtained by doubling the tax on beer, which had been unchanged at $1 a barrel since the end of Prohibition.

Unrest in Madison. Two major disorders occurred in the University of Wisconsin area at Madison. For 12 days in February, students attempted to promote a strike in support of a list of black students' demands. The disorders that resulted were quelled by 1,900 National Guardsmen. Early in May, students and hippies near the campus battled police for three consecutive nights.

Economy. Manufacturing employment reached an all-time high of 531,000 in 1969 and total employment of 1,871,600 also set a record. Personal incomes ran more than 9% ahead of 1968, and the unemployment rate was under the national average until late fall, when it turned up slightly.

PAUL SALSINI
The Milwaukee "Journal"

WOOL

World wool production in 1969–70 expanded less than 1% over the previous production year to a new peak of 6,132,000,000 pounds (greasy basis). Significant increases in Australia, South Africa, and Argentina, and a further increase in New Zealand, more than offset declines in the United States, Uruguay, the USSR, and Britain. The U. S. wool clip, declining for years, still ranked sixth.

U. S. Wool Textile Industry. In contrast to a world trend, wool consumption declined in U. S. textile mills. This situation reflected the impact of inflated retail clothing and textile prices on consumer demand and the higher costs that retailers, manufacturers, and mills met in carrying inventories.

Two indicators of demand for apparel wool in the United States—retail clothing sales and unfilled orders in textile mills—suggest that 1969 apparel wool consumption declined about 8% to 220 million pounds (scoured basis) from the previous year. In the first 10 months of 1969, imports of raw apparel

WORLD PRODUCTION OF VIRGIN WOOL
(Million pounds, greasy basis)

Country and types	Average 1956–57 to 1960–61	1968–69	1969–70 Forecast	% of Total
Australia	1,582	1,952	2,023	33
USSR	690	911	860	14
New Zealand	539	732	740	12
Argentina	414	397	405	7
South Africa	296	317	331	5
United States	309	214	200	3
Uruguay	181	187	176	3
Other countries	1,333	1,401	1,397	23
Total	5,344	6,111	6,132	100
Of which:				
Merino (fine)	2,177	2,477	2,498	41
Crossbred (medium to coarse)	1,955	2,333	2,330	38
Total apparel type	4,132	4,810	4,828	79
Other (mostly carpet type)	1,212	1,301	1,304	21

Source: Commonwealth Secretariat.

wool—which supplement U. S. wool production—were 32% under 1968 imports for the same period.

Imports of semi-processed and manufactured wool textile products have become increasingly important in U. S. markets. In the first eight months of 1969, net imports of wool textile products declined 13% from the same period in 1968 and, when added to raw wool consumption in U. S. mills, indicated a 9% decline in the consumption of apparel wool by consumers.

Mill consumption of carpet wool was expected to run about 95 million pounds in 1969, up 4 million pounds from 1968. Imports of carpet wool, which is not produced domestically, apparently dropped about 23% from the 120 million pounds imported in 1968.

World Wool Consumption. In 1969 world wool consumption appeared to be a record 3.5 million pounds (clean basis). U. S. raw wool consumption annually accounts for slightly more than 9% of the world total.

RUTH JACKENDOFF
The Wool Bureau, Inc.

WORLD BANK. See INTERNATIONAL FINANCE.
WORLD HEALTH ORGANIZATION. See UNITED NATIONS.
WRESTLING. See SPORTS.

WYOMING

Republican Gov. Stanley K. Hathaway, beginning his third year in office, obtained support for most of his programs in 1969. The Legislature reorganized several branches of the state government and increased some taxes. Mineral production rose considerably during the year, and industrial development progressed slowly.

Legislature. The 40th Legislature met in regular biennial session in January and February. The Republican party, as usual, controlled both houses, with a majority of 18–12 in the Senate and 45–16 in the House of Representatives.

General fund appropriations totaled $64,595,066. The Legislature adopted a 6.25% severance tax on extractive minerals, but gave producers a credit of 52.5 mills, per $1 for property taxes. The net effect was to augment existing taxes on mineral production by 1%, about $4 million a year. The gasoline tax was raised from 6 cents to 7 cents a gallon.

To eliminate duplication and centralize executive authority, Governor Hathaway requested and obtained: a Department of Economic Planning and Development to replace the Natural Resource Board and several other agencies; a Department of Health and Social Services to replace the Health Department, the Welfare Department, and the vocational rehabilitation division of the Education Department; and a state planning coordinator to sit with state boards and commissions as his liaison officer.

Education. By past standards education fared well in the 1969 legislative session. The University of Wyoming received an appropriation of $25,796,-987 and the junior colleges, $3,547,000. Public school laws were recodified. The public school classroom unit allowance was raised from $8,200 to $10,500.

Minerals. The state enjoyed record mineral production. Led by oil—with more than 140 million barrels—output levels were also high in natural gas, trona, uranium, coal, and iron ore. Meanwhile, exploration for minerals was expanded. Wyoming, as usual, led the states of the Rocky Mountain region drilling for oil and gas, with more than 1,500 well completions. A large uranium deposit was discovered in the Powder River Basin.

Industrial Development. The most noteworthy additions to Wyoming's industry were new units built at the huge coal-fired electrical power plants at Glenrock and Kemmerer, and a Control Data Corporation plant at Casper that will have a work force of about 200 to make electronic components.

Agriculture. Several thousand sheep died in an April blizzard. On July 8, a 9,300-acre-foot reservoir of the Wheatland Irrigation District burst, submerging 10,000 acres of farm and ranch land and causing more than $1 million in damage.

T. A. LARSON
University of Wyoming

YAHYA KHAN, A. M. See biographical sketch under PAKISTAN.

——————— WYOMING • Information Highlights ———————

Area: 97,914 square miles (253,598 sq km).
Population: 314,000 (1969, est.).
Chief Cities (1969, est.): Cheyenne, the capital, 42,000; Casper, 35,500; Laramie, 21,000; Sheridan, 11,200.
Government: *Chief Officers*—governor, Stanley K. Hathaway (Rep.); secy. of state, Mrs. Thyra Thomson (Rep.); atty. gen., James E. Barrett (Rep.); treas., Mrs. Minnie Mitchell; supt. of pub. instr., Harry Roberts; chief justice, Norman B. Gray. *Legislature*—Senate, 30 members (12 Democrats, 18 Republicans); House of Representatives, 61 members (16 D, 45 R).
Education: *School enrollment* (1968–69)—public elementary, 50,000 pupils (2,300 teachers); public secondary, 38,000 pupils (2,200 teachers); nonpublic schools, 3,800 pupils (190 teachers); college and university (fall 1968), 12,010 students. *Public school expenditures* (1967–68)—$63,050,-000 ($775 per pupil); average teacher's salary, $7,277.
Public Finance (fiscal year 1968): *Revenues*, $189,289,000 (general sales and gross receipts taxes, $24,198,000; motor fuel tax, $14,172,000; federal funds, $72,474,000). *Expenditures*, $179,894,000 (education, $34,829,000; highways, $63,279,000). State debt, $53,538,000.
Personal Income (1968): $1,005,000,000; average annual income per person, $3,190.
Public Assistance (fiscal year 1968): $7,021,619 to 5,049 recipients.
Labor Force (employed persons, 139,200 (1968): *Agricultural*, 16,880; *nonagricultural* (wage and salary earners), 117,010 (5.8% manufacturing, 19.2% trade, 24.6% government). *Unemployed persons* (Dec. 31, 1968)—5,330.
Manufacturing (1965): Value added by manufacture, $93,882,-000 (petroleum and coal products, $44,253,000; stone, clay, and glass products, $9,264,000).
Agriculture (1967): *Cash farm income*, $211,915,000 (livestock, $166,267,000; crops, $34,550,000; govt. payments, $11,-098,000). *Chief crops* (tons)—Hay, 1,946,000; sugar beets, 845,000; wheat, 230,610; barley, 108,288; oats, 64,768.
Mining (1968): *Production value*, $576,200,000. *Chief minerals* (tons)—Sand and gravel, 8,630,000; bituminous coal, 3,-829,000; iron ore, 1,967,000; clays, 1,828,000; natural gas, 248,481,000,000 cubic feet; petroleum, 140,945,000 barrels.
Transportation: *Roads* (1968), 40,338 miles (64,916 km); *motor vehicles* (1968), 273,942; *railroads* (1968), 3,214 track miles (5,172 km); *airports* (1969), 7.
Communications (1968): *Telephones* (1969), 180,500; *television stations* (1967), 3; *radio stations* (1967), 30.

YEMEN

The civil war between republicans and royalists in Yemen basically came to an end in 1969. The conflict had erupted in 1962 when a military group revolted against the royalist regime of Imam (ruler) Muhammad al-Badr and established a republic. By mid-1969, after seven years of fighting, the republican government was in control of most of the country.

End of the Civil War. Following the defeat of the United Arab Republic in the Israeli-Arab War of 1967, UAR troops supporting Yemeni republican forces were withdrawn. The UAR withdrawal led to the gradual acceptance by many of the royalist tribes of the purely Yemeni republican forces. In February 1969, Imam al-Badr announced the appointment of a new royalist cabinet with himself as prime minister. But in the following month, Saudi Arabia halted its arms and financial aid to the royalists; Imam al-Badr and his brothers, uncles, and cousins abandoned Yemen and gave up the struggle.

In May republican president Abd al-Rahman al-Iryani declared that the "royalists are finished" and that "not one single shot has been fired anywhere in Yemen" for many months. In the course of the civil war several hundreds of thousands of Yemenis and about 25,000 Egyptians were killed.

The civil war generated a strong nationalist feeling in Yemen and initiated a cohesiveness that hardly existed before. After the UAR troops withdrew, Soviet personnel, who had come with them, were in disfavor and most had left by year end.

Government. The first session of the newly established National Assembly was held in Sana on March 17. The Assembly has 57 seats, of which 12 are reserved for representatives of Southern Yemen and will remain vacant until a merger between the two countries can be effected.

Al-Iryani was reelected as president. On April 3, Prime Minister Hasan al-Amri announced the formation of a new cabinet, with Ahmed Said Barrakat as foreign minister. The new government received several million dollars from Kuwait to bolster the economy. Press censorship was lifted and many steps were taken to develop the country. Prime Minister al-Amri resigned on July 8 and was succeeded in September by Abdallah al-Karshumi, a young engineer.

Relations with Southern Yemen. It had been the hope and expectation of Yemeni republican leaders that the Republic of Southern Yemen would join with Yemen to form a united state. But Southern Yemeni leaders decreed severe punishment for any of their countrymen who participated in the Yemeni government or National Assembly.

Relations with the West. Diplomatic relations were resumed with West Germany in July. Both Prime Minister al-Karshumi and Foreign Minister Barrakat stated that the Yemeni government wished to resume diplomatic relations with the United States, which were broken by Yemen in 1966. Barrakat also declared that Yemen wished to establish relations with Britain and France.

The new government is a mixture of western educated young men and representatives of the old distinguished families and tribes. Since the new Yemeni leaders are not socialists, seem able and willing to suppress leftist movements, and seek better relations with the West, the Soviet Union is less eager to provide material support.

Economy. The civil war left Yemen with a disrupted economy, but large sums were channeled into the hands of tribesmen for the first time during the fighting. Throughout 1969, Yemeni cabinet ministers visited Iraq, Syria, the United Arab Republic, Algeria, and Kuwait to seek aid and arrange trade agreements. West Germany gave Yemen a $12 million loan for economic development.

SYDNEY NETTLETON FISHER
The Ohio State University

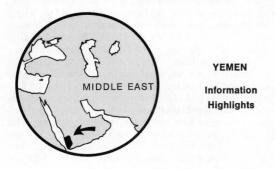

YEMEN

Information Highlights

Area: 75,290 square miles (195,000 sq km).
Population: 5,000,000 (1968 est.).
Chief Cities (1963 est.): Sana, the capital, 100,000; Taiz, 80,000; Hopeida, 45,000.
Government: *President*—Abd al-Rahman al-Iryani (took office Nov. 5, 1967); *Prime Minister*—Abdallah al-Karshumi (took office in September 1969). *Parliament*—National Assembly, 57 seats, 12 left vacant.
Religious Faith: Muslims, 99% of population.
Education: *Literacy rate* (1969), 5% of population. *Total school enrollment* (1965)—71,428 (primary, 69,139; secondary, 2,119; teacher-training, 125; technical/vocational, 45).
Finance (1964–65): Budget est. $27,300,000; *monetary unit,* rial (1.071 rials equal U. S.$1).
Chief Crop (metric tons, 1967–68 crop year): Coffee, 3,000.
Chief Mineral (metric tons, 1966): Salt, 100,000.
Foreign Trade (1967): *Chief Exports:* coffee, hides and skins, salt, kat (a narcotic drug); *chief imports:* textiles, sugar, glass.
Transportation: *Roads* (1960), 750 miles (1,200 km): *motor vehicles* (1965), 2,930; *national airline,* Yemeni Airline Co.
Communications: *Telephones* (1968): 1,650; *radio stations* (1965), 1; *newspapers* (1965), 3.

YUGOSLAVIA

In 1969 the League of Communists of Yugoslavia reorganized its top leadership committees. The country's economy showed contradictory trends. Yugoslavia's foreign policy was primarily aimed at improving relations with the Soviet Union.

Political Developments. The 9th Congress of the League of Communists of Yugoslavia (LCY) took place in Belgrade on March 11–15. The Communist parties of the Warsaw Pact nations, with the exception of Rumania, boycotted the congress.

An unexpected feature of the congress was the creation of an Executive Bureau to serve as the new "collective" leadership organ of the LCY. The 15 members of the bureau were top leaders representing each of the six federal republics that make up Yugoslavia. The establishment of the Executive Bureau was seen as a measure against disunity in LCY leadership, as well as against other domestic centrifugal tendencies. A 52-member Presidium, replacing the Central Committee, was also established.

The congress was dominated by domestic problems. It did not initiate any new internal or external policies but reaffirmed the LCY policy of socioeconomic reform.

On May 17, Mitja Ribičič, a 50-year-old Slovene, was elected Yugoslavia's new prime minister. Ribičič's political record has not been liberal; he was the chief of secret police in Slovenia.

————————————— YUGOSLAVIA • Information Highlights —————————————

Area: 98,766 square miles (255,804 sq km).

Population: 20,186,000 (1968 est.).

Chief Cities (1961 census): Belgrade, the capital, 585,234; Zagreb, 430,802; Skopje, 165,529; Sarajevo, 143,117.

Government: *President*—Josip Broz Tito (first elected Jan. 14, 1953); *President of the Federal Executive Council*—Mitja Ribičič (took office May 1969). *Parliament*—Federal Assembly, 670 members.

Religious Faiths: Serbian Orthodox Catholics, 41% of population; Roman Catholics, 33%; Muslims, 12%.

Education: *Literacy rate* (1969), 80% of population aged 10 and over. *Total school enrollment* (1965)—3,641,714 (primary, 2,945,520; secondary, 177,237; teacher-training, 27,908; university/higher, 184,923).

Finance (1969 est.): *National budget,* $924,000,000; *monetary unit,* dinar (12.5 dinars equal U. S.$1).

Gross National Product (1968 est.): $9,000,000,000.

National Income (1968): $8,144,000,000; *average annual income per person,* $403.

Economic Indexes (1967): *Industrial production* (1968), 139 (1963=100); *agricultural production,* 115 (1963=100); *cost of living,* 197 (1963=100).

Manufacturing (metric tons, 1967): Cement, 3,312,000; wheat flour, 1,980,000; crude steel, 1,836,000.

Crops (metric tons, 1967–68 crop year): Maize, 7,200,000; wheat, 4,870,000; sugar beets, 3,680,000; potatoes, 2,790,000; grapes, 1,050,000; barley, 606,000.

Minerals (metric tons, 1967): Lignite, 25,560,000 (ranks 5th among world producers); iron ore, 2,580,000; crude petroleum, 2,376,000; bauxite, 2,136,000; lime (1966), 1,138,000; coal, 912,000; magnesite, 424,800.

Foreign Trade (1968): *Exports,* $1,264,000,000 (chief exports, 1967: transport equipment, $106,000,000; meat, $103,000,000; nonferrous metals, $75,592,000; ships and boats, $58,880,000); *imports,* $1,797,000,000 (chief imports, 1967: nonelectrical machinery, $297,600,000; iron and steel, $137,600,000; cereals and preparations, $36,000,000). *Chief trading partners* (1967): Italy (took 18% of exports, supplied 13% of imports); USSR (took 18% of exports, supplied 10% of imports); West Germany.

Transportation: *Roads* (1969), 49,048 miles (78,933 km); *motor vehicles* (1967), 422,000 (automobiles 355,300); *railways* (1965), 7,366 miles (11,852 km); *merchant vessels* (1967), 181 (1,174,000 gross registered tons); *national airline,* Jugoslovenski Aerotransport (JAT).

Communications: *Telephones* (1968), 506,039; *television stations* (1967), 29; *television sets* (1967), 850,000; *radios* (1967), 3,059,000; *newspapers* (1967), 23.

A sharp conflict between the Slovenian republic and the federal government occurred in July over postponement in modernizing a major highway in Slovenia.

The critical mood of the country's writers and intellectuals, as well as nationality strifes, particularly in Kosovo and Metohija, caused government reprisals and angry comments in President Tito's speeches. On October 25, Tito denounced a play entitled "When the Pumpkins Were Blooming," which criticized Yugoslavia's anti-Soviet campaign of 1948–53. Zoran Gluščević, editor-in-chief of the literary weekly *Književne Novine,* was sentenced to six months imprisonment on October 28 for writing an article considered "libelous toward a friendly country," in this case the Soviet Union. Milovan Djilas' latest book, *The Unperfect Society,* published in New York, was banned in Yugoslavia.

Economy. One positive economic development was the growth of industrial production, which was 12.5% higher in the first nine months of 1969 than

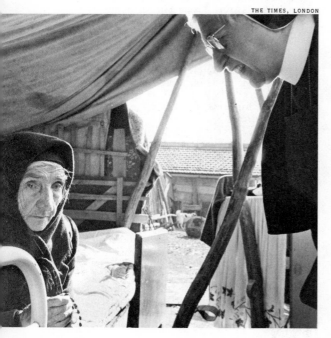

YUGOSLAVIAN EARTHQUAKE survivor in Banja Luka is comforted by nun as she rests in a makeshift tent.

THE TIMES, LONDON

in the same period in 1968. Agricultural production as a whole increased by 12%, although livestock decreased by 5%. Excellent weather conditions contributed to a near record harvest. The best results were achieved in the production of maize and of such crops as sunflower and potato.

Negative trends in Yugoslavia's economy were also conspicuous. The country's foreign trade deficit grew, as exports increased by 16% in comparison to 1968 but imports increased by 26%. Industry showed a high degree of insolvency, with 57% of the enterprises unable to meet their financial obligations regularly. Prices rose during 1969. The high level of unemployment continued, and more than 350,000 Yugoslavs were working abroad in June.

The Presidium of the LCY decided on October 14 to abolish the central government investment funds and to reform the banking, financial, and fiscal systems.

In October the International Financial Corporation, one of the three institutions of the World Bank, decided to join with several Yugoslav banks to establish a new investment company in Yugoslavia. The company's initial capital of $12 million will be provided by 40 banks and financial institutions in Europe, the United States, and Japan.

Foreign Affairs. Yugoslavia showed its interest in acting as an informal leader of the nonaligned countries by holding a consultative meeting in Belgrade on July 8–12. Fifty-one nonaligned governments sent representatives to the meeting. The participants agreed on the desirability of holding, with adequate preparations, a conference of the top leaders of the nonaligned countries. However, they disagreed about the proper role to be played by the nonaligned countries in world politics.

The Soviet and Yugoslav press engaged in polemical arguments earlier in the year, and the LCY boycotted the International Communist Conference in Moscow in June. But the visit to Yugoslavia of Soviet Foreign Minister Andrei Gromyko in September indicated willingness on both sides to improve relations. The communiqué issued at the end of Gromyko's visit emphasized the across-the-board cooperation between Yugoslavia and the Soviet Union. In a speech on October 4, Tito stated that Yugoslavia and the USSR had "arrived at the common conclusion that it is best to forget the past and cooperate in those things which are of common interest to us." He said the case of Czechoslovakia would therefore be put aside and that "we no longer wish to raise and dramatize this question."

PRESIDENT TITO of Yugoslavia is congratulated by young woman in uniform on his 77th birthday, May 25.

TITO (JOSIP BROZ), president of Yugoslavia, was reelected secretary-general of the Yugoslav Communist party in March 1969. In his address to the congress he reaffirmed Yugoslavia's ideological independence and criticized Soviet efforts to subordinate the interests of Yugoslavia to the demands of Soviet policy. In August, Tito announced a purge to remove "antiparty and antisocialist elements" from the party leadership and reaffirmed Yugoslavia's determination to adhere to socialist policies.

Tito was born on May 25, 1892, at Kumrovac, Croatia. After serving in the Austro-Hungarian Army in World War I he joined the Red Army and took part in the Russian Revolution. He played an active role in the Yugoslav Communist party in the 1920's and 1930's. In World War II he organized partisan forces that helped defeat the Axis powers. In 1945, Tito became premier of Yugoslavia, and since 1953 he has been the nation's president.

Yugoslavia's relations with Bulgaria and Albania remained unsatisfactory, but Yugoslav-Rumanian relations continued to be close. Tito met with Rumanian chief of state Nicolae Ceauşescu twice, in February and in September.

On June 12, Yugoslavia was among the first countries to recognize the provisional revolutionary government of South Vietnam, which had formed early in June.

Yugoslavia also cultivated relations with western European states. Yugoslav Premier Mika Špiljak visited France in January, the first visit to a top Yugoslav official there in 12 years. Yugoslav Foreign Minister Mirko Tepavac paid an official visit to West Germany on July 27–29. It was the first postwar visit by a Yugoslav foreign minister to West Germany. On October 2–6, Italian President Giuseppe Saragat visited Yugoslavia.

MILORAD M. DRACHKOVITCH
The Hoover Institution, Stanford University

YUKON TERRITORY

Economic activity in the Yukon in 1969 continued to center around the mining of metal, the territory's major industry. A new mine began production, and its first shipment of ore concentrates went to Japan in early December.

Political Affairs. The federal Ministry of Indian Affairs and Northern Development, in a major policy change, announced that it would shift responsibility for various government departments from appointed civil servants to elected members of the Territorial Council. The announcement, which came in response to the demands of the 7-member council, brought new interest to the field of politics and resulted in new hopes for business.

Mining. Anvil Mining Corporation, which runs the largest mine in the Yukon, started operations in 1969. By the end of the year the mine was on the way to reaching the highest anticipated level of production. Present production of 700 tons of concentrate daily has already had an effect on the Yukon's economy.

High production levels in the mining industry as a whole continued, and, with world mineral prices holding at very satisfactory levels, the outlook for 1970 also seemed favorable. Oldtimers in the field, such as United Keno Hills Mines, continued to produce, and newcomers, such as the Cassiar Asbestos Corporation and New Imperial Mines, made an impact on the economy with very substantial production. The level of mining production led to high employment in the mining and milling processes and allied industries, such as transportation.

Prospectors were very active during 1969, and it may prove to be the greatest period of claim-staking in the history of the territory.

Communications. Communications were greatly expanded in 1969. A private radio station was added in Whitehorse, and a Canadian Press wire hookup for the daily newspaper provided the Yukon with its first direct news service.

Transportation. Air traffic was increased, mainly because of the greater volume of goods moving from Whitehorse to Alaska's North Slope. Vehicle registration was 13% higher than in 1968, and construction began on 45 miles (72 km) of new road.

JIM MURDOCH
Yukon "Daily News"

YUKON TERRITORY · Information Highlights

Area: 207,076 square miles (536,327 sq km).
Population: 15,000 (Jan. 1, 1969 est.).
Chief Cities (1966 census): Whitehorse, the capital, 4,771.
Government: Chief Officers—*Commissioner*, James Smith; *judges of the territorial court*, Harry C. B. Maddison, W. G. Morrow. *Territorial Council* (convened March 10, 1964); 7 elected members: speaker, John O. Livesey, Donald E. Taylor, George O. Shaw, Mrs. Jean Gordon, N. S. Chamberlist, J. K. McKinnon, John Dumas.
Education: *School enrollment* (1968–69 est.)—public elementary and secondary, 3,603 pupils (214 teachers); Indian (federal) schools, 40 pupils (4 teachers); vocational training center, 214 students (15 teachers).
Public Finance (fiscal year 1967 est.): *Revenues*, $13,528,463; *expenditures*, $13,923,457.
Personal Income (including Northwest Terr., 1966 est.): $64,000,000.
Manufacturing (incl. Northwest Terr., 1966): *Value added by manufacture*, $1,489,000 (wood industries, $327,000; food and products, $181,000).
Mining (1967 est.): *Production value*, $15,575,684. *Chief minerals* (tons)—silver, 3,894,431 troy ounces (ranks 4th among the provinces); lead, 7,735 (ranks 5th).
Transportation (1968): *Roads*, 2,285 miles (3,677 km); *motor vehicles*, 9,735; *railroads*, 58 track miles (93 km).
Communications (1966): *Telephones*, 5,308; *television stations*, 1; *radio stations*, 2; *newspapers*, 2.
All figures given in Canadian dollars equal to U. S.93¢.

ZAMBIA

Events in Zambia in 1969 were dominated by the announcement of terms for the nationalization of copper producing companies, a crisis in the ruling political party, a delay in the proposed railway link with Tanzania, and the framing of labor and management legislation.

Copper Nationalization. On November 17, President Kenneth David Kaunda announced terms for the government's acquisition of a majority interest in Zambia's two major mining companies. The government-owned Industrial Development Corporation (Indeco) will pay $292 million for a 51% interest in two new companies to be formed from the seven subsidiaries of Roan Selection Trust and the Anglo American Corporation. The Anglo American Corporation will receive $179.5 million, and Roan Selection Trust will receive $112.5 million, in semi-annual installments over eight years at an annual interest rate of 6%. The terms were accepted by the mining companies, whose officers will negotiate with their subsidiaries on future management policies. It is believed that these policies will be similar to those followed in the past.

Two Swiss companies announced on November 15 their intention to finance a new copper mine in Zambia. The new mine will go into production in 1971, with Indeco in control of 51% of the shares.

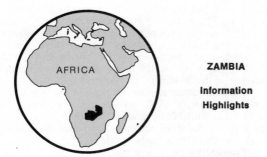

ZAMBIA

Information Highlights

Area: 290,584 square miles (752,614 sq km).
Population: 4,080,000 (1968 est.).
Chief Cities (1966 urban area est.): Lusaka, the capital, 152,000; Kitwe, 146,000; Ndola, 108,000.
Government: *President*—Kenneth David Kaunda (reelected Dec. 19, 1968). *Parliament*—Legislative Assembly, 105 members (party seating, 1969: United National Independence party, 81; African National Congress, 23; independents, 1).
Religious Faiths: Roman Catholics, 17% of population.
Education: *Literacy* (1969), over 90% of children receive 4 years of schooling. *Total school enrollment* (1965–66)—478,534 (primary, 473,432; teacher-training, 1,510; vocational, 3,245; higher, 347).
Finance (1969 est.): *Revenues*, $415,700,000; *expenditures*, $279,400,000; *monetary unit*, kwacha (0.7143 kwacha equals U.S.$1).
Gross National Product (1967): $1,100,000,000.
National Income (1967): $1,772,612,710; *average annual income per person*, $434.
Economic Indexes: *Industrial production* (1968), 124 (1963= 100); *cost of living* (1967), 129 (1963=100).
Manufacturing (metric tons, 1967): Smelter copper, 616,200; cement, 246,000; meat, 16,000.
Crops (metric tons, 1967–68 crop year): Maize, 280,000.
Minerals (metric tons, 1967): Copper, 663,000 (ranks 4th among world producers); limestone (1966), 570,254; zinc ore, 54,400; manganese, 13,700.
Foreign Trade (1968): *Exports*, $762,000,000 (chief exports, 1967: copper, $605,060,000; maize, $12,240,000; tobacco, $5,170,000); *imports*, $456,000,000 (chief imports, 1967: transport equipment, $77,310,000; nonelectrical machinery, $69,850,000; electrical machinery, $29,690,000). *Chief trading partners* (1967): Britain (took 27% of exports, supplied 21% of imports); Japan; U. S.
Transportation: *Roads* (1969), 22,000 miles (35,000 km); *motor vehicles* (1967), 69,700.
Communications: *Telephones* (1968): 43,267; *television stations* (1968), 2; *television sets* (1967), 11,000; *radios* (1966), 55,000; *newspapers* (1966), 1.

On November 19, President Kaunda said that he hopes all foreign-owned industries in Zambia eventually will be nationalized. Observers believe that Kaunda has been compelled to nationalize Zambia's industrial assets because of internal pressures such as tribal dissention, underemployment, political unrest, and Zambia's uneasy border position between African-ruled and white-ruled countries. He reportedly believes that a state-owned copper industry will train Africans for key jobs more diligently than would private companies. The added state income will also help finance national development projects.

Political Affairs. The resignation of Vice President Simon Kapwepwe on August 25 briefly plunged the country into its most serious political crisis since independence. The alleged reason for Kapwepwe's resignation was his disenchantment over the loss of political power by his numerically strong northern Bemba people. President Kaunda, however, prevailed on Kapwepwe to withdraw his resignation two days later.

Kapwepwe's return to office prevented a showdown over tribal grievances in the ruling United National Independence party (UNIP). In a further move to head off difficulty, President Kaunda appointed a commission on September 10 to review the UNIP constitution. The commission's recommendations are expected to be submitted to the National Council in early 1970.

Railway Link to Tanzania. A delay was announced on November 16 in a final decision on the financing and construction by Communist China of the proposed 1,200-mile (1,931-km) railway line between Zambia and Tanzania. Landlocked Zambia must now ship its copper ore through white-ruled Rhodesia. The proposed railway will provide an alternate route through Tanzania to the port of Dar es Salaam. Some 3,000 Communist Chinese technicians have been at work in Zambia and Tanzania on the initial survey.

No reason was given for the delay in accepting Chinese financial aid to construct the rail line. The communiqué said, however, that further meetings will be held in 1970, after the completion of the survey and design. Western advisers as well as the International Bank for Reconstruction and Development earlier declined to make loans on the project, calling it impractical.

Economic Affairs. Speaking before a trade union congress in Kitwe on December 13, President Kaunda announced pending legislation designed to give workers representation on all company boards, including those of state enterprises. He said that work councils were to be established to provide machinery for worker participation in management decisions. He also disclosed that the legislation will formulate a price and income policy in order to hold down prices while increasing productivity. Included in the legislation will be an industrial court for settling wage disputes and making wage determinations. Kaunda said that wage increases will not be allowed to exceed 5%.

The government announced in mid-November that the Zambian Railway Company has placed a $7.2 million contract with the General Electric Company of the United States for the purchase of 20 diesel locomotives.

FRANKLIN PARKER
West Virginia University

ZANZIBAR. See TANZANIA.

ZOOLOGY

The most noteworthy events in 1969, both to zoologists and to the general public, were the various developments in the area of environmental contamination, or pollution. Not so widely publicized, but of potentially great importance, is the continuing International Biological Programme.

Ecology. On Jan. 28, 1969, a blowout from the Union Oil Company's well A-21, in the Santa Barbara Channel off the coast of southern California, caused extensive contamination of offshore waters and the seacoast. This unexpected accident, with its locally spectacular effects on animal and plant life, helped make the public more aware of the gross contamination of the marine environment that has long been increasing. (See also CONSERVATION.)

The Santa Barbara oil well is situated on the outer continental shelf, a relatively shallow portion of the ocean floor. The outer-shelf area bordering the United States totals about 800,000 square miles (2,072,000 sq km) and is under control of the federal government. It is a region rich in petroleum and mineral resources and the location of important fishing grounds. To date, less than 1% of this area has been leased for commercial exploitation. Similar areas, such as off northern South America and in the Indonesian region, are currently being explored for commercial exploitation. The impact of such activities on the marine environment remains to be seen.

On May 21, 1969, Army representatives officially conceded, after repeated denials, that nerve gas tested by the Army at the Dugway Proving Ground in Utah on March 13, 1968, had killed 6,000 sheep.

Pesticides. Many of the environmental contaminants, if they continue to accumulate at the ever-accelerating rate of the past few years, will so decimate the world that many thousands of species of wildlife will vanish and man will survive only in completely artificial environments. Even the present levels of environmental contamination by the chlorinated hydrocarbons—the so-called deadly seven: DDT, dieldrin, aldrin, endrin, heptachlor, chlordane, and lindane—may cause the extinction of certain birds. DDT upsets calcium metabolism, and birds carrying high levels of DDT lay thin-shelled eggs that never hatch. Pelicans in California, eagles in Michigan, peregrine falcons in North America (especially the eastern United States) and parts of Europe, duck hawks in England—all are known to be severely affected.

Chlorinated Biphenyls. In addition to the adverse effects of the chlorinated hydrocarbon insecticides, it has been discovered that the chlorinated biphenyls, used in industry as lubricants, heat-transfer media, and insulators, may have similar effects. European biologists have demonstrated that fishes, mussels, and birds from the Rhine River and the Netherlands coastal area have significant or critical levels of chlorinated biphenyls, presumably from materials that escaped or were dumped as industrial wastes into the Rhine.

International Biological Programme. About 10 years ago, Sir Rudolph Peters, then president of the International Council of Scientific Unions, and Professor G. Montalenti, then president of the International Union of Biological Sciences, began discussions that led to the approval by the 10th General Assembly of the International Council, 1963, of an International Biological Programme (IBP).

As envisioned, the program would involve a worldwide study of "(1) organic production on the land, in fresh waters, and in the seas, so that adequate estimates may be made of the potential yield of new as well as existing natural resources; and (2) human adaptability to the changing conditions." By 1965, preliminary planning for the participation of the United States in the IBP was underway. Originally scheduled for activation by late 1967, various problems, mainly financial in nature, resulted in a slow start in the United States. With the central theme of man's survival in a changing world, various teams of scientists, including representatives from a spectrum of specialties, have joined forces to study in detail the effects of various uses of land on the balance of nature in specific areas. Some programs, such as the Grasslands Biome Study, were underway in late 1968; others, such as the Desert Biome study, are scheduled to be launched in 1970.

Physiology. D. E. Aiken of the Fisheries Research Board of Canada demonstrated that because of differences in photoperiods, endocrine levels, and other physiological control mechanisms, animals living in natural populations often react differently than individuals kept under laboratory conditions. This may explain some of the conflicting data obtained by various investigations, utilizing presumably identical animals and experimental procedures.

Evolution. J. L. King and T. H. Jukes summarized evidence indicating that most evolutionary changes in proteins result from non-Darwinian evolutionary causes such as neutral mutations (neither harmful nor helpful to the organism) and genetic drift (accidental events). In their view, natural selection, that is, Darwinian evolution, is the editor, not the composer, of genetic messages carried on the DNA molecule, and one thing the editor does not do is remove changes (mutations) that it cannot perceive.

Taxonomy. As pointed out by R. H. Whittaker (*Science*, 163:150), for the past three decades biologists have been gradually abandoning the classical two-kingdom (plants and animals) system of classifying living organisms. Instead, most now use a four- or five-kingdom system that appears better to reflect modern knowledge of the origin, evolution, and structure of living organisms. As long as we are simply distinguishing between a flowering plant and butterfly, we have no difficulties with the classical two-kingdom system. Problems arise, however, in classifying the "primitive" groups. The single-celled *Euglena* is generally studied as a "primitive" *animal* and classified as a protozoan by zoologists; yet, because *Euglena* may contain chlorophyll and manufacture its own food, it is generally studied as a "primitive" *plant* by botanists.

The five-kingdom system that probably will be widely used recognizes the following: Kingdom Monera, with primitive structures, including blue-green algae and bacteria; Kingdom Protista, with unicellular or colonial unicellular forms, including certain algae and Protozoans; Kingdom Plantae, with multicellular, generally photosynthetic forms, including complex algae, stonewarts, and all higher plants; Kingdom Fungi, with multinucleate organisms without chlorophyll, including the molds and fungi; and Kingdom Animalia, including the typical animals.

E. LENDELL COCKRUM
University of Arizona

contributors

Following is a list of the distinguished authorities who contributed articles to this edition of THE AMERICANA ANNUAL. Their professional affiliations are shown, together with the titles of their articles.

ADAMS, GEORGE, Legislative Reference Librarian, Connecticut State Library: CONNECTICUT

AKERMAN, ROBERT H., Chairman, Department of History and Government, Florida Southern College: FLORIDA

ALEXANDER, MYRL E., Director, U. S. Bureau of Prisons: PRISONS

ALEXANDER, ROBERT J., Professor of Economics, Rutgers University: COSTA RICA; DOMINICAN REPUBLIC; GUYANA; JAMAICA

ALEXANDER, WILLIAM M., Director, Institute for Curriculum Improvement, University of Florida: EDUCATION—*Curriculum Developments*

ALVEY, EDWARD, JR., Professor of Education, Mary Washington College of the University of Virginia: EDUCATION

ANDERSON, JOSEPH, Secretary to the First Presidency, The Church of Jesus Christ of Latter-day Saints: CHURCH OF JESUS CHRIST OF LATTER-DAY SAINTS

ANDERSON, SAMUEL K., Associate Professor of History, Oregon College of Education: OREGON

ARMSTRONG, FREDERICK H., Associate Professor of History, Talbot College, University of Western Ontario: TORONTO

BAILEY, HARRY A., JR., Chairman, Department of Political Science, Temple University: PENNSYLVANIA; PHILADELPHIA

BAKER, RICHARD T., Professor of Journalism, Columbia University: NEWSPAPERS

BALL, ROBERT M., Commissioner, Social Security Administration: SOCIAL SECURITY

BALLINGER, RONALD B., Professor of History, Rhode Island College: SOUTH AFRICA

BANKS, RONALD F., Assistant to the President, University of Maine: MAINE

BARKER, TWILEY W., JR., Professor of Political Science, University of Illinois at Chicago Circle: CHICAGO; ILLINOIS

BARR, LOIS F., Reporter, The Denver *Post:* COLORADO

BARRETT, RUSSELL H., Professor of Political Science, University of Mississippi: AUSTRALIA

BEATTIE, A. J., Lecturer in Political Science, London School of Economics and Political Science: GREAT BRITAIN; WILSON, HAROLD

BENEDICT, BURTON, Professor of Anthropology, University of California, Berkeley: MAURITIUS

BENFEY, THEODOR, Professor of Chemistry, Earlham College; Editor, *Chemistry:* CHEMISTRY

BERGEN, DAN, Associate Professor of Library Science, University of Mississippi: LIBRARIES

BERGER, BERNARD B., Director, Water Resources Research Center, University of Massachusetts: POLLUTION

BILKEY, WARREN J., Professor of Business, University of Wisconsin: CONSUMER AFFAIRS

BISCHOFF, RALPH F., Charles L. Denison Professor of Law, New York University: CIVIL RIGHTS AND LIBERTIES

BLACK, KENNETH, JR., Regents Professor of Insurance and Dean, School of Business Administration, Georgia State College; Coauthor, *Life Insurance* and *Cases in Life Insurance:* INSURANCE

BLUE, GARTH, Librarian, Western Region, Canada Department of Regional Economic Expansion: SASKATCHEWAN

BOGARDUS, EMORY S., Professor Emeritus of Sociology, University of Southern California; Editor Emeritus, *Sociology and Social Research:* SOCIOLOGY

BOILY, ROBERT, Département de Science Politique, Université de Montréal: QUEBEC

BOK, BART J., Head, Department of Astronomy; Director, Steward Observatory, University of Arizona: ASTRONOMY

BOND, DONOVAN H., Director of Development and Professor of Journalism, West Virginia University: WEST VIRGINIA

BOVEY, JOHN A., Provincial Archivist of Manitoba: MANITOBA

BOWERS, Q. DAVID, Columnist, *Coin World;* Author, *Coins and Collectors:* COIN COLLECTING

BOYLAN, JAMES R., Editor, *Columbia Journalism Review:* MAGAZINES

BRADDOCK, BILL, Sports Department, *The New York Times:* SPORTS

BRADLEY, C. PAUL, Professor of Political Science, Flint College, University of Michigan: MALAYSIA; SINGAPORE

BRAMMER, DANA B., Assistant Director, Bureau of Governmental Research, University of Mississippi: MISSISSIPPI

BRESNAHAN, WILLIAM A., Managing Director, American Trucking Associations, Inc.: MOTOR TRANSPORTATION

BRIDGE, LAWRENCE, Chief, Business Structure Division, Office of Business Economics, U. S. Department of Commerce: ECONOMY OF THE U. S.—*Wholesale Selling*

BRODIN, PIERRE, Director of Studies, Lycée Français de New York: FRENCH LITERATURE

BRONNER, EDWIN B., Curator of the Quaker Collection, Haverford College: FRIENDS, RELIGIOUS SOCIETY OF

BURDETTE, FRANKLIN L., Professor and Director, Bureau of Governmental Research, University of Maryland: ELECTIONS; POLITICAL PARTIES

BURKS, ARDATH W., Director of International Programs, Rutgers University: JAPAN

BURLINGAME, MERRILL G., Professor of History, Montana State University: MONTANA

BUSH, GRAHAM, Lecturer in Political Studies, The University of Auckland: NEW ZEALAND

BUSTIN, EDOUARD, Associate Professor of Government, Boston University: BURUNDI; CONGO (BRAZZAVILLE); CONGO (KINSHASA); GABON; RWANDA

BUTLER, ALEXANDER R., Professor, Department of Humanities, Michigan State University: MIES VAN DER ROHE, LUDWIG

BUTWELL, RICHARD, Professor of Southeast Asian Politics, The American University; Author, *Southeast Asia Today —and Tomorrow:* BURMA; CAMBODIA; LAOS; VIETNAM; VIETNAM WAR

CAIRNS, JOHN C., Professor of History, University of Toronto: FRANCE; POMPIDOU, GEORGES

CANNON, LEE, Managing Editor, *Interior Design:* INTERIOR DESIGN

CARMONY, DONALD F., Professor of History, Indiana University; Editor, *Indiana Magazine of History:* INDIANA

CASTAGNO, A. A., Director, African Studies Program, Boston University: SOMALIA

CHALMERS, J. W., Faculty of Education, University of Alberta: ALBERTA

CHING, FRANK, Foreign News Desk, *The New York Times:* COMMUNISM—*Sino-Soviet Relations*

CHINN, RONALD E., Head, Department of Political Science, University of Alaska: ALASKA

CHRIEN, ROBERT E., Physicist, Brookhaven National Laboratory: ATOMIC ENERGY

CHRISTENSEN, C. DIANE, Institute of African Studies, Columbia University: GHANA; IVORY COAST; SIERRA LEONE

CHRISTENSON, REO M., Professor of Political Science, Miami University, Ohio: POVERTY

CLARK, J. STANLEY, Department of History, Oklahoma City University; Author, *The Oil Century, from the Drake Well to the Conservation Era:* OKLAHOMA

CLARK, ROBERT S., Associate Editor, *Stereo Review:* MUSIC

CLARKE, JAY, Sunday Editor, The Miami *Herald:* TOURISM

COCKRUM, E. LENDELL, Professor, Department of Biological Sciences, University of Arizona: ZOOLOGY

COHEN, SIDNEY, Director, Division of Narcotic Addiction and Drug Abuse, National Institute of Mental Health: NARCOTICS AND HALLUCINOGENS

COLLINS, ROBERT O., Associate Professor of History, University of California, Santa Barbara: KENYA; SUDAN; TANZANIA; UGANDA

COOPER, JOHN I., Professor of History, McGill University: MONTREAL

COOPER, RICHARD N., Professor of Economics, Yale University: INTERNATIONAL FINANCE

COYNE, ROBERT W., President, Distilled Spirits Institute, Inc.: ALCOHOLIC BEVERAGES—*Distilling Industry*

CRITCHFIELD, HOWARD J., Professor and Chairman, Department of Geography, Western Washington State College: PACIFIC ISLANDS; WESTERN SAMOA

CROW, PAUL A., JR., General Secretary, Consultation on Church Union: RELIGION—*Protestantism*

CURTIS, L. PERRY, JR., Associate Professor of History, University of California, Berkeley: IRELAND

DAUSTER, FRANK N., Professor of Romance Languages, Rutgers University: LATIN AMERICAN LITERATURE

DAVID, HEATHER M., Pentagon Correspondent, Fairchild Publications and Fairchild Broadcast News: MISSILES

DAVIS, CHARLES M., Professor of Geography, University of Michigan: MICHIGAN

DAVIS, PETER G., Music Editor, *High Fidelity* Magazine: RECORDINGS—*Classical Records*

DAWSON, RICHARD E., Associate Professor of Political Science, Washington University: MISSOURI; ST. LOUIS

DEL GATTO, JOSEPH V., Executive Editor, *Rubber World:* RUBBER

DELZELL, CHARLES F., Professor of History, Vanderbilt University: ITALY

DIGGES, DUDLEY P., Editorial Writer, The Baltimore *Evening Sun:* BALTIMORE

DOBLER, CLIFFORD, Professor of Business Law, University of Idaho: IDAHO

DORPALEN, ANDREAS, Professor of History, The Ohio State University: GERMANY

DRACHKOVITCH, MILORAD M., Senior Staff Member, The Hoover Institution, Stanford University: YUGOSLAVIA

DRIGGS, DON W., Chairman, Department of Political Science, University of Nevada, Reno: NEVADA

DuBOIS, RUTH MARY (PACKARD), Fashion Lecturer, Fashion Institute of Technology, New York City: FASHION

DUCHON, M. L., Ophthalmologist and Author: EYE DISEASES

DUFF, ERNEST A., Professor of Political Science, Randolph-Macon Woman's College: COLOMBIA

DUFFY, JOSEPH A., Executive Director, American Booksellers Association, Inc.: BOOK PUBLISHING

DUPREE, LOUIS, American Universities Field Staff: AFGHANISTAN

DUPREE, NANCY HATCH, American Universities Field Staff: AFGHANISTAN

ELLIOTT, GORDON R., Department of English, Simon Fraser University: CANADIAN LITERATURE

ENGLISH, JOSEPH T., Administrator, Health Services and Mental Health Administration, U. S. Public Health Service: PUBLIC HEALTH

ETCHESON, WARREN W., Professor of Business Administration, University of Washington: WASHINGTON

FAIRBROTHERS, DAVID E., Professor of Botany, Rutgers University: BOTANY

FARRELL, RAYMOND F., Commissioner of Immigration and Naturalization, U. S. Department of Justice: IMMIGRATION

FARROW, MOIRA, Reporter, The Vancouver *Sun:* VANCOUVER

FEINBERG, SAMUEL, Columnist, *Women's Wear Daily:* CLOTHING INDUSTRY

FERRAR, HAROLD, Assistant Professor of English and Comparative Literature, Columbia University: THEATER

FISHER, ROBERT W., Economist, Bureau of Labor Statistics, U. S. Department of Labor: LABOR

FISHER, SIDNEY NETTLETON, Professor of History, The Ohio State University: KUWAIT; YEMEN

FOLMSBEE, STANLEY J., Professor of History, University of Tennessee: TENNESSEE

FORD, JOSEPH P., Department of Political Science, University of New Hampshire: NEW HAMPSHIRE

FOWLER, JOHN, Architect: ARCHITECTURE

FRANKEL, CHARLES, Old Dominion Professor of Philosophy and Public Affairs, Columbia University: THE YEAR OF THE MOON (part)

FREEMAN, ARTHUR, Editor, Journal of the American Veterinary Medical Association: VETERINARY MEDICINE

FRIEDLY, ROBERT L., Director, Office of Interpretation, Christian Church (Disciples of Christ): CHRISTIAN CHURCH

GAIGE, FREDERICK H., Instructor of Asian Studies, Davidson College: NEPAL

GAILEY, HARRY A., Professor of History, San Jose State College: GAMBIA; GUINEA; NIGERIA; SENEGAL

GALLOWAY, DAVID D., Associate Professor of Modern Literature, Case Western Reserve University: ENGLISH LITERATURE

GEIS, GILBERT, Visiting Professor, School of Criminal Justice, State University of New York at Albany: CRIME; POLICE

GEOGHEGAN, JOHN T., News Services Manager, American Telephone & Telegraph Co.: TELEPHONE

GIBBONS, CHARLES A., Statistician, Foreign Regional Analysis Division, Economic Research Service, U. S. Department of Agriculture: FOOD—*World Food Supply*

GILLETTE, GERALD W., Research Historian, The Presbyterian Historical Society: PRESBYTERIAN CHURCHES

GINTZIG, LEON, Professor and Chairman, Department of Health Care Administration, The George Washington University: HOSPITALS

GJESTER, THOR, City Editor, *Norwegian Journal of Commerce and Shipping,* Oslo: NORWAY

GOLD, LEON, Vice President–Directing Editor, Tax Research Institute of America: TAXATION

GORDON, MAYNARD M., Editor, *Motor News Analysis* and *The Imported Car Reports:* AUTOMOBILES

GORMAN, JOHN A., Associate Chief, National Income Division, Office of Business Economics, U. S. Department of Commerce: ECONOMY OF THE U. S.—*National Income and Product*

GRACE, JOHN, National Chief Secretary, The Salvation Army: SALVATION ARMY

GROTH, ALEXANDER J., Associate Professor of Political Science, University of California, Davis: POLAND

GUILBERT, CHARLES M., Secretary, The Executive Council, Episcopal Church Center: EPISCOPAL CHURCH

GULICK, LEWIS, Diplomatic Affairs Reporter, The Associated Press: FOREIGN AID

GUNN, JOHN M., Television Producer and Professor in Speech and Dramatic Art, State University of New York at Albany: TELEVISION AND RADIO—*Television Broadcasting; Radio Broadcasting*

HALL, FRANCES L., Director, International Trade Analysis Division, Bureau of International Commerce, U. S. Department of Commerce: INTERNATIONAL TRADE—*Trade Developments*

HALPERIN, ERNST, Professor of Political Science, Massachusetts Institute of Technology: CUBA

HAMILTON, CHARLES V., Professor of Political Science, Columbia University: CIVIL RIGHTS MOVEMENT

HANNA, PAUL L., Professor of Social Sciences, University of Florida: IRAN; IRAQ; ISRAEL; JORDAN; LEBANON; SYRIA

HANSON, EARL PARKER, Geographer; Former Consultant to the Puerto Rico Department of State: PUERTO RICO

HARVEY, ANDREW S., Economic Research Associate, Institute of Public Affairs, Dalhousie University: NOVA SCOTIA

HARWOOD, RICHARD, National Editor—National Correspondent, The Washington *Post:* UNITED STATES—*Domestic Affairs*

HAYES, JOHN D., Rear Admiral, USN (Ret.); U. S. Naval Academy Alumni Association: NAVY; SHIPPING

HEAD, HOWARD T., Consulting Radio Engineer: TELEVISION AND RADIO—*Television and Radio Engineering*

HECKMAN, DON, Contributing Editor, *Stereo Review;* Columnist, *The Village Voice:* RECORDINGS—*Popular Records*

HEDGPETH, JOEL W., Resident Director, Marine Science Center, Oregon State University: MARINE BIOLOGY

HELMREICH, E. C., Thomas B. Reed Professor of History and Political Science, Bowdoin College: AUSTRIA

HELMREICH, PAUL C., Associate Professor of History, Wheaton College, Norton, Mass.: SWITZERLAND

HENDERSHOT, LELAND N., Editor-in-Chief, American Dental Association: DENTISTRY

HENDERSHOTT, MYRL C., Assistant Professor of Oceanography, Scripps Institution of Oceanography: OCEANOGRAPHY

HENDERSON, GERALD M., Associate Professor of Anthropology, Brooklyn College, City University of New York: ANTHROPOLOGY

HERBER, LEWIS, Specialist on City Planning; Author, *Crisis in Our Cities:* CITIES AND URBAN AFFAIRS

HERSHKOWITZ, LEO, Department of History, Queens College, City University of New York: NEW YORK CITY; NEW YORK STATE

HIRT, FRANCIS L., Business Economist, U. S. Department of Commerce: ECONOMY OF THE U. S.—*Industrial Production*

HODGES, RALPH W., Assistant Technical Editor, *Stereo Review:* RECORDINGS—*Audio Equipment and Techniques*

HODGSON, STUART M., Commissioner, Northwest Territories: NORTHWEST TERRITORIES

HOLLAND, JAMES R., Special Assistant to the Postmaster General: POST OFFICE

HOOVER, HERBERT T., Professor of History, The University of South Dakota: SOUTH DAKOTA

HOPKINS, JAMES F., Head, Department of History, University of Kentucky: KENTUCKY

HOVET, THOMAS, JR., Professor of Political Science, University of Oregon: THANT, U; UNITED NATIONS

HOWARD, HARRY N., Adjunct Professor of Middle East Studies, School of International Service, The American University: TURKEY

HUFFARD, ELZA, President, Northeastern Christian Junior College: CHURCHES OF CHRIST

HUNKINS, KENNETH L., Senior Research Associate, Lamont–Doherty Geological Observatory: ARCTIC REGIONS

HUNT, STANLEY B., President, Textile Economics Bureau, Inc.: TEXTILE INDUSTRY

HUTCHINSON, C. ALAN, Associate Professor of History, University of Virginia: EL SALVADOR; NICARAGUA

HUTH, JOHN F., JR., Columnist and Reporter, *The Plain Dealer:* CLEVELAND

IGLAUER, ARNOLD, Associate Clinical Professor of Medicine, College of Medicine, University of Cincinnati: HEART DISEASE

INGRAM, HELEN M., Assistant Professor of Political Science, University of New Mexico: NEW MEXICO

JACKENDOFF, RUTH, Director, Department of Economics and Statistics, The Wool Bureau, Inc.: WOOL

JACOBS, WALTER DARNELL, Professor of Government and Politics, University of Maryland: LAIRD, MELVIN ROBERT; ROGERS, WILLIAM PIERCE

JENSEN, J. GRANVILLE, Professor of Geography, Oregon State University: CONSERVATION

JONES, DOROTHEA S., Statistician, Office of Business Economics, U. S. Department of Commerce: ECONOMY OF THE U. S.—*Retail Sales*

JOYCE, WALTER, Editor, *Marketing/Communications:* ADVERTISING

KANTOR, HARRY, Professor of Political Science, Marquette University: PERU

KARSKI, JAN, Department of Government, Georgetown University: BULGARIA; HUNGARY

KEHR, ERNEST A., Director, Stamp News Bureau; Executive Chairman, Philatelic Press Club: STAMP COLLECTING

KELLER, EUGENIA, Managing Editor, *Chemistry:* CHEMISTRY

KENEFICK, DONALD P., Director, Research and Professional Affairs, National Association for Mental Health, Inc.: MENTAL HEALTH

KING, HENRY B., President, United States Brewers Association: ALCOHOLIC BEVERAGES—*Brewing Industry*

KING, PETER J., Associate Professor of History, Carleton University: OTTAWA

KLAWITER, RANDOLPH J., Department of Modern and Classical Languages, University of Notre Dame: GERMAN LITERATURE

KLEIN, STANLEY, Science Moderator, WEVD Radio: COMPUTERS

KNORR, N. H., President, Watch Tower Bible and Tract Society of Pennsylvania: JEHOVAH'S WITNESSES

KOENIG, LOUIS W., Professor of Government, New York University; Author, *The Chief Executive:* EISENHOWER, DWIGHT DAVID

KOLEHMAINEN, JOHN I., Chairman, Department of Political Science, Heidelberg College, Tiffin, Ohio: FINLAND

KOMINUS, NICHOLAS, Director of Information, U. S. Cane Sugar Refiners Association; Kominus Agri-Info Associates: AGRICULTURE—*Fruits, Grains, Vegetables;* COFFEE; COTTON; SUGAR; TEA; TOBACCO

KREITZMAN, STEPHEN, Assistant Professor of Dental Research, Emory University: BIOCHEMISTRY

KREPS, CLIFTON H., JR., Wachovia Professor of Banking, University of North Carolina: BANKING

KUDRLE, ALBERT E., Director of Information, American Hotel & Motel Association: TOURISM—*Hotels and Motels*

KUFLIK, ABIGAIL L., Music Reporter, *Newsweek:* MUSIC—*Woodstock Rock Festival*

KURTZ, PAUL, Professor of Philosophy, State University of New York at Buffalo; Director, U. S. A., *Bibliography of Philosophy:* PHILOSOPHY

LAI, DAVID CHUEN-YAN, Assistant Professor of Geography, University of Victoria, B. C.: HONG KONG

LAIDLER, HARRY W., Executive Director Emeritus, League for Industrial Democracy; Author, *History of Socialism:* SOCIALISM

LANDSBERG, H. E., Research Professor, Institute for Fluid Dynamics and Applied Mathematics, University of Maryland: METEOROLOGY

LARSEN, WILLIAM, Professor of History, Radford College: VIRGINIA

LARSON, ARTHUR, Director, Rule of Law Research Center, Duke University: INTERNATIONAL LAW

LARSON, T. A., Professor of History, University of Wyoming; Author, *History of Wyoming:* WYOMING

LAWRENCE, ROBERT M., Associate Professor of Government, University of Arizona: DEFENSE FORCES

LEE, CHAE-JIN, Assistant Professor of Political Science, University of Kansas: KOREA

LEFEVER, ERNEST W., Senior Fellow, Foreign Policy Studies, The Brookings Institution: DISARMAMENT AND ARMS CONTROL

LEFLER, HUGH T., Kenan Professor of History, University of North Carolina; Coauthor, *North Carolina: The History of a Southern State:* NORTH CAROLINA

LEIDEN, CARL, Professor of Government, University of Texas: PAKISTAN; THAILAND; UNITED ARAB REPUBLIC

LELYVELD, JOSEPH, Reporter, *The New York Times:* KENNEDY, EDWARD MOORE

LEONARD, OLEN E., Rural Sociologist, The Ohio State University, São Paulo, Brazil: BOLIVIA

LE VINE, VICTOR T., Professor of Political Science, University of Ghana: CAMEROON; CENTRAL AFRICAN REPUBLIC; CHAD; LIBERIA; UPPER VOLTA

LEVY, JAMES R., Assistant Professor of History, Pomona College: ARGENTINA

LEWIS, FRANK M., Chairman, Department of Political Science, University of Toledo: CHILE

LEWIS, OSCAR, Author, *San Francisco: Mission to Metropolis, The Big Four,* and other books: SAN FRANCISCO

LINDGREN, RAYMOND E., Professor of History, California State College, Long Beach: DENMARK; ICELAND; SWEDEN

LINDSEY, ROBERT H., Aviation Reporter, *The New York Times:* AEROSPACE INDUSTRY; AIR TRANSPORTATION

LIVINGSTONE, WILLIAM, Reviewer, *Ballet Review;* Managing Editor, *Stereo Review:* DANCE

LOHMANN, LAWRENCE C., City Hall Reporter, The Milwaukee *Journal:* MILWAUKEE

LONG, ERNEST E., Secretary of the General Council, United Church of Canada: UNITED CHURCH OF CANADA

LOTT, LEO B., Professor and Chairman, Department of Political Science, University of Montana: PARAGUAY; VENEZUELA

LUTHER, ERNEST W., Economist; Author, *Ethiopia Today:* ETHIOPIA

LYLES, CHARLES H., Chief, Branch of Fishery Statistics, U. S. Fish and Wildlife Service: FISHERIES

LYNCH, J. JOSEPH, S. J., Director, Fordham Seismic Observatory: EARTHQUAKES

McANALLY, THOMAS S., Director, Nashville Office, United Methodist Information: UNITED METHODIST CHURCH

McCLESKEY, CLIFTON, Professor of Government, University of Texas: TEXAS

McCORQUODALE, SUSAN, Assistant Professor of Political Science, Memorial University of Newfoundland: NEWFOUNDLAND

McFARLAND, M. CARTER, Assistant Commissioner for Programs, Federal Housing Administration: BUILDING AND CONSTRUCTION

McGUIRE, JOHNSON, Professor of Medicine, College of Medicine, University of Cincinnati; Director, Cardiac Laboratory, Cincinnati General Hospital: HEART DISEASE

McLEAN, W. PAUL, Assistant Professor of Religion, Southern Methodist University: RELIGION—*Islam*

McNASPY, C. J., S. J., Associate Editor, *America* Magazine: PAUL VI, POPE; RELIGION—*Roman Catholicism;* ROMAN CATHOLIC CHURCH

MacNUTT, W. S., Professor of History, University of New Brunswick: NEW BRUNSWICK

MAJOR, ANDRÉ, Literary Critic, *Le Devoir,* Montreal: CANADIAN LITERATURE—*French Canadian Literature*

MARCOPOULOS, GEORGE J., Assistant Professor of History, Tufts University: CYPRUS; GREECE

MARKE, JULIUS J., Law Librarian and Professor of Law, New York University: LAW

MARTIN, J. A., JR., Professor of Religion, Columbia University: RELIGION—*General Survey*

MARTY, MARTIN E., Associate Editor, *The Christian Century;* Professor of Modern Church History, University of Chicago: PIKE, JAMES ALBERT

MARWICK, CHARLES S., Washington Bureau Science Correspondent, *Medical World News:* MEDICINE

MATHESON, NEIL A., Agricultural Editor, *The Guardian,* Charlottetown, P. E. I.: PRINCE EDWARD ISLAND

MATHEWS, THOMAS G., Director, Institute of Caribbean Studies, University of Puerto Rico: BARBADOS; CARIBBEAN; TRINIDAD AND TOBAGO

MECHAM, J. LLOYD, Professor Emeritus of Government, University of Texas: BRAZIL

MEREDITH, J. R., Director, Bureau of Economics and Statistics, British Columbia: BRITISH COLUMBIA

METCALF, GEORGE S., Museum Specialist, Department of Anthropology, U. S. National Museum: ARCHAEOLOGY—*Western Hemisphere*

MICKELSEN, OLAF, Department of Foods and Nutrition, Michigan State University; Secretary, American Institute of Nutrition: NUTRITION

MIESEL, VICTOR H., Associate Professor, Department of the History of Art, University of Michigan: ART

MILLER, LUTHER S., Editor, *Railway Age:* RAILROADS

MILLER, NYLE H., Secretary, Kansas State Historical Society: KANSAS

MILLEVILLE, HOWARD P., Extension Food Technologist, Oregon State University: FOOD—*Food Industry*

MITCHELL, GARY, Associate Professor of Physics, North Carolina State University at Raleigh: PHYSICS

MODEAN, ERIK W., Director, News Bureau, Lutheran Council in the USA: LUTHERAN CHURCHES

MOIR, JOHN S., Professor of History, Scarborough College, University of Toronto: CANADA; TRUDEAU, PIERRE ELLIOTT

MORGAN, CHARLES S., General Manager, National Fire Protection Association: FIRES

MOSS, ROBERT V., President, United Church of Christ: UNITED CHURCH OF CHRIST

MUNROE, JOHN A., H. Rodney Sharp Professor of History, University of Delaware: DELAWARE

MURDOCH, JIM, The Yukon *Daily News*, Whitehorse: YUKON TERRITORY

MUSTE, JOHN M., Associate Professor of English, The Ohio State University: AMERICAN LITERATURE

NELSON, RALPH L., Professor of Economics, Queens College, City University of New York: PHILANTHROPY

NEWMAN, LOUIS E., Director, Institute of Government Research, Louisiana State University: LOUISIANA; NEW ORLEANS

NEWSOM, DONALD W., Professor and Head, Department of Horticulture, Louisiana State University: GARDENING AND HORTICULTURE

NOLAN, WILLIAM C., Associate Professor of Political Science, Southern State College: ARKANSAS

NORMAN, JOHN, Professor of History and Government, Pace College Westchester: LIBYA; TUNISIA

NOSS, JOHN B., Author, *Man's Religions:* RELIGION—*Oriental Religions*

NUQUIST, ANDREW E., Professor of Political Science, University of Vermont: VERMONT

NYSTROM, J. WARREN, Executive Secretary. Association of American Geographers: GEOGRAPHY

O'LEARY, JOHN F., Director, U. S. Bureau of Mines: MINING—*Mining Technology*

ORDWAY, FREDERICK I., III, Professor of Science and Technology Applications, Research Institute, University of Alabama, Huntsville: THE YEAR OF THE MOON (part)

OVERTON, LEONARD C., Southeast Asia Study Program, Yale University: HO CHI MINH

PAINE, THOMAS O., Administrator, National Aeronautics and Space Administration: THE YEAR OF THE MOON (part)

PALMER, NORMAN D., Professor of Political Science and South Asian Studies, University of Pennsylvania: CEYLON; INDIA

PANO, NICHOLAS C., Assistant Professor of History, Western Illinois University: ALBANIA

PARKER, FRANKLIN, Benedum Professor of Education, West Virginia University: BOTSWANA; EQUATORIAL GUINEA; LESOTHO; MALAGASY REPUBLIC; MALAWI; RHODESIA; SWAZILAND; ZAMBIA

PETERSEN, WILLIAM, Robert Lazarus Professor of Social Demography, The Ohio State University; Author, *Population* (2d ed.): POPULATION

PHILLIPS, JACKSON, Director of Municipal Research, Dun & Bradstreet, Inc.: ECONOMY OF THE U. S.—*Economic Review*

PIPPIN, LARRY L., Associate Professor of Political Science, Elbert Covell College, University of the Pacific: GUATEMALA; HONDURAS; PANAMA

POLK, IRWIN J., Director of Children's Allergy Service, St. Luke's Hospital, New York City: ALLERGIES

PORTER, J. R., Professor and Chairman, Department of Microbiology, College of Medicine, University of Iowa: MICROBIOLOGY

PORTNOY, BERNARD, Associate Professor of Pediatrics and Community Medicine and Public Health, University of Southern California: RESPIRATORY DISEASES

PRITCHETT, C. HERMAN, Professor of Political Science, University of California, Santa Barbara: SUPREME COURT

PRITIKIN, ROLAND I., Eye Surgeon and Consulting Ophthalmologist; Author, *Essentials of Ophthalmology:* EYE DISEASES ·

PUMPHREY, RALPH E., Professor of Social Work, Washington University, St. Louis: SOCIAL WELFARE

PYLE, HOWARD, President, National Safety Council: ACCIDENTS AND DISASTERS

QUARLES, BENJAMIN, Professor of History, Morgan State College, Md.; Founding Member, Black Academy of Arts and Letters: CIVIL RIGHTS MOVEMENT—*Black Academy of Arts and Letters*

QUIRK, WILLIAM H., Editorial Director, *Contractors & Engineers:* BRIDGES; DAMS; TUNNELS

RAKOVE, MILTON, Professor of Political Science, University of Illinois at Chicago Circle: DIRKSEN, EVERETT MCKINLEY

RANDALL, CHARLES E., Forestry Information Specialist: FORESTRY AND LUMBERING

RATHBONE, ROBERT B., Director, Information Division, Agricultural Research Service: AGRICULTURE—*U. S. Agricultural Research*

RAYBACK, JOSEPH G., Professor of History, Temple University: LEWIS, JOHN LLEWELLYN

RAYMOND, ELLSWORTH, Head of Russian Area Studies, New York University; Author, *The Soviet State:* COMMUNISM; KOSYGIN, ALEKSEI; UNION OF SOVIET SOCIALIST REPUBLICS

RAYMOND, JACK, President, Thomas J. Deegan Co., Inc.; Author, *Power at the Pentagon:* ARMY; MARINE CORPS; NATIONAL GUARD

RENTZ, GEORGE, Curator of the Middle East Collection, The Hoover Institution, Stanford University: MUSCAT AND OMAN; PERSIAN GULF STATES; SAUDI ARABIA; SOUTHERN YEMEN

REOCK, ERNEST C., JR., Director, Bureau of Government Research, Rutgers University: NEW JERSEY

RIGBY, GERALD, Professor of Political Science, California State Polytechnic College, Pomona: CALIFORNIA; LOS ANGELES

RODRIGUEZ, ALFRED, Professor of Spanish and Portuguese, University of Wisconsin, Milwaukee: SPANISH LITERATURE

ROMAN, JAMES R., JR., Assistant Professor of Business Administration, The George Washington University: HIGHWAYS; TRANSPORTATION

RONNE, EDITH M., Antarctic Specialist: ANTARCTICA

ROSS, RUSSELL M., Professor of Political Science, University of Iowa: IOWA

ROTHMAN, FRANK G., Associate Professor of Biology, Brown University: GENETICS

ROUTH, PORTER W., Executive Secretary, Executive Committee, Southern Baptist Convention: BAPTIST CHURCHES —*Southern Baptist Convention*

ROWLETT, RALPH M., Assistant Professor of Anthropology, University of Missouri: ARCHAEOLOGY—*Eastern Hemisphere*

RUPEN, ROBERT A., Professor of Political Science, University of North Carolina: MONGOLIA

SAGAN, CARL, Director, Laboratory for Planetary Studies, and Associate Professor of Astronomy, Cornell University: ASTRONOMY (part)

SALSINI, PAUL, State Desk Reporter, The Milwaukee *Journal:* WISCONSIN

SANBORN, STEPHEN, Associate Director of Institutional Services, Kohlmeyer & Co.: STOCKS AND BONDS

SARRIS, ANDREW, Associate Professor of Cinema, Columbia University: MOTION PICTURES

SCHAAR, STUART, Associate Professor of History, Brooklyn College, City University of New York: ALGERIA; MOROCCO

SCHMEIDLER, GERTRUDE R., Professor of Psychology, The City College, City University of New York: PSYCHOLOGY

SCHMITT, KARL M., Professor of Government, University of Texas: HAITI

SCHNEIDERMAN, RONALD A., Communications Editor, *Electronic News:* ELECTRONICS

SCOTT, MARTIN L., Eastman Kodak Company: PHOTOGRAPHY

SEGAR, WILLIAM E., Department of Pediatrics, Mayo Clinic and Mayo Graduate School of Medicine, Rochester, Minn.: PEDIATRICS

SHAFER, ROBERT JONES, Professor of History, Syracuse University: MEXICO

SHEATSLEY, PAUL B., Director, Survey Research Service, National Opinion Research Center, University of Chicago: PUBLIC OPINION RESEARCH

SHOGAN, ROBERT, Washington Bureau, *Newsweek:* AGNEW, SPIRO THEODORE; NIXON, RICHARD MILHOUS

SIEGEL, SEYMOUR, Professor of Theology, Jewish Theological Seminary: RELIGION—*Judaism*

SINGLETON, VERNON L., Professor of Enology, University of California, Davis: ALCOHOLIC BEVERAGES—*Wine Industry*

SINNEN, JEANNE, Senior Editor, University of Minnesota Press: MINNESOTA

SKELDING, FRANK H., President, AMDEC Corp., Mineral Industry Consultants: MINING—*World Mineral Production*

SKURNIK, W. A. E., Associate Professor of Political Science, University of Colorado: MALI; MAURITANIA

SLOAN, HENRY S., Associate Editor, *Current Biography:* NECROLOGY (in part); Special Biographies

SLONIM, MARC, Director, Sarah Lawrence College Foreign Studies: ITALIAN LITERATURE; SOVIET LITERATURE

SMITH, ARTHUR A., Senior Vice President and Economist, First National Bank, Dallas: DALLAS

SMITH, GENE, Reporter, *The New York Times:* ELECTRICAL INDUSTRIES; GAS

SMITH, RHEA MARSH, Professor of History, Rollins College: PORTUGAL; SPAIN

SMITH, WILLARD J., Admiral, USCG; Commandant, U. S. Coast Guard: COAST GUARD

SPANIER, JOHN W., Professor of Political Science, University of Florida: UNITED STATES—*Foreign Affairs*

SPECTOR, SHERMAN D., Professor of History, Russell Sage College: RUMANIA

SPENCER, JEAN E., Assistant Professor of Government, University of Maryland: MARYLAND; WASHINGTON, D. C.

SPITZ, ALLAN A., Professor of International Relations and Director of Field Experience Program, James Madison College, Michigan State University: HAWAII

STEHLING, KURT R., Aerospace Consultant, Executive Office of the President: SPACE EXPLORATION—*Advances in Space Technology*

STEPHENS, GENE, Political and Investigative Reporter, The Atlanta *Constitution:* GEORGIA

STOKES, J. BUROUGHS, Manager, Committees on Publication, First Church of Christ, Scientist: CHRISTIAN SCIENCE

STOKES, W. LEE, Professor of Geology, University of Utah: GEOLOGY

STOUDEMIRE, ROBERT H., Assistant Director, Bureau of Governmental Research, University of South Carolina: SOUTH CAROLINA

STOUMPAS, GEORGE N., Metallurgical Engineer, American Iron and Steel Institute: STEEL

SUBER, HOWARD, Assistant Professor, Motion Picture Division, Department of Theater Arts, University of California, Los Angeles: GARLAND, JUDY; TAYLOR, ROBERT

SULLIVAN, WALTER, Science Editor, *The New York Times:* THE YEAR OF THE MOON (part)

SUTTON, GLENN W., Commissioner, U. S. Tariff Commission: INTERNATIONAL TRADE—*Tariffs*

SWANSON, CURTIS E., Manager, Public Relations Division, American Library Association: AMERICAN LIBRARY ASSOCIATION

SWINTON, WILLIAM E., Centennial Professor, University of Toronto; Fellow of Massey College, Toronto: PALEONTOLOGY

TABORSKY, EDWARD, Professor of Government, University of Texas: CZECHOSLOVAKIA

TAN, CHESTER C., Professor of History, New York University: CHINA; MAO TSE-TUNG

TANAKA, KASHIHI, Assistant Professor of Japanese, University of California, Santa Barbara: JAPANESE LITERATURE

TAYLOR, PHILIP B., JR., Professor of Political Science; Director, of Latin American Studies, University of Houston: ECUADOR; URUGUAY

TAYLOR, ZACK, Boats Editor, *Sports Afield;* Regional Editor, *Waterway Guide:* BOATING

THEISEN, CHARLES, Staff Writer, The Detroit *News:* DETROIT

THOMAS, JAMES D., Associate Professor of Political Science, University of Alabama: ALABAMA

THOME, PITT G., Director of Advanced Programs, Office of Space Science and Applications, National Aeronautics and Space Administration: SPACE EXPLORATION—*Manned Space Flight; Earth Satellites and Space Probes*

THOMFORD, NEIL R., Assistant Professor, Department of Surgery, The Ohio State University: SURGERY

TIBBITTS, CLARK, Director, Training Grant Programs, Administration on Aging, Department of Health, Education, and Welfare: OLDER POPULATION

TINKLEPAUGH, JAMES R., Associate Professor and Director of Technical Services, College of Ceramics at Alfred University, State University of New York: MATERIALS

TRAVIS, MARTIN B., Chairman, Department of Political Science, State University of New York, Stony Brook: LATIN AMERICA

TROMBLEY, KENNETH E., Editor, *Professional Engineer:* CANALS

TULLER, EDWIN H., General Secretary, American Baptist Convention: BAPTIST CHURCHES—*American Baptist Convention*

TURNER, ARTHUR C., Professor of Political Science, University of California, Riverside: AFRICA; ASIA; EUROPE; MIDDLE EAST

UHL, WILLIAM, Editorial Director, *World Petroleum:* PETROLEUM

UPJOHN, EVERARD M., Professor of Art History, Columbia University: GROPIUS, WALTER

VANDENBOSCH, AMRY, Professor Emeritus of Political Science, University of Kentucky: BELGIUM; INDONESIA; LUXEMBOURG; NETHERLANDS

VASILIADIS, BASIL G., Chief Secretary, Greek Orthodox Archdiocese of North and South America: RELIGION—*Eastern Orthodoxy*

von BRAUN, WERNHER, Deputy Associate Administrator for Planning, National Aeronautics and Space Administration; Former Director, George C. Marshall Space Flight Center: THE YEAR OF THE MOON (part)

VONDRACEK, FELIX J., Professor of History, University of North Dakota: NORTH DAKOTA

WAMSLEY, GARY L., Assistant Professor of Political Science, Vanderbilt University: SELECTIVE SERVICE

WARREN, DAVID D., Professor of Political Science, University of Rhode Island: RHODE ISLAND

WASHBURN, WILCOMB E., Chairman, Department of American Studies, Smithsonian Institution; Adjunct Professor, The American University: INDIANS, AMERICAN

WEAVER, ELLSWORTH E., Director, Institute of Government, University of Utah: UTAH

WEBB, RICHARD E., Director, Reference and Library Division, British Information Services: COMMONWEALTH OF NATIONS; MALTA

WEISENBURGER, FRANCIS P., Professor of History, The Ohio State University: OHIO

WELCH, CLAUDE E., JR., Dean of University College, State University of New York at Buffalo: DAHOMEY; NIGER; TOGO

WESTERN, JOE, Kominus Agri-Info Associates: AGRICULTURE—*World Agriculture, U. S. Agriculture, Dairy Products, U. S. Farm Services, Livestock and Poultry*

WILSON, JOHN S., Reviewer of Jazz Records, *The New York Times* and *High Fidelity* Magazine; Author, *Jazz: The Transition Years—1940-1960:* RECORDINGS—*Jazz Records*

WILSON, R. NORRIS, Executive Vice President, United States Committee for Refugees: REFUGEES

WOODS, GEORGE A., Children's Books Editor, *The New York Times:* CHILDREN'S LITERATURE

YANG, M. G., Department of Foods and Nutrition, Michigan State University: NUTRITION

YOUNG, CHARLES W., Sloan-Kettering Institute for Cancer Research: CANCER

ZABEL, ORVILLE H., Professor of History, Creighton University: NEBRASKA

ZAFRA, NICOLAS, Professor Emeritus of History, University of the Philippines: PHILIPPINES

ZISK, BETTY H., Associate Professor of Government, Boston University: BOSTON; MASSACHUSETTS

ZUBKOFF, HARRY M., Writer-Editor, Office of the Secretary of the Air Force: AIR FORCE

necrology·1969

The following is a selected list of over 350 prominent persons who died during 1969. Separate articles on those persons whose names are preceded by an asterisk (*) may be found in the text under their own heading. Cross references in this list are to articles in the text where biographical sketches of the subject will be found.

Adler, Clarence (83), U. S. musician; was a concert pianist appearing in the U. S. and Europe for over 60 years: d. New York, N. Y., Dec. 24.

al-Azhari, Ismail (69), Sudanese political leader; served as Sudan's 1st prime minister (1954–56); was president of the country from 1964 until a military coup in May 1969: d. Khartoum, Sudan, Aug. 27.

Alexander of Tunis, Earl (Harold Rupert Leofric George Alexander) (77), retired British military officer: b. Castle Caledon, County Tyrone, Northern Ireland, Dec. 10, 1891; d. Slough, Buckinghamshire, June 16, 1969. He was noted for his humane approach to warfare, as well as for his brilliant strategy that led to World War II Allied victories in North Africa, Sicily, and Italy. A graduate of Sandhurst Royal Military College, he led the evacuation of British forces from Dunkirk in 1940, and two years later he commanded British troops in a fighting retreat from Burma to India that delayed advancing Japanese forces for four months. Appointed British commander in chief in the Middle East in 1942, he directed the strategy for Gen. Bernard L. Montgomery's decisive victory over German Field Marshal Erwin Rommel's Afrika-Korps at El Alamein. In February 1943 he became deputy commander in chief to Gen. Dwight D. Eisenhower, with responsibility for the invasions of Sicily and Italy. He attained the rank of field marshal in July 1944 and was appointed Supreme Allied Commander for the Mediterranean Theater. From 1946 to 1952 he was governor general of Canada.

Allen, Terry (81), U. S. military officer; World War II hero who led divisions in the North African and Sicily campaigns and helped Allied offensives into Germany: d. El Paso, Texas, Sept. 12.

Almeida, Guilherme de (78), Brazilian poet; was known as the "Prince of Brazilian poetry"; d. São Paulo, Brazil, July 11.

Andrew, Princess of Greece (84), mother of Britain's Prince Philip and granddaughter of Queen Victoria; was married to Prince Andrew of Greece (1903–44): d. London, England, Dec. 5.

Annadurai, Conjeevaram Natarajan (59), Indian public official; founded the Dravidian Progressive party (1949) and was chief minister of Tamil Nadu (formerly Madras State) since 1967: d. Madras, India, Feb. 1.

Ansermet, Ernest (Alexander) (86), Swiss orchestra conductor: b. Vevey, Switzerland, Nov. 11, 1883; d. Geneva, Feb. 20, 1969. As conductor of the world-renowned Orchestre de la Suisse Romande, which he founded in 1918, he became one of the foremost representatives of the French school and was noted for his interpretations of such modern composers as Debussy and Stravinsky. His style was marked by finesse, strength, and precision. He retired as conductor of the Orchestre de la Suisse Romande in 1967.

Arenales (Catalán), Emilio (46), Guatemalan public official: b. Guatemala City, May 10, 1922; d. Guatemala City, April 17, 1969. He served as president of the United Nations General Assembly in its 23d session, which opened in September 1968. From 1955 to 1958 he was Guatemala's permanent representative at the United Nations. After serving in 1958 as president of the UN Trusteeship Council, he returned to the private practice of law in Guatemala. In 1966 he was appointed Guatemala's minister of foreign affairs.

Arnold, Thurman Wesley (78), U. S. lawyer and legal scholar: b. Laramie, Wyo., June 2, 1891; d. Alexandria, Va., Nov. 7, 1969. Arnold was the government's chief trustbuster from 1938 to 1943. As assistant attorney general in charge of the antitrust division of the Department of Justice, he instituted 130 suits against business and labor monopolies. A former dean of the West Virginia University Law School and former Yale professor, he served as an associate justice of the U. S. Court of Appeals for the District of Columbia from 1943 to 1945. In recent years he was senior partner in the Washington law firm of Arnold and Porter, and he argued for the defense in many civil liberties cases, often without fee.

Asquith, Baroness Helen Violet (Lady Violet Bonham Carter) (81), British political figure; was the daughter of Prime Minister Herbert Asquith and an influential leader of the Liberal party; author of *Winston Churchill As I Knew Him* (1965): d. London, England, Feb. 19.

Auerbach, Josef (85), Polish-born movie producer; was pioneer screen producer; won an Oscar for his film *Chagall* (1963): d. Hollywood, Calif., Mar. 29.

Ayres, Mitchell (58), U. S. musician and composer; well-known leader of dance bands in the 1930's: d. (auto accident) Las Vegas, Nev., Sept. 5.

Backhaus, Wilhelm (85), German-born pianist: b. Leipzig, Germany, March 26, 1884; d. Villach, Austria, July 5, 1969. One of the world's foremost interpreters of Beethoven, he was best known for his recordings of that composer's works. His playing has been described as "immense, monolithic, carved out of granite." He made his debut at the age of 8 and met Brahms three years later. He taught at the Royal Manchester College of Music in England and won the Rubinstein piano prize in 1905. Between 1912 and 1962 he made several tours of the United States. His repertoire also included works of Brahms, Schumann, Mozart, and Chopin. A citizen of Switzerland, he had been making his home in Lugano since 1930.

Baer, Arthur (Bugs) (83), U. S. newspaper columnist; was a well known humorist who wrote a daily syndicated column: d. New York, N. Y., May 17.

Baggs, William C. (48), U. S. journalist; was editor of the *Miami News* since 1957 and won recognition as a Southern crusader for civil rights; served as unofficial peace envoy to Hanoi (1967, 1968): d. Miami, Fla., Jan. 7.

Bakopoulos, Nicholas (82), Greek political leader; became interim leader of the Center Union party in 1968; was elected to Parliament 9 times and served in 5 liberal cabinets: d. Athens, Greece, April 22.

Barbarin, Paul (67), U. S. musician; noted jazz drummer of the 1920's–30's; made over 20 recordings with Louis Armstrong: d. New Orleans, La., Feb. 17.

Barbeau, Marius (85), Canadian folklorist and ethnologist; served on the staff of National Museum of Canada (1911–48); collected the texts and melodies of thousands of folk songs: d. Ottawa, Canada, Feb. 27.

Barbey, Daniel (79), U. S. naval officer; was known as the "father" of the U. S. Navy's amphibious fleet in the Southwest Pacific in World War II: d. Bremerton, Wash., April 11.

Barrientos Ortuño, René (49), Bolivian statesman: b. Tunary, department of Cochabamba, Bolivia, May 30, 1919; d. (helicopter crash in Bolivian interior) April 27, 1969. As president of Bolivia since 1964 he instituted social and economic reforms and became immensely popular among the country's impoverished Indian peasants. He grew up in a Franciscan orphanage and graduated from the Colegio Militar de Ejército in 1937. After flight training at Randolph Field, Texas, in 1945, he held various posts in the Bolivian air force. An early supporter of the National Revolutionary Movement of Victor Paz Estenssoro, he rapidly rose after Paz came to power in 1952 and eventually became air force chief of staff. Disillusioned with corruption in the Paz regime, Barrientos joined army commander Gen. Alfredo Ovando Candia in a military coup in 1964 and was installed as president. In 1966 he was elected president with 61% of the vote.

Bates, William Henry (52), U. S. congressman; was a representative from Massachusetts since 1950: d. Washington, D. C., June 22.

Beal, Royal (69), U. S. actor; played comedy roles on the stage, screen, and television: d. Keene, N. H., May 20.

Beall, Lester (66), U. S. artist; designed posters and murals for government and business organizations; was first graphic designer to have a special exhibit at the Museum of Modern Art: d. New York, N. Y., June 20.

Benjamin, Harold (75), U. S. educator and author; was dean of the University of Maryland College of Education (1939–51); helped draft charter for UNESCO: d. Baltimore, Md., Jan. 12.

Bentley, Alvin M. (50), U. S. congressman and diplomat; represented Michigan in Congress (1953–61); seriously injured in an attack in the House chamber by Puerto Rican Nationalists (1954): d. Tucson, Ariz., Apr. 10.

Beran, Joseph Cardinal (80), Roman Catholic prelate; named archbishop of Prague in 1946 and was imprisoned by the Communists for 12 years; in exile in Rome since 1965: d. Rome, Italy, May 18.

Blaiberg, Philip (60), South African dentist; was the world's longest surviving heart transplant patient; lived for 19 months and 15 days after receiving the world's third heart transplant on Jan. 2, 1968: d. Cape Town, South Africa, Aug. 17.

Boehm, Edward M. (56), U. S. artist; noted sculptor whose porcelain birds became world famous as collector's items and gifts of state: d. Trenton, N. J., Jan. 29.

Boles, John (73), U. S. actor; won fame as the actor-singer star of the film *The Desert Song* (1929): d. San Angelo, Texas, Feb. 27.

Boni, Charles (74), U. S. publisher; was a major figure in the literary life of New York since 1913; helped found the Little Leather Library and the Modern Library and published the first popular paperback book series: d. New York, N. Y., Feb. 14.

Booth, Mary (84), British Salvation Army leader; was the head of the Salvation Army in Belgium at outbreak of World War II and was imprisoned by the Germans: d. Finchampstead, England, Sept. 1.

Bouché, Louis (73), U. S. painter: b. New York City, March 18, 1896; d. Pittsfield, Mass., Aug. 7, 1969. Bouché made a reputation first as a muralist, then as a painter of realistic scenes of daily life in American cities and small towns. His loose brushwork and bright colors are in the French impressionist tradition. He has murals in the Radio City Music Hall and in the buildings of the departments of Justice and of the Interior in Washington, D. C. His paintings include *Ten Cents a Ride* in the Metropolitan Museum of Art, New York City.

Boykin, Frank W. (84), U. S. political figure; was a member of the House of Representatives from Alabama (1935–62); convicted of conspiracy and conflict of interest (1963) and pardoned in 1965: d. Washington, D. C., March 12.

Bracken, John (85), Canadian public official and agriculturalist; was premier of Manitoba (1922–43); led the federal Progressive Conservative party (1942–57) and was a member of the federal Parliament (1945–48): d. Ottawa, Canada, March 18.

Brackett, Charles (76), U. S. screenwriter and film producer; his Oscar-winning movies (often made in collaboration with Billy Wilder) include *The Lost Weekend, Sunset Boulevard,* and *The Titanic:* d. Hollywood, Calif., March 10.

Breeskin, Elias (73), Russian-born U. S. conductor; conducted the Pittsburgh Symphony orchestra (1928–31) and the Hollywood Bowl Symphony (1935–40): d. Mexico City, Mexico, May 6.

Briscoe, Robert (74), Irish nationalist and political leader; played a leading role in Ireland's war of independence against Britain; served in Parliament (1927–65) and was the first Jewish lord mayor of Dublin (1956–57, 1961–62): d. Dublin, Ireland, May 30.

Brooks, Ned (67), U. S. journalist; was moderator of the TV and radio program *Meet the Press* until 1967: d. Washington, D. C., April 13.

Brown, Dillard Houston (57), U. S. church official; was one of four Negro bishops of the Episcopal church and served as Episcopal bishop of Liberia since 1964: d. Monrovia, Liberia, Nov. 19.

Brown, John Mason (68), U. S. critic, author, and lecturer: b. Louisville, Ky., July 3, 1900; d. New York City, March 16, 1969. Once described as "the greatest lecturer of the present day," he was also a leading drama critic and the author of 19 books, ranging from interpretations of the theater to accounts of his World War II Navy experiences. A graduate of Harvard University, he was drama critic with the New York *Evening Post* from 1929 to 1941 and with the New York *World-Telegram* in 1941–42. In 1944 he became associate editor and drama critic with the *Saturday Review,* for which he wrote the column "Seeing Things." Works he wrote or edited include *The Modern Theatre in Revolt* (1929); *The Art of Playgoing* (1936); *Two on the Aisle* (1938); *Broadway in Review* (1940); *Seeing Things* (1946); *The Portable Charles Lamb* (1949); and the first volume of an uncompleted biography of Robert E. Sherwood (1965).

Brownlee, John (68), Australian-born opera singer; was a leading opera baritone for 32 years until his retirement in 1958: d. New York, N. Y., Jan. 10.

Bruce, Ailsa Mellon (65), U. S. philanthropist; was regarded as the wealthiest woman in the U. S.: d. New York, N. Y., Aug. 25.

Bruguière, Margaret Louise (Mrs. Louis S.) (92), U. S. society figure; considered one of the wealthiest women in the U. S. and known for her baronial life-style: d. Newport, R. I., Jan. 20.

Bunker, Zaddie (81), U. S. pilot; learned to fly at 65 and was known as "the flying grandmother"; at 73 flew an Air Force jet faster than the speed of sound: d. Palm Springs, Calif., Aug. 21.

Burger, Ralph W. (79), U. S. executive; was president and board chairman of the A & P food chain (1950–63): d. Daytona Beach, Fla., April 2.

Cameron, Helen de Young (86), U. S. society figure; was a grande dame of San Francisco society: d. Hillsborough, Calif., July 23.

Cantril, Hadley (62), U. S. psychologist; established the Office of Public Opinion Research at Princeton University (1939) and was its head until 1957: d. Princeton, N. J., May 29.

Carr, Lawrence (48), U. S. theatrical producer; brought to the stage such hits as *The Desk Set* (1955), *Advise and Consent* (1960), and *Mame* (1966): d. New York, N. Y., Jan. 17.

Carrigan, William, Sr. (85), U. S. athlete; was the manager of the Boston Red Sox when they won two World Series victories (1915, 1916): d. Lewiston, Me., July 8.

Carter, Kenneth (62), Canadian accountant; was chairman of the commission that produced a controversial report on Canada's tax structure (1967): d. Toronto, Canada, May 12.

Casson, Lewis (93), British actor and producer; produced and appeared with his wife, Dame Sybil Thorndike, in several hit plays: d. London, England, May 16.

Castle, Irene (75), U. S. ballroom dancer: b. New Rochelle, N. Y., 1894 (?); d. Eureka Springs, Ark., Jan. 25, 1969. As the internationally famous dance team of Vernon and Irene Castle, her husband and she captured the imagination of the romantically minded of the World War I era. The Castles achieved their first success shortly after their marriage in 1911, when they appeared as entertainers in a Paris café at the request of a Russian count. Their popularity followed them back to the United States, where they introduced such ballroom steps as the Castle Walk and the maxixe.

Catroux, Georges (92), French military officer and diplomat; was a leader of the Free French forces during World War II; held top posts in many French colonial areas: d. Paris, France, Dec. 21.

Caudle, T. Lamar (64), U. S. government official; was assistant attorney general in the Truman administration until removal (1951) and later imprisonment for conspiring to defraud the government: d. Wadesboro, N. C., April 1.

Chadwick, Henry (97), U. S. doctor; noted tuberculosis fighter and originator of the Chadwick clinics for TB control: d. Waltham, Mass., March 31.

Chaney, Stewart (59), U. S. stage designer; designed the sets for many Broadway plays including *Life With Father, The Voice of the Turtle,* and *Ghosts:* d. East Hampton, N. Y., Nov. 9.

Chang, Carsun (82), Chinese political leader and Confucian scholar; was a founder and leader of the Chinese Democratic Socialist party (1940's) and helped draft the constitution of the Republic of China (1946): d. San Francisco, Calif., Feb. 23.

Chukovsky, Kornei I. (87), Soviet author and translator; wrote many children's books, best known of which was *From Two to Five;* translated adult literature such as Walt Whitman into Russian: d. Moscow, USSR, Oct. 28.

Ciannelli, Eduardo (80), Italian-born U. S. actor; was a character actor who portrayed criminals and comics; was best known for his role in the stage and screen versions of *Winterset:* d. Rome, Italy, Oct. 8.

Cicotte, Eddie (84), U. S. athlete; was banned from baseball after the Black Sox scandal of 1919, in which he and 7 other players admitted throwing the World Series: d. Farmington, Mich., May 5.

Clement, Frank G(oad) (49), U. S. public official: b. Dickson, Tenn., June 2, 1920; d. (automobile crash) near Nashville, Tenn., Nov. 4, 1969. As Democratic governor of Tennessee for three terms he fought corruption and generally followed a liberal policy. Noted for his colorful oratory, he delivered the keynote speech at the 1956 Democratic national convention, castigating the Eisenhower-Nixon administration. After graduating from Vanderbilt University Law School in 1942 he became a special agent with the Federal Bureau of Investigation. He saw World War II service in the army and later was appointed general counsel for the Tennessee railroad and public utilities commission. Campaigning on a platform pledging "government in a goldfish bowl," he was elected in 1952 to a 2-year term as governor of Tennessee, becoming the youngest state governor in the United States. In 1954 he was reelected for four years, and in 1962 he won another 4-year term.

Clement, Gaston C. (66), Argentine naval officer; was a leader of the revolution that overthrew Juan Perón (1955): d. Buenos Aires, Argentina, Nov. 30.

Collyer, Bud (61), U. S. TV personality; was master of ceremonies on many quiz programs including *Beat the Clock* and *To Tell the Truth:* d. Greenwich, Conn., Sept. 8.

Compton-Burnett, Ivy (85), British novelist: b. London, June 5, 1884 (?); d. London, Aug. 27, 1969. In her 19 novels, in which she presented a witty, sardonic, and sometimes lurid view of British upper-class family life in the late 19th and early 20th centuries, she sought to puncture human vanity and pomposity. Her books are long on dialogue but short on descriptions of scenes and characters. She took a degree in classics at the University of London and published her first novel, *Dolores,* in 1911. Among her other works are *Pastors and Masters* (1925), *Brothers and Sisters* (1929), *Daughters and Sons* (1937), *Elders and Betters* (1944), *A Heritage and Its History* (1959), and *A God and His Gifts* (1963).

Connolly Brinker, Maureen (Catherine) (34), U. S. tennis player: b. San Diego, Calif., Sept. 17, 1934; d. Dallas, Tex., June 21, 1969. Known as "Little Mo," she became the only woman in the history of tennis to achieve the grand slam when she won the British, French, Australian, and United States women's singles championships in 1953.

Constantine of Bavaria, Prince (48), West German public official; was a deputy in the Bundestag since 1965: d. Hechingen, West Germany, July 31.

Conway, Granville (71), U. S. public official; was Atlantic Coast director of the War Shipping Administration in World War II and head of the agency in 1946: d. New York, N. Y., Sept. 5.

Conway, Herbert (65), U. S. plastic surgeon; was director of the plastic surgery department of New York Hospital-Cornell Medical Center; clinical professor of surgery at Cornell University Medical College since 1955: d. New Rochelle, N. Y., Aug. 25.

Cooley, Donnell (Spade) (59), U. S. musician; was once known as the "king of Western swing"; died during his first public performance since his 1961 conviction for murdering his wife: d. Oakland, Calif., Nov. 23.

Corrigan, Lloyd (69), U. S. actor, movie writer, and director; wrote the first of the Fu Manchu mystery series: d. Hollywood, Calif., Nov. 7.

Costa e Silva, Artur da (67), Brazilian statesman: b. Taquarí, Rio Grande do Sul, Brazil, Oct. 3, 1902; d. Rio de Janeiro, Dec. 17, 1969. As president of Brazil from 1967 to 1969 he was pledged to a program of "social humanism" but met with only moderate success in bringing about economic and social reforms. He attended the military school of Pôrto Alegre, graduated from the Escola Militar do Realengo, and received additional military training in the United States and Argentina. After becoming a brigadier general in 1952 he held various infantry command posts and acquired a knowledge of the country's regional problems. As army commander in chief he was a key figure in the military coup of April 1964 that ousted the civilian government of President João Goulart. In the new revolutionary regime headed by a colleague, Marshal Humberto Castello Branco, he served as minister of war. In 1966 he resigned from the army with the rank of marshal and was elected president. After his inauguration in March 1967 he introduced some liberal reforms. But in late 1968, in a move to curb civilian critics of the military, he dissolved the national congress and ruled by decree. In August 1969 he suffered a stroke and was succeeded by a military triumvirate.

Costello, William (65), U. S. radio and television correspondent; wrote *The Facts About Nixon: an Unauthorized Biography* (1960); was ambassador to Trinidad and Tobago (1967–69): d. Port-of-Spain, Trinidad, June 20.

Cox, Wiffy (72), U. S. athlete; was a star golfer in the 1930's and was the professional at the Congressional Country Club in Washington (1938–68): d. Washington, D. C., Feb. 20.

Craven, Thomas (81), U. S. art critic and lecturer; championed indigenous American art and criticized French painters; his books included *Men of Art* (1931) and *A Treasury of Art Masterpieces From the Renaissance to the Present Day* (1939): d. Boston, Mass., Feb. 27.

Csokor, Franz Theodor (83), Austrian dramatist and author; best known for his play *Third of November, 1918;* awarded the Austrian national prize for literature (1956): d. Vienna, Austria, Jan. 5.

Cummings, Vicki (50), U. S. actress; was best known for her roles as a comedienne and musical comedy actress on the stage: d. New York, N. Y., Nov. 30.

Cvetkovic, Dragisha, Yugoslav public official; was ousted as Yugoslav premier two days after signing pact with Germany (1941): d. Paris, France, Feb. 8.

Dahlgrun, Rolf (61), German public official; was finance minister of West Germany (1962–66): d. Hamburg, West Germany, Dec. 19.

Dameshek, William (69), U. S. doctor; pioneered in the study of blood and was credited with establishing hematology as a separate medical specialty: d. New York, N. Y., Oct. 6.

Daniell, Raymond (68), U. S. journalist; covered domestic and foreign news as reporter and correspondent for the New York *Times* for 39 years until he retired in 1967: d. Ottawa, Canada, April 12.

Dao, S. Y. (50), Chinese public official; became Nationalist China's minister of economic affairs in 1969: d. New York, N. Y., Sept. 27.

David-Neel, Alexandra (100), French-born writer and traveler; was the first European woman to enter the Tibetan capital of Lhasa: d. Digne, France, Sept. 8.

Davis, Hallie Flanagan (78), U. S. educator and theatrical producer; was director of the Federal Theater Project (1935–39); founded and directed the experimental theater at Vassar College (1925–42); was dean at Smith College (1942–55): d. Old Tappan, N. J., July 23.

Davis, John Kerr (87), U. S. diplomat; served in many posts (primarily in China) for the U. S. Foreign Service for 30 years until he retired in 1942: d. Vancouver, British Columbia, July 15.

Dejoie, Louise (72), Haitian political leader; was forced into exile after losing 1957 presidential election to François Duvalier: d. New York, N. Y., July 11.

de-Shalit, Amos (42), Israeli nuclear physicist; was known for his studies in the field of nuclear structure; directed the Weizmann Institute of Science (1966–68): d. Rehovoth, Israel, Sept. 2.

*Dirksen, Everett McKinley (73), U. S. legislator: d. Washington, D. C., Sept. 7.

Dix, Otto (77), German painter; a leader of the "New Objectivity," a form of social realism in Germany after World War I; his painting *Parents of the Artist* (1921) was in a mode of "magic realism"; taught art in Dresden (1927–

Maureen Connolly   Allen W. Dulles   Max Eastman   H. E. Fosdick   Walter Hagen

33); was forbidden to exhibit during Nazi era; after World War II he turned to a form of mystical religious expression: d. Singen, West Germany, July 28.

Dornier, Claude (85), German aviation engineer and industrialist: b. Kempten, Germany, May 14, 1884; d. Zug, Switzerland, Dec. 5, 1969. He headed the Dornier-Werke and built many of Germany's World War I fighter planes and World War II bombers. He graduated from the Munich Technical University in 1907 and worked for several years with the airship designer, Ferdinand, Count von Zeppelin. In 1911 he designed the world's first all-metal aircraft. After World War I he became head of his own firm, and in the 1920's he concentrated on transatlantic seaplanes. His DO-X, developed in 1929, was at the time the world's largest airplane. In World War II he developed the Dornier 17 "Flying Pencil" bomber, used in raids on Britain. Exonerated by an Allied denazification court after the war, he opened a factory in 1955. It produced the Dornier Skyservant and the DO-31, the world's first jet vertical take-off and landing transport.

Douglas, William Sholto (75), British Air Force officer; was marshal of the Royal Air Force (1946–47); headed British occupation forces in Germany; served as chairman of British European Airways (1949–64): d. London, England, Oct. 29.

Douglass, Truman B(artlett) (67), U. S. Protestant clergyman: b. Grinnell, Iowa, July 15, 1901; d. New York City, May 27, 1969. A leading figure in modern Protestantism and in the 20th century ecumenical movement, he played an important role in the establishment, in 1957, of the United Church of Christ, a merger of the Congregationalists with the Evangelical and Reformed denomination. Douglass was a vice president of the National Council of Churches and vice-chairman of the information department of the World Council of Churches.

Dowling, Constance (49), U. S. actress; appeared on Broadway and in such films as *Up in Arms* and *The Well Groomed Bride:* d. Los Angeles, Calif., Oct. 28.

Draper, Dorothy (79), U. S. decorator; designed interiors of many well-known buildings including Hampshire House in New York; wrote newspaper column "Ask Dorothy Draper" (1959–67): d. White Sulphur Springs, W. Va., March 10.

du Pont, Henry Francis (88), U. S. chemical executive; was a director of E. I. du Pont de Nemours & Co. since 1915; a collector of early American decorative art, he turned his family home into the Winterthur Museum (1951): d. Wilmington, Del., April 10.

Dudley, Earl of (William Humble Eric Ward) (75), British industrialist; reputed to be one of the richest men in Britain: d. Paris, France, Dec. 26.

Duff, James H. (86), U. S. public official; was Republican governor of Pennsylvania (1947–51) and U. S. senator (1951–57): d. Washington, D. C., Dec. 20.

Duke, Vernon (65), Russian-born U. S. composer; wrote score for Broadway hit *Cabin in the Sky* (1940) and many popular songs; composed symphonies and ballets under his real name, Vladimir Dukelsky: d. Santa Monica, Calif., Jan. 17.

Dulles, Allen W(elsh) (75), U. S. public official: b. Watertown, N. Y., April 7, 1893; d. Washington, D. C., Jan. 29, 1969. As director (1953–61) of the U. S. Central Intelligence Agency, which he had helped to establish in 1950, he headed the government's espionage network of the Cold War era. He studied at Princeton (M. A., 1916) and George Washington University (LL. B., 1926) and served in diplomatic posts during and after World War I. He attended the Paris Peace Conference in 1919 and was chief of the State Department's division of Near Eastern affairs from 1922 to 1926. As a member of the Wall Street law firm of Sullivan & Cromwell he continued his public service and was an adviser at the Three-Power Naval Conference (1927) and the Geneva Disarmament Conference (1932–33). From 1942 to 1945 he headed the U. S. Office of Strategic Services in Switzerland, directing intelligence operations that helped bring about Germany's surrender. He was deputy director of the CIA from 1950 to 1953. Under his direction, the agency engineered successful coups in Iran (1953) and Guatemala (1954), but it also met such setbacks as the Soviet capture of a U-2 reconnaissance plane in 1960 and the ill-fated Bay of Pigs invasion by anti-Castro Cubans in 1961.

Dupuy, Pierre (72), Canadian diplomat; served as Canada's ambassador to France (1958–1963); became commissioner general of Expo 67 in Montreal in 1963: d. Cannes, France, May 21.

Eastman, Max (Forrester) (86), U. S. author: b. Canandaigua, N. Y., Jan. 4, 1883; d. Bridgetown, Barbados, March 25, 1969. One of the most influential American leftist intellectuals of the World War I era and the 1920's,

he was best known for his critical studies of Soviet Marxism. He also wrote extensively about literary subjects. He studied at Williams College (B. A., 1905) and completed Ph. D. requirements at Columbia but did not take the degree. A cofounder of the radical *Masses* magazine in 1913, he was its editor until 1917, when it was suppressed by the government. From 1918 to 1922 he edited *Liberator* magazine. A visit to Russia in the early 1920's made him increasingly critical of the Soviet system, and especially of Joseph Stalin. For a time he was closely associated with Leon Trotsky, but by the mid-1930's he had become totally disillusioned with communism. In 1941 he became a roving editor for *Reader's Digest.* His political books include *Marxism: Is It Science?* (1940).

Eberstadt, Ferdinand (79), U. S. investment banker; founded the investment firm of F. Eberstadt & Co. (1931) and the Chemical Fund, Inc. (1938); was vice chairman of the War Production Board during World War II: d. Washington, D. C., Nov. 11.

Egbert, Sherwood H. (49), U. S. auto executive; as president of Studebaker Corp. (1961–63) tried unsuccessfully to salvage the firm: d. West Los Angeles, Calif., July 30.

*Eisenhower, Dwight David (78), U. S. president: d. Washington, D. C., March 28.

Erlanger, Alene Stern (74), U. S. dog breeder; founded the U. S. Canine Corps during World War II: d. Long Branch, N. J., June 25.

Eshkol, Levi (73), Israeli political leader: d. Jerusalem, Israel, Feb. 26. (See ISRAEL.)

Ettinger, Karl (69), U. S. business expert; was a specialist in marketing research and management; his books include *Management Primer* and *Research in Public Relations:* d. Paris, France, Sept. 23.

Fay, William P. (60), Irish diplomat; was Ireland's ambassador to France, Canada, and, since 1964, to the U. S.: d. Dublin, Ireland, Sept. 7.

Fickes, Robert O. (60), U. S. business executive; was president (1964–68) and chairman of the board (1966–68) of the Philco-Ford Corp.: d. Philadelphia, Pa., June 17.

Field, Winston J. (64), English-born Rhodesian public official; was prime minister of Southern Rhodesia (1962–64) and leader of the rightist Rhodesian Front party: d. Salisbury, Rhodesia, March 17.

Finer, Herman (71), Rumanian-born political scientist; was professor of political science at the University of Chicago (1946–63); his books include *Mussolini's Italy* and *The Theory and Practice of Modern Government:* d. Chicago, Ill., March 4.

Fitzpatrick, Daniel R. (78), U. S. cartoonist; won Pulitzer prizes (1926, 1954) for his editorial cartoons in the St. Louis *Post-Dispatch:* d. St. Louis, Mo., May 18.

Flanagan, William, Jr. (46), U. S. composer and music critic; wrote the incidental music for the plays *Ballad of the Sad Café* and *The Death of Bessie Smith:* d. New York, N. Y., Aug. 31.

Fleischmann, Raoul H(erbert) (83), U. S. publisher: b. Bad Ischl, Austria, Aug. 17, 1885; d. New York City, May 11, 1969. With Harold Ross he founded the *New Yorker* magazine and built it into a flourishing enterprise. A member of the family that developed Fleischmann's yeast, he went to the U. S. as an infant and was educated at Princeton and at Williams College. He entered the family baking business in 1907, and after it merged into the General Baking Company in 1911 he became a company director and plant manager. His associations with leading literary figures brought him into contact with Ross, and together they conceived of a high-quality humor magazine, which began publication as the *New Yorker* in 1925.

Foord, Archibald (54), U. S. historian; authority on European history and author of award-winning *His Majesty's Opposition, 1714–1830* (1964); professor of history at Yale since 1965: d. London, England, March 14.

Forbes, Edward (95), U. S. art curator; under his directorship (1909–44) the Fogg Museum at Harvard became a leading art institution; innovator in the use of X-rays to detect art forgeries: d. Belmont, Mass., March 11.

Ford, Corey (67), U. S. humorist; was a literary parodist who wrote many magazine articles and books including his autobiography, *A Time for Laughter:* d. Hanover, N. H., July 27.

Fosdick, Harry Emerson (91), U. S. Protestant clergyman: b. Buffalo, N. Y., May 24, 1878; d. Bronxville, N. Y., Oct. 5, 1969. A proponent of liberal Protestantism and critic of fundamentalism, he was the founding pastor of Riverside Church in New York City. Educated at Colgate University and Union Theological Seminary, he was ordained in 1903. After his open opposition to fundamentalism compelled him to resign as minister of New York's First Presbyterian Church in 1925, he became minister of the Park Avenue Baptist Church at the request of John D. Rockefeller, Jr. Six years later he took over the pulpit of the interdenominational Riverside Church, which Rockefeller built at his urging, and he served as its pastor until his retirement in 1946. From 1915 to 1946 he was also a professor at Union Theological Seminary, and for years he conducted a radio program. A liberal on social and political issues, he tried to relate Christian doctrine to modern civilization and was an outspoken pacifist and exponent of birth control.

Foulkes, Charles (66), Canadian military officer; led Canadian forces on the Western and Italian fronts during World War II; was chairman of Canada's Chiefs of Staff Committee (1951–60): d. Ottawa, Canada, Sept. 12.

Francis, Thomas, Jr. (69), U. S. virologist; was credited with developing the first effective vaccine against influenza; directed field tests of the Salk polio vaccine (1954): d. Ann Arbor, Mich., Oct. 1.

Freedley, Vinton (77), U. S. theatrical producer; produced many Broadway musical comedy hits in the 1920's and 1930's including *Lady, Be Good; Anything Goes;* and *Red, Hot and Blue:* d. New York, N. Y., June 5.

Freyse, William (70), U. S. cartoonist; drew the "Our Boarding House" cartoon panel since 1939: d. Tucson, Ariz., March 3.

Friedman, William F. (78), U. S. cryptanalyst; led the Army task force that broke the Japanese "Purple" code before the U. S. entered World War II: d. Washington, D. C., Nov. 2.

Gallegos, Rómulo (84), Venezuelan public official and author; became the first popularly elected president of Venezuela (1948) but was deposed by a military coup: d. Caracas, Venezuela, April 4.

*****Garland, Judy** (47), U. S. singer and actress: d. London, England, June 22.

Gaus, John M. (74), U. S. political scientist; an expert on regional planning, he was professor of political science at Harvard (1927–61): d. Utica, N. Y., May 28.

Gauthier, Maurice (67), U. S. architect-designer; designed the rebuilt Times Tower in New York for the Allied Chemical Corp.: d. New York, N. Y., Sept. 22.

Genovese, Vito (71), Italian-born U. S. underworld figure; was Mafia chief in New York area since 1957 and reportedly directed Mafia operations from prison where he was serving a 15-year sentence (1958) for smuggling narcotics: d. Springfield, Mo., Feb. 14.

Georgiev, Kimon (87), Bulgarian public official; was twice premier of Bulgaria (1934–35, 1944–46); was a leader of the 1944 coup d'etat that led to Bulgaria's Communist government: d. Sofia, Bulgaria, Sept. 28.

Gerstmann, Josef (81), Austrian-born U. S. neurologist and psychiatrist; was the author of numerous papers on neuropsychiatry and first to describe a brain disorder that caused right-left disorientation (now called Gerstmann syndrome): d. New York, N. Y., March 23.

Gimbel, Adam (Long) (75), U. S. business executive: b. Milwaukee, Wis., Dec. 21, 1893; d. New York City, Sept. 9, 1969. As president of Saks Fifth Avenue from 1926 until his retirement in 1969 he built it into the largest chain of specialty stores in the U. S. A grandson of the founder of the Gimbel department store empire, he joined the family business in 1916, after studying architecture at Yale University. Described as a "renaissance man," Gimbel also tried his hand at playwriting, and he was a noted sportsman, art collector, and philanthropist.

Goetz, William (66), U. S. movie producer; was a founder and vice president of 20th Century-Fox (1935–43) and was production head at Universal-International (1945–53); produced over 100 films including *Sayonara, Song of Bernadette,* and *The Glenn Miller Story:* d. Holmby Hills, Calif., Aug. 15.

Gombrowicz, Witold (64), Polish-born novelist; lived in exile in Argentina and then France; his works were translated into as many as 30 languages and his novel *Cosmos* won the 1967 International Prize for Literature: d. Nice, France, July 25.

Gorcey, Leo (49), U. S. actor; played in the Dead End Kids movies: d. Oakland, Calif., June 2.

Gordon, Donald (67), Canadian business executive; was chairman of the Wartime Prices and Trade Board in World War II; was president of the government-owned Canadian National Railways (1950–66): d. Westmount, Canada, May 2.

Grau San Martín, Ramón (86), Cuban public official; was president of Cuba (1933–34 and 1944–48); was a foe of the dictator Fulgencio Batista: d. Havana, Cuba, July 28.

Gray, Bowman (62), U. S. business executive; was chairman of the board of the R. J. Reynolds Tobacco Co. (1959–67): d. Winston-Salem, N. C., April 11.

Greene, Harry (64), U. S. pathologist; was chairman of the department of pathology of Yale Medical School since 1950; made numerous contributions in the field of tissue transplant and cancer research: d. New Haven, Conn., Feb. 14.

Greene, Theodore (72), U. S. philosopher, theologian, and author; was professor of philosophy at Princeton (1938–45) and Yale (1946–55) universities; his books include *Our Cultural Heritage* (1956) and *Liberalism* (1957): d. Christmas Cove, Me., Aug. 13.

*****Gropius, Walter** (86), German-born architect and designer: d. Boston, Mass., July 5.

Groves, Harold M. (72), U. S. economist; wrote Wisconsin's 1930 unemployment compensation law, the first in the U. S.; was professor of economics at the University of Wisconsin (1927–68): d. Madison, Wis., Dec. 2.

Guenter, Siegfried (69), German aircraft designer; helped develop the world's first jet plane: d. Munich, West Germany, June 19.

Grunitsky, Nicolas (56), Togolese public official; was the first premier of French Togoland (1956–58) and the second president of independent Togo (1963–67): d. (auto accident) Paris, France, Sept. 28.

Hagen, Walter (76), U. S. professional golfer: b. Rochester, N. Y., Dec. 21, 1892; d. Traverse City, Mich., Oct. 6, 1969. He was noted for his powerful mashie shots and his putting skill. Between 1914, when he won his first U. S. Open title, and 1929, when he retired from competition, he attained 17 major championships. He won the U. S. Open twice, the Canadian Open once, the Professional Golf Association title five times, the British Open four times, and the Western Open five times. He was seven times captain of American Ryder Cup teams. A friend of royalty, he did much to elevate the status of the professional golfer, and he is credited with revolutionizing the style of dress on the golf course.

Hailey, William Malcolm (97), British colonial administrator; aided in the transition of India and British Africa from imperial rule: d. London, England, June 1.

Hale, Robert Lee (85), U. S. educator and author; was professor of law at Columbia University (1935–54); his books include *Freedom Through Law* (1952): d. Stamford, Conn., Aug. 30.

Hamilton, Roy (40), U. S. pop singer; his hit records include *You'll Never Walk Alone, Unchained Melody,* and *Ebb Tide:* d. New Rochelle, N. Y., July 20.

Hargrave, Eugene (Bubbles) (76), U. S. baseball player; was the National League's batting champion in 1926: d. Cincinnati, Ohio, Feb. 23.

Harman, Harvey (69), U. S. sports figure; was football coach at Rutgers University (1937–41, 1946–57); became executive director of the National Football Foundation in 1957: d. Highland Park, N. J., Dec. 17.

Harris, John H. (70), U. S. showman; organized and headed the Ice Capades (1940–63): d. Pittsburgh, Pa., Feb. 12.

Hartley, Fred A. (67), U. S. legislator; was a U. S. congressman from New Jersey (1929–49); coauthor of the Taft-Hartley labor act: d. Linwood, N. J., May 11.

Hawkins, Coleman (64), U. S. jazz musician: b. St. Joseph, Mo., Nov. 21, 1904; d. New York City, May 19, 1969. A pioneer in the development of jazz, he was the first to develop a serious jazz style for the tenor saxophone, and he greatly influenced later saxophonists. From 1923 to 1934 he played with Fletcher Henderson's band, appearing mainly in New York's Roseland ballroom. His 1939 recording of *Body and Soul* is considered a classic.

Hawley, Cameron (63), U. S. novelist; left a successful business career (1951) to write about businessmen and their lives; his novels include *Executive Suite* (1952) and *Cash McCall* (1955): d. Marathon, Fla., Feb. 9.

Hay, Clarence (84), U. S. archaeologist; was secretary of the board of the American Museum of Natural History (1931–60): d. Paris, France, June 4.

Hayek, Heinrich von (68), Austrian scientist; was a crusader against pollution; taught and conducted research in Germany, China, and since 1952 at the University of Vienna: d. Vienna, Austria, Sept. 29.

Hayes, George (Gabby) (83), U. S. actor; was best known for his role as Hopalong Cassidy's sidekick in movies and later on television: d. Burbank, Calif., Feb. 9.

Hayes, Paul (86), Irish-born actor; was best known for his folk tales: d. New York, N. Y., July 29.

Hearne, John (75), Irish diplomat; served as Ireland's first ambassador to the U. S. (1950–60): d. Dublin, Ireland, March 29.

Heath, Edward (Ted) (69), British musician; was one of Britain's best known dance band leaders: d. Virginia Water, England, Nov. 18.

Heller, Walter E. (78), U. S. financier; founded Walter E. Heller & Co. (1919), an international commercial finance business that broadened the concept of small business loans: d. Chicago, Ill., April 12.

THE NEW YORK TIMES

SONJA HENIE, Norwegian skater and actress.

Henie, Sonja (57), Norwegian ice-skating star: b. Oslo, April 8, 1912: d. (on ambulance plane en route to Oslo) Oct. 12, 1969. Noted for her graceful ballet style, she won most of the major world ice-skating championships between 1927 and 1936, when she became a professional. She began skating at the age of 6, studied in Germany, England, Austria, and Switzerland, and took ballet training in London. When she was 8 she won the children's figure skating title of Oslo, and two years later she became figure skating champion of Norway. She made her debut in the Olympic Winter Games in 1924. In 1927 she won the first of her 10 consecutive world skating championships. She won Olympic figure skating titles at St. Moritz in 1928, at Lake Placid in 1932, and at Garmisch-Partenkirchen, Germany, in 1936. After turning professional she toured the United States and starred in several successful Hollywood films, beginning with *One in a Million* (1936). She also staged and performed in ice shows, including the Hollywood Ice Revues. She and her husband, shipowner Neils Onstad, contributed an art museum to Norway in 1968.

Herber, Arnie (59), U. S. football player; was one of the first passers in pro football; played for the Green Bay Packers (1930–40) and was named to the Hall of Fame (1966): d. Green Bay, Wis., Oct. 14.

Hess, Harry H. (63), U. S. geologist; headed the geology department of Princeton University since 1950; was one of the scientists analyzing lunar samples from the Apollo 11 mission: d. Woods Hole, Mass., Aug. 25.

Higgins, Pinky (Michael Franklin) (59), U. S. baseball player and manager: b. Red Oak, Texas, May 27, 1909; d. Dallas, Texas, March 21, 1969. Noted for his easygoing nature, he was manager of the Boston Red Sox from 1955 (when he was named American League manager of the year) through 1962, except for a period in 1959 and 1960. As a third baseman for the Red Sox in 1938, he set a major league record with 12 consecutive hits. He played on two American League championship teams—the Detroit Tigers in 1940 and the Red Sox in 1946. His batting average, for 15 years in the majors, was .292.

Hilton, Conrad (Nicky) (42), U. S. executive; was chairman of the executive committee of the Hilton International Co.; was first husband of actress Elizabeth Taylor (1950): d. West Los Angeles, Calif., Feb. 5.

Hilton, Violet and Daisy (60), British-born Siamese twins; were a well-known vaudeville act in 1920's–1930's: d. Charlotte, N. C., Jan. 4.

Hitchcock, Charles (63), U. S. geographer and explorer; was director of the American Geographical Society (1953–

66) and president of the Explorers Club (1959–61): d. Somers, N. Y., March 26.

Hlasko, Marek (35), Polish author; his best-known work was the novel *The Eighth Day* (Eng. tr., 1958): d. (suicide) Wiesbaden, West Germany, June 14 or 15.

*Ho Chi Minh (79), Communist revolutionary leader and president of North Vietnam: d. Hanoi, North Vietnam, Sept. 3.

Hoak, Don (41), U. S. baseball player; was third baseman for the Pittsburgh Pirates and helped them win the pennant in 1960: d. Pittsburgh, Pa., Oct. 9.

Hodges, Nancy (81), Canadian politician, journalist, and clubwoman; was the first woman of the Commonwealth to sit as speaker of a legislative assembly, the British Columbia House: d. Victoria, B. C., Dec. 15.

Holborn, Hajo (67), U. S. historian; was Sterling Professor of history at Yale University; was the author of the 3-volume *History of Modern Germany* (1969): d. Bonn, West Germany, June 30.

Homan, Paul T. (76), U. S. economist and educator; was head of the first Council of Economic Advisers: d. Washington, D. C., July 3.

Hoover, Herbert, Jr. (65), U. S. undersecretary of state in the Eisenhower administration (1954–57); was son of the former U. S. president: d. Pasadena, Calif., July 9.

Horsbrugh, Florence (80), British political figure; was minister of education under Winston Churchill, the only woman ever to have reached cabinet rank in a Conservative government: d. Edinburgh, Scotland, week of Dec. 6.

Hromadka, Josef (80), Czech theologian; served as a member of the Executive Board of the Protestant World Council of Churches and established the Christian Peace Prize (1958): d. Prague, Czechoslovakia, Dec. 26.

Hughes, Emrys (75), Welsh Labour M. P., journalist, author, and teacher; supported pacifist causes and attacked the monarchy: d. Ayrshire, Scotland, Oct. 18.

Hunt, Martita (69), Argentine-born English actress; her most memorable portrayals include the title role in the play *The Madwoman of Chaillot* (1948) and the part of Miss Havisham in the film *Great Expectations* (1947): d. London, England, June 13.

Hunter, Jeffrey (43), U. S. film actor; remembered for his interpretation of the role of Jesus in the film *King of Kings* (1961): d. Hollywood, Calif., May 27.

Husain, Zakir (72), Indian political leader and educator; was an early follower of Mahatma Gandhi and served as president of India from 1967, the first Muslim ever to hold that post; founded Moslem National University (1927) and worked to reform India's educational system: d. New Delhi, India, May 3.

Hyman, Libbie (80), U. S. zoologist and world authority on invertebrates; wrote 6-volume reference work, *The Invertebrates* (1967), incomplete at her death: d. New York City, Aug. 3.

Ingram, Rex (73), U. S. stage and screen actor; best known for his role in the 1936 movie *The Green Pastures:* d. Hollywood, Calif., Sept. 19.

Innes, William T. (95), U. S. author and expert on tropical fish; founder and former publisher and editor of *The Aquarium;* author of *Exotic Aquarium Fishes* (1935): d. Philadelphia, Pa., Feb. 27.

Iturbi, Amparo (70), Spanish-born, U. S. concert pianist; the younger sister of José Iturbi, she made her New York debut in 1937: d. Los Angeles, Calif., April 21.

Jabotinsky, Eri (60), Israeli mathematician; was professor at the Haifa Technion and director of the Jabotinsky Publishing House; was a member of the Knesset (Parliament) from 1949–51: d. Haifa, Israel, June 6.

Jaques, Francis Lee (81), U. S. artist; painted background murals for the American Museum of Natural History's Hall of Birds in New York City; illustrated and wrote natural history books: d. New York, N. Y., July 24.

Jaspers, Karl (86), German philosopher: b. Oldenburg, Germany, Feb. 23, 1883; d. Basel, Switzerland, Feb. 26, 1969. A leading architect of modern existentialist philosophy, he went beyond religious idealism and scientific rationalism, and turned to man's inner self for an approach to answers to the questions of human existence. Because of his outspoken opposition of Nazism, he was dismissed as a professor at Heidelberg University in 1937, but after the defeat of Hitler he was reinstated. He emerged as a leading spokesman for the German conscience after World War II. In 1949 he took a chair in philosophy at the University of Basel. His books include *The Atomic Bomb and the Future of Man* (1958).

Jones, Brian (26), English pop musician; guitarist for the rock group "The Rolling Stones," his records sold 43 million copies around the world: d. (suicide) Hartfield, England, July 3.

UPI

JOSEPH P. KENNEDY, the financier father of a President, with John at the inaugural on Jan. 20, 1961.

Kagan, Henry Enoch (62), U. S. rabbi and leader in combating anti-Semitism; was consultant to the drafting of the Vatican Council's decrees on ecumenism and religious liberty: d. Pittsburgh, Pa., Aug. 16.

Kallio, Kalervo (60), Finnish sculptor, whose models included such leading figures as Albert Einstein and Harry Truman: d. Helsinki, Finland, Nov. 3.

Karloff, Boris (81), British actor: d. Midhurst, England, Feb. 2. (See MOTION PICTURES.)

Katchen, Julius (42), U. S. pianist and specialist in the music of Brahms; a child prodigy, he made many successful concert tours in the U. S. and Europe: d. Paris, France, April 29.

Kellogg, Charles W. (89), U. S. executive; as president of the Edison Electric Institute (1936–46), he was spokesman for the nation's electric utilities: d. Easton, Md., March 31.

Kennedy, Joseph P(atrick) (81), U. S. financier and diplomat: b. Boston, Sept. 6, 1888; d. Hyannis Port, Mass., Nov. 18, 1969. As patriarch of one of America's foremost political families he experienced several tragedies, including the World War II death of his oldest son, Joseph, Jr. (1944), and the assassinations of his second and third sons, President John F. Kennedy (1963) and Sen. Robert F. Kennedy (1968). The son of an Irish Roman Catholic immigrant who had acquired some wealth, Joseph Kennedy attended Boston Latin School, graduated from Harvard in 1912, and was president of the Columbia Trust Company by 1914. He engaged in a variety of business ventures and amassed a vast fortune through investments. His holdings included New York and Florida real estate, Texas oil properties, and Chicago's Merchandise Mart, which he acquired in 1945. A staunch supporter of Franklin D. Roosevelt, he served as chairman of the Securities and Exchange Commission in 1934–35 and as ambassador to Britain from 1938 to 1940. He resigned from the latter post because his isolationism and his support of British Prime Minister Neville Chamberlain's Munich policy conflicted with Roosevelt's views.

Kerouac, Jack (47), U. S. novelist: b. Lowell, Mass., March 12, 1922; d. St. Petersburg, Fla., Oct. 21, 1969. In his best-selling novel *On the Road* (1957), an account of cross-country travels with various companions, written in a free-wheeling style, he gave the "beat generation" its name and popularized its life-style, which includes emphasis on sensual pleasure, freedom from middle-class conventions, closeness to nature, affinity for such Eastern religions as Zen Buddhism, and experimentation with drugs. He has been called the godfather of the hippie movement of the 1960's. He briefly attended Columbia University on a football scholarship and served with the merchant marine in World War II.

Kerr, Andy (90), U. S. sports figure; was head football coach at Colgate University (1926–46) and annually coached the East team in the Shrine East-West game (1927–67): d. Tucson, Ariz., Feb. 16.

King, A. D. Williams (38), Baptist minister and civil rights activist; the younger brother of Martin Luther King, Jr., he was active in the Southern Christian Leadership Conference: d. (drowned) Atlanta, Ga., July 21.

King, Frank (86), U. S. cartoonist; best known for his comic strip "Gasoline Alley," which he created in 1919: d. Winter Park, Fla., June 24.

King, Slater (41), U. S. civil rights leader; active in the Urban League, the Southern Christian Leadership Conference and helped found the Albany Movement; first Negro candidate for mayor in Albany, Ga.: d. (auto accident) Albany, Ga., March 6.

Kirkland, Jack (66), U. S. dramatist; best known for his adaptation of Erskine Caldwell's novel *Tobacco Road* into the Broadway hit that ran from 1933 to 1941: d. New York, N. Y., Feb. 22.

Kline, Allan B. (73), U. S. farmer and president of the Farm Bureau Federation from 1947 to 1954: d. Vinton, Iowa, June 14.

Kocher, A. Lawrence (83), U. S. architect; an authority on colonial architecture and history, he supervised the restoration of colonial Williamsburg and other historic monuments: d. Williamsburg, Va., June 6.

Kohlmar, Fred (64), U. S. motion picture producer; his films included *Picnic, Pal Joey,* and *How To Steal a Million:* d. Hollywood, Calif., Oct. 13.

Korotchenko, Demyan S. (74), Soviet public official; was chairman of the Presidium of the Ukrainian Supreme Soviet and president of the Ukraine since 1954: d. April 7.

Kreizer, Yakov G. (64), Soviet military commander; was army commander on the Soviet western front during World War II: d. Moscow, USSR, Nov. 30.

Kritz, Karl (63), U. S. musician; was conductor of the Syracuse Symphony since its founding in 1961; former member of the conducting staff of the Metropolitan Opera, New York: d. Syracuse, N. Y., Dec. 17.

Larsen, Agnew E. (73), U. S. aeronautical engineer; received the Collier award from the National Aeronautical Association in 1930 for perfecting the autogiro, predecessor of the helicopter: d. Willow Grove, Pa., Aug. 16.

Lawton, Frank (64), British actor; played in British and U. S. films, including *Cavalcade, David Copperfield,* and *A Night to Remember:* d. London, England, June 10.

Lebedev, Aleksandr (75), Soviet scientist; designed the first Soviet electron microscope (1947); was deputy chairman of the Supreme Soviet (1953–56): d. Moscow, USSR, March 15.

Lee, Ulysses Grant, Jr. (55), U. S. historian; was professor of English at Morgan State College since 1959; authority on Negro history and culture; author of *The Employment of Negro Troops in World War II* (1966): d. Baltimore, Md., Jan. 7.

Lehman, Robert (77), U. S. investment banker: b. New York City, Sept. 29, 1891; d. Sands Point, Long Island, N. Y., Aug. 9, 1969. As senior partner of the Wall Street firm of Lehman Brothers he built it into one of the nation's top investment banking organizations. A graduate of Yale University, he joined the family banking firm in 1919, and by 1925 he had assumed top responsibilities. He was instrumental in the founding of American Airlines and the early expansion of Pan American and Trans-World Airlines, and he pioneered in the underwriting of television enterprises. The owner of art treasures valued at more than $50 million, Lehman became chairman of the board of trustees of the Metropolitan Museum of Art in 1967. He was also noted as a breeder of racehorses and as a philanthropist.

LeTourneau, Robert G. (80), U. S. manufacturer; developed and manufactured world's largest earth-moving machinery and other heavy equipment: d. Longview, Texas, June 1.

Lewis, D(ominic) **B**(evan) **Wyndham** (?78), British author: b. Wales, 1891 or 1894; d. Altea, Spain, Nov. 23(?), 1969. A humorist, journalist, and author of historical biographies, he was known for his sharp satirical comments on modern civilization and his criticisms of what he regarded as a steady cultural decline since the Middle Ages. A member of a distinguished family, he studied at Oxford and later wrote for the London *Daily Express, Daily Mail,* and *News Chronicle.* His books range from *A London Farrago* (1922) to *The World of Goya* (1968).

*Lewis, John L. (89), U. S. labor leader: d. Washington, D. C., June 11.

Ley, Willy (62), German-born U. S. author and educator; prolific writer and lecturer on space travel whose books include *Engineers' Dreams* (1959) and *Rockets, Missiles, and Space Travel* (1960): d. New York, N. Y., June 24.

Li Tsung-jen (78), Chinese official; defected to Communist China (1965) after a government career in Nationalist China (including vice president, 1948–49) and self-imposed exile in U. S. (1949–65): d. Peking, China (reported), Jan. 30.

Lockheed (Loughead), **Allan Haines** (80), U. S. pioneer aviator; cofounder of Lockheed Aircraft Corporation; designed and built first successful tractor seaplane (1911–12): d. Tucson, Ariz., May 26.

Loesser, Frank (Henry) (59), U. S. composer and lyricist: b. New York City, June 29, 1910; d. there, July 28, 1969. One of Broadway's top creative talents, he was responsible for such musical hit shows as *Where's Charley?* (1948), *Guys and Dolls* (1950), *The Most*

Happy Fella (1956), and *How to Succeed in Business Without Really Trying,* which won a Pulitzer Prize in 1962. He also wrote many hit songs, including "Baby, It's Cold Outside," which won a 1948 Motion Picture Academy award. In World War II he turned out "Praise the Lord and Pass the Ammunition." After the war he collaborated with George Abbott on *Where's Charley?,* for which he wrote both music and lyrics. With *Guys and Dolls,* he began his long collaboration with Abe Burrows. His most popular hit songs include "Once in Love with Amy" and "Two Sleepy People."

Logan, Ella (56), Scottish-born U. S. singer and actress; appeared in numerous films and in nightclubs; starred in *Finian's Rainbow* (1947) on Broadway: d. Burlingame, Calif., May 1.

Lopez Mateos, Adolfo (59), Mexican president (1958–64): d. Mexico City, Sept. 22. (See MEXICO.)

Lusher, David (59), Canadian-born U. S. economist; was member of the president's Council of Economic Advisers since 1951: d. Washington, D. C., June 15.

McCarey, Leo (71), U. S. film writer and director; won Oscar awards for writing and directing *Going My Way* (1944) and for directing *The Awful Truth* (1937): d. Santa Monica, Calif., July 5.

McCloskey, Robert G. (53), U. S. historian and educator; professor of American history and government at Harvard University; author of *The American Supreme Court* (1960): d. Boston, Mass., Aug. 4.

McCobb, Paul (51), U. S. designer; pioneered in modern design for the home; the phrase "McCobb furniture" came to mean clean-cut styles, often in natural woods: d. New York, N. Y., March 10.

McCown, Theodore D. (61), U. S. anthropologist; authority on the identification of human fossils; found the skeletal remains of Mount Carmel Man (60,000 to 100,000 years old); professor of anthropology, University of California (1951–69): d. Berkeley, Calif., Aug. 17.

McGill, Ralph (Emerson) (70), U. S. journalist: b. Soddy, Tenn., Feb. 5, 1898; d. Atlanta, Ga., Feb. 3, 1969. As editor and publisher of the Atlanta *Constitution* he championed civil rights and liberal causes and was known as the "conscience of the South." He won the 1959 Pulitzer Prize for editorial writing and was awarded the Presidential Medal of Freedom in 1964. After studying medicine at Vanderbilt University he turned to journalism and served as a reporter and sports editor with the Nashville *Banner* from 1922 to 1928. He joined the Atlanta *Constitution* as sports editor and columnist in 1929 and became its executive editor in 1938, editor in 1942, and publisher in 1960. His book *The South and the Southerners* (1963) won an Atlantic nonfiction prize. He was director of the Fund for the Advancement of Education and a trustee of the Carnegie Endowment for International Peace.

McHugh, Jimmy (74), U. S. composer; composed the scores for 55 films and many Broadway musicals; wrote over 500 songs, including *The Sunny Side of the Street* and *Comin' in on a Wing and a Prayer:* d. Beverly Hills, Calif., May 23.

MacLane, Barton (66), U. S. actor; played role of the outlaw, villain, convict, and gangster in numerous motion pictures: d. Santa Monica, Calif., Jan. 1.

MacMichael, Sir Harold (86), British colonial administrator; was high commissioner of Palestine from 1937 to 1944; author of *The History of Arabs in the Sudan* (1922): d. Folkestone, England, Sept. 19.

McMillan, Donald (82), English-born U. S. evangelist; was national commander of The Salvation Army (1953–57): d. New York, N. Y., Dec. 3.

Madrazo, Carlos Alberto (53), Mexican political figure; was president of the Institutional Revolutionary party since 1964; governor of Tabasco, Mexico (1958–65): d. (plane crash) near Monterrey, Mexico, June 4.

Manger, Itzik (67), Rumanian-born Yiddish poet and playwright; his *Megilla of Itzik Manger* was staged in Israel in 1965 and on Broadway in 1968: d. Gedera, Israel, Feb. 21.

Manley, Norman W. (76), West Indian public official; was prime minister of Jamaica from 1959 to 1962; worked to establish the West Indian Federation: d. Kingston, Jamaica, Sept. 2.

Mann, Erika (63), German-born U. S. writer; daughter of Thomas Mann and wife of poet W. H. Auden; anti-Nazi writer and lecturer; among her books describing conditions in Nazi Germany was *The Lights Go Down* (1940): d. Zurich, Switzerland, Aug. 27.

Marceau, Henri (73), U. S. scholar and curator; director of Philadelphia Museum of Art (1955–64); authority on Renaissance art and curator of the John G. Johnson Collection (1927–33): d. Philadelphia, Pa., Sept. 15.

Marciano, Rocky (45), U. S. boxing champion: d. (in airplane crash) near Des Moines, Iowa, Aug. 31. (See SPORTS.)

Marshall, George Preston (72), U. S. sportsman; owner and former president of the Washington Redskins football team; promoted spectacular half-time shows and the Pro Bowl playoff games: d. Washington, D. C., Aug. 9.

Marshall, Walter P. (67), U. S. business executive; president and chairman of Western Union Telegraph Co. (1948–66); he moved the company into field of computerized communications: d. Manhasset, N. Y., May 5.

Martin, Kingsley (71), British journalist; was editor of *The New Statesman* (1930–60) and built it into an influential journal of radical opinion: d. Cairo, UAR, Feb. 16.

Martinelli, Giovanni (83), opera singer: b. Montagnana, Italy, Oct. 22, 1885; d. New York City, Feb. 2, 1969. The Metropolitan Opera's leading dramatic tenor for 33 years, he was noted for his brilliant and powerful voice, effervescent style, and cheerful temperament. Enrico Caruso referred to him as his "crown prince." The son of a cabinetmaker, he began his career as a choirboy and made his operatic debut at a theater in Milan in 1910. Among the 57 roles in his repertoire were the title role of *Otello* and Rodolfo in *La Bohème.*

Maschwitz, Eric (68), British playwright and composer; wrote for movies, theater, and radio and television; wrote screenplay of *Goodbye, Mr. Chips* (1939); among his hit songs was *These Foolish Things:* d. London, England, Oct. 27.

Maxwell, Gavin (55), Scottish naturalist and author; his most popular books were a trilogy about otters: *Ring of Bright Water* (1960), *The Rocks Remain* (1963), and *Raven Seek Thy Brother* (1969): d. Inverness, Scotland, Sept. 6.

Mboya, Tom (38), Kenyan political leader and minister of economic affairs: d. (assassinated) Nairobi, Kenya, July 5. (See KENYA.)

Meretskov, Kirill (71), Soviet army officer; was chief of the General Staff (1940–41); decorated military hero: d. death announced on Dec. 30.

Merlot, Joseph-Jean (55), Belgian public official; was a Walloon Socialist leader; served as deputy premier and minister for economic affairs since 1968: d. Liège, Belgium, Jan. 20.

Meyers, Sidney (63), U. S. film director and editor; his movies included *The Savage Eye* (1959) and *Man-Made Man* (1967), which won the Lasker award for the best medical film: d. New York, N. Y., Dec. 4.

*Mies van der Rohe, Ludwig (83), German-born U. S. architect: d. Chicago, Ill., Aug. 17.

Karl Jaspers	Jack Kerouac	Ralph McGill	Rafael Osuna	Drew Pearson

Miller, Gilbert (84), U. S. theatrical producer; his plays, equally successful in New York and London, include *Victoria Regina, Journey's End, Under Milk Wood,* and *Daddy Long-Legs:* d. New York, N. Y., Jan. 2.

Millikan, Max F. (56), U. S. economist; was director of the Center for International Studies at Massachusetts Institute of Technology since 1952; an expert on the economic development of underdeveloped countries: d. Boston, Mass., Dec. 14.

Mirakovic, Bora (80), Yugoslav military figure; was commander in chief of Yugoslav air forces in World War II; organized coup that placed King Peter II on throne (1941): d. London, England, Aug. 21.

Mirza, Iskander (70), Pakistani public official; was first president of Pakistan (1956–58); turned over government to Gen. Ayub Khan (1958) after threatened coup: d. London, England, Nov. 13.

Modesto Guilloto, Juan (63), Spanish general; during the Spanish civil war he headed the Republican forces that crossed the Ebro River and saved Madrid (1937); member of central committee of the exiled Spanish Communist party: d. Prague, Czechoslovakia, April 19.

Monaghan, Frank (64), U. S. historian and author; professor of history at Yale from 1933; archivist for New York World's Fair (1940); author of *John Jay, Defender of Liberty* (1935): d. Washington, D. C., July 17.

Morgan, Russ (65), U. S. band leader; trombonist and pianist; wrote popular songs, including *Somebody Else is Taking My Place* and *So Long:* d. Las Vegas, Nev., Aug. 7.

Morse, Samuel F. B. (83), U. S. realtor; founded Del Monte Properties Company in 1919 and developed Pebble Beach, Calif., as a golf resort area: d. Monterey, Calif., May 10.

Mowbray, Alan (72), British-born U. S. actor; was a popular character actor on screen and television; was a founder of the Screen Actors Guild (1933): d. Hollywood, Calif., March 25.

Murchison, Clint (on Williams) (73), U. S. entrepreneur: b. Athens, Texas, Oct. 17, 1895; d. there, June 20, 1969. One of the world's richest men, he had a fortune estimated at $500 million and at one time controlled about 115 companies. He joined his father's small-town bank after briefly attending college. After World War I, in partnership with Sid W. Richardson, he made his first fortune trading oil leases in west Texas. Later he expanded his interests into life insurance, railroads, steamships, taxicabs, bus companies, magazine and book publishing, real estate, theaters, restaurants, grocery chains, racetracks, candy manufacturing, chemicals, household appliances, sporting goods, and cattle ranches.

Mus, Paul (67), U. S. educator; specialist on Indochina; professor of civilization of Southeast Asia at Yale University since 1952, and at the Collège de France: d. Avignon, France, Aug. 12.

Mutesa, Sir Edward (45), Uganda public official; king of Buganda, and president of Uganda (1963–66): d. London, England, Nov. 21.

Northrop, Eugene P. (60), U. S. educator; was professor of mathematics at University of Chicago (1953–60) and an originator of the "new math": d. New York, N. Y., Jan. 5.

O'Daniel, W. Lee (79), U. S. political leader; Democratic governor of Texas (1939–41); elected to U. S. Senate during his second term as governor and served a second senatorial term (1941–48): d. Dallas, Texas, May 11.

Odone, Angelo (77), Italian army officer; led the underground resistance against the Germans in occupied Rome during World War II: d. Naples, Italy, Jan. 31.

O'Doul, Lefty (Frank Joseph) (72), U. S. baseball player and manager: b. San Francisco, Calif., March 4, 1897; d. there, Dec. 7, 1969. O'Doul attained a lifetime batting average of .349, the highest of any living major leaguer. He is credited with having introduced baseball into Japan when he visited there with Babe Ruth in 1931. He won National League batting titles with the Philadelphia Phillies in 1929, with an average of .398, and with the Brooklyn Dodgers in 1932, when he batted .368.

O'Hara, Barratt (87), U. S. legislator; Democratic representative to Congress from Illinois (1948 and 1952–68); U. S. delegate to the 20th UN General Assembly (1965); d. Washington, D. C., Aug. 11.

Oktyabrsky, Filipp S. (69), Soviet admiral; commander of the Soviet Black Sea Fleet in World War II; led the defense of the naval base of Sevastopol against the Germans (1941–42): d. Moscow, USSR, July 8.

Oldham, Joseph (94), English interfaith leader; an organizer of the Edinburgh Missionary Conference (1910); honorary president of the World Council of Churches (1961–69): d. Sussex, England, May 16.

Orlich, Francisco (62), Costa Rican public official; representative to the Costa Rican Congress (1940); president of Costa Rica (1962–66): d. San José, Costa Rica, Oct. 29.

Osborn, Fairfield (82), U. S. conservationist; president of the New York Zoological Society (1940–68); founder (1947) and president of the Conservation Foundation; wrote *Our Plundered Planet* (1948) and *The Limits of the Earth* (1953): d. New York, N. Y., Sept. 15.

Osorio, Oscar (58), Salvadoran political leader; army major who was president of Salvador (1950–56): d. Houston, Texas, March 6.

Ostrovityanov, Kostantin V. (76), Soviet economist; was prominent during postwar Stalin period; author of the theory of the eventual replacement of barter for money in Communist countries: d. Moscow, USSR, Feb. 9.

Osuna, Rafael (31), Mexican tennis player: b. Mexico City(?), 1938(?); d. (air crash, near Monterrey, Mexico) June 4, 1969. Noted for his technical skill and swiftness, he was several times the tennis champion of Mexico, and he won the U. S. Open title at Forest Hills in 1963.

Papen, Franz von (89), German public official: b. Werl, Germany, Oct. 29, 1879; d. Obersasbach, West Germany, May 2, 1969. One of the last chancellors of the German Weimar Republic, he was a key figure in the intrigues that led to Hitler's rise to power in 1933, and he became the first vice-chancellor of the Nazi regime. The son of a Westphalian landowner, he became an imperial page in 1897 and rose to the rank of captain and member of the army general staff in 1913. While serving as military attaché in Washington, D. C., he became involved in espionage and sabotage and was expelled in 1916. After World War I he published a Catholic political journal and served in the Prussian Landtag. As German chancellor from June to November 1932 he lifted restrictions on Nazi stormtroopers, arrested Socialists, and instituted martial law. Although a falling-out with Hitler over the dictator's persecution of the Catholic Church led to his resignation as vice-chancellor in 1934, he accepted the post of ambassador to Austria shortly thereafter and paved the way for that country's takeover by Germany in 1938. From 1939 to 1944 he was ambassador to Turkey, where he coordinated German espionage activities. Cleared of war crimes by the Nuremberg tribunal, he was for a time imprisoned under sentence by a West German denazification court. He spent his last years on his Saarland estate, writing his memoirs.

Pastor, Tony (62), U. S. bandleader; started as a jazz singer and saxophonist; formed his own band (1940–57); wrote novelty hit songs including *Dance With a Dolly* and *Bell Bottom Trousers:* d. New London, Conn., Oct. 31.

Patterson, Graham C. (87), U. S. publisher; built *Farm Journal,* which he published (1935–51), into nation's largest agricultural magazine: d. Chicago, Ill., Nov. 23.

Pearson, Drew (Andrew Russell) (71), U. S. journalist: b. Evanston, Ill., Dec. 13, 1897; d. Washington, D. C., Sept. 1, 1969. Pearson exposed the activities of top government and military officials in his syndicated daily newspaper column, "Washington Merry-Go-Round" which he wrote with Robert S. Allen from 1932 to 1942, and later with Jack Anderson. Pearson's revelations brought him into conflict with President Harry S Truman and Sen. Joseph McCarthy, among others. The son of a professor, he graduated from Swarthmore College (B.A., 1919) and was director of the American Friends Service Committee in Yugoslavia and Albania after World War I. After World War II he organized the Friendship Trains for European relief.

Pegler, (James) **Westbrook** (74), U. S. journalist: b. Minneapolis, Minn., Aug. 2, 1894; d. Tucson, Ariz., June 24, 1969. A master of vituperative prose, he left few persons in high places unscathed by the caustic comments in his syndicated newspaper columns, which appeared from 1933 to 1962. In 1941 he won a Pulitzer Prize for his exposés of corruption in labor unions. In 1933 he began to write his column of national affairs, "Fair Enough," for the United Features Syndicate. He changed over in 1944 to the Hearst-owned King Features Syndicate and renamed his column "As Pegler Sees It." Increasingly right-wing in his orientation, he concentrated much of his fire against President Franklin D. Roosevelt and members of the New Deal administration.

Perez, Leander (77), U. S. political figure; a New Orleans political leader known for his defiance of civil rights orders, he became a symbol of resistance to desegregation in the 1960's: d. New Orleans, La., March 19.

Pickering, James (71), U. S. astronomer; was associated with the Hayden Planetarium, New York (1951–65); was the author of numerous books: d. Milburn, N. J., Feb. 13.

*Pike, James A. (56), former U. S. Episcopal bishop of California: d. Judean hills near Jordan-Israel border, Sept. 7.

Pire, Dominique (Georges Henri) (58), Belgian Roman Catholic priest: b. Dinant, Belgium, Feb. 10, 1910; d. Louvain, Belgium, Jan. 30, 1969. For his work in behalf of refugees and displaced persons in post–World War II Europe he was awarded the 1958 Nobel Peace Prize. During World War II he served as chaplain to the Belgian underground and as an intelligence officer with the resistance, and after the war he set up refugee camps for French and Belgian children. In 1949 he established Aid to Displaced Persons to provide for the needs of some 150,000 homeless persons in Europe.

Pope, Arthur (88), U. S. educator and author; authority on Iranian history, archaeology, and art; wrote *Survey of Persian Art* (1938): d. Teheran, Iran, Sept. 3.

Portman, Eric (66), English stage and screen actor; appeared in over 100 plays in London (1926–47); is best known in the U. S. for his role in *Separate Tables* (1956) and in the British film *One of Our Aircraft Is Missing* (1942): d. Cornwall, England, Dec. 7.

Powell, Cecil Frank (65), British nuclear physicist; won Nobel Prize (1950) for development of photographic methods of studying nuclear processes and for discovering the subatomic pi-meson particles: d. Lake Como, Italy, Aug. 9.

Priest, Alan (70), U. S. art collector; was curator of Far Eastern Art at the New York Metropolitan Museum of Art (1928–63); wrote *Aspects of Chinese Painting* (1954): d. New York, N. Y., Jan. 21.

Rademacher, Hans (76), German-born U. S. mathematician; professor of mathematics at the University of Pennsylvania (1934–62); known for his work in analytic number theory and functions: d. Haverford, Pa., Feb. 7.

Reik, Theodor (81), Austrian-born psychoanalyst: b. Vienna, May 12, 1888; d. New York City, Dec. 31, 1969. An early student and protégé of Sigmund Freud, he devoted much of his career to the interpretation of Freudian concepts of sexuality and the development of theories and techniques of psychoanalysis. The son of a civil servant, he studied at the University of Vienna, where he met Freud in 1910 and obtained his doctorate in 1912. His books include *Masochism in Modern Man* (1941), *Listening With the Third Ear* (1948), *Sex in Man and Woman* (1960), and *The Need to Be Loved* (1963).

Rinehart, Stanley M., Jr. (71), U. S. publisher; was senior vice president and director of Holt, Rinehart and Winston, Inc., until 1963; was cofounder of the original company of Farrar & Rinehart: d. South Miami, Fla., April 26.

Ritter, Thelma (63), U. S. actress: b. Brooklyn, N. Y., Feb. 14, 1905; d. Queens, N. Y., Feb. 5, 1969. Miss Ritter was famous for her brassy and astringent characterizations in motion pictures and on the stage.

Robinson, William E. (68), U. S. executive; retired board chairman of the Coca-Cola Company; publisher of the New York *Herald Tribune* (1953–54): d. Miami, Fla., June 6.

Rolfe, Red (Robert A.) (60) U. S. baseball player and athletic manager: b. Penacook, N. H., Oct. 17, 1908; d. Laconia, N. H., July 8, 1969. Designated all-time third baseman of the New York Yankees in 1969, he had served as manager of the Detroit Tigers from 1949 to 1952 and had been named manager of the year in 1950. From 1954 until his retirement in 1967 he was athletic director of Dartmouth College, his alma mater. During his nine seasons with the Yankees beginning in 1934, the team won 6 pennants and five World Series. In 1939 he led the American League in runs, hits, and doubles, and achieved a batting average of .329.

Rose, Sir David (46), governor general of Guyana; governor of British Guiana (1964–66); became governor of independent nation in 1966; knighted in 1966: d. (accident) London, England, Nov. 10.

Rosenthal, Jean (57), U. S. theatrical lighting designer: b. New York City, March 16, 1912; d. there, May 1, 1969. Through her skillful application of stage lighting she enhanced the atmosphere of many leading Broadway shows as well as opera, ballet, and repertory theater productions.

Russell, Pee Wee (Charles) (62), U. S. musician; a leading jazz clarinetist for more than 40 years with numerous Dixieland bands: d. Alexandria, Va., Feb. 15.

Sabin, Robert (57), U. S. music and dance critic; editor of the 9th edition of the *International Cyclopedia of Music and Musicians;* chief editor of *Musical America* (1936–62): d. New York, N. Y., May 17.

Sakharov, Vladimir (66), Soviet geneticist; pioneered in the study of the mutation process in plants and animals (1920–30's): d. Moscow, USSR, Jan. 10.

Sardi, Vincent, Sr. (83), Italian-born U. S. restaurateur; in 1921 he opened The Little Restaurant, later called Sardi's, in the New York theater district; Sardi's became a famous meeting place for theater personalities: d. Saranac Lake, N. Y., Nov. 18.

Saud (Ibn Abd al-Aziz Al Faisal Al Saud) (67), King of Saudi Arabia: b. Kuwait, Jan. 12, 1902; d. Athens, Greece, Feb. 23, 1969. As king of Saudi Arabia from 1953 to 1964 he was technically the absolute ruler of his vast, oil-rich nation, but he left much of the governing power to his brother Faisal, who succeeded him. The oldest surviving son of King Ibn Saud, he was designated crown prince in 1933, became commander in chief of the army in 1939, and succeeded to the throne on his father's death in 1953. His rivalry with Egypt's Gamal Abdel Nasser for leadership of the Arab world impelled him toward friendship with Jordan and with the United States. which he visited several times. Although he initiated some social reforms and public work projects, his lavish style of living at times brought the country close to bankruptcy. Family differences forced him to abdicate in favor of Faisal in 1964. He spent his last years in exile in Athens.

Schenck, Nicholas M. (87), U. S. motion picture executive: b. Rybinsk, Russia, Nov. 14, 1881; d. Miami Beach, Fla., March 3, 1969. As president of Metro-Goldwyn-Mayer from 1927 to 1955, he was one of the central figures in the Hollywood motion picture industry.

Schmitt, Bernadotte E. (82), U. S. historian; authority on modern diplomatic history; his major work, *The Coming of the War, 1914* (1930), won the 1930 Pulitzer Prize for history: d. Alexandria, Va., March 22.

Seneca, Cornelius V. (72), U. S. Indian leader; was twice president of the Seneca Indian nation and led losing fight against the Kinzua Dam project in Pennsylvania: d. Gowanda, N. Y., July 26.

Sewell, Wilbur P. (Bill Sands) (49), U. S. author; wrote about his life in prison in *My Shadow Ran Fast* (1964) and *The Seventh Step* (1967); formed the Seventh Step Foundation (1962) to prepare convicts for parole: d. Los Angeles, Calif., Oct. 28.

Shahn, Ben (70), Lithuanian-born U. S. artist: d. New York, N. Y., March 14. (See ART.)

Shapiro, Arthur (59), U. S. scientist; pioneered in psychophysiology, using machines to study the meaning of dreams and origins of sleep: d. Philadelphia, Pa., Sept. 28.

Shaughnessy, Frank (86), U. S. athlete and sports executive; was president of baseball's International League (1936–60); originated the playoff system in baseball that bears his name: d. Montreal, Canada, May 15.

Westbrook Pegler   Saud   Gladys Swarthout   Moïse Tshombe   Josh White

WIDE WORLD   UPI   THE NEW YORK TIMES   LONDON DAILY EXPRESS   CULVER PICTURES

Shaw, Mark (47), U. S. photographer; was White House photographer for President Kennedy; filmed award-winning television commercials and was a leading magazine fashion photographer: d. New York, N. Y., Jan. 26.

Sheil, Bernard J(ames) (83), U. S. Roman Catholic prelate: b. Chicago, Ill., Feb. 18, 1886; d. Tucson, Ariz., Sept. 13, 1969. A militant crusader for civil rights and social justice, he had been auxiliary bishop of the Chicago archdiocese since 1928 and founded the Catholic Youth Organization in 1930.

Shermarke, Abdirashid Ali (49), president of Somalia; doctorate from Rome University (1958); deputy in Somalia National Assembly (1959–1960); first premier of independent nation (1960–1964); elected president in 1964: d. (assassinated) Las Anod, Somalia, Oct. 15.

Shoriki, Matsutaro (84), Japanese publisher and politician; published one of Japan's leading newspapers, the Yomiuri Shimbun; introduced baseball to Japan; was a Conservative member of Diet: d. Tokyo, Japan, Oct. 9.

Sierpinski, Wacław (87), Polish mathematician; founded the Warsaw school of mathematics and published studies dealing with set theory and functions, including Theory of Numbers (1914): d. Warsaw, Poland, Oct. 19.

Simon, Abe (56), U. S. athlete; was heavyweight boxer who was knocked out twice by Joe Louis (1940's): d. Westbury, N. Y., Oct. 24.

Singstad, Ole (87), Norwegian-born U. S. engineer; designed and built numerous tunnels including New York's Holland Tunnel, Queens Midtown Tunnel, Lincoln Tunnel: d. New York, N. Y., Dec. 8.

Sitwell, Sir Osbert (76), British poet and essayist; wrote five-volume autobiography bearing the general title of Left Hand, Right Hand! (1945): d. Montagnana, Italy, May 4.

Slim, Mongi (61), Tunisian diplomat; was ambassador to U. S. (1956–61) and president of the UN General Assembly (1961–62); active in Tunisian independence movement: d. Tunis, Tunisia, Oct. 23.

Slipher, Vesto M(elvin) (93), U. S. astronomer: b. Mulberry, Ind., Nov. 11, 1875; d. Flagstaff, Ariz., Nov. 8, 1969. One of the nation's leading astronomers, he was director of the Lowell Observatory in Flagstaff from 1926 until his retirement in 1952 and headed the team that discovered the trans-Neptunian planet Pluto in 1930. A pioneer in spectroscopy, he discovered the existence of calcium and sodium in interstellar space and was the first to observe molecular bands in the spectra of major planets. He devised methods for accurately determining the rotation periods of planets. His discovery of the rotation speeds and space velocities of spiral nebulas helped furnish the basis for the expanding-universe theory.

Smith, Courtney C. (52), U. S. educator; president, Swarthmore College (1953–69); directed selection of U. S. Rhodes scholarship students: d. Swarthmore, Pa., Jan. 16.

Smith, William S. (61), U. S. art curator and author; was authority on Middle Eastern and Egyptian archaeology, art, and history; curator of Egyptian Art at Museum of Fine Arts, Boston (1956–69): d. Cambridge, Jan. 13.

Southworth, Billy (76), U. S. athlete; major league baseball player (1913–29); managed St. Louis Cardinals to two World Series victories (1942, 1944): d. Columbus, Ohio, Nov. 15.

Spruance, Raymond A(mes) (83), U. S. naval officer: b. Baltimore, Md., July 3, 1886; d. Pebble Beach, Calif., Dec. 13, 1969. The foremost tactician of the U. S. Navy in World War II, he led the defeat of Japanese forces in the Battle of Midway (1942), a turning point of the war in the Pacific. After the Midway victory, Spruance, an Annapolis graduate, became chief of staff to Admiral Chester W. Nimitz. Then he was appointed commander of the Central Pacific force, and planned and executed the invasion of the Gilbert and Marshall islands.

Stern, Gustav (65), German-born U. S. philanthropist; founded the Hartz Mountain Pet Food Company; established the Gustav Stern Foundation to aid in the study of virology: d. New York, N. Y., May 5.

Stern, Otto (81), German-born U. S. scientist; was awarded Nobel Prize for physics (1943) for his use of the molecular beam in the study of atomic structure of various elements: d. Berkeley, Calif., Aug. 17.

Stillman, Lou (82), U. S. sports figure; owned Stillman's Gymnasium in New York City, considered a school for prizefighters (1921–59): d. Santa Barbara, Calif., Aug. 19.

Stratemeyer, George E(dward) (78), U. S. air force officer: b. Cincinnati, Ohio, Nov. 24, 1890; d. Winter Park, Fla., Aug. 9, 1969. As chief of air staff and commander of Army Air Forces in the China-Burma-India theater in World War II and commander of Far East Air Forces in the Korean War, he was noted as one of the nation's most skillful tacticians.

Stulginskis, Aleksandras (84), Lithuanian political figure; signed the Lithuanian Declaration of Independence (1918) and served as president of the republic (1922–26): d. Kaunas, Lithuania, Sept. 22.

Sullivan, Brian (49), U. S. operatic tenor; was leading artist at the Metropolitan Opera (1948–64): d. (suicide) Geneva, Switzerland, June 17.

Sutliff, Vincent E. (69). U. S. executive; was a director of Grolier, Inc., and president and board chairman of the Americana Corporation, publisher of THE ENCYCLOPEDIA AMERICANA: d. Gaithersburg, Md., Oct. 29.

Swarthout, Gladys (64), U. S. opera singer: b. Deepwater, Mo., Dec. 25, 1904; d. near Florence, Italy, July 7, 1969. One of the most popular stars of the Metropolitan Opera, she was noted for her rich mezzo-soprano voice and her glamour and acting skill. From 1929 to 1945 she sang with the Metropolitan Opera Company in New York, where she was a protégée of soprano Mary Garden. She also appeared in concert recitals, on radio and television, and in such Hollywood films as Rose of the Rancho (1936), Champagne Waltz (1937), and Romance in the Dark (1938). Best known for her portrayal of Carmen, she also appeared in major roles in such operas as La Gioconda, Norma, and Faust. She retired in 1956.

Swing, Betty Gram (76), U. S. women's rights leader; participated in suffrage movement (1920's) and was often arrested; helped organize for the UN the Commission on the Status of Women: d. Norwalk, Conn., Sept. 1.

Swope, Tom (80), U. S. journalist; was president of the Baseball Writers Association (1941); sports writer for the Cincinnati Post (1915–69) and a noted baseball statistician: d. Cincinnati, Ohio, Feb. 11.

Talmadge, Natalie (70), U. S. actress; was silent screen star (1920's) and one of the three famous Talmadge sisters: d. Santa Monica, Calif., June 19.

Tannenbaum, Frank (76), Austrian-born U. S. scholar; founded (1945) and directed the seminar program at Columbia University, an interdisciplinary approach to education; professor of Latin American history (1945–61): d. New York, N. Y., June 1.

Tate, Sharon (26), U. S. actress: d. (murdered) Benedict Canyon, Calif., Aug. 9.

*Taylor, Robert (57), U. S. actor: d. Santa Monica, Calif., June 8.

Testa, Gustavo Cardinal (82), Italian Roman Catholic prelate; spent most of his career in the Vatican diplomatic service: d. Rome, Italy, Feb. 28.

Thayer, Charles (59), U. S. diplomat and author; directed the Voice of America (1948–49); noted authority on Soviet affairs and author of many books based on his experiences as a diplomat: d. Salzburg, Austria, Aug. 27.

Thye, Edward John (73), U. S. political figure; served as Republican governor of Minnesota (1943–47) and later as U. S. senator (1947–59): d. Northfield, Minn., Aug. 28.

Torrance, Jack (57), U. S. athlete; was world shotput champion (1934); boxed professionally and played football with the Chicago Bears (1939–40): d. Baton Rouge, La., Nov. 11.

Torsvan, Traven (79), U. S.-born author; identified by friends as "B. Traven," mysterious author of numerous best sellers including The Treasure of the Sierra Madre: d. Mexico City, Mexico, March 27.

Tshombe, Moïse (49), Congolese political leader: b. Musumba, Belgian Congo, Nov. 10, 1919; d. Algeria, June 29, 1969. A skillful manipulator of power, he led the secession of the Congo's wealthy Katanga province in 1960, in defiance of United Nations authorities, and served as its president until its collapse in 1963. He was premier of the unified Congo in 1964–65. The son of a well-to-do businessman, he was educated at an American Methodist mission school and took over his father's business in 1951. Aided by Belgian financial interests and foreign mercenary troops, he declared Katanga's secession from the newly independent Congo in July 1960 and maintained its independence until UN troops brought an end to the secession in January 1963. Returning from exile in July 1964 he served as premier of the Congo until October 1965, when a power struggle with President Joseph Kasavubu forced him into exile in Spain. Kidnapped on a flight over the Mediterranean in June 1967, he spent his last two years in imprisonment in Algeria, while Congolese authorities unsuccessfully tried to extradite him.

Tykociner, Joseph T. (91), Polish-born U. S. scientist; invented the first talking motion picture process (1922); was professor of electrical engineering at University of Illinois (1922–49): d. Champaign, Ill., June 4.

Urbani, Giovanni Cardinal (69), Roman Catholic prelate; patriarch of Venice; a leader of Italian Catholic Action and, since 1966, president of the Italian Bishops' Conference: d. Venice, Sept. 17.

Vajda, Imre (69), Hungarian economist and government official; was head of the national economic planning office and a member of the Communist party Politburo: d. Vienna, Aug. 30.

Victoria Eugenia (81), former queen of Spain; was a granddaughter of Queen Victoria of Britain; wife of the late King Alfonso XIII; grandmother of Franco's designated heir, Prince Juan Carlos: d. Lausanne, Switzerland, April 15.

von Sternberg, Josef (Jo Sternberg) (75), U. S. motion picture director: b. Vienna, Austria, 1894; d. Los Angeles, Calif., Dec. 22, 1969. A master craftsman who sought to elevate the artistic level of film-making, he was best known for discovering Marlene Dietrich and furthering her·development as an actress. He began his career at 17 as an assistant in a New Jersey film studio. In World War I he made realistic training films for the War College, and in 1924 he obtained his first Hollywood job, as an assistant director. Departing from conventional film-making techniques, he ·made *The Salvation Hunters* (1925) independently. He was more successful with a series of films he directed for Paramount, including *The Exquisite Sinner* (1926) and *The Last Command* (1928). After directing Miss Dietrich in *The Blue Angel* (1930) in Germany, he made six more films with her in Hollywood, including *Morocco* (1930) and *The Devil Is a Woman* (1935).

Voroshilov, Kliment Y(efremovich) (88), Soviet public official: b. Verkhneye, Ukraine, Feb. 4, 1881; d. in the USSR, Dec. 2, 1969. A close associate of Josef Stalin, he was chairman of the Presidium of the Supreme Soviet (nominal chief of state) from 1953 to 1960. The son of a railroad watchman, he worked in coal mines at the age of 7, took part in revolutionary activities as a factory apprentice in his teens, and led a local uprising in the abortive 1905 revolution. He played an important role in the 1917 revolution and as a commander of Red forces in the civil war that followed. Elected to the Central Committee of the Communist party in 1921, he served for three years as commander of the North Caucasus military district and was appointed in 1925 as war commissar (or defense minister), a post he held for 15 years. As commander of part of the western sector in World War II he failed to distinguish himself. He was appointed deputy premier in 1946. A member of the "anti-party group" that sought to oust Premier Nikita S. Khrushchev in 1957, he later repudiated his position but was forced by Khrushchev to resign as Presidium chairman in 1960.

Wales, Nathaniel B., Jr. (54), U. S. nuclear physicist and inventor; his inventions include the polycathodic counting tube (an early kind of Geiger counter) and a computer tape printer and reader: d. Red Bank, N. Y., June 13.

Walker, Fred (82), U. S. military figure; commanded the 36th Infantry Division in North Africa and Italy during World War II: d. Washington, D. C., Oct. 6.

Warburg, James P. (72), U. S. financier, author, and critic of U. S. foreign policy; his books include *Germany: Key to Peace* (1953) and *Cross Currents in the Middle East* (1968): d. Greenwich, Conn., June 3.

Ward, Angus (75), U. S. diplomat; imprisoned by the Chinese Communists in 1948–49 while he was consul general at Mukden, Manchuria: d. Málaga, Spain, May 22.

Weill, Al (75), U. S. boxing manager; among the fighters whose careers he managed were Joey Archibald, Marty Servo, and Rocky Marciano: d. Miami, Fla., Oct. 20.

Weinberg, Sidney J(ames) (77), U. S. investment banker: b. Brooklyn, N. Y., Oct. 12, 1891; d. New York City, July 23, 1969. Known as "Mr. Wall Street," he engineered the sale of $650 million worth of Ford Motor Company stock for the Ford Foundation in 1956 and was the underwriter for $350 million worth of Sears Roebuck debentures in 1958. He finished his formal education with the eighth grade, joined Goldman, Sachs & Co. as an assistant janitor in 1907, and became a partner in the firm in 1926. At one time he was a director in 31 companies. He served as an unofficial adviser to Presidents Roosevelt, Truman, Eisenhower, Kennedy, and Johnson.

Weinstock, Jack (62), U. S. urologist, professor of medicine, and playwright; was coauthor ·with Willie Gilbert of prize-winning musical *How to Succeed in Business Without Really Trying* (1961): d. New York City, May 23.

Welch, Herbert (106), U. S. religious figure; was president of Ohio Wesleyan University from 1905 until 1916, when he became a bishop of the Methodist Church: d. New York, N. Y., April 4.

Werth, Alexander (68), British journalist and specialist on Soviet affairs; wrote *Russia at War: 1941–1945* (1964): d. Paris, France, March 5.

White, Josh(ua) (61), U. S. folk singer: b. Greenville, S. C., Feb. 11, 1908; d. Manhasset, Long Island, N. Y., Sept. 5, 1969. One of the earliest professional folk artists, he was noted for his virtuosity as a guitarist, his smooth baritone voice, and the easy style in which he presented his blues, spirituals, folk ballads, and prison songs at night clubs, concert halls, and colleges, and on his many recordings. In the early 1930's he went to New York, where he worked with a folk singing group and recorded an album of spirituals. His *Chain Gang* album of Southern prison songs, recorded in the early 1940's, became immensely popular. At the request of President Roosevelt he gave three performances at the White House.

White, Ruth (55), U. S. stage, film, and television actress; appeared in Beckett's play *Happy Days* and in the film *Midnight Cowboy:* d. Perth Amboy, N. J., Dec. 3.

Whitney, Courtney (71), U. S. general; was chief aide and close friend of Gen. Douglas MacArthur; wrote *MacArthur, His Rendezvous With History* (1956): d. Washington, D. C., March 21.

Wiedemann, Guillermo Egon (63), German-born Colombian artist; noted figurative painter of the 1940's who later turned to abstract art: d. Key Biscayne, Fla., Jan. 25.

Wierzynski, Kazimierz (74), Polish-born poet; wrote 25 books of poetry, biography, and literary criticism including *The Life and Death of Chopin* (1949): d. London, England Feb. 14.

Winninger, Charles (84), U. S. actor; created the role of Cap'n Andy in the stage (1927) and movie (1929, 1936) versions of *Show Boat:* d. Palm Springs, Calif., Jan. 27.

Winters, Robert (59), Canadian political leader; held various cabinet posts in Liberal governments from 1948; in 1968 lost leadership bid to Prime Minister Trudeau: d. Monterey, Calif., Oct. 10.

Witebsky, Ernest (68), German-American biologist; discovered a combination of substances of blood groups "A" and "B" that when added to type "O" produced a universal type useful for emergency transfusions to patients with unknown blood types: d. Buffalo, N. Y., Dec. 7.

Wood, Robert E(lkington) (90), U. S. business executive: b. Kansas City, Mo., June 13, 1879; d. Lake Forest, Ill., Nov. 6, 1969. As vice president (1924–28), president (1928–39), and board chairman (1939–54) of Sears, Roebuck and Co., he built it from a strictly mail-order business into the world's largest merchandising organization. with more than 800 retail stores and 11 mail-order plants. A graduate of the U. S. Military Academy in the class of 1900, he served in the Philippines, Panama, and France before retiring from the Army in 1918 as a brigadier general. After World War I he became a vice president with Montgomery Ward, where his proposals that the company expand into retailing failed to gain acceptance. He was more successful at Sears, which he joined in 1924 as a vice president and head of factory operations.

Woolf, Leonard (88), British author and intellectual; was a leader of London's famous Bloomsbury group and the husband of novelist Virginia Woolf: d. Rodmell, England, Aug. 14.

Wright, John (78), U. S. geographer; was director of the American Geographical Society (1938–49); wrote many works on geography and cartography: d. Hanover, N. H., March 24.

Wuorinen, John H. (71), Finnish-born U. S. historian; was chairman of Department of History at Columbia (1949–58); wrote studies of Scandinavian history including *History of Finland* (1965): d. Gardner, Mass., April 10.

Wyatt, Bowden (54), U. S. football coach; was head coach at Tennessee, Wyoming, and Arkansas and led conference title winners at these three universities: d. Sweetwater, Tenn., Jan. 21.

Wyman, Willard (71), U. S. general; was aide to General Eisenhower and led Normandy invasion force (1944); helped organize the Turkish and Greek armies for NATO (1952): d. Washington, D. C., March 29.

Yablonski, Joseph A. (59), U. S. labor leader; was an official in the United Mine Worker's of America (1942–69) and had recently lost an election for UMW president after a bitter campaign: d. (murdered, along with wife and daughter) Clarksville, Pa., Dec. 31.

Young, Edward (83), U. S. surgeon; was a founder of White Cross (the precursor of Blue Cross and Blue Shield) and a pioneer in the Medicare idea: d. Brookline, Mass., Feb. 19.

Zachary, Tom (72), U. S. athlete; a major league baseball player, he is remembered as the Washington Senators' pitcher who in 1927 served up Babe Ruth's 60th home run ball: d. Graham, N. C., Jan. 23.

Zomosa, Maximiliano (31), Chilean-born dancer; was a principal dancer with the New York City Center Joffrey Ballet (1966–69): d. Woodbridge, N. J., Jan. 9.

A

Main article headings appear in this Index as bold-faced capitals; subjects within articles appear as lower-case entries. Main article page numbers and general references are listed first under each entry; the sub-entries which follow them on separate lines direct the reader to related topics appearing elsewhere. Both the general references and the subentries should be consulted for maximum usefulness of this Index. Illustrations are indexed herein. Cross references are to the entries in this Index.

D